Black's Law Dictionary®

Seventh Edition

Black's Law Dictionary®

Seventh Edition

Bryan A. Garner
Editor in Chief

ST. PAUL, MINN., 1999

610 Opperman Drive
P.O. Box 64526
St. Paul, MN 55164–0526
1–800–328–9352

Printed in the United States of America

ISBN 0–314–22864–0
ISBN 0–314–24130–2—deluxe

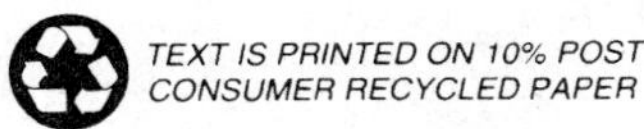
TEXT IS PRINTED ON 10% POST CONSUMER RECYCLED PAPER

Editorial Staff

Bryan A. Garner
Editor in Chief

David W. Schultz
Senior Assistant Editor

Lance A. Cooper
Assistant Editor

Elizabeth C. Powell
Assistant Editor

Academic Consultants

Hans W. Baade
Professor of Law
University of Texas

Tony Honoré
Professor Emeritus
University of Oxford

Joseph F. Spaniol, Jr.
Former Clerk
U.S. Supreme Court

David M. Walker
Professor Emeritus
University of Glasgow

Contributing Editors

Michael L. Atchley

Beverly Ray Burlingame

Elizabeth S. Kerr

Ann Taylor Schwing

Charles Harrington Elster
Pronunciation Editor

Karen Magnuson
Copyeditor

Contents

Preface ix
Guide to the Dictionary xvii
List of Abbreviations xxiii

Dictionary 1

Appendixes

A. Legal Maxims 1615
B. The Constitution of the United States of America 1703
C. Universal Declaration of Human Rights 1717
D. Time Chart of the United States Supreme Court 1721
E. Federal Circuits Map 1725
F. British Regnal Years 1727
G. List of Works Cited 1729

Preface

When Henry Campbell Black published the first edition of *Black's Law Dictionary* back in 1891, the *Oxford English Dictionary* had not yet been completed. Nor was the *OED* finished when Black prepared his second edition in 1910. By today's standards, the "gentle art of lexicography,"[1] as it has been called, was yet to experience the tremendous dictionary-making developments that the 20th century had in store, the highlights being the *OED* (1928), *Webster's Second* (1934), *Webster's Third* (1961), and the second edition of the *OED* (1989). Largely through the influence of these major works, dictionaries today are much better than they used to be.

Legal scholarship has also made tremendous strides — even in describing pre-19th-century law. The great legal historians Pollock, Maitland, and Holdsworth had not yet produced their monumental works when Black put out the first edition. Our understanding of Roman law is better today than it was a century ago. Our understanding of feudal law is much better. Meanwhile, our precedent-based system still has not entirely escaped the influence of Roman and feudal law.

At the same time, modern law hurtles headlong into decade after decade of new statutes, new doctrines, and new tripartite tests. The world — as well as the law that tries to govern it — is changing at a dizzying pace. If you want evidence of this change, look inside for the hundreds of new entries such as *cyberstalking*, *jurimetrics*, *parental kidnapping*, *quid pro quo sexual harassment*, *reproductive rights*, and *viatical settlement*.

Given all these developments — both in lexicography and in law — it is hardly surprising that, by the end of the 20th century, *Black's Law Dictionary* had come to need a major overhaul. This edition is the result of that effort.

New Features in the Seventh Edition

Significant strides have been made both in modernizing this edition and in improving its historical depth. The editors' goal was to make it at once the most scholarly and the most practical edition ever published. More than 4,500 entries in the book are entirely new. (Some of the new entries are surprising: previous editions had omitted some commonplace terms such as *act of Congress*, *circuit judge*, *motion for summary judgment*, *senatorial courtesy*, and *sidebar comment*.) Of the remaining 20,000 entries, all have been thoroughly revised: sharpened and tightened.

Aside from the thousands of new entries and subentries, the differences between earlier editions and this one are many. The headwords show whether a term should be uppercase or lowercase, roman or italic.

[1] Eric Partridge, *The Gentle Art of Lexicography, as Pursued and Experienced by an Addict* (1963).

The pronunciation symbols are easy to understand. For the first time ever, etymologies systematically appear. Senses of words are analytically broken down and given numbers — as never before. Definitions are clearer than ever (though the battle for clarity, when the subject is feudal law, can never be completely won). Bullets now appear within definitions to help differentiate definitional information (before the bullet) from encyclopedic information (after the bullet). More than 2,000 newly added quotations from some 400 important works of Anglo-American legal scholarship appear throughout the text to help convey the nuances of the legal vocabulary. (More about these in a moment.) The 2,200 legal maxims (mostly Latin) are conveniently collected in an appendix, instead of cluttering the main lexicon. In addition, my colleagues and I have:

- Attempted a thorough marshaling of the language of the law from original sources.
- Examined the writings of specialist scholars rather than looking only at judicial decisions.
- Considered entries entirely anew rather than merely accepting what previous editions have said. We have often checked Westlaw and other sources when trying to decide which of two competing forms now predominates in legal usage.
- Imposed analytical rigor on entries by avoiding duplicative definitions and by cataloguing and numbering senses.
- Ensured that specialized vocabularies are included — from bankruptcy to securities law, from legal realism to critical legal studies.

This modern approach to legal lexicography is only a beginning. To its great credit, the West Group has now made the editing of *Black's Law Dictionary*, in its various editions, an ongoing project. This means that *Black's*, like all major dictionaries outside the law, will be a continuing work in progress. As the law continues its rapid evolution, *Black's Law Dictionary* will keep apace.

The Inclusion of Scholarly Quotations

In a novel feature, more than 2,000 quotations from scholarly works appear throughout the text to help round out the treatment of various terms. In selecting these quotations, my colleagues and I have sought a blend of characteristics: temporal and geographic range, aptness, and insight. Some scholars show great astuteness in discussing terminology — particularly Blackstone (English law), Glanville Williams (criminal law and jurisprudence), Rollin Perkins (criminal law), and Charles Alan Wright (federal procedure). Although Blackstone and Wright are well known to American lawyers, Williams and Perkins are not: their work deserves more widespread attention.

The List of Works Cited (Appendix G) sets forth the 400-plus lawbooks cited in these pages. We have tried to locate the best scholarly discussions of legal terminology and to give snippets of them. In future editions, we intend to continue this practice, and we encourage readers to submit published quotations for this purpose.

The Challenge of Legal Lexicography

Law dictionaries have a centuries-old tradition of apologizing in advance for errors and omissions. Some of the apologies are moving — especially to one who understands the arduousness of lexicography — and a few border on the humorous:

1607: "[I]f I have either omitted any hard word within my circuit, or set it downe not expounded, I give you good leave to impute the one to my negligence, the other to mine ignorance: and so commend these my paines to your best profit, and you unto God."[2]

1670: "If I have sometimes committed a *Jeofaile*, or hunted Counter in any explication or Etymology, in so large a field of words, and stor'd with such variety of Game, it will be no wonder, and, I hope, will draw no censure upon me from the Ingenuous . . . . [I]f I leave some words with a *Quaere* . . . to be resolved or corrected by the more learned; it is but what Cowell frequently, and Spelman has sometimes done."[3]

1732: "[W]here there is such great Variety of Learning and abundant Quantity of Nice Matter, with the utmost Care, there must be some Faults and Failings to be Pardon'd by the Reader."[4]

1839: "To those who are aware of the difficulties of the task, the author deems it unnecessary to make any apology for the imperfections which may be found in the work. His object has been to be useful; if that has been accomplished in any degree, he will be amply rewarded for his labour; and he relies upon the generous liberality of the members of the profession to overlook the errors which may have been committed in his endeavours to serve them."[5]

1848: "It is not without very considerable diffidence, that this Lexicon is submitted to the indulgence of the Profession and the Public, for no man can be more conscious of the difficulties besetting such a subject — of the many requisites of the task — and above all, of the great discrepancy usually exhibited between what a book *ought to be*, and what it *is* — than the Author of the present undertaking."[6]

1859: "[T]he work is now submitted to the examination of the profession. That its execution has fallen far short of its design, is already but too apparent to the author's own observation. Of the defects that may be discovered in its pages, some seem to be inseparable from the task of first compiling any matter of the kind from sources so numerous, and scattered over so wide a field."[7]

---

[2] John Cowell, *The Interpreter* 5 (1607).

[3] Thomas Blount, *Nomo-Lexicon: A Law-Dictionary* [n.p.] (1670).

[4] Giles Jacob, *A New Law-Dictionary* 4 (2d ed. 1732).

[5] John Bouvier, *A Law Dictionary* viii (1839).

[6] J.J.S. Wharton, *The Legal Lexicon, or Dictionary of Jurisprudence* iii (1st Am. ed. 1848).

[7] Alexander M. Burrill, *A Law Dictionary and Glossary* xv (1859).

1874: "[W]ithout craving the indulgence of the public, whose servant he is, and to whom, therefore, if he serve up anything he should in all conscience serve up a proper dish, [the Author] is reluctant to acknowledge that an unaccustomed feeling of diffidence has once or twice assailed him, lest his work should not prove so absolutely faultless or so generally useful as it has been his wish to make it."[8]

In the first edition of this book (1891), Henry Campbell Black broke the tradition, boldly asserting the exhaustiveness of his work:

> "The dictionary now offered to the profession is the result of the author's endeavor to prepare a concise and yet comprehensive book of definitions of the terms, phrases, and maxims used in American and English law and necessary to be understood by the working lawyer and judge, as well as those important to the student of legal history or comparative jurisprudence. . . . Of the most esteemed law dictionaries now in use, each will be found to contain a very considerable number of words not defined in any other. None is quite comprehensive in itself. The author has made it his aim to include *all* these terms and phrases here, together with some not elsewhere defined." Henry Campbell Black, *A Dictionary of Law* iii (1891).

There is no lack of confidence expressed anywhere in his preface.

Yet in putting forth this seventh edition, I confess that my feelings incline more to those of Black's predecessors than to those of Black himself.

A Lot of Help from Our Friends

Diffidence, though, can lead to safeguards. And so it has in this work. I engaged several distinguished scholars who thoroughly vetted the entire manuscript:

- Tony Honoré, former holder of the Regius Professorship in Civil Law at Oxford University, and author of many important books, including *Causation in the Law* (with H.L.A. Hart).
- Joseph F. Spaniol, Jr., former Clerk of the Supreme Court of the United States, whose wide-ranging experience includes decades of service in federal rulemaking as a consultant to the Standing Committee on Rules of Practice and Procedure.
- David M. Walker, former holder of the Regius Professorship in Law at Glasgow University, perhaps the most prolific legal writer in the British Isles, and author of the renowned *Oxford Companion to Law* (1980).

Additionally, in about a third of the manuscript, we had the help of Hans W. Baade, holder of the Hugh Lamar Stone Chair in Civil Law at the University of Texas. He is a comparativist of the first rank whose expertise ranges from domestic relations to international transactions to conflict of laws.

---

[8] Archibald Brown, *A New Law Dictionary* vi (1874).

On the editorial side, several of my colleagues at LawProse, Inc. played crucial roles. David W. Schultz, a seasoned editor who joined the *Black's* team in 1995, was invaluable in producing both the pocket edition (which appeared in 1996) and this unabridged edition. His editorial judgments have improved every page. Lance A. Cooper, an aspiring legal historian, joined the team in 1997, working skillfully on thousands of entries for more than 18 months. Elizabeth C. Powell arrived in 1998, bringing with her a keen intellect, ten years of lawyerly experience, and an amazing capacity for hard work. All three — Schultz, Cooper, and Powell — are splendid lawyers who, not so long ago, never imagined they would one day be legal lexicographers. Yet they learned dictionary-making as the best lexicographers do: on the job. And they've become quite accomplished.

When it came to pronunciations, though, I knew we needed someone already expert in the art. This dictionary presents extraordinary challenges to a pronunciation editor, being full of Latin and French as well as Law Latin (the impure Latin of Renaissance lawyers) and Law French (the Norman French of medieval lawyers). Fortunately, Charles Harrington Elster of San Diego, an orthoepist with several excellent books to his credit, was willing to take on the task. He wisely guided us through the confusing mazes of Anglo-Latin, the only type of Latin with a continuous tradition in Anglo-American law. Even if some of the pronunciations strike you at first as odd, you can be sure that there is sound authority for them.

On translating Greek, Latin, and French, we had the benefit of many scholars' expertise. Professors Honoré and Walker supplied many of our etymologies. So did Edwin Carawan and Alison Parker, both of whom hold Ph.D.s in Classics; they examined all the maxims listed in Appendix A and supplied new translations and annotations for them.

As the manuscript deadline approached, I asked 30 judges, lawyers, and academics — mostly practicing lawyers — to read and comment on a batch of 150 pages of manuscript each. All of them generously agreed. I am enormously grateful to each of these learned lawyers:

Paul H. Anderson
Beverly Ray Burlingame
Jordan B. Cherrick
Charles Dewey Cole, Jr.
Dana Fabe
Stephen F. Fink
Neal Goldfarb
C. Kenneth Grosse
Molly H. Hatchell
Lynn N. Hughes
Harriet Lansing
Clyde D. Leland
James K. Logan
Margaret I. Lyle
Susan L. Karamanian
Joseph Kimble
Edward J. Kionka
Kent N. Mastores
Lann G. McIntyre
Paul G. McNamara
John W. McReynolds
Wayne Moore
James L. Nelson
R. Eric Nielsen
George C. Pratt
Carol Marie Stapleton
Scott Patrick Stolley
Randall M. Tietjen
Carla L. Wheeler
Richard C. Wydick

What I hadn't fully reckoned, when sending out batches of manuscript, was how challenging it would be to integrate more than 4,500 pages of lightly to heavily edited text. Evaluating and entering the edits into our database took three full-time lawyers the better part of six weeks. Fortunately, Beverly Ray Burlingame of Dallas, an immensely talented editor and prodigiously hard worker, took time off from her busy law practice to help complete the project. She made huge contributions during the final stage.

But hers was not the only extraordinary act on behalf of the cause. During the final months, Michael L. Atchley of Dallas, upon learning of our deadline, began sending us draft entries for several hundred terms that were missing from the sixth edition. His broad legal knowledge, as well as his natural aptitude for lexicography, showed in all his work. Then he generously read and commented on large stacks of manuscript.

Several lawyers made important contributions beyond those I've already described. Ann Taylor Schwing of Sacramento painstakingly culled through the 90 volumes of *Words and Phrases* for possible inclusions, and she read large portions of the manuscript. Elizabeth Sturdivant Kerr of Fort Worth contributed drafts of many entries for the letters E, H, and T, and she read much of the manuscript. Michelle D. Monse of Dallas contributed drafts of many L entries. Stephen W. Kotara of Dallas contributed to the letters F and G. Meanwhile, Terrence W. Kirk of Austin submitted many useful drafts of criminal-law definitions.

As the work progressed, I occasionally ran queries by scholars in various legal specialties, and they all responded helpfully. Many thanks to J.H. Baker, Peter Butt, Robert W. Hamilton, Herbert J. Hammond, Geoffrey C. Hazard, Jr., Gideon Kanner, Robert E. Keeton, John S. Lowe, Neil MacCormick, Joseph W. McKnight, Sir Robert Megarry, Richard A. Posner, William C. Powers, Jr., Thomas M. Reavley, Christoph Schreuer, Sir David Williams, and Charles Alan Wright. In a specialized review, Marc I. Steinberg commented on the business-law terms throughout the book.

Several universities provided significant assistance. While working on the project, I was an adjunct professor at Southern Methodist University School of Law. Meanwhile, I had stints as a visiting scholar at the University of Glasgow (July 1996), under the sponsorship of Professor David M. Walker; at the University of Cambridge (July 1997), under the sponsorship of Vice-Chancellor Emeritus Sir David Williams; and at the University of Salzburg (July 1998), under the sponsorship of Professors Wolfram Karl and Christoph Schreuer. I used the libraries at each of those universities to good advantage. I also made good use of the renowned Tarlton Law Library at the University of Texas (thanks to Professor Roy M. Mersky and his colleagues). And the entire *Black's* team constantly used the Underwood Law Library at Southern Methodist University (thanks to Professor Gail Daly and her colleagues). Also, I was able to carry out some research at the Langdell Law Library at Harvard University. To all of these libraries and their staffs, I am grateful for the cordial help they unfailingly gave.

Professor Mersky helped in another notable way: he and several of his colleagues — Beth Youngdale, Marlyn Robinson, and Monika Szakasits — generously verified the accuracy of our List of Works Cited (Appendix G).

Five research assistants — extraordinarily talented law students at Southern Methodist University School of Law — verified citations throughout the book. The editors are much indebted to Daniel Alexander, Julie Buffington, Nicole Schauf Gambrell, Peggy Glenn-Summitt, and Kenneth E. Shore. I especially thank Julie Buffington for organizing this team and ensuring the timely completion of a complex task.

Karen Magnuson of Portland, who has worked on several of my other books, courageously proofread the entire 3,500-page single-spaced manuscript as we worked through the final draft. Her talents as a proofreader are, in my experience, unmatched.

Many others contributed to the book in various ways: the late Alexander Black of Rochester began a reading program to gather illustrative quotations for our files; Thomas M. Fleming of Rochester continued that program for most of its duration; Caroline B. Garner of Dallas located historical legal terms in early dictionaries; E.N. Genovese of San Diego helped supply some foreign pronunciations; Tanya Glenn of Dallas typed the initial list of maxims; Michael Greenwald of Philadelphia helped on terms relating to the American Law Institute; and Tinh T. Nguyen of Dallas, with unusual enthusiasm, carried out the tedious but necessary task of checking cross-references and alphabetization.

While the project has been housed at LawProse, Inc. — as it will be through at least the next edition — Pan Garner, vice president of the company, has handled its business operations with energy, enthusiasm, and care. This included, over several years, working with me to acquire one of the most comprehensive collections of law-related dictionaries anywhere to be found. This collection has been invaluable in our work.

At the West Group, David J. Oliveiri, Doug Powell, John Perovich, and Brendan Bauer had the imagination and the forcefulness to make the book a reality. Their logistical support, not to mention their moral support, helped everyone involved in the project. In the production department, Kathy Walters worked wonders to produce the book within a tight deadline.

Tremendous amounts of talent and toil have gone into the making of this book. Yet the worries of early lexicographers have a haunting ring: this work might not prove as absolutely faultless as it has been my wish to make it. If that turns out to be so, as it inevitably will, I can only hope that readers will recognize the genuine merits residing in these pages.

Bryan A. Garner
Dallas, Texas
June 1999

Guide to the Dictionary

1. Alphabetization

All headwords, including abbreviations, are alphabetized letter by letter, not word by word. Spaces, apostrophes, hyphens, virgules, and the like do not count. For example:

co-
co
c/o
COA
coadjutor
coal note
Coase Theorem
co-assignee
coasting trade
coast water

Numbers in headwords are ordered as follows: spelled-out numbers are alphabetized letter by letter; numbers written as numerals are arranged in ascending numerical order. Thus:

Nineteenth Amendment
1933 Act
1934 Act
ninety-day letter
Ninth Amendment
nisi

Commas break the letter-by-letter alphabetization if they are backward-looking (e.g., *perpetuities, rule against*), but not if they are forward-looking (e.g., *right, title, and interest*).

2. Pronunciations

A word may have more than one acceptable pronunciation. When that is so, the preferred pronunciation appears first. Pronunciations are separated by *or* if each of them is standard among English-speaking lawyers. A pronunciation is introduced by *also* if it is either nonstandard or not as widely accepted as the first pronunciation. Thus:

lessor (**les**-or *or* le-**sor**).
voir dire (vwahr **deer** *also* vor **deer** *or* vor **dɪr**), *n.*

Boldface syllables receive primary stress. For variably pronounced syllables, often only the changed syllables are included. For example:

scienter (sɪ-**en**-tər *or* see-), *n.*

Brackets in a pronunciation indicate an optional sound, as in *fiduciary* (fi-**d**[**y**]**oo**-shee-er-ee).

For handy reference, the pronunciation guide is located inside the front cover.

3. Etymologies

The origins of most foreign words and phrases are given in brackets. By far the most frequent etymologies are "Latin" (i.e., the classical Latin used during the time of ancient Rome) and "Law Latin" (i.e., the Anglicized Latin formerly used in legal documents and proceedings). Essentially, the *Law Latin* tag corresponds to what some dictionaries call *Late Latin*, and others *Medieval Latin*. Other languages of origin are listed as well, including French, Law French, Old English, Greek, German, and Dutch.

4. Tags

Two types of tags appear. First, there are usage tags:

Hist. = historical; no longer current in law
Archaic = old-fashioned and declining in use
Rare = very infrequent in modern usage
Slang = very informal

Second, there are many subject-matter tags that identify the field of law that a particular term or sense belongs to (e.g., *Antitrust*, *Commercial law*, and *Wills & estates*). Two of these tags deserve special mention. *Roman law* indicates a term that can be traced back to the legal system of the ancient Romans. *Civil law* indicates a term that is used in modern civil-law systems, including much of the law in Louisiana.

5. Angle Brackets

Contextual illustrations of a headword are given in angle brackets:

> **taxable,** *adj.* **1.** Subject to taxation <interest earned on a checking account is taxable income>. **2.** (Of legal costs or fees) assessable <expert-witness fees are not taxable court costs>.

6. Bullets

Bullets are used to separate definitional information (before the bullet) from information that is not purely definitional (after the bullet), such as encyclopedic information or usage notes.

7. Cognate Forms

This dictionary lists corresponding parts of speech. For example, under the definition of *confirmation*, the corresponding verb (*confirm*) and adjective (*confirmatory*) are listed.

If a cognate form applies to only one sense of a headword, that form is denoted as follows:

construction, *n.* **1.** The act of building by combining or arranging parts or elements; the thing so built. **2.** The act or process of interpreting or explaining the sense or intention of something (usu. a statute, opinion, or instrument). — **construct** (for sense 1), *vb.* — **construe** (for sense 2), *vb.*

delegation, *n.* **1.** The act of entrusting another with authority or empowering another to act as an agent or representative <delegation of contractual duties>. **2.** A group of representatives <a large delegation from Texas>. — **delegate** (**del**-ə-gayt) (for sense 1), *vb.* — **delegable** (**del**-ə-gə-bəl) (for sense 1), *adj.*

8. Cross-references

a. See

The signal "See" is used in three ways:

(1) To indicate that the definition is at another location in the dictionary:

secondary boycott. See BOYCOTT.

assembly, right of. See RIGHT OF ASSEMBLY.

(2) To refer to closely related terms:

mercy. Compassionate treatment, as of criminal offenders or of those in distress; esp., imprisonment, rather than death, imposed as punishment for capital murder. See CLEMENCY.

investment banker. A person or institution that underwrites, sells, or assists in raising capital for businesses, esp. for new issues of stocks or bonds; a trader at an investment bank. See *investment bank* under BANK.

(3) To refer to a synonymous subentry:

pure easement. See *easement appurtenant* under EASEMENT.

b. Cf.

"Cf." is used to refer to related but contrastable terms:

strategic alliance. A coalition formed by two or more persons in the same or complementary businesses to gain long-term financial, operational, and marketing advantages without jeopardizing competitive independence <through their strategic alliance, the manufacturer and distributor of a co-developed product shared development costs>. Cf. JOINT VENTURE; PARTNERSHIP.

testacy (**tes**-tə-see), *n.* The fact or condition of leaving a valid will at one's death. Cf. INTESTACY.

c. Also termed

The phrase "also termed" at the end of an entry signals a synonymous word or phrase. Variations on "also termed" include "also spelled," "also written," and "often shortened to."

d. Terms with multiple senses

If the cross-referenced term has multiple senses, the particular sense referred to is indicated in parentheses:

appropriation bill. See BILL (3).

common mistake. See *mutual mistake* (2) under MISTAKE.

9. Quotations

Quotations are set off in small type. Most quotations are included because they provide nuances that would otherwise not be available within the strict confines of a traditional definition. Older quotations show what scholars said about legal terminology at particular points in history. The editors have selected quotations on the basis of aptness, insight, and clarity. Please note that some of the older quotations might not fully reflect current law.

10. Subentries

Many terms in this dictionary are collected by topic. For example, the different types of contracts, such as *bilateral contract* and *gratuitous contract*, are defined under the main term *contract*. (Cross-references in B and G will refer readers who look up *bilateral contract* and *gratuitous contract* to *contract*.) If a term has more than one sense, then the corresponding subentries are placed under the appropriate sense of that term.

11. Typefaces

Most of the typefaces used in this dictionary are self-explanatory. For instance, all headwords and cognate forms are in boldface type and all subentries are italicized. As for headwords of foreign origin, those that are fully naturalized are in boldface Roman type, while those that are not fully naturalized are in boldface italics. Generally, small caps are used with "See" and "Cf." cross-references. Three other uses of small caps deserve special mention:

a. Small caps refer to a synonymous headword. In the following example, the small caps suggest that you review the definition at *contiguous* for more information:

adjoining (ə-**joyn**-ing), *adj*. Touching; sharing a common boundary; CONTIGUOUS. — **adjoin** (ə-**joyn**), *vb*. Cf. ADJACENT.

b. Small caps also refer to the predominant form when it may be phrased or spelled in more than one way. For example, the following uses of small caps direct you to the entries at *perjury* and *payor*:

> **false swearing.** See PERJURY.
>
> **payer.** See PAYOR.

c. Small caps also refer to the spelled-out form of abbreviations (the term is defined at the spelled-out headword, not the abbreviated form). For example:

> **FDIC.** *abbr*. FEDERAL DEPOSIT INSURANCE CORPORATION.
>
> **Federal Deposit Insurance Corporation.** An independent governmental agency that insures bank deposits up to a statutory amount per depositor at each participating bank. ● The insurance fund is financed by a premium paid by the participating banks. — Abbr. FDIC.

List of Abbreviations

abbr.	=	abbreviated as; abbreviation for
adj.	=	adjective
adv.	=	adverb
BrE	=	British English
ca.	=	circa
cap.	=	capitalized
cf.	=	(*confer*) compare with
ch.	=	chapter
conj.	=	conjunction
ed.	=	edition; editor
e.g.	=	(*exempli gratia*) for example
esp.	=	especially
et seq.	=	(*et sequentes*) and those (pages or sections) that follow
fr.	=	from; derived from
id.	=	(*idem*) in the same work
i.e.	=	(*id est*) that is
l.c.	=	lowercase
n.	=	noun; note
no.	=	number
¶	=	paragraph
pl.	=	plural
pp.	=	pages
p.pl.	=	past participle
prep.	=	preposition
prob.	=	probably
pt.	=	part
repr.	=	reprinted
rev.	=	revised by; revision
§	=	section
sing.	=	singular
specif.	=	specifically
usu.	=	usually
vb.	=	verb

a. **1.** (*usu. cap. & often ital.*) A hypothetical person <A deeds Blackacre to B>. **2.** [Latin] From; by; in; on; of; at. **3.** [Law Latin] With. **4.** [Law French] Of; at; to; for; in; with. **5.** *Securities.* A letter used in a newspaper stock-transaction table to indicate that a cash payment in addition to regular dividends was paid during the year. **6.** *Securities.* A letter used in a newspaper mutual-fund transaction table to indicate a yield that may include capital gains and losses as well as current interest. **7.** (*cap.*) *Securities.* A letter used in a newspaper corporate earnings report to identify the American Stock Exchange as the primary market of a firm's common stock. **8.** (*cap.*) *Securities.* An above-average grade given to a debt obligation by a rating agency. • The grades, as ranked by Standard & Poor's, range from AAA (highest) down to C. The equivalent standards from Moody's are Aaa, Aa, A, Baa, and so on down to C. **9.** *Marine insurance.* A rating assigned in *Lloyd's Register of Shipping* to ships considered to be in first-class condition. **10.** *abbr.* ADVERSUS. **11.** (*cap.*) *Hist.* A scarlet letter worn as punishment by a person convicted of adultery. **12.** *Roman law.* An abbreviation for *absolvo* written on wooden tablets by criminal-court judges to indicate a vote for acquittal. **13.** *Roman law.* An abbreviation for *antiquo* ("for the old law") written on wooden tablets by the participants in a popular assembly to indicate a vote against a proposed bill.

AAA. *abbr.* **1.** AMERICAN ARBITRATION ASSOCIATION. **2.** AMERICAN ACCOUNTING ASSOCIATION. **3.** AMERICAN ACADEMY OF ACTUARIES. **4.** AGRICULTURAL ADJUSTMENT ACT. **5.** See *accumulated-adjustments account* under ACCOUNT.

A.A.C. *abbr.* ANNO ANTE CHRISTUM.

A.A.C.N. *abbr.* ANNO ANTE CHRISTUM NATUM.

AALS. *abbr.* ASSOCIATION OF AMERICAN LAW SCHOOLS.

a aver et tener (ay **ay**-vər [*or* ah **ah**-vər] et **ten**-ər). [Law French] To have and to hold. See HABENDUM CLAUSE.

AB. See *able-bodied seaman* under SEAMAN.

ab, *prep.* [Latin] From; by; of.

ABA. *abbr.* **1.** AMERICAN BAR ASSOCIATION. **2.** AMERICAN BANKERS ASSOCIATION.

abacinate (ə-**bas**-ə-nayt), *vb.* To blind (a person) by placing a red-hot iron or metal plate in front of the eyes.

abaction (ab-**ak**-shən). See ABIGEATUS.

ab actis (ab **ak**-tis), *n.* [Latin "in relation to proceedings"] *Roman law.* An officer responsible for public records (*acta*), registers, journals, or minutes; a court clerk; a notary.

abactor (ab-**ak**-tər *or* -tor). See ABIGEUS.

ab agendo (ab ə-**jen**-doh), *adj.* [Latin] Unable to act; incapacitated for business or transactions of any kind.

abalienation (ab-**ayl**-yə-nay-shən), *n.* [fr. Latin *abalienare* "to alienate"] *Civil law.* The transfer of an interest or title in property; ALIENATION (2). • In Roman law, the term was *abalienatio* ("a perfect conveyance from one Roman citizen to another"), which was anglicized to *abalienation.* — **abalienate,** *vb.*

abamita (ə-**bam**-ə-tə). [Latin] *Civil law.* A great-great-great aunt.

abandoned property. See PROPERTY.

abandonee (ə-ban-də-**nee**). One to whom property rights are relinquished; one to whom something is formally or legally abandoned.

abandonment, *n.* **1.** The relinquishing of a right or interest with the intention of never again claiming it. • In the context of contracts for the sale of land, courts sometimes use the term *abandonment* as if it were synonymous with *rescission,* but the two should be distinguished. An abandonment is merely the acceptance by one party of the situation that a nonperforming party has caused. But a rescission due to a material breach by the other party is a termination or discharge of the contract for all purposes. **2.** *Family law.* The act of leaving a spouse or child willfully and without an intent to return. Cf. DESERTION.

> "The lines of distinction between abandonment and the many forms of child neglect are often not very clear so that failure to support or to care for a child may sometimes be characterized as abandonment and sometimes as neglect." Homer H. Clark, Jr., *The Law of Domestic Relations in the United States* § 20.6, at 895 (1988).

malicious abandonment. The desertion of a spouse without just cause. See *criminal desertion* under DESERTION.

voluntary abandonment. **1.** As a ground for divorce, a final departure without the consent of the other spouse, without sufficient reason, and without the intention to return. **2.** In the law of adoption, a natural parent's willful act or course of conduct that implies a conscious disregard of or indifference to a child, as if no parental obligation existed.

3. *Criminal law.* RENUNCIATION (2). **4.** *Bankruptcy.* A trustee's court-approved release of property that is burdensome or of inconsequential value to the estate, or the trustee's release of nonadministered property to the debtor when the case is closed. **5.** *Contracts.* RESCISSION (2). **6.** *Intellectual property.* Disuse of a trademark, copyright, or patent, with or without an intent to resume use, resulting in loss of the protected right. **7.** *Insurance.* An insured's relinquishing of damaged or lost property to the insurer as a constructive total loss. Cf. SALVAGE (2). — **abandon,** *vb.*

abandum (ə-**ban**-dəm), *n.* [Law Latin] *Hist.* A thing that has been forfeited. — Also spelled *abandun*; *abandonum.*

ab ante (ab **an**-tee), *adv.* [Latin] *Hist.* Before; beforehand; in advance. — Also termed *ab antecedente.*

ab antiquo (ab an-**tI**-kwoh), *adv.* [Law Latin] *Hist.* From ancient times; of old. — Also termed *ab antiqua.*

abarnare (ab-ahr-**nair**-ee), *vb.* [Law Latin] *Hist.* To detect or disclose a secret crime; to bring to judgment.

abatable nuisance. See NUISANCE.

abatamentum (ə-bay-tə-**men**-təm), *n.* [Law Latin] *Hist.* See ABATEMENT (5).

abatare (ab-ə-**tair**-ee), *vb.* [Law Latin] *Hist.* To abate.

abatement (ə-**bayt**-mənt), *n.* **1.** The act of eliminating or nullifying <abatement of a nuisance> <abatement of a writ>. **2.** The suspension or defeat of a pending action for a reason unrelated to the merits of the claim <the defendant sought abatement of the suit because of misnomer>. See *plea in abatement* under PLEA.

> "Although the term 'abatement' is sometimes used loosely as a substitute for 'stay of proceedings,' the two may be distinguished on several grounds. For example, when grounds for abatement of an action exist, the abatement of the action is a matter of right, but a stay is granted in the court's discretion. And in proper circumstances a court may stay a proceeding pending the outcome of another proceeding although a strict plea in abatement could not be sustained." 1 Am. Jur. 2d *Abatement, Survival, and Revival* § 3 (1994).

3. The act of lessening or moderating; diminution in amount or degree <abatement of the debt>. **4.** The reduction of a legacy, general or specific, as a result of the estate's being insufficient to pay all debts and legacies <the abatement of legacies resulted from the estate's insolvency>. **5.** *Archaic.* The act of thrusting oneself tortiously into real estate after the owner dies and before the legal heir enters <abatement of freehold>. — Also termed (in sense 5) *abatamentum.* — **abate,** *vb.* — **abatable,** *adj.*

abatement clause. A lease provision that releases the tenant from the rent obligation when an act of God precludes occupancy.

abator (ə-**bay**-tər *or* -tor). **1.** A person who eliminates a nuisance. See ABATEMENT (1). **2.** *Hist.* A person who tortiously intrudes on an heir's freehold before the heir takes possession. See ABATEMENT (5).

abatuda (ab-ə-**t[y]oo**-də), *n.* [fr. Law Latin *abatudus* "debased"] *Hist.* A thing diminished, such as money reduced in value by clipping (*moneta abatuda*).

abavia (ə-**bay**-vee-ə), *n.* [Latin] *Civil law.* A great-great-great grandmother.

abavunculus (ab-ə-**vəng**-kyə-ləs), *n.* [Latin] *Civil law.* A great-great-great uncle. — Also termed *avunculus maximus.*

abavus (**ab**-ə-vəs), *n.* [Latin] *Civil law.* A great-great grandfather.

abbacy (**ab**-ə-see). *Eccles. law.* An abbot's jurisdiction or term of tenure.

abbess (**ab**-is). *Eccles. law.* A female spiritual superior of a convent. Cf. ABBOT.

abbey (**ab**-ee). *Eccles. law.* A monastery governed by an abbot, or a convent governed by an abbess.

abbey land. (*usu pl.*) *Hist.* Real property held by an abbey in mortmain and therefore exempt from tithes. See MORTMAIN.

abbot (**ab**-ət). *Eccles. law.* A spiritual superior or governor of an abbey. Cf. ABBESS.

abbreviated term sheet. See TERM SHEET.

Abbreviatio Placitorum (ə-bree-vee-**ay**-shee-oh plas-i-**tor**-əm), *n.* [Law Latin "summary of the pleas"] *Hist.* An abstract of pleadings culled from the rolls of the *Curia Regis*, Parliament, and common-law courts from the 12th to 14th centuries, compiled in the 17th century, printed in 1811, attributed to Arthur Agarde, Deputy Chamberlain of the Exchequer, and other keepers of the records. Cf. YEAR BOOKS.

abbreviator. 1. One who abbreviates, abridges, or shortens. **2.** *Eccles. law.* An officer in the court of Rome appointed as assistant to the vice-chancellor for drawing up the Pope's briefs and reducing petitions, when granted, into proper form to be converted into papal bulls.

abbroachment (ə-**brohch**-mənt), *n. Hist.* The act of forestalling the market by buying wholesale merchandise to sell at retail as the only vendor. — Also spelled *abbrochment*; *abbrochement*. — **abbroach,** *vb.*

ABC test. The rule that an employee is not entitled to unemployment insurance benefits if the employee (A) is free from the control of the employer, (B) works away from the employer's place of business, and (C) is engaged in an established trade. • The name derives from the A, B, and C commonly used in designating the three parts of the test.

ABC transaction. *Oil & gas.* A sale of a working interest from an owner (A) to an operator (B) in return for a cash payment and the right to another (usu. larger) payment when the well produces, followed by A's sale of the right to the production payment to a corporation (C), which pays A in cash borrowed from a lender on C's pledge of the production payment. • Thus A receives cash taxed at capital-gains rates, and B pays part of the purchase price with nontaxable production income. The tax advantages of this transaction were eliminated by the Tax Reform Act of 1969.

abdication (ab-di-**kay**-shən), *n.* The act of renouncing or abandoning privileges or duties, esp. those connected with high office <Edward VIII's abdication of the Crown in 1936> <the court's abdication of its judicial responsibility>. — **abdicate** (**ab**-di-kayt), *vb.* — **abdicable** (**ab**-di-kə-bəl), *adj.* — **abdicator** (**ab**-di-kay-tər), *n.*

abditory (**ab**-di-tor-ee), *n.* [Law Latin *abditorium* "box, receptacle"] A repository used to hide and preserve goods or money. — Also termed *abditorium* (ab-di-**tor**-ee-əm).

abduction (ab-**dək**-shən), *n.* **1.** The act of leading someone away by force or fraudulent persuasion. • Some jurisdictions have various elements added to this basic definition, such as that the abductor must have the intent to marry or defile the person, that the abductee must be an underage child, or that the abductor must have the intent to subject the abductee to concubinage or prostitution. **2.** *Archaic.* At common law, the crime of taking away a female person without her consent by use of persuasion, fraud, or violence, for the purpose of marriage, prostitution, or illicit sex. — **abduct,** *vb.* — **abductor,** *n.* — **abductee,** *n.* See KIDNAPPING.

> "There was no such crime as abduction known to the English common law, but a statute [3 Hen. 7, ch. 2 (1487)], passed a few years before Columbus discovered America, created a felony which is the forerunner of all the present statutes on abduction." Rollin M. Perkins & Ronald N. Boyce, *Criminal Law* 183 (3d ed. 1982).

abearance (ə-**bair**-ənts), *n. Archaic.* Behavior; conduct.

> "The other species of recognizance, with sureties, is for the *good abearance*, or *good behaviour*. This includes security for the peace . . . ." 4 William Blackstone, *Commentaries on the Laws of England* 253 (1769).

ab epistolis (ab ee-**pis**-tə-lis), *n.* [Latin] *Hist.* An officer who maintained the correspondence (*epistolae*) for a superior; a secretary.

aberrant behavior (a-**ber**-ənt). A single act of unplanned or thoughtless criminal behavior. • Many courts have held that aberrant behavior justifies a downward departure — that is, a more lenient sentence — under the federal sentencing guidelines, based on a comment in the introduction to the *Guidelines Manual* to the effect that the guidelines do not deal with single acts of aberrant behavior. *U.S. Sentencing Guidelines Manual*, ch. 1, pt. A, ¶ 4.

abesse (ab-**es**-ee), *vb.* [Law Latin] *Roman & civil law.* To be absent; to be away from a place where one is supposed to be (as before a court). Cf. ADESSE.

abet (ə-**bet**), *vb.* **1.** To encourage and assist (someone), esp. in the commission of a crime <abet a known felon>. **2.** To support (a crime) by active assistance <abet a burglary>. — **abetment,** *n.* See AID AND ABET. Cf. INCITE.

abettator (ab-ə-**tay**-tər), *n.* [Law Latin] *Archaic.* See ABETTOR.

abettor. A person who encourages or assists in the commission of a crime. — Also spelled *abetter.* — Also termed *principal in the second degree*; (archaically) *abettator.*

ab extra (ab **ek**-strə), *adv.* [Latin] From outside; extra; beyond.

abeyance (ə-**bay**-ənts), *n.* **1.** Temporary inactivity; suspension. **2.** *Property.* A lapse in succession during which no person is vested with title. — **abeyant,** *adj.*

> "Abeyance, from the French *bayer*, to expect, is that which is in expectation, remembrance, and intendment of law. By a principle of law, in every land there is a fee simple in somebody, or else it is in *abeyance*; that is, though for the present it be in no man, yet it is in expectancy belonging to him that is next to enjoy the land." 1 Richard Burn, *A New Law Dictionary* 4 (1792).

abiaticus (ab-ee-**ay**-tə-kəs), *n.* [Law Latin "descended from a grandfather"] *Hist.* A grandson in the male line; a son's son. — Also spelled *aviaticus.*

abide, *vb.* **1.** To tolerate or withstand <the widow found it difficult to abide the pain of losing her husband>. **2.** To obey <try to abide the doctor's order to quit smoking>. **3.** To await <the death-row prisoners abide execution>. **4.** To perform or execute (an order or judgment) <the trial court abided the appellate court's order>. **5.** To stay or dwell <the right to abide in any of the 50 states>.

abide by, *vb.* To act in accordance with or in conformity to.

abiding conviction. See CONVICTION.

abigeatus (ə-bij-ee-**ay**-təs), *n.* [Latin] *Roman law.* The act of stealing cattle by driving them away (*abigere*). • This was known in the later civil law as *abaction.*

abigeus (ə-**bij**-ee-əs), *n.* [Latin] *Roman law.* One who steals cattle, esp. in large numbers; a cattle rustler. • This was known in the later civil law as an *abactor.*

ability. The capacity to perform an act or service; esp., the power to carry out a legal act <ability to enter into a contract>.

present ability. The actual, immediate power to do something (esp. to commit a crime).

ab inconvenienti (ab in-kən-vee-nee-**en**-tɪ), *adv.* [Law Latin] From hardship or inconvenience. See *argumentum ab inconvenienti* under ARGUMENTUM.

ab initio (ab i-**nish**-ee-oh), *adv.* [Latin] From the beginning <the injunction was valid *ab initio*>. Cf. IN INITIO.

ab intestato (ab in-tes-**tay**-toh), *adv.* [Latin] By intestacy <succession *ab intestato* is often treated as being necessary because of the neglect or misfortune of the deceased proprietor>. Cf. EX TESTAMENTO.

ab invito (ab in-**vɪ**-toh), *adv.* [Latin] By or from an unwilling party; against one's will <a transfer *ab invito*>. Cf. IN INVITUM.

ab irato (ab ɪ-**ray**-toh), *adv.* [Latin] By one who is angry. • This phrase usu. refers to a gift or devise made adversely to an heir's interests, out of anger. An action to set aside this type of conveyance was known at common law as an action *ab irato.*

abishering. See MISKERING.

abjudge (ab-**jəj**), *vb. Archaic.* To take away or remove (something) by judicial decision. Cf. ADJUDGE.

> "As a result of the trial a very solemn judgment is pronounced. The land is adjudged to the one party and his heirs, and abjudged (*abiudicata*) from the other party and his heirs for ever." 2 Frederick Pollock & Frederic W. Maitland, *The History of English Law Before the Time of Edward I* 63 (2d ed. 1899).

abjudicatio (ab-joo-di-**kay**-shee-oh), *n.* [Law Latin] The act of depriving a person of a thing by judicial decision.

abjuration (ab-juu-**ray**-shən), *n.* A renouncing by oath.

abjuration of the realm. An oath taken to leave the realm forever.

oath of abjuration. English law. An oath renouncing all right of descendants of a pretender to the Crown.

abjure (ab-**joor**), *vb.* **1.** To renounce formally or on oath <abjure one's citizenship>. **2.** To avoid or abstain from <abjure one's civic duties>. — **abjuratory** (ab-**joor**-ə-tor-ee), *adj.*

ablative fact. See *divestitive fact* under FACT.

able-bodied seaman. See SEAMAN.

ablegate (**ab**-lə-gayt), *n.* A papal envoy on a special mission, such as carrying a newly appointed cardinal's insignia of office.

able seaman. See *able-bodied seaman* under SEAMAN.

able to work. *Labor law.* (Of a worker) released from medical care and capable of employment; esp., not qualified to receive unemployment benefits on grounds of illness or injury.

ablocation (ab-loh-**kay**-shən). *Archaic.* The leasing of property for money. Cf. LOCATIO.

abmatertera (ab-mə-**tər**-tər-ə), *n.* [Latin] *Civil law.* A great-great-great aunt. See MATERTERA MAXIMA.

abnepos (ab-**nep**-ahs *or* -ohs), *n.* [Latin] *Civil law.* A great-great grandson; the grandson of a grandson or granddaughter.

abneptis (ab-**nep**-tis), *n.* [Latin] *Civil law.* A great-great granddaughter; the granddaughter of a grandson or granddaughter.

abnormal law. The law as it applies to persons who are under legal disabilities such as infancy, alienage, insanity, criminality, and (formerly) coverture.

abnormally dangerous activity. An undertaking that cannot be performed safely even if reasonable care is used while performing it, and for which the actor may face strict liability for any harm caused; esp., an activity (such as dynamiting) for which the actor is held strictly liable because the activity (1) involves the risk of serious harm to persons or property, (2) cannot be performed without this risk, regardless of the precautions taken, and (3) does not ordinarily occur in the community. • Under the *Restatement (Second) of Torts*, determining whether an activity is abnormally dangerous includes analyzing whether there is a high degree of risk of harm, whether any harm caused will be substantial, whether the exercise of reasonable care will eliminate the risk, whether the activity is a matter of common usage, whether the activity is appropriate to the place in which it occurs, and whether the activity's value to society outweighs its dangerousness. Restatement (Second) of Torts § 520 (1977). — Also termed *ultrahazardous activity.* See *strict liability* under LIABILITY.

abode. A home; a fixed place of residence. See DOMICILE.

abogado (ah-boh-**gah**-thoh), *n.* [Spanish] *Spanish law.* An advocate; a lawyer.

ab olim (ab **oh**-lim), *adj.* [Law Latin] Of old.

abolish, *vb.* To annul or destroy, esp. an ongoing practice or thing.

abolition. 1. The act of abolishing. **2.** The state of being annulled or abrogated. **3.** (*usu. cap.*) The legal termination of slavery in the United States. **4.** *Civil law.* A sovereign's remission of punishment for a crime.

abominable and detestable crime against nature. See SODOMY.

a bon droit (ay *or* a bawn **drwah**), *adv.* [Law French] With good reason; justly; rightfully.

aboriginal cost. See COST (1).

aboriginal title. See INDIAN TITLE.

abortee (ə-bor-**tee**). A woman who undergoes an abortion.

abortifacient (ə-bor-tə-**fay**-shənt), *n.* A drug, article, or other thing designed or intended for producing an abortion. — **abortifacient,** *adj.*

abortion, *n.* **1.** The spontaneous or artificially induced expulsion of an embryo or fetus. • In *Roe v. Wade*, the Supreme Court first recognized a woman's right to choose to end her pregnancy as a privacy right stemming from the Due Process Clause of the 14th Amendment. 410 U.S. 113, 93 S.Ct. 1409 (1973). **2.**

Archaic. At common law, the misdemeanor of causing a miscarriage or premature delivery of a fetus by means of any instrument, medicine, drug, or other means. • Many American states made this a statutory felony until the *Roe v. Wade* decision. — Also termed *procuring an abortion.* — **abort,** *vb.* — **abortionist,** *n.*

> "The word 'abortion,' in the dictionary sense, means no more than the expulsion of a fetus before it is capable of living. In this sense it is a synonym of 'miscarriage.' With respect to human beings, however, it has long been used to refer to an intentionally-induced miscarriage as distinguished from one resulting naturally or by accident. There has been some tendency to use the word to mean a criminal miscarriage, and there would be distinct advantages in assigning this meaning to it; but there are so many references to lawful abortion or justification for abortion that it is necessary to speak of 'criminal abortion' or the 'crime of abortion' to emphasize the element of culpability." Rollin M. Perkins & Ronald N. Boyce, *Criminal Law* 186–87 (3d ed. 1982).

therapeutic abortion. An abortion carried out for medical reasons.

> "Until recently it was common to speak of 'therapeutic abortion.' The literal meaning of the term is an abortion induced for medical reasons, but it was commonly understood to mean one for the purpose of saving the mother's life . . . ." Rollin M. Perkins & Ronald N. Boyce, *Criminal Law* 193 (3d ed. 1982).

aboutissement (a-boo-tees-**mahn**), *n.* [Law French] An abuttal or abutment.

above, *adv.* In a higher court <the court above>. Cf. BELOW.

above-mentioned, *adj.* See AFORESAID.

above-stated, *adj.* See AFORESAID.

above-the-line, *adj.* (Of a deduction) taken after calculating gross income and before calculating adjusted gross income. • Examples of above-the-line deductions are IRA contributions and moving expenses. Formerly, individual tax returns had a dark line above which these deductions were written. Cf. BELOW-THE-LINE.

abpatruus (ab-**pa**-troo-əs), *n.* [Latin] *Roman & civil law.* A great-great-great uncle. — Also termed *patruus maximus.*

abridge, *vb.* **1.** To reduce or diminish <abridge one's civil liberties>. **2.** To condense (as a book or other writing) <the author abridged the treatise before final publication>. — **abridgment,** *n.*

abridgment. *Hist.* A legal digest or encyclopedia.

abridgment of damages. The right of a court to reduce the damages in certain cases. Cf. REMITTITUR.

abroad, *adv.* Outside a country; esp., other than in a forum country.

abrogate (**ab**-rə-gayt), *vb.* To abolish (a law or custom) by formal or authoritative action; to annul or repeal. — **abrogation,** *n.* Cf. OBROGATE.

ABS. See *able-bodied seaman* under SEAMAN.

abscond (ab-**skond**), *vb.* To depart secretly or suddenly, esp. to avoid service of process; to conceal oneself. — **abscondence** (ab-**skon**-dənts), *n.*

absconding debtor. See DEBTOR.

absence, *n.* **1.** The state of being away from one's usual place of residence. **2.** A failure to appear when expected.

absente (ab-**sen**-tee). [Latin] In the absence of. • This term formerly appeared in law reports to note the absence of a judge <the court, *absente* Ellis, J., was unanimous>.

absentee, *n.* **1.** A person who is away from his or her usual residence; a person who is absent. **2.** A person who is not present where expected.

absentee, *adj.* Having the characteristics of an absentee <absentee voter>.

absentee, *adv.* In an absentee manner <Debby voted absentee>.

absentee ballot. See BALLOT (3).

absentee landlord. See LANDLORD.

absentee management. See *absentee landlord* under LANDLORD.

absentee voting. See VOTING.

absente reo (ab-**sen**-tee **ree**-oh). [Latin] The defendant being absent.

absoile (ab-**soyl**), *vb.* See ASSOIL.

absolute, *adj.* **1.** Free from restriction, qualification, or condition <absolute ownership>. **2.** Conclusive and not liable to revision <absolute delivery>. **3.** Unrestrained in the exercise of governmental power <absolute monarchy>.

absolute assignment. See ASSIGNMENT (2).

absolute auction. See *auction without reserve* under AUCTION.

absolute-bar rule. The principle that, when a creditor sells collateral without giving reasonable notice to the debtor, the creditor may not obtain a deficiency judgment for any amount of the debt that is not satisfied by the sale.

absolute contraband. See CONTRABAND.

absolute conveyance. See CONVEYANCE.

absolute covenant. See COVENANT (1).

absolute deed. See DEED.

absolute defense. See *real defense* under DEFENSE (4).

absolute delivery. See DELIVERY.

absolute disparity. *Constitutional law.* The difference between the percentage of a group in the general population and the percentage of that group in the pool of prospective jurors on a venire. • For example, if African–Americans make up 12% of a county's population and 8% of the potential jurors on a venire, the absolute disparity of African–American veniremembers is 4%. The reason for calculating the disparity is to analyze a claim that the jury was not impartial because the venire from which it was chosen did not represent a fair cross-section of the jurisdiction's population. Some courts criticize the absolute-disparity analysis, favoring instead the comparative-disparity analysis, in the belief that the absolute-disparity analysis understates the deviation. See FAIR-CROSS-SECTION REQUIREMENT; DUREN TEST; STATISTICAL-DECISION THEORY. Cf. COMPARATIVE DISPARITY.

absolute duty. See DUTY (1).

absolute estate. See ESTATE.

absolute gift. See *inter vivos gift* under GIFT.

absolute guaranty. See GUARANTY.

absolute immunity. See IMMUNITY (1).

absolute interest. See INTEREST (2).

absolute law. A supposed law of nature thought to be unchanging in principle, although circumstances may vary the way in which it is applied. See NATURAL LAW.

absolute legacy. See LEGACY.

absolute liability. See *strict liability* under LIABILITY.

absolute majority. See MAJORITY.

absolute martial law. See MARTIAL LAW.

absolute nuisance. See NUISANCE.

absolute nullity. See NULLITY.

absolute obligation. See OBLIGATION.

absolute pardon. See PARDON.

absolute pollution exclusion. See *pollution exclusion* under EXCLUSION (3).

absolute presumption. See *conclusive presumption* under PRESUMPTION.

absolute-priority rule. *Bankruptcy.* The rule that a confirmable reorganization plan must provide for full payment to a class of dissenting unsecured creditors before a junior class of claimants will be allowed to receive or retain anything under the plan. • Some jurisdictions recognize an exception to this rule when a junior class member, usu. a partner or shareholder of the debtor, contributes new capital in exchange for an interest in the debtor. 11 USCA § 1129(b)(2)(B)(ii).

absolute privilege. See PRIVILEGE (1).

absolute property. See PROPERTY.

absolute right. See RIGHT.

absolute sale. See SALE.

absolute title. See TITLE (2).

absolute veto. See VETO.

absolution (ab-sə-**loo**-shən). **1.** Release from a penalty; the act of absolving. **2.** *Civil law.* An acquittal of a criminal charge. **3.** *Eccles. law.* Official forgiveness of sins.

absolutism (**ab**-sə-loo-tiz-əm), *n.* In politics, the atmosphere surrounding a dictator whose power has no restrictions, checks, or balances; the belief in such a dictator. — **absolutist** (**ab**-sə-loo-tist), *adj.* & *n.*

absolve (ab- *or* əb-**zolv**), *vb.* **1.** To release from an obligation, debt, or responsibility. **2.** To free from the penalties for misconduct.

absorbable risk. See RISK.

absorption, *n.* **1.** The act or process of including or incorporating a thing into something else; esp., the application of rights guaranteed by the U.S. Constitution to actions by the states. **2.** *Int'l law.* The merger of one nation into another, whether voluntarily or by subjugation. **3.** *Labor law.* In a post-merger collective-bargaining agreement, a provision allowing seniority for union members in the resulting entity. **4.** *Real estate.* The rate at which property will be leased or sold on the market at a given time. **5.** *Commercial law.* A sales method by which a manufacturer pays the seller's freight costs, which the manufacturer accounts for before quoting the seller a price. — Also termed (in sense 5) *freight absorption.* — **absorb,** *vb.*

absque (**abs**-kwee), *adv.* [Latin] Without.

absque aliquo inde reddendo (**abs**-kwee **al**-ə-kwoh **in**-dee ri-**den**-doh), *adv.* [Law Latin] *Hist.* Without rendering anything therefrom. • This phrase appeared in royal grants in which no tenure was reserved.

absque consideratione curiae (**abs**-kwee kən-sid-ə-ray-shee-**oh**-nee **kyoor**-ee-ee), *adv.* [Law Latin] Without the consideration of the court; without judgment.

absque dubio (**abs**-kwee **d[y]oo**-bee-oh), *adv.* [Latin] Without doubt.

absque hoc (**abs**-kwee **hok**), *adv.* [Latin] *Archaic.* Without this. • The phrase was formerly used in common-law pleading to introduce the denial of allegations. — Also termed *sans ce que.* See TRAVERSE.

absque impetitione vasti (**abs**-kwee im-pə-tish-ee-**oh**-nee **vas**-tɪ), *adv.* [Law Latin] *Hist.* See WITHOUT IMPEACHMENT OF WASTE.

absque tali causa (**abs**-kwee **tay**-lɪ **kaw**-zə), *adv.* [Law Latin] Without such cause. • In common-law pleading, this was part of the larger phrase *de injuria sua propria, absque tali causa* ("of his own wrong, without such cause") appearing in a reply that a trespass plaintiff made to counter a defendant's claim of excuse. In an assault case, for example, if a defendant pleaded that he had struck the plaintiff in self-defense, the plaintiff could reply that the defendant was guilty of his own wrong committed without such cause as alleged. Cf. DE INJURIA.

abstain, *vb.* **1.** To refrain from doing something. **2.** (Of a federal court) to refrain from exercising jurisdiction over a matter.

abstention. **1.** The act of withholding or keeping back (something or oneself). **2.** A federal court's relinquishment of jurisdiction when necessary to avoid needless conflict with a state's administration of its own affairs. **3.** The legal principle underlying such a relinquishment of jurisdiction. Cf. COMITY.

Burford abstention. A federal court's refusal to review a state court's decision in cases involving a complex regulatory scheme and sensitive areas of state concern. *Burford v. Sun Oil Co.,* 319 U.S. 315, 63 S.Ct. 1098 (1943).

Colorado River abstention. A federal court's decision to abstain while relevant and parallel state-court proceedings are underway. *Colorado River Water Conservation Dist. v. United States,* 424 U.S. 800, 96 S.Ct. 1236 (1976).

equitable abstention. A federal court's refraining from interfering with a state administrative agency's decision on a local matter when the aggrieved party has adequate relief in the state courts.

permissive abstention. Abstention that a bankruptcy court can, but need not, exercise in a dispute that relates to the bankruptcy estate but that can be litigated, or is being litigated, in another forum. • In deciding whether to abstain, the bankruptcy court must consider (1) the degree to which state law governs the case, (2) the appropriateness of the procedure to be followed in the other forum, (3) the remoteness of the dispute to the issues in the bankruptcy case, and (4) the presence of nondebtor parties in the dispute. 28 USCA § 1334(c)(1).

Pullman abstention. A federal court's decision to abstain so that state courts will have an opportunity to settle an underlying state-law question whose resolution may avert the need to decide a federal constitutional question. *Railroad Comm'n v. Pullman Co.*, 312 U.S. 496, 61 S.Ct. 643 (1941).

Thibodaux abstention (**tib**-ə-doh). A federal court's decision to abstain so that state courts can decide difficult issues of public importance that, if decided by the federal court, could result in unnecessary friction between state and federal authorities. *Louisiana Power & Light Co. v. City of Thibodaux*, 360 U.S. 25, 79 S.Ct. 1070 (1959).

Younger abstention. **1.** A federal court's decision not to interfere with an ongoing state criminal proceeding by issuing an injunction or granting declaratory relief, unless the prosecution has been brought in bad faith or merely as harassment. *Younger v. Harris*, 401 U.S. 37, 91 S.Ct. 746 (1971). — Also termed *equitable-restraint doctrine*. **2.** By extension, a federal court's decision not to interfere with a state-court civil proceeding used to enforce the criminal law, as to abate an obscene nuisance. See OUR FEDERALISM.

abstinence (**ab**-stə-nənts). The practice of refraining completely from indulgence in some act; esp., the practice of not having sex or of not consuming alcoholic beverages.

abstract, *n.* A concise statement of a text, esp. of a legal document; a summary. See ABSTRACT OF JUDGMENT; ABSTRACT OF TITLE.

abstract compromis. See *general compromis* under COMPROMIS.

abstracter. See ABSTRACTOR.

abstraction (ab- *or* əb-**strak**-shən), *n.* **1.** The mental process of considering something without reference to a concrete instance <jurisprudence is largely the abstraction of many legal particulars>. **2.** A theoretical idea not applied to any particular instance <utopia in any form is an abstraction>. **3.** The summarizing and recording of a legal instrument in public records <abstraction of the judgment in Tarrant County>. **4.** The act of taking with the intent to injure or defraud <the abstraction of funds was made possible by the forged signature on the check>. — **abstract** (ab-**strakt**), *vb.*

abstraction-filtration-comparison test. *Copyright.* A judicially created test for determining whether substantial similarity exists between the nonliteral elements of two or more computer programs. • Under this test, a program is first dissected according to its varying levels of generality ("abstractions test"). Then each level of abstraction is examined to filter out program elements that are unprotectable, such as ideas, processes, facts, public-domain information, merger material, scenes a faire, and other unprotectable elements ("filtration test"). Finally, the remaining protectable elements are compared with the allegedly infringing program to determine whether substantial elements of the plaintiff's program have been misappropriated ("comparison test").

abstractions test. *Copyright.* A means of comparing copyrighted material with material that is claimed to infringe on the copyright, by examining whether the actual substance has been copied or whether the two works merely share the same abstract ideas. • The primary authority for the abstractions test is Judge Learned Hand's opinion in *Nichols v. Universal Pictures Corp.*, 45 F.2d 119 (2d Cir. 1930).

abstract of a fine. See NOTE OF A FINE.

abstract of conviction. A summary of the court's finding on an offense, esp. a moving violation.

abstract of judgment. A copy or summary of a judgment that, when filed with the appropriate public office, creates a lien on the judgment debtor's nonexempt property. See *judgment lien* under LIEN.

abstract of record. An abbreviated case history that is complete enough to show an appellate court that the questions presented for review have been preserved.

abstract of title. A concise statement, usu. prepared for a mortgagee or purchaser of real property, summarizing the history of a piece of land, including all conveyances, interests, liens, and encumbrances that affect title to the property. — Also termed *brief*.

good and merchantable abstract of title. An abstract of title showing clear, good, and marketable title, rather than showing only the history of the property. See *clear title*, *good title*, and *marketable title* under TITLE (2).

abstractor (ab- *or* əb-**strak**-tər). A person who prepares abstracts of title. — Also spelled *abstracter*.

abstract question. See HYPOTHETICAL QUESTION.

ab urbe condita (ab **ər**-bee **kon**-di-tə). [Latin] From the founding of the city (esp. Rome in 753 B.C.). • This term is sometimes used in abbreviated form in classical dates. For example, the date "23 A.U.C." means "23 years after the founding of Rome," or 730 B.C. — Abbr. A.U.C.

abuse (ə-**byoos**), *n.* **1.** A departure from legal or reasonable use; misuse. **2.** Physical or mental maltreatment.

abuse of the elderly. Physical or psychological abuse of an elderly person by a caretaker. • Examples include deprivation of food or medication, beatings, oral assaults, and isolation. — Also termed *elder abuse*.

carnal abuse. See *sexual abuse*.

child abuse. An intentional or neglectful physical or emotional injury imposed on a child, including sexual molestation. — Also termed *cruelty to a child*; *cruelty to children*. See BATTERED-CHILD SYNDROME.

elder abuse. See *abuse of the elderly*.

sexual abuse. **1.** An illegal sex act, esp. one performed against a minor by an adult. — Also termed *carnal abuse*. **2.** RAPE (2).

spousal abuse. Physical, sexual, or psychological abuse inflicted by one spouse on the other spouse. See BATTERED-WOMAN SYNDROME.

abuse (ə-**byooz**), *vb.* **1.** To depart from legal or reasonable use in dealing with (a person or thing); to misuse. **2.** To injure (a person) physically or mentally. **3.** To damage (a thing).

abuse excuse. *Criminal law.* The defense that a defendant is unable to tell right from wrong, having been physically or mentally abused as a child. • Like the traditional criminal-law excuse of insanity, the abuse excuse is asserted by a defendant in an effort to avoid all culpability for the crime charged.

abuse of discovery. See DISCOVERY ABUSE.

abuse of discretion. **1.** An adjudicator's failure to exercise sound, reasonable, and legal decision-making. **2.** An appellate court's standard for reviewing a decision that is asserted to be grossly unsound, unreasonable, or illegal. See DISCRETION.

abuse of process. The improper and tortious use of a legitimately issued court process to obtain a result that is either unlawful or beyond the process's scope. — Also termed *abuse of legal process*; *malicious abuse of process*; *malicious abuse of legal process*; *wrongful process*; *wrongful process of law*. Cf. MALICIOUS PROSECUTION.

abuse of rights. *Int'l law.* A country's exercise of a right either in a way that impedes the enjoyment by other countries of their own rights or for a purpose different from that for which the right was created (e.g., to harm another country).

abuse-of-rights doctrine. *Civil law.* The principle that a person may be liable for harm caused by doing something the person has a right to do, if the right (1) is exercised for the purpose or primary motive of causing harm, (2) is exercised without a serious and legitimate interest that is deserving of judicial protection, (3) is exercised against moral rules, good faith, or elementary fairness, or (4) is exercised for a purpose other than the one it was granted for.

abuse of the elderly. See ABUSE.

abuse-of-the-writ doctrine. *Criminal law.* The principle that a petition for a writ of habeas corpus may not raise claims that could have been, but were not, asserted in a previous petition.

abusive (ə-**byoo**-siv), *adj.* **1.** Characterized by wrongful or improper use <abusive discovery tactics>. **2.** (Of a person) that treats another badly <abusive parent>. — **abusively,** *adv.*

abut (ə-**bət**), *vb.* To join at a border or boundary; to share a common boundary with <the company's land in Arizona abuts the Navajo Indian reservation>. — **abutment** (ə-**bət**-mənt), *n.*

abuttals (ə-**bət**-əlz). Land boundaries; the boundary lines of a piece of land in relation to other contiguous lands. — Also termed (archaically) *buttals*.

abutter (ə-**bət**-ər). **1.** The owner of adjoining land; one whose property abuts another's.

> "The major right of [an abutter] is that of access to his property — a right of reasonable ingress and egress. He

"... is entitled to compensation for any substantial impairment of this reasonable access. The right normally includes the right to have, at some point, a driveway onto his premises. An abutter does *not* have the right to the continued flow of traffic in the same amount or pattern past his premises." Osborne M. Reynolds, Jr., *Handbook of Local Government Law* § 180, at 620 (1982).

2. Land that adjoins the land in question.

abutting foot. See FRONT FOOT.

a/c. *abbr.* ACCOUNT (1).

academic, *adj.* **1.** Of or relating to a school or a field of study; esp., of or relating to a field of study that is not vocational or commercial, such as the liberal arts <academic courses>. **2.** Theoretical; specif., not practical or immediately useful <academic question>.

academic freedom. The right (esp. of a university teacher) to speak freely about political or ideological issues without fear of loss of position or other reprisal.

academic lawyer. A law professor, usu. one who maintains a law practice on the side.

Académie de Droit International de La Haye. See HAGUE ACADEMY OF INTERNATIONAL LAW.

academy. **1.** An institution of higher learning. **2.** An association dedicated to the advancement of knowledge in a particular field, such as the American Academy of Matrimonial Lawyers. **3.** A private high school. **4.** (*cap.*) A garden near Athens where Plato taught; hence, the school of philosophy that he led.

a cancellando (ay kan-sə-**lan**-doh). [Law Latin] From canceling.

"It has its name of chancery, *cancellaria*, from the judge who presides here, the lord chancellor or *cancellarius*; who, Sir Edward Coke tells us, is so termed *a cancellando*, from cancelling the king's letters patents when granted contrary to law...." 3 William Blackstone, *Commentaries on the Laws of England* 46 (1768).

a cancellis (ay kan-**sel**-is), *n.* [Law Latin] *Hist.* A chancellor, so called because he performed the duties of office behind a *cancelli* ("lattice").

a cancellis curiae explodi (ay kan-**sel**-is **kyoor**-ee-I ek-**sploh**-dI). [Law Latin] *Hist.* To be expelled from the bar of the court.

a cause de cy (ay **kaw**-zə də **see**), *adv.* [Law French] For this reason.

accedas ad curiam (ak-**see**-dəs ad **kyoor**-ee-əm), *n.* [Law Latin "you are to go to the court"] *Hist.* An original writ for removing a replevin action to a royal court from either of two feudal courts — a court baron or a hundred court. • It is a *recordare facias loquelam* for replevin actions. See RECORDARE FACIAS LOQUELAM.

accede (ak-**seed**), *vb.* To consent or agree. — **accession,** *n.* — **accedence** (ak-**see**-dənts), *n.*

Accelerated Cost Recovery System. An accounting method that is used to calculate asset depreciation and that allows for the faster recovery of costs by assigning the asset a shorter useful life than was previously permitted under the Internal Revenue Code. • This system applies to property put into service from 1981 to 1986. It was replaced in 1986 by the Modified Accelerated Cost Recovery System. — Abbr. ACRS.

accelerated depreciation method. See DEPRECIATION METHOD.

accelerated remainder. See REMAINDER.

acceleration, *n.* **1.** The advancing of a loan agreement's maturity date so that payment of the entire debt is due immediately. **2.** The shortening of the time for vesting in possession of an expectant interest. — Also termed *acceleration of remainder*. **3.** *Property.* The hastening of an owner's time for enjoyment of an estate because of the failure of a preceding estate. **4.** *Securities.* The SEC's expediting of a registration statement's effective date so that the registrant bypasses the required 20-day waiting period. — **accelerate,** *vb.*

acceleration clause. A loan-agreement provision that requires the debtor to pay off the balance sooner than the due date if some specified event occurs, such as failure to pay an installment or to maintain insurance. Cf. INSECURITY CLAUSE.

acceleration of remainder. See ACCELERATION (2).

acceptance, *n.* **1.** An agreement, either by express act or by implication from conduct, to the terms of an offer so that a binding contract is formed. • If an acceptance modifies the terms or adds new ones, it generally operates as a counteroffer. Cf. OFFER.

acceptance by silence. Acceptance of an offer not by explicit words but through the lack of an offeree's response in circumstances in which the relationship between the offeror and the offeree justifies both the offeror's expectation of a reply and the offeror's reasonable conclusion that the lack of one signals acceptance. • Ordinarily, silence does not give rise to an acceptance of an offer, but this exception arises when the offeree has a duty to speak.

qualified acceptance. A conditional or partial acceptance that varies the original terms of an offer and operates as a counteroffer; esp., in negotiable instruments, an acceptor's variation of the terms of the instrument.

2. A buyer's assent that the goods are to be taken in performance of a contract for sale. • Under UCC § 2–606, a buyer's acceptance consists in (1) signifying to the seller that the goods are conforming ones or that the buyer will take them despite nonconformities, (2) not making an effective rejection, or (3) taking any action inconsistent with the seller's ownership. If the contract is for the sale of goods that are not identified when the contract is entered into, there is no acceptance until the buyer has had a reasonable time to examine the goods. But if the buyer deals with them as owner, as by reselling them, a court may find constructive acceptance.

> "Acceptance means communicated acceptance.... [It] must be something more than a mere mental assent." William R. Anson, *Principles of the Law of Contract* 34 (Arthur L. Corbin ed., 3d Am. ed. 1919). [But Corbin adds:] "This use of the word 'communicated' is open to some objection. To very many persons the word means that knowledge has been *received*. Frequently a contract is made even though the offeror has no such knowledge. In such case the acceptance is not 'communicated' and yet it consummates the contract." *Id.* n.2.

> "Acceptance of a conveyance or of a document containing a promise is a manifestation of assent to the terms thereof made, either before or after delivery, in accordance with any requirements imposed by the grantor or promisor. If the acceptance occurs before delivery and is not binding as an option contract, it is revocable until the moment of delivery." Restatement (Second) of Contracts § 106 (1981).

3. The formal receipt of and agreement to pay a negotiable instrument. **4.** A negotiable instrument, esp. a bill of exchange, that has been accepted for payment.

acceptance au besoin (oh bə-**zwan**). [French "in case of need"] An acceptance by one who has agreed to pay the draft in case the drawee fails to do so.

acceptance for honor. An acceptance or undertaking not by a party to the instrument, but by a third party, for the purpose of protecting the honor or credit of one of the parties, by which the third party agrees to pay the debt when it becomes due if the original drawee does not. • This type of acceptance inures to the benefit of all successors to the party for whose benefit it is made. — Also termed *acceptance supra protest*.

accommodation acceptance. The acceptance of an offer to buy goods for current or prompt shipment by shipping nonconforming goods after notifying the buyer that the shipment is intended as an accommodation. • This type of "acceptance" is not truly an acceptance under contract law, but operates instead as a counteroffer if the buyer is duly notified.

banker's acceptance. A bill of exchange drawn on and accepted by a commercial bank. • Banker's acceptances are often issued to finance the sale of goods in international trade. — Abbr. BA. — Also termed *bank acceptance*.

blank acceptance. Acceptance by a bill-of-exchange drawee before the bill is made, as indicated by the drawee's signature on the instrument.

conditional acceptance. An agreement to pay a draft on the occurrence or nonoccurrence of a particular event.

express acceptance. A written or oral expression indicating that the drawee has seen the instrument and does not dispute its sufficiency. • While a written acceptance is typically signified by the stamped or written word "accepted" or "presented" usu. on the instrument itself, an oral acceptance must be made directly to a drawer or holder who has waived the right to a written acceptance.

implied acceptance. An acceptance implied by a drawee whose actions indicate an intention to comply with the request of the drawer; conduct by the drawee from which the holder is justified in concluding that the drawee intends to accept the instrument.

special acceptance. An acceptance that departs from either the terms of a bill or the terms added to but not otherwise expressed in a bill. • An example is an acceptance of a draft as payable in a particular place even though the draft contains no such limitation.

trade acceptance. A bill of exchange for the amount of a specific purchase, drawn on and accepted by the buyer for payment at a specified time.

5. An insurer's agreement to issue a policy of insurance. — **accept,** *vb.*

> "And in some instances, insurance companies have even specified in the application forms that acceptance of an applicant's offer will not occur until the insurance policy is literally delivered to the applicant — that is, the insurer chooses to structure the arrangement so that acceptance is to be manifested by the physical delivery of the insurance policy to the applicant." Robert E. Keeton & Alan I. Widiss, *Insurance Law: A Guide to Fundamental Principles, Legal Doctrines, and Commercial Practices* § 2.1, at 39–40 (1988).

acceptance au besoin. See ACCEPTANCE (4).

acceptance by silence. See ACCEPTANCE (1).

acceptance company. See *sales finance company* under FINANCE COMPANY.

acceptance credit. See *time letter of credit* under LETTER OF CREDIT.

acceptance doctrine. *Construction law.* The principle that, once an owner accepts the work of a contractor, the contractor is not liable to third parties for an injury arising from the contractor's negligence in performing under the contract, unless the injury results from a hidden, imminently dangerous defect that the contractor knows about and the owner does not know about. — Also termed *accepted-work doctrine.*

acceptance for honor. See ACCEPTANCE (4).

acceptance-of-the-benefits rule. The doctrine that a party may not appeal a judgment after having voluntarily and intentionally received the relief provided by it.

acceptance sampling. The practice of examining only a few items from a shipment to determine the acceptability of the whole shipment.

acceptance supra protest. See *acceptance for honor* under ACCEPTANCE.

acceptare (ak-sep-**tair**-ee), *vb.* [Latin] *Civil law.* To accept or assent to, as a promise made by another.

accepted-work doctrine. See ACCEPTANCE DOCTRINE.

acceptilation (ak-sep-tə-**lay**-shən). *Civil law.* An oral release from an obligation even though payment has not been made in full; a complete discharge. Cf. APOCHA.

acceptor. A person or entity that accepts a negotiable instrument and agrees to be primarily responsible for its payment or performance.

acceptor supra protest. One who accepts a bill that has been protested, for the honor of the drawer or an indorser.

access, *n.* **1.** An opportunity or ability to enter, approach, pass to and from, or communicate with <access to the courts>. **2.** *Copyright.* An opportunity to view or copy a copyrighted work <the duplication of the error proved that the defendant had access>. — **access,** *vb.*

> "Since direct evidence of copying is rarely available, a plaintiff can rely upon circumstantial evidence to prove this essential element; the most important component of such circumstantial evidence to support a copyright infringement claim is proof of access. Evidence of access and substantial similarity create an inference of copying and establish a prima facie case of copying." 18 Am. Jur. 2d *Copyright and Literary Property* § 206 (1985).

multiple access. *Family law.* In a paternity suit, the defense that the mother had lovers other than the defendant around the time of conception.

access easement. See EASEMENT.

accession (ak-**sesh**-ən). **1.** The act of acceding or agreeing <the family's accession to the kidnapper's demands>. **2.** A coming into possession of a right or office <as promised, the state's budget was balanced within two years after the governor's accession>. **3.** *Int'l law.* The process by which a nation becomes a party to a treaty that has already been agreed on by other nations <Italy became a party to the nuclear-arms treaty by accession>. — Also termed *adherence*; *adhesion.* **4.** The acquisition of title to personal property by bestowing labor on a raw material to convert it to another thing <the owner's accession to the lumber produced from his land>. — Also termed (in Roman law) *accessio.* See ADJUNCTION (2).

> "*Accessio* is the combination of two chattels belonging to different persons into a single article: as when A's cloth is used to patch B's coat, or a vehicle let on hire-purchase has new accessories fitted to it." R.F.V. Heuston, *Salmond on the Law of Torts* 113 (17th ed. 1977).

5. A property owner's right to all that is added to the land, naturally or by labor, including land left by floods and improvements made by others <the newly poured concrete driveway became the homeowner's property by accession>. Cf. ANNEXATION. **6.** An improvement to existing personal property, such as new shafts on golf clubs.

"The problem of accessions arises infrequently, judging from reported cases, but an obvious instance of the difficulty arises where a motor vehicle is being financed by a secured party and the debtor in possession of necessity acquires a new engine or new tires for the vehicle. . . . If the seller of the engine or tires reserved a security interest at the time the goods were installed, the seller should prevail over the vehicle's secured party, with a right to remove the accessions. Conversely, if the sale were on open credit with no security interest reserved, or if the seller acquired a security interest after installation of the goods, then the financer of the vehicle should prevail." Ray D. Henson, *Handbook on Secured Transactions Under the Uniform Commercial Code* § 4–22, at 93 (2d ed. 1979).

7. ACCESSORYSHIP.

accessorial (ak-sə-**sor**-ee-əl), *adj.* **1.** (Of a promise) made for the purpose of strengthening another's credit <an accessorial pledge by way of guaranty>. — Also termed *accessory.* **2.** *Criminal law.* Of or relating to the accessory in a crime <accessorial guilt>.

accessorial obligation. See COLLATERAL OBLIGATION.

accessory (ak-**ses**-ə-ree), *n.* **1.** Something of secondary or subordinate importance. **2.** A person who aids or contributes in the commission of a crime. • An accessory is usu. liable only if the crime is a felony. — **accessory,** *adj.* — **accessoryship,** *n.* Cf. PRINCIPAL (2).

"In most jurisdictions, the common-law distinctions between principals and accessories have largely been abolished, although the pertinent statutes vary in form and substance. Conceptually, the common-law pattern remains the same: The person who aids, abets, commands, counsels, or otherwise encourages another to commit a crime is still regarded as a party to the underlying crime as at common law, even though the labels principal in the first degree, principal in the second degree, and accessory before the fact are no longer used, and even though it usually does not matter whether the aider and abettor is or is not present at the scene of the crime." 1 Charles E. Torcia, *Wharton's Criminal Law* § 35, at 202–03 (15th ed. 1993).

accessory after the fact. An accessory who knows that a crime has been committed and who helps the offender try to escape arrest or punishment. • The liability of such an accessory is still treated separately under most penal statutes. There are four requirements: (1) someone else must have committed a felony, and it must have been completed before the accessory's act; (2) the accessory must not be guilty as a principal; (3) the accessory must personally help the principal try to avoid the consequences of the felony; and (4) the accessory's assistance must be rendered with guilty knowledge. — Sometimes shortened to *accessory after.*

"At common law, an accessory after the fact is one who, knowing that a felony has been committed by another, receives, relieves, comforts, or assists the felon, or in any manner aids him to escape arrest or punishment. To be guilty as an accessory after the fact one must have known that a completed felony was committed, and that the person aided was the guilty party. The mere presence of the defendant at the scene of the crime will not preclude a conviction as an accessory after the fact, where the evidence shows the defendant became involved in the crime after its commission." 21 Am. Jur. 2d *Criminal Law* § 209, at 275–76 (1998).

accessory at the fact. See *principal in the second degree* under PRINCIPAL (2).

"A principal in the second degree is one by whom the actual perpetrator of the felony is aided and abetted at the very time when it is committed; for instance, a car-owner sitting beside the chauffeur who kills someone by over-fast driving, or a passenger on a clandestine joy-riding expedition which results in manslaughter; or a bigamist's second 'wife', if she *knows* he is committing bigamy. (In early law he was not ranked as a principal at all, but only as a third kind of accessory — the accessory *at* the fact.)" J.W. Cecil Turner, *Kenny's Outlines of Criminal Law* 86 (16th ed. 1952).

accessory before the fact. An accessory who assists or encourages another to commit a crime but who is not present when the offense is actually committed. • Most jurisdictions have abolished this category of accessory and instead treat such an offender as an accomplice. — Sometimes shortened to *accessory before.* See ACCOMPLICE.

"An accessory before the fact is a person who procures or advises one or more of the principals to commit the felony. This definition requires from him an instigation so active that a person who is merely shown to have acted as the stake-holder for a prize-fight, which ended fatally, would not be punishable as an accessory. The fact that a crime has been committed in a manner different from the mode which the accessory had advised will not excuse him from liability for it. Accordingly if *A* hires *B* to poison *C*, but *B* instead kills *C* by shooting him, *A* is none the less liable as accessory before the fact to *C*'s murder. But a man who has counselled a crime does not become liable as accessory if, instead of any form of the crime suggested, an entirely different offence is committed." J.W. Cecil Turner, *Kenny's Outlines of Criminal Law* 88 (16th ed. 1952).

accessory contract. See CONTRACT.

accessory obligation. See OBLIGATION.

accessory right. See RIGHT.

accessoryship. The status or fact of being an accessory. — Also termed (loosely) *accession.*

accessory use. See USE (1).

access to counsel. See RIGHT TO COUNSEL.

accident, *n.* **1.** An unintended and unforeseen injurious occurrence; something that does not occur in the usual course of events or that could not be reasonably anticipated. **2.** *Equity practice.* An unforeseen and injurious occurrence not attributable to mistake, neglect, or misconduct. — **accidental,** *adj.*

"The word 'accident,' in accident policies, means an event which takes place without one's foresight or expectation. A result, though unexpected, is not an accident; the means or cause must be accidental. Death resulting from voluntary physical exertions or from intentional acts of the insured is not accidental, nor is disease or death caused by the vicissitudes of climate or atmosphere the result of an accident; but where, in the act which precedes an injury, something unforeseen or unusual occurs which produces the injury, the injury results through accident." 1A John Alan Appleman & Jean Appleman, *Insurance Law and Practice* § 360, at 455 (rev. vol. 1981).

"Policies of liability insurance as well as property and personal injury insurance frequently limit coverage to losses that are caused by 'accident.' In attempting to accommodate the layman's understanding of the term, courts have broadly defined the word to mean an occurrence which is unforeseen, unexpected, extraordinary, either by virtue of the fact that it occurred at all, or because of the extent of the damage. An accident can be either a sudden happening or a slowly evolving process like the percolation of harmful substances through the ground. Qualification of a particular incident as an accident seems to depend on two criteria: 1. the degree of foreseeability, and 2. the state of mind of the actor in intending or not intending the result." John F. Dobbyn, *Insurance Law in a Nutshell* 128 (3d ed. 1996).

culpable accident. An accident due to negligence. • A culpable accident, unlike an unavoidable accident, is no defense except in those few cases in which wrongful intent is the exclusive and necessary basis for liability.

unavoidable accident. An accident that cannot be avoided because it is produced by an irresistible physical cause that cannot be prevented by human skill or reasonable foresight. • Examples include accidents resulting from lightning or storms, perils of the sea, inundations or earthquakes, or sudden illness or death. Unavoidable accident has been considered a means of avoiding both civil and criminal liability. — Also termed *inevitable accident*; *pure accident*; *unavoidable casualty.* Cf. ACT OF GOD.

"An unavoidable accident is an occurrence which was not intended and which, under all the circumstances, could not have been foreseen or prevented by the exercise of reasonable precautions. That is, an accident is considered unavoidable or inevitable at law if it was not proximately caused by the negligence of any party to the action, or to the accident." W. Page Keeton et al., *The Law of Torts* § 29, at 162 (5th ed. 1984).

accidental-death benefit. An insurance-policy provision that allows for a payment (often double the face amount of the policy) if the insured dies as a result of some mishap or sudden external force. — Abbr. ADB.

accidental injury. See INJURY.

accidental killing. Homicide resulting from a lawful act performed in a lawful manner under a reasonable belief that no harm would be possible. — Also termed *death by misadventure*; *homicide by misadventure*; *killing by misadventure*; *homicide per infortunium.* See *justifiable homicide* under HOMICIDE. Cf. *involuntary manslaughter* under MANSLAUGHTER.

accidental stranding. See STRANDING.

accident and health insurance. See *health insurance* under INSURANCE.

accident insurance. See INSURANCE.

accident policy. See INSURANCE POLICY.

accidere (ak-**sid**-ər-ee), *vb.* [Latin] *Civil law.* **1.** To fall down. **2.** By extension, to befall or happen to.

accipere (ak-**sip**-ər-ee), *vb.* [Latin] *Civil law.* To receive; esp., to take under a will.

accipitare (ak-sip-ə-**tair**-ee), *vb.* [Law Latin] *Hist.* To pay (a lord) in order to become a vassal; esp., to pay relief upon succeeding to an estate.

accola (**ak**-ə-lə), *n.* [Latin "person living nearby"] **1.** *Roman law.* A person who inhabits or occupies land near a certain place, such as one who dwells near a river. **2.** *Hist.* An agricultural tenant; a tenant of a manor.

accomenda (ak-ə-**men**-də). *Hist. Maritime law.* A contract between a cargo owner and a shipmaster whereby the parties agree to sell the cargo and divide the profits (after deducting the owner's costs). • This contract actually consists of two agreements: a *mandatum*, by which the owner gives the shipmaster the power to dispose of the cargo, and a partnership contract, by which the parties divide any profits arising from the sale. See MANDATE (5).

accommodated party. A party for whose benefit an accommodation party signs and incurs liability. Cf. ACCOMMODATION PARTY.

accommodation, *n.* **1.** A loan or other financial favor. **2.** The act of signing an accommodation paper as surety for another. See ACCOMMODATION PAPER. **3.** The act or an instance of making a change or provision for someone or something; an adaptation or adjustment. See PUBLIC ACCOMMODATION; REASONABLE ACCOMMODATION.

accommodation acceptance. See ACCEPTANCE (4).

accommodation bill. See ACCOMMODATION PAPER.

accommodation indorsement. See INDORSEMENT.

accommodation indorser. See INDORSER.

accommodation land. See LAND.

accommodation line. *Insurance.* One or more policies that an insurer issues to retain the business of a valued agent, broker, or customer, even though the risk would not be accepted under the insurer's usual standards.

accommodation loan. See LOAN.

accommodation maker. See MAKER.

accommodation note. See NOTE (1).

accommodation paper. A negotiable instrument that one party cosigns, without receiving any consideration, as surety for another party who remains primarily liable. • An accommodation paper is typically used when the cosigner is more creditworthy than the principal debtor. — Also termed *accommodation bill*; *accommodation note.*

accommodation party. A person who, without recompense or other benefit, signs a negotiable instrument for the purpose of being a surety for another party (called the *accommodated party*) to the instrument. • The accommodation party can sign in any capacity (i.e., as maker, drawer, acceptor, or indorser). An accommodation party is liable to all parties except the accommodated party, who impliedly agrees to pay the note or draft and to indemnify the accommodation party for all losses incurred in having to pay it. See SURETY.

accommodation surety. See *voluntary surety* under SURETY.

accommodatum (ə-kom-ə-**day**-təm), *n.* See COMMODATUM.

accompany, *vb.* To go along with (another); to attend. • In automobile-accident cases, an unlicensed driver is not considered accompanied by a licensed driver unless the latter is close enough to supervise and help the former.

accomplice (ə-**kom**-plis). **1.** A person who is in any way concerned with another in the commission of a crime, whether as a principal in the first or second degree or as an accessory. • Although the definition includes an accessory before the fact, not all authorities include an accessory after the fact.

> "There is some authority for using the word 'accomplice' to include all principals and all accessories, but the preferred usage is to include all principals and accessories before the fact, but to exclude accessories after the fact. If this limitation is adopted, the word 'accomplice' will embrace all perpetrators, abettors and inciters." Rollin M. Perkins & Ronald N. Boyce, *Criminal Law* 727 (3d ed. 1982).

> "A person is an 'accomplice' of another in committing a crime if, with the intent to promote or facilitate the commission of the crime, he solicits, requests, or commands the other person to commit it, or aids the other person in planning or committing it." 1 Charles E. Torcia, *Wharton's Criminal Law* § 38, at 220 (15th ed. 1993).

2. A person who knowingly, voluntarily, and intentionally unites with the principal offender in committing a crime and thereby becomes punishable for it. See ACCESSORY. Cf. PRINCIPAL (2).

> "By definition an accomplice must be a person who acts with the purpose of promoting or facilitating the commission of the substantive offense for which he is charged as an accomplice. State v. White, N.J. 1984, 484 A.2d 691, 98 N.J. 122." Model Penal Code § 2.06 annot. (1997).

accomplice liability. See LIABILITY.

accomplice witness. See WITNESS.

accord, *n.* **1.** An amicable arrangement between parties, esp. between peoples or nations; COMPACT; TREATY. **2.** An offer to give or to accept a stipulated performance in the future to satisfy an obligor's existing duty, together with an acceptance of that offer. • The performance becomes what is known as a *satisfaction.* — Also termed *executory accord*; *accord executory.* See ACCORD AND SATISFACTION; SATISFACTION. Cf. NOVATION.

"An accord is a contract under which an obligee promises to accept a stated performance in satisfaction of the obligor's existing duty. Performance of the accord discharges the original duty." Restatement (Second) of Contracts § 281(1) (1981).

"The term *executory accord* is sometimes used to underscore the point that the accord itself does not discharge the duty. It also reflects an historical anachronism, now generally rejected, under which an unperformed accord was not a defense to an action on the underlying duty." E. Allan Farnsworth, *Contracts* § 4.24, at 285 n.8 (1982).

3. A signal used in a legal citation to introduce a case clearly supporting a proposition for which another case is being quoted directly.

accord, *vb.* **1.** To furnish or grant, esp. what is suitable or proper <accord the litigants a stay of costs pending appeal>. **2.** To agree <they accord in their opinions>.

accord and satisfaction. An agreement to substitute for an existing debt some alternative form of discharging that debt, coupled with the actual discharge of the debt by the substituted performance. • The new agreement is called the *accord*, and the discharge is called the *satisfaction*. Cf. NOVATION; SETTLEMENT.

" 'Accord and satisfaction' means an agreement between the parties that something shall be given to, or done for, the person who has the right of action, in satisfaction of the cause of action. There must be not only agreement ('accord') but also consideration ('satisfaction'). Such an arrangement is really one of substituted performance." 1 E.W. Chance, *Principles of Mercantile Law* 101 (P.W. French ed., 13th ed. 1950).

accordant (ə-**kor**-dənt), *adj.* In agreement <accordant with these principles>.

accouchement (ə-**koosh**-mənt *or* ak-oosh-**mawn**). [French] Childbirth.

account, *n.* **1.** A detailed statement of the debits and credits between parties to a contract or to a fiduciary relationship; a reckoning of monetary dealings <the trustee balanced the account at the end of each month>. • In wills and estates, an account is a brief financial statement of the manner in which an executor or administrator has performed the official duties of collecting the estate's assets and paying those who are entitled. An account charges the executor or administrator with the value of the estate as shown by the inventory, plus any increase, and credits the executor with expenses and costs, duly authorized disbursements, and the executor's commission. — Abbr. acct.; a/c. **2.** A course of business dealings or other relations for which records must be kept <open a brokerage account>. **3.** ACCOUNTING (3) <the principal filed an action for account against his agent>. — Also spelled (archaically) *accompt*.

"The action of account lies where one has received goods or money for another in a fiduciary capacity, to ascertain and recover the balance due. It can only be maintained where there is such a relationship between the parties, as to raise an obligation to account, and where the amount due is uncertain and unliquidated." Benjamin J. Shipman, *Handbook of Common-Law Pleading* § 56, at 144 (Henry Winthrop Ballantine ed., 3d ed. 1923).

4. ACCOUNTING (4) <the contractor filed an action for account against the nonpaying customer>. **5.** A statement by which someone seeks to explain an event <Fred's account of the holdup differed significantly from Martha's>.

account in trust. An account established by an individual to hold the account's assets in trust for someone else.

account payable. (*usu. pl.*) An account reflecting a balance owed to a creditor; a debt owed by an enterprise in the normal course of business dealing. — Often shortened to *payable*. — Also termed *note payable*. Pl. *accounts payable*.

account receivable. (*usu. pl.*) An account reflecting a balance owed by a debtor; a debt owed by a customer to an enterprise for goods or services. — Often shortened to *receivable*. — Also termed *note receivable*. Pl. *accounts receivable*.

account rendered. An account produced by the creditor and presented for the debtor's examination and acceptance.

account settled. An account with a paid balance.

account stated. **1.** A balance that parties to a transaction or settlement agree on, either expressly or by implication. • The phrase also refers to the agreement itself or to the assent giving rise to the agreement.

"An account stated is a manifestation of assent by debtor and creditor to a stated sum as an accurate computation of an amount due the creditor." Restatement (Second) of Contracts § 282(1) (1981).

"If a creditor and a debtor wish to compromise or liquidate a disputed or unliquidated debt, they may do so by either a substituted contract or an accord. If, however, their agreement is in the nature of a computation, it is called an *account stated*. An account stated, then, is a manifestation of assent by both parties to the stated sum as an accurate computation of the debt." E. Allan Farnsworth, *Contracts* § 4.24, at 286 (1982).

2. A plaintiff's claim in a suit for such a balance. **3.** *Equity practice.* A defendant's plea in response to an action for an accounting. • The defendant states that the balance due on the statement of the account has been discharged and that the defendant holds the plaintiff's release. — Also termed *stated account.*

accumulated-adjustments account. *Tax.* An item on the books of an S corporation (usu. an equity item on the corporation's balance sheet) to account for taxable-income items passed through to shareholders, such as accumulated earnings — earned before the corporation converted from a C corporation to an S corporation — that would have been distributed as a dividend to the shareholders if the corporation had remained a C corporation. • One of the theories underlying the accumulated-adjustments account is that the shareholders should not be permitted to avoid dividend-tax treatment on a corporation's accumulated earnings just because the corporation converts from C status to S status. IRC (26 USCA) § 1368(e)(1). — Abbr. AAA.

adjunct account. An account that accumulates additions to another account.

assigned account. A pledge of an account receivable to a bank or factor as security for a loan.

bank account. A deposit or credit account with a bank, such as a demand, time, savings, or passbook account. UCC § 4–104(a).

blocked account. An account at a bank or other financial institution, access to which has been restricted either by the government or by an authorized person. • An account may be blocked for a variety of reasons, as when hostilities erupt between two countries and each blocks access to the other's accounts. — Also termed *frozen account.*

book account. A detailed statement of debits and credits giving a history of an enterprise's business transactions.

capital account. An account on a partnership's balance sheet representing a partner's share of the partnership capital.

charge account. See CHARGE ACCOUNT.

closed account. An account that no further credits or debits may be added to but that remains open for adjustment or setoff.

community account. An account consisting of commingled and community funds. See COMMUNITY PROPERTY.

contra account (**kon**-trə). An account that serves to reduce the gross valuation of an asset.

custodial account. An account opened on behalf of someone else, such as one opened by a parent for a minor child.

deposit account. A demand, time, savings, passbook, or similar account maintained with a bank, savings-and-loan association, credit union, or like organization, other than investment property or an account evidenced by an instrument. UCC § 9–102(a)(20). — Abbr. D.A.

escrow account. **1.** A bank account, generally held in the name of the depositor and an escrow agent, that is returnable to the depositor or paid to a third person on the fulfillment of specified conditions. — Also termed *escrow deposit.* See ESCROW. **2.** See *impound account.*

frozen account. See *blocked account.*

impound account. An account of accumulated funds held by a lender for payment of taxes, insurance, or other periodic debts against real property. — Also termed *escrow*; *escrow account*; *reserve account.* See ESCROW.

intermediate account. An account filed by an executor, administrator, or guardian after the initial account and before the final account.

joint account. A bank or brokerage account opened by two or more people, by which each party has a present right to all funds in the account and, upon the death of one party, the survivors become the owners of the account, with no right of the deceased party's heirs or devisees to share in it. — Abbr. JA. — Also termed *joint-and-survivorship account.*

lien account. A statement of claims that fairly informs the owner and public of the amount and nature of a lien.

long account. An account involving numerous items or complex transactions in an equitable action, usu. referred to a master or commissioner.

margin account. A brokerage account that allows an investor to buy or sell securities on credit, with the securities usu. serving as collateral for the broker's loan.

multiple-party account. An account that has more than one owner with a current interest in the account. • Multiple-party accounts include joint accounts, payable-on-death (P.O.D.) accounts, and trust accounts. Uniform Probate Code § 6–201(5).

mutual account. An account showing mutual transactions between parties, as by showing debits and credits on both sides of the account.

> "[E]ach party to a mutual account occupies both a debtor and creditor relation with regard to the other party. A mutual account arises where there are mutual dealings,

and the account is allowed to run with a view to an ultimate adjustment of the balance. In order to establish a mutual account, it is not enough that the parties to the account have cross demands or cross open accounts; there must be an actual mutual agreement, express or implied, that the claims are to be set off against each other." 1 Am. Jur. 2d *Accounts and Accounting* § 6, at 564 (1994).

negotiable-order-of-withdrawal account. See *NOW account.*

nominal account (**nahm**-ə-nəl). An income-statement account that is closed into surplus at the end of the year when the books are balanced.

NOW account (now). An interest-bearing savings account on which the holder may write checks. — Also termed *negotiable-order-of-withdrawal account.*

offset account. One of two accounts that balance against each other and cancel each other out when the books are closed.

open account. **1.** An unpaid or unsettled account. **2.** An account that is left open for ongoing debit and credit entries and that has a fluctuating balance until either party finds it convenient to settle and close, at which time there is a single liability.

pledged account. A mortgagor's account pledged to a lender in return for a loan bearing interest at a below-market rate.

profit-and-loss account. A transfer account of all income and expense accounts, closed into the retained earnings of a corporation or the capital account of a partnership.

real account. An account that records assets and liabilities rather than receipts and payments.

reserve account. See *impound account.*

revolving charge account. See *revolving credit* under CREDIT (4).

running account. An open, unsettled account that exhibits the reciprocal demands between the parties.

sequestered account. An account (such as a joint bank account) that a court has ordered to be separated, frozen, and impounded.

share-draft account. An account that a member maintains at a credit union and that can be drawn on through the use of share drafts payable to third parties. • A share-draft account operates much like a checking account operates at a bank. — Also termed *share account.*

accountable, *adj.* Responsible; answerable <the company was held accountable for the employee's negligence>. — **accountability,** *n.*

accountable receipt. See RECEIPT.

accountant. 1. A person authorized under applicable law to practice public accounting; a person whose business is to keep books or accounts, to perform financial audits, to design and control accounting systems, and to give tax advice. • For some purposes, the term includes a professional accounting association, a corporation, and a partnership, if they are so authorized.

certified public accountant. An accountant who has satisfied the statutory and administrative requirements to be registered or licensed as a public accountant. — Abbr. CPA.

2. A defendant in an action of account.

accountant-client privilege. See PRIVILEGE (3).

accountant's lien. See LIEN.

account book. A journal in which a business's transactions are recorded. See SHOP BOOKS.

account debtor. See DEBTOR.

account executive. See STOCKBROKER.

account for. 1. To furnish a good reason or convincing explanation for; to explain the cause of. **2.** To render a reckoning of (funds held, esp. in trust). **3.** To answer for (conduct).

accounting. 1. The act or a system of establishing or settling financial accounts; esp., the process of recording transactions in the financial records of a business and periodically extracting, sorting, and summarizing the recorded transactions to produce a set of financial records. — Also termed *financial accounting.* **2.** A rendition of an account, either voluntarily or by court order. • The term frequently refers to the report of all items of property, income, and expenses prepared by a personal representative, trustee, or guardian and given to heirs, beneficiaries, and the probate court. **3.** A legal action to compel a defendant to account for and pay over money owed to the plaintiff but held by the defendant (often the plaintiff's agent); ACCOUNTING FOR PROFITS. — Also termed *account render*; *account.* **4.** More broadly, an action for the recovery of money for services performed, property sold and delivered, money loaned, or damages for the nonperformance of simple contracts. • Such an action is available when the rights of parties will be adequately protected by the payment of money. — Also termed *action on account*; *account*; *action of book debt*. **5.** *Commercial law*. An equitable proceeding for a complete settlement of all partnership affairs, usu. in connection with partner misconduct or with a winding up. See WINDING UP. **6.** *Secured transactions*. A record that (1) is authenticated by a secured party, (2) indicates the aggregate unpaid secured obligation as of a date no more than 35 days before or after the date of the record, and (3) identifies the components of the obligations in reasonable detail. UCC § 9–102(a)(2).

accounting for profits. An action for equitable relief against a person in a fiduciary relationship to recover profits taken in a breach of the relationship. — Often shortened to *accounting*.

> "The term accounting, or accounting for profits, is used in several ways. In its most important meaning, it is a restitutionary remedy based upon avoiding unjust enrichment. In this sense it reaches monies owed by a fiduciary or other wrongdoer, including profits produced by property which in equity and good conscience belonged to the plaintiff. It resembles a constructive trust in that tracing may be used to reach profits. But even if tracing fails, the plaintiff may recover a judgment for the profits due from use of his property." Dan B. Dobbs, *Law of Remedies* § 4.3(5), at 408 (2d ed. 1993).

accounting method. A system for determining income and expenses for tax purposes.

accrual accounting method (ə-**kroo**-əl). An accounting method that records entries of debits and credits when the liability arises, rather than when the income or expense is received or disbursed.

capitalization accounting method. A method of determining an asset's present value by discounting its stream of expected future benefits at an appropriate rate.

cash-basis accounting method. An accounting method that considers only cash actually received as income and cash actually paid out as an expense.

completed-contract accounting method. A method of reporting profit or loss on certain long-term contracts by recognizing gross income and expenses in the tax year that the contract is completed.

cost accounting method. The practice of recording the value of assets in terms of their cost. — Also termed *cost accounting*.

direct charge-off accounting method. A system of accounting by which a deduction for bad debts is allowed when an account has become partially or completely worthless.

equity accounting method. A method of accounting for long-term investment in common stock based on acquisition cost, investor income, net losses, and dividends.

fair-value accounting method. The valuation of assets at present actual or market value.

installment accounting method. A method by which a taxpayer can spread the recognition of gains from a sale of property over the payment period by computing the gross-profit percentage from the sale and applying it to each payment.

percentage-of-completion method. An accounting method in which revenue is recognized gradually during the completion of the subject matter of the contract.

physical-inventory accounting method. A method of counting a company's goods at the close of an accounting period.

purchase accounting method. A method of accounting for mergers whereby the total value paid or exchanged for the acquired firm's assets is recorded on the acquiring firm's books, and any difference between the fair market value of the assets acquired and the purchase price is recorded as goodwill.

accounting period. A regular span of time used for accounting purposes; esp., a period used by a taxpayer in determining income and related tax liability.

Accounting Research Bulletin. A publication containing accounting practices recommended by the American Institute of Certified Public Accountants. — Abbr. ARB.

Accounting Series Release. A bulletin providing the Securities and Exchange Commission's requirements for accounting and auditing procedures to be followed in reports filed with that agency. — Abbr. ASR.

account in trust. See ACCOUNT.

account party. The customer in a letter-of-credit transaction. — Also termed *applicant*.

account payable. See ACCOUNT.

account receivable. See ACCOUNT.

account render. See ACCOUNTING (3).

account rendered. See ACCOUNT.

account representative. See STOCKBROKER.

account settled. See ACCOUNT.

accounts-receivable insurance. See INSURANCE.

account stated. See ACCOUNT.

account statement. See STATEMENT OF ACCOUNT.

accouple, *vb. Archaic.* To unite; to marry.

accredit (ə-**kred**-it), *vb.* **1.** To give official authorization or status to. **2.** To recognize (a school) as having sufficient academic standards to qualify graduates for higher education or for professional practice. **3.** *Int'l law.* To send (a person) with credentials as an envoy. — **accreditation** (ə-kred-i-**tay**-shən), *n.*

accredited investor. An investor treated under the Securities Act of 1933 as being knowledgeable and sophisticated about financial matters, esp. because of the investor's large net worth. • In a securities offering that is exempt from registration, an accredited investor (which can be a person or an entity) is not entitled to protection under the Act's disclosure provisions, although the investor does keep its remedies for fraud.

accredited law school. See LAW SCHOOL.

accredited representative. See REPRESENTATIVE.

accredulitare (ə-kred-yə-lə-**tair**-ee), *vb.* [Law Latin] *Hist.* To purge an offense by an oath.

accretion (ə-**kree**-shən). **1.** The gradual accumulation of land by natural forces, esp. as alluvium is added to land situated on the bank of a river or on the seashore. Cf. ALLUVION; AVULSION (2); DELICTION; EROSION. **2.** *Civil law.* The right of heirs or legatees to unite their shares of the estate with the portion of any coheirs or legatees who do not accept their portion, fail to comply with a condition, or die before the testator. **3.** Any increase in trust property other than increases ordinarily considered as income.

accroach (ə-**krohch**), *vb.* To exercise power without authority; to usurp. — **accroachment** (ə-**krohch**-mənt), *n.*

accrocher (a-kroh-**shay**), *vb.* [Law French] **1.** ACCROACH. **2.** To delay.

accrocher un procès (a-kroh-**shay** ən proh-**say**). [French] To stay the proceedings in a suit.

accrual, clause of. See CLAUSE OF ACCRUAL.

accrual accounting method. See ACCOUNTING METHOD.

accrual bond. See BOND (3).

accrue (ə-**kroo**), *vb.* **1.** To come into existence as an enforceable claim or right; to arise <the plaintiff's cause of action for silicosis did not accrue until the plaintiff knew or had reason to know of the disease>.

> "The term 'accrue' in the context of a cause of action means to arrive, to commence, to come into existence, or to become a present enforceable demand or right. The time of accrual of a cause of action is a question of fact." 2 Ann Taylor Schwing, *California Affirmative Defenses* § 25:3, at 17–18 (2d ed. 1996).

2. To accumulate periodically <the savings-account interest accrues monthly>. — **accrual,** *n.*

accrued asset. See ASSET.

accrued compensation. See COMPENSATION.

accrued depreciation. See *accumulated depreciation* under DEPRECIATION.

accrued dividend. See *accumulated dividend* under DIVIDEND.

accrued expense. See EXPENSE.

accrued income. See INCOME.

accrued interest. See INTEREST (3).

accrued liability. See LIABILITY.

accrued right. See RIGHT.

accrued salary. See SALARY.

accrued tax. See TAX.

accruer. See CLAUSE OF ACCRUAL.

accruing costs. See COST (3).

acct. *abbr.* ACCOUNT (1).

accumulated-adjustments account. See ACCOUNT.

accumulated depreciation. See DEPRECIATION.

accumulated dividend. See DIVIDEND.

accumulated-earnings credit. See CREDIT (7).

accumulated-earnings tax. See TAX.

accumulated income. See INCOME.

accumulated legacy. See LEGACY.

accumulated profit. See PROFIT.

accumulated surplus. See SURPLUS.

accumulated taxable income. See INCOME.

accumulation, *n.* The increase of a thing by repeated additions to it; esp., the increase of a fund by the repeated addition of the income that it creates. — **accumulate,** *vb.*

accumulations, rule against. A rule rendering void any accumulation of income beyond the period of perpetuities.

accumulation trust. See TRUST.

accumulative (ə-**kyoo**-myə-lay-tiv *or* -lə-tiv), *adj.* Increasing by successive addition; cumulative.

accumulative damages. See DAMAGES.

accumulative dividend. See *cumulative dividend* under DIVIDEND.

accumulative judgment. See JUDGMENT.

accumulative legacy. See LEGACY.

accumulative sentences. See *consecutive sentences* under SENTENCE.

accusation, *n.* **1.** A formal charge of criminal wrongdoing. • The accusation is usu. presented to a court or magistrate having jurisdiction to inquire into the alleged crime. **2.** An informal statement that a person has engaged in an illegal or immoral act.

> ***malicious accusation.*** An accusation against another for an improper purpose and without probable cause. See MALICIOUS PROSECUTION.

accusator (ak-yoo-**say**-tər), *n.* [Latin] *Roman law.* A complainant in a criminal prosecution.

accusatorial system. See ADVERSARY SYSTEM.

accusatory (ə-**kyoo**-zə-tor-ee), *adj.* Accusing; having the nature of an accusation.

accusatory body. A body, such as a grand jury, charged with the duty to hear evidence and determine whether a person should be charged with a crime.

accusatory instrument. See CHARGING INSTRUMENT.

accusatory part. The section of an indictment in which the offense is named.

accusatory pleading. See PLEADING (1).

accusatory procedure. See ADVERSARY SYSTEM.

accusatory stage. The point in a criminal proceeding when the suspect's right to counsel attaches. • This occurs usu. after arrest and once interrogation begins.

accuse, *vb.* To charge (a person) judicially or publicly with an offense; to make an accusation against <she accused him of the crime> <he was accused as an accomplice>.

accused, *n.* **1.** A person who has been blamed for wrongdoing <many people believed that the accused was incapable of committing such a brutal act>. **2.** Specifically, a person who has been subjected to actual restraints on liberty through an arrest or a person against whom a formal indictment or information has been returned <although Jordan was being vigorously questioned, he did not actually become an accused until the officer arrested him>.

accuser. A person who accuses another of a crime.

accusing jury. See GRAND JURY.

a ce (a **sə**), *adv.* [Law French] For this purpose.

a cel jour (ə sel **zhoor**), *adv.* [Law French] At this day.

ac etiam (ak **ee**-shee-əm *or* **esh**-ee-əm). [Law Latin] **1.** And also. • These words introduced a genuine claim in a pleading in a common-law case in which a fictitious claim had to be alleged to give the court jurisdiction. In other words, the phrase *ac etiam* directed the court to the real cause of action. — Also spelled *acetiam.*

> "[T]o remedy this inconvenience, the officers of the king's bench devised a method of adding what is called a clause of *ac etiam* to the usual complaint of trespass; the bill of Middlesex commanding the defendant to be brought in to answer the plaintiff of a plea of trespass, *and also* to a bill of debt: the complaint of trespass giving cognizance to the court, and that of debt authorizing the arrest." 3 William Blackstone, *Commentaries on the Laws of England* 288 (1768).

2. *Common-law pleading.* The clause that introduced the real allegation after a fictitious allegation of trespass. — Also termed (in sense 2) *ac etiam clause.*

acid-test ratio. See QUICK-ASSET RATIO.

acknowledge, *vb.* **1.** To recognize (something) as being factual <acknowledge the federal court's jurisdiction>. **2.** To show that one accepts responsibility for <acknowledge paternity of the child>. **3.** To make known the receipt of <acknowledged the plaintiff's letter>. **4.** To confirm as genuine before an authorized officer <acknowledged before a notary public>. **5.** (Of a notary public or other officer) to certify as genuine <the notary acknowledged the genuineness of the signature>.

acknowledgment. 1. A recognition of something as being factual. **2.** An acceptance of responsibility. **3.** The act of making it known that one has received something. **4.** A formal declaration made in the presence of an authorized officer, such as a notary public, by someone who signs a document and confirms that the signature is authentic. • In most states, the officer certifies that (1) he or she personally knows the document signer or has established the signer's identity through satisfactory evidence, (2) the signer appeared before the officer on the date and in the place (usu. the county) indicated, and (3) the signer acknowledged signing the document freely. Cf. VERIFICATION (1).

> "An acknowledgment is a verification of the fact of execution, but is not a verification of the contents of the instrument executed; in other words, an acknowledgment is the method of authenticating an instrument by showing it was the act of the person executing it, while a verification is a sworn statement as to the truth of the facts stated within an instrument." 1A C.J.S. *Acknowledgments* § 2 (1985).

5. The officer's certificate that is affixed to the document. — Also termed (in sense 5) *certificate of acknowledgment*; (loosely) *verification.* See PROOF OF ACKNOWLEDGMENT.

acknowledgment money. See LAUDEMIUM.

ACLU. *abbr.* AMERICAN CIVIL LIBERTIES UNION.

a confectione (ay kən-fek-shee-**oh**-nee). [Law Latin] From the making.

a confectione praesentium (ay kən-fek-shee-**oh**-nee pri-**zen**-shee-əm). [Law Latin] From the making of the indentures.

a consiliis (ay kən-**sil**-ee-is), *n.* [Law Latin "of counsel"] See APOCRISARIUS.

a contrario sensu (ay kən-**trair**-ee-oh **sen**-s[y]oo), *adv.* [Law Latin] On the other hand; in the opposite sense.

acquaintance rape. See *date rape* under RAPE.

acquest (ə-**kwest**). See ACQUET.

acquet (a-**kay** *or* ə-**kwet**). [French *acquêt* "acquisition"] (*usu. pl.*) *Civil law.* Property acquired by purchase, gift, or any means other than inheritance; profits or gains of property between husband and wife. — Also termed *acquest.*

acquiesce (ak-wee-**es**), *vb.* To accept tacitly or passively; to give implied consent to (an act) <in the end, all the partners acquiesced in the settlement>. — **acquiescent,** *adj.*

acquiescence (ak-wee-**es**-ənts). **1.** A person's tacit or passive acceptance; implied consent to an act. **2.** *Int'l law.* Passivity and inaction on foreign claims that, according to customary international law, usu. call for protest to assert, preserve, or safeguard rights. • The result is that binding legal effect is given to silence and inaction. Acquiescence, as a principle of substantive law, is grounded in the concepts of good faith and equity.

acquietandis plegiis (ə-kwI-ə-**tan**-dis **plee**-jee-is), *n.* [Law Latin "for acquitting sureties"] *Hist.* A writ to force a creditor to discharge a surety when the debt has been satisfied.

acquietatus (ə-kwI-ə-**tay**-təs), *adj.* [Law Latin] *Hist.* Pronounced innocent by a jury; acquitted.

acquieto. See ADQUIETO.

acquire, *vb.* To gain possession or control of; to get or obtain.

acquired allegiance. See ALLEGIANCE.

acquired corporation. See CORPORATION.

acquired right. See RIGHT.

acquired servitude. See SERVITUDE (1).

acquired surplus. See SURPLUS.

acquisition, *n.* **1.** The gaining of possession or control over something <acquisition of the target company's assets>. **2.** Something acquired <a valuable acquisition>.

derivative acquisition. An acquisition obtained from another, as by sale or gift.

new acquisition. An estate not originating from descent, devise, or gift from the parental or maternal line of the owner. • For example, an estate acquired from a nonrelative is a new acquisition. See *nonancestral estate* under ESTATE.

original acquisition. An acquisition that has never been the property of anyone else, such as a copyright owned by an author.

acquisition cost. See COST (1).

acquisitive offense. See OFFENSE (1).

acquisitive prescription. See PRESCRIPTION (2).

acquit, *vb.* To clear (a person) of a criminal charge. **2.** To pay or discharge (a debt or claim).

acquittal, *n.* **1.** The legal certification, usu. by jury verdict, that an accused person is not guilty of the charged offense.

acquittal in fact. An acquittal by a jury verdict of not guilty.

acquittal in law. An acquittal by operation of law, as of someone who has been charged merely as an accessory after the principal has been acquitted.

implied acquittal. An acquittal in which a jury convicts the defendant of a lesser-included offense without commenting on the greater offense. • Double jeopardy bars the retrial of a defendant who has received an implied acquittal.

2. *Contracts.* A release or discharge from debt or other liability; ACQUITTANCE. **3.** *Hist.* The obligation of a middle lord to protect a tenant from a claim, entry, or molestation by a paramount lord arising out of service that the middle lord owes the paramount lord.

acquittance, *n.* A document by which one is discharged from a debt or other obligation; a receipt or release indicating payment in full. — **acquit,** *vb.*

acquitted, *adj.* **1.** Judicially discharged from an accusation; absolved. **2.** Released from a debt.

acre. An area of land measuring 43,560 square feet.

acre-foot. A volume measurement in irrigation, equal to the amount of water that will cover one acre of land in one foot of water (325,850 gallons).

acre right. *Hist.* In New England, a citizen's share in the common lands. • The value of the acre right varied among towns but was fixed in each town. A 10–acre lot in a certain town was equivalent to 113 acres of upland and 12 acres of meadow, and an exact proportion was maintained between the acre right and salable land.

across-the-board, *adj.* Applying to all classes, categories, or groups <an across-the-board tax cut>.

ACRS. *abbr.* ACCELERATED COST-RECOVERY SYSTEM.

act, *n.* **1.** Something done or performed, esp. voluntarily; a deed.

> " '[A]ct' or 'action' means a bodily movement whether voluntary or involuntary ...." Model Penal Code § 1.13.

2. The process of doing or performing; an occurrence that results from a person's will being exerted on the external world; ACTION (1). — Also termed *positive act*; *act of commission.*

> "The term act is one of ambiguous import, being used in various senses of different degrees of generality. When it

is said, however, that an act is one of the essential conditions of liability, we use the term in the widest sense of which it is capable. We mean by it any event which is subject to the control of the human will. Such a definition is, indeed, not ultimate, but it is sufficient for the purpose of the law." John Salmond, *Jurisprudence* 367 (Glanville L. Williams ed., 10th ed. 1947).

"The word 'act' is used throughout the Restatement of this Subject to denote an external manifestation of the actor's will and does not include any of its results, even the most direct, immediate, and intended." Restatement (Second) of Torts § 2 (1965).

act in pais (in **pay**). [Law French] An act performed out of court, such as a deed made between two parties on the land being transferred. See IN PAIS.

act in the law. An act that is intended to create, transfer, or extinguish a right and that is effective in law for that purpose; the exercise of a legal power. — Also termed *juristic act*; *act of the party*; *legal act*.

act of omission. See *negative act*.

act of the law. The creation, extinction, or transfer of a right by the operation of the law itself, without any consent on the part of the persons concerned. — Also termed *legal act*.

act of the party. See *act in the law*.

administrative act. An act made in a management capacity; esp., an act made outside the actor's usual field (as when a judge supervises court personnel). • An administrative act is often subject to a greater risk of liability than an act within the actor's usual field. See IMMUNITY (1).

bilateral act. An act that involves the consenting wills of two or more distinct parties, as with a contract, a conveyance, a mortgage, or a lease; AGREEMENT (1).

external act. An act involving bodily activity, such as speaking.

intentional act. An act resulting from the actor's will directed to that end. • An act is intentional when foreseen and desired by the doer, and this foresight and desire resulted in the act through the operation of the will.

internal act. An act of the mind, such as thinking.

judicial act. An act involving the exercise of judicial power.

"The distinction between a judicial and a legislative act is well defined. The one determines what the law is, and what the rights of parties are, with reference to transactions already had; the other prescribes what the law shall be in future cases arising under it." *Union Pacific R.R. v. United States*, 99 U.S. 700, 721 (1878) (Field, J., dissenting).

jural act (**joor**-əl). An act taken in the context of or in furtherance of a society's legal system. — Also termed *jural activity*.

"In order to identify an act as a jural act, it must be the kind of act that would be engaged in by someone who is enforcing a law, determining an infraction of the law, making or changing a law, or settling a dispute." Martin P. Golding, *Philosophy of Law* 23 (1975).

juristic act. See *act in the law*.

negative act. The failure to do something that is legally required; a nonoccurrence that involves the breach of a legal duty to take positive action. • This takes the form of either a forbearance or an omission. — Also termed *act of omission*.

unilateral act. An act in which there is only one party whose will operates, as in a testamentary disposition, the exercise of a power of appointment, or the voidance of a voidable contract.

unintentional act. An act not resulting from the actor's will toward what actually takes place.

verbal act. An act performed through the medium of words, either spoken or written.

3. The formal product of a legislature or other deliberative body; esp., STATUTE.

construction act. A legislative directive included in a statute, intended to guide or direct a court's interpretation of the statute. • A construction act can, for example, be a simple statement such as "The word 'week' means seven consecutive days" or a broader directive such as "Words and phrases are to be read in context and construed according to the rules of grammar and common usage. Words and phrases that have acquired a technical or particular meaning, whether by legislative definition or otherwise, are to be construed accordingly."

acta diurna (**ak**-tə dɪ-**ər**-nə), *n.* [Latin "daily proceedings"] *Roman law.* A public register of the daily proceedings of the senate, assemblies of the people, or the courts.

acta publica (**ak**-tə **pəb**-li-kə), *n.* [Latin] *Roman & civil law.* Things of general knowledge and concern; matters transacted before certain public officers.

acte (akt), *n.* [French] *French law.* **1.** An instrument; a proof in writing, such as a deed, bill of sale, or birth certificate.

acte authentique (**akt** oh-taw*n*-**teek**). A deed executed with certain prescribed formalities, in the presence of a notary or other official.

acte de décès (**akt** də day-**say**). A death certificate.

acte de francisation (**akt** də frangk-ə-za-**syawn**). A certificate confirming that a ship is of French nationality.

acte de mariage (**akt** də mar-**yahzh**). A marriage certificate.

acte de naissance (**akt** də **nay**-sənts). A birth certificate.

acte extrajudiciaire (**akt** eks-trə-zhuu-dee-**syair**). A document served by a *huissier* at the request of one party on another party without legal proceedings. See HUISSIER (1).

l'acte de l'état civil (**lakt** də lay-**tah** see-**veel**). A public document relating to status (e.g., birth, divorce, death).

2. An act; conduct.

acte d'héritier (**akt** day-ri-**tyay**). [French "act of an heir"] Conduct by an heir indicating an intent to accept the succession.

acting, *adj*. Holding an interim position; serving temporarily <an acting director>.

acting chargé d'affaires. See CHARGÉ D'AFFAIRES.

acting executor. See EXECUTOR.

acting officer. See OFFICER (1).

act in pais. See ACT (2).

act in the law. See ACT (2).

actio (**ak**-shee-oh *also* **ak**-tee-oh), *n*. [Latin] **1.** *Roman & civil law*. An action; a right or claim. **2.** A right of action. **3.** *Hist*. At common law, a lawsuit. Pl. ***actiones.***

actio ad exhibendum (**ak**-shee-oh ad ek-si-**ben**-dəm). An action to compel a defendant to produce property so as to establish that it is in the defendant's possession.

actio aestimatoria. See DE AESTIMATO.

actio arbitraria (**ak**-shee-oh ahr-bi-**trair**-ee-ə). An action in which the judge orders the defendant to do something (such as restoring property to the plaintiff) on pain of a monetary judgment payable to the plaintiff.

actio bonae fidei (**ak**-shee-oh **boh**-nee **fI**-dee-I). One of a class of actions in which a judge could take equitable considerations into account in rendering a decision.

actio calumniae (**ak**-shee-oh kə-**ləm**-nee-ee). An action to retrain, or collect damages for, a malicious civil suit.

actio civilis (**ak**-shee-oh sə-**vI**-lis). A civil action.

actio commodati (**ak**-shee-oh kom-ə-**day**-tI). [Latin "action on loan"] *Roman law*. An action for the recovery of a thing gratuitously lent but not returned to the lender. — Also termed *commodati actio*. See COMMODATUM.

actio commodati contraria (**ak**-shee-oh kom-ə-**day**-tI kən-**trair**-ee-ə). An action by a gratuitous borrower against a lender to compel the performance of, or for damages for the breach of, the contract.

actio commodati directa (**ak**-shee-oh kom-ə-**day**-tI di-**rek**-tə). An action by a lender against a borrower for restitution for an item gratuitously lent to another.

actio condictio indebiti (**ak**-shee-oh kən-**dik**-shee-oh in-**deb**-ə-tI). See *condictio indebiti* under CONDICTIO. • Strictly speaking, the headword is a solecism, since a *condictio* is a type of *actio*, but it is occasionally found in legal literature.

actio conducti (**ak**-shee-oh kən-**dək**-tI). [Latin "action for the thing hired"] *Roman law*. An action that a hirer of a thing (the *conductor*) might have against a lessor. Cf. *actio locati*.

actio confessoria (**ak**-shee-oh kon-fə-**sor**-ee-ə). [Latin "action based on an admission"] *Roman law*. **1.** See *vindicatio servitutis* under VINDICATIO. **2.** An action in which the defendant admits liability but does not express it in a fixed sum. • A judge therefore assesses the damages.

actio contraria (**ak**-shee-oh kən-**trair**-ee-ə). A counterclaim. Cf. *actio directa*.

actio criminalis (**ak**-shee-oh kri-mə-**nay**-lis). A criminal action.

actio damni injuriae (**ak**-shee-oh **dam**-nI in-**joor**-ee-ə). An action for damages for tortiously causing pecuniary loss.

actio de communi dividendo. See DE COMMUNI DIVIDUNDO.

actio de dolo malo (**ak**-shee-oh dee **doh**-loh **mal**-oh). An action of fraud. • This type of action was widely applied in cases involving deceitful conduct. — Also termed *actio doli*.

actio de in rem verso (**ak**-shee-oh dee **in rem vər**-soh). See *action de in rem verso* under ACTION.

actio de peculio (**ak**-shee-oh dee pə-**kyoo**-lee-oh). An action against a paterfamilias or slave owner concerning the child or slave's separate fund (*peculium*).

actio de pecunia constituta (**ak**-shee-oh dee pə-**kyoo**-nee-ə kon-sti-**t[y]oo**-tə). An action on a promise to pay a preexisting debt.

actio depositi contraria (**ak**-shee-oh di-**poz**-ə-tɪ kən-**trair**-ee-ə). An action that a depositary has against the depositor for unpaid expenses.

actio depositi directa (**ak**-shee-oh di-**poz**-ə-tɪ di-**rek**-tə). An action that a depositor has against a depositary for the return of the deposited item.

actio de tigno juncto (**ak**-shee-oh dee **tig**-noh **jəngk**-toh). An action by the owner of material incorporated without payment into the defendant's building.

actio directa (**ak**-shee-oh di-**rek**-tə). **1.** An action founded on strict law and conducted according to fixed forms; an action based on clearly defined obligations actionable at law. **2.** A direct action, as opposed to a counterclaim (*actio contrario*). Cf. *actio utilis*.

actio empti (**ak**-shee-oh **emp**-tɪ). An action by a buyer to compel a seller to deliver the item sold or for damages for breach of contract.

actio ex conducto (**ak**-shee-oh eks kən-**dək**-toh). An action by the lessee of a thing or the hirer of another's services to enforce the contract or claim damages for breach.

actio ex contractu (**ak**-shee-oh eks kən-**trak**-t[y]oo). An action arising out of a contract. • This term had a similar meaning at common law.

actio ex delicto (**ak**-shee-oh eks də-**lik**-toh). An action founded on a tort. — Also termed *actio poenalis*.

actio exercitoria (**ak**-shee-oh eg-zər-si-**tor**-ee-ə). An action against the owner or lessee (*exercitor*) of a vessel, esp. for contracts made by the master. — Also termed *exercitoria actio*.

actio ex locato. See *actio locati*.

actio ex stipulatu (**ak**-shee-oh eks stip-yə-**lay**-t[y]oo). An action brought to enforce a *stipulatio*. See STIPULATIO.

actio familiae erciscundae (**ak**-shee-oh fə-**mil**-ee-ee ər-sis-**kən**-dee). [Latin "to divide an estate"] *Roman law*. An action for the partition of the inheritance among heirs. — Sometimes shortened to *familiae erciscundae*.

actio furti (**ak**-shee-oh **fər**-tɪ). *Roman law*. An action by which the owner of stolen goods can recover twice their value from the thief by way of penalty, without prejudice to a further action to recover the goods themselves or their value.

actio honoraria (**ak**-shee-oh on-ə-**rair**-ee-ə). A praetorian action; a class of equitable actions introduced by the praetors to prevent injustices.

actio in factum (**ak**-shee-oh in **fak**-təm). *Roman law*. An action granted by the praetor when no standard action was available. • The closest Anglo–American equivalent is *action on the case* or *trespass on the case*. See *trespass on the case* under TRESPASS.

actio in personam (**ak**-shee-oh in pər-**soh**-nəm). See *action in personam* under ACTION.

actio in rem (**ak**-shee-oh in **rem**). See *action in rem* under ACTION.

actio institoria (**ak**-shee-oh in-sti-**tor**-ee-ə). [Latin] *Roman law*. An action against a principal by one who contracted with the principal's business agent. See INSTITOR.

actio judicati (**ak**-shee-oh joo-di-**kay**-tɪ). An action to enforce a judgment by execution on the defendant's property.

actio legis Aquiliae (**ak**-shee-oh **lee**-jis ə-**kwil**-ee-ee). An action under the Aquilian law; an action to recover damages for intentional or negligent injury to another's property.

actio locati (**ak**-shee-oh loh-**kay**-tɪ). [Latin "action for what has been hired out"] *Roman law*. An action that a lessor of a thing (the *locator*) might have against the hirer. — Also termed *actio ex locato*. Cf. *actio conducti*.

actio mandati (**ak**-shee-oh man-**day**-tɪ). An action to enforce a contract for gratuitous services (i.e., a *mandatum*).

actio mixta (**ak**-shee-oh **mik**-stə). A mixed action; an action in which two or more features are combined, as an action for damages and for a penalty, or an action *in rem* and *in personam*.

actio negatoria (**ak**-shee-oh neg-ə-**tor**-ee-ə). An action brought by a landowner against anyone claiming a servitude in the landowner's property. — Also termed *actio negativa*.

actio negotiorum gestorum (**ak**-shee-oh nə-goh-shee-**or**-əm jes-**tor**-əm). An action either by a *gestor* for the recovery of expenses incurred in looking after another's property or against the *gestor* for the mismanagement of the person's property. See NEGOTIORUM GESTOR.

actio non accrevit infra sex annos (**ak**-shee-oh non ə-**kree**-vit seks **an**-ohs), *n.* [Latin "the action did not accrue within six years"] *Hist.* A plea to the statute of limitations by which the defendant asserts that the plaintiff's cause of action has not accrued within the last six years.

actio non ulterius (**ak**-shee-oh non əl-**teer**-ee-əs), *n.* [Latin "an action no further"] *Hist.* The distinctive clause in a plea to abate further maintenance of the action. • This plea replaced the *puis darrein continuance*. Cf. *plea to further maintenance to the action* under PLEA; PUIS DARREIN CONTINUANCE.

actio perpetua (**ak**-shee-oh pər-**pech**-oo-ə). An action that is not required to be brought within a specified time. Cf. *actio temporalis*.

actio personalis (**ak**-shee-oh pər-sə-**nay**-lis). A personal action.

actio pignoratitia (**ak**-shee-oh pig-nə-rə-**tish**-ee-ə). An action of pledge; an action founded on a contract of pledge. See PIGNUS.

actio poenalis. See *actio ex delicto*.

actio praejudicialis (**ak**-shee-oh pree-joo-dish-ee-**ay**-lis). A preliminary action; an action begun to determine a preliminary matter on which other litigated matters depend.

actio praetoria (**ak**-shee-oh pri-**tor**-ee-ə). A praetorian action; one introduced by a praetor.

actio pro socio (**ak**-shee-oh proh **soh**-shee-oh). An action brought by one partner against another.

actio Publiciana (**ak**-shee-oh pə-blish-ee-**ay**-nə). An action allowing a person who had acquired bonitarian ownership of property to recover it, so that the person would in due course acquire full title by prescription. • This action is named for Publicius, the praetor who first granted it. — Also termed *actio Publiciana in rem*. See *bonitarian ownership* under OWNERSHIP.

actio quod jussu (**ak**-shee-oh kwod **jəs**-[y]oo). An action against a master for enforcement of a debt contracted on the master's behalf by a slave.

actio quod metus causa (**ak**-shee-oh kwod **mee**-təs **kaw**-zə). An action to penalize someone who wrongfully compelled the plaintiff to assume an obligation. • The plaintiff could obtain damages of four times the value of the extorted property.

actio realis (**ak**-shee-oh ree-**ay**-lis). [Law Latin] A real action.

actio redhibitoria (**ak**-shee-oh red-i-bi-**tor**-ee-ə). An action to cancel a sale because of defects in the thing sold.

actio rerum amotarum (**ak**-shee-oh **reer**-əm am-ə-**tair**-əm). An action to recover items stolen by a spouse shortly before a divorce.

actio rescissoria (**ak**-shee-oh re-si-**sor**-ee-ə). An action to restore the plaintiff to property lost by prescription. • This action was available to minors and other persons exempt from prescriptive claims against their property.

actio serviana (**ak**-shee-oh sər-vee-**ay**-nə). An action by which a lessor could seize, in satisfaction of unpaid rent, the lessee's personal property brought onto the leased premises.

actio stricti juris (**ak**-shee-oh **strik**-tɪ **joor**-is). A class of personal actions enforceable exactly as stated in the *formula* without taking equitable considerations into account; an action of strict right. See FORMULA (1).

actio temporalis (**ak**-shee-oh tem-pə-**ray**-lis). An action that must be brought within a specified time. Cf. *actio perpetua*.

actio tutelae (**ak**-shee-oh t[y]oo-**tee**-lee). An action arising from a breach of the duty owed by a guardian (*tutor*) to the ward, such as mismanagement of the ward's property.

actio utilis (**ak**-shee-oh **yoo**-tə-lis). An action founded on utility rather than strict right, available esp. to persons having an interest in property less than ownership. • This type of action was modeled after the *actio directa*. Cf. *actio directa* (1).

actio venditi (**ak**-shee-oh **ven**-də-tɪ). An action by which a seller could enforce a contract of sale.

actio vi bonorum raptorum (**ak**-shee-oh **vɪ** bə-**nor**-əm rap-**tor**-əm). A penal action to recover goods taken by force. • A successful plaintiff would also receive three times the value of the taken property. Cf. INTERDICTUM QUOD VI AUT CLAM.

actio vulgaris (**ak**-shee-oh vəl-**gair**-is). An ordinary action, as opposed to one granted in special circumstances.

action. 1. The process of doing something; conduct or behavior. **2.** A thing done; ACT (1). **3.** A civil or criminal judicial proceeding.

> "An action has been defined to be an ordinary proceeding in a court of justice, by which one party prosecutes another party for the enforcement or protection of a right, the redress or prevention of a wrong, or the punishment of a public offense. But in some sense this

definition is equally applicable to special proceedings. More accurately, it is defined to be any judicial proceeding, which, if conducted to a determination, will result in a judgment or decree. The action is said to terminate at judgment." 1 Morris M. Estee, *Estee's Pleadings, Practice, and Forms* § 3, at 1 (Carter P. Pomeroy ed., 3d ed. 1885).

"The terms 'action' and 'suit' are nearly if not quite synonymous. But lawyers usually speak of proceedings in courts of law as 'actions,' and of those in courts of equity as 'suits.' In olden time there was a more marked distinction, for an action was considered as terminating when judgment was rendered, the execution forming no part of it. A suit, on the other hand, included the execution. The word 'suit,' as used in the Judiciary Act of 1784 and later Federal statutes, applies to any proceeding in a court of justice in which the plaintiff pursues in such court the remedy which the law affords him." Edwin E. Bryant, *The Law of Pleading Under the Codes of Civil Procedure* 3 (2d ed. 1899).

" 'Action' in the sense of a judicial proceeding includes recoupment, counterclaim, set-off, suit in equity, and any other proceedings in which rights are determined." UCC § 1–201(1).

action de die in diem (dee **dɪ**-ee in **dɪ**-em). [Law Latin "from day to day"] *Hist.* **1.** An action occurring from day to day; a continuing right of action. **2.** An action for trespass for each day that an injury continues.

"That trespass by way of personal entry is a continuing injury, lasting as long as the personal presence of the wrongdoer, and giving rise to actions *de die in diem* so long as it lasts, is sufficiently obvious." R.F.V. Heuston, *Salmond on the Law of Torts* 42 (17th ed. 1977).

action de in rem verso (dee **in rem vər**-soh). [Latin "action for money applied to (the defendant's) advantage"] *Roman & civil law.* An action for unjust enrichment, in which the plaintiff must show that an enrichment was bestowed, that the enrichment caused an impoverishment, that there is no justification for the enrichment and impoverishment, and that the plaintiff has no other adequate remedy at law, including no remedy under an express or implied contract. — Also termed *actio de in rem verso.*

action ex contractu (eks kən-**trak**-t[y]oo). A personal action arising out of a contract.

"*Actions ex contractu* were somewhat illogically classified thus: *covenant, debt, assumpsit, detinue,* and *account.* The *action of covenant* lay where the party claimed damages for a breach of contract or promise under seal. The *writ of debt* lay for the recovery of a debt; that is, a liquidated or certain sum of money alleged to be due from defendant to plaintiff. The *writ of detinue* was the ancient remedy where the plaintiff claimed the specific recovery of goods, chattels, deeds, or writings detained from him. This remedy fell into disuse by reason of the unsatisfactory mode of trial of 'wager of law,' which the defendant could claim; and recourse was had to the action of replevin. In the American States an action of replevin founded upon statute provisions is almost universally the remedy for the recovery of specific personal property." Edwin E. Bryant, *The Law of Pleading Under the Codes of Civil Procedure* 5 (2d ed. 1899).

action ex delicto (eks də-**lik**-toh). A personal action arising out of a tort.

"The actions *ex delicto* were originally the action of *trespass* and the action of *replevin.*" Edwin E. Bryant, *The Law of Pleading Under the Codes of Civil Procedure* 5 (2d ed. 1899).

action for money had and received. At common law, an action by which the plaintiff could recover money paid to the defendant, the money usu. being recoverable because (1) the money had been paid by mistake or under compulsion, or (2) the consideration was insufficient.

"The *action for money had and received* lay to recover money which the plaintiff had paid to the defendant, on the ground that it had been paid under a mistake or compulsion, or for a consideration which had wholly failed. By this action the plaintiff could also recover money which the defendant had received from a third party, as when he was accountable or had attorned to the plaintiff in respect of the money, or the money formed part of the fruits of an office of the plaintiff which the defendant had usurped." Robert Goff & Gareth Jones, *The Law of Restitution* 3 (3d ed. 1986).

action for money paid. At common law, an action by which the plaintiff could recover money paid to a third party — not to the defendant — in circumstances in which the defendant had benefited.

"The *action for money paid* was the appropriate action when the plaintiff's claim was in respect of money paid, not to the defendant, but to a third party, from which the defendant had derived a benefit. Historically, the plaintiff had to show that the payment was made at the defendant's request; but we shall see that the law was prepared to 'imply' such a request on certain occasions, in particular where the payment was made under compulsion of law or, in limited circumstances, in the course of intervention in an emergency on the defendant's behalf, which in this book we shall call necessitous intervention." Robert Goff & Gareth Jones, *The Law of Restitution* 3 (3d ed. 1986).

action for poinding. *Hist.* A creditor's action to obtain sequestration of the land rents and goods of the debtor to satisfy the debt or enforce a distress.

action for the loss of services. *Hist.* A husband's lawsuit against one who has taken away, imprisoned, or physically harmed his wife in circumstances in which (1) the act is wrongful to the wife, and (2) the husband is deprived of her society or services.

action for the recovery of land. See EJECTMENT.

action in equity. An action that seeks equitable relief, such as an injunction or specific performance, as opposed to damages.

action in personam (in pər-**soh**-nəm). An action determining the rights and interests of the parties themselves in the subject matter of the case. — Also termed *personal action*; (in Roman law) *actio in personam*; *actio personalis*. See IN PERSONAM.

action in rem (in **rem**). An action determining the title to property and the rights of the parties, not merely among themselves, but also against all persons at any time claiming an interest in that property. — Also termed (in Roman law) *actio in rem*; *actio realis*. See IN REM.

action of assize. *Hist.* A real action by which the plaintiff proves title to land merely by showing an ancestor's possession. See ASSIZE.

action of book debt. See ACCOUNTING (4).

action of reprobator. See REPROBATOR.

action on account. See ACCOUNTING (4).

action on expenditure. An action for payment of the principal debt by a personal surety.

action on the case. See *trespass on the case* under TRESPASS.

action per quod servitium amisit (pər kwod sər-**vish**-ee-əm ə-**mI**-sit). [Latin] *Hist.* An action for the loss of a servant's services.

action quasi in rem (**kway**-sI in **rem** *or* **kway**-zI). An action brought against the defendant personally, with jurisdiction based on an interest in property, the objective being to deal with the particular property or to subject the property to the discharge of the claims asserted. See *quasi in rem* under IN REM.

action to quiet title. A proceeding to establish a plaintiff's title to land by compelling the adverse claimant to establish a claim or be forever estopped from asserting it. — Also termed *quiet-title action*.

amicable action. See *test case* (1) under CASE.

civil action. An action brought to enforce, redress, or protect a private or civil right; a noncriminal litigation.

> "The code of New York, as originally adopted, declared, 'the distinctions between actions at law and suits in equity, and the forms of all such actions and heretofore existing, are abolished; and there shall be in this State hereafter but one form of action for the enforcement or protection of private rights and the redress of private wrongs, which shall be denominated a civil action.' With slight verbal changes the above provision has been enacted in most of the States and Territories which have adopted the reformed procedure." Edwin E. Bryant, *The Law of Pleading Under the Codes of Civil Procedure* 106 (2d ed. 1899).

class action. See CLASS ACTION.

collusive action. An action between two parties who have no actual controversy, being merely for the purpose of determining a legal question or receiving a precedent that might prove favorable in related litigation. — Also termed *fictional action*.

common-law action. An action governed by common law, rather than statutory, equitable, or civil law.

criminal action. An action instituted by the government to punish offenses against the public.

derivative action. See DERIVATIVE ACTION.

direct action. See DIRECT ACTION.

fictional action. See *collusive action*.

fictitious action. An action, usu. unethical, brought solely to obtain a judicial opinion on an issue of fact or law, rather than for the disposition of a controversy.

joint action. **1.** An action brought by two or more plaintiffs. **2.** An action brought against two or more defendants.

local action. An action that can be brought only in the jurisdiction where the cause of action arose, as when the action's subject matter is a piece of real property.

matrimonial action. An action relating to the state of marriage, such as an action for separation, annulment, or divorce.

mixed action. An action that has some characteristics of both a real action and a personal action.

> "In early times the only mixed actions were those for the partition of lands, for which a writ was provided in the common-law courts. The remedy was further enlarged by the statute of 31 Hen. VII c. 1, and 32 Hen. VIII c. 32, which gave compulsory partition, by writ at common law. These statutes formed the basis of partition in the American States; but in England and here courts of Chancery have been found most convenient, and their procedure most favorable for the division of estates in land. The statutes at the present time, in most of the States, prescribe a procedure which is quite similar to that in equity practice." Edwin E. Bryant, *The Law of Pleading Under the Codes of Civil Procedure* 10–11 (2d ed. 1899).

nonpersonal action. An action that proceeds within some category of territorial jurisdiction other than in personam — that is, jurisdiction in rem, quasi in rem, or over status.

penal action. **1.** A criminal prosecution. **2.** A civil proceeding in which either the state or a common informer sues a defendant who has violated a statute and seeks to recover a penalty. • Although civil in nature, a penal action resembles a criminal proceeding because the result of a successful action is a monetary penalty intended, like a fine, to punish the defendant. See COMMON INFORMER.

"At one time it was a frequent practice, when it was desired to repress some type of conduct thought to be harmful, to do so by the machinery of the civil rather than of the criminal law. The means so chosen was called a penal action, as being brought for the recovery of a penalty; and it might be brought, according to the wording of the particular statute creating the penal action, either by the Attorney-General on behalf of the state, or by a common informer on his own account. A common informer was anyone who should first sue the offender for the penalty. Penal actions are still possible in a few cases, and their existence renders invalid several suggested distinctions between civil wrongs and crimes." John Salmond, *Jurisprudence* 107 (Glanville L. Williams ed., 10th ed. 1947).

"For in 'penal actions', unless the statute expressly authorizes private persons to act as informers, the State alone can sue and recover the penalty; and yet there is full authority for ranking such suits by it as merely civil proceedings." J.W. Cecil Turner, *Kenny's Outlines of Criminal Law* 538 (16th ed. 1952).

3. A civil lawsuit by an aggrieved party seeking recovery of a statutory fine or a penalty, such as punitive damages.

"[T]here exists a well-known class of proceedings called 'penal actions', by which pecuniary penalties can be recovered — in some cases by any person who will sue for them — from the doers of various prohibited acts; these acts being thus prohibited, and visited with penalties, solely on account of their tendency to cause evil to the community at large, 'considered as a community.' For example, a person who, in advertising a reward for the return of lost property, adds that 'no questions will be asked' incurs by the Larceny Act, 1861, a penalty of £50 recoverable by anyone who will sue for it." J.W. Cecil Turner, *Kenny's Outlines of Criminal Law* 533–34 (16th ed. 1952).

personal action. **1.** An action brought for the recovery of debts, personal property, or damages arising from any cause.

"*Personal actions* are those brought (1) for specific recovery of goods or chattels, (2) or for damages or other redress for breach of contract, (3) or every other kind of injury. They are *ex contractu* when they arise out of contract, *ex delicto* when they arise out of the wrong or delict of the defendant." Edwin E. Bryant, *The Law of Pleading Under the Codes of Civil Procedure* 5 (2d ed. 1899).

"Personal actions are subdivided into those brought for the recovery of a debt or of damages for the breach of a contract, or for tort, for some injury to the person or to relative rights or to personal or real property. The most common of these actions are debt, covenant, assumpsit, detinue, trespass, trespass on the case, trover, and replevin." Benjamin J. Shipman, *Handbook of Common-Law Pleading* § 34, at 65 (Henry Winthrop Ballantine ed., 3d ed. 1923).

2. See *action in personam.*

petitory action (**pet**-ə-tor-ee). An action to establish and enforce title to property independently of the right to possession. — Also termed *petitorium.*

plenary action (**plee**-nə-ree *or* **plen**-). A full hearing or trial on the merits, as opposed to a summary proceeding. Cf. *summary proceeding* under PROCEEDING.

possessory action (pə-**zes**-ə-ree). **1.** An action to obtain, recover, or maintain possession of property but not title to it, such as an action to evict a nonpaying tenant. — Also termed *possessorium.*

"The possessory action affords a remedy against a disturbance, in fact or in law, of possession. The function of the possessory action is to aid the 'disturbed' possessor of immovable property or a real right in maintaining his possession of the property or the enjoyment of the right, or to restore the 'evicted' possessor to the possession of the property or enjoyment of the right." James D. Johnson, Jr., *Guide to Louisiana Real Actions, Ten Year and Thirty Year Prescriptions* 5 (1961).

2. *Maritime law.* An action brought to recover possession of a ship under a claim of title.

real action. An action brought for the recovery of land or other real property; specif., an action to recover the possession of a freehold estate in real property, or seisin. See SEISIN.

"If the question be asked why it was that a large part of the really English law which Bracton undertook to expound is found in connection with the subject of real actions, while in Blackstone's treatise only the personal actions are deemed worthy of attention, the answer must be that the former were dying out. When Chitty wrote (1808) the old real actions were practically obsolete, and in the succeeding generation such vestiges of them as remained were abolished by statute." Hannis Taylor, *The Science of Jurisprudence* 574 (1908).

"The principal real actions formerly in use were (1) the writs of right; (2) the writs of entry; (3) the possessory assizes, such as novel disseisin and mort d'ancestor. Real actions are those in which the demandant seeks to recover seisin from one called a tenant, because he holds the land. They are real actions at common law because the judgment is in rem and awards the seisin or possession." Benjamin J. Shipman, *Handbook of Common-Law Pleading* § 32, at 63 (Henry Winthrop Ballantine ed., 3d ed. 1923).

redhibitory action. *Civil law.* An action brought to void a sale of an item having a defect that renders it either useless or so flawed that the buyer would not have bought it in the first place. See REDHIBITION.

remedial action. See REMEDIAL ACTION.

representative action. **1.** CLASS ACTION. **2.** DERIVATIVE ACTION (1).

separate action. **1.** An action brought alone by each of several complainants who are all involved in the same transaction but cannot legally join the suit. **2.** One of several distinct actions brought by a single plaintiff against each of two or more parties who are all liable to a plaintiff with respect to the same subject matter. — Also termed *several action.*

several action. See *separate action.*

statutory action. An action governed by statutory law rather than equitable, civil, or common law.

test action. See *test case* (2) under CASE.

third-party action. An action distinct from the main claim, whereby the defendant brings in an entity that is not directly involved in the lawsuit but that may be liable to the defendant for all or part of the plaintiff's claim. • A common example is an action for indemnity or contribution.

transitory action. An action that can be brought in any venue where the defendant can be personally served with process.

> "Transitory actions are universally founded on the supposed violation of rights which, in contemplation of law, have no locality. They are personal actions, that is, they are brought for the enforcement of purely personal rights or obligations. If the transaction on which the action is founded could have taken place anywhere, the action is generally regarded as transitory; but if the transaction could only have happened in a particular place . . . the action is local. Some authorities, considering the effect of the distinction, define transitory actions as actions which may be tried wherever defendant may be found and served." 92 C.J.S. *Venue* § 8, at 678–79 (1955).

action, cause of. See CAUSE OF ACTION.

action, form of. See FORM OF ACTION.

action, right of. See RIGHT OF ACTION.

actionable, *adj.* Furnishing the legal ground for a lawsuit or other legal action <intentional interference with contractual relations is an actionable tort>.

actionable negligence. See NEGLIGENCE.

actionable nuisance. See NUISANCE (3).

actionable word. A term that is defamatory in itself. See *libel per se* under LIBEL.

actionare (ak-shee-ə-**nair**-ee), *vb.* [Law Latin] To bring an action; to sue.

action de die in diem. See ACTION.

action de in rem verso. See ACTION.

actio negativa. See *actio negatoria* under ACTIO.

actio negatoria. See ACTIO.

actio negotiorum gestorum. See ACTIO.

actiones legis (ak-shee-**oh**-neez **lee**-jis), *n. pl.* [Latin] *Roman law.* Legal or lawful actions; actions at law requiring the use of fixed forms of words. • This phrase is the plural of *actio legis* (more commonly termed *legis actio*).

actiones nominatae (ak-shee-**oh**-neez nom-ə-**nay**-tee), *n. pl.* [Latin "named actions"] *Hist.* Actions for which the Chancery had well-established forms. See CONSIMILI CASU.

actiones poenales (ak-shee-**oh**-neez pee-**nay**-leez), *n. pl.* [Latin "penal actions"] *Roman law.* Actions in which a plaintiff sues for a penalty.

action ex contractu. See ACTION.

action ex delicto. See ACTION.

action for money had and received. See ACTION.

action for money paid. See ACTION.

action for poinding. See ACTION.

action for the loss of services. See ACTION.

action for the recovery of land. See EJECTMENT.

action in equity. See ACTION.

action in personam. See ACTION.

action in rem. See ACTION.

action of assize. See ACTION.

action of book debt. See ACCOUNTING (4).

action of reprobator. See REPROBATOR.

actio non (**ak**-shee-oh **non**). [Latin "an action not"] *Hist.* A declaration in a special plea denying the plaintiff's right to maintain the action. See *special plea* under PLEA.

action on account. See ACCOUNTING (4).

actio non accrevit infra sex annos. See ACTIO.

action on decision. A legal memorandum from attorneys in the Internal Revenue Service's litigation division to the Service's Chief Counsel, containing advice on whether the Service should acquiesce, appeal, or take some other action regarding a court's decision that is unfavorable to the Service. — Abbr. AOD.

action on expenditure. See ACTION.

action on the case. See *trespass on the case* under TRESPASS.

actio non ulterius. See ACTIO.

actio noxalis (**ak**-shee-oh nok-**say**-lis), *n.* See NOXAL ACTION.

action *per quod servitium amisit.* See ACTION.

action quasi in rem. See ACTION.

action to quiet title. See ACTION.

actio perpetua. See ACTIO.

actio pignoratitia. See ACTIO.

actio poenalis. See *actio ex delicto* under ACTIO.

actio praejudicialis. See ACTIO.

actio praetoria. See ACTIO.

actio pro socio. See ACTIO.

actio Publiciana. See ACTIO.

actio Publiciana in rem. See *actio Publiciana* under ACTIO.

actio quod jussu. See ACTIO.

actio quod metus causa. See ACTIO.

actio realis. See ACTIO.

actio redhibitoria. See ACTIO.

actio rerum amotarum. See ACTIO.

actio rescissoria. See ACTIO.

actio serviana. See ACTIO.

actio stricti juris. See ACTIO.

actio temporalis. See ACTIO.

actio tutelae. See ACTIO.

actio utilis. See ACTIO.

actio venditi. See ACTIO.

actio vi bonorum raptorum. See ACTIO.

actio vulgaris. See ACTIO.

active breach of contract. See BREACH OF CONTRACT.

active case. See CASE.

active concealment. See CONCEALMENT.

active-control-of-vessel duty. See ACTIVE-OPERATIONS DUTY.

active debt. See DEBT.

active duty. *Military law.* The full-time status of being in any of the U.S. armed forces.

active euthanasia. See EUTHANASIA.

active income. See INCOME.

active inducement. See INDUCEMENT.

active negligence. See NEGLIGENCE.

active-operations duty. *Maritime law.* A shipowner's obligation to provide safe working conditions, in the work areas controlled by the shipowner, for the stevedore and longshoremen who are loading or unloading the ship. — Also termed *active-control-of-vessel duty.* Cf. TURNOVER DUTY; INTERVENTION DUTY.

active supervision. *Antitrust.* Under the test for determining whether a private entity may claim a state-action exemption from the antitrust laws, the right of the state to review the entity's anticompetitive acts and to disapprove those acts that do not promote state policy. See STATE-ACTION DOCTRINE; MIDCAL TEST.

"The active supervision requirement stems from the recognition that where a private party is engaging in the anticompetitive activity, there is a real danger that he is acting to further his own interests, rather than the governmental interests of the State. The requirement is designed to ensure that the state-action doctrine will shelter only the particular anticompetitive acts that, in the judgment of the State, actually further state regulatory policies. To accomplish this purpose, the active supervision requirement mandates that the State exercise ultimate control over the challenged anticompetitive conduct." *Patrick v. Burget*, 486 U.S. 94, 100–01, 108 S.Ct. 1658, 1663 (1988).

active trust. See TRUST.

active waste. See *commissive waste* under WASTE.

activity. See MARKET VOLUME.

activity incident to service. An act undertaken by a member of the armed forces as a part of a military operation or as a result of the actor's status as a member of the military. • For example, if a member of the military takes advantage of that status by flying home on a military aircraft, the flight is activity incident to service, and a claim against the government for any injuries received may be barred under the *Feres* doctrine. See FERES DOCTRINE.

act of attainder. See BILL OF ATTAINDER.

act of bankruptcy. An event, such as a debtor's fraudulent conveyance of property, that triggers an involuntary bankruptcy proceeding against a debtor. • The 1978 Bankruptcy Reform Act abolished this requirement as a condition to an involuntary bankruptcy proceeding.

act of commission. See ACT (2).

act of Congress. A law that is formally enacted in accordance with the legislative power granted to Congress by the U.S. Constitution. • To become a law, or an act of Congress, a bill or resolution must be passed by a majority of the members of both the House of Representatives and the Senate. Bills or resolutions may generally be introduced in either chamber, except that bills for generating revenue must be introduced in the House of Representatives. When a bill or resolution is introduced in a chamber, it is usu. assigned to a committee. If it is passed by the committee, it is reported to the full chamber. If it passes in the full chamber, it is reported to the other chamber, which then usu. assigns it to a committee in that chamber. If it passes by majority votes of the committee and full body in that chamber, it is reported back to the originating chamber. If its terms have changed in the second chamber, it is submitted to a conference committee, consisting of members from both chambers, to work out a compromise. When the bill or resolution is passed, with the same terms, by both chambers, it is signed by the Speaker of the House and the President of the Senate (usu. the President Pro Tempore), and is presented to the President of the United States for signature. If the President signs it or fails to return it to Congress within ten days, the bill or resolution becomes law. But if the President vetoes the bill or resolution, it must be passed by a two-thirds majority of the House of Representatives and the Senate to become law. U.S. Const. art. I, § 7; 3 *The Guide to American Law* 165–66 (West 1983).

act of God. An overwhelming, unpreventable event caused exclusively by forces of nature, such as an earthquake, flood, or tornado. • The definition has been statutorily broadened to include all natural phenomena that are exceptional, inevitable, and irresistible, the effects of which could not be prevented or avoided by the exercise of due care or foresight. 42 USCA § 9601(1). — Also termed *act of nature*; *act of providence*. Cf. FORCE MAJEURE; *unavoidable accident* under ACCIDENT.

"[A]ll natural agencies, as opposed to human activities, constitute acts of God, and not merely those which attain an extraordinary degree of violence or are of very unusual occurrence. The distinction is one of kind and not one of degree. The violence or rarity of the event is relevant only in considering whether it could or could not have been prevented by reasonable care; if it could not, then it is an act of God which will relieve from liability, howsoever trivial or common its cause may have been. If this be correct, then the unpredictable nature of the occurrence will go only to show that the act of God in question was one which the defendant was under no duty to foresee or provide against. It is only in such a case that the act of God will provide a defence." R.F.V. Heuston, *Salmond on the Law of Torts* 330 (17th ed. 1977).

act of grace. An act of clemency; esp., such an act performed at the beginning of a monarch's reign or at some other significant occasion.

act of honor. *Commercial law.* A transaction, memorialized in an instrument prepared by a notary public, evidencing a third person's agreement to accept, for the credit of one or more of the parties, a bill that has been protested. • The UCC eliminated this type of transaction.

act of nature. See ACT OF GOD.

act of omission. See *negative act* under ACT (2).

act of Parliament. A law made by the British sovereign, with the advice and consent of the lords and the commons; a British statute.

act of Parliament of Scotland. 1. A law passed by the Parliament of Scotland between its creation about the 17th century and 1707. **2.** A law passed (from 1999 onward) by the new Parliament of Scotland created by the Scotland Act of 1998.

act of petition. *Hist.* A summary proceeding in which litigants provide brief statements supported by affidavit. • This procedure was used in the English High Court of Admiralty.

act of possession. Conduct indicating an intent to claim the property in question as one's own; esp., conduct that supports a claim of adverse possession.

act of providence. See ACT OF GOD.

act of sale. An official record of a sale of property; esp., a document drawn up by a notary, signed by the parties, and attested by witnesses.

Act of Settlement. *Hist.* An act of Parliament (12 & 13 Will. 3, ch. 2, 1700) that resolved the question of royal succession unsettled after the Glorious Revolution of 1688. • The question was resolved by limiting the Crown to members of the House of Hanover who were Protestant. The Act also provided that the sovereign must be a member of the Church of England, and it established that judges would hold office during good behavior rather than at the will of the sovereign.

act-of-state doctrine. The common-law principle that prevents U.S. courts from questioning the validity of a foreign country's sovereign acts within its own territory. • As originally formulated by the U.S. Supreme Court in 1897, the doctrine provides that "the courts of one country will not sit in judgment on the acts of the government of another done within its own territory." *Underhill v. Hernandez*, 168 U.S. 250, 252, 18 S.Ct. 83, 84 (1897).

Act of Supremacy. *Hist.* A statute that named the English sovereign as supreme head of the Church of England (26 Hen. 8, ch. 1). • The Act was passed in 1534 during Henry VIII's reign and confirmed in 1559 (1 Eliz., ch. 1) to counteract pro-Catholic legislation enacted during the reign of Mary Tudor.

act of the law. See ACT (2).

act of the party. See *act in the law* under ACT (2).

Act of Uniformity. *Hist.* Any of several 16th- and 17th-century acts mandating uniform religious practices in England and Ireland; specif., an act requiring the use of the *Book of Common Prayer*.

Act of Union. Any of several acts of Parliament uniting various parts of Great Britain. • The term applies to (1) the Laws in Wales Act (1535), which united Wales with England and made that principality subject to English law, and (2) the Union with Ireland Act (1800), which abolished the Irish Parliament and incorporated Ireland into the United Kingdom of Great Britain and Ireland. It is also, but quite mistakenly, used in reference to the Union with Scotland in 1707, which was not made by statute but by treaty, approved by separate acts of Parliament of Scotland and of England, which by the treaty dissolved themselves and created the new state of Great Britain with one parliament, the Parliament of Great Britain.

actor. 1. One who acts; a person whose conduct is in question. **2.** *Archaic.* A male plaintiff. **3.** *Hist.* An advocate or pleader; one who acted for another in legal matters. Cf. REUS (1).

actrix (**ak**-triks). *Archaic.* A female plaintiff.

acts of assembly. See SESSION LAWS.

actual, *adj.* Existing in fact; real <actual malice>. Cf. CONSTRUCTIVE.

actual agency. See AGENCY (1).

actual allegiance. See ALLEGIANCE.

actual authority. See AUTHORITY (1).

actual bailment. See BAILMENT.

actual capital. See CAPITAL.

actual cash value. See *fair market value* under VALUE.

actual cause. See *but-for cause* under CAUSE (1).

actual change of possession. A real, rather than constructive, transfer of ownership. • A creditor of the transferor cannot reach property that has actually changed possession.

actual controversy. See CONTROVERSY (2), (3).

actual damages. See DAMAGES.

actual delivery. See DELIVERY.

actual escape. See ESCAPE (2).

actual eviction. See EVICTION.

actual-evidence test. See SAME-EVIDENCE TEST.

actual force. See FORCE.

actual fraud. See FRAUD.

actual-injury trigger. *Insurance.* The point at which an insured suffers damage or injury (such as the time of an automobile accident), so that there is an occurrence invoking coverage under an insurance policy. — Also termed *injury-in-fact trigger.* Cf. EXPOSURE THEORY; MANIFESTATION THEORY; TRIPLE TRIGGER.

actual innocence. See INNOCENCE.

actual knowledge. See KNOWLEDGE.

actual loss. See LOSS.

actually litigated. (Of a claim that might be barred by collateral estoppel) properly raised in an earlier lawsuit, submitted to the court for a determination, and determined. • A party is barred by the doctrine of collateral estoppel from relitigating an issue that was actually litigated — usu. including by summary judgment but not necessarily by default judgment — in an earlier suit involving the same parties, even if that suit involved different claims. Restatement (Second) of Judgments § 27 cmt. d (1982).

actual malice. See MALICE.

actual market value. See *fair market value* under VALUE.

actual notice. See NOTICE.

actual physical control. Direct bodily power over something, esp. a vehicle. • Many jurisdictions require a showing of "actual physical control" of a vehicle by a person charged with driving while intoxicated.

actual possession. See POSSESSION (3).

actual reduction to practice. See REDUCTION TO PRACTICE.

actual-risk test. The doctrine that, for an injured employee to be entitled to workers'-compensation benefits, the employee must prove that the injury arose from, and occurred in the course and scope of, employment.

actual seisin. See *seisin in deed* under SEISIN.

actual service. See PERSONAL SERVICE (1).

actual taking. See TAKING (2).

actual total loss. See LOSS.

actual value. See *fair market value* under VALUE.

actuarial equivalent. The amount of accrued pension benefits to be paid monthly or at some other interval so that the total amount of benefits will be paid over the expected remaining lifetime of the recipient.

actuarially sound retirement system. A retirement plan that contains sufficient funds to pay future obligations, as by receiving contributions from employees and the employer to be invested in accounts to pay future benefits. Cf. NONACTUARIALLY SOUND RETIREMENT SYSTEM.

actuarial method. A means of determining the amount of interest on a loan by using the loan's annual percentage rate to separately calculate the finance charge for each payment period, after crediting each payment, which is credited first to interest and then to principal.

actuarial present value. The amount of money necessary to purchase an annuity that would generate a particular monthly payment, or whatever periodic payment the plan provides, for the expected remaining life span of the recipient.

actuarial surplus. An estimate of the amount by which a pension plan's assets exceed its expected current and future liabilities, including the amount expected to be needed to fund future benefit payments.

actuarial table. An organized chart of statistical data indicating life expectancies for people in various categories (such as age, family history, and exposure to chemicals). • Actuarial tables are usu. admissible in evidence. — Also termed *expectancy table*; *mortality table*; *mortuary table*. Cf. LIFE TABLE.

actuarius (ak-choo-**air**-ee-əs *or* ak-tyoo-), *n.* [Latin] *Roman law.* **1.** A notary or clerk; a shorthand writer. **2.** A keeper of public records.

actuary (**ak**-choo-air-ee), *n.* A statistician who determines the present effects of future contingent events; esp., one who calculates insurance and pension rates on the basis of empirically based tables. — **actuarial** (ak-choo-**air**-ee-əl), *adj.*

actum (**ak**-təm), *n.* [Latin] A thing done; an act or deed.

actus (**ak**-təs), *n.* [Latin] **1.** An act or action; a thing done. **2.** *Hist.* An act of Parliament; esp., one passed by both houses but not yet approved by the monarch. Cf. STATUTUM (1). **3.** *Roman law.* A servitude for driving cattle or a carriage across another's land. Cf. ITER (1).

actus reus (**ak**-təs **ree**-əs *also* **ray**-əs). [Law Latin "guilty act"] The wrongful deed that comprises the physical components of a crime and that generally must be coupled with *mens rea* to establish criminal liability; a forbidden act <the *actus reus* for theft is the taking of or unlawful control over property without the owner's consent>. — Also termed *deed of crime*; *overt act*. Cf. MENS REA.

> "The word *actus* connotes a 'deed', a physical result of human conduct. When criminal policy regards such a deed as sufficiently harmful it prohibits it and seeks to prevent its occurrence by imposing a penalty for its commission. It has long been the custom of lawyers to describe a deed so prohibited by law in the words *actus reus*. Thus *actus reus* may be defined as 'Such result of human conduct as the law seeks to prevent'. It is important to note that the *actus reus*, which is the result of conduct, and therefore an event, must be distinguished from the conduct which produced the result. For example, in a simple case of murder it is the victim's death (brought about by the conduct of the murderer) which is the *actus reus*; the *mens rea* is the murderer's intention to cause that death. In other words, the crime is constituted by the event, and not by the activity (or in certain cases, as we shall see, by the omission to act) which caused the event." J.W. Cecil Turner, *Kenny's Outlines of Criminal Law* 13 (16th ed. 1952).

> "The phrase 'deed of crime' [= *actus reus*] as so used does not indicate the crime itself but merely one of the ingredients of crime; and this ingredient may be present without any crime at all, just as hydrogen is one of the ingredients of water but may be present without water. The words 'deed of crime' are so suggesting of the crime itself, however, that perhaps the Latin phrase '*actus reus*' is less likely to cause confusion. The *actus reus* is essential to crime but is not sufficient for this purpose without the necessary mens rea, just as mens rea is essential to crime but is insufficient without the necessary *actus reus*." Rollin M. Perkins & Ronald N. Boyce, *Criminal Law* 831 (3d ed. 1982).

A.D. *abbr.* ANNO DOMINI.

ad (ad), *prep.* [Latin] At; by; for; near; on account of; to; until; upon; with relation to; concerning.

ADA. *abbr.* AMERICANS WITH DISABILITIES ACT.

ad abundantiorem cautelam (ad ab-ən-dan-shee-**or**-əm kaw-**tee**-ləm). [Law Latin] *Hist.* For more abundant caution. — Also termed *ad cautelam ex superabundanti* (ad kaw-**tee**-ləm eks s[y]oo-pər-ab-ən-**dan**-tI).

ad admittendum clericum (ad ad-mi-**ten**-dəm **kler**-ə-kəm). [Law Latin] See DE CLERICO ADMITTENDO.

ad aliud examen (ad **ay**-lee-əd eg-**zay**-mən), *adv.* [Law Latin] To another tribunal.

ad alium diem (ad **ay**-lee-əm **dI**-əm), *adv.* [Law Latin] To another day.

adaptation right. *Copyright.* A copyright holder's exclusive right to prepare derivative works based on the protected work. • For example, before a movie studio can make a film version of a book, it must secure the author's adaptation right. See DERIVATIVE WORK.

ad assisas capiendas (ad ə-**sIz**-əs kap-ee-**en**-dəs). [Law Latin] To take assizes; to hold assizes.

a dato (ay **day**-toh), *adv.* [Law Latin] From the date. — Also termed *a datu*.

ad audiendam considerationem curiae (ad aw-dee-**en**-dəm kən-sid-ə-ray-shee-**oh**-nəm **kyoor**-ee-I), *vb.* [Law Latin] To hear the judgment of the court.

ad audiendum et determinandum (ad aw-dee-**en**-dəm et di-tər-mi-**nan**-dəm), *vb.* [Law Latin] To hear and determine. See OYER ET TERMINER.

ADB. *abbr.* ACCIDENTAL-DEATH BENEFIT.

ad barram (ad **bahr**-əm), *adv.* [Law Latin] To the bar; at the bar.

ad barram evocatus (ad **bahr**-əm ee-voh-**kay**-təs). [Law Latin] Called to the bar. See CALL TO THE BAR.

ad campi partem (ad **kam**-pɪ **pahr**-təm *or* -tem). [Law Latin] For a share of the field or land.

ad captum vulgi (ad **kap**-təm **vəl**-jɪ). [Law Latin] Adapted to the common understanding.

ad colligendum (ad kol-i-**jen**-dəm). [Law Latin] For collecting <administrator *ad colligendum*>.

ad colligendum bona defuncti (ad kol-i-**jen**-dəm **boh**-nə di-**fəngk**-tɪ). [Law Latin "for collecting the goods of the deceased"] Special letters of administration authorizing a person to collect and preserve a decedent's property.

ad communem legem (ad kə-**myoo**-nəm **lee**-jəm), *n.* [Law Latin "to common law"] *Hist.* A writ of entry available after the death of a life tenant to recover a reversionary interest in land alienated by the tenant. — Also termed *entry ad communem legem.*

ad commune nocumentum (ad kə-**myoo**-nee nok-yə-**men**-təm), *adv.* [Law Latin] To the common nuisance.

ad comparendum (ad kom-pə-**ren**-dəm), *vb.* [Law Latin] To appear. • This term is part of the larger phrase *ad comparendum, et ad standum juri* ("to appear and to stand to the law"). — Also termed (in standard Latin) *ad comparandum.*

ad computum reddendum (ad kəm-**pyoo**-təm ri-**den**-dəm), *vb.* [Law Latin] To render an account.

adcordabilis denarii (ad-kor-**day**-bə-lis di-**nair**-ee-ɪ), *n.* [Latin] *Hist.* Money paid by a vassal to the lord upon the sale or exchange of a feud.

ad culpam (ad **kəl**-pəm), *adv.* [Law Latin] Until misconduct.

ad curiam (ad **kyoor**-ee-əm), *adv.* [Law Latin] At a court; to court.

ad curiam vocare (ad **kyoor**-ee-əm voh-**kair**-ee), *vb.* [Law Latin] To summon to court.

ad custagia (ad kə-**stay**-jee-ə), *adv.* [Law Latin] At the costs.

ad custum (ad **kəs**-təm), *adv.* [Law Latin] At the cost.

***ad damnum* clause** (ad **dam**-nəm). [Latin "to the damage"] A clause in a prayer for relief stating the amount of damages claimed. See PRAYER FOR RELIEF.

> "Where the amount the plaintiff is entitled to recover appears from the statement of facts — as where the amount due the plaintiff is alleged on breach of a money demand, the demand of judgment may take the place of an *ad damnum* clause." Edwin E. Bryant, *The Law of Pleading Under the Codes of Civil Procedure* 209 (2d ed. 1899).

added damages. See *punitive damages* under DAMAGES.

ad defendendum (ad di-fen-**den**-dəm), *vb.* [Latin] To defend.

addendum (ə-**den**-dəm). Something to be added, esp. to a document; a supplement.

addicere (ə-**dis**-ər-ee), *vb.* [Latin] *Roman law.* To adjudge, allot, or condemn.

addict (**a**-dikt), *n.* A person who habitually uses a substance, esp. a narcotic drug. — **addict** (ə-**dikt**), *vb.* — **addictive,** *adj.* — **addiction,** *n.*

drug addict. A person who is psychologically or physiologically dependent on a narcotic drug.

addictio (ə-**dik**-shee-oh), *n.* [Latin] *Roman law.* The awarding by a magistrate of a person or thing to another, as the property of a debtor to a creditor.

addictive drug. See DRUG.

ad diem (ad **dɪ**-əm). [Latin] At a day; at the appointed day.

addition. 1. A structure that is attached to or connected with another building that predates the structure; an extension or annex. • Although some courts have held that an addition is merely an appurtenant structure that might not actually be in physical contact with the other building, most courts hold that there must be physical contact. **2.** A title or appellation appended to a person's name to show rank, occupation, or place of residence. • In English law, there are traditionally four kinds of additions: (1) those of estate, such as yeoman, gentleman, or esquire; (2) those of degree (or dignity), such as knight, baron, earl, marquis, or duke; (3) those of trade or occupation, such as scrivener, painter, mason, or carpenter; and (4) those of place of residence, such as London, Bath, or Chester. It was formerly required by the statute of additions (1 Hen. 5, ch. 5) that original writs and indictments state a person's addition, but the practice has long since been abolished.

additional-consideration rule. *Employment law.* An exception to the employment-at-will principle, whereby an employee who does not have a written contract but who undertakes substantial hardship in addition to the normal job duties — as by relocating to a different city based on oral assurances of job security — can maintain a breach-of-contract claim if the employer does not fulfill its agreement.

additional damages. See DAMAGES.

additional extended coverage. *Insurance.* A policy endorsement providing supplemental residential coverage for a variety of perils, including vandalism, damage from falling trees, and water damage from the plumbing system.

additional grand jury. See *special grand jury* under GRAND JURY.

additional instruction. See JURY INSTRUCTION.

additional insurance. See INSURANCE.

additional insured. See INSURED.

additional legacy. See LEGACY.

additional servitude. See SERVITUDE (1).

additional standard deduction. See DEDUCTION.

additional term. See TERM (5).

additional work. See WORK.

additur (**ad**-ə-tur). [Latin "it is added to"] A trial court's order, issued usu. with the defendant's consent, that increases the damages awarded by the jury to avoid a new trial on grounds of inadequate damages. • The term may also refer to the increase itself, the procedure, or the court's power to make the order. — Also termed *increscitur.* Cf. REMITTITUR.

add-on clause. An installment-contract provision that converts earlier purchases into security for new purchases.

addone (ə-**doh**-nee), *p.pl.* [Law French] Given to. — Also spelled *addonne.*

add-on interest. See INTEREST (3).

add-on loan. See LOAN.

address, *n.* **1.** The place where mail or other communication is sent. **2.** In some states, a legislature's formal request to the executive to do a particular thing, as to remove a judge from office. **3.** *Equity practice.* The part of a bill in which the court is identified. See DIRECTION (5).

address to the Crown. Upon a reading of a royal speech in Parliament, the ceremonial resolution by Parliament expressing thanks to the sovereign for the gracious speech. • Formerly, two members were selected in each house for moving and seconding the address. With the commencement of the 1890–1891 session, a single resolution was adopted.

adduce (ə-**d**[**y**]**oos**), *vb.* To offer or put forward for consideration (something) as evidence or authority <adduce the engineer's expert testimony>. — **adduction** (ə-**dək**-shən), *n.* — **adducible** (ə-**d**[**y**]**oo**-sə-bəl), *adj.*

ADEA. *abbr.* AGE DISCRIMINATION IN EMPLOYMENT ACT.

ad effectum (ad i-**fek**-təm). [Law Latin] To the effect.

ad effectum sequentem (ad i-**fek**-təm si-**kwen**-təm). [Law Latin] To the effect following.

ademptio (ə-**demp**-shee-oh), *n.* [Latin] *Roman law.* See ADEMPTION.

ademption (ə-**demp**-shən), *n.* *Wills & estates.* The destruction or extinction of a legacy or bequest by reason of a bequeathed asset's ceasing to be part of the estate at the time of the testator's death; a beneficiary's forfeiture of a legacy or bequest that is no longer operative. — Also termed *extinguishment of legacy.* — **adeem** (ə-**deem**), *vb.* Cf. ADVANCEMENT; LAPSE (2).

ademption by extinction. An ademption that occurs because the property specifically described in the will is not in the estate at the testator's death.

ademption by satisfaction. An ademption that occurs because the testator, while alive, has already given property to the beneficiary with the intention of rendering the testamentary gift inoperative.

adeo (**ad**-ee-oh). [Latin] So; as.

adequacy test. See IRREPARABLE-INJURY RULE.

adequate, *adj.* Legally sufficient <adequate notice>.

adequate assurance. *Bankruptcy.* Evidence that a debtor will probably be able to perform its obligations under a contract, such as the posting of a bond or a showing that the debtor will generate sufficient income to pay any arrearages and future payment obligations.

adequate care. See *reasonable care* under CARE.

adequate cause. See ADEQUATE PROVOCATION.

adequate compensation. See *just compensation* under COMPENSATION.

adequate consideration. See CONSIDERATION.

adequate notice. See *due notice* under NOTICE.

adequate protection. *Bankruptcy.* The protection afforded to a holder of a secured claim against the debtor, such as a periodic cash payment or an additional lien <the bankruptcy court permitted the lender to foreclose on the debtor's home after finding a lack of adequate protection of the lender's property interest>. 11 USCA § 361.

> "Bankruptcy intends to safeguard secured creditors' encumbrances, but the stay threatens them by preventing the secured creditors from foreclosing or taking other actions to apply the property's value against the secured debt. Bankruptcy aims to guard against this threat by ordering relief . . . for lack of adequate protection of the secured interest." David G. Epstein et al., *Bankruptcy* § 3–27, at 140 (1993).

adequate provocation. Something (such as the heat of passion) that affects a person's reason and self-control, causing the person to impulsively commit a crime. • In certain circumstances, adequate provocation can reduce a charge from murder to manslaughter. — Also termed *adequate cause.* Cf. SELF-DEFENSE (1).

adequate remedy at law. See REMEDY.

adequate representation. A close alignment of interests between actual parties and potential parties in a lawsuit, so that the interests of potential parties are sufficiently protected by the actual parties. • The concept of adequate representation is often used in procedural contexts. For example, if a case is to be certified as a class action, there must be adequate representation by the named plaintiffs of all the potential class members. Fed. R. Civ. P. 23(a)(4). And if a nonparty is to intervene in a lawsuit, there must not already be adequate representation of the nonparty by an existing party. Fed. R. Civ. P. 24(a)(2).

adequate-state-grounds doctrine. A judge-made principle that prevents the Supreme Court from reviewing a state-court decision based partially on state law if a decision on a federal issue would not change the result.

adequate warning. *Products liability.* Notice of the potential dangers involved in using a product, provided in a way that is reasonably calculated to reach the product's consumers and to catch their attention, and written so that it is comprehensible to the average user of the product and fairly conveys the nature and extent of any danger involved in using the product and the way to avoid the danger. Restatement (Third) of Torts: Products Liability § 2(c) cmt. i (1998).

adesse (ad-**es**-ee), *vb. Civil law.* To be present. Cf. ABESSE.

adeu (ə-**dyoo**), *adv.* [Law French] Without day. • This is a common term in the Year Books, indicating a final dismissal from court (*alez adeu* "go hence without day"). See GO HENCE WITHOUT DAY; ALLER SAN JOUR.

ad eversionem juris nostri (ad i-vər-shee-**oh**-nəm **joor**-is **nos**-trɪ). [Law Latin] To the overthrow of our right.

ad excambium (ad eks-**kam**-bee-əm). [Law Latin] For exchange; for compensation.

ad exhaeredationem (ad eks-heer-ə-day-shee-**oh**-nəm). [Law Latin] To the disinheritance; to the injury of the inheritance.

"The writ of waste calls upon the tenant to appear and shew cause why he hath committed waste and destruction in the place named, *ad exhaeredationem*, to the disinherison of the plaintiff." 3 William Blackstone, *Commentaries on the Laws of England* 228 (1768).

ad exitum (ad **ek**-si-təm). [Law Latin] At issue; at the end (usu. of pleadings).

ad faciendam juratam illam (ad fay-shee-**en**-dəm jə-**ray**-təm **il**-əm). [Law Latin] To make up that jury.

ad faciendum (ad fay-shee-**en**-dəm). [Latin] To do; to make.

ad feodi firmam (ad **fee**-ə-dɪ **fər**-məm). [Law Latin] To fee farm. See FEE FARM.

ad fidem (ad **fɪ**-dəm), *adv.* [Law Latin] In allegiance; under allegiance; owing allegiance. • This term appeared in a variety of phrases, including *ad fidem regis* ("under the king's allegiance") and *natus ad fidem regis* ("born in allegiance to the king").

ad filum aquae (ad **fɪ**-ləm **ak**-wee), *adv.* [Law Latin] To the thread of the water; to the central line or middle of a stream. • This refers to the ownership reach of a riparian proprietor. — Also termed *ad medium filum aquae*.

ad filum viae (ad **fɪ**-ləm **vɪ**-ee), *adv.* [Law Latin] To the middle of the way; to the central line of the road. — Also termed *ad medium filum viae*.

ad finem (ad **fɪ**-nəm), *adv.* [Latin] To the end. • This citation signal, abbreviated in text *ad fin.*, formerly provided only the first page of the section referred to, but now usu. directs the reader to a stated span of pages.

ad firmam tradidi (ad **fər**-məm **tray**-də-dɪ), *n.* [Law Latin] See FARM LET.

ad fundandam jurisdictionem (ad fən-**dan**-dəm joor-is-dik-shee-**oh**-nəm), *vb.* [Law Latin] To make the basis of jurisdiction.

ad gaolam deliberandam (ad **jay**-ləm di-lib-ə-**ran**-dəm), *vb.* [Law Latin] To deliver the jail; to make jail delivery. See COMMISSION OF GAOL DELIVERY; JAIL DELIVERY.

ad gravamen (ad grə-**vay**-mən), *adv.* [Latin] To the grievance, injury, or oppression of (another person).

adherence. See ACCESSION (3).

adhesion. See ACCESSION (3).

adhesionary contract. See *adhesion contract* under CONTRACT.

adhesion contract. See CONTRACT.

adhesory contract. See *adhesion contract* under CONTRACT.

adhibere (ad-hə-**bair**-ee), *vb.* [Latin] *Civil law.* To apply; to use; to exercise.

adhibere diligentiam (ad-hə-**bair**-ee dil-ə-**jen**-shee-əm), *vb.* [Latin] *Civil law.* To use care.

ad hoc (ad **hok**), *adj.* [Latin "for this"] Formed for a particular purpose <the board created an ad hoc committee to discuss funding for the new arena>. — **ad hoc,** *adv.*

ad hoc arbitration. See ARBITRATION.

ad hoc compromis. See COMPROMIS.

ad hominem (ad **hom**-ə-nəm), *adj.* [Latin "to the person"] Appealing to personal prejudices rather than to reason; attacking an opponent's character rather than the opponent's assertions <the brief was replete with ad hominem attacks against opposing counsel>. — **ad hominem,** *adv.*

ad hunc diem (ad **həngk dɪ**-əm), *adv.* [Law Latin] To this day.

ad idem (ad **ɪ**-dəm). [Latin] To the same point or matter; of the same mind <the parties reached a consensus *ad idem* and agreed to consummate a sale>.

a die confectionis (ay **dɪ**-ee kən-fek-shee-**oh**-nis), *adv.* [Law Latin] From the day of the making.

a die datus (ay **dɪ**-ee **day**-təs), *n.* [Latin "given from (such-and-such) a day"] A lease provision establishing the beginning of the rental period.

adieu (ə-**dyoo**). [Law French "to God"] Farewell. • This term, although etymologically distinct, appears sometimes in the Year Books in place of *adeu*. See ADEU; ALLER A DIEU.

ad inde (ad **in**-dee), *adv.* [Law Latin] To that or them; thereto.

ad infinitum (ad in-fə-**nI**-təm). [Latin "without limit"] To an indefinite extent <a corporation has a duration *ad infinitum* unless the articles of incorporation specify a shorter period>.

ad inquirendum (ad in-kwə-**ren**-dəm), *n.* [Law Latin "to inquire"] *Hist.* A writ instructing the recipient to investigate something at issue in a pending case.

ad instantiam partis (ad in-**stan**-shee-əm **pahr**-tis), *adv.* [Law Latin] At the instance of a party.

ad interim (ad **in**-tər-im), *adv.* [Latin] In the meantime; temporarily.

adiratus (ad-ə-**ray**-təs), *adj.* [Law Latin] Lost; strayed; removed.

adjacent, *adj.* Lying near or close to, but not necessarily touching. Cf. ADJOINING.

adjective law (**aj**-ik-tiv). The body of rules governing procedure and practice; PROCEDURAL LAW. — Also termed *adjectival law.*

> "The body of law in a State consists of two parts, *substantive* and *adjective* law. The former prescribes those rules of civil conduct which declare the rights and duties of all who are subject to the law. The latter relates to the remedial agencies and procedure by which rights are maintained, their invasion redressed, and the methods by which such results are accomplished in judicial tribunals." Edwin E. Bryant, *The Law of Pleading Under the Codes of Civil Procedure* 1 (2d ed. 1899).

adjoining (ə-**joyn**-ing), *adj.* Touching; sharing a common boundary; CONTIGUOUS. — **adjoin** (ə-**joyn**), *vb.* Cf. ADJACENT.

adjoining owner. See OWNER.

adjourn (ə-**jərn**), *vb.* To recess or postpone.

adjourn sine die (**sI**-nee [*or* **sin**-ay] **dI**-ee). [Latin "without date"] To postpone action of a convened court or legislative body indefinitely.

adjournatur (aj-ər-**nay**-tər). [Latin] It is adjourned. • This word formerly appeared at the end of reported decisions.

adjourned term. See TERM (5).

adjournment (ə-**jərn**-mənt), *n.* **1.** A putting off of a court session or other meeting or assembly until a later time. **2.** The period or interval during which a session is put off.

adjournment day. See DAY.

adjournment day in error. See DAY.

adjudge (ə-**jəj**), *vb.* **1.** ADJUDICATE (1). **2.** To deem or pronounce to be. **3.** To award judicially.

adjudicate (ə-**joo**-di-kayt), *vb.* **1.** To rule upon judicially. **2.** ADJUDGE (2). **3.** ADJUDGE (3).

adjudicatee (ə-joo-di-kə-**tee**). *Civil law.* A purchaser at a judicial sale.

adjudicatio (ə-joo-di-**kay**-shee-oh), *n.* [Latin] *Roman & civil law.* A part of a formula (i.e., the praetor's statement of an issue for a judex) directing the judex to apportion property in a divisory action such as an *actio de communi dividundo.* See FORMULA (1).

adjudication (ə-joo-di-**kay**-shən), *n.* **1.** The legal process of resolving a dispute; the process of judicially deciding a case. **2.** JUDGMENT. **3.** *Scots law.* A method of transferring heritable land to a creditor as security for or in satisfaction of a debt.

adjudicative (ə-**joo**-di-kə-tiv), *adj.* **1.** Of or relating to adjudication. **2.** Having the ability to judge. — Also termed *adjudicatory*; *judicative.*

adjudicative-claims arbitration. See ARBITRATION.

adjudicative fact. See FACT.

adjudicative law. See CASELAW.

adjudicator (ə-**joo**-di-kay-tər). A person whose job is to render binding decisions; one who makes judicial pronouncements.

adjudicatory. See ADJUDICATIVE.

adjudicatory hearing. See HEARING.

ad judicium provocare (ad joo-**dish**-ee-əm proh-və-**kair**-ee), *vb.* [Latin] To summon to court; to commence an action.

adjunct (**aj**-əngkt), *adj.* Added as an accompanying object or circumstance; attached in a subordinate or temporary capacity <an adjunct professor>. — **adjunct,** *n.*

adjunct account. See ACCOUNT.

adjunction (ə-**jəngk**-shən). **1.** The act of adding to. **2.** *Civil law.* The union of an item of personal property owned by one person with that owned by another. See ACCESSION (4).

adjunctum accessorium (ə-**jəngk**-təm ak-sə-**sor**-ee-əm), *n.* [Law Latin] An accessory or appurtenance.

ad jungendum auxilium (ad jən-**jen**-dəm awg-**zil**-ee-əm), *vb.* [Law Latin] To join in aid.

ad jura regis (ad **joor**-ə **ree**-jis), *n.* [Law Latin "for the rights of the king"] *Hist.* A writ brought against a person seeking to eject the holder of a royal benefice. • The writ was available to the holder of the benefice.

adjure (ə-**juur**), *vb.* To charge or entreat solemnly <the President adjured the foreign government to join the alliance>. — **adjuration** (aj-ə-**ray**-shən), *n.* — **adjuratory** (ə-**juur**-ə-tor-ee), *adj.* — **adjurer, adjuror** (ə-**juur**-ər), *n.*

adjust, *vb.* **1.** To determine the amount that an insurer will pay an insured to cover a loss. **2.** To arrive at a new agreement with a creditor for the payment of a debt.

adjustable-rate mortgage. See MORTGAGE.

adjusted basis. See BASIS.

adjusted book value. See BOOK VALUE.

adjusted cost basis. See BASIS.

adjusted gross estate. See ESTATE.

adjusted gross income. See INCOME.

adjusted ordinary gross income. See INCOME.

adjusted present value. See PRESENT VALUE.

adjuster. One appointed to ascertain, arrange, or settle a matter; esp., an independent agent or employee of an insurance company who negotiates and settles claims against the insurer. — Also termed *claims adjuster.*

independent adjuster. An adjuster who solicits business from more than one insurance company; one who is not employed by, and does not work exclusively for, one insurance company.

adjusting entry. An accounting entry made at the end of an accounting period to record previously unrecognized revenue and expenses, as well as changes in assets and liabilities.

adjustment board. An administrative agency charged with hearing and deciding zoning appeals. — Also termed *board of adjustment*; *board of zoning appeals.*

adjustment bond. See BOND (3).

adjustment security. See SECURITY.

adjutant general (**aj**-ə-tənt), *n.* (*usu. cap.*) **1.** The administrative head of a military unit having a general staff. **2.** An officer in charge of the National Guard of a state.

ad largum (ad **lahr**-gəm), *adj.* [Law Latin] At large; at liberty; unconfined.

adlegiare (ad-lee-jee-**air**-ee), *vb.* [Law Latin] To purge (oneself) of a crime by oath. See PURGATION.

ad libellum rescribere (lə-**bel**-əm ri-**skrI**-bə-ree), *vb.* [Latin] *Roman law.* To write an answer to a petition, esp. one to the emperor.

ad libitum (ad **lib**-i-təm), *adv.* [Law Latin] At pleasure. • The modern term *ad-lib* (adj. & vb.), borrowed from drama and music, is essentially the same; it means "at the performer's pleasure," and allows the performer discretion in innovating a part impromptu.

> "[B]ut in actions where the damages are precarious, being to be assessed *ad libitum* by a jury, as in actions for words, ejectment, or trespass, it is very seldom possible for a plaintiff to swear to the amount of his cause of action; and therefore no special bail is taken thereon. . . ." 3 William Blackstone, *Commentaries on the Laws of England* 292 (1768).

ad litem (ad **lI**-tem *or* -təm). [Latin "for the suit"] For the purposes of the suit; pending the suit. See GUARDIAN AD LITEM.

ad lucrandum vel perdendum (ad loo-**kran**-dəm vel pər-**den**-dəm), *adv.* [Law Latin] For gain or loss. • These were emphatic words in a warrant of attorney. It is sometimes expressed "to lose and gain." See WARRANT OF ATTORNEY.

ad majorem cautelam (ad mə-**jor**-əm kaw-**tee**-ləm), *adv.* [Law Latin] For greater security.

admanuensis (ad-man-yoo-**en**-sis), *n.* [Law Latin fr. Latin *ad-* + *manus* "a hand"] *Hist.* An oath-taker who places a hand on the Bible.

ad manum (ad **may**-nəm), *adj.* [Latin] At hand; ready for use.

admeasurement (ad-**mezh**-ər-mənt), *n.* **1.** Ascertainment, assignment, or apportionment by a fixed quantity or value, or by certain limits <the ship's admeasurement is based on its crew, engine, and capacity>. **2.** A writ obtained for purposes of ascertaining, assigning, or apportioning a fixed quantity or value or to establish limits; esp., a writ available against persons who usurp more than their rightful share of property. — **admeasure** (ad-**mezh**-ər), *vb.*

admeasurement of dower. *Hist.* A writ to recover property from a widow who held more than she was entitled to. — Also termed *admensuratione dotis.*

admeasurement of pasture. *Hist.* A writ against a person whose cattle have overgrazed a common pasture.

ad medium filum aquae. See AD FILUM AQUAE.

ad medium filum viae. See AD FILUM VIAE.

ad melius inquirendum (ad **mee**-lee-əs in-kwə-**ren**-dəm), *n.* [Law Latin "for making better inquiry"] *Hist.* A writ commanding a coroner to hold a second inquest.

admensuratio (ad-men-shə-**ray**-shee-oh), *n.* [Law Latin] *Hist.* Admeasurement.

admensuratione dotis. See *admeasurement of dower* under ADMEASUREMENT.

adminicle (ad-**min**-i-kəl), *n.* Corroborative or explanatory proof. — Also termed *adminiculum.*

adminicular (ad-mə-**nik**-yə-lər), *adj.* Corroborative or auxiliary <adminicular evidence>.

adminiculate (ad-mə-**nik**-yə-layt), *vb. Scots law.* To give corroborating evidence.

adminiculum (ad-mə-**nik**-yə-ləm), *n.* [Latin "support"] *Roman law.* Legal or evidentiary means of supporting one's case; ADMINICLE.

administration, *n.* **1.** The management or performance of the executive duties of a government, institution, or business. **2.** In public law, the practical management and direction of the executive department and its agencies. **3.** A judicial action in which a court undertakes the management and distribution of property. • Examples include the administration of a trust, the liquidation of a company, and the realization and distribution of a bankrupt estate. **4.** The management and settlement of the estate of an intestate decedent, or of a testator who has no executor, by a person legally appointed and supervised by the court. — **administer,** *vb.* — **administrative,** *adj.* — **administrator,** *n.*

administration cum testamento annexo (kəm tes-tə-**men**-toh ə-**nek**-soh). [Latin "with the will annexed"] An administration granted when a testator's will does not name any executor or when the executor named is incompetent to act, is deceased, or refuses to act. — Abbr. c.t.a. — Also termed *administration with the will annexed.*

administration de bonis non (dee **boh**-nis **non**). [Latin "of the goods not administered"] An administration granted for the purpose of settling the remainder of an estate that was not administered by the former executor or administrator. — Abbr. d.b.n.

administration de bonis non cum testamento annexo (de **boh**-nis non kəm tes-tə-**men**-toh ə-**neks**-oh). An administration granted to settle the remainder of an estate not settled by a previous administrator or executor. • This type of administration arises when there is a will, as opposed to an *administration de bonis non,* which is granted when there is no will. — Abbr. d.b.n. c.t.a.

administration durante absentia (d[y]uu-**ran**-tee ab-**sen**-shee-ə). An administration granted during the absence of either the executor or the person who has precedence as administrator.

administration durante minore aetate (d[y]uu-**ran**-tee mi-**nor**-ee ee-**tay**-tee). An administration granted during the minority of either a child executor or the person who has precedence as administrator.

administration pendente lite (pen-**den**-tee **lɪ**-tee). An administration granted during the pendency of a suit concerning a will's validity. — Also termed *pendente lite administration; special administration.* See PENDENTE LITE.

administration with the will annexed. See *administration cum testamento annexo.*

ancillary administration (**an**-sə-ler-ee). An administration that is auxiliary to the administration at the place of the decedent's domicile, such as one in a foreign state, the purpose being to collect assets and pay debts in that locality. — Also termed *foreign administration*.

"The object of ancillary administration is to collect assets of nonresident decedents found within the state and remit the proceeds to the domiciliary executor or administrator, and historically it has been the only feasible way of doing this, although statutes in some jurisdictions permit simpler solutions today, such as permitting the domiciliary representative to act as local representative if he complies with certain requirements . . . ." 31 Am. Jur. 2d *Executors and Administrators* § 1168, at 558 (1989).

caeterorum administration (set-ə-**ror**-əm). [Latin "of the rest"] An administration granted when limited powers previously granted to an administrator are inadequate to settle the estate's residue.

domiciliary administration (dom-ə-**sil**-ee-er-ee). The handling of an estate in the state where the decedent was domiciled at death.

foreign administration. See *ancillary administration*.

general administration. An administration with authority to deal with an entire estate. Cf. *special administration*.

limited administration. An administration for a temporary period or for a special purpose.

pendente lite administration. See *administration pendente lite*.

public administration. In some jurisdictions, an administration by an officer appointed to administer for an intestate who has left no person entitled to apply for letters (or whose possible representatives refuse to serve).

special administration. **1.** An administration with authority to deal with only some of a decedent's effects, as opposed to administering the whole estate. **2.** See *administration pendente lite*. Cf. *general administration*.

temporary administration. An administration in which the court appoints a fiduciary to administer the affairs of a decedent's estate for a short time before an administrator or executor can be appointed and qualified.

administration expense. *Tax.* A necessary expenditure made by an administrator in managing and distributing an estate. • These expenses are deductible even if not actually incurred by the time the return is filed.

administration letters. See LETTERS OF ADMINISTRATION.

administration of justice. The maintenance of right within a political community by means of the physical force of the state; the state's application of the sanction of force to the rule of right.

administration pendente lite. See ADMINISTRATION.

administration with the will annexed. See *administration cum testamento annexo* under ADMINISTRATION.

administrative act. See ACT (2).

administrative adjudication. The process used by an administrative agency to issue regulations through an adversary proceeding. Cf. RULEMAKING.

administrative agency. See AGENCY (3).

administrative collateral estoppel. See COLLATERAL ESTOPPEL.

administrative-control rule. *Tax.* The rule making the grantor of a trust liable for tax if the grantor retains control that may be exercised primarily for the grantor's own benefit. IRC (26 USCA) § 675.

administrative-convenience exception. *Bankruptcy.* A provision permitting a bankruptcy plan to have a separate classification for small, unsecured claims, to the extent that the separate classification will assist in a more efficient disposition of the estate, as by paying or eliminating the small claims earlier than other claims. 11 USCA § 1122(b).

administrative crime. See CRIME.

administrative deviation. A trustee's unauthorized departure from the terms of the trust.

administrative discharge. See DISCHARGE (8).

administrative discretion. See DISCRETION.

administrative expense. **1.** OVERHEAD. **2.** *Bankruptcy.* A cost incurred by the debtor, after filing a bankruptcy petition, that is necessary for the debtor to continue operating its business. • Administrative expenses are entitled to payment on a priority basis when the estate is distributed. 11 USCA § 503(b). See *general administrative expense* under EXPENSE.

administrative freeze. *Bankruptcy.* The refusal by a debtor's bank to permit withdrawals from the debtor's bank account after the bank learns that the debtor has filed bankruptcy, usu. because the debtor owes money to the bank in addition to maintaining funds on deposit.

administrative hearing. An administrative-agency proceeding in which evidence is offered for argument or trial.

administrative interpretation. See INTERPRETATION.

administrative law. The law governing the organization and operation of the executive branch of government (including independent agencies) and the relations of the executive with the legislature, the judiciary, and the public. • Administrative law is divided into three parts: (1) the statutes endowing agencies with powers and establishing rules of substantive law relating to those powers; (2) the body of agency-made law, consisting of administrative rules, regulations, reports or opinions containing findings of fact, and orders; and (3) the legal principles governing the acts of public agents when those acts conflict with private rights.

> "Administrative law deals with the field of legal control exercised by law-administering agencies other than courts, and the field of control exercised by courts over such agencies." Felix Frankfurter, *The Task of Administrative Law*, 75 U. Pa. L. Rev. 614, 615 (1927).

international administrative law. **1.** The internal law and rules of international organizations. **2.** The substantive rules of international law that directly refer to the administrative matters of individual states. **3.** Domestic administrative law specifically concerned with international problems or situations. — Also termed *administrative international law.*

administrative-law judge. An official who presides at an administrative hearing and who has the power to administer oaths, take testimony, rule on questions of evidence, and make factual and legal determinations. 5 USCA § 556(c). — Abbr. ALJ. — Also termed *hearing examiner*; *hearing officer*; *trial examiner.*

Administrative Office of the United States Courts. A federal agency that carries out the nonjudicial business of the federal courts. • The Administrative Office collects statistics on the courts, supervises the administrative personnel, disburses the payroll, and performs other similar functions.

administrative officer. See OFFICER (1).

administrative order. See ORDER (2).

administrative procedure. See PROCEDURE.

Administrative Procedure Act. **1.** A federal statute establishing practices and procedures to be followed in rulemaking and adjudication. • The Act was designed to give citizens basic due-process protections such as the right to present evidence and to be heard by an independent hearing officer. **2.** A similar state statute.

administrative proceeding. A hearing, inquiry, investigation, or trial before an administrative agency, usu. adjudicatory in nature but sometimes quasi-legislative. — Also termed *evidentiary hearing*; *full hearing*; *trial-type hearing*; *agency adjudication.*

administrative process. **1.** The procedure used before administrative agencies. **2.** The means of summoning witnesses to an agency hearing.

administrative remedy. See REMEDY.

administrative review. See REVIEW.

administrative rule. A broadly applicable agency statement that interprets a law or policy or describes the agency's requirements.

administrative rulemaking. See RULEMAKING.

administrative search. See SEARCH.

administrative tribunal. An administrative agency before which a matter may be heard or tried, as distinguished from a purely executive agency; an administrative agency exercising a judicial function.

administrative warrant. See WARRANT (1).

administrator (ad-**min**-ə-stray-tər). **1.** A person appointed by the court to manage the assets and liabilities of an intestate decedent. • This term once referred to males only (as opposed to *administratrix*), but legal writers now generally use *administrator* to refer to someone of either sex. Cf. EXECUTOR (2).

administrator ad litem (ad **lI**-tem *or* -təm). A special administrator appointed by the court to represent the estate's interest in an action usu. either because there is no administrator of the estate or because the current administrator has an interest in the action adverse to that of the estate.

administrator ad prosequendum (ad prahs-ə-**kwen**-dəm). An administrator appointed to prosecute or defend a certain action or actions involving the estate.

administrator c.t.a. See *administrator cum testamento annexo.*

administrator cum testamento annexo (kəm tes-tə-**men**-toh ə-**nek**-soh). An administrator appointed by the court to carry out the provisions of a will when the testator has named no executor, or the executors named refuse, are incompetent to act, or have died before performing their duties. — Also termed *administrator c.t.a.*; *administrator with the will annexed.*

administrator de bonis non (dee **boh**-nis **non**). An administrator appointed by the court to administer the decedent's goods that were not administered by an earlier administrator or executor. • If there is no will, the administrator bears the name *administrator de bonis non* (abbr. *administrator d.b.n.*), but if there is a will, the full name is *administrator de bonis non cum testamento annexo* (abbr. *administrator d.b.n. c.t.a.*).

administrator pendente lite. See *special administrator.*

administrator with the will annexed. See *administrator cum testamento annexo.*

ancillary administrator (**an**-sə-ler-ee). A court-appointed administrator who oversees the distribution of the part of a decedent's estate located in a jurisdiction other than that of the main administration, where the decedent was domiciled.

foreign administrator. An administrator appointed in another jurisdiction.

general administrator. A person appointed to administer an intestate decedent's entire estate.

public administrator. A state-appointed officer who administers intestate estates that are not administered by the decedent's relatives. • This officer's right to administer is usu. subordinate to the rights of creditors, but in a few jurisdictions the creditors' rights are subordinate.

special administrator. **1.** A person appointed to administer only a specific part of an intestate decedent's estate. **2.** A person appointed to serve as administrator of an estate solely because of an emergency or an unusual situation, such as a will contest. — Also termed (in sense 2) *administrator pendente lite.*

2. A person who manages or heads a business, public office, or agency.

court administrator. An official who supervises the nonjudicial functions of a court, esp. the court's calendar, judicial assignments, budget, and nonjudicial personnel.

administrator ad litem. See ADMINISTRATOR (1).

administrator ad prosequendum. See ADMINISTRATOR (1).

administrator c.t.a. See *administrator cum testamento annexo* under ADMINISTRATOR (1).

administrator cum testamento annexo. See ADMINISTRATOR (1).

administrator d.b.n. See *administrator de bonis non* under ADMINISTRATOR (1).

administrator de bonis non. See ADMINISTRATOR (1).

administrator pendente lite. See *special administrator* (2) under ADMINISTRATOR (1).

administrator's deed. See DEED.

administrator with the will annexed. See *administrator cum testamento annexo* under ADMINISTRATOR (1).

administratrix (ad-min-ə-**stray**-triks *or* ad-**min**-ə-strə-triks). *Archaic.* A female administrator. See ADMINISTRATOR (1).

admiralitas (ad-mə-**ral**-ə-tas), *n.* [Law Latin] **1.** Admiralty; an admiralty court. **2.** SOCIETAS NAVALIS.

admiralty (**ad**-mə-rəl-tee), *n.* **1.** A court that exercises jurisdiction over all maritime contracts, torts, injuries, or offenses. • The federal courts are so called when exercising their admiralty jurisdiction, which is conferred by the U.S. Constitution (art. III, § 2, cl. 1). — Also termed *admiralty court*; *maritime court.* **2.** The system of jurisprudence that has grown out of the practice of admiralty courts; MARITIME LAW. **3.** Narrowly, the rules governing contract, tort, and workers'-compensation claims arising out of commerce on or over water. — Also termed (in senses 2 & 3) *admiralty law*. — **admiralty,** *adj.*

Admiralty, First Lord. See FIRST LORD OF THE ADMIRALTY.

Admiralty Clause. The clause of the U.S. Constitution giving the federal courts jurisdiction over maritime cases. U.S. Const. art. III, § 2, cl. 1.

admiralty court. See ADMIRALTY (1).

admiralty law. See MARITIME LAW.

admissibility (ad-mis-ə-**bil**-ə-tee), *n.* The quality or state of being allowed to be entered into evidence in a hearing, trial, or other proceeding.

> "'Admissibility' can best be thought of as a concept consisting of two quite different aspects: disclosure to the trier of fact and express or implied permission to use as 'evidence.' If we think of admissibility as a question of disclosure or nondisclosure, it is usually easy to say whether or not an item of evidence has been admitted. When we consider the question of permissible use, the concept seems much more complex. In the first place, evidence may be 'admissible' for one purpose but not for another. . . . In the second place, questions of the permissible use of evidence do not arise only at the time of disclosure to the trier of fact. The court may have to consider admissibility in deciding whether to give the jury a limiting instruction, whether or not an opponent's rebuttal evidence is relevant, and whether or not counsel can argue to the jury that the evidence proves a particular point." 22 Charles Alan Wright & Kenneth W. Graham, Jr., *Federal Practice and Procedure* § 5193, at 184 (1978).

conditional admissibility. The evidentiary rule that when a piece of evidence is not itself admissible, but is admissible if certain other facts make it relevant, the evidence becomes admissible on condition that counsel later introduce the connecting facts. • If counsel does not satisfy this condition, the opponent may ask the judge to strike from the record the conditionally admitted piece of evidence and to instruct the jury to disregard it.

curative admissibility. The rule that an inadmissible piece of evidence may be admitted if offered to cure or counteract the effect of some similar piece of the opponent's evidence that itself should not have been admitted.

limited admissibility. The principle that testimony or exhibits may be admitted into evidence for a restricted purpose. • Common examples are admitting prior contradictory testimony to impeach a witness but not to establish the truth, and admitting evidence against one party but not another. The trial court must instruct the jury properly about the applicable limits when admitting the evidence. Fed. R. Evid. 105.

multiple admissibility. The evidentiary rule that, though a piece of evidence is inadmissible under one rule for the purpose given in offering it, it is nevertheless admissible if relevant and offered for some other purpose not forbidden by the rules of evidence.

admissible (ad-**mis**-ə-bəl), *adj.* **1.** Allowable; permissible <admissible evidence>. **2.** Worthy of gaining entry or being admitted <a person is admissible to the bar upon obtaining a law degree and passing the bar exam>.

admissible evidence. See EVIDENCE.

admission (ad-**mish**-ən), *n.* **1.** A voluntary acknowledgment of the existence of facts relevant to an adversary's case. — **admit,** *vb.* Cf. CONFESSION.

admission against interest. A person's statement acknowledging a material fact that is harmful to the person's position as a litigant. • An admission against interest must be made either by a litigant or by one in privity with or occupying the same legal position as the litigant; as an exception to the hearsay rule, it is admissible whether or not the person is available as a witness. A declaration against interest, by contrast, is made by a nonlitigant who is not in privity with a litigant; a declaration against interest is also admissible as an exception to the hearsay rule, but only when the declarant is unavailable as a witness.

admission by employee or agent. An admission made by a party-opponent's agent during employment and concerning a matter either within the scope of the agency or authorized by the party-opponent.

admission by party-opponent. An opposing party's admission, which is not considered hearsay if it is offered against that party and is (1) the party's own statement, in either an individual or a representative capacity; (2) a statement of which the party has manifested an adoption or belief in its truth; (3) a statement by one authorized by the party to make such a statement; (4) a statement by the party's agent concerning a matter within the scope of the agency or employment and made during the existence of the relationship; or (5) a statement by a coconspirator of the party during the course of and in furtherance of the conspiracy. Fed. R. Evid. 801(d)(2).

admission by silence. The failure of a party to speak after an assertion of fact by another party that, if untrue, would naturally compel a person to deny the statement.

admission in judicio. See *judicial admission.*

adoptive admission. An action by a party that indicates approval of a statement made by another, and thereby acceptance of the truth of the statement.

extrajudicial admission. An admission made outside court proceedings.

implied admission. An admission reasonably inferable from a party's action or statement, or a party's failure to act or speak. — Also termed *tacit admission.*

incidental admission. An admission made in some other connection or involved in the admission of some other fact.

incriminating admission. An admission of facts tending to establish guilt.

judicial admission. A formal waiver of proof that relieves an opposing party from having to prove the admitted fact and bars the party who made the admission from disputing it. — Also termed *solemn admission*; *admission in judicio*; *true admission.*

quasi-admission. An act or utterance, usu. extrajudicial, that creates an inconsistency with and discredits, to a greater or lesser degree, a present claim or other evidence of the person creating the inconsistency.

solemn admission. See *judicial admission.*

tacit admission. See *implied admission.*

true admission. See *judicial admission.*

2. Acceptance of a lawyer by the established licensing authority, such as a state bar association, as a member of the practicing bar, usu. after the lawyer passes a bar examination and supplies adequate character references <admission to the bar>.

admission on motion. Permanent admission of a lawyer who is in good standing in the bar of a different state without the need for a full bar examination.

admission pro hac vice (proh hak **vI**-see *or* proh hak **vee**-chay). Temporary admission of an out-of-jurisdiction lawyer to practice before a court in a specified case or set of cases. See PRO HAC VICE.

admission against interest. See ADMISSION (1).

admission by employee or agent. See ADMISSION (1).

admission by party-opponent. See ADMISSION (1).

admission by silence. See ADMISSION (1).

admission in judicio. See *judicial admission* under ADMISSION.

admission tax. See TAX.

admission to sufficient facts. See SUBMISSION TO A FINDING.

admittance. 1. The act of entering a building, locality, or the like. **2.** Permission to enter. **3.** *Hist.* The act of giving seisin of a copyhold estate. • Admittance corresponded with livery of seisin of a freehold. Copyhold estates were abolished by the Law of Property Act of 1922. See COPYHOLD.

admitted asset. See ASSET.

admitted corporation. See CORPORATION.

admittendo clerico (ad-mi-**ten**-doh **kler**-ə-koh). See DE CLERICO ADMITTENDO.

admittendo in socium (ad-mi-**ten**-doh in **soh**-shee-əm). [Latin] *Hist.* A writ for associating certain persons, such as knights, to justices of assize on the circuit.

admixture (ad-**miks**-chər). **1.** The mixing of things. **2.** A substance formed by mixing.

admonition (ad-mə-**nish**-ən), *n.* **1.** Any authoritative advice or caution from the court to the jury regarding their duty as jurors or the admissibility of evidence for consideration <the judge's admonition that the jurors not discuss the case until they are charged>. **2.** A reprimand or cautionary statement addressed to counsel by a judge <the judge's admonition that the lawyer stop speaking out of turn>. — **admonish** (ad-**mon**-ish), *vb.* — **admonitory** (ad-**mon**-ə-tor-ee), *adj.*

admonitio trina (ad-mə-**nish**-ee-oh **trI**-nə), *n.* [Law Latin "triple warning"] *Hist.* A threefold warning advising a defendant charged with a capital crime that refusal to answer questions about the offense would in itself be considered a capital crime punishable by death. See PEINE FORT ET DURE.

ad mordendum assuetus (ad mor-**den**-dəm ə-**swee**-təs), *adj.* [Law Latin] *Hist.* Accustomed to bite. • This phrase was a common charge in a declaration of damage done by a dog to a person or to another animal.

admortization (ad-mor-tə-**zay**-shən). *Hist.* The reduction of property of lands or tenements to mortmain.

adnepos (ad-**nep**-ohs), *n.* [Latin] A great-great grandson.

adneptis (ad-**nep**-tis), *n.* [Latin] A great-great granddaughter.

adnihilare (ad-nI-hə-**lair**-ee), *vb.* [Law Latin] To annul; to make void.

ad nocumentum (ad nok-yoo-**men**-təm), *adv.* [Law Latin] To the nuisance; to the hurt or injury.

ad non executa (ad non ek-sə-**kyoo**-tə), *adv.* [Latin] For the things not executed (as by an executor).

adnotatio (ad-noh-**tay**-shee-oh), *n.* [Latin] *Roman law.* A note written in the margin of a document; esp., the reply of the emperor in his own hand to a petition addressed to him. See RESCRIPT (3).

adoption, *n.* **1.** *Family law.* The statutory process of terminating a child's legal rights and duties toward the natural parents and substituting similar rights and duties toward adoptive parents.

adoption by estoppel. An equitable adoption of a child by a person's promises and acts that preclude the person and his or her estate from denying adopted status to the child. — Also termed *equitable adoption*; *virtual adoption*.

de facto adoption. An adoption that falls short of the statutory requirements in a particular state. • The adoption agreement may ripen to a de jure adoption when the statutory formalities have been met.

2. *Contracts.* The process by which a person agrees to assume a contract previously made for that person's benefit, such as a newly formed corporation's acceptance of a preincorporation contract. — **adopt,** *vb.* — **adoptive,** *adj.*

adoption by reference. See INCORPORATION BY REFERENCE.

adoptive admission. See ADMISSION (1).

adoptive parent. See PARENT.

ad opus (ad **oh**-pəs), *adv.* [Law Latin] For the benefit; for the use. • This term indicated an intent to create a use to benefit another. See USE (4).

ad ostendendum (ad ah-sten-**den**-dəm), *vb.* [Law Latin] To show.

ad ostium ecclesiae (ad **ah**-stee-əm e-**klee**-z[h]ee-ee), *adv.* [Law Latin] At the church door. See *dower ad ostium ecclesiae*.

ad pios usus (ad **pI**-ohs **yoo**-səs *or* **yoo**-zəs), *adv.* [Law Latin] For pious (religious or charitable) uses or purposes. • This phrase was used in reference to gifts and bequests.

adpromission (ad-prə-**mish**-ən). *Roman law.* **1.** A suretyship contract. • Roman law had five types of adpromission: (1) sponsion; (2) fidepromission; (3) fidejussion; (4) mandatum; and (5) pactum de constituto. **2.** A suretyship relation. — Also termed *adpromissio*. — **adpromissor,** *n.*

ad prosequendam (ad prahs-ə-**kwen**-dəm), *vb.* [Law Latin] To prosecute.

ad punctum temporis (ad **pəngk**-təm **tem**-pə-ris), *adv.* [Law Latin] At the point of time.

ad quaerimoniam (ad kweer-ə-**moh**-nee-əm), *adv.* [Law Latin] On complaint of.

ad quem (ad **kwem**), *adv.* [Latin] To whom. • This term is used as a correlative to *a quo* in computation of time or distance. For example, the *terminus a quo* is the point of beginning or departure; the *terminus ad quem* is the end of the period or point of arrival.

ad quod curia concordavit (ad kwod **kyoor**-ee-ə kon-kor-**day**-vit). [Law Latin] To which the court agreed.

ad quod damnum (ad kwod **dam**-nəm). [Latin "to what damage"] *Hist.* A writ directing the sheriff to inquire of jurors under oath to what damage a grant (as of a fair, market, liberty, or other franchise) would be to various people if the king were to make the grant. • The writ was issuable from the court of chancery. — Also termed *writ of ad quod damnum.*

ad quod non fuit responsum (ad kwod non **fyoo**-it ri-**spon**-səm). [Law Latin] To which there was no answer. • This phrase was used in law reports to indicate an unresponded-to argument or objection.

ADR. *abbr.* **1.** ALTERNATIVE DISPUTE RESOLUTION. **2.** ASSET-DEPRECIATION RANGE. **3.** AMERICAN DEPOSITORY RECEIPT.

ad rationem ponere (ad ray-shee-**oh**-nəm **poh**-nə-ree), *vb.* [Law Latin "to give a reason"] To cite (a person) to appear. • The Exchequer summoned persons to appear and explain a charge with this phrase.

ad recognoscendum (ad ree-kog-nə-**sen**-dəm), *vb.* [Law Latin] To recognize. • These were formal words in writs.

adrectare (ad-rek-**tair**-ee), *vb.* [Law Latin] *Hist.* To do right; to satisfy.

ad rectum (ad **rek**-təm), *vb.* [Law Latin] To right; to meet an accusation.

ad reparationem et sustentationem (ad rep-ə-ray-shee-**oh**-nəm et sə-sten-tay-shee-**oh**-nəm), *adv.* [Law Latin] For repairing and keeping in suitable condition.

ad respondendum (ad ree-spon-**den**-dəm). [Latin] To answer. See *capias ad respondendum* under CAPIAS; *habeas corpus ad respondendum* under HABEAS CORPUS.

adrogate (**ad**-roh-gayt), *vb. Roman law.* (Of a man) to adopt a son or daughter who is not already under another father's power (*patria potestas*).

adrogation (ad-roh-**gay**-shən), *n. Roman law.* An adoption of a person of full capacity (*sui juris*) into another family. — Also termed *adrogatio* (ad-roh-**gay**-shee-oh).

ads. *abbr.* AD SECTAM.

ad satisfaciendum (ad sat-is-fay-shee-**en**-dəm). [Latin] To satisfy. See *capias ad satisfaciendum* under CAPIAS.

adscendentes (ad-sen-**den**-teez), *n. pl.* [Latin] *Civil law.* Ascendants.

adscripti glebae (ad-**skrip**-tɪ **glee**-bee), *n.* [Latin "(tenants) tied to the soil"] *Roman law.* Tenants or serfs bound to the land. • If the land was conveyed, the serfs were conveyed along with it. — Also termed *glebae ascriptitii.*

adscriptitius (ad-skrip-**tish**-ee-əs), *n.* [Latin] *Roman law.* **1.** A supernumerary soldier. **2.** A tenant bound to the land. — Also spelled *ascripticius.*

adscriptus (ad-**skrip**-təs), *adj.* [Latin] *Roman law.* Added, annexed, or bound by or in writing; enrolled or registered; generally bound, as in *servus colonae adscriptus* (a tenant bound to an estate as a cultivator) or *fundus adscriptus* (an estate bound to or burdened with a duty).

ad sectam (ad **sek**-təm), *adj.* [Law Latin] At the suit of. • This term, in abbreviated form, was used in indexing the names of cases by defendant — for example, "B *ads.* A" if B is the defendant. — Abbr. *ads.*

adsessor (ad-**ses**-ər), *n.* [Latin] **1.** *Roman law.* A legally qualified assistant or adviser to a judge. **2.** *Hist.* Assessor. • This was a title of a master in chancery.

adstipulator (ad-**stip**-yə-lay-tər), *n.* [Latin] *Roman law.* An additional party to a contract who could enforce the contract along with the principal (i.e., the *stipulator*). • An *adstipulator* who enforced an agreement would have to, in turn, pay the *stipulator*. An *adstipulator* was brought in to avoid the rule that a person could not directly stipulate for payment after death.

ad terminum annorum (ad **tər**-mə-nəm ə-**nor**-əm), *adv.* [Law Latin] For a term of years.

ad terminum qui praeteriit (ad **tər**-mə-nəm kwɪ pri-**ter**-ee-it). [Law Latin "for a term which has passed"] A writ of entry to recover land leased out to a holdover tenant. — Also termed *entry ad terminum qui praeteriit.*

ad testificandum (ad tes-ti-fi-**kan**-dəm). [Latin] To testify. See *habeas corpus ad testificandum* under HABEAS CORPUS; *subpoena ad testificandum* under SUBPOENA.

ad tunc et ibidem (ad **təngk** et i-**bɪ**-dəm *or* **ib**-i-dəm), *adv.* [Latin] *Hist.* Then and there being found. • This phrase was formerly used in indictments.

adult (ə-**dəlt** *or* **ad**-əlt), *n.* A person who has attained the legal age of majority, generally 18. • In criminal cases, the age of majority is typically 17. — Also termed *major.* — **adult** (ə-**dəlt**), *adj.*

adult correctional institution. See PRISON.

adulter (ə-**dəl**-tər), *n.* [Latin] *Roman law.* An adulterer; a man guilty of adultery.

adultera (ə-**dəl**-tə-rə), *n.* [Latin] *Roman law.* An adulteress; a woman guilty of adultery.

adulterate (ə-**dəl**-tə-rayt), *vb.* To debase or make impure by adding a foreign or inferior substance. — **adulteration,** *n.*

adulterated drug. See DRUG.

adulterator (ə-**dəl**-tə-ray-tər), *n.* [Latin fr. *adulterare* "to adulterate"] *Civil law.* A corrupter; a forger; a counterfeiter, as in *adulteratores monetae* ("counterfeiters of money").

adulterine (ə-**dəl**-tə-rin), *adj.* **1.** Characterized by adulteration. **2.** Illegal; unlicensed. **3.** Born of adultery. **4.** Of or involving adultery.

adulterine, *n. Archaic.* An illegitimate child.

adulterine guild. *Hist.* A group of traders who act like a corporation without a charter and who pay an annual fine for permission to exercise their usurped privileges.

adulterini (ə-dəl-tə-**rɪ**-nɪ). [Law Latin] *Hist.* Children begotten adulterously. Cf. INCESTUOSI.

adulterium (ad-əl-**teer**-ee-əm), *n.* [Latin] *Roman & civil law.* **1.** The crime of adultery. **2.** A punishment imposed for the offense of adultery.

> "Adulterium. A statutory punishment of adultery, which was considered a criminal offense only when committed by a married woman (*adultera*) .... [Before the statute *Lex Julia de adulteriis coercendis* of 18 B.C.], customary law admitted only immediate revenge of the husband .... Under the Julian statute, the father of the adulterous woman was permitted to kill her and her partner (*adulter*) if he surprised them in his or her husband's house. The husband's rights were rather limited; he was forced to divorce her, for otherwise he made himself guilty of matchmaking .... Besides, he or his father had to accuse the adulteress of *adulterium* which now became a public crime prosecuted before a criminal court." Adolf Berger, *Encyclopedic Dictionary of Roman Law* 352 (1953).

adultery (ə-**dəl**-tə-ree), *n.* Voluntary sexual intercourse between a married person and a person other than the offender's spouse. — Formerly also termed *spouse-breach.* — **adulterous,** *adj.* Cf. FORNICATION; INFIDELITY.

> "Returning to the question of adultery, evidently this word cannot be interpreted today in precisely the meaning it bore for the Old Testament patriarchs. On Old Testament principles one may marry several wives, even two sisters; and a married man may and should beget children for his dead brother. When Sarah found herself childless, she advised her husband Abraham to go in unto her maid, so that she might obtain children by the maid. Such acts, though evidently not adulterous within the original meaning of the Decalogue, would be regarded as adulterous by the laws and customs of Western society at the present day." Glanville Williams, *The Sanctity of Life and the Criminal Law* 134 (1957).

> "If a statute provided for the punishment of adultery without definition of the term, this gave rise to a difficulty as to the meaning of the word. In England, (1) the common-law meaning of the word was sex with another's wife, but this was not a common-law offense; (2) as the name of an offense it referred to sex by a married person with one other than the spouse, but that was recognized only in the ecclesiastical court." Rollin M. Perkins & Ronald N. Boyce, *Criminal Law* 455 (3d ed. 1982).

> "In some states, sexual intercourse between two married persons, who are not married to each other, constitutes adultery on the part of both; sexual intercourse between a married person and an unmarried person likewise constitutes adultery on the part of both. In other states, adultery can be committed only by a married person. Thus, sexual intercourse between two married persons, who are not married to each other, constitutes adultery on the part of both; but if only one party to the sexual intercourse is married, the intercourse constitutes adultery on the part of the married person and fornication on the part of the unmarried person. In other states, sexual intercourse constitutes adultery only where the woman is the married party. Thus, sexual intercourse between a married woman and a married man other than her spouse or sexual intercourse between a married woman and an unmarried man constitutes adultery on the part of both; but if the woman is unmarried, neither party is guilty of adultery even if the man is married." 2 Charles E. Torcia, *Wharton's Criminal Law* § 211, at 531 (15th ed. 1994).

double adultery. Adultery between persons who are both married to other persons.

incestuous adultery. Adultery between relatives; adultery committed by persons who are closely related.

open and notorious adultery. *Archaic.* An offense in which the parties reside together publicly, as if conjugal relations existed between them, and the community is generally aware of the living arrangement and the fact that the couple is not married.

single adultery. Adultery in which only one party is married to another person.

adult offender. See OFFENDER.

ad usum et commodum (ad **yoo**-səm [*or* -zəm] et **kom**-ə-dəm), *adv.* [Law Latin] To the use and benefit.

ad valentiam (ad və-**len**-shee-əm), *adv.* [Law Latin] To the value.

ad valorem (ad və-**lor**-əm), *adj.* [Latin "according to the value"] (Of a tax) proportional to the value of the thing taxed. — **ad valorem,** *adv.*

ad valorem tax. See TAX.

advance, *n.* **1.** The furnishing of money or goods before any consideration is received in return. **2.** The money or goods furnished.

advance bill. See BILL (6).

advance-decline index. See INDEX (2).

advance directive. 1. A durable power of attorney that takes effect upon one's incompetency and designates a surrogate decision-maker for healthcare matters. See POWER OF ATTORNEY. **2.** A legal document explaining one's wishes about medical treatment if one becomes incompetent or unable to communicate. — Also termed *medical directive*; *physician's directive*; *written directive.* Cf. LIVING WILL.

advancement, *n.* A payment or gift to an heir (esp. a child) during one's lifetime as an advance share of one's estate, with the intention of extinguishing the heir's claim to the estate under intestacy laws. — **advance,** *vb.* Cf. ADEMPTION.

advance payment. See PAYMENT.

advance premium. See PREMIUM (1).

advance sheets. A softcover pamphlet containing recently reported opinions by a court or set of courts. • Advance sheets are published during the interim between an opinion's announcement and its inclusion in a bound volume of law reports. Cf. *slip opinion* (1) under OPINION; REPORT (3).

> "As a bound volume of any series of reports is not published until sufficient matter has accumulated to fill it, it necessarily results in the holding of the first decisions rendered after the preceding volume has been issued, until there are enough more to justify the publication of the next volume. Even after enough material has been accumulated to fill a volume, there is necessarily considerable time consumed in its printing, indexing, and binding before the book is ready for delivery. Hence, it is customary, as soon as a part of the volume has come from the press, to issue such part in pamphlet form; and these paper-bound copies are known as 'advance sheets.' They are portions of the next volume issued in advance of final publication, being paged as they will appear in the bound volume. Advance sheets enable the enterprising lawyer to obtain the decisions right down almost to the date of his search for the law." Frank Hall Childs, *Where and How to Find the Law* 21 (1922).

advancing market. See *bull market* under MARKET.

advantagium (ad-van-**tay**-jee-əm), *n.* [Law Latin] *Hist.* An advantage.

advena (**ad**-və-nə), *n.* [Latin] *Roman law.* One who has come from abroad, esp. for a temporary stay; a sojourner. — Also termed *albanus.*

adventitia bona (ad-ven-**tish**-ee-ə **boh**-nə), *n.* [Latin] **1.** *Roman law.* Goods acquired by free persons in some way other than through their paterfamilias, or by slaves in a way other than through their owner. **2.** *Civil law.* Goods acquired fortuitously, but not by inheritance.

adventitia dos (ad-ven-**tish**-ee-ə **dohs**), *n.* [Latin] *Civil law.* A dowry given by someone other than the wife's paterfamilias.

ad ventrem inspiciendum (ad **ven**-trəm in-spish-ee-**en**-dəm), *n.* [Latin] See DE VENTRE INSPICIENDO.

adventura (ad-ven-**t[y]oor**-ə), *n.* [Law Latin] *Hist.* An adventure. • Flotsam, jetsam, and lagan were styled *adventurae maris* ("adventures of the sea").

adventure. 1. A commercial undertaking that has an element of risk; a venture. Cf. JOINT VENTURE. **2.** *Marine insurance.* A voyage involving financial and insurable risk, as to a shipment of goods.

gross adventure. A loan on bottomry, so called because the lender will be liable for the gross (or general) average. See BOTTOMRY.

joint adventure. See JOINT ADVENTURE.

adventurer. A person who undertakes a hazardous action or enterprise; one with a stake in a commercial adventure.

adversarius (ad-vər-**sair**-ee-əs), *n.* [Latin] *Roman law.* An adversary in a lawsuit.

adversary (**ad**-vər-ser-ee), *n.* An opponent; esp., opposing counsel. — **adversary, adversarial,** *adj.*

adversary procedure. See ADVERSARY SYSTEM.

adversary proceeding. 1. A hearing involving a dispute between opposing parties <Judge Adams presided over the adversary proceeding between the landlord and tenant>. **2.** *Bankruptcy.* A lawsuit that is brought within a bankruptcy proceeding, governed by special procedural rules, and based on conflicting claims usu. between the debtor (or the trustee) and a creditor or other interested party <the Chapter 7 trustee filed an adversary proceeding against the party who received $100,000 from the debtor one week before the bankruptcy filing>.

adversary system. A procedural system, such as the Anglo–American legal system, involving active and unhindered parties contesting with each other to put forth a case before an independent decision-maker. — Also termed *adversary procedure* and (in criminal cases) *accusatorial system* or *accusatory procedure.* Cf. INQUISITORIAL SYSTEM.

adverse-agent doctrine. The rule that an agent's knowledge will not be imputed to the principal if the agent is engaged in fraudulent activities that are concealed as part of the fraud.

adverse authority. See AUTHORITY (4).

adverse-domination doctrine. The equitable principle that the statute of limitations on a breach-of-fiduciary-duty claim against officers and directors is tolled as long as a corporate plaintiff is controlled by the alleged wrongdoers. • The statute is tolled until a majority of the disinterested directors discover or are put on notice of the claim against the wrongdoers. This doctrine is available to benefit only the corporation.

adverse dominion. The doctrine that tolls the limitations period for claims against wrongdoing directors and officers of a corporation while they are in control of the corporation. • The purpose of this doctrine is to prevent a director or officer from successfully hiding wrongful or fraudulent conduct during the limitations period. *FDIC v. Shrader & York*, 991 F.2d 216, 227 (5th Cir. 1993).

adverse easement. See *prescriptive easement* under EASEMENT.

adverse employment action. An employer's decision that substantially and negatively affects an employee's job, such as a termination, demotion, or pay cut. — Also termed *adverse job action.*

adverse enjoyment. See ENJOYMENT.

adverse impact. See DISPARATE IMPACT.

adverse-inference rule. See ADVERSE-INTEREST RULE.

adverse interest. An interest that is opposed or contrary to that of someone else.

adverse-interest rule. The principle that if a party fails to produce a witness who is within its power to produce and who should have been produced, the judge may instruct the jury to infer that the witness's evidence is unfavorable to the party's case. — Also termed *empty-chair doctrine*; *adverse-inference rule.*

adverse job action. See ADVERSE EMPLOYMENT ACTION.

adverse opinion. See OPINION (2).

adverse party. See PARTY (2).

adverse possession. A method of acquiring title to real property by possession for a statutory period under certain conditions, esp. a nonpermissive use of the land with a claim of right when that use is continuous, exclusive, hostile, open, and notorious. Cf. PRESCRIPTION (2).

> ***constructive adverse possession.*** Adverse possession in which the claim arises from the claimant's payment of taxes under color of right rather than by actual possession of the land.

adverse title. See TITLE (2).

adverse use. See USE (1).

adverse witness. See *hostile witness* under WITNESS.

adversus (ad-**vər**-səs), *prep.* [Latin] Against. • The first letter of this term was formerly used in law reports in place of the more commonly used *v.* ("versus"). — Abbr. a.

adversus bonos mores. See CONTRA BONOS MORES.

advertent negligence. See NEGLIGENCE.

advertising. **1.** The action of drawing the public's attention to something to promote its sale. **2.** The business of producing and circulating advertisements.

comparative advertising. Advertising that specifically compares the advertised brand with another brand of the same product.

competitive advertising. Advertising that contains little information about the advertised product, and that is used only to help a producer maintain a share of the market for that product.

informative advertising. Advertising that gives information about the suitability and quality of a product.

advertising substantiation. A doctrine of the Federal Trade Commission making it an unfair and deceptive act to put out an advertisement unless the advertiser first has a reasonable basis for believing that each claim in the advertisement is true.

advice (ad-**vIs**). **1.** Guidance offered by one person, esp. a lawyer, to another. See ADVICE OF COUNSEL. **2.** Notice of the drawing of a draft for goods or services. See LETTER OF ADVICE. — **advise** (ad-**vIz**), *vb.*

remittance advice. Notice that a sum of money has been sent (esp. by mail) for goods or services. See REMITTANCE.

advice and consent. The right of the U.S. Senate to participate in making treaties and appointing federal officers, provided by U.S. Const. art II, § 2. • As to treaties, the Senate's advice and consent generally includes Senate involvement in the negotiation process, and the need for a two-thirds majority of the Senate for ratification. As to public officers, the Senate's advice and consent generally includes the right to vote on approval of an appointment.

advice of counsel. **1.** The guidance given by lawyers to their clients. **2.** In a malicious-prosecution lawsuit, a defense requiring both a complete presentation of facts by the defendant to his or her attorney and honest compliance with the attorney's advice. **3.** A defense in which a party seeks to avoid liability by claiming that he or she acted reasonably and in good faith on the attorney's advice. • Such a defense usu. requires waiver of the attorney-client privilege, and the attorney cannot have knowingly participated in implementing an illegal plan.

"Advice of counsel is a defense to a limited number of torts involving lack of probable cause, bad faith, or malice as an element of the cause of action. By far the most frequent cause of action against which the defense is asserted is malicious prosecution. The defense may also be asserted to avoid liability for punitive damages on the reasoning that good faith reliance on advice of counsel defeats the malice necessary to an award of punitive damages. In civil matters, the advice is typically obtained from the defendant's own attorney; when the underlying proceeding is criminal, the advice may be obtained from the district attorney's office or similar source and may take the form of action by that officer rather than advice followed by action by the defendant." 4 Ann Taylor Schwing, *California Affirmative Defenses* § 41:26, at 82 (2d ed. 1996).

advice of credit. Notice by an advising bank of the issuance of a letter of credit.

advisare (ad-vi-**zair**-ee), *vb.* [Law Latin] To consult, deliberate, or consider. See CURIA ADVISARI VULT.

advisement (ad-**vIz**-mənt). Careful consideration; deliberation <the judge took the matter under advisement and promised a ruling by the next day>.

advising bank. See BANK.

advisory committee. A committee formed to make suggestions to some other body or to an official; esp., any one of five committees that propose to the Standing Committee on Rules of Practice and Procedure amendments to federal court rules, the five committees being responsible for appellate, bankruptcy, civil, criminal, and evidence rules.

advisory counsel. See COUNSEL.

advisory jury. See JURY.

advisory opinion. See OPINION (1).

ad vitam (ad **vI**-təm), *adj.* [Latin] For life.

ad vitam aut culpam (ad **vI**-təm awt **kəl**-pəm), *adj.* [Law Latin] For life or until misbehavior. • This phrase described a tenure of office.

advocacy. **1.** The work or profession of an advocate. **2.** The act of pleading for or actively supporting a cause or proposal.

advocare (ad-və-**kair**-ee), *vb.* [Law Latin] **1.** To advocate, defend, or protect. **2.** To acknowledge or admit openly, as to acknowledge a child (*advocare filium*).

advocassie (**ad**-və-kə-see), *n.* [Law French] Advocacy.

advocata (ad-və-**kay**-tə), *n.* [Law Latin] *Hist.* A patroness; a woman holding the right to present to a church.

advocate (**ad**-və-kit), *n.* **1.** A person who assists, defends, pleads, or prosecutes for another.

public advocate. An advocate who purports to represent the public at large in matters of public concern, such as utility rates or environmental quality.

2. *Civil & Scots law.* A barrister. See BARRISTER. — **advocate** (**ad**-və-kayt), *vb.* — **advocacy** (**ad**-və-kə-see), *n.*

advocate-witness rule. See LAWYER-WITNESS RULE.

advocati ecclesiae (ad-və-**kay**-tI e-**klee**-z[h]ee-ee), *n. pl.* [Latin "church advocates"] *Hist. Eccles. law.* **1.** Church patrons who had a right to present a clerk to a benefice. See ADVOWSON. **2.** Legal advocates retained to argue cases relating to a church.

advocatio (ad-və-**kay**-shee-oh), *n.* [Law Latin] *Hist.* **1.** An inferior's management of a business for a superior. **2.** The defense of a religious establishment. **3.** ADVOWSON. **4.** *Civil law.* The quality, function, privilege, or office of an advocate.

advocatione decimarum (ad-və-kay-shee-**oh**-nee des-ə-**mair**-əm), *n.* [Law Latin] *Hist.* A writ to collect a tithe belonging to the church.

advocator (ad-voh-**kay**-tər), *n.* [Law Latin] *Hist.* **1.** A person who calls on another to warrant a title. **2.** A warrantor. **3.** The patron of a benefice.

advocatus (ad-voh-**kay**-təs). [Latin "advocate"] **1.** *Roman law.* A legal adviser; a person who assists clients with cases before judicial tribunals. Cf. CAUSIDICUS. **2.** *Hist.* The patron who has an advowson; PATRONUS. — Also termed *advowee*; *avowee.* See ADVOWSON. **3.** *Hist.* A person called on by another to warrant a title.

advocatus diaboli (ad-voh-**kay**-təs dI-**ab**-ə-lI), *n.* [Latin "devil's advocate"] *Eccles. law.* An official who argues against a person's beatification or canonization.

advocatus fisci (ad-voh-**kay**-təs **fisk**-I), *n.* [Latin] *Roman law.* An official responsible for representing the emperor in cases involving the public fisc.

ad voluntatem (ad vol-ən-**tay**-təm), *adv.* & *adj.* [Law Latin] At will.

advoutrer (ad-**vow**-trər), *n.* [Law French] *Hist.* An adulterer. — Also termed *advouter*; *advouterer*; *advoutre.*

advoutry (ad-**vow**-tree), *n.* [Law French] *Hist.* Adultery between two married persons. — Also spelled *advowtry.*

advowee (ad-vow-**ee**). A patron who holds an advowson; ADVOCATUS (2). — Also spelled *avowee.*

advowee paramount. The sovereign, or highest patron.

advowson (ad-**vow**-zən). *Eccles. law.* The right of presenting or nominating a person to a vacant benefice in the church. • The person enjoying this right is called the "patron" (*patronus*) of the church, and was formerly termed "advocatus," the advocate or defender, or in English, the "advowee." The patron presents the nominee to the bishop (or, occasionally, another church dignitary). If there is no patron, or if the patron neglects to exercise the right within six months, the right lapses and a title is given to the ordinary (a diocesan officer) to appoint a cleric to the church. Cf. PRESENTATION; INSTITUTION.

> "Advowson is the right of presentation to a church, or ecclesiastical benefice.... For, when lords of manors first built churches on their own demesnes, and appointed the tithes of those manors to be paid to the officiating ministers, which before were given to the clergy in common ... the lords, who thus built a church, and endowed it with glebe or land, had of common right a power annexed of nominating such minister as he pleased ... to officiate in that church of which he was the founder, endower, maintainer, or, in one word, the patron. This instance of an advowson will completely illustrate the nature of an incorporeal hereditament. It is not itself the bodily possession of the church and its appendages; but it is a right to give some other man a title to such bodily possession. The advowson is the object of neither the sight, nor the touch; and yet it perpetually exists in the mind's eye, and in contemplation of law.... The patronage can therefore be only conveyed by operation of law ...." 2 William Blackstone, *Commentaries on the Laws of England* 21–22 (1766).

advowson appendant (ə-**pen**-dənt). An advowson annexed to a manor, and passing as incident to it, whenever the manor is conveyed to another. • The advowson passes with the manor even if it is not mentioned in the grant.

advowson collative (kə-**lay**-tiv). An advowson for which there is no separate presentation to the bishop because the bishop happens to be the patron as well. • In this case, the one act by which the benefice is conferred is called "collation."

advowson donative (**don**-ə-tiv *or* **doh**-nə-tiv). An advowson in which the patron has the right to put a cleric in possession by a mere gift, or deed of donation, without any presentation to the bishop. • This type of advowson was converted into the *advowson presentative* by the Benefices Act of 1898. — Also termed *donative advowson.*

> "An advowson donative is when the king, or any subject by his licence, doth found a church or chapel, and ordains that it shall be merely in the gift or disposal of the patron; subject to his visitation only, and not to that of the ordinary; and vested absolutely in the clerk by the patron's deed of donation, without presentation, institution, or induction. This is said to have been anciently the only way of conferring ecclesiastical benefices in England; the method of institution by the bishop not being established more early than the time of archbishop Becket in the reign of Henry II." 2 William Blackstone, *Commentaries on the Laws of England* 23 (1766).

advowson in gross. An advowson that is separated from the manor and annexed to a person. • All advowsons that have been separated from their original manors are advowsons in gross.

advowson presentative (pri-**zen**-tə-tiv). The usual kind of advowson, in which the patron has the right to make the presentation to the bishop and to demand that the nominee be instituted, if the bishop finds the nominee canonically qualified.

aedes (**ee**-deez), *n.* [Latin] *Roman law.* A building; esp., a temple (*aedes sacra*).

aedificare (ee-də-fi-**kair**-ee), *vb.* [Latin] *Roman law.* To erect a building.

aedile (**ee**-dɪl). *Roman law.* A magistrate charged with policing the city, managing public buildings and services, supervising markets, and arranging public games. — Also spelled *edile.*

aedilitium edictum (ee-də-**lish**-ee-əm ee-**dik**-təm), *n.* [Latin] *Roman law.* An edict giving remedies for fraudulent sales; the Aedilitian Edict. • This edict was enforced by the *aediles curules*, who were municipal officers with police duties and jurisdiction over markets.

aegrotus (ee-**groh**-təs), *adj.* [Latin] Sick; indisposed by illness.

aequitas (**ek**-wə-tas *or* **ee**-kwə-tas), *n.* [Latin] *Roman law.* Equity, as opposed to *jus strictum* or *jus summum.*

aequus (**ee**-kwəs), *adj.* [Latin] Equal; even. • A provision in a will, for example, might divide the residuary estate *ex aequis* (the adverbial form) among the legatees.

aerarium (i-**rair**-ee-əm), *n.* [Latin fr. *aes* "money"] *Roman law.* The treasury.

aes (ees), *n.* [Latin] *Roman law.* Metallic money, including gold.

aes alienum (**eez** ay-lee-**ee**-nəm *or* al-ee-), *n.* [Latin "another's money"] *Roman law.* Money owed to another; borrowed money.

aesnecia (ees-**neesh**-ee-ə). [Law Latin] See ESNECY.

aes suum (**ees s[y]oo**-əm), *n.* [Latin "one's own money"] *Roman law.* Money lent to a borrower.

aesthetic functionality. See FUNCTIONALITY.

aesthetic zoning. See ZONING.

aetas (**ee**-tas), *n.* [Latin] *Roman law.* Age.

aetas infantiae proxima (**ee**-tas in-**fan**-shee-ee **prok**-sə-mə), *n.* [Latin] *Roman law.* The first part of the period of childhood between infancy (up to 7 years) and puberty (12 to 14 years); esp., for males, the period between 7 and 10½ years of age. Cf. AETAS PUBERTATI PROXIMA; PUERITIA.

aetas legitima (**ee**-tas lə-**jit**-ə-mə), *n.* [Latin] *Roman law.* Lawful age.

aetas perfecta (**ee**-tas pər-**fek**-tə), *n.* [Latin] *Roman law.* Complete age; the age of majority.

aetas prima (**ee**-tas **prɪ**-mə), *n.* [Latin] *Roman law.* First age. See INFANTIA.

aetas pubertati proxima (**ee**-tas pyoo-bər-**tay**-tɪ **prok**-sə-mə), *n.* [Latin] *Roman law.* The second period of childhood, (for males) from 10½ to 14 years of age. Cf. AETAS INFANTIAE PROXIMA; PUERITIA.

aetate probanda (ee-**tay**-tee proh-**ban**-də). See DE AETATE PROBANDA.

aff'd. *abbr.* Affirmed.

affectation doctrine. See AFFECTS DOCTRINE.

affecting commerce. (Of an industry, activity, etc.) touching or concerning business, industry, or trade; esp., under the Labor–Management Relations Act, burdening or obstructing commerce, or having led or tending to lead to a labor dispute that burdens or obstructs the free flow of commerce. 29 USCA § 152(7).

affection. 1. Fond attachment, devotion, or love <alienation of affections>. **2.** *Hist.* The pawning or mortgaging of a thing to ensure the payment of money or performance of some other obligation.

affects doctrine. *Constitutional law.* The principle allowing Congress to regulate intrastate activities that have a substantial effect on interstate commerce. • The doctrine is so called because the test is whether a given activity "affects" interstate commerce. — Also termed *effects doctrine* or (erroneously) *affectation doctrine.*

affectus (ə-**fek**-təs), *n.* [Latin] *Hist.* Intent; disposition of mind.

affeer (ə-**feer**), *vb. Hist.* To fix the amount of an amercement.

affeeror (ə-**feer**-ər), *n. Hist.* An official responsible for assessing amercements in cases in which no precise penalty is given by statute.

affermer (a-fər-**may**), *vb.* [Law French] **1.** To let to farm. **2.** To make sure; to confirm.

aff'g. *abbr.* Affirming.

affiance (ə-**fI**-ənts). **1.** *Archaic.* The act of confiding. **2.** The pledging of faith; specif., the act of promising to wed.

affiant (ə-**fI**-ənt). **1.** One who makes an affidavit. — Also termed *deponent.* **2.** COMPLAINANT (2).

affidare (af-ə-**dair**-ee), *vb.* [Law Latin] To swear faith to; esp., a tenant's pledge of faith to a lord.

affidatio dominorum (af-ə-**day**-shee-oh dom-ə-**nor**-əm), *n.* [Law Latin] *Hist.* An oath taken by lords in Parliament.

affidatus (af-ə-**day**-təs), *n.* [Law Latin] *Hist.* A tenant by fealty.

affidavit (af-ə-**day**-vit). A voluntary declaration of facts written down and sworn to by the declarant before an officer authorized to administer oaths. • A great deal of evidence is submitted by affidavit, esp. in pretrial matters such as summary-judgment motions. Cf. DECLARATION (8).

affidavit of defense. See *affidavit of merits.*

affidavit of increase. *Hist.* An affidavit that lists — and seeks reimbursement from the opposing party for — the additional costs (above the filing fee and other basic fees charged by the court clerk) incurred by a party in taking a matter through trial. • Attorney fees, witness payments, and the like were included in this affidavit. See COSTS OF INCREASE.

affidavit of inquiry. An affidavit, required in certain states before substituted service of process on an absent defendant, in which the plaintiff's attorney or a person with knowledge of the facts indicates that the defendant cannot be served within the state.

affidavit of merits. An affidavit in which a defendant asserts that he or she has a meritorious defense. — Also termed *affidavit of defense.*

affidavit of notice. An affidavit stating that the declarant has given proper notice of hearing to other parties to the action.

affidavit of service. An affidavit certifying the service of a notice, summons, writ, or process.

counteraffidavit. An affidavit made to contradict and oppose another affidavit.

IFP affidavit. See *poverty affidavit.*

in forma pauperis affidavit. See *poverty affidavit.*

pauper's affidavit. See *poverty affidavit.*

poverty affidavit. An affidavit made by an indigent person seeking public assistance, appointment of counsel, waiver of court fees, or other free public services. 28 USCA § 1915. — Also termed *pauper's affidavit*; *in forma pauperis affidavit*; *IFP affidavit.*

self-proving affidavit. An affidavit attached to a will and signed by witnesses, indicating that the testator was of sound mind and under no duress when signing the will. • The effect is to make live testimony or other evidence unnecessary when the will is offered for probate.

sham affidavit. An affidavit that contradicts clear testimony previously given by the same witness, usu. used in an attempt to create an issue of fact in response to a motion for summary judgment.

supplemental affidavit. An affidavit made in addition to a previous one, usu. to supply additional facts.

affidavit of defense. See *affidavit of merits* under AFFIDAVIT.

affilare (af-ə-**lair**-ee), *vb.* [Law Latin] To put on record; to file.

affile (ə-**fīl**), *vb. Archaic.* To file.

affiliate (ə-**fil**-ee-it), *n.* **1.** A corporation that is related to another corporation by shareholdings or other means of control; a subsidiary, parent, or sibling corporation. **2.** *Securities.* One who controls, is controlled by, or is under common control with an issuer of a security. SEC Rule 10b–18(a)(1) (17 CFR § 240.10b–18(a)(1)). See CONTROL PERSON. — **affiliate** (ə-**fil**-ee-ayt), *vb.* — **affiliation** (ə-fil-ee-**ay**-shən), *n.*

affiliated director. See *outside director* under DIRECTOR.

affiliated group. A chain of corporations that can elect to file a consolidated tax return because at least 80% of each corporation is owned by others in the group.

affiliated purchaser. See PURCHASER (1).

affine (ə-**fīn**). A relative by marriage.

affinitas (ə-**fin**-ə-tas). [Latin] *Roman law.* Relationship by marriage.

affinitas affinitatis (ə-**fin**-i-tas ə-fin-i-**tay**-tis), *n.* [Latin] *Civil law.* The connection between parties arising from marriage; remote relationship by marriage.

affinity (ə-**fin**-ə-tee). **1.** A close agreement. **2.** The relation that one spouse has to the blood relatives of the other spouse; relationship by marriage. **3.** Any familial relation resulting from a marriage. Cf. CONSANGUINITY.

> "There is no affinity between the blood relatives of one spouse and the blood relatives of the other. A husband is related by affinity to his wife's brother, but not to the wife of his wife's brother. There is no affinity between the husband's brother and the wife's sister; this is called affinitas affinitatis." 2 Charles E. Torcia, *Wharton's Criminal Law* § 242, at 573 (15th ed. 1994).

collateral affinity. The relationship of a spouse's relatives to the other spouse's relatives. • An example is a wife's brother and her husband's sister.

direct affinity. The relationship of a spouse to the other spouse's blood relatives. • An example is a wife and her husband's brother.

quasi-affinity. *Civil law.* The affinity existing between two persons, one of whom has been engaged to a relative of the other.

secondary affinity. The relationship of a spouse to the other spouse's marital relatives. • An example is a wife and her husband's sister-in-law.

affirm, *vb.* **1.** To confirm (a judgment) on appeal. **2.** To solemnly declare rather than swear under oath.

affirmance, *n.* **1.** A ratification, reacceptance, or confirmation.

> "A party who has the power of avoidance may lose it by action that manifests a willingness to go on with the contract. Such action is known as 'affirmance' and has the effect of ratifying the contract. See Restatement of Restitution § 68. The rule stated in this Section is a special application of that stated in § 85, under which a promise to perform a voidable duty is binding. On ratification, the affirming party is bound as from the outset and the other party continues to be bound." *Restatement (Second) of Contracts* § 380 cmt. a (1981).

2. The formal approval by an appellate court of a lower court's judgment, order, or decree. — **affirm,** *vb.*

affirmance day general. See DAY.

affirmant. A person who testifies under affirmation and not under oath.

affirmation, *n.* A pledge equivalent to an oath but without reference to a supreme being or to "swearing." • While an oath is "sworn to," an affirmation is merely "affirmed," but either type of pledge may subject the person making it to the penalties for perjury. — **affirm,** *vb.* — **affirmatory,** *adj.* Cf. OATH.

affirmative, *adj.* **1.** That supports the existence of certain facts <affirmative evidence>. **2.**

That involves or requires effort <an affirmative duty>.

affirmative action. A set of actions designed to eliminate existing and continuing discrimination, to remedy lingering effects of past discrimination, and to create systems and procedures to prevent future discrimination. See *reverse discrimination* under DISCRIMINATION.

affirmative charge. See *affirmative instruction* under JURY INSTRUCTION.

affirmative condition. See *positive condition* under CONDITION (2).

affirmative converse instruction. See JURY INSTRUCTION.

affirmative covenant. See COVENANT (1), (4).

affirmative defense. See DEFENSE (1).

affirmative duty. See DUTY (1).

affirmative easement. See EASEMENT.

affirmative injunction. See *mandatory injunction* under INJUNCTION.

affirmative instruction. See JURY INSTRUCTION.

affirmative misconduct. See MISCONDUCT.

affirmative plea. See *pure plea* under PLEA (2).

affirmative pregnant. A positive statement that ambiguously implies a negative; a statement that does not explicitly deny a charge, but instead answers an unasked question and thereby implies culpability, as when a person says "I returned your car yesterday" to the charge "You stole my car!" Cf. NEGATIVE PREGNANT.

affirmative proof. See PROOF.

affirmative relief. See RELIEF.

affirmative representation. See REPRESENTATION.

affirmative statute. See STATUTE.

affirmative testimony. See TESTIMONY.

affirmative warranty. See WARRANTY (3).

affirmative waste. See *commissive waste* under WASTE (1).

affix (ə-**fiks**), *vb.* To attach, add to, or fasten on permanently. — **affixation** (af-ik-**say**-shən), *n.* See FIXTURE.

affixus (ə-**fik**-səs). [Latin] *Roman law.* Affixed or fastened to.

afforare (af-ə-**rair**-ee), *vb.* [Law Latin] To set a price or value on a thing.

afforce (ə-**fors**), *vb.* To strengthen (a jury) by adding new members.

afforcement (ə-**fors**-mənt), *n.* [Law Latin] *Hist.* **1.** A reinforcement or fortification; esp., the reinforcing of a court on a solemn or extraordinary occasion. **2.** A fortress. — Also termed *afforciament* (ə-**for**-shə-mənt); *afforciamentum* (ə-for-shee-ə-**men**-təm).

afforcing the assize. *Hist.* A method of securing a jury verdict from a hung jury either by denying food and drink to the members until they reached a verdict or by bringing in new jurors until 12 would agree.

afforest, *vb.* To convert (land) into a forest, esp. by subjecting it to forest law. — **afforestation,** *n.*

affranchir (a-frah*n*-**sheer**). See AFFRANCHISE.

affranchise (ə-**fran**-chɪz), *vb. Archaic.* To set free; to liberate from servitude or an obligation. • The equivalent verb in Law French was *affranchir*.

affray (ə-**fray**). The fighting, by mutual consent, of two or more persons in some public place, to the terror of onlookers. • The fighting must be mutual. If one person unlawfully attacks another who resorts to self-defense, the first is guilty of assault and battery, but there is no affray. — Also termed *fray*.

> "The word 'affray' comes from the same source as the word 'afraid,' and the tendency to alarm the community is the very essence of this offense." Rollin M. Perkins & Ronald N. Boyce, *Criminal Law* 479 (3d ed. 1982).

casual affray. See CHANCE-MEDLEY.

mutual affray. See MUTUAL COMBAT.

affrectamentum (ə-frek-tə-**men**-təm). See AFFREIGHTMENT.

affreightment (ə-**frayt**-mənt). The hiring of a ship to carry cargo. — Also termed (in French law) *affretement*; (in Law Latin) *affrectamentum*. See CONTRACT OF AFFREIGHTMENT.

affretement. See AFFREIGHTMENT.

a fine force (ay fIn **fors**). [Law French] Of pure necessity.

AFL-CIO. *abbr.* AMERICAN FEDERATION OF LABOR AND CONGRESS OF INDUSTRIAL ORGANIZATIONS.

a force (ay **fors**). [Law French] Of necessity.

a force et armes (ay **fors** et **ahr**-mis). [Law French] With force and arms. — Also spelled *a force et armis*. See VI ET ARMIS.

aforesaid (ə-**for**-sed), *adj.* Mentioned above; referred to previously. — Also termed *aforementioned*; *above-mentioned*; *above-stated*; *said*.

aforethought (ə-**for**-thawt), *adj.* Thought of in advance; deliberate; premeditated <malice aforethought>. See MALICE AFORETHOUGHT.

a fortiori (ay for-shee-**or**-I *or* ah for-shee-**or**-ee), *adv.* [Latin] By even greater force of logic; even more so <if a 14–year-old child cannot sign a binding contract, then, *a fortiori*, a 13–year-old cannot>. Cf. A MULTO FORTIORI.

after-acquired domicile. See DOMICILE.

after-acquired-evidence doctrine. *Employment law.* The rule that, if an employer discharges an employee for an unlawful reason and later discovers misconduct sufficient to justify a lawful discharge, the employee cannot win reinstatement. • The doctrine either shields the employer from liability or limits the available relief when, after an employee has been terminated, the employer learns for the first time that the employee engaged in wrongdoing that would have resulted in a discharge anyway. *McKennon v. Nashville Banner Publ'g Co.*, 513 U.S. 352, 115 S.Ct. 879 (1995).

after-acquired property. **1.** *Secured transactions.* A debtor's property that is acquired after a security transaction and becomes additional security for payment of the debt. UCC § 9–204. — Also termed *future-acquired property*. **2.** *Bankruptcy.* Property that the bankruptcy estate acquires after commencement of the bankruptcy proceeding. 11 USCA § 541(a)(7). **3.** *Wills & estates.* Property acquired by a person after making a will. • The old rule was that a testamentary gift of personal property spoke at the time of the testator's death, whereas a gift of lands spoke from the date of the will's execution (so that after-acquired property was not disposed of), but this has been changed by legislation in most states.

after-acquired-property clause. A mortgage provision that makes any later-acquired real estate subject to the mortgage.

after-acquired title. See TITLE.

after-acquired-title doctrine. The principle that title to property automatically vests in a person who bought the property from a seller who acquired title only after purporting to sell the property to the buyer.

after-born child. See CHILD.

after-born heir. See HEIR.

aftercare. See *juvenile parole* under PAROLE.

after cost. See COST (1).

aftermarket. See *secondary market* under MARKET.

after the fact. Subsequent to an event of legal significance <accessory after the fact>.

AG. *abbr.* ATTORNEY GENERAL.

against the form of the statute. Contrary to the statutory requirements. • This formal phrase, which traditionally concludes an indictment, indicates that the conduct alleged contravenes the cited statute and therefore constitutes a criminal offense. In modern contexts, the full conclusion often reads: "against the form of the statute in such case made and provided." The phrase is a translation of the Law Latin *contra formam statuti*.

against the peace and dignity of the state. A concluding phrase in an indictment, used to condemn the offending conduct generally (as opposed to the specific charge of wrongdoing contained in the body of the instrument). • This phrase derives from the Law Latin *contra pacem domini regis* ("against the peace of the lord the king"), a charging phrase formerly used in indictments and in civil actions of trespass. See KING'S PEACE.

against the weight of the evidence. (Of a verdict or judgment) contrary to the credible evidence; not sufficiently supported by the evidence in the record. See WEIGHT OF THE EVIDENCE.

against the will. Contrary to a person's wishes. • Indictments use this phrase to indicate that the defendant's conduct was without the victim's consent.

agalma (ə-**gal**-mə). A figure or design on a seal.

agard (ə-**gahrd**). [Law French] An award. See NUL FAIT AGARD.

agarder (ah-gahr-**day**), *vb.* [Law French] To award, adjudge, or determine; to sentence or condemn.

age, *n.* A period of time; esp., a period of individual existence or the duration of a person's life.

age of capacity. The age, usu. defined by statute as 18 years, at which a person is legally capable of agreeing to a contract, executing a will, maintaining a lawsuit, or the like. — Also termed *age of majority*; *legal age*; *lawful age*. See CAPACITY.

age of consent. The age, usu. defined by statute as 16 years, at which a person is legally capable of agreeing to marriage (without parental consent) or to sexual intercourse. See CONSENT.

age of majority. **1.** The age, usu. defined by statute as 18 years, at which a person attains full legal rights, esp. civil and political rights such as the right to vote. — Also termed *lawful age*. **2.** See *age of capacity*.

age of reason. The age at which a person becomes able to distinguish right from wrong and is thus legally capable of committing a crime or tort. • The age of reason varies from jurisdiction to jurisdiction, but 7 years is usu. the age below which a child is conclusively presumed not to have committed a crime or tort, while 14 years is usu. the age below which a rebuttable presumption applies.

fighting age. The age at which a person becomes eligible to serve in (or liable to conscription into) a military unit.

lawful age. **1.** See *age of capacity*. **2.** See *age of majority* (1).

age discrimination. See DISCRIMINATION.

Age Discrimination in Employment Act. A federal law prohibiting job discrimination based on a person's age, esp. unfair and discriminatory employment decisions that negatively affect someone who is 40 years old or older. 29 USCA §§ 621–634. • Passed in 1967, the Act applies to businesses with more than 20 employees and to all governmental entities. — Abbr. ADEA.

agency. 1. A fiduciary relationship created by express or implied contract or by law, in which one party (the *agent*) may act on behalf of another party (the *principal*) and bind that other party by words or actions. See AUTHORITY (1).

> "The basic theory of the agency device is to enable a person, through the services of another, to broaden the scope of his activities and receive the product of another's efforts, paying such other for what he does but retaining for himself any net benefit resulting from the work performed." Harold Gill Reuschlein & William A. Gregory, *The Law of Agency and Partnership* § 1, at 3 (2d ed. 1990).

actual agency. An agency in which the agent is in fact employed by a principal.

agency by estoppel. An agency created by operation of law and established by a principal's actions that would reasonably lead a third person to conclude that an agency exists. — Also termed *apparent agency*; *ostensible agency*; *agency by operation of law*.

agency by necessity. See *agency of necessity*.

agency by operation of law. See *agency by estoppel*.

agency coupled with an interest. An agency in which the agent is granted not only the power to act on behalf of a principal but also a legal interest in the estate or property involved. See *power coupled with an interest* under POWER.

agency from necessity. See *agency of necessity*.

agency in fact. An agency created voluntarily, as by a contract. • Agency in fact is distinguishable from an agency relationship created by law, such as agency by estoppel.

agency of necessity. An agency arising during an emergency that necessitates the agent's acting without authorization from the principal; the relation between a person who in exigent circumstances acts in the interest of another without being authorized to do so. • It is a quasi-contractual relation formed by the operation of legal rules and not by the agreement of the parties. — Also termed *agency from necessity*; *agency by necessity*. See NEGOTIORUM GESTIO.

apparent agency. See *agency by estoppel.*

exclusive agency. The right to represent a principal — esp. either to sell the principal's products or to act as the seller's real-estate agent — within a particular market free from competition. — Also termed *exclusive franchise.*

"Contracts involving the element of exclusive agency generally fall into three classes: (1) where the contract does not prevent the principal from making direct sales but deprives him of the right to appoint other agents; (2) where the agent is the only one with any right to sell; and (3) where the exclusive agency is accompanied with a stipulated right to commissions on all sales whether made through the agent or not." 3 Am. Jur. 2d *Agency* § 268, at 768 (1986).

express agency. An actual agency arising from the principal's written or oral authorization of a person to act as the principal's agent. Cf. *implied agency.*

financing agency. A bank, finance company, or other entity that in the ordinary course of business (1) makes advances against goods or documents of title, or (2) by arrangement with either the seller or the buyer intervenes to make or collect payment due or claimed under a contract for sale, as by purchasing or paying the seller's draft, making advances against it, or taking it for collection, regardless of whether documents of title accompany the draft. UCC § 2–102(a)(20).

general agency. A principal's delegation to an agent, without restriction, to take any action connected with a particular trade, business, or employment. — Also termed *universal agency.*

implied agency. An actual agency arising from the conduct by the principal that implies an intention to create an agency relationship. Cf. *express agency.*

ostensible agency. See *agency by estoppel.*

special agency. An agency in which the agent is authorized only to conduct a single transaction or a series of transactions not involving continuous service.

undisclosed agency. An agency relationship in which an agent deals with a third party who has no knowledge that the agent is acting on a principal's behalf. • The fact that the agency is undisclosed does not prohibit the third party from seeking redress from the principal or the agent.

universal agency. See *general agency.*

2. An agent's place of business. **3.** A governmental body with the authority to implement and administer particular legislation. — Also termed (in sense 3) *government agency*; *administrative agency*; *public agency*; *regulatory agency.*

federal agency. A department or other instrumentality of the executive branch of the federal government, including a government corporation and the Government Printing Office. • The Administrative Procedure Act defines the term *agency* negatively as being any U.S. governmental authority that does not include Congress, the courts, the government of the District of Columbia, the government of any territory or possession, courts-martial, or military authority. 5 USCA § 551. The caselaw on this definition focuses on authority: generally, an entity is an agency if it has authority to take binding action. Other federal statutes define agency to include any executive department, government corporation, government-controlled corporation, or other establishment in the executive branch, or federal regulatory board.

independent agency. A federal agency, commission, or board that is not under the direction of the executive, such as the Federal Trade Commission or the National Labor Relations Board. — Also termed *independent regulatory agency*; *independent regulatory commission.*

quasi-governmental agency. A government-sponsored enterprise or corporation (sometimes called a *government-controlled corporation*), such as the Federal National Mortgage Corporation.

agency adjudication. See ADMINISTRATIVE PROCEEDING.

agency by operation of law. See *agency by estoppel* under AGENCY (1).

agency records. Under the Freedom of Information Act, documents that are created or obtained by a government agency, and that are in the agency's control at the time the information request is made. 5 USCA § 552; *United States Dep't of Justice v. Tax Analysts*, 492 U.S. 136, 109 S.Ct. 2841 (1989).

agency regulation. See REGULATION (2).

agency security. See *government security* under SECURITY.

agency shop. See SHOP.

agenda. A list of things to be done, as items to be discussed at a meeting.

agens (**ay**-jenz). [Latin] **1.** One who acts or does an act; an agent. Cf. PATIENS. **2.** A plaintiff.

agent. 1. One who is authorized to act for or in place of another; a representative <a professional athlete's agent>. Cf. PRINCIPAL (1); EMPLOYEE. **2.** Something that produces an effect <an intervening agent>. See CAUSE (1).

> "Generally speaking, anyone can be an agent who is *in fact* capable of performing the functions involved. The agent normally binds not himself but his principal by the contracts he makes; it is therefore not essential that he be legally capable to contract (although his duties and liabilities to his principal might be affected by his status). Thus an infant or a lunatic may be an agent, though doubtless the court would disregard either's attempt to act as if he were so young or so hopelessly devoid of reason as to be completely incapable of grasping the function he was attempting to perform." Floyd R. Mechem, *Outlines of the Law of Agency* 8–9 (Philip Mechem ed., 4th ed. 1952).

> "The etymology of the word agent or agency tells us much. The words are derived from the Latin verb, *ago, agere*; the noun *agens, agentis*. The word agent denotes one who acts, a doer, force or power that accomplishes things." Harold Gill Reuschlein & William A. Gregory, *The Law of Agency and Partnership* § 1, at 2–3 (2d ed. 1990).

apparent agent. A person who reasonably appears to have authority to act for another, regardless of whether actual authority has been conferred. — Also termed *ostensible agent.*

bargaining agent. A labor union in its capacity of representing employees in collective bargaining.

co-agent. A person who shares with another agent the authority to act for the principal. — Also termed *dual agent.*

corporate agent. An agent authorized to act on behalf of a corporation; broadly, all employees and officers who have the power to bind the corporation.

del credere agent (del **kred**-ə-ray *or* **kray**-də-ray). An agent who guarantees the solvency of the third party with whom the agent makes a contract for the principal. • A del credere agent receives possession of the principal's goods for purposes of sale and guarantees that anyone to whom the agent sells the goods on credit will pay promptly for them. For this guaranty, the agent receives a higher commission for sales. The promise of such an agent is almost universally held not to be within the statute of frauds. — Also termed *del credere factor.*

diplomatic agent. A national representative in one of four categories: (1) ambassadors, (2) envoys and ministers plenipotentiary, (3) ministers resident accredited to the sovereign, or (4) chargés d'affaires accredited to the minister of foreign affairs.

dual agent. See *co-agent.*

emigrant agent. One engaged in the business of hiring laborers for work outside the country or state.

fiscal agent. A bank or other financial institution that collects and disburses money and services as a depository of private and public funds on another's behalf.

foreign agent. A person who registers with the federal government as a lobbyist representing the interests of a foreign nation or corporation.

forwarding agent. **1.** A person or company whose business is to receive and ship goods for others. — Also termed *freight-forwarder.* **2.** A freight-forwarder who assembles less-than-carload shipments (small shipments) into carload shipments, thus taking advantage of lower freight rates.

general agent. An agent authorized to transact all the principal's business of a particular kind or in a particular place. • Among the common types of general agents are factors, brokers, and partners.

> "Although the distinction between general and special agents can be difficult to apply, the terminology is sometimes used by courts and the distinction plays a major role in the Restatement of Agency. A general agent . . . is an integral part of the principal's business and does not need fresh authorization for each separate transaction. A manager of a store is an example of a general agent." J. Dennis Hynes, *Agency, Partnership, and the LLC in a Nutshell* 21 (1997).

government agent. **1.** An employee or representative of a governmental body. **2.** A law-enforcement official, such as a police officer or an FBI agent. **3.** An informant, esp. an inmate, hired by law enforcement to obtain incriminating statements from another inmate. • An accused's Sixth Amendment right to counsel is triggered when the accused is questioned by a government agent.

high-managerial agent. An agent of a corporation or other business, having authority to formulate corporate policy or supervise employees. — Also termed *superior agent.*

independent agent. An agent who exercises personal judgment and is subject to the principal only for the results of the work performed.

local agent. An agent appointed to act as another's (esp. a company's) representative and to transact business within a specified district.

managing agent. A person with general power involving the exercise of judgment and discretion, as opposed to an ordinary agent who acts under the direction and control of the principal. — Also termed *business agent.*

mercantile agent. An agent employed to sell goods or merchandise on behalf of the principal.

ostensible agent. See *apparent agent.*

private agent. An agent acting for an individual in that person's private affairs.

process agent. A person authorized to accept service of process on behalf of another.

public agent. A person appointed to act for the public in matters pertaining to governmental administration or public business.

real-estate agent. An agent who represents a buyer or seller (or both, with proper disclosures) in the sale or lease of real property. • A real-estate agent can be either a broker (whose principal is a buyer or seller) or a salesperson (whose principal is a broker).

registered agent. A person authorized to accept service of process for another person, esp. a corporation, in a particular jurisdiction. — Also termed *resident agent.*

soliciting agent. **1.** *Insurance.* An agent with limited authority relating to the solicitation or submission of applications to an insurance company but usu. without authority to bind the insurer, as by accepting the applications on behalf of the company. **2.** An agent who solicits orders for goods or services for a principal. **3.** A managing agent of a corporation for purposes of service of process.

special agent. An agent employed to conduct a particular transaction or to perform a specified act.

statutory agent. An agent designated by law to receive litigation documents and other legal notices for a nonresident corporation. • In most states, the secretary of state is the statutory agent for such corporations.

stock-transfer agent. An organization that oversees and maintains records of transfers of shares for a corporation.

subagent. A person appointed by an agent to perform some duty relating to the agency. — Also termed *subservant.*

superior agent. See *high-managerial agent.*

transfer agent. An organization (such as a bank or trust company) that handles transfers of shares for a publicly held corporation by issuing new certificates and overseeing the cancellation of old ones and that usu. also maintains the record of shareholders for the corporation and mails dividend checks. • Generally, a transfer agent ensures that certificates submitted for transfer are properly indorsed and that the right to transfer is appropriately documented.

undercover agent. **1.** An agent who does not disclose his or her role as an agent. **2.** A police officer who gathers evidence of criminal activity without disclosing his or her identity to the suspect.

universal agent. An agent authorized to perform all acts that the principal could personally perform.

agent provocateur (**ay**-jənt prə-vok-ə-**tər** *or* **a**-zhawn praw-vaw-kə-**tuur**), *n.* **1.** An undercover agent who instigates or participates in a crime, often by infiltrating a group involved in suspected illegal conduct, to expose and punish criminal activity. **2.** A person who entraps or entices another to break the law and then informs against the other as a lawbreaker.

agent's lien. See LIEN.

age of capacity. See AGE.

age of consent. See AGE.

age of majority. See AGE.

age of reason. See AGE.

ager (**ay**-jər), *n.* [Latin] *Roman law.* Land or territory; esp., a portion of land enclosed by definite boundaries.

ager publicus (**ay**-jər **pəb**-li-kəs). Land of the people; public land.

aggravated, *adj.* **1.** (Of a crime) made worse or more serious by circumstances such as violence, the presence of a deadly weapon, or the intent to commit another crime <aggravated robbery>. Cf. SIMPLE (1). **2.** (Of a tort) made worse or more serious by circumstances such as intention to cause harm or reckless disregard for another's safety <the defendant's negligence was aggravated by malice>. **3.** (Of an injury) harmful to a part of the body previously injured or debilitated <an aggravated bone fracture>. See AGGRAVATION RULE.

aggravated arson. See ARSON.

aggravated assault. See ASSAULT.

aggravated battery. See BATTERY.

aggravated damages. See *punitive damages* under DAMAGES.

aggravated kidnapping. See KIDNAPPING.

aggravated larceny. See LARCENY.

aggravated robbery. See ROBBERY.

aggravated sodomy. See SODOMY.

aggravating circumstance. See CIRCUMSTANCE.

aggravation rule. *Workers' compensation.* The principle that when an on-the-job injury combines with a preexisting injury, resulting in a greater disability than that which would have resulted from the on-the-job injury alone, the entire disability is compensable as if it had occurred at work.

aggregate (**ag**-rə-git), *adj.* Formed by combining into a single whole or total <aggregate income>.

aggregate (**ag**-rə-git), *n.* An assemblage of particulars; an agglomeration <aggregate of interests>.

aggregate (**ag**-rə-gayt), *vb.* To collect into a whole <aggregate the claims>.

aggregate concept. An approach to taxing business organizations whereby an organization is viewed as a collection of its individual owners, not as a separate taxable entity.

aggregate corporation. See CORPORATION.

aggregate demand. See DEMAND (3).

aggregate income. See INCOME.

aggregate sentence. See SENTENCE.

aggregate supply. See SUPPLY.

aggregate theory of partnership. The theory that a partnership does not have a separate legal existence (as does a corporation), but rather is only the totality of the partners who make it up. Cf. ENTITY THEORY OF PARTNERSHIP.

aggregatio mentium (ag-rə-**gay**-shee-oh **men**-shee-əm). [Latin "gathering together of minds"] See MEETING OF THE MINDS.

aggregation. *Patents.* A combination of two or more elements in a patent claim, each one unrelated and each one performing separately and without cooperation — as a result of which the combination does not define a composite integrated mechanism. — Also termed *juxtaposition.*

aggregation doctrine. The rule that precludes a party from totaling all claims for purposes of meeting the minimum amount necessary to give rise to federal diversity jurisdiction under the amount-in-controversy requirement. See *diversity jurisdiction* under JURISDICTION; AMOUNT IN CONTROVERSY.

aggression. *Int'l law.* The use of armed force by a country against the sovereignty, territorial integrity, or political independence of another country, or in a manner inconsistent with the Charter of the United Nations. • Acts falling within this definition include declaring war against, invading, attacking, blockading, or landing troops on another country's territory.

aggressor corporation. See CORPORATION.

aggressor doctrine. *Civil law.* The principle precluding tort recovery for a plaintiff who acts in a way that would provoke a reasonable person to use physical force for protection from the plaintiff, unless the defendant uses excessive force to repel the plaintiff.

aggrieved party. See PARTY (2).

AGI. See *adjusted gross income* under INCOME.

agillarius (aj-ə-**lair**-ee-əs), *n.* [Law Latin] *Hist.* A keeper of a herd of cattle in a common field; a hayward.

aging of accounts. A process of classifying accounts receivable by the time elapsed since the claim came into existence for the purpose of estimating the balance of uncollectible accounts as of a given date.

agio (**aj**-ee-oh *or* **ay**-jee-oh). The premium paid for the exchange of one kind of money for another, such as paper currency for coin or one country's currency for another's.

agiotage (**aj**-ee-ə-tij). **1.** The business of dealing in foreign exchange. **2.** Speculative buying and selling of securities.

agist (ə-**jist**), *vb.* To allow animals to graze on one's pasture for a fee.

agister (ə-**jis**-tər). One who takes and pastures grazing animals for a fee; a person engaged in the business of agistment. • An agister is a type of bailee for hire. — Also spelled *agistor*.

agister's lien. See LIEN.

agistment (ə-**jist**-mənt). **1.** A type of bailment in which a person, for a fee, allows animals to graze on his or her pasture; the taking in of cattle or other livestock to feed at a per-animal rate. **2.** A charge levied upon the owner or occupier of land. See TITHE OF AGISTMENT.

> ***agistment of sea-banks.*** *Hist.* A charge on land used to pay for the upkeep of dikes that prevent the encroachment of the sea.

agnate (**ag**-nayt), *adj.* Related or akin through male descent or on the father's side.

agnate, *n.* A blood relative whose connection is through the male line. Cf. COGNATE.

agnatic, *adj.* (Of a relationship) restricted to affiliations through the male line.

agnatio (ag-**nay**-shee-oh). [Latin] *Roman law.* A relationship extended to a person through males only; an affiliation of free persons of either sex in the power (*patria potestas*) of the senior living male or of a male who would be in his power if he were living. • An agnatic relationship could be created either by adoption or by a blood relationship (*cognatio*) traced solely through the male side of a family. See COGNATIO; *patria potestas* under POTESTAS.

agnatus (ag-**nay**-təs), *n.* [Latin] *Roman law.* A person related through the male line. Cf. COGNATUS.

> "[*Agnati* were] all individuals subject for the time being to the same *patria potestas*, or who would be so subject were the common ancestor alive. Brothers and sisters, with their uncles, aunts, nephews, nieces, and other collaterals (not having been received into another family), if related through males, were agnates. The civil issue of the state was the Agnatic Family. Cognates were all persons who could trace their blood to a single ancestor or ancestress, and agnates were those cognates who traced their connection exclusively through males." John Bouvier, *Bouvier's Law Dictionary* (8th ed. 1914).

agnomen (ag-**noh**-mən). [Latin] **1.** An additional name or title; a nickname. **2.** *Roman law.* An additional name, given in recognition of some achievement or to reflect adoption by a different *gens*. See NOMEN.

agrarian (ə-**grair**-ee-ən), *adj.* Of or relating to land, land tenure, or a division of landed property. — **agrarian,** *n.*

agrarian law. *Roman & civil law.* The body of law governing the ownership, use, and distribution of land.

agrarium (ə-**grair**-ee-əm). [Law Latin] *Hist.* A tax upon, or tribute payable out of, land.

a gratia (ay **gray**-shee-ə). [Law Latin] EX GRATIA.

agreamentum (ə-gree-ə-**men**-təm). [Law Latin] Agreement; an agreement.

agreed-amount clause. An insurance-policy provision that the insured will carry a stated amount of coverage.

agreed-boundary doctrine. The principle that owners of contiguous land may agree on the boundary between the parcels, as long as the actual boundary is uncertain, there is agreement between the two owners about the boundary line, there is acquiescence in the agreed line for a time exceeding the statute of limitations, and the agreed boundary is identifiable on the ground.

agreed judgment. See JUDGMENT.

agreed price. See PRICE.

agreed statement of facts. See STATEMENT OF FACTS.

agreed statement on appeal. See *agreed statement of facts* under STATEMENT OF FACTS.

agreed value. See VALUE.

agreement. 1. A mutual understanding between two or more persons about their relative rights and duties regarding past or future performances; a manifestation of mutual assent by two or more persons. **2.** The parties' actual bargain as found in their language or by implication from other circumstances, including course of dealing or usage of trade or course of performance. UCC § 1–201(3).

"An agreement, as the courts have said, 'is nothing more than a manifestation of mutual assent' by two or more parties legally competent persons to one another. Agreement is in some respects a broader term than contract, or even than bargain or promise. It covers executed sales, gifts, and other transfers of property." Samuel Williston, *A Treatise on the Law of Contracts* § 2, at 6 (Walter H.E. Jaeger ed., 3d ed. 1957).

agreement of sale. An agreement that obligates someone to sell and that may include a corresponding obligation for someone else to purchase.

agreement to agree. **1.** An unenforceable agreement that purports to bind two parties to negotiate and enter into a contract; esp., a proposed agreement negotiated with the intent that the final agreement will be embodied in a formal written document and that neither party will be bound until the final agreement is executed. **2.** A fully enforceable agreement containing terms that are sufficiently definite as well as adequate consideration, but leaving some details to be worked out by the parties.

"[I]t has been many times reiterated that the law does not recognize 'an agreement to agree' as a valid contract. So an agreement under which a builder was to construct a building for a developer was held not to be binding because no price was fixed, it being simply agreed that fair and reasonable sums would be negotiated. An 'agreement to agree' would be unobjectionable if the parties had definitely agreed to enter into a contract on terms which were themselves sufficiently definite. What they cannot do is to bind themselves to negotiate *and reach agreement*, for the negotiations may quite genuinely fail to lead to an agreement." P.S. Atiyah, *An Introduction to the Law of Contract* 89 (3d ed. 1981).

agreement to sell. An agreement that obligates someone to sell.

binding agreement. An enforceable contract. See CONTRACT.

closing agreement. *Tax.* A written contract between a taxpayer and the Internal Revenue Service to resolve a tax dispute.

formal agreement. An agreement in which the law requires not only the consent of the parties but also a manifestation of the agreement in some particular form, in default of which the agreement is null.

integrated agreement. See INTEGRATED CONTRACT.

invalid agreement. See *invalid contract* under CONTRACT.

outsourcing agreement. See OUTSOURCING AGREEMENT.

point-and-click agreement. See POINT-AND-CLICK AGREEMENT.

simple agreement. An agreement in which the law requires nothing for its effective operation beyond some manifestation that the parties have consented.

subordination agreement. An agreement by which one who holds an otherwise senior interest agrees to subordinate that interest to a normally lesser interest, usu. when a seller agrees to subordinate a purchase-money mortgage so that the buyer can obtain a first-mortgage loan to improve the property.

unconscionable agreement (ən-**kon**-shə-nə-bəl). An agreement that no promisor with any sense, and not under a delusion, would make, and that no honest and fair promisee would accept. — Also termed *unconscionable contract.*

underwriting agreement. An agreement between a corporation and an underwriter covering the terms and conditions of a new securities issue.

valid agreement. See *valid contract* under CONTRACT.

voidable agreement. See *voidable contract* under CONTRACT.

void agreement. See *void contract* under CONTRACT.

agreement of imperfect obligation. See *unenforceable contract* under CONTRACT.

agreement of rescission. See RESCISSION (2).

agreement of sale. See AGREEMENT.

Agreement Relating to Liability Limitation of the Warsaw Convention and The Hague Protocol. See MONTREAL AGREEMENT.

agreement to agree. See AGREEMENT.

agreement to sell. See AGREEMENT.

agri (**ag**-rɪ), *n. pl.* [Latin] Lands.

agribusiness. The pursuit of agriculture as an occupation or profit-making enterprise, including labor, land-use planning, and financing the cost of land, equipment, and other necessary expenses.

Agricultural Adjustment Act. A federal statute, enacted in 1933, that paid farmers to not produce crops in an effort to raise crop prices. • The U.S. Supreme Court declared the act unconstitutional in 1936 on grounds that Congress had overstepped its power to regulate commerce. A second, more limited Agricultural Adjustment Act was enacted in 1938. — Abbr. AAA.

agricultural labor. Work that is performed on a farm or ranch, or that pertains to the production of commodities, such as harvesting crops, raising livestock, or obtaining milk, honey, or other animal products. • Agricultural labor is often excluded from certain labor laws, such as unemployment insurance and workers' compensation.

agricultural lien. See LIEN.

agriculture. The science or art of cultivating soil, harvesting crops, and raising livestock.

> " 'Agriculture' is broader in meaning than 'farming'; and while it includes the preparation of soil, the planting of seeds, the raising and harvesting of crops, and all their incidents, it also includes gardening, horticulture, viticulture, dairying, poultry, bee raising, and ranching." 3 Am. Jur. 2d *Agriculture* § 1, at 934–35 (1986).

agri limitati (**ag**-rɪ lim-i-**tay**-tɪ). [Latin "fields limited" or "lands enclosed by boundaries"] *Roman & civil law.* Lands whose boundaries have been fixed by a surveyor. • They included land belonging to the state by right of conquest, and granted and sold in individual plots.

***Aguilar–Spinelli* test** (ah-gee-**lahr** spi-**nel**-ee *or* **ag**-wə-lahr). *Criminal procedure.* A standard for determining whether hearsay (such as an informant's tip) is sufficiently reliable to establish probable cause for an arrest or search warrant. • Under this two-pronged test — which has been replaced by a broader, totality-of-the-circumstances approach — the reliability of both the information and the informant must be independently shown. *Aguilar v. Texas*, 378 U.S. 108, 84 S.Ct. 1509 (1964); *Spinelli v. United States*, 393 U.S. 410, 89 S.Ct. 584 (1969). Cf. TOTALITY-OF-THE-CIRCUMSTANCES TEST.

ahupuaa (ah-hoo-poo-**ah**-ah). A variable measure of Hawaiian land, traditionally understood to stretch from the sea to the mountains, to allow the people to obtain the various materials needed for subsistence offered at different elevations. — Also spelled *ahupua'a.*

AICPA. *abbr.* American Institute of Certified Public Accountants.

aid, *n. Hist.* **1.** A subsidy or tax granted to the king for an extraordinary purpose. — Also termed *grant-in-aid.* **2.** A benevolence or tribute (i.e., a sum of money) granted by the tenant to his lord in times of difficulty and distress. • Over time, these grants grew from being discretionary to matters of right. The three principal aids were: (1) to ransom the lord's person if he was taken prisoner; (2) to contribute toward the ceremony of knighting the lord's eldest son; and (3) to provide a suitable portion to the lord's eldest daughter when she married. **3.** Assistance in defending a lawsuit in which the plaintiff also has a claim against an unsued third party having a joint interest in the defense.

aid and abet, *vb.* To assist or facilitate the commission of a crime, or to promote its accomplishment. • Aiding and abetting is a crime in most jurisdictions. — Also termed *aid or abet*; *counsel and procure.* — **aider and abettor,** *n.*

> "The phrase 'aid and abet' and 'aider and abettor' seem unnecessarily verbose. . . . [A]ny aid given with mens rea is abetment; hence to add the word 'aid' to the word 'abet' is not necessary and is sometimes misleading." Rollin M. Perkins & Ronald N. Boyce, *Criminal Law* 724–25 (3d ed. 1982).

> "In connection with the principal in the second degree or accessory before the fact, the terms 'aid' and 'abet' are frequently used interchangeably, although they are not synonymous. To 'aid' is to assist or help another. To 'abet' means, literally, to bait or excite, as in the case of an animal. In its legal sense, it means to encourage, advise, or instigate the commission of a crime." 1 Charles E. Torcia, *Wharton's Criminal Law* § 29, at 181 (15th ed. 1993).

aid and comfort. Help given by someone to a national enemy in such a way that the help amounts to treason.

> "Aid and comfort may be given in various ways, such as buying a vessel and fitting it for service in aid of the enemy, delivering prisoners and deserters to the enemy, or selling critical materials with knowledge of the fact that the purchaser buys them to use in the manufacture of gunpowder for the enemy, or otherwise to aid him in his prosecution of the war. And the courts have given short shrift to the claim that such a sale was not intended to aid the enemy but only to make a profit." Rollin M. Perkins & Ronald N. Boyce, *Criminal Law* 502 (3d ed. 1982).

aide-mémoire (ayd-mem-**wahr**). *Int'l law.* A diplomatic document that a diplomatic agent leaves with the receiving state's department of foreign affairs on the occasion of a *démarche.* • The *aide-mémoire* presents the receiving state with a precise record of the substance of the diplomatic agent's mission. It is typically written in an impersonal style, without mentioning either the addressee or the author. It appears on printed letterhead and is dated, but it is not signed, initialed, or embossed with a seal. See DÉMARCHE.

aider, *n.* **1.** An act of aiding; the curing of a defect. **2.** One who aids another.

aider by pleading over. The cure of a pleading defect by an adversary's answering the pleading without an objection, so that the objection is waived.

aider by verdict. The cure of a pleading defect by a trial verdict, based on the presumption that the record contains adequate proof of the necessary facts even if those facts were not specifically alleged.

> "AIDER BY VERDICT. Wherever a pleading states the essential requisites of a cause of action or ground of defense, it will be held sufficient after a general verdict in favor of the party pleading, though the statement be informal or inaccurate; but a verdict will never aid the statement of a title or cause of action inherently defective." Benjamin J. Shipman, *Handbook of Common-Law Pleading* § 332, at 531 (Henry Winthrop Ballantine ed., 3d ed. 1923).

aiding an escape. The crime of helping a prisoner escape custody.

aid of the king. *Hist.* A request of the king made by a tenant for relief from another's demand for rent.

aid or abet. See AID AND ABET.

aid prayer. *Hist.* A plea by a life tenant or other holder of less than a fee simple to bring into the action another who holds an interest in the estate (such as a reversioner or remainderman) to help defend the title. — Also termed *prayer in aid.*

aids. See AID (2).

aiel (**ay**-əl), *n.* [Law French] *Hist.* **1.** A grandfather. **2.** A writ by an heir of a grandfather for recovery of the grandfather's estate, which had been wrongfully possessed by a stranger. — Also termed (in sense 2) *writ of aiel.* — Also spelled *aile*; *ayel*; *ayle.* Cf. BESAYEL; COSINAGE.

aimable compositeur (ay-**mah**-blə ko*n*-poh-zee-**tuur**). [French] See AMIABLE COMPOSITOR.

airbill. A document serving as a bill of lading for goods transported by air. • The term includes air consignment notes and air waybills.

aircraft piracy. See *air piracy* under PIRACY (2).

air law. The part of law, esp. international law, relating to civil aviation.

airman's certificate. A license that every aircraft pilot must have to operate an aircraft in U.S. airspace. 49 USCA §§ 44701–44711; 14 CFR § 61.3.

Airman's Information Manual. A publication of the Federal Aviation Administration, providing the fundamental requirements of any pilot who flies in national airspace.

air piracy. See PIRACY.

air pollution. Any harmful substance or energy emitted directly or indirectly into the air, esp. if the harm is to the environment or to the public health or welfare.

air-quality-control region. *Environmental law.* A federally designated area in which communities share an air-pollution problem, often involving several states; an interstate area or major intrastate area that the Environmental Protection Agency designates for monitoring and ameliorating ambient air-quality standards. 42 USCA § 7407(c).

air-quality criteria. *Environmental law.* The legal limits that the Environmental Protection Agency sets for pollutants in a defined area and at a specified time.

air right. The right to use all or a portion of the airspace above real property.

air-services agreement. See AIR-TRANSPORT AGREEMENT.

air-transport agreement. A contract governing the operation of air services; esp., an intergovernmental agreement governing the operation of international air services between their territories. — Also termed *air-services agreement.*

aisiamentum (ay-shee-ə-**men**-təm). [Law Latin] An easement or privilege.

aisne. See EIGNE.

a issue (ah is[h]-**yoo**). [Law French] At issue.

a.k.a. *abbr.* Also known as.

al (ahl), *prep.* [Law French] At.

a la grande grevaunce (ah lə **grawnd** grə-**vawns**). [Law French] To the great grievance.

a large (ah **lahrzh**). [Law French] Free; at large.

a latere (ay **lat**-ə-ree). [Latin] From the side; collaterally. • This term was formerly used to denote collateral succession rather than lineal succession.

alba firma (**al**-bə **fər**-mə). [Law Latin] See WHITE RENT.

albanus (al-**bay**-nəs), *n.* [Law Latin] See ADVENA.

al barre (ahl **bahr**). [Law French] At the bar.

album breve (**al**-bəm breev *or* **bree**-vee). See BREVE.

albus liber (**al**-bəs **lɪ**-bər). [Law Latin "white book"] *Hist.* An ancient book containing a compilation of the laws and customs of the city of London. — Also termed *White Book.*

alcalde (al-**kal**-dee *or* ahl-**kahl**-thay). [fr. Arabic *al-qadi* "the Cadi" or "the judge"] *Spanish law.* **1.** *Hist.* A judicial officer. • The alcalde's functions typically resembled those of a justice of the peace. **2.** The mayor of a Spanish or Spanish–American town, usu. with a judicial element. • This is the modern sense.

alcoholometer. See BREATHALYZER.

alderman. A member of a city council or other local governing body. — Also termed *alderperson.*

aldermannus (al-dər-**man**-əs). [Law Latin] *Hist.* An alderman.

aldermannus civitatis vel burgi (siv-i-**tay**-tis vel **bər**-jɪ). An alderman of a city or borough.

aldermannus hundredi seu wapentachii (**hən**-dri-dɪ **syoo** wahp-ən-**tay**-kee-ɪ). An alderman of a hundred or wapentake.

aldermannus regis (**ree**-jis). An alderman of the king, so called because he is appointed by the king or gives the king's judgment in the premises allotted to him.

aldermannus totius Angliae (**toh**-shee-əs **ang**-glee-ee). An alderman of all England, similar to the chief justiciary of England in later times. See JUSTICIARY.

alderperson. See ALDERMAN.

alderwoman. A female member of a city council or other local governing body.

alea (**ay**-lee-ə), *n.* [Latin] *Roman law.* **1.** A game of chance. **2.** The chance of gain or loss in a contract.

aleator (ay-lee-**ay**-tər). [Latin] *Roman law.* A gambler; dice player.

aleatory (**ay**-lee-ə-tor-ee), *adj.* Dependent on uncertain contingencies. — Also termed *aleatoric.*

aleatory contract. See CONTRACT.

aleatory promise. See PROMISE.

alegal, *adj.* Outside the sphere of law; not classifiable as being legal or illegal <the law often treats the promises of unmarried cohabitants as contractual words rather than alegal words of commitment>. — **alegality,** *n.*

aler a dieu. See ALLER A DIEU.

aler sans jour. See ALLER SANS JOUR.

ale silver. *Hist.* A rent or tribute paid annually to the lord mayor of London by persons who sold ale within the city.

alez adeu (ah-**lay** ah-**duu**). See ADEU.

alfet (**al**-fet). *Hist.* A cauldron filled with boiling water, used to scald the arm of a person undergoing an ordeal. See *ordeal by water* (2) under ORDEAL.

Alford **plea.** A guilty plea entered into by a defendant in connection with a plea bargain, without actually admitting guilt. • This plea is not considered compelled within the language of the Fifth Amendment if the plea represents a voluntary, knowing, and intelligent choice between the available options <the defendant — realizing the strength of the prosecution's evidence and not wanting to risk receiving the death penalty — entered into an *Alford* plea>. *North Carolina v. Alford,* 400 U.S. 25, 91 S.Ct. 160 (1970).

algorithm. *Patents.* A statement or conclusion based on a sequence of steps involving mathematical, logical, or natural rules or principles.

ALI. *abbr.* AMERICAN LAW INSTITUTE.

alia enormia (**ay**-lee-ə i-**nor**-mee-ə). [Law Latin "other serious wrongs"] *Hist.* A general allegation of injuries made at the conclusion of the declaration by a plaintiff in a trespass action.

aliamenta (al-ee-ə-**men**-tə). [Latin] A liberty of passage or open way, such as a path through another's hedge or drainage for a waterway.

alias (**ay**-lee-əs), *adv.* **1.** Otherwise called or named; also known as <James Grimsley, alias the Grim Reaper>. **2.** At another time.

alias, *n.* **1.** An assumed or additional name that a person has used or is known by. — Also termed *assumed name.* **2.** *Hist.* A second writ issued after the first has failed. See *alias writ* under WRIT.

alias, *adj.* Issued after the first instrument has not been effective or resulted in action.

alias dictus (**ay**-lee-əs **dik**-təs), *adv.* [Latin] Otherwise called; ALIAS (1).

alias execution. See EXECUTION.

alias subpoena. See SUBPOENA.

alias summons. See SUMMONS.

alias writ. See WRIT.

a libellis (ay li-**bel**-is). [Law Latin] *Roman law.* **1.** An officer having charge of petitions (*libelli*) addressed to the emperor or sovereign. **2.** CHANCELLOR OF THE EXCHEQUER.

alibi (**al**-ə-bɪ), *n.* [Latin "elsewhere"] **1.** A defense based on the physical impossibility of a defendant's guilt by placing the defendant in a location other than the scene of the crime at the relevant time. Fed. R. Crim. P. 12.1. **2.** The fact or state of having been elsewhere when an offense was committed.

alibi, *vb.* To offer or provide an alibi for <the conspirators alibied for each other>.

alibi witness. See WITNESS.

alien (**ay**-lee-ən *or* **ayl**-yən), *n.* A person who resides within the borders of a country but is not a citizen or subject of that country; a person not owing allegiance to a particular nation. • In the United States, an alien is a person who was born outside the jurisdiction of the United States, who is subject to some foreign government, and who has not been naturalized under U.S. law.

alien ami. See *alien friend.*

alien amy. See *alien friend.*

alien enemy. A citizen or subject of a country at war with the country in which the citizen or subject is living or traveling. — Also termed *enemy alien.*

> "In its natural meaning, the term 'alien enemy' indicates a subject of a State with which this country is at war; but in considering the enforcement of civil rights, the test is not nationality, but residence or place of business. Hence, if a person is voluntarily resident in or is carrying on business in an enemy country, then he is an alien enemy even though he be a British subject or the subject of a neutral State ...." 1 E.W. Chance, *Principles of Mercantile Law* 52–53 (P.W. French ed., 13th ed. 1950).

alien friend. An alien who is a citizen or subject of a friendly power. — Also termed (in Law French) *alien amy*; *alien ami.*

alien immigrant. See IMMIGRANT.

enemy alien. See *alien enemy.*

illegal alien. An alien who enters a country at the wrong time or place, eludes an examination by officials, obtains entry by fraud, or enters into a sham marriage to evade immigration laws. — Also termed *undocumented alien.*

nonresident alien. A person who is neither a resident nor a citizen of the United States.

resident alien. An alien who has a legally established domicile in the United States. See NATURALIZATION.

undocumented alien. See *illegal alien.*

alien, *vb.* See ALIENATE.

alienable, *adj.* Capable of being transferred to the ownership of another; transferable <an alienable property interest>. — **alienability,** *n.*

alienage (**ay**-lee-ə-nij *or* **ayl**-yə-nij), *n.* The condition or status of being an alien.

declaration of alienage. The declaration of a citizen or subject having dual citizenship that the person wishes to renounce the citizenship of one state. • For the declaration to be effective, the person making it must be of full age and not under any disability.

alien ami. See *alien friend* under ALIEN.

alien amy. See *alien friend* under ALIEN.

Alien and Sedition Acts. *Hist.* Four statutes passed in 1798 designed to silence critics of the Federalist party by tightening residency requirements for citizenship, granting to the President the power to jail aliens considered dangerous to the country, and restricting freedoms of the press and speech by criminalizing speech hostile to the government. • All the acts had expired or been repealed by 1802.

alienate (**ay**-lee-ə-nayt *or* **ayl**-yə-nayt), *vb.* To transfer or convey (property or a property right) to another. — Also termed *alien.*

alienation (ay-lee-ə-**nay**-shən *or* ayl-yə-**nay**-shən), *n.* **1.** Withdrawal from former attachment; estrangement <alienation of affections>. **2.** Conveyance or transfer of property to another <alienation of one's estate>. — **alienative** (**ay**-lee-ə-nay-tiv), *adj.*

> "[A]ny transfer of real estate short of a conveyance of the title is not an alienation of the estate." 4A John Alan Appleman & Jean Appleman, *Insurance Law and Practice* § 2741, at 325 n.12 (rev. vol. 1969).

involuntary alienation. Alienation against the wishes of the transferor, as by attachment. — Also termed *involuntary conveyance.*

alienation clause. 1. A deed provision that either permits or prohibits the further conveyance of the property. **2.** A clause in an insurance policy voiding coverage if the policyholder alienates the insured property.

alienation of affections. A tort claim for willful or malicious interference with a marriage by a third party without justification or excuse. • The tort has been abolished in most states. See CONSORTIUM.

alienation office. See OFFICE.

alienative fact. See FACT.

alien corporation. See *foreign corporation* under CORPORATION.

alienee (ay-lee-ə-**nee** *or* ayl-yə-**nee**), *n.* One to whom property is transferred or conveyed. — Also termed *disponee.*

fraudulent alienee. One who knowingly receives an asset by means of fraudulent alienation.

alien enemy. See ALIEN.

alien friend. See ALIEN.

alienigena (ay-lee-ə-**nij**-ə-nə). [Latin] *Hist.* An alien. Cf. INDIGENA.

alieni generis (ay-lee-**ee**-nI [*or* al-ee-] **jen**-ə-ris). [Latin] Of another kind; of a foreign kind.

alieni juris (ay-lee-**ee**-nI [*or* al-ee-] **joor**-is), *adj.* [Latin] *Roman law.* Subject to the power or authority of another. — Also spelled *alieni iuris.*

alien immigrant. See IMMIGRANT.

alienism. The state, condition, or character of an alien.

alienist. A psychiatrist, esp. one who assesses a criminal defendant's sanity or capacity to stand trial.

alienor (**ay**-lee-ə-nər *or* -nor), *n.* One who transfers or conveys property to another. — Also termed *disponor.*

alienus (ay-lee- *or* al-ee-**ee**-nəs), *adj.* [Latin] *Roman law.* Belonging to another. • *Alienus homo* means "another's slave."

alimenta (al-ə-**men**-tə). [Latin] *Roman law.* Things necessary to sustain life, such as food and clothing.

alimony (**al**-ə-moh-nee). A court-ordered allowance that one spouse pays to the other spouse for maintenance and support while they are separated, while they are involved in a matrimonial lawsuit, or after they are divorced. — Also termed *spousal support*; *maintenance*; *estover.* Cf. CHILD SUPPORT.

alimony in gross. Alimony in the form of a single and definite sum not subject to modification. — Also termed *lump-sum alimony.*

alimony pendente lite (pen-**den**-tee **lI**-tee). See *temporary alimony.*

lump-sum alimony. See *alimony in gross.*

permanent alimony. Alimony payable in usu. weekly or monthly installments either indefinitely or until a time specified by court order. • This kind of alimony may usu. be modified for changed circumstances of either party. — Also termed *periodic alimony.*

rehabilitative alimony. Alimony necessary to assist a divorced person in regaining a useful and constructive role in society through vocational or other training.

reimbursement alimony. Alimony designed to repay a spouse who during the marriage made financial contributions that directly enhanced the future earning capacity of the other spouse. • An example is alimony for a wife who worked full-time supporting herself and her husband while he attended medical school and earned a medical degree.

temporary alimony. Temporary alimony ordered by the court pending an action for divorce or separation. — Also termed *alimony pendente lite*; *allowance pendente lite*.

alimony trust. See TRUST.

alio intuitu (**ay**-lee-oh in-**t[y]oo**-ə-t[y]oo), *adv.* [Latin "under a different aspect"] In a different view; with respect to another case or condition.

aliquot (**al**-ə-kwot), *adj.* Contained in a larger whole an exact number of times; fractional <5 is an aliquot part of 30>.

aliquot-part rule. The principle that a person must intend to acquire a fractional part of the ownership of property before a court can declare a resulting trust in the person's favor.

aliter (**al**-ə-tər). [Latin] Otherwise; it would be otherwise.

> "If I trespass on another's land, and make an excavation there without leaving any rubbish on the land, the trespass ceases as soon as I leave the land, and does not continue until I have filled the excavation up again. Consequently only one action will lie, and in it full damages are recoverable for both the past and the future. *Aliter* if I have brought a heap of soil and left it on the plaintiff's land." R.F.V. Heuston, *Salmond on the Law of Torts* 42 (17th ed. 1977).

ALI test. See SUBSTANTIAL-CAPACITY TEST.

aliud (**ay**-lee-əd). [Latin] Something else; another thing.

aliud examen (**ay**-lee-əd ig-**zay**-mən). [Latin "another investigation" or "another trial"] A different or foreign mode of trial.

aliunde (ay-lee-**yən**-dee), *adj.* [Latin] From another source; from elsewhere <evidence aliunde>. See *extrinsic evidence* under EVIDENCE.

aliunde rule. The doctrine that a verdict may not be impeached by evidence of a juror unless a foundation to introduce such evidence is first made by competent evidence from another source.

ALJ. *abbr.* ADMINISTRATIVE-LAW JUDGE.

all and singular. Collectively and individually.

allegata (al-ə-**gay**-tə). [Latin] *pl.* ALLEGATUM.

allegation, *n.* **1.** The act of declaring something to be true. **2.** Something declared or asserted as a matter of fact, esp. in a legal pleading; a party's formal statement of a factual matter as being true or provable, without its having yet been proved. — **allege,** *vb.*

disjunctive allegation. A statement in a pleading or indictment that expresses something in the alternative, usu. with the conjunction "or" <a charge that the defendant murdered or caused to be murdered is a disjunctive allegation>.

material allegation. In a pleading, an assertion that is essential to the claim or defense <a material allegation in a battery case is harmful or offensive contact with a person>.

primary allegation. **1.** The principal charge made against an adversary in a legal proceeding. **2.** *Eccles. law.* The opening pleading in an action in ecclesiastical court. — Also termed *primary plea*.

allegation of faculties. *Family law.* A statement of the husband's property, made by the wife to obtain alimony. See FACULTIES.

allegations-of-the-complaint rule. See EIGHT-CORNERS RULE.

allegatum (al-ə-**gay**-təm), *n.* [Latin] A fact alleged in a pleading; ALLEGATION. Pl. ***allegata.*** Cf. PROBATUM.

alleged (ə-**lejd**), *adj.* **1.** Asserted to be true as described <alleged offenses>. **2.** Accused but not yet tried <alleged murderer>.

allegiance. 1. A citizen's obligation of fidelity and obedience to the government or sovereign in return for the benefits of the protection of the state. • Allegiance may be either an absolute and permanent obligation or a qualified and temporary one.

acquired allegiance. The allegiance owed by a naturalized citizen.

actual allegiance. The obedience owed by one who resides temporarily in a foreign country to that country's government. • Foreign sovereigns, their representatives, and military personnel are typically excepted from this requirement. — Also termed *local allegiance*.

natural allegiance. The allegiance that native-born citizens or subjects owe to their nation.

permanent allegiance. The lasting allegiance owed to a state by citizens or subjects.

temporary allegiance. The impermanent allegiance owed to a state by a resident alien during the period of residence.

2. *Hist.* A vassal's obligation to the liege lord. See LIEGE.

Allen **charge.** *Criminal procedure*. A supplemental jury instruction given by the court to encourage a deadlocked jury, after prolonged deliberations, to reach a verdict. *Allen v. United States*, 164 U.S. 492, 17 S.Ct. 154 (1896). — Also termed *dynamite charge*; *dynamite instruction*; *nitroglycerine charge*; *shotgun instruction*; *third-degree instruction*.

aller a dieu (a-**lay** ə **dyuu** *or* **dyoo**). [Law French] To go to God. • This phrase prays for the case to be dismissed from court. — Sometimes spelled *aler a dieu*. Cf. ADIEU.

aller sans jour (a-**lay** san **zhoor**). [Law French] To go without day. • This phrase prays for a final dismissal of a case. — Also spelled *aler sans jour*. See GO HENCE WITHOUT DAY; ADEU.

all-events test. *Tax*. A requirement that all events fixing an accrual-method taxpayer's right to receive income or incur expense must occur before the taxpayer can report an item of income or expense.

alleviare (ə-lee-vee-**air**-ee), *vb*. [Law Latin] To levy or pay a fine or composition.

all faults, with. See AS IS.

all fours. See ON ALL FOURS.

all-holders rule. 1. An SEC rule that prohibits a public offering by the issuer of shares to some, but fewer than all, of the holders of a class of shares. **2.** An SEC rule requiring a tender offeror to make its offer to all the target company's shareholders.

alliance. 1. A bond or union between persons, families, states, or other parties. **2.** *Int'l law*. A union or association of two or more states or nations, formed by league or treaty, esp. for jointly waging war or mutually protecting against and repelling hostile attacks. Cf. DETENTE; ENTENTE. See STRATEGIC ALLIANCE.

allied offenses. *Criminal law*. Two or more crimes with elements so similar that the commission of one is automatically the commission of the other.

all-inclusive mortgage. See *wraparound mortgage* under MORTGAGE.

allision (ə-**lizh**-ən), *n*. *Maritime law*. The sudden impact of a vessel with a stationary object such as an anchored vessel or a pier. — **allide** (ə-**lɪd**), *vb*. Cf. COLLISION.

allocable (**al**-ə-kə-bəl), *adj*. That can be assigned or allocated.

allocation, *n*. A designation or apportionment for a specific purpose; esp., the crediting of a receipt or the charging of a disbursement to an account <allocation of funds>. — **allocate,** *vb*. — **allocable,** *adj*. — **allocator,** *n*.

allocatione facienda (al-ə-kay-shee-**oh**-nee fay-shee-**en**-də), *n*. See DE ALLOCATIONE FACIENDA.

allocatur (al-ə-**kay**-tər). [Law Latin] It is allowed. • This word formerly indicated that a writ, bill, or other pleading was allowed. It is still used today in Pennsylvania to denote permission to appeal. — Also termed *allogatur*.

special allocatur. An allowance of a writ (such as a writ of error) that is legally required in certain cases.

allocute (**al**-ə-kyoot), *vb*. To deliver in court a formal, exhortatory address; to make an allocution.

allocution (al-ə-**kyoo**-shən), *n*. *Criminal procedure*. **1.** A trial judge's formal address to a convicted defendant, asking him or her to speak in mitigation of the sentence to be imposed. • This address is required under Fed. R. Crim. P. 32(c)(3)(C). **2.** An unsworn statement from a convicted defendant to the sentencing judge or jury in which the defendant can ask for mercy, explain his or her conduct, apologize for the crime, or say anything else in an effort to lessen the impending sentence. • This statement is not subject to cross-examination.

victim allocution. A crime victim's address to the court before sentencing, usu. urging a harsher punishment.

allocutory (ə-**lok**-yə-tor-ee), *adj.* Of or relating to an allocution <allocutory pleas for mercy>.

allod (**al**-əd), *n. Hist.* The domain of a household.

allodial (ə-**loh**-dee-əl), *adj.* Held in absolute ownership; pertaining to an allodium. — **allodially,** *adv.*

allodium (ə-**loh**-dee-əm), *n.* An estate held in fee simple absolute. — Also spelled *alodium.* — Also termed *alod*; *alode.*

> "In this country, one who has full ownership of land is said to own it allodially — that is, free of feudal services and incidents." Thomas F. Bergin & Paul G. Haskell, *Preface to Estates in Land and Future Interests* 18 (2d ed. 1984).

allogatur. See ALLOCATUR.

allograph (**al**-ə-graf). An agent's writing or signature for the principal.

allonge (a-**lawnzh**). A slip of paper sometimes attached to a negotiable instrument for the purpose of receiving further indorsements when the original paper is filled with indorsements.

all-or-none offering. See OFFERING.

all-or-none order. See ORDER (4).

all-or-nothing rule. A gloss on the rule against perpetuities holding that a class gift is invalid in its entirety if it is invalid in part. • The effect of this principle is to invalidate a class member's interest if it vests in interest within the period of the rule because it may be subject to partial divestment by the remote interest of another class member.

allotment, *n.* **1.** A share or portion of something, such as property previously held in common or shares in a corporation. **2.** In American Indian law, the selection of specific land awarded to an individual allottee from a common holding. — **allot,** *vb.*

allotment certificate. *Securities.* A document that records the essential elements of a subscription of shares, as how many shares are to be purchased, the price to be paid, and the payment and delivery schedule.

allotment note. *English law.* A seaman's written assignment of a portion of his wages to a wife, parent, grandparent, or sibling. • These notes are governed by the Merchant Shipping Act of 1970, § 13(1).

allotment system. *English law.* The practice of dividing land into small portions for cultivation by agricultural laborers and others.

allottee. One to whom an allotment is made; a recipient of an allotment.

allowance. 1. A share or portion, esp. of money that is assigned or granted.

backhaul allowance. A price discount given to customers who get their goods from a seller's warehouse as a reflection of the seller's freight-cost savings.

family allowance. A portion of a decedent's estate set aside by statute for a surviving spouse, children, or parents, regardless of any testamentary disposition or competing claims.

gratuitous allowance. A pension voluntarily granted by a public entity. • The gratuitous (rather than contractual) nature of this type of allowance gives the pensioner no vested rights in the allowance.

spousal allowance. A portion of a decedent's estate set aside by statute for a surviving spouse, regardless of any testamentary disposition or competing claims. • This allowance is superior to the claims of general creditors. In some states, it is even preferred to the expenses of administration, funeral, and last illness of the spouse. — Also termed *widow's allowance*; *widower's allowance.*

2. The sum awarded by a court to a fiduciary as payment for services. **3.** A deduction.

depletion allowance. A tax deduction for the owners of oil, gas, mineral, or timber resources corresponding to the reduced value of the property resulting from the removal of the resource.

allowance pendente lite. See *alimony pendente lite* under ALIMONY.

alloynour (ə-**loy**-nər). [Law French] *Hist.* One who conceals, steals, or furtively carries off something.

all-risk insurance. See INSURANCE.

all-the-estate clause. *English law.* The provision in a conveyance transferring "all the estate, right, title, interest, claims, and demand" of the grantor in the property conveyed.

allurement. *Torts.* An attractive object that tempts a trespassing child to meddle when the child ought to abstain.

alluvial mining. The practice of removing sand and gravel from a riverbed.

alluvio maris (ə-**loo**-vee-oh **mar**-is). [Latin "alluvion of the sea"] The formation of soil or land from the sea.

alluvion (ə-**loo**-vee-ən). [fr. Latin *alluvio* "flood"] *Roman & civil law.* **1.** Strictly, the flow or wash of water against a shore or riverbank. **2.** A deposit of soil, clay, or other material caused by running water; esp., in land law, an addition of land caused by the buildup of deposits from running water, the added land then belonging to the owner of the property to which it is added. — Also termed (in sense 2) *alluvium.* Cf. ACCRETION (1); AVULSION (2); DELICTION; EROSION.

alluvium. See ALLUVION (2).

All Writs Act. A federal statute that gives the U.S. Supreme Court and all courts established by Congress the power to issue writs in aid of their jurisdiction and in conformity to the usages and principles of law. 28 USCA § 1651(a).

ally. *Int'l law.* **1.** A nation tied to another by treaty or alliance. **2.** A citizen or subject of an allied nation.

almaria (al-**mair**-ee-ə). [Latin "cupboard, bookcase"] The archives of a church or library. — Also termed *armaria.*

almoign (al-**moyn**). [Law French "alms"] **1.** Alms; a church treasury; an ecclesiastical possession. **2.** FRANKALMOIN.

almoin. See FRANKALMOIN.

almoner (**al**-mə-nər). A person charged with distributing the alms of a monarch, religious house, or other institution. • This office was first instituted in religious houses and although formerly one of importance is now almost a sinecure.

alms (ahmz). Charitable donations; any type of relief bestowed on the poor.

almshouse. *Archaic.* A dwelling for the publicly or privately supported poor of a city or county.

alnager (**al**-nə-jər). [Law Latin] *Hist.* A royal official responsible for collecting taxes (the *alnage*) on woolen cloth. • The tax was abolished in 1699.

alod. See ALLODIUM.

alode. See ALLODIUM.

alodium. See ALLODIUM.

a lour foy (ah loor **fwah**). [Law French "in their faith"] In their allegiance.

ALTA. *abbr.* American Land Title Association.

alta proditio (**al**-tə proh-**dish**-ee-oh). [Law Latin] See TREASON.

altarage (**awl**-tər-ij). *Eccles. law.* **1.** The offerings made upon an altar or to a church. **2.** An endowment or honorarium received by a priest for services performed at the altar.

alta via (**al**-tə **vɪ**-ə). [Law Latin] A highway.

alteration. **1.** A substantial change to real estate, esp. to a structure, not involving an addition to or removal of the exterior dimensions of a building's structural parts. • Although any addition to or improvement of real estate is by its very nature an alteration, real-estate lawyers habitually use *alteration* in reference to a lesser change. Still, to constitute an alteration, the change must be substantial — not simply a trifling modification. **2.** An act done to an instrument, after its execution, whereby its meaning or language is changed; esp., the changing of a term in a negotiable instrument without the consent of all parties to it. • Material alterations void an instrument, but immaterial ones do not. An alteration is material if it (1) changes the burden of a party (as by changing the date, time, place, amount, or rate of interest), (2) changes the liabilities or duties of any party (as by adding or removing the name of a maker, drawer, indorser, payee, or co-surety), or (3) changes the operation of the instrument or its effect in evidence (as by adding words or negotiability, changing the form of an indorsement, or changing the liability from joint to several).

"With respect to written instruments, 'alteration' generally means a change in an instrument's sense of language caused by a party to the instrument, and does not include such changes by non-parties or 'strangers' to the instrument. Although the distinction is not always observed, technically an alteration by a non-party or stranger to the instrument is a 'spoliation,' not an alteration, which does not invalidate it or change the rights or liabilities of the parties in interest, so long as the original writing remains legible." 4 Am. Jur. 2d *Alteration of Instruments* § 1 (1995).

material alteration. **1.** A significant change in something; esp., a change in a legal instrument sufficient to alter the instrument's legal meaning or effect. **2.** An unauthorized change in an instrument or an addition to an incomplete instrument resulting in the modification of a party's obligations. UCC § 3–407.

structural alteration. A significant change to a building or other structure, essentially creating a different building or structure.

altercation. A vehement dispute; a noisy argument.

"**altercation.** The traditional view is that this word refers to 'a noisy brawl or dispute,' not rising to the seriousness of physical violence.... But in AmE, the word now often denotes some type of scuffling or fighting, especially in police jargon." Bryan A. Garner, *A Dictionary of Modern American Usage* 34 (1998).

alter ego. A corporation used by an individual in conducting personal business, the result being that a court may impose liability on the individual by piercing the corporate veil when fraud has been perpetrated on someone dealing with the corporation. See PIERCING THE CORPORATE VEIL.

alter-ego rule. **1.** *Corporate law.* The doctrine that shareholders will be treated as the owners of a corporation's property, or as the real parties in interest, whenever it is necessary to do so to prevent fraud or to do justice. **2.** *Criminal law.* The common-law doctrine limiting the use of force when defending another person to the amount of force that the other person would be privileged to use in self-defense.

altering or amending a judgment. A trial court's act of correcting a substantive mistake in a judgment, as by correcting a manifest error of law or fact. Fed. R. Civ. P. 59(e).

alternat (**awl**-tər-nit *or* al-ter-**nah**). [French] The rotation in precedence among states, diplomats, etc., esp. in the signing of treaties. • This practice gives each diplomat a copy of the treaty with the diplomat's signature appearing first.

alternate legacy. See LEGACY.

alternate valuation date. *Tax law.* The date six months after a decedent's death. • Generally, the estate can elect to appraise the decedent's property either on the date of the decedent's death or on the alternate valuation date. See BASIS.

alternatim (al-tər-**nay**-tim *or* awl-), *adv.* [Latin] Interchangeably; by turns.

alternative constituency. See NONSHAREHOLDER CONSTITUENCY.

alternative contract. See CONTRACT.

alternative dispute resolution. A procedure for settling a dispute by means other than litigation, such as arbitration, mediation, or minitrial. — Abbr. ADR.

alternative judgment. See JUDGMENT.

alternative liability. See LIABILITY.

alternative mandamus. See MANDAMUS.

alternative-means doctrine. *Criminal law.* The principle that, when a crime may be committed in more than one way, jury unanimity is required on the defendant's guilt, but is not required on the possible different methods of committing the crime, as long as each possible method is supported by substantial evidence.

alternative-methods-of-performance contract. See *alternative contract* under CONTRACT.

alternative minimum tax. See TAX.

alternative obligation. See OBLIGATION.

alternative order. See ORDER (4).

alternative pleading. See PLEADING (2).

alternative promise. See PROMISE.

alternative relief. See RELIEF.

alternative remainder. See REMAINDER.

alternative writ. See WRIT.

alterum non laedere (**al**-tər-əm [*or* **awl-**] non **lee**-də-ree). [Latin "not to injure another"] *Roman & civil law.* To hurt no one by word or deed. • This is a fundamental principle of tort law and, according to Justinian, of law in general. Cf. HONESTE VIVERE; SUUM CUIQUE TRIBUERE.

alteruter (al-tər-**yoo**-tər *or* awl-). [Law Latin] One of two; either.

altius non tollendi (**al**-shee-əs non tə-**len**-dɪ). [Latin "of not raising higher"] *Roman & civil law.* A servitude prohibiting a landowner from building a house above a certain height.

altius tollendi (**al**-shee-əs tə-**len**-dɪ). [Latin "of raising higher"] *Roman & civil law.* A servitude that allows a landowner to build a house as high as desired.

alto et basso. See DE ALTO ET BASSO.

altum mare (**al**-təm **mair**-ee *or* **mahr**-ee), *n.* [Law Latin] *Hist.* The high seas; the deep seas.

a lui et a ses heritiers pour toujours (a **lwee** ay a **sayz** e-ree-**tyay** poor too-**zhoor**). [Law French] To him and his heirs forever. See *and his heirs* under HEIR.

alveus (**al**-vee-əs), *n.* [Law Latin] *Hist.* The bed or channel through which a stream flows in its ordinary course.

a.m. *abbr.* ANTE MERIDIEM.

AMA. *abbr.* American Medical Association.

a ma intent (ah mah *an*-**tawn**). [Law French] On my action.

amalgamation (ə-mal-gə-**may**-shən), *n.* The act of combining or uniting; consolidation <amalgamation of two small companies to form a new corporation>. — **amalgamate,** *vb.* — **amalgamator,** *n.* See MERGER.

Amalphitan Code (ə-**mal**-fə-tən). *Hist.* A code of maritime law compiled late in the 11th century at the port of Amalfi near Naples. • The Code was regarded as a primary source of maritime law throughout the Mediterranean to the end of the 16th century. — Also termed *Amalphitan Table*; *Laws of Amalfi.*

a manibus (ay **man**-ə-bəs), *n.* [Law Latin] *Hist.* A royal scribe.

amanuensis (ə-man-yoo-**en**-sis), *n.* [fr. Latin *ab-* "from" + *manus* "hand"] One who takes dictation; a scribe or secretary.

a manu servus (ay **man**-yoo **sər**-vəs). [Latin] A handservant; scribe; secretary.

ambactus (am-**bak**-təs). [Latin] *Hist.* **1.** A messenger. **2.** A servant whose services are hired out by the master.

ambasciator (am-**bash**-ee-ay-tər). [Law Latin] *Hist.* A person sent about in the service of another; an ambassador.

ambassador. 1. A diplomatic officer of the highest rank, usu. designated by a government as its resident representative in a foreign state. • Ambassadors represent the sovereign as well as the nation and enjoy many privileges while abroad in their official capacity, including immunity. Ambassadors are distinguished from ministers and envoys, who represent only the state where they are from and not the sovereign. Ambassadors are also generally distinguished from certain legates who have only ecclesiastical authority. But the papal nuncio and some legates, such as the *legate a latere*, bear the rank of ambassador. See NUNCIO; LEGATE. **2.** A representative appointed by another. **3.** An unofficial or nonappointed representative. — Also spelled (archaically) *embassador.* — **ambassadorial,** *adj.* — **ambassadorship,** *n.*

ambiguitas latens (am-bi-**gyoo**-ə-tas **lay**-tenz). See *latent ambiguity* under AMBIGUITY.

ambiguitas patens (am-bi-**gyoo**-ə-tas **pay**-tenz). See *patent ambiguity* under AMBIGUITY.

ambiguity (am-bi-**gyoo**-ə-tee), *n.* An uncertainty of meaning or intention, as in a contractual term or statutory provision. — **ambiguous** (am-**big**-yoo-əs), *adj.*

> "In the context of statutory interpretation the word most frequently used to indicate the doubt which a judge must entertain before he can search for and, if possible, apply a secondary meaning is 'ambiguity'. In ordinary language this term is often confined to situations in which the same word is capable of meaning two different things, but, in relation to statutory interpretation, judicial usage sanctions the application of the word 'ambiguity' to describe any kind of doubtful meaning of words, phrases or longer statutory provisions. *Hinchy's* case prompted the suggestion that if, in a particular context, words convey to different judges a different range of meanings 'derived from, not fanciful speculations or mistakes about linguistic usage, but from true knowledge

about the use of words, they are ambiguous'." Rupert Cross, *Statutory Interpretation* 76–77 (1976).

ambiguity on the factum. An ambiguity relating to the foundation of an instrument, such as a question relating to whether a testator intended for a particular clause to be part of an agreement, whether a codicil was intended to republish a former will, or whether the residuary clause was accidentally omitted.

latent ambiguity. An ambiguity that does not readily appear in the language of a document, but instead arises from a collateral matter when the document's terms are applied or executed <the contract contained a latent ambiguity because the shipping terms stated that the goods would arrive on the ship *Peerless*, but two ships have that name>. — Also termed *extrinsic ambiguity*; *equivocation*; *ambiguitas latens*.

"Instead of this word 'equivocation,' the phrase 'latent ambiguity' is sometimes used by courts, — 'latent' because it does not develop until we seek to apply it and then discover the equivocation. This phrase was invented by Lord Bacon, in one of his maxims, and it long held sway; but it has only served to confuse discussion, and his other word for the same thing, 'equivocation,' is more suitable, and has come into general use since Professor Thayer's masterly analysis of the subject some fifty years ago." John H. Wigmore, *A Students' Textbook of the Law of Evidence* 529 (1935). — In fact, the usual term today is *latent ambiguity*. — Eds.

patent ambiguity (**payt**-ənt). An ambiguity that clearly appears on the face of a document, arising from the language itself <the nonperformance was excused because the two different prices expressed in the contract created a patent ambiguity>. — Also termed *intrinsic ambiguity*; *ambiguitas patens*.

"[L]*atent* ambiguity ... must be carefully distinguished from *patent* ambiguity, where words are omitted, or contradict one another; for in such cases explanatory evidence is not admissible. Where a bill of exchange was expressed in words to be drawn for 'two hundred pounds' but in figures for '£245,' evidence was not admitted to show that the figures expressed the intention of the parties." William R. Anson, *Principles of the Law of Contract* 401 (Arthur L. Corbin ed., 3d Am. ed. 1919).

ambiguity doctrine. See CONTRA PROFERENTEM.

ambiguity on the factum. See AMBIGUITY.

ambit (**am**-bit). **1.** A space surrounding a house or town. **2.** A boundary line; an enclosing line or limit.

ambitus (**am**-bi-təs), *n.* [Latin *ambitus* "deviousness, corruption"] *Hist.* The procuring of a public office by money or gifts; the unlawful buying and selling of a public office.

ambulance chaser. 1. A lawyer who approaches victims of accidents in hopes of persuading them to sue for damages. **2.** A lawyer's agent who engages in this activity. — **ambulance-chasing,** *n.*

ambulatory (**am**-byə-lə-tor-ee), *adj.* **1.** Able to walk <the accident victim is still ambulatory>. **2.** Capable of being altered or revised <a will is ambulatory because it is revocable until the testator's death>.

ambulatory automatism. See AUTOMATISM.

ambulatory disposition. See DISPOSITION.

ambulatory will. See WILL.

a me (ay mee). [Latin] From me. ● This phrase was used in feudal grants to denote tenure held directly of the chief lord. The phrase is short for *a me de superiore meo* (ay mee dee s[y]oo-peer-ee-**or**-ee **mee**-oh), meaning "from me of my superior." Cf. DE ME.

ameliorate (ə-**meel**-yə-rayt), *vb.* **1.** To make better <the charity tries to ameliorate the conditions of the homeless>. **2.** To become better <with time, the situation ameliorated>.

ameliorating waste. See WASTE (1).

amelioration, *n.* **1.** The act of improving something; the state of being made better. **2.** An improvement. — **ameliorative,** *adj.*

ameliorative waste. See *ameliorating waste* under WASTE (1).

amenable (ə-**mee**-nə-bəl *or* -**men**-), *adj.* Legally answerable; liable to being brought to judgment <amenable to process>. — **amenability,** *n.*

amend, *vb.* **1.** To make right; to correct or rectify <amend the order to fix a clerical error>. **2.** To change the wording of; specif., to alter (a statute, constitution, etc.) formally by adding or deleting a provision or by modifying the wording <amend the legislative bill>.

amendatory (ə-**men**-də-tor-ee), *adj.* Designed or serving to amend; corrective <an amendatory rider to an insurance policy>.

amended complaint. See COMPLAINT.

amended pleading. See PLEADING (1).

amended return. See TAX RETURN.

amende honorable (ə-**mend on**-ə-rə-bəl *or* a-**mawnd** on-ə-**rah**-bəl). [French "honorable reparation"] *Hist.* A formal reparation for an offense or injury, done by making an open and usu. humiliating acknowledgment and apology so as to restore the victim's honor. • This apology could be accomplished, for example, by walking into church with a rope around the neck and a torch in hand, begging forgiveness from the injured party.

amendment. 1. A formal revision or addition proposed or made to a statute, constitution, or other instrument.

hostile amendment. A legislative amendment intended to antagonize potential supporters of a bill.

killer amendment. A legislative amendment that has the effect (intended or not) of antagonizing potential supporters of a bill.

perfecting amendment. A legislative amendment that either corrects one or more minor problems with a bill or makes minor adjustments to attract more support for the bill.

substitute amendment. A legislative amendment that seeks to change provisions in a bill.

2. The process of making such a revision. **3.** A change made by addition, deletion, or correction; an alteration in wording. — Abbr. amend.

amendment on court's own motion. A change to a pleading or other document by the judge without a motion from a party.

nunc pro tunc amendment (**nəngk** proh **təngk** *or* **nuungk** proh **tuungk**). An amendment that is given retroactive effect, usu. by court order.

amendment of indictment. The alteration of the charging terms of an indictment, either literally or in effect, after the grand jury has made a decision on it. • The indictment usu. cannot legally be amended at trial in a way that would prejudice the defendant by having a trial on matters that were not contained in the indictment.

amendment on court's own motion. See AMENDMENT (3).

amends, *n.* Compensation given for a loss or injury; reparation.

amenity. [fr. Latin *amoenitas* "pleasantness"] Something tangible or intangible that increases the enjoyment of real property, such as location, view, landscaping, security, or access to recreational facilities.

a mensa et thoro (ay **men**-sə et **thor**-oh). [Latin "from board and hearth"] (Of a divorce decree) effecting a separation of the parties rather than a dissolution of the marriage <a separation *a mensa et thoro* was the usual way for a couple to separate under English law up until 1857>. See *divorce a menso et thoro* under DIVORCE; SEPARATION; A VINCULO MATRIMONII.

amerce (ə-**mərs**), *vb.* **1.** To impose a fine or penalty that is not fixed but is left to the court's discretion; to punish by amercement. **2.** To fine or punish in any manner. — **amerceable** (ə-**mər**-sə-bəl), **amerciable** (ə-**mər**-see-ə-bəl), *adj.*

amercement (ə-**mərs**-mənt), *n.* [fr. Law French *estre à merci* "to be at the mercy (of another)," fr. Latin *merces* "payment"] **1.** The imposition of a discretionary fine or penalty by a court, esp. on an official for misconduct <an amercement proceeding>. **2.** The fine or penalty so imposed <an amercement charged to the sheriff for failing to return the writ of execution>. — Also termed *cashlite*; (archaically) *amerciament*; *merciament.*

American Academy of Actuaries. A national organization of actuaries who must meet specified educational requirements and have at least three years of actuarial work experience. • Created in 1965, the Academy promotes public awareness of the actuarial profession, represents the profession before federal and state governments, and sponsors continuing-education conferences. — Abbr. AAA. See ACTUARY.

American Accounting Association. An organization of accounting practitioners, educators, and students. • The Association, founded in 1916, promotes accounting as an academic discipline by sponsoring research projects and continuing-education seminars. — Abbr. AAA.

American Arbitration Association. A national organization that maintains a panel of arbitrators to hear labor and commercial disputes. — Abbr. AAA.

American Bankers Association. A voluntary trade association of banking institutions, including banks, trust companies, and savings banks and associations, whose members represent the vast majority of banking deposits in the United States. • The association was founded in 1875. Abbr. ABA.

American Bar Association. A voluntary national organization of lawyers. • Among other things, it participates in law reform, law-school accreditation, and continuing legal education in an effort to improve legal services and the administration of justice. — Abbr. ABA.

American Bar Foundation. An outgrowth of the American Bar Association involved with sponsoring and funding projects in law-related research, education, and social studies.

American Civil Liberties Union. A national organization whose primary purpose is to help enforce and preserve individual rights and liberties guaranteed by federal and state constitutions. — Abbr. ACLU.

American clause. *Marine insurance.* A policy provision that prevents an insurer from claiming contribution from a policy later purchased by the insured.

American depository receipt. A receipt issued by an American bank as a substitute for stock shares in a foreign-based corporation. • ADRs are the most common method by which foreign companies secure American shareholders. Companies that offer ADRs maintain a stock listing in their domestic market in their domestic currency, while the ADRs are held in U.S. dollars and listed on a U.S. stock exchange, usu. the New York Stock Exchange. — Abbr. ADR. — Also termed *American depositary receipt.*

American Experience Table of Mortality. *Insurance.* A chart developed by insurers in the 1860s to predict mortality rates and thereby more accurately set insurance rates. • The Table was widely used by insurers to establish rates until the 1950s.

American Federation of Labor and Congress of Industrial Organizations. A voluntary affiliation of more than 100 labor unions that operate autonomously yet benefit from the affiliation's political activities and its establishment of broad policies for the national labor movement. — Abbr. AFL–CIO.

American Inns of Court Foundation. See INN OF COURT (2).

American Law Institute. An organization of lawyers, judges, and legal scholars who promote consistency and simplification of American law by publishing restatements of the law and other model codes and treatises, as well as promoting continuing legal education. — Abbr. ALI.

American Law Institute test. See SUBSTANTIAL-CAPACITY TEST.

American Lloyd's. See LLOYD'S UNDERWRITERS.

American rule. 1. The requirement that each litigant must pay its own attorney's fees, even if the party prevails in the lawsuit. • The rule is subject to bad-faith and other statutory and contractual exceptions. Cf. ENGLISH RULE. **2.** The doctrine that a witness cannot be questioned on cross-examination about any fact or circumstance not connected with the matters brought out in the direct examination.

American Stock Exchange. An organized stock exchange and self-regulating organization under the Securities Exchange Act of 1934, located in New York City and engaged in national trading of corporate stocks. • It often trades in the securities of young or small companies because its listing requirements are less strict than those of the New York Stock Exchange. — Abbr. AMEX; ASE.

Americans with Disabilities Act. A federal statute that prohibits discrimination — in employment, public services, and public accommodations — against any person with a disability ("a physical or mental impairment that substantially limits one or more of the major life activities"). 42 USCA §§ 12101–12213. • Under the ADA, major life activities include any activity that an average person in the general population can perform with little or no difficulty, such as seeing, hearing, sleeping, eating, walking, traveling, and working. The statute applies to both private and governmental entities. — Abbr. ADA.

AMEX (**am**-eks). *abbr.* AMERICAN STOCK EXCHANGE.

amiable compositor. *Int'l law.* An unbiased third party, often a king or emperor, who suggests a solution that disputing countries might accept of their own volition; a mediator in a dispute between subjects of international law. — Also termed *aimable compositeur.*

> "When the King of the Netherlands, to whom Great Britain and the United States resorted in the Northeast Boundary Dispute, by a treaty of 1827, handed down an award in the manner of an 'amiable compositor,' both parties agreed to reject the award on the ground that under the treaty he had been authorized merely to decide on the legal merits of the respective territorial claims." Philip C. Jessup, *The Use of International Law* 35 (1959).

amicable action. See *test case* (1) under CASE.

amicable compounder. See COMPOUNDER (1).

amicable scire facias to revive a judgment. See SCIRE FACIAS.

amicus curiae (ə-**mee**-kəs **kyoor**-ee-I *or* ə-**mI**-kəs **kyoor**-ee-ee *also* **am**-i-kəs). [Latin "friend of the court"] A person who is not a party to a lawsuit but who petitions the court or is requested by the court to file a brief in the action because that person has a strong interest in the subject matter. — Often shortened to *amicus*. — Also termed *friend of the court*. Pl. **amici curiae** (ə-**mee**-kee *or* ə-**mI**-sI *or* ə-**mI**-kI).

amita (**am**-ə-tə). [Latin] *Civil law.* The sister of one's father; an aunt on the father's side.

amitina (am-ə-**tI**-nə). [Latin] *Civil law.* The daughter of a paternal aunt or maternal uncle; a female first cousin.

amitinus (am-ə-**tI**-nəs). [Latin] *Civil law.* The son of a paternal aunt or maternal uncle; a male first cousin.

amittere curiam (ə-**mit**-ə-ree **kyoor**-ee-əm), *vb.* [Law Latin] *Hist.* To lose the privilege of attending court.

amittere legem terrae (ə-**mit**-ə-ree **lee**-jəm **ter**-ee). See LIBERAM LEGEM AMITTERE.

amittere liberam legem (ə-**mit**-ə-ree **lib**-ər-əm **lee**-jəm). See LIBERAM LEGEM AMITTERE.

amnesty, *n.* A pardon extended by the government to a group or class of persons, usu. for a political offense; the act of a sovereign power officially forgiving certain classes of persons who are subject to trial but have not yet been convicted <the 1986 Immigration Reform and Control Act provided amnesty for undocumented aliens already present in the country>. • Unlike an ordinary pardon, amnesty is usu. addressed to crimes against state sovereignty — that is, to political offenses with respect to which forgiveness is deemed more expedient for the public welfare than prosecution and punishment. Amnesty is usu. general, addressed to classes or even communities. — Also termed *general pardon.* — **amnesty,** *vb.* See PARDON.

express amnesty. Amnesty granted in direct terms.

implied amnesty. Amnesty indirectly resulting from a peace treaty executed between contending parties.

amnesty clause. A clause, esp. one found in a peace treaty, that wipes out past offenses such as treason, sedition, rebellion, and even war crimes. • A sovereign may grant amnesty to all guilty persons or only to certain categories of offenders.

Amnesty International. An international nongovernmental organization founded in the early 1960s to protect human rights throughout the world. • Its mission is to "secure throughout the world the observance of the Universal Declaration of Human Rights." Amnesty Int'l Statute, art. 1.

amortization (am-ər-tə-**zay**-shən), *n.* **1.** The act or result of gradually extinguishing a debt, such as a mortgage, usu. by contributing payments of principal each time a periodic interest payment is due.

negative amortization. An increase in a loan's principal balance caused by monthly payments insufficient to pay accruing interest.

2. The act or result of apportioning the initial cost of a usu. intangible asset, such as a patent, over the asset's useful life. Cf. DEPRECIATION.

amortization reserve. See RESERVE.

amortization schedule. A schedule of periodic payments of interest and principal owed on a debt obligation; specif., a loan schedule showing both the amount of principal and interest that is due at regular intervals over the loan term and the remaining unpaid principal balance after each scheduled payment is made.

amortize, *vb.* **1.** To extinguish (a debt) gradually, often by means of a sinking fund. **2.** To arrange to extinguish (a debt) by gradual increments. **3.** *Hist.* To alienate or convey lands to a corporation (that is, in mortmain). — Also spelled *amortise*. See MORTMAIN.

amortized loan. See LOAN.

amortized mortgage. See MORTGAGE.

amotion. 1. A turning out, as the eviction of a tenant or the removal of a person from office. **2.** The common-law procedure available to shareholders to remove a corporate director for cause. **3.** The wrongful moving or carrying away of another's personal property.

amount in controversy. The damages claimed or relief demanded by the injured party in a lawsuit. • For a federal court to have diversity jurisdiction, the amount in controversy must exceed $75,000. 28 USCA § 1332(a). — Also termed *jurisdictional amount*; *matter in controversy*. See DIVERSITY OF CITIZENSHIP; AGGREGATION DOCTRINE.

amount realized. *Tax.* The amount received by a taxpayer for the sale or exchange of an asset, such as cash, property, services received, or debts assumed by a buyer. Cf. GAIN (3); LOSS (4).

amove, *vb.* To remove (a person) from an office or position.

amoveas manus (ay-**moh**-vee-əs **man**-əs). [Law Latin "that you remove your hands"] *Hist.* **1.** A judgment ordering the Crown to relinquish possession of land to the complainant. • The judgment is so called from the emphatic words *quod manus domini regis amoveantur* ("that the hands of the king be removed"). **2.** The writ issued on the judgment.

ampliatio (am-plee-**ay**-shee-oh). [Latin] *Roman law.* **1.** The act of deferring or reserving judgment. **2.** In a criminal trial, the repeating of evidence at the jury's request.

ampliation (am-plee-**ay**-shən). *Civil law.* A postponement of the decision in a case.

amplius (**am**-plee-əs). [Latin] *Roman law.* More; further. • This word prefaced a statement made by a praetor to defer a case to a later date if an obscurity prevented the judex from reaching a decision.

AMT. See *alternative minimum tax* under TAX.

a multo fortiori (ay **məl**-toh for-shee-**or**-I). [Latin] By far the stronger reason. Cf. A FORTIORI.

amusement tax. See TAX.

anaconda clause. See MOTHER HUBBARD CLAUSE (1).

anacrisis (an-ə-**krI**-sis). *Civil law.* An investigation or inquiry, esp. one conducted by torture.

analogous art. See ART.

analytical jurisprudence. See JURISPRUDENCE.

anarchist, *n.* One who advocates the overthrow of organized government by force or who believes in the absence of government as a political ideal. — **anarchism** (the philosophy), *n.*

anarchy, *n.* Absence of government; lawlessness. — **anarchic,** *adj.*

anathema (ə-**nath**-ə-mə), *n.* An ecclesiastical curse that prohibits a person from receiving communion (as in excommunication) and bars the person from contact with members of the church. — **anathematize,** *vb.*

anatocism (ə-**nat**-ə-siz-əm). *Civil law.* Compound interest.

anatomical gift. See GIFT.

ancestor. See ASCENDANT.

ancestral debt. See DEBT.

ancestral estate. See ESTATE.

ancestry. A line of descent; lineage.

anchorage. A duty paid by shipowners for the use of a port; a toll for anchoring.

ancient, *adj. Evidence.* Existing for a long time, usu. at least 20 to 30 years <ancient deed> <ancient map>. • Ancient items are usu. presumed to be valid even if proof of validity cannot be made. Fed. R. Evid. 901(b)(8).

ancient, *n.* A senior member of an Inn of Court or of Chancery.

ancient demesne. See DEMESNE.

ancient document. See DOCUMENT.

ancient house. See HOUSE.

ancient law. The law of antiquity, considered esp. either from an anthropological standpoint or from the standpoint of tracing precursors to modern law.

> "Ancient law uniformly refuses to dispense with a single gesture, however grotesque; with a single syllable, however its meaning may have been forgotten; with a single witness, however superfluous may be his testimony. The entire solemnities must be scrupulously completed by persons legally entitled to take part in them, or else the conveyance is null, and the seller is re-established in the rights of which he had vainly attempted to divest himself." Henry S. Maine, *Ancient Law* 225–26 (17th ed. 1901).

ancient-lights doctrine. The common-law principle by which a landowner acquired, after 20 years of uninterrupted use, an easement preventing a neighbor from building an obstruction that blocks light from passing through the landowner's window. • The window (or other opening) is termed an *ancient light*. This doctrine has rarely been applied in the United States. — Also termed *ancient-windows doctrine*.

> "Under the English doctrine of ancient lights, which has been soundly repudiated in this country, if a landowner had received sunlight across adjoining property for a specified period of time, the landowner was entitled to continue to receive unobstructed access to sunlight across the adjoining property; the landowner acquired a negative prescriptive easement and could prevent the adjoining landowner from obstructing access to light." 1 Am. Jur. 2d *Adjoining Landowners* § 90, at 889 (1994).

ancient readings. *Hist.* Lectures on ancient English statutes, formerly having substantial legal authority.

ancient rent. *Hist.* The rent reserved at the time the lease is made, if the estate was not then under lease.

ancients. *Hist.* Certain members of seniority in the Inns of Court and Chancery. • In Gray's Inn, the society consisted of benchers, ancients, barristers, and students under the bar, with the ancients being the oldest barristers. In the Middle Temple, those who passed the readings were termed *ancients*. The Inns of Chancery consisted of both ancients and students or clerks.

ancient serjeant. *Hist. English law.* The eldest of the Crown's serjeants. • The last serjeant to hold this office died in 1866.

ancient wall. See WALL.

ancient watercourse. See WATERCOURSE.

ancient-windows doctrine. See ANCIENT-LIGHTS DOCTRINE.

ancient writing. See *ancient document* under DOCUMENT.

ancilla (an-**sil**-ə), *n.* [Latin] *Hist.* A female auxiliary or assistant.

ancillary (**an**-sə-ler-ee), *adj.* Supplementary; subordinate <ancillary claims>. — **ancillarity** (an-sə-**la**[**i**]**r**-ə-tee), *n.*

ancillary administration. See ADMINISTRATION.

ancillary administrator. See ADMINISTRATOR (1).

ancillary attachment. See ATTACHMENT (3).

ancillary bill. See *ancillary suit* under SUIT.

ancillary claim. A claim that is collateral to, dependent on, or auxiliary to another claim, such as a state-law claim that is sufficiently related to a federal claim to permit federal jurisdiction over it. • The concept of ancillary federal jurisdiction is now contained in the supplemental-jurisdiction statute, 28 USCA § 1367. See *ancillary jurisdiction* and *supplemental jurisdiction* under JURISDICTION.

ancillary jurisdiction. See JURISDICTION.

ancillary legislation. See LEGISLATION.

ancillary proceeding. See *ancillary suit* under SUIT.

ancillary process. See *ancillary suit* under SUIT.

ancillary receiver. See RECEIVER.

ancillary suit. See SUIT.

ancipitis usus. See *conditional contraband* under CONTRABAND.

***Anders* brief.** *Criminal procedure.* A brief filed by a court-appointed defense attorney who wants to withdraw from the case on appeal based on a belief that the appeal is frivolous. • In an *Anders* brief, the attorney seeking to withdraw must identify anything in the record that might arguably support the appeal. The court then decides whether the appeal is frivolous and whether the attorney should be permitted to withdraw. *Anders v. California*, 386 U.S. 738, 87 S.Ct. 1396 (1967). — Also termed *no-merit brief*.

> "*Anders* requires an attorney to assume two somewhat contradictory roles when filing a no-merit brief. The first, and most important, role is that of an advocate. *Anders* makes clear that the first duty of appellate counsel is to study the record and to consult with the defendant to ascertain whether there is anything in the record to support an appeal. Counsel should not consider the case with a view toward finding no merit or of acting as a neutral party. Only if counsel can find no issue of even arguable merit does he change hats and become an amicus curiae." Jonathan M. Purver & Lawrence E. Taylor, *Handling Criminal Appeals* § 138, at 285 (1980).

and his heirs. See HEIR.

and other good and valuable consideration. See *other consideration* under CONSIDERATION.

androlepsy (**an**-drə-lep-see). [fr. Greek "seizure of men"] *Hist.* The taking by one nation of citizens or subjects of another nation either in reprisal or to enforce some claim (as to surrender or punish a fugitive). — Also termed *androlepsia* (an-drə-**lep**-see-ə).

anecius (ə-**nee**-shee-əs), *n.* [Law Latin] *Hist.* The eldest; the firstborn; the senior, as contrasted with *puisne* ("the younger").

angaria (ang-**gair**-ee-ə). **1.** ANGARY. **2.** *Roman law.* A compulsory service consisting in the transport of goods or persons for the imperial post. **3.** *Hist.* A service exacted by a lord beyond what is due.

angary (**ang**-gə-ree). *Int'l law.* A country's right, in war or other urgent circumstances, to seize — for temporary use — neutral merchant ships in its inland or territorial waters as well as aircraft within its territory, with full indemnity by the country. — Also termed *right of angary*; *jus angariae*.

> "In many respects the content and scope of the right of angary remain unclear and there is little evidence of State practice on several controversial questions. In practice, the right has been exercised mainly in wartime. Nevertheless, several writers consider it to be applicable in times of peace and in cases of absolute necessity, such as the evacuation of the population in the event of a national emergency." Rainer Lagoni, "Angary, Right of," in 1 *Encyclopedia of Public International Law* (1992).

Anglicé (**ang**-glə-see), *adv.* [French] In English. • This term formerly appeared in pleadings to signal an English translation or restatement of a previous Latin word or phrase <*panis*, Anglicé, bread>.

Anglo-Saxon law. The body of royal decrees and customary laws developed by the Germanic peoples who dominated England from the 5th century to 1066.

anhlote, *n. Hist.* A single tribute or tax paid according to custom, such as scot and lot. See SCOT AND LOT.

aniente (**an**-ee-ənt *or* an-ee-**ent**), *adj.* [Law French] (Of a law, etc.) having no force or effect; void. — Also spelled *anient.* — Also termed *aniens.*

animo (**an**-ə-moh). [Latin] See ANIMUS (2).

animo et corpore (**an**-ə-moh et **kor**-pə-ree), *adv.* [Latin] By the mind and by the body; by the intention and by the physical act <possession is acquired *animo et corpore*>.

animo felonico (**an**-ə-moh fə-**lon**-ə-koh), *adv.* [Latin] With felonious intent; with the intention to commit a felony.

animus (**an**-ə-məs). [Latin] **1.** Ill will; animosity.

class-based animus. A prejudicial disposition toward a discernible, usu. constitutionally protected, group of persons. • A *class-based animus* is an essential element of a civil-rights conspiracy case.

2. Intention. • All the following Latin "animus" phrases have analogous adverbial forms beginning with "animo" (the definition merely needing "with" at the outset) — for example, *animo furandi* means "with the intention to steal," *animo testandi* means "with testamentary intention," etc.

animus belligerendi (**an**-ə-məs bə-lij-ə-**ren**-dɪ). The intention to wage war.

animus cancellandi (**an**-ə-məs kan-sə-**lan**-dɪ). [Latin] The intention to cancel. • This phrase usu. refers to a will.

animus capiendi (**an**-ə-məs kap-ee-**en**-dɪ). [Latin] The intention to take or capture.

animus dedicandi (**an**-ə-məs ded-ə-**kan**-dɪ). [Latin] The intention to donate or dedicate.

animus defamandi (**an**-ə-məs def-ə-**man**-dɪ). [Latin] The intention to defame.

animus derelinquendi (**an**-ə-məs dee-rel-ing-**kwen**-dɪ). [Latin] The intention to abandon.

animus deserendi (**an**-ə-məs des-ə-**ren**-dɪ). [Latin] The intention to desert (usu. a spouse, child, etc.).

animus differendi (**an**-ə-məs dif-ə-**ren**-dɪ). [Latin] The intention to obtain delay.

animus domini (**an**-ə-məs **dom**-ə-nɪ). [Latin] *Roman law.* The intent to exercise dominion over a thing; the intent to own something. Cf. *animus possidendi.*

"All possession has two elements, a physical and a mental, which the Romans distinguish as corpus and animus. The first is the physical relation of the possessor to the object. The second is his sense of that relation. If he is minded to deal with the thing as his own (animus domini — animus sibi habendi), no matter whether rightfully or wrongfully, he possesses in the fullest sense." R.W. Lee, *The Elements of Roman Law* 179–80 (4th ed. 1956).

animus donandi (**an**-ə-məs doh-**nan**-dɪ). The intention to give.

animus et factum (**an**-ə-məs et **fak**-təm). [Latin "mind and deed"] The intention and the deed. • This phrase can refer to a person's intent to reside in a given country permanently or for an indefinite period.

animus felonicus (**an**-ə-məs fe-**loh**-ni-kəs). The intention to commit a felony.

animus furandi (**an**-ə-məs fyuu-**ran**-dɪ). The intention to steal. — Also termed *furandi animus.*

"[An] intent to deprive the owner of his property permanently, or an intent to deal with another's property unlawfully in such a manner as to create an obviously unreasonable risk of permanent deprivation, [is] all that is required to constitute the *animus furandi* — or intent to steal." Rollin M. Perkins & Ronald N. Boyce, *Criminal Law* 332–33 (3d ed. 1982).

animus injuriandi (**an**-ə-məs in-joor-ee-**an**-dɪ). The intention to injure, esp. to insult.

animus lucrandi (**an**-ə-məs loo-**kran**-dɪ). [Latin] The intention to make a gain or profit.

animus malus (**an**-ə-məs **mal**-əs). [Latin] Evil intent.

animus manendi (**an**-ə-məs mə-**nen**-dɪ). [Latin "will to remain"] The intention to remain; the intention to establish a permanent residence.

animus morandi (**an**-ə-məs mə-**ran**-dɪ). [Latin "will to tarry"] The intention to remain. • Although *animus morandi* is broadly synonymous with *animus manendi, morandi* suggests less permanency.

animus nocendi (**an**-ə-məs noh-**sen**-dɪ). [Latin] The intention to harm.

animus possidendi (**an**-ə-məs pah-sə-**den**-dɪ). [Latin] *Roman law.* The intent to possess a thing. Cf. *animus domini.*

animus quo (**an**-ə-məs **kwoh**). [Latin] The intent with which.

animus recipiendi (**an**-ə-məs ri-sip-ee-**en**-dɪ). [Latin] The intention to receive.

animus recuperandi (**an**-ə-məs ri-k[y]oo-pə-**ran**-dɪ). [Latin] The intention to recover.

animus republicandi (**an**-ə-məs ree-pub-lə-**kan**-dɪ). [Latin] The intention to republish.

animus restituendi (**an**-ə-məs rə-sti-tyoo-**en**-dɪ). [Latin] The intention to restore.

animus revertendi (**an**-ə-məs ree-vər-**ten**-dɪ). The intention to return (to a place).

animus revocandi (**an**-ə-məs rev-oh-**kan**-dɪ). [Latin] The intention to revoke (a will) <her destruction of the will indicated that she had animus revocandi>.

animus signandi (**an**-ə-məs sig-**nan**-dɪ). [Latin] The intention to sign.

animus testandi (**an**-ə-məs tes-**tan**-dɪ). [Latin] Testamentary intention.

ann, jour, et wast (an, zhoor, ay wayst). [Law French] See YEAR, DAY, AND WASTE.

annates (**an**-ayts *or* **an**-its), *n.* [fr. Law Latin *annata*] *Hist. Eccles. law.* First fruits paid out of spiritual benefices, initially to the Pope and later to the Crown under Henry VIII.

annex, *n.* Something that is attached, such as a document to a report or an addition to a building.

annexation, *n.* **1.** The act of attaching; the state of being attached. **2.** *Property.* The point at which a fixture becomes a part of the realty to which it is attached. **3.** A formal act by which a nation, state, or municipality incorporates land within its dominion. • In international law, the usual formalities of announcing annexation involve having specially commissioned officers hoist the national flag and read a proclamation. **4.** The annexed land itself. — **annex,** *vb.* Cf. ACCESSION (5).

cherry-stem annexation. **1.** Annexed land that resembles (on a map) a cherry because the annexed territory — the cherry — is not contiguous to the acquiring municipality, and the narrow corridor of annexed land leading to the targeted area resembles a stem. **2.** The process of annexing land with this configuration.

anniversary date. *Insurance.* The annually recurring date of the initial issuance of a policy. Cf. POLICY YEAR.

anno ante Christum (**an**-oh **an**-tee **kris**-təm), *adv.* [Latin] In the year before Christ. — Abbr. A.A.C.

anno ante Christum natum (**an**-oh **an**-tee **kris**-təm **nay**-təm), *adv.* [Latin] In the year before the birth of Christ. — Abbr. A.A.C.N.

Anno Domini (**an**-oh **dom**-ə-nI *or* -nee). [Latin "in the year of the Lord"] Of the modern era. • This phrase denotes the method of calculating time from the birth of Christ <A.D. 1776>. — Abbr. A.D. — Also termed *Year of Our Lord.*

annonae civiles (ə-**noh**-nee sə-**vI**-leez), *n.* [Latin] *Hist.* Yearly rents issuing out of particular lands and payable to certain monasteries.

anno orbis conditi (**an**-oh **or**-bis **kon**-di-tI), *n.* [Latin] The year of the creation of the world. — Abbr. A.O.C.

Anno Regni (**an**-oh **reg**-nI). [Latin] In the year of the reign. • A.R.V.R. 22, for example, is an abbreviated reference to *Anno Regni Victoriae Reginae vicesimo secundo* ("in the twenty-second year of the reign of Queen Victoria"). — Abbr. A.R.

annotatio (an-oh-**tay**-shee-oh). [Latin] RESCRIPT (3).

annotation (an-ə-**tay**-shən), *n.* **1.** A brief summary of the facts and decision in a case, esp. one involving statutory interpretation. **2.** A note that explains or criticizes a source of law, usu. a case. • Annotations appear, for example, in the *United States Code Annotated* (USCA). **3.** A volume containing such explanatory or critical notes. — **annotate** (**an**-ə-tayt), *vb.* — **annotative** (**an**-ə-tay-tiv), *adj.* — **annotator** (**an**-ə-tay-tər), *n.* Cf. NOTE (2).

> "One of the most important classes of Search Books is those included in the category of Annotations. They are important and valuable, in that they often purport to give, in very condensed form, some indication of the law, deduced from the cases or statutes, as well as to point out where similar cases can be found." William M. Lile et al., *Brief Making and the Use of Law Books* 84 (3d ed. 1914).

announce, vb. To make publicly known; to proclaim formally <the judge announced her decision in open court>.

annoyance. See NUISANCE (1).

annual depreciation. See DEPRECIATION.

annual exclusion. See EXCLUSION (1).

annual gift-tax exclusion. See *annual exclusion* under EXCLUSION.

annual meeting. See MEETING.

annual message. See MESSAGE.

annual percentage rate. See INTEREST RATE.

annual permit. A permit, required by some states, that must be paid each year by a corporation that does business in the state. • In some states, the permit fee is set according to the corporation's capitalization.

annual report. A yearly corporate financial report for shareholders and other interested parties. • The Securities Exchange Act of 1934 requires registered corporations to file an annual report on the SEC's Form 10–K. An annual report includes a balance sheet, income statement, statement of changes in financial position, reconciliation of changes in owners' equity accounts, a summary of significant accounting principles, other explanatory notes, the auditor's report, and comments from management about prospects for the coming year. — Also termed *annual statement*; *financial report.*

annual value. See VALUE.

annua pensione. See DE ANNUA PENSIONE.

annuitant (ə-**n[y]oo**-ə-tənt), *n.* A beneficiary of an annuity.

annuity (ə-**n[y]oo**-ə-tee). **1.** An obligation to pay a stated sum, usu. monthly or annually, to a stated recipient. • These payments terminate upon the death of the designated beneficiary. **2.** A fixed sum of money payable periodically. **3.** A right, often acquired under a life-insurance contract, to receive fixed payments periodically for a specified duration. Cf. PENSION. **4.** A savings account with an insurance company or investment company, usu. established for retirement income. • Payments into the account accumulate tax-free, and the account is taxed only when the annuitant withdraws money in retirement.

annuity certain. An annuity payable over a specified period, regardless of whether the annuitant dies.

annuity due. An annuity that makes payments at the beginning of each pay period. Cf. *ordinary annuity.*

cash-refund annuity. An annuity providing for a lump-sum payment after the annuitant's death of the difference between the total received and the price paid.

contingent annuity. **1.** An annuity that begins making payments when some future event occurs, such as the death of a person other than the annuitant. **2.** An annuity that makes an uncertain number of payments, depending on the outcome of a future event.

deferred annuity. An annuity that begins making payments on a specified date if the annuitant is alive at that time. — Also termed *deferred-payment annuity.* Cf. *immediate annuity.*

fixed annuity. An annuity that guarantees fixed payments, either for life or for a specified period.

group annuity. An annuity payable to members of a group, esp. employees, who are covered by a single annuity contract, such as a group pension plan.

immediate annuity. An annuity paid for with a single premium and that begins to pay benefits within the first payment interval. Cf. *deferred annuity.*

joint annuity. An annuity payable to two annuitants until one of them dies, at which time the annuity terminates for the survivor (unless the annuity also provides for survivorship rights). See *survivorship annuity.*

life annuity. An annuity payable only during the annuitant's lifetime, even if the annuitant dies prematurely.

life-income period-certain annuity. An annuity that pays a specified number of payments even if the annuitant dies before the minimum amount has been paid.

nonrefund annuity. An annuity with guaranteed payments during the annuitant's life, but with no refund to anyone at death. — Also termed *straight life annuity*; *pure annuity.*

ordinary annuity. An annuity that makes payments at the end of each pay period. Cf. *annuity due.*

private annuity. An annuity from a private source rather than from a public or life-insurance company.

pure annuity. See *nonrefund annuity.*

refund annuity. An annuity that, upon the annuitant's death, pays to the annuitant's estate the difference between the purchase price and the total payments received during the annuitant's lifetime.

retirement annuity. An annuity that begins making payments only after the annuitant's retirement. • If the annuitant dies before retirement, an agreed amount will usu. be refunded to the annuitant's estate.

straight annuity. An annuity that makes payments in fixed amounts at periodic intervals. Cf. *variable annuity.*

straight life annuity. See *nonrefund annuity.*

survivorship annuity. An annuity providing for continued payments to a survivor, usu. a spouse, after the original annuitant dies.

tax-deferred annuity. See *403(b) plan* under EMPLOYEE BENEFIT PLAN.

variable annuity. An annuity that makes payments in varying amounts depending on the success of investment strategy. Cf. *straight annuity.* See *variable annuity contract* under CONTRACT.

annuity bond. See BOND (3).

annuity certain. See ANNUITY.

annuity depreciation method. See DEPRECIATION METHOD.

annuity due. See ANNUITY.

annuity insurance. See INSURANCE.

annuity policy. An insurance policy providing for monthly or periodic payments to the insured to begin at a fixed date and continue through the insured's life.

annuity trust. See TRUST.

annulment (ə-**nəl**-mənt), *n.* **1.** The act of nullifying or making void. **2.** A judicial or ecclesiastical declaration that a marriage is void. • Unlike a divorce, an annulment establishes that marital status never existed in law. — **annul** (ə-**nəl**), *vb.* Cf. DIVORCE.

annum luctus (**an**-əm **lək**-təs), *n.* [Latin "year of mourning"] *Roman law.* The year following the death of a married man during which his widow could not remarry, because of the confusion that would ensue in determining the parentage of a child born a few months after a second marriage within that year. — Also sometimes termed *year in mourning.*

annus (**an**-əs). [Latin] A year.

annus, dies, et vastum (**an**-əs, **dI**-eez, et **vas**-təm). [Law Latin] See YEAR, DAY, AND WASTE.

annus et dies (**an**-əs et **dI**-eez). [Law Latin] A year and a day. See YEAR-AND-A-DAY RULE.

annus utilis (**an**-əs **yoo**-tə-lis), *n.* [Latin] *Roman law.* A year made up of the available days for conducting legal business and deducting the remaining days, such as days when the courts are closed or when the opposing party is absent.

annuus reditus (**an**-əs **red**-ə-təs). [Law Latin] A yearly rent.

anomalous indorsement. See *irregular indorsement* under INDORSEMENT.

anomalous jurisdiction. See JURISDICTION.

anomalous-jurisdiction rule (ə-**nom**-ə-ləs). The principle that a court of appeals has provisional jurisdiction to review the denial of a motion to intervene in a case, and if the court of appeals finds that the denial was correct, then its jurisdiction disappears — and it must dismiss the appeal for want of jurisdiction — because an order denying a motion to intervene is not a final, appealable order. • This rule has been criticized by courts and commentators. Many appellate courts, upon finding that the trial court properly denied a motion to intervene, will affirm the denial instead of dismissing the appeal for want of jurisdiction. — Also termed *anomalous rule.*

anomalous plea. See PLEA (3).

anomalous pleading. See PLEADING (1).

anomalous rule. See ANOMALOUS-JURISDICTION RULE.

anonymous, *adj.* Not named or identified <the police arrested the defendant after a tip from an anonymous informant>. — **anonymity** (an-ə-**nim**-ə-tee), *n.*

anoysance (ə-**noy**-zənts), *n.* [Law French] *Hist.* An annoyance or nuisance. See NUISANCE.

answer, *n.* A defendant's first pleading that addresses the merits of the case, usu. by denying the plaintiff's allegations. • An answer usu. sets forth the defendant's defenses and counterclaims.

answer, *vb.* **1.** To respond to a pleading or a discovery request <the company failed to answer the interrogatories within 30 days>. **2.** To assume the liability of another <a guarantor answers for another person's debt>. **3.** To pay (a debt or other liability) <she chose to promise to answer damages out of her own estate>.

answer date. See *answer day* under DAY.

answer day. See DAY.

antapocha (ant-**ap**-ə-kə). [Latin "counter-receipt"] *Roman & civil law.* A counterpart to a receipt (i.e., an *apocha*), signed by the debtor and delivered to the creditor. Cf. APOCHA.

ante (**an**-tee), *prep.* [Latin] Before. Cf. POST.

antea (**an**-tee-ə), *adv.* [Latin] Formerly; heretofore.

antecedent (an-tə-**seed**-ənt), *adj.* Earlier; preexisting; previous. — **antecedent** (preceding thing), *n.* — **antecedence** (quality or fact of going before), *n.*

antecedent claim. A preexisting claim. • Under the UCC, a holder takes an instrument for value if it is taken for an antecedent claim. UCC § 3–303.

antecedent debt. See DEBT.

antecessor (an-tə-**ses**-ər *or* **an**-), *n.* [Latin] **1.** *Roman law.* A professor of law. **2.** *Hist.* An ancestor. **3.** *Hist.* A predecessor to an office.

antedate (**an**-ti-dayt), *vb.* **1.** To affix with a date earlier than the true date; BACKDATE (1) <antedate a check>. **2.** To precede in time <the doctrine antedates the *Smith* case by many years>. — Also termed *predate.* — **antedate,** *n.* Cf. POSTDATE.

ante exhibitionem billae (**an**-tee ek-si-bish-ee-**oh**-nəm **bil**-ee). Before the exhibition of the bill; i.e., before a suit has begun.

ante litem motam (**an**-tee **lI**-təm **moh**-təm). [Law Latin "before the lawsuit was started"] Before a legal dispute arose — i.e., at a time when the declarant has no motive to lie.

ante meridiem (**an**-tee mə-**rid**-ee-əm). [Latin] Before noon. — Abbr. a.m.; A.M.

ante mortem interest (**an**-tee **mor**-təm). [Latin] An interest existing before (but not after) a transferor's death.

ante natus (**an**-tee **nay**-təs). [Law Latin] A person born before a certain political event that affected the person's political rights; esp., a person born before the signing of the Declaration of Independence. Cf. POST NATUS.

antenuptial (an-ti-**nəp**-shəl), *adj*. See PRENUPTIAL.

antenuptial agreement. See PRENUPTIAL AGREEMENT.

antenuptial gift. See *prenuptial gift* under GIFT.

antenuptial will. See *prenuptial will* under WILL.

anthropometry (an-thrə-**pom**-ə-tree). A system of measuring the human body, esp. the size relationships among the different parts. • Before the advent of fingerprinting, minute measurements of the human body — taken and compared to other persons' measurements — were used to identify criminals and deceased persons. Cf. BERTILLON SYSTEM.

antichresis (an-ti-**kree**-sis). [Latin "in place of interest"] *Roman & civil law*. A mortgage in which the mortgagee retains possession of the mortgaged property and takes the fruits (such as rents) of the property in lieu of interest on the debt.

anticipated compromis. See *general compromis* under COMPROMIS.

anticipation. *Patents*. The previous use, knowledge, documentation, or patenting of an invention. • Any of these will negate the invention's novelty, thereby preventing a patent or providing a defense to an infringement claim. See NOVELTY.

anticipatory breach. See BREACH OF CONTRACT.

anticipatory nuisance. See NUISANCE.

anticipatory offense. See *inchoate offense* under OFFENSE.

anticipatory replication. See REPLICATION.

anticipatory repudiation. See REPUDIATION.

anticipatory search warrant. See SEARCH WARRANT.

anticompetitive conduct. *Antitrust*. An act that harms or seeks to harm the market or the process of competition among businesses, and that has no legitimate business purpose.

antideficiency legislation. See LEGISLATION.

antidestruction clause. A provision in a security protecting a shareholder's conversion rights, in the event of a merger, by granting the shareholder a right to convert the securities into the securities that will replace the company's stock when the merger is complete. — See *convertible security* under SECURITY.

antidilution provision. A convertible-security provision that safeguards the conversion privilege from share splits, share dividends, or other transactions that might affect the conversion ratio. See CONVERSION RATIO; DILUTION (2).

antidumping law. A statute designed to protect domestic companies by preventing the sale of foreign goods at less than fair value, as defined in the statute (for example, at a price below that of the domestic market). See DUMPING.

antidumping tariff. See TARIFF (2).

antifraud rule. See RULE 10B-5.

antigraph (**an**-ti-graf). *Archaic*. A copy or counterpart of an instrument.

antigraphus (an-**tig**-rə-fəs), *n*. [Law Latin] *Hist*. An officer who maintains tax revenues; a comptroller.

Anti-Injunction Act. A federal statute providing that a federal court may not enjoin state-court proceedings unless an injunction is (1) expressly authorized by Congress, (2) necessary for the federal court's in rem jurisdiction, or (3) necessary to prevent relitigation of a judgment rendered by the federal court. 28 USCA § 2283.

anti-john law. A criminal-law statute punishing prostitutes' customers.

antilapse statute. *Wills & estates.* A statute that passes a bequest to the heirs of the beneficiary if the beneficiary dies before the testator dies. — Also termed *lapse statute*; *nonlapse statute*.

antimanifesto. *Int'l law.* A proclamation in which a belligerent power asserts that the war is a defensive one for that power.

antimarital-facts privilege. See *marital privilege* (2) under PRIVILEGE (3).

antinomia (an-ti-**noh**-mee-ə). [Greek] *Roman law.* See ANTINOMY.

antinomy (an-**tin**-ə-mee), *n.* A contradiction in law or logic; esp., a conflict of authority, as between two decisions <antinomies in the caselaw>. — **antinomic** (an-ti-**nom**-ik), *adj.*

antiqua custuma (an-**tI**-kwə **kəs**-t[y]oo-mə), *n.* [Law Latin "ancient customs"] *Hist.* A tax on wool, woolfells, and leather, under St. 3 Edw. • The distinction between *antiqua custuma* and *nova custuma* arose when the king imposed new taxes on the same articles in the 22nd year of his reign. Cf. NOVA CUSTUMA.

antiquare (an-ti-**kwair**-ee), *vb.* [Latin] *Roman law.* **1.** To reject a proposal for a new law. • Those who voted against a proposed law wrote on their ballots the letter "A" for *antiquo* ("I am for the old law"). **2.** To repeal a law.

antiqua statuta (an-**tI**-kwə stə-**t[y]oo**-tə). See VETERA STATUTE.

antiquum dominicum (an-**tI**-kwəm də-**min**-i-kəm). [Law Latin] Ancient demesne. See DEMESNE.

antisubrogation rule (an-tee-səb-roh-**gay**-shən). *Insurance.* The principle that an insurance carrier has no right of subrogation — that is, no right to assert a claim on behalf of the insured or for payments made under the policy — against its own insured for the risk covered by the policy. See SUBROGATION.

antitakeover statute. A state law designed to protect companies based in the state from hostile takeovers.

antithetarius (an-tith-ə-**tair**-ee-əs). [Law Latin] *Hist.* An accused person who asserts that his or her accuser is guilty of the crime. Cf. APPROVER (1).

Antitrust Civil Process Act. A federal law prescribing the procedures for an antitrust action by way of a petition in U.S. District Court. 15 USCA §§ 1311 et seq.

antitrust law. The body of law designed to protect trade and commerce from restraints, monopolies, price-fixing, and price discrimination. • The principal federal antitrust laws are the Sherman Act (15 USCA §§ 1–7) and the Clayton Act (15 USCA §§ 12–27).

> "As legislative history and case law both disclose, the general objective of the antitrust laws is the maintenance of competition. Competition per se thus becomes a goal of the legal order. Yet, competition is not a concept which defines itself; notions about the desirability of competition may shape judgments about how the law should apply, at least at its indistinct edges." Lawrence A. Sullivan, *Handbook of the Law of Antitrust* § 5, at 20 (1977).

A.O.C. *abbr.* **1.** ANNO ORBIS CONDITI. **2.** And other consideration. See *other consideration* under CONSIDERATION.

AOD. *abbr.* ACTION ON DECISION.

AOGI. See *adjusted ordinary gross income* under INCOME.

a pais (ah **pay** *or* **pays**). [Law French] *Hist.* At or to the country; at issue.

apartheid (ə-**pahrt**-hayt *or* ə-**pahr**-tIt). Racial segregation; specif., a policy of discrimination and segregation against blacks in South Africa.

apertum breve. See BREVE.

apertum factum (ə-**pər**-təm **fak**-təm). [Latin "open deed"] An overt act.

apertura testamenti (ap-ər-**t[y]oor**-ə tes-tə-**men**-tI), *n.* [Latin "opening of the testament"] *Roman law.* A procedure for proving a will by which the witnesses acknowledged their signatures and seal before a magistrate and the will was opened and publicly read.

apex deposition. See DEPOSITION.

apex juris (**ay**-peks **joor**-is). [Latin "summit of law"] *Roman law.* An extreme point or subtlety of law, such as a merely technical objection in pleading or an extreme interpretation of a doctrine. Cf. APICES LITIGANDI.

apex rule. *Mining law.* The principle that a vein of ore may be mined if it extends beyond the vertical boundaries of the surface claim on which the vein apexes. — Also termed *extralateral right.* Cf. INTRALIMINAL RIGHT.

apices litigandi (**ay**-pi-seez lit-i-**gan**-dI). [Law Latin] Extremely fine points (or subtleties) of litigation. Cf. APEX JURIS.

apocha (**ap**-ə-kə). *Roman & civil law.* A receipt acknowledging payment. • An apocha discharges only the obligation represented by the payment, in contrast to an acceptilation, which discharges an entire debt. — Also spelled *apoca.* Cf. ACCEPTILATION; ANTAPOCHA.

apochae oneratoriae (**ap**-ə-kee oh-nər-ay-**tor**-ee-ee). [Law Latin "cargo receipt"] *Hist.* Bills of lading.

apocrisarius (ə-pok-ri-**sair**-ee-əs), *n.* [Latin] *Hist. Eccles. law.* **1.** An ambassador; a messenger, such as a Pope's legate. **2.** One who answers for another; esp., an officer who presented church matters to the emperor and conveyed the answers to the petitioners. **3.** One who, upon consultation, gives advice in ecclesiastical matters. — Also termed *responsalis*; *a responsis*; *secretarius*; *consiliarius*; *referendarius*; *a consiliis.*

apographa (ə-**pog**-rə-fə), *n.* [fr. Greek *apographein* "to copy"] **1.** *Civil law.* An examination and enumeration of things possessed; an inventory. **2.** Copies; transcripts. — **apographal,** *adj.*

apostasy (ə-**pos**-tə-see). *Hist.* A crime against religion consisting in the total renunciation of Christianity by one who had previously embraced it.

apostata capiendo. See DE APOSTATA CAPIENDO.

apostate (ə-**pos**-tayt). A person who has forsaken religion or a particular religion. — Also termed (archaically) *apostata* (ap-ə-**stay**-tə).

a posteriori (ay pos-teer-ee-**or**-I *or* ah pos-teer-ee-**or**-ee), *adv.* [Latin "from what comes after"] Inductively; from the particular to the general, or from known effects to their inferred causes <as a legal analyst, she reasoned a posteriori — from countless individual cases to generalized rules that she finally applied>. — **a posteriori,** *adj.* Cf. A PRIORI.

apostille (ə-**pos**-til). [French "postscript, footnote"] *Int'l law.* A marginal note or observation; esp., a standard certification provided under the Hague Convention for authenticating documents used in foreign countries. — Also spelled *apostil.* See CERTIFICATE OF AUTHORITY.

apostle (ə-**pos**-əl), *n. Civil & maritime law.* **1.** A letter sent from a trial court to an appellate court, stating the case for the appeal. **2.** The record or papers sent up on appeal. — Also termed *apostoli.*

apostolus (ə-**pos**-tə-ləs), *n.* [fr. Greek *apostolos* "one sent from another"] *Hist.* A messenger, ambassador, legate, or nuncio. Pl. ***apostoli*** (ə-**pos**-tə-lI).

apotheca (ap-ə-**thee**-kə), *n.* [fr. Greek *apotheke* "store"] *Civil law.* A repository, as for wine or books.

apparent, *adj.* Visible; manifest; obvious.

apparent agency. See *agency by estoppel* under AGENCY (1).

apparent agent. See AGENT.

apparent authority. See AUTHORITY (1).

apparent danger. See DANGER.

apparent defect. See *patent defect* under DEFECT.

apparent easement. See EASEMENT.

apparent heir. See *heir apparent* under HEIR.

apparent servitude. See SERVITUDE (1).

apparent title. See COLOR OF TITLE.

apparitor (ə-**par**-ə-tər *or* -tor). **1.** *Roman law.* An officer who served a court, esp. as secretary, messenger (*viator*), or herald. — Also termed *viator.* **2.** *Civil law.* An officer who attends court to execute judicial orders. **3.** *Eccles. law.* An officer who executes orders and decrees, esp. by serving summonses.

apparlement (ə-**pahrl**-mənt), *n.* [Law French] *Hist.* Likelihood, as in the *apparlement* of war.

apparura (ap-ə-**ruur**-ə), *n.* [fr. Law Latin *apparare* "to furnish"] *Hist.* Furniture, apparel, implements, or tackle.

appeal, *n.* A proceeding undertaken to have a decision reconsidered by bringing it to a higher authority; esp., the submission of a lower court's or agency's decision to a higher court for review and possible reversal <the case is on appeal>. Cf. CERTIORARI.

appeal as of right. See *appeal by right.*

appeal by application. An appeal for which permission must first be obtained from the reviewing court. — Also termed *appeal by leave.*

appeal by right. An appeal to a higher court from which permission need not be first obtained. — Also termed *appeal as of right; appeal of right.*

appeal de novo. An appeal in which the appellate court uses the trial court's record but reviews the evidence and law without deference to the trial court's rulings. — Also termed *de novo review.*

appeal in forma pauperis (in **for**-mə **paw**-pər-is). An appeal by an indigent party, for whom court costs are waived. Fed. R. App. P. 24. See IN FORMA PAUPERIS.

consolidated appeal. An appeal in which two or more parties, whose interests were similar enough to make a joinder practicable, proceed as a single appellant.

cross-appeal. An appeal by the appellee, usu. heard at the same time as the appellant's appeal.

delayed appeal. An appeal that takes place after the time for appealing has expired, but only when the reviewing court has granted permission because of special circumstances.

devolutive appeal (di-**vol**-yə-tiv). An appeal that does not suspend the execution of the underlying judgment.

direct appeal. An appeal from a trial court's decision directly to the jurisdiction's highest court, thus bypassing review by an intermediate appellate court. • Such an appeal may be authorized, for example, when the case involves the constitutionality of a state law.

duplicitous appeal. An appeal from two separate judgments, from a judgment and an order, or from two orders.

interlocutory appeal. An appeal that occurs before the trial court's final ruling on the entire case. • Some interlocutory appeals involve legal points necessary to the determination of the case, while others involve collateral orders that are wholly separate from the merits of the action. Cf. FINAL-JUDGMENT RULE.

limited appeal. An appeal from only certain portions of a decision, usu. only the adverse or unfavorable portions.

suspensive appeal. An appeal that stays the execution of the underlying judgment.

appeal, *vb.* To seek review (from a lower court's decision) by a higher court <petitioner appeals the conviction>. — **appealability,** *n.*

appealable decision. See DECISION.

appeal as of right. See *appeal by right* under APPEAL.

appeal bond. See BOND (2).

appeal by leave. See *appeal by application* under APPEAL.

appeal court. See *appellate court* under COURT.

appeal de novo. See APPEAL.

appealer. *Archaic.* APPELLANT.

appeal in forma pauperis. See APPEAL.

appeal of felony. *Hist.* A procedure by which a person accused another of a crime, demanded proof of innocence by wager of battle, or informed against an accomplice. — Also termed *appellum de felonia.*

appeal of right. See *appeal by right* under APPEAL.

appeals council. A commission that hears appeals of rulings by administrative-law judges in social-security matters.

appeals court. See *appellate court* under COURT.

appearance, *n. Procedure.* A coming into court as a party or interested person, or as a lawyer on behalf of a party or interested person. — **appear,** *vb.*

"The English courts did not, until modern times, claim jurisdiction over the person of the defendant merely by service of summons upon him. It was deemed necessary to resort to further process by attachment of his property and arrest of his person to compel 'appearance,' which is not mere presence in court, but some act by which a person who is sued submits himself to the authority and jurisdiction of the court. Any steps in the action, such as giving bail upon arrest, operated as an appearance or submission." Benjamin J. Shipman, *Handbook of Common-Law Pleading* § 5, at 24 (Henry Winthrop Ballantine ed., 3d ed. 1923).

"The term 'appearance' is used particularly to signify or designate the overt act by which one against whom suit has been commenced submits himself to the court's jurisdiction, although in a broader sense it embraces the act of either plaintiff or defendant in coming into court .... An appearance may be expressly made by formal written or oral declaration, or record entry, or it may be implied from some act done with the intention of appearing and submitting to the court's jurisdiction." 4 Am. Jur. 2d *Appearance* § 1, at 620 (1995).

appearance de bene esse. See *special appearance.*

appearance pro hac vice (proh hak **vɪ**-see *or* proh hahk **vee**-chay). [Latin] An appearance made by an out-of-state lawyer for one particular case, usu. by leave of court. • For more on the pronunciation of this term, see PRO HAC VICE.

compulsory appearance. An appearance by one who is required to appear by having been served with process.

general appearance. An appearance for general purposes, which waives a party's ability later to dispute the court's personal jurisdiction.

initial appearance. A criminal defendant's first appearance in court to hear the charges read, to be advised of his or her rights, and to have bail determined. • The initial appearance is usu. required by statute to occur without undue delay. In a misdemeanor case, the initial appearance may be combined with the arraignment. See ARRAIGNMENT.

special appearance. **1.** A defendant's pleading that either claims that the court lacks personal jurisdiction over the defendant or objects to improper service of process. **2.** A defendant's showing up in court for the sole purpose of contesting the court's assertion of personal jurisdiction over the defendant. — Also termed *limited appearance*; *appearance de bene esse.*

voluntary appearance. An appearance entered by a party's own will, without the service of process.

appearance bond. See *bail bond* under BOND (2).

appearance date. See *answer day* under DAY.

appearance day. See *answer day* under DAY.

appearance de bene esse. See *special appearance* under APPEARANCE.

appearance docket. See DOCKET (1).

appearance doctrine. In the law of self-defense, the rule that a defendant's use of force is justified if the defendant reasonably believed it to be justified.

appearance pro hac vice. See APPEARANCE.

appellant (ə-**pel**-ənt). A party who appeals a lower court's decision, usu. seeking reversal of that decision. — Formerly also termed *appealer*. Cf. APPELLEE.

appellate (ə-**pel**-it), *adj.* Of or relating to an appeal or appeals generally.

appellate counsel. See COUNSEL.

appellate court. See COURT.

appellate division. A department of a superior court responsible for hearing appeals; an intermediate appellate court in some states, such as New York and New Jersey.

appellate jurisdiction. See JURISDICTION.

appellate record. See RECORD ON APPEAL.

appellate review. See REVIEW.

appellate rules. A body of rules governing appeals from lower courts.

appellatio (ap-ə-**lay**-shee-oh). [Latin] *Roman law.* An appeal from a lower court.

appellator (ap-ə-**lay**-tər). [Latin] *Roman & civil law.* **1.** An appellant. **2.** The judge to whom an appeal is taken.

appellee (ap-ə-**lee**). A party against whom an appeal is taken and whose role is to respond to that appeal, usu. seeking affirmance of the lower court's decision. Cf. APPELLANT.

appello (ə-**pel**-oh). [Latin] *Roman law.* I appeal. • This was the form of making an appeal *apud acta* (in the presence of the judge).

appellor (ə-**pel**-or *or* **ap**-ə-lor). *Hist. English law.* A person who formally accuses another of a crime, challenges a jury, or informs against an accomplice.

appellum de felonia. See APPEAL OF FELONY.

appendant (ə-**pen**-dənt), *adj.* Attached or belonging to property as an additional but subsidiary right. — **appendant,** *n.*

appendant easement. See *easement appurtenant* under EASEMENT.

appendant power. See POWER (5).

appenditia (ap-en-**dish**-ee-ə), *n.* [Law Latin] *Hist.* The appendages or appurtenances of an estate.

appendix, *n.* A supplementary document attached to the end of a writing <the brief includes an appendix of exhibits>. Pl. **appendixes, appendices.**

appensura (ap-en-**s[y]oor**-ə), *n.* [fr. Latin *appendere* "to weigh out"] *Hist.* The payment of money by weight rather than by count.

applicant. 1. One who requests something; a petitioner, such as a person who applies for letters of administration. **2.** ACCOUNT PARTY.

application. 1. MOTION. **2.** *Bankruptcy.* A request for an order not requiring advance notice and an opportunity for a hearing before the order is issued.

application for leave to appeal. A motion requesting an appellate court to hear a party's appeal from a judgment when the party has no appeal by right or when the party's time limit for an appeal by right has expired. • The reviewing court has discretion whether to grant or reject such a motion.

applied cost. See COST (1).

apply, *vb.* **1.** To make a formal request or motion <apply for a loan> <apply for injunctive relief>. **2.** To employ for a limited purpose <apply the payments to a reduction in interest>. **3.** To put to use with a particular subject matter <apply the law to the facts> <apply the law only to transactions in interstate commerce>.

appointee. 1. One who is appointed. **2.** One who receives the benefit of a power of appointment. See POWER OF APPOINTMENT.

permissible appointee. A person to whom appointive property may be assigned under a power of appointment. — Also termed *object of the power of appointment; object of the power.*

appointive asset. See ASSET.

appointive property. A property interest that is subject to a power of appointment.

appointment, *n.* **1.** The act of designating a person, such as a nonelected public official, for a job or duty <Article II of the U.S. Constitution grants the President the power of appointment for principal federal officials, subject to senatorial consent>.

public appointment. An appointment to a public office.

2. An office occupied by someone who has been appointed <a high appointment in the federal government>. **3.** The act of disposing of property, in exercise of a power granted for that purpose <the tenant's appointment of lands>. See POWER OF APPOINTMENT. — **appoint,** *vb.* — **appointer** (for senses 1 & 2), *n.* — **appointor** (for sense 3), *n.*

illusory appointment. A nominal, unduly restrictive, or conditional transfer of property under a power of appointment.

> "Like many other theories which are very plausible in the abstract, experience has shown that the doctrine of illusory appointments is difficult in application, since the term 'illusory' is vague and indefinite. And, because of the difficulty of formulating rules for determining what is an illusory appointment and the evils resulting from attempts to substitute the judicial will for the intent of the donor and donee of the power, the doctrine has been condemned or rejected by many courts." 62 Am. Jur. 2d *Powers of Appointment* § 186 (1990).

Appointments Clause. The clause of the U.S. Constitution giving the President the power to nominate federal judges and various other officials. U.S. Const. art. II, § 2.

apport (ə-**port**), *n.* [Law French] *Hist.* A tax, expense, tribute, or payment.

apportionment, *n.* **1.** Division into proportionate shares. **2.** The act of allocating or attributing moneys or expenses in a given way, as when a taxpayer allocates part of profits to a particular tax year or part of the use of a personal asset to a business. **3.** Distribution of legislative seats among districts that are entitled to representation; esp., the allocation of congressional representatives among the states based on population, as required by the 14th Amendment. • The claim that a state is denying the right of representation to its citizens through improper apportionment presents a justiciable issue. — Also termed *legislative apportionment*. See REAPPORTIONMENT. **4.** The division (by statute or by the testator's instruction) of an estate-tax liability among persons interested in an estate. — **apportion,** *vb.*

apportionment clause. *Insurance.* A policy provision that distributes insurance proceeds in proportion to the total coverage.

apportionment of liability. *Torts.* The parceling out of liability for an injury among multiple tortfeasors, and possibly the plaintiff as well. • Apportionment of liability encompasses such legal doctrines as joint and several liability, comparative responsibility, indemnity, and settlements. See Restatement (Third) of Torts: Apportionment of Liability (1999).

apportum (ə-**por**-təm), *n.* [Law Latin] *Hist.* The revenue, profit, or emolument that something brings to its owner. • This was often used in reference to a pension.

apposer. See FOREIGN APPOSER.

apposite (**ap**-ə-zit), *adj.* Suitable; appropriate.

appraisal, *n.* **1.** The determination of what constitutes a fair price; valuation; estimation of worth. **2.** The report of such a determination. — Also termed *appraisement*. — **appraise,** *vb.* Cf. ASSESSMENT (3).

appraisal clause. An insurance-policy provision allowing either the insurer or the insured to demand an independent estimation of a claimed loss.

appraisal remedy. The statutory right of corporate shareholders who oppose some extraordinary corporate action (such as a merger) to have their shares judicially appraised and to demand that the corporation buy back their shares at the appraised value. — Also termed *appraisal right*; *dissenters' right*; *right of dissent and appraisal*.

appraisal trinity. The three most commonly accepted methods of appraising real property: the market approach, the cost approach, and the income approach. See MARKET APPROACH; COST APPROACH; INCOME APPROACH.

appraisement. **1.** APPRAISAL. **2.** An ADR method used for resolving the amount or extent of liability on a contract when the issue of liability itself is not in dispute. • Unlike arbitration, appraisement is not a quasi-judicial proceeding but instead an informal determination of the amount owed on a contract.

appraiser. An impartial person who estimates the value of something, such as real estate, jewelry, or rare books. — Also termed *valuer*.

appreciable, *adj.* Capable of being measured or perceived.

appreciate, *vb.* **1.** To understand the significance or meaning of. **2.** To increase in value.

appreciation, *n.* An increase in an asset's value, usu. because of inflation. — **appreciate,** *vb.* — **appreciable,** *adj.* Cf. DEPRECIATION.

appreciation surplus. See *revaluation surplus* under SURPLUS.

appreciation test. *Criminal law.* A test for the insanity defense requiring proof by clear and convincing evidence that at the time of the crime, the defendant suffered from a severe mental disease or defect preventing him or her from appreciating the wrongfulness of the conduct. • This test, along with the accompanying plea of *not guilty by reason of insanity*, was established by the Insanity Defense Reform Act of 1984. 18 USCA § 17. — Also termed *Insanity Defense Reform Act of 1984 test*. See INSANITY DEFENSE.

apprehensio (ap-ri-**hen**-see-oh). [Latin] **1.** APPREHENSION (1). **2.** *Civil law.* A mode of acquisition of things belonging to no one; a type of *occupatio*.

apprehension, *n.* **1.** Seizure in the name of the law; arrest <apprehension of a criminal>. **2.** Perception; comprehension <the tort of assault requires apprehension by the plaintiff of imminent contact>. **3.** Fear; anxiety <most people approach public speaking with some apprehension>. — **apprehend,** *vb.*

apprentice. **1.** *Hist.* A person bound by an indenture to work for an employer for a specified period to learn a craft, trade, or profession.

2. A learner in any field of employment or business.

apprentice of the law. *Hist.* **1.** A law student. **2.** A barrister. — Also termed *apprentice en la ley*; *apprenticius ad legem.*

apprenticius ad legem (a-pren-**tish**-ee-əs ad **lee**-jəm). [Law Latin] APPRENTICE OF THE LAW.

approach, right of. See RIGHT OF APPROACH.

appropriated retained earnings. See EARNINGS.

appropriated surplus. See SURPLUS; *appropriated retained earnings* under EARNINGS.

appropriation, *n.* **1.** The exercise of control over property; a taking of possession. **2.** A legislative body's act of setting aside a sum of money for a public purpose. **3.** The sum of money so voted. **4.** *Torts.* An invasion of privacy whereby one person takes the name or likeness of another for commercial gain. — **appropriate,** *vb.* — **appropriable,** *adj.* — **appropriator,** *n.* Cf. EXPROPRIATION; MISAPPROPRIATION.

appropriation bill. See BILL (3).

appropriator, *n. Hist.* The possessor of an appropriated benefice, that is, a benefice that has been perpetually annexed to a spiritual corporation.

approval sale. See *sale on approval* under SALE.

approve, *vb.* To give formal sanction to; to confirm authoritatively. — **approval,** *n.*

approved indorsed note. See NOTE (1).

approved list. See LEGAL LIST.

approvement. 1. *English law.* The right of an owner of common lands to enclose them partially and receive income arising from them. • This right — originally granted by the Statute of Merton (1235) — is still available, but a landowner seeking to approve land must receive the government's consent to do so. **2.** *Hist.* The act of avoiding a capital conviction by accusing an accomplice; turning king's evidence.

approver (ə-**proo**-vər), *n. Hist.* **1.** One who offers proof; esp., a criminal who confesses and testifies against his or her accomplices. Cf. ANTITHETARIUS. **2.** An agent or bailiff; esp., one who manages a farm or estate for another.

approximation, doctrine of. See DOCTRINE OF APPROXIMATION.

appruare (ap-roo-**air**-ee), *vb.* [Law Latin] *Hist.* To obtain a benefit from land by making improvements.

appurtenance (ə-**pərt**-[ə-]nənts), *n.* Something that belongs or is attached to something else <the garden is an appurtenance to the land>.

appurtenant, *adj.* Annexed to a more important thing.

appurtenant easement. See *easement appurtenant* under EASEMENT.

APR. See *annual percentage rate* under INTEREST RATE.

à prendre (ah **prawn**-drə *or* -dər). [French] For taking; for seizure. See PROFIT À PRENDRE.

a priori (ay prɪ-**or**-ɪ *or* ah pree-**or**-ee), *adv.* [Latin "from what is before"] Deductively; from the general to the particular <as an analyst, he reasoned a priori — from seemingly self-evident propositions to particular conclusions>. — **a priori,** *adj.* Cf. A POSTERIORI.

a provisione viri (ay prə-vizh-ee-**oh**-nee **vɪ**-rɪ). [Latin] By the provision of a man (i.e., a husband).

apud acta (**ap**-əd **ak**-tə). [Latin] *Roman & civil law.* Among the acts; among the judicial proceedings recorded in writing. • This phrase refers to appeals taken orally in the presence of the judge.

apud iudicem. See IN JUDICIO.

APV. See *adjusted present value* under PRESENT VALUE.

a qua (ay **kway** *or* **kwah**). [Latin] See A QUO.

aqua (**ak**-wə), *n.* [Latin] *Roman law.* **1.** Water. **2.** A watercourse. Pl. ***aquae*** (**ak**-wee).

aqua aestiva (**ak**-wə es-**tɪ**-və), *n.* Summer water; water used only in the summer.

aqua currens (**ak**-wə **kər**-enz). See *aqua profluens.*

aqua dulcis (**ak**-wə **dəl**-sis), *n.* Fresh water. — Also termed *aqua frisca.*

aqua fontanea (**ak**-wə fon-**tay**-nee-ə), *n.* Springwater.

aqua profluens (**ak**-wə **prof**-loo-enz), *n.* Flowing or running water. — Also termed *aqua currens.*

aqua quotidiana (**ak**-wə kwoh-tid-ee-**ay**-nə), *n.* Daily water; water that can be drawn at all times of the year.

aqua salsa (**ak**-wə **sal**-sə), *n.* Salt water.

aquaeductus (ak-wee-**dək**-təs), *n.* [Latin "conveying of water"] A servitude consisting in the right to conduct water (as through pipes) over or through another's land.

aquaehaustus (ak-wee-**haws**-təs), *n.* [Latin "drawing of water"] A servitude consisting in the right to draw water from a well, pool, spring, or stream on another's land.

aquae immittendae (**ak**-wee im-ə-**ten**-dee), *n.* [Latin "waters to be thrown out"] A servitude consisting in the right of one whose house is surrounded by other buildings to cast wastewater on the neighboring roofs or yards. • This is similar to common-law drip rights. — Also termed *stillicidium.* Cf. *servitus stillicidii* under SERVITUS; DRIP RIGHTS.

aqua frisca. See *aqua dulcis* under AQUA.

aquagium (ə-**kway**-jee-əm), *n.* [Law Latin] *Hist.* **1.** A canal for draining water, esp. from marshy land. **2.** A payment for supplying water to a mill or carrying goods by water.

aquatic right. See WATER RIGHT.

Aquilian law. See LEX AQUILIA.

a quo (ah *or* ay **kwoh**), *adv.* [Latin] From which. — Also termed *a qua.* See AD QUEM; *court a quo* under COURT.

A.R. *abbr.* ANNO REGNI.

arabant (ə-**ray**-bənt). [Latin] They plowed. • This term was applied to those who held by the tenure of plowing and tilling the lord's lands within the manor.

arable land. See LAND.

arator (ə-**ray**-tər), *n.* [Law Latin] *Hist.* A farmer of arable land.

aratrum terrae (ə-**ray**-trəm **ter**-ee), *n.* [Law Latin] *Hist.* The amount of land that can be plowed with a single plow; plowland.

araturia (ar-ə-**t[y]oor**-ee-ə), *n.* [Law Latin] See *arable land* under LAND.

ARB. *abbr.* ACCOUNTING RESEARCH BULLETIN.

arbiter (**ahr**-bə-tər). One with the power to decide disputes, such as a judge <the Supreme Court is the final arbiter of legal disputes in the United States>. Cf. ARBITRATOR.

arbitrage (**ahr**-bə-trahzh), *n.* The simultaneous buying and selling of identical securities in different markets, with the hope of profiting from the price difference in those markets. — Also termed *space arbitrage.* — **arbitrager** (**ahr**-bə-trazh-ər), **arbitrageur** (ahr-bə-trah-zhər), *n.*

kind arbitrage. Purchase of a security that, having no restriction other than the payment of money, is exchangeable or convertible within a reasonable time to a second security, with a simultaneous offsetting sale of the second security. — Also termed *convertible arbitrage.*

risk arbitrage. Arbitrage of assets that are probably, but not necessarily, equivalent; esp., arbitrage of corporate stock in a potential merger or takeover, whereby the target company's stock is bought and the acquiring company's stock is sold simultaneously.

time arbitrage. Purchase of a commodity against a present sale of the identical commodity for a future delivery; esp., the simultaneous buying and selling of securities for immediate delivery and future delivery, with the hope of profiting from the difference in prices.

arbitrage bond. See BOND (3).

arbitrament (ahr-**bi**-trə-mənt). **1.** The power to decide for oneself or others; the power to decide finally and absolutely. **2.** The act of deciding or settling a dispute that has been referred to arbitration. **3.** AWARD. — Also spelled (archaically) *arbitrement.*

arbitrament and award. A plea that the same matter has already been decided in arbitration.

arbitrary, *adj.* **1.** Depending on individual discretion; specif., determined by a judge rather than by fixed rules, procedures, or law. **2.** (Of a judicial decision) founded on prejudice or preference rather than on reason or fact. • This type of decision is often termed *arbitrary and capricious.*

arbitrary mark. See *arbitrary trademark* under TRADEMARK.

arbitrary trademark. See TRADEMARK.

arbitration, *n.* A method of dispute resolution involving one or more neutral third parties who are usu. agreed to by the disputing parties and whose decision is binding. — Also termed (redundantly) *binding arbitration.* — **arbitrate,** *vb.* — **arbitral,** *adj.* Cf. MEDIATION (1).

ad hoc arbitration. Arbitration of only one issue.

adjudicative-claims arbitration. Arbitration designed to resolve matters usu. handled by courts (such as a tort claim), in contrast to arbitration of labor issues, international trade, and other fields traditionally associated with arbitration.

compulsory arbitration. Arbitration required by law or forced by law on the parties.

final-offer arbitration. Arbitration in which both parties are required to submit their "final offer" to the arbitrator, who may choose only one. • This device gives each party an incentive to make a reasonable offer or risk the arbitrator's accepting the other party's offer. The purpose of this type of arbitration is to counteract arbitrators' tendency to make compromise decisions halfway between the two parties' demands.

grievance arbitration. **1.** Arbitration that involves the violation or interpretation of an existing contract. • The arbitrator issues a final decision regarding the meaning of the contractual terms. **2.** *Labor law.* Arbitration of an employee's grievance, usu. relating to an alleged violation of the employee's rights under a collective-bargaining agreement. • The arbitration procedure is set out in the collective-bargaining agreement. Grievance arbitration is the final step in grievance procedure. — Also termed *rights arbitration.* See GRIEVANCE PROCEDURE.

> "The great majority of today's collective bargaining agreements provide for an impartial arbitrator to hear and decide grievances under the bargaining agreement. The details of grievance arbitration vary considerably among agreements." Douglas L. Leslie, *Labor Law in a Nutshell* 264 (3d ed. 1992).

interest arbitration. Arbitration that involves settling the terms of a contract being negotiated between the parties; esp., in labor law, arbitration of a dispute concerning what provisions will be included in a new collective-bargaining agreement. • When the parties cannot agree on contractual terms, an arbitrator decides. This type of arbitration is most common in public-sector collective bargaining.

judicial arbitration. Court-referred arbitration that is final unless a party objects to the award.

rights arbitration. See *grievance arbitration.*

voluntary arbitration. Arbitration by the agreement of the parties.

arbitration act. A federal or state statute providing for the submission of disputes to arbitration.

arbitration and award. An affirmative defense asserting that the subject matter of the action has already been settled in arbitration.

arbitration board. A panel of arbitrators appointed to hear and decide a dispute according to the rules of arbitration.

arbitration clause. A contractual provision mandating arbitration — and thereby avoiding litigation — of disputes about the contracting parties' rights, duties, and liabilities.

arbitration of exchange. The simultaneous buying and selling of bills of exchange in different international markets, with the hope of profiting from the price difference of the currencies in those markets. See ARBITRAGE; DRAFT (1).

arbitrator, *n.* A neutral person who resolves disputes between parties, esp. by means of formal arbitration. — **arbitratorship,** *n.* Cf. ARBITER.

arbitrement. *Archaic.* See ARBITRAMENT.

arbitrium (ahr-**bi**-tree-əm). [Law Latin] An award; a decision of an arbitrator.

arbor civilis (**ahr**-bər **siv**-ə-lis). [Latin "civil tree"] A genealogical tree.

arbor finalis (**ahr**-bər fi-**nay**-lis). [Latin] *Hist.* A boundary tree; a tree used for marking a boundary line.

arcana imperii (ahr-**kay**-nə im-**peer**-ee-I). [Latin] State secrets.

arcarius (ahr-**kair**-ee-əs). [Latin] *Hist.* A treasurer; a keeper of public money.

Archaionomia (ahr-kee-ə-**noh**-mee-ə). A Latin translation of Saxon laws, published in 1568 by William Lambarde.

archdeaconry. *Eccles. law.* **1.** The circuit of an archdeacon's jurisdiction. **2.** The office or rank of an archdeacon.

Archdeacon's Court. See COURT OF ARCHDEACON.

Archdiaconal Court. See COURT OF ARCHDEACON.

Arches Court of Canterbury. See COURT OF ARCHES.

archicapellanus (ahr-kee-kap-ə-**lay**-nəs). [Law Latin] *Hist.* A chief or high chancellor.

architect's lien. See LIEN.

architectural review. See DESIGN REVIEW.

architectural work. *Copyright.* The design of a building, as embodied in any tangible medium of expression, including plans and drawings (which are protected as pictorial or graphic works) or the building itself (which is protected, if built after December 1, 1990, under the Berne Convention).

arcifinious (ahr-sə-**fin**-ee-əs), *adj.* [fr. Latin *arcifinius* "having irregular boundaries"] *Civil law.* (Of a landed estate) having natural boundaries such as woods, mountains, or rivers.

arcta et salva custodia (**ahrk**-tə et **sal**-və kə-**stoh**-dee-ə). [Law Latin] *Hist.* In close and safe custody. • A defendant arrested under the writ of *capias ad satisfaciendum* was said to be kept *arcta et salva custodia.*

ardour. [Law French] *Hist.* An arsonist.

area bargaining. Negotiation by a union of collective-bargaining agreements with several employers in a particular geographic area.

area-standards picketing. *Labor law.* The practice that a union undertakes to protect its members in a particular region by picketing employers that may undercut the market through the potentially lower labor costs of a nonunion workforce.

area variance. See VARIANCE (2).

Areeda-Turner test. *Antitrust.* An economic test for predatory pricing whereby a price below average variable cost is presumed to be predatory and therefore illegal. • This test is widely accepted by federal courts. Its name derives from the coauthors of an influential law-review article: Phillip Areeda & Donald F. Turner, *Predatory Pricing and Practices Under Section 2 of the Sherman Act*, 88 Harv. L. Rev. 692 (1975). They reformulated their test in 3 Phillip Areeda & Donald F. Turner, *Antitrust Law* ¶¶ 710–722 (1978). See PREDATORY PRICING.

à rendre (ah **rawn**-drə *or* -dər). [Law French] To render; to yield.

arentare (ar-ən-**tair**-ee). [Law Latin] To rent out; to let out at a certain rent.

A reorganization. See REORGANIZATION (2).

arere (ə-**reer**), *adj.* [Law French] Behind in payment (as of rent); in arrears.

a responsis (ay ri-**spon**-sis), *n.* [Law Latin] See APOCRISARIUS.

arg. *abbr.* ARGUENDO (2).

argentarius (ahr-jən-**tair**-ee-əs). [Latin] *Roman law.* A moneylender; a banker.

argentarius miles (ahr-jən-**tair**-ee-əs **mI**-leez), *n.* [Law Latin] *Hist.* A money porter who carries money from the lower to the upper Exchequer to be examined and tested.

argentum (ahr-**jen**-təm), *n.* [Latin] Silver; esp., silver coinage.

argentum dei (ahr-**jen**-təm **dee**-I), *n.* [Law Latin] See DENARIUS DEI.

arguendo (ahr-gyoo-**en**-doh). [Latin "in arguing"] **1.** For the sake of argument <assuming arguendo that discovery procedures were correctly followed, the court still cannot grant the defendant's motion to dismiss>. **2.** During the course of argument <counsel mentioned arguendo that the case has been followed in three other decisions>. — Abbr. arg.

argument. 1. A statement that attempts to persuade; esp., the remarks of counsel in analyzing and pointing out or repudiating a desired inference, for the assistance of a decision-maker. **2.** The act or process of attempting to persuade. See ORAL ARGUMENT; CLOSING ARGUMENT.

argumentative, *adj.* **1.** Of or relating to argument or persuasion <an argumentative tone of voice>. **2.** Stating not only facts, but also inferences and conclusions drawn from facts <the judge sustained the prosecutor's objection to the argumentative question>.

argumentative instruction. See JURY INSTRUCTION.

argumentative question. A question in which the examiner interposes a viewpoint under the guise of asking a question. • This is considered an abuse of interrogation.

argumentum (ahr-gyoo-**men**-təm), *n.* [Latin] An argument. Pl. ***argumenta.***

argumentum ab auctoritate (ahr-gyoo-**men**-təm ab awk-tor-ə-**tay**-tee). [Latin] An argument from authority (of a statute or case).

argumentum ab impossibili (ahr-gyoo-**men**-təm ab im-pah-**sib**-ə-lI). [Latin] An argument from impossibility.

argumentum ab inconvenienti (ahr-gyoo-**men**-təm ab in-kən-vee-nee-**en**-tI). [Latin] An argument from inconvenience; an argument that emphasizes the harmful consequences of failing to follow the position advocated.

argumentum a contrario (ahr-gyoo-**men**-təm ay kən-**trair**-ee-oh). [Latin] An argument for contrary treatment.

argumentum ad baculum (ahr-gyoo-**men**-təm ad **bak**-yə-ləm). [Latin] An argument depending on physical force to back it up.

argumentum ad captandum (ahr-gyoo-**men**-təm ad kap-**tan**-dəm). [Latin] An argument appealing to the emotions of a crowd.

argumentum ad crumenam (ahr-gyoo-**men**-təm ad kroo-**mee**-nəm). [fr. Latin *crumena* "purse"] An argument appealing to the purse (or one's desire to save money).

argumentum ad hominem (ahr-gyoo-**men**-təm ad **hom**-ə-nəm). [Latin "argument to the man"] An argument based on disparagement or praise of another in a way that obscures the real issue.

argumentum ad ignorantiam (ahr-gyoo-**men**-təm ad ig-nə-**ran**-shee-əm). [Latin] An argument based on an adversary's ignorance of the matter in dispute.

argumentum ad invidiam (ahr-gyoo-**men**-təm ad in-**vid**-ee-əm). [Latin] An argument appealing to one's hatreds or prejudices.

argumentum ad judicium (ahr-gyoo-**men**-təm ad joo-**dish**-ee-əm). [Latin] An argument addressed to the judgment; a proof based on knowledge or probability.

argumentum ad misericordiam (ahr-gyoo-**men**-təm ad miz-ə-ri-**kor**-dee-əm). [Latin] An argument appealing to pity.

argumentum ad populum (ahr-gyoo-**men**-təm ad **pop**-yə-ləm). [Latin] An argument appealing to the crowd.

argumentum ad rem (ahr-gyoo-**men**-təm ad **rem**). [Latin] An argument on the point at issue.

argumentum ad verecundiam (ahr-gyoo-**men**-təm ad ver-ə-**kən**-dee-əm). [Latin] An argument appealing to the listener's modesty; an argument based on the opinions of people who are considered authorities.

argumentum a simili (ahr-gyoo-**men**-təm ay **sim**-ə-lI). [Latin "argument from a like case"] An argument by analogy or similarity.

argumentum baculinum (ahr-gyoo-**men**-təm bak-yə-**lI**-nəm). [fr. Latin *baculus* "a rod or scepter"] An argument appealing to force.

argumentum ex concesso (ahr-gyoo-**men**-təm eks kən-**ses**-oh). [Latin] An argument based on an earlier admission by the adversary.

argumentum ex silentio (ahr-gyoo-**men**-təm eks si-**len**-shee-oh). [Latin] An argument from silence — i.e., based on the absence of express evidence to the contrary.

arimanni (ar-ə-**man**-I), *n.* [Law Latin] *Hist.* A fine for not joining the army when summoned.

arise, *vb.* **1.** To originate; to stem (from) <a federal claim arising under the U.S. Constitution>. **2.** To result (from) <litigation routinely arises from such accidents>. **3.** To emerge in one's consciousness; to come to one's attention <the question of appealability then arose>.

arising-in jurisdiction. See JURISDICTION.

aristocracy. 1. A privileged class of persons, esp. the hereditary nobility. **2.** A government ruled by a privileged class.

aristodemocracy. A government consisting of both democratic and aristocratic elements; a government in which power is divided between the nobility (or more powerful group) and the rest of the people.

Arkansas rule. *Secured transactions.* The principle that the collateral securing a loan is presumed to be worth at least as much as the loan's balance, and that the creditor has the burden to prove that a sale of the collateral would not satisfy the loan amount. *Norton v. National Bank of Commerce*, 398 S.W.2d 538 (Ark. 1966).

ARM. See *adjustable-rate mortgage* under MORTGAGE.

arma (**ahr**-mə), *n.* [Latin] *Roman law.* **1.** Arms; weapons. **2.** Military service.

arma moluta (**ahr**-mə mə-**loo**-tə), *n.* [Law Latin] Sharp weapons that cut, as contrasted with blunt instruments that bruise or break.

arma reversata (**ahr**-mə ree-vər-**say**-tə), *n.* [Law Latin] Reversed arms. • This was a punishment for a felon or traitor.

arma vis (**ahr**-mə **vis**), *n.* [Latin] Armed force.

armaria. See ALMARIA.

armed, *adj.* **1.** Equipped with a weapon <an armed robber>. **2.** Involving the use of a weapon <armed robbery>.

armed neutrality. See NEUTRALITY.

armed peace. See PEACE.

armed robbery. See ROBBERY.

armiger (**ahr**-mə-jər), *n.* [Latin fr. *arma* "arms" + *gerere* "to bear"] *Hist.* **1.** One who bears arms; an armor-bearer; an esquire. **2.** A servant who carried the armor of a knight. **3.** A tenant by scutage; a valet.

arm-in-arm, *adj.* Of, relating to, or involving a transaction between parties whose personal interests are involved. Cf. ARM'S-LENGTH.

armiscara (ahr-mə-**skair**-ə), *n.* [Law Latin] *Hist.* **1.** A punishment consisting of carrying a saddle on one's back as a sign of subjection. **2.** A fine.

armistice. See TRUCE.

arm of the sea. The portion of a river or bay in which the tide ebbs and flows. • It may extend as far into the interior as the water of the river is propelled backward by the tide.

arm of the state. An entity created by a state and operating as an alter ego or instrumentality of the state, such as a state university or a state department of transportation. • The 11th Amendment of the U.S. Constitution generally bars suits in federal court by individuals against states. The Amendment has been interpreted as protecting arms of the state as well as the state itself. Courts usu. find an entity to be an arm of the state if it operates without substantial autonomy from state regulation. For example, cities and local school districts have been held not to be arms of the state.

arms, law of. 1. Rules concerning conditions of war, such as the treatment of prisoners. **2.** The law relating to the right to bear arms. **3.** The law relating to armorial bearings, i.e., coats of arms granted by the College of Heralds in England, Lord Lyon King of Arms in Scotland, and corresponding officers in some other countries.

arms, right to bear. See RIGHT TO BEAR ARMS.

arms control. *Int'l law.* A policy of minimizing instabilities in the military field by lessening the possibility of the outbreak of war while reducing in number a country's weapons of mass destruction. Cf. DISARMAMENT.

arm's-length, *adj.* Of or relating to dealings between two parties who are not related or not on close terms and who are presumed to have roughly equal bargaining power; not involving a confidential relationship <an arm's-length transaction does not create fiduciary duties between the parties>. Cf. ARM-IN-ARM.

army. 1. A military force, esp. of ground troops. **2.** Any substantial group of individuals armed for combat. **3.** A vast, organized group.

regular army. The permanent military establishment, maintained during both war and peacetime.

arra (**ar**-ə), *n.* [Latin "earnest, deposit"] *Roman & civil law.* Earnest money; evidence of a completed bargain. See DENARIUS DEI.

arraignment, *n.* The initial step in a criminal prosecution whereby the defendant is brought before the court to hear the charges and to enter a plea. — **arraign,** *vb.* Cf. PRELIMINARY HEARING; *initial appearance* under APPEARANCE.

arrangement with creditors. *Bankruptcy.* A debtor's agreement with creditors for the settlement, satisfaction, or extension of time for payment of debts. See BANKRUPTCY PLAN.

arranger for disposal. *Environmental law.* An entity that owns or possesses hazardous substances, and either disposes of them or has an obligation to control them. • An arranger for disposal can be held liable for environmental cleanup costs under CERCLA.

array, *n.* **1.** A panel of potential jurors; VENIRE (1) <the array of mostly wealthy professionals seemed to favor the corporate defendant>. **2.** The jurors actually impaneled <the array hearing the case consisted of seven women and five men>. **3.** A list or roster of impaneled jurors <the plaintiff obtained a copy of the array to help prepare for voir dire>. **4.** Order; arrangement <the array of jurors from oldest to youngest>. **5.** A militia <the array organized antigovernment rallies>. **6.** A series of statistics or a group of elements <a mathematical array>.

array, *vb.* **1.** To impanel a jury for trial. **2.** To call out the names of jurors, one by one, as they are impaneled.

arrear, *n.* (*usu. pl.*) **1.** The state of being behind in the payment of a debt or the discharge of an obligation <the creditor filed a lawsuit against the debtor who was in arrears>. — Also termed *arrearage.* **2.** An unpaid or overdue debt <the creditor reached an agreement with the debtor on settling the arrears>. **3.** An unfinished duty <the arrears of work have accumulated>. See IN ARREARS.

arrearage. See ARREAR (1).

arrent (ə-**rent**), *vb. Hist.* To let at a fixed rent; specif., royal permission to enclose a portion of public land in exchange for annual rent.

arrest, *n.* **1.** A seizure or forcible restraint. **2.** The taking or keeping of a person in custody by legal authority, esp. in response to a criminal charge. — **arrest,** *vb.*

arrest in execution. See *arrest on final process.*

arrest in quarters. *Military law.* A nonjudicial punishment that can be given to officers and warrant officers only by a general, a flag officer in command, or an officer exercising general court-martial jurisdiction. See BREACH OF ARREST.

arrest on final process. *Hist.* Arrest in a civil case after the conclusion of a trial. — Also termed *arrest in execution.*

arrest on mesne process (meen). *Hist.* Arrest in a civil case before trial takes place.

citizen's arrest. An arrest of a private person by another private person on grounds that (1) a public offense was committed in the arrester's presence, or (2) the arrester has reasonable cause to believe that the arrestee has committed a felony.

civil arrest. *Hist.* An arrest and detention of a civil-suit defendant until bail is posted or a judgment is paid. • Civil arrest is prohibited in most states.

false arrest. An arrest made without proper legal authority. Cf. FALSE IMPRISONMENT.

house arrest. See HOUSE ARREST.

lawful arrest. The taking of a person into legal custody either under a valid warrant or on probable cause that the person has committed a crime.

malicious arrest. An arrest made without probable cause and for an improper purpose; esp., an abuse of process by which a person procures the arrest (and often the imprisonment) of the plaintiff by means of judicial process, without any reasonable cause. • Malicious arrest can be grounds for an action for abuse of process, false imprisonment, or malicious prosecution.

parol arrest (pə-**rohl** *or* **par**-əl). An arrest ordered by a judge or magistrate from the bench, without written complaint, and executed immediately, such as an arrest of a person who breaches the peace in open court. See CONTEMPT.

pretextual arrest. An arrest of a person for a minor offense for the opportunity to investigate the person's involvement in a more serious offense for which there are no lawful grounds to make an arrest. — Also termed *pretext arrest.*

rearrest. A warrantless arrest of a person who has escaped from custody, violated parole or probation, or failed to appear in court as ordered.

warrantless arrest. An arrest, without a warrant, based on probable cause of a felony, or for a misdemeanor committed in a police officer's presence. See WARRANT.

3. *Maritime law.* The taking of a ship into custody by virtue of a court's warrant.

arrestable offense. See OFFENSE (1).

arrestandis bonis ne dissipentur. See DE ARRESTANDIS BONIS NE DISSIPENTUR.

arrestando ipsum qui pecuniam recepit. See DE ARRESTANDO IPSUM QUI PECUNIAM RECEPIT.

arrestatio (ar-ə-**stay**-shee-oh), *n.* [Law Latin] *Hist.* An arrest.

arrest in execution. See *arrest on final process* under ARREST.

arrest in quarters. See ARREST.

arresto facto super bonis mercatorum alienigenorum (ə-**res**-toh **fak**-toh **s**[y]**oo**-pər **boh**-nis mər-kə-**tor**-əm ay-lee-**ee**-nɪ-jə-**nor**-əm *or* al-ee-). [Latin "seizure of the goods of foreign merchants"] *Hist.* A writ to seize the goods of an alien, taken in recompense of goods taken from an English subject living abroad.

arrest of inquest. A plea that a matter proposed for inquiry has already been investigated and should therefore not be reexamined.

arrest of judgment. The staying of a judgment after its entry; esp., a court's refusal to render or enforce a judgment because of a defect apparent from the record. • At common law, courts have the power to arrest judgment for intrinsic causes appearing on the record, as when the verdict differs materially from the pleadings or when the case alleged in the pleadings is legally insufficient. Today, this type of defect must typically be objected to before trial or before judgment is entered, so that the motion in arrest of judgment has been largely superseded.

> "An arrest of judgment [under common law] was the technical term describing the act of a trial judge refusing to enter judgment on the verdict because of an error appearing on the face of the record that rendered the judgment invalid." *United States v. Sisson*, 399 U.S. 267, 280–81, 90 S.Ct. 2117, 2125 (1970).

arrest on final process. See ARREST.

arrest on mesne process. See ARREST.

arrest record. **1.** A form completed by a police officer when a person is arrested. **2.** A cumulative list of the instances when a person has been arrested. — Also termed *police blotter*; *bench blotter*; *blotter*.

arrest warrant. See WARRANT (1).

arret (ah-**ret** *or* -**ray**). [French] *Civil law.* A judgment, sentence, or decree of a court with competent jurisdiction.

arretted (ə-**ret**-id), *adj.* [Law French] (Of an accused) brought before a judge and charged with a crime.

arriage and carriage (**ar**-ij). *Hist.* Indefinite services formerly demandable from tenants, but prohibited by statute in the 18th century.

arrière-ban (ah-ree-air-**bahn** *or* **ar**-ee-air-**ban**), *n.* [French] *Hist.* **1.** A king's proclamation summoning vassals to military service. **2.** The group of vassals so summoned.

arriere fee. See *arriere fee* under FEE (2).

arriere fief. See FIEF.

arriere vassal. See VASSAL.

arrogation (ar-ə-**gay**-shən), *n.* **1.** The act of claiming or taking something without the right to do so <some commentators argue that limited military actions unilaterally ordered by the President are an arrogation of Congress's power to declare war>. **2.** *Roman & civil law.* The adoption of an adult; specif., the adoption of a person sui juris, as a result of which the adoptee loses independence and comes within the paternal power (*patria potestas*) of the adopting father. — **arrogate,** *vb.*

arser in le main (ahr-**say** a*n* lə **ma*n*** *or* an lə **man**), *n.* [French "burning in the hand"] *Hist.* A punishment of burning or branding the left thumb of a lay offender who falsely claimed and was allowed the benefit of clergy, so that the offender would be distinguished if he tried to claim the benefit again. — Also termed *arsure en le main* (ahr-**soor** aw*n* lə **ma*n*** *or* awn lə **man**).

arson, *n.* **1.** At common law, the malicious burning of someone else's dwelling house or outhouse that is either appurtenant to the dwelling house or within the curtilage.

> "At common law, arson is the wilful and malicious burning of the dwelling house of another. It may occur during the nighttime or the daytime, and it is an offense against the security of habitation or occupancy, rather than against ownership or property." 3 Charles E. Torcia, *Wharton's Criminal Law* § 334, at 324–25 (15th ed. 1995).

2. Under modern statutes, the intentional and wrongful burning of someone else's property (as to destroy a building) or one's own property (as to fraudulently collect insurance). — Also termed (in sense 2) *statutory arson.* Cf. HOUSEBURNING.

> "The term 'statutory arson' is employed to designate the entire area of statutory proscription which is analogous to, but does not constitute, common-law arson. It is important to have mutually-exclusive labels here not only for the reasons mentioned in the preceding section, but because some of the state statutes provide a penalty for arson without defining the word and hence adopt the common-law definition." Rollin M. Perkins & Ronald N. Boyce, *Criminal Law* 287 (3d ed. 1982).

> "(1) Arson. A person is guilty of arson, a felony of the second degree, if he starts a fire or causes an explosion with the purpose of: (a) destroying a building or occupied structure of another; or (b) destroying or damaging any property, whether his own or another's, to collect insurance for such loss. It shall be an affirmative defense to prosecution under this paragraph that the actor's conduct did not recklessly endanger any building or occupied structure of another or place any other person in danger of death or bodily injury." Model Penal Code § 220.1 (1997).

aggravated arson. Arson accompanied by some aggravating factor, as when the offender foresees or anticipates that one or more persons will be in or near the property being burned.

arsonable, *adj.* (Of property) of such a nature as to give rise to a charge of arson if maliciously burned <only real property, and not personal property, is arsonable>.

arson clause. An insurance-policy provision that excludes coverage of a loss due to fire if the insured intentionally started the fire.

arsonist. One who commits arson; INCENDIARY (1).

arsonous, *adj.* Of, relating to, or involving arson <an arsonous purpose>.

arsura (ahr-**s**[**y**]**oor**-ə), *n.* [Law Latin] *Hist.* **1.** The trial of money by heating it after it is coined. **2.** The loss in weight from this process.

arsure en la main (ahr-**soor** aw*n* lah **ma*n***), *n.* [Law French] See ARSER IN LE MAIN.

art. 1. The methodical application of knowledge or skill in creating something. **2.** An occupation or business that requires skill; a craft. **3.** *Patents.* A process or method that produces a beneficial physical effect.

analogous art. The technique or method that is reasonably related to the problem addressed by the invention, and with which the inventor is assumed to be familiar. — Also termed *pertinent art.* See NONOBVIOUSNESS.

prior art. Knowledge that is available, including what would be obvious from it, at a given time to a person of ordinary skill in an art; esp., the body of previously patented inventions that the patent office or court analyzes before granting or denying a patent to a comparable invention.

relevant art. Art to which one can reasonably be expected to look for a solution to the problem that a patented device attempts to solve. • The term includes not only knowledge about a problem in a particular industry, but also knowledge accumulated in scientific fields whose techniques have been commonly employed to solve similar problems. — Also termed *pertinent art.*

4. *Hist.* In a seduction case, the skillful and systematic coaxing of another to engage in sexual activity.

artful pleading. See PLEADING (2).

article, *n.* **1.** Generally, a particular item or thing <article of clothing>.

proprietary article. (*often pl.*) A product manufactured under an exclusive right to sell it.

2. A separate and distinct part (as a clause or stipulation) of a writing, esp. in a contract, statute, or constitution <Article III>. **3.** (*pl.*) An instrument containing a set of rules or stipulations <articles of war> <articles of incorporation>. **4.** A nonfictional literary composition forming an independent part of a publication, such as a law review or journal <a well-researched article>.

article, *vb.* **1.** To bring charges against by an exhibition of articles. **2.** To be an articled clerk.

Article I court. See *legislative court* under COURT.

Article II judge. A U.S. bankruptcy judge or magistrate judge appointed for a term of years as authorized by Congress under Article II of the U.S. Constitution. 28 USCA §§ 151 et seq., 631 et seq.

Article III Court. A federal court that, deriving its jurisdiction from U.S. Const. art. III, § 2, hears cases arising under the Constitution and the laws and treaties of the United States, cases in which the United States is a party, and cases between the states and between citizens of different states.

Article III judge. A U.S. Supreme Court, Court of Appeals, or District Court judge appointed for life under Article III of the U.S. Constitution.

Article 15. See *nonjudicial punishment* under PUNISHMENT.

articled clerk. *English law.* A clerk who works for a solicitor in exchange for learning the profession; a clerk bound by articles of apprenticeship.

article of manufacture. See MANUFACTURE.

articles of amendment. A document filed to effectuate an amendment or change to a corporation's articles of incorporation.

articles of apprenticeship. *Hist.* A contract under which a minor agrees to work for a master for a specified time in exchange for learning a trade.

articles of association. **1.** ARTICLES OF INCORPORATION. **2.** A document — similar to articles of incorporation — that legally creates a nonstock or nonprofit organization.

Articles of Confederation. The instrument that governed the association of the 13 original states from March 1, 1781 until the adoption of the U.S. Constitution. • They were prepared by the Continental Congress, submitted to the states in 1777, and later ratified by representatives of the states empowered by their respective legislatures for that purpose.

articles of dissolution. A document that a dissolving corporation must file with the appropriate governmental agency, usu. the secretary of state, after the corporation has settled all its debts and distributed all its assets.

articles of impeachment. A formal document alleging the specific charges against a public official and the reasons for removing that official from office. • It is similar to an indictment in a criminal proceeding. See IMPEACHMENT.

articles of incorporation. A document that sets forth the basic terms of a corporation's existence, including the number and classes of shares and the purposes and duration of the corporation. • In most states, the articles of incorporation are filed with the secretary of state as part of the process of forming the corporation. In some states, the articles serve as a certificate of incorporation and are the official recognition of the corporation's existence. In other states, the government issues a certificate of incorporation after approving the articles and other required documents. — Also termed *articles of association*; *articles of organization*; *certificate of incorporation*. Cf. BYLAW (1); CHARTER (3).

articles of organization. See ARTICLES OF INCORPORATION.

articles of partnership. See PARTNERSHIP AGREEMENT.

Articles of the Clergy. *Hist.* A statute enacted in 1315 to settle the jurisdictions of the ecclesiastical and temporal courts. — Also termed *Articuli Cleri*.

articles of the eyre (air). *Hist.* A series of questions put to the members of a community by the justices in eyre to discover what breaches of the law had occurred during the court's absence. • The inquiry enabled the justices to fine criminal behavior and to raise revenue for the Crown through the levying of penalties. See EYRE. Cf. CHAPITER.

articles of the peace. *English law.* A sworn complaint in which a person alleges that a named person poses a threat to the complainant's person, family, or property.

articles of union. *Hist.* The 25 articles agreed to by the English and Scottish parliaments in 1707 for the union of the two kingdoms.

Articles of War. The body of laws and procedures that governed the U.S. military until replaced in 1951 by the Uniform Code of Military Justice.

articulated pleading. See PLEADING (1).

articuli (ahr-**tik**-yə-lI), *n.* [Latin] Articles; items. • This term was applied to several English statutes and treatises.

Articuli Cleri (ahr-**tik**-yə-lI **kleer**-I). [Law Latin] See ARTICLES OF THE CLERGY.

articuli magnae chartae (ahr-**tik**-yə-lI **mag**-nee **kahr**-tee), *n.* [Latin] *Hist.* The 49 preliminary articles on which Magna Carta was founded.

Articuli super Cartas (ahr-**tik**-yə-lI **s[y]oo**-pər **kahr**-təs). [Law Latin "articles upon the charters"] *Hist.* A statute passed in 1300 to confirm and enlarge many particulars of Magna Carta and the Forest Charter.

articulo mortis. See IN ARTICULO MORTIS.

artifice (**ahr**-tə-fis). A clever plan or idea, esp. one intended to deceive.

artificer. 1. A skilled worker, such as a mechanic or craftsman; an artisan. **2.** One who builds or contrives; an inventor.

artificial condition. See CONDITION (5).

artificial day. See DAY.

artificial force. *Patents.* A natural force so transformed in character or energies by human power that it is something new.

artificial person. See PERSON.

artificial presumption. See *presumption of law* under PRESUMPTION.

artificial succession. See SUCCESSION (4).

artificial watercourse. See WATERCOURSE.

artisan's lien. See *mechanic's lien* under LIEN.

a rubro ad nigrum (ay **roo**-broh ad **nI**-grəm). [Latin] From the red to the black — i.e., from the title of a statute (formerly often printed in red letters) to its body (often printed in black letters).

as. [Latin] **1.** *Roman law.* A pound weight or a coin weighing a pound, divisible into 12 parts, called *unciae.* • *As* and the multiples of its *unciae* were used to denote interest rates. See UNCIA. **2.** *Roman & civil law.* A whole inheritance; the whole of an asset.

as-applied challenge. See CHALLENGE (1).

ascendant (ə-**sen**-dənt), *n.* One who precedes in lineage, such as a parent or grandparent. — Also termed *ancestor.* — **ascendant,** *adj.* Cf. DESCENDANT.

collateral ascendant. Loosely, an aunt, uncle, or other relative who is not strictly an ancestor. — Also termed *collateral ancestor.*

ascent. The passing of an estate upwards to an heir in the ascending line. Cf. DESCENT.

ascriptitius (as-krip-**tish**-ee-əs), *n.* [Latin] *Roman law.* An alien who had been registered and naturalized in the colony where the person resided. — Also spelled *ascripticius.*

ASE. *abbr.* AMERICAN STOCK EXCHANGE.

as-extracted collateral. See COLLATERAL.

Ashwander **rules.** A set of principles outlining the U.S. Supreme Court's policy of deciding constitutional questions only when necessary, and of avoiding a constitutional question if the case can be decided on the basis of another issue. • These rules were outlined in Justice Brandeis's concurring opinion in *Ashwander v. Tennessee Valley Authority,* 297 U.S. 288, 56 S.Ct. 466 (1936). They include the policy that the court should not decide a constitutional question in a friendly suit, should not anticipate a question of constitutional law, should not create a rule of constitutional law that is broader than that called for by the facts of the case, should not decide a constitutional issue if the case can be decided on another ground, should not rule on the constitutionality of a statute unless the plaintiff is harmed by the statute or if the plaintiff has accepted the benefits of the statute, and should not rule on the constitutionality of an act of Congress without first analyzing whether the act can be fairly construed in a way that would avoid the constitutional question. — Also termed *Brandeis rules.*

as is, *adv. & adj.* In the existing condition without modification <the customer bought the car as is>. • Under UCC § 2–316(3)(a), a seller can disclaim all implied warranties by stating that the goods are being sold "as is" or "with all faults." Generally, a sale of property "as is" means that the property is sold in its existing condition, and use of the phrase *as is* relieves the seller from liability for defects in that condition. — Also termed *with all faults*.

as-is warranty. See WARRANTY (2).

asked price. See PRICE.

asking price. See PRICE.

as of. On; at. • This is often used to signify the effective legal date of a document, as when the document is backdated or the parties sign at different times <the lease commences as of June 1>.

as of right. By virtue of a legal entitlement <the case is not one triable to a jury as of right>.

as per. In accordance with; PER (3). • This phrase has traditionally been considered a barbarism, *per* being the preferred form in commercialese <per your request>. But even *per* can be improved on <as you requested>.

asportation (as-pər-**tay**-shən), *n.* The act of carrying away or removing (property or a person). • Asportation is a necessary element of larceny. — Also termed *carrying away.* — **asport,** *vb.* See LARCENY.

> "There is no larceny unless the personal goods of another which have been taken by trespass are 'carried away,' but this technical requirement may be satisfied by a very slight movement. There must be 'asportation,' to use the word commonly found in the early cases, but the slightest start of the carrying-away movement constitutes asportation." Rollin M. Perkins & Ronald N. Boyce, *Criminal Law* 323 (3d ed. 1982).

> "To constitute larceny, there must be a taking or caption and carrying away or asportation of the property of another. There is a caption when the defendant takes possession. He takes possession when he exercises dominion and control over the property. There is an asportation when he carries away the property; any carrying away movement, however slight, is sufficient. An asportation presupposes a prior caption; therefore, there can be no asportation unless there has first been a caption." 3 Charles E. Torcia, *Wharton's Criminal Law* § 357, at 412–13 (15th ed. 1995).

asportavit (as-por-**tay**-vit). [Law Latin] He carried away.

ASR. *abbr.* ACCOUNTING SERIES RELEASE.

assart. *Hist.* **1.** The action of pulling up trees and bushes in a forest to make the land arable. • This was a crime if done without a license. **2.** A piece of land made arable by clearing a forest.

assassination, *n.* The act of deliberately killing someone, esp. a public figure, usu. for hire or for political reasons. — **assassinate,** *vb.* — **assassin,** *n.*

assault, *n.* **1.** *Criminal & tort law.* The threat or use of force on another that causes that person to have a reasonable apprehension of imminent harmful or offensive contact; the act of putting another person in reasonable fear or apprehension of an immediate battery by means of an act amounting to an attempt or threat to commit a battery. **2.** *Criminal law.* An attempt to commit battery, requiring the specific intent to cause physical injury. — Also termed (in senses 1 and 2) *simple assault.* **3.** Loosely, a battery. **4.** Popularly, any attack. — **assault,** *vb.* — **assaultive,** *adj.* Cf. BATTERY.

> "Ordinary usage creates a certain difficulty in pinning down the meaning of 'assault.' Etymologically, the word is compounded of the Latin *ad* + *saltare,* to jump at. In popular language, it has always connoted a physical attack. When we say that D assaults V, we have a mental picture of D attacking V, by striking or pushing or stabbing him. In the middle ages, however, the terms 'assault' and 'battery' were given technical meanings which they have retained ever since. It became settled that though an assault could be committed by physical contact, it did not require this, since a show of force raising an apprehension in the mind of the victim was sufficient. Also, a 'battery' did not require an actual beating; the use of any degree of force against the body would suffice. The acts of spitting on a person and kissing without consent are both batteries." Glanville Williams, *Textbook of Criminal Law* 135–36 (1978).

> "In addition to the classic definitions of assault, some jurisdictions have used assault as a generic term to describe either assault or battery. Thus, a defendant who intentionally injures somebody may be convicted of assault rather than battery." Arnold H. Loewy, *Criminal Law in a Nutshell* 57 (2d ed. 1987).

aggravated assault. Criminal assault accompanied by circumstances that make it more severe, such as the use of a deadly weapon, the intent to commit another crime, or the intent to cause serious bodily harm.

> "The common law did not include any offense known as 'aggravated assault.' However, it did make provision for certain situations in this field, under other names. If, for example, the intended application of force to the person would have resulted in murder, mayhem, rape or robbery, if successful, and the scheme proceeded far enough to constitute an attempt the prosecution was for an attempt to commit the intended felony." Rollin M. Perkins & Ronald N. Boyce, *Criminal Law* 180 (3d ed. 1982).

assault purpensé (ə-**sawlt** poor-paw*n*-**say**). *Hist.* Premeditated assault. — Also termed *assultus premeditatus* (ə-**səl**-təs pree-med-ə-**tay**-tis).

"Even before the conquest, . . . deliberately planned assassinations came to be distinguished and put into the list of Crown pleas as *forsteal*. The original sense of this word was lying in wait to ambush the victim. After the conquest this is expressed in various terms in French and Latin, but frequently takes the form of *assault purpensé*, or *assultus premeditatus*. In time this yields before *malitia excogitata*, and so introduces us to the very troublesome word 'malice'." Theodore F.T. Plucknett, *A Concise History of the Common Law* 444 (5th ed. 1956).

assault to rape. See *assault with intent to commit rape*.

assault with a deadly weapon. An aggravated assault in which the defendant, controlling a deadly weapon, threatens the victim with death or serious bodily injury. — Also termed *felonious assault*.

assault with intent. Any of several assaults that are carried out with an additional criminal purpose in mind, such as assault with intent to murder, assault with intent to rob, assault with intent to rape, and assault with intent to inflict great bodily injury. • These are modern statutory inventions that are often found in state criminal codes.

assault with intent to commit rape. An assault carried out with the additional criminal purpose of intending to rape the victim. — Also termed *assault to rape*.

attempted assault. An attempt to commit an assault. — Also termed *attempt to assault*.

"[I]t is apparent that reference may be made to an 'attempt to assault' without logical absurdity. There is nothing absurd in referring to an attempt to frighten, which would constitute, if successful, a criminal assault in most jurisdictions. . . . It is not surprising, therefore, that there is a tendency to break away from the ancient view that there is no such offense known to the law as an attempt to commit an assault." Rollin M. Perkins & Ronald N. Boyce, *Criminal Law* 168 (3d ed. 1982).

"By far the most interesting cases in this area are the attempted assault cases. Where assault is defined as intentionally putting another in fear of a battery, there is of course no basis for denying the possibility of an attempt. Where, however, assault is defined as an attempted battery, attempted assault looks very much like the forbidden 'attempt to attempt' a battery. For this reason some courts have held that there is no such crime as attempted assault. Other courts, however, have held that an attempted assault can exist, defining it as an attempted battery which has not progressed far enough to be an assault." Arnold H. Loewy, *Criminal Law in a Nutshell* 223–24 (2d ed. 1987).

civil assault. An assault considered as a tort and not as a crime. • Although the same assaultive conduct can be both a tort and a crime, this term isolates the legal elements that give rise to civil liability.

conditional assault. An assault expressing a threat on condition, such as "your money or your life."

criminal assault. An assault considered as a crime and not as a tort. • This term isolates the legal elements that give rise to criminal liability even though the act might also have been tortious.

excusable assault. An assault committed by accident or while doing a lawful act by lawful means, with ordinary caution and without any unlawful intent.

felonious assault. An assault that is of sufficient severity to be classified and punished as a felony. See *aggravated assault*.

indecent assault. See *sexual assault*.

malicious assault with a deadly weapon. An aggravated assault in which the victim is threatened with death or serious bodily harm from the defendant's use of a deadly weapon. • Malice is inferred from both the nature of the assault and the weapon used.

sexual assault. **1.** Sexual intercourse with another person without that person's consent. • Several state statutes have abolished the crime of rape and replaced it with the offense of sexual assault. **2.** Offensive sexual contact with another person, exclusive of rape. — Also termed (in sense 2) *indecent assault*. Cf. RAPE.

simple assault. **1.** ASSAULT (1). **2.** ASSAULT (2).

"(1) Simple Assault. A person is guilty of assault if he: (a) attempts to cause or purposely, knowingly or recklessly causes bodily injury to another; or (b) negligently causes bodily injury to another with a deadly weapon; or (c) attempts by physical menace to put another in fear of imminent serious bodily injury." Model Penal Code § 211.1 (1997).

assault and battery. Loosely, a criminal battery. See BATTERY.

assaultee. A person who is assaulted.

assaulter. A person who assaults another.

assault purpensé. See ASSAULT.

assault to rape. See *assault with intent to commit rape* under ASSAULT.

assault with a deadly weapon. See ASSAULT.

assault with intent. See ASSAULT.

assault with intent to commit rape. See ASSAULT.

assay, *n.* **1.** A proof or trial, by chemical experiments, of the purity of metals, esp. gold and silver. **2.** An examination of weights and measures.

assayator regis. See ASSAYER OF THE KING.

assayer. One who makes assays of precious metals.

assayer of the king. *Hist.* An officer of the royal mint, appointed by St. 2 Hen. 6, ch. 12, who receives and tests bullion taken in for coining. — Also termed *assayator regis.*

assecurare (ə-sek-yə-**rair**-ee), *vb.* [Law Latin] *Hist.* To make secure, as by pledges.

assecuration (ə-sek-yə-**ray**-shən). *Marine insurance.* Insurance.

assecurator (ə-**sek**-yə-ray-tər). *Marine insurance.* An insurer.

assembly. 1. A group of persons organized and united for some common purpose.

riotous assembly. *Hist.* An unlawful assembly of 12 or more persons causing a disturbance of the peace.

unlawful assembly. A meeting of three or more persons who intend either to commit a violent crime or to carry out some act, lawful or unlawful, that will constitute a breach of the peace. Cf. RIOT.

> "An unlawful assembly differs from a riot in that if the parties assemble in a tumultuous manner, and actually execute their purpose with violence, it is a riot; but if they merely meet on a purpose, which, if executed, would make them rioters, and, having done nothing, they separate without carrying their purpose into effect, it is an unlawful assembly." 77 C.J.S. *Riot; Insurrection* § 2, at 565 (1994).

2. In many states, the lower house of a legislature.

assembly, right of. See RIGHT OF ASSEMBLY.

assent, *n.* Agreement, approval, or permission. — **assent,** *vb.* See CONSENT.

> "The requirement of 'assent,' which is fundamental to the formation of a binding contract, implies in a general way that both parties to an exchange shall have a reasonably clear conception of what they are getting and what they are giving up." Marvin A. Chirelstein, *Concepts and Case Analysis in the Law of Contracts* 66 (1990).

constructive assent. Assent imputed to someone based on conduct.

express assent. Assent that is clearly and unmistakably communicated.

implied assent. Assent inferred from one's conduct rather than from direct expression.

mutual assent. See MUTUAL ASSENT.

assented stock. See STOCK.

assenting-silence doctrine. The principle that an accusation will be taken as true, despite silence by the accused, if the accusation was made under circumstances in which silence can be fairly said to be an agreement. • This doctrine is usu. held to be invalid as a measure of a criminal defendant's guilt.

assertion, *n.* A declaration or allegation. — **assert,** *vb.* — **assertor,** *n.*

assertive conduct. See CONDUCT.

assertive question. *Civil law.* A question asked of a witness at a criminal trial, by which inadmissible evidence is sought, to provide the jury with details regarding another crime. Cf. INTERROGATIVE QUESTION.

assertory covenant. See COVENANT (1).

assertory oath (ə-**sər**-tə-ree). See OATH.

assessable insurance. See INSURANCE.

assessable policy. See INSURANCE POLICY.

assessable security. See SECURITY.

assessable stock. See STOCK.

assessed valuation. See VALUATION.

assessment, *n.* **1.** Determination of the rate or amount of something, such as a tax or damages <assessment of the losses covered by insurance>. **2.** Imposition of something, such as a tax or fine, according to an established rate; the tax or fine so imposed <assessment of a luxury tax>.

> "There is a distinction between public improvements, which benefit the entire community, and local improvements, which benefit particular real estate or limited areas of land. The latter improvements are usually fi-

nanced by means of special, or local, assessments. These assessments are, in a certain sense, taxes. But an assessment differs from a general tax in that an assessment is levied only on property in the immediate vicinity of some local municipal improvement and is valid only where the property assessed receives some special benefit differing from the benefit that the general public enjoys." Robert Kratovil, *Real Estate Law* 465 (6th ed. 1974).

assessment for benefits. See *special assessment.*

deficiency assessment. An assessment by the IRS — after administrative review and tax-court adjudication — of additional tax owed by a taxpayer who underpaid. See TAX DEFICIENCY.

erroneous assessment. An assessment that deviates from the law and creates a jurisdictional defect, and that is therefore invalid.

excessive assessment. A tax assessment that is grossly disproportionate as compared with other assessments.

jeopardy assessment. An assessment by the IRS — without the usual review procedures — of additional tax owed by a taxpayer who underpaid, based on the IRS's belief that collection of the deficiency would be jeopardized by delay.

local assessment. A tax to pay for improvements (such as sewers and sidewalks) in a designated area, levied on property owners who will benefit from the improvements. — Also termed *local-improvement assessment.*

"Since there is [an] important and fundamental distinction between the tax in the more limited sense and the local assessment, the question often arises whether provisions in constitutions and statutes which refer by name to taxes, include also local assessments. This is primarily a question of legislative intention. In the absence of anything to show the specific intention of the legislature, the general rule is that the local assessment possesses such marked peculiarities differentiating it from the tax in the more limited sense of the term, that the use of the term 'tax' does not *prima facie* show an intention to include local assessments." 1 William H. Page & Paul Jones, *A Treatise on the Law of Taxation by Local and Special Assessments* § 39, at 67 (1909).

maintenance assessment. A charge for keeping an improvement in working condition or a residential property in habitable condition. — Also termed *maintenance fee.*

political assessment. *Hist.* A charge levied on officeholders and political candidates by a political party to defray the expenses for a political canvass.

special assessment. The assessment of a tax on property that benefits in some important way from a public improvement. — Also termed *assessment for benefits.*

3. Official valuation of property for purposes of taxation <assessment of the beach house>. — Also termed *tax assessment.* Cf. APPRAISAL. **4.** An audit or review <internal financial assessment> <environmental site assessment>. — **assess,** *vb.*

assessment bond. See BOND (3).

assessment company. An association that offers its members life insurance, and then pays for death losses by levying an assessment on the surviving members of the association.

assessment contract. See CONTRACT.

assessment district. See DISTRICT.

assessment for benefits. See *special assessment* under ASSESSMENT.

assessment fund. The balance of the assessments of a mutual benefit association, minus expenses, from which beneficiaries are paid.

assessment insurance. See INSURANCE.

assessment list. See ASSESSMENT ROLL.

assessment period. A taxable period.

assessment ratio. For property tax purposes, the ratio of assessed value to fair market value.

assessment roll. A record of taxable persons and property, prepared by a tax assessor. — Also termed *assessment list.*

assessment work. *Mining law.* The annual labor (such as improvements) that must be performed on an unpatented mining claim to continue to hold the claim.

assessor. 1. One who evaluates or makes assessments, esp. for purposes of taxation. — Also termed (specif.) *tax assessor.* **2.** A person who advises a judge or magistrate about scientific or technical matters during a trial. See MASTER (2). — **assessorial** (as-ə-**sor**-ee-əl), *adj.* — **assessorship,** *n.*

asset. 1. An item that is owned and has value. **2.** (*pl.*) The entries on a balance sheet showing the items of property owned, including cash, inventory, equipment, real estate, accounts receivable, and goodwill. **3.** (*pl.*) All the property of a person (esp. a bankrupt or deceased person) available for paying debts.

accrued asset. An asset arising from revenues earned but not yet due.

admitted asset. An asset that by law may be included in evaluating the financial condition of an insurance company. Cf. *nonadmitted asset.*

appointive asset. An asset distributed under a power of appointment.

assets by descent. The portion of an estate that passes to an heir and is sufficient to charge the heir with the decedent's specialty debts. — Also termed *assets per descent.*

assets in hand. The portion of an estate held by an executor or administrator for the payment of debts chargeable to the executor or administrator. — Also termed *assets entre main*; *assets entre mains.*

asset under management. A securities portfolio for which an investment adviser provides ongoing, regular supervisory or management services.

capital asset. **1.** A long-term asset used in the operation of a business or used to produce goods or services, such as equipment, land, or an industrial plant. — Also termed *fixed asset.* **2.** For income-tax purposes, any of most assets held by a taxpayer except those assets specifically excluded by the Internal Revenue Code. • Excluded from the definition are, among other things, stock in trade, inventory, and property held by the taxpayer primarily for sale to customers in the ordinary course of trade or business.

commercial assets. The aggregate of available property, stock in trade, cash, and other assets belonging to a merchant.

current asset. An asset that is readily convertible into cash, such as a marketable security, a note, or an account receivable. — Also termed *liquid asset*; *quick asset*; *near money.*

> "*Current assets* are assets expected to be converted to cash, sold, or consumed during the next twelve months, or within the business's normal operating cycle if the cycle is longer than a year. The *operating cycle* is the period from the time that cash is used to acquire goods and services, these goods and services are sold to customers, and the accounts receivable from these customers are collected in cash. For a small retail store, the operating cycle may be only a few weeks or months. For a shipbuilding company, however, the normal operating cycle could run several years." Jay Alix & Elmer E. Heupel, *Financial Handbook for Bankruptcy Professionals* § 9.2, at 354 (1991).

dead asset. A worthless asset that has no realizable value, such as an uncollectible account receivable.

earning asset. (*usu. pl.*) An asset (esp. of a bank) on which interest is received. • Banks consider loans to be earning assets.

equitable asset. An asset that is subject to payment only in a court of equity.

frozen asset. An asset that is difficult to convert into cash because of court order or other legal process.

hidden asset. An asset carried on the books at a substantially reduced or understated value that is considerably less than market value.

illiquid asset. An asset that is not readily convertible into cash, usu. because of (1) the lack of demand, (2) the absence of an established market, or (3) the substantial cost or time required for liquidation (such as for real property, even when it is desirable).

individual asset. (*usu. pl.*) Property belonging to a member of a partnership as personal property, apart from the firm's property.

intangible asset. An asset that is not a physical object, such as a patent, a trademark, or goodwill.

legal asset. A decedent's asset that by law is subject to the claims of creditors or legacies. — Also termed *probate asset.*

liquid asset. See *current asset.*

mass asset. An intangible asset, such as a dominant market position, that is made up of several components but that is considered a single entity for purposes of depreciation, because the loss of any component of the asset is replaced by new components, so that the whole asset has little or no fluctuation in value. • An entity with a dominant market position might lose a vendor, but because of its dominant market position is able to replace the loss with a new vendor. The market position is therefore considered a mass asset.

net assets. See NET WORTH.

net quick assets. The excess of quick assets less current liabilities. See QUICK-ASSET RATIO.

new asset. *Wills & estates.* In the administration of a decedent's estate, property that the administrator or executor receives after the time has expired to file claims against the estate.

nominal asset. An asset whose value is difficult to assess, such as a judgment or claim.

nonadmitted asset. An asset that by law may not be included in evaluating the financial condition of an insurance company because it cannot be converted quickly into cash without a financial loss. Cf. *admitted asset.*

personal asset. An asset in the form of money or chattels.

probate asset. See *legal asset.*

quick asset. **1.** Cash and other current assets other than inventory. **2.** See *current asset.*

real asset. An asset in the form of land.

tangible asset. An asset that has a physical existence and is capable of being assigned a value.

wasting asset. An asset exhausted through use or the loss of value, such as an oil well or a coal deposit.

asset acquisition. Acquisition of a corporation by purchasing all its assets directly from the corporation itself, rather than by purchasing shares from its shareholders. — Also termed *asset purchase.* Cf. SHARE ACQUISITION.

asset allocation. The spreading of funds between different types of investments with the intention of decreasing risk and increasing return.

asset-backed security. See SECURITY.

asset-based financing. See FINANCING.

asset-coverage test. *Accounting.* A bond-indenture restriction that permits additional borrowing only if the ratio of assets (typically net tangible assets) to debt (typically long-term debt) does not fall below a specified minimum.

asset-depreciation range. The IRS's range of depreciation lifetimes allowed for assets placed in service between 1970 and 1980 and for assets depreciated under the Modified Accelerated Cost Recovery System under the Tax Reform Act of 1986. — Abbr. ADR. See ACCELERATED COST RECOVERY SYSTEM.

asset dividend. See DIVIDEND.

asset purchase. See ASSET ACQUISITION.

assets by descent. See ASSET.

assets entre main. See *assets in hand* under ASSET.

assets in hand. See ASSET.

assets per descent. See *assets by descent* under ASSET.

asset under management. See ASSET.

asset value. See NET ASSET VALUE.

asseverate (ə-**sev**-ə-rayt), *vb.* To state solemnly or positively; to aver. — **asseveration** (ə-sev-ə-**ray**-shən), *n.* See AVERMENT.

assign, *n.* (*usu. pl.*) See ASSIGNEE.

assignable, *adj.* That can be assigned; transferable from one person to another, so that the transferee has the same rights as the transferor had <assignable right>. Cf. NEGOTIABLE.

assignable lease. See LEASE.

assigned account. See ACCOUNT.

assigned counsel. See COUNSEL.

assigned risk. See RISK.

assignee (ə-SI-**nee** *or* as-ə-**nee**). One to whom property rights or powers are transferred by another. • Use of the term is so widespread that it is difficult to ascribe positive meaning to it with any specificity. Courts recognize the protean nature of the term and are therefore often forced to look to the intent of the assignor and assignee in making the assignment — rather than to the formality of the use of the term *assignee* — in defining rights and responsibilities. — Also termed *assign.*

absolute assignee. A person who is assigned an unqualified interest in property in a transfer of some or all of the incidents of ownership.

assignee ad interim. An assignee appointed between the time of bankruptcy and the appointment of a regular assignee.

collateral assignee. A lender who is assigned an interest in property (usu. real property) as security for a loan.

assignee clause. A provision of the Judiciary Act of 1789 that prevented a litigant without diversity of citizenship from assigning a claim to another who did have the required diversity. • In 1948 the assignee clause was replaced by 28 USCA § 1359, which denies federal jurisdiction when a party is improperly or collusively joined, by assignment or otherwise, merely to invoke jurisdiction.

assigner. See ASSIGNOR.

assignment, *n.* **1.** The transfer of rights or property <assignment of stock options>. **2.** The rights or property so transferred <the creditor took the assignment>.

> "An *assignment* is a transfer or setting over of property, or of some right or interest therein, from one person to another; the term denoting not only the *act* of transfer, but also the instrument by which it is effected. In these senses the word is variously applied in law." Alexander M. Burrill, *A Treatise on the Law and Practice of Voluntary Assignments for the Benefit of Creditors* § 1, at 1 (James Avery Webb ed., 6th ed. 1894).

> "Negotiability differs from assignment, with which it has obvious affinities, in at least two respects. In the first place no notice need be given of the transfer of a negotiable instrument, and in the second place the transfer of such an instrument is not subject to equities. Thus whereas an assignor only transfers his rights subject to any defences which could be pleaded against him, a transfer of a negotiable instrument to someone in good faith passes a good title, free from any such defences. For instance a person who receives a cheque in good faith obtains a good title, even though the cheque may have been stolen. It is not, of course, any document which has the attributes of negotiability. Only those documents recognized by the custom of trade to be transferable by delivery (or endorsement) are negotiable. Other documents can only be transferred by assignment." P.S. Atiyah, *An Introduction to the Law of Contract* 278–79 (3d ed. 1981).

absolute assignment. An assignment that leaves the assignor no interest in the assigned property or right.

assignment in gross. A transfer of a company's trademark separately from the goodwill of the business. • Courts often hold that such an assignment passes nothing of value to the transferee.

assignment of account. An assignment that gives the assignee the right to funds in an account, usu. to satisfy a debt.

assignment of dower (**dow**-ər). The act of setting apart a widow's share of her deceased husband's real property.

assignment of income. See *assignment of wages.*

assignment of lease. An assignment in which a lessee transfers the entire unexpired remainder of the lease term, as distinguished from a sublease transferring only a portion of the remaining term.

assignment of wages. A transfer of the right to collect wages from the wage earner to a creditor. — Also termed *assignment of income.*

assignment pro tanto. An assignment that results when an order is drawn on a third party and made payable from a particular fund that belongs to the drawer. • The drawee becomes an assignee with respect to the drawer's interest in that fund.

collateral assignment. An assignment of property as collateral security for a loan.

common-law assignment. An assignment for the benefit of creditors made under the common law, rather than by statute.

conditional assignment. An assignment of income (such as rent payments or accounts receivable) to a lender, made to secure a loan. • The lender receives the assigned income only if the assignor defaults on the underlying loan.

effective assignment. An assignment that terminates the assignor's interest in the property and transfers it to the assignee.

equitable assignment. An assignment that, although not legally valid, will be recognized and enforced in equity — for example, an assignment of a chose in action or of future acquisitions of the assignor. • To accomplish an "equitable assignment," there must be an absolute appropriation by the assignor of the debt or fund sought to be assigned.

fly-power assignment. A blank written assignment that, when attached to a stock certificate, renders the stock transferable.

foreign assignment. An assignment made in a foreign country or in another jurisdiction.

general assignment. Assignment of a debtor's property for the benefit of all the assignor's creditors, instead of only a few. — Also termed *voluntary assignment.* See ASSIGNMENT FOR THE BENEFIT OF CREDITORS.

gratuitous assignment. An assignment given or taken in either of two ways: (1) in exchange for a performance or return promise that would be consideration for a promise; or (2) as security for — or in total or partial satisfaction of — a preexisting obligation.

mesne assignment (meen). A middle or intermediate assignment; any assignment before the last one.

partial assignment. The immediate transfer of part but not all of the assignor's right.

preferential assignment. See PREFERENTIAL TRANSFER.

total assignment. An assignment empowering the assignee to enforce the entire right for the benefit of the assignor or others. • Examples are assignment to secure an obligation and assignment to a trustee.

voluntary assignment. See *general assignment.*

wage assignment. An assignment by an employee of a portion of the employee's pay to another (such as a creditor).

3. The instrument of transfer <the assignment was appended to the contract>. **4.** A task, job, or appointment <the student's math assignment> <assignment as ambassador to a foreign country>. **5.** In litigation practice, a point that a litigant advances <the third assignment of error>.

new assignment. *Hist.* A plaintiff's restatement of a claim because the first complaint did not contain sufficient details. • The purpose was to allow a plaintiff to reply to a defendant's responsive plea that did not address the plaintiff's specific claim because the complaint was too general. New assignment has been replaced by amended pleadings. — Also termed *novel assignment.*

> "A new assignment is a restatement in the replication of the plaintiff's cause of action. Where the declaration in an action is ambiguous and the defendant pleads facts which are literally an answer to it, but not to the real claim set up by the plaintiff, the plaintiff's course is to reply by way of new assignment; that is, to allege that he brought his action, not for the cause supposed by the defendant, but for some other cause, to which the plea has no application." Benjamin J. Shipman, *Handbook of Common-Law Pleading* § 214, at 370 (Henry Winthrop Ballantine ed., 3d ed. 1923).

assignment for the benefit of creditors. Assignment of a debtor's property to another person in trust so as to consolidate and liquidate the debtor's assets for payment to creditors, any surplus being returned to the debtor. • This procedure serves as a state-law substitute for federal bankruptcy proceedings. The debtor is not discharged from unpaid debts by this procedure since creditors do not agree to any discharge.

assignment of error. A specification of the trial court's alleged errors on which the appellant relies in seeking an appellate court's reversal, vacation, or modification of an adverse judgment. Pl. **assignments of error.** See ERROR. Cf. WRIT OF ERROR.

assignment of income. See *assignment of wages* under ASSIGNMENT (2).

assignment of lease. See ASSIGNMENT (2).

assignment-of-rents clause. A mortgage provision or separate agreement that entitles the lender to collect rents from the mortgaged premises if the borrower defaults.

assignment of rights. *Contracts.* The transfer of rights from a party to a contract to a third party.

assignment of wages. See ASSIGNMENT (2).

assignment pro tanto. See ASSIGNMENT (2).

assignor (as-ə-**nor** *or* ə-**sɪ**-nər *or* ə-sɪ-**nor**). One who transfers property rights or powers to another. — Also spelled *assigner.*

assignor estoppel. See ESTOPPEL.

assisa armorum (ə-**sɪ**-zə ahr-**mor**-əm). [Law Latin "assize of arms"] *Hist.* A statute requiring the keeping of arms for the common defense.

assisa cadere (ə-**sɪ**-zə **kad**-ə-ree), *vb.* [Law Latin] *Hist.* To fail in the assize, as by being nonsuited.

assisa continuanda (ə-**sɪ**-zə kən-tin-yoo-**an**-də) [Law Latin] *Hist.* A writ addressed to the justices of assize for the continuation of a case.

assisa de foresta (ə-**sɪ**-zə dee for-**es**-tə), *n.* [Law Latin "assize of the forest"] *Hist.* A statute concerning orders to be observed in the royal forest. — Also termed *ordinatio forestae*; *assisa forestae.*

assisa de mensuris (ə-**sɪ**-zə dee men-**s[y]oor**-is), *n.* [Law Latin "assize of measures"] *Hist.* A common rule for weights and measures, established by Richard I in the eighth year of his reign.

assisa de morte antecessoris. See *assize of mort d'ancestor* under ASSIZE (6).

assisa de nocumento (ə-**sɪ**-zə dee nok-yə-**men**-toh), *n.* [Law Latin "assize of nuisance"]. See *assize of nuisance* under ASSIZE (8).

assisa de utrum (ə-**sɪ**-zə dee **yoo**-trəm), *n.* [Law Latin "assize of utrum"] See ASSIZE UTRUM.

assisa forestae. See ASSISA DE FORESTAE.

assisa friscae fortiae. See *assize of fresh force* under ASSIZE (7).

assisa mortis d'ancestoris (ə-**sɪ**-zə **mor**-tis dan-ses-**tor**-is), *n.* [Law Latin] See *assize of mort d'ancestor* under ASSIZE (6).

assisa novae disseysinae (ə-**sI**-zə **noh**-vee di-**see**-zin-ee), *n.* [Law Latin] See ASSIZE OF NOVEL DISSEISIN.

assisa panis et cerevisiae (ə-**sI**-zə **pan**-is et ser-ə-**vish**-ee-ee), *n.* [Law Latin "assize of bread and ale"] *Hist.* A statute passed in the 51st year of the reign of Henry III, regulating the sale of bread and ale. — Also termed *statute of bread and ale.*

assisa proroganda. See DE ASSISA PROROGANDA.

assisa ultimae praesentationis (ə-**sI**-zə **əl**-ti-mee pree-zən-tay-shee-**oh**-nis *or* prez-ən-), *n.* [Law Latin] See *assize of darrein presentment* under ASSIZE (7).

assisa venalium (ə-**sI**-zə və-**nay**-lee-əm), *n.* [Law Latin] *Hist.* The assize of salable commodities.

assise. See ASSIZE.

assiser. See ASSIZER.

assistance, writ of. See WRIT OF ASSISTANCE.

assistance of counsel. Representation by a lawyer, esp. in a criminal case. See RIGHT TO COUNSEL.

effective assistance of counsel. A conscientious, meaningful legal representation, whereby the defendant is advised of all rights and the lawyer is given reasonable opportunity to perform assigned tasks.

ineffective assistance of counsel. A representation in which the lawyer cannot devote full effort to the defendant, usu. because of a conflict of interest.

> "The Sixth Amendment right to assistance of counsel has been held to imply the 'right to the effective assistance of counsel.' The Court has often said that the converse — ineffective assistance of counsel — is a constitutional denial of the Sixth Amendment right, even if the lawyer has been retained by rather than appointed for the defendant. 'Ineffective' does not necessarily mean incompetent or unprepared; it means an inability to perform as an independent lawyer devoted to the defendant.... However, counsel's assistance is not necessarily ineffective because the lawyer made mistakes. Only very serious errors, such as would likely have produced an entirely different outcome at trial, will suffice to require a new trial." Jethro K. Lieberman, *The Evolving Constitution* 263–64 (1992).

assisted self-determination. See *assisted suicide* under SUICIDE.

assisted suicide. See SUICIDE.

assize (ə-**sIz**), *n.* **1.** A session of a court or council.

maiden assize. *Hist.* **1.** An assize in which no prisoner is sentenced. **2.** An assize in which the sheriff presents the judges with white gloves because there are no prisoners to try. • This practice stemmed from a custom in which a prisoner who was convicted of murder but pardoned by the Crown presented gloves to the judges as a fee.

2. A law enacted by such a body, usu. one setting the measure, weight, or price of a thing.

Assize of Clarendon (**klar**-ən-dən). *Hist.* A decree issued in 1166 by Henry II to the justices in eyre and sheriffs concerning criminal procedure. • The Assize expanded the reach of the king's courts by asserting royal jurisdiction over serious crimes. See CONSTITUTIONS OF CLARENDON.

Assize of Northampton. *Hist.* A decree issued in 1176 by Henry II as an expansion and reissue of the Assize of Clarendon, instructing judges esp. on questions of tenure, relief, and dower.

3. The procedure provided for by such an enactment. **4.** The court that hears cases involving that procedure. **5.** A jury.

grand assize. (*often cap.*) A sworn panel summoned by judicial writ to resolve disputes concerning real property. • Henry II instituted the Grand Assize in the 12th century as an alternative to trial by battle. — Also termed *magna assisa.*

petite assize. A jury convened to decide questions of possession.

6. A jury trial.

assize of mort d'ancestor (**mor**[**t**] **dan**-ses-tər). An action for the recovery of land belonging to the claimant's ancestor. • Mort d'ancestor was abolished in the early 19th century. — Also termed *assisa mortis d'ancestoris*; *assisa de morte antecessoris.*

judicial assize. An assize begun by judicial writ and deriving from pleas of *gage*, *mort d'ancestor*, and *darrein presentment.*

petty assize. An assize begun by an original writ. • Petty assizes were characterized by the form of the writ, which specified the questions to be put to the panel, and ordered that a panel be assembled. The petty assizes were *novel disseisin*, *mort d'ancestor*, *utrum*, and *darrein presentment.*

"The word 'Assisa' means originally the sitting of a court or assembly. It then comes to denote the things done, the enactments passed, at such a court or assembly. Thus we speak of the Assize of Clarendon, or the Assize of Northampton. Certain of these enactments in Henry II's reign introduced a new procedure for the trial of questions as to the ownership or possession of lands held by free tenure. The Grand Assize introduced this new procedure for the determination of questions of ownership; the possessory assizes for the determination of question of possession." 1 William Holdsworth, *A History of English Law* 275 (7th ed. 1956).

7. A jury's finding. **8.** A writ. — Also spelled *assise*; *assisa*.

assize of darrein presentment (**dar**-ayn pri-**zent**-mənt), *n.* [fr. French *dernier présentation* "last presentment"] *Hist.* A writ of assize allowing a person with a right of advowson that has been disturbed by another claimant to have a jury determine who had the last right to present a clerk to a benefice and then to allow that person to present again and to recover damages for interference. • This was abolished by the Real Property Limitation Act of 1833 and was replaced by the *quare impedit* action. — Also termed *darreign presentment*; *assize of last presentation*; *assisa ultimae praesentationis*; *assize de ultima presentatione*. — Also spelled *darreign*. See ADVOWSON; QUARE IMPEDIT.

"An assise of *darrein presentment*, or last presentation, lies when a man, or his ancestors, under whom he claims, have presented a clerk to a benefice, who is instituted; and afterwards upon the next avoidance a stranger presents a clerk, and thereby disturbs him that is the real patron. In which case the patron shall have this writ, directed to the sheriff to summon an assise or jury, to enquire who was the last patron that presented to the church now vacant, of which the plaintiff complains that he is deforced by the defendant: and, according as the assise determines that question, a writ shall issue to the bishop; to institute the clerk of that patron, in whose favour the determination is made, and also to give damages ...." 3 William Blackstone, *Commentaries on the Laws of England* 245 (1768).

"[A]t some time or another during his reign Henry gave a possessory action, the assize of darrein presentment ... which stands to the writ of right of advowson in somewhat the same relation as that in which the novel disseisin stands to the writ of right for land. If the church is vacant and two persons are quarrelling about the advowson, it is very necessary that some provisional, some possessory judgment should be given .... The principle of the new assize is, simply stated, this: 'He who presented last time, let him present this time also; but this without prejudice to any question of right.' An inquest of neighbours is summoned to declare who it was that presented the last parson." 1 Frederick Pollock & Frederic W. Maitland, *The History of English Law Before the Time of Edward I* 148–49 (2d ed. 1898).

assize of fresh force. *Hist.* A writ available in urban areas to disseise another's land. • This writ is so called because it was available only within the first 40 days after title accrued to the person seeking it. — Also termed *assisa friscae fortiae*.

assize of novel disseisin. *Hist.* A writ for a tenant who has been disseised of lands and tenements. — Also termed *assisa novae disseysinae*.

assize of nuisance. *Hist.* A judicial writ directing a sheriff of the county where an alleged nuisance occurred to summon a jury to view the premises and do justice. • A successful plaintiff is entitled to abate the nuisance and recover damages. — Also termed *assisa de nocumento*.

assizer, *n. Hist.* **1.** A member of a grand assize. See *grand assize* under ASSIZE (5). **2.** *Scots law.* A juror. **3.** One having custody of the standards of weight and measure; esp., one who fixes the assize of bread, ale, and other items of general consumption. — Also spelled *assizor*; *assiser*; *assisor*.

Assizes de Jerusalem (ə-**sIz**-əz də jə-**roo**-sə-ləm). A code of feudal law intended to serve as the law of the lands conquered by the Crusaders. • The code was prepared in the 12th century after the 1099 conquest of Jerusalem.

assize utrum (**yoo**-trəm). [Latin] *Hist.* A writ to determine whether land claimed by a church was a lay or spiritual tenure. • This writ is named after its emphatic word, which required the fact-finder to determine whether (*utrum*) the land belonged to the church. — Also termed (erroneously) *assize of utrum*.

"In the assize utrum a jury was summoned to decide whether land was held by lay or spiritual tenure — a preliminary question to any litigation about it, for the Church claimed jurisdiction over spiritual land. Later the Church was to lose this jurisdiction, and the assize utrum became the parson's substitute for the writ of right. This curious development was brought about in this way. A parson could not use the writs of right, for, like a life tenant, he could not trace his title back to the seisin of an ancestor. The assize utrum could be made to serve the parson, however, for the question asked in the writ was whether certain land in a parish was 'the free alms of the Church of X.' If the answer was 'yes,' then it followed that it was the parson of the parish's land." Brian Simpson, *An Introduction to the History of the Land Law* 30–31 (1961).

"[T]he 'assize utrum' ... is important as being the first instance known to us of the general use of the royal procedure by way of inquest in a matter of private litigation. If the answer of the inquest was that this land was held in frankalmoign, then the case went to the ecclesiastical court; if that it was lay fee, then to the appropriate lay tribunal. In the course of the thirteenth century the ecclesiastical courts lost their jurisdiction over land held by spiritual tenure, and the 'assize utrum' came to be used not as a merely preliminary procedure but as a mode of deciding in royal courts a question of title to glebe land." Geoffrey Radcliffe & Geoffrey Cross, *The English Legal System* 33–34 (G.J. Hand & D.J. Bentley eds., 6th ed. 1977).

assizor. See ASSIZER.

associate, *n.* **1.** A colleague or companion. **2.** A junior member of an organization or profession; esp., a lawyer in a law firm, usu. with fewer than a certain number of years in practice, who may, upon achieving the requisite seniority, receive an offer to become a partner or shareholder. **3.** *English law.* An officer of a common-law court responsible for maintaining the court's records, attending jury trials, and entering verdicts. • In 1894, associates' duties were taken over by the staff of the Central Office. See CLERK OF ASSIZE; CENTRAL OFFICE.

associated person. *Securities.* **1.** A partner, officer, director, branch manager of a broker or dealer, or any person performing similar functions or occupying a similar status, any person directly or indirectly controlling, controlled by, or under common control with the broker or dealer, or any employee of the broker or dealer — with two exceptions: (1) those whose functions are solely clerical or ministerial, and (2) those required to register under state law as a broker or dealer solely because they are issuers of securities or associated with an issuer of securities. **2.** A natural person who is a partner, officer, director, or employee of: (1) the issuer; (2) a general partner of a limited partnership issuer; (3) a company or partnership that controls, is controlled by, or is under common control with the issuer; or (4) a registered investment adviser to a registered investment company issuer.

associate judge. See JUDGE.

associate justice. See JUSTICE (2).

association. 1. The process of mentally collecting ideas, memories, or sensations. **2.** A gathering of people for a common purpose; the persons so joined. **3.** An unincorporated business organization that is not a legal entity separate from the persons who compose it. • If an association has sufficient corporate attributes, such as centralized management, continuity of existence, and limited liability, it may be classified and taxed as a corporation. — Also termed *unincorporated association*; *voluntary association.*

benevolent association. An unincorporated, nonprofit organization that has a philanthropic or charitable purpose. — Also termed *beneficial association, benefit association, benevolent society, fraternal society, friendly society.*

homeowners' association. **1.** An association of people who own homes in a given area and have united to improve or maintain the area's quality. **2.** An association formed by a land developer or homebuilder to manage and maintain property in which they own an undivided, common interest. • Homeowners' associations — which are regulated by statute in many states — are commonly formed by restrictive covenant or a declaration of restrictions. — Also spelled *homeowners association.*

professional association. **1.** A group of professionals organized to practice their profession together, though not necessarily in corporate or partnership form. **2.** A group of professionals organized for education, social activity, or lobbying, such as a bar association. — Abbr. P.A.

trade association. An association of business organizations having similar concerns and engaged in similar fields, formed for mutual protection, the interchange of ideas and statistics, and the establishment and maintenance of industry standards. • A trade association may be composed of members of a single industry (e.g., the Chemical Manufacturers Association) or members having a common interest or purpose (e.g., the Consumer Mortgage Coalition). Among the joint actions that a trade association often takes are collecting industry data, advertising, marketing, and engaging in public relations and government relations.

association-in-fact enterprise. Under RICO, a group of people or entities that have not formed a legal entity, but that have a common or shared purpose, and maintain an ongoing organizational structure through which the associates function as a continuing unit. • A RICO violation is not shown merely by proving that an enterprise, including an association-in-fact, exists. A pattern of racketeering activity must also be proved. 18 USCA § 1961(4); *United States v. Turkette*, 452 U.S. 576, 101 S.Ct. 2524 (1981).

Association of American Law Schools. An organization of law schools that have each graduated at least three annual classes of students. — Abbr. AALS.

assoil (ə-**soyl**), *vb.* [Law French] *Hist.* To acquit or absolve; to deliver from excommunication. — Also spelled *assoile.* — Also termed *absoile*; *assoilyie.*

assultus premeditatus. See *assault purpensé* under ASSAULT.

assumed bond. See *guaranteed bond* under BOND (3).

assumed name. 1. ALIAS (1). **2.** The name under which a business operates or by which it is commonly known <Antex Corporation's assumed name is Computer Warehouse>. • Many states require an individual or business operating under an assumed name to file an assumed-name certificate, usu. in the secretary of state's office or the county clerk's office where the principal place of business is located. See D/B/A. Cf. *corporate name* under NAME.

assumpsit (ə-**səm**[**p**]-sit). [Law Latin "he undertook"] **1.** An express or implied promise, not under seal, by which one person undertakes to do some act or pay something to another <an assumpsit to pay a debt>. **2.** A common-law action for breach of such a promise or for breach of a contract <the creditor's assumpsit against the debtor>.

> "It was early known as 'trespass on the case upon promises,' but in time came to be designated *assumpsit* (he assumed or promised), and lies for damages for breach of all contracts, parol or simple, whether written or verbal, express or implied." Edwin E. Bryant, *The Law of Pleading Under the Codes of Civil Procedure* 9–10 (2d ed. 1899).

> "In its origin an action of tort, [assumpsit] was soon transformed into an action of contract, becoming afterwards a remedy where there was neither tort nor contract. Based at first only upon an express promise, it was afterwards supported upon an implied promise, and even upon a fictitious promise. Introduced as a special manifestation of the action on the case, it soon acquired the dignity of a distinct form of action, which superseded Debt, became concurrent with Account, with Case upon a bailment, a warranty, and bills of exchange, and competed with Equity in the case of the essentially equitable quasi-contracts growing out of the principle of unjust enrichment. Surely, it would be hard to find a better illustration of the flexibility and power of self-development of the Common Law." James Barr Ames, "The History of Assumpsit," in 3 *Select Essays in Anglo-American Legal History* 298 (1909).

general assumpsit. An action based on the defendant's breach of an implied promise to pay a debt to the plaintiff. — Also termed *common assumpsit*; *indebitatus assumpsit.*

> "General assumpsit is brought for breach of a fictitious or implied promise raised by law from a debt founded upon an executed consideration. The basis of the action is the promise implied by law from the performance of the consideration, or from a debt or legal duty resting upon the defendant." Benjamin J. Shipman, *Handbook of Common-Law Pleading* § 59, at 153 (Henry Winthrop Ballantine ed., 3d ed. 1923).

indebitatus assumpsit (in-deb-i-**tay**-təs ə-**səm**[**p**]-sit). [Latin "being indebted, he undertook"] **1.** *Hist.* A form of action in which the plaintiff alleges that the defendant contracted a debt and, as consideration, had undertaken (i.e., promised) to pay. • The action was equivalent to the common-law action for debt (an action based on a sealed instrument), but could be used to enforce an oral debt. *Indebitatus assumpsit* was abolished in 1873 by the Judicature Act. See CONCESSIT SOLVERE. **2.** See *general assumpsit.*

> "[I]f I verbally agree to pay a man a certain price for a certain parcel of goods, and fail in the performance, an action of debt lies against me; for this is a *determinate* contract: but if I agree for no settled price, I am not liable to an action of debt, but a special action on the case, according to the nature of my contract. And indeed actions of debt are now seldom brought but upon special contracts under seal .... [T]he plaintiff must recover the whole debt he claims, or nothing at all. For the debt is one single cause of action, fixed and determined; and which therefore, if the proof varies from the claim, cannot be looked upon as the same ... action of debt.... But in an action on the case, on what is called an *indebitatus assumpsit*, which is not brought to compel a specific performance of the contract, but to recover damages for its non-performance, the implied *assumpsit*, and consequently the damages for the breach of it, are in their nature indeterminate; and will therefore adapt and proportion themselves to the truth of the case which shall be proved, without being confined to the precise demand stated in the declaration." 3 William Blackstone, *Commentaries on the Laws of England* 154 (1768).

special assumpsit. An action based on the defendant's breach of an express contract. — Also termed *express assumpsit.*

> "Special assumpsit lies for the recovery of damages for the breach of simple contract, either express or implied in fact. The term 'special contract' is often used to denote an express or explicit contract as contrasted with a promise implied in law." Benjamin J. Shipman, *Handbook of Common-Law Pleading* § 58, at 148 (Henry Winthrop Ballantine ed., 3d ed. 1923).

assumption, *n.* **1.** A fact or statement taken for granted; a supposition <a logical assumption>. **2.** The act of taking (esp. someone else's debt or other obligation) for or on oneself; the agreement to so take <assumption of a debt>. — **assume,** *vb.*

implied assumption. The imposition of personal liability on a land purchaser who buys subject to a mortgage and who deducts the mortgage amount from the purchase price, so that the purchaser is treated as having assumed the debt.

assumption clause. **1.** A mortgage provision that prohibits another from assuming the mortgage without the permission of the mortgagee. **2.** A provision by which the transferee of an instrument agrees to assume an obligation of the transferor.

assumption fee. A lender's charge for processing records for a new buyer's assumption of an existing mortgage.

assumption of the risk. *Torts.* **1.** The act or an instance of a prospective plaintiff's taking on the risk of loss, injury, or damage <the skydiver's assumption of the risk>. — Also termed *assumption of risk.*

> "[Assumption of risk] has been a subject of much controversy, and has been surrounded by much confusion, because 'assumption of risk' has been used by the courts in several different senses, which traditionally have been lumped together under the one name, often without realizing that any differences exist. There are even courts which have limited the use of the term 'assumption of risk' to cases in which the parties stand in the relation of master and servant, or at least some other contractual relation; but they have been compelled to invent other names for other cases, such as 'incurred risk,' or 'volenti non fit injuria.' This appears to be largely a distinction without a difference; and most courts have made general use of the one term.... In its most basic sense, assumption of risk means that the plaintiff, in advance, has given his express consent to relieve the defendant of an obligation of conduct toward him, and to take his chances of injury from a known risk arising from what the defendant is to do or leave undone." W. Page Keeton et al., *The Law of Torts* § 68, at 480–81 (5th ed. 1984).

2. The principle that one who has taken on oneself the risk of loss, injury, or damage consequently cannot maintain an action against the party having caused the loss <assumption of the risk was not a valid defense>. • Assumption of the risk was originally an affirmative defense, but in most jurisdictions it has now been wholly or largely subsumed by the doctrine of contributory or comparative negligence. The risk assumed by the person was often termed an *incurred risk.*

assurance, *n.* **1.** Something that gives confidence; the state of being confident or secure <self-assurance>. **2.** A pledge or guarantee <adequate assurances of the borrower's solvency>. **3.** The act of transferring real property; the instrument by which it is transferred <the owner's assurance of the farm to his son>. **4.** *English law.* See *life insurance* under INSURANCE <she obtained assurance before traveling abroad, naming her husband as the beneficiary>. — **assure,** *vb.*

collateral assurance. A pledge made in addition to the principal assurance of an agreement.

common assurance. See MUNIMENT OF TITLE.

further assurance. A covenant contained in a warranty deed whereby the grantor promises to execute any document that might be needed in the future to perfect the title that the original deed purported to transfer.

assured, *n. Insurance.* One who is indemnified against loss; INSURED.

assurer. See INSURER.

as their interests may appear. See ATIMA.

astipulation (as-tip-yə-**lay**-shən). *Archaic.* Agreement; assent.

astitution (as-tə-**t**[**y**]**oo**-shən). *Archaic.* See ARRAIGNMENT.

astrarius (as-**trair**-ee-əs), *n.* [Law Latin "hearth owner"] *Hist.* The owner or occupant of a house. — Also termed *astrer* (**as**-trər). See *heres astrarius* under HERES.

astronomical day. See *solar day* (2) under DAY.

asylee (ə-sɪ-**lee**). A refugee applying for asylum; an asylum-seeker.

asylum. **1.** A sanctuary or shelter. **2.** Protection of usu. political refugees from arrest by a foreign jurisdiction; a nation or embassy that affords such protection. — Also termed *political asylum.* **3.** An institution for the protection and relief of the unfortunate, esp. the mentally ill. — Also termed (in sense 3) *insane asylum.*

atamita (ə-**tam**-i-tə), *n.* [Latin] *Civil law.* A great-great-great-grandfather's sister.

atavia (ə-**tay**-vee-ə), *n.* [Latin] *Roman & civil law.* A great-great-great grandmother.

atavunculus (at-ə-**vəngk**-yə-ləs), *n.* [Latin] *Civil law.* A great-great-great-grandfather's brother.

atavus (**at**-ə-vəs), *n.* [Latin] *Roman & civil law.* The male ascendant in the fifth degree; a great-grandfather's or great-grandmother's grandfather; a fourth grandfather.

at bar. Now before the court <the case at bar>. — Also termed *at bench*; *at the bar*.

at bench. See AT BAR.

at equity. According to equity; by, for, or in equity.

a terme (a **tairm**). [Law French] For a term.

a terme de sa vie (a **tairm** də sa **vee**). [Law French] For the term of his life.

a terme que n'est mye encore passe (a **tairm** kə nay mee **awn**-kor **pahs**). [Law French] For a term that has not yet passed.

a terme que passe est (a **tairm** kə **pahs ay**). [Law French] For a term that has passed.

Atilian law. See LEX ATILIA.

ATIMA (ə-**tee**-mə). *abbr*. As their interests may appear. • The phrase is sometimes used in insurance policies to show that the named insured has an interest, usu. an unspecified one, in the property covered by the policy and is entitled to benefits to the extent of that interest. The phrase is also used in a policy's mortgage clause to protect the mortgagee's real-property interest. See INSURABLE INTEREST; MORTGAGE CLAUSE.

Atinian law. See LEX ATINIA.

at issue. Taking opposite sides; under dispute; in question <the federal appeals courts are at issue over a question of law>.

at-issue waiver. An exemption from the attorney-client privilege, whereby a litigant is considered to have waived the privilege by taking a position that cannot be effectively challenged without analyzing privileged information. Cf. OFFENSIVE-USE WAIVER.

Atlantic Reporter. A set of regional lawbooks that, being part of the West Group's National Reporter System, contain every published decision from Connecticut, Delaware, Maine, Maryland, New Hampshire, New Jersey, Pennsylvania, Rhode Island, and Vermont, as well as the decisions of the District of Columbia Municipal Court of Appeals, from 1885 to date. • The first series ran from 1885 to 1938; the second series is the current one. — Abbr. A.; A.2d.

at large. 1. Free; unrestrained; not under control <the suspect is still at large>. **2.** Not limited to any particular place, person, matter, or question <at-large election>. **3.** Chosen by the voters of an entire political entity, such as a state, county, or city, rather than from separate districts within the entity <councilmember at large>. **4.** Not ordered in a topical way; at random <statutes at large>. **5.** Fully; in detail; in an extended form <there wasn't time to discuss the issue at large>.

at-large election. See *election at large* under ELECTION.

at law. According to law; by, for, or in law.

atmatertera (at-may-**tər**-tər-ə), *n*. [Latin] *Civil law*. A great-great-great-grandmother's sister. — Also termed *abmatertera magna* (ab-may-**tər**-tər-ə **mag**-nə).

atort (a-**tor**), *adv*. [Law French] *Hist*. Wrongfully.

a tort et a travers (a **tor** tay a tra-**vair**). [Law French] Without consideration or discernment.

a tort ou a droit (a **tor** oo a **drwah**). [Law French] Right or wrong.

at par, *adj*. (Of a stock or bond) issued or selling at face value.

atpatruus (at-**pa**-troo-əs), *n*. [Latin] *Civil law*. A brother of a great-great-grandfather.

at-risk rules, *n. pl*. Statutory limitations of a taxpayer's deductible losses to the amount the taxpayer could actually lose, to prevent the taxpayer from sheltering income.

ATS. *abbr*. At the suit of.

attach, *vb*. **1.** To annex, bind, or fasten <attach the exhibit to the pleading>. **2.** To take or seize under legal authority <attach the debtor's assets>. **3.** To become attributed; to adhere <jeopardy attaches when the jury is sworn>.

attaché (at-ə-**shay** *or* a-ta-**shay**), *n*. A person who serves as a technical adviser to an embassy.

attachiamenta bonorum (ə-tach-ee-ə-**men**-tə bə-**nor**-əm), *n*. [Law Latin] *Hist*. A distress taken on goods and chattels by bailiffs, as security to answer an action for debt.

attachiamentum (ə-tach-ee-ə-**men**-təm), *n.* [Law Latin] An attachment. Pl. ***attachiamenta.***

attaching creditor. See CREDITOR.

attachment. 1. The seizing of a person's property to secure a judgment or to be sold in satisfaction of a judgment. — Also termed (in civil law) *provisional seizure.* Cf. GARNISHMENT; SEQUESTRATION (1).

attachment of wages. The attachment by a plaintiff of a defendant's earnings as an employee. • In some jurisdictions, an attachment-of-earnings order requires the defendant's employer to deduct a specified sum from the defendant's wages or salary and to pay the money into court. The court then sends the money to the plaintiff. — Also termed *attachment of earnings.* Cf. GARNISHMENT.

provisional attachment. A prejudgment attachment in which the debtor's property is seized so that if the creditor ultimately prevails, the creditor will be assured of recovering on the judgment through the sale of the seized property. • Ordinarily, a hearing must be held before the attachment takes place, and most courts require the creditor to post a bond for any damages that result from the seizure (esp. if the creditor ultimately loses in the lawsuit).

2. The arrest of a person who either is in contempt of court or is to be held as security for the payment of a judgment. **3.** A writ ordering legal seizure of property (esp. to satisfy a creditor's claim) or of a person. — Also termed *writ of attachment.*

ancillary attachment. An attachment that results in seizure and holding of property pending a resolution of the plaintiff's claim.

4. The creation of a security interest in property, occurring when the debtor agrees to the security, receives value from the secured party, and obtains rights in the collateral. UCC § 9–203. Cf. PERFECTION. **5.** The act of affixing or connecting; something (as a document) that is affixed or connected to something else.

attachment bond. See BOND (2).

attachment lien. See LIEN.

attachment of earnings. See *attachment of wages* under ATTACHMENT (1).

attachment of risk. The point when the risk of loss of purchased goods passes from the seller to the buyer. UCC § 2–509.

attachment of wages. See ATTACHMENT (1).

attainder (ə-**tayn**-dər), *n.* At common law, the act of extinguishing a person's civil rights when sentenced to death or declared an outlaw for committing a felony or treason. — **attaint** (ə-**taynt**), *vb.* See BILL OF ATTAINDER.

> "The word *attainder* is derived from the Latin term *attinctus*, signifying *stained* or *polluted*, and includes, in its meaning, all those disabilities which flow from a capital sentence. On the attainder, the defendant is disqualified to be a witness in any court; he can bring no action, nor perform any of the legal functions which before he was admitted to discharge; he is, in short, regarded as dead in law." 1 Joseph Chitty, *A Practical Treatise on the Criminal Law* 725 (2d ed. 1826).

attaint (ə-**taynt**), *adj.* Stained or blackened reputationally; under an attainder for crime.

attaint, *n. Hist.* A writ to inquire whether a 12–member jury gave a false verdict. • If it was so found (by a 24–member jury), the judgment based on the verdict was overturned. The writ was abolished in England in 1826.

attempt, *n.* **1.** The act or an instance of making an effort to accomplish something, esp. without success. **2.** *Criminal law.* An overt act that is done with the intent to commit a crime but that falls short of completing the crime. • Attempt is an inchoate offense distinct from the attempted crime. — Also termed (in sense 2) *criminal attempt*; *offer.* See DANGEROUS-PROXIMITY TEST; INDISPENSABLE-ELEMENT TEST; LAST-PROXIMATE-ACT TEST; PHYSICAL-PROXIMITY TEST; PROBABLE-DESISTANCE TEST. Cf. CONSPIRACY; SOLICITATION (2). — **attempt,** *vb.*

> "An attempt to commit an indictable offence is itself a crime. Every attempt is an act done with intent to commit the offence so attempted. The existence of this ulterior intent or motive is the essence of the attempt.... [Yet] [a]lthough every attempt is an act done with intent to commit a crime, the converse is not true. Every act done with this intent is not an attempt, for it may be too remote from the completed offence to give rise to criminal liability, notwithstanding the criminal purpose of the doer. I may buy matches with intent to burn a haystack, and yet be clear of attempted arson; but if I go to the stack and there light one of the matches, my intent has developed into a criminal attempt." John Salmond, *Jurisprudence* 387 (Glanville L. Williams ed., 10th ed. 1947).

> "Attempt ... is the most common of the preliminary crimes. It consists of steps taken in furtherance of an indictable offence which the person attempting intends to carry out if he can. As we have seen there can be a

long chain of such steps and it is necessary to have some test by which to decide that the particular link in the chain has been reached at which the crime of attempt has been achieved; that link will represent the *actus reus* of attempt . . . ." J.W. Cecil Turner, *Kenny's Outlines of Criminal Law* 79 (16th ed. 1952).

attempted assault. See ASSAULT.

attempted monopolization. See MONOPOLIZATION.

attempted suicide. See SUICIDE.

attempt to assault. See *attempted assault* under ASSAULT.

attendance officer. See TRUANCY OFFICER.

attendant, *adj.* Accompanying; resulting <attendant circumstances>.

attendant term. See TERM (4).

attenuation doctrine (ə-ten-yə-**way**-shən). *Criminal procedure.* The rule providing — as an exception to the fruit-of-the-poisonous-tree doctrine — that evidence obtained by illegal means may nonetheless be admissible if the connection between the evidence and the illegal means is sufficiently attenuated or remote. See FRUIT-OF-THE-POISONOUS-TREE DOCTRINE.

atterminare (ə-tər-mi-**nair**-ee), *vb.* [Law Latin] **1.** To put off to a succeeding term; to adjourn. **2.** To prolong the time to pay a debt.

atterminement (ə-**tər**-min-mənt). The granting of a delay for some purpose; esp., the extension of time to pay a debt.

attermoiement (at-ər-**moy**-ə-mənt). [Law French] *Eccles. law.* COMPOSITION (1).

attest (ə-**test**), *vb.* **1.** To bear witness; testify <attest to the defendant's innocence>. **2.** To affirm to be true or genuine; to authenticate by signing as a witness <attest the will>. — **attestation** (a-te-**stay**-shən), *n.* — **attestative** (ə-**tes**-tə-tiv), *adj.*

attestation clause. A provision at the end of an instrument (esp. a will) that is signed by the instrument's witnesses and that recites the formalities required by the jurisdiction in which the instrument might take effect (such as where the will might be probated). • The attestation strengthens the presumption that all the statutory requirements for executing the will have been satisfied. Cf. TESTIMONIUM CLAUSE.

attested copy. See *certified copy* under COPY.

attester (ə-**tes**-tər). One who attests or vouches for. — Also spelled *attestant*; *attestator*; *attestor*.

attesting witness. See WITNESS.

at the bar. See AT BAR.

at the courthouse door. (Of the posting of a notice of judicial sale, etc.) on the courthouse door, or in direct proximity to the door, as on a bulletin board that is located just outside the door and that is regularly used for the posting of legal notices. • Some statutes may specify that the notice be actually posted on the door. See POSTING (5).

at-the-market price. See PRICE.

attorn (ə-**tərn**), *vb.* **1.** To agree to be the tenant of a new landlord. **2.** To transfer (money, goods, etc.) to another.

attornatus (at-ər-**nay**-təs). [Law Latin] One who is attorned, or put in the place of another; an attorney.

attorney. 1. Strictly, one who is designated to transact business for another; a legal agent. — Also termed *attorney-in-fact*; *private attorney*. **2.** A person who practices law; LAWYER. — Also termed (in sense 2) *attorney-at-law*; *public attorney*. Cf. COUNSEL. — Abbr. att'y. Pl. **attorneys.**

attorney, power of. See POWER OF ATTORNEY.

attorney-at-law. See ATTORNEY (2).

attorney-client privilege. See PRIVILEGE (3).

attorney fees. See ATTORNEY'S FEES.

attorney general. The chief law officer of a state or of the United States, responsible for advising the government on legal matters and representing it in litigation. — Abbr. AG. Pl. **attorneys general.**

attorney general's opinion. 1. An opinion furnished by the U.S. Attorney General to the President or another executive official on a request concerning a question of law. **2.** A written opinion by a state attorney general, usu. given at the request of a public official, interpreting a legal provision.

attorney in charge. See *lead counsel* under COUNSEL.

attorney-in-fact. See ATTORNEY (1).

attorney malpractice. See *legal malpractice* under MALPRACTICE.

attorney of record. The lawyer who appears for a party in a lawsuit and who is entitled to receive, on the party's behalf, all pleadings and other formal documents from the court and from other parties. — Also termed *counsel of record*. See OF RECORD (1).

attorney's fees. The charge to a client for services performed for the client, such as an hourly fee, a flat fee, or a contingent fee. — Also spelled *attorneys' fees*. — Also termed *attorney fees*. Cf. RETAINER (2).

attorney's lien. See LIEN.

attorney-witness rule. See LAWYER-WITNESS RULE.

attorney work product. See WORK PRODUCT.

attornment (ə-**tərn**-mənt), *n.* **1.** A tenant's agreement to hold the land as the tenant of a new landlord. **2.** A constructive delivery involving the transfer of mediate possession while a third person has immediate possession; esp., a bailee's acknowledgment that he or she will hold the goods on behalf of someone other than the bailor. • For the other two types of constructive delivery, see CONSTITUTUM POSSESSORIUM; TRADITIO BREVI MANU. — **attorn,** *vb.*

> "[Another] form of constructive delivery is that which is known to English lawyers as attornment. . . . The mediate possessor of a thing may deliver it by procuring the immediate possessor to agree with the transferee to hold it for the future on his account, instead of on account of the transferor. Thus if I have goods in the warehouse of A and sell them to B, I have effectually delivered them to B so soon as A has agreed with B to hold them for him, and no longer for me." John Salmond, *Jurisprudence* 306–07 (Glanville L. Williams ed., 10th ed. 1947).

attractive nuisance. See NUISANCE.

attractive-nuisance doctrine. *Torts.* The rule that a person who owns property on which there is a dangerous thing or condition that will foreseeably lure children to trespass is under a duty to protect those children from the danger <the attractive-nuisance doctrine imposed a duty on the school to protect the children from the shallow, polluted pond on school property>. — Also termed *turntable doctrine*; *torpedo doctrine*. See DANGEROUS INSTRUMENTALITY.

attribution, *n.* The process — outlined in the Internal Revenue Code — by which a person's or entity's stock ownership is assigned to a related family member or entity for tax purposes. — Also termed *stock attribution*. — **attribute,** *vb.* — **attributive,** *adj.*

attribution right. See MORAL RIGHT.

att'y. *abbr.* ATTORNEY.

at will. Subject to one's discretion; as one wishes or chooses; esp. (of a legal relationship), able to be terminated or discharged by either party without cause <employment at will>.

at-will employment. See *employment at will* under EMPLOYMENT.

at-will tenancy. See *tenancy at will* under TENANCY.

***Atwood* doctrine.** The principle that, to the extent an ERISA plan and its summary-plan description conflict regarding the circumstances under which benefits may be denied, the summary-plan description controls. *Atwood v. Newmont Gold Co.*, 45 F.3d 1317 (9th Cir. 1995); 29 USCA § 1022. See SUMMARY-PLAN DESCRIPTION.

au besoin (oh bə-**zwan**). [French "in case of need"] A designation in a bill of exchange stating who is responsible for payment if the drawee fails or refuses to pay. • *Au besion* is part of the phrase *au besion, chez Messrs. Garnier et DuCloux* (meaning "in case of need, apply to Messrs. Garnier and DuCloux").

A.U.C. *abbr.* AB URBE CONDITA.

auction, *n.* A sale of property to the highest bidder. • Under the UCC, a sale at auction is complete when the auctioneer so announces in a customary manner, as by pounding a hammer. — Also termed *auction sale*. — **auction,** *vb.*

auction without reserve. An auction in which the property will be sold to the highest bidder, no minimum price will limit bidding, the owner may not withdraw property after the first bid is received, the owner may not reject any bids, and the owner may not nullify the bidding by outbidding all other bidders. • In an auction without reserve, the owner essentially becomes an offeror, and each successively higher bid creates a contingent contract, with the highest bid creating an enforceable agreement. — Also termed *absolute auction*. See WITHOUT RESERVE.

auction with reserve. An auction in which the property will not be sold unless the highest bid exceeds a minimum price. See WITH RESERVE.

Dutch auction. **1.** An auction in which property is initially offered at an excessive price that is gradually lowered until the property is sold. **2.** A method of tendering stock shares, by which a corporation provides a price range, shareholders indicate how many shares they will sell and at what price, and the corporation buys however many shares it wants at the lowest prices offered. — Also termed *Dutch-auction tender method*.

auctioneer, *n.* A person legally authorized to sell goods or lands of other persons at public auction for a commission or fee. • The auctioneer is the property owner's agent up to the moment when a purchaser's bid is accepted, when the auctioneer becomes the purchaser's agent. — Formerly also termed *vendue master*.

auction market. See MARKET.

auction sale. See AUCTION.

audience, *n.* A hearing before judges. See RIGHT OF AUDIENCE.

audit, *n.* A formal examination of an individual's or organization's accounting records, financial situation, or compliance with some other set of standards. — **audit,** *vb.* — **auditor,** *n.* See GENERALLY ACCEPTED AUDITING STANDARDS.

audit of return. See *tax audit*.

compliance audit. An audit conducted by a regulatory agency, an organization, or a third party to assess compliance with one or more sets of laws and regulations.

correspondence audit. An IRS audit of a taxpayer's return conducted by mail or telephone.

desk audit. A review of a civil-service position to determine whether its duties and responsibilities fit the prescribed job classification and pay scale.

field audit. An IRS audit conducted at the taxpayer's business premises or lawyer's offices.

independent audit. An audit conducted by an outside person or firm not connected with the person or organization being audited.

internal audit. An audit performed by an organization's personnel to ensure that internal procedures, operations, and accounting practices are in proper order.

office audit. An IRS audit of a taxpayer's return conducted in the IRS agent's office.

post audit. An audit of funds spent on a completed capital project, the purpose being to assess the efficiency with which the funds were spent and to compare expected cash-flow estimates with actual cash flows.

tax audit. The review of a taxpayer's return by the IRS, including an examination of the taxpayer's books, vouchers, and records supporting the return. — Also termed *audit of return*.

audita querela (aw-**dI**-tə kwə-**ree**-lə). [Law Latin "the complaint having been heard"] A writ available to a judgment debtor who seeks a rehearing of a matter on grounds of newly discovered evidence or newly existing legal defenses.

> "The writ of audita querela (= quarrel having been heard) . . . , introduced during the time of Edward III, was available to re-open a judgment in certain circumstances. It was issued as a remedy to defendant where an important matter concerning his case had arisen since the judgment. Its issue was based on equitable, rather than common law principles." L.B. Curzon, *English Legal History* 103 (2d ed. 1979).

> "Audita querela is distinguished from coram nobis in that coram nobis attacks the judgment itself, whereas audita querela may be directed against the enforcement, or further enforcement, of a judgment which when rendered was just and unimpeachable." 7A C.J.S. *Audita Querela* § 2, at 901 (1980).

audit letter. A client's written request for its attorney to give its financial auditors information about matters such as pending or threatened litigation. • The attorney usu. sends the response (called an *audit response*) directly to the financial auditors. See AUDIT RESPONSE.

audit-letter response. See AUDIT RESPONSE.

audit of return. See *tax audit* under AUDIT.

audit opinion. See OPINION (2).

auditor. A person or firm, usu. an accountant or an accounting firm, that formally examines an individual's or entity's financial records or status.

county auditor. An official who examines a county's accounts and financial records.

audit report. An outside auditor's written statement, usu. accompanying a company's financial statement, expressing the auditor's opinion of the accuracy of the company's financial condition as set forth in the financial statement.

audit response. A letter that an attorney provides to a client's financial auditors, usu. at the client's request, regarding matters such as pending or threatened litigation. • Audit responses should comply with the American Bar Association's Statement of Policy Regarding Lawyer's Responses to Auditors' Requests for Information, published in December 1975. — Also termed *audit-letter response.* See AUDIT LETTER.

audit trail. The chain of evidence connecting account balances to original transactions and calculations.

augmented estate. See ESTATE.

aula regis (**aw**-lə **ree**-jis). [Latin "king's hall"] *Hist.* See CURIA REGIS.

Aunt Jemima **doctrine.** *Trademarks.* The principle that a trademark is protected not only from an act of direct copying, but also from the use of any similar mark that would likely make a buyer think that the item bearing the similar mark comes from the same source as the trademarked item. *Aunt Jemima Mills Co. v. Rigney & Co.*, 247 F. 407 (2d Cir. 1917); 15 USCA § 1114.

aural acquisition. *Criminal law.* Under the Federal Wiretapping Act, hearing or tape-recording a communication, as opposed to tracing its origin or destination. 18 USCA § 2510(4).

Australian ballot. See BALLOT (4).

authentic act. *Civil law.* **1.** A writing signed before a notary public or other public officer. **2.** A certified copy of a writing.

authenticate, *vb.* **1.** To prove the genuineness of (a thing). **2.** To render authoritative or authentic, as by attestation or other legal formality. See UCC § 9–102(a)(5).

authentication, *n.* **1.** Broadly, the act of proving that something (as a document) is true or genuine, esp. so that it may be admitted as evidence; the condition of being so proved <authentication of the handwriting>. **2.** Specif., the assent to or adoption of a writing as one's own.

self-authentication. Authentication without extrinsic evidence of truth or genuineness. • In federal courts, certain writings, such as notarized documents and certified copies of public records, may be admitted into evidence by self-authentication. Fed. R. Evid. 902.

authentic interpretation. See INTERPRETATION.

authenticum (aw-**then**-tə-kəm). *Roman & civil law.* **1.** An original instrument. **2.** A collection of Justinian's laws from A.D. 535 to 556.

authoritative precedent. See *binding precedent* under PRECEDENT.

authority. 1. The right or permission to act legally on another's behalf; the power delegated by a principal to an agent <authority to sign the contract>. See AGENCY.

"The term 'authority,' like the term 'contract,' may easily be used in three senses, and is therefore a term to be avoided when accurate reasoning is desirable. It may be used to mean (1) the operative acts of the principal, (2) a physical document executed by the principal, or (3) the legal relations consequent upon the preceding operative facts (1) and (2), and especially the legal *power* conferred upon the agent to bring the principal into new legal relations without any further action by the principal. The operative facts may be spoken words, a document together with the acts necessary to execute it, or other conduct by the principal apparently expressing an intention to create a power. Hereafter, the word 'authority' will be used to denote these operative facts; in other cases the word *power* will usually be substituted. This latter word is not so likely to be taken in shifting senses, in spite of the fact that 'power of attorney' generally means a physical document under seal." William R. Anson, *Principles of the Law of Contract* 508 n.1 (Arthur L. Corbin ed., 3d Am. ed. 1919).

actual authority. Authority that a principal intentionally confers on an agent, including the authority that the agent reasonably believes he or she has as a result of the agent's dealings with the principal. • Actual authority can be either express or implied. — Also termed *real authority.*

"Actual authority is such as a principal intentionally confers upon the agent, or intentionally, or by want of ordinary care, allows the agent to believe himself to possess." Cal. Civ. Code § 2316.

apparent authority. Authority that a third party reasonably believes an agent has, based on the third party's dealings with the principal. • Apparent authority can be created by law even when no actual authority has been conferred. — Also termed *ostensible authority; authority by estoppel.*

"The term 'apparent authority' means that a legal power is vested in the agent in the absence of any intention by the principal that it should exist, or even in spite of his intention that it should *not* exist. The operative facts causing this power to exist are acts of the principal which, considered along with surrounding facts, induce the third person with whom the agent deals to believe reasonably that the principal intended the power to exist. The power is real and not merely *apparent.* The agent is indeed a wrongdoer in exercising the power. He possesses the power but not the legal privilege of using it. Likewise, the *authority* (meaning the action of the principal creating the agent's power) is real. It is only the intention of the principal to create such a power that is merely apparent (i.e., *non-existent*)." William R. Anson, *Principles of the Law of Contract* 510 n.1 (Arthur L. Corbin ed., 3d Am. ed. 1919).

" 'Apparent authority' of an insurance agent means such authority as an insurer knowingly permits the agent to assume, or which it holds him out as possessing, that is, such authority as he appears to have by reason of actual authority or such authority as a reasonably prudent man would suppose the agent to possess." John Alan Appleman & Jean Appleman, *Insurance Law and Practice* § 8674 (1981).

authority coupled with an interest. Authority given to an agent for valuable consideration. • This authority cannot be unilaterally terminated by the principal.

constructive authority. Authority that is inferred because of an earlier grant of authority.

express authority. Authority given to the agent by explicit agreement, either orally or in writing. — Also termed *stipulated authority.*

general authority. A general agent's authority, intended to apply to all matters arising in the course of business.

implied authority. Authority given to the agent as a result of the principal's conduct, such as the principal's earlier acquiescence to the agent's actions. — Also termed *presumptive authority.*

incidental authority. Authority needed to carry out actual or apparent authority. • For example, the actual authority to borrow money includes the incidental authority to sign commercial paper to bring about the loan. — Also termed *inferred authority.*

inherent authority. Authority of an agent arising from the agency relationship.

naked authority. Authority delegated solely for the principal's benefit, without giving any consideration to the agent. • This authority can be revoked by the principal at any time.

ostensible authority. See *apparent authority.*

presumptive authority. See *implied authority.*

real authority. See *actual authority.*

special authority. Authority limited to an individual transaction.

stipulated authority. See *express authority.*

2. Governmental power or jurisdiction <within the court's authority>. **3.** A governmental agency or corporation that administers a public enterprise <transit authority>. — Also termed *public authority.*

constituted authority. (*often pl.*) The legislative, executive, and judicial departments officially and rightfully governing a nation, people, municipality, or other governmental unit; an authority properly appointed or elected under organic law, such as a constitution or charter.

examining authority. A self-regulatory organization registered with the Securities and Exchange Commission and vested with the authority to examine, inspect, and otherwise oversee the activities of a registered broker or dealer.

4. A legal writing taken as definitive or decisive; esp., a judicial or administrative decision cited as a precedent <that case is good authority in Massachusetts>. • The term includes not only the decisions of tribunals but also statutes, ordinances, and administrative rulings.

adverse authority. Authority that is unfavorable to an advocate's position. • Most ethical codes require counsel to disclose adverse authority in the controlling jurisdiction even if the opposing counsel has not cited it.

imperative authority. Authority that is absolutely binding on a court. — Also termed *binding authority.* Cf. *binding precedent* under PRECEDENT.

persuasive authority. Authority that carries some weight but is not binding on a court.

"It may be well to call attention to the fact that the word 'authority' is used by lawyers in at least two senses, one abstract and the other concrete. The word [in its concrete sense] refer[s] to the book or other repository to which one resorts to find propositions of law, and sometimes the word is used in an even narrower sense to mean reported cases. In its abstract sense, however, 'authority' is substantially equivalent to 'influence' or 'power,' and in this sense 'authority' may be divided into two grades, in that the force of a statement of law is either imperative (that is to say, absolutely binding upon the courts) or simply persuasive. The use of the terms 'primary' and 'secondary' authority, as applied in the concrete sense, must not be confused with the use of the terms 'imperative' and 'persuasive' authority, as used in the abstract sense. That is to say, a book of primary authority may be either imperative or persuasive, according to the circumstances . . . , or it may be of no force at all. Books of secondary authority are, in the nature of things, usually merely of persuasive authority." William M. Lile et al., *Brief Making and the Use of Law Books* 12 (3d ed. 1914).

primary authority. Authority that issues directly from a law-making body; legislation and the reports of litigated cases.

secondary authority. Authority that explains the law but does not itself establish it, such as a treatise, annotation, or law-review article.

5. A source, such as a statute, case, or treatise, cited in support of a legal argument <the brief's table of authorities>.

authority by estoppel. See *apparent authority* under AUTHORITY (1).

authority coupled with an interest. See AUTHORITY (1).

authorize, *vb.* **1.** To give legal authority; to empower <he authorized the employee to act for him>. **2.** To formally approve; to sanction <the city authorized the construction project>. — **authorization,** *n.*

authorized capital. See *nominal capital* under CAPITAL.

authorized capital stock. See *capital stock* (1) under STOCK.

authorized committee. See SPECIAL LITIGATION COMMITTEE.

authorized shares. See *capital stock* (1) under STOCK.

authorized stock. See *capital stock* (1) under STOCK.

autocracy (aw-**tok**-rə-see), *n.* Government by one person with unlimited power and authority; unlimited monarchy. — **autocratic** (aw-tə-**krat**-ik), *adj.* — **autocrat** (**aw**-tə-krat), *n.*

autolimitation, *n.* An authority's establishment of rules that, in effect, limit the authority's own power. — **autolimit,** *vb.*

"The theory of Jellinek (*Allgemeine Staatslehre*), so far as the writer understands it, is not an explanation either. In his view something which he calls the State, not defined, but, as it seems, a group of persons, finds itself in possession of power, and establishes rules. These are the law. This process he calls 'autolimitation.' It is true that a body with supreme power does make law. An autocrat, man or group, without rules, may do justice, though it probably will not, but it does not make law — there is no *Rechtsstaat*. But autolimitation is, as Professor Brierly notes . . . , a contradiction in terms. If the State's power is limited, it must be by some superior power. But even accepting the analysis, we are no better off." W.W. Buckland, *Some Reflections on Jurisprudence* 24 (1945).

automated transaction. A contract formed or performed, in whole or in part, by electronic means or by electronic messages in which either party's electronic actions or messages establishing the contract are not intended to be reviewed in the ordinary course by an individual. UCC § 2A–102(a)(3).

automatic-adjustment clause. A provision in a utility-rate schedule that allows a public utility to increase its rates without a public hearing or state review, if certain operating costs, such as the price of fuel, increase. *Federal Energy Regulatory Comm'n v. Mississippi*, 456 U.S. 742, 102 S.Ct. 2126 (1982).

automatic perfection. See PERFECTION.

automatic stay. See STAY.

automatic suspension. See *automatic stay* under STAY.

automatism (aw-**tom**-ə-tiz-əm), *n.* **1.** Action or conduct occurring without will, purpose, or reasoned intention, such as sleepwalking; behavior carried out in a state of unconsciousness or mental dissociation without full awareness. • Automatism may be asserted as a defense to negate the requisite mental state of voluntariness for commission of a crime. **2.** The state of a person who, though capable of action, is not conscious of his or her actions. — **automaton,** *n.*

"How far is automatism a defence? It has been defined as involuntary action performed in a state of unconsciousness not amounting to insanity. Theoretically the defence is that no act in the legal sense took place at all — the plea is that there was no volition or psychic awareness." George Whitecross Paton, *A Textbook of Jurisprudence* 315 (G.W. Paton & David P. Derham eds., 4th ed. 1972).

ambulatory automatism. Automatism that consists in irresponsible or purposeless wanderings.

automobile exception. An exemption from the requirement of a search warrant, whereby the police may search a vehicle without a warrant when there is probable cause to suspect that the vehicle contains contraband or evidence of a crime. *Carroll v. United States*, 267 U.S. 132, 45 S.Ct. 280 (1925); *California v. Acevedo*, 500 U.S. 565, 111 S.Ct. 1982 (1991).

automobile exclusion. See EXCLUSION (3).

automobile guest statute. See GUEST STATUTE.

automobile insurance. See INSURANCE.

autonomic law (aw-tə-**nom**-ik). The type of enacted law that has its source in various forms of subordinate and restricted legislative authority possessed by private persons and bodies of persons. • Examples are corporate bylaws, university regulations, and the rules of the International Monetary Fund.

autonomous tariff. See TARIFF (2).

autonomy (aw-**tahn**-ə-mee), *n.* **1.** The right of self-government. **2.** A self-governing state. — **autonomous** (aw-**tahn**-ə-məs), *adj.*

autopsy (**aw**-top-see). **1.** An examination of a dead body to determine the cause of death, esp. in a criminal investigation. — Also termed *post-mortem*; *necropsy*. **2.** The evidence of one's own senses.

"To a rational man of perfect organization, . . . the best and highest proof of which any fact is susceptible is the evidence of his own senses. Hence *autopsy*, or the evidence of one's own senses, furnishes the strongest probability and indeed the only perfect and indubitable certainty of the existence of any sensible fact." *Gentry v. McMinnis*, 3 Dana 382 (1835) (as quoted in John H. Wigmore, *A Students' Textbook of the Law of Evidence* 214 (1935)).

autoptic evidence (aw-**top**-tik). See *demonstrative evidence* under EVIDENCE.

autoptic proference (proh-**fər**-ənts). The presentation of an item for inspection by the court. See *demonstrative evidence* under EVIDENCE.

"Yet another form of proof that may present difficulties in defining evidence is what Wigmore calls 'autoptic proference.' By this barbarism, the learned author was referring to those few cases in which it is possible to bring before the jury the material fact itself, rather than evidence of the fact." 22 Charles Alan Wright & Kenneth W. Graham, Jr., *Federal Practice and Procedure* § 5163, at 33 (1978).

autre action pendant (**oh**-trə ak-see-**awn** pah*n*-**dahn**). [Law French] Another action pending. • This phrase was formerly used in pleas of abatement.

autre droit (**oh**-trə **drwah**). [Law French] In right of another. • This phrase describes the manner in which a trustee holds property for a beneficiary.

autrefois (oh-trə-**fwah** *or* **oh**-tər-foyz). [Law French] On another occasion; formerly.

autrefois acquit (ə-**kwit** *or* a-**kee**). A plea in bar of arraignment that the defendant has been acquitted of the offense. — Also termed *former acquittal*. See DOUBLE JEOPARDY.

"Suppose that a transgressor is charged and acquitted for lack of evidence, and evidence has now come to light showing beyond doubt that he committed the crime. Even so, he cannot be tried a second time. He has what is termed, in legal Frenglish, the defence of autrefois acquit. Similarly, if he is convicted, even though he is let off very lightly, he cannot afterwards be charged on fresh evidence, because he will have the defence of autrefois convict. These uncouth phrases have never been superseded, though they might well be called the defence of 'previous acquittal' and 'previous conviction'; and 'double jeopardy' makes an acceptable generic name for both." Glanville Williams, *Textbook of Criminal Law* 24 (1978).

autrefois attaint (ə-**taynt**). *Hist.* A plea in bar that the defendant has already been attainted for one felony and therefore cannot be prosecuted for another.

autrefois convict. A plea in bar of arraignment that the defendant has been convicted of the offense. See DOUBLE JEOPARDY.

autre vie (**oh**-trə **vee**). [Law French] Another's life. See PUR AUTRE VIE; VIE.

auxiliary, *adj.* **1.** Aiding or supporting. **2.** Subsidiary.

auxiliary covenant. See COVENANT (1).

auxiliator (awg-**zil**-ee-ay-tər), *n.* [Latin] *Hist.* A helper; an assistant.

auxilium (awg-**zil**-ee-əm), *n.* [Latin] *Hist.* Aid; esp., compulsory aid such as a tax or tribute to be paid by a vassal to a lord as an incident of the tenure by knight's service.

auxilium ad filium militem faciendum et filiam maritandam (awg-**zil**-ee-əm ad **fil**-ee-əm **mil**-ə-tem fay-shee-**en**-dəm et **fil**-ee-am mar-ə-**tan**-dəm), *n.* [Law Latin] *Hist.* A writ ordering a sheriff to levy a tax toward the knighting of a son and the marrying of a daughter of tenants *in capite* of the Crown.

auxilium curiae (awg-**zil**-ee-əm **kyoor**-ee-I *or* **kyoor**-ee-ee). [Latin] *Hist.* A court order summoning a party to appear and assist a party already before the court.

auxilium regis (awg-**zil**-ee-əm **ree**-jis), *n.* [Latin] *Hist.* The Crown's tax levied for royal use and public service, such as a tax granted by Parliament.

auxilium vice comiti (awg-**zil**-ee-əm **vI**-see **kom**-ə-tI), *n.* [Latin] *Hist.* An ancient tax paid to sheriffs.

avail, *n.* **1.** Use or advantage <of little or no avail>. **2.** (*pl.*) Profits or proceeds, esp. from a sale of property <the avails of the trust fund>.

available for work, *adj.* (Of a person) ready, willing, and able to accept temporary or permanent employment when offered.

availment, *n.* The act of making use or taking advantage of something for oneself <availment of the benefits of public office>. — **avail,** *vb.*

avail of marriage. See VALOR MARITAGII.

aver (ə-**vər**), *vb.* To assert positively, esp. in a pleading; to allege.

average, *n.* **1.** A single value that represents a broad sample of subjects; esp., in mathematics, the mean, median, or mode of a series. **2.** The ordinary or typical level; the norm. **3.** *Maritime law.* Liability for partial loss or damage to an insured ship or its cargo during a voyage; the apportionment of such liability. — **average,** *vb.* & *adj.*

extraordinary average. A contribution by all the parties concerned in a commercial voyage — whether for vessel or cargo — toward a loss sustained by some of the parties in interest for the benefit of all.

general average. Average resulting from an intentional partial sacrifice of ship or cargo to avoid total loss. • The liability is shared by all parties who had an interest in the voyage. — Abbr. GA. — Also termed *gross average*; *general-average contribution*.

> "[G]eneral average refers to certain extraordinary sacrifices made or expenses incurred to avert a peril that threatens the entire voyage. In such a case the party sustaining the loss confers a common benefit on all the parties to the maritime venture. As a result the party suffering the loss has a right — apart from contract or tort — to claim contribution from all who participate in the venture. The doctrine of general average is thus an equitable principle derived from the general maritime law. General average is an exception to the principle of particular average that losses lie where they fall; rather the loss becomes 'general,' meaning that it is spread ratably among all the parties involved in the maritime adventure. The doctrine of general average is of ancient vintage, and can be traced back to remotest antiquity." Thomas J. Schoenbaum, *Admiralty and Maritime Law* § 16–1, at 522–23 (1987).

particular average. Average resulting from an accidental partial loss or damage. • The liability is borne solely by the person who suffered the loss. — Also termed *simple average*; *partial average*.

average bond. See BOND (2).

average cost. See COST (1).

average daily balance. See DAILY BALANCE.

average gross sales. See SALE.

average tax rate. See TAX RATE.

average variable cost. The average cost per unit of output, arrived at by dividing the total cost (fixed cost and variable cost) by output. Cf. LONG-RUN INCREMENTAL COST.

averaging down. *Securities.* An investment strategy in which shares in the same company are purchased at successively lower prices to achieve a lower average cost than the first purchase.

averaging up. *Securities.* An investment strategy in which shares in the same company are purchased at successively higher prices to accumulate an increasingly larger position at an average cost that is lower than the market price. • The investor will earn significant profits only if the stock's price continues to rise.

averment (ə-**vər**-mənt), *n.* A positive declaration or affirmation of fact; esp., an assertion or allegation in a pleading <the plaintiff's averment that the defendant ran a red light>. Cf. ASSEVERATE.

immaterial averment. An averment that alleges something in needless detail; a statement that goes far beyond what is in issue. • This type of averment may be ordered struck from the pleading.

negative averment. An averment that is negative in form but affirmative in substance and that must be proved by the alleging party. • An example is the statement "she was not old enough to enter into the contract," which is more than just a simple denial. Cf. TRAVERSE.

averment of notice. A statement in a pleading that someone else has been properly notified about some fact. See NOTICE.

aviation easement. See *avigational easement* under EASEMENT.

aviation insurance. See INSURANCE.

avigational easement. See EASEMENT.

avigation easement. See *avigational easement* under EASEMENT.

a vinculo matrimonii (ay **ving**-kyə-loh ma-trə-**moh**-nee-I). [Latin] From the bond of matrimony. See *divorce a vinculo matrimonii* under DIVORCE.

avoid, *vb.* To render void <because the restrictive covenant was overbroad, the court avoided it>. • Because this legal use of *avoid* can be easily confused with the ordinary sense of the word, the verb *to void* is preferable.

avoidable-consequences doctrine. See MITIGATION-OF-DAMAGES DOCTRINE.

avoidable cost. See COST (1).

avoidance, *n.* **1.** The act of evading or escaping <avoidance of tax liability>. See TAX AVOIDANCE. **2.** The act of refraining from (something) <avoidance of an argument>. **3.** VOIDANCE <avoidance of the agreement>. **4.** CONFESSION AND AVOIDANCE <the defendant filed an avoidance in an attempt to avert liability>. — **avoid,** *vb.*

avoucher (ə-**vow**-chər). *Hist.* A tenant's calling upon a warrantor of title to the land to help the tenant defend the title.

avowal (ə-**vow**-əl), *n.* **1.** An open declaration. **2.** OFFER OF PROOF. — **avow,** *vb.*

avowant (ə-**vow**-ənt), *n.* A person who makes avowry in an action of replevin.

avowee. See ADVOCATUS.

avowry (ə-**vow**-ree), *n.* *Common-law pleading.* An acknowledgment — in an answer to a replevin action — that one has taken property, and a justification for that taking <the defendant's avowry was based on alleged damage to the property by the plaintiff>. — **avow,** *vb.* Cf. COGNIZANCE (4).

avulsion (ə-**vəl**-shən), *n.* **1.** A forcible detachment or separation. **2.** A sudden removal of land caused by change in a river's course or by flood. • Land removed by avulsion remains the property of the original owner. Cf. ALLUVION; ACCRETION (1); DELICTION; EROSION. **3.** A tearing away of a body part surgically or accidentally. — **avulse,** *vb.*

avunculus (ə-**vəngk**-yə-ləs), *n.* [Latin] *Roman & civil law.* A maternal uncle; one's mother's brother.

avunculus maximus (**mak**-sə-məs). See ABAVUNCULUS.

avus (**av**-əs *or* **ay**-vəs), *n.* [Latin] *Roman & civil law.* A grandfather.

award, *n.* A final judgment or decision, esp. one by an arbitrator or by a jury assessing damages. — Also termed *arbitrament.*

award, *vb.* To grant by formal process or by judicial decree <the company awarded the contract to the low bidder> <the jury awarded punitive damages>.

AWOL. *abbr.* Absent without leave; missing without notice or permission.

axiom (**ak**-see-əm), *n.* An established principle that is universally accepted within a given framework of reasoning or thinking <"innocent until proven guilty" is an age-old axiom of criminal law>. — **axiomatic** (ak-see-ə-**mat**-ik), *adj.*

ayant cause (**ay**-ənt). *Civil law.* One to whom a right has been assigned by will, gift, sale, or exchange; an assignee.

ayel (**ay**-əl). See AIEL.

ayle (ayl). See AIEL.

B. *abbr.* BARON (3).

BA. See *banker's acceptance* under ACCEPTANCE (4).

baby act, pleading the. *Slang.* Asserting a person's infancy as a defense to a contract claim made by a minor.

baby bond. See BOND (3).

Baby Doe. A generic pseudonym for a very young child involved in litigation, esp. in the context of medical care.

Baby FTC Act. A state statute that, like the Federal Trade Commission Act, outlaws deceptive and unfair trade practices.

baby-snatching. See *child-kidnapping* under KIDNAPPING.

BAC. *abbr.* BLOOD ALCOHOL CONTENT.

bachelor. 1. An unmarried man. **2.** The usual title of the first degree that is conferred on a university graduate. **3.** *English law.* A member of one of the orders of chivalry, such as the Order of the Bath. — Also termed (in sense 3) *knight bachelor.*

bachelor of laws. See LL.B.

back, *vb.* **1.** To indorse; to sign the back of an instrument. **2.** To sign so as to show acceptance or approval. **3.** To sign so as to indicate financial responsibility for. **4.** *Hist.* (Of a magistrate) to sign a warrant issued in one county to permit its execution in the signing magistrate's county.

> "[Although] the warrant of the judge of the Court of King's Bench extends over the whole realm, . . . that of a justice of the peace cannot be executed out of his county, unless it be *backed*, that is, indorsed by a justice of the county, in which it is to be carried into execution. It is said, that formerly there ought in strictness to have been a fresh warrant in every fresh county, but the practice of backing warrants has long been observed, and was at last sanctioned by the statute 23 Geo. 2. c. 26. s. 2, and 24 Geo. 2. c. 55." 1 Joseph Chitty, *A Practical Treatise on the Criminal Law* 45 (2d ed. 1826).

backadation. See BACKWARDATION.

backberend (**bak**-ber-ənd). [Old English] *Hist.* **1.** The bearing of stolen goods upon the back or about the person. • *Backberend* is sometimes modernized to *backbearing.* **2.** A person caught carrying stolen goods. — Also spelled *bacberende*; *backberinde.* Cf. HANDHABEND.

> "*Backberinde* signifieth bearing upon the Back, or about a Man. *Bracton* useth it for a Sign or Circumstance of Theft apparent, which the Civilians call *Furtum manifestum* . . . ." Giles Jacob, *A New Law-Dictionary* (8th ed. 1762).

back carry. *Hist.* The crime of carrying, on one's back, unlawfully killed game.

backdate, *vb.* **1.** To put a date earlier than the actual date on (something, as an instrument). • Under UCC § 3–113(a), backdating does not affect an instrument's negotiability. Cf. POSTDATE. **2.** To make (something) retroactively valid.

backhaul allowance. See ALLOWANCE (1).

backing. Endorsement, esp. of a warrant by a magistrate. See BACK (4).

back-in right. *Oil & gas.* A reversionary interest in an oil-and-gas lease entitling an assignor to a share of the working interest after the assignee has recovered specified costs from production.

back lands. Generally, lands lying away from — not next to — a highway or a watercourse.

backpay award. A judicial or quasi-judicial body's decision that an employee or ex-employee is entitled to accrued but uncollected wages or benefits. — Sometimes shortened to *backpay.*

backspread. *Securities.* In arbitrage, a less than normal price difference in the price of a currency or commodity. See ARBITRAGE; SPREAD (3).

back taxes. Taxes that, though assessed for a previous year or years, remain due and unpaid.

back-title letter. A letter from a title insurer advising an attorney of the condition of title to land as of a certain date. • With this information, the attorney can begin examining the title from that date forward.

back-to-back loan. See LOAN.

back-to-work agreement. A contract between a union and an employer covering the terms under which the employees will return to work after a strike.

backwardation. *Securities.* A fee paid by the seller of securities so that the buyer will allow delivery after their original delivery date. — Also termed *backadation*; *inverted market.*

backward integration. See INTEGRATION (4).

backwater. See WATER.

baculus (**bak**-yə-ləs *or* **bak**-ə-ləs). *Hist.* A rod or staff used to symbolize the conveyance of unimproved land. See LIVERY OF SEISIN. See FESTUCA.

bad-boy disqualification. An issuer's disqualification from certain SEC-registration exemptions as a result of the issuer's securities-law violations.

bad-boy provision. *Securities.* A statutory or regulatory clause in a blue-sky law stating that certain persons, because of their past conduct, are not entitled to any type of exemption from registering their securities. • Such clauses typically prohibit issuers, officers, directors, control persons, or broker-dealers from being involved in a limited offering if they have been the subject of an adverse proceeding concerning securities, commodities, or postal fraud.

bad character. A person's predilection toward evil. • In limited circumstances, proof of bad character may be introduced into evidence to discredit a witness. Fed. R. Evid. 608, 609. See *character evidence* under EVIDENCE.

bad check. See CHECK.

bad-conduct discharge. See DISCHARGE (8).

bad debt. See DEBT.

bad-debt loss ratio. The ratio of uncollectible debt to a business's total receivables.

bad-debt reserve. See RESERVE.

bad faith, *n.* **1.** Dishonesty of belief or purpose <the lawyer filed the pleading in bad faith>. — Also termed *mala fides* (**mal**-ə **fɪ**-**deez**).

> "A complete catalogue of types of bad faith is impossible, but the following types are among those which have been recognized in judicial decisions: evasion of the spirit of the bargain, lack of diligence and slacking off, willful rendering of imperfect performance, abuse of a power to specify terms, and interference with or failure to cooperate in the other party's performance." Restatement (Second) of Contracts § 205 cmt. d (1981).

2. *Insurance.* An insurance company's unreasonable and unfounded (though not necessarily fraudulent) refusal to provide coverage in violation of the duties of good faith and fair dealing owed to an insured. • Bad faith often involves an insurer's failure to pay the insured's claim or a claim brought by a third party. **3.** An insured's claim against an insurance company for an unreasonable and unfounded refusal to provide coverage. — **bad-faith,** *adj*. Cf. GOOD FAITH.

badge of fraud. A circumstance that the courts generally interpret as a reliable indicator that a party to a transaction was trying to hinder or defraud the other party, such as a transfer in anticipation of litigation, a transaction outside the usual course of business, or a false statement. See FRAUD.

badge of slavery. 1. Strictly, a legal disability suffered by a slave, such as the inability to vote or to own property. **2.** Broadly, any act of racial discrimination — public or private — that Congress can prohibit under the 13th Amendment.

badger game. A scheme to extort money or some other benefit by catching someone in a compromising position and threatening to make that person's behavior public.

> "The 'badger game' is a blackmailing trick, usually in the form of enticing a man into a compromising position with a woman whose real or pretended husband comes upon the scene and demands payment under threat of prosecution or exposure." Rollin M. Perkins & Ronald N. Boyce, *Criminal Law* 451 (3d ed. 1982).

bad-man theory. The jurisprudential doctrine or belief that a bad person's view of the law represents the best test of what the law actually is because that person will carefully calculate precisely what the rules allow and operate up to the rules' limits. • This theory was first espoused by Oliver Wendell Holmes in his essay *The Path of the Law*, 10 Harv. L. Rev. 457 (1897). In the essay, Holmes maintained that a society's legal system is defined by predicting how the law will affect a person, as opposed to considering the ethics or morals supposedly underlying the law. Under Holmes's theory, the prediction is best made by viewing the law as would a "bad man" who is unconcerned with morals. Such a person is not concerned with acting morally or in accord with a grand philosophical scheme. Rather, that person is concerned with whether and to what degree certain acts will incur punishment by the public force of the law. See LEGAL REALISM. — Also termed *prediction theory*.

bad motive. See MOTIVE.

bad title. See *unmarketable title* under TITLE (2).

baga (**bag**-ə). [Law Latin] *Hist.* A bag or purse, esp. one in which original writs were kept by the Chancery.

bagman. A person who collects and distributes illegally obtained money; esp., an intermediary who collects a bribe for a public official.

bail, *n.* **1.** A security such as cash or a bond; esp., security required by a court for the release of a prisoner who must appear at a future time <bail is set at $500>. Cf. RECOGNIZANCE.

bail absolute. A type of fiduciary bond conditioning a surety's liability on the failure of an estate administrator, executor, or guardian to properly account for estate funds. See *fiduciary bond* under BOND (2).

cash bail. A sum of money (rather than a surety bond) posted to secure a prisoner's release from jail. — Also termed *stationhouse bail*.

civil bail. A bond or deposit of money given to secure the release of a person arrested for failing to pay a court-ordered civil debt. • The bail is conditioned on the payment of the debt.

excessive bail. Bail that is unreasonably high considering both the offense with which the accused is charged and the risk that the accused will not appear for trial. • The Eighth Amendment prohibits excessive bail.

2. Release of a prisoner on security for a future appearance <the court refused bail for the accused serial killer>. **3.** One or more sureties for a criminal defendant <the attorney stood as bail for her client>. See BAILER (1).

"As a noun, and in its strict sense, bail is the person in whose custody the defendant is placed when released from jail, and who acts as surety for defendant's later appearance in court.... The term is also used to refer to the undertaking by the surety, into whose custody defendant is placed, that he will produce defendant in court at a stated time and place." 8 C.J.S. *Bail* § 2 (1988).

bail above. See *bail to the action*.

bail below. See *bail to the sheriff*.

bail common. *Hist.* A fictitious surety filed by a defendant in a (usu. minor) civil action. — Also termed *common bail*; *straw bail*.

"[T]he *Common Pleas* made a distinction between *common* and *special* bail, allowing the former, in cases where the defendant voluntarily appeared to the process, or where the damage expressed in it appeared to be but of a trifling amount, and requiring the latter only, when the plaintiff's demand or the damage he had sustained appeared to be something considerable. In time therefore, in common cases, every defendant took the liberty of offering *John Doe* and *Richard Roe*, for his bail...." 1 George Crompton, *Practice Common-Placed: Rules and Cases of Practice in the Courts of King's Bench and Common Pleas* lxi (3d ed. 1787).

bail to the action. *Hist.* A surety for a civil defendant arrested by a mesne process (i.e., a process issued during the lawsuit). • If the defendant lost the lawsuit, the *bail to the action* was bound either to pay the judgment or to surrender the defendant into custody. — Also termed *bail above*; *special bail*. Cf. *bail to the sheriff*.

bail to the sheriff. *Hist.* A person who pledged to the sheriff that a defendant served with process during a civil action would appear on the writ's return day. — Also termed *bail below*. Cf. *bail to the action*.

"This kind of bail is called bail *to the sheriff*, because given to that officer, and for his security; and bail *below*, because subordinate or preliminary to bail to the action or special bail, which is termed bail *above*." 1 Alexander M. Burrill, *A Law Dictionary and Glossary* 174 (2d ed. 1867).

common bail. See *bail common*.

special bail. See *bail to the action*.

straw bail. See *bail common*.

bail, *vb.* **1.** To obtain the release of (oneself or another) by providing security for future appearance <his parents bailed him out of jail>. **2.** To release (a person) after receiving such security <the court bailed the prisoner>. **3.** To place (personal property) in someone else's charge or trust <bail the goods with the warehouse>.

bailable, *adj.* (Of an offense or person) eligible for bail.

bailable offense. A criminal charge for which a defendant may be released from custody after providing proper security <misdemeanor theft is a bailable offense>.

bailable process. See PROCESS (2).

bail above. See *bail to the action* under BAIL (3).

bail absolute. See BAIL (1).

bail below. See *bail to the sheriff* under BAIL (3).

bail bond. See BOND (2).

bail bondsman. See BAILER (1).

bail common. See BAIL (3).

Bail Court. *Hist.* An ancillary court of Queen's Bench responsible for ensuring that bail sureties were worth the sums pledged (i.e., hearing *justifications*) and handling other procedural matters. • The court was established in 1830 and abolished in 1854. — Also termed *Practice Court*.

bail dock. A small compartment in a courtroom used to hold a criminal defendant during trial.

bailee. A person who receives personal property from another as a bailment. See BAILMENT.

bailee policy. See INSURANCE POLICY.

bail-enforcement agent. See BOUNTY HUNTER.

bailer. 1. One who provides bail as a surety for a criminal defendant's release. — Also spelled *bailor*. — Also termed *bail bondsman*; *bailsman*. **2.** BAILOR (1).

bailiff. 1. A court officer who maintains order during court proceedings. **2.** A sheriff's officer who executes writs and serves processes.

bailiff-errant. *Hist.* A bailiff appointed by the sheriff to deliver writs and other process within a county. Cf. *bailiffs of franchises*.

bailiff of franchises. *Hist.* A bailiff who executes writs and performs other duties in privileged districts that are outside the Crown's (and therefore the sheriff's) jurisdiction. Cf. *bailiff-errant*.

> "*Bailiffs of Franchises* are those who are appointed by every Lord within his Liberty, to do such Offices therein, as the *Bailiff Errant* does at large in the County." Thomas Blount, *Nomo-Lexicon: A Law–Dictionary* (1670).

bailiffs of hundreds. *Hist.* Bailiffs appointed by a sheriff to collect fines, summon juries, attend court sessions, and execute writs and process in the county district known as a *hundred*. See HUNDRED.

bailiffs of manors. *Hist.* Persons appointed to superintend the estates of the nobility. • These bailiffs collected fines and rents, inspected buildings, and took account of waste, spoils, and misdemeanors in the forests and demesne lands.

bound bailiff. *Hist.* A deputy sheriff placed under bond to ensure the faithful performance of assigned duties.

high bailiff. *Hist.* A bailiff attached to a county court, responsible for attending court sessions, serving summonses, and executing orders, warrants, and writs.

special bailiff. *Hist.* A deputy sheriff appointed at a litigant's request to serve or execute some writ or process related to the lawsuit.

bail in error. Security given by a defendant who intends to bring a writ of error on a judgment and desires a stay of execution in the meantime. See *appeal bond* & *supersedeas bond* under BOND (2).

bailivia. See BAILIWICK.

bailiwick (**bay**-lə-wik). The office, jurisdiction, or district of a bailiff; esp., a bailiff's territorial jurisdiction. — Also termed *bailivia*; *baliva*; *balliva*.

> "In the early days a village was called a 'wick.' Each village had a bailiff who was its peace officer. His authority was limited to the territory of the wick. A bailiff was popularly referred to as a 'bailie,' and before long a bailie's wick was expressed as his 'bailiwick.' And in time this word came to be used to indicate the special territory over which a peace officer exercises his authority as such. Although it may be changed by statute, the normal situation is that the bailiwick of a policeman is his city, the bailiwick of a sheriff is his county and the bailiwick of a state officer, such as a member of the Highway Patrol, is the state." Rollin M. Perkins & Ronald N. Boyce, *Criminal Law* 1096 (3d ed. 1982).

bail-jumping, *n.* The criminal offense of defaulting on one's bail. — **bail-jumper,** *n.* — **jump bail,** *vb.* See JUMP BAIL.

bailment. 1. A delivery of personal property by one person (the *bailor*) to another (the *bailee*) who holds the property for a certain purpose under an express or implied-in-fact contract. •

Unlike a sale or gift of personal property, a bailment involves a change in possession but not in title. Cf. PAWN.

> "The customary definition of a bailment considers the transaction as arising out of contract. Thus Justice Story defines a bailment as 'a delivery of a thing in trust for some special object or purpose, and upon a contract express or implied, to conform to the object or purpose of the trust' [Joseph Story, *Bailments* 5 (9th ed. 1878)]. There has, however, been a vigorous dissent to this insistence on the contractual element in bailments. Professor Williston ... defines bailments broadly 'as the rightful possession of goods by one who is not the owner' [4 Samuel Williston, *Law of Contracts* 2888 (rev. ed. 1936)].... It is obvious that the restricted definition of a bailment as a delivery of goods on a contract cannot stand the test of the actual cases. The broader definition of Professor Williston is preferable." Ray Andrews Brown, *The Law of Personal Property* § 73, at 252, 254 (2d ed. 1955).

> "Although a bailment is ordinarily created by the agreement of the parties, resulting in a consensual delivery and acceptance of the property, such a relationship may also result from the actions and conduct of the parties in dealing with the property in question. A bailment relationship can be implied by law whenever the personal property of one person is acquired by another and held under circumstances in which principles of justice require the recipient to keep the property safely and return it to the owner." 8A Am. Jur. 2d *Bailment* § 1 (1997).

actual bailment. A bailment that arises from an actual or constructive delivery of property to the bailee.

bailment for hire. A bailment for which the bailee is compensated, as when one leaves a car with a parking attendant. — Also termed *lucrative bailment*.

bailment for mutual benefit. A bailment for which the bailee is compensated and from which the bailor receives some additional benefit, as when one leaves a car with a parking attendant who will also wash the car while it is parked.

constructive bailment. A bailment that arises when the law imposes an obligation on a possessor of personal property to return the property to its rightful owner, as with an involuntary bailment.

gratuitous bailment. A bailment for which the bailee receives no compensation, as when one borrows a friend's car. • A gratuitous bailee is liable for loss of the property only if the loss is caused by the bailee's gross negligence. — Also termed *naked bailment*; *depositum*; *naked deposit*; *gratuitous deposit*; *deposit*.

involuntary bailment. A bailment that arises when a person accidentally, but without any negligence, leaves personal property in another's possession. • An involuntary bailee who refuses to return the property to the owner can be liable for conversion. — Also termed *involuntary deposit*. See *abandoned property*, *lost property*, *mislaid property* under PROPERTY.

lucrative bailment. See *bailment for hire*.

naked bailment. See *gratuitous bailment*.

2. The personal property delivered by the bailor to the bailee. **3.** The contract or legal relation resulting from such a delivery. **4.** The act of posting bail for a criminal defendant. **5.** The documentation for the posting of bail for a criminal defendant.

bailor (bay-**lor** *or* **bay**-lər). **1.** A person who delivers personal property to another as a bailment. — Also spelled *bailer*. **2.** BAILER (1).

bailout, *n.* **1.** A rescue of an entity, usu. a corporation, from financial trouble. **2.** An attempt by a business to receive favorable tax treatment of its profits, as by withdrawing profits at capital-gain rates rather than distributing stock dividends that would be taxed at higher ordinary-income rates.

bailout stock. See STOCK.

bail piece. *Hist.* A document recording the nature of the bail granted to a defendant in a civil action. • The bail piece was filed with the court and usu. signed by the defendant's sureties. See BAIL (2); RECOGNIZANCE.

bail-point scale. A system for determining a criminal defendant's eligibility for bail, whereby a defendant either will be released on personal recognizance or will have a bail amount set according to the total number of points given, based on the defendant's background and behavior.

bailsman. See BAILER (1).

bail to the action. See BAIL (3).

bail to the sheriff. See BAIL (3).

bait advertising. See BAIT AND SWITCH.

bait and switch. A sales practice whereby a merchant advertises a low-priced product to lure customers into the store only to induce them to buy a higher-priced product. • Most states prohibit the bait and switch when the original product is not actually available as advertised. — Also termed *bait advertising*.

balance, *vb.* **1.** To compute the difference between the debits and credits of (an account) <the accountant balanced the company's books>. **2.** To equalize in number, force, or effect; to bring into proportion <the company tried to balance the ratio of mid-level managers to assembly-line workers>. **3.** To measure competing interests and offset them appropriately <the judge balanced the equities before granting the motion>. — **balance,** *n.*

balanced economy. See ECONOMY.

balanced fund. See MUTUAL FUND.

balance of power. *Int'l law.* A relative equality of force between countries or groups of countries, as a result of which peace is encouraged because no country is in a position to predominate.

balance of probability. See PREPONDERANCE OF THE EVIDENCE.

balance sheet. A statement of an entity's current financial position, disclosing the value of the entity's assets, liabilities, and owners' equity. — Also termed *statement of financial condition*; *statement of condition*; *statement of financial position*. Cf. INCOME STATEMENT.

balance-sheet insolvency. See INSOLVENCY.

balance-sheet test. See *balance-sheet insolvency* under INSOLVENCY.

balancing test. A judicial doctrine, used esp. in constitutional law, whereby a court measures competing interests — as between individual rights and governmental powers, or between state authority and federal supremacy — and decides which interest should prevail.

bale. A package of goods wrapped in cloth and marked so as to be identifiable on a bill of lading.

baliva. See BAILIWICK.

ballistics. 1. The science of the motion of projectiles, such as bullets. **2.** The study of a weapon's firing characteristics, esp. as used in criminal cases to determine a gun's firing capacity and whether a particular gun fired a given bullet.

balliva. See BAILIWICK.

ballivo amovendo (bə-**lı**-voh ay-moh-**ven**-doh). [Latin "a bailiff to be removed"] *Hist.* A writ to remove from office a bailiff who does not have sufficient land in the bailiwick as required by the Statute of Westminster (1285).

balloon note. See NOTE (1).

balloon payment. See PAYMENT.

balloon-payment mortgage. See MORTGAGE.

ballot, *n.* **1.** A small ball or ticket used for indicating a vote. **2.** The system of choosing persons for office by marking a paper or by drawing papers with names on them from a receptacle. **3.** The formal record of a person's vote.

absentee ballot. A ballot that a voter submits, sometimes by mail, before an election. See *absentee voting* under VOTING.

joint ballot. *Parliamentary practice.* A vote by legislators of both houses sitting together as one body.

secret ballot. A vote cast in such a way that the person voting cannot be identified.

> "The secret ballot, when used to protect citizens when choosing their representatives, is a hallmark of a democratic system of government; but, when it is used to conceal a public official's vote, it violates the fundamental tenet of an elected or appointed official's ultimate accountability to the electorate." Op. Tex. Att'y Gen. H–1163 (1978).

4. A list of candidates running for office. — **ballot,** *vb.*

Australian ballot. A ballot characterized by a variety of safeguards designed to maintain secrecy in voting. • Australian ballots are widely used in various forms in the United States.

Massachusetts ballot. A ballot in which, under each office, the names of candidates and party designations are printed in alphabetical order. • This is a type of Australian ballot.

office-block ballot. A ballot that lists the candidates' names under the title of the office sought without mentioning the candidates' party affiliations.

party-column ballot. A ballot that lists the candidates' names in separate columns by political party regardless of the offices sought by the candidates.

ballot box. A locked box into which ballots are deposited.

ban, *n.* **1.** *Hist.* A public proclamation or summons. • *Bans* dealt with a variety of matters, such as the calling to arms of a lord's vassals or the proclamation that an offender was henceforth to be considered an outlaw. **2.** *Eccles. law.* An authoritative ecclesiastical prohibition; an interdiction. **3.** BANNS OF MATRIMONY. — Also spelled *bann.*

ban, *vb.* To prohibit, esp. by legal means.

banc (bangk *or* bongk). [French] Bench. See EN BANC.

banco (**bang**-koh). **1.** A seat or bench of justice. See EN BANC. **2.** A tract of land cut off by the shifting of a river's course; esp., land that has become cut off in such a manner from the country it originally belonged to. See AVULSION (2).

bancus (**bang**-kəs). [Law Latin "bench"] *Hist. English law.* A court or tribunal.

bancus reginae (**bang**-kəs rə-**jɪ**-nee). See QUEEN'S BENCH.

bancus regis (**bang**-kəs **ree**-jəs). See KING'S BENCH.

bancus superior (**bang**-kəs sə-**peer**-ee-ər). Upper bench. • The King's Bench was so called during the Protectorate (1653–1659). — Abbr. b.s. — Also termed *bancus publicus* ("public bench").

B and E. *abbr.* Breaking and entering. See BURGLARY (2).

bane. *Hist.* A malefactor or murderer; a person whose criminal act calls for the raising of the hue and cry.

banish. See EXILE.

bank. 1. A financial establishment for the deposit, loan, exchange, or issue of money and for the transmission of funds; esp., a member of the Federal Reserve System. • Under securities law, a bank includes any banking institution, whether or not incorporated, doing business under federal or state law, if a substantial portion of the institution's business consists of receiving deposits or exercising fiduciary powers similar to those permitted to national banks and if the institution is supervised and examined by a state or federal banking authority; or a receiver, conservator, or other liquidating agent of any of the above institutions. 15 USCA § 78c(a)(6). **2.** The office in which such an establishment conducts transactions.

"A bank is a quasi public institution, for the custody and loan of money, the exchange and transmission of the same by means of bills and drafts, and the issuance of its own promissory notes, payable to bearer, as currency, or for the exercise of one or more of these functions, not always necessarily chartered, but sometimes so, created to subserve public ends, or a financial institution regulated by law .... A bank is wholly a creature of statute doing business by legislative grace and the right to carry on a banking business through the agency of a corporation is a 'franchise' which is dependent on a grant of corporate powers by the state." 1A *Michie on Banks and Banking* § 2, at 5–6 (1993).

bank for cooperatives. A bank within a system of banks established to provide a permanent source of credit to farmers' cooperatives and supervised by the Farm Credit Administration.

collecting bank. In the check-collection process, any bank handling an item for collection, except for the payor bank or the depositary bank. UCC § 4–105(5).

commercial bank. A bank authorized to receive both demand and time deposits, to engage in trust services, to issue letters of credit, to rent time-deposit boxes, and to provide similar services.

correspondent bank. A bank that acts as an agent for another bank, or engages in an exchange of services with that bank, in a geographical area to which the other bank does not have direct access.

custodian bank. A bank or trust company that acts as custodian for a clearing corporation and that is supervised and examined by a state or federal authority. UCC § 8–102(4).

depositary bank. The first bank to which an item is transferred for collection. UCC § 4–105(2).

drawee bank. See *payor bank.*

Federal Home Loan Bank. See FEDERAL HOME LOAN BANK.

federal land bank. See FEDERAL LAND BANK.

intermediary bank. A bank to which an item is transferred in the course of collection, even though the bank is not the depositary or payor bank. UCC § 4–105(4).

investment bank. A bank whose primary purpose is to acquire financing for businesses, esp. through the sale of securities. • An investment bank does not accept deposits and, apart from selling securities, does not deal with the public at large. See INVESTMENT BANKER.

member bank. A bank that is a member of the Federal Reserve System. — Also termed *reserve bank.* See FEDERAL RESERVE SYSTEM.

mutual savings bank. A bank that has no capital stock and in which the depositors are the owners. See SAVINGS-AND-LOAN ASSOCIATION.

national bank. A bank incorporated under federal law and governed by a charter approved by the Comptroller of the Currency. • A national bank is permitted to use the abbreviation n.a. (national association) as part of its name.

nonbank bank. A financial institution that either accepts demand deposits or makes commercial loans, but, unlike banks, does not do both at the same time and therefore can avoid federal regulations on bank ownership. • Nonbank banks were esp. prolific in the 1980s, but amendments to the definition of a bank under federal law have essentially closed this loophole.

nonmember bank. A bank that is not a member of the Federal Reserve System. See FEDERAL RESERVE SYSTEM.

payor bank. A bank that is requested to pay the amount of a negotiable instrument and, on the bank's acceptance, is obliged to pay that amount; a bank by which an item is payable as drawn or accepted. UCC § 4–105(3). — Also termed *drawee bank*.

presenting bank. A nonpayor bank that presents a negotiable instrument for payment. UCC § 4–105.

private bank. An unincorporated banking institution owned by an individual or partnership and, depending on state statutes, subject to or free from state regulation.

remitting bank. A payor or intermediary bank that pays or transfers an item.

reserve bank. See *member bank*.

respondent bank. A bank, association, or other entity that exercises fiduciary powers, that holds securities on behalf of beneficial owners, and that deposits the securities for safekeeping with another bank, association, or other entity exercising fiduciary powers. SEC Rule 14a–1(k) (17 CFR § 240.14a–1(k)).

savings-and-loan bank. See SAVINGS-AND-LOAN ASSOCIATION.

savings bank. A bank that receives deposits, pays interest on them, and makes certain types of loans, but does not provide checking services.

state bank. A bank chartered by a state and supervised by the state banking department. • For a state bank to have FDIC insurance on deposits, it must become a member of the Federal Reserve System.

bank, *vb.* **1.** To keep money at <he banks at the downtown branch>. **2.** To deposit (funds) in a bank <she banked the prize money yesterday>. **3.** *Slang.* To loan money to facilitate (a transaction) <who banked the deal?>. • The lender's consideration usu. consists of a fee or an interest in the property involved in the transaction.

bankable paper. See PAPER.

bank acceptance. See *banker's acceptance* under ACCEPTANCE (4).

bank account. See ACCOUNT.

bank-account trust. See *Totten trust* under TRUST.

bank bill. See BANKNOTE.

bankbook. See PASSBOOK.

bank charter. See CHARTER (3).

bank credit. See CREDIT (4).

bank discount. The interest that a bank deducts in advance on a note. See DISCOUNT (2).

bank draft. See DRAFT.

banker. A person who engages in the business of banking.

bankerout, *adj. Archaic.* Indebted beyond the means of payment; bankrupt. — Also spelled *bankrout*.

banker's acceptance. See ACCEPTANCE (4).

banker's bill. See *finance bill* under BILL (6).

banker's lien. See LIEN.

bank examiner. A federal or state official who audits banks with respect to their financial condition, management, and policies.

bank for cooperatives. See BANK.

bank fraud. The criminal offense of knowingly executing, or attempting to execute, a scheme or artifice to defraud a financial institution, or to obtain property owned by or under the control of a financial institution, by means of false or fraudulent pretenses, representations, or promises. 18 USCA § 1344.

bank holding company. A company that owns or controls one or more banks. • Ownership or control of 25 percent is usu. enough for this purpose. — Abbr. BHC.

banking. The business carried on by or with a bank.

Banking Act of 1933. See GLASS-STEAGALL ACT.

banking day. **1.** Banking hours on a day when a bank is open to the public for carrying on substantially all its banking functions. • Typically, if the bookkeeping and loan departments are closed by a certain hour, the remainder of that day is not part of that bank's banking day. **2.** A day on which banks are open for banking business.

"'Banking day' is defined in [UCC §] 4–104(1)(c) [now 4–104(a)(3)]. The definition was designed to exclude from the 'banking day' all bank holidays (although some states added specifics on holidays) as well as the portions of a day on which one or more of the substantial departments of the bank closed off their services to the public, even though it remained open for accepting deposits and withdrawing funds as well as continuously processing items for payment or for dispatch. Clearly, when night depositaries came into vogue, their existence did not extend the 'banking day.' The present existence and growing use of so-called 24-hour teller machines also does not extend the banking day. The nature of the banking day is sufficiently tenuous that banks would do well to fix a definite cutoff hour under subsection 4–107(1)." William D. Hawkland, *Uniform Commercial Code Series* § 4–104:01, at 4–43 (1984).

banking game. A gambling arrangement in which the house (i.e., the bank) accepts bets from all players and then pays out winning bets and takes other bettors' losses.

bank night. A lottery in which a prize is awarded to a person (often a theater patron) whose name is drawn randomly from a hopper.

banknote. A bank-issued promissory note that is payable to bearer on demand and that may circulate as money. — Also written *bank note*. — Also termed *bank bill*.

spurious banknote. **1.** A banknote that is legitimately made from a genuine plate but that has forged signatures of the issuing officers, or the names of fictitious officers. **2.** A banknote that is not a legitimate impression from a genuine plate, or is made from a counterfeit plate, but that is signed by the persons shown on it as the issuing officers. — Also termed *spurious bank bill*.

bank rate. See INTEREST RATE.

Bankr. Rep. *abbr.* Bankruptcy Reporter.

bankrupt, *adj.* Indebted beyond the means of payment; insolvent. — Also spelled (archaically) *bankerout*; *bankrout*.

bankrupt, *n.* **1.** A person who cannot meet current financial obligations; an insolvent person. **2.** DEBTOR (2).

cessionary bankrupt. *Archaic.* A person who forfeits all property so that it may be divided among creditors. • For the modern near-equivalent, see CHAPTER 7.

bankruptcy. **1.** The statutory procedure, usu. triggered by insolvency, by which a person is relieved of most debts and undergoes a judicially supervised reorganization or liquidation for the benefit of that person's creditors. • For various types of bankruptcy under federal law, see the entries at CHAPTER. — Also termed *bankruptcy proceeding*; *bankruptcy case*.

"There are two general forms of bankruptcy: (1) liquidation and (2) rehabilitation. Chapter 7 of the Code is entitled 'Liquidation.' The terms 'straight bankruptcy' and 'bankruptcy' often are used to describe liquidation cases under the bankruptcy laws because the vast majority of bankruptcy cases are liquidation cases. In a typical Chapter 7 liquidation case, the trustee collects the nonexempt property of the debtor, converts that property to cash, and distributes the cash to the creditors. The debtor gives up all the nonexempt property she owns at the time of the filing of the bankruptcy petition and hopes to obtain a discharge. Chapters 11, 12, and 13 of the Bankruptcy Code contemplate debtor rehabilitation. In a rehabilitation case, creditors look to future earnings of the debtor, not to the property of the debtor at the time of the initiation of the bankruptcy proceeding, to satisfy their claims. The debtor generally retains its assets and makes payments to creditors, usually from postpetition earnings, pursuant to a court-approved plan." David G. Epstein et al., *Bankruptcy* § 1–5, at 8–9 (1993).

involuntary bankruptcy. A bankruptcy proceeding initiated by creditors (usu. three or more) to force the debtor to declare bankruptcy or be legally declared bankrupt. 11 USCA § 303(b).

voluntary bankruptcy. A bankruptcy proceeding initiated by the debtor. 11 USCA § 301.

2. The fact of being financially unable to pay one's debts and meet one's obligations; insolvency. — Also termed *failure to meet obli-*

gations. **3.** The status of a party who has declared bankruptcy under a bankruptcy statute. **4.** The fact of having declared bankruptcy under a bankruptcy statute. **5.** The field of law dealing with the rights and entitlements of debtors and creditors in bankruptcy.

Bankruptcy Act. The Bankruptcy Act of 1898, which governed bankruptcy cases filed before October 1, 1979.

bankruptcy case. See BANKRUPTCY (1).

bankruptcy clause. See IPSO FACTO CLAUSE.

Bankruptcy Code. The Bankruptcy Reform Act of 1978 (as amended and codified in 11 USCA), which governs bankruptcy cases filed on or after October 1, 1979.

Bankruptcy Court. 1. A U.S. district court that is exclusively concerned with administering bankruptcy proceedings. **2.** The bankruptcy judges within a given district, considered as making up a court that is a subunit of a U.S. district court.

bankruptcy estate. A debtor's legal and equitable interests in property as of the commencement of a bankruptcy case.

bankruptcy judge. A judicial officer appointed by a U.S. Court of Appeals to preside over a bankruptcy court in a designated judicial district for a term of 14 years. • A bankruptcy judge is called an Article II judge. 28 USCA §§ 151 et seq. See ARTICLE II JUDGE.

bankruptcy plan. A detailed program of action formulated by a debtor or its creditors to govern the debtor's rehabilitation, continued operation or liquidation, and payment of debts. • The bankruptcy court and creditors must approve the plan before it is implemented. — Often shortened to *plan.* — Also termed *plan of reorganization* (for Chapter 11); *plan of rehabilitation* (for Chapter 13). See ARRANGEMENT WITH CREDITORS.

bankruptcy proceeding. 1. BANKRUPTCY (1). **2.** Any judicial or procedural action (such as a hearing) related to a bankruptcy.

bankruptcy-remote entity. A business, usu. a special-purpose entity, established to perform limited functions and to have one or a few primary creditors. • This type of entity is sometimes established to protect lenders on large, complex projects, when the lender is to be paid solely or almost exclusively out of the money generated when the project becomes operational. This business is established to have no function other than to develop, own, and operate the project, and to have no principal creditors other than the project lenders. In this way, the lenders have additional protection because there are fewer creditors to compete for the money generated by the project, and there is less likelihood that the project will be forced into bankruptcy. A bankruptcy-remote entity will sometimes issue securities instead of just receiving a direct loan. See SINGLE-PURPOSE PROJECT; SPECIAL-PURPOSE ENTITY; *project financing* under FINANCING.

bankruptcy trustee. The person appointed by the U.S. Trustee and approved by the bankruptcy court to take charge of and administer the debtor's estate during bankruptcy proceedings. — Also termed *trustee in bankruptcy.* See UNITED STATES TRUSTEE.

Bank Secrecy Act of 1970. A federal law requiring banks to maintain records of all transactions with depositors and to report to the U.S. Treasury all deposits of more than $10,000.

bank statement. See STATEMENT OF ACCOUNT (1).

bank-statement rule. *Commercial law.* The principle that if a bank customer fails to examine a bank statement within a reasonable time (usu. no more than a year for a forged drawer's signature or alteration, and no more than three years for a forged indorsement), the customer is precluded from complaining about a forgery or material alteration. UCC § 4–406.

bannitio (bə-**nish**-ee-oh *or* ba-). [Law Latin] *Hist.* Expulsion by a ban or public proclamation; banishment. See EXILE; BAN (1).

bannitus (**ban**-ə-təs). [Law Latin] *Hist.* A person under a ban; an outlaw. See BAN (1).

banns of matrimony. *Hist.* Public notice of an intended marriage. • The notice was given to ensure that objections to the marriage would be voiced before the wedding. — Also spelled *bans of matrimony.*

bar, *n.* **1.** In a courtroom, the railing that separates the front area, where the judge, court personnel, lawyers, and witnesses conduct court business, from the back area, which provides seats for observers; by extension, a similar railing in a legislative assembly <the spectator stood behind the bar>. **2.** The whole body of lawyers qualified to practice in a given court or jurisdiction; the legal profession, or an organized subset of it <the attorney's outrageous misconduct disgraced the bar>. See BAR ASSOCIATION.

integrated bar. A bar association in which membership is a statutory requirement for the practice of law. — Also termed *unified bar*.

specialty bar. A voluntary bar association for lawyers with special interests, specific backgrounds, or common practices.

voluntary bar. A bar association that lawyers need not join to practice law.

3. A particular court or system of courts <case at bar>. ● Originally, *case at bar* referred to an important case tried "at bar" at the Royal Courts of Justice in London. **4.** BAR EXAMINATION <Pendarvis passed the bar>. **5.** A preventive barrier to or the destruction of a legal action or claim; the effect of a judgment for the defendant <a bar to any new lawsuit>. Cf. MERGER (5). **6.** A plea arresting a lawsuit or legal claim <the defendant filed a bar>. See *plea in bar* under PLEA.

bar, *vb.* To prevent, esp. by legal objection <the statute of limitations barred the filing of the stale claims>.

bar association. An organization of members of the legal profession <several state bar associations sponsor superb CLE programs>. See BAR (2).

state bar association. An association or group of attorneys that have been admitted to practice law in a given state. ● State bar associations are usu. created by statute, and membership is often mandatory for those who practice law in the state. Unlike voluntary, professional-development bar associations such as the American Bar Association, state bar associations often have the authority to regulate the legal profession, by undertaking such matters as disciplining attorneys and bringing lawsuits against those who participate in the unauthorized practice of law.

bareboat charter. See CHARTER (4).

barebones indictment. See INDICTMENT.

bare license. See LICENSE.

bare licensee. See LICENSEE.

bare ownership. See *trust ownership* under OWNERSHIP.

bare possibility. See *naked possibility* under POSSIBILITY.

bare promise. See *gratuitous promise* under PROMISE.

bare trustee. See TRUSTEE (1).

bar examination. A written test that a person must pass before being licensed to practice law. ● The content and format of bar examinations vary from state to state. — Often shortened to *bar*.

Multistate Bar Examination. A part of every state's bar examination given in the form of a multiple-choice test covering broad legal subjects, including constitutional law, contracts, criminal law, evidence, property, and torts. — Abbr. MBE.

bar examiner. One appointed by the state to test applicants (usu. law graduates) by preparing and administering the bar examination.

bargain, *n.* An agreement between parties for the exchange of promises or performances. ● A bargain is not necessarily a contract because the consideration may be insufficient or the transaction may be illegal. — **bargain,** *vb.*

> "A bargain is an agreement of two or more persons to exchange promises, or to exchange a promise for a performance. Thus defined, 'bargain' is at once narrower than 'agreement' in that it is not applicable to all agreements, and broader than 'contract,' since it includes a promise given in exchange for insufficient consideration. It also covers transactions which the law refuses to recognize as contracts because of illegality." Samuel Williston, *A Treatise on the Law of Contracts* § 2A, at 7 (Walter H.E. Jaeger ed., 3d ed. 1957).

bargain and sale. A written agreement for the sale of land whereby the buyer would give valuable consideration (recited in the agreement) without having to enter the land and perform livery of seisin, so that the parties equitably "raised a use" in the buyer. ● The result of the bargain and sale was to leave the legal estate in fee simple in the seller and to create an equitable estate in fee simple in the buyer.

bargain-and-sale deed. See DEED.

bargainee. The buyer in a bargained-for exchange.

bargaining agent. See AGENT.

bargaining unit. A group of employees authorized to engage in collective bargaining on behalf of all the employees of a company or an industry sector.

bargain money. See EARNEST MONEY.

bargainor (bahr-gən-**or** *or* **bahr**-gə-nər). The seller in a bargained-for exchange.

bargain purchase. See BARGAIN SALE.

bargain sale. A sale of property for less than its fair market value. • For tax purposes, the difference between the sale price and the fair market value must be taken into account. And bargain sales between family members may lead to gift-tax consequences. — Also termed *bargain purchase*.

bargain theory of consideration. The theory that a promise in exchange for a promise is sufficient consideration for a contract. • This theory underlies all bilateral contracts. See *bilateral contract* under CONTRACT.

> "We saw earlier that classical contract theory tended to associate the doctrine of consideration with the concept of bargain. The emphasis of classical law shifted away from actual benefits and detriments to the mutual promises which constitute a wholly executory contract. American lawyers developed from this trend a 'bargain theory of consideration' and similarly in English law a more modern basis for the doctrine of consideration was found by some lawyers in the notion that a contract is a bargain in which the consideration is the price of the bargain. Allied to this is the supposed rule that nothing can be treated as a consideration unless it is seen by the parties as the 'price' of the bargain." P.S. Atiyah, *An Introduction to the Law of Contract* 119 (3d ed. 1981).

barometer stock. See STOCK.

baron. 1. *Hist.* A man holding land directly from the Crown in exchange for military service. **2.** *Hist.* A husband. See BARON ET FEME. **3.** One of the judges of the English or Scottish Courts of Exchequer. — Abbr. B. See BARONS OF THE EXCHEQUER. **4.** A noble rank; specif., the lowest rank in the British peerage. **5.** Generally, a lord or nobleman.

barones scaccarii. See BARONS OF THE EXCHEQUER.

baronet. *Hist.* A non-noble hereditary title that descends in the male line only. • Baronets originated in 1611 when James I began selling the title as a way to raise revenue.

baron et feme (**bar**-ən ay **fem**). [Law French] *Hist.* Husband and wife. See COVERTURE; FEME COVERT.

baronial court. *Hist.* A feudal court established by the owner of extensive lands held directly of the king under military tenure.

Baron Parke's rule. See GOLDEN RULE.

Barons of the Exchequer. *Hist.* The six judges of the Court of Exchequer. • After the 1873 transfer of the Court's jurisdiction to the High Court of Justice, the judges were known as *justices of the High Court*. — Also termed *barones scaccarii*. See COURT OF EXCHEQUER.

barony (**bar**-ən-ee). See TENURE (2).

barra (**bah**-rə). [Law French "bar"] *Hist.* **1.** See *plea in bar* under PLEA. **2.** A barrister. — Also spelled *barre*.

barrator (**bar**-ə-tər), *n.* A fomenter of quarrels and lawsuits; one who excites dissension and litigation among people. — Also spelled *barretor*. Cf. CHAMPERTOR.

> "*Barrator* or *Barater* (Fr. *Barateur*, a Deceiver) Is a common mover or maintainer of Suits, Quarrels, or Parts, either in Courts or elswhere in the Country, and is himself never quiet, but at variance with one or other." Thomas Blount, *Nomo-Lexicon: A Law-Dictionary* (1670).

barratry (**bar**-ə-tree *or* **bair**-), *n.* **1.** Vexatious incitement to litigation, esp. by soliciting potential legal clients. • Barratry is a crime in most jurisdictions. **2.** *Maritime law.* Fraudulent or grossly negligent conduct (by a master or crew) that is prejudicial to a shipowner. **3.** The buying or selling of ecclesiastical or governmental positions. — **barratrous** (**bar**-ə-trəs), *adj.*

barrier to entry. An economic factor that makes it difficult for a business to enter a market and compete with existing suppliers.

> "Strictly speaking, a barrier to entry is a condition that makes the long-run costs of a new entrant into a market higher than the long-run costs of the existing firms in the market; a good example is a regulatory limitation on entry. The term is also used, more questionably, as a synonym for heavy start-up costs." Richard A. Posner, *Economic Analysis of Law* § 10.8, at 227 (2d ed. 1977).

barring of entail. The freeing of an estate from the limitations imposed by an entail and permitting its free disposition. • This was anciently done by means of a fine or common recovery, but later by deed in which the tenant and next heir join. — Also termed *breaking of entail*. See ENTAIL.

barrister (**bar**-is-tər), *n*. In England or Northern Ireland, a lawyer who is admitted to plead at the bar and who may argue cases in superior courts. — **barristerial** (bar-ə-**steer**-ee-əl), *adj*. Cf. SOLICITOR (4).

inner barrister. **1.** QUEEN'S COUNSEL. **2.** A student member of an Inn of Court.

outer barrister. A barrister called to the bar, but not called to plead from within it, as a Queen's Counsel or (formerly) serjeant-at-law is permitted to do; a barrister belonging to the outer bar. — Also termed *utter barrister*. See OUTER BAR.

vacation barrister. A counselor who, being newly called to the bar, is to attend for six long vacations the exercises of the house.

barter, *n*. The exchange of one commodity for another without the use of money. — **barter,** *vb*.

base court. See COURT.

base estate. See ESTATE.

base fee. See FEE (2); *fee simple determinable* under FEE SIMPLE.

baseline. *Int'l law.* The line that divides the land from the sea, by which the extent of a coastal jurisdiction is measured.

basement court. *Slang.* A low-level court of limited jurisdiction, such as a police court, traffic court, municipal court, or small-claims court.

base-point pricing. A freight-charge calculation based on the distance from a geographical location that differs from the goods' shipment point of origin (often where a major competitor is located). • The purpose is to reduce freight charges and enhance the shipper's competitive position, or to have customers incur freight charges not paid by the seller.

base service. *Hist.* Work of an agricultural nature performed by a villein tenant in exchange for permission from the lord to hold the land. Cf. KNIGHT SERVICE.

base tenure. See TENURE.

basic crops. See CROPS.

basic-form policy. See INSURANCE POLICY.

basic norm. See NORM.

basic patent. See PATENT (3).

Basilica (bə-**sil**-i-kə). A 60-book Greek summary of Justinian's *Corpus Juris Civilis*, with comments (*scholia*). • The *Basilica* ("royal law") was begun by the Byzantine emperor Basil I, and it served as a major source of the law of the Eastern Empire from the early 10th century until Constantinople's fall in 1453.

basis. 1. A fundamental principle; an underlying condition. **2.** *Tax.* The value assigned to a taxpayer's investment in property and used primarily for computing gain or loss from a transfer of the property. • When the assigned value represents the cost of acquiring the property, it is also called *cost basis*. — Also termed *tax basis*. Pl. **bases.**

adjusted basis. Basis increased by capital improvements and decreased by depreciation deductions.

> "[I]t is well to consider the word 'adjusted' in the term 'adjusted basis.' Often, after property is acquired, certain adjustments (increases or decreases to the dollar amount of the original basis) must be made. After these adjustments, the property then has an 'adjusted basis.' " Michael D. Rose & John C. Chommie, *Federal Income Taxation* § 6.04, at 300 (3d ed. 1988).

adjusted cost basis. Basis resulting from the original cost of an item plus capital additions minus depreciation deductions.

carryover basis. The basis of property transferred by gift or in trust, equaling the transferor's basis. — Also termed *substituted basis*.

stepped-up basis. The basis of property transferred by inheritance. • Stepped-up basis equals the fair market value of property on the date of the decedent's death (or on the alternate valuation date).

substituted basis. **1.** The basis of property transferred in a tax-free exchange or other specified transaction. **2.** See *carryover basis*.

basis point. One-hundredth of 1%; .01%. • Basis points are used in computing investment yields (esp. of bonds) and in apportioning costs and calculating interest rates in real-estate transactions.

Basket Clause. See NECESSARY AND PROPER CLAUSE.

basse justice (**bahs** zhoo-**stees**). [Latin "low justice"] *Hist.* A feudal lord's right to personally try a person charged with a minor offense.

bastard. **1.** ILLEGITIMATE CHILD. **2.** A child born to a married woman whose husband could not possibly be the father.

bastard eisne. See EISNE.

bastardy. See ILLEGITIMACY.

bastardy proceeding. See PATERNITY SUIT.

batable ground (**bay**-tə-bəl). Land of uncertain ownership. • *Batable* (or *debatable*) *ground* originally referred to certain lands on the border of England and Scotland before the 1603 union of the two kingdoms.

bathtub conspiracy. See *intra-enterprise conspiracy* under CONSPIRACY.

Batson **challenge.** See CHALLENGE (1).

battered-child syndrome. The medical and psychological condition of a child who has suffered continuing injuries that could not be accidental and are therefore presumed to have been inflicted by someone close to the child.

battered-woman syndrome. The medical and psychological condition of a woman who has suffered physical, sexual, or emotional abuse at the hands of a spouse or lover. • This syndrome is sometimes proposed as a defense to justify a woman's killing of a man. — Sometimes (more specifically) termed *battered-wife syndrome*; (more broadly) *battered-spouse syndrome*.

battery, *n.* **1.** *Criminal law.* The application of force to another, resulting in harmful or offensive contact. • It is a misdemeanor under most modern statutes. — Also termed *criminal battery.*

> "Criminal battery, sometimes defined briefly as the unlawful application of force to the person of another, may be divided into its three basic elements: (1) the defendant's conduct (act or omission); (2) his 'mental state,' which may be an intent to kill or injure, or criminal negligence, or perhaps the doing of an unlawful act; and (3) the harmful result to the victim, which may be either a bodily injury or an offensive touching." Wayne R. LaFave & Austin W. Scott, Jr., *Criminal Law* § 7.15, at 685 (2d ed. 1986).

aggravated battery. A criminal battery accompanied by circumstances that make it more severe, such as the use of a deadly weapon or the fact that the battery resulted in serious bodily harm.

sexual battery. The forced penetration of or contact with another's sexual organs or the sexual organs of the perpetrator. See RAPE.

simple battery. A criminal battery not accompanied by aggravating circumstances and not resulting in serious bodily harm.

2. *Torts.* An intentional and offensive touching of another without lawful justification. — Also termed *tortious battery.* — **batter,** *vb.* Cf. ASSAULT.

battle of the forms. The conflict between the terms of standard forms exchanged between a buyer and a seller during contract negotiations. • UCC § 2–207 attempts to resolve battles of the forms by abandoning the common-law requirement of mirror-image acceptance and providing that an acceptance with additional terms is normally valid. — Also termed *UCC battle of the forms.* See MIRROR-IMAGE RULE.

> "The rules of offer and acceptance are difficult to apply in certain circumstances known as the 'battle of the forms' where parties want to enter into a contract, but jockey for position in an attempt to use the rules of law so as to ensure that the contract is on terms of their choosing." P.S. Atiyah, *An Introduction to the Law of Contract* 54 (3d ed. 1981).

batture (bə-**tyoor** *or* ba-**toor**). [French] Soil, stone, or other material that builds under water and may or may not break the surface. • If batture builds against a bank and breaks the surface, it becomes alluvion. See ALLUVION (2).

bawd. *Archaic.* A person, usu. a woman, who solicits customers for a prostitute; a madam. See DISORDERLY HOUSE (2). Cf. PIMP.

bawdy house. See DISORDERLY HOUSE.

bay. *Int'l law.* An inlet of the sea, over which the coastal country exercises its jurisdiction to enforce its environmental, immigration, and customs laws.

historic bay. A bay that, because of its shape, would not be considered a bay subject to the coastal country's jurisdiction, except for that country's long-standing unilateral claim over it; a bay over which the coastal country has traditionally asserted and maintained dominion.

BCD. See *bad-conduct discharge* under DISCHARGE.

BCD special court-martial. See COURT-MARTIAL.

beadle (**beed**-əl). **1.** *Hist.* A court crier with duties similar to those of a constable. **2.** *Hist. Eccles. law.* A minor parish officer who serves the vestry's needs in various ways, including giving notice of the vestry's meetings, executing its orders, and attending its inquests. **3.** A macebearer at Oxford University or Cambridge University. — Also spelled *bedel.*

beak. *BrE Slang.* A magistrate or justice of the peace.

bean counter. *Slang.* A person who makes decisions using numerical calculations; esp., an accountant.

bear, *vb.* **1.** To support or carry <bear a heavy load>. **2.** To produce as yield <bear interest>. **3.** To give as testimony <bear witness>.

bear drive. See BEAR RAID.

bearer. One who possesses a negotiable instrument marked "payable to bearer" or indorsed in blank.

bearer bond. See BOND (3).

bearer document. See *bearer paper* under PAPER.

bearer instrument. See *bearer paper* under PAPER.

bearer paper. See PAPER.

bearer security. See SECURITY.

bear hug. *Slang.* A takeover offer that is much higher than the target company's market value.

bear market. See MARKET.

bear raid. *Slang.* High-volume stock selling by a large trader in an effort to drive down a stock price in a short time. • Bear raids are prohibited by federal law. — Also termed *bear drive.*

beat, *n.* **1.** A law-enforcement officer's patrol territory. **2.** A colloquial term for the principal county subdivision in some southern states, such as Alabama, Mississippi, and South Carolina. **3.** A voting precinct.

beaupleader (boh-**plee**-dər). [Law French "fair pleading"] *Hist.* **1.** A fine imposed for bad or unfair pleading. **2.** A writ of prohibition that prevented a sheriff from taking a fine for bad pleading. • The Statute of Marlbridge (1267) prohibited the taking of fines for this type of pleading. See WRIT OF PROHIBITION.

beauty contest. *Slang.* A meeting at which a major client interviews two or more law firms to decide which firm will get its business.

before-and-after theory. *Antitrust.* A method of determining damages for lost profits (and sometimes overcharges), whereby the plaintiff's profits are examined before, during, and after the violation to estimate the reduction in profits due to the defendant's violation. — Also termed *before-and-after method.* Cf. YARDSTICK THEORY; MARKET-SHARE THEORY.

> "In its simplest form, the [before-and-after] theory looks at the plaintiff's net profits before and after the injury period, discounts all dollars to their present value, and gives the plaintiff a sum that, before trebling, will bring its earnings during the injury period up to the same average level as its earnings during the noninjury periods." Herbert Hovenkamp, *Economics and Federal Antitrust Law* § 16.7, at 450 (1985).

before the fact. Prior to an event of legal significance.

behavioral science. The body of disciplines (psychology, sociology, anthropology) that study human behavior.

behoof, *n. Archaic.* A use, profit, or advantage that is part of a conveyance <to his use and behoof>. — **behoove,** *vb.*

belief-action distinction. *Constitutional law.* In First Amendment law, the Supreme Court's distinction between allowing a person to follow any chosen belief and allowing the state to intervene if necessary to protect others from the practices of that belief.

belief-cluster. In critical legal studies, a group of unconnected ideas or opinions that appear to be related when considered together in reference to a specific subject, such as racism, sexism, or religious intolerance.

belligerency. *Int'l law.* **1.** The status assumed by a nation that wages war against another nation. **2.** The quality of being belligerent; the act or state of waging war.

belligerent, *n.* A country involved in a war or other hostile action. — **belligerent,** *adj.* Cf. NEUTRAL.

bellum (**bel**-əm). [Latin] See WAR (1).

bellum justum (**bel**-əm **jəs**-təm). [Latin] *Int'l law.* A just war; one that the proponent considers morally and legally justifiable, such as a war against an aggressive, totalitarian regime. • Under Roman law, before war could be declared, the *fetiales* (a group of priests who monitored international treaties) had to certify to the Senate that just cause for war existed. Thomas Aquinas and other medieval theologian-jurists debated the circumstances that justified war; some canonists supported the notion of a just war against non-Catholics. Over time, debating the justness of war had little practical effect, and most belligerents now simply declare the validity of their warlike behavior.

bellwether stock. See *barometer stock* under STOCK.

belong, *vb.* **1.** To be the property of a person or thing <this book belongs to the judge>. See OWNERSHIP. **2.** To be connected with as a member <they belong to the state bar>.

below, *adv.* In a lower court <as the court noted below, the defendant's confession was not tape-recorded>. Cf. ABOVE.

below-market loan. See *interest-free loan* under LOAN.

below-the-line, *adj.* (Of a deduction) taken after calculating adjusted gross income and before calculating taxable income. • Examples of below-the-line deductions are medical payments and local taxes. Cf. ABOVE-THE-LINE.

Ben Avon **doctrine.** The principle that due process entitles public utilities to judicial review of rates set by public-service commissions. *Ohio Valley Water Co. v. Borough of Ben Avon*, 253 U.S. 287, 40 S.Ct. 527 (1920).

bench. 1. The raised area occupied by the judge in a courtroom <approach the bench>. **2.** The court considered in its official capacity <remarks from the bench>. **3.** Judges collectively <bench and bar>. **4.** The judges of a particular court <the Fifth Circuit bench>.

bench blotter. See ARREST RECORD (2).

bench conference. See SIDEBAR CONFERENCE (1).

bencher. A governing officer of an English Inn of Court; one of the Masters of the Bench. See INN OF COURT (1).

bench legislation. See JUDGE-MADE LAW (2).

benchmark. A standard unit used as a basis for comparison.

bench memo. 1. A short brief submitted by a lawyer to a trial judge, often at the judge's request. **2.** A legal memorandum prepared by an appellate judge's law clerk to help the judge in preparing for oral argument and perhaps in drafting an opinion. • A trial-court judge may similarly assign a bench memo to a law clerk, for use in preparing for hearing or trial or in drafting an opinion.

bench ruling. An oral ruling issued by a judge from the bench.

bench trial. See TRIAL.

bench warrant. See WARRANT (1).

benefice (**ben**-ə-fis). **1.** *Hist.* A feudal estate in land, held during the life of the tenant. See BENEFICIUM (3).

> "[T]he vassal no longer owns the land, but 'holds' it 'of' the lord — the vassal has become a 'tenant' (from the Latin, 'tenere', to hold). The vassal's interest in the land so held, first called a 'benefice', is now a 'feudum', anglicised in modern law as 'fee.'" Peter Butt, *Land Law* 52 (3d ed. 1996).

2. *Hist. Eccles. law.* An estate held by the Catholic Church in feudal tenure. **3.** An ecclesiastical office such as a bishopric; a preferment.

bénéfice (bay-nay-**fees**). [French "benefit"] *French law.* A benefit or advantage; esp., a privilege given by law rather than by agreement of the parties.

bénéfice de discussion. [French] BENEFIT OF DISCUSSION.

bénéfice de division. [French] BENEFIT OF DIVISION.

bénéfice d'inventaire. [French] BENEFIT OF INVENTORY.

beneficial, *adj.* **1.** Favorable; producing benefits <beneficial ruling>. **2.** Consisting in a right that derives from something other than legal title <beneficial interest in a trust>.

beneficial association. See *benevolent association* under ASSOCIATION.

beneficial enjoyment. See ENJOYMENT.

beneficial holder of securities. A holder of equitable title to corporate stock. • The stock is not registered under the holder's name in the corporation's records.

beneficial interest. A right or expectancy in something (such as a trust or an estate), as opposed to legal title to that thing. • For example, a person with a beneficial interest in a trust receives income from the trust but does not hold legal title to the trust property.

beneficial owner. See OWNER.

beneficial ownership. See OWNERSHIP.

beneficial power. See POWER (4).

beneficial use. See USE (1).

beneficiary (ben-ə-**fish**-ee-er-ee *or* ben-ə-**fish**-ə-ree), *n.* A person who is designated to benefit from an appointment, disposition, or assignment (as in a will, insurance policy, etc.); one designated to receive something as a result of a legal arrangement or instrument. — **beneficiary,** *adj.*

contingent beneficiary. The person designated in a life-insurance policy to receive the proceeds if the primary beneficiary is unable to do so. — Also termed *secondary beneficiary.*

creditor beneficiary. A third-party beneficiary who is owed a debt that is to be satisfied by performing the contract.

direct beneficiary. See *intended beneficiary.*

donee beneficiary. A third-party beneficiary who is intended to receive the benefit of the contract's performance as a gift from the promisee.

favored beneficiary. See FAVORED BENEFICIARY.

incidental beneficiary. A third-party beneficiary who is not intended to benefit from a contract and thus does not acquire rights under the contract. Cf. *intended beneficiary.*

income beneficiary. A person entitled to income from property; esp., a person entitled to receive trust income.

intended beneficiary. A third-party beneficiary who is intended to benefit from a contract and thus acquires rights under the contract as well as the ability to enforce the contract once those rights have vested. — Also termed *direct beneficiary.* Cf. *incidental beneficiary.*

primary beneficiary. The person designated in a life-insurance policy to receive the proceeds when the insured dies.

secondary beneficiary. See *contingent beneficiary.*

third-party beneficiary. A person who, though not a party to a contract, stands to benefit from the contract's performance. • For example, if Ann and Bob agree to a contract under which Bob will render some performance to Chris, then Chris is a third-party beneficiary.

unborn beneficiary. A person named in a general way as sharing in an estate or gift though not yet born.

beneficiary heir. See HEIR.

beneficio primo ecclesiastico habendo (ben-ə-**fish**-ee-oh **pry**-moh ə-klee-z[h]ee-**as**-tə-koh hə-**ben**-doh). [Latin "to have the first ecclesiastical benefice"] *Hist.* A writ from the king to the lord chancellor ordering the appointment of a named person to the first vacant benefice.

beneficium (ben-ə-**fish**-ee-əm). [Latin "benefit"] **1.** *Roman law.* A privilege, remedy, or benefit granted by law, such as the *beneficium abstinendi* ("privilege of abstaining"), by which an heir could refuse to accept an inheritance (and thereby avoid the accompanying debt). **2.** *Hist.* A lease, generally for life, given by a ruler or lord to a freeman. • *Beneficium* in this sense arose on the continent among the German tribes after the collapse of the Roman Empire.

> "All those to whom the Frankish king had given land and to whom the Frankish emperor had granted political authority had received it on certain conditions. They were the recipients of royal favor — a *beneficium.* Their holding came to be so styled." Max Radin, *Handbook of Anglo-American Legal History* 126 (1936).

3. *Hist. English law.* An estate in land granted by the king or a lord in exchange for services.

• Originally, a *beneficium* could not be passed to the holder's heirs, in contrast to *feuds*, which were heritable from an early date. Tenants, however, persisted in attempting to pass the property to their heirs, and over time the *beneficium* became a heritable estate. As this process occurred, the meaning of *beneficium* narrowed to a holding of an ecclesiastical nature. See BENEFICE (1).

> "*Beneficia* were formerly Portions of Land, etc. given by Lords to their Followers for their Maintenance; but afterwards as these Tenures became Perpetual and Hereditary, they left their Name of *Beneficia* to the Livings of the Clergy, and retained to themselves the Name of *Feuds*. And *Beneficium* was an estate in land at first granted for Life only, so called, because it was held *ex mero Beneficio* of the Donor ... [b]ut at Length, by the Consent of the Donor, or his Heirs, they were continued for the Lives of the Sons of the Possessors, and by Degrees past into an Inheritance. . . ." Giles Jacob, *A New Law-Dictionary* (8th ed. 1762).

> "In England from almost, if not quite, the earliest moment of its appearance, the word *feodum* seems not merely to imply, but to denote, a heritable, though a dependent right. But if on the continent we trace back the use of this word, we find it becoming interchangeable with *beneficium*, and if we go back further we find *beneficium* interchangeable with *precarium*. A tenancy at will has, we may say, become a tenancy in fee. . . . The Norman conquest of England occurs at a particular moment in the history of this process. It has already gone far; the words *feum*, *feudum*, *feodum* are fast supplanting *beneficium*. . . ." 1 Frederick Pollock & Frederic W. Maitland, *The History of English Law Before the Time of Edward I* 67–68 (2d ed. 1898).

4. *Hist. Eccles. law.* A feudal tenure for life in church-owned land, esp. land held by a layperson. • Over time, this sense of *beneficium* faded, and it came to be restricted to that of an ecclesiastical living, i.e., a benefice.

> "The pope became a feodal lord; and all ordinary patrons were to hold their right of patronage under this universal superior. Estates held by feodal tenure, being originally gratuitous donations, were at that time denominated *beneficia*: their very name as well as constitution was borrowed, and the care of the souls of a parish thence came to be denominated a *benefice*." 4 William Blackstone, *Commentaries on the Laws of England* 106 (1769).

5. *Hist.* A benefit or favor; any particular privilege, such as benefit of clergy (*beneficium clericale*). **6.** BENEFICE (3).

beneficium abstinendi (ben-ə-**fish**-ee-əm ab-sti-**nen**-dI). [Latin "privilege of abstaining"] *Roman law.* The right of an heir to refuse an inheritance and thus avoid liability for the testator's debts.

> "[T]hese heirs came also to be protected by the praetor, viz. by the *jus* or *beneficium abstinendi*. Provided they took care not to act as heir in any kind of way, then, whether they formally demanded the privilege or not, their own property could not be made liable for their ancestor's debts." R.W. Leage, *Roman Private Law* 220 (C.H. Ziegler ed., 2d ed. 1930).

beneficium cedendarum actionum (ben-ə-**fish**-ee-əm see-den-**day**-rəm ak-shee-**oh**-nəm). [Latin "privilege of having actions made over"] *Roman & Scots law.* The right of a cosurety who might or might not have paid the debt to compel the creditor to give over the right of action against the other cosurety. • Under Scots law, a cosurety's (or *cocautioner's*) right of action against the nonpaying cosurety arises on payment, without the necessity of compelling the creditor to assign the action. But in Roman law, the right of action arose before the paying of the debt.

beneficium competentiae (ben-ə-**fish**-ee-əm kom-pə-**ten**-shi-ee). [Latin "privilege of competency"] *Roman & Scots law.* A debtor's right to be ordered to pay only as much as the debtor reasonably could, so that after assigning his or her estate to creditors, the debtor kept enough to live on. See *assignment for the benefit of creditors* under ASSIGNMENT.

beneficium divisionis (ben-ə-**fish**-ee-əm di-vizh-ee-**oh**-nis). See BENEFIT OF DIVISION.

beneficium inventarii (ben-ə-**fish**-ee-əm in-ven-**tay**-ree-I *or* in-ven-**tair**-ee-I). See BENEFIT OF INVENTORY.

beneficium ordinis (ben-ə-**fish**-ee-əm **or**-də-nis). [Latin "privilege of order"] *Roman & Scots law.* A surety's right to require a creditor to seek payment from the principal debtor before seeking payment from the surety. See BÉNÉFICE DE DISCUSSION.

> "*Beneficium Ordinis* ... by the civil law and our own, a cautioner, simply bound *as such*, is entitled to insist that the principal be first discussed by extreme diligence." Hugh Barclay, *A Digest of the Law of Scotland* 76 (3d ed. 1865).

beneficium separationis (ben-ə-**fish**-ee-əm sep-ə-ray-shee-**oh**-nis). [Latin "privilege of separation"] *Roman law.* The right of a creditor of the deceased to have the property of the deceased separated from an heir's property. • This separation protected the deceased's creditors by ensuring that the deceased's property was not used to pay the heir's creditors.

benefit, *n.* **1.** Advantage; privilege <the benefit of owning a car>. **2.** Profit or gain <a benefit received from the sale>.

fringe benefit. A benefit (other than direct salary or compensation) received by an employee from an employer, such as insurance, a company car, or a tuition allowance. — Often shortened (esp. in pl.) to *benefit.*

general benefit. *Eminent domain.* The whole community's benefit as a result of a taking. • It cannot be considered to reduce the compensation that is due the condemnee.

pecuniary benefit. A benefit capable of monetary valuation.

special benefit. *Eminent domain.* A benefit that accrues to the owner of the land in question and not to any others. • Any special benefits justify a reduction in the amount of damages payable to the owner of land that is partially taken by the government during a public project.

3. Financial assistance that is received from an employer, insurance, or a public program (such as social security) in time of sickness, disability, or unemployment <a benefit from the welfare office>. — **benefit,** *vb.*

benefit association. See *benevolent association* under ASSOCIATION.

benefit certificate. A written obligation to pay a named person a specified amount upon stipulated conditions. • Benefit certificates are often issued by fraternal and beneficial societies.

benefit-of-bargain rule. See BENEFIT-OF-THE-BARGAIN RULE.

benefit of cession. *Civil law.* A debtor's immunity from imprisonment for debt. • The immunity arises when the debtor's property is assigned to the debtor's creditors.

benefit of clergy. 1. At common law, the right of a cleric not to be tried for a felony in the King's Court <in the Middle Ages, anyone who could recite the "neck verse" was granted the benefit of clergy>. • It was abolished in England in 1827 but survived even longer in some American states, such as South Carolina, where it was successfully claimed in 1855. *State v. Bosse*, 42 S.C.L. (3 Rich.) 276 (1855). See NECK VERSE.

> "Benefit of clergy was a remarkable privilege which, although now obsolete, was for centuries of great importance in criminal law. Some knowledge of it is even now essential for a proper understanding of common law crimes. After William the Conqueror separated the ecclesiastical from the secular courts, the clergy put forward the claim that all persons in holy orders should be exempt from secular jurisdiction in all proceedings, civil or criminal. Eventually the rule was established that 'clerks' of all kinds, who committed any of the serious crimes termed felonies, could be tried only in an ecclesiastical court, and therefore were only amenable to such punishments as that court could inflict. Any clerk accused of such crime was accordingly passed over to the bishop's court. He was there tried before a jury of clerks by the oaths of twelve compurgators; a mode of trial which usually ensured him an acquittal." J.W. Cecil Turner, *Kenny's Outlines of Criminal Law* 75 (16th ed. 1952).

> " 'Benefit of clergy,' in its origin, was the right of a clergyman not to be tried for felony in the King's Court. In ancient times, when the Church was at the peak point of its power, it preempted jurisdiction over felony charges against clergymen. It demanded that in any case in which a clergyman was charged with felony, the case be transferred to the Ecclesiastical Court for trial. The benefit was extreme because conviction of felony in the King's Court resulted in the sentence of death, whereas the Ecclesiastical Court did not make use of capital punishment." Rollin M. Perkins & Ronald N. Boyce, *Criminal Law* 4 (3d ed. 1982).

2. Loosely, religious approval as solemnized in a church ritual <the couple had several children without benefit of clergy>.

benefit of discussion. *Civil law.* A guarantor's right to require a creditor to seek payment from the principal debtor before seeking payment from the guarantor. — Also termed *bénéfice de discussion.*

> "*Benefit of Discussion.* By common law a cautioner, bound simply as such, had right to insist that the creditor should *discuss* the principal debtor, that is, exhaust his estate by diligence, before coming upon him for payment of the debt." William K. Morton & Dale A. Whitman, *Manual of the Law of Scotland* 299 (1896).

benefit of division. *Civil law.* A surety's right to be sued only for a part of the debt proportionate to the number of solvent cosureties. — Also termed *bénéfice de division.*

benefit of inventory. *Civil law.* The principle that an heir's liability for estate debts is limited to the value of what is inherited, if the heir so elects and files an inventory of the estate's assets. — Also termed *bénéfice d'inventaire.*

benefit-of-the-bargain damages. See DAMAGES.

benefit-of-the-bargain rule. 1. The principle that a party who breaches a contract must provide the aggrieved party everything the aggrieved party would have received, including profits, had the contract been fully performed. **2.** The principle that a defrauded buyer may recover from the seller as damages the difference between the misrepresented value of the property and the actual value received. — Also termed *benefit-of-bargain rule*. Cf. OUT-OF-POCKET RULE.

benevolent association. See ASSOCIATION.

benevolentia regis habenda (ben-ə-və-**len**-shee-ə **ree**-jis hə-**ben**-də). [Latin "the king's benevolence to be had"] *Hist.* A fine paid to receive the king's pardon and a restoration of place, title, or estate.

benevolent society. See *benevolent association* under ASSOCIATION.

Benthamism. See *hedonistic utilitarianism* under UTILITARIANISM.

Benthamite, *adj.* Of or relating to the utilitarian theory of Jeremy Bentham. See *hedonistic utilitarianism* under UTILITARIANISM.

bequeath (bə-**kweeth**), *vb.* To give property (usu. personal property) by will.

bequest (bə-**kwest**), *n.* **1.** The act of giving property (usu. personal property) by will. **2.** Property (usu. personal property other than money) disposed of in a will. — Also termed *bequeathal* (bə-**kwee**-thəl). Cf. DEVISE; LEGACY.

charitable bequest. A bequest given to a charitable organization. See CHARITABLE ORGANIZATION.

conditional bequest. A bequest whose effectiveness or continuation depends on the occurrence or nonoccurrence of a particular event.

demonstrative bequest. A bequest that, by its terms, must be paid out of a specific source, such as a stock fund.

executory bequest. A bequest of a future, deferred, or contingent interest in personalty.

general bequest. A bequest payable out of the general assets of the estate.

pecuniary bequest. A bequest of money; a legacy. — Also termed *monetary bequest*; *money bequest*.

residuary bequest. A bequest of the remainder of the testator's estate, after the payment of the debts, legacies, and specific bequests. — Also termed *remainder bequest*.

specific bequest. A bequest of a specific item or cash amount.

Berne Convention. An international copyright treaty — drawn up in Berne in 1886 and revised in Berlin in 1908, now administered by the World Intellectual Property Organization — providing that works created by citizens of one signatory nation will be protected in other signatory nations, without the need for local formalities. • The United States ratified the Berne Convention in 1989 and modified several aspects of U.S. copyright law to comply with the treaty's terms.

***Berry* rule.** The doctrine that a defendant seeking a new trial on grounds of newly discovered evidence must show that (1) the evidence is newly discovered and was unknown to the defendant at the time of trial; (2) the evidence is material rather than merely cumulative or impeaching; (3) it will probably produce an acquittal; and (4) the failure to learn of the evidence was not due to the defendant's lack of diligence. *Berry v. State*, 10 Ga. 511 (1851).

bertillon system (**bər**-tə-lon *or* bair-tee-**yawn**). A system of anthropometry once used to identify criminals by measuring and describing them. • The bertillon system is named for Alphonse Bertillon, the French anthropologist who developed the technique early in the 20th century. Fingerprinting has largely replaced the bertillon system. Cf. ANTHROPOMETRY.

bes (bes). [Latin] **1.** *Roman law.* Two-thirds of the Roman *as*, or pound, consisting of eight *unciae* (ounces) out of twelve. See AS; UNCIA. **2.** *Civil law.* Two-thirds of an inheritance.

besayel (bes-**ay**-əl). [Law French] *Hist.* **1.** A writ of right used by a great-grandfather's heirs to recover property held by the great-grandfather. See *assize of mort d'ancestor* under ASSIZE (6). **2.** A great-grandfather. — Also spelled *besaiel*; *besaile*; *bisaile*; *besayle*. Cf. AIEL; COSINAGE.

best bid. See BID (1).

best efforts. Diligent attempts to carry out an obligation <the contractor must use best efforts to complete its work within the stated time>. • As a standard, a best-efforts obligation is stronger than a good-faith obligation. — Also termed *best endeavors*. Cf. *due diligence* (1) under DILIGENCE; GOOD FAITH.

best-efforts contract. See CONTRACT.

best-efforts underwriting. See UNDERWRITING.

best endeavors. See BEST EFFORTS.

best evidence. See EVIDENCE.

best-evidence rule. The evidentiary rule providing that, to prove the contents of a writing (or a recording or photograph), a party must produce the original writing unless it is unavailable, in which case secondary evidence — such as copies, notes, or testimony — may be admitted. Fed. R. Evid. 1001–1004. — Also termed *documentary-originals rule*; *original-writing rule*; *original-document rule*.

> "Down to a century or more ago, the term 'best evidence' was a good deal used; 'the best evidence that the nature of the thing will afford' was said to be required. But this loose expression never represented a concrete rule. The only positive and concrete rules of the kind are those above named. And today, though the cant phrase is sometimes invoked, and though an inference may be made against a party who fails to produce what might be better evidence, yet no court will in general exclude relevant evidence because there might be better evidence available." John H. Wigmore, *A Students' Textbook of the Law of Evidence* 219 (1935).

bestiality (bes-chee-**al**-ə-tee). Sexual activity between a human and an animal. • Some authorities restrict the term to copulation between a human and an animal of the opposite sex. See SODOMY.

best-mode requirement. *Patents.* The requirement that a patent application show the best physical method known to the inventor for using the invention. Cf. ENABLEMENT REQUIREMENT.

bestow, *vb.* To convey as a gift <bestow an honor on another>. — **bestowal,** *n.*

best use. See *highest and best use* under USE.

bet, *n.* Something (esp. money) staked or pledged as a wager.

layoff bet. A bet placed by a bookmaker to protect against excessive losses or to equalize the total amount placed on each side of the wager.

betterment. An improvement that increases the value of real property. See IMPROVEMENT.

betterment act. A statute requiring a landowner to compensate an occupant who improves the land under a mistaken belief that the occupant is the real owner. • The compensation usu. equals the increase in the land's value generated by the improvements. — Also termed *occupying-claimant act*.

beyond a reasonable doubt. See REASONABLE DOUBT.

beyond seas. (Of a person) being absent from a jurisdiction or nation. • Some jurisdictions toll the statute of limitations during a defendant's absence. — Also termed *beyond the seas*; *out of the state*; *ultra mare*.

> "[I]t has been provided that if any person or persons *against* whom there shall be any cause of action shall at the time of its accrual be beyond seas, then the person or persons entitled to any such cause of action shall be at liberty to bring the same against such person or persons within such time as before limited, after his or their return from beyond seas." John Indermaur, *Principles of the Common Law* 240 (Edmund H. Bennett ed., 1st Am. ed. 1878).

b.f. *abbr.* BONUM FACTUM.

BFOQ. *abbr.* BONA FIDE OCCUPATIONAL QUALIFICATION.

BFP. See *bona fide purchaser* under PURCHASER (1).

BHC. *abbr.* BANK HOLDING COMPANY.

bias, *n.* Inclination; prejudice <the juror's bias prompted a challenge for cause>. — **bias,** *vb.* — **biased,** *adj.*

judicial bias. Bias that a judge develops during a trial. • Judicial bias is usu. insufficient to justify disqualifying a judge from presiding over a case. To justify disqualification or recusal, the judge's bias usu. must be personal or based on some extrajudicial reason.

bicameral, *adj.* (Of a legislature) having two legislative houses (usu. called the House of Representatives and the Senate). • The federal government and all states except Nebraska have bicameral legislatures. — **bicameralism,** *n.*

bid, *n.* **1.** A buyer's offer to pay a specified price for something that may or may not be for sale <a bid at an auction> <a takeover bid>.

best bid. The highest auction bid; in the letting of a contract, the lowest bid by a qualified bidder.

bid in. A bid made by the owner of auctioned property to ensure that the property is not sold below actual value.

bid off. To purchase by bid at auction or judicial sale.

upset bid. A bid in a judicial sale made for more than the purchaser's bid so that the sale will be set aside (i.e., upset).

2. A submitted price at which one will perform work or supply goods <the subcontractor's bid>. — **bid,** *vb.* See BID SHOPPING.

competitive bid. A bid submitted in response to public notice of an intended sale or purchase.

firm bid. A bid that, by its terms, remains open and binding until accepted or rejected. • A firm bid usu. contains no unusual conditions that might defeat acceptance.

open bid. A bid that the bidder may alter after submission so as to meet competing bids.

sealed bid. A bid that is not disclosed until all submitted bids are opened and considered simultaneously.

bid and asked. *Securities.* A notation describing the range of prices quoted for securities in an over-the-counter stock exchange. • *Bid* denotes the buying price, and *asked* denotes the selling price. See SPREAD (2).

bid bond. See BOND (2).

bidding up. The act or practice of raising the price for an auction item by making a series of progressively higher bids. • *Bidding up* is unlawful if the bids are made collusively by persons with an interest in raising the bids. Cf. BY-BIDDING.

bid in. See BID (1).

bid off. See BID (1).

bid peddling. See BID SHOPPING.

bid price. See PRICE.

bid quote. *Securities.* The price a broker will pay for a security or commodity.

bid shopping. A general contractor's effort — after being awarded a contract — to reduce its own costs by finding a subcontractor that will submit a lower bid than that used in calculating the total contract price. • If a lower bid is secured, the general contractor will receive a windfall profit because the savings are usu. not passed on to the property owner. The subcontractor whose bid is used in the initial proposal can seek to avoid bid shopping by insisting that it be irrevocably named in the contract as the project's subcontractor.

bid wanted. *Securities.* A dealer's notation that bids are being sought from anyone on a security for sale. • The notation appears in the pink sheets. — Abbr. BW. See PINK SHEET.

biennial session. See SESSION.

biennium (bɪ-**en**-ee-əm). **1.** A two-year period. **2.** The period for which many state legislatures make appropriations.

biens (beenz *or* byenz). [French] *Hist.* Goods; property. • *Biens* includes real property in most civil-law jurisdictions. Cf. BONA.

bifactoral obligation. See OBLIGATION.

bifurcated divorce. See *divisible divorce* under DIVORCE.

bifurcated trial. See TRIAL.

bigamous (**big**-ə-məs), *adj.* **1.** (Of a person) guilty of bigamy. **2.** (Of a marriage) involving bigamy.

bigamus (**big**-ə-məs), *n. Hist.* **1.** One who commits bigamy; a bigamist. **2.** A man who marries a widow, or who remarries. • Under ecclesiastical law, a bigamus could be denied benefit of clergy.

bigamy, *n.* The act of marrying one person while legally married to another. • Bigamy is a criminal offense if it is committed knowingly. — **bigamist,** *n.* Cf. POLYGAMY; MONOGAMY.

big bath. *Slang.* A write-off of significant costs, taken to shed an unprofitable business line or to remove the necessity for future write-offs.

Big Board. 1. The New York Stock Exchange. • This sense of *Big Board* may have derived from the former name of the NYSE — New York Stock and Exchange Board. **2.** A quotation display showing the current prices of securities listed on the New York Stock Exchange.

big pot. See MAIN POT.

bilagines (bɪ-**lay**-jə-neez). [Law Latin] *Hist.* Town bylaws; laws made by a town's inhabitants for their own government.

bilan (bee-**lahn**). [French "balance sheet"] *Civil law.* A book used by bankers and merchants to record all that they owe and all that is owed to them; a balance sheet.

bilanciis deferendis (bə-**lan**-shee-is def-ər-**en**-dis). *Hist.* An obsolete writ ordering a corporation to carry weights to a given place to weigh wool licensed for transportation.

bilateral, *adj.* Affecting or obligating both parties <a bilateral contract>.

bilateral act. See ACT (2).

bilateral contract. See CONTRACT.

bilateral mistake. See *mutual mistake* (1) under MISTAKE.

bilateral monopoly. See MONOPOLY.

bilboes (**bil**-bohz). *Hist.* **1.** A device for punishment at sea consisting of a board with holes that secure an offender's hands and feet. Cf. STOCKS. **2.** An iron bar with sliding shackles for confining the ankles of prisoners, esp. on shipboard.

bill, *n.* **1.** A formal written complaint, such as a court paper requesting some specific action for reasons alleged. **2.** An equitable pleading by which a claimant brings a claim in a court of equity. • Before the merger of law and equity, the bill in equity was analogous to a declaration in law. The nine parts of every equitable bill are (1) the address to the person holding the great seal, (2) the introduction, which identifies the parties, (3) the premises, which state the plaintiff's case, (4) the confederating part, in which the defendants are charged with combination, (5) the charging part, in which the plaintiff may try to overcome defenses that the defendants may allege, (6) the jurisdictional clause, showing that the court has jurisdiction, (7) the interrogating part, inserted to try to compel a full and complete answer, (8) the prayer for relief, and (9) the prayer for process to compel the defendants to appear and answer. — Also termed *bill in equity.* See DECLARATION (7).

> "The statement of the plaintiff's cause of action in equity is called the *bill.* To this bill the defendant (unless he could protect himself by a demurrer or a plea) was obliged to put in an *answer* under oath." George Tucker Bispham, *The Principles of Equity: A Treatise on the System of Justice Administered in Courts of Chancery* § 9, at 12 (11th ed. 1931).

bill for a new trial. A bill in equity to enjoin a judgment and to obtain a new trial because of some fact that would render enforcement of the judgment inequitable. • The fact must have been either unavailable or unknown to the party at trial due to fraud or accident. Cf. MOTION FOR NEW TRIAL.

bill in aid of execution. A bill to set aside a fraudulent encumbrance or conveyance.

bill in perpetuam rei memoriam. See *bill to perpetuate testimony.*

bill in the nature of a bill of review. A postjudgment bill of review filed by a person who was neither a party to the original suit nor bound by the decree sought to be reversed. — Also termed *supplemental bill in nature of bill of review.*

bill in the nature of a bill of revivor. A bill filed when a litigant dies or becomes incapacitated before the litigant's interest in property could be determined. • The purpose of the bill is to resolve who holds the right to revive the original litigation in the deceased's stead.

bill in the nature of a supplemental bill. A bill bringing to court new parties and interests arising from events happening after the filing of the suit. • A *supplemental bill,* in contrast, involves parties or interests already before the court.

bill in the nature of interpleader. A bill of interpleader filed by a person claiming an interest in interpleaded property.

bill of certiorari. A bill in equity seeking removal of an action to a higher court. See CERTIORARI.

bill of complaint. An original bill that begins an action in a court of equity. See COMPLAINT (1).

> "A suit in equity, under the procedure of the English Court of Chancery, which was generally adopted in the American States prior to the code, is instituted by the plaintiff filing a bill of complaint. The plaintiff is usually called the complainant, in the Federal courts the complainant or plaintiff indifferently. The bill is in substance a petition to the chancellor, or judge of the court of equity, setting forth at large the grounds of the suit, and praying the process of the court, its subpoena, to bring the defendant into court and compel him to answer the plaintiff's bill, and, also, for such relief by decree or interlocutory remedy, by way of injunction, etc., as the plaintiff supposes himself entitled to." Edwin E. Bryant, *The Law of Pleading Under the Codes of Civil Procedure* 55 (2d ed. 1899).

bill of conformity. A bill filed by an executor or administrator who seeks the court's guidance in administering an involved estate.

• The bill is usu. filed to adjust creditors' claims.

bill of costs. A certified, itemized statement of the amount of costs owed by one litigant to another.

bill of discovery. A bill in equity seeking disclosure of facts within the adverse party's knowledge. See DISCOVERY.

bill of evidence. A transcript of testimony heard at trial.

bill of exceptions. **1.** A formal written statement — signed by the trial judge and presented to the appellate court — of a party's objections or exceptions taken during trial and the grounds on which they are founded. • These bills have largely been replaced by straight appeals under the Federal Rules of Civil Procedure. See EXCEPTION (1). **2.** In some jurisdictions, a record made to preserve error after the judge has excluded evidence.

bill of foreclosure. A bill in equity filed by a lender to have mortgaged property sold to satisfy all or part of the secured, unpaid debt.

bill of interpleader. An original bill filed by a party against two or more persons who claim from that party the same debt or duty. • The requesting party asks the court to compel the contenders to litigate their rights to establish to whom the debt or duty is due. See INTERPLEADER.

> "The common law offered the stakeholder no relief, in that if he paid in good faith to one claimant, he might nevertheless be sued by and required to pay another claimant. And a judgment at law in favor of one claimant against the stakeholder was no defense to an action against the stakeholder by another claimant. However, in equity the bill or suit of interpleader offers him a remedy in that he may interplead (bring) into one action all of the claimants, turn the money or property over to the court, be himself dismissed from the proceeding, and have the court decide which of the claimants is entitled to the fund or property. . . ." William Q. de Funiak, *Handbook of Modern Equity* § 108, at 241–42 (2d ed. 1956).

bill of peace. An equitable bill filed by one who is threatened with multiple suits involving the same right, or with recurrent suits on the same right, asking the court to determine the question once and for all, and to enjoin the plaintiffs from proceeding with the threatened litigation. • One situation involves many persons having a common claim but threatening to bring separate suits; another involves one person bringing a second action on the same claim.

> "By a bill of peace we are to understand a bill brought by a person to establish and perpetuate a right which he claims, and which, from its nature, may be controverted by different persons, at different times, and by different actions; or, where separate attempts have already been unsuccessfully made to overthrow the same right, and justice requires that the party should be quieted in the right, if it is already sufficiently established; or if it should be sufficiently established under the direction of the court. The obvious design of such a bill is to procure repose from perpetual litigation, and therefore, it is justly called a bill of peace." Joseph Story, *Commentaries on Equity Jurisprudence* § 853, at 567 (W.E. Grigsby ed., 1st English ed. 1884).

> "If there was a dispute as to some right involving a multiplicity of persons (e.g., as to a man's right to take tolls, or to a right of way traversing many estates), a bill of peace could be brought in equity to establish the right and so secure repose from the prospect of incessant or multifarious litigation. Bills of peace have now in practice been superseded by modern procedural provisions for the joinder of parties and for representative actions." Robert E. Megarry & P.V. Baker, *Snell's Principles of Equity* 570 (27th ed. 1973).

bill of review. A bill in equity requesting that a court reverse or revise a prior decree.

bill of revivor. A bill filed for the purpose of reviving and continuing a suit in equity when there has been an abatement of the suit before final consummation. • The most common cause of such an abatement is the death of either the plaintiff or the defendant.

bill of revivor and supplement. A compound of a supplemental bill and a bill of revivor, joined for convenience. • Its distinct parts must be framed and proceeded on separately.

bill quia timet. An equitable bill used to guard against possible or prospective injuries and to preserve the means by which existing rights are protected from future or contingent violations. • It differs from an injunction, which corrects past and present — or imminent and certain — injuries. One example is a bill to perpetuate testimony. See QUIA TIMET.

bill to carry a decree into execution. A bill brought when a decree could not be enforced without further court order due to the parties' neglect or for some other reason.

bill to perpetuate testimony. An original bill to preserve the testimony of a material witness who may die or leave the jurisdiction before a suit is commenced, or to prevent or avoid future litigation. — Also termed *bill in perpetuam rei memoriam*.

bill to suspend a decree. A bill brought to set aside a decree.

bill to take testimony de bene esse (dee *or* də **bee**-nee **es**-ee *also* day **ben**-ay **es**-ay). A bill brought to take testimony pertinent to pending litigation from a witness who may be unavailable at the time of trial.

cross-bill. A bill brought by the defendant against the plaintiff in the same suit, or against other defendants in the same suit, relating to the matters alleged in the original bill.

nonoriginal bill. A bill relating to some matter already litigated by the same parties. • It is an addition to or a continuation of an original bill.

original bill. A bill relating to some matter that has never before been litigated by the same parties having the same interests.

skeleton bill of exceptions. A bill of exceptions that, in addition to the formal parts, contains only the court's directions to the clerk to copy or insert necessary documents into the record for appellate review, but does not contain the actual evidence or trial-court rulings. • For example, the statement "the clerk will insert the official transcript here" is typically a skeleton bill.

supplemental bill. A bill filed for the purpose of adding something to an original bill. • This addition usu. results from the discovery of new facts or from a new understanding of facts after the defendant has put on a defense.

supplemental bill in nature of bill of review. See *bill in the nature of a bill or review.*

3. A legislative proposal offered for debate before its enactment.

appropriation bill. A bill that authorizes governmental expenditures. • The federal government cannot spend money unless Congress has appropriated the funds. U.S. Const. art. I, § 9, cl. 7. See APPROPRIATION (2), (3).

clean bill. A bill that has been changed so much by a legislative committee that it is better to introduce a new bill (a "clean" one) than to explain the changes made.

deficiency bill. An appropriation bill covering expenses omitted from the general appropriation bills, or for which insufficient appropriations were made. • An *urgent deficiency bill* covers immediate expenses usu. for one item, and a *general deficiency bill* covers a variety of items.

engrossed bill. A bill passed by one house of the legislature.

enrolled bill. A bill passed by both houses of the legislature and signed by their presiding officers. See ENROLLED-BILL RULE.

house bill. (*often cap.*) A legislative bill being considered by a house of representatives. — Abbr. H.B.

money bill. See *revenue bill.*

omnibus bill. **1.** A single bill containing various distinct matters, usu. drafted in this way to force the executive either to accept all the unrelated minor provisions or to veto the major provision. **2.** A bill that deals with all proposals relating to a particular subject, such as an "omnibus judgeship bill" covering all proposals for new judgeships or an "omnibus crime bill" dealing with different subjects such as new crimes and grants to states for crime control.

private bill. A bill relating to a matter of personal or local interest only. Cf. SPECIAL LAW.

> "A private Bill is a measure for the interest of some person or class of persons, whether an individual, a corporation, or the inhabitants of a county, town, parish, or other locality, and originates on the motion of some member of the [legislature] in which the Bill is introduced." Courtenay P. Ilbert, *Legislative Methods and Forms* 28 (1901).

public bill. A bill relating to public policy in the whole community.

revenue bill. A bill that levies or raises taxes. • Federal revenue bills must originate in the House of Representatives. U.S. Const. art. I, § 7, cl. 1. — Also termed *money bill.*

senate bill. (*often cap.*) A legislative bill being considered by a senate. — Abbr. S.B.

4. An enacted statute <the GI Bill>. **5.** An itemized list of charges; an invoice <hospital bill>. See FEE STATEMENT.

bill of parcels. **1.** A seller's itemized list of goods and prices, intended to assist a buyer in detecting any mistakes or omissions in a shipment of goods. **2.** INVOICE.

bill payable. See *account payable* under ACCOUNT.

bill receivable. See *account receivable* under ACCOUNT.

bill rendered. See *account rendered* under ACCOUNT.

6. A bill of exchange; a draft <the bank would not honor the unsigned bill>. See DRAFT (1).

advance bill. A bill of exchange drawn before the shipment of the goods.

banker's bill. See *finance bill.*

blank bill. A bill with the payee's name left blank. Cf. DRAFT (1).

domestic bill. **1.** A bill of exchange that is payable in the state or country in which it is drawn. **2.** A bill on which both the drawer and drawee reside within the same state or country. — Also termed (in sense 2) *inland bill of exchange*. Cf. *foreign bill*.

finance bill. A bill of exchange drawn by a bank in one country on a bank in another country for the purpose of raising short-term credit. • Finance bills are often issued in tight money periods, and usu. have maturity dates of more than 60 days. — Also termed *banker's bill*; *working capital acceptance*.

foreign bill. A bill of exchange drawn in one state or country and payable in another. Cf. *domestic bill*.

inland bill of exchange. See *domestic bill*.

investment bill. A bill of exchange purchased at a discount and intended to be held to maturity as an investment.

7. A formal document or note; an instrument <bill of sale>.

> "The expression 'bill of sale' includes bills of sale, assignments, transfers, declarations of trust without transfer, inventories of goods with receipts thereto attached, or receipts for purchase-monies of goods, and other assurances of personal chattels, and also powers of attorney, authorities, or licences to take possession of personal chattels as security for any debt, and also any agreement, whether intended or not to be followed by the execution of any other instrument, by which a right in equity to any personal chattels, or to any charge or security thereon, shall be conferred . . . ." Joshua Williams, *Principles of the Law of Personal Property* 60 (11th ed. 1881) (tracking the definition in the [U.K.] Bills of Sale Act of 1878).

> "A transfer may be either an absolute assignment by way of gift or sale, or an assignment by way of mortgage or security only; but in either case when a written document of any sort is used to effect the transfer, the document is called technically a 'bill of sale.' " Arthur Weldon & H. Gibson Rivington, *Gibson's Conveyancing* 302 (14th ed. 1933).

bill obligatory. A written promise to pay; a promissory note under seal. — Also termed *single bond*. See NOTE (1).

bill of debt. A debt instrument, such as a bill obligatory or promissory note.

bill of lading. See BILL OF LADING.

bill penal. A written promise to pay that carries a penalty in excess of the underlying debt for failure to pay. Cf. *bill single*.

bill single. A written promise to pay that is not under seal and has no penalty for failure to pay. — Also termed *single bill*. Cf. *bill penal*.

grand bill of sale. **1.** *Hist.* An instrument used to transfer title to a ship that is at sea. **2.** An instrument used to transfer title of a ship from the builder to the first purchaser.

single bill. See *bill single*.

skeleton bill. A bill drawn, indorsed, or accepted in blank.

8. A piece of paper money <a $10 bill>. **9.** A promissory note <the debtor signed a bill for $7,000>.

billable hour. A unit of time used by an attorney or paralegal to account for work performed and chargeable to a client. • Billable hours are usu. divided into quarters or tenths of an hour.

billable time. An attorney's or paralegal's time that is chargeable to a client. Cf. NONBILLABLE TIME.

billa cassetur (**bil**-ə kə-**see**-tər). See CASSETUR BILLA.

billa excambii (**bil**-ə eks-**kam**-bee-I). [Latin] See BILL OF EXCHANGE.

billa exonerationis (**bil**-ə ig-zon-ə-ray-shee-**oh**-nis). [Latin] See BILL OF LADING.

billa vera (**bil**-ə **veer**-ə). [Latin] See TRUE BILL.

bill broker. A middleman who negotiates the purchase or sale of commercial paper.

billeta (**bil**-ə-tə). *Hist.* A proposed statute or petition presented in Parliament.

bill for a new trial. See BILL (2).

billhead. A printed invoice containing a business's name and address.

bill in aid of execution. See BILL (2).

bill in equity. See BILL (2).

billing cycle. The period in which creditors regularly submit bills to customers or debtors.

bill *in perpetuam rei memoriam.* See *bill to perpetuate testimony* under BILL (2).

bill in the nature of a bill of review. See BILL (2).

bill in the nature of a bill of revivor. See BILL (2).

bill in the nature of a supplemental bill. See BILL (2).

bill in the nature of interpleader. See BILL (2).

bill obligatory. See BILL (7).

bill of adventure. *Maritime law.* A shipper's written statement that the shipped property belongs to another and is conveyed at the owner's risk.

bill of attainder. A special legislative act prescribing capital punishment, without a trial, for a person guilty of a high offense such as treason or a felony. • Bills of attainder are prohibited by the U.S. Constitution (art. I, § 9, cl. 3; art. I, § 10, cl. 1). — Also termed *act of attainder*. See ATTAINDER; BILL OF PAINS AND PENALTIES.

bill of certiorari. See BILL (2).

bill of complaint. See BILL (2).

bill of conformity. See BILL (2).

bill of costs. See BILL (2).

bill of credit. 1. Legal tender in the form of paper, issued by a state and involving the faith of the state, designed to circulate as money in the ordinary uses of business. **2.** LETTER OF CREDIT.

bill of debt. See BILL (7).

bill of discovery. See BILL (2).

bill of entry. *Maritime law.* A written description of goods filed by an importer with customs officials to obtain permission to unload a ship's goods.

bill of evidence. See BILL (2).

bill of exceptions. See BILL (2).

bill of exchange. See DRAFT (1).

bill of foreclosure. See BILL (2).

bill of health. *Maritime law.* A statement certifying the healthy condition of a ship's cargo and crew. • The bill is issued by the port authority from which a vessel sails and is shown to the port authority at the ship's destination as proof that the ship's cargo and crew are disease-free. A "clean" bill states that no contagious or infectious diseases were present at the port; a "touched" or "foul" bill states that the named disease was suspected, anticipated, or actually present.

bill of indemnity. 1. *Hist.* An act of Parliament passed annually to protect officeholders who unwittingly fail to take an oath necessary for officeholding from liability for acts done in an official capacity. • A more general statute, the Promissory Oaths Act, replaced the bill of indemnity in 1868. **2.** A law protecting a public official from liability for official acts. **3.** An initial pleading by which a plaintiff seeks to require another (often an insurance company) to discharge the plaintiff's liability to a third person.

bill of indictment. An instrument presented to a grand jury for the jury's determination whether sufficient evidence exists to formally charge the accused with a crime. See INDICTMENT; NO BILL; TRUE BILL.

bill of information. 1. INFORMATION. **2.** *Hist.* A civil suit begun by the Crown or by those under its protection, such as a charity.

bill of interpleader. See BILL (2).

bill of lading (**layd**-ing). A document of title acknowledging the receipt of goods by a carrier or by the shipper's agent; a document that indicates the receipt of goods for shipment and that is issued by a person engaged in the business of transporting or forwarding goods. • An airbill is usu. included within the definition of the term. — Abbr. B/L. — Also termed *waybill*.

> "A bill of lading may be regarded in three several aspects. (1) It is a receipt given by the master of a ship acknowledging that the goods specified in the bill have been put on board; (2) it is the document [that] contains the terms of the contract for the carriage of the goods agreed upon between the shipper of the goods and the shipowner (whose agent the master of the ship is); and (3) it is a 'document of title' to the goods, of which it is the symbol. It is by means of this document of title that the goods themselves may be dealt with by the owner of them while they are still on board ship and upon the high seas." William R. Anson, *Principles of the Law of Contract* 380 (Arthur L. Corbin ed., 3d Am. ed. 1919).

***clean bill of lading.* 1.** A bill of lading containing no clause or notation qualifying the bill's terms. **2.** *Maritime law.* A bill of lading that, by not providing for storage of goods on a ship's deck, implies that the goods are to be stowed belowdecks.

destination bill of lading. A bill procured to be issued at the shipping or other destination rather than at the place of shipment. UCC § 7–305.

foul bill of lading. A bill of lading that shows on its face that the goods were damaged or that there was a shortage of goods at the time of shipment.

negotiable bill of lading. A bill of lading calling for the delivery of goods to the bearer or to a named person's order. UCC § 7–104.

ocean bill of lading. A negotiable bill of lading used in shipment by water. — Often shortened to *ocean bill.*

onboard bill of lading. A bill of lading reflecting that goods have been loaded onto a ship. — Often shortened to *onboard bill.*

order bill of lading. A negotiable bill of lading stating that the goods are consigned to the order of the person named in the bill.

overseas bill of lading. A bill of lading used for overseas shipment by water or air. UCC § 2–323. — Often shortened to *overseas bill.*

straight bill of lading. A nonnegotiable bill of lading that specifies a consignee to whom the carrier is contractually obligated to deliver the goods. — Also termed *nonnegotiable bill of lading.*

through bill of lading. A bill of lading by which a carrier transports goods to a designated destination, even though the carrier will have to use a connecting carrier for part of the passage. UCC § 7–302. — Often shortened to *through bill.*

bill of Middlesex. *Hist.* A process by which the Court of the King's Bench in Middlesex obtains jurisdiction over a defendant who resides in a county outside the jurisdiction of the Court, by alleging a fictitious trespass in a county over which the court has jurisdiction. • Once the sheriff returns the bill noting that the defendant is not in the county where the trespass occurred, a *latitat* is issued to the sheriff of the defendant's actual residence. See LATITAT.

> "The bill of Middlesex ... is a kind of *capias*, directed to the sheriff of that county, and commanding him to take the defendant and have him before our lord the king at Westminster on a day prefixed, to answer to the plaintiff of a plea of trespass. For this accusation of trespass it is, that gives the court of king's bench jurisdiction in other civil causes, as was formerly observed; since when once the defendant is taken into custody ... of this court, may here be prosecuted for any other species of injury." 3 William Blackstone, *Commentaries on the Laws of England* 285 (1768).

bill of mortality. *Hist.* A record of the number of deaths occurring in a given district. • Bills of mortality were compiled — often week to week — in England from late in the 16th century to the 19th century as a way to keep track of the plague and other highly contagious diseases.

bill of pains and penalties. A legislative act that, though similar to a bill of attainder, prescribes punishment less severe than capital punishment. • Bills of pains and penalties are included within the U.S. Constitution's ban of bills of attainder. U.S. Const. art I, § 9.

bill of parcels. See BILL (5).

bill of particulars. A formal, detailed statement of the claims or charges brought by a plaintiff or a prosecutor, usu. filed in response to the defendant's request for a more specific complaint. — Also termed *statement of particulars.* See MOTION FOR MORE DEFINITE STATEMENT.

> "Although it has been said that the bill of particulars is not a discovery device, it seems plain that it is a means of discovery, though of a limited nature. It is the one method open to a defendant in a criminal case to secure the details of the charge against him." 1 Charles Alan Wright, *Federal Practice and Procedure* § 129, at 646–47 (3d ed. 1999).

bill of peace. See BILL (2).

bill of review. See BILL (2).

bill of revivor. See BILL (2).

bill of revivor and supplement. See BILL (2).

bill of rights. 1. (*usu. cap.*) A section or addendum, usu. in a constitution, defining the situations in which a politically organized society will permit free, spontaneous, and individual activity, and guaranteeing that governmental powers will not be used in certain ways; esp., the first ten amendments to the U.S. Constitution. **2.** (*cap.*) One of the four great charters of English liberty (1 W. & M., 1689), embodying in statutory form all the principles of the other three charters, namely, Magna Carta, the Petition of Right (3 Car., 1628), and the Habeas Corpus Act (31 Car. 2, 1679).

bill of sale. An instrument for the conveyance of title to personal property, absolutely or by way of security. Cf. DEED.

bill of sight. *Maritime law.* A declaration made to a customs officer by an importer who is unsure about what is being shipped. • The bill of sight allows an importer to inspect the goods before paying duties.

bill payable. See *account payable* under ACCOUNT.

bill penal. See BILL (7).

bill quia timet. See BILL (2).

bill receivable. See *account receivable* under ACCOUNT.

bill rendered. See *account rendered* under ACCOUNT.

bills and notes. See PAPER.

bills in a set. A bill of lading made up of a series of independent parts, each bearing a number and providing that goods delivered against any one part void the other parts. • Traditionally, in overseas-goods shipments, the parts of this type of bill were sent under separate cover so that if one was lost, the buyer could take delivery of the goods with another one. UCC § 7–304.

bill single. See BILL (7).

bill taken *pro confesso* (proh kən-**fes**-oh). [Latin "as if admitted"] *Hist.* An order issued by a court of equity when a defendant fails to file an answer.

bill to carry a decree into execution. See BILL (2).

bill to perpetuate testimony. See BILL (2).

bill to suspend a decree. See BILL (2).

bill to take testimony de bene esse. See BILL (2).

bimetallism. A monetary system in which currency is defined in terms of two metals (usu. gold and silver), both being legal tender and with a fixed rate of exchange between them. • The American money system was based on a bimetallic standard from 1792 to 1873.

bind, *vb.* To impose one or more legal duties on (a person or institution) <the contract binds the parties> <courts are bound by precedent>. — **binding,** *adj.* — **bindingness,** *n.*

binder. 1. A document in which the buyer and the seller of real property declare their common intention to bring about a transfer of ownership, usu. accompanied by the buyer's initial payment. **2.** Loosely, the buyer's initial payment in the sale of real property. Cf. EARNEST MONEY. **3.** An insurer's memorandum giving the insured temporary coverage while the application for an insurance policy is being processed or while the formal policy is being prepared. — Also termed *binding receipt*; *binding slip*.

binding, *adj.* **1.** (Of an agreement) that binds <a binding contract>. **2.** (Of an order) that requires obedience <the temporary injunction was binding on the parties>.

binding agreement. See AGREEMENT.

binding arbitration. See ARBITRATION.

binding authority. See *binding precedent* under PRECEDENT.

binding instruction. See *mandatory instruction* under JURY INSTRUCTION.

binding precedent. See PRECEDENT.

binding receipt. See BINDER.

binding slip. See BINDER.

bind over, *vb.* **1.** To put (a person) under a bond or other legal obligation to do something, esp. to appear in court. **2.** To hold (a person) for trial; to turn (a defendant) over to a sheriff or warden for imprisonment pending further judicial action. • A court may bind over a defendant if it finds at a preliminary examination that enough evidence exists to require a trial on the charges made against the defendant. — **binding over,** *n.* — **bindover,** *adj.*

bindover hearing. See PRELIMINARY HEARING.

biological child. See *natural child* under CHILD.

biological father. See *natural father* under FATHER.

biological warfare. See WARFARE.

bipartite, *adj.* (Of an instrument) executed in two parts by both parties.

birretum (bə-**ret**-əm). [Law Latin] A cap or coif formerly worn by British judges and serjeants-at-law.

birth. The complete extrusion of a newborn baby from the mother's body.

> "For purposes of criminal law — and also for those of property law, e.g. to become a holder of property and so transmit it again to new heirs, or to enable the father to obtain curtesy of his wife's lands — *birth* consists in extrusion from the mother's body, i.e. in having 'come into the world.' If but a foot be unextricated, there can be no murder, the extrusion must be complete, the whole body of the infant must have been brought into the world. But it is not necessary that the umbilical cord should have been severed. And to be born alive the child must have been still in a living state after having wholly quitted the body of the mother." J.W. Cecil Turner, *Kenny's Outlines of Criminal Law* 104 (16th ed. 1952).

birth certificate. A formal document that records a person's birthdate, birthplace, and parentage.

birth mother. A biological mother, as opposed to an adoptive mother.

birth record. Statistical data kept by a governmental entity concerning persons' birthdates, birthplaces, and parentage.

bi-scot. *Hist. English law.* A fine imposed for not repairing banks, ditches, and causeways.

bishop. The chief superintendent and highest-ranking member of the clergy within a diocese. • The bishop is subject to the archbishop of a province.

> "[A] bishop ... has several courts under him, and may visit at pleasure every part of his diocese. His chancellor is appointed to hold his courts for him, and to assist him in matters of ecclesiastical law...." 1 William Blackstone, *Commentaries on the Laws of England* 370 (1765).

bishopric (**bish**-ə-prik). **1.** DIOCESE. **2.** The office of a bishop.

Bishop's Court. *Hist. Eccles. law.* A court held in the cathedral of each diocese, the judge being the bishop's chancellor, who applied civil canon law. • The jurisdiction included appeals from the Court of Archdeacon. In a large diocese, the bishop's chancellor would have commissaries in remote parts who held consistory courts. See CONSISTORY COURT.

biting rule. A rule of construction that once a deed or will grants a fee simple, a later provision attempting to cut down, modify, or qualify the grant will be held void.

***Bivens* action.** A lawsuit brought to redress a federal official's violation of a constitutional right. *Bivens v. Six Unknown Named Agents of the Federal Bureau of Narcotics*, 403 U.S. 388, 91 S.Ct. 1999 (1971). • A *Bivens* action allows federal officials to be sued in a manner similar to that set forth at 42 USCA § 1983 for state officials who violate a person's constitutional rights under color of state law.

B/L. *abbr.* BILL OF LADING.

blackacre. A fictitious tract of land used in legal discourse (esp. law-school hypotheticals) to discuss real-property issues. • When another tract of land is needed in a hypothetical, it is often termed "whiteacre."

> "Blackacre is the most celebrated tract of land in the world of the law.... Blackacre is wholly mythical, yet totally real. It is a concept, living in the realm of the mind and doubly valuable since much of the law of property has the same type of reality." John E. Cribbet, *Principles of the Law of Property* 2 (2d ed. 1975).

Black Act. *Hist.* An English statute (9 Geo. ch. 22) establishing the death penalty for the unlawful killing or maiming of animals. • The statute was passed in 1722 in the wake of crimes committed by persons with faces blackened or otherwise disguised. The statute was repealed in 1827. The classic study of this law is E.P. Thompson, *Whips and Hunters: The Origins of the Black Act* (1975).

Black Acts. *Scots law.* Statutes of the Scottish Parliament passed from 1535 to 1594 and recorded in a book printed in black letter.

Black Book of the Exchequer. *Hist.* A record book containing treaties, conventions, charters, papal bulls, and other English state documents. • It dates from the 13th century. — Also termed *Liber Niger Parvus*.

black cap. A square cap worn by English judges on certain state or solemn occasions. • The black cap was formerly worn by a judge when handing down a death sentence.

black codes. (*usu. cap.*) *Hist.* **1.** Antebellum state laws enacted to regulate the institution of slavery. **2.** Laws enacted shortly after the Civil War in the ex-Confederate states to restrict the liberties of the newly freed slaves to ensure a supply of inexpensive agricultural labor and to maintain white supremacy.

> "Clearly, leaders of the old South who survived the war were in no mood for racial equality. It was a bitter enough pill that the slaves were legally free; there was no inclination to go beyond the formal status. The Black Codes of 1865, passed in almost all of the states of the old Confederacy, were meant to replace slavery with some kind of caste system and to preserve as much as possible of the prewar way of life." Lawrence M. Friedman, *A History of American Law* 504 (2d ed. 1985).

blackletter law. One or more legal principles that are old, fundamental, and well settled. • The term refers to the law printed in books set in Gothic type, which is very bold and black. — Also termed *hornbook law*.

blacklist, *vb.* To put the name of (a person) on a list of those who are to be boycotted or punished <the firm blacklisted the former employee>. — **blacklist,** *n.*

blackmail, *n.* A threatening demand made without justification; EXTORTION (1). — **blackmail,** *vb.* Cf. GRAYMAIL; GREENMAIL; FEEMAIL.

> "[Blackmail is] a certain rate of Money, Corn, Cattle, or other consideration, paid to some inhabiting upon, or near the borders, being persons of name and power, allied with . . . known Robbers . . . to be thereby by them freed and protected from the danger of those Spoiltakers." Thomas Blount, *Nomo-Lexicon: A Law-Dictionary* (1670).

> " 'Black-mail' (black rent) was anciently used to indicate 'rents reserved in work, grain or baser money' (i.e. baser than silver). It was also employed at one time to refer to 'a tribute formerly exacted in the north of England and in Scotland by freebooting chiefs for protection from pillage.' [Quoting *American College Dictionary* (1948).] Such practice was extortion, in the literal sense, and hence 'blackmail' is frequently used to indicate statutory extortion or sometimes an extorsive threat. And the federal statute forbidding the sending of an extorsive threat by mail has been referred to as the 'blackmail statute.' " Rollin M. Perkins & Ronald N. Boyce, *Criminal Law* 451 (3d ed. 1982).

blackmail suit. See SUIT.

black maria. *Slang.* A locked van used by the police to transport prisoners to and from jail.

black market. See MARKET.

black-rage insanity defense. See INSANITY DEFENSE.

black rent. *Hist.* Feudal rents paid in work, grain, or money baser than silver. Cf. WHITE RENT.

Blackstone lawyer. *Slang.* **1.** A lawyer with a broad knowledge of blackletter principles. **2.** A self-educated lawyer (esp. in antebellum America) whose legal training consists primarily of reading Blackstone's *Commentaries*.

black ward. *Hist.* A subvassal; a vassal of the king's vassal.

blame, *n.* **1.** An act of attributing fault; an expression of disapproval <the judge said all the plaintiff's attorneys were to blame>. **2.** Responsibility for something wrong <blame rested with all the defendants>. — **blame,** *vb.* — **blameworthy, blamable,** *adj.*

blanc seign (blahnk **sayn**). [Law French] *Civil law.* A signed paper entrusted to someone with the power to bind the signer within the limits of the agreement between the signer and the grantee. See POWER OF ATTORNEY (1).

blank acceptance. See ACCEPTANCE (4).

blank bar. *Hist.* A plea in bar interposed by a defendant in a trespass action. • This type of plea was filed to compel the plaintiff to state exactly where the alleged trespass occurred. — Also termed *common bar*.

blank bill. See BILL (6).

blank bond. See BOND (2).

blank check. See CHECK.

blank contract. See CONTRACT.

blanket agreement. *Labor law.* A collective-bargaining agreement that applies to workers throughout an organization, industry, or geographical area.

blanket bond. See BOND (2).

blanket lien. See LIEN.

blanket mortgage. See MORTGAGE.

blanket policy. See INSURANCE POLICY.

blanket search warrant. See SEARCH WARRANT.

blank indorsement. See INDORSEMENT.

blank lien. See LIEN.

blank stock. See STOCK.

blasphemy (**blas**-fə-mee), *n.* Irreverence toward God, religion, a religious icon, or something else considered sacred. • Blasphemy was a crime at common law and remains so in some U.S. jurisdictions, but it is rarely if ever enforced because of its questionable constitutionality under the First Amendment. — **blaspheme** (blas-**feem** *or* **blas**-feem), *vb.* — **blasphemous** (**blas**-fə-məs), *adj.* — **blasphemer** (**blas**-fee-mər), *n.*

> "Blasphemy is the malicious revilement of God and religion. In England blasphemy was the malicious revilement of the Christian religion.... Blasphemy has been held to be a common-law crime [in the United States] because of its tendency to stir up breaches of the peace. It is expressly made punishable by some of the statutes." Rollin M. Perkins & Ronald N. Boyce, *Criminal Law* 474, 475 (3d ed. 1982).

blended fund. See FUND (1).

blended trust. See TRUST.

blending clause. A provision in a will disposing of both the testator's own property and the property over which the testator has a power of appointment, so that the two types of property are treated as a unit.

blind entry. See ENTRY (2).

blind pig. See BLIND TIGER.

blind plea. See PLEA (1).

blind selling. The sale of goods without giving a buyer the opportunity to examine them.

blind tiger. *Slang.* A place where intoxicants are illegally sold. • This term was commonly used during Prohibition. — Also termed *blind pig.* See PROHIBITION (3).

blind trust. See TRUST.

bloc. A group of persons or countries aligned with a common interest or purpose, even if only temporarily <voting bloc>.

block, *n.* **1.** A municipal area enclosed by streets <three blocks away>. See LOT (1). **2.** A quantity of things bought or sold as a unit <a block of preferred shares>.

blockade. *Int'l law.* A belligerent's prevention of access to or egress from an enemy's ports by stationing ships or squadrons in such a position that they can intercept vessels attempting to enter or leave those ports. • To be binding, a blockade must be effective — that is, it must be maintained by a force sufficient to prevent access to ports.

blockage rule. *Tax.* The principle that a large block of stock shares may be valued at less than the sum of the values of the individual shares because such a large block may be difficult to sell at full price.

***Blockburger* test.** See SAME-EVIDENCE TEST.

blockbusting. The act or practice, usu. by a real-estate broker, of persuading property owners to sell their property quickly, and often at a loss, to avoid an imminent influx of members of minority groups. • Blockbusting is illegal in many states.

blocked account. See ACCOUNT.

blocked currency. See CURRENCY.

blocked income. See INCOME.

block grant. An unrestricted grant of federal funds.

block interest. See *add-on interest* under INTEREST (3).

block policy. See INSURANCE POLICY.

block voting. A shareholders' agreement to cast their votes in a single block. See *voting trust* under TRUST (4).

blood. The relationship arising by descent from a common ancestor. See RELATIVE.

full blood. The relationship existing between persons having the same two parents; unmixed ancestry. — Also termed *whole blood; entire blood.*

half blood. The relationship existing between persons having the same father or mother, but not both parents in common.

inheritable blood. *Hist.* A relationship between an ancestor and an heir that the law recognizes for purposes of passing good title to property.

mixed blood. The relationship between persons whose ancestors are of different races or nationalities.

"The term 'mixed bloods,' as used in treaties and statutes, has been held to include persons of half, or more or less than half, Indian blood, derived either from the father or from the mother." 42 C.J.S. *Indians* § 3 (1991).

whole blood. See *full blood*.

blood, corruption of the. See CORRUPTION OF BLOOD.

blood alcohol content. The concentration of alcohol in one's bloodstream, expressed as a percentage. • Blood alcohol content is used to determine whether a person is legally intoxicated, esp. under a driving-while-intoxicated law. In many states, a blood alcohol content of .08% is enough to charge a person with an offense. — Abbr. BAC. — Also termed *blood alcohol count*; *blood alcohol concentration*. See DRIVING UNDER THE INFLUENCE; DRIVING WHILE INTOXICATED.

blood feud. A state of hostility between families in which one family seeks to avenge the killing of one of its members by killing a member of the other family.

"Anglo-Saxon polity preserved, even down to the Norman Conquest, many traces of a time when kinship was the strongest of all bonds. Such a stage of society, we hardly need add, is not confined to any one region of the world or any one race of men.... When it puts on the face of strife between hostile kindreds, it is shown in the war of tribal factions, and more specifically in the blood-feud. A man's kindred are his avengers; and, as it is their right and honour to avenge him, so it is their duty to make amends for his misdeeds, or else maintain his cause in fight. Step by step, as the power of the State waxes, the self-centred and self-helping autonomy of the kindred wanes. Private feud is controlled, regulated, put, one may say, into legal harness; the avenging and the protecting clan on the slain and the slayer are made pledges and auxiliaries of public justice." 1 Frederick Pollock & Frederic W. Maitland, *The History of English Law Before the Time of Edward I* 31 (2d ed. 1898).

blood-grouping test. A test used in paternity and illegitimacy cases to determine whether a particular man could be the father of a child. • The test does not establish paternity; rather, it eliminates men who could not be the father. See PATERNITY TEST.

blood money. 1. *Hist.* A payment given by a murderer's family to the next of kin of the murder victim. **2.** A reward given for the apprehension of a person charged with a crime, esp. capital murder.

bloodwite. See EFFUSIO SANGUINIS.

blotter. 1. See ARREST RECORD. **2.** See WASTE BOOK.

blue-blue-ribbon jury. See *blue-ribbon jury* under JURY.

Blue Book. 1. A compilation of session laws. See SESSION LAWS (2). **2.** A volume formerly published to give parallel citation tables for a volume in the National Reporter System. **3.** *English law.* A government publication, such as a Royal Commission report, issued in blue paper covers.

Bluebook. The citation guide — formerly titled *A Uniform System of Citation* — that is generally considered the authoritative reference for American legal citations. • The book's complete title is *The Bluebook: A Uniform System of Citation*. Although it has been commonly called the *Bluebook* for decades, the editors officially included *Bluebook* in the title only in the mid–1990s. The book is compiled by the editors of the *Columbia Law Review*, the *Harvard Law Review*, the *University of Pennsylvania Law Review*, and *The Yale Law Journal*.

blue books. See SESSION LAWS.

blue chip, *n.* A corporate stock that is considered a safe investment because the corporation has a history of stability, consistent growth, and reliable earnings. — Also termed *blue-chip stock*. — **blue-chip,** *adj.*

blue law. A statute regulating or prohibiting commercial activity on Sundays. • Although blue laws were formerly common, they have declined since the 1980s, when many courts held them invalid because of their origin in religion (i.e., Sunday being the Christian Sabbath). Blue laws usu. pass constitutional challenge if they are enacted to support a nonreligious purpose, such as a day of rest for workers. — Also termed *Sunday law*; *Sunday-closing law*; *Sabbath law*; *Lord's Day Act*.

Blue List. *Securities.* A daily listing (on blue paper) of secondary-market offerings of municipal bonds.

"Municipal bonds available for resale in the *secondary* market are listed by state in *The Blue List*, along with such information as the number of bonds offered, issuer, maturity date, coupon rate, price, and dealer making the offering. Ratings are *not* included. But there are sections on settlement dates of recent new offerings, prerefunded bonds, and miscellaneous offerings (some U.S. government and agency obligations, railroad equipment trust certificates, corporate bonds, and even preferred stocks). The dollar value of listings, referred to as the *floating supply*, gives an indication of the size and liquidity of the secondary municipal market." The New York Institute of Finance, *How the Bond Market Works* 185 (1988).

blue note. See NOTE (1).

blue-pencil test. A judicial standard for deciding whether to invalidate the whole contract or only the offending words. • Under this standard, only the offending words are invalidated if it would be possible to delete them simply by running a blue pencil through them, as opposed to changing, adding, or rearranging words.

blue-ribbon jury. See JURY.

blue-sky, *vb.* To approve (the sale of securities) in accordance with blue-sky laws <the company's IPO has not yet been blue-skyed>.

blue-sky, *adj.* (Of a security) having little value.

blue-sky law. A state statute establishing standards for offering and selling securities, the purpose being to protect citizens from investing in fraudulent schemes or unsuitable companies.

"The first legislative attempts to regulate securities transactions were effected on the state level, with the first general securities law being said to have been enacted by the State of Kansas in 1911, and with 48 jurisdictions having enacted such statutes by 1933. These statutes were said to be enacted to stop the sale of stock in fly-by-night concerns, visionary oil wells, distant gold mines, and other fraudulent exploitations. A similar description of the early legislative purpose is that such acts were aimed at 'speculative schemes which have no more basis than so many feet of blue sky,' and this description has had a lasting influence in that state securities acts are commonly referred to as 'blue sky laws.' " 69A Am. Jur. 2d *Securities Regulation — State* § 1 (1993).

"The state legislatures entered the arena of securities regulation more than twenty years before Congress. . . . [T]he statutes, which vary widely in their terms and scope, are commonly referred to as 'blue sky' laws, an appellation with several suggested origins. It has been said, for example, that the Kansas legislature was spurred by the fear of fast-talking eastern industrialists selling everything including the blue sky." 1 Thomas Lee Hazen, *Treatise on the Law of Securities Regulation* § 8.1, at 490–92 (3d ed. 1995).

bluewater seaman. See *able-bodied seaman* under SEAMAN.

board. 1. A group of persons having managerial, supervisory, or advisory powers <board of directors>. **2.** Daily meals (and sometimes lodging) furnished to a guest at an inn, boardinghouse, or other lodging <room and board>.

board-certified, *adj.* (Of a professional) recognized by an official body as a specialist in a given field of law or medicine <board-certified in civil litigation>. See BOARD OF LEGAL SPECIALIZATION.

board lot. See *round lot* under LOT (3).

board of adjustment. See ADJUSTMENT BOARD.

board of aldermen. See CITY COUNCIL.

board of directors. 1. The governing body of a corporation, elected by the shareholders to establish corporate policy, appoint executive officers, and make major business and financial decisions. — Also termed (esp. in charitable organizations) *board of trustees*. See DIRECTOR.

staggered board of directors. A board of directors in which a fraction of the board is elected each year to serve for two or three years.

2. The governing body of a partnership, association, or other unincorporated group. — Also termed *board of trustees*.

board of education. A state or local agency that governs and manages public schools within a state or local district. Cf. SCHOOL BOARD.

board of equalization. See EQUALIZATION BOARD.

board of examiners. See EXAMINING BOARD.

board of fire underwriters. An unincorporated voluntary association made up of fire insurers.

Board of Governors. See FEDERAL RESERVE BOARD OF GOVERNORS.

Board of Green Cloth. *Hist.* A group of persons responsible for governing the royal-household staff, esp. in financial matters such as accounting for expenses and paying servants' wages. • The Board consisted of the Lord Steward and inferior officers, and its name derived from the green cloth that covered the table used by the Board to conduct its duties. In more ancient times, it kept the peace and maintained courts of justice within the area around the royal household (i.e., the *verge*). — Also termed *Counting House of the King's Household*; *Green Cloth*.

board of health. A municipal or state agency charged with protecting the public health.

Board of Immigration Appeals. The highest administrative tribunal for matters arising under U.S. immigration law, charged with hearing appeals from the Immigration and Naturalization Service. • The Board is made up of five permanent members appointed by the Attorney General and two immigration judges who serve on a temporary basis. Most cases are heard by panels of two permanent judges and one temporary judge. — Also termed *Immigration Appeals Board*.

board of legal specialization. A body, usu. an arm of a state bar association, that certifies qualified lawyers as specialists within a given field. • Typically, to qualify as a specialist, a lawyer must meet a specified level of experience, pass an examination, and provide favorable recommendations from peers.

board of pardons. A state agency, of which the governor is usu. a member, authorized to pardon persons convicted of crimes.

board of parole. See PAROLE BOARD.

Board of Patent Appeals and Interferences. A quasi-judicial body that reviews rejected patent applications and determines priority between rival patent applicants. See INTERFERENCE (2).

board of regents. A group of persons appointed to supervise an educational institution, esp. a university.

board of registration. A state agency authorized to license and discipline members of a trade or profession.

board of review. **1.** A body that reviews administrative-agency decisions. **2.** A body that reviews property-tax assessments. **3.** In some cities, a board that reviews allegations of police misconduct.

Board of Tax Appeals. See TAX COURT, U.S.

board of trade. **1.** A federation of business executives dedicated to advancing and protecting business interests. **2.** An organization that runs a commodities exchange. See CHICAGO BOARD OF TRADE. **3.** *Hist.* The Lords of the Committee of the Privy Council that had jurisdiction over trade and foreign plantations. • Today, the responsibilities once assigned to this committee are carried out by the ministry for trade and industry.

board of trustees. See BOARD OF DIRECTORS.

board of zoning appeals. See ADJUSTMENT BOARD.

bockland. See BOOKLAND.

bocland. See BOOKLAND.

bodily harm. See HARM.

bodily heir. See *heir of the body* under HEIR.

bodily injury. See INJURY.

body. **1.** The main part of a written instrument. **2.** A collection of laws. — Also termed *body of laws*. See CORPUS JURIS. **3.** An artificial person created by a legal authority. See CORPORATION. **4.** An aggregate of individuals or groups.

body corporate. See CORPORATION.

body execution. See CAPIAS; EXECUTION.

body of a county. A county as a whole.

body of laws. See BODY (2).

body politic. A group of people regarded in a political (rather than private) sense and organized under a single governmental authority.

bogus check. See *bad check* under CHECK.

boilerplate, *n.* **1.** Ready-made or all-purpose language that will fit in a variety of documents. **2.** Fixed or standardized contractual language that the proposing party views as relatively nonnegotiable. — **boilerplate,** *adj.*

boiler-room transaction. *Slang.* A high-pressure telephone sales pitch, often of a fraudulent nature.

bolster, *vb.* To enhance (unimpeached evidence) with additional evidence. • This practice is often considered improper.

bolts. *Hist.* Student-argued cases in the Inns of Court. • These practice cases were held privately, in contrast to the more formal and public *moots.* — Also termed *boltings.*

bombardment. *Int'l law.* An attack from land, sea, or air with weapons that are capable of destroying enemy targets at a distance with bombs, missiles, or projectiles.

bona (**boh**-nə), *n.* [Latin "goods"] Chattels; personal property. Cf. BIENS (2).

bona confiscata (**boh**-nə kon-fi-**skay**-tə). Goods confiscated by — or forfeited to — the Crown.

bona felonum (**boh**-nə fə-**loh**-nəm). Personal property belonging to a convicted felon.

bona forisfacta (**boh**-nə for-is-**fak**-tə). Forfeited goods.

bona fugitivorum (**boh**-nə fyoo-jə-ti-**vor**-əm). Goods belonging to a fugitive. — Also termed *bona utlagatorum.*

bona immobilia (**boh**-nə i-moh-**bil**-ee-ə). Immovable property.

bona mobilia (**boh**-nə moh-**bil**-ee-ə). [Latin] Movable property. See MOVABLE.

bona notabilia (**boh**-nə noh-tə-**bil**-ee-ə). Notable goods; property worth accounting for in a decedent's estate.

bona paraphernalia (**boh**-nə par-ə-fər-**nay**-lee-ə). Clothes, jewelry, and ornaments not included in a married woman's dowry.

bona peritura (**boh**-nə per-ə-**t[y]uur**-ə). Perishable goods; goods that an executor or trustee must diligently convert into money.

bona utlagatorum (**boh**-nə ət-lay-gə-**tor**-əm). See *bona fugitivorum.*

bona vacantia (**boh**-nə və-**kan**-shee-ə). [Latin "vacant goods"] **1.** Property not disposed of by a decedent's will and to which no relative is entitled under intestacy laws. See ESCHEAT. **2.** Ownerless property; goods without an owner. • *Bona vacantia* often resulted when a deceased person died without an heir willing and able to make a claim. The property either belonged to the finder or escheated to the Crown. — Also termed *vacantia bona.* — Sometimes shortened to *vacantia.*

bona waviata (**boh**-nə way-vee-**ay**-tə). Stolen goods thrown away in flight by a thief. • The goods escheated to the Crown as a penalty to the owner for failing to pursue the thief and recover the goods.

vacantia bona. See *bona vacantia.*

bona activa (**boh**-nə ak-**tI**-və). [Latin "active goods"] Assets. See ASSET (1).

bona confiscata. See BONA.

bonae fidei (**boh**-nee **fI**-dee-I). [Latin] Of good faith; in good faith.

***bonae fidei* possessor** (**boh**-nee **fI**-dee-I pə-**zes**-ər). [Latin] *Roman law.* A good-faith possessor of property owned by another. • Unless the owner sued to recover the property, the possessor became the rightful owner after a specified time elapsed, unless the property had been stolen or taken by force. See ADVERSE POSSESSION.

bona et catalla (**boh**-nə et kə-**tal**-ə). [Law Latin] Goods and chattels.

bona felonum. See BONA.

bona fide (**boh**-nə fId *or* **boh**-nə **fI**-dee), *adj.* [Latin "in good faith"] **1.** Made in good faith; without fraud or deceit. **2.** Sincere; genuine. See GOOD FAITH. — **bona fide,** *adv.*

bona fide contract. See CONTRACT.

bona fide emptor (**boh**-nə fId **emp**-tər). [Latin] Good-faith purchaser. See *good-faith purchaser* under PURCHASER.

bona fide holder for value. See HOLDER FOR VALUE.

bona fide judgment creditor. See JUDGMENT CREDITOR.

bona fide occupational qualification. An employment qualification that, although it may discriminate against a protected class (such as sex, religion, or national origin), relates to an essential job duty and is considered reasonably necessary to the operation of the particular business. • Such a qualification is not illegal under federal employment-discrimination laws. — Abbr. BFOQ.

> "The bona fide occupational qualification is a complete defense. It is invoked when the defendant makes a distinction expressly forbidden by Title VII, such as the refusal to hire women or women with preschool-age children, the reassignment of pregnant employees, or the exclusion of particular ethnic groups from particular jobs.... The employer's motivation for excluding the protected class is not significant in evaluating the BFOQ defense. The inquiry focuses on the necessity of using an expressly forbidden classification. The fact that the employer adopted the exclusion for invidious reasons, rather

than for the business consideration on which the defense is based, is not material. Thus, if the exclusion, in fact, is proved to be necessary it may be used, even if invidiously motivated." Mack A. Player, *Employment Discrimination Law* § 5.29, at 282–83 (1988).

bona fide operation. A real, ongoing business.

bona fide possession. See POSSESSION (3).

bona fide purchaser. See PURCHASER (1).

bona fide purchaser for value. See PURCHASER (1).

bona fides (**boh**-nə **fI**-deez), *n.* [Latin] See GOOD FAITH.

bona fide sale. See SALE.

bona forisfacta. See BONA.

bona fugitivorum. See BONA.

bona gratia matrimonium dissolvitur (**boh**-nə **gray**-shee-ə ma-trə-**moh**-nee-əm di-**sol**-və-tər). [Law Latin "the marriage is dissolved with good grace"] *Hist.* A consensual divorce.

bona immobilia. See BONA.

bona memoria (**boh**-nə mə-**mor**-ee-ə). [Latin] Good memory. • *Bona memoria,* as used in the phrase *sanae mentis et bonae memoria* (of sound mind and good memory), refers to a testator's mental capacity. See MIND AND MEMORY.

bona mobilia. See BONA.

bona notabilia. See BONA.

bona paraphernalia. See BONA.

bona peritura. See BONA.

bona utlagatorum. See *bona fugitivorum* under BONA.

bona vacantia. See BONA.

bona waviata. See BONA.

bond, *n.* **1.** An obligation; a promise.

"[A]n obligation, or in English a 'bond,' is a document written and sealed containing a confession of a debt; in later times 'contract' is the genus, 'obligation' the species." 2 Frederick Pollock & Frederic W. Maitland, *The History of English Law* 207 (2d ed. 1899).

2. A written promise to pay money or do some act if certain circumstances occur or a certain time elapses; a promise that is defeasible upon a condition subsequent.

"The fact that an instrument is called a 'bond' is not conclusive as to its character. It is necessary to disregard nomenclature and look to the substance of the bond itself. The distinguishing feature of a bond is that it is an obligation to pay a fixed sum of money, at a definite time, with a stated interest, and it makes no difference whether a bond is designated by that name or by some other, if it possesses the characteristics of a bond. There is no distinction between bonds and certificates of indebtedness which conform to all the characteristics of bonds." 1 Silvester E. Quindry, *Bonds & Bondholders Rights & Remedies* § 2, at 3–4 (1934).

appeal bond. A bond that an appellate court may require from an appellant in a civil case to ensure payment of the costs of appeal; a bond required as a condition to bringing an appeal or staying execution of the judgment appealed from. Fed. R. App. P. 7. Cf. *supersedeas bond.*

appearance bond. See *bail bond.*

attachment bond. A bond that a defendant gives to recover attached property. • The plaintiff then looks to the bond issuer to satisfy a judgment against the defendant.

average bond. *Marine insurance.* A bond given to the captain of a ship by consignees of cargo subject to general average, guaranteeing payment of their contribution once it is ascertained, on condition that their goods be promptly delivered.

bail bond. A bond given to a court by a criminal defendant's surety, guaranteeing that the defendant will duly appear in court in the future; a bond given to obtain a prisoner's release and to secure the prisoner's appearance to answer legal process. • The effect of the release on bail bond is to transfer custody of the prisoner from the officers of the law to the custody of the surety on the bail bond, whose undertaking is to redeliver the defendant to legal custody at the time and place appointed in the bond. — Also termed *appearance bond.* See BAIL.

bid bond. A bond filed in public construction projects to ensure that the bidding contractor will enter into the contract. • The *bid bond* is a type of performance bond.

blank bond. *Archaic.* A bond in which the space for the creditor's name is left blank.

blanket bond. **1.** A bond covering several persons or projects that require performance bonds. **2.** See *fidelity bond.*

bond for land. A bond given by the seller of land to a buyer, binding the seller to convey once the buyer tenders the agreed price. — Also termed *bond for a deed.* Cf. BINDER (1).

bond of corroboration. An additional obligation undertaken to corroborate the debtor's original obligation.

bottomry bond. A contract for the loan of money on a ship, usu. at extraordinary interest, for maritime risks encountered during a certain period or for a certain voyage. • The loan can be enforced only if the vessel survives the voyage. — Also termed *bottomage bond.* Cf. *respondentia bond.*

"A bottomry bond, strictly speaking, is a mortgage or pledge of a ship by the owner or agent, to secure the repayment of money lent for the use of the ship; and the conditions of it are, that if the ship is lost, the lender loses his money; but if it arrives, then, not only the ship itself is liable, but also the person of the borrower." John Indermaur, *Principles of the Common Law* 169 (Edmund H. Bennett ed., 1st Am. ed. 1878).

"[T]he bottomry bond ... is a sort of mortgage on a ship, entered into for the purpose of raising money in case of necessity in a foreign port. The advance of communications has caused bottomry and respondentia bonds to pass virtually out of use." Grant Gilmore & Charles L. Black, Jr., *The Law of Admiralty* § 1–10, at 25 n.85 (2d ed. 1975).

claim-property bond. See *replevin bond.*

common-defeasance bond. See *penal bond.*

common-law bond. A performance bond given by a construction contractor. • A common-law bond exceeds the requirements of a statutory performance bond because it provides additional coverage for construction projects. Cf. PERFORMANCE BOND.

common money bond. A promise to pay money as a penalty for failing to perform a duty or obligation.

cost bond. A bond given by a litigant to secure the payment of court costs.

counterbond. A bond to indemnify a surety.

delivery bond. See *forthcoming bond.*

depository bond. A bond given by a bank to protect a public body's deposits should the bank become insolvent.

discharging bond. A bond that both permits a defendant to regain possession of attached property and releases the property from the attachment lien. — Also termed *dissolution bond.* See *forthcoming bond.*

executor's bond. A bond given to ensure the executor's faithful administration of the estate. See *fiduciary bond.*

"The English law did not require an executor to give bond because he was appointed by the testator and his authority was derived from the will rather than court appointment. Some American jurisdictions do not require a bond of an executor. In the majority of our states a testator may by will dispense with the executor's bond, but in absence of such testamentary provision a bond will be required." Thomas E. Atkinson, *Handbook of the Law of Wills* § 113, at 621 (2d ed. 1953).

fidelity bond. A bond to indemnify an employer or business for loss due to embezzlement, larceny, or gross negligence by an employee or other person holding a position of trust. — Also termed *blanket bond.*

fiduciary bond. A type of surety bond required of a trustee, administrator, executor, guardian, conservator, or other fiduciary to ensure the proper performance of duties.

forthcoming bond. **1.** A bond guaranteeing that something will be produced or forthcoming at a particular time, or when called for. **2.** A bond (usu. given to a sheriff) to permit a person to repossess attached property in exchange for that person's commitment to surrender the property in the event of an adverse judgment. — Also termed *delivery bond.* Cf. *replevin bond.*

general-average bond. *Maritime law.* A cargo owner's bond exacted by a carrier to ensure that the owner will pay the general average contribution. • When the contribution amounts are disputed, the carrier requires this bond before agreeing to unload the ship. — Also termed *average bond.* See *general average* under AVERAGE (3).

guaranty bond. A bond combining the features of a fidelity and a surety bond, securing both payment and performance.

heritable bond. *Scots law.* A bond secured by land.

hypothecation bond. A bond given in the contract of bottomry or respondentia.

indemnity bond. A bond to reimburse the holder for any actual or claimed loss caused by the issuer's or some other person's conduct.

injunction bond. A bond required of an injunction applicant to cover the costs incurred by a wrongfully enjoined party. Fed. R. Civ. P. 65(c).

interim bond. **1.** A bond set by a police officer when a person is arrested for a minor offense, such as a misdemeanor, without a warrant. • Although the bond allows the arrestee to be released, it requires that the person be available for arraignment. **2.** A bond set by a judge or magistrate and attached to a misdemeanor warrant.

judicial bond. A bond to indemnify an adverse party in a lawsuit against loss occasioned by delay or by deprivation of property resulting from the lawsuit. • Judicial bonds are usu. classified according to the nature of the action in which they are required, as with appeal bonds, injunction bonds, attachment bonds, replevin bonds, forthcoming or redelivery bonds, and bail bonds. A bond of a fiduciary — such as a receiver, administrator, executor, or guardian — is often required as a condition to appointment.

liability bond. A bond intended to protect the assured from a loss arising from some event specified in the bond.

license bond. A bond required of a person seeking a license to engage in a specified business or to receive a certain privilege. — Also termed *permit bond.*

maintenance bond. A bond guaranteeing against construction defects for a period after the completion of the contracted-for work.

negotiable bond. A bond that can be transferred from the original holder to another.

official bond. A bond given by a public officer, conditioned on the faithful performance of the duties of office. • *Official bond* may also refer to a bond filed by an executor, guardian, trustee, or other fiduciary. See *fiduciary bond.*

payment bond. A bond given by a surety to cover any amounts that, because of the general contractor's default, are not paid to a subcontractor or materialman.

> "[T]he bond serves two purposes: it assures the owner a lien-free project, and it induces suppliers and subcontractors to accept work on the project, perhaps at a lower price, because of the assurance that they will be paid. Since no additional charge is generally made for a payment bond when a performance bond is being purchased, the two are usually issued simultaneously." Grant S. Nelson, *Real Estate Finance Law* § 12.2, at 881 (3d ed. 1994).

peace bond. A bond required by a court from a person who has breached or threatened to breach the peace. See BREACH OF THE PEACE.

penal bond. A bond requiring the obligor to pay a specified sum as a penalty if the underlying obligation is not performed. — Also termed *penal bill*; *common-defeasance bond.*

performance bond. See PERFORMANCE BOND.

permit bond. See *license bond.*

personal bond. **1.** See *bail bond*; BAIL. **2.** A written document in which an obligor formally recognizes an obligation to pay money or to do a specified act.

probate bond. A bond, such as that filed by an executor, required by law to be given during a probate proceeding to ensure a faithful performance by the person under bond.

redelivery bond. See *replevin bond.*

refunding bond. A bond given to assure an executor that a legatee will return an estate distribution should the remaining estate assets be insufficient to pay the other legacies.

registered bond. A governmental or corporate obligation to pay money, represented by a single certificate delivered to the creditor. • The obligation is registered in the holder's name on the books of the debtor.

removal bond. **1.** A bond to cover possible duties owed by a person who removes goods from a warehouse for export. **2.** A bond required in some states when a litigant seeks to remove an action to another court.

replevin bond (ri-**plev**-in). **1.** A bond given by a plaintiff to replevy or attach property in the defendant's possession before judgment is rendered in a replevin action. • The bond protects the attaching officer and ensures the property's safekeeping until the court decides whether it should be returned to the defendant. — Also termed *replevy bond.* See REPLEVIN. **2.** A bond given by a defendant in a replevin action to regain attached property pending the outcome of litigation. • The bond does not discharge the attachment lien. — Also termed *replevy bond*; *claim-property bond*; *redelivery bond.* Cf. *forthcoming bond.*

respondentia bond (re-spon-**den**-shee-ə *or* ree-). A contract containing the pledge of a ship's cargo; a mortgage of a ship's cargo. Cf. *bottomry bond.*

simple bond. **1.** A bond without a penalty. **2.** A bond payable to a named obligee on demand or on a certain date.

statutory bond. A bond that literally or substantially meets the requirements of a statute.

straw bond. A bond, usu. a bail bond, that carries either a fictitious name or the name of a person who is unable to pay the sum guaranteed; a worthless or inadequate bond.

submission bond. A bond given by a litigant who agrees to submit a lawsuit to arbitration and to be bound by an arbitrator's award.

supersedeas bond (soo-pər-**see**-dee-əs). An appellant's bond to stay execution on a judgment during the pendency of the appeal. Fed. R. Civ. P. 62(d); Fed. R. App. P. 8(b). — Often shortened to *supersedeas*. See SUPERSEDE (2). Cf. *appeal bond*.

surety bond. See PERFORMANCE BOND.

ten-percent bond. A bail bond in the amount of 10% of the bond otherwise required for a defendant's release. • This type of bond usu. allows a defendant to arrange a bond without the services of a bondsman or other surety.

unsecured bail bond. A bond that holds a defendant liable for a breach of the bond's conditions (such as failure to appear in court), but that is not secured by a deposit of or lien on property. See RECOGNIZANCE.

3. A long-term, interest-bearing debt instrument issued by a corporation or governmental entity usu. to provide for a particular financial need; esp., such an instrument in which the debt is secured by a lien on the issuer's property. Cf. DEBENTURE.

"Typically debt securities are notes, debentures, and bonds. Technically a 'debenture' is an unsecured corporate obligation while a 'bond' is secured by a lien or mortgage on corporate property. However, the word 'bond' is often used indiscriminately to cover both bonds and debentures.... A 'bond' is a long term debt security while a 'note' is usually a shorter term obligation. Bonds are historically bearer instruments, negotiable by delivery, issued in multiples of $1,000 with interest payments represented by coupons that are periodically clipped and submitted for payment." Robert W. Hamilton, *The Law of Corporations in a Nutshell* 128 (3d ed. 1991).

accrual bond. A bond — usu. the last collateralized-mortgage-obligation issue — from which no principal or interest payment will be made until any bonds issued earlier have been fully paid. — Also termed *Z-bond*.

adjustment bond. A bond issued when a corporation is reorganized. — Also termed *reorganization bond*.

annuity bond. A bond that lacks a maturity date and that perpetually pays interest. — Also termed *consol*; *perpetual bond*; *continued bond*; *irredeemable bond*.

arbitrage bond. A municipal bond, the proceeds of which are invested in bonds paying a higher yield than that paid by the municipality on its own bonds. • Under the Internal Revenue Code, the tax-free aspect of municipal-bond income may be lost if the bonds are classified as arbitrage bonds. See ARBITRAGE.

assessment bond. A municipal bond repaid from property assessment taxes.

assumed bond. See *guaranteed bond* (1).

baby bond. A bond usu. having a face value of $1,000 or less.

bearer bond. A bond payable to the person holding it. • The transfer of possession transfers the bond's ownership. Cf. *registered bond*.

bond and mortgage. A bond that is backed by a mortgage on realty. — Also termed *mortgage bond*. Cf. DEBENTURE.

book-entry bond. A bond for which no written certificate is issued to reflect ownership.

callable bond. See *redeemable bond*.

chattel-mortgage bond. A bond secured by a mortgage on personal property.

closed-end mortgage bond. A mortgage bond with provisions prohibiting the debtor from issuing additional bonds against the bond's collateral.

collateral trust bond. **1.** A bond representing a debt secured by the deposit of another security with a trustee. — Also termed *collateral trust certificate*. **2.** A long-term corporate bond that is secured by other companies' mortgage bonds held by the corporation, which pledges and deposits the mortgage bonds in trust. • The interest on these collateral trust bonds is typically lower than that received on the bonds pledged; the surplus is used to form a sinking fund to redeem the collateral trust bonds. A holding company often issues these bonds by pledging the stock of a subsidiary.

commodity-backed bond. A bond with interest payments or principal repayment tied to the price of a specific commodity, such as gold. • This type of bond, which has a low interest rate but provides a hedge against inflation because the commodity price will usu. rise, is often issued by a firm with a stake in the commodity.

consolidated bond. **1.** A railroad bond secured by a mortgage on the entire railroad line formed by several consolidated railroads. Cf. *divisional bond*. **2.** A single bond that replaces two or more outstanding issues.

construction bond. A bond issued by a governmental entity for a building project.

continued bond. See *annuity bond*.

convertible bond. A bond that can be exchanged for stock shares in the corporation that issued the bond.

corporate bond. **1.** An interest-bearing instrument containing a corporation's promise to pay a fixed sum of money at some future time. • A corporate bond may be secured or unsecured. **2.** A bond issued by a corporation, usu. having a maturity of ten years or longer.

county bond. A county-issued bond paid through a levy on a special taxing district, whether or not the district is coextensive with the county.

coupon bond. A bond with attached interest coupons that the holder may present to receive interest payments. See BOND COUPON.

cushion bond. A bond paying an uncommonly high interest rate.

debenture bond. See DEBENTURE (3).

deferred-interest bond. A bond whose interest payments are postponed for a time.

discount bond. A bond sold at its current market value, which is less than its face value. — Also termed *non-interest-bearing bond.*

divisional bond. A railroad bond secured by a mortgage on a specific segment of a consolidated railroad system. Cf. *consolidated bond.*

endorsed bond. See *guaranteed bond* (1).

equipment trust bond. A bond secured by tangible property, such as an airplane. • A trustee usu. holds title to the equipment, which is leased to the issuer. — Also termed *equipment trust certificate.*

first-mortgage bond. A long-term bond that has the first claim on specified assets.

flat bond. A bond that trades without accrued interest.

floating-interest bond. A bond with an interest rate that moves up and down with changing economic conditions.

flower bond. A Treasury bond redeemable before maturity if used to settle federal estate taxes. • Flower bonds were issued before April 1971 and reached final maturity in 1998.

foreign bond. A bond issued in a currency different from that used where the issuer is located, such as a Canadian-government bond that is denominated in U.S. dollars and issued in the United States.

full-faith-and-credit bond. See *general-obligation bond.*

general-mortgage bond. A corporate bond secured by a blanket mortgage on property. • The general-mortgage bond, however, is often less valuable because it is subordinate to prior mortgages.

general-obligation bond. A municipal bond payable from general revenue rather than from a special fund. • Such a bond has no collateral to back it other than the issuer's taxing power. — Often shortened to *obligation bond.* — Also termed *full-faith-and-credit bond.*

> "There are two main types of bonds issued by local governments: general obligation bonds and revenue bonds.... Bonds will be assumed to be general obligation unless they themselves contain a clear promise to pay *only* out of a special fund." Osborne M. Reynolds, Jr., *Handbook of Local Government Law* § 104, at 323 (1982).

gold bond. **1.** *Hist.* A bond payable in gold coin or U.S. currency at the election of the bondholder. • This type of bond existed until 1933, when the U.S. monetary system abandoned the gold standard. **2.** A commodity-backed bond that is secured by gold and issued by a gold-mining company.

government bond. See *savings bond*; *government security* under SECURITY (4).

guaranteed bond. **1.** A bond issued by a corporation and guaranteed by a third party. • This type of bond is common among railroads. — Also termed *endorsed bond*; *assumed bond*; *joint bond.* **2.** A bond issued by a subsidiary corporation whose parent corporation guarantees the principal and interest payments.

improvement bond. See *revenue bond.*

income bond. A corporate bond secured by the corporation's net income, after the payment of interest on senior debt. • Sometimes this type of bond is a *cumulative-income bond*, in which case, if the income in any year is insufficient to pay the full interest, the deficit is carried forward as a lien on any future income.

indeterminate bond. A callable bond with no set maturity date.

industrial-development bond. **1.** A type of revenue bond in which interest and principal payments are backed by a corporation rather than a municipality. • This type of bond usu. finances a private business facility. **2.** A tax-exempt municipal bond that finances a usu. local industry. — Also termed *industrial-revenue bond.*

interchangeable bond. A bond that can be exchanged for a different type of bond, such as a coupon bond that may be exchanged for a registered bond.

interest bond. A bond paid in lieu of interest due on other bonds.

investment-grade bond. A bond with a rating of BBB or better by the leading bond rating services. See INVESTMENT-GRADE RATING.

irredeemable bond. See *annuity bond.*

joint and several bond. A bond in which the principal and interest are guaranteed by two or more obligors.

joint bond. A bond signed by two or more obligors. • In contrast to a joint and several bond, all the obligors must be joined if an action is brought on the bond.

junior bond. A bond subordinate in priority to another bond.

junk bond. A high-risk, high-yield subordinated bond issued by a corporation with a below-standard industry rating.

leasehold-mortgage bond. A bond issued by a lessee and secured by the lessee's leasehold interest.

Lloyd's bond. *Hist. English law.* A corporate bond issued on work done or goods delivered. • A bond issued in this manner avoids any restriction on indebtedness existing either in law or in corporate bylaws. The term supposedly derives from an English lawyer named Lloyd, who is credited with devising the method.

mortgage bond. A bond secured by the issuer's real property.

multimaturity bond. See *put bond.*

municipal bond. A bond issued by a nonfederal government or governmental unit, such as a state bond to finance local improvements. • The interest received from a municipal bond may be exempt from federal, state, and local taxes. — Often shortened (in pl.) to *municipals*; *munies.* — Also termed *municipal security.*

noncallable bond. See *noncallable security* under SECURITY.

non-interest-bearing bond. See *discount bond.*

nonstatutory bond. See *voluntary bond.*

obligation bond. See *general-obligation bond.*

open-end mortgage bond. A mortgage bond that can be used as security for another bond issue.

optional bond. A bond that the holder may redeem before its maturity date if the issuer agrees.

option tender bond. See *put bond.*

participating bond. A bond that entitles the holder to a share of corporate profits but does not have a fixed interest rate.

passive bond. A bond bearing no interest. See *passive debt* under DEBT.

perpetual bond. See *annuity bond.*

post-obit bond. An agreement by which a borrower promises to pay to the lender a lump sum (exceeding the amount advanced) upon the death of a person whose property the borrower expects to inherit. • Equity traditionally enforces such bonds only if the terms are just and reasonable.

premium bond. A bond with a selling price above face or redemption value. See PREMIUM (3).

put bond. A bond that gives the holder the right to redeem it for full value at specified times before maturity. — Also termed *multimaturity bond*; *option tender bond.* Cf. *put option* under OPTION (4).

railroad-aid bond. A bond issued by a public body to fund railway construction.

redeemable bond. A bond that the issuer may call for payment. — Also termed *callable bond.*

re-funding bond. A bond that retires an outstanding bond.

registered bond. A bond that only the holder of record may redeem, enjoy benefits from, or transfer to another. Cf. *bearer bond.*

reorganization bond. See *adjustment bond.*

revenue bond. A government bond repayable from public funds.

savings bond. A nontransferable bond issued by the U.S. government.

school bond. A bond issued by a city or school district to fund school construction.

secured bond. A bond backed by some type of security. Cf. DEBENTURE (2).

serial bond. A bond issued concurrently with other bonds having different maturity dates.

series bonds. A group of bonds issued under the authority of the same indenture, but offered publicly at different times and with different maturity dates and interest rates.

single bond. See *bill obligatory* under BILL (7).

sinking-fund bond. A bond backed by a sinking fund for bond redemption. See *sinking fund* under FUND (1).

special-tax bond. A municipal bond secured by taxes levied for a specific governmental purpose, usu. improvements. — Also termed *special-assessment bond.*

state bond. A bond issued by a state.

statutory bond. A bond given in accordance with a statute.

subordinated bond. See *junior bond.*

tax-exempt bond. A bond that pays tax-free interest.

term bond. A bond that matures concurrently with other bonds in that issue.

Treasury bond. See TREASURY BOND.

unsecured bond. See DEBENTURE (2).

voluntary bond. A bond not required by statute but given anyway. — Also termed *nonstatutory bond.*

zero-coupon bond. A bond paying no interest. • It is sold at a discount price and later redeemed at face value, the profit being the difference. — Also termed *passive bond.* See *zero-coupon security* under SECURITY (4).

bond, *vb.* **1.** To secure payment by providing a bond <at the creditor's insistence, Gabriel consolidated and bonded his various loans>. **2.** To provide a bond for (a person) <the company bonded its off-site workers>.

bond and mortgage. See BOND (3).

bond conversion. The exchange of a convertible bond for another asset, usu. stock.

bond coupon. The part of a coupon bond that is clipped by the holder and surrendered to obtain an interest payment. See *coupon bond* under BOND (3).

bond covenant. A bond-indenture provision that protects bondholders by specifying what the issuer may or may not do, as by prohibiting the issuer from issuing more debt. See BOND INDENTURE (1).

bond creditor. See CREDITOR.

bond discount. See DISCOUNT (3).

bond dividend. See DIVIDEND.

bonded, *adj.* (Of a person or entity) acting under, or placed under, a bond <a bonded court official>.

bonded debt. See DEBT.

bonded warehouse. See WAREHOUSE.

bond for a deed. See *bond for land* under BOND (2).

bond for deed. See CONVEYANCE (6); BOND FOR TITLE.

bond for land. See BOND (2).

bond for title. *Real estate.* The seller's retention of legal title until the buyer pays the purchase price. — Also termed *bond for deed.* Cf. *contract for deed* under CONTRACT.

bond fund. See MUTUAL FUND.

bondholder. One who holds a government or business bond.

bond indenture. 1. A contract between a bond issuer and bondholder outlining a bond's face value, interest rate, maturity date, and other features. **2.** A mortgage held on specified corporate property to secure payment of the bond.

bonding company. See COMPANY.

bond issue. See ISSUE (2).

bondman. See BONDSMAN (2).

bond of corroboration. See BOND (2).

bond premium. See PREMIUM (3).

bond rating. A system of evaluating and appraising the investment value of a bond issue.

bond retirement. The cancellation of a bond that has been called or paid.

bondsman. 1. One who guarantees a bond; a surety. **2.** A serf or peasant; VILLEIN. — Also termed (in sense 2) *bondman.*

bond table. A schedule used in determining a bond's current value by its coupon rate, its time to maturity, and its effective yield if held to maturity.

bond trust. See TRUST.

bones gents (bohn **jents**). [Law French "good men"] *Hist.* Qualified or competent persons; esp., men qualified to serve on a jury.

bonification (bahn-ə-fi-**kay**-shən). A tax remission, usu. on goods intended for export. • Bonification enables a commodity to be sold in a foreign market as if it had not been taxed.

boni homines (**boh**-nI **hom**-ə-neez). [Law Latin "good men"] *Hist.* Free tenants who judged each other in their lord's court.

> "[W]e may find traces of juries in the laws of all those nations which adopted the feodal system, as in Germany, France, and Italy; who had all of them a tribunal composed of twelve good men and true, *'boni homines'*. . . ." 3 William Blackstone, *Commentaries on the Laws of England* 349 (1768).

bonis cedere (**boh**-nis **see**-də-ree). [Latin "to cede one's goods"] *Civil law.* A transfer or surrender of property, usu. from a debtor to a creditor.

bonis non amovendis. See DE BONIS NON AMOVENDIS.

bonitarian (bahn-ə-**tair**-ee-in), *adj.* Equitable. — Also termed *bonitary*. Cf. QUIRITARIAN.

bonitarian ownership. See OWNERSHIP.

bonitary. See BONITARIAN.

bono et malo (**boh**-noh et **mal**-oh). See DE BONO ET MALO.

bonorum possessio contra tabulas (bə-**noh**-rəm pə-**zesh**-ee-oh **kahn**-trə **tab**-yə-ləs). [Latin "possession of goods against the testament"] *Roman law.* An order authorizing the applicant to take possession of an estate contrary to the testator's will. • Magistrates made such orders in certain cases, as where a testator passed over a son who was not expressly disinherited. — Also termed *contra tabulas*.

> "The Praetor could not affect the civil validity of a will; he could not make or unmake a *heres*. He could, however, give *bonorum possessio* to a person, *heres* or not at civil law, which gave him power to take possession of the goods by appropriate steps, *bonorum possessio contra tabulas* . . . ." W.W. Buckland, *A Textbook of Roman Law: From Augustus to Justinian* 324 (Peter Stein ed., 3d ed. 1963).

bonum factum (**boh**-nəm **fak**-təm). [Latin] A good or proper act or deed. — Abbr. *b.f.*

bonus. 1. A premium paid in addition to what is due or expected <year-end bonus>. • In the employment context, workers' bonuses are not a gift or gratuity; they are paid for services or on consideration in addition to or in excess of the compensation that would ordinarily be given. **2.** *Oil & gas.* A payment made to the lessee for the execution of an oil-and-gas lease <the lessee received a large bonus at closing>.

> "The amount of bonus paid, usually referred to as a per acre amount, may fluctuate widely between properties. The amount paid depends upon the nature of the development activity in the vicinity. If the land is located in a semi-proven area, or in a logical extension of a proven field, the bonus paid may be substantial." Richard W. Hemingway, *The Law of Oil and Gas* § 2.5, at 57 (3d ed. 1991).

bonus share. See *bonus stock* under STOCK.

bonus stock. See STOCK.

bonus zoning. See *incentive zoning* under ZONING.

boodle. *Slang.* Money paid as a bribe, usu. to a public official.

book, *vb.* **1.** To record in a book (as a sale or accounting item) <Jenkins booked three sales that day>. **2.** To record the name of (a person arrested) in a sequential list of police arrests, with details of the person's identity (usu. including a photograph and a fingerprint), particulars about the alleged offense, and the name of the arresting officer <the defendant was booked immediately after arrest>. **3.** To engage (someone) contractually as a performer or guest <although the group was booked for two full performances, the lead singer, Raven, canceled and this action ensued>. See BOOKING CONTRACT.

book account. See ACCOUNT.

book entry. 1. A notation made in an accounting journal. **2.** The method of reflecting ownership of publicly traded securities whereby a customer of a brokerage firm receives confirmations of transactions and monthly statements, but not stock certificates. See CENTRAL CLEARING SYSTEM.

book-entry bond. See BOND (3).

book equity. The percentage of a corporation's book value allocated to a particular class of stock. Cf. BOOK VALUE; MARKET EQUITY.

bookie. See BOOKMAKER.

booking contract. An agreement by which an actor or other performer is engaged.

bookkeeping, *n.* The mechanical recording of debits and credits or the summarizing of financial information, usu. about a business enterprise. Cf. ACCOUNTING.

double-entry bookkeeping. A method of bookkeeping in which every transaction recorded by a business involves one or more "debit" entries and one or more "credit" entries. • The debit entries must equal the credit entries for each transaction recorded.

single-entry bookkeeping. A method of bookkeeping in which each transaction is recorded in a single record, such as a record of cash or credit accounts.

bookland (**buuk**-land). *Hist.* Land held under charter or deed; freehold land. • This was a privileged form of ownership (usu. free of the customary burdens on land) generally reserved for churches and leaders. — Also spelled *bocland*; *bockland*. — Also termed *charter-land*. Cf. LOANLAND; FOLKLAND.

"Charter-land is such as a man holds by charter, that is, by evidence in writing, which otherwise is called freehold.... [T]his land was held with more easy and commodious conditions, than folkland and copy-hold land held without writing; ... it is a free and absolute inheritance; whereas land without writing is charged with payment and bondage; so that for the most part noblemen and persons of quality possess the former, and rustics the other. The first we call freehold and by charter: the other, land at the will of the lord." *Termes de la Ley* 80 (1st. Am. ed. 1812).

"Prior to the Conquest, property in land was divided into *bocland*, *folcland*, and *laenland*. The exact nature of these rights has been disputed, but probably *bocland* was held by owners of high station claiming under a charter of privileges originally granted by the King, while *folcland* was held by ordinary owners according to the custom of the district in which the land lay. *Laenland*, or loanland, appears to have represented something in the nature of a tenancy of a less enduring character. It derived its existence from the loan of land by one person to another, and hence emphasises the relation later known as that of feudal landlord and tenant. Furthermore, as *bocland* became more common, a tendency for *laenland* and *bocland* to coalesce appeared." A.K.R. Kiralfy, *Potter's Outlines of English Legal History* 195 (5th ed. 1958).

bookmaker. A person who determines odds and receives bets on the outcome of events, esp. sports events. See BOOKMAKING.

bookmaking. Gambling that entails the taking and recording of bets on an event, such as a horse race.

book of original entry. A day-to-day record in which a business's transactions are first recorded.

books of account. See SHOP BOOKS.

Books of Adjournal. *Scots law.* The records of the High Court of Justiciary.

book value. The value at which an asset is carried on a balance sheet. Cf. BOOK EQUITY.

adjusted book value. Inventory value adjusted to reflect the inventory's current actual value.

book-value stock. See STOCK.

boomage. 1. A fee charged by a company for collecting and distributing logs that have accumulated in its boom (i.e., a line of sawed logs collected and stored on a stream's surface). **2.** A right to enter on riparian lands to fasten booms. **3.** An anchorage fee charged by a canal proprietor.

boon day. (*usu. pl.*) *Hist.* One of several days in the year when copyhold tenants were obliged to perform base services for the lord (such as reaping corn) without pay. — Also termed *due day*.

boot, *n.* **1.** *Tax.* Supplemental money or property subject to tax in an otherwise tax-free exchange. **2.** *Corporations.* In a corporate reorganization, anything received other than the stock or securities of a controlled corporation. **3.** *Commercial law.* Cash or other consideration used to balance an otherwise unequal exchange. **4.** *Hist.* ESTOVERS (1).

boot camp. 1. A camp for basic training of Navy or Marine Corps recruits. **2.** See *shock incarceration* under INCARCERATION.

boothage (**boo**-thij). See BOTHAGIUM.

bootleg, *vb.* To manufacture, reproduce, or distribute (something) illegally or without authorization <he was bootlegging copyrighted videotapes>.

bootlegger, *n.* A person who manufactures, transports, or sells something illegally, esp. alcoholic beverages. See MOONSHINE.

bootstrap, *vb.* **1.** To make a success despite sparse resources. **2.** To reach an unsupported conclusion.

bootstrap doctrine. *Conflict of laws.* The doctrine that forecloses collateral attack on the jurisdiction of another state's court that has rendered final judgment. • The doctrine applies when a court in an earlier case has taken jurisdiction over a person, over status, or over land. It is based on the principle that under res judicata, the parties are bound by the judgment, whether the issue was the court's jurisdiction or something else. The bootstrap doctrine, however, cannot give effectiveness to a judgment by a court that had no subject-matter jurisdiction. For example, parties cannot, by appearing before a state court, "bootstrap" that court into having jurisdiction over a federal matter.

> "If the court which rendered the judgment has, with the parties before it, expressly passed upon the jurisdictional question in the case, or had opportunity to do so because the parties could have raised the question, that question is res judicata, and is therefore not subject to collateral attack in the state in which the judgment is sued on. This has been called the 'bootstrap doctrine,' the idea being that a court which initially had no jurisdiction can when the issue is litigated lift itself into jurisdiction by its own incorrect but conclusive finding that it does have jurisdiction." Robert A. Leflar, *American Conflicts Law* § 79, at 159 (3d ed. 1977).

bootstrap sale. See SALE.

booty. 1. *Int'l law.* Movables taken from the enemy as spoils in the course of warlike operations. — Also termed *spoils of war.* **2.** Property taken by force or piracy; prize or loot.

bordage (**bor**-dij). *Hist.* A type of tenure in which a tenant holds a cottage and a few acres in exchange for providing customary services to the lord.

bordarii (bor-**dair**-ee-I). *Hist.* Bordage tenants. • The status of these tenants was less servile than that of villein tenants. See BORDAGE; VILLEINAGE.

border. A boundary between one nation (or a political subdivision) and another.

border control. *Int'l law.* A country's physical manifestation of its territorial sovereignty, by which it regulates which people and goods may enter and leave. • As a practical matter, border controls are often used to contain plant and animal diseases, fight terrorism, and detect the movement of criminals.

bordereau (bor-də-**roh**), *n.* **1.** A description of reinsured risks; esp., a periodic report provided by a cedent to a treaty reinsurer, consisting of basic information affecting the reinsurance treaty, such as the underlying insureds, the types of risks covered, policies, and dates of loss. See REINSURANCE TREATY. **2.** A detailed note of account. Pl. **bordereaux.** — **bordereau,** *vb.*

border search. See SEARCH.

bord-halfpenny (bord-**hay**-pə-nee). See BOTHAGIUM.

bordlands. *Hist.* Land used by the nobility to produce food. • Bordlands remained under the nobility's direct control or were given to tenants who produced provisions for the landowner. Cf. BORDAGE.

bork (bork), *vb. Slang.* **1.** (Of the U.S. Senate) to reject a nominee for the U.S. Supreme Court or other governmental position because of the nominee's unorthodox political and legal philosophy. • The term derives from the name of Robert Bork, President Ronald Reagan's unsuccessful nominee for the Court in 1987. **2.** (Of political and legal activists) to embark on a media campaign that helps pressure U.S. Senators into rejecting a President's nominee for the U.S. Supreme Court. **3.** Generally, to smear a political opponent.

borough. 1. A town or township with a municipal charter, such as one of the five political divisions of New York City. **2.** *English law.* A chartered town that originally sent a member to Parliament. **3.** *Hist.* A fortified or important town.

borough court. *English law.* An inferior civil court of record, usu. presided over by the municipal recorder. • Most borough courts were abolished by Parliament in 1972. Cf. BOROUGH SESSIONS; RECORDER (1).

borough English. *Hist.* A common-law rule of descent whereby the youngest son inherited all his father's lands. — Also termed *burgh English*; *burgh Engloys.* See PRIMOGENITURE.

borough fund. *English law.* The revenue generated by a municipal borough.

borough-holder. See BORSHOLDER.

borough sessions. Criminal court sessions held before a municipal recorder. Cf. BOROUGH COURTS; RECORDER (1).

borrow, *vb.* **1.** To take something for temporary use. **2.** To receive money with the understanding or agreement that it must be repaid, usu. with interest. See LOAN.

borrowed capital. Funds lent to a corporation or other entity to finance its operations, such as cash dividends that are declared by a corporation but temporarily retained (with stockholder approval) to provide operating funds.

borrowed employee. See EMPLOYEE.

borrowed servant. See *borrowed employee* under EMPLOYEE.

borrowed-statutes doctrine. The principle that if one state adopts a statute identical to that of another state, any settled judicial construction of that statute by the courts of the other state is binding on the courts of the state that later enacts the statute.

borrower. A person or entity to whom money or something else is lent.

borrowhead. See BORSHOLDER.

borrowing statute. A legislative exception to the conflict-of-laws rule holding that a forum state must apply its own statute of limitations. • A borrowing statute specifies the circumstances in which a forum state will apply another state's statute of limitations.

borsholder (**bors**-hohl-dər). *Hist.* **1.** The chief of a tithing or frankpledge. **2.** A petty constable. — Also termed *borough-holder*; *borrowhead*; *headborough*.

Boston interest. See INTEREST (3).

bote (boht). *Hist.* **1.** A compensation or profit. — Also spelled *bot*; *boot*.

cart-bote. See *plowbote*.

fire-bote. See *housebote*.

haybote. See HAYBOTE.

hedgebote. See HAYBOTE.

housebote. An allowance of wood from the estate used to repair a house or to burn in the fireplace. — Also termed *fire-bote*.

plowbote. An allowance of wood for the construction and repair of farm equipment. — Also termed *cart-bote*.

wainbote. An allowance of wood for the repair of wagons.

2. A compensatory payment for causing an injury. Cf. BOTELESS.

God-bote. A church fine paid for offenses against God.

man-bote. Compensation for killing someone.

theft-bote. The acceptance of a payment from a thief in exchange for an agreement not to prosecute; COMPOUNDING A CRIME. • The payment might be either a bribe or a return of the stolen goods themselves. This was a form of compounding a felony.

> "Another offence of this class is *theftbote* or composition with a thief by which the person robbed takes his goods again and by contract suppresses the robbery and defrauds justice. This crime is punishable by fine and imprisonment." 1 Sir Robert Chambers, *A Course of Lectures on the English Law: 1767–1773* 448 (Thomas M. Curley ed., 1986).

3. A tenant's right to use as much wood from the estate as necessary for fuel, fences, and other agricultural operations. • *Bote* in this sense is an earlier form of *estovers*.

boteless (**boht**-ləs), *adj. Hist.* Without relief or remedy; without the privilege of making satisfaction for a crime by pecuniary payment. • The modern word *bootless* is derived from this term. Cf. BOTE (2).

bothagium (bah-**thay**-jee-əm). *Hist.* Customary dues paid to a lord for placing a booth in a fair or market. — Also termed *bord-halfpenny*; *boothage*.

botiler of the king. *Hist.* An officer who provided the king's wines. • By virtue of office, the *botiler* could choose two casks from every wine-laden ship. The modern word *butler* is derived from *botiler*.

bottomage bond. See *bottomry bond* under BOND (2).

bottom-hole contract. *Oil & gas.* An agreement requiring a payment from the well owner to the well's lessee after the lessee drills to a specified depth, whether or not the well produces.

bottomland. Low-lying land, often located in a river's floodplain.

bottomry. A contract by which a shipowner pledges the ship as security for a loan to finance a voyage (as to equip or repair the ship), the lender losing the money if the ship is lost during the voyage. • The term refers to the idea that the shipowner pledges the ship's bottom, or keel. Cf. RESPONDENTIA.

bottomry bond. See BOND (2).

bought and sold notes. Two memoranda prepared by a broker to record the sale of a note. • The broker sends the *bought note* to the purchaser, and sends the *sold note* to the seller.

bought note. See NOTE (3).

boulevard rule. The principle that the driver of a vehicle approaching a highway from a smaller road must stop and yield the right-of-way to all highway traffic.

boulwarism. *Labor law.* A bargaining tactic in which an employer researches the probable outcome of collective bargaining and uses the information to make a firm settlement offer to a union on a take-it-or-leave-it basis, so that there is no real negotiation. • *Boulwarism* is now considered to be an unfair labor practice by the National Labor Relations Board. The practice takes its name from Lemuel Boulware, vice president for employee relations at General Electric Company, who used the technique during the mid–20th century.

bounced check. See *bad check* under CHECK.

bound, *n.* (*usu. pl.*) **1.** BOUNDARY <metes and bounds>. **2.** A limitation or restriction on action <within the bounds of the law>.

bound, *vb.* To delineate a property boundary <property bounded by the creek>. Cf. BIND.

bound, *adj.* **1.** Constrained by a contractual or other obligation <they are bound to make the payments by the first of each month>. **2.** (Of a court) constrained to follow a precedent <bound by a Supreme Court decision>.

boundary. 1. A natural or artificial separation that delineates the confines of real property <the creek serves as a boundary between the two properties>. See METES AND BOUNDS.

> "The object of all rules for the establishment of boundaries is to ascertain the actual location of the boundary as made at the time. The important and controlling consideration, where there is a conflict as to a boundary, is the parties intention, whether express or shown by surrounding circumstances . . . ." 11 C.J.S. *Boundaries* § 3 (1995).

natural boundary. Any nonartificial thing (such as a river or ocean) that forms a boundary of a nation, a political subdivision, or a piece of property. — Also termed *natural object*.

private boundary. An artificial boundary marker.

public boundary. A natural formation that marks the beginning of a boundary line. — Also termed *natural boundary*.

2. *Int'l law.* A line marking the limit of the territorial jurisdiction of a state or other entity having an international status.

boundary by acquiescence. See DOCTRINE OF PRACTICAL LOCATION.

boundary by agreement. See DOCTRINE OF PRACTICAL LOCATION.

boundary traffic. The movement of persons or goods across an international boundary.

bound bailiff. See BAILIFF.

bounded tree. A tree that marks a corner of a property's boundary.

bounder. A visible mark that indicates a territorial limit in a land survey.

bounty. 1. A premium or benefit offered or given, esp. by a government, to induce someone to take action or perform a service <a bounty for the killing of dangerous animals>. **2.** A gift, esp. in a will; generosity in giving <the court will distribute the testator's bounty equally>.

bounty hunter. A person who for a fee pursues someone charged with, or suspected of committing, a crime; esp., a person hired by a bail-bond company to find and arrest a criminal defendant who has breached the bond agreement by failing to appear in court as ordered. — Also termed *bail-enforcement agent*.

bounty land. See LAND.

bourse (buurs). [French] *French law.* An exchange; a stock exchange. — Also termed *bourse de commerce*.

boutique (boo-**teek**). A small specialty business; esp., a small law firm specializing in one particular aspect of law practice <a tax boutique>.

bovata terrae (boh-**vay**-tə **ter**-ee). [Law Latin] *Hist.* See OXGANG.

bow-bearer. *Hist.* An officer responsible for apprehending trespassers and poachers in the king's forest.

box-top license. See *shrink-wrap license* under LICENSE.

boycott, *n.* **1.** An action designed to achieve the social or economic isolation of an adversary. • The term derives from Captain Charles C. Boycott, an English landowner in famine-plagued Ireland of the 1870s; because of his ruthless treatment of Irish tenant farmers, the Irish Land League ostracized him. **2.** A concerted refusal to do business with a party to express disapproval of that party's practices. **3.** A refusal to deal in one transaction in an effort to obtain terms desired in a second transaction. • Under the Sherman Antitrust Act, even peaceful persuasion of a person to refrain from dealing with another can amount to a boycott. See 15 USCA §§ 1–7. — **boycott,** *vb.* Cf. PICKETING; STRIKE.

consumer boycott. A boycott by consumers of products or services to show displeasure with the manufacturer, seller, or provider.

group boycott. *Antitrust.* **1.** CONCERTED REFUSAL TO DEAL. **2.** A type of secondary boycott by two or more competitors who refuse to do business with one firm unless it refrains from doing business with an actual or potential competitor of the boycotters. • A group boycott can violate the Sherman Act and is analyzed under either the per se rule or the rule of reason, depending on the nature of the boycott. See PER SE RULE; RULE OF REASON.

> "Since early in this century, courts have interpreted Section 1 [of the Sherman Act] to limit the ability of competing firms to agree not to deal with or to isolate another firm. Unlike many cartels, where all competitors voluntarily join to fix prices (and share monopoly rewards), concerted refusals to deal usually involve a subset of all market participants who band together to gain market power by destroying or coercing their rivals. Such organized refusals to deal with a particular firm are usually given the pejorative label of 'group boycotts.'" Ernest Gellhorn & William E. Kovacic, *Antitrust Law and Economics in a Nutshell* 204 (4th ed. 1994).

primary boycott. A boycott by union members who stop dealing with a former employer.

secondary boycott. A boycott of the customers or suppliers of a business so that they will withhold their patronage from that business. • For example, a group might boycott a manufacturer who advertises on a radio station that broadcasts messages considered objectionable by the group.

B.R. *abbr.* **1.** Bankruptcy Reporter. — Also abbreviated *Bankr. Rep.* **2.** *Bancus Regis* [Latin "King's Bench"]. **3.** *Bancus Reginae* [Latin "Queen's Bench"]. • This abbreviation has been replaced by the English initials of these courts, K.B. and Q.B.

bracery. *Hist.* **1.** The offense of selling pretended rights or title to land. • This practice was outlawed by statute of 32 Hen. 8, ch. 9. **2.** EMBRACERY.

bracket creep. The process by which inflation or increased income pushes individuals into higher tax brackets.

bracket system. A system for collecting a sales tax based on an index providing for a graduated payment depending on the purchase price of the item, the purpose being fourfold: (1) to avoid having the seller collect a tax less than one cent; (2) to avoid requiring the state to figure the exact amount of tax on each sale; (3) to allow the seller to have a ready means for fixing the tax to be collected; and (4) to allow the state to collect about the right amount of tax. • This system may be provided for either by statute or by administrative regulation.

Bracton. The common title of one of the earliest books of English law, *De Legibus et Consuetudinibus Angliae* (ca. 1250). • Henry of Bratton (also known as *Bracton*), a judge of the Court of King's Bench and of Assize, is credited with writing the work, though he may have merely revised an earlier version.

> "Bracton's book is the crown and flower of English medieval jurisprudence.... Romanesque in form, English in substance — this perhaps is the best brief phrase that we can find for the outcome of his labours; but yet it is not very good. He had at his command and had diligently studied ... various parts of the Corpus Iuris Civilis, of the Decretum, and the Decretals, and he levied contributions from the canonist Tancred.... Bracton's debt — and therefore our debt — to the civilians is inestimably great. But for them, his book would have been impossible; but for them ... we should have missed not only the splendid plan, the orderly arrangement, the keen dilemmas, but also the sacerdotal spirit of the work. On the other hand, the main matter of his treatise is genuine English law laboriously collected out of the plea rolls of the king's court.... [H]is endeavor is to state the practice, the best and most approved practice, of the king's court, and of any desire to romanize the law we must absolutely acquit him." 1 Frederick Pollock & Frederic W. Maitland, *The History of English Law Before the Time of Edward I* 206–09 (2d ed. 1898).

Brady Act. A federal law establishing a national system for quickly checking the background of a prospective handgun purchaser. • The formal name of the law is the Brady Handgun Violence Prevention Act. The U.S. Supreme Court held unconstitutional the law's interim provision, which required chief state law-enforcement officers (usu. sheriffs) to conduct background checks until the national system was in place. The act is named for James Brady, a campaigner for gun-control laws who, as a member of President Ronald Reagan's staff, was wounded by gunfire during an attempted presidential assassination in 1981. 18 USCA §§ 921–930.

***Brady* material.** Information or evidence that is favorable to a criminal defendant's case and that the prosecution has a duty to disclose. • The prosecution's withholding of such information violates the defendant's due-process rights. *Brady v. Maryland*, 373 U.S. 83, 83 S.Ct. 1194 (1963). Cf. JENCKS MATERIAL.

brain death. See DEATH.

brake. See DUKE OF EXETER'S DAUGHTER.

branch. 1. An offshoot, lateral extension, or division of an institution <the executive, legislative, and judicial branches of government>. **2.** A line of familial descent stemming from a common ancestor <the Taylor branch of the Bradshaw family>. — Also termed *stock*.

Brandeis brief (**bran**-dɪs). A brief, usu. an appellate brief, that makes use of social and economic studies in addition to legal principles and citations. • The brief is named after Supreme Court Justice Louis D. Brandeis, who as an advocate filed the most famous such brief in *Muller v. Oregon*, 208 U.S. 412, 28 S.Ct. 324 (1908), in which he persuaded the Court to uphold a statute setting a maximum ten-hour workday for women.

Brandeis rules. See ASHWANDER RULES.

branding. 1. The act of marking cattle with a hot iron to identify their owner. **2.** Formerly, the punishment of marking an offender with a hot iron.

brand name. See TRADENAME.

branks (brangks). *Hist.* An instrument used to punish scolds, consisting of an iron framework that surrounded the head and entered the mouth to keep the offender's tongue depressed. — Also termed *scolding bridle*. See SCOLD. Cf. CASTIGATORY; DUCKING STOOL.

brassage (**bras**-ij). *Hist.* A government charge for the actual cost of coining metals. • Any profit is termed *seigniorage*. See SEIGNIORAGE (2).

breach, *n.* A violation or infraction of a law or obligation <breach of warranty> <breach of duty>. — **breach,** *vb.*

breach of arrest. A military offense committed by an officer who, being under arrest in quarters, leaves those quarters without a superior officer's authorization. See *arrest in quarters* under ARREST.

breach of close. The unlawful or unauthorized entry on another person's land; a common-law trespass. — Also termed *breaking a close*. See CLOSE.

breach of contract. Violation of a contractual obligation, either by failing to perform one's own promise or by interfering with another party's performance.

> "A breach may be one by non-performance, or by repudiation, or by both. Every breach gives rise to a claim for damages, and may give rise to other remedies. Even if the injured party sustains no pecuniary loss or is unable to show such loss with sufficient certainty, he has at least a claim for nominal damages. If a court chooses to ignore a trifling departure, there is no breach and no claim arises." Restatement (Second) of Contracts § 236 cmt. a (1981).

active breach of contract. *Civil law.* The negligent performance of a contractual obligation, to the point of acting outside the contract's terms. • Under Louisiana law, active breach of contract is contrasted with passive breach of contract, which is a failure to perform the obligations created by the contract. Unlike a passive breach, an active breach of contract may give rise to claims in contract and in tort. Cf. *passive breach of contract*.

anticipatory breach. A breach of contract caused by a party's anticipatory repudiation, i.e., unequivocally indicating that the party will not perform when performance is due. • Under these circumstances, the nonbreaching party may elect to treat the repudiation as an immediate breach and sue for damages. — Also termed *constructive breach*. See REPUDIATION.

> "A repudiation by one party may occur before the time for performance has arrived. Such a repudiation is called an anticipatory breach, and it gives the innocent party the option of treating the contract as terminated at once and suing for damages immediately if he chooses or, alternatively, of waiting until the time of performance has arrived, and then again calling on the other party to

perform. Should he choose the latter course he runs the risk that the contract may possibly become frustrated in the interim, in which case he will have lost his right to damages." P.S. Atiyah, *An Introduction to the Law of Contract* 298 (3d ed. 1981).

continuing breach. A breach of contract that endures for a considerable time or is repeated at short intervals.

efficient breach. An intentional breach of contract and payment of damages by a party who would incur greater economic loss by performing under the contract. See EFFICIENT-BREACH THEORY.

immaterial breach. See *partial breach*.

immediate breach. A breach that entitles the nonbreaching party to sue for damages immediately.

material breach. A substantial breach of contract, usu. excusing the aggrieved party from further performance and affording it the right to sue for damages.

"In determining whether a failure to render or to offer performance is material, the following circumstances are significant: (a) the extent to which the injured party will be deprived of the benefit which he reasonably expected; (b) the extent to which the injured party can be adequately compensated for the part of that benefit of which he will be deprived; (c) the extent to which the party failing to perform or to offer to perform will suffer forfeiture; (d) the likelihood that the party failing to perform or to offer to perform will cure his failure, taking account of all the circumstances including any reasonable assurances; (e) the extent to which the behavior of the party failing to perform or to offer to perform comports with standards of good faith and fair dealing." Restatement (Second) of Contracts § 241 (1981).

partial breach. A breach of contract that is less significant than a material breach and that gives the aggrieved party a right to damages, but does not usu. excuse that party from performance. — Also termed *immaterial breach*.

passive breach of contract. *Civil law.* A failure to perform the requirements of a contract. • Under Louisiana law, passive breach of contract is contrasted with active breach of contract, which is negligence in performing a contractual obligation. While an active breach of contract may give rise to claims in contract and in tort, a passive breach of contract usu. does not give rise to a tort claim. Cf. *active breach of contract*.

total breach. A material breach of contract that gives rise to a claim for damages based on the injured party's remaining rights to performance under the contract.

breach of covenant. The violation of an express or implied promise, usu. in a contract, either to do or not to do an act. See COVENANT.

breach of duty. The violation of a legal or moral obligation; the failure to act as the law obligates one to act. See NEGLIGENCE.

breach of peace. See BREACH OF THE PEACE.

breach of prison. See PRISON BREACH.

breach of promise. The violation of one's word or undertaking, esp. a promise to marry. See HEARTBALM STATUTE.

breach of the peace. The criminal offense of creating a public disturbance or engaging in disorderly conduct, particularly by making an unnecessary or distracting noise. — Also termed *breach of peace*; *disturbing the peace*; *disturbance of the peace*. See DISORDERLY CONDUCT.

"A breach of the peace takes place when either an assault is committed on an individual or public alarm and excitement is caused. Mere annoyance or insult is not enough: thus at common law a householder could not give a man into custody for violently and persistently ringing his door-bell. It is the particular duty of a magistrate or police officer to preserve the peace unbroken; hence if he has reasonable cause to believe that a breach of the peace is imminent he may be justified in committing an assault or effecting an arrest." R.F.V. Heuston, *Salmond on the Law of Torts* 131 (17th ed. 1977).

"The beginning of our criminal justice ... was concerned very largely with the problem of keeping the peace. Because of this fact all early indictments included some such phrase as 'against the peace of the King'; and until recently statutory provisions for simplification, indictments in this country were thought to be incomplete without some such conclusion as 'against the peace and dignity of the state.' As a result of this history all indictable offenses are sometimes regarded as deeds which violate the public peace, and hence in a loose sense the term 'breach of the peace' is regarded as a synonym for crime." Rollin M. Perkins & Ronald N. Boyce, *Criminal Law* 477 (3d ed. 1982).

breach of trust. A trustee's violation of either the trust's terms or the trustee's general fiduciary obligations; the violation of a duty that equity imposes on a trustee, whether the violation was willful, fraudulent, negligent, or inadvertent. • A breach of trust subjects the trustee to removal and creates personal liability.

breach of warranty. **1.** A breach of an express or implied warranty relating to the title, quality, content, or condition of goods sold. UCC § 2–312. **2.** *Insurance*. WARRANTY (3).

bread acts. *Hist.* Laws providing for the sustenance of persons kept in prison for debt. • These laws were formerly on the books in both England and the United States.

break. *vb.* **1.** To violate or disobey (a law) <to break the law>. **2.** To nullify (a will) by court proceeding <Samson, the disinherited son, successfully broke the will>. **3.** To escape from (a place of confinement) without permission <break out of prison>. **4.** To open (a door, gate, etc.) and step through illegally <he broke the close>.

breakage. **1.** An allowance given by a manufacturer to a buyer for goods damaged during transit or storage. **2.** Insignificant amounts of money retained by racetrack promoters from bets. • The retention of these small sums avoids the inconvenience of counting and paying out inconsequential winnings.

breaking, *n. Criminal law.* In the law of burglary, the act of entering a building without permission.

> "[T]o constitute a breaking at common law, there had to be the creation of a breach or opening; a mere trespass at law was insufficient. If the occupant of the dwelling had created the opening, it was felt that he had not entitled himself to the protection of the law, as he had not properly secured his dwelling.... In the modern American criminal codes, only seldom is there a requirement of a breaking. This is not to suggest, however, that elimination of this requirement has left the 'entry' element unadorned, so that any type of entry will suffice. Rather, at least *some* of what was encompassed within the common law 'breaking' element is reflected by other terms describing what kind of entry is necessary. The most common statutory term is 'unlawfully,' but some jurisdictions use other language, such as 'unauthorized,' by 'trespass,' 'without authority,' 'without consent,' or 'without privilege.'" Wayne R. LaFave & Austin W. Scott, Jr., *Criminal Law* § 8.13, at 793–94 (2d ed. 1986).

breaking a case. **1.** The voicing by one appellate judge to another judge on the same panel of a tentative view on how a case should be decided. • These informal expressions assist the judges in ascertaining how close they are to agreement. **2.** The solving of a case by the police.

breaking a close. See BREACH OF CLOSE.

breaking and entering. See BURGLARY (2).

breaking bulk, *n.* **1.** The act of dividing a large shipment into smaller units. **2.** Larceny by a bailee, esp. a carrier, who opens containers, removes items from them, and converts the items to personal use. — Also termed *breaking bale*. — **break bulk,** *vb.*

breaking of entail. See BARRING OF ENTAIL.

breast of the court. A judge's conscience, mind, or discretion. • This phrase is a loan translation (or calque) of the Latin phrase *in pectore judicis*. See IN PECTORE JUDICIS.

Breathalyzer. A device used to measure the blood alcohol content of a person's breath, esp. when the police suspect that the person was driving while intoxicated. • Breathalyzer test results are admissible as evidence if the test was properly administered. — Also termed *alcoholometer*; *drunkometer*; *intoxilyzer*; *intoximeter*. — **breathalyze,** *vb.* See BLOOD ALCOHOL CONTENT.

breathing room. *Slang.* The post-bankruptcy period during which a debtor may formulate a debt-repayment plan without harassment or interference by creditors.

bredwite (**bred**-wət). *Hist.* A penalty for not complying with regulations relating to the weight or quantity of bread.

brehon (**bree**-hən). *Hist.* In Ireland, a judge.

Brehon law (**bree**-hən law). *Hist.* The ancient system of law in Ireland at the time of its conquest by Henry II. • This law was formally abolished in 1366. — Sometimes spelled *Brehon Law*.

> "[T]he Irish were governed by what they called the Brehon law, so stiled from the Irish name of judges, who were denominated Brehons. But king John in the twelfth year of his reign went into Ireland, and carried over with him many able sages of the law; and there by his letters patent, in right of the dominion of conquest, is said to have ordained and established that Ireland should be governed by the laws of England .... But to this ordinance many of the Irish were averse to conform, and still stuck to their Brehon law: so that both Henry the third and Edward the first were obliged to renew the injunction.... And yet, even in the reign of queen Elizabeth, the wild natives still kept and preserved their Brehon law...." 1 William Blackstone, *Commentaries on the Laws of England* 100–01 (1765).

B reorganization. See REORGANIZATION (2).

brephotrophi (bre-**fah**-trə-fī). *Civil law.* Persons who manage institutions that receive and care for poor or abandoned children. • The word is Greek in origin and was used in late Roman law, but it first appeared in English in the 18th century.

brethren (**breth**-rən), *n. pl.* Brothers, esp. those considered spiritual kin (such as male colleagues on a court) <my brethren argue in the dissent that my statutory interpretation is faulty>. • The use of this collegial term has naturally dwindled as more women have entered law and esp. into the judiciary. Cf. SISTREN.

Bretts and Scotts, Laws of the. A system of laws used by the Celtic tribes of Scotland until the beginning of the 14th century, when Edward I of England abolished those laws.

breve (breev *or* **bree**-vee), *n.* [Law Latin] *Hist.* Writ. • The word *brevis* meant "short," and *brevia* were short writs, unlike charters. Pl. ***brevia*** (**bree**-vee-ə).

album breve (**al**-bəm breev *or* **bree**-vee). A blank writ; a writ with a blank or omission in it.

apertum breve (ə-**pər**-təm breev *or* **bree**-vee). [Latin "open writ"] An open, unsealed writ. See *patent writ* under WRIT. Cf. CLAUSUM.

breve de bono et malo (breev *or* **bree**-vee dee **boh**-noh et **mal**-oh). See DE ODIO ET ATIA.

breve de conventione (breev *or* **bree**-vee dee kən-ven-shee-**oh**-nee). See WRIT OF COVENANT.

breve de recto (breev *or* **bree**-vee dee **rek**-toh). See DE RECTO.

breve de transgressione super casum (breev *or* **bree**-vee dee trans-gres[h]-ee-**oh**-nee **s[y]oo**-pər **kay**-səm). See TRESPASS ON THE CASE.

breve innominatum (breev *or* **bree**-vee i-nom-ə-**nay**-təm). [Latin "innominate writ"] A writ that recites a cause of action only in general terms.

breve magnum de recto (breev *or* **bree**-vee **mag**-nəm dee **rek**-toh). See DE RECTO PATENS.

breve perquirere (breev *or* **bree**-vee pər-**kwɪ**-rə-ree). [Latin "to obtain a writ"] To purchase a writ or license of trial in the king's courts.

breve rebellionis. See COMMISSION OF REBELLION.

breve testatum (breev *or* **bree**-vee tes-**tay**-təm). [Latin "a witnessed writ"] A written memorandum used to memorialize the terms of a conveyance and investiture of land. • Witnesses to the conveyance did not sign the document, but their names were recorded. *Brevia testata* were introduced to reduce disputes concerning the terms of oral grants.

brevia amicabilia (**bree**-vee-ə am-ə-kə-**bil**-ee-ə). [Latin "writs with agreement"] Writs obtained with the agreement or consent of the opposing party in an action.

brevia anticipantia (**bree**-vee-ə an-tis-ə-**pan**-shee-ə). [Latin "anticipatory writs"] Anticipatory or preventive writs. • Six were included in this category: writs of *mesne*; *warrantia chartae*; *monstraverunt*; *audita querela*; *curia claudenda*; and *ne injuste vexes*. See QUIA TIMET.

brevia formata (**bree**-vee-ə for-**may**-tə). [Latin "writs of approved form"] Writs of established and approved form, issued as a matter of course. Cf. *brevia magistralia*.

brevia judicialia (**bree**-vee-ə joo-dish-ee-**ay**-lee-ə). [Latin "judicial writs"] Writs that issue during an action or afterward in aid of judgment. • A court issued such a writ after an original writ had issued out of Chancery. Cf. *brevia originale*.

brevia magistralia (**bree**-vee-ə maj-i-**stray**-lee-ə). [Latin "masters' writs"] Writs issued by the masters or clerks of chancery according to the circumstances of particular cases. • These writs, unlike some others, might be varied in accordance with the complainant's particular situation. Cf. *brevia formata*.

brevia originale (**bree**-vee-ə ə-rij-i-**nay**-lee). [Latin] Original writ. • This writ began a judicial action. Cf. *brevia judicialia*.

brevia selecta (**bree**-vee-ə sə-**lek**-tə). [Latin "selected writs"] Choice or selected writs or processes. — Abbr. *brev. sel.*

brevet (brə-**vet** *or* **brev**-it). **1.** *Military law.* A commission promoting an officer to a higher rank, esp. during wartime, but without a corresponding pay increase. **2.** *French law.* A privilege or warrant granted by the government to a private person, authorizing a special benefit or the exercise of an exclusive privilege. • For example, a *brevet d'invention* is a patent for an invention.

brevet officer. See OFFICER (2).

brevia amicabilia. See BREVE.

brevia anticipantia. See BREVE.

brevia formata. See BREVE.

brevia judicialia. See BREVE.

brevia magistralia. See BREVE.

brevia originale. See BREVE.

Breviarium Alaricanum (bree-vee-**air**-ee-əm al-ə-ri-**kay**-nəm). [Latin] An abridgment (or *breviary*) of Roman law compiled by order of the Visigoth king Alaric II, published for the use of his Roman subjects in the year 506. • The compilation was known before the 16th century as the *Lex Romana Visigothorum*. It was also termed the *Breviarium Aniani* after Alaric's chancellor, Anian, who edited and distributed the work. — Also termed *Breviary of Alaric* (**bree**-vee-er-ee əv **al**-ə-rik).

> "Though the *Breviarium* was later replaced by the *Lex Visigothorum* in the Visigothic kingdom, it continued in use in southern France and Lombardy, which had meantime passed under the dominion of the Franks. Its qualities made the *Breviarium* a book of high authority throughout the whole of western Europe during the Middle Ages and it was one of the main channels through which Roman law entered western European law prior to the Reception." David M. Walker, *The Oxford Companion to Law* 151–52 (1980).

brevia selecta. See BREVE.

breviate (**bree**-vee-ət). [Latin] *Hist.* An abstract of a writing; esp., a short statement attached to a Parliamentary bill summarizing the contents of the bill.

brevia testata (**bree**-vee-ə tes-**tay**-tə). [Latin] *Hist.* See *breve testatum* under BREVE.

brevibus et rotulis liberandis (**bree**-və-bəs et **roch**-ə-ləs lib-ər-**an**-dis). [Latin "breves and rolls to be freed"] *Hist.* A writ ordering a sheriff to turn over to a successor all paraphernalia of office.

brev. sel. See *brevia selecta* under BREVE.

bribe, *n.* A price, reward, gift, or favor bestowed or promised with a view to pervert the judgment of or influence the action of a person in a position of trust.

> "The core concept of a bribe is an inducement improperly influencing the performance of a public function meant to be gratuitously exercised." John T. Noonan, Jr., *Bribes* xi (1984).

bribee. One who receives a bribe. — Also termed *bribe-taker*.

bribe-giver. See BRIBER.

briber. One who offers a bribe. — Also termed *bribe-giver*.

bribery, *n.* The corrupt payment, receipt, or solicitation of a private favor for official action. • Bribery is a felony in most jurisdictions. — **bribe,** *vb.*

> "If money has been corruptly paid and corruptly received, for the purpose of influencing official action, do we have one crime of which two are guilty, or two different crimes? No uniform answer is possible under existing statutes. Under some of the provisions bribery is one offense and references to (1) giving or offering a bribe, or (2) to receiving or soliciting a bribe, are merely factual statements in regard to the guilt of one party or the other. Under another plan 'bribery' is employed as a generic term to cover two different offenses: (1) giving or offering a bribe, and (2) receiving or soliciting a bribe. A third plan uses the word 'bribery' to indicate the offense of the briber and 'receiving a bribe' for the other side of the transaction." Rollin M. Perkins & Ronald N. Boyce, *Criminal Law* 537 (3d ed. 1982).

commercial bribery. Corrupt dealing with the agents or employees of prospective buyers to secure an advantage over business competitors.

bribe-taker. See BRIBEE.

bribour (**brɪ**-bər). [fr. French *bribeur*] *Hist.* A thief.

bridge bank. A national bank chartered to operate an insolvent bank for up to three years or until the bank is sold.

bridge loan. See LOAN.

brief, *n.* **1.** A written statement setting out the legal contentions of a party in litigation, esp. on appeal; a document prepared by counsel as the basis for arguing a case, consisting of legal and factual arguments and the authorities in support of them. — Also termed *legal brief*.

Anders brief. See ANDERS BRIEF.

Brandeis brief. See BRANDEIS BRIEF.

proof brief. A preliminary appellate brief to be reviewed by the clerk of the court for compliance with applicable rules. • Proof briefs are required by local rules of the U.S. Court of Appeals for the Sixth Circuit. A proof brief in full compliance will be accepted and filed. If not in compliance, it will be returned for corrections to be made, and a deadline will be set for refiling. After all proof briefs have been accepted in a case, a date is set for filing a final brief, which may be modified only to include joint-appendix references, repagination, or updated citations.

reply brief. A brief that responds to issues and arguments raised in the brief previously filed by one's opponent.

2. *English law.* A solicitor's document that abstracts the pleadings and facts to inform a barrister about the case. **3.** ABSTRACT OF TITLE. — **brief,** *vb.*

brief-writing. The art or practice of preparing legal briefs. — Also termed *brief-making.*

brigandage (**brig**-ən-dij). *Archaic.* Plundering and banditry carried out by bands of robbers. • Piracy is sometimes called "maritime brigandage."

bright-line rule. A judicial rule of decision that tends to resolve issues, esp. ambiguities, simply and straightforwardly, sometimes sacrificing equity for certainty.

bring to book. To arrest and try (an offender) <the fugitives were brought to book and convicted>.

British subject. The status conferred on a citizen of the United Kingdom and the Commonwealth countries such as Canada, Australia, New Zealand, and India by the British Nationality Act 1981. • Although this is the current sense, the phrase *British subject* has had many different meanings over the years, under different statutes.

broad-form insurance. See INSURANCE.

broad-form policy. See INSURANCE POLICY.

broad interpretation. See *liberal construction* under CONSTRUCTION (2).

broadside objection. See OBJECTION.

brocard (**brahk**-ərd *or* **broh**-kərd). An elementary legal principle or maxim, esp. one deriving from Roman law or ancient custom.

brocarius (broh-**kair**-ee-əs). [Law Latin] *Hist.* A broker; a middleman between buyer and seller.

broker, *n.* **1.** An agent who acts as an intermediary or negotiator, esp. between prospective buyers and sellers; a person employed to make bargains and contracts between other persons in matters of trade, commerce, and navigation. • A broker differs from a factor because the broker usu. does not have possession of the property. Cf. FACTOR. **2.** *Securities.* A person engaged in the business of conducting securities transactions for the accounts of others. — **broker,** *vb.*

> "The most important determining factor of what constitutes a 'broker' is whether the party is dealing for itself or for another. A broker may, by contract, have title to property pass through it (though usually it does not), and it may, by contract, collect from the consumer, but a broker does not deal on its account. Two preliminary requirements must be met for a finding that an individual is acting as a broker: (1) the person is acting for compensation; and (2) the person is acting on behalf of someone else." 12 Am. Jur. 2d *Brokers* § 1 (1997).

broker-agent. **1.** A person who acts as an intermediary between parties to a transaction, and as a representative of one of them. **2.** A person licensed both as a broker and as an agent.

broker-dealer. A brokerage firm that engages in the business of trading securities for its own account (i.e., as a principal) before selling them to customers. • Such a firm is usu. registered with the SEC and with the state in which it does business. See DEALER (2).

> "Since many broker-dealers maintain custody of funds and securities belonging to their customers, safeguards are required to assure that the customers can recover those funds and securities in the event the broker-dealer becomes insolvent. The three principal techniques that have been utilized are (a) financial responsibility standards for broker-dealers, (b) requirements for segregation of customers' funds and securities, and (c) maintenance of an industry-wide fund to satisfy the claims of customers whose brokerage firms become insolvent." David L. Ratner, *Securities Regulation in a Nutshell* 182–83 (4th ed. 1992).

broker for sale. A broker retained to sell something, but having neither possession of the goods nor any right of action in the broker's own name on contracts that the broker enters into.

broker's broker. A municipal securities broker or dealer that routinely effects transactions for the account of other brokers, dealers, and municipal securities dealers.

commercial broker. A broker who negotiates the sale of goods without having possession or control of the goods. Cf. FACTOR (2).

commission broker. A member of a stock or commodity exchange who executes buy and sell orders.

customhouse broker. A broker who prepares paperwork for the entry or clearance of ships, and for the import or export of goods. — Also termed *customs broker.*

discount broker. **1.** A broker who discounts bills of exchange and promissory notes, and advances money on securities. **2.** A broker who executes buy and sell orders at commission rates lower than those of full-service brokers.

government-securities interdealer broker. A broker engaged exclusively in the business of transacting in government securities for parties that are themselves government brokers or dealers.

institutional broker. A broker who trades securities for institutional clients such as banks, mutual funds, pension funds, and insurance companies.

insurance broker. *Insurance.* A person who, for compensation, brings about or negotiates contracts of insurance as an agent for someone else, but not as an officer, salaried employee, or licensed agent of an insurance company. • The broker acts as an intermediary between the insured and the insurer. — Also termed *producer.*

"The term 'insurance broker' is often used to characterize an individual who is thought to act primarily on behalf of a purchaser in an insurance transaction. This delineation . . . is employed by some courts and writers even though almost all insurance brokers are actually compensated for their services through commissions that are paid by the insurers. Because brokers receive compensation from the insurer, it seems evident that a persuasive argument can be made for not treating a broker as an agent of the insurance purchaser." Robert E. Keeton & Alan I. Widiss, *Insurance Law: A Guide to Fundamental Principles, Legal Doctrines, and Commercial Practices* § 2.5, at 83–84 (1988).

loan broker. A person who is in the business of lending money, usu. to an individual, and taking as security an assignment of wages or a security interest in the debtor's personal property.

merchandise broker. One who negotiates the sale of merchandise without possessing it. • A merchandise broker is an agent with very limited powers.

money broker. A broker who negotiates the lending or raising of money for others.

mortgage broker. An individual or organization that markets mortgage loans and brings lenders and borrowers together. • A mortgage broker does not originate or service mortgage loans.

note broker. A broker who negotiates the discount or sale of commercial paper.

real-estate broker. A broker who negotiates contracts of sale and other agreements (such as mortgages or leases) between buyers and sellers of real property. • Real-estate brokers must be licensed in the states where they conduct business.

registered broker. A broker registered or required to be registered under the Securities Exchange Act of 1934.

responsible broker-dealer. A broker-dealer who communicates bids or offers on the floor of a stock exchange at the designated location for trading in a reported security or who, in an off-exchange transaction, communicates the bid or offer as either a principal or an agent, for its own or another's account. SEC Rule 11Ac1–1(a)(21) (17 CFR § 240.11Ac1–1(a)(21)).

securities broker. A broker employed to buy or sell securities for a customer, as opposed to a securities dealer, who trades as a principal before selling the securities to a customer. See DEALER (2).

brokerage. 1. The business or office of a broker <a profitable stock brokerage>. **2.** A broker's fee <collect the brokerage after the house sells>.

brokerage contract. An agency agreement employing a broker to make contracts in the name of and on behalf of the principal and for which the broker receives a commission.

brokerage listing. See LISTING (1).

broker-agent. See BROKER.

broker call loan. See *call loan* under LOAN.

broker-dealer. See BROKER.

broker for sale. See BROKER.

broker's broker. See BROKER.

brother. A male having one parent or both parents the same as another person.

consanguine brother (kahn-**sang**-gwin). *Civil law.* A brother descended from the same father as another, but from a different mother.

half brother. See HALF BROTHER.

uterine brother (**yoo**-tər-in). *Civil law.* A brother descended from the same mother as another, but from a different father.

brother-german. See GERMAN.

brother-in-law. The brother of one's spouse or the husband of one's sister. • Additionally, the husband of one's spouse's sister is also sometimes considered a brother-in-law. Pl. *brothers-in-law.*

brother-sister corporation. See *sister corporation* under CORPORATION.

***Bruton* error** (**broot**-ən). The violation of a criminal defendant's constitutional right of confrontation by admitting into evidence a nontestifying codefendant's confession that implicates a defendant who claims innocence. *Bruton v. United States*, 391 U.S. 123, 88 S.Ct. 1620 (1968).

brutum fulmen (**broo**-təm **fəl**-men *or* -mən). [Latin "inert thunder"] **1.** An empty noise; an empty threat; something ineffectual. **2.** A judgment void on its face; one that is, in legal effect, no judgment at all.

Bryan treaties. *Int'l law*. Any of 48 treaties designed to avert war by requiring the signatories to submit disputes of any kind to standing peace commissions. • The first of these treaties, named after Secretary of State William Jennings Bryan, was signed between the United States and Great Britain in 1914.

b.s. *abbr*. See *bancus superior* under BANCUS.

BTA. *abbr*. Board of Tax Appeals. See TAX COURT.

bubble. *Slang*. A dishonest or insubstantial business project, generally founded on a fictitious or exaggerated prospectus, designed to ensnare unwary investors.

Bubble Act. An English statute passed in 1720 to prevent corporate fraud.

bucketing. *Securities*. The illegal practice of receiving an order to buy or sell stock but not immediately performing the order. • The perpetrator profits by executing the order when the stock market goes down, but confirming the order to the customer at the original price.

bucket shop. *Securities*. An establishment that is nominally engaged in stock-exchange transactions or some similar business, but in fact engages in registering bets or wagers, usu. for small amounts, on the rise or fall of the prices of stocks and commodities. • A bucket shop uses the terms and outward forms of the exchanges, but differs from exchanges because there is no delivery of — and no expectation or intention to deliver or receive — the securities or commodities nominally exchanged.

budget. 1. A statement of an organization's estimated revenues and expenses for a specified period, usu. a year. **2.** A sum of money allocated to a particular purpose or project.

buffer-zone. *Land-use planning*. An area of land separating two different zones or areas to help each blend more easily with the other, such as a strip of land between industrial and residential areas.

buggery, *n*. Sodomy or bestiality. — **bugger,** *vb*. — **bugger,** *n*. See SODOMY.

bugging, *n*. A form of electronic surveillance by which conversations may be electronically intercepted, overheard, and recorded, usu. covertly; eavesdropping by electronic means. See WIRETAPPING.

building-and-loan association. A quasi-public corporation that accumulates funds through member contributions and lends money to the members buying or building homes. Cf. SAVINGS-AND-LOAN ASSOCIATION.

building codes. Laws and regulations setting forth standards for the construction, maintenance, occupancy, use, or appearance of buildings and dwelling units. — Also termed (for dwelling units) *housing codes*.

building lien. See *mechanic's lien* under LIEN.

building line. A boundary drawn along a curb or the edge of a municipality's sidewalks to establish how far a building must be set away from the street to maintain a uniform appearance. • This is often referred to as a setback requirement.

building loan. See LOAN.

building permit. A license granted by a government agency (esp. a municipality) for the construction of a new building or a substantial alteration of an existing structure.

building restrictions. Regulations governing the type of structures that can be constructed on certain property. • The restrictions are usu. listed in zoning ordinances or restrictive covenants in deeds. Cf. BUILDING CODE; *restrictive covenant* under COVENANT (4).

built-in obsolescence. See *planned obsolescence* under OBSOLESCENCE.

bulk, *adj.* (Of goods) not divided into parts <a bulk shipment of grain>.

bulk discount. See *volume discount* under DISCOUNT.

bulk mortgage. See MORTGAGE.

bulk sale. A sale of a large quantity of inventory outside the ordinary course of the seller's business. • Bulk sales are regulated by Article 6 of the UCC, which is designed to prevent sellers from defrauding unsecured creditors by making these sales and then dissipating the sale proceeds. — Also termed *bulk transfer.*

bulk transfer. See BULK SALE.

bull. *Eccles. law.* **1.** A document issued by a Pope, so called from the leaden seal attached to it. **2.** A seal attached to an official document, esp. a papal edict.

bulla (**buul**-ə or **bəl**-ə). [Law Latin] A metal or wax papal seal or document.

bulletin des lois (buul-ə-**tan** day **lwah**). *French law.* The publication that provides official notice of the text and effective date of a law or decree.

bullion (**buul**-yən). An uncoined solid mass of gold or silver.

bullion fund. Public money used by a mint to purchase precious metals for coinage and to pay bullion depositors.

bull market. See MARKET.

bullpen. *Slang.* **1.** An area in a prison where inmates are kept in close confinement. **2.** A detention cell where prisoners are held until they are brought into court.

bumbershoot insurance. See INSURANCE.

bum-marriage doctrine. The principle that the marital-witness privilege may not be asserted by a partner in a marriage that is in fact moribund, though legally valid. See *marital privilege* (2) under PRIVILEGE (3).

bumping. **1.** Displacement of a junior employee's position by a senior employee. **2.** An airline-industry practice of denying seats to passengers because of overbooking.

bunco. A swindling game or scheme; any trick or ploy calculated to win a person's confidence in an attempt to deceive that person.

bundle, *vb.* To sell related products or services in one transaction at an all-inclusive price.

bunkhouse rule. The principle that an employee's injury suffered while living in an employer's housing is compensable even if the injury occurs during off-duty hours.

burden, *n.* **1.** A duty or responsibility <the seller's burden to insure the shipped goods>. **2.** Something that is oppressive <a burden on interstate commerce>. **3.** A restriction on the use or value of land; an encumbrance <the easement created a burden on the estate>. — **burden,** *vb.* — **burdensome,** *adj.*

burden of allegation. A party's duty to plead a matter for that matter to be heard in the lawsuit. — Also termed *burden of pleading.*

burden of going forward with evidence. See BURDEN OF PRODUCTION.

burden of persuasion. A party's duty to convince the fact-finder to view the facts in a way that favors that party. • In civil cases, the plaintiff's burden is usu. "by a preponderance of the evidence," while in criminal cases the prosecution's burden is "beyond a reasonable doubt." — Also termed *persuasion burden*; *risk of nonpersuasion*; *risk of jury doubt.* — Also loosely termed *burden of proof.*

burden of pleading. See BURDEN OF ALLEGATION.

burden of production. A party's duty to introduce enough evidence on an issue to have the issue decided by the fact-finder, rather than decided against the party in a peremptory ruling such as a summary judgment or a directed verdict. — Also termed *burden of going forward with evidence*; *burden of producing evidence*; *production burden*; *degree of proof.*

burden of proof. **1.** A party's duty to prove a disputed assertion or charge. • The burden of proof includes both the *burden of persuasion* and the *burden of production.* — Also termed *onus probandi.* **2.** Loosely, BURDEN OF PERSUASION.

> "In the past the term 'burden of proof' has been used in two different senses. (1) The burden of going forward with the evidence. The party having this burden must introduce some evidence if he wishes to get a certain

issue into the case. If he introduces enough evidence to require consideration of this issue, this burden has been met. (2) Burden of proof in the sense of carrying the risk of nonpersuasion. The one who has this burden stands to lose if his evidence fails to convince the jury — or the judge in a nonjury trial. The present trend is to use the term 'burden of proof' only with this second meaning ...." Rollin M. Perkins & Ronald N. Boyce, *Criminal Law* 78 (3d ed. 1982).

"The expression 'burden of proof' is tricky because it has been used by courts and writers to mean various things. Strictly speaking, burden of proof denotes the duty of establishing by a fair preponderance of the evidence the truth of the operative facts upon which the issue at hand is made to turn by substantive law. Burden of proof is sometimes used in a secondary sense to mean the burden of going forward with the evidence. In this sense it is sometimes said that a party has the burden of countering with evidence a prima facie case made against that party." William D. Hawkland, *Uniform Commercial Code Series* § 2A–516:08 (1984).

Bureau Veritas. See VERITAS.

***Burford* abstention.** See ABSTENTION.

burgage-tenure (**bər**-gij **ten**-yər). *Hist.* **1.** A type of socage tenure in which tenants paid annual rents to the lord of the borough. See SOCAGE. **2.** *Scots law.* The tenure by which a burgh held its land of the king, the service due being watching and warding. See WATCH AND WARD.

burgator (bər-**gay**-tər). *Hist.* A burglar; a person who breaks into a house or an enclosed space.

burgess (**bər**-jis). *Hist.* **1.** An inhabitant or freeman of a borough or town. **2.** A magistrate of a borough. **3.** A person entitled to vote at elections. **4.** A representative of a borough or town in Parliament.

"[Burgesses] are properly Men of Trade, or the Inhabitants of a Borow or Walled Town; yet we usually apply this name to the Magistrates of such a Town, as the Bailiff and *Burgesses of Leominster*. But we do now usually call those *Burgesses* who serve in Parliament, for any such Borow or Corporation." Thomas Blount, *Nomo-Lexicon: A Law-Dictionary* (1670).

burgh English (**bərg ing**-glish). See BOROUGH ENGLISH.

burgh Engloys (**bərg** ing-**gloiz**). See BOROUGH ENGLISH.

burglar, *n.* One who commits burglary.

burglarious (bər-**glair**-ee-əs), *adj.* Of or relating to burglary <burglarious intent>. — **burglariously,** *adv.*

burglarize, *vb.* To commit a burglary <the defendant burglarized three houses>. — Also termed (esp. in BrE) *burgle.*

burglary, *n.* **1.** The common-law offense of breaking and entering another's dwelling at night with the intent to commit a felony. **2.** The modern statutory offense of breaking and entering any building — not just a dwelling, and not only at night — with the intent to commit a felony. • Some statutes make petit larceny an alternative to a felony for purposes of proving burglarious intent. — Also termed (in sense 2) *breaking and entering*; *statutory burglary.* Cf. ROBBERY.

burglary tool. (*often pl.*) An implement designed to assist a person in committing a burglary. • In many jurisdictions, it is illegal to possess such a tool if the possessor intends to commit a burglary.

burgle. See BURGLARIZE.

burial insurance. See INSURANCE.

buried-facts doctrine. *Securities.* The rule that a proxy-statement disclosure is inadequate if a reasonable shareholder could fail to understand the risks presented by facts scattered throughout the proxy. • In applying this rule, a court will consider a securities disclosure to be false and misleading if its overall significance is obscured because material information is buried in footnotes, appendixes, and the like.

burking, *n.* The crime of murdering someone, usu. by smothering, for the purpose of selling the corpse. • This term arose from the Scottish murder team of Burke and Hare, whose practice in 1828 of suffocating their victims while leaving few visible marks made the corpses more salable to medical schools. — **burke,** *vb.*

burlaw. See BYRLAW.

burlaw court. See BYRLAW COURT.

bursting-bubble theory. *Evidence.* The principle that a presumption disappears once the presumed facts have been contradicted by credible evidence.

business. A commercial enterprise carried on for profit; a particular occupation or employment habitually engaged in for livelihood or gain.

business agent. 1. See *managing agent* under AGENT. **2.** A labor-union representative selected to deal with employers.

business associations. See BUSINESS ENTERPRISES.

business combination. 1. The consolidation, for accounting purposes, of a corporation and one or more incorporated or unincorporated businesses. **2.** The two entities considered as one entity for accounting purposes.

business compulsion. See *economic duress* under DURESS (1).

business corporation. See CORPORATION.

business court. See COURT.

business cycle. The recurrent expansion and contraction of economic activity.

business day. See DAY.

business enterprises. The field of law dealing with various forms of business, such as corporations, limited-liability companies, and partnerships. — Also termed *business entities*; *business associations*.

business entry. A writing admissible under the business-records exception. See BUSINESS-RECORDS EXCEPTION.

business-entry rule. See BUSINESS-RECORDS EXCEPTION.

business expense. See EXPENSE.

business gain. See GAIN (2), (3).

business guest. See GUEST.

business homestead. See HOMESTEAD.

business-interruption insurance. See INSURANCE.

business invitee. See INVITEE.

business-judgment rule. *Corporations.* The presumption that in making business decisions not involving direct self-interest or self-dealing, corporate directors act on an informed basis, in good faith, and in the honest belief that their actions are in the corporation's best interest. • The rule shields directors and officers from liability for unprofitable or harmful corporate transactions if the transactions were made in good faith, with due care, and within the directors' or officers' authority.

> "The business judgment rule is a presumption protecting conduct by directors that can be attributed to any rational business purpose. In order to plead and prove a claim, a plaintiff must plead and prove facts overcoming this presumption. Where the presumption is overcome, directors bear the burden of proving the fairness of the challenged conduct. The difference between these two levels of judicial scrutiny — a presumption in favor of directors that protects conduct that is rational, versus a burden of proving fairness — frequently is outcome determinative." 1 Dennis J. Block et al., *The Business Judgment Rule* 18–19 (5th ed. 1998).

business loss. See *ordinary loss* under LOSS.

business plan. A written proposal explaining a new business or business idea and usu. covering financial, marketing, and operational plans.

business-purpose doctrine. *Tax.* The principle that a transaction must serve a bona fide business purpose (i.e., not just for tax avoidance) to qualify for beneficial tax treatment.

business record. A report, memorandum, or other record made usu. in the ordinary course of business. • It may be ordered produced as part of discovery in a lawsuit.

business-records exception. *Evidence.* A hearsay exception allowing business records (such as reports or memoranda) to be admitted into evidence if they were prepared in the ordinary course of business. Fed. R. Evid. 803(6). — Also termed *business-entry rule*.

business-risk exclusion. See EXCLUSION (3).

business trust. See TRUST.

bust-up merger. See MERGER.

but-for cause. See CAUSE (1).

but-for test. *Tort & criminal law.* The doctrine that causation exists only when the result would not have occurred without the party's conduct. — Also termed (in criminal law) *had-not test*. See *but-for cause* under CAUSE (1).

butlerage. *Hist.* A duty on wine imported into England, payable to the royal butler. Cf. PRISAGE.

but see. See SED VIDE.

buttals (**bət**-əlz). *Archaic.* See ABUTTALS.

butts and bounds. See METES AND BOUNDS.

buy. See PURCHASE (1).

buy-and-sell agreement. See BUY-SELL AGREEMENT.

buy-down, *n.* Money paid by the buyer of a house to reduce the mortgage-interest payments.

buyer. One who makes a purchase. See PURCHASER.

buyer in ordinary course of business. A person who — in good faith and without knowledge that the sale violates a third party's ownership rights or security interest in the goods — buys from a person regularly engaged in the business of selling goods of that kind. • Pawnbrokers are excluded from the definition. UCC § 1–201(9).

qualified institutional buyer. *Securities.* An institution with more than $100 million in invested assets.

buyer's market. See MARKET.

buying in, *n.* The purchase of property by the original owner or an interested party at an auction or foreclosure sale. — **buy in,** *vb.*

buying on margin. See MARGIN TRANSACTION.

buying syndicate. See SYNDICATE.

buy order. See ORDER (4).

buyout, *n.* The purchase of all or a controlling percentage of the assets or shares of a business. — **buy out,** *vb.* Cf. MERGER (7).

leveraged buyout. The purchase of a publicly held corporation's outstanding stock by its management or outside investors, financed mainly with funds borrowed from investment bankers or brokers and usu. secured by the corporation's assets. — Abbr. LBO.

management buyout. **1.** A buyout of a corporation by its own directors and officers. **2.** A leveraged buyout of a corporation by an outside entity in which the corporation's management has a material financial interest. — Abbr. MBO. See GOING PRIVATE.

buy-sell agreement. **1.** An arrangement between owners of a business by which the surviving owners agree to purchase the interest of a withdrawing or deceased owner. Cf. CONTINUATION AGREEMENT. **2.** *Corporations.* A share-transfer restriction that commits the shareholder to sell, and the corporation or other shareholders to buy, the shareholder's shares at a fixed price when a specified event occurs. — Also termed *buy-and-sell agreement.* Cf. OPTION AGREEMENT.

BW. *abbr.* BID WANTED.

by-bidder. At an auction, a person employed by the seller to bid on property for the sole purpose of stimulating bidding by potential genuine buyers. — Also termed *puffer.*

by-bidding. The illegal practice of employing a person to bid at an auction for the sole purpose of stimulating bidding on the seller's property. — Also termed *puffing.* Cf. BIDDING UP.

by God and my country. *Hist.* A customary reply for a criminal defendant when asked at arraignment, "Culprit, how wilt thou be tried?"

bylaw. **1.** A rule or administrative provision adopted by an association or corporation for its internal governance. • Corporate bylaws are usu. enacted apart from the articles of incorporation. — Also termed *regulation.* **2.** ORDINANCE. — Sometimes spelled *by-law*; *byelaw.* See ARTICLES OF INCORPORATION.

bylaw man. *Hist.* One of the chief men of a town, usu. appointed for some purpose under the town's corporate bylaws.

by operation of law. See OPERATION OF LAW.

bypass trust. See TRUST.

byrlaw (**bir**-law). *Hist. Scots law.* A law made by the members of a local community. — Also spelled *burlaw.*

byrlaw court. *Hist. Scots law.* A community assembly that judged minor disputes arising in the community. — Also spelled *burlaw court.*

bystander. One who is present when an event takes place, but who does not become directly involved in it.

C

c. *abbr.* **1.** CIRCA. **2.** COPYRIGHT.

ca. *abbr.* CIRCA.

cabal (kə-**bal** *or* kə-**bahl**). A small group of political schemers or conspirators. • The term is sometimes said to have originated as an acronym from a committee of five ministers of Charles II, whose surnames began with C, A, B, A, and L (Clifford, Arlington, Buckingham, Ashley, and Lauderdale). Though colorful, this etymology is false: the term came into English directly from the French *cabale* "intrigue," which derives ultimately from Hebrew *qabbalah* "received lore."

cabala (**kab**-ə-lə *or* kə-**bahl**-ə). An esoteric or obscure doctrine.

caballeria (kah-bah-ye-**ree**-ah). [Spanish] *Spanish law.* An allotment of land in regions formerly conquered by Spain, such as Mexico and the southwestern United States. • Originally a Spanish feudal tenure held by a soldier, a *caballeria* eventually came to refer to an area of land. It usu. measures 100 by 200 feet in the United States, and between 30 and 200 acres in Mexico and other former Spanish territories.

cabinet. (*often cap.*) The advisory council to an executive officer, esp. the President. • The President's cabinet is a creation of custom and tradition, dating back to the term of George Washington. The U.S. Constitution alludes to a group of presidential advisers — the President "may require the Opinion, in writing, of the principal Officer in each of the executive Departments, upon any Subject relating to the Duties of their respective Offices" (art. II, § 2, cl. 1) — but the term *cabinet* is not specifically mentioned. The cabinet today comprises the heads of the 14 executive departments: the Secretary of State, the Secretary of the Treasury, the Secretary of Defense, the Attorney General, the Secretary of the Interior, the Secretary of Agriculture, the Secretary of Commerce, the Secretary of Labor, the Secretary of Health and Human Services, the Secretary of Housing and Urban Development, the Secretary of Transportation, the Secretary of Energy, the Secretary of Education, and the Secretary of Veterans Affairs. Other officials, such as the U.S. ambassador to the United Nations and the director of the Office of Management and the Budget, have been accorded cabinet rank.

inner cabinet. The heads of the departments of State, Treasury, Defense, and Justice. • This group is so called because in most administrations they tend to be closer to the President and more influential than the rest of the cabinet (the *outer cabinet*).

kitchen cabinet. An unofficial and informal body of noncabinet advisers who often have more sway with the executive than the real cabinet does. • This term was first used derisively in reference to some of President Andrew Jackson's advisers, who, because of their reputation for unpolished manners, were supposedly not important enough to meet in the formal rooms of the White House.

> "The term [*kitchen cabinet*] began to lose its sting after Jackson's time. But because most Presidents do have circles of personal friends, the idea remains. Theodore Roosevelt had his 'tennis cabinet.' Jonathan Daniels referred to Warren Harding's 'poker cabinet.' Herbert Hoover had an exercise-loving 'medicine ball cabinet.' Even governors can play the game. In writing of New York's Alfred Smith, Ed Flynn mentions the 'golfing cabinet.' " William Safire, *Safire's New Political Dictionary* 389 (1993).

cabotage (**kab**-ə-tij). *Int'l law.* **1.** The carrying on of trade along a country's coast; the transport of goods or passengers from one port or place to another in the same country. • The privilege to carry on this trade is usu. limited to vessels flying the flag of that country. **2.** The privilege of carrying traffic between two ports in the same country. **3.** The right of a foreign airline to carry passengers and cargo between airports in the same country.

> "*Cabotage* meant originally navigation and trade along the same stretch of coast between the parts thereof, such coast belonging to one and the same State. However, the term *cabotage* or coasting trade as used in commercial treaties comprises now sea trade between any two parts of the same country, whether on the same coasts or different coasts, provided always that the different coasts are all of them the coasts of one and the same country as a political and geographical unit in contra-distinction to the coasts of colonies or dominions of such countries." 1 F.L. Oppenheim, *International Law* 493 (Hersch Lauter ed., 8th ed. 1955).

"Some writers maintain [that *cabotage*] should be applied only to maritime navigation; in this context one can distinguish between petit cabotage — transport between ports situated on the same sea (e.g. Bordeaux–Le Havre) — and grand cabotage — transport between ports situated on different seas (e.g. Bordeaux–Marseille). However, the term is also properly applied to transport between two inland points on an international river within one State, although the term grand cabotage is sometimes incorrectly applied to transnational transport between the inland ports of different riparian States on the same waterway. River cabotage properly so called is sometimes also referred to as local transport. Finally, the term has also been adopted to describe commercial air transport between airports situated in the same State." Robert C. Lane, "Cabotage," in 1 *Encyclopedia of Public International Law* 519–20 (1992).

ca'canny strike. See STRIKE.

cacicazgos (kah-see-**kahs**-gohs). Land held in entail by *caciques* (leaders of Indian villages) and their descendants in Spanish America.

cadastre (kə-**das**-tər). A survey and valuation of real estate in a county or region compiled for tax purposes. — Also spelled *cadaster*.

cadena (kə-**deen**-ə). [Spanish "chain"] *Spanish law*. Imprisonment; formerly, confinement at hard labor while chained from waist to ankle.

cadena perpetua. Life imprisonment.

cadena temporal. Imprisonment for a term less than life.

cadere (**kad**-ə-ree). [Latin "to fail"] *Hist.* **1.** To end, cease, or fail. • This term usu. refers to the failure of a writ action. *Cadit breve*, for example, means "the writ fails." **2.** To be changed or turned into. • *Cadit assisa in juratum* means "the assise is changed into a jury."

caduca (kə-**d**[**y**]**oo**-kə). [Latin "fallen things"] **1.** *Civil law*. Inheritable property; property descending to an heir. **2.** *Roman law*. Property formerly belonging to an intestate owner who has died without heirs or to someone who has suffered forfeiture for crime. • The property escheated to the state. See ESCHEAT. **3.** *Roman law*. Testamentary gifts that lapse. See LAPSE.

caducary (kə-**d**[**y**]**oo**-kə-ree). (Of a bequest or estate) subject to, relating to, or by way of escheat, lapse, or forfeiture of property <the statute was intended to waive the rights of the caducary heirs>.

caduce (kə-**d**[**y**]**oos**), *vb*. To take by escheat or lapse <the government caduced the unclaimed mineral royalties>.

caducity (kə-**d**[**y**]**oo**-sə-tee), *n*. The lapse of a testamentary gift <the testator failed to provide a contingency for the caducity of the legacy>.

caeteris paribus. See CETERIS PARIBUS.

caeteris tacentibus. See CETERIS TACENTIBUS.

caeterorum administration. See ADMINISTRATION.

c.a.f. Cost, assurance, and freight. • This term is synonymous with C.I.F.

"[I]n a French contract the term 'C.A.F.' does not mean 'Cost and Freight' but has exactly the same meaning as the term 'C.I.F.,' since it is merely the French equivalent of that term. The 'A' does not stand for 'and' but for 'assurance,' which means insurance." William D. Hawkland, *Uniform Commercial Code Series* § 2–320 (1984).

cafeteria plan. An employee fringe-benefit plan allowing a choice of basic benefits up to a certain dollar amount.

cahoots (kə-**hoots**). *Slang*. Partnership, esp. in an illegal act; collusion <the lawyer was in cahoots with her client>.

Cairns's Act (**kairn**-zəz). *Hist*. An 1858 statute that expanded the relief available in England's chancery courts to include monetary damages in addition to injunctive relief. • Cairns's Act was superseded by the Judicature Acts of 1873–1875. — Also spelled *Cairns' Act*. Cf. JUDICATURE ACTS.

***Calandra* rule** (kə-**lan**-drə). The doctrine that a grand-jury witness may be compelled to answer questions about certain items, even though the items were obtained by the police illegally. *United States v. Calandra*, 414 U.S. 338, 94 S.Ct. 613 (1974).

calendar, *n*. **1.** A systematized ordering of time into years, months, weeks, and days; esp., the Gregorian calendar established by Pope Gregory XIII in 1582 and adopted in Great Britain in 1752. • The Gregorian calendar is used throughout the Western world.

Gregorian calendar. See NEW STYLE.

Julian calendar. See OLD STYLE.

2. A court's list of civil or criminal cases.

court calendar. See COURT CALENDAR.

special calendar. A calendar marked with court cases that have been specially set for hearing or trial. See *special setting* under SETTING.

3. A list of bills reported out of a legislative committee for consideration by the entire legislature.

calendar, *vb.* **1.** To place an important event on a calendar, esp. so that the event will be remembered. **2.** To place a case on a calendar.

calendar call. A court session in which the judge calls each case awaiting trial, determines its status, and assigns a trial date.

calendar day. See DAY.

calendar month. See MONTH.

calendar motion. See MOTION.

calendar year. See YEAR.

calends (**kal**-əndz). *Roman law.* In the ancient Roman calendar, the first day of the month. — Also spelled *kalends*. Cf. NONES.

call, *n.* **1.** A request or command to come or assemble; an invitation or summons. **2.** A demand for payment of money.

margin call. A securities broker's demand that a customer put up money or stock as collateral when the broker finances a purchase of securities. • A margin call usu. occurs when the market prices of the securities are falling. — Also termed *maintenance call.*

3. See *call option* under OPTION. **4.** A demand for the presentation of a security (esp. a bond) for redemption before the maturity date. **5.** A landmark designating a property boundary. • The landmarks are chosen by the surveyor and recorded in his field notes or in the accompanying deed. See METES AND BOUNDS.

call, *vb.* **1.** To summon. **2.** To demand payment of money. **3.** To redeem (a bond) before maturity.

callable, *adj.* (Of a security) redeemable by the issuing corporation before maturity. See REDEMPTION.

callable bond. See *redeemable bond* under BOND (3).

callable preferred stock. See STOCK.

callable security. See *redeemable security* under SECURITY.

called meeting. See *special meeting* under MEETING.

call equivalent position. *Securities.* A security position that increases in value as the value of the underlying equity increases. • It includes a long convertible security, a long call option, and a short put option. SEC Rule 16a–1(b) (17 CFR § 240.16a–1(b)).

calling to the bar. See CALL TO THE BAR.

call loan. See LOAN.

call option. See OPTION.

call patent. See PATENT (2).

call premium. The percentage amount of a bond's face value that a company pays, along with the face value, to redeem a callable bond; the difference between a bond's call price and its par value.

call price. See PRICE.

call-protection clause. A clause in a bond issue or a callable preferred stock issue prohibiting the issuer from recalling the security during a specified period.

call to the bar, *n.* The admission of a person to practice law. • This common phrase is a loan translation of the Latin *ad barram evocatus* ("called to the bar"). See AD BARRAM EVOCATUS. — Also termed *calling to the bar.*

calumniae judicium (kə-**ləm**-nee-ee joo-**dish**-ee-əm). [Latin "action for vexation"] *Roman law.* A countersuit that a defendant maliciously sued could bring after winning a judgment in the principal action. — Also spelled *calumniae iudicium.*

calumniae jusjurandum (kə-**ləm**-nee-ee jəs-jə-**ran**-dəm). [Law Latin "oath of calumny"] *Roman law.* An oath given by a litigant that he is not suing or defending vexatiously.

calumniate (kə-**ləm**-nee-ayt), *vb.* To slander or make false charges against.

calumny (**kal**-əm-nee), *n. Archaic.* **1.** The act of maliciously misrepresenting someone's words or actions in a way that is calculated to injure that person's reputation. **2.** A false charge or imputation. — **calumnious** (kə-**ləm**-nee-əs), *adj.* — **calumniator** (kə-ləm-nee-ay-tər), *n.*

Calvin's case. The decision establishing that persons born in Scotland after the 1603 accession of James I to the English throne were deemed natural-born subjects of the King of England and could inherit English land. *Calvin v. Smith*, 7 Eng. Rep. 1, 2 S.T. 559 (1608).

Calvo clause (**kahl**-voh). A contractual clause by which an alien waives his right to invoke diplomatic immunity. • Such a clause typically appears in a contract between a national government and an alien.

Calvo doctrine. *Int'l law.* The rule that resident aliens have the same rights to protection as citizens, but no more. • This doctrine, which establishes a minimum international standard for the treatment of aliens, was developed by the Argentinian jurist Carlos Calvo in his treatise *Le droit international théorique et pratique* (5th ed. 1896). The doctrine is intended to prevent aliens from abusing their right of diplomatic protection.

cambiale jus (kam-bee-**ay**-lee **jəs**). [Latin "law of exchange"] The law of commercial exchange.

cambiator (**kam**-bee-ay-tər). *Hist.* An exchanger, usu. of money (*cambiatores monetae*).

cambist (**kam**-bist). [fr. Latin *cambiare* "to exchange"] A broker whose trades are promissory notes or bills of exchange. — Also termed *cambiator*.

cambium (**kam**-bee-əm). [Law Latin "exchange"] *Hist.* **1.** An exchange of money, debt, or land.

> ***cambium locale.*** A contract of exchange in which a person agrees to pay a sum of money at one location in consideration of money received at another location. — Also termed *cambium mercantile*; *cambium trajectitium.*
>
> ***cambium reale.*** An exchange of land. — Also termed *cambium manuale.*

2. A mercantile contract in which the parties agree to exchange money for money; a bill of exchange. — Also termed *escambium.*

camera (**kam**-ə-rə). [Latin] Chamber; room. See IN CAMERA.

camera regis (**kam**-ə-rə **ree**-jis). [Latin "chambers of the king"] *Hist.* A locale that the king takes a particular interest in, usu. expressed as a royal privilege benefiting a city.

camerarius (kam-ə-**rair**-ee-əs). [fr. Latin *camera* "chamber"] *Hist.* **1.** A chamberlain or other treasurer in charge of public money. **2.** BAILIFF.

Camera Stellata (**kam**-ə-rə stə-**lay**-tə). [Law Latin] See STAR CHAMBER, COURT OF.

campers. *Hist.* The share of a lawsuit's proceeds payable to a champertor. See CHAMPERTY.

campipartitio (kam-pə-pahr-**tish**-ee-oh). [Law Latin] See CHAMPERTY.

can, *vb.* **1.** To be able to do something <you can lift 500 pounds>. **2.** To have permission (as often interpreted by courts); MAY <no appeal can be filed until the filing fee is paid>.

cancel, *vb.* **1.** To destroy a written instrument by defacing or obliterating it <she canceled her will by marking through it>. **2.** To terminate a promise, obligation, or right <the parties canceled the contract>.

canceled check. See CHECK.

cancellaria (kan-sə-**lair**-ee-ə). [Law Latin] See CHANCERY (1). — Also termed *curia cancellaria.*

cancellarius (kan-sə-**lair**-ee-əs). [Law Latin] **1.** A chancellor, scrivener, or notary. **2.** See *Lord High Chancellor* under CHANCELLOR.

cancellation, *n.* **1.** The act of defacing or obliterating a writing (as by marking lines across it), thereby rendering it void. **2.** An annulment or termination of a promise or an obligation.

> ***flat cancellation.*** The cancellation of an insurance policy without any charge to the insured.

3. An equitable remedy by which courts call in and annul outstanding void or rescinded instruments because they may either spawn vexatious litigation or cloud someone's title to property. — **cancel,** *vb.* — **cancelable,** *adj.*

cancellation clause. A contractual provision allowing one or both parties to annul their obligations under certain conditions.

cancellatura. *Hist.* See CANCELLATION.

cancelled check. See CHECK.

cancelli (kan-**sel**-I). [Latin "lattice, grille"] *Archaic.* **1.** Lines drawn on a writing, esp. a will, indicating its revocation. See CANCELLATION (1). **2.** *Hist.* The rails or latticework enclosing the bar of a court.

C & F. *abbr.* COST AND FREIGHT. — Also spelled *CandF.*

canfara (**kan**-fə-rə). [Law Latin] *Hist.* A trial by hot iron, formerly used in England. See *ordeal by fire* under ORDEAL.

canon (**kan**-ən), *n.* **1.** A rule or principle, esp. one accepted as fundamental.

canon of construction. A rule used in construing legal instruments, esp. contracts and statutes. • Although a few states have codified the canons of construction — examples of which are *contra proferentem* and *ejusdem generis* — most jurisdictions treat the canons as mere customs not having the force of law. — Often shortened to *canon.* — Also termed *rule of construction*; *rule of interpretation.*

> "A frequent criticism of the canons [of construction], made forcefully by Professor Llewellyn many years ago, is that for every canon one might bring to bear on a point there is an equal and opposite canon. This is an exaggeration; but what is true is that there is a canon to support every possible result." Richard A. Posner, *The Federal Courts: Crisis and Reform* 276 (1985).

canon of descent. (*usu. pl.*) A common-law rule governing intestate succession. • In England, canons of descent tended to concentrate landholdings in the hands of a few people, an approach generally rejected in the United States. — Also termed *canon of inheritance.*

> "The common-law canons of descent tended to prevent the diffusion of landed property, and to promote its accumulation in the hands of a few. The principles sprang from the martial genius of the feudal system. In the United States the English common law of descents, in its essential features, has been rejected; each State has established a law for itself." William C. Anderson, *A Dictionary of Law* 349 (1889).

2. (*usu. cap.*) A maxim stating in general terms the standards of professional conduct expected of lawyers. • The Model Code of Judicial Conduct (1990) contains five canons and hundreds of specific rules. **3.** A rule of ecclesiastical law. **4.** A corpus of writings. **5.** A clergy member on the staff of a cathedral.

honorary canon. A canon who serves without pay or other benefits.

6. A fixed regular payment or tribute made as a contribution payable to the church.

canonical (kə-**non**-ə-kəl), *adj.* **1.** (Of a rule or decree) prescribed by, in conformity with, or relating to canon law. **2.** Orthodox; conforming to accepted rules or conventions.

canonical disability. A canonical impediment (usu. impotence). See CANONICAL IMPEDIMENT.

canonical impediment. A condition rendering a marriage subject to annulment. • The canonical impediments are consanguinity, affinity, and impotence.

canonical law. See CANON LAW.

canonical purgation. See PURGATION.

canonist (**kan**-ən-ist), *n.* An expert in canon law; esp., a canon lawyer or professor.

canon law. 1. A body of Roman ecclesiastical law that was not compiled until the 12th to 14th centuries. • It has grown steadily since that time, and is now codified in the *Codex Juris Canonici* of 1983, replacing that of 1918. — Also termed *corpus juris canonici*; *papal law*; *jus canonicum.* **2.** A body of law developed within a particular religious tradition. — Also termed *church law*; *canonical law.* Cf. ECCLESIASTICAL LAW.

> "The indirect contributions of the canon law to the development of English law were as great as, and the direct contributions far greater than, those made by the civil law. Indirectly the canon lawyers gave much even to the purely secular law of England, because, during the early Middle Ages, most of the judges or the royal courts were ecclesiastics acquainted with the chief doctrines of canon law.... The direct influence of the canon law in England resulted from its being the law which was administered in the courts of the Church." W.J.V. Windeyer, *Lectures on Legal History* 41 (2d ed. 1949).

canon of construction. See CANON (1).

canon of descent. See CANON (1).

canon of inheritance. See *canon of descent* under CANON (1).

cant (kant). *Civil law.* A method of dividing commonly held property by awarding it to the highest-bidding owner on condition that the successful bidder must buy out each coowner's interest. — Also termed *licitation.*

cantred (**kan**-tred). [fr. Welsh *cant* "hundred" + *tref* "village"] See HUNDRED.

canum (**kay**-nəm). [Law Latin] *Hist.* A duty or tribute payable from a tenant to a lord, usu. consisting of produce from the land.

canvass, *vb.* **1.** To examine in detail; scrutinize <that issue has been repeatedly canvassed by our state's courts>. **2.** To solicit political support from voters or a voting district; to take stock of public opinion <the candidate is actively canvassing the Western states>. — **canvass,** *n.*

cap, *n.* An upper limit, such as a statutory limit on the recovery in a tort action or on the interest a bank can charge. — **cap,** *vb.*

capacitate (kə-**pas**-ə-tayt), *vb.* To qualify; to make legally competent. — **capacitation** (kə-pas-ə-**tay**-shən), *n.*

capacity. 1. The role in which one performs an act <in her corporate capacity>.

proprietary capacity. The capacity of a city or town when it engages in a business-like venture rather than a governmental function. See PROPRIETARY FUNCTION.

2. A legal qualification, such as legal age, that determines one's ability to sue or be sued, to enter into a binding contract, and the like <she had full capacity to bind the corporation with her signature>. • Unless necessary to show the court's jurisdiction, a plaintiff's pleadings need not assert the legal capacity of any party. A party wishing to raise the issue of capacity must do so by specific negative pleading. Fed. R. Civ. P. 9(a). — Also termed (specif.) *capacity to sue.* See STANDING. **3.** The mental ability to understand the nature and effect of one's acts <his acute pain reduced his capacity to understand the hospital's admission form>. — Also termed *mental capacity.* See COMPETENCY.

criminal capacity. The mental ability that a person must possess to be held accountable for a crime; the ability to understand right from wrong. See INSANITY; INFANCY.

diminished capacity. An impaired mental condition — short of insanity — that is caused by intoxication, trauma, or disease and that prevents the person from having the mental state necessary to be held responsible for a crime. • In some jurisdictions, a defendant's diminished capacity can be used to determine the degree of the offense or the severity of the punishment. — Also termed *diminished responsibility.* Cf. INSANITY.

testamentary capacity. The mental ability a person must have to prepare a valid will. • This capacity is often described as the ability to recognize the natural objects of one's bounty, the nature and extent of one's estate, and the fact that one is making a plan to dispose of the estate after death. — Also termed *disposing capacity.*

capacity defense. See DEFENSE (1).

capacity to sue. See CAPACITY (2).

capax doli (**kay**-paks **doh**-lɪ). See DOLI CAPAX.

capax negotii (**kay**-paks ni-**goh**-shee-ɪ), *adj.* [Latin "capable of entering into a transaction"] (Of a person) having capacity to enter into a contract; capable of transacting business.

cape (**kay**-pee). *Hist.* [Latin "take"] A writ filed to recover possession of land.

cape magnum (**kay**-pee **mag**-nəm). [Latin "grand" cape] A writ granting possession of land before a tenant's appearance in the action. — Also termed *grand cape.*

cape parvum (**kay**-pee **pahr**-vəm). [Latin "little" cape] A writ for the recovery of land issuing after the appearance of the tenant in the action. — Also termed *petit cape.*

> "*Cape* is a writ judiciall touching plee of land or tenements, so tearmed (as most writs be) of that word in itselfe, which carieth the especiallest intention or end thereof. And this writ is divided in (*Cape magnum,* & *Cape parvum*:) both which . . . take hold of things immoveable, and seeme to differ betweene themselves in these points. First, because (*cape magnum*) or the (*grand Cape*) lyeth before appearance, and (*Cape parvum*) afterward. Secondly, the (*Cape magnum*) summoneth the tenent to aunswer to the default, and over to the demaundant: (*Cape parvum*) summoneth the tenent to aunswer to the default onely: and therefore is called (*Cape parvum*) or in French English (*petit Cape.*)" John Cowell, *The Interpreter* (1607).

capias (**kay**-pee-əs *or* **kap**-ee-əs). [Latin "that you take"] Any of various types of writs that require an officer to take a named defendant into custody. — Also termed *writ of capias; body execution.*

capias ad audiendum judicium (ad aw-dee-**en**-dəm joo-**dish**-ee-əm). [Latin "that you take to hear the judgment"] In a misdemeanor case, a writ issued to bring the defendant to hear the judgment to be imposed after having failed to appear.

capias ad computandum (ad kom-pyoo-**tan**-dəm). [Latin "that you take for computation"] *Hist.* A writ issued when a debtor has failed to appear and make account after losing in an action of account render. See ACCOUNTING (3).

capias ad respondendum (ad ree-spon-**den**-dəm). [Latin "that you take to answer"] A writ commanding the sheriff to take the defendant into custody to ensure that the defendant will appear in court. — Abbr. *ca. resp.*

capias ad satisfaciendum (ad sat-is-fay-shee-**en**-dəm). [Latin "that you take to satisfy"] *Hist.* A postjudgment writ commanding the sheriff to imprison the defendant until the judgment is satisfied. — Abbr. *ca. sa.*

capias extendi facias (ek-**sten**-dɪ **fay**-shee-əs). [Latin "take for extending"] *Hist.* A writ of execution issued against one who is indebted to the Crown, commanding the sheriff to arrest the debtor.

capias in withernam (**kay**-pee-əs in **with**-ər-nahm). [Law Latin "taking again"] A writ authorizing the sheriff to seize the goods or cattle of a wrongful distrainor. See WITHERNAM.

capias pro fine (**kay**-pee-əs proh **fɪ**-nee). [Latin "that you take for the fine"] A writ for the arrest of a person who had not paid an imposed fine. — Also termed *capiatur pro fine.*

capias utlagatum (**kay**-pee-əs ət-lə-**gay**-təm). [Latin "you take the outlaw"] A writ commanding the arrest of an outlawed person.

capita. See PER CAPITA.

capital, *adj.* **1.** Of or relating to economic or financial capital <capital market>. **2.** Punishable by execution; involving the death penalty <a capital offense>.

capital, *n.* **1.** Money or assets invested, or available for investment, in a business. **2.** The total assets of a business, esp. those that help generate profits. **3.** The total amount or value of a corporation's stock; corporate equity. See *capital stock* under STOCK.

actual capital. Funds generated by the sale of stock. See *authorized stock* under STOCK.

authorized capital. See *nominal capital.*

circulating capital. See *floating capital.*

debt capital. Funds raised by issuing bonds.

equity capital. Funds provided by a company's owners in exchange for evidence of ownership, such as stock.

fixed capital. **1.** The amount of money invested in fixed assets, such as land and machinery. **2.** Fixed assets.

floating capital. **1.** Funds not allocated to a particular class of the corporation's capital stock. **2.** Funds not presently invested or committed; esp., money retained for the purpose of meeting current expenditures. — Also termed *circulating capital.*

impaired capital. Corporate funds consisting of assets that are less than the sum of the corporation's legal capital and its liabilities.

legal capital. An amount equal to the aggregate "par" or stated value of all outstanding shares of a corporation, or, in the case of stock without par value, an amount set by the board of directors. • A minority of states require this amount to remain in the corporation to protect creditors. — Also termed *stated capital.*

moneyed capital. Money that is invested with the intent of making a profit.

nominal capital. The minimum value of the shares that a company is authorized by its association documents to issue. — Also termed *authorized capital.*

paid-in capital. The money paid for the capital stock of a corporation.

proprietary capital. Money that represents the initial investment in a sole proprietorship.

risk capital. **1.** Money or property invested in a business venture, esp. one in which the investor has no managerial control. **2.** See *venture capital.*

stated capital. **1.** See *legal capital.* **2.** The total equity of a corporation as it appears on the balance sheet.

subscribed capital. The total value of stock for which there are subscriptions (contracts of purchase).

venture capital. Funds invested in a new enterprise that has high risk and the potential for a high return. — Also termed *risk capital.* See SEED MONEY.

working capital. Current assets (such as cash, inventory, and accounts receivable) less current liabilities. • Working capital measures liquidity and the ability to discharge short-term obligations.

capital account. See ACCOUNT.

capital asset. See ASSET.

capital contribution. 1. Cash, property, or services contributed by partners to a partnership. **2.** Funds made available by a shareholder, usu. without an increase in stock holdings.

capital crime. See *capital offense* under OFFENSE (1).

capitale (kap-i-**tay**-lee). [Latin "a thing"] *Hist.* **1.** Movable property, esp. animals (such as 100 head of cattle). • Over time, *chattel* became the more common term. **2.** A stolen thing, or its equivalent value. Pl. ***capitalia.***

capital expenditure. An outlay of funds to acquire or improve a fixed asset. — Also termed *capital improvement*; *capital outlay*.

capital expense. See EXPENSE.

capital flight. The sending of large amounts of investment money out of a country, usu. as a result of panic caused by political turmoil or a severe recession.

capital gain. The profit realized when a capital asset is sold or exchanged. — Also termed *capital gains*. Cf. *ordinary gain* under GAIN (3); *capital loss* under LOSS.

> "Throughout most of the history of income taxation in the U.S., a distinction has been drawn between the rate of taxation on 'ordinary income' (or ordinary loss) and 'capital gain' (or capital loss). 'Capital gain' refers to the income from certain transactions in some assets, called capital assets, or from other transactions that Congress has said should be taxed as capital gain.... The most common form of capital gain or loss transaction is a sale of an asset such as a share of stock or a parcel of land, for cash." John K. McNulty, *Federal Income Taxation of Individuals in a Nutshell* 420 (5th ed. 1995).

long-term capital gain. The profit realized from selling or exchanging a capital asset held for more than a specified period, usu. one year.

short-term capital gain. The profit realized from selling or exchanging a capital asset held for less than a specified period, usu. one year. • It is treated as ordinary income under current federal tax law.

capital-gain distribution. See *capital-gain dividend* under DIVIDEND.

capital-gain dividend. See DIVIDEND.

capital gains. See CAPITAL GAIN.

capital-gains tax. See TAX.

capital goods. See GOODS.

capital impairment. The financial condition of a corporation whose assets are less than the sum of its legal capital and its liabilities.

capital improvement. See CAPITAL EXPENDITURE.

capitalis (kap-i-**tay**-lis), *adj.* [Latin] **1.** *Roman law.* (Of a crime) punishable by death, loss of liberty, or loss of citizenship. See CAPUT. **2.** *Hist.* (Of a person or judicial proceeding) that is principal or chief.

capitalis, *n.* [Latin "chief"] *Hist.* A principal (or chief) person, object, or judicial proceeding.

capitalis baro (kap-i-**tay**-lis **bar**-oh). [Latin "chief baron"] *Hist.* The chief baron of the Court of Exchequer. See CHIEF BARON.

capitalis custos (kap-i-**tay**-lis **kəs**-tohs). [Latin "chief guardian"] *Hist.* **1.** A chief warden or magistrate. **2.** Loosely, a mayor.

capitalis dominus (kap-i-**tay**-lis **dom**-ə-nəs). [Latin "chief lord"] *Hist.* A tenant's immediate lord; CHIEF LORD.

capitalis justiciarius (kap-i-**tay**-lis jəs-tish-ee-**air**-ee-əs). [Latin "chief justiciary"] *Hist.* The principal minister of state who governed when the king traveled abroad. • By the 13th century the duties of office were more judicial than political. See JUSTICIARY (2).

capitalis justiciarius ad placita coram rege tenenda (kap-i-**tay**-lis jəs-tish-ee-**air**-ee-əs ad **plas**-ə-tə **kor**-əm **ree**-jee tə-**nen**-də). [Latin] *Hist.* Chief justice for holding pleas before the king. • This phrase — which dates from the 13th century — referred to the chief justice of the King's Bench.

capitalis justiciarius banci (kap-i-**tay**-lis jəs-tish-ee-**air**-ee-əs **ban**-sI). [Latin] Chief justice of the bench. • This phrase — which dates from the 13th century — referred to the chief justice of the Court of Common Pleas.

capitalis justiciarius totius Angliae (kap-i-**tay**-lis jəs-tish-ee-**air**-ee-əs **toh**-shee-əs **ang**-glee-ee). [Latin] *Hist.* Chief justice of all England. • This was the title of the presiding justice in the court of aula regis.

capitalism, *n.* An economic system that depends on the private ownership of the means of production and on competitive forces to determine what is produced. — **capitalist,** *adj.* & *n.*

capitalis plegius (kap-i-**tay**-lis **plee**-jee-əs). [Latin "chief pledge"] *Hist.* **1.** A chief pledge or surety. **2.** BORSHOLDER.

capitalis terra (kap-i-**tay**-lis **ter**-ə). [Latin "head-land"] *Hist.* A piece of land lying before, or at the head of, other land.

capitalization, *n.* **1.** The act or process of capitalizing or converting something into capital. **2.** The amount or sum resulting from this act or process. **3.** The total amount of long-term financing used by a business, including stocks, bonds, retained earnings, and other funds. **4.** The total par value or stated value of the authorized or outstanding stock of a corporation.

thin capitalization. The financial condition of a firm that has a high ratio of liabilities to capital.

undercapitalization. The financial condition of a firm that does not have enough capital to carry on its business.

capitalization accounting method. See ACCOUNTING METHOD.

capitalization rate. The interest rate used in calculating the present value of future periodic payments. — Also termed *cap rate*; *income yield.*

capitalization ratio. The ratio between the amount of capital raised and the total capitalization of the firm. — Also termed *capital ratio.*

capitalize, *vb.* **1.** To convert (earnings) into capital. **2.** To treat (a cost) as a capital expenditure rather than an ordinary and necessary expense. **3.** To determine the present value of (long-term income). **4.** To supply capital for (a business).

capitalized expense. See EXPENSE.

capital lease. See LEASE-PURCHASE AGREEMENT.

capital leverage. The use of borrowed funds in a business to obtain a return greater than the interest rate. See LEVERAGE.

capital loss. See LOSS.

capital market. See MARKET.

capital offense. See OFFENSE (1).

capital outlay. **1.** CAPITAL EXPENDITURE. **2.** Money expended in acquiring, equipping, and promoting a business.

capital punishment. See DEATH PENALTY (1).

capital ratio. See CAPITALIZATION RATIO.

capital recovery. The collection of charged-off bad debt that has been previously written off against the allowance for doubtful accounts.

capital return. See RETURN.

capital-risk test. *Securities.* A method of determining whether a transaction constitutes an investment contract (subject to securities laws), whereby if a substantial portion of the capital used by a franchiser to start its operations is provided by a franchisee, then the transaction is treated as an investment contract.

capital stock. See STOCK.

capital-stock tax. See TAX.

capital structure. The mix of debt and equity by which a business finances its operations; the relative proportions of short-term debt, long-term debt, and capital stock.

capital surplus. See SURPLUS.

capital transaction. A purchase, sale, or exchange of a capital asset.

capitaneus (kap-i-**tay**-nee-əs). [Law Latin "tenant in chief"] **1.** *Hist.* A tenant *in capite*; one who holds title directly from the king. — Also termed *cataneus.* **2.** *Maritime law.* A ship captain or naval commander. **3.** A ruler or leader.

capitation. See *poll tax* under TAX.

capitation tax. See *poll tax* under TAX.

capitis aestimatio (**kap**-i-tis es-ti-**may**-shee-oh). [Latin "valuing of a head"] *Hist.* A monetary estimate of a person's life, made to assess a penalty for the person's slaying. See WERGILD.

capitis deminutio (**kap**-i-tis dem-i-**n[y]oo**-shee-oh). [Latin "reduction of status"] *Roman* *law*. A diminution or abridgment of a person's legal status. — Also spelled *capitis diminutio*. Pl. ***capitis deminutiones.***

> "Capitis deminutio is the destruction of the 'caput' or legal personality. Capitis deminutio, so to speak, wipes out the former individual and puts a new one in his place, and between the old and the new individual there is, legally speaking, nothing in common. A juristic personality may be thus destroyed in one of three ways: (1) by loss of the status libertatis. This is the capitis deminutio maxima; (2) by loss of the status civitatis. This is the capitis deminutio media (magna); (3) by severance from the agnatic family. This entails capitis deminutio minima." Rudolph Sohm, *The Institutes: A Textbook of the History and System of Roman Private Law* 178–79 (James Crawford Ledlie trans., 3d ed. 1907).

capitula (kə-**pich**-ə-lə). [Law Latin "chapters"] *Hist.* **1.** Collections of laws or ordinances organized under various headings. — Also termed *capitulary*. **2.** Chapters or assemblies of ecclesiastical persons.

capitula coronae (kə-**pich**-ə-lə kə-**roh**-nee). [Latin "chapters of the Crown"] *Hist.* A more detailed form of the articles of the eyre. See ARTICLES OF THE EYRE.

capitula de judaeis (kə-**pich**-ə-lə dee joo-**dee**-is). [Latin "chapters on the Jews"] *Hist.* **1.** Laws concerning the Jews. **2.** Questions posed by the justices in eyre to determine the amount a Jew would pay to receive the king's protection and a license to conduct business. • The *capitula de judaeis* reflected the pervasive anti-Semitism of medieval England. Cf. ARTICLES OF THE EYRE.

capitula itineris (kə-**pich**-ə-lə I-**tin**-ə-ris). [Law Latin "chapters of the eyre"] See ARTICLES OF THE EYRE.

capitulary (kə-**pich**-ə-ler-ee). [Latin "chapter *or* section (of a code)"] Any orderly and systematic collection or code of laws. See CAPITULA (1).

capitulation (kə-pich-ə-**lay**-shən), *n.* **1.** The act of surrendering or giving in. **2.** *Int'l law.* An agreement to surrender a fortified place or a military or naval force. • A commander in control may generally make such an agreement for the place or force. **3.** *Hist.* An agreement between a Christian state and a non-Christian one (such as the Ottoman Empire) giving subjects of the former certain privileges in the territory of the latter. — **capitulate,** *vb.* — **capitulatory,** *adj.*

cap rate. See CAPITALIZATION RATE.

caprice (kə-**prees**), *n.* **1.** Arbitrary or unfounded motivation. **2.** The disposition to change one's mind impulsively.

capricious (kə-**prish**-əs), *adj.* **1.** (Of a person) characterized by or guided by unpredictable or impulsive behavior. **2.** (Of a decree) contrary to the evidence or established rules of law. Cf. ARBITRARY.

captain-of-the-ship doctrine. In medical-malpractice law, the doctrine imposing liability on a surgeon for the actions of assistants who are under the surgeon's control but who are employees of the hospital, not the surgeon.

captain's mast. *Military law.* The nonjudicial punishment of an enlisted person by a military commanding officer. • This type of punishment is usu. for a minor offense. See *nonjudicial punishment* under PUNISHMENT.

captation (kap-**tay**-shən). *Civil law.* Coercion of a testator resulting in the substitution of another person's desires for those of the testator. • The term formerly applied to the first stage of a hypnotic trance. Cf. UNDUE INFLUENCE.

captator (kap-**tay**-tər). *Civil law.* A person who obtains a gift or legacy through artifice. Cf. UNDUE INFLUENCE.

captio (**kap**-shee-oh). *Hist.* **1.** An arrest of a person, or a seizure of a thing. **2.** The holding of court.

caption. 1. The introductory part of a court paper stating the names of the parties, the name of the court, the docket or file number, and the title of the action. Cf. STYLE (1). **2.** The arrest or seizure of a person by legal process.

captive-audience doctrine. 1. *Constitutional law.* The principle that when the listener cannot, as a practical matter, escape from intrusive speech, the speech can be restricted. **2.** *Labor law.* The rule that prohibits either party to a union election from making a speech on company time to a mass assembly of employees within 24 hours of an election. — Also termed *captive-audience rule*.

captive insurance. See INSURANCE.

captive insurance company. See INSURANCE COMPANY.

captive insurer. See *captive insurance company* under INSURANCE COMPANY.

capture. See RULE OF CAPTURE.

caput (**kap**-ət). [Latin "head"] **1.** *Hist.* A head, chief, or principal person. **2.** *Roman law.* A person. **3.** *Roman law.* A person's condition or status.

> "A 'natural,' as opposed to an 'artificial,' person is such a human being as is regarded by the law as capable of rights or duties: in the language of Roman law as having a 'status.' ... Besides possessing this general legal capacity, or status, a man may also possess various special capacities, such as the 'tria capita' of liberty, citizenship, and family rights. A slave having, as such, neither rights nor liabilities, had in Roman law, strictly speaking, no 'status,' 'caput,' or 'persona.' ... It must however be remembered that the terms 'persona' and 'caput' were also used in popular language as nearly equivalent to 'homo,' and in this sense were applied to slaves as well as to freemen." Thomas E. Holland, *The Elements of Jurisprudence* 80–81 (4th ed. 1888).

caput comitatus (**kap**-ət kom-ə-**tay**-təs). [Latin "head of the county"] *Hist.* The head of a county; a sheriff.

caput gerat lupinum (**kap**-ət **jeer**-ət loo-**pI**-nəm). [Latin "let him bear the head of a wolf"] *Hist.* An outlawed felon considered a pariah — a lone wolf — open to attack by anyone. See OUTLAWRY.

> "He who breaks the law has gone to war with the community; the community goes to war with him. It is the right and duty of every man to pursue him, to ravage his land, to burn his house, to hunt him down like a wild beast and slay him; for a wild beast he is; not merely is he a 'friendless man,' he is a wolf.... *Caput gerat lupinum* — in these words the court decreed outlawry." 2 Frederick Pollock & Frederic W. Maitland, *The History of English Law Before the Time of Edward I* 449 (2d ed. 1899).

carcanum (kahr-**kay**-nəm). [Latin "iron collar, pillory"] *Hist.* A prison or workhouse.

carcelage (**kahr**-sə-lij). [fr. Latin *carcer* "prison"] *Hist.* Prison fees.

carcer (**kahr**-sər). [Latin "jail, prison"] *Hist.* A prison or jail, esp. one used to detain rather than punish. • *Carcer*, as used in English law and Roman law, usu. referred to a jail used as a place of detention during trial or after sentence pending execution, rather than as a place of punishment. The modern term *incarceration* derives from this word.

cardinal-change doctrine. *Contracts.* The principle that if the government makes a fundamental, unilateral change to a contract beyond the scope of what was originally contemplated, the other party (usu. a contractor) will be released from the obligation to continue work under the contract. • A contractor's allegation of *cardinal change* is essentially an assertion that the government has breached the contract.

care, *n.* **1.** Serious attention; heed <written with care>. **2.** Under the law of negligence, the conduct demanded of a person in a given situation. • Typically, this involves a person's giving attention both to possible dangers, mistakes, and pitfalls and to ways of ensuring that these risks do not materialize <standard of care>. See DEGREE OF CARE; REASONABLE PERSON.

adequate care. See *reasonable care.*

due care. See *reasonable care.*

great care. **1.** The degree of care that a prudent person exercises in dealing with very important personal affairs. **2.** The degree of care exercised in a given situation by the person most competent to deal with the situation.

ordinary care. See *reasonable care.*

proper care. See *reasonable care.*

reasonable care. As a test of liability for negligence, the degree of care that a prudent and competent person engaged in the same line of business or endeavor would exercise under similar circumstances. — Also termed *due care*; *ordinary care*; *adequate care*; *proper care.* See REASONABLE PERSON.

slight care. The degree of care a person gives to matters of minor importance; the degree of care given by a person of limited accountability.

career criminal. See RECIDIVIST.

career vice-consul. See VICE-CONSUL.

careless, *adj.* **1.** (Of a person) not exercising reasonable care. **2.** (Of an action or behavior) engaged in without reasonable care. Cf. RECKLESS.

carelessness, *n.* **1.** The fact, condition, or instance of a person's either not having done what he or she ought to have done, or having done what he or she ought not to have done. **2.** A person's general disposition not to do something that ought to be done.

"The word 'carelessness' as a synonym for negligence can be committed by those who care deeply. A man may take all the care of which he is capable, and yet be accounted negligent for failing to reach the objective standard. He may honestly ... believe that the facts are such that he is not imperilling anyone; but he may be held to have been negligent in arriving at that belief. An incompetent driver may be convicted of driving 'without due care and attention' even though he was doing his level best. The careless person is the person who does not *take* the care he ought to take: never mind whether he *felt* careful. He can be held to be negligent in making a perfectly honest mistake." Glanville Williams, *Textbook of Criminal Law* 44–45 (1978).

ca. resp. See *capias ad respondendum* under CAPIAS.

cargo insurance. See INSURANCE.

carjacking. The forcible theft of a vehicle from a motorist.

carnal abuse. See *sexual abuse* under ABUSE.

carnal knowledge. *Archaic.* Sexual intercourse, esp. with an underage female.

"The ancient term for the act itself was 'carnal knowledge' and this is found in some of the recent cases and statutes. The phrase 'sexual intercourse,' more common today apart from legal literature, is also found in recent cases and statutes. Either term, when the reference is to rape, is sometimes coupled with the word 'ravish.' And unlawful intercourse with a girl under the age of consent is often characterized as 'carnal knowledge and abuse.'" Rollin M. Perkins & Ronald N. Boyce, *Criminal Law* 201 (3d ed. 1982).

carnet (kahr-**nay**). A customs document allowing an item (esp. an automobile) to be exported temporarily from one country into another country.

carriage. Transport of freight or passengers.

Carriage of Goods by Sea Act. *Maritime law.* A 1936 federal act defining, for goods damaged in transit, the rights and responsibilities of issuers and holders of ocean bills of lading. 46 USCA §§ 1300 et seq.

carrier. 1. An individual or organization (such as a railroad or an airline) that transports passengers or goods for a fee.

common carrier. A carrier that is required by law to transport passengers or freight, without refusal, if the approved fare or charge is paid. — Also termed *public carrier.*

"[A] 'common carrier' is bound to take all goods of the kind which he usually carries, unless his conveyance is full, or the goods be specially dangerous; but may charge different rates to different customers." Thomas E. Holland, *The Elements of Jurisprudence* 299 (13th ed. 1924).

marine carrier. A carrier operating on navigable waters subject to the jurisdiction of the United States.

private carrier. A carrier that is not bound to accept business from the general public and is therefore not considered a common carrier. — Also termed *contract carrier.*

2. INSURER.

carrier's lien. See LIEN.

***Carroll* doctrine.** The principle that a broadcast licensee has standing to contest any grant of a competitive license by the Federal Communications Commission because the grant could lead to a diminution in broadcast service by causing economic injury to an existing licensee. *Carroll Broadcasting Co. v. FCC*, 258 F.2d 440 (D.C. Cir. 1958).

carryback. *Tax.* An income-tax deduction (esp. for a net operating loss) that cannot be taken entirely in a given period but may be taken in an earlier period (usu. the previous three years). — Also termed *loss carryback*; *tax-loss carryback.* Cf. CARRYOVER.

carryforward. See CARRYOVER.

carrying away. See ASPORTATION.

carrying charge. 1. A cost, in addition to interest, paid to a creditor for carrying installment credit. **2.** Expenses incident to property ownership, such as taxes and upkeep.

carrying cost. See COST (1).

carryover. An income-tax deduction (esp. for a net operating loss) that cannot be taken entirely in a given period but may be taken in a later period (usu. the next five years). — Also termed *loss carryover*; *tax-loss carryover*; *carryforward*; *loss carryforward*; *tax-loss carryforward.* Cf. CARRYBACK.

carryover basis. See BASIS.

carta (**kahr**-tə). [Latin] *Hist.* A charter, deed, or other written instrument.

Carta Mercatoria (**kahr**-tə mər-kə-**tor**-ee-ə). *Hist.* An English statute (enacted in 1303) establishing various rules that favored certain foreign merchants. • In exchange for paying customs duties, merchants received extensive trading rights throughout England, the power to export their merchandise, the liberty to dwell where they pleased, and certain legal rights. — Also termed *Statutum de Nova Custuma.*

cart-bote. See *plowbote* under BOTE (1).

carte blanche (kahrt **blawnsh**). [French "blank card"] **1.** A signed, blank instrument that is filled out at an agent's discretion. **2.** Full discretionary power; unlimited authority.

cartel (kahr-**tel**), *n.* **1.** A combination of producers or sellers that join together to control a product's production or price. **2.** An association of firms with common interests, seeking to prevent extreme or unfair competition, allocate markets, or share knowledge. **3.** *Int'l law.* An agreement between belligerents about the means of conducting whatever relations they allow during wartime; esp., such an agreement regarding the exchange of prisoners. — Also spelled *chartel.* — **cartelize** (**kahr**-tə-lIz *or* kahr-**tel**-Iz), *vb.*

car trust certificate. See EQUIPMENT TRUST CERTIFICATE.

carucage (**kar**-ə-kij). [Law Latin] *Hist.* A tax imposed either on a carucate or on the plows used on the land. — Also termed *carvage.*

carucate (**kar**-ə-kayt). [Law Latin] *Hist.* A measure of land for assessment purposes, usu. considered about 120 acres. • This amount was thought to be as much land as one plow with eight oxen could plow in a year. A *carucate* was used to assess taxes. — Also termed *carucata*; *carve*; *plowland.* Cf. HIDE (1); OXGANG.

carvage. See CARUCAGE.

carve (karv), *n.* See CARUCATE.

carve out, *vb.* **1.** To create an explicit exception to a broad rule. **2.** *Tax.* To separate from property the income derived from the property.

carveout, *n.* **1.** An explicit exception to a broad rule. **2.** *Tax.* For tax purposes, the separation from property of the income derived from the property.

ca. sa. See *capias ad satisfaciendum* under CAPIAS.

casata (kə-**say**-tə). *Hist.* A house with enough land to support one family.

casatus (kə-**zay**-təs). *Hist.* A vassal or feudal tenant possessing a casata.

case. 1. A proceeding, action, suit, or controversy at law or in equity <the parties settled the case>.

active case. A case that is still pending.

case at bar. A case under the immediate consideration of the court. — Also termed *case at bench*; *instant case*; *present case.*

case made. See *case reserved.*

case of first impression. A case that presents the court with issues of law that have not previously been decided in that jurisdiction.

case reserved. **1.** A written statement of the facts proved at trial and drawn up and stipulated to by the parties, so that certain legal issues can be decided by an appellate court. — Also termed *case made*; *special case.* **2.** *Hist.* An agreement between litigants to submit the case to a judge rather than to a jury.

> "It should have come as no surprise ... that in most cases 'merchants were not fond of juries.' For one of the leading measures of the growing alliance between bench and bar on the one hand and commercial interests on the other is the swiftness with which the power of the jury is curtailed after 1790.... [D]uring the last years of the eighteenth century American lawyers vastly expanded the 'special case' or 'case reserved,' a device designed to submit points of law to the judges while avoiding the effective intervention of a jury. In England, Lord Mansfield had used a similar procedure to bring about an alliance between common lawyers and mercantile interests." Morton J. Horwitz, *The Transformation of American Law, 1780–1860* 141–42 (1977).

case stated. **1.** A formal written statement of the facts in a case, submitted to the court jointly by the parties so that a decision may be rendered without trial. — Also termed *case agreed on.* **2.** *Hist.* A procedure used by the Court of Chancery to refer difficult legal questions to a common-law court. • This procedure was abolished in 1852. **3.** *English law.* An appeal from a Magistrates' Court to the Divisional Court of Queen's Bench on a point of criminal law. • After ruling, the magistrate states the facts for the appeal and the Queen's Bench rules on the question of law presented by the magistrate's ruling.

inactive case. A pending case that is not proceeding toward resolution. • This may occur for several reasons, such as nonservice, want of prosecution, or (in a criminal case) the defendant's having absconded.

instant case. See *case at bar*.

present case. See *case at bar*.

special case. See *case reserved*.

test case. **1.** A lawsuit brought to establish an important legal principle or right. • Such an action is frequently brought by the parties' mutual consent on agreed facts — when that is so, a test case is also sometimes termed *amicable action*; *amicable suit*. **2.** An action selected from several suits that are based on the same facts and evidence, that raise the same question of law, and that have a common plaintiff or a common defendant. • Sometimes, when all parties agree, the court orders a consolidation and all parties are bound by the decision in the test case. — Also termed *test action*.

2. A criminal investigation <the Manson case>. **3.** An individual suspect or convict in relation to any aspect of the criminal-justice system <the probation officer said he considers Mr. Jones a difficult case>. **4.** An argument <the debater made a compelling case for gun control>. **5.** An instance, occurrence, or situation <a case of mistaken identity> <a terminal case of cancer>. **6.** TRESPASS ON THE CASE <the actions of trover and case are not entirely defunct>.

case agreed on. See *case stated* under CASE.

case at bar. See CASE.

case at bench. See *case at bar* under CASE.

casebook. A compilation of extracts from instructive cases on a particular subject, usu. with commentary and questions about the cases, designed as a teaching aid. Cf. HORNBOOK.

casebook method. An inductive system of teaching law in which students study specific cases to learn general legal principles. • Professor Christopher C. Langdell introduced the technique at Harvard Law School in 1869. The casebook method is now the most widely used form of instruction in American law schools. — Also termed *case method*; *case system*; *Langdell method*. Cf. HORNBOOK METHOD.

caseflow. **1.** The movement of cases through the judicial system, from the initial filing to the final appeal. **2.** An analysis of that movement.

case-in-chief. **1.** The evidence presented at trial by the party with the burden of proof. **2.** The part of a trial in which a party presents evidence to support its claim or defense. Cf. REBUTTAL.

caselaw. The collection of reported cases that form the body of law within a given jurisdiction. — Also written *case law*; *case-law*. — Also termed *decisional law*; *adjudicative law*; *jurisprudence*; *organic law*.

case lawyer. An attorney whose knowledge is largely confined to a specific field of expertise.

> "A working lawyer cannot expect to keep abreast of all this output of ideas, but he can at least study some portion so as to liberalize his views of law and to avoid the reproach of being a mere case lawyer." Lord Wright, *The Study of Law*, 54 Law Q. Rev. 185, 185 (1938).

caseload. The volume of cases assigned to a given court, agency, officer, judge, law firm, or lawyer.

case made. See *case reserved* under CASE.

case-management order. A court order designed to control the procedure in a case on the court's docket, esp. by limiting pretrial discovery. — Abbr. CMO.

case method. See CASEBOOK METHOD.

case of first impression. See CASE.

case-or-controversy requirement. The constitutional requirement that, for a federal court to hear a case, the case must involve an actual dispute. See CONTROVERSY (3).

> "The courts of the United States do not sit to decide questions of law presented in a vacuum, but only such questions as arise in a 'case or controversy.' The two terms can be used interchangeably, for, we are authoritatively told, a 'controversy,' if distinguishable at all from a 'case,' is distinguishable only in that it is a less comprehensive term, and includes only suits of a civil nature." Charles Alan Wright, *The Law of Federal Courts* 60 (5th ed. 1994).

case reserved. See CASE.

case stated. See CASE.

case system. See CASEBOOK METHOD.

case-within-a-case rule. *Torts.* The requirement that in a legal-malpractice action, the plaintiff must show that, but for the attorney's negligence, the plaintiff would have won the case underlying the malpractice action.

cas fortuit (**kah** for-**twee**). [French "fortuitous case"] *Insurance.* A fortuitous event; an inevitable accident.

cash, *n.* **1.** Money or its equivalent. **2.** Currency or coins, negotiable checks, and balances in bank accounts. — **cash,** *vb.*

petty cash. Currency kept on hand for incidental expenditures.

cash-against-documents sale. See *documentary sale* under SALE.

cash-and-carry clause. *Int'l law.* A regulation that, before U.S. involvement in World War II, allowed belligerent countries to pay cash for goods whose export was prohibited. • Formally, this regulation was entirely neutral, but in practice it favored Great Britain.

cash bail. See BAIL (1).

cash-basis accounting method. See ACCOUNTING METHOD.

cash book. An account book of all cash received and paid out by a business.

cash budget. A period-by-period schedule of a business's opening cash on hand, estimated cash receipts, cash disbursements, and cash balance. • A cash budget is used to project a business's cash receipts and disbursements over some future period.

cash collateral. See COLLATERAL.

cash cycle. The time it takes for cash to flow into and out of a business, such as the time between the purchase of raw materials for manufacture and the sale of the finished product.

cash discount. See DISCOUNT.

cash dividend. See DIVIDEND.

cash equivalent. A short-term security that is liquid enough to be considered equivalent to cash.

cash-equivalent doctrine. *Tax.* The doctrine requiring income to be reported even if it is not cash, as when the taxpayer barters to receive in-kind payments.

cash-expenditure method. *Tax.* A technique used by the IRS to reconstruct a taxpayer's unreported income by comparing the amount spent on goods and services during a given period with the income reported for that period. • If the expenditures exceed the reported revenue, the IRS treats the difference as taxable income.

cash flow. 1. The movement of cash through a business, as a measure of profitability or liquidity. **2.** The cash generated from a business or transaction. **3.** Cash receipts minus cash disbursements for a given period. — Sometimes spelled *cashflow*.

cash flow per common share. The cash flow from operations minus preferred stock dividends, divided by the number of outstanding common shares.

discounted cash flow. A method of evaluating a capital investment by comparing its projected income and costs with its current value. — Abbr. DCF.

incremental cash flow. The net increase in cash flow attributable to a particular capital investment.

negative cash flow. A financial situation in which cash outflow exceeds cash inflow. See INSOLVENCY.

net cash flow. Cash inflow minus cash outflow.

cashier, *n.* **1.** One who receives and records payments at a business. **2.** A bank's or trust company's executive officer, who is responsible for banking transactions.

cashier, *vb.* To dismiss from service dishonorably <after three such incidents, Jones was cashiered>.

cashier's check. See CHECK.

cashlite. See AMERCEMENT.

cash merger. See MERGER.

cash or deferred arrangement. A retirement-plan provision permitting an employee to have a certain amount of compensation paid in cash or contributed, on behalf of the employee, to a profit-sharing or stock-bonus plan. • A 401(k) plan is a type of cash or deferred arrangement. — Abbr. CODA.

cashout, *n.* An arrangement by a seller to receive the entire amount of equity in cash rather than retain an interest in the property. — **cash out,** *vb.*

cash-out merger. See *cash merger* under MERGER.

cash-refund annuity. See ANNUITY.

cash sale. See SALE.

cash surrender value. See VALUE.

cash tender offer. See TENDER OFFER.

cash-transaction report. IRS Form 4789, which requires banks and other financial institutions to report cash transactions above a certain amount.

cash value. 1. See *fair market value* under VALUE. **2.** See *full cash value* under VALUE.

cash-value option. See OPTION.

cassare (kə-**sair**-ee), *vb.* [Law Latin fr. Latin *cassus* "void"] *Hist.* To quash or nullify. • *Cassare* was usu. used in reference to voiding an agreement, law, or writ. See CASSETUR BILLA; CASSETUR BREVE.

cassation (ka-**say**-shən), *n.* A quashing. See COURT OF CASSATION.

cassetur billa (kə-**see**-tər **bil**-ə). [Latin "that the bill be quashed"] *Hist.* **1.** A judgment quashing a plea in abatement. **2.** A plaintiff's on-the-record admission that a defendant's plea in abatement cannot be avoided. • This statement discontinues the action. — Also termed *billa cassetur*; *quod billa cassetur.*

cassetur breve (kə-**see**-tər **bree**-vee). [Latin "that the writ be quashed"] *Hist.* A judgment quashing an action begun by writ.

castigatory (**kas**-ti-gə-tor-ee). *Hist.* A device for punishing scolds by repeatedly plunging them underwater. — Also termed *ducking stool*; *cucking stool*; *trebucket.* See SCOLD. Cf. BRANKS.

> "[A] *common scold*, ... if convicted, shall be sentenced to be placed in a certain engine of correction called the trebucket, castigatory, or *cucking* stool, which in the Saxon language signifies the scolding stool; though now it is frequently corrupted into *ducking* stool, because the residue of the judgment is, that, when she is so placed therein, she shall be plunged in the water for her punishment." 4 William Blackstone, *Commentaries on the Laws of England* 169 (1769).

casting vote. 1. A deciding vote cast by the presiding officer of a deliberative body when the votes are tied. • The U.S. Constitution gives the Vice President the casting vote in the Senate. U.S. Const. art. I, § 3. **2.** VOTE (3).

cast-iron-pipe doctrine. See DIVIDEND-CREDIT RULE.

castle doctrine. *Criminal law.* An exception to the retreat rule allowing the use of deadly force by a person who is protecting his or her home and its inhabitants from attack, esp. from a trespasser who intends to commit a felony or inflict serious bodily harm. — Also termed *dwelling defense*; *defense of habitation.* See RETREAT RULE.

castle-guard, *n. Hist.* **1.** The protection of a castle. **2.** A form of knight service in which a tenant must protect the lord's castle. **3.** The tenure giving rise to this knight service. **4.** A tax once imposed in lieu of this knight service. **5.** The territory that is chargeable with the tax imposed in lieu of the knight service. — Also termed (in senses 2–5) *ward.*

casual, *adj.* **1.** (Of employment) occurring without regularity; occasional <a casual employee>. See *casual employment* under EMPLOYMENT. **2.** (Of an event or occurrence) not expected, foreseen, or planned; fortuitous <a casual deficit>.

casual affray. See CHANCE-MEDLEY.

casual condition. See CONDITION (2).

casual deficit. An unforeseen shortfall of funds.

casual ejector. See EJECTOR.

casual employment. See EMPLOYMENT.

casualty. 1. A serious or fatal accident. **2.** A person or thing injured, lost, or destroyed.

casualty gain. *Insurance.* The profit realized by an insured when the benefits paid exceed the insured property's adjusted value.

casualty insurance. See INSURANCE.

casualty loss. See LOSS.

casualty pot. *Tax.* A step in evaluating tax liability in which casualty gains and losses are compared to determine whether a net loss or gain has occurred. Cf. MAIN POT.

casu consimili (**kay**-s[y]oo kən-**sim**-ə-lI). [Latin "in a like case"] *Hist.* A writ of entry allowing the holder of a reversionary interest to take possession of land alienated by a life tenant. • This writ originated in the Statute of Westminster 2 (13 Edw. ch. 24 (1285)), which expanded the writs available to litigants by authorizing the Chancery to issue a writ for any situation that called for a writ similar to one that had previously issued *casu consimili* ("in a like case"). Many other writs were framed under Westminster 2, but this particular writ's close association with the statute led to the term's becoming generic. — Also termed *consimili casu*; *entry in casu consimili.*

casu proviso (**kay**-s[y]oo prə-**vI**-zoh). [Latin "in the case provided"] *Hist.* A writ of entry to recover a reversion in land alienated by a tenant in dower, i.e., a widow with a life estate in the alienated land.

casus (**kay**-səs). [Latin] **1.** A chance accident; an event without human intervention or fault. Cf. CULPA; DOLUS. **2.** A situation actually contemplated by the legislature in enacting a statute that applies to the situation. • In this sense, the term is opposed to *casus omissus.*

casus belli (**kay**-səs **bel**-I). [Latin] An act or circumstance that provokes or justifies war.

casus foederis (**kay**-səs **fed**-ər-is). [Latin "the case of the treaty" *or* "the case of the agreement"] **1.** *Int'l law.* A provocative act by one nation toward another, entitling the latter to call upon an ally to fulfill the terms of an alliance. **2.** A clause within a treaty of alliance specifying such provocative acts. **3.** *Contracts.* A case or an event falling within the terms of a contract.

casus fortuitus (**kay**-səs for-**t[y]oo**-ə-təs). [Latin] **1.** A fortuitous event. **2.** A loss not attributable to human fault.

casus major (**kay**-səs **may**-jər). [Latin] An extraordinary casualty.

casus male inclusus (**kay**-səs **mal**-ee in-**kloo**-səs). [Latin "case wrongly included"] A situation literally provided for by a statute or contract, but wrongly so because the provision's literal application has unintended consequences.

casus omissus (**kay**-səs ə-**mis**-əs). [Latin "case omitted"] A situation not provided for by a statute or contract, and therefore governed by caselaw or new judge-made law. Pl. ***casus omissi.***

> "At times a state of war appears to exist between the courts and the parliamentary draftsman. The courts decline to come to the rescue when a *casus omissus* is revealed, so words appropriate to cover the *casus omissus* are added to the statute. More frequently the draftsman gets in first and, anticipating a strict construction by the courts coupled with a total lack of sympathy if there should happen to be a *casus omissus*, he produces a statute which is nothing less than horrific in its detail." Rupert Cross, *Statutory Interpretation* 11–12 (1976).

catalla (kə-**tal**-ə). [Law Latin "chattels"] *Hist.* **1.** CHATTEL. — Also termed *catals.*

> "*Catals (catalla) alias chatels,* cometh of the *Normans.* For . . . all movable goods . . . are called chatels: the contrary whereof is *(fief)* which we do call fee." John Cowell, *The Interpreter* (1607).

2. Cattle used for plowing.

catalla otiosa (kə-**tal**-ə oh-shee-**oh**-sə). [Law Latin "nonworking chattels"] *Hist.* **1.** Chattels that are not animals. **2.** Cattle not used for plowing.

catallis captis nomine districtionis (kə-**tal**-is **kap**-tis **nahm**-ə-nee di-strik-shee-**oh**-nis). [Latin "chattels taken in name of distress"] *Hist.* A writ permitting a landlord who is owed rent to distrain (i.e., seize) the doors, windows, and gates of the tenant's house.

catallis reddendis (kə-**tal**-is ri-**den**-dis). See DE CATALLIS REDDENDIS.

catals. See CATALLA.

cataneus. See CAPITANEUS.

catchpoll (**kach**-pohl). *Hist.* A sheriff's deputy or bailiff. — Also spelled *catchpol*; *catchpole.*

> "Catchpol . . . (One that *catches* by the *Poll*) Though now taken as a word of Contempt, yet in ancient times, it was used, without reproach, for such as we now call *Sergeants of the Mace*, Bailiffs, or any other that use to Arrest Men upon any Action." Thomas Blount, *Nomo-Lexicon: A Law-Dictionary* (1670).

catch-time charter. See *time charter* under CHARTER (4).

categorical question. See QUESTION (1).

cater cousin (**kay**-tər). A distant relative. • The term derives from the French *quatrecousin*, meaning a cousin in the fourth degree.

cathedral. *Eccles. law.* The principal church of a diocese, in which the bishop's throne, or *cathedra*, is situated.

cathedral preferment. *Eccles. law.* In a cathedral church, a deanery, archdeaconry, canonry, or other office below the rank of bishop.

Catoniana regula (kə-toh-nee-**ay**-nə **reg**-yə-lə). [Latin "rule attributed to Cato"] *Roman law.* The principle that the lapse of time does not cure something void at the outset. • It was typically used to set aside a bequest in which the testator did not have the requisite power or capacity when executing the will.

cats and dogs. *Slang.* **1.** Nonperforming securities. **2.** Highly speculative securities.

> "Wall Street disdainfully regards most penny stocks as *cats and dogs*, a popular phrase in use since 1879 to describe low-priced, often worthless, speculative securities. The single word *dog* also means a worthless security, and the related *pup* meant a low-priced, inactive stock during the 1940s and 1950s." Kathleen Odean, *High Steppers, Fallen Angels, and Lollipops: Wall Street Slang* 10 (1988).

cattle rustling. The stealing of cattle.

caucus (**kaw**-kəs), *n.* **1.** Representatives from a political party who assemble to nominate candidates and decide party policy. **2.** A meeting of a group of people to formulate a policy or strategy. — **caucus,** *vb.*

separate caucus. A confidential mediation session that a mediator holds with an individual party to elicit settlement offers and demands. • When separate caucuses are used, the mediator typically shuttles between the two (or more) sides of a dispute to communicate offers and demands.

causa (**kaw**-zə), *n.* [Latin] **1.** CAUSE (1).

> "One of the vaguest terms of the Roman juristic language. Starting from the basic meaning of cause, reason, inducement, the jurists use it in very different senses.... *Causa* is the reason for which some judicial measures (actions, exceptions, interdicts) were introduced by the praetor.... Sometimes *causa* is roughly identical with animus when it alludes to the subjective motive, intention, or purpose of a person." Adolf Berger, *Encyclopedic Dictionary of Roman Law* 382–83 (1953).

causa causans (**kaw**-zə **kaw**-zanz). An immediate or effective cause. See *immediate cause* under CAUSE.

causa jactitationis maritagii (**kaw**-zə jak-ti-tay-shee-**oh**-nis mar-ə-**tay**-jee-I). [Latin "cause of assertion of marriage"] See JACTITATION OF MARRIAGE.

causa matrimonii praelocuti (**kaw**-zə ma-trə-**moh**-nee-I pree-lə-**kyoo**-tI). [Latin "cause of prearranged marriage"] *Hist.* A writ of entry available to a woman who had given land to a suitor who refused to marry her within a reasonable time. — Also termed *entry for marriage in speech.*

causa proxima (**kaw**-zə **prok**-si-mə). The immediate or latest cause. See *proximate cause* under CAUSE.

causa remota (**kaw**-zə ri-**moh**-tə). A remote or indirect cause. See *remote cause* under CAUSE.

causa sine qua non (**kaw**-zə **sI**-nee kway **non** *also* **sin**-ay kwah **nohn**). A necessary cause; the cause without which the thing cannot be or the event could not have occurred. See *but-for cause* under CAUSE.

2. *Civil law.* A consideration or inducement.

> "The revolution of the ancient law of Contract was consummated when the Praetor of some one year announced in his Edict that he would grant equitable actions upon Pacts which had never been matured at all into Contracts, provided only that the Pacts in question had been founded on a consideration (*causa*)." Henry S. Maine, *Ancient Law* 28 (17th ed. 1901).

> "Article 1131 of the French Civil Code provides that: 'L'obligation sans cause, ou sur une fausse cause, ou sur une cause illicte, ne peut avoir aucun effet.' This *cause* or *causa* is a synonym for consideration, and we find the terms used interchangeably in the earlier English authorities." John Salmond, *Jurisprudence* 361 (Glanville L. Williams ed., 10th ed. 1947).

causa non secuta (**kaw**-zə non sə-**kyoo**-tə). [Latin "the (expected) consideration not having followed"] *Roman law.* A consideration that has failed; failure of consideration.

falsa causa (**fal**-sə [*or* **fawl**-sə] **kaw**-zə). [Latin "mistaken reason or motive"] *Roman law.* Falsity of consideration. • This might result from several things, such as a mistaken reason for making a gift or bequest.

causa causae est causa causati (**kaw**-zə **kaw**-zee est **kaw**-zə kaw-**zay**-tI). [Latin "the cause of a cause is the cause of the thing caused"]. *Torts.* The principle that the cause of the cause (rather than only the immediate cause) should also be considered as the cause of the effect.

causa causans. See CAUSA (1).

causa jactitationis maritagii. See CAUSA (1).

causal (**kaw**-zəl), *adj.* **1.** Of, relating to, or involving causation <a causal link exists between the defendant's action and the plaintiff's injury>. **2.** Arising from a cause <a causal symptom>. Cf. CAUSATIVE.

causal challenge. See *challenge for cause* under CHALLENGE (2).

causality (kaw-**zal**-ə-tee), *n.* The principle of causal relationship; the relation between cause and effect <the foreseeability test is one of duty and of causality>. — Also termed *causation.* — **causal,** *adj.*

causa matrimonii praelocuti. See CAUSA (1).

causam nobis significes quare (**kaw**-zəm **noh**-bis sig-**nif**-ə-seez **kwair**-ee). [Latin "that you signify to us the cause why"] *Hist.* A writ ordering a town's mayor to give seisin of land to a grantee of the king.

causa mortis (**kaw**-zə **mor**-tis), *adj.* Done or made in contemplation of one's own death. See *gift causa mortis* under GIFT.

causa non secuta. See CAUSA (2).

causa proxima. See CAUSA (1).

causare (kaw-**zair**-ee), *vb.* [fr. Latin *causari* "to litigate"] To litigate; to show cause against.

causa remota. See CAUSA (1).

causa sine qua non. See CAUSA (1).

causation (kaw-**zay**-shən). **1.** The causing or producing of an effect <the plaintiff must prove causation>. **2.** CAUSALITY.

negative causation. *Securities.* The defense that part of the plaintiff's damages were caused by factors other than the depreciation in value of the securities resulting from registration-statement defects. • If negative causation is proved, the plaintiff's damages should be reduced. 15 USCA § 77k(e).

transaction causation. *Securities.* The fact that an investor would not have engaged in a given transaction if the other party had made truthful statements at the required time.

causative (**kaw**-zə-tiv), *adj.* **1.** Effective as a cause or producing a result <causative factor of the accident>. **2.** Expressive of causation <the causative relationship between drinking and assault>. Cf. CAUSAL.

causator (kaw-**zay**-tər). [Latin "promoter of litigation"] *Hist.* **1.** A litigant. **2.** A person who manages or litigates a cause for another.

cause, *n.* **1.** Something that produces an effect or result <the cause of the accident>.

but-for cause. The cause without which the event could not have occurred. — Also termed *actual cause*; *cause in fact*; *factual cause.*

concurrent cause. **1.** One of two or more causes that simultaneously create a condition that no single cause could have brought about. **2.** One of two or more causes that simultaneously create a condition that any one cause could have created alone.

contributing cause. A factor that — though not the primary cause — plays a part in producing a result.

cooperative cause. *Archaic.* A person who is contributorily or comparatively negligent.

direct and proximate cause. See *proximate cause.*

direct cause. See *proximate cause.*

efficient adequate cause. See *proximate cause.*

efficient cause. See *proximate cause.*

efficient intervening cause. See *intervening cause.*

efficient proximate cause. See *proximate cause.*

factual cause. See *but-for cause.*

immediate cause. The last event in a chain of events, though not necessarily the proximate cause of what follows. — Also termed *effective cause.*

intervening cause. An event that comes between the initial event in a sequence and the end result, thereby altering the natural course of events that might have connected a wrongful act to an injury. • If the intervening cause is strong enough to relieve the wrongdoer of any liability, it becomes a *superseding cause.* A *dependent intervening cause* is one that is not an act and is never a superseding cause. An *independent intervening cause* is one that operates on a condition produced by an antecedent cause but in no way resulted from that cause. — Also termed *intervening act*; *intervening agency*; *intervening force*; *in-*

dependent intervening cause; *efficient intervening cause*; *supervening cause*; *novus actus interveniens*; *nova causa interveniens*. See *superseding cause*.

jural cause. See *proximate cause*.

legal cause. See *proximate cause*.

primary cause. See *proximate cause*.

procuring cause. **1.** See *proximate cause* (2). **2.** *Real estate*. The efforts of the agent or broker who effects the sale of realty and who is therefore entitled to a commission.

proximate cause. **1.** A cause that is legally sufficient to result in liability. **2.** A cause that directly produces an event and without which the event would not have occurred. — Also termed *direct cause*; *direct and proximate cause*; *efficient proximate cause*; *efficient cause*; *efficient adequate cause*; *legal cause*; *procuring cause*; *producing cause*; *primary cause*; *jural cause*.

"The four 'tests' or 'clues' of proximate cause in a criminal case are (1) expediency, (2) isolation, (3) foreseeability and (4) intention." Rollin M. Perkins & Ronald N. Boyce, *Criminal Law* 823 (3d ed. 1982).

" 'Proximate cause' — in itself an unfortunate term — is merely the limitation which the courts have placed upon the actor's responsibility for the consequences of the actor's conduct. In a philosophical sense, the consequences of an act go forward to eternity, and the causes of an event go back to the dawn of human events, and beyond. But any attempt to impose responsibility upon such a basis would result in infinite liability for all wrongful acts, and would 'set society on edge and fill the courts with endless litigation.' [*North v. Johnson*, 58 Minn. 242, 59 N.W. 1012 (1894).] As a practical matter, legal responsibility must be limited to those causes which are so closely connected with the result and of such significance that the law is justified in imposing liability. Some boundary must be set to liability for the consequences of any act, upon the basis of some social idea of justice or policy." W. Page Keeton et al., *Prosser and Keeton on Torts* § 41, at 264 (5th ed. 1984).

remote cause. A cause that does not necessarily or immediately produce an event or injury.

sole cause. The only cause that, from a legal viewpoint, produces an event or injury. • If it comes between a defendant's action and the event or injury at issue, it is treated as a *superseding cause*.

"When this one dominant cause is found it is treated as the 'sole cause' for the purposes of the particular case, even if it might not be so treated in a different kind of cause of action. A 'sole cause' which intervenes between defendant's act and the result in question is spoken of as a 'superseding cause.' . . . The phrase 'sole cause,' meaning the only cause which will receive juridical recognition for the purposes of the particular case, is convenient to give emphasis to three points: (1) If defendant's act was the sole cause of the death or other socially-harmful occurrence, it is by definition a proximate cause thereof; (2) if something other than his act was the sole cause of the harm there need be no further inquiry so far as he is concerned; (3) it is not necessary that defendant's act should have been the sole cause of the harm, — which is merely another form of stating that a contributory cause is sufficient." Rollin M. Perkins & Ronald N. Boyce, *Criminal Law* 781–82 (3d ed. 1982).

superseding cause. An intervening act that the law considers sufficient to override the cause for which the original tortfeasor was responsible, thereby exonerating that tortfeasor from liability. — Also termed *sole cause*. Cf. *intervening cause*.

supervening cause. See *intervening cause*.

unavoidable cause. A cause that a reasonably prudent person would not anticipate or be expected to avoid.

2. A ground for legal action <the plaintiff does not have cause to file suit>.

good cause. A legally sufficient reason. • Good cause is often the burden placed on a litigant (usu. by court rule or order) to show why a request should be granted or an action excused. The term is often used in employment-termination cases. — Also termed *good cause shown*; *just cause*; *lawful cause*; *sufficient cause*.

"Issues of 'just cause,' or 'good cause,' or simply 'cause' arise when an employee claims breach of the terms of an employment contract providing that discharge will be only for just cause. Thus, just cause is a creature of contract. By operation of law, an employment contract for a definite term may not be terminated without cause before the expiration of the term, unless the contract provides otherwise." Mark A. Rothstein et al., *Employment Law* § 9.7, at 539 (1994).

probable cause. See PROBABLE CAUSE.

3. A lawsuit; a case <the court has 50 causes on the motion docket>. **4.** CAUSA (2).

cause, *vb*. To bring about or effect <dry conditions caused the fire>.

cause-and-prejudice rule. *Criminal law*. The doctrine that a prisoner attacking the conviction or sentence (as by a petition for writ of habeas corpus) on the basis of a constitutional challenge that was not presented to the trial court, must show good cause for failing to preserve the objection at trial, and must show that the trial court's error actually prejudiced the defendant. • The cause that will excuse the defendant's procedural lapse must ordinarily be some objective factor that made presentation of the defense impractical at trial, such as the reasonable unavailability of the legal or factual basis of the defense at trial, or wrongful governmental interference. As for the prejudice element, the defendant must show that some actual prejudice, such as a constitutionally invalid sentence, resulted from the trial court's error. The cause-and-prejudice rule creates a higher burden than the defendant would face in a direct appeal because it is intended to provide protection from fundamental miscarriages of justice rather than from minor trial-court errors. But in death-penalty cases in which the defendant proves actual innocence, the court may grant relief even when the standards of the cause-and-prejudice rule have not been met. See *actual innocence* under INNOCENCE.

cause célèbre (**kawz** sə-**leb** *or* **kawz** say-**leb**-rə). [French "celebrated case"] A trial or decision in which the subject matter or the characters are unusual or sensational <the O.J. Simpson trial was a cause célèbre in the 1990s>.

cause in fact. See *but-for cause* under CAUSE (1).

cause list. See DOCKET (2).

cause of action. 1. A group of operative facts giving rise to one or more bases for suing; a factual situation that entitles one person to obtain a remedy in court from another person; CLAIM (4) <after the crash, Aronson had a cause of action>.

"What is a cause of action? Jurists have found it difficult to give a proper definition. It may be defined generally to be a situation or state of facts that entitles a party to maintain an action in a judicial tribunal. This state of facts may be — (*a*) a primary right of the plaintiff actually violated by the defendant; or (*b*) the threatened violation of such right, which violation the plaintiff is entitled to restrain or prevent, as in case of actions or suits for injunction; or (*c*) it may be that there are doubts as to some duty or right, or the right beclouded by some apparent adverse right or claim, which the plaintiff is entitled to have cleared up, that he may safely perform his duty, or enjoy his property." Edwin E. Bryant, *The Law of Pleading Under the Codes of Civil Procedure* 170 (2d ed. 1899).

2. A legal theory of a lawsuit <a malpractice cause of action>. Cf. RIGHT OF ACTION. — Also termed (in senses 1 & 2) *ground of action*.

new cause of action. A claim not arising out of or relating to the conduct, occurrence, or transaction contained in the original pleading. • An amended pleading often relates back to the date the original pleading was filed. Thus, a plaintiff may add claims to a suit without facing a statute-of-limitations bar, as long as the original pleading was filed in time to satisfy the statute. But if the amended pleading adds a claim that arises out of a different transaction or occurrence, or out of different alleged conduct, the amendment does not relate back to the date the original pleading was filed. Fed. R. Civ. P. 15(c).

3. Loosely, a lawsuit <there are four defendants in the pending cause of action>.

cause-of-action estoppel. See COLLATERAL ESTOPPEL.

causidicus (kaw-**zid**-ə-kəs). [Latin "pleader"] *Roman law.* A speaker or pleader who pleaded cases orally for others. Cf. ADVOCATUS.

cautio (**kaw**-shee-oh). [Latin "security"] *Roman & civil law.* **1.** Security given to ensure the performance of an obligation. See BAIL; BOND (2). **2.** A surety.

cautio fideiussoria (**kaw**-shee-oh fī-dee-yə-**sor**-ee-ə). [Latin "security from a third party"] Security given by a third party. — Also spelled *cautio fidejussoria*.

cautio judicatem solvi (**kaw**-shee-oh joo-di-**kay**-təm **sol**-vī). [Latin] A plaintiff's security for court costs.

cautio Muciana (**kaw**-shee-oh myoo-shee-**ay**-nə). [Latin "security introduced by Mucius Scaevola"] Security given by an heir or legatee to obtain immediate possession of a conditional inheritance. • The condition in the will usu. required an heir to refrain from doing some act, such as marriage or overseas travel.

cautio pignoratitia (**kaw**-shee-oh pig-nər-ə-**tish**-[ee]-ə). [Latin "security by pledge"] Security given by pledging goods. Cf. PIGNORATITIA ACTIO.

cautio pro expensis (**kaw**-shee-oh proh ek-**spen**-sis). [Latin "security for costs"] Security for court costs.

cautio usufructuaria (**kaw**-shee-oh yooz-yə-frək-choo-**air**-ee-ə). [Latin "tenant's security"] Security given by a tenant for life or a term for years against waste of the rented property. See USUFRUCT.

caution (**kay**-shən). *Civil & Scots law.* **1.** Security given to ensure performance of some obligation. **2.** The person who gives the security. See BAIL.

cautionary instruction. See JURY INSTRUCTION.

cautione admittenda. See DE CAUTIONE ADMITTENDA.

caution money. See EARNEST MONEY.

c.a.v. *abbr.* CURIA ADVISARI VULT.

caveat (**kav**-ee-aht *or* **kay**-vee-at *or* **kav**-ee-at). [Latin "let him or her beware"] **1.** A warning or proviso <he sold the car to his friend with the caveat that the brakes might need repairs>.

caveat actor (**kay**-vee-at **ak**-tor). [Latin] Let the doer, or actor, beware.

caveat emptor (**kay**-vee-at **emp**-tor). [Latin "let the buyer beware"] A doctrine holding that purchasers buy at their own risk. • Modern statutes and cases have greatly limited the importance of this doctrine.

> "It [*caveat emptor*] is one of that tribe of anonymous Latin maxims that infest our law ... they fill the ear and sound like sense, and to the eye look like learning; while their main use is to supply the place of either or both." Gulian C. Verplanck, *An Essay on the Doctrine of Contracts* 218 (1825).

> "*Caveat emptor* is the ordinary rule in contract. A vendor is under no duty to communicate the existence even of latent defects in his wares unless by act or implication he represents such defects not to exist." William R. Anson, *Principles of the Law of Contract* 245 (Arthur L. Corbin ed., 3d Am. ed. 1919).

caveat venditor (**kay**-vee-at **ven**-di-tor). [Latin] Let the seller beware.

caveat viator (**kay**-vee-at vI-**ay**-tor). [Latin "let the traveler beware"]. The duty of a traveler on a highway to use due care to detect and avoid defects in the way.

2. A formal notice or warning given by a party to a court or court officer requesting a suspension of proceedings <the decedent's daughter filed a caveat stating the facts on which her will contest is based>. **3.** Under the Torrens system of land titles, a formal notice of an unregistered interest in land. • Once lodged with the register of deeds, this notice prevents the register from recording any dealing affecting the estate or the interest claimed. See TORRENS SYSTEM. — **caveat,** *vb.*

caveatable (kay-vee-**at**-ə-bəl), *adj.* Of or relating to a legal or equitable interest that is protectable by a caveat. See CAVEAT (2), (3).

caveatee (kay-vee-at-**ee**). One whose interest is challenged by a caveat.

caveat emptor. See CAVEAT.

caveator (**kay**-vee-ay-tər). One who files a caveat, esp. to challenge the validity of a will; CONTESTANT.

caveat venditor. See CAVEAT.

caveat viator. See CAVEAT.

C.B. *abbr.* **1.** COMMON BENCH. **2.** *Hist.* Chief Baron of the Exchequer.

CBOE. *abbr.* CHICAGO BOARD OPTIONS EXCHANGE.

CBOT. *abbr.* CHICAGO BOARD OF TRADE.

CBT. *abbr.* CHICAGO BOARD OF TRADE.

C.C. *abbr.* **1.** Circuit, city, civil, or county court. **2.** Chancery, civil, criminal, or Crown cases. **3.** CIVIL CODE.

CCC. *abbr.* **1.** COMMODITY CREDIT CORPORATION. **2.** CUSTOMS COOPERATION COUNCIL.

C corporation. See CORPORATION.

CD. *abbr.* CERTIFICATE OF DEPOSIT.

CEA. *abbr.* COUNCIL OF ECONOMIC ADVISORS.

ceap (cheep). *Hist.* Anything for sale; a chattel (usu. cattle) used as a medium for barter.

ceapgild (**cheep**-gild). *Hist.* A tax or fine paid with an animal rather than with money.

cease, *vb.* **1.** To stop, forfeit, suspend, or bring to an end. **2.** To become extinct; to pass away. — **cessation** (se-**say**-shən), *n.*

cease-and-desist order. A court's or agency's order prohibiting a person from continuing a particular course of conduct. See INJUNCTION; RESTRAINING ORDER.

ceasefire. See TRUCE.

cedant. See REINSURED.

cede (seed), *vb.* **1.** To surrender or relinquish. **2.** To assign or grant. — **cession** (**sesh**-ən), *n.* — **cessionary** (**sesh**-ən-er-ee), *adj.*

cedent. See REINSURED.

cédula (**say**-thoo-lah). [Spanish] *Spanish law.* **1.** An official document used to identify someone; an identity card. **2.** A promissory note. **3.** A citation requiring a fugitive to appear in court to face criminal charges. • The citation is usu. affixed to the fugitive's door.

ceiling price. See PRICE.

ceiling rent. See RENT (1).

cenegild (**kay**-nə-gild). *Hist.* An expiatory fine paid by a murderer to the victim's relatives.

censere (sen-**seer**-ee), *vb.* [Latin "to express an opinion"] *Roman law.* To decree or resolve.

censo (**sen**-soh). [Spanish] *Spanish law.* **1.** Ground rent. **2.** An annuity or payment for the use of land.

censo al quitar (ahl kee-**tahr**). A redeemable annuity. — Also termed *censo redimible.*

censo consignativo (**sen**-soh kawn-seeg-nah-**tee**-voh). A transferable annuity, backed by a lien on the debtor's real property. • The debtor retains full legal title to the real property.

censo enfiteutico (en-fee-**tay**-oo-tee-koh). A real property owner's annuity from a usufructuary tenant; an emphyteutic annuity. See EMPHYTEUSIS.

censo redimible. See *censo al quitar.*

censo reservatio (ray-ser-vah-**tee**-oh). An annuity payable by a grantee of land to the grantor. • The annuity is reserved when the land is transferred to the grantee.

censor, *n.* **1.** *Roman law.* A Roman officer who acted as a census taker, assessor, and reviewer of public morals. **2.** A person who inspects publications, films, and the like for objectionable content. **3.** In the armed forces, someone who reads letters and other communications and deletes material considered a security threat. — **censorial,** *adj.* — **censorship,** *n.*

censor (**sen**-sər), *vb.* To officially inspect (esp. a book or film) and delete material considered offensive.

censo redimible. See *censo al quitar* under CENSO.

censo reservatio. See CENSO.

censorial jurisprudence. See LAW REFORM.

censumethidus (sen-sə-**meth**-ə-dəs). [Law Latin] See MORTMAIN. — Also spelled *censumorthidus.*

censure (**sen**-shər), *n.* An official reprimand or condemnation; harsh criticism <the judge's careless statements subjected her to the judicial council's censure>. — **censorious,** *adj.*

censure, *vb.* To reprimand; to criticize harshly <Congress censured the senator for his inflammatory remarks>.

census. The official counting of people to compile social and economic data for the political subdivision to which the people belong. Pl. **censuses.**

federal census. A census of a state or territory, or a portion of either, taken by the Census Bureau of the United States. • The Constitution (art. I, § 2) requires only a simple count of persons for purposes of apportioning congressional representation among the states. Under Congress's direction, however, the census has evolved to include a wide variety of information that is useful to businesses, historians, and others not affiliated with the federal government.

centena (sen-**tee**-nə). [fr. Latin *centum* "hundred"] *Hist.* A district containing 100 freemen, established among the Germans, Franks, Goths, and Lombards. • The *centena* corresponds to the Saxon *hundred.*

centenarius (sen-tə-**nair**-ee-əs). [fr. Latin *centum* "hundred-man"] *Hist.* A petty judge or under-sheriff of a hundred. See HUNDRED.

center-of-gravity doctrine. *Conflict of laws.* The rule that, in choice-of-law questions, the law of the jurisdiction with the most significant relationship to the transaction or event applies. — Also termed *significant-relationship theory*; *grouping-of-contacts theory.*

centesima (sen-**tes**-ə-mə). [Latin "one-hundredth"] *Roman law.* The hundredth part; 1%. See USURAE CENTESIMAE.

Central American Court of Justice. A court created by a 1908 convention between Costa Rica, El Salvador, Guatemala, Honduras, and Nicaragua, to guarantee the rights of the various republics to maintain peace and harmony in their relations and to prevent recourse to the use of force. • The convention expired after ten years, and the court ceased to exist in 1918.

central clearing system. A method of facilitating securities transactions in which an agent or subsidiary of an exchange acts as a clearinghouse for member brokerage firms by clearing their checks, settling their accounts, and delivering their payments. • Most transactions are reflected solely by computerized book entries, and clearinghouse statements are submitted showing the net balance to be paid to reconcile the member firm's accounts.

Central Criminal Court. The Crown Court sitting in London, formerly known as the Old Bailey. • The Central Criminal Court, created in 1834, has jurisdiction to try all indictable offenses committed in London. See CROWN COURT.

Central Criminal Court Act. See PALMER'S ACT.

central government. See *federal government* under GOVERNMENT.

Central Intelligence Agency. A U.S. federal agency responsible for gathering, analyzing, and sometimes acting on information relating to national security, esp. foreign intelligence and counterintelligence activities. — Abbr. CIA.

Central Office. The primary office for most of England's courts. • The Central Office was established in 1879 to consolidate the masters and associates of the common-law courts, and the clerical functions of the Crown Office of the Queen's Bench Division, the Report and Enrollment offices of the Chancery Division, and several other offices.

centumviri (sen-**təm**-və-rɪ). [Latin "hundred men"] *Roman law.* A court with jurisdiction to hear important cases, esp. those relating to inheritances, wills, and property. • The court originally consisted of 105 judges — 3 from each of the 35 tribes.

CEO. *abbr.* CHIEF EXECUTIVE OFFICER.

ceorl (chorl). *Hist.* A Saxon freeman who either possessed no landed property or held land of a thane by paying rent or providing services. • After the Norman Conquest, ceorls were reduced to the status of unfree villeins. Under Norman rule, the variant form of the word, *churl*, became associated with a base peasant, and soon acquired the connotation of a surly, coarse person (hence the modern meaning). — Also termed *churl*; *cirliscus*.

cepi (**see**-pɪ). [Latin] *Hist.* I have taken. • *Cepi* was often used in a capias return by an arresting sheriff, as in *cepi corpus et est in custodia* ("I have taken the defendant [or body] and he is in custody").

> "But for injuries committed *with force* to the person, property, or possession, of the plaintiff, the law, to punish the breach of the peace, and prevent its disturbance in the future, provided also a process against the defendant's *person*.... This process was called a *capias ad respondendum*, which at once authorised the sheriff to take the defendant, and imprison him till the return-day, and then produce him in court.... If by this process the defendant was arrested, the sheriff returned it with *cepi corpus* indorsed. But notwithstanding this writ commanded the sheriff to take and secure him till the return-day, he might, at his own peril, have let the defendant continue at large; thought he was liable, in case of his non appearance in court, to make amends to the plaintiff in an action for an escape, or to be amerced by the court for the contempt, in not producing the body pursuant to the return he had made on the writ." George Crompton, *Practice Common-Placed: Rules and Cases of Practice in the Courts of King's Bench and Common Pleas* xlii–xliii (3d ed. 1787).

cepi corpus et bail (**see**-pɪ **kor**-pəs et **bayl**). I have arrested and then released the defendant on a bail bond.

cepi corpus et committitur (**see**-pɪ **kor**-pəs et kə-**mit**-ə-tər). I have arrested and committed the defendant (to prison).

cepi corpus et est languidus (**see**-pɪ **kor**-pəs et est **lang**-gwə-dəs). I have arrested the defendant and he is sick. • This notation in a sheriff's return indicated that the defendant was too sick to be moved safely from the place of arrest.

cepi corpus et paratum habeo (**see**-pɪ **kor**-pəs et pə-**ray**-təm **hay**-bee-oh). I have made an arrest and am ready to produce the defendant.

cepit (**see**-pit). [Latin] *Hist.* He took. • This was the main verb in a declaration in an action for trespass or replevin.

cepit et abduxit (**see**-pit et ab-**duk**-sit). [Latin] *Hist.* He took and led away. • This declaration appeared in either a writ of trespass or a larceny indictment for theft of an animal.

cepit et asportavit (**see**-pit et as-por-**tay**-vit). [Latin] *Hist.* He took and carried away. • This declaration appeared in either a writ of trespass or a larceny indictment for a defendant's wrongfully carrying away goods.

cepit in alio loco (**see**-pit in **ay**-lee-oh **loh**-koh). [Latin] *Hist.* He took in another place. • This phrase appeared in a replevin-action pleading in which a defendant asserted that the property had been taken at a place other than that named in the plaintiff's declaration.

cerage (**seer**-ij). See WAX SCOT.

cera impressa (**seer**-ə im-**pres**-ə). [Latin "impressed wax"] *Hist.* An impressed seal. ● *Cera impressa* originally referred only to wax seals, but later came to include any impressed seal, regardless of the substance impressed. See SEAL.

> "The courts have held that an impression made on wafers or other adhesive substance capable of receiving an impression comes within the definition of '*cera impressa*.' If then wax be construed to be merely a general term including any substance capable of receiving and retaining the impression of a seal, paper, if it has that quality, may well be included in the category. The machine now used to impress public seals does not require any substance to receive or retain the impression, which is as well defined, as durable — less likely to be defaced than that made on wax. It is the seal which authenticates, not the substance impressed." William C. Anderson, *A Dictionary of Law* 926 (1889).

ceratium (si-**ray**-shee-əm). See WAX SCOT.

CERCLA (**sər**-klə). *abbr.* Comprehensive Environmental Response, Compensation, and Liability Act of 1980. ● This statute holds responsible parties liable for the cost of cleaning up hazardous-waste sites. 42 USCA §§ 9601 et seq. See SUPERFUND.

> "CERCLA is probably the most controversial environmental law ever enacted. Supporters praise it as a vital program to safeguard human health and the environment from the toxic consequences of decades of irresponsible waste handling. Citing cost estimates ranging up to $750 billion, critics deride it as an extraordinarily expensive measure which imposes crippling liability on innocent parties to fund clean-ups which are either unnecessary or largely ineffective." John G. Sprankling & Gregory S. Weber, *The Law of Hazardous Wastes and Toxic Substances in a Nutshell* 256 (1997).

ceremonial marriage. See MARRIAGE (2).

cert. *abbr.* CERTIORARI.

certain contract. See CONTRACT.

certificando de recognitione stapulae (sər-ti-fi-**kan**-doh dee rek-əg-nish-ee-**oh**-nee **stay**-pyə-lee). [Law Latin "by certifying the recognition of the statute staple"] *Hist.* A writ commanding the holder of certain commercial debt instruments (i.e., the mayor of the staple) to certify to the lord chancellor the existence and terms of a statute staple (i.e., a bond for commercial debt) wrongfully detained by a party to the bond. See STATUTE STAPLE.

certificate, *n.* **1.** A document in which a fact is formally attested <death certificate>.

face-amount certificate. *Securities.* **1.** A certificate, investment contract, or other security representing an obligation by its issuer to pay a stated or determinable sum, at a fixed or determinable date or dates more than 24 months after the date of issuance, in consideration of the payment of periodic installments of a stated or determinable amount. — Also termed *face-amount certificate of the installment type.* **2.** A security representing a similar obligation on the part of the issuer of a face-amount certificate, the consideration for which is the payment of a single lump sum. See 15 USCA § 80a–2(a)(15). — Also termed *fully paid face-amount certificate.*

periodic-payment-plan certificate. A certificate, investment contract, or other security providing for a series of periodic payments by the holder and representing an undivided interest in certain specified securities or in a unit or fund of securities purchased wholly or partly with the proceeds of those payments. ● The term also includes any security whose issuer is also issuing the certificates described above and whose holder has substantially the same rights and privileges as those holders have upon completing the periodic payments for which the securities provide. See 15 USCA § 80a–2(a)(27).

2. A document certifying the bearer's status or authorization to act in a specified way <nursing certificate>. **3.** A notice by one court to another court of the action it has taken <when issuing its opinion, the Seventh Circuit sent a certificate to the Illinois Supreme Court>.

certificate creditor. See CREDITOR.

certificated security. See SECURITY.

certificate into chancery. *English law.* The decision of a common-law court on a legal question submitted by the chancery court.

certificate land. See LAND.

certificate of acknowledgment. See ACKNOWLEDGMENT (5).

certificate of amendment. A document filed with a state corporation authority, usu. the secretary of state, reflecting changes made to a corporation's articles of incorporation.

certificate of assize. *Hist.* In England, a writ granting a retrial. • The certificate of assize has been replaced by a court order granting a motion for new trial.

certificate of authority. **1.** A document authenticating a notarized document that is being sent to another jurisdiction. • The certificate assures the out-of-state or foreign recipient that the notary public has a valid commission. — Also termed *certificate of capacity*; *certificate of official character*; *certificate of authentication*; *certificate of prothonotary*; *certificate of magistracy*; *apostille*; *verification*. **2.** A document issued by a state agency, usu. the secretary of state, granting an out-of-state corporation the right to do business in the state.

certificate of conference. A section of a pleading or motion filed with the court, usu. contained separately on a page near the end of the document, whereby the party filing the pleading or motion certifies to the court that the parties have attempted to resolve the matter, but that a judicial determination is needed because an agreement could not be reached. • Courts require some motions to have a certificate of conference attached to them. This compels the parties to try to resolve the issue themselves, without burdening the court unless absolutely necessary.

certificate of convenience and necessity. A certificate issued by an administrative agency granting operating authority to a utility or transportation company. — Also termed *certificate of public convenience and necessity*.

certificate of deposit. **1.** A banker's certificate acknowledging the receipt of money and promising to repay the depositor. **2.** A bank document showing the existence of a time deposit, usu. one that pays interest. — Abbr. CD.

certificate of discharge. See SATISFACTION PIECE.

certificate of dissolution. A document issued by a state authority (usu. the secretary of state) certifying that a corporation has been dissolved.

certificate of election. A document issued by a governor, board of elections, or other competent authority certifying that the named person has been duly elected.

certificate of holder of attached property. A certificate given by a person who holds — but does not own — property attached by a sheriff. • The certificate sets forth the holder's interest in the property.

certificate of incorporation. **1.** A document issued by a state authority (usu. the secretary of state) granting a corporation its legal existence and the right to function as a corporation. — Also termed *charter*; *corporate charter*. **2.** ARTICLES OF INCORPORATION.

certificate of indebtedness. **1.** DEBENTURE. **2.** TREASURY BILL. **3.** CERTIFICATE OF DEPOSIT.

certificate of insurance. A document acknowledging that an insurance policy has been written, and setting forth in general terms what the policy covers.

certificate of interest. *Oil & gas.* A document evidencing a fractional or percentage ownership in oil-and-gas production.

certificate of magistracy. See CERTIFICATE OF AUTHORITY.

certificate of occupancy. A document indicating that a building complies with zoning and building ordinances. • A certificate of occupancy is often required before title can be transferred and the building occupied.

certificate of official character. See CERTIFICATE OF AUTHORITY.

certificate of proof. See *proof of acknowledgment* under ACKNOWLEDGMENT.

certificate of prothonotary. See CERTIFICATE OF AUTHORITY.

certificate of public convenience and necessity. See CERTIFICATE OF CONVENIENCE AND NECESSITY.

certificate of purchase. A document reflecting a successful bid for property at a judicial sale. • The bidder receives a property deed if the land is not redeemed or if the sale is confirmed by court order. — Also termed *certificate of sale*.

certificate of registry. *Maritime law.* A document certifying that a ship has been registered as required by law. See REGISTRY (2).

certificate of sale. See CERTIFICATE OF PURCHASE.

certificate of service. A section of a pleading or motion filed with the court, usu. contained separately on the last page, whereby the party filing the pleading or motion certifies to the court that a copy has been sent to the opposing party. • A certificate of service is usu. not included with the initial pleading that the plaintiff files to begin a suit, because that pleading is usu. served with a formal summons, unless the defendant waives service. But other pleadings and motions filed in a suit are usu. required to have a certificate of service attached to them. Fed. R. Civ. P. 5(d).

certificate of stock. See STOCK CERTIFICATE.

certificate of title. A document indicating ownership of real or personal property. • This document usu. identifies any liens or other encumbrances.

certification, *n.* **1.** The act of attesting. **2.** The state of having been attested. **3.** An attested statement. **4.** The writing on the face of a check by which it is certified. **5.** A procedure by which a U.S. court of appeals asks the U.S. Supreme Court or the highest state court to review a question of law arising in a case pending before it on which the court of appeals needs guidance. See 15 USCA § 1254(2). Cf. CERTIORARI.

certification mark. A word, symbol, or device used on goods or services to certify the place of origin, material, mode of manufacture, quality, or other characteristic. See 15 USCA § 1127. — Also termed *certification trademark*. See TRADEMARK. Cf. COLLECTIVE MARK.

certification of bargaining agent. See UNION CERTIFICATION.

certification of labor union. See UNION CERTIFICATION.

certification to state court. The procedure by which a federal court of appeals defers deciding a novel question of state law by certifying the question to the highest court of the state. See CERTIFICATION (5).

certification trademark. See CERTIFICATION MARK.

certified check. See CHECK.

certified copy. See COPY.

certified financial statement. See FINANCIAL STATEMENT.

certified mail. See MAIL.

certified military lawyer. See LAWYER.

certified public accountant. See ACCOUNTANT.

certified question. 1. CERTIFICATION (5). **2.** A point of law on which a U.S. court of appeals seeks guidance from either the U.S. Supreme Court or the highest court in a state.

certify, *vb.* **1.** To authenticate or verify in writing. **2.** To attest as being true or as meeting certain criteria. **3.** (Of a court) to issue an order allowing a class of litigants to maintain a class action; to create (a class) for purposes of a class action. See CERTIFICATION. Cf. DECERTIFY.

certiorari (sər-shee-ə-**rair**-I *or* -**rair**-ee *or* -**rah**-ree). [Law Latin "to be more fully informed"] An extraordinary writ issued by an appellate court, at its discretion, directing a lower court to deliver the record in the case for review. • The U.S. Supreme Court uses certiorari to review most of the cases that it decides to hear. — Abbr. cert. — Also termed *writ of certiorari*. Cf. CERTIFICATION (5).

> "The established method by which the Court of King's Bench from the earliest times exercised superintendence over the due observance of their limitations by inferior courts, checked the usurpation of jurisdiction, and maintained the supremacy of the royal courts, was by writs of prohibition and certiorari. A proceeding by writ of certiorari (cause to be certified) is a special proceeding by which a superior court requires some inferior tribunal, board, or judicial officer to transmit the record of its proceedings for review, for excess of jurisdiction. It is similar to a writ of error, in that it is a proceeding in a higher court to superintend and review judicial acts, but it only lies in cases not appealable by writ of error or otherwise." Benjamin J. Shipman, *Handbook of Common-Law Pleading* § 340, at 541 (Henry Winthrop Ballantine ed., 3d ed. 1923).

> "The discretionary writ of certiorari has come to control access to almost all branches of Supreme Court jurisdiction. Appeal jurisdiction has been narrowly limited, and certification of questions from federal courts of appeals has fallen into almost complete desuetude. Certiorari control over the cases that come before the Court enables the Court to define its own institutional role." Charles Alan Wright et al., *Federal Practice and Procedure* § 4004, at 22 (2d ed. 1996).

certiorari facias (sər-shee-ə-**rair**-I **fay**-shee-əs). [Latin "cause to be certified"] The command of a writ of certiorari, referring to certification of the court record for review.

certworthy, *adj. Slang.* (Of a case or issue) deserving of review by writ of certiorari. — **certworthiness,** *n.*

cess (ses), *n. Hist.* **1.** *English law.* An assessment or tax. **2.** *Scots law.* A land tax. — Also spelled *cesse*; *sess.*

cessation-of-production clause. *Oil & gas.* A lease provision that temporarily extends a lease under which production has stopped. • The clause extends the lease for a specified period during which, to keep the lease alive, the lessee must resume operations.

> "Many oil and gas leases contain provisions intended to give lessees more certainty than is given by the temporary cessation of production doctrine. Usually, such provision takes the form of a temporary cessation of production clause, a provision in the lease that states that the lease will be maintained so long as production does not cease for more than an agreed period of time, usually sixty to ninety days.... So long as sixty days does not elapse without operations on the property, the lease will not terminate even though there is no production." John S. Lowe, *Oil and Gas Law in a Nutshell* 258 (3d ed. 1995).

cessavit per biennium (se-**say**-vit pər bɪ-**en**-ee-əm). [Latin "he ceased for two years"] *Hist.* A writ of right available to a landlord to recover land from a tenant who has failed to pay rent or provide prescribed services for a two-year period. • The writ could also be used to recover land donated to a religious order if the order has failed to perform certain spiritual services. — Also termed *cessavit.*

cesse. See CESS.

cesser (**ses**-ər). **1.** *Hist.* A tenant whose failure to pay rent or perform prescribed services gives the landowner the right to recover possession of the land. — Also spelled *cessor*; *cessure.* **2.** The termination of a right or interest.

cesset executio (**ses**-ət ek-sə-**kyoo**-shee-oh). [Latin "let execution stay"] An order directing a stay of execution.

cesset processus (**ses**-ət proh-**ses**-əs). [Latin "let process stay"] An order directing a stay of a legal proceeding.

cessio (**sesh**-ee-oh). [Latin "cession"] A relinquishment or assignment; CESSION.

cessio actionum (**sesh**-ee-oh ak-shee-**oh**-nəm). [Latin] *Roman law.* The assignment of an obligation by allowing a third party to (1) sue on the obligation in the name of the party entitled to it, and (2) retain the proceeds.

cessio bonorum (**sesh**-ee-oh bə-**nor**-əm). [Latin "cession of goods"] *Roman law.* An assignment of a debtor's property to creditors.

> "It was the Roman equivalent of modern bankruptcy.... [O]ne who thus made *cessio bonorum* would not become *infamis*, was never liable in future beyond his means, for the old debts, and was not liable to personal seizure thereafter in respect of them." W.W. Buckland, *A Manual of Roman Private Law* 388 (1953).

cessio in jure (**sesh**-ee-oh in **joor**-ee). [Latin "transfer in law"] *Roman law.* A fictitious action brought to convey property, whereby the claimant demanded certain property, the owner did not contest the claim, and a magistrate awarded the property to the claimant. • *Cessio in jure* resembled the English *common recovery.* See COMMON RECOVERY.

cession (**sesh**-ən). **1.** The act of relinquishing property rights. **2.** The relinquishment or transfer of land from one state to another, esp. when a state defeated in war gives up the land as part of the price of peace. **3.** The land so relinquished or transferred.

cessionary bankrupt. See BANKRUPT.

cessment (**ses**-mənt). *Hist.* An assessment or tax.

cessor. See CESSER.

cessure. See CESSER.

cestui (**set**-ee *or* **ses**-twee). [French "he who"] A beneficiary. — Also spelled *cestuy.*

cestui que trust (**set**-ee [*or* **ses**-twee] kee [*or* kə] **trəst**). [Law French] One who possesses equitable rights in property and receives the rents, issues, and profits from it; BENEFICIARY. — Also termed *fide-commissary*; *fidei-commissarius.* Pl. **cestuis que trust** or (erroneously) **cestuis que trustent.**

> "[A]n alternative name for the beneficiary is '*cestui que trust*,' an elliptical phrase meaning 'he [for]= whose [benefit the] trust [was created].' In this phrase *cestui* is pronounced 'settee' (with the accent on the first syllable), *que* is pronounced 'kee,' and trust as in English. Grammatically the plural should be *cestuis que trust* (pronounced like the singular); but by an understandable mistake it is sometimes written *cestuis que trustent*, as if

trust were a verb." Glanville Williams, *Learning the Law* 10 (11th ed. 1982).

cestui que use (**set**-ee [*or* **ses**-twee] kee [*or* kə] **yoos**). The person for whose use and benefit property is being held by another, who holds the legal title to the property. Pl. **cestuis que use** or (erroneously) **cestuis que usent.**

"The basis of this institution was the transfer of property to a trusted friend, who was to hold it not for personal benefit but for the purpose of carrying out the transferor's instructions. The person to whom the land was conveyed for this purpose was the 'feoffee to uses'; the person for whose benefit the land was conveyed — the beneficiary — was the 'cestui que use' . . . , from the law French 'cestui a que use le feoffment fuit fait'." Peter Butt, *Land Law* § 702, at 97 (3d ed. 1996).

cestui que vie (**set**-ee [*or* **ses**-twee] kee [*or* kə] **vee**). The person whose life measures the duration of a trust, gift, estate, or insurance contract.

"[L]et us assume that A instead transfers 'to E *for the life of* A.' Since A has used his own life as the measuring life of E's estate, A has given away all that he had. Because E's estate is measured by the life of someone other than himself, his estate is called an estate *pur autre vie.* A, whose life is the measuring life, is called the *cestui que vie.*" Thomas F. Bergin & Paul G. Haskell, *Preface to Estates in Land and Future Interests* 36 (2d ed. 1984).

ceteris paribus (**set**-ə-ris **par**-ə-bəs). [Latin] Other things being equal. — Also spelled *caeteris paribus*.

ceteris tacentibus (**set**-ə-ris ta-**sen**-tə-bəs). [Latin] *Hist.* The others being silent. • This phrase appeared in serially printed law reports after an opinion by one judge. It referred to the judges who did not vote or express an opinion. — Also spelled *caeteris tacentibus*. See SERIATIM.

cf. *abbr.* [Latin *confer*] Compare.

C.F. *abbr.* COST AND FREIGHT.

CFC. See *controlled foreign corporation* under CORPORATION.

CFP. *abbr.* Certified financial planner. See FINANCIAL PLANNER.

CFR. *abbr.* CODE OF FEDERAL REGULATIONS.

CFTC. *abbr.* COMMODITY FUTURES TRADING COMMISSION.

CGL policy. See *comprehensive general liability policy* under INSURANCE POLICY.

ch. *abbr.* **1.** Chapter. **2.** Chancellor. **3.** Chancery. **4.** Chief.

chafewax (**chayf**-waks). *Hist.* A chancery officer who heated (or *chafed*) wax to seal writs, commissions, and other instruments. • The office was abolished in 1852. — Also spelled *chaffwax*.

chain-certificate method. The procedure for authenticating a foreign official record by the party seeking to admit the record as evidence at trial. See Fed. R. Civ. P. 44.

chain conspiracy. See CONSPIRACY.

chain gang. A group of prisoners chained together to prevent their escape while working outside a prison.

chain of causation. 1. A series of events each caused by the previous one. **2.** The causal connection between a cause and its effects. Cf. CAUSATION.

chain-of-causation rule. *Workers' compensation.* The principle that an employee's suicide is compensable under workers' compensation statutes if the employee suffered an earlier work-related injury that led to a mental disorder resulting in the suicide.

chain of custody. 1. The movement and location of real evidence from the time it is obtained to the time it is presented in court.

"Chain of custody requires testimony of continuous possession by each individual having possession, together with testimony by each that the object remained in substantially the same condition during its presence in his possession. All possibility of alteration, substitution or change of condition need not be eliminated. For example, normally an object may be placed in a safe to which more than one person had access without each such person being produced. However the more authentication is genuinely in issue, the greater the need to negate the possibility of alteration or substitution." Michael H. Graham, *Federal Rules of Evidence in a Nutshell* 402 (3d ed. 1992).

2. The history of a chattel's possession. — Also termed *chain of possession*.

chain of title. 1. The ownership history of a piece of land, from its first owner to the present one. — Also termed *line of title*. **2.** The ownership history of commercial paper, traceable through the indorsements. • For the holder to have good title, every prior negotiation must have been proper. If a necessary indorsement is missing or forged, the chain of title is broken and no later transferee can become a holder.

chain-referral scheme. See PYRAMID SCHEME.

chair. The person who presides over a committee, convention, assembly, or other deliberative body. — Also termed *chairman*; *chairwoman*; *chairperson*.

Chairman of Committees of the Whole House. The member of Parliament who presides over the House of Commons when it is sitting in committee.

chairperson. See CHAIR.

chairwoman. See CHAIR.

challenge, *n.* **1.** An act or instance of formally questioning the legality or legal qualifications of a person, action, or thing <a challenge to the opposing party's expert witness>.

as-applied challenge. A lawsuit claiming that a law or governmental policy, though constitutional on its face, is unconstitutional as applied, usu. because of a discriminatory effect; a claim that a statute is unconstitutional on the facts of a particular case or to a particular party.

Batson challenge. *Criminal procedure.* A defendant's objection to peremptory challenges of jurors whereby the defendant raises an inference that the prosecution used peremptory challenges to exclude potential jurors on the basis of race (*Batson v. Kentucky*, 476 U.S. 79, 106 S.Ct. 1712 (1986)). • *Edmonson v. Leesville Concrete Company* extended *Batson* challenges to civil cases. 500 U.S. 614, 111 S.Ct. 2077 (1991).

constitutional challenge. A lawsuit claiming that a law or governmental action is unconstitutional.

facial challenge. A claim that a statute is unconstitutional on its face — that is, that it always operates unconstitutionally.

2. A party's request that a judge disqualify a potential juror or an entire jury panel <the personal-injury plaintiff used his last challenge to disqualify a neurosurgeon>. — Also termed *jury challenge*.

causal challenge. See *challenge for cause*.

challenge for cause. A party's challenge supported by a specified reason, such as bias or prejudice, that would disqualify that potential juror. — Also termed *causal challenge*; *general challenge*; *challenge to the poll*.

challenge propter affectum (**prop**-tər ə-**fek**-təm). A challenge because some circumstance, such as kinship with a party, renders the potential juror incompetent to serve in the particular case.

challenge propter defectum (**prop**-tər də-**fek**-təm). A challenge based on a claim that the juror is incompetent to serve on any jury for reasons such as alienage, infancy, or nonresidency.

challenge propter delictum (**prop**-tər də-**lik**-təm). A challenge based on a claim that the potential juror has lost citizenship rights, as by being convicted of an infamous crime. See CIVIL DEATH (1).

challenge to the array. A legal challenge to the manner in which the entire jury panel was selected, usu. for a failure to follow prescribed procedures designed to produce impartial juries. • Such a challenge is either a principal challenge (if some defect renders the jury prima facie incompetent, as where the officer selecting veniremembers is related to the prosecutor or defendant) or a challenge for favor (as where the defect does not amount to grounds for a principal challenge, but there is a probability of partiality). — Also termed *challenge to the jury array*.

challenge to the poll. See *challenge for cause*.

general challenge. See *challenge for cause*.

peremptory challenge. One of a party's limited number of challenges that need not be supported by any reason, although a party may not use such a challenge in a way that discriminates against a protected minority. — Often shortened to *peremptory*. — Also termed *peremptory strike*. See STRIKE (2).

3. *Military law.* An objection to a member of the court serving in a court-martial case. • A military judge can be challenged only for cause.

challenge, *vb.* **1.** To dispute or call into question <the columnist challenged the wisdom of the court's ruling>. **2.** To formally object to the legality or legal qualifications of <the defendant challenged the person's eligibility for jury duty>.

challenge to the jury array. See *challenge to the array* under CHALLENGE (2).

challenge to the poll. See *challenge for cause* under CHALLENGE (2).

chamber, *n.* **1.** A room or compartment <gas chamber>. **2.** A legislative or judicial body; the hall or room where such a body conducts business <the senate chamber>. — **chamber,** *adj.*

judge's chamber. (*usu. pl.*) **1.** The private room or office of a judge. **2.** Any place that a judge transacts official business when not holding a session of the court. See IN CAMERA.

lower chamber. In a bicameral legislature, the larger of the two legislative bodies, such as the House of Representatives or the House of Commons.

upper chamber. In a bicameral legislature, the smaller of the two legislative bodies, such as the Senate or the House of Lords.

chamber, *vb.* (Of a judge) to sit in one's chambers at a given location <Judge Kaye chambers sometimes in New York and sometimes in Albany>.

chamber business. A judge's official business that is conducted outside the courtroom.

chamberlain (**chaym**-bər-lin). A treasurer; originally, the keeper of the royal treasure chamber. • The term has been used for several high offices in England, such as the Lord Great Chamberlain, Lord Chamberlain of the Household, and Chamberlain of the Exchequer.

chamberlaria (chaym-bər-**lair**-ee-ə). [Law Latin] Chamberlainship; the office of chamberlain.

chamber of accounts. *French law.* A court responsible for adjudicating disputes concerning public-revenue collection. Cf. COURT OF EXCHEQUER.

chamber of commerce. An association of merchants and other business leaders who organize to promote the commercial interests in a given area and whose group is generally affiliated with the national organization of the same name.

champertor (**cham**-pər-tər), *n.* A person who engages in champerty; one who supports and promotes another person's lawsuit for pecuniary gain.

champertous (**cham**-pər-təs), *adj.* Of, relating to, or characterized by champerty; constituting champerty <a champertous contract>.

"In England and many other countries, the contingent fee is prohibited as a form of champerty because it permits a client to carry on litigation in exchange for a promise to the lawyer of a share in the recovery. Although most states in the United States prohibit a lawyer from accepting an assignment of a percentage of the client's cause of action as a legal fee, they do not similarly condemn, as champertous, contingent fees whereby the lawyer receives a percentage of the recovery as a fee and no fee at all if there is no recovery." Robert H. Aronson & Donald T. Weckstein, *Professional Responsibility in a Nutshell* 271–72 (2d ed. 1991).

champerty (**cham**-pər-tee), *n.* **1.** An agreement between a stranger to a lawsuit and a litigant by which the stranger pursues the litigant's claim as consideration for receiving part of any judgment proceeds. **2.** The act or fact of maintaining, supporting, or promoting another person's lawsuit. Cf. MAINTENANCE (6).

"There is disagreement in the American courts as to what constitutes champerty. (1) Some courts hold that an agreement to look to the proceeds of the suit for compensation is champerty.... (2) Some courts hold that in addition the attorney must prosecute the suit at his own cost and expense to constitute champerty.... (3) Some courts hold even in a case like (2) that there is no champerty.... (4) All authorities agree that a contract for a contingent fee is not champerty if it is not to be paid out of the proceeds of the suit.... (5) In some states it is declared that the common law doctrines of maintenance and champerty are unknown ... ; in some the matter is regulated wholly by statute.... [A]nd in most there is a marked tendency to narrow the doctrines of champerty or to evade them." William R. Anson, *Principles of the Law of Contract* 294 n.2 (Arthur L. Corbin ed., 3d Am. ed. 1919).

"The rule as to champerty has been generally relaxed under modern decisions and a majority of courts now recognize that an agreement by which the attorney is to receive a contingent fee, i.e., a certain part of the avails of a suit or an amount fixed with reference to the amount recovered, is valid as long as the attorney does not agree to pay the expenses and costs of the action." Walter Wheeler Cook, "Quasi-Contracts," in 1 *American Law and Procedure* 129 (1952).

chance, *n.* **1.** A hazard or risk. **2.** The unforeseen, uncontrollable, or unintended consequences of an act. **3.** An accident.

chancellor, *n.* **1.** A judge serving on a court of chancery. **2.** A university president or CEO of an institution of higher education. — **chancellorship,** *n.*

Chancellor, Lord. See LORD CHANCELLOR.

chancellor of the diocese. *Eccles. law.* The sole judge of the consistory court of a diocese.

Chancellor of the Exchequer. In England, a government minister who controls revenue and expenditures. • Formerly, the Chancellor sat in the Court of Exchequer.

chancellor's foot. A symbol of the variability of equitable justice. • John Selden, the 17th-century jurist, is thought to have coined the phrase in this passage, from his best-known book: "Equity is a roguish thing. For law we have a measure, know what to trust to: equity is according to the conscience of him that is Chancellor, and as that is larger or narrower, so is equity. 'Tis all one as if they should make the standard for the measure the Chancellor's foot. What an uncertain measure would this be! One Chancellor has a long foot, another a short foot, a third an indifferent foot; 'tis the same thing in the Chancellor's conscience." *Table Talk* (1689).

chance-medley. [fr. Anglo-Norman *chance medlee* "chance scuffle"] A spontaneous fight during which one participant kills another participant in self-defense. — Also termed *chaud-medley*; *casual affray*. Cf. MEDLEY.

> "But the self-defence, which we are now speaking of, is that whereby a man may protect himself from an assault, or the like, in the course of a sudden brawl or quarrel, by killing him who assaults him. And this is what the law expresses by the word *chance-medley*, or (as some rather choose to write it) *chaud-medley*; the former of which in its etymology signifies a *casual* affray, the latter an affray in the *heat* of blood or passion: both of them of pretty much the same import; but the former is in common speech too often erroneously applied to any manner of homicide by misadventure; whereas it appears . . . that it is properly applied to such killing, as happens in self-defence upon a sudden rencounter." 4 William Blackstone, *Commentaries on the Laws of England* 184 (1769).

chance-of-survival doctrine. The principle that a wrongful-death plaintiff need only prove that the defendant's conduct was a substantial factor in causing the death — that is, that the victim might have survived but for the defendant's conduct.

chancer (**chan**-sər), *vb*. To adjust according to equitable principles, as a court of chancery would. • The practice arose in parts of New England when the courts had no equity jurisdiction, and were compelled to act on equitable principles.

> "The practice of 'chancering' is a very old one. A forfeiture could be 'chancered' under a law of 1699. . . . Adjudged cases in 1630–1692 may be found in the Records of the Court of Assistants of Massachusetts Bay Colony. The early laws of Massachusetts provided for 'chancering' the forfeiture of any penal bond. . . . In Rhode Island an act of 1746 provided for 'chancerizing' the forfeiture 'where any penalty is forfeited, or conditional estate recovered, or equity of redemption sued for, whether judgment is confessed or otherwise obtained.' " 1 John Bouvier, *Bouvier's Law Dictionary* 456–57 (8th ed. 1914).

chancery (**chan**-sər-ee). **1.** A court of equity; collectively, the courts of equity. — Also termed *court of chancery*; *chancery court*.

> "Chancery's jurisdiction was complementary to that of the courts of common law — it sought to do justice in cases for which there was no adequate remedy at common law. It had originated in the petition, not the writ, of the party who felt aggrieved to the Lord Chancellor as 'keeper of the King's conscience.' In its origins, therefore, Chancery's flexible concern for justice complemented admirably the formalism of a medieval system of common law which had begun to adhere strictly, perhaps overstrictly on occasion, to prescribed forms. By 1800, however, Chancery's system was itself regarded as being both consistent and certain." A.H. Manchester, *Modern Legal History of England and Wales, 1750–1950* 135–36 (1980).

2. The system of jurisprudence administered in courts of equity. See EQUITY. **3.** *Int'l law*. The place where the head of a diplomatic mission and staff have their offices, as distinguished from the embassy (where the ambassador lives).

Chancery Court of York. *Eccles. law*. The ecclesiastical court of the province of York, responsible for appeals from provincial diocesan courts. Cf. COURT OF ARCHES.

chancery guardian. See GUARDIAN.

chance verdict. See VERDICT.

changed circumstances. See *change of circumstances* under CIRCUMSTANCE.

change of circumstances. See CIRCUMSTANCE.

change of condition. **1.** *Workers' compensation*. A substantial worsening of an employee's physical health occurring after an award, as a result of which the employee merits an increase in benefits. **2.** *Family law*. A change of circumstances justifying a modification to a custody, child support, or alimony order. Cf. *change of circumstances* under CIRCUMSTANCE.

change of venue. **1.** The transfer of a lawsuit from one locale to another. **2.** The transfer of a lawsuit begun in one court to another court in the same district, usu. because of questions of fairness. — Also termed *transfer of venue*. See VENUE.

change order. A directive issued by the federal government to a contractor to alter the specifications of an item the contractor is producing for the government.

changing fund. See FUND (1).

channel. 1. The bed of a stream of water; the groove through which a stream flows <digging a deeper channel was thought to help protect the river from flooding>.

main channel. The bed over which the principal volume of water flows; the deepest and most navigable part of a channel.

natural channel. The naturally formed bed and banks of a stream.

natural flood channel. A channel through which floodwaters naturally accumulate and flow downstream.

2. The line of deep water that vessels follow <a shipping channel>. **3.** A water route between two islands or an island and a continent <the English Channel>. **4.** A mode of transmitting something <the news channel>.

chantry (**chan**-tree), *n. Hist. Eccles. law.* **1.** A benefice endowed for the saying of Mass by chantry priests for the soul of the founder or his designees. • This practice was abolished in England by the Chantry Acts of 1545 and 1547. **2.** A chapel or part of a church so endowed. — Also spelled *chauntry*.

chapiter (**chap**-ə-tər). [Law French] *Hist.* A list of matters drawn up by the king to be presented before the justices in eyre, justices of assise, or justices of the peace. — Also spelled *chapitre*. Cf. ARTICLES OF THE EYRE.

Chapter 7. 1. The chapter of the Bankruptcy Code allowing a trustee to collect and liquidate a debtor's property, either voluntarily or by court order, to satisfy creditors. **2.** A bankruptcy case filed under this chapter. • An individual debtor who undergoes this type of liquidation (the most common type of bankruptcy) usu. gets a fresh financial start by receiving a discharge of all debts. — Also termed (in sense 2) *straight bankruptcy*.

> "A Chapter 7 case has five stages: (1) getting the debtor into bankruptcy court; (2) collecting the debtor's property; (3) selling this property; (4) distributing the proceeds of the sale to creditors; and (5) determining whether the debtor is discharged from further liability to these creditors." David G. Epstein et al., *Bankruptcy* § 1–7, at 9 (1993).

Chapter 9. 1. The chapter of the Bankruptcy Code governing the adjustment of a municipality's debts. **2.** A bankruptcy case filed under this chapter.

Chapter 11. 1. The chapter of the Bankruptcy Code allowing an insolvent business, or one that is threatened with insolvency, to reorganize itself under court supervision while continuing its normal operations and restructuring its debt. • Although the Code does not expressly prohibit the use of Chapter 11 by an individual nonbusiness debtor, the vast majority of Chapter 11 cases involve business debtors. **2.** A business reorganization conducted under this chapter; REORGANIZATION (2).

Chapter 12. 1. The chapter of the Bankruptcy Code providing for a court-approved debt-payment relief plan for family farmers with a regular income. **2.** A bankruptcy case filed under this chapter. — Also termed (in sense 2) *family-farmer bankruptcy*; *farmer bankruptcy*.

Chapter 13. 1. The chapter of the Bankruptcy Code allowing a person's future earnings to be collected by a trustee and paid to unsecured creditors. • A plan filed under Chapter 13 is sometimes called a *wage-earner's plan*, a *wage-earner plan*, or an *income-based plan*. A Chapter 13 debtor does not receive a discharge of debts; rather, Chapter 13 allows the debtor to propose a plan of rehabilitation to extend or reduce the balance of any obligations. A plan made in good faith will be confirmed if the creditors acquiesce, if they receive the fair value of their claims, or if the plan pledges all of the debtor's disposable income for three years. **2.** A bankruptcy case filed under this chapter.

chapter surfing. *Slang.* A debtor's movement from a filing under one Bankruptcy Code chapter to a filing under another.

character evidence. See EVIDENCE.

characterization. 1. *Conflict of laws.* The classification, qualification, and interpretation of laws that apply to the case. — Also termed *qualification*; *classification*; *interpretation*.

> "In a conflict-of-laws situation, a court must determine at the outset whether the problem presented to it for solution relates to torts, contracts, property, or some other field, or to a matter of substance or procedure, in order to refer to the appropriate law. In other words, the court must initially, whether consciously or not, go through the process of determining the nature of the problem; otherwise, the court will not know which choice-of-law rule to apply to the case. This process is generally called 'characterization,' and sometimes 'classi-

fication,' 'qualification,' or 'interpretation.' " 16 Am. Jur. 2d *Conflict of Laws* § 3, at 12 (1998).

2. The process of classifying marital property as either separate or community property.

character witness. See WITNESS.

charge, *n.* **1.** A formal accusation of a crime as a preliminary step to prosecution <a murder charge>. — Also termed *criminal charge.* **2.** An instruction or command <a mother's charge to her son>. **3.** JURY CHARGE <review the charge for appealable error>. **4.** An assigned duty or task; a responsibility <the manager's charge to open and close the office>. **5.** An encumbrance, lien, or claim <a charge on property>. **6.** A person or thing entrusted to another's care <a charge of the estate>. **7.** Price, cost, or expense <free of charge>.

delinquency charge. A charge assessed against a borrower for failing to timely make a payment.

noncash charge. A cost (such as depreciation or amortization) that does not involve an outlay of cash.

charge, *vb.* **1.** To accuse (a person) of criminal conduct <the police charged him with murder>. **2.** To instruct or command <the dean charged the students to ensure that the entire group acted ethically>. **3.** To instruct a jury on matters of law <the judge charged the jury on self-defense>. **4.** To impose a lien or claim; to encumber <charge the land with a tax lien> **5.** To entrust with responsibilities or duties <charge the guardian with the ward's care>. **6.** To demand a fee; to bill <the clerk charged a small filing fee>.

chargeable, *adj.* (Of an act) capable or liable of being charged as a criminal offense <taking that money for personal use would be chargeable>.

charge account. A credit arrangement by which a customer purchases goods and services and pays for them periodically or within a specified time. See CREDIT (4).

charge and discharge. *Equity practice.* Court-ordered account filings by a plaintiff and a defendant. • The plaintiff's account (*charge*) and the defendant's response (*discharge*) were filed with a master in chancery.

charge and specification. *Military law.* A written description of an alleged offense.

charge-back, *vb.* A bank's deducting of sums it had provisionally credited to a customer's account, occurring usu. when a check deposited in the account has been dishonored. UCC § 4–214.

charge conference. A meeting between a trial judge and the parties' attorneys to develop a jury charge.

chargé d'affaires (shahr-**zhay** də-**fair**). [French "one in charge of affairs"] A diplomat who is the second in command in a diplomatic mission (hence, subordinate to an ambassador or minister). — Also spelled *chargé des affaires.* Pl. **chargés d'affaires.**

acting chargé d'affaires. A chargé d'affaires who performs mission functions when the leader of the mission is not available to do so or when the position is vacant. — Also termed *chargés d'affaires ad interim.*

permanent chargé d'affaires. A chargé d'affaires with a high enough rank to head a mission (if there is no ambassador or minister). — Also termed *chargé d'affaires en pied*; *chargé d'affaires en titre.*

chargee (chahr-**jee**). **1.** The holder of a charge on property or of a security on a loan. **2.** One charged with a crime.

charge off, *vb.* To treat (an account receivable) as a loss or expense because payment is unlikely; to treat as a bad debt. See *bad debt* under DEBT.

charge sheet. **1.** A police record showing the names of each person brought into custody, the nature of the accusations, and the identity of the accusers. **2.** *Military law.* A four-part charging instrument containing (1) information about the accused and the witnesses, (2) the charges and specifications, (3) the preferring of charges and their referral to a summary, special, or general court-martial for trial, and (4) for a summary court-martial, the trial record.

charging instrument. A formal document — usu. either an indictment or an information — that sets forth an accusation of a crime. — Also termed *accusatory instrument.*

charging lien. See LIEN.

charging order. *Partnership.* A statutory procedure whereby an individual partner's creditor can satisfy its claim from the partner's interest in the partnership.

charitable, *adj.* **1.** Dedicated to a general public purpose, usu. for the benefit of needy people who cannot pay for benefits received <charitable contribution>. **2.** Involved in or otherwise relating to charity <charitable foundation>.

charitable bequest. See BEQUEST.

charitable contribution. 1. A contribution of money or property to an organization engaged in charitable activities. **2.** A contribution to a qualified nonprofit charitable organization. • Charitable contributions are deductible for certain tax purposes.

charitable corporation. See CORPORATION.

charitable deduction. See DEDUCTION.

charitable immunity. See IMMUNITY (2).

charitable organization. *Tax.* A tax-exempt organization that (1) is created and operated exclusively for religious, scientific, literary, educational, athletic, public-safety, or community-service purposes, (2) does not distribute earnings for the benefit of private individuals, and (3) does not interfere in any way with political campaigns and decision-making processes. IRC (26 USCA) § 501(c)(3). — Also termed *charity*; *501(c)(3) organization.*

charitable purpose. *Tax.* The purpose for which an organization must be formed so that it qualifies as a charitable organization under the Internal Revenue Code. — Also termed *charitable use.*

charitable remainder. See REMAINDER.

charitable remainder annuity trust. See TRUST.

charitable-remainder trust. See TRUST.

charitable trust. See TRUST.

charitable use. See *charitable trust* under TRUST.

charity, *n.* **1.** CHARITABLE ORGANIZATION. **2.** Aid given to the poor, the suffering, or the general community for religious, educational, economic, public-safety, or medical purposes. **3.** Goodwill.

charlatan (**shahr**-lə-tən), *n.* A person who pretends to have more knowledge or skill than he or she actually has; a quack or faker. — **charlatanism, charlatanry,** *n.*

charta (**kahr**-tə). [Law Latin] *Hist.* **1.** A charter or deed. **2.** A token by which an estate is held. **3.** A royal grant of privileges or liberties.

chartae libertatum (**kahr**-tee lib-ər-**tay**-təm). [Latin] Charters of liberties. • This term refers to the two great sources of English liberties: *Magna Carta* and the *Charta de Foresta.*

chartel. See CARTEL.

charter, *n.* **1.** An instrument by which a governmental entity (such as a city or state) grants rights, liberties, or powers to its citizens. **2.** *Hist.* The writing that accompanies a livery of seisin. • Rather than being an operative element of transfer, the writing was merely evidence of it. **3.** A legislative act that creates a business or defines a corporate franchise. Cf. ARTICLES OF INCORPORATION.

bank charter. A document issued by a governmental authority permitting a bank to conduct business.

corporate charter. **1.** CERTIFICATE OF INCORPORATION (1). **2.** A document that one files with the secretary of state upon incorporating a business. • The corporate charter is often the articles of incorporation.

home-rule charter. A municipal corporation's organizational plan or framework, analogous to a constitution, drawn by the municipality itself and adopted by popular vote of the citizenry.

municipal charter. A charter by which a municipality is constituted.

> "Municipal Charters. — The charter issued to a municipality is in the nature of a constitution to it, being superior to all ordinances enacted by that municipality, though inferior in rank to all State laws of every kind." Frank Hall Childs, *Where and How to Find the Law* 8 (1922).

4. The leasing or hiring of an airplane, ship, or other vessel.

bareboat charter. A charter under which the shipowner provides the ship, and the charterer provides the personnel, insurance, and other materials necessary to operate it. — Also termed *demise charter.*

catch-time charter. See *time charter.*

demise charter. A charter under which the shipowner surrenders possession and control of the vessel to the charterer, who then succeeds to many of the shipowner's rights and obligations. • The charterer is known either as a *demise charterer* or as an *owner pro hac vice*.

gross charter. A charter under which the shipowner provides all personnel and pays all expenses.

time charter. A charter for a specified period, rather than for a specific task or voyage; a charter under which the shipowner continues to manage and control the vessel, but the charterer designates the ports of call and the cargo carried. • Each party bears the expenses related to its functions and for any damage it causes. — Also termed *catch-time charter*.

voyage charter. A charter under which the shipowner provides a ship and crew, and places them at the disposal of the charterer for the carriage of cargo to a designated port. • The voyage charterer may lease the entire vessel for a voyage or series of voyages — or may (by "space charter") lease only part of the vessel.

charter, *vb.* **1.** To establish or grant by charter <charter a bank>. **2.** To hire or rent for temporary use <charter a boat>.

charter agreement. See CHARTERPARTY.

chartered life underwriter. See UNDERWRITER.

chartered ship. See SHIP.

charter-land. *Hist.* See BOOKLAND.

charter of affreightment. See AFFREIGHTMENT.

charterparty. A contract by which a ship, or a principal part of it, is leased by the owner, esp. to a merchant for the conveyance of goods on a predetermined voyage to one or more places; a special contract between the shipowner and charterer, esp. for the carriage of goods at sea. — Also written *charter-party*; *charter party*. — Also termed *charter agreement*.

"*Charter partie* (*charta partita*) is nothing but that which we call a paire of indentures, conteining the covenants and agreements made betweene merchants, or sea faring men touching their marine affaires." John Cowell, *The Interpreter* (1607).

"The instrument by which a vessel is leased is a charter party. The term is derived from *charta partita*, i.e., a deed of writing divided; in earlier times the *charta partita*, like the indenture agreement, was prepared in two parts, the ship owner retaining one part and the charterer the other.... While a charter party need not be in writing, most charters today are detailed written documents drawn to accommodate the particular needs of shipper and carrier in a certain type of trade or commerce." Frank L. Maraist, *Admiralty in a Nutshell* 44–45 (3d ed. 1996).

chartis reddendis (**kahr**-tis ri-**den**-dis). [Latin "for returning charters"] *Hist.* A writ seeking the return of a charter of feoffment from a person who has been entrusted with the charter but who has refused to deliver it as instructed. See FEOFFMENT.

chartophylax (kahr-**tof**-ə-laks). *Hist.* A keeper of records or public instruments; a registrar.

chase. *Hist.* A franchise granted by the Crown empowering the grantee to keep, within a certain district, animals for hunting, i.e., the objects of the chase. • This franchise was also known as a *free chase* to contrast it with a *chase royal* — a chase held by the Crown.

common chase. A chase in which everyone is entitled to hunt.

chattel (**chat**-əl). (*usu. pl.*) Movable or transferable property; esp., personal property.

"That Money is not to be accounted Goods or *Chattels*, because it is not of it self valuable.... *Chattels* are either *personal* or *real*. *Personal*, may be so called in two respects: One, because they belong immediately to the person of a Man, as a Bow, Horse, etc. The other, for that being any way injuriously withheld from us, we have no means to recover them, but Personal Actions. *Chattels real*, are such as either appertain not immediately to the person, but to some other thing, by way of dependency, as a Box with Charters of Land, Apples upon a Tree, or a Tree it self growing on the Ground.... [O]r else such as are issuing out of some immoveable thing to a person, as a Lease or Rent for the term of years." Thomas Blount, *Nomo-Lexicon: A Law-Dictionary* (1670).

chattel personal. A tangible good or an intangible right (such as a patent). — Also termed *personal chattel*.

chattel real. A real-property interest that is less than a freehold or fee, such as a leasehold estate. • The most important chattel real is an estate for years in land, which is considered a chattel because it lacks the indefiniteness of time essential to real property. — Also termed *real chattel*.

chattel vegetable. A movable article of a vegetable origin, such as timber, undergrowth, corn, or fruit.

personal chattel. See *chattel personal*.

real chattel. See *chattel real*.

chattel lien. See *mechanic's lien* under LIEN.

chattel mortgage. See MORTGAGE.

chattel-mortgage bond. See BOND (3).

chattel paper. A writing that shows both a monetary obligation and a security interest in or a lease of specific goods. • Chattel paper is generally used in a consumer transaction when the consumer buys goods on credit. The consumer typically promises to pay for the goods by executing a promissory note, and the seller retains a security interest in the goods. See SECURITY AGREEMENT.

> " 'Chattel paper' means a record or records that evidence both a monetary obligation and a security interest in or a lease of specific goods or of specific goods and software used in the goods. The term does not include a charter or other contract involving the use or hire of a vessel. If a transaction is evidenced both by a security agreement or lease and by an instrument or series of instruments, the group of records taken together constitutes chattel paper." UCC § 9–102(a)(8).

electronic chattel paper. Chattel paper evidenced by a record or records consisting of information stored in an electronic medium and retrievable in perceivable form. UCC § 9–102(a)(22).

tangible chattel paper. Chattel paper evidenced by a record or records consisting of information that is inscribed on a tangible medium. UCC § 9–102(a)(54).

chattel personal. See CHATTEL.

chattel real. See CHATTEL.

chattel vegetable. See CHATTEL.

chaud-medley (**showd**-med-lee). See CHANCE-MEDLEY.

chauntry (**chon**-tree), *n.* See CHANTRY.

cheat, *n.* **1.** CHEATING. **2.** A person who habitually cheats; a swindler.

cheat, *vb.* To defraud; to practice deception.

cheater. 1. A person who cheats. **2.** ESCHEATOR.

cheating. The fraudulent obtaining of another's property by means of a false symbol or token, or by other illegal practices. — Also termed *cheating at common law*; *common-law cheat*; *cheat*. See FRAUD.

cheating by false pretenses. The act of purposely obtaining both the possession and ownership of money, goods, wares, or merchandise by means of misrepresentations, with the intent to defraud. See FALSE PRETENSES. Cf. *larceny by trick* under LARCENY.

check, *n.* A draft signed by the maker or drawer, drawn on a bank, payable on demand, and unlimited in negotiability. • Under UCC § 3–104(4), an instrument may be a check even though it is described on its face by another term, such as "money order." — Also spelled *cheque*. See DRAFT.

bad check. A check that is not honored because the account either contains insufficient funds or does not exist. — Also termed *hot check*; *worthless check*; *rubber check*; *bounced check*; *cold check*; *bogus check*; *false check*; *dry check*.

blank check. A check signed by the drawer but left blank as to the payee or the amount, or both.

bogus check. See *bad check*.

canceled check. A check bearing a notation that it has been paid by the bank on which it was drawn. • A canceled check is often used as evidence of payment. — Also spelled *cancelled check*.

cashier's check. A check drawn by a bank on itself, payable to another person, and evidencing the payee's authorization to receive from the bank the amount of money represented by the check; a draft for which the drawer and drawee are the same bank, or different branches of the same bank.

certified check. A depositor's check drawn on a bank that guarantees the availability of funds for the check. • The guarantee may be by the drawee's signed agreement to pay the draft or by a notation on the check that it is certified.

cold check. See *bad check*.

depository-transfer check. An unsigned, nonnegotiable check that is used by a bank to transfer funds from its branch to the collection bank.

dry check. See *bad check*.

false check. See *bad check*.

hot check. See *bad check*.

memorandum check. A check that a borrower gives to a lender for the amount of a short-term loan, with the understanding that it is not to be presented for payment but will be redeemed by the borrower when the loan falls due.

personal check. A check drawn on a person's own account.

postdated check. A check that bears a date after the date of its issue and is payable on or after the stated date.

raised check. A check whose face amount has been increased, usu. without the knowledge of the issuer — an act that under the UCC is considered a material alteration. UCC § 3–407. See RAISING AN INSTRUMENT.

registered check. A check purchased at a bank and drawn on bank funds that have been set aside to pay that check.

rubber check. See *bad check*.

stale check. A check that has been outstanding for an unreasonable time — more than six months under the UCC. • Banks in jurisdictions adopting the UCC may choose not to honor such a check. UCC § 4–404.

teller's check. A draft drawn by a bank on another bank or payable at or through a bank.

traveler's check. A cashier's check that must be signed by the purchaser at the time of purchase and countersigned when cashed; an instrument that (1) is payable on demand, (2) is drawn on or payable at or through a bank, (3) is designated by the term "traveler's check" or by a substantially similar term, and (4) requires, as a condition to payment, a countersignature by a person whose specimen signature appears on the instrument. UCC § 3–104(i). • Traveler's checks, which are available in various denominations, are typically purchased from a bank or financing company.

worthless check. See *bad check*.

check, *vb.* **1.** To control or restrain <handcuffs checked the defendant's movement>. **2.** To verify or audit <an accountant checked the invoices>. **3.** To investigate <the police checked up on the suspect>.

check-kiting. The illegal practice of writing a check against a bank account with insufficient funds to cover the check, in the hope that the funds from a previously deposited check will reach the account before the bank debits the amount of the outstanding check. — Also termed *kiting*; *check-flashing*.

check-off system. The procedure by which an employer deducts union dues directly from the employees' wages and remits those dues to the union.

checkpoint search. See SEARCH.

checks and balances. The theory of governmental power and functions whereby each branch of government has the ability to counter the actions of any other branch, so that no single branch can control the entire government. • For example, the executive branch can check the legislature by exercising its veto power, but the legislature can, by a sufficient majority, override any veto. See SEPARATION OF POWERS.

chefe (chef). [Law French fr. French *chef* "head"] See WERGILD.

cheque. See CHECK.

cherry-stem annexation. See ANNEXATION.

chevage (**chee**-vij). [fr. French *chef* "head"] *Hist.* An annual tribute payment from a villein to a lord. • Chevage was commonly exacted from villeins for permission to marry or permission to work outside a lord's domain. — Also spelled *chivage*; *chiefage*.

> "*Chevage*, (*chevagium*) commeth of the French (*chef*.i. *caput*). It signifieth with us, a summe of money paid by villeins to their Lords, in acknowledgment of their slaverie.... It seemeth also to be used, for a summe of a mony, yearely given by a man to another of might & power, for his avowement, maintenance, and protection, as to their head or leader." John Cowell, *The Interpreter* (1607).

chevantia (chə-**van**-shee-ə). [Law French] *Hist.* A loan of money.

chevisance (**chev**-ə-zints). [Law French] *Hist.* **1.** A composition; an agreement between a creditor and a debtor. See COMPOSITION. **2.** An unlawful or usurious contract; esp., a contract intended to evade the statutes prohibiting usury.

cheze (shayz). [French *chez* "at the home of"] *Hist.* **1.** HOMESTEAD. **2.** A homestall; a farmyard.

Chicago Board of Trade. The commodities exchange where futures contracts in a large number of agricultural products are made. — Abbr. CBT; CBOT.

Chicago Board Options Exchange. The predominant organized marketplace in the United States for trading options. — Abbr. CBOE.

chicanery (shi-**kay**-nər-ee), *n.* Trickery; deception. — Also termed *chicane.* — **chicanerous,** *adj.*

chief, *n.* **1.** A person who is put above the rest; the leader <chief of staff>. **2.** The principal or most important part or position <commander-in-chief>. — **chief,** *adj.*

chief baron. *Hist.* The presiding judge of the English Court of Exchequer. • The office has been superseded by the Lord Chief Justice of England. See BARONS OF THE EXCHEQUER.

chief executive. See EXECUTIVE.

chief executive officer. A corporation's highest-ranking administrator who manages the firm day by day and reports to the board of directors. — Abbr. CEO.

chief judge. See JUDGE.

chief justice. See JUSTICE (2).

Chief Justice of England. The former title of the Lord Chief Justice of England.

Chief Justice of the Common Pleas. *Hist.* Formerly, the presiding judge in the Court of Common Pleas. • The Judicature Act of 1875 merged the Common Pleas Division into the Queen's Bench Division, at which time the Lord Chief Justice assumed the office of the Chief Justice of the Common Pleas. Cf. LORD CHIEF JUSTICE OF ENGLAND.

chief justiciar. See JUSTICIARY (2).

chief lease. See HEADLEASE.

chief lord. *Hist.* The immediate lord of a fee, to whom the tenants were directly and personally responsible.

chief magistrate. See MAGISTRATE (1).

chief pledge. See BOROUGH-HEAD.

chief rents. *Hist.* A small, fixed, annual rent payable to the lord by a freeholder of a manor; annual quit rent. • Chief rents were abolished in 1922. See QUIT RENT.

chiefry (**cheef**-ree). *Hist.* A small rent paid to the sovereign by a feudal landholder. — Also spelled *chiefrie*; *chiefery.*

chief use. A standard for determining a proper tariff classification in which a commodity's use is understood by examining the intended users as a whole, rather than individually.

child. **1.** At common law, a person who has not reached the age of 14, though the age now varies from jurisdiction to jurisdiction. **2.** A boy or girl; a young person. **3.** A son or daughter. **4.** A baby or fetus. See JUVENILE; MINOR.

afterborn child. A child born after execution of a will or after the time in which a class gift closes. See *after-born heir* under HEIR.

biological child. See *natural child* (1).

child out of wedlock. See *illegitimate child.*

delinquent child. A legal infant who has either violated criminal laws or engaged in disobedient or indecent conduct, and is in need of treatment, rehabilitation, or supervision. See JUVENILE DELINQUENT.

disobedient child. See *incorrigible child.*

foster child. A child whose care and upbringing are entrusted to an adult other than the child's natural or adoptive parents. — Also termed (archaically) *fosterling.* See *foster parent* under PARENT.

illegitimate child. A child that was neither born nor begotten in lawful wedlock nor later legitimized. • At common law, such a child was considered the child of nobody (*nullius filius*) and had no name except what was gained by reputation. Being no one's child, an illegitimate child could not inherit, even from the mother, but statutes in most states changed this rule to allow maternal inheritance. — Also termed *bastard*; *child out of wedlock*; *nonmarital child.* Cf. BASTARD.

incorrigible child. A child who refuses to obey his or her parents or guardians or has been adjudicated delinquent under laws governing unruly children. — Also termed *disobedient child.*

legitimate child. **1.** At common law, a child born or begotten in lawful wedlock. **2.** Modernly, a child born or begotten in lawful wedlock or legitimized by the parents' later marriage.

natural child. **1.** A child by birth, as distinguished from an adopted child. — Also termed *biological child.* **2.** An illegitimate child acknowledged by the father. **3.** An illegitimate child.

neglected child. **1.** A child whose parents or legal custodians are unfit to care for him or her for reasons of cruelty, immorality, or incapacity. **2.** A child whose parents or legal custodians refuse to provide the necessary care and medical services for the child.

nonmarital child. See *illegitimate child.*

posthumous child. A child born after the father's death.

quasi-posthumous child. *Civil law.* A child who becomes a direct heir of a grandfather or other male ascendant because of the death of the child's father.

unborn child. A child not yet born, esp. at the happening of some event.

child abuse. See ABUSE.

child- and dependent-care tax credit. See TAX CREDIT.

child-care fund. State-government funds set aside to reimburse counties for part of the payments for children's foster care and expenses.

child-care rules. Administrative rules for the care of foster children.

child destruction. See FETICIDE.

child endangerment. The placing of a child in a place or position that exposes him or her to danger to life or health.

child-kidnapping. See KIDNAPPING.

child-labor law. A state or federal statute that protects children by prescribing the necessary working conditions for children in a workplace.

child molestation. See MOLESTATION.

child neglect. The failure of a person responsible for a minor to care for the minor's emotional or physical needs.

child out of wedlock. See *illegitimate child* under CHILD.

child pornography. See PORNOGRAPHY.

children's court. See *juvenile court* under COURT.

child-sexual-abuse-accommodation syndrome. The medical and psychological condition of a child who has suffered repeated instances of sexual abuse, usu. from a relative or family friend. — Also termed *child-sexual-abuse syndrome.*

child's income tax. See *kiddie tax* under TAX.

child-slaying. See INFANTICIDE.

child's part. An inheritance that, by statute in some states, a widow may claim in lieu of dower or what she would receive under her husband's will. • The amount is the same as the amount that the decedent's child is entitled to receive, subject to payments to estate creditors and the costs of administration.

child-stealing. See *child-kidnapping* under KIDNAPPING.

child support. *Family law.* **1.** A parent's legal obligation to contribute to the economic maintenance and education of a child. • The obligation is enforceable both civilly and criminally. **2.** In a custody or divorce action, the money legally owed by one parent to the other for the expenses incurred for children of the marriage. Cf. ALIMONY.

chill, *vb.* To inhibit or discourage <chill one's free-speech rights>.

chilling a sale. The act of bidders or others who combine or conspire to discourage others from attempting to buy an item so that they miggr buy the item themselves for a lower price.

chilling effect. **1.** *Constitutional law.* The result of a law or practice that seriously discourages the exercise of a constitutional right, such as the right to appeal or the right of free speech. **2.** Broadly, the result when any practice is discouraged.

***Chimel* search.** See *protective search* under SEARCH (1).

chimney money. See HEARTH MONEY.

Chinese Wall. See ETHICAL WALL.

chirograph (**kI**-rə-graf), *n.* **1.** *Civil law.* A handwritten instrument signed by the party who writes it. **2.** A written deed, subscribed and witnessed. **3.** Such a deed in two parts from a single original document separated by an indented line through the word "chirographum," each party retaining one part. **4.** *Hist.* FOOT OF THE FINE. — Also termed (in sense 4) *cyrographarius*. — **chirographic,** *adj.*

"Formerly, when deeds were more concise than at present, it was usual to write both parts on the same piece of parchment, with some word or letters of the alphabet written between them; through which the parchment was cut, either in a straight or indented line, in such a manner as to leave half the word on one part and half on the other. Deeds thus made were denominated *syngrapha* by the canonists; and with us *chirographa*, or handwritings." 2 William Blackstone, *Commentaries on the Laws of England* 295–96 (1766).

chirographer of fines. *Hist.* A Court of Common Pleas officer who engrossed court-ordered fines and delivered indentures of the fines to the parties. See INDENTURE OF A FINE.

"*Chirographer of fynes* . . . signifieth in our common lawe, him in the common bench office, that ingrosseth fines in that court acknowledged, into a perpetuall record, after they be acknowledged, and fully passed by those officers, by whome they are formerly examined; and that writeth and delivereth the indentures of them unto the party. This officer also maketh two indentures, one for the buier, another for the seller; and maketh one other indented peece, containing also the effect of the fine, which he delivereth over to the *custos brevium*, that is called the foote of the fine." John Cowell, *The Interpreter* (1607).

chirographum (kI-**rog**-rə-fəm). *Roman law.* **1.** A handwritten document, usu. an undertaking or acknowledgment of debt written in the debtor's own hand. **2.** A right of action for debt. Pl. **chirographa.**

chit. 1. A signed voucher for money received or owed, usu. for food, drink, or the like. **2.** A slip of paper with writing on it.

chivalry (**shiv**-əl-ree). *Hist.* Tenure held by knight-service; tenure in which a person held land in exchange for military service. See KNIGHT-SERVICE.

"Chivalry is a tenure of land by knight's service: for the better understanding whereof it is to be known, that there is no land but is held mediately or immediately of the crown by some service or other; and therefore all our free-holds that are to us and our heirs are called fees, as proceeding from the bounty of the king for some small yearly rent, and the performance of such services as originally were imposed upon the land at the giving thereof. . . . And these services are all by Littleton divided into two sorts, chivalry and soccage: the one martial and military; the other clownish and rustical." *Termes de la Ley* 83–84 (1st Am. ed. 1812).

choate (**koh**-it), *adj.* **1.** Complete in and of itself. **2.** Having ripened or become perfected. — **choateness,** *n.* Cf. INCHOATE.

choate lien. See LIEN.

choice of evils. See NECESSITY (1).

choice of jurisdiction. *Conflict of laws.* The choice of the state (or country) that should exercise jurisdiction over a case.

choice of law. The question of which jurisdiction's law should apply in a given case. See CONFLICT OF LAWS.

choice-of-law clause. A contractual provision by which the parties designate the jurisdiction whose law will govern any disputes that may arise between the parties. Cf. FORUM-SELECTION CLAUSE.

chop-shop, *n.* A garage where stolen automobiles are dismantled so that their parts can be sold separately.

chose (shohz), *n.* [French] A thing, whether tangible or intangible; a personal article; a chattel. See THING.

chose in action. **1.** A proprietary right in personam, such as a debt owed by another person, a share in a joint-stock company, or a claim for damages in tort. **2.** The right to bring an action to recover a debt, money, or thing. **3.** Personal property that one person owns but another person possesses, the owner being able to regain possession through a lawsuit. — Also termed *thing in action*.

"Chose, or, thing in action is, when a man hath cause, or may bring an action for some duty due to him; as an action of debt . . . and because they are things whereof a man is not possessed, but for recovery of them is driven to his action, they are called things in action." *Termes de la Ley* 85 (1st Am. ed. 1812).

"The term *chose in action* has been in common use for a long time, but some doubts have been recently raised as to its precise meaning. (See *Law Quarterly Review* for 1893, 1894, 1895.) A Divisional Court, however, has now given us the following definition: " 'chose in action' " is a known legal expression used to describe all personal rights of property which can only be claimed or enforced by action, and not by taking physical possession.' Torkington v. Magee, [1902] 2 K.B. p. 430. The phrase 'rights *of property*' does not seem a very happy one, but it is quite clear that the court meant to include under the term *chose in action* rights under a contract and rights of action arising from breach of contract." William R. Anson, *Principles of the Law of Contract* 362 n.(b) (Arthur L. Corbin ed., 3d Am. ed. 1919).

chose in possession. Personal property for which title and possession unite in the same person. — Also termed *thing in possession*.

chose local. A fixed chattel.

chose transitory. A movable chattel.

christianitatis curia (kris-tee-an-ə-**tay**-tis **kyoor**-ee-ə). [Latin "Christian court"] See *ecclesiastical court* (2) under COURT.

church court. See *ecclesiastical court* under COURT.

church law. See CANON LAW (2).

churl (chərl). See CEORL.

churn, burn, and bury. (Of a stockbroker) to make numerous risky trades in (an account) and, as a result, squander the customer's money. • The term denotes the action involved in particularly reckless churning.

churning, *n. Securities.* A stockbroker's excessive trading of a customer's account to earn more commissions rather than to further the customer's interests; an abuse of a customer's confidence for personal gain by frequent and numerous transactions, disproportionate to the size and nature of the customer's account. • Under securities laws, the practice is illegal — a violation of § 10(b) of the Exchange Act (15 USCA § 78j(b)). But because the fraud is the activity as a whole and there is no communication between the broker and the customer about a specific sale of securities, there is not normally a right of action for fraud based on churning. — **churn,** *vb.*

CIA. *abbr.* CENTRAL INTELLIGENCE AGENCY.

C.I.F. *abbr.* COST, INSURANCE, AND FREIGHT.

C.I.F. destination. See COST, INSURANCE, AND FREIGHT.

C.I.F. place of destination. See *C.I.F. destination* under COST, INSURANCE, AND FREIGHT.

cinque ports (singk ports). [Fr. "five ports"] The five English ports — Hastings, Romney, Hythe, Dover, and Sandwich — that were important defenses against French invasion. • They received special privileges and were obliged to furnish a certain number of ships for use in war.

CIO. *abbr.* The Congress of Industrial Organizations, which merged with the AFL in 1955. See AMERICAN FEDERATION OF LABOR AND CONGRESS OF INDUSTRIAL ORGANIZATIONS.

CIP. *abbr.* CONTINUATION IN PART.

cippi (**sip**-I). [Law Latin] *Hist.* See STOCKS.

circa (**sər**-kə), *prep.* [Latin] About or around; approximately <the book was written circa 1938–1941>. — Abbr. ca.; c.

circle conspiracy. See *wheel conspiracy* under CONSPIRACY.

circuit, *n.* **1.** A judicial division in which hearings occur at several locations, as a result of which judges often travel to different courthouses. **2.** A judicial division of the United States — that is, the 13 circuits where the U.S. courts of appeals sit.

circuit court. See COURT.

circuit judge. See JUDGE.

circuit justice. See JUSTICE (2).

circuit-riding, *n. Hist.* The practice of judges' traveling within a legislatively defined circuit to hear cases in one place for a time, then another, and so on.

> "The Judiciary Act of 1789 required that the justices of the Supreme Court serve also as judges of the circuit courts. The justices complained that circuit riding caused serious physical hardships and diverted them from more important duties in the nation's capital.... Congress in 1801 abolished circuit riding on grounds of efficiency, but a year later a new Jeffersonian Republican majority restored the practice, obliging each justice to hold circuit court along with a district judge. Gradually, however, improved communications, increasing business in the nation's capital, and the strengthening of American nationhood following the Civil War rendered circuit riding anachronistic. Congress in the Judiciary Act of 1869 established a separate circuit court judiciary, although the justices retained nominal circuit riding duties until the Circuit Court of Appeals Act of 1891. Congress officially ended the practice in 1911." *The Oxford Companion to the Supreme Court of the United States* 145 (Kermit L. Hall ed., 1992).

circuity of action. A procedure allowing duplicative lawsuits, leading to unnecessarily lengthy and indirect litigation, as when a defendant fails to bring a counterclaim, but later brings a separate action to recover what could have been awarded in the original lawsuit. • Civil-procedure rules have eliminated many problems associated with circuity of action.

> "Circuity of action is, when an action is rightfully brought for a duty, but yet about the bush, as it were, for that it might as well have been otherwise answered and determined, and the suit saved: and because the

same action was more than needful, it is called circuity of action." *Termes de la Ley* 87 (1st Am. ed. 1812).

circular letter of credit. See LETTER OF CREDIT.

circular note. See LETTER OF CREDIT.

circulating capital. See *floating capital* under CAPITAL.

Circumspecte agatis (sər-kəm-**spek**-tee ə-**gay**-tis). [Latin "that you act circumspectly"] *Hist.* A directive from the king to his justices detailing the boundaries of ecclesiastical jurisdiction. • The directive, issued circa 1285, was originally in the form of a writ, but over time acquired statutory authority. The title *Circumspecte agatis* derives from the first few words of the writ: "*Rex talibus judicibus salutem; Circumspecte agatis. . . .*"

circumstance, *n.* (*often pl.*) An accompanying or accessory fact, event, or condition, such as a piece of evidence that indicates the probability of an event. — **circumstantial,** *adj.*

aggravating circumstance. **1.** A fact or situation that increases the degree of liability or culpability for a tortious or criminal act. **2.** A fact or situation that relates to a criminal offense or defendant and that is considered by the court in imposing punishment (esp. a death sentence). • Aggravating circumstances in death-penalty cases are usu. prescribed by statute. — Also termed *aggravating element*; *aggravating factor.* Cf. *mitigating circumstance.*

change of circumstances. *Family law.* A modification in the physical, emotional, or financial condition of one or both parents, used to show the need to modify a custody or support order. — Also termed *changed circumstances.*

exigent circumstances. A situation that demands unusual or immediate action and that may allow people to circumvent usual procedures, as when a neighbor breaks through a window of a burning house to save someone inside.

extenuating circumstance. See *mitigating circumstance.*

extraordinary circumstances. A highly unusual set of facts that are not commonly associated with a particular thing or event.

mitigating circumstance. **1.** A fact or situation that does not justify or excuse a wrongful act or offense but that reduces the degree of culpability and thus may reduce the damages (in a civil case) or the punishment (in a criminal case). **2.** A fact or situation that does not bear on the question of a defendant's guilt but that is considered by the court in imposing punishment and esp. in lessening the severity of a sentence. **3.** *Contracts.* An unusual or unpredictable event that prevents performance, such as a labor strike. — Also termed *extenuating circumstance.* Cf. *aggravating circumstance.*

circumstantial evidence. See EVIDENCE.

cirliscus (sər-**lis**-kəs). See CEORL.

citatio ad reassumendam causam (sɪ-**tay**-shee-oh ad ree-as-yoo-**men**-dəm **kaw**-zəm). [Latin "citation to take up a cause again"] *Civil law.* A citation issued to revive an action that was abated upon one party's death. • The citation issues against the deceased party's heir. Cf. *bill of revivor* under BILL (2).

citation, *n.* **1.** A court-issued writ that commands a person to appear at a certain time and place to do something demanded in the writ, or to show cause for not doing so. **2.** A police-issued order to appear before a judge on a given date to defend against a stated charge, such as a traffic violation. **3.** A reference to a legal precedent or authority, such as a case, statute, or treatise, that either substantiates or contradicts a given position. — Often shortened to (in sense 3) *cite.*

parallel citation. An additional reference to a case that has been reported in more than one reporter. • For example, whereas a *Bluebook* citation reads "*Morgan v. United States*, 304 U.S. 1 (1938)," the same reference including parallel citations reads "*Morgan v. United States*, 304 U.S. 1, 58 S.Ct. 773, 82 L.Ed. 1129 (1938)," in which the main citation is to the *U.S. Reports* and the parallel citations are to the *Supreme Court Reporter* and to the *Lawyer's Edition.*

pinpoint citation. The page on which a quotation or relevant passage appears, as opposed to the page on which a case or article begins. • For example, the number 217 is the pinpoint citation in *Baker v. Carr*, 369 U.S. 186, 217 (1962). — Also termed *jump citation*; *dictum page*; *pincite.*

citational, *adj.* Of or relating to a citation (esp. a reference citation) <citational analysis>.

citation order. The appropriate ranking of the various authorities marshaled in support of a legal proposition.

Citations, Law of. *Roman law.* An A.D. 426 decree of Emperor Valentinian listing Papinian, Paul, Gaius, Ulpian, and Modestinus as the only juristic writers who could be cited authoritatively in court. • If a majority of the writers agreed on an issue, the judge was bound to follow the majority view. The Law of Citations allowed the judge to use discretion only if the writers were equally divided and Papinian (whose view prevailed in a tie) was silent on the issue.

> "In 426 came the famous *lex de responsis prudentium* — the Law of Citations.... This law lessened the difficulties of the courts in dealing with juristic literature. It excluded a huge mass of conflicting doctrine, the relative value of which had not been determined, and which yet had to be used by the judges as a source of principle on which to base their decisions." W.W. Buckland, *A Text-book of Roman Law: From Augustus to Justinian* 35 (1921).

citation signal. See SIGNAL (2).

citator (sI-tay-tər). A book or section of a book containing tables of cases or statutes that have been judicially cited in later cases.

> "A citator is a compilation showing where certain cases have been cited in other cases, and whether the provisions of constitutions and statutes have been repealed, amended, or otherwise affected, or have been judicially construed, or have been cited." Frank Hall Childs, *Where and How to Find the Law* 61 (1922).

citatory (sI-tə-tor-ee), *adj.* Of, relating to, or having the power of a citation or summons <letters citatory>.

cite, *n.* See CITATION (3).

cite, *vb.* **1.** To summon before a court of law <the witness was cited for contempt>. **2.** To refer to or adduce as precedent or authority <counsel then cited the appropriate statutory provision>. **3.** To commend or honor <the soldier was cited for bravery>.

citizen, *n.* **1.** A person who, by either birth or naturalization, is a member of a political community, owing allegiance to the community and being entitled to enjoy all its civil rights and protections; a member of the civil state, entitled to all its privileges. Cf. RESIDENT; DOMICILIARY.

federal citizen. A citizen of the United States.

natural-born citizen. A person born within the jurisdiction of a national government.

naturalized citizen. A foreign-born person who attains citizenship by law.

2. For diversity-jurisdiction purposes, a corporation that was incorporated within a state or has its principal place of business there.

citizen-informant. A witness who, without expecting payment and with the public good in mind, comes forward and volunteers information to the police or other authorities.

citizen's arrest. See ARREST.

citizenship, *n.* **1.** The status of being a citizen. **2.** The quality of a person's conduct as a member of a community.

Citizenship Clause. The clause of the U.S. Constitution providing that all persons born or naturalized in the United States are citizens of the United States and the state they reside in. U.S. Const. art. XIV, § 1, cl. 1.

citizen suit. An action under a statute giving citizens the right to sue violators of the law (esp. environmental law) and to seek injunctive relief and penalties. • In the 1970s, during the heyday of antipollution statutes such as the Clean Water Act and the Clean Air Act, legislators believed that regulators sometimes become too close to the industries they oversee and, as a result, lack the aggressiveness that individual citizens would be able to bring to litigation. The statutes therefore included provisions authorizing people to be "private attorneys general" to protect the environment, seeking not only injunctions to stop pollution but also penalties to be paid to the U.S. Treasury.

citology. See LEGAL CITOLOGY.

city. 1. A municipal corporation, usu. headed by a mayor and governed by a city council. **2.** The territory within a city's corporate limits. **3.** Collectively, the people who live within this territory. Cf. TOWN.

city attorney. An attorney employed by a city to advise it and represent it in legal matters. — Also termed *municipal attorney*; *city counsel*; *corporation counsel*; *city solicitor*.

> "There may have been a time in this country when the function of the City Attorney of the average city consisted mainly of advising the Council, preparing an occasional ordinance or handling an infrequent lawsuit. The legal business of the average city is no longer so simple, so

> infrequent and so nonconsuming of the time of the City Attorney. Every action of the City must be justified by its legal powers, and the City Attorney is the municipal officer whose responsibility it is to decide whether any act or action is within the city's legal powers. The demands of citizens for augmented municipal services, and the resulting diversification of city operations have increased the volume of work to the point where the City Attorney, in many cities, has become a central consultant of the city officers and employees on a day-to-day, hour-to-hour basis." Allen Grimes, *The City Attorney: A Practice Manual* 6 (1978).

city clerk. See CLERK (1).

city council. A city's legislative body, usu. responsible for passing ordinances, levying taxes, appropriating funds, and generally administering city government. — Also termed (in some states) *board of aldermen*.

city counsel. See CITY ATTORNEY.

city court. See *municipal court* under COURT.

city judge. See *municipal judge* under JUDGE.

city solicitor. See CITY ATTORNEY.

Civ. Ct. See *civil court* under COURT.

civic, *adj.* **1.** Of or relating to citizenship or a particular citizen <civic responsibilities>. **2.** Of or relating to a city <civic center>.

civil, *adj.* **1.** Of or relating to the state or its citizenry <civil rights>. **2.** Of or relating to private rights and remedies that are sought by action or suit, as distinct from criminal proceedings <civil litigation>. **3.** Of or relating to any of the modern legal systems derived from Roman law <Louisiana is a civil-law jurisdiction>.

civil action. See ACTION.

civil arrest. See ARREST.

civil assault. See ASSAULT.

civil-authority clause. *Insurance.* A clause, esp. in a fire insurance policy, insuring against damages caused by firefighters, police, or other civil authority.

civil bail. See BAIL (1).

Civil Code. 1. The code that embodied the law of Rome. **2.** The code that embodies the law of France, from which a great part of the Louisiana Civil Code is derived. — Abbr. C.C. — Also termed *Code Civil*. See NAPOLEONIC CODE. **3.** A codification of noncriminal statutes.

civil cognation. See COGNATION.

civil commitment. See COMMITMENT.

civil commotion. A public uprising by a large number of people who, acting together, cause harm to people or property. • A civil commotion usu. involves many more people than a riot. Cf. RIOT.

civil conspiracy. See CONSPIRACY.

civil contempt. See CONTEMPT.

civil corporation. See CORPORATION.

civil court. See COURT.

civil day. See *artificial day* under DAY.

civil death. 1. *Archaic.* At common law, the loss of rights — such as the rights to vote, make contracts, inherit, and sue — by a person who has been outlawed or convicted of a serious crime, or who is considered to have left the temporal world for the spiritual by entering a monastery.

> "In one large department of law the fiction [civil death] is elegantly maintained. A monk or nun can not acquire or have any proprietary rights. When a man becomes 'professed in religion,' his heir at once inherits from him any land that he has, and, if he has made a will, it takes effect at once as though he were naturally dead." 1 Frederick Pollock & Frederic W. Maitland, *History of English Law* 434 (2d ed. 1898).

> "Civil death arises from outlawry; it seems doubtful whether there are any other circumstances to which the phrase is now applicable." William R. Anson, *Principles of the Law of Contract* 193 n.(b) (Arthur L. Corbin ed., 3d Am. ed. 1919).

2. In some states, the loss of rights — such as the rights to vote and hold public office — by a person serving a life sentence. Cf. *civil disability* under DISABILITY (2). **3.** The state of a corporation that has formally dissolved or become bankrupt, leaving an estate to be administered for the benefit of shareholders and creditors. — Also termed *legal death*.

civil defense. 1. The practice of protecting civilians from dangers caused by hostilities or disasters and helping them recover from the immediate effects of such events. **2.** The policies that underlie this practice.

civil disability. See DISABILITY (2).

civil disobedience. A deliberate but nonviolent act of lawbreaking to call attention to a particular law or set of laws of questionable legitimacy or morality.

> "Social protest and even civil disobedience serve the law's need for growth. Ideally, reform would come according to reason and justice without self-help and disturbing, almost violent, forms of protest .... Still, candor compels one here again to acknowledge the gap between the ideal and the reality. Short of the millennium, sharp changes in the law depend partly upon the stimulus of protest." Archibald Cox, *Civil Rights, the Constitution, and the Courts*, 40 N.Y. State B.J. 161, 169 (1968).

civil disorder. A public disturbance involving three or more people who commit violent acts that cause immediate danger or injury to people or property. See RIOT.

civil forfeiture. See FORFEITURE.

civil fraud. See FRAUD.

civil fruit. See FRUIT.

civilian, *n.* **1.** A person not serving in the military. **2.** A lawyer practicing in a civil-law jurisdiction. — **civilian,** *adj.*

civil infraction. See INFRACTION.

civil injury. See INJURY.

civilis (sə-**vɪ**-lis), *adj.* [Latin] Of or according to civil law.

civilista (siv-ə-**lis**-tə). [Latin] *Hist.* See CIVILIAN (2).

civiliter (sə-**vil**-ə-tər), *adv.* [Latin "civilly"] **1.** By a civil, as distinguished from a criminal, proceeding. Cf. CRIMINALITER. **2.** Civilly; as a citizen.

civiliter mortuus (sə-**vil**-ə-tər **mor**-choo-əs). [Latin] Civilly dead <the wife of a man *civiliter mortuus* had similar rights>. See CIVIL DEATH (1).

civilization. The transformation of a criminal matter to a civil one by law or judgment. Cf. CRIMINALIZATION.

civil justice. The methods by which a society redresses civil wrongs. Cf. CRIMINAL JUSTICE (1).

civil law. 1. (*usu. cap.*) One of the two prominent legal systems in the Western World, originally administered in the Roman Empire and still influential in continental Europe, Latin America, Scotland, and Louisiana, among other parts of the world. — Also termed *jus civile*; *Roman law*; *Romanesque law*. Cf. COMMON LAW (2). **2.** ROMAN LAW (1). **3.** The body of law imposed by the state, as opposed to moral law. **4.** The law of civil or private rights, as opposed to criminal law or administrative law. — Abbr. CL.

> "The difference between civil law ... and criminal law turns on the difference between two different objects which the law seeks to pursue — redress or punishment. The object of civil law is the redress of wrongs by compelling compensation or restitution: the wrongdoer is not punished, he only suffers so much harm as is necessary to make good the wrong he has done. The person who has suffered gets a definite benefit from the law, or at least he avoids a loss. On the other hand, in the case of crimes, the main object of the law is to punish the wrongdoer; to give him and others a strong inducement not to commit the same or similar crimes, to reform him if possible, and perhaps to satisfy the public sense that wrongdoing ought to meet with retribution." William Geldart, *Introduction to English Law* 146 (D.C.M. Yardley ed., 9th ed. 1984).

civil liability. See LIABILITY.

civil-liability act. See DRAM-SHOP LIABILITY.

civil liberty. (*usu. pl.*) Freedom from undue governmental interference or restraint. • This term usu. refers to freedom of speech or religion. — Also termed *civil right*.

civil list. An annual sum granted by Parliament for the expenses of the royal household.

civil marriage. See MARRIAGE (2).

civil month. See MONTH (1).

civil offense. See *public tort* under TORT.

civil penalty. See PENALTY.

civil possession. See POSSESSION (3).

civil power. See POLITICAL POWER.

civil procedure. 1. The body of law — usu. rules enacted by the legislature or courts — governing the methods and practices used in civil litigation. • An example is the Federal Rules of Civil Procedure. **2.** A particular method or practice used in carrying on civil litigation.

civil process. See PROCESS.

civil right. (*usu. pl.*) **1.** The individual rights of personal liberty guaranteed by the Bill of Rights and by the 13th, 14th, 15th, and 19th Amendments, as well as by legislation such as the Voting Rights Act. • Civil rights include esp. the right to vote, the right of due process, and the right of equal protection under the law. **2.** CIVIL LIBERTY.

civil-rights act. One of several federal statutes enacted after the Civil War (1861–1865) and, much later, during and after the civil-rights movement of the 1950s and 1960s, and intended to implement and give further force to the basic rights guaranteed by the Constitution, and esp. prohibiting discrimination in employment and education on the basis of race, sex, religion, color, or age.

civil-rights removal. See REMOVAL.

civil service, *n.* **1.** The administrative branches of a government. **2.** The group of people employed by these branches. — **civil servant,** *n.*

Civil Service Commission. A defunct federal board created in 1883 to ensure that civil-service employees are hired on the basis of merit rather than personal preference or political considerations. • In 1978, the Commission's functions were split between the Office of Personnel Management and the Merit Systems Protection Board.

civil society. See SOCIETY.

civil war. See WAR.

civil wrong. See WRONG; TORT.

civis (**siv**-is). [Latin] *Roman law.* A Roman citizen; a person entitled to the public and private rights associated with Roman citizenship. — Also termed *civis Romanus.*

civitas (**siv**-ə-tas). [Latin] *Roman law.* **1.** A state; a group of people living under a given body of law. **2.** The rights of a citizen.

C.J. *abbr.* **1.** See *chief justice* under JUSTICE (2). **2.** See *chief judge* under JUDGE. **3.** See *circuit judge* under JUDGE. **4.** CORPUS JURIS.

CJE. *abbr.* CONTINUING JUDICIAL EDUCATION.

C.J.S. *abbr. Corpus Juris Secundum.* — Also written CJS.

CL. *abbr.* CIVIL LAW.

Claflin trust. See *indestructible trust* under TRUST.

Claflin-trust principle. The doctrine that a trust cannot be terminated by the beneficiaries if the termination would defeat one of the settlor's material purposes in establishing the trust. • If the settlor is alive and consents, however, the trust may be terminated. Trusts in the "Claflin" category are spendthrift trusts, support trusts, trusts in which the trustee has discretion to make distributions, and trusts in which the beneficiary is entitled to income until a certain age and the principal at that age.

claim, *n.* **1.** The aggregate of operative facts giving rise to a right enforceable by a court <the plane crash led to dozens of wrongful-death claims>. **2.** The assertion of an existing right; any right to payment or to an equitable remedy, even if contingent or provisional <the spouse's claim to half of the lottery winnings>. **3.** A demand for money or property to which one asserts a right <an insurance claim>.

liquidated claim. A claim for an amount previously agreed on by the parties or that can be precisely determined by operation of law or by the terms of the parties' agreement. — Also termed *liquidated demand.*

matured claim. A claim based on a debt that is due for payment.

unliquidated claim. A claim in which the liability of the party or the amount of the claim is in dispute.

4. An interest or remedy recognized at law; the means by which a person can obtain a privilege, possession, or enjoyment of a right or thing; CAUSE OF ACTION (1) <claim against the employer for wrongful termination>.

colorable claim. **1.** A claim that is legitimate and that may reasonably be asserted, given the facts presented and the current law (or a reasonable and logical extension or modification of the current law). **2.** A claim in which the debtor and property holder are, as a matter of law, not adverse. • One example of a colorable claim is one made by a person holding property as an agent or bailee of the bankrupt.

contingent claim. A claim that has not yet accrued and is dependent on some future event that may never happen.

counterclaim. See COUNTERCLAIM.

cross-claim. See CROSS-CLAIM.

supplemental claim. A claim for further relief made after the original claim.

5. A right to payment or to an equitable remedy for breach of performance if the breach gives rise to a right to payment. • It does not matter whether the right has been reduced to judgment or whether it is fixed or contingent, matured or unmatured, disputed or undisputed, or secured or unsecured.

creditor's claim. *Bankruptcy.* A claim that a creditor has against a debtor.

involuntary gap claim. *Bankruptcy.* A claim that accrues in the ordinary course of business after an involuntary bankruptcy petition has been filed but before the order for relief or the appointment of a trustee. • The Bankruptcy Code gives priority to creditors with claims of this type to encourage creditors to continue dealing with a debtor until the debtor has a chance to challenge the involuntary petition.

priority claim. *Bankruptcy.* An unsecured claim that, under bankruptcy law, must be paid before other unsecured claims. • The Bankruptcy Code sets forth eight classes of claims, to be paid in order of priority: (1) administrative expenses of the bankruptcy estate, (2) involuntary gap claims, (3) wage claims, (4) contributions to employee benefit plans, (5) claims of grain farmers and fishermen, (6) consumer deposits, (7) tax claims, and (8) capital requirements of an insured depository institution.

secured claim. A claim held by a creditor who has a lien or a right of setoff against the debtor's property.

unsecured claim. **1.** A claim by a creditor who does not have a lien or a right of setoff against the debtor's property. **2.** A claim by a creditor who has a lien on or right of setoff against the debtor's property worth less than the amount of the debt.

6. *Patents.* A formal statement describing the novel features of an invention and defining the scope of the patent's protection <claim no. 3 of the patent describes an electrical means for driving a metal pin>. Cf. SPECIFICATION (3).

dependent claim. A patent claim that refers to and further limits another claim or set of claims in the same patent application.

multiple dependent claim. A dependent claim that refers to more than one other claim.

claim and delivery. A claim for the recovery of specific personal property wrongfully taken or detained, as well as for any damages caused by the taking or detention. • This claim derives from the common-law action of replevin.

claimant, *n.* One who asserts a right or demand, esp. formally.

claim check. A receipt obtained for bailed or checked property and surrendered by the holder when the bailee returns the property.

claim dilution. *Bankruptcy.* The reduction in the likelihood that a debtor's claimants will be fully repaid, including considerations of the time value of money.

claim for relief. The part of a complaint in a civil action specifying what relief the plaintiff asks of the court.

claim in equity. *Hist.* A summary proceeding created to eliminate protracted pleading procedure in simple cases. • The claim in equity was established in England in 1850 and abolished in 1860.

claim-jumping. 1. The extension of the borders of a mining claim to infringe on other areas or claims. **2.** The filing of a duplicate claim to take advantage of a flaw in the original claim.

claim of appeal. See NOTICE OF APPEAL.

claim of cognizance. *Hist.* An intervention seeking the return of a case to the claimant's own court. • Cognizance may be claimed by a person, city, or public corporation granted the right to hold court. — Also termed *claim of conusance.* See COGNIZANCE; CONUSANCE.

claim of conusance. See CLAIM OF COGNIZANCE.

claim of liberty. *Hist.* A petition to the Crown, filed in the Court of Exchequer, seeking the Attorney General's confirmation of liberties and franchises.

claim of ownership. 1. The possession of a piece of property with the intention of claiming it in hostility to the true owner. **2.** A party's manifest intention to take over land, regardless of title or right. — Also termed *claim of right*; *claim of title*.

claim of right. *Hist.* A criminal plea, usu. to a theft charge, by a defendant asserting that the property was taken under the honest (but mistaken) belief that the defendant had a superior right to the property. • The claim of right could also be raised in defense against bigamy if a defendant honestly believed that an earlier marriage had been legally dissolved. It has been superseded by a *defense of honesty*.

claim-of-right doctrine. *Tax.* The rule that any income constructively received must be reported as income, whether or not the taxpayer has an unrestricted claim to it.

claim of title. See CLAIM OF OWNERSHIP.

claim preclusion. See RES JUDICATA.

> "[T]he principal distinction between claim preclusion and issue preclusion is . . . that the former forecloses litigation of matters that have never been litigated. This makes it important to know the dimensions of the 'claim' that is foreclosed by bringing the first action, but unfortunately no precise definition is possible." Charles Alan Wright, *The Law of Federal Courts* § 100A, at 723 (5th ed. 1994).

claim-property bond. See *replevin bond* under BOND (2).

claims adjuster. See ADJUSTER.

claims-consciousness, *n.* The quality characterizing a legal culture in which people have firm expectations of justice and are willing to take concrete steps to see that justice is done <claims-consciousness in the United States has resulted from certain social changes, not from any character deficiency>. — Also termed *rights-consciousness*. — **claims-conscious,** *adj*.

Claims Court, U.S. See UNITED STATES COURT OF FEDERAL CLAIMS.

claims-made policy. See INSURANCE POLICY.

clam (klam), *adv.* [Latin] *Civil law.* Secretly; covertly. • Under Roman law, an act (such as occupying or altering the condition of someone else's property) was committed *clam* when it was done with the intent to conceal it in an effort to avoid liability. See INTERDICTUM QUOD VI AUT CLAM.

clamea admittenda in itinere per attornatum (**klay**-mee-ə ad-mə-**ten**-də in I-**tin**-ə-ree pər ə-tor-**nay**-təm). [Latin "claim to be admitted at the eyre by an attorney"] *Hist.* A writ from the king commanding the justices in eyre to permit by attorney the claim of a person employed in the king's service who cannot attend court in person.

clameur de haro (klah-**mər** dah-**roh**). [French] An outcry recognized in the Channel Islands as a protest against trespass to land. • The *clameur de haro* is a legal remnant of when the Duchy of Normandy held the islands before England took control in the 13th century. The victim's cry of *haro* (repeated 3 times) is popularly supposed to be an abbreviation of *Ha Rollo*, the first Duke of Normandy. The full cry, *Haro, Haro, Haro, a l'aide, mon prince, on me fait tort*, when registered at the local records office, enjoins the offender from possessing the land. See HARO; HUE AND CRY; GRAND COUTUMIER DE PAYS ET DUCHÉ DE NORMANDIE.

clamor. **1.** *Hist.* A lawsuit; a claim. **2.** HUE AND CRY (1). **3.** *Civil law.* A claimant. **4.** *Civil law.* The thing claimed from another.

clandestine (klan-**des**-tin), *adj.* Secret or concealed, esp. for illegal or unauthorized purposes.

clandestine marriage. See MARRIAGE (1).

class, *n.* **1.** A group of people, things, qualities, or activities that have common characteristics or attributes <a class of common-stock shares> <the upper-middle class>.

protected class. A class of people who benefit from protection by statute, such as Title VII of the Civil Rights Act of 1964, which prohibits discrimination based on race, sex, national origin, or religion.

2. The order or rank that people or things are arranged in <she flew first class to Chicago>. **3.** A group of people, uncertain in number <a class of beneficiaries>.

testamentary class (tes-tə-**men**-tə-ree *or* -tree). A group of beneficiaries who are uncertain in number but whose number will be ascertainable in the future, when each will take an equal or other proportionate share of the gift.

4. *Civil procedure.* A group of people who have a common legal position, so that all their claims can be efficiently adjudicated in a single proceeding <a class of asbestos plaintiffs>.

settlement class. Numerous similarly situated people for whom a claimant's representative and an adversary propose a contract liquidating the claims of all class members. • During the 1980s and 1990s, mass-tort defendants began using settlement classes as a means of foreclosing claims by some unknown number of future claimants.

class action. A lawsuit in which a single person or a small group of people represents the interests of a larger group. • Federal procedure has several requirements for maintaining a class action: (1) the class must be so large that individual suits would be impracticable, (2) there must be legal or factual questions common to the class, (3) the claims or defenses of the representative parties must be typical of those of the class, and (4) the representative parties must adequately protect the interests of the class. Fed. R. Civ. P. 23. — Also termed *class suit*; *representative action*.

"The class action was an invention of equity . . . mothered by the practical necessity of providing a procedural device so that mere numbers would not disable large groups of individuals, united in interest, from enforcing their equitable rights nor grant them immunity from their equitable wrongs. . . . By rule 23 the Supreme Court has extended the use of the class action device to the entire field of federal civil litigation by making it applicable to all civil actions." *Montgomery Ward & Co. v. Langer*, 168 F.2d 182, 187 (8th Cir. 1948).

hybrid class action. A type of action in which the rights to be enforced are several and varied, but the object is to adjudicate claims that do or may affect the specific property in the action.

spurious class action. A former category of class action in which the interests of class members are several, not interdependent, and joinder is allowed to avoid multiplicity of suits.

class-based animus. See ANIMUS (1).

class director. See DIRECTOR.

class gift. See GIFT.

classification. See CHARACTERIZATION (1).

classified information. Data or material that, having been designated as secret or confidential, only a limited number of authorized persons may know about.

classified risk. See RISK.

classified tax. See TAX.

class legislation. See *local and special legislation* under LEGISLATION.

class lottery. See *Dutch lottery* under LOTTERY.

class of stock. A category of corporate shares used when more than one type of stock is issued. See *preferred stock* and *common stock* under STOCK.

class-one insured. See INSURED.

class rate. See RATE.

class representative. See REPRESENTATIVE.

class suit. See CLASS ACTION.

class-two insured. See INSURED.

class voting. See VOTING.

clausa rebus sic stantibus (**klawz**-ə **ree**-bəs sik **stan**-tə-bəs). [Law Latin] *Int'l law.* **1.** A treaty provision stating that the treaty is binding only as long as the circumstances in existence when the treaty was signed remain substantially the same. **2.** A doctrine by which the law supplies such a provision to a treaty that does not expressly contain one; REBUS SIC STANTIBUS. — Often shortened to *clausa*. — Also termed *clausula rebus sic stantibus*; *clausula*.

"[T]he problem of the attitude of international law to oppressive or obsolete treaty obligations remains, and an attempt has been made by many writers to solve it by the doctrine known as the *clausula rebus sic stantibus*. In every treaty, it is said, there is implied a clause which provides that the treaty is to be binding only 'so long as things stand as they are'; the expressed terms may be absolute, but a treaty is never more than conditional, and when a 'vital change of circumstances' has occurred, the condition of the treaty's validity has failed, and it ceases to be binding. Such a doctrine, if it is to be accepted into the law, clearly needs careful definition. Otherwise it is capable of being used, and it often has been used, merely to excuse the breach of a treaty obligation that a state finds it inconvenient to fulfil." J.L. Brierly, *The Law of Nations* 260 (5th ed. 1955).

clause, *n.* **1.** A distinct section or provision of a legal document or instrument. **2.** ITEM (3). — **clausal,** *adj*.

clause of accrual. A provision, usu. found in a gift by will or in a deed between tenants in common, that grants a decedent beneficiary's shares to the surviving beneficiary. — Also termed *clause of accruer*.

clause paramount. *Maritime law.* A provision in a charterparty incorporating the Carriage of Goods by Sea Act into the charter. See CHARTERPARTY; CARRIAGE OF GOODS BY SEA ACT.

clause potestative (**poh**-tes-tay-tiv). *French law.* A contractual provision in which one party reserves the right to annul the contract.

clause rolls. *Hist.* Sealed rolls containing royal writs (*close writs*) and other documents that the sovereign deemed inappropriate for the public record. — Also termed *close rolls.* See *close writ* under WRIT.

clausula (**klawz**-yə-lə). [Latin] A clause; a sentence or part of a sentence in a written instrument or statute.

clausula derogativa (**klawz**-yə-lə də-rog-ə-**tɪ**-və). [Latin] See DEROGATORY CLAUSE.

clausula rebus sic stantibus (**klawz**-yə-lə **ree**-bəs sik **stan**-tə-bəs). See CLAUSA REBUS SIC STANTIBUS.

clausum (**klawz**-əm). [Latin "close; closed"] *Hist.* **1.** CLOSE (1). — Also termed *clausura.* **2.** See *close writ* under WRIT.

clausum fregit (**klawz**-əm **free**-jit). [Latin "he broke the close"] See TRESPASS QUARE CLAUSUM FREGIT.

clausura (klaw-**zhuur**-ə). See CLAUSUM.

clawback, *n.* Money taken back; esp., retrieval or recovery of tax allowances by additional forms of taxation. — **claw back,** *vb.*

Clayton Act. A federal statute — enacted in 1914 to amend the Sherman Act — that prohibits price discrimination, tying arrangements, and exclusive-dealing contracts, as well as mergers and interlocking directorates, if their effect might substantially lessen competition or create a monopoly in any line of commerce. 15 USCA §§ 12–27.

Cl. Ct. *abbr.* CLAIMS COURT, U.S.

CLE. *abbr.* CONTINUING LEGAL EDUCATION.

clean bill. See BILL (3).

clean bill of lading. See BILL OF LADING.

clean draft. See DRAFT.

clean-hands doctrine. The principle that a party cannot seek equitable relief or assert an equitable defense if that party has violated an equitable principle, such as good faith. • Such a party is described as having "unclean hands." — Also termed *unclean-hands doctrine.*

clean house, *vb. Slang.* **1.** To discharge a considerable number of employees, usu. in management, so that new employees may be brought in. **2.** To sell securities not meeting an investor's requirements.

clean letter of credit. See LETTER OF CREDIT.

clean-slate rule. *Criminal procedure.* The doctrine that the double-jeopardy prohibition does not apply to the retrial of a defendant who appealed and obtained a reversal of an earlier conviction.

cleanup clause. In a loan agreement, a clause that calls for a loan to be repaid in full within a given period, after which no further loans will be afforded the debtor for a specified "cleanup" period.

cleanup doctrine. The jurisdictional principle that once an equity court has acquired jurisdiction over a case, it may decide both equitable and legal issues as long as the legal issues are ancillary to the equitable ones.

clear, *adj.* **1.** Free from encumbrances or claims. **2.** Free from doubt; sure. **3.** Unambiguous.

clear, *vb.* **1.** To acquit or exonerate <she was cleared of all wrongdoing>. **2.** (Of a drawee bank) to pay (a check or draft) out of funds held on behalf of the maker <the bank cleared the employee's check>. **3.** (Of a check or draft) to be paid by the drawee bank out of funds held on behalf of the maker <the check cleared yesterday>.

clearance. 1. *Maritime law.* The right of a ship to leave port, or the certificate issued by the port collector evidencing the ship's right to leave port. **2.** The time that must elapse between runs of the same movie within a particular area; a theater's exclusive right of exhibition over competing theaters.

clearance card. A letter given by an employer to a departing employee, stating the duration and nature of the employment and reasons for leaving. • The clearance card is not necessarily a recommendation.

clear and convincing evidence. See EVIDENCE.

clear and convincing proof. See *clear and convincing evidence* under EVIDENCE.

clear-and-present-danger test. *Constitutional law.* The doctrine allowing the government to restrict the First Amendment freedoms of speech and press if necessary to prevent immediate and severe danger to interests that the government may lawfully protect. • This test was formulated by Justice Oliver Wendell Holmes in *Schenck v. United States*, 249 U.S. 47, 39 S.Ct. 247 (1919).

clear annual value. See VALUE.

clear chance. See LAST-CLEAR-CHANCE DOCTRINE.

clear error. See ERROR (2).

***Clearfield Trust* doctrine.** The doctrine describing the federal courts' power to make federal common law when there is both federal lawmaking power to do so and a strong federal interest in a nationally uniform rule. *Clearfield Trust Co. v. United States*, 318 U.S. 363, 63 S.Ct. 573 (1943). Cf. ERIE DOCTRINE.

clearing. 1. *Banking.* The exchanging of checks and balancing of accounts. **2.** *Maritime law.* The departure of a ship from port, after complying with customs, health laws, and other local regulations. See CLEARANCE (1).

clearing account. *Banking.* An account (usu. a temporary one) containing amounts to be transferred to another account before the end of an accounting period.

clearing agent. *Securities.* A person or company acting as an intermediary in a securities transaction or providing facilities for comparing data with respect to securities transactions. • The term includes a custodian of securities in connection with the central handling of securities. Securities Exchange Act § 3(a)(23)(A) (15 USCA § 78c(a)(23)(A)). — Also termed *clearing agency*.

clearing agreement. A contract whose purpose is to facilitate the collective settlement of monetary claims between creditors and debtors in different currency areas, without resort to foreign-exchange reserves.

clearing corporation. See CORPORATION.

clearinghouse. 1. A place where banks exchange checks and drafts and settle their daily balances; an association of banks or other payors regularly clearing items. See UCC § 4–104(a)–(d). **2.** A stock-and-commodity exchange where the daily transactions of the brokers are cleared. **3.** Any place for the exchange of specialized information.

clearing loan. See LOAN.

clearings. *Banking.* Checks or other items drawn on a local bank and presented for payment through a clearinghouse or directly to the drawee bank. See CLEARINGHOUSE (1).

clearly-erroneous standard. The standard of review that an appellate court usu. applies in judging a trial court's treatment of factual issues. • Under this standard, a judgment is reversible if the appellate court is left with the firm conviction that an error has been committed.

clear market value. See *fair market value* under VALUE.

clear-reflection-of-income standard. *Tax.* An income-accounting method that the IRS can force on a taxpayer if the method used does not clearly reflect income. IRC § 446(b).

clear residue. The income deriving from funds used to pay a decedent's debts, administration expenses, and general legacies. — Also termed *true residue*.

clear title. See TITLE (2).

clear value. See VALUE.

clear-view doctrine. See PLAIN-VIEW DOCTRINE.

clemency (**klem**-ən-see), *n.* Mercy or leniency; esp., the power of the President or a governor to pardon a criminal or commute a criminal sentence. — Also termed *executive clemency.* — **clement** (**klem**-ənt), *adj.* See PARDON; COMMUTATION.

Clementines (**klem**-ən-tinz *or* -tɪnz *or* -teenz). *Eccles. law.* A collection of decretals of Pope Clement V, published in 1317 by his successor, Pope John XXII, and forming the fourth of the six parts of the *Corpus Juris Canonici*, completed in 1502. — Also termed *Clementine Constitutions*.

Clement's Inn. See INN OF CHANCERY.

clergy, benefit of. See BENEFIT OF CLERGY.

clergyable, *adj. Archaic.* (Of an offense or person) admitting benefit of clergy.

clergyman-penitent privilege. See *priest-penitent privilege* under PRIVILEGE (3).

clergy privilege. See BENEFIT OF CLERGY (1).

clericale privilegium (kler-ə-**kay**-lee priv-ə-**lee**-jee-əm). [Law Latin "clerical privilege"] See BENEFIT OF CLERGY.

clerical error. See ERROR (2).

clerical misprision. See MISPRISION.

clerici de cancellaria (**kler**-ə-sI dee kan-sə-**lair**-ee-ə). [Law Latin "clerks of the chancery"] Cursitors. — Also termed *clerici de cursu.* See CURSITOR.

clerici praenotarii (**kler**-ə-sI pree-nə-**tair**-ee-I). [Law Latin "prenotary clerks"] See SIX CLERKS.

clerico capto per statutum mercatorium. See DE CLERICO CAPTO PER STATUTUM MERCATORIUM.

clerico convicto commisso gaolae in defectu ordinarii deliberando. See DE CLERICO CONVICTO COMMISSO GAOLAE IN DEFECTU ORDINARII DELIBERANDO.

clerico infra sacros ordines constituto, non eligendo in officium. See DE CLERICO INFRA SACROS ORDINES CONSTITUTO, NON ELIGENDO IN OFFICIUM.

clericus (**kler**-ə-kəs). [Law Latin "clergyman"] *Hist.* **1.** *Eccles. law.* A person in holy orders; a priest. **2.** A court clerk or officer of the royal household. **3.** AMANUENSIS.

clericus mercati (**kler**-ə-kəs mər-**kay**-tI). [Law Latin] See CLERK OF THE MARKET.

clerk, *n.* **1.** A public official whose duties include keeping records or accounts.

city clerk. A public official who records a city's official proceedings and vital statistics.

2. A court officer responsible for filing papers, issuing process, and keeping records of court proceedings as generally specified by rule or statute. — Also termed *clerk of court.*

district clerk. The clerk of a district court within a state or federal system. See *district court* under COURT.

3. An employee who performs general office work. **4.** A law student who assists a lawyer or judge with legal research, writing, and other tasks. — Also termed *law clerk*; *extern*; or (depending on the time of year) *summer clerk*; *summer associate.* See INTERN. **5.** A lawyer who assists a judge with research, writing, and case management.

> "[M]odern American judging in all courts of national significance — the federal courts and the more prominent state appellate courts — staggers along despite the burden of bloated caseloads and the shortcomings of distinctly human judges only by the delegation of a great deal of the labor of judging to law clerks: subordinate, anonymous, but often quite powerful lawyers who function as the noncommissioned officers in the army of the judiciary." John Bilyeu Oakley & Robert S. Thompson, *Law Clerks and the Judicial Process* 2 (1980).

6. *Hist.* A cleric.

> "Eventually the rule was established that 'clerks' of all kinds, who committed any of the serious crimes termed felonies, could be tried only in an ecclesiastical court, and therefore were only amenable to such punishments as that court could inflict. Any clerk accused of such crime was accordingly passed over to the bishop's court. He was there tried before a jury of clerks by the oaths of twelve compurgators; a mode of trial which usually ensured him an acquittal." J.W. Cecil Turner, *Kenny's Outlines of Criminal Law* 75 (16th ed. 1952).

clerk, *vb.* To work as a clerk <she clerked for a Chicago law firm last summer>.

clerk of arraigns (ə-**raynz**). *Hist.* A deputy of the clerk of assize responsible for arraigning defendants and putting the formal questions to the jurors as they deliver their verdict. • The office was abolished in England in 1946.

clerk of assize (ə-**sIz**). *Hist.* An assize associate responsible for record-keeping and other clerical and administrative functions. See ASSOCIATE (3).

clerk of court. See CLERK (2).

clerk of enrollments. *Hist.* The former chief of the Enrollment Office, which the British Parliament abolished in 1879, reassigning its duties to the Central Office. See ENROLLMENT OFFICE; CENTRAL OFFICE.

clerk of indictment. *Hist.* An officer of England's Central Criminal Court, responsible for preparing indictments and assisting the Clerk of Arraigns. • The office was abolished in 1946, when its duties were moved to the Central Office.

Clerk of Nichils. See NICHIL.

clerk of records and writs. *Hist.* Officers of the English Court of Chancery responsible for filing documents and sealing bills of complaint and writs of execution. • The office was abolished in 1879, when its duties were moved to the Central Office.

clerk of the corporation. See SECRETARY.

Clerk of the Crown in Chancery. The head of the permanent staff of the Crown Office in Chancery (of the Central Office), responsible for reading the title of Bills in the House of Lords, sending out writs of summons to peers, and issuing election writs.

Clerk of the House of Commons. *English law.* An officer of the House of Commons who keeps the House journal, signs orders, indorses bills sent to the House of Lords, and has custody of all records. • The Clerk is appointed for life by the Crown.

clerk of the market. *Hist.* The overseer of a public market, responsible for witnessing oral contracts, inquiring into weights and measures, measuring land, and settling disputes between people dealing there. • The office has become obsolete as a result of various statutes regulating weights and measures.

Clerk of the Parliaments. The principal permanent official of the House of Lords, responsible for the House's minutes and documents, and for advising the members on procedure.

Clerk of the Peace. *Hist.* An officer of the Quarter Sessions responsible for maintaining the courts' records, preparing indictments, entering judgments, issuing process, and other clerical and administrative functions. • The office was abolished in England in 1971, when the Quarter Sessions' jurisdiction was transferred to the Crown Courts. See QUARTER SESSIONS.

Clerk of the Pells. *Hist.* An Exchequer officer who entered tellers' bills on the parchment rolls (*pells*), one for receipts and the other for disbursements. — Also termed *Master of the Pells*.

Clerk of the Pipe. *Hist.* An Exchequer officer responsible for the Pipe Rolls. • The office was abolished in 1833. — Also termed *Engrosser of the Great Roll*. See PIPE ROLLS.

Clerk of the Privy Seal (**priv**-ee **seel**). *Hist.* An officer responsible for preparing documents for the Lord Privy Seal. • The use of the Privy Seal was abolished in 1884. See PRIVY SEAL.

Clerk of the Signet (**sig**-nit). *Hist.* An officer who kept the privy signet and attended the sovereign's principal secretary. • The signet was used to seal royal letters and other documents until the office was abolished in England in 1851. See PRIVY SIGNET.

clerkship. 1. A type of internship in which a law student or recent law-school graduate assists a lawyer or judge with legal writing, research, and other tasks. **2.** *Hist.* A law student's employment as an attorney's apprentice before gaining admission to the bar.

cliens (**klɪ**-enz). [Latin "client"] *Roman law.* A dependent; a person who depended on another for defense in suits at law and other difficulties. • A *cliens* was often a freed slave or immigrant. Pl. ***clientes*** (klɪ-**en**-teez).

client, *n.* A person or entity that employs a professional for advice or help in that professional's line of work. — **cliental,** *adj.*

clientela (klɪ-ən-**tee**-lə). [Latin] *Roman law.* **1.** Clientship; the relationship between a *cliens* and a patron. **2.** A person's dependents.

client security fund. See FUND (1).

client's privilege. See *attorney-client privilege* under PRIVILEGE (3).

client state. A country that is obliged in some degree to share in the control of its external relations with some foreign power or powers. — Also termed *satellite state*. Cf. SOVEREIGN STATE.

***Clifford* trust.** See TRUST.

clinical diagnosis. See DIAGNOSIS.

clinical legal studies. Law-school training in which students participate in actual cases under the supervision of a practicing attorney or law professor. — Often shortened to *clinical studies*.

clog on the equity of redemption. An agreement or condition that prevents a defaulting mortgagor from getting back the property free from encumbrance upon paying the debt or performing the obligation for which the security was given. See EQUITY OF REDEMPTION.

close, *n.* **1.** An enclosed portion of land. **2.** The interest of a person in a particular piece of land, enclosed or not. **3.** The final price of a stock at the end of the exchange's trading day.

close, *vb.* **1.** To conclude; to bring to an end <the case was closed>. **2.** To conclude discussion or negotiation about <close on a house>. See CLOSING.

close-connectedness doctrine. A doctrine used by some courts to deny an assignee of a negotiable note holder-in-due-course status if the assignee is too closely connected to the original holder-mortgagee. — Also termed *close-connection doctrine*.

close corporation. See CORPORATION.

closed, *adj.* **1.** (Of a class or organization) confined to a limited number <a closed mass-tort class> <nonunion workers were excluded from the closed shop>. **2.** (Of a proceeding or gathering) conducted in secrecy <a closed hearing> <a closed shareholders' meeting>.

closed account. See ACCOUNT.

closed corporation. See *close corporation* under CORPORATION.

closed court. *Hist.* The English Court of Common Pleas, open only to serjeants-at-law. • The monopoly of the serjeants-at-law was abolished in 1845.

closed-end fund. See MUTUAL FUND.

closed-end mortgage. See MORTGAGE.

closed-end mortgage bond. See BOND (3).

closed insurance contract. See *closed policy* under INSURANCE POLICY.

closed mortgage. See MORTGAGE.

closed policy. See INSURANCE POLICY.

closed session. See SESSION.

closed shop. See SHOP.

closed-shop contract. A labor agreement requiring an employer to hire and retain only union members and to discharge nonunion members.

closed testament. See *mystic will* under WILL.

closed transaction. See TRANSACTION.

closed union. See UNION.

closed will. See *mystic will* under WILL.

close-jail execution. See EXECUTION.

closely held corporation. See *close corporation* under CORPORATION.

close-nexus test. See NEXUS TEST.

close rolls. See CLAUSE ROLLS.

close writ. See WRIT.

closing. The final meeting between the parties to a transaction, at which the transaction is consummated; esp., in real estate, the final transaction between the buyer and seller, whereby the conveyancing documents are concluded and the money and property transferred. — Also termed *settlement*.

closing agreement. See AGREEMENT.

closing argument. In a trial, a lawyer's final statement to the judge or jury before deliberation begins, in which the lawyer requests the judge or jury to consider the evidence and to apply the law in his or her client's favor. • Usu. in a jury trial, the judge afterwards instructs the jury on the law that governs the case. — Also termed *closing statement*; *final argument*; *jury summation*; *summing up*.

closing costs. *Real estate.* The expenses that must be paid, usu. in a lump sum at closing, apart from the purchase price and interest.

closing of estate. *Wills & estates.* The completion of the administration of a decedent's estate, brought about by the administrator's distribution of estate assets, payment of taxes, and filing of necessary accounts with the probate court.

closing price. See PRICE.

closing statement. **1.** CLOSING ARGUMENT. **2.** A written breakdown of the costs involved in a particular real-estate transaction, usu. prepared by a lender or an escrow agent. — Also termed *settlement sheet*; *settlement statement.*

cloture (**kloh**-chər), *n.* The procedure of ending debate in a legislative body and calling for an immediate vote. — **cloture,** *vb.*

cloud on title. A defect or potential defect in the owner's title to a piece of land arising from some claim or encumbrance, such as a lien, an easement, or a court order. See *action to quiet title* under ACTION.

CLS. *abbr.* CRITICAL LEGAL STUDIES.

CLSer. See CRIT.

CLU. See *chartered life underwriter* under UNDERWRITER.

club-law. Government by clubs (big sticks) or violence; the use of illegal force in place of law.

cluster zoning. See ZONING.

CMO. *abbr.* **1.** CASE-MANAGEMENT ORDER. **2.** COLLATERALIZED MORTGAGE OBLIGATION.

CMR. *abbr.* **1.** Court of Military Review. See COURT OF CRIMINAL APPEALS (1). **2.** COURT-MARTIAL REPORTS.

CN. *abbr.* Code Napoléon. See NAPOLEONIC CODE (1).

co-. *prefix.* Jointly or together with <coowner> <codefendant>.

co. *abbr.* (*usu. cap.*) **1.** COMPANY. **2.** COUNTY.

c/o. *abbr.* Care of.

COA. *abbr.* CONTRACT OF AFFREIGHTMENT.

coadjutor (koh-ə-**joo**-tər *or* koh-**aj**-ə-tər), *n.* A coworker or assistant, esp. one appointed to assist a bishop who, because of age or infirmity, is unable to perform all duties of the office. — **coadjutor,** *adj.*

co-administrator. *Wills & estates.* A person appointed to jointly administer an estate with one or more other administrators.

co-adventurer. See COVENTURER.

co-agent. See AGENT.

coal note. See NOTE (1).

coal notice. In Pennsylvania, a notice that must be included in deeds and other instruments relating to the sale of surface property (excepting mortgages or quitclaim deeds) detailing any severance of the ownership of coal under the land.

Coase Theorem (kohs). An economic proposition describing the relationship between legal rules about entitlements and economic efficiency. • The theorem, innovated by Ronald Coase, holds that if there are no transaction costs — such as the costs of bargaining or acquiring information — then any legal rule will produce an efficient result. Coase's seminal article was *The Problem of Social Cost*, 3 J. Law & Econ. 1 (1960).

> "Nothing is more central to the study of law and economics nor more responsible for its growth than the Coase Theorem. What the Coase Theorem says, in effect, is that in many instances, the assignment of rights by courts or legal authorities may have little to do with who eventually possesses those rights. In the words of Mark Kelman, 'the market, like an untameable river, will knock out attempts to alter its mighty course.' " Jeffrey L. Harrison, *Law and Economics in a Nutshell* 56 (1995).

co-assignee. A person who, along with one or more others, is an assignee of the same subject matter.

coasting trade. *Maritime law.* Commerce among different coastal ports or navigable rivers of the United States, in contrast to commerce carried on between nations. — Also termed *coastwise trade.*

coast water. See WATER.

coastwise trade. See COASTING TRADE.

COB clause. *Insurance.* A coordination-of-benefits clause, which provides that the total sums paid for medical and hospital care will not exceed the benefits receivable from all combined sources of insurance.

COBRA (**koh**-brə) *abbr.* CONSOLIDATED OMNIBUS BUDGET RECONCILIATION ACT OF 1985.

coconspirator. A person who engages in a criminal conspiracy with another; a fellow conspirator. See CONSPIRATOR.

unindicted coconspirator. See *unindicted conspirator* under CONSPIRATOR.

coconspirator's exception. An exception to the hearsay rule whereby one conspirator's acts and statements, if made during and in furtherance of the conspiracy, are admissible against a defendant even if the statements are made in the defendant's absence. — Also termed *coconspirator's rule.* See HEARSAY.

C.O.D. *abbr.* **1.** Cash on delivery; collect on delivery. • By consenting to this delivery term, the buyer agrees to pay simultaneously with delivery and appoints the carrier as the buyer's agent to receive and transmit the payment to the seller. With C.O.D. contracts, the practice of carriers has traditionally been to disallow inspection before payment. **2.** Costs on delivery. **3.** Cash on demand. — Sometimes written *c.o.d.*

CODA. *abbr.* CASH OR DEFERRED ARRANGEMENT.

code. 1. A complete system of positive law, carefully arranged and officially promulgated; a systematic collection or revision of laws, rules, or regulations <the Uniform Commercial Code>. • Strictly, a code is a compilation not just of existing statutes, but also of much of the unwritten law on a subject, which is newly enacted as a complete system of law. — Also termed *consolidated laws.*

> "A code is not only a collection of the existing statutory law, but also of much of the unwritten law on any subject, and is composed partly of such materials as might be at hand from all sources — from statutes, cases, and from customs — supplemented by such amendments, alterations, and additions as are deemed by the codifiers necessary to harmonize and perfect the existing system. In fact, in making a code, new laws may be added and old laws repealed in order to constitute a complete system." William M. Lile et al., *Brief Making and the Use of Law Books* 18–19 (3d ed. 1914).

2. (*usu. cap.*) The collection of laws and constitutions made by order of the Roman Emperor Justinian and first authoritatively published in A.D. 529 (with a second edition in 534). • Contained in 12 books, the Code is one of four works that make up what is now called the *Corpus Juris Civilis.* — Also termed (in sense 2) *Legal Code.* See CODEX; CORPUS JURIS CIVILIS.

Code Civil. The code embodying the civil law of France, dating from 1804. • It was known from the beginning as the *Code Civil,* to distinguish it from the other four Codes promoted by Napoleon, but is sometimes called *Code Napoléon.* In 1870, the official name became *Code Civil.* Cf. NAPOLEONIC CODE. See CIVIL CODE (2).

coded communications. Messages that are encoded or enciphered by some method of transposition or substitution so that they become unintelligible to anyone who does not have the key to the code or cipher.

Code de commerce (**kohd** də kaw-**mairs**). A codification of French commercial law, enacted in 1807, dealing with commercial transactions, bankruptcy, and the jurisdiction and procedure of the courts handling these subjects. • This code supplemented the *Code Napoléon.* See NAPOLEONIC CODE.

Code de procédure civil (**kohd** də praw-se-**door** see-**veel**). A French civil-procedure code, enacted in 1806 and appended to the *Code Napoléon.* See NAPOLEONIC CODE.

Code d'instruction criminelle (**kohd** d*an*-struuk-see-**awn** kri-mi-**nel**). A French criminal-procedure code, enacted in 1811 and appended to the *Code Napoléon.* See NAPOLEONIC CODE.

codefendant. One of two or more defendants sued in the same litigation or charged with the same crime. — Also termed *joint defendant.* Cf. COPLAINTIFF.

Code Napoléon (**kohd** na-poh-lay-**awn**). See NAPOLEONIC CODE.

Code Noir (kohd **nwahr**). [French "black code"] *Hist.* A body of laws issued by Louis XIV and applied in French colonies. • The Code regulated slavery and banned Jews and non-Catholic religious practices from the colonies.

code of conduct. A written set of rules governing the behavior of specified groups, such as lawyers, government employees, or corporate employees.

Code of Federal Regulations. The annual collection of executive-agency regulations published in the daily Federal Register, combined with previously issued regulations that are still in effect. — Abbr. CFR.

Code of Hammurabi (hah-mə-**rah**-bee *or* ham-ə-). The oldest known written legal code, produced in Mesopotamia during the rule of Hammurabi (who reigned from 1792 to 1750 B.C.). • The code consisted of nearly 300 provisions, arranged under headings such as family, trade, real property, personal property, and labor.

Code of Justinian. See JUSTINIAN CODE.

Code of Military Justice. The collection of substantive and procedural rules governing the discipline of members of the armed forces. 10 USCA §§ 801 et seq. — Also termed *Uniform Code of Military Justice* (UCMJ).

Code of Professional Responsibility. See MODEL CODE OF PROFESSIONAL RESPONSIBILITY.

Code pénal (**kohd** pay-**nal**). The fourth of five codes promoted by Napoleon, enacted in 1810, setting forth the penal code of France. See NAPOLEONIC CODE.

code pleading. See PLEADING (2).

code state. *Hist.* A state that, at a given time, had already procedurally merged law and equity, so that equity was no longer administered as a separate system. • This term was current primarily in the early to mid-20th century.

codex (**koh**-deks). [Latin] *Archaic.* **1.** A code, esp. the Justinian Code. **2.** A book written on paper or parchment; esp., a volume of an ancient text.

Codex Gregorianus (**koh**-deks gri-gor-ee-**ay**-nəs). [Latin] *Roman law.* A collection of imperial constitutions compiled by the Roman jurist Gregorius and published in A.D. 291. — Also termed *Gregorian Code.*

> "The imperial enactments, rapidly increasing in number, covering, at hazard, the whole range of law, and, by reason of difficulties of communication and imperfect methods of promulgation, not always readily ascertainable, created a burden for the practitioner almost as great as that of the unmanageable juristic literature. Something was done to help him by two collections published privately about the end of the third century, the *Codex Gregorianus* and *Codex Hermogenianus.* These collections do not now exist: what is known of them is from citations in later literature...." W.W. Buckland, *A Manual of Roman Private Law* 20–21 (2d ed. 1953).

Codex Hermogenianus (**koh**-deks hər-mə-jee-nee-**ay**-nəs). [Latin] *Roman law.* A collection of imperial constitutions compiled by the Roman jurist Hermogenianus and published in A.D. 295. • The *Codex Hermogenianus* supplemented the *Codex Gregorianus.* — Also termed *Hermogenian Code.*

Codex Justinianeus. See JUSTINIAN CODE.

Codex Repetitae Praelectionis (**koh**-deks rep-ə-**tɪ**-tee pri-lek-shee-**oh**-nis). [Latin "code of the resumed reading"] *Roman law.* A revised version of the Justinian Code, published in A.D. 534. • This code is divided into 12 books, and deals with ecclesiastical law, criminal law, administrative law, and private law. — Also termed *Codex Iustinianus Repetitae Praelectionis.* See JUSTINIAN CODE.

> "By the time when the *Digest* and *Institutes* had been completed it was obvious that the *Codex*, published little more than four years earlier, was incomplete, since in the interval Justinian ... had promulgated other new constitutions. Tribonian, therefore, was appointed to revise the Code, so as to bring it fully up to date, and at the end of the year A.D. 534 this new Code, known as the *Codex Repetitae Praelectionis*, was promulgated, and is the only Code which survives to the present day. Justinian seem to have laboured under the erroneous impression that the system he had framed would be adequate for all time. But as there is nothing static about law, further legislative enactments, termed *Novellae Constitutiones*, were issued during his reign.... In modern times Justinian's various compilations came to be called collectively the *Corpus Juris Civilis*: the *Corpus* being regarded as a single work, made up of the *Institutes*, the *Digest*, the *Codex Repetitae Praelectionis*, and the *Novels.*" R.W. Leage, *Roman Private Law* 44 (C.H. Ziegler ed., 2d ed. 1930).

Codex Theodosianus (**koh**-deks thee-ə-doh-shee-**ay**-nəs). [Latin] *Roman law.* A compilation of imperial enactments prepared at the direction of the emperor Theodosius and published in A.D. 438. • The *Codex Theodosianus* replaced all other imperial legislation from the time of Constantine I (A.D. 306–337), and remained the basis of Roman law until it was superseded by the Justinian Code in A.D. 529. — Also termed *Theodosian Code.*

codicil (**kod**-ə-səl *or* -sil). A supplement or addition to a will, not necessarily disposing of the entire estate but modifying, explaining, or otherwise qualifying the will in some way. • When admitted to probate, the codicil becomes a part of the will.

> "A Schedule or supplement to a Will, or some other writing; some Writers, conferring a Testament, and a *Codicil* together, call a Testament a great Will, and a *Codicil* a little one; and compare a Testament to a Ship, and the *Codicil* to the Boat tied to the Ship." Thomas Blount, *Nomo-Lexicon: A Law-Dictionary* (1670).

> "A codicil, from *codicillus*, a small *codex*, a little book or writing, may be defined as a writing by the testator

intended as a supplement or addition to his will, the effect of which may be either to enlarge or restrict it, or to annul or revoke it altogether. It may add to or subtract from provisions of the will, may explain or alter, confirm or revoke them wholly or in part; or, when the will itself is invalid, may by a valid re-execution and republication revive and renew the will." 1 H.C. Underhill, *A Treatise on the Law of Wills* § 7, at 11 (1900).

codicillus (kod-ə-**sil**-əs). [Latin "little document"] *Roman law.* **1.** An informal document instructing an heir to carry out a certain performance, usu. the payment of money or the transfer of property to a third person. • During the reign of Augustus (27 B.C.–A.D. 14), directives (*fideicommissa*) contained in *codicilli* became legally binding. See FIDEICOMMISSUM. **2.** An imperially granted appointment or special privilege.

codification (kod-ə-fi-**kay**-shən), *n.* **1.** The process of compiling, arranging, and systematizing the laws of a given jurisdiction, or of a discrete branch of the law, into an ordered code. **2.** The code that results from this process. — **codify** (**kod**-ə-fɪ), *vb.* — **codifier** (**kod**-ə-fɪ-ər), *n.*

codifying statute. See STATUTE.

Coefficient Clause. See NECESSARY AND PROPER CLAUSE.

coemptio (koh-**emp**-shee-oh). [Latin] *Roman law.* A form of civil marriage in which the husband "purchased" from a woman's father — by fictitious sale — the right to exercise marital power (*manus*) over the woman. • The importance of *coemptio* as a method of civil marriage had faded by the end of the Republic period. Cf. CONFARREATIO; USUS (2).

coemption (koh-**emp**-shən), *n.* **1.** The act of purchasing the entire quantity of any commodity. **2.** COEMPTIO. — **coemptional, coemptive,** *adj.*

coerce (koh-**ərs**), *vb.* To compel by force or threat <coerce a confession>.

coerced confession. See CONFESSION.

coercion (koh-**ər**-shən), *n.* **1.** Compulsion by physical force or threat of physical force. • An act such as signing a will is not legally valid if done under coercion.

criminal coercion. Coercion intended to restrict another's freedom of action by: (1) threatening to commit a criminal act against that person; (2) threatening to accuse that person of having committed a criminal act; (3) threatening to expose a secret that either would subject the victim to hatred, contempt, or ridicule or would impair the victim's credit or goodwill, or (4) taking or withholding official action or causing an official to take or withhold action.

2. Conduct that constitutes the improper use of economic power to compel another to submit to the wishes of one who wields it. — Also termed *economic coercion.* **3.** *Hist.* A husband's actual or supposed control or influence over his wife's actions. • Under the common-law doctrine of coercion, a wife who committed a crime in her husband's presence was presumed to have been coerced by him and thus had a complete defense. Courts have abolished this doctrine. — **coercive,** *adj.* — **coercer,** *n.*

"Although as an abstract statement any action or restraint imposed upon one by another may be spoken of as coercion, there has been a tendency in the criminal law to employ the word 'compulsion' for the general field and to reserve the word 'coercion' to indicate the exercise of such influence (actual or presumed) over a married woman by her husband. And since the latter is not merely a specific instance of the former, but is something which differs from it in kind so far as common-law consequences are concerned, there are important reasons for retaining this difference in the meaning to be assigned to these terms." Rollin M. Perkins & Ronald N. Boyce, *Criminal Law* 1018 (3d ed. 1982).

coercive relief. See RELIEF.

coexecutor (koh-eg-**zek**-yə-tər). See *joint executor* under EXECUTOR.

coexistence. *Int'l law.* The peaceful continuation of nations, peoples, or other entities or groups within an effective political-military equilibrium.

cogent (**koh**-jənt), *adj.* Compelling or convincing <cogent reasoning>. — **cogency,** *n.*

cognate, *adj.* See COGNATIC.

cognate, *n.* One who is kin to another. • In Roman law, the term implies that the kinship derives from a lawful marriage. In Scots and later civil law, the term implies kinship from the mother's side. Cf. AGNATE.

cognate nuisance. See NUISANCE.

cognate offense. See OFFENSE (1).

cognati. See COGNATUS.

cognatic (kog-**nat**-ik), *adj.* (Of a relationship) existing between cognates. — Also termed *cognate.*

cognatio (kog-**nay**-shee-oh). [Latin] *Roman law.* The relationship between people having a common ancestor; a blood relationship. Cf. AGNATIO.

cognation (kog-**nay**-shən), *n.* **1.** Relationship by blood rather than by marriage; relationship arising through common descent from the same man and woman, whether the descent is traced through males or females.

> " 'Cognation' is . . . a relative term, and the degree of connexion in blood which it indicates depends on the particular marriage which is selected as the commencement of the calculation." Henry S. Maine, *Ancient Law* 122 (17th ed. 1901).

2. *Civil law.* A relationship existing between two people by blood, by family, or by both.

civil cognation. A relationship arising by law, such as that created by adoption.

mixed cognation. A relationship that combines the ties of blood and family, such as that existing between brothers who are born of the same marriage.

natural cognation. A blood relationship, usu. arising from an illicit connection.

3. Relationship between persons or things of the same or similar nature; likeness.

cognatus (kog-**nay**-təs), *n.* [Latin] *Roman law.* A cognatic relative; a person related to another by a common ancestor. — Also termed *cognate.* Cf. AGNATUS.

cognitio (kog-**nish**-ee-oh). [fr. Latin *cognoscere* "to know"] **1.** *Hist.* The acknowledgment of a fine, or the certificate of such an acknowledgment. **2.** *Roman law.* A judicial examination or hearing of a case by a magistrate or juror. • *Cognitio* includes everything that the judicial authority did during the proceedings to establish the facts relevant to the controversy.

cognitionibus mittendis (kog-nish-ee-**oh**-nə-bəs mi-**ten**-dis). [Latin "cognizance of pleas to be released"] *Hist.* A writ ordering a justice of the Common Pleas to certify a fine that the justice had imposed but refused to certify.

cognitive test. *Criminal law.* A test of the defendant's ability to know certain things, specifically the nature of his or her conduct and whether the conduct was right or wrong. • This test is used in assessing whether a defendant may rely on an insanity defense.

cognitor (**kog**-ni-tor). *Roman law.* A person formally appointed to represent another in a civil trial. Cf. PROCURATOR (1).

cognizable (**kog**-ni-zə-bəl), *adj.* **1.** Capable of being known or recognized; esp., capable of being identified as a group because of a common characteristic or interest that cannot be represented by others <American Indians qualify as a cognizable group for jury-selection purposes>. **2.** Capable of being judicially tried or examined before a designated tribunal; within the court's jurisdiction <the tort claims are not cognizable under the consumer-protection statute>.

cognizance (**kog**-ni-zəns), *n.* **1.** The right and power to try and determine cases; JURISDICTION. **2.** The taking of judicial or authoritative notice. **3.** Acknowledgment or admission of an alleged fact; esp. (*hist.*), acknowledgment of a fine. See FINE (1); FINE SUR COGNIZANCE DE DROIT. **4.** *Common-law pleading.* In a replevin action, a plea by the defendant that the goods are held in bailment for another. Cf. AVOWRY.

cognizee (kog-ni-**zee**). *Hist.* The grantee of land in a conveyance by fine. — Also termed *conusee; conuzee.* See FINE (1).

cognizor (**kog**-ni-zər *or* -zor). *Hist.* The grantor of land in a conveyance by fine. — Also termed *conusor; conuzor.* See FINE (1).

> "Next comes the *concord*, or agreement itself, after leave obtained from the court; which is usually an acknowledgment . . . that the lands in question are the right of the complainant. And from this acknowledgment, or recognition of right, the party levying the fine is called the *cognizor*, and he to whom it is levied the *cognizee*." 2 William Blackstone, *Commentaries on the Laws of England* 350–51 (1766).

cognovit (kog-**noh**-vit). [Latin "he has conceded (a debt or an action)"] An acknowledgment of debt or liability in the form of a confessed judgment. • Formerly, credit contracts often included a cognovit clause in which the consumer relinquished, in advance, any right to be notified of court hearings in any suit for nonpayment — but such clauses are now generally illegal. See CONFESSION OF JUDGMENT. Cf. WARRANT OF ATTORNEY.

> "A cognovit is an instrument signed by a defendant in an action actually commenced confessing the plaintiff's demand to be just, and empowering the plaintiff to sign judgment against him in default of his paying the plaintiff the sum due to him within the time mentioned in the

cognovit." John Indermaur, *Principles of the Common Law* 8 (Edmund H. Bennett ed., 1st Am. ed. 1878).

cognovit actionem (kog-**noh**-vit ak-shee-**oh**-nəm). [Law Latin "he has confessed the action"] A defendant's written acknowledgment of the plaintiff's claim, authorizing the plaintiff to take a judgment for a named sum; a cognovit.

cognovit clause. A contractual provision by which a debtor agrees to jurisdiction in certain courts, waives notice requirements, and authorizes the entry of an adverse judgment in the event of a default or breach. • Cognovit clauses are outlawed or restricted in most states.

cognovit judgment. See JUDGMENT.

cognovit note. A promissory note containing a cognovit clause. — Also termed *judgment note.*

cohabitation (koh-hab-ə-**tay**-shən), *n.* The fact or state of living together, esp. as partners in life, usu. with the suggestion of sexual relations. — **cohabit** (koh-**hab**-it), *vb.* — **cohabitative** (koh-**hab**-ə-tay-tiv), *adj.* — **cohabitant** (koh-**hab**-ə-tənt), *n.*

illicit cohabitation. At common law, the act of a man and a woman openly living together without being married to each other. — Also termed *lewd and lascivious cohabitation.*

matrimonial cohabitation. The living together of husband and wife.

notorious cohabitation. The act of a man and a woman openly living together under circumstances that make the arrangement illegal under statutes that are now rarely enforced.

cohabitation agreement. A contract outlining the property and financial arrangements between persons who live together. Cf. PRENUPTIAL AGREEMENT.

cohabiting unmarried person of the opposite sex. See CUPOS.

***Cohan* rule** (**koh**-han). *Tax.* A former rule that a taxpayer may approximate travel and entertainment expenses where no records exist if the taxpayer has taken all possible steps to provide documentation. • Since 1962, travel and entertainment expenses have been only partly deductible and must be carefully documented, but courts may apply the *Cohan* reasoning to other items. *Cohan v. Commissioner*, 39 F.2d 540 (2d Cir. 1930).

coheir (koh-**air**). One of two or more persons to whom an inheritance descends. See HEIR.

coheiress (koh-**air**-is). *Hist.* A female coheir.

***Cohen* doctrine** (**koh**-ən). See COLLATERAL-ORDER DOCTRINE.

cohort analysis (**koh**-hort). A method of measuring racial discrimination in the workplace by comparing, at several points in time, the pay and promotions of employees of different races. • Cohort analyses are often used in employment-discrimination cases.

coif (koyf). **1.** A white linen headpiece formerly worn by serjeants at law (barristers of high standing) in common-law courts. **2.** The rank or order of serjeants-at-law. See ORDER OF THE COIF.

Coinage Clause. The provision in the U.S. Constitution (art. I, § 8, cl. 5) granting to Congress the power to coin money.

coincident indicator. See INDICATOR.

coindictee. One of two or more persons who have been jointly indicted. Cf. *joint indictment* under INDICTMENT.

coined term. See *fanciful trademark* under TRADEMARK.

coinsurance. See INSURANCE.

coinsurance clause. A provision in an insurance policy requiring a property owner to carry separate insurance up to an amount stated in the policy to qualify for full coverage. — Also termed *contribution clause.*

coinsurer. An insurer who shares losses sustained under an insurance policy. See *coinsurance* under INSURANCE.

cojudices. *Archaic.* In England, associate judges.

cold blood. A killer's state of mind when committing a willful and premeditated homicide <a shooting in cold blood>. See COOL BLOOD. Cf. HEAT OF PASSION.

cold check. See *bad check* under CHECK.

cold-water ordeal. See ORDEAL.

colegatee. A joint legatee; one of two or more persons who receive a legacy under a will. Cf. LEGATEE.

colibertus (kol-i-**bər**-təs). [Law Latin] *Hist.* A serf in free socage; that is, a serf who is nominally freed but is still subject to certain servile conditions. • A *colibertus* occupied a position in society between servile and free tenants. — Also spelled *collibertus*. Pl. ***coliberti.*** See SOCAGE.

collapsible corporation. See CORPORATION.

collapsible partnership. See PARTNERSHIP.

collate (kə-**layt**), *vb. Civil law.* To return (inherited property) to an estate for division <the grandchildren collated the property they had received>.

collateral (kə-**lat**-ər-əl), *adj.* **1.** Supplementary; accompanying, but secondary and subordinate to <whether or not the accident victim was wearing a seat belt is a collateral issue>. **2.** Not direct in line, but on a parallel or diverging line <my uncle is in my collateral line of descent>. Cf. LINEAL. — **collaterality** (kə-lat-ər-**al**-ə-tee), *n.*

collateral (kə-**lat**-ər-əl), *n.* **1.** A person collaterally related to a decedent. **2.** Property that is pledged as security against a debt; the property subject to a security interest. See UCC § 9–102(a)(9). — Also termed (in sense 2) *collateral security*.

as-extracted collateral. **1.** Oil, gas, or other minerals that are subject to a security interest that is created by a debtor having an interest in the minerals before extraction and that attaches to the minerals as they are extracted. UCC § 9–102(a)(4)(A). **2.** An account arising out of the sale at the wellhead or minehead of oil, gas, or other minerals in which the debtor had an interest before extraction. UCC § 9–102(a)(4)(B).

cash collateral. Collateral consisting of cash, negotiable instruments, documents of title, securities, deposit accounts, or other cash equivalents.

cross-collateral. **1.** Security given by all parties to a contract. **2.** *Bankruptcy.* Bargained-for security that protects a creditor's postpetition extension of credit in addition to the creditor's prepetition unsecured claims that, as a result of this security, obtain priority over other creditors' prepetition unsecured claims. • Some courts allow this procedure, which is known as *cross-collateralization*.

collateral act. Any act (usu. excluding the payment of money) for which a bond or recognizance is given as security.

collateral affinity. See AFFINITY.

collateral ancestor. See *collateral ascendant* under ASCENDANT.

collateral ascendant. See ASCENDANT.

collateral assignment. See ASSIGNMENT (2).

collateral assurance. See ASSURANCE.

collateral attack. An attack on a judgment entered in a different proceeding. • A petition for a writ of habeas corpus is one type of collateral attack. — Also termed *indirect attack*. Cf. DIRECT ATTACK.

collateral-benefit rule. See COLLATERAL-SOURCE RULE.

collateral condition. See CONDITION (2).

collateral consanguinity. See CONSANGUINITY.

collateral consequence. A penalty for committing a crime — in addition to the penalties included in the criminal sentence. • An example is the loss of a professional license.

collateral contract. See CONTRACT.

collateral-contract doctrine. The principle that in a dispute concerning a written contract, proof of a second (but oral) agreement will not be excluded under the parol-evidence rule if the oral agreement is independent of and not inconsistent with the written contract, and if the information in the oral agreement would not ordinarily be expected to be included in the written contract.

collateral covenant. See COVENANT (1).

collateral defense. See DEFENSE (1).

collateral descent. See DESCENT.

collateral estoppel (e-**stop**-əl). An affirmative defense barring a party from relitigating an issue determined against that party in an earlier action, even if the second action differs significantly from the first one. — Also termed *issue preclusion*; *issue estoppel*; *direct estoppel*; *estoppel by judgment*; *estoppel by record*; *estoppel by verdict*; *cause-of-action estoppel*; *estoppel per rem judicatam*. Cf. RES JUDICATA.

administrative collateral estoppel. Estoppel that arises from a decision made by an agency acting in a judicial capacity.

defensive collateral estoppel. Estoppel asserted by a defendant to prevent a plaintiff from relitigating an issue previously decided against the plaintiff and for another defendant.

offensive collateral estoppel. Estoppel asserted by a plaintiff to prevent a defendant from relitigating an issue previously decided against the defendant and for another plaintiff.

collateral fact. See FACT.

collateral fraud. See *extrinsic fraud* (1) under FRAUD.

collateral heir. See HEIR.

collateral-inheritance tax. See TAX.

collateral issue. See ISSUE (1).

collateralize (kə-**lat**-ər-əl-ɪz), *vb.* **1.** To serve as collateral for <the purchased property collateralized the loan agreement>. **2.** To make (a loan) secure with collateral <the creditor insisted that the loan be collateralized>. — **collateralization** (kə-lat-ər-əl-ə-**zay**-shən), *n.*

collateralized mortgage obligation. *Securities.* A bond secured by a group of mortgage obligations or pass-through securities and paid according to the payment schedule of its class (or *tranche*). • CMOs are issued by the Federal Home Loan Mortgage Corporation, and benefit from predictable payments of interest and principal. — Abbr. CMO. See *pass-through security* under SECURITY; TRANCHE.

collateral limitation. See LIMITATION.

collateral line. See LINE.

collateral loan. See *secured loan* under LOAN.

collateral matter. *Evidence.* Any matter on which evidence could not have been introduced for a relevant purpose. • If a witness has erred in testifying about a detail that is collateral to the relevant facts, then another party cannot call witnesses to contradict that point — cross-examination alone must suffice.

collateral mistake. See *unessential mistake* under MISTAKE.

collateral mortgage. See MORTGAGE.

collateral negligence. See NEGLIGENCE.

collateral-negligence doctrine. The rule holding that one who engages an independent contractor is not liable for physical harm that the contractor causes if (1) the contractor's negligence consists solely of the improper manner in which the contractor's work is performed, (2) the risk of harm created is not normal to the work, and (3) the employer had no reason to contemplate the contractor's negligence when the contract was made.

collateral note. See *secured note* under NOTE.

collateral obligation. A liability undertaken by a person who becomes bound for another's debt. — Also termed *accessorial obligation*.

collateral-order doctrine. A doctrine allowing appeal from an interlocutory order that conclusively determines an issue wholly separate from the merits of the action and effectively unreviewable on appeal from a final judgment. — Also termed *Cohen doctrine* (fr. *Cohen v. Beneficial Indus. Loan Corp.*, 337 U.S. 541, 69 S.Ct. 1221 (1949)). See *appealable decision* under DECISION.

collateral power. See POWER.

collateral proceeding. See PROCEEDING.

collateral promise. See PROMISE.

collateral relative. See RELATIVE.

collateral security. See SECURITY.

collateral-source rule. *Torts.* The doctrine that if an injured party receives compensation for its injuries from a source independent of the tortfeasor, the payment should not be deducted from the damages that the tortfeasor must pay. • Insurance proceeds are the most common collateral source. — Also termed *collateral-benefit rule*.

collateral trust bond. See BOND (3).

collateral trust certificate. See *collateral trust bond* (1) under BOND (3).

collateral use. See USE (1).

collateral warranty. See WARRANTY (1).

collatio bonorum (kə-**lay**-shee-oh bə-**nor**-əm). [Latin "collation of goods"] *Civil law.* The bringing into hotchpot of goods or money advanced by a parent to a child, so that the parent's personal estate will be equally distributed among the parent's children. See HOTCHPOT.

> "[I]f the estates so given them, by way of advancement, are not quite equivalent to the other shares, the children so advanced shall now have so much as will make them equal. This just and equitable provision hath been also said to be derived from the *collatio bonorum* of the imperial law: which it certainly resembles in some points, though it differs widely in others. But it may not be amiss to observe, that, with regard to goods and chattels, this is part of . . . the common law of England, under the name of *hotchpot*." 2 William Blackstone, *Commentaries on the Laws of England* 516–17 (1766).

collation (kə-**lay**-shən), *n.* **1.** The comparison of a copy with its original to ascertain its correctness; the report of the officer who made the comparison. **2.** An estimate of the value of advancements made by an intestate to his or her children so that the estate may be divided in accordance with the intestacy statute. **3.** *Eccles. law.* The act (by a bishop) of conferring a benefice where the bishop holds the right of advowson, thus combining the acts of *presentation* and *institution*. — Also termed *collation to a benefice*. See *advowson collative* under ADVOWSON. — **collate** (kə-**layt**), *vb.* — **collator** (kə-**lay**-tər), *n.*

collatione facta uni post mortem alterius (kə-lay-shee-**oh**-nee **fak**-tə **yoo**-nI pohst **mor**-təm al-**teer**-ee-əs [*or* awl-]). [Law Latin "collation to a benefice made to one after the death of the other"] *Hist.* A writ directed to the Court of Common Pleas, requesting that the court order a bishop to appoint a clerk in place of another who had died pending appointment.

collatione heremitagii (kə-lay-shee-**oh**-nee her-ə-mə-**tay**-jee-I). [Law Latin "collation of hermitage"] *Hist.* A writ by which the Crown conferred the keeping of a hermitage on a clerk.

collation to a benefice. See COLLATION.

collatio signorum (kə-**lay**-shee-oh sig-**nor**-əm). [Law Latin "comparison of signs"] *Hist.* A method of testing a seal's genuineness by comparing it with another known to be genuine.

collative fact. See *investitive fact* under FACT.

collectability. The relative ability of a judgment creditor to make a judgment debtor pay the amount of the judgment; the degree to which a judgment can be satisfied through collection efforts against the defendant.

collecting bank. See BANK.

collection. *Banking.* The process through which an item (such as a check) passes in a payor bank. See *payor bank* under BANK (1).

collection indorsement. See *restrictive indorsement* under INDORSEMENT.

collection item. An item (such as a documentary draft) taken by a bank for a customer's account, but not credited until payment for the item has actually been received. See *documentary draft* under DRAFT (1).

collective bargaining. Negotiations between an employer and the representatives of organized employees to determine the conditions of employment, such as wages, hours, and fringe benefits. See CONCESSION BARGAINING.

> "Collective bargaining means the joint determination by employees and employers of the problems of the employment relationship. Such problems include wage rates and wage systems, hours and overtime, vacations, discipline, work loads, classification of employees, layoffs, and worker retirement. The advent of collective bargaining does not give rise to these problems. Rather they are germane to the industrial relations environment, and exist with or without unionization." Benjamin J. Taylor & Fred Whitney, *Labor Relations Law* 3 (1971).

collective-bargaining agreement. *Labor law.* A contract that is made between an employer and a labor union and that regulates employment conditions. — Also termed *collective labor agreement*; *trade agreement*.

collective mark. A trademark or servicemark used by an association, union, or other group either to identify the group's products or services or to signify membership in the group. • Collective marks — such as "Realtor" or "American Peanut Farmers" — can be federally registered under the Lanham Act. — Also termed *collective trademark*. Cf. CERTIFICATION MARK. See TRADEMARK.

collective measure. *Int'l law*. An activity undertaken by more than one country to achieve an agreed-upon end. • The countries involved may undertake a collective measure either in an ad hoc manner or through an institutionalized association.

collective punishment. A penalty inflicted on a group of persons without regard to individual responsibility for the conduct giving rise to the penalty. • Collective punishment was outlawed in 1949 by the Geneva Convention.

collective trademark. See COLLECTIVE MARK.

collective work. *Copyright*. **1.** A publication (such as a periodical issue, anthology, or encyclopedia) in which several contributions, constituting separate and independent works in themselves, are assembled into a copyrightable whole. **2.** A selection and arrangement of brief portions of different movies, television shows, or radio shows into a single copyrightable work. • If the selecting and arranging involves any originality, the person who selects and arranges the clips may claim a copyright even if copyright cannot be claimed in the individual component parts. Cf. COMPILATION (1).

> "If a work is not joint and not derivative but nevertheless consists of works of authorship created by more than one person, it is a compilation of some sort except for the possibility that it is a work for hire. . . . If the component parts have an independent identity, that is, they are works of authorship, then the compilation is a collective work, a type of compilation." Arthur R. Miller & Michael H. Davis, *Intellectual Property in a Nutshell* 374 (2d ed. 1990).

collector of decedent's estate. A person temporarily appointed by a probate court to collect assets and payments due to a decedent's estate, and to settle other financial matters requiring immediate attention. • A collector is often appointed to look after an estate when there is a will contest or a dispute about who should be appointed administrator. The collector's duties end when an administrator is appointed.

collega (kə-**lee**-gə). [Latin] *Roman law*. A person invested with joint authority; a colleague or associate. • *Collega* usu. referred to a member of an association (*collegium*) or a coheir. See COLLEGIUM.

collegatarius (kə-leg-ə-**tair**-ee-əs). [Latin] *Roman law*. A co-legatee.

collegatary (kə-**leg**-ə-ter-ee). A co-legatee; a person who shares a common legacy with one or more other persons. — Also termed *collegatarius* (kə-leg-ə-**ter**-ee-əs).

college. 1. An institution of learning that offers instruction in the liberal arts, humanities, and sciences, but not in the technical arts or in studies preparatory to admission to a profession. **2.** An assembly of people, established by law to perform some special function or to promote some common purpose, usu. of an educational, political, ecclesiastical, or scientific nature.

College of Arms. See HERALDS' COLLEGE.

collegium (kə-**lee**-jee-əm). [Latin] *Roman law*. An association of at least three people having the right to assemble and enact rules concerning membership, organization, and the rights and duties of members. • *Collegia* were formed for professional, cultural, charitable, and religious purposes. Pl. *collegia*.

collegium illicitum (kə-**lee**-jee-əm i-**lis**-ə-təm). A collegium that either is not sanctioned by law or assembles for some purpose other than that expressed in its charter.

collegium licitum (kə-**lee**-jee-əm **lis**-ə-təm). An assemblage of people empowered to act as a juristic person in the pursuit of some useful purpose or business.

collision. *Maritime law*. **1.** The crashing together of two vessels.

fortuitous collision. The accidental crashing of two vessels.

2. ALLISION.

collision insurance. See INSURANCE.

colliterales et socii (kə-lit-ə-**ray**-leez et **soh**-shee-ɪ). [Law Latin "assistants and associates"] *Hist*. In England, the former title of assistants to the Chancery judges (i.e., *masters in chancery*).

collobium (kə-**loh**-bee-əm). [Law Latin] *Hist*. A hood or covering for the shoulders, formerly worn by serjeants-at-law.

colloquium (kə-**loh**-kwee-əm). **1.** The offer of extrinsic evidence to show that an alleged defamatory statement referred to the plaintiff even though it did not explicitly mention the plaintiff. **2.** The introductory averments in a plaintiff's pleading setting out all the special circumstances that make the challenged words defamatory. Pl. **colloquiums, colloquia.** Cf. INDUCEMENT (4); INNUENDO (2).

colloquy (**kol**-ə-kwee). Any formal discussion, such as an oral exchange between a judge, the prosecutor, the defense counsel, and a criminal defendant in which the judge ascertains the defendant's understanding of the proceedings and of the defendant's rights.

collusion (kə-**loo**-zhən), *n.* An agreement to defraud another or to obtain something forbidden by law. • For example, before the no-fault concept in divorce proceedings, a husband and wife might agree to make it appear that one of them had committed an act that was grounds for divorce. — **collude,** *vb.* — **collusive,** *adj.* — **colluder,** *n.*

collusive action. See ACTION.

collusive joinder. See JOINDER.

***Collyer* doctrine** (**kol**-yər). *Labor law.* The principle under which the National Labor Relations Board will refer an issue brought before it to arbitration if the issue is arbitrable under the collective-bargaining agreement. *Collyer Insulated Wire*, 192 NLRB 837 (1971). Cf. SPIELBERG DOCTRINE.

colonial law. 1. Law governing a colony or colonies. **2.** The body of law in force in the 13 original U.S. colonies before the Declaration of Independence.

colony, *n. Int'l law.* **1.** A dependent territorial entity subject to the sovereignty of an independent country, but considered part of that country for purposes of relations with third countries. **2.** A group of people who live in a new territory but retain ties with their parent country. **3.** The territory inhabited by such a group. — **colonize,** *vb.* — **colonial,** *adj.* Cf. MOTHER COUNTRY.

color, *n.* **1.** Appearance, guise, or semblance; esp., the appearance of a legal claim to a right, authority, or office <color of title> <under color of state law>. **2.** *Common-law pleading.* An apparent, but legally insufficient, ground of action, admitted in a defendant's pleading to exist for the plaintiff; esp., a plaintiff's apparent (and usu. false) right or title to property, the existence of which is pleaded by the defendant as a confession and avoidance to remove the case from the jury by turning the issue from one of fact to one of law. See GIVE COLOR.

> "It is a rule of pleading, that no man be allowed to plead specially such a plea as amounts only to the general issue, or a total denial of the charge; but in such case he shall be driven to plead the general issue in terms, whereby the whole question is referred to a jury. But if the defendant, in an assise or action of trespass, be desirous to refer the validity of his title to the court rather than the jury, he may state his title specially, and at the same time *give colour* to the plaintiff, or suppose him to have an appearance or colour of title, bad indeed in point of law, but of which the jury are not competent judges. As if his own true title be, that he claims by feoffment with livery from A, by force of which he entered on the lands in question, he cannot plead this by itself, as it amounts to no more than the general issue . . . *not guilty* in an action of trespass. But he may allege this specially, provided he goes farther and says, that the plaintiff claiming by *colour* of a prior deed of feoffment, without livery, entered; upon whom he entered; and may then refer himself to the judgment of the court which of these two titles is the best in point of law." 3 William Blackstone, *Commentaries on the Laws of England* 309 (1768).

express color. A feigned matter pleaded by the defendant in an action of trespass, from which the plaintiff seems to have a good claim while in truth the plaintiff has only the appearance of one. • This pleading was abolished by the Common-Law Procedure Act of 1852, 15 & 16 Vict., ch. 76, § 64.

> "Express color is a fictitious allegation, not traversable, to give an appearance of right to the plaintiff, and thus enable the defendant to plead specially his own title, which would otherwise amount to the general issue. It is a licensed evasion of the rule against pleading contradictory matter specially." Benjamin J. Shipman, *Handbook of Common-Law Pleading* § 202, at 351 (Henry Winthrop Ballantine ed., 3d ed. 1923).

implied color. An apparent ground of action that arises from the nature of the defense, as when the defense consists of a confession and avoidance in which the defendant admits the facts but denies their legal sufficiency. • This is a quality inherent in all pleadings in confession and avoidance.

colorable, *adj.* **1.** (Of a claim or action) appearing to be true, valid, or right <the pleading did not state a colorable claim>. **2.** Intended to deceive; counterfeit <the court found the conveyance of exempt property to be a colorable transfer, and so set it aside>.

colorable alteration. *Intellectual property.* A modification that effects no real or substantial change, but is made only to distinguish an invention or work from an existing patent or copyright.

colorable claim. See CLAIM (4).

colorable-imitation test. *Trademarks.* A test for a trademark violation in which a court determines whether an ordinary person who is not allowed to compare the two items side by side could recognize the difference between the two.

colorable transaction. See TRANSACTION.

***Colorado River* abstention.** See ABSTENTION.

color book. *Archaic. Int'l law.* An official compilation of diplomatic documents and internal papers and reports of a government, the purpose of which is to inform the legislature and the public about foreign policy, esp. during foreign crises. • Color books reached their height of popularity in the late 19th and early 20th centuries. They are now little used in most countries.

colore officii (kə-**lor**-ee ə-**fish**-ee-I). [Latin "by color of office"] See COLOR OF OFFICE.

color of authority. The appearance or presumption of authority sanctioning a public officer's actions. • The authority derives from the officer's apparent title to the office or from a writ or other apparently valid process the officer bears.

color of law. The appearance or semblance, without the substance, of a legal right. • The term usu. implies a misuse of power made possible because the wrongdoer is clothed with the authority of the state. *State action* is synonymous with *color of law* in the context of federal civil-rights statutes or criminal law. See STATE ACTION.

color of office. The authority or power that is inherent in an office, esp. a public office. • Acts taken under the color of an office are vested with, or appear to be vested with, the authority entrusted to that office.

> "The starting point in the law of bribery seems to have been when a judge, for doing his office or acting under color of his office, took a reward or fee from some person who had occasion to come before him, — and apparently guilt attached only to the judge himself and not to the bribe-giver." Rollin M. Perkins & Ronald N. Boyce, *Criminal Law* 527 (3d ed. 1982).

color of title. A written instrument or other evidence that appears to give title, but does not do so. — Also termed *apparent title.*

com. *abbr.* **1.** COMPANY. **2.** COMMONWEALTH.

comaker. One who participates jointly in borrowing money on a promissory note; esp., one who acts as surety under a note if the maker defaults. — Also termed *cosigner.* Cf. MAKER.

combatant (kəm-**bat**-ənt *or* **kom**-bə-tənt). *Int'l law.* A person who participates directly in hostilities. • "Legitimate" combatants are members of the armed forces or uniformed members of a militia or volunteer corps, under military command and subject to the laws of war.

combination. 1. An alliance of individuals or corporations working together to accomplish a common (usu. economic) goal. See COMBINATION IN RESTRAINT OF TRADE. **2.** CONSPIRACY. **3.** *Patents.* A union of elements that may be partly old and partly new. • The term encompasses not only a combination of mechanical elements but also a combination of substances in a composition claim or steps in a process claim. **4.** STRADDLE.

combination in restraint of trade. An express or tacit agreement between two or more persons or entities designed to raise prices, reduce output, or create a monopoly.

combination patent. See PATENT (3).

combustio domorum (kəm-**bus**-tee-oh də-**mor**-əm). [Latin "houses burning"] *Hist.* See HOUSEBURNING.

comes (**koh**-meez). [Latin] *Hist.* **1.** A count or earl. **2.** A person who is part of a high government official's retinue. Pl. **comites.** See COMITATUS.

comes and defends. *Archaic.* Traditionally, the standard commencement of a defendant's plea or demurrer. • The phrase, now rarely used, announces the defendant's appearance in court and intent to defend against the action.

comes now. *Archaic.* Traditionally, the standard commencement in pleadings <Comes now the plaintiff, Gilbert Lewis, by and through his attorneys of record, and would show unto the court the following>. • For a plural subject, the phrase is *come now* <Come now the plaintiffs, Bob and Louise Smith>. — Also termed *now comes.* — Sometimes shortened to *comes* <Comes the State of Tennessee>.

comfort letter. 1. *Securities.* A letter from a certified public accountant certifying that no false or misleading information has been used in preparing a financial statement accompanying a securities offering. **2.** *Corporations.* A letter, esp. from a parent corporation on behalf of a subsidiary, stating its support (but short of a guarantee) for the activities and commitments of another corporation.

comingle, *vb.* See COMMINGLE.

coming-to-rest doctrine. *Insurance.* The principle that coverage of shipped goods ends when the goods are unloaded and any cables or other links to the transporting vehicle have been disconnected. • The coming-to-rest doctrine covers only the movement of goods from the shipping vehicle to a place of rest outside the vehicle, in contrast to the broader coverage of the complete-operation rule. Cf. COMPLETE-OPERATION RULE.

comitas (**kom**-ə-təs). [Latin "courtesy"] See COMITY.

comitas gentium. See COMITY.

comitatu commisso (kom-ə-**tay**-t[y]oo kə-**mis**-oh). [Latin "county commission"] *Hist.* A writ or commission authorizing a sheriff to take charge of a county.

comitatu et castro commisso (kom-ə-**tay**-t[y]oo et **kas**-troh kə-**mis**-oh). [Latin "county and castle commission"] *Hist.* A writ authorizing a sheriff to take charge of a county and a castle.

comitatus (kom-ə-**tay**-təs). [Latin] *Hist.* **1.** A county or shire. **2.** The territorial jurisdiction of a count or earl. **3.** A county court. **4.** The retinue accompanying a prince or high government official.

comites (**kom**-ə-teez). See COMES.

comites paleys (**kom**-ə-teez-pa-**lays**). [Law French] *Hist.* Counts or earls palatine; those who exercise royal privileges in a county palatine. See COUNTY PALATINE.

comitia (kə-**mish**-ee-ə). [Latin "assembly"] *Roman law.* An assembly of the Roman people, gathered together for legislative or judicial purposes.

comitia centuriata (kə-**mish**-ee-ə sen-tyoor-ee-**ay**-tə). An assembly of the entire populace, voting by centuries (that is, military units) empowered to elect magistrates and to act as a court of appeal in a capital matter.

comitia curiata (kə-**mish**-ee-ə kyoor-ee-**ay**-tə). An assembly of (originally) patricians whose chief function was to authorize private acts of citizens, such as declaring wills and adoptions. • The *comitia curiata* engaged in little legislative activity.

> "[I]n Rome the patrician will, recorded before the Comitia Curiata, was a variety of adoption but disappeared gradually, while the plebeian will, which proved the permanent form, was made by a formal sale, or *mancipatio.*" John Henry Wigmore, *Problems of Law* 46–47 (1920).

comitia tributa (kə-**mish**-ee-ə tri-**byoo**-tə). An assembly of tribes convened to elect lower-ranking officials. • The *comitia tributa* undertook a great deal of legislative activity in the later Roman republic. Cf. CONCILIUM PLEBIS.

> "Of the various popular assemblies the oldest was the *Comitia Curiata.* This was an assembly of the whole people, or rather of all heads of families, grouped in 30 *curiae,* the *curia* being the voting unit.... It is doubtful whether this body ever exercised legislative power in the ordinary sense. Important as its functions were, they belong, in the main and apart from formalities, to an age before legislation was thought of as an ordinary method of law reform. The *Comitia Centuriata* was, in historical times, a much more important body. The centuriate organisation, which was existing, at the latest, soon after the foundation of the Republic, was a grouping of the whole people, patrician and plebeian.... [I]t could vote only on propositions submitted by the presiding magistrate ... in addition a *lex* of the *centuriae* required *auctoritas patrum,* which is commonly supposed to mean approval of the patrician members of the Senate.... A third assembly of the whole people was the *Comitia Tributa.* The voting unit of this body was the *tribus,* a subdivision, essentially local, of the territory of the State.... As in the case of the *Comitia Centuriata,* the proposal by the presiding magistrate was usually submitted for the previous approval of the Senate, and *auctoritas patrum* was required." W.W. Buckland, *A Textbook of Roman Law: From Augustus to Justinian* 2–4 (1921).

comity (**kom**-ə-tee). **1.** Courtesy among political entities (as nations, states, or courts of different jurisdictions), involving esp. mutual recognition of legislative, executive, and judicial acts. — Also termed *comitas gentium*; *courtoisie internationale.* Cf. ABSTENTION.

> "A great deal of misconception about the nature of conflict of laws is due to the loose use of the term 'comity.' The laws of another state or nation, it has been sometimes said, can have no operation in another sovereignty except by comity. In the dictionary definition, comity means 'courtesy between equals; friendly civility.' Such a conception of the matter supposes one sovereign, as a matter of courtesy, allowing the law of another to operate within the territory of the first. If this were true, the determination of when, by comity, recognition would be given to foreign law would not be a predictable matter.... Courts use it, often loosely, and in cases correctly decided despite looseness of terms. It is clear

that the reference to foreign law in appropriate cases is dependent not upon a mere courtesy which a court may grant or withhold at will, but upon the need to achieve justice among parties to a controversy having foreign contacts." Herbert F. Goodrich & Eugene F. Scoles, *Handbook of the Conflict of Laws* § 7, at 7–8 (4th ed. 1964).

"The comity principle is most accurately characterized as a golden rule among nations — that each must give the respect to the laws, policies and interests of others that it would have others give to its own in the same or similar circumstances." Thomas Buergenthal & Harold G. Maier, *Public International Law in a Nutshell* 178 (2d ed. 1990).

judicial comity. The respect a court of one state or jurisdiction shows to another state or jurisdiction in giving effect to the other's laws and judicial decisions.

2. A rule of law having its origin in courtesy among political entities. **3.** INTERNATIONAL LAW. • This sense is considered a misusage: "[I]n Anglo–American jurisprudence, . . . the term is also misleadingly found to be used as a synonym for international law." Peter Macalister–Smith, "Comity," in 1 *Encyclopedia of Public International Law* 672 (1992).

Comity Clause. The clause of the U.S. Constitution giving citizens of one state the right to all privileges and immunities enjoyed by citizens of the other states. U.S. Const. art. IV, § 2, cl. 1. See PRIVILEGES AND IMMUNITIES CLAUSE.

command. 1. An order; a directive. **2.** In legal positivism, the sovereign's express desire that a person act or refrain from acting a certain way, combined with the threat of punishment for failure to comply.

"Commands are orders backed by threats. It is in virtue of threatened evils, sanctions, that expressions of desire not only constitute commands but also impose an obligation or duty to act in the prescribed ways." Martin P. Golding, *Philosophy of Law* 26 (1975).

command, *vb.* To direct authoritatively; to order.

commander-in-chief. 1. One who holds supreme or highest command of armed forces. **2.** (*cap.*) The title of the U.S. President when acting as the constitutionally designated leader of the nation's military. U.S. Const. art. II, § 2.

Commander in Chief Clause. The clause of the U.S. Constitution appointing the President as supreme commander of the military. U.S. Const. art. I, § 8, cl. 3.

commandment. *Hist.* **1.** An authoritative order of a judge or magisterial officer. **2.** The offense of inducing another to commit a crime.

commencement. See INTRODUCTORY CLAUSE.

commencement of infringement. *Copyright.* The first of a series of discrete copyright violations, such as the first of many separate sales of infringing items. See INFRINGEMENT.

commenda (kə-**men**-də). A business association in which one person has responsibility for managing all business property.

commendam (kə-**men**-dam *or* -dəm). **1.** *Eccles. law.* A vacant benefice held by a clerk until a regular pastor can be appointed. • Commendams were abolished in 1836. See BENEFICE. **2.** PARTNERSHIP IN COMMENDAM.

commendation. *Hist.* The act of becoming a lord's feudal tenant to receive the lord's protection.

commendator (**kom**-ən-day-tər). *Eccles. law.* A person holding a commendam (a benefice) as a trustee. • Commendators are so called because benefices are commended to their supervision. See COMMENDAM.

commendatus (kom-ən-**day**-təs). *Hist.* A person who, by voluntary oath of homage, was placed under a lord's protection.

comment, *n.* **1.** NOTE (2). **2.** An explanatory statement made by the drafters of a particular statute, code section, or rule. — **commentator,** *n.*

commentators. See POSTGLOSSATORS.

commenter. One who comments; esp., one who sends comments to an agency about a proposed administrative rule or regulation. See NOTICE-AND-COMMENT PERIOD.

comment on the evidence. A statement made to the jury by the judge or by counsel on the probative value of certain evidence. • Lawyers typically make such comments in closing argument — and judges may make such comments in federal court — but most state-court judges are not permitted to do so when examining a witness, instructing the jury, and the like (in which case the comment is sometimes termed an *impermissible comment on the evidence*).

comment period. See NOTICE-AND-COMMENT PERIOD.

commerce. The exchange of goods and services, esp. on a large scale involving transportation between cities, states, and nations.

interstate commerce. Trade and other business activities between those located in different states; esp., traffic in goods and travel of people between states. • For purposes of this phrase, most statutory definitions include a territory of the United States as a state. Some statutory definitions of *interstate commerce* include commerce between a foreign country and a state.

intrastate commerce. Commerce that begins and ends entirely within the borders of a single state.

Commerce Clause. U.S. Const. art. I, § 8, cl. 3, which gives Congress the exclusive power to regulate commerce among the states, with foreign nations, and with Indian tribes.

Dormant Commerce Clause. The constitutional principle that the Commerce Clause prevents state regulation of interstate commercial activity even when Congress has not acted under its Commerce Clause power to regulate that activity. — Also termed *Negative Commerce Clause.*

Commerce Court. See COURT.

commercia belli (kə-**mər**-shee-ə **bel**-I). [Latin "commerce of war"] Commercial dealings or contracts between nations at war, or between the subjects of nations at war, under which arrangements for nonhostile dealings are made.

commercial-activity exception. An exemption from the rule of sovereign immunity, permitting a claim against a foreign state if the claim arises from private acts undertaken by the foreign state, as opposed to the state's public acts. See RESTRICTIVE PRINCIPLE OF SOVEREIGN IMMUNITY; JURE GESTIONIS; JURE IMPERII.

commercial agent. 1. BROKER. **2.** A consular officer responsible for the commercial interests of his or her country at a foreign port.

commercial assets. See ASSET.

commercial bank. See BANK.

commercial bribery. See BRIBERY.

commercial broker. See BROKER.

commercial court. See COURT.

commercial credit company. See *commercial finance company* under FINANCE COMPANY.

commercial division. See *business court* under COURT.

commercial domicile. See DOMICILE.

commercial finance company. See FINANCE COMPANY.

commercial frustration. See FRUSTRATION.

commercial general liability policy. See *comprehensive general liability policy* under INSURANCE POLICY.

commercial impracticability. See IMPRACTICABILITY.

commercial insurance. See INSURANCE.

commercial law. 1. The substantive law dealing with the sale and distribution of goods, the financing of credit transactions on the security of the goods sold, and negotiable instruments. • Most American commercial law is governed by the Uniform Commercial Code. — Also termed *mercantile law.*

> "Although the term *commercial law* is not a term of art in American law it has become synonymous in recent years with the legal rules contained in the Uniform Commercial Code." Jonathan A. Eddy & Peter Winship, *Commercial Transactions* 1 (1985).

2. LAW MERCHANT.

commercial-law notice. See NOTICE.

commercial letter of credit. See LETTER OF CREDIT.

commercial loan. See LOAN.

commercially reasonable, *adj.* (Of a property sale) conducted in good faith and in accordance with commonly accepted commercial practice. • Under the UCC, a sale of collateral by a secured party must be done in a commercially reasonable manner, or the sale may be rescinded. UCC § 9–504.

> "[Section] 9–504 does impose two requirements upon the reselling creditor: (1) the creditor must send notice; and (2) every aspect of the sale including the method, man-

ner, time, place, and terms must be 'commercially reasonable.' The notice requirement is easy to understand and apply.... The second condition is both more important and more difficult to define in operational terms. Its importance lies in the fact that the amount of the deficiency judgment will be inversely proportional to the sales price; if the price is high, the amount of the judgment will be low, and vice versa. The 'method, manner, time, place and terms' tests are really proxies for 'insufficient price,' and their importance lies almost exclusively in the extent they protect against an unfairly low price." James J. White & Robert S. Summers, *Uniform Commercial Code* § 25–10, at 918 (4th ed. 1995).

commercial name. See TRADENAME.

commercial paper. See PAPER.

commercial partnership. See *trading partnership* under PARTNERSHIP.

commercial set. The primary documents covering shipment of goods, usu. including an invoice, bill of lading, bill of exchange, and certificate of insurance.

commercial speech. See SPEECH.

commercial surety. See *compensated surety* under SURETY.

commercial tort claim. A claim arising in tort when the claimant is either (1) an organization, or (2) an individual whose claim arose in the course of the claimant's business or profession, and the claim does not include damages arising out of personal injury or death. UCC § 9–102(a)(10).

commercial-traveler rule. The principle that an accident will be treated as occurring during the course of employment if it was caused by an employee whose job requires travel, and the employee was not on a personal errand. • The commercial-traveler rule is an exception to the going-and-coming rule.

commercial treaty. See TREATY.

commercial unit. A unit of goods that by commercial usage is a single whole for purposes of lease and whose division materially impairs its character or value in the relevant market or in use. UCC § 2–102(a)(7). • Under the UCC, "a commercial unit may be a single article, such as a machine; a set of articles, such as a suite of furniture or a line of machinery; a quantity, such as a gross or carload; or any other unit treated in use or in the relevant market as a single whole." *Id.*

comminatorium (kə-min-ə-**tor**-ee-əm). [Latin *comminari* "threaten"] *Hist.* A clause often included at the end of a writ, admonishing the sheriff to be faithful in the writ's execution.

commingle (kə-**ming**-gəl), *vb.* To put together in one mass, as when one mixes separate funds or properties into a common fund. — Also spelled *comingle.*

commingling (kə-**ming**-gling), *n.* A mixing together; esp., a fiduciary's mixing of personal funds with those of a beneficiary or client. • Commingling is usu. considered a breach of the fiduciary relationship. Under the Model Rules of Professional Conduct, a lawyer is prohibited from commingling personal funds with those of a client. — Also spelled *comingling.*

commissary (**kom**-i-ser-ee), *n.* **1.** A person who is delegated or commissioned to perform some duty, usu. as a representative of a superior. **2.** A general store, esp. on a military base; also, a lunchroom. — **commissary,** *adj.*

commission, *n.* **1.** A warrant or authority, from the government or a court, that empowers the person named to execute official acts <the student received his commission to the U.S. Navy after graduation>. **2.** The authority under which a person transacts business for another <the client gave her attorney express commission to sign the contract>. **3.** A body of persons acting under lawful authority to perform certain public services <the Federal Communications Commission>.

public-service commission. A commission created by a legislature to regulate public utilities or public-service corporations.

4. The act of doing or perpetrating (as a crime) <the perpetrator fled to Mexico after commission of the assault>. **5.** A fee paid to an agent or employee for a particular transaction, usu. as a percentage of the money received from the transaction <a real-estate agent's commission>.

double commission. A commission paid by both a seller and a buyer to the same person acting in different capacities, as when a person acts as both executor and trustee.

commission broker. See BROKER.

commission del credere (del **kred**-ər-ay). The commission received by the seller's agent for guaranteeing a buyer's debt.

commissioned officer. See OFFICER (2).

commissioner. **1.** A person who directs a commission; a member of a commission. **2.** The administrative head of an organization, such as a professional sport.

commissioner of bail. An officer appointed to take bail bonds.

commissioner of deeds. An officer authorized by a state to take acknowledgments of deeds and other papers while residing in another state. • The acknowledgments are recognized in the state that licensed the commissioner. Cf. NOTARY PUBLIC.

commissioner of highways. A public officer responsible for overseeing the construction, alteration, and repair of highways.

commissioner of woods and forests. *Hist.* An officer who, by an 1817 Act of Parliament, assumed the jurisdiction of the Chief Justice of the Forest.

county commissioner. A county officer charged usu. with the management of the county's financial affairs, its police regulations, and its corporate business. — Also termed *county supervisor*.

court commissioner. An officer appointed by the court esp. to hear and report facts, or to conduct judicial sales.

United States Commissioner. *Hist.* A judicial officer appointed by a U.S. district court to hear a variety of pretrial matters in criminal cases. • Commissioners' duties have been transferred to U.S. Magistrate Judges. Cf. UNITED STATES MAGISTRATE JUDGE.

commissioner's court. See COURT.

commission government. A type of municipal government in which the legislative power is in the hands of a few people.

commission merchant. See FACTOR.

commission of appraisement and sale. *Maritime law.* A court order requiring the sale of property in an in-rem admiralty action.

commission of assize. *Hist.* A royal authorization empowering a person to hold court and try cases arising while the justices in eyre held court elsewhere. Cf. EYRE.

> "[B]oth the presentment of crimes and the conduct of trials by assize or jury — which rapidly became a common feature of royal justice — required the presence of twelve or more men from the vicinity where the matter in question occurred.... The means of achieving this reconciliation was the frequent issue of commissions to perform judicial functions in the country.... [A]ssize commissioners had original jurisdiction to hear a case from beginning to end.... But the assizes, though moulded into a regular routine, never became a distinct 'court' in the permanent sense. The jurisdiction of the judges rested entirely on the commissions which issued for each circuit: the judges could therefore be regularly interchanged, and after 1340 it was quite normal for a Common Plea case to be tried at nisi prius by a King's Bench judge, and vice versa." J.H. Baker, *An Introduction to English Legal History* 67 (3d ed. 1990).

commission of charitable uses. *Hist.* An authorization issuing out of the Court of Chancery to a bishop or other person authorizing the appointee to investigate allegations of fraud or other disputed matters concerning charitable land grants.

commission of delegates. *Hist.* A commission appointing a person (usu. a lord, bishop, or judge) to sit with several other appointees to hear an appeal of an ecclesiastical judgment in the Court of Chancery. • This commission was abolished in 1832, and its functions transferred to the Judicial Committee of the Privy Council.

Commission of Gaol Delivery. *Hist.* A royal appointment authorizing a judge to go on the assize circuit and hear all criminal cases of those held in county jails. See JAIL DELIVERY. Cf. COMMISSION OF OYER AND TERMINER.

commission of lieutenancy. *Hist.* A commission issued to send officers into every county to establish military order over the inhabitants. • This commission superseded the former *commission of array*, which provided the same powers. The commissions became obsolete with the establishment of the militia system.

commission of lunacy. See DE LUNATICO INQUIRENDO.

Commission of Oyer and Terminer (**oy**-ər an[d] **tər**-mə-nər). [Law French *oyer et terminer* "to hear and determine"] *Hist.* A royal appointment authorizing a judge (often a serjeant-at-law) to go on the assize circuit and hear felony and treason cases. Cf. COMMISSION OF GAOL DELIVERY; COURT OF OYER AND TERMINER.

> "[U]nder the commission of *Oyer and Terminer*, as the judges are directed to *inquire* as well as to hear and determine the same, they can only proceed upon an indictment found at the same assize, and before themselves; for they must first *inquire* by means of the grand jury or inquest, before they are empowered to hear and determine by the intervention of the petit jury." 1 Joseph Chitty, *A Practical Treatise on the Criminal Law* 142 (2d ed. 1826).

commission of partition. An authorization appointing a person to sit with several other appointees for the purpose of dividing land held by tenants in common who desire a partition.

commission of rebellion. *Hist.* An attaching process that empowered a layperson to arrest and bring a defendant to Chancery to enforce obedience to a writ of subpoena or decree. • The commission of rebellion was abolished in 1841. — Also termed *writ of rebellion*; *commissio rebellionis*; *breve rebellionis*.

> "*Commission of rebellion* (*Commissio rebellionis*) is otherwise called a writte of rebellion, (*breve rebellionis*) and it hath use, when a man after proclamation made by the Shyreeve upon an order of the channcerie, or court of Starre chamber, under penaltie of his allegance, to present himselfe to the court by a certaine day, appeareth not. And this commission is directed by way of command to certain persons, to this end, that they ... apprehend, or cause to be apprehended, the party as a rebell and contemner of the kings lawes." John Cowell, *The Interpreter* (1607).

commission of review. *Hist.* In England, an authorization sometimes granted in an extraordinary case to review a judgment of the Court of Delegates. • The commission of review is no longer used because the Privy Council was substituted for the Court of Delegates as the appellate court in ecclesiastical cases in 1832. See COURT OF DELEGATES.

commission of the peace. *Hist.* An appointment of a person to keep the peace (i.e., provide police protection) on a local level. • Over time the recipients of these commissions began to acquire judicial responsibilities, and became known as justices of the peace.

commission of unlivery (ən-**liv**-ər-ee). *Hist.* A court order requiring the unloading of goods from a ship so that they may be appraised.

commission plan. A form of municipal government whereby both legislative and executive power is vested in a small group of elected officials. • Today, commission plans are used in only a few cities.

commission to examine a witness. A judicial commission directing that a witness beyond the court's territorial jurisdiction be deposed. Cf. LETTER OF REQUEST.

commissio rebellionis. See COMMISSION OF REBELLION.

commissive waste. See WASTE (1).

commissoria lex (kom-i-**sor**-ee-ə **leks**). [Latin "forfeiture clause"] *Roman law.* **1.** An agreement in which a seller could rescind the sale if the purchaser failed to pay for the item at the appointed time. **2.** A clause allowing a creditor to take a debtor's collateral if the debtor failed to pay the debt.

commit, *vb.* **1.** To perpetrate (a crime). **2.** To send (a person) to prison or to a mental health facility, esp. by court order.

commitment, *n.* **1.** An agreement to do something in the future, esp. to assume a financial obligation <the shipper had a firm commitment>. **2.** The act of entrusting or giving in charge <commitment of money to the bank>. **3.** The act of confining a person in a prison, mental hospital, or other institution <commitment of the felon to prison>. **4.** The order directing an officer to take a person to a penal or mental institution; MITTIMUS <the judge signed the commitment after ruling that it was in the best interest of the troubled teen>.

civil commitment. A confinement order for a person who is ill, incompetent, drug-addicted, or the like, as contrasted with a criminal sentence; the confinement itself.

commitment fee. An amount paid to a lender by a potential borrower for the lender's promise to lend money at a stipulated rate and within a specified time. • Commitment fees are common in real estate transactions. See LOAN COMMITMENT.

commitment letter. A lender's written offer to grant a mortgage loan. • The letter generally outlines the loan amount, the interest rate, and other terms.

commitment warrant. See *warrant of commitment* under WARRANT (1).

committee. 1. (kə-**mit**-ee) A group of people appointed or elected to consider, determine, or manage a matter <the bill was sent to legislative committee>.

conference committee. A joint legislative committee that meets to adjust differences in a bill passed in different versions by both houses.

congressional committee. A committee of the House of Representatives or the Senate, or a joint committee formed for some particular purpose.

joint committee. A legislative committee composed of members of both houses of a legislature.

legislative committee. A group of legislators appointed to help a legislature conduct its business, esp. by providing careful consideration of proposals for new legislation within a particular field so that the entire body can handle its work efficiently without wasting time and effort on unmeritorious submissions.

permanent committee. See *standing committee.*

special committee. A temporary legislative committee appointed for a nonlegislative purpose, such as writing memorials, procuring chaplains, determining the qualifications of members, and settling election disputes. — Also termed *select committee.*

standing committee. A permanent legislative committee concerned with a specific field of legislation. • A standing committee usu. considers basic questions of legislative policy, holds hearings on legislation, eliminates unwanted bills, and prepares favored measures for passage. — Also termed *permanent committee.*

2. (kom-i-**tee**) A person who is civilly committed, usu. to a psychiatric hospital <the board determined that the committee was dangerous and should not be released>. **3.** (kom-i-**tee**) The guardian for the person so committed <the patient's lawyer objected to the appointment of the committee>.

committee of the whole. An entire legislative house sitting as a committee and operating under informal procedural rules.

committing magistrate. See MAGISTRATE.

committitur (kə-**mit**-ə-tər). [Latin "he is committed"] An order or minute stating that the person named in it is to be committed to the custody of the sheriff.

committitur piece. *Hist.* An instrument used to civilly charge a debtor already in prison, esp. by the plaintiff who had brought about the debtor's imprisonment. • The committitur piece was rendered obsolete by the 1869 Debtors Act, which abolished imprisonment for debt.

commixtio (kə-**miks**-tee-oh). [Latin "mixture"] *Roman law.* A mixture of dry or solid items belonging to different owners, the resulting mixture being held in common or divided in proportion to the shares contributed. Cf. CONFUSIO. See CONFUSION OF GOODS.

commodati actio (kom-ə-**day**-tI **ak**-shee-oh). See *actio commodati* under ACTIO.

commodatum (kom-ə-**day**-təm), *n.* [Latin *commodare* "to lend"] *Roman & civil law.* A bailment involving the gratuitous loan of goods to be used by the bailee and then returned to the bailor. • This type of bailment is for the sole benefit of the bailee. This is one of three types of contracts for permissive use, the other two being *locatio conductio* and *mutuum.* — Also termed *accommodatum.*

commodity. 1. An article of trade or commerce. • The term embraces only tangible goods, such as products or merchandise, as distinguished from services. **2.** An economic good, esp. a raw material or an agricultural product.

commodity-backed bond. See BOND (3).

Commodity Credit Corporation. A federal agency that, through loan subsidies and loan purchases, supports prices of agricultural products to help sell the products in domestic and foreign markets. — Abbr. CCC.

Commodity Futures Trading Commission. A federal agency that supervises the trading of commodity futures and commodity options. — Abbr. CFTC.

commodity loan. See LOAN.

commodity option. See OPTION.

commodity paper. See PAPER.

common, *n.* **1.** A legal right to use another person's property, such as an easement. See PROFIT A PRENDRE.

common appendant (ə-**pen**-dənt). *Hist.* A tenant's right to graze animals on the landowner's land as a result of longstanding practice.

common appurtenant (ə-**pər**-tə-nənt). *Hist.* A landowner's right to graze animals on another's land as a result of a written grant relating to the ownership or occupancy of land.

common in gross. *Hist.* A right to graze animals on another's land as a result of a written grant unrelated to ownership or occupancy of land. — Also termed *common at large*.

common in the soil. *Hist.* The right to dig and take away earth from another's land. — Also termed *common of digging*.

common of estovers (e-**stoh**-vərz). *Hist.* A tenant's right to take necessary supplies, esp. wood, from the lord's estate; the right to estovers. See ESTOVER (1).

common of fishery. See *common of piscary*.

common of pasture. *Hist.* A right to pasture one's cattle on another's land. • The common of pasture may be appendant, appurtenant, or in gross.

common of piscary (**pis**-kə-ree). *Hist.* A right to fish in waters on another's land. — Often shortened to *piscary*. — Also termed *common of fishery*.

common of shack. *Hist.* The right of people occupying land in a common field to release their cattle to graze after harvest.

common of turbary (**tər**-bə-ree). *Hist.* The right to dig turf (for use as fuel in a house) from another's land.

2. A tract of land set aside for the general public's use.

commonable, *adj.* **1.** (Of an animal) allowed to graze on common land. **2.** (Of land) that can be held in common.

commonality test. The principle that a group seeking to be certified as a class in a class-action suit must share at least one issue whose resolution will affect all or a significant number of the putative class members.

common and notorious thief. See *common thief* under THIEF.

common appendant. See COMMON.

common appurtenant. See COMMON.

common area. 1. *Landlord-tenant law.* The realty that all tenants may use though the landlord retains control and responsibility over it. **2.** An area owned and used in common by the residents of a condominium, subdivision, or planned-unit development. — Also termed *common elements*.

common assumpsit. See *general assumpsit* under ASSUMPSIT.

common assurance. See MUNIMENT OF TITLE.

common at large. See *common in gross* under COMMON.

common-authority rule. The principle that a person may consent to a law officer's search of another's property if both persons use, control, or have access to the property.

common bail. See *bail common* under BAIL (3).

common bar. See BLANK BAR.

Common Bench. *Hist.* The former name of the English Court of Common Pleas. • The court was so called because it was the forum for the common people, that is, for cases between two or more subjects when the Crown had no interest. — Abbr. C.B.

common-bond doctrine. The rule that prospective members of a credit union must share some connection (such as common employment) other than a desire to create a credit union.

common business purpose. Related activity by two or more associated businesses. • If one of the businesses comes within the jurisdiction of the Fair Labor Standards Act, then another business that shares a common business purpose will also.

common calling. 1. An ordinary occupation that a citizen has a right to pursue under the Privileges and Immunities Clause. **2.** A commercial enterprise that offers services to the general public, with a legal duty to serve anyone who requests the services.

> "It was only in a very few cases indeed that a person was under a legal obligation to enter into a contract; virtually the only example of such an obligation in fact was the person exercising a 'common calling' such as the innkeeper and the common carrier who were (subject to certain safeguards) legally bound to contract with any member of the public who required their services." P.S. Atiyah, *An Introduction to the Law of Contract* 8 (3d ed. 1981).

common carrier. See CARRIER.

common cause. See *common plea* under PLEA (3).

common-character requirement. The rule that for a group of persons to qualify as a class in a class-action lawsuit, the appointment of the class must achieve economies of time, effort, and expense, and must promote uniformity of decision for persons similarly situated in addition to sharing common questions of fact and law.

common cost. See *indirect cost* under COST.

common council. See COUNCIL.

common count. See COUNT.

common court. See COURT.

common day. See DAY.

common-defeasance bond. See *penal bond* under BOND (2).

common descriptive name. See GENERIC NAME.

common design. **1.** The intention by two or more people to join in committing an unlawful act. **2.** An intention to commit more than one crime. **3.** The general design or layout of plots of land surrounding a particular tract. — Also termed *common scheme*; *common plan*. See ZONING.

common disaster. An event that causes two or more persons with related property interests (such as an insured and the beneficiary) to die at very nearly the same time, with no way to tell who died first. See SIMULTANEOUS-DEATH ACT.

common-disaster clause. A provision in a dispositive instrument, such as an insurance policy or a will, that seeks to cover the situation in which the transferor and transferee die in a common disaster.

common duty of care. A landowner's obligation to take reasonable care under the circumstances to see that a lawful visitor will be reasonably safe in using the premises for the purposes for which the visitor is permitted to be there.

common easement. See EASEMENT.

common elements. See COMMON AREA (2).

common-employment doctrine. See FELLOW-SERVANT RULE.

common-enemy doctrine. *Property.* The rule that a landowner may repel surface waters as necessary (as during a flood), without having to consider the consequences to upper landowners. • The doctrine takes its name from the idea that the floodwater is every landowner's common enemy.

common enterprise. See JOINT ENTERPRISE.

commoner. **1.** *BrE.* An ordinary citizen; one not a peer. **2.** *Archaic.* A member of the House of Commons. **3.** *Archaic.* A common lawyer. **4.** *Archaic.* A person having a right of common — that is, a right to pasture on a lord's land. **5.** A person who shares a right in common.

common error. *Copyright.* A mistake found both in a copyrighted work and in an alleged infringing work, the mistake being persuasive evidence of unauthorized copying.

common fine. See FINE (4).

common fishery. See FISHERY (2).

common-fund doctrine. The principle that if a plaintiff or his or her attorney creates, discovers, increases, or preserves a fund to which others also have a claim, then the plaintiff is entitled to recover from the fund the litigation costs and attorney's fees. — Also termed *equitable-fund doctrine*.

common heritage of mankind. *Int'l law.* The parts of the earth and cosmos that can be said to belong to human posterity, without regard for geographic location. • The term embraces the ocean floor and its subsoil, and outer space. — Also termed *common heritage of humankind*.

common highway. See HIGHWAY.

common informer. A person who sues to recover a penalty in a penal action. • In some jurisdictions, such an action may be instituted either by the attorney general on behalf of the state or by a common informer. See INFORMER; *penal action* under ACTION.

common in gross. See COMMON.

common intendment. See INTENDMENT.

common-interest doctrine. See *joint-defense privilege* under PRIVILEGE (3).

common in the soil. See COMMON.

common jury. See *petit jury* under JURY.

common knowledge. A fact that is so generally known that a court may accept it as true without proof. See JUDICIAL NOTICE.

common-knowledge exception. The principle that lay testimony concerning routine or simple medical procedures is admissible to establish negligence in a medical-malpractice action. • This is a narrow exception in some jurisdictions to the rule that a medical-malpractice plaintiff must present expert testimony to establish negligence.

common law, *n.* [fr. Law French *commen ley* "common law"] **1.** The body of law derived from judicial decisions, rather than from statutes or constitutions; CASELAW <federal common law>. Cf. STATUTORY LAW.

> "Historically, [the common law] is made quite differently from the Continental code. The code precedes judgments; the common law follows them. The code articulates in chapters, sections, and paragraphs the rules in accordance with which judgments are given. The common law on the other hand is inarticulate until it is expressed in a judgment. Where the code governs, it is the judge's duty to ascertain the law from the words which the code uses. Where the common law governs, the judge, in what is now the forgotten past, decided the case in accordance with morality and custom and later judges followed his decision. They did not do so by construing the words of his judgment. They looked for the reason which had made him decide the case the way he did, the *ratio decidendi* as it came to be called. Thus it was the principle of the case, not the words, which went into the common law. So historically the common law is much less fettering than a code." Patrick Devlin, *The Judge* 177 (1979).

federal common law. The judge-made law of federal courts, excluding the law in all cases governed by state law. • An example is the nonstatutory law applying to interstate streams of commerce.

general federal common law. *Hist.* In the period before *Erie v. Tompkins* (304 U.S. 64, 58 S.Ct. 817 (1938)), the judge-made law developed by federal courts in deciding disputes in diversity cases. • Since *Erie* was announced in 1938, a federal court has been bound to apply, as a general matter, the law of the state in which it sits. Thus, although there is a "federal common law," there is no *general* federal common law applicable to all disputes heard in federal court.

2. The body of law based on the English legal system, as distinct from a civil-law system <all states except Louisiana have the common law as their legal system>. Cf. CIVIL LAW (1). **3.** General law common to the country as a whole, as opposed to special law that has only local application <the issue is whether the common law trumps our jurisdiction's local rules>. — Also termed *jus commune.*

> "In its historical origin the term common law (*jus commune*) was identical in meaning with the term general law .... The *jus commune* was the general law of the land — the *lex terrae* — as opposed to *jus speciale*. By a process of historical development, however, the common law has now become, not the entire general law, but only the residue of that law after deducting equity and statute law. It is no longer possible, therefore, to use the expression common law and general law as synonymous." John Salmond, *Jurisprudence* 97 (Glanville L. Williams ed., 10th ed. 1947).

> "[I]t is necessary to dispose briefly of a problem of nomenclature. European equivalents of the expression 'common law' have been used, especially in Germany, to describe an emergent system of national law, based on the Roman model, that came into existence before national parliaments undertook to enact laws for the nation as a whole. In this use, 'the common law' (*gemeines Recht*) was used to distinguish the commonly shared tradition of Roman law from local statutes and customs." Lon L. Fuller, *Anatomy of the Law* 133 (1968).

4. The body of law deriving from law courts as opposed to those sitting in equity <a mortgage founded in common law>. • The common law of England was one of the three main historical sources of English law. The other two were legislation and equity. The common law evolved from custom and was the body of law created by and administered by the king's courts. Equity developed to overcome the occasional rigidity and unfairness of the common law. Originally the king himself granted or denied petitions in equity; later the task fell to the chancellor, and later still to the Court of Chancery. **5.** The body of law to which no constitution or statute applies <the common law used by lawyers to settle disputes>.

common-law action. See ACTION.

common-law assignment. See ASSIGNMENT (2).

common-law bond. See BOND (2).

common-law cheat. See CHEATING.

common-law contempt. See *criminal contempt* under CONTEMPT.

common-law copyright. See COPYRIGHT.

common-law corporation. See *corporation by prescription* under CORPORATION.

common-law crime. See CRIME.

common-law dedication. See DEDICATION.

common-law extortion. See EXTORTION (1).

common-law fraud. See *promissory fraud* under FRAUD.

common-law jurisdiction. See JURISDICTION.

common-law lawyer. A lawyer who is versed in or practices under a common-law system. — Also termed *common lawyer.*

common-law lien. See LIEN.

common-law malice. See MALICE.

common-law marriage. See MARRIAGE (1).

common-law pleading. See PLEADING (2).

common-law rule. 1. A judge-made rule as opposed to a statutory one. **2.** A legal as opposed to an equitable rule. **3.** A general rule as opposed to one deriving from special law (such as a local custom or a rule of foreign law that, based on choice-of-law principles, is applied in place of domestic law). **4.** An old rule of English law.

common-law state. 1. See NONCODE STATE. **2.** Any state that is not a community-property state. Cf. COMMUNITY-PROPERTY STATE.

common-law trust. See *business trust* under TRUST.

common lawyer. See COMMON-LAW LAWYER.

common market. See MARKET.

Common Market. The European Economic Community. • *Common Market* is a colloquial term — not a formal designation.

common mistake. See *mutual mistake* (2) under MISTAKE.

common money bond. See BOND (2).

common-nucleus-of-operative-fact test. The doctrine that a federal court will have jurisdiction over state-law claims that arise from the same facts as the federal claims providing a basis for subject-matter jurisdiction.

> "The modern doctrine of pendent jurisdiction, as announced by the Supreme Court in United Mine Workers v. Gibbs (1966), is much broader.... Pendent jurisdiction, the Court said, existed whenever 'the state and federal claims ... derive from a common nucleus of operative fact,' and when considerations of judicial economy dictate having a single trial." David P. Currie, *Federal Jurisdiction in a Nutshell* 106 (3d ed. 1990).

common nuisance. See *public nuisance* under NUISANCE.

common occupant. See *general occupant* under OCCUPANT.

common of digging. See *common in the soil* under COMMON.

common of estovers. See COMMON.

common of fishery. See *common of piscary* under COMMON.

common of pasture. See COMMON.

common of piscary. See COMMON.

common of shack. See COMMON.

common of turbary. See COMMON.

common plan. See COMMON DESIGN.

common plea. See PLEA (3).

Common Pleas, Court of. See COURT OF COMMON PLEAS.

common property. See PROPERTY.

common recovery. *Hist.* An elaborate proceeding, full of legal fictions, by which a tenant in tail disentailed a fee-tail estate. • The action facilitated land transfer by allowing a potential transferee who was barred by law from receiving land to "recover" the land by suing the actual owner. Common recoveries, which were abolished early in the 19th century, were originally concocted by the clergy as a way to avoid the land-conveyance restrictions imposed by mortmain acts. — Also termed *feigned recovery.* See MORTMAIN STATUTE. Cf. CESSIO IN JURE; PRAECIPE QUOD REDDAT.

> "Here's how [the common recovery] worked. B, with the connivance of A, would bring a real action against A claiming falsely that he, B, owned the land and demanding recovery of it. A responded by claiming, just as falsely, that he had acquired the land from C and that C had warranted title to the land. When A demanded of C,

also an accomplice of A, that he defend the title, C admitted falsely that he had, indeed, warranted the title. C allowed B to take a default judgment against A for the recovery of the land, and allowed A to obtain a default judgment against himself, C, for the recovery of land of equal value. The result of this fancy feudal footwork was to leave B with title to the land in fee simple and to leave A with his judgment against C. The judgment against C was viewed by the court as an adequate substitute for the entailed land. But when it came time for O or A's lineal heirs to enforce the judgment, it would transpire that C had been selected by A because he had no land at all! (Why else would C have played along?) Did the court have any suspicion that A, B, and C were colluding? Of course they did — but how else, in the face of *De Donis*, could they unshackle land from the chains of the fee tail?" Thomas F. Bergin & Paul G. Haskell, *Preface to Estates in Land and Future Interests* 31–32 (2d ed. 1984).

common-return days. See *dies communes in banco* under DIES.

common scheme. See COMMON DESIGN.

common school. See *public school* under SCHOOL.

common scold. See SCOLD.

common-situs picketing. See PICKETING.

common-source doctrine. The principle that a defendant in a trespass-to-try-title action who claims under a source common to both the defendant and the plaintiff may not demonstrate title in a third source that is paramount to the common source, because doing so amounts to an attack on the source under which the defendant claims title.

common stock. See STOCK.

common-stock equivalent. A security that is exchangeable for common stock, and thus is considered to be the same as common stock. • Common-stock equivalents include certain types of convertible securities, stock options, and warrants.

common-stock fund. See MUTUAL FUND.

common-stock ratio. The relationship of outstanding common stock to the corporation's total capitalization. • The common-stock ratio measures the relative claims of stockholders to earnings (earnings per share and payout ratio), cash flow (cash flow per share), and equity (book value per share). Cf. PAYOUT RATIO.

common substitution. See SUBSTITUTION (3).

common suit. See *common plea* under PLEA (2).

common tenancy. See *tenancy in common* under TENANCY.

common thief. See THIEF.

common traverse. See TRAVERSE.

common trust fund. See TRUST FUND.

common wall. See *party wall* under WALL.

commonweal (**kom**-ən-weel). The general welfare; the common good.

commonwealth. 1. A nation, state, or other political unit <the Commonwealth of Pennsylvania>. **2.** A political unit that has local autonomy but is voluntarily united with the United States <Puerto Rico and the Northern Mariana Islands are commonwealths>. Cf. DEPENDENCY; TERRITORY. **3.** A loose association of countries that recognize one sovereign <the British Commonwealth>. • In this context, in Great Britain, the term *British* has been dropped from *British Commonwealth*; BrE speakers refer simply to *the Commonwealth*. — Abbr. Commw.; comm. **4.** The central (federal) power in Australia. — Abbr. (in sense 4) Cwth.

commonwealth court. See COURT.

commorancy (**kom**-ə-rən-see). **1.** A temporary residency. **2.** *English law.* Permanent residency in a certain place.

commorant (**kom**-ə-rənt). **1.** A person who dwells in a place temporarily. **2.** *English law.* A person who resides permanently in a certain place.

commorientes (kə-mor-ee-**en**-teez). [fr. Latin *commorior* "to die together"] **1.** Persons who die at the same time, such as spouses who die in an accident. **2.** *Civil law.* The rule of succession regarding such persons. See *simultaneous death* under DEATH; SIMULTANEOUS-DEATH ACT.

commune (**kom**-yoon), *n.* A community of people who share property.

commune forum (kə-**myoo**-nee **for**-əm). [Latin "common place of justice"] *Hist.* The seat of the principal English courts, esp. those that do not go on circuit.

commune placitum (kə-**myoo**-nee **plas**-ə-təm). [Latin "common plea"] *Hist.* A common plea between persons, as opposed to a plea of the Crown (i.e., a criminal action). Pl. ***communia placita.***

commune vinculum (kə-**myoo**-nee **ving**-kyə-ləm). [Latin "common bond"] *Hist.* A relationship or link between persons; esp., the bond between lord and tenant, or the relationship between relatives.

communia (kə-**myoo**-nee-ə). [Latin] *Hist.* Things owned in common, such as running water, the air, and the sea.

communia placita non tenenda in scaccario (kə-**myoo**-nee-ə **plas**-ə-tə non tə-**nen**-də in skə-**kair**-ee-oh). [Law Latin "common pleas are not held in the Exchequer"] *Hist.* A writ directed to the Treasurer and Barons of the Exchequer, forbidding them from holding pleas between common persons, i.e., pleas in which the Crown was not a party.

communication. 1. The expression or exchange of information by speech, writing, or gestures. **2.** The information so expressed or exchanged.

conditionally privileged communication. A defamatory statement made in good faith by a person with an interest in a subject to someone who also has an interest in the subject, as an employer giving a poor but accurate job review of a former employee to a potential future employer. • The privilege may be lost on a showing of malice or bad faith.

confidential communication. A communication made within a certain protected relationship — such as husband-wife, attorney-client, or priest-penitent — and legally protected from forced disclosure.

privileged communication. A communication that is protected by law from forced disclosure. See PRIVILEGE (3).

communicative evidence. See *testimonial evidence* under EVIDENCE.

communi consensu (kə-**myoo**-nɪ kən-**sen**-s[y]oo). [Latin] By common consent.

communi dividundo. See DE COMMUNI DIVIDUNDO.

communio bonorum (kə-**myoo**-nee-oh bə-**nor**-əm). [Latin "community of goods"] *Civil law.* Commonly owned goods, esp. those held in common by a husband and wife.

communis opinio (kə-**myoo**-nis ə-**pin**-ee-oh). [Latin "common opinion"] *Hist.* A generally accepted belief about a point of law. • If held unanimously by those learned in the law, this common belief had the force of law in classical Rome.

> "*Communis opinio* is evidence of what the law is, — not where it is an opinion merely speculative and theoretical, floating in the minds of persons, but where it has been made the ground-work and *substratum* of practice." 1 Alexander M. Burrill, *A Law Dictionary and Glossary* 330 (2d ed. 1867) (quoting Lord Ellenborough).

communis opinio doctorum (kə-**myoo**-nis ə-**pin**-ee-oh dok-**tor**-əm). [Latin "learned common opinion"] *Hist.* Scholarly agreement on points of Roman law, collected by the glossators of Justinian's texts in the later Middle Ages.

communis paries (kə-**myoo**-nis **par**-ee-eez). [Latin "common wall"] *Civil law.* See PARTY WALL.

communis scriptura (kə-**myoo**-nis skrip-**t[y]oor**-əkəm-**myoo**-nəs-skrip-**tyuur**-ə). [Latin "common writing"] *Hist.* See CHIROGRAPH.

communis stipes (kə-**myoo**-nis **stɪ**-peez). [Latin "common trunk"] *Hist.* A common ancestor.

communitization (kə-myoo-nə-tə-**zay**-shən), *n. Oil & gas.* The aggregating of small tracts sufficient for the granting of a well permit under applicable well-spacing rules. — Also termed *pooling*. — **communitize** (kə-**myoo**-nə-tɪz), *vb.* Cf. UNITIZATION.

community. 1. A neighborhood, vicinity, or locality. **2.** A society or group of people with similar rights or interests. **3.** A collection of common interests that arise from an association.

community account. See ACCOUNT.

community debt. See DEBT.

community lease. See LEASE.

community of interest. 1. Participation in a joint venture characterized by shared liability and shared opportunity for profit. See JOINT VENTURE. **2.** A common grievance that must be shared by all class members to maintain the class action. See CLASS ACTION. **3.** *Labor law.* A criterion used by the National Labor Relations Board in deciding whether a group of employees should be allowed to act as a bargaining unit. • The Board considers whether the employees have similar duties, wages, hours, benefits, skills, training, supervision, and working conditions. See BARGAINING UNIT.

community property. Property owned in common by husband and wife as a result of its having been acquired during the marriage by means other than an inheritance or a gift to one spouse, each spouse holding a one-half interest in the property. • Only nine states have community-property systems: Arizona, California, Idaho, Louisiana, Nevada, New Mexico, Texas, Washington, and Wisconsin. See *marital property* under PROPERTY. Cf. SEPARATE PROPERTY.

community-property state. A state in which spouses hold property that is acquired during marriage (other than property acquired by inheritance or individual gift) as community property. See COMMUNITY PROPERTY. Cf. COMMON-LAW STATE.

community trust. An agency organized to permanently administer funds placed in trust for public-health, educational, and charitable purposes.

commutation (kom-yə-**tay**-shən), *n.* **1.** An exchange or replacement. **2.** *Criminal law.* The executive's substitution in a particular case of a less severe punishment for a more severe one that has already been judicially imposed on the defendant. Cf. PARDON; REPRIEVE. **3.** *Commercial & civil law.* The substitution of one form of payment for the other. — **commute,** *vb.* — **commutative,** *adj.*

commutation of taxes. A tax exemption resulting from a taxpayer's paying either a lump sum or a specific sum in lieu of an ad valorem tax.

commutative contract. See CONTRACT.

commutative justice. See JUSTICE (1).

commuted value (kə-**myoo**-tid). **1.** In the assessment of damages, the present value of a future interest in property. **2.** The value of future payments when discounted to present value.

Commw. *abbr.* COMMONWEALTH.

compact (**kom**-pakt), *n.* An agreement or covenant between two or more parties, esp. between governments or states.

interstate compact. A voluntary agreement between states enacted into law in the participating states upon federal congressional approval. Cf. INTERSTATE AGREEMENT.

Compact Clause. U.S. Const. art. I, § 10, cl. 3, which disallows a state from entering into a contract with another state or a foreign country without congressional approval.

companionship services. Assistance provided to someone who needs help with personal matters such as bathing and dressing. • This type of service (in contrast to housecleaning) is exempt from the Federal Labor Standards Act's minimum-wage and overtime requirements.

company. A corporation — or, less commonly, an association, partnership, or union — that carries on a commercial or industrial enterprise; a corporation, partnership, association, joint-stock company, trust, fund, or organized group of persons, whether incorporated or not, and (in an official capacity) any receiver, trustee in bankruptcy, or similar official, or liquidating agent, for any of the foregoing. Investment Company Act § 2(a)(8) (15 USCA § 80a–2(a)(8)). — Abbr. co.; com.

bonding company. A company that insures a party against a loss caused by a third party.

controlled company. A company that is under the control of an individual, group, or corporation that owns most of the company's voting stock. Cf. *subsidiary corporation* under CORPORATION.

dead-and-buried company. A business that has dissolved, leaving no assets.

deposit company. An institution whose business is the safekeeping of securities or other valuables deposited in boxes or safes leased to the depositors. See DEPOSITARY; DEPOSITORY.

development-stage company. *Securities.* A company that devotes substantially all of its efforts to establishing a new business in which the principal operations either have not yet begun or have begun but without significant revenue.

diversified holding company. A holding company that controls several unrelated companies or businesses.

diversified investment company. An investment company that by law must invest 75% of its assets, but may not invest more than 5% of its assets in any one company or hold more than 10% of the voting shares in any one company.

face-amount certificate company. An investment company that is engaged or proposes to engage in the business of issuing face-amount certificates of the installment type, or that has been engaged in this business and has such a certificate outstanding. See *investment company*.

growth company. A company whose earnings have increased at a rapid pace and that usu. directs a high proportion of income back into the business.

guaranty company. See *surety company*.

holding company. A company formed to control other companies, usu. confining its role to owning stock and supervising management.

investment company. A company formed to acquire and manage a portfolio of diverse assets by investing money collected from different sources. • The Investment Company Act of 1940 defines the term as an issuer of securities that (1) is, holds itself out to be, or proposes to be engaged primarily in the business of investing, reinvesting, or trading in securities; (2) is engaged or proposes to engage in the business of issuing face-amount certificates of the installment type, or has been engaged in this business and has such a certificate outstanding; or (3) is engaged or proposes to engage in the business of investing, reinvesting, owning, holding, or trading in securities, and owns or proposes to acquire investment securities having a value exceeding 40% of the value of the issuer's total assets (exclusive of government securities and cash items) on an unconsolidated basis. 15 USCA § 80a–2(a)(16). — Also termed *investment trust*. See REAL-ESTATE INVESTMENT TRUST; MUTUAL FUND.

joint-stock company. **1.** An unincorporated association of individuals possessing common capital, the capital being contributed by the members and divided into shares, of which each member possesses a number of shares proportionate to the member's investment. **2.** A partnership in which the capital is divided into shares that are transferable without the express consent of the partners. — Also termed *joint-stock association*; *stock association*.

"The joint stock association or company developed early in English company law, the term being used to distinguish companies which operated on a joint account and with a 'joint stock' (in trade) of their members from companies (now obsolete) each member of whom traded on one's separate account with one's own stock in trade.... In American jurisdictions, the joint stock association is generally an unincorporated business enterprise with ownership interests represented by shares of stock." Henry G. Henn & John R. Alexander, *Laws of Corporations* § 50, at 109 (3d ed. 1983).

limited company. A company in which the liability of each shareholder is limited to the amount individually invested. • A corporation is the most common example of a limited company.

limited-liability company. A company — statutorily authorized in certain states — that is characterized by limited liability, management by members or managers, and limitations on ownership transfer. — Abbr. L.L.C. — Also termed *limited-liability corporation*.

management company. Any investment company that is neither a face-amount certificate company nor a unit-investment trust. See *investment company*; *face-amount certificate company*; *unit-investment trust* under TRUST.

mutual company. A company that is owned by its customers rather than by a separate group of stockholders. • Many insurance companies are mutual companies, as are many federal savings-and-loan associations. See MUTUAL INSURANCE COMPANY.

personal holding company. A holding company that is subject to special taxes and that usu. has a limited number of shareholders, with most of its revenue originating from passive income such as dividends, interest, rent, and royalties.

reporting company. See REPORTING COMPANY.

surety company. A company authorized to engage in the business of entering into guaranty and suretyship contracts and acting as a surety on bonds, esp. bail, fidelity, and judicial bonds. — Also termed *guaranty company*.

title company. A company that examines real-estate titles for any encumbrances, claims, or other flaws, and issues title insurance. — Also termed *title-guaranty company*. See TITLE SEARCH.

trust company. A company that acts as a trustee for people and entities and that sometimes also operates as a commercial bank. See TITLE.

company union. See UNION.

comparable (**kom**-pər-ə-bəl), *n.* (*usu. pl.*) A piece of property used as a comparison to determine the value of a similar piece of property.

comparable accommodation. A standard used for determining the maximum allowable rent in rent-regulated housing. • In applying this standard, a court reviews the prevailing rent for substantially similar housing units in the same area.

comparable worth. **1.** The analogous value that two or more employees bring to a business through their work. **2.** The idea that employees who perform identical work should receive identical pay, regardless of their sex; the doctrine that men and women who perform work of equal value should receive comparable pay.

comparatio literarum (kom-pə-**ray**-shee-oh lit-ə-**rair**-əm). [Latin "comparison of writings"] *Roman law.* The act of comparing writings to ascertain authorship. • Even under Roman law, handwriting experts (*comparatores*) sometimes testified about a document's authenticity.

comparative advertising. See ADVERTISING.

comparative disparity. *Constitutional law.* The percentage of underrepresentation of a particular group among potential jurors on a venire, in comparison with the group's percentage of the general population. • Comparative disparity is calculated by subtracting a group's percentage of representation on the venire from the group's percentage of the population — that is, calculating the group's absolute-disparity representation — then dividing that percentage by the group's percentage-representation in the population, and multiplying the result by 100. For example, if African-Americans make up 12% of a county's population, and 8% of the potential jurors on the venire, the absolute disparity of African-Americans is 4%. And the comparative disparity is 33%, because 4 divided by 12 is .33, or 33%. Many courts criticize the comparative-disparity analysis, and favor an absolute-disparity analysis, because the comparative-disparity analysis is said to exaggerate the deviation. The reason for calculating the disparity is to analyze a claim that the jury was not impartial because it was not selected from a pool of jurors that fairly represented the makeup of the jurisdiction. See DUREN TEST; FAIR-CROSS-SECTION REQUIREMENT; STATISTICAL-DECISION THEORY. Cf. ABSOLUTE DISPARITY.

comparative fault. See *comparative negligence* under NEGLIGENCE.

comparative-impairment test. *Conflict of laws.* A test that asks which of two or more forums would have its policies most impaired by not having its law applied in the case.

comparative interpretation. A method of statutory interpretation by which parts of the statute are compared to each other, and the statute as a whole is compared to other documents from the same source on a similar subject.

comparative jurisprudence. See JURISPRUDENCE.

comparative law. See *comparative jurisprudence* under JURISPRUDENCE.

comparative negligence. See NEGLIGENCE.

comparative-negligence doctrine. *Torts.* The principle that reduces a plaintiff's recovery proportionally to the plaintiff's degree of fault in causing the damage, rather than barring recovery completely. • Most states have statutorily adopted the comparative-negligence doctrine. See NEGLIGENCE. Cf. CONTRIBUTORY-NEGLIGENCE DOCTRINE.

comparative-rectitude doctrine. *Family law.* Before the advent of no-fault divorce, the rule providing that when both spouses show grounds for divorce, the party least at fault is granted the requested relief.

comparative-sales approach. See MARKET APPROACH.

comparator (kəm-**par**-ə-tər *or* kom-pə-**ray**-tər). Something with which something else is compared <the female plaintiffs alleged illegal wage discrimination and contrasted their pay with that of male comparators>.

compassing (**kəm**-pə-sing). *Hist.* The act of contriving or plotting, esp. of something underhanded. • The Treason Act of 1351 criminalized the act of compassing the sovereign's death.

compel, *vb.* **1.** To cause or bring about by force or overwhelming pressure <a lawyer cannot be compelled to testify about a privileged communication>. **2.** (Of a legislative mandate or judicial precedent) to convince (a court) that there is only one possible resolution of a legal dispute <the wording of the statute compels us to affirm>.

compellable, *adj*. Capable of or subject to being compelled, esp. to testify <an accused person's spouse is not a compellable witness for the prosecution>.

compellativus (kəm-pel-ə-**tɪ**-vəs). [fr. Latin *compellare* "to accuse"] *Hist*. An adversary or accuser.

compelling-state-interest test. *Constitutional law*. A method for determining the constitutional validity of a law, whereby the government's interest in the law is balanced against the individual's constitutional right to be free of the law, and only if the government's interest is strong enough will the law be upheld. • The compelling-state-interest test is used most commonly in equal-protection analysis when the disputed law requires strict scrutiny. See STRICT SCRUTINY.

compensable (kəm-**pen**-sə-bəl), *adj*. Able or entitled to be compensated for <a compensable injury>. — Also termed *recompensable*.

compensable death. *Workers' compensation*. A death that, because it occurred in the course of employment, entitles the employee's heirs to compensation.

compensable injury. See INJURY.

compensate (**kom**-pən-sayt), *vb*. **1.** To pay (another) for services rendered <the lawyer was fairly compensated for her time and effort>. **2.** To make an amendatory payment to; to recompense (for an injury) <the court ordered the defendant to compensate the injured plaintiff>.

compensated surety. See SURETY.

compensating balance. The amount of money a borrower from a bank is required to keep on deposit as a condition for a loan or a line of credit.

compensatio (kom-pen-**say**-shee-oh). [Latin "weighing; balancing"] *Roman law*. A defendant's claim to have the plaintiff's demand reduced by the amount that the plaintiff owes the defendant. See SETOFF (2).

compensatio criminis (kom-pen-**say**-shee-oh **krim**-ə-nis). [Latin] *Eccles. law*. A defendant's plea in a divorce action, alleging that the complainant is guilty of the same conduct that the defendant is charged with, esp. adultery. See RECRIMINATION.

compensation (kom-pən-**say**-shən), *n*. **1.** Remuneration and other benefits received in return for services rendered; esp., salary or wages.

> "*Compensation* consists of wages and benefits in return for services. It is payment for work. If the work contracted for is not done, there is no obligation to pay. [Compensation] includes wages, stock option plans, profit-sharing, commissions, bonuses, golden parachutes, vacation, sick pay, medical benefits, disability, leaves of absence, and expense reimbursement." Kurt H. Decker & H. Thomas Felix II, *Drafting and Revising Employment Contracts* § 3.17, at 68 (1991).

2. Payment of damages, or any other act that a court orders to be done by a person who has caused injury to another and must therefore make the other whole. **3.** See SETOFF (2). — **compensatory** (kəm-**pen**-sə-tor-ee), **compensational** (kom-pən-**say**-shə-nəl), *adj*.

accrued compensation. Remuneration that has been earned but not yet paid.

adequate compensation. See *just compensation*.

deferred compensation. **1.** Payment for work performed, to be paid in the future or when some future event occurs. **2.** An employee's earnings that are taxed when received or distributed and not when earned, such as contributions to a qualified pension or profit-sharing plan.

just compensation. Under the Fifth Amendment, a fair payment by the government for property it has taken under eminent domain — usu. the property's fair market value, so that the owner is no worse off after the taking. — Also termed *adequate compensation*; *due compensation*; *land damages*.

unemployment compensation. Compensation paid at regular intervals by a state agency to an unemployed person, esp. one who has been laid off.

unreasonable compensation. Under the Internal Revenue Code, pay that is out of proportion to the actual services rendered and is therefore not deductible.

compensation period. The time fixed by unemployment or workers'-compensation law during which an unemployed or injured worker is entitled to receive compensation.

compensatory damages. See DAMAGES.

compensatory time. See COMP TIME.

comperendinatio (kom-pər-en-də-**nay**-shee-oh). [Latin "to remand to the next day but one"] *Roman law.* An adjournment of an action to hear the parties or their advocates a second time; a second hearing of the parties to a case. • The judge (*judex*) would decide the case at the conclusion of the second hearing.

competence, *n.* **1.** A basic or minimal ability to do something; qualification, esp. to testify <competence of a witness>. **2.** The capacity of an official body to do something <the court's competence to enter a valid judgment>. **3.** Authenticity <the documents were supported by a business-records affidavit, leaving their competence as evidence beyond doubt>. — **competent,** *adj.* Cf. COMPETENCY.

competency, *n.* **1.** The mental ability to understand problems and make decisions. **2.** A criminal defendant's ability to stand trial, measured by the capacity to understand the proceedings, to consult meaningfully with counsel, and to assist in the defense. — Also termed *competency to stand trial.* — **competent,** *adj.* Cf. COMPETENCE.

competency hearing. See PATE HEARING.

competency proceeding. See PROCEEDING.

competency to stand trial. See COMPETENCY.

competent evidence. See EVIDENCE.

competent witness. See WITNESS.

competition. The effort or action of two or more commercial interests to obtain the same business from third parties.

fair competition. Open, equitable, and just competition between business competitors.

horizontal competition. Competition between a seller and its competitors. • The Sherman Act prohibits unreasonable restraints on horizontal competition, such as price-fixing agreements between competitors. — Also termed *primary-line competition.*

perfect competition. A completely efficient market situation characterized by numerous buyers and sellers, a homogeneous product, perfect information for all parties, and complete freedom to move in and out of the market. • Perfect competition rarely if ever exists, but antitrust scholars often use the theory as a standard for measuring market performance.

primary-line competition. See *horizontal competition.*

vertical competition. Competition between participants at different levels of distribution, such as manufacturer and distributor. — Also termed *secondary-line competition.*

competitive advertising. See ADVERTISING.

competitive bid. See BID (2).

competitive civil-service examination. A test designed to evaluate a person's qualifications for a civil-service position. • This type of examination may be open to all those seeking civil-service employment, or it may be restricted to those civil servants seeking a promotion. See CIVIL SERVICE.

compilation (kom-pə-**lay**-shən), *n.* **1.** *Copyright.* A collection of literary works arranged in an original way; esp., a work formed by collecting and assembling preexisting materials or data that are selected, coordinated, or arranged in such a way that the resulting product constitutes an original work of authorship. Cf. COLLECTIVE WORK; DERIVATIVE WORK.

> "A compilation consists of an original work of authorship that incorporates other pre-existing material.... The author who finally assembles the components into a compilation is the owner of the copyright of the compilation — but not of the component parts." Arthur R. Miller & Michael H. Davis, *Intellectual Property in a Nutshell* 374–75 (2d ed. 1990).

2. A collection of statutes, updated and arranged to facilitate their use. — Also termed *compiled statutes.* **3.** A financial statement that does not have an accountant's assurance of conformity with generally accepted accounting principles. • In preparing a compilation, an accountant does not gather evidence or verify the accuracy of the information provided by the client; rather, the accountant reviews the compiled reports to ensure that they are in the appropriate form and are free of obvious errors. — **compile,** *vb.*

compiled statutes. See COMPILATION (2); STATUTE.

complainant (kəm-**playn**-ənt). **1.** The party who brings a legal complaint against another; esp., the plaintiff in a civil suit.

> "A suit in equity, under the procedure of the English Court of Chancery, which was generally adopted in the American States prior to the code, is instituted by the

plaintiff filing a bill of complaint. The plaintiff is usually called the complainant, in the Federal courts the complainant or plaintiff indifferently. The bill is in substance a petition to the chancellor, or judge of the court of equity, setting forth at large the grounds of the suit, and praying the process of the court, its subpoena, to bring the defendant into court and compel him to answer the plaintiff's bill, and, also, for such relief by decree or interlocutory remedy, by way of injunction, etc., as the plaintiff supposes himself entitled to." Edwin E. Bryant, *The Law of Pleading Under the Codes of Civil Procedure* 55 (2d ed. 1899).

2. A person who, under oath, signs a statement (called a "complaint") establishing reasonable grounds to believe that some named person has committed a crime. — Also termed *affiant*.

complaint. 1. The initial pleading that starts a civil action and states the basis for the court's jurisdiction, the basis for the plaintiff's claim, and the demand for relief. • In some states, this pleading is called a *petition*. **2.** *Criminal law*. A formal charge accusing a person of an offense. Cf. INDICTMENT; INFORMATION.

amended complaint. A complaint that modifies and replaces the original complaint by adding relevant matters that occurred before or at the time the action began. • In some circumstances, a party must obtain the court's permission to amend its complaint.

preliminary complaint. A complaint issued by a court to obtain jurisdiction over a criminal suspect for a hearing on probable cause or on whether to bind the suspect over for trial.

supplemental complaint. An additional complaint that either corrects a defect in the original complaint or adds relevant matters that occurred after the action began. • Generally, a party must obtain the court's permission to file a supplemental complaint.

third-party complaint. A complaint filed by the defendant against a third party, alleging that the third party may be liable for some or all of the damages that the plaintiff is trying to recover from the defendant.

well-pleaded complaint. An original or initial pleading that sufficiently sets forth a claim for relief — by including the grounds for the court's jurisdiction, the basis for the relief claimed, and a demand for judgment — so that a defendant may draft an answer that is responsive to the issues presented. • A well-pleaded complaint must raise a controlling issue of federal law for a federal court to have federal-question jurisdiction over the lawsuit.

completed-contract accounting method. See ACCOUNTING METHOD.

completed gift. See GIFT.

complete diversity. See DIVERSITY OF CITIZENSHIP.

completed-operations policy. See INSURANCE POLICY.

complete in itself, *adj*. (Of a legislative act) fully covering an entire subject.

complete integration. See INTEGRATION (2).

complete interdiction. See *full interdiction* under INTERDICTION (2).

completely integrated contract. See INTEGRATED CONTRACT.

completeness doctrine. See RULE OF OPTIONAL COMPLETENESS.

complete-operation rule. *Insurance*. The principle that goods are covered against damage at any time during the shipping process, including the loading and unloading of the goods. Cf. COMING-TO-REST DOCTRINE.

complete-preemption doctrine. The rule that a federal statute's preemptive force may be so extraordinary and all-encompassing that it converts an ordinary state-common-law complaint into one stating a federal claim for purposes of the well-pleaded-complaint rule.

complete voluntary trust. See *executed trust* under TRUST.

completion bond. See PERFORMANCE BOND.

complex trust. See TRUST.

complicated larceny. See *mixed larceny* under LARCENY.

complice (**kom**-plis). *Archaic*. An accomplice or accessory to a crime or immoral behavior.

complicity (kəm-**plis**-ə-tee), *n*. Association or participation in a criminal act; the act or state of being an accomplice. — **complicitous** (kəm-**plis**-ə-təs), *adj*. See ACCOMPLICE.

composite state. See STATE (1).

composite work (kəm-**poz**-it). *Copyright*. An original publication that relates to a variety of subjects and that includes discrete selections from many authors. • Although the distinguishable parts are separately protectable, the owner of the work — not the author — owns the renewal term, if any. 17 USCA § 304(a).

composition, *n.* **1.** An agreement between a debtor and two or more creditors for the adjustment or discharge of an obligation for some lesser amount; an agreement among the debtor and two or more creditors that the debtor will pay the creditors less than their full claims in full satisfaction of their claims. • The preexisting-duty rule is not a defense to this type of agreement because consideration arises from the agreement by each creditor with each other to take less than full payment. Through this agreement, the debtor is discharged in full for the debts of the participating creditors. — Also termed *creditors' composition*; *attermoiement.* **2.** The compensation paid as part of such an agreement. **3.** *Hist.* A payment of money or chattels as satisfaction for an injury. • In Anglo-Saxon and other early societies, a *composition* with the injured party was recognized as a way to deter acts of revenge by the injured party. — **compose,** *vb.*

> "[T]he first theory of liability was in terms of a duty to buy off the vengeance of him to whom an injury had been done whether by oneself or by something in one's power. The idea is put strikingly in the Anglo-Saxon proverb, 'Buy spear from side or bear it,' that is, buy off the feud or fight it out.... As the social interest in peace and order — the general security in its lowest terms — comes to be secured more effectively by regulation and ultimate putting down of feud as a remedy, payment of composition becomes a duty rather than a privilege.... The next step is to measure the composition not in terms of the vengeance to be bought off but in terms of the injury. A final step is to put it in terms of reparation." Roscoe Pound, *An Introduction to the Philosophy of Law* 74 (rev. ed. 1954).

composition deed. See DEED.

composition of matter. *Patents.* A patentable compound of material composed of two or more different substances; a product containing two or more substances, including all composite articles, whether resulting from chemical union or from mechanical mixture, and whether the substances are gases, fluids, powders, or solids.

> "[A] composition of matter describes what most people imagine to be the goal of the typical laboratory inventor, since it is usually a new chemical invention, although it can be any composition of materials, not limited solely to chemicals." Arthur R. Miller & Michael H. Davis, *Intellectual Property in a Nutshell* 21 (2d ed. 1990).

compos mentis (**kom**-pəs **men**-tis), *adj.* [Latin "master of one's mind"] Of sound mind; having use and control over one's own mental faculties. Cf. NON COMPOS MENTIS.

compossessio (kom-pə-**zes**[**h**]-ee-oh). [Latin] *Civil law.* Possession by two or more persons of the same thing in common.

compos sui (**kom**-pəs **s**[**y**]**oo**-I), *adj.* [Latin "master of one's self"] (Of a person) having control over one's own limbs, or the power of bodily motion.

compound (kom- *or* kəm-**pownd**), *vb.* **1.** To put together, combine, or construct. **2.** To compute (interest) on the principal and the accrued interest. **3.** To settle (a matter, esp. a debt) by a money payment, in lieu of other liability; to adjust by agreement. **4.** To agree for consideration not to prosecute (a crime). • Compounding a felony in this way is itself a felony. **5.** Loosely, to aggravate; to make (a crime, etc.) more serious by further bad conduct.

compounder (kom- *or* kəm-**pown**-dər). **1.** One who settles a dispute; the maker of a composition. — Also termed *amicable compounder.* See COMPOSITION (1). **2.** One who knows of a crime by another and agrees, for a promised or received reward, not to prosecute.

compounding a crime. The offense of either agreeing not to prosecute a crime that one knows has been committed or agreeing to hamper the prosecution. — Also termed *theft-bote.*

> "If a prosecuting attorney should accept money from another to induce the officer to prevent the finding of an indictment against that person this would be *compounding a crime* if the officer knew the other was guilty of an offense, but would be bribery whether he had such knowledge or not." Rollin M. Perkins & Ronald N. Boyce, *Criminal Law* 539 (3d ed. 1982).

compound interest. See INTEREST (3).

compound journal entry. See ENTRY (2).

compound larceny. See *mixed larceny* under LARCENY.

comprehensive general liability policy. See INSURANCE POLICY.

comprehensive insurance. See INSURANCE.

comprehensive nonliteral similarity. See SUBSTANTIAL SIMILARITY.

comprehensive zoning plan. A general plan to control and direct the use and development of a large piece of property. See ZONING.

comprint (**kom**-print). A surreptitious and illegal printing of another bookseller's copy of a work. See INFRINGEMENT.

compromis (kom-prə-**mee**). [French] *Int'l law.* An agreement between two or more countries to submit an existing dispute to the jurisdiction of an arbitrator, an arbitral tribunal, or an international court.

ad hoc compromis (ad hok kom-prə-**mee**). An agreement in which countries submit a particular dispute that has arisen between them to an ad hoc or institutionalized arbitral tribunal or to an international court. — Also termed *compromis proper*; *special agreement.*

general compromis. An agreement in which countries submit all or a definite class of disputes that may arise between them to an arbitral institution, a court, or an ad hoc arbitral tribunal by concluding a general arbitration treaty or by including an arbitration clause in a treaty. — Also termed *abstract compromis*; *anticipated compromis.*

compromise, *n.* **1.** An agreement between two or more persons to settle matters in dispute between them. **2.** A debtor's partial payment coupled with the creditor's promise not to claim the rest of the amount due or claimed. — **compromise,** *vb.*

compromise verdict. See VERDICT.

compromis proper. See *ad hoc compromis* under COMPROMIS.

compromissarius (kom-prə-mi-**sair**-ee-əs). [Latin] *Roman law.* See ARBITRATOR.

compromissum (kom-prə-**mis**-əm). [Latin "mutual agreement"] *Roman law.* An agreement to submit a controversy to arbitration.

compte arrêté (**kawnt** a-ray-**tay**). [French "settled account"] An account stated in writing, and acknowledged to be correct on its face by the party against whom it is stated.

comp time. Time that an employee is allowed to take off from work instead of being paid for overtime already worked. — Also termed *compensatory time.*

comptroller (kən-**troh**-lər). An officer of a business or a private, state, or municipal corporation who is charged with duties usu. relating to fiscal affairs, including auditing and examining accounts and reporting the financial status periodically. — Also spelled *controller.*

compulsion, *n.* **1.** The act of compelling; the state of being compelled.

> "Compulsion can take other forms than physical force; but in whatever form it appears the courts have been indisposed to admit that it can be a defence for any crime committed through yielding to it and the law of the matter is both meagre and vague. It can best be considered under the heads of obedience to orders, martial coercion, duress *per minas*, and necessity." J.W. Cecil Turner, *Kenny's Outlines of Criminal Law* 54 (16th ed. 1952).

2. An uncontrollable inclination to do something. **3.** Objective necessity; duress. — **compel,** *vb.*

compulsory (kəm-**pəl**-sə-ree), *adj.* Compelled; mandated by legal process or by statute <compulsory counterclaim>.

compulsory, *n. Eccles. law.* A writ that compels the attendance of a witness.

compulsory appearance. See APPEARANCE.

compulsory arbitration. See ARBITRATION.

compulsory-attendance law. A statute requiring minors of specified ages to attend school.

compulsory condition. See CONDITION (2).

compulsory counterclaim. See COUNTERCLAIM.

compulsory disclosure. See DISCLOSURE.

compulsory insurance. See INSURANCE.

compulsory joinder. See JOINDER.

compulsory labor. See FORCED LABOR.

compulsory license. See LICENSE.

compulsory nonsuit. See NONSUIT.

compulsory pilot. *Maritime law.* A ship pilot entitled by law to guide a ship for a particular purpose, such as piloting the ship into harbor. • The compulsory nature of the appointment relieves the vessel's owner of personal liability if the pilot causes a collision. Cf. VOLUNTARY PILOT.

> "The compulsory pilot presents a special problem. Statutes that impose a fine or imprisonment for the failure to take a pilot obviously create compulsory pilotage. Some statutes, however, allow the ship to refuse the pilot provided she pays his fee or half of it ('half-pilotage'). The Supreme Court has indicated that it does not regard the tendering of this alternative as amounting to compulsion. It makes a difference, because it is pretty well settled that if the pilotage is 'compulsory' the *respondeat superior* nexus is broken, and the shipowner cannot be held personally liable for the fault of the pilot resulting in collision. The ship's liability *in rem*, however, is unaffected by the fact that the pilotage is compulsory. This is one of the more striking consequences of the endowment of the ship with a juristic personality independent of that of her owner." Grant Gilmore & Charles L. Black, Jr., *The Law of Admiralty* § 7-16, at 520–21 (2d ed. 1975).

compulsory process. See PROCESS.

Compulsory Process Clause. The clause of the Sixth Amendment to the U.S. Constitution giving criminal defendants the subpoena power for obtaining witnesses in their favor.

compulsory sale. See SALE.

compurgation (kom-pər-**gay**-shən), *n.* [Latin *con-* "together" + *purgare* "to clear or purge"] *Hist.* A trial by which a defendant could have supporters (called *compurgators*), frequently 11 in number, testify that they thought the defendant was telling the truth. — Also termed *wager of law*; *trial by oath*. — **compurgatory,** *adj.*

> "If a defendant on oath and in a set form of words will deny the charge against him, and if he can get a certain number of other persons (compurgators) to back his denial by their oaths, he will win his case. If he cannot get the required number, or they do not swear in proper form, 'the oath bursts,' and he will lose. Though oaths were used in the Roman law of procedure, this institution of compurgation was not known to it. It was, however, common to the laws of many of the barbarian tribes who overran the Roman empire. Because it was so common and so widespread the church adopted it .... The case of *King v. Williams* in 1824 was the last instance of its use. It was finally abolished in 1833." 1 William Holdsworth, *A History of English Law* 305–08 (7th ed. 1956).

compurgator (**kom**-pər-gay-tər). *Hist.* A person who appeared in court and made an oath in support of a civil or criminal defendant. — Also termed OATH-HELPER. See COMPURGATION.

computer crime. See CRIME.

computus (**kom**-pyə-təs). [Latin *computo* "to count up; to reckon"] *Hist.* A writ to compel a guardian, bailiff, receiver, or accountant to render an accounting. — Also spelled *compotus*.

comstockery (**kom**-stok-ər-ee). (*often cap.*) Censorship or attempted censorship of art or literature that is supposedly immoral or obscene.

Comstock law (**kom**-stok). An 1873 federal statute that tightened rules against mailing "obscene, lewd, or lascivious" books or pictures, as well as "any article or thing designed for the prevention of conception or procuring of abortions." • Because of the intolerance that led to this statute, the law gave rise to an English word roughly equivalent to *prudery* — namely, *comstockery*.

con. *abbr.* **1.** Confidence <con game>. **2.** Convict <ex-con>. **3.** Contra <pros and cons>. **4.** (*cap.*) Constitutional <Con. law>.

con. See CONFIDENCE GAME.

concealed weapon. See WEAPON.

concealment, *n.* **1.** The act of refraining from disclosure; esp., an act by which one prevents or hinders the discovery of something. **2.** The act of removing from sight or notice; hiding. **3.** *Insurance.* The insured's intentional withholding from the insurer material facts that increase the insurer's risk and that in good faith ought to be disclosed. — **conceal,** *vb.*

> "Concealment is an affirmative act intended or known to be likely to keep another from learning of a fact of which he would otherwise have learned. Such affirmative action is always equivalent to a misrepresentation and has any effect that a misrepresentation would have ...." Restatement (Second) of Contracts § 160 cmt. a (1981).

active concealment. The concealment by words or acts of something that one has a duty to reveal.

fraudulent concealment. The affirmative suppression or hiding, with the intent to deceive or defraud, of a material fact or circumstance that one is legally (or, sometimes, morally) bound to reveal.

passive concealment. The act of maintaining silence when one has a duty to speak.

concealment rule. The principle that a defendant's conduct that hinders or prevents a plaintiff from discovering the existence of a claim tolls the statute of limitations until the plaintiff discovers or should have discovered the claim. — Also termed *fraudulent-concealment rule*.

concedo (kən-**see**-doh). [Latin] *Hist.* I grant. • This was formerly a term of conveyance.

concentration account. A single centralized bank account into which funds deposited at or collected at out-of-area locations are periodically transferred.

conception of invention. The formation in the inventor's mind of a definite and permanent idea of a complete invention that is thereafter applied in practice. • Courts usu. consider conception when determining priority of invention.

conceptum (kən-**sep**-təm). [Latin "seized"] *Civil law.* A theft in which the stolen item was searched for and found in someone's possession and in the presence of witnesses. See FURTUM CONCEPTUM.

concerted action. An action that has been planned, arranged, and agreed on by parties acting together to further some scheme or cause, so that all involved are liable for the actions of one another. — Also termed *concert of action*.

concerted activity. *Labor law.* Action by employees concerning wages or working conditions. • Concerted activity is protected by the National Labor Relations Act and cannot be used as a basis for disciplining or discharging an employee.

> "Typical protected concerted activity involves union organizing, the discussion of unionization among employees, or the attempt by one employee to solicit union support from another employee. But concerted activity need not involve a union. Activities by groups of employees unaffiliated with a union to improve their lot at their work place are deemed protected concerted activities." Douglas L. Leslie, *Labor Law in a Nutshell* 84 (3d ed. 1992).

concerted refusal to deal. *Antitrust.* An agreement between two or more persons or firms to not do business with a third party. • The parties to the agreement may or may not be competitors. Concerted refusals to deal may violate § 1 of the Sherman Act and are analyzed under either the per se rule or the rule of reason, depending on the nature of the agreement. See BOYCOTT; PER SE RULE; RULE OF REASON.

concert of action. See CONCERTED ACTION.

concert-of-action rule. See WHARTON RULE.

concessi (kən-**ses**-I). [Latin] *Hist.* I have granted. • *Concessi* grants a covenant in a lease for years; it does not warrant title. *Concessi* often appeared in the phrase *demisi, concessi, et ad firmam tradidi* ("demised, granted, and let to farm"). Cf. DEDI.

> "Concessi (a word much used in Conveyances). In Law it creates a *Covenant*, as *Dedi* does a *Warranty*." Thomas Blount, *Nomo-Lexicon: A Law–Dictionary* (1670).

concessimus (kən-**ses**-ə-məs). [Latin] *Hist.* We have granted. • *Concessimus* is a term of conveyance that creates a joint covenant on the part of the grantors.

concessio (kən-**sesh**-ee-oh). [Latin] *Hist.* A grant. • A term of conveyance used to convey incorporeal property. Pl. ***concessiones.***

> "Grants, *concessiones*; the regular method by the common law of transferring the property of *incorporeal* hereditaments, or, such things whereof no livery can be had. For which reason all corporeal hereditaments, as lands and houses, are said to lie *in livery*; and the others, as advowsons, commons, rents, reversions, etc., to lie *in grant*. . . . These therefore pass merely by the delivery of the deed." 2 William Blackstone, *Commentaries on the Laws of England* 317 (1766).

concession, *n.* **1.** A government grant for specific privileges. **2.** The voluntary yielding to a demand for the sake of a settlement. **3.** A rebate or abatement. **4.** *Int'l law.* A contract in which a country transfers some rights to a foreign enterprise, which then engages in an activity (such as mining) contingent on state approval and subject to the terms of the contract. — **concede,** *vb.* — **concessive,** *adj.*

concession bargaining. *Labor law.* A type of collective bargaining in which the parties negotiate the employees' giving back previously gained improvements in wages, benefits, or working conditions in exchange for some form of job security, such as protection against layoffs. — Also termed *employee givebacks*; *union givebacks*. See COLLECTIVE BARGAINING.

concessit solvere (kən-**ses**-it **sol**-və-ree). [Latin "he agreed to pay"] *Hist.* A form of debt action on a simple contract. • The plaintiff alleged that the defendant had granted and agreed to pay to the plaintiff the sum sued for, but had not done so. The defendant responded with a plea of *nunquam indebitatus* ("never indebted"). See *indebitatus assumpsit* under ASSUMPSIT; NUNQUAM INDEBITATUS; COMMON COUNT.

concessor (kən-**ses**-ər). *Hist.* A grantor. Cf. CONCESSUS.

concessum (kən-**ses**-əm), *p.pl.* [fr. Latin *concedere* "to grant"] *Hist.* Granted. • Judges used this term to signify their assent to a point made in argument; for example, a court might state that a particular proposition was *concessum per totam curiam* ("granted by the whole court").

concessus (kən-**ses**-əs). *Hist.* A grantee. Cf. CONCESSOR.

conciliation, *n.* **1.** A settlement of a dispute in an agreeable manner. **2.** A process in which a neutral person meets with the parties to a dispute (often labor) and explores how the dispute might be resolved; MEDIATION (1). — **conciliate,** *vb.* — **conciliative, conciliatory,** *adj.* — **conciliator,** *n.*

conciliation court. See *small-claims court* under COURT.

concilium (kən-**sil**-ee-əm). [Latin "council"] **1.** *Hist.* The sitting of a court to hear argument in a case; a motion requesting a day to present an argument. **2.** CONCILIUM PLEBIS.

concilium plebis (kən-**sil**-ee-əm **plee**-bis). [Latin "assembly of the people"] *Roman law.* An assembly of the plebs gathered together to enact legislation. — Often shortened to *concilium.* See PLEBISCITUM. Cf. COMITIA TRIBUTA.

> "Legislation was carried on to some extent by the *Comitia Tributa* and in an increasing degree by the assembly of the *plebs* alone, *concilium plebis*, which, in historical times, was also based on the tributal organisation. This assembly, presided over by a tribune of the *plebs*, was active from early times and there was early legislation on constitutional questions, enacted by that body and approved by the Senate, which was regarded as binding on the whole community. Its enactments, properly called *plebiscita*, were often called, as binding on the whole community, leges...." W.W. Buckland, *A Textbook of Roman Law: From Augustus to Justinian* 4 (1921).

concilium regis (kən-**sil**-ee-əm **ree**-jis). [Latin "assembly of the king"] *Hist.* A tribunal that, during the reigns of Edward I and Edward II, heard cases of extraordinary difficulty.

conclude, *vb.* **1.** To ratify or formalize (a treaty, convention, or contract) <it can be difficult to amend a contract that the parties have already concluded>. **2.** To bind; estop <the admissions concluded the party as a matter of law>.

conclusion, *n.* **1.** The final part of a speech or writing (such as a jury argument or a pleading). **2.** A judgment arrived at by reasoning; an inferential statement. **3.** The closing, settling, or final arranging (as of a treaty or contract). **4.** *Archaic.* An act by which one estops oneself from doing anything inconsistent with it.

> "Conclusion is, when a man by his own act upon record hath charged himself with a duty or other thing.... So if the sheriff, upon a *capias* to him directed, returns that he hath taken the body, and yet hath not the body in court at the day of the return, he shall be amerced...." *Termes de la Ley* 102–03 (1st Am. ed. 1812).

conclusional, *adj.* See CONCLUSORY.

conclusionary, *adj.* See CONCLUSORY.

conclusion of fact. A factual deduction drawn from observed or proven facts; an evidentiary inference. Cf. FINDING OF FACT.

conclusion of law. An inference on a question of law, made as a result of a factual showing, no further evidence being required; a legal inference. Cf. FINDING OF FACT; LEGAL CONCLUSION.

conclusion to the country. *Archaic.* The closing part of a pleading that requests the trial of an issue by a jury. Cf. GOING TO THE COUNTRY.

conclusive, *adj.* Authoritative; decisive; convincing <her conclusive argument ended the debate>. Cf. CONCLUSORY.

conclusive evidence. See EVIDENCE.

conclusive presumption. See PRESUMPTION.

conclusive proof. See *conclusive evidence* (1) under EVIDENCE.

conclusory (kən-**kloo**-zə-ree *or* -sə-ree), *adj.* Expressing a factual inference without stating the underlying facts on which the inference is based <because the plaintiff's allegations lacked any supporting evidence, they were merely conclusory>. — Also termed *conclusional*; *conclusionary*. Cf. CONCLUSIVE.

concomitant (kən-**kom**-ə-tənt), *adj.* Accompanying; incidental <concomitant actions>. — **concomitant,** *n.*

concomitant evidence. See EVIDENCE.

concord (**kon**-kord *or* **kong**-), *n.* **1.** An amicable arrangement between parties, esp. between peoples or nations; a compact or treaty. **2.** *Archaic.* An agreement to compromise and settle an action in trespass.

> "Concord is an Agreement made between two or more, upon a Trespass committed; and is divided into *Concord executory*, and *Concord executed* ... one binds not, as being imperfect, but the other is absolute, and ties the Party." Giles Jacob, *A New Law-Dictionary* (8th ed. 1762).

3. *Archaic.* An in-court agreement in which a person who acquired land by force acknowledges that the land in question belongs to the complainant. See DEFORCE.

> "Next comes the *concord*, or agreement itself, after leave obtained from the court; which is usually an acknowledgment from the deforciants (or those who keep the other out of possession) that the lands in question are the right of the complainant." 2 William Blackstone, *Commentaries on the Laws of England* 350 (1766).

4. *Hist.* The settlement of a dispute.

final concord. A written agreement between the parties to an action by which they settle the action in court, with the court's permission. — Also termed *finalis concordia*; *final peace*.

concordat (kon- *or* kən-**kor**-dat). **1.** An agreement between a government and a church, esp. the Roman Catholic Church.

> "The qualification of a treaty as a concordat depends only upon its object and purpose, not upon the name or outward form chosen by the parties. Although the term originally was also used for treaties between States, it has increasingly become restricted to only those treaties concluded with the Holy See." Heribert Franz Köck, "Concordats," in 1 *Encyclopedia of Public International Law* 164 (1992).

2. *Hist. Eccles. law.* An agreement between ecclesiastical persons concerning a benefice, such as a resignation or promotion. See BENEFICE. **3.** An agreement between secular persons or entities.

concordatory (kən-**kor**-də-tor-ee), *adj.* Of or relating to a concordat, esp. one between church and state in France.

Concordia discordantium canonum (kon-**kor**-dee-ə dis-kor-**dan**-shee-əm kə-**nohn**-əm). [Latin "the harmony of the discordant canons"] *Hist.* A collection of ecclesiastical authorities compiled by Gratian, an Italian monk, ca. 1140. • Gratian analyzed questions of law by drawing conclusions from side-by-side comparisons of a variety of texts. Later canonist scholarship usu. proceeded from Gratian's work. — Also termed *Decretum Gratiani*; *Decretum*.

> "Another body of jurisprudence was coming into being. From humble beginnings the canon law had grown into a mighty system. Already it asserted its right to stand beside or above the civil law. The civil law might be the law of earth, *ius soli*; here was the law of heaven, *ius poli*.... Many men had been endeavouring to state that law, but the fame of earlier labourers was eclipsed by that of Gratian. A monk of Bologna, that city which was the centre of the new secular jurisprudence, he published ... a book which he called *Concordia discordantium canonum*, but which was soon to become for all mankind simply the *Decretum Gratiani*, or yet more simply the *Decretum*. It is a great law-book. The spirit which animated its author was not that of a theologian, not that of an ecclesiastical ruler, but that of a lawyer.... The Decretum soon became an authoritative text-book and the canonist seldom went behind it.... The canonist had for it rather that reverence which English lawyers have paid to Coke upon Littleton...." 1 Frederick Pollock & Frederic W. Maitland, *The History of English Law Before the Time of Edward I* 112–13 (2d ed. 1898).

concourse (**kon**-kors *or* **kong**-). *Scots law.* **1.** The simultaneous existence of two actions based on the same facts, esp. a civil action and a criminal action. **2.** The concurrence of the public prosecutor to a criminal prosecution by a private person.

> "A private party may prosecute for the punishment of an offence perpetrated against himself, and for which the public prosecutor may refuse to prosecute at the public expense; but the concourse of the public prosecutor is necessary, and it cannot be refused; or if refused, the case may proceed at the instance of the private party. *Concourse* is distinguished from *Instance*. In the former case the public prosecutor merely concurs or consents, whilst in the latter case he is also a principal party prosecuting for the public interest." Hugh Barclay, *A Digest of the Law of Scotland* 162 (3d ed. 1865).

3. A conflict among creditors or claimants. See CONCURSUS (1).

concubinage (kon-**kyoo**-bə-nij), *n.* **1.** The relationship of a man and woman who cohabit without the benefit of marriage. **2.** The state of being a concubine. **3.** *Hist.* A plea in a dower action made by a defendant who asserts that the plaintiff is the defendant's concubine rather than wife.

> "*Concubinage*, in common Acceptation is the Keeping of a Whore or Concubine: But in a legal Sense, it is used as an Exception against her that sueth for Dower, alledging thereby that she was not a Wife lawfully married to the Party, in whose Lands she seeks to be endowed, but his *Concubine*." Giles Jacob, *A New Law-Dictionary* (8th ed. 1762).

concubinatus (kon-kyoo-bi-**nay**-təs). [Latin "concubinage"] *Roman law.* A permanent, monogamous union of a man and a woman who are not legally married. • *Concubinatus* was not prohibited by law, but carried fewer benefits than a legal marriage. Cf. JUSTAE NUPTIAE.

> "[C]oncubinage (*concubinatus*) ... was something to which we have no precise analogue in modern law, for, so far from being prohibited by the law, it was regulated thereby, being treated as a lawful connexion. It is almost a sort of unequal marriage (and is practically so described by some of the jurists) existing between persons of different station — the man of superior rank, the woman of a rank so much inferior that it is not to be presumed that his union with her was intended to be a marriage." James Bryce, "Marriage and Divorce under Roman and English Law," in 3 *Select Essays in Anglo-American Legal History* 806–07 (1909).

concubine (**kong**-kyə-bIn). A woman who cohabits with a man to whom she is not married.

concur (kən-**kər**), *vb.* **1.** To agree; to consent. **2.** In a judicial opinion, to agree with the judgment in the case (usu. as expressed in the opinion of another judge), or the opinion of another judge, but often for different reasons or through a different line of reasoning. **3.** *Civil law.* To join with other claimants in presenting a demand against an insolvent estate.

concurator (kon- *or* kən-**kyuur**-ə-tər). *Civil law.* A guardian or co-curator. See CURATOR.

concurrence. 1. Agreement; assent. **2.** A vote cast by a judge in favor of the judgment reached, often on grounds differing from those expressed in the opinion or opinions explaining the judgment. **3.** A separate written opinion explaining such a vote. — Also termed (in sense 3) *concurring opinion.*

concurrency, *n.* **1.** *Archaic.* The quality or fact of being concurrent in jurisdiction; joint right or authority. **2.** *Criminal procedure.* (Of a criminal sentence) concurrent in duration.

concurrent, *adj.* **1.** Operating at the same time; covering the same matters <concurrent interests>. **2.** Having authority on the same matters <concurrent jurisdiction>.

concurrent cause. See CAUSE (1).

concurrent condition. See CONDITION (2).

concurrent consideration. See CONSIDERATION.

concurrent covenant. See COVENANT (1).

concurrent estate. See ESTATE.

concurrent finding. See FINDING OF FACT.

concurrent interest. See *concurrent estate* under ESTATE (4).

concurrent jurisdiction. See JURISDICTION.

concurrent lease. See LEASE.

concurrent lien. See LIEN.

concurrent negligence. See NEGLIGENCE.

concurrent policy. See INSURANCE POLICY.

concurrent power. See POWER.

concurrent remedy. See REMEDY.

concurrent resolution. See RESOLUTION (1).

concurrent-sentence doctrine. The principle that an appellate court affirming a conviction and sentence need not hear a challenge to a conviction on another count if the conviction on the other count carries a sentence that is equal to or less than the affirmed conviction.

concurrent sentences. See SENTENCE.

concurrent tortfeasors. See TORTFEASOR.

concurrent writ. See WRIT.

concurring opinion. See CONCURRENCE (3).

concurso (kon- *or* kən-**kər**-soh). *Civil law.* An action in which a creditor seeks to enforce a claim against an insolvent debtor.

concursus (kon- *or* kən-**kər**-səs). [Latin "a running together"] **1.** *Civil & Scots law.* A proceeding in which two or more creditors claim, usu. adversely to each other, an interest in a fund or estate so that they can sort out and adjudicate all the claims on the fund. See CONCOURSE (3). **2.** *Civil law.* INTERPLEADER. **3.** *Eccles. law.* An examination to determine a person's fitness for parochial office.

concursus in delicto (kon- *or* kən-**kər**-səs in də-**lik**-toh). [Latin] Cooperation in crime.

concussio (kən-**kəsh**-ee-oh). [Latin] *Roman law.* The offense of extorting money or gifts by threat of violence. • In modern civil-law contexts, the term is often anglicized to *concussion*. — **concuss,** *vb.*

concussionary. *Archaic.* A person who extorts from others under guise of authority; one who practices concussion.

condedit (kən-**dee**-dit *or* -**ded**-it). [Latin "he made (a will)"] *Eccles. law.* A defensive plea filed by a party in response to an ecclesiastical-court libel (i.e., complaint) questioning the veracity of a will. — Also spelled *condidit.*

condemn, *vb.* **1.** To judicially pronounce (someone) guilty. **2.** To determine and declare that certain property is assigned to public use. See EMINENT DOMAIN. **3.** To adjudge (a building) as being unfit for habitation. **4.** To adjudge (food or drink) as being unfit for human consumption. **5.** *Maritime law.* To declare that a vessel (1) is forfeited to the government, (2) is a prize, or (3) is unfit for service.

condemnation (kon-dem-**nay**-shən), *n.* **1.** The act of judicially pronouncing someone guilty; conviction. **2.** The determination and declaration that certain property (esp. land) is assigned to public use, subject to reasonable compensation; the exercise of eminent domain by a governmental entity. See EMINENT DOMAIN.

excess condemnation. The taking of property beyond what is needed for public use.

inverse condemnation. An action brought by a property owner for compensation from a governmental entity that has taken the owner's property without bringing formal condemnation proceedings. — Also termed *condemnation blight.*

quick condemnation. The immediate taking of private property for public use, whereby the estimated reasonable compensation is placed in escrow until the actual amount of compensation can be established.

3. An official pronouncement that a thing (such as a building) is unfit for use or consumption; the act of making such a pronouncement.

condemnation money. **1.** Damages that a losing party in a lawsuit is condemned to pay. **2.** Compensation paid by an expropriator of land to the landowner for taking the property.

condemnatory (kən-**dem**-nə-tor-ee), *adj.* **1.** Condemning; expressing condemnation or censure. **2.** Of or relating to the use of eminent domain or expropriation.

condemnee (kon-dem-**nee**). One whose property is expropriated for public use or taken by a public-works project.

condemnor (kon-dem-**nor** *or* kən-**dem**-nər). A public or semipublic entity that expropriates property for public use.

condescendence (kon-di-**sen**-dənts). *Scots law.* A statement of facts in a civil pleading, set out in consecutively numbered paragraphs, that the claimant relies on to justify the claim for relief.

condictio (kən-**dik**-shee-oh). [fr. Latin *condicere* "to demand back"] *Roman & civil law.* A personal action in the nature of demanding something back; an action of debt. • In the sense here used, *debt* must be understood broadly to cover not only contractual but also noncontractual claims. *Condictio* is usu. founded on an obligation to give or do a certain thing or service. — Also termed *condiction*; *action of debt.* — **condictitious, condictious,** *adj.*

> "The principal *actio stricti juris* was the *condictio*, a general term with many applications. It might be brought for a certain sum of money (*condictio certae pecuniae*), or for some other certain thing (*condictio triticaria*), or to assert an illiquid claim (*condictio incerti*). The various forms of *condictio* were also distinguished according to the cause which gave rise to them, as *condictio furtiva*, *condictio indebiti*, and others. . . ." R.W. Lee, *The Elements of Roman Law* 435 (4th ed. 1956).

condictio certi (kən-**dik**-shee-oh **sər**-tɪ). [Latin "claim for recovery of a certain sum or thing"] An action based on a promise to do a thing, where the promise is certain.

condictio ex causa furtiva. See *conductio rei furtivae.*

condictio ex lege (kən-**dik**-shee-oh eks **lee**-jee). [Latin "claim for recovery under a statute"] An action arising where a statute creates an obligation but provides no remedy.

condictio furtiva. See *condictio rei furtivae.*

condictio incerti (kən-**dik**-shee-oh in-**sər**-tɪ). [Latin "claim for recovery of an uncertain amount"] An action to recover an uncertain amount.

condictio indebiti (kən-**dik**-shee-oh in-**deb**-ə-tɪ). [Latin "claim for recovery of something not due"] An action to prevent the unjust enrichment of a defendant who had received money or property from the plaintiff by mistake. — Also termed *actio condictio indebiti.*

condictio rei furtivae (kən-**dik**-shee-oh **ree**-ɪ fər-**tɪ**-vee). [Latin "claim for recovery of a stolen thing"] An action to recover a stolen thing. • A *condictio rei furtivae* could be brought against the thief or the thief's heirs. — Also termed *condictio furtiva*; *condictio ex causa furtiva*.

condictio sine causa (kən-**dik**-shee-oh **sɪ**-nee **kaw**-zə). [Latin "claim for recovery of money or a thing given without consideration"] An action for the recovery of a thing given without consideration and in contemplation of a specific event that did not occur, such as a dowry made in view of a marriage that does not take place.

condictio triticaria (kən-**dik**-shee-oh trɪ-ti-**kair**-ee-ə). [Latin "claim for recovery of wheat"] An action for the recovery of a specified quantity of a named commodity.

conditio (kən-**dish**-ee-oh). [Latin] A condition.

condition, *n.* **1.** A future and uncertain event on which the existence or extent of an obligation or liability depends; an uncertain act or event that triggers or negates a duty to render a promised performance. • For example, if Jones promises to pay Smith $500 for repairing a car, Smith's failure to repair the car (a condition) relieves Jones of the promise to pay.

"A condition is an event, not certain to occur, which must occur, unless its non-occurrence is excused, before performance under a contract becomes due." Restatement (Second) of Contracts § 224 (1981).

" 'Condition' is used in this Restatement to denote an event which qualifies a duty under a contract. It is recognized that 'condition' is used with a wide variety of other meanings in legal discourse. Sometimes it is used to denote an event that limits or qualifies a transfer of property. In the law of trusts, for example, it is used to denote an event such as the death of the settlor that qualifies his disposition of property in trust. Sometimes it is used to refer to a term in an agreement that makes an event a condition, or more broadly to refer to any term in an agreement (e.g., 'standard conditions of sale'). For the sake of precision, 'condition' is not used here in these other senses." *Id.* cmt. a.

"Strictly, a condition is a fact or event on the occurrence of which some legal right or duty comes into existence; a party may promise that this fact is so, or that the event will take place, but it is equally possible that no party to the contract promises this. An insurance company promises to pay £10,000 to an insured person if his house is destroyed by fire; the destruction of the house by fire is a condition of the insurer's promise to pay, but neither party promises to burn the house." P.S. Atiyah, *An Introduction to the Law of Contract* 146 (3d ed. 1981).

2. A stipulation or prerequisite in a contract, will, or other instrument, constituting the essence of the instrument. • If a court construes a contractual term to be a condition, then its untruth or breach will entitle the party to whom it is made to be discharged from all liabilities under the contract.

"Promises and the duties they generate can be either unconditional ('I promise to pay you $100,000') or conditional ('I promise to pay you $100,000 if your house burns down'). Lawyers use the word *condition* in several senses. Sometimes they use it to refer to the term in the agreement that makes the promise conditional. . . . However, lawyers also use the word *condition* to refer to an operative fact rather than to a term. According to the Restatement Second a condition is 'an event, not certain to occur, which must occur, unless occurrence is excused, before performance under a contract becomes due.' This use of the word has the support of leading writers." E. Allan Farnsworth, *Contracts* § 8.2, at 563 (2d ed. 1990).

"The terms 'warranty' and 'condition' are generally used interchangeably, for all practical purposes, and they refer to representations or promises by the insured, incorporated into the contract itself, on the truthfulness or fulfillment of which it is agreed that the rights of the insured shall depend. The primary differences between a mere representation and a warranty or condition are (1) while the insurer has the burden of proving the materiality of a misrepresentation before it will be grounds for avoidance, the materiality of a warranty or condition is conclusively presumed; and (2) while a representation will not be grounds for avoidance as long as it is substantially true, a warranty or condition must be strictly complied with in order to preclude avoidance. As with the majority view in representations, good or bad faith on the part of the insured is irrelevant." John F. Dobbyn, *Insurance Law in a Nutshell* 201 (3d ed. 1996).

affirmative condition. See *positive condition.*

casual condition. *Civil law.* A condition that depends on chance; one that is not within the power of either party to an agreement.

collateral condition. A condition that requires the performance of an act having no relation to an agreement's main purpose.

compulsory condition. A condition expressly requiring that a thing be done, such as a tenant's paying rent on a certain day.

concurrent condition. A condition that must occur or be performed at the same time as another condition, the performance by each party separately operating as a condition precedent; a condition that is mutually dependent on another, arising when the parties to a contract agree to exchange performances simultaneously. — Also termed *condition concurrent.*

"*Conditions concurrent* are acts that the parties to a contract are under duties of performing concurrently, the act of each party being separately operative as a condition precedent. The act is not concurrent with the legal relation affected, but only with the act of the other party." William R. Anson, *Principles of the Law of Contract* 412–13 (Arthur L. Corbin ed., 3d Am. ed. 1919).

condition implied by law. See *constructive condition.*

condition implied in law. See *constructive condition.*

condition precedent. An act or event, other than a lapse of time, that must exist or occur before a duty to perform something promised arises. • If the condition does not occur and is not excused, the promised performance need not be rendered. The most common condition contemplated by this phrase is the immediate or unconditional duty of performance by a promisor.

> "Now the most important type of conditional clause, i.e. *a clause on which the entire operation of the contract depends*, is called a condition precedent. The vital thing about such a condition is that it is not a promise, and if a contract is subject to a condition precedent it may properly be called a conditional contract. A much-quoted example of such a contract is found in *Pym* v. *Campbell*, where the defendants agreed to buy from the plaintiffs a share of an invention, provided that the invention was approved by a third party. This proviso was held to be a condition precedent to the operation of the entire contract, and in the absence of the approval specified, the contract never came into operation." P.S. Atiyah, *An Introduction to the Law of Contract* 146 (3d ed. 1981).

> "Before one gets too confused by the precedent and subsequent classifications, it might be helpful to know that in contract law there is no substantive difference between the two.... However, in the area of pleading and procedure significance may be placed upon the difference between a condition precedent and subsequent in terms of who has the burden of pleading and proof, the party seeking to enforce the promise usually being required to plead and prove a condition precedent and the party seeking to avoid liability for breach of promise sometimes being required to plead and prove the occurrence of the condition subsequent that would terminate his duty." Claude Rohwer & Gordon D. Schaber, *Contracts in a Nutshell* 313 (4th ed. 1997).

condition subsequent. A condition that, if it occurs, will bring something else to an end; an event the existence of which, by agreement of the parties, discharges a duty of performance that has arisen.

> "It must also be observed that lawyers sometimes refer to a condition subsequent, i.e. a condition on the happening of which the whole contract is dissolved. A condition subsequent is simply a statement of the circumstances in which the contract may be prematurely brought to an end, and is usually more readily recognized than a condition precedent. Like a condition precedent, however, a condition subsequent differs from terms which are promises, because the occurrence of such a condition involves the parties in no liability." P.S. Atiyah, *An Introduction to the Law of Contract* 147 (3d ed. 1981).

> "If ... the deed or will uses such words as 'but if,' 'on condition that,' 'provided, however,' or 'if, however,' it will generally be assumed that a condition subsequent was intended." Thomas F. Bergin & Paul G. Haskell, *Preface to Estates in Land and Future Interests* 50 (2d ed. 1984).

constructive condition. A condition contained in an essential contractual term that, though omitted by the parties from their agreement, a court has supplied as being reasonable in the circumstances; a condition imposed by law to do justice. • The cooperation of the parties to a contract, for example, is a constructive condition. — Also termed *implied-in-law condition*; *condition implied by law*; *condition implied in law*.

> "[C]onstructive conditions are imposed by law to do justice.... The dividing line between an express condition ... and constructive conditions is often quite indistinct. Yet, the distinction is often of crucial importance. The general rule governing an express condition is that it must be strictly performed. The general rule as to constructive conditions is that substantial compliance is sufficient." John D. Calamari & Joseph M. Perillo, *The Law of Contracts* § 11.8, at 402 (4th ed. 1998).

copulative condition (**kop**-yə-lə-tiv *or* -lay-tiv). A condition requiring the performance of more than one act. Cf. *disjunctive condition*; *single condition*.

dependent condition. A mutual covenant that goes to the consideration on both sides of a contract.

disjunctive condition. A condition requiring the performance of one of several acts. Cf. *copulative condition*; *single condition*.

dissolving condition. See *resolutory condition*.

express condition. A condition that is explicitly stated in an instrument; esp., a contractual condition that the parties have reduced to writing.

implied condition. A condition that is not expressly mentioned, but is imputed by law from the nature of the transaction or the conduct of the parties to have been tacitly understood between them as a part of the agreement.

implied-in-fact condition. A contractual condition that the parties have implicitly agreed to by their conduct or by the nature of the transaction.

implied-in-law condition. See *constructive condition*.

inherent condition. A condition that is an intrinsic part of an agreement; a condition that is not newly imposed but is already present in an agreement.

lawful condition. A condition that can be fulfilled without violating the law.

mixed condition. *Civil law*. A condition that depends either on the will of one party and the will of a third person, or on the will of one party and the happening of a causal event.

negative condition. A condition forbidding a party from doing a certain thing, such as prohibiting a tenant from subletting leased property; a promise not to do something, usu. as part of a larger agreement. — Also termed *restrictive condition*. See *negative easement* under EASEMENT.

positive condition. A condition that requires some act, such as paying rent. — Also termed *affirmative condition*.

potestative condition (**poh**-tes-tə-tiv). *Civil law*. A condition that will be fulfilled only if the obligated party chooses to do so. • Louisiana no longer uses this term, instead providing that this type of condition will render the obligation null. Cf. *suspensive condition*; *resolutory condition*.

preexisting condition. *Insurance*. A physical or mental condition evident during the period before the effective date of a medical-insurance policy. • Typically, coverage for later treatment for such a condition is excluded if symptoms of the condition were present during the period before the policy was effective.

promissory condition. A condition that is also a promise.

> "The distinction between a condition which is also a promise, and a condition which is not the subject of a promise, is often one of great difficulty and importance, especially where the term is implied and not expressed, and it is unfortunate that legal usage has sanctioned the word 'condition' for two such different concepts. It would at least be desirable if lawyers could be persuaded to refer to conditions which are the subject of a promise as 'promissory conditions', a usage which it is proposed to adopt here." P.S. Atiyah, *An Introduction to the Law of Contract* 147 (3d ed. 1981).

resolutory condition (rə-**zol**-yə-tor-ee). *Civil law*. A condition that upon fulfillment terminates an already enforceable obligation and entitles the parties to be restored to their original positions. — Also termed *resolutive condition*; *dissolving condition*. Cf. *potestative condition*.

restrictive condition. See *negative condition*.

single condition. A condition requiring the performance of a specified thing. Cf. *copulative condition*; *disjunctive condition*.

suspensive condition. *Civil law*. A condition that must be fulfilled before an obligation is enforceable. Cf. *potestative condition*.

unlawful condition. A condition that cannot be fulfilled without violating the law.

3. Loosely, a term, provision, or clause in a contract.

> "This term *condition* is generally used to describe any fact, subsequent to the formation of a contract, which operates to make the duty of a promisor immediately active and compelling. Such a fact may be described as such in a term of the contract or it may not. In either event, the *term* of the contract should not itself be called the *condition*.... It is not uncommon, popularly, to speak of a condition of the contract as synonymous with *term* or *provision* of the contract. This should be avoided." William R. Anson, *Principles of the Law of Contract* 226 n.1 (Arthur L. Corbin ed., 3d Am. ed. 1919).

> "The word 'condition' is used in the law of property as well as in the law of contract and it is sometimes used in a very loose sense as synonymous with 'term,' 'provision,' or 'clause.' In such a sense it performs no useful service." *Id.* at 409.

4. A qualification attached to the conveyance of property providing that if a particular event does or does not take place, the estate will be created, enlarged, defeated, or transferred. **5.** A state of being; an essential quality or status. — **condition,** *vb*.

artificial condition. A physical characteristic of real property, brought about by a person's affirmative act instead of by natural forces.

dangerous condition. **1.** A property defect creating a substantial risk of injury when the property is used in a reasonably foreseeable manner. • A dangerous condition may result in waiver of sovereign immunity. **2.** A property risk that children, because of their immaturity, cannot appreciate or avoid.

conditional, *adj*. Subject to or dependent on a condition <a conditional sale>.

conditional acceptance. See ACCEPTANCE (4).

conditional admissibility. See ADMISSIBILITY.

conditional agreement. See AGREEMENT.

conditional assault. See ASSAULT.

conditional assignment. See ASSIGNMENT (2).

conditional bequest. See BEQUEST.

conditional contraband. See CONTRABAND.

conditional contract. See CONTRACT.

conditional conveyance. See CONVEYANCE.

conditional covenant. See COVENANT (1).

conditional creditor. See CREDITOR.

conditional delivery. See DELIVERY.

conditional devise. See DEVISE.

conditional guaranty. See GUARANTY.

conditional indorsement. See INDORSEMENT.

conditional legacy. See LEGACY.

conditional limitation. See LIMITATION.

conditionally privileged communication. See COMMUNICATION.

conditional obligation. See OBLIGATION.

conditional pardon. See PARDON.

conditional payment. See PAYMENT.

conditional presumption. See *rebuttable presumption* under PRESUMPTION.

conditional privilege. See *qualified privilege* under PRIVILEGE (1).

conditional promise. See PROMISE.

conditional proof. See PROOF.

conditional purpose. **1.** An intention to do something, conditions permitting. **2.** *Criminal law.* A possible defense against a crime if the conditions make committing the crime impossible (e.g., "I will steal the money if it's there," and the money is not there).

conditional right. See RIGHT.

conditional sale. See SALE.

conditional sales contract. See *retail installment contract* under CONTRACT.

conditional sentence. See SENTENCE.

conditional use. See USE (1).

conditional-use permit. See SPECIAL-USE PERMIT.

conditional will. See WILL.

conditional zoning. See ZONING.

condition concurrent. See *concurrent condition* under CONDITION (2).

condition implied by law. See *constructive condition* under CONDITION (2).

condition implied in law. See *constructive condition* under CONDITION (2).

conditioning the market. See GUN-JUMPING.

condition of employment. A qualification or circumstance required for obtaining or keeping a job.

condition precedent. See CONDITION (2).

conditions of sale. The terms under which auctions are to be conducted. • The conditions of sale are usu. placed in the auction room for public viewing before the sale.

condition subsequent. See CONDITION (2).

condominia (kon-də-**min**-ee-ə). *Civil law.* Coownerships or limited ownerships. • *Condominia* are considered part of the *dominium* of the property, and thus are more than mere rights in the property (i.e., *jure in re aliena*); examples of *condominia* include *emphyteusis*, *superficies*, *pignus*, *hypotheca*, *usufructus*, *usus*, and *habitatio*.

condominium (kon-də-**min**-ee-əm). **1.** Ownership in common with others. **2.** A single real-estate unit in a multi-unit development in which a person has both separate ownership of a unit and a common interest, along with the development's other owners, in the common areas. Cf. COOPERATIVE (2). Pl. (for sense 2) **condominiums.**

> "The condominium concept is not new, despite its relatively recent introduction in the United States. Ownership of individual units in buildings can be traced back to ancient Babylon; it was quite common in ancient Rome and in medieval Europe. The earliest condominium statute is Article 664 of the Code Napoleon of 1804, a very brief provision which was later substantially expanded. Condominium statutes were adopted in most nations in Europe, and in Central and South America, before any were adopted in the United States." Roger A. Cunningham et al., *The Law of Property* § 2.2, at 34 n.26 (2d ed. 1993).

3. Joint sovereignty by two or more nations. **4.** A politically dependent territory under such sovereignty. Pl. **condominia** (senses 3 & 4).

condonation (kon-də-**nay**-shən), *n.* A victim's implied forgiveness of an offense by treating the offender as if there had been no offense; esp., before the advent of no-fault divorce, a spouse's forgiveness implied by continuing to live normally with the other spouse after that spouse has committed an offense that would otherwise be grounds for divorce.

condone (kən-**dohn**), *vb.* To voluntarily pardon or overlook (esp. an act of adultery). — **condonable** (kən-**dohn**-ə-bəl), *adj.*

conduct, *n.* Personal behavior, whether by action or inaction; the manner in which a person behaves. — **conduct,** *vb.*

"The word 'conduct' ... covers both acts and omissions.... In cases in which a man is able to show that his conduct, whether in the form of action or of inaction, was involuntary, he must not be held liable for any harmful result produced by it ...." J.W. Cecil Turner, *Kenny's Outlines of Criminal Law* 13 n.2, 24 (16th ed. 1952).

assertive conduct. *Evidence.* Nonverbal behavior that is intended to be a statement, such as pointing one's finger to identify a suspect in a police lineup. • Assertive conduct is a statement under the hearsay rule, and thus it is not admissible unless a hearsay exception applies. Fed. R. Evid. 801(a)(2). — Also termed *implied assertion.*

contumacious conduct (kon-t[y]oo-**may**-shəs). A willful disobedience of a court order. See CONTUMACY.

disorderly conduct. Behavior that tends to disturb the public peace, offend public morals, or undermine public safety. See BREACH OF THE PEACE.

disruptive conduct. Disorderly conduct in the context of a governmental proceeding. See CONTEMPT.

nonassertive conduct. *Evidence.* Nonverbal behavior that is not intended to be a statement, such as fainting while being questioned as a suspect by a police officer. • Nonassertive conduct is not a statement under the hearsay rule, and thus it is admissible. Fed. R. Evid. 801.

outrageous conduct. Conduct so extreme that it exceeds all reasonable bounds of human decency. See EMOTIONAL DISTRESS.

unprofessional conduct. Behavior that is immoral, unethical, or dishonorable, either generally or when judged by the standards of the actor's profession.

conductio (kən-**dək**-shee-oh). [Latin "a hiring"] *Roman law.* The act of hiring or leasing, usu. of property or services. See LOCATIO-CONDUCTIO.

conductor (kən-**dək**-tər *or* -tor). [Latin "one who hires"] *Roman law.* **1.** A person who leases property or hires the services of another. **2.** A person who engages himself to make a specific work.

conductor operarum (kən-**dək**-tər [*or* -tor] op-ə-**rair**-əm). [Latin "a hirer of labor"] *Roman law.* A person who engages another to perform specified work for another at a stated price; a contractor.

conductus (kən-**dək**-təs). [fr. Latin *conducere* "hired"] *Roman law.* A person or thing hired by a *conductor.*

conduit taxation. See *pass-through taxation* under TAXATION.

confarreatio (kən-far-ee-**ay**-shee-oh). [Latin] *Roman law.* A religious ceremony used to wed patricians. • By this ceremony, the wife was brought into the husband's family and placed under the husband's protection (*manus*). See MANUS. Cf. COEMPTIO; USUS (2).

"Anciently, there were three modes in which marriage might be contracted according to Roman usage, one involving a religious solemnity, the other two the observance of certain secular formalities. By the religious marriage of *Confarreation*; by the higher form of civil marriage, which was called *Coemption*; and by the lower form, which was termed *Usus*, the Husband acquired a number of rights over the person and property of his wife, which were on the whole in excess of such as are conferred on him in any system of modern jurisprudence. But in what capacity did he acquire them? Not as *Husband*, but as *Father*. By the Confarreation, Coemption, and Usus, the woman passed *in manum viri*, that is, in law she became the *Daughter* of her husband. She was included in his Patria Potestas.... These three ancient forms of marriage fell, however, gradually into disuse, so that, at the most splendid period of Roman greatness, they had almost entirely given place to a fashion of wedlock — old apparently, but not hitherto considered reputable — which was founded on a modification of the lower form of civil marriage." Henry S. Maine, *Ancient Law* 149 (10th ed. 1884).

confectio (kən-**fek**-shee-oh). [Latin "a completing"] *Hist.* The act of making or executing a written instrument.

confederacy, *n.* **1.** A league of states or countries that have joined for mutual support or joint action; an alliance. **2.** An association of two or more persons, usu. for unlawful purposes; CONSPIRACY. **3.** The fact or condition of being an ally or accomplice.

confederacy clause. *Archaic.* A clause in a complaint charging that the defendant or defendants have combined with others (who may yet be named as defendants) to defraud or deprive the plaintiff of personal rights.

confederate, *n.* An ally; esp., a coconspirator or accomplice.

confederation. A league or union of states or nations, each of which retains its sovereignty but also delegates some rights and powers to a central authority. Cf. FEDERATION.

confederation of states. A confederation involving a central government that exists and exercises certain powers but does not control all the external relations of the member states. • For international purposes there exists not one but a number of states. Cf. *federal state* under STATE.

conferee (kon-fər-**ee**). See MANAGER (2).

conference committee. See COMMITTEE.

confess, *vb.* To admit (an allegation) as true; to make a confession. — **confessor,** *n.*

confessed judgment. See CONFESSION OF JUDGMENT.

confessing error. A plea admitting to an assignment of error. See ASSIGNMENT OF ERROR.

confessio in judicio (kən-**fesh**-ee-oh in joo-**dish**-ee-oh). [Latin "confession in court"] *Hist.* An in-court confession.

confession, *n.* A criminal suspect's acknowledgment of guilt, usu. in writing and often including details about the crime. Cf. ADMISSION; STATEMENT.

> "A confession is an acknowledgment in express words, by the accused in a criminal case, of the truth of the main fact charged or of some essential part of it." 3 John H. Wigmore, *Evidence in Trials at Common Law* § 821, at 308 (James H. Chadbourn ed., 4th rev. ed. 1970).

> "The distinction between admissions in criminal cases and confessions by the accused is the distinction in effect between admissions of fact from which the guilt of the accused may be inferred by the jury and the express admission of guilt itself." William P. Richardson, *The Law of Evidence* § 394, at 268 (3d ed. 1928).

coerced confession. A confession that is obtained by threats or force.

direct confession. A statement in which an accused person acknowledges having committed the crime.

extrajudicial confession. A confession made out of court, and not as a part of a judicial examination or investigation. • Such a confession must be corroborated by some other proof of the corpus delicti, or else it is insufficient to warrant a conviction. Cf. *judicial confession.*

implied confession. A confession in which the person does not plead guilty but invokes the mercy of the court and asks for a light sentence.

indirect confession. A confession that is inferred from the defendant's conduct.

interlocking confessions. Confessions by two or more suspects whose statements are substantially the same and consistent concerning the elements of the crime. • Such confessions are admissible in a joint trial.

involuntary confession. A confession induced by the police or other law-enforcement authorities who make promises to, coerce, or deceive the suspect.

judicial confession. A plea of guilty or some other direct manifestation of guilt in court or in a judicial proceeding. Cf. *extrajudicial confession.*

naked confession. A confession unsupported by any evidence that a crime has been committed, and therefore usu. highly suspect.

oral confession. A confession that is not made in writing. • Oral confessions are admissible, though as a practical matter police interrogators prefer to take written or recorded confessions since juries typically view these as being more reliable.

plenary confession (**plee**-nə-ree *or* **plen**-ə-). A complete confession; one that is believed to be conclusive against the person who made it.

confession and avoidance. A plea in which a defendant admits allegations but pleads additional facts that deprive the admitted facts of an adverse legal effect. • For example, a plea of contributory negligence (before the advent of comparative negligence) was a confession and avoidance. — Also termed *avoidance*; *plea in confession and avoidance*; *plea of confession and avoidance.*

confession of judgment. 1. A person's agreeing to the entry of judgment upon the occurrence or nonoccurrence of an event, such as making a payment. **2.** A judgment taken against a debtor by the creditor, based on the debtor's written consent. **3.** The paper on which the person so agrees, before it is entered. — Also termed *confessed judgment*; *cog-*

novit judgment; *statement of confession*. See COGNOVIT. Cf. WARRANT OF ATTORNEY.

confidence. 1. Assured expectation; firm trust; faith <the partner has confidence in the associate's work>. **2.** Reliance on another's discretion; a relation of trust <she took her coworker into her confidence>. **3.** A communication made in trust and not intended for public disclosure; specif., a communication protected by the attorney-client or similar privilege <the confidences between lawyer and client>. • Under the ABA Code of Professional Responsibility, a lawyer cannot reveal a client's confidence unless the client consents after full disclosure. DR 4–101. Cf. SECRET (2). — **confide,** *vb.*

confidence game. A means of obtaining money or property whereby a person intentionally misrepresents facts to gain the victim's trust so that the victim will transfer money or property to the person. — Also termed *con game*; *con*.

confidential, *adj.* **1.** (Of information) meant to be kept secret <confidential settlement terms>. **2.** (Of a relationship) characterized by trust and a willingness to confide in the other <a confidential relationship between attorney and client>.

confidential communication. See COMMUNICATION.

confidentiality, *n.* **1.** Secrecy; the state of having the dissemination of certain information restricted. **2.** The relation between lawyer and client or guardian and ward, or between spouses, with regard to the trust that is placed in the one by the other.

confidential relationship. See FIDUCIARY RELATIONSHIP.

confidential source. A person who provides information to a law-enforcement agency or to a journalist on the express or implied guarantee of anonymity. • Confidentiality is protected both under the Federal Freedom of Information Act (for disclosures to law enforcement) and under the First Amendment (for disclosures to journalists).

confinee. A person held in confinement.

confinement, *n.* The act of imprisoning or restraining someone; the state of being imprisoned or restrained <solitary confinement>. — **confine,** *vb.*

confirm, *vb.* **1.** To give formal approval to <confirm the bankruptcy plan>. **2.** To verify or corroborate <confirm that the order was signed>. **3.** To make firm or certain <the judgment confirmed the plaintiff's right to possession>.

confirmatio (kon-fər-**may**-shee-oh). [Latin "confirmation"] *Hist.* A confirmation of a voidable estate. See CONFIRMATION (4).

confirmatio crescens (kon-fər-**may**-shee-oh **kres**-enz). [Latin "growing confirmation"] A confirmation that enlarges an estate.

confirmatio diminuens (kon-fər-**may**-shee-oh di-**min**-yoo-enz). [Latin "diminishing confirmation"] A confirmation that decreases the services that a tenant must perform.

confirmatio perficiens (kon-fər-**may**-shee-oh pər-**fish**-ee-enz). [Latin "perfecting confirmation"] A confirmation that ratifies a wrongful and defeasible title, or makes a conditional estate absolute. See CONFIRMATION (4).

Confirmatio Chartarum (kon-fər-**may**-shee-oh kahr-**tair**-əm). [Latin "confirmation of the charters"] *Hist.* A declaration first made by Henry III in 1225 confirming the guarantees of Magna Carta and the Charter of the Forest. • It was not enrolled until 1297, when, during the reign of Edward I, it was enacted, thus introducing these charters into the common law. — Also spelled *Confirmatio Cartarum*.

> "For lawyers, the really important date is neither 1215 nor 1225, when Henry's Charter took its final form, but 1297, when Edward I, in his *Inspeximus*, confirmed the Charter of 1225 and the Forest Charter, which was issued at the same time (*Confirmatio Chartarum*). The important element in the *Confirmatio* is the statement that the Charter might be pleaded in every royal court, either to support a claim or a defense. The Charter becomes in this way part of the law — the Common Law — which, in 1297, was already a definite concept although it was not yet quite the equivalent of the law of England. Until then, the political aspects of the Charter had been much the more important." Max Radin, *Handbook of Anglo–American Legal History* 156 (1936).

confirmation, *n.* **1.** The act of giving formal approval <Senate confirmation hearings>. **2.** The act of verifying or corroborating; a statement that verifies or corroborates <the journalist sought confirmation of the district attorney's remarks>. **3.** The act of ratifying a voidable estate; a type of conveyance in which a voidable estate is made certain or a particular estate is increased <deed of confirmation>. **4.** *Civil law.* A declaration that corrects a null provision of an obligation in order to make the provision enforceable. **5.** *Commercial law.* A bank's agreement to honor a letter of credit issued by another bank. — **confirmatory** (kən-**fər**-mə-tor-ee), *adj.* Cf. RATIFICATION.

silent confirmation. A bank's confirmation based on the request of the beneficiary of the credit rather than the issuing bank.

confirmation of sale. A court's approval — usu. in the form of a docket entry or order — of the terms of a court-ordered sale.

confirmation slip. The form verifying a purchase or sale of a security, usu. mailed by the broker to the investor. — Also termed *transaction slip*; *sold note.*

confirmatio perficiens. See CONFIRMATIO.

confirmavi (kon-fər-**may**-vI). [Latin] *Hist.* I have confirmed. • The emphatic word in a deed of confirmation. See CONFIRMATION (3).

confirmed letter of credit. See LETTER OF CREDIT.

confirmee (kon-fər-**mee**). *Hist.* The grantee of a deed of confirmation. See CONFIRMATION (3).

confirming bank. See BANK.

confirmor (kən-**fər**-mər *or* -mor). *Hist.* The grantor of a deed of confirmation. See CONFIRMATION (3).

confiscable (kən-**fis**-kə-bəl *or* **kon**-fə-skə-bəl), *adj.* (Of property) liable to confiscation; subject to forfeiture <confiscable contraband>.

confiscare (kon-fi-**skair**-ee), *vb.* [Latin *con* "together" + *fiscus* "treasury"] *Hist.* To seize (property) for the government.

confiscate (**kon**-fə-skayt), *vb.* **1.** To appropriate (property) as forfeited to the government. **2.** To seize (property) by authority of law.

confiscation (kon-fi-**skay**-shən), *n.* **1.** Seizure of property for the public treasury. **2.** Seizure of property by actual or supposed authority. — **confiscatory** (kən-**fis**-kə-tor-ee), *adj.* — **confiscator** (**kon**-fə-skay-tər), *n.*

confiscatory rate. See RATE.

confitens reus (**kon**-fə-tenz **ree**-əs). [Latin "confessing accused"] *Hist.* An accused person who admits committing the offense.

conflicting evidence. See EVIDENCE.

conflicting presumption. See PRESUMPTION.

conflict of authority. 1. A disagreement between two or more courts, often courts of coordinate jurisdiction, on a point of law. **2.** A disagreement between two or more treatise authors or other scholars, esp. in an area in which scholarly authority is paramount, such as public or private international law.

conflict of interest. 1. A real or seeming incompatibility between one's private interests and one's public or fiduciary duties. **2.** A real or seeming incompatibility between the interests of two of a lawyer's clients, such that the lawyer is disqualified from representing both clients if the dual representation adversely affects either client or if the clients do not consent.

conflict of laws. 1. A difference between the laws of different states or countries in a case in which a transaction or occurrence central to the case has a connection to two or more jurisdictions. — Often shortened to *conflict.*

conflict of personal laws. **1.** A difference of laws between a jurisdiction's general laws and the laws of a racial or religious group, such as a conflict between federal law and American Indian tribal law. **2.** A difference between personal laws. See PERSONAL LAW.

false conflict of laws. **1.** A situation resembling but not embodying an actual conflict because the potentially applicable laws do not differ, because the laws' underlying policies have the same objective, or because one of the laws is not meant to apply to the case before the court. **2.** The situation in which, although a case has a territorial connection to two or more states whose laws conflict with one another, there is no real conflict because one state has a dominant interest in having its law chosen to govern the case — hence there is no real conflict. **3.** The situation in which the laws of all states that are relevant to the facts in dispute either are the same or would produce the same decision in the case. — Often shortened to *false conflict.*

2. The body of jurisprudence that undertakes to reconcile such differences or to decide what law is to govern in these situations; the principles of choice of law. — Often shortened (in sense 2) to *conflicts.* — Also termed (in international contexts) *private international law*; *international private law.*

"The phrase [conflict of laws], although inadequate, because it does not cover questions as to jurisdiction, or as to the execution of foreign judgments, is better than any other." Thomas E. Holland, *The Elements of Jurisprudence* 421 (13th ed. 1924).

conflict out, *vb.* To disqualify (a lawyer or judge) on the basis of a conflict of interest <the judge was conflicted out of the case by his earlier representation of one of the litigants>.

conformed copy. See COPY.

conforming, *adj.* Being in accordance with contractual obligations <conforming goods> <conforming conduct>. UCC § 2–102(a)(8).

conforming use. See USE (1).

Conformity Act. *Hist.* An 1872 federal statute providing that the practice and procedure in federal district courts (other than in equity and admiralty matters) must conform to the practice and procedure used by the state courts for like cases. • The Federal Rules of Civil Procedure (effective in 1938) superseded the Conformity Act.

"[E]ven where there was conformity, it was to be 'as near as may be,' and this was understood by the Court to make the Conformity Act 'to some extent only directory and advisory' and to permit the federal judge to disregard a state practice that would, in his view, 'unwisely encumber the administration of the law, or tend to defeat the ends of justice.' With all these exceptions to conformity, and with the judge left somewhat at large to decide when he would conform, it is hardly surprising that the result was, in the view of a distinguished commentator, 'a mixture of conflicting decisions, which have served to cloud the whole subject in hideous confusion and shifting certainty.' " Charles Alan Wright, *The Law of Federal Courts* § 61, at 425–26 (5th ed. 1994) (quoting *Indianapolis & St. Louis Ry. Co. v. Horst*, 93 U.S. 291, 300–01 (1876)).

conformity hearing. 1. A court-ordered hearing to determine whether the judgment or decree prepared by the prevailing party conforms to the decision of the court. **2.** A hearing before a federal agency or department to determine whether a state-submitted plan complies with the requirements of federal law. • This type of hearing is common in cases involving social services.

Confrontation Clause. The Sixth Amendment provision guaranteeing a criminal defendant's right to directly confront an accusing witness and to cross-examine that witness.

confusio (kən-**fyoo**-zhee-oh). [fr. Latin *confundere* "to pour together"] **1.** *Roman law.* An inseparable mixture of liquid property belonging to different owners. Cf. COMMIXTIO. **2.** *Scots law.* A doctrine whereby a lesser right is absorbed into a greater right and is thus extinguished.

confusion. 1. CONFUSION OF GOODS. **2.** MERGER (8).

"Confusion is the intermingling of two or more pieces of personal property so that the property rights in each can no longer be distinguished. Thereafter, no specific identification or separation of the formerly separate chattel is possible. Such an intermingling occurs most often with fungible goods like gas, oil, grain, mineral ore, or unmarked timber." Barlow Burke, *Personal Property in a Nutshell* 379 (2d ed. 1993).

confusion of boundaries. *Hist.* The branch of equity that deals with the settlement of disputed or uncertain boundaries.

confusion of debts. See MERGER (8).

confusion of goods. The mixture of things of the same nature but belonging to different owners so that the identification of the things is no longer possible. • If this occurs by common consent of the owners, they are owners in common, but if the mixture is done willfully by one person alone, that person loses all right in the property unless (1) the goods can be distinguished and separated among owners, or (2) the mixing person's goods are equal in value to the goods with which they were intermingled. *Confusion of goods* combines the civil-law concepts of *confusio* (a mixture of liquids) and *commixtio* (a mixture of dry items). — Also termed *intermixture of goods*.

confusion of rights. See MERGER (8).

confusion of titles. *Civil law.* The merger of two titles to the same land in the same person. Cf. MERGER (8).

con game. See CONFIDENCE GAME.

congeable (**kon**-jee-ə-bəl), *adj.* [fr. French *congé* "permission"] *Hist.* Lawful; permissible.

congé d'accorder (kawn-**zhay** da-kor-**day**). [Law French] *Hist.* Leave to accord. • Courts used this phrase in fictitious land-title lawsuits to grant the defendant permission to agree with the plaintiff's allegations. See FINE (1).

congé d'emparler (kawn-**zhay** dawm-pahr-**lay**). [French] *Hist.* Leave to imparl. • This phrase was formerly used by a defendant to request leave of court for additional time to file a responsive pleading. See IMPARLANCE.

congeries (kon-**jeer**-eez *or* **kon**-jə-reez). A collection or aggregation <a congeries of rights>.

conglomerate (kən-**glom**-ər-it), *n.* A corporation that owns unrelated enterprises in a wide variety of industries. — **conglomerate** (kən-**glom**-ə-rayt), *vb.* — **conglomerate** (kən-**glom**-ər-it), *adj.*

conglomerate merger. See MERGER.

congress, *n.* **1.** A formal meeting of delegates or representatives. **2.** (*cap.*) The legislative body of the federal government, created under U.S. Const. art. I, § 1 and consisting of the Senate and the House of Representatives. — **congressional,** *adj.*

congressional committee. See COMMITTEE.

congressional district. See DISTRICT.

Congressional Globe. A privately issued record of the proceedings in Congress. • The *Globe* was the sole record of congressional speeches and statements from 1833 until the publicly printed *Congressional Record* appeared in 1873.

congressional immunity. See IMMUNITY (1).

congressional intent. See LEGISLATIVE INTENT.

congressional power. See POWER.

Congressional Record. The published record of the daily proceedings in the U.S. Senate and House of Representatives. • Members of Congress are allowed to edit their speeches before printing, and they may insert material never actually spoken by obtaining permission from their respective houses to print or extend their remarks.

congressional survey. See *government survey* under SURVEY.

conjectio (kən-**jek**-shee-oh), *vb.* [Latin "to infer"] *Roman law.* (Of a court) to draw a conclusion from evidence; to infer a fact from the evidence presented.

conjectio causae (kən-**jek**-shee-oh **kaw**-zee). [Latin "putting together of a cause"] *Roman law.* A summary presentation of a case before the court by the parties or their advocates.

conjectural choice, rule of. The principle that no basis for recovery is presented when all theories of causation rest only on conjecture.

conjecture (kən-**jek**-chər), *n.* A guess; supposition; surmise. — **conjecture** (kən-**jek**-chər), *vb.* — **conjectural** (kən-**jek**-chər-əl), *adj.*

conjoint (kən-**joynt**). A person connected with another in a joint interest or obligation, such as a cotenant or spouse.

conjoint robbery. See ROBBERY.

conjoint will. See *joint will* under WILL.

conjudex (kon-**joo**-deks). [fr. Latin *con* "together" + *judex* "judge"] *Hist.* An associate judge.

conjugal (**kon**-jə-gəl), *adj.* Of or relating to the married state, often with an implied emphasis on sexual relations between spouses <the prisoner was allowed a private bed for conjugal visits>.

conjugal rights. The rights and privileges arising from the marriage relationship, including the mutual rights of companionship, support, and sexual relations. • Loss of conjugal rights amounts to loss of consortium. See CONSORTIUM.

conjugium (kən-**joo**-jee-əm), *n.* [fr. Latin *con* "together" + *jugum* "yoke"] *Roman law.* The condition of being married.

conjuncta (kən-**jəngk**-tə). [Latin] *Civil law.* Things (usu. words or phrases) that are joined together. Cf. DISJUNCTA.

conjunctim (kən-**jəngk**-tim), *adv.* [Latin] *Roman law.* Conjointly. • Heirs instituted *conjunctim,* for example, became coheirs with equal shares. Cf. DISJUNCTIM.

conjunctim et divisim (kən-**jəngk**-timet də-**VI**-zim *or* -sim). [Latin] *Hist.* Jointly and severally.

conjunctive denial. See DENIAL.

conjuratio (kon-juu-**ray**-shee-oh). [Latin] CONJURATION.

conjuration (kon-jə-**ray**-shən). *Hist.* **1.** A plot or compact made by persons who swear to each other to do something that will result in public harm. **2.** The offense of attempting a conference with evil spirits to discover some secret or effect some purpose; witchcraft; sorcery.

> "*Coniuration* (*coniuratio*) is the very French word drawne from the latine, which as it is compounded of (*con* & *iuro*) so it signifieth a compact or plot, made by men combining themselves together by oath or promise, to do some publique harme. But in our common lawe, it is especially used for such as have personall conference with the devill or evill spirit, to know any secret, or to effect any purpose. And the difference that I have observed (how truly let those judge that be beter skilled in these maters) betweene coniuration and witchcraft, is because the one seemeth, by prayers and invocation of Gods powerfull names, to compell the devill, to say or doe what he commandeth him: the other dealeth rather by a friendly and voluntarie conference or agreement betweene him or her and the devill or familiar, to have her or his desires and turnes served in lieu of blood, or other gift offered unto him, especially of his or her soule." John Cowell, *The Interpreter* (1607).

conjurator (**kon**-jə-ray-tər). *Hist.* A person who swears an oath with others; a coconspirator.

connecting factors. *Conflict of laws.* Factual or legal circumstances that help determine the choice of law by linking an action or individual with a state or jurisdiction. • An example of a connecting factor is a party's domicile within a state.

connecting-up doctrine. The rule allowing evidence to be admitted on condition that the party offering it will adduce other evidence to show relevance.

connexity (kə-**nek**-sə-tee). Connectedness; the quality of being connected. • In some states, *connexity* expresses the relationship that must exist between a foreign party (such as a corporation) and the state for a plaintiff to maintain personal jurisdiction over the party; generally, the claim must arise from a transaction connected with the activities of the party in the state.

connivance (kə-**nI**-vənts), *n.* **1.** The ignoring of a wrongdoer's illegal conduct; esp., a secret or indirect condonation of another's unlawful act. **2.** *Family law.* In a divorce action, a defense that points to the plaintiff's corrupt consent, implied or express, to the action being complained of.

connive (kə-**nIv**), *vb.* **1.** To knowingly overlook another's wrongdoing. **2.** Loosely, to conspire.

connubium (kə-**n**[**y**]**oo**-bee-əm), *n.* [fr. Latin *con* "together" + *nubere* "to marry"] *Roman law.* **1.** The legal capacity to wed. **2.** The collection of rights that accompany a marriage between persons who have the capacity to marry. — Also spelled *conubium.* — Also termed *jus connubii.* See CONCUBINATUS; JUSTAE NUPTIAE.

> "The word *connubium* denotes properly the right to intermarry with Roman citizens; and hence to contract a Roman marriage, according to the peculiar forms and with the peculiar incidents and effects of marriage between Roman citizens. Chief among these incidents or effects was the *patria potestas*, or life-long control of the father over his children, which, as we shall soon see, was among the most remarkable peculiarities of the Roman system. In general, *connubium* embraces the peculiar rights of Roman citizens, so far as they pertain to family relations." James Hadley, *Introduction to Roman Law* 116 (1881).

conqueror, *n.* [fr. Law French *conquerir* "to acquire"] *Hist.* The first person who acquired land by purchase; one who first brought an estate into a family. See CONQUEST (2); PURCHASE (2).

conqueror, *vb.* [Latin] To complain. • *Conqueror* served as a declaratory statement in petitions, often by introducing the complaint: *Conqueror quod* .... ("I complain that....").

conquest. **1.** *Int'l law.* An act of force by which, during a war, a belligerent occupies territory within an enemy country with the intention of extending its sovereignty over that territory. • That intention is usu. explained in a proclamation or some other legal act. **2.** *Hist.* The acquisition of land by any method other than descent, esp. by purchase. **3.** *Hist.* The land so acquired. Cf. PURCHASE (2).

> "What we call *purchase*, *perquisitio*, the feudists called *conquest*, *conquaestus*, or *conquisitio*: both denoting any means of acquiring an estate out of the common course of inheritance. And this is still the proper phrase in the law of Scotland: as it was, among the Norman jurists, who stiled the first purchasor (that is, he who first brought the estate into the family which at present owns it) the conqueror or *conquereur*. Which seems to be all that was meant by the appellation which was given to William the Norman, when his manner of ascending the throne of England was, in his own and his successors' charters, and by the historians of the times, entitled *conquaestus*, and himself *conquaestor* or *conquisitor*; signifying, that he was the first of his family who acquired the crown of England, and from whom therefore all future claims by descent must be derived: though now, from our disuse of the feodal sense of the word, together with the reflection on his forcible method of acquisition, we are apt to annex the idea of *victory* to this name of *conquest* or *conquisition*; a title which, however just with regard to the *crown*, the conqueror never pretended with

regard to the *realm* of England; nor, in fact, ever had." 2 William Blackstone, *Commentaries on the Laws of England* 242–43 (1766).

conquisitio (kən- *or* kəng-kwi-**zish**-ee-oh). [Latin "search"] See CONQUEST (2). — Also termed *conquisition*.

conquisitor (kən- *or* kəng-**kwiz**-ə-tər). [Latin "one who searches"] See CONQUEROR (1).

consanguine brothers. See BROTHERS.

consanguineo. See COSINAGE.

consanguineus (kon-sang-**gwin**-ee-əs), *n.* [Latin "related by blood"] *Hist.* A person related to another by blood; a consanguineous relative.

consanguineus frater (kon-sang-**gwin**-ee-əs **fray**-tər). [Latin "blood brother"] *Hist.* A half-brother by the same father.

consanguineus uterinus (kon-sang-**gwin**-ee-əs yoo-tə-**rI**-nəs). [Latin "blood relative by the uterus"] *Hist.* A half-brother by the same mother.

consanguinitas (kon-sang-**gwin**-ə-tas). [Latin "relationship by blood"] *Roman law.* The relationship between siblings who have the same father.

consanguinity (kon-sang-**gwin**-ə-tee), *n.* The relationship of persons of the same blood or origin. — **consanguineous,** *adj.* See *prohibited degree* under DEGREE. Cf. AFFINITY.

collateral consanguinity. The relationship between persons who have the same ancestor but do not descend or ascend from one another (for example, uncle and nephew, etc.).

lineal consanguinity. The relationship between persons who are directly descended or ascended from one another (for example, mother and daughter, great-grandfather and grandson, etc.).

conscience. 1. The moral sense of right or wrong; esp., a moral sense applied to one's own judgment and actions. **2.** In law, the moral rule that requires justice and honest dealings between people.

conscience of the court. 1. The court's equitable power to decide issues based on notions of fairness and justice. **2.** A standard applied by the court in deciding whether the parties or a jury has acted within limits. • Thus, in some cases, a jury's award of damages is upset because it is said to "shock the conscience of the court."

conscientious objector. A person who for moral or religious reasons is opposed to participating in any war, and who is therefore deferred from military conscription but is subject to serving in civil work for the nation's health, safety, or interest. Cf. PACIFIST.

conscionable (**kon**-shə-nə-bəl), *adj.* Conforming with good conscience; just and reasonable <a conscionable bargain>. — **conscionableness, conscionability,** *n.* Cf. UNCONSCIONABLE.

consciously parallel. *Antitrust.* Of, relating to, or characterizing the conduct of a party who has knowledge of a competitor's action (such as raising prices) and who makes an independent decision to take the same action. • In some cases this is viewed as evidence of a conspiracy.

conscious parallelism. *Antitrust.* An act of two or more businesses intentionally engaging in monopolistic conduct.

conscription. See DRAFT (2).

consecratio capitis (kon-sə-**kray**-shee-oh **kap**-i-tis). [Latin "consecrating the body"] *Roman law.* The act of declaring a wrongdoer an outlaw who could be killed on sight; the punishing of criminal behavior by relegating an offender to the gods, i.e., leaving the person outside divine and human protection. See SACER; OUTLAWRY.

consecutive sentences. See SENTENCE.

consecutive tortfeasors. See TORTFEASOR.

consensual (kən-**sen**-shoo-əl), *adj.* Having, expressing, or occurring with full consent. — Also termed *consentaneous*; *consentient*.

consensual contract. See CONTRACT.

consensual crime. See *victimless crime* under CRIME.

consensual marriage. See MARRIAGE (1).

consensus ad idem (kən-**sen**-səs ad **I**-dem). [Latin] An agreement of parties to the same thing; a meeting of minds. — Also termed *consensus in idem*.

"Agreement between the parties or *consensus in idem* is the basis of contractual obligation. . . ." 2 David M. Walker, *Principles of Scottish Private Law* 11 (4th ed. 1988).

consent, *n.* Agreement, approval, or permission as to some act or purpose, esp. given voluntarily by a competent person. • Consent is an affirmative defense to assault, battery, and related torts, as well as such torts as defamation, invasion of privacy, conversion, and trespass. — **consent,** *vb.* — **consensual,** *adj.*

"The consent [to a contract] is none the less 'genuine' and 'real,' even though it be induced by fraud, mistake, or duress. Consent may be induced by a mistaken hope of gain or a mistaken estimate of value or by the lie of a third person, and yet there is a contract and we do not doubt the 'reality of the consent.' Fraud, mistake, and duress are merely collateral operative facts that co-exist with the expressions of consent and have a very important effect upon the resulting legal relations." William R. Anson, *Principles of the Law of Contract* 199 n.1 (Arthur L. Corbin ed., 3d Am. ed. 1919).

express consent. Consent that is clearly and unmistakably stated.

implied consent. Consent inferred from one's conduct rather than from one's direct expression.

informed consent. **1.** A person's agreement to allow something to happen, made with full knowledge of the risks involved and the alternatives. **2.** A patient's knowing choice about treatment or a procedure, made after a physician or other healthcare provider discloses whatever information a reasonably prudent provider in the medical community would provide to a patient regarding the risks involved in the proposed treatment.

consentaneous, *adj.* See CONSENSUAL.

consent calendar. **1.** A schedule of informal hearings involving a child, usu. arranged when it appears that the child's best interests will be served, if the case is heard informally. • The child and all interested parties must first consent before the case goes on the consent calendar. **2.** A list of legislative bills that, having no anticipated objection, may be enacted into law without a vote. • The term also applies to a similar list maintained by an administrative agency. — Also termed (in sense 2) *unanimous-consent calendar.*

consent decree. See DECREE.

consent dividend. See DIVIDEND.

consentient, *adj.* See CONSENSUAL.

consent judgment. See *agreed judgment* under JUDGMENT.

consent jurisdiction. See JURISDICTION.

consent order. See *consent decree* under DECREE.

consent search. See SEARCH.

consent to be sued. Agreement in advance to be sued in a particular forum. See COGNOVIT CLAUSE.

consent to notice. A provision stating that notice required by a document may be given beforehand or to a designated person.

consequential contempt. See CONTEMPT.

consequential damages. See DAMAGES.

consequential economic loss. See ECONOMIC LOSS.

consequential loss. See LOSS.

conservation. *Environmental law.* The supervision, management, and maintenance of natural resources; the protection, improvement, and use of natural resources in a way that ensures the highest social as well as economic benefits.

conservator (kən-**sər**-və-tər *or* **kon**-sər-vay-tər), *n.* A guardian, protector, or preserver. — **conservatorship,** *n.*

managing conservator. **1.** A person appointed by a court to manage the estate or affairs of someone who is legally incapable of doing so; GUARDIAN (1). **2.** *Family law.* In the child-custody laws of some states, the parent who has primary custody of a child, with the right to establish the child's primary domicile. See CUSTODY.

possessory conservator. *Family law.* In the child-custody laws of some states, the parent who has visitation rights, but not the primary custody rights, of the child.

conservator of the peace. See PEACE OFFICER.

consideration, *n.* **1.** Something of value (such as an act, a forbearance, or a return promise) received by a promisor from a promisee. • Consideration, or a substitute such as promissory estoppel, is necessary for an agreement to be enforceable. **2.** *Hist.* A court's judgment. — Also termed (in Roman law) *consideratio.*

"A 'consideration' has been explained to be 'any act of the plaintiff from which the defendant, or a stranger, derives a benefit or advantage, or any labour, detriment, or inconvenience sustained by the plaintiff, however small the detriment or inconvenience may be, if such act is performed, or inconvenience suffered by the plaintiff with the assent, express or implied, of the defendant, or, in the language of pleading, at the special instance and request of the defendant'." Thomas E. Holland, *The Elements of Jurisprudence* 286 (13th ed. 1924).

"A consideration in its widest sense is the reason, motive, or inducement, by which a man is moved to bind himself by an agreement. It is not for nothing that he consents to impose an obligation upon himself, or to abandon or transfer a right. It is in *consideration* of such and such a fact that he agrees to bear new burdens or to forgo the benefits which the law already allows him." John Salmond, *Jurisprudence* 359 (Glanville L. Williams ed., 10th ed. 1947).

"The word 'consideration' has been around for a long time, so it is tempting to think we have had a theory of consideration for a long time. In fact until the nineteenth century the word never acquired any particular meaning or stood for any theory." Grant Gilmore, *The Death of Contract* 18 (1974).

adequate consideration. Consideration that is fair and reasonable under the circumstances of the agreement. Cf. *sufficient consideration.*

"It is helpful to observe precision in use of vocabulary when analyzing consideration issues. Distinguish carefully between 'adequate' consideration and 'sufficient' consideration. 'Adequacy' refers to whether there was a fair bargain involving an exchange of equal values. 'Sufficiency' refers to whether the consideration is legally sufficient to enforce a promise, and this requires only that there be some legal detriment incurred as a bargained exchange for the other party's promise." Claude Rohwer & Gordon D. Schaber, *Contracts in a Nutshell* 83 (4th ed. 1997).

and other good and valuable consideration. See *other consideration.*

concurrent consideration. Consideration arising at the same time as other consideration, or where the promises are simultaneous.

continuing consideration. An act or performance extending over time.

due consideration. See *sufficient consideration.*

executed consideration. A consideration that has been wholly given; past consideration as opposed to present or future consideration.

executory consideration (eg-**zek**-yə-tor-ee). A consideration that is to be given only after formation of the contract; present or future consideration as opposed to past consideration.

express consideration. Consideration that is specifically stated in an instrument.

fair consideration. **1.** Consideration that is equal in value to the thing being exchanged; consideration given for property or for an obligation in either of the following circumstances: (1) when given in good faith as an exchange for the property or obligation, or (2) when the property or obligation is received in good faith to secure a present advance or prior debt in an amount not disproportionately small as compared with the value of the property or obligation obtained. — Also termed *fair and valuable consideration.* **2.** Consideration that is honest, reasonable, and free from suspicion, but not strictly adequate or full.

future consideration. **1.** Consideration to be given in the future; esp., consideration that is due after the other party's performance. **2.** Consideration that is a series of performances, some of which will occur after the other party's performance. **3.** Consideration the specifics of which have not been agreed on between the parties. Cf. *past consideration.*

good and valuable consideration. See *legal consideration.*

good consideration. **1.** Consideration based on natural love or affection or on moral duty <good consideration, being based purely on affection, does not amount to valuable consideration>. • Such consideration is usu. not valid for the enforcement of a contract. — Also termed *meritorious consideration*; *moral consideration.*

"A good consideration is that of *blood*, or the natural love and affection which a person has to his children, or any of his relatives.... A good consideration is not of itself sufficient to support a promise, any more than the moral obligation which arises from a man's passing his word; neither will the two together make a binding contract; thus a promise by a father to make a gift to his child will not be enforced against him. The consideration of natural love and affection is indeed good for so little in law, that it is not easy to see why it should be called a *good* consideration ...." Joshua Williams, *Principles of the Law of Personal Property* 95–96 (11th ed. 1881).

"Stated simply, good or meritorious consideration is nothing more than motive or moral obligation." 3 Richard A. Lord, *Williston on Contracts* § 7:16, at 325–26 (4th ed. 1992).

2. Loosely, valuable consideration; consideration that is adequate to support the bargained-for exchange between the parties <his agreement to pay the offering price was good consideration for the sale>.

gratuitous consideration (grə-**t**[**y**]**oo**-i-təs). Consideration that, not being founded on any detriment to the party who gives it, will not support a contract; a performance for which a party was already obligated.

illegal consideration. Consideration that is contrary to the law or public policy, or prejudicial to the public interest. • Such consideration does not support a contract.

immoral consideration. A consideration that so offends societal norms as to be invalid. • A contract supported by immoral consideration is usu. voidable or unenforceable.

implied consideration. Consideration that is inferred by law from the parties' actions.

impossible consideration. Consideration stemming from a promise or performance that cannot be fulfilled.

inadequate consideration. Consideration that does not involve an exchange of equal values.

invented consideration. Fictional consideration created by a court to prevent the invalidation of a contract that lacks consideration.

legally sufficient consideration. See *sufficient consideration.*

meritorious consideration. See *good consideration.*

moral consideration. See *good consideration.*

nominal consideration. Consideration that is so insignificant as to bear no relationship to the value of what is being exchanged (e.g., $10 for a piece of real estate). • Such consideration can be valid, since courts do not ordinarily examine the adequacy of consideration (although they do often inquire into such issues as fraud and duress). — Also termed *peppercorn.*

> "Offers made in consideration of one dollar paid or promised are often irrevocable .... The irrevocability of an offer may be worth much or little to the offeree, and the courts do not ordinarily inquire into the adequacy of the consideration bargained for. Hence a comparatively small payment may furnish consideration for the irrevocability of an offer proposing a transaction involving much larger sums. But gross disproportion between the payment and the value of the option commonly indicates that the payment was not in fact bargained for but was a mere formality or pretense. In such a case there is no consideration .... Nevertheless, such a nominal consideration is regularly held sufficient to support a short-time option proposing an exchange on fair terms. The fact that the option is an appropriate preliminary step in the conclusion of a socially useful transaction provides a sufficient substantive basis for enforcement, and a signed writing taking a form appropriate to a bargain satisfies the desiderata of form. In the absence of statute, however, the bargaining form is essential: a payment of one dollar by each party to the other is so obviously not a bargaining transaction that it does not provide even the form of an exchange." Restatement (Second) of Contracts § 87 cmt. b (1981).

other consideration. Additional things of value to be provided under the terms of a contract, usu. unspecified in the contract, deed, or bill of sale, because they are too numerous to conveniently list, or to avoid public knowledge of the total amount of consideration. — Also termed *other good and valuable consideration.*

past consideration. An act done or a promise given by a promisee before making a promise sought to be enforced. • Past consideration is not consideration for the new promise because it has not been given in exchange for this promise (although exceptions exist for new promises to pay debts barred by limitations or debts discharged in bankruptcy). See PREEXISTING-DUTY RULE. Cf. *future consideration.*

> "A past consideration is, in effect, no consideration at all; that is to say, it confers no benefit on the promisor, and involves no detriment to the promisee in respect of his promise. It is some act or forbearance in time past by which a man has benefited without thereby incurring any legal liability." William R. Anson, *Principles of the Law of Contract* 149 (Arthur L. Corbin ed., 3d Am. ed. 1919).

sufficient consideration. Enough consideration — as a matter of law — to support a contract. — Also termed *due consideration*; *legally sufficient consideration.* Cf. *adequate consideration.*

valuable consideration. Consideration that is valid under the law; consideration that either confers a pecuniarily measurable benefit on one party or imposes a pecuniarily measurable detriment on the other. — Also termed *good and valuable consideration*; *legal consideration.*

> "By a valuable consideration is meant something of value given or promised by one party in exchange for the promise of the other .... The thing thus given by way of consideration must be of some *value.* That is to say, it must be material to the interests of one or the other or both of the parties. It must either involve some gain or benefit to the promisor by way of recompense for the burden of his promise, or it must involve some loss or disadvantage to the promisee for which the benefit of the promise is a recompense." John Salmond, *Jurisprudence* 360 (Glanville L. Williams ed., 10th ed. 1947).

consideration, failure of. See FAILURE OF CONSIDERATION.

consideration, want of. See WANT OF CONSIDERATION.

consideratum est per curiam (kən-sid-ə-**ray**-təm est pər **kyoor**-ee-əm). [Latin] *Hist.* It is considered by the court. • This was the formal language preceding the judgment of a common-law court. Cf. IDEO CONSIDERATUM EST.

> "A judgment is the decision or sentence of the law, given by a court of justice, as the result of proceedings instituted therein for the redress of an injury. The language of the judgment is not, therefore, that 'it is decreed,' or 'resolved,' by the court, but that 'it is considered by the court,' *consideratum est per curiam*, that the plaintiff recover his debt, etc. In the early writers, *considerare*, *consideratio* always means the judgment of a court." 1 John Bouvier, *Bouvier's Law Dictionary* 619 (8th ed. 1914).

consign (kən-**sIn**), *vb.* **1.** To transfer to another's custody or charge. **2.** To give (goods) to a carrier for delivery to a designated recipient. **3.** To give (merchandise or the like) to another to sell, usu. with the understanding that the seller will pay the owner for the goods from the proceeds.

consignee (kon-sI-**nee** *or* kən-). One to whom goods are consigned.

consignment (kən-**sIn**-mənt). **1.** The act of consigning goods for custody or sale. **2.** A quantity of goods delivered by this act, esp. in a single shipment. **3.** Under the UCC, a transaction in which a person delivers goods to a merchant for the purpose of sale, and (1) the merchant deals in goods of that kind under a name other than the name of the person making delivery, is not an auctioneer, and is not generally known by its creditor to be substantially engaged in selling others' goods, (2) with respect to each delivery, the aggregate value of the goods is $1,000 or more at the time of delivery, (3) the goods are not consumer goods immediately before delivery, and (4) the transaction does not create a security interest that secures an obligation. UCC § 9–102(a)(13).

consignment sale. See SALE.

consignor (kən-**sI**-nər *or* kon-sI-**nor**). One who dispatches goods to another on consignment.

consiliarius (kən-sil-ee-**air**-ee-əs). [fr. Latin *consilium* "advice"] **1.** *Roman law.* A person who advises a magistrate; one who sits with the judge and assists in deciding cases. See CONCILIUM (1). **2.** *Hist.* A counselor learned in law. See APOCRISARIUS.

consimili casu (kən-**sim**-ə-**lI kay**-s[y]oo), *n.* [Latin "in a like case"] *Hist.* A writ of entry allowing the holder of a reversionary interest in land to sue for the return of land alienated by a life tenant or a tenant by the curtesy. • This writ originated in the Statute of Westminster 2 (13 Edw. I) ch. 24 (1285), which expanded the writs available to litigants by requiring the Chancery to issue a writ for any situation that called for a writ similar to one that had previously issued *consimili casu* ("in a like case"). Specifically, the statute provided (in Latin) that "as often as it shall happen in chancery that in one case a writ is found, and in a like case [*in consimili casu*], falling under the same right, and requiring like remedy, no writ is to be found, the clerks of chancery shall agree in making a writ ...." Many other writs were framed under Westminster 2, but this particular writ's close association with the statute led to its taking the generic name. See ACTIONES NOMINATAE.

Consistorium (kon-sis-**tor**-ee-əm). [Latin] *Roman law.* An imperial council that functioned both as a general council of state and as a supreme court of law.

consistory court (kən-**sis**-tər-ee). *Eccles. law.* In England, a diocesan court exercising jurisdiction over church property, such as a cemetery, and other ecclesiastical matters. • Consistory courts are presided over by the bishop's chancellor or the chancellor's commissary. In some instances, appeals may be taken to the High Court of Justice. Cf. BISHOP'S COURT.

consobrini (kon-sə-**brI**-nI). [Latin] *Roman law.* First cousins; children of brothers or sisters.

consol (**kon**-sol *or* kən-**sol**). See *annuity bond* under BOND (3).

Consolato del Mare (kawn-soh-**lah**-toh del **mah**-ray). [Italian "consolate of the sea"] *Hist. Maritime law.* An influential collection of European maritime customs, referred to by commercial judges (*consuls*) in ports of the kingdom of Aragon and other Mediterranean maritime towns. • The *Consolato del Mare* was published in Barcelona in the 15th century and soon became one of the leading maritime codes of Europe.

consolidate, *vb.* **1.** To combine or unify into one mass or body. **2.** *Corporations.* To unite (two or more corporations) to create one new corporation. **3.** *Civil procedure.* To combine, through court order, two or more actions involving the same parties or issues into a single action ending in a single judgment or, sometimes, in separate judgments. Cf. MERGER (7).

consolidated appeal. See APPEAL.

consolidated bond. See BOND (3).

consolidated financial statement. See FINANCIAL STATEMENT.

consolidated laws. See CODE (1).

consolidated mortgage. See MORTGAGE.

Consolidated Omnibus Budget Reconciliation Act of 1985. A federal statute that requires employers who offer group health coverage to their employees to continue to do so for a prescribed period (usu. 18 to 36 months) after employment has terminated so that the employee can continue to benefit from group-health rates until becoming a member of another health-insurance plan. • The statute temporarily continues group coverage for a person no longer entitled to receive it, such as a terminated employee or an overage dependent. — Abbr. COBRA.

> "In the absence of any type of statutory vesting provision (which would render benefits nonforfeitable), terminated employees were generally left without health care coverage while they were looking for another job. While some state insurance laws provide for limited continuation coverage or individual conversion options, these alternatives were not available in all states .... Thus, COBRA was designed to fill this void, by providing a statutorily mandated mechanism for enabling terminated employees (and their eligible family members) to continue to have access to group health coverage at group rates until they can get another job or otherwise arrange for replacement coverage." I.M. Golub et al., *COBRA Handbook* § 1.1, at 1–2 (1994).

consolidated return. See TAX RETURN.

consolidated school district. See SCHOOL DISTRICT.

consolidated security. See SECURITY.

consolidating statute. See STATUTE.

consolidation, *n.* **1.** The act or process of uniting; the state of being united. **2.** *Corporations.* The unification of two or more corporations by dissolving the existing ones and creating a single new corporation. — Also termed *consolidation of corporations.* Cf. MERGER (7). **3.** *Corporations. Archaic.* A union of the stock, property, or franchises of two or more companies whereby the conduct of their affairs is permanently — or for a long period — put under one management, whether the agreement between them is by lease, sale, or other form of contract, and whether the effect is the dissolution of one, both, or neither of the companies. **4.** *Civil procedure.* The court-ordered unification of two or more actions, involving the same parties and issues, into a single action resulting in a single judgment or, sometimes, in separate judgments. — Also termed *consolidation of actions.* Cf. JOINDER. — **consolidate,** *vb.* — **consolidatory** (kən-**sol**-ə-day-tər-ee), *adj.*

__procedural consolidation.__ See JOINT ADMINISTRATION.

__substantive consolidation.__ *Bankruptcy.* The merger of two or more bankruptcy cases, usu. pending against the same debtor or related debtors, into one estate for purposes of distributing the assets, usu. resulting in the two estates sharing assets and liabilities, and in the extinguishment of duplicate claims and claims between the debtors.

consolidation loan. See LOAN.

consolidation of actions. See CONSOLIDATION.

consolidation of corporations. See CONSOLIDATION.

consonant statement. See STATEMENT.

consortium (kən-**sor**-shee-əm). **1.** The benefits that one person, esp. a spouse, is entitled to receive from another, including companionship, cooperation, affection, aid, and (between spouses) sexual relations <a claim for loss of consortium>. See LOSS OF CONSORTIUM.

__filial consortium__ (**fil**-ee-əl). A child's society, affection, and companionship given to a parent.

__parental consortium.__ A parent's society, affection, and companionship given to a child.

__spousal consortium.__ A spouse's society, affection, and companionship given to the other spouse.

2. *Hist.* The services of a wife or daughter, the loss of which gives rise to a cause of action. • A husband could, for example, bring an action against a person who had injured his wife, "whereby he lost the help or companionship (of his wife)" (*per quod consortium amisit*). **3.** A group of companies that join or associate in an enterprise <several high-tech businesses formed a consortium to create a new supercomputer>. **4.** *Roman law.* A community of undivided goods existing among coheirs after the death of the head of their family (*paterfamilias*). Pl. **consortiums, consortia.**

consortship (**kon**-sort-ship). *Maritime law.* An agreement by which salvors agree to work together to salvage wrecks, the recovery being apportioned among the salvors. • Consortships reduce interference from other salvors, and help to prevent collisions at sea between operators attempting to salvage the same wreck.

conspicuous, *adj.* (Of a term or clause) clearly visible or obvious. • Whether a printed clause is conspicuous as a matter of law usu. depends on the size and style of the typeface. Under the UCC, a term or clause is conspicuous if it is written in a way that a reasonable person against whom it is to operate ought to notice it. UCC § 1–201(10). See FINE PRINT.

conspicuous place. For purposes of posting notices, a location that is reasonably likely to be seen.

conspiracy, *n.* An agreement by two or more persons to commit an unlawful act; a combination for an unlawful purpose. • In criminal law, conspiracy is a separate offense from the crime that is the object of the conspiracy. — Also termed *criminal conspiracy.* — **conspiratorial,** *adj.* Cf. ATTEMPT (2); SOLICITATION (2).

"*Conspiracie* (*conspiratio*) though both in Latine and French it be used for an agreement of men, to doe any thing either good or bad: yet in our lawyers bookes, it is alway taken in the evill part." John Cowell, *The Interpreter* (1607).

"[Conspiracy is an] elastic, sprawling and pervasive offense, ... so vague that it almost defies definition. Despite certain elementary and essential elements, it also, chameleon-like, takes on a special coloration from each of the many independent offenses on which it may be overlaid. It is always 'predominantly mental in composition' because it consists primarily of a meeting of minds and an intent." *Krulewitch v. United States,* 336 U.S. 440, 445–48, 69 S.Ct. 716, 719–20 (1949) (Jackson, J., concurring).

bathtub conspiracy. See *intra-enterprise conspiracy.*

chain conspiracy. A single conspiracy in which each person is responsible for a distinct act within the overall plan, such as an agreement to produce, import, and distribute narcotics in which each person performs only one function. • All participants are interested in the overall scheme and liable for all other participants' acts in furtherance of that scheme.

"In a 'chain' conspiracy, the court looks to whether the parties serve as links in a chain. In *Blumenthal v. United States* (1947), the Supreme Court found that the parties had agreed to sell liquor at prices exceeding the ceiling set by regulations of the Office of Price Administration. The Court found that the agreements were steps in the formulation of one larger general conspiracy. By reason of all having knowledge of the plan's general scope and common end, the disposing of whiskey, they could be drawn together in a single conspiracy." Ellen S. Podgor & Jerold H. Israel, *White Collar Crime in a Nutshell* 52 (2d ed. 1997).

circle conspiracy. See *wheel conspiracy.*

civil conspiracy. An agreement between two or more persons to commit an unlawful act that causes damage to a person or property.

conspiracy in restraint of trade. See RESTRAINT OF TRADE.

hub-and-spoke conspiracy. See *wheel conspiracy.*

intra-enterprise conspiracy. *Antitrust.* A conspiracy existing between two subsidiaries, divisions, or other parts of the same firm. — Also termed *bathtub conspiracy.*

seditious conspiracy. A criminal conspiracy to forcibly (1) overthrow or destroy the U.S. government, (2) oppose its authority, (3) prevent the execution of its laws, or (4) seize or possess its property. 18 USCA § 2384.

wheel conspiracy. A conspiracy in which a single member or group (the "hub") separately agrees with two or more other members or groups (the "spokes"). • The person or group at the hub is the only part liable for all the conspiracies. — Also termed *circle conspiracy*; *hub-and-spoke conspiracy.*

conspirator, *n.* A person who takes part in a conspiracy.

unindicted conspirator. A person who has been identified by law enforcement as a member of a conspiracy, but who has not been named in the indictment charging the person's fellow conspirator with conspiracy. • Prosecutors often name someone an unindicted conspirator because any statement that the unindicted conspirator has made in the course and furtherance of the conspiracy is admissible against the indicted defendants. — Also termed *unindicted coconspirator.*

conspire, *vb.* To engage in conspiracy; to join in a conspiracy.

constable (**kon**-stə-bəl), *n.* **1.** A peace officer responsible for minor judicial duties, such as serving writs and warrants, but with less authority and smaller jurisdiction than a sheriff. **2.** In the United Kingdom, a police officer; also, the title of a police officer. — **constabulary** (kən-**stab**-yə-ler-ee), *adj.* — **constabulary** (body or force), *n.*

constablewick (**kon**-stə-bəl-wik). *Hist.* In the United Kingdom, the territorial jurisdiction of a constable. Cf. BAILIWICK.

constant dollars. The value of current money expressed as a percentage of its buying power in a previous year as determined by the consumer price index.

constat (**kon**-stat). [Latin "it is settled"] *Hist.* A certificate made by the Clerk of the Pipe and the auditors of the Exchequer at the request of a person intending to plead in the Court of Exchequer for the discharge of some item. • The *constat* certified what appeared on record.

constate (kən-**stayt**), *vb.* To establish, constitute, or ordain. • *Constate* usu. appears in relation to corporate documents; for example, the *constating* instruments of a corporation are its charter, organic law, or grant of powers to it.

constituency. The residents of an electoral district.

constituent, *adj.* **1.** (Of a component) that helps make up or complete a unit or a whole <a constituent element of the criminal offense>. **2.** (Of an assembly) able to frame or amend a constitution <a constituent council>.

constituent, *n.* **1.** A person who gives another the authority to act as a representative; a principal who appoints an agent. **2.** Someone who is represented by a legislator or other elected official. **3.** One part of something that makes up a whole; an element. — **constituency,** *n.*

constituent element. An essential component of a crime or cause of action.

constituere (kon-sti-**tyoo**-ə-ree), *vb.* [Latin "to appoint"] *Hist.* To appoint (someone). • *Constituere* was used principally in powers of attorney: *attornavi et in loco meo constitui* ("I have attorned and put in my place").

constituted authority. See AUTHORITY (3).

constitutio (kon-sti-**t[y]oo**-shee-oh). [Latin "a decree"] **1.** *Roman law.* An imperial decree; a law issued by the emperor; later, a collection of laws. • The *constitutiones* took various forms, including *orationes* (laws submitted to the Senate), *edicta* (laws — usu. of a general character — put forth by the emperor without Senate approval), *mandata* (administrative directives to imperial officials), *decreta* (decisions by the emperor in legal cases), and *rescripta* (the emperor's responses to questions posed by litigants or imperial officials). Over time, the rapidly increasing number of *constitutiones* prompted their arrangement into collections such as the Theodosian Code and the Code of Justinian. Pl. ***constitutiones*** (kon-sti-t[y]oo-shee-**oh**-neez). See CODEX THEODOSIANUS; JUSTINIAN CODE.

> "The name *constitutiones*, applied to the law-making utterances of the Roman emperors, had a very different meaning from our word 'constitution,' used to denote the fundamental, organic law of the state. Every official public document issuing from the emperor, and creating, declaring, or modifying law, was a *constitutio*. . . . [A]nd it is hardly necessary to say that, although professing to come from the person of the emperor, they were actually composed by jurists, and usually by those who stood first in their profession." James Hadley, *Introduction to Roman Law* 6–7 (1881).

2. *Civil law.* A settlement achieved without a trial; the sum paid according to the settlement. **3.** *Hist.* In England, a statute; a provision of a statute.

constitution. 1. The fundamental and organic law of a nation or state, establishing the conception, character, and organization of its government, as well as prescribing the extent of its sovereign power and the manner of its exercise.

flexible constitution. A constitution that is not defined or set apart in a distinct document and that is not distinguishable from other law in the way in which its terms can be legislatively altered. • The British constitution is of this type.

rigid constitution. A constitution embodied in a special and distinct enactment, the terms of which cannot be altered by ordinary forms of legislation. • The U.S. Constitution, which cannot be changed without the consent of three-fourths of the state legislatures or through a constitutional convention, is of this type.

unwritten constitution. The customs and values, some of which are expressed in statutes, that provide the organic and fundamental law of a state or country that does not have a single written law functioning as a constitution.

2. The written instrument embodying this fundamental law.

constitutional, *adj.* **1.** Of or relating to a constitution <constitutional rights>. **2.** Proper under a constitution <constitutional actions>.

constitutional challenge. See CHALLENGE (1).

constitutional convention. An assembly of state or national delegates who meet to frame, amend, or revise their constitution.

constitutional court. See COURT.

constitutional-fact doctrine. 1. The rule that federal courts are not bound by an administrative agency's findings of fact when the facts involve whether the agency has exceeded constitutional limitations on its power, esp. regarding personal rights. • Instead, the courts are charged with making an independent inquiry based on the record. **2.** The now discredited rule that a federal appellate court is not bound by a trial court's findings of fact when constitutional rights are implicated. Cf. JURISDICTIONAL-FACT DOCTRINE.

constitutional freedom. A basic liberty guaranteed by the Constitution or Bill of Rights, such as the freedom of speech. — Also termed *constitutional protection*.

constitutional homestead. See HOMESTEAD.

constitutional immunity. See IMMUNITY (1).

constitutionality, *n.* The quality or state of being constitutional <the constitutionality of the senator's bill is questionable>.

constitutionalize, *vb.* **1.** To provide with a constitution <constitutionalize the new government>. **2.** To make constitutional; to bring in line with a constitution <the court plans to constitutionalize the segregated school district>. **3.** To make a constitutional question out of a question of law <the dissenter accused the majority of unnecessarily constitutionalizing its decision>.

constitutional law. 1. The body of law deriving from the U.S. Constitution and dealing primarily with governmental powers, civil rights, and civil liberties. **2.** The body of legal rules that determine the constitution of a state with a flexible constitution.

constitutional limitation. A constitutional provision that restricts the powers of a governmental branch, department, agency, or officer.

constitutional monarchy. See *limited monarchy* under MONARCHY.

constitutional office. A public position that is created by a constitution, rather than by a statute.

constitutional officer. A government official whose office is created by a constitution, rather than by a statute; one whose term of office is fixed and defined by a constitution.

constitutional protection. See CONSTITUTIONAL FREEDOM.

constitutional question. A legal issue resolvable by the interpretation of a constitution, rather than a statute.

constitutional right. A right guaranteed by a constitution; esp., one guaranteed by the U.S. Constitution or by a state constitution.

constitutional taking. See TAKING (2).

constitutional tort. See TORT.

constitutiones principum. [Latin] *Roman law.* Roman imperial enactments, which were the sole form of legislation in the third century A.D.

Constitutions of Clarendon. *Hist.* Statutes enacted in 1164, during the reign of Henry II, by which the jurisdiction of the ecclesiastical courts was limited and the clerics' exemptions from secular jurisdiction were greatly narrowed.

> "During the first half of the twelfth century the claims of the church were growing, and the duty of asserting them passed into the hands of men who were not mere theologians but expert lawyers. Then, as all know, came the quarrel between Henry and Becket. In the Constitutions of Clarendon (1164) the king offered to the prelates a written treaty, a treaty which, so he said, embodied the 'customs' of his ancestors, more especially of his grandfather. Becket, after some hesitation, rejected the constitutions. The dispute waxed hot; certain of the customs were condemned by the pope. The murder followed .... [F]rom [Henry's] time onwards the lay courts, rather than the spiritual, are the aggressors and the victors in almost every contest." 1 Frederick Pollock & Frederic W. Maitland, *The History of English Law* 124–25 (2d ed. 1898).

constitutor (**kon**-stə-t[y]oo-tər). [Latin "an orderer, arranger"] *Roman law.* A person who, by agreement, becomes responsible for the payment of another's debt.

constitutum (kon-sti-**t[y]oo**-təm). [Latin "agreed arrangement"] *Roman law.* **1.** An agreement to pay (one's own or another's) existing debt. • A *constitutum* was not a novation;

the creditor could still sue the original debtor. It differed from a stipulation because it had to be for an existing debt. **2.** The fixing of a day for the repayment of money owed.

constitutum debiti (kon-sti-**t[y]oo**-təm **deb**-ə-tɪ). [Latin "debt agreement"] *Roman law.* A promise to discharge an existing liability that is either one's own (*constitutum debiti proprii*) or another's (*constitutum debiti alieni*).

constitutum possessorium (kon-sti-**t[y]oo**-təm pah-ses-**sor**-ee-əm). [Latin "possessory agreement"] *Roman law.* A type of constructive delivery in which mediate possession is transferred while the immediate possession remains in the transferor; the agreement by which this transfer is brought about. • In the context of a security interest, the pledged property may remain in the possession of the debtor, but as bailee of the creditor. For the other two types of constructive delivery, see ATTORNMENT; TRADITIO BREVI MANU.

> "[Another] form of constructive delivery is that which the commentators on the civil law have termed *constitutum possessiorum* .... Any thing may be effectually delivered by means of an agreement that the possessor of it shall for the future hold it no longer on his own account but on account of someone else.... [I]f I buy goods from a warehouseman, they are delivered to me so soon as he has agreed with me that he will hold them as warehouseman on my account. The position is then exactly the same as if I had first taken actual delivery of them, and then brought them back to the warehouse, and deposited them there for safe custody." John Salmond, *Jurisprudence* 306 (Glanville L. Williams ed., 10th ed. 1947).

construction, *n.* **1.** The act of building by combining or arranging parts or elements; the thing so built. **2.** The act or process of interpreting or explaining the sense or intention of a writing (usu. a statute, opinion, or instrument). — **construct** (for sense 1), *vb.* — **construe** (for sense 2), *vb.*

> "Construction, as applied to written law, is the art or process of discovering and expounding the meaning and intention of the authors of the law with respect to its application to a given case, where that intention is rendered doubtful either by reason of apparently conflicting provisions or directions, or by reason of the fact that the given case is not explicitly provided for in the law." Henry Campbell Black, *Handbook on the Construction and Interpretation of the Laws* 1 (1896).

> "Some authors have attempted to introduce a distinction between 'interpretation' and 'construction.' Etymologically there is, perhaps, such a distinction; but it has not been accepted by the profession. For practical purposes any such distinction may be ignored, in view of the real object of both interpretation and construction, which is merely to ascertain the meaning and will of the lawmaking body, in order that it may be enforced." William M. Lile et al., *Brief Making and the Use of Law Books* 337 (3d ed. 1914).

> "There is no explanation of the distinction between interpretation and construction [in Blackstone], nor can it be inferred from the matters dealt with under each head. The distinction is drawn in some modern works, but it is not taken in this book because it lacks an agreed basis. Some writers treat interpretation as something which is only called for when there is a dispute about the meaning of statutory words, while speaking of construction as a process to which all statutes, like all other writings, are necessarily subject when read by anyone. Others treat interpretation as something which is mainly concerned with the meaning of statutory words, while regarding construction as a process which mainly relates to the ascertainment of the intention of the legislature." Rupert Cross, *Statutory Interpretation* 18 (1976).

contemporaneous construction. An interpretation given at or near the time when a writing was prepared, usu. by one or more persons involved in its preparation. — Also termed *contemporaneous and practical interpretation.*

liberal construction. An interpretation that applies a writing in light of the situation presented and that tends to effectuate the spirit and purpose of the writing. — Also termed *equitable construction*; *loose construction*; *broad interpretation.*

> "Liberal construction ... expands the meaning of the statute to embrace cases which are clearly within the spirit or reason of the law, or within the evil which it was designed to remedy, provided such an interpretation is not inconsistent with the language used. It resolves all reasonable doubts in favor of the applicability of the statute to the particular case." William M. Lile et al., *Brief Making and the Use of Law Books* 343 (3d ed. 1914).

literal construction. See *strict construction.*

purposive construction (**pər**-pə-siv). An interpretation that looks to the "evil" that the statute is trying to correct (i.e., the statute's purpose). — Also termed *teleological interpretation.*

strict construction. **1.** An interpretation that considers only the literal words of a writing. — Also termed *literal construction*; *literal interpretation.* See STRICT CONSTRUCTIONISM. **2.** A construction that considers words narrowly, usu. in their historical context. • This type of construction treats statutory and contractual words with highly restrictive readings. — Also termed *strict interpretation.* **3.** The philosophy underlying strict interpretation of statutes; STRICT CONSTRUCTIONISM.

> "Strict construction of a statute is that which refuses to expand the law by implications or equitable considerations, but confines its operation to cases which are clearly within the letter of the statute, as well as within

its spirit or reason, not so as to defeat the manifest purpose of the Legislature, but so as to resolve all reasonable doubts against the applicability of the statute to the particular case." William M. Lile et al., *Brief Making and the Use of Law Books* 343 (3d ed. 1914).

"Strict interpretation is an equivocal expression, for it means either literal or narrow. When a provision is ambiguous, one of its meanings may be wider than the other, and the strict (i.e., narrow) sense is not necessarily the strict (i.e., literal) sense." John Salmond, *Jurisprudence* 171 n.(t) (Glanville L. Williams ed., 10th ed. 1947).

construction act. See ACT (3).

construction bond. See BOND (3).

construction contract. See CONTRACT.

construction financing. See *interim financing* under FINANCING.

construction lien. See *mechanic's lien* under LIEN.

construction mortgage. See MORTGAGE.

construction warranty. See WARRANTY (2).

constructive, *adj*. Legally imputed; having an effect in law though not necessarily in fact. • Courts usu. give something a constructive effect for equitable reasons <the court held that the shift supervisor had constructive knowledge of the machine's failure even though he did not actually know until two days later>. See LEGAL FICTION. Cf. ACTUAL.

constructive adverse possession. See ADVERSE POSSESSION.

constructive assent. See ASSENT.

constructive authority. See AUTHORITY (1).

constructive bailment. See BAILMENT.

constructive breach. See *anticipatory breach* under BREACH OF CONTRACT.

constructive breaking into a house. A breaking made out by construction of law, as when a burglar gains entry by threat or fraud.

constructive condition. See CONDITION (2).

constructive contempt. See CONTEMPT.

constructive contract. See *implied-in-law contract* under CONTRACT.

constructive conversion. See CONVERSION (2).

constructive custody. See CUSTODY (1).

constructive delivery. See DELIVERY.

constructive desertion. See DESERTION.

constructive discharge. See DISCHARGE (7).

constructive dividend. See DIVIDEND.

constructive escape. See ESCAPE (2).

constructive eviction. See EVICTION.

constructive force. See FORCE.

constructive fraud. See FRAUD.

constructive intent. See INTENT (1).

constructive knowledge. See KNOWLEDGE.

constructive larceny. See LARCENY.

constructive loss. See *constructive total loss* (1) under LOSS.

constructive malice. See *implied malice* under MALICE.

constructive murder. See *felony murder* under MURDER.

constructive notice. See NOTICE.

constructive payment. See PAYMENT.

constructive possession. See POSSESSION.

constructive-receipt doctrine. The rule that gross income under a taxpayer's control before it is actually received (such as accumulated interest income that has not been withdrawn) must be included by the taxpayer in gross income, unless the actual receipt is subject to significant constraints. IRC (26 USCA) § 451.

constructive reduction to practice. See REDUCTION TO PRACTICE.

constructive search. See SEARCH.

constructive seisin. See *seisin in law* under SEISIN.

constructive service. See SERVICE (2).

constructive taking. See TAKING (1).

constructive total loss. See LOSS.

constructive transfer. See TRANSFER.

constructive trust. See TRUST.

construe (kən-**stroo**), *vb.* To analyze and explain the meaning of (a sentence or passage) <the court construed the language of the statute>.

constuprate (**kon**-st[y]ə-prayt). *Archaic.* To rape or violate (a person).

consuetudinarius (kon-swə-t[y]oo-di-**nair**-ee-əs). [fr. Latin *consuetudo* "custom"] *Hist. Eccles. law.* A book containing the rites and forms of divine offices or customs of abbeys and monasteries.

consuetudinary law. See LAW.

Consuetudines Feudorum (kon-swə-**t**[**y**]**oo**-di-neez fyoo-**dor**-əm). [Law Latin "the customs of fiefs"] *Hist.* FEUDORUM LIBRI.

consuetudinibus et serviciis (kon-swə-t[y]oo-**din**-ə-bəs et sər-**vish**-ee-is). [Law Latin "customs and services"] *Hist.* A writ of right that lay against a tenant who withheld rent or services from the lord.

consuetudo (kon-swə-**t**[**y**]**oo**-doh). [Latin "custom"] **1.** *Roman law.* Custom; long-established usage or practice. **2.** *Hist.* Customary law. • *Consuetudo* generally bears this sense, referring to law that has been long approved by the will of the people. It is a broad term that includes both the common law and the statutory law of England. **3.** *Hist.* A duty or tax.

consuetudo anglicana (kon-swə-**t**[**y**]**oo**-doh ang-gli-**kay**-noh). [Law Latin "the custom of England"] *Hist.* The English common law, as distinguished from Roman or civil law.

consuetudo curiae (kon-swə-**t**[**y**]**oo**-doh **kyoor**-ee-ee). [Latin] *Hist.* The custom or practice of a court.

consuetudo mercatorum (kon-swə-**t**[**y**]**oo**-doh mər-kə-**tor**-əm). [Latin "the custom of merchants"] *Hist.* See LAW MERCHANT. — Also termed *consuetudo mercatoria.*

consul (**kon**-səl), *n.* **1.** A governmental representative living in a foreign country to oversee commercial and other matters involving the representative's home country and its citizens in that foreign country. • Because they are not diplomatic agents, consuls are subject to local law and jurisdiction. — **consular** (**kon**-sə-lər), *adj.* — **consulship** (**kon**-səl-ship), *n.*

> "Consuls are commercial, not diplomatic agents. They reside abroad for the purpose of protecting the individual interests of traders, travellers, and mariners belonging to the State which employs them.... They exercise jurisdiction over their countrymen, their persons are inviolable, their residences may be used as asylums in the case of war or tumult, and in fact they possess more than the ordinary diplomatic immunities." T.J. Lawrence, *A Handbook of Public International Law* 86–87 (10th ed. 1925).

> "Consuls are not diplomatic agents; they perform various services for a state or its subjects in another state, without, however, representing the former in the full sense. They may be nationals of either state, and generally they are made subject to the authority of the diplomatic representative of the state for which they act. They watch over commercial interests of the state for which they act; collection information for it; help its nationals with advice, administer their property if they die abroad, and register their births, deaths, and marriages; they authenticate documents for legal purposes, take depositions from witnesses, visa passports, and the like." J.L. Brierly, *The Law of Nations* 216 (5th ed. 1955).

> "The usual criterion used for the distinction between diplomats and consuls is the representative character of the former of which the latter are devoid. However, this distinction is not altogether correct. Undoubtedly diplomatic agents have a general representative character since in all matters and relations they represent their country in the state to which they are accredited. Consuls, on the other hand, as state organs, also represent their country in another state, but only in matters within their competence. Thus, the representative character of consuls is, like their competence, specific, and secondary to that of diplomatic agents." Constantin Economidès, "Consuls," in 1 *Encyclopedia of Public International Law* 770 (1992).

consul general. A high-ranking consul appointed to a strategically important region and often having supervisory powers over other regions or other consuls.

2. *Roman law.* One of two chief magistrates elected annually during the Republic to exercise supreme authority. • Under the Empire, the consulship was reduced to a sinecure, held by appointees of the emperor or the emperor himself.

"The principal inheritors of the royal authority and dignity were the two consuls elected by the comitia centuriata. They enjoyed equal powers. In the calendar the year was distinguished by their names. They convoked and initiated legislation in either comitia. In special emergencies, particularly in times of grave crisis, either consul might appoint a dictator who exercised supreme authority, but not beyond six months, unless reappointed.... It was abolished by Justinian in A.D. 541, though later emperors continued to assume the title." R.W. Lee, *The Elements of Roman Law* 14 (4th ed. 1956).

consular court. See COURT.

consular invoice. See INVOICE.

consular jurisdiction. The exercise of a judicial function by a consul in a foreign territory, as by performing a wedding ceremony between nationals of the country represented by the consul.

consular law. The law relating to consuls, developed through custom and multitudes of bilateral consular agreements.

consular marriage. See MARRIAGE (1).

consular relations. *Int'l law.* The aggregate of relations established between two countries through the exercise of consuls' functions on behalf of a sending state within the territory of a receiving state. See SENDING STATE; RECEIVING STATE.

consulate (**kon**-sə-lit). **1.** The office or jurisdiction of a consul <the senator advised the businessman to notify the U.S. consulate in Kuwait before visiting the country>. **2.** The location of a consul's office or residence <the family was staying on the second floor, just above the Turkish consulate>.

foreign consulate. The consulate of a foreign country in the receiving state.

3. Government by consuls <after the French Revolution, the Directory was overthrown and the Consulate was created>. • This sense of *consulate* is based on the original Roman meaning ("chief magistrate") — not on the modern sense of an overseas representative of a country.

consul general. See CONSUL.

consultation, *n.* **1.** The act of asking the advice or opinion of someone (such as a lawyer). **2.** A meeting in which parties consult or confer. **3.** *Int'l law.* The interactive methods by which states seek to prevent or resolve disputes. — **consult,** *vb.* — **consulting, consultative,** *adj.*

consulting expert. See EXPERT.

consumable, *n.* A thing (such as food) that cannot be used without changing or extinguishing its substance. Cf. NONCONSUMABLE.

consumer. A person who buys goods or services for personal, family, or household use, with no intention of resale; a natural person who uses products for personal rather than business purposes. 40 CFR § 721(b)(1).

consumer boycott. See BOYCOTT.

consumer-contemplation test. A method of imposing product liability on a manufacturer if the evidence shows that a product's danger is greater than what a reasonable consumer would expect. — Also termed *consumer-user-contemplation test*; *consumer-expectation test.* Cf. RISK-UTILITY TEST.

consumer credit. See CREDIT (4).

Consumer Credit Code. See UNIFORM CONSUMER CREDIT CODE.

Consumer Credit Protection Act. A federal statute that safeguards the consumer in connection with the use of credit by (1) requiring full disclosure of the terms of the loan agreement, including finance charges, (2) restricting the garnishment of wages, and (3) regulating the use of credit cards (15 USCA §§ 1601–1693). • Many states have adopted consumer-credit-protection acts. — Also termed *Truth in Lending Act* (abbr. TILA). See UNIFORM CONSUMER CREDIT CODE.

consumer-credit sale. See SALE.

consumer-credit transaction. A transaction by which a person receives a loan for buying consumer goods or services. • Consumer-credit transactions are usu. subject to regulations enacted for the consumer's protection.

consumer debt. See DEBT.

consumer-expectation test. See CONSUMER-CONTEMPLATION TEST.

consumer finance company. See FINANCE COMPANY.

consumer goods. See GOODS.

consumer-goods transaction. *Secured transactions.* A transaction in which (1) an individual incurs an obligation primarily for person, family, or household purposes, and (2) a security interest in consumer goods secures the obligation. UCC § 9–102(a)(16).

consumer law. The area of law dealing with consumer transactions — that is, a person's obtaining credit, goods, real property, or services for personal, family, or household purposes. — Also termed *consumer-transactions law*.

consumer lease. See LEASE.

consumer loan. See LOAN.

consumer price index. An index that tracks the price of goods and services purchased by the average consumer and that is published monthly by the U.S. Bureau of Labor Statistics. — Abbr. CPI. — Also termed *cost-of-living index*. Cf. PRODUCER PRICE INDEX.

consumer product. An item of personal property that is distributed in commerce and is normally used for personal, family, or household purposes. 15 USCA § 2301(1).

consumer-protection law. A state or federal statute designed to protect consumers against unfair trade and credit practices involving consumer goods, as well as to protect consumers against faulty and dangerous goods.

consumer transaction. A bargain or deal in which a party acquires property or services primarily for a personal, family, or household purpose.

consumer-transactions law. See CONSUMER LAW.

consumer-user-contemplation test. See CONSUMER-CONTEMPLATION TEST.

consummate (kən-**səm**-it), *adj.* Completed; fully accomplished. • *Consummate* was used frequently at common law to describe the status of a contract or an estate, such as the transformation of a husband's interest in his wife's inheritance from that of a tenant by the curtesy *initiate* to a tenant by curtesy *consummate* upon her death (assuming that a child had been born during the marriage). See *curtesy consummate* under CURTESY.

consummate (**kon**-sə-mayt), *vb.* **1.** To bring to completion; esp., to make (a marriage) complete by sexual intercourse. **2.** To achieve; fulfill. **3.** To perfect; carry to the highest degree.

consummate dower. See DOWER.

consummate lien. See LIEN.

consumption. The act of destroying a thing by using it; the use of a thing in a way that thereby exhausts it.

consumption tax. See TAX.

containment. *Int'l law.* The policy of restricting the ideological and territorial expansion of one's enemy. • This was the basic philosophy of the United States during the Cold War.

contango (kən-**tang**-goh). *Securities.* **1.** A market in which long-term futures or options contracts sell at a premium over short-term contracts. — Also termed *normal market.* **2.** The premium so paid. • The premium paid for securities with longer maturities reflects the cost of holding the commodity for future delivery.

contemn (kən-**tem**), *vb.* To treat (as laws or court orders) with contemptuous disregard. See CONTEMPT.

contemner (kən-**tem**-ər *or* -nər). A person who is guilty of contempt before an instrumentality of government, such as a court or legislature. — Also spelled *contemnor*.

contemplation of bankruptcy. The thought of declaring bankruptcy because of the inability to continue current financial operations, often coupled with action designed to thwart the distribution of assets in a bankruptcy proceeding. — Also termed *contemplation of insolvency*.

contemplation of death. The thought of dying, not necessarily from an imminent danger, but as the compelling reason to transfer property to another. See *gift causa mortis* under GIFT.

contemplation of insolvency. See CONTEMPLATION OF BANKRUPTCY.

contemporanea expositio (kən-tem-pə-**ray**-nee-ə eks-pə-**zish**-ee-oh). [Latin "contemporaneous exposition"] The doctrine that the best meaning of a statute or document is the one given by those who enacted it or signed it, and that the meaning publicly given by contemporary or long professional usage is presumed to be the true one, even if the language may have a popular or an etymological meaning that is very different.

contemporaneous and practical interpretation. See *contemporaneous construction* under CONSTRUCTION.

contemporaneous construction. See CONSTRUCTION.

contemporaneous-construction doctrine. The rule that the initial interpretation of an ambiguous statute by an administrative agency or lower court is entitled to great deference if the interpretation has been used over a long period.

contemporaneous-objection rule. The doctrine that a proper objection to the admission of evidence must be made at trial for the issue of admissibility to be considered on appeal.

contemporary community standard. The gauge by which a fact-finder decides whether material is obscene, judging by its patent offensiveness and its pruriency in the locale at a given time. See OBSCENITY (1).

> "Both pruriency and patent offensiveness are determined by 'contemporary community standards.' But what is the relevant community? In *Miller*, the Court rejected the contention that only a national community standard, free of local biases, would provide adequate First Amendment protection and allowed lower courts to use local standards in defining what is obscene. Subsequent cases have made it clear that the state may choose to omit reference to any particular geographic community, state or local, although it may do so. If a geographic reference is omitted, each jury is free to ascertain the contemporary community standard." Jerome A. Barron & C. Thomas Dienes, *Constitutional Law in a Nutshell* 396 (3d ed. 1995).

contempt, *n.* **1.** The act or state of despising; the condition of being despised. **2.** Conduct that defies the authority or dignity of a court or legislature. • Because such conduct interferes with the administration of justice, it is punishable, usu. by fine or imprisonment. See CONTUMACY. — Also termed *contempt of court* — **contemptuous,** *adj.*

> "Contempt is a disregard of, or disobedience to, the rules or orders of a legislative or judicial body, or an interruption of its proceedings by disorderly behavior or insolent language, in its presence or so near thereto as to disturb the proceedings or to impair the respect due to such a body." Edward M. Dangel, *Contempt* § 1, at 2 (1939).

civil contempt. The failure to obey a court order that was issued for another party's benefit. • A civil-contempt proceeding is coercive or remedial in nature. The usual sanction is to confine the contemner until he or she complies with the court order.

consequential contempt. **1.** Contempt that, although not amounting to gross insolence or direct opposition, tends to create a universal disregard of the power and authority of courts and judges. **2.** See *constructive contempt.*

constructive contempt. Contempt that is committed outside of court, as when a party disobeys a court order. — Also termed *consequential contempt*; *indirect contempt.*

contempt of Congress. Deliberate interference with the duties and powers of Congress, such as a witness's refusal to answer a question from a congressional committee. • Contempt of Congress is a criminal offense. 2 USCA § 192.

criminal contempt. An act that obstructs justice or attacks the integrity of the court. • A criminal-contempt proceeding is punitive in nature. — Also termed *common-law contempt.*

> "Criminal contempt is a crime in the ordinary sense; it is a violation of the law, a public wrong which is punishable by fine or imprisonment or both." *Bloom v. Illinois,* 391 U.S. 194, 201, 88 S.Ct. 1477, 1481 (1968).

direct contempt. Contempt that is committed in open court, as when a lawyer insults a judge on the bench.

indirect contempt. See *constructive contempt.*

contempt power. The power of a public institution (as Congress or a court) to punish someone who shows contempt for the process, orders, or proceedings of that institution.

contempt proceeding. See PROCEEDING.

contenement (kən-**ten**-ə-mənt). *Hist.* **1.** Freehold land held by a feudal tenant, esp. land used to support the tenant. • Magna Carta exempted this property from seizure.

> "*Contenement,* (*contenementum*) seemeth to be the free hould land, which lyeth to a mans tenement or dwelling house, that is in his owne occupation. For *magna carta. ca.* 14. you have these words: A free man shall not be amerced for a small fault, but after the quantity of the fault: and for a great fault, after the maner thereof, saving to him his contenement or free hould. And a merchant likewise shal be amerced saving to him his

merchandies: and any other villaine then owers, shal be amerced saving his wainage. . . ." John Cowell, *The Interpreter* (1607).

2. A person's reputation or standing in the community. • Though *contenement* as used in this sense is also rooted in the ownership of land, it may stem from the Law French *contenance* ("countenance") rather than the Law Latin *contenementum* ("with tenement"), as used in sense 1.

"Contenement signifies his Countenance, Credit, or Reputation, which he hath, together with, and by reason of his Freehold; and in this sense does the Statute of 1 Edw. 3 and *Old Nat. Br.* use it, where *Countenance* is used for *Contenement*: The Armor of a Soldier is his Countenance; the Books of a Schollar, his Countenance; and the like." Thomas Blount, *Nomo-Lexicon: A Law-Dictionary* (1670).

content-based restriction. *Constitutional law.* A restraint on the substance of a particular type of speech. • This type of restriction can survive a challenge only if it is based on a compelling state interest and its measures are narrowly drawn to accomplish that end. See SPEECH (1).

contentious jurisdiction. See JURISDICTION.

contentious possession. See *hostile possession* under POSSESSION.

contents unknown. A statement placed on a bill of lading to show that the carrier does not know what is inside shipped containers. • Carriers use this phrase in an attempt to limit their liability for damage to the goods shipped.

content-valid test. A job-applicant examination that bears a close relationship to the skills required by the job. • Content-validation studies are often performed in employment-discrimination cases that contest the validity of an examination.

"The simplest form of test validation is where the test replicates major portions of the job, as for example, where a test measuring typing or computer literacy is used to select a secretarial support person. . . . A content valid test must measure or replicate a 'representative sample' of the job's duties. It is not valid if it measures only a small portion of those duties. For example, fire fighters may need to write reports, but a grammar test is too narrow to be content valid." Mack A. Player, *Federal Law of Employment Discrimination in a Nutshell* 101 (3d ed. 1992).

conterminous, *adj.* **1.** Sharing a common boundary <the surveyor set a new line between the conterminous counties>. **2.** Enclosed within a common boundary <all 48 conterminous states of this country>.

contest (kən-**test**), *vb.* **1.** To strive to win or hold; contend <he chose to contest for the prize>. **2.** To litigate or call into question; challenge <they want to contest the will>. **3.** To deny an adverse claim or assert a defense to it in a court proceeding <she contests that charge>. — **contest** (**kon**-test), *n.*

contestability clause (kən-tes-tə-**bil**-ə-tee). *Insurance.* A policy provision setting forth when and under what conditions the insurer may contest a claim or void the policy based on a representation or omission made when the policy was issued. • Contestability clauses usu. lapse after two years. — Also termed *contestable clause*. Cf. INCONTESTABILITY CLAUSE.

contestant. One who contests the validity of a will. — Also termed *objectant*; *caveator*.

contestatio litis (kon-tes-**tay**-shee-oh **lI**-tis). [Latin "contestation of suit"] **1.** *Roman law.* A position statement in an action, given by the litigants to the praetor for approval and submission to a judge (*judex*) for a decision.

"Both parties being present, or represented, before the praetor, the plaintiff stated the nature of his claim and asked for an action. It lay in the discretion of the praetor to give or to refuse it. . . . If, in the event, the praetor refused any action at all, or any action which the plaintiff was willing to accept, the matter was at an end. . . . If, on the other hand, subject to the direction and approval of the praetor, the parties agreed upon the issues to be referred . . . [a] document framed in identical terms was issued to the judex by the praetor as his authority to act. This ceremonial in which three persons concurred (plaintiff, defendant, praetor) was the litis contestatio." R.W. Lee, *The Elements of Roman Law* 179–80 (4th ed. 1956).

2. *Hist.* The development in a lawsuit — brought about by the litigants' alternating statements — of a point in controversy. **3.** *Hist.* An issue developed by the litigants' alternating statements. **4.** CONTESTATION OF SUIT. — Also termed *litis contestatio*. See LITISCONTESTATION.

contestation of suit (kon-tes-**tay**-shən). *Eccles. law.* The point in an action when the defendant answers the plaintiff's libel (i.e., complaint); the plea and joinder of an issue. — Also termed *contestatio litis*.

context, *n.* **1.** The surrounding text of a word or passage, used to determine the meaning of that word or passage <his remarks were taken out of context>. **2.** Setting or environment <in the

context of foreign relations>. — **contextual,** *adj.*

contiguity (kon-ti-**gyoo**-ə-tee), *n.* The state or condition of being contiguous <contiguity existed between the two adjoining tracts of land>.

contiguous (kən-**tig**-yoo-əs), *adj.* **1.** Touching at a point or along a boundary; ADJOINING <Texas and Oklahoma are contiguous>. **2.** Near in time or sequence; successive <contiguous thunder and lightning>.

contiguous zone. *Int'l law.* An area abutting and extending beyond the territorial sea, in which countries have limited powers to enforce customs as well as fiscal, sanitary, and immigration laws.

Continental Congress. The first national governmental assembly in the United States, formed in 1774 to protest British treatment of the colonies. • The Second Continental Congress, commencing in 1775, adopted the Declaration of Independence and served as the national government until the Articles of Confederation were ratified in 1781.

contingency (kən-**tin**-jən-see). **1.** An event that may or may not occur; a possibility. **2.** The condition of being dependent on chance; uncertainty. **3.** CONTINGENT FEE.

contingency fee. See CONTINGENT FEE.

contingency reserve. See *contingent fund* under FUND.

contingency with a double aspect. A contingent remainder existing along with a second remainder, the latter taking the remainder only if the first fails. • In the following example, this type of remainder would arise if A never has children: "to A for life, and if A has children, then to the children and their heirs forever; and if A dies without children, then to B and B's heirs forever." See *contingent remainder* under REMAINDER.

contingent (kən-**tin**-jənt), *adj.* **1.** Possible; uncertain; unpredictable <the trust was contingent, and the contingency never occurred>. **2.** Dependent on something else; conditional <her acceptance of the position was contingent upon the firm's agreeing to guarantee her husband a position as well>.

contingent annuity. See ANNUITY.

contingent beneficiary. See BENEFICIARY.

contingent claim. See CLAIM (4).

contingent debt. See DEBT.

contingent estate. See ESTATE.

contingent fee. A fee charged for a lawyer's services only if the lawsuit is successful or is favorably settled out of court. • Contingent fees are usu. calculated as a percentage of the client's net recovery (such as 25% of the recovery if the case is settled, and 33% if the case is won at trial). — Also termed *contingency fee*; *contingency*.

reverse contingent fee. A fee in which a defense lawyer's compensation depends in whole or in part on how much money the lawyer saves the client, given the client's potential liability — so that the lower the settlement or judgment, the higher the lawyer's fee. • For example, if a client might be liable for up to $2 million, and agrees to pay the lawyer 40% of the difference between $1 million and the amount of the settlement or judgment, then a settlement of $800,000 would result in a fee of $80,000 (40% of the $200,000 under the threshold amount of $1 million). — Also termed *negative contingent fee*; *defense contingent fee*; *reverse bonus*.

contingent fund. See FUND (1).

contingent guaranty. See GUARANTY.

contingent interest. See INTEREST (2).

contingent-interest mortgage. See MORTGAGE.

contingent legacy. See LEGACY.

contingent liability. See LIABILITY.

contingent ownership. See OWNERSHIP.

contingent remainder. See REMAINDER.

contingent trust. See TRUST.

contingent use. See USE (4).

contingent will. See WILL.

continual claim. *Hist.* A formal claim to a tract of land made by an out-of-possession owner who is deterred from taking possession by a menace of some type. • The claim — called *continual* because it had to be renewed annually — preserved the claimant's right to the land. The owner had to make the claim as near to the land as could be done safely. This procedure gave the disseised person the same benefits (such as the right to devise the land) as a legal entry. The continual claim was abolished early in the 19th century.

> "Continual claim is, where a man hath right to enter into certain lands whereof another is seised in fee, or fee tail, and dares not enter for fear of death or beating, but approaches as nigh as he dares, and makes claim thereto within the year and day before the death of him that hath the lands ...." *Termes de la Ley* 114 (1st Am. ed. 1812).

continual injury. See INJURY.

continuance, *n.* **1.** The act of keeping up, maintaining, or prolonging <continuance of the formal tradition>. **2.** Duration; time of continuing <the senator's continuance in office>. **3.** *Procedure.* The adjournment or postponement of a trial or other proceeding to a future date <motion for continuance>. — **continue,** *vb.* Cf. RECESS (1).

continuando (kən-tin-yoo-**an**-doh). [Law Latin "by continuing"] *Hist.* An allegation charging that the trespass or other wrongful act complained of constitutes a continuing tort against the plaintiff's property.

> "In trespasses of a permanent nature, where the injury is continually renewed, (as by spoiling or consuming the herbage with the defendant's cattle) the declaration may allege the injury to have been committed by *continuation* from one given day to another, (which is called laying the action with a *continuando*) and the plaintiff shall not be compelled to bring separate actions for every day's separate offence." 3 William Blackstone, *Commentaries on the Laws of England* 212 (1768).

continuation agreement. *Partnership.* An agreement among the partners that, in the event of dissolution, the business of the partnership can be continued without the necessity of liquidation. Cf. BUY-SELL AGREEMENT (1).

> "Normally, a continuation agreement would have some type of provision for purchasing the interest of a deceased or expelled partner. However, such a provision is not necessary. Courts have enforced agreements that give the estate of the deceased partner nothing." Harold Gill Reuschlein & William A. Gregory, *The Law of Agency and Partnership* § 269, at 461 (2d ed. 1990).

continuation in part. A patent application filed during the lifetime of an earlier application by the same applicant, repeating a substantial part of the earlier application but adding to or subtracting from it. 35 USCA § 120. — Abbr. CIP.

continued bond. See *annuity bond* under BOND (3).

continuing, *adj.* **1.** (Of an act or event) that is uninterrupted <a continuing offense>. **2.** (Of status or power) that needs no renewal; enduring <continuing stockholders> <continuing jurisdiction>.

continuing breach. See BREACH OF CONTRACT.

continuing consideration. See CONSIDERATION.

continuing contract. See CONTRACT.

continuing covenant. See COVENANT (1).

continuing damages. See DAMAGES.

continuing guaranty. See GUARANTY.

continuing injury. See INJURY.

continuing judicial education. Continuing legal education for judges, usu. organized and sponsored by a governmentally subsidized body and often involving topics such as judicial writing, efficient decision-making, caseload management, and the like. — Abbr. CJE.

continuing jurisdiction. See JURISDICTION.

continuing-jurisdiction doctrine. **1.** The rule that a court retains power to enter and enforce a judgment over a party even though that party is no longer subject to a new action. **2.** *Family law.* The rule that once a court has acquired jurisdiction over a child-custody or support case, that court continues to have jurisdiction to modify orders, even if the child or a parent moves to another state.

continuing legal education. **1.** The process or system through which lawyers extend their learning beyond their law-school studies, usu. by attending seminars designed to sharpen lawyering skills or to provide updates on legal developments within particular practice areas. • In some jurisdictions, lawyers have annual or biennial requirements to devote a given number of hours (usu. 12–15) to continuing legal education. **2.** The enhanced skills or knowledge derived from this process. **3.** The business field in which educational providers supply the demand for legal seminars, books, audiotapes, and videotapes designed to further the education of lawyers. — Abbr. CLE.

continuing nuisance. See NUISANCE.

continuing objection. See OBJECTION.

continuing offense. See OFFENSE (1).

continuing part-time judge. See JUDGE.

continuing trespass. See TRESPASS.

continuing warranty. See *promissory warranty* under WARRANTY (3).

continuing wrong. See WRONG.

continuity (kon-ti-**n**[**y**]**oo**-ə-tee). *Int'l law.* The principle that upheavals and revolutions within a country — as well as changes in governmental forms, the extent of a country's territory, and measures taken during a military occupation — do not affect the existence of the country and therefore cannot lead to its extinction.

continuity of business enterprise. A doctrine covering acquisitive reorganizations whereby the acquiring corporation must continue the target corporation's historical business or must use a significant portion of the target's business assets in a new business to qualify the exchange as a tax-deferred transaction.

continuity-of-enterprise doctrine. See SUBSTANTIAL-CONTINUITY DOCTRINE.

continuity-of-entity doctrine. See MERE-CONTINUATION DOCTRINE.

continuity of existence. See CONTINUITY-OF-LIFE DOCTRINE.

continuity of interest. 1. A doctrine covering acquisitive reorganizations whereby a target corporation's shareholders must retain a share in the acquiring corporation to qualify the exchange as a tax-deferred transaction. **2.** A judicial requirement for divisive reorganizations whereby a target corporation's shareholders must retain an interest in both the distributing and the controlled corporations to qualify the exchange as a tax-deferred transaction.

continuity-of-life doctrine. The principle that the withdrawal, incapacity, bankruptcy, or death of the owner of an entity (esp. a corporation) does not end the entity's existence. — Also termed *continuity of existence*.

continuous-adverse-use principle. The rule that the uninterrupted use of land — along with the other elements of adverse possession — will result in a successful claim for adverse possession. — Also termed *uninterrupted-adverse-use principle*. See ADVERSE POSSESSION.

continuous easement. See EASEMENT.

continuous injury. See *continual injury* under INJURY.

continuous-representation doctrine. The principle that the limitations period for bringing a legal-malpractice action is tolled as long as the lawyer continues the representation that is related to the negligent act or omission.

continuous-treatment doctrine. The principle that the limitations period for bringing a medical-malpractice action is tolled while the patient continues treatment that is related to the negligent act or omission.

continuous trigger. See TRIPLE TRIGGER.

contort (**kon**-tort), *n.* **1.** (*usu. pl.*) The overlapping domain of contract law and tort law.

> "I have occasionally suggested to my students that a desirable reform in legal education would be to merge the first-year courses in Contracts and Torts into a single course which we could call Contorts." Grant Gilmore, *The Death of Contract* 90 (1974).

2. A specific wrong that falls within that domain.

contra (**kon**-trə), *prep.* Against or contrary to. • As a citation signal, *contra* denotes that the cited authority supports a contrary view.

> "Observe in the note citing cases in support of a proposition mentioned in the text whether any of the cases follow the word *contra*, which means that a contrary rule has been laid down in them." Frank Hall Childs, *Where and How to Find the Law* 78–79 (1922).

contra account. See ACCOUNT.

contraband (**kon**-trə-band), *n.* **1.** Illegal or prohibited trade; smuggling. **2.** Goods that are unlawful to import, export, or possess. — **contraband,** *adj.*

absolute contraband. Goods used primarily for war, such as arms and ammunition, as well as clothing and equipment of a military character.

conditional contraband. Goods susceptible of being used for warlike and peaceful purposes, such as coal and food. — Also termed *ancipitis usus.*

contraband per se. Property whose possession is unlawful regardless of how it is used. Cf. *derivative contraband.*

derivative contraband. Property whose possession becomes unlawful when it is used in committing an illegal act. Cf. *contraband per se.*

contra bonos mores (**kon**-trə **boh**-nohs **mor**-eez). [Latin "against good morals"] Offensive to the conscience and to a sense of justice. • Contracts *contra bonos mores* are voidable. — Also termed *contra bonos mores et decorum*; *adversus bonos mores.*

> "Whatever is *contra bonos mores et decorum*, the principles of our law prohibit, and the King's court, as the general censor and guardian of the public manners, is bound to restrain and punish." *Jones v. Randall*, 98 E.R. 706, 707 (1774) (per Mansfield, C.J.).

contracausator (kon-trə-kaw-**zay**-tər). *Hist.* A criminal; a person prosecuted for a crime.

contraceptivism. *Hist.* The criminal offense of distributing or prescribing contraceptives.

contract, *n.* **1.** An agreement between two or more parties creating obligations that are enforceable or otherwise recognizable at law <a binding contract>. **2.** The writing that sets forth such an agreement <a contract is valid if valid under the law of the residence of the party wishing to enforce the contract>.

> "The term contract has been used indifferently to refer to three different things: (1) the series of operative acts by the parties resulting in new legal relations; (2) the physical document executed by the parties as the lasting evidence of their having performed the necessary operative acts and also as an operative fact in itself; (3) the legal relations resulting from the operative acts, consisting of a right or rights *in personam* and their corresponding duties, accompanied by certain powers, privileges, and immunities. The sum of these legal relations is often called 'obligation.' The present editor prefers to define contract in sense (3) ...." William R. Anson, *Principles of the Law of Contract* 13 n.2 (Arthur L. Corbin ed., 3d Am. ed. 1919).

> "A contract is a promise, or a set of promises, for breach of which the law gives a remedy, or the performance of which the law in some way recognizes as a duty. This definition may not be entirely satisfactory since it requires a subsequent definition of the circumstances under which the law does in fact attach legal obligation to promises. But if a definition were attempted which should cover these operative facts, it would require compressing the entire law relating to the formation of contracts into a single sentence." Samuel Williston, *A Treatise on the Law of Contracts* § 1, at 1–2 (Walter H.E. Jaeger ed., 3d ed. 1957) (footnote omitted).

> "The term 'contract' is also used by lay persons and lawyers alike to refer to a document in which the terms of a contract are written. Use of the word in this sense is by no means improper so long as it is clearly understood that rules of law utilizing the concept 'contract' rarely refer to the writing itself. Usually, the reference is to the agreement; the writing being merely a memorial of the agreement." John D. Calamari & Joseph M. Perillo, *The Law of Contracts* § 1.1, at 3 (4th ed. 1998).

3. Loosely, an unenforceable agreement between two or more parties to do or not to do a thing or set of things; a compact <when they finally agreed, they had a contract>. **4.** A promise or set of promises by a party to a transaction, enforceable or otherwise recognizable at law; the writing expressing that promise or set of promises <when the lessor learned that the rooms were to be used for the delivery of blasphemous lectures, he declined to carry out his contract>.

> "The promissory element present in every contract is stressed in a widely quoted definition: 'A contract is a promise, or set of promises, for breach of which the law gives a remedy, or the performance of which the law in some way recognizes as a duty.' [1 Samuel Williston, *Contracts* § 1.1 (4th ed. 1990).] This, like similar definitions, is somewhat misleading. While it is true that a promise, express or implied, is a necessary element in every contract, frequently the promise is coupled with other elements such as physical acts, recitals of fact, and the immediate transfer of property interests. In ordinary usage the contract is not the promise alone, but the entire complex of these elements." John D. Calamari & Joseph M. Perillo, *The Law of Contracts* § 1.1, at 1–2 (4th ed. 1998).

5. Broadly, any legal duty or set of duties not imposed by the law of tort; esp., a duty created by a decree or declaration of a court <an obligation of record, as a judgment, recognizance, or the like, is included within the term "contract">. **6.** The body of law dealing with agreements and exchange <the general theory of contract>. **7.** The terms of an agreement, or any particular term <there was no express contract about when the money was payable>. — **contract,** *vb.* — **contractual,** *adj.*

accessory contract. A contract entered into primarily for the purpose of carrying out a principal contract. • The principal types are suretyship, indemnity, pledge, warranty, and ratification. Cf. *principal contract.*

adhesion contract. A standard-form contract prepared by one party, to be signed by the party in a weaker position, usu. a consumer, who has little choice about the terms. — Also termed *contract of adhesion*; *adhesory contract*; *adhesionary contract*; *take-it-or-leave-it contract*; *leonine contract*.

"Some sets of trade and professional forms are extremely one-sided, grossly favoring one interest group against others, and are commonly referred to as contracts of adhesion. From weakness in bargaining position, ignorance, or indifference, unfavored parties are willing to enter transactions controlled by these lopsided legal documents." Quintin Johnstone & Dan Hopson, Jr., *Lawyers and Their Work* 329–30 (1967).

aleatory contract (**ay**-lee-ə-tor-ee). A contract in which at least one party's performance depends on some uncertain event that is beyond the control of the parties involved. • Most insurance contracts are of this type. — Also termed *hazardous contract*. Cf. *certain contract*.

alternative contract. A contract in which the performing party may elect to perform one of two or more specified acts to satisfy the obligation; a contract that provides more than one way for a party to complete performance, usu. permitting that party to choose the manner of performance. — Also termed *alternative-methods-of-performance contract*.

assessment contract. A contract in which the payment of a benefit is dependent on the collection of an assessment levied on persons holding similar contracts. See *assessment insurance* under INSURANCE.

best-efforts contract. A contract in which a party undertakes to use best efforts to fulfill the promises made; a contract in which the adequacy of a party's performance is measured by the party's ability to fulfill the specified obligations. • Although the obligor must use best efforts, the risk of failure lies with the obligee. To be enforceable, a best-efforts term must generally set some kind of goal or guideline against which the efforts may be measured. See BEST EFFORTS.

bilateral contract. A contract in which each party promises a performance, so that each party is an obligor on that party's own promise and an obligee on the other's promise. — Also termed *mutual contract*; *reciprocal contract*.

"In a bilateral contract a promise, or set of promises on one side, is exchanged for a promise or a set of promises on the other side. In a unilateral contract, on the other hand, a promise on one side is exchanged for an act (or a forbearance) on the other side. Typical examples of bilateral contracts are contracts of sale, the buyer promising to pay the price and the seller promising to deliver the goods. A typical example of a unilateral contract is a promise of a reward for the finding of lost property followed by the actual finding of the property." P.S. Atiyah, *An Introduction to the Law of Contract* 32 (3d ed. 1981).

blanket contract. A contract covering a group of products, goods, or services for a fixed period.

bona fide contract (**boh**-nə fīd *or* **fī**-dee). A contract in which equity may intervene to correct inequalities and to adjust matters according to the parties' intentions.

certain contract. A contract that will be performed in a stipulated manner. Cf. *aleatory contract*.

collateral contract. A side agreement that relates to a contract, which, if unintegrated, can be supplemented by evidence of the side agreement; an agreement made before or at the same time as, but separately from, another contract. See COLLATERAL-CONTRACT DOCTRINE.

"The term 'collateral contract' has no very precise meaning in the law. It is generally used as a label for a contract which is collateral, or by the side of, another contract. A great many examples of implied or constructive contracts created by the Courts are collateral in a broad sense.... [A]lthough the normal presumption is that the parties intend a written contract to be exclusive evidence of their intentions, it is always open to a party to show that in fact the writing did not exclusively represent their intentions, because of a 'collateral' contract made during the negotiations but not incorporated in the written instrument." P.S. Atiyah, *An Introduction to the Law of Contract* 80–81, 161 (3d ed. 1981).

commutative contract (kə-**myoo**-tə-tiv *or* **kom**-yə-tay-tiv). *Civil law*. A contract in which one party's performance is correlative to the performance of the other, so that nonperformance by either affords a defense to the other. Cf. *independent contract*; *synallagmatic contract*.

conditional contract. An agreement that is enforceable only if another agreement is performed or if another particular prerequisite or condition is satisfied.

conditional sales contract. See *retail installment contract*.

consensual contract. *Hist*. A contract arising from the mere consensus of the parties, without any formal or symbolic acts performed to fix the obligation. • Although the consensual contract was known to the common law, it originated in Roman law, where it embraced four types of contracts in which informal consent alone was sufficient: (1) an agency agreement (*mandatum*), (2) a partnership agreement (*societas*), (3) a sale (*emptio venditio*), or (4) a letting or hiring (*locatio conductio*). Cf. *real contract*.

"[T]he peculiarity of these Consensual Contracts is that *no* formalities are required to create them out of the Pact. Much that is indefensible, and much more that is obscure, has been written about the Consensual Contracts, and it has even been asserted that in them the *consent* of the Parties is more emphatically given than in any other species of agreement. But the Consensual merely indicates that the Obligation is here annexed at once to the *Consensus*. The Consensus, or mutual assent of the parties, is the final and crowning ingredient in the Convention, and it is the special characteristic of agreements falling under one of the four heads of Sale, Partnership, Agency, and Hiring, that, as soon as the assent of the parties has supplied this ingredient, there is *at once* a Contract. The Consensus draws with it the Obligation, performing, in transactions of the sort specified, the exact functions which are discharged, in the other contracts, by the *Res* or Thing...." Henry S. Maine, *Ancient Law* 322–23 (10th ed. 1884).

construction contract. A contract setting forth the specifications for a building project's construction. • This type of contract is usu. secured by performance and payment bonds to protect both the owner and the subcontractors.

constructive contract. See *implied-in-law contract*.

continuing contract. A contract calling for periodic performances.

contract for deed. A conditional sales contract for the sale of real property. — Also termed *installment land contract*; *land sales contract*; *land contract*.

contract for sale. **1.** A contract for the present transfer of property for a price. — Also termed *contract of sale*. **2.** A contract to sell goods at a future time. — Also termed (in sense 2) *contract to sell*.

contract implied in fact. See *implied-in-fact contract*.

contract implied in law. See *implied-in-law contract*.

contract of adhesion. See *adhesion contract*.

contract of beneficence. See *gratuitous contract*.

contract of benevolence. See *gratuitous contract*.

contract of insurance. See INSURANCE POLICY.

contract of record. A contract that is declared by a court and entered into the court's record. • Contracts of record include judgments, recognizances, and (in England) statutes staple.

"Contracts of record are not really contracts at all, but are transactions which, being entered on the records of certain courts called 'courts of record,' are conclusive proof of the facts thereby appearing, and could formerly be enforced by action of law as if they had been put in the shape of a contract." 1 Stewart Rapalje & Robert L. Lawrence, *A Dictionary of American and English Law* 282 (1883).

"A contract of record is in point of fact no contract at all, and has nothing whatever to do with the law of contracts. These so-called contracts are the obligations incurred by a judgment or recognizance of a Court of Record. They came to be called contracts only because they were enforceable by the same type of action as was used for genuinely contractual cases in the old common-law system of procedure." P.S. Atiyah, *An Introduction to the Law of Contract* 31 (3d ed. 1981).

contract of sale. See *contract for sale* (1).

contract to satisfaction. See *satisfaction contract*.

contract to sell. See *contract for sale* (2).

contract uberrimae fidei (yoo-**ber**-ə-mee **fI**-dee-I). A contract in which the parties owe each other duties with the utmost good faith.

"In a certain restricted group of contracts good faith is peculiarly necessary owing to the relationship between the parties, and in these cases — known as contracts *uberrimae fidei* — there is a full duty to disclose all material facts. The typical instance of such contracts is the contract of insurance. Here the duty to disclose all material facts to the insurer arises from the fact that many of the relevant circumstances are within the exclusive knowledge of one party, and it would be impossible for the insurer to obtain the facts necessary for him to make a proper calculation of the risk he is asked to assume without this knowledge." P.S. Atiyah, *An Introduction to the Law of Contract* 221–22 (3d ed. 1981).

contract under seal. A formal contract that requires no consideration and has the seal of the signer attached. • Modern statutes have mostly eliminated the special effects of a sealed contract. It must be in writing or printed on paper or parchment and is conclusive between the parties when signed, sealed, and delivered. Delivery is made either by actually handing it to the other party (or party's representative) or by stating an intention that the deed be operative even though it is retained in the possession of the party executing it. — Also termed *sealed contract*; *special contract*; *specialty contract*; *specialty*; *deed*; *covenant*.

"The only formal contract of English law is the *contract under seal*, sometimes also called a deed and sometimes a specialty. It is the only *formal contract*, because it derives its validity neither from the fact of agreement, nor from the consideration which may exist for the promise of either party, but from the *form* in which it is expressed." William R. Anson, *Principles of the Law of Contract* 82 (Arthur L. Corbin ed., 3d Am. ed. 1919).

"Contracts under seal also bear little resemblance to ordinary contracts, although here at least the liability is based on a promise. A contract under seal, that is to say a deed, ... is a written promise or set of promises which derives its validity from the form, and the form alone, of the executing instrument. In point of fact the 'form' of the deed is nowadays surprisingly elastic. The only necessities are that the deed should be intended as such, and should be signed, sealed, and delivered. The sealing, however, has now become largely a fiction, an adhesive wafer simply being attached to the document in place of a genuine seal. Similarly, 'delivery' is not literally necessary, provided that there is a clear intention that the deed should be operative." P.S. Atiyah, *An Introduction to the Law of Contract* 31 (3d ed. 1981).

cost-plus contract. A contract in which payment is based on a fixed fee or a percentage added to the actual cost incurred.

de facto contract of sale. A contract purporting to pass property but defective in some element.

dependent contract. A contract conditioned or dependent on another contract.

deposit contract. An agreement between a financial institution and its customer governing the treatment of deposited funds and the payment of checks and other demands against the customer's account.

destination contract. A contract in which a seller bears the risk of loss until the goods arrive at the destination. UCC § 2–509. Cf. *shipment contract.*

discharged contract. See *void contract* (2).

divisible contract. See *severable contract.*

dual contract. A contract between parties who have made two contracts for the same transaction, sometimes so that one may be used to defraud another (such as a lender) as to the terms of the parties' actual agreement.

employment contract. A contract between an employer and employee in which the terms and conditions of employment are stated.

engineering, procurement, and construction contract. A fixed-price, schedule-intensive construction contract — typically used in the construction of single-purpose projects, such as energy plants — in which the contractor agrees to a wide variety of responsibilities, including the duties to provide for the design, engineering, procurement, and construction of the facility; to prepare start-up procedures; to conduct performance tests; to create operating manuals; and to train people to operate the facility. — Abbr. EPC contract. — Also termed *turnkey contract.* See SINGLE-PURPOSE PROJECT.

entire-output contract. See *output contract.*

escrow contract. The agreement among buyer, seller, and escrow holder, setting forth the rights and responsibilities of each. See ESCROW.

evergreen contract. A contract that renews itself from one term to the next in the absence of contrary notice by one of the parties.

executed contract. **1.** A contract that has been fully performed by both parties. **2.** A signed contract.

executory contract (eg-**zek**-yə-tor-ee). **1.** A contract that remains wholly unperformed or for which there remains something still to be done on both sides, often as a component of a larger transaction and sometimes memorialized by an informal letter agreement, by a memorandum, or by oral agreement.

"If a contract is wholly executory, and the legal duties of the parties are as yet unfulfilled, it can be discharged by mutual consent, the acquittance of each from the other's claims being the consideration for the promise of each to waive his own." William R. Anson, *Principles of the Law of Contract* 138 (Arthur L. Corbin ed., 3d Am. ed. 1919).

2. *Bankruptcy.* A contract under which debtor and nondebtor each have unperformed obligations and the debtor, if it ceased further performance, would have no right to the other party's continued performance.

express contract. A contract whose terms the parties have explicitly set out. — Also termed *special contract.* Cf. *implied contract.*

financial contract. *Securities.* An arrangement that (1) takes the form of an individually negotiated contract, agreement, or option to buy, sell, lend, swap, or repurchase, or other similar individually negotiated transaction commonly entered into by participants in the financial markets; (2) involves securities, commodities, currencies, interest or other rates, other measures of value, or any other financial or economic interest similar in purpose or function; and (3) is entered into in response to a request from a counterparty for a quotation, or is otherwise entered into and structured to accommodate the objectives of the counterparty to the arrangement.

fixed-price contract. A contract in which the buyer agrees to pay the seller a definite and predetermined price regardless of increases in the seller's cost or the buyer's ability to acquire the same goods in the market at a lower price.

formal contract. *Hist.* A written contract under seal.

futures contract. See FUTURES CONTRACT.

gambling contract. An agreement to engage in a gamble; a contract in which two parties wager something, esp. money, for a chance to win a prize. — Also termed *gaming contract.*

"Generally, under or apart from statutes so providing, or prohibiting such contracts or transactions, gambling contracts and transactions are illegal and void and cannot be enforced; and such contracts are void ab initio.... A gambling contract is invalid, no matter what outward form it may assume, and no ingenuity can make it legal." 38 C.J.S. *Gaming* § 26, at 138–39 (1996).

government contract. See *procurement contract.*

gratuitous contract (grə-t[y]oo-i-təs). A contract made for the benefit of a promisee who does not give consideration to the promisor. — Also termed *contract of beneficence; contract of benevolence.* Cf. *onerous contract.*

grubstake contract. A contract between two parties in which one party provides the grubstake — money and supplies — and the other party prospects for and locates mines on public land. • Each party acquires an interest in the mine as agreed to in the contract. Grubstake contracts are used chiefly in the western United States. In some states, such as Alaska, a request for grubstake money is considered the offer of a security and must be registered. — Also termed *grubstaking contract.*

guaranteed-sale contract. A contract between a real-estate agency and a property owner in which the agency agrees to buy the property at a guaranteed price after a specified length of time if it has not been sold under the listing agreement. • The guaranteed price is usu. a substantial discount from the listed price. — Also termed *guaranteed-purchase contract.*

hazardous contract. See *aleatory contract.*

illegal contract. A promise that is prohibited because the performance, formation, or object of the agreement is against the law. • Technically speaking, an illegal contract is not a contract at all, so the phrase is a misnomer.

"An illegal contract is exceptionally difficult to define. It does not merely mean a contract contrary to the criminal law, although such a contract would indubitably be illegal. But a contract can well be illegal without contravening the criminal law, because there are certain activities which the law does not actually prohibit, but at the same time regards as contrary to the public interest and definitely to be discouraged, for instance, prostitution. While a void contract is not necessarily illegal, an illegal contract is often void. However, the consequences of an illegal contract differ somewhat from those usually produced by a simply void contract, so illegal contracts are usually accorded separate treatment." P.S. Atiyah, *An Introduction to the Law of Contract* 38 (3d ed. 1981).

illusory contract. An agreement in which one party gives as consideration a promise that is so insubstantial as to impose no obligation. • The insubstantial promise renders the contract unenforceable.

immoral contract. A contract that so flagrantly violates societal norms as to be unenforceable.

implied contract. **1.** An implied-in-law contract. **2.** An implied-in-fact contract. Cf. *express contract.*

implied-in-fact contract. A contract that the parties presumably intended, either by tacit understanding or by the assumption that it existed. — Also termed *contract implied in fact.*

implied-in-law contract. An obligation imposed by law because of the conduct of the parties, or some special relationship between them, or because one of them would otherwise be unjustly enriched. • An implied-in-law contract is not actually a contract, but instead a remedy that allows the plaintiff to recover a benefit conferred on the defendant. — Also termed *contract implied in law; quasi-contract; constructive contract.* See UNJUST ENRICHMENT.

"[A]dventurous courts have turned to the idea of a 'contract implied in law,' a 'quasi-contract' — not really a contract, a legal fiction necessary to promote the ends of justice and, in particular, to prevent 'unjust enrichment.'" Grant Gilmore, *The Death of Contract* 73–74 (1974).

"Since ... claims for the redress of unjust enrichment did not fit comfortably into either the category of contract or that of tort, they came to be described as claims in *quasi-contract.* Some of them were originally characterized as being in *quantum meruit* (as much as he deserved), a form of action used for claims to payment for services. This procedural term has persisted and is sometimes used inexactly as a synonym for the more general term *quasi-contract,* which refers to any money claim for the redress of unjust enrichment." E. Allan Farnsworth, *Contracts* § 2.20, at 103 (2d ed. 1990).

impossible contract. A contract that the law will not enforce because there is no feasible way for one of the parties to perform. See IMPOSSIBILITY (3).

independent contract. A contract in which the mutual acts or promises of the parties have no relation to each other, either as equivalents or as considerations. Cf. *commutative contract.*

informal contract. See *parol contract* (2).

innominate contract (i-**nom**-ə-nit). *Civil law.* A contract not classifiable under any particular name; a contract for which the law supplies nothing in addition to the express agreement of the parties. — Also termed *innominate real contract*. Cf. *nominate contract*.

installment contract. A contract requiring or authorizing the delivery of goods in separate lots, or payments in separate increments, to be separately accepted. • Under the UCC, this type of agreement will be considered one contract even if it has a clause stating that each delivery is a separate contract. UCC § 2–612.

installment land contract. See *contract for deed*.

integrated contract. See INTEGRATED CONTRACT.

invalid contract. A contract that is either void or voidable. — Also termed *invalid agreement*.

investment contract. See INVESTMENT CONTRACT.

joint contract. A contract in which two or more promisors are together bound to fulfill its obligations, or one in which two or more promisees are together entitled to performance. Cf. *severable contract*.

land contract. See *contract for deed*.

land sales contract. See *contract for deed*.

leonine contract. See *adhesion contract*.

letter contract. In federal contract law, a written contract with sufficient provisions to permit the contractor to begin performance.

leverage contract. See LEVERAGE CONTRACT.

literal contract. **1.** *Roman law*. A type of written contract originally created by — and later evidenced by — an entry of the sum due on the debit side of a ledger, binding a signatory even though the signatory receives no consideration. See LITERIS OBLIGATIO.

> "Though an obligation could be created by a literal contract in the time of Gaius, the so-called literal contract of Justinian was not, in itself, a means of *creating* an obligation, but was the *evidence* of an obligation created in some other way .... The true literal contract, as described by Gaius, may be defined as a means of creating an obligation to pay money by a fictitious entry ... in the creditor's account book ... with the consent of the intended debtor. A, with B's consent, enters the fact that B is indebted to him ... and thereupon B is under an obligation to pay, though no money has passed between them." R.W. Leage, *Roman Private Law* 316–17 (C.H. Ziegler ed., 2d ed. 1930).

2. *Civil law*. A contract fully evidenced by a writing and binding on the signatory.

marine contract. A contract relating to maritime affairs, including navigation, marine insurance, affreightment, maritime loans, and shipping. — Also termed *maritime contract*.

maritime contract. A contract that relates to a vessel in its use as such, to navigation on navigable waters, to transportation by sea, or to maritime employment. • An action on a maritime contract falls within the admiralty jurisdiction.

marketing contract. **1.** A business's agreement with an agency or other association for the promotion of sales of the business's goods or services. **2.** An agreement between a cooperative and its members, by which the members agree to sell through the cooperative, and the cooperative agrees to obtain an agreed price.

mixed contract. **1.** *Civil law*. A contract in which the respective benefits conferred are unequal. **2.** A contract for both the sale of goods and services. • The UCC may apply to a mixed contract if the primary contract purpose is for the sale of goods.

mutual contract. See *bilateral contract*.

naked contract. See NUDUM PACTUM.

nominate contract (**nom**-ə-nit). *Civil law*. A contract distinguished by a particular name, such as sale, insurance, or lease, the very use of which determines some of the rules governing the contract and the contractual rights of the parties, without the need for special stipulations. • The contracts are generally divided into four types: (1) real (arising from something done), (2) oral (arising from something said), (3) literal (arising from something written), and (4) consensual (arising from something agreed to). Cf. *innominate contract*.

nude contract. See NUDUM PACTUM.

onerous contract. *Civil law*. A contract in which each party is obligated to perform in exchange for each party's promise of performance. Cf. *gratuitous contract*.

option contract. See OPTION (2).

oral contract. See *parol contract* (1).

output contract. A contract in which a buyer promises to buy all the goods or services that a seller can supply during a specified period and at a set price. • The quantity term is measured by the seller's output. — Also termed *entire-output contract*. Cf. *requirements contract*.

parol contract (pə-**rohl** *or* **par**-əl). **1.** A contract or modification of a contract that is not in writing or is only partially in writing. — Also termed *oral contract*; *parol agreement*; (loosely) *verbal contract*. **2.** At common law, a contract not under seal, although it could be in writing. — Also termed *informal contract*; *simple contract*. See PAROL-EVIDENCE RULE.

pignorative contract (**pig**-nə-ray-tiv). *Civil law.* A contract in which the seller of real property, instead of relinquishing possession of the property that is theoretically sold, gives the buyer a lien; a contract of pledge, hypothecation, or mortgage of realty.

precontract. A contract that precludes a party from entering into a comparable agreement with someone else. Cf. LETTER OF INTENT.

principal contract. A contract giving rise to an accessory contract, as an agreement from which a secured obligation originates. Cf. *accessory contract*.

procurement contract. A contract in which a government receives goods or services. • A procurement contract, including the bidding process, is subject to government regulation. See FEDERAL ACQUISITION REGULATION. — Also termed *government contract*.

public contract. A contract that, although it involves public funds, may be performed by private persons and may benefit them.

quasi-contract. See *implied-in-law contract*.

real contract. **1.** *Hist.* A contract in which money or other property passes from one party to another. • This term, derived from the Roman law, referred to contracts concerning both personal and real property. **2.** *Roman law.* A contract requiring something more than mere consent, such as the lending of money or the delivery of a thing. Cf. *consensual contract*.

> "The essence of ... *the real contracts*, was that, at the time the agreement was made, one party, by delivering something belonging to him to the other party to the contract, imposed on that other an obligation to return the thing itself or, in the case of things intended to be consumed, an equivalent in kind. As the Roman lawyers expressed it, the contractual obligation was created by something being handed over...." R.W. Leage, *Roman Private Law* 292 (C.H. Ziegler ed., 2d ed. 1930).

> "The term 'real contract' is in common use in the Civil law, and though not commonly used by judges or writers in the common law, nevertheless describes certain obligations enforced in England from very early times. A real contract is an obligation arising from the possession or transfer of a res." Samuel Williston, *A Treatise on the Law of Contracts* § 8, at 19 (Walter H.E. Jaeger ed., 3d ed. 1957).

reciprocal contract. See *bilateral contract*.

requirements contract. A contract in which a seller promises to supply all the goods or services that a buyer needs during a specific period and at a set price, and in which the buyer promises (explicitly or implicitly) to obtain those goods or services exclusively from the seller. • The quantity term is measured by the buyer's requirements. Cf. *output contract*.

retail installment contract. A contract for the sale of goods under which the buyer makes periodic payments and the seller retains title to or a security interest in the goods. — Also termed *retail installment contract and security agreement*; *conditional sales contract*. Cf. *chattel mortgage* under MORTGAGE.

satisfaction contract. A contract by which one party agrees to perform to the reasonable satisfaction of the other. — Also termed *contract to satisfaction*.

sealed contract. See *contract under seal*.

self-determination contract. Under the Indian Self–Determination and Education Assistance Act, an agreement by which the federal government provides funds to an Indian tribe and allows the tribe to plan and administer a program that would otherwise be administered by the federal government. 25 USCA § 450b(j).

service contract. A contract to perform a service; esp., a written agreement to provide maintenance or repairs on a consumer product for a specified term. 15 USCA § 2301(8).

severable contract. A contract that includes two or more promises each of which can be enforced separately, so that failure to perform one of the promises does not necessarily put the promisor in breach of the entire contract. — Also termed *divisible contract*; *several contract*. See SEVERABILITY CLAUSE. Cf. *joint contract*.

> "A *severable* contract ... is one the consideration of which is, by its terms, susceptible of apportionment on either side, so as to correspond to the unascertained consideration on the other side, as a contract to pay a person the worth of his services so long as he will do certain work; or to give a certain price for every bushel of so much corn as corresponds to a sample." Ivan Horniman, *Wharton's Law Lexicon* 215 (13th ed. 1925).

shipment contract. A contract in which a seller bears the risk of damage to the items sold only until they are brought to the place of shipment. • If a contract for the sale of goods does not address the terms of delivery, it is presumed to be a shipment contract. UCC §§ 2–319, 2–504, 2–509. Cf. *destination contract*.

> "In the jargon of commercial lawyers, a contract that requires or authorizes the seller to send the goods to the buyer but does not require that he deliver them at any

particular destination is called a 'shipment contract.' Generally, in shipment contracts, risk of loss passes to the buyer at the point of shipment, which is also the point of 'delivery,' while in 'destination contracts' (seller must deliver at a particular destination) risk passes upon seller's tender at destination." 1 James J. White & Robert S. Summers, *Uniform Commercial Code* § 3–5, at 128–29 (4th ed. 1995).

simple contract. See *parol contract* (2).

simulated contract. *Civil law.* A contract that, although clothed in concrete form, has no existence in fact; a sham contract. • A simulated contract can be declared a sham and avoided by an interested party, including a creditor of one of the parties to the contract. — Also termed *simulation*.

special contract. **1.** See *contract under seal*. **2.** A contract with peculiar provisions that are not ordinarily found in contracts relating to the same subject matter. **3.** See *express contract*.

specialty contract. See *contract under seal*.

standard-form contract. A usu. preprinted contract containing set clauses, used repeatedly by a business or within a particular industry with only slight additions or modifications to meet the specific situation.

stock-option contract. A negotiable instrument that gives the holder the right to buy or sell — for a specified price within a fixed time limit — a certain number of shares of the corporation's stock. See *stock option* under OPTION.

subcontract. A contract made by a party to another contract for carrying out the other contract, or a part of it.

subscription contract. See SUBSCRIPTION (3).

substituted contract. A contract between parties to a prior contract that takes the place of and discharges the previous obligation. • A substituted contract differs from a novation (as "novation" is traditionally defined) in that the latter requires the substitution for the original obligor of a third person not a party to the original agreement; when the obligee accepts the third party, the agreement is immediately discharged. In contrast to both substituted contract and novation, an executory accord does not immediately discharge an obligation; rather, the obligation is discharged on performance, often by a third person rather than the original obligor. Cf. NOVATION; ACCORD (2).

"[A] substituted contract immediately discharges the prior claim which is merged into the new agreement. Consequently, in the absence of an express agreement to the contrary, the original claim can no longer be enforced. In the event of a breach, any action would have to be brought on the substituted agreement.... The concept of 'substituted contract' was created largely to circumvent the unsatisfactory rules that until recently governed executory accords. Now that these rules have been modernized, the next step should be the reabsorption of the substituted contract into the executory accord.... [T]he untidy distinction between executory accords and substituted contracts should not be allowed to complicate litigation about routine claim settlements." John D. Calamari & Joseph M. Perillo, *The Law of Contracts* § 21.6, at 803 (4th ed. 1998).

synallagmatic contract (sin-ə-lag-**mat**-ik). [fr. Greek *synallagma* "mutual agreement"] *Civil law.* A contract in which the parties obligate themselves reciprocally, so that the obligation of each party is correlative to the obligation of the other. • A synallagmatic contract is characterized by correlative obligations, whereas a commutative contract is characterized by correlative performances. The term *synallagmatic contract* is essentially the civil-law equivalent of the common law's *bilateral contract*. Cf. *commutative contract*.

tacit contract. A contract in which conduct takes the place of written or spoken words in the offer or acceptance (or both).

take-it-or-leave-it contract. See *adhesion contract*.

take-or-pay contract. A contract requiring the buyer to either purchase and receive a minimum amount of a product at a set price ("take") or pay for this minimum without taking immediate delivery ("pay"). • These contracts are often used in the energy and oil-and-gas businesses.

third-party-beneficiary contract. A contract that directly benefits a third party and that gives the third party a right to sue any of the original contracting parties for breach.

unconscionable contract. See *unconscionable agreement* under AGREEMENT.

unenforceable contract. A valid contract that, because of some technical defect, cannot be enforced; a contract having some legal consequences, but that may not be enforced in an action for damages or specific performance in the face of certain defenses, such as the statute of frauds. • Unenforceable contracts share many features with voidable contracts, but unlike the latter, in some instances they may be enforced indirectly. Restatement (Second) of Contracts § 8 cmt. a (1981). — Also termed *agreement of imperfect obligation*.

"The difference between what is voidable and what is unenforceable is mainly a difference between substance and procedure. A contract may be good, but incapable of proof owing to lapse of time, want of written form, or failure to affix a revenue stamp. Writing in the first cases, a stamp in the last, may satisfy the requirements of law and render the contract enforceable, but it is never at any time in the power of either party to avoid the transaction. The contract is unimpeachable, only it cannot be proved in court." William R. Anson, *Principles of the Law of Contract* 19–20 (Arthur L. Corbin ed., 3d Am. ed. 1919).

"An unenforceable contract is a somewhat anomalous concept, fortunately now of small importance. We have already mentioned that certain types of contract are required by statute to be evidenced in writing, and that if this requirement is not satisfied, the contracts are regarded as unenforceable, but not void. There are, in fact, only two such contracts left now, namely a contract of guarantee and a contract for the sale of an interest in land. For most practical purposes an unenforceable contract is not much better than a void contract, since the most important characteristic of a valid contract is that it is enforceable." P.S. Atiyah, *An Introduction to the Law of Contract* 38 (3d ed. 1981).

unilateral contract. A contract in which only one party makes a promise or undertakes a performance.

"[M]any unilateral contracts are in reality gratuitous promises enforced for good reason with no element of bargain." P.S. Atiyah, *An Introduction to the Law of Contract* 126 (3d ed. 1981).

"If A says to B, 'If you walk across the Brooklyn Bridge I will pay you $100,' A has made a promise but has not asked B for a return promise. A has asked B to perform, not a commitment to perform. A has thus made an offer looking to a unilateral contract. B cannot accept this offer by promising to walk the bridge. B must accept, if at all, by performing the act. Because no return promise is requested, at no point is B bound to perform. If B does perform, a contract involving two parties is created, but the contract is classified as unilateral because only one party is ever under an obligation." John D. Calamari & Joseph M. Perillo, *The Law of Contracts* § 2–10(a), at 64–65 (4th ed. 1998).

valid contract. A contract that is fully operative in accordance with the parties' intent. — Also termed *valid agreement*.

variable annuity contract. *Securities*. An annuity whose payments vary according to how well the fund (usu. made up of common stocks) that backs it is performing. SEC Rule 0–1(e)(1) (17 CFR § 270.0–1(e)(1)). See *variable annuity* under ANNUITY.

verbal contract. See *parol contract* (1).

voidable contract. A contract that can be affirmed or rejected at the option of one of the parties; a contract that is void as to the wrongdoer but not void as to the party wronged, unless that party elects to treat it as void.

"A voidable contract is a contract which, in its inception, is valid and capable of producing the results of a valid contract, but which may be 'avoided', i.e. rendered void at the option of one (or even, though rarely, of both) of the parties." P.S. Atiyah, *An Introduction to the Law of Contract* 37–38 (3d ed. 1981).

void contract. **1.** A contract that is of no legal effect, so that there is really no contract in existence at all.

"Strictly speaking, a 'void contract' is a contradiction in terms; for the words describe a state of things in which, despite the intention of the parties, no contract has been made. Yet the expression, however faulty, is a compendious way of putting a case in which there has been the outward semblance without the reality of contract." William R. Anson, *Principles of the Law of Contract* 18 (Arthur L. Corbin ed., 3d Am. ed. 1919).

"A valid contract is, of course, simply a contract of full force and effect, not vitiated in any way. A so-called void contract, on the other hand, is really a contradiction in terms inasmuch as a contract has already been defined in terms applicable only to a valid contract. However, the term is convenient and is universally used. For purposes of exposition, it is convenient to treat void contracts as falling, broadly speaking, into main categories. On the one hand, are cases where one of the normal requirements for the creation of a contract is absent, while, on the other hand, are cases where all the normal requirements are satisfied, but the contract is void because the law disapproves of its purpose or the terms by which it seeks to achieve that purpose. Typical examples of contracts which are void because one of the normal requirements is absent are contracts in which the acceptance of an offer has not been communicated or in which a promise is given gratuitously. Typical examples of contracts which are void because of their terms or objects are wagering contracts, and contracts prejudicial to family relations." P.S. Atiyah, *An Introduction to the Law of Contract* 36–37 (3d ed. 1981).

2. A contract that has been fully performed. — Also termed *discharged contract*.

"Not only is the term 'void contract' in itself technically inaccurate, but a contract is sometimes said to be void, not because it was destitute of legal effect from its commencement, but because it has been fully performed, and so has ceased to have legal operation. It would be more proper to describe such a contract as 'discharged.' " William R. Anson, *Principles of the Law of Contract* 20 (Arthur L. Corbin ed., 3d Am. ed. 1919).

3. Loosely, a voidable contract.

"Again the word 'void' has been used, even by judges and the framers of statutes, where 'voidable' is meant. One illustration will suffice. By 17 *Geo. III*, c. 50, failure to pay certain duties at an auction is stated to make a bidding 'nul and void to all intents,' but this does not entitle a purchaser who has repented of his bargain to avoid the contract by his own wrong, that is by refusal to pay the statutory duty. The contract is voidable at the option of the party who has not broken the condition imposed by law." William R. Anson, *Principles of the Law of Contract* 20–21 (Arthur L. Corbin ed., 3d Am. ed. 1919).

wagering contract. **1.** A contract the performance of which depends on the happening of an uncertain event, made entirely for sport. **2.** A contract in which an uncertain event affects or results from a business transaction. • With this type of wagering contract, a business person is protected from a trade risk.

written contract. A contract whose terms have been reduced to writing.

"Written contracts are also commonly signed, but a written contract may consist of an exchange of correspondence, of a letter written by the promisee and assented to by the promisor without signature, or even of a memorandum or printed document not signed by either party. Statutes relating to written contracts are often expressly limited to contracts signed by one or both parties. Whether such a limitation is to be implied when not explicit depends on the purpose and context." Restatement (Second) of Contracts § 95 cmt. c (1981) (citations omitted).

contract, freedom of. See FREEDOM OF CONTRACT.

contract bond. See PERFORMANCE BOND.

contract carrier. See *private carrier* under CARRIER.

Contract Clause. See CONTRACTS CLAUSE.

contract demurrage. See DEMURRAGE.

contractee. *Rare.* A person with whom a contract is made.

contract for deed. See CONTRACT.

contract for sale. See CONTRACT.

contract implied in fact. See *implied-in-fact contract* under CONTRACT.

contract implied in law. See *implied-in-law contract* under CONTRACT.

contract loan. See *add-on loan* under LOAN.

contract not to compete. See *noncompetition covenant* under COVENANT (1).

contract not to sue. See *covenant not to sue* under COVENANT (1).

contract of adhesion. See *adhesion contract* under CONTRACT.

contract of affreightment (ə-**frayt**-mənt). *Maritime law.* An agreement for carriage of goods by water. • This type of contract usu. takes the form of a bill of lading or charterparty. — Abbr. COA. See *bareboat charter* under CHARTER; CHARTERPARTY.

contract of beneficence (bə-**nef**-ə-sənts). See *gratuitous contract* under CONTRACT.

contract of benevolence. See *gratuitous contract* under CONTRACT.

contract of insurance. See INSURANCE POLICY.

contract of record. See CONTRACT.

contract of sale. See *contract for sale* (1) under CONTRACT.

contractor. 1. A party to a contract. **2.** More specif., one who contracts to do work or provide supplies for another.

general contractor. One who contracts for the completion of an entire project, including purchasing all materials, hiring and paying subcontractors, and coordinating all the work. — Also termed *original contractor*; *prime contractor*.

independent contractor. See INDEPENDENT CONTRACTOR.

subcontractor. See SUBCONTRACTOR.

contract rate. See INTEREST RATE.

Contracts Clause. The clause of the U.S. Constitution prohibiting states from passing a law that would impair private contractual obligations. • The Supreme Court has generally interpreted this clause so that states can regulate private contractual obligations if the regulation is reasonable and necessary. U.S. Const. art. I, § 10, cl. 1. — Also termed *Contract Clause*; *Obligation of Contracts Clause*.

contract system. *Hist.* The practice of leasing prisoners out to private individuals for the prisoners' labor.

contract to satisfaction. See *satisfaction contract* under CONTRACT.

contract to sell. See *contract for sale* (2) under CONTRACT.

contractual duty. See DUTY (1).

contract *uberrimae fidei*. See CONTRACT.

contract under seal. See CONTRACT.

contractus (kən-**trak**-təs). [Latin] *Roman law.* A contract; an agreement between two or more parties, usu. to create an actionable bond between them. See CONTRAHERE.

> "The texts of the Roman Law do not supply a definition of contract. The words contractus — contrahere — like 'contract' in English, are used in various senses, sometimes wider, sometimes narrower. Labeo gives contractus the meaning of a reciprocal obligation, such as purchase and sale, hire, partnership. But when the Romans speak of obligation arising from contract, they mean obligations arising from convention or agreement. In Roman law it was far from being the case that all agreements which might be expected to produce a legal obligation did so." R.W. Lee, *The Elements of Roman Law* 285 (4th ed. 1956).

contractus bonae fidei (kən-**trak**-təs **boh**-nee **fI**-dee-I). [Latin "contract of good faith"] *Roman law.* A contract requiring that the parties perform their duties in good faith. • In an action brought on a *contractus bonae fidei*, the plaintiff had to assert that he had not acted in bad faith. All consensual contracts were considered *contractus bonae fidei*. Essentially, then, the phrase was typically used when a remedy was being sought for a breach.

contract zoning. See ZONING.

contradictory motion. See MOTION.

contrafactio (kon-trə-**fak**-shee-oh). [Law Latin] *Hist.* The act of counterfeiting. • The word appeared frequently in the phrase *contrafactio sigilli regis* ("counterfeiting the king's seal").

contra formam collationis (**kon**-trə **for**-məm kə-lay-shee-**oh**-nis). [Latin "against the form of a collation"] *Hist.* A writ to regain lands given to a religious society in exchange for perpetual alms. • The writ was usu. sought by an heir of the person who had given the land away.

contra formam feoffmenti (**kon**-trə **for**-məm feef-**men**-tI). [Latin "contrary to the form of the feoffment"] *Hist.* A writ that commanded a landowner to stop demanding from a tenant more services than those included in the tenant's deed to the land. — Also spelled *contra formam feoffamenti.*

> "Contra formam feoffamenti is a writ that lies where a man before the statute of *quia emptores terrarum*, made 18 Ed. 1, infeoffed another by deed to do certain service; if the feoffor or his heirs distrain him to do other service than is comprised in the deed, then the tenant shall have this writ, commanding him not to distrain him to do other service than is comprised in the deed." *Termes de la Ley* 116 (1st Am. ed. 1812).

contra formam statuti (**kon**-trə **for**-məm stə-**tyoo**-tI). [Law Latin] Contrary to the form of the statute. See AGAINST THE FORM OF THE STATUTE.

contrahere (kən-**tray**-hə-ree), *vb.* [Latin "draw together"] *Roman law.* **1.** To establish or enter into a formal relationship, as between husband and wife, creditor and debtor, by mutual agreement. **2.** To commit a crime. **3.** To accept an inheritance. **4.** Generally, to perform any act of legal significance. See CONTRACTUS.

contra jus belli (**kon**-trə jəs **bel**-I). [Latin] Against the law of war.

contra jus commune (**kon**-trə jəs kə-**myoo**-nee). [Latin] Against common right or law; contrary to the rule of the common law.

contra legem terrae (**kon**-trə **lee**-jəm **ter**-ee). [Latin] Against the law of the land.

contra non valentem. See DOCTRINE OF CONTRA NON VALENTEM.

contra omnes gentes (**kon**-trə **om**-neez **jen**-teez). [Latin] *Hist.* Against all people. • These were the traditional words of warranty in a deed.

contra pacem (**kon**-trə **pay**-səm). [Latin] Against the peace. • This term was formerly used in indictments to signify that the alleged offense is against the public peace.

contraplacitum (kon-trə-**plas**-ə-təm). [Latin] *Hist.* A counterplea.

contra proferentem (**kon**-trə prof-ə-**ren**-təm). [Latin "against the offeror"] The doctrine that, in interpreting documents, ambiguities are to be construed unfavorably to the drafter. — Also spelled *contra proferentes.* — Also termed *ambiguity doctrine.*

contrarotulator (kon-trə-roch-yə-**lay**-tər *or* kon-trə-**roh**-tyə-lay-tər). [Latin "controller"] *Hist.* A person responsible for collecting and managing funds on behalf of the Crown or other government office. • A variety of controllers existed in England, including the *contrarotulator custumarum* (controller of the customs), *contrarotulator hospitii domini regis* (controller of the king's household), and *contrarotulator pipae* (controller of the pipe — i.e., an officer who collected debts due to the Exchequer).

contrary to law. 1. (Of an act or omission) illegal. **2.** (Of a jury verdict) in conflict with established law.

contrary to the evidence. (Of an argument) that is counter to the weight of the evidence presented at a contested hearing.

contra tabula. See BONORUM POSSESSIO CONTRA TABULAS.

contravene (kon-trə-**veen**), *vb.* **1.** To violate or infringe; to defy <the soldier contravened the officer's order, and then went AWOL>. **2.** To come into conflict with; to be contrary to <the court held that the regulation contravenes public policy>.

contravening equity. See EQUITY.

contravention (kon-trə-**ven**-shən). **1.** An act violating a legal condition or obligation; esp., an entail heir's act that conflicts with the entail provision. **2.** *French law.* A criminal breach of a law, treaty, or agreement; a minor violation of the law. • A contravention is traditionally punishable by *peines de police*, usu. a fine not exceeding 15 francs and imprisonment not exceeding three days. See *public-welfare offense* under OFFENSE.

> "We might get [terminological] help from the practice of Continental Europe in which three classes of punishable offenses are maintained — crimes, delicts, and contraventions. The last word is used for those minor violations of regulations, all of them necessary enough for public safety and convenience, which are so numerous and so detailed in our lives. It is a convenient term and is widely used in the United States for just such acts, but it has not yet been made official. The Continental practice has the advantage of using the word crimes only for really serious offenses, which is in conformity with popular feeling on the subject." Max Radin, *The Law and You* 92 (1948).

3. *Scots law.* An action brought for breach of a peace bond. See LAWBURROWS. **4.** *Hist. Scots law.* An act committed in violation of a legal condition or obligation, esp. one done by an entail heir contrary to a deed.

contrectatio (kon-trek-**tay**-shee-oh), *n.* [fr. Latin *contrectare* "to touch or handle"] *Hist.* The act of laying hands on another's property with the intent of taking, misappropriating, or misusing it. • This term implied a greater culpability than simply taking property without the owner's permission and, under the Roman law, could rise to the level of theft (*furtum*).

contributing cause. See CAUSE (1).

contributing to the delinquency of a minor. The offense of an adult's engaging in conduct involving a minor — or in the presence of a minor — likely to result in delinquent conduct. • Examples include encouraging a minor to shoplift, to lie under oath, or to commit vandalism. — Also termed *contributing to delinquency*. See JUVENILE DELINQUENCY. Cf. IMPAIRING THE MORALS OF A MINOR.

contribution. 1. The right that gives one of several persons who are liable on a common debt the ability to recover ratably from each of the others when that one person discharges the debt for the benefit of all; the right to demand that another who is jointly responsible for a third party's injury supply part of what is required to compensate the third party. — Also termed *right of contribution*. **2.** A tortfeasor's right to collect from others responsible for the same tort after the tortfeasor has paid more than his or her proportionate share, the shares being determined as a percentage of fault. **3.** The actual payment by a joint tortfeasor of a proportionate share of what is due. Cf. INDEMNITY. **4.** WAR CONTRIBUTION.

contribution bar. Preclusion of a defendant having contribution rights against other defendants, who have settled their dispute with the plaintiff, from seeking contribution from them. • The bar is usu. allowed in exchange for a credit against any judgment the plaintiff obtains against the nonsettling defendant.

contribution clause. See COINSURANCE CLAUSE.

contributione facienda (kon-tri-byoo-shee-**oh**-nee fay-shee-**en**-də). [Latin "writ for making contribution"] *Hist.* A writ to compel a tenant in common to contribute to a fellow tenant who has paid more than the tenant's share of a sum for which all the tenants are liable.

> "*Contributione facienda* is a writ that lieth in case where more are bound to one thing, & one is put to the whole burden. . . . If tenents in comon or joynt, hold a mill (*pro indiviso*) & equally take the profits therof, the mill falling to decay, & one or more of them refusing to contribute toward the reparation therof, the rest shall have this writ. . . ." John Cowell, *The Interpreter* (1607).

contribution margin. The difference between a product's selling price and its cost of production. • The contribution margin indicates the amount of funds available for profit and payment of fixed costs.

contributory (kən-**trib**-yə-tor-ee), *adj.* **1.** Tending to bring about a result. **2.** (Of a pension fund) that receives contributions from both the employer and the employees.

contributory, *n.* **1.** One who contributes or who has a duty to contribute. **2.** A contributing factor. **3.** *Hist.* A person who, as a result of being or representing a past or present member of a corporation, is liable to contribute to the corporation's debts upon its winding up.

contributory infringement. See INFRINGEMENT.

contributory negligence. See NEGLIGENCE.

contributory-negligence doctrine. *Torts.* The principle that completely bars a plaintiff's recovery if the damage suffered is partly the plaintiff's own fault. • Most states have abolished this doctrine and have adopted instead a comparative-negligence scheme. See NEGLIGENCE. Cf. COMPARATIVE-NEGLIGENCE DOCTRINE.

contributory pension plan. See PENSION PLAN.

control, *n.* The direct or indirect power to direct the management and policies of a person or entity, whether through ownership of voting securities, by contract, or otherwise; the power or authority to manage, direct, or oversee <the principal exercised control over the agent>.

> ***superintending control.*** The general supervisory control that a higher court in a jurisdiction has over the administrative affairs of a lower court within that jurisdiction.
>
> ***working control.*** The effective control of a corporation by a person or group who owns less than 50% of the stock.

control, *vb.* **1.** To exercise power or influence over <the judge controlled the proceedings>. **2.** To regulate or govern <by law, the budget office controls expenditures>. **3.** To have a controlling interest in <the five shareholders controlled the company>.

control group. The persons with authority to make decisions on a corporation's behalf.

control-group test. A method of determining whether the attorney-client privilege protects communications made by corporate employees, by providing that those communications are protected only if made by an employee who is a member of the group with authority to direct the corporation's actions as a result of that communication. • The U.S. Supreme Court rejected the control-group test in *Upjohn Co. v. United States*, 449 U.S. 383, 101 S.Ct. 677 (1981). Cf. SUBJECT-MATTER TEST.

controlled company. See COMPANY.

controlled corporate groups. See CONTROLLED GROUP.

controlled corporation. See CORPORATION.

controlled foreign corporation. See CORPORATION.

controlled group. *Tax.* Two or more corporations whose stock is substantially held by five or fewer persons. • The Internal Revenue Code subjects these entities (such as parent-subsidiary or brother-sister groups) to special rules for computing tax liability. — Also termed *controlled corporate groups.* IRC (26 USCA) §§ 851(c)(3), 1563(a).

controlled-securities-offering distribution. See *securities-offering distribution* under DISTRIBUTION.

controlled substance. Any type of drug whose possession and use is regulated by law, including a narcotic, a stimulant, or a hallucinogen. See DRUG.

controlled-substance act. A federal or state statute that is designed to control the distribution, classification, sale, and use of certain drugs. • Most states have enacted these laws, which are usu. modeled on the Uniform Controlled Substances Act.

controller. See COMPTROLLER.

controlling interest. See INTEREST (2).

controlling person. See CONTROL PERSON.

controlling shareholder. See SHAREHOLDER.

control person. *Securities.* A person who has actual control or significant influence over the issuer of securities, as by directing corporate policy. • The control person is subject to many of the same requirements applicable to the sale of securities by the issuer. — Also termed *controlling person.*

> "[T]he question of who is a control person is highly factual and is not dependent upon ownership of any specific percentage. For example, it has been held that someone owning eight percent of a company's stock was

not a control person. . . ." 1 Thomas Lee Hazen, *The Law of Securities Regulation* § 4.24, at 279 (3d ed. 1995).

control premium. See PREMIUM (3).

control stock. Stock belonging to a control person at the time of a given transaction. — Also termed *control shares*.

control test. See IRRESISTIBLE-IMPULSE TEST.

control-your-kid law. See PARENTAL-RESPONSIBILITY STATUTE.

controver (kən-**troh**-vər). *Hist.* A person who concocts false news.

controversy. 1. A disagreement or a dispute, esp. in public. **2.** A justiciable dispute. **3.** *Constitutional law.* A case that requires a definitive determination of the law on the facts alleged for the adjudication of an actual dispute, and not merely a hypothetical, theoretical, or speculative legal issue. — Also termed (in senses 2 & 3) *actual controversy.* See CASE-OR-CONTROVERSY REQUIREMENT.

"What is a 'case or controversy' that is justiciable in the federal courts? The answer of Chief Justice Hughes is classic if cryptic. He said: 'A *controversy* in this sense must be one that is appropriate for judicial determination. A justiciable controversy is thus distinguished from a difference or dispute of a hypothetical character; from one that is academic or moot. The controversy must be definite and concrete, touching the legal relations of parties having adverse legal interests. It must be a real and substantial controversy admitting of specific relief through a decree of a conclusive character, as distinguished from an opinion advising what the law would be upon a hypothetical state of facts.' [*Aetna Life Ins. Co. v. Haworth*, 300 U.S. 227, 240–41, 57 S.Ct. 461, 464 (1937) (Hughes, C.J.).] Unfortunately, this definition, though often quoted, turns upon labels that the Court had used in the past to describe cases before it, and the labels themselves are 'elastic, inconstant, and imprecise.' " Charles Alan Wright, *The Law of Federal Courts* § 12, at 60–61 (5th ed. 1994).

public controversy. A controversy involving issues that are debated publicly and that have substantial ramifications for persons other than those engaged in it. • A participant in a public controversy may be deemed a public figure for purposes of a defamation suit arising from the controversy. See PUBLIC FIGURE.

"The nature and extent of an individual's involvement in a public controversy is determined by three factors: (1) the extent to which participation in it is voluntary; (2) the extent to which there is access to channels of effective communication in order to counteract false statements; and (3) the prominence of the role played in the public controversy." 50 Am. Jur. 2d *Libel and Slander* § 75, at 390 (1995).

controvert (**kon**-trə-vərt *or* kon-trə-**vərt**), *vb.* To dispute or contest; esp., to deny (as an allegation in a pleading) or oppose in argument <the allegations in Peck's pleadings were never adequately controverted>.

contubernium (kon-t[y]uu-**bər**-nee-əm). [Latin] *Roman law.* A marriage-like union between slaves.

"No such thing as marriage among slaves was, or could be, recognized by the law. As slaves were wholly subject to the disposal of their masters, no unions having the character of permanence or sacredness could exist among them: such a union, if it existed, would abridge the master's power of absolute control. Among slaves there could only be *contubernium*, cohabitation of the sexes for a longer or shorter time, but no legal *matrimonium*." James Hadley, *Introduction to Roman Law* 111 (1881).

contumace capiendo. See DE CONTUMACE CAPIENDO.

contumacious conduct. See CONDUCT.

contumacy (**kon**-t[y]uu-mə-see), *n.* Contempt of court; the refusal of a person to follow a court's order or direction. — **contumacious,** *adj.* See CONTEMPT.

contumax. *Hist.* **1.** A person found to be in contempt of court. **2.** A person who is accused of a crime but refuses to appear and answer the charge.

contumely (**kon**-t[y]uu-mə-lee *or* kən-**t[y]oo**-mə-lee), *n.* Insulting language or treatment; scornful rudeness.

contutor (kən-**t[y]oo**-tər). [Latin] *Roman law.* A co-guardian of a ward. • Appointment as a co-guardian could be accomplished by testament or by court order.

conusance (**kon**-yə-zənts). *Hist.* **1.** Cognizance; jurisdiction. • The word *conusance* is actually an archaic form of *cognizance*. See COGNIZANCE (1); CLAIM OF COGNIZANCE. **2.** JUDICIAL NOTICE. **3.** An acknowledgment (of a debt, act, or opposing claim). • Examples of *conusance* include an acknowledgment in replevin that the defendant took the sued-for goods, or an acknowledgment in a land transfer (by *fine*) that the grantee is entitled to the land. See FINE (1).

conusant (**kon**-yə-zənt), *adj.* (Of a person) having cognizance or knowledge. See COGNIZANCE.

conusee (kon-yə-**zee**). See COGNIZEE.

conusor (**kon**-yə-zər *or* -zor). See COGNIZOR.

convene, *vb.* **1.** To call together; to cause to assemble. **2.** *Eccles. law.* To summon to respond to an action. See CONVENTIO (1).

> "When the defendant was brought to answer, he was said to be convened, — which the canonists called *conventio,* because the plaintiff and defendant met to contest." 1 John Bouvier, *Bouvier's Law Dictionary* 668 (8th ed. 1914).

3. *Civil law.* To bring an action.

convening authority. *Military law.* An officer (usu. a commanding officer) with the power to convene, or who has convened, a court-martial.

convening order. *Military law.* An instrument that creates a court-martial. • The convening order specifies (1) the type of court-martial and its time and place, (2) the names of the members and the trial and defense counsel, (3) the name of the military judge, if one has been detailed, and (4) if necessary, the authority by which the court-martial has been created.

conventicle (kən-**ven**-tə-kəl). [fr. Latin *conventiculum* "small assembly"] **1.** An assembly of a clandestine or unlawful character. **2.** An assembly for religious worship; esp., a secret meeting for worship not sanctioned by law. **3.** A place where such meetings are held.

conventio (kən-**ven**-shee-oh). [fr. Latin *convenire* "to come together"] **1.** *Eccles. law.* The act of convening the parties to an action by summoning the defendant. **2.** *Hist.* An agreement or convention; an agreement between two or more persons respecting a legal relation between them. See CONVENTION (1).

> "Conventio is a word much used both in Ancient and Modern Law-pleadings, for an Agreement or Covenant." Thomas Blount, *Nomo-Lexicon: A Law–Dictionary* (1670).

convention. 1. An agreement or compact, esp. one among nations; a multilateral treaty <the Geneva Convention>. See TREATY. **2.** An assembly or meeting of members belonging to an organization or having a common objective <an ABA convention>. **3.** A generally accepted rule or practice; usage or custom <the court dispensed with the convention of having counsel approach the bench>.

conventional, *adj.* **1.** Customary; orthodox; traditional <conventional motion practice>. **2.** Depending on, or arising from, the agreement of the parties, as distinguished from something arising by law <conventional subrogation>. **3.** Arising by treaty or convention <conventional international law>.

conventional custom. See CUSTOM.

conventional interest. See INTEREST (3).

conventionalism. A jurisprudential conception of legal practice and tradition holding that law is a matter of respecting and enforcing legal and social rules.

> "Conventionalism makes two postinterpretive, directive claims. The first is positive: that judges must respect the established legal conventions of their community except in rare circumstances. It insists, in other words, that they must treat as law what convention stipulates as law. Since convention in Britain establishes that acts of Parliament are law, a British judge must enforce even acts of Parliament he considers unfair or unwise. This positive part of conventionalism most plainly corresponds to the popular slogan that judges should follow the law and not make new law in its place. The second claim, which is at least equally important, is negative. It declares that there is no law — no right flowing from past political decisions — apart from the law drawn from those decisions by techniques that are themselves matters of convention, and therefore that on some issues there is no law either way." Ronald Dworkin, *Law's Empire* 116 (1986).

conventional law. A rule or system of rules agreed on by persons for the regulation of their conduct toward one another; law constituted by agreement as having the force of special law between the parties, by either supplementing or replacing the general law of the land. • The most important example is conventional international law, but there are many lesser examples such as rules and regulations of a country club or professional association, or the rules of golf, basketball, or any other game. — Also termed (in international law) *treaty-made law*; *treaty-created law*.

conventional lien. See LIEN.

conventional loan. See *conventional mortgage* under MORTGAGE.

conventional mortgage. See MORTGAGE.

conventional obligation. See OBLIGATION.

conventional remission. See REMISSION.

conventional sequestration. See SEQUESTRATION.

conventional subrogation. See SUBROGATION.

conventione (kən-ven-shee-**oh**-nee). [Latin] *Hist.* A writ for the breach of a written covenant. • This writ was often used when parties wished to convey land by fine. — Also termed *writ of covenant*. See FINE (1).

conventus (kən-**ven**-təs). [Latin] *Roman law.* **1.** An assembly. • *Conventus magnatum vel procerum* ("the assembly of the nobles") was an ancient name for Parliament. **2.** A judicial assize held within a province.

conventus juridicus (kən-**ven**-təs juu-**rid**-i-kəs). [Latin "judicial assembly"] *Roman law.* A court session held by a provincial governor in the leading cities of the province.

conversion, *n.* **1.** The act of changing from one form to another; the process of being exchanged.

equitable conversion. The act of treating real property as personal property, or vice versa, in certain circumstances. • Courts usu. apply the doctrine of equitable conversion to recognize the transfer of land when a party dies after the signing of an agreement to sell real property but before the transfer of title. Equitable conversion is based on the maxim that equity regards as done that which ought to be done.

forced conversion. The conversion of a convertible security, after a call for redemption, when the value of the security that it may be converted to is greater than the amount that will be received if the holder permits the security to be redeemed.

2. *Tort & criminal law.* The wrongful possession or disposition of another's property as if it were one's own; an act or series of acts of willful interference, without lawful justification, with any chattel in a manner inconsistent with another's right, whereby that other person is deprived of the use and possession of the chattel. — **convert,** *vb.*

"There are three distinct methods by which one man may deprive another of his property, and so be guilty of a conversion and liable in an action for trover — (1) by wrongly taking it, (2) by wrongly detaining it, and (3) by wrongly disposing of it. The term conversion was originally limited to the third of these cases. To convert goods meant to dispose of them, or make away with them, to deal with them, in such a way that neither owner nor wrongdoer had any further possession of them: for example, by consuming them, or by destroying them, or by selling them, or otherwise delivering them to some third person. Merely to take another's goods, however wrongfully, was not to convert them. Merely to detain them in defiance of the owner's title was not to convert them. The fact that conversion in its modern sense includes instances of all three modes in which a man may be wrongfully deprived of his goods, and not of one mode only, is the outcome of a process of historical development whereby, by means of legal fictions and other devices, the action of trover was enabled to extend its limits and appropriate the territories that rightly belonged to other and earlier forms of action." R.F.V. Heuston, *Salmond on the Law of Torts* 94 (17th ed. 1977).

"By conversion of goods is meant any act in relation to goods which amounts to an exercise of dominion over them, inconsistent with the owner's right of property. It does not include mere acts of damage, or even an asportation which does not amount to a denial of the owner's right of property; but it does include such acts as taking possession, refusing to give up on demand, disposing of the goods to a third person, or destroying them." William Geldart, *Introduction to English Law* 143 (D.C.M. Yardley ed., 9th ed. 1984).

constructive conversion. Conversion consisting of an action that in law amounts to the appropriation of property. • Constructive conversion could be, for example, an appropriation that was initially lawful.

conversion by detention. Conversion by detaining a chattel in a way that is adverse to the owner or other lawful possessor. • The mere possession of a chattel without title is not conversion. The defendant must have shown an intention to keep it in defiance of the plaintiff.

conversion by estoppel. A judicial determination that a conversion has taken place — though in truth one has not — because a defendant is estopped from offering a defense. • This occurs, for example, under the traditional rule that a bailee is estopped from denying the bailor's title even if the bailor has no title to the chattel.

conversion by taking. Conversion by taking a chattel out of the possession of another with the intention of exercising a permanent or temporary dominion over it, despite the owner's entitlement to use it at all times.

conversion by wrongful delivery. Conversion by depriving an owner of goods by delivering them to someone else so as to change the possession.

conversion by wrongful destruction. Conversion by willfully consuming or otherwise destroying a chattel belonging to another person.

conversion by wrongful disposition. Conversion by depriving an owner of goods by giving some other person a lawful title to them.

direct conversion. The act of appropriating the property of another to one's own benefit, or to the benefit of another. • A direct conversion is per se unlawful, and the traditional requirements of demand and refusal of the property do not apply.

fraudulent conversion. Conversion that is committed by the use of fraud, either in obtaining the property or in withholding it.

involuntary conversion. The loss or destruction of property through theft, casualty, or condemnation.

conversion premium. *Securities.* The surplus at which a security sells above its conversion price.

conversion price. *Securities.* The contractually specified price per share at which a convertible security can be converted into shares of common stock.

conversion ratio. 1. The number of common shares into which a convertible security may be converted. **2.** The ratio of the face amount of the convertible security to the conversion price.

conversion security. See SECURITY.

conversion value. A convertible security's value as common stock. • For example, a bond that can be converted into ten shares of stock worth $40 each has a conversion value of $400. See BOND CONVERSION.

convertible arbitrage. See *kind arbitrage* under ARBITRAGE.

convertible bond. See BOND (3).

convertible collision insurance. See INSURANCE.

convertible debenture. See DEBENTURE.

convertible debt. See DEBT.

convertible insurance. See INSURANCE.

convertible security. See SECURITY.

convertible stock. See *convertible security* under SECURITY.

convertible subordinated debenture. See DEBENTURE.

convey, *vb.* To transfer or deliver (something, such as a right or property) to another, esp. by deed or other writing.

conveyance (kən-**vay**-ənts), *n.* **1.** The voluntary transfer of a right or of property.

absolute conveyance. A conveyance in which a right or property is transferred to another free of conditions or qualifications (i.e., not as a security). Cf. *conditional conveyance.*

conditional conveyance. A conveyance that is based on the happening of an event, usu. payment for the property; a mortgage. Cf. *absolute conveyance.*

derivative conveyance. See *secondary conveyance.*

innocent conveyance. *Hist.* A leaseholder's conveyance of the leaseholder's property interest — that is, something less than a fee simple. • It is a conveyance of an equitable interest.

mesne conveyance (meen). An intermediate conveyance; one occupying an intermediate position in the chain of title between the first grantee and the present holder.

original conveyance. See *primary conveyance.*

present conveyance. A conveyance made with the intent that it take effect at once rather than in the future.

primary conveyance. A conveyance that creates an estate. • Examples of primary conveyances include feoffment, gift, grant, lease, exchange, and partition. — Also termed *original conveyance.* Cf. *secondary conveyance.*

> "Of conveyances by the common law, some may be called *original*, or *primary* conveyances; which are those by means whereof the benefit or estate is created or first arises: others are *derivative* or *secondary*; whereby the benefit or estate, originally created, is enlarged, restrained, transferred, or extinguished." 2 William Blackstone, *Commentaries on the Laws of England* 309 (1766).

secondary conveyance. A conveyance that follows an earlier conveyance and that serves only to enlarge, confirm, alter, restrain, restore, or transfer the interest created by the primary conveyance. — Also termed *derivative conveyance.* Cf. *primary conveyance.*

voluntary conveyance. A conveyance made without valuable consideration, such as a deed in favor of a relative.

2. The transfer of a property right that does not pass by delivery of a thing or merely by agreement. **3.** The transfer of an interest in real property from one living person to another, by means of an instrument such as a deed. **4.** The document (usu. a deed) by which such a transfer occurs. **5.** A means of transport; a vehicle. **6.** *Bankruptcy.* A transfer of an interest in real or personal property, including an assignment, release, monetary payment, or the creation of a lien or encumbrance. — Also termed (in sense 6) *bond for deed.* See FRAUDULENT CONVEYANCE; PREFERENTIAL TRANSFER.

conveyancer (kən-**vay**-ən-sər). A lawyer who specializes in real-estate transactions. • In England, a *conveyancer* is a solicitor or licensed conveyancer who examines title to real estate, prepares deeds and mortgages, and performs other functions relating to the transfer of real property.

conveyancing (kən-**vay**-ən-sing). The act or business of drafting and preparing legal instruments, esp. those (such as deeds or leases) that transfer an interest in real property.

> "*Conveyancing* is the art or science of preparing documents and investigating title in connection with the creation and assurance of interests in land. Despite its connection with the word 'conveyance', the term in practice is not limited to use in connection with old system title but is used without discrimination in the context of all types of title." Peter Butt, *Land Law* 7 (2d ed. 1988).

conveyancing counsel. Three to six lawyers who are appointed by the Lord Chancellor to assist the High Court of Justice with opinions in matters of property titles and conveyancing. — Also termed *conveyancing counsel of the Supreme Court*; (formerly) *conveyancing counsel to the Court of Chancery.*

conveyee (kən-vay-**ee**). One to whom property is conveyed.

conveyor (kən-**vay**-ər *or* -or). One who transfers or delivers title to another.

convicium (kən-**vish**-ee-əm). [Latin] *Roman law.* Reproach, abuse, reviling, or insult.

convict (**kon**-vikt), *n.* A person who has been found guilty of a crime and is serving a sentence of confinement for that crime; a prison inmate.

convict (kən-**vikt**), *vb.* To find (a person) guilty of a criminal offense upon a criminal trial, a plea of guilty, or a plea of nolo contendere (no contest).

conviction (kən-**vik**-shən), *n.* **1.** The act or process of judicially finding someone guilty of a crime; the state of having been proved guilty. **2.** The judgment (as by a jury verdict) that a person is guilty of a crime. **3.** A strong belief or opinion.

abiding conviction. A settled conviction; a definite conviction based on a thorough examination of the case.

summary conviction. A conviction of a person for a violation or minor misdemeanor as the result of a trial before a magistrate sitting without a jury.

conviction rate. Within a given area or for a given time, the number of convictions (including plea bargains) as a percentage of the total number of prosecutions undertaken.

convivium (kən-**viv**-ee-əm). [Latin "banquet"] *Hist.* Tenure that binds the tenant to provide meat and drink for the lord at least once a year.

convocation. See *provincial synod* under SYNOD.

convoy, *n.* A protective escort, esp. for ships. — **convoy,** *vb.*

co-obligee. One of two or more persons to whom an obligation is owed. See OBLIGEE.

co-obligor. One of two or more persons who have undertaken an obligation. See OBLIGOR.

cool blood. *Criminal law.* In the law of homicide, the finding that the defendant's emotions were not in such an excited state that they interfered with his or her faculties and reason. — Also termed *cool state of blood.* See COLD BLOOD. Cf. HEAT OF PASSION.

***Cooley* doctrine.** *Constitutional law.* The principle that Congress has exclusive power under the Commerce Clause to regulate the national as well as the local aspects of national commercial matters, and that the states may regulate those aspects of interstate commerce so local in character as to require diverse treatment. • The Supreme Court has abandoned the *Cooley* doctrine in favor of a balancing test for Commerce Clause cases. *Cooley v. Port Board of Wardens*, 53 U.S. (12 How.) 299 (1851).

cooling-off period. 1. During a dispute, a period during which no action may be taken by either side. **2.** A period during which a buyer may cancel a purchase. **3.** An automatic delay in some states between the filing of divorce papers and the divorce hearing. **4.** *Securities.* A period (usu. at least 20 days) between the filing of a registration and the effective registration.

cooling time. *Criminal law.* Time to recover cool blood after great excitement, stress, or provocation, so that one is considered able to contemplate, comprehend, and act with reference to the consequences that are likely to follow. See COOL BLOOD.

> "[O]ne who controls his temper time after time, following repeated acts of provocation, may have his emotion so bottled-up that the final result is an emotional explosion.... [I]n such a case the 'cooling time' begins to run not from earlier acts, but from 'the last straw.' ... As was the position in regard to the adequacy of the provocation, so the early holding was that the cooling time was a matter of law for the court." Rollin M. Perkins & Ronald N. Boyce, *Criminal Law* 100 (3d ed. 1982).

cool state of blood. See COOL BLOOD.

cooperation. **1.** An association of individuals who join together for a common benefit. **2.** *Patents.* A unity of action to a common end or result, not merely joint or simultaneous action. **3.** *Int'l law.* The voluntary coordinated action of two or more countries occurring under a legal régime and serving a specific objective.

cooperation clause. *Insurance.* A policy provision requiring that the insured assist the insurer in investigating and defending a claim.

cooperative, *n.* **1.** An organization or enterprise (as a store) owned by those who use its services. **2.** A dwelling (as an apartment building) owned by its residents, to whom the apartments are leased. — Often shortened to *coop*; *co-op*.

cooperative cause. See CAUSE (1).

cooperative corporation. See CORPORATION.

cooperative federalism. Distribution of power between the federal government and the states in which each recognizes the powers of the other but shares those powers to jointly engage in governmental functions.

co-opt, *vb.* **1.** To add as a member. **2.** To assimilate; absorb.

co-optation (koh-ahp-**tay**-shən), *n.* The act of selecting a person to fill a vacancy (usu. in a close corporation). — **co-optative,** *adj.*

coordinate jurisdiction. See *concurrent jurisdiction* under JURISDICTION.

coordination-of-benefits clause. See COB CLAUSE.

coowner, *n.* A person who is in concurrent ownership, possession, and enjoyment of property with one or more others; a tenant in common, a joint tenant, or a tenant by the entirety. — **coown,** *vb.* — **coownership,** *n.*

cop a plea, *vb. Slang.* (Of a criminal defendant) to plead guilty to a lesser charge as a means to avoid standing trial for a more serious offense. See PLEA BARGAIN.

coparcenary (koh-**pahr**-sə-ner-ee), *n.* An estate that arises when two or more persons jointly inherit from one ancestor, the title and right of possession being shared equally by all. • Coparcenary was a form of coownership created by common-law rules of descent upon intestacy when two or more persons together constituted the decedent's heir. Typically, this situation arose when the decedent was survived by no sons but by two or more daughters, so that the daughters took as coparceners. — Also termed *parcenary*; *tenancy in coparcenary*. — **coparcenary,** *adj.*

coparcener (koh-**pahr**-sə-nər). A person to whom an estate descends jointly, and who holds it as an entire estate. — Also termed *parcener*.

> "But sometimes two or more persons together constituted the heir, and in this case they took the land as 'parceners' or 'coparceners,' the latter expression being the more common.... In theory of law coparceners together constituted a single heir: 'they be but one heire, and yet severall persons.' They were called parceners because, as already seen, every coparcener had a common law right to have a partition made." Robert E. Megarry & H.W.R. Wade, *The Law of Real Property* 456–57 (5th ed. 1984).

coparticeps (koh-**pahr**-tə-seps). [fr. Latin *particeps* "sharing"] See COPARCENER.

copartner. A member of a partnership; PARTNER.

copartnership. See PARTNERSHIP. • The terms *copartnership* and *partnership* are equally old — each having first appeared in the 1570s.

coparty. A litigant or participant in a legal transaction who has a like status with another party; a party on the same side of a lawsuit. See CODEFENDANT; COPLAINTIFF.

copayment. A fixed amount that a patient pays to a healthcare provider according to the terms of the patient's health plan. — Often shortened to *copay*.

copia libelli deliberanda. See DE COPIA LIBELLI DELIBERANDA.

coplaintiff. One of two or more plaintiffs in the same litigation. Cf. CODEFENDANT.

coprincipal. 1. One of two or more participants in a criminal offense who either perpetrate the crime or aid a person who does so. **2.** One of two or more persons who have appointed an agent whom they both have the right to control.

copulative condition. See CONDITION (2).

copy, *n.* An imitation or reproduction of an original. • In the law of evidence, a copy is generally admissible to prove the contents of a writing. Fed. R. Evid. 1003. See BEST-EVIDENCE RULE.

> "The noun 'copy' ordinarily connotes a tangible object that is a reproduction of the original work; the courts have generally found no reason to depart from this usage in the law of copyright." 1 Melville B. Nimmer & David Nimmer, *Nimmer on Copyright* § 4.08[B], at 4–47 (Supp. 1995).

certified copy. A duplicate of an original (usu. official) document, certified as an exact reproduction usu. by the officer responsible for issuing or keeping the original. — Also termed *attested copy*; *exemplified copy*; *verified copy*; *verification*.

conformed copy. An exact copy of a document bearing written explanations of things that were not or could not be copied, such as a note on the document indicating that it was signed by a person whose signature appears on the original.

examined copy. A copy (usu. of a record, public book, or register) that has been compared with the original or with an official record of an original.

exemplified copy. See *certified copy*.

true copy. A copy that, while not necessarily exact, is sufficiently close to the original that anyone can understand it.

verified copy. See *certified copy*.

copycat drug. See *generic drug* under DRUG.

copyhold. *Hist.* A base tenure requiring the tenant to provide the customary services of the manor, as reflected in the manor's court rolls. • Copyhold tenure descended from pure villeinage; over time, the customs of the manor, as reflected on the manor's rolls, dictated what services a lord could demand from a copyholder. This type of tenure was abolished by the Law of Property Act of 1922, which converted copyhold land into freehold or leasehold land. — Also termed *copyhold tenure*; *customary estate*; *customary freehold*; *tenancy by the verge*; *tenancy par la verge*; *tenancy by the rod*. See *base tenure* under TENURE; VILLEINAGE.

> "Out of the tenure by villeinage, copyhold tenure developed.... By the end of the fifteenth century, to hold by copy of the court roll, to be a 'copyholder,' was a definite advantage, and, in most cases the holders had for many generations been personally free. The fusing of several different types of payment had also gone on, so that there was little difference between a holder in socage who had commuted the services for a sum of money and a copyholder who had done the same, except the specific dues of *heriot* and *merchet*. In Coke's time, a very large part of the land of England was still held by copyhold." Max Radin, *Handbook of Anglo-American Legal History* 371 (1936).

copyholder. *Hist.* A tenant by copyhold tenure. — Also termed *tenant by the verge*; *tenant par la verge*.

copyright, *n.* **1.** A property right in an original work of authorship (such as a literary, musical, artistic, photographic, or film work) fixed in any tangible medium of expression, giving the holder the exclusive right to reproduce, adapt, distribute, perform, and display the work. **2.** The body of law relating to such works. • Federal copyright law is governed by the Copyright Act of 1976. 17 USCA §§ 101–1332. — Abbr. c. — **copyright,** *vb.* — **copyrighted,** *adj.*

> "The development of copyright law in England was shaped by the efforts of mercantile interests to obtain monopoly control of the publishing industry — similar to those of the guilds that were instrumental in shaping patent and trademark law.... American copyright law came to distinguish between the 'common law' right of an author to his unpublished creations, and the statutory copyright that might be secured upon publication. Until recently, therefore, an author had perpetual rights to his creation, which included the right to decide when, if, and how to publish the work, but that common law right terminated upon publication at which time statutory rights become the sole rights, if any, to which the author was entitled. This distinction was altered by the Copyright Act of 1976, which shifts the line of demarcation between common law and statutory copyright from the moment of publication to the moment of fixation of the work into tangible form." Arthur R. Miller & Michael H. Davis, *Intellectual Property in a Nutshell* 280–82 (2d ed. 1990).

> "What is copyright? From copyright law's beginnings close to three centuries ago, the term has meant just what it says: the right to make copies of a given work — at first it meant simply written work — and to stop others from making copies without one's permission." Paul Goldstein, *Copyright's Highway* 3 (1994).

"Before the 1976 Copyright Act swept virtually all copyrightable subject matter within the exclusive domain of federal protection, the term 'copyright' implied a statutory right created by Congress in order to 'Promote the Progress of Science.' Our first copyright act, in 1790, protected only maps, charts, and books. Protection gradually was extended to musical compositions and graphic works. In the middle of the nineteenth century, photography was developed and then protected, followed at the end of the century by motion pictures (although they were protected as photographs). As the twentieth century comes to a close, digital technology and multimedia forms of authorship seriously challenge the gradual, compartmentalized approach to granting new rights and new subject matter ...." 1 William F. Patry, *Copyright Law and Practice* 1 (1994).

common-law copyright. A property right that arose when the work was created, rather than when it was published. • Under the Copyright Act of 1976, which was effective on January 1, 1978, common-law copyright was largely abolished for works created after the statute's effective date, but it still applies in a few areas. Notably, a common-law copyright received before January 1, 1978, remains entitled to protection.

Copyright Clause. U.S. Const. art. I, § 8, cl. 8, which gives Congress the power to secure to authors the exclusive rights to their writings for a limited time.

copyright infringement. See INFRINGEMENT.

copyright notice. A notice that a work is copyright-protected, usu. placed in each published copy of the work. • Since March 1, 1989, such notice is not required for a copyright to be valid (although it continues to provide certain procedural advantages).

copyright owner. One who holds exclusive rights to copyrighted material. 17 USCA § 101.

coram (**kor**-əm), *prep.* [Latin] (Of a person) before; in the presence of.

coram domino rege (**kor**-əm **dom**-ə-noh **ree**-jee). [Latin] *Hist.* Before our lord the king.

coram ipso rege (**kor**-əm **ip**-soh **ree**-jee). [Latin] *Hist.* Before the king himself. — Also termed *coram ipso domino rege*.

"The court of king's bench (so called because the king used formerly to sit there in person, the style of the court still being *coram ipso rege*) is the supreme court of common law in the kingdom ...." 3 William Blackstone, *Commentaries on the Laws of England* 41 (1768).

coram nobis (**kor**-əm **noh**-bis). [Latin "before us"] *Hist.* **1.** A writ of error taken from a judgment of the King's Bench. • "Before us" refers to the sovereign, in contrast to the writ *coram vobis* ("before you"), which refers to any court other than King's Bench, esp. the Court of Common Pleas. **2.** A writ of error directed to a court for review of its own judgment and predicated on alleged errors of fact. — Also termed *writ of error coram nobis*; *writ of coram nobis*.

coram non judice (**kor**-əm non **joo**-di-see). [Latin "not before a judge"] **1.** Outside the presence of a judge. **2.** Before a judge or court that is not the proper one or that cannot take legal cognizance of the matter.

coram paribus (**kor**-əm **par**-ə-bəs). [Latin] *Hist.* Before the peers. • This phrase appeared in deed attestations.

Coram Rege Court. See KING'S BENCH.

coram sectatoribus (**kor**-əm sek-tə-**tor**-ə-bəs). [Law Latin] *Hist.* Before the suitors.

coram vobis (**kor**-əm **voh**-bis), *n.* [Latin "before you"] *Hist.* **1.** A writ of error directed to a court other than the King's Bench, esp. the Court of Common Pleas, to review its judgment.

"Certain errors in the process of the court, committed by the defaults of the clerks, or as to matters of fact, could be remedied by the court itself. The writ issued for this purpose was called a writ of error 'coram vobis' if the error was in the Common Pleas; 'coram nobis' if it was in the King's Bench." 1 William Holdsworth, *A History of English Law* 224 (7th ed. 1956).

2. A writ of error sent by an appellate court to a trial court to review the trial court's judgment based on an error of fact. — Also termed *writ of error coram vobis*.

core proceeding. *Bankruptcy.* A proceeding involving claims that substantially affect the debtor-creditor relationship, such as an action to recover a preferential transfer. • In such a proceeding, the bankruptcy court, as opposed to the district court, conducts the trial or hearing and enters a final judgment. Cf. RELATED PROCEEDING.

corespondent. **1.** A coparty who responds to a petition, such as a petition for a writ of certiorari. **2.** In some states, a coparty who responds to an appeal. **3.** *Family law.* In a divorce suit based on adultery, the person with whom the spouse is accused of having committed adultery. See RESPONDENT.

corium forisfacere (**kor**-ee-əm for-is-**fay**-sə-ree). [Law Latin "to forfeit skin"] *Hist.* To whip (a person, esp. a servant) as punishment. — Also termed *corium perdere*.

corium redimere (**kor**-ee-əm ri-**dim**-ər-ee). [Latin] *Hist.* To redeem one's skin. • This referred to a person who paid restitution for an offense.

cornage (**kor**-nij). [fr. Anglo–French *corne* "horn"] *Hist.* **1.** A type of grand-serjeanty military tenure in which the tenant was bound to blow a horn to alert others whenever an enemy approached. **2.** A form of tenure entitling a landowner to rent based on the number of horned cattle owned by the tenant. • Cornage may have developed into a type of serjeanty or knight-service tenure that obligated the tenant to blow a horn to warn of invaders, esp. along the border with Scotland. See KNIGHT-SERVICE; SERJEANTY. — Also termed (in senses 1 & 2) *horn tenure*. **3.** A tribute of corn due only on special occasions, as distinguished from a regularly provided service. • This term has often been spelled *coraage* or *coraagium*, stemming perhaps from a spelling error in the 1569 edition of Bracton's *De Legibus et Consuetudinibus Angliae*.

Cornelian law. See LEX CORNELIA.

corner, *n.* **1.** The common end of two survey lines; an angle made by two boundary lines.

existent corner. A corner whose location can be verified by an original landmark, a surveyor's field notes, or other reliable evidence.

lost corner. A point in a land description, such as a landmark or natural object, whose position cannot be reasonably determined from traces of the original marks or other acceptable evidence. • The location can be determined by reference to one or more independent points remaining in the description.

obliterated corner. A corner that can be located only with evidence other than that put in place by the original surveyor.

2. The acquisition of control over all or a dominant quantity of a commodity with the purpose of artificially enhancing the price, carried out by purchases and sales of the commodity — and of options and futures — in a way that depresses the market price so that the participants are enabled to purchase the commodity at satisfactory prices and withhold it from the market for a time, thereby inflating its price. • A corner accomplished by confederation, with the purpose of raising or depressing prices and operating on the market, is a criminal conspiracy if the means are unlawful.

cornering the market. The act or process of acquiring ownership or control of a large portion of the available supply of a commodity or security, permitting manipulation of the commodity's or security's price.

Corn Products **doctrine.** *Tax.* The principle that a capital asset should be narrowly defined to exclude inventory-related property that is integrally tied to the day-to-day operations of a business. *Corn Products Refining Co. v. C.I.R.*, 350 U.S. 46, 76 S.Ct. 20 (1955).

corody (**kor**- *or* **kahr**-ə-dee). *Hist.* An allowance of money, accommodation, food, or clothing given by a religious house to a royal servant. • The Crown was entitled to these benefits only from houses it had founded. — Also spelled *corrody*.

> "Corrody is a partition for one's sustenance. Be it bread, ale, herring, a yearly robe, or sum of money for the robe. So of a chamber, and stable for my horses, when the same is coupled with other things ...." Sir Henry Finch, *Law, or a Discourse Thereof* 162 (1759).

corollary (**kor**- *or* **kahr**-ə-ler-ee), *n.* A proposition that follows from a proven proposition with little or no additional proof; something that naturally follows.

corona (kə-**roh**-nə). [Latin] *Hist.* The Crown. • This term formerly appeared in criminal pleadings, e.g., *placita coronae* ("pleas of the Crown").

coronation case. Any of the many lawsuits for breach of contract resulting from the postponement of the coronation of Edward VII because of his illness. • In one case, for example, the defendant had agreed to hire a ship for watching the naval review by King Edward VII and for a day's cruise around the fleet. The court held that the contract was not frustrated by the cancellation of the naval review — the day's cruise around the fleet was still possible, and indeed, the ship could have been used for many other purposes.

coronator (**kor**- *or* **kahr**-ə-nay-tər). [fr. Latin *corona* "crown"] A coroner. See CORONER (2).

> "The formal title of *custos* (or occasionally *conservator*) *placitorum corone* continued to be used throughout the Middle Ages, but the more convenient shorter forms

coronarius, which was confined to a short period around 1200, and CORONATOR rapidly gained greater currency. The English form was 'coroner' or 'crowner.' " R.F. Hunnisett, *The Medieval Coroner* 1 n.1 (1961).

coronatore eligendo. See DE CORONATORE ELIGENDO.

coronatore exonerando. See DE CORONATORE EXONERANDO.

coroner (**kor**- *or* **kahr**-ə-nər). **1.** A public official whose duty is to investigate the causes and circumstances of any death that occurs suddenly, suspiciously, or violently. See MEDICAL EXAMINER. **2.** *Hist.* A royal official with countywide jurisdiction to investigate deaths, to hold inquests, and to assume the duties of the sheriff if need be. • The coroner acted as a check on the sheriff, a local officer whose growing power threatened royal control over the counties. The coroner reported criminal activity to the king's justices in eyre. When the eyre court arrived in a county, it collected the coroner's roll to learn what had occurred in the county during the eyre's absence. The justices fined the coroner if he failed to produce the roll, or if they learned of criminal activity in the county from a source other than the roll.

"The office of coroner was established in September 1194, when the justices in eyre were required to see that three knights and one clerk were elected in every county as 'keepers of the pleas of the crown.' These were the first county coroners.... Throughout the Middle Ages the coroner could be ordered to perform almost any duty of an administrative or inquisitorial nature within his bailiwick, either alone or with the sheriff, but there were other duties which belonged more specifically to his office and which he performed without being ordered. These consisted of holding inquests upon dead bodies, receiving adjurations of the realm made by felons in sanctuary, hearing appeals, confessions of felons and appeals of approvers, and attending and sometimes organising exactions and outlawries promulgated in the county court. These were the 'crown pleas' which the coroner had to 'keep'...." R.F. Hunnisett, *The Medieval Coroner* 1 (1961).

coroner's court. See COURT.

coroner's inquest. See INQUEST.

coroner's jury. See JURY.

corpnership. [Portmanteau word probably formed fr. *corporation* + *partnership*] A limited partnership (usu. having many public investors as limited partners) whose general partner is a corporation.

corporale sacramentum (kor-pə-**ray**-lee sak-rə-**men**-təm). Corporal oath. See OATH.

corporal oath. See OATH.

corporal punishment. See PUNISHMENT.

corporate, *adj.* Of or relating to a corporation, esp. a business corporation <corporate bonds>.

corporate acquisition. The takeover of one corporation by another if both parties retain their legal existence after the transaction. Cf. MERGER (7).

corporate agent. See AGENT.

corporate authority. **1.** The power rightfully wielded by officers of a corporation. **2.** In some jurisdictions, a municipal officer, esp. one empowered to represent the municipality in certain statutory matters.

corporate body. See CORPORATION.

corporate bond. See BOND (3).

corporate books. Written records of a corporation's activities and business transactions.

corporate charter. See CHARTER (3).

corporate citizenship. Corporate status in the state of incorporation, though a corporation is not a citizen for the purposes of the Privileges and Immunities Clause of the U.S. Constitution.

corporate counsel. See COUNSEL.

corporate crime. See CRIME.

corporate distribution. See DISTRIBUTION.

corporate domicile. See DOMICILE.

corporate entity. See ENTITY.

corporate franchise. See FRANCHISE (2).

corporate immunity. See IMMUNITY (2).

corporate indenture. See INDENTURE.

corporate-mortgage trust. A financing device in which debentures are issued and secured by property held in trust. • An independent trustee protects the interests of those who purchase the debentures.

corporate name. See NAME.

corporate officer. See OFFICER (1).

corporate-opportunity doctrine. The rule that a corporation's directors, officers, and employees are precluded from using information gained as such to take personal advantage of any business opportunities that the corporation has an expectancy right or property interest in, or that in fairness should otherwise belong to the corporation. • In a partnership, the analogous principle is the *firm-opportunity doctrine.*

corporate purpose. The general scope of the business objective for which a corporation was created. • A statement of corporate purpose is commonly required in the articles of incorporation.

corporate raider. A person or business that attempts to take control of a corporation, against its wishes, by buying its stock and replacing its management. — Often shortened to *raider.* — Also termed *hostile bidder*; *unfriendly suitor*. Cf. WHITE KNIGHT.

corporate seal. See SEAL.

corporate speech. See SPEECH.

corporate stock. See STOCK.

corporate trustee. See TRUSTEE (1).

corporate veil. The legal assumption that the acts of a corporation are not the actions of its shareholders, so that the shareholders are exempt from liability for the corporation's actions. See PIERCING THE CORPORATE VEIL.

corporate welfare. See WELFARE.

corporation, *n.* An entity (usu. a business) having authority under law to act as a single person distinct from the shareholders who own it and having rights to issue stock and exist indefinitely; a group or succession of persons established in accordance with legal rules into a legal or juristic person that has legal personality distinct from the natural persons who make it up, exists indefinitely apart from them, and has the legal powers that its constitution gives it. — Also termed *corporation aggregate*; *aggregate corporation*; *body corporate*; *corporate body.* — **incorporate,** *vb.* — **corporate,** *adj.* See COMPANY.

"A corporation is an artificial being, invisible, intangible, and existing only in contemplation of law.... [I]t possesses only those properties which the charter of its creation confers upon it." *Trustees of Dartmouth College v. Woodward*, 17 U.S. (4 Wheat.) 518, 636 (1819) (Marshall, J.).

acquired corporation. The corporation that no longer exists after a merger or acquisition.

admitted corporation. A corporation licensed or authorized to do business within a particular state.

aggressor corporation. A corporation that attempts to obtain control of a publicly held corporation by (1) a direct cash tender, (2) a public exchange offer to shareholders, or (3) a merger, which requires the agreement of the target's management.

alien corporation. See *foreign corporation.*

brother-sister corporation. See *sister corporation.*

business corporation. A corporation formed to engage in commercial activity for profit. Cf. *nonprofit corporation.*

C corporation. A corporation whose income is taxed through it rather than through its shareholders. • Any corporation not electing S-corporation tax status under the Internal Revenue Code is a C corporation by default. — Also termed *subchapter-C corporation.* Cf. *S corporation.*

charitable corporation. A nonprofit corporation that is dedicated to benevolent purposes and thus entitled to special tax status under the Internal Revenue Code. — Also termed *eleemosynary corporation.* See CHARITABLE ORGANIZATION.

civil corporation. Any corporation other than a charitable or religious corporation.

clearing corporation. A corporation whose capital stock is held by or for a national security exchange or association registered under federal law such as the Securities Exchange Act of 1934.

close corporation. A corporation whose stock is not freely traded and is held by only a few shareholders (often within the same family). • The requirements and privileges of close corporations vary by jurisdiction. — Also termed *closely held corporation*; *closed corporation.*

collapsible corporation. A corporation formed to give a short-term venture the appearance of a long-term investment in order to portray income as capital gain, rather than profit. • The corporation is typically formed for the sole purpose of purchasing property. The corporation is usu. dissolved before the property has generated substantial income. The Internal Revenue Service treats the income earned through a collapsible corporation as ordinary income rather than as capital gain. IRC (26 USCA) § 341(a). Cf. *collapsible partnership* under PARTNERSHIP.

controlled corporation. A corporation in which the majority of the stock is held by one individual or firm.

controlled foreign corporation. *Tax.* A foreign corporation in which more than 50% of the stock is owned by U.S. citizens who each own 10% or more of the voting stock. • These shareholders (known as *U.S. shareholders*) are required to report their pro rata share of certain passive income of the corporation. — Abbr. CFC. IRC (26 USCA) §§ 951–964.

cooperative corporation. An entity that has a corporate existence, but is primarily organized for the purpose of providing services and profits to its members and not for corporate profit. • The most common kind of cooperative corporation is formed to purchase real property, such as an apartment building, so that its shareholders may lease the apartments. See COOPERATIVE (1).

corporation aggregate. *Hist.* A corporation made up of a number of individuals. Cf. *corporation sole.*

> "The first division of corporations is into *aggregate* and *sole*. Corporations aggregate consist of many persons united together into one society, and are kept up by a perpetual succession of members, so as to continue forever: of which kind are the mayor and commonalty of a city, the head and fellows of a college, the dean and chapter of a cathedral church." 1 William Blackstone, *Commentaries on the Laws of England* 457 (1765).

> "The corporation aggregate is the typical corporation, which, at any given time, normally contains a number of individuals as members. This number may be great or small, varying from the hundreds of thousands of burgesses of a large borough to the two members of a private joint-stock company. It is even said that a corporation aggregate would not necessarily cease to exist if all its members died, leaving no successors; and this is, probably, sound doctrine." Edward Jenks, *The Book of English Law* 118 (P.B. Fairest ed., 6th ed. 1967).

corporation by estoppel. A business that is deemed, by operation of law, to be a corporation because a third party dealt with the business as if it were a corporation, thus preventing the third party from holding a shareholder or officer of the corporation individually liable. See ESTOPPEL.

corporation by prescription. A corporation that, though lacking a charter, has acquired its corporate status through a long period of operating as a corporation. • Such an entity may engage in any enterprises that are not manifestly inconsistent with the purposes for which it is assumed to have been created. — Also termed *common-law corporation.*

corporation de facto. See *de facto corporation.*

corporation de jure. See *de jure corporation.*

corporation for profit. See *for-profit corporation.*

corporation sole. A series of successive persons holding an office; a continuous legal personality that is attributed to successive holders of certain monarchical or ecclesiastical positions, such as kings, bishops, rectors, vicars, and the like. • This continuous personality is viewed, by legal fiction, as having the qualities of a corporation. Cf. *corporation aggregate.*

> "It would have been quite possible to explain in the same way the devolution of the lands of the Crown, or of a bishopric, or of a rectory, from the sovereign, bishop, or rector, to his successor; but English law has preferred to introduce for this purpose the fiction, peculiar to itself, of a 'corporation sole.' " Thomas E. Holland, *The Elements of Jurisprudence* 350–51 (13th ed. 1924).

> "But English Law knows another kind of corporation, the 'corporation sole', in which the group consists, not of a number of contemporary members, but of a succession of single members, of whom only one exists at any given time. This kind of corporation has been described by eminent legal writers as a 'freak'; but it is a freak which undoubtedly has a legal existence. It has been said that the Crown is the only common law lay corporation sole; though the Master of Trinity College, Cambridge, has been claimed as another example, and statutory examples, such as the Public Trustee and the Treasury Solicitor, are conspicuous. But the examples of ecclesiastical corporations sole are numerous. Every diocesan bishop, every rector of a parish, is a corporation sole, and can acquire and hold land (and now also personal property) even during the vacancy of the see or living, for the benefit of his successors, and can bind his successors by his lawful conveyances and contracts. But, obviously, the distinction between the bishop or rector, in his personal and in his corporate character, is even harder to grasp than that between the members of a corporation aggregate and the corporation itself . . . ." Edward Jenks, *The Book of English Law* 118–19 (P.B. Fairest ed., 6th ed. 1967).

de facto corporation (di **fak**-toh). An incompletely formed corporation whose existence operates as a defense to personal liability of the directors, officers, and shareholders who in good faith thought they were operating the business as a duly formed corporation. — Also termed *corporation de facto.*

de jure corporation (di **juur**-ee). A corporation formed in accordance with all applicable laws and recognized as a corporation for liability purposes. — Also termed *corporation de jure*.

domestic corporation. **1.** A corporation that is organized and chartered under the laws of a state. • The corporation is considered *domestic* by the chartering state. Cf. *foreign corporation*. **2.** *Tax.* A corporation created or organized in the United States or under federal or state law. IRC (26 USCA) § 7701(a)(4).

dormant corporation. **1.** An inactive corporation; a legal corporation that is presently not operating. **2.** A corporation whose authority to do business has been revoked or suspended either by operation of law (as by failure to pay franchise taxes) or by an act of the government official responsible for the corporation's authority.

dummy corporation. A corporation whose only function is to hide the principal's identity and to protect the principal from liability.

ecclesiastical corporation (i-klee-zee-**as**-tə-kəl). *English law.* A corporation that is organized for spiritual purposes or for the administration of property held for religious uses. • This type of corporation is composed exclusively of ecclesiastics. — Also termed *religious corporation*. Cf. *lay corporation*.

> "Ecclesiastical corporations. Corporations created for the furtherance of religion.... They are of two kinds: (1) corporations sole, *i.e.*, bishops, certain deans, parsons and vicars; and (2) corporations aggregate, *i.e.*, deans and chapters, and formerly prior and convent, abbot and monks, and the like. Such corporations are called 'religious corporations,' or 'religious societies,' in the United States." 1 Stewart Rapalje & Robert L. Lawrence, *A Dictionary of American and English Law* 432 (1883).

eleemosynary corporation. See *charitable corporation*.

foreign corporation. A corporation that was organized and chartered under the laws of another state, government, or country <in Arizona, a California corporation is said to be a foreign corporation>. — Also termed *alien corporation*. Cf. *domestic corporation*.

> " 'Foreign' is defined as 'not native or domestic.' This is the meaning given to the word in the various judicial definitions of foreign corporations. With respect to a particular state or country, a corporation created by or under the laws of that state or country is a 'domestic corporation,' and any corporation that owes its existence to the laws of another state, government or country is a 'foreign corporation.' The difference between a domestic and a foreign corporation of the same kind is one of status, determined by considerations that are external to the corporation and not internal or organic. Moreover, foreign corporations of all classes fall equally within the definition. In many jurisdictions foreign corporations are defined by statute, and the statutory definitions do not differ in substance from that stated above." 17 *Fletcher Cyclopedia on the Law of Private Corporations* § 8290, at 6–7 (1998).

for-profit corporation. A corporation organized for the purpose of making a profit; a business corporation. — Also termed *corporation for profit*; *moneyed corporation*.

government corporation. See *public corporation* (3).

joint-venture corporation. A corporation that has joined with one or more individuals or corporations to accomplish some specified project.

lay corporation. *English law.* A corporation made up of laypersons, and existing for a business or charitable purpose. Cf. *ecclesiastical corporation*.

limited-liability corporation. See *limited-liability company* under COMPANY.

migratory corporation. A corporation formed under the laws of another state than that of the incorporators' residence for the purpose of carrying on a significant portion of its business in the state of the incorporators' residence or in a state other than where it was incorporated.

moneyed corporation. **1.** A corporation that uses money capital in its business, esp. one (such as a bank) that engages in the exchange or lending of money. **2.** See *for-profit corporation*.

multinational corporation. A company with operations in two or more countries, generally allowing it to transfer funds and products according to price and demand conditions, subject to risks such as changes in exchange rates or political instability.

multistate corporation. A corporation incorporated under the laws of two or more states.

municipal corporation. See MUNICIPAL CORPORATION.

municipal corporation de facto. See MUNICIPAL CORPORATION.

nonprofit corporation. A corporation organized for some purpose other than making a profit, and usu. afforded special tax treatment. — Also termed *not-for-profit corporation*. Cf. *business corporation*.

nonstock corporation. A corporation that does not issue shares of stock as evidence of ownership but instead is owned by its members in accordance with a charter or agreement. • Examples are mutual insurance companies, charitable organizations, and private clubs.

not-for-profit corporation. See *nonprofit corporation.*

parent corporation. A corporation that has a controlling interest in another corporation (called a *subsidiary corporation*), usu. through ownership of more than one-half the voting stock. — Often shortened to *parent.* — Also termed *parent company.*

political corporation. See *public corporation* (2).

private corporation. A corporation founded by and composed of private individuals principally for a nonpublic purpose, such as manufacturing, banking, and railroad corporations (including charitable and religious corporations).

professional corporation. A corporation that provides services of a type that requires a professional license. • A professional corporation may be made up of architects, accountants, physicians, veterinarians, or the like. — Abbr. P.C.

public corporation. **1.** A corporation whose shares are traded to and among the general public. — Also termed *publicly held corporation.* **2.** A corporation that is created by the state as an agency in the administration of civil government. — Also termed *political corporation.* **3.** A government-owned corporation that engages in activities that benefit the general public, usu. while remaining financially independent. • Such a corporation is managed by a publicly appointed board. — Also termed (in sense 3) *government corporation*; *public-benefit corporation.*

public-service corporation. A corporation whose operations serve a need of the general public, such as public transportation, communications, gas, water, or electricity. • This type of corporation is usu. subject to extensive governmental regulation.

quasi-corporation. An entity that exercises some of the functions of a corporation but that has not been granted corporate status by statute; esp., a public corporation with limited authority and powers (such as a county or school district). — Also sometimes termed *quasi-municipal corporation.* Cf. MUNICIPAL CORPORATION.

quasi-public corporation. A for-profit corporation providing an essential public service. • An example is an electric company or other utility.

railroad corporation. A company organized to construct, maintain, and operate railroads. — Also termed *railroad company.*

> "A railroad company or corporation is usually regarded as a private corporation, and justly so, as contrasted with a strictly public corporation, such as a city, county, township, or the like governmental subdivision, but it is not a private corporation in the strict sense that an ordinary business corporation is, for it is charged with duties of a public nature that distinguish it from a purely and strictly private corporation." 1 Byron K. Elliott & William F. Elliott, *A Treatise on the Law of Railroads* § 3, at 7 (3d ed. 1921).

registered corporation. A publicly held corporation a security of which is registered under § 12 of the Securities Exchange Act of 1934. • The corporation is subject to the Act's periodic disclosure requirements and proxy regulations. 15 USCA § 78l.

religious corporation. A corporation created to carry out some religious purpose.

S corporation. A corporation whose income is taxed through its shareholders rather than through the corporation itself. • Only corporations with a limited number of shareholders can elect S-corporation tax status under Subchapter S of the Internal Revenue Code. — Also termed *subchapter-S corporation*; *tax-option corporation.* Cf. *C corporation.*

shell corporation. A corporation that has no active business and usu. exists only in name as a vehicle for another company's business operations.

sister corporation. One of two or more corporations controlled by the same, or substantially the same, owners. — Also termed *brother-sister corporation.*

small-business corporation. **1.** A corporation having 75 or fewer shareholders and otherwise satisfying the requirements of the Internal Revenue Code provisions permitting a subchapter S election. IRC (26 USCA) § 1361. See *S corporation.* **2.** A corporation receiving money for stock (as a contribution to capital and paid-in surplus) totaling not more than $1,000,000, and otherwise satisfying the requirements of the Internal Revenue Code section 1244(c), thereby enabling the shareholders to claim an ordinary loss on worthless stock. IRC (26 USCA) § 1244(c).

sole corporation. A corporation having or acting through only a single member.

spiritual corporation. A corporation whose members are spiritual persons, such as bishops, rectors, and abbots.

stock corporation. A corporation in which the capital is contributed by the shareholders and divided into shares represented by certificates.

subchapter-C corporation. See *C corporation.*

subchapter-S corporation. See *S corporation.*

subsidiary corporation. A corporation in which a parent corporation has a controlling share. — Often shortened to *subsidiary.*

surviving corporation. A corporation that acquires the assets and liabilities of another corporation by a merger or takeover.

target corporation. A corporation over which control is being sought by another party. See TAKEOVER.

thin corporation. A corporation with an excessive amount of debt in its capitalization. See *thin capitalization* under CAPITALIZATION.

trading corporation. A corporation whose business involves the buying and selling of goods.

tramp corporation. A corporation chartered in a state where it does not conduct business.

U.S.-owned foreign corporation. A foreign corporation in which 50% or more of the total combined voting power or total value of the stock is held directly or indirectly by U.S. citizens. IRC (26 USCA) § 904(g)(6). • If the dividend or interest income paid by a U.S. corporation is classified as a foreign source, the U.S. corporation is treated as a U.S.-owned foreign corporation. IRC (26 USCA) § 861.

Corporation Act. *Hist.* A 1661 English statute (13 Car. 2, St. 2, ch. 1) prohibiting the holding of public office by anyone who would not take the Anglican sacrament and the oaths of supremacy and allegiance. • The Act was repealed by the Promissory Oaths Act of 1871.

corporation aggregate. See CORPORATION.

corporation by estoppel. See CORPORATION.

corporation by prescription. See CORPORATION.

corporation counsel. See COUNSEL.

corporation court. See COURT.

corporation de facto. See *de facto corporation* under CORPORATION.

corporation de jure. See *de jure corporation* under CORPORATION.

corporation for profit. See *for-profit corporation* under CORPORATION.

corporation sole. See CORPORATION.

corporator (**kor**-pə-ray-tər). **1.** A member of a corporation. **2.** INCORPORATOR.

> "Usually, a member of a corporation, in which sense it includes a stockholder; also, one of the persons who are the original organizers or promoters of a new corporation. The corporators are not the corporation, for either may sue the other." William C. Anderson, *A Dictionary of Law* 266 (1889).

corporeal (kor-**por**-ee-əl), *adj.* Having a physical, material existence; tangible <land and fixtures are corporeal property>. — **corporeality,** *n.* Cf. INCORPOREAL.

corporeal hereditament. See HEREDITAMENT.

corporeal ownership. See OWNERSHIP.

corporeal possession. See POSSESSION.

corporeal property. See PROPERTY.

corporeal thing. See THING.

corps diplomatique (**kor** dee-plə-ma-**teek**). DIPLOMATIC CORPS.

corpus (**kor**-pəs), *n.* [Latin "body"] **1.** An abstract collection or body. **2.** The property for which a trustee is responsible; the trust principal. — Also termed *res*; *trust estate*; *trust fund*; *trust property*; *trust res.* **3.** Principal (as of a fund or estate), as opposed to interest or income. Pl. **corpora** (**kor**-pə-rə), **corpuses** (**kor**-pə-səz).

corpus comitatus (**kor**-pəs kom-ə-**tay**-təs). [Latin "the body of a county"] *Hist.* Places not part of the "high seas" and hence where admiralty jurisdiction did not originally extend.

corpus corporatum (**kor**-pəs kor-pə-**ray**-təm). [Latin] *Hist.* A corporate body; a corporation.

corpus cum causa (**kor**-pəs kəm **kaw**-zə). [Law Latin "the body with the cause"] *Hist.* A writ issuing out of Chancery to remove both a person and a record from an inferior court in order to review a judgment issued by the inferior court.

> "The first use of the writ to challenge imprisonment was in cases of privilege; an officer of a central court, or a litigant there, could be released from imprisonment in another court by writ of privilege in habeas corpus form. The Court of Chancery at the same time developed a similar procedure for reviewing the cause of imprisonment in an inferior tribunal; this species of writ was called *corpus cum causa*, and it became a common remedy against the misuse of borough jurisdiction in the fifteenth century." J.H. Baker, *An Introduction to English Legal History* 168 (3d ed. 1990).

corpus delicti (**kor**-pəs də-**lik**-tɪ *or* -tee). [Latin "body of the crime"] **1.** The fact of a transgression; ACTUS REUS.

> "[T]he definition of 'corpus delicti' often becomes important. (a) Essentially it signifies merely the fact of the specific loss or injury sustained, e.g., death of a victim or burning of a house. (b) To this is added also, by most courts, the criminal agency of some person (i.e., not mere accident). (c) A few courts also include evidence of the accused's identity with the deed; but this is absurd, for it virtually signifies making 'corpus delicti' synonymous with the whole charge. — Many courts treat this rule with a pedantic and unpractical strictness." John H. Wigmore, *A Students' Textbook of the Law of Evidence* 310 (1935).

> "One of the important rules of evidence in criminal cases is that which requires proof of the *corpus delicti*. Literally defined this term means 'the body of the offense,' or 'the substance of the crime.' In popular language it is used to describe the visible evidence of the crime, such as the dead body of a murdered person. Properly used, however, it is applicable to any crime and relates particularly to the act element of criminality; that is, that a certain prohibited act has been committed or result accomplished and that it was committed or accomplished by a criminal human agency." Justin Miller, "The Criminal Act," in *Legal Essays in Tribute to Orrin Kip McMurray* at 469, 478 (1935).

> "The phrase 'corpus delicti' does not mean dead body, but body of the crime, and every offense has its corpus delicti. Its practical importance, however, has been very largely limited to the homicide cases. It concerns the usability in a criminal case of a confession made by the defendant outside of court." Rollin M. Perkins & Ronald N. Boyce, *Criminal Law* 140 (3d ed. 1982).

2. Loosely, the material substance on which a crime has been committed; the physical evidence of a crime, such as the corpse of a murdered person.

***corpus delicti* rule.** *Criminal law.* The doctrine that prohibits a prosecutor from proving the corpus delicti based solely on a defendant's extrajudicial statements. • The prosecution must establish the *corpus delicti* with corroborating evidence to secure a conviction.

corpus juris (**kor**-pəs **joor**-is). [Latin "body of law"] The law as the sum or collection of laws <*Corpus Juris Secundum*>. — Abbr. C.J.

corpus juris Angliae (**kor**-pəs **joor**-is **ang**-glee-ee). The entire body of English law, comprising the common law, statutory law, equity, and special law in its various forms.

Corpus Juris Canonici (**kor**-pəs **joor**-is kə-**non**-ə-sɪ). [Latin] *Hist.* The body of the canon law, compiled from the decrees and canons of the Roman Catholic Church. • The *Corpus Juris Canonici* emerged during the 12th century, beginning with the publication of Gratian's *Decretum* (1141–1150). In addition to the *Decretum*, it includes Raymond of Pennaforte's *Liber Extra* (1234), the *Liber Sextus* of Pope Boniface VIII (1298), the *Clementines* of Pope Clement V (1313), the *Extravagantes Joannis* of Pope John XXII (1325), and *extravagantes* published by Pope John's successors (1499–1502). In 1582, the entire collection was edited by a commission of church dignitaries and officially named the *Corpus Juris Canonici*. It remained the Catholic Church's primary body of law until the promulgation of the Code of Canon Law in 1917, now replaced by that of 1983.

> "After Gratian, later papal enactments, called 'decretals,' were collected and issued by the authority of various popes.... A revised edition of such 'decretals' ... was presented to Pope Gregory IX in 1234 — only a short while, therefore, after the final form of Magna Carta in 1225 — and issued by him with statutory force. The revision freely made changes in the text of the enactments and the resulting compilation in four 'books' was regarded as a 'Code,' corresponding to the 'Code' of Justinian, just as the *Decretum* of Gratian corresponded to the Digest.... All these compilations and collections were, from the sixteenth century on, known as the *Corpus Juris Canonici*, the 'Body of Canon Law,' and formed the basis of the law administered in the Church courts." Max Radin, *Handbook of Anglo-American Legal History* 33–34 (1936).

Corpus Juris Civilis (**kor**-pəs **joor**-is sə-**vil**-is *or* sə-**vɪ**-lis). The body of the civil law, compiled and codified under the direction of the Roman emperor Justinian in A.D. 528–534. • The collection includes four works — the Institutes, the Digest (or Pandects), the Code, and the Novels. The title *Corpus Juris Civilis* was not original, or even early, but was modeled on the *Corpus Juris Canonici* and given in the 16th century and later to editions of the texts of the four component parts of the Roman law. See ROMAN LAW (1).

corpus possessionis (**kor**-pəs pə-zes[h]-ee-**oh**-nis). [Latin] *Roman law.* A thing possessed by someone. See *animus possidendi* under ANIMUS.

corpus pro corpore (**kor**-pəs proh **kor**-pə-ree). [Latin] *Hist.* Body for body. • This phrase commonly expressed the liability of a surety in a civil action (a mainpernor). See MAINPRISE.

correal (**kor**-ee-əl *or* kə-**ree**-əl), *adj.* Of or relating to liability that is joint and several. • Under Roman law, a *correal* debtor who paid an entire obligation had no right of action against a co-debtor. See CORREUS; SOLIDARY.

> "If Aulus, having first obtained from Titius the promise of a hundred aurei, turned to Seius and said, *Spondesne mihi, Sei, cosdem centum aureos dare?* (Do you engage, Seius, to give me the same one hundred aurei?), then if Seius answered, *Spondeo*, there was one single obligation for a hundred aurei, binding in full on each of the two debtors. Aulus could demand a hundred from Titius or a hundred from Seius, and in case of non-payment could sue either one, taking his choice between them, for the full amount. If either paid the hundred, whether willingly or by compulsion, the other was released: for there was but one debt, and that was now discharged. This kind of obligation is called correal obligation (correal, from *con*, and *reus* or *rei*, connected parties, parties associated in a common debt or credit)." James Hadley, *Introduction to Roman Law* 258 (1881).

correality (kor-ee-**al**-ə-tee), *n.* The quality or state of being correal; the relationship between parties to an obligation that terminates when an entire payment is made by one of two or more debtors to a creditor, or a payment is made by a debtor to one of two or more creditors.

> "But there were circumstances, apart from indivisibility, in which each of the parties might be liable in full. . . . Several were liable or entitled, each *in solidum*, under an obligation, but the thing was due only once. Satisfaction by, or to, one of those liable, or entitled, ended the whole obligation, and action by one of the joint creditors, or against one of the debtors, not only 'novated' the obligation between the actual parties, but destroyed it altogether as against the others. This relation is commonly called correality (*correi debendi vel credendi*)." W.W. Buckland, *A Manual of Roman Private Law* 349–50 (2d ed. 1953).

correal obligation. See OBLIGATION.

corrected policy. See INSURANCE POLICY.

correction, *n.* **1.** Generally, the act or an instance of making right what is wrong <mark your corrections in red ink>. **2.** A change in business activity or market price following and counteracting an increase or decrease in the activity or price <the broker advised investors to sell before the inevitable stock-market correction>. See DOWN REVERSAL. **3.** (*usu. pl.*) The punishment and treatment of a criminal offender through a program of imprisonment, parole, and probation <Department of Corrections>. — **correct,** *vb.* — **corrective** (for senses 1 & 2), **correctional** (for sense 3), *adj.*

correction, house of. See PRISON.

correctional institution. See PRISON.

correctional system. A network of governmental agencies that administer a jurisdiction's prisons and parole system.

corrective advertising. Advertising that informs consumers that earlier advertisements contained a deceptive claim, and that provides consumers with corrected information. • This type of advertising may be ordered by the Federal Trade Commission.

corrector of the staple. *Hist.* A clerk who records merchants' transactions at a staple. See STAPLE (2).

correi credendi (**kor**-ee-I kri-**den**-dI). [Latin] *Roman law.* Joint creditors. — Also termed *correi stipulandi* (stip-yə-**lan**-dI). See STIPULATIO.

> "The mode for *stipulatio* is stated in the Institutes. Of several stipulators (*correi credendi*, active correality) each asks the debtor and he answers once for all. Of several promisors (*correi debendi*, passive correality) the creditor asks each and they answer together." W.W. Buckland, *A Manual of Roman Private Law* 350 (2d ed. 1953).

correi debendi (**kor**-ee-I di-**ben**-dI). [Latin] *Roman & Scots law.* Joint debtors. — Also termed *correi promittendi* (proh-mi-**ten**-dI). See STIPULATIO.

> "*Correi Debendi* — The name given by the Roman law to persons *jointly* bound. . . . In the Scotch law, if bound *severally*, and not *jointly and severally*, each is bound only for *his share*, whatever be the responsibility of the others." Hugh Barclay, *A Digest of the Law of Scotland* 196 (3d ed. 1865).

correi stipulandi. See CORREI CREDENDI.

correlative (kə-**rel**-ə-tiv), *adj.* **1.** Related or corresponding; analogous. **2.** Having or involving a reciprocal or mutually interdependent relationship <the term *right* is correlative with *duty*>.

correlative-rights doctrine. *Water law.* The principle that adjoining landowners must limit their use of a common water source to a reasonable amount.

> "Under the correlative rights doctrine . . . rights to groundwater are determined by land ownership. However, owners of land overlying a single aquifer are each limited to a reasonable share of the total supply of groundwater. The share is usually based on the acreage owned." David H. Getches, *Water Law in a Nutshell* 249 (3d ed. 1997).

correspondence audit. See AUDIT.

correspondent, *n.* **1.** The writer of a letter or letters. **2.** A person employed by the media to report on events. **3.** A securities firm or financial institution that performs services for another in a place or market that the other does not have direct access to. — **correspond,** *vb.*

correspondent bank. See BANK.

correus (**kor**-ee-əs), *n.* [Latin] *Roman law.* A codebtor to a contract (*stipulatio*); a joint debtor. Pl. ***correi*** (**kor**-ee-I). See STIPULATIO.

corrigendum (kor-ə-**jen**-dəm), *n.* [Latin "correction"] An error in a printed work discovered after the work has gone to press. — Also termed *erratum.* Pl. **corrigenda** (kor-ə-**jen**-də).

corroborate (kə-**rob**-ə-rayt), *vb.* To strengthen or confirm; to make more certain <the witness corroborated the plaintiff's testimony>.

corroborating evidence. See EVIDENCE.

corroborating witness. See WITNESS.

corroboration (kə-rob-ə-**ray**-shən), *n.* **1.** Confirmation or support by additional evidence or authority <corroboration of the witness's testimony>. **2.** Formal confirmation or ratification <corroboration of the treaty>. — **corroborate,** *vb.* — **corroborative** (kə-**rob**-ə-rə-tiv), *adj.* — **corroborator** (kə-**rob**-ə-ray-tər), *n.*

corroborative evidence. See *corroborating evidence* under EVIDENCE.

corrupt, *adj.* **1.** *Archaic.* (Of a person) subject to corruption of blood.

> "[T]here are divers offences made Treason by Act of Parliament, whereof, though a Man be Attaint, yet his Blood, by Provisoes therein, is not corrupt, nor shall he forfeit any thing. . . ." Thomas Blount, *Nomo-Lexicon: A Law-Dictionary* (1670).

2. Having an unlawful or depraved motive; esp., influenced by bribery.

corrupt, *vb.* **1.** *Archaic.* To impose corruption of blood on (a person). **2.** To change (a person's morals or principles) from good to bad.

corruption. 1. Depravity, perversion, or taint; an impairment of integrity, virtue, or moral principle; esp., the impairment of a public official's duties by bribery.

> "The word 'corruption' indicates impurity or debasement and when found in the criminal law it means depravity or gross impropriety." Rollin M. Perkins & Ronald N. Boyce, *Criminal Law* 855 (3d ed. 1982).

2. The act of doing something with an intent to give some advantage inconsistent with official duty and the rights of others; a fiduciary's or official's use of a station or office to procure some benefit either personally or for someone else, contrary to the rights of others.

corruption in office. See *official misconduct* under MISCONDUCT.

corruption of blood. A defunct doctrine, now considered unconstitutional, under which a person loses the ability to inherit or pass property as a result of an attainder or of being declared civilly dead. — Also termed *corruption of the blood.* See ATTAINDER; CIVIL DEATH.

> "Corruption of blood is, when any one is attainted of felony or treason, then his blood is said to be corrupt; by means whereof neither his children, nor any of his blood, can be heirs to him, or to any other ancestor, for that they ought to claim by him. And if he were a noble or gentleman before, he and all his children are made thereby ignoble and ungentle. . . ." *Termes de la Ley* 125 (1st Am. ed. 1812).

corruptly, *adv.* In a corrupt or depraved manner; by means of corruption or bribery. • As used in criminal-law statutes, *corruptly* usu. indicates a wrongful desire for pecuniary gain or other advantage.

corrupt-motive doctrine. *Criminal law.* The rule that conspiracy is punishable only if the agreement was entered into with an evil purpose, not merely with an intent to do the illegal act. • This doctrine — which originated in *People v. Powell,* 63 N.Y. 88 (1875) — has been rejected by the Model Penal Code. — Also termed *Powell doctrine.*

corrupt-practices act. A federal or state statute that regulates campaign contributions and expenditures as well as their disclosure.

corvée seigneuriale (kor-**vay** sen-yuu-ree-**ahl**). [French] *Hist.* Services due the lord of the manor. — Often shortened to *corvée.*

cosen, *vb.* See COZEN.

cosign, *vb.* To sign a document along with another person, usu. to assume obligations and to supply credit to the principal obligor. — **cosignature,** *n.*

cosigner. See COMAKER.

cosinage (**kəz**-ən-ij). *Hist.* A writ used by an heir to secure the right to land held by a great-great-grandfather or certain collateral relatives. — Also spelled *cosenage*; *cousinage.* — Also termed *consanguineo*; *de consanguineo*; *de consanguinitate.* Cf. AIEL; BESAYEL.

> "This remedy, by writ of assise, is only applicable to two species of injury by ouster, viz. *abatement*, and a recent or *novel disseisin* .... If the abatement happened on the death of one's grandfather or grandmother, then an assise of *mort d'ancestor* no longer lies, but a writ of *ayle*, or *de avo*; if on the death of the great grandfather or great grandmother, then a writ of *besayle*, or *de proavo*; but if it mounts one degree higher, to the *tresayle*, or grandfather's grandfather, or if the abatement happened upon the death of any collateral relation, other than those before-mentioned, the writ is called a writ of *cosinage*, or *de consanguineo*." 3 William Blackstone, *Commentaries on the Laws of England* 185–86 (1768).

cost, *n.* **1.** The amount paid or charged for something; price or expenditure. Cf. EXPENSE.

aboriginal cost. The cost of an asset incurred by the first company to use it for public utilities.

acquisition cost. An asset's net price; the original cost of an asset. — Also termed *historical cost*; *original cost.*

after cost. A delayed expense; an expense, such as one for repair under a warranty, incurred after the principal transaction.

applied cost. A cost appropriated to a project before it has been incurred.

average cost. The sum of the costs of beginning inventory costs and the costs of later additions divided by the total number of available units.

avoidable cost. A cost that can be averted if production is held below a certain level so that additional expenses will not be incurred.

carrying cost. *Accounting.* The variable cost of stocking one unit of inventory for one year. • Carrying cost includes the opportunity cost of the capital invested in the inventory. — Also termed *cost of carrying.*

common cost. See *indirect cost.*

cost of completion. *Contracts.* A measure of damages based on the expense incurred by the party not in breach to finish the promised performance.

direct cost. The amount of money for material, labor, and overhead to produce a product.

distribution cost. Any cost incurred in marketing a product or service, such as advertising, storage, and shipping.

fixed cost. A cost whose value does not fluctuate with changes in output or business activity; esp., overhead expenses such as rent, salaries, and depreciation. — Also termed *fixed charge*; *fixed expense.*

flotation cost. (*usu. pl.*) A cost incurred in issuing additional stock.

historical cost. See *acquisition cost.*

implicit cost. See *opportunity cost.*

indirect cost. A cost that is not specific to the production of a particular good or service, but that arises from production activity in general, such as overhead allocations for general and administrative activities. — Also termed *common cost.*

manufacturing cost. The cost incurred in the production of goods, including direct and indirect costs.

marginal cost. The additional cost incurred in producing one more unit of output.

mixed cost. A cost that includes fixed and variable costs.

net cost. The cost of an item, arrived at by subtracting any financial gain from the total cost.

opportunity cost. The cost of acquiring an asset measured by the value of an alternative investment that is forgone <her opportunity cost of $1,000 in equipment was her consequent inability to invest that money in bonds>. — Also termed *implicit cost.*

original cost. See *acquisition cost.*

prime cost. The true price paid for goods on a bona fide purchase.

replacement cost. The cost of acquiring an asset that is as equally useful or productive as an asset currently held.

social cost. The cost to society of any particular practice or rule <although automobiles are undeniably beneficial to society, they carry a certain social cost in the lives that are lost every year on the road>.

sunk cost. A cost that has already been incurred and that cannot be recovered.

tangible cost. *Oil & gas.* A particular expense associated with drilling, such as the costs incurred for materials and land. • Drilling and testing costs are considered intangible.

transaction cost. (*usu. pl.*) A cost connected with a process transaction, such as a broker's commission, the time and effort expended to arrange a deal, or the cost involved in litigating a dispute.

unit cost. The cost of a single unit of a product or service; the total manufacturing cost divided by the number of units.

variable cost. The cost that varies in the short run in close relationship with changes in output.

2. (*pl.*) The charges or fees taxed by the court, such as filing fees, jury fees, courthouse fees, and reporter fees. — Also termed *court costs.* **3.** (*pl.*) The expenses of litigation, prosecution, or other legal transaction, esp. those allowed in favor of one party against the other. — Also termed (in sense 3) *litigation costs.*

accruing costs. Costs and expenses incurred after judgment.

costs of increase. See COSTS OF INCREASE.

costs of the day. Costs incurred in preparing for trial.

costs to abide event. Costs incurred by a successful party who is entitled to an award of those costs incurred at the conclusion of the matter.

cost accounting. See *cost accounting method* under ACCOUNTING METHOD.

cost accounting method. See ACCOUNTING METHOD.

cost and freight. A term in a quoted sales price indicating that the quoted price includes the cost of the goods and freight charges to the named destination, but not insurance or other special charges. • During shipment, the risk of loss is on the buyer. — Abbr. C.F.; C & F; CandF.

cost approach. A method of appraising real property, based on the cost of building a new property with the same utility, assuming that an informed buyer would pay no more for the property than it would cost to build a new property having the same usefulness. Cf. MARKET APPROACH; INCOME APPROACH.

cost basis. See BASIS (2).

cost-benefit analysis. An analytical technique that weighs the costs of a proposed decision, holding, or project against the expected advantages, economic or otherwise.

cost bond. See BOND (2).

cost-book mining company. An association of persons organized for the purpose of working mines or lodes, whose capital stock is divided into shares that are transferable without the consent of other members. • The management of the mine is entrusted to an agent called a purser.

cost depletion. *Oil & gas.* The recovery of an oil-and-gas producer's basis (i.e., investment) in a producing well by deducting the basis proportionately over the producing life of the well. Treas. Reg. § 1.611–2.

> "Under cost depletion, the taxpayer in an oil and gas property deducts the basis in the property from the income as oil and gas are produced and sold. Cost depletion is calculated by a formula ... [that] relates the recovery of the taxpayer's investment to the proportion that the current unit sales of oil and gas bear to the total anticipated sales of oil and gas from the property. The investment is recovered ratably over the life of the reserves." John S. Lowe, *Oil and Gas Law in a Nutshell* 353 (3d ed. 1995).

cost, insurance, and freight. A term in a quoted sales price indicating that the price includes the cost of the goods as well as freight and insurance charges to the named destination. • During shipment, the risk of loss is on the buyer. But the seller must provide insurance at a specified amount (usu. at a minimum of 110%). — Abbr. C.I.F. Cf. FREE ALONGSIDE SHIP; FREE ON BOARD.

> " 'C.i.f.' is a mercantile symbol that is commonly used in international sales contracts. It is defined by section 2–320 of the UCC and by the Incoterms — 1953 and the Revised American Foreign Trade Definitions — 1941. Under all of these definitions the letters 'c.i.f.' mean that the price covers the cost of the goods, the cost of insuring them for the benefit of the order of the buyer, and the cost of carrying them to the named point, almost always the destination. Like the other mercantile symbols, the meaning of 'C.I.F.' may be varied by agreement." William D. Hawkland, *Uniform Commercial Code Series* § 2–320:01 (1984).

C.I.F. destination. A contractual term denoting that the price includes in a lump sum the cost of the goods and the insurance and freight to the named destination. — Also termed *C.I.F. place of destination.*

cost justification. Under the Robinson–Patman Act, an affirmative defense against a charge of price discrimination dependent on the seller's showing that it incurs lower costs in serving those customers who are paying less. 15 USCA § 13(a).

cost-of-capital method. A means of measuring a utility's cost of acquiring debt and equity capital. • Regulatory commissions often use this method to determine a fair rate of return for the utility's investors.

cost of carrying. See *carrying cost* under COST.

cost of completion. See COST (1).

cost-of-living clause. A provision (as in a contract or lease) that gives an automatic wage, rent, or benefit increase tied in some way to cost-of-living rises in the economy. • A cost-of-living clause may also cover a decrease, though this is rare. See INFLATION.

cost-of-living index. See CONSUMER PRICE INDEX.

cost-plus contract. See CONTRACT.

cost-push inflation. See INFLATION.

costs de incremento. See COSTS OF INCREASE.

costs of collection. Expenses incurred in receiving payment of a note; esp., attorney's fees created in the effort to collect a note.

costs of increase. *Hist.* Costs of court that are awarded in addition to what a jury awards. • Juries usu. awarded the successful party only a small sum for costs. A party wishing to recoup the additional costs had to file an affidavit of increase setting forth what further costs were incurred by taking the matter through trial. — Also termed *costs de incremento*. See *affidavit of increase* under AFFIDAVIT.

costs of the day. See COST (3).

costs to abide event. See COST (3).

cosurety. A surety who shares the cost of performing suretyship obligations with another. See SURETY.

cotarius (kə-**tair**-ee-əs). [Law Latin] *Hist.* A socage-tenure serf who holds land by paying rent and providing some personal services to the lord. • Both *cotarius* and *coterellus* serfs were also known as *cottagers*. Cf. COTERELLUS.

cotenancy. See TENANCY.

coterellus (kot-ə-**rel**-əs). [Law Latin] *Hist.* A serf who inhabits a cottage; a servile tenant whose person, issue, and goods are at the disposal of the lord. — Also spelled *coterell*. Cf. COTARIUS.

> "Coterellus.... A cottager. Considered by Spelman and others, the same with *cotarius*. But Cowell makes the distinction that the *cotarius* had free socage tenure, and paid a stated firm (rent) in provisions or money, with some occasional customary service; whereas the *coterellus* seemed to have held in mere villenage, and had his person and issue and goods disposed at the pleasure of the lord." 1 Alexander M. Burrill, *A Law Dictionary and Glossary* 387 (2d ed. 1867).

coterminous (koh-**tər**-mə-nəs), *adj.* **1.** CONTERMINOUS (1). **2.** (Of ideas or events) coextensive in time or meaning <Judge Smith's tenure was coterminous with Judge Jasper's>.

cotland (**kot**-lənd). *Hist.* Land held by a cottager, whether in socage or villeinage tenure.

cotortfeasor (koh-**tort**-fee-zər). One who, together with another, has committed a tort. See TORTFEASOR.

cotrustee. One of two or more persons in whom the administration of a trust is vested. • The cotrustees form a collective trustee and exercise their powers jointly. — Also termed *joint trustee*. See TRUSTEE.

cotset (**kot**-set). *Hist.* A villein who provides labor to a lord in exchange for a cottage and plot of land. — Also termed *cotsetus*.

cottier (**kot**-ee-ər). **1.** *Hist.* A serf who lives in a cottage; a cottager. • Over time, *cottier* has come to refer to a day laborer or a rural dweller. **2.** *Hist. Irish law.* A tenant who leases a house and a small (usu. two acre or less) plot of land.

couchant and levant (**kow**-chənt / **lev**-ənt), *adj.* See LEVANT AND COUCHANT.

council. **1.** A deliberative assembly <the U.N. Security Council>.

common council. **1.** In some cities, the lower branch of a city council. **2.** In some cities, the city's governing board.

select council. In some states, the upper branch of a city council.

2. An administrative or executive body <a parish council>.

councillor. See COUNCILOR.

Council of Economic Advisors. A select group of economists who advise the U.S. President on economic issues. — Abbr. CEA.

Council of the North. *Hist.* A body used by the Tudors to administer the northern parts of England (esp. Yorkshire) during the 16th and 17th centuries. • The council probably predated the Tudors, but Henry VIII revived it. In addition to enforcing Crown policy in the northern territories, the appointees (many of whom were lawyers) exercised wide criminal and civil jurisdiction. The Council disbanded ca. 1640.

councilor, *n.* A person who serves on a council, esp. at the local level. — Also spelled *councillor.* — **councillorship,** *n.*

counsel, *n.* **1.** Advice or assistance <the lawyer's counsel was to petition immediately for a change of immigration status>. **2.** One or more lawyers who represent a client <the client acted on advice of counsel>. — In the singular, also termed *counselor.* Cf. ATTORNEY; LAWYER. **3.** *English law.* A member of the bar; BARRISTER.

advisory counsel. An attorney retained merely to give advice on a particular matter, as distinguished from one (such as trial counsel) actively participating in a case.

appellate counsel. A lawyer who represents a party on appeal. • The term is often used in contrast with *trial counsel.*

assigned counsel. An attorney appointed by the court to represent a person, usu. an indigent person. — Also termed *court-appointed attorney.*

corporate counsel. An in-house attorney for a corporation.

corporation counsel. A city attorney in an incorporated municipality.

counsel of record. See ATTORNEY OF RECORD.

general counsel. **1.** A lawyer or law firm that represents a client in all or most of the client's legal matters, but that sometimes refers extraordinary matters — such as litigation and intellectual-property cases — to other lawyers. **2.** The most senior lawyer in a corporation's legal department, usu. also a corporate officer.

house counsel. See *in-house counsel.*

independent counsel. An attorney hired to provide an unbiased opinion about a lawsuit or to conduct an impartial investigation; esp., an attorney appointed by a governmental branch or agency to investigate alleged misconduct within that branch or agency. See *special prosecutor* under PROSECUTOR. Cf. *special counsel.*

in-house counsel. One or more lawyers employed by a company. — Also termed *house counsel.*

junior counsel. **1.** The younger or lower-ranking of two or more attorneys employed on the same side of a case, esp. someone charged with the less important aspects of the case. **2.** *English law.* The barrister who assists Queen's Counsel.

King's Counsel. See KING'S COUNSEL.

lead counsel. **1.** The more highly ranked lawyer if two or more are retained; the lawyer who manages or controls the case or cases, esp. in class actions or multidistrict litigation. — Also termed *senior counsel*; *attorney in charge.* **2.** QUEEN'S COUNSEL. — Also termed *leading counsel.*

of counsel. **1.** A lawyer employed by a party in a case; esp., one who — although not the principal attorney of record — is employed to assist in the preparation or management of the case or in its presentation on appeal. **2.** A lawyer who is affiliated with a law firm, though not as a member, partner, or associate.

Queen's Counsel. See QUEEN'S COUNSEL.

senior counsel. **1.** See *lead counsel.* **2.** See KING'S COUNSEL; QUEEN'S COUNSEL.

special counsel. An attorney employed by the state or political subdivision to assist in a particular case when the public interest so requires. — Also termed *special attorney.* Cf. *independent counsel.*

standby counsel. An attorney who is appointed to be prepared to represent a pro se criminal defendant if the defendant's self-representation ends. • The standby counsel may also provide some advice and guidance to the defendant during the self-representation. — Also termed *advisory counsel.*

trial counsel. **1.** A lawyer who represents a party at trial. • The term is often used in contrast with *appellate counsel.* **2.** *Military law.* The person who prosecutes a case on the government's behalf.

counsel, assistance of. See ASSISTANCE OF COUNSEL.

counsel, right to. See RIGHT TO COUNSEL.

counsel and procure. See AID AND ABET.

counsel of record. See ATTORNEY OF RECORD.

counselor. See COUNSEL (2).

count, *n. Procedure.* **1.** The part of an indictment charging the suspect with a distinct offense. **2.** In a complaint or similar pleading, the statement of a distinct claim. Cf. DECLARATION (7).

"This word . . . is in our old law-books used synonymously with declaration . . . . But when the suit embraces two or more causes of action (each of which of course requires a different statement), or when the plaintiff makes two or more different statements of one and the same cause of action, each several statement is called a count, and all of them, collectively, constitute the declaration." 1 John Bouvier, *A Law Dictionary* 245 (1839).

common count. *Hist.* In a plaintiff's pleading in an action for debt, boilerplate language that is not founded on the circumstances of the individual case but is intended to guard against a possible variance and to enable the plaintiff to take advantage of any ground of liability that the proof may disclose. • In the action for indebitatus assumpsit, the common count stated that the defendant had failed to pay a debt as promised. See *indebitatus assumpsit* under ASSUMPSIT.

general count. A count that states the plaintiff's claim without undue particularity.

money count. *Hist.* A count, usu. founded on a simple contract, giving rise to a claim for payment of money.

"Simple contracts, express or implied, resulting in mere debts, are of so frequent occurrence as causes of action, that certain concise forms of counts were devised for suing upon them. These are called the '*indebitatus*' or 'money counts.'" 2 Stewart Rapalje & Robert L. Lawrence, *A Dictionary of American and English Law* 833 (1883).

multiple counts. Several separate causes of action or charged offenses contained in a single pleading or indictment.

omnibus count (**ahm**-ni-bəs). A count that combines into one count all money claims, claims for goods sold and delivered, claims for work and labor, and claims for an account stated.

separate count. One of two or more criminal charges contained in one indictment, each charge constituting a separate indictment for which the accused may be tried.

several count. One of two or more counts in a pleading, each of which states a different cause of action.

special count. A section of a pleading in which the plaintiff's claim is stated with great particularity — usu. employed only when the pleading rules require specificity.

3. *Hist.* The plaintiff's declaration, or initial pleading, in a real action. See DECLARATION (7). **4.** *Patents.* The part of a patent application that defines the subject matter in a priority contest (i.e., an *interference*) between two or more applications or between one or more applications and one or more patents. See INTERFERENCE (2).

count, *vb.* **1.** In pleading, to declare or state; to narrate the facts that state a claim. **2.** *Hist.* To plead orally; to plead or argue a case in court.

counter. *Hist.* An advocate or professional pleader; one who counts (i.e., orally recites) for a client. • Counters had coalesced into an identifiable group practicing before the Common Bench by the beginning of the 13th century. They were the leaders of the medieval legal profession, and over time came to be known as *serjeants-at-law*. — Also spelled *countor*; *contor*; *counteur*. See SERJEANT-AT-LAW.

counteraction. See COUNTERCLAIM.

counteraffidavit. See AFFIDAVIT.

counterbond. See BOND (2).

counterclaim, *n.* A claim for relief asserted against an opposing party after an original claim has been made; esp., a defendant's claim in opposition to or as a setoff against the plaintiff's claim. — Also termed *counteraction*; *countersuit*; *cross-demand*. — **counterclaim,** *vb.* — **counterclaimant,** *n.* Cf. CROSS-CLAIM.

"Under [Fed. R. Civ. P.] Rule 13 the court has broad discretion to allow claims to be joined in order to expedite the resolution of all controversies between the parties in one suit. Rule 13(c) specifically provides that the counterclaimant is not limited by recovery sought by the opposing party but may claim relief in excess of that amount. Further, the general legal rule is that it is immaterial whether a counterclaim is legal or equitable for purposes of determining whether it properly is brought under Rule 13. . . . The expectation is that this liberal joinder policy will further the elimination of circuity of action and multiple litigation." 6 Charles Alan Wright et al., *Federal Practice and Procedure* § 1403, at 15–16 (2d ed. 1990).

compulsory counterclaim. A counterclaim that must be asserted to be cognizable, usu. because it relates to the opposing party's claim and arises out of the same subject matter. • If a defendant fails to assert a compulsory counterclaim in the original action, that claim may not be brought in a later, separate action (with some exceptions).

permissive counterclaim. A counterclaim that need not be asserted to be cognizable, usu. because it does not arise out of the same subject matter as the opposing party's claim or involves third parties over which the court does not have jurisdiction. • Permissive counterclaims may be brought in a later, separate action.

counterdeed. See DEED.

counterfeisance (**kown**-tər-fee-zənts). *Archaic.* The act of counterfeiting.

counterfeit, *vb.* To forge, copy, or imitate (something) without a right to do so and with the purpose of deceiving or defrauding; esp., to manufacture fake money (or other security) that might be used in place of the genuine article. • Manufacturing fake food stamps is considered counterfeiting. — **counterfeit,** *n.* — **counterfeit,** *adj.*

> "Literally a *counterfeit* is an imitation intended to pass for an original. Hence it is spurious or false, and *to counterfeit* is to make false. For this reason the verbs *counterfeit* and *forge* are often employed as synonyms and the same is true to some extent of the corresponding nouns. No error is involved in this usage but it is important to distinguish between the words as far as possible when used as the labels of criminal offenses. In the most restricted sense, [c]ounterfeiting is the unlawful making of false money in the similitude of the genuine. At one time under English statutes it was made treason. Under modern statutes it is a felony." Rollin M. Perkins & Ronald N. Boyce, *Criminal Law* 431–32 (3d ed. 1982).

counterfeiter. A person who makes an unauthorized imitation of something (esp. a document, currency, or another's signature) with the intent to deceive or defraud.

counterfoil (**kown**-tər-foyl), *n.* A detachable part of a writing on which the particulars of the main part are summarized. • The most common example is a check stub, on which the date, the payee, and the amount are typically noted.

counterletter. *Civil law.* A document by which a record owner of real property acknowledges that another actually owns the property. • Counterletters are used when the property is to be reconveyed after a period. See *simulated contract* under CONTRACT.

countermand (**kown**-tər-mand), *n.* An action that has the effect of voiding something previously ordered; a revocation. — **countermand** (kown-tər-**mand** *or* **kown**-), *vb.*

counteroffer, *n. Contracts.* An offeree's new offer that varies the terms of the original offer and that therefore rejects the original offer. — **counteroffer,** *vb.* — **counterofferor,** *n.* See MIRROR-IMAGE RULE.

counterpart. 1. In conveyancing, a corresponding part of an instrument <the other half of the indenture — the counterpart — could not be found>. **2.** One of two or more copies or duplicates of a legal instrument <this lease may be executed in any number of counterparts, each of which is considered an original>.

> "Formerly 'part' was used as the opposite of 'counterpart,' in respect to covenants executed in duplicate, but now each copy is called a 'counterpart.'" 2 Stewart Rapalje & Robert L. Lawrence, *A Dictionary of American and English Law* 927 (1883).

counterpart writ. See WRIT.

counterpromise, *n.* A promise made in exchange for another party's promise <a promise supported by a counterpromise is binding in its inception>. — **counterpromise,** *vb.*

counter-roll. *Hist.* A record kept by an officer as a check on another officer's record, esp. the rolls maintained by a sheriff and a coroner.

countersign, *vb.* To write one's own name next to someone else's to verify the other signer's identity. — **countersignature,** *n.*

countersuit. See COUNTERCLAIM.

countertrade. A type of international trade in which purchases made by an importing nation are linked to offsetting purchases made by the exporting nation.

> "Countertrade is barter in modern clothes. It developed rapidly as a form of doing business with the USSR and Eastern European nations in the 1970s and 1980s, before the major economic and political reforms tended to diminish its emphasis as a means of doing business." Ralph H. Folsom & Michael W. Gordon, *International Business Transactions* § 2.1, at 46 (1995).

countervailable subsidy (kown-tər-**vayl**-ə-bəl **səb**-sə-dee). A foreign government's subsidy on the manufacture of goods exported to another country, giving rise to the importing country's entitlement to impose a countervailing duty on the goods if their import caused or threatens to cause material injury to domestic industry. See *countervailing duty* under DUTY (4).

countervailing duty. See DUTY (4).

countervailing equity. See EQUITY.

counter will. See *mutual will* under WILL.

countez (**kawn**-teez). [Law French] *Hist.* A direction given by a clerk of a court to a crier, after a jury was sworn, to count the jury members.

> "Of this ignorance we may see daily instances, in the abuse of two legal terms of ancient French; one, the prologue to all proclamations, '*oyez*, or hear ye,' which is generally pronounced most unmeaningly, 'O yes:' the other, a more pardonable mistake, viz., when a jury are all sworn, the officer bids the crier number them, for which the word in law-french is, '*countez*;' but we now hear it pronounced in very good English, 'count these.' " 4 William Blackstone, *Commentaries on the Laws of England* 334 n.s (1769).

Counting House of the King's Household. See BOARD OF GREEN CLOTH.

country. 1. A nation or political state. **2.** The territory of such a nation or state.

county. The largest territorial division for local government within a state, generally considered to be a political subdivision and a quasi-corporation. • Every county exists as a result of a sovereign act of legislation, either constitutional or statutory, separating it from the rest of the state as an integral part of its territory and establishing it as one of the primary divisions of the state for purposes of civil administration. — Abbr. co.

> "A county is a part of the realm, intirely governed by one sheriff under the king, but all subject to the general government of the realm; and therefore every county is as it were an intire body of itself, so that upon a feoffment of lands in many towns in one county, livery of seisin made in one parcel in any one of the towns in the name of all, sufficeth for all the lands in all the other towns within the same county: but upon a feoffment of lands in divers counties, there must be livery of seisin in every county." Sir Henry Finch, *Law, or a Discourse Thereof* 79 (1759).

foreign county. Any county separate from that of a county where matters arising in the former county are called into question, though both may lie within the same state or country.

county agent. See JUVENILE OFFICER.

county attorney. An attorney who represents a county in civil matters. • In some jurisdictions, county attorneys prosecute criminal offenders.

county auditor. See AUDITOR.

county bond. See BOND (3).

county commissioner. See COMMISSIONER.

county court. See COURT.

county judge. See JUDGE.

county officer. See OFFICER.

county palatine (**pal**-ə-tIn *or*-tin). *Hist.* A county in which the lord held certain royal privileges, such as the right to pardon a felon or to have indictments recite that offenses were committed against the lord's — rather than the king's — peace. • In England, there were three such counties: Chester, Durham, and Lancaster. The separate legal systems in these counties was slowly eliminated; the last vestiges of a separate system were abolished by the Courts Act (1971). Cf. *proprietary government* under GOVERNMENT.

county property. Property that a county is authorized to acquire, hold, or sell.

county purpose. An objective pursued by a county; esp., one that a county levies taxes for.

county seat. The municipality where a county's principal offices are located. — Also termed *county town*.

county supervisor. See *county commissioner* under COMMISSIONER.

county town. See COUNTY SEAT.

county warrant. See WARRANT (3).

coup d'état (koo day-**tah**). [French "stroke of state"] A sudden, usu. violent, change of government through seizure of power.

coupon (**koo**-pon). An interest or dividend certificate that is attached to another instrument, such as a bond, and that may be detached and separately presented for payment of a definite sum at a specified time.

coupon bond. See BOND (3).

coupon interest rate. See *coupon rate* under INTEREST RATE.

coupon note. See NOTE (1).

coupon rate. See INTEREST RATE.

coupon security. See SECURITY.

coupon yield. See YIELD.

Cour de Cassation. See COURT OF CASSATION.

courier. A messenger, esp. one who delivers parcels, packages, and the like. • In international law, the term denotes a messenger duly authorized by a sending state to deliver a diplomatic pouch.

course of business. The normal routine in managing a trade or business. — Also termed *ordinary course of business*; *regular course of business*; *ordinary course*; *regular course.*

course of dealing. An established pattern of conduct between the parties to a particular transaction. • If a dispute arises, the parties' course of dealing can be used as evidence of how they intended to carry out the transaction. Cf. COURSE OF PERFORMANCE; *trade usage* under USAGE.

> "A course of dealing is distinguishable from a course of performance. As defined by the [UCC], 'course of dealing' relates to conduct under other transactions which occurred with regularity prior to the formation of the present contract, while 'course of performance' relates to the conduct of the parties under the contract in question subsequent to its formation. However, in meaning the two expressions are essentially equivalent." Ronald A. Anderson, *Uniform Commercial Code* § 1–205:86 (1997).

course of employment. Events that occur or circumstances that exist as a part of one's employment; esp., the time during which an employee furthers an employer's goals through employer-mandated directives.

course of performance. A sequence of previous performance by either party after an agreement has been entered into, when a contract involves repeated occasions for performance and both parties know the nature of the performance and have an opportunity to object to it. • A course of performance accepted or acquiesced in without objection is relevant to determining the meaning of the agreement. UCC § 2–208; § 2A–301(a). Cf. COURSE OF DEALING; *trade usage* under USAGE.

> "[C]ommon law courts have recognized the necessity of learning how people usually talk and what they usually mean by their language before one interprets their contracts. . . . '[C]ourse of performance' refers to a pattern of performance of the contract that is the subject of the dispute, as contrasted to 'course of dealing' which refers to the pattern of performance in prior contracts between the same parties." Claude Rohwer & Gordon D. Schaber, *Contracts in a Nutshell* 171–73 (4th ed. 1997).

> "The phrase 'course of performance' relates to the way the parties have acted in performance of the particular contract in question. The judicial inquiry on this point is limited to the way the parties have acted in carrying out the particular contract that is in controversy, as distinguished from a general pattern of dealing that may embrace many other contracts or transactions between the parties." Ronald A. Anderson, *Uniform Commercial Code* § 1–205:74 (1997).

course of trade. See *trade usage* under USAGE.

court, *n.* **1.** A governmental body consisting of one or more judges who sit to adjudicate disputes and administer justice <a question of law for the court to decide>.

> "A court . . . is a permanently organized body, with independent judicial powers defined by law, meeting at a time and place fixed by law for the judicial public administration of justice." 1 William J. Hughes, *Federal Practice, Jurisdiction & Procedure* § 7, at 8 (1931).

2. The judge or judges who sit on such a governmental body <the court asked the parties to approach the bench>. **3.** A legislative assembly <in Massachusetts, the General Court is the legislature>. **4.** The locale for a legal proceeding <an out-of-court statement>. **5.** The building where the judge or judges convene to adjudicate disputes and administer justice <the lawyers agreed to meet at the court at 8:00 a.m.>. — Also termed (in sense 5) *courthouse.*

admiralty court. See ADMIRALTY (1).

appellate court. A court with jurisdiction to review decisions of lower courts or administrative agencies. — Also termed *appeals court*; *appeal court*; *court of appeals*; *court of appeal*; *court of review.*

> "Appellate courts are among the most important institutions of governance in the United States. Through their review of trial court and administrative agency decisions they ensure that those bodies function lawfully and that litigants receive justice under law. Moreover, they provide authoritative interpretations of statutory and constitutional provisions and control the shaping of the common law in response to ever-changing circumstances; they are thus major sources of law." Daniel John Meador & Jordana Simone Bernstein, *Appellate Courts in the United States* v (1994).

Article I Court. See *legislative court.*

Article III Court. See ARTICLE III COURT.

bankruptcy court. See BANKRUPTCY COURT.

base court. *Archaic.* An inferior court.

basement court. See BASEMENT COURT.

business court. A court that handles exclusively commercial litigation. • In the late 20th century, business courts emerged as a way to unclog the general dockets and to dispose of commercial cases more efficiently and consistently. — Also termed *commercial court*; *commercial division.*

church court. See *ecclesiastical court.*

circuit court. A court usu. having jurisdiction over several counties, districts, or states, and holding sessions in all those areas.

civil court. A court with jurisdiction over noncriminal cases. — Abbr. Civ. Ct.

claims court. See *court of claims.*

Commerce Court. *Hist.* A federal court having the power to review and enforce determinations of the Interstate Commerce Commission. • The Commerce Court existed from 1910 to 1913.

commercial court. **1.** See *business court.* **2.** *English law.* A court that hears business disputes under simplified procedures designed to expedite the trials. • This court was created in 1971 as part of the Queen's Bench Division of the High Court of Justice.

commissioner's court. In certain states, a court having jurisdiction over county affairs and often functioning more as a managerial group than as a judicial tribunal.

common pleas court. See COURT OF COMMON PLEAS.

commonwealth court. **1.** In some states, a court of general jurisdiction. **2.** In Pennsylvania, a court that hears suits against the state and reviews decisions of state agencies and officials.

conciliation court. See *small-claims court.*

constitutional court. A court named or described and expressly protected in a constitution.

consular court (**kon**-sə-lər). A court held by the consul of one country within the territory of another. • Consular courts are created by treaty, and their jurisdiction is usu. limited to civil cases. The last of the U.S. consular courts (Morocco) was abolished in 1956.

coroner's court. *English law.* A common-law court that holds an inquisition if a person died a violent or unnatural death, died in prison, or died suddenly when the cause is not known. • The court also has jurisdiction over treasure trove.

corporation court. In some jurisdictions, a court that serves an incorporated municipality. See *municipal court.*

county court. A court with powers and jurisdiction dictated by a state constitution or statute. • The county court may govern administrative or judicial matters, depending on state law. — Also termed (in Louisiana) *parish court.*

court above. A court to which a case is appealed. — Also termed *higher court*; *upper court.*

court a quo (ay **kwoh**). A court from which a case has been removed or appealed.

court below. A trial court or intermediate appellate court from which a case is appealed. — Also termed *lower court.*

court christian. See *ecclesiastical court.*

court of appeals. **1.** An intermediate appellate court. — Also termed (as in California and England) *court of appeal.* **2.** In New York and Maryland, the highest appellate court within the jurisdiction.

court of chivalry. See HIGH COURT OF CHIVALRY.

court of claims. A court with the authority to hear claims made against a state (or its political subdivision) for cases in which the state has waived sovereign immunity. — Also termed *claims court.*

court of competent jurisdiction. A court that has the power and authority to do a particular act; one recognized by law as possessing the right to adjudicate a controversy.

court of domestic relations. See *family court.*

court of equity. A court that (1) has jurisdiction in equity, (2) administers and decides controversies in accordance with the rules, principles, and precedents of equity, and (3) follows the forms and procedures of chancery. Cf. *court of law.*

court of first instance. See *trial court.*

court of general jurisdiction. A court having unlimited or nearly unlimited trial jurisdiction in both civil and criminal cases.

court of inquiry. **1.** *Hist.* In English law, a court appointed by the monarch to ascertain whether it was proper to use extreme measures against someone who had been court-martialed. **2.** *Hist.* In American law, an agency created under articles of war and vested with the power to investigate the nature of a transaction or accusation of an officer or soldier. **3.** In some jurisdictions, a procedure that allows a magistrate to examine witnesses in relation to any offense that the magistrate has a good-faith reason to believe was committed.

court of last resort. The court having the authority to handle the final appeal of a case, such as the U.S. Supreme Court.

court of law. **1.** Broadly, any judicial tribunal that administers the laws of a state or nation. **2.** A court that proceeds according to the course of the common law, and that is governed by its rules and principles. Cf. *court of equity.*

court of limited jurisdiction. A court with jurisdiction over only certain types of cases, or cases in which the amount in controversy is limited.

court of ordinary. See *probate court.*

court of original jurisdiction. A court where an action is initiated and first heard.

court of record. A court that is required to keep a record of its proceedings and that may fine and imprison people for contempt. • The court's records are presumed accurate and cannot be collaterally impeached. See OF RECORD (2).

court of review. See *appellate court.*

court of special session. A court that has no stated term and is not continuous, but is organized only for hearing a particular case.

de facto court (di **fak**-toh). **1.** A court functioning under the authority of a statute that is later adjudged to be invalid. **2.** A court established and acting under the authority of a *de facto* government.

diocesan court. *Eccles. law.* A court exercising general or limited jurisdiction (as determined by patent, local custom, or legislation) of matters arising within a bishop's diocese. • Diocesan courts include the consistorial court, the courts of the commissaries, and the courts of archdeacons.

district court. A trial court having general jurisdiction within its judicial district. — Abbr. D.C.

divisional court. An English court made up of two or more judges from the High Court of Justice sitting in special cases that cannot be disposed of by one judge. • Each division of the High Court has a divisional court, e.g., the Divisional Court of the Family Division. With the exception of the Divisional Court of the Chancery Division, which has jurisdiction to review land-registration appeals from the county court, almost all judicial appeals are from decisions of a magistrates' court. The Divisional Court of the Queen's Bench Division hears appeals from the Crown Court or the magistrates' court by way of case stated in criminal prosecutions, which is the most frequent use of a divisional court.

domestic court. **1.** A court having jurisdiction at the place of a party's residence or domicile. **2.** See *family court.*

domestic-relations court. See *family court.*

ecclesiastical court (i-klee-zee-**as**-ti-kəl). **1.** A religious court that hears matters concerning a particular religion. **2.** In England, a court having jurisdiction over matters concerning the Church of England (the established church) as well as the duties and rights of the people serving it, but whose modern jurisdiction is limited to matters of ecclesiastical discipline and church property. — Also termed *church court*; *court christian*; *spiritual court.*

examining court. A lower court (usu. presided over by a magistrate) that determines probable cause and sets bail at a preliminary hearing in a criminal case.

family court. A court having jurisdiction over matters involving divorce, child custody and support, paternity, domestic violence, and other family-law issues. — Also termed *domestic-relations court*; *court of domestic relations*; *domestic court.*

federal court. A court having federal jurisdiction, including the U.S. Supreme Court, courts of appeals, district courts, bankruptcy courts, and tax courts. — Also termed *United States court.*

foreign court. **1.** The court of a foreign nation. **2.** The court of another state.

full court. A court session that is attended by all the court's judges; an en banc court. — Also termed *full bench.*

higher court. See *court above.*

hot court. A court, esp. an appellate court, that is familiar with the briefs filed in the case, and therefore with the issues, before oral argument. • Typically, a hot court controls the oral argument with its questioning, as opposed to listening passively to set presentations of counsel.

housing court. A court dealing primarily with landlord-and-tenant matters, including disputes over maintenance, lease terms, and building and fire codes.

hundred court. *Hist.* In England, a larger court baron, held for all inhabitants of a particular hundred rather than a manor, in which the free suitors were the judges (jurors) and the steward the register. • A hundred court was not a court of record, and it resembled a court-baron in all respects except for its larger territorial jurisdiction. The last hundred court was abolished in 1971. — Also termed *hundred moot.* See COURT BARON.

inferior court. **1.** Any court that is subordinate to the chief appellate tribunal within a judicial system. **2.** A court of special, limited, or statutory jurisdiction, whose record must show the existence of jurisdiction in any given case to give its ruling presumptive validity. — Also termed *lower court.*

instance court. **1.** See *trial court.* **2.** *Hist.* The admiralty court in England exercising original jurisdiction in all cases except those involving prizes.

insular court. A federal court with jurisdiction over U.S. island territories, such as the Virgin Islands.

intermediate court. An appellate court that is below a court of last resort.

justice court. A court, presided over by a justice of the peace, that has jurisdiction to hear cases involving small amounts of money or certain specified claims (such as forcible-entry-and-detainer suits). — Also termed *justice-of-the-peace court*; *J.P. court.*

juvenile court. A court having jurisdiction over cases involving children under a specified age, usu. 18. — Also termed *children's court.*

kangaroo court. **1.** A self-appointed tribunal or mock court in which the principles of law and justice are disregarded, perverted, or parodied. • Kangaroo courts may be assembled by various groups, such as prisoners in a jail (to settle disputes between inmates) and players on a baseball team (to "punish" teammates who commit fielding errors). **2.** A court or tribunal characterized by unauthorized or irregular procedures, esp. so as to render a fair proceeding impossible. **3.** A sham legal proceeding.

land court. A court having jurisdiction over land-related matters including: (1) exclusive original jurisdiction of applications for registration of land titles and related questions, writs of entry and petitions to clear title to real estate, petitions to determine the validity and extent of municipal zoning ordinances, bylaws, and regulations, and proceedings for foreclosure and redemption from tax titles; (2) original concurrent jurisdiction of declaratory judgment proceedings, shared with the supreme judicial, superior, and probate courts; and (3) original concurrent equity jurisdiction in land-related matters, except for cases of specific performance of land contracts. • Land courts today exist in the United States only in Massachusetts and Hawaii.

landed-estates court. *Hist. English law.* A statutorily established tribunal to dispose of encumbered real estate more promptly and easily than could be accomplished through the ordinary judicial machinery. • This type of court was first established in Ireland by acts of 11 & 12 Vict., ch. 48 and 12 & 13 Vict., ch. 77. The purpose of the court was to enable the owner, or any lessee of an unexpired term of 63 years or less, of encumbered land to apply to commissioners to direct a sale. The court served as a court of record and was called the Incumbered Estates Court. A later act abolished that court and created a new permanent tribunal called the Landed Estates Court. 21 & 22 Vict., ch. 72.

legislative court. A court created by a statute, as opposed to one authorized by a constitution. — Also termed (in federal law) *Article I court.*

levy court. *Hist.* A court that once existed in the District of Columbia, exercising many of the functions typical of county commissioners or county supervisors in the states, such as constructing and repairing roads and bridges.

limited court. A court having special jurisdiction conferred by statute, such as a probate court.

local court. A court whose jurisdiction is limited to a particular territory, such as a state, municipal, or county court.

lord mayor's court. A court of law and equity having jurisdiction in civil cases arising within the city of London and acting as the appellate court from the Chamberlain Court. • It was abolished by the Court Act of 1971.

lower court. See *court below.*

magistrate's court (**maj**-i-strayts *or* -strits). **1.** A court with jurisdiction over minor criminal offenses. • Such a court also has the power to bind over for trial persons accused of more serious offenses. — Also termed *police court.* **2.** A court with limited jurisdiction over minor criminal and civil matters. — Sometimes spelled (esp. in England) *magistrates' court.* — Also termed (in England) *court of petty sessions*; *court of summary jurisdiction*.

mayor's court. A municipal court in which the mayor presides as the judge, with jurisdiction over minor criminal (and sometimes civil) matters, traffic offenses, and the like.

moot court. See MOOT COURT.

municipal court. A court having jurisdiction (usu. civil and criminal) over cases arising within the municipality in which it sits. • A municipal court's civil jurisdiction to issue a judgment is often limited to a small amount.

naturalization court. See NATURALIZATION COURT.

orphan's court. See *probate court*.

parish court. See *county court*.

piepowder court. See PIEPOWDER COURT.

pretorial court. *Hist.* A colonial court in Maryland with jurisdiction of capital crimes, consisting of the lord proprietary or his lieutenant-general and the council.

prize court. A court having jurisdiction to adjudicate the captures made at sea in time of war. See PRIZE (2).

probate court. A court with the power to declare wills valid or invalid, to oversee the administration of estates, and in some states to appoint guardians and approve the adoption of minors. — Also termed *surrogate's court*; *court of ordinary*; *county court*; *orphan's court* (abbr. o.c.). See PROBATE.

provisional court. A federal court with jurisdiction and powers governed by the order granting its authority, such as a temporary court established in a conquered or occupied territory.

small-claims court. A court that informally and expeditiously adjudicates claims that seek damages below a specified monetary amount, usu. claims to collect small accounts or debts. — Also termed *small-debts court*; *conciliation court*.

spiritual court. See *ecclesiastical court*.

state court. A court of the state judicial system, as opposed to a federal court.

superior court. **1.** In some states, a trial court of general jurisdiction. **2.** In Pennsylvania, an intermediate court between the trial court and the chief appellate court.

supreme court. See SUPREME COURT.

surrogate's court. See *probate court*.

territorial court. A U.S. court established in a U.S. territory (such as the Virgin Islands) and serving as both a federal and state court. • The court was created under U.S. Const. art. IV, § 3, cl. 2.

three-judge court. A court made up of three judges; esp., a panel of three federal judges convened to hear a trial in which a statute is challenged on constitutional grounds. • Three-judge courts were virtually abolished in 1976 when Congress restricted their jurisdiction to constitutional challenges to congressional reapportionments.

trial court. A court of original jurisdiction where the evidence is first received and considered. — Also termed *court of first instance*; *instance court*.

United States court. See *federal court*.

upper court. See *court above*.

court administrator. See ADMINISTRATOR (1).

court-appointed attorney. See *assigned counsel* under COUNSEL.

court-appointed expert. See *impartial expert* under EXPERT.

court a quo. See COURT.

court baron. *Hist.* A manorial court with jurisdiction over amounts in controversy of 40 shillings or less. • According to some authorities, the court baron developed into two courts: the customary court baron for disputes involving copyholders, and the court baron proper (also known as the freeholders' court baron), in which freeholders were allowed to hold court concerning minor disputes.

> "In Coke's day it was said that the lord of a manor had one court, 'a court baron,' for his freeholders and another court, 'a customary court,' for his copyholders, and that in the latter the lord or his steward was the judge. Now over his unfree men the lord had, according to the law of the king's court, almost unlimited power; short of maiming them he might do what he liked with them; and every tenant of an unfree tenement was a tenant at will. Nevertheless in the court rolls and the manuals for stewards which come to us from the thirteenth and fourteenth centuries we cannot discover two courts or two methods of constituting the court. Freeholders and serfs are said to owe suit to the same halimoot, and so far as we can see, the *curia* which pronounces judgment is always the same body." 1 Frederick Pollock & Frederic W. Maitland, *The History of English Law Before the Time of Edward I* 593 (2d ed. 1898).

court below. See COURT.

court calendar. A list of matters scheduled for trial or hearing; DOCKET (2).

court christian. See *ecclesiastical court* under COURT.

court commissioner. See COMMISSIONER.

court costs. See COST (2).

court day. See DAY.

courtesy supervision. Oversight of a parolee by a correctional agency located in a jurisdiction other than where the parolee was sentenced. • Courtesy supervision is usu. arranged informally between correctional authorities in cases in which the offense is not serious and the rehabilitative needs of the parolee are better served in another jurisdiction.

Court for Consideration of Crown Cases Reserved. *Hist.* A court established in 1848 to review questions of law arising in criminal cases. • Trial judges posed the postverdict questions of law to the Court, which decided whether error had been committed. The Court was abolished in 1907, and its jurisdiction was transferred to the Court of Criminal Appeal. — Also termed *Court for Crown Cases Reserved.*

> "It was an old practice for the judge, in case of a conviction, if he felt a doubt as to the law, to respite judgment or sentence, and discuss the matter informally with the other judges. If they thought that the prisoner had been improperly convicted, he was pardoned. Statutory authority was given to this practice in 1848 by the establishment of the court for Crown Cases Reserved. All the judges were members of this court; and five, of whom the Lord Chief Justice must be one, formed a quorum." 1 William Holdsworth, *A History of English Law* 217 (7th ed. 1956).

Court for Divorce and Matrimonial Causes. *Hist.* A court exercising jurisdiction over family issues, such as legitimacy and divorce. • The Court, which was established in 1857, acquired the matrimonial jurisdiction previously exercised by the ecclesiastical courts. It consisted of the Lord Chancellor, the Chief Justices of the Queen's Bench and Common Pleas, the Chief Baron of Exchequer, the senior puisne judges of the last three courts, and the Judge Ordinary. In most instances, the Judge Ordinary heard the cases. The Judicature Act of 1873 abolished the Court and transferred its jurisdiction to the Probate Divorce and Admiralty Division (now Family Division) of the High Court of Justice.

Court for the Correction of Errors. A court having jurisdiction to review a lower court. • The name was formerly used in New York and South Carolina.

Court for the Relief of Insolvent Debtors. *Hist.* A court located in London with jurisdiction over bankruptcy matters. • The Bankruptcy Act of 1861 abolished the Court.

court for the trial of impeachments. A tribunal empowered to try a government officer or other person brought before it by the process of impeachment. • The U.S. Senate and the British House of Lords have this authority, as do the upper houses of most state legislatures. — Also termed *impeachment court*; *court of impeachment.*

court hand. *Hist.* A script style used by English court clerks, the words being abbreviated and contracted according to a set of common principles for maintaining brevity and uniformity. • This type of writing, along with the use of Latin (except for technical or untranslatable phrases), was banned early in the 18th century in an effort to make court records more accessible to nonlawyers.

> "[T]echnical Latin continued in use from the time of its first introduction, till the subversion of our ancient constitution under Cromwell; when, among many other innovations in the law, some for the better and some for the worse, the language of our records was altered and turned into English. But, at the restoration of king Charles, this novelty was no longer countenanced; the practicers finding it very difficult to express themselves so concisely or significantly in any other language but the Latin. And thus it continued without any sensible inconvenience till about the year 1730, when it was again thought proper that the proceedings at law should be done into English, and it was accordingly so ordered by statute 4 Geo. II. c. 26. . . . What is said of the alteration of language by the statute 4 Geo. II. c. 26 will hold equally strong with respect to the prohibition of using the ancient immutable *court hand* in writing the records of other legal proceedings; whereby the reading of any record that is forty years old is now become the object of science, and calls for the help of an antiquarian." 3 William Blackstone, *Commentaries on the Laws of England* 322–23 (1768).

courthouse. See COURT (5).

court lands. *Hist.* The part of a manor used for the lord's household.

court leet (**kort** leet). *Hist.* A feudal court responsible for receiving frankpledges and notices of criminal accusations. • Courts leet exercised both governmental and judicial powers, but declined after the justices in eyre began to take over serious criminal cases. The court met once or twice a year, and was presided over by the lord's steward, a lawyer who acted as judge.

court-martial, *n.* An ad hoc military court, convened under military authority, to try and punish those who violate the Uniform Code of Military Justice, particularly members of the armed forces. Pl. **courts-martial.** — **court-martial,** *vb.*

> "Courts-martial are not a part of the federal judiciary system, and the procedure in such courts is regulated by the Articles of War, Army Regulations, orders of the President, and Military custom." *Altmayer v. Sanford*, 148 F.2d 161 (5th Cir. 1945).

BCD special court-martial. A special court-martial in which a possible punishment is a bad-conduct discharge (a "BCD").

general court-martial. A proceeding that is presided over by a military judge, and no fewer than five members (who serve as jurors), and that has jurisdiction over all the members of the armed forces. • It is the highest military trial court.

special court-martial. A proceeding that is presided over by a military judge and no fewer than three members (who serve as jurors) to hear noncapital offenses and prescribe a sanction of hard labor, dismissal, or extended confinement (up to six months). • It is the intermediate level of courts-martial.

summary court-martial. A proceeding presided over by a single commissioned officer who is jurisdictionally limited in what sanctions can be imposed. • It is the lowest level of courts-martial.

court-martial order. A written order containing the result of a court-martial trial.

Court-Martial Reports. A publication containing the opinions of the U.S. Court of Military Appeals and select decisions of the Courts of Military Review. • This publication appeared during the years 1951–1975. — Abbr. CMR.

Court of Admiralty. See HIGH COURT OF ADMIRALTY.

court of ancient demesne. *Hist.* A court made up of freeholders of land held by the Crown (i.e., an *ancient demesne*). • The freeholders acted as judges much the same way that freeholders of an ordinary manor would in a court baron. See *ancient demesne* under DEMESNE; COURT BARON.

Court of Appeal. An English court of civil and criminal appellate jurisdiction established by the Judicature Acts of 1873 and 1875. • The court is made up of the Lord Chancellor, Lord Chief Justice, Master of the Rolls, President of the Family Division, Vice-Chancellor of the Chancery Division, former Lord Chancellors, Lords of Appeal in Ordinary, and Lords Justices of Appeal. In practice it is made up of the Master of Rolls and the Lords Justices. It sits in several divisions, each having three members.

Court of Appeal in Chancery. *Hist.* An English court of intermediate appeal in equity cases, established in 1851 and abolished in 1873–1875, when its jurisdiction was transferred to the Court of Appeal.

court of appeals. See COURT.

Court of Appeals, U.S. See UNITED STATES COURT OF APPEALS.

Court of Appeals for the Armed Forces. See UNITED STATES COURT OF APPEALS FOR THE ARMED FORCES.

Court of Appeals for the Federal Circuit. See UNITED STATES COURT OF APPEALS FOR THE FEDERAL CIRCUIT.

Court of Appeals in Cases of Capture. *Hist.* A court responsible for reviewing state-court decisions concerning British ships captured by American privateers during the War of Independence. • The Court was established by Congress under the Articles of Confederation and served as the chief U.S. court from 1780 to 1787. It was the first federal court in the United States.

Court of Archdeacon (ahrch-**dee**-kən). *Hist. Eccles. law.* An inferior ecclesiastical court with jurisdiction over cases arising within the archdeaconry and probate matters. • Appeal was to the Bishop's Court. The Court of Archdeacon was abolished in 1967. — Also termed *Archdeacon's Court*; *Archdiaconal Court* (ahr-kə-dI-**ak**-ən-əl).

Court of Arches. *Eccles. law.* The ecclesiastical court of the province of Canterbury, responsible for various appeals from provincial diocesan courts. • The court handled probate cases until the Court of Probate acquired jurisdiction in 1857. The Pope heard appeals from the Court of Arches until the break with Rome prompted a transfer of the appellate jurisdiction to the royal courts. The Judicial Committee of the Privy Council now hears certain appeals from the Court of Arches. — Also termed *Arches Court of Canterbury*; *Court of Canterbury*; *Court of the Official Principal*. Cf. CHANCERY COURT OF YORK.

"The Court of Arches is the provincial court of the Archbishop of Canterbury. It is held by a judge generally called the *Dean of the Arches*. Its jurisdiction was important while testamentary cases were dealt with in the Ecclesiastical Courts. The name is derived from the fact that the court was originally held in the Church of St. Mary-Le-Bow (*Ecclesia Beatae Mariae de Arcubus*), the steeple of which is raised on stone pillars formed archwise like bent bows." W.J.V. Windeyer, *Lectures on Legal History* 184 n.11 (2d ed. 1949).

Court of Assistants. *Hist.* A colonial body organized in Massachusetts Bay Colony in 1630 to act as a legislature and court for the colony. See GENERAL COURT.

"The court of assistants, made up of governor, deputy governor, and magistrates, heard appeals from lower courts, and took original jurisdiction in certain cases — for example, cases of divorce. Below it were the county courts." Lawrence M. Friedman, *A History of American Law* 40 (2d ed. 1985).

Court of Attachments. *Hist.* An inferior forest court with jurisdiction over trespasses of the royal forests. • The judges of this court (the *verderers*) met every 40 days to hear charges made by the royal foresters. Major trespass cases were heard by the justices in eyre. — Also termed *wood-mote*. See VERDERER.

Court of Audience. *Hist. Eccles. law.* A court in which the two archbishops exercise personal jurisdiction. • This court was abolished in 1963.

"Just as the bishop did not deprive himself of all jurisdiction by delegation to an official or commissary, so the archbishop did not originally deprive himself of all jurisdiction by delegation to the official principal. He possessed a jurisdiction concurrent with that of the court of the Arches, which was exercised in the court of Audience. In later times this jurisdiction was exercised by the judge of the court of Audience. At one time the archbishop may have exercised a considerable part of this jurisdiction in this court." 1 William Holdsworth, *A History of English Law* 601 (7th ed. 1956).

Court of Augmentations. *Hist.* A court established in 1536 by Henry VIII to determine controversies arising from the royal policy of taking over property owned by monasteries. • The court was merged into the Court of Exchequer in 1554.

Court of Canterbury. See COURT OF ARCHES.

Court of Cassation (ka-**say**-shən). The highest court of France. • The court's name derives from its power to quash (*casser*) the decrees of inferior courts. — Also termed (more formally) *Cour de Cassation*.

court of chancery. See CHANCERY (1).

court of chivalry. See HIGH COURT OF CHIVALRY.

Court of Civil Appeals. An intermediate appellate court in some states, such as Alabama and (formerly) Texas.

court of claims. **1.** See COURT. **2.** (*cap.*) See UNITED STATES COURT OF FEDERAL CLAIMS.

Court of Common Pleas. **1.** *Hist.* A superior court having jurisdiction of all real actions and common pleas (i.e., actions between subjects). • The Court was presided over by a chief justice with four (later five) puisne judges. In 1873 it became the Common Pleas Division of the High Court of Justice. In 1881 it merged into the Queen's Bench Division. **2.** An intermediate-level court in some states, such as Arkansas. **3.** A trial court of general jurisdiction in some states, such as Ohio, Pennsylvania, and South Carolina. — Also termed *Court of Common Bench*. — Abbr. C.P.

"*Common pleas* is the kings Court now held in *Westminster* hall, but in auncient time moveable, as appeareth by the statute called *Magna charta*.... [U]ntill the time that *Henry* the third granted the great charter, there were but two courts in all, called the Kings courts: whereof one was the Exchequer, and the other, the kings bench, which was then called (*curia Domini regis*) and (*aula regis*) because it followed the court or king: and that upon the grant of that charter, the court of common pleas was erected and setled in one place certaine: viz. at *Westminster*.... All civill causes both reall and personall are, or were in former times, tryed in this court, according to the strict lawe of the realme: and by *Fortescue, cap. 50* it seemeth to have bene the onely court for reall causes." John Cowell, *The Interpreter* (1607).

court of competent jurisdiction. See COURT.

court of conscience. *Hist.* A local English court with jurisdiction of small-debt cases. • The court was so called because its judgments were supposed to reflect equity and good conscience. County courts assumed the jurisdiction of the courts of conscience in 1846.

Court of Convocation. *Eccles. law.* An assembly of high-ranking provincial officials and minor clergy having jurisdiction over cases of heresy, schism, and other purely ecclesiastical matters.

Court of Criminal Appeals. **1.** For each armed service, an intermediate appellate court that reviews court-martial decisions. • The court was established by the Military Justice Act of 1968. 10 USCA §§ 859–876. — Formerly termed *Court of Military Review* (abbr. CMR). **2.** In some jurisdictions, such as Texas and Oklahoma, the highest appellate court that hears criminal cases.

Court of Customs and Patent Appeals. *Hist.* An Article III court created in 1929 to hear appeals in customs and patent cases. • This court was abolished in 1982 and was superseded by the U.S. Court of Appeals for the Federal Circuit.

Court of Delegates. *Hist. Eccles. law.* A court serving as the final court of appeal for admiralty and ecclesiastical matters. • The Court was established in 1534 to serve in the stead of the Papal Curia when the English Church severed its ties with the Papacy. Six delegates made up the Court, usu. three persons trained in common law and three in civil law. This mixture led to confused rulings and unreliable precedents that hindered the Court's credibility and ultimately led to its dissolution. The Court was abolished in 1833 and its jurisdiction transferred to the Judicial Committee of the Privy Council. — Also termed *High Court of Delegates*.

> "The crown had an absolute discretion as to the person to be appointed. But, as the lawyers of Doctors' Commons were the only lawyers acquainted with canon or civil law, certain of them were usually included in the commission. . . . It is not surprising to find that the [Court of Delegates] was unsatisfactory. It was a shifting body, so that no general rules of procedure could be established. It did not as a rule give reasons for its decisions. Its members were only paid a guinea a day; and consequently it was usually composed of the junior civilians. On them, the judges of the common law courts, appointed as delegates, were obliged to rely for their law. In consequence of the dissatisfaction felt at its working the Ecclesiastical Commission of 1832, in a special report, recommended the transfer of its jurisdiction to the Privy Council. . . ." 1 William Holdsworth, *A History of English Law* 605 (7th ed. 1956).

court of domestic relations. See *family court* under COURT.

Court of Earl Marshal. See HIGH COURT OF CHIVALRY.

court of equity. See COURT.

court of error. **1.** *Hist.* Formerly, the Court of Exchequer Chamber and the House of Lords. • Appeals from common-law courts lay to the Court of Exchequer Chamber, and then to the House of Lords until 1873, when the Judicature Act gave jurisdiction of superior-court appeals to the Court of Appeal. Cf. COURT OF EXCHEQUER CHAMBER. **2.** Generally, a court having jurisdiction to review a lower court's rulings.

Court of Errors and Appeals. *Hist.* Formerly, the court of last resort in New Jersey and New York. — Also termed *High Court of Errors and Appeals*.

Court of Exchequer (eks-**chek**-ər *or* **eks**-chek-ər). *Hist.* A former English superior court responsible primarily for adjudicating disputes about the collection of public revenue. • In 1873 it became the Exchequer Division of the High Court of Justice. In 1881 that Division was merged into the Queen's Bench Division. See QUEEN'S BENCH DIVISION. Cf. CHAMBER OF ACCOUNTS.

Court of Exchequer Chamber. *Hist.* **1.** An informal assembly of common-law judges who (sometimes with the Lord Chancellor) gathered to discuss important cases that have adjourned pending an opinion from the Court. • This body never became a court of law in a technical sense, but judges gave great weight to its decisions. The last reported decision of this body is from 1738.

> "Earlier than these two statutory courts was the practice, which apparently originated about the time of Edward I, of informal meetings of the judges in the Exchequer Chamber to decide matters connected with litigation. . . . The purpose of the meeting was to bring before the judges a point of law which caused difficulty and which had arisen in a case being heard before one or other of the courts. Any resolution passed did not constitute a judgment; it was left to the court concerned to make the appropriate decree, and the official record made no reference to the informal decision. . . . Civil cases were debated in the Exchequer Chamber as late as the seventeenth century, and criminal cases continued to be 'reserved' for full discussion by all the common law judges until the nineteenth century." A.K.R. Kiralfy, *Potter's Outlines of English Legal History* 202–04 (5th ed. 1958).

2. A court created by statute in 1357 to hear appeals from the Court of Exchequer. **3.** A court created by statute in 1585 to hear appeals from the King's Bench. • This court consisted of all the justices of the Common Pleas and the Barons of Exchequer who were serjeants. At least six judges were necessary to render a judgment.

> "Parliament was only occasionally summoned in the sixteenth century; and as Parliament was the only court which could amend errors of the King's Bench, the want of a court which could hold regular sessions was much felt. To supply this want a new court of Exchequer Chamber was created in 1585 for the purpose of amend-

ing the errors of the King's Bench." 1 William Holdsworth, *A History of English Law* 244 (7th ed. 1956).

4. A court charged with hearing appeals from the common-law courts of record. • This court was created in 1830 by combining the courts created by the statutes of 1357 and 1585. Appeals from one common-law court were heard by judges from the other two courts.

"This complicated system of appellate courts was abolished in 1830, when a new Court of Exchequer Chamber was set up as the court of error from each of the three common law courts. It was composed of the judges of the two common law courts other than those of the court appealed from. At the same time the right of the King's Bench to hear error from the Common Pleas was abolished. From the judgment of this new court a further appeal still lay to the House of Lords. This court was thus, until the Judicature Act, 1873, a court of intermediate appeals. Its jurisdiction after the Judicature Act passed to the Court of Appeal which was then created." W.J.V. Windeyer, *Lectures on Legal History* 144 (2d ed. 1949).

Court of Faculties. *Eccles. law.* An archbishop's tribunal that grants special dispensations (such as a marriage license) and decides questions relating to monuments and mortuary matters. See MASTER OF THE FACULTIES.

Court of Federal Claims, U.S. See UNITED STATES COURT OF FEDERAL CLAIMS.

court officer. See OFFICER OF THE COURT.

court of first instance. See *trial court* under COURT.

court of general jurisdiction. See COURT.

Court of General Quarter Sessions of the Peace. *Hist.* **1.** *English law.* A court of criminal jurisdiction held in each county (or borough) once in every quarter of a year. • The court was made up of a county's justices of the peace. It committed certain cases to the Assizes. Quarter Sessions were abolished in 1971, with most jurisdiction transferred to the Crown Court. — Often shortened to *Quarter Sessions*; *Sessions.*

"The court of general *quarter sessions* of the peace is a court that must be held in every county, once in every quarter of a year.... It is held before two or more justices of the peace, one of which must be of the *quorum*. The jurisdiction of this court, by statute 34 Edw. III. c. I. extends to the trying and determining all felonies and trespasses whatsoever, though they seldom, if ever, try any greater offence than small felonies within the benefit of clergy...." 4 William Blackstone, *Commentaries on the Laws of England* 268 (1769).

2. A court held in some states four times a year with jurisdiction over misdemeanors and occasionally tasks of an administrative nature, such as the care of public roads and bridges. — Often shortened to *Quarter Session Court.* — Also termed *Court of Quarter Sessions of the Peace.*

Court of Great Sessions in Wales. *Hist.* A common-law court established in 1543 in Wales with jurisdiction equivalent to that of the English assizes. • The Court of Great Sessions was bound to follow English law, but not necessarily English case precedent. — Also termed *King's Great Sessions in Wales.*

"There was no outcry when, in 1536, 'the sinister usages and customs' of the Welsh were abrogated and Welsh subjects were granted the same laws and liberties as the English.... A new system of courts, called the Great Sessions in Wales, was set up. The courts were to sit twice a year in four circuits, each comprising three counties, and to each circuit were appointed justices 'learned in the laws of this realm'. These courts operated alongside the English courts, and they had the same jurisdiction in Wales as the King's Bench and Common Pleas had in England.... In 1830 the Great Sessions were abolished, and by complete procedural assimilation England and Wales became at last one unified jurisdiction, two extra circuits being added to the English assize system." J.H. Baker, *An Introduction to English Legal History* 37–38 (3d ed. 1990).

Court of High Commission. *Hist. Eccles. law.* A tribunal responsible for inquiring into religious offenses such as adultery, the holding of heretical opinions, and absence from church. • The High Commission was created to prosecute violations of the Acts of Supremacy and Uniformity (1559), the statutes that gave the Crown supreme power over the Church of England. From about 1580 on, the High Commission functioned as a court. The Court's broad powers and use of civil-law procedures in ways counter to the common law (such as compelling suspects to testify against themselves) sparked opposition to its existence. Its close relationship with the Court of Star Chamber hastened its demise (along with the Star Chamber) in 1641. — Also termed *High Commission Court.*

"[T]he court of the king's *high commission* in causes ecclesiastical ... was intended to vindicate the dignity and peace of the church, by reforming, ordering, and correcting the ecclesiastical state and persons, and all manner of errors, heresies, schisms, abuses, offences, contempts, and enormities. Under the shelter of which very general words, means were found in that and the two succeeding reigns, to vest in the high commissioners extraordinary and almost despotic powers, of fining and imprisoning; which they exerted much beyond the degree of the offence itself, and frequently over offences by no means of spiritual cognizance. For these reasons this court was justly abolished by Statute 16 Car. I, c. 11.

And the weak and illegal attempt that was made to revive it, during the reign of King James the second, served only to hasten that infatuated prince's ruin." 3 William Blackstone, *Commentaries on the Laws of England* 67–68 (1768).

Court of Honor. *Hist.* **1.** *English law.* A feudal court of the manor. **2.** *English law.* A court with jurisdiction to hear complaints concerning either affronts to honor or encroachments in precedence rights, heraldry, or coat-armor. **3.** A tribunal of army officers convened to review and punish any dereliction from a code of honor.

Court of Hustings (**həs**-tingz). *Hist.* **1.** *English law.* A local court with jurisdiction over real and mixed actions, held in the Guildhall of London before the Recorder, the Lord Mayor, and Sheriff (the latter two officials serving as honorary judges). • This court dates from before the Conquest. **2.** Formerly, a local court in Virginia. — Also termed *curia burgi.* See HUSTING.

court of impeachment. See COURT FOR THE TRIALS OF IMPEACHMENT.

court of inquiry. See COURT.

Court of International Trade, U.S. See UNITED STATES COURT OF INTERNATIONAL TRADE.

Court of Justice Seat. See COURT OF THE CHIEF JUSTICE IN EYRE.

Court of Justiciary, High. See HIGH COURT OF JUSTICIARY.

Court of King's Bench. See KING'S BENCH.

court of last resort. See COURT.

court of law. See COURT.

court of limited jurisdiction. See COURT.

Court of Magistrates and Freeholders. *Hist.* A South Carolina court with criminal jurisdiction over alleged offenses committed by slaves and free persons of color.

Court of Military Appeals. See UNITED STATES COURT OF APPEALS FOR THE ARMED FORCES.

Court of Military Review. See COURT OF CRIMINAL APPEALS (1).

court of nisi prius. See NISI PRIUS.

Court of Official Principal. See COURT OF ARCHES.

Court of Ordinary. *Hist.* A Georgia court of probate jurisdiction.

court of original jurisdiction. See COURT.

Court of Orphans. *Hist.* In Maryland and Pennsylvania, a court exercising probate jurisdiction.

Court of Oyer and Terminer. **1.** *Hist.* An assize court commissioned by the Crown to pass through the counties two or more times a year and hear felonies and treason cases. • The judges sat by virtue of several commissions, each of which, strictly speaking, created a separate and distinct court. A judge with an *oyer and terminer* commission, for example, was allowed to hear only cases of felony and treason; he could not try persons charged with other criminal offenses. But if the judge also carried a commission of *gaol delivery* (as most did), he could try all prisoners held in gaol for any offense; in this way most Courts of Oyer and Terminer gathered full criminal jurisdiction. The jurisdiction of the assize courts was taken over by the Crown Court in 1971. See ASSIZE (1); COMMISSION OF OYER AND TERMINER; COMMISSION OF GAOL DELIVERY. **2.** In some states, a court of higher criminal jurisdiction.

Court of Oyer and Terminer and General Gaol Delivery. *Hist.* **1.** A court that carries the commissions of *oyer and terminer* and *gaol delivery.* **2.** In Pennsylvania, a court of criminal jurisdiction.

Court of Peculiars. *Hist. Eccles. law.* A branch of the Court of Arches that had jurisdiction over the provincial parishes of Canterbury that were exempt from the jurisdiction of the diocesan bishop and responsible to the metropolitan only. • The Court of Peculiars was abolished in the 19th century. See COURT OF ARCHES.

court of petty sessions. See *magistrate's court* under COURT.

court of piepowder. See PIEPOWDER COURT.

Court of Pleas. *Hist.* A court of the county palatine of Durham, having a local common-law jurisdiction. • It was abolished in 1873, and its jurisdiction was transferred to the High

Court. — Also termed *Court of Pleas of Durham.*

Court of Policies of Insurance. *Hist.* A court that determines in a summary way insurance-policy issues arising between merchants. • The Court's jurisdiction extended only to London, and appeal was taken to the Court of Chancery. The Court was abolished in 1863. — Also termed *Court of Policies of Assurance.*

Court of Private Land Claims. *Hist.* A federal court — in existence from 1891 to 1895 — with jurisdiction to hear private parties' claims to public-domain land located in the southwestern part of the United States and deriving from Spanish or Mexican grants.

Court of Probate. 1. *Hist.* A court established in 1857 to receive the testamentary jurisdiction formerly held by the ecclesiastical courts. • In 1873 the Court was merged into the High Court of Justice, where its jurisdiction was exercised by the Probate Divorce and Admiralty (now Family) Division. **2.** See *probate court* under COURT.

Court of Quarter Sessions of the Peace. See COURT OF GENERAL QUARTER SESSIONS OF THE PEACE.

Court of Queen's Bench. See QUEEN'S BENCH.

court of record. See COURT.

Court of Regard. *Hist.* A forest court responsible for looking into matters of waste and encroachment onto forest land (i.e., *purpresture*). • The Court also ensured that the feet of all mastiffs — a breed allowed in royal forests as guard dogs — within the forest were declawed and cut so as to prevent them from chasing deer.

Court of Requests. *Hist.* A royal court whose jurisdiction was mainly civil, though it exercised quasi-criminal jurisdiction in offenses such as riot and forgery. • Dating from 1483, the Court of Requests was a part of the Privy Council. It was disbanded in 1641 when Parliament limited the Privy Council's judicial functions. Cf. MASTER OF REQUESTS

> "The establishment of the court of Requests was due to the large increase in the judicial business of the Council and the Chancery under the Tudors.... It was related both to the judicial side of the Council, which, as we shall see, came, in the course of the Tudor period, to be known as the court of Star Chamber, and to the court of Chancery.... [F]rom the end of Henry VIII's reign onwards, the legal assessors of the court assumed entire control, with the result that it became a court which was quite separate from the court of Star Chamber. These legal assessors were styled Masters of Requests, and from their title the court got its name." 1 William Holdsworth, *A History of English Law* 412–13 (7th ed. 1956).

court of review. See *appellate court* under COURT.

Court of Session. 1. *Scots law.* The supreme Scottish civil court, having divisions for trials and for hearing appeals. • Its jurisdiction corresponds generally to the English High Court of Justice. It has two appellate chambers, the First and Second Division, and several Lords Ordinary, who sit singly as trial judges. **2.** In a few states, a court with jurisdiction over criminal cases.

Court of Shepway. *Hist.* The Court of the Lord Warden of the Cinque Ports, exercising civil jurisdiction. • The civil jurisdiction of the Cinque Ports was abolished in 1855.

court of special session. See COURT.

Court of Star Chamber. See STAR CHAMBER (1).

court of summary jurisdiction. See *magistrate's court* under COURT.

Court of Swanimote. See COURT OF SWEINMOTE.

Court of Sweinmote (**swayn**-moht). *Hist.* A medieval forest court with jurisdiction over a variety of matters, esp. the right to graze animals during the summer when deer were fawning. • The forest freeholders (the *sweins*) made up the jury of the Court. By the 14th century, the Court's jurisdiction had expanded, and it acquired a form similar to the eyre courts. During this period, the Court came to be referred to as the *Court of Swanimote* rather than the *Court of Sweinmote.*

Court of the Chief Justice in Eyre (air). *Hist.* An eyre court responsible for trying offenses against the forest laws. • The jurisdiction of this Court was similar to that of the Court of Sweinmote. — Also termed *Court of Justice Seat.*

Court of the Earl Marshal. See HIGH COURT OF CHIVALRY.

Court of the Lord High Constable and Earl Marshal. *Hist.* A court having jurisdiction over diverse military matters, such as treason, prisoners of war, and disputed coats of arms. • The Lord High Constable and the Earl Marshal were the top military officials of the Norman kings. After the office of Lord High Constable was forfeited in 1521, the court continued on as the *Court of the Earl Marshal*, but its jurisdiction was reduced to questions of chivalry only. Cf. HIGH COURT OF CHIVALRY.

Court of the Lord High Admiral. See HIGH COURT OF ADMIRALTY.

Court of the Lord High Steward. *Hist.* A court commissioned to try a peer indicted for treason or a felony. • The Court met only if the House of Lords was not in session. The Lord High Steward sat as a judge and decided questions of law, and the peers decided facts only. The Court last sat in 1688.

Court of the Lord High Steward of the Universities. *Hist.* A court convened to try scholars, esp. Oxford or Cambridge students, who have been indicted for treason, felony, or mayhem.

Court of the Marshalsea (**mahr**-shəl-see). *Hist.* A court that moved about with the king, and had jurisdiction over certain cases arising within 12 miles of the king's residence (an area known as the *verge*). • The Court's steward and marshal acted as judges of the Court, and heard criminal cases and the common pleas of debt, covenant, and certain trespasses. The court's migratory nature made it inconvenient for litigants, and prompted its abolition in 1849. — Also termed *Court of the Steward and Marshal*. Cf. PALACE COURT.

> "Coke points out that all the Acts passed concerning this court restrained, or explained, but never added to its jurisdiction. He decided, in the *Case of the Marshalsea*, that it could not try the newer forms of action such as assumpsit and trover. Its once general jurisdiction had passed to the court of King's Bench, and the attitude of that court to the more limited court of the Marshalsea made the court of the Marshalsea almost useless. There were complaints in the seventeenth century of the conduct of its officials; and, as it was obliged to follow the king in his progresses, it was a court extremely inconvenient to use." 1 William Holdsworth, *A History of English Law* 208 (7th ed. 1956).

Court of the Official Principal. See COURT OF ARCHES.

Court of the Steward of the King's Household. *Hist.* A court having jurisdiction over criminal cases involving a member of the royal household. • This court's jurisdiction was at first limited to acts of violence by the king's servants toward a member of the king's council, but it was later given broader criminal authority. The Court was abolished in 1828.

Court of Verge. See VERGE.

Court of Veterans Appeals, U.S. See UNITED STATES COURT OF VETERANS APPEALS.

Court of Wards and Liveries. *Hist.* A court created in 1540 to assert the Crown's right to income from a variety of feudal tenures. • The Court's unpopularity led to its abolition in 1660.

> "[I]nquests of office were more frequently in practice than at present, during the continuance of the military tenures among us: when, upon the death of every one of the king's tenants, an inquest of office was held, called an *inquisitio post mortem*, to enquire of what lands he died seised, who was his heir, and of what age, in order to entitle the king to his marriage, wardship, relief, *primer-seisin*, or other advantages, as the circumstances of the case might turn out. To superintend and regulate these enquiries, the court of wards and liveries was instituted by statute 32 Hen. VIII c. 46 which was abolished at the restoration of king Charles the second, together with the oppressive tenures upon which it was founded." 3 William Blackstone, *Commentaries on the Laws of England* 258 (1768).

courtoisie internationale. See COMITY.

court order. See ORDER (2).

court-packing plan. An unsuccessful proposal — made in 1937 by President Franklin D. Roosevelt — to increase the number of U.S. Supreme Court justices from nine to fifteen. • The ostensible purpose of the proposal was to increase the Court's efficiency, but President Roosevelt wanted to appoint justices who would not block his administration's New Deal programs.

court papers. All documents that a party files with the court, including pleadings, motions, notices, and the like. — Often shortened to *papers*. — Also termed *suit papers*.

court recorder. See RECORDER.

court reporter. 1. A person who records testimony, stenographically or by electronic or other means, and when requested prepares a transcript <the deposition could not start until the court reporter arrived>. Cf. *court recorder* under RECORDER. **2.** REPORTER OF DECISIONS.

court roll. *Hist.* A record of a manor's tenures; esp., a record of the terms by which the various tenants held their estates. • Copyhold tenure, for example, developed from the practice of maintaining court rolls. See COPYHOLD.

courtroom. The part of a courthouse where trials and hearings take place. Cf. *judge's chamber* under CHAMBER.

court rules. Regulations having the force of law and governing practice and procedure in the various courts, such as the Federal Rules of Civil Procedure, Federal Rules of Criminal Procedure, the U.S. Supreme Court Rules, and the Federal Rules of Evidence, as well as any local rules that a court promulgates. — Also termed *rules of court.*

courts of the franchise. See FRANCHISE COURT.

court system. The network of courts in a jurisdiction.

cousin. 1. A child of one's aunt or uncle. — Also termed *first cousin*; *full cousin*; *cousin-german.* **2.** A relative descended from one's ancestor (such as a grandparent) by two or more steps in a diverging line. **3.** Any distant relative by blood or marriage; a kinsman or kinswoman.

cousin-in-law. **1.** A husband or wife of one's cousin. **2.** A cousin of one's husband or one's wife.

cousin once removed. **1.** A child of one's cousin. **2.** A cousin of one's parent.

cousin twice removed. **1.** A grandchild of one's cousin. **2.** A cousin of one's grandparent.

second cousin. A person related to another by descending from the same great-grandfather or great-grandmother.

third cousin. A person related to another by descending from the same great-great-grandfather or great-great-grandmother.

cousin-german. See GERMAN.

covenant (**kəv**-ə-nənt), *n.* **1.** A formal agreement or promise, usu. in a contract.

absolute covenant. A covenant that is not qualified or limited by any condition. Cf. *conditional covenant.*

affirmative covenant. A covenant that obligates a party to do some act; esp., an agreement that real property will be used in a certain way. • An affirmative covenant is more than a restriction on the use of property; it requires the owner to undertake certain specified acts.

assertory covenant. One that affirmatively states certain facts; an affirming promise under seal.

auxiliary covenant (awg-**zil**-yə-ree). A covenant that does not relate directly to the primary subject of the agreement, but to something connected to it. Cf. *principal covenant.*

collateral covenant (kə-**lat**-ə-rəl). A covenant entered into in connection with the grant of something, but that does not relate immediately to the thing granted; esp., a covenant in a deed or other sealed instrument not pertaining to the conveyed property. Cf. *inherent covenant.*

concurrent covenant. A covenant that requires performance by one party at the same time as another's performance.

conditional covenant. A covenant that is qualified by a condition. Cf. *absolute covenant.*

continuing covenant. A covenant that requires the successive performance of acts, such as an agreement to pay rent in installments.

covenant in deed. See *express covenant.*

covenant in law. See *implied covenant.*

covenant not to compete. See *noncompetition covenant.*

covenant not to sue. A covenant in which a party having a right of action agrees not to assert that right in litigation. — Also termed *contract not to sue.*

> "A covenant not to sue is a promise by the creditor not to sue either permanently or for a limited period. If the promise is one never to sue it operates as a discharge just as does a release. The theory is that should the creditor sue despite his promise not to, the debtor has a counterclaim for damages for breach of the creditor's covenant not to sue which is equal to and cancels the original claim.... If the covenant is not to sue for a limited time, the modern view is that the covenant may be raised as an affirmative defense to any action brought in violation of the covenant." John D. Calamari & Joseph M. Perillo, *The Law of Contracts* § 21-11, 878-79 (3d ed. 1987).

dependent covenant. A covenant that depends on a party's prior performance of some act or condition. • Until the performance, the other party does not have to perform. Cf. *concurrent covenant*; *independent covenant.*

executed covenant. A covenant that has been fully performed.

executory covenant (eg-**zek**-yə-tor-ee). A covenant that remains unperformed in whole or in part.

express covenant. A covenant created by the words of the parties. — Also termed *covenant in deed*. Cf. *implied covenant*.

implied covenant. A covenant that can be inferred from the whole agreement and the conduct of the parties. — Also termed *covenant in law*. Cf. *express covenant*.

implied covenant of good faith and fair dealing. An implied covenant to cooperate with the other party to an agreement so that both parties may obtain the full benefits of the agreement; an implied covenant to refrain from any act that would injure a contracting party's right to receive the benefit of the contract.

implied negative covenant. A covenant binding a grantor not to permit use of any reserved right in a manner that might destroy the benefits that would otherwise inure to the grantee.

independent covenant. A covenant that makes each party independently liable for its promises, regardless of the other party's actions.

inherent covenant. A covenant that relates directly to land, such as a covenant of quiet enjoyment. Cf. *collateral covenant*.

intransitive covenant. A covenant whose performance does not pass from the original covenantor to the covenantor's representatives. Cf. *transitive covenant*.

joint covenant. A covenant that binds two or more covenantors together. Cf. *several covenant*.

negative covenant. A covenant that requires a party to refrain from doing something; esp., in a real-estate financing transaction, the borrower's promise to the lender not to encumber or transfer the real estate as long as the loan remains unpaid.

noncompetition covenant. A contractual provision — typically found in employment, partnership, or sale-of-business agreements — in which one party agrees to refrain from conducting business similar to that of the other party. • Courts generally enforce these clauses for the duration of the original business relationship, but clauses extending beyond termination must usu. be reasonable in scope, time, and territory. — Also termed *noncompete covenant*; *covenant not to compete*; *restrictive covenant*; *promise not to compete*; *contract not to compete*.

positive covenant. A covenant that requires a party to do something (such as to erect a fence within a specified time).

principal covenant. A covenant that relates directly to the principal matter of an agreement. Cf. *auxiliary covenant*.

restrictive covenant. See *noncompetition covenant*.

several covenant. A covenant that binds two or more covenantors separately. — Also termed *separate covenant*. Cf. *joint covenant*.

transitive covenant. A covenant whose duty of performance passes from the original covenantor to the covenantor's representatives. Cf. *intransitive covenant*.

2. TREATY. **3.** A common-law action to recover damages for breach of contract under seal. **4.** A promise made in a deed or implied by law; esp., an obligation in a deed burdening or favoring a landowner.

> "A *covenant* is properly defined as a promise made in deed, although in practice the term is used rather more loosely to mean simply an obligation affecting a landowner whether created by deed or not." Peter Butt, *Land Law* 334–35 (2d ed. 1988).

> "In their nature, covenants are first cousins to easements appurtenant. The burdened land corresponds to a servient tenement, the benefitted land, to a dominant tenement. In concept, the main difference between easements and covenants is that, whereas an easement allows its holder to go upon and to do something upon the servient tenement, the beneficiary of a covenant may not enter the burdened land, but may require the owner of that land to do, or more likely not to do, something on that land." Roger A. Cunningham et al., *The Law of Property* § 8.13, at 467 (2d ed. 1993).

affirmative covenant. An agreement that real property will be used in a certain way. • An affirmative covenant is more than a restriction on the use of property. It requires the owner to undertake certain acts on the property.

covenant against encumbrances. A grantor's promise that the property has no visible or invisible encumbrances. • In a special warranty deed, the covenant is limited to encumbrances made by the grantor. — Also termed *general covenant against encumbrances*. Cf. *special covenant against encumbrances*.

covenant appurtenant (ə-**pər**-tə-nənt). A covenant that is connected with the grantor's land; a covenant running with the land. Cf. *covenant in gross*.

covenant for further assurances. A covenant to do whatever is reasonably necessary to perfect the title conveyed if it turns out to be imperfect. See *further assurance* under ASSURANCE.

covenant for possession. A covenant giving a grantee or lessee possession of land.

covenant for quiet enjoyment. **1.** A covenant insuring against the consequences of a defective title or any other disturbance of the title. **2.** A covenant ensuring that the tenant will not be evicted or disturbed by the grantor or a person having a lien or superior title. • This covenant is sometimes treated as being synonymous with *covenant of warranty*. — Also termed *covenant of quiet enjoyment*.

covenant for title. A covenant that binds the grantor to ensure the completeness, security, and continuance of the title transferred. • This covenant usu. includes the covenants for seisin, against encumbrances, for the right to convey, for quiet enjoyment, and of warranty.

covenant in gross. A covenant that does not run with the land. Cf. *covenant appurtenant*.

covenant of good right to convey. See *covenant of seisin*.

covenant of habitability (hab-ə-tə-**bil**-ə-tee). See *implied warranty of habitability* under WARRANTY (2).

covenant of nonclaim. A covenant barring a grantor or the grantor's heirs from claiming title in the conveyed land.

covenant of quiet enjoyment. See *covenant for quiet enjoyment*.

covenant of seisin (**see**-zin). A covenant, usu. appearing in a warranty deed, stating that the grantor has an estate, or the right to convey an estate, of the quality and size that the grantor purports to convey. • For the covenant to be valid, the grantor must have both title and possession at the time of the grant. — Also termed *covenant of good right to convey*; *right-to-convey covenant*.

covenant of warranty. A covenant by which the grantor agrees to defend the grantee against any lawful or reasonable claims of superior title by a third party and to indemnify the grantee for any loss sustained by the claim. • This covenant is sometimes treated as being synonymous with *covenant for quiet enjoyment*. See WARRANTY (1).

covenant running with the land. A covenant that, because it relates to the land, binds successor grantees indefinitely. • The land cannot be conveyed without the covenant. — Also termed *real covenant*.

"The important consequence of a covenant running with the land is that its burden or benefit will thereby be imposed or conferred upon a subsequent owner of the property who never actually agreed to it. Running covenants thereby achieve the transfer of duties and rights in a way not permitted by traditional contract law." Roger Bernhardt, *Real Property in a Nutshell* 212 (3d ed. 1993).

covenant running with the title. A covenant that is specific to the conveyance of title between a grantor and a grantee.

covenant to convey. A covenant in which the covenantor agrees to transfer an estate's title to the covenantee.

covenant to renew. An executory contract that gives a lessee the right to renew the lease.

covenant to stand seised (seezd). *Hist.* A covenant to convey land to a relative. • This covenant could not be used to convey land to a stranger; the only consideration that supports the covenant is the relationship by blood or marriage.

future covenant. A covenant that can be breached only upon interference with the possession of the grantee or the grantee's successors. • The covenants in this class are the covenant for further assurances, the covenant for quiet enjoyment, and the covenant of warranty. The distinction between future and present covenants becomes important in determining when the statute of limitations begins to run. Cf. *present covenant*.

general covenant against encumbrances. See *covenant against encumbrances*.

implied reciprocal covenant. A presumption that a promisee has, in return for a promise made respecting land, impliedly made a promise to the promisor respecting other land. — Also termed *implied reciprocal servitude*.

present covenant. A covenant that can be breached only at the time of conveyance. • The three covenants in this class are the covenant against encumbrances, the covenant of right to convey, and the covenant of seisin. Cf. *future covenant*.

real covenant. See *covenant running with the land*.

restrictive covenant. **1.** A private agreement, usu. in a deed or lease, that restricts the use or occupancy of real property, esp. by specifying lot sizes, building lines, architectural styles, and the uses to which the property may be put. — Also termed *restrictive covenant in equity*; *equitable easement*; *equitable servitude*. **2.** See *noncompetition covenant* under COVENANT (1).

right-to-convey covenant. See *covenant of seisin*.

special covenant against encumbrances. A grantor's promise that the property is free of encumbrances created by the grantor only, not the grantor's predecessors. See *special warranty deed* under WARRANTY DEED. Cf. *covenant against encumbrances*.

covenant, *vb.* To promise or undertake in a covenant; to agree formally.

covenant against encumbrances. See COVENANT (4).

covenant appurtenant. See COVENANT (4).

covenantee (kəv-ə-nən-**tee**). The person to whom a promise by covenant is made; one entitled to the benefit of a covenant.

covenant for further assurances. See COVENANT (4).

covenant for possession. See COVENANT (4).

covenant for quiet enjoyment. See COVENANT (4).

covenant for title. See COVENANT (4).

covenant in deed. See *express covenant* under COVENANT (1).

covenant in gross. See COVENANT (4).

covenant in law. See *implied covenant* under COVENANT (1).

covenant marriage. See MARRIAGE (1).

covenant not to compete. See *noncompetition covenant* under COVENANT (1).

covenant not to sue. See COVENANT (1).

covenant of good right to convey. See *covenant of seisin* under COVENANT (4).

covenant of habitability. See *implied warranty of habitability* under WARRANTY (2).

covenant of quiet enjoyment. See *covenant for quiet enjoyment* under COVENANT (4).

covenant of seisin. See COVENANT (4).

covenant of warranty. See COVENANT (4).

covenantor (**kəv**-ə-nən-tər *or* kəv-ə-nən-**tor**). The person who makes a promise by covenant; one subject to the burden of a covenant. — Also spelled *covenanter*.

covenant running with the land. See COVENANT (4).

covenant running with the title. See COVENANT (4).

covenant to convey. See COVENANT (4).

covenant to renew. See COVENANT (4).

covenant to stand seized. See COVENANT (4).

Coventry Act (**kəv**-ən-tree *or* **kov**-). An 1803 English statute establishing the death penalty for anyone who, with malice aforethought, did "cut out or disable the tongue, put out an eye, slit the nose, cut off a nose or lip, or cut off or disable any limb or member of any subject; with the intention in so doing to maim or disfigure him."

> "[At common law,] an injury such as cutting off [a man's] ear or nose did not constitute mayhem . . . , because it did not result in permanent disablement, but merely disfigured the victim. This was corrected by an early English statute. It seems that an assault was made upon Sir John Coventry on the street by persons who waylaid him and slit his nose in revenge for obnoxious words uttered by him in Parliament. This emphasized the weakness of the law of mayhem, and the so-called 'Coventry Act' was passed [in 1803]." Rollin M. Perkins & Ronald N. Boyce, *Criminal Law* 239–40 (3d ed. 1982).

coventurer (koh-**ven**-chər-ər). A person who undertakes a joint venture with one or more persons. — Also termed *co-adventurer*. Cf. JOINT VENTURE.

cover, *n.* The purchase on the open market, by the buyer in a breach-of-contract dispute, of goods to substitute for those promised but never delivered by the seller. • Under UCC § 2–712, the buyer can recover from the seller the difference between the cost of the substituted goods and the original contract price.

coverage, *n.* **1.** Inclusion of a risk under an insurance policy; the risks within the scope of an insurance policy. — **cover,** *vb.*

dependent coverage. An insurance provision for protection of an insured's dependents.

full coverage. Insurance protection that pays for the full amount of a loss with no deduction.

2. The ratio between corporate pretax income and corporate liability for bond interest payments.

coverage opinion. See OPINION (2).

coverage ratio. A measurement of a firm's ability to cover its financing charges.

cover-all clause. See MOTHER HUBBARD CLAUSE (2).

covered wages. See WAGE.

cover letter. See TRANSMITTAL LETTER.

cover note. A written statement by an insurance agent confirming that coverage is in effect. • The cover note is distinguished from a binder, which is prepared by the insurance company.

covert baron (**kəv**-ərt **bar**-ən). [Law French] *Hist.* The condition or status of a married woman at common law. — Also written *cover-baron*. — Also termed *covert de baron*.

> "By marriage, the husband and wife are one person in law: that is, the very being or legal existence of the woman is suspended during the marriage, or at least is incorporated and consolidated into that of the husband: under whose wing, protection, and *cover*, she performs every thing; and is therefore called in our law-french a *feme-covert*; is said to be *covert-baron*, or under the protection and influence of her husband, her *baron*, or lord; and her condition during her marriage is called her *coverture*." 1 William Blackstone, *Commentaries on the Laws of England* 430 (1765).

coverture (**kəv**-ər-chər *also* -tyoor), *n. Archaic.* The condition of being a married woman <under former law, a woman under coverture was allowed to sue only through the personality of her husband>. — **covert** (**kəv**-ərt), *adj.*

> "*Coverture*, is a french word signifying any thing that covereth, as apparell, a coverlet.... It is particularly applied in our common lawe, to the estate and condition of a maried woman, who by the lawes of our realme, is in (*potestate viri*) and therefore disabled to contract with any, to the preiudice of her selfe or her husband, without his consent and privity; or at the least, without his allowance and confirmation." John Cowell, *The Interpreter* (1607).

> "*Coverture* is by law applied to the state and condition of a married woman, who is *sub potestati viri*, (under the power of her husband) and therefore unable to contract with any to the damage of herself or husband, without his consent and privity, or his allowance and confirmation thereof. When a woman is married she is called a *Femme couvert*, and whatever is done concerning her during marriage is said to be done during coverture." *The Pocket Lawyer and Family Conveyancer* 96 (3d ed. 1833).

covin (**kəv**-ən). *Hist.* A secret conspiracy or agreement between two or more persons to injure or defraud another.

> "Covin is a secret assent determined in the hearts of two or more, to the prejudice of another: As if a tenant for term of life, or tenant in tail, will secretly conspire with another, that the other shall recover against the tenant for life the land which he holds, & c. in prejudice of him in the reversion." *Termes de la Ley* 129 (1st Am. ed. 1812).

covinous (**kəv**-ə-nəs), *adj. Hist.* Of a deceitful or fraudulent nature.

cozen (**kəz**-ən), *vb. Hist.* To cheat or defraud. — Also spelled *cosen*.

cozening (**kəz**-ən-ing). *Hist.* A deceitful practice; the offense of cheating, or fraudulent dealing. — Also spelled *cosening*. Cf. STELLIONATUS.

> "*Cosening* is an offence unnamed, whereby any thing is done guilefully in or out of contracts, which cannot be fitly termed by any speciall name. It is called *stellionatus* in the civile law...." John Cowell, *The Interpreter* (1607).

C.P. *abbr.* COURT OF COMMON PLEAS.

CPA. See *certified public accountant* under ACCOUNTANT.

CPI. *abbr.* CONSUMER PRICE INDEX.

C.R. *abbr.* CURIA REGIS.

cracking, *n.* A gerrymandering technique in which a geographically concentrated political or racial group that is large enough to constitute a district's dominant force is broken up by district lines and dispersed throughout two or more districts. Cf. PACKING; STACKING (2).

craft union. See UNION.

cramdown, *n.* Court confirmation of a Chapter 11 bankruptcy plan despite the opposition of certain creditors. • Under the Bankruptcy Code, a court may confirm a plan — even if it has not been accepted by all classes of creditors — if the plan (1) has been accepted by at least one impaired class, (2) does not discriminate unfairly, and (3) is fair and equitable. 11 USCA § 1129(b). — **cram down,** *vb.* See IMPAIRMENT.

crashworthiness doctrine. *Products liability.* The principle that the manufacturer of a product will be held strictly liable for injuries occurring in a collision, even if the collision results from an independent cause, to the extent that a defect in the product causes injuries above and beyond those that would have occurred in the collision itself. — Also termed *second-collision doctrine*; *second-impact doctrine*.

crastino (**kras**-tə-noh). [Law Latin] *Hist.* Tomorrow; on the morrow. • The return day of writs, so-called because the court terms always began on a saint's day; writs were therefore returnable the day after.

creancer (**kree**-ən-sər). [Law French] *Hist.* A creditor. — Also spelled *creansour*.

creativity. *Copyright.* The degree to which a work displays imaginativeness beyond what a person of very ordinary talents might create. Cf. ORIGINALITY.

> "Where creativity refers to the nature of the work itself, originality refers to the nature of the author's contribution to the work. Thus, a public domain painting may evince great creativity, but if a copyright claimant adds nothing of his own to it, by way of reproduction or otherwise, then copyright will be denied on the basis of lack of originality. Conversely, a work may be entirely the product of the claimant's independent efforts, and hence original, but may nevertheless be denied protection as a work of art if it is completely lacking in any modicum of creativity." 1 Melville B. Nimmer & David Nimmer, *Nimmer on Copyright* § 2.08[B][2], at 2–88 (Supp. 1995).

creator. See SETTLOR (1).

creature of statute. A doctrine, governmental agency, etc. that would not exist but for a legislative act that brought it into being.

credibility, *n.* The quality that makes something (as a witness or some evidence) worthy of belief. — **credible,** *adj.*

credible evidence. See EVIDENCE.

credible witness. See WITNESS.

credit, *n.* **1.** Belief; trust <the jury gave credit to Benson's version>. **2.** One's ability to borrow money; the faith in one's ability to pay debts <a customer with good credit>. **3.** The time that a seller gives the buyer to make the payment that is due <30 days' credit>. **4.** The availability of funds either from a financial institution or under a letter of credit <the bank extended a line of credit to the customer>.

bank credit. Credit that a bank makes available to a borrower.

consumer credit. Credit extended to an individual to facilitate the purchase of consumer goods and services.

installment credit. Consumer credit scheduled to be repaid in two or more payments, usu. at regular intervals. • The seller ordinarily exacts finance charges.

noninstallment credit. Consumer credit arranged to be repaid in a single payment. • Examples include doctors' and plumbers' bills.

revolving credit. A consumer-credit arrangement that allows the borrower to buy goods or secure loans on a continuing basis as long as the outstanding balance does not exceed a specified limit. — Also termed *open credit*; *revolving charge account.* Cf. *revolver loan* under LOAN.

5. LETTER OF CREDIT <the bank issued a credit in favor of the exporter>. **6.** A deduction from an amount due; an accounting entry reflecting an addition to revenue or net worth <confirm that the credit was properly applied to my account>. Cf. DEBIT. **7.** TAX CREDIT <the $500 credit reduced his income-tax liability by $500>.

accumulated-earnings credit. *Tax.* A deduction allowed in arriving at a corporation's accumulated taxable income. • It offsets the base on which the tax is assessed by reducing the taxable base by the greater of $250,000 or the accumulated earnings retained for the reasonable needs of the corporation, reduced by the net capital gain. IRC (26 USCA) § 535. See *accumulated-earnings tax* under TAX.

credit, *vb.* **1.** To believe <the jury did not credit his testimony>. **2.** To enter (as an amount) on the credit side of an account <her account was credited with $500>.

credit balance. *Accounting.* The status of an account when the sum of the credit entries exceeds the sum of the debit entries.

credit bureau. An organization that compiles information on people's creditworthiness and publishes it in the form of reports that are used chiefly by merchants and service-providers who deal directly with customers. • The practices of credit bureaus are regulated by federal (and often state) law. Most bureaus are members of the Associated Credit Bureaus of America. Cf. CREDIT-REPORTING BUREAU.

credit card. An identification card used to obtain items on credit, usu. on a revolving basis. See *revolving credit* under CREDIT. Cf. DEBIT CARD.

credit-card crime. The offense of using a credit card to purchase something with knowledge that (1) the card is stolen or forged, (2) the card has been revoked or canceled, or (3) the card's use is unauthorized.

credit freeze. See FREEZE.

credit insurance. See INSURANCE.

credit life insurance. See INSURANCE.

credit line. See LINE OF CREDIT.

credit memorandum. A document issued by a seller to a buyer confirming that the seller has credited (i.e., reduced) the buyer's account because of an error, return, or allowance.

credit mobilier. A company or association that carries on a banking business by making loans on the security of personal property.

creditor. 1. One to whom a debt is owed; one who gives credit for money or goods. — Also termed *debtee*. **2.** A person or entity with a definite claim against another, esp. a claim that is capable of adjustment and liquidation. **3.** *Bankruptcy*. A person or entity having a claim against the debtor predating the order for relief concerning the debtor. **4.** *Roman law*. One to whom any obligation is owed, whether contractual or otherwise. Cf. DEBTOR.

attaching creditor. A creditor who has caused an attachment to be issued and levied on the debtor's property.

bond creditor. A creditor whose debt is secured by a bond.

certificate creditor. A creditor of a municipal corporation who receives a certificate of indebtedness rather than payment because the municipality cannot pay the debt. Cf. *warrant creditor*.

conditional creditor. *Civil law*. A creditor who has either a future right of action or a right of action in expectancy.

creditor at large. A creditor who has not established the debt by reducing it to judgment, or who has not otherwise secured a lien on any of the debtor's property.

domestic creditor. A creditor who resides in the same state or country as the debtor or the debtor's property.

double creditor. A creditor who has a lien on two funds. Cf. *single creditor*.

execution creditor. A judgment creditor who has caused an execution to issue on the judgment.

foreign creditor. A creditor who resides in a different state or country from that of the debtor or the debtor's property.

gap creditor. *Bankruptcy*. A creditor who extends credit to, lends money to, or has a claim arise against the debtor in the period between the filing of an involuntary bankruptcy petition and the entry of the order for relief. • Under the Bankruptcy Code, a gap creditor's claim receives second priority, immediately below administrative claims. 11 USCA §§ 502(f), 507(a)(2).

general creditor. See *unsecured creditor*.

hypothetical creditor. *Bankruptcy*. An actual or code-created judicial-lien creditor or bona fide purchaser who establishes a bankruptcy trustee's status under the Bankruptcy Code's priority scheme, claiming property through the debtor at the time of the bankruptcy filing. 11 USCA § 544. — Also termed *hypothetical lien creditor*.

joint creditor. A creditor who is entitled, along with another creditor, to demand payment from a debtor.

judgment creditor. See JUDGMENT CREDITOR.

junior creditor. A creditor whose claim accrued after that of another creditor; a creditor who holds a debt that is subordinate to another's.

known creditor. A creditor whose identity or claim is either known or reasonably ascertainable by the debtor. • Known creditors are entitled to notice of the debtor's bankruptcy or corporate dissolution, as well as notice of any deadline for filing proofs of claim.

lien creditor. A creditor whose claim is secured by a lien on the debtor's property. UCC § 9–301(3).

preferred creditor. A creditor with a superior right to payment, such as a holder of a perfected security interest as compared to a holder of an unsecured claim. UCC § 9–301(1).

principal creditor. A creditor whose claim or demand greatly exceeds the claims of other creditors.

prior creditor. A creditor who is given priority in payment from the debtor's assets.

secondary creditor. A creditor whose claim is subordinate to a preferred creditor's.

secured creditor. A creditor who has the right, on the debtor's default, to proceed against collateral and apply it to the payment of the debt. — Also termed *secured party.*

"'Secured party' means (A) a person in whose favor a security interest is created or provided for under a security agreement, whether or not any obligation to be secured is outstanding; (B) a person that holds an agricultural lien; (C) a consignor; (D) a person to which accounts, chattel paper, payment intangibles, or promissory notes have been sold; or (E) if a security interest or agricultural lien is created or provided for in favor of a trustee, agent, collateral agent, or other representative, that representative." UCC § 9-102(a)(50).

single creditor. In the marshaling of assets, a creditor with a lien on one fund. Cf. *double creditor.*

subsequent creditor. A creditor whose claim comes into existence after a given fact or transaction, such as the recording of a deed or the execution of a voluntary conveyance.

unsecured creditor. A creditor who, upon giving credit, takes no rights against specific property of the debtor. — Also termed *general creditor.*

warrant creditor. A creditor of a municipal corporation who is given a municipal warrant for the amount of the claim because the municipality lacks the funds to pay the debt. Cf. *certificate creditor.*

creditor at large. See CREDITOR.

creditor beneficiary. See BENEFICIARY.

creditor's bill. An equitable suit in which a judgment creditor seeks to reach property that cannot be reached by the process available to enforce a judgment. — Also termed *creditor's suit.*

creditor's claim. See CLAIM (5).

creditors' committee. *Bankruptcy.* A committee comprising representatives of the creditors in a Chapter 11 proceeding, formed to negotiate the debtor's plan of reorganization. • Generally, a committee has no fewer than 3 and no more than 11 members and serves as an advisory body. 11 USCA § 1102.

creditors' composition. See COMPOSITION.

creditors' meeting. See MEETING.

creditor's suit. See CREDITOR'S BILL.

credit rating. An evaluation of a potential borrower's ability to repay debt, prepared by a credit bureau at the request of a lender.

credit report. 1. A credit bureau's report on a person's financial status, usu. including the approximate amounts and locations of a person's bank accounts, charge accounts, loans, and other debts, bill-paying habits, defaults, bankruptcies, foreclosures, marital status, occupation, income, and lawsuits. See CREDIT BUREAU. **2.** The report of a credit-reporting bureau, usu. including highly personal information gathered through interviews with a person's friends, neighbors, and coworkers. See CREDIT-REPORTING BUREAU.

credit-reporting bureau. An organization that, on request, prepares investigative reports not just on people's creditworthiness but also on personal information gathered from various sources, including interviews with neighbors, friends, and coworkers. • These reports are used chiefly by employers (for prospective employees), insurance companies (for applicants), and landlords (for prospective tenants). — Also termed *investigating bureau.* Cf. CREDIT BUREAU.

creditrix (**kred**-ə-triks), *n.* [fr. Latin *credere* "to lend, entrust"] *Archaic. Civil law.* A female creditor.

credit sale. See SALE.

credit service charge. See SERVICE CHARGE.

credit-shelter trust. See *bypass trust* under TRUST.

credit slip. A document that allows a store customer to either purchase another item or receive cash or credit for merchandise the customer has returned to the store.

credit union. A cooperative association that offers low-interest loans and other consumer banking services to persons sharing a common bond — often fellow employees and their family members. • Most credit unions are regulated by the National Credit Union Administration. State-chartered credit unions are also subject to regulation by the chartering state, and they may be regulated by state banking boards.

"Credit unions were the last major thrift institutions developed in the United States .... What distinguished credit unions from mutual savings banks and savings and loan associations was their emphasis on a common bond of workers, church members, or people in a local area, wanting to borrow relatively small amounts at reasonable interest rates from each other, and help each other save to meet these short-term needs. Their goal was to provide a low interest rate alternative (6–9 percent and preferably the lower) to loan sharks and pawnbrokers." William A. Lovett, *Banking and Financial Institutions Law in a Nutshell* 284 (1997).

creditworthy, *adj.* (Of a borrower) financially sound enough that a lender will extend credit in the belief that the chances of default are slight; fiscally healthy. — **creditworthiness,** *n.*

creeping tender offer. See TENDER OFFER.

C reorganization. See REORGANIZATION (2).

cretion (**kree**-shən). [fr. Latin *cernere* "to decide"] *Roman law.* **1.** A method or form of accepting an inheritance by an heir who is appointed in a testament. • *Cretion* usu. had to be declared within 100 days from the date an heir received notice of the appointment. *Cretion* was formally abolished in A.D. 407.

"In the old law it was the practice to fix a time limit, usually of one hundred days, within which the heir was to make a formal acceptance, with the addition that if he failed to do so, he was to be disinherited and a substitute was to take the inheritance in his place. This formal acceptance was known as cretio from the Latin verb cernere=to decide. The practice had fallen into disuse before Justinian, who formally abolished it." R.W. Lee, *The Elements of Roman Law* 199 (4th ed. 1956).

2. The period within which an heir might decide whether to accept an inheritance. — Also termed *cretio* (**kree**-shee-oh). — **cretionary** (**kree**-shən-er-ee), *adj.*

CRF. *abbr.* CRIMINAL-REFERRAL FORM.

crier (**krɪ**-ər). **1.** An officer of the court who makes public pronouncements as required by the court. See BAILIFF. **2.** An auctioneer. — Also spelled *cryer.*

criez la peez (**krɪ**-eez lə **pees**). [Law French] *Hist.* Rehearse the concord (or peace). • This phrase was used to confirm the conveyance of land by fine. The serjeant or countor in attendance read the phrase aloud in court. See FINE (1).

crim. con. *abbr.* CRIMINAL CONVERSATION.

crime. A social harm that the law makes punishable; the breach of a legal duty treated as the subject-matter of a criminal proceeding. — Also termed *criminal wrong.* See OFFENSE.

"Understanding that the conception of *Crime*, as distinguished from that of *Wrong* or *Tort* and from that of *Sin*, involves the idea of injury to the State of collective community, we first find that the commonwealth, in literal conformity with the conception, itself interposed directly, and by isolated acts, to avenge itself on the author of the evil which it had suffered." Henry S. Maine, *Ancient Law* 320 (17th ed. 1901).

"It is a curious fact that all the minor acts enumerated in the penal code of a state like, say, New York are in law called crimes, which term includes both murder and overparking. It is a strong term to use for the latter, and of course the law has for centuries recognized that there are more serious and less serious crimes. At the common law, however, only two classes were recognized, serious crimes or felonies, and minor crimes or misdemeanors." Max Radin, *The Law and You* 91 (1948).

administrative crime. An offense consisting of a violation of an administrative rule or regulation that carries with it a criminal sanction.

capital crime. See *capital offense* under OFFENSE.

common-law crime. A crime that is punishable under the common law, rather than by force of statute. Cf. *statutory crime.*

computer crime. A crime requiring knowledge of computer technology, such as sabotaging or stealing computer data or using a computer to commit some other crime.

consensual crime. See *victimless crime.*

corporate crime. A crime committed either by a corporate body or by its representatives acting on its behalf. • Examples include price-fixing and consumer fraud.

crime against nature. See SODOMY.

crime malum in se. See MALUM IN SE.

crime malum prohibitum. See MALUM PROHIBITUM.

crime of omission. An offense that carries as its material component the failure to act.

crime of passion. A crime committed in the heat of an emotionally charged moment, with no opportunity to reflect on what is happening. See HEAT OF PASSION.

crime of violence. See *violent crime.*

crime without victims. See *victimless crime.*

federal crime. See FEDERAL CRIME.

hate crime. A crime motivated by the victim's race, color, ethnicity, religion, or national origin. • Certain groups have lobbied to expand the definition by statute to include a crime motivated by the victim's disability, gender, or sexual orientation. Cf. *hate speech* under SPEECH.

high crime. A crime that is offensive to public morality, though not necessarily a felony. • Under the U.S. Constitution, a civil officer's committing of a "high crime" is, along with treason and bribery, grounds for removal from office. U.S. Const. art. II, § 4. See IMPEACHABLE OFFENSE.

index crime. See *index offense* under OFFENSE.

infamous crime (**in**-fə-məs). **1.** At common law, a crime for which part of the punishment was infamy, so that one who committed it would be declared ineligible to serve on a jury, hold public office, or testify. • Examples are perjury, treason, and fraud. **2.** A crime punishable by imprisonment in a penitentiary. • The Fifth Amendment requires a grand-jury indictment for the prosecution of infamous (or capital) crimes, which include all federal felony offenses. See *indictable offense* under OFFENSE.

instantaneous crime. A crime that is fully completed by a single act, as arson or murder, rather than a series of acts. • The statute of limitations for an instantaneous crime begins to run with its completion.

noninfamous crime. A crime that does not qualify as an infamous crime. Cf. *infamous crime.*

organized crime. See ORGANIZED CRIME.

political crime. A crime (such as treason) directed against the government.

quasi-crime. **1.** An offense not subject to criminal prosecution (such as contempt or violation of a municipal ordinance) but for which penalties or forfeitures can be imposed. • The term includes offenses that give rise to *qui tam* actions and forfeitures for the violation of a public duty. **2.** An offense for which someone other than the actual perpetrator is held liable, the perpetrator being presumed to act on the command of the responsible party. See *quasi-delict* (1) under DELICT.

signature crime. A distinctive crime so similar in pattern, scheme, or modus operandi to previous crimes that it identifies a particular defendant as the perpetrator.

status crime. A type of crime of which a person is guilty by being in a certain condition or of a specific character, such as vagrancy. — Also termed *status offense.*

statutory crime. A crime punishable by statute. Cf. *common-law crime.*

street crime. Crime generally directed against a person in public, such as mugging, theft, or robbery.

strict-liability crime. A crime that does not require a *mens rea* element, such as speeding or attempting to carry a weapon aboard an aircraft.

vice crime. A crime of immoral conduct, such as gambling or prostitution.

victimless crime. A crime that is considered to have no direct victim, usu. because only consenting adults are involved. • Examples are possession of drugs and deviant sexual intercourse between consenting adults. — Also termed *consensual crime*; *crime without victims.*

> "When a man's house has been robbed or his brother murdered, he is likely to take this complaint vigorously to the police and demand action. His presence on the scene dramatizes the need for law enforcement and gives sense and purpose to the work of the police and district attorney. In contrast, the absence of a prosecuting witness surrounds 'crimes without victims' with an entirely different atmosphere. Here it is the police who must assume the initiative. If they attempt to work without the aid of informers, they must resort to spying, and this spying is rendered all the more distasteful because what is spied upon is sordid and pitiable." Lon L. Fuller, *Anatomy of the Law* 44 (1968).

violent crime. A crime that has as an element the use, attempted use, threatened use, or substantial risk of use of physical force against the person or property of another. 18 USCA § 16. — Also termed *crime of violence.*

white-collar crime. See WHITE-COLLAR CRIME.

crime against humanity. *Int'l law.* A brutal crime that is not an isolated incident but that involves large and systematic actions, often cloaked with official authority, and that shocks the conscience of humankind. • Among the specific crimes that fall within this category are mass murder, extermination, enslavement, deportation, and other inhumane acts perpetrated against a population, whether in wartime or not.

crime against international law. See CRIME AGAINST THE LAW OF NATIONS.

crime against nature. See SODOMY.

crime against peace. *Int'l law.* An international crime in which the offenders plan, prepare, initiate, or wage a war of aggression or a war in violation of international peace treaties, agreements, or assurances.

crime against the law of nations. *Int'l law.* **1.** A crime punishable under internationally prescribed criminal law or defined by an international convention and required to be made punishable under the criminal law of the member states. **2.** A crime, such as piracy or a war crime, punishable under international criminal law. **3.** A crime punishable under international law; an act that is internationally agreed to be of a criminal nature, such as genocide, piracy, or engaging in the slave trade. — Also termed *crime against international law.*

crime against the person. See CRIMES AGAINST PERSONS.

crime-fraud exception. The doctrine that neither the attorney-client privilege nor the attorney-work-product privilege protects attorney-client communications that are in furtherance of a current or planned crime or fraud. *Clark v. United States*, 289 U.S. 1, 53 S.Ct. 465 (1933); *In re Grand Jury Subpoena Duces Tecum*, 731 F.2d 1032 (2d Cir. 1984).

crime insurance. See INSURANCE.

crime malum in se. See MALUM IN SE.

crime malum prohibitum. See MALUM PROHIBITUM.

crimen (**krɪ**-mən), *n.* [Latin] **1.** An accusation or charge of a crime. **2.** A crime. Pl. ***crimina*** (**krim**-ə-nə).

crimen falsi (**krɪ**-mən **fal**-sɪ *or* **fawl**-sɪ). [Latin "the crime of falsifying"] **1.** A crime in the nature of perjury. **2.** Any other offense that involves some element of dishonesty or false statement. See Fed. R. Evid. 609(a)(2).

> "The starting point [for perjury] seems to have been the so-called *crimen falsi*, — crime of falsifying. In the beginning, perhaps, one convicted of perjury was deemed too untrustworthy to be permitted to testify in any other case, and the idea grew until the term '*crimen falsi*' included any crime involving an element of deceit, fraud or corruption." Rollin M. Perkins & Ronald N. Boyce, *Criminal Law* 26 (3d ed. 1982).

crimen furti (**krɪ**-mən **fər**-tɪ). [Latin "the crime of stealing"] See THEFT.

crimen incendii (**krɪ**-mən in-**sen**-dee-ɪ). [Latin "the crime of burning"] See ARSON.

crimen innominatum (**krɪ**-mən i-nom-ə-**nay**-təm). [Latin "the nameless crime"] See SODOMY.

crimen majestatis (**krɪ**-mən maj-ə-**stay**-tis). [Latin "crime against majesty"] *Hist.* High treason; any crime against the king's person or dignity; LESE MAJESTY. • Under Roman law, *crimen majestatis* denoted any enterprise by a Roman citizen or other person against the emperor or the republic. — Also spelled *crimen maiestatis.* — Also termed *crimen laesae majestatis.* Cf. PERDUELLIO.

crimen raptus (**krɪ**-mən **rap**-təs). [Latin "the crime of rape"] See RAPE.

crimen repetundarum (**krɪ**-mən rep-ə-tən-**dair**-əm). [Latin] *Roman law.* The crime of bribery or extortion.

crimen roberiae (**krɪ**-mən rə-**beer**-ee-ee). [Latin "the crime of robbery"] ROBBERY.

crime of omission. See CRIME.

crime of passion. See CRIME.

crime of violence. See *violent crime* under CRIME.

crimes against persons. A category of criminal offenses in which the perpetrator uses or threatens to use force. • Examples include murder, rape, aggravated assault, and robbery. — Also termed *crimes against the person.* Cf. *offense against the person* under OFFENSE.

crimes against property. A category of criminal offenses in which the perpetrator seeks to derive an unlawful benefit from — or do damage to — another's property without the use or threat of force. • Examples include burglary, theft, and arson (even though arson may result in injury or death). — Also termed *property crimes.* Cf. *offense against property* under OFFENSE.

crimes against the person. See CRIMES AGAINST PERSONS.

crime statistics. Figures compiled by a governmental agency to show the incidence of various types of crime within a defined geographic area during a specified time.

crime without victims. See *victimless crime* under CRIME.

crimina extraordinaria (**krim**-ə-nə ek-stror-də-**nair**-ee-ə). [Latin] *Roman law.* Extraordinary crimes.

criminal, *adj.* **1.** Having the character of a crime; in the nature of a crime <criminal mischief>. **2.** Connected with the administration of penal justice <the criminal courts>.

criminal, *n.* **1.** One who has committed a criminal offense. **2.** One who has been convicted of a crime.

dangerous criminal. A criminal who has either committed a violent crime or used force in trying to escape from custody.

state criminal. **1.** A person who has committed a crime against the state (such as treason); a political criminal. **2.** A person who has committed a crime under state law.

criminal action. See ACTION.

criminal anarchy. The doctrine that advocates the violent overthrow of government. • To promote this doctrine is a criminal offense. 18 USCA § 2385.

criminal anthropology. See CRIMINOLOGY.

criminal assault. See ASSAULT.

criminal attempt. See ATTEMPT.

criminal battery. See BATTERY.

criminal behavior. Conduct that causes social harm and is defined and punished by law.

criminal capacity. See CAPACITY (3).

criminal charge. See CHARGE (1).

criminal code. A code, usu. enacted by a legislature, setting out the elements of crimes and specifying punishments for their commission.

criminal coercion. See COERCION.

criminal conspiracy. See CONSPIRACY.

criminal contempt. See CONTEMPT.

criminal conversation. *Hist.* A tort action for adultery, brought by a husband against a third party who engaged in sexual intercourse with his wife. — Abbr. crim. con.

> "An action (whether of trespass or case is uncertain, but probably trespass) formerly lay against one who had committed adultery with the wife of the plaintiff. It was known as an action for criminal conversation. The wife's consent was irrelevant. The action was distinct from that of enticement: one may commit adultery without enticing a wife away from her husband. The action was no doubt a necessity when divorce could only be obtained by Act of Parliament: as Parliament was not a tribunal suitable for trying allegations of adultery it was reasonable to require the petitioner to establish the truth of his allegations before a court of law. The action might also have been justified on the ground that the plaintiff is in substance complaining of the invasion of privacy of his marriage, and the insult thereby caused to his honour as a husband." R.F.V. Heuston, *Salmond on the Law of Torts* 358 (17th ed. 1977).

criminal damage to property. 1. Injury, destruction, or substantial impairment to the use of property (other than by fire or explosion) without the consent of a person having an interest in the property. **2.** Injury, destruction, or substantial impairment to the use of property (other than by fire or explosion) with the intent to injure or defraud an insurer or lienholder. Cf. ARSON.

criminal defendant. The accused in a criminal proceeding.

criminal desertion. See DESERTION.

criminal forfeiture. See FORFEITURE.

criminal fraud. See FRAUD.

criminal homicide. See HOMICIDE.

criminal infringement. See INFRINGEMENT.

criminal-instrumentality rule. The principle that when a criminal act is committed, that act — rather than the victim's negligence that made the crime possible — will be considered to be the crime's proximate cause.

criminal intent. 1. MENS REA. **2.** An intent to commit an actus reus without any justification, excuse, or other defense.

> "The phrase 'criminal intent' is one that has been bandied about with various meanings not carefully distinguished. At times it has been used in the sense of the 'intent to do wrong' (the *outline* of the mental pattern which is necessary for crime in general), — as, for example, in the phrase 'the mental element commonly called criminal intent.' At times it has been used in the sense of mens rea as the mental element requisite for guilt of the very offense charged, 'a varying state of mind which is the contrary of an innocent state of mind, whatever may be pointed out by the nature of the crime

as an innocent state of mind.' Often it is used to include criminal negligence as well as an actual intent to do the harmful deed, although at other times such negligence is referred to as a substitute, so to speak, for criminal intent in connection with certain offenses. Occasionally it is found in the sense of an intent to violate the law, — implying a knowledge of the law violated. On the other hand, as such knowledge is a factor not ordinarily required for conviction it has been pointed out that to establish ignorance of the law does not disprove criminal intent. Thus it has been said (assuming the absence of any circumstance of exculpation) 'whenever an act is criminal, the party doing the act is chargeable with criminal intent.' . . . This suggests a helpful guide for the use of the phrase 'criminal intent.' Some other term such as mens rea or guilty mind should be employed for more general purposes, and 'criminal intent' be restricted to those situations in which there is (1) an intent to do the *actus reus*, and (2) no circumstance of exculpation." Rollin M. Perkins & Ronald N. Boyce, *Criminal Law* 832–34 (3d ed. 1982).

criminalism. 1. A pathological tendency toward criminality. **2.** *Archaic.* The branch of psychiatry dealing with habitual criminals.

criminalist (**krim**-ə-nəl-ist). **1.** A person who practices criminalistics as a profession. **2.** *Archaic.* One versed in criminal law. **3.** *Archaic.* A psychiatrist who treats criminals. **4.** *Archaic.* A habitual criminal.

criminalistics (krim-ə-nə-**lis**-tiks), *n.* The science of crime detection, usu. involving the subjection of physical evidence to laboratory analysis, including ballistic testing, blood-fluid and tissue analysis, and other tests that are helpful in determining what happened. Cf. CRIMINOLOGY.

criminaliter (krim-ə-**nay**-lə-tər), *adv.* [Latin] Criminally. Cf. CIVILITER.

criminality (krim-ə-**nal**-ə-tee). **1.** The state or quality of being criminal. **2.** An act or practice that constitutes a crime.

criminalization (**krim**-ə-nəl-ə-**zay**-shən), *n.* **1.** The act or an instance of making a previously lawful act criminal, usu. by passing a statute. Cf. DECRIMINALIZATION; CIVILIZATION. **2.** The process by which a person develops into a criminal.

criminalize (**krim**-ə-nəl-IZ), *vb.* To make illegal; to outlaw.

criminal jurisdiction. See JURISDICTION.

criminal justice. 1. The methods by which a society deals with those who are accused of having committed crimes. See LAW ENFORCEMENT (1). **2.** The field of study pursued by those seeking to enter law enforcement as a profession. ● Many colleges offer degrees in criminal justice, typically after two to four years of study. — Also termed (in sense 2) *police science*; *law enforcement.*

criminal-justice system. The collective institutions through which an accused offender passes until the accusations have been disposed of or the assessed punishment concluded. ● The system typically has three components: law enforcement (police, sheriffs, marshals), the judicial process (judges, prosecutors, defense lawyers), and corrections (prison officials, probation officers, parole officers). — Also termed *law-enforcement system.*

criminal law. The body of law defining offenses against the community at large, regulating how suspects are investigated, charged, and tried, and establishing punishments for convicted offenders.

"The criminal law represents the pathology of civilization." Morris R. Cohen, *Reason and Law* 70 (1961).

"Often the term 'criminal law' is used to include all that is involved in 'the administration of criminal justice' in the broadest sense. As so employed it embraces three different fields, known to the lawyer as (1) the substantive criminal law, (2) criminal procedure, and (3) special problems in the administration and enforcement of criminal justice. . . . The phrase 'criminal law' is more commonly used to include only that part of the general field known as the substantive criminal law. . . ." Rollin M. Perkins & Ronald N. Boyce, *Criminal Law* 1, 5 (3d ed. 1982).

criminal lawyer. See LAWYER.

criminal libel. See LIBEL.

criminally negligent homicide. See *negligent homicide* under HOMICIDE.

criminal mischief. See MALICIOUS MISCHIEF.

criminal negligence. See NEGLIGENCE.

criminal policy. The branch of criminal science concerned with limiting harmful conduct in society. ● It draws on information provided by criminology, and its subjects for investigation are (1) the appropriate measures of social organization for preventing harmful activities, and (2) the treatment to be accorded to those who have caused harm, whether the offenders are to be given warnings, supervised probation, medical treatment, or more serious deprivations of life or liberty, such as imprisonment or capital punishment.

criminal procedure. The rules governing the mechanisms under which crimes are investigated, prosecuted, adjudicated, and punished. • It includes the protection of accused persons' constitutional rights.

criminal proceeding. See PROCEEDING.

criminal process. See PROCESS.

criminal prosecution. See PROSECUTION (2).

criminal protector. An accessory after the fact to a felony; one who aids or harbors a wrongdoer after the commission of a crime.

criminal-referral form. A form once required (from 1988 to 1996) for reporting every instance when a bank employee or affiliate committed or aided in committing a crime such as credit-card fraud, employee theft, or check-kiting. • This form, like the suspicious-transaction report, has since been superseded by the suspicious-activity report. — Abbr. CRF.

criminal registration. See REGISTRATION (1).

criminal responsibility. See RESPONSIBILITY (1), (2).

criminal sanction. See SANCTION.

criminal science. The study of crime with a view to discovering the causes of criminality, devising the most effective methods of reducing crime, and perfecting the means for dealing with those who have committed crimes. • The three main branches of criminal science are criminology, criminal policy, and criminal law.

criminal solicitation. See SOLICITATION.

criminal statute. See STATUTE.

criminal syndicalism. See SYNDICALISM.

criminal trespass. See TRESPASS.

criminal wrong. See CRIME.

criminate, *vb.* INCRIMINATE.

crimination (krim-ə-**nay**-shən), *n.* **1.** INCRIMINATION. **2.** An accusation or strong censure.

criminative (**krim**-ə-nay-tiv), *adj.* Of, relating to or involving incrimination or accusation. Cf. INFIRMATIVE.

criminogenic, *adj.* Tending to cause crime or criminality. — **criminogenesis,** *n.*

criminology, *n.* The study of crime and criminal punishment as social phenomena; the study of the causes of crime, comprising (1) criminal biology, which examines causes that may be found in the mental and physical constitution of an offender (such as hereditary tendencies and physical defects), and (2) criminal sociology, which deals with inquiries into the effects of environment as a cause of criminality. — Also termed *criminal anthropology.* — **criminological,** *adj.* — **criminologist,** *n.* Cf. CRIMINALISTICS.

crimping. *Hist.* The offense of decoying and confining persons to force them into military service. Cf. IMPRESSMENT (3).

crit. An adherent to the critical-legal-studies school of thought. — Also termed *CLSer*; *Critic*; *critter.*

fem-crit. A feminist adherent of critical legal studies.

critical evidence. See EVIDENCE.

Critical Legal Studies. 1. A school of thought advancing the idea that the legal system's manipulative nature masks its true function, which, according to the predominant Marxist wing of this school, is to perpetuate the socioeconomic status quo. **2.** The body of work produced by adherents to this school of thought. — Abbr. CLS.

critical limitation. *Patents.* A limitation essential either to the operativeness of an invention or to the patentability of a patent claim for the invention.

Critical Race Theory. 1. A reform movement within the legal profession, particularly within academia, whose adherents believe that the legal system has disempowered racial minorities. • The term first appeared in 1989. Critical race theorists observe that even if the law is couched in neutral language, it cannot be neutral because those who fashioned it had their own subjective perspectives that, once enshrined in law, have disadvantaged minorities and even perpetuated racism. **2.** The body of work produced by adherents to this theory. — Abbr. CRT.

critical stage. **1.** The point in a criminal prosecution when the accused's rights may be prejudiced by the absence of legal representation. • A defendant is entitled to counsel at critical stages, such as trial or a preliminary hearing, when the defendant's rights could be prejudiced. **2.** The point in a criminal prosecution when jeopardy attaches, when the jury is empaneled, or when a witness is sworn.

critter. See CRIT.

crop insurance. See INSURANCE.

crops. Products that are grown, raised, and harvested. • Crops usu. are from the soil, but fruit grown on trees are also considered crops.

basic crops. Crops (such as wheat and corn) that are usu. subject to government-price supports.

growing crops. Crops that are in the process of growth. • Judicial decisions vary on the growth stage at which a crop becomes a growing crop and on whether pasturage grass is a growing crop. Growing crops are goods under UCC § 2–105(1). Cf. FARM PRODUCT.

cross, *n.* **1.** CROSS-EXAMINATION. **2.** A sale of a large amount of stock privately traded between two parties. • Although the transaction does not happen on the exchange floor, it typically requires exchange permission.

cross-action. See CROSS-CLAIM.

cross-appeal. See APPEAL.

cross-bill. See BILL (2).

cross-claim, *n.* A claim asserted between codefendants or coplaintiffs in a case and that relates to the subject of the original claim or counterclaim. — Also termed *cross-action.* — **cross-claim,** *vb.* — **cross-claimant,** *n.* Cf. COUNTERCLAIM.

> "The courts have not always distinguished clearly between a cross-claim and a counterclaim, and have used one name where the other is proper under the rules, perhaps because in some states, and in the old equity practice, the term cross-complaint or cross-bill is used for what the rules regard as a counterclaim. Under Rule 13 a counterclaim is a claim against an opposing party, while a cross-claim is against a co-party. Further there is not the same freedom in asserting cross-claims that the rules provide for counterclaims. An unrelated claim against an opposing party may be asserted as a permissive counterclaim, but only claims related to the subject matter of the original action, or property involved therein, are appropriate as cross-claims." Charles Alan Wright, *The Law of Federal Courts* § 80, at 574 (5th ed. 1994).

cross-collateral. See COLLATERAL.

cross-collateral clause. An installment-contract provision allowing the seller, if the buyer defaults, to repossess not only the particular item sold but also every other item bought from the seller on which a balance remained due when the last purchase was made. — Also termed *dragnet clause.*

cross-complaint. **1.** A claim asserted by a defendant against another party to the action. **2.** A claim asserted by a defendant against a person not a party to the action for a matter relating to the subject of the action.

cross-default. A provision under which default on one debt obligation triggers default on another obligation.

cross-demand. See DEMAND (3).

cross-elasticity of demand. *Antitrust.* A relationship between two products, usu. substitutes for each other, in which a price change for one product affects the price of the other.

cross-error. See ERROR (2).

cross-examination, *n.* The questioning of a witness at a trial or hearing by the party opposed to the party who called the witness to testify. • The purpose of cross-examination is to discredit a witness before the fact-finder in any of several ways, as by bringing out contradictions and improbabilities in earlier testimony, by suggesting doubts to the witness, and by trapping the witness into admissions that weaken the testimony. The cross-examiner is typically allowed to ask leading questions but is traditionally limited to matters covered on direct examination and to credibility issues. — Also termed *cross-interrogation.* — **cross-examine,** *vb.* Cf. DIRECT EXAMINATION; RECROSS-EXAMINATION.

cross-interrogatory. See INTERROGATORY.

cross-licensing. *Patents.* The act, by two or more license holders, of exchanging licenses so that each may use or benefit from the other's patent.

cross-marriage. See MARRIAGE (1).

cross-offer, *n. Contracts.* An offer made to another in ignorance that the offeree has made the same offer to the offeror. — **cross-offer,** *vb.* — **cross-offeror,** *n.*

cross-purchase buy-sell agreement. 1. BUY-SELL AGREEMENT (1). **2.** A partnership insurance plan in which each partner individually buys and maintains enough insurance on the life or lives of other partners to purchase a deceased or expelled partner's equity.

cross-question. See QUESTION (1).

cross-rate. The exchange rate between two currencies expressed as the ratio of two foreign exchange rates in terms of a common third currency (usu. the U.S. dollar). • Foreign-exchange-rate dealers use cross-rate tables to look for arbitrage opportunities. See ARBITRAGE.

cross-remainder. See REMAINDER.

Crown. See KING.

Crown case. *English law.* A criminal action.

Crown Court. An English court having jurisdiction over major criminal cases. • Crown Courts date from 1971, when they assumed the criminal jurisdiction of the Assize Courts and all the jurisdiction of the Courts of Quarter Sessions.

crown jewel. A company's most valuable asset, esp. as valued when the company is the subject of a hostile takeover. • A common antitakeover device is for the target company to sell its crown jewel to a third party so that the company will be less attractive to an unfriendly suitor. See SCORCHED-EARTH DEFENSE.

Crown land. See LAND.

Crown loan. See LOAN.

CRT. *abbr.* CRITICAL RACE THEORY.

cruel and inhumane treatment. A ground for divorce consisting in unjustifiably abusive conduct by one spouse toward the other.

cruel and unusual punishment. See PUNISHMENT.

cruelty. The intentional and malicious infliction of mental or physical suffering on a living creature, esp. a human; abusive treatment; outrage.

cruelty to animals. A malicious or criminally negligent act that causes an animal to suffer pain or death.

extreme cruelty. As a ground for divorce, one spouse's physical violence toward the other spouse, or conduct that destroys or severely impairs the other spouse's mental health.

legal cruelty. Cruelty that will justify granting a divorce to the injured party; specif., conduct by one spouse that endangers the life, person, or health of the other spouse, or creates a reasonable apprehension of bodily or mental harm.

mental cruelty. As a ground for divorce, one spouse's course of conduct that creates such anguish that it endangers the life, physical health, or mental health of the other spouse. See EMOTIONAL DISTRESS.

physical cruelty. As a ground for divorce, actual personal violence committed by one spouse against the other.

cruelty to a child. See *child abuse* under ABUSE.

cruelty to children. See *child abuse* under ABUSE.

cry de pais (krI də **pay**). [Law French] *Hist.* The cry of the country. • The hue and cry after an offender, as raised by the country (i.e., the people). — Also spelled *cri de pais.* See HUE AND CRY (1).

cryer. See CRIER.

CSV. See *cash surrender value* under VALUE.

c.t.a. See *administration cum testamento annexo* under ADMINISTRATION.

cucking stool. See CASTIGATORY.

cui ante divortium (kI [*or* kwI *or* kwee] **an**-tee də-**vor**-shee-əm). [Law Latin "to whom before divorce"] *Hist.* A writ of entry enabling a divorced woman to recover land that she had held in fee but that her husband had sold without her permission during the marriage. • The name of this writ derives from the words within it: *cui ipsa ante divortium inter eos celebratum, contradicere non potuit* ("whom she, before the divorce between them, could not gainsay"). The writ was abolished in 1833. — Also termed *sur cui ante divortium*.

cui in vita (kI [*or* kwI *or* kwee] in **vI**-tə). [Law Latin "to whom in the life"] *Hist.* A writ of entry enabling a woman to recover land that she had held in fee but that her deceased husband had sold without her permission. ● It is so called from the words of the writ: *cui ipsa in vita sua contradicere non potuit* ("whom she, in his lifetime, could not gainsay"). — Also termed *sur cui in vita*.

> "Cui in vita, is a writ of entry, which a Widow hath against him, to whom her Husband alienated her Lands or Tenements in his life time, which must specifie, that *During his life*, she could not withstand it." Thomas Blount, *Nomo-Lexicon: A Law-Dictionary* (1670).

culpa (**kəl**-pə). [Latin] *Roman & civil law.* Fault, neglect, or negligence; unintentional wrong. See NEGLIGENCE. Cf. CASUS; DOLUS.

lata culpa (**lay**-tə **kəl**-pə). [Latin "grave fault"] Gross negligence. ● This phrase occurs most commonly in bailment law and in the law of the transport of persons. — Also termed *culpa lata*. See *gross negligence* under NEGLIGENCE.

levis culpa (**lee**-vis **kəl**-pə). [Latin "slight fault"] Ordinary negligence. — Also termed *culpa levis*. See *ordinary negligence* under NEGLIGENCE.

levissima culpa (lə-**vis**-ə-mə **kəl**-pə). [Latin "the slightest fault"] Slight negligence. — Also termed *culpa levissima*. See *slight negligence* under NEGLIGENCE.

culpabilis (kəl-**pay**-bə-lis), *adj.* [Latin] *Hist.* Guilty.

culpability (kəl-pə-**bil**-ə-tee), *n.* Blameworthiness; the quality of being culpable. ● Except in cases of absolute liability, criminal culpability requires a showing that the person acted purposely, knowingly, recklessly, or negligently with respect to each material element of the offense.

> "The concept of culpability is used as a reference point to assess the defendant's guilt and punishment even though, in the two contexts, culpability denotes different aspects of the defendant and the murder. At the guilt phase, culpability is most often used to refer to the state of mind that the defendant must possess. Also at the guilt phase, culpability may reflect a broader judgment about the defendant: when he is culpable for his conduct, it means that he is blameworthy and deserves punishment. At the punishment phase, the concept of culpability stands as the benchmark for when the death penalty is an appropriate punishment." Phyllis L. Crocker, *Concepts of Culpability and Deathworthiness*, 66 Fordham L. Rev. 21, 35–36 (1997).

culpable (**kəl**-pə-bəl), *adj.* **1.** Guilty; blameworthy. **2.** Involving the breach of a duty.

culpable accident. See ACCIDENT.

culpable intoxication. See *voluntary intoxication* under INTOXICATION.

culpable neglect. See NEGLECT.

culpable negligence. See NEGLIGENCE.

***culpa-in-contrahendo* doctrine.** [Law Latin "fault in contracting"] The principle that parties must act in good faith during preliminary contract negotiations; esp., the principle that a breach by the offeror after the offeree has begun performance of a unilateral contract and is stopped by the offeror before completion will give rise to liability in tort.

culpa lata. See *lata culpa* under CULPA.

culpa levis. See *levis culpa* under CULPA.

culpa levissima. See *levissima culpa* under CULPA.

culprit. 1. A person accused or charged with the commission of a crime. **2.** A person who is guilty of a crime. ● *Culprit* may be a running together of *cul*, shortened from the Latin *culpabilis* ("guilty"), and *prit*, from Old French *prest* ("ready"), two words formerly used to orally plead at the outset of a criminal case.

> "When the prisoner hath thus pleaded not guilty, *non culpabilis* ... the clerk of the assise, or clerk of the arraigns, on behalf of the crown replies, that the prisoner is guilty, and that he is ready to prove him so. This is done by two monosyllables in the same spirit of abbreviation, '*cul. prit.*' which signifies first that the prisoner is guilty, (*cul. culpable*, or *culpabilis*) and then that the king is ready to prove him so; *prît, praesto sum*, or *paratus verificare*.... How our courts came to express a matter of this importance in so odd and obscure a manner ... can hardly be pronounced with certainty. It may perhaps, however, be accounted for by supposing that these were at first short notes, to help the memory of the clerk, and remind him what he was to reply; or else it was the short method of taking down in court, upon the minutes, the replication and averment; '*cul. prît*': which afterwards the ignorance of succeeding clerks adopted for the very words to be by them spoken. But however it may have arisen, the joining of issue ... seems to be clearly the meaning of this obscure expression; which has puzzled our most ingenious etymologists, and is commonly understood as if the clerk of the ar-

raigns, immediately on plea pleaded, had fixed an opprobrious name on the prisoner, by asking him, '*culprit*, how wilt thou be tried?' " 4 William Blackstone, *Commentaries on the Laws of England* 333–34 (1769).

cultural agreement. *Int'l law.* A bilateral or multilateral agreement between nations for the purpose of furthering cultural or intellectual relations.

cultural property. *Int'l law.* Movable and immovable property that has cultural significance, whether in the nature of antiquities and monuments of a classical age or important modern items of fine arts, decorative arts, and architecture. • Some writers prefer the term *cultural heritage*, which more broadly includes intangible cultural things such as folklore, crafts, and skills.

cum dividend. With dividend. • Stocks purchased cum dividend entitle the buyer to any pending declared dividends. Cf. EX DIVIDEND.

cum grano salis (kəm **gray**-noh **say**-lis *or* kuum **grah**-noh **sah**-lis). [Latin] With a grain of salt; with allowance for exaggeration; with reservations.

cum onere (kəm **on**-ə-ree). [Latin] With the burden. • An item acquired *cum onere* is taken subject to existing burdens and charges.

cum pertinentiis (kəm pər-tə-**nen**-shee-is). [Latin] With the appurtenances.

cum rights. With rights. • A *cum rights* purchaser of stock is entitled to rights that have been declared but not distributed, such as the right to purchase additional shares at a stated price. — Also termed *rights on*.

cum testamento annexo (kəm tes-tə-**men**-toh ə-**nek**-soh). See *administration cum testamento annexo* under ADMINISTRATION.

cumulative dividend. See DIVIDEND.

cumulative-effects doctrine. The rule that a transaction affecting interstate commerce in a trivial way may be taken together with other similar transactions to establish that the combined effect on interstate commerce is not trivial and can therefore be regulated under the Commerce Clause.

cumulative evidence. See EVIDENCE.

cumulative legacies. See LEGACY.

cumulative offense. See OFFENSE (1).

cumulative preference share. See *cumulative preferred stock* under STOCK.

cumulative preferred stock. See STOCK.

cumulative punishment. See PUNISHMENT.

cumulative remedy. See REMEDY.

cumulative sentences. See *consecutive sentences* under SENTENCE.

cumulative stock. See *cumulative preferred stock* under STOCK.

cumulative testimony. See TESTIMONY.

cumulative-to-the-extent-earned dividend. See DIVIDEND.

cumulative traverse. See TRAVERSE.

cumulative voting. See VOTING.

cumulative zoning. See ZONING.

CUPOS. *abbr.* Cohabiting unmarried person of the opposite sex. • Although this term is intended to be synonymous with POSSLQ (a person of the opposite sex sharing living quarters), it is more literally precise because it excludes married persons. See POSSLQ.

cur. *abbr.* CURIA (3).

cura (**kyoor**-ə), *n.* [Latin] *Roman law.* A guardianship that protects the interests of youths (from puberty to the age of 25) or incapacitated persons. Cf. TUTELA. Pl. ***curae.***

"*Cura* was a form of guardianship indicated by the necessities of the case, with respect to persons who, though *sui juris*, were in need of protection. It was not regarded as a substitute for *patria potestas* as *tutela* was. . . . It extended to the person as well as the property, and in the latter respect is much the same as in the case of the *tutela* of infants." R.W. Leage, *Roman Private Law* 122 (C.H. Ziegler ed., 2d ed. 1930).

cura furiosi (**kyoor**-ə fyoor-ee-**oh**-sI). A guardianship for a person who was completely incapacitated from all acts.

"The cura furiosi empowered and bound the curator to manage the property of the lunatic on the lunatic's behalf." Rudolph Sohm, *The Institutes: A Textbook of the*

History and System of Roman Private Law 492 (James Crawford Ledlie trans., 3d ed. 1907).

cura minorum (**kyoor**-ə mi-**nor**-əm). A guardianship for a minor whose capacity of action was complete.

cura prodigi (**kyoor**-ə **prah**-də-jI). A guardianship for a person whose capacity of action was imperfect.

"The cura prodigi differed from the cura furiosi in that the prodigus, unlike the furiosus, was himself capable of performing any act by which he acquired a right or benefit. The appointment of a curator, however, precluded the prodigus from performing any act which operated to alienate property or to subject him to a liability; any such act, in order to be effectual, had to be concluded either by the curator on behalf of the prodigus or by the prodigus with the approval of the curator." Rudolph Sohm, *The Institutes: A Textbook of the History and System of Roman Private Law* 492 (James Crawford Ledlie trans., 3d ed. 1907).

cur. adv. vult. *abbr.* CURIA ADVISARI VULT.

curate (**kyuur**-it). *Eccles. law.* **1.** A person in charge of a parish; a pastor. **2.** A member of the clergy who receives a stipend or salary to assist a vicar, rector, or pastor; an assistant to a parish priest.

curatio (kyə-**ray**-shee-oh). [fr. Latin *cura* "care"] *Roman law.* **1.** The power or duty of managing the property of a youth or incompetent person. **2.** The office of a curator. See CURA.

curative admissibility. See ADMISSIBILITY.

curative-admissibility doctrine. The rule that otherwise inadmissible evidence will be admitted to rebut inadmissible evidence placed before the fact-finder by the adverse party. • The doctrine applies when a motion to strike cannot cure the prejudice created by the adverse party.

curative instruction. See JURY INSTRUCTION.

curator (**kyuur**-ə-tər *or* **kyuur**-ay-tər *or* kyuu-**ray**-tər), *n.* **1.** *Roman law.* A person who manages the affairs of another; a guardian. See CURA.

"One of the very oldest monuments of Roman legislation . . . placed all free males who were of full years and rights under the temporary control of new class of guardians, called *Curatores*, whose sanction was required to validate their acts or contracts." Henry S. Maine, *Ancient Law* 134 (17th ed. 1901).

curator ad litem (kyuu-**ray**-tər ad **lI**-təm). A curator appointed by a court to represent the interests of a youth or incapacitated person during the proceedings before the court.

curator bonorum (kyuu-**ray**-tər bə-**nor**-əm). A person appointed by a court to administer the estate of an insolvent person.

2. A temporary guardian or conservator appointed by a court to care for the property or person of a minor or incapacitated person.

interim curator. *Hist.* A person appointed by a justice of the peace to hold a felon's property until a royal administrator could be assigned the task.

3. *Civil law.* A guardian who manages the estate of a minor, an absent person, or an incapacitated person. Pl. ***curatores.***

curator ad hoc (kyuu-**ray**-tər ad **hok**). A court-appointed curator who manages a single matter or transaction; a special guardian.

curatorship. The office of a curator or guardian.

curatrix (kyuu-**ray**-triks). *Archaic.* A female curator.

cure, *vb.* **1.** To remove legal defects or correct legal errors. • For example, curing title involves removing defects from title to unmarketable land so that title becomes marketable. **2.** The right of a seller under the UCC to correct a nonconforming delivery of goods, usu. within the contract period. — **curative,** *adj.*

cure by verdict. See AIDER BY VERDICT.

curfew (**kər**-fyoo). **1.** *Hist.* A law requiring that all fires be extinguished at a certain time in the evening, usu. announced by the ringing of a bell. **2.** A regulation that forbids people (or certain classes of them) from being outdoors between certain hours.

curia (**kyoor**-ee-ə). [Latin] **1.** *Roman law.* One of 30 divisions (three tribes of ten *curiae*) into which the Roman people were said to be divided by Romulus. **2.** *Roman law.* A legislative gathering, esp. of the Roman Senate; the building used for the assembly. Cf. *comitia curiata* under COMITIA. **3.** *Hist.* A judicial tribunal held in the sovereign's palace; a royal court. — Abbr. *cur.* **4.** *Hist.* A court. **5.** The papal court, including its functionaries and officials.

"The word *curia* in classical Latin is used in a number of ways. Apparently, it meant at first a subdivision of the people. It was also used, by a transfer which is not too clear, for the building in which the Roman Senate met. By an almost inevitable development it became the word for the Senate itself and later the ordinary designation for the Council in municipalities of the later Empire.... How much of this was still recalled in Medieval times, we cannot tell, but ... in the early Middle Ages, *curia* was a common word to describe both the groups of men who generally were found in attendance on pope, emperor, king or prince, and the groups which were summoned by him to give him counsel. The *curia* in the latter sense, however, was not really a casual group of persons, summoned spasmodically to advise the king or any other person. It had come to be in Feudal Europe the ordinary Latin word for the general meeting of the lord's vassals, which itself grew out of the Germanic *mot* or *thing*.... The *Curia* of the king was in theory a larger and more important example of the same kind of assemblage." Max Radin, *Handbook of Anglo-American Legal History* 46–48 (1936).

curia admiralitatis (**kyoor**-ee-ə ad-mə-ral-ə-**tay**-tis). [Law Latin] See HIGH COURT OF ADMIRALTY.

curia advisari vult (**kyoor**-ee-ə ad-və-**sair**-I **vəlt**). [Latin] The court will be advised; the court will consider. • This phrase signaled a court's decision to delay judgment pending further consideration. In England, the phrase is still used in all Court of Appeal decisions when the judgment is reserved; that is, not delivered after the hearing. — Abbr. *cur. adv. vult*; *c.a.v.*

curia baronis (**kyoor**-ee-ə bə-**roh**-nis). [Law Latin] See COURT BARON.

curia burgi (**kyoor**-ee-ə **bər**-jI). See COURT OF HUSTINGS.

curia cancellaria. See CANCELLARIA.

curia christianitatis (**kyoor**-ee-ə kris-tee-an-ə-**tay**-tis). [Law Latin] See COURT CHRISTIAN.

curia claudenda (**kyoor**-ee-ə klaw-**den**-də). See DE CURIA CLAUDENDA.

curia comitatus (**kyoor**-ee-ə kom-ə-**tay**-təs). [Law Latin] See COUNTY COURT.

curia domini (**kyoor**-ee-ə **dom**-ə-nI). [Law Latin "lord's court"] *Hist.* A lord's house or hall, used as a meeting place for tenants during court sessions.

curia magna (**kyoor**-ee-ə **mag**-nə). [Law Latin "great court"] *Hist.* An ancient name for Parliament.

curia palatii (**kyoor**-ee-ə pə-**lay**-shee-I). [Law Latin "court of the palace"] PALACE COURT.

curia regis (**kyoor**-ee-ə **ree**-jis). [Latin "king's court"] *Hist.* (*usu. cap.*) The chief court in early Norman England, established by William the Conqueror. • The *curia regis* was a body of advisers who traveled with the king, advising him on political matters and acting as an appellate court in important or complicated cases. Over time the functions of the *curia regis* became exclusively judicial in nature. — Also termed *King's Court*; *aula regis*. — Abbr. *C.R.*

"[W]e are tempted to use terms which are more precise than those that were current in the twelfth century. In particular we are wont to speak of *the* Curia Regis without remembering that the definite article is not in our documents. Any court held in the king's name by the king's delegates is Curia Regis. Thus the institution of what in course of time will be a new tribunal, a Court of King's Bench or a Court of Common Pleas, may be found in some small rearrangement, some petty technical change, which at the moment passes unnoticed." 1 Frederick Pollock & Frederic W. Maitland, *The History of English Law Before the Time of Edward I* 153 (2d ed. 1898).

"The focal point of royal government was the *curia regis* (king's court), the body of advisers and courtiers who attended the king and supervised the administration of the realm. It was not a specific court of law, any more than the eyre was, but rather was the descendant of the Anglo-Saxon *witengemot* (meeting with the *witan*, or royal advisers) and the ancestor of the king's council which later subdivided into parliament and the privy council." J.H. Baker, *An Introduction to English Legal History* 20 (3d ed. 1990).

curing title. The act of removing defects from a land title to make it marketable.

currency. An item (such as a coin, government note, or banknote) that circulates as a medium of exchange. See LEGAL TENDER.

blocked currency. Currency or bank deposits that, by government restriction, may be used only within the country where they are located.

fractional currency. Paper money worth less than one dollar; esp., the currency issued by the federal government from 1863 to 1876.

hard currency. Currency backed by reserves, esp. gold and silver reserves.

postal currency. A fractional currency bearing a facsimile of postage stamps during the Civil War.

soft currency. Currency not backed by reserves and therefore subject to sharp fluctuations in value.

United States currency. Currency issued under the authority of the federal government.

currency swap. See SWAP.

current account. See *open account* under ACCOUNT.

current asset. See ASSET.

current-cost accounting. A method of measuring assets in terms of replacement cost. • This approach accounts for inflation by recognizing price changes in a company's assets and restating the assets in terms of their current cost.

current expense. See *operating expense* under EXPENSE.

current funds. See FUNDS (2).

current income. See INCOME.

current liabilities. See *short-term debt* under DEBT.

current liability. See LIABILITY.

current market value. The price at which an asset can be sold within the present accounting period.

current money. See MONEY.

current obligation. See OBLIGATION.

current revenue. See *current income* under INCOME.

current wages. See WAGE.

current yield. See YIELD.

currit quattuor pedibus (**kər**-it **kwah**-too-ər **ped**-ə-bəs). [Law Latin] It runs on four feet; it runs on all fours. See ON ALL FOURS.

cursitor (**kər**-sə-tər). *Hist.* A chancery clerk responsible for making out original writs. • *Cursitor* derives from the writs *de cursu* that the clerks wrote out.

cursitor baron. *Hist.* An officer of the Court of Exchequer with administrative, but not judicial, duties. • Over time, as the Barons of the Exchequer took on more judicial rather than fiscal duties, the need for someone with financial experience became apparent. So in 1610 a cursitor baron was appointed to sit alongside the judges. The office was abolished in 1856.

cursor (**kər**-sər). *Eccles. law.* An inferior officer of the papal court.

curtesy (**kər**-tə-see). At common law, a husband's right, upon his wife's death, to a life estate in the land that his wife owned during their marriage, assuming that a child was born alive to the couple. • This right has been largely abolished. Traditionally, the full phrase was *estate by the curtesy of England*. Cf. DOWER.

curtesy consummate (**kər**-tə-see kən-**səm**-it). The interest the husband has in his wife's estate after her death.

curtesy initiate (**kər**-tə-see i-**nish**-ee-it). The interest the husband has in his wife's estate after the birth of issue capable of inheriting, and before the death of the wife.

curtilage (**kər**-tə-lij). The land or yard adjoining a house, usu. within an enclosure. • Under the Fourth Amendment, the curtilage is an area usu. protected from warrantless searches. See OPEN-FIELDS DOCTRINE. Cf. MESSUAGE.

curtiles terrae (kər-**tɪ**-leez **ter**-ee). [Law Latin] COURT LANDS.

curtillium (kər-**til**-ee-əm). [Law Latin] CURTILAGE.

cushion. See EQUITY (7).

cushion bond. See BOND (3).

custode admittendo (kə-**stoh**-dee ad-mi-**ten**-doh). See DE CUSTODE ADMITTENDO.

custode amovendo (kə-**stoh**-dee ay-moh-**ven**-doh). See DE CUSTODE AMOVENDO.

custodes libertatis angliae auctoritate parliamenti (kə-**stoh**-deez lib-ər-**tay**-tis **ang**-glee-ee awk-tor-ə-**tay**-tee parl-[y]ə-**men**-tɪ). [Latin] *Hist.* Guardians of the liberty of England by the authority of Parliament. • The style of all writs and judicial process that issued during the period between the execution of Charles I (January 1649) and the proclamation of Oliver Cromwell as Lord Protector (December 1653).

custodes pacis (kə-**stoh**-deez **pay**-sis). [Latin] *Hist.* Guardians (or *conservators*) of the peace. See PEACE OFFICER.

custodial account. See ACCOUNT.

custodia legis. See IN CUSTODIA LEGIS.

custodial interrogation. See INTERROGATION.

custodial trust. See TRUST.

custodian, *n.* **1.** A person or institution that has charge or custody of property, papers, or other valuables; GUARDIAN. **2.** *Bankruptcy.* A prepetition agent who has taken charge of any asset belonging to the debtor. 11 USCA § 101(11). — **custodianship,** *n.*

custodian bank. See BANK.

custodia terrae et haeredis. See DE CUSTODIA TERRAE ET HAEREDIS.

custody, *n.* **1.** The care and control of a thing or person for inspection, preservation, or security.

constructive custody. Custody of a person (such as a parolee or probationer) whose freedom is controlled by legal authority but who is not under direct physical control.

penal custody. Custody intended to punish a criminal offender.

physical custody. Custody of a person (such as an arrestee) whose freedom is directly controlled and limited.

preventive custody. Custody intended to prevent further dangerous or criminal behavior.

protective custody. The government's confinement of a person for that person's own security or well-being, such as a witness whose safety is in jeopardy or an incompetent person who may harm others.

2. The care, control, and maintenance of a child awarded by a court to a relative, usu. one of the parents, in a divorce or separation proceeding. — Also termed *managing conservatorship*; *legal custody.*

divided custody. An arrangement by which each parent has custody and full control of and responsibility for the child part of the time, with reciprocal visitation rights.

joint custody. An arrangement by which both parents share the responsibility for and authority over the child at all times. — Also termed *shared custody.*

"The statutes, and the cases as well, differ over the definition of joint custody. It is most often defined as meaning only that both parents will share in the decisions concerning the child's care, education, religion, medical treatment and general welfare." Homer H. Clark, Jr., *The Law of Domestic Relations in the United States* § 19.5, at 815 (2d ed. 1988).

physical custody. The right to have the child live with the person awarded custody by the court.

shared custody. See *joint custody.*

sole custody. An arrangement by which one parent has full control and responsibility to the exclusion of the other.

3. The detention of a person by virtue of lawful process or authority. — Also termed *legal custody.* — **custodial,** *adj.*

custody hearing. A judicial examination of the facts relating to parental custody in a divorce or separation proceeding.

custody of the law. The condition of property or a person being under the control of legal authority (as a court or law officer). See IN CUSTODIA LEGIS.

custom, *n.* **1.** A practice that by its common adoption and long, unvarying habit has come to have the force of law. See USAGE.

conventional custom. A custom that operates only indirectly through the medium of agreements, so that it is accepted and adopted in individual instances as conventional law between the parties to those agreements. — Also termed *usage.* See USAGE.

general custom. **1.** A custom that prevails throughout a country and constitutes one of the sources of the law of the land. **2.** A custom that businesses recognize and follow. See *trade usage* under USAGE.

legal custom. A custom that operates as a binding rule of law, independently of any agreement on the part of those subject to it. — Often shortened to *custom.*

local custom. A custom that prevails in some defined locality only, such as a city or county, and constitutes a source of law for that place only. — Also termed *particular custom*; *special custom.*

2. (*pl.*) Duties imposed on imports or exports. **3.** (*pl.*) The agency or procedure for collecting such duties. — **customary** (for sense 1), *adj.*

custom and usage. General rules and practices that have become generally adopted through unvarying habit and common use. Cf. CUSTOM (1); USAGE.

customary, *n.* A record of all the established legal and quasi-legal practices within a community.

customary court baron. See COURT BARON.

customary dispatch. See DISPATCH.

customary estate. See COPYHOLD.

customary freehold. See COPYHOLD.

customary international law. See INTERNATIONAL LAW.

customary interpretation. See INTERPRETATION.

customary law. Law consisting of customs that are accepted as legal requirements or obligatory rules of conduct; practices and beliefs that are so vital and intrinsic a part of a social and economic system that they are treated as if they were laws. — Also termed *consuetudinary law*.

> "In contrast with the statute, *customary law* may be said to exemplify *implicit law*. Let us, therefore, describe customary law in terms that will reveal to the maximum this quality of implicitness. A custom is not declared or enacted, but grows or develops through time. The date when it first came into full effect can usually be assigned only within broad limits. Though we may be able to describe in general the class of persons among whom the custom has come to prevail as a standard of conduct, it has no definite author; there is no person or defined human agency we can praise or blame for its being good or bad. There is no authoritative verbal declaration of the terms of the custom; it expresses itself not in a succession of words, but in a course of conduct." Lon L. Fuller, *Anatomy of the Law* 71 (1968).

customary seisin. See *quasi seisin* under SEISIN.

customary tenant. See TENANT.

customer's goods. See GOODS.

customer's man. See *registered representative* under REPRESENTATIVE.

customer's person. See *registered representative* under REPRESENTATIVE.

customhouse. A building or office, esp. at a port, where duties or customs are collected and where ships are cleared for entering or leaving the port. — Also termed *customshouse*.

customhouse broker. See BROKER.

custom of York. See YORK, CUSTOM OF.

Customs and Patent Appeals, Court of. See COURT OF CUSTOMS AND PATENT APPEALS.

customs broker. See *customhouse broker* under BROKER.

Customs Cooperation Council. A specialized intergovernmental organization for the study of customs questions. • Established in 1952, the Council has its headquarters in Brussels. — Abbr. CCC.

Customs Court, U.S. See UNITED STATES CUSTOMS COURT.

customs duty. See DUTY (4).

customs frontier. *Int'l law.* The territorial boundary at which a country imposes customs duties.

customs union. *Int'l law.* A combination of two or more countries within a single customs area with a common external tariff, though each participating country remains politically independent. • The effect is that tariffs originally levied on the traffic of goods between those countries are abolished or else successively dismantled according to an agreed-upon scheme, and that common tariffs are imposed on imports from nonmembers.

custos (**kəs**-tahs *also* **kəs**-təs). [Latin] *Hist.* A keeper, protector, or guardian.

Custos Brevium (**kəs**-tahs **bree**-vee-əm). [Law Latin "keeper of the writs"] *Hist.* A clerk who receives and files the writs returnable to the Courts of King's Bench and Common Pleas. • The office was abolished in 1837. — Also termed *Keeper of the Briefs*.

custos maris (**kəs**-tahs **mar**-is). [Law Latin "warden of the sea"] *Hist.* A high-ranking naval officer; an admiral. — Also termed *seaward*; *seward*.

custos morum (**kəs**-tahs **mor**-əm). [Law Latin] Custodian of morals <H.L.A. Hart believed that courts should not be seen as the *custos morum*>. • This name was sometimes used in reference to the Court of King's Bench.

> "[H]e [Viscount Simonds] approved the assertion of Lord Mansfield two centuries before that the Court of King's Bench was the *custos morum* of the people and had the superintendency of offences *contra bonos mores*." Patrick Devlin, *The Enforcement of Morals* 88 (1968).

custos placitorum coronae (**kəs**-tahs plas-ə-**tor**-əm kə-**roh**-nee). [Law Latin] See CORONATOR.

Custos Rotulorum (**kəs**-tahs roch-yə-**lor**-əm *or* rot-yə-**lor**-əm). [Law Latin "keeper of the pleas of the Crown"] *Hist.* The principal justice of the peace in a county, responsible for the rolls of the county sessions of the peace. — Also termed *Keeper of the Rolls*.

Custos Sigilli. See KEEPER OF THE GREAT SEAL.

custos spiritualium (**kəs**-tahs spir-i-choo-**ay**-lee-əm *or* -tyoo-**ay**-lee-əm). [Law Latin "keeper of the spiritualities"] *Eccles. law.* A member of the clergy responsible for a diocese's spiritual jurisdiction during the vacancy of the see.

custos terrae (**kəs**-tahs **ter**-ee). [Law Latin "keeper of the land"] *Hist.* Guardian, warden, or keeper of the land.

custuma (**kəs**-chə-mə *or* **kəs**-tyə-mə). [French *coustum* "toll" or "tribute"] *Hist.* A duty or impost.

cutpurse. *Hist.* A person who steals by cutting purses; a pickpocket.

CVA. *abbr.* UNITED STATES COURT OF VETERANS APPEALS.

CVSG. *abbr.* A call for the view of the Solicitor General — an invitation from the U.S. Supreme Court for the Solicitor General's views on a pending petition for writ of certiorari in a case in which, though the government is not a party, governmental interests are involved.

Cwth. *abbr.* COMMONWEALTH (4).

cyberlaw (**sI**-bər-law). The field of law dealing with computers and the Internet, including such issues as intellectual-property rights, freedom of expression, and free access to information.

cybersquatting. The act of reserving a domain name on the Internet, esp. a name that would be associated with a company's trademark, and then seeking to profit by selling or licensing the name to the company that has an interest in being identified with it.

cyberstalking. The act of threatening, harassing, or annoying someone through multiple e-mail messages, as through the Internet, esp. with the intent of placing the recipient in fear that an illegal act or an injury will be inflicted on the recipient or a member of the recipient's family or household.

cybertheft. The act of using an online computer service, such as one on the Internet, to steal someone else's property or to interfere with someone else's use and enjoyment of property. • Examples of cybertheft are hacking into a bank's computer records to wrongfully credit one account and debit another, and interfering with a copyright by wrongfully sending protected material over the Internet.

cyclical (**sI**-klə-kəl *or* **sik**-lə-kəl), *adj.* (Of a stock or an industry) characterized by large price swings that occur because of government policy, economic conditions, and seasonal changes.

cy pres (see **pray** *also* sI). [Law French "as near as"] The equitable doctrine under which a court reforms a written instrument with a gift to charity as closely to the donor's intention as possible, so that the gift does not fail. • Courts use *cy pres* esp. in construing charitable gifts when the donor's original charitable purpose cannot be fulfilled. Cf. DOCTRINE OF APPROXIMATION.

> "The *cy pres* doctrine has been much discussed, if not a little severely criticised, and in many cases misunderstood.... The *cy pres* doctrine is one under which Courts of Chancery act, when a gift for charitable uses cannot be applied according to the exact intention of the donor. In such cases the courts will apply the gift, as nearly as possible (*cy pres*) in conformity with the presumed general intention of the donor; for it is an established maxim in the interpretation of wills, that a court is bound to carry the will into effect if it can see a general intention consistent with the rules of law, even if the particular mode or manner pointed out by the testator cannot be followed." George T. Bispham, *The Principles of Equity* § 104, at 113–14 (11th ed. 1931).

> "Although the reason for the adoption of the cy pres rule by the English chancery court in the middle ages is not known, various hypotheses as to the motives of the court have been suggested. The most plausible theory is that the chancellors, being ecclesiastics and trained in Roman law, resurrected this civil law doctrine in order to save gifts made for religious purposes and thereby subject the property to church control. Justification for the use of the doctrine was laid on the shoulders of the donor, the idea being that since the object of the testator in donating the money to charity was to obtain an advantageous position in the kingdom of heaven, he ought not to be frustrated in this desire because of an unexpected or unforeseen failure." Edith L. Fisch, *The Cy Pres Doctrine in the United States* 4 (1950).

cyrographarius (sI-roh-grə-**fair**-ee-əs). [Law Latin] *Hist.* See CHIROGRAPH (4).

cyrographum (sI-**rog**-rə-fəm). [Law Latin] See CHIROGRAPH (2).

D

D. *abbr.* **1.** DISTRICT. **2.** DEFENDANT. **3.** DIGEST.

D.A. *abbr.* **1.** DISTRICT ATTORNEY. **2.** See *deposit account* under ACCOUNT.

dactylography (dak-tə-**log**-rə-fee), *n.* The scientific study of fingerprints as a method of identification. — **dactylographic** (dak-til-ə-**graf**-ik), *adj.*

dailia. See DALUS.

dailus. See DALUS.

daily balance. The final daily accounting for a day on which interest is to be accrued or paid.

average daily balance. The average amount of money in an account (such as a bank account or credit-card account) during a given period. • This amount serves as the basis for computing interest or a finance charge for the period.

daily newspaper. See NEWSPAPER.

daisy chain. A series of purchases and sales of the same stock by a small group of securities dealers attempting to drive up the stock's price to attract unsuspecting buyers' interest. • Once the buyers have invested (i.e., are caught up in the chain), the traders sell for a quick profit, leaving the buyers with overpriced stock. This practice is illegal.

dalus (**day**-ləs), *n.* [Law Latin "a dale"] *Hist.* **1.** A dale; a ditch. **2.** A measure of land being a thin strip of pasture between two plowed furrows. — Also termed *dailus*; *dailia*.

damage, *adj.* Of or relating to monetary compensation for loss or injury to a person or property <a damage claim> <a damage award>. — Also termed *damages* <a damages claim>. Cf. DAMAGES.

damage, *n.* Loss or injury to person or property <actionable damage resulting from negligence>.

damage-cleer (**dam**-ij **kleer**), *n.* [fr. Latin *damna clericorum* "clerk's compensation"] *Hist.* A set fee payable by a plaintiff to the Court of the Common Pleas, King's Bench, or Exchequer before execution on an award of damages. • The fee — later abolished by statute — was originally a gratuity to the court clerks for preparing special pleadings. — Also spelled *damage cleere.* — Also termed *damna clericorum.*

> "Damage cleere, *damna clericorum*, was assessed by the tenth part in the common pleas, and by the twentieth part in the king's bench and exchequer, of all damages, exceeding five marks, recovered either by verdict, confession, or judgment of the court, in all actions upon the case, covenant, trespass, battery, false imprisonment, dower, and all others, wherein the damages were uncertain, which the plaintiff was obliged to pay to the prothonotary, or chief officer of that court, wherein they were recovered before he could have execution for them. But this is taken away by 17 Car. 2, c. 6." *Termes de la Ley* 141 (1st Am. ed. 1812).

damage feasant (**dam**-ij **fez**-ənt *or* **fee**-zənt), *n.* [fr. French *faisant dommage*] *Hist.* Doing damage. • This phrase usu. refers to injury to a person's land caused by another person's animals trespassing on the property and eating the crops or treading the grass. By law, the owner of the damaged property could distrain and impound the animals until compensated by the animals' owner. But the impounder had to feed the animals and could not sell or harm them. The term was introduced during the reign of Edward III. — Also spelled *damage faisant*. — Also termed *damnum facientes*.

damage rule. See LEGAL-INJURY RULE.

damages, *n. pl.* Money claimed by, or ordered to be paid to, a person as compensation for loss or injury <the plaintiff seeks $8,000 in damages from the defendant>. — **damage,** *adj.*

> "Damages are the sum of money which a person wronged is entitled to receive from the wrongdoer as compensation for the wrong." Frank Gahan, *The Law of Damages* 1 (1936).

accumulative damages. Statutory damages allowed in addition to amounts available under the common law. — Also termed *enhanced damages*.

actual damages. An amount awarded to a complainant to compensate for a proven injury or loss; damages that repay actual losses. — Also termed *compensatory damages.*

added damages. See *punitive damages.*

additional damages. Damages usu. provided by statute in addition to direct damages. • Additional damages can include expenses resulting from the injury, consequential damages, or punitive damages.

benefit-of-the-bargain damages. Damages that a breaching party to a contract must pay to the aggrieved party, equal to the amounts that the aggrieved party would have received, including profits, if the contract had been fully performed.

compensatory damages (kəm-**pen**-sə-tor-ee). **1.** Damages sufficient in amount to indemnify the injured person for the loss suffered. — Often shortened to *compensatories.* **2.** See *actual damages.*

consequential damages. Losses that do not flow directly and immediately from an injurious act, but that result indirectly from the act.

continuing damages. **1.** Damages arising from the same injury. **2.** Damages arising from the repetition of similar acts within a definite period.

damages for lost expectations. See *expectation damages.*

damages ultra (**əl**-trə). Additional damages claimed by a plaintiff who is not satisfied with the amounts the defendant paid into court.

direct damages. See *general damages.*

discretionary damages. Damages (such as mental anguish or pain and suffering) that are not definitive but are measurable by the enlightened conscience of an impartial juror.

double damages. Damages that, by statute, are twice the amount that the fact-finder determines is owed, or twice the amount of actual damages awarded. • In some cases, double damages are awarded in addition to actual damages, so the effect is the same as treble damages.

enhanced damages. **1.** See *accumulative damages.* **2.** *Patents.* Damages for patent infringement in an amount up to three times that of compensatory damages, at the discretion of the court, based on the egregiousness of the defendant's conduct, including the willfulness of the infringement.

estimated damages. See *liquidated damages.*

excess damages. Damages awarded to an insured — beyond the coverage provided by an insurance policy — because the insurer did not settle the claim within policy limits. • If the insurer acted in bad faith in not settling, the insured may have a claim to recover the excess damages from the insurer. — Also termed *excess-liability damages.*

excessive damages. A jury award that grossly exceeds the amount warranted by law based on the facts and circumstances of the case; unreasonable or outrageous damages, which are subject to reduction by remittitur. See REMITTITUR.

exemplary damages. See *punitive damages.*

expectation damages. Compensation awarded for the loss of what a person reasonably anticipated from a transaction that was not completed. — Also termed *expectancy damages*; *loss-of-bargain damages*; *lost-expectation damages*; *damages for lost expectations.*

> "[I]f a person contracts to buy a new car, and then changes his mind overnight and cancels the contract, the seller is in principle entitled to recover his anticipated profit on the transaction even though he has not, at the time of the cancellation, done anything whatever in pursuance of the contract. A person who books a room in a hotel would in theory be liable to pay for the hotel's loss of profit even though he cancels in sufficient time for the hotel to be able to relet the room, so long only as the room in fact remains unlet because there are no takers. Damages of this kind are often called damages for lost expectations, or 'expectation damages', or 'loss of bargain damages'." P.S. Atiyah, *An Introduction to the Law of Contract* 310 (3d ed. 1981).

fee damages. Damages awarded to the owner of abutting property for injury caused by the construction and operation of an elevated railroad. • The term is used because the damage is to the property owner's easements of light, air, and access, which are parts of the fee.

foreseeable damages. Damages that a breaching party knew or should have been aware of when the contract was made.

future damages. Money awarded to an injured party for an injury's residual or projected effects that reduce the person's ability to function. • Examples are expected pain and suffering, loss or impairment of earning capacity, and projected medical expenses.

general damages. Damages that the law presumes follow from the type of wrong complained of. • General damages do not need to be specifically claimed or proved to have been sustained. — Also termed *direct damages*; *necessary damages*.

hedonic damages (hi-**don**-ik). Damages that attempt to compensate the loss of the pleasure of being alive. • Such damages are not allowed in most jurisdictions.

imaginary damages. See *punitive damages*.

inadequate damages. Damages insufficient to fully and fairly compensate the parties; damages bearing no reasonable relation to the plaintiff's injuries, indicating prejudice, mistake, or other fact to support setting aside a jury's verdict.

incidental damages. **1.** Losses reasonably associated with or related to actual damages. **2.** A seller's commercially reasonable expenses incurred in stopping delivery or in transporting and caring for goods after a buyer's breach. UCC § 2–710. **3.** A buyer's expenses reasonably incurred in caring for goods after a seller's breach. UCC § 2–715(1).

"What are incidental damages? The Code does not define incidental damages; rather 2–715(1) lists many expenses that are included as incidental damages. However, Comment 1 to 2–715 stresses that those listed 'are not intended to be exhaustive' but are merely illustrative of the typical kinds of incidental expenses that can be recovered under 2–715: (1) those associated with rightful rejection (for instance, inspection and storage); (2) those associated with a proper revocation of acceptance; and (3) those involved in effecting cover." 1 James J. White & Robert S. Summers, *Uniform Commercial Code* § 10–3, at 561–62 (4th ed. 1995).

irreparable damages (i-**rep**-ə-rə-bəl). Damages that cannot be easily ascertained because there is no fixed pecuniary standard of measurement, e.g., damages for a repeated public nuisance.

land damages. See *just compensation* under COMPENSATION.

lawful damages. Those damages fixed by law and ascertained in a court of law.

liquidated damages. An amount contractually stipulated as a reasonable estimation of actual damages to be recovered by one party if the other party breaches. • If the parties to a contract have agreed on liquidated damages, the sum fixed is the measure of damages for a breach, whether it exceeds or falls short of the actual damages. — Also termed *stipulated damages*; *estimated damages*. See LIQUIDATED-DAMAGES CLAUSE. Cf. *unliquidated damages*; PENALTY CLAUSE.

"Where the terms of a contract specify a sum payable for non-performance, it is a question of construction whether this sum is to be treated as a *penalty* or as *liquidated damages*. The difference in effect is this: The amount recoverable in case of a penalty is not the sum named, but the damage actually incurred. The amount recoverable as liquidated damages is the sum named as such. In construing these terms a judge will not accept the phraseology of the parties; they may call the sum specified 'liquidated damages,' but if the judge finds it to be a penalty, he will treat it as such." William R. Anson, *Principles of the Law of Contract* 470 (Arthur L. Corbin ed., 3d Am. ed. 1919).

"The distinction between a penalty and genuine liquidated damages, as they are called, is not always easy to apply, but the Courts have made the task simpler by laying down certain guiding principles. In the first place, if the sum payable is so large as to be far in excess of the probable damage on breach, it is almost certainly a penalty. Secondly, if the same sum is expressed to be payable on any one of a number of different breaches of varying importance, it is again probably a penalty, because it is extremely unlikely that the same damage would be caused by these varying breaches. Thirdly, where a sum is expressed to be payable on a certain date, and a further sum in the event of default being made, this latter sum is prima facie a penalty, because mere delay in payment is unlikely to cause damage. Finally, it is to be noted that the mere use of the words 'liquidated damages' is not decisive, for it is the task of the Court and not of the parties to decide the true nature of the sum payable." P.S. Atiyah, *An Introduction to the Law of Contract* 316–17 (3d ed. 1981).

loss-of-bargain damages. See *expectation damages*.

lost-expectation damages. See *expectation damages*.

moratory damages (**mor**-ə-tor-ee *or* **mahr**-). *Civil law.* Damages for a delay in performing an obligation. • There must be a default before these damages can be recovered, while compensatory damages are recoverable for both a failure of performance and for a defective performance.

multiple damages. Statutory damages (such as double or treble damages) that are a multiple of the amount that the fact-finder determines to be owed. — Also termed *multiplied damages*. See *double damages*; *treble damages*.

"[T]he statutory multiple damages differ from the common law punitive damages in that punitive damages involved no fixed sum or limit. The fixed limit of multiple damages not only reduces their threat to the defendant and the potential for abuse, it also reduces the possibility of a measured deterrence. Likewise, because the enhancement of the award is fixed by the statutory multiple, there is no occasion for introducing evidence of the defendant's wealth as there is in the case of common law punitive damages .... Perhaps a more important distinction is that multiple damages statutes may be enacted for entirely non-punitive purposes. Specifically, some double or treble damages statutes, and also specified 'civil penalties,' are intended to provide a kind of liquidated damages for actual losses that cannot be proved or that are otherwise unrecognized by the law." Dan B. Dobbs, *Law of Remedies* § 3.12, at 359 (2d ed. 1993).

necessary damages. See *general damages.*

nominal damages. A trifling sum awarded when a legal injury is suffered but when there is no substantial loss or injury to be compensated. Cf. *substantial damages.*

"Nominal damages are damages awarded for the infraction of a legal right, where the extent of the loss is not shown, or where the right is one not dependent upon loss or damage, as in the case of rights of bodily immunity or rights to have one's material property undisturbed by direct invasion. The award of nominal damages is made as a judicial declaration that the plaintiff's right has been violated." Charles T. McCormick, *Handbook on the Law of Damages* § 20, at 85 (1935).

particular damages. See *special damages.*

pecuniary damages (pə-**kyoo**-nee-er-ee). Damages that can be estimated and monetarily compensated. • Although this phrase appears in many old cases, it is now widely considered a redundancy — since damages are always pecuniary.

presumptive damages. See *punitive damages.*

prospective damages. Future damages that, based on the facts pleaded and proved by the plaintiff, can reasonably be expected to occur.

proximate damages. Damages directly, immediately, and naturally flowing from the act complained of. Cf. *speculative damages* (1).

punitive damages. Damages awarded in addition to actual damages when the defendant acted with recklessness, malice, or deceit. • Punitive damages, which are intended to punish and thereby deter blameworthy conduct, are generally not recoverable for breach of contract. The Supreme Court has held that three guidelines help determine whether a punitive-damages award violates constitutional due process: (1) the reprehensibility of the conduct being punished; (2) the reasonableness of the relationship between the harm and the award; and (3) the difference between the award and the civil penalties authorized in comparable cases. *BMW of North America, Inc. v. Gore,* 517 U.S. 559, 116 S.Ct. 1589 (1996). — Also termed *exemplary damages*; *vindictive damages*; *punitory damages*; *presumptive damages*; *added damages*; *aggravated damages*; *speculative damages*; *imaginary damages*; *smart money*; *punies.*

reliance damages. Damages awarded for losses incurred by the plaintiff in reliance on the contract.

"Reliance damages are ... 'real' losses in a much more tangible way than losses of expectations. The distinction is nicely illustrated by *McRae v. Commonwealth Disposals Commission* .... In this case, ... the defendants sold a shipwrecked tanker which they advertised as lying on a certain reef in the Pacific, and the plaintiffs spent a substantial sum of money equipping a salvage expedition to go in search of the ship. The ship was wholly nonexistent, and the plaintiffs were held entitled to damages. Here it was clear that the plaintiffs had incurred substantial expenses — real losses — in reliance on the contract, and the Australian High Court awarded these reliance damages to the plaintiffs." P.S. Atiyah, *An Introduction to the Law of Contract* 311 (3d ed. 1981).

reliance-loss damages. A reimbursement for losses or expenses that the plaintiff suffers in reliance on the defendant's contractual promise that has been breached.

remote damages. See *speculative damages* (1).

rescissory damages (ri-**sis**-ə-ree *or* ri-**siz**-). Damages contemplated to restore a plaintiff to the position occupied before the defendant's wrongful acts. • An award of rescissory damages may mean returning property to the original owner or, if that is not possible, paying the owner the monetary value of the property.

restitution damages. Damages awarded to a plaintiff when the defendant has been unjustly enriched at the plaintiff's expense.

"Suppose A pays money to B in pursuance of a contract which turns out to be void, or perhaps is subsequently frustrated: clearly A cannot sue B for breach of contract. B's promise to perform his side of the bargain is vitiated by the mistake or the frustrating event, so A's lost expectations are losses which he must just put up with. But his claim to repayment of the money is evidently much stronger: for this money is a tangible loss to A and a tangible enrichment to B. So in this sort of case the money will often be recoverable, though English lawyers think of this as a quasi-contractual claim to recover money as on a total failure of consideration, and not a contractual claim to restitution damages. There is, however, no strong reason for refusing to call this a contractual action, any more than there is a reason for calling an action for damages quasi-contractual." P.S. Atiyah, *An Introduction to the Law of Contract* 312 (3d ed. 1981).

severance damages. In a condemnation case, damages awarded to a property owner for diminution in the fair market value of land as a result of severance from the land of the property actually condemned; compensation awarded to a landowner for the loss in value of the tract that remains after a partial taking of the land.

special damages. Damages that are alleged to have been sustained in the circumstances of a particular wrong. • To be awardable, special damages must be specifically claimed and proved. — Also termed *particular damages.*

speculative damages. **1.** Damages that are so uncertain that they will not be awarded. —

Also termed *remote damages*. **2.** See *punitive damages*.

statutory damages. Damages provided by statute (such as a wrongful death and survival statute), as distinguished from damages provided under the common law.

stipulated damages. See *liquidated damages*.

substantial damages. A considerable sum awarded to compensate for a significant loss or injury. Cf. *nominal damages*.

"Substantial damages ... are the result of an effort at measured compensation, and are to be contrasted with nominal damages which are in no sense compensatory, but merely symbolic." Charles T. McCormick, *Handbook on the Law of Damages* § 20, at 85 (1935).

temporary damages. Damages allowed for an intermittent or occasional wrong, such as a real-property injury whose cause can be removed or abated.

treble damages. Damages that, by statute, are three times the amount that the fact-finder determines is owed. — Also termed *triple damages*.

uncertain damages. Damages that are not clearly the result of a wrong. • The rule against allowing recovery of uncertain damages refers to these damages, not damages that are uncertain only in amount.

unliquidated damages. Damages that have been established by a verdict or award but cannot be determined by a fixed formula, so they are left to the discretion of the judge or jury. Cf. *liquidated damages*.

vindictive damages. See *punitive damages*.

damages, mitigation of. See MITIGATION-OF-DAMAGES DOCTRINE.

damages for detention. See *noncontract demurrage* under DEMURRAGE.

damages for lost expectations. See *expectation damages* under DAMAGES.

damages ultra. See DAMAGES.

dame. 1. The legal title of the wife of a knight or baronet. **2.** The female equivalent of a knight. **3.** A form of address to a woman of high rank. **4.** A matron. **5.** *Slang*. A woman. — Also termed (in senses 1 & 2) *domina*.

damna (**dam**-nə), *n.* [fr. Latin *damnum* "damage; loss"] *Hist.* **1.** Damages, exclusive of costs. **2.** Damages, inclusive of costs. **3.** The abbreviation of *damna clericorum*, the Latin equivalent to *damage-cleer*, being a portion of damages constituting the clerk's fee. See DAMAGE-CLEER.

damna clericorum (**dam**-nə kler-ə-**kor**-əm), *n.* See DAMAGE-CLEER.

damnatus (dam-**nay**-təs). [fr. Latin *damnare* "to condemn"] **1.** *Roman law*. A person condemned, esp. in a capital case. **2.** *Hist.* Something prohibited by law; something that is unlawful, as in *damnatus coitus* ("unlawful sexual connection").

damn-fool doctrine. *Insurance*. The principle that an insurer may deny (esp. liability) coverage when an insured engages in behavior that is so ill-conceived that the insurer should not be compelled to bear the loss resulting from the insured's actions. — Also termed *damned-fool doctrine*.

"The 'damn foolish acts' concept is not a perfect predictor of judicial decisions, both because of its own imprecision and because other considerations, such as a desire to assure an innocent third party a source of indemnification, may influence a court. However, especially when ... the insured who acted foolishly has sufficient resources to provide compensation to the injured persons, analysis of a coverage issue on the basis of a 'damn fool' doctrine is frequently a very effective approach both to predicting and to understanding outcomes." Robert E. Keeton & Alan I. Widiss, *Insurance Law: A Guide to Fundamental Principles, Legal Doctrines, and Commercial Practices* § 5.4, at 541 (1988).

damnification, *n.* Something that causes damage <damnification in the form of a penalty>.

damnify, *vb.* To cause loss or damage to; to injure <the surety was damnified by the judgment obtained against it>.

damni injuriae actio (**dam**-nI in-**joor**-ee-ee **ak**-shee-oh), *n.* [Latin "an action for wrongful damage"] *Roman law*. A person's right to sue someone who wrongfully injured or killed that person's slave or beast or wrongfully inflicted loss in some other way.

damnosa hereditas (dam-**noh**-sə hə-**red**-i-tas), *n.* [Latin "a losing inheritance"] **1.** *Roman & civil law*. An inheritance more onerous than beneficial, esp. because it is burdened with debt. **2.** *English law*. Property of a bankrupt that creditors will disclaim under the bankruptcy laws because income from the property will exceed revenues. **3.** Generally, anything that is acquired but turns out to be disadvantageous. — Also spelled *damnosa haereditas*.

damnum (**dam**-nəm), *n.* [Latin] A loss; damage suffered. Pl. **damna.** See AD DAMNUM.

damnum absque injuria (**dam**-nəm **ab**-skwee in-**joor**-ee-ə). See DAMNUM SINE INJURIA.

damnum emergens (**dam**-nəm i-**mər**-jenz), *n.* [Latin "damage arising"] *Roman law.* An actual realized loss (such as a decline in the value of property) as opposed to an expected future loss (such as loss of profit).

> "These kinds of damage are distinguished by the commentators as damnum emergens and lucrum cessans, which may be rendered 'positive damage' and 'loss of profit.' The first may be immediate (*e.g.*, my slave is killed or has lost an eye), or consequential (I have lost his services — I have incurred medical expenses — he was one of a troupe of singers and the whole troupe is less valuable in consequence of his death or injury). Where there is no pecuniary loss there is no action. An action does not lie ... for striking a slave if his value to me has not been depreciated by the blow nor for trespass to land unattended by damage." R.W. Lee, *The Elements of Roman Law* 394 (4th ed. 1956).

damnum facientes (**dam**-nəm fay-shee-**en**-teez), *n.* See DAMAGE FEASANT.

damnum fatale (**dam**-nəm fə-**tay**-lee), *n.* [Latin "accidental damage"] *Roman law.* Damage caused by an unavoidable circumstance, such as a storm or a shipwreck, for which bailees or others will not be held liable. • But an exception was made for damages resulting from theft.

> "The liability of innkeepers, carriers, and stable keepers, at Roman law, was provided for in the praetor's edict. They were under an obligation to restore all goods which the guests or passengers had with them, or left in their charge, and they could not defend themselves by showing the utmost degree of diligence. Unavoidable accident, which no human prudence would avert or provide against, *damnum fatale*, or overwhelming force, *vis maior*, were, however, an adequate defense .... It was particularly noted that theft by a third person would not be permitted as a defense and the reason assigned was the fact that travelers have scarcely any chance to protect themselves against collusion between the innkeeper and the thief." Max Radin, *Handbook of Roman Law* 254 (1927).

damnum infectum (**dam**-nəm in-**fek**-təm). [Latin] *Roman law.* Loss not yet suffered but threatened or apprehended, as when a neighbor's building is about to collapse onto one's property.

damnum injuria datum (**dam**-nəm in-**joor**-ee-ə **day**-təm). [Latin] *Roman law.* The willful or negligent damage to corporeal property.

damnum sine injuria (**dam**-nəm **sı**-nee in-**joor**-ee-ə *or* **sin**-ay). [Latin "damage without wrongful act"] Loss or harm for which there is no legal remedy. — Also termed *damnum absque injuria.* Cf. INJURIA ABSQUE DAMNO.

> "There are cases in which the law will suffer a man knowingly and wilfully to inflict harm upon another, and will not hold him accountable for it. Harm of this description — mischief that is not wrongful because it does not fulfil even the material conditions of responsibility — is called *damnum sine injuria*, the term *injuria* being here used in its true sense of an act contrary to law (*in jus*), not in its modern and corrupt sense of harm." John Salmond, *Jurisprudence* 372–73 (Glanville L. Williams ed., 10th ed. 1947).

> "There are many forms of harm of which the law takes no account. Damage so done and suffered is called *damnum sine injuria*, and the reasons for its permission by the law are various and not capable of exhaustive statement. For example, the harm done may be caused by some person who is merely exercising his own rights; as in the case of the loss inflicted on individual traders by competition in trade, or where the damage is done by a man acting under necessity to prevent a greater evil." R.F.V. Heuston, *Salmond on the Law of Torts* 13 (17th ed. 1977).

Dan (dan), *n.* [fr. Latin *dominus*] *Archaic.* In England, an honorable title for a man; the English equivalent to the Spanish *Don.* • The term evolved into the terms *Master*, *Mister*, and *Sir.*

D & O liability insurance. See *directors' and officers' liability insurance* under INSURANCE.

danelaw (**dayn**-law). *Hist.* **1.** A system of rules, introduced by the Danes during their invasions of England primarily in the ninth century and maintained principally in the midland and eastern counties where the invasions occurred. • Danelaw was the prevailing law in these regions from the reign of King Edgar to Edward the Confessor, who compiled a uniform law that included some Danelaw components. **2.** The counties in England where the Danish law was enforced primarily in the ninth and tenth centuries — Also termed *danelage*; *lex Danorum.*

> "The Danish invasions of the ninth century subjected the eastern parts of the island to new Scandinavian influences. Where the Danes conquered, their 'Danelaw' prevailed. The very word 'law' is believed to have been given to the English language by the Danes." J.H. Baker, *An Introduction to English Legal History* 3 (3d ed. 1990).

danger. 1. Peril; exposure to harm, loss, pain, or other negative result. **2.** A cause of peril; a menace.

apparent danger. **1.** Obvious danger; real danger. **2.** *Criminal law.* The danger resulting from a person's overt demonstration of the intent to seriously injure or kill another, making it necessary for the threatened person to kill the offender. See SELF-DEFENSE.

deterrent danger. An obvious danger that an occupier of land creates to discourage trespassers, such as a barbed-wire fence or spikes on the top of a wall.

imminent danger. **1.** An immediate, real threat to one's safety that justifies the use of force in self-defense. **2.** *Criminal law.* The danger resulting from an immediate threatened injury sufficient to cause a reasonable and prudent person to defend himself or herself.

retributive danger. A concealed danger that an occupier of land creates to injure trespassers. • A retributive danger is lawful only to the extent that it could be justified if the occupier had inflicted the injury personally or directly to the trespasser. Thus, a spring gun or a landmine is an unlawful means of defending land against a trespasser.

unavoidable danger. **1.** Inescapable danger. **2.** A danger that is unpreventable, esp. by a person operating a vessel.

danger-creation doctrine. The theory that if a state's affirmative conduct places a person in jeopardy, then the state may be liable for the harm inflicted on that person by a third party. • This is an exception to the general principle that the state is not liable for an injury that a third party inflicts on a member of the public. — Also termed *danger-creation exception.* Cf. SPECIAL-RELATIONSHIP DOCTRINE.

dangeria, *n. Hist.* Payment by forest tenants to the lord so that they can plow and sow in time of mast feeding by swine in the forest.

danger-invites-rescue doctrine. The principle holding a defendant liable not only for injuries to the person that the defendant has imperiled, but also for injuries that a third person receives while trying to rescue the imperiled person.

> "Danger invites rescue. The cry of distress is the summons to relief. The law does not ignore these reactions of the mind in tracing conduct to its consequences. It recognizes them as normal. It places their effects within the range of the natural and probable. The wrong that imperils life is a wrong to the imperiled victim; it is a wrong also to his rescuer .... The railroad company whose train approaches without signal is a wrongdoer toward the traveler surprised between the rails, but a wrongdoer also to the bystander who drags him from the path .... The emergency begets the man. The wrongdoer may not have foreseen the coming of a deliverer. He is accountable as if he had." *Wagner v. International Ry. Co.,* 133 N.E. 437, 437–38 (N.Y. 1921).

danger of navigation. See PERIL OF THE SEA.

danger of river. See PERIL OF THE SEA.

dangerous, *adj.* **1.** (Of a condition, situation, etc.) perilous; hazardous; unsafe <a dangerous intersection>. **2.** (Of a person, an object, etc.) likely to cause serious bodily harm <a dangerous weapon> <a dangerous criminal>.

dangerous condition. See CONDITION (5).

dangerous criminal. See CRIMINAL.

dangerous drug. See DRUG.

dangerous instrumentality. An instrument, substance, or condition so inherently dangerous that it may cause serious bodily injury or death without human use or interference. • It may serve as the basis for strict liability. See ATTRACTIVE-NUISANCE DOCTRINE. Cf. *deadly weapon* under WEAPON.

dangerous-propensity test. See DANGEROUS-TENDENCY TEST.

dangerous-proximity test. *Criminal law.* A common-law test for the crime of attempt, focusing on whether the defendant is dangerously close to completing the offense. • Factors include the gravity of the potential crime, the apprehension of the victim, and the uncertainty of the crime's occurrence. See ATTEMPT (2).

dangerous situation. Under the last-clear-chance doctrine, the circumstance in which a plaintiff operating a motor vehicle has reached a position (as on the path of an oncoming train) that cannot be escaped by the exercise of ordinary care. — Also termed *situation of danger.* See LAST-CLEAR-CHANCE DOCTRINE.

dangerous-tendency test. A propensity of a person or animal to inflict injury. • The test is used, esp. in dog-bite cases, to determine whether an owner will be held liable for injuries caused by the owner's animal. — Also termed *dangerous-propensity test.*

dangerous weapon. See WEAPON.

danger-utility test. See RISK-UTILITY TEST.

danism (**dan**-iz-əm), *n.* [fr. Greek *daneismos* "a loan"] *Hist.* The lending of money on usury.

***Darden* hearing.** *Criminal procedure.* An ex parte proceeding to determine whether disclosure of an informer's identity is pertinent to establishing probable cause when there is otherwise insufficient evidence to establish probable cause apart from the arresting officer's testimony about an informer's communications. • The defense attorney may be excluded from the hearing but can usu. submit questions to be used by the judge in the examination. *People v. Darden*, 313 N.E.2d 49 (N.Y. 1974).

dare (**dair**-ee), *vb.* [Latin "to give"] *Roman law.* **1.** To give; to transfer (something, esp. property). • The transfer can be made to discharge a debt, to create an obligation, or to make a gift. **2.** To appoint a representative.

dare ad remanentiam (**dair**-ee ad rem-ə-**nen**-shee-əm), *vb.* [Latin "to give in fee or forever"] To transfer (esp. a remainder) in fee or forever.

darraign (də-**rayn**), *vb.* [fr. Latin *derationare*; fr. French *disrener*] *Hist.* **1.** To displace; to disarrange. **2.** To respond to an accusation; to settle a dispute. — Also spelled *deraign*; *dereyne.*

darrein (**dar**-ayn), *adj.* [fr. French *dernier* "the last"] The last, as in *darrein presentment* ("the last presentment"). See DARREIN CONTINUANCE; ASSIZE OF DARREIN PRESENTMENT.

darrein continuance (**dar**-ayn kən-**tin**-yoo-ənts), *n.* [fr. French *dernier continuance* "the last continuance"] *Hist.* Every plea of a new matter after the last entry of a plea on the record. • Every entry of a pleading after the first pleading on the record was called a *continuance.* — Also spelled *dareyne continuance.*

darrein presentment (**dar**-ayn pri-**zent**-mənt), *n.* See ASSIZE OF DARREIN PRESENTMENT.

darrein seisin (**dar**-ayn **see**-zin), *n.* [French "last seisin"] *Hist.* A tenant's plea in a writ of right. See SEISIN.

date. 1. The day when an event happened or will happen <date of trial>. **2.** A period of time in general <at a later date>. **3.** An appointment at a specified time <no dates are available>.

date of bankruptcy. The date when a court declares a person to be bankrupt; the date of bankruptcy adjudication. • This date may coincide with the voluntary-filing date.

date of cleavage. The filing date of a voluntary-bankruptcy petition. • With a few exceptions, only the debts existing at this time are dischargeable.

date of injury. The inception date of an injury; the date of an accident causing an injury.

***date of issue.* 1.** *Commercial law.* An arbitrary date (for notes, bonds, and other documents in a series) fixed as the beginning of the term for which they run; the date that a stock or bond bears on its face, not the date on which it is actually signed, delivered, or put into circulation. • When a bond is delivered to a purchaser, it is considered "issued." But this concept is distinguishable from the "date of issue," which remains fixed, regardless of the date of sale or delivery. **2.** *Insurance.* The date specified in the policy as the "date of issue," not the date on which the policy is executed or delivered, and regardless of other dates that may be specified in the policy or elsewhere, such as the date that the policy is to "take effect."

date of maturity. The date when a debt falls due, such as a debt on a promissory note or bond.

declaration date. The date when corporate directors declare a dividend. Cf. DIVIDEND DATE; EX-DIVIDEND DATE.

dividend date. See DIVIDEND DATE.

payable date. The official date on which shareholder dividends or distributions become payable. — Also termed *record date.*

payment date. The date on which stock dividends or interest checks are paid to shareholders.

record date. The date on which a stockholder must own shares to be entitled to vote or receive a dividend. — Also termed *date of record.* See EX-DIVIDEND DATE.

***settlement date.* 1.** The date on which an investor must pay the broker for securities purchased. **2.** The date on which a seller must deliver negotiable certificates for securities sold.

***submission date.* 1.** The date that a case is to be submitted to a court for determination. **2.** The date on which an investor must pay the broker for securities purchased. **3.** The date on which a seller must deliver negotiable certificates for securities sold.

date certain. A fixed or appointed day; a specified day, esp. a date fixed by an instrument such as a deed. — Also termed (in French law) *date certaine* (**dat** sair-**tayn**).

date of bankruptcy. See DATE.

date of cleavage. See DATE.

date of injury. See DATE.

date of issue. See DATE.

date of maturity. See DATE.

date of record. See *record date* under DATE.

date rape. See RAPE.

datio (**day**-shee-oh), *n.* [fr. Latin *dare* "to give"] *Roman law.* **1.** An act of giving, as in *datio in solutum* ("giving in payment"). **2.** An appointment, as in *datio tutoris* ("appointment of a guardian").

datio in solutum (**day**-shee-oh in sə-**l**[**y**]**oo**-təm). *Roman law.* The discharging of an obligation by the giving and acceptance of something other than the thing due.

dation (**day**-shən), *n.* [fr. Latin *dare* "to give"] *Civil law.* A grant of something the recipient is actually entitled to, such as an office.

dation en paiement (**day**-shən in **pay**-mənt *or* da-**syon** ah*n* pay-**mon**), *n.* [French "a giving in payment"] *Civil law.* **1.** An exchange of something instead of money to satisfy a debt. See ACCORD AND SATISFACTION. **2.** A method of satisfying a mortgage debt by transferring the mortgaged property when the mortgage exceeds the property's value and the mortgage-holder is willing to accept the property in satisfaction of the debt. • *Dation en paiement* requires court approval after petition and notice.

dative (**day**-tiv), *n.* [fr. French *datif* "of giving"] **1.** *Roman & civil law.* An appointment made by judicial or magisterial authority; esp., something granted that is not provided by law or a will. • In Scotland, an executor-dative is a court-appointed executor. **2.** *Hist.* Something that can be given or retracted at will, such as an appointment to a nonperpetual office. — Also spelled *datif.*

datum (**day**-təm), *n.* [fr. Latin *dare* "to give"] **1.** A piece of information. **2.** *Hist.* Something given or executed. **3.** A date.

Daubert **hearing** (**daw**-bərt *or* doh-**ber**). A hearing conducted by federal district courts, usu. before trial, to determine whether proposed expert testimony meets the federal requirements for relevance and reliability, as clarified by the Supreme Court in *Daubert v. Merrell Dow Pharms., Inc.*, 509 U.S. 579, 113 S.Ct. 2786 (1993). See DAUBERT TEST.

Daubert **test.** A method that federal district courts use to determine whether expert testimony is admissible under Federal Rule of Evidence 702, which generally requires that expert testimony consist of scientific, technical, or other specialized knowledge that will assist the fact-finder in understanding the evidence or determining a fact in issue. • In its role as "gatekeeper" of the evidence, the trial court must decide whether the proposed expert testimony meets the requirements of relevance and reliability. The court applies the test outside the jury's presence, usu. during a pretrial *Daubert* hearing. At the hearing, the proponent must show that the expert's underlying reasoning or methodology, and its application to the facts, are scientifically valid. In ruling on admissibility, the court considers a flexible list of factors, including (1) whether the theory can be or has been tested, (2) whether the theory has been subjected to peer review or publication, (3) the theory's known or potential rate of error and whether there are standards that control its operation, and (4) the degree to which the relevant scientific community has accepted the theory. *Daubert v. Merrell Dow Pharms., Inc.*, 509 U.S. 579, 113 S.Ct. 2786 (1993). The Supreme Court has held that similar scrutiny must be applied to nonscientific expert testimony. *Kumho Tire Co. v. Carmichael*, 119 S.Ct. 1167 (1999). Variations of the *Daubert* test are applied in the trial courts of most states. See *scientific knowledge* under KNOWLEDGE.

daughter. **1.** A parent's female child. **2.** A female descendant. **3.** A female child in a parent-child relationship.

daughter-in-law. The wife of one's son.

Davis-Bacon Act. A federal law originally enacted in 1931 to regulate the minimum-wage rates payable to employees of federal public-works projects. 40 USCA § 276a.

day. 1. Any 24-hour period; the time it takes the earth to revolve once on its axis <we have a day to prepare a mandamus petition>. **2.** The period between the rising and the setting of the sun <day or night>. — Also termed *natural day*. **3.** Sunlight <we can see it in the day>. **4.** The period when the sun is above the horizon, along with the period in the early morning and late evening when a person's face is discernible. **5.** Any specified time period, esp. as distinguished from other periods <the good old days> <a day's work>. — Also termed (in senses 2, 3, and 4) *daytime*. Cf. NIGHT.

adjournment day. **1.** The day on which an organization, such as a court or legislature, adjourns. **2.** *Hist.* A later day appointed by the judges at regular sittings at *nisi prius* to try an issue of fact not then ready for trial.

adjournment day in error. *Hist.* A day scheduled for completion of matters not finished on the affirmance day of the term.

affirmance day general. *Hist.* In the Court of Exchequer, a day appointed after the beginning of every term to affirm or reverse judgments.

answer day. The last day for a defendant to file and serve a responsive pleading in a lawsuit. • Under the Federal Rules of Civil Procedure, a defendant generally must serve an answer (1) within 20 days after being served with the summons and complaint, or (2) if a defendant timely waives service at the plaintiff's request, within 60 days after the request for waiver was sent. Fed. R. Civ. P. 4(d), 12(a). — Also termed *answer date*; *appearance date*; *appearance day*.

artificial day. The period from the rising to the setting of the sun. — Also termed *solar day*; *dies solaris*.

astronomical day. See *solar day* (2).

banking day. See BANKING DAY.

business day. A day that most institutions are open for business, usu. a day on which banks and major stock exchanges are open, excluding Saturdays and Sundays.

calendar day. A consecutive 24-hour day running from midnight to midnight. — Also termed *natural day*.

common day. In England, an ordinary court day.

court day. A day on which a particular court is open for court business.

dedication day. *Hist.* A day on which people from several villages gathered in one place to celebrate the feast day of the saint and patron of a church.

entire day. An undivided day, rather than parts of two or more days aggregated to form a 24-hour period. • An entire day must have a legal, fixed, precise time to begin and end. A statute referring to an *entire day* contemplates a 24-hour period beginning and ending at midnight.

ferial day (**feer**-ee-əl). *Hist.* **1.** A day free from labor, pleading, and service of process; a holiday. **2.** A working day, under a 1449 statute (27 Hen. 6, ch. 5).

juridical day (juu-**rid**-i-kəl). A day on which legal proceedings can be held. — Also termed *judicial day*. Cf. *nonjudicial day*; NONJURIDICAL.

law day. See LAW DAY.

lay day. *Maritime law.* A day allowed for loading and unloading cargo without penalty to the parties chartering the vessel.

love day. *Hist.* **1.** A day when neighbors amicably settled a dispute. **2.** A day when one neighbor helped another without payment.

natural day. **1.** The 24-hour period from midnight to midnight. — Also termed *calendar day*. **2.** The period between sunrise and sunset. — Also termed *artificial day*.

nonjudicial day. A day when courts do not sit or when legal proceedings cannot be conducted, such as a Sunday or legal holiday. See LEGAL HOLIDAY; NON JURIDICUS. Cf. *juridical day*.

peremptory day. A day assigned for trial or hearing, without further opportunity for postponement.

quarter day. *Hist.* One of four days during a year that money owed (such as rent) was legally or customarily payable.

return day. **1.** A day on which a defendant must appear in court (as for an arraignment). **2.** A day on which a defendant must file an answer. **3.** A day on which a proof of service must be returned to court. **4.** A day on which a writ of execution must be returned to court. **5.** A day specified by law for counting votes in an election. — Also termed *return date*.

solar day. **1.** See *artificial day*. **2.** The 24-hour period from noon to noon. — Also termed *astronomical day*.

daybook. A merchant's original record of daily transactions.

day in court. 1. The right and opportunity, in a judicial tribunal, to litigate a claim, seek relief, or defend one's rights. **2.** The right to be notified and given an opportunity to appear and to be heard when one's case is called.

day loan. See LOAN.

day order. See ORDER (4).

day rule. See DAY WRIT.

days in bank. Particular days set aside by the Court of Common Pleas for specific matters, including the appearance of parties and service of process. — Also termed *dies in banco.*

> "There are in each of these terms stated days called *days in bank, dies in banco;* that is, days of appearance in the court of common pleas. They are generally at the distance of about a week from each other, and regulated by some festival of the church. On some one of these days in bank all original writs must be made returnable . . . ." 3 William Blackstone, *Commentaries on the Laws of England* 277 (1768).

daysman (**dayz**-mən). *Hist.* **1.** An arbitrator; an elected judge; an umpire. **2.** A day laborer. — Also spelled *deiesman.*

days of grace. 1. GRACE PERIOD. **2.** *Int'l law.* A timed exemption from prize law that is granted to enemy merchant ships when they are caught unawares by the outbreak of war.

daytime. See DAY (2), (3), (4).

daywork. 1. Short-term employment that is intended to last only for a day, or for a few days. **2.** *Hist.* In England, a measure of land being the amount of arable land that can be plowed in a day. — Also termed *daywere.*

day writ. *English law.* A Queen's Bench writ allowing a prisoner to leave prison to conduct business (such as attending trial at the Court of Assizes), as long as the prisoner returns by 9:00 p.m. — Also termed *day rule.*

D.B. *abbr.* DOMESDAY BOOK.

d/b/a. *abbr.* Doing business as. • The abbreviation usu. precedes a person's or business's assumed name <Paul Smith d/b/a Paul's Dry Cleaners>.

d.b.e. *abbr.* DE BENE ESSE.

d.b.n. See *administration de bonis non* under ADMINISTRATION.

d.b.n. c.t.a. See *administration de bonis non cum testamento annexo* under ADMINISTRATION.

D.C. *abbr.* **1.** DISTRICT OF COLUMBIA. **2.** See *district court* under COURT.

DCF. See *discounted cash flow* under CASH FLOW.

de (də *or* duu). [French] Of; about. • This is a French preposition often used to show the genitive case, as in *brefe de droit* ("writ of right").

de (dee *or* day). [Latin] Of; about; concerning; respecting; by; from; out of; affecting. • This preposition is used in the titles of English statutes, of original and judicial writs, and of court proceedings.

deacon. 1. *Eccles. law.* In certain churches, a member of the clerical order who assists the priest in various duties, including the presentation of the sacrament. • It is the third order of the Church of England below bishops and priests. A deacon is not allowed to consecrate the Holy Communion or pronounce absolution but can perform most of the other priestly duties. **2.** An elected or appointed officer of a church who assists a minister or priest in various duties.

dead asset. See ASSET.

deadbeat. *Slang.* A person who does not pay debts or financial obligations, usu. with the suggestion that the person is also adept or experienced at evading creditors.

dead freight. See FREIGHT.

deadhand control. The use of executory interests that vest at some indefinite and remote time in the future to restrict alienability and to ensure that property remains in the hands of a particular family or organization. • The rule against perpetuities restricts this activity, which is sometimes referred to either as the power of the dead hand (*mortua manus*) or as trying to retain property *in mortua manu.* See MORTMAIN.

dead letter. 1. A law or practice that, although not formally abolished, is no longer used, observed, or enforced. **2.** A piece of mail that can be neither delivered nor returned because it lacks correct addresses for both the intended recipient and the sender.

deadlock, *n.* **1.** A state of inaction resulting from opposition or lack of compromise. **2.** *Corporations.* The blocking of corporate action by one or more factions of shareholders or directors who disagree about a significant aspect of corporate policy. — **deadlock,** *vb.*

deadlocked jury. See *hung jury* under JURY.

deadly force. See FORCE.

deadly weapon. See WEAPON.

deadly weapon per se. See WEAPON.

dead man's part. *Hist.* By custom in certain places, the portion of a dead man's estate given to the administrator. • That portion ranged from one-third (if the deceased had a wife and children) to the entire estate amount (if the deceased had no wife or children). — Also termed *death's part*; (in Scots law) *dead's part.*

> "If the deceased leaves a widow and children, his substance ... is divided into three parts; one of which belongs to the widow, another to the children, and the third to the administrator: if only a widow, or only children, they shall respectively, in either case, take one moiety, and the administrator the other: if neither widow nor child, the administrator shall have the whole. And this portion, or *dead man's* part, the administrator was wont to apply to his own use, till the statute I Jac. II. c. 17 declared that the same should be subject to the statute of distributions." 2 William Blackstone, *Commentaries on the Laws of England* 518 (1766).

dead man's statute. A law prohibiting the admission of a decedent's statement as evidence in certain circumstances, as when an opposing party or witness seeks to use the statement to support a claim against the decedent's estate. — Also termed *dead person's statute.*

de admensuratione dotis (dee ad-men-s[y]uu-ray-shee-**oh**-nee **doh**-tis), *n.* [Law Latin "of the admeasurement of dower"] *Hist.* A writ available to an heir (or the heir's guardian if the heir is an infant) to reduce the dower of the ancestor's widow who, while the heir was an infant, was assigned more dower than she was entitled to.

> "If the heir or his guardian do not assign her dower within the term of quarantine, or do assign it unfairly, she has her remedy at law, and the sheriff is appointed to assign it. Or if the heir (being under age) or his guardian assign more than she ought to have, it may be afterwards remedied by writ of *admeasurement* of dower." 2 William Blackstone, *Commentaries on the Laws of England* 136 (1766).

dead person's statute. See DEAD MAN'S STATUTE.

dead pledge. *Archaic.* See MORTGAGE (1).

dead rent. A mining-lease payment, either in addition to or as part of the royalty, that must be made whether or not the mine is working. • The purpose of the provision is to secure the working of the mine. See *delay rental* under RENTAL.

dead-ship doctrine. *Maritime law.* The rule that admiralty law no longer applies to a ship when its purpose has been so changed that it is no longer a vessel because it has no further navigation function.

dead's part. See DEAD MAN'S PART.

dead stock. Goods that remain in inventory because there is no market for them.

dead storage. The stowage of goods, esp. motor vehicles, for a long time in a public storage area, as opposed to the daily or regular stowage of goods in active use. Cf. LIVE STORAGE.

dead time. Time that does not count for a particular purpose, such as time not included in calculating an employee's wages or time not credited toward a prisoner's sentence.

dead use. A future use.

de advisamento consilii nostri (dee ad-vɪ-zə-**men**-toh kən-**sil**-ee-ɪ **nos**-trɪ). [Law Latin] With or by the advice of our council. • This phrase was formerly used in writs of summons to Parliament.

de aequitate (dee ee-kwə-**tay**-tee). [Latin] In equity.

de aestimato (dee es-ti-**may**-toh), *n.* [Latin "for the estimation of something in money"] *Roman law.* An action available to an owner of goods against a person who received the goods but failed, after a certain period, to either pay the owner an agreed price after finding a purchaser or return the goods to the owner. • The transaction, or *aestimatum*, was an innominate contract often used by traveling merchants or second-hand dealers who, after purchasing items, could then resell them at higher prices or return them to the owner. — Also termed *actio aestimatoria.*

de aetate probanda (dee ee-**tay**-tee proh-**ban**-də), *n.* [Law Latin "of (about) proving age"] *Hist.* A writ ordering the sheriff to summon a jury to determine whether an heir of a tenant holding an estate directly of the Crown was old enough to receive the estate.

deafforest. See DISAFFOREST.

deal, *n.* **1.** An act of buying and selling; the purchase and exchange of something for profit <a business deal>. **2.** An arrangement for mutual advantage <the witness accepted the prosecutor's deal to testify in exchange for immunity>. **3.** An indefinite quantity <a great deal of money>.

deal, *vb.* **1.** To distribute (something) <to deal drugs>. **2.** To transact business with (a person or entity) <to deal with the competitor>. **3.** To conspire with (a person or entity) <to deal for the account>.

dealer, *n.* **1.** A person who purchases goods or property for sale to others; a retailer. **2.** A person or firm that buys and sells securities for its own account as a principal, and then sells to a customer. See DEAL, *n.* & *vb.*

registered dealer. A dealer registered or required to be registered under the Securities Exchange Act of 1934.

dealer's talk. See PUFFING.

de allocatione facienda (dee al-ə-kay-shee-**oh**-nee fay-shee-**en**-də), *n.* [Law Latin "for making allowance"] *Hist.* A writ directed to the treasurer and barons of the Exchequer allowing certain officers (such as accountants and customs collectors) to have in their accounts the funds necessary to make certain payments.

de alto et basso (dee **al**-toh et **bas**-oh), *n.* [fr. French *haut et de bass* "of high and low"] *Hist.* The total submission of all differences — great or small — to arbitration.

de ambitu (dee **am**-bi-tyoo). [Latin "of going around"] Of devious methods of securing a position, as through bribery. • Several Roman laws (such as the *Lex Julia de Ambitu*) dealt with this problem.

de ampliori gratia (dee am-plI-**or**-I **gray**-shee-ə). [Latin] Of more abundant or more full grace.

dean. 1. *Eccles. law.* An officer who leads a chapter, parish, or other subdivision of a church, usu. upon a bishop's request or appointment.

> "A dean and chapter are the council of the bishop, to assist him with their advice in affairs of religion, and also in the temporal concerns of his see .... All ancient deans are elected by the chapter, by *conge d'eslire* from the king, and letters missive of recommendation; in the same manner as bishops: but in those chapters, that were founded by Henry VIII out of the spoils of the dissolved monasteries, the deanery is donative .... The chapter, consisting of canons or prebendaries, are sometimes appointed by the king, sometimes by the bishop, and sometimes elected by each other." 1 William Blackstone, *Commentaries on the Laws of England* 370–71 (1765).

2. In a school, college, or university, the administrative or academic head. • In larger schools, there may be several kinds of deans, such as a dean of admissions and a dean of student affairs. Within a university, there may be deans of specific schools. **3.** The head or commander of a group of ten, such as ten soldiers or ten monks.

de anno bissextili (dee **an**-oh bis-sek-**stI**-lI), *n.* [Law Latin "of the bissextile year"] *Hist.* A law of Henry III advising the justices of the bench that in a case requiring something to be done within a year, the leap-year day and the day before should be counted as one day.

de annua pensione (dee **an**-yoo-ə pen-shee-**oh**-nee), *n.* [Law Latin "of annual pension"] *Hist.* A royal writ demanding payment from an abbey or prior, of a yearly pension for the king's chaplain named in the writ.

de annuo reditu (dee **an**-yoo-oh **red**-i-tyoo), *n.* [Law Latin "for a yearly rent"] *Hist.* A writ to recover an annuity payable in goods or money.

Dean of the Arches. *English law.* The presiding judge of the Court of Arches. See COURT OF ARCHES.

de apostata capiendo (dee ə-**pos**-tə-tə kap-ee-**en**-doh), *n.* [Law Latin "of the taking of an apostate"] *Hist.* A writ ordering a sheriff to apprehend and return to an abbey a person who had entered the abbey, professed the religious order, and then left and wandered around the country.

de arbitratione facto (dee ahr-bi-tray-shee-**oh**-nee **fak**-toh), *n.* [Law Latin "of arbitration had"] *Hist.* A writ staying an action already settled by arbitration.

de arrestandis bonis ne dissipentur (dee ar-ə-**stan**-dis **boh**-nis nee dis-ə-**pen**-tər), *n.* [Law Latin "of goods arrested lest they be dispersed"] *Hist.* A writ to seize goods from a party to ensure that the goods do not disappear while a lawsuit is pending.

de arrestando ipsum qui pecuniam recepit (dee ar-ə-**stan**-doh **ip**-səm kwɪ pə-**kyoo**-nee-əm ri-**see**-pit), *n.* [Law Latin "for the apprehension of one who took the king's money"] *Hist.* A writ ordering the arrest of a person who took the king's money for war service, and then hid to keep from serving.

de asportatis religiosorum (dee as-por-**tay**-tis ri-lij-ee-oh-**sor**-əm), *n.* [Law Latin "concerning the property of religious persons carried away"] *Hist.* A statute of Edward I passed to curb abuses of clerical possessions, including the removal of those possessions to foreign countries.

de assisa proroganda (dee ə-**sɪ**-zə proh-rə-**gan**-də), *n.* [Law Latin "of the proroguing of an assize"] *Hist.* A writ ordering justices to postpone an assize because a party is busy in the Crown's service.

death. The ending of life; the cessation of all vital functions and signs. — Also termed *decease*; *demise*.

brain death. The bodily condition of showing no response to external stimuli, no spontaneous movements, no breathing, no reflexes, and a flat reading (usu. for a full day) on a machine that measures the brain's electrical activity. — Also termed *legal death*.

civil death. See CIVIL DEATH.

immediate death. **1.** See *instantaneous death*. **2.** A death occurring within a short time after an injury or seizure, but not instantaneously.

> "A distinction has been made between 'instantaneous' and 'immediate' death .... As an example of 'immediate' rather than 'instantaneous' death ... the situation in which a blow on the head produces unconsciousness and renders the victim incapable of intelligent thought, speech, or action for several minutes until he dies." 22A Am. Jur. 2d *Death* § 43, at 159 (1988).

instantaneous death. Death occurring in an instant or within an extremely short time after an injury or seizure. • It is a factor in determining an award of damages for the victim's pain and suffering. — Sometimes also termed *immediate death*.

> "Although the possibility of a death that is truly simultaneous with the injury that caused it has been denied, it has been pointed out that death may be so contemporaneous with the fatal injury as to be instantaneous in the sense that there could be no recovery for the victim's pain and suffering. Ordinarily, death is not regarded as instantaneous if an appreciable length of time elapsed between the injury and the death. Indeed, even where the injury causing the death is necessarily fatal and death results therefrom in a few moments, it has been held that although it would commonly be called an instantaneous death, still if the injured person survives the injury for a brief period, it may not be said that the death is instantaneous .... In such case it is immaterial that the period of time between the injury and death is short." 22A Am. Jur. 2d *Death* § 43, at 158 (1988).

legal death. See *brain death*.

natural death. **1.** Bodily death, as opposed to civil death. **2.** Death from causes other than accident or violence; death from natural causes. — Also termed *mors naturalis*. Cf. *violent death*. See NATURAL-DEATH ACT.

presumptive death. Death inferred from proof of the person's long, unexplained absence, usu. after seven years.

simultaneous death. The death of two or more persons in the same mishap, under circumstances that make it impossible to determine who died first. See SIMULTANEOUS-DEATH ACT; COMMORIENTES.

violent death. Death accelerated by human intervention and resulting from a sharp blow, explosion, gunfire, or the like. Cf. *natural death*.

death, contemplation of. See CONTEMPLATION OF DEATH.

death action. See WRONGFUL-DEATH ACTION.

deathbed declaration. See *dying declaration* under DECLARATION (6).

death benefits. An amount paid to a beneficiary on the death of an insured.

death by misadventure. See ACCIDENTAL KILLING.

death case. **1.** A criminal case in which the death penalty may be or has been imposed. **2.** WRONGFUL-DEATH ACTION.

death certificate. An official document issued by a public registry verifying that a person has died, with information such as the date and time of death, the cause of death, and the signature of the attending or examining physician.

death-knell doctrine. A rule allowing an interlocutory appeal if precluding an appeal until final judgment would moot the issue on appeal and irreparably injure the appellant's rights. • Once recognized as an exception to the final-judgment rule, the doctrine was limited by the U.S. Supreme Court in *Coopers & Lybrand v. Livesay*, 437 U.S. 463, 98 S.Ct. 2454 (1978). There, the Court held that the death-knell doctrine does not permit an immediate appeal of an order denying class certification. But the doctrine still applies in some contexts. For example, the doctrine allows an immediate appeal of the denial of a temporary restraining order when the lack of an appeal would leave nothing to be considered in the trial court. *Woratzeck v. Arizona Bd. of Executive Clemency*, 117 F.3d 400 (9th Cir. 1997). — Also termed *death-knell exception*. See FINAL-JUDGMENT RULE.

Death on the High Seas Act. A federal law, enacted in 1920, permitting a wrongful-death action to be filed in U.S. district court for a death occurring on the high seas (i.e., seas beyond any state or territory's waters). 46 USCA app. §§ 761–767. — Abbr. DOHSA.

death penalty. 1. State-imposed death as punishment for a serious crime. — Also termed *capital punishment*. **2.** A penalty that makes a person or entity ineligible to participate in an activity that the person or entity previously participated in. • The penalty is usu. imposed because of some type of gross misconduct.

death-penalty sanction. See SANCTION.

death-qualified jury. See JURY.

death row. The area of a prison where those who have been sentenced to death are confined.

death sentence. See SENTENCE.

deathsman. An executioner; a hangman.

death's part. See DEAD MAN'S PART.

death statute. A law that protects the interests of a decedent's family and other dependents, who may recover in damages what they would reasonably have received from the decedent if the death had not occurred. Cf. SURVIVAL STATUTE.

death tax. See TAX.

death trap. 1. A structure or situation involving an imminent risk of death. **2.** A situation that is seemingly safe but actually quite dangerous.

death warrant. See WARRANT (1).

de attornato recipiendo (dee a-tor-**nay**-toh ri-sip-ee-**en**-doh), *n.* [Law Latin "of receipt of an attorney"] *Hist.* A writ requiring a court to receive and admit an attorney for a party.

de audiendo et terminando (dee aw-dee-**end**-doh et tər-mi-**nan**-doh), *n.* [Law Latin "for hearing and determining"] *Hist.* A writ or commission directing certain justices to hear and resolve particular cases resulting from a riot, including those involving heinous misdemeanors, breaches of the peace, and trespass. Cf. COMMISSION OF OYER AND TERMINER.

de averiis captis in withernamium (dee ə-**veer**-ee-is **kap**-tis in wi*th*-ər-**nay**-mee-əm), *n.* [Law Latin "for taking cattle in withernam"] *Hist.* A writ directing a sheriff to detain a defendant's cattle because the defendant had unlawfully taken the plaintiff's cattle out of the county. • The defendant's cattle would be detained until the sheriff could replevy the plaintiff's cattle.

de averiis replegiandis (dee ə-**veer**-ee-is ri-plee-jee-**an**-dis), *n.* [Law Latin "of replevying beasts"] *Hist.* A writ ordering a sheriff to replevy someone's beasts or chattels that had been unlawfully taken and detained. • This is the old writ of replevin.

de banco (dee *or* də **bang**-koh). [Law Latin] Of the bench. • In England, the term applied to justices of the Court of Common Pleas.

debarment, *n.* The act of precluding someone from having or doing something; exclusion or hindrance. — **debar,** *vb.*

debasement. 1. The act of reducing the value, quality, or purity of something; esp., the act of lowering the value of coins by either reducing the weight of gold and silver in the coins or increasing the coins' alloy amounts. **2.** Degradation. **3.** The state of being degraded.

debauch (di-**bawch**), *vb.* **1.** *Archaic.* To draw (a person) away from duty; to lead (a person) astray. **2.** To corrupt (a person) with lewdness; to seduce (someone). **3.** To mar or spoil (a person or thing).

debauchery (di-**bawch**-ə-ree), *n.* Excessive indulgence in sensual pleasures; sexual immorality or excesses. — **debauch,** *vb.*

debellatio (deb-ə-**lay**-shee-oh). [Latin] *Int'l law.* A means of ending a war and acquiring territory when one of the belligerent countries has been so soundly defeated that its adversary is able to decide alone the fate of the defeated country's territory; conquest followed by annexation. — Also termed *subjugation.*

> "[There are] three possible alternative meanings of *debellatio* in international law. The first is that *debellatio* denotes the change wrought by the conquest and total subjugation of a State together with that State's annexation by the conqueror. The second view is that *debellatio* corresponds to the total defeat of an enemy State, its occupation, and the elimination of a vital component of Statehood; in this view, *debellatio* implies the extinction of the old State, but it leaves open the legal future of the occupied territory (annexation or the founding of one or more new States). The third view is that *debellatio* only describes a factual situation and that even the elimination of all the State organs combined with the occupation of the territory does not exclude the continuing existence of that State. It is mainly the second and the third meanings of *debellatio* which have been advocated for the situation of Germany since the end of World War II." Karl-Ulrich Meyn, "*Debellatio,*" in 1 *Encyclopedia of Public International Law* 166 (1992).

de bene esse (dee **bee**-nee **es**-ee *also* day **ben**-ay **es**-ay), *adv.* [Law Latin "of well-being"] As conditionally allowed for the present; in anticipation of a future need <Willis's deposition was taken *de bene esse*>. — Abbr. *d.b.e.* — ***de bene esse,*** *adj.*

debenture (di-**ben**-chər). **1.** A debt secured only by the debtor's earning power, not by a lien on any specific asset. **2.** An instrument acknowledging such a debt. **3.** A bond that is backed only by the general credit and financial reputation of the corporate issuer, not by a lien on corporate assets. — Also termed *debenture bond*; *unsecured bond*; *naked debenture*; *plain bond.* Cf. BOND (3).

convertible debenture. A debenture that the holder may change or convert into some other security, such as stock.

convertible subordinated debenture. A debenture that is subordinate to another debt but can be converted into a different security.

sinking-fund debenture. A debenture that is secured by periodic payments into a fund established to retire long-term debt.

subordinate debenture. A debenture that is subject to the prior payment of ordinary debentures and other indebtedness.

4. *English law.* A company's security for a monetary loan. • The security usu. creates a charge on company stock or property. **5.** A customhouse certificate providing for a refund of the duties on imported goods when the importer reexports the goods rather than selling them in the country where they were imported.

debenture bond. See DEBENTURE (3).

debenture indenture. An indenture containing obligations not secured by a mortgage or other collateral. • It is a long-term financing vehicle that places the debenture holder in substantially the same position as a bondholder secured by a first mortgage.

debenture stock. 1. *English law.* A type of bond representing money borrowed by a company using its property or other fixed assets as security. **2.** Stock that is issued under a contract providing for periodic, fixed payments.

debet et detinet (**dee**-bet *or* **deb**-et et **det**-i-net *or* **det**-ə-nət). [Law Latin] *Hist.* He owes and detains. • This phrase was used in declarations in actions for debt when the original creditor sued the original debtor. The declaration stated that the defendant "owes to" as well as "detains from" the plaintiff the debt or thing in question; thus, the action was said to be "in the *debet et detinet.*" But if the action was brought against someone other than the original debtor (such as an executor, for a debt due from the testator), then the action was said to be "in the *detinet* alone." Cf. DETINET.

debet sine breve (**dee**-bet *or* **deb**-et **sI**-nee **breev** *or* **bree**-vee), *n.* [Law Latin "debt without a writ"] **1.** An action for debt commenced under a bill rather than a writ. **2.** A debt confessed by judgment. — Abbr. *d.s.b.* — Also termed *debitum sine breve*; *debit sans breve.* See CONFESSION OF JUDGMENT.

de bien et de mal (də **byen** ay də **mal**). [Law French]. See DE BONO ET MALO.

de biens le mort (də **beenz** lə **mor**[**t**]). [Law French] *Hist.* Of the goods of the deceased.

de bigamis (dee **big**-ə-mis), *n.* [Law Latin "concerning men twice married"] *Hist.* The statute of 4 Edw. I. st. 3, so called from the opening words of the fifth chapter. See BIGAMUS.

debit. 1. A sum charged as due or owing. **2.** In bookkeeping, an entry made on the left side of a ledger or account, noting an increase in assets or a decrease in liabilities. **3.** An account balance showing that something remains due to the holder of the account. Cf. CREDIT (6).

debita laicorum (**deb**-i-tə lay-ə-**kor**-əm), *n.* [Law Latin "debts of laity"] *Hist.* The debts recoverable in civil courts.

debit card. A card used to pay for purchases by electronic transfer from the purchaser's bank account. Cf. CREDIT CARD.

debitor. *Roman law.* Someone who has a legal obligation to someone else. Cf. CREDITOR (1).

debitor non praesumitur donare (**deb**-i-tor non pri-**zyoo**-mi-tur doh-**nair**-ee), *n.* [Law Latin "a debtor is not presumed to make a gift"] *Hist.* The presumption that any payment from a debtor is intended to satisfy the debt, unless the disposition clearly shows the debtor's intent to make a donation.

debitrix (**deb**-ə-triks), *n.* [Latin] *Archaic. Civil law.* A female debtor.

debit sans breve. See DEBET SINE BREVE.

debitum (**deb**-i-təm), *n.* [Latin] Something owing; a debt. Cf. INDEBITUM.

debitum in praesenti solvendum in futuro (**deb**-ə-təm in pri-**zen**-tɪ sol-**ven**-dəm in fyoo-**t[y]oor**-oh). [Latin] A present debt (or obligation) to be paid at a future time; a debt or obligation complete when contracted, but of which the performance cannot be required until some future period.

debitum sine breve. See DEBET SINE BREVE.

de bonis asportatis (dee **boh**-nis as-pər-**tay**-tis). See *trespass de bonis asportatis* under TRESPASS.

de bonis non (dee **boh**-nis **non**). See *administration de bonis non* under ADMINISTRATION.

de bonis non administratis (dee **boh**-nis **non** ad-min-ə-**stray**-tis). [Law Latin] *Hist.* Of the goods not administered. • When the first administrator of an intestate estate dies or is removed, the second administrator is called an administrator *bonis non,* who administers the goods not administered by the previous executor.

de bonis non amovendis (dee **boh**-nis non ay-moh-**ven**-dis), *n.* [Latin "of goods not to be moved"] *Hist.* A writ directing the sheriffs of London to make sure that a defendant's goods are not removed while the defendant's writ of error on a judgment is pending.

de bonis propriis (dee **boh**-nis **proh**-pree-is), *n.* [Law Latin "of his own goods"] *Hist.* A judgment allowing execution on an administrator's individual property rather than the property of an estate, as when the administrator mismanages the estate. Cf. DE BONIS TESTATORIS.

de bonis testatoris (dee **boh**-nis tes-tə-**tor**-is), *n.* [Law Latin "of the goods of the testator"] *Hist.* A judgment awarding execution on a testator's property, rather than the individual property of an administrator. Cf. DE BONIS PROPRIIS.

de bonis testatoris ac si (dee **boh**-nis tes-tə-**tor**-is ak **sɪ**). [Law Latin "from the goods of the testator if he has any, and if not, from those of the executor"]. *Hist.* A judgment holding an executor responsible if the testator's estate is insufficient or if the executor falsifies a pleading as a release.

de bonne memoire (də **bawn** **mem**-wahr). [Law French] Of sound mind; of good memory. — Also spelled *de bone memorie.* See MIND AND MEMORY; COMPOS MENTIS.

de bono et malo (dee **boh**-noh et **mal**-oh), *n.* [Law Latin "for good and evil"] *Hist* **1.** For good and evil. • A criminal defendant indicated full submission to the jury's verdict by placing himself or herself at the jury's mercy *de bono et malo.* — Also termed *de bien et de mal.* **2.** A special writ of jail delivery issued by the justices of assize to enable them to try all criminal defendants who were in jail where the court traveled. • Formerly, the judges were required to issue a separate writ for every prisoner. This was replaced by a general commission of jail delivery.

> "[T]hey have . . . a commission of general *gaol delivery;* which empowers them to try and deliver every prisoner, who shall be in the gaol when the judges arrive at the circuit town, whenever indicted, or for whatever crime committed. It was anciently the course to issue special writs of gaol delivery for each particular prisoner, which were called the writs *de bono et malo*: but, these being found inconvenient and oppressive, a *general* commission for all the prisoners has long been established in their stead. So that, one way or other, the gaols are cleared, and all offenders tried, punished, or delivered, twice in every year: a constitution of singular use and excel-

lence." 4 William Blackstone, *Commentaries on the Laws of England* 267 (1769).

de bono gestu (dee **boh**-noh **jes**-t[y]oo). [Law Latin] For good behavior.

debt. 1. Liability on a claim; a specific sum of money due by agreement or otherwise <the debt amounted to $2,500>. **2.** The aggregate of all existing claims against a person, entity, or state <the bank denied the loan application after analyzing the applicant's outstanding debt>. **3.** A nonmonetary thing that one person owes another, such as goods or services <her debt was to supply him with 20 international first-class tickets on the airline of his choice>. **4.** A common-law writ by which a court adjudicates claims involving fixed sums of money <he brought suit in debt>. — Also termed (in sense 4) *writ of debt*.

"The action of debt lies where a party claims the recovery of a debt; that is, a liquidated or certain sum of money due him. The action is based upon contract, but the contract may be implied, either in fact or in law, as well as express; and it may be either a simple contract or a specialty. The most common instances of its use are for debts: (a) Upon unilateral contracts express or implied in fact. (b) Upon quasi-contractual obligations having the force and effect of simple contracts. (c) Upon bonds and covenants under seal. (d) Upon judgments or obligations of record. (e) Upon obligations imposed by statute." Benjamin J. Shipman, *Handbook of Common-Law Pleading* § 52, at 132 (Henry Winthrop Ballantine ed., 3d ed. 1923).

active debt. *Civil law.* A debt due to another person.

ancestral debt. An ancestor's debt that an heir can be compelled to pay.

antecedent debt. **1.** *Contracts.* An old debt that may serve as consideration for a new promise if the statute of limitations has run on the old debt. See PREEXISTING-DUTY RULE. **2.** *Bankruptcy.* A debtor's prepetition obligation that existed before a debtor's transfer of an interest in property. • For a transfer to be preferential, it must be for or on account of an antecedent debt. See PREFERENTIAL TRANSFER.

bad debt. A debt that is uncollectible and that may be deductible for tax purposes.

bonded debt. A debt secured by a bond; a business or government debt represented by issued bonds.

community debt. A debt that is chargeable to the community of husband and wife rather than to either individually. See COMMUNITY PROPERTY.

consumer debt. A debt incurred by someone primarily for a personal, family, or household purpose.

"What are 'consumer' debts? Section 101(8) defines a consumer debt as follows: 'consumer debt means debt incurred by an individual primarily for a personal, family, or household purpose.' The touchstone is the debtor's use of the money. The nature of the collateral, the business of the creditor and the form of the loan are all irrelevant. A loan of $25,000 from a Credit Union to pay for a child's education is a consumer debt, but the same loan used to finance the opening of an accounting business is not a consumer debt. This is so irrespective of the nature of the collateral put up for the debt." David G. Epstein et al., *Bankruptcy* § 7-45, at 579 (1993).

contingent debt. A debt that is not presently fixed but that may become fixed in the future with the occurrence of some event.

convertible debt. A debt whose security may be changed by a creditor into another form of security.

debt by simple contract. See *simple-contract debt*.

debt by special contract. See *special-contract debt*.

debt by specialty contract. See *special-contract debt*.

debt of record. A debt evidenced by a court record, such as a judgment.

exigible debt. A liquidated and demandable debt; a matured claim.

fixed debt. Generally, a permanent form of debt commonly evidenced by a bond or debenture; long-term debt. — Also termed *fixed liability*.

floating debt. Short-term debt that is continuously renewed to finance the ongoing operations of a business or government.

fraudulent debt. A debt created by fraudulent practices.

funded debt. **1.** A state or municipal debt to be paid out of an accumulation of money or by future taxation. **2.** Secured long-term corporate debt meant to replace short-term, floating, or unsecured debt.

general debt. A governmental body's debt that is legally payable from general revenues and is backed by the full faith and credit of the governmental body.

hypothecary debt. A lien on an estate.

individual debt. (*usu. pl.*) Debt personally owed by a partner, rather than by the partnership.

installment debt. A debt that is to be repaid in a series of payments at regular times over a specified period.

judgment debt. A debt that is evidenced by a legal judgment or brought about by a successful lawsuit against the debtor.

legal debt. A debt recoverable in a court of law.

liquidated debt. A debt whose amount has been determined by agreement of the parties or by operation of law.

liquid debt. A debt that is due immediately and unconditionally.

long-term debt. Generally, a debt that will not come due within the next year.

mutual debts. Cross-debts of the same kind and quality between two persons.

national debt. See NATIONAL DEBT.

nondischargeable debt. See NONDISCHARGEABLE DEBT.

passive debt. A debt that, by agreement between the debtor and creditor, is interest-free.

preferential debt. A debt that is legally payable before others, such as an employee's wages.

privileged debt. A debt that has priority over other debts if a debtor becomes insolvent; a secured debt.

public debt. A debt owed by a municipal, state, or national government.

secured debt. A debt backed by collateral.

short-term debt. Collectively, all debts and other liabilities that are payable within one year. — Also termed *current liability.*

simple-contract debt. A debt that is either oral or written but is not of record and not under seal. — Also termed *debt by simple contract.*

special-contract debt. A debt due, or acknowledged to be due, by an instrument under seal, such as a deed of covenant or sale, a lease reserving rent, or a bond. — Also termed *debt by special contract*; *debt by specialty contract*; *specialty debt.*

"Any contract in short whereby a determinate sum of money becomes due to any person, and is not paid but remains in action merely, is a contract of debt. And, taken in this light, it comprehends a great variety of acquisition; being usually divided into debts of *record*, debts by *special*, and debts by simple contract." 2 William Blackstone, *Commentaries on the Laws of England* 464 (1766).

subordinate debt. A debt that is junior or inferior to other types or classes of debt.

unliquidated debt. A debt that has not been reduced to a specific amount, and about which there may be a dispute.

unsecured debt. A debt not supported by collateral or other security.

debt adjustment. See DEBT POOLING.

debt by simple contract. See *simple-contract debt* under DEBT.

debt by special contract. See *special-contract debt* under DEBT.

debt by specialty contract. See *special-contract debt* under DEBT.

debt capital. See CAPITAL.

debt consolidation. See DEBT POOLING.

debtee. *Archaic.* See CREDITOR (1).

debt-equity ratio. See DEBT-TO-EQUITY RATIO.

debt financing. See FINANCING.

debt instrument. A written promise to repay a debt, such as a promissory note, bill, bond, or commercial paper.

debt limitation. A ceiling placed on borrowing by an individual, business, or government. • The constitutions of many states prohibit the states from incurring debt in excess of a stated amount. Other state constitutions allow states to incur debt above a stated amount only through a vote of the people. — Also termed *limitation on indebtedness.*

debt of record. See DEBT.

debtor. 1. One who owes an obligation to another, esp. an obligation to pay money. **2.** *Bankruptcy.* A person who files a voluntary petition or against whom an involuntary petition is filed. — Also termed *bankrupt.* **3.** *Secured transactions.* A person who either (1) has a property interest — other than a security interest or other lien — in collateral, even if the person is not an obligor, or (2) is a seller of accounts, chattel paper, payment intangibles, or promissory notes. UCC § 9–102(a)(19). — Abbr. Dr.

absconding debtor. A debtor who flees from creditors to avoid having to pay a debt. •

Absconding from a debt was formerly considered an act of bankruptcy. See ACT OF BANKRUPTCY.

account debtor. A person obligated on an account, chattel paper, or general intangible. • The UCC exempts from the definition of *account debtor* a person obligated to pay a negotiable instrument, even if the instrument constitutes chattel paper. UCC § 9–105(1)(a).

joint debtor. One of two or more debtors jointly liable for the same debt.

judgment debtor. See JUDGMENT DEBTOR.

new debtor. *Secured transactions.* A person that becomes bound as debtor under a security agreement previously entered into by another person. UCC §§ 9–102(a)(39), 9–203(c).

debtor-in-possession. *Bankruptcy.* A Chapter 11 or 12 debtor that continues to operate its business as a fiduciary to the bankruptcy estate. • With certain exceptions, the debtor-in-possession has all the rights, powers, and duties of a Chapter 11 trustee. — Abbr. DIP.

debtor rehabilitation. See REHABILITATION (3).

Debtor's Act of 1869. An English statute that, among other things, (1) abolished imprisonment for debt except in certain cases, as when a debtor owed a debt to the Crown or a debtor had money but refused to pay a debt, (2) abolished arrest by mesne process, that is, by compelling the defendant to appear and give bail unless it was believed that the defendant would leave the country, (3) made it a misdemeanor to obtain credit under false pretenses or to defraud creditors, and (4) defined how warrants and judgment orders would be executed.

debt pooling. An arrangement by which a person's debts are consolidated and creditors agree to accept lower monthly payments or to take less money. — Also termed *debt consolidation*; *debt adjustment*.

debt ratio. A corporation's total long-term and short-term liabilities divided by the firm's total assets. • A low debt ratio indicates conservative financing and thus usu. an enhanced ability to borrow in the future. — Also termed *debt-to-total-assets ratio*.

debt retirement. Repayment of debt; RETIREMENT (3).

debt security. See SECURITY.

debt service. 1. The funds needed to meet a long-term debt's annual interest expenses, principal payments, and sinking-fund contributions. **2.** Payments due on a debt, including interest and principal.

debt-to-equity ratio. A corporation's long-term debt divided by its owners' equity, calculated to assess its capitalization. — Also termed *debt-equity ratio*; *debt-to-net-worth ratio*.

debt-to-total-assets ratio. See DEBT RATIO.

de caetero (dee **see**-tə-roh) [Latin "about the other"] Henceforth; in the future. — Also spelled *de cetero*.

de calceto reparando (dee **kal**-sə-toh rep-ə-**ran**-doh), *n.* [Law Latin "for repairing a causeway"] *Hist.* A writ directing a sheriff to distrain residents of a place to repair a road.

decanatus (dek-ə-**nay**-təs), *n.* [Law Latin] *Hist.* A group of ten people; a decenary. See DECANUS.

decania (di-**kay**-nee-ə), *n.* [Law Latin] *Hist.* A dean's office; a dean's territory.

decanus (di-**kay**-nəs), *n.* [fr. Greek *dekanos* "a dean"] **1.** *Roman law.* An officer commanding ten soldiers. **2.** *Eccles. & Civil law.* A leader of ten people, as in *decanus monasticus* ("dean of ten monks"). **3.** The dean of a cathedral.

de capitalibus dominus feodi (dee kap-ə-**tay**-lə-bəs **dom**-ə-nəs **fee**-ə-dɪ). [Law Latin] *Hist.* From the highest lord of the fee. • This term was primarily used in old charters to state that the tenure of an estate was to be held of the chief lord of the fee, rather than of the immediate grantor.

decapitation (dee-kap-ə-**tay**-shən). *Hist.* The act of cutting off a head; a beheading. • This was once a common method of capital punishment.

de capite minutis (dee **kap**-ə-tee mi-**n[y]oo**-tis), *n.* [Latin "of those who have lost their status"] *Roman law.* A title in the *Pandects*, referring to people who lost their civil status.

de cartis reddendis (dee **kahr**-tis ri-**den**-dis), *n.* [Law Latin "for restoring charters"] *Hist.* A writ ordering redelivery of a charter or deed; a writ of detinue. See DETINUE.

de catallis reddendis (dee kə-**tal**-is ri-**den**-dis), *n.* [Law Latin "of chattels to be restored"] *Hist.* A writ ordering a bailee to deliver chattels kept from the owner. • This was replaced by the writ of detinue. See DETINUE.

de cautione admittenda (dee kaw-shee-**oh**-nee ad-mi-**ten**-də), *n.* [Law Latin "of security to be taken"] *Hist.* A writ ordering a bishop who had imprisoned an excommunicated person for contempt, even though the prisoner had offered bail and promised to obey the church in the future, to take the offered security and release the prisoner.

decease, *n.* See DEATH.

decease, *vb.* To die; to depart from life.

decedent (di-**see**-dənt), *n.* A dead person, esp. one who has died recently. — Also termed *deceased.*

nonresident decedent. A decedent who was domiciled outside the jurisdiction in question (such as probate jurisdiction) at the time of death.

decedent's estate. See ESTATE.

deceit, *n.* **1.** The act of intentionally giving a false impression <the juror's deceit led the lawyer to believe that she was not biased>. **2.** A tort arising from a false representation made knowingly or recklessly with the intent that another person should detrimentally rely on it <the new homeowner sued both the seller and the realtor for deceit after discovering termites>. **3.** See *fraudulent misrepresentation* under MISREPRESENTATION. — **deceive,** *vb.* See FRAUD; MISREPRESENTATION.

> "The tort of deceit consists in the act of making a wilfully false statement with the intent that the plaintiff shall act in reliance on it, and with the result that he does so act and suffers harm in consequence.... There are four main elements in this tort: (1) there must be a false representation of fact; (2) the representation must be made with knowledge of its falsity; (3) it must be made with the intention that it should be acted on by the plaintiff, or by a class of persons which includes the plaintiff, in the manner which resulted in damage to him; (4) it must be proved that the plaintiff has acted upon the false statement and has sustained damage by so doing." R.F.V. Heuston, *Salmond on the Law of Torts* 387 (17th ed. 1977).

decem tales (**des**-em **tay**-leez), *n.* [Law Latin "ten such people"] *Hist.* A writ directing a sheriff to summon ten people for a jury panel when a sufficient number have not already appeared.

decemviri litibus judicandis (di-**sem**-və-rɪ **lɪ**-ti-bəs joo-də-**kan**-dis), *n.* [Latin "ten persons to decide lawsuits"] *Roman law.* A group of five senators and five knights who assisted the elected magistrate in deciding legal disputes.

decenary. *Hist.* A town or district consisting of ten freeholding families. • A freeholder of the decenary (a *decennarius*) was bound by frankpledge to produce any wrongdoer living in the decenary. — Also spelled *decennary.* — Also termed *decenna*; *tithing*. Cf. FRANKPLEDGE.

> "The civil division of the territory of England is into counties, of those counties into hundreds, of those hundreds into tithings or towns. Which division, as it now stands, seems to owe its original to king Alfred; who, to prevent the rapines and disorders which formerly prevailed in the realm, instituted tithings; so called from the Saxon, because *ten* freeholders, with their families, composed one. These all dwelt together, and were sureties or free pledges to the king for the good behavior of each other; and, if any offence was committed in their district, they were bound to have the offender forthcoming. And therefore anciently no man was suffered to abide in England above forty days, unless he were enrolled in some tithing or decennary." 1 William Blackstone, *Commentaries on the Laws of England* 110 (1765).

decency. The state of being proper, as in speech or dress; the quality of being seemly.

decenna (di-**sen**-ə), *n.* [fr. Latin *decem* "ten"] See DECENARY.

decennarius (des-ə-**nair**-ee-əs), *n.* [Law Latin "a deciner"] One of ten families of freeholders comprising a decennary. See DECENARY.

decennary. See DECENARY.

deceptive act. As defined by the Federal Trade Commission and most state statutes, conduct that is likely to deceive a consumer acting reasonably under similar circumstances. — Also termed *deceptive practice*; *deceptive sales practice.*

deceptive advertising. Advertising containing false or misleading statements <a fictitious testimonial about a product or service may constitute deceptive advertising>.

deceptive practice. See DECEPTIVE ACT.

deceptive sales practice. See DECEPTIVE ACT.

deceptive warranty. See WARRANTY (2).

de certificando (dee sər-ti-fi-**kan**-doh), *n.* [Law Latin "about something to be certified"] A writ requiring something to be certified, similar to certiorari. See CERTIFICANDO DE RECOGNITIONE STAPULAE.

decertify, *vb.* **1.** To revoke the certification of. **2.** To remove the official status of (a labor union) by withdrawing the right to act as a collective-bargaining agent. **3.** (Of a court) to overrule a previous order that created a class for purposes of a class action; to officially undo (a class). — **decertification,** *n.* Cf. CERTIFY.

de certiorando (dee sər-shee-ə-**ran**-doh), *n.* [Law Latin "about certification"] A writ ordering a sheriff to certify a fact.

decessus (di-**ses**-əs), *n.* [fr. Latin *decedere* "to depart"] **1.** *Roman law.* A death. **2.** A departure. • This term has been used in both the civil and common law, esp. in reference to the desertion of a ground in a previous pleading in favor of another. See DEPARTURE.

de champertia (dee kam-**pər**-shee-ə), *n.* [Law Latin "about champerty"] *Hist.* A writ ordering justices of the bench to enforce the champerty laws. See CHAMPERTOR; CHAMPERTY.

de char et de sank (də **shahr** ay də **sangk**). [Law French] *Hist.* Of flesh and blood.

de chimino (dee **kim**-ə-noh), *n.* [Law Latin "writ of way"] *Hist.* A writ to enforce a right-of-way.

de cibariis utendis (dee si-**bair**-ee-əs yoo-**ten**-dis), *n.* [Law Latin "of victuals to be used"] *Hist.* The statute of 10 Edw. 3 ch. 3 restraining entertainment expenses. • This was one of several statutes limiting luxury spending.

decies tantum (**desh**-ee-eez *or* **dee**-shee-eez **tan**-təm), *n.* [Law Latin "ten times as much"] *Hist.* A writ ordering a juror who accepted a bribe for a verdict to pay ten times the bribery amount, half to the suing party and half to the Crown.

> "Decies tantum is a writ that lies where a juror in any inquest takes money of the one part or other, to give his verdict; then he shall pay ten times as much as he hath received: and every one that will sue may have this action, and shall have the one half, and the king the other .... And the same law is of all other actions popular, where one part is to the king, the other to the party that sues. Also the embracers, who procure such inquests, shall be punished in the same manner, and they shall have imprisonment a year. But no justice shall inquire thereof *ex officio*, but only at the suit of the party." *Termes de la Ley* 146 (1st Am. ed. 1812).

decimae (**des**-ə-mee), *n.* [fr. Latin *decem* "ten"] *Eccles. law.* **1.** The tenth part of the annual profits of a benefice originally payable to the Pope, and later to the Crown by 26 Hen. 8, ch. 3.

> "The tenths, or *decimae*, were the tenth part of the annual profit of each living ... which was also claimed by the holy see .... But this claim of the pope met with a vigorous resistance from the English parliament; and a variety of acts were passed to prevent and restrain it .... But the popish clergy, blindly devoted to the will of a foreign master, still kept it on foot; sometimes more secretly, sometimes more openly and avowedly .... And, as the clergy expressed this willingness to contribute so much of their income to the head of the church, it was thought proper (when in the same reign the papal power was abolished, and the king was declared the head of the church of England) to annex this revenue to the crown ...." 1 William Blackstone, *Commentaries on the Laws of England* 274 (1765).

2. Tithes paid to the church, often in grain or wool.

decimation (des-ə-**may**-shən). **1.** A major destruction of people; a great loss of life. **2.** *Hist.* A tithing; a payment of the tenth part. **3.** *Hist.* A punishment, esp. by death, of every tenth person by lot. • Under Roman law, *decimatio legonis* referred to the execution by lot of every tenth soldier for mutiny or other neglect of duty.

decision, *n.* A judicial determination after consideration of the facts and the law; esp., a ruling, order, or judgment pronounced by a court when considering or disposing of a case. — **decisional,** *adj.* See JUDGMENT; OPINION.

appealable decision. A decree or order that is sufficiently final to receive appellate review (such as an order granting summary judgment), or an interlocutory decree or order that is immediately appealable, usu. by statute (such as an order denying immunity to a police officer in a civil-rights suit). — Also termed *reviewable issue.* See COLLATERAL-ORDER DOCTRINE.

final decision. See *final judgment* under JUDGMENT.

interlocutory decision. See *interlocutory order* under ORDER (2).

decisional law. See CASELAW.

decision on the merits. See *judgment on the merits* under JUDGMENT.

decisive oath. See OATH.

decisory oath. See *decisive oath* under OATH.

***Decker* test.** See SUBJECT-MATTER TEST.

declarant (di-**klair**-ənt), *n.* **1.** One who has made a statement <in accordance with the rules of evidence, the statement was offered to prove the declarant's state of mind>. **2.** One who has signed a declaration, esp. one stating an intent to become a U.S. citizen <the declarant grew up in Italy>.

declaration, *n.* **1.** A formal statement, proclamation, or announcement, esp. one embodied in an instrument.

declaration of dividend. A company's setting aside of a portion of its earnings or profits for distribution to its shareholders. See DIVIDEND.

declaration of homestead. A statement required to be filed with a state or local authority, to prove property ownership to claim homestead-exemption rights. See HOMESTEAD.

declaration of intention. An alien's formal statement resolving to become a U.S. citizen and to renounce allegiance to any other government or country.

declaration of legitimacy. A formal pronouncement that a child is legitimate.

declaration of trust. **1.** The act by which the person who holds legal title to property or an estate acknowledges that the property is being held in trust for another person or for certain specified purposes. **2.** The instrument that creates a trust. — Also termed (in sense 2) *trust instrument*; *trust deed*; *trust agreement.*

2. *Int'l law.* The part of a treaty containing the stipulations under which the parties agree to conduct their actions; TREATY. **3.** *Int'l law.* A country's unilateral pronouncement that affects the rights and duties of other countries.

declaration of war. A country's announcement that it is officially engaged in war against another country.

4. A document that governs legal rights to certain types of real property, such as a condominium or a residential subdivision. **5.** A listing of the merchandise that a person intends to bring into the United States. • This listing is given to U.S. Customs when one enters the country. **6.** *Evidence.* An unsworn statement made by someone having knowledge of facts relating to an event in dispute.

declaration against interest. A statement by a person who is not a party to a suit and is not available to testify at trial, discussing a matter that is within the declarant's personal knowledge and is adverse to the declarant's interest. • Such a statement is admissible into evidence as an exception to the hearsay rule. Fed. R. Evid. 804(b)(3). See *admission against interest* under ADMISSION.

declaration of pain. A person's exclamation of present pain, which operates as an exception to the hearsay rule. Fed. R. Evid. 803(3).

declaration of state of mind. A person's state-of-mind statement that operates as an exception to the hearsay rule. Fed. R. Evid. 803(3).

dying declaration. A statement by a person who believes that death is imminent, relating to the cause or circumstances of the person's impending death. • The statement is admissible in evidence as an exception to the hearsay rule. — Also termed *deathbed declaration.*

self-serving declaration. An out-of-court statement made to benefit one's own interest.

7. *Common-law pleading.* The plaintiff's first pleading in a civil action. • It is an amplification of the original writ on which the action is founded, with the additional circumstances of the time and place of injury. In a real action, the declaration is called a *count.* Today the equivalent term in English law is *statement of claim*; in most American jurisdictions, it is called a *petition* or *complaint.* — Also termed *narratio.* See COUNT (3). Cf. PLEA (2).

> "The declaration is a statement of all material facts constituting the plaintiff's cause of action in a methodical and legal form. It consists of the following parts: (a) Statement of title of court. (b) Statement of venue in the margin. (c) The commencement. (d) The body, or statement of the cause of action. (e) The conclusion." Benjamin J. Shipman, *Handbook of Common-Law Pleading* § 76, at 192 (Henry Winthrop Ballantine ed., 3d ed. 1923).

declaration in chief. A declaration for the principal cause of action.

8. A formal, written statement — resembling an affidavit but not notarized or sworn to — that attests, under penalty of perjury, to facts known by the declarant. • Such a declaration, if properly prepared, is admissible in federal court with the same effect as an affidavit. 28 USCA § 1746. — Also termed *declaration under penalty of perjury*; *unsworn declaration under penalty of perjury.* Cf. AFFIDAVIT. **9.** *Int'l law.* An oral or written statement, unilaterally made, by which a state expresses its will, intent, or opinion when acting in the field of international relations. **10.** See *declaratory judgment* under JUDGMENT. — **declare,** *vb.* — **declaratory,** *adj.*

declaration date. See DATE.

declaration of a desire for a natural death. See LIVING WILL.

declaration of alienage. See ALIENAGE.

declaration of dividend. See DECLARATION (1).

declaration of estimated tax. A required IRS filing by certain individuals and businesses of current estimated tax owed, accompanied by periodic payments of that amount. • The requirement ensures current collection of taxes from taxpayers (such as self-employed persons) whose incomes are not fully taxed by payroll withholding. IRC (26 USCA) §§ 6315, 6654.

declaration of homestead. See DECLARATION (1).

Declaration of Independence. The formal proclamation of July 4, 1776, in the name of the people of the American colonies, asserting their independence from the British Crown and announcing themselves to the world as an independent nation.

declaration of legitimacy. See DECLARATION (1).

declaration of no defenses. See WAIVER OF DEFENSES.

declaration of pain. See DECLARATION (6).

Declaration of Paris. An international agreement, signed by Great Britain, France, Turkey, Sardinia, Austria, Prussia, and Russia in 1856 (at the end of the Crimean War), providing that (1) privateering is illegal, (2) with the exception of contraband, a neutral flag covers an enemy's goods, (3) with the exception of contraband, neutral goods cannot be confiscated under a hostile flag, and (4) a blockade must work to be binding. • The agreement was later adopted by most other maritime powers, except the United States and a few others.

> "The Declaration of Paris is one of the greatest triumphs won by commercial interests over the strict rules of maritime warfare. Its importance resides in its first three articles. Article 4 did no more than formulate a principle acknowledged for more than a century. Construed strictly it requires an impossibility; for no blockade, however strict, can always 'prevent access to the coast of the enemy.' But it is clear that the words were meant to be understood in a reasonable sense as merely prohibitory of ineffective or 'paper' blockades .... Article 1 struck at a most objectionable practice. The current of opinion had long been running strongly against the use of privateers.... Article 2 ... has provoked an enormous amount of controversy. Together with Article 3 it amounted to a new departure in the law of maritime capture. Up to 1856 the great naval powers had been divided between the old principle that the liability of goods to capture should be determined by the character of their owner, and the more modern principle ... that the character of the ship in which the goods were laden should settle their fate." 1 R.H. Inglis Palgrave, *Palgrave's Dictionary of Political Economy* 520–21 (Henry Higgs ed., 2d ed. 1925).

declaration of rights. An action in which a litigant requests a court's assistance not because any rights have been violated but because those rights are uncertain. • Examples include suits for a declaration of legitimacy, of nullity of marriage, of the legality or illegality of the conduct of state officers, and of the authoritative interpretation of wills. See *declaratory judgment* under JUDGMENT.

declaration of state of mind. See DECLARATION (6).

Declaration of Taking Act. The federal law regulating the government's taking of private property for public use under eminent domain. 40 USCA § 258a. • Fair compensation must be paid for the property.

declaration of trust. See DECLARATION (1).

declaration of war. See DECLARATION (3).

declaration under penalty of perjury. See DECLARATION (8).

declarator of trust (di-**klar**-ə-tər *or* di-**klair**-ə-tər *or* -tor). A common-law action against a trustee who holds property under a title *ex facie* for the trustee's own benefit.

declaratory (di-**klar**-ə-tor-ee *or* di-**klair**-), *adj.* **1.** Clearly; manifestly <a declaratory statute>. **2.** Explanatory <a declaratory judgment>.

declaratory decree. See *declaratory judgment* under JUDGMENT.

declaratory judgment. See JUDGMENT.

declaratory-judgment act. A federal or state law permitting parties to bring an action to determine their legal rights and positions regarding a controversy not yet ripe for adjudication, as when an insurance company seeks a determination of coverage before deciding whether to cover a claim. See *declaratory judgment* under JUDGMENT.

declaratory part of a law. A portion of a law clearly defining rights to be observed or wrongs to be avoided.

declaratory precedent. See PRECEDENT.

declaratory statute. See STATUTE.

declaratory theory. The belief that judges' decisions never make law but instead merely constitute evidence of what the law is. • This antiquated view — held by such figures as Coke and Blackstone — is no longer accepted.

> "There are ... at least three good reasons why the declaratory theory should have persisted for some time after the modern English doctrine [of precedent] had begun to take shape. In the first place, it appealed to believers in the separation of powers, to whom anything in the nature of judicial legislation would have been anathema. Secondly, it concealed a fact which Bentham was anxious to expose, namely, that judge-made law is retrospective in its effect. If in December a court adjudges that someone is liable, in consequence of his conduct during the previous January, it would certainly appear to be legislating retrospectively, unless the liability is based on an earlier Act of Parliament, or unless the court is simply following a previous decision. A way of disguising the retrospective character of such a judgment would be to maintain the doctrine that the court really was doing no more than state a rule which anyone could have deduced from well-known principles or common usage, for the conduct in question would then have been prohibited by the law as it stood in January. The third reason for the persistence of the declaratory theory may be thought to justify its retention in a revised form today. When confronted with a novel point, judges always tend to speak as though the answer is provided by the common law." Rupert Cross & J.W. Harris, *Precedent in English Law* 30 (4th ed. 1991).

de claro die (dee **klair**-oh **dI**-ee). [Law Latin "by clear day"] By daylight.

de clauso fracto (dee **klaw**-zoh **frak**-toh). [Law Latin] Of a breach of close. See CLAUSUM FREGIT.

de clerico admittendo (dee **kler**-ə-koh ad-mi-**ten**-doh), *n.* [Law Latin "for admitting a clerk"] *Hist.* A writ of execution commanding a bishop to accept a nominee for a vacant benefice. • A benefice's patron could enforce the right to fill a vacancy (the right of *presentation*) in the Court of Common Pleas by writ of *quare impedit*. — Also termed *admittendo clerico*; *ad admittendum clericum*. Cf. ADVOWSON; PRESENTATION; QUARE IMPEDIT.

de clerico capto per statutum mercatorium deliberando (dee **kler**-ə-koh **kap**-toh pər stə-**tyoo**-təm mər-kə-**tor**-ee-əm di-lib-ə-**ran**-doh), *n.* [Law Latin "for delivering a clerk arrested on a statute merchant"] *Hist.* A writ ordering the release of a clerk imprisoned for breaching a statute merchant. — Often shortened to *de clerico capto per statutum mercatorium*.

de clerico convicto commisso gaolae in defectu ordinarii deliberando (dee **kler**-ə-koh kən-**vik**-toh kə-**mis**-oh **jay**-[ə]-lee in di-**fek**-t[y]oo di-lib-ə-**ran**-doh). [Law Latin "for delivering a cleric convicted and committed to gaol in defect of his ordinary"] *Hist.* A writ ordering the delivery of a cleric to his ordinary (i.e., superior) when the cleric did not claim benefit of clergy and consequently was convicted of a felony. See ORDINARY (1); BENEFIT OF CLERGY (1).

de clerico infra sacros ordines constituto, non eligendo in officium (dee **kler**-ə-koh **in**-frə **sak**-rohs **or**-di-neez kon-sti-**tyoo**-toh, non el-i-**jen**-doh in ə-**fish**-ee-əm). [Law Latin "for not electing a clerk in holy orders to office"] *Hist.* A writ ordering a cleric's release from secular office. • The writ was addressed to the bailiff or other person who had forced a cleric to take a bailiwick or other secular office.

de clero (dee **kleer**-oh), *n.* [Law Latin "concerning the clergy"] The statute of 25 Edw. 3 addressing clerical matters, including presentations and indictments.

declination (dek-lə-**nay**-shən). **1.** A deviation from proper course <declination of duty>. **2.** An act of refusal <declination of a gift>. **3.** A document filed by a fiduciary who chooses not to serve. **4.** At common law, a plea to the court's jurisdiction by reason of the judge's personal interest in the lawsuit.

declinatory exception (di-**klIn**-ə-tor-ee). A dilatory objection to a court's jurisdiction.

declinatory plea. *Hist.* A pretrial plea claiming benefit of clergy. — Also termed *plea of sanctuary*. See BENEFIT OF CLERGY.

declining-balance depreciation method. See DEPRECIATION METHOD.

decoctor (di-**kok**-tər *or* -tor), *n.* [fr. Latin *deciquere* "to waste"] *Roman law.* A bankrupt; a defaulting debtor.

de coelo usque ad inferos (dee **see**-loh **əs**-kwee ad in-**fər**-nohs). [Latin] From heaven to the center of the earth. • This phrase expressed a common-law maxim about the extent of a real-property owner's ownership interest in the property.

decollatio (dee-kah-**lay**-shee-oh), *n.* [fr. Latin *de* "off" + *collum* "neck"] *Hist.* In England and Scotland, an act of beheading. See DECAPITATION.

decolonization. *Int'l law.* The process by which a colonial power divests itself of sovereignty over a colony — whether a territory, a protectorate, or a trust territory — so that the colony is granted autonomy and eventually attains independence.

de communi dividundo (dee kə-**myoo**-nɪ di-vi-**dən**-doh), *n.* [Latin "for dividing a thing held in common"] *Roman & civil law.* An action to partition common property. — Also termed *actio de communi dividendo.*

de comon droit (də **kah**-mən **droyt**). [Law French] *Hist.* By the common law; of common right. See COMMON LAW.

de computo (dee **kom**-pyə-toh), *n.* [Law Latin "of account"] *Hist.* A writ ordering a defendant to either give a reasonable accounting to the plaintiff or explain why such an accounting should not be required. • This was the foundation for an action of account. See ACCOUNT (3).

de concilio curiae (dee kən-**sil**-ee-oh **kyoor**-ee-ee). [Law Latin] By the advice of the court; by the direction of the court. — Also spelled *de consillio curiae.*

De Conflictu Legum (dee kən-**flik**-too **lee**-gəm), *n.* [Latin] Concerning the conflict of laws. • This is a title to several works on the conflict of laws.

De Conjunctim Feoffatis (dee kən-**jəngk**-təm fee-**fay**-tis), *n.* [Law Latin "concerning persons jointly enfeoffed"] *Hist.* The title of the statute of Edward I preventing delays caused by tenants pleading, in novel disseisins or other actions, that someone else was jointly seised with them.

de consanguineo (dee kon-sang-**gwin**-ee-oh), *n.* See COSINAGE.

de consanguinitate (dee kon-sang-gwin-i-**tay**-tee), *n.* See COSINAGE.

de consilio (dee kən-**sil**-ee-oh). [Law Latin] Of counsel. • This term often referred to the advice or counsel to commit a crime.

deconstruction, *n.* In critical legal studies, a method of analyzing legal principles or rules by breaking down the supporting premises to show that these premises might also advance the opposite rule or result. — Also termed *trashing.* — **deconstructionist,** *adj.* & *n.*

de continuando assisam (dee kən-tin-yoo-**an**-doh ə-**sɪ**-zəm), *n.* [Law Latin "for continuing an assize"] A writ to continue an assize.

de contumace capiendo (dee kon-tyə-**may**-see kap-ee-**en**-doh), *n.* [Law Latin "for arresting a contumacious person"] *Hist.* A writ issuing out of the Court of Chancery at the request of an ecclesiastical court that has found a person to be in contempt. • This writ came into use after the Ecclesiastical Courts Act of 1813 removed ecclesiastical courts' power to excommunicate litigants who failed to comply with a court order. Cf. EXCOMMUNICATO CAPIENDO.

> "In 1812 the case of Mary Ann Dix — a woman not of age, who was imprisoned for two years on a writ de excommunicato capiendo for not paying costs in a suit for defamation — aroused the Legislature. In the following year it was enacted that excommunication should cease to exist as part of the process of the ecclesiastical courts to enforce appearance, and as a punishment for contempt. . . . [F]or the writ de excommunicato capiendo was substituted the writ de contumace capiendo; and the rules applying to the older writ were made applicable to the new." 1 William Holdsworth, *A History of English Law* 632 (7th ed. 1956).

de copia libelli deliberanda (dee **koh**-pee-ə li-**bel**-ɪ di-lib-ə-**ran**-də), *n.* [Law Latin "for delivering a copy of a libel"] *Hist. Eccles. law.* A writ ordering an ecclesiastical-court judge (such as the Dean of Arches) to provide the defendant with a copy of the plaintiff's complaint.

de coronatore eligendo (dee kor-ə-nə-**tor**-ee el-i-**jen**-doh), *n.* [Law Latin "for electing a coroner"] *Hist.* A writ ordering a sheriff to call an election of a coroner to fill a vacant office. See CORONER (2).

de coronatore exonerando (dee kor-ə-nə-**tor**-ee eg-zon-ə-**ran**-doh), *n.* [Law Latin "for removing a coroner"] A writ ordering the sheriff to remove a coroner from office for a reason stated in the writ. See CORONER (2).

> "The coroner is chosen for life: but may be removed, either by being made sheriff, or chosen verderor, which are offices incompatible with the other; or by the king's writ *de coronatore exonerando*, for a cause to be therein assigned, as that he is engaged in other business, is incapacitated by years or sickness, hath not a sufficient estate in the county, or lives in an inconvenient part of it." 1 William Blackstone, *Commentaries on the Laws of England* 336 (1765).

de corpore comitatus (dee **kor**-pə-ree kom-ə-**tay**-təs). [Law Latin] From the body of the county. • This term was esp. used to distinguish a body of the county at large from a smaller area or *de vicineto* ("from a neighborhood").

de corrodio habendo (dee kə-**roh**-dee-oh hə-**ben**-doh), *n.* [Law Latin "writ for having a corody"] *Hist.* A writ to obtain an allowance, esp. of meat or other sustenance, from a religious house for a royal servant living there.

decoy, *vb.* To entice (a person) without force; to inveigle <the victim was decoyed out of her home> <the defendant was decoyed into the county and then served with process>. Cf. ENTRAPMENT.

decoy letter. A letter prepared and mailed to detect a criminal who has violated the postal or revenue laws.

decreasing term insurance. See INSURANCE.

decree, *n.* **1.** Traditionally, a judicial decision in a court of equity, admiralty, divorce, or probate — similar to a judgment of a court of law <the judge's decree in favor of the will's beneficiary>. **2.** Any court order, but esp. one in a matrimonial case <divorce decree>. See JUDGMENT; ORDER (2); DECISION.

consent decree. A court decree that all parties agree to. — Also termed *consent order.*

decree absolute. A ripened decree nisi; a court's decree that has become unconditional because the time specified in the decree nisi has passed. — Also termed *order absolute*; *rule absolute.*

decree nisi (**nI**-sI). A court's decree that will become absolute unless the adversely affected party shows the court, within a specified time, why it should be set aside. — Also termed *nisi decree*; *order nisi*; *rule nisi.* See NISI.

decree of distribution. An instrument by which heirs receive the property of a deceased person.

decree of insolvency. A probate-court decree declaring an estate's insolvency.

decree of nullity. A decree declaring a marriage to be void *ab initio.* See NULLITY OF MARRIAGE.

decree pro confesso (proh kən-**fes**-oh). *Equity practice.* A decree entered in favor of the plaintiff as a result of the defendant's failure to timely respond to the allegations in the plaintiff's bill.

> "A decree pro confesso in equity is similar to a default judgment in an action at law. If a defendant in an equity suit fails to answer the plaintiff's petition within the prescribed time period, the bill will be taken pro confesso, and a decree entered in favor of the plaintiff .... However, whereas a default judgment in an action at law effects an admission of pleaded facts and conclusions of law ... a decree pro confesso in an equity action admits only the material and well pleaded facts in the petition and does not admit the legal claims upon which the plaintiff seeks relief." 27A Am. Jur. 2d *Equity* § 249, at 733–34 (1996).

deficiency decree. See *deficiency judgment* under JUDGMENT.

final decree. See *final judgment* under JUDGMENT.

interlocutory decree. See *interlocutory judgment* under JUDGMENT.

decreet (di-**kreet**), *n.* [fr. Latin *decretum*] *Scots law.* A court's final judgment; a decree.

decreet absolvitor (ab-**zol**-vi-tər *or* -tor), *n.* *Scots law.* A judgment for a defendant, either by a dismissal of a claim or by an acquittal.

decreet arbitral (**ahr**-bi-trəl), *n.* *Scots law.* **1.** An arbitration award. **2.** A form for an arbitration award. — Also termed *decree arbitral.*

decreet cognitionis causa (kog-nish-ee-**oh**-nis **kaw**-zə), *n.* *Scots law.* A judgment in a suit involving a plaintiff creditor suing a debtor's heir to attach the heir's lands.

decreet condemnator (kon-dem-**nay**-tər *or* -tor), *n.* *Scots law.* A judgment for the plaintiff.

decreet of valuation of teinds (teendz), *n.* *Scots law.* A court of sessions judgment determining the proper amount of tithes to be paid to church officers for their services.

decrementum maris (dek-rə-**men**-təm **mar**-is). [Latin "decrease of the sea"] The receding of the sea from the land.

decrepit (di-**krep**-it), *adj.* (Of a person) disabled; physically or mentally incompetent to such an extent that the individual would be helpless in a personal conflict with a person of ordinary health and strength.

decreta (di-**kree**-tə), *n.* [Latin "decisions"] *Roman law.* Judgments of magistrates; esp., sentences pronounced by the emperor as the supreme judge. See DECRETUM.

> "*Decreta.* In Roman law decisions of magistrates given after investigation of a case by *cognitio* ... and in particular, decisions of the emperor as judge of first instance after trial by *cognitio*, or as a judge of appeal. As the highest authority in the State the emperor could interpret the law freely and even introduce new principles. Consequently imperial decisions were authoritative interpretations of the law or even innovatory and regarded as statements binding for the future, and as such quoted by the jurists. They were not only communicated to the parties but recorded in the records of the imperial court and private persons might obtain copies of them." David M. Walker, *The Oxford Companion to Law* 343 (1980).

decretal (di-**kree**-təl), *adj.* Of or relating to a decree.

decretal interdict. See INTERDICT (1).

decretal order. See ORDER (2).

decretals (di-**kree**-təlz), *n. Eccles. law.* Canonical epistles written either by the Pope or by the Pope and his cardinals to settle controversial matters; esp., the second part of the *Corpus Juris Canonici*, canonical epistles consisting mainly of: (1) *Decretales Gregorii Noni*, a collection by Raymundus Barcinius, chaplain to Gregory IX, dating from about 1227; (2) *Decretales Bonifacii Octavi*, a collection by Boniface VIII in the year 1298; (3) *Clementinae*, a collection of Clement V, published in the year 1308; and (4) the *Extravagantes*, a collection by John XXII and other bishops. — Also (in Law Latin) *Decretales*. See CANON LAW.

decretist (di-**kree**-tist), *n.* In medieval universities, a law student; esp., a student of the decretals.

decretum (di-**kree**-təm), *n.* [Latin "a decision having mandatory force"] **1.** *Roman law.* An emperor's judgment in a matter; a type of imperial constitution. **2.** *Eccles. law.* An ecclesiastical law, as distinguished from a secular law. Pl. ***decreta.*** See DECRETA.

Decretum Gratiani (di-**kree**-təm gray-shee-**ay**-nI), *n.* [Latin "Gratian's decree"] See CONCORDIA DISCORDANTIUM CANONUM.

decriminalization, *n.* The legislative act or process of legalizing an illegal act <many doctors seek the decriminalization of euthanasia>. — **decriminalize,** *vb.* Cf. CRIMINALIZATION (1).

decrowning. The act of depriving someone of a crown.

decry (di-**krI**), *vb.* To speak disparagingly about (someone or something).

de cujus (dee **kyoo**-jəs *or* **kI**-əs). [Latin] From whom. • This term is used to designate (1) the person by or through whom another claimed something, or (2) the person whose legal position is in issue.

de curia claudenda (dee **kyoor**-ee-ə klaw-**den**-də), *n.* [Law Latin "of enclosing a court"] *Hist.* A writ ordering a person to build a wall or fence around his or her house to avoid disturbing a neighbor.

decurio (di-**kyoor**-ee-oh), *n.* [Latin "a decurion"] *Roman law.* A municipal senator belonging to a municipal council responsible for managing the internal affairs of the municipality.

de cursu (dee **kər**-s[y]oo). [Law Latin] Of course. • This term usu. refers to regular, formal proceedings as distinguished from incidental, summary proceedings.

de custode admittendo (dee kə-**stoh**-dee ad-mi-**ten**-doh), *n.* [Law Latin "of admitting a guardian"] *Hist.* A writ to admit a guardian.

de custode amovendo (dee kə-**stoh**-dee ay-moh-**ven**-doh), *n.* [Law Latin "of removing a guardian"] *Hist.* A writ to remove a guardian.

de custodia terrae et haeredis (dee kə-**stoh**-dee-ə **ter**-ee et **her**-ə-dis), *n.* [Law Latin "of right of ward"] *Hist.* A writ allowing a guardian in a knight's service to obtain custody of an infant ward.

de debito (dee **deb**-i-toh), *n.* [Law Latin "of debt"] *Hist.* A writ of debt. — Sometimes shortened to *debito.*

de debitore in partes secando (dee deb-i-**tor**-ee in **pahr**-teez si-**kan**-doh), *n.* [Latin "of cutting a debtor in pieces"] *Roman law.* The title of a law in the Twelve Tables, meaning either literally to cut a debtor into pieces or merely to divide the debtor's estate. See TWELVE TABLES.

> "DE DEBITORE IN PARTES SECANDO .... [S]ome writers contending for the literal signification, while others have supposed it to be only a figurative expression .... The latter view has been adopted by Montesquieu, Bynkershoek, Heineccius and Taylor .... The literal meaning, on the other hand, is advocated by Aulus Gellius and other writers of antiquity, and receives support from an expression (*semoto omni cruciatu*) in the Roman Code itself .... This is also the opinion of Gibbon, Gravina, Pothier, Hugo and Niebuhr." 1 Alexander Burrill, *A Law Dictionary and Glossary* 432 (2d ed. 1867).

de deceptione (dee di-sep-shee-**oh**-nee), *n.* [Law Latin "of deceit"] *Hist.* A writ available to a party who was deceived and damaged by someone acting in the party's name.

de deoneranda pro rata portionis (dee dee-on-ə-**ran**-də proh **ray**-tə por-shee-**oh**-nis), *n.* [Law Latin "of the disburdening of a pro rata share"] *Hist.* A writ for someone who is forced to pay rent that others are supposed to proportionately contribute to.

dedi (**dee**-dI). [Latin] *Hist.* I have given. • *Dedi* is a conveyancing term that implies a warranty of title. Cf. CONCESSI.

> "Dedi is a warranty in law to the feoffee and his heirs: as if it be said in a feoffment A. B. hath given and granted, & c. it is a warranty." *Termes de la Ley* 148 (1st Am. ed. 1812).

dedication, *n. Property.* The donation of land or creation of an easement for public use. — **dedicate,** *vb.* — **dedicatory,** *adj.*

common-law dedication. A dedication made without a statute, consisting in the owner's appropriation of land, or an easement in it, for the benefit or use of the public, and the acceptance, by or on behalf of the land or easement. — Often shortened to *dedication.*

dedication by adverse user. A dedication arising from the adverse, exclusive use by the public with the actual or imputed knowledge and acquiescence of the owner.

express dedication. A dedication explicitly manifested by the owner.

implied dedication. A dedication presumed by reasonable inference from the owner's conduct.

statutory dedication. A dedication for which the necessary steps are statutorily prescribed, all of which must be substantially followed for an effective dedication.

tacit dedication. A dedication of property for public use arising from silence or inactivity and without an express agreement.

dedication and reservation. A dedication made with reasonable conditions, restrictions, and limitations.

dedication day. See DAY.

de die in diem (dee **dI**-ee in **dI**-em). [Law Latin] From day to day; daily.

dedi et concessi (**dee**-dI et kən-**ses**-I). [Law Latin] I have given and conveyed. • These were the words generally used to convey a gift.

dedimus et concessimus (**ded**-ə-məs et kən-**ses**-i-məs). [Law Latin] We have given and granted. • These words were used in a conveyance when there was more than one grantor or when the grant was from the Crown.

dedimus potestatem (**ded**-ə-məs poh-tes-**tay**-təm). [Law Latin "we have given power"] **1.** A commission issuing from the court before which a case is pending, authorizing a person named in the commission to compel the attendance of certain witnesses, to take their testimony on the written interrogatories and cross-interrogatories attached to the commission, to reduce the answers to writing, and to send it sealed to the court issuing the commission. **2.** In England, a chancery writ commissioning the persons named in the writ to take certain actions, including administering oaths to defendants and justices of the peace. • The writ was formerly used to commission a person to take action such as acknowledging a fine and appointing an attorney for representation in court. Before the Statute of Westminster (1285), an attorney could not appear on behalf of a party without this writ. — Also termed *dedimus potestatem de attorno faciendo.*

> "Dedimus potestatem is a writ that lies where a man sues in the king's court, or is sued, and cannot well travel, then he shall have this writ directed to some justice, or other discreet person in the country, to give him power to admit some man for his attorney, or to levy a fine, or to take his confession, or his answer, or other examination, as the matter requires." *Termes de la Ley* 148 (1st Am. ed. 1812).

dediticii (ded-i-**tish**-ee-I *or* dee-di-**tI**-shee-I), *n.* [Latin "those who have surrendered"] *Roman law.* Enemies who on surrender were granted their freedom or by the Lex Aelia Sentia, slaves (esp. criminals) who on being freed were denied citizenship. • Justinian abolished this status. — Also spelled *dedititii.*

> "Slaves who before manumission had been subjected to degrading punishment (*e.g.* had been branded or made to fight in the arena) were given, on manumission, a special status, viz. that of enemies surrendered at discretion (*dediticii*). A *dediticius*, though free and not a slave, had none of the rights of a citizen, could never under any circumstances better his position (*e.g.* become a citizen), and was not allowed to live within 100 miles of Rome." R.W. Leage, *Roman Private Law* 67 (C.H. Ziegler ed., 2d ed. 1942).

dedition (di-**dish**-ən), *n.* [fr. Latin *deditio* "give up"] A surrender of something, such as property.

de diversis regulis juris antiqui (dee di-**vər**-sis **reg**-yə-lis **joor**-is an-**tɪ**-kwɪ), *n.* [Latin "of various rules of ancient law"] *Roman law.* The last in the collection of Digest titles containing 211 maxims. See DIGEST.

de dolo malo (dee **doh**-loh **mal**-oh). [Latin] Of or based on fraud. See *ACTIO DE DOLO MALO.*

de domo reparanda (dee **doh**-moh rep-ə-**ran**-də), *n.* [Law Latin "to repair a house"] *Hist.* A writ ordering a cotenant to contribute to the expenses of maintaining common property.

De Donis Conditionalibus (dee **doh**-nis kən-dish-ee-ə-**nal**-i-bəs). An English statute, enacted in 1285, that gave rise to the ability to create a fee tail. — Often shortened to *De Donis.*

> "[A]fter *De Donis*, the formula 'to A and the heirs of his body' gave to A an estate known as an *estate in fee tail.* Because A had no power to transfer an estate in fee simple absolute, it became theoretically possible for persons like O to tie up the ownership of land in a single family for hundreds of years. We say *theoretically possible* because by 1472 a way would be found for the tenant in tail (as A was called) to transfer an estate in fee simple absolute despite *De Donis.*" Thomas F. Bergin & Paul G. Haskell, *Preface to Estates in Land and Future Interests* 29 (2d ed. 1984).

de dote assignanda (dee **doh**-tee as-ig-**nan**-də), *n.* [Law Latin "for assigning dower"] *Hist.* A writ ordering a royal escheater to provide dower to a widow of a tenant holding an estate directly from the Crown.

de dote unde nil habet (dee **doh**-tee **ən**-dee nil **hay**-bet), *n.* [Law Latin "of dower whereof she has none"] A writ ordering a tenant interfering with a widow's right to dower to provide a reasonable dower. — Also termed *writ of dower.*

> "DE DOTE UNDE NIL HABET. This is a writ of right in its nature .... It must be brought by the widow as demandant, against the tenant of the freehold, that is, the heir or his alienee, and its effect is to enable the former to recover from the latter the seisin of a third part of the tenements in demand, to be set forth to her in severalty by metes and bounds, together with damages and costs." 1 Alexander M. Burrill, *A Law Dictionary and Glossary* 433 (2d ed. 1867).

deductible, *adj.* Capable of being subtracted, esp. from taxable income. See DEDUCTION (2).

deductible, *n.* **1.** Under an insurance policy, the portion of the loss to be borne by the insured before the insurer becomes liable for payment. Cf. SELF-INSURED RETENTION.

straight deductible. A deductible that is a specified, fixed amount.

2. The insurance-policy clause specifying the amount of this portion.

deduction, *n.* **1.** The act or process of subtracting or taking away. **2.** *Tax.* An amount subtracted from gross income when calculating adjusted gross income, or from adjusted gross income when calculating taxable income. — Also termed *tax deduction.* Cf. EXEMPTION (3); TAX CREDIT.

additional standard deduction. The sum of the additional amounts that a taxpayer who turns 65 or becomes blind before the close of the taxable year is entitled to deduct.

charitable deduction. A deduction for a contribution to a qualified charity or other tax-exempt institution. See CHARITABLE CONTRIBUTION (2); CHARITABLE ORGANIZATION.

deduction in respect of a decedent. A deduction that accrues to the point of death but is not recognizable on the decedent's final income-tax return because of the accounting method used, such as an accrued-interest expense of a cash-basis debtor.

itemized deduction. An expense (such as a medical expense, home-mortgage interest, or a charitable contribution) that can be subtracted from adjusted gross income to determine taxable income.

marital deduction. A federal tax deduction allowed for lifetime and testamentary transfers from one spouse to another. IRC (26 USCA) §§ 2056, 2523.

miscellaneous itemized deduction. Generally, an itemized deduction of job or investment expenses; a deduction other than those allowable in computing adjusted gross income, those enumerated in IRC (26 USCA)

§ 67(b), and personal exemptions. • This type of deduction is allowed only to an itemizing taxpayer whose total miscellaneous itemized deductions exceed a statutory percentage of adjusted gross income.

standard deduction. A specified dollar amount that a taxpayer can deduct from adjusted gross income, instead of itemizing deductions, to determine taxable income.

3. The portion of a succession to which an heir is entitled before a partition. **4.** The act or process of reasoning from general propositions to a specific application or conclusion. Cf. INDUCTION (2). — **deduct** (for senses 1–3), *vb.* — **deduce** (for sense 4), *vb.*

deduction for new. See NEW-FOR-OLD (1).

de ea re ita censuere (dee **ee**-ə ree **ɪ**-tə sen-**s[y]oo**-ə-ree). [Latin] Concerning that matter they have so decreed. • This phrase was used to record decrees of the Roman senate. — Abbr. *d.e.r.i.c.*

deed, *n.* **1.** Something that is done or carried out; an act or action. **2.** A written instrument by which land is conveyed. **3.** At common law, any written instrument that is signed, sealed, and delivered and that conveys some interest in property. — **deed,** *vb.* Cf. CONVEYANCE; BILL OF SALE.

> "A deed is a writing sealed and delivered. For if either a parchment without writing be delivered as one's deed, yet it is not his deed, though an obligation be afterwards written in it: or if it be a writing but not sealed at the time of the delivery of it as his deed, it is a scrole and not his deed. Or if I make and seal a deed, and the party take it without my delivery, I may plead it is not my deed." Sir Henry Finch, *Law, or a Discourse Thereof* 108 (1759).

> "All deeds are documents, but not all documents are deeds. For instance, a legend chalked on a brick wall, or a writing tattooed on a sailor's back may be documents but they are not deeds. A deed is, therefore, a particular kind of document. It must be a *writing* and a writing on *paper* or its like, e.g., vellum or parchment. Any instrument under seal is a deed if made between private persons. It must be *signed, sealed,* and *delivered.* A deed must either (a) effect the transference of an interest, right or property, or (b) create an obligation binding on some person or persons, or (c) confirm some act whereby an interest, right, or property has already passed." Gerald Dworkin, *Odgers' Construction of Deeds and Statutes* 1 (5th ed. 1967).

absolute deed. A deed that conveys title without condition or encumbrance. — Also termed *deed absolute.*

administrator's deed. A document that conveys property owned by a person who has died intestate.

bargain-and-sale deed. A deed that conveys property to a buyer for valuable consideration but that lacks any guarantee from the seller about the validity of the title. See BARGAIN AND SALE.

composition deed. A deed reflecting the terms of an agreement between a debtor and a creditor to discharge or adjust a debt.

counterdeed. A secret deed, executed either before a notary or under a private seal, that voids, invalidates, or alters a public deed.

deed absolute. See *absolute deed.*

deed in fee. A deed conveying the title to land in fee simple, usu. with covenants.

deed in lieu of foreclosure. A deed by which a borrower conveys fee-simple title to a lender in satisfaction of a mortgage debt and as a substitute for foreclosure. • This deed is often referred to simply as "deed in lieu."

deed of covenant. A deed to do something, such as a document providing for periodic payments by one party to another (usu. a charity) for tax-saving purposes. • The transferor can deduct taxes from the payment and, in some cases, the recipient can reclaim the deducted tax.

deed of distribution. A fiduciary's deed conveying a decedent's real estate.

deed of gift. A deed executed and delivered without consideration. — Also termed *gratuitous deed.*

deed of inspectorship. *Hist.* An instrument reflecting an agreement between a debtor and creditor to appoint a receiver to oversee the winding-up of the debtor's affairs on behalf of the creditor.

deed of partition. A deed that divides land held by joint tenants, tenants in common, or coparceners.

deed of release. A deed that surrenders full title to a piece of property upon payment or performance of specified conditions.

deed of separation. An instrument governing a spouse's separation and maintenance.

deed of settlement. **1.** A deed to settle something, such as the distribution of property in a marriage. **2.** *English law.* A deed formerly used to form a joint-stock company.

deed of trust. A deed conveying title to real property to a trustee as security until the grantor repays a loan. • This type of deed resembles a mortgage. — Also termed *trust deed*; *trust indenture.*

deed poll. A deed made by and binding on only one party, or on two or more parties having similar interests. • It is so called because, traditionally, the parchment was "polled" (that is, shaved) so that it would be even at the top (unlike an indenture). — Also spelled *deed-poll*. Cf. INDENTURE.

deed to lead uses. A common-law deed prepared before an action for a fine or common recovery to show the object of those actions.

deed without covenants. See *quitclaim deed*.

defeasible deed. A deed containing a condition subsequent causing title to the property to revert to the grantor or pass to a third party.

disentailing deed. *Hist.* A tenant-in-tail's assurance that the estate tail will be barred and converted into an estate in fee. • The Fines and Recoveries Act (3 & 4 Will. 4 ch. 74) introduced this way of barring an entail. It authorized nearly every tenant in tail, if certain conditions were met, to dispose of the land in fee simple absolute and thus to defeat the rights of all persons claiming under the tenant.

full-covenant-and-warranty deed. See *warranty deed*.

general warranty deed. See *warranty deed*.

gift deed. A deed given for a nominal sum or for love and affection.

grant deed. A deed containing, or having implied by law, some but not all of the usual covenants of title; esp., a deed in which the grantor warrants that he or she (1) has not previously conveyed the estate being granted, (2) has not encumbered the property except as noted in the deed, and (3) will convey to the grantee any title to the property acquired after the date of the deed.

latent deed. A deed kept in a strongbox or other secret place, usu. for 20 years or more.

mineral deed. A conveyance of an interest in the minerals in or under the land.

mortgage deed. The instrument creating a mortgage. • A mortgage deed typically must contain (1) the name of the mortgagor, (2) words of grant or conveyance, (3) the name of the mortgagee, (4) a property description sufficient to identify the mortgaged premises, (5) the mortgagor's signature, and (6) an acknowledgment. To be effective and binding, a mortgage deed must also be delivered.

quitclaim deed. A deed that conveys a grantor's complete interest or claim in certain real property but that neither warrants nor professes that the title is valid. — Often shortened to *quitclaim*. — Also termed *deed without covenants*. Cf. *warranty deed*.

> "A quitclaim deed purports to convey only the grantor's *present interest in the land*, if any, rather than the land itself. Since such a deed purports to convey whatever interest the grantor has at the time, its use excludes any implication that he has good title, or any title at all. Such a deed in no way obligates the grantor. If he has no interest, none will be conveyed. If he acquires an interest after executing the deed, he retains such interest. If, however, the grantor in such deed has complete ownership at the time of executing the deed, the deed is sufficient to pass such ownership. . . . A seller who knows that his title is bad or who does not know whether his title is good or bad usually uses a quitclaim deed in conveying." Robert Kratovil, *Real Estate Law* 49 (6th ed. 1974).

release deed. A deed that is issued once a mortgage has been discharged, explicitly releasing and reconveying to the mortgagor the entire interest conveyed by an earlier deed of trust.

sheriff's deed. A deed that gives ownership rights in property bought at a sheriff's sale.

special warranty deed. **1.** A deed in which the grantor covenants to defend the title against only those claims and demands of the grantor and those claiming by and under the grantor. **2.** In a few jurisdictions, a quitclaim deed. Cf. *warranty deed*.

statutory deed. A warranty-deed form prescribed by state law and containing certain warranties and covenants even though they are not included in the printed form.

support deed. A deed by which a person (usu. a parent) conveys land to another (usu. a son or daughter) with the understanding that the grantee will support the grantor for life. • Support deeds often result in litigation.

tax deed. A deed showing the transfer of title to real property sold for the nonpayment of taxes. See *office grant* under GRANT; *tax sale* under SALE. Cf. TAX CERTIFICATE.

title deed. A deed that evidences a person's legal ownership of property. See TITLE.

trust deed. See *deed of trust*.

warranty deed. A deed containing one or more covenants of title; esp., a deed that expressly guarantees the grantor's good, clear title and that contains covenants concerning the quality of title, including warranties of seisin, quiet enjoyment, right to convey, freedom from encumbrances, and defense of title against all claims. — Also termed *general warranty deed*; *full-covenant-and-warranty deed*. See WARRANTY (1). Cf. *quitclaim deed*; *special warranty deed*.

wild deed. A recorded deed that is not in the chain of title, usu. because a previous instrument connected to the chain of title has not been recorded.

deed box. *Archaic.* A box in which deeds of land title are traditionally kept. • Such a box is considered an heirloom in the strict sense. See HEIRLOOM (1).

deed of agency. A revocable, voluntary trust for payment of a debt.

deed of crime. See ACTUS REUS.

deed of feoffment. See FEOFFMENT.

deed without covenants. See *quitclaim deed* under DEED.

de ejectione custodiae (dee ee-jek-shee-**oh**-nee kəs-**toh**-dee-ee). [Latin *ejectment de gard* "ejectment of a ward"] *Hist.* A writ available to a guardian after being ejected from the ward's land during the ward's minority. • The writ lay to recover the land or person of the ward, or both. The French equivalent was *ejectment de garde.*

de ejectione firmae (dee ee-jek-shee-**oh**-nee **fər**-mee). [Latin "ejectment of farm"] *Hist.* A writ or action of trespass to obtain the return of lands or tenements to a lessee for a term of years that had been ousted by the lessor or by a reversioner, remainderman, or stranger. • The lessee was then entitled to a writ of ejection to recover, at first, damages for the trespass only, but later the term itself, or the remainder of it, with damages. This action is the foundation of the modern action of ejectment. See EJECTMENT.

> "A writ then of *ejectione firmae*, or action of trespass in *ejectment*, lieth, where lands or tenements are let for a term of years; and afterwards the lessor, reversioner, remainder-man, or any stranger, doth eject or oust the lessee of his term. In this case he shall have his writ of *ejection*, to call the defendant to answer for entering on the lands so demised to the plaintiff for a term that is not yet expired, and ejecting him. And by this writ the plaintiff shall recover back his term, or the remainder of it, with damages." 3 William Blackstone, *Commentaries on the Laws of England* 199 (1768).

deem, *vb.* **1.** To treat (something) as if (1) it were really something else, or (2) it has qualities that it doesn't have <although the document was not in fact signed until April 21, it explicitly states that it must be deemed to have been signed on April 14>. **2.** To consider, think, or judge <she deemed it necessary>.

> "'Deem' is a useful word when it is necessary to establish a legal fiction either positively by 'deeming' something to be something it is not or negatively by 'deeming' something not to be something which it is.... All other uses of the word should be avoided. Phrases like 'if he deems fit' or 'as he deems necessary' or 'nothing in this Act shall be deemed to ...' are objectionable as unnecessary deviations from common speech. 'Thinks' or 'considers' are preferable in the first two examples and 'construed' in the third.... 'Deem' is useful but dangerous. It creates an artificiality and artificiality should not be resorted to if it can be avoided." G.C. Thornton, *Legislative Drafting* 83–84 (2d ed. 1979).

deemed transferor. *Tax.* A person who holds an interest in a generation-skipping trust on behalf of a beneficiary, and whose death will trigger the imposition of a generation-skipping transfer tax. • A *deemed transferor* is often a child of the settlor. For example, a grandfather could establish a trust with income payable for life to his son (who, because he is only one generation away from his father, is also known as a *nonskip person*) with the remainder to his grandson, a beneficiary also known as the *skip person.* When the son dies, the trust will be included in his gross estate for determining the generation-skipping transfer tax. IRC (26 USCA) §§ 2601–2663. See GENERATION-SKIPPING TRANSFER; *generation-skipping transfer tax* under TAX; *generation-skipping trust* under TRUST; SKIP PERSON; NONSKIP PERSON.

deep issue. See ISSUE (1).

deep pocket. 1. (*pl.*) Substantial wealth and resources <the plaintiff nonsuited the individuals and targeted the corporation with deep pockets>. **2.** A person or entity with substantial wealth and resources against which a claim may be made or a judgment may be taken <that national insurance company is a favorite deep pocket among plaintiff's lawyers>.

Deep Rock doctrine. *Bankruptcy.* The principle by which unfair or inequitable claims presented by controlling shareholders of bankrupt corporations may be subordinated to claims of general or trade creditors. • The doctrine is named for a corporation that made fraudulent transfers to its parent corporation in *Taylor v. Standard Gas & Elec. Co.,* 306 U.S. 307, 59 S.Ct. 543 (1939).

de escaeta (dee es-**kee**-tə), *n.* [Law Latin "of escheat"] *Hist.* A writ authorizing a lord to recover land when the lord's tenant died without an heir. See ESCHEAT.

de escambio monetae (dee es-**kam**-bee-oh mə-**nee**-tee), *n.* [Law Latin "of exchange of money"] *Hist.* A writ authorizing a merchant to prepare a bill of exchange.

de essendo quietum de theolonio (dee e-**sen**-doh kwI-**ee**-təm dee thee-ə-**loh**-nee-oh), *n.* [Law Latin "of being quit of toll"] *Hist.* A writ authorizing a person who is exempt from paying a toll to enforce the exemption without harassment. — Also spelled *de essendo quietum de tolonio.*

de essonio de malo lecti (dee e-**soh**-nee-oh dee **mal**-oh **lek**-tI), *n.* [Law Latin "of essoin of *malum lecti* (sickness of bed)"] *Hist.* A writ ordering a determination whether a person is truly sick after the person has issued an essoin claiming sickness as an excuse for not appearing in court.

de estoveriis habendis (dee es-tə-**veer**-ee-is hə-**ben**-dis), *n.* [Law Latin "for having estovers"] *Hist.* A writ allowing a wife divorced *a mensa et thoro* ("from bed and board") to recover alimony.

> "In case of divorce *a mensa et thoro*, the law allows alimony to the wife which is that allowance, which is made to a woman for her support out of her husband's estate; being settled at the discretion of the ecclesiastical judge, on consideration of all the circumstances of the case. This is sometimes called her *estovers* for which, if he refuses payment, there is; (besides the ordinary process of excommunication) a writ at common law *de estoveriis habendis*, in order to recover it .... It is generally proportioned to the rank and quality of the parties. But in case of elopement, and living with an adulterer, the law allows her no alimony." 1 William Blackstone, *Commentaries on the Laws of England* 429 (1765).

de estrepamento (dee e-strep-ə-**men**-toh), *n.* [Law Latin "of enstrepment"] *Hist.* A writ to prevent waste by a tenant while a suit to recover the land is pending against the tenant. • Because this writ was only auxiliary to a real action to recover land, and because equity afforded the same relief by injunction, the writ fell into disuse and was abolished by 3 & 4 Will. 4, ch. 27. — Also termed *writ of estrepement.* See ESTREPEMENT.

de eu et trene (də **yoo** ay **trayn**). [French] *Hist.* Of water and whip of three cords. • This term referred to a neife who, as a servant, could be corporally punished. See NEIFE.

de eve et de treve (də **ev** ay də **trev**). [Law French] *Hist.* From grandfather and great-grandfather's great-grandfather. • This phrase described the ancestral rights of lords to their villeins.

de excommunicato capiendo (dee eks-kə-myoo-ni-**kay**-toh kap-ee-**en**-doh), *n.* [Law Latin "for taking an excommunicated person"] *Hist. Eccles. law.* A writ ordering a sheriff to imprison an excommunicated person until the person reconciled with the church. • It was replaced by the writ *de contumace capiendo.* See DE CONTUMACE CAPIENDO.

de excommunicato deliberando (dee eks-kə-myoo-ni-**kay**-toh di-lib-ə-**ran**-doh), *n.* [Law Latin "for delivering an excommunicated person"] *Hist. Eccles. law.* A writ releasing an excommunicated person from prison upon a certification by the person's superior that the person has reconciled with the church.

de excommunicato recapiendo (dee eks-kə-myoo-ni-**kay**-toh ri-kap-ee-**en**-doh), *n.* [Law Latin "for retaking an excommunicated person"] *Hist. Eccles. law.* A writ ordering the rearrest of an excommunicated person who had been released but had not reconciled with the church or given security for a reconciliation.

de excusationibus (dee ek-skyoo-zay-shee-**oh**-ni-bəs), *n.* [Latin "of excuses"] *Roman law.* The first title of the 27th book of the Digest, containing a person's legal excuses from serving as *tutor* or *curator.* • It is primarily made up of part of the Greek work of Herennius Modestinus. See DIGEST.

de executione facienda in withernamium (dee ek-sə-kyoo-shee-**oh**-nee fay-shee-**en**-də in with-ər-**nay**-mee-əm), *n.* [Law Latin "for making execution in withernam"] *Hist.* A writ of execution in withernam. • This is a type of *capis in withernam* directing the sheriff to take from the defendant goods equal in value to the goods that the defendant took from the plaintiff.

de executione judicii (dee ek-sə-kyoo-shee-**oh**-nee joo-**dish**-ee-I), *n.* [Law Latin "of execution of judgment"] *Hist.* A writ ordering a sheriff or bailiff to execute a judgment.

de exemplificatione (dee ig-zem-pli-fi-kay-shee-**oh**-nee), *n.* [Law Latin "of exemplification"] A writ ordering the transcription of an original record.

de exoneratione sectae (dee ig-zon-ə-ray-shee-**oh**-nee **sek**-tee), *n.* [Law Latin "of exoneration of suit"] *Hist.* A writ exempting the king's ward from being sued in any court lower than the Court of Common Pleas (such as a county court, hundred court, leet, or court baron) during the time of the wardship.

de expensis civium et burgensium (dee ek-**spen**-sis **siv**-ee-əm et bər-**jen**-see-əm), *n.* [Law Latin "for levying the expenses of burgesses"] *Hist.* A writ ordering the sheriff to levy the expenses of each citizen and burgess of Parliament.

de expensis militum levandis (dee ek-**spen**-sis **mil**-ə-təm lə-**van**-dis), *n.* [Law Latin "for levying the expenses of knights"] *Hist.* A writ ordering the sheriff to levy an allowance for knights of the shire in Parliament.

deface (di-**fays**), *vb.* **1.** To mar or destroy (a written instrument, signature, or inscription) by obliteration, erasure, or superinscription. **2.** To detract from the value of (a coin) by punching, clipping, cutting, or shaving. **3.** To mar or injure (a building, monument, or other structure). — **defacement,** *n.*

defacere. See DIFFACERE.

de facto (di **fak**-toh *also* dee *or* day), *adj.* [Law Latin "in point of fact"] **1.** Actual; existing in fact; having effect even though not formally or legally recognized <a de facto contract> **2.** Illegitimate but in effect <a de facto government>. Cf. DE JURE.

de facto adoption. See ADOPTION.

de facto contract of sale. See CONTRACT.

de facto corporation. See CORPORATION.

de facto court. See COURT.

de facto dissolution. See DISSOLUTION.

de facto government. See GOVERNMENT.

de facto judge. See JUDGE.

de facto marriage. See MARRIAGE (1).

de facto merger. See MERGER.

de facto officer. See *officer de facto* under OFFICER (1).

de facto segregation. See SEGREGATION.

de facto taking. See TAKING (2).

defalcation (dee-fal-**kay**-shən), *n.* **1.** EMBEZZLEMENT. **2.** Loosely, the failure to meet an obligation; a nonfraudulent default. **3.** *Archaic.* A deduction; a setoff. — **defalcate** (di-**fal**-kayt *or* dee-), *vb.* — **defalcator,** *n.*

defalk (di-**fawlk**), *vb. Archaic.* To deduct (a debt); to set off (a claim).

de falso judicio (dee **fal**-soh *or* **fawl**-soh joo-**dish**-ee-oh), *n.* [Law Latin "of false judgment"] *Hist.* A writ of false judgment; a writ to reverse an inferior court's ruling.

de falso moneta (dee **fal**-soh *or* **fawl**-soh mah-**nee**-tə), *n.* [Law Latin "of false money"] *Hist.* The statute of Edward I providing that persons importing certain coins (called "pollards" and "crokards") would forfeit both their goods and their lives.

defamacast (di-**fam**-ə-kast). Defamation by television or radio broadcast. See DEFAMATION.

defamation, *n.* **1.** The act of harming the reputation of another by making a false statement to a third person. • If the alleged defamation involves a matter of public concern, the plaintiff is constitutionally required to prove both the statement's falsity and the defendant's fault. **2.** A false written or oral statement that damages another's reputation. — **defame,** *vb.* See LIBEL; SLANDER. Cf. DISPARAGEMENT.

> "The wrong of defamation consists in the publication of a false and defamatory statement concerning another person without lawful justification. That person must be in being. Hence not only does an action of defamation not survive for or against the estate of a deceased person, but a statement about a deceased or unborn person is not actionable at the suit of his relatives, however great their pain and distress, unless the statement is in some way defamatory of them." R.F.V. Heuston, *Salmond on the Law of Torts* 138 (17th ed. 1977).

> "Defamation ... is involved in two related harms, libel and slander. A familiar statement is that libel is written whereas slander is oral. This covers the idea in a general way but tends to mislead because defamation may be published without the use of words and hence be neither written nor oral. Thus libel may be perpetrated by hanging a person in effigy and slander, by sign or gesture." Rollin M. Perkins & Ronald N. Boyce, *Criminal Law* 489 (3d ed. 1982).

defamation per quod. Defamation that either (1) is not apparent but is proved by extrinsic evidence showing its injurious meaning or (2) is apparent but is not a statement that is actionable per se.

defamation per se. A statement that is defamatory in and of itself and is not capable of an innocent meaning.

defamatory, *adj.* (Of a statement or communication) tending to harm a person's reputation, usu. by subjecting the person to public contempt, disgrace, or ridicule, or by adversely affecting the person's business.

> "No exhaustive definition of 'defamatory' emerges from the cases for, as Lord Reid once said, it is not for the judges to 'frame definitions or to lay down hard and fast rules. It is their function to enunciate principles and much that they say is intended to be illustrative or explanatory and not to be definitive' [*Cassell & Co. Ltd. v. Broome* (1972) AC 1027, 1085]. One can nevertheless achieve a working description by combining two statements, namely: a defamatory statement is one which injures the reputation of another by exposing him to hatred, contempt, or ridicule, or which tends to lower him in the esteem of right-thinking members of society." R.W.M. Dias & B.S. Markesinis, *Tort Law* 423–24 (2d ed. 1989).

defamatory libel. See LIBEL.

defamatory statement. A statement that tends to injure the reputation of a person referred to in it. • The statement is likely to lower that person in the estimation of reasonable people and in particular to cause that person to be regarded with feelings of hatred, contempt, ridicule, fear, or dislike.

defames (di-**fay**-meez or di-**fahm**), *adj.* [Law French] Infamous.

default, *n.* The omission or failure to perform a legal or contractual duty; esp., the failure to pay a debt when due. — **default,** *vb.* — **defaulter,** *n.*

defaulter. 1. A person who is in default. **2.** A person who misappropriates or fails to account for money held in the person's official or fiduciary capacity.

default judgment. 1. A judgment entered against a defendant who has failed to plead or otherwise defend against the plaintiff's claim, often by failing to appear at trial. **2.** A judgment entered as a penalty against a party who does not comply with an order, esp. an order to comply with a discovery request. — Also termed *judgment by default.* See JUDGMENT.

nil-dicit default judgment (nil **dI**-sit). [Latin "he says nothing"] A judgment for the plaintiff entered after the defendant fails to file a timely answer, often after appearing in the case by filing a preliminary motion. — Also termed *nihil-dicit default judgment.* — Often shortened to *nihil dicit.*

no-answer default judgment. A judgment for the plaintiff entered after the defendant fails to timely answer or otherwise appear.

post-answer default judgment. A judgment for the plaintiff entered after the defendant files an answer, but fails to appear at trial or otherwise provide a defense on the merits.

defeasance (di-**feez**-ənts), *n.* **1.** An annulment or abrogation; VOIDANCE. **2.** The fact or an instance of bringing an estate or status to an end, esp. by conditional limitation. **3.** A condition upon the fulfillment of which a deed or other instrument is defeated or made void; a contractual provision containing such a condition. — Also termed *defeasance clause.* **4.** *Hist.* A collateral deed made simultaneously with a conveyance and containing a condition by which the main deed might be defeated or made void. — Also spelled *defeazance.* — **defease,** *vb.*

> "A defeazance is a collateral deed, made at the same time with a feoffment or other conveyance, containing certain conditions, upon the performance of which the estate then created may be *defeated* or totally undone." 2 William Blackstone, *Commentaries on the Laws of England* 327 (1766).

defeasance clause. A mortgage provision stating that the conveyance to the mortgagee will be ineffective if the mortgagor pays the debt on time.

defeasible, *adj.* (Of an act, right, agreement, or position) capable of being annulled or avoided <defeasible deed>. See *fee simple defeasible* under FEE SIMPLE.

defeasible deed. See DEED.

defeasible estate. See ESTATE.

defeasible fee simple. See *fee simple defeasible* under FEE SIMPLE.

defeasible remainder. See REMAINDER.

defeasible title. See TITLE (2).

defeasive, *adj. Rare.* Capable of defeating <a counterclaim defeasive of the plaintiff's right to recovery>.

defeat, *vb.* **1.** To deprive (someone) of something expected, usu. by an antagonistic act <to defeat the opponent in an election>. **2.** To annul or render (something) void <to defeat title>. **3.**

To vanquish; to conquer (someone or something) <to defeat the armies>. **4.** To frustrate (someone or something) <the expenditures defeat the bill's purpose>.

defect, *n.* An imperfection or shortcoming, esp. in a part that is essential to the operation or safety of a product. — **defective,** *adj.*

apparent defect. See *patent defect.*

design defect. A product imperfection occurring when the seller or distributor could have reduced or avoided a foreseeable risk of harm by adopting a reasonable alternative design, and when, as a result of not using the alternative, the product is not reasonably safe.

fatal defect. A serious defect capable of nullifying a contract.

hidden defect. A product imperfection that is not discoverable by reasonable inspection and for which a seller or lessor is generally liable if the flaw causes harm. • Upon discovering a hidden defect, a purchaser may revoke a prior acceptance. UCC § 2–608(1)(b). — Also termed *latent defect*; *inherent defect.*

manufacturing defect. An imperfection in a product that departs from its intended design even though all possible care was exercised in its assembly and marketing.

marketing defect. **1.** The failure to adequately warn of a potential risk of harm that is known or should have been known about a product or its foreseeable use. **2.** The failure to adequately instruct the user about how to use a product safely.

patent defect. A defect that is apparent to a normally observant person, esp. a buyer on a reasonable inspection. — Also termed *apparent defect.*

product defect. An imperfection in a product that has a manufacturing defect or design defect, or is faulty because of inadequate instructions or warnings.

defective, *adj.* **1.** (Of a position, right, act, or process) lacking in legal sufficiency <defective execution of documents> <defective service of process>. **2.** (Of a product) containing an imperfection or shortcoming in a part essential to the product's safe operation <defective wiring caused the accident>.

defective condition. An unreasonably dangerous state that might well cause physical harm beyond that contemplated by the ordinary user or consumer who purchases the product. See PRODUCTS LIABILITY.

defective performance. See PERFORMANCE.

defective pleading. See PLEADING (1).

defective product. See PRODUCT.

defective record. See RECORD.

defective title. See TITLE (2).

defective verdict. See VERDICT.

defect of form. An imperfection in the style, manner, arrangement, or nonessential parts of a legal document, as distinguished from a substantive defect. Cf. DEFECT OF SUBSTANCE.

defect of parties. A failure to include all necessary parties in a lawsuit.

defect of substance. An imperfection in the substantive part of a legal document, as by omitting an essential term. Cf. DEFECT OF FORM.

defectus (di-**fek**-təs), *n.* [fr. Latin *deficere* "to be deficient"] *Hist.* A defect; a deficiency.

defectus sanguinis (di-**fek**-təs **sang**-gwi-nis). [Latin "defect of blood"] *Hist.* A failure of issue, often resulting in an escheat. See ESCHEAT.

defence. See DEFENSE.

defend, *vb.* **1.** To deny, contest, or oppose (an allegation or claim) <the corporation vigorously defended against the shareholder's lawsuit>. **2.** To represent (someone) as an attorney <the accused retained a well-known lawyer to defend him>.

defendant (di-**fen**-dənt). A person sued in a civil proceeding or accused in a criminal proceeding. — Abbr. D. Cf. PLAINTIFF.

defendant in error. *Archaic.* In a case on appeal, the prevailing party in the court below. See APPELLEE; RESPONDENT (1).

defendant's gain. The amount of money or the value of property that a criminal defendant has obtained by committing a crime. • Some states, such as New York, consider the defendant's gain when assessing a criminal fine or ordering restitution.

defendemus (di-**fen**-də-məs). [fr. Latin *defendere*] We will defend. • This term was used in conveyancing to require the donor and the donor's heirs to defend the donee against any attempted encumbrance not specifically agreed to. Although *defendum* was not a warranty, it became part of the warranty clause "shall and will warrant and forever defend."

defender. One who defends, such as the defendant in a lawsuit, a person using self-defense, or defense counsel.

defendere (di-**fen**-də-ree), *vb.* [Law Latin] To deny; to defend.

defendere se per corpus suum (di-**fen**-də-ree see pər **kor**-pəs **s[y]oo**-əm), *vb.* [Law Latin "to defend himself by his own body"] *Hist.* To agree to a trial by judicial combat; to agree to a duel.

defendere unica manu (di-**fen**-də-ree **yoo**-nə-kə **man**-yoo), *n.* [Law Latin "to defend with one hand"] *Hist.* A denial of an accusation under oath.

Defender of the Faith. See DEFENSOR FIDEI.

defendour (day-fon-**duur**), *n.* [Law French] *Hist.* A defendant; the party accused in an appeal.

defeneration (dee-fen-ə-**ray**-shən), *n.* [fr. Latin *de* "of" + *foenero* "to lend upon usury"] *Hist.* The act of lending money at a usurious interest rate.

defenestration (dee-fen-ə-**stray**-shən). The act of throwing someone or something out a window.

defense (di-**fen[t]s**). **1.** A defendant's stated reason why the plaintiff or prosecutor has no valid case; esp., a defendant's answer, denial, or plea <her defense was that she was 25 miles from the building at the time of the robbery>.

> "**Defence** is defined to be that which is alleged by a party proceeded against in an action or suit, as a reason why the plaintiff should not recover or establish that which he seeks by his complaint or petition." Edwin E. Bryant, *The Law of Pleading Under the Codes of Civil Procedure* 240 (2d ed. 1899).

affirmative defense. A defendant's assertion raising new facts and arguments that, if true, will defeat the plaintiff's or prosecution's claim, even if all allegations in the complaint are true. • Examples of affirmative defenses include duress and contributory negligence (in a civil case) and insanity and self-defense (in a criminal case).

capacity defense. A defense based on the defendant's inability to be held accountable for an illegal act or the plaintiff's inability to prosecute a lawsuit (as when the plaintiff was a corporation, but has lost its corporate charter). See CAPACITY.

collateral defense (kə-**lat**-ə-rəl). *Criminal law.* A defense of justification or excuse not involving a rebuttal of the allegation and therefore collateral to the elements that the prosecutor must prove. See EXCUSE (2); JUSTIFICATION (2).

dilatory defense (**dil**-ə-tor-ee). A defense that temporarily obstructs or delays a lawsuit but does not address the merits.

equitable defense. A defense formerly available only in a court of equity but now maintainable in a court of law. • Examples include mistake, fraud, illegality, and failure of consideration.

frivolous defense. A defense that has no basis in fact or law.

full defense. A technical common-law defensive plea, stated at length and without abbreviation. • The plea is obsolete because of the pleading requirements in federal and state rules of civil procedure.

inconsistent defense. A defense so contrary to another defense that the acceptance of one requires abandonment of the other. • For example, a person accused of murder cannot claim both self-defense and the alibi of having been in a different city when the murder took place.

insanity defense. See INSANITY DEFENSE.

issuable defense. *Common-law pleading.* A plea on the merits setting forth a legal defense. Cf. *issuable plea* under PLEA.

justification defense. See JUSTIFICATION DEFENSE.

legal defense. A complete and adequate defense in a court of law.

meritorious defense (mer-ə-**tor**-ee-əs). **1.** A defense that addresses the substance or essentials of a case rather than dilatory or technical objections. **2.** A defense that appears likely to succeed or has already succeeded.

partial defense. A defense going either to part of the action or toward mitigation of damages.

peremptory defense (pər-**emp**-tər-ee). A defense that questions the plaintiff's legal right to sue or contends that the right to sue has been extinguished.

pretermitted defense (pree-tər-**mit**-id). A defense available to a party that must be pleaded at the right time or be waived.

sham defense. A fictitious, untrue defense, made in bad faith.

2. A defendant's method and strategy in opposing the plaintiff or the prosecution; a doctrine giving rise to such a method or strategy <the lawyer advised her client to adopt a passive defense and to avoid taking the witness stand>.

derivative defense. A defense that rebuts the criminal elements that a prosecutor must establish to justify the submission of a criminal case to a jury.

dwelling defense. See CASTLE DOCTRINE.

empty-chair defense. See EMPTY-CHAIR DEFENSE.

3. One or more defendants in a trial <the defense rests>. **4.** *Commercial law.* A basis for avoiding liability on a negotiable instrument <the drawer asserted a real defense against the holder in due course>.

personal defense. An ordinary defense in a contract action — such as failure of consideration or nonperformance of a condition — that the maker or drawer of a negotiable instrument is precluded from raising against a person who has the rights of a holder in due course. • A personal defense can be asserted only against a transferee who is not a holder in due course. — Also termed *limited defense.*

real defense. A type of defense that is good against any possible claimant, so that the maker or drawer of a negotiable instrument can raise it even against a holder in due course. • The ten real defenses are (1) fraud in the factum, (2) forgery of a necessary signature, (3) adjudicated insanity that, under state law, renders the contract void from its inception, (4) material alteration of the instrument, (5) infancy, which renders the contract voidable under state law, (6) illegality that renders the underlying contract void, (7) duress, (8) discharge in bankruptcy, or any discharge known to the holder in due course, (9) a suretyship defense (for example, if the holder knew that one indorser was signing as a surety or accommodation party), and (10) a statute of limitations (generally three years after dishonor or acceptance on a draft and six years after demand or other due date on a note). — Also termed *absolute defense*; *universal defense.*

5. Measures taken by a country or individual to protect against an attack. See SELF-DEFENSE; NATIONAL DEFENSE (1).

self-defense. See SELF-DEFENSE.

6. A country's military establishment. See NATIONAL DEFENSE (2). — Also spelled (esp. in BrE) *defence.*

defense attorney. A lawyer who represents a defendant in a civil or criminal case. — Also termed *defense counsel*; *defense lawyer.*

defense contingent fee. See *reverse contingent fee* under CONTINGENT FEE.

defense counsel. See DEFENSE ATTORNEY.

Defense Department. An executive department of the federal government, responsible for coordinating and overseeing military affairs and the agencies responsible for national security. • The Department was established as the National Military Establishment in 1947, by combining the War and the Navy Departments. Its name was changed to Department of Defense in 1949. The Department's components include the Army, the Air Force, the Navy, the Marine Corps, and the Joint Chiefs of Staff. It is headed by the Secretary of Defense, who is answerable to the President as Commander-in-Chief. — Also termed *Department of Defense* (abbr. DOD).

defense lawyer. See DEFENSE ATTORNEY.

defense-month. See FENCE-MONTH.

defense of habitation. See CASTLE DOCTRINE.

defense of others. A justification defense available if one harms or threatens another when defending a third person. See JUSTIFICATION (2).

defense of property. A justification defense available if one harms or threatens another when defending one's property. See JUSTIFICATION (2).

defense of self. See SELF-DEFENSE.

defensiva (dee-fen-**sɪ**-və), *n.* [Latin "a protector"] *Hist.* A warden of the Marches, being one of many lords appointed by the Crown to defend England's borders.

defensive allegation. *Hist. Eccles. law.* A defendant's pleading of the facts relied upon that require the plaintiff's response under oath.

> "The proceedings in the ecclesiastical courts are therefore regulated according to the practice of the civil and canon laws .... [T]heir ordinary course of proceeding is; first, by *citation*, to call the party injuring before them. Then ... to set forth the complainant's ground of complaint. To this succeeds the *defendant's answer* upon oath; when, if he denies or extenuates the charge, they proceed to *proofs* by witnesses examined, and their depositions taken down in writing, by an officer of the court. If the defendant has any circumstances to offer in his defence, he must also propound them in what is called his *defensive allegation*, to which he is entitled in his turn to the *plaintiff's answer* upon oath, and may from thence proceed to *proofs* as well as his antagonist." 3 William Blackstone, *Commentaries on the Laws of England* 100 (1768).

defensive collateral estoppel. See COLLATERAL ESTOPPEL.

defensor (di-**fen**-sər *or* -sor), *n.* [fr. Latin *defendere* "to forbid"] **1.** *Roman law.* A defender of another's interests in court; an advocate, esp. for a corporation. Cf. PROCURATOR LITIS. **2.** *Roman law.* DEFENSOR CIVITATIS. **3.** *Hist. Eccles. law.* An advocate or patron of a church; a church warden. **4.** *Hist.* A guardian; a protector; a defender.

defensor civitatis (di-**fen**-sər siv-i-**tay**-tis), *n.* [Latin "defender of the city"] *Roman law.* An officer conducting public business, including protecting people, esp. the poor, from legal injustices, adjudicating certain minor offenses and pecuniary matters, and acting as a notary in the execution of a will or other transfer. — Often shortened to *defensor*.

defensor fidei (di-**fen**-sər **fɪ**-dee-ɪ), *n.* [Latin "defender of the faith"] A unique title of the sovereign of England, first granted by Pope Leo X to Henry VIII for writing against Martin Luther. • The Pope later withdrew the title because of Henry's harsh regulation of the church, but the title was again bestowed on the King by Parliament. The term is similar to the application of "Catholic" to the Spanish sovereign and "Most Christian" to the French sovereign. — Also termed *Defender of the Faith.*

defensum (di-**fen**-səm), *n.* [Law Latin "an inclosure"] *Hist.* **1.** A portion of an open field allotted for corn or hay but not for feeding. **2.** A wood partially enclosed to prevent the cattle from damaging the undergrowth. **3.** A prohibition.

defer, *vb.* **1.** To postpone; to delay <to defer taxes to another year>. **2.** To show deference to (another); to yield to the opinion of <because it was a political question, the courts deferred to the legislature>.

deferment, *n.* **1.** The act of delaying; postponement <deferment of a judicial decision>. **2.** *Military law.* A delay in serving in the military. **3.** *Military law.* A delay in serving confinement that results from a court-martial until the sentence has been approved and its execution has been ordered. • The convening authority may grant a deferment. — **defer,** *vb.*

deferral of taxes. The postponement of paying a tax from one year to another, as by contributing money to an IRA, for which earnings and contributions will be taxed only when the money is withdrawn.

deferral state. Under the Age Discrimination in Employment Act (ADEA), a state that has its own antidiscrimination legislation and enforcement mechanism, so that the time to file a federal lawsuit under the ADEA is postponed until state remedies have been exhausted.

deferred adjudication. See *deferred judgment* under JUDGMENT.

deferred-adjudication probation. See *deferred judgment* under JUDGMENT.

deferred annuity. See ANNUITY.

deferred charge. An expense not currently recognized on an income statement but carried forward on the balance sheet as an asset to be written off in the future <insurance premiums are a deferred charge>.

deferred claim. A claim postponed to a future accounting period.

deferred compensation. See COMPENSATION.

deferred credit. A credit (such as a premium on an issued bond) that is required to be spread over later accounting periods.

deferred dividend. See DIVIDEND.

deferred expense. See EXPENSE.

deferred income. See INCOME.

deferred-interest bond. See BOND (3).

deferred judgment. See JUDGMENT.

deferred lien. See LIEN.

deferred payment. A principal-and-interest payment that is postponed; an installment payment.

deferred-payment annuity. See *deferred annuity* under ANNUITY.

deferred prosecution. See *deferred judgment* under JUDGMENT.

deferred revenue. See *prepaid income* under INCOME.

deferred sentence. See SENTENCE.

deferred stock. See STOCK.

deficiency, *n.* **1.** A lack, shortage, or insufficiency. **2.** A shortfall in paying taxes; the amount by which the tax properly due exceeds the sum of the amount of tax shown on a taxpayer's return. — Also termed *tax deficiency*; *income-tax deficiency*; *deficiency in tax.* **3.** The amount still owed when the property secured by a mortgage is sold at a foreclosure sale for less than the outstanding debt; esp., the shortfall between the proceeds from a foreclosure sale and an amount consisting of the principal debt plus interest plus the foreclosure costs. See *deficiency judgment* under JUDGMENT.

deficiency assessment. See ASSESSMENT.

deficiency bill. See BILL (3).

deficiency decree. See *deficiency judgment* under JUDGMENT.

deficiency dividend. See DIVIDEND.

deficiency in tax. See DEFICIENCY (2).

deficiency judgment. See JUDGMENT.

deficiency letter. An SEC letter to a registrant of a securities offering, detailing the ways in which the registration statement fails to meet federal disclosure requirements. — Also termed *letter of comment*; *letter of comments.*

deficiency notice. See NINETY-DAY LETTER.

deficiency suit. An action to recover the difference between a mortgage debt and the amount realized on foreclosure. See *deficiency judgment* under JUDGMENT.

deficit. 1. A deficiency or disadvantage; a deficiency in the amount or quality of something.

trade deficit. In economics, the excess of merchandise imports over merchandise exports during a specific period. — Also termed *trade gap.* Cf. *trade surplus* under SURPLUS.

2. An excess of expenditures or liabilities over revenues or assets.

deficit spending. Expenditures in excess of income, usu. from borrowed funds rather than actual revenues or surplus.

defile (di-**fɪl**), *vb.* **1.** To make dirty; to physically soil. **2.** To figuratively tarnish; to dishonor. **3.** To make ceremonially unclean; to desecrate. **4.** To morally corrupt (someone). **5.** *Archaic.* To debauch (a person); to deprive (a person) of chastity.

defilement (di-**fɪl**-mənt), *n.* 1. An act of defiling. **2.** A condition of being defiled.

define, *vb.* **1.** To state or explain explicitly. **2.** To fix or establish (boundaries or limits). **3.** To set forth the meaning of (a word or phrase).

defined-benefit plan. See EMPLOYEE BENEFIT PLAN.

defined-contribution plan. See EMPLOYEE BENEFIT PLAN.

defined pension plan. See PENSION PLAN.

defined term. In legal drafting, a word or phrase given a specific meaning for purposes of the document in which it appears; a definiendum.

de fine force (dee **fɪ**-nee fors). [Law French] Of pure necessity.

de fine non capiendo pro pulchre placitando (dee **fɪ**-nee non kap-ee-**en**-doh proh **pəl**-kree plas-ə-**tan**-doh), *n.* [Law Latin "of not taking a fine for amending a bad pleading"] *Hist.* A writ prohibiting the imposition of a fine for bad pleading. See BEAUPLEADER.

de fine pro redisseisina capiendo (dee **fɪ**-nee proh ree-dis-**see**-zin-ə kap-ee-**en**-doh), *n.* [Law

Latin "of a fine paid for one imprisoned for redisseisin"] *Hist.* A writ releasing a person who paid a reasonable fine after being imprisoned for a redisseisin.

de finibus levatis (dee **fɪ**-nə-bəs lə-**vay**-tis), *n.* [Law Latin "concerning fines levied"] *Hist.* The statute requiring any levied fines to be read solemnly in open court. 27 Edw. 1.

definite sentence. See *determinate sentence* under SENTENCE.

definitio (def-ə-**nish**-ee-oh), *n.* [fr. Latin *definire* "definition"] *Civil law.* **1.** A definition; an explanation of something. **2.** The establishment of a general rule. **3.** A boundary.

definition. The meaning of a term as explicitly stated in a drafted document such as a contract, a corporate bylaw, an ordinance, or a statute; a definiens.

lexical definition. A dictionary-style definition of a word, purporting to give the full meaning of a term.

stipulative definition. A definition that, for purposes of the document in which it appears, arbitrarily clarifies a term with uncertain boundaries or that includes or excludes specified items from the ambit of the term.

definitive judgment. See *final judgment* under JUDGMENT.

definitive partition. See PARTITION.

definitive sentence. See *determinate sentence* under SENTENCE.

deflation, *n.* A general decline in the price of goods and services. — **deflate,** *vb.* — **deflationary,** *adj.* Cf. INFLATION; DISINFLATION.

deforce, *vb.* **1.** To keep (lands) from the true owner by means of force. **2.** To oust (another) from possession by means of force. **3.** To detain (a creditor's money) unjustly and forcibly. — **deforciant,** *n.*

> "The character of the action of debt is well illustrated by the form of the writ as given by Glanville. It directs the sheriff to order the debtor to render a stated sum which he owes to the plaintiff, 'and whereof the plaintiff complains that the defendant unjustly deforces him,' and, if he will not obey, he is to be summoned before the King's Court. The plaintiff is 'deforced' of money just as in a writ of right he is 'deforced' of land. It is true that the term 'deforces' disappeared from the writ shortly after Glanville's time, the word *debet* taking its place; but this seems to have been a matter of form, not of substance. The plaintiff sought to recover the money due as his property." William F. Walsh, *Outlines of the History of English and American Law* 411 (1924).

deforcement. 1. An act of keeping lands from the true owner by force. **2.** An act of ousting another from possession by means of force. **3.** An act of detaining a creditor's money unjustly and forcibly.

deforciant (di-**for**-shənt), *n.* [fr. Law Latin *deforcians* "a deforcer"] A person who prevents another from taking possession of property; the defendant in an action of fine. See FINE (1).

deforciare (di-for-shee-**air**-ee), *vb.* [fr. Law Latin *defortiare* "to deforce"] *Hist.* To withhold property (such as land and tenements) from the true owner.

deforciatio (di-for-shee-**ay**-shee-oh), *n.* [Law Latin "a distress"] *Hist.* A seizure of goods to satisfy a debt.

de forisfactura maritagii (dee for-is-fak-**tyoor**-ə mar-ə-**tay**-jee-ɪ), *n.* [Law Latin "of forfeiture of marriage"] *Hist.* A writ forfeiting a marriage.

defossion (di-**fosh**-in), *n.* [fr. Latin *de* "down" + *fodere* "dig"] The punishment of being buried alive.

de frangentibus prisonam (dee fran-**jen**-ti-bəs **priz**-ə-nəm), *n.* [Latin "of those who break prison"] *Hist.* The statute providing that an escaped prisoner will not be put to death or forfeit a limb simply for escaping from prison unless the original crime required that penalty upon conviction. 1 Edw. 2.

defraud, *vb.* To cause injury or loss to (a person) by deceit. See FRAUD.

defraudation. An act of privation by fraud.

defrauder. See FRAUDFEASOR.

defunct, *adj.* Dead; extinct <defunct corporation>.

defunct marriage. A marriage in which both parties, by their conduct, indicate their intent to no longer be married.

defunctus (di-**fəngk**-təs), *adj.* [Latin] Dead, as in *defunctus sine prole* ("dead without (leaving) issue").

de furto (dee **fər**-toh), *n.* [Latin "of theft"] *Hist.* In England, a type of criminal appeal.

degaster (day-gas-**tay**), *vb.* [fr. Old French *dégaster* "to spoil"] To waste.

de gestu et fama (dee **jes**-ty[y]oo et **fay**-mə), *n.* [Law Latin "of behavior and reputation"] *Hist.* A writ available to a person whose character and reputation had been impeached.

degradation (deg-rə-**day**-shən). **1.** A reduction in rank, degree, or dignity; specif., censure of a clergy member by divestiture of holy orders, either by word or by a solemn divestiture of robes and other insignia. **2.** A moral or intellectual decadence or degeneration; a lessening of a person's or thing's character or quality <degradation of resources>. **3.** A wearing down of something, as by erosion.

de gratia (dee **gray**-shee-ə). [Latin] Of favor; by grace, as in *de speciali gratia* ("of special grace or favor").

degree. 1. Generally, a classification or specification <degrees of proof>. **2.** An incremental measure of guilt or negligence; a level based on the seriousness of an offense <murder in the first degree>. **3.** A stage in a process; a step in a series of steps toward an end <the statute went through several degrees of development>. **4.** A stage in intensity <a high degree of legal skill is required>. **5.** In the line of descent, a measure of removal determining the proximity of a blood or marital relationship <the judge was recused because she was related to the plaintiff within the second degree of affinity> <the council member did not participate in the vote because he was related to one of the bidders within the first degree of consanguinity>. — Also termed *degree of kin.* See AFFINITY (2); CONSANGUINITY.

equal degree. A relationship between two or more relatives who are the same number of steps away from a common ancestor.

prohibited degree. A degree of relationship so close (as between brother and sister) that marriage between the persons is forbidden by law. • Generally, with slight variations from jurisdiction to jurisdiction, the law forbids marriages between all persons lineally related and within the third civil-law degree of relationship. — Also termed *forbidden degree.*

6. A title conferred on a graduate of a school, college, or university, either after the completion of required studies or in honor of special achievements <she began studying for the bar exam the day after receiving her law degree>. Cf. DIPLOMA (3).

degree of care. A standard of care to be exercised in a given situation. See CARE.

***highest degree of care.* 1.** The degree of care exercised commensurate with the danger involved. **2.** The degree of care applied by people in the business or profession of dealing with the given situation. — Also termed *extraordinary care*; *utmost care.*

degree of crime. 1. A division or classification of a single crime into several grades of guilt, according to the circumstances surrounding the crime's commission, such as aggravating factors present or the type of injury suffered. **2.** A division of crimes generally, such as felonies or misdemeanors.

degree of kin. See DEGREE.

degree of negligence. One of the varying levels of negligence typically designated as slight negligence, ordinary negligence, and gross negligence. See NEGLIGENCE.

> "Although the common law concept of degrees of negligence has been criticized or repudiated in many jurisdictions, the usefulness of the view at common law that degrees of negligence exist is still recognized in a number of jurisdictions, particularly in regard to the distinction between ordinary and gross negligence. Furthermore, legislators have not been dissuaded from using the degrees of negligence concept when it is helpful to achieve a legislative purpose." 57A Am. Jur. 2d *Negligence* § 233, at 274 (1989).

degree of proof. See BURDEN OF PRODUCTION.

de haerede deliberando illi qui habet custodiam terrae (dee hi-**ree**-dee di-lib-ə-**ran**-doh **il**-I kwI **hay**-bət kə-**stoh**-dee-əm **ter**-ee), *n.* [Law Latin "for delivering an heir to him who has wardship of the land"] *Hist.* A writ ordering the sheriff to deliver an heir to a person who had wardship.

de haerede rapto et abducto (dee hi-**ree**-dee **rap**-toh et ab-**dək**-toh), *n.* [Law Latin "of an heir ravished and carried away"] *Hist.* A writ allowing a lord to recover a ward who had been taken by another person.

de haeretico comburendo (dee hi-**ret**-i-koh kom-byə-**ren**-doh), *n.* [Law Latin "of burning a heretic"] *Hist.* **1.** A writ ordering the execution by burning of a heretic who, after having already been convicted of heresy by the bishop and recanted, was again convicted by a secular court. — Also termed *writ de haeretico comburendo.*

"And . . . we find among our ancient precedents a writ *de haeretico comburendo*, which is thought by some to be as ancient as the common law itself. However, it appears from thence, that the conviction of heresy by the common law was not in any petty ecclesiastical court, but before the archbishop himself in a provincial synod; and that the delinquent was delivered over to the king to do as he should please with him: so that the crown had a control over the spiritual power, and might pardon the convict by issuing no process against him; the writ *de haeretico comburendo* being not a writ of course, but issuing only by the special direction of the king in council." 4 William Blackstone, *Commentaries on the Laws of England* 46–47 (1769).

"But the case of Sawtre (1400) is a clear case in which the rule of the canon law was applied. He was convicted of heresy before the Bishop of Norwich and recanted his heresy. He fell again into heresy, and was condemned by the archbishop and his provincial Council, as a relapsed heretic. On this conviction the king issued a writ de haeretico comburendo. This case clearly shows that the common law recognized the rule of the canon law . . . ." 1 William Holdsworth, *A History of English Law* 617 (7th ed. 1956).

2. The first English penal law against heresy, enacted in 1401 (2 Hen. 4, ch. 15). • The law authorized the burning of defendants who relapsed or refused to abandon their heretical opinions.

"The first English statute that denounced the penalty of death against heretics was passed in the year 1401. Whether before that statute the law that was in force in our land demanded or suffered that such persons should be burnt is a question that has been eagerly debated; on it in the days of Elizabeth and James I depended the lives of Anabaptists and Arians; it has not yet lost its interest; but it is a question that buzzes in a vacuum, for until Lollardy became troublesome there was too little heresy in England to beget a settled course of procedure." 2 Frederick Pollock & Frederic Maitland, *The History of English Law Before the Time of Edward I* 544 (1899).

de homagio respectuando (dee hə-**may**-jee-oh ri-spek-tyoo-**an**-doh), *n.* [Law Latin "for respiting or postponing homage"] *Hist.* A writ to postpone an homage. See HOMAGE.

de homine capto in withernamium (dee **hom**-ə-nee **kap**-toh in with-ər-**nay**-mee-əm), *n.* [Law Latin "for taking a man in withernam"] *Hist.* A writ to seize and jail a person who took a bondman out of the county to keep the bondman from being replevied. • The defendant was jailed without bail until the bondman was returned. See WITHERNAM.

de homine replegiando (dee **hom**-ə-nee ri-plee-jee-**an**-doh), *n.* [Law Latin "for replevying a man"] A writ to replevy a person out of jail or out of the custody of another person after giving security that the replevied person will answer any charge.

"The writ *de homine replegiando* lies to replevy a man out of prison, or out of the custody of any private person, (in the same manner that chattels taken in distress may be replevied . . .) upon giving security to the sheriff that the man shall be forthcoming to answer any charge against him. And, if the person be conveyed out of the sheriff's jurisdiction, the sheriff may return that he is eloigned . . . upon which a process issues . . . to imprison the defendant himself, without bail . . . till he produces the party. But this writ is guarded with so many exceptions, that it is not an effectual remedy in numerous instances, especially where the crown is concerned." 3 William Blackstone, *Commentaries on the Laws of England* 129 (1768).

dehors (də-**hor** *or* də-**horz**). [Law French] Outside; beyond the scope of <the court cannot consider the document because it is dehors the record>.

de identitate nominis (dee ɪ-den-tə-**tay**-tee **nom**-ə-nis), *n.* [Law Latin "of identity of name"] *Hist.* A writ to free a person mistaken for someone else with the same name and then falsely arrested and imprisoned. — Also termed *de idemptitate nominis.*

de idiota inquirendo (dee id-ee-**oh**-tə in-kwɪ-**ren**-doh *or* in-kwə-**ren**-doh). [Latin "of inquiring concerning an idiot"] *Hist.* A writ directing the sheriff to open an inquiry before a jury of 12 into whether a person is an idiot, that is, mentally incapable of managing personal affairs.

Dei gratia (**dee**-ɪ **gray**-shee-ə). [Latin] By the grace of God. • This phrase was often used in rulers' titles to show that their authority was by divine right. It was also formerly used in titles of magistrates and other officers.

de iis qui ponendi sunt in assisis (dee **ɪ**-əs kwɪ pə-**nen**-dɪ sənt in ə-**sɪ**-zəz), *n.* [Law Latin "of those who are to be put on assises"] *Hist.* The statute establishing juror qualifications. 21 Edw. 1.

de incremento (dee in-krə-**men**-toh). [Law Latin "of increase"] *Hist.* Additional. • Costs *de incremento* are costs awarded by a court in addition to costs awarded by the jury.

de ingressu (dee in-**gres**-[y]oo), *n.* [Law Latin "of entry"] *Hist.* A writ allowing entry into lands or tenements.

de injuria (dee in-**joor**-ee-ə). [Law Latin "of injury"] *Hist.* Of injury. • A traverse *de injuria*, contained in a replication in a trespass action, denies the defendant's excuse for the wrong done. See TRAVERSE.

de inofficioso testamento (dee in-ə-fish-ee-**oh**-soh tes-tə-**men**-toh). [Latin] *Hist.* Concerning an inofficious or undutiful will. • This was a title of Roman law. See INOFFICIOSUS.

de integro (dee **in**-tə-groh), *n.* [Latin] Again; a second time.

de intrusione (dee in-troo-zhee-**oh**-nee), *n.* [Law Latin "of intrusion"] *Hist.* A writ available to a reversioner when the tenant dies and a stranger occupies the land.

dejeration (dej-ə-**ray**-shən). The act of taking a solemn oath.

de jure (di **juur**-ee *also* dee *or* day), *adj.* [Law Latin "as a matter of law"] Existing by right or according to law <de jure segregation during the pre-*Brown* era>. Cf. DE FACTO; DE GRATIA.

de jure corporation. See CORPORATION.

de jure officer. See *officer de jure* under OFFICER (1).

de jure segregation. See SEGREGATION.

delantal (di-**lan**-təl). [Old English] *Hist.* See UTLAND.

de la plus belle (də lah ploo **bel**), *adj.* [Law French] *Hist.* Of the most fair. • This term described a form of dower assigned out of the husband's best tenements. The term was used in military tenures but was abolished by St. 12 Car. 2, ch. 24. — Also termed *de la pluis beale.*

de latere (dee **lat**-ər-ee). [Latin] Of collaterals; from the side.

delatio (di-**lay**-shee-oh), *n.* [fr. Latin *deferre* "to denounce"] *Roman & civil law.* **1.** An accusation. **2.** Information.

delator (di-**lay**-tər *or* -tor), *n.* [fr. Latin *deferre* "to denounce"] *Roman & civil law.* **1.** An accuser. **2.** An informer.

delatura (del-ə-**tyoor**-ə), *n.* [fr. Latin *deferre* "to denounce"] *Hist.* A reward given to an informer.

delay, *n.* **1.** The act of postponing or slowing <the continuance was sought for no purpose other than delay>. **2.** An instance at which something is postponed or slowed <the delay in starting the trial made it difficult for all the witnesses to attend>. **3.** The period during which something is postponed or slowed <during the delay, the case settled>. **4.** *Civil law.* The period within which a party to a suit must take some action, such as perfecting an appeal or responding to a written-discovery request <the delay for responding to written interrogatories is 15 days after the date they are served on the responding party>.

delayed appeal. See APPEAL.

delayed-compliance order. *Environmental law.* An order issued by the Environmental Protection Agency or by a state agency to an existing source of pollutants, whereby the deadline for complying with an implementation plan is postponed. See IMPLEMENTATION PLAN.

delayed funds availability. A hold that a bank places on uncollected funds that are represented by a deposited check. — Abbr. DFA.

delayed rental. See RENTAL.

del bien estre (del **been es**-tər). [Law French] *Hist.* Of well-being. See DE BENE ESSE.

del credere (del **kred**-ə-ray *or* **kray**-də-ray), *adj.* [Italian] Of belief or trust.

> " '*Del credere*' agents for the sale of goods, in consideration of a higher payment than usual, become responsible for the solvency of the person to whom they sell them." Thomas E. Holland, *The Elements of Jurisprudence* 304 (13th ed. 1924).

***del credere* agent.** See AGENT.

***del credere* bailiff.** See FACTOR.

***del credere* commission.** A factor's commission that is increased because the factor guarantees the payment to the principal of all debts that become due through the agency relationship.

***del credere* factor.** See *del credere agent* under AGENT.

delectus personae (di-**lek**-təs pər-**soh**-nee). [Latin "choice of the person"] The rule that when personal relations are important, a person cannot be compelled to associate with another person. • Based on this principle, a partner has the right to accept or reject a candidate proposed as a new partner.

delegable duty. See DUTY (1).

delegate (**del**-ə-git), *n.* One who represents or acts for another person or a group.

delegated legislation. See REGULATION (3).

delegatee (del-ə-gə-**tee**). An agent or representative to whom a matter is delegated.

delegation, *n.* **1.** The act of entrusting another with authority or empowering another to act as an agent or representative <delegation of contractual duties>. **2.** A group of representatives <a large delegation from Texas>. — **delegate** (**del**-ə-gayt) (for sense 1), *vb.* — **delegable** (**del**-ə-gə-bəl) (for sense 1), *adj.*

delegation doctrine. *Constitutional law.* The principle (based on the separation-of-powers concept) limiting Congress's ability to transfer its legislative power to another governmental branch, esp. the executive branch. • Delegation is permitted only if Congress prescribes an intelligible principle to guide an executive agency in making policy. — Also termed *nondelegation doctrine.* See *legislative veto* under VETO.

delegation of duties. *Contracts.* A transaction by which a party to a contract arranges to have a third party perform the party's contractual duties.

delegation of powers. A transfer of authority by one branch of government to another branch or to an administrative agency. See DELEGATION DOCTRINE.

de legatis et fidei commissis (dee li-**gay**-tis et **fɪ**-dee-ɪ kə-**mis**-is). [Latin] Of legacies and trusts. • This is a title in the Pandects.

de lege ferenda (dee **lee**-jee fə-**ren**-də). [Latin "from law to be passed"] *Int'l law.* A principle created to apply to a given situation, rather than from existing precedents; law created for changing circumstances. Cf. DE LEGE LATA.

> "It is not sufficient for the codifiers of international law to study the subject matter solely from the juridical aspect, or to rely only on the 'state practice, precedent and doctrine.' ... [T]he systematic development of sociological inquiries concerning international law is indispensable for the human future, at any rate, insofar as the human future is deemed to depend on the role of international law. It seems indispensable, moreover, not only for the development of international law *de lege ferenda*, but also for the clarification of its present content *de lege lata*." R.P. Dhokalia, *The Codification of Public International Law* 334–35 (1970).

de lege lata (dee **lee**-jee **lay**-tə). [Latin "from law passed"] *Int'l law.* **1.** Existing law. **2.** The principle that a court should decide based on actual law and not on how it thinks the law ought to be. Cf. DE LEGE FERENDA.

deleterious (del-ə-**teer**-ee-əs), *adj.* **1.** Poisonous <deleterious toxins>. **2.** Unwholesome; psychologically or physically harmful <deleterious influence>.

de libera falda (dee **lib**-ər-ə **fal**-də *or* **fawl**-də), *n.* [Law Latin "of free fold"] *Hist.* A writ allowing a free feeding, esp. of sheep on land. • This was a form of *quod permittat.*

de libera piscaria (dee **lib**-ər-ə pi-**skair**-ee-ə), *n.* [Law Latin "of free fishery"] *Hist.* A writ allowing an exclusive right to fish on public navigable water. • This was a form of *quod permittat.*

deliberate (di-**lib**-[ə]-rit), *adj.* **1.** Intentional; premeditated; fully considered. **2.** Unimpulsive; slow in deciding.

deliberate elicitation. *Criminal procedure.* The purposeful yet covert drawing forth of an incriminating response (usu. not during a formal interrogation) from a suspect whose Sixth Amendment right to counsel has attached but who has not waived that right. • Deliberate elicitation may occur, for example, when a police officer engages an arrested suspect in conversation on the way to the police station. Deliberate elicitation violates the Sixth Amendment. *Massiah v. United States*, 377 U.S. 201, 84 S.Ct. 1199 (1964).

deliberate-indifference instruction. See JEWELL INSTRUCTION.

deliberate speed, with all. As quickly as the maintenance of law and order and the welfare of the people will allow, esp. with respect to the desegregation of public schools. *Brown v. Board of Educ.*, 347 U.S. 483, 74 S.Ct. 686 (1954).

deliberation, *n.* The act of carefully considering issues and options before making a decision or taking some action; esp., the process by which a jury reaches a verdict, as by analyzing, discussing, and weighing the evidence. — **deliberate** (di-**lib**-ə-rayt), *vb.*

deliberative-process privilege. See PRIVILEGE (1).

de libero passagio (dee **lib**-ər-oh pə-**say**-jee-oh), *n.* [Law Latin "of free passage"] *Hist.* A writ allowing free passage over water. • This was a form of *quod permittat.*

de libertate probanda (dee lib-ər-**tay**-tee proh-**ban**-də), *n.* [Law Latin "for proving liberty"] *Hist.* A writ directing a sheriff to take security from a person accused of being a villein and to protect that person from harassment until the person's status was determined by the justices of assize.

de libertatibus allocandis (dee lib-ər-**tay**-tə-bəs al-ə-**kan**-dis), *n.* [Law Latin "for allowing liberties"] *Hist.* A writ allowing a person entitled to certain liberties to obtain them.

de licentia transfretandi (dee lɪ-**sen**-shee-ə trans-frə-**tan**-dɪ), *n.* [Law Latin "of permission to cross the sea"] *Hist.* A writ ordering wardens of seaports, on certain conditions, to permit any person named in the writ to cross the sea.

delict (di-**likt**), *n.* [Latin *delictum* "an offense"] A violation of the law; a tort; a wrong. — Also termed (in Roman law) *delictum*; (in French law) *délit.*

> "A delict is a civil wrong. It is an infringement of another's interests that is wrongful irrespective of any prior contractual undertaking to refrain from it — though there may also be one. It entitles the injured party to claim compensation in civil proceedings — though criminal proceedings aimed at punishing the wrongdoer may also ensue." 1 P.Q.R. Boberg, *The Law of Delict* 1 (1984).

private delict. A wrong regarded primarily as a matter of compensation between individuals.

public delict. A wrong for which the community as a whole takes steps to punish the offender. Cf. *public tort* under TORT.

quasi-delict. **1.** *Roman law.* An offense for which some person other than the actual perpetrator is held responsible, such as a master for the wrongdoing of a slave.

> "QUASI-DELICT .... Justinian enumerates four cases of obligations said to arise quasi ex delicto. The implication seems to be that in all of them the law creates a liability though the defendant may not in fact be to blame. The cases are the following: — (1) The judge who 'makes the case his own' ... incurs a penalty fixed by the magistrate at discretion .... (2) If anything was thrown, or poured, from an upper room ... the occupier was liable for double the damage .... (3) If a thing was kept placed or suspended over a way used by the public ... there was a penalty ... which might be recovered from the occupier .... (4) Ship-owners, innkeepers and stable-keepers were liable for damage or theft committed by slaves or free persons in their employ ...." R.W. Lee, *The Elements of Roman Law* 401–02 (4th ed. 1956).

2. See *quasi-offense* under OFFENSE (2).

delictal. See DELICTUAL.

deliction (di-**lik**-shən). The loss of land by gradual, natural changes, such as erosion resulting from a change in the course of a river or stream. Cf. ACCRETION (1); ALLUVION; AVULSION (2); EROSION.

delictual (di-**lik**-chə-wəl), *adj.* Of, relating to, or involving a delict; TORTIOUS. — Also termed *delictal.*

delictual fault. *Civil law.* A legal obligation arising between people independent of any prior contractual or other legal relationship between them, such as the obligation arising when one person commits a tort against another person.

delictum. See DELICT.

delimination. The act of marking a boundary or fixing a limit.

delimit (di-**lim**-it), *vb.* To mark (a boundary); to fix (a limit).

delimitation. A fixing of limits or boundaries.

delinquency, *n.* **1.** A failure or omission; a violation of a law or duty. See JUVENILE DELINQUENCY. **2.** A debt that is overdue in payment.

delinquency charge. See CHARGE.

delinquent, *adj.* **1.** (Of a person) failing to perform an obligation. **2.** (Of a person) guilty of serious antisocial or criminal conduct. **3.** (Of an obligation) past due or unperformed.

delinquent, *n.* **1.** A person who fails to perform an obligation. **2.** A person guilty of serious antisocial or criminal conduct. See JUVENILE DELINQUENT.

delinquent child. See CHILD.

delinquent minor. See JUVENILE DELINQUENCY.

delinquent tax. See TAX.

delirium. 1. A disordered mental state, often occurring during illness. **2.** Exaggerated excitement. **3.** A delusion; a hallucination.

delisting, *n.* The suspension of the privilege of having a security listed on an exchange. • Delisting results from failing to meet the exchange's listing requirements, as by not complying with the minimum net-asset requirement. — **delist,** *vb.* Cf. DEREGISTRATION.

délit. See DELICT.

deliverance. 1. A jury's verdict. **2.** A judicial opinion or judgment. **3.** A court's order directing that a person in custody be released; esp., such an order by an ecclesiastical court. — Also termed *writ of deliverance.* **4.** *Archaic.* In a replevin action, a writ ordering the redelivery to the owner of goods.

second deliverance. *Hist.* A second replevin remedy after the plaintiff has been nonsuited and the distrained property has been returned to the defendant. — Also termed *writ of second deliverance.*

"And at the common law, the plaintiff might have brought another replevin, and so *in infinitum*, to the intolerable vexation of the defendant. Wherefore the statute of Westm. 2, c. 2 restrains the plaintiff, when nonsuited, from suing any fresh replevin, but allows him a *judicial* writ issuing out of the original record, and called a writ of *second deliverance*, in order to have the same distress again delivered to him, on giving the like security as before. And, if the plaintiff be a second time nonsuit, or if the defendant has judgment upon verdict . . . he shall have a writ or *return irreplevisable*; after which no writ of second deliverance shall be allowed." 3 William Blackstone, *Commentaries on the Laws of England* 150 (1767).

5. Such a release (as in sense 3) or redelivery (as in sense 4).

delivery, *n.* **1.** The formal act of transferring or conveying something, such as a deed; the giving or yielding possession or control of something to another. **2.** The thing so transferred or conveyed. — **deliver,** *vb.* Cf. LIVERY.

absolute delivery. A delivery that is complete upon the actual transfer of the instrument from the grantor's possession. • Such a delivery usu. does not depend on recordation.

actual delivery. The act of giving real and immediate possession to the buyer or the buyer's agent.

conditional delivery. A delivery that passes possession only upon the happening of a specified event.

constructive delivery. An act that amounts to a transfer of title by operation of law when actual transfer is impractical or impossible. • For example, the delivery of a deposit-box key by someone who is ill and immobile amounts to a constructive delivery of the box's contents even though the box may be miles away. For the three traditional types of constructive delivery, see ATTORNMENT; CONSTITUTUM POSSESSORIUM; TRADITIO BREVI MANU.

good delivery. *Securities.* The basic conditions for delivery of a security, including that (1) the certificate is in good condition, (2) the certificate belongs to the person transferring it, (3) the certificate is properly indorsed, and (4) any legal documents necessary for negotiability must accompany the certificate.

second delivery. A legal delivery by the depositary of a deed placed in escrow.

symbolic delivery. The constructive delivery of the subject matter of a sale by the actual delivery of an article that represents the item, that renders access to it possible, or that provides evidence of the purchaser's title to it, such as the key to a warehouse or a bill of lading for goods on shipboard.

unconditional delivery. A delivery that immediately passes both possession and title and that takes effect immediately.

delivery bond. See *forthcoming bond* under BOND (2).

delivery in escrow. The physical transfer of something to an escrow agent to be held until some condition is met, at which time the agent will release it. • An example of such a delivery is a stock buyer's transfer of cash to a bank that will give the seller the cash upon receiving the stock certificates. This type of delivery creates immediate conditional rights in the promisee. The device may be used to create an option contract in which the promisee has the option. See ESCROW.

delivery of deed. The placing of a deed in the grantee's hands or within the grantee's control. • By this act, the grantor shows an intention that the deed operates immediately as a conveyance.

delivery order. A written order to deliver goods, directed to a warehouseman, carrier, or other person who ordinarily issues warehouse receipts or bills of lading. UCC § 7-102(1)(d).

de lunatico inquirendo (dee loo-**nat**-ə-koh in-kwə-**ren**-doh), *n.* [Law Latin "for inquiring about a lunatic"] *Hist.* A writ or commission to determine whether a person is a lunatic. — Also termed *commission of lunacy.*

dem. *abbr.* DEMISE.

de magna assisa eligenda (dee **mag**-nə ə-**sI**-zə el-i-**jen**-də), *n.* [Law Latin "of choosing the grand assize"] *Hist.* A writ ordering a sheriff to first summon 4 knights to give oaths before the justices of assize and then choose 12 more knights to form a grand assize to determine who had the right in a writ of right.

de malo (dee **mal**-oh). [Law Latin] Of illness. • This term defined certain legal excuses, such as *de malo lecti* ("of illness in bed"), *de malo veniendi* ("of illness or misfortune in coming where the court is"), and *de malo villae* ("of illness in town where the court is").

demand, *n.* **1.** The assertion of a legal right.

cross-demand. A party's demand opposing an adverse party's demand. See COUNTERCLAIM; CROSS-CLAIM.

incidental demand. *Civil law.* A plea by which a party other than the plaintiff asserts a claim that is related to the plaintiff's suit. • Examples include a cross-claim, a demand against a third party, an intervention, and a reconventional demand. La. Code Civ. Proc. art. 1031.

legal demand. A lawful demand made by an authorized person.

main demand. *Civil law.* A plaintiff's principal or primary claim against one or more defendants, contained in an original or validly amended pleading. — Also termed *principal demand*; *principal action.*

reconventional demand. *Civil law.* A plea by which a defendant asserts any claim that it has against the plaintiff, or any offset against the plaintiff's claim. • This plea is similar to the common-law counterclaim. La. Code Civ. Proc. 1061 et seq.

2. A request for payment of a debt or an amount due.

personal demand. An in-person demand for payment upon the drawer, maker, or acceptor of a bill or note.

3. In economics, the intensity of buyer pressure on the availability and cost of a commodity or service.

aggregate demand. **1.** The total amount spent on goods and services in an economy during a specific period. **2.** The total demand for a firm's products and services during a specific period.

derived demand. Product demand that is related to another product's demand.

demand, *vb.* **1.** To claim as one's due; to require; to seek relief. **2.** To summon; to call into court.

demandant. *Archaic.* The plaintiff in a real action (the defendant being called a *tenant*). See *real action* under ACTION.

demand clause. A provision in a note allowing the holder to compel full payment if the maker fails to meet an installment.

demand deposit. See DEPOSIT (2).

demand draft. See *sight draft* under DRAFT.

demand for document inspection. See REQUEST FOR PRODUCTION.

demand for relief. See PRAYER FOR RELIEF.

demand instrument. An instrument payable on demand, at sight, or on presentation, as opposed to an instrument that is payable at a set future date. — Also termed *demand note.*

demand letter. A letter by which one party explains its legal position in a dispute and requests that the recipient take some action (such as paying money owed), or else risk being sued. • Under some statutes (esp. consumer-protection laws), a demand letter is a prerequisite for filing a lawsuit.

demand loan. See *call loan* under LOAN.

demand note. See NOTE (1); DEMAND INSTRUMENT.

demand of oyer. *Hist.* The assertion of a party's right to hear, read, or inspect a deed of which profert is made by the opposing party in a pleading. See OYER (3).

demand of view. *Hist.* In a real action, a defendant's request to see the thing at issue to ascertain its identity and the circumstances of the claim. • If a real action was brought against a tenant who did not know what land was at issue, the tenant might demand a view. See VIEW (4).

demand-pull inflation. See INFLATION.

demandress. *Archaic.* A female demandant.

de manucaptione (dee man-yə-kap-shee-**oh**-nee), *n.* [Law Latin "of manucaption"] *Hist.* A writ ordering a sheriff to release on sufficient bail an accused felon whose initial offer of bail had been rejected.

de manutenendo (dee man-yə-tə-**nen**-doh), *n.* [Law Latin "of maintenance"] *Hist.* A writ against a person who has wrongfully meddled in a lawsuit by providing assistance to a party to continue the litigation. See MAINTENANCE (6).

demarcation line. *Int'l law.* A provisional border having the function of separating territories under different jurisdictions, usu. established when the political situation does not admit a final boundary arrangement. — Also termed *line of demarcation.*

démarche (day-**mahrsh**). [French "gait; walk"] An oral or written diplomatic statement, esp. one containing a demand, offer, protest, threat, or the like. — Also spelled *demarche.*

de maritagio amisso per defaltam (dee mar-ə-**tay**-jee-oh ə-**mis**-oh pər də-**fawl**-təm), *n.* [Law Latin] *Hist.* A writ available to a tenant of a frankmarriage to regain land lost by default.

de me (dee mee). [Latin] Of me. • This phrase appeared in feudal grants to confirm that a superior lord's permission was not needed for the conveyance. This was distinguished from a conveyance *a me de superiore meo* ("from me of my superior"), in which the estate is to be held of the superior, and is invalid unless confirmed by the superior. Cf. A ME.

demeanor. Outward appearance or behavior, such as facial expressions, tone of voice, gestures, and the hesitation or readiness to answer questions. • In evaluating a witness's credibility, the jury may consider the witness's demeanor.

demeanor evidence. See EVIDENCE.

demease (di-**meez**), *n. Hist.* Death.

de medietate linguae (dee mee-dee-ə-**tay**-tee **ling**-gwee). [Law Latin] Of half-tongue. • This term describes a jury made up of an equal number of natives and aliens. Edward III originally provided for such a jury in commercial cases when one party was an alien. It was later extended to criminal cases. If enough aliens could not be found, trial proceeded with the available number.

de medio (dee **mee**-dee-oh), *n.* [Law Latin "of mesne"] *Hist.* A writ against a mesne (i.e., middle) lord to protect an undertenant from harassment by a paramount lord for rent actually due from the mesne lord. — Also termed *writ of mesne.*

de melioribus damnis (dee mee-lee-**or**-ə-bəs **dam**-nis). [Law Latin] Of the better damages. • This term describes a plaintiff's election of the defendant against which to take judgment when the jury has mistakenly awarded separate damages against two or more defendants for a joint tort. Under these circumstances, the plaintiff could take a judgment against the defendant that had been assessed the greatest damages, and then enter a *nolle prosequi* against the others.

demented, *adj.* Not of sound mind; insane.

dementenant en avant (də-men-tə-**nahnt** on ə-**vahnt**). [Law French] From this time forward.

de mercatoribus (dee mər-kə-**tor**-ə-bəs), *n.* [Latin "of merchants"] *Hist.* The title of two statutes enacted in the 11th and 13th years of the reign of Edward I, providing that the land of a business debtor could be held by a creditor as security until the debt was paid.

> "But by the statute *de mercatoribus* . . . the whole of a man's lands was liable to be pledged in a statute merchant, for a debt contracted in trade; though one-*half* of them was liable to be taken in execution for any other debt of the owner." 1 William Blackstone, *Commentaries on the Laws of England* 161 (1765).

demesne (di-**mayn** *or* di-**meen**), *n.* [French] **1.** At common law, land held in one's own right, and not through a superior. **2.** Domain; realm. — Also spelled *demain.*

ancient demesne. *Hist.* A manor that was held by the Crown at the time of William the Conqueror and was recorded in the Domesday Book.

demesne as of fee. *Hist.* Complete ownership of something.

"But there is this distinction between the two species of hereditaments: that, of a corporeal inheritance a man shall be said to be seised *in his demesne, as of fee*; of an incorporeal one, he shall only be said to be seised *as of fee*, and not in his demesne. For, as incorporeal hereditaments are in their nature collateral to, and issue out of, lands and houses, their owner hath no property, *dominicum*, or demesne, in the *thing* itself, but hath only something derived out of it; resembling the *servitutes*, or services, of the civil law." 2 William Blackstone, *Commentaries on the Laws of England* 106 (1766).

demesne land. See LAND.

demesne land of the Crown. See *Crown land* under LAND.

demesnial (di-**may**-nee-əl *or* di-**meen**-ee-əl), *adj.* Of or relating to a demesne.

demi (**dem**-ee), *n.* [French] Half; the half. • The term is most often a combining form, as in *demi-sangue.*

demidietas (dem-ee-**dɪ**-ə-tas), *n.* [Law Latin] A half; a moiety.

demilitarization. *Int'l law.* The process by which a country obligates itself not to station military forces — or to maintain military installations — in specified areas or zones within its territory.

demilitarized zone. *Int'l law.* A territorial area in which a country is obligated not to station military forces or maintain military installations.

demimark. *Hist.* Half a mark; money equal to ten shillings and eight pence, required to be tendered in a writ of right to force the demandant to prove seisin.

de minimis (də **min**-ə-mis), *adj.* [Latin "of the least"] **1.** Trifling; minimal. **2.** (Of a fact or thing) so insignificant that a court may overlook it in deciding an issue or case. **3.** DE MINIMIS NON CURAT LEX.

de minimis non curat lex (də **min**-ə-mis non **kyoor**-at **leks**). [Latin] The law does not concern itself with trifles. — Often shortened to *de minimis.*

de minis (dee **min**-is), *n.* [Latin "of threats"] *Hist.* A writ ordering a person to keep the peace when the person has threatened another person with bodily harm or property destruction.

deminutio (dee-mi-**n[y]oo**-shee-oh), *n.* [fr. Latin *deminuere* "taking away"] *Roman law.* A deprivation or loss. • The term appeared, for example, in the phrase *capitis deminutio* "the loss of civil status." — Also spelled *diminutio.*

demi-sangue (**dem**-ee-sang). [Law French] Half-blood; blood on either the father's or the mother's side. — Also termed *demy-sangue.*

demise (di-**mɪz**), *n.* **1.** The conveyance of an estate by will or lease <the demise of the land for one year>. **2.** The instrument by which such a conveyance is accomplished <the demise set forth the terms of the transfer>. **3.** The passing of property by descent or bequest <a testator's demise of $100,000 to charity>. **4.** The death of a person or (figuratively) of a thing <the corporation's untimely demise>. — Abbr. dem. — **demise,** *vb.*

demise of the Crown. The immediate, automatic transfer of a kingdom to a successor upon a sovereign's death or long absence from the throne.

"The king never dies. Henry, Edward, or George may die; but the king survives them all. For immediately upon the decease of the reigning prince in his natural capacity, his kingship or imperial dignity, by act of law, without any ... interval, is vested at once in his heir; who is, *eo instanti*, king to all intents and purposes. And so tender is the law of supposing even a possibility of his death, that his natural dissolution is generally called his *demise* ... an expression which signifies merely a transfer of property; for ... when we say the demise of the crown, we mean only that, in consequence of the disunion of the king's body natural from his body politic, the kingdom is transferred or demised to his successor; and so the royal dignity remains perpetual." 1 William Blackstone, *Commentaries on the Laws of England* 242 (1765).

joint demise. In an ejectment action, a demise made by two or more persons in one declaration.

separate demise. In an ejectment action, a demise made solely by the lessor.

several demise. (*often pl.*) *Hist.* In an ejectment action, a list of demises by all people potentially owning the property at issue, used to ensure that the plaintiff had proved a lease from the person actually having title. See EJECTMENT.

single demise. In an ejectment action, a declaration containing one demise. See EJECTMENT.

demise charter. See CHARTER (4).

demise charterer. See *demise charter* under **charter.**

demised premises. Property that has been leased.

demisi (di-**mI**-zI). [fr. Latin *demittere*] I have demised. • This was the operative phrase in a lease.

demissio (di-**mish**-ee-oh), *n.* [fr. Latin *demittere* "to demise"] *Hist.* A lease or other transfer. • In an ejectment action, this term was used in the phrase *ex demissione* ("on the demise") to show that a nominal plaintiff (a fictitious person) held an estate on a demise from the real plaintiff.

de mittendo tenorem recordi (dee mi-**ten**-doh tə-**nor**-əm ri-**kor**-dI), *n.* [Law Latin "of sending the tenor of a record"] *Hist.* A writ to certify a record under seal.

demobilization. A dismissal of troops from active service.

democracy, *n.* Government by the people, either directly or through representatives. — **democratic,** *adj.* Cf. REPUBLIC.

de moderata misericordia capienda (dee mod-ə-**ray**-tə miz-ə-ri-**kor**-dee-ə kap-ee-**en**-də), *n.* [Law Latin "for taking a moderate amercement"] *Hist.* A writ ordering a bailiff to take a moderate penalty from a party who had been excessively penalized in a court not of record. • The writ was founded on Magna Carta.

de modo decimandi (dee **moh**-doh des-ə-**man**-dI), *n.* [Law Latin] *Eccles. law.* Of a mode of tithing. • This refers to any special kind of tithing by custom that is different from the general law that usu. required the tenth part of an annual increase. For example, it could mean a twelfth part of a quantity of hay rather than a tenth part or a couple of hens instead of a normal tithing of eggs. — Also termed *modus decimandi*; *modus.*

demonetization. A disuse of a metal in coinage; a withdrawal of the value of a metal as money <the demonetization of gold in the United States>.

demonstratio (dem-ən-**stray**-shee-oh). [fr. Latin *demonstrare* "to show"] *Roman law.* **1.** A description, as in *falsa demonstratio* (a false description of something or someone in a will). **2.** The statement of facts in a formula, forming the basis of a claim. See FORMULA (1).

demonstrative bequest. See BEQUEST.

demonstrative evidence. See EVIDENCE.

demonstrative legacy. See LEGACY.

demote, *vb.* To lower (a person) in rank, position, or pay. See DEGRADATION.

demur (di-**mər**), *vb.* To file a demurrer; to object to the legal sufficiency of a claim alleged in a pleading without admitting or denying the truth of the facts stated. See DEMURRER.

demurrable (di-**mər**-ə-bəl), *adj.* (Of a claim, pleading, etc.) subject to a demurrer <a demurrable pleading>. See DEMURRER.

demurrage (di-**mər**-ij). (*usu. pl.*) *Maritime law.* A liquidated penalty owed by a charterer to a shipowner for the charterer's failure to load or unload cargo by a certain time.

contract demurrage. A demurrage paid by a vessel's charterer if the time to unload the vessel at port takes longer than that agreed upon in the charterer's contract with the shipowner. Cf. DISPATCH MONEY.

> "The contract may also provide that if ... the loading time exceeds that fixed by the charter, the charterer will pay a liquidated compensation termed 'contract demurrage.'" Frank L. Maraist, *Admiralty in a Nutshell* 56 (2d ed. 1988).

noncontract demurrage. Demurrage not provided by contract, but ordered by a court. — Also termed *damages for detention.*

> "After the ... days on contract demurrage have expired, the charterer of course still remains liable for further delay, but the liability now is one for noncontract demurrage, which will be fixed by the court just as would any other unliquidated claim for damages. Non-contract demurrage may also be referred to as 'damages for detention.'" Grant Gilmore & Charles L. Black, Jr., *The Law of Admiralty* § 4–8, at 212 (2d ed. 1975).

demurrage lien. See LIEN.

demurrant (di-**mər**-ənt). A party who interposes a demurrer. See DEMURRER.

demurrer (di-**mər**-ər). [Law French *demorer* "to wait or stay"] A pleading stating that although the facts alleged in a complaint may be true, they are insufficient for the plaintiff to state a claim for relief and for the defendant to frame an answer. • In most jurisdictions, such a pleading is now termed a *motion to dismiss*, but the demurrer is still used in a few states, including California, Nebraska, and Pennsylvania. Cf. DENIAL (1).

> "The word 'demurrer,' derived from the Latin *demorari*, or the French *demorrer*, meaning to 'wait or stay,' imports that the party demurring waits or stays in his proceedings in the action until the judgment of the court is given whether he is bound to answer to so insufficient a pleading. Each party may demur to what he deems an insufficient pleading of the other. The demurrer was *general* when it was to matter of substance; it was *special* when it was made to matter of form, and must specifically point out the defect." Edwin E. Bryant, *The Law of Pleading Under the Codes of Civil Procedure* 15 (2d ed. 1899).

demurrer ore tenus. An oral demurrer. See ORE TENUS.

> "The codes either expressly or by implication require all pleadings to be in writing. To this proposition there is the apparent exception that objections to the jurisdiction of the court, or to the sufficiency of a pleading, that it does not state a cause of action or defence, may be raised on the trial by what is sometimes called a demurrer *ore tenus* (that is, orally, — by word of mouth)." Edwin E. Bryant, *The Law of Pleading Under the Codes of Civil Procedure* 179 (2d ed. 1899).

general demurrer. See *general exception* (1) under EXCEPTION (1).

parol demurrer. *Hist.* A suspension of proceedings during the minority of an infant.

speaking demurrer. A demurrer that cannot be sustained because it introduces new facts not contained in the original complaint.

special demurrer. An objection that questions the form of the pleading and states specifically the nature of the objection, such as that the pleading violates the rules of pleading or practice.

demurrer book. A record of the demurrer issue used by the court and counsel in argument.

demurrer to evidence. A party's objection or exception that the evidence is legally insufficient to make a case. • Its effect, upon joinder in the demurrer by the opposite party, is that the jury is discharged and the demurrer is entered on record and decided by the court. A demurrer to evidence admits the truth of all the evidence and the legal deductions from that evidence.

demurrer to interrogatories. The objection or reason given by a witness for failing to answer an interrogatory.

demutualization, *n.* The process of converting a mutual insurance company (which is owned by its policyholders) to a stock insurance company (which is owned by outside shareholders), usu. as a means of increasing the insurer's capital by allowing the insurer to issue shares. • About half the states have demutualization statutes authorizing such a conversion. — **demutualize,** *vb.*

demy-sangue. See DEMI-SANGUE.

den and strond (**den** an[d] **strond**). *Hist.* Permission for a ship to run aground or strand itself.

denarius (di-**nair**-ee-əs), *n.* [Law Latin "penny"] **1.** *Roman law.* The principal silver coin used by the Romans. **2.** *Hist.* An English penny; a pence. **3.** (*pl.*) *Slang.* Money in general. Pl. ***denarii.*** — Also termed *denier.*

denarius Dei (di-**nair**-ee-əs **dee**-I), *n.* [Law Latin "God's penny"] *Hist.* Earnest money exchanged by contracting parties, so called because the money was originally given either to the church or to the poor. • The *denarius Dei* was not part of the consideration. See ARRA.

denationalization. 1. *Int'l law.* The unilateral act of a country in depriving a person of nationality, whether by administrative decision or by operation of law. • Strictly, the term does not cover a person's renunciation of citizenship. **2.** The act of returning government ownership and control of an industry or function to private ownership and control. — **denationalize,** *vb.*

de nativo habendo (dee nə-**tI**-voh hə-**ben**-doh), *n.* [Law Latin "about a serf to be held"] *Hist.* A writ directing a sheriff to apprehend and return a runaway serf to the serf's lord. • A trial on the writ would determine the lord's ownership status.

de natura brevium (dee nə-**tyoor**-ə **bree**-vee-ə). [Latin] Concerning the nature of writs. • This was a common title of textbooks on English medieval law.

denial, *n.* **1.** A refusal or rejection; esp., a court's refusal to grant a request presented in a motion or petition <denial of the motion for summary judgment>. **2.** A defendant's response controverting the facts that a plaintiff has alleged in a complaint; a repudiation <the worker's denial that physical contact occurred>. Cf. DEMURRER.

conjunctive denial. A response that controverts all the material facts alleged in a complaint.

disjunctive denial. A response that controverts the truthfulness of two or more allegations of a complaint in the alternative.

general denial. A response that puts in issue all the material assertions of a complaint or petition. — Also termed *general plea*.

qualified general denial. A general denial of all the allegations except the allegations that the pleader expressly admits.

> "The qualified general denial most frequently is used when a limited number of allegations in the complaint are to be admitted. This form of denial also is employed when defendant cannot expressly deny an averment in his opponent's pleading and therefore cannot submit a general denial, although defendant wants to put plaintiff to his proof on that averment by interposing a denial of knowledge or information sufficient to form a belief or a denial on information and belief." 5 Charles Alan Wright & Arthur Miller, *Federal Practice and Procedure* § 1266, at 405 (1990).

specific denial. A separate response applicable to one or more particular allegations in a complaint.

3. A refusal or rejection <denial of an employment application>. **4.** A deprivation or withholding <denial of due process>. — **deny,** *vb.*

denial of justice. *Int'l law.* A defect in a country's organization of courts or administration of justice, resulting in the country's violating its international legal duties to protect aliens. • A denial of justice is a wrongful act under international law. — Also termed *justitia denegata*; *déni de justice*; *refus de justice*.

denier, *n.* **1.** (də-**nyay**) [French fr. Latin *denarius*] DENARIUS (1), (3). **2.** (di-**nI**-ər). [Law French] *Hist.* Denial; refusal, as in refusal to pay rent when demanded.

Denier à Dieu (də-**nyay** ah **dyuu** *or* **dyoo**). [French "God's money"] *French law.* Earnest money exchanged by contracting parties. See DENARIUS DEI.

denization (den-ə-**zay**-shən). The act of making a person a denizen. See DENIZEN.

denize (**den**-Iz *or* di-**nIz**), *vb.* To make (a person) a denizen. See DENIZEN.

denizen (**den**-ə-zən). **1.** A person given certain rights in a foreign nation or living habitually in a foreign nation. **2.** *English law.* A person who holds a position midway between being an alien and a natural-born or naturalized subject.

Denman's Act. *Hist.* **1.** The (English) Evidence Act of 1843, providing that no person offered as a witness can be excluded because of incapacity due to a past crime or an interest in the proceedings. — Also termed *Lord Denman's Act.* **2.** The (English) Criminal Procedure Act of 1865 that allowed defense counsel to sum up evidence as allowed in a civil trial, to prove contradictory statements of an adverse witness, to prove a previous criminal conviction of an adverse witness, and to compare disputed handwriting. — Also termed *Mr. Denman's Act.*

denomination. 1. An act of naming. **2.** A collective designation, esp. of a religious sect.

de non decimando (dee **non** des-ə-**man**-doh), *n.* [Law Latin "of not paying tithes"] *Eccles. law.* A claim for release from paying a tithe. — Also termed *modus de non decimando.*

> "A prescription *de non decimando* is a claim to be entirely discharged of tithes, and to pay no compensation in lieu of them. Thus the king by his prerogative is discharged from all tithes. So a vicar shall pay no tithes to the rector, nor the rector to the vicar .... But these privileges are personal to both the king and the clergy; for their tenant or lessee shall pay tithes .... And from this original have sprung all the lands, which, being in lay hands, do at present claim to be tithe-free: for, if a man can show his lands to have been such abbey lands, and also immemorially discharged of tithes ... this is now a good prescription, *de non decimando.* But he must show both these requisites for abbey lands, without a special ground of discharge, are not discharged of course; neither will any prescription *de non decimando* avail in total discharge of tithes, unless it relates to such abbey lands." 2 William Blackstone, *Commentaries on the Laws of England* 31–32 (1766).

de non procedendo ad assisam (dee **non** proh-sə-**den**-doh ad ə-**sI**-zəm), *n.* [Law Latin "of not proceeding to take an assize"] *Hist.* A writ ordering justices not to hold an assize in a particular case.

de non residentia clerici regis (dee **non** rez-ə-**den**-shee-ə **kler**-ə-sI **ree**-jis), *n.* [Law Latin "of the nonresidence of a parson employed in royal service"] *Hist.* A writ to excuse a parson from nonresidence because the parson is busy serving the Crown. See NONRESIDENCE (1).

de non sane memorie (dee **non** sayn **mem**-ə-ree). [Law French] Of unsound memory; of unsound mind. See MIND AND MEMORY; NON COMPOS MENTIS.

denotative fact. See FACT.

denounce, *vb.* **1.** To condemn openly, esp. publicly. **2.** To declare (an act or thing) to be a crime and prescribe a punishment for it. **3.** To accuse or inform against. **4.** To give formal notice to a foreign country of the termination of (a treaty).

denouncement. 1. An act of accusation or condemnation <denouncement of a thief>. **2.** A declaration of a threatened action <denouncement of war> <denouncement of a treaty>. **3.** In Mexican law, an application for a grant to work a mine that is either newly discovered or forfeited <the denouncement was granted>. **4.** *Archaic.* A formal announcement; a declaration <a denouncement of a doctrine>. — Also termed *denunciation.* — **denunciatory, denunciative,** *adj.*

de novi operis nuntiatione. See NOVI OPERIS NUNTIATIO.

de novo (di **noh**-voh or dee-), *adj.* Anew.

hearing de novo. See HEARING.

trial de novo. See TRIAL DE NOVO.

venire facias de novo (və-**nI**-ree **fay**-shee-əs dee **noh**-voh). See VENIRE FACIAS.

de novo review. See *appeal de novo* under APPEAL.

density zoning. See *cluster zoning* under ZONING.

denumeration. An act of making a present payment.

denunciation. See DENOUNCEMENT.

denuntiatio (di-nən-shee-**ay**-shee-oh), *n.* [Latin] **1.** *Roman & civil law.* A declaration intended to protect or set in motion the enforcement of the declarer's right; esp., a report of a crime. **2.** *Hist.* A summons; a public notice. **3.** *Scots law.* A report of someone to be a rebel.

deodand (**dee**-ə-dand). *Hist.* An old English practice of forfeiting to the Crown a thing (such as an animal) that has done wrong. • This practice was abolished in 1846.

> "[W]hen in 1716 the coroner's jury of Yarmouth declared a stack of timber which had fallen on a child to be forfeited as a deodand, it was ransomed for 30*s.*, which was paid over to the child's father." J.W. Cecil Turner, *Kenny's Outlines of Criminal Law* 7 (16th ed. 1952).

de odio et atia (dee **oh**-dee-oh et **ay**-shee-ə), *n.* [Law Latin "of hatred and malice"] *Hist.* A writ ordering a sheriff to summon a 12–member jury to inquire whether a prisoner jailed for murder was charged for a good reason or only because of ill-will and to determine whether bail should be set. • If the prisoner was accused out of spite or had committed the crime in self-defense, then another writ called *tradas in ballim* would have been issued ordering the sheriff to release the prisoner on bail if the sheriff could find 12 good citizens of the county to vouch for the prisoner. This writ, similar to *habeas corpus*, was first mentioned in Magna Carta. — Also termed *breve de bono et malo.*

de onerando pro rata portione (dee on-ə-**ran**-doh proh **ray**-tə por-shee-**oh**-nee), *n.* [Law Latin "of charging according to a ratable proportion"] *Hist.* A writ for a joint tenant or cotenant who is distrained for more rent than is proportionately required.

de pace et legalitate tenenda (dee **pay**-see et lə-gal-ə-**tay**-tee tə-**nen**-də). [Latin] *Hist.* A writ for keeping the peace and adherence to the laws (or good behavior). — Also termed *de pace et legalitate tuenda.*

de pace et plagis (dee **pay**-see et **play**-jis), *n.* [Law Latin "of breach of peace and wounds"] *Hist.* A type of criminal appeal used in cases of assault, wounding, and breach of the peace.

de pace et roberia (dee **pay**-see et roh-**beer**-ee-ə), *n.* [Law Latin "of breach of peace and robbery"] *Hist.* A type of criminal appeal used in cases of robbery and breach of the peace.

de parco fracto (dee **pahr**-koh **frak**-toh), *n.* [Law Latin "of pound breach"] *Hist.* A writ against someone, esp. an owner, who breaks into a pound to rescue animals that have been legally distrained and impounded.

> "And, being thus in the custody of the law, the taking them back by force is looked upon as an atrocious injury, and denominated a *rescous*, for which the distreinor has a remedy in damages, either by writ of *rescous,* in case they were going to the pound, or by writ *de parco fracto*, or *pound-breach*, in case they were actually impounded." 3 William Blackstone, *Commentaries on the Laws of England* 146 (1768).

de partitione facienda (dee pahr-tish-ee-**oh**-nee fay-shee-**en**-də), *n.* [Law Latin] *Hist.* A writ to partition lands or tenements.

department, *n.* **1.** A division of a greater whole; a subdivision <a legal department>. **2.** A country's division of territory, usu. for governmental and administrative purposes, as in the division of a state into counties <France has regional departments similar to states>. **3.** A principal branch or division of government <legislative department>; specif., a division of the executive branch of the U.S. government, headed by a secretary who is a member of the President's cabinet <Department of Labor>. — **departmental,** *adj.*

Department of Defense. See DEFENSE DEPARTMENT.

Department of Energy. A federal department that oversees a comprehensive national energy plan, including the research, development, and demonstration of energy technology; energy conservation; the nuclear-weapons program; and pricing and allocation. — Abbr. DOE.

Department of Justice. The federal executive division that is responsible for federal law enforcement and related programs and services. • The U.S. Attorney General heads this department, which has separate divisions for prosecuting cases under federal antitrust laws, tax laws, environmental laws, and criminal laws. The department also has a civil division that represents the U.S. government in cases involving tort claims and commercial litigation. — Abbr. DOJ.

Department of State. See STATE DEPARTMENT.

Department of the Interior. A federal department responsible for managing federally owned land and natural resources, and for overseeing American Indian reservations. • The Department administers a number of agencies, including the Bureau of Land Management, the Bureau of Indian Affairs, the U.S. Fish and Wildlife Service, and the U.S. Geological Survey. — Also termed *Interior Department.*

Department of Transportation. The federal executive division that is responsible for programs and policies concerning transportation. • Through a series of specialized agencies, this department oversees aviation, highways, railroads, mass transit, the U.S. merchant marine, and other programs. — Abbr. DOT.

departure, *n.* **1.** A deviation or divergence from a standard rule, regulation, measurement, or course of conduct <an impermissible departure from sentencing guidelines>.

downward departure. In the federal sentencing guidelines, a court's imposition of a sentence more lenient than the standard guidelines propose, as when the court concludes that a criminal's history is less serious than it appears.

lateral departure. In the federal sentencing guidelines, a sentence that allows a defendant to avoid incarceration through community or home confinement. — Also termed *lateral sentencing.*

upward departure. In the federal sentencing guidelines, a court's imposition of a sentence harsher than the standard guidelines propose, as when the court concludes that a criminal's history did not take into account additional offenses committed while the prisoner was out on bail.

2. A variance between a pleading and a later pleading or proof <the departure between the plaintiff's pleadings and the actual evidence was significant>. **3.** A party's desertion of the ground (either legal or factual) taken in the immediately preceding pleading and resort to another ground <the defendant's departure from the asserted alibi necessitated a guilty plea>. — **depart,** *vb.*

departure in despite of court. *Hist.* A failure of a tenant in a real action to appear on demand. • A tenant, having once appeared in a real action, was considered to be constructively present until again called. So if the tenant failed to appear when demanded, the tenant was said to have departed in despite (in contempt) of court.

dépeçage (dep-ə-**sahzh**). [French "dismemberment"] A court's application of different state laws to different issues in a legal dispute; choice of law on an issue-by-issue basis.

depeculation (dee-pek-yə-**lay**-shən). *Hist.* An embezzlement from the public treasure. Cf. PECULATION.

dependency. 1. A land or territory geographically distinct from the country governing it, but belonging to the country and governed by its laws. • The Philippines was formerly a dependency of the United States. Cf. COMMONWEALTH; TERRITORY. **2.** A relationship between two persons or things whereby one is sustained by the other or relies on the other for support or necessities.

dependency exemption. See EXEMPTION.

dependent, *n.* **1.** One who relies on another for support; one not able to exist or sustain oneself without the power or aid of someone else.

lawful dependent. **1.** One who receives an allowance or benefits from the public, such as social security. **2.** One who qualifies to receive a benefit from private funds as determined within the terms of the laws governing the distribution.

legal dependent. A person who is dependent according to the law; a person who derives principal support from another and usu. may invoke laws to enforce that support.

partial dependent. *Workers' compensation.* A person whose partial reliance on an employee covered under workers'-compensation law for support entitles him or her to receive death benefits if the employee is killed on the job.

2. *Tax.* A relative, such as a child or parent, for whom a taxpayer may claim a personal exemption if the taxpayer provides more than half the person's support during the taxable year. — Also termed *lawful dependent.* — **dependent,** *adj.*

dependent claim. See CLAIM (6).

dependent condition. See CONDITION (2).

dependent contract. See CONTRACT.

dependent covenant. See COVENANT (1).

dependent coverage. See COVERAGE.

dependent intervening cause. A cause of an accident or injury that occurs between the defendant's behavior and the injurious result, but that does not change the defendant's liability.

dependent promise. See PROMISE.

dependent relative revocation. The doctrine that regards as mutually dependent the acts of destroying a will and substituting a new one when both acts are the result of one plan, so that, if a testator fails to complete the substitution, it is presumed that the testator would have preferred the old will to take effect. • This doctrine is a specific application of the rule that the testator's intent governs.

dependent state. See *nonsovereign state* under STATE (1).

de perambulatione facienda (dee pə-ram-byə-lay-shee-**oh**-nee fay-shee-**en**-də), *n.* [Law Latin "for making perambulation"] *Hist.* A writ ordering the sheriff to go with 12 knights of the county to settle a boundary dispute by walking about to determine the proper boundary between adjacent towns or lordships.

de placito (dee **plas**-ə-toh), *n.* [Law Latin] Of a plea. • These words were used in a declaration describing the particular action being brought, as in *de placito debit* ("of a plea of debt").

de plagis et mahemio (dee **play**-jis et mə-**hee**-mee-oh), *n.* [Law Latin "of wounds and mayhem"] *Hist.* A type of criminal appeal used in cases of wounding and maiming.

de plano (dee **play**-noh). [Latin "from ground level"] **1.** *Roman law.* Informally; in a summary manner. • The praetor would administer justice *de plano* when he stood on the same level with the parties instead of sitting on an elevated bench. **2.** *Hist.* Clearly; manifestly, as in *de bigamis.* See DE BIGAMIS. **3.** *Hist.* By collusion. **4.** *Scots law.* Forthwith.

de plegiis acquietandis (dee **plee**-jee-is ə-kwI-ə-**tan**-dis), *n.* [Law Latin "for acquitting or releasing pledges"] *Hist.* A writ ordering repayment to a surety by a principal who had failed to make a required payment that the surety then had to cover.

depletable economic interest. A mineral-land interest subject to depletion by the removal (by drilling or mining) of the mineral that is the subject of the interest.

depletion, *n.* An emptying, exhausting, or wasting of an asset, esp. of a finite natural resource such as oil. — **deplete,** *vb.* — **depletive,** *adj.*

depletion allowance. See ALLOWANCE (3).

depletion reserve. *Accounting.* A charge to income reflecting the decrease in the value of a wasting asset, such as an oil reserve.

depone (di-**pohn**), *vb. Scots law.* To testify. See DEPOSE.

de ponendo sigillum ad exceptionem (dee pə-**nen**-doh si-**jil**-əm ad ek-sep-shee-**oh**-nəm), *n.* [Law Latin "for putting a seal to an exception"] *Hist.* A writ directing justices of assize to preserve exceptions taken by a party in a case.

deponent (di-**poh**-nənt), *n.* **1.** One who testifies by deposition. **2.** A witness who gives written testimony for later use in court; AFFIANT. — **depone,** *vb.*

depopulatio agrorum (dee-pop-yoo-**lay**-shee-oh ə-**gror**-əm), *n.* [Law Latin "depopulating the county"] *Hist.* The crime of destroying or ravaging a country. • A person could not claim the benefit of clergy for this crime.

depopulation. 1. A reduction in population. **2.** *Hist.* A species of waste by which the kingdom's population was diminished. See DEPOPULATIO AGRORUM.

deportatio (dee-por-**tay**-shee-oh), *n.* [fr. Latin *deportare* "to carry away"] *Roman law.* Permanent exile of a condemned criminal. • The person's legal rights were virtually eliminated, all property was forfeited, and the person was "taken out of the number of Roman citizens" (*ex numero civium Romanorum tollitur*). Cf. RELEGATIO.

> "Deportatio. Perpetual banishment of a person condemned for a crime. It was the severest form of banishment since it included additional penalties, such as seizure of the whole property, loss of Roman citizenship, confinement to a definite place. Under the Principate it replaced the former *interdictio aqua et igni*. The emperor could grant the deportee full amnesty, which restored him to his former rights (*postliminium*). Places of *deportatio* were islands (*in insulam*) near the Italian shore or an oasis in the Libyan desert." Adolf Berger, *Encyclopedic Dictionary of Roman Law* 432 (1953).

deportation (dee-por-**tay**-shən), *n.* The act or an instance of removing a person to another country; esp., the expulsion or transfer of an alien from a country. — **deport,** *vb.*

depose (di-**pohz**), *vb.* **1.** To examine (a witness) in a deposition <the defendant's attorney will depose the plaintiff on Tuesday>. **2.** To testify; to bear witness <the affiant deposes and states that he is at least 18 years old>. **3.** To remove from office or from a position of power; dethrone <the rebels sought to depose the dictator>.

deposit, *n.* **1.** The act of giving money or other property to another who promises to preserve it or to use it and return it in kind; esp., the act of placing money in a bank for safety and convenience. **2.** The money or property so given.

demand deposit. A bank deposit that the depositor may withdraw at any time without prior notice to the bank.

direct deposit. The payment of wages by transferring the payment directly into the employee's bank account, usu. by electronic transfer.

frozen deposit. A bank deposit that cannot be withdrawn, as when the financial institution is insolvent.

general deposit. **1.** A bank deposit of money that is commingled with other depositors' money. **2.** A bank deposit that is to the depositor's credit, thus giving the depositor a right to the money and creating a debtor-creditor relationship between the bank and the depositor. • A bank is not required to return the actual money deposited as a general deposit, as it must with a special deposit; the bank need return only an equivalent sum.

special deposit. A bank deposit that is made for a specific purpose, that is kept separately, and that is to be returned to the depositor. • The bank serves as a bailee or trustee for a special deposit. — Also termed *specific deposit.*

time deposit. A bank deposit that is to remain for a specified period or on which notice must be given to the bank before withdrawal.

3. Money placed with a person as earnest money or security for the performance of a contract. • The money will be forfeited if the depositor fails to perform. — Also termed *security deposit.* **4.** *Copyright.* The placing of two copies of a published work with the Library of Congress within three months of publication. • This requirement is independent of copyright registration. **5.** *Civil law.* A bailment of goods to be kept by the bailee without payment; a gratuitous caretaking of an object. — Also termed *depositum*; *naked deposit*; *gratuitous deposit.* See *gratuitous bailment* under BAILMENT.

involuntary deposit. A deposit made by accidentally leaving or placing personal property in another's possession. See *involuntary bailment* under BAILMENT.

necessary deposit. A bailment, usu. made by reason of emergency or other necessity, that prevents the depositor from freely choosing the depositary. • A necessary deposit occurs, for example, when a person entrusts goods to a stranger during a fire.

quasi-deposit. An involuntary deposit made when one party lawfully possesses property merely by finding it.

voluntary deposit. A deposit made by the mutual consent of the bailor and bailee.

deposit account. See ACCOUNT.

depositary. **1.** A person or institution that one leaves money or valuables with for safekeeping <a title-insurance officer is the depositary of the funds>. • When a depositary is a company, it is often termed a *safe-deposit company*. Cf. DEPOSITORY. **2.** A gratuitous bailee. See DEPOSIT (6).

depositary bank. See BANK.

deposit box. See SAFE-DEPOSIT BOX.

deposit company. See COMPANY.

deposit contract. See CONTRACT.

deposit in court. The placing of money or other property that represents a person's potential liability in the court's temporary custody, pending the outcome of a lawsuit. — Also termed *deposit into the registry of the court*.

deposit insurance. See INSURANCE.

deposit into the registry of the court. See DEPOSIT IN COURT.

deposition (dep-ə-**zish**-ən). **1.** A witness's out-of-court testimony that is reduced to writing (usu. by a court reporter) for later use in court or for discovery purposes. **2.** The session at which such testimony is recorded.

apex deposition. The deposition of a person whose position is at the highest level of a company's hierarchy. • Courts often preclude an apex deposition unless (1) the person to be deposed has particular knowledge regarding the claim, and (2) the requesting party cannot obtain the requested — and discoverable — information through less intrusive means.

deposition de bene esse (dee **bee**-nee **es**-ee *also* day **ben**-ay **es**-ay). A deposition taken from a witness who will likely be unable to attend a scheduled trial or hearing. • If the witness is not available to attend trial, the testimony is read at trial as if the witness were present in court. See *testimony de bene esse* under TESTIMONY.

deposition on written questions. A deposition given in response to a prepared set of written questions, as opposed to a typical oral deposition. — Formerly also termed *deposition on written interrogatories*.

"The advantage of a deposition on written questions is that counsel for the parties need not go to some distant place to be present at the taking of the deposition. Instead they serve on each other questions and cross questions — and even redirect and recross questions — that they wish to have put to the deponent. These are then sent to the officer who is to take the deposition. The officer puts the questions to the witness, records the answers, and transcribes and files the deposition as with an oral deposition. The officer is merely to record what the witness says in response to the various questions propounded to him or her." Charles Alan Wright, *The Law of Federal Courts* § 85, at 618–19 (5th ed. 1994).

oral deposition. A deposition given in response to oral questioning by a lawyer.

30(b)(6) deposition. Under the Federal Rules of Civil Procedure, the deposition of an organization, through the organization's designated representative. • Under Rule 30(b)(6), a party may take the deposition of an organization, such as a corporation. The notice of deposition (or subpoena) may name the organization and may specify the matters to be covered in the deposition. The organization must then designate a person to testify about those matters on its behalf. Fed. R. Civ. P. 30(b)(6). Most states authorize a similar procedure under state-court procedural rules.

deposit of title deeds. A pledge of real property as security for a loan, by placing with the lender, as pledgee, the title-deed to the land.

depositor, *n.* One who makes a deposit. See DEPOSIT.

depository (di-**poz**-ə-tor-ee), *n.* A place where one leaves money or valuables for safekeeping <the grade school's depository for used books>. Cf. DEPOSITARY.

depository bond. See BOND (2).

depository institution. **1.** An organization formed under state or federal law, authorized by law to receive deposits, and supervised and examined by a government agency for the protection of depositors. **2.** A trust company or other institution authorized by law to exercise fiduciary powers similar to those of a national bank. • The term does not include an insurance company, a Morris Plan bank, an industrial loan company, or a similar bank unless its deposits are insured by a federal agency.

depository-transfer check. See CHECK.

Depository Trust Corporation. The principal central clearing agency for securities transactions on the public markets. — Abbr. DTC.

deposit premium. The initial premium paid by an insured pending the final premium adjustment.

deposit ratio. The ratio of total deposits to total capital.

deposit slip. A bank's acknowledgment of an amount received on a certain date by a depositor.

depositum (di-**poz**-i-təm). See *gratuitous bailment* under BAILMENT; DEPOSIT (5).

deposit warrant. See WARRANT (2).

de post disseisina (dee **pohst** dis-**see**-zin-ə), *n.* [Law Latin "of past disseisin"] *Hist.* A writ for recovery of land by a person who had previously recovered the land from a disseisor by a *praecipe quod reddat* or on a default or reddition, but who was again disseised by the same disseisor.

de praerogativa regis (dee pri-rog-ə-**tɪ**-və **ree**-jis). See PRAEROGATIVA REGIS.

de praesenti (dee pri-**zen**-tɪ). [Law Latin] In the present tense; of the present.

depraved, *adj.* (Of a person or crime) corrupt; perverted; heinous.

depraved-heart murder. See MURDER.

depreciable life. See USEFUL LIFE.

depreciation (di-pree-shee-**ay**-shən), *n.* A decline in an asset's value because of use, wear, or obsolescence. — **depreciate,** *vb.* — **depreciable,** *adj.* Cf. APPRECIATION; AMORTIZATION (2).

accumulated depreciation. The total depreciation currently recorded on an asset. • On the balance sheet, an asset's total cost less accumulated depreciation reflects the asset's book value. — Also termed *accrued depreciation.*

annual depreciation. The annual loss to property due to regular wear and tear.

functional depreciation. Depreciation that results from the replacement of equipment that is not yet worn out, but that is obsolete in light of a new invention or improved machinery allowing more efficient and satisfactory production.

depreciation method. A set formula used in estimating an asset's use, wear, or obsolescence over the asset's useful life. • This method is useful in calculating the allowable annual tax deduction for depreciation. See USEFUL LIFE.

accelerated depreciation method. A depreciation method that yields larger deductions in the earlier years of an asset's life and smaller deductions in the later years.

annuity depreciation method. A depreciation method that allows for a return of imputed interest on the undepreciated balance of an asset's value. • The imputed interest is subtracted from the current depreciation amount before it is credited to the accumulated depreciation accounts.

declining-balance depreciation method. A method of computing the annual depreciation allowance by multiplying the asset's undepreciated cost each year by a uniform rate that may not exceed double the straight-line rate or 150 percent.

double-declining depreciation method. A depreciation method that spreads over time the initial cost of a capital asset by deducting in each period twice the percentage recognized by the straight-line method and applying that double percentage to the undepreciated balance existing at the start of each period.

replacement-cost depreciation method. A depreciation method that fixes an asset's value by the price of its substitute.

sinking-fund depreciation method. A depreciation method that accounts for the time value of money by setting up a depreciation-reserve account that earns interest, resulting in a gradual yearly increase in the depreciation deduction.

straight-line depreciation method. A depreciation method that writes off the cost or other basis of the asset by deducting the expected salvage value from the initial cost of the capital asset, and dividing the difference by the asset's estimated useful life.

sum-of-the-years'-digits depreciation method. A method of calculating the annual depreciation allowance by multiplying the depreciable cost basis (cost minus salvage value) by a constantly decreasing fraction, which is represented by the remaining years of useful life at the beginning of each year divided by the total number of years of useful life at the time of acquisition. — Sometimes shortened to *SYD method.*

unit depreciation method. A depreciation method — directly related to the productivity of the asset — that divides the asset's value by the estimated total number of units to be produced, and then multiplies the unit cost by the number of units sold during the year, representing the depreciation expense for the year.

units-of-output depreciation method. A method by which the cost of a depreciable asset, minus salvage value, is allocated to the accounting periods benefited based on output (as miles, hours, number of times used, and the like).

depreciation reserve. An account, esp. of a public utility, built up to offset the depreciation of property because of time and use, so that at the end of the property's service, there is enough money to replace the property.

depredation. The act of plundering; pillaging.

depression. A period of economic stress that persists over an extended period, accompanied by poor business conditions and high unemployment. Cf. RECESSION.

deprivation. 1. An act of taking away <deprivation of property>. **2.** A withholding of something <deprivation of food>. **3.** The state of being without something; wanting <deprivation from lack of food>. **4.** A removal or degradation from office <deprivation of the bishop>.

***Deprizio* doctrine.** *Bankruptcy.* The rule that a debtor's payment to an outside creditor more than 90 days before a bankruptcy filing is voidable as a preferential transfer if it benefits an inside creditor. *Levit v. Ingersoll Rand Fin. Corp. (In re V.N. Deprizio Constr. Co.)*, 874 F.2d 1186 (7th Cir. 1989).

de procedendo ad judicium (dee proh-sə-**den**-doh ad joo-**dish**-ee-əm), *n.* [Law Latin "for proceeding in an assise"] *Hist.* A chancery writ ordering a lower court to proceed to judgment in a case that had been wrongfully stayed. • If the lower-court justices refused, they could be punished for contempt.

de proprietate probanda (dee prə-prɪ-ə-**tay**-tee prə-**ban**-də), *n.* [Law Latin "for proving property"] *Hist.* A writ ordering a sheriff to investigate the ownership of distrained goods claimed by a defendant in a replevin action.

> "If therefore the distreinor claims any such property, the party replevying must sue out a writ *de proprietate probanda*, in which the sheriff is to try, by an inquest, in whom the property previous to the distress subsisted. And if it be found to be in the distreinor, the sheriff can proceed no farther; but must return the claim of property to the court of king's bench or common pleas, to be there farther prosecuted, if thought advisable, and there finally determined." 3 William Blackstone, *Commentaries on the Laws of England* 148 (1768).

deputy, *n.* A person appointed or delegated to act as a substitute for another, esp. for an official. — **deputize, depute,** *vb.*

***general deputy.* 1.** A deputy appointed to act in another officer's place and execute all ordinary functions of the office. **2.** See *deputy sheriff* under SHERIFF.

special deputy. A deputy specially appointed to serve a particular purpose, such as keeping the peace during a riot.

deputy sheriff. See SHERIFF.

de quarantina habenda (dee kwahr-ən-**tɪ**-nə hə-**ben**-də), *n.* [Law Latin "of return of quarantine"] *Hist.* A writ ordering a sheriff to give a widow possession of part of her husband's estate, after she had been wrongfully ejected but before dower is assigned. See QUARANTINE.

de quo (dee **kwoh**). [Latin] Of which. • These were formal words used in a writ of entry, as in a writ of entry "in the quo" or "in the *quibus*." — Also termed *de quibus*.

de raptu virginum (dee **rap**-t[y]oo **vər**-jə-nəm), *n.* [Latin "of the ravishment of virgins"] *Hist.* A writ for taking an appeal in a rape case.

de rationabilibus divisis (dee rash-ən-ə-**bil**-i-bəs di-**vɪ**-sis), *n.* [Law Latin "of the fixing of reasonable boundaries"] *Hist.* A writ to settle the boundaries between property owners of different towns when one owner claimed a trespass by the other.

de rationabili parte bonorum (dee rash-[ee]-ə-**nay**-bə-lɪ **pahr**-tee bə-**nor**-əm), *n.* [Law Latin "of reasonable share of goods"] *Hist.* A writ allowing the wife and children of a dead man to recover a reasonable share of his goods from his executors after his debts were paid. • This writ was usu. founded on custom rather than the general law.

de recordo et processu mittendis (dee ri-**kor**-doh et proh-**ses**-[y]oo mi-**ten**-dis), *n.* [Law Latin "of the sending of the record and process of a cause to a superior court"] A type of writ of error.

de recto (dee **rek**-toh), *n.* [Law Latin] A writ of right to recover both the seisin and the property. — Also termed *breve de recto.* See WRIT OF RIGHT.

de recto de advocatione (dee **rek**-toh dee ad-və-kay-shee-**oh**-nee), *n.* [Law Latin "of the right of advowson"] *Hist.* A writ restoring a person's right to present a clerk to a benefice when that right had been interfered with. • It was abolished by St. 3 & 4 Will. 4, ch. 27.

de recto de rationabili parte (dee **rek**-toh dee rash-[ee]-ə-**nay**-bə-lɪ **pahr**-tee), *n.* [Law Latin "of right of reasonable part"] *Hist.* A writ allowing one coparcener or blood relative owning land in fee simple to obtain a rightful share from the other. • It was abolished by St. 3 & 4 Will. 4, ch. 27.

de recto patens (dee **rek**-toh **pay**-tenz), *n.* [Law Latin "of right patent"] *Hist.* The highest writ of right under the law given to an owner in fee simple to recover the possession and use of land from the freehold tenant. — Also termed *breve magnum de recto.*

de redisseisina (dee ree-dis-**see**-zin-ə), *n.* [Law Latin "of redisseisin"] *Hist.* A writ for recovery of land or rent by a person who had previously recovered the land or rent by an assize of novel disseisin, but who was again disseised by the same disseisor. • This writ is similar to *de post disseisina.* See *DE POST DISSEISINA*; DISSEISIN.

deregistration, *n.* The point at which an issuer's registration under section 12 of the Securities Exchange Act of 1934 is no longer required because of a decline in the number of holders of the issuer's securities. 15 USCA § 78*l*. — **deregister,** *vb.* Cf. DELISTING.

deregulation, *n.* The reduction or elimination of governmental control of business, esp. to permit free markets and competition. — **deregulate,** *vb.*

derelict (**der**-ə-likt), *adj.* **1.** Forsaken; abandoned; cast away <derelict property>.

quasi-derelict. (Of a ship or similar vessel) temporarily or involuntarily deserted or abandoned, as when the crew is dead or otherwise incapable of navigating the ship.

2. Lacking a sense of duty; in breach of a legal or moral obligation <the managers were unquestionably derelict in their duties>.

derelict, *n.* **1.** Personal property abandoned or thrown away by the owner with an intent to no longer claim it, such as a boat deserted or abandoned at sea by a master or crew.

quasi-derelict. A ship that has been abandoned temporarily or involuntarily.

2. Land uncovered by receding water from its former bed. **3.** A street person or vagrant; a hobo.

dereliction (der-ə-**lik**-shən), *n.* **1.** Abandonment, esp. through neglect or moral wrong.

dereliction in the performance of duties. *Military law.* Willful or negligent failure to perform assigned duties; culpable inefficiency in performing assigned duties.

2. An increase of land caused by the receding of a sea, river, or stream from its usual watermark. See RELICTION.

de replegiore de averiis. See DE AVERIIS REPLEGIANDIS.

de rescussu (dee ri-**skəs**-[y]oo), *n.* [Law Latin "of rescue"] *Hist.* A writ available when cattle were distrained or persons were arrested, and then rescued.

de retorno habendo (dee ri-**tor**-noh hə-**ben**-doh). [Law Latin] For having a return. • This term applied to (1) a judgment for a defendant in a replevin action, (2) a writ of execution for a defendant awarded judgment in a replevin action, and (3) a surety provided by a plaintiff at the beginning of a replevin action.

d.e.r.i.c. *abbr.* DE EA RE ITA CENSUERE.

de rien culpable (də **reen kəl**-pə-bəl). [Law French] Guilty of nothing; not guilty.

derivative, *n.* A volatile financial instrument whose value depends on or is derived from the performance of a secondary source such as an underlying bond, currency, or commodity. — Also termed *derivative instrument.*

> "Derivatives transactions may be based on the value of foreign currency, U.S. Treasury bonds, stock indexes, or interest rates. The values of these underlying financial instruments are determined by market forces, such as movements in interest rates. Within the broad panoply of derivatives transactions are numerous innovative financial instruments whose objectives may include a hedge against market risks, management of assets and liabilities, or lowering of funding costs; derivatives may also be used as speculation for profit." *Procter & Gamble Co. v. Bankers Trust Co.*, [1996–1997 Transfer Binder]

Fed. Sec. L. Rep. (CCH) ¶ 99,229, at 95,238 (S.D. Ohio 1996).

derivative acquisition. See ACQUISITION.

derivative action. 1. A suit by a beneficiary of a fiduciary to enforce a right belonging to the fiduciary; esp., a suit asserted by a shareholder on the corporation's behalf against a third party (usu. a corporate officer) because of the corporation's failure to take some action against the third party. — Also termed *derivative suit*; *shareholder derivative suit*; *stockholder derivative suit*; *representative action*. Cf. DIRECT ACTION (3). **2.** A lawsuit arising from an injury to another person, such as a husband's action for loss of consortium arising from an injury to his wife caused by a third person.

derivative contraband. See CONTRABAND.

derivative conveyance. See *secondary conveyance* under CONVEYANCE.

derivative defense. See DEFENSE (1).

derivative estate. See ESTATE.

derivative evidence. See EVIDENCE.

derivative instrument. See DERIVATIVE.

derivative-jurisdiction doctrine. The principle that a case is not properly removable unless it is within the subject-matter jurisdiction of the state court from which it is removed.

derivative liability. See LIABILITY.

derivative possession. See POSSESSION.

derivative suit. See DERIVATIVE ACTION (1).

derivative title. See TITLE (2).

derivative-use immunity. See *use immunity* under IMMUNITY (3).

derivative work. *Copyright.* A copyrightable creation that is based on a preexisting product, such as a translation, musical arrangement, fictionalization, motion-picture version, abridgment, or any other recast or adapted form, and that only the holder of the copyright on the original form can produce or give permission to another to produce. Cf. COMPILATION (1).

"[W]hile a compilation consists merely of the selection and arrangement of pre-existing material without any internal changes in such material, a derivative work involves recasting or transformation, i.e., changes in the pre-existing material, whether or not it is juxtaposed in an arrangement with other pre-existing materials. A catalog constitutes a compilation, and a translation of a pre-existing work constitutes a derivative work." 1 Melville B. Nimmer & David Nimmer, *Nimmer on Copyright* § 3.02, at 3–5 (Supp. 1997).

derived demand. See DEMAND (3).

derogation (der-ə-**gay**-shən), *n.* **1.** The partial repeal or abrogation of a law by a later act that limits its scope or impairs its utility and force <statutes in derogation of the common law>. **2.** Disparagement; depreciation in value or estimation <some argue that the derogation of family values has caused an increase in crime>. **3.** Detraction, prejudice, or destruction (of a grant or right) <an attorney may be punished for derogation from professional integrity>. — **derogate** (**der**-ə-gayt), *vb.*

derogation from grant. A provision in an instrument of transfer (such as a deed) that diminishes, avoids, or otherwise operates against the grant itself.

derogatory clause. *Wills & estates.* A clause that a testator inserts secretly in a will, containing a provision that any later will not having that precise clause is invalid. • A derogatory clause seeks to protect against a later will extorted by undue influence, duress, or violence.

de salva gardia (dee **sal**-və **gahr**-dee-ə), *n.* [Law Latin "of safeguard"] A writ issued to protect strangers from harm while pursuing their legal rights in England.

de salvo conductu (dee **sal**-voh kən-**dək**-t[y]oo). [Law Latin "of safe conduct"] A writ of safe conduct.

de sa vie (də sa **vee**). [Law French] Of one's own life, as distinguished from *pur autre vie* ("for another's life").

descendant (di-**sen**-dənt), *n.* One who follows in lineage, such as a child or grandchild — but not a collateral relative. Cf. ASCENDANT.

descendibility of future interests. The legal possibility that a future interest (such as a remainder or an executory interest) can legally pass by inheritance.

descendible, *adj.* (Of property) capable of passing by descent or being inherited.

descent, *n.* **1.** The acquisition of real property by law, as by inheritance; the passing of intestate real property to heirs. See SUCCESSION (2). Cf. DISTRIBUTION (1); PURCHASE (2). **2.** The fact or process of originating from a common ancestor. — **descend,** *vb.*

collateral descent. Descent in a collateral or oblique line, from brother to brother or cousin to cousin. • With collateral descent, the donor and donee are related through a common ancestor.

direct-line descent. See *lineal descent.*

immediate descent. **1.** A descent directly to an heir, as from a grandmother to granddaughter, brought about by the earlier death of the mother. **2.** A direct descent without an intervening link in consanguinity, as from mother to daughter.

lineal descent. Descent in a direct or straight line, as from father or grandfather to son or grandson. — Also termed *direct-line descent.*

maternal-line descent. Descent between two persons, traced through the mother of the younger.

mediate descent. **1.** A descent not occurring immediately, as when a granddaughter receives land from her grandmother, which first passed to the mother. **2.** A direct descent occurring through a link in consanguinity, as when a granddaughter receives land from her grandfather directly.

> "The law categorizes descents as either lineal or collateral, and as mediate or immediate. The term mediate or immediate descent may denote either the passing of the estate, or the relationship between the intestate and the heir. The classification of descents as mediate or immediate describes the proximity of the descent, while the characterization as lineal or collateral refers to the direction of the descent." 23 Am. Jur. 2d, *Descent and Distribution* § 49, at 787–88 (1983).

paternal-line descent. Descent between two persons, traced through the father of the younger.

descent cast. *Hist.* The devolution of realty that has been acquired by disseisin, abatement, or intrusion, upon an heir whose ancestor died intestate. • This tolled the real owner's right of entry until the owner brought a legal action. — Also termed *descent which tolls entry.*

descriptio personae (di-**skrip**-shee-oh pər-**soh**-nee). [Law Latin] Description of the person. • This phrase, typically used to identify or describe a person in a contract or deed, is not essential to a document's validity. Cf. *designatio personae.*

description. **1.** A delineation or explanation of something by an account setting forth the subject's characteristics or qualities <description of a patentable process>. **2.** A representation by words or drawing of something seen or heard or otherwise experienced <description of the criminal> <description of the accident>. **3.** An enumeration or specific identification of something <description of items in the estate>. **4.** LEGAL DESCRIPTION.

descriptive mark. A trademark merely describing the goods to which it is affixed. • The trademark will be protected only if the user can demonstrate secondary meaning. — Also termed *descriptive trademark.* See SECONDARY MEANING.

> "The bar against descriptive marks simply reflects the requirement of distinctiveness. 15 U.S.C.A. § 1052(e)(1). It often is said that a mark should not be analyzed in a piecemeal fashion. Instead, the mark as a whole must be tested for descriptiveness or secondary meaning. A mark that merely describes a product cannot possibly distinguish one producer from another. As an obvious example, 'apple' would be a descriptive name for that fruit, and, as a mark, would serve only to confuse the consumer, for it would tell nothing about the different origins of a selection of apples produced by different producers. Moreover, to allow an owner to pre-empt the term 'apple' would afford the owner a monopoly of something that is necessary to describe the goods for sale." Arthur Miller & Michael Davis, *Intellectual Property: Patents, Trademarks, and Copyright in a Nutshell* 163 (2d ed. 1990).

de scutagio habendo (dee skyoo-**tay**-jee-oh hə-**ben**-doh), *n.* [Law Latin "for having scutage"] *Hist.* **1.** A writ ordering a tenant-in-chief by knight's service to serve in a war, send a substitute, or pay a sum of money. **2.** A writ authorizing a lord who had served in the war or paid the required fine, to recover the scutage from his knights' fees. See SCUTAGE.

> "Such a baron, having proved that he fulfilled his contract or paid his fine, will have a royal writ *de scutagio habendo*, whereby the sheriff will be ordered to cause him to have the scutage due from his tenants. Still, before he can get his scutage, he has to obtain something that the king is apt to treat as a favour." 1 Frederick Pollock & Frederic W. Maitland, *The History of English Law Before the Time of Edward I* 270 (2d ed. 1898).

desecrate, *vb.* To divest (a thing) of its sacred character; to defile or profane (a sacred thing).

de secta ad molendinum (dee **sek**-tə ad mə-**len**-di-nəm), *n.* [Law Latin "of suit at mill"]

Hist. A writ forcing a person to continue grinding corn at a particular mill, as was customary, or to give a good reason why the custom should not be continued.

> "There are also other services, due by ancient *custom* and *prescription* only. Such is that of doing suit to another's mill: where the persons, resident in a particular place, by usage time out of mind have been accustomed to grind their corn at a certain mill; and afterwards any of them go to another mill, and withdraw their suit ... from the ancient mill. This is not only a damage, but an injury, to the owner .... And for this injury the owner shall have a writ *de secta ad molendinum* commanding the defendant to do his suit at that mill ... or show good cause to the contrary: in which action the validity of the prescription may be tried, and if it be found for the owner, he shall recover damages against the defendant." 3 William Blackstone, *Commentaries on the Laws of England* 234–35 (1768).

de sectis non faciendis (dee **sek**-tis non fay-shee-**en**-dis), *n.* [Law Latin "of not doing services"] *Hist.* A writ exempting a ward or dowress from performing certain services.

desegregation, *n.* **1.** The abrogation of policies that separate people of different races into different institutions and facilities (such as public schools). **2.** The state of having had such policies abrogated. — **desegregate,** *vb.* Cf. INTEGRATION (3).

de seisina habenda (dee **see**-zin-ə hə-**ben**-də), *n.* [Law Latin "of holding seisin"] *Hist.* A writ ordering the sovereign to deliver seisin of lands and tenements to a lord, after holding them for the allowed year and a day because the lord's tenant committed a felony.

deserter. *Int'l law.* A soldier who unilaterally leaves national military service with the intention of reneging on military obligations either permanently or for the duration of a military operation; a person who illegally abandons a military force, often by seeking refuge in a foreign territory or by joining enemy forces.

desertion, *n.* The willful and unjustified abandonment of a person's duties or obligations, esp. to military service or to a spouse or family. • In family law, the five elements of spousal desertion are (1) a cessation of cohabitation, (2) the lapse of a statutory period, (3) an intention to abandon, (4) a lack of consent from the abandoned spouse, and (5) a lack of spousal misconduct that might justify the abandonment. — Also termed *gross neglect of duty.* — **desert,** *vb.*

constructive desertion. One spouse's misconduct that forces the other spouse to leave the marital abode.

criminal desertion. One spouse's willful failure without just cause to provide for the care, protection, or support of the other spouse who is in ill health or needy circumstances.

obstinate desertion. Desertion by a spouse who persistently refuses to return to the marital home, so that the other spouse has grounds for divorce. • Before the advent of no-fault divorce, this term was commonly used in divorce statutes. The term was often part of the longer phrase *willful, continued, and obstinate desertion.*

deserts. See JUST DESERTS.

design, *n.* **1.** A plan or scheme. **2.** Purpose or intention combined with a plan.

formed design. *Criminal law.* The deliberate and fixed intention to kill, though not necessarily a particular person. See PREMEDITATION.

3. The pattern or configuration of elements in something, such as a work of art. **4.** *Patents.* The drawing or the depiction of an original plan for a novel pattern, model, shape, or configuration that is chiefly decorative or ornamental. — **design,** *vb.*

designate, *n.* See DESIGNEE.

designated public forum. See PUBLIC FORUM.

designating petition. A document used to designate a candidate for a party nomination at a primary election or for election to a party position.

designatio personae (dez-əg-**nay**-shee-oh pər-**soh**-nee). [Law Latin] Designation of the person. • This phrase was used to specifically identify a person in a contract or deed, often as a word of limitation (e.g., "to my eldest son"). Cf. DESCRIPTIO PERSONAE.

design defect. See DEFECT.

design-defect exclusion. See EXCLUSION (3).

designedly, *adv.* Willfully; intentionally.

designee. A person who has been designated to perform some duty or carry out some specific role. — Also termed *designate* (**dez**-ig-nət), *n.*

designer drug. See DRUG.

design patent. See PATENT (3).

design review. A process by which a building permit is not issued until the proposed building meets the architectural standards established by land-use regulations. — Also termed *architectural review*.

desist. To stop or leave off. See CEASE-AND-DESIST ORDER.

desk audit. See AUDIT.

de son tort (də sawn [*or* son] **tor**[**t**]). [Law French "by his own wrongdoing"] Wrongful.

executor de son tort. See EXECUTOR.

trustee de son tort. See TRUSTEE.

de son tort demesne (də sawn **tor**[**t**] di-**mayn**). [Law French] Of a person's own wrong. • This is the law French equivalent of the Latin phrase *de injuria*. See DE INJURIA.

despitus (di-**spɪ**-təs *or* **des**-pi-təs). [Law Latin] **1.** Contempt. **2.** A contemptible person.

despoil (di-**spoil**), *vb.* To deprive (a person) of possessions illegally by violence or by clandestine means; to rob. — **despoliation** (di-spoh-lee-**ay**-shən), *n.* — **despoilment,** *n.*

desponsation (dee-spon-**say**-shən). *Archaic.* The act of betrothal; the act of contracting for marriage.

despot (**des**-pət), *n.* **1.** A ruler with absolute power and authority. **2.** A tyrant. — **despotic** (di-**spot**-ik), *adj.*

despotism (**des**-pə-tiz-əm). **1.** A government by a ruler with absolute, unchecked power. **2.** Total power or controlling influence.

de statuto mercatorio (dee stə-**tyoo**-toh mər-kə-**tor**-ee-oh), *n.* [Law Latin "of statute merchant"] *Hist.* A writ ordering the imprisonment of someone who forfeits a statute-merchant bond until the debt has been paid. See STATUTE MERCHANT.

de statuto stapulae (dee stə-**tyoo**-toh **stay**-pyə-lee), *n.* [Law Latin "of statute staple"] *Hist.* A writ to seize the property of and imprison a person who forfeits a staple-statute bond. See STATUTE STAPLE.

destination bill of lading. See BILL OF LADING.

destination contract. See CONTRACT.

destination du père de famille (des-tee-nah-**syawn** doo **pair** də fa-**mee**). [French "destination of the father of the family"] *Hist.* A property use that the owner has intentionally established on one part of the property in favor of another part.

destitute (**des**-ti-t[y]oot), *adj.* Not possessing the necessaries of life; lacking possessions and resources; indigent.

destitutive fact. See *divestitive fact* under FACT.

destructibility, *n.* The capability of being destroyed by some action, turn of events, or operation of law. — **destructible,** *adj.*

destructibility of contingent remainders. *Property.* The common-law doctrine requiring a future interest to vest by the time it is to become possessory or else suffer total destruction (the interest then reverting to the grantor). • This doctrine has been abolished in all but a few American jurisdictions; the abolishing statutes are commonly termed *anti-destructibility statutes*. — Also termed *destructibility rule*.

> "The destructibility rule still exists in its old common-law form in Florida. Various authors have suggested that it also exists unchanged in Arkansas, North Carolina, Oregon, Pennsylvania, South Carolina, and Tennessee; but there are no statutes or recent decisions to clarify the rule's status in these states." Thomas F. Bergin & Paul G. Haskell, *Preface to Estates in Land and Future Interests* 79 n.46 (2d ed. 1984).

destructible trust. See TRUST.

desuetude (**des**-wə-t[y]ood). **1.** Lack of use; obsolescence through disuse. **2.** The doctrine holding that if a statute or treaty is left unenforced long enough, the courts will no longer regard it as having any legal effect even though it has not been repealed.

> "[T]he doctrine of desuetude has had in all legal systems a very limited and cautious application. For the anachronistic statute a better remedy may be found through reinterpretation in the light of new conditions; as Gray remarks with some irony. 'It is not as speedy or as simple a process to interpret a statute out of existence as to repeal it, but with time and patient skill it can often be done.' " Lon L. Fuller, *Anatomy of the Law* 38 (1968) (quoting John Chipman Gray, *The Nature and Sources of Law* 192 (1921)).

> "There is no doctrine of desuetude in English law, so a statute never ceases to be in force merely because it is

obsolete. Normally there must be an express repeal, but the whole or part of an enactment may be impliedly repealed by a later statute." Rupert Cross, *Statutory Interpretation* 3 (1976).

de superoneratione pasturae (dee soo-pə-roh-nə-ray-shee-**oh**-nee **pas**-tyə-ree), *n.* [Law Latin "of surcharge of pasture"] *Hist.* A judicial writ against a person who was initially brought into county court for putting too many cattle on pasture, and later was impleaded in the same court on the same charge, and the cause was removed to the superior court at Westminster.

de tabulis exhibendis (dee **tab**-yə-lis ek-si-**ben**-dis), *n.* [Latin] *Roman law.* Of producing the tablets of a will. • This was a subject covered under Roman exhibitory interdicts governing the production of documents. A will of a deceased person had to be produced and opened to determine whether the applicant had rights under it.

detachiare (di-tak-ee-**air**-ee *or* di-tash-ee-**air**-ee), *vb.* [Law Latin] *Hist.* To seize a person or property by a writ of attachment or other legal remedy.

detainer. 1. The action of detaining, withholding, or keeping something in one's custody.

forcible detainer. See FORCIBLE DETAINER.

unlawful detainer. The unjustifiable retention of the possession of real property by one whose original entry was lawful, as when a tenant holds over after lease termination despite the landlord's demand for possession.

2. The confinement of a person in custody. **3.** A writ authorizing a prison official to continue holding a prisoner in custody.

de tallagio non concedendo (dee tə-**lay**-jee-oh non kon-sə-**den**-doh), *n.* [Law Latin "of not granting tallage"] *Hist.* The title of a statute declaring that no taxes will be imposed by the king or his heirs without the consent of the archbishops, bishops, earls, barons, knights, and other freemen of the realm. • The statute has been used to support the constitutional doctrine disallowing taxation except by Parliament. 34 Edw. 1 st. 4.

detection. The act of discovering or revealing something that was hidden, esp. to solve a crime.

"There is a clear distinction between inducing a person to do an unlawful act and setting a trap to catch him in the execution of a criminal plan of his own conception. There is also a distinction between the terms 'detection' and 'entrapment,' as applied to the activities of law enforcement officers. Legitimate detection of crime occurs when officers test a suspected person by offering him an opportunity to transgress the law in such manner as is usual in the activity alleged to be unlawful. On the other hand, entrapment occurs when officers induce a person to violate the law when he would not otherwise do so." 21 Am. Jur. 2d *Criminal Law* § 202 (1981).

de tempore cujus contrarium memoria hominum non existit (dee **tem**-pə-ree **k[y]oo**-jəs kən-**trair**-ee-əm mə-**mor**-ee-ə **hom**-ə-nəm non eg-**zis**-tit). [Latin] From time whereof the memory of man does not exist to the contrary. See LEGAL MEMORY.

de tempore in tempus et ad omnia tempora (dee **tem**-pə-ree in **tem**-pəs et ad **om**-nee-ə **tem**-pə-rə). [Latin] From time to time, and at all times.

de temps dont memorie ne court (də **tahn** daw*n* **mem**-ə-ree nə **koor**). [Law French] From time whereof memory does not run; time out of human memory. See LEGAL MEMORY.

détente (day-**tahnt**). [French] **1.** The relaxation of tensions between two or more parties, esp. nations. **2.** A policy promoting such a relaxation of tensions. **3.** A period during which such tensions are relaxed. Cf. ENTENTE; ALLIANCE.

detentio (di-**ten**-shee-oh), *n.* [Latin] **1.** *Roman law.* NATURALIS POSSESSIO. **2.** *Hist.* Detention; detainment, as opposed to *captio* ("taking").

detention, *n.* **1.** The act or fact of holding a person in custody; confinement or compulsory delay. — **detain,** *vb.*

investigative detention. The holding of a suspect without formal arrest during the investigation of the suspect's participation in a crime. • Detention of this kind is constitutional only if probable cause exists.

pretrial detention. The holding of a defendant before trial on criminal charges either because the established bail could not be posted or because release was denied. — Also termed *temporary detention*.

preventive detention. Confinement imposed usu. on a criminal defendant who has threatened to escape or has otherwise violated the law while awaiting trial, or on a mentally ill person who may cause harm.

2. An employee's custody of the employer's property without being considered as having legal possession of it.

detention hearing. See HEARING.

detention in a reformatory. A juvenile offender's sentence of being sent to a reformatory school for some period.

determinable, *adj.* **1.** Liable to end upon the happening of a contingency; terminable <fee simple determinable>. **2.** Able to be determined or ascertained <the delivery date is determinable because she kept the written invoice>.

determinable easement. See EASEMENT.

determinable estate. See ESTATE.

determinable fee. 1. See *fee simple determinable* under FEE SIMPLE. **2.** See *base fee* under FEE (2).

determinate hospitalization. A fixed period of hospitalization, usu. by civil commitment.

determinate obligation. See OBLIGATION.

determinate sentence. See SENTENCE.

determination, *n.* **1.** A final decision by a court or administrative agency <the court's determination of the issue>.

initial determination. The first determination made by the Social Security Administration of a person's eligibility for benefits.

2. The ending or expiration of an estate or interest in property, or of a right, power, or authority <the easement's determination after four years>. — **determine,** *vb.*

determination letter. A letter issued by the Internal Revenue Service in response to a taxpayer's request, giving an opinion about the tax significance of a transaction, such as whether a nonprofit corporation is entitled to tax-exempt status. — Also termed *ruling letter.*

determinative judgment. See *final judgment* under JUDGMENT.

determinism. (*sometimes cap.*) A philosophy that human behavior is governed primarily by preexisting conditions, such as family or environmental factors, and is not influenced by will. — **deterministic,** *adj.*

deterrence, *n.* The act or process of discouraging certain behavior, particularly by fear; esp., as a goal of criminal law, the prevention of criminal behavior by fear of punishment. — **deter,** *vb.* — **deterrent,** *adj.* Cf. REHABILITATION (1); RETRIBUTION (1).

general deterrence. A goal of criminal law generally, or of a specific conviction and sentence, to discourage people from committing crimes.

special deterrence. A goal of a specific conviction and sentence to dissuade the offender from committing crimes in the future.

deterrent, *n.* Something that impedes; something that prevents <a deterrent to crime>.

deterrent danger. See DANGER.

deterrent punishment. See PUNISHMENT.

de theolonio (dee thee-ə-**loh**-nee-oh), *n.* [Law Latin "of toll"] *Hist.* A writ of trespass available to a person prevented from taking toll. See TOLL.

detinet (**det**-i-net). [Latin] He detains. • An action in debt may be in detinet when the plaintiff alleges that the defendant wrongfully kept goods, as distinguished from wrongfully taking them. An action in debt may also be in *detinet* when it is brought by or against someone other than an original party to the debt, such as an executor. An action of replevin is in *detinet* when the defendant retains possession of the property until after the judgment. Cf. DEBET ET DETINET.

detinue (**det**-i-nyoo *or* -noo). A common-law action to recover personal property wrongfully taken by another. Cf. REPLEVIN; TROVER.

> "A claim in detinue lies at the suit of a person who has an immediate right to the possession of the goods against a person who is in actual possession of them, and who, upon proper demand, fails or refuses to deliver them up without lawful excuse. Detinue at the present day has two main uses. In the first place, the plaintiff may desire the specific restitution of his chattels and not damages for their conversion. He will then sue in detinue, not in trover. In the second place, the plaintiff will have to sue in detinue if the defendant sets up no claim of ownership and has not been guilty of trespass; for the original acquisition in *detinue sur bailment* was lawful." R.F.V. Heuston, *Salmond on the Law of Torts* 111 (17th ed. 1977).

detinue of goods in frankmarriage. *Hist.* A writ allowing a divorced wife to obtain the goods given to her during the marriage.

detinue sur bailment (**det**-i-nyoo sər **bayl**-mənt) [Law French] *Hist.* An action to recover property that the defendant acquired by bailment but refuses to return.

detinuit (di-**tin**-yoo-it). [Latin] He has detained. • An action is said to be *in the detinuit* when the plaintiff finally recovers possession of the property claimed under a writ of replevin.

detour, *n. Torts.* An employee's minor deviation from the employer's business for personal reasons. • Because a detour falls within the scope of employment, the employer is still vicariously liable for the employee's actions. Cf. FROLIC.

detournement (di-**tuurn**-mənt), *n.* An employee's misappropriation of the employer's funds.

detraction, *n.* The removal of property from one state to another after transfer of title by a will or inheritance.

de transgressione (dee trans-gresh-ee-**oh**-nee), *n.* [Law Latin "of trespass"] The general name of various writs of trespass. See TRESPASS.

de transgressione, ad audiendum et terminandum (dee trans-gresh-ee-**oh**-nee, ad aw-dee-**en**-dəm et tər-mi-**nan**-dəm), *n.* [Law Latin "of determining and hearing a misdemeanor"] *Hist.* A commission for hearing and determining an outrage or misdemeanor.

detriment. 1. Any loss or harm suffered by a person or property. **2.** *Contracts.* The relinquishment of some legal right that a promisee would have otherwise been entitled to exercise.

> "A promise or an act may be a detriment although *on balance* the promisor is making a good bargain. Thus a promise to pay £10,000 for a Rolls Royce worth £12,000, is none the less a detriment, and a good consideration for a promise to deliver the car." P.S. Atiyah, *An Introduction to the Law of Contract* 101 (3d ed. 1981).

detriment to a promisee. *Contracts.* Consideration offered by a promisee to a promisor, esp. in a unilateral contract requiring an act from the promisee though the promisor has the power to revoke the promise.

detrimental reliance. See RELIANCE.

detunicari (di-tyoo-ni-**kair**-ɪ), *vb.* [Latin "to be revealed"] To discover; to lay open.

de una parte (dee **yoo**-nə **pahr**-tee), *n.* [Latin] Of one party. • A deed is *de una parte* when only one party grants something to another, as distinguished from a deed *inter partes.* See INTER PARTES.

deuterogamy (d[y]oo-tər-**og**-ə-mee). [fr. Greek *deuterogamia* "second marriage"] A second marriage after the death of, or annulment or divorce from, the first spouse. — Also termed *digama; digamy.*

de uxore rapta et abducta (dee ək-**sor**-ee **rap**-tə et ab-**dək**-tə), *n.* [Law Latin "of seizing and carrying away a man's wife"] *Hist.* A writ of trespass for a man whose wife had been raped and carried away.

devadiatus (di-vad-ee-**ay**-təs), *n.* [Law Latin] *Hist.* A defendant without a surety. — Also termed *divadiatus.*

devaluation, *n.* The reduction in the value of one currency in relation to another currency. — **devalue,** *vb.* Cf. REVALUATION.

devastation. 1. An executor's squandering or mismanagement of the deceased's estate. **2.** An act of destruction.

devastaverunt (di-vas-tə-**veer**-ənt). [Latin pl. of *devastavit* "he (or she) has wasted"] They have wasted. • This word usu. referred to both an executor's waste of a decedent's property and the action against the executor for that waste.

devastavit (dev-ə-**stay**-vit). [Latin "he (or she) has wasted"] A personal representative's failure to administer a decedent's estate promptly and properly, esp. by spending extravagantly or misapplying assets. • A personal representative who commits waste in this way becomes personally liable to those having claims on the assets, such as creditors and beneficiaries.

de vasto (dee **vas**-toh), *n.* [Law Latin "of waste"] A writ allowing a reversioner or remainderman to compel a tenant for life or for years to appear and answer for the waste and resulting damage to the plaintiff's inheritance.

developed water. See WATER.

developing country. *Int'l law.* A country that is not as economically or politically advanced as the main industrial powers. • They are located mostly in Africa, Asia, Eastern Europe, the Middle East, and South America. — Also termed *developing state; underdeveloped country; less-developed country; Third World country.*

> "Pertinent terminology has undergone extensive changes in the past 40 years. At the very start, before the category found its way into official texts, economic and political writings referred mainly to 'poor' or 'backward'

countries. In the late 1940s, the term 'underdeveloped countries' came into common usage in economic literature and in the jargon of international organizations. It was replaced in the 1950s by the term 'less developed countries,' for which the current 'developing countries' was eventually substituted. These terms are essentially interchangeable as they refer to the same group and kind of countries. However, variations in the use of the term reflect significant changes in the perception of the central issue, namely, economic development, as well as responses to justified sensitivities on the part of the countries principally concerned." A.A. Fatouros, "Developing States," in 1 *Encyclopedia of Public International Law* 1017 (1992).

development. 1. A human-created change to improved or unimproved real estate, including buildings or other structures, mining, dredging, filing, grading, paving, excavating, and drilling. **2.** An activity, action, or alteration that changes undeveloped property into developed property.

development disability. See DISABILITY (1).

development-stage company. See COMPANY.

de ventre inspiciendo (dee **ven**-tree in-spish-ee-**en**-doh), *n.* [Law Latin "of (or for) inspecting the belly"] **1.** A writ allowing a presumptive heir to summon a jury of matrons to verify the pregnancy of a widow suspected of feigning the pregnancy to produce a supposed heir. — Also termed *ad ventrem inspiciendum*. See *venire facias tot matronas* under VENIRE FACIAS.

"And this gives occasion to a proceeding at common law, where a widow is suspected to feign herself with child, in order to produce a supposititious heir to the estate: an attempt which the rigor of the Gothic constitutions esteemed equivalent to the most atrocious theft, and therefore punished with death. In this case with us the heir presumptive may have a writ *de ventre inspiciendo* to examine whether she be with child, or not . . . and, if the widow be upon due examination found not pregnant, any issue she may afterwards produce, though within nine months, will be bastard." 1 William Blackstone, *Commentaries on the Laws of England* 444 (1765).

2. A writ providing a temporary stay of execution if a jury of matrons determines that a woman scheduled for execution and claiming pregnancy is "quick with child." • The execution would be postponed until after the birth, but if the woman became pregnant a second time before execution, she had no remedy. — Sometimes shortened to *ventre inspiciendo*. — Also spelled *de ventre in spiciendo*.

de verbo in verbum (dee **vər**-boh in **vər**-bəm). [Law Latin] Word for word.

devest (di-**vest**), *vb.* **1.** *Hist.* To deprive (a person) of possession, title, or property. **2.** To take; to draw away.

deviance, *n.* The quality or state of departing from established norms, esp. in social customs. — **deviate** (**dee**-vee-ayt), *vb.* — **deviant,** *adj.* & *n.* — **deviate** (**dee**-vee-ət), *n.*

deviation. *Marine insurance.* **1.** An unnecessary departure from the course fixed by express agreement, by maritime custom, or by the discretion of a reasonably careful and skillful navigator. **2.** An unreasonable delay in pursuing this course.

deviation doctrine. 1. A principle allowing variation from a term of a will or trust to avoid defeating the document's purpose. **2.** A principle allowing an agent's activity to vary slightly from the scope of the principal's permission. **3.** The rule that an insurance policy covering a ship's voyage is canceled if the ship deviates unreasonably from its course.

deviation-well survey. An examination to determine whether a well is bottomed under another person's land.

device. 1. An invention or contrivance; any result of design. **2.** A scheme to trick or deceive; a stratagem or artifice, as in the law relating to fraud.

de vicineto (dee vi-**sin**-ə-toh *or* -**sI**-nə-toh). [Law Latin] From a vicinage; from a neighborhood. • This term was generally used in reference to a jury pool. See DE CORPORE COMITATUS.

de vi laica amovenda (dee **vI lay**-ə-kə ay-moh-**ven**-də), *n.* [Law Latin "of removing a lay force"] *Hist.* A writ allowing a parson claiming rights to a church to order a sheriff to remove a group of laymen who had gathered with another parson at the church and prevented the new parson from entering.

deviling (**dev**-ə-ling). **1.** The act of a barrister handing a brief over to another to handle a case. **2.** The practice of a junior barrister who drafts pleadings or other documents for a senior barrister who approves them, signs them, and is ultimately responsible for the work. — Also spelled *devilling*.

devil on the neck. *Hist.* A torture device made of irons that fastened to a person's neck and legs and then wrenched together to either gradually or quickly break the person's back. • It was often used to coerce confessions.

devisable, *adj.* **1.** Capable of being bequeathed by a will. **2.** Capable of being invented. **3.** Feigned.

devisavit vel non (dev-ə-**say**-vit [*or* -**zay**-vit] vel **non**), *n.* [Law Latin "he (or she) devises or not"] *Hist.* An issue directed from a chancery court to a court of law to determine the validity of a will that has been contested, as by an allegation of fraud or testamentary incapacity. See VEL NON.

devise (di-**vɪz**), *n.* **1.** The act of giving property (usu. real property) by will. **2.** The provision in a will containing such a gift. **3.** Property (usu. real property) disposed of in a will. **4.** A will disposing of real property. Cf. TESTAMENT (1). — **devise,** *vb.* Cf. BEQUEST; LEGACY.

conditional devise. A devise that depends on the occurrence of some uncertain event.

executory devise. An interest in land, created by will, that takes effect in the future and depends on a future contingency; a limitation, by will, of a future estate or interest in land when the limitation cannot, consistently with legal rules, take effect as a remainder. • An executory devise, which is a type of conditional limitation, differs from a remainder in three ways: (1) it needs no particular estate to support it, (2) with it a fee simple or lesser estate can be limited after a fee simple, and (3) with it a remainder can be limited in a chattel interest after a particular estate for life is created in that interest. See *conditional limitation* under LIMITATION.

general devise. A devise that passes the testator's lands without specifically enumerating or describing them.

lapsed devise. A devise that fails because the devisor outlives the named recipient.

residuary devise. A devise of the remainder of the testator's real property left after other specific devises are taken.

specific devise. A devise that passes a particular piece of property.

devisee (dev-ə-**zee** *or* di-vɪ-**zee**). A recipient of property (usu. real property) by will.

first devisee. The first devisee designated to receive an estate under a will.

next devisee. The devisee who receives the remainder of an estate in tail, as distinguished from the first devisee.

residuary devisee. The person named in a will who takes the testator's real property that remains after the other devises.

deviser. One who invents or contrives <the deviser of these patents>.

devisor. One who disposes of property (usu. real property) in a will.

devoir (də-**vwahr** *or* **dev**-wahr). *Hist.* A duty; a tax. — Also spelled *devoire.*

> "Devoire is as much as to say a duty. It is used in the statute of 2 R. 2, cap. 3, where it is provided, that all the western merchants, being of the king's amity, shall pay all manner of customs and subsidies, and other *devoire of Calais.*" *Termes de la Ley* 168 (1st Am. ed. 1812).

devolution (dev-ə-**loo**-shən), *n.* The act or an instance of transferring one's rights, duties, or powers to another; the passing of such rights, duties, or powers by transfer or succession <the federal government's devolution of police power to the states>. — **devolutionary,** *adj.*

devolutive appeal. See APPEAL.

devolve (di-**vahlv**), *vb.* **1.** To transfer (rights, duties, or powers) to another. **2.** To pass (rights, duties, or powers) by transmission or succession. See DEVOLUTION.

devy (də-**vɪ**), *vb.* [Law French] To die.

de warrantia chartae (dee wə-**ran**-shee-ə **kahr**-tee), *n.* [Law Latin "of a warranty of charter"] *Hist.* A writ allowing a tenant enfeoffed with a warranty, who was impleaded in an assize or other action in which the tenant could not call upon the warranty, to compel the feoffor to assist the tenant with a plea or defense, or else to pay damages and the value of the land, if it is recovered against the tenant.

> "This we still make use of in the form of common recoveries, which are grounded on a writ of entry; a species of action that we may remember relies chiefly on the weakness of the tenant's title, who therefore vouches another person to warrant it .... In assises indeed, where the principal question is whether the demandant or his ancestors were or were not in possession till the ouster happened, and the title of the tenant is little (if at all) discussed, there no voucher is allowed; but the tenant may bring a writ of *warrantia chartae* against the warrantor, to compel him to assist him with a good plea or defence, or else to render damages and the value of the land, if recovered against the tenant." 3 William Blackstone, *Commentaries on the Laws of England* 299 (1768).

de warrantia diei (dee wə-**ran**-shee-ə dɪ-**ee**-ɪ), *n.* [Law Latin "of warranty of day"] *Hist.* A writ ordering a judge not to default a party for nonappearance because the Crown warranted that the party was busy in its service.

dextrarius (dek-**strair**-ee-əs). *Hist.* One at the right hand of another.

dextras dare (**dek**-strəs **dair**-ee), *vb.* [Latin "to give right hands"] **1.** To shake hands to show friendship. **2.** To give oneself up to the power of another.

DFA. *abbr.* DELAYED FUNDS AVAILABILITY.

diaconate (dɪ-**ak**-ə-nit), *n.* [Law Latin] A deacon's office.

diaconus (dɪ-**ak**-ə-nəs), *n.* [Law Latin] A deacon. See DEACON.

diagnosis (dɪ-əg-**noh**-sis). **1.** The determination of a medical condition (such as a disease) by physical examination or by study of its symptoms. **2.** The result of such an examination or study. Cf. PROGNOSIS.

clinical diagnosis. A diagnosis from a study of symptoms only.

physical diagnosis. A diagnosis from physical examination only.

dialectic (dɪ-ə-**lek**-tik), *n.* **1.** A school of logic that teaches critical examination of the truth of an opinion, esp. by discussion or debate. • The method was applied by ancient philosophers, such as Plato and Socrates, primarily in the context of conversational discussions involving questions and answers, and also by more modern philosophers, such as Immanuel Kant, who viewed it as a theory of fallacies, and G.W.F. Hegel, who applied the term to his philosophy proceeding from thesis, to antithesis, to synthesis. **2.** An argument made by critically examining logical consequences. **3.** A logical debate. **4.** A disputant; a debater. Pl. **dialectics.**

diallage (dɪ-**al**-ə-jee), *n.* [fr. Greek *diallagê* "interchange"] A rhetorical figure of speech in which arguments are placed in several points of view, and then brought to bear on one point.

Dialogus de Scaccario (dɪ-**al**-ə-gəs dee skə-**kair**-ee-oh), *n.* [Law Latin "a dialogue of or about the Exchequer"] *Hist.* A treatise, written during the reign of Henry II, on the Court of Exchequer, set up in imaginary dialogue form between a master and a disciple. • Although some originally attributed the work to Gervase of Tilbury, it was probably written by Richard Fitz Nigel, the bishop of London under Richard I, and the former Treasurer of the Exchequer.

> "The Dialogus de Scaccario is an anonymous book, but there can be little doubt that we are right in ascribing it to Richard Fitz Neal: that is to say, to Richard the son of that Nigel, bishop of Ely .... The book stands out as an unique book in the history of medieval England, perhaps in the history of medieval Europe. A high officer of state, the trusted counsellor of a powerful king, undertakes to explain to all whom it may concern the machinery of government. He will not deal in generalities, he will condescend to minute details. Perhaps the book was not meant for the general public so much as for the numerous clerks who were learning their business in the exchequer, but still that such a book should be written, is one of the wonderful things of Henry's wonderful reign." 1 Frederick Pollock & Frederic W. Maitland, *The History of English Law Before the Time of Edward I* 161–62 (2d ed. 1898).

dianatic (dɪ-ə-**nat**-ik). See DIANOETIC.

dianoetic (dɪ-ə-noh-**et**-ik), *n.* [Greek *dianoetikos*, fr. *dia-* "through" + *noein* "to revolve in the mind"] *Archaic.* A form of logical reasoning that proceeds from one subject to another. — Also termed (erroneously) *dianatic.*

diarchy. See DYARCHY.

diarium (dɪ-**air**-ee-əm), *n.* [fr. Latin *dies* "day"] *Roman law.* An allowance (usu. of food) needed for a day; a daily allowance of food or pay. Pl. ***diaria*** (dɪ-**air**-ee-ə).

diatim (dɪ-**ay**-təm). [fr. Latin *dies* "day"] Every day; daily.

dica (**dɪ**-kə), *n.* [Law Latin] An account tally. See TALLY (1).

dicast (**dɪ**-kast *or* **dik**-ast), *n.* [Greek *dikastes*] *Hist.* An ancient Greek officer sitting as both judge and juror. • Each dicast was generally a free citizen over the age of 30. The dicasts sat together in groups of between 100 to 500, according to each case's importance, and decided cases by a majority.

dictate, *vb.* **1.** To pronounce orally for transcription. **2.** To order; to command authoritatively.

dictation. **1.** The act of speaking words to be transcribed. **2.** The words so transcribed.

dictator. **1.** *Roman law.* An absolute ruler appointed in an emergency for a term of six months and subject to reappointment.

"In special emergencies, particularly in times of grave crisis, either consul might appoint a dictator who exercised supreme authority, but not beyond six months, unless reappointed. This was, in effect, a temporary reversion to monarchy." R.W. Lee, *The Elements of Roman Law* 14 (4th ed. 1956).

2. A person, esp. a ruler, with absolute authority.

dictum (**dik**-təm), *n.* **1.** A statement of opinion or belief considered authoritative because of the dignity of the person making it. **2.** A familiar rule; a maxim. **3.** OBITER DICTUM. Pl. **dicta.**

"As a dictum is by definition no part of the doctrine of the decision, and as the citing of it as a part of the doctrine is almost certain to bring upon a brief maker adverse comment, lawyers are accustomed to speak of a dictum rather slightingly, and sometimes they go so far as to intimate a belief that the pronouncing of a dictum is the doing of a wrong. Yet it must not be forgotten that dicta are frequently, and indeed usually, correct, and that to give an occasional illustration, or to say that the doctrine of the case would not apply to some case of an hypothetical nature, or to trace the history of a doctrine, even though it be conceded, as it must, that such passages are not essential to the deciding of the very case, is often extremely useful to the profession." William M. Lile et al., *Brief Making and the Use of Law Books* 307 (3d ed. 1914).

dictum proprium (**dik**-təm **proh**-pree-əm). A personal or individual dictum that is given by the judge who delivers an opinion but that is not necessarily concurred in by the whole court and is not essential to the disposition. — Also termed (loosely) *dictum propria.*

gratis dictum (**gray**-tis **dik**-təm). **1.** A voluntary statement; an assertion that a person makes without being obligated to do so. **2.** A court's stating of a legal principle more broadly than is necessary to decide the case. **3.** A court's discussion of points or questions not raised by the record or its suggestion of rules not applicable in the case at bar.

judicial dictum. An opinion by a court on a question that is directly involved, briefed, and argued by counsel, and even passed on by the court, but that is not essential to the decision. Cf. OBITER DICTUM.

obiter dictum. See OBITER DICTUM.

simplex dictum (**sim**-pleks **dik**-təm). An unproved or dogmatic statement. See IPSE DIXIT.

dictum de Kenilworth (**dik**-təm dee **ken**-əl-wərth), *n.* [Law Latin "edict of Kenilworth"] *Hist.* A declaration of an agreement between Edward I and the barons who had opposed him under the leadership of Simon de Montfort. • The agreement, which concerned rent on the lands forfeited in the rebellion, was so called because it was made at Kenilworth castle in Warwickshire in A.D. 1266. It was published in the *Statutes of the Realm* and 52 Hen. 3.

dictum page. See *pinpoint citation* under CITATION.

dictum propria. See *dictum proprium* under DICTUM.

diei dictio (dɪ-**ee**-ɪ **dik**-shee-oh), *n.* [Latin "appointing a day"] *Roman law.* **1.** A magistrate's notice appointing a day for trial. **2.** The service of a summons.

diem clausit extremum (**dɪ**-əm **klaw**-zit ek-**stree**-məm), *n.* [Law Latin "he closed his last day"] *Hist.* **1.** A chancery writ, founded on the statute of Marlbury, ordering the county escheator, after the death of a chief tenant of the Crown, to summon a jury to determine the amount and value of land owned by the chief tenant, to determine the next heir, and to reclaim the property for the Crown. • It was a type of inquisition post mortem.

"Diem clausit extremum is a writ that lies where the king's tenant that holds in chief, dies; then this writ shall be directed to the excheator, to inquire of what estate he was seised, who is next heir, and his age, and of the certainty and value of the land, and of whom it is holden; and the inquisition shall be returned into the chancery, which is commonly called *the office after the death of that person.*" *Termes de la Ley* 169 (1st Am. ed. 1812).

2. An Exchequer writ ordering a sheriff to summon a jury to investigate a Crown debtor's place of death and amount of property owned, and to levy the property of the deceased's heirs and executors. • It was established by the Crown Suits Act of 1865 and repealed by the Crown Proceedings Act of 1947.

"And there is another writ of diem clausit extremum awarded out of the exchequer, after the death of an accomptant or debtor of his majesty, to levy the debt of his heir, executor, administrator's lands or goods." *Termes de la Ley* 169 (1st Am. ed. 1812).

dies (**dɪ**-eez), *n.* [Latin] A day; days.

dies ad quem (**dɪ**-eez ad **kwem**), *n.* [Latin "the day to which"] *Civil law.* An ending date for a transaction; the ending date for computing time, such as the day on which interest no longer accrues.

dies amoris (**dɪ**-eez ə-**mor**-is), *n.* [Law Latin] *Hist.* A day of favor; esp., a day set by the court for the defendant to make an appearance. • This was usu. the fourth day of the term, which was the first day the court normally sat for business. In addition, the defendant usu. had three days of grace from the summons to appear, but an appearance on the fourth day *quarto die post* ("on the fourth day thereafter") was usu. sufficient.

dies a quo (**dɪ**-eez ay **kwoh**), *n.* [Latin "the day from which"] *Civil law.* A transaction's commencement date; the date from which to compute time, such as a day when interest begins to accrue.

dies cedit (**dɪ**-eez **see**-dit), *n.* [Latin "the time begins to run"] *Roman & Scots law.* The day on which an interest, esp. a legacy, vests; the day on which a condition obligation becomes due. — Also termed *dies cedens.* Cf. *dies venit.*

> "A legacy was due, or became a valid right, either at the death of the testator or the occurrence of a condition precedent. This vesting of the property or the accruing of an obligation determined the content and nature of the interests involved. What the legatary got was discovered by examining what the legacy actually carried with it on the day when it became vested. To express the fact that the legacy had become vested, the technical expression *dies cedit* was used." Max Radin, *Handbook of Roman Law* 434–35 (1927).

dies comitiales (**dɪ**-eez kə-mish-ee-**ay**-leez), *n.* [Latin] *Roman law.* The 190 days in the year when an election could be held or the people could assemble as a legislative body. • The praetors could not hold court while a legislative assembly was in session.

dies communes in banco (**dɪ**-eez kə-**myoo**-neez in **bang**-koh), *n.* [Law Latin "common days in banc"] **1.** Regular appearance dates in court. — Also termed *common-return days.* **2.** An enactment printed under the Statutes of Henry III, regulating continuances and writ return dates. • Examples include the *Statutes of the Realm*, *Statutes of Uncertain Date*, and *Statutes at Large.*

dies datus (**dɪ**-eez **day**-təs), *n.* [Law Latin "a given day"] A continuance, esp. for a defendant before a declaration is filed; a time of respite in a case. • A continuance granted after the filing of the declaration is called an *imparlance.* See IMPARLANCE.

dies datus in banco (**dɪ**-eez **day**-təs in **bang**-koh), *n.* [Law Latin "a day given in the bench"] A day given in bank, as distinguished from a day at *nisi prius.*

dies datus partibus (**dɪ**-eez **day**-təs **pahr**-tə-bəs), *n.* [Law Latin "a day given to the parties"] A continuance; an adjournment.

dies datus prece partium (**dɪ**-eez **day**-təs **pree**-see **pahr**-shee-əm), *n.* [Law Latin "a day given at the prayer of the parties"] A day given at the parties' request.

dies Dominicus (**dɪ**-eez də-**min**-i-kəs), *n.* [Latin] The Lord's day; Sunday.

dies excrescens (**dɪ**-eez ek-**skree**-sənz), *n.* [Law Latin "the increasing day"] The additional day in a leap year.

dies fasti (**dɪ**-eez **fas**-tɪ), *n.* [Latin] *Roman law.* A day when justice could be administered; a day when the praetor could officially pronounce the three words "*do*," "*dico*," and "*addico*." — Also called *triverbial days.* See *dies juridicus.* Cf. NEFASTUS.

dies feriati (**dɪ**-eez fer-ee-**ay**-tɪ), *n.* [Latin] *Roman & civil law.* A holiday; holidays.

dies gratiae (**dɪ**-eez **gray**-shee-ee), *n.* [fr. Law French *jour de grace*] *Hist.* A day of grace, usu. granted to the plaintiff.

dies in banco. See DAYS IN BANK.

dies intercisi (**dɪ**-eez in-tər-**sɪ**-zɪ), *n.* [Latin "divided days"] *Roman law.* A day when the courts were open for only part of the day.

dies juridicus (**dɪ**-eez juu-**rid**-i-kəs), *n.* [Latin] A day when justice can be administered. • This term was derived from the civil-law term *dies fasti.*

dies legitimus (**dɪ**-eez lə-**jit**-i-məs), *n.* [Latin] *Roman law.* A lawful day; a law day.

dies marchiae (**dɪ**-eez **mahr**-kee-ee), *n.* [Law Latin "a day of the march"] *Hist.* In the reign of Richard II, the annual day set aside for the wardens of the English and Scottish borders to hold peace talks and resolve differences.

dies nefasti (**dɪ**-eez nee-**fas**-tɪ), *n.* See NEFASTUS; *dies non juridicus.*

dies non (**dɪ**-eez non). See *dies non juridicus.*

dies non juridicus (**dɪ**-eez non juu-**rid**-i-kəs), *n.* [Law Latin "a day not juridical"] A day exempt from court proceedings, such as a holiday or a Sunday. — Often shortened to *dies non.*

dies pacis (**dɪ**-eez **pay**-sis), *n.* [Law Latin "day of peace"] *Hist.* A day of peace. • The days were originally divided into two categories: *dies pacis ecclesiae* ("a day of the peace of the church") and *dies pacis regis* ("a day of the Crown's peace").

dies religiosi (**dɪ**-eez ri-lij-ee-**oh**-sɪ). [Latin] *Roman law.* Religious days on which it was unlawful to transact legal or political business.

dies solaris (**dɪ**-eez sə-**lair**-is), *n.* [Law Latin "a solar day"] See *solar day* under DAY.

dies solis (**dɪ**-eez **soh**-lis), *n.* [Latin "day of the sun"] *Roman law.* Sunday.

dies utiles (**dɪ**-eez **yoo**-tə-leez), *n.* [Latin "available days"] *Roman law.* A day when something can be legally done, such as a day a person can apply to the court to claim an inheritance.

dies venit (**dɪ**-eez **vee**-nit), *n.* [Latin "the day has come"] *Roman & Scots law.* The date when an interest is both vested and actionable. • It is usu. the day when a legatee can claim payment of a legacy. — Also termed *dies veniens*. Cf. *dies cedit*.

> "But the legacy, though vested, is not yet so completely the property of the legatary that he may bring an action for it. To express the fact that such a right of action accrues, the term *dies venit* was used. In general, it may be said that *dies veniens* occurred when, and not until, the *heres* has actually entered upon the inheritance. But, of course, if the legacy was conditional, the *heres* may enter before the condition happens. In that case, *dies veniens* will occur simultaneously with *dies cedens*; i.e., the legacy will vest and the bequest become actionable at the same moment." Max Radin, *Handbook of Roman Law* 435 (1927).

dies votorum (**dɪ**-eez voh-**tor**-əm), *n.* [Latin "a day of vows"] A wedding day.

diet. 1. A regimen, esp. of food. **2.** A governing body's meeting day for legislative, political, or religious purposes; specif., a national assembly of various European countries, such as the diet of the German empire, which was summoned by the emperor regularly to perform various functions, including levying taxes, enacting laws, and declaring war. **3.** *Scots law.* A day to perform a duty, such as a court sitting day, an appearance day, and a criminal pleading or trial day. — Also spelled *dyet*.

> "In procedure on indictment there are two diets, the pleading diet, when the accused is called to plead, and the trial diet when, if he has pled not guilty, he is tried." David M. Walker, *The Oxford Companion to Law* 357 (1980).

dieta (dɪ-**ee**-tə), *n.* [fr. Latin *dies* "day"] *Hist.* **1.** A day's journey. **2.** A day's work. **3.** A day's expenses.

dietary law. Any of the body of laws observed by orthodox Jews regulating which foods may be eaten, how the foods must be prepared and served, and what combinations and contacts (as between meat and milk) are prohibited.

di. et fi. (**dɪ** et **fɪ**). *abbr.* DILECTO ET FIDELI.

Dieu et mon droit (**dyuu** ay maw*n* **drwah**). [French "God and my right"] The motto of the royal arms of England. • It was first used by Richard I and, with the exception of Elizabeth I, was continually used from Edward III to William III, who used the motto *je maintiendrey*. Queen Anne used Elizabeth I's motto, *semper eadem*, but *Dieu et mon droit* has been used since her death.

Dieu son acte (**dyuu** saw*n* **akt**), *n.* [Law Latin "an act of God"] *Hist.* An act of God, beyond human control.

diffacere (di-**fay**-sə-ree), *vb.* [fr. Old French *deffacer*] *Hist.* To deface; to mutilate. — Also termed *disfacere*; *defacere*.

differential pricing. The setting of the price of a product or service differently for different customers. See PRICE DISCRIMINATION.

difforciare (di-for-shee-**air**-ee), *vb.* [Law Latin "to deny"] *Hist.* To keep (something) from someone; to deny (something) to someone.

diffused surface water. See WATER.

DIF system. See DISCRIMINANT FUNCTION.

digama (**dig**-ə-mə). See DEUTEROGAMY.

digamy (**dig**-ə-mee). See DEUTEROGAMY.

digest, *n.* **1.** An index of legal propositions showing which cases support each proposition; a collection of summaries of reported cases, arranged by subject and subdivided by jurisdiction and court. • The chief purpose of a digest is to make the contents of reports available and to separate, from the great mass of caselaw, those cases bearing on some specific point. The American Digest System covers the decisions of all American courts of last resort, state and federal, from 1658 to present. — Abbr. D.

> "An important and numerous class of books included in the general division designated as books of secondary authority is the group known by the generic name of 'Digests.' A Digest is essentially an index to Cases. But it is much more than an ordinary index, for it indicates the holdings and (in some, though not all, publications) the facts of each case. Any particular digest is a summary of the case law coming within its scope, and its units are summaries of particular points of particular cases. What the syllabi of a reported case are to that case, a digest is to many cases. Were a digest simply a collection of citations to cases, arranged logically according to the contents of such cases, it would be a search book; but, being a summary of the case law, it is a book of secondary authority." William M. Lile et al., *Brief Making and the Use of Law Books* 68 (3d ed. 1914).

2. *Civil law.* A compilation and systematic discussion of the various areas of law; chiefly, the Pandects of Justinian in 50 books, known as the *Digest*. — Also termed *digesta*; *digests*. See PANDECT.

digital signature. See SIGNATURE.

dignatory tort. See TORT.

dignitary. 1. A person who holds a high rank or honor. **2.** *Eccles. law.* A person who, by virtue of holding a benefice (such as a cathedral), is preeminent over ordinary priests and canons.

dignity, *n.* **1.** The state of being noble; the state of being dignified. **2.** An elevated title or position. **3.** A person holding an elevated title; a dignitary. **4.** A right to hold a title of nobility, which may be hereditary or for life.

> "Dignities may be hereditary, such as peerages . . . or for life, such as life peerages and knighthoods. The dignities of peerages and baronetcies are created by writ or letters patent, that of knighthood by dubbing as knight. A dignity of inheritance may also exist by prescription. Dignities of inheritance are incorporeal hereditaments having been originally annexed to the possession of certain lands or created by a grant of those lands and are generally limited to the grantee and his heirs or his heirs of the body. If heirs are not mentioned, the grantee holds for life only. The heirs are determined by the rules which governed the descent of land prior to 1926." David M. Walker, *The Oxford Companion to Law* 358 (1980).

dijudication (dɪ-joo-də-**kay**-shən). *Archaic.* A judicial determination.

dilapidations, action for (də-lap-ə-**day**-shənz). *Hist.* A tort action brought by a new incumbent of a benefice for the disrepair of the houses or buildings on the benefice. • The incumbent — whether of a rectory, a vicarage, or a chapel — sued the executors or administrators of the incumbent's deceased predecessor (who was not liable while living). The incumbent of a benefice was bound to maintain the parsonage, farm buildings, and chancel in good and substantial repair, restoring and rebuilding when necessary, according to the original plan. But the incumbent need not supply or maintain anything in the nature of ornament.

dilatory (**dil**-ə-tor-ee), *adj.* Tending to cause delay <the judge's opinion criticized the lawyer's persistent dilatory tactics>.

dilatory defense. See DEFENSE (1).

dilatory exception. See EXCEPTION (1).

dilatory fiduciary. See FIDUCIARY.

dilatory motion. See MOTION.

dilatory plea. See PLEA (3).

dilecto et fideli (di-**lek**-toh et fi-**dee**-lɪ). [Law Latin] To his beloved and faithful. • This phrase was used in various writs. — Abbr. *di. et fi.*

diligence. 1. A continual effort to accomplish something. **2.** Care; caution; the attention and care required from a person in a given situation. • The Roman-law equivalent is *diligentia*. See DILIGENTIA.

> "Care, or the absence of *negligentia*, is *diligentia*. The use of the word diligence in this sense is obsolete in modern English, though it is still retained as an archaism of legal diction. In ordinary usage, diligence is opposed to idleness, not to carelessness." John Salmond, *Jurisprudence* 393 n.(i) (Glanville L. Williams ed., 10th ed. 1947).

***due diligence.* 1.** The diligence reasonably expected from, and ordinarily exercised by, a person who seeks to satisfy a legal requirement or to discharge an obligation. — Also termed *reasonable diligence*. **2.** *Corporations & securities.* A prospective buyer's or broker's investigation and analysis of a target company, a piece of property, or a newly issued security. • A failure to exercise due diligence may sometimes result in liability, as when a broker recommends a security without first investigating it adequately.

extraordinary diligence. Extreme care that a person of unusual prudence exercises to secure rights or property.

great diligence. The diligence that a very prudent person exercises in handling his or her own property like that at issue. — Also termed *high diligence*.

low diligence. See *slight diligence*.

necessary diligence. The diligence that a person is required to exercise to be legally protected.

ordinary diligence. The diligence that a person of average prudence would exercise in handling his or her own property like that at issue.

***reasonable diligence.* 1.** A fair degree of diligence expected from someone of ordinary prudence under circumstances like those at issue. **2.** See *due diligence* (1).

slight diligence. The diligence that a person of less than common prudence takes with his or her own concerns. — Also termed *low diligence*.

special diligence. The diligence expected from a person practicing in a particular field of specialty under circumstances like those at issue.

3. *Scots law.* A court-issued warrant to compel something, such as the attendance of a witness. **4.** The legal process of attaching property for the payment of debt.

diligent, *adj.* Careful; attentive; persistent in doing something.

diligentia (dil-ə-**jen**-shee-ə), *n.* [Latin] *Roman law.* Carefulness; diligence. • The failure to exercise *diligentia* might make a person liable if contractually obliged to look after another's interests, or it might result in tort liability. Cf. NEGLIGENTIA. See DILIGENCE.

diligentia exactissima (dil-ə-**jen**-shee-ə eks-ak-**tis**-ə-mə), *n.* [Latin] Extraordinary diligence that a head of a family habitually exercises in business. — Also termed *diligentia exacta*; *diligentia boni patrisfamilias.* See *extraordinary diligence* under DILIGENCE.

diligentia quam suis rebus (dil-ə-**jen**-shee -ə kwam **s[y]oo**-is **ree**-bəs), *n.* [Latin] The care that an ordinary person exercises in managing his or her affairs. See *ordinary diligence* under DILIGENCE.

"The texts distinguish two standards of diligence, a higher and a lower. The higher is the diligence which the good father of a family habitually exhibits in his own affairs (diligentia exacta or exactissima — diligentia boni patrisfamilias). The lower is the diligence which the person in question exhibits in his own affairs (diligentia quam suis rebus). This may, in fact, reach a high degree of diligence or it may not. But, at least, where this standard is applied nothing extraordinary is expected. It is a concrete standard. It is enough that the person in question pursues his normal course. According to a traditional terminology, where the first standard is applied, there is said to be liability for culpa levis in abstracto — slight negligence in the abstract; in the second case there is liability for culpa levis in concreto — slight negligence in the concrete." R.W. Lee, *The Elements of Roman Law* 288 (4th ed. 1956).

diligent inquiry. A careful and good-faith probing to ascertain the truth of something.

diligiatus (də-lij-ee-**ay**-təs), *n.* [fr. Latin *dis-* "apart" + *ligius* "under legal protection"] A person cast out of the law's protection; an outlaw.

Dillon's rule. The doctrine that a unit of local government may exercise only those powers that the state expressly grants to it, the powers necessarily and fairly implied from that grant, and the powers that are indispensable to the existence of the unit of local government. • For the origins of this rule, see 1 John F. Dillon, *The Law of Municipal Corporations* § 89, at 115 (3d ed. 1881).

dilution. 1. The act or an instance of diminishing a thing's strength or lessening its value. **2.** *Corporations.* The reduction in the monetary value or voting power of stock by increasing the total number of outstanding shares. **3.** *Constitutional law.* The limitation of the effectiveness of a particular group's vote by legislative reapportionment or political gerrymandering. • Such dilution violates the Equal Protection Clause. — Also termed *vote dilution.* **4.** *Trademarks.* The impairment of a trademark's strength or effectiveness caused by the use of the mark on an unrelated product, usu. blurring the trademark's distinctive character or tarnishing it with an unsavory association. • Trademark dilution may occur even when the use is not competitive and when it creates no likelihood of confusion.

dilution doctrine. *Trademarks.* The rule protecting a trademark from a deterioration in strength, as when a person seeks to use the mark for an unrelated product.

dimidietas (dim-ə-**dɪ**-ə-tas), *n.* [Law Latin] *Hist.* Half of something; a moiety.

dimidium (di-**mid**-ee-əm), *n.* [Latin "half"] *Hist.* **1.** Half; a half — as in *dimidium unius libratae* ("half a pound"). **2.** An undivided half of something.

dimidius (di-**mid**-ee-əs), *adj.* [Latin "half"] *Hist.* **1.** Half; doubled. **2.** Loosely, incomplete.

diminished capacity. See CAPACITY (3).

diminished responsibility. See *diminished capacity* under CAPACITY (3).

diminutio. See DEMINUTIO.

diminution (dim-ə-**n[y]oo**-shən), *n.* **1.** The act or process of decreasing, lessening, or taking away. **2.** An incompleteness or lack of certification in a court record sent from a lower court to a higher one for review. — **diminish** (for sense 1), *vb.*

diminution-in-value method. A way of calculating damages for breach of contract based on a reduction in market value that is caused by the breach.

dimissoriae litterae (dim-ə-**sor**-ee-ee **lit**-ər-ee), *n.* [Latin "dimissory letters"] *Eccles. law.* Dimissory letters; apostles. See APOSTLE.

dimissory letters (**dim**-ə-sor-ee). **1.** *Hist. Eccles. law.* Documents allowing a clergy member to leave one diocese for another. **2.** *Eccles. law.* Documents provided by one bishop to enable another bishop to ordain a candidate already ordained in the former bishop's diocese.

diocesan (dI-**os**-ə-sən), *adj.* Of or belonging to a diocese; of or relating to the relationship between a bishop and the clergy within the diocese.

diocesan court. See COURT.

diocesan mission. A mission performing its work in a single diocese.

diocesan synod. See SYNOD.

diocese (**dI**-ə-sees *or* -sis). **1.** *Roman law.* The division of the Roman empire into provinces. **2.** *Eccles. law.* An archbishop's jurisdiction, including governance over several bishops, who each control a parish. **3.** *Eccles. law.* A bishop's jurisdiction. • Several dioceses together are governed by an archbishop.

dioichia (dI-**oy**-kee-ə), *n.* [fr. Latin *diocesis* "a diocese"] A district over which a bishop exercises his spiritual functions.

DIP. *abbr.* DEBTOR-IN-POSSESSION.

diploma. 1. *Roman law.* A letter giving permission to use the imperial post. **2.** *Hist.* A royal charter; letters patent. **3.** A document that evidences or memorializes graduation from a school or society. Cf. DEGREE (6). **4.** A document that evidences a license or privilege to practice a profession, such as medicine.

diplomacy, *n. Int'l law.* **1.** The art and practice of conducting negotiations between national governments.

open diplomacy. Diplomacy carried on with free access to interested observers and members of the press.

parliamentary diplomacy. The negotiations and discussions carried out in international organizations according to their rules of procedure.

secret diplomacy. Diplomacy carried on behind closed doors. — Also termed *quiet diplomacy.*

shuttle diplomacy. Diplomatic negotiations assisted by emissaries, who travel back and forth between negotiating countries. • In legal contexts, the term usu. refers to a similar approach used by a mediator in negotiating the settlement of a lawsuit. The mediator travels back and forth between different rooms, one of which is assigned to each side's decision-makers and counsel. The mediator relays offers and demands between the rooms and, by conferring with the parties about their positions and about the uncertainty of litigation, seeks to reach an agreed resolution of the case.

2. Loosely, foreign policy. **3.** The collective functions performed by a diplomat. — **diplomatic,** *adj.* — **diplomat,** *n.*

diplomatic agent. See AGENT.

diplomatic bag. See DIPLOMATIC POUCH.

diplomatic corps. *Int'l law.* The ambassador and other diplomatic personnel assigned by their government to a foreign capital.

diplomatic immunity. See IMMUNITY (1).

diplomatic pouch. 1. A bag containing official correspondence, documents, or articles intended exclusively for official communications of a nation with its missions, consular posts, or delegations. **2.** The contents of the bag. — Also termed *diplomatic bag*; *valise diplomatique.*

diplomatic protection. Protection given by one country's representatives to a person, usu. an individual, against another country's violation of international law.

> "The term diplomatic protection is not altogether precise. First, not only diplomatic agents and missions and other foreign offices may and do exercise diplomatic protection, but also, at a different level, consuls, and, although very rarely, military forces. Secondly, the term diplomatic protection does not clearly denote the boundary line to other diplomatic activities for the benefit of individuals, such as mere promotion of interests in one's own nationals in a foreign State, or friendly intercessions with foreign authorities. Thus, diplomatic or consular actions to obtain concessions or other government contracts for nationals from the receiving State, or the arrangement of legal defense for a justly imprisoned national are not diplomatic protection in our sense; they are usually neither directed against the other State nor

based on a real or alleged violation of international law. All these last-mentioned activities may be called diplomatic protection only if the term is taken in a very broad sense." William Karl Geck, "Diplomatic Protection," in 1 *Encyclopedia of Public International Law* 1046 (1992).

diplomatic relations. *Int'l law.* The customary form of permanent contact and communication between sovereign countries.

diplomatics. The science of deciphering and authenticating ancient writings. • The principles were largely developed by the Benedictine Dom Mabillon in his 1681 work entitled *De re diplomatica.* — Also termed *diplomatic* (*n.*).

"Diplomatics, the science derived from the study of ancient diplomas, so called from being written on two leaves, or on double tablets. The Romans used the term more specially for the letters of license to use the public conveyances provided at the different stations, and generally for public grants. Subsequently it attained a more extended signification, and in more modern times has been used as a general term for ancient imperial and ecclesiastical acts and grants, public treaties, deeds of conveyance, letters, wills, and similar instruments, drawn up in forms and marked with peculiarities varying with their dates and countries. With the revival of literature, the importance of such documents in verifying facts and establishing public and private rights led to their being brought together from the historical works and the monastic registers in which they had been copied, or, in rarer instances, from public and ecclesiastical archives where the originals were still preserved. Then arose questions of authenticity, and doubts of the so-called originals; disputants defended or condemned them; and, in order to establish principles for distinguishing the genuine from the forged, treatises were written on the whole subject of these diplomas." 7 *Encyclopaedia Britannica* 220 (9th ed. 1907).

Diplomatic Security Service. A bureau of the U.S. Department of State having responsibility for protecting the Secretary of State and domestic and foreign dignitaries, as well as for investigating criminal activities such as identity-document fraud involving U.S. passports and visas. • The Service now employs some 800 special agents (members of the U.S. Foreign Service), who are located throughout the United States and in scores of embassies worldwide.

diptych (**dip**-tik), *n.* [fr. Latin *diptycha* fr. Greek *diptycha* "two-leaved"] **1.** *Roman law.* Two tablets usu. made of wood or metal and tied with string through holes at the edges so that they could fold over (like a book with two leaves). • Diptychs were often used to send letters, and the text was sometimes written using a stylus, once on the inside waxed leaves and again on the outside, so that it could be read without opening the tablets. **2.** *Hist. Eccles. law.* Tablets used by the church, esp. to register names of those making supplication, and to record births, marriages, and deaths. **3.** *Hist. Eccles. law.* The registry of those names.

"The recitation of the name of any prelate or civil ruler in the diptychs was a recognition of his orthodoxy; its omission, the reverse. The mention of a person after death recognized him as having died in the communion of the church, and the introduction of his name into the list of saints or martyrs constituted canonization. In liturgics the diptychs are distinguished as *the diptychs of the living* and the *diptychs of the dead*, the latter including also the commemoration of the saints .... In the Western Church the use of the diptychs died out between the ninth and the twelfth century; in the Eastern Church it still continues." 2 *The Century Dictionary and Cyclopedia* (1895).

"Diptychs were used in the time of the Roman empire for sending letters .... The consula and quaestors used, on assuming office, to send diptychs containing their names and portraits to their friends .... The early Christians used tablets thus made in the celebration of divine worship .... They were placed on ... the pulpits, or reading desks, which may still be seen in ancient basilicas at the west end of the choir or presbytery; and from them were read to the congregation of the faithful the names of the celebrating priests, of those who occupied the superior positions in the Christian hierarchy, of the saints, martyrs, and confessors, and, in process of time, also of those who had died in the faith.... The inscription on the diptychs of deaths and baptisms, naturally led to the insertion of *dates*, and the diptychs seem thus to have grown into calendars, and to have been the germ from which necrologies, lists of saints, and almanacs have been developed." 7 *Encyclopaedia Britannica* 223–24 (9th ed. 1907).

dirationare (di-ray-shee-ə-**nair**-ee), *vb.* [fr. Latin *dis* "thoroughly" + *ratiocinari* "to reason"] *Hist.* **1.** To prove; to establish one's right. **2.** To disprove; to refute (an allegation).

direct (di-**rekt**), *adj.* **1.** (Of a thing) straight; undeviating <a direct line>. **2.** (Of a thing or a person) straightforward <a direct manner> <direct instructions>. **3.** Free from extraneous influence; immediate <direct injury>. **4.** Of or relating to passing in a straight line of descent, as distinguished from a collateral line <a direct descendant> <a direct ancestor>. **5.** (Of a political action) effected by the public immediately, not through representatives <direct resolution> <direct nomination>.

direct, *n.* See DIRECT EXAMINATION.

direct, *vb.* **1.** To aim (something or someone). **2.** To cause (something or someone) to move on a particular course. **3.** To guide (something or someone); to govern. **4.** To instruct (someone) with authority. **5.** To address (something or someone).

direct action. **1.** A lawsuit by an insured against his or her own insurance company rather than against the tortfeasor and the tortfeasor's insurer. **2.** A lawsuit by a person claiming against an insured but suing the insurer directly instead of pursuing compensation indirectly through the insured. **3.** A lawsuit to enforce a shareholder's rights against a corporation. Cf. DERIVATIVE ACTION (1).

direct-action statute. A statute that grants an injured party direct standing to sue an insurer instead of the insured tortfeasor. • Under Rhode Island's direct-action statute, for example, an injured party may bring a direct action against an insurer when good-faith efforts to serve process on the insured are unsuccessful. These statutes exist in several states, including Alabama, Arkansas, Louisiana, Minnesota, New York, Pennsylvania, and Wisconsin.

direct affinity. See AFFINITY.

direct and proximate cause. See *proximate cause* under CAUSE (1).

direct appeal. See APPEAL.

direct attack. An attack on a judgment made in the same proceeding as the one in which the judgment was entered. • Examples of direct attacks are appeals and motions for new trial. Cf. COLLATERAL ATTACK.

direct beneficiary. See *intended beneficiary* under BENEFICIARY.

direct cause. See *proximate cause* under CAUSE (1).

direct charge-off accounting method. See ACCOUNTING METHOD.

direct confession. See CONFESSION.

direct contempt. See CONTEMPT.

direct conversion. See CONVERSION (2).

direct cost. See COST (1).

direct damages. See *general damages* under DAMAGES.

direct deposit. See DEPOSIT (2).

direct economic loss. See ECONOMIC LOSS.

directed verdict. See VERDICT.

direct estoppel. See COLLATERAL ESTOPPEL.

direct evidence. See EVIDENCE.

direct examination. The first questioning of a witness in a trial or other proceeding, conducted by the party who called the witness to testify. — Often shortened to *direct*. — Also termed *examination-in-chief*. Cf. CROSS-EXAMINATION; REDIRECT EXAMINATION.

direct financing. See FINANCING.

direct infringement. See *patent infringement* under INFRINGEMENT.

direct injury. See INJURY.

direct interest. See INTEREST (2).

direction (di-**rek**-shən). **1.** The course taken in relation to the point toward which something or someone is moving; a point to or from which a person or thing moves <the storm moved in a northerly direction>. **2.** The course on which something is aimed <the direction of the trial>. **3.** An act of guidance <under the chair's direction>. **4.** An order; an instruction on how to proceed <the judge's direction to the jury>. See JURY INSTRUCTION. **5.** The address to the court contained on a bill of equity <the direction on the bill>. **6.** A board of directors; a board of managers <the direction met on Wednesday>.

directive to physicians. See LIVING WILL.

direct line. See LINE.

direct-line descent. See *lineal descent* under DESCENT.

direct loss. See LOSS.

directly, *adv.* **1.** In a straightforward manner. **2.** In a straight line or course. **3.** Immediately.

direct notice. See NOTICE.

director (di-**rek**-tər). **1.** One who manages, guides, or orders; a chief administrator. **2.** A person appointed or elected to sit on a board that manages the affairs of a corporation or company by electing and exercising control over its officers. See BOARD OF DIRECTORS. Cf. OFFICER (1).

affiliated director. See *outside director.*

class director. **1.** A director whose term on a corporate board is staggered with those of the other directors to make a hostile takeover more difficult. **2.** A director elected or appointed to a corporate board to represent a special-interest group, e.g., the preferred stockholders.

dummy director. A board member who is a mere figurehead and exercises no real control over the corporation's business.

inside director. A director who is also an employee, officer, or major shareholder of the corporation.

interlocking director. A director who simultaneously serves on the boards of two or more corporations that deal with each other or have allied interests.

outside director. A nonemployee director with little or no direct interest in the corporation. — Also termed *affiliated director.*

provisional director. A director appointed by a court to serve on a close corporation's deadlocked board of directors.

direct order of alienation. *Real estate.* The principle that a grantee who assumes the debt on a mortgaged property is required to pay the mortgage debt if the original mortgagor defaults.

Director of Public Prosecutions. An officer (usu. a barrister or solicitor of ten years' standing) who advises the police and prosecutes criminal cases in England and Wales under the supervision of the Attorney General.

Director of the Mint. An officer appointed by the President, with the advice and consent of the Senate, to control and manage the U.S. Mint and its branches.

directors' and officers' liability insurance. — Also termed *D & O insurance.* See INSURANCE.

directory, *n.* **1.** A book containing an alphabetical list of names, addresses, and telephone numbers, esp. those of a city's or area's residents and businesses. **2.** Any organization's publication containing information on its members or business, such as a legal directory. **3.** *Eccles. law.* A church's book of directions for conducting worship. ● One of the primary directories is the *Directory for the Public Worship of God,* prepared by the Assembly of Divines in England in 1644 to take the place of the Book of Common Prayer that had been abolished by Parliament. It was ratified by Parliament in 1645 and adopted by the Scottish Parliament and General Assembly of the Church of Scotland that same year. A directory in the Roman Catholic Church contains instructions for saying the mass and offices each day of the year. **4.** A small governing body; specif., the five-member executive body that governed France from 1795–1799 during the French Revolution until it was overthrown by Napoleon and succeeded by the consulate.

directory call. *Property.* In a land description, a general description of the areas in which landmarks or other calls are found. See CALL (5); LOCATIVE CALLS.

directory provision. A statutory or contractual sentence or paragraph in which a directory requirement appears.

directory requirement. A statutory or contractual instruction to act in a way that is advisable, but not absolutely essential — in contrast to a mandatory requirement. ● A directory requirement is frequently introduced by the word *should* or, less frequently, *shall.*

directory statute. See STATUTE.

directory trust. See TRUST.

direct-participation program. An investment vehicle that is financed through the sale of securities not traded on an exchange or quoted on NASDAQ and that provides flow-through tax consequences to the investors.

direct payment. See PAYMENT.

direct placement. **1.** The sale by a company, such as an industrial or utility company, of an entire issue of securities directly to a lender (such as an insurance company or group of investors), instead of through an underwriter. ● This type of offering is exempt from SEC filing requirements. **2.** PRIVATE PLACEMENT (1).

direct possession. See *immediate possession* under POSSESSION (3).

direct question. See QUESTION (1).

direct-reduction mortgage. See MORTGAGE.

direct selling. 1. Selling to a customer without going through a dealer. **2.** Selling to a retailer without going through a wholesaler.

direct skip. *Tax.* A generation-skipping transfer of assets, either directly or through a trust. • A direct skip may be subject to a generation-skipping transfer tax — either a gift tax or an estate tax. IRC (26 USCA) §§ 2601–2602. See GENERATION-SKIPPING TRANSFER; *generation-skipping transfer tax* under TAX; SKIP PERSON.

direct tax. See TAX.

direct trust. See *express trust* under TRUST.

diribitores (di-rib-ə-**tor**-eez), *n.* [Latin "sorters of votes"] *Roman law.* Officers who distributed voting ballots to the public.

diriment impediment (**dir**-ə-mənt im-**ped**-ə-mənt), *n.* [fr. Latin *dirimens impedimentum* "nullifying impediment"] *Hist.* A bar to marriage (such as a close familial relationship) that annuls a marriage as a matter of law.

dirt-for-debt transfer. A transaction in which a bankrupt debtor satisfies all or part of a secured debt by transferring the collateral to the creditor.

disability. 1. The inability to perform some function; an objectively measurable condition of impairment, physical or mental <his disability entitled him to workers'-compensation benefits>. — Also termed *incapacity.*

developmental disability. An impairment of general intellectual functioning or adaptive behavior.

partial disability. A worker's inability to perform all the duties that he or she could do before an accident, even though the worker can still engage in some gainful activity on the job.

permanent disability. A disability that will indefinitely prevent a worker from performing some or all of the duties that he or she could do before an accident.

physical disability. An incapacity caused by a physical defect or infirmity, or by bodily imperfection or mental weakness.

temporary disability. A disability that exists until an injured worker is as far restored as the nature of the injury will permit.

temporary total disability. Total disability that is not permanent.

total disability. A worker's inability to perform employment-related duties because of a physical or mental impairment.

2. Incapacity in the eyes of the law <most of a minor's disabilities are removed when he or she turns 18>. — Also termed *incapacity.*

civil disability. The condition of a person who has had a legal right or privilege revoked as a result of a criminal conviction, as when a person's driver's license is revoked after a DWI conviction. Cf. CIVIL DEATH (2).

disability benefits. See DISABILITY COMPENSATION.

disability clause. A life-insurance-policy provision providing for a waiver of premiums during the policyholder's period of disability, and sometimes providing for monthly payments equal to a percentage of the policy's face value.

disability compensation. Payments from public or private funds to a disabled person who cannot work, such as social-security or workers'-compensation benefits. — Also termed *disability benefits.*

disability insurance. See INSURANCE.

disability retirement plan. See EMPLOYEE BENEFIT PLAN.

disable, *vb.* **1.** To deprive (someone or something) of the ability to function; to weaken the capability of (someone or something). **2.** To impair; to diminish. **3.** To legally disqualify (someone); to render (someone) legally incapable.

disabled person. See PERSON.

disablement, *n.* **1.** The act of incapacitating or immobilizing. **2.** The imposition of a legal disability.

disabling restraints. Limits on the alienation of property. • These restraints are sometimes void as being against public policy.

disabling statute. See STATUTE.

disadvocare (dis-ad-və-**kair**-ee), *vb.* [Law Latin] To deny; to disavow.

disaffirm (dis-ə-**fərm**), *vb.* **1.** To repudiate; to revoke consent; to disclaim the intent to be bound by an earlier transaction. **2.** To declare (a voidable contract) to be void.

disaffirmance (dis-ə-**fərm**-ənts). An act of denial; a repudiation, as of an earlier transaction. **2.** A declaration that a voidable contract (such as one entered into by a minor) is void. — Also termed *disaffirmation*.

"Disaffirmance is an operative act whereby the legal relations created by an infant's contract are terminated and discharged and other legal relations substituted. Inasmuch as the infant's executory promise does not operate to create any legal duty in him (the infant being at all times at liberty or *privileged* not to perform), his disaffirmance is not the discharge of such a duty. A return promise by an adult, however, creates a legal duty and the infant has a correlative right *in personam*. A disaffirmance terminates these." William R. Anson, *Principles of the Law of Contract* 181 (Arthur L. Corbin ed., 3d Am. ed. 1919).

disafforest (dis-ə-**for**-əst *or* -**fahr**-əst), *vb*. [fr. French *desaforester*] *Hist.* To free lands from the restrictions of the forest laws and return them to the status of ordinary lands. — Also termed *deafforest*.

disagreement. 1. A difference of opinion; a lack of agreement. **2.** A quarrel. **3.** An annulment; a refusal to accept something, such as an interest in an estate.

disallow, *vb*. **1.** To refuse to allow (something). **2.** To reject (something).

disalt (dis-**awlt**), *vb. Hist.* To disable (a person).

disappeared person. A person who has been absent from home for at least seven continuous years and who, during that period, has not communicated with the person most likely to know his or her whereabouts. See SEVEN-YEARS'-ABSENCE RULE; MISSING PERSON.

disappropriation. 1. *Eccles. law.* The alienation of church property from its original use; the severance of property from church ownership or possession. **2.** The release of property from individual ownership or possession.

disapprove, *vb*. **1.** To pass unfavorable judgment on (something). **2.** To decline to sanction (something).

disarmament. *Int'l law.* The negotiated or voluntary reduction of military arms, esp. nuclear weapons, to a greatly reduced level or to nil. Cf. ARMS CONTROL.

disaster. A calamity; a catastrophic emergency.

disaster area. A region officially declared to have suffered a catastrophic emergency, such as a flood or hurricane, and therefore eligible for government aid.

disaster loss. See LOSS.

disavow (dis-ə-**vow**), *vb*. To disown; to disclaim knowledge of; to repudiate <the company disavowed the acts of its agent>. — **disavowal,** *n*.

disbarment, *n*. The action of expelling a lawyer from the bar or from the practice of law, usu. because of some disciplinary violation. — Also termed *striking off the roll*. — **disbar,** *vb*.

disbocatio (dis-bə-**kay**-shee-oh), *n*. [fr. Law Latin *dis-* + *boscus* "wood"] *Hist.* The conversion of forest to pasture.

disbursement (dis-**bərs**-mənt), *n*. The act of paying out money, commonly from a fund or in settlement of a debt or account payable <dividend disbursement>. — **disburse,** *vb*.

DISC. *abbr.* DOMESTIC INTERNATIONAL SALES CORPORATION.

discarcare (dis-kahr-**kair**-ee), *vb*. [fr. Latin *dis-* + *carcare* "to charge"] *Hist.* To unload (cargo), usu. from a ship. — Also termed *discargare*.

disceptatio causae (di-sep-**tay**-shee-oh **kaw**-zee), *n*. [Latin "debate about a case"] *Roman law.* The argument by the advocates of both sides of a dispute.

discharge (**dis**-chahrj), *n*. **1.** The payment of a debt or satisfaction of some other obligation. **2.** The release of a debtor from monetary obligations upon adjudication of bankruptcy; RELEASE (1). **3.** The dismissal of a case. **4.** The canceling or vacating of a court order. **5.** The release of a prisoner from confinement. **6.** The relieving of a witness, juror, or jury from further responsibilities in a case. **7.** The firing of an employee.

constructive discharge. A termination of employment brought about by making the employee's working conditions so intolerable that the employee feels compelled to leave.

"Most constructive discharges fall into one of two basic fact patterns. First, the employer can cause a constructive discharge by breaching the employee's contract of employment in some manner short of termination. Second, the employer can make working conditions so intolerable that the employee feels compelled to quit." Mark A. Rothstein et al., *Employment Law* § 9.7, at 539 (1994).

retaliatory discharge. A discharge that is made in retaliation for the employee's conduct (such as reporting unlawful activity by the employer to the government) and that clearly violates public policy. • Most states have statutes allowing an employee who is dismissed by retaliatory discharge to recover damages.

unconditional discharge. **1.** A release from an obligation without any conditions attached. **2.** A release from confinement without any parole requirements to fulfill.

wrongful discharge. A discharge for reasons that are illegal or that violate public policy.

8. The dismissal of a member of the armed services from military service <the sergeant was honorably discharged>. — **discharge** (dis-**chahrj**), *vb.*

administrative discharge. A military-service discharge given by administrative means and not by court-martial.

bad-conduct discharge. A punitive discharge that a court-martial can give a member of the military, usu. as punishment for repeated minor offenses. — Abbr. BCD.

dishonorable discharge. The most severe punitive discharge that a court-martial can give to a member of the military. • A dishonorable discharge may result from conviction for an offense recognized in civilian law as a felony or of a military offense requiring severe punishment. Only a general court-martial can give a dishonorable discharge.

general discharge. One of the administrative discharges given to a member of the military who does not qualify for an honorable discharge.

honorable discharge. A formal final judgment passed by the government on a soldier's entire military record, and an authoritative declaration that he or she has left the service in a status of honor. • Full veterans' benefits are given only to a person honorably discharged.

undesirable discharge. One of the administrative discharges given to a member of the military who does not qualify for an honorable discharge.

dischargeability proceeding. *Bankruptcy.* A hearing to determine whether a debt is dischargeable or is subject to an exception to discharge. 11 USCA § 523.

dischargeable claim. *Bankruptcy.* A claim that can be discharged in bankruptcy.

discharged contract. See *void contract* under CONTRACT.

discharge hearing. *Bankruptcy.* A hearing at which the court informs the debtor either that a discharge has been granted or the reasons why a discharge has not been granted. See REAFFIRMATION HEARING.

discharge in bankruptcy. **1.** The release of a debtor from personal liability for prebankruptcy debts. **2.** A bankruptcy court's decree releasing a debtor from that liability.

discharging bond. See BOND (2).

disciplinary proceeding. An action brought to reprimand, suspend, or expel a licensed professional or other person from a profession or other group because of unprofessional, unethical, improper, or illegal conduct. • A disciplinary proceeding against a lawyer may result in the lawyer's being suspended or disbarred from practice.

disciplinary rule. (*usu. cap.*) A mandatory regulation stating the minimum level of professional conduct that a professional must sustain to avoid being subject to disciplinary action. • For lawyers, the disciplinary rules are found chiefly in the Model Code of Professional Responsibility. — Abbr. DR. Cf. ETHICAL CONSIDERATION.

discipline, *n.* **1.** Punishment intended to correct or instruct; esp., a sanction or penalty imposed after an official finding of misconduct. **2.** Control gained by enforcing compliance or order. **3.** *Military law.* A state of mind inducing instant obedience to a lawful order, no matter how unpleasant or dangerous such compliance might be. — **discipline,** *vb.* — **disciplinary,** *adj.*

disclaimer, *n.* **1.** A renunciation of one's legal right or claim. **2.** A repudiation of another's legal right or claim. **3.** A writing that contains such a renunciation or repudiation. — **disclaim,** *vb.*

disclaimer of warranty. An oral or written statement intended to limit a seller's liability for defects in the goods sold. • In some circumstances, printed words must be specific and conspicuous to be effective.

patent disclaimer. A patent applicant's amendment of a specification to relinquish part of the claim to the invention. • When part of the invention is not patentable, such a disclaimer can be filed to help ensure the validity of the rest of the patent. See SPECIFICATION (3).

qualified disclaimer. A person's refusal to accept an interest in property so that he or she can avoid having to pay estate or gift taxes. • To be effective under federal tax law, the refusal must be in writing and must be executed no later than nine months from the time when the interest was created. IRC (26 USCA) § 2518.

disclosed principal. See PRINCIPAL (1).

disclosure, *n.* The act or process of making known something that was previously unknown; a revelation of facts <a lawyer's disclosure of a conflict of interest>. — **disclose,** *vb.* — **disclosural,** *adj.* See DISCOVERY; INITIAL DISCLOSURE.

compulsory disclosure. A mandatory disclosure of information, as of matters within the scope of the discovery rules. See DISCOVERY (2).

full disclosure. A complete revelation of all material facts.

discommon (dis-**kom**-ən), *vb.* **1.** To deprive of the right of common (e.g., the right to pasture). **2.** To deprive (something, esp. land) of commonable character. • A person could discommon land by separating or enclosing it. **3.** To deprive (someone) of the privileges of a place, such as the right to a church fellowship.

discontinuance (dis-kən-**tin**-yoo-ənts), *n.* **1.** The termination of a lawsuit by the plaintiff; a voluntary dismissal or nonsuit. See DISMISSAL; NONSUIT. **2.** The termination of an estate-tail by a tenant in tail who conveys a larger estate in the land than is legally allowed.

> "Such is . . . the injury of *discontinuance*; which happens when he who hath an estate-tail, maketh a larger estate of the land than by law he is entitled to do: in which case the estate is good, so far as his power extends who made it, but no farther. As if tenant in tail makes a feoffment in fee-simple, or for the life of the feoffee, or in tail; all which are beyond his power to make, for that by the common law extends no farther than to make a lease for his own life: the entry of the feoffee is lawful during the life of the feoffer; but if he retains the possession after the death of the feoffor, it is an injury, which is termed a discontinuance; the ancient legal estate, which ought to have survived to the heir in tail, being gone, or at least suspended, and for a while discontinued." 3 William Blackstone, *Commentaries on the Laws of England* 171–72 (1768).

discontinuee, *n.* A person who receives an entailed estate from the tenant in tail; one whose acquisition of an entailed estate causes a discontinuance of the fee tail heirs' right to the estate. Cf. DISCONTINUOR.

discontinuing easement. See *discontinuous easement* under EASEMENT.

discontinuor, *n.* A tenant in tail whose conveyance of the entailed estate causes a discontinuance. Cf. DISCONTINUEE.

discontinuous easement. See EASEMENT.

disconvenable (dis-kən-**vee**-nə-bəl), *adj.* [Law French] *Archaic.* Unfit; improper.

discount, *n.* **1.** A reduction from the full amount or value of something, esp. a price. **2.** An advance deduction of interest when a person lends money on a note, bill of exchange, or other commercial paper, resulting in its present value. See PRESENT VALUE. **3.** The amount by which a security's market value is below its face value. Cf. PREMIUM (3). — **discount,** *vb.*

bulk discount. See *volume discount.*

cash discount. **1.** A seller's price reduction in exchange for an immediate cash payment. **2.** A reduction from the stated price if the bill is paid on or before a specified date.

functional discount. **1.** A supplier's price discount given to a purchaser based on the purchaser's role (such as warehousing or advertising) in the supplier's distributive system. • This type of discount typically reflects the value of services performed by the purchaser for the supplier. If a functional discount constitutes a reasonable reimbursement for the purchaser's actual marketing functions, it does not constitute unlawful price discrimination and does not violate antitrust laws. **2.** A supplier's price discount based on the purchaser's relative distance from the supplier in the chain of distribution. • For example, a wholesaler or distributor usu. receives a greater discount than a retailer.

quantity discount. See *volume discount.*

trade discount. **1.** A discount from list price offered to all customers of a given type — for example, a discount offered by a lumber dealer to building contractors. **2.** The difference between a seller's list price and the price at which the dealer actually sells goods to the trade.

volume discount. A price decrease based on a large-quantity purchase. — Also termed *bulk discount*; *quantity discount*.

discount bond. See BOND (3).

discount broker. See BROKER.

discounted cash flow. See CASH FLOW.

discount interest. See INTEREST (3).

discount loan. See LOAN.

discount market. See MARKET.

discount rate. See INTEREST RATE.

discount share. See *discount stock* under STOCK.

discount stock. See STOCK.

discount yield. See YIELD.

discoverable, *adj.* Subject to pretrial discovery <the defendant's attorney argued that the defendant's income-tax returns were not discoverable during the liability phase of the trial>.

discovered-peril doctrine. See LAST-CLEAR-CHANCE DOCTRINE.

discovert (dis-**kəv**-ərt), *adj.* **1.** *Archaic.* Uncovered; exposed. **2.** Not married, esp. a widow or a woman who has never married.

discovery, *n.* **1.** The act or process of finding or learning something that was previously unknown <after making the discovery, the inventor immediately applied for a patent>. **2.** Compulsory disclosure, at a party's request, of information that relates to the litigation <the plaintiff filed a motion to compel discovery>. • The primary discovery devices are interrogatories, depositions, requests for admissions, and requests for production. Although discovery typically comes from parties, courts also allow limited discovery from nonparties. **3.** The facts or documents disclosed <the new associate spent all her time reviewing discovery>. — **discover,** *vb.* — **discoverable,** *adj.*

"Discovery has broad scope. According to Federal Rule 26, which is the model in modern procedural codes, inquiry may be made into 'any matter, not privileged, that is relevant to the subject matter of the action.' Thus, discovery may be had of facts incidentally relevant to the issues in the pleadings even if the facts do not directly prove or disprove the facts in question." Geoffrey C. Hazard, Jr. & Michele Taruffo, *American Civil Procedure: An Introduction* 115 (1993).

postjudgment discovery. Discovery conducted after judgment has been rendered, usu. to determine the nature of the judgment debtor's assets or to obtain testimony for use in future proceedings. — Also termed *posttrial discovery*.

pretrial discovery. Discovery conducted before trial to reveal facts and develop evidence. • Modern procedural rules have broadened the scope of pretrial discovery to prevent the parties from surprising each other with evidence at trial.

discovery abuse. 1. The misuse of the discovery process, esp. by making overbroad requests for information that is unnecessary or beyond the scope of permissible disclosure. **2.** The failure to respond adequately to proper discovery requests. — Also termed *abuse of discovery*.

"The term 'discovery abuse' has been used as if it were a single concept, but it includes several different things. Thus, it is useful to subdivide 'abuse' into 'misuse' and 'overuse.' What is referred to as 'misuse' would include not only direct violation of the rules, as by failing to respond to a discovery request within the stated time limit, but also more subtle attempts to harass or obstruct an opponent, as by giving obviously inadequate answers or by requesting information that clearly is outside the scope of discovery. By 'overuse' is meant asking for more discovery than is necessary or appropriate to the particular case. 'Overuse,' in turn, can be subdivided into problems of 'depth' and of 'breadth,' with 'depth' referring to discovery that may be relevant but is simply excessive and 'breadth' referring to discovery requests that go into matters too far removed from the case." Charles Alan Wright, *The Law of Federal Courts* § 81, at 580 (5th ed. 1994).

discovery immunity. A (usu. statutory) prohibition that excludes certain documents or information from discovery.

discovery policy. See *claims-made policy* under INSURANCE POLICY.

discovery rule. *Civil procedure.* The rule that a limitations period does not begin to run until the plaintiff discovers (or reasonably should have discovered) the injury giving rise to the claim. • The discovery rule usu. applies to injuries that are inherently difficult to detect, such as those resulting from medical malpractice. See STATUTE OF LIMITATIONS. Cf. OCCURRENCE RULE.

discovery vein. See VEIN.

discredit, *vb.* To destroy or impair the credibility of (a witness, a piece of evidence, or a theory); to lessen the degree of trust to be accorded to (a witness or document). — **discredit,** *n.*

discreet (di-**skreet**), *adj.* Exercising discretion; prudent; judicious; discerning.

discrete (di-**skreet**), *adj.* Individual; separate; distinct.

discretion (di-**skresh**-ən). **1.** A public official's power or right to act in certain circumstances according to personal judgment and conscience. — Also termed *discretionary power.*

administrative discretion. A public official's or agency's power to exercise judgment in the discharge of its duties.

judicial discretion. The exercise of judgment by a judge or court based on what is fair under the circumstances and guided by the rules and principles of law; a court's power to act or not act when a litigant is not entitled to demand the act as a matter of right. — Also termed *legal discretion.*

prosecutorial discretion. A prosecutor's power to choose from the options available in a criminal case, such as filing charges, prosecuting, plea-bargaining, and recommending a sentence to the court.

2. *Criminal & tort law.* The capacity to distinguish between right and wrong, sufficient to make a person responsible for his or her own actions. **3.** Wise conduct and management; cautious discernment; prudence.

discretion, abuse of. See ABUSE OF DISCRETION.

discretionary (di-**skresh**-ə-ner-ee), *adj.* (Of an act or duty) involving an exercise of judgment and choice, not an implementation of a hard-and-fast rule. • Such an act by a court may be overturned only after a showing of abuse of discretion.

discretionary account. An account that allows a broker access to a customer's funds to purchase and sell securities or commodities for the customer based on the broker's judgment and without first having to obtain the customer's consent to the purchase or sale.

discretionary act. A deed involving an exercise of personal judgment and conscience. — Also termed *discretionary function.* See DISCRETION; ABUSE OF DISCRETION.

discretionary damages. See DAMAGES.

discretionary function. See DISCRETIONARY ACT.

discretionary immunity. See IMMUNITY (1).

discretionary order. See ORDER (4).

discretionary power. See DISCRETION (1).

discretionary review. See REVIEW.

discretionary trust. See TRUST.

discriminant function (di-**skrim**-ə-nənt). An IRS method of selecting tax returns to be audited. • The method consists of (1) using a computer program to identify returns with a high probability of error (such as those showing a disproportionate amount of deductible expenses), and (2) having examiners manually review the selected returns to determine which ones should be audited. — Also termed *DIF system.*

discriminatee (di-skrim-ə-nə-**tee**). A person unlawfully discriminated against.

discrimination, *n.* **1.** The effect of a law or established practice that confers privileges on a certain class or that denies privileges to a certain class because of race, age, sex, nationality, religion, or handicap. • Federal law, including Title VII of the Civil Rights Act, prohibits employment discrimination based on any one of those characteristics. Other federal statutes, supplemented by court decisions, prohibit discrimination in voting rights, housing, credit extension, public education, and access to public facilities. State laws provide further protections against discrimination. **2.** Differential treatment; esp., a failure to treat all persons equally when no reasonable distinction can be found between those favored and those not favored.

> "The dictionary sense of 'discrimination' is neutral while the current political use of the term is frequently non-neutral, pejorative. With both a neutral and a non-neutral use of the word having currency, the opportunity for confusion in arguments about racial discrimination is enormously multiplied. For some, it may be enough that a practice is called discriminatory for them to judge it wrong. Others may be mystified that the first group condemns the practice without further argument or inquiry. Many may be led to the false sense that they have

actually made a moral argument by showing that the practice discriminates (distinguishes in favor of or against). The temptation is to move from '*X* distinguishes in favor of or against' to '*X* discriminates' to '*X* is wrong' without being aware of the equivocation involved." Robert K. Fullinwider, *The Reverse Discrimination Controversy* 11–12 (1980).

age discrimination. Discrimination based on age. • Federal law prohibits age discrimination in employment against people who are age 40 or older.

gender discrimination. See *sex discrimination*.

invidious discrimination (in-**vid**-ee-əs). Discrimination that is offensive or objectionable, esp. because it involves prejudice or stereotyping.

racial discrimination. Discrimination based on race.

reverse discrimination. Preferential treatment of minorities, usu. through affirmative-action programs, in a way that adversely affects members of a majority group. See AFFIRMATIVE ACTION.

sex discrimination. Discrimination based on gender, esp. against women. — Also termed *gender discrimination*.

3. The effect of state laws that favor local interests over out-of-state interests. • Such a discriminatory state law may still be upheld if it is narrowly tailored to achieve an important state interest. — **discriminate,** *vb.* — **discriminatory,** *adj.* Cf. FAVORITISM.

discriminatory tariff. See TARIFF (2).

discussion. 1. The act of exchanging views on something; a debate. **2.** *Civil law.* A creditor's act of exhausting all remedies against the principal debtor before proceeding against the guarantor. See BENEFIT OF DISCUSSION.

disease. 1. A deviation from the healthy and normal functioning of the body <the drug could not be linked to his disease>. **2.** (*pl.*) Special classes of pathological conditions with similar traits, such as having similar causes and affecting similar organs <respiratory diseases> <occupational diseases>. **3.** Any disorder; any depraved condition.

functional disease. A disease that prevents, obstructs, or interferes with an organ's special function, without anatomical defect or abnormality in the organ itself.

industrial disease. See OCCUPATIONAL DISEASE.

occupational disease. See OCCUPATIONAL DISEASE.

organic disease. A disease that is caused by an injury to, or lesion or malfunction in, an organ.

disembarrass, *vb.* To free from embarrassment; to extricate or disentangle one thing from another.

disenfranchise (dis-ən-**fran**-chɪz), *vb.* To deprive (a person) of the right to exercise a franchise or privilege, esp. to vote. — Also termed *disfranchise*.

disenfranchisement (dis-ən-**fran**-chiz-mənt *or* -**fran**-chɪz-mənt). **1.** The act of depriving a member of a corporation or other organization of a right, as by expulsion. **2.** The act of taking away the right to vote in public elections from a citizen or class of citizens. — Also termed *disfranchisement*.

disentailing deed. See DEED.

disentailing statute (dis-ən-**tayl**-ing). A statute regulating or prohibiting disentailing deeds. See *disentailing deed* under DEED.

disentailment (dis-ən-**tayl**-mənt), *n.* The act or process by which a tenant in tail bars the entail on an estate and converts it into a fee simple, thereby nullifying the rights of any later claimant to the fee tail. — **disentail,** *vb.*

disentitle (dis-ən-**tɪt**-əl), *vb.* To deprive (someone) of a title or claim <the plaintiff's actions disentitled her from recovering damages>.

disfacere. See DIFFACERE.

disfigurement (dis-**fig**-yər-mənt). An impairment or injury to the appearance of a person or thing.

disfranchise. See DISENFRANCHISE.

disfranchisement. See DISENFRANCHISEMENT.

disgavel (dis-**gav**-əl), *vb. Hist.* To convert (gavelkind land) into ordinary freehold land. See GAVELKIND.

disgorgement, *n.* The act of giving up something (such as profits illegally obtained) on demand or by legal compulsion. — **disgorge,** *vb.*

disgrading. *Hist.* **1.** The act of degrading. **2.** The depriving of an order; the depriving of a dignity.

> "Disgrading, or degrading, is when a man having taken upon him a dignity temporal or spiritual, is afterwards thereof deprived, be he knight, clerk or other. Whereof if a clerk be delivered to his ordinary, and cannot clear himself of the offence whereof he is convicted by the jury, he shall be disgraded for it; which is nothing else but the deprivation of him from those orders he hath taken upon him, as priesthood, deaconship, or otherwise.... In like manner there is disgrading of a knight .... And it is worthy the observation, that by the canon law there are two kinds of disgradings; the one summary, by word only, and the other solemn, by devesting the party disgraded from those ornaments and rites which are the ensigns of his order or degree." *Termes de la Ley* 175–76 (1st Am. ed. 1812).

disguised dividend. See *informal dividend* under DIVIDEND.

disguised installment sale. See INSTALLMENT SALE.

disherison (dis-**her**-ə-zən). See DISINHERITANCE.

disheritor (dis-**her**-ə-tər *or* -tor). *Archaic.* A person who deprives someone of an inheritance.

dishonest act. See FRAUDULENT ACT.

dishonor, *vb.* **1.** To refuse to accept or pay (a negotiable instrument) when presented. See NOTICE OF DISHONOR; WRONGFUL DISHONOR. **2.** To deface or defile (something, such as a flag). — **dishonor,** *n.*

dishonorable discharge. See DISCHARGE (8).

disincarcerate, *vb.* To release (a person) from jail; to set free.

disincentive, *n.* A deterrent (to a particular type of conduct), often created, intentionally or unintentionally, through legislation <federal tax law creates a disincentive to marriage> <sales taxes provide a disincentive to excessive consumer spending>.

disinflation. A period or process of slowing down the rate of inflation. Cf. DEFLATION.

disinherison (dis-in-**her**-ə-zən), *n.* See DISINHERITANCE.

disinheritance, *n.* **1.** The act by which an owner of an estate deprives a would-be heir of the expectancy to inherit the estate. **2.** The state of being disinherited. — Also termed *disherison*; *disinherison.* — **disinherit,** *vb.*

disinter (dis-in-**tər**), *vb.* **1.** To exhume (a corpse). **2.** To remove (something) from obscurity. — **disinterment** (dis-in-**tər**-mənt), *n.*

disinterested, *adj.* Free from bias, prejudice, or partiality; not having a pecuniary interest <a disinterested witness>. — **disinterest, disinterestedness,** *n.*

disinterested witness. See WITNESS.

disintermediation. The process of bank depositors' withdrawing their funds from accounts with low interest rates to put them into investments that pay higher returns.

disinvestment, *n.* **1.** The consumption of capital. **2.** The withdrawal of investments, esp. on political grounds. — Also termed (in sense 2) *divestment.* — **disinvest,** *vb.*

disjoinder (dis-**joyn**-dər). The undoing of the joinder of parties or claims. See JOINDER. Cf. MISJOINDER; NONJOINDER.

disjuncta (dis-**jəngk**-tə), *n.* [Latin] *Roman & civil law.* Things (usu. words or phrases) that are separated or opposed. — Also spelled *disiuncta.* Cf. CONJUNCTA.

disjunctim (dis-**jəngk**-təm), *adv.* [Latin] *Roman law.* Separately; severally. • A condition imposed *disjunctim,* for example, would bind the persons severally, rather than jointly. — Also spelled *disiunctim.* Cf. CONJUNCTIM.

disjunctive allegation. See ALLEGATION.

disjunctive condition. See CONDITION (2).

disjunctive denial. See DENIAL.

disme (dɪm), *n.* [Law French] A tithe; a tenth part, as in a tithe due the clergy equal to the tenth of all spiritual livings as required by the statute 25 Edw. 3, st. 7. • This is the Law French equivalent to the Latin *decimae.* Pl. ***dismes.*** See DECIMAE.

dismemberment. *Archaic. Int'l law.* **1.** The disappearance of a country as a result of a treaty or an annexation, whereby it becomes part of one or more other countries. **2.** The reduction of a country's territory by annexation or cession, or the secession of one part. **3.** The extinguishment of a country and the creation of two or more new countries from the former country's territory.

dismiss, *vb.* **1.** To send (something) away; specif., to terminate (an action or claim) without further hearing, esp. before the trial of the issues involved. **2.** To release or discharge (a person) from employment. See DISMISSAL.

dismissal, *n.* **1.** Termination of an action or claim without further hearing, esp. before the trial of the issues involved.

dismissal for failure to prosecute. See *dismissal for want of prosecution.*

dismissal for want of equity. A court's dismissal of a lawsuit on substantive, rather than procedural, grounds, usu. because the plaintiff's allegations are found to be untrue or because the plaintiff's pleading does not state an adequate claim.

dismissal for want of prosecution. A court's dismissal of a lawsuit because the plaintiff has failed to pursue the case diligently toward completion. — Abbr. DWOP. — Also termed *dismissal for failure to prosecute.*

dismissal without prejudice. A dismissal that does not bar the plaintiff from refiling the lawsuit within the applicable limitations period.

dismissal with prejudice. A dismissal, usu. after an adjudication on the merits, barring the plaintiff from prosecuting any later lawsuit on the same claim. • If, after a dismissal with prejudice, the plaintiff files a later suit on the same claim, the defendant in the later suit can assert the defense of res judicata (claim preclusion). See RES JUDICATA.

involuntary dismissal. A court's dismissal of a lawsuit because the plaintiff failed to prosecute or failed to comply with a procedural rule or court order. Fed. R. Civ. P. 41(b).

voluntary dismissal. A plaintiff's dismissal of a lawsuit at the plaintiff's own request or by stipulation of all the parties. Fed. R. Civ. P. 41(a).

2. A release or discharge from employment. See DISCHARGE (7).

dismissal for cause. A dismissal of a contract employee for a reason that the law or public policy has recognized as sufficient to warrant the employee's removal.

3. *Military law.* A court-martial punishment for an officer, commissioned warrant officer, cadet, or midshipman, consisting of separation from the armed services with dishonor. • A dismissal can be given only by a general court-martial and is considered the equivalent of a dishonorable discharge. — **dismiss,** *vb.*

dismissal compensation. See SEVERANCE PAY.

dismissal for cause. See DISMISSAL (2).

dismissal for failure to prosecute. See *dismissal for want of prosecution* under DISMISSAL (1).

dismissal for want of equity. See DISMISSAL (1).

dismissal for want of prosecution. See DISMISSAL (1).

dismissal without prejudice. See DISMISSAL (1).

dismissal with prejudice. See DISMISSAL (1).

dismissed for want of equity. (Of a case) removed from the court's docket for substantive reasons, usu. because the plaintiff's allegations are found to be untrue or because the plaintiff's pleading does not state an adequate claim. See *dismissal for want of equity* under DISMISSAL (1).

dismissed for want of prosecution. (Of a case) removed from the court's docket because the plaintiff has failed to pursue the case diligently toward completion. See *dismissal for want of prosecution* under DISMISSAL (1).

dismissed without prejudice. (Of a case) removed from the court's docket in such a way that the plaintiff may refile the same suit on the same claim. See *dismissal without prejudice* under DISMISSAL (1); WITHOUT PREJUDICE.

dismissed with prejudice. (Of a case) removed from the court's docket in such a way that the plaintiff is foreclosed from filing a suit again on the same claim or claims. See *dismissal with prejudice* under DISMISSAL (1); WITH PREJUDICE.

dismission. *Archaic.* **1.** An act of dismissing <dismission of the jury>. **2.** A removal, esp. from office or position <dismission of the employee>. **3.** A decision that a suit cannot be maintained <dismission of the case>.

dismortgage. See REDEMPTION (4).

disobedient child. See *incorrigible child* under CHILD.

disorder. 1. A lack of proper arrangement <disorder of the files>. **2.** An irregularity <a disorder in the proceedings>. **3.** A public disturbance; a riot <civil disorder>. **4.** A disturbance in mental or physical health <an emotional disorder> <a liver disorder>.

disorderly conduct. See CONDUCT.

disorderly house. 1. A dwelling where people carry on activities that are a nuisance to the neighborhood. **2.** A dwelling where people conduct criminal or immoral activities. • Examples are brothels and drug houses. — Also termed *bawdy house*; *house of prostitution*; *house of ill fame*; *lewd house*.

> "The keeping of one type of disorderly house — the bawdy house — is punished because it violates the social interest in maintaining proper standards of morality and decency.... As included here a house may be disorderly for other reasons. Any house in which disorderly persons are permitted to congregate, and to disturb the tranquillity of the neighborhood by fighting, quarreling, swearing or any other type of disorder, is a disorderly house; and the keeping thereof is a misdemeanor at common law." Rollin M. Perkins & Ronald N. Boyce, *Criminal Law* 487 (3d ed. 1982).

disorderly person. 1. A person guilty of disorderly conduct. **2.** A person who breaches the peace, order, decency, or safety of the public, as defined by statute.

> "Ordinarily, a person who is guilty of disorderly conduct is a 'disorderly person,' but where statutes define 'a disorderly person' and distinguish acts which may constitute the offense of disorderly conduct, the distinction is to be preserved and the different provisions relative to the different offenses particularly followed." 27 C.J.S. *Disorderly Conduct* § 1(1), at 509 (1959).

disparagare (di-spar-ə-**gair**-ee), *vb.* [Law Latin fr. Law French *disparager* "to disparage"] *Hist.* **1.** To disparage. **2.** To bring together unequal persons, as in a marriage between persons of unequal lineage. Cf. PARAGE.

disparagatio (di-spar-ə-**gay**-shee-oh), *n.* [Law Latin] *Hist.* Disparagement in marriage.

disparagation (di-spar-ə-**gay**-shən), *n.* [Law French] *Hist.* **1.** Disparagement. **2.** A marriage below one's station.

disparage (di-**spar**-ij), *vb.* **1.** *Hist.* To connect unequally (e.g., to marry below one's status). **2.** To dishonor (something or someone) by comparison. **3.** To unjustly discredit or detract from the reputation of (another's property, product, or business).

disparagement (di-**spar**-ij-mənt), *n.* A false and injurious statement that discredits or detracts from the reputation of another's property, product, or business. • To recover in tort for disparagement, the plaintiff must prove that the statement caused a third party to take some action resulting in specific pecuniary loss to the plaintiff. — Also termed *injurious falsehood*. — More narrowly termed *slander of title*; *trade libel*; *slander of goods*. Cf. DEFAMATION.

disparaging instruction. A jury charge that discredits or defames a party to a lawsuit.

disparate impact (**dis**-pə-rit). The adverse effect of a facially neutral practice (esp. an employment practice) that nonetheless discriminates against persons because of their race, sex, national origin, age, or disability and that is not justified by business necessity. • Discriminatory intent is irrelevant in a disparate-impact claim. — Also termed *adverse impact*.

disparate treatment. The practice, esp. in employment, of intentionally dealing with persons differently because of their race, sex, national origin, age, or disability. • To succeed on a disparate-treatment claim, the plaintiff must prove that the defendant acted with discriminatory intent or motive.

disparity (di-**spar**-ə-tee). Inequality; a difference in quantity or quality between two or more things.

dispatch (di-**spach** *also* **dis**-pach), *n.* **1.** A prompt sending off of something <a dispatch of the letter agreement>. **2.** A prompt completion of something <dispatch of a business transaction>. **3.** Something quickly sent <the dispatch was mailed>. **4.** *Maritime law.* The required diligence in discharging cargo <dispatch is required on all charters>.

customary dispatch. Dispatch that follows the rules, customs, and usages of the port where cargo is discharged.

quick dispatch. A speedy dispatch that does not strictly follow the customs of the port, esp. to avoid delays resulting from a crowded wharf.

5. *Maritime law.* DISPATCH MONEY.

dispatch money. *Maritime law.* An amount paid by a shipowner to a vessel's charterer if the vessel's cargo is unloaded at the port sooner than provided for in the agreement between the charterer and the shipowner. — Also termed *dispatch*. Cf. *contract demurrage* under DEMURRAGE.

> "Some charters contain a provision for 'dispatch money,' which is in the nature of a reward to the charterer for loading or unloading more rapidly than provided for — *i.e.*, in less time than the stipulated 'lay days.' Dispatch, where payable, is usually stated, just as is demurrage, in terms of a rate per day and pro rata part thereof." Grant Gilmore & Charles L. Black, Jr., *The Law of Admiralty* § 4–8, at 212 (2d ed. 1975).

dispauper (dis-**paw**-pər), *vb.* To disqualify from being a pauper; to deprive (a person) of the ability to sue *in forma pauperis*. See IN FORMA PAUPERIS.

dispensary (di-**spen**-sər-ee), *n.* **1.** A place where drugs are prepared or distributed. **2.** An institution, usu. for the poor, where medical advice and medicines are distributed for free or at a discounted rate.

dispensation (dis-pen-**say**-shən). An exemption from a law, duty, or penalty; permission to do something that is ordinarily forbidden.

dispersonare (dis-pər-sə-**nair**-ee), *vb.* [Latin] *Hist.* To scandalize, disparage, or slander.

displacement. 1. Removal from a proper place or position <displacement of a file> <displacement of an officer>. **2.** A replacement; a substitution <displacement of the lawyer with another>. **3.** A forced removal of a person from the person's home or country, esp. because of war <displacement of refugees>. **4.** A shifting of emotional emphasis from one thing to another, esp. to avoid unpleasant or unacceptable thoughts or tendencies <emotional displacement>.

display right. *Copyright.* A copyright holder's exclusive right to show or exhibit a copy of the protected work publicly, whether directly or by technological means. • For example, this right makes it illegal to transmit a copyrighted work over the Internet without permission.

dispone (dis-**pohn**), *vb.* [fr. Middle English *disponen* fr. Old French *disponer* "dispose"] **1.** *Archaic.* To dispose; to arrange. **2.** *Scots law.* To convey, transfer, or otherwise alienate (property).

disponee. See ALIENEE.

dispono (dis-**poh**-noh), *vb.* [Latin] *Scots law.* To grant or convey (land, etc.).

disponor. See ALIENOR.

disposable earnings. See *disposable income* under INCOME.

disposable income. See INCOME.

disposable portion. The portion of property that can be willed to anyone the testator chooses.

disposing capacity. See *testamentary capacity* under CAPACITY (3).

Disposing Clause. The clause of the U.S. Constitution giving Congress the power to dispose of property belonging to the federal government. U.S. Const. art. IV, § 3, cl. 2.

disposition (dis-pə-**zish**-ən), *n.* **1.** The act of transferring something to another's care or possession, esp. by deed or will; the relinquishing of property <a testamentary disposition of all the assets>. **2.** A final settlement or determination <the court's disposition of the case>.

ambulatory disposition. A judgment or sentence that is subject to amendment or revocation.

3. Temperament or character; personal makeup <a surly disposition>. — **dispose,** *vb.* — **dispositive,** *adj.*

disposition hearing. See HEARING.

disposition without a trial. The final determination of a criminal case without a trial on the merits, as when a defendant pleads guilty or admits sufficient facts to support a guilty finding without a trial.

dispositive (dis-**poz**-ə-tiv), *adj.* Being a deciding factor; (of a fact or factor) bringing about a final determination.

dispositive clause. *Scots law.* In a deed, the clause of conveyance by which the grantor directs how to dispose of the property.

dispositive fact. See FACT.

dispositive treaty. See TREATY.

dispossess (dis-pə-**zes**), *vb.* To oust or evict (someone) from property. See DISPOSSESSION.

dispossession (dis-pə-**zesh**-ən), *n.* Deprivation of, or eviction from, possession of property; ouster.

dispossessor. A person who dispossesses.

dispossess proceeding. A summary procedure initiated by a landlord to oust a defaulting tenant and regain possession of the premises. See FORCIBLE ENTRY AND DETAINER.

disprove, *vb.* To refute (an assertion); to prove (an allegation) false.

dispunishable, *adj. Hist.* (Of an offense) not punishable; not answerable.

disputable presumption. See *rebuttable presumption* under PRESUMPTION.

disputatio fori (dis-pyoo-**tay**-shee-oh **for**-I), *n.* [Latin] *Roman law.* Argument before a court; the practice of legal advocacy.

dispute, *n.* A conflict or controversy, esp. one that has given rise to a particular lawsuit. — **dispute,** *vb.*

major dispute. *Labor law.* Under the Railway Labor Act, a disagreement about basic working conditions, often resulting in a new collective-bargaining agreement or a change in the existing agreement. • Under the Act, two classes of disputes — major and minor — are subject to mandatory arbitration. 45 USCA § 155. — Also termed *new-contract dispute.*

minor dispute. *Labor law.* Under the Railway Labor Act, a disagreement about the interpretation or application of a collective-bargaining agreement, as opposed to a disagreement over the formation of a new agreement. 45 USCA § 155.

disqualification, *n.* **1.** Something that makes one ineligible; esp., a bias or conflict of interest that prevents a judge or juror from impartially hearing a case, or that prevents a lawyer from representing a party.

vicarious disqualification. Disqualification of all the lawyers in a firm or in an office because one of the lawyers is ethically disqualified from representing the client at issue. — Also termed *imputed disqualification.*

"In general, disqualification of a lawyer from representation, at least in multiple client-conflict scenarios, means disqualification of that lawyer's entire firm from the same representation. When a lawyer has been exclusively or chiefly responsible for the representation of a client and that lawyer changes jobs, there is little question but that the imputed-disqualification rule will apply to disqualify the new firm from representing the opponent of the first client. But because lawyers often work for large organizations, . . . a question may arise about the application of the imputation rule when a lawyer has left employment . . . . If the lawyer had little or no responsibility in the first organization for the representation or if the lawyer can be effectively shielded from the representation in the new organization, or both, there may be no useful purpose served by imputing the lawyer's disqualification to the new organization . . . ." James E. Moliterno & John M. Levy, *Ethics of the Lawyer's Work* 151 (1993).

2. The act of making ineligible; the fact or condition of being ineligible. — **disqualify,** *vb.* Cf. RECUSAL.

disrate, *vb.* To reduce to a lower rank; esp., to reduce a ship or petty officer's rank.

disrationare (dis-ray-shee-ə-**nair**-ee), *n.* [Law Latin fr. Law French *desreigner* "to deraign"] *Hist.* To prove; to establish a title.

disregarding the corporate entity. See PIERCING THE CORPORATE VEIL.

disrepair. A state of being in need of restoration after deterioration or injury.

disrepute. A loss of reputation; dishonor.

disruptive conduct. See CONDUCT.

disseise (dis-**seez**), *vb.* To wrongfully deprive (a person) of the freehold possession of property.

disseisee (dis-see-**zee**). A person who is wrongfully deprived of the freehold possession of property. — Also termed *disseisitus.*

disseisin (dis-**see**-zin), *n.* The act of wrongfully depriving someone of the freehold possession of property; DISPOSSESSION. — Also spelled *disseizin.*

fresh disseisin. The right at common law of a person disseised of land to forcefully eject the disseisor from the land without resort to law, as long as the ejection occurred soon after the disseisin.

disseisitrix. See DISSEISORESS.

disseisitus. See DISSEISEE.

disseisor (dis-**see**-zər *or* -zor). A person who wrongfully deprives another of the freehold possession of property.

disseisoress (dis-**see**-zər-is). *Hist.* A female disseisor. — Also termed *disseisitrix*.

dissemble (di-**sem**-bəl), *vb.* **1.** *Archaic.* To physically disguise <to dissemble by wearing a mask>. **2.** To give a false impression about (something); to cover up (something) by deception <to dissemble the facts>.

dissensus (di-**sen**-səs), *n.* [Latin "disagreement"] *Roman law.* A mutually agreed annulment of a contractual obligation; an undoing of the *consensus* that created the obligation.

dissent (di-**sent**), *n.* **1.** A disagreement with a majority opinion, esp. among judges. **2.** See *dissenting opinion* under OPINION (1). **3.** A withholding of assent or approval. — **dissent** (di-**sent**), *vb.*

dissent and appraisal, right of. See APPRAISAL REMEDY.

dissenters' right. See APPRAISAL REMEDY.

dissentiente (di-sen-shee-**en**-tee). [Latin] Dissenting. • When used with a judge's name, it indicates a dissenting opinion.

dissenting opinion. See OPINION (1).

dissignare (di-sig-**nair**-ee), *vb.* [Law Latin] To break open a seal.

dissipation. The use of an asset for an illegal or inequitable purpose, such as a spouse's use of community property for personal benefit when a divorce is imminent.

dissolute, *adj.* (Of a person or thing) loosed from restraint; wanton; devoted to pleasure <dissolute person> <a dissolute lifestyle>.

dissolution (dis-ə-**loo**-shən), *n.* **1.** The act of bringing to an end; termination. **2.** The cancellation or abrogation of a contract, with the effect of annulling the contract's binding force and restoring the parties to their original positions. See RESCISSION. **3.** The termination of a corporation's legal existence by expiration of its charter, by legislative act, by bankruptcy, or by other means; the event immediately preceding the liquidation or winding-up process.

de facto dissolution. The termination and liquidation of a corporation's business, esp. because of an inability to pay its debts.

involuntary dissolution. The termination of a corporation administratively (for failure to file reports or pay taxes), judicially (for abuse of corporate authority, management deadlock, or failure to pay creditors), or through involuntary bankruptcy.

voluntary dissolution. A corporation's termination initiated by the board of directors and approved by the shareholders.

4. The termination of a previously existing partnership upon the occurrence of an event specified in the partnership agreement, such as a partner's withdrawal from the partnership. Cf. WINDING UP. — **dissolve,** *vb.*

dissolution bond. See *discharging bond* under BOND (2).

dissolution of marriage. See DIVORCE.

dissolving condition. See *resolutory condition* under CONDITION (2).

dissuade, *vb.* To persuade (someone) not to do something <to dissuade the expert from testifying>.

distincte et aperte (dis-**tingk**-tee et ə-**pər**-tee). [Law Latin] Distinctly; openly. • This phrase was formerly used in writs of error to refer to the return required to be made.

distinctive name. See NAME.

distinctiveness, *n.* The quality of a trademarked word, symbol, or device that identifies the goods of a particular merchant and distinguishes them from the goods of others. — **distinctive,** *adj.*

distinguish, *vb.* **1.** To note a significant factual, procedural, or legal difference in (an earlier case), usu. to minimize the case's precedential effect or to show that it is inapplicable <the lawyer distinguished the cited case from the case at bar>.

> "In practice, courts do not concede to their predecessors the power of laying down very wide rules; they reserve to themselves the power to narrow such rules by introducing into them particular facts of the precedent case that were treated by the earlier court as irrelevant. This process is known as 'distinguishing.'" John Salmond, *Jurisprudence* 192 (Glanville L. Williams ed., 10th ed. 1947).

2. To make a distinction <the court distinguished between willful and reckless conduct>. — **distinction,** *n.*

distinguishable, *adj.* (Of a case or law) different from, and thereby not controlling or applicable in, a given case or situation.

distinguishing mark. A physical indication or feature that identifies or delineates one person or thing from another <the voting ballots contained distinguishing marks so that they could not be counted>. See DISTINCTIVENESS.

distracted, *adj.* **1.** (Of a person) not concentrating. **2.** (Of a person) disordered.

distractio (di-**strak**-shee-oh), *n.* [Latin fr. *distrahere* "to draw apart"] *Roman law.* A separation or division into parts; an alienation or sale, such as a creditor's sale of a pledge.

distractio bonorum (di-**strak**-shee-oh bə-**nor**-əm), *n.* [Latin "the sale of goods"] *Roman law.* A curator's sale of the property of an insolvent estate to satisfy creditors' claims.

distraction doctrine. The rule that a plaintiff may not be guilty of contributory negligence if the plaintiff's attention was diverted from a known danger by a sufficient cause. See *contributory negligence* under NEGLIGENCE.

distractio pignoris (di-**strak**-shee-oh pig-**nor**-is), *n.* [Latin "the sale of something pledged"] *Roman law.* A creditor's sale of something pledged or hypothecated to obtain satisfaction on a debt.

distrahere (dis-**tray**-hə-ree), *vb.* [fr. Latin *dis* "apart" + *trahere* "to draw"] To draw apart; to sell; to dissolve, as in a contract.

distrain, *vb.* **1.** To force (a person, usu. a tenant), by the seizure and detention of personal property, to perform an obligation (such as paying overdue rent). **2.** To seize (goods) by distress, a legal remedy entitling the rightful owner to recover property wrongfully taken. — **distraint,** *n.*

distrainee. One who is, or whose property is, distrained.

distrainer. Someone who seizes property under a distress. — Also spelled *distrainor.*

distraint. See DISTRESS.

distress, *n.* **1.** The seizure of another's property to secure the performance of a duty, such as the payment of overdue rent. **2.** The legal remedy authorizing such a seizure; the procedure by which the seizure is carried out.

distress damage feasant. The right to seize animals or inanimate chattels that are damaging or encumbering land and to keep them as security until the owner pays compensation.

distress infinite. A distress that the sheriff can repeat from time to time to enforce the performance of something, as in summoning a juror or compelling a party to appear in court. • The goods must be returned after the delinquent person performs his or her duty.

> "And, for the most part it is provided that distresses be reasonable and moderate; but, in the case of distress for fealty or suit of court, no distress can be unreasonable, immoderate, or too large: for this is the only remedy to which the party aggrieved is entitled, and therefore it ought to be such as is sufficiently compulsory; and, be it of what value it will, there is no harm done, especially as it cannot be sold or made away with, but must be restored immediately on satisfaction made. A distress of this nature, that has no bounds with regard to its quantity, and may be repeated from time to time until the stubbornness of the party is conquered, is called a *distress infinite.*" 3 William Blackstone, *Commentaries on the Laws of England* 231 (1768).

grand distress. *Hist.* In a *quare impedit* action in which the defendant has failed to appear, a distress of the defendant's goods and lands to compel the defendant's appearance.

second distress. A supplementary distress allowed when goods seized under the first distress are insufficient to satisfy the claim.

3. The property seized. — Also termed *distraint.*

distressed goods. See GOODS.

distressed property. See PROPERTY.

distress sale. See SALE.

distress warrant. See WARRANT (1).

distributable net income. The amount of distributions from estates and trusts that the beneficiaries will have to include in income.

distribute (di-**strib**-yoot), *vb.* **1.** To apportion; to divide among several. **2.** To arrange by class or order. **3.** To deliver. **4.** To spread out; to disperse.

distributee (di-strib-yoo-**tee**), *n.* **1.** A beneficiary entitled to payment. **2.** An heir, esp. one who obtains personal property from the estate of an intestate decedent.

legal distributee. A person whom the law would entitle to take property under a will.

distribution, *n.* **1.** At common law, the passing of personal property to an intestate decedent's heirs. Cf. DESCENT (1). **2.** The act or process of apportioning or giving out. — **distribute,** *vb.*

controlled-securities-offering distribution. See *securities-offering distribution* (1).

corporate distribution. A corporation's direct or indirect transfer of money or other property, or incurring of indebtedness to or for the benefit of its shareholders, such as a dividend payment out of current or past earnings.

liquidating distribution. A distribution of trade or business assets by a dissolving corporation or partnership. — Also termed *distribution in liquidation.*

nonliquidating distribution. A distribution of assets by a corporation or partnership that is not going out of business, such as a distribution of excess capital not necessary for current operations.

partnership distribution. A partnership's payment of cash or property to a partner out of earnings or as an advance against future earnings, or a payment of the partners' capital in partial or complete liquidation of the partner's interest.

probate distribution. The judicially supervised apportionment and division — usu. after the payment of debts and charges — of assets of an estate among those legally entitled to share.

secondary distribution. **1.** The public sale of a large block of previously issued stock. — Also termed *secondary offering.* See OFFERING. **2.** The sale of a large block of stock after the close of the exchange.

securities-offering distribution. **1.** An issuer's public offering of securities through a formal underwriting agreement with a broker-dealer. — Also termed *controlled-securities-offering distribution.* **2.** An issuer's public offering of securities on an informal basis, with or without brokers. — Also termed *uncontrolled-securities-offering distribution.*

trust distribution. The cash or other property paid or credited to a trust beneficiary.

uncontrolled-securities-offering distribution. See *securities-offering distribution* (2).

distribution cost. See COST (1).

distribution in kind. A transfer of property in its original state, such as a distribution of land instead of the proceeds of its sale.

distribution in liquidation. See *liquidating distribution* under DISTRIBUTION.

distribution right. *Copyright.* A copyright holder's exclusive right to sell, lease, or otherwise transfer copies of the protected work to the public. See FIRST-SALE DOCTRINE.

distributive (di-**strib**-yə-tiv), *adj.* Of or relating to apportioning, dividing, and assigning in separate items or shares; of or relating to distributing.

distributive clause. A will or trust provision governing the distribution of income and gifts.

distributive deviation. A trustee's transfer of principal to the income beneficiaries when the income is inadequate to carry out the settlor's scheme of distribution, and without the permission of a remainderman who owns a future interest in the principal. • This practice is usu. impermissible except when life-income beneficiaries need the money to buy necessaries.

distributive finding. A jury's decision partly in favor of one party and partly in favor of another.

distributive justice. See JUSTICE (1).

distributive share. **1.** The share that an heir or beneficiary receives from the legal distribution of an estate. **2.** The portion (as determined in the partnership agreement) of a partnership's income, gain, loss, or deduction that is passed through to a partner and reported on the partner's tax return. **3.** The share of assets or liabilities that a partner or partner's estate acquires after the partnership has been dissolved.

distributor. A wholesaler, jobber, or other manufacturer or supplier that sells chiefly to retailers and commercial users.

distributorship. A franchise held by a person or company who sells merchandise, usu. in a specific area to individual customers <a car distributorship>.

dual distributorship. A business structure in which one party operates a branch or dealership on the same market level as one or more of its customers.

district. **1.** A territorial area into which a country, state, county, municipality, or other political subdivision is divided for judicial, political, electoral, or administrative purposes. **2.** A territorial area in which similar local businesses or entities are concentrated, such as a theater district or an arts district. — Abbr. D.

assessment district. *Tax.* A usu. municipal subdivision in which separate assessments of taxable property are made.

congressional district. A geographical unit of a state from which one member of the U.S. House of Representatives is elected.

floterial district (floh-**teer**-ee-əl). A legislative district that includes several separate districts or political subdivisions that independently would not be entitled to additional representation, but whose conglomerate population entitles the district to another seat in the legislative body being apportioned.

land district. A federally created state or territorial division containing a U.S. land office that manages the disposition of the district's public lands.

legislative district. A geographical subdivision of a state for the purpose of electing legislative representatives.

metropolitan district. A special district, embracing parts of or entire cities and towns in a metropolitan area, created by a state to provide unified administration of one or more common services, such as water supply or public transportation.

municipal utility district. A publicly owned corporation, or a political subdivision, that provides the public with a service or services, such as water, electricity, gas, transportation, or telecommunications. — Abbr. MUD. — Also termed *public utility district.*

school district. See SCHOOL DISTRICT.

special district. A political subdivision that is created to bypass normal borrowing limitations, to insulate certain activities from traditional political influence, to allocate functions to entities reflecting particular expertise, and to provide a single service within a specified area <a transit authority is a special district>.

district attorney. A public official appointed or elected to represent the state in criminal cases in a particular judicial district; PROSECUTOR (1). — Abbr. D.A. — Also termed *public prosecutor*; *state's attorney*; *prosecuting attorney*. Cf. UNITED STATES ATTORNEY.

district clerk. See CLERK (2).

district court. See COURT.

district-court magistrate. See MAGISTRATE.

districting. The act of drawing lines or establishing boundaries between geographic areas to create voting districts. See APPORTIONMENT; GERRYMANDERING.

districtio (di-**strik**-shee-oh), *n.* [Law Latin "distraint"] *Hist.* **1.** A distress; a distraint. **2.** The right of distress. **3.** Something (such as a good or animal) that can be distrained. **4.** A territory within which distraint can be exercised. **5.** Any compulsory proceeding.

district judge. See JUDGE.

District of Columbia. The seat of the U.S. government, situated on the Potomac River between Maryland and Virginia. • Though neither a state nor a territory, it is constitutionally subject to the exclusive jurisdiction of Congress. — Abbr. D.C.

district parish. See PARISH.

district school. See SCHOOL.

distringas (di-**string**-gas), *n.* [Law Latin "you are to distrain"] **1.** A writ ordering a sheriff to distrain a defendant's property to compel the defendant to perform an obligation, such as appearing in court or giving up a chattel to a plaintiff awarded judgment in a detinue action. **2.** A writ ordering the sheriff to seize jurors' goods to compel them to appear for jury service. **3.** An equitable process of execution against a corporate body that has refused to obey a summons. **4.** *Hist.* An order, issued initially from the Court of Exchequer, then the Court of Chancery, and finally the High Court of Justice, for someone interested in purchasing Bank of England stock, temporarily restraining the bank officers from transferring the stock or paying a dividend on it. • This proceeding was used to prevent fraudulent dealing by a trustee or other stockholder. The relief was only temporary, and if the bank received a request from the stockholder to permit a stock deal, the bank had to warn the distringing party to promptly obtain a restraining order or a writ of injunction, or else the stock deal would go through.

distringas juratores (di-**string**-gas joor-ə-**tor**-eez), *n.* [Law Latin "you are to distrain the jurors"] *Hist.* A writ ordering the sheriff to distrain jurors or their property to compel their appearance before the judges of assize and *nisi prius* for jury duty on an appointed day.

distringas nuper vicecomitem (di-**string**-gas **n[y]oo**-pər **vI**-see-**kom**-i-təm), *n.* [Law Latin "you are to distrain the late sheriff"] *Hist.* **1.** A writ ordering a sheriff's successor to distrain the former sheriff's property until the former sheriff brings in a defendant to answer the plaintiff's charge, sells goods attached under a *fieri facias*, or performs some other obligation that the former sheriff should have completed while still in office. **2.** A writ calling on an ex-sheriff to account for the proceeds taken in execution.

distringas vice comitem (di-**string**-gas **vI**-see **kom**-i-təm), *n.* [Law Latin "you are to distrain the sheriff"] *Hist.* A *distringas* writ ordering the coroner to distrain the sheriff for not executing a writ of *venditioni exponas*. See VENDITIONI EXPONAS.

distringere (di-**strinj**-ə-ree), *vb.* [Latin] To distrain; to coerce; to compel. • The first-person form of the verb was *distringo* ("I distrain").

disturbance, *n.* **1.** An act causing annoyance or disquiet, or interfering with a person's pursuit of a lawful occupation or the peace and order of a neighborhood, community, or meeting. **2.** At common law, a wrong done to an incorporeal hereditament by hindering the owner's enjoyment of it.

disturbance of common. At common law, a wrongful interference with, or impediment to, another's right to commonable property, such as a wrongful fencing or surcharge on the common.

> "The disturbance of *common* comes next to be considered; where any act is done, by which the right of another to his common is incommoded or diminished. This may happen, in the first place, where one who hath no right of common, puts his cattle into the land; and thereby robs the cattle of the commoners of their respective shares of the pasture. Or if one, who hath a right of common, puts in cattle which are not commonable, as hogs and goats; which amounts to the same inconvenience" 3 William Blackstone, *Commentaries on the Laws of England* 237 (1768).

disturbance of franchise. At common law, a wrongful interference with a liberty or privilege.

> "Disturbance of *franchises* happens when a man has the franchise of holding a court-leet, of keeping a fair or market, of free-warren, of taking toll, of seizing waifs or estrays, or (in short) any other species of franchise whatsoever, and he is disturbed or incommoded in the lawful exercise thereof." 3 William Blackstone, *Commentaries on the Laws of England* 236 (1768).

disturbance of patronage. A wrongful obstruction of a patron from presenting a clerk to a benefice.

disturbance of public meetings. The unlawful interference with the proceedings of a public assembly.

> "Generally speaking, any conduct which, being contrary to the usages of the particular sort of meeting and class of persons assembled, interferes with its due progress and services, or is annoying to the congregation in whole or in part, is a disturbance; and a meeting may be said to be 'disturbed' when it is agitated, aroused from a state of repose, molested, interrupted, hindered, perplexed, disquieted, or diverted from the object of the assembly." 27 C.J.S. *Disturbance of Public Meetings* § 1, at 817 (1959).

disturbance of public worship. Any conduct that interferes with the peaceful, lawful assembly of people for religious exercises.

disturbance of tenure. A stranger's ouster of a tenant from a tenancy. • The tenant's lord could recover damages for the ouster.

disturbance of the peace. See BREACH OF THE PEACE.

disturbance of ways. An impediment to a person's lawful right-of-way, as by an obstruction.

disturber. See IMPEDITOR.

disturbing the peace. See BREACH OF THE PEACE.

divadiatus. See DEVADIATUS.

diverse, *adj.* **1.** Of or relating to different types <the attorney handles diverse cases ranging from probate matters to criminal law>. **2.** (Of a person or entity) having a different citizenship from the party or parties on the other side of the lawsuit <the parties are diverse because the plaintiffs are citizens of Illinois and the defendant is a New York citizen>. See *diversity jurisdiction* under JURISDICTION. **3.** (Of a group of people) including people of different races, sexes, nationalities, and cultural backgrounds <the school has a diverse student body>.

diversification, *n.* **1.** A company's movement into a broader range of products, usu. by buying firms already serving the market or by expanding existing operations <the soft-drink company's diversification into the potato-chip market has increased its profits>. **2.** The act of investing in a wide range of companies to reduce the risk if one sector of the market suffers losses <the prudent investor's diversification of the portfolio among 12 companies>. — **diversify,** *vb.*

diversified holding company. See COMPANY.

diversified investment company. See COMPANY.

diversion, *n.* **1.** A deviation or alteration from the natural course of things; esp., the unauthorized alteration of a watercourse to the prejudice of a lower riparian owner, or the unauthorized use of funds. **2.** A distraction or pastime. — **divert,** *vb.*

diversion program. A program that refers certain criminal defendants before trial to community programs on job training, education, and the like, which if successfully completed may lead to the dismissal of the charges. — Also termed *pretrial diversion*; *pretrial intervention*. Cf. *deferred judgment* under JUDGMENT.

Diversité des courts (di-vər-si-**tay** də **koort**). [Law French] A treatise on courts written in French, supposedly by Fitzherbert during the reign of Edward III. • It was printed initially in 1525 and again in 1534. — Also spelled *Diversité des courtes*.

> "[F]or in the ancient treatise, entitled *diversité de courtes* ... we have a catalogue of the matters of conscience then cognizable by *subpoena* in chancery, which fall within a very narrow compass." 3 William Blackstone, *Commentaries on the Laws of England* 53 (1768).

diversity, *n.* **1.** DIVERSITY OF CITIZENSHIP. **2.** *Hist.* A plea that a prisoner to be executed is not the one that was accused and found guilty, at which point a jury is immediately impaneled to try the issue of the prisoner's identity.

diversity, *adj.* Of, relating to, or involving diversity jurisdiction <a diversity case>.

diversity jurisdiction. See JURISDICTION.

diversity of citizenship. A basis for federal-court jurisdiction that exists when (1) a case is between citizens of different states, or between a citizen of a state and an alien, and (2) the matter in controversy exceeds a specific value (now $75,000). 28 USCA § 1332. • For purposes of diversity jurisdiction, a corporation is considered a citizen of both the state of incorporation and the state of its principal place of business. An unincorporated association, such as a partnership, is considered a citizen of each state of which at least one of its members is a citizen. — Often shortened to *diversity*. See *diversity jurisdiction* under JURISDICTION.

complete diversity. In a multiparty case, diversity between both sides to the lawsuit so that all plaintiffs have different citizenship from all defendants. • Complete diversity must exist for a federal court to have diversity jurisdiction over the matter. The rule of complete diversity was first laid down by Chief Justice Marshall in *Strawbridge v. Curtiss*, 7 U.S. (3 Cranch) 267 (1806).

manufactured diversity. Improper or collusively created diversity of citizenship for the sole or primary purpose of creating federal jurisdiction. • Manufactured diversity is prohibited by 28 USCA § 1359.

dives costs (dɪ-veez), *n.* Ordinary court costs granted to a successful party, as distinguished from limited costs (such as out-of-pocket costs) allowed to a successful pauper who sued or defended *in forma pauperis*. • The term derives from the name of Dives, the supposed name of the rich man in the parable of the rich man and Lazarus (*Luke* 16:19–31). *Dives* is a Latin word meaning "rich."

divestitive fact. See FACT.

divestiture (di-**ves**-tə-chər *or* dɪ-), *n.* **1.** The loss or surrender of an asset or interest. **2.** A court order to a party to dispose of assets or property. **3.** *Antitrust.* A court order to a defendant to rid itself of property, securities, or other assets to prevent a monopoly or restraint of trade. — **divest,** *vb.*

divestment, *n.* **1.** *Property.* The cutting short of an interest in property before its normal termination. **2.** The complete or partial loss of an interest in an asset, such as land or stock. **3.** DISINVESTMENT (2). — **divest,** *vb.*

divide-and-pay-over rule. *Wills & estates.* The principle that if the only provisions in a testamentary disposition are words ordering that payment be made at some time after the testator's death, time will be of the essence and the interest is future and contingent rather than vested and immediate.

divided court. An appellate court whose opinion or decision in a particular case is not unanimous, esp. when the majority is slim, as in a 5–to–4 decision of the U.S. Supreme Court.

divided custody. See CUSTODY (2).

divided-damages rule. *Maritime law.* The obsolete principle that when two parties are jointly liable to a third party for a tort, each party is liable for only half the damages. • The courts now apply a comparative-negligence standard.

> "For over a hundred years admiralty law embraced the rule of 'divided damages' in collision cases .... In 1975, in *United States v. Reliable Transfer Co.*, 421 U.S. 397, 95 S.Ct. 1708, 44 L.Ed.2d 251 (1975), the Supreme Court jettisoned that inequitable and illogical rule in favor of proportionate allocation of fault among joint-tortfeasors in collision cases. Each vessel now is liable to the other offending vessel in contribution for that part of the total damages proportionate to its fault, and is liable for its per capita (virile) share only when the respective faults of the vessels are equal, or when proportionate fault can not be ascertained." Frank L. Maraist, *Admiralty in a Nutshell* 165 (2d ed. 1988).

dividend. A portion of a company's earnings or profits distributed pro rata to its shareholders, usu. in the form of cash or additional shares.

accumulated dividend. A dividend that has been declared but not yet paid. — Also termed *accrued dividend.*

accumulative dividend. See *cumulative dividend.*

asset dividend. A dividend paid in the form of property, usu. the company's product, rather than in cash or stock. — Also termed *property dividend.*

bond dividend. A dividend in which a shareholder receives a bond instead of scrip, property, or money.

capital-gain dividend. A taxable payment to a mutual-fund shareholder. • The payment is the shareholder's proportional share of the net capital gains realized by securities sales from the mutual fund's portfolio. — Also termed *capital-gain distribution.*

cash dividend. A dividend paid to shareholders in the form of money.

consent dividend. A dividend that is not actually paid to the shareholders, but is taxed to the shareholders and increases the basis in their stock investment. • A corporation declares a consent dividend to avoid or reduce an accumulated-earnings or personal-holding-company penalty tax.

constructive dividend. A taxable benefit derived by a shareholder from the corporation even though the benefit was not designated a dividend. • Examples include excessive compensation, bargain purchases of corporate property, and shareholder use of corporate property.

cumulative dividend. A dividend that grows from year to year when not paid. • A cumulative dividend is usu. on preferred shares, and it must be paid in full before common shareholders may receive any dividend. If the corporation does not pay a dividend in a particular year or period, it is carried over to the next year or period and must be paid before the common shareholders receive any payment. — Also termed *accumulative dividend.* Cf. *noncumulative dividend.*

deferred dividend. A dividend that is declared, but is payable at a future date.

deficiency dividend. A dividend paid to reduce or avoid personal-holding-company tax in a prior year.

disguised dividend. See *informal dividend.*

extraordinary dividend. A dividend paid in addition to a regular dividend, usu. because of exceptional corporate profits during the dividend period. — Also termed *extra dividend*; *nonrecurring dividend*; *special dividend.*

fixed-return dividend. A dividend that is constant throughout the investment's life.

informal dividend. A payment of salary, rent, interest, or the like to or for a shareholder as a substitute for a dividend. — Also termed *disguised dividend.*

liability dividend. See *scrip dividend.*

liquidation dividend. A dividend paid to a dissolving corporation's shareholders, usu. from the capital of the corporation, upon the decision to suspend all or part of its business operations. — Also termed *liquidating dividend.*

nimble dividend. A dividend paid out of current earnings when there is a deficit in the account from which dividends may be paid. • Some state statutes prohibit nimble dividends.

noncumulative dividend. A dividend that does not accrue for the benefit of a preferred shareholder if there is a passed dividend in a particular year or period. Cf. *cumulative dividend.*

nonrecurring dividend. See *extraordinary dividend.*

passed dividend. A dividend that is not paid when due by a company that has a history of paying regular dividends.

preferred dividend. A dividend paid to preferred shareholders, who are generally paid a fixed amount and take priority over common shareholders.

property dividend. See *asset dividend.*

reinvested dividend. A dividend that is used to purchase additional shares in the corporation, instead of being taken in cash by the shareholder. See DIVIDEND-REINVESTMENT PLAN.

scrip dividend. A dividend paid in certificates entitling the holder to ownership of capital stock to be issued in the future. • This type of dividend usu. signals that the corporation's cash flow is poor. — Also termed *liability dividend.*

special dividend. See *extraordinary dividend.*

stock dividend. A dividend paid in stock expressed as a percentage of the number of shares already held by a shareholder.

unpaid dividend. A declared but unpaid dividend.

year-end dividend. An extra dividend paid at the end of the fiscal year depending on the amount of the profits.

dividenda (div-i-**den**-də), *n.* [fr. Latin *dividere* "to divide"] *Hist.* Something to be divided; an indenture.

dividend addition. An amount added to the face value of a life-insurance policy and purchased by using a dividend as a single premium payment.

dividend-credit rule. The principle that a corporate reserve fund amassed from unpaid dividends on preferred stock must be used to pay subsequent dividends on preferred stock before dividend payments on common stock. — Also termed *cast-iron-pipe doctrine.*

dividend date. The date on which a corporation distributes dividends to record owners of stock shares. See *record date* under DATE. Cf. EX-DIVIDEND DATE.

dividend income. See INCOME.

dividend-payout ratio. A profitability ratio computed by dividing annual dividends per share by earnings per share.

dividend preference. The right of a holder of preferred shares to receive a dividend before the company pays dividends to holders of common shares. See *preferred stock* under STOCK.

dividend-received deduction. A deduction allowed to a corporate shareholder for dividends received from a domestic corporation. IRC (26 USCA) §§ 243–247.

dividend-reinvestment plan. A company-sponsored program that enables common shareholders to reinvest their dividends, plus additional voluntary payments, into shares of the entity's common stock, usu. with no sales charge, and sometimes at a discount from the stock's market price.

dividend yield. The current annual dividend divided by the market price per share.

divinare (div-i-**nair**-ee), *vb.* [Latin] To foretell or divine (something).

divine law. God's law, as distinguished from human law. See NATURAL LAW.

divine right of kings. The political theory that the sovereign is a direct representative of God and has the right to rule absolutely by virtue of birth.

> "Divine Right of Kings .... It originated in the mediaeval concept of God's award of temporal power to civil rulers and spiritual power to the Church. It was claimed by the earlier Stuart kings in England, and explains many of their attitudes in the struggle which developed between them and Parliament for political sovereignty .... The principle of divine right was submerged during the Commonwealth but re-emerged under James II, but disappeared with his flight and abdication." David M. Walker, *The Oxford Companion to Law* 366 (1980).

divine service. 1. *Hist.* A feudal tenure in which the tenants were obligated to perform special divine functions, such as singing at a certain number of masses or distributing a specified amount in alms. **2.** A public worship service.

divisa (di-**vɪ**-zə), *n.* [fr. French *diviser* "to divide"] **1.** A division, as of goods by a will; a devise. **2.** A boundary of neighboring lands. **3.** A court held on such a boundary to settle the tenants' disputes.

divisible contract. See *severable contract* under CONTRACT.

divisible divorce. See DIVORCE.

divisible offense. See OFFENSE (1).

divisim (di-**vI**-zəm). [Law Latin] *Hist.* Severally; separately.

divisional bond. See BOND (3).

divisional court. See COURT.

divisional security. See SECURITY.

division of fees. See FEE-SPLITTING.

division of powers. The allocation of power between the national government and the states. • Under the Tenth Amendment, powers not delegated to the federal government are reserved to the states or to the people. But today the Tenth Amendment provides only a limited check on Congress's power to regulate the states. Cf. SEPARATION OF POWERS.

division order. *Oil & gas.* A sales contract for the purchase of oil or gas, directing the purchaser to pay for the value of the products in the proportions set out in the contract. • The purchaser usu. asks the lessee to provide complete abstracts of title, which the purchaser uses to obtain a title examination and a title opinion. The purchaser then prepares the division order, usu. requiring it to be executed by the operator, the royalty owners, and anyone else with an interest in production. Once the division order is executed and returned to the purchaser, payments begin for the products removed.

divisum imperium (di-**vI**-zəm im-**peer**-ee-əm), *n.* [Latin "a divided empire"] Divided jurisdiction; alternate jurisdiction, as of courts.

> "This main sea begins at the low-water-mark. But between the high-water-mark and the low-water-mark, where the sea ebbs and flows, the common law and admiralty have *divisum imperium*, an alternate jurisdiction; one upon the water, when it is full sea; the other upon the land, when it is an ebb." 1 William Blackstone, *Commentaries on the Laws of England* 107 (1765).

divorce. The legal dissolution of a marriage by a court. — Also termed *marital dissolution*; *dissolution of marriage*. Cf. ANNULMENT.

divisible divorce. A divorce whereby the marriage itself is dissolved but the issues incident to the divorce, such as alimony, child custody, and visitation, are reserved until a later proceeding. • This type of divorce can be granted when the court has subject-matter jurisdiction but lacks personal jurisdiction over the defendant-spouse. — Also termed *bifurcated divorce*.

divorce a mensa et thoro (ay **men**-sə et **thor**-oh). [Latin "(divorce) from board and bed"] A partial or qualified divorce by which the parties are separated and forbidden to live or cohabit together, without affecting the marriage itself. • This type of divorce, abolished in England in 1857, was the forerunner of modern judicial separation. — Also termed *separation a mensa et thoro*; *separation from bed and board*.

> "[The Ecclesiastical Courts] grant also what is called a divorce *a mensa et thoro*, or rather what we should call a judicial separation, i.e. they release the parties from the duty of living together on grounds of cruelty or misconduct . . . ." William Geldart, *Introduction to English Law* 38 (D.C.M. Yardley ed., 9th ed. 1984).

divorce a vinculo matrimonii (ay **ving**-kyə-loh ma-trə-**moh**-nee-I). [Latin "(divorce) from the chains of marriage"] A total divorce of husband and wife, dissolving the marriage tie and releasing the parties wholly from their matrimonial obligations. • This type of common-law divorce, which bastardizes any children from the marriage, is granted on grounds that existed before the marriage. In England, the Matrimonial Causes Act of 1857 introduced statutory divorce *a vinculo matrimonii*.

ex parte divorce (eks **pahr**-tee). A divorce proceeding in which only one spouse participates or appears in court.

foreign divorce. A divorce obtained outside the state or country in which one spouse resides.

hotel divorce. A form of collusive divorce — occurring before widespread passage of no-fault divorce laws — in which the spouses agree to fake an adultery scene to create "fault." Cf. *no-fault divorce*.

> "Clearly a lawyer may not originate or participate in a scheme to make it appear to the court that a ground for divorce has occurred when this is not the fact. Such is the case in the so-called 'hotel divorces,' prevalent in jurisdictions where adultery is the only ground for divorce, and based on the principle that intercourse will be presumed from apparently uninhibited opportunity." Henry S. Drinker, *Legal Ethics* 123–24 (1953).

legislative divorce. *Hist.* **1.** The legal termination of a particular marriage, enacted by the legislature rather than by a court. • Legislative divorces once existed in New England, but now courts perform all divorces. **2.** See *parliamentary divorce*.

limited divorce. **1.** A divorce with no provision that one spouse must provide financial support to the other. **2.** Loosely, a legal separation.

mail-order divorce. A divorce obtained by parties who are not physically present or domiciled in the jurisdiction purporting to grant the divorce. • Such a divorce is not recognized in the United States because of the absence of the usual bases for jurisdiction.

Mexican divorce. A divorce obtained in Mexico by mail order or by the appearance of one spouse who does not have a Mexican domicile. • Neither type is recognized in the United States.

migratory divorce. A divorce obtained by a spouse who moves to, or temporarily resides in, another state or country to get the divorce.

no-fault divorce. A divorce in which the parties are not required to prove fault or grounds beyond a showing of the irretrievable breakdown of the marriage or irreconcilable differences. • The system of no-fault divorce was adopted throughout the United States during the late 1960s and the 1970s.

Parliamentary divorce. A divorce decreed by Parliament or a legislative act, as opposed to a court. — Also termed *legislative divorce*.

pro-con divorce. An uncontested divorce granted after only the plaintiff appears at the proceeding (since the defendant contests nothing).

rabbinical divorce. A divorce granted under the authority of a rabbi.

divorce proctor. A person (such as a guardian) who is appointed to protect the interest of the state or children in a divorce action.

D.J. See *district judge* under JUDGE.

DJIA. *abbr.* DOW JONES INDUSTRIAL AVERAGE.

DL/C. See *documentary letter of credit* under LETTER OF CREDIT.

DNA identification. A method of comparing a person's deoxyribonucleic acid (DNA) — a patterned chemical structure of genetic information — with the DNA in a biological specimen (such as blood, tissue, or hair) to determine if the person is the source of the specimen. — Also termed *DNA fingerprinting*; *genetic fingerprinting*. Cf. HLA TEST.

do (doh). [Latin] *Hist.* I give. • This phrase was considered the oldest and aptest words of a feoffment and gift.

dock, *n.* **1.** A structure that encloses water, often between two piers, in which ships are received for loading, unloading, safekeeping, or repair. **2.** The part of a warehouse or other building (usu. elevated with oversized doors) at which trucks are received for loading and unloading. **3.** *English law.* In a criminal court, the enclosure in which the prisoner is placed during trial <it was through his own deliberate choice that Mr. Bourne found himself in the dock at the Old Bailey, charged with a felony>.

dockage. A charge for the use of a dock, esp. while a vessel is undergoing repairs.

docket, *n.* **1.** A formal record in which a judge or court clerk briefly notes all the proceedings and filings in a court case <review the docket to determine the filing date>. — Also termed *judicial record*.

appearance docket. A list of the parties and lawyers participating in an action, together with a brief abstract of the successive steps in the action.

judgment docket. A book that a court clerk keeps for the entry or recordation of judgments, giving official notice of existing judgment liens to interested parties. — Also termed *judgment book*; *judgment file*; *judgment record*; *judgment roll*.

2. A schedule of pending cases <the case is third on Monday's trial docket>. — Also termed *court calendar*; *cause list*; *trial calendar*.

DWOP docket. A list of cases that the court has set for possible dismissal for want of prosecution. — Also termed *doowop docket*. See *dismissal for want of prosecution* under DISMISSAL (1).

preferred docket. A list of cases set for trial, arranged in order of priority. • Criminal cases are, for example, generally given precedence over civil cases on the preferred docket because of the constitutional right to a speedy trial.

3. DOCKET CALL <the agreed judgment was signed at the court's uncontested docket call on May 24>. **4.** A written abstract that provides specific information (usu. about something attached); esp., a label <check the docket to determine the goods' destination and value>.

docket, *vb.* **1.** To make a brief entry in the docket of the proceedings and filings in a court case <to docket the filing date>. **2.** To abstract and enter in a book <to docket a judgment>.

3. To schedule (a case) for trial or some other event <the case was docketed for a May trial>. See DOCKET, *n*.

docket call. A court session in which attorneys (and sometimes parties) appear in court to report the status of their cases. • For example, they may announce readiness for trial or report the suit's settlement.

docket fee. See FEE (1).

docket number. A number that the court clerk assigns to a case on the court's docket.

dockmaster. *English law.* An officer who directs the mooring and removal of ships to avoid the obstruction of commerce.

dock receipt. An interim certificate issued by a maritime shipping company for the delivery of goods at the dock. • A dock receipt entitles the designated person to receive a bill of lading. — Also termed *dock warrant.* See DOCUMENT OF TITLE.

dock sale. See SALE.

dock warrant. See DOCK RECEIPT.

doctor. **1.** *Hist.* In Roman Catholic canon law, an honorary title for exceptional scholars. **2.** A title of a person who has acquired an advanced degree in academics, or has achieved an honorable distinction. **3.** A physician. — Abbr. Dr.

Doctor of Juridical Science. A graduate law degree, beyond the J.D. and the LL.M. — Abbr. S.J.D.; J.S.D. — Also termed *Doctor of Judicial Science*; *Doctor of the Science of Jurisprudence*; *Doctor of the Science of Law.*

Doctor of Jurisprudence. See JURIS DOCTOR.

Doctor of Law. See JURIS DOCTOR.

Doctor of Laws. An honorary degree bestowed on one who has achieved great distinction. Cf. JURIS DOCTOR; MASTER OF LAWS.

Doctor of the Science of Jurisprudence. See DOCTOR OF JURIDICAL SCIENCE.

Doctor of the Science of Law. See DOCTOR OF JURIDICAL SCIENCE.

doctor-patient privilege. See PRIVILEGE (3).

doctrine. **1.** A principle, esp. a legal principle, that is widely adhered to. **2.** *Archaic.* HOLDING (1).

doctrine of adverse domination. A rule allowing the statute of limitations to be tolled in an action against corporate officers and directors (esp. a corporation's action against its own officers and directors) until the alleged wrongdoers no longer control the corporation. — Also termed *adverse domination doctrine.*

doctrine of approximation. A doctrine that authorizes a court to vary the details of a trust's administration to preserve the trust and to carry out the donor's intentions. — Also termed *equitable doctrine of approximation.* Cf. CY PRES.

doctrine of capture. See RULE OF CAPTURE.

doctrine of completeness. See RULE OF OPTIONAL COMPLETENESS.

doctrine of *contra non valentem* (**kon**-trə non və-**len**-təm). The rule that a limitations or prescriptive period does not begin to run against a plaintiff who is unable to act, usu. because of the defendant's culpable act, such as concealing material information that would give rise to the plaintiff's claim. — Also termed *contra non valentem.*

doctrine of *contra proferentem*. See CONTRA PROFERENTEM.

doctrine of curative admissibility. A rule allowing a party to introduce otherwise inadmissible evidence to remove the prejudice caused by the improper admission of evidence that was offered by the opposing party. — Also termed *curative-admissibility doctrine.*

doctrine of entireties (en-**tI**-ər-teez). In customs law, the rule that when an entry consists of parts that assemble to form an article different from any of the parts, the proper classification will be of the whole article, rather than the individual components.

doctrine of equivalents. *Patents.* A judicially created theory for finding patent infringement when the accused process or product falls outside the literal scope of the patent claims. • The doctrine evolved to prevent parties from evading liability for patent infringement by making trivial changes to avoid the literal language of the patent claims. *Graver Tank &*

Mfg. Co. v. Linde Air Prods. Co., 339 U.S. 605, 70 S.Ct. 854 (1950). In determining whether infringement exists under the doctrine, the court must first determine whether "the accused product or process contain[s] an element identical or equivalent to each claimed element of the patented invention." *Warner-Jenkinson Co. v. Hilton Davis Chem. Co.*, 117 S.Ct. 1040, 1054 (1997). Then, if a correspondence is found between the elements of the accused device and of at least one patent claim, infringement under the doctrine turns on (1) whether the accused device substitutes an element that performs the same function, in a substantially similar way, to accomplish substantially the same result as each claimed element, or (2) whether the substitute element plays a role substantially different from the claimed element. — Also termed *equivalents doctrine*; *doctrine of equivalence*; *doctrine of equivalency*; *doctrine of substantial equivalents*; *nonliteral infringement*. Cf. *literal infringement* under INFRINGEMENT.

reverse doctrine of equivalents. The doctrine preventing infringement liability when the invention is substantially described by the claims of another's patent but performs the same or similar function in a substantially different way.

doctrine of finality. See FINALITY DOCTRINE.

doctrine of general average. A rule allowing a carrier to require cargo owners and the shipowner to contribute pro rata to the cost of protecting the ship and its cargo.

doctrine of illusory coverage. A rule requiring an insurance policy to be interpreted so that it is not merely a delusion to the insured.

doctrine of incontrovertible physical facts. See PHYSICAL-FACTS RULE.

doctrine of necessaries. *Archaic.* The common-law rule holding a husband or father liable to one who sells goods to his wife or child if the goods are required for sustenance or support. See NECESSARIES.

doctrine of notice. See NOTICE DOCTRINE.

doctrine of optional completeness. See RULE OF OPTIONAL COMPLETENESS.

doctrine of *parens patriae*. See PARENS PATRIAE (2).

doctrine of practical location. The principle by which adjacent landowners resolve uncertainties over land boundaries by permanently fixing the boundaries by agreement. — Also termed *boundary by agreement*; *boundary by acquiescence*.

doctrine of precedent. 1. The rule that precedents not only have persuasive authority, but must be followed when similar circumstances arise. • This rule developed in the 19th century and prevails today. See STARE DECISIS. **2.** A rule that precedents are reported, may be cited, and will probably be followed by courts. • This is the rule that prevailed in England until the 19th century.

doctrine of preclusion of inconsistent positions. See *judicial estoppel* under ESTOPPEL.

doctrine of revestment. A rule by which a court regains jurisdiction after the entry of final judgment when the former opposing parties have actively participated in proceedings inconsistent with the court's judgment.

doctrine of scrivener's error. A rule permitting a typographical error in a document to be reformed by parol evidence, if the evidence is precise, clear, and convincing. See *clerical error* under ERROR (2).

doctrine of specialty. *Int'l law.* The principle, included as a provision in most extradition treaties, under which a person who is extradited to a country to stand trial for certain criminal offenses may be tried only for those offenses and not for any other pre-extradition offenses. — Also termed *specialty doctrine*. See EXTRADITION.

doctrine of substantial equivalents. See DOCTRINE OF EQUIVALENTS.

doctrine of superior equities. *Insurance.* A rule by which an insurer is unable to recover from anyone whose equities are equal or superior to the insured's; esp., a rule that a right of subrogation may be invoked against another party only if that party's guilty conduct renders the party's equity inferior to that of the insured.

doctrine of the conclusiveness of the judgment. See *judicial estoppel* under ESTOPPEL.

doctrine of the last antecedent. See RULE OF THE LAST ANTECEDENT.

doctrine of the last preceding antecedent. RULE OF THE LAST ANTECEDENT.

doctrine of worthier title. See WORTHIER-TITLE DOCTRINE.

document, *n.* **1.** Something tangible on which words, symbols, or marks are recorded. **2.** (*pl.*) The deeds, agreements, title papers, letters, receipts, and other written instruments used to prove a fact.

ancient document. *Evidence.* A document that is presumed to be authentic because its physical condition strongly suggests authenticity, it has existed for 20 or more years, and it has been maintained in proper custody (as by coming from a place where it is reasonably expected to be found). Fed. R. Evid. 901(b)(8). — Also termed *ancient writing.*

foreign document. A document that originated in, or was prepared or executed in, a foreign state or country.

hot document. A document that directly supports a litigant's allegation.

public document. A document of public interest issued or published by a political body or otherwise connected with public business. Cf. *public record* under RECORD.

3. *Evidence.* Under the best-evidence rule, a physical embodiment of information or ideas, such as a letter, contract, receipt, account book, blueprint, or X-ray plate; esp., the original of such an embodiment.

document, *vb.* **1.** To support with records, instruments, or other evidentiary authorities <document the chain of custody>. **2.** To record; to create a written record of <document a file>.

documentary credit. 1. Credit extended on a document of title or any other legal document. **2.** A financing arrangement in which a financial institution authorizes or makes a payment to a third party (usu. an exporter) at a customer's request. • This financing method facilitates international transactions by providing the importer with necessary credit and the exporter with an expedited cash payment.

documentary draft. See DRAFT.

documentary evidence. See EVIDENCE.

documentary instruction. A written agreement between an importer and exporter covering the relegation of various documents relating to the shipment and disposition of goods.

documentary letter of credit. See LETTER OF CREDIT.

documentary-originals rule. See BEST-EVIDENCE RULE.

documentary sale. See SALE.

documentary stamp. A stamp required to be affixed to a deed or other instrument before it is recorded.

documentary stamp tax. See *stamp tax* under TAX.

document of title. A written description, identification, or declaration of goods authorizing the holder (usu. a bailee) to receive, hold, and dispose of the document and the goods it covers. • Documents of title, such as bills of lading, warehouse receipts, and delivery orders, are generally governed by Article 7 of the UCC. See BAILMENT.

negotiable document of title. A document of title that actually stands for the goods it covers, so that any transfer of the goods requires a surrender of the document. UCC § 7–104(1).

nonnegotiable document of title. A document of title that merely serves as evidence of the goods it covers. UCC § 7–104(2).

documentum (dok-yə-**men**-təm). [Latin] *Roman law.* **1.** Proof. **2.** A document. • This term appeared in postclassical imperial constitutions.

DOD. *abbr.* Department of Defense. See DEFENSE DEPARTMENT.

do, dico, addico (**doh**, **dɪ**-koh, ə-**dɪ**-koh *or* **dik**-oh, ə-**dik**-oh). [Latin] I give, I say, I adjudge. • These formal words were spoken by the Roman praetor in the exercise of his jurisdiction on certain days, such as *dies fasti.* They could not be officially spoken on *dies nefasti. Do* refers to the granting of actions, exceptions, and the appointment of judges; *dico* refers to the pronouncement of judgments; and *addico* refers to the adjudication of controverted property.

DOE. *abbr.* DEPARTMENT OF ENERGY.

Doe, Jane. See JANE DOE.

Doe, John. See JOHN DOE.

***D'Oench Duhme* doctrine** (dench **doom**). The rule that estops a borrower from asserting a claim or defense against a federal successor to a failed financial institution — if the claim or defense is based on a side or secret agreement or representation — unless the agreement or representation has been (1) put into writing, (2) executed by the financial institution and borrower when the loan was issued, (3) approved by the financial institution's board of directors or loan committee, and (4) made a permanent part of the financial institution's records. *D'Oench, Duhme & Co. v. FDIC*, 315 U.S. 447, 62 S.Ct. 676 (1942) (now partially codified at 12 USCA § 1823(e), and otherwise of questionable standing in light of *O'Melveny & Myers v. FDIC*, 512 U.S. 79, 114 S.Ct. 2048 (1994)).

d'office (daw-**fees**). [Law French] Of office; officially. • This is similar to the Latin phrase *ex officio*.

dog. *Slang.* **1.** Something undesirable, esp. a lawsuit <the cases assigned to the new lawyer were all dogs>. **2.** *Securities.* A stock or other investment that suffers public disdain and repeated price declines or poor performance.

dog-draw. *Hist.* The apprehension of someone chasing a deer in a forest with a dog.

> "Dog-draw is an apparent deprehension of an offender against venison in the forest. There are four kinds of them observed by Manwood, part. 2, cap. 18, num. 9, of his Forest Laws, that is, dog-draw, stable-stand, back-bear, and bloody-hand. Dog-draw is, when one is found drawing after a deer by the scent of a hound led in his hand." *Termes de la Ley* 181 (1st Am. ed. 1812).

dogma (**dawg**-mə *or* **dahg**-), *n.* A philosophy, opinion, or tenet that is strongly held, is believed to be authoritative, and is followed steadfastly, usu. to the exclusion of other approaches to the same subject matter; a formally stated and proclaimed doctrine of faith. Pl. **dogmas, dogmata** (-mə-tə).

DOHSA (**doh**-sə). *abbr.* DEATH ON THE HIGH SEAS ACT.

doing business. The act of engaging in business activities; esp., a nonresident's participation in sufficient business activities in a foreign state to allow the state's courts to exercise personal jurisdiction over the nonresident. See DOING-BUSINESS STATUTE; LONG-ARM STATUTE; MINIMUM CONTACTS.

doing-business statute. A state law defining the acts that constitute undertaking business there, usu. for the purpose of establishing the circumstances under which the state's courts may exercise personal jurisdiction over a nonresident. See MINIMUM CONTACTS; LONG-ARM STATUTE.

DOJ. *abbr.* DEPARTMENT OF JUSTICE.

dol (dohl *or* dol), *n.* [French "deceit; fraud"] *Civil law.* Fraud committed in inducing another to enter into a contract. See *fraud in the inducement* under FRAUD. Cf. FRAUDE.

do, lego (**doh**, **lee**-goh). [Latin] *Hist.* I give and bequeath. • In Roman law, this was the phrase used to make a bequest.

doli capax (**doh**-lɪ **kay**-paks), *adj.* [Latin "capable of wrong"] *Roman law.* Capable of committing a crime or tort; esp., old enough to determine right from wrong. — Also termed *capax doli*. Cf. DOLI INCAPAX.

> "In criminal cases, an infant of the age of *fourteen* years may be capitally punished for any capital offence: but under the age of *seven* he cannot. The period between *seven* and *fourteen* is subject to much incertainty: for the infant shall, generally speaking, be judged *prima facie* innocent; yet if he was *doli capax*, and could discern between good and evil at the time of the offence committed, he may be convicted and undergo judgment and execution of death, though he hath not attained to years of puberty or discretion." 1 William Blackstone, *Commentaries on the Laws of England* 452–53 (1765).

doli incapax (**doh**-lɪ in-**kay**-paks), *adj.* [Latin "incapable of wrong"] *Roman law.* Incapable of committing a crime or tort. — Also termed *incapax doli*. Cf. DOLI CAPAX.

dollar-cost averaging, *n.* The investment practice of purchasing a fixed dollar amount of a type of security at regular intervals.

dolo (**doh**-loh), *n.* [Spanish] *Spanish law.* Bad or mischievous design, as in *dolo malo pactum se non servaturum* ("an agreement induced by fraud cannot stand").

dolus (**doh**-ləs). [Latin "device; artifice"] *Roman & civil law.* **1.** Fraud or deceit; conduct intended to deceive someone. • Although there may be *dolus* without fraud, fraud always includes *dolus*. Cf. CASUS; CULPA. **2.** Intentional aggression; willful injury, esp. to another's property. — Also termed *dolus malus*; *fraus*.

> "In the twelfth century the resuscitated Roman law introduced some new ideas. Men began to contrast, as

Glanvill does, civil with criminal causes, to speak of *dolus* and *culpa* and *casus*, and to lay stress on the psychical element in crime." 2 Frederick Pollock & Frederic W. Maitland, *History of English Law Before the Time of Edward I* 477 (2d ed. 1899).

"Although the word *malitia* is not unknown to the Roman lawyers, the usual and technical name for wrongful intent is *dolus*, or more specifically *dolus malus*. *Dolus* and *culpa* are two forms of *mens rea*. In a narrower sense, however, *dolus* includes merely that particular variety of wrongful intent which we term fraud — that is to say, the intent to deceive. From this limited sense it was extended to cover all forms of wilful wrongdoing. The English term fraud has never received an equally wide extension." John Salmond, *Jurisprudence* 385 (Glanville L. Williams ed., 10th ed. 1947).

dolus bonus (**doh**-ləs **boh**-nəs). [Latin "good deceit"] Shrewdness or justifiable deceit, as when a person lies to an attacker to prevent an assault. • *Dolus bonus* does not produce any legal consequences.

dolus dans locum contractui (**doh**-ləs danz **loh**-kəm kən-**trak**-choo-I). [Latin] Fraud (or deceit) giving rise to the contract; specif., a fraudulent misrepresentation that, having been made by one of the parties to the contract and relied on by the other, was actually instrumental in inducing the latter to enter into the contract.

dolus malus (**doh**-ləs **mal**-əs). [Latin "bad *or* evil deceit"] Evil or fraudulent design or intent; an unjustifiable deceit.

domain (doh-**mayn**), *n.* **1.** The territory over which sovereignty is exercised <the 19th-century domains of the British Empire>. **2.** An estate in land <the family domain is more than 6,000 acres>. **3.** The complete and absolute ownership of land <his domain over this land has now been settled>. See EMINENT DOMAIN; PUBLIC DOMAIN.

domain-name infringement. See INFRINGEMENT.

domboc. See DOME BOOK.

***Dombrowski* doctrine.** The rule entitling a person to a federal-court injunction to prevent prosecution under a broad or vague state statute that affects rights guaranteed by the First Amendment. *Dombrowski v. Pfister*, 380 U.S. 479, 85 S.Ct. 1116 (1965).

dome book (**doom** buuk), *n.* [fr. Saxon *dombec*] *Hist.* A code, compiled under Alfred, containing maxims of common law, judicial forms, and criminal penalties.• The code existed until the reign of Edward IV when it was lost. — Also termed *doombook*; *domboc*; *liber judicialis of Alfred*.

Domesday Book (**doomz**-day). The census or survey, ordered by William the Conqueror and substantially completed in 1086, of England's landholdings, buildings, people, and livestock. — Abbr. D.B. — Also spelled *Doomsday Book*.

domestic, *adj.* **1.** Of or relating to one's own country <domestic affairs>. **2.** Of or relating to one's own jurisdiction <in Alaska, a domestic corporation is an Alaskan one>. **3.** Of or relating to the family or the household <a domestic dispute>.

domestic authority. A defense allowing a person responsible for another (such as a parent responsible for a child) to use nondeadly force when reasonably necessary to protect the person being cared for.

domestic bill. See BILL (6).

domestic corporation. See CORPORATION.

domestic court. See COURT.

domestic creditor. See CREDITOR.

domestic dispute. A disturbance, usu. at a residence and usu. within a family, involving violence and often resulting in a call to a law-enforcement agency. — Also termed *domestic disturbance*; *family disturbance*. See *domestic violence* under VIOLENCE.

domestic export. See EXPORT (1).

domestic guardian. See GUARDIAN.

Domestic International Sales Corporation. A U.S. corporation, esp. a subsidiary whose income is primarily attributable to exports. • Income tax on part of a DISC's income is usu. deferred, resulting in a lower overall corporate tax for the parent than it would otherwise incur. IRC (26 USCA) §§ 991–997. — Abbr. DISC.

domestic judgment. See JUDGMENT.

domestic relations. See FAMILY LAW.

domestic-relations court. See *family court* under COURT.

domestic-relations law. See FAMILY LAW.

domestic servant. A household servant. — Often shortened to *domestic*.

domesticus (də-**mes**-ti-kəs), *n.* [Latin] *Hist.* Steward; judge's assistant; assessor.

domestic violence. See VIOLENCE.

domicellus (dom-ə-**sel**-əs), *n.* [Law Latin] *Hist.* **1.** A king's natural son in France. **2.** A young lord.

"*Domicellus*, Is an old obsolete ... Word, anciently given as an Appellation or Addition to the King's natural Sons in *France*, and sometimes to the eldest Sons of Noblemen there; from whence we borrowed these Additions: As several natural Children of *John of Gaunt*, Duke of *Lancaster*, are stiled *Domicelli* by the Charter of Legitimation.... But according to *Thorn*, the *Domicelli* were only the better Sort of Servants in Monasteries." Giles Jacob, *A New Law–Dictionary* (8th ed. 1762).

domicile (**dom**-ə-sɪl), *n.* **1.** The place at which a person is physically present and that the person regards as home; a person's true, fixed, principal, and permanent home, to which that person intends to return and remain even though currently residing elsewhere. — Also termed *permanent abode.*

"By domicile we mean home, the permanent home; and if you do not understand your permanent home, I am afraid that no illustration drawn from foreign writers or foreign languages will very much help you to it." *Whicker v. Hume* (1858) 7 H.L.C. 124, 160 (per Lord Cranworth).

"It is difficult to give a definition of domicil that will cover at once domicil by operation of law and domicil by choice. The idea of domicil certainly includes the idea of place and the idea of settled connection with the place. Domicil of choice is so closely connected with the idea of home that it seems desirable to include that idea in any definition, and yet the idea is not applicable to many kinds of domicil by operation of law. It has therefore seemed best to state this element in the alternative. If a home is in the place, that is sufficient. If there is no home, or if the party is not *sui juris*, then the place is assigned by law without his will." 1 Joseph H. Beale, *A Treatise on the Conflict of Laws* § 9.1, at 89–90 (1935).

"Though the idea of permanent home is the central practical feature of domicile, Lord Cranworth's definition has a deceptive simplicity; for domicile ... is a conception of law employed for the purpose of establishing a connection for certain legal purposes between an individual and the legal system of the territory with which he either has the closest connection in fact or is considered by law so to have because of his dependence on some other person." R.H. Graveson, *Conflict of Laws* 185 (7th ed. 1974).

2. The residence of a person or corporation for legal purposes. — Also termed (in sense 2) *legal residence*. Cf. RESIDENCE; PLACE OF BUSINESS.

after-acquired domicile. A domicile established after the facts relevant to an issue arose. • An after-acquired domicile cannot be used to establish jurisdiction or choice of law.

commercial domicile. **1.** A domicile acquired by a nonresident corporation conducting enough activities to permit taxation of the corporation's property or activities located outside the bounds of the taxing state. **2.** A domicile acquired by a person or company freely residing or carrying on business in enemy territory or enemy-occupied territory. — Also termed *quasi-domicile*.

corporate domicile. The place considered by law as the center of corporate affairs, where the corporation's functions are discharged; the legal home of a corporation, usu. its state of incorporation or the state in which it maintains its principal place of business. • For purposes of determining whether diversity jurisdiction exists in federal court, a corporation is considered a citizen of both its state of incorporation and the state of its principal place of business. See DIVERSITY OF CITIZENSHIP.

domicile of choice. **1.** A domicile established by physical presence within a state or territory, coupled with the intention to make it home. **2.** The domicile that a person chooses after reaching majority or being emancipated.

domicile of origin. The domicile of a person at birth, derived from the custodial parent or imposed by law. — Also termed *natural domicile*.

domicile of succession. The domicile that determines the succession of a person's estate.

domicile of trustee. The domicile where a trustee is appointed.

elected domicile. A contractually agreed domicile between parties for purposes of the contract.

foreign domicile. A domicile established by a citizen or subject of one sovereignty within the territory of another.

matrimonial domicile. A domicile that a husband and wife, as a married couple, have established as their home. — Also termed *matrimonial home*.

municipal domicile. A person's residence in a county or municipality, as distinguished from the person's state or national domicile.

national domicile. A domicile considered in terms of a particular nation rather than a locality or subdivision of a nation.

natural domicile. See *domicile of origin.*

necessary domicile. A domicile legally fixed and independent of choice, as in the domicile of origin. See *domicile of origin.*

quasi-domicile. See *commercial domicile.*

quasi-national domicile. A person's state of residence, as distinguished from the person's national or local domicile.

domiciliary (dom-ə-**sil**-ee-er-ee), *adj.* Of or relating to domicile <domiciliary jurisdiction>.

domiciliary (dom-ə-**sil**-ee-er-ee), *n.* A person who resides in a particular place with the intention of making it a principal place of abode; one who is domiciled in a particular jurisdiction. Cf. RESIDENT; CITIZEN.

domiciliary administration. See ADMINISTRATION.

domiciliate (dom-ə-**sil**-ee-ayt), *vb.* To establish a domicile; to fix a place of residence.

domicilium (dom-ə-**sil**-ee-əm), *n.* [Law Latin] *Roman law.* DOMICILE.

domigerium (dom-ə-**jeer**-ee-əm), *n.* [Law Latin] *Hist.* **1.** Power over someone. **2.** Danger.

domina (**dom**-ə-nə), *n.* [Law Latin] **1.** A lady. **2.** A peeress. Cf. DAME (1), (2).

dominant estate. See ESTATE.

dominant-jurisdiction principle. The rule that the court in which a case is first filed maintains the suit, to the exclusion of all other courts that would also have jurisdiction.

dominant property. See *dominant estate* under ESTATE.

dominant tenant. See TENANT.

dominant tenement. See *dominant estate* under ESTATE (4).

dominate, *vb.* **1.** To master (someone or something); to control (someone or something). **2.** Predominate.

dominatio (dom-ə-**nay**-shee-oh), *n.* [Latin] *Hist.* Lordship; rule.

dominical (də-**min**-ə-kəl), *adj.* Of or relating to a Sunday; of or relating to the Lord's day.

dominicide (də-**min**-ə-sɪd), *n.* [fr. Latin *dominus* "master" + *caedo* "to kill"] *Hist.* **1.** The crime of killing one's master. **2.** A person who kills his or her master.

dominicum (də-**min**-ə-kəm), *n.* [Latin "domain"] **1.** *Hist.* Domain; lordship. **2.** *Hist.* Land ownership, esp. that retained by a lord for his own possession, as distinguished from the rights given to a tenant. **3.** *Eccles. law.* A church or other religious building.

dominicum antiquum (də-**min**-ə-kəm an-**tɪ**-kwəm), *n.* [Law Latin] *Hist.* Ancient domain.

dominion. 1. Control; possession <dominion over the car>. **2.** Sovereignty <dominion over the nation>. **3.** FOREIGN DOMINION.

dominium (də-**min**-ee-əm), *n.* [fr. Latin *dominus* "lord"] **1.** *Roman law.* Absolute ownership including the right to possession and use. • This term gradually came to also mean merely ownership of property, as distinguished from the right to possession or use.

> "*Dominium* is the Roman term for the rights of an owner against all the world: and the contrast of *dominium* and *obligatio* is the nearest approach that can be made, in classical Roman language, to the distinction marked by the modern terms *in rem* and *in personam.*" Frederick Pollock, *A First Book of Jurisprudence* 83 (1896).

> "The one word *dominium* has to assume so many shades of meaning. The tenant *qui tenet terram in dominico,* is *dominus rei* and has *dominium rei;* but then he has above him one who is his *dominus,* and for the rights of this lord over him and over his land there is no other name than *dominium.*" 2 Frederick Pollock & Frederic W. Maitland, *The History of English Law Before the Time of Edward I* 4 (2d ed. 1899).

dominium directum (də-**min**-ee-əm di-**rek**-təm), *n.* [Law Latin] *Civil law.* Legal, not equitable, ownership.

dominium directum et utile (də-**min**-ee-əm di-**rek**-təm et **yoo**-tə-lee), *n.* [Law Latin] *Civil law.* Complete ownership of property, including both title and exclusive use.

dominium eminens (də-**min**-ee-əm **em**-ə-nenz), *n.* [Law Latin] *Civil law.* Eminent domain. See EMINENT DOMAIN.

dominium plenum (də-**min**-ee-əm **plee**-nəm), *n.* [Law Latin] *Civil law.* Full ownership combining *dominium directum* and *dominium utile*. — Also termed *plenum dominium*.

dominium utile (də-**min**-ee-əm **yoo**-tə-lee), *n.* [Law Latin] *Civil law.* Equitable ownership; a beneficial right to use property; the right of a tenant to use the soil and its profits.

> "The special characteristic of Feudal land was that ownership in it was split into two kinds, the *dominium directum* of the superior (lord) and the *dominium utile* of the vassal. The feudists correctly insisted that this was not a form of joint ownership, not yet of ownership burdened with an easement or a 'usufruct,' but that two kinds of ownership were present, and that each of these persons, the lord and the vassal, was properly called 'owner' or *dominus*. The lord's *dominium directum* gave him a reversion in the case of forfeiture of failure of issue and the enjoyment of whatever the *naturalia* and *accidentalia* were. The vassal's *dominium utile* gave him the immediate enjoyment of the land itself." Max Radin, *Handbook of Anglo-American Legal History* 148 (1936).

plenum dominium. See *dominium plenum*.

2. *Hist.* Lordship; sovereignty.

> "The Latin word for ownership, *dominium*, is particularly confusing, since in medieval times it is also the word for lordship." J.H. Baker, *An Introduction to English Legal History* 255 (3d ed. 1990).

domino volente (**dom**-ə-noh və-**len**-tee). [Law Latin "the owner being willing"] With the owner's consent.

dominus (**dom**-ə-nəs), *n.* [Latin "lord"] **1.** *Roman law.* An owner of a thing or inheritance. **2.** *Roman law.* The title of the emperor in the later empire. **3.** *Hist.* A lord; a feudal superior, as in *dominus rex* ("the lord of the king"), *dominus capitalis* ("a chief lord"), *dominus medius* ("an intermediate lord"), and *dominus ligius* ("a liege lord"). **4.** *Hist. Eccles. law.* Lord; sir. • This is a title of distinction usu. given to a knight, a clergyman, a lord of a manor, or another gentleman of quality. **5.** *Civil law.* Someone who possesses something by right. Pl. ***domini.***

dominus litis (**dom**-ə-nəs **lɪ**-tis), *n.* [Latin] **1.** *Civil law.* The party who makes the decisions in a lawsuit, usu. as distinguished from the attorney. **2.** *Maritime law.* A third person who represents an absent party in a case. — Also termed *litis dominium*.

dominus navis (**dom**-ə-nəs **nay**-vis), *n.* [Latin] *Civil law.* The absolute owner of a shipping vessel.

domitae naturae (**dom**-ə-tee nə-**tyoor**-ee). [Latin] *Hist.* Of a tame nature; not wild. • This term usu. refers to long-domesticated animals, such as sheep or cattle, in which a person has absolute property rights. But it can also refer to naturally wild animals that have been tamed.

dommage survenu (daw-**mazh** suur-və-**noo**). [French] Damage sustained. • This is from article 17 of the Warsaw Convention providing for compensatory damages, rather than awards for loss of society or punitive damages, for bodily injury that a passenger suffers while on board an aircraft, or while boarding or disembarking.

domo reparanda (**doh**-moh rep-ə-**ran**-də), *n.* [Latin "to repair a house"] *Hist.* A writ available to a person to force a neighbor who owns a decrepit house to repair it because the person is worried that the neighbor's house will fall and cause injury.

Dom. Proc. *abbr.* DOMUS PROCERUM.

domus (**doh**-məs), *n.* [Latin] A house; an abode.

domus conversorum (**doh**-məs kon-vər-**sor**-əm), *n.* [Law Latin "house of the converts"] *Hist.* An institution, established by Henry III for converted Jews, that continued until Edward III expelled Jews from the kingdom and converted the institution to a chancery record office.

domus Dei (**doh**-məs **dee**-ɪ), *n.* [Law Latin] House of God. • This term was applied to various hospitals and religious houses, such as the Hospital of St. Julian in Southampton.

Domus Procerum (**doh**-məs **pros**-ə-rəm), *n.* [Latin "house of nobles"] The House of Lords. — Abbr. *Dom. Proc.*; *D.P.*

donatarius (doh-nə-**tair**-ee-əs), *n.* [Latin] A donee; a gift recipient.

donate, *vb.* To give (property or money) without receiving consideration for the transfer. — **donation,** *n.* — **donative** (**doh**-nə-tiv), *adj.*

donated stock. See STOCK.

donated surplus. See SURPLUS.

donatio (doh-**nay**-shee-oh). [Latin] A gift.

donatio causa mortis (doh-**nay**-shee-oh **kaw**-zə **mor**-tis), *n.* See *gift causa mortis* under GIFT. Pl. ***donationes causa mortis.***

donatio inofficiosa (doh-**nay**-shee-oh in-ə-fish-ee-**oh**-sə). [Latin "inofficious gift"] A gift so large that it diminishes an heir's birthright portion of the donor's property.

donatio inter vivos (doh-**nay**-shee-oh **in**-tər **vI**-vohs). See *inter vivos gift* under GIFT.

donatio mortis causa, *n.* See *gift causa mortis* under GIFT. Pl. ***donationes mortis causa.***

donation. 1. A gift. **2.** *Eccles. law.* A method of acquiring a benefice by deed of gift alone, without presentation, institution, or induction.

donation land. See LAND.

donatio propter nuptias (doh-**nay**-shee-oh **prahp**-tər **nəp**-shee-əs). [Latin "a gift on account of marriage"] *Roman law.* A gift from a husband to his wife equivalent to her dowry and subject to similar conditions. • It was formerly called *donatio ante nuptias* ("gift before marriage") because it was not allowed after the marriage celebration. Justinian later changed the law and the name. See DOS.

donative (**don**-ə-tiv *or* **doh**-nə-tiv), *adj.* **1.** Of, relating to, or characterized by a donation <a donative transfer>. **2.** Subject to a donation <an advowson donative>.

donative advowson. See ADVOWSON.

donative trust. See TRUST.

donator (**doh**-nay-tər *or* doh-**nay**-tər *also* -tor), *n.* [Latin] A donor; a person who makes a gift.

donatory (**don**-ə-tor-ee *or* **doh**-nə-tor-ee), *n.* *Scots law.* A recipient of a gift; specif., a donee of the Crown.

> "A donatory is the donee or receiver of a gift or donation. In practice, the term is applied exclusively to the person to whom the Crown makes a gift, as of escheat, *ultimus haeres*, or the like." William Bell, *Bell's Dictionary and Digest of the Law of Scotland* 299 (George Watson ed., 1882).

donec (**doh**-nek). [Latin] *Hist.* As long as; while; until; within a certain time. • This term was used in old conveyances.

donec probetur in contrarium (**doh**-nek proh-**bee**-tər in kən-**trair**-ee-əm). [Latin] Until proof is given to the contrary.

donee (doh-**nee**). One to whom a gift is made.

donee beneficiary. See BENEFICIARY.

donee of power. The recipient of a power of appointment.

donor. 1. One who gives something without receiving consideration for the transfer. **2.** SETTLOR (1).

donum (**doh**-nəm), *n.* [Latin "a gift"] *Roman law.* A gift.

donum gratuitum. See *gratuitous gift* under GIFT.

doombook. See DOME BOOK.

Doomsday book. See DOMESDAY BOOK.

door-closing statute. A state law closing or denying access to local courts unless a plaintiff meets specified conditions; esp., a statute requiring a foreign corporation to "qualify" before doing business in the state, including registering with the secretary of state, paying a fee or tax, and appointing an agent to receive service of process.

doowop docket. *Slang.* See *DWOP docket* under DOCKET (2).

dope. 1. A thick liquid used esp. for medicinal purposes. **2.** *Slang.* A drug, esp. a narcotic.

dormant (**dor**-mənt), *adj.* Inactive; suspended; latent <a dormant judgment>. — **dormancy,** *n.*

dormant claim. A claim that is in abeyance.

Dormant Commerce Clause. See COMMERCE CLAUSE.

dormant corporation. See CORPORATION.

dormant execution. See EXECUTION.

dormant judgment. See JUDGMENT.

dormant legislative intent. See LEGISLATIVE INTENT.

dormant partner. See *silent partner* under PARTNER.

dormant title. See TITLE (2).

dorsum (**dor**-səm). [Latin] *Hist.* The back. • This term usu. appeared as part of the phrase *in dorso* to indicate that an instrument had been signed on the back. *In dorso recordi,* for example, meant "on the back of the record."

> "In the first place then the payee, or person to whom or whose *order* such bill of exchange or promissory note is payable, may by endorsement, or writing his name in *dorso* or on the back of it, assign over his whole property to the bearer, or else to another person by name...." 2 William Blackstone, *Commentaries on the Laws of England* 468 (1766).

dos (dos *or* dohs), *n.* [Latin] **1.** *Roman law.* Dowry. **2.** *Hist.* Dower.

> "Dos was a gift made to the husband on the part of the wife as her contribution towards the expenses of the joint establishment. It was made by the wife or by another person on her behalf, usually before marriage and conditionally on the marriage taking place; but it might also be made or increased after marriage." R.W. Lee, *The Elements of Roman Law* 150 (4th ed. 1956).

dos rationabilis (dohs rash-[ee]-ə-**nay**-bə-lis), *n.* [Latin] See *dower by the common law* under DOWER.

dossier (**dos**-ee-ay), *n.* [French] A file or brief; a bundle of papers pertaining to a particular matter.

DOT. *abbr.* DEPARTMENT OF TRANSPORTATION.

dot (dot *or* dawt), *n.* [French fr. Latin *dos*] *Civil law.* Dowry; the property that a woman brings to the marriage to help with marriage expenses. • The income is usu. controlled by the husband, while the principal remains the wife's separate property.

dotage (**doh**-tij). **1.** Senility; feebleness of a person's mind in old age. **2.** Foolish affection; excessive fondness.

dotal (**doht**-əl), *adj.* Of or relating to dowry. See DOWRY.

dotalitium (doh-tə-**lish**-ee-əm), *n.* [Law Latin] *Hist.* Dower.

> "[S]ome have ascribed the introduction of dower to the Normans, as a branch of *their* local tenures; though we cannot expect any feodal reason for its invention, since it was not a part of the pure, primitive, simple law of feuds, but was first of all introduced into that system (wherein it was called ... *dotalitium*) by the emperor Frederick the second; who was contemporary with our king Henry III. It is possible therefore that it might be with us the relic of a Danish custom: since, according to the historians of that country, dower was introduced into Denmark by Swein, the father of our Canute the great, out of gratitude to the Danish ladies, who sold all their jewels to ransom him when taken prisoner by the Vandals." 2 William Blackstone, *Commentaries on the Laws of England* 129–30 (1766).

dotal property. *Civil law.* Separate property that the wife brings to the marriage to assist the husband with the marriage expenses.

dotation (doh-**tay**-shən), *n.* **1.** The act of giving a dowry. **2.** An endowment, esp. of funds for a charitable institution such as a hospital.

dote (doht), *vb.* **1.** To be silly due to old age. **2.** To bestow excessive fondness.

dote assignanda (**doh**-tee as-ig-**nan**-də). See DE DOTE ASSIGNANDA.

dote unde nil habet (**doh**-tee **ən**-dee nil **hay**-bet). See DE DOTE UNDE NIL HABET.

dotis administratio (**doh**-tis ad-min-ə-**stray**-shee-oh). See DE ADMENSURATIONE DOTIS.

dotissa (doh-**tis**-ə), *n.* [Law Latin] A dowager.

double adultery. See ADULTERY.

double assessment. The act of requiring that tax be paid twice for the same property. See *double taxation* under TAXATION.

double-bill, *vb.* To charge two different clients or customers the same charge; to charge two different customers for services rendered to each customer at the same time.

double-breasted operation. An arrangement in which a business owner operates both a union business and a similar nonunion business, to compete for both types of business contracts. — Also termed *open-shop–closed-shop operation.*

double commission. See COMMISSION (5).

double complaint. See DUPLEX QUERELA.

double creditor. See CREDITOR.

double damages. See DAMAGES.

double-declining depreciation method. See DEPRECIATION METHOD.

double-dipping, *n.* An act of seeking or accepting essentially the same benefit twice, either from the same source or from two different sources, as in simultaneously accepting retirement and unemployment benefits. — **double-dipper,** *n.*

double-entry bookkeeping. See BOOKKEEPING.

double forgery. See FORGERY.

double gibbet. See GIBBET.

double hearsay. See HEARSAY.

double indemnity. See INDEMNITY.

double insurance. See INSURANCE.

double jeopardy. The fact of being prosecuted twice for substantially the same offense. • Double jeopardy is prohibited by the Fifth Amendment. Cf. FORMER JEOPARDY.

Double Jeopardy Clause. The Fifth Amendment provision stating, "nor shall any person be subject for the same offence to be twice put in jeopardy of life or limb." • The amendment was ratified in 1791.

double patenting. 1. The issuance of two patents covering the same invention. • An inventor is not allowed to receive more than one patent on one invention. — Also termed *same-invention double patenting.* **2.** The issuance of a second patent claiming an invention that differs from an already patented invention only in some unpatentable particular. — Also termed *obviousness double patenting.*

double plea. See PLEA (3).

double pleading. See DUPLICITY (2).

double proof. See PROOF.

double quarrel. See DUPLEX QUERELA.

double recovery. See RECOVERY.

double rent. See RENT (1).

double standard. A set of principles permitting greater opportunity or greater lenience for one class of people than for another, usu. based on differences such as gender or race. See DISCRIMINATION.

double taxation. See TAXATION.

double use. See USE (1).

double value. Twice the value of something; specif., a penalty payable by a tenant to a landlord of twice the yearly value of lands held by the tenant, who refused to leave when the landlord provided written notice of intent to possess the property. • The penalty was provided under the Landlord and Tenant Act (1730). St. 4 Geo. 2. ch. 28, s. 1.

double voucher. In a common-recovery suit, a voucher first by the fictitious tenant to the real tenant, and then by the real tenant to the common vouchee. See COMMON RECOVERY.

> "The recovery, here described, is with a *single* voucher only; but sometimes it is with *double* ... or farther voucher, as the exigency of the case may require. And indeed it is now usual always to have a recovery with double voucher at the least; by first conveying an estate of freehold to any indifferent person, against whom the *praecipe* is brought; and then he vouches the tenant in tail, who vouches over the common vouchee. For, if a recovery be had immediately against tenant in tail, it bars only such estate in the premises of which he is then actually seised; whereas if the recovery be had against another person, and the tenant in tail be vouched, it bars every latent right and interest which he may have in the lands recovered." 2 William Blackstone, *Commentaries on the Laws of England* 359 (1766).

double waste. See WASTE (1).

double will. See *mutual will* under WILL.

doubt, reasonable. See REASONABLE DOUBT.

doubtful title. See TITLE (2).

doun (doon *or* dohn), *n.* [Law French] A gift.

do ut des (**doh** ət **deez**). [Latin "I give that you may give"] *Roman law.* An innominate contract in which a party gives something in exchange for something that the other party is to give. See *innominate contract* under CONTRACT.

do ut facias (**doh** ət **fay**-shee-əs). [Latin "I give that you may do"] *Roman law.* An innominate contract in which a person gives something to another person who is to do or perform certain work. See *innominate contract* under CONTRACT.

dovetail seniority. The combination of seniority lists from merging companies into one list that allows employees to keep their premerger seniority.

Dow (dow). See DOW JONES INDUSTRIAL AVERAGE.

dowable (**dow**-ə-bəl), *adj.* **1.** Capable of being endowed <the widow received the dowable estate>. **2.** Capable of receiving dower <the woman was dowable of the estate>.

dowager (**dow**-ə-jər). A widow holding property or title — esp. a life estate in real property — received from her deceased husband.

dowager-queen. The widow of the king of England. — Also termed *queen dowager*; *queen mother*.

> "A queen *dowager* is the widow of the king, and as such enjoys most of the privileges belonging to her as queen consort. But it is not high treason to conspire her death; or to violate her chastity ... because the succession to the crown is not thereby endangered. Yet still, ... no man can marry a queen dowager without special licence from the king, on pain of forfeiting his lands and goods.... A queen dowager, when married again to a subject, doth not lose her regal dignity, as peeresses dowager do their peerage when they marry commoners." 1 William Blackstone, *Commentaries on the Laws of England* 217 (1765).

dower (**dow**-ər). At common law, the right of a wife, upon her husband's death, to a life estate in one-third of the land that he owned in fee. • With few exceptions, the wife could not be deprived of dower by any transfer made by her husband during his lifetime. Although most states have abolished dower, many states retaining the concept have expanded the wife's share to a life estate in all the land that her husband owned in fee. — Also termed *dowment*. Cf. CURTESY.

consummate dower (kən-**səm**-it). A wife's interest in her deceased husband's estate until that interest is legally assigned to her.

dower ad ostium ecclesiae (ad **ahs**-tee-əm e-**klee**-z[h]ee-ee), *n.* [Law Latin "dower at the church door"] *Hist.* An endowment of dower made by a man to his wife at the church door or porch, usu. as part of the marriage ceremony.

> "DOWER AD OSTIUM ECCLESIAE .... This appears to have been the original English dower .... It was formerly the most usual species of dower, and, though latterly fallen into disuse, was not abolished until the statute of 3 & 4 Will. IV. c. 105, s. 13 .... The wife might be endowed of personalty or goods as well as of lands, and a trace of this ancient kind of dower is still distinctly preserved in the marriage ritual of the church of England, in the expression 'with all my worldly goods I thee endow.'" 1 Alexander M. Burrill, *A Law Dictionary and Glossary* 520 (2d ed. 1867).

dower by custom. *Hist.* Dower that is determined by custom rather than the general law.

> "Dower by ... *custom*; as that the wife shall have half the husband's lands, or in some places the whole, and in some only a quarter." 2 William Blackstone, *Commentaries on the Laws of England* 132 (1766).

dower by the common law. The regular dower, consisting of a life interest in one-third of the lands that the husband held in fee. — Also termed *dos rationabilis*.

dower ex assensu patris (eks ə-**sen**-s[y]oo **pa**-tris), *n.* [Law Latin "dower by the father's assent"] *Hist.* A type of dower *ad ostium ecclesiae* made while the husband's father is alive and consents to the endowment to his son's wife.

inchoate dower (in-**koh**-it). A wife's interest in her husband's estate while both are living.

doweress. See DOWRESS.

Dow Jones Industrial Average. A stock-market-performance indicator that consists of the price movements in the stocks of 30 leading industrial companies in the United States. — Abbr. DJIA. — Often shortened to *Dow*. — Also termed *Dow Jones Average*.

dowle stones (dohl). Rocks used as land boundaries.

dowment. See DOWER.

down market. See *bear market* under MARKET.

down payment. See PAYMENT.

down reversal. *Securities.* A sudden market-price decline after a rising trend. • The term applies to the early stage of the decline; if the decline continues for several months, it is termed a *bear market*. Also termed *correction*; *market correction*.

downside. *Securities.* A period of declining stock prices.

downside risk. *Securities.* A likely risk that stock prices will drop.

downside trend. *Securities.* The portion of the market cycle that shows declining stock prices. — Also termed *down trend*.

downsizing. Reducing the number of employees, usu. to decrease labor costs and to increase efficiency.

downstream merger. See MERGER.

down trend. See DOWNSIDE TREND.

downward departure. See DEPARTURE.

dowress (**dow**-ris). *Archaic.* **1.** A woman legally entitled to dower. **2.** A tenant in dower. — Also spelled *doweress.*

dowry (**dow**-ree). *Archaic.* The money, goods, or property that a woman brings to her husband in marriage. — Also termed *marriage portion*; *maritagium* (mar-ə-**tay**-jee-əm).

dozen peers. *Hist.* During the reign of Henry III, 12 peers assembled by the barons to be the King's advisers.

D.P. *abbr.* DOMUS PROCERUM.

Dr. *abbr.* **1.** DEBTOR. **2.** DOCTOR.

DR. *abbr.* DISCIPLINARY RULE.

draconian (dray- *or* drə-**koh**-nee-in), *adj.* (Of a law) harsh; severe. • This term derives from *Draco*, the name of the ancient Athenian lawgiver. — Also termed *draconic.*

draff (draf). Refuse; dregs; sweepings of dust and dirt. • In weighing commodities, it is not included as part of the waste allowance for goods sold by weight.

draft, *n.* **1.** An unconditional written order signed by one person (the *drawer*) directing another person (the *drawee* or *payor*) to pay a certain sum of money on demand or at a definite time to a third person (the *payee*) or to bearer. • A check is the most common example of a draft. — Also termed *bill of exchange*; *letter of exchange*. Cf. NOTE (1).

bank draft. A draft drawn by one financial institution on another.

clean draft. A draft with no shipping documents attached.

demand draft. See *sight draft.*

documentary draft. A payment demand conditioned on the presentation of a document, such as a document of title, invoice, certificate, or notice of default.

export draft. A draft drawn by a domestic seller on a foreign buyer, directing the buyer to pay the trade amount to the seller or the seller's bank.

foreign draft. A draft drawn in one country or state but payable in another. — Also termed *foreign bill of exchange*; *international bill of exchange.*

inland draft. A draft drawn and payable in the same state or country.

overdraft. See OVERDRAFT.

share draft. A demand that a member draws against a credit-union share account, payable to a third party. • A share draft is similar to a check that is written to draw funds out of a checking account at a bank.

sight draft. A draft that is payable on the bearer's demand or on proper presentment to the drawer. — Also termed *demand draft.*

time draft. A draft that contains a specified payment date. UCC § 3–108. — Also termed *time bill.*

2. The compulsory enlistment of persons into military service <his illness disqualified him from the draft>. — Also termed *conscription.* **3.** An initial or preliminary version <the second draft of the contract>.

draft, *vb.* **1.** To write or compose <to draft a contract>. **2.** To recruit or select (someone) <to draft someone to run for political office> <to draft someone into the armed services>.

draft board. A civilian board that registers and selects persons for mandatory military service. See SELECTIVE SERVICE SYSTEM.

drafter. A person who draws or frames a legal document, such as a will, contract, or legislative bill. — Also termed *draftsman.*

drafting. The practice, technique, or skill involved in preparing legal documents — such as statutes, rules, regulations, contracts, and wills — that set forth the rights, duties, liabilities, and entitlements of persons and legal entities.

draftsman. See DRAFTER.

dragnet clause. 1. See MOTHER HUBBARD CLAUSE (1). **2.** See CROSS-COLLATERAL CLAUSE.

dragnet lien. See LIEN.

Drago doctrine. The principle asserted by Luis Drago, Minister of Foreign Affairs of the Argentine Republic, in a December 29, 1902 letter to the Argentine Minister in Washington, in which Drago, in response to the forcible coercion of Venezuela's unpaid loans by Great Britain and others, argued that no public debt should be collected from a sovereign state by force or through the occupation of American territory by a foreign power. • The subject was presented at the Hague Conference of 1907, when a modified version of the Drago doctrine was adopted.

drain, *n.* **1.** The act of drawing a liquid off gradually; the act of emptying. **2.** The act of gradually exhausting. **3.** A conduit for draining liquid, as a ditch or a pipe.

drain, *vb.* **1.** To draw (a liquid) off gradually <the farmer drained water from the property>. **2.** To exhaust gradually <the facility has drained the area's natural resources>. **3.** To empty gradually <the water drained>.

drainage district. A political subdivision authorized to levy assessments for making drainage improvements within its area.

> "In the United States there are numerous special districts that administer drainage projects. They are typically formed under state law after a local election or petition showing consent of a majority of affected landowners. The projects are usually publicly financed, and assessments are made against all property benefited, whether or not all individual landowners have consented. Such projects can increase the agricultural capacity of drained lands and provide 'new' land for buildings and other improvements .... Special statutes governing drainage districts generally exempt them from restraints.... But if private property rights are taken or if others are damaged, compensation must be paid." David H. Getches, *Water Law in a Nutshell* 301 (3d ed. 1997).

drainage rights. The interest that a property owner has in the natural drainage and flow of water on the land.

dram (dram). **1.** An apothecary measurement of fluid equal to an eighth of an ounce. **2.** A small amount of anything, esp. liquor.

drama, *n.* **1.** A presentation of a story portrayed by words and actions or actions alone; a play. Cf. DRAMATIC COMPOSITION.

> "The term [*drama*] is applied to compositions which imitate action by representing the personages introduced in them as real and as employed in the action itself. The varieties of the drama differ more or less widely, both as to the objects imitated and as to the means used in the imitation. But they all agree as to the *method* or *manner* which is essential to the dramatic art, viz., *imitation in the way of action.*" 7 *Encyclopaedia Britannica* 338 (9th ed. 1907).

2. An event or series of events having conflicting and exciting elements that capture people's attention.

dramatic composition. *Copyright.* A literary work setting forth a story, incident, or scene intended to be performed by actors, often with a musical accompaniment. Cf. DRAMA (1).

dram shop. *Archaic.* A place where alcoholic beverages are sold; a bar or saloon. — Also spelled *dram-shop*; *dramshop*. — Also termed *grog-shop*; *drinking shop*.

dram-shop act. A statute allowing a plaintiff to recover damages from a commercial seller of alcoholic beverages for the plaintiff's injuries caused by a customer's intoxication. — Also termed *civil-liability act*.

> "Largely at the behest of the temperance movement, statutes (called 'dram shop acts') were enacted in many states which imposed some form of civil liability on those engaged in the business of selling such beverages in favor of third persons injured thereby .... At one time, almost half the states had such laws; today, that number seems to be declining.... A growing minority of states have overthrown the common law rule and have created a common law dram shop action. In most of these jurisdictions, liability is predicated on statutes which regulate the liquor business and prohibit certain sales by liquor licensees (to minors, intoxicated persons, etc.) thus, where the sale is unlawful, it is negligence per se ...." Edward J. Kionka, *Torts in a Nutshell* 293–94 (2d ed. 1992).

dram-shop liability. Civil liability of a commercial seller of alcoholic beverages for personal injury caused by an intoxicated customer. • Claims based on a similar type of liability have been brought against private citizens for personal injury caused by an intoxicated social guest.

draw, *vb.* **1.** To create and sign (a draft) <draw a check to purchase goods>. **2.** To prepare or frame (a legal document) <draw up a will>. **3.** To take out (money) from a bank, treasury, or depository <she then drew $6,000 from her account>. **4.** To select (a jury) <the lawyers then began voir dire and had soon drawn a jury>.

drawback. A government allowance or refund on import duties when the importer reexports imported products rather than selling them domestically. 19 USCA § 1313.

drawee (draw-**ee**). The person or entity that a draft is directed to and that is requested to pay the amount stated on it. • The drawee is usu. a bank that is directed to pay a sum of money on an instrument. — Also termed *payor*.

drawee bank. See *payor bank* under BANK.

drawer. One who directs a person or entity, usu. a bank, to pay a sum of money stated in an instrument — for example, a person who writes a check; the maker of a note or draft. See MAKER.

drawing account. See ACCOUNT.

drawing lots. An act of selection or decision-making based on pure chance, with the result depending on the particular lot drawn. • Jurors are usu. instructed by the court not to base their verdict on drawing lots or similar methods of chance.

drawlatch. *Hist.* A thief; a robber who waits until homes are empty, then draws the homes' door latches to steal what is inside.

drayage. A charge for transporting property.

dread-disease insurance. See INSURANCE.

dreit dreit. See DROIT-DROIT.

D reorganization. See REORGANIZATION (2).

drift of the forest. *Hist.* A periodic examination of forest cattle by officers who drive them to an enclosed place to determine their ownership or common status.

> "Drift of the forest is nothing else but an exact view or examination taken once, twice, or oftener in a year as occasion shall require, what beasts there are in the forest, to the end that the common in the forest be not overcharged, that the beasts of foreigners that have no common there be not permitted, and that beasts not commonable may be put out." *Termes de la Ley* 185–87 (1st Am. ed. 1812).

drift-stuff. Any material floating at random in water without a discoverable source. • Drift-stuff is usu. the property of the riparian owner.

drilling-delay rental clause. *Oil & gas.* A clause in an oil-and-gas lease providing for periodic payments by the lessee to postpone exploration during the primary lease term. • This clause is usu. used to negate any requirement of drilling a test well.

> "The purpose of the lease drilling-delay rental clause is to ensure that the lessee has no obligation to drill during the primary term by negating any implied obligation to test the premises. Before drilling-delay rental clauses became common in oil and gas leases, many courts held that lessees had an implied duty to drill a test well on the leased premises within a reasonable time after grant of the lease. The rationale for the implied covenant was that the major consideration for the grant of the lease by the lessor was the expectation that the property would be tested within a reasonable time. The courts' determination of what was a reasonable time ranged from a few months to several years, depending upon the circumstances. Lessees found that they could not rely upon a long stated term alone to preserve their rights." John S. Lowe, *Oil and Gas Law in a Nutshell* 195–96 (3d ed. 1995).

drinking shop. See DRAM SHOP.

drip rights. A servitude allowing water dripping off a person's roof to fall on a neighbor's land.

driver. 1. A person who steers and propels a vehicle. **2.** A person who herds animals; a drover.

driver's license. The state-issued certificate authorizing a person to operate a motor vehicle.

driving, *n.* The act of directing the course of something, such as an automobile or a herd of animals.

driving under the influence. The offense of operating a motor vehicle in a physically or mentally impaired condition, esp. after consuming alcohol or drugs. • Generally, this is a lesser offense than driving while intoxicated. But in a few jurisdictions the two are synonymous. — Abbr. DUI. — Also termed (in N.Y.) *driving while ability-impaired* (DWAI); *driving under the influence of liquor* (DUIL); *driving while intoxicated* (DWI); *operating under the influence* (OUI); *operating while intoxicated* (OWI); *operating a motor vehicle while intoxicated* (OMVI); *operating a motor vehicle under the influence* (OMVUI). Cf. DRIVING WHILE INTOXICATED.

driving while ability-impaired. See DRIVING UNDER THE INFLUENCE.

driving while intoxicated. The offense of operating a motor vehicle in a physically or mentally impaired condition after consuming enough to raise one's blood alcohol content above the statutory limit (.08% in many states), or after consuming drugs. • Penalties vary widely; for example, the maximum penalty in Missouri and Louisiana is a $500 fine and six months in jail, while the penalties in New York range from $500 to $5,000 in fines and up to four years in jail. — Abbr. DWI. Cf. DRIVING UNDER THE INFLUENCE.

DRM. See *direct-reduction mortgage* under MORTGAGE.

droit (drwah *or* droyt). [French "right"] **1.** A legal right or claim. **2.** The whole body of law.

droit-close (droyt **klohz**), *n.* [Law French] *Hist.* A writ against a lord on behalf of a tenant in ancient demesne holding land by charter in fee simple, in fee-tail, for life, or in dower.

droit common (droyt **kom**-ən), *n.* [Law French] The common law. — Also termed *droit coutumier*. See COMMON LAW (2).

droit coutumier. See DROIT COMMON.

droit d'accession (**drwah** dak-ses-**syawn**), *n.* [French "right of accession"] *French law.* A property right acquired by making, from existing material, something new that cannot be reduced to the original material's shape. • This is the equivalent to the Roman *specificatio*. See ACCESSION (4).

> "DROIT D'ACCESSION .... The civil law rule is that if the thing can be reduced to the former matter it belongs to the owner of the matter, *e.g.* a statue made of gold; but if it cannot so be reduced it belongs to the person who made it, *e.g.* a statue made of marble." 1 John Bouvier, *Bouvier's Law Dictionary* 941 (8th ed. 1914).

droit d'accroissement (**drwah** da-krwas-**mawn**), *n.* [French] *French law.* A right of survivorship by which an heir's interest is combined with the interest of a coheir who either has refused or is unable to accept the interest.

droit d'aubaine (**drwah** doh-**ben**), *n.* [Law French "right of alienage"] *Hist.* With certain exceptions, a sovereign's right to a deceased alien's property, regardless of whether the alien had a will. • This right was primarily exercised in France where it was revived in some form by Napoleon after its initial abolishment in 1790. It was ultimately abolished in 1819. — Also spelled *droit d'aubaigne*; *droit d'aubenage*. — Also termed *jus albanagii*; *jus albinatus*.

> "Under the French rule of law, known as the *droit d'aubaine* ... the whole property of an alien dying in France without leaving children born in that country escheated to the crown. The royal right was not universally exacted, and at a very early period special exceptions were introduced in favour of certain classes. Thus Louis XI exempted merchants of Brabant, Flanders, Holland, and Zealand from the operation of the law, and a similar privilege was extended by Henri II to merchants of the Hanse towns, and from Scotland." 1 R.H. Inglis Palgrave, *Palgrave's Dictionary of Political Economy* 68 (Henry Higgs ed., 2d ed. 1925).

> "In France by the fourteenth century it was accepted that a stranger might acquire and possess but not inherit or transmit by will or on intestacy. In 1386 the French king assumed the seigneurial *droit d'aubaine* or right to inherit. In treaties in the seventeenth and eighteenth centuries the right was frequently renounced. Louis XVI in 1787 abolished the right as against subjects of Great Britain without reciprocity. The constituent Assembly abolished the right in 1790 and it was commonly abolished elsewhere in the early nineteenth century." David M. Walker, *The Oxford Companion to Law* 378 (1980).

droit de bris (**drwah** də **bree**), *n.* [Law French "right of a wreck"] *Hist.* A right claimed by lords of the coasts of France to fragments of shipwrecks, including persons or property that had washed ashore. • The right was exercised primarily in Bretagne but was abrogated by Henry III as duke of Normandy, Aquitaine, and Guienne, in a charter granted in A.D. 1226. — Also termed *droit de bris sur le naufrages*. Cf. DROIT DE NAUFRAGE.

droit de détraction (**drwah** də day-trak-**syawn**), *n.* [French "the right of withdrawal"] *Int'l law.* A tax on property acquired by succession or by will and then removed to another state or country.

droit de garde (**drwah** də **gahrd**), *n.* [French "right of ward"] *Hist. French law.* A king's right to wardship of a noble vassal who has not reached majority.

droit de gite (**drwah** də **zheet**), *n.* [French "right of lodging"] *Hist. French law.* A duty of a commoner holding land in the royal domain to provide lodging and food to a royal party traveling on royal business.

droit de greffe (**drwah** də **gref**), *n.* [French "a right concerning the clerk's office"] *Hist. French law.* The Crown's privilege to sell offices connected with the custody of judicial records or official acts.

droit de maitrise (**drwah** də may-**treez**), *n.* [French "a right of mastership"] *Hist. French law.* A required payment to the Crown by an apprentice who has become a master worker.

droit de naufrage (**drwah** də noh-**frazh**), *n.* [French] *Hist. French law.* The right of a sovereign or a lord owning a seashore to seize the wreckage of a shipwreck and kill the crew or sell them as slaves. Cf. DROIT DE BRIS.

droit de prise (**drwah** də **preez**), *n.* [French "a right of prize"] *Hist. French law.* A commoner's duty to supply articles on credit to the royal household for domestic consumption.

droit de quint (**drwah** də **kant**), *n.* [French "the right of a fifth"] *Hist. French law.* A required payment made by a noble vassal to the king each time ownership of the vassal's fief changed.

droit de suite (**drwah** də **sweet**), *n.* [French "right to follow"] A creditor's right to recover a debtor's property after it passes to a third party.

droit d'exécution (**drwah** dek-say-kyoo-**syawn**), *n.* [French "right of execution"] *French law.* **1.** A stockbroker's right to sell the stock bought for a client who later refuses it. **2.** A stockbroker's right to sell deposited securities to secure the broker against a loss in buying for a client.

droit-droit (drwah-drwah), *n.* [Law French "double right"] *Hist.* The unification of the right of possession with the right of property. — Also termed *jus duplicatum*; *dreit dreit.*

> "A complete title to lands, tenements, and hereditaments. For it is an ancient maxim of the law, that no title is completely good, unless the right of possession be joined with the right of property; which right is then denominated a double right, *jus duplicatum*, or *droit droit*. And when to this double right the actual possession is also united . . . then, and then only, is the title completely legal." 2 William Blackstone, *Commentaries on the Laws of England* 199 (1766).

droit du seigneur (**drwah** də sen-**yuur**). [French "right of the lord"] *Hist.* **1.** A supposed customary right of a feudal lord to have sexual intercourse with a tenant's bride on her wedding night. **2.** A supposed custom requiring sexual abstinence by a couple on their wedding night. — Also spelled *droit de seigneur.* — Also termed *jus primae noctis.*

droit écrit (**drwaht** ay-**kree**), *n.* [French "the written law"] *French law.* The civil law; the *corpus juris civilis.*

droit international (**drwaht** a*n*-tair-nah-syoh-**nahl**), *n.* [French] International law.

droit maritime (**drwah** ma-ree-**teem**). [French] Maritime law.

droit moral (**drwah** maw-**ral**). [French] The doctrine of moral right, which entitles artists to prevent others from altering their works. • The basic rights protected by this doctrine are (1) the right to create, (2) the right to disclose or publish, (3) the right to withdraw from publication, (4) the right to be identified with the work, and (5) the right to ensure the integrity of the work, including the right to object to any mutilation or distortion of the work. These rights are sometimes called *moral rights.* See MORAL RIGHT.

droit naturel (**drwah** na-tuu-**rel**), *n.* [French] Natural law.

droits civils (**drwah** see-**veel**), *n.* [French] *French law.* Private rights not connected to a person's civil status. • Foreigners had certain rights that could be enforced when there was reciprocity with the foreigner's home country.

droits of admiralty (droyts), *n.* The Lord High Admiral's rights in connection with the sea, such as the right to recover proceeds from shipwrecks, enemy goods confiscated at the beginning of hostilities, jetsam, flotsam, treasure, deodand, fines, forfeitures, sturgeons, whales, and other large fishes. • The droit proceeds are paid to the Exchequer's office for the public's use. See PRIZE (2).

> "The crown had originally certain rights to property found upon the sea, or stranded upon the shore. The chief kinds of property to which the crown was thus entitled were, great fish (such as whales or porpoises), deodands, wreck of the sea, flotsam, jetsam, and lagan, ships or goods of the enemy found in English ports or captured by uncommissioned vessels, and goods taken or retaken from pirates . . . . After the rise of the court of Admiralty the Lord High Admiral became entitled to these droits by royal grant . . . . The right to droits carried with it a certain jurisdiction. Inquisitions were held into these droits at the ports, or the Vice-Admirals or droit gatherers reported them to the Admiral. The large terms of the Admiral's Patents incited them, or their grantees, to frequent litigation with private persons or other grantees of the crown . . . . The Admiralty droits . . . are now transferred to the consolidated fund." 1 William Holdsworth, *A History of English Law* 559–61 (7th ed. 1956).

droitural (**droy**-chə-rəl), *adj.* [fr. Old French *droiture* "right"] Of or relating to an interest in property, as distinguished from actual possession.

dromones (drə-**moh**-neez), *n. pl. Hist.* **1.** Large ships. **2.** War vessels of recognized navies, usu. prepared for hostilities. — Also termed *dromos*; *dromunda.*

drop. *English law.* A rule *nisi* that is not adopted because the members of a court are equally divided on the issue. • The rule is dropped rather than discharged or made absolute.

drop-down clause. An insurance-policy provision requiring an excess insurer to provide coverage to the insured even though the underlying coverage has not been exhausted, usu. because the underlying insurers are insolvent.

drop letter. A letter addressed to someone in the delivery area of the post office where the letter was posted.

drop-shipment delivery. A manufacturer's shipment of goods directly to the consumer rather than initially to a wholesaler. • If the wholesaler takes the order, it may receive part of the profit from the sale.

drop shipper. A wholesaler who arranges to have goods shipped directly from a manufacturer to a consumer. See DROP-SHIPMENT DELIVERY.

dropsy testimony. See TESTIMONY.

drove, *n.* **1.** A group of animals driven in a herd. **2.** A large group of people in motion.

drover's pass. A free pass issued by a railroad company to the cattle's drover, who accompanies the cattle on the train.

drug, *n.* **1.** A substance intended for use in the diagnosis, cure, treatment, or prevention of disease. **2.** A natural or synthetic substance that alters one's perception or consciousness. — **drug,** *vb.* See CONTROLLED SUBSTANCE.

addictive drug. A drug (such as heroin or nicotine) that, usu. after repeated consumption, causes physical dependence and results in well-defined physiological symptoms upon withdrawal.

adulterated drug. A drug that does not have the strength, quality, or purity represented or expected.

copycat drug. See *generic drug.*

dangerous drug. A drug that has potential for abuse or injury, usu. requiring a label warning that it cannot be dispensed without a prescription.

designer drug. A chemical substance that is created to duplicate the pharmacological effects of controlled substances, often by using the same chemicals contained in controlled substances, but manipulating their formulas.

ethical drug. A drug that can be dispensed only with a doctor's prescription. Cf. *proprietary drug.*

generic drug. A drug containing the active ingredient but not necessarily the same excipient substances (such as binders or capsules) as the pioneer drug marketed under a brand name. — Also termed *copycat drug.* See *pioneer drug.*

new drug. A drug that experts have not recognized as safe and effective for use under the conditions prescribed. 21 USCA § 321(p)(1). • The Food and Drug Administration must approve all new drugs before they can be marketed.

orphan drug. A prescription drug developed to treat diseases affecting fewer than 200,000 people in the United States (such as AIDS or rare cancers) or whose developmental costs are not reasonably expected to be recovered from the drug's sales. 21 USCA § 360bb.

pioneer drug. The first drug that contains a particular active ingredient that is approved by the FDA for a specified use.

precompounded prescription drug. A drug that is distributed from the manufacturer, to the pharmacist, and then to the consumer without a change in form.

proprietary drug. A drug that is prepared and packaged for the public's immediate use. • Proprietary drugs may be sold over the counter. Cf. *ethical drug.*

drug abuse. The detrimental state produced by the repeated consumption of a narcotic or other potentially dangerous drug, other than as prescribed by a doctor to treat an illness or other medical condition.

drug addict. See ADDICT.

drug dependence. Psychological or physiological need for a drug.

drug-free zone. An area in which the possession or distribution of a controlled substance results in an increased penalty. • Drug-free zones are often established, for example, around public schools.

druggist. A person who mixes, compounds, dispenses, or otherwise deals in drugs and medicines, usu. either as a proprietor of a drugstore or as a pharmacist.

drug kingpin. An organizer, leader, manager, financier, or supervisor of a drug conspiracy; a person who has more authority than others in running an illegal drug operation.

drug paraphernalia. Any thing used, intended for use, or designed for use with a controlled substance. • Possession of drug paraphernalia is a crime.

drummer. 1. A commercial agent who travels around taking orders for goods to be shipped from wholesale merchants to retail dealers; a traveling sales representative. **2.** A traveling salesperson.

drungarius (drəng-**gair**-ee-əs), *n.* [Law Latin] *Hist.* **1.** A commander of a band of soldiers. **2.** A naval commander.

drungus (**drəng**-gəs), *n.* [Law Latin] *Hist.* A band of soldiers.

drunk, *adj.* Intoxicated; (of a person) under the influence of intoxicating liquor to such a degree that the normal capacity for rational thought and conduct is impaired.

drunkard. A person who is habitually or often intoxicated.

drunkenness. 1. A state of intoxication; inebriation; the condition resulting from a person's ingestion of excessive amounts of intoxicating liquors sufficient to affect the person's normal capacity for rational thought and conduct. **2.** A habitual state of intoxication.

excessive drunkenness. A state of drunkenness in which a person is so far deprived of reason and understanding that the he or she is incapable of understanding the character and consequences of an act.

drunkometer (drəng-**kom**-ə-tər). See BREATHALYZER.

dry, *adj.* **1.** Free from moisture; desiccated <dry land>. **2.** Unfruitful; destitute of profitable interest; nominal <a dry trust>. **3.** (Of a jurisdiction) prohibiting the sale or use of alcoholic beverages <a dry county>.

dry check. See *bad check* under CHECK.

dry exchange. Something that pretends to pass on both sides of a transaction, but passes on only one side.

"Dry exchange ... seems to be a subtil term invented to disguise usury, in which something is pretended to pass on both sides, whereas in truth nothing passes on the one side." *Termes de la Ley* 185 (1st Am. ed. 1812).

"DRY EXCHANGE .... A euphemism applied to the 'coverture' or 'colouring' of the stringent statutes passed during the tudor period against usury .... Usury, which was condemned by religion and law alike during the middle ages, was from the middle of the 16th century no longer to be confounded with the legitimate employment of capital; but the sentiment which inspired the above enactments was that of governing classes associated with the landed interest." 1 R.H. Inglis Palgrave, *Palgrave's Dictionary of Political Economy* 643 (Henry Higgs ed., 2d ed. 1925).

dry mortgage. See MORTGAGE.

dry receivership. See RECEIVERSHIP.

dry rent. See RENT (1).

dry trust. See TRUST.

d.s.b. *abbr.* DEBET SINE BREVE.

DTC. *abbr.* DEPOSITORY TRUST CORPORATION.

dual agent. See *co-agent* under AGENT (1).

dual-capacity doctrine. The principle that makes an employer — who is normally shielded from tort liability by workers'-compensation laws — liable in tort to an employee if the employer and employee stand in a secondary relationship that confers independent obligations on the employer. Cf. DUAL-PURPOSE DOCTRINE.

dual citizenship. 1. A person's status as a citizen of two countries, as when the person is born in the United States to parents who are citizens of another country, or one country still recognizes a person as a citizen even though that person has acquired citizenship in another country. **2.** The status of a person who is a citizen of both the United States and the person's country of residence.

dual contract. See CONTRACT.

dual-criminality principle. A rule prohibiting the extradition of a fugitive unless the offense involves conduct that is criminal in both countries.

dual distributor. A firm that sells goods simultaneously to buyers on two different levels of the distribution chain; esp., a manufacturer that sells directly to both wholesalers and retailers.

dual distributorship. See DISTRIBUTORSHIP.

dual employment. See MOONLIGHTING.

dual fund. See MUTUAL FUND.

dual listing. See LISTING (2).

dual-persona doctrine (**d**[**y**]**oo**-əl pər-**soh**-nə). The principle that makes an employer (who is normally shielded from tort liability by workers'-compensation laws) liable in tort to an employee if the liability stems from a second persona unrelated to the employer's status as an employer.

dual-priorities rule. The principle that partnership creditors have priority for partnership assets and that individual creditors have priority for a partner's personal assets. • This rule has been abandoned by the bankruptcy laws and the Revised Uniform Partnership Act. The bankruptcy code now allows partnership creditors access to all assets of bankrupt partners, not just those remaining after payment to individual creditors. — Also termed *jingle rule*.

dual-prosecution rule. The principle that the federal and state governments may both prosecute a defendant for the same offense because both governments are separate and distinct entities. See DUAL-SOVEREIGNTY DOCTRINE.

dual-purpose doctrine. The principle that an employer is liable for an employee's injury that occurs during a business trip even though the trip also serves a personal purpose. Cf. DUAL-CAPACITY DOCTRINE.

dual-purpose fund. See *dual fund* under MUTUAL FUND.

dual-sovereignty doctrine. The rule that the federal and state governments may both prosecute someone for a crime, without violating the constitutional protection against double jeopardy, if the person's act violated both jurisdictions' laws. See DUAL-PROSECUTION RULE.

duarchy (**d**[**y**]**oo**-ahr-kee), *n.* [fr. Greek *duo* "two" + *archia* "rule"] See DYARCHY.

dubitante (d[y]oo-bi-**tan**-tee). [Latin] Doubting. • This term was usu. placed in a law report next to a judge's name, indicating the judge doubted a legal point but was unwilling to state that it was wrong. — Also termed *dubitans*.

> "[E]xpressing the epitome of the common law spirit, there is the opinion entered *dubitante* — the judge is unhappy about some aspect of the decision rendered, but cannot quite bring himself to record an open dissent." Lon L. Fuller, *Anatomy of the Law* 147 (1968).

dubitatur (d[y]oo-bi-**tay**-tər). [Latin] It is doubted. • This phrase indicates that a point of law is doubtful. — Also termed *dubitavit*.

ducat (**dək**-it). A gold coin used as currency, primarily in Europe and first appearing in Venice in the early 1100s, with the motto *sit tibi, Christe, dato, quem tu regis, iste Ducatus* ("let this duchy which thou rulest be dedicated to thee, O Christ"). • It survived into the 20th century in several countries, including Austria and the Netherlands.

ducatus (d[y]ə-**kay**-təs), *n.* [Law Latin] A duchy; a dukedom.

duces tecum (**d**[**y**]**oo**-səs **tee**-kəm *also* **tay**-kəm). [Latin] Bring with you. See *subpoena duces tecum* under SUBPOENA.

duces tecum licet languidus (**d**[**y**]**oo**-səs **tee**-kəm **lI**-set **lang**-gwə-dəs), *n.* [Law Latin "bring with you, although sick"] *Hist.* A habeas corpus writ ordering a sheriff to bring someone into court despite a return by the sheriff noting that the person was too ill to come.

Duchy Court of Lancaster (**dəch**-ee **kort** əv **lang**-kə-stər). *Hist. English law.* A court with special equity jurisdiction, similar to the equity courts of chancery, in which the Duchy of Lancaster's chancellor or deputy presides over issues primarily relating to land held by the Crown in right of the Duchy.

Duchy of Lancaster (**dəch**-ee əv **lang**-kə-stər). Land, in the county of Lancaster, the Savoy in London, and around Westminster, that originally belonged to the Duke of Lancaster and later belonged to the Crown in right of the Duchy.

ducking stool. See CASTIGATORY.

due, *adj.* **1.** Just, proper, regular, and reasonable <due care> <due notice>. **2.** Immediately enforceable <payment is due on delivery>. **3.** Owing or payable; constituting a debt <the tax refund is due from the IRS>.

due-bill. See IOU.

due care. See *reasonable care* under CARE.

due compensation. See *just compensation* under COMPENSATION.

due consideration. 1. The degree of attention properly paid to something, as the circumstances merit. **2.** *Sufficient consideration* under CONSIDERATION.

due course, payment in. See PAYMENT IN DUE COURSE.

due-course holder. See HOLDER IN DUE COURSE.

due course of law. 1. The regular and customary administration of law through the legal system. **2.** DUE PROCESS.

due days. See BOON DAY.

due diligence. See DILIGENCE.

due-diligence information. *Securities.* Information that a broker-dealer is required to have on file and make available to potential customers before submitting quotations for over-the-counter securities. • The informational requirements are set out in SEC Rule 15c2–11 (17 CFR § 240.15c2–11).

due influence. The sway that one person has over another, esp. as a result of persuasion, argument, or appeal to the person's affections. Cf. UNDUE INFLUENCE.

duel. 1. TRIAL BY COMBAT. **2.** A single combat; specif., a prearranged combat with deadly weapons fought between two or more persons under prescribed rules, usu. in the presence of at least two witnesses, to resolve a previous quarrel or avenge a deed. • In England and the United States, death resulting from a duel is treated as murder, and seconds may be liable as accessories. — Also termed *monomachy*; *single combat*. Cf. MUTUAL COMBAT.

> "Dueling is distinguished from other offenses in that it has none of the elements of sudden heat and passion, and is usually carried out with some formality. A duel has been distinguished from an 'affray' in that an affray occurs on a sudden quarrel while a duel is always the result of design." 28A C.J.S. *Dueling* § 2, at 154 (1996).

dueling, *n.* The common-law offense of fighting at an appointed time and place after an earlier disagreement. • If one of the participants is killed, the other is guilty of murder, and all who are present, abetting the crime, are guilty as principals in the second degree.

> "Dueling is prearranged fighting with deadly weapons, usually under certain agreed or prescribed rules. . . . It is a misdemeanor at common law to fight a duel, even though no death result, to challenge another to a duel, intentionally to provoke such a challenge, or knowingly to be the bearer of such a challenge." Rollin M. Perkins & Ronald N. Boyce, *Criminal Law* 243 (3d ed. 1982).

duellum (d[y]oo-**el**-əm), *n.* [fr. Latin *duo* "two"] *Hist.* See TRIAL BY COMBAT.

due negotiation. See NEGOTIATION.

due notice. See NOTICE.

due-on-encumbrance clause. A mortgage provision giving the lender the option to accelerate the debt if the borrower further mortgages the real estate without the lender's consent.

due-on-sale clause. A mortgage provision that gives the lender the option to accelerate the debt if the borrower transfers or conveys any part of the mortgaged real estate without the lender's consent.

due posting. 1. The stamping and placing of letters or packages in the U.S. mail. **2.** The proper entry of an item into a ledger. **3.** Proper publication; proper placement of an item (such as an announcement) in a particular place, as on a particular wall.

due process. The conduct of legal proceedings according to established rules and principles for the protection and enforcement of private rights, including notice and the right to a fair hearing before a tribunal with the power to decide the case. — Also termed *due process of law*; *due course of law*.

> "The words '*due process*' have a precise technical import, and are only applicable to the process and proceedings of the courts of justice; they can never be referred to an act of legislature." Alexander Hamilton, Remarks on an Act for Regulating Elections, New York Assembly, 6 Feb. 1787, in 4 *Papers of Alexander Hamilton* 34, 35 (Harold C. Syrett ed., 1962).

> "The words, 'due process of law,' were undoubtedly intended to convey the same meaning as the words, 'by the law of the land,' in *Magna Charta*." *Murray's Lessee v. Hoboken Land & Improvement Co.*, 59 U.S. (18 How.) 272, 276 (1856) (Curtis, J.).

> "Due process of law in each particular case means, such an exertion of the powers of government as the settled maxims of law sanction, and under such safeguards for the protection of individual rights as those maxims prescribe for the class of cases to which the one in question

belongs." Thomas M. Cooley, *A Treatise on the Constitutional Limitations* 356 (1868).

"An elementary and fundamental requirement of due process in any proceeding which is to be accorded finality is notice reasonably calculated, under all the circumstances, to apprise interested parties of the pendency of the action and afford them an opportunity to present their objections.... The notice must be of such nature as reasonably to convey the required information." *Mullane v. Central Hanover Bank & Trust Co.*, 339 U.S. 306, 314, 70 S.Ct. 652, 657 (1950) (Jackson, J.).

economic substantive due process. The doctrine that certain social policies, such as the freedom of contract or the right to enjoy property without interference by government regulation, exist in the Due Process Clause of the 14th Amendment, particularly in the words "liberty" and "property."

procedural due process. The minimal requirements of notice and a hearing guaranteed by the Due Process Clauses of the 5th and 14th Amendments, esp. if the deprivation of a significant life, liberty, or property interest may occur.

substantive due process. The doctrine that the Due Process Clauses of the 5th and 14th Amendments require legislation to be fair and reasonable in content and to further a legitimate governmental objective.

Due Process Clause. The constitutional provision that prohibits the government from unfairly or arbitrarily depriving a person of life, liberty, or property. • There are two Due Process Clauses in the U.S. Constitution, one in the 5th Amendment applying to the federal government, and one in the 14th Amendment applying to the states (although the 5th Amendment's Due Process Clause also applies to the states under the incorporation doctrine). Cf. EQUAL PROTECTION CLAUSE.

due process of law. See DUE PROCESS.

due-process rights. The rights (as to life, liberty, and property) so fundamentally important as to require compliance with due-process standards of fairness and justice. See DUE PROCESS; DUE PROCESS CLAUSE.

due proof. Sufficient and properly submitted evidence to produce a result or support a conclusion, such as an entitlement to benefits supported by an insurance policy.

DUI. *abbr.* DRIVING UNDER THE INFLUENCE.

DUIL. *abbr.* Driving under the influence of liquor. See DRIVING UNDER THE INFLUENCE.

duke. 1. A sovereign prince; a ruler of a duchy. **2.** The first order of nobility in Great Britain below the royal family.

"But after the Norman conquest, which changed the military policy of the nation, the kings themselves continuing for many generations *dukes* of Normandy, they would not honour any subjects with that title, till the time of Edward III; who, claiming to be the king of France, and thereby losing the ducal in the royal dignity, in the eleventh year of his reign created his son, Edward the black prince, duke of Cornwall: and many, of the royal family especially, were afterwards raised to the honour. However, in the reign of queen Elizabeth, A.D. 1572, the whole order became utterly extinct: but it was revived about fifty years afterwards by her successor, who was remarkably prodigal of honours, in the person of George Villiers duke of Buckingham." 1 William Blackstone, *Commentaries on the Laws of England* 385 (1765).

Duke of Exeter's Daughter. A torture rack in the Tower of London, named after the Duke of Exeter, Henry VI's minister who assisted in introducing it to England. — Also termed *brake*.

"The rack ... to extort a confession from criminals, is a practice of a different nature .... And the trial by rack is utterly unknown to the law of England; though once when the dukes of Exeter and Suffolk ... had laid a design to introduce the civil law into this kingdom as the rule of government, for a beginning thereof they erected a rack for torture; which was called in derision the duke of Exeter's daughter, and still remains in the tower of London: where it was occasionally used as an engine of state, not of law, more than once in the reign of queen Elizabeth." 4 William Blackstone, *Commentaries on the Laws of England* 320–21 (1769).

Duke of York's Laws. A body of laws compiled in 1665 by Governor Nicholls for the more orderly government of the New York colony. • The laws were gradually extended to the entire province.

dulocracy (d[y]oo-**lok**-rə-see), *n.* [fr. Greek *doulos* "servant" + *kratein* "to rule"] A government in which servants or slaves have so many privileges that they essentially rule. — Also spelled *doulocracy*.

duly, *adv.* In a proper manner; in accordance with legal requirements.

dum (dəm). [Latin] While; provided that.

dumb bidding. An auction bidding process in which the minimum acceptance price is placed under the object for sale — unbeknown to the bidders — and no bids are accepted until they meet that price. • Dumb bidding was initially intended to avoid the taxes imposed on auction sales by the statute of 1779, 19 Geo. 3, ch. 56, §§ 5–6, but the courts determined that the practice was fraudulent.

dum fervet opus (dəm **fər**-vet **oh**-pəs). [Latin] While the action is fresh; in the heat of action. • This term usu. referred to matters of testimony.

dum fuit infra aetatem (dəm **fyoo**-it **in**-frə ee-**tay**-təm), *n.* [Law Latin "while he was within age"] *Hist.* A writ allowing a person of full age to recover lands feoffed while the person was an infant. • The remedy was also available to the person's heirs. It was later replaced by the action of ejectment. See EJECTMENT.

dum fuit in prisona (dəm **fyoo**-it in **priz**-ə-nə), *n.* [Law Latin "while he was in prison"] *Hist.* A writ restoring a man to his estate after he transferred the estate under duress of imprisonment. See DURESS OF IMPRISONMENT.

dummodo (**dəm**-ə-doh). [Latin] So that. • This term was used as a limitation in conveyances, as in *dummodo solverit talem redditum* (**dəm**-ə-doh **sol**-və-rit **tay**-lem **red**-i-təm), meaning "provided he shall pay such a rent."

dummy, *n.* **1.** A party who has no interest in a transaction, but participates to help achieve a legal goal. **2.** A party who purchases property and holds legal title for another.

dummy, *adj.* Sham; make-believe; pretend <dummy corporation>.

dummy corporation. See CORPORATION.

dummy director. See DIRECTOR.

dummy shareholder. See SHAREHOLDER.

dum non fuit compos mentis (dəm non **fyoo**-it **kom**-pəs **men**-tis), *n.* [Law Latin "while he was of unsound mind"] *Hist.* A writ allowing heirs to recover an estate transferred by someone of unsound mind.

dump, *vb.* **1.** To drop (something) down, esp. in a heap; to unload. **2.** To sell (products) at an extremely low price; specif., to sell (products) in a foreign market at a lower price than at home.

dumping. 1. The act of selling a large quantity of goods at less than fair value. **2.** Selling goods abroad at less than the market price at home. See ANTIDUMPING LAW.

> "Dumping involves selling abroad at a price that is less than the price used to sell the same goods at home (the 'normal' or '*fair*' value). To be unlawful, dumping must threaten or cause material injury to an industry in the export market, the market where prices are lower. Dumping is recognized by most of the trading world as an unfair practice (akin to price discrimination as an antitrust offense)." Ralph H. Folsom & Michael W. Gordon, *International Business Transactions* § 6.1 (1995).

3. The disposal of waste matter into the environment.

Dumping Act. A federal antidumping law requiring the Secretary of the Treasury to notify the U.S. International Trade Commission (USITC) whenever the Secretary determines that goods are likely to be sold abroad at less than their fair value, so that the USITC can take appropriate action. 19 USCA § 1673.

dum sola (dəm **soh**-lə). [Latin] While single. • This phrase was used to limit conveyances, esp. to women, as in *dum sola fuerit* ("while she remains single"), *dum sola et casta vixerit* ("while she remains single and chaste"), and *dum sola et casta* ("while she is unmarried and lives chastely").

dun (dən), *vb.* To demand payment from (a delinquent debtor) <his creditors are dunning him daily>. — **dun,** *n.*

dungeon. 1. The bottom part of a fortress or tower, often used as a prison. — Also termed *dungeon-keep.* **2.** A dark underground prison.

dunnage (**dən**-ij). Anything, esp. pieces of wood, that are put underneath or between cargo on a vessel to prevent the cargo from bruising or getting wet from water leaking into the hold.

duodecemvirale judicium (d[y]oo-oh-des-əm-və-**ray**-lee joo-**dish**-ee-əm). [Latin] A trial by 12 persons; a trial by jury.

duodecima manus (d[y]oo-oh-**des**-ə-mə **man**-əs). [Latin] Twelve men.

> "The manner of waging and making law is this. He that has waged, or given security, to make his law, brings with him into court eleven of his neighbours: . . . for by the old Saxon constitution every man's credit in courts of law depended upon the opinion which his neighbours had of his veracity. The defendant then, standing at the end of the bar, is admonished by the judges of the nature and danger of a false oath. . . . And thereupon his eleven neighbours or compurgators shall avow upon their oaths that they believe in their consciences that he saith the truth . . . . It is held indeed by later authorities . . . that fewer than eleven compurgators will do: but Sir Edward Coke is positive that there must be this number . . . for

as wager of law is equivalent to a verdict in the defendant's favor, it ought to be established by the same or equal testimony, namely, by the oath of *twelve* men. And so indeed Glanvil expresses it, ... *'jurabit duodecima manu'* ...." 3 William Blackstone, *Commentaries on the Laws of England* 343 (1768).

duodena (d[y]oo-ə-**dee**-nə). [Latin] **1.** A jury of twelve. **2.** A dozen of anything.

duopoly (d[y]oo-**ahp**-ə-lee). A market in which there are only two sellers of a product.

duopsony (d[y]oo-**op**-sə-nee). A market in which there are only two buyers of a product.

duoviri (d[y]oo-**oh**-və-rɪ *or* d[y]oo-oh **vɪ**-rɪ). See DUUMVIRI.

duplex querela (**d[y]oo**-pleks kwə-**ree**-lə). **1.** *Hist. Eccles. law.* An appeal by a clerk to the archbishop in response to the bishop's delaying or wrongfully refusing to do justice. • It is a double quarrel in that sometimes the archbishop orders a judge considering parallel proceedings not to take any action against the complainant during the pendency of the suit. **2.** *Eccles. law.* An appeal to a person's immediate superior, as when a bishop appeals to an archbishop. — Also termed *double quarrel*; *double complaint*.

duplex valor maritagii (**d[y]oo**-pleks **val**-ər mar-ə-**tay**-jee-ɪ), *n.* [Law Latin "double the value of a marriage"] *Hist.* A ward's forfeiture of double the value of a marriage made without the guardian's consent. • In the quotation that follows, Blackstone uses the accusative form (*duplicem valorem maritagii*) because the phrase follows the verb *forfeited*.

"For, while the infant was in ward, the guardian had the power of tendering him or her a suitable match, without *disparagement*, or inequality: which if the infants refused, they forfeited the value of the marriage ... to their guardian; that is, so much as a jury would assess, or any one would *bona fide* give to the guardian for such an alliance: ... and, if the infants married themselves without the guardian's consent, they forfeited double the value, *duplicem valorem maritagii*. This seems to have been one of the greatest hardships of our ancient tenures." 2 William Blackstone, *Commentaries on the Laws of England* 70 (1766).

duplicate (**d[y]oo**-pli-kit), *n.* **1.** A reproduction of an original document having the same particulars and effect as the original. **2.** A new original, made to replace an instrument that is lost or destroyed. — Also termed (in sense 2) *duplicate original*. — **duplicate** (**d[y]oo**-pli-kit), *adj.*

"A 'duplicate' is defined for purposes of the best evidence rule as a counterpart produced by the same impression as the original, or from the same matrix, or by means of photography including enlargements and miniatures, by mechanical or electronic recording, by chemical reproduction, or by other equivalent techniques which accurately reproduce the original; copies subsequently produced manually, either handwritten or typed, are not within this definition." 29A Am. Jur. 2d *Evidence* § 1085 (1994).

duplicate (**d[y]oo**-pli-kayt), *vb.* **1.** To copy exactly <he duplicated the original document>. **2.** To double; to repeat <she duplicated the performance>.

duplicate will. See WILL.

duplicatio (d[y]oo-pli-**kay**-shee-oh), *n.* [fr. Latin *duplicare* "to double"] **1.** *Roman & civil law.* A defendant's answer to the plaintiff's replication, similar to a rejoinder in common law. — Also termed (in Scots law) *duply*. See REPLICATION. **2.** The fourth in a series. **3.** A duplication of a transaction.

duplicatum jus (d[y]oo-pli-**kay**-təm **jəs**), *n.* [Law Latin "double right"] A double right, such as *droit droit* (both the "right of possession and right of property").

duplicitous (d[y]oo-**plis**-i-təs), *adj.* **1.** (Of a person) deceitful; double-dealing. **2.** (Of a pleading, esp. an indictment) alleging two or more matters in one plea; characterized by double pleading.

duplicitous appeal. See APPEAL.

duplicitous indictment. See INDICTMENT.

duplicitous information. See *duplicitous indictment* under INDICTMENT.

duplicity (d[y]oo-**plis**-i-tee), *n.* **1.** Deceitfulness; double-dealing. **2.** The pleading of two or more distinct grounds of complaint or defense for the same issue. • In criminal law, this takes the form of joining two or more offenses in the same count of an indictment. — Also termed *double pleading*. Cf. *alternative pleading* under PLEADING (2); *double plea* under PLEA (3).

duplum (**d[y]oo**-pləm). [Latin] *Civil law.* Double the price of something. Cf. SIMPLUM.

duply. See DUPLICATIO (1).

durable goods. See GOODS.

durable lease. See LEASE.

durable power of attorney. See POWER OF ATTORNEY.

durables. See *durable goods* under GOODS.

durante (d[y]ə-**ran**-tee). [Law Latin] While; during, as in *durante minore aetate* ("during minority"), *durante viduitate* ("during widowhood"), *durante virginitate* ("during virginity"), and *durante vita* ("during life"). • The term was often used in conveyancing.

durante absentia (d[y]ə-**ran**-tee ab-**sen**-shee-ə). [Law Latin] During absence. • This term referred to the administration of an estate while the executor was out of the county or otherwise absent. During the executor's absence, the administration sometimes continued because a delay until the executor's return would impair the estate settlement.

durante bene placito (d[y]ə-**ran**-tee **bee**-nee **plas**-ə-toh). [Law Latin] During good pleasure. • This phrase was used in the royal writ granting tenure *durante bene placito* to the king' judges.

duration. 1. The length of time something lasts <the duration of the lawsuit>.

duration of interest. The length of time a property interest lasts.

duration of trust. The length of time a trust exists.

2. A length of time; a continuance in time <an hour's duration>.

durational-residency requirement. The requirement that one be a state resident for a certain time, such as one year, as a precondition to the exercise of a specified right or privilege. • When applied to voting, this requirement has been held to be an unconstitutional denial of equal protection because it burdens voting rights and impairs the fundamental personal right of travel.

Duren **test.** *Constitutional law.* A test to determine whether a jury's composition violates the fair-cross-section requirement and a criminal defendant's Sixth Amendment right to an impartial jury. • Under the test, a constitutional violation occurs if (1) in the venire from which the jury was selected, a distinctive group is not fairly and reasonably represented in relation to the group's population in the community, (2) the underrepresentation is the result of a systematic exclusion of the group from the jury-selection process, and (3) the government cannot reasonably justify the discrepancy. *Duren v. Missouri*, 439 U.S. 357, 99 S.Ct. 664 (1979). See FAIR-CROSS-SECTION REQUIREMENT; STATISTICAL-DECISION THEORY; ABSOLUTE DISPARITY; COMPARATIVE DISPARITY.

duress (d[y]uu-**res**). **1.** Strictly, the physical confinement of a person or the detention of a contracting party's property. • In the field of torts, duress is considered a species of fraud in which compulsion takes the place of deceit in causing injury.

> "Duress consists in actual or threatened violence or imprisonment; the subject of it must be the contracting party himself, or his wife, parent, or child; and it must be inflicted or threatened by the other party to the contract, or else by one acting with his knowledge and for his advantage." William R. Anson, *Principles of the Law of Contract* 261–62 (Arthur L. Corbin ed., 3d Am. ed. 1919).

> "Few areas of the law of contracts have undergone such radical changes in the nineteenth and twentieth centuries as has the law governing duress. In Blackstone's time relief from an agreement on grounds of duress was a possibility only if it was coerced by actual (not threatened) imprisonment or fear of loss of life or limb. 'A fear of battery ... is no duress; neither is the fear of having one's house burned, or one's goods taken away or destroyed'; he wrote, 'because in these cases, should the threat be performed, a man may have satisfaction by recovering equivalent damages: but no suitable atonement can be made for the loss of life, or limb.' Today the general rule is that any wrongful act or threat which overcomes the free will of a party constitutes duress. This simple statement of the law conceals a number of questions, particularly as to the meaning of 'free will' and 'wrongful.' " John D. Calamari & Joseph M. Perillo, *The Law of Contracts* § 9–2, at 337 (3d ed. 1987).

2. Broadly, the threat of confinement or detention, or other threat of harm, used to compel a person to do something against his or her will or judgment. • Duress is a recognized defense to a crime, contractual breach, or tort. See COERCION; EXTORTION.

> "[In most states,] the age-old rule of duress — that the doing of a prohibited act is not a crime if reasonably believed to be necessary to save from death or great bodily injury — together with the equally ancient exception in the form of the 'inexcusable choice,' are as firm today as ever except for the realization that they cover only part of the field." Rollin M. Perkins & Ronald N. Boyce, *Criminal Law* 1064 (3d ed. 1982).

duress of circumstances. See NECESSITY (1).

duress of goods. **1.** The act of seizing personal property by force, or withholding it from an entitled party, and then extorting something as the condition for its release. **2.** Demanding and taking personal property under color of legal authority that either is void or for some other reason does not justify the demand.

duress of imprisonment. The wrongful confining of a person to force the person to do something.

duress of the person. Compulsion of a person by imprisonment, by threat, or by a show of force that cannot be resisted.

duress per minas (pər **mɪ**-nəs). [Law Latin] Duress by threat of loss of life, loss of limb, mayhem, or other harm to a person.

> "Duress *per minas* is either for fear of loss of life, or else for fear of mayhem, or loss of limb. And this fear must be upon sufficient reason .... A fear of battery, or being beaten, though never so well grounded, is no duress; neither is the fear of having one's house burned, or one's goods taken away and destroyed; because in these cases, should the threat be performed, a man may have satisfaction by recovering equivalent damages: but no suitable atonement can be made for the loss of life, or limb." 1 William Blackstone, *Commentaries on the Laws of England* 127 (1765).

> "Duress *per minas* is a very rare defence; so rare that Sir James Stephen, in his long forensic experience, never saw a case in which it was raised. It has, however, been thought that threats of the immediate infliction of death, or even of grievous bodily harm, will excuse *some* crimes that have been committed under the influence of such threats." J.W. Cecil Turner, *Kenny's Outlines of Criminal Law* 58 (16th ed. 1952).

economic duress. An unlawful coercion to perform by threatening financial injury at a time when one cannot exercise free will. — Also termed *business compulsion*.

> "Courts have shown a willingness to recognize the concept of 'economic duress.' For instance it has been held that a defence on these grounds may be available to the purchaser of a ship from a shipbuilder, if the latter extracts a promise of extra payment as a condition of delivery of the ship." P.S. Atiyah, *An Introduction to the Law of Contract* 230 (3d ed. 1981).

moral duress. An unlawful coercion to perform by unduly influencing or taking advantage of the weak financial position of another. • Moral duress focuses on the inequities of a situation while economic duress focuses on the lack of will or capacity of the person being influenced.

duressor (d[y]ə-**res**-ər). A person who coerces another person to do something against his or her will or judgment.

Durham (**dər**-əm). One of the three remaining county palatines in England, the others being Chester and Lancaster. • Its jurisdiction was vested in the Bishop of Durham until the statute 6 & 7 Will. 4, ch. 19 vested it as a separate franchise and royalty in the Crown. The jurisdiction of the Durham Court of Pleas was transferred to the Supreme Court of Judicature by the Judicature Act of 1873, but Durham continued to maintain a Chancery Court according to the Palatine Court of Durham Act of 1889. See COUNTY PALATINE.

***Durham* rule.** *Criminal law.* A test for the insanity defense, holding that a defendant is not criminally responsible for an act that was the product of mental disease or defect (*Durham v. United States*, 214 F.2d 862 (D.C. Cir. 1954)). • Formerly used in New Hampshire and the District of Columbia, the *Durham* rule has been criticized as being too broad and is no longer accepted in any American jurisdiction. — Also termed *product test*. See INSANITY DEFENSE.

***Durrett* rule.** *Bankruptcy.* The principle that a transfer of property in exchange for less than 70% of the property's value should be invalidated as a preferential transfer. *Durrett v. Washington Nat'l Ins. Co.*, 621 F.2d 201 (5th Cir. 1980); 11 USCA § 548. • This rule has been applied most frequently to foreclosure sales. But it has essentially been overruled by the U.S. Supreme Court, which has held that, at least for mortgage foreclosure sales, the price received at a regularly conducted, noncollusive sale represents a reasonably equivalent value of the property, and the transfer is presumed valid. *BFP v. Resolution Trust Corp.*, 511 U.S. 531, 114 S.Ct. 1757 (1994).

Dutch auction. See AUCTION.

Dutch-auction tender method. See *Dutch auction* (2) under AUCTION.

Dutch lottery. See LOTTERY.

dutiable (**d[y]oo**-tee-ə-bəl), *adj.* Subject to a duty <dutiable goods>.

duty. 1. A legal obligation that is owed or due to another and that needs to be satisfied; an obligation for which somebody else has a corresponding right.

> "There is a duty if the court says there is a duty; the law, like the Constitution, is what we make it. Duty is only a word with which we state our conclusion that there is or is not to be liability; it necessarily begs the essential question.... [M]any factors interplay: the hand of history, our ideas of morals and justice, the convenience of administration of the rule, and our social ideas as to where loss should fall." William L. Prosser, *Palsgraf Revisited*, 52 Mich. L. Rev. 1, 15 (1953).

"A classic English definition [of *duty*] from the late nineteenth century holds that, when circumstances place one individual in such a position with regard to another that thinking persons of ordinary sense would recognize the danger of injury to the other if ordinary skill and care were not used, a duty arises to use ordinary skill and care to avoid the injury. A much quoted American judicial definition of duty emphasizes its relational aspects, with a focus on the foreseeability of risk to those 'within the range of apprehension.' At about the same time, one of the most creative of American law teachers defined duty as a complex of factors, including administrative, economic, and moral ones, to be applied by judges in their analyses of the legal strength of personal injury cases." Marshall S. Shapo, *The Duty to Act* xi–xii (1977).

"While courts frequently say that establishing 'duty' is the first prerequisite in an individual tort case, courts commonly go on to say that there is a 'general duty' to 'exercise reasonable care,' to avoid subjecting others to 'an unreasonable risk of harm,' or to comply with the 'legal standard of reasonable conduct.' Though cast in the language of duty, these formulations merely give the expression to the point that negligence is the standard of liability." Restatement (Third) of Torts § 6 cmt. a (Discussion Draft 1999).

absolute duty. A duty to which no corresponding right attaches. • According to John Austin's legal philosophy, there are four kinds of absolute duties: (1) duties not regarding persons (such as those owed to God and to lower animals), (2) duties owed to persons indefinitely (i.e., to the community as a whole), (3) self-regarding duties (such as the duty not to commit suicide), and (4) duties owed to the sovereign. 1 John Austin, *The Providence of Jurisprudence Determined* 400 (Sarah Austin ed., 2d ed. 1861).

active duty. See *positive duty.*

affirmative duty. A duty to take a positive step to do something.

contractual duty. **1.** A duty arising under a particular contract. **2.** A duty imposed by the law of contracts.

delegable duty. A duty that may be transferred to another to perform. See ASSIGNMENT.

duty to act. A duty to take some action to prevent harm to another, and for the failure of which one may be liable depending on the relationship of the parties and the circumstances.

duty to speak. A duty to say something to correct another's false impression. • For example, a duty to speak may arise when a person has, during the course of negotiations, said something that was true at the time but that has ceased to be true before the contract is signed.

imperfect duty. **1.** A duty that, though recognized by law, is not enforceable against the person who owes it. **2.** A duty that is not fit for enforcement but should be left to the discretion and conscience of the person whose duty it is.

implied duty of cooperation. A duty existing in every contract, obligating each party to cooperate with, or at least not to wrongfully hinder, the other party's performance. • Breach of this implied duty excuses performance.

legal duty. A duty arising by contract or by operation of law; an obligation the breach of which would be a legal wrong <the legal duty of parents to support their children>.

moral duty. A duty the breach of which would be a moral wrong. — Also termed *natural duty.*

negative duty. A duty that forbids someone to do something; a duty that requires someone to abstain from something. — Also termed *passive duty.*

noncontractual duty. A duty that arises independently of any contract.

nondelegable duty (non-**del**-ə-gə-bəl). **1.** *Contracts.* A duty that cannot be delegated by a contracting party to a third party. • If the duty is transferred, the other contracting party can rightfully refuse to accept performance by the third party. **2.** *Torts.* A duty that may be delegated to an independent contractor by a principal, who retains primary (as opposed to vicarious) responsibility if the duty is not properly performed. • For example, a landlord's duty to maintain common areas, though delegated to a service contractor, remains the landlord's responsibility if someone is injured by improper maintenance.

perfect duty. A duty that is not merely recognized by the law but is actually enforceable.

positive duty. A duty that requires a person either to do some definite action or to engage in a continued course of action. — Also termed *active duty.*

preexisting duty. A duty that one is already legally bound to perform. See PREEXISTING-DUTY RULE.

2. Any action, performance, task, or observance owed by a person in an official or fiduciary capacity.

duty of candor (**kan**-dər). A duty to disclose material facts; esp., a duty of a director seeking shareholder approval of a transaction to disclose to the shareholders all known material facts about the transaction.

duty of fair representation. A labor union's duty to represent its member employees fairly, honestly, and in good faith.

duty of good faith and fair dealing. A duty that is implied in some contractual relationships, requiring the parties to deal with each other fairly, so that neither prohibits the other from realizing the agreement's benefits. • This duty is most commonly implied in insurance contracts, and usu. against the insurer, regarding matters such as the insurer's obligation to settle reasonable demands that are within the policy's coverage limits. See GOOD FAITH; BAD FAITH.

duty of loyalty. A person's duty not to engage in self-dealing or otherwise use his or her position to further personal interests rather than those of the beneficiary. • For example, directors have a duty not to engage in self-dealing to further their own personal interests rather than the interests of the corporation.

fiduciary duty (fi-**d**[**y**]**oo**-shee-er-ee). A duty of utmost good faith, trust, confidence, and candor owed by a fiduciary (such as a lawyer or corporate officer) to the beneficiary (such as a lawyer's client or a shareholder); a duty to act with the highest degree of honesty and loyalty toward another person and in the best interests of the other person (such as the duty that one partner owes to another). See FIDUCIARY; FIDUCIARY RELATIONSHIP.

strictly ministerial duty. A duty that is absolute and imperative, requiring neither the exercise of official discretion nor judgment.

3. *Torts.* A legal relationship arising from a standard of care, the violation of which subjects the actor to liability. — Also termed *duty of care.* **4.** A tax imposed on a commodity or transaction, esp. on imports; IMPOST. • A duty in this sense is imposed on things, not persons.

countervailing duty. A duty that protects domestic industry by offsetting subsidies given by foreign governments to manufacturers of imported goods.

customs duty. A duty levied on an imported or exported commodity; esp., the federal tax levied on goods shipped into the United States.

duty of detraction. A tax on property acquired by succession or will and then removed from one state to another.

import duty. **1.** A duty on the importation of a product. **2.** A duty on the imported product. — Also termed *duty on import.*

probate duty. A duty assessed by the government either on every will admitted to probate or on the gross value of the decedent's personal property.

unascertained duty. A preliminary, estimated payment to a customs collector of the duty that will be due on final accounting. • An importer pays this duty to receive permission to land and sale the goods.

duty-bound, *adj.* Required by legal or moral obligation to do something <Jones is duty-bound to deliver the goods by Friday>.

duty-free, *adj.* Of or relating to products of foreign origin that are not subject to import or export taxes.

duty of candor. See DUTY (2).

duty of care. See DUTY (3).

duty of detraction. See DUTY (4).

duty of fair representation. See DUTY (2).

duty of loyalty. See DUTY (2).

duty of the flag. *Hist.* A maritime ceremony by which a foreign vessel struck her flag and lowered her topsail upon meeting the British flag. • The ceremony was an acknowledgment of British sovereignty over the British seas.

duty of tonnage (**tən**-ij). A charge imposed on a commercial vessel for entering, remaining in, or leaving a port.

duty of water. The amount of water necessary to irrigate a given tract.

duty on import. See *import duty* under DUTY (4).

duty to act. See DUTY (1).

duty-to-defend clause. A liability-insurance provision obligating the insurer to take over the defense of any lawsuit brought by a third party against the insured on a claim that falls within the policy's coverage.

duty to mitigate (**mit**-i-gayt). *Contracts.* A nonbreaching party's duty to make reasonable efforts to limit losses resulting from the other party's breach. • Not doing so precludes the party from collecting damages that might have been avoided. See MITIGATION-OF-DAMAGES DOCTRINE.

duty to speak. See DUTY (1).

duumviri (d[y]oo-**əm**-və-rI), *n.* [fr. Latin *due* "two" + *viri* "men"] **1.** *Roman law.* Magistrates elected or appointed in pairs to hold an office or perform a function.

duumviri municipales (d[y]oo-**əm**-və-rI myoo-nis-ə-**pay**-leez), *n.* [Latin] Two judicial magistrates annually elected in towns and colonies.

duumviri navales (d[y]oo-**əm**-və-rI nə-**vay**-leez), *n.* [Latin] Two officers appointed to man, equip, and refit the navy.

2. Two peers in authority. — Also termed *duoviri.*

dux (dəks), *n.* [fr. Latin *ducere* "to lead"] **1.** *Roman law.* An army commander. **2.** *Roman law.* A military governor of a province. • This term was eventually used also as a title of distinction. **3.** *Hist.* Duke; a title of nobility. See DUKE.

DWAI. *abbr.* Driving while ability-impaired. See DRIVING UNDER THE INFLUENCE.

dwell, *vb.* **1.** To remain; to linger <the case dwelled in her memory>. **2.** To reside in a place permanently or for some period <he dwelled in California for nine years>.

dwelling defense. See CASTLE DOCTRINE.

dwelling-house. 1. The house or other structure in which a person lives; a residence or abode. **2.** *Real estate.* The house and all buildings attached to or connected with the house. **3.** *Criminal law.* A building, a part of a building, a tent, a mobile home, or another enclosed space that is used or intended for use as a human habitation. • The term has referred to connected buildings in the same curtilage but now typically includes only the structures connected either directly with the house or by an enclosed passageway. — Often shortened to *dwelling.* — Also termed (archaically) *mansion house.*

> "A 'dwelling house' or 'dwelling' has been defined in connection with the crime of arson as any house intended to be occupied as a residence, or an enclosed space, permanent or temporary, in which human beings usually stay, lodge, or reside. If a building is not used exclusively as a dwelling, it is characterized as a dwelling if there is internal communication between the two parts of the building. Dwellings include mobile homes and a boat, if the person resides on it." 5 Am. Jur. 2d *Arson and Related Offenses* § 13, at 789 (1995).

DWI. *abbr.* DRIVING WHILE INTOXICATED.

DWOP (**dee**-wop). See *dismissal for want of prosecution* under DISMISSAL (1).

DWOP docket. See DOCKET (2).

dyarchy (**dI**-ahr-kee), *n.* [fr. Greek *dy* "two" + *archein* "rule"] A government jointly ruled by two people, such as William and Mary of England. — Also termed *diarchy.*

> "Dyarchy. A term applied by Mommsen to the Roman principate . . . a period in which he held that sovereignty was shared between the princes and the senate. The term has also been given to a system of government, promoted as a constitutional reform in India by Montagu and Chelmsford and introduced by the Government of India Act, 1919. It marked the introduction of democracy into the executive of the British administration of India by dividing the provincial executives into authoritarian and popularly responsible sections composed respectively of councillors appointed by the Crown and ministers appointed by the governor and responsible to the provincial legislative councils . . . . The system ended when full provincial autonomy was granted in 1935." David M. Walker, *The Oxford Companion to Law* 386 (1980).

Dyer Act. A federal law, originally enacted in 1919, making it unlawful either (1) to transport a stolen motor vehicle across state lines, knowing it to be stolen, or (2) to receive, conceal, or sell such a vehicle, knowing it to be stolen. 18 USCA §§ 2311–2313. — Also termed *National Motor Vehicle Theft Act.*

dyet. See DIET.

dying declaration. See DECLARATION (6).

dying without issue. See FAILURE OF ISSUE.

dynamite charge. See ALLEN CHARGE.

dynamite instruction. See ALLEN CHARGE.

dynasty. 1. A powerful family line that continues for a long time <an Egyptian dynasty>. **2.** A powerful group of individuals who control a particular industry or field and who control their successors <a literary dynasty> <a banking dynasty>.

dysnomy (**dis**-nə-mee), *n.* [fr. Greek *dys* "bad" + *nomos* "law"] Bad laws; the enactment of bad legislation.

ea intentione (**ee**-ə in-ten-shee-**oh**-nee). [Latin] With that intent.

EAJA. *abbr.* EQUAL ACCESS TO JUSTICE ACT.

E & O insurance. See *errors-and-omissions insurance* under INSURANCE.

earl. A title of nobility, formerly the highest in England but now the third highest, ranking between a marquis and a viscount. • This title corresponds with the French *comte* and the German *graf.* Originating with the Saxons, this title is the most ancient of the English peerage. William the Conqueror first made the title hereditary, giving it in fee to his nobles. No territorial, private, or judicial rights now accompany the title; it merely confers nobility and a hereditary seat in the House of Lords.

earldom. The dignity or jurisdiction of an earl. • Only the dignity remains now, the jurisdiction having been given over to the sheriff. See DIGNITY.

earles-penny. *Hist.* Money given in part payment; EARNEST. — Also termed *earl's penny.*

Earl Marshal of England. A great officer of state, who historically had jurisdiction over several courts, including the court of chivalry and the court of honor. • Under this office is the herald's office, or college of arms. The Earl Marshal was also a judge of the Marshalsea court, now abolished. This office is quite ancient. Since 1672, it has been hereditary in the family of Howards, Dukes of Norfolk. — Often shortened to *Earl Marshal.*

earl's penny. See EARLES-PENNY.

earmark, *n.* **1.** Originally, a mark upon the ear — a mode of marking sheep and other animals. **2.** A mark put on something (such as a coin) to distinguish it from another.

earmark, *vb.* **1.** To mark with an earmark. **2.** To set aside for a specific purpose or recipient.

earmarking doctrine. *Bankruptcy.* An equitable principle that when a new lender makes a loan to enable a debtor to pay off a specified creditor, the funds are specifically set aside for that creditor so that, if the debtor lacks control over the disposition of the funds, they do not become part of the debtor's estate and thus subject to a preference.

earn, *vb.* **1.** To acquire by labor, service, or performance. **2.** To do something that entitles one to a reward or result, whether it is received or not.

earned income. See INCOME.

earned-income credit. See TAX CREDIT.

earned premium. See PREMIUM (1).

earned surplus. See *retained earnings* under EARNINGS.

earned time. *Criminal procedure.* A credit toward a sentence reduction awarded to a prisoner who takes part in activities designed to lessen the chances that the prisoner will commit a crime after release from prison. • Earned time, which is usu. awarded for taking educational or vocational courses, working, or participating in certain other productive activities, is distinct from good time, which is awarded simply for refraining from misconduct. Cf. GOOD TIME.

earner. 1. One who produces income through personal efforts or property or both. **2.** Property or an asset that produces income for its owner.

earnest, *n.* **1.** A nominal payment or token act that serves as a pledge or a sign of good faith, esp. as the partial purchase price of property. • Though not legally necessary, an earnest may help the parties come to an agreement. **2.** EARNEST MONEY.

earnest money. A deposit paid (usu. in escrow) by a prospective buyer (esp. of real estate) to show a good-faith intention to complete the transaction, and ordinarily forfeited if the buyer defaults. • Although earnest money has traditionally been a nominal sum (such as a nickel or a dollar) used in the sale of goods, it is not a mere token in the real-estate context: it may amount to many thousands of dollars. — Also termed *earnest*; bargain money; *caution money*; *hand money*. Cf. BINDER (2); *down payment* under PAYMENT.

> "The amount of earnest money deposited rarely exceeds 10 percent of the purchase price, and its primary purpose is to serve as a source of payment of damages should the buyer default. Earnest money is *not* essential to make a purchase agreement binding if the buyer's and seller's exchange of mutual promises of performance (that is, the buyer's promise to purchase and the seller's promise to sell at a specified price and terms) constitutes the consideration for the contract." John W. Reilly, *The Language of Real Estate* 131 (4th ed. 1993).

earning asset. See ASSET.

earning capacity. A person's ability or power to earn money, given the person's talent, skills, training, and experience. • Earning capacity is one element considered when measuring the damages recoverable in a personal-injury lawsuit. And in family law, earning capacity is considered when awarding child support and spousal maintenance (or alimony) and in dividing property between spouses upon divorce. — Also termed *earning power*. See LOST EARNING CAPACITY.

earnings. Revenue gained from labor or services, from the investment of capital, or from assets. See INCOME. Cf. PROFIT.

appropriated retained earnings. Retained earnings that a company's board designates for a distinct use, and that are therefore unavailable to pay dividends or for other uses. — Also termed *appropriated surplus*; *surplus revenue*; *suspense reserve*.

future earnings. See *lost earnings*.

gross earnings. See *gross income* under INCOME.

lost earnings. Wages, salary, or other income that a person could have earned if he or she had not lost a job, suffered a disabling injury, or died. • Lost earnings are typically awarded as damages in personal-injury and wrongful-termination cases. There can be past lost earnings and future lost earnings. Both are subsets of this category, though legal writers sometimes loosely use *future earnings* as a synonym for *lost earnings*. Cf. LOST EARNING CAPACITY.

net earnings. See *net income* under INCOME.

pretax earnings. Net earnings before income taxes.

real earnings. Earnings that are adjusted for inflation so that they reflect actual purchasing power.

retained earnings. A corporation's accumulated income after dividends have been distributed. — Also termed *earned surplus*; *undistributed profit*.

surplus earnings. The excess of corporate assets over liabilities within a given period, usu. a year.

earnings and profits. *Corporations*. In corporate taxation, the measure of a corporation's economic capacity to make a shareholder distribution that is not a return of capital. • The distribution will be dividend income to the shareholders to the extent of the corporation's current and accumulated earnings and profits. Cf. *accumulated-earnings tax* under TAX; *accumulated taxable income* under INCOME.

earnings per share. *Corporations*. A measure of corporate value by which the corporation's net income is divided by the number of outstanding shares of common stock. • Investors benefit from calculating a corporation's earnings per share, because it helps the investor determine the fair market value of the corporation's stock. — Abbr. EPS.

fully diluted earnings per share. A corporation's net income — assuming that all convertible securities had been transferred to common equity and all stock options had been exercised — divided by the number of shares of the corporation's outstanding common stock.

earnings-price ratio. See *earnings yield* under YIELD.

earnings report. See INCOME STATEMENT.

earnings yield. See YIELD.

earnout agreement. An agreement for the sale of a business whereby the buyer first pays an agreed amount up front, leaving the final purchase price to be determined by the business's future profits. • Usu. the seller helps manage the business for a period after the sale. — Sometimes shortened to *earnout*.

earwitness. A witness who testifies about something that he or she heard but did not see. Cf. EYEWITNESS.

easement (**eez**-mənt). An interest in land owned by another person, consisting in the right to use or control the land, or an area above or below it, for a specific limited purpose (such as to cross it for access to a public road). • The land benefiting from an easement is called the *dominant estate*; the land burdened by an easement is called the *servient estate*. Unlike a lease or license, an easement may last forever, but it does not give the holder the right to possess, take from, improve, or sell the land. The primary recognized easements are (1) a right-of-way, (2) a right of entry for any purpose relating to the dominant estate, (3) a right to the support of land and buildings, (4) a right of light and air, (5) a right to water, (6) a right to do some act that would otherwise amount to a nuisance, and (7) a right to place or keep something on the servient estate. See SERVITUDE. Cf. PROFIT À PRENDRE.

access easement. An easement allowing one or more persons to travel across another's land to get to a nearby location, such as a road. • The access easement is a common type of easement by necessity. — Also termed *easement of access*.

adverse easement. See *prescriptive easement*.

affirmative easement. An easement that forces the servient-estate owner to permit certain actions by the easement holder, such as discharging water onto the servient estate. — Also termed *positive easement*. Cf. *negative easement*.

> "Positive easements give rights of entry upon the land of another, not amounting to profits, to enable something to be done on that land. Some are commonplace, examples being rights of way across the land of another and rights to discharge water on to the land of another. Others are more rare, such as the right to occupy a pew in a church, the right to use a kitchen situated on the land of another for the purpose of washing and drying clothes, and the right to use a toilet situated on the land of another." Peter Butt, *Land Law* 305 (2d ed. 1988).

apparent easement. A visually evident easement, such as a paved trail or a sidewalk.

appendant easement. See *easement appurtenant*.

appurtenant easement. See *easement appurtenant*.

avigational easement. An easement permitting unimpeded aircraft flights over the servient estate. — Also termed *avigation easement*; *aviation easement*; *flight easement*; *navigation easement*.

common easement. An easement allowing the servient landowner to share in the benefit of the easement. — Also termed *nonexclusive easement*.

continuous easement. An easement that may be enjoyed without an interfering act by the party claiming it, such as an easement for drains, sewer pipes, lateral support of a wall, or light and air. Cf. *discontinuous easement*.

determinable easement. An easement that terminates on the happening of a specific event.

discontinuous easement. An easement that can be enjoyed only if the party claiming it interferes in some way with the servient estate. • An example is a right-of-way. — Also termed *discontinuing easement*; *noncontinuous easement*; *nonapparent easement*. Cf. *continuous easement*.

easement appurtenant. An easement created to benefit another tract of land, the use of the easement being incident to the ownership of that other tract. — Also termed *appurtenant easement*; *appendant easement*; *pure easement*; *easement proper*. Cf. *easement in gross*.

easement by estoppel. A court-ordered easement created from a voluntary servitude after a person, mistakenly believing the servitude to be permanent, acted in reasonable reliance on the mistaken belief.

easement by implication. See *implied easement*.

easement by necessity. An easement created by operation of law because the easement is indispensable to the reasonable use of nearby property, such as an easement connecting a parcel of land to a road. — Also termed *easement of necessity*; *necessary way*.

easement by prescription. See *prescriptive easement*.

easement in gross. An easement benefiting a particular person and not a particular piece of land. • The beneficiary need not, and usu. does not, own any land adjoining the servient estate. Cf. *easement appurtenant*.

easement of access. See *access easement*.

easement of convenience. An easement that increases the facility, comfort, or convenience of enjoying the dominant estate or some right connected with it.

easement of natural support. See *lateral support* under SUPPORT.

easement of necessity. See *easement by necessity*.

easement proper. See *easement appurtenant*.

equitable easement. **1.** An implied easement created by equity when adjacent lands have been created out of a larger tract. • Such an easement is usu. created to allow implied privileges to continue. **2.** See *restrictive covenant* (1) under COVENANT (4).

exclusive easement. An easement that the holder has the sole right to use. Cf. *common easement.*

flight easement. See *avigational easement.*

floating easement. An easement that, when created, is not limited to any specific part of the servient estate.

flowage easement. A common-law easement that gives the dominant-estate owner the right to flood a servient estate, as when land near a dam is flooded to maintain the dam or to control the water level in a reservoir.

implied easement. An easement created by law after an owner of two parcels of land uses one parcel to benefit the other to such a degree that, upon the sale of the benefited parcel, the purchaser could reasonably expect the use to be included in the sale. — Also termed *easement by implication.*

intermittent easement. An easement that is usable or used only from time to time, not regularly or continuously.

light-and-air easement. A negative easement preventing an adjoining landowner from constructing a building that would prevent light or air from reaching the dominant estate. See *negative easement.* Cf. *solar easement.*

mineral easement. An easement that permits the holder to enter the property to remove minerals from it.

navigation easement. **1.** An easement giving the federal government the right to regulate navigable waters, even when the regulation interferes with private water rights. **2.** See *avigational easement.*

negative easement. An easement that prohibits the servient-estate owner from doing something, such as building an obstruction. Cf. *affirmative easement.*

> "Negative easements ... confer no right of entry, but consist essentially of the right to prevent something being done; examples are the right to the flow of air through defined aperture, the right to receive light for a building, the right to the support of a building, and (possibly) the right to require a neighbouring landowner to repair fences." Peter Butt, *Land Law* 305 (2d ed. 1988).

nonapparent easement. See *discontinuous easement.*

noncontinuous easement. See *discontinuous easement.*

nonexclusive easement. See *common easement.*

positive easement. See *affirmative easement.*

prescriptive easement. An easement created from an open, adverse, and continuous use over a statutory period. — Also termed *easement by prescription; adverse easement.*

private easement. An easement whose enjoyment is restricted to one specific person or a few specific people.

public easement. An easement for the benefit of an entire community, such as the right to travel down a street or a sidewalk.

pure easement. See *easement appurtenant.*

quasi-easement. **1.** An easement-like right occurring when both tracts of land are owned by the same person. • A quasi-easement may become a true easement if the landowner sells one of the tracts. **2.** An obligation or license that relates to land but that is not a true easement — for example, a landowner's obligation to maintain the fence between the landowner's tract and someone else's tract.

reciprocal negative easement. An easement created when a landowner sells part of the land and restricts the buyer's use of that part, and, in turn, that same restriction is placed on the part kept by the landowner. • Such an easement usu. arises when the original landowner creates a common scheme of development for smaller tracts that are carved out of the original tract.

reserved easement. An easement created by the grantor of real property to benefit the grantor's retained property and to burden the granted property.

secondary easement. An easement that is appurtenant to the primary or actual easement; the right to do things that are necessary to fully enjoy the easement itself.

solar easement. An easement created to protect the dominant estate's exposure to the direct rays of the sun. • A solar easement is often created to prevent the servient-estate owner from constructing any building that would cause shadows on the dominant estate, thus interfering with the use of a solar-energy system. Cf. *light-and-air easement.*

> "Solar easements ... remain difficult to describe because of the relationship of the sun to the earth. Shadow variables include land slope, terrain, solar orientation, latitude, time of day, and height of potential obstructions. Lawyers, engineers, land planners, title companies and others have expressed concern over the complexity

required to write a solar easement containing highly detailed, technical information often included in these easements." Sandy F. Kraemer, *Solar Law* 42 (1978).

timber easement. An easement that permits the holder to cut and remove timber from another's property.

easement appurtenant. See EASEMENT.

easement by estoppel. See EASEMENT.

easement by necessity. See EASEMENT.

easement in gross. See EASEMENT.

easement of convenience. See EASEMENT.

easement of natural support. See *lateral support* under SUPPORT.

Easter-offerings. *Eccles. law.* Small sums of money paid as personal tithes to the parochial clergy by the parishioners at Easter. • Under the Recovery of Small Tithes Act (1695), Easter-offerings were recoverable before justices of the peace. St. 7 & 8 Will. 3, ch. 6. — Also termed *Easter-dues.*

Easter sittings. *English law.* A term of court beginning on April 15 of each year and usu. ending on May 8, but sometimes extended to May 13. • This was known until 1875 as *Easter term.* Cf. HILARY SITTINGS; MICHAELMAS SITTING.

East Greenwich (eest **gren**-ich). *Hist.* The name of a royal manor in the county of Kent, England. • Historically, this manor was mentioned in royal grants or patents as descriptive of the tenure of free socage.

East India Company. *Hist.* The company that was originally established to pursue exclusive trade between England and India, and that later became more active in political affairs than in commerce. • In 1858, by the Government of India Act, the government of the company's territories was transferred to the Crown. The company was dissolved in 1874. St. 21 & 22 Vict., ch. 106.

EAT. *abbr.* Earnings after taxes.

eat inde sine die (**ee**-ət **in**-dee **sɪ**-nee **dɪ**-ee) [Latin] Let him go thence without day. • These words were used on a defendant's acquittal, or when a prisoner was to be discharged, to signify that the matter be dismissed without any further judicial proceedings. See GO HENCE WITHOUT DAY.

eaves-drip. 1. The dripping of water from the eaves of a house onto adjacent land. **2.** An easement permitting the holder to allow water to drip onto the servient estate. See DRIP RIGHTS; STILLICIDIUM.

eavesdropping. The act of secretly listening to the private conversation of others without their consent. Cf. BUGGING; WIRETAPPING.

ebba et fluctus (**eb**-ə et **flək**-təs), *n.* [Latin "ebb and flow"] *Hist.* The ebb and flow of tide; ebb and flood. • The time of one ebb and flood, plus an additional 40 days, was anciently granted to a person who was excused from court for being beyond seas. See EBB AND FLOW; ESSOIN; BEYOND SEAS.

ebb and flow. The coming in and going out of tide. • This expression was formerly used to denote the limits of admiralty jurisdiction.

ebdomadarius (eb-dom-ə-**dair**-ee-əs), *n.* [Latin "weekly"] *Eccles. law.* An officer in a cathedral church who supervises the regular performance of divine service and prescribes the duties of choir members.

EBIT. *abbr.* Earnings before interest and taxes.

EC. *abbr.* **1.** ETHICAL CONSIDERATION. **2.** European Community. See EUROPEAN UNION.

ecclesia (i-**klee**-z[h]ee-ə), *n.* [Latin "assembly"] **1.** A place of religious worship. **2.** A Christian assembly; a church.

ecclesiarch (i-**klee**-zee-ahrk), *n.* The ruler of a church.

ecclesiastic (i-klee-zee-**as**-tik), *n.* A clergyman; a priest; one consecrated to the service of the church.

ecclesiastical (i-klee-zee-**as**-ti-kəl), *adj.* Of or relating to the church, esp. as an institution. — Also termed *ecclesiastic.*

ecclesiastical authorities. The church's hierarchy, answerable to the Crown, but set apart from the rest of the citizens, responsible for superintending public worship and other religious ceremonies and for administering spiritual counsel and instruction. • In England, the several orders of the clergy are (1) archbishops and bishops, (2) deans and chapters, (3) archdeacons, (4) rural deans, (5) parsons (under whom are included appropriators) and vicars, and (6) curates. Church-wardens, sidesmen, parish clerks, and sextons are also considered types of ecclesiastical authorities because their duties are connected with the church. Cf. *ecclesiastical courts* under COURTS.

ecclesiastical commissioners. *Hist. English law.* A group of people empowered to suggest measures to improve the established church's efficiency, to be ratified by orders in council. • This body of commissioners, established by the Ecclesiastical Commissioners Act (1836), has been dissolved. Its functions, rights, and property are now vested in church commissioners. St. 6 & 7 Will. 4, ch. 77.

ecclesiastical corporation. See CORPORATION.

ecclesiastical court. See COURT.

ecclesiastical jurisdiction. Jurisdiction over ecclesiastical cases and controversies, such as that exercised by ecclesiastical courts.

ecclesiastical law. 1. The body of law derived largely from canon and civil law and administered by the ecclesiastical courts. **2.** The law governing the doctrine and discipline of a particular church; esp., Anglican canon law. — Also termed *jus ecclesiasticum*; *law spiritual*. Cf. CANON LAW.

ecclesiastical matter. A matter that concerns church doctrine, creed, or form of worship, or the adoption and enforcement, within a religious association, of laws and regulations to govern the membership, including the power to exclude from such an association those deemed unworthy of membership.

ecclesiastical sentence. The judgment in an ecclesiastical case.

ecclesiastical things. Property (such as buildings and cemeteries) given to a church to support the poor or for any other pious use.

ecdicus (**ek**-də-kəs), *n.* [Greek *ekdikos* "legal representative"] *Hist.* The attorney, proctor, or advocate of an organization. • A church's attorney, for example, was known as an *episcoporum ecdicus*.

echevin (esh-ə-**van**), *n. French law.* A municipal officer corresponding with the position of alderman or burgess, and sometimes having civil jurisdiction to hear and determine certain minor cases.

echouement (ay-shoo-**mawn**), *n.* In French marine law, stranding. See STRANDING.

ECJ. *abbr.* European Court of Justice.

e-commerce. The practice of buying and selling goods and services through online consumer services on the Internet. • The *e*, a shortened form of *electronic*, has become a popular prefix for other terms associated with electronic transactions. See ELECTRONIC TRANSACTION.

econometrics (ee-kon-ə-**me**-triks). The branch of economics that expresses economic theory in mathematical terms and that seeks to verify theory through statistical methods.

economic coercion. See COERCION (2).

economic discrimination. Any form of discrimination within the field of commerce, such as boycotting a particular product or price-fixing. See BOYCOTT; PRICE DISCRIMINATION; PRICE-FIXING.

economic duress. See DURESS.

economic frustration. See *commercial frustration* under FRUSTRATION.

economic-harm rule. See ECONOMIC-LOSS RULE.

economic indicator. A statistical measure (such as housing starts) used to describe the state of the economy or to predict its direction. See INDICATOR.

lagging economic indicator. An economic indicator (such as new-home sales) that tends to respond to the direction of the economy. — Often shortened to *lagging indicator*.

leading economic indicator. An economic indicator (such as interest rates) that tends to predict the future direction of the economy. — Often shortened to *leading indicator*.

economic life. The duration of an asset's profitability, usu. shorter than its physical life.

economic loss. A monetary loss such as lost wages or lost profits. • The term is usu. used to refer to the damages recoverable in a lawsuit. For example, in a products-liability suit, economic loss includes the cost of repair or replacement of defective property, as well as commercial loss for the property's inadequate value and consequent loss of profits or use.

consequential economic loss. Economic loss that proximately results from a defective product and that is beyond direct economic loss. • Examples include lost profits and loss of goodwill or business reputation.

direct economic loss. Economic loss flowing directly from insufficient product quality. • The most common type is loss-of-bargain damages — the difference between the actual value of goods accepted and the value they would have had if they had been delivered as promised or warranted.

economic-loss rule. *Torts.* The principle that a plaintiff cannot sue in tort to recover for purely monetary loss — as opposed to physical injury or property damage — caused by the defendant. • Many states recognize an exception to this rule when the defendant commits fraud or negligent misrepresentation, or when a special relationship exists between the parties (such as an attorney-client relationship). — Also termed *economic-harm rule*; *economic-loss doctrine*.

> "One way the courts have attempted to draw a line between tort and warranty is to bar recovery for 'economic loss' in tort. In some states this common law doctrine has achieved the status of the 'economic loss doctrine,' meaning that once loss is defined as 'economic' it cannot be recovered at least in negligence or strict tort and perhaps not in fraud or misrepresentation." 1 James J. White & Robert S. Summers, *Uniform Commercial Code* § 10-5, at 581 (4th ed. 1995).

economic obsolescence. See OBSOLESCENCE.

economic-realities test. A method by which a court determines the true nature of a business transaction or situation by examining the totality of the commercial circumstances. • Courts often use this test to determine whether a person is an employee or an independent contractor. Factors include whether the alleged employer controls the details of the work and whether taxes are withheld from payments made to the worker.

economic rent. **1.** The return gained from an economic resource (such as a worker or land) above the minimum cost of keeping the resource in service. **2.** Rent that yields a fair return on capital and expenses.

economics. The social science dealing with the production, distribution, and consumption of goods and services.

economic strike. See STRIKE.

economic substantive due process. See DUE PROCESS.

economic warfare. See WARFARE.

economic waste. Overproduction or excessive drilling of oil or gas.

economist. A professional who studies economics and the economy; a specialist in economics.

economy. **1.** The management or administration of the wealth and resources of a community (such as a city, state, or country). **2.** The sociopolitical organization of a community's wealth and resources. **3.** Restrained, thrifty, or sparing use of resources; efficiency.

balanced economy. An economy in which the monetary values of imports and exports are equal.

judicial economy. See JUDICIAL ECONOMY.

overheated economy. An economy that, although it has a high level of economic activity, has the capacity to cause interest rates and inflation to rise.

political economy. A social science dealing with the economic problems of government and the relationship between political policies and economic processes.

economy of scale. (*usu. pl.*) A decline in a product's per-unit production cost resulting from increased output, usu. due to increased production facilities; savings resulting from the greater efficiency of large-scale processes.

e contra (ee **kon**-trə). [Latin] On the contrary.

e converso (ee kən-**vər**-soh). [Latin] Conversely; on the other hand; on the contrary.

ECU. *abbr.* EUROPEAN CURRENCY UNIT.

ecumenical (ek-yə-**men**-ə-kəl), *adj.* **1.** General; universal. **2.** Interreligious; interdenominational.

E.D. *abbr.* Eastern District, in reference to U.S. judicial districts.

edge lease. See LEASE.

EDI agreement. *abbr.* Electronic Data Interchange agreement; an agreement that governs the transfer or exchange of data, such as purchase orders, between parties by computer. • Electronic data transmitted under an EDI agreement is usu. formatted according to an agreed standard, such as the American National Standards Institute ANSI X12 standard or the U.N. EDIFACT standard.

edict (**ee**-dikt), *n.* A formal decree, demand, or proclamation issued by the sovereign of a country. • An edict has legal force equivalent to that of a statute. — **edictal** (ee-**dik**-təl), *adj.*

perpetual edict. *Roman law.* The praetor's edict republished into legislation and intended to exist in perpetuity or until abrogated by a later enactment. • This term originally had the narrower sense of the praetors' general edicts as opposed to edicts issued in specific cases.

praetorian edict (pri-**tor**-ee-ən). *Roman law.* One of the yearly proclamations by which the new praetors made known the legal rules that they would apply in the administration of justice.

edictal interdict. See INTERDICT (1).

Edicts of Justinian. *Roman law.* The 13 constitutions or laws of Justinian, appended to the Greek collection of the Novels. • The Edicts were confined to police matters in the provinces of the Roman Empire.

edictum (ə-**dik**-təm), *n.* [Latin] *Roman law.* An edict or mandate; an ordinance or law enacted by the emperor without the senate, belonging to the class of *constitutiones principis.* • An edict was a constitution of the emperor acting on his own initiative, differing from a rescript in not being returned in the way of answer; from a decree in not being given in judgment; and from both in not being founded upon solicitation.

edictum annuum (**an**-yoo-əm). The annual edict or system of rules promulgated by a Roman praetor immediately upon assuming office, setting forth the principles by which the praetor would be guided in determining cases and administering justice while in office.

edictum perpetuum (pər-**pech**-oo-əm). The permanent part of the urban praetor's edict, edited in its final form by Julian in A.D. 131.

edictum provinciale (prə-vin-shee-**ay**-lee). An edict or system of rules for the administration of justice, similar to the edict of the praetor, set forth by the proconsuls and propraetors in the provinces of the Roman Empire.

Edictum Theodorici (thee-ə-də-**rɪ**-sɪ). A collection of Roman laws applicable to both Romans and Goths, promulgated by Theodoric, king of the Ostrogoths, at Rome about A.D. 500, or perhaps in the time of Theodoric III of the Visigoths in Gaul about A.D. 460.

edictum tralatitium (tral-ə-**tish**-ee-əm). A praetor's edict that retained all or a principal part of the predecessor's edict, with only such additions as appeared necessary to adapt it to changing social conditions or juristic ideas.

edile (**ee**-dɪl). See AEDILE.

editorial privilege. See *journalist's privilege* (2) under PRIVILEGE (3).

editus (**ed**-ə-təs), *adj. Hist.* **1.** (Of a statute or rule) enacted; promulgated. **2.** (Of a child) born; brought forth.

Edmunds–Tucker Act. An 1882 federal law enacted to punish polygamy. 48 USCA § 1480a. — Sometimes shortened to *Edmunds Act.*

educational expense. See EXPENSE.

educational institution. 1. A school, seminary, college, university, or other educational facility, though not necessarily a chartered institution. **2.** As used in a zoning ordinance, all buildings and grounds necessary to accomplish the full scope of educational instruction, including those things essential to mental, moral, and physical development.

educational trust. See TRUST.

EEC. *abbr.* European Economic Community. See EUROPEAN UNION.

EEOC. *abbr.* EQUAL EMPLOYMENT OPPORTUNITY COMMISSION.

effect, *n.* **1.** That which is produced by an agent or cause; a result, outcome, or consequence. **2.** The result that an instrument between parties will produce on their relative rights, or that a statute will produce on existing law, as discovered from the language used, the forms employed, or other materials for construing it.

effect, *vb.* To bring about; to make happen <the improper notice did not effect a timely appeal>.

effective assignment. See ASSIGNMENT (2).

effective assistance of counsel. See ASSISTANCE OF COUNSEL.

effective cause. See *immediate cause* under CAUSE (1).

effective date. The date on which a statute, contract, insurance policy, or other such instrument becomes enforceable or otherwise takes effect, which sometimes differs from the date on which it was enacted or signed.

effective possession. See *constructive possession* under POSSESSION.

effective rate. See INTEREST RATE.

effects, *n. pl.* Movable property; goods <personal effects>.

effects doctrine. See AFFECTS DOCTRINE.

effets (e-**fe** *or* e-**fets**), *n. pl.* [French] **1.** Bills of exchange. **2.** Goods; movables; chattels.

effets mobiliers (moh-beel-**yay** *or* moh-bə-**leerz**). Funds; stocks.

efficient adequate cause. See *proximate cause* under CAUSE (1).

efficient breach. See BREACH OF CONTRACT.

efficient-breach theory. *Contracts.* The view that a party should be allowed to breach a contract and pay damages, if doing so would be more economically efficient than performing under the contract. • This relatively modern theory stems from the law-and-economics movement. See BREACH OF CONTRACT.

efficient cause. See *proximate cause* under CAUSE (1).

efficient intervening cause. See *intervening cause* under CAUSE (1).

efficient proximate cause. See *proximate cause* under CAUSE (1).

effigy (**ef**-ə-jee), *n.* A figure, image, or other representation; esp., a crude representation of someone who is disliked. • Effigies are sometimes hanged, burned, or otherwise abused to express public disapproval or ridicule.

effluent (**ef**-loo-ənt), *n.* Liquid waste that is discharged into a river, lake, or other body of water.

effluxion of time (i-**fluk**-shən). The expiration of a lease term resulting from the passage of time rather than from a specific action or event. — Also termed *efflux of time.*

efforcialiter (e-for-shee-**ay**-lə-tər), *adv.* [Latin] *Hist.* Forcibly. • This adverb referred primarily to military force.

effraction (ə-**frak**-shən). A breach made by the use of force.

effractor (ə-**frak**-tər). One who breaks through; one who commits a burglary.

effusio sanguinis (e-**fyoo**-zhee-oh **sang**-gwi-nis). [Latin] *Hist.* **1.** The shedding of blood. **2.** The fine or penalty imposed for the shedding of blood. • The Crown granted to many lords of manors the power to collect this fine. — Also termed *bloodwite*; *bloodwit*. Cf. WERGILD.

EFT. *abbr.* Electronic funds transfer. See FUNDS TRANSFER.

e.g. *abbr.* [Latin *exempli gratia*] For example <an intentional tort, e.g., battery or false imprisonment>. Cf. I.E.

eggshell-skull rule. *Torts.* The principle that a defendant is liable for a plaintiff's unforeseeable and uncommon reactions to the defendant's negligent or intentional act. • Under this rule, for example, if one person negligently scrapes another who turns out to be a hemophiliac, the negligent defendant is liable for the full extent of the plaintiff's injuries even though the harm to another plaintiff would have been minor. — Also termed *eggshell-plaintiff rule*; *thin-skull rule*; *special-sensitivity rule*; *old-soldier's rule.*

ego, talis (**ee**-goh, **tay**-lis). [Latin] I, such a one. • This phrase was used in describing the forms of old deeds.

egrediens et exeuns (e-**gree**-dee-enz et **ek**-see-ənz). [Latin "stepping out and exiting"] *Common-law pleading.* Going forth and issuing out of (land).

egregious (i-**gree**-jəs), *adj.* Extremely or remarkably bad; flagrant <the defendant's egregious behavior>.

egress (**ee**-gres). **1.** The act of going out or leaving. **2.** The right or ability to leave; a way of exit. Cf. INGRESS.

eight-corners rule. *Insurance.* The principle that a liability insurer's duty to defend its insured — generally triggered if the plaintiff's claims against the insured are within the policy's coverage — is assessed by reviewing the claims asserted in the plaintiff's complaint, without reference to matters outside the four corners of the complaint plus the four corners of the policy. — Also termed *allegations-of-the-complaint rule*. Cf. FOUR-CORNERS RULE.

Eighteenth Amendment. The constitutional amendment — ratified in 1919 and repealed by the 21st Amendment in 1933 — that prohibited the manufacture, sale, transportation, and possession of alcoholic beverages in the United States. See PROHIBITION (3).

Eighth Amendment. The constitutional amendment, ratified as part of the Bill of Rights in 1791, prohibiting excessive bail, excessive fines, and cruel and unusual punishment.

eight-hour law. A law (such as the federal Fair Labor Standards Act) that establishes the standard working day for certain types of employment at eight hours and that usu. requires overtime pay (such as time-and-a-half compensation) for hours worked beyond this period. See WAGE-AND-HOUR LAW.

8–K. An SEC form that a registered corporation must file if a material event affecting its financial condition occurs between the due dates for regular SEC filings. — Also termed *Form 8–K*. Cf. 10–K.

eigne (ayn), *n.* [Law French] The eldest or firstborn. — Also spelled *eygne*; *aisne*. — Also termed (in Law Latin) *einetius*.

eignesse (ay-**nes**), *n.* [French] See ESNECY.

einecia (I-**nee**-shee-ə), *n.* [Law Latin fr. French *einé* "being born before"] Eldership. See ESNECY.

einetia. See EISNETIA.

einetius (I-**nee**-shee-əs), *n.* See EIGNE.

EIR. *abbr.* Environmental-impact report. See ENVIRONMENTAL-IMPACT STATEMENT.

eire (air), *n. Hist.* A journey; route; circuit. See EYRE.

eirenarcha (I-rə-**nahr**-kə), *n.* [Latin "peace ruler"] *Roman law.* A justice of the peace; a person charged with maintaining order. — Also spelled (in Justinian's Digest) *irenarcha*.

EIS. *abbr.* ENVIRONMENTAL-IMPACT STATEMENT.

eisne (ayn), *adj.* [Law French] *Hist.* Eldest; firstborn. — Also spelled *eigne, einsne, aisne, eign*.

bastard eisne. *Hist.* An illegitimate son whose parents afterward marry and have a second son (*mulier puisne*) for lawful issue.

eisnetia (IZ-**nee**-shee-ə), *n.* [Law Latin] The share of the oldest son; the portion of an estate acquired by primogeniture. — Also spelled *einetia*.

either-or order. See *alternative order* under ORDER (4).

eiusdem generis. See EJUSDEM GENERIS.

eject, *vb.* **1.** To cast or throw out. **2.** To oust or dispossess; to put or turn out of possession. **3.** To expel or thrust out forcibly (e.g., disorderly patrons). — **ejector,** *vb.*

ejection, *n.* An expulsion by action of law or by actual or threatened physical force. See OUSTER.

ejectione custodiae. See DE EJECTIONE CUSTODIAE.

ejectione firmae. See DE EJECTIONE FIRMAE.

ejectment. 1. The ejection of an owner or occupier from property. **2.** A legal action by which a person wrongfully ejected from property seeks to recover possession and damages. • The essential allegations in an action for ejectment are that (1) the plaintiff has title to the land, (2) the plaintiff has been wrongfully dispossessed or ousted, and (3) the plaintiff has suffered damages. — Also termed *action for the recovery of land*. See FORCIBLE ENTRY AND DETAINER. Cf. EVICTION; OUSTER.

"The evolution of the action of ejectment from its primitive form as a mere action of trespass, enabling a lessee of lands to recover damages when ousted of his possession, through a series of most ingenious fictions, which were afterwards added to enable him to recover possession as well, until its final establishment as the proper method of trying all disputed titles to real property, presents to the student of legal science one of the most interesting studies that the history of the law affords. Few remedies have passed through so many changes of form, both in pleading and practice, and yet retained the same distinctive character that marked their origin." George W. Warvelle, *A Treatise on the Principles and Practice of the Action of Ejectment* § 4, at 4–5 (1905).

"Any person wrongfully dispossessed of land may sue for the specific restitution of it in an action of ejectment. Originally this action was a special variety of trespass and available only to leaseholders. But in time and by the aid of the most elaborate fictions it came to be used by freeholders also. All these fictions have now been swept away; in theory even the term ejectment has been replaced by the term action for the recovery of land. The older term is, however, replaced in practice." R.F.V. Heuston, *Salmond on the Law of Torts* 41 (17th ed. 1977).

equitable ejectment. A proceeding brought to enforce specific performance of a contract for the sale of land and for other purposes. • Though in the form of an ejectment action, this proceeding is in reality a substitute for a bill in equity.

justice ejectment. A statutory proceeding to evict a tenant who has held over after termination of the lease or breach of its conditions.

ejectment bill. *Equity practice.* A bill in equity brought to recover real property and an accounting of rents and profits, without setting out a distinct ground of equity jurisdiction (and thus demurrable).

ejectmente de garde. See DE EJECTIONE CUSTODIAE.

ejector. One who ejects, puts out, or dispossesses another.

casual ejector. The nominal defendant in an ejectment action who, under a legal fiction, is supposed to come casually or by accident upon the premises and to eject the lawful possessor.

ejectum (i-**jek**-təm), *n.* Something that is cast out, esp. by the sea. See FLOTSAM. Cf. JETSAM; LAGAN.

ejectus (ee-**jek**-təs), *n.* [Latin] *Hist.* A whoremonger; a pimp.

ejercitoria (ay-hair-see-**tor**-ee-ə), *n.* [Spanish] In Spain, the name of an action lying against a ship's owner upon the contracts or obligations made by the master for repairs or supplies. • This action corresponds to the *actio exercitoria* of Roman law.

ejidos (e-**hee**-thohs), *n.* [Spanish] In Spain, lands used in common by inhabitants of a city, pueblo, or town for such things as pasture, wood, and threshing-ground; commons. — Also termed *exidos*; *exedos*.

ejuration (ej-ə-**ray**-shən). The renouncing or resigning of one's place.

ejusdem generis (ee-**jəs**-dəm **jen**-ə-ris *also* ee-**joos**- *or* ee-**yoos**-). [Latin "of the same kind or class"] A canon of construction that when a general word or phrase follows a list of specific persons or things, the general word or phrase will be interpreted to include only persons or things of the same type as those listed. • For example, in the phrase *horses, cattle, sheep, pigs, goats, or any other barnyard animal*, the general language *or any other barnyard animal* — despite its seeming breadth — would probably be held to include only four-legged, hoofed mammals (and thus would exclude chickens). — Also spelled *eiusdem generis*. — Also termed *ejusdem generis rule*; *Lord Tenterden's rule*. Cf. EXPRESSIO UNIUS EST EXCLUSIO ALTERIUS; NOSCITUR A SOCIIS; RULE OF RANK.

elaborare (i-lab-ə-**rair**-ee), *vb.* [Latin] *Hist.* To gain, acquire, or purchase, as by labor and industry.

elaboratus (i-lab-ə-**ray**-təs), *n.* [Latin] Property acquired by labor.

Elastic Clause. See NECESSARY AND PROPER CLAUSE.

elder abuse. See ABUSE.

elder brethren. A distinguished body of men elected as masters of Trinity House, an institution incorporated in the reign of Henry VIII and charged with many duties in marine affairs, such as superintending lighthouses. • The full title of the corporation is Elder Brethren of the Holy and Undivided Trinity.

elder law. The field of law dealing with the elderly, including such issues as estate planning, retirement benefits, social security, age discrimination, and healthcare.

elder title. A title of earlier date but one that becomes operative simultaneously with, and prevails over, a title of newer origin.

elected domicile. See DOMICILE.

electee. 1. A person chosen or elected. **2.** A person to whom the law gives a choice about status.

election, *n.* **1.** The exercise of a choice; esp., the act of choosing from several possible rights or remedies in a way that precludes the use of other rights or remedies <the taxpayers' election to file jointly instead of separately>. See ELECTION OF REMEDIES. **2.** The doctrine by which a person is compelled to choose between accepting a benefit under a legal instrument or retaining some property right to which the person is already entitled; an obligation imposed on a party to choose between alternative rights or claims, so that the party is entitled to enjoy only one <the prevailing plaintiff was put to an election between out-of-pocket damages and lost profits>. — Also termed *equitable election*. See RIGHT OF ELECTION. **3.** The process of selecting a person to occupy a position or office, usu. a public office <the 1994 congressional election>. — **elect,** *vb.* — **elective,** *adj.*

by-election. An election specially held to fill a vacant post. — Also spelled *bye-election*. Cf. *general election*.

election at large. An election in which a public official is selected from a major election district rather than from a subdivision of the larger unit. — Also termed *at-large election*.

free election. An election in which the political system and processes guarantee that each voter will be allowed to vote according to conscience.

general election. **1.** An election that occurs at a regular interval of time. — Also termed *regular election*. **2.** An election for all seats, as contrasted with a by-election. Cf. *by-election*.

municipal election. The election of municipal officers.

off-year election. An election conducted at a time other than the presidential election year.

popular election. An election by people as a whole, rather than by a select group.

primary election. A preliminary election in which a political party's registered voters nominate the candidate who will run in the general election. — Often shortened to *primary*.

recall election. An election in which voters have the opportunity to remove a public official from office.

regular election. See *general election*.

representation election. An election held by the National Labor Relations Board to decide whether a certain union will represent employees in a specific bargaining unit. See BARGAINING UNIT.

runoff election. An election held after a general election, in which the two candidates who received the most votes — neither of whom received a majority — run against each other so that the winner can be determined.

special election. An election that occurs in an interim between general elections, usu. to fill a sudden vacancy in office.

election, doctrine of. A doctrine holding that when a person has contracted with an agent without knowing of the agency and later learns of the principal's identity, the person may enforce the contract against either the agent or the principal, but not both. See ELECTION (1).

election, estoppel by. See *estoppel by election* under ESTOPPEL.

election board. 1. A board of inspectors or commissioners appointed in each election precinct to determine voter qualification, to supervise the polling, and often to ascertain and report the results. **2.** A local agency charged with the conduct of elections.

election by spouse. See RIGHT OF ELECTION.

election contest. A challenge by an election's loser against the winner, calling for an analysis of the election returns, which may include reviewing voter qualifications or re-counting the ballots.

election district. A subdivision of a state, county, or city that is established to facilitate an election or to elect governmental representatives for that subdivision.

election dower. A name sometimes given to a law specifying a widow's statutory share of her deceased husband's estate if she chooses to reject her share under a will. See RIGHT OF ELECTION.

election fraud. Illegal conduct committed in an election, usu. in the form of fraudulent voting (such as a person's voting twice, voting under another person's name (usu. a deceased person), or voting while ineligible).

election judge. **1.** A person appointed to supervise an election at the precinct level; a local representative of an election board. **2.** *English law.* One of two puisne judges of the Queen's Bench Division of the High Court selected to try election petitions.

election of remedies. **1.** A claimant's act of choosing between two or more concurrent but inconsistent remedies based on a single set of facts. **2.** The affirmative defense barring a litigant from pursuing a remedy inconsistent with another remedy already pursued, when that other remedy has given the litigant an advantage over, or has damaged, the opposing party. • This doctrine has largely fallen into disrepute and is now rarely applied. **3.** The affirmative defense that a claimant cannot simultaneously recover damages based on two different liability findings if the injury is the same for both claims, thus creating a double recovery. Cf. *alternative relief* under RELIEF (3).

election petition. *English law.* A petition for inquiry into the validity of a Parliament member's election, when the member's return is allegedly invalid for bribery or other reason.

election returns. The report made to the board of canvassers or the election board, by those charged with tallying votes, of the number of votes cast for a particular candidate or proposition.

elective franchise. See FRANCHISE (1).

elective office. An office that is filled by popular election rather than by appointment.

elective share. *Wills & estates.* The percentage of a deceased spouse's estate, set by statute, that a surviving spouse (or sometimes a child) may choose to receive instead of taking under a will or in the event of being unjustifiably disinherited. — Also termed *forced share*; *statutory share*; *statutory forced share.* See RIGHT OF ELECTION.

> "In many states today, common-law dower and curtesy have been wholly replaced by statutes that make the surviving spouse an 'heir' of the deceased spouse and fix a *minimum* percentage of the decedent's estate (real and personal) to which the survivor will be entitled regardless of efforts of the deceased spouse to prevent it *by will.* This statutory minimum — called the *statutory forced share* — is typically an estate in fee simple, not merely a life estate. A serious disadvantage to the surviving spouse under many of these statutes, however, is that the minimum percentage applies only to property owned by the decedent *at death.* Both husbands and wives can, under such statutes, defeat their spouses' forced shares by *inter vivos* transfer." Thomas F. Bergin & Paul G. Haskell, *Preface to Estates in Land and Future Interests* 37–38 (2d ed. 1984).

elector. **1.** A member of the electoral college chosen to elect the President and Vice President. — Also termed *presidential elector.* **2.** One who is qualified to vote; a voter. **3.** A person who chooses between alternative rights or claims. **4.** *Hist.* The title of certain German princes who had a voice in electing the Holy Roman Emperors. • This office sometimes became hereditary and was connected with territorial possessions.

electoral college. (*often cap.*) The body of electors chosen from each state to formally elect the U.S. President and Vice President by casting votes based on the popular vote.

electoral process. **1.** A method by which a person is elected to public office. **2.** The taking and counting of votes.

electric chair. A chair that is wired so that electrodes can be fastened to a condemned person's head and one leg and a lethal charge passed through the body. • The electric chair was first used in 1890 at the Auburn State Prison in New York.

electronic chattel paper. See CHATTEL PAPER.

Electronic Data Interchange agreement. See EDI AGREEMENT.

electronic funds transfer. See FUNDS TRANSFER.

electronic surveillance. See EAVESDROPPING; WIRETAPPING.

electronic transaction. A transaction formed by electronic messages in which the messages of one or both parties will not be reviewed by an individual as an expected step in forming a contract. UCC § 2A–102(a)(16).

eleemosynae (el-ə-**mos**-ə-nee), *n. pl. Eccles. law.* Possessions belonging to the church.

eleemosynaria (el-ə-mos-ə-**nair**-ee-ə), *n. Hist.* **1.** The place in a religious house where the common alms were deposited, to be distributed to the poor by the almoner. **2.** The office of almoner.

eleemosynarius (el-ə-mos-ə-**nair**-ee-əs), *n. Hist.* [Law Latin] **1.** An almoner, or chief officer, who received the eleemosynary rents and gifts and distributed them to pious and charitable uses. **2.** The name of an officer (lord almoner) of the English kings, in former times, who distributed the royal alms or bounty.

eleemosynary (el-ə-**mos**-ə-ner-ee), *adj.* Of, relating to, or assisted by charity; not-for-profit <an eleemosynary institution>.

eleemosynary corporation. See *charitable corporation* under CORPORATION.

eleemosynary defense. See *charitable immunity* under IMMUNITY (2).

eleganter (el-ə-**gan**-tər), *adv. Civil law.* Accurately; with discrimination; neatly.

elegit (ə-**lee**-jit). [Latin "he has chosen"] *Hist.* A writ of execution (first given by 13 Edw., ch. 18) either upon a judgment for a debt or damages or upon the forfeiture of a recognizance taken in the king's court. • Under it, the defendant's goods and chattels were appraised and, except for plow beasts, delivered to the plaintiff to satisfy the debt. If the goods were not sufficient to pay the debt, then the moiety of the defendant's freehold lands held at the time of judgment was also delivered to the plaintiff, to hold until the debt was satisfied out of rents and profits or until the defendant's interest expired. During this period the plaintiff was called *tenant by elegit*, and the estate an *estate by elegit*. The writ was abolished in 1956.

element. 1. A constituent part of a claim that must be proved for the claim to succeed <Burke failed to prove the element of proximate cause in prosecuting his negligence claim>. **2.** *Patents.* A discretely claimed component of a patent claim. • To recover for patent infringement, the plaintiff must prove that the accused product infringes every element of at least one claim, either literally or under the doctrine of equivalents. — Also termed (in sense 2) *limitation*. See DOCTRINE OF EQUIVALENTS.

elemental fact. See *ultimate fact* under FACT.

elements of crime. The constituent parts of a crime — usu. consisting of the actus reus, mens rea, and — that the prosecution must prove to sustain a conviction. • The term is more broadly defined by the Model Penal Code in § 1.13(9) to refer to each component of the actus reus, causation, the mens rea, any grading factors, and the negative of any defense.

Eleventh Amendment. The constitutional amendment, ratified in 1795, prohibiting a federal court from hearing an action between a state and a person who is not a citizen of that state. See *sovereign immunity* under IMMUNITY (1).

eligible, *adj.* Fit and proper to be selected or to receive a benefit; legally qualified for an office, privilege, or status. — **eligibility,** *n.*

elimination. *Hist.* The act of banishing or turning out of doors; rejection.

elinguation (ee-ling-**gway**-shən). *Hist.* The punishment of cutting out a person's tongue. — **elinguate,** *vb.*

elisor (i-**lɪ**-zər). A person appointed by a court to assemble a jury, serve a writ, or perform other duties of the sheriff or coroner if either is disqualified. — Also spelled *eslisor*.

Elkins Act. A 1903 federal law that strengthened the Interstate Commerce Act by prohibiting rebates and other forms of preferential treatment to large carriers. 49 USCA §§ 41–43 (superseded).

ell (el). *Hist.* A measure of length corresponding to the modern yard.

Ellenborough's Act (**el**-ən-brəz). An English law (the Malicious Shooting and Stabbing Act) of 1803 punishing offenses against the person. St. 43 Geo. 3, ch. 58.

elogium (i-**loh**-jee-əm), *n. Civil law.* A will or testament.

eloign (i-**loyn**), *vb.* **1.** To remove (a person or property) from a court's or sheriff's jurisdiction. **2.** To remove to a distance; conceal. — Also spelled *eloin*. — **eloigner,** *n.*

eloignment (i-**loyn**-mənt), *n.* The getting of a thing or person out of the way, or removing it to a distance, so as to be out of reach.

elongata (ee-lawng-**gay**-tə). [Latin] **1.** *adj.* Eloigned; carried away to a distance. **2.** ELONGATUS.

elongatus (ee-lawng-**gay**-təs). [Latin "eloigned"] A return made by a sheriff to a writ *de homine replegiando*, stating that the party to be replevied has been eloigned, or conveyed out of the sheriff's jurisdiction. — Also termed *elongata*.

elongavit (ee-lawng-**gay**-vit). [Latin "he has eloigned"] In a proceeding by foreign attachment, the serjeant-at-mace's return that the garnishee has eloigned the goods, so that they cannot be appraised. • Upon such a return, judgment was given for the plaintiff that an inquiry be made into the eloigned goods. The inquiry was then set for trial and an assessment made by a jury.

elope, *vb.* **1.** *Archaic.* To run away; escape. **2.** *Archaic.* To abandon one's husband and run away with a lover. **3.** To run away secretly for the purpose of getting married, often without parental consent. — **elopement,** *n.*

elsewhere, *adv.* In another place. • In shipping articles, this term, following the designation of the port of destination, must be construed either as void for uncertainty or as subordinate to the principal voyage stated in the preceding words.

eluviation (i-loo-vee-**ay**-shən). Movement of soil caused by excessive water in the soil.

e-mail. A communication exchanged between people by computer, either through a local area network or the Internet.

emanation. 1. The act of coming or flowing forth from something. **2.** That which flows or comes forth from something; an effluence.

emancipate, *vb.* **1.** To set free from legal, social, or political restraint; esp., to free from slavery or bondage. **2.** To release (a child) from the control, support, and responsibility of a parent or guardian. — **emancipative, emancipatory,** *adj.* — **emancipator,** *n.*

emancipated minor. See MINOR.

emancipation. 1. The act by which one who was under another's power and control is freed. **2.** A surrender and renunciation of the correlative rights and duties concerning the care, custody, and earnings of a child; the act by which a parent (historically a father) frees a child and gives the child the right to his or her own earnings. • This act also frees the parent from all legal obligations of support. Emancipation may take place by agreement between the parent and child, by operation of law (as when the parent abandons or fails to support the child), or when the child gets legally married. A "partial emancipation" frees a child for only a part of the period of minority, or from only a part of the parent's rights, or for only some purposes. **3.** *Roman law.* The enfranchisement of a son by his father, accomplished through the formality of an imaginary sale. • Justinian substituted the simpler proceeding of a manumission before a magistrate. Cf. MANCIPATION.

emancipation proclamation. (*usu. cap.*) An executive proclamation, issued by President Abraham Lincoln on January 1, 1863, declaring that all persons held in slavery in certain designated states and districts were freed.

embargo, *n.* **1.** A government's wartime or peacetime detention of an offending nation's private ships found in the ports of the aggrieved nation <the President called off the embargo of Iraq's ships after the war ended>. — Also termed *hostile embargo.* **2.** A nation's detention of its own ships in its own ports to promote safety and to preclude transportation to an offending nation <the embargo of all U.S. ships traveling to Iraq remained in effect until hostilities subsided>. **3.** The unilateral or collective restrictions on the import or export of goods, materials, capital, or services into or from a specific country or group of countries for political or security reasons <for a time, the industrialized nations placed an embargo on all goods from Libya>. — Also termed *trade embargo.* **4.** The conscription of private property for governmental use, such as to transport troops <the Army's embargo of the company jet to fly General White to Washington>. **5.** A temporary prohibition on disclosure <the embargo on the press release expired at 11:59 p.m.>. — **embargo,** *vb.*

embassador. See AMBASSADOR.

embassy. 1. The building in which a diplomatic body is located; esp., the residence of the ambassador. **2.** A body of diplomatic representatives headed by an ambassador; a diplomatic mission on the ambassadorial level. **3.** The mission, business, and function of an ambassador. Cf. LEGATION.

Ember Days. *Eccles. law.* The days — which the ancient church fathers called *quatuor tempora jejunii* — that are observed on the Wednesday, Friday, and Saturday following (1) Quadragesima Sunday (the first Sunday in Lent), (2) Whitsuntide, or Holyrood Day, in September, and (3) St. Lucy's Day, about the middle of December. • Almanacs refer to the weeks in which these days fall as *Ember Weeks*; they are now chiefly noticed because, by tradition, the Sundays following Ember Days are used to ordain priests and deacons, although the canon allows bishops to ordain on any Sunday or holiday.

embezzlement, *n.* The fraudulent taking of personal property with which one has been entrusted, esp. as a fiduciary. • The criminal intent for embezzlement — unlike larceny and false pretenses — arises after taking possession (not before or during the taking). — Also termed *defalcation*; *peculation*. — **embezzle,** *vb.* See LARCENY; FALSE PRETENSES.

> "Embezzlement is not a common-law crime. It is the result of legislative efforts to make provision for an unreasonable gap which appeared in the law of larceny as it developed. Under the early English statute embezzlement was made a misdemeanor, but under most modern American statutes it is either a felony or a misdemeanor depending upon the value of the property converted." Rollin M. Perkins & Ronald N. Boyce, *Criminal Law* 351 (3d ed. 1982).

> "Embezzlement can be defined as the fraudulent conversion of the property of another by one who has lawful possession of the property and whose fraudulent conversion has been made punishable by the statute." Arnold H. Loewy, *Criminal Law in a Nutshell* 94 (2d ed. 1987).

emblem. **1.** A flag, armorial bearing, or other symbol of a country, organization, or movement. **2.** Loosely, something that is used to symbolize something else.

emblemata Triboniani (em-**blee**-mə-tə trə-boh-nee-**ay**-nɪ). [Latin] *Roman law.* Alterations, modifications, and additions to the writings of the older jurists, combined to form the Pandects. • Justinian appointed a commission over which Tribonian presided to harmonize contradictions, delete obsolete matter, and bring the law up to date.

emblements (**em**-blə-mənts). **1.** The growing crop annually produced by labor, as opposed to a crop occurring naturally. • Emblements are considered personal property that the executor or administrator of a deceased tenant may harvest and take regardless of who may have since occupied the land. — Also termed *fructus industriales*. **2.** The tenant's right to harvest and take away such crops after the tenancy has ended.

> "At common law those products of the earth which are annual, and are raised by yearly manurance and labor, and essentially owe their annual existence to the cultivation by man, [are] termed 'emblements' and sometimes '*fructus industriales*.'" *Sparrow v. Pond*, 52 N.W. 36 (Minn. 1892).

> "The law of emblements has its origin and matrix, in the privilege, recognized at least as early as the fifteenth century, of the tenant for an uncertain term, to harvest and remove, even after the tenancy had terminated, the annual crop, which he had planted and nurtured." Ray Andrews Brown, *The Law of Personal Property* § 159, at 806 (2d ed. 1955).

emblers de gentz (**em**-blərz də **jents**). [Law French] A theft from the people. • The phrase occurs in the old English rolls of Parliament — for example, "Whereas divers murders, *emblers de gentz*, and robberies are committed . . . ."

embossed seal. See NOTARY SEAL.

embracee (em-bray-**see**). The bribe-taker in the offense of embracery.

embracer (im-**brays**-ər). The bribe-giver in the offense of embracery. — Also spelled *embraceor*.

embracery (im-**brays**-ə-ree), *n.* The attempt to corrupt or instruct a jury to reach a particular conclusion by means other than presenting evidence or argument in court, as by bribing or threatening jurors; a corrupt or wrongful attempt to influence a juror's vote on a verdict. — Also termed *jury-tampering*; *laboring a jury*. Cf. JURY-FIXING; JURY-PACKING.

> "The word 'embracery' . . . has tended to disappear. It is included in some of the codes but the tendency has been to divide this common-law offense into two parts, placing that which is appropriate thereto in sections on bribery and the remainder in provisions dealing with obstruction of justice." Rollin M. Perkins & Ronald N. Boyce, *Criminal Law* 552 (3d ed. 1982).

embryo (**em**-bree-oh). A developing but unborn or unhatched animal; esp., an unborn human from conception until the development of organs (i.e., until about the eighth week of pregnancy).

embryo formatus (for-**may**-təs). *Eccles. law.* A human embryo organized into human shape and endowed with a soul. • Though rejected in the early doctrine of the Christian church, the distinction between the embryo *formatus* and *informatus* was accepted by Gratian (regarded as the founder of canon law) in his *Decretum* (ca. 1140), in which he said that abortion is not murder if the fetus has not yet been infused with a soul. Though he did not specify the time of formation or animation, by the 16th century canonists accepted that the time of formation and animation was the 40th day after conception for the male fetus and the 80th day for the female. — Also termed *embryo animatus*.

embryo informatus (in-for-**may**-tәs). *Eccles. law.* A human embryo before it has been endowed with a soul. — Also termed *embryo inanimatus.*

emend (i-**mend**), *vb.* To correct or revise; esp., to edit or change (a text).

emenda (ee-**men**-dә), *n. pl.* [Latin "amends"] Things given in reparation for a trespass.

emendatio (ee-men-**day**-shee-oh), *n.* [Latin] *Hist.* The power of amending and correcting abuses, according to certain rules and measures.

emendatio panis et cerevisiae (ee-men-**day**-shee-oh **pan**-is et ser-ә-**vizh**-ee-ee). [Latin "the correction of bread and ale"] The power of supervising and correcting (assizing) the weights and measures of bread and ale.

emendation (ee-men-**day**-shәn). **1.** Correction or revision, esp. of a text. **2.** *Hist.* The correction of an error or wrongdoing; atonement for a criminal offense. • As criminal law developed over time, emendation by payment of *wer* or *wite* gradually faded away and was replaced by harsher punishments.

e mera gratia (ee **meer**-ә **gray**-shee-ә). [Latin] Out of mere grace or favor.

Emergency Court of Appeals. A temporary court, established during World War II, whose purpose is to review wage- and price-control matters.

emergency doctrine. 1. A legal principle exempting a person from the ordinary standard of reasonable care if that person acted instinctively to meet a sudden and urgent need for aid. — Also termed *imminent-peril doctrine*; *sudden-emergency doctrine*; *sudden-peril doctrine.* **2.** A legal principle by which consent to medical treatment in a dire situation is inferred when neither the patient nor a responsible party can consent but a reasonable person would do so. — Also termed (in sense 2) *emergency-treatment doctrine.* Cf. GOOD SAMARITAN DOCTRINE; RESCUE DOCTRINE.

emergency-employment doctrine. The principle that an employee may enlist another's help in dealing with an emergency that falls within the scope of the employee's duties and that could not be overcome without the assistance of the other person.

emergency-treatment doctrine. See EMERGENCY DOCTRINE (2).

emigrant (**em**-ә-grәnt), *n.* One who leaves his or her country for any reason with the intent to establish a permanent residence elsewhere. Cf. IMMIGRANT.

emigrant agent. See AGENT.

emigration (em-ә-**gray**-shәn), *n.* The act of leaving a country with the intent to not return and to maintain a residence elsewhere. — **emigrate,** *vb.* Cf. IMMIGRATION.

> "Emigration is usually defined as the voluntary removal of an individual from his home State with the intention of residing abroad. However, not all emigration is voluntary; there sometimes exists forced emigration, even mass emigration. Emigration may also be due to flight for political reasons or expulsion. One then speaks of refugees or exiles." Paul Weis, "Emigration," in 2 *Encyclopedia of Public International Law* 76 (1995).

emigré (**em**-ә-gray *or* em-ә-**gray**), *n.* [French] One who is forced to leave his or her country for political reasons. — Also spelled *émigré.*

eminence (**em**-ә-nәnts). (*usu. cap.*) *Eccles. law.* An honorary title given to cardinals of the Catholic Church. • Until the pontificate of Urban VIII, cardinals were called *illustrissimi* and *reverendissimi.*

eminent domain. The inherent power of a governmental entity to take privately owned property, esp. land, and convert it to public use, subject to reasonable compensation for the taking. See CONDEMNATION (2); EXPROPRIATION; TAKING (2).

> "The term 'eminent domain' is said to have originated with Grotius, the seventeenth century legal scholar. Grotius believed that the state possessed the power to take or destroy property for the benefit of the social unit, but he believed that when the state so acted, it was obligated to compensate the injured property owner for his losses. Blackstone, too, believed that society had no general power to take the private property of landowners, except on the payment of a reasonable price. The just compensation clause of the fifth amendment to the Constitution was built upon this concept of a moral obligation to pay for governmental interference with private property. . . . No provision for the power of eminent domain appears in the federal Constitution. The Supreme Court, however, has said that the power of eminent domain is an incident of federal sovereignty and an 'offspring of political necessity.' The Court has also noted that the fifth amendment's limitation on taking private property is a tacit recognition that the power to take private property exists." John E. Nowak & Ronald D. Rotunda, *Constitutional Law* § 11.11, at 424–25 (4th ed. 1991) (quoting

Bauman v. Ross, 167 U.S. 548, 574, 17 S.Ct. 966, 976 (1897)).

Eminent Domain Clause. The Fifth Amendment provision providing that private property cannot be taken for public use without just compensation.

emissary. One sent on a special mission as another's agent or representative, esp. to promote a cause or to gain information.

emit, *vb.* **1.** To give off or discharge into the air <emit light>. **2.** To issue with authority <emit a new series of currency>. — **emission,** *n.*

emolument (i-**mol**-yə-mənt), *n.* (*usu. pl.*) Any advantage, profit, or gain received as a result of one's employment or one's holding of office.

Emolument Clause. The clause of the U.S. Constitution prohibiting titles of nobility and the acceptance of a gift, title, or other benefit from a foreign power. U.S. Const. art. I, § 9, cl. 8.

emotional distress. A highly unpleasant mental reaction (such as anguish, grief, fright, humiliation, or fury) that results from another person's conduct; emotional pain and suffering. • Emotional distress, when severe enough, can form a basis for the recovery of tort damages. — Also termed *emotional harm*; *mental anguish*; *mental distress*; *mental suffering*. See INTENTIONAL INFLICTION OF EMOTIONAL DISTRESS; NEGLIGENT INFLICTION OF EMOTIONAL DISTRESS.

> "Emotional distress passes under various names, such as mental suffering, mental anguish, mental or nervous shock, or the like. It includes all highly unpleasant mental reactions, such as fright, horror, grief, shame, humiliation, embarrassment, anger, chagrin, disappointment, worry, and nausea. It is only where it is extreme that the liability arises. Complete emotional tranquility is seldom attainable in this world, and some degree of transient and trivial emotional distress is a part of the price of living among people. The law intervenes only where the distress inflicted is so severe that no reasonable man could be expected to endure it. The intensity and the duration of the distress are factors to be considered in determining its severity. Severe distress must be proved; but in many cases the extreme and outrageous character of the defendant's conduct is in itself important evidence that the distress has existed." Restatement (Second) of Torts § 46 cmt. j (1965).

emotional insanity. See INSANITY.

empanel, *vb.* To swear in (a jury) to try an issue or case. — Also spelled *impanel*. — **empanelment, empaneling,** *n.*

emparnours (em-**pahr**-nərz), *n. pl.* [French] *Hist.* Persons who undertook lawsuits on behalf of others.

emperor. 1. The title of the sovereign ruler of an empire. **2.** The chief of a confederation of states of which kings are members. • The rulers of the Roman world adopted the designation *emperor* after the fall of the republic. The title was later assumed by those — including Napoleon — who claimed to be their successors in the Holy Roman Empire. The sovereigns of Japan and Morocco are often called *emperors*, as were, in Western speech, the former sovereigns of Turkey and China. The title denotes a power and dignity superior to that of a king. It appears to be the appropriate style of the executive head of a federal government constructed on the monarchial principle and comprising several distinct kingdoms or other quasi-sovereign states, as with the German empire from 1871 to 1918.

emphasis added. A citation signal indicating that the writer quoting another's words has italicized or otherwise emphasized some of them. — Also termed *emphasis supplied*.

emphyteusis (em-fi-**t[y]oo**-sis), *n.* [Greek "implanting"] *Roman & civil law.* A hereditary leasehold; a nonowner's right to use land in perpetuity, subject to forfeiture for nonpayment of a fixed rent or for certain other contingencies.

emphyteuta (em-fi-**t[y]oo**-tə), *n.* [Latin] *Roman & civil law.* The person to whom an *emphyteusis* is granted; the lessee or tenant under a contract of *emphyteusis*. See FEE FARM.

emphyteutic (em-fi-**t[y]oo**-tik), *adj.* [Latin] *Civil law.* Founded on, growing out of, or having the character of an *emphyteusis*; held under an *emphyteusis*.

empire. The dominion or jurisdiction of an emperor; the region over which an emperor's dominion extends.

empirical (em-**pir**-i-kəl), *adj.* Of, relating to, or based on experience, experiment, or observation <the expert's theory was not supported by empirical data>. — Also termed *empiric*.

emplazamiento (em-plah-sah-**myen**-toh), *n.* [Spanish] *Spanish law.* A summons or citation, issued by authority of a judge, requiring the addressee to appear before the tribunal at a designated time.

emploi (om-**plwah**), *n.* [French] *French law.* Equitable conversion. • When property covered by the *régime dotal* is sold, the purchaser must ensure that the sale proceeds are reinvested for the wife's benefit. See *régime dotal* under RE-GIME.

employ, *vb.* **1.** To make use of. **2.** To hire. **3.** To use as an agent or substitute in transacting business. **4.** To commission and entrust with the performance of certain acts or functions or with the management of one's affairs.

employee. A person who works in the service of another person (the employer) under an express or implied contract of hire, under which the employer has the right to control the details of work performance. — Also spelled *employe.* Cf. AGENT; INDEPENDENT CONTRACTOR.

borrowed employee. An employee whose services are, with the employee's consent, lent to another employer who temporarily assumes control over the employee's work. • Under the doctrine of respondeat superior, the borrowing employer is vicariously liable for the employee's acts. But the employer may also be entitled to assert immunity under workers'-compensation laws. — Also termed *borrowed servant*; *loaned employee*; *loaned servant*; *employee pro hac vice*; *special employee.* See RESPONDEAT SUPERIOR.

statutory employee. *Workers' compensation.* An employee who is covered, or required to be covered, by the employer's workers'-compensation insurance and who therefore has no independent tort claim against the employer for unintentional injuries suffered on the job. See *statutory employer* under EMPLOYER.

employee benefit plan. A written stock-purchase, savings, option, bonus, stock-appreciation, profit-sharing, thrift, incentive, pension, or similar plan solely for employees, officers, and advisers of a company. • The term includes an employee-welfare benefit plan, an employee-pension benefit plan, or a combination of those two. But the term excludes any plan, fund, or program (other than an apprenticeship or training program) in which no employees are plan participants. — Often shortened to *plan.* Cf. PENSION PLAN.

defined-benefit plan. A plan established and maintained by an employer primarily to provide systematically for the payment of definitely determinable benefits to employees over a period of years, usu. for life, after retirement. • Retirement benefits under a defined-benefit plan are measured by and based on various factors such as years of service rendered and compensation earned. The amount of benefits and the employer's contributions do not depend on the employer's profits. The employer has the entire investment risk, and must cover any funding shortfall. Any plan that is not a defined-contribution plan is a defined-benefit plan. 29 USCA § 1002(35). Cf. *defined-contribution plan.*

defined-contribution plan. Under ERISA, an employee retirement plan in which each employee has a separate account — funded by the employee's contributions and the employer's contributions (usu. in a preset amount), the employee being entitled to receive the benefit generated by the individual account. 29 USCA § 1002(34). — Also termed *individual account plan.* Cf. *defined-benefit plan.*

disability retirement plan. **1.** A plan that is invoked when a covered person is disabled from working to normal retirement age. **2.** A plan that provides increased benefits if a person retires because of a disability.

employee-stock-ownership plan. A profit-sharing plan designed primarily to give an employee retirement benefits and a stake in the company, but also used to allow employees to purchase their employer company if it is closing. IRC (26 USCA) § 4975(e)(7)(A). — Abbr. ESOP.

excess benefit plan. An employee benefit plan maintained by an employer solely for the purpose of providing benefits for certain employees in excess of the statutory limitations on contributions and benefits.

401(k) plan. A retirement and savings plan that allows an employee to invest pretax contributions from a certain portion of gross wages. • Many employers match the employee's contributions. The contributions and their earnings are accumulated tax-free until they are withdrawn. The contributions are invested, usu. in investments that the employees choose from a list of options. The employer's contributions and the growth on those contributions are usu. not fully vested in the employee unless the employee has achieved a certain duration of service with the employer. IRC (26 USCA) § 401(k).

403(b) plan. A tax-deferred retirement plan for employees of public educational systems and certain tax-exempt organizations, funded primarily with employee contributions (through deferred compensation) and the employer's matching contributions. • The contributions accumulate earnings on a tax-deferred basis, so that neither the contributions nor the earnings are taxed until they are distributed to the employee. IRC (26 USCA) § 403(b). — Also termed *tax-sheltered annuity*; *tax-deferred annuity*.

governmental plan. An employee benefit plan established and maintained by the government for its employees at any level, including plans established or maintained in accordance with collective-bargaining agreements between governmental entities and labor unions if those plans are funded by, and cover only employees of, governmental entities. — Also termed *governmental employee benefit plan*; *government plan*.

individual account plan. See *defined-contribution plan*.

Keogh plan. See KEOGH PLAN.

money-purchase plan. An employee benefit plan that provides a benefit based on the total amount of employer contributions in a participant's account. • A money-purchase plan can be a qualified plan if the contributions are fixed and not geared to profits.

nonqualified deferred-compensation plan. A compensation arrangement (such as providing stock options), frequently offered to executives, that defers the recognition of taxable income to a later date.

> "Generally, a nonqualified deferred compensation plan is an agreement or promise by an employer to certain individuals to pay compensation to those individuals at some future date. A nonqualified plan may also be a series of deferred compensation agreements between an employer and certain individuals that are considered to be a plan of benefits. These types of plans do not qualify for the special tax treatment afforded to plans that meet the qualification requirements of Section 401(a) of the Internal Revenue Code ...." Bruce J. McNeil, *Nonqualified Deferred Compensation Plans* 1 (1994).

retirement plan. An employee benefit plan — such as a pension plan or Keogh plan — provided by an employer (or a self-employed person) for an employee's retirement.

simplified employee pension plan. An individual retirement account or annuity established for an employee and funded by employee contributions and by discretionary contributions from the employer. • A simplified employee pension plan operates much like a 401(k) plan, in that the employee contributions can be made by deferred compensation and the employer can contribute. But the plan is attractive to small employers because it is much easier to administer than a 401(k) plan and gives the employer complete discretion on whether to make an annual contribution. IRC (26 USCA) § 408(k). — Abbr. SEP.

split-funded plan. A retirement plan combining elements of both life insurance and investment plans.

target benefit plan. A money-purchase plan that sets a "targeted" benefit to be met by actuarially determined contributions.

employee givebacks. See CONCESSION BARGAINING.

employee-liability exclusion. See EXCLUSION (3).

employee pro hac vice. See *borrowed employee* under EMPLOYEE.

Employee Retirement Income Security Act. A federal statute that regulates private pension plans and employee benefit plans and that established the Pension Benefit Guaranty Corporation. 29 USCA §§ 1001 et seq. — Abbr. ERISA.

employee stock option. See STOCK OPTION (2).

employee-stock-ownership plan. See EMPLOYEE BENEFIT PLAN.

Employee's Withholding Allowance Certificate. See W-4 FORM.

employer. A person who controls and directs a worker under an express or implied contract of hire and who pays the worker's salary or wages. Cf. PRINCIPAL (1).

equal-opportunity employer. An employer who agrees not to discriminate against any job applicant or employee on the basis of race, color, religion, sex, natural origin, age, or disability. — Abbr. EOE.

general employer. An employer who transfers an employee to another employer for a limited period. See *borrowed employee* under EMPLOYEE.

special employer. An employer who has borrowed an employee for a limited period and has temporary responsibility and control over the employee's work.

statutory employer. *Workers' compensation.* One who employs a statutory employee. See *statutory employee* under EMPLOYEE.

employers' liability. See WORKERS' COMPENSATION.

employers'-liability insurance. See INSURANCE.

employment. 1. The act of employing; the state of being employed. **2.** Work for which one has been hired and is being paid by an employer.

casual employment. Work that is occasional, irregular, or for a limited, temporary purpose.

employment at will. Employment that is usu. undertaken without a contract and that may be terminated at any time, by either the employer or the employee, without cause. — Also termed *at-will employment*; *hiring at will*.

"Surprisingly, the employment at will doctrine is not an ancient one. On the contrary, it dates only from the period in the mid-nineteenth century that saw the transformation of the employment relation from one of status to one of contract. The relentless logic of the contract approach dictated the rule that the employee had only such rights as were expressly agreed to in his contract of employment — no more and no less. This meant that there was no implication that an indefinite hiring would last for a year or any other presumed period, since if the parties had wanted a particular term they would have expressly agreed to it." 1 Lex K. Larson, *Unjust Dismissal* § 1.01, at 1–3 (1992).

"The doctrine of employment at will prescribed that an employee without a contract for a fixed term could be hired or fired for any reason or no reason at all.... [The] rule provided that employees categorized as 'at will' had no legal interest in continuing job security. Whereas early American masters had some responsibility to the public as well as to their servants when they turned dependent servants out on the world, under [this] formulation, masters could simply fire employees who had no contracts." Mark A. Rothstein et al., *Employment Law* § 1.4, at 9–10 (1994).

gainful employment. Work that a person can pursue and perform for money.

hazardous employment. High-risk work; work involving extra peril. • In the context of workers' compensation, hazardous employment often requires an employer to carry workers'-compensation coverage or its equivalent, regardless of the number of employees.

joint employment. A job in which the essential terms and conditions of the employee's work are controlled by two or more entities, as when a company hires a contractor to perform a task and retains control over the contractor's employees in matters such as hiring, firing, discipline, conditions of employment, promulgation of work rules, assignment of day-to-day job duties, and issuance of operating instructions.

permanent employment. Work that, under a contract, is to continue indefinitely until either party wishes to terminate it for some legitimate reason.

seasonal employment. An occupation possible only during limited parts of the year, such as a summer-camp counselor, a baseball-park vendor, or a shopping-mall Santa.

employment agency. A business that procures, for a fee, employment for others and employees for employers. • Whether the employer or the employee pays the fee depends on the terms of the agreement. See FINDER (1).

employment at will. See EMPLOYMENT.

employment contract. See CONTRACT.

employment-practices-liability insurance. See INSURANCE.

employment-related-practices exclusion. See EXCLUSION (3).

emporium (em-**por**-ee-əm), *n.* A place for wholesale trade in commodities carried by sea. • The term is sometimes applied to a seaport town, but properly signifies only a particular place in such a town.

empresario (em-pri-**sahr**-ee-oh), *n.* [Spanish] **1.** *Mexican law.* A businessperson; a person who invests in or manages a business. **2.** *Hist.* A person receiving extensive land grants in consideration of bringing people into Mexico (esp. into what would become Texas) and settling them on the land with a view toward increasing the population and developing the country's resources.

emptio (**emp**-shee-oh), *n.* [Latin "purchase"] *Roman & civil law.* The act of buying; a purchase. — Also spelled *emtio*.

emptio bonorum (bə-**nor**-əm). [Latin "purchase of goods"] A type of forced assignment for the benefit of creditors, involving a public sale of an insolvent debtor's estate whereby the purchaser succeeded to all the debtor's property, rights, and claims, and became responsible for the debtor's debts and liabilities to an extent fixed before the transfer.

emptio et venditio (et ven-**dish**-ee-oh). [Latin "purchase and sale"] A contract of sale. — Also termed *emptio venditio*. See VENDITIO.

emptio rei speratae (**ree**-I spə-**ray**-tee). [Latin "purchase of a hoped-for thing"] The purchase of a thing not yet in existence or not yet in the seller's possession; e.g., a future crop. • The price of such a purchase typically depended on the actual yield and thus could fluctuate.

emptio spei (**spee**-I). [Latin "purchase of a hope"] An *emptio rei speratae* in which the price is fixed, regardless of actual gain.

emptio venditio. See *emptio et venditio*.

emptor (**emp**-tor *or* -tər), *n.* [Latin] *Civil law.* A buyer. — Also spelled *emtor*. See *caveat emptor* under CAVEAT.

emptor familiae. See FAMILIAE EMPTOR.

empty-chair defense. A trial tactic in a multiparty case, whereby one defendant attempts to put all the fault on a defendant who settled before trial or who was not named as a party.

empty-chair doctrine. See ADVERSE-INTEREST RULE.

emtio. See EMPTIO.

emtor. See EMPTOR.

emtrix (**em**[**p**]-trəks), *n.* [Latin] *Civil law.* A female buyer.

enable, *vb.* To give power to do something; to make able.

enablement requirement. *Patents.* The rule that the specification of a patent application must describe the invention so that a person with ordinary skill in the art could make and use the invention without experimenting unduly. • A specification that meets this requirement is referred to as *enabling*. Cf. ENABLING SOURCE.

enabling act. See *enabling statute* under STATUTE.

enabling clause. The part of a statute or constitution that gives governmental officials the power and authority to put the law into effect and enforce it. See ENACTING CLAUSE.

enabling power. See POWER OF APPOINTMENT.

enabling source. *Patents.* A document that defeats the patentability of an invention because the information provided made it possible — before the patent application was filed — for a person skilled in the art to make the invention. Cf. ENABLEMENT REQUIREMENT.

enabling statute. 1. See STATUTE. **2.** *Hist.* The Lease Act (1540), by which tenants in tail, husbands seised in right of their wives, and others were empowered to make leases for their lives or for 21 years. St. 32 Hen. 8, ch. 28.

enact, *vb.* **1.** To make into law by authoritative act; to pass <the statute was enacted shortly before the announced deadline>. **2.** (Of a statute) to provide <the statute of frauds enacts that no action may be brought on certain types of contracts unless the plaintiff has a signed writing to prove the agreement>. — **enactor,** *n.*

enacted law. See LAW.

enacting clause. The part of a statute stating the legislative authority by which it is made and when it takes effect. • In codifications of statutes, enacting clauses generally appear not in the text of the statutes but in historical or legislative notes.

enactment, *n.* **1.** The action or process of making into law <enactment of a legislative bill>. **2.** A statute <a recent enactment>.

enajenación (e-nah-hen-ah-**syohn**), *n.* [Spanish] In Spain and Mexico, alienation; conveyance of property.

en arere (en ə-**reer**). [Law French] In time past.

en autre droit (en **oh**-trə **droyt** *or* on **noh**-trə **drwah**). [French] In the right of another, as when an executor sues on behalf of the estate. — Also spelled *in autre droit*. See AUTRE DROIT.

en banc (en **bangk** *or* on **bongk**). [Law French "on the bench"] *adv.* & *adj.* With all judges present and participating; in full court <the court heard the case en banc> <an en banc rehearing>. — Also spelled *in banc*; *in bank*. — Also termed *in banco*.

en banc sitting. See SITTING.

enbancworthy, *adj. Slang.* Worthy of being considered en banc <the Fifth Circuit conclud-

ed that two of the four issues are truly enbancworthy>. — **enbancworthiness,** *n.*

en bloc (en **blok**). [French] As a whole; as a unit.

enbrever (en-**bree**-vər), *vb.* [Law French] **1.** To abbreviate. **2.** To put into a schedule.

encheson (en-**chee**-zən), *n.* [Law French] The occasion, cause, or reason for which something is done. — Also spelled *encheason.*

enclave (**en**-klayv). *Int'l law.* An isolated part of a country's territory entirely surrounded by the territory of one foreign country, so that any communication with the main part of the country must pass through the territory of the foreign country. • Although international enclaves were once common, they are now relatively rare; examples include Baarle–Hertog, a Belgian enclave in the Netherlands, and Büsingen, a German enclave in Switzerland. — Also termed *international enclave.*

quasi-enclave. An isolated part of a country's territory that, though not entirely surrounded by the territory of a foreign country, is inaccessible by way of the country's own territory because of topographical features such as impassable mountains.

enclose, *vb.* **1.** To surround or encompass; to fence or hem in on all sides. **2.** To place (something) in a parcel or envelope. — Also spelled *inclose.*

enclosed land. See LAND.

enclosed please find. See TRANSMITTAL LETTER.

enclosure. 1. Something enclosed in a parcel or envelope. **2.** Land surrounded by some visible obstruction; CLOSE (1). **3.** An artificial fence around one's estate. — Also spelled *inclosure.*

encomienda (en-koh-mee-**en**-də), *n.* [Spanish] *Spanish law.* **1.** A royal grant to a private person of a certain portion of territory in the Spanish colonies, together with the concession of a certain number of the native inhabitants, on the feudal principle of commendation. **2.** A royal grant of privileges to the military orders of Spain.

encourage, *vb. Criminal law.* To instigate; to incite to action; to embolden; to help. See AID AND ABET.

encroach, *vb.* **1.** To enter by gradual steps or stealth into the possessions or rights of another; to trespass or intrude. **2.** To gain or intrude unlawfully upon another's lands, property, or authority. — Formerly also spelled *incroach.*

encroachment, *n.* An infringement of another's rights or intrusion on another's property <the court remedied the encroachment by ordering the defendant to cut down the tree limb hanging over the plaintiff's yard>. — Formerly also spelled *incroachment.* See TRESPASS.

encumbrance, *n.* A claim or liability that is attached to property or some other right and that may lessen its value, such as a lien or mortgage; any property right that is not an ownership interest. • An encumbrance cannot defeat the transfer of possession, but it remains after the property or right is transferred. — Also spelled *incumbrance.* — **encumber,** *vb.*

> "Encumbrances are not confined to the law of property, but pertain to the law of obligations also. Choses in action may be mortgaged, settled in trust, or otherwise made the subject-matter of *jura in re aliena*, no less than land and chattels." John Salmond, *Jurisprudence* 435–36 n.(k) (Glanville L. Williams ed., 10th ed. 1947).

> " 'Encumbrance' means a right, other than an ownership interest, in real property. The term includes a mortgage or other lien on real property." UCC § 9–102(a)(23).

mesne encumbrance (meen). An intermediate encumbrance; an encumbrance that first occurred both earlier and later than other encumbrances.

encumbrancer. One having a legal claim, such as a lien or mortgage, against property.

end, *n.* **1.** An object, goal, or purpose. **2.** A result; a termination point.

endangered species. See SPECIES.

endangerment, *n.* The act or an instance of putting someone or something in danger; exposure to peril or harm. — **endanger,** *vb.* See CHILD ENDANGERMENT; RECKLESS ENDANGERMENT.

endeavor, *n.* A systematic or continuous effort to attain some goal.

endeavor, *vb.* To exert physical or intellectual strength toward the attainment of an object or goal.

en déclaration de simulation (on dek-lah-rah-**syawn** də sim-[y]ə-lah-**syawn**). [French "in order to declare (something) a pretence"] *Civil law.* An action to void a contract; esp., one brought to remove a cloud from title and bring back, for any legal purpose, to the true owner's estate the thing sold.

en demeure (*on* də-**myuur**). [French "in default"] *Civil law.* Of a debtor who fails to pay on demand according to the terms of the obligation.

endenizen (en-**den**-ə-zən), *vb.* To recognize as a legal resident; to naturalize. — Also spelled *endenize*; *indenizen*; *indenize.*

endless-chain scheme. See PYRAMID SCHEME.

end lines. *Mining law.* A claim's lines, as platted or laid down on the ground, that mark its boundaries on the shorter dimension, where the claim crosses the vein, in contrast to side lines, which mark the longer dimension and follow the course of the vein. • With reference to the apex rule, if the claim as a whole crosses the vein instead of following its course, the end lines will become the side lines and vice versa. Cf. SIDE LINES; APEX RULE.

endnote. A note that, instead of appearing at the bottom of the page (as a footnote does), appears at the end of the book, chapter, or paper.

endorsed bond. See *guaranteed bond* under BOND (3).

endorsee. See INDORSEE.

endorsement, *n.* **1.** INDORSEMENT. **2.** An amendment to an insurance policy; a rider. — **endorse,** *vb.*

endorser. See INDORSER.

endow, *vb.* **1.** To give money or property to, esp. as a source of continuing or permanent income. **2.** *Hist.* To provide (a woman) with a dower.

endowment. 1. A gift of money or property to an institution (such as a university) for a specific purpose, esp. one in which the principal is kept intact indefinitely and only the interest income from that principal is used. **2.** *Hist.* The assigning or giving of a dower to a woman.

endowment insurance. See INSURANCE.

endowment policy. See INSURANCE POLICY.

end position. One's legal and financial position on the signing of a contract, including the choices now available, such as renewal and renegotiation.

end user. See USER.

Enelow–Ettelson **rule** (**en**-ə-loh–**et**-əl-sən). The defunct doctrine that an order staying federal-court proceedings pending the determination of an equitable defense (such as arbitration) is an injunction appealable under 28 USCA § 1292(a)(1) if the proceeding stayed was an action that could have been maintained as an action at law before the merger of law and equity. *Enelow v. New York Life Ins. Co.*, 293 U.S. 379, 55 S.Ct. 310 (1935); *Ettelson v. Metropolitan Life Ins. Co.*, 317 U.S. 188, 63 S.Ct. 163 (1942).

enemy. 1. One who opposes or inflicts injury on another; an antagonist. **2.** An opposing military force. **3.** A state with which another state is at war. — Also termed *public enemy.* **4.** A person possessing the nationality of the state with which one is at war. — Also termed *enemy subject.* **5.** A foreign state that is openly hostile to another whose position is being considered.

alien enemy. See ALIEN.

public enemy. **1.** A notorious criminal who is a menace to society; esp., one who seems more or less immune from successful prosecution. **2.** ENEMY (3). **3.** A social, health, or economic condition or problem that affects the public at large and is difficult to control <teenage smoking has been declared a public enemy in this country>.

enemy alien. See *alien enemy* under ALIEN.

enemy's property. *Int'l law.* Property used in illegal commerce or trading with a public enemy, whether that property belongs to an ally or a citizen. • This term is esp. common in prize courts. The illegal traffic makes the property hostile, and allows penal consequences to attach to the property itself.

enemy subject. See ENEMY (4).

Energy, Department of. See DEPARTMENT OF ENERGY.

en fait (*on* **fay**), *adv.* [French] In fact; actually.

enfeoff (en-**fef** *or* en-**feef**), *vb.* To put (a person) in legal possession of a freehold interest; to transfer a fief to. — Formerly spelled *infeoff*. — Also termed *feoff*; *infeudate*.

enfeoffment (en-**fef**- *or* en-**feef**-mənt), *n.* **1.** At common law, the act or process of transferring possession and ownership of an estate in land. — Also termed *infeudation*. **2.** The property or estate so transferred. **3.** The instrument or deed by which one obtains such property or estate. — Also spelled *infeoffment*. — Also termed *feoffment*.

enforce, *vb.* **1.** To give force or effect to (a law, etc.); to compel obedience to. **2.** Loosely, to compel a person to pay damages for not complying with (a contract).

enforcement, *n.* The act or process of compelling compliance with a law, mandate, or command.

extrajudicial enforcement. See SELF-HELP.

law enforcement. See LAW ENFORCEMENT.

remedial enforcement. See *secondary right* under RIGHT.

sanctional enforcement. See *secondary right* under RIGHT.

secondary enforcement. See *secondary right* under RIGHT.

selective enforcement. See SELECTIVE ENFORCEMENT.

specific enforcement. See *primary right* under RIGHT.

Enforcement of Foreign Judgments Act. A uniform law, adopted by several states, that gives the holder of a foreign judgment essentially the same rights to levy and execute on the judgment as the holder of a domestic judgment. • The Act defines a *foreign judgment* as any judgment, decree, or order (of a court in the United States or of any other court) that is entitled to full faith and credit in the state. See FULL FAITH AND CREDIT.

enforcement power. The authority by which Congress may enforce a particular constitutional amendment's provisions by appropriate legislation. • Enforcement power is granted to Congress under the 13th, 14th, 15th, 19th, 23rd, 24th, and 26th Amendments.

enfranchise, *vb.* **1.** To grant voting rights or other rights of citizenship to (a person or class). **2.** To set free, as from slavery.

enfranchisement (en-**fran**-chiz-mənt *or* -chɪz-mənt), *n.* **1.** The granting of voting rights or other rights of citizenship to a class of persons. **2.** The act of making free, as from slavery.

enfranchisement of copyhold. *Hist.* The conversion of copyhold into freehold tenure, by (1) a conveyance of the fee simple from the lord of the manor to the copyholder, (2) a release from the lord of all seigniorial rights, or (3) a release by the copyholder to the lord of the copyholder's interest in the estate. See COPYHOLD.

engage, *vb.* To employ or involve oneself; to take part in; to embark on.

engagement, *n.* **1.** A contract or agreement involving mutual promises. **2.** An agreement to marry; the period after which a couple has agreed to marry but before they do so.

engagement slip. A note sent by a lawyer to a court informing the court that the lawyer is professionally engaged in a second court on a given day and thus cannot appear before the first court on that day as scheduled. • The term is used in Pennsylvania.

engender, *vb.* To cause; to bring about; to occasion.

engineering, procurement, and construction contract. See CONTRACT.

***England* procedure.** A procedure by which — after a federal court has referred a case back to state court under the *Pullman* abstention doctrine, and the state court has adjudicated the state-court issues — a litigant may return to federal court to have the federal claims adjudicated. *England v. Louisiana State Bd. of Med. Examiners*, 375 U.S. 411, 84 S.Ct. 461 (1964). See *Pullman abstention* under ABSTENTION.

English rule. The requirement that a losing litigant must pay the winner's costs and attorney's fees. — Also termed *loser-pays rule*. Cf. AMERICAN RULE.

Englishry, presentment of. PRESENTMENT OF ENGLISHRY.

en gros (on **groh**). [French] In gross; total; by wholesale.

engross, *vb.* **1.** *Hist.* To handwrite a document, esp. a deed, in a style characterized by large letters. • This method of writing, which was derived from ancient court hand, was also used in transcribing wills well into the 19th century. Cf. COURT HAND. **2.** To prepare a copy of (a legal document, such as a deed) for execution. **3.** To prepare a copy of (a bill or mandate) before a final legislative vote. **4.** To buy large quantities of (a stock or commodity) in an effort to corner the market and control the price. **5.** To absorb or fully occupy. — Formerly also spelled *ingross*. Cf. ENROLL.

engrossed bill. See BILL (3).

engrosser, *n. Hist.* A person who engages in or is guilty of engrossing.

Engrosser of the Great Roll. See CLERK OF THE PIPE.

engrossing, *n. Hist.* The practice of buying large quantities of commodities or merchandise with the intent of gaining a monopoly and selling them at a very high price. • Engrossing was a misdemeanor in England until 1834. — Also termed *engrossment*. See CORNERING THE MARKET.

> "Engrossing . . . is the getting into one's possession, or buying up, of corn or other dead victuals, with intent to sell them again. This must of course be injurious to the public, by putting it in the power of one or two rich men to raise the price of provisions at their own discretion." 4 William Blackstone, *Commentaries on the Laws of England* 158 (1769).

engrossment, *n.* **1.** The preparation of a legal document (such as a deed) for execution. **2.** The drafting of a resolution or bill just before a final vote on the matter in the legislature. **3.** ENGROSSING.

enhanced, *adj.* Made greater; increased <because of his recidivism, Monte was subject to an enhanced sentence after his latest conviction>.

enhanced damages. See DAMAGES.

enhancement. The act of augmenting; the state of being enhanced <the use of a deadly weapon led to an enhancement of the sentence>.

enheritance (*on*-nair-ee-**tah*n*s**), *n.* [Law French] See INHERITANCE.

enitia pars (ə-**nish**-ee-ə **pahrz**). [Latin] The share of the eldest. • In English law, this describes the lot or share chosen by the eldest of coparceners when they make a voluntary partition. The first choice (*primer election*) belongs to the eldest.

enjoin, *vb.* **1.** To legally prohibit or restrain by injunction <the company was enjoined from selling its stock>. **2.** To prescribe, mandate, or strongly encourage <the graduating class was enjoined to uphold the highest professional standards>. — **enjoinment** (for sense 1), *n.* — **enjoinder** (for sense 2), *n.*

enjoinable, *adj.* Capable of being prohibited by injunction <an enjoinable nuisance>.

enjoy, *vb.* To have, possess, and use (something) with satisfaction; to occupy or have the benefit of (property).

enjoyment, *n.* **1.** Possession and use, esp. of rights or property. **2.** The exercise of a right.

adverse enjoyment. The possession or use of land under a claim of right against the owner of the property from which the easement derives.

beneficial enjoyment. The possession and benefit of property, but without legal title.

present enjoyment. The immediate possession and use of an estate.

quiet enjoyment. The possession of real property with the assurance that the possession will not be disturbed by a superior title. See *covenant for quiet enjoyment* under COVENANT (4).

en juicio (en **hwee**-syoh), *adv.* [Spanish] Judicially; in a court of law; in a suit at law.

enlarge, *vb.* **1.** To increase in size or extend in scope or duration <the court enlarged the time allotted for closing arguments>. **2.** To free from custody or imprisonment <at common law, an action for escape lay when a prisoner was wrongly enlarged>. — **enlargement,** *n.*

enlargement of time. A usu. court-ordered extension of the time allowed to perform an action, esp. a procedural one.

enlarger l'estate (en-**lahr**-jər lə-**stayt**). [Law French] A release that enlarges an estate and consists of a conveyance of the ulterior interest to the particular tenant. • If an estate is held by a tenant for life or years, with the remainder to another in fee, and if the one in remainder releases all rights to the particular tenant and his or her heirs (through an *enlarger l'estate*), the tenant then holds the estate in fee.

enlisted member. *Military law.* A person in an enlisted grade; a person in military service below the grade of officer or warrant officer.

enlistment, *n.* Voluntary entry into a branch of the armed services. — **enlist,** *vb.*

en masse (en **mas**). [French] In a mass; in a large group all at once; all together.

en mort mayne (en **mort** mayn). [French "in dead hand"] In mortmain. See MORTMAIN.

Enoch Arden law (**ee**-nək **ahrd**-ən). A statute that grants a divorce or an exemption from liability so that a person can remarry when his or her spouse has been absent without explanation for a specified number of years (usu. five or seven). • This type of law is named after a Tennyson poem, in which the eponymous hero, having been shipwrecked for years on a desert island, returns home to find that his wife has remarried. He selflessly conceals his identity from her so that she can remain with her new husband. — Also spelled *Enoc Arden law.* See *presumptive death* under DEATH; ABANDONMENT (2).

enormia (i-**nor**-mee-ə), *n.* [Latin] *Common-law pleading.* Unlawful or wrongful acts; wrongs. • This word, esp. as part of the phrase *et alia enormia* ("and other outrages"), appeared regularly in writs and declarations of trespass.

enormious (i-**nor**-mee-əs), *adj. Archaic.* Made without a rule or against law.

enormous, *adj.* Aggravated; excessively large <enormous crimes>.

en owel main (en **ow**-əl **mayn**). [Law French] In equal hand.

enpleet (en-**pleet**), *vb. Hist.* See IMPLEAD.

enquête (on-**ket**), *n.* [French] *Eccles. law.* An examination of witnesses (taken down in writing) by or before an authorized judge for the purpose of gathering testimony to be used on a trial. — Also termed *enquest* (on[g]-**kwes**[**t**]).

en recouvrement (on ray-koo-vrə-**mon**). [French "for purpose of recovery"] *French law.* An indorsement on a bill of exchange that does not transfer the property in the bill of exchange but merely gives the indorsee the authority to recover the amount of the bill.

enrégistrement (on-ray-zhees-trə-**mon**), *n.* [French] *French law.* Registration. • This is a formality that consists in inscribing, on a register kept by the government, a summary analysis of certain deeds and documents. When the analysis is so inscribed, the clerk places on the document a note indicating the date on which it was registered; alongside the memorandum the clerk makes an impression with a stamp.

enroll, *vb.* **1.** To register or transcribe (a legal document, as a deed) into an official record on execution. — Formerly also spelled *inroll.* **2.** To prepare (a bill passed by the legislature) for the executive's signature. Cf. ENGROSS.

enrolled, *adj.* Registered; recorded.

enrolled agent. One who, though neither a certified public accountant nor an attorney, has been admitted to practice before the IRS, either by passing an examination or by working for the IRS in a technical area for at least five years. • The enrolled agent is one of four types of persons who are allowed to practice before the IRS, the other three being attorneys, certified public accountants, and persons who are admitted to represent either themselves or others in a particular case.

enrolled bill. See BILL (3).

enrolled-bill rule. The conclusive presumption that a statute, once formalized, appears precisely as the legislature intended, thereby preventing any challenge to the drafting of the bill.

enrollment, *n.* The act of recording or registering.

enrollment of vessels. *Maritime law.* The recording and certification of vessels used in coastal or inland navigation, as distinguished from the "registration" of vessels used in foreign commerce. • *Enrollment* and *registry* are used to distinguish certificates granted to two classes of vessels. Enrollment evidences the national character of a vessel engaged in coasting trade or home traffic; registry is used to declare the nationality of a vessel engaged in foreign trade. Cf. REGISTRY (2).

Enrollment Office. *Hist.* A department of the Court of Chancery responsible for storing enrolled deeds and judgments. • The Enrollment Office was abolished in 1879; its duties were transferred to the Central Office.

en route (en *or* on **root**). [French] On the way; in the course of transportation or travel.

enschedule, *vb. Archaic.* To insert in a list, account, or writing.

enseal, *vb. Archaic.* To seal (a document).

enserver (en-**sər**-vər), *vb.* [Law French] To make subject to a service or servitude.

ens legis (enz **lee**-jis). [Law Latin] A creature of the law; an artificial being as opposed to a natural person. • The term describes a corporation, which derives its existence entirely from the law.

entail, *n.* A fee abridged or limited to the owner's issue or class of issue rather than descending to all the heirs. See BARRING OF ENTAIL.

> "*Entail* is fee entailed, viz; abridged, limited, and tied to certain conditions at the will of the donor; where lands are given to, or settled on others." *The Pocket Lawyer and Family Conveyancer* 97 (3d ed. 1833).

quasi-entail. An estate *pur autre vie* that is granted to a person and the heirs of the person's body. • The interest so granted is not properly an estate-tail (because it is not granted by inheritance), but it is similar enough that the interest will go to the heir of the body as special occupant during the life of the *cestui que vie,* in the same manner as an estate of inheritance would descend if limited to the grantee and the heirs of his body.

entail, *vb.* **1.** To make necessary; to involve <responding to this onerous discovery will entail countless hours of work>. **2.** To limit the inheritance of (an estate) to only the owner's issue or class of issue, so that none of the heirs can transfer the estate <the grantor entailed the property through a so-called "tail female">. See FEE TAIL.

entailed, *adj.* Settled or limited to specified heirs or in tail <entailed gifts>.

entailed estate. See FEE TAIL.

entailment, *n.* **1.** The act of entailing an estate. **2.** An estate so entailed.

entencion (en-**ten**-shən), *n.* [Law French] *Hist.* A plaintiff's count or declaration.

entendment. *Archaic.* See INTENDMENT.

entente (ahn-**tahnt**). [French "intent, understanding"] *Int'l law.* **1.** An understanding that two or more nations have for carrying out a common policy or course of action. • An *entente* is looser than an alliance but stronger than the nations' merely having good relations. **2.** The nations having such an understanding. Cf. ALLIANCE; DETENTE.

enter, *vb.* **1.** To come or go into; esp., to go onto (real property) by right of entry so as to take possession <the landlord entered the defaulting tenant's premises>. **2.** To put formally before a court or on the record <the defendant entered a plea of no contest>. **3.** To become a party to <they entered into an agreement>. See ENTRY.

enterceur (en-tər-**sər**), *n.* [Law French] A party claiming goods; one who has placed goods in the hands of a third party.

enterpleder. *Archaic.* See INTERPLEADER (1).

enterprise, *n.* **1.** An organization or venture, esp. for business purposes.

governmental enterprise. An enterprise undertaken by a governmental body, such as a parks department that creates a public park.

2. Under federal anti-racketeering law, an individual, partnership, corporation, association, union, other legal entity, or group of individuals associated in fact, although not a legal entity. • The enterprise must be ongoing and must exist as an entity separate from the allegedly illegal activity that it engages in. 18 USCA § 1961(4). See RACKETEER INFLUENCED AND CORRUPT ORGANIZATIONS ACT. **3.** One or more persons or organizations that have related activities, unified operation or common control, and a common business purpose. • Under the Fair Labor Standards Act, an employee who is employed by an enterprise is entitled to minimum-wage and overtime benefits. 29 USCA §§ 201 et seq.

enterprise liability. See LIABILITY.

entertain, *vb.* **1.** To bear in mind or consider; esp., to give judicial consideration to <the court then entertained motions for continuance>. **2.** To amuse or please. **3.** To receive (a person) as a guest or provide hospitality to (a person).

entertainment expense. See EXPENSE.

entertainment law. The field of law dealing with the legal and business issues in the entertainment industry (such as film, music, and theater), and involving the representation of artists and producers, the negotiation of contracts, and the protection of intellectual-property rights.

entice, *vb.* To lure or induce; esp., to wrongfully solicit (a person) to do something.

enticement, *n.* **1.** The act or an instance of wrongfully soliciting or luring a person to do something.

enticement of a child. *Criminal law.* The act or offense of inviting, persuading, or attempting to persuade a child to enter a vehicle, building, room, or secluded place with the intent of committing an unlawful sexual act against the child.

2. *Hist.* The tort of inducing a man's wife to leave him or to remain away from him against his will.

entire, *adj.* **1.** Whole; complete in all its parts. **2.** Not divisible into parts.

entire benefit. See *entire use* under USE (4).

entire blood. See FULL BLOOD.

entire-contract clause. 1. INTEGRATION CLAUSE. **2.** A provision in an insurance contract stating that the entire agreement between the insured and insurer is contained in the contract, often including the application (if attached), declarations, insuring agreement, exclusions, conditions, and endorsements.

entire-controversy doctrine. The principle that a plaintiff or defendant who does not assert all claims or defenses related to the controversy in a legal proceeding is not entitled to assert those claims or defenses in a later proceeding. — Also termed *single-controversy doctrine.* Cf. *compulsory counterclaim* under COUNTERCLAIM; RES JUDICATA (2).

entire day. See DAY.

entire interest. See INTEREST (2).

entire-output contract. See *output contract* under CONTRACT.

entire tenancy. See TENANCY.

entirety (en-tɪ-ər-tee). **1.** The whole, as opposed to a moiety or part. **2.** Something (such as certain judgments and contracts) that the law considers incapable of being divided into parts.

entirety, tenancy by the. See *tenancy by the entirety* under TENANCY.

entire use. See USE (4).

entitle, *vb.* **1.** To grant a legal right to or qualify for. **2.** *Eccles. law.* To ordain as a minister. — Formerly also spelled *intitle.*

entitlement. An absolute right to a (usu. monetary) benefit, such as social security, granted immediately upon meeting a legal requirement.

entity. An organization (such as a business or a governmental unit) that has a legal identity apart from its members.

corporate entity. A corporation's status as an organization existing independently of its shareholders. • As a separate entity, a corporation can, in its own name, sue and be sued, lend and borrow money, and buy, sell, lease, and mortgage its property.

public entity. A governmental entity, such as a state government or one of its political subdivisions.

entity assumption. The presumption that a business is a unit separate from its owners and from other firms.

entity theory of partnership. The theory that a partnership is an entity with a legal existence apart from the partners who make it up. Cf. AGGREGATE THEORY OF PARTNERSHIP.

entrapment, *n.* **1.** A law-enforcement officer's or government agent's inducement of a person to commit a crime, by means of fraud or undue persuasion, in an attempt to later bring a criminal prosecution against that person. **2.** The affirmative defense of having been so induced. • To establish entrapment (in most states), the defendant must show that he or she would not have committed the crime but for the fraud or undue persuasion. — **entrap,** *vb.*

> "Entrapment, so-called, is a relatively simple and very desirable concept which was unfortunately misnamed, with some resulting confusion. It is socially desirable for criminals to be apprehended and brought to justice. And there is nothing whatever wrong or out of place in setting traps for those bent on crime, provided the traps are not so arranged as likely to result in offenses by persons other than those who are ready to commit them.

What the State cannot tolerate is having crime instigated by its officers who are charged with the duty of enforcing the law.... Obviously 'entrapment' is not the appropriate word to express the idea of official investigation of crime, but it is so firmly entrenched that it seems wiser to accept it with due explanation than attempt to supplant it...." Rollin M. Perkins & Ronald N. Boyce, *Criminal Law* 1161 (3d ed. 1982).

derivative entrapment. Entrapment in which the government uses a private person, acting either as an agent of the government or as an unwitting participant, to induce the subject of the entrapment to commit a crime.

sentencing entrapment. Entrapment of a defendant who is predisposed to commit a lesser offense but who is unlawfully induced to commit a more serious offense that carries a more severe sentence. — Also termed *sentence-factor manipulation*.

entrebat (on-trə-**ba**), *n.* [Law French] An intruder or interloper.

entrepôt (on-trə-**poh**), *n.* [French] *French law.* A building or place where goods from abroad may be deposited and from which those goods may then be exported to another country without paying a duty.

entrepreneur (on-trə-prə-**nər**), *n.* One who initiates and assumes the financial risks of a new enterprise and who usu. undertakes its management.

entrust, *vb.* To give (a person) the responsibility for something, usu. after establishing a confidential relationship. — **entrustment,** *n.* See NEGLIGENT ENTRUSTMENT.

entrusting, *n. Commercial law.* The transfer of possession of goods to a merchant who deals in goods of that type and who may in turn transfer the goods and all rights to them to a purchaser in the ordinary course of business. UCC § 2–403(2).

entry, *n.* **1.** The act, right, or privilege of entering real property <they were given entry into the stadium>.

lawful entry. **1.** The entry onto real property by a person not in possession, under a claim or color of right, and without force or fraud. **2.** The entry of premises under a search warrant. See EJECTION; EVICTION; *search warrant* under WARRANT.

open entry. A conspicuous entry onto real estate to take possession; an entry that is neither clandestine nor carried out by secret artifice or stratagem and that (by law in some states) is accomplished in the presence of two witnesses.

reentry. See REENTRY.

2. An item written in a record; a notation <Forney made a false entry in the books on March 3>.

blind entry. An accounting entry that indicates only the debited and credited amounts without any explanation.

compound journal entry. A journal entry requiring more than one debit and credit (as when revenue is received partly in cash and partly in security).

journal entry. An entry in an accounting journal of equal debits and credits, with occasional explanations of the recorded transactions.

3. The placement of something before the court or on the record. **4.** *Copyright.* The deposit of a title of work with the Register of Copyrights to secure its protection. **5.** *Immigration.* Any entrance of an alien into the United States, whether voluntary or involuntary. **6.** *Criminal law.* The unlawful coming into a building to commit a crime.

entry, right of. See POWER OF TERMINATION.

entry, writ of. See WRIT OF ENTRY.

entry *ad communem legem* (ad kə-**myoo**-nəm **lee**-jəm). [Latin] *Hist.* **1.** Entry at common law. **2.** AD COMMUNEM LEGEM.

entry *ad terminum qui praeteriit* (ad **tər**-mə-nəm kwI pri-**ter**-ee-it). See AD TERMINUM QUI PRAETERIIT.

entry for marriage in speech. See *causa matrimonii praelocuti* under CAUSA (1).

entry in *casu consimili* (**en**-tree in **kay**-s[y]oo kən-**sim**-ə-lI). [Latin] See CASU CONSIMILI.

entry of judgment. The ministerial recording of a court's final decision, usu. by noting it in a judgment book or civil docket. Cf. RENDITION OF JUDGMENT.

entry on the roll. *Hist.* **1.** A clerk's notation on a parchment roll of the proceedings and issues in a particular case. • Before parties began submitting written pleadings, they would appear (in person or through counsel) in open court and state their respective contentions orally until they settled on the issue or precise point in dispute. During the progress of these oral statements, an appointed officer of the court would make minutes of the various proceedings on a parchment roll that then became the official record of the suit. Even after the practice of oral pleadings had fallen into disuse, proceedings continued to be entered "on the roll." This practice was abolished early in the 19th century. H.T. 4 Will. 4. **2.** A future interest created in a transferor who conveys an estate on condition subsequent.

enumerate (i-**n**[**y**]**oo**-mə-rayt), *vb.* To count off or designate one by one; to list. — **enumeration,** *n.*

enumerated power. See POWER.

enumerator. A person appointed to collect census papers or schedules.

enunciate (i-**nən**-see-ayt), *vb.* **1.** To state publicly; to announce or proclaim <the court enunciated a new doctrine yesterday>. **2.** To articulate or pronounce <enunciate your syllables more clearly when you speak>. — **enunciation,** *n.* — **enunciable,** *adj.* — **enunciator,** *n.*

enure. See INURE.

en ventre sa mere (*on* **von**-trə sa **mair**). [Law French "in utero"] (Of a fetus) in the mother's womb <child *en ventre sa mere*>. • This phrase refers to an unborn child, usu. in the context of a discussion of that child's rights. — Also spelled *in ventre sa mere*. See VENTER.

> "An infant *in ventre sa mere*, or in the mother's womb, is supposed in law to be born for many purposes." 1 William Blackstone, *Commentaries on the Laws of England* 126 (1765).

en vie (*on* **vee**). [Law French "in life"] Alive.

environmental effect. *Environmental law.* A natural or artificial disturbance of the physical, chemical, or biological components that make up the environment.

environmental-impact statement. *Environmental law.* A document that the National Environmental Policy Act (42 USCA § 4332(2)(c)) requires a federal agency to produce for a major project or legislative proposal so that better decisions can be made about the positive and negative environmental effects of an undertaking. — Abbr. EIS. — Also termed *environmental-impact report* (EIR).

environmental law. The field of law dealing with the maintenance and protection of the environment, including preventive measures such as the requirements of environmental-impact statements, as well as measures to assign liability and provide cleanup for incidents that harm the environment. • Because most environmental litigation involves disputes with governmental agencies, environmental law is heavily intertwined with administrative law.

Environmental Protection Agency. A federal agency created in 1970 to coordinate governmental action to protect the environment. — Abbr. EPA.

envoy (**en**-voy). **1.** A high-ranking diplomat sent to a foreign country to execute a special mission or to serve as a permanent diplomatic representative. — Also termed *envoy extraordinary*. **2.** A messenger or representative.

envoy extraordinary. *Int'l law.* A person who heads a legation rather than an embassy. • In current usage, the term is honorific and has no special significance.

eo die (**ee**-oh **dɪ**-ee). [Latin] On that day; on the same day.

EOE. *abbr.* **1.** See *equal-opportunity employer* under EMPLOYER. **2.** Errors and omissions excepted. • This phrase is sometimes appended to an account stated to allow for slight errors. See *errors-and-omissions insurance* under INSURANCE.

eo instante (**ee**-oh in-**stan**-tee). [Latin] At that very instant.

eo intuitu (**ee**-oh in-**t**[**y**]**oo**-ə-too). [Latin] With or in that view; with that intent or object.

eo ipso (**ee**-oh **ip**-soh). [Latin] By that very act.

eo loci (**ee**-oh **loh**-sɪ). [Latin] *Civil law.* In that state; in that condition.

eo loco (**ee**-oh **loh**-koh). [Latin] In that place.

E.O.M. *abbr.* End of month. • This appears as a payment term in some sales contracts.

eo nomine (**ee**-oh **nahm**-ə-nee). [Latin] By or in that name <interest *eo nomine*>.

EPA. *abbr.* ENVIRONMENTAL PROTECTION AGENCY.

EPC contract. See *engineering, procurement, and construction contract* under CONTRACT.

e pili ana (ay **pee**-lee **ah**-nah). [Hawaiian] Adjoining. • This term usu. refers to land that adjoins a stream.

epimenia (ep-ə-**mee**-nee-ə), *n. pl.* [Latin] Expenses; gifts.

epiqueya (ep-ee-**kay**-ah), *n.* [Spanish] *Spanish law.* An equitable principle calling for the benign and prudent interpretation of the law according to the circumstances of the time, place, and person.

episcopacy (i-**pis**-kə-pə-see), *n. Eccles. law.* **1.** The office of a bishop. **2.** A form of church government by diocesan bishops. **3.** An office of overlooking or overseeing.

episcopalia (i-pis-kə-**pay**-lee-ə), *n. pl. Eccles. law.* Synodals, pentecostals, and other customary payments from the clergy to their diocesan bishop, collected by rural deans and forwarded to the bishop.

episcopate (i-**pis**-kə-pit), *n. Eccles. law.* **1.** A bishopric. **2.** The dignity or office of a bishop.

episcoporum ecdicus (i-pis-kə-**por**-əm **ek**-di-kəs). [Latin] *Eccles. law.* A bishop's proctor; a church lawyer.

episcopus (i-**pis**-kə-pəs), *n.* [Latin fr. Greek] **1.** *Roman law.* An overseer; an inspector, such as the municipal officer responsible for oversight of the bread and other provisions that served as the citizens' daily food. **2.** A bishop.

episcopus puerorum (i-**pis**-kə-pəs pyoo-ər-**or**-əm). [Latin "bishop of the boys"] *Hist Eccles. law.* A layperson who would, on certain feasts, braid his hair, dress like a bishop, and act ludicrous. • This custom lasted in England long after several laws were passed to abolish it.

epistola (i-**pis**-tə-lə), *n.* [Latin "letter"] A charter; a written instrument to convey lands or to assure contracts. See ASSURANCE.

epistolae (i-**pis**-tə-lee), *n. pl.* [Latin "letters"] *Roman law.* **1.** Rescripts; opinions given by the emperors in cases submitted to them for decision. **2.** Opinions of *juris consulti*, such as Neratius, on questions of law in the form of letters to those consulting them. — Also spelled *epistulae*.

EPL insurance. See *employment-practices-liability insurance* under INSURANCE.

e pluribus unum (ee **ploor**-ə-bəs [y]**oo**-nəm). [Latin] One out of many. • This is the motto on the official seal of the United States and on several U.S. coins.

epoch (**ep**-ək), *n.* **1.** A period of time marked by distinctive features or noteworthy events. **2.** A time when a new computation is begun; a time from which memorable dates are counted. — **epochal** (**ep**-ə-kəl), *adj.*

EPS. *abbr.* EARNINGS PER SHARE.

equal-access rule. *Criminal law.* The doctrine that contraband found on a defendant's premises will not support a conviction if other persons have the same access to the premises as the defendant. • To invoke this defense successfully, the defendant must show that other persons did in fact have equal access to the premises; speculative evidence that trespassers might have come onto the premises will not bar a conviction.

Equal Access to Justice Act. A federal statute enacted in 1980 to allow the prevailing party in certain actions against the government to recover attorney's or expert-witness fees. Pub. L. No. 96–481, title II, 94 Stat. 2325 (codified as amended in scattered sections of 5, 15, and 28 USCA). — Abbr. EAJA.

equal and uniform taxation. See TAXATION.

Equal Credit Opportunity Act. A federal statute prohibiting a creditor from discriminating against an applicant on the basis of race, color, religion, national origin, age, sex, or marital status with respect to any aspect of a credit transaction. 15 USCA §§ 1691 et seq.

equal degree. See DEGREE.

equal-dignities rule. *Agency.* The doctrine that an agent can perform all acts requiring a writing signed by the principal only if the agent's authority is set forth in a writing. • This rule is an adjunct to the statute of frauds and applies when one or more of the signatories to a contract acted through an agent.

Equal Employment Opportunity Commission. A federal agency created under the Civil Rights Act of 1964 to end discriminatory employment practices and to promote nondiscriminatory employment programs. • The EEOC investigates alleged discriminatory employment practices and encourages mediation and other nonlitigious means of resolving employment disputes. A claimant is required to file a charge of discrimination with the EEOC before pursuing a claim under Title VII of the Civil Rights Act and certain other employment-related statutes. — Abbr. EEOC.

equal-footing doctrine. The principle that a state admitted to the Union after 1789 enters with the same rights, sovereignty, and jurisdiction within its borders as did the original 13 states.

equality. The quality or state of being equal; esp., likeness in power or political status. See EQUAL PROTECTION.

> "We need not repeat the burning irony of Anatole France: 'The law in its majesty draws no distinction but forbids rich and poor alike from begging in the streets or from sleeping in the public parks.' Equality is meaningless under unequal conditions." Morris R. Cohen, *Reason and Law* 101 (1961).

equality before the law. The status or condition of being treated fairly according to regularly established norms of justice; esp., in British constitutional law, the notion that all persons are subject to the ordinary law of the land administered by the ordinary law courts, that officials and others are not exempt from the general duty of obedience to the law, that discretionary governmental powers must not be abused, and that the task of superintending the operation of law rests with an impartial, independent judiciary.

> "A number of distinct meanings are normally given to the provision that there should be equality before the law. One meaning is that equality before the law only connotes the equal subjection of all to a common system of law, whatever its content.... A second theory asserts that equality before the law is basically a procedural concept, pertaining to the application and enforcement of laws and the operation of the legal system.... A third meaning normally borne by declarations that all are equal before the law, perhaps no more than a variant of the second, is that State and individual before the law should be equal." Polyvios G. Polyviou, *The Equal Protection of the Laws* 1–2 (1980).

equality of states. *Int'l law.* The doctrine that all fully independent nations are equal under international law. • This doctrine does not, of course, mean that all nations are equal in power or influence, but merely that, as nations, they all have the same legal rights.

equalization, *n.* **1.** The raising or lowering of assessed values to achieve conformity. **2.** *Tax.* The adjustment of an assessment or tax to create a rate uniform with another. — Also termed *equalization of taxes*; *fair and proper legal assessment*.

equalization board. A local governmental agency responsible for adjusting the tax rates in different districts to ensure an equitable distribution of the tax burden. — Also termed *board of equalization*.

equalization of taxes. See EQUALIZATION (2).

equalize, *vb.* To make equal; to cause to correspond or be the same in amount or degree.

equally divided. 1. (Of property) apportioned per capita — not per stirpes — among heirs on the testator's death. • A provision in a will calling for property to be divided "share and share alike" has the same effect. **2.** (Of a court, legislature, or other group) having the same number of votes on each side of an issue or dispute.

equal-opportunity employer. See EMPLOYER.

Equal Pay Act. A federal law mandating that all who perform substantially the same work must be paid equally. 29 USCA § 206.

equal protection. The constitutional guarantee under the 14th Amendment that the government must treat a person or class of persons the same as it treats other persons or classes in like circumstances. • In today's constitutional jurisprudence, equal protection means that legislation that discriminates must have a rational basis for doing so. And if the legislation affects a fundamental right (such as the right to vote) or involves a suspect classification (such as race), it is unconstitutional unless it can withstand strict scrutiny. — Also termed *equal protection of the laws*; *equal protection under the law*. See RATIONAL-BASIS TEST; STRICT SCRUTINY.

> "Equal protection does not require that all persons be dealt with identically, but it does require that a distinction made have some relevance to the purpose for which the classification is made." *Baxstrom v. Herold*, 383 U.S. 107, 111, 86 S.Ct. 760, 763 (1966).

> "As in all equal protection cases, ... the crucial question is whether there is an appropriate governmental interest suitably furthered by the differential treatment." *Police Dep't v. Mosley*, 408 U.S. 92, 95, 92 S.Ct. 2286, 2290 (1972).

> "[T]he equal protection principle is exclusively associated with written Constitutions and embodies guarantees of equal treatment normally applied not only to the procedural enforcement of laws but also to the substan-

tive content of their provisions. In other words, the equal protection of the laws is invariably treated as a substantive constitutional principle which demands that laws will only be legitimate if they can be described as just and equal." Polyvios G. Polyviou, *The Equal Protection of the Laws* 4 (1980).

Equal Protection Clause. The 14th Amendment provision requiring the states to give similarly situated persons or classes similar treatment under the law. Cf. DUE PROCESS CLAUSE.

equal protection of the laws. See EQUAL PROTECTION.

equal protection under the law. See EQUAL PROTECTION.

Equal Rights Amendment. A failed constitutional amendment that, had it been ratified, would have constitutionally prohibited entirely sex-based discrimination. • Congress passed the Amendment in 1972, but it failed in 1982, having been ratified by only 35 of the required 38 states. — Abbr. ERA.

equal-shares clause. *Insurance.* A clause requiring an insurer to pay its proportionate share of a claimed loss.

Equal Time Act. A federal law requiring that a broadcasting-facility licensee who permits a legally qualified candidate for public office to use the facility for broadcasting must afford an equal opportunity to all other candidates for the office. 47 USCA § 315.

equal-time doctrine. See FAIRNESS DOCTRINE.

eques (**ee**-kweez), *n.* [Latin] *Hist.* A knight.

equilocus (ee-kwə-**loh**-kəs), *n.* [Latin] An equal.

equinox (**ee**-kwə-noks *or* **ek**-wə-noks), *n.* One of the two periods of the year when the time from the sun's rising to its setting is equal to that from its setting to its rising. • The *vernal equinox* is about March 21, and the *autumnal equinox* is about September 22.

equip, *vb.* To furnish for service or against a need or exigency; to fit out; to supply with whatever is necessary for efficient action.

equipment, *n.* The articles or implements used for a specific purpose or activity (esp. a business operation). • Under the UCC, *equipment* includes goods if (1) the goods are used in or bought for a business enterprise (including farming or a profession) or by a debtor that is a nonprofit organization or a governmental subdivision or agency, and (2) the goods are not inventory, farm products, or consumer goods. UCC § 9–109(2).

equipment trust. A financing device commonly used by railroads in which a trustee and the railroad together buy equipment from a manufacturer, with the trustee providing most of the purchase price, and the trustee then leases the equipment to the railroad, which pays a rental fee comprising interest, amortization for serial retirement, and the trustee's fee.

equipment trust bond. See BOND (3).

equipment trust certificate. A security, usu. issued by a railroad, to pay for new equipment. • Title to the equipment is held by a trustee until the note has been paid off. — Also termed *car trust certificate*; *trust certificate*.

equitable (**ek**-wi-tə-bəl), *adj.* **1.** Just; conformable to principles of justice and right. **2.** Existing in equity; available or sustainable by an action in equity, or under the rules and principles of equity.

equitable abstention. See ABSTENTION.

equitable action. See *action in equity* under ACTION.

equitable-adjustment theory. The doctrine that in settling a federal contract dispute, the contracting officer should make a fair adjustment within a reasonable time before the contractor has to settle with its subcontractors, suppliers, and other creditors.

equitable adoption. See *adoption by estoppel* under ADOPTION (1).

equitable asset. See ASSET.

equitable assignment. See ASSIGNMENT (2).

equitable-benefit doctrine. *Bankruptcy.* The principle that allows a bankruptcy court to grant preferred status to claims for service rendered by persons other than bankruptcy officers, to the extent that the service benefited the estate, when the person filing the claim acted primarily for the benefit of the estate as a whole.

equitable construction. See *liberal construction* under CONSTRUCTION.

equitable conversion. See CONVERSION (1).

equitable defense. See DEFENSE (1).

equitable distribution. *Family law.* The division of marital property by a court in a divorce proceeding, under statutory guidelines that provide for a fair, but not necessarily equal, allocation of the property between the spouses. • The court can take into account a variety of factors, including the relative earning capacity of the spouses and (in a state that does not allow for no-fault divorce) the fault of either of the spouses. Equitable distribution is applied in 41 states (i.e., all the states that do not have a community-property system). — Also termed *equitable division.*

equitable doctrine of approximation. See DOCTRINE OF APPROXIMATION.

equitable easement. See EASEMENT.

equitable ejectment. See EJECTMENT.

equitable election. See ELECTION (2).

equitable estate. See ESTATE.

equitable estoppel. See ESTOPPEL.

equitable foreclosure. See FORECLOSURE.

equitable fraud. See *constructive fraud* under FRAUD.

equitable-fund doctrine. See COMMON-FUND DOCTRINE.

equitable interest. See INTEREST (2).

equitable lien. See LIEN.

equitable life estate. An interest in real or personal property that lasts for the life of the holder of the estate and that is equitable as opposed to legal in its creation. • An example is a life estate held by a trust beneficiary.

equitable life tenant. See LIFE TENANT.

equitable mortgage. See MORTGAGE.

equitable owner. See *beneficial owner* under OWNER.

equitable recoupment. *Tax.* **1.** A doctrine allowing a taxpayer to offset previously overpaid taxes against current taxes due, even though the taxpayer is time-barred from claiming a refund on the previous taxes. **2.** A doctrine allowing the government to offset taxes previously uncollected from a taxpayer against the taxpayer's current claim for a refund, even though the government is time-barred from collecting the previous taxes. • In both senses, this type of recoupment can be asserted only if the statute of limitations has created an inequitable result. See RECOUPMENT (2).

equitable-recoupment doctrine. A principle that diminishes a party's right to recover a debt to the extent that the party holds money or property of the debtor to which the party has no right. • This doctrine is ordinarily a defensive remedy going only to mitigation of damages. The doctrine is sometimes applied so that a claim for a tax refund that is barred by limitations may nonetheless be recouped against a tax claim of the government.

equitable relief. See *equitable remedy* under REMEDY.

equitable remedy. See REMEDY.

equitable rescission. See RESCISSION.

equitable-restraint doctrine. See *Younger abstention* (1) under ABSTENTION.

equitable reversion. See REVERSION.

equitable right. See RIGHT.

equitable right to setoff. The right to cancel cross-demands, usu. used by a bank to take from a customer's deposit accounts the amount equal to the customer's debts that have matured and that are owed to that bank. See SETOFF.

equitable seisin. See *seisin in law* under SEISIN.

equitable servitude. See *restrictive covenant* under COVENANT (4).

equitable subrogation. See *legal subrogation* under SUBROGATION.

equitable title. See TITLE (2).

equitable tolling. The doctrine that the statute of limitations will not bar a claim if the plaintiff, despite diligent efforts, did not discover the injury until after the limitations period had expired. • Equitable tolling does not require misconduct by the defendant.

equitable waste. See WASTE (1).

equity, *n.* **1.** Fairness; impartiality; evenhanded dealing <the company's policies require managers to use equity in dealing with subordinate employees>. **2.** The body of principles constituting what is fair and right; natural law <the concept of "inalienable rights" reflects the influence of equity on the Declaration of Independence>. **3.** The recourse to principles of justice to correct or supplement the law as applied to particular circumstances <the judge decided the case by equity because the statute did not fully address the issue>. — Also termed *natural equity*. **4.** The system of law or body of principles originating in the English Court of Chancery and superseding the common and statute law (together called "law" in the narrower sense) when the two conflict <in appealing to the equity of the court, she was appealing to the "king's conscience">.

> "Equity is that system of justice which was developed in and administered by the High Court of Chancery in England in the exercise of its extraordinary jurisdiction. This definition is rather suggestive than precise; and invites inquiry rather than answers it. This must necessarily be so. Equity, in its technical and scientific legal sense, means neither natural justice nor even all that portion of natural justice which is susceptible of being judicially enforced. It has, when employed in the language of English law, a precise, definite and limited signification, and is used to denote a system of justice which was administered in a particular court — the nature and extent of which system cannot be defined in a single sentence, but can be understood and explained only by studying the history of that court, and the principles upon which it acts. In order to begin to understand what equity is, it is necessary to understand what the English High Court of Chancery was, and how it came to exercise what is known as its extraordinary jurisdiction. Every true definition of equity must, therefore, be, to a greater or less extent, a history." George T. Bispham, *The Principles of Equity* 1–2 (Joseph D. McCoy ed., 11th ed. 1931).

> "The term 'equity' is an illustration of Mr. Towkington's proposition that some words have a legal meaning very unlike their ordinary one. In ordinary language 'equity' means natural justice; but the beginner must get that idea out of his head when dealing with the system that the lawyers call equity. Originally, indeed, this system was inspired by ideas of natural justice, and that is why it acquired its name; but nowadays equity is no more (and no less) natural justice than the common law, and it is in fact nothing else than a particular branch of the law of England. Equity, therefore, is law. The student should not allow himself to be confused by the lawyer's habit of contrasting 'law' and 'equity,' for in this context 'law' is simply an abbreviation for the common law. Equity *is* law in the sense that it is part of the law of England; it is not law only in the sense that it is not part of the common law." Glanville Williams, *Learning the Law* 25–26 (11th ed. 1982).

5. A right, interest, or remedy recognizable by a court of equity <there was no formal contract formation, so they sued for breach in equity>.

contravening equity (kon-trə-**veen**-ing). A right or interest that is inconsistent with or contrary to a right sought to be enforced.

countervailing equity (kown-tər-**vayl**-ing). A contrary and balancing equity, equally deserving of consideration.

latent equity (**lay**-tənt). An equitable claim or right known only by the parties for and against whom it exists, or that has been concealed from one who is interested in the subject matter. — Also termed *secret equity*.

perfect equity. An equitable title or right that, to be a legal title, lacks only the formal conveyance or other investiture that would make it cognizable at law; esp., the equity of a real-estate purchaser who has paid the full amount due but has not yet received a deed.

secret equity. See *latent equity*.

6. The right to decide matters in equity; equity jurisdiction <the court decided that the wrong was egregious enough to ignore the statute of limitations and decide the case in equity>. **7.** The amount by which the value of or an interest in property exceeds secured claims or liens; the difference between the value of the property and all encumbrances upon it <thanks to the real-estate boom, the mortgaged house still had high equity>. — Also termed *cushion*. **8.** An ownership interest in property, esp. in a business <the founders gave her equity in the business in return for all her help>. See OWNERS' EQUITY. **9.** A share in a publicly traded company <he did not want to cash in his equity>.

equity, bill in. See BILL (2).

equity, court of. See COURT.

equity accounting method. See ACCOUNTING METHOD.

equity capital. See CAPITAL.

equity financing. See FINANCING.

equity insolvency. See INSOLVENCY.

equity jurisdiction. See JURISDICTION.

equity jurisprudence. See JURISPRUDENCE.

equity kicker. See EQUITY PARTICIPATION.

equity loan. See *home equity loan* under LOAN.

equity of exoneration (eg-**zon**-ə-ray-shən). The right of a person who is secondarily liable on a debt to make the primarily liable party discharge the debt or reimburse any payment that the secondarily liable person has made. • One example is the right of a surety to call on the principal for reimbursement after the surety has paid the debt. Unlike contribution, which exists when the parties are equally liable, the equity of exoneration exists when parties are successively liable. — Also termed *right of exoneration*. See EXONERATION.

equity of partners. The right of each partner to have the firm's property applied to the firm's debts.

equity of redemption. *Real estate*. The right of a mortgagor in default to recover property before a foreclosure sale by paying the principal, interest, and other costs that are due. • A defaulting mortgagor with an equity of redemption has the right, until the foreclosure sale, to reimburse the mortgagee and cure the default. In many jurisdictions, the mortgagor also has a statutory right to redeem within six months after the foreclosure sale, and the mortgagor becomes entitled to any surplus from the sale proceeds above the amount of the outstanding mortgage. — Also termed *right of redemption*. See CLOG ON THE EQUITY OF REDEMPTION.

equity of subrogation. The right of a person who is secondarily liable on a debt, and who pays the debt, to personally enforce any right that the original creditor could have pursued against the debtor, including the right to foreclose on any security held by the creditor and any right that the creditor may have to contribution from others who are liable for the debt. — Also termed *right of subrogation*. See SUBROGATION.

equity-of-the-statute rule. In statutory construction, the principle that a statute should be interpreted according to the legislators' purpose and intent, even if this interpretation goes beyond the literal meaning of the text. • Under this little-used rule, for example, if a statute defines jury-tampering to include a party's "giving a juror food or drink," the giving of cigars to a juror would also fall within that definition. Cf. GOLDEN RULE; MISCHIEF RULE; PLAIN-MEANING RULE.

equity participation. The inclusion of a lender in the equity ownership of a project as a condition of the lender's granting a loan. — Also termed *equity kicker*.

equity ratio. 1. The percentage relationship between a purchaser's equity value (esp. the amount of a down payment) and the property value. **2.** The measure of a shareholder's equity divided by total equity.

equity security. See SECURITY.

equity stock. See STOCK.

equity term. The period during which a court tries only equity cases.

equity to a settlement. A wife's equitable right, arising when her husband sues in equity for the reduction of her equitable estate to his own possession, to have all or part of that estate settled upon herself and her children. — Also termed *wife's equity*; *wife's settlement*.

equivalent, *adj*. **1.** Equal in value, force, amount, effect, or significance. **2.** Corresponding in effect or function; nearly equal; virtually identical.

equivalents doctrine. See DOCTRINE OF EQUIVALENTS.

equivocal (i-**kwiv**-ə-kəl), *adj*. **1.** Of doubtful character; questionable. **2.** Having more than one meaning or sense; ambiguous.

equivocality (i-kwiv-ə-**kal**-ə-tee). See RES IPSA LOQUITUR (2).

equivocation (i-kwiv-ə-**kay**-shən). See *latent ambiguity* under AMBIGUITY.

equuleus (i-**kwoo**-lee-əs), *n*. [Latin] *Roman law*. A rack in the shape of a horse, used for torture.

ERA. *abbr*. EQUAL RIGHTS AMENDMENT.

erase, *vb.* **1.** To rub or scrape out (something written); to obliterate. **2.** To obliterate (recorded material). **3.** To seal (criminal records) from disclosure. — **erasure,** *n.*

Erastian (i-**ras**-chən *or* i-**ras**-tee-ən). *Hist.* A follower of Thomas Erastus (1524–1583), who thought that offenses against religion and morality should be punished by the civil power and not by the censures of the church. • As a sect, Erastians had great influence in England, particularly among 17th-century common-law lawyers.

erasure of record. See EXPUNGEMENT OF RECORD.

erciscundus (er-sis-**kən**-dəs), *adj.* [Latin] *Civil law.* To be divided. • A suit *judicium familiae erciscundae* was one to partition an inheritance.

erect, *vb.* **1.** To construct. **2.** To establish. • In England, *erect* is one of the formal words of incorporation in a royal charter, being part of the phrase, "We do incorporate, erect, ordain, name, constitute, and establish." See ERIGIMUS.

E reorganization. See REORGANIZATION (2).

ergo (**ər**-goh *or* **air**-goh). [Latin] Therefore; thus.

ergolabus (ər-goh-**lay**-bəs), *n.* [Latin] *Civil law.* A person who contracts to perform work by personally furnishing the materials and labor.

***Erie*-bound,** *adj.* (Of a federal court) required to apply the *Erie* doctrine.

***Erie* doctrine** (**eer**-ee). The principle that a federal court exercising diversity jurisdiction over a case that does not involve a federal question must apply the substantive law of the state where the court sits. *Erie R.R. v. Tompkins*, 304 U.S. 64, 58 S.Ct. 817 (1938).

***Erie/Klaxon* doctrine.** See KLAXON DOCTRINE.

erigimus (i-**rij**-ə-məs). [Latin] *Hist.* We erect. • This was one of the words used in a corporation's royal charter. See ERECT (2).

ERISA (ee- *or* ə-**ris**-ə). *abbr.* EMPLOYEE RETIREMENT INCOME SECURITY ACT.

eristic (e-**ris**-tik), *adj.* Of or relating to controversy or disputation. — Also termed *eristical.*

ermine (**ər**-min), *n.* The station of a judge; judgeship. • The term refers to the fur trimmings (made from the coats of white weasels called "ermine") adorning official robes of English judges.

erosion. The wearing away of something by action of the elements; esp., the gradual eating away of soil by the operation of currents or tides. Cf. ACCRETION (1); DELICTION; AVULSION (2); ALLUVION.

err (ər), *vb.* To make an error; to be incorrect or mistaken <the court erred in denying the motion for summary judgment>.

errant (**er**-ənt), *adj.* **1.** Fallible; incorrect; straying from what is proper <an errant judicial holding>. **2.** Traveling <a knight errant>.

errata sheet. An attachment to a deposition transcript containing the deponent's corrections upon reading the transcript and the reasons for those corrections. — Also termed *errata page.*

erratum (i-**ray**-təm *or* i-**rah**-təm), *n.* [Latin "error"] An error that needs correction. Pl. **errata.** See CORRIGENDUM.

erroneous (i-**roh**-nee-əs), *adj.* Involving error; deviating from the law.

erroneous assessment. See ASSESSMENT.

erroneous judgment. See JUDGMENT.

erroneous tax. See TAX.

erronice (i-**roh**-nə-see), *adv.* [Law Latin] Erroneously; through error or mistake.

error, *n.* **1.** A psychological state that does not conform to objective reality; a belief that what is false is true or that what is true is false; MISTAKE.

error in corpore (**kor**-pə-ree). A mistake involving the identity of a particular object, as when a party buys a horse believing it to be the one that the party had already examined and ridden, when in fact it is a different horse.

error in negotio (ni-**goh**-shee-oh). A mistake about the type of contract that the parties actually wanted to enter.

error in qualitate (kwah-lə-**tay**-tee). A mistake affecting the quality of the contractual object.

error in quantitate (kwahn-tə-**tay**-tee). A mistake affecting the amount of the contractual object.

2. A mistake of law or of fact in a court's judgment, opinion, or order.

clear error. A trial judge's decision or action that appears to a reviewing court to have been unquestionably erroneous. • Even though a clear error occurred, it may not warrant reversal.

clerical error. An error resulting from a minor mistake or inadvertence, esp. in writing or copying something on the record, and not from judicial reasoning or determination. • Among the boundless examples of clerical errors are omitting an appendix from a document; typing an incorrect number; mistranscribing a word; and failing to log a call. A court can correct a clerical error at any time, even after judgment has been entered. — Also termed *scrivener's error*; *vitium clerici*. See VITIUM SCRIPTORIS.

cross-error. An error brought by the party responding to a writ of error.

error apparent of record. See *plain error*.

fatal error. See *reversible error*.

fundamental error. See *plain error*.

harmless error. An error that does not affect a party's substantive rights or the case's outcome. • A harmless error is not grounds for reversal. — Also termed *technical error*; *error in vacuo*.

invited error. An error that a party cannot complain of on appeal because the party, through conduct, encouraged or prompted the trial court to make the erroneous ruling.

manifest constitutional error. An error by the trial court that has an identifiably negative impact on the trial to such a degree that the constitutional rights of a party are compromised. • A manifest constitutional error can be reviewed by a court of appeals even if the appellant did not object at trial.

manifest error. An error that is plain and indisputable, and that amounts to a complete disregard of the controlling law or the credible evidence in the record.

plain error. An error that is so obvious and prejudicial that an appellate court should address it despite the parties' failure to raise a proper objection. • A plain error is often said to be so obvious and substantial that failure to correct it would infringe a party's due-process rights and damage the integrity of the judicial process. — Also termed *fundamental error*; *error apparent of record*.

reversible error. An error that affects a party's substantive rights or the case's outcome, and thus is grounds for reversal if the party properly objected. — Also termed *harmful error*; *prejudicial error*; *fatal error*.

technical error. See *harmless error*.

3. An appeal <a proceeding in error>.

error, writ of. See WRIT OF ERROR.

error *de persona* (dee pər-**soh**-nə). [Latin "error of the person"] A mistake about a person's identity. Cf. ERROR NOMINIS.

error in corpore. See ERROR (1).

error in fact. See *mistake of fact* under MISTAKE.

error in law. See *mistake of law* under MISTAKE.

error in negotio. See ERROR (1).

error in qualitate. See ERROR (1).

error in quantitate. See ERROR (1).

error *in vacuo* (in **vak**-yoo-oh). [Latin "error in a void"] See *harmless error* under ERROR.

error *nominis* (**nahm**-ə-nis). [Latin "error of name"] A mistake of detail in a person's name. Cf. ERROR DE PERSONA.

error of fact. See *mistake of fact* under MISTAKE.

error-of-judgment rule. The doctrine that a professional is not liable to a client for advice or an opinion given in good faith and with an honest belief that the advice was in the client's best interests, but that was based on a mistake either in judgment or in analyzing an unsettled area of the professional's business. • For example, an attorney who makes an error in trial tactics involving an unsettled area of the law may, under certain circumstances, defeat a malpractice claim arising from the tactical error. — Also termed *judgmental immunity*.

error of law. See *mistake of law* under MISTAKE.

errors, assignment of. See ASSIGNMENT OF ERRORS.

errors-and-omissions insurance. See INSURANCE.

escalator clause. A contractual provision that increases or decreases the contract price according to changing market conditions, such as higher or lower taxes or operating costs. — Also termed *escalation clause*; *fluctuating clause*.

escambium. See CAMBIUM.

escape, *n.* **1.** The act or an instance of breaking free from confinement, restraint, or an obligation. **2.** An unlawful departure from legal custody without the use of force. — Also termed *actual escape*. Cf. PRISON BREACH.

> "In the technical sense an 'escape' is an unauthorized departure from legal custody; in a loose sense the word is used to indicate either such an unlawful departure or an avoidance of capture. And while the word is regularly used by the layman in the broader sense it usually is limited to the narrower meaning when used in the law, — although this is not always so." Rollin M. Perkins & Ronald N. Boyce, *Criminal Law* 559 (3d ed. 1982).

constructive escape. A prisoner's obtaining more liberty than the law allows, while not fully regaining freedom.

3. At common law, a criminal offense committed by a peace officer who allows a prisoner to depart unlawfully from legal custody. — Also termed *voluntary escape*. — **escape,** *vb.*

negligent escape. A prisoner's departure from legal custody as a result of an officer's negligence.

> "Escapes are either voluntary, or negligent. Voluntary are such as are by the express consent of the keeper, after which he never can retake his prisoner again, (though the plaintiff may retake him at any time) but the sheriff must answer for the debt. Negligent escapes are where the prisoner escapes without his keeper's knowledge or consent; and then upon fresh pursuit the defendant may be retaken, and the sheriff shall be excused, if he has him again before any action brought against himself for the escape." 3 William Blackstone, *Commentaries on the Laws of England* 415–16 (1768).

escape clause. A contractual provision that allows a party to avoid performance under specified conditions; specif., an insurance-policy provision — usu. contained in the "other insurance" section of the policy — requiring the insurer to provide coverage only if there is no other coverage available. Cf. EXCESS CLAUSE; PRO RATA CLAUSE.

escapee. A prisoner or other inmate who has escaped from lawful custody.

> "The word 'escapee' is employed at times by those who are not careful in the use of language. They probably think this word is comparable to 'arrestee' or 'employee.' But the arrestee did not do the arresting and the employee did not do the employing. The employee does the work but that makes him a worker, not a workee." Rollin M. Perkins & Ronald N. Boyce, *Criminal Law* 560 (3d ed. 1982).

escape period. *Labor law.* A time agreed upon in some union contracts during which workers may withdraw from the union near the end of one term covered by the contract and before the start of the next.

escape warrant. See WARRANT (1).

escapium (e-**skay**-pee-əm), *n.* [Law Latin] That which comes by chance or accident. • In medieval Latin, the term often referred to the escape of a prisoner or the straying of cattle.

escheat (es-**cheet**), *n.* **1.** *Hist.* The reversion of land ownership back to the lord when the immediate tenant dies without heirs. See WRIT OF ESCHEAT. **2.** Reversion of property (esp. real property) to the state upon the death of an owner who has neither a will nor any legal heirs. **3.** Property that has so reverted. — **escheat,** *vb.*

escheator (es-**cheet**-ər). *Hist.* A royal officer appointed to assess the value of property escheating to the Crown. • Corrupt officers led many to associate the escheator with fraudulent conduct, giving rise to the word *cheat* as used in the modern sense. — Also termed *cheater*.

escheccum (es-**chek**-əm), *n.* [Latin] *Hist.* A jury or inquisition.

***Escobedo* rule** (es-kə-**bee**-doh). *Criminal procedure.* The principle that a statement by an unindicted, targeted suspect in police custody is inadmissible at trial unless the police warn the suspect of the right to remain silent and provide an opportunity for the suspect to consult with retained or appointed counsel. • This rule was a precursor to the *Miranda* rule. *Escobedo v. Illinois*, 378 U.S. 478, 84 S.Ct. 1758 (1964). See MIRANDA RULE.

escot (e-**skot**), *n.* *Hist. English law.* A tax paid in boroughs and corporations to support the community.

escribano (es-kree-**bah**-noh), *n.* [Spanish] *Spanish law.* An officer — resembling a notary in French law — who has authority to set down in writing, and attest to, transactions and contracts between private persons, as well as judicial acts and proceedings.

escritura (es-kree-**toor**-ah), *n.* [Spanish] *Spanish law.* **1.** A written instrument. **2.** A deed prepared by an *escribano* or notary of a corporation or council (*concejo*), or that is sealed with the seal of the king or other authorized person.

escroquerie (es-**kroh**-kə-ree), *n.* [French] Fraud; swindling; cheating.

escrow (**es**-kroh), *n.* **1.** A legal document or property delivered by a promisor to a third party to be held by the third party for a given amount of time or until the occurrence of a condition, at which time the third party is to hand over the document or property to the promisee <the agent received the escrow two weeks before the closing date>. **2.** An account held in trust or as security <the earnest money is in escrow>. — Also termed *escrow account*; *impound account*; *reserve account*. See *escrow account* under ACCOUNT. **3.** The holder of such a document, property, or deposit <the attorney performed the function of escrow>. — Also termed *escrow agent*. **4.** The general arrangement under which a legal document or property is delivered to a third person until the occurrence of a condition <creating an escrow>. — **escrow,** *vb.*

> "Like 'scroll' and 'scrawl,' the word 'escrow' is derived from the Norman–French word for a writing or a written instrument. It has come in practice to refer to a security device: one or both parties to a transaction deposit property or an instrument with a third party until some condition has occurred. The property or instrument may be referred to as 'the escrow'; the delivery is said to be 'in escrow.'" Restatement (Second) of Contracts § 103 cmt. a (1981).

escrow account. See ACCOUNT.

escrow agent. The third-party depositary of an escrow; ESCROW (3). — Also termed *escrow holder*; *escrowee*.

escrow agreement. The instructions given to the third-party depositary of an escrow.

escrow contract. See CONTRACT.

escrow deposit. See *escrow account* under ACCOUNT.

escrowee. See ESCROW AGENT.

escrow holder. See ESCROW AGENT.

escrowl (es-**krohl**), *n. Hist.* **1.** An escrow. **2.** A scroll.

escuage (**es**-kyoo-ij). [French, fr. Latin *escuagium*] See SCUTAGE.

esketores (es-kə-**tor**-eez), *n. pl. Hist.* Robbers; destroyers of others' lands or fortunes.

eskipper (ə-**skip**-ər), *vb.* To ship. — Also termed *eskippare* (es-kə-**pair**-ee).

eskippeson (ə-**skip**-[ə]-sən), *n.* Shippage; passage by sea. — Also termed *skippeson*.

eslisor (es-**lɪ**-zər). See ELISOR.

esne (**ez**-nee), *n. Hist.* A hireling of servile condition; a hired laborer or a slave.

esnecy (**es**-ni-see), *n.* Seniority; the condition or right of the eldest; the privilege of the eldest-born. • The term esp. applied to the privilege of the eldest among coparceners to make a first choice of shares upon a voluntary partition. — Also termed *aesnecia*.

ESOP (**ee**-sop). *abbr.* See *employee-stock-ownership plan* under EMPLOYEE BENEFIT PLAN.

espera (**es**-pə-rə), *n.* A period fixed by law or by a court within which certain acts are to be performed (such as payment of a debt).

espionage (**es**-pee-ə-nahzh). The practice of using spies to collect information about what another government or company is doing or plans to do.

industrial espionage. One company's spying on another to steal the other company's trade secrets or other proprietary information.

Espionage Act. A federal law that criminalizes and punishes espionage, spying, and related crimes. 18 USCA §§ 793 et seq.

esplees (es-**pleez**), *n. pl. Archaic.* **1.** Products yielded from land. **2.** Rents or other payments derived from land. **3.** Land itself. — Also termed *explees*.

espousals (ə-**spow**-zəlz), *n.* A mutual promise between a man and a woman to marry one another.

esquire (**es**-kwIr *or* e-**skwIr**). (*usu. cap.*) A title of courtesy commonly appended after the name of a lawyer. — Abbr. Esq.

essence, of the. See OF THE ESSENCE.

essence test. *Labor law.* A test under which an arbitrator's interpretation of a collective-bargaining agreement must be upheld if it derives in any rational way from the agreement, viewed in light of the agreement's language, its context, and any other evidence of the parties' intention.

essendi quietum de tolonio (e-**sen**-dI kwI-**ee**-təm dee tə-**loh**-nee-oh). [Latin "a writ to be free of a toll"] *Hist.* A writ available to a citizen or a burgess of any city or town who, by charter or prescription, is exempt from a particular toll.

essential finding. See FINDING OF FACT.

essential mistake. See MISTAKE.

essential term. See *fundamental term* under TERM (2).

essoin (e-**soyn**), *n.* [fr. Old French *essoi(g)ne* "excuse"] *Hist.* **1.** An excuse for not appearing in court on an appointed day in obedience to a summons. **2.** The offering or presentation of such an excuse. — Also spelled *essoign.*

> "The first return-day of every term, properly speaking, is the first day of that term; and on that day the court used formerly to sit ... to hear the *essoigns*, or excuses, of such as did not appear according to the summons of the writ. This day therefore came to be called the *essoign*-day of the term." 1 George Crompton, *Practice Common-Placed: Rules and Cases of Practice in the Courts of King's Bench and Common Pleas* liv (3d ed. 1787).

essoin, *vb.* [fr. Old French *essoi(g)nier* "to excuse"] *Hist.* To present an excuse for not appearing in court as ordered.

> "Upon the summons, the defendant either appeared, or *essoigned*, or made default. If he did the former, the plaintiff declared against him, and the cause was proceeded in by the court; and if he did the latter, the plaintiff had liberty to take out further process against him. But if he *essoigned*, that is, sent an excuse to the court why he could not attend, he was to send it by the *return day of the writ* which if he did, a further process did not issue against him." 1 George Crompton, *Practice Common-Placed: Rules and Cases of Practice in the Courts of King's Bench and Common Pleas* liv (3d ed. 1787).

essoin day. *Hist. English law.* The first general return day of the term, when the courts sat to receive essoins. • By the Law Terms Act (1830), essoin days were eliminated as a part of the term. St. 11 Geo. 4; 1 Will. 4, ch. 70, § 6.

essoin *de malo villae* (dee **mal**-oh **vil**-ee). *Hist.* A procedure by which a defendant, who was in court the first day but was then taken ill without pleading, would send two essoiners to state in court that the defendant was detained by sickness in a particular village and thus unable to attend. • This essoin would be accepted unless the plaintiff could show its falsity.

essoiner (e-**soyn**-ər), *n. Hist.* A person making an essoin. — Also termed *essoiniator* (e-**soyn**-ee-ay-tər).

essoin roll. *Hist.* A roll upon which essoins were entered, together with the day to which they were adjourned.

establish, *vb.* **1.** To settle, make, or fix firmly; to enact permanently <one object of the Constitution was to establish justice>. **2.** To make or form; to bring about or into existence <Congress has the power to establish Article III courts>. **3.** To prove; to convince <the House managers tried to establish the President's guilt>.

establishment, *n.* **1.** The act of establishing; the state or condition of being established. **2.** An institution or place of business. **3.** A group of people who are in power or who control or exercise great influence over something.

Establishment Clause. The First Amendment provision that prohibits the government from creating or favoring a particular religion. U.S. Const. amend. I. Cf. FREE EXERCISE CLAUSE.

estadal (es-tah-**dahl**), *n.* [Spanish] *Hist.* In Spanish America, a measure of land of 16 square varas, or yards.

estadia (es-tah-**thee**-ah), *n.* [Spanish] *Spanish law.* **1.** A delay in a voyage, or in the delivery of cargo, caused by the charterer or consignee and for which demurrage is payable. **2.** The time for which the party who has chartered a vessel, or is bound to receive the cargo, has to pay demurrage because of a delay in executing the contract. — Also termed *sobrestadia* (soh-bray-stah-**thee**-ah).

estandard (ə-**stan**-dərd), *n.* [Law French] A standard of weights and measures.

est a scavoir (ay ah skah-**vwahr**). [Law French, prob. fr. Latin *est sciendum* "it is to be known"] It is to be understood or known; to wit. • This expression is common in Sir Thomas de Littleton's 15th-century *Treatise on Tenures*, written in Law French. See SCIENDUM EST.

estate. 1. The amount, degree, nature, and quality of a person's interest in land or other property. **2.** All that a person or entity owns, including both real and personal property. **3.** The property that one leaves after death; the collective assets and liabilities of a dead person. **4.** A tract of land, esp. one affected by an easement.

> "The old definitions of this word [*estate*] generally confine it to lands or realty. Thus, according to Lord Coke, '*state* or *estate* signifieth such inheritance, freehold, term for years, & c., as any man hath in *lands* or tenements.' *Co.Litt.* 345a. So Cowell defines it to be 'that title or interest which a man hath in *lands* or tenements,' and the same definition is given in the *Termes de la Ley*. And this limited sense of the word has been relied on, in argument, in some cases .... But, according to the settled modern doctrine, the term *estate* is of much more extensive import and application, being indeed *genus generalissimum*, and clearly comprehending things personal as well as real; person as well as real estate." 1 Alexander M. Burrill, *A Law Dictionary and Glossary* 561 (2d ed. 1867).

absolute estate. A full and complete estate that cannot be defeated.

***adjusted gross estate.* 1.** The total value of a decedent's property after subtracting administration expenses, funeral expenses, creditors' claims, and casualty losses. • The value of the adjusted gross estate is used in computing the federal estate tax. Cf. *net estate*. **2.** See *gross estate* (1).

ancestral estate. An estate that is acquired by descent or by operation of law with no other consideration than that of blood.

augmented estate. A statutory forced share that is enlarged for the benefit of a surviving spouse to include any transfer made by the decedent during the marriage. Uniform Probate Code § 2–202. See FORCED SHARE.

bankruptcy estate. See BANKRUPTCY ESTATE.

base estate. *Hist.* An estate held at the will of the lord, as distinguished from a freehold.

concurrent estate. Ownership or possession of property by two or more persons at the same time. • In modern practice, there are three types of concurrent estates: tenancy in common, joint tenancy, and tenancy by the entirety. — Also termed *concurrent interest*.

> "A concurrent estate is simply an estate — whether present or future, defeasible or non-defeasible, in fee simple, in tail, for life, or for years — that is owned by *two or more persons at the same time*. O transfers 'to A and B and their heirs.' A and B own a present concurrent estate in fee simple absolute." Thomas F. Bergin & Paul G. Haskell, *Preface to Estates in Land and Future Interests* 53 (2d ed. 1984).

contingent estate. An estate that vests only if a certain event does or does not happen. See *estate on condition*.

decedent's estate. The real and personal property that a person possesses at the time of death and that descends to the heirs subject to the payment of debts and claims.

defeasible estate. An estate that may come to an end before its maximum duration has run by reason of the operation of a special limitation, a condition subsequent, or an executory limitation. • If an estate is defeasible by operation of a special limitation, it is called a *determinable estate*.

derivative estate. A particular interest that has been carved out of another, larger estate. Cf. *original estate*.

determinable estate. An estate that is defeasible by operation of a special limitation.

dominant estate. An estate that benefits from an easement. — Also termed *dominant tenement*; *dominant property*; *upper estate*. Cf. *servient estate*.

equitable estate. An estate recognized in equity, such as a trust beneficiary's interest. See EQUITY.

estate ad remanentiam (ad rem-ə-**nen**-shee-əm). An estate in fee simple.

estate at sufferance. See *tenancy at sufferance* under TENANCY.

estate at will. See *tenancy at will* under TENANCY.

estate by curtesy. An estate owned by a wife, to which the husband is entitled upon her death. See CURTESY.

estate by elegit. An estate held by a judgment creditor, entitling the creditor to the rents and profits from land owned by the debtor until the debt is paid. See ELEGIT.

estate by purchase. An estate acquired in any manner other than by descent. See PURCHASE.

estate by statute staple. An estate in a defendant's land held by a creditor under the statute staple until the debt was paid. See STATUTE STAPLE.

estate by the entirety. See *tenancy by the entirety* under TENANCY.

estate for a term. See *tenancy for a term* under TENANCY.

estate for life. See *life estate.*

estate for years. See *tenancy for a term* under TENANCY.

estate in fee simple. See FEE SIMPLE.

estate in partnership. A joint estate that is vested in the members of a partnership when real estate is purchased with partnership funds and for partnership purposes.

estate in possession. An estate in which a present interest passes to the tenant without any contingency; an estate in which the tenant is entitled to receive the rents and other profits arising from the estate.

estate in reversion. See REVERSION.

estate in severalty (**sev**-ə-rəl-tee). An estate held by a tenant separately, without any other person being joined or connected in interest.

estate in vadio (in **vad**-ee-oh). An estate in gage or pledge. See MORTGAGE.

estate less than freehold. An estate for years, an estate at will, or an estate at sufferance.

estate of inheritance. An estate that may descend to heirs.

estate on condition. An estate that vests, is modified, or is defeated upon the occurrence or nonoccurrence of some specified event. • While an estate on limitation can revert without any action by the grantor or the grantor's heirs, an estate on condition requires the entry of the grantor or the grantor's heirs to end the estate whenever the condition occurs. — Also termed *contingent estate*; *estate on conditional limitation*.

estate on conditional limitation. See *contingent estate*.

estate on condition expressed. A contingent estate in which the condition upon which the estate will fail is stated explicitly in the granting instrument.

estate on condition implied. A contingent estate having some condition that is so inseparable from the estate's essence that it need not be expressed in words.

estate on limitation. An estate that automatically reverts back to the grantor according to a provision, usu. regarding the passage of a determined time period, designated by words like "during," "while," and "as long as." See *fee simple determinable* under FEE SIMPLE.

estate tail. See FEE TAIL.

estate tail quasi. An estate granted by a life tenant, who, despite using language of conveyance that is otherwise sufficient to create an estate tail, is unable to grant in perpetuity.

freehold estate. See FREEHOLD.

future estate. See FUTURE INTEREST.

gross estate. **1.** The total value of a decedent's property without any deductions. **2.** Loosely, adjusted gross estate.

heirless estate. The property of a person who dies intestate and without heirs. See ESCHEAT.

joint estate. Any of the following five types of estates: (1) a joint tenancy, (2) a tenancy in common, (3) an estate in coparcenary, (4) a tenancy by the entirety, or (5) an estate in partnership.

landed estate. An interest in real property, esp. suburban or rural land, as distinguished from real estate situated in a city. — Also termed *landed property*.

leasehold estate. See LEASEHOLD.

legal estate. An interest enforced in law rather than in equity.

life estate. An estate held only for the duration of a specified person's life, usu. the possessor's. • Most life estates — created, for example, by a grant "to Jane for life" — are beneficial interests under trusts, the corpus being personal property, not real property. — Also termed *estate for life*; *legal life estate*; *life tenancy*.

life estate pur autre vie (pər **oh**-trə **vee**). A life estate for which the measuring life — the life whose duration determines the duration of the estate — is someone other than the life tenant. — Also spelled *life estate per autre vie*.

lower estate. See *servient estate*.

minor's estate. A minor's property that must be administered by a court-appointed fiduciary.

net estate. The portion of an estate left after payment of state and federal estate taxes. Cf. *adjusted gross estate*.

next eventual estate. An estate taking effect upon an event that terminates the accumulation of undisposed rents and profits; an estate taking effect when the existing estate terminates.

nonancestral estate. An estate from any source other than the owner's ancestors.

nonfreehold estate. Any estate in real property without seisin, such as an estate for years, from period to period, at will, or at sufferance; any estate except the fee simple, fee tail, or life estate.

original estate. An estate that is the first of one or more derivative estates, bearing to each other the relation of a particular estate and a reversion.

particular estate. An estate of limited duration, such as a fee tail, a life estate, or an estate for years.

periodic estate. See *periodic tenancy* under TENANCY.

possessory estate. An estate giving the holder the right to possess the property, with or without an ownership interest in the property.

present estate. An estate in immediate possession; one vested at the present time, as distinguished from a future estate.

qualified estate. Any estate that is not absolute and unconditional; a limited or conditional estate.

real estate. See *real property* under PROPERTY.

residuary estate. The part of a decedent's estate remaining after all debts, expenses, taxes, and specific bequests and devises have been satisfied. — Also termed *residual estate*; *residue*; *residuary*; *residuum*.

separate estate. The individual property of one of two persons who stand in a marital or business relationship. See SEPARATE PROPERTY.

servient estate (**sər**-vee-ənt). An estate burdened by an easement. — Also termed *servient tenement*; *servient property*; *lower estate*. Cf. *dominant estate*.

settled estate. An estate created or limited under a settlement; an estate in which the powers of alienation, devising, and transmission according to the ordinary rules of descent are restrained by the settlement's terms.

stipendiary estate (stɪ-**pen**-dee-er-ee). *Hist.* An estate granted in return for services, usu. of a military kind.

taxable estate. A decedent's gross estate reduced by allowable deductions (such as administration costs and ESOP deductions). IRC (26 USCA) § 2051. • The taxable estate is the amount that is subject to the federal unified transfer tax at death.

upper estate. See *dominant estate*.

vested estate. An estate with a present right of enjoyment or a present fixed right of future enjoyment.

estate ad remanentiam. See ESTATE.

estate at sufferance. See *tenancy at sufferance* under TENANCY.

estate at will. See *tenancy at will* under TENANCY.

estate by curtesy. See ESTATE.

estate by elegit. See ESTATE.

estate by purchase. See ESTATE.

estate by statute staple. See ESTATE.

estate by the entirety. See *tenancy by the entirety* under TENANCY.

estate duty. A duty imposed on the principal value of all property that passed on death. • In Britain, this duty was replaced by inheritance tax.

estate for a term. See *tenancy for a term* under TENANCY.

estate for life. See *life estate* under ESTATE.

estate for years. See *tenancy for a term* under TENANCY.

estate freeze. An estate-planning maneuver whereby an owner of a closely held business exchanges common stock for dividend-paying preferred stock and gives the common stock to his or her children, thus guaranteeing a pension and avoiding estate tax.

estate from period to period. See *periodic tenancy* under TENANCY.

estate in common. See *tenancy in common* under TENANCY.

estate in expectancy. See FUTURE INTEREST.

estate in fee simple. See FEE SIMPLE.

estate in lands. **1.** Property that one has in lands, tenements, or hereditaments. **2.** The conditions or circumstances under which a tenant stands in relation to the leased property.

estate in partnership. See ESTATE.

estate in possession. See ESTATE.

estate in reversion. See REVERSION.

estate in severalty. See ESTATE.

estate in vadio. See ESTATE.

estate less than freehold. See ESTATE.

estate of inheritance. See ESTATE.

estate on condition. See ESTATE.

estate on conditional limitation. See *estate on condition* under ESTATE.

estate on condition expressed. See ESTATE.

estate on condition implied. See ESTATE.

estate on limitation. See ESTATE.

estate planning. **1.** The preparation for the distribution and management of a person's estate at death through the use of wills, trusts, insurance policies, and other arrangements, esp. to reduce estate-tax liability. **2.** A branch of law that involves the arrangement of a person's estate, taking into account the laws of wills, taxes, insurance, property, and trusts.

estates of the realm. **1.** The lords spiritual, the lords temporal, and the commons of Great Britain. — Also termed *the three estates.* **2.** In feudal Europe, the clergy, nobles, and commons. • Because the lords spiritual had no separate assembly or negative in their political capacity, some authorities reduce the estates in Great Britain to two, the lords and commons. In England (until about the 14th century), the three estates of the realm were the clergy, barons, and knights. In legal practice, the lords spiritual and lords temporal are usu. collectively designated simply as *lords*.

estate tail. See FEE TAIL.

estate tail quasi. See ESTATE.

estate tax. See TAX.

estate trust. See TRUST.

***ester* in judgment** (**es**-tər). [Law French] To appear before a tribunal, as either plaintiff or defendant.

estimated damages. See *liquidated damages* under DAMAGES.

estimated tax. See TAX.

estimated useful life. See USEFUL LIFE.

estop (e-**stop**), *vb.* To bar or prevent by estoppel.

estoppage (e-**stop**-ij), *n.* The state or condition of being estopped.

estoppel (e-**stop**-əl), *n.* **1.** A bar that prevents one from asserting a claim or right that contradicts what one has said or done before or what has been legally established as true. **2.** A bar that prevents the relitigation of issues. **3.** An affirmative defense alleging good-faith reliance on a misleading representation and an injury or detrimental change in position resulting from that reliance. Cf. WAIVER (1).

> " 'Estoppe,' says Lord Coke, 'cometh of the French word *estoupe*, from whence the English word stopped; and it is called an estoppel or conclusion, because a man's own act or acceptance stoppeth or closeth up his mouth to allege or plead the truth.' [Co. Litt. 352a.] Estoppel may also be defined to be a legal result or 'conclusion' arising from an admission which has either been actually made, or which the law presumes to have been made, and which is binding on all persons whom it affects." Lancelot Feilding Everest, *Everest and Strode's Law of Estoppel* 1 (3d ed. 1923).

> "In using the term 'estoppel,' one is of course aware of its kaleidoscopic varieties. One reads of estoppel by conduct, by deed, by laches, by misrepresentation, by negligence, by silence, and so on. There is also an estoppel by judgment and by verdict; these, however, obviously involve procedure. The first-named varieties have certain aspects in common. But these aspects are not always interpreted by the same rules in all courts. The institution seems to be flexible." John H. Wigmore, "The Scientific Role of Consideration in Contract," in *Legal Essays in Tribute to Orrin Kip McMurray* 641, 643 (1935).

administrative collateral estoppel. See COLLATERAL ESTOPPEL.

assignor estoppel. *Patents.* Estoppel barring someone who has assigned the rights to a patent from later attacking the patent's validity. *Westinghouse Elec. & Mfg. Co. v. Formica*

Insulation Co., 266 U.S. 342, 45 S.Ct. 117 (1924).

collateral estoppel. See COLLATERAL ESTOPPEL.

***equitable estoppel.* 1.** A defensive doctrine preventing one party from taking unfair advantage of another when, through false language or conduct, the person to be estopped has induced another person to act in a certain way, with the result that the other person has been injured in some way. • This doctrine is founded on principles of fraud. The five essential elements for this type of estoppel are (1) that there was a false representation or concealment of material facts, (2) that the representation must have been known to be false by the party making it, or the party must have been negligent in not knowing its falsity, (3) that it was believed to be true by the person to whom it was made, (4) that the party making the representation must have intended that it be acted on, or the person acting on it must have been justified in assuming this intent, and (5) that the party asserting estoppel acted on the representation in a way that will result in substantial prejudice unless the claim of estoppel succeeds. — Also termed *estoppel by conduct*; *estoppel in pais*. **2.** See *promissory estoppel*.

estoppel by conduct. See *equitable estoppel*.

estoppel by contract. A bar against a person' denying a term, fact, or performance arising from a contract that the person has entered into.

estoppel by deed. Estoppel that prevents a party to a deed from denying anything recited in that deed if the party has induced another to accept or act under the deed; esp., estoppel that prevents a grantor of a warranty deed, who does not have title at the time of the conveyance but who later acquires title, from denying that he or she had title at the time of the transfer. See AFTER-ACQUIRED-TITLE DOCTRINE.

estoppel by election. The intentional exercise of a choice between inconsistent alternatives that bars the person making the choice from the benefits of the one not selected.

estoppel by inaction. See *estoppel by silence*.

estoppel by judgment. See COLLATERAL ESTOPPEL.

estoppel by laches. An equitable doctrine by which some courts deny relief to a claimant who has unreasonably delayed or been negligent in asserting a claim.

estoppel by negligence. An estoppel arising when a negligent person induces someone to believe certain facts, and then the other person reasonably and detrimentally relies on that belief.

estoppel by record. See COLLATERAL ESTOPPEL.

estoppel by representation. An estoppel that arises when one makes a statement or admission that induces another person to believe something and that results in that person's reasonable and detrimental reliance on the belief; esp., equitable estoppel.

estoppel by silence. Estoppel that arises when a party is under a duty to speak but fails to do so. — Also termed *estoppel by standing by*; *estoppel by inaction*.

estoppel by verdict. See COLLATERAL ESTOPPEL.

estoppel in pais. See *equitable estoppel*.

file-wrapper estoppel. See PROSECUTION-HISTORY ESTOPPEL.

judicial estoppel. Estoppel that prevents a party from contradicting previous declarations made during the same or a later proceeding if the change in position would adversely affect the proceeding or constitute a fraud on the court. — Also termed *doctrine of preclusion of inconsistent positions*; *doctrine of the conclusiveness of the judgment*.

legal estoppel. Estoppel recognized in law, such as an estoppel resulting from a recital or other statement in a deed or official record, and precluding any denial or assertion concerning a fact, as distinguished from equitable estoppel or estoppel in pais.

marking estoppel. *Patents.* Estoppel that prevents a party from asserting that a product is not covered by a patent if that party has marked the product with a patent number. • This type of estoppel has been called into question in recent years, and has been sharply limited by some courts.

promissory estoppel. The principle that a promise made without consideration may nonetheless be enforced to prevent injustice if the promisor should have reasonably expected the promisee to rely on the promise and if the promisee did actually rely on the promise to his or her detriment. — Also termed (inaccurately) *equitable estoppel*.

> "The doctrine of promissory estoppel is equitable in origin and nature and arose to provide a remedy through the enforcement of a gratuitous promise. Promissory is distinct from equitable estoppel in that the representation at issue is promissory rather than a representation of fact. 'Promissory estoppel and estoppel by conduct are

two entirely distinct theories. The latter does not require a promise.' " Ann Taylor Schwing, *California Affirmative Defenses* § 34:16, at 35 (2d ed. 1996) (quoting *Division of Labor Law Enforcement v. Transpacific Transp. Co.*, 88 Cal. App. 3d 823, 829 (Cal. Ct. App. 1979)).

prosecution-history estoppel. See PROSECUTION-HISTORY ESTOPPEL.

quasi-estoppel. An equitable doctrine preventing one from repudiating an act or assertion if it would harm another who reasonably relied on the act or assertion.

estoppel by conduct. See *equitable estoppel* (1) under ESTOPPEL.

estoppel by contract. See ESTOPPEL.

estoppel by deed. See ESTOPPEL.

estoppel by election. See ESTOPPEL.

estoppel by inaction. See *estoppel by silence* under ESTOPPEL.

estoppel by judgment. See COLLATERAL ESTOPPEL.

estoppel by laches. See ESTOPPEL.

estoppel by negligence. See ESTOPPEL.

estoppel by record. See COLLATERAL ESTOPPEL.

estoppel by representation. See ESTOPPEL.

estoppel by silence. See ESTOPPEL.

estoppel by standing by. See *estoppel by silence* under ESTOPPEL.

estoppel by verdict. See COLLATERAL ESTOPPEL.

estoppel certificate. 1. A signed statement by a party (such as a tenant or a mortgagee) certifying for another's benefit that certain facts are correct, as that a lease exists, that there are no defaults, and that rent is paid to a certain date. • A party's delivery of this statement estops that party from later claiming a different state of facts. **2.** See WAIVER OF CLAIMS AND DEFENSES.

estoppel in pais (in **pays** *or* **pay**). See *equitable estoppel* (1) under ESTOPPEL.

estoppel per rem judicatam (pər rem joo-di-**kay**-təm). See COLLATERAL ESTOPPEL.

estover (e-**stoh**-vər). (*usu. pl.*) **1.** Wood that a tenant is allowed to take for fuel, the manufacture or repair of agricultural instruments, and the erection and maintenance of fences and hedges; necessary supplies. See *common of estovers* under COMMON. **2.** The tenant's right to obtain that wood. **3.** ALIMONY.

estoveriis habendis (es-tə-**veer**-ee-is hə-**ben**-dis). [Latin] *Hist.* A writ for a wife who was judicially separated to recover her alimony or estovers.

estray (e-**stray**), *n.* **1.** A valuable tame animal found wandering and ownerless; an animal that has escaped from its owner and wanders about. • At common law, an estray belonged to the Crown or to the lord of the manor, but today the general rule is that it passes to the state in trust for the true owner, who may regain it by proving ownership. An animal cannot be an estray when on the range where it was raised and where its owner permits it to run, and esp. when the owner is known to the party who takes the animal. **2.** FLOTSAM.

estreat (e-**street**), *n.* A copy or duplicate of some original writing or record, esp. of a fine or amercement imposed by a court, extracted from the record, and certified to one who is authorized and required to collect it.

estreat, *vb.* To take out a forfeited recognizance from the recordings of a court and return it to the court to be prosecuted.

estrepe (e-**streep**), *vb.* **1.** To strip; to despoil; to commit waste upon an estate, as by cutting down trees or removing buildings. **2.** To injure the value of a reversionary interest by stripping or spoiling the estate. See WASTE.

estrepement (e-**streep**-mənt), *n.* A species of aggravated waste, by stripping or devastating land to the injury of the reversioner, esp. pending a suit for possession. See DE ESTREPAMENTO.

et, *conj.* [Latin] And. • This conjunction was the introductory word of several Latin and Law French phrases that were once common.

et adjournatur (et aj-ər-**nay**-tər). [Latin] *Hist.* And it is adjourned. • This phrase was used in the old reports, when argument of a case was adjourned to another day, or where a second argument was had.

et al. (et **al** *or* **ahl**). *abbr.* **1.** [Latin *et alii* or *et alia*] And other persons <the office of Thomas Webb et al.>. **2.** [Latin *et alibi*] And elsewhere.

et alii e contra (et **ay**-lee-I ee **kon**-trə). [Latin "and others on the other side"] *Hist.* A phrase often used in the Year Books, describing a joinder in issue.

et alius (et **ay**-lee-əs). [Latin] And another.

et allocatur (et al-ə-**kay**-tər). [Latin] And it is allowed.

etc. *abbr.* ET CETERA.

et cetera (et **set**-ər-ə). [Latin "and others"] And other things. • The term usu. indicates additional, unspecified items in a series. — Abbr. etc.

et de ceo se mettent en le pays (ay də **say**-oh sə me-**tawn** *on* lə **pay**). [Law French] *Hist.* And of this they put themselves upon the country. See CONCLUSION TO THE COUNTRY; GOING TO THE COUNTRY.

et de hoc ponit se super patriam (et dee hok **poh**-nit see **s[y]oo**-pər **pay**-tree-əm). [Latin] *Hist.* And of this he puts himself upon the country. • This was the formal conclusion of a common-law plea in bar by way of traverse.

et ei legitur in haec verba (et **ee**-I **lee**-jə-tər in **heek vər**-bə). [Latin] *Hist.* And it is read to him in these words. • This phrase was formerly used in entering the prayer of oyer on the record.

eternal law. See NATURAL LAW.

et habeas ibi tunc hoc breve (et **hay**-bee-əs **ib**-I təngk hok **bree**-vee). [Latin] *Hist.* And that you have then and there this writ. • These were the formal words directing the return of a writ. The literal translation was retained in the later form of a considerable number of writs.

et habuit (et **hab**-yoo-it). [Latin "and he had [it]"] *Hist.* A common phrase in the Year Books, indicating that a party's application or demand was granted.

ethical, *adj.* **1.** Of or relating to moral obligations that one person owes another; esp., in law, of or relating to legal ethics <the ethical rules regarding confidences>. See LEGAL ETHICS. **2.** In conformity with moral norms or standards of professional conduct <the judge's recusal was a perfectly ethical act>.

ethical absolutism. See MORAL ABSOLUTISM.

ethical consideration. (*often cap.*) An aspirational goal or principle intended to guide a lawyer's professional conduct. • A lawyer's violation of these considerations (which are contained in the Model Code of Professional Responsibility) does not necessarily subject the lawyer to discipline. — Abbr. EC. Cf. DISCIPLINARY RULE.

ethical drug. See DRUG.

ethical jurisprudence. See JURISPRUDENCE.

ethical relativism. See MORAL RELATIVISM.

ethical wall. A screening mechanism that protects client confidences by preventing one or more lawyers within an organization from participating in any matter involving that client. • This mechanism is designed to allow a lawyer to move to a new law firm without the fear of vicariously disqualifying that firm from representing certain clients. Creating an ethical wall generally entails (1) prohibiting certain lawyers and paralegals from having any connection with the matter; (2) banning discussions with or the transfer of documents to those individuals; (3) restricting access to files; and (4) educating all members of the firm, corporation, or entity about the separation of the lawyers and paralegals (both organizationally and physically) from the pending matter. — Also termed *Chinese wall*; *screening mechanism*.

ethics. See LEGAL ETHICS.

et hoc paratus est verificare (et hok pə-**ray**-təs est ver-ə-fi-**kair**-ee). [Latin "and this he is prepared to verify"] *Archaic.* A phrase that concluded a plea in confession and avoidance, or any pleading that contained new affirmative matter. • A pleading containing this phrase was technically said to "conclude with a verification," as opposed to a simple denial.

et hoc petit quod inquiratur per patriam (et hok **pet**-it kwod in-kwə-**ray**-tər pər **pay**-tree-əm). [Latin "and this he prays may be inquired of by the country"] *Archaic.* The conclusion of a plaintiff's pleading that tendered an issue to the country. See CONCLUSION TO THE COUNTRY.

et inde petit judicium (et **in**-dee **pet**-it joo-**dish**-ee-əm). [Latin "and thereupon he prays judgment"] *Archaic.* A clause found at the end of a pleading, requesting judgment in that party's favor.

etiquette of the profession. See LEGAL ETHICS (1).

et modo ad hunc diem (et **moh**-doh ad **həngk dI**-əm). [Latin "and now at this day"] *Archaic.* The formal beginning of an entry of appearance or of a continuance.

et non (et **non**). [Latin "and not"] *Archaic.* A phrase formerly used in pleading to introduce the negative averments of a special traverse. See ABSQUE HOC.

et seq. (et **sek**). *abbr.* [Latin *et sequentes*] And those (pages or sections) that follow <11 USCA §§ 101 et seq.>.

et sic (et **sik**). [Latin "and so"] *Archaic.* The introductory words of a special conclusion to a plea in bar, intending to render the plea positive and not argumentative.

et sic ad judicium (et **sik** ad joo-**dish**-ee-əm). [Latin] *Archaic.* And so to judgment.

et sic ad patriam (et **sik** ad **pay**-tree-əm). [Latin] *Hist.* And so to the country. • This phrase was used in the Year Books to record an issue to the country.

et sic fecit (et **sik fee**-sit). [Latin] *Archaic.* And he did so.

et sic pendet (et **sik pen**-dit). [Latin] *Hist.* And so it hangs. • This phrase was used in the old reports to signify that a point was left undetermined.

et sic ulterius (et **sik** əl-**teer**-ee-əs). [Latin] *Archaic.* And so on; and so further; and so forth.

et uxor (et **ək**-sor). [Latin] *Archaic.* And wife. • This phrase was formerly common in case names and legal documents (esp. abstracts of title) involving a husband and wife jointly. It usu. appears in its abbreviated form, *et ux.* <conveyed the land to Donald Baird et ux.>.

et vir (et **veer**). [Latin] *Archaic.* And husband.

EU. *abbr.* EUROPEAN UNION.

Euclidean zoning. See ZONING.

eundo et redeundo (ee-**ən**-doh et red-ee-**ən**-doh). [Latin] *Hist.* Going and returning. • This phrase was once used to describe vessels in transit.

eundo, morando, et redeundo (ee-**ən**-doh, mə-**ran**-doh, et red-ee-**ən**-doh). [Latin] *Hist.* Going, remaining, and returning. • This phrase was once used to describe a person (for example, a witness or legislator) who is privileged from arrest while traveling to the place where assigned duties are to be performed, while remaining there, and while returning.

eunomy (**yoo**-nə-mee), *n.* A system of good laws that lead to civil order and justice. — Also termed *eunomia.* — **eunomic,** *adj.*

euro (**yuur**-oh). The official currency of 11 countries in the European Union. • On January 1, 1999, the euro became the single currency of the 11 participating countries — Austria, Belgium, Finland, France, Germany, Ireland, Italy, Luxembourg, Netherlands, Portugal, and Spain. Euro notes and coins will be issued on January 1, 2002.

Eurobank. A bank that participates in the Eurocurrency market by accepting deposits and providing loans in foreign currencies.

Eurobond. An international bond issued in a country other than the one in whose currency the bond is denominated.

Eurodollar. A U.S. dollar deposited in a foreign bank and used in European money markets.

European Community. See EUROPEAN UNION.

European Court of Human Rights. The judicial body — established in 1950 and sitting at Strasbourg — of the Council of Europe. • The Convention on Human Rights of 1950, in force as of 1953, does not necessarily form part of the domestic law of member nations, nor is a member nation obliged to accept this court's jurisdiction.

European Currency Unit. A monetary unit whose value is calculated as a weighted average of currencies from ten member-nations of the European Union. • The European Currency Unit was created in 1979 to promote currency stability. The unit was a hypothetical currency. — Abbr. ECU; ecu.

European Economic Community. See EUROPEAN UNION.

European law. **1.** The law of the European Union. **2.** More broadly, the law of the European Union, together with the conventions of the Council of Europe and the European Convention on Human Rights. **3.** More broadly still, all the law current in Europe, including the law of European organizations such as the Western European Union, the Benelux Economic Union, the Organization for Economic Cooperation and Development, the North Atlantic Treaty Organization, and all the bilateral and multilateral conventions in effect, as well as European customary law.

European Union. An association of European nations, with the purpose of achieving full economic unity (and eventual political union) by agreeing to eliminate barriers to the free movement of capital, goods, and labor among the member-nations. • The European Union was formed as the European Economic Community (EEC) by the Treaty of Rome in 1957, and later renamed the European Community (EC). The European Community became the European Union when the Maastricht Treaty on European Union took effect in November 1993. As of 1999, Austria, Belgium, Denmark, Finland, France, Germany, Great Britain, Greece, Ireland, Italy, Luxembourg, Netherlands, Portugal, Spain, and Sweden had full membership privileges. — Abbr. EU.

euthanasia (yoo-thə-**nay**-zhə), *n.* The act or practice of killing or bringing about the death of a person who suffers from an incurable disease or condition, esp. a painful one, for reasons of mercy. • Euthanasia is sometimes regarded by the law as second-degree murder, manslaughter, or criminally negligent homicide. — Also termed *mercy killing*. — **euthanasic** (yoo-thə-**nay**-zik), *adj.* See LIVING WILL; ADVANCE DIRECTIVE. Cf. *assisted suicide* under SUICIDE.

active euthanasia. Euthanasia performed by a facilitator (usu. a physician) who not only provides the means of death but also carries out the final death-causing act.

involuntary euthanasia. Euthanasia of a competent, nonconsenting person.

nonvoluntary euthanasia. Euthanasia of an incompetent, and therefore nonconsenting, person.

passive euthanasia. The act of allowing a terminally ill person to die by either withholding or withdrawing life-sustaining support such as a respirator or feeding tube.

voluntary euthanasia. Euthanasia performed with the terminally ill person's consent.

euthanize (**yoo**-thə-nIz), *vb.* To put to death by euthanasia. • This term is used chiefly in reference to animals. — Also termed *euthanatize*.

evaluative fact. See FACT.

Evarts Act (**ev**-ərts). An 1891 federal statute that established the circuit courts of appeals (now U.S. courts of appeals) and fixed the contemporary method of federal appellate review.

evasion. See TAX EVASION.

evasive, *adj.* Tending or seeking to evade; elusive; shifting. • If a pleading requiring a response is evasive, the responding party may move for a more definite statement. Fed. R. Civ. P. 12(e).

evasive answer. A response that neither directly admits nor denies a question. • In pleading, this is considered a failure to answer. Fed. R. Civ. P. 37(3).

even date. The same date. • This jargonistic phrase is sometimes used in one instrument to refer to another instrument with the same date, esp. when both relate to the same transaction (as a deed and a mortgage).

evenings. *Hist.* The delivery at evening or night to a customary tenant of a gratuity in the form of a portion of the grass, corn, or other crop that the tenant cuts, mows, or reaps for the lord.

even lot. See *round lot* under LOT (3).

evergreen contract. See CONTRACT.

evict, *vb.* **1.** To expel (a person, esp. a tenant), from real property, usu. by legal process. **2.** *Archaic.* To recover (property or title) from a person by legal process. — **evictor,** *n.*

eviction. The act or process of legally dispossessing a person of land or rental property. See FORCIBLE ENTRY AND DETAINER. Cf. EJECTMENT.

actual eviction. A physical expulsion of a person from land or rental property.

constructive eviction. **1.** A landlord's act of making premises unfit for occupancy, often with the result that the tenant is compelled to leave. **2.** The inability of a land purchaser to obtain possession because of paramount outstanding title. • Such an eviction usu. constitutes a breach of the covenants of warranty and quiet enjoyment.

partial eviction. An eviction, either constructive or actual, from a portion of a tenant's premises.

retaliatory eviction. An eviction — nearly always illegal — commenced in response to a tenant's complaints or involvement in activities with which the landlord does not agree.

summary eviction. An eviction accomplished through a simplified legal procedure, without the formalities of a full trial.

total eviction. An eviction that wholly deprives the tenant of any right in the premises.

evidence, *n.* **1.** Something (including testimony, documents and tangible objects) that tends to prove or disprove the existence of an alleged fact <the bloody glove is the key piece of evidence for the prosecution>. **2.** See *fact in evidence* under FACT. **3.** The collective mass of things, esp. testimony and exhibits, presented before a tribunal in a given dispute <the evidence will show that the defendant breached the contract>. **4.** The body of law regulating the burden of proof, admissibility, relevance, and the weight and sufficiency of what should be admitted into the record of a legal proceeding <under the rules of evidence, the witness's statement is inadmissible hearsay that is not subject to any exception>. — **evidence,** *vb.*

> "Evidence is any matter of fact which is furnished to a legal tribunal, otherwise than by reasoning or a reference to what is noticed without proof, as the basis of inference in ascertaining some other matter of fact." James B. Thayer, *Presumptions and the Law of Evidence*, 3 Harv. L. Rev. 141, 142 (1889).

> "Evidence, broadly defined, is the means from which an inference may logically be drawn as to the existence of a fact; that which makes evident or plain. Evidence is the demonstration of a fact; it signifies that which demonstrates, makes clear, or ascertains the truth of the very fact or point in issue, either on the one side or on the other. In legal acceptation, the term 'evidence' includes all the means by which any alleged matter of fact, the truth of which is submitted to investigation, is established or disproved. 'Evidence' has also been defined to mean any species of proof legally presented at the trial of an issue, by the act of the parties and through the medium of witnesses, records, documents, concrete objects, and the like." 31A C.J.S. *Evidence* § 3, at 67–68 (1996).

admissible evidence. Evidence that is relevant and is of such a character (e.g., not unfairly prejudicial or based on hearsay) that the court should receive it. — Also termed *competent evidence*; *proper evidence*.

autoptic evidence. See *demonstrative evidence*.

best evidence. Evidence of the highest quality available, as measured by the nature of the case rather than the thing being offered as evidence. — Also termed *primary evidence*; *original evidence*. See BEST-EVIDENCE RULE. Cf. *secondary evidence*.

> "In some circumstances, 'best evidence' may mean that evidence which is more specific and definite as opposed to that which is merely general and indefinite or descriptive. However, 'best evidence' or 'primary evidence' is variously defined as that particular means of proof which is indicated by the nature of the fact under investigation as the most natural and satisfactory, or as that kind of proof which under any possible circumstances affords the greatest certainty of the fact in question; or as evidence which carries on its face no indication that better remains behind." 32A C.J.S. *Evidence* § 1054, at 417 (1996).

character evidence. Evidence regarding someone's personality traits; evidence of a person's moral standing in a community, based on reputation or opinion. Fed. R. Evid. 404, 405, 608.

circumstantial evidence. **1.** Evidence based on inference and not on personal knowledge or observation. — Also termed *indirect evidence*; *oblique evidence*. Cf. *direct evidence* (1). **2.** All evidence that is not given by testimony.

> "*Indirect* evidence (called by the civilians, *oblique*, and more commonly known as *circumstantial* evidence) is that which is applied to the principal fact, indirectly, or through the medium of other facts, by establishing certain circumstances or minor facts, already described as evidentiary, from which the principal fact is extracted and gathered by a process of special inference ...." Alexander M. Burrill, *A Treatise on the Nature, Principles and Rules of Circumstantial Evidence* 4 (1868).

> "Some circumstantial evidence is very strong, as when you find a trout in the milk." Henry David Thoreau, Journal, 11 Nov. 1850, in 2 *Journal of Henry D. Thoreau* 94 (Bradford Torrey & Francis H. Allen eds., 1962).

> "Evidence of some collateral fact, from which the existence or non-existence of some fact in question may be inferred as a probable consequence, is termed circumstantial evidence." William P. Richardson, *The Law of Evidence* § 111, at 68 (3d ed. 1928).

> "Testimonial evidence readily defines itself by its name; it is any assertion by a human being, offered to evidence the truth of the matter asserted. Circumstantial evidence is any and all other evidence. Scientifically the term 'circumstantial' is indefensible, for it does not correlate with 'testimonial'; a more correct equivalent would be 'nontestimonial.' But no one has yet invented an acceptable substitute for 'circumstantial.' " John H. Wigmore, *A Students' Textbook of the Law of Evidence* 38 (1935).

clear and convincing evidence. Evidence indicating that the thing to be proved is highly probable or reasonably certain. • This is a greater burden than preponderance of the evidence, the standard applied in most civil trials, but less than evidence beyond a reasonable doubt, the norm for criminal trials. — Also termed *clear and convincing proof*. Cf. PREPONDERANCE OF THE EVIDENCE.

communicative evidence. See *testimonial evidence*.

competent evidence. **1.** See *admissible evidence*. **2.** See *relevant evidence*.

conclusive evidence. **1.** Evidence so strong as to overbear any other evidence to the contrary. — Also termed *conclusive proof*. **2.** Evidence that, though not irrebuttable, so preponderates as to oblige a fact-finder to come to a certain conclusion.

concomitant evidence. Evidence that, at the time of the act, the alleged doer of the act was present and actually did it.

conflicting evidence. Irreconcilable evidence that comes from different sources.

corroborating evidence. Evidence that differs from but strengthens or confirms other evidence (esp. that which needs support). — Also termed *corroborative evidence*. Cf. *cumulative evidence*.

credible evidence. Evidence that is worthy of belief; trustworthy evidence.

critical evidence. Evidence strong enough that its presence could tilt a juror's mind. • Under the Due Process Clause, an indigent criminal defendant is usu. entitled to an expert opinion of the merits of critical evidence.

cumulative evidence. Additional evidence of the same character as existing evidence and that supports a fact established by the existing evidence (esp. that which does not need further support). Cf. *corroborating evidence*.

demeanor evidence. The behavior of a witness on the witness stand, to be considered by the fact-finder on the issue of credibility.

demonstrative evidence (di-**mon**-strə-tiv). Physical evidence that one can see and inspect (such as a model or photograph) and that, while of probative value and usu. offered to clarify testimony, does not play a direct part in the incident in question. — Also termed *illustrative evidence*; *real evidence*; *tangible evidence*; *autoptic evidence*; *autoptic proference*. See *nonverbal testimony* under TESTIMONY. Cf. *testimonial evidence*.

> "There remains a source of proof, distinct from either circumstantial or testimonial evidence, viz., what the tribunal *sees or hears* by its own senses. Whether this should be termed 'evidence' or not is a question of words, open to difference of view. But it is universally conceded to be an available source of proof. Bentham's term for it, 'real evidence,' came into wide vogue, but is ambiguous. The term 'autoptic proference' (etymologically meaning 'showing to the tribunal's own vision') is preferable." John H. Wigmore, *A Students' Textbook of the Law of Evidence* 39 (1935).

derivative evidence. Evidence that is discovered as a result of illegally obtained evidence and is therefore inadmissible because of the primary taint. See EXCLUSIONARY RULE; FRUIT-OF-THE-POISONOUS-TREE DOCTRINE.

direct evidence. **1.** Evidence that is based on personal knowledge or observation and that, if true, proves a fact without inference or presumption. — Also termed *positive evidence*. Cf. *circumstantial evidence*; *negative evidence*. **2.** See *original evidence* (1).

> "A little reflection shows that no disputed case will ordinarily be proved solely by circumstantial or solely by testimonial evidence. Ordinarily there is evidence of *both kinds*. The matter has been obscured by the use of the term 'direct evidence,' — a term sometimes used to mean testimonial evidence in general, but sometimes also limited to apply only to testimony directly asserting the fact-in-issue.... The term 'direct' evidence has no utility." John H. Wigmore, *A Students' Textbook of the Law of Evidence* 40 (1935).

documentary evidence. Evidence supplied by a writing or other document, which must be authenticated before the evidence is admissible.

evidence aliunde. See *extrinsic evidence*.

evidence-in-chief. Evidence used by a party in making its case-in-chief.

exclusive evidence. The only facts that have any probative force at all on a particular matter in issue.

> "[T]here is an important class of rules declaring certain facts to be exclusive evidence, none other being admissible. The execution of a document which requires attestation can be proved in no other way than by the testimony of an attesting witness, unless owing to the death or some other circumstance his testimony is unavailable. A written contract can generally be proved in no other way than by the production of the writing itself, whenever its production is possible." John Salmond, *Jurisprudence* 485 (Glanville L. Williams ed., 10th ed. 1947).

exculpatory evidence (ik-**skəl**-pə-tor-ee). Evidence tending to establish a criminal defendant's innocence. • The prosecution has a duty to disclose exculpatory evidence in its possession or control when the evidence may be material to the outcome of the case.

expert evidence. Evidence about a scientific, technical, or professional issue given by a person qualified to testify because of familiarity with the subject or special training in the field. — Also termed *expert testimony*. Fed. R. Evid. 702–705. See DAUBERT TEST.

extrajudicial evidence. Evidence that does not come directly under judicial cognizance but nevertheless constitutes an intermediate link between judicial evidence and the fact requiring proof. • It includes all facts that are known to the tribunal only by way of inference from some form of judicial evidence. See JUDICIAL NOTICE.

extrinsic evidence. **1.** Evidence relating to a contract but not appearing on the face of the contract because it comes from other sources, such as statements between the parties or the circumstances surrounding the agreement. • Extrinsic evidence is usu. not admissible to contradict or add to the terms of an unambiguous document. — Also termed *extraneous evidence*; *parol evidence*; *evidence aliunde*. **2.** Evidence that is not legitimately before the court. Cf. *intrinsic evidence*.

fabricated evidence. False or deceitful evidence that is unlawfully created, usu. after the relevant event, in an attempt to avoid liability or conviction. — Also termed *fabricated fact*.

forensic evidence. Evidence used in court; esp., evidence arrived at by scientific means, such as ballistic or medical evidence.

habit evidence. Evidence of one's regular response to a repeated specific situation. Fed. R. Evid. 406.

hearsay evidence. See HEARSAY.

illegally obtained evidence. Evidence obtained by violating a statute or a person's Fourth Amendment guarantee against unreasonable searches or Fifth Amendment right to remain silent.

illustrative evidence. See *demonstrative evidence*.

immaterial evidence. **1.** Evidence lacking in probative value. **2.** Evidence offered to prove a matter that is not in issue.

impeachment evidence. Evidence used to undermine a witness's credibility. Fed. R. Evid. 607–610.

incompetent evidence. Evidence that is for any reason inadmissible.

incriminating evidence. Evidence tending to establish guilt or from which a fact-trier can infer guilt.

inculpatory evidence (in-**kəl**-pə-tor-ee). Evidence showing or tending to show one's involvement in a crime.

indirect evidence. See *circumstantial evidence*.

indispensable evidence. Evidence without which a particular fact cannot be proved.

insufficient evidence. Evidence that is inadequate to prove something, so that no presumption — even a conditional one — is raised.

intrinsic evidence. **1.** Evidence brought out by the examination of the witness testifying. **2.** Evidence existing within a writing. Cf. *extrinsic evidence*.

judicial evidence. Evidence produced in court, consisting of all facts brought to the attention of or admitted into evidence before the tribunal.

legal evidence. All admissible evidence, both oral and documentary, of such a character that it reasonably and substantially proves the point rather than merely raising suspicion or conjecture.

material evidence. Evidence having some logical connection with the consequential facts or the issues. Cf. *relevant evidence*.

mathematical evidence. Loosely, evidence that establishes its conclusions with absolute certainty.

mediate evidence. See *secondary evidence*.

medical evidence. Evidence furnished by a doctor, nurse, or other qualified medical person testifying in a professional capacity as an expert, or by a standard treatise on medicine or surgery.

moral evidence. Loosely, evidence that depends on a belief, rather than complete and absolute proof. • Generally, such evidence is testimonial.

multiple evidence. Evidence with probative value on more than one issue but usu. admitted into evidence for one specific purpose.

negative evidence. Evidence suggesting that an alleged fact does not exist, such as a witness's testifying that he or she did not see an event occur. • Negative evidence is generally regarded to be weaker than positive evidence, because a positive assertion that a witness saw an event is a stronger statement than an assertion that a witness did not see it. But a negative assertion will sometimes be considered positive evidence, depending on the witness's opportunity to see the event. For instance, testimony that the witness watched the entire game and saw no riot in the stands is stronger than testimony stating only that the witness did not see a riot. —

Also termed *negative testimony*. Cf. *direct evidence* (1).

newly discovered evidence. Evidence existing at the time of a motion or trial but then unknown to a party, who, upon later discovering it, may assert it as grounds for reconsideration or a new trial.

no evidence. See NO EVIDENCE.

oblique evidence. See *circumstantial evidence*.

opinion evidence. A witness's belief, thought, or inference about a disputed fact. Fed. R. Evid. 701–705. See OPINION (3); OPINION RULE.

> "In a sense all testimony to matter of fact is opinion evidence; i.e. it is a conclusion formed from phenomena and mental impressions." James B. Thayer, *A Preliminary Treatise on Evidence at the Common Law* 524 (1898).

original evidence. **1.** A witness's statement that he or she perceived a fact in issue by one of the five senses, or that the witness was in a particular physical or mental state. — Also termed *direct evidence*. Cf. HEARSAY. **2.** See *best evidence*.

parol evidence (pə-**rohl** *or* **par**-əl). **1.** Evidence given orally. **2.** See *extrinsic evidence* (1). See PAROL-EVIDENCE RULE.

partial evidence. Evidence that establishes one of a series of facts.

personal evidence. See TESTIMONY.

positive evidence. See *direct evidence* (1).

preappointed evidence. Evidence prescribed in advance (as by statute) for the proof of certain facts.

preliminary evidence. Evidence that is necessary to begin a hearing or trial and that may be received conditionally in anticipation of other evidence linking it to issues in the case. Fed. R. Evid. 104.

presumptive evidence. **1.** Evidence deemed true and sufficient unless discredited by other evidence. **2.** *Archaic.* Circumstantial evidence as distinct from testimonial evidence. — Also termed *probable evidence*.

prima facie evidence (**prɪ**-mə **fay**-shə). Evidence that will establish a fact or sustain a judgment unless contradictory evidence is produced.

> "The legislative branch may create an evidential presumption, or a rule of 'prima facie' evidence, i.e., a rule which does not shut out evidence, but merely declares that certain conduct shall suffice as evidence until the opponent produces contrary evidence." John H. Wigmore, *A Students' Textbook of the Law of Evidence* 237 (1935).

primary evidence. See *best evidence*.

privileged evidence. Evidence that is exempt from production to an opposing party (with certain, limited exceptions) because it is covered by one or more statutory and common-law protections, such as the attorney-client privilege. See *privileged communication* under COMMUNICATION.

probable evidence. See *presumptive evidence*.

probative evidence (**proh**-bə-tiv). Evidence that tends to prove or disprove a point in issue.

proffered evidence (**prof**-ərd). **1.** Evidence that is offered to the court to obtain a ruling on its admissibility. **2.** Evidence whose admissibility depends on the existence or nonexistence of a preliminary fact.

proper evidence. See *admissible evidence*.

prospectant evidence (prə-**spek**-tənt). Evidence that, before someone does an act, suggests that the person might or might not do the act. • This evidence typically falls into any of five categories: (1) moral character or disposition, (2) physical and mental capacity, (3) habit or custom, (4) emotion or motive, and (5) plan, design, or intention.

Queen's evidence. *English law.* Testimony provided by one criminal defendant, usu. under a promise of pardon, against another criminal defendant. — Also termed (when a king reigns) *King's evidence*. See *state's evidence*.

real evidence. **1.** Physical evidence (such as a knife wound) that itself plays a direct part in the incident in question. **2.** See *demonstrative evidence*.

> "Anything which is believed for any other reason than that someone has said so, is believed on real evidence." John Salmond, *Jurisprudence* 480 (Glanville L. Williams ed., 10th ed. 1947).

rebuttal evidence. Evidence offered to disprove or contradict the evidence presented by an opposing party.

relevant evidence. Evidence tending to prove or disprove a matter in issue. • Relevant evidence is both probative and material and is admissible unless excluded by a specific statute or rule. Fed. R. Evid. 401–403. — Also termed *competent evidence*. Cf. *material evidence*.

reputation evidence. Evidence of what one is thought by others to be. • Reputation evidence may be introduced as proof of character when character is in issue or is used circumstantially. Fed. R. Evid. 405(a). — Also termed *reputational evidence.*

retrospectant evidence (re-trə-**spek**-tənt). Evidence that, although it occurs after an act has been done, suggests that the alleged doer of the act actually did it <when goods have been stolen, and the thief is sought, a person's later possession of those goods amounts to retrospectant evidence that this person took them>. — Also termed *traces.*

satisfactory evidence. Evidence that is sufficient to satisfy an unprejudiced mind seeking the truth. — Also termed *sufficient evidence; satisfactory proof.*

scientific evidence. Testimony or opinion evidence that draws on technical or specialized knowledge and relies on scientific method for its evidentiary value. See DAUBERT TEST.

secondary evidence. Evidence that is inferior to the primary or best evidence and that becomes admissible when the primary or best evidence is lost or inaccessible. • Examples include a copy of a lost instrument or testimony regarding the contents of a lost document. — Also termed *mediate evidence; mediate testimony; substitutionary evidence.* Cf. *best evidence.*

secondhand evidence. See HEARSAY.

signature evidence. Evidence of a person's prior bad acts that, while ordinarily inadmissible, will be admitted if it shows, for example, that two crimes were committed through the same planning, design, scheme, or modus operandi, and in such a way that the prior act and the current act are uniquely identifiable as those of the defendant.

slight evidence. Inconsiderable evidence; a trifling quantity of evidence; esp., the small amount sufficient for a rational fact-finder to conclude that the state failed to disprove an affirmative defense beyond a reasonable doubt.

state's evidence. Testimony provided by one criminal defendant — under a promise of immunity or reduced sentence — against another criminal defendant. See TURN STATE'S EVIDENCE.

substantial evidence. Evidence that a reasonable mind would accept as adequate to support a conclusion; evidence beyond a scintilla. See SUBSTANTIAL-EVIDENCE RULE.

substantive evidence (**səb**-stən-tiv). Evidence offered to support a fact in issue, as opposed to impeachment or corroborating evidence.

substitutionary evidence. See *secondary evidence.*

sufficient evidence. See *satisfactory evidence.*

tainted evidence. Evidence that is inadmissible because it was directly or indirectly obtained by illegal means. See FRUIT-OF-THE-POISONOUS-TREE DOCTRINE.

tangible evidence. See *demonstrative evidence.*

testimonial evidence. A person's testimony offered to prove the truth of the matter asserted; esp., evidence elicited from a witness. — Also termed *communicative evidence.* Cf. *demonstrative evidence.*

> "An assertion is testimonial evidence whether made out of court or in court, if it is offered with a view to persuading the tribunal of the matter asserted." John H. Wigmore, *A Students' Textbook of the Law of Evidence* 120 (1935).

traditionary evidence. Evidence derived from a deceased person's former statements or reputation. • Traditionary evidence is admissible to prove ancestry, ancient boundaries, or similar facts, usu. when no living witnesses are available to testify.

unwritten evidence. Evidence given orally, in court or by deposition.

evidence by inspection. See *demonstrative evidence* under EVIDENCE.

evidence code. A codified set of statutory provisions governing the admissibility of evidence and the burden of proof at hearings and trials.

evidence-in-chief. See EVIDENCE.

evidence of debt. 1. BOND. **2.** DEBENTURE.

evidence of insurability. Information — such as medical records or a medical examination — that an insurer may require to establish a potential insured's qualification for a particular insurance policy.

evidence of title. The means by which the ownership of land is satisfactorily demonstrated within a given jurisdiction. See DEED.

> "There are four kinds of evidence of title: *abstract and opinion, certificate of title, title insurance* and *Torrens certificate.* The certificate of title is used extensively in the Eastern states, and some Southern states. In urban centers in a great many sections of the country, title insurance occupies a dominant position in real estate transactions. In farm areas the abstract and opinion method is common. To a great extent, the acceptability

of a particular kind of evidence of title depends on the local custom." Robert Kratovil, *Real Estate Law* 170 (6th ed. 1974).

evidence rules. See EVIDENCE (4).

evidentia (ev-i-**den**-shee-ə), *n.* [Law Latin] Evidence.

evidential, *adj.* Of, relating to, relying on, or constituting evidence; EVIDENTIARY (1).

evidential fact. See *evidentiary fact* (2) under FACT.

evidentiary (ev-i-**den**-shə-ree), *adj.* **1.** Having the quality of evidence; constituting evidence; evidencing. **2.** Pertaining to the rules of evidence or the evidence in a particular case.

evidentiary fact. See FACT.

evidentiary hearing. See HEARING.

evince, *vb.* To show, indicate, or reveal <in abstaining from the vote, Hariden evinced misgivings about the nomination>.

evocation (ev-ə-**kay**-shən). *French law.* The act of withdrawing a case from an inferior court and bringing it before a superior court.

evolution statute. *Hist.* Legislation that forbids the teaching of the theory of evolution in schools. • Such statutes were held unconstitutional as violative of the Establishment Clause in *Epperson v. Arkansas*, 393 U.S. 97, 89 S.Ct. 266 (1968).

ewage (**yoo**-ij), *n.* [Law French] *Hist.* A toll paid for water passage.

ex. **1.** Former <ex-wife>. **2.** Without <ex rights>. **3.** From <*ex cathedra*>. **4.** (*usu. cap.*) *abbr.* Exhibit <Ex. 4>. **5.** *abbr.* Example <this is but one ex. of several that might be cited>. **6.** *abbr.* EXCHEQUER.

ex abundanti (eks ab-ən-**dan**-tɪ). [Latin "out of abundance"] *Archaic.* Abundantly; superfluously.

ex abundanti cautela (eks ab-ən-**dan**-tɪ kaw-**tee**-lə). [Latin] *Archaic.* Out of abundant caution; to be on the safe side.

exacta diligentia (eg-**zak**-tə dil-ə-**jen**-shee-ə). [Latin] *Roman law.* Great care.

exaction, *n.* **1.** The act of demanding more money than is due; extortion. **2.** A fee, reward, or other compensation arbitrarily or wrongfully demanded. — **exact,** *vb.*

exactor. **1.** *Civil law.* A tax collector; a gatherer or receiver of money. **2.** *Hist.* A collector of public funds; a tax collector.

ex adverso (eks ad-**vər**-soh). [Latin] On the other side. • This term is sometimes applied to opposing counsel.

ex aequitate (eks ee-kwə-**tay**-tee). [Latin] According to equity; in equity.

ex aequo et bono (eks **ee**-kwoh et **boh**-noh). [Latin] According to what is equitable and good. • A decision-maker (esp. in international law) who is authorized to decide *ex aequo et bono* is not bound by legal rules and may instead follow equitable principles.

ex altera parte (eks **al**-tər-ə [*or* **awl**-] **pahr**-tee). [Latin] Of the other part.

examen (eg-**zay**-mən), *n.* [Law Latin] A trial; investigation.

examen computi (eg-**zay**-mən kəm-**pyoo**-tɪ). [Latin] The balance of an account.

examination. **1.** The questioning of a witness under oath. See DIRECT EXAMINATION; CROSS-EXAMINATION. **2.** *Bankruptcy.* The questioning of a bankrupt, esp. at the first meeting of creditors, concerning such matters as the bankrupt's debts and assets. **3.** *Patents.* An inquiry made at the Patent and Trademark Office, upon application for a patent, into the alleged invention's novelty and utility, and whether it interferes with any other patented invention. **4.** PRELIMINARY HEARING. **5.** A test, such as a bar examination.

examination-in-chief. See DIRECT EXAMINATION.

examination on the voir dire. See VOIR DIRE.

examination *pro interesse suo* (**proh** in-tər-**es**-ee **s**[**y**]**oo**-oh). [Latin "according to his interest"] A judicial inquiry into the merits of a person's claim to sequestered property.

"In practice, an examination pro interesse suo is an inquiry described as follows: When any person claims to be entitled to an estate or other property sequestered, whether by mortgage or judgment, lease or otherwise, or has a title paramount to the sequestration, he should apply to the court to direct an inquiry whether the applicant has any and what interest in the property sequestered." 79A C.J.S. *Sequestration* § 31, at 589 (1995).

examined copy. See COPY.

examiner. 1. One authorized to conduct an examination; esp., a person appointed by the court to administer an oath and take testimony. See MASTER (2). **2.** A patent officer responsible for determining the patentability of an invention submitted to the patent office. **3.** MEDICAL EXAMINER.

examining authority. See AUTHORITY (3).

examining board. An appointed group of public officials responsible for conducting the tests required by those applying for occupational and professional licenses. — Also termed *board of examiners*.

examining court. See COURT.

examining trial. See PRELIMINARY HEARING.

exannual roll (eks-**an**-yoo-əl). *Hist.* In England, a roll into which illeviable fines and desperate debts were transcribed and that was annually read to the sheriff upon his accounting to see what might be gotten.

ex ante (eks **an**-tee), *adj.* & *adv.* [Latin "from before"] Based on assumption and prediction; subjective; prospective <from an *ex ante* perspective>. Cf. EX POST.

ex arbitrio judicis (eks ahr-**bi**-tree-oh **joo**-di-sis). [Latin] *Civil law.* At, from, or upon the discretion of the judge.

ex assensu curiae (eks ə-**sen**-s[y]oo **kyoor**-ee-ee *or* -I). [Latin] By or with the consent of the court.

ex assensu patris (eks ə-**sen**-s[y]oo **pay**-tris). [Latin "by or with the consent of the father"] *Hist.* A species of dower *ad ostium ecclesiae*, under which a husband, by his father's express consent, would endow his wife with a parcel of the father's lands. • This type of dower was abolished in England by the Dower Act (1833). St. 3 & 4 Will. 4, ch. 105, § 13.

ex assensu suo (eks ə-**sen**-s[y]oo **s[y]oo**-oh). [Latin "with his assent"] Formal words in a default judgment for damages.

ex bonis (eks **boh**-nis). [Latin] *Civil law.* Of or relating to goods or property.

excambiator (eks-kam-bee-**ay**-tər), *n.* [Latin] *Hist.* An exchanger of lands; a broker.

excambium (eks-**kam**-bee-əm), *n.* [Latin] **1.** An exchange; a place where merchants meet to transact their business. — Also termed (in Scots law) *excambion*. **2.** An equivalent in recompense; a recompense in lieu of dower *ad ostium ecclesiae*.

ex capite (eks **kap**-i-tee). [Latin] On the ground of; by reason of.

ex cathedra (eks kə-**thee**-drə *or* **kath**-ə-drə), *adv.* & *adj.* [Latin "from the chair"] By virtue of one's high office or position; with authority <ex cathedra pronouncements>.

ex causa (eks **kaw**-zə). [Latin] By title.

excellency. (*usu. cap.*) A title of honor given to certain high officials or dignitaries, such as governors, ambassadors, and Roman Catholic bishops or archbishops.

exceptio (ek-**sep**-shee-oh), *n.* [Latin] *Hist.* **1.** An exception, plea, or objection. **2.** *Roman & civil law.* A defendant's plea admitting the claim in principle, but alleging facts or legal provisions that negate it in this instance. **3.** A defense to a claim that is justly brought but that unjustly accuses the particular defendant named.

exceptio dilatoria (dil-ə-**tor**-ee-ə). A dilatory exception; an exception that defeated the action for a time and creates a delay, such as an agreement not to sue within a certain time.

exceptio doli mali (**doh**-lI **mal**-I). An exception or plea of fraud.

exceptio dominii (də-**min**-ee-I). A claim of ownership by the defendant in an action to recover property not in the plaintiff's possession.

exceptio dotis cautae non numeratae (**doh**-tis **kaw**-tee non n[y]oo-mə-**ray**-tee). A defense to an action for the restitution of dowry, asserting that, although promised, dowry was never paid.

exceptio in factum (in **fak**-təm). An exception on the fact; an exception or plea founded on the peculiar circumstances of a case.

exceptio in personam (in pər-**soh**-nəm). A plea or defense of a personal nature that only the person to whom it is granted by law may assert.

exceptio in rem (in **rem**). A plea or defense that is not of a personal nature but is connected with the legal circumstances on which the suit is founded, and that may therefore be alleged by any party in interest, such as an heir or surety of the proper or original debtor.

exceptio jurisjurandi (**joor**-is-juu-**ran**-dI). An exception of oath; an exception or plea that the matter had been sworn to. • This kind of exception was allowed if a debtor, at a creditor's instance, had sworn that nothing was due the creditor, but the creditor sued anyway.

exceptio metus (**met**-əs). An exception or plea of fear or compulsion.

exceptio non adimpleti contractus (non ad-im-**plee**-tI kən-**trak**-təs). An exception in a contract action involving mutual duties or obligations, to the effect that the plaintiff may not sue if the plaintiff's own obligations have not been performed.

exceptio non solutae pecuniae (non sə-**loo**-tee pi-**kyoo**-nee-ee). A plea that the debt at issue in the suit was not discharged by payment (as the adverse party alleged), notwithstanding the existence of a receipt or acquittance reflecting payment.

exceptio pacti conventi (**pak**-tI-kən-**ven**-tI). An exception of compact; an exception or plea that the plaintiff had agreed not to sue.

exceptio pecuniae non numeratae (pi-**kyoo**-nee-ee non n[y]oo-mə-**ray**-tee). An exception or plea of money not paid; a defense by a party who was sued on a promise to repay money that was never received.

exceptio peremptoria (pər-emp-**tor**-ee-ə). A peremptory exception that forever destroyed the subject matter or ground of the action, such as the *exceptio doli mali* and the *exceptio metus*. — Also termed *exceptio perpetua*.

exceptio plurium concubentium (**ploor**-ee-əm kon-kyoo-**ben**-shee-əm). The plea or defense in a paternity action that the plaintiff had several lovers.

exceptio rei judicatae (**ree**-I joo-də-**kay**-tee). An exception or plea of matter adjudged; a plea that the subject matter of the action had been determined in a previous action.

exceptio rei venditae et traditae (**ree**-I **ven**-də-tee et **trad**-ə-tee). An exception or plea of the sale and delivery [of a thing]. • This exception presumes a valid sale but, because no one can transfer a right greater than what is possessed, no valid transfer of property occurred, yet the real owner is nonetheless estopped from contesting the sale.

exceptio senatusconsulti Macedoniani (sə-**nay**-təs-kən-**səl**-tI mas-ə-doh-nee-**ay**-nI). A defense to an action for the recovery of money loaned, on the ground that the loan was made to a minor or a person under another person's paternal power. • This defense is so named from the decree of the senate that forbade the recovery of such loans.

exceptio senatusconsulti Velleiani (sə-**nay**-təs-kən-**səl**-tI vel-ee-**ay**-nI). A defense to an action on a contract of suretyship, on the ground that the surety was a woman and thus incapable of becoming bound for another. • This defense is so named from the decree of the senate forbidding such sureties.

exceptio temporis (**tem**-pə-ris). An exception or plea that the time prescribed by law for bringing a particular action has expired.

exception, *n.* **1.** A formal objection to a court's ruling by a party who wants to preserve the objection for appeal <the prosecutor stated her exception to the court's ruling disallowing the witness's testimony>. • In federal courts and most state courts, the term *exception* has been superseded by *objection*.

> The following quotation reflects former practice: "The exception must be distinguished from the objection. Many counsel are heard carelessly saying 'I except' when the thing they are doing is 'I object.' The exception serves an entirely distinct purpose from the objection, — a double purpose, in fact. It warns the judge and the other party that the excepter is not satisfied with the ruling and takes issue with a view to appeal; and it sums up and preserves the precise terms of the ruling. The proponent of the evidence is the excepter if the ruling excludes the evidence; but if it admits the evidence, the opponent of the evidence is the excepter. Thus the excepter and the objector are not necessarily the same parties." John H. Wigmore, *A Students' Textbook of the Law of Evidence* 421 (1935).

dilatory exception (**dil**-ə-tor-ee). An exception intended to delay but not dismiss an action.

general exception. **1.** An objection pointing out a substantive defect in an opponent's pleading, such as the insufficiency of the claim or the court's lack of subject-matter jurisdiction; an objection to a pleading for want of substance. — Also termed *general demurrer*. Cf. SPECIAL EXCEPTION (1). **2.** An objection in which the excepting party does not specify the grounds of the objection.

peremptory exception. A defensive pleading asserting that no legal remedy exists for the plaintiff's alleged injury, that res judicata or prescription bars the claim, or that an indispensable party has not been included in the litigation.

special exception. See SPECIAL EXCEPTION.

2. Something that is excluded from a rule's operation <employers with fewer than five employees are an exception to the rule>.

statutory exception. A provision in a statute exempting certain persons or conduct from the statute's operation.

3. The retention of an existing right or interest, by and for the grantor, in real property being granted to another. Cf. RESERVATION (1). — **except,** *vb.*

exceptis excipiendis (ek-**sep**-tis ek-sip-ee-**en**-dis). [Latin] With all necessary exceptions.

exceptor, *n.* One who takes exception; an objector. — Also spelled *excepter*.

excerpta (ek-**sərp**-tə), *n. pl.* [Latin] Extracts.

ex certa scientia (eks **sər**-tə sI-**en**-shee-ə). [Latin] Of certain or sure knowledge. • This phrase was anciently used in patents, and imported full knowledge of the subject matter on the part of the sovereign.

excès de pouvoir (ek-**say** də poo-**vwahr**). [French "excess of power"] **1.** *Int'l law.* Beyond the powers (of a tribunal). **2.** *Administrative law.* Beyond the powers of an official.

excess benefit plan. See EMPLOYEE BENEFIT PLAN.

excess clause. An insurance-policy provision — usu. contained in the "other insurance" section of the policy — that limits the insurer's liability to the amount exceeding other available coverage. • This clause essentially requires other insurers to pay first. Cf. ESCAPE CLAUSE; PRO RATA CLAUSE.

excess condemnation. See CONDEMNATION.

excess damages. See DAMAGES.

excess insurance. See INSURANCE.

excessive assessment. See ASSESSMENT.

excessive bail. See BAIL (1).

excessive damages. See DAMAGES.

excessive drunkenness. See DRUNKENNESS.

excessive fine. See FINE (5).

Excessive Fines Clause. The clause of the Eighth Amendment to the U.S. Constitution prohibiting the imposition of excessive fines.

excessive force. See FORCE.

excessive punishment. See PUNISHMENT.

excessive verdict. See VERDICT.

excess judgment. See JUDGMENT.

excess jurisdiction. See EXCESS OF JURISDICTION (1).

excess-liability damages. See *excess damages* under DAMAGES.

excess limits. Insurance coverage against losses in excess of a specified limit.

excess-lines insurance. See *surplus-lines insurance* under INSURANCE.

excess of jurisdiction. 1. A court's acting beyond the limits of its power, usu. in one of three ways: (1) when the court has no power to deal with the kind of matter at issue, (2) when the court has no power to deal with the particular person concerned, or (3) when the judgment or order issued is of a kind that the court has no power to issue. **2.** A court's departure from recognized and established requirements of law, despite apparent adherence to procedural form, the effect of which is a deprivation of one's constitutional right. — Also termed *excess jurisdiction*.

excess of privilege. 1. An excessive publication of a privileged statement — that is, beyond the limits of the privilege. **2.** The improper and malicious use of the privilege to publish a statement.

excess policy. See *excess insurance* under INSURANCE.

excess-profits tax. See TAX.

excess reinsurance. See REINSURANCE.

excess theory. *Insurance.* The principle that a tortfeasor will be considered underinsured if the injured party's damages exceed the tortfeasor's liability-insurance coverage. • This principle allows an injured party to invoke underinsured-motorist coverage. Cf. GAP THEORY.

excess water. See WATER.

exchange, *n.* **1.** The act of transferring interests, each in consideration for the other. **2.** The payment of a debt using a bill of exchange or credit rather than money. **3.** An organization that brings together buyers and sellers of securities, commodities, and the like to promote uniformity in the customs and usages of merchants, to facilitate the speedy adjustment of business disputes, to gather and disseminate valuable commercial and economic information, and to secure to its members the benefits of cooperation in the furtherance of their legitimate pursuits. • The best-known exchanges are stock, produce, livestock, cotton, and grain exchanges. **4.** The building or hall where members of an exchange meet every business day to buy and sell for themselves, or as brokers for their customers, for present and future delivery. See SECURITIES EXCHANGE. — **exchange,** *vb.*

Exchange Act. See SECURITIES EXCHANGE ACT OF 1934.

exchange broker. One who negotiates money or merchandise transactions for others.

exchange rate. The ratio for converting one country's money into another country's money. See FOREIGN EXCHANGE.

exchange ratio. The number of shares that an acquiring company must give for each share of an acquired company.

Exchequer (eks-**chek**-ər *or* **eks**-chek-ər). **1.** *English law.* The government department charged with collecting the national revenue; the treasury department. • The name is said to have derived from the checkered cloth, resembling a chessboard, that anciently covered the table on which certain of the king's accounts were tallied, the sums being marked and scored with counters. **2.** COURT OF EXCHEQUER. — Abbr. Ex.

Exchequer bill. A bill of credit issued in England by the authority of Parliament; an instrument issued at the Exchequer, usu. under the authority of an act of Parliament passed for that specific purpose, containing an engagement on the part of the government to repay, with interest, the principal sums advanced.

Exchequer Chamber. An English court of intermediate appeal from the common-law courts, namely, the Court of King's Bench, the Court of Common Pleas, and the Court of Exchequer. • It was established in 1822.

Exchequer Division. *Hist.* A division of the English high court of justice, to which the business of the Court of Exchequer was specially assigned by section 34 of the Judicature Act of 1873, and later merged into the Queen's Bench Division in 1881.

excise, *n.* A tax imposed on the manufacture, sale, or use of goods (such as a cigarette tax), or on an occupation or activity (such as a license tax or an attorney occupation fee). — Also termed *excise tax.* Cf. *income tax* and *property tax* under TAX.

excise lieu property tax. See TAX.

excise tax. See EXCISE.

excited utterance. A statement about a startling event made under the stress and excitement of the event. • An excited utterance may be admissible as a hearsay exception. Fed. R. Evid. 803(2). Cf. PRESENT SENSE IMPRESSION.

excludable, *adj.* (Of evidence) subject to exclusion <excludable hearsay>.

exclusion, *n.* **1.** *Tax.* An item of income excluded from gross income. — Also termed *income exclusion.*

> ***annual exclusion.*** The amount (such as $10,000) allowed as nontaxable gift income during the calendar year. • The purpose of the annual exclusion is both to serve as an estate-planning mechanism (so that gifts made during the donor's lifetime remain nontestamentary and nontaxable) and to eliminate the administrative inconvenience of taxing relatively small gifts. For an individual, the first $10,000 in gifts can be excluded; for married persons, the exclusion is $20,000 per donee for joint gifts, regardless of which spouse supplied the donated property. IRC (26 USCA) § 2503. — Also termed *annual gift-tax exclusion.*

2. *Evidence.* A trial judge's determination that an item offered as evidence may not be presented to the trier of fact (esp. the jury). **3.** *Insurance.* An insurance-policy provision that excepts certain events or conditions from coverage. — **exclude,** *vb.* — **exclusionary,** *adj.*

automobile exclusion. A provision in some commercial general liability policies, excluding coverage for damages arising from the use (including loading and unloading) of an automobile, aircraft, or other motor vehicle owned, operated, rented, or borrowed by the insured.

business-risk exclusion. An exclusion in some commercial general liability policies, excluding coverage for common risks of doing business, including harm to the insured's product or work, damages arising from a product recall, damages arising from the insured's failure to perform under a contract, or damages arising from a failure of the insured's product to perform as intended.

design-defect exclusion. A provision in some umbrella policies and some older commercial general liability policies, excluding coverage for bodily injury arising from the failure of the insured's product to perform its intended function because of a defect or deficiency in its design, formula, specifications, instructions, or advertising materials.

employee-liability exclusion. A provision in some commercial general liability policies, excluding coverage for injury to an employee (or a member of the employee's family), arising from and in the course of employment with the insured. • This exclusion is generally intended to exclude from coverage all injuries covered by the workers'-compensation laws.

employment-related-practices exclusion. A provision in some commercial general liability policies, excluding coverage for damages arising from an insured's employment practices, including any policy, action, or omission — such as coercion, demotion, evaluation, reassignment, discipline, defamation, harassment, humiliation, or discrimination — that is directed at the person injured.

expected/intended exclusion. A provision in some commercial general liability policies, excluding coverage for property damage or bodily injury that is expected or intended by the insured, except any harm arising from the use of reasonable force to protect a person or property. • This exclusion is sometimes referred to as "exclusion a" because it is the first exclusion listed on most policies. — Also termed *exclusion a*; *intentional-injury exclusion.*

failure-to-perform exclusion. A provision in some commercial general liability policies, excluding coverage for (1) the loss of use of undamaged property resulting from the insured's delay or failure in performing an obligation, or (2) a design defect or failure in the insured's product. — Also termed *loss-of-use exclusion.*

knowledge-of-falsity exclusion. A provision in some commercial general liability policies, excluding coverage for damages arising from an oral or written communication made by the insured with knowledge that it is false.

named-insured exclusion. An exclusion limiting liability-insurance coverage to a named insured whose injuries were caused by another named insured under the same insurance policy.

owned-property exclusion. A provision in some commercial general liability policies, excluding coverage for damage to any of the following: (1) property owned, rented, occupied, sold, given away, or abandoned by the insured, (2) personal property in the care, custody, or control of the insured, or (3) property located where the insured and its employees work.

own-product exclusion. A provision in some commercial general liability policies, excluding coverage for property damage to a product that is manufactured, sold, handled, distributed, or disposed of by the insured.

own-work exclusion. A provision in some commercial general liability policies, excluding coverage for damage to the work or services performed by the insured.

pollution exclusion. A provision in some commercial general liability policies, excluding coverage for bodily injury or property damages arising from the discharge, dispersal, release, or escape of chemicals, waste, acid, and other pollutants. • Pollution-exclusion clauses may take one of two forms: (1) sudden and accidental, and (2) absolute. The sudden-and-accidental clause, usu. limited to polices issued before 1985, contains an exception under which the damages are covered (i.e., exempted from the exclusion) if the discharge or other release was sudden and accidental. The absolute pollution exclusion, in most policies issued since 1985, does not contain this exception.

sistership exclusion. A provision in some commercial general liability policies, excluding coverage for damages arising from the withdrawal, inspection, repair, replacement, or loss of use of the insured's product or work, to the extent that the product or work is withdrawn or recalled from the market because of a known or suspected defect or deficiency. — Also termed *recall exclusion.*

exclusion a. See *expected/intended exclusion* under EXCLUSION (3).

exclusionary hearing. See HEARING.

exclusionary rule. 1. *Evidence.* Any rule that excludes or suppresses evidence that does not satisfy a minimum standard of probative value <despite many exceptions, hearsay has long been inadmissible under an exclusionary rule>. **2.** *Criminal procedure.* A rule that excludes or suppresses evidence obtained in violation of an accused person's constitutional rights <in accordance with the exclusionary rule, the court did not admit the drugs into evidence because they had been obtained during a warrantless search of the defendant's home>. See FRUIT-OF-THE-POISONOUS-TREE DOCTRINE; GOOD-FAITH EXCEPTION.

> "The deterrence of unreasonable searches and seizures is a major purpose of the exclusionary rule.... But the rule serves other purposes as well. There is, for example, ... 'the imperative of judicial integrity,' namely, that the courts do not become 'accomplices in willful disobedience of a Constitution they are sworn to uphold.' ... A third purpose of the exclusionary rule ... is that of 'assuring the people — all potential victims of unlawful government conduct — that the government would not profit from its lawless behavior, thus minimizing the risk of seriously undermining popular trust in the government.' " Wayne R. LaFave & Jerold H. Israel, *Criminal Procedure* § 3.1, at 107 (2d ed. 1992) (quoting *Elkins v. United States*, 364 U.S. 206, 80 S.Ct. 1437 (1960); *United States v. Calandra*, 414 U.S. 338, 94 S.Ct. 613 (1974) (dissent)).

> "In the simplest of exclusionary rule cases, the challenged evidence is quite clearly 'direct' or 'primary' in its relationship to the prior arrest, search, interrogation, lineup or other identification procedure. Such is the case when that evidence is an identification occurring at the confrontation between suspect and victim or witness, a confession or admission made in response to questioning, or physical evidence obtained by search or arrest. Not infrequently, however, challenged evidence is 'secondary' or 'derivative' in character. This occurs when, for example, a confession is obtained after an illegal arrest, physical evidence is located after an illegally obtained confession, or an in-court identification is made following an illegally conducted pretrial identification. In these situations, it is necessary to determine whether the derivative evidence is 'tainted' by the prior constitutional or other violation." Wayne R. LaFave & Jerold H. Israel, *Criminal Procedure* § 9.3, at 471 (2d ed. 1992).

exclusionary zoning. See ZONING.

exclusive agency. See AGENCY (1).

exclusive-agency listing. See LISTING (1).

exclusive authorization-to-sell listing. See *exclusive-agency listing* under LISTING (1).

exclusive contract. See EXCLUSIVE-DEALING ARRANGEMENT.

exclusive control. Under the doctrine of res ipsa loquitur, a defendant's sole management of and responsibility for the instrumentality causing harm. • Exclusive control is a prerequisite to the doctrine's applicability. See RES IPSA LOQUITUR.

exclusive-dealing arrangement. An agreement requiring a buyer to purchase all needed goods from one seller. — Also termed *exclusive dealing.* See *requirements contract* under CONTRACT.

exclusive easement. See EASEMENT.

exclusive economic zone. *Int'l law.* An area just beyond the territorial sea, extending up to 200 nautical miles from the baseline of the territorial sea, in which the coastal country enjoys special authority for economic purposes.

exclusive evidence. See EVIDENCE.

exclusive franchise. See *exclusive agency* under AGENCY (1).

exclusive jurisdiction. See JURISDICTION.

exclusive license. See LICENSE.

exclusive listing. See LISTING (1).

exclusive ownership. See FEE SIMPLE.

exclusive possession. See POSSESSION.

exclusive sale. See SALE.

exclusive use. See USE (1).

ex colore (eks kə-**lor**-ee). [Latin] By color; under color of; under pretense, show, or protection of.

ex comitate (eks kom-ə-**tay**-tee). [Latin] Out of comity or courtesy.

excommengement (eks-kə-**menj**-mənt), *n.* See EXCOMMUNICATION.

ex commodato (eks kom-ə-**day**-toh). [Latin "out of loan"] *Hist.* (Of a right of action) arising out of a loan.

excommunicant (eks-kə-**myoo**-ni-kənt), *n. Eccles. law.* **1.** An excommunicated person. **2.** *Rare.* An excommunicator.

excommunication, *n. Eccles. law.* A sentence of censure pronounced by a spiritual court for an offense falling under ecclesiastical cognizance; expulsion from religious society or community. • In England, an excommunicated person was formerly subject to various civil disabilities, such as an inability to be a juror, to be a witness in any court, or to sue to recover lands or money due. These penalties were abolished by the Ecclesiastical Courts Act (1813). St. 53 Geo. 3, ch. 127. — **excommunicate,** *vb.*

excommunicato capiendo (eks-kə-myoo-ni-**kay**-toh kap-ee-**en**-doh). [Latin] *Hist. Eccles. law.* A writ that, being founded on a bishop's certificate of excommunication, required the sheriff to arrest and imprison the defendant. • The writ issued out of chancery and was returnable to the King's Bench. Cf. DE CONTUMACE CAPIENDO.

excommunicator. A person who excommunicates.

excommunicato recapiendo (eks-kə-myoo-ni-**kay**-toh ri-kap-ee-**en**-doh). [Latin] *Hist. Eccles. law.* A writ commanding that an excommunicant — who had been committed to prison for obstinacy but who was unlawfully freed before agreeing to obey the church's authority — should be found, retaken, and imprisoned again.

ex comparatione scriptorum (eks kom-pə-ray-shee-**oh**-nee skrip-**tor**-əm). [Latin] By a comparison of writings or handwritings. • This term was formerly used in the law of evidence.

ex concessis (eks kən-**ses**-is). [Latin] From the premises granted; according to what has already been allowed.

ex consulto (eks kən-**səl**-toh). [Latin] With consultation or deliberation.

ex continenti (eks kon-tə-**nen**-tI). [Latin] *Civil law.* Immediately; without any interval or delay.

ex contractu (eks kən-**trak**-t[y]oo). [Latin "from a contract"] Arising from a contract <action *ex contractu*>. Cf. EX DELICTO.

exculpate (**ek**-skəl-payt *or* ek-**skəl**-payt), *vb.* To free from blame or accusation. — **exculpation** (ek-skəl-**pay**-shən), *n.* — **exculpatory** (ek-**skəl**-pə-tor-ee), *adj.* Cf. EXONERATE (1).

exculpatory clause. A contractual provision relieving a party from any liability resulting from a negligent or wrongful act. See EXEMPTION CLAUSE.

exculpatory evidence. See EVIDENCE.

exculpatory-no doctrine. *Criminal law.* The principle that a person cannot be charged with making a false statement for falsely denying guilt in response to an investigator's question. • This principle is based on the Fifth Amendment's privilege against self-incrimination.

ex curia (eks **kyoor**-ee-ə). [Latin] Out of court; away from the court.

excusable, *adj.* (Of an illegal act or omission) not punishable under the specific circumstances <excusable neglect>.

excusable assault. See ASSAULT.

excusable homicide. See HOMICIDE.

excusable neglect. See NEGLECT.

excusatio (ek-skyoo-**zay**-shee-oh), *n.* [Latin] *Roman & civil law.* An excuse or reason that exempts someone from some duty or obligation.

excusator (ek-skyoo-**zay**-tər), *n.* **1.** *Hist.* An excuser. **2.** In old German law, a defendant; one who wholly denies the plaintiff's claim.

excuse (eks-**kyoos**), *n.* **1.** A reason that justifies an act or omission or that relieves a person of a duty. **2.** *Criminal law.* A defense that arises because the defendant is not blameworthy for having acted in a way that would otherwise be criminal. • The following defenses are the traditional excuses: duress, entrapment, infancy, insanity, and involuntary intoxication. — Also termed *legal excuse.* Cf. JUSTIFICATION (2). — **excuse** (ek-**skyooz**), *vb.* — **excusatory** (ek-**skyooz**-ə-tor-ee), *adj.*

excuss (ek-**skəs**), *vb.* To seize and detain by law.

excussio (ek-**skə**-s[h]ee-oh), *n.* [Latin] *Roman & civil law.* A diligent prosecution of a remedy against a debtor; the exhausting of a remedy against a principal debtor before resorting to a surety.

ex-date. See EX-DIVIDEND DATE.

ex debito justitiae (eks **deb**-i-toh jəs-**tish**-ee-ee). [Latin] From or as a debt of justice; in accordance with the requirement of justice; of right; as a matter of right.

ex defectu sanguinis (eks di-**fek**-t[y]oo **sang**-gwə-nis). [Latin] From failure of blood; for want of issue.

ex delicto (eks də-**lik**-toh). [Latin "from a tort"] Arising from a tort <action *ex delicto*>. Cf. IN DELICTO; EX CONTRACTU.

ex delicto trust. See TRUST.

ex demissione (eks də-mish-ee-**oh**-nee). [Latin "upon the demise"] *Hist.* A phrase forming part of the title of the old action of ejectment. — Abbr. *ex dem.*

ex directo (eks di-**rek**-toh). [Latin] Directly; immediately.

ex distribution. Without distribution. • Shares are traded ex distribution when they no longer carry the right to receive a distribution to be made to holders. — Abbr. X; XDIS.

ex dividend. Without dividend. • Shares are traded ex dividend when the seller, not the purchaser, is entitled to the next dividend payment because it will be made before the stock transfer is completed. The first day on which shares are traded ex dividend, the stock price will drop by an amount usu. approximating the amount of the dividend. — Abbr. XD.; X. Cf. CUM DIVIDEND.

ex-dividend date. The date on or after which the buyer of a security does not acquire the right to receive a recently declared dividend. — Also termed *ex-date*. Cf. DIVIDEND DATE.

ex dolo malo (eks **doh**-loh **mal**-oh). [Latin] Out of fraud; out of deceitful or tortious conduct.

exeat (**ek**-see-ət), *n.* **1.** Generally, permission to go outside (a place). **2.** Permission that a bishop grants to a priest to go out of his diocese. Cf. NE EXEAT REPUBLICA.

execute, *vb.* **1.** To perform or complete (a contract or duty) <once the contract was fully executed, the parties owed no further contractual duties to each other>. **2.** To change (as a legal interest) from one form to another <the shifting use was executed into a valid legal estate>. **3.** To make (a legal document) valid by signing; to bring (a legal document) into its final, legally enforceable form <each party executed the contract without a signature witness>. **4.** To put to death, esp. by legal sentence <Johnson was executed shortly after midnight>. **5.** To enforce and collect on (a money judgment) <Williams asked the sheriff to execute on the judgment>.

executed, *adj.* **1.** (Of a document) that has been signed <an executed will>. **2.** That has been done, given, or performed <executed consideration>.

> "[T]he term 'executed' is a slippery word. Its use is to be avoided except when accompanied by explanation. *Executed* consideration is also used to mean *past* consideration as opposed to *present* or *future*. A contract is frequently said to be *executed* when the document has been signed, or has been signed, sealed, and delivered. Further, by executed contract is frequently meant one that has been fully performed by both parties." William R. Anson, *Principles of the Law of Contract* 26 n.* (Arthur L. Corbin ed., 3d Am. ed. 1919).

executed consideration. See CONSIDERATION.

executed contract. See CONTRACT.

executed covenant. See COVENANT (1).

executed fine. See FINE (1).

executed note. See NOTE (1).

executed remainder. See *vested remainder* under REMAINDER.

executed trust. See TRUST.

executed use. See USE (4).

executio (ek-sə-**kyoo**-shee-oh), *n.* [Latin] **1.** The performance or completion of a thing; the act of following through on a commitment. **2.** The doing of something thoroughly. **3.** Management or administration. **4.** *Hist.* Execution; the final process in an action.

executio bonorum (bə-**nor**-əm). [Latin] *Hist.* The management or administration of goods.

execution, *n.* **1.** The act of carrying out or putting into effect (as a court order) <execution of the court's decree>. **2.** Validation of a written instrument, such as a contract or will, by fulfilling the necessary legal requirements <delivery of the goods completed the contract's execution>. **3.** Judicial enforcement of a money judgment, usu. by seizing and selling the judgment debtor's property <even if the plaintiff receives a judgment against the foreign debtor, execution is unlikely>. **4.** A court order directing a sheriff or other officer to enforce a judgment, usu. by seizing and selling the judgment debtor's property <the court issued the execution authorizing seizure of the car>. — Also termed *writ of execution*; *judgment execution*; *general execution*.

> "A writ of execution is an authorization to an executive officer, issued from a court in which a final judgment has been rendered, for the purpose of carrying such judgment into force and effect. It is founded upon the judgment, must generally be conformed to it in every respect, and the plaintiff is always entitled to it to obtain a satisfaction of his claim, unless his right has been suspended by proceedings in the nature of an appeal or by his own agreement." Benjamin J. Shipman, *Handbook of Common-Law Pleading* § 26, at 50 (Henry Winthrop Ballantine ed., 3d ed. 1923).

alias execution. A second execution issued to enforce a judgment not fully satisfied by the original writ. Cf. *alias writ* under WRIT.

body execution. A court order requiring an officer to take a named person into custody, usu. to bring the person before the court to pay a debt; CAPIAS.

close-jail execution. A body execution stating that the person to be arrested should be confined in jail without the privilege of movement about the jailyard.

dormant execution. An execution authorizing an officer to seize and hold property rather than sell it, until further notice.

junior execution. An execution that is subordinate to another execution issued from an earlier judgment against the same debtor.

malicious execution. An abuse of process by which a person, maliciously and without reasonable cause, issues an execution against the property of a judgment debtor.

special execution. An execution authorizing a judgment to be satisfied from specified property.

speedy execution. An execution issuing quickly (esp. by judges at nisi prius) after a trial.

5. *Criminal law.* The carrying out of a death sentence <the Supreme Court stayed the execution>. — **execute,** *vb.*

execution clause. The part of a deed containing the date, seal (if required), and signatures of the grantor, grantor's spouse, and witnesses.

execution creditor. See CREDITOR.

executione facienda in withernamium (ek-sə-kyoo-shee-**oh**-nee fay-shee-**en**-də in with-ər-**nay**-mee-əm). [Latin] *Hist.* A writ that lay for taking cattle of a person who had taken someone else's cattle out of the county so that the sheriff could not replevy them.

executione judicii (ek-sə-kyoo-shee-**oh**-nee joo-**dish**-ee-I). [Latin] *Hist.* A writ directed to a judge of an inferior court to issue execution upon a judgment in that court, or to return some reasonable cause why the judge has delayed execution.

executioner. A person who puts another person to death to carry out a death sentence; a person who carries out capital punishment on the state's behalf.

execution lien. See LIEN.

exécution parée (eg-zay-koo-**syawn** pa-**ray**). [French] *French law.* A right founded on an act approved and verified before a notary, by which a creditor may immediately — without citation or summons — seize and cause to be sold the debtor's property and keep the proceeds of the sale (to the extent of the indebtedness).

execution-proof. See JUDGMENT-PROOF.

execution sale. See SALE.

executive, *n.* **1.** The branch of government responsible for effecting and enforcing laws; the person or persons who constitute this branch. • The executive branch is sometimes said to be the residue of all government after subtracting the judicial and legislative branches. Cf. LEGISLATURE; JUDICIARY (1).

chief executive. The head of the executive branch of a government, such as the President of the United States.

2. A corporate officer at the upper levels of management. — **executive,** *adj.*

executive administration. Collectively, high public officials who administer the chief departments of the government.

executive agency. An executive-branch department whose activities are subject to statute and whose contracts are subject to judicial review. • One example is the Army and Air Force Exchange Service.

executive agreement. *Int'l law.* An international agreement entered into by the President, without the need for approval by the Senate, and usu. involving routine diplomatic matters. Cf. TREATY.

executive branch. The branch of government charged with administering and carrying out the law; EXECUTIVE (1). Cf. JUDICIAL BRANCH; LEGISLATIVE BRANCH.

executive clemency. See CLEMENCY.

executive committee. The group of principal officers and directors who directly manage business operations between meetings of the board of directors.

executive department. See EXECUTIVE (1).

executive employee. An employee whose duties include some form of managerial authority and active participation in the control, supervision, and management of the business. — Often shortened to *executive*.

executive immunity. See IMMUNITY (1).

executive officer. See EXECUTIVE.

executive order. An order issued by or on behalf of the President, usu. intended to direct or instruct the actions of executive agencies or government officials, or to set policies for the executive branch to follow. — Abbr. ex. ord.

executive pardon. See PARDON.

executive power. *Constitutional law.* The power to see that the laws are duly executed and enforced. • Under federal law, this power is vested in the President; in the states, it is vested in the governors. The President's enumerated powers are found in the U.S. Constitution, art. II, § 2; governors' executive powers are provided for in state constitutions. The other two great powers of government are the legislative power and the judicial power.

executive privilege. See PRIVILEGE (3).

executive session. A session of a board or governmental body that is closed to the public and that only invited persons may attend.

> "Virtually all open meeting statutes expressly authorize the use of executive sessions, typically specifying the particular circumstances in which executive sessions are permitted. When the specific circumstances are specified, generally no other exceptions are permitted .... Use of the executive session to discuss matters not properly hidden from the public is a clear violation of the open meeting law. Many states expressly or implicitly forbid use of the executive session as a subterfuge to defeat the purposes of the open meeting law." Ann Taylor Schwing, *Open Meeting Laws* § 7.1 (2d ed. 1999).

executor, *n.* **1.** (**ek**-sə-kyoo-tər) One who performs or carries out some act. **2.** (eg-**zek**-yə-tər) A person named by a testator to carry out the provisions in the testator's will. Cf. ADMINISTRATOR (1).

acting executor. One who assumes the role of executor — usu. temporarily — but is not the legally appointed executor or the executor-in-fact.

coexecutor. See *joint executor*.

executor ab episcopo constitutus (ab ə-**pis**-kə-poh kon-sti-**t**[**y**]**oo**-təs). [Law Latin] *Eccles. law.* An executor appointed by a bishop; an administrator to an intestate. — Also termed *executor dativus*.

executor a lege constitutus (ay [*or* ah] **lee**-jee kon-sti-**t**[**y**]**oo**-təs). [Law Latin] *Eccles. law.* One authorized by law to be an executor; the ordinary of the diocese.

executor a testatore constitutus (ay [*or* ah] tes-tə-**tor**-ee kon-sti-**t**[**y**]**oo**-təs). [Law Latin] *Eccles. law.* An executor appointed by a testator. — Also termed *executor testamentarius*.

executor dative. See DATIVE (1).

executor dativus. See *executor ab episcopo constitutus*.

executor de son tort (də sawn [*or* son] **tor**[**t**]). [Law French "executor of his own wrong"] A person who, without legal authority, takes on the responsibility to act as an executor or administrator of a decedent's property, usu. to the detriment of the estate's beneficiaries or creditors.

> "*Executor de son tort* — or, executor of his own wrong. Is he that takes upon him the office of an executor by intrusion, not being so constituted by the testator." *The Pocket Lawyer and Family Conveyancer* 98 (3d ed. 1833).

executor lucratus (loo-**kray**-təs). An executor who has assets of the testator, the latter having become liable by wrongfully interfering with another's property.

executor testamentarius. See *executor a testatore constitutus.*

executor to the tenor. *Eccles. law.* A person who is not named executor in the will but who performs duties similar to an executor.

general executor. An executor who has the power to administer a decedent's entire estate until its final settlement.

independent executor. An executor who, unlike an ordinary executor, can administer the estate with very little supervision by the probate court. • Only a few states — mostly in the West and Southwest — allow testators to designate independent executors. — Also termed *nonintervention executor.*

joint executor. One of two or more persons named in a will as executor of an estate. — Also termed *coexecutor.*

limited executor. An executor whose appointment is restricted in some way, such as time, place, or subject matter.

nonintervention executor. See *independent executor.*

special executor. An executor whose power is limited to a portion of the decedent's estate.

substituted executor. An executor appointed to act in the place of an executor who cannot or will not perform the required duties.

3. (eg-**zek**-yə-tər) *Patents.* One who represents a legally incapacitated inventor. — **executorial,** *adj.* — **executorship,** *n.*

executor fund. See FUND (1).

executor's bond. See BOND (2).

executor testamentarius. See *executor a testatore constitutus* under EXECUTOR.

executory (eg-**zek**-yə-tor-ee), *adj.* **1.** Taking full effect at a future time <executory judgment>. **2.** To be performed at a future time; yet to be completed <executory contract>.

executory accord. See ACCORD (2).

executory bequest. See BEQUEST.

executory consideration. See CONSIDERATION.

executory contract. See CONTRACT.

executory covenant. See COVENANT (1).

executory devise. See DEVISE.

executory interest. A future interest, held by a third person, that either cuts off another's interest or begins after the natural termination of a preceding estate. Cf. REMAINDER.

> "What is an executory interest? Here is a pretty good definition: *An executory interest is any future interest created in a person other than the transferor that is not a remainder.* Here are five classic examples of executory interest: (1) O transfers 'to A for life; then, one day after A's death, to the heirs of A.' The transfer creates a springing executory interest in those who will be A's heirs. (2) O transfers 'to A for 200 years if he shall so long live, then to the heirs of A.' This transfer also creates a springing executory interest in A's prospective heirs. (3) O transfers 'to A and his heirs five years from the date of this deed.' A owns a springing executory interest. (4) O, when B is fifteen, transfers 'to A for life; then no sooner than one day after A's death, to B and his heirs if B ever reaches 21.' B owns a springing executory interest. (5) O transfers 'to A and his heirs; but if A marries X, to B and his heirs.' B owns a shifting executory interest." Thomas F. Bergin & Paul G. Haskell, *Preface to Estates in Land and Future Interests* 80 (2d ed. 1984).

executory judgment. See JUDGMENT.

executory limitation. See LIMITATION.

executory process. *Civil law.* **1.** A process that can be resorted to either (1) when the right of a creditor arises from an act importing a confession of judgment, and that contains a privilege or mortgage in the creditor's favor, or (2) when the creditor demands the execution of a judgment that has been rendered by a different tribunal. **2.** An accelerated procedure, summary in nature, by which the holder of a mortgage or privilege evidenced by a confession of judgment seeks to effect an ex parte seizure and sale of the subject property.

executory remainder. See *contingent remainder* under REMAINDER.

executory sale. See SALE.

executory trust. See TRUST.

executory unilateral accord. An offer to enter a contract; OFFER (2).

executory use. See *springing use* under USE (4).

executory warranty. See WARRANTY (3).

executress. See EXECUTRIX.

executrix (eg-**zek**-yə-triks), *n. Archaic.* A female executor. — Abbr. exrx. — Also termed *executress*. Pl. **executrixes** (eg-**zek**-yə-trik-səz), **executrices** (eg-zek-yə-**trI**-seez). See EXECUTOR.

exedos (e-**he**-thohs), *n.* See EJIDOS.

exemplar (eg-**zem**-plər *or* -plahr), *n.* An ideal or typical example; a standard specimen <handwriting exemplars>.

exemplary, *adj.* **1.** Serving as an ideal example; commendable <exemplary behavior>. **2.** Serving as a warning or deterrent; admonitory <exemplary damages>.

exemplary damages. See *punitive damages* under DAMAGES.

exemplary substitution. See SUBSTITUTION (4).

exemplification, *n.* An official transcript of a public record, authenticated as a true copy for use as evidence. — **exemplify,** *vb.*

exemplificatione (eg-zem-plə-fə-**kay**-shee-oh-nee). [Latin] A writ granted for the exemplification or transcript of an original record.

exemplified copy. See *certified copy* under COPY.

exempli gratia (eg-**zem**-plI **gray**-shee-ə *or* ek-**sem**-plee **grah**-tee-ə). [Latin] For example; for instance. — Abbr. *e.g.* or (rarely) *ex. gr.*

exemplum (eg-**zem**-pləm), *n.* [Latin] *Civil law.* A copy; a written authorized copy.

exempt, *adj.* Free or released from a duty or liability to which others are held <persons exempt from military service> <property exempt from sequestration>. — **exempt,** *vb.* — **exemptive,** *adj.*

exempt income. See INCOME.

exemption. 1. Freedom from a duty, liability, or other requirement. See IMMUNITY. **2.** A privilege given to a judgment debtor by law, allowing the debtor to retain certain property without liability. **3.** *Tax.* An amount allowed as a deduction from adjusted gross income, used to determine taxable income. Cf. DEDUCTION (2).

dependency exemption. An exemption granted to an individual taxpayer for each dependent whose gross income is less than the exemption amount and for each child who is younger than 19 or, if a student, younger than 24.

personal exemption. An amount allowed as a deduction from an individual taxpayer's adjusted gross income.

exemption clause. A contractual provision providing that a party will not be liable for damages for which that party would otherwise have ordinarily been liable. Cf. INDEMNITY CLAUSE.

> "An exemption clause may take many forms, but all such clauses have one thing in common in that they exempt a party from a liability which he would have borne had it not been for the clause. In some cases an exemption clause merely relieves a party from certain purely contractual obligations, for example, the duties of a seller in a contract of sale regarding the quality and fitness of the goods. In other cases exemption clauses go further and protect the party not merely from contractual liability but even from liability which would otherwise have arisen in tort. For example, a shipping company's ticket may exempt the company from liability to the passenger for any injuries, however caused. Now if the passenger is injured as a result of the negligence of the company's employees, that would, in the normal way, give rise to an action in tort for negligence, quite apart from the contract." P.S. Atiyah, *An Introduction to the Law of Contract* 167 (3d ed. 1981).

exemption equivalent. The maximum value of assets that one can transfer to another before incurring a federal gift and estate tax.

exemption law. A law describing what property of a debtor cannot be attached by a judgment creditor or trustee in bankruptcy to satisfy a debt. See EXEMPT PROPERTY (1).

ex empto (eks **emp**-toh). [Latin] *Roman & civil law.* Out of purchase; founded on purchase.

exempt organization. An organization that is either partially or completely exempt from federal income taxation. See CHARITABLE ORGANIZATION.

exempt property. 1. A debtor's holdings and possessions that, by law, a creditor cannot attach to satisfy a debt. • All the property that creditors may lawfully reach is known as *nonexempt property*. Many states provide a homestead exemption that excludes a person's house and household items, up to a certain amount, from the liens of most creditors. The purpose of the exemption is to prevent debtors from becoming destitute. See HOMESTEAD. **2.** Personal property that a surviving spouse is automatically entitled to receive from the decedent's estate.

exempt security. See SECURITY.

exempt transaction. A securities sale that falls outside the scope of the Securities Act of 1933 and the Securities Exchange Act of 1934.

exennium (eg-**zen**-ee-əm), *n.* [Latin] *Hist.* A gift, esp. one given at the new year.

exequatur (ek-sə-**kway**-tər). [Latin "let it be executed"] A written official recognition and authorization of a consular officer, issued by the government to which the officer is accredited.

exercise, *vb.* **1.** To make use of; to put into action <exercise the right to vote>. **2.** To implement the terms of; to execute <exercise the option to buy the commodities>. — **exercise,** *n.*

Exercise Clause. See FREE EXERCISE CLAUSE.

exercise of judgment. The use of sound discretion — that is, discretion exercised with regard to what is right and equitable rather than arbitrarily or willfully.

exercise price. See *strike price* under PRICE.

exercise value. The value to an optionholder of using the option.

exercitalis (eg-zər-si-**tay**-lis), *n.* [Latin] A soldier; a vassal.

exercitor (eg-**zər**-si-tor), *n.* [Latin "an exercisor"] *Civil law.* The person to whom the profits of a ship temporarily belong, whether that person is the owner, charterer, or mortgagee. — Also termed *exercitor maris*; *exercitor navis.* Cf. SHIP'S HUSBAND.

exercitoria actio. See *actio exercitoria* under ACTIO.

exercitorial power (eg-zər-si-**tor**-ee-əl). The trust given to a shipmaster.

exercitor maris (eg-**zər**-si-tər **mar**-is). See EXERCITOR.

exercitor navis (eg-**zər**-si-tər **nay**-vis). See EXERCITOR.

exercituale (eg-zər-sich-oo-**ay**-lee), *n.* [Law Latin, fr. Latin *exercitus* "an army"] *Hist.* A heriot paid only in arms, horses, or military accouterments. See HERIOT.

exercitus (eg-**zər**-si-təs), *n.* [Latin "an army"] *Hist.* An army; an armed force. • Of indefinite number, the term was applied on various occasions to a gathering of 42 armed men, of 35, or even of 4.

ex facie (eks **fay**-shə *or* -shee). [Latin "from the face"] Apparently; evidently; facially.

ex facto (eks **fak**-toh). [Latin "from a fact"] From or in consequence of a fact or action; actually; DE FACTO.

exfestucare (eks-fes-tə-**kair**-ee), *vb.* [Latin] *Hist.* To abdicate or resign; to surrender (an estate, office, or dignity) by the symbolic delivery of a staff or rod (*festuca*) to the transferee.

ex fictione juris (eks fik-shee-**oh**-nee **joor**-is). [Latin] By a fiction of law.

exfrediare (eks-free-dee-**air**-ee), *vb.* [Latin] To break the peace; to commit open violence.

ex. gr. *abbr.* EXEMPLI GRATIA.

ex gratia (eks **gray**-shee-ə *or* **grah**-tee-ə). [Latin "by favor"] As a favor; not legally necessary. — Also termed *a gratia.*

ex gratia payment. A payment not legally required; esp., an insurance payment not required to be made under an insurance policy.

ex gravi querela (eks **gray**-vɪ kwə-**ree**-lə). [Latin "from or on the grievous complaint"] *Hist.* A writ that lay for a person to whom any lands or tenements in fee were devised by will (within any city, town, or borough in which lands were devisable by custom), against an heir of the devisor who entered and detained them from the devisee. • The writ was abolished by the Real Property Limitation Act (1833). St. 3 & 4 Will. 4, ch. 27, § 36.

exhaustion of remedies. The doctrine that, if an administrative remedy is provided by statute, a claimant must seek relief first from the administrative body before judicial relief is available. • The doctrine's purpose is to maintain comity between the courts and administrative agencies and to ensure that courts will not be burdened by cases in which judicial relief is unnecessary. — Also termed *exhaustion of administrative remedies.*

"The traditional rule can . . . be fairly simply stated. A litigant must normally exhaust state 'legislative' or 'administrative' remedies before challenging the state action in federal court. He or she need not normally exhaust state 'judicial' remedies. The rationale for this distinction is that until the administrative process is complete, it cannot be certain that the party will need judicial relief, but when the case becomes appropriate for judicial determination, he or she may choose whether to resort to a state or federal court for that relief. The word 'normally' is required in both branches of the rule." Charles Alan Wright, *The Law of Federal Courts* § 49, at 313 (5th ed. 1994).

exhaustion of state remedies. The doctrine that an available state remedy must be exhausted in certain types of cases before a party can gain access to a federal court. • For example, a state prisoner must exhaust all state remedies before a federal court will hear a petition for habeas corpus.

exhibere (ek-sə-**beer**-ee), *vb.* [Latin] **1.** To present (a tangible thing) so that it may be handled. **2.** To appear personally to defend against an action at law.

exhibit, *n.* **1.** A document, record, or other tangible object formally introduced as evidence in court. **2.** A document attached to and made part of a pleading, motion, contract, or other instrument.

exhibitio billae (ek-sə-**bish**-ee-oh **bil**-ee). [Latin] *Hist.* The commencement of a suit by presenting or exhibiting a bill to the court.

exhibitionism, *n.* The indecent display of one's body. — **exhibitionist,** *adj.* & *n.*

exhibition value. In the motion-picture industry, the minimum receipts that distributors expect to realize from showing a particular film. — Also termed *minimum sale*; *price expectancy*.

exhibit list. A pretrial filing that identifies by number and description the exhibits a party intends to offer into evidence at trial. • Courts often require the exchange of exhibit lists before trial so that evidentiary disputes can be resolved with minimal disruption in the course of a jury trial.

exhibitory interdict. See INTERDICT (1).

exhumation (eks-hyoo-**may**-shən *or* eg-zyoo-), *n.* The removal from the earth of something buried, esp. a human corpse; disinterment.

ex hypothesi (eks hI-**poth**-ə-sI). [Latin] Hypothetically; by hypothesis; on the assumption <conviction for a felony is *ex hypothesi* impossible in the case of suicide>.

exidos (e-**hee**-thohs), *n.* See EJIDOS.

exigency (**ek**-sə-jən-see), *n.* A demand for immediate action or performance arising from a circumstance or condition <exigency of a bond> <exigency of a writ>. — **exigent,** *adj.*

exigendary (ek-sə-**jen**-də-ree), *n.* See EXIGENTER.

exigent, *adj.* Requiring immediate action or aid; urgent <exigent circumstances>.

exigent (**ek**-sə-jənt), *n. Hist.* A judicial writ employed in the process of outlawry, commanding the sheriff to demand the defendant's appearance, from county court to county court, until he was outlawed — or, if the defendant appeared, to take him before the court to answer the plaintiff's action. See EXIGI FACIAS.

exigent circumstances. See CIRCUMSTANCE.

exigenter (**ek**-sə-jen-tər), *n. Hist.* An officer of the court of common pleas responsible for preparing exigents and proclamations in the process of outlawry. • This office was abolished in 1837 by the Superior Courts (Officers) Act, St. 7 Will. 4, and 1 Vict., ch. 30. — Also termed *exigendary*.

exigent list. A list of cases set down for hearing upon various incidental and ancillary motions and rules.

exigent search. See SEARCH.

exigible debt. See DEBT.

exigi facias (**ek**-sə-jI **fay**-shee-əs). [Latin] That you cause to be demanded. • These were the emphatic words of the Latin form of the writ of exigent; the phrase was sometimes used as the name of the writ. See EXIGENT.

exile, *n.* **1.** Expulsion from a country, esp. from the country of one's origin or longtime residence; banishment. **2.** A person who has been banished. — **exile,** *vb.*

forced exile. Compelled removal or banishment from one's native country.

exilium (eg-**zil**-ee-əm), *n.* [Latin "exile"] *Hist.* **1.** Exile; the act of driving away or despoiling. **2.** A type of waste consisting in the driving away of an estate's bondservants and tenants by demolishing their homes or by enfranchising the bondservants and then turning them out of their homes.

Ex-Im Bank. See EXPORT-IMPORT BANK.

ex industria (eks in-**dəs**-tree-ə). [Latin] With contrivance or deliberation; designedly; on purpose.

ex integro (eks **in**-tə-groh). [Latin] Anew; afresh.

existent corner. See CORNER.

existimatio (eg-zis-tə-**may**-shee-oh), *n.* [Latin] *Roman law.* **1.** The civil reputation belonging to a Roman citizen of unimpeached dignity or character; the highest standing of a Roman citizen. **2.** *Hist.* The decision or award of an arbiter.

exit, *n.* **1.** A way out. See EGRESS. **2.** In a docket entry, an issuance of something (as a writ or process). • For example, *exit attachment* denotes that a writ of attachment has been issued in the case. — **exit,** *vb.*

exitus (**ek**-si-təs), *n.* [Latin] *Hist.* **1.** Children; offspring. **2.** The rents, issues, and profits of lands and tenements. **3.** An export duty. **4.** The conclusion of a pleading.

ex jure (eks **juur**-ee). [Latin] Of or by legal right.

ex justa causa (eks **jəs**-tə **kaw**-zə). [Latin] From a just or lawful cause; by a just or legal title.

ex justitia (eks jəs-**tish**-ee-ə). [Latin] From justice; as a matter of justice.

exlegalitas (eks-lə-**gay**-lə-tas), *n.* [Law Latin] *Hist.* **1.** Outlawry; outside the law's protection. **2.** A person who is prosecuted as an outlaw.

exlegare (eks-lə-**gair**-ee), *vb.* [Law Latin] *Hist.* To outlaw; to deprive of the benefit and protection of the law.

ex lege (eks **lee**-jee *or* **lay**-gay). [Latin] By virtue of law; as a matter of law <property forfeited *ex lege*>.

> "Antecedent rights 'in personam' ... either arise or do not arise out of a contract.... In the latter case, since they arise from facts of various kinds to which it pleases the Law to affix similar results, we shall describe them as rights 'ex lege'; and it will be convenient to consider the rights which arise thus variously before treating of those which arise solely from contract.... The rights which we describe as arising 'ex lege' were described by the Roman lawyers as arising 'quasi ex contractu,' and more simply, 'ex variis causarum figuris.' " Thomas E. Holland, *The Elements of Jurisprudence* 246–47 (13th ed. 1924).

ex legibus (eks **lee**-jə-bəs). [Latin "according to the laws"] *Roman law.* According to both the letter and the spirit of the law.

exlex (**eks**-leks), *n.* [Law Latin] *Hist.* An outlaw; one who is outside the law's protection.

ex licentia regis (eks lɪ-**sen**-shee-ə **ree**-jis). [Latin] By the king's license.

ex locato (eks loh-**kay**-toh). [Latin] From lease; out of letting. • In Roman law, this term referred to an action or right of action arising out of a contract of hiring, bailment for reward, or employment.

ex maleficio (eks mal-ə-**fish**-ee-oh), *adv.* [Latin] By malfeasance.

ex maleficio, *adj.* [Latin] Tortious.

ex malitia (eks mə-**lish**-ee-ə). [Latin] From malice; maliciously. • In the law of defamation, the term refers to a publication that is false and without legal excuse.

ex mero motu (eks **meer**-oh **moh**-tyoo). [Latin "on his mere motion"] Voluntarily; without suggestion or influence from another person. • The phrase was formerly sometimes used in reference to a court, as an equivalent of *sua sponte* or *on its own motion.* See SUA SPONTE.

ex mora (eks **mor**-ə). [Latin] *Civil law.* From or in consequence of delay. • Interest is allowed *ex mora* — that is, if there has been delay in repaying borrowed money.

ex more (eks **mor**-ee). [Latin] According to custom.

ex mutuo (eks **myoo**-choo-oh). [Latin] From or out of loan. • In old English law, a debt was said to arise *ex mutuo* when one lent another anything that consisted in number, weight, or measure.

ex necessitate (eks nə-ses-i-**tay**-tee). [Latin] Of or from necessity.

ex necessitate legis (eks nə-ses-i-**tay**-tee **lee**-jis). From or by necessity of law.

ex necessitate rei (eks nə-ses-i-**tay**-tee **ree**-I). From the necessity or urgency of the thing or case.

ex nihilo (eks **nI**-hi-loh). [Latin] From nothing.

ex nobili officio (eks **nob**-i-lI ə-**fish**-ee-oh). [Latin "by virtue of its noble office"] *Scots law.* (Of a judicial act) done as a matter of equity.

ex officio (eks ə-**fish**-ee-oh), *adv.* & *adj.* [Latin] By virtue or because of an office; by virtue of the authority implied by office.

ex officio information. *English law.* A criminal information filed by the attorney general ex officio on behalf of the Crown, in the Court of King's Bench, for offenses more immediately affecting the government, as distinguished from informations in which the Crown is the nominal prosecutor.

ex officio justice. A judge who serves on a commission or board only because the law requires the presence of a judge rather than because the judge was selected for the position.

ex officio service. A service that the law imposes on an official by virtue of the office held, such as a local sheriff's duty to perform marriage ceremonies.

exoine (e-**soyn**), *n.* [French "excuse"] *French law.* An act or instrument in writing containing the reasons why a party in a civil suit, or a person accused, has not appeared after being summoned. See ESSOIN.

exonerate (eg-**zon**-ə-rayt), *vb.* **1.** To free from responsibility <exonerate from the payment of the debt>. Cf. EXCULPATE. **2.** To free from encumbrances <exonerate the property from the mortgage lien>. — **exonerative** (eg-**zon**-ər-ay-tiv *or* -ə-tiv), *adj.*

exoneration. **1.** The removal of a burden, charge, responsibility, or duty. **2.** The right to be reimbursed by reason of having paid money that another person should have paid. **3.** The equitable right of a surety — confirmed by statute in many states — to proceed to compel the principal debtor to satisfy the obligation when, even though the surety would have a right of reimbursement, it would be inequitable for the surety to be compelled to perform if the principal debtor can satisfy the obligation. See EQUITY OF EXONERATION; QUIA TIMET.

exoneration, suit for. See SUIT FOR EXONERATION.

exoneratione sectae (eg-zon-ə-ray-shee-**oh**-nee **sek**-tee). [Latin] *Hist.* A writ that lay for the Crown's ward, to be free from all suit during wardship.

exoneratione sectae ad curiam baron (eg-zon-ə-ray-shee-**oh**-nee **sek**-tee ad **kyoor**-ee-əm **bar**-ən). [Latin "by exoneration of the suit to the lord's court"] *Hist.* A writ issued by the guardian of the Crown's ward, forbidding the sheriff or steward of a particular court from distraining or taking other action against the ward.

exonerative fact. See FACT.

exoneretur (eg-zon-ə-**ree**-tər). *Hist.* [Latin "let him be relieved or discharged"] An entry made on a bailpiece whereby a surety is relieved or discharged from further obligation when the condition is fulfilled.

ex. ord. (*often cap.*) *abbr.* EXECUTIVE ORDER.

exordium (eg-**zor**-dee-əm). [Latin] See INTRODUCTORY CLAUSE.

ex parte (eks **pahr**-tee), *adv.* [Latin "from the part"] On or from one party only, usu. without notice to or argument from the adverse party <the judge conducted the hearing ex parte>.

ex parte, *adj.* Done or made at the instance and for the benefit of one party only, and without notice to, or argument by, any person adversely interested <an ex parte hearing> <an ex parte injunction>.

ex parte communication. A generally prohibited communication between counsel and the court when opposing counsel is not present.

ex parte divorce. See DIVORCE.

ex parte hearing. See *ex parte proceeding* under PROCEEDING.

ex parte injunction. See INJUNCTION.

ex parte materna (eks **pahr**-tee mə-**tər**-nə). [Latin] On the mother's side; of the maternal line.

ex parte motion. See MOTION.

ex parte order. See ORDER (2).

ex parte paterna (eks **pahr**-tee pə-**tər**-nə). [Latin] On the father's side; of the paternal line.

ex parte proceeding. See PROCEEDING.

expatriate (eks-**pay**-tree-it), *n.* An expatriated person; esp., a person who lives permanently in a foreign country.

expatriate (eks-**pay**-tree-ayt), *vb.* **1.** To withdraw (oneself) from residence in or allegiance to one's native country; to leave one's home country to live elsewhere. **2.** To banish or exile (a person). — **expatriation,** *n.*

expectancy, *n.* **1.** *Property.* An estate with a reversion, a remainder, or an executory interest. **2.** *Wills & estates.* The possibility that an heir apparent, an heir presumptive, or a presumptive next-of-kin will acquire property by devolution on intestacy, or the possibility that a presumptive legatee or devisee will acquire property by will. **3.** *Insurance.* The probable number of years in one's life. See LIFE EXPECTANCY.

expectancy damages. See *expectation damages* under DAMAGES.

expectancy table. See ACTUARIAL TABLE.

expectant, *adj.* Having a relation to, or being dependent on, a contingency; CONTINGENT.

expectant estate. See ESTATE.

expectant heir. See HEIR.

expectant right. See RIGHT.

expectation, *n.* **1.** The act of looking forward; anticipation. **2.** A basis on which something is expected to happen; esp., the prospect of receiving wealth, honors, or the like.

> "[E]xpectation does not in itself amount to intention. An operating surgeon may know very well that his patient will probably die of the operation; yet he does not intend the fatal consequence which he expects. He intends the recovery which he hopes for but does not expect." John Salmond, *Jurisprudence* 379–80 (Glanville L. Williams ed., 10th ed. 1947).

expectation damages. See DAMAGES.

expectation interest. See INTEREST (2).

expectation of life. See LIFE EXPECTANCY.

expectation of privacy. A belief in the existence of the right to be free of governmental intrusion in regard to a particular place or thing. • To suppress a search on privacy grounds, a defendant must show the existence of the expectation and that the expectation was reasonable.

expected/intended exclusion. See EXCLUSION (3).

expediente (ek-spe-thee-**en**-te), *n.* [Spanish] **1.** A historical record of proceedings relating to a grant of land by the sovereign. **2.** *Mexican law.* The papers or documents constituting a grant or title to land from the government.

expediment (ek-**sped**-ə-mənt), *n.* The whole of one's goods and chattels.

expedited proceeding. See SHOW-CAUSE PROCEEDING.

expeditio brevis (ek-spə-**dish**-ee-oh **bree**-vəs). [Latin] *Archaic.* The service of a writ.

expel, *vb.* To drive out or away; to eject, esp. with force. See EJECT; EVICT.

expenditor (ek-**spen**-də-tər). One who expends or disburses certain taxes; a paymaster.

expenditure. 1. The act or process of paying out; disbursement. **2.** A sum paid out.

expensae litis (ek-**spen**-see **lɪ**-tis). [Latin] Costs or expenses of a lawsuit, for which a successful party is usu. reimbursed.

expense, *n.* An expenditure of money, time, labor, or resources to accomplish a result; esp., a business expenditure chargeable against revenue for a specific period. — **expense,** *vb.* Cf. COST (1).

accrued expense. An expense incurred but not yet paid.

administrative expense. See *general administrative expense.*

business expense. An expense incurred to operate and promote a business; esp., an expenditure made to further the business in the taxable year in which the expense is incurred. • Most business expenses — unlike personal expenses — are tax-deductible.

capital expense. An expense made by a business to provide a long-term benefit; a capital expenditure. • A capital expense is not deductible, but it can be used for depreciation or amortization.

capitalized expense. An amortized expense.

current expense. See *operating expense.*

deferred expense. A cost incurred by a business when the business expects to benefit from that cost over a period beyond the current year. • An example is a prepaid subscription to a business periodical the cost of which will be recognized as an expense over a multiyear subscription period.

educational expense. A deductible expense incurred either to maintain or improve an existing job skill or to meet a legally imposed job requirement.

entertainment expense. An expense incurred while providing entertainment relating directly to or associated with a business purpose. • Entertainment expenses are partially tax-deductible.

extraordinary expense. An unusual or infrequent expense, such as a write-off of goodwill or a large judgment. • As used in a constitutional provision authorizing a state to incur extraordinary expenses, the term denotes an expense for the general welfare compelled by an unforeseen condition such as a natural disaster or war.

fixed expense. See *fixed cost* under COST.

funeral expense. (*usu. pl.*) An expense necessarily and reasonably incurred in procuring the burial, cremation, or other disposition of a corpse, including the funeral or other ceremonial rite, a coffin and vault, a monument or tombstone, a burial plot and its care, and a wake.

general administrative expense. (*usu. pl.*) An expense incurred in running a business, as distinguished from an expense incurred in manufacturing or selling; overhead. • Examples include executive and clerical salaries, rent, utilities, and legal and accounting services. — Also termed *administrative expense*; *general expense.*

medical expense. **1.** An expense for medical treatment or healthcare, such as drug costs and health-insurance premiums. • Medical expenses are tax-deductible to the extent that the amounts (less insurance reimbursements) exceed a certain percentage of adjusted gross income. **2.** (*usu. pl.*) In civil litigation, any one of many possible medical costs that the plaintiff has sustained because of the defendant's allegedly wrongful act, including charges for visits to physicians' offices, medical procedures, hospital bills, medicine, and recuperative therapy. — Often shortened (in pl.) to *medicals.*

moving expense. An expense incurred in changing one's residence. • If incurred for business reasons (as when one's job requires relocation), most moving expenses are tax-deductible.

operating expense. An expense incurred in running a business and producing output. — Also termed *current expense.*

ordinary and necessary expense. An expense that is normal or usual and helpful or appropriate for the operation of a particular trade or business and that is paid or incurred during the taxable year. • Ordinary and necessary expenses are tax-deductible. — Also termed *ordinary and necessary business expense.*

organizational expense. An expense incurred while setting up a corporation or other entity.

out-of-pocket expense. An expense paid from one's own funds.

prepaid expense. An expense (such as rent, interest, or insurance) that is paid before the due date or before a service is rendered.

travel expense. An expense (such as for meals, lodging, and transportation) incurred while away from home in the pursuit of a trade or business. See TAX HOME.

expense loading. See LOADING.

expense ratio. *Accounting.* The proportion or ratio of expenses to income.

expenses of administration. Expenses incurred by a decedent's representatives in administering the estate.

expenses of receivership. Expenses incurred by a receiver in conducting the business, including rent and fees incurred by the receiver's counsel and by any master, appraiser, and auditor.

expense stop. A lease provision establishing the maximum expenses to be paid by the landlord, beyond which the tenant must bear all remaining expenses.

expensis militum non levandis (ek-**spen**-sis mi-**lit**-əm non lə-**van**-dis). [Latin] *Hist.* A writ to prohibit the sheriff from levying any allowance for knights of the shire on persons who held lands in ancient demesne. See *ancient demesne* under DEMESNE.

experience rating. *Insurance.* A method of determining the amount of the premium by analyzing the insured's loss record over time to assess (1) the risk that covered events will occur, and (2) the amount of probable damages if they do.

experimental use. See USE (1).

expert, *n.* A person who, through education or experience, has developed skill or knowledge in a particular subject, so that he or she may form an opinion that will assist the fact-finder. Fed. R. Evid. 702. See DAUBERT TEST. — **expertise** (ek-spər-**teez**), *n.*

consulting expert. An expert who, though retained by a party, is not expected to be called as a witness at trial. • A consulting expert's opinions are generally exempt from the scope of discovery. — Also termed *nontestifying expert.* Fed. R. Civ. P. 26(b)(4)(B).

impartial expert. An expert who is appointed by the court to present an unbiased opinion. — Also termed *court-appointed expert.* Fed. R. Evid. 706.

testifying expert. An expert who is identified by a party as a potential witness at trial. • As a part of initial disclosures in federal court, a party must provide to all other parties a wide range of information about a testifying expert's qualifications and opinion, including all information that the witness considered in forming the opinion. Fed. R. Civ. P. 26(a)(2)(b).

expert evidence. See EVIDENCE.

expert testimony. See *expert evidence* under EVIDENCE.

expert witness. See WITNESS.

expert-witness fee. See FEE (1).

expilare (eks-pə-**lair**-ee), *vb.* [Latin] *Roman law.* In the law of inheritance, to spoil; to rob; to plunder.

expilatio (eks-pə-**lay**-shee-oh), *n.* [Latin] *Roman law.* The offense of unlawfully appropriating goods belonging to a succession. • This offense was not technically theft (*furtum*) because the property belonged to neither the decedent nor an heir, since the latter had not yet taken possession.

expilator (eks-pə-**lay**-tər), *n.* [Latin] *Roman law.* A robber; a spoiler or plunderer.

expiration, *n.* A coming to an end; esp., a formal termination on a closing date <expiration of the insurance policy>. — **expire,** *vb.*

expiration date. The date on which an offer, option, or the like ceases to exist.

explecia (ek-**splee**-shee-ə). [Law Latin] See EXPLETA.

explees (eks-**pleez**). See ESPLEES.

expleta (ek-**splee**-tə), *n. pl.* [Law Latin] *Hist.* The rents and profits of an estate. — Also termed *expletia*; *explecia.*

explicatio (eks-plə-**kay**-shee-oh), *n.* [Law Latin] *Civil law.* The fourth pleading in an action, consisting of the plaintiff's response to the defendant's rejoinder. • This is the civil-law equivalent of the common-law *surrejoinder.*

exploitation, *n.* The act of taking advantage of something; esp., the act of taking unjust advantage of another for one's own benefit. — **exploit,** *vb.* — **exploitative,** *adj.*

exploration manager. See LAND MANAGER.

export, *n.* **1.** A product or service created in one country and transported to another.

domestic export. A product originally grown or manufactured in the United States, as distinguished from a product originally imported into the United States and then exported.

2. The process of transporting products or services to another country.

export, *vb.* **1.** To send or carry abroad. **2.** To send, take, or carry (a good or commodity) out of the country; to transport (merchandise) from one country to another in the course of trade. **3.** To carry out or convey (goods) by sea.

exportation. The act of sending or carrying goods and merchandise from one country to another.

Export Clause. See IMPORT-EXPORT CLAUSE.

export declaration. A document — required by federal law — containing details of an export shipment.

export draft. See DRAFT.

Export-Import Bank. A federal agency, established in 1934, that encourages trade with foreign countries by financing exports and imports with funds borrowed from the U.S. Treasury. — Abbr. Ex–Im Bank.

export letter of credit. See LETTER OF CREDIT.

export quota. See QUOTA.

export tax. See TAX.

exposé (ek-spoh-**zay**), *n.* [French] **1.** A statement or account; an explanation. • In diplomatic language, the term describes a written explanation of the reasons for a certain act or course of conduct. **2.** Exposure of discreditable matter.

expositio (eks-pə-**zish**-ee-oh), *n.* [Latin] An explanation or interpretation; an exposition.

exposition de part (eks-poh-zee-**syawn** də **pahr**). [French] *French law.* The abandonment, in either a public or a private place, of a child that is unable to take care of itself.

expository jurisprudence. See JURISPRUDENCE.

expository statute. See STATUTE.

ex post, *adj.* [Latin "from after"] Based on knowledge and fact; objective; retrospective. Cf. EX ANTE.

ex post facto (eks pohst **fak**-toh), *adv.* [Latin "from a thing done afterward"] After the fact; retroactively.

ex post facto, *adj.* Done or made after the fact; having retroactive force or effect.

Ex Post Facto Clause. One of two clauses in the U.S. Constitution forbidding the enactment of ex post facto laws. U.S. Const. art. I, § 9; art. I, § 10.

ex post facto law. A law that applies retroactively, esp. in a way that negatively affects a person's rights, as by criminalizing an action that was legal when it was committed. • Ex post facto criminal laws are prohibited by the U.S. Constitution.

exposure. The amount of liability or other risk to which a person is subject <the client wanted to know its exposure before it made a settlement offer>.

exposure of person. See INDECENT EXPOSURE.

exposure theory. *Insurance.* A theory of coverage providing that an insurer must cover a loss if the insurance was in effect when the claimant was exposed to the product that caused the injury. Cf. MANIFESTATION THEORY; ACTUAL-INJURY TRIGGER; TRIPLE TRIGGER.

express, *adj.* Clearly and unmistakably communicated; directly stated. — **expressly,** *adv.* Cf. IMPLIED.

express abrogation. The repeal of a law or provision by a later one that refers directly to it; abrogation by express provision or enactment.

express acceptance. See ACCEPTANCE (4).

express active trust. See TRUST.

express actual knowledge. See *actual knowledge* under KNOWLEDGE.

express agency. See AGENCY (1).

express amnesty. See AMNESTY.

express assent. See ASSENT.

express assumpsit. See *special assumpsit* under ASSUMPSIT.

express authority. See AUTHORITY (1).

express color. See COLOR.

express condition. See CONDITION (2).

express consent. See CONSENT.

express consideration. See CONSIDERATION.

express contract. See CONTRACT.

express covenant. See COVENANT (1).

express dedication. See DEDICATION.

express dissatisfaction. *Wills & estates.* A beneficiary's contesting of a will or objecting to any provision of the will in a probate proceeding.

expressed, *adj.* Declared in direct terms; stated in words; not left to inference or implication.

expression, freedom of. See FREEDOM OF EXPRESSION.

expressio unius est exclusio alterius (ek-**spres**[**h**]-ee-oh yoo-**nI**-əs est eks-**kloo**-zhee-oh al-tə-**rI**-əs). [Law Latin] A canon of construction holding that to express or include one thing implies the exclusion of the other, or of the alternative. • For example, the rule that "each citizen is entitled to vote" implies that noncitizens are not entitled to vote. — Also termed *inclusio unius est exclusio alterius*; *expressum facit cessare tacitum*. Cf. EJUSDEM GENERIS; NOSCITUR A SOCIIS; RULE OF RANK.

> "Several Latin maxims masquerade as rules of interpretation while doing nothing more than describing results reached by other means. The best example is probably *expressio unius est exclusio alterius*, which is a rather elaborate, mysterious sounding, and anachronistic way of describing the negative implication. Far from being a rule, it is not even lexicographically accurate, because it is simply not true, generally, that the mere express conferral of a right or privilege in one kind of situation implies the denial of the equivalent right or privilege in other kinds. Sometimes it does and sometimes it does not, and whether it does or does not depends on the particular circumstances of context. Without contextual support, therefore, there is not even a mild presumption here. Accordingly, the maxim is at best a description, after the fact, of what the court has discovered from context." Reed Dickerson, *The Interpretation and Application of Statutes* 234–35 (1975).

> "The canon *expressio unius est exclusio alterius* is ... based on the assumption of legislative omniscience, because it would make sense only if all omissions in legislative drafting were deliberate. Although this canon seemed dead for a while, it has been resurrected by the Supreme Court to provide a basis for refusing to create private remedies for certain statutory violations. Its recent disparagement by a unanimous Court [in *Herman & MacLean v. Huddleston*, 459 U.S. 375, 386 n.23, 103 S.Ct. 683, 690 n. 23 (1983)] puts its future in some doubt but more likely confirms that judicial use of canons of construction is opportunistic." Richard A. Posner, *The Federal Courts: Crisis and Reform* 282 (1985).

express malice. See MALICE.

express notice. See NOTICE.

express power. See *enumerated power* under POWER.

express private passive trust. See TRUST.

express repeal. See REPEAL.

express republication. A testator's repeating of the acts essential to a will's valid execution, with the avowed intent of republishing the will. See REPUBLICATION (2).

express trust. See TRUST.

expressum facit cessare tacitum. See EXPRESSIO UNIUS EST EXCLUSIO ALTERIUS.

express waiver. See WAIVER (1).

express warranty. See WARRANTY (2).

expromissio (eks-prə-**mis**[**h**]-ee-oh), *n. Roman law.* A type of novation by which a creditor accepts a new debtor in place of a former one, who is then released.

expromissor (eks-prə-**mis**-ər), *n. Roman law.* One who assumes another's debt and becomes solely liable for it, by a stipulation with the creditor.

expromittere (eks-prə-**mit**-ə-ree), *vb. Roman law.* To undertake for another with the view of becoming liable in his place.

expropriation, *n.* **1.** A governmental taking or modification of an individual's property rights, esp. by eminent domain; CONDEMNATION (2). Cf. APPROPRIATION. **2.** A voluntary surrender of rights or claims; the act of renouncing or divesting oneself of something previously claimed as one's own. — **expropriate,** *vb.* — **expropriator,** *n.*

ex proprio motu (eks **proh**-pree-oh **moh**-tyoo). [Latin] Of one's own accord.

ex proprio vigore (eks **proh**-pree-oh vi-**gor**-ee). [Latin] By their or its own force.

ex provisione hominis (eks prə-vizh-ee-**oh**-nee **hom**-ə-nis). [Latin] By the provision of man; by the limitation of the party, as distinguished from the disposition of the law.

ex provisione mariti (eks prə-vizh-ee-**oh**-nee mə-**rI**-tI *or* **mar**-ə-tI). [Latin] From the provision of the husband.

expulsion, *n.* An ejectment or banishment, either through depriving a person of a benefit or by forcibly evicting a person. — **expulsive,** *adj.*

expunction of record. See EXPUNGEMENT OF RECORD.

expunge (ek-**spənj**), *vb.* To erase or destroy <the trustee wrongfully expunged the creditor's claim against the debtor>. — **expungement** (ek-**spənj**-mənt), **expunction** (ek-**spəngk**-shən), *n.*

expungement of record. The removal of a conviction (esp. for a first offense) from a person's criminal record. — Also termed *expunction of record*; *erasure of record*.

expurgation (ek-spər-**gay**-shən), *n.* The act or practice of purging or cleansing, as by publishing a book without its obscene passages. — **expurgate** (**eks**-pər-gayt), *vb.* — **expurgator** (**eks**-pər-gay-tər), *n.*

ex quasi contractu (eks **kway**-zI kən-**trak**-t[y]oo). [Latin] From quasi-contract.

ex rel. *abbr.* [Latin *ex relatione* "by or on the relation of"] On the relation or information of. • A suit *ex rel.* is typically brought by the government upon the application of a private party (called a *relator*) who is interested in the matter. See RELATOR (1).

ex re nata (eks ree **nay**-tə). [Latin] According to a case that has arisen.

ex rights, *adv.* Without rights. • Shares are traded ex rights when the value of the subscription privilege has been deducted, giving the purchaser no right to buy shares of a new stock issue. — Abbr. X; XR. — Also termed *rights off*.

ex-rights date. The date on which a share of common stock no longer offers privilege subscription rights.

ex rigore juris (eks ri-**gor**-ee **joor**-is). [Latin] According to the rigor or strictness of the law; in strictness of law.

exrogare (eks-rə-**gair**-ee), *vb.* [Latin] *Roman law.* To remove something from an old law by a new law.

exrx. *abbr.* EXECUTRIX.

ex scriptis olim visis (eks **skrip**-tis **oh**-ləm **vI**-zis *or* -sis). [Latin "from writings formerly seen"] A method of handwriting proof available when a witness has seen other documents purporting to be in the party's handwriting and either has had further correspondence with the party about the documents' subject matter or has had some other type of communication with the party that would lead to a reasonable presumption that the documents were in the party's handwriting.

ex ship. Of or referring to a shipment of goods for which the liability or risk of loss passes to the buyer once the goods leave the ship.

ex statuto (eks stə-**tyoo**-toh). [Latin] According to the statute.

ex stipulatu actio (eks stip-yə-**lay**-t[y]oo **ak**-shee-oh). [Latin] *Roman & civil law.* An action on a stipulation; an action given to recover marriage portions.

ex tempore (eks **tem**-pə-ree), *adv.* [Latin "out of time"] **1.** By lapse of time. **2.** Without any preparation; extemporaneously.

extended-coverage clause. *Insurance.* A policy provision that insures against hazards beyond those covered (or excluded) in the basic policy.

extended family. See FAMILY.

extended first mortgage. See *wraparound mortgage* under MORTGAGE.

extended insurance. See INSURANCE.

extended policy. See INSURANCE POLICY.

extended service contract. See *extended warranty* under WARRANTY (2).

extended service warranty. See *extended warranty* under WARRANTY (2).

extended-term insurance. See INSURANCE.

extended warranty. See WARRANTY (2).

extendi facias (ek-**sten**-dɪ **fay**-shee-əs). [Latin "you are to cause to be executed"] See EXTENT (3).

extension, *n.* **1.** The continuation of the same contract for a specified period. Cf. RENEWAL. **2.** *Patents.* A continuation of the life of a patent for an additional statutorily allowed period. **3.** *Tax.* A period of additional time to file an income-tax return beyond its due date. **4.** A period of additional time to take an action, make a decision, accept an offer, or complete a task. — **extend,** *vb.*

extension agreement. An agreement providing additional time for the basic agreement to be performed.

extensive interpretation. See INTERPRETATION.

extensores (ek-sten-**sor**-eez), *n. pl. Hist.* Officers appointed to appraise and divide or apportion land; extenders or appraisers.

extent. *Hist.* **1.** A seizure of property in execution of a writ. **2.** A writ issued by the Exchequer to recover a debt owed to the Crown, under which the debtor's lands, goods, or body could all be seized to secure payment. — Also termed *writ of extent*; *extent in chief.* **3.** A writ giving a creditor temporary possession of the debtor's property (esp. land). — Also termed *extendi facias.*

extenta manerii (ek-**sten**-tə mə-**neer**-ee-ɪ). [Latin "the extent of a manor"] An English statute (4 Edw., St. 1) directing the making of a survey of a manor and all its appendages.

extent in aid. *Hist.* A writ that a Crown debtor could obtain against a person indebted to the Crown debtor so that the Crown debtor could satisfy the debt to the Crown. • This writ, having been much abused because of some peculiar privileges that Crown debtors enjoyed, was abolished in 1947 by the Crown Proceedings Act.

extent in chief. See EXTENT (2).

extenuate (ek-**sten**-yoo-ayt), *vb.* To make less severe; to mitigate.

extenuating circumstance. See *mitigating circumstance* under CIRCUMSTANCE.

extenuation (ek-sten-yoo-**ay**-shən), *n.* The act or fact of making the commission of a crime or tort less severe.

extern. See CLERK (4).

external act. See ACT (2).

externality. (*usu. pl.*) A social or monetary consequence or side effect of one's economic activity, causing another to benefit without paying or to suffer without compensation. — Also termed *spillover*; *neighborhood effect.*

> ***negative externality.*** An externality that is detrimental to another, such as water pollution created by a nearby factory.
>
> ***positive externality.*** An externality that benefits another, such as the advantage received by a neighborhood when a homeowner attractively landscapes the property.

external sovereignty. See SOVEREIGNTY.

exterritorial. See EXTRATERRITORIAL.

exterritoriality. See EXTRATERRITORIALITY.

exterus (**ek**-stər-əs), *n.* [Latin] A foreigner or alien; one born abroad.

ex testamento (eks tes-tə-**men**-toh), *adv.* [Latin] By, from, or under a will or testament <succession *ex testamento* is the mode of devolution that the property of deceased persons ought primarily to follow>. Cf. AB INTESTATO.

extinct, *adj.* **1.** No longer in existence or use. **2.** (Of a debt) lacking a claimant.

extinctive fact. See FACT.

extinctive prescription. See PRESCRIPTION (3).

extinguish, *vb.* **1.** To bring to an end; to put an end to. **2.** To terminate or cancel. **3.** To put out or stifle.

extinguishment, *n.* The cessation or cancellation of some right or interest. • For example, the extinguishment of a legacy occurs when the item bequeathed no longer exists or no longer belongs to the testator's estate.

extinguishment of copyhold. The destruction of copyhold by a uniting of freehold and copyhold interests in the same person and in the same right. • In England, under the 1922 Law of Property Act, copyholds were enfranchised and became either leasehold or, more often, freehold. See COPYHOLD.

extinguishment of legacy. See ADEMPTION.

extinguishment of lien. A lien's discharge by operation of law.

extirpation (ek-stər-**pay**-shən), *n.* **1.** The act of completely removing or destroying something. **2.** Damage to land intentionally done by a person who has lost the right to the land.

extirpatione (ek-stər-pay-shee-**oh**-nee), *n.* [Latin] *Hist.* A writ issued either before or after judgment to restrain a person from maliciously damaging any house or extirpating any trees on land that the person had lost the right to possess.

extort, *vb.* **1.** To compel or coerce (a confession, etc.) by means that overcome one's power to resist. **2.** To gain by wrongful methods; to obtain in an unlawful manner; to exact wrongfully by threat or intimidation. — **extortive,** *adj.*

extortion, *n.* **1.** The offense committed by a public official who illegally obtains property under the color of office; esp., an official's collection of an unlawful fee. — Also termed *common-law extortion.*

> "The dividing line between bribery and *extortion* is shadowy. If one other than the officer corruptly takes the initiative and offers what he knows is not an authorized fee, it is bribery and not extortion. On the other hand, if the officer corruptly makes an unlawful demand which is paid by one who does not realize it is not the fee authorized for the service rendered, it is extortion and not bribery. In theory it would seem possible for an officer to extort a bribe under such circumstances that he would be guilty of either offense whereas the outraged citizen would be excused." Rollin M. Perkins & Ronald N. Boyce, *Criminal Law* 538 (3d ed. 1982).

2. The act or practice of obtaining something or compelling some action by illegal means, as by force or coercion. — Also termed *statutory extortion.* — **extortionate,** *adj.*

extortionate credit transaction. See LOANSHARKING.

extra (**ek**-strə), *prep.* [Latin] Beyond; except; without; out of; additional.

extra allowance. In New York practice, a sum in addition to costs that may, in the court's discretion, be awarded to the successful party in an unusually difficult case.

extra commercium (**eks**-trə kə-**mər**-shee-əm). [Latin] Outside commerce. • This phrase was used in Roman and civil law to describe property dedicated to public use and not subject to private ownership.

extract (**ek**-strakt), *n.* A portion or segment, as of a writing.

extract (ek-**strakt**), *vb.* To draw out or forth; to pull out from a fixed position.

extracta curiae (ek-**strak**-tə **kyoor**-ee-ee). *Hist.* The issues or profits of holding a court, arising from customary dues, fees, and amercements.

extradite (**ek**-strə-dɪt), *vb.* **1.** To surrender or deliver (a fugitive) to another jurisdiction. **2.** To obtain the surrender of (a fugitive) from another jurisdiction.

extradition (ek-strə-**dish**-ən). The official surrender of an alleged criminal by one state or nation to another having jurisdiction over the crime charged; the return of a fugitive from justice, regardless of consent, by the authorities where the fugitive resides. Cf. RENDITION (2).

international extradition. Extradition in response to a demand made by the executive of one nation on the executive of another nation. • This procedure is regulated by treaties.

interstate extradition. Extradition in response to a demand made by the governor of one state on the governor of another state. • This procedure is provided for by the U.S. Constitution, by federal statute, and by state statutes.

Extradition Clause. The clause of the U.S. Constitution providing that any accused person who flees to another state must, on request of the executive authority of the state where the crime was committed, be returned to that state. U.S. Const. art. IV, § 2, cl. 2.

extradition treaty. A treaty governing the preconditions for, and exceptions to, the surrender of a fugitive from justice by the fugitive's country of residence to another country claiming criminal jurisdiction over the fugitive.

extradition warrant. See WARRANT (1).

extra dividend. See *extraordinary dividend* under DIVIDEND.

extradotal property (eks-trə-**doh**-təl). *Civil law.* Property that forms no part of a woman's dowry. — Also termed *paraphernal property.*

extra feodum (**eks**-trə **fee**-ə-dəm). [Latin] Out of his fee; out of the seigniory.

extrahazardous, *adj.* Especially or unusually dangerous. • This term is often applied to exceptionally dangerous railroad crossings.

extrahura (ek-strə-**hyoor**-ə), *n.* [Law Latin] *Hist.* An animal that wanders about or strays without its owner; ESTRAY.

extrajudicial, *adj.* Outside court; outside the functioning of the court system <extrajudicial confessions>. — Also termed *out-of-court.*

extrajudicial admission. See ADMISSION (1).

extrajudicial confession. See CONFESSION.

extrajudicial enforcement. See SELF-HELP.

extrajudicial evidence. See EVIDENCE.

extrajudicial oath. See OATH.

extrajudicial remedy. See REMEDY.

extrajudicial statement. Any utterance made outside of court. • It is usu. treated as hearsay under the rules of evidence.

extra judicium (**ek**-strə joo-**dish**-ee-əm). [Latin] Extrajudicial; out of court; beyond the jurisdiction.

extra jus (**ek**-strə **jəs**). [Latin] Beyond the law; more than the law requires.

extralateral right. See APEX RULE.

extralegal, *adj.* Beyond the province of law.

extra legem (**ek**-strə **lee**-jəm). [Latin] Out of the law; out of the protection of the law.

extramural powers (ek-strə-**myuur**-əl). Powers exercised by a municipality outside its corporate limits.

extranational, *adj.* Beyond the territorial and governing limits of a country.

extraneous evidence. See *extrinsic evidence* (1) under EVIDENCE.

extraneous offense. See OFFENSE (1).

extraneous question. A question that is beyond or beside the point to be decided.

extraneus (ek-**stray**-nee-əs), *n.* [Latin "outside"] **1.** *Hist.* A person who is foreign-born; a foreigner. **2.** *Roman law.* An heir not born in the family of the testator; a citizen of a foreign state.

extraordinary average. See AVERAGE.

extraordinary care. See *highest degree of care* under DEGREE OF CARE.

extraordinary circumstances. See CIRCUMSTANCE.

extraordinary danger. See HAZARD (1).

extraordinary diligence. See DILIGENCE.

extraordinary dividend. See DIVIDEND.

extraordinary expense. See EXPENSE.

extraordinary flood. A flood whose occurrence is not predictable and whose magnitude and destructiveness could not have been anticipated or provided against by the exercise of ordinary foresight; a flood so unusual that a person of ordinary prudence and experience could not have foreseen it. See ACT OF GOD.

extraordinary gain. See GAIN (3).

extraordinary grand jury. See *special grand jury* under GRAND JURY.

extraordinary hazard. See HAZARD (1).

extraordinary majority. See *supermajority* under MAJORITY.

extraordinary remedy. See REMEDY.

extraordinary repair. As used in a lease, a repair that is made necessary by some unusual or unforeseen occurrence that does not destroy the building but merely renders it less suited to its intended use; a repair that is beyond the usual, customary, or regular kind.

extraordinary risk. See *extraordinary hazard* under HAZARD (1).

extraordinary session. See *special session* under SESSION.

extraordinary writ. See WRIT.

extraparochial (ek-strə-pə-**roh**-kee-əl), *adj.* Out of a parish; not within the bounds or limits of any parish.

extrapolate (ek-**strap**-ə-layt), *vb.* **1.** To estimate an unknown value or quantity on the basis of the known range, esp. by statistical methods. **2.** To deduce an unknown legal principle from a known case. **3.** To speculate about possible results, based on known facts. — **extrapolative** (-lay-tiv *or* -lə-tiv), **extrapolatory** (-lə-tor-ee), *adj.* — **extrapolator** (-lay-tər), *n.*

extrapolation (ek-strap-ə-**lay**-shən), *n.* **1.** The process of estimating an unknown value or quantity on the basis of the known range of variables. **2.** The process by which a court deduces a legal principle from another case. **3.** The process of speculating about possible results, based on known facts.

extra praesentiam mariti (**eks**-trə pri-**zen**-shee-əm mə-**rI**-tI *or* **mar**-ə-tI). [Latin] Out of her husband's presence.

extra quatuor maria (**eks**-trə **kwah**-too-ər **mar**-ee-ə). [Latin] **1.** Beyond the four seas. **2.** Out of the kingdom of England.

extra regnum (**eks**-trə **reg**-nəm). [Latin] Out of the realm.

extra session. See *special session* under SESSION.

extraterritorial, *adj.* Beyond the geographic limits of a particular jurisdiction. — Also termed *exterritorial.*

extraterritoriality. The freedom of diplomats, foreign ministers, and royalty from the jurisdiction of the country in which they temporarily reside. — Also termed *exterritoriality.* See *diplomatic immunity* under IMMUNITY (1).

extraterritorial jurisdiction. See JURISDICTION.

extra territorium (**eks**-trə ter-ə-**tor**-ee-əm). [Latin] Beyond or outside the territory.

Extravagantes (ek-strav-ə-**gan**-teez), *n. pl.* [Law Latin "wandering"] *Eccles. law.* Papal constitutions and decretal epistles of Pope John XXII and his successors. • These epistles were so called because they were not digested or arranged with the other papal constitutions, but appeared detached from canon law; the term remained even after the epistles were later included in the body of canon law.

extra viam (**eks**-trə **vI**-əm). [Latin "out of the way"] A plaintiff's responsive pleading in a trespass action, asserting that the defendant's claim of a right-of-way across the plaintiff's land is not a defense to the action because the defendant strayed from the supposed right-of-way.

extra vires (**eks**-trə **vI**-reez *or* **veer**-eez). See ULTRA VIRES.

extra work. See WORK.

extreme cruelty. See CRUELTY.

extreme force. See *deadly force* under FORCE.

extrinsic, *adj.* From outside sources.

extrinsic ambiguity. See *latent ambiguity* under AMBIGUITY.

extrinsic evidence. See EVIDENCE.

extrinsic fraud. See FRAUD.

ex turpi causa (eks **tər**-pI **kaw**-zə). [Latin] From an immoral consideration. • This phrase, a shortened form of the maxim *ex turpi causa non oritur actio* ("from an immoral consideration an action does not arise"), expresses the principle that a party does not have a right to enforce performance of an agreement founded on a consideration that is contrary to the public interest.

> "The doctrine *ex turpi causa* has made its way into the law as an extension of a moral principle. If it is misused, the principle suffers. Moreover, its misuse is a symptom of a disease of thought that debilitates the law and morals. This is the failure to recognize that there is a fundamental difference between the law that expresses a moral principle and the law that is only a social regulation. If only in the growth of English law that distinction had been maintained, much of the arbitrariness and the absurdities in the cases I have cited would have been avoided. There is a dictum of Lord Wright's which may

some day be used as a foundation for a change of heart. Speaking of the maxim *ex turpi causa*, he said: 'In these days there are many statutory offences which are the subject of the criminal law and in that sense are crimes, but which would, it seems, afford no moral justification for a court to apply the maxim'. *Beresford* v. *Royal Insurance* (1937), 2 KB. at 220." Patrick Devlin, *The Enforcement of Morals* 60 (1968).

exuere patriam (eg-**z**[**y**]**oo**-ə-ree **pay**-tree-əm), *vb*. [Latin] To renounce one's country or native allegiance; to expatriate oneself.

exulare (eks-[y]ə-**lair**-ee), *vb*. [Latin] *Hist*. To exile or banish.

ex una parte (eks [**y**]**oo**-nə **pahr**-tee). [Latin] Of one part or side; on one side.

exuperare (eg-z[y]oo-pə-**rair**-ee), *vb*. [Latin] To overcome; to apprehend or take.

ex utraque parte (eks yoo-**tray**-kwee **pahr**-tee). [Latin] On both sides.

ex utriusque parentibus conjuncti (eks yoo-tree-**əs**-kwee pə-**ren**-ti-bəs kən-**jəngk**-tɪ). [Latin] Related on the side of both parents; of the whole blood.

ex visceribus (eks vi-**ser**-ə-bəs). [Latin "from the bowels"] From the vital part; from the very essence of (a thing).

ex visceribus verborum (eks vi-**ser**-ə-bəs vər-**bor**-əm). [Latin] From the mere words (and nothing else); from the words themselves.

ex visitatione Dei (eks viz-ə-tay-shee-**oh**-nee **dee**-ɪ). [Latin] **1.** By the dispensation of God; by reason of physical incapacity. • Anciently, when a prisoner who was being arraigned stood silently instead of pleading, a jury was impaneled to inquire whether the prisoner obstinately stood mute or was dumb *ex visitatione Dei*. **2.** By natural causes as opposed to violent ones. • This phrase sometimes appears in a coroner's report when death results from a disease or another natural cause.

ex visu scriptionis (eks **vɪ**-s[y]oo [*or* -z[y]oo] skrip-shee-**oh**-nis). [Latin] From the sight of the writing; from having seen a person write. • This phrase describes a method of proving handwriting.

ex vi termini (eks vɪ **tər**-mə-nɪ). [Law Latin] From or by the force of the term; from the very meaning of the expression used.

ex voluntate (eks vol-ən-**tay**-tee). [Latin] Voluntarily; from free will or choice.

EXW. *abbr*. EX WORKS.

ex warrants, *adv*. Without warrants. • Shares are traded ex warrants when they no longer carry the right to receive declared warrants that have been distributed to holders. — Abbr. X; XW.

ex works. From the factory. • This trade term defines the obligations of a buyer and a seller of goods with respect to delivery, payment, and risk of loss. — Abbr. EXW.

ex-works price. See *ex-works price* under PRICE.

eyde (ayd), *n*. [Law French] Aid; assistance; relief; subsidy.

eye for an eye. See LEX TALIONIS.

eye of the law. The law as a personified thinker; legal contemplation <dead people are no longer persons in the eye of the law>.

eyewitness. One who personally observes an event. Cf. EARWITNESS.

eyewitness identification. A naming or description by which one who has seen an event testifies from memory about the person or persons involved.

eygne (ayn), *n*. See EIGNE.

eyre (air). [Old French *eire* "journey, march"] *Hist*. A system of royal courts sent out into the counties by the Crown to investigate allegations of wrongdoing, to try cases, and to raise revenue for the Crown through the levy of fines. • The eyre system was abolished in the 13th century. See ARTICLES OF THE EYRE; JUSTICE IN EYRE.

"In 1176 the itinerant justices were organised into six circuits.... The justices assigned to these circuits, who numbered as many as twenty or thirty at a time in the 1180s, were known as *justiciae errantes* (later *justiciarii in itinere*, justices in eyre); and the French word 'eyre' became the name of one of the most prominent forms of royal justice until the time of Edward III. Every so often a 'general eyre' would visit a county, bringing the king's government with it.... The general eyres were not merely law courts; they were a way of supervising local government through itinerant central government." J.H. Baker, *An Introduction to English Legal History* 19 (3d ed. 1990).

eyrer (**air**-ər), *vb*. [Law French] *Hist*. To travel or journey; to go about.

F. **1.** *abbr.* The first series of the Federal Reporter, which includes federal decisions (trial and appellate) from 1880 to 1924. **2.** *Hist.* A letter branded on a felon who claimed benefit of clergy so that the felon could claim the benefit only once. • Additionally, those convicted for an affray (fray) or falsity were so branded.

> "He that shall maliciously strike any person with a Weapon in Church or Churchyard, or draw any Weapon there with intent to strike, shall have one of his Ears cut off; and, if he have no Ears, then shall be marked on the Cheek with a hot Iron, having the Letter F, whereby he may be known for a *Fray-maker* or *Fighter*." Thomas Blount, *Nomo-Lexicon: A Law–Dictionary* (1670).

> "F, Is a Letter wherewith *Felons*, & c. are branded and marked with an hot Iron, on their being admitted to the Benefit of Clergy." Giles Jacob, *A New Law–Dictionary* (8th ed. 1762).

F.2d. *abbr.* The second series of the Federal Reporter, which includes federal appellate decisions from 1924 to 1993.

F.3d. *abbr.* The third series of the Federal Reporter, which includes federal appellate decisions from 1993.

FAA. *abbr.* **1.** FEDERAL AVIATION ADMINISTRATION. **2.** The Federal Arbitration Act, 9 USCA §§ 1–16. **3.** FREE OF ALL AVERAGE.

fabricare (fab-rə-**kair**-ee), *vb.* [Law Latin "to make"] *Hist.* **1.** To make a coin lawfully or unlawfully. **2.** To forge, esp. a bill of lading. • The term sometimes appeared in indictments: *fabricavit et contrafecit* ("[he] forged and counterfeited").

fabricate, *vb.* To invent, forge, or devise falsely. • To fabricate a story is to create a plausible version of events that is advantageous to the person relating those events. The term is softer than *lie*. See LIE (1).

fabricated evidence. See EVIDENCE.

fabric land. See LAND.

fabula (**fab**-yə-lə). [Law Latin] *Hist.* A contract or covenant, esp. a nuptial contract.

FAC. *abbr.* Failure to answer a (traffic) citation. • In some jurisdictions, if someone fails to respond after receiving a ticket, the court notifies the relevant administrative agency, which records this information and suspends the defendant's driver's license until the FAC is vacated and any fines or fees are paid.

face, *n.* **1.** The surface of anything, esp. the front, upper, or outer part <the face of a clock>. **2.** By extension, the apparent or explicit part of a writing or record <the fraud must appear on the face of the record>. **3.** The inscribed side of a document, instrument, or judgment <although the contract appeared valid on its face, the buyer did not have the legal capacity to enter into it>.

face amount. **1.** PAR VALUE. **2.** *Insurance.* The amount payable under an insurance policy. — Also termed *face value*; *face amount insured by the policy*; *face of policy*.

face-amount certificate. See CERTIFICATE.

face-amount certificate of installment type. See *face-amount certificate* (1) under CERTIFICATE.

face amount insured by the policy. See FACE AMOUNT.

face of policy. See FACE AMOUNT.

face rate. See *nominal rate* under INTEREST RATE.

face value. See FACE AMOUNT.

facial, *adj.* Apparent; on the face of things; prima facie <a facial challenge to the statute>.

facial attack. A challenge to the sufficiency of a complaint, such as a motion to dismiss in federal practice.

facial challenge. See CHALLENGE (1).

facially sufficient, *adj.* (Of a document) appearing valid on its face. • A search-warrant affidavit's facial sufficiency will not protect it from attack if the affidavit is based on false testimony by the officer making the affidavit. See FRANKS HEARING.

facially void. See VOID.

facias (**fay**-shee-əs). [Law Latin] That you cause. • *Facias* is used in writs as an emphatic word. See FIERI FACIAS; LEVARI FACIAS; SCIRE FACIAS. It also appears in the phrase *ut facias* ("so that you do"). See DO UT FACIAS; FACIO UT DES; FACIO UT FACIAS.

facies (**fay**-shee-eez). [Latin] The outward appearance or surface (of a thing).

facilitate, *vb. Criminal law.* To make the commission of a crime easier. • Property (such as a vehicle or home) that facilitates the commission of certain offenses may be forfeited. — **facilitator,** *n.*

facilitation, *n.* The act or an instance of aiding or helping; esp., in criminal law, the act of making it easier for another person to commit a crime.

facility-of-payment clause. An insurance-policy provision allowing the appointment of a person to receive payment from the insurer on the beneficiary's behalf.

facio ut des (**fay**-shee-oh ət **deez**). [Latin "I do so that you give"] *Civil law.* **1.** An innominate contract in which a person agrees to do something for recompense. See *innominate contract* under CONTRACT. **2.** The consideration in such a contract.

facio ut facias (**fay**-shee-oh ət **fay**-shee-əs). [Latin "I do that you may do"] *Civil law.* **1.** An innominate contract in which a person agrees to do something for another person who agrees to do something in return, such as an agreement to marry. **2.** The consideration in such a contract. See *innominate contract* under CONTRACT.

> "These valuable considerations are divided by the civilians into four species.... The second species is, *facio, ut facias*: as when I agree with a man to do his work for him, if he will do mine for me; or if two persons agree to marry together; or to do any positive acts on both sides. Or, it may be to forbear on one side in consideration of something done on the other; as, that in consideration A, the tenant, will repair his house, B, the landlord, will not sue him for waste." 2 William Blackstone, *Commentaries on the Laws of England* 444 (1766).

facsimile (fak-**sim**-ə-lee). **1.** An exact copy. **2.** FAX.

facsimile signature. See SIGNATURE.

facsimile transmission. See FAX.

fact. 1. Something that actually exists; an aspect of reality <it is a fact that all people are mortal>. **2.** An actual or alleged event or circumstance, as distinguished from its legal effect, consequence, or interpretation <the jury made a finding of fact>. **3.** An evil deed; a crime <an accessory after the fact>.

> "A *fact* is any act or condition of things, assumed (for the moment) as happening or existing." John H. Wigmore, *A Students' Textbook of the Law of Evidence* 7 (1935).

ablative fact. See *divestitive fact.*

adjudicative fact (ə-**joo**-di-kay-tiv *or* -kə-tiv). A controlling or operative fact, rather than a background fact; a fact that concerns the parties to a judicial or administrative proceeding and that helps the court or agency determine how the law applies to those parties. • For example, adjudicative facts include those that the jury weighs. Cf. *legislative fact.*

alienative fact (**ay**-lee-ə-nay-tiv *or* **ay**-lee-ə-nə-tiv). A fact that divests a person of a right by transferring it to another.

collateral fact. A fact not directly connected to the issue in dispute, esp. because it involves a different transaction from the one at issue.

collative fact. See *investitive fact.*

denotative fact (**dee**-noh-tay-tiv *or* di-**noh**-tə-tiv). A fact relevant to the use of a nonlegal term in a legal rule.

destitutive fact. See *divestitive fact.*

dispositive fact (dis-**poz**-ə-tiv). **1.** A fact that confers rights or causes the loss of rights. • A dispositive fact may be either an investitive or a divestitive fact. — Also termed *vestitive fact* (**ves**-tə-tiv). **2.** A fact that is decisive of a legal matter; evidence that definitively resolves a legal issue or controversy. See DISPOSITION.

divestitive fact (di-**ves**-tə-tiv *or* dɪ-). A fact that causes the loss of rights; an act or event modifying or extinguishing a legal relation. — Also termed *destitutive fact*; *ablative fact.*

elemental fact. See *ultimate fact.*

evaluative fact. A fact used to assess an action as being reasonable or negligent.

evidentiary fact (ev-i-**den**-shə-ree). **1.** A fact that is necessary for or leads to the determination of an ultimate fact. — Also termed *predicate fact*. **2.** A fact that furnishes evidence of the existence of some other fact. — Also termed *evidential fact*. **3.** See *fact in evidence*.

exonerative fact (eg-**zon**-ər-ə-tiv *or* -ay-tiv). A divestitive fact that extinguishes a duty.

extinctive fact. A fact that divests a right by destroying it. — Also termed *destitutive fact*; *ablative fact*.

fabricated fact. See *fabricated evidence* under EVIDENCE.

fact in evidence. A fact that a tribunal considers in reaching a conclusion; a fact that has been admitted into evidence in a trial or hearing. — Sometimes written *fact-in-evidence*. — Also termed *evidentiary fact*.

> "A *fact-in-evidence*, or, briefly, *evidence*, signifies any facts considered by the tribunal as data to persuade them to reach a reasoned belief upon a probandum. This process of thought by which the tribunal reasons from fact to probandum is termed *inference*." John H. Wigmore, *A Students' Textbook of the Law of Evidence* 7 (1935).

fact in issue. (*usu. pl.*) **1.** *Hist.* A fact that the plaintiff alleges and that the defendant controverts. **2.** A fact to be determined by a fact-trier; PROBANDUM. — Also written *fact-in-issue*. — Also termed *principal fact*.

> "A *fact-in-issue* is a fact as to the correctness of which the tribunal, under the law of the case, must be persuaded; the term 'probandum' (thing to be proved) will here be used as the convenient single word." John H. Wigmore, *A Students' Textbook of the Law of Evidence* 7 (1935).

fact material to risk. *Insurance.* A fact that may increase the risk and that, if disclosed, might induce the insurer either to decline to insure or to require a higher premium.

foundational fact. See *predicate fact*.

immaterial fact. A fact that is not essential to a matter in issue.

impositive fact. An investitive fact that imposes duties.

inferential fact. A fact established by conclusions drawn from other evidence rather than from direct testimony or evidence; a fact derived logically from other facts.

investitive fact (in-**ves**-tə-tiv). A fact that confers rights. — Also termed *collative fact* (kə-**lay**-tiv).

judicial fact. A fact that the court accepts as proved without hearing evidence. See JUDICIAL NOTICE.

jurisdictional fact. (*usu. pl.*) A fact that must exist for a court to properly exercise its jurisdiction over a case, party, or thing. See JURISDICTIONAL-FACT DOCTRINE.

legal fact. A fact that triggers a particular legal consequence.

legislative fact. A fact that explains a particular law's rationality and that helps a court or agency determine the law's content and application. • Legislative facts are not ordinarily specific to the parties in a proceeding. Cf. *adjudicative fact*.

material fact. A fact that is significant or essential to the issue or matter at hand.

minor fact. A subordinate fact or circumstance.

operative fact. A fact that affects an existing legal relation, esp. a legal claim.

physical fact. A fact having a physical existence, such as a fingerprint left at a crime scene.

predicate fact (**pred**-ə-kit). A fact from which a presumption or inference arises. — Also termed *foundational fact*; *evidentiary fact*.

primary fact. A fact that can be established by direct testimony and from which inferences are made leading to ultimate facts. See *ultimate fact*.

principal fact. **1.** A fact on which the plaintiff's right of recovery depends. **2.** See *fact in issue*.

private fact. A fact that has not been made public. • Whether a fact is private often arises in invasion-of-privacy claims. Cf. *public fact*.

probative fact (**proh**-bə-tiv). A fact in evidence used to prove an ultimate fact, such as skid marks used to show speed as a predicate to a finding of negligence.

public fact. For the purpose of an invasion-of-privacy claim, a fact that is in a public record or in the public domain. Cf. *private fact*.

relative fact. A fact incidental to another fact; a minor fact.

translative fact (trans- *or* tranz-**lay**-tiv). A fact by means of which a right is transferred from one person to another; a fact that fulfills the double function of terminating one person's right to an object and of originating another's right to it.

ultimate fact. A fact essential to the claim or the defense. — Also termed *elemental fact*; *principal fact*.

undisputed fact. An uncontested or admitted fact, esp. one that a court has not deemed necessary to include in a finding of fact.

vestitive fact. See *dispositive fact* (1).

facta (**fak**-tə). [Latin] *pl.* FACTUM.

fact-finder. One or more persons — such as jurors in a trial or administrative-law judges in a hearing — who hear testimony and review evidence to rule on a factual issue. — Also termed *finder of fact*; *fact-trier* or *trier of fact* (in a judicial proceeding); *fact-finding board* (for a group or committee). See FINDING OF FACT.

fact-finding. 1. The process of taking evidence to determine the truth about a disputed point. **2.** *Int'l law.* A method of gathering information for purposes of international relations, including legislative tours, the peaceful settlement of disputes, the supervision of international agreements, and the acquisition of information required for making decisions at an international level. — Also termed *inquiry*. **3.** A method of alternative dispute resolution in which an impartial third party determines and studies the facts and positions of disputing parties that have reached an impasse, with a view toward clarifying the issues and helping the parties work through their dispute.

fact-finding board. See FACT-FINDER.

fact in evidence. See FACT.

fact in issue. See FACT.

fact material to risk. See FACT.

facto. See DE FACTO; IPSO FACTO.

facto et animo (**fak**-toh et **an**-ə-moh). [Latin] In fact and intent <taking possession *facto et animo*>.

factor, *n.* **1.** An agent or cause that contributes to a particular result <punishment was a factor in the court's decision>. **2.** An agent who is employed to sell property for the principal and who possesses or controls the property; a person who receives and sells goods for a commission <a factor was employed to sell goods for the company>. • A factor differs from a broker because the factor possesses or controls the property. — Also termed *commission merchant*; *del credere bailiff*. Cf. BROKER.

> "A factor by the rules of common law and of mercantile usage is an agent to whom goods are consigned for the purpose of sale, and he has possession of the goods, power to sell them in his own name, and a general discretion as to their sale. He may sell them on the usual terms of credit, may receive the price, and give a good discharge to the buyer." William R. Anson, *Principles of the Law of Contract* 523 (Arthur L. Corbin ed., 3d Am. ed. 1919).

3. One who buys accounts receivable at a discount <the company sold its receivables to a factor at only 5% of their stated value>. **4.** A garnishee <the factor held $400 of the debtor's property when the writ of garnishment was served>.

factorage. 1. The compensation paid to a factor for his or her services. **2.** The business of a factor.

factoring, *n.* The buying of accounts receivable at a discount. • The price is discounted because the factor (who buys them) assumes the risk of delay in collection and loss on the accounts receivable.

factorize, *vb.* See GARNISH.

factorizing process. A procedure or legal process by which a third party, rather than the creditor, attaches a debtor's property; GARNISHMENT. — Also termed *trustee process*; *process by foreign attachment*.

> "In Vermont and Connecticut, the [garnishee] is also sometimes called the factor, and the process [of garnishing], factorizing process." Charles D. Drake, *A Treatise on the Law of Suits by Attachment in the United States* § 451, at 386 (7th ed. 1891).

factor's act. A statute protecting one who buys goods from a factor or agent by creating the presumption that the agent was acting on the owner's behalf and with the owner's approval.

factor's lien. See LIEN.

factory act. A statute that regulates workers' hours, health, and safety. See FAIR LABOR STANDARDS ACT.

fact pleading. See *code pleading* under PLEADING (2).

fact question. See QUESTION OF FACT.

fact-trier. See FACT-FINDER.

factual cause. See *but-for cause* under CAUSE (1).

factual impossibility. See IMPOSSIBILITY.

factual presumption. See *presumption of fact* under PRESUMPTION.

factum (**fak**-təm), *n.* [Latin] **1.** A fact, such as a person's physical presence in a new domicile. **2.** An act or deed, such as the due execution of a will. • Over time, *factum* in this sense came to mean "charter" — that is, the act or deed of conveying land, reduced to written form. See *fraud in the factum* under FRAUD.

> "[I]t is only a short step to holding as a matter of law that a 'deed' — and by a deed (*fet, factum*) men are beginning to mean a sealed piece of parchment — has an operative force of its own which intentions expressed, never so plainly, in other ways have not. The sealing and delivering of the parchment is the contractual act. Further, what is done by 'deed' can only be undone by 'deed.'" 2 Frederick Pollock & Frederic W. Maitland, *The History of English Law Before the Time of Edward I* 220 (2d ed. 1899).

factum juridicum (**fak**-təm juu-**rid**-i-kəm). [Latin] A juridical fact.

factum probandum (**fak**-təm prə-**ban**-dəm). [Latin] A fact to be proved.

factum probans (**fak**-təm **proh**-banz). [Latin] A probative or evidentiary fact.

3. A statement of facts. **4.** BRIEF (1). Pl. **facta.**

facultative certificate (**fak**-əl-tay-tiv). *Reinsurance.* A contract of reinsurance separately negotiated to cover risks under a single insurance policy. • Facultative reinsurance allows the reinsurer the "faculty" of assessing and possibly rejecting a particular risk (esp. if underwriting information is inadequate).

facultative reinsurance. See REINSURANCE.

faculties. *Hist. Eccles. law.* **1.** An authorization granted to a person to do what otherwise would not be allowed. **2.** The extent of a husband's estate; esp., the ability to pay alimony. See ALLEGATION OF FACULTIES.

Faculties, Court of. See COURT OF FACULTIES.

Faculties, Master of the. See MASTER OF THE FACULTIES.

faderfium (**fah**-thər-fee-əm). *Hist.* A marriage gift to the bride from her father or brother.

faeder-feoh (**fah**-thər-fee). *Hist.* Property brought by a wife to her husband at marriage. • If the husband died, the property reverted to the widow if the heir of the deceased husband refused consent to her second marriage. The property reverted to the widow's family if she returned to them.

faggot. *Hist.* **1.** A piece of firewood used to burn a heretic alive. **2.** An embroidered figure of a faggot, required to be worn by heretics who had recanted.

fail, *n.* A transaction between securities brokers in which delivery and payment do not occur at the prescribed time, usu. on the settlement date. — Also termed *fail contract.*

fail to deliver. The nondelivery of securities from a selling broker to a buying broker by the settlement date.

fail to receive. The failure of a buying broker to receive delivery of securities from the selling broker by the settlement date.

fail, *vb.* **1.** To be deficient or unsuccessful; to fall short <they failed to settle the dispute>. **2.** To become insolvent or bankrupt <two banks failed last week>. **3.** To lapse <the bequest failed as a result of ademption>.

failing circumstances. See INSOLVENCY.

failing-company doctrine. *Antitrust.* The rule that allows an otherwise proscribed merger or acquisition between competitors when one is bankrupt or near failure. 15 USCA §§ 12–27. — Also termed *failing-firm defense.*

> "The 1992 guidelines provide a limited defense for failing firms and failing divisions of firms. The defense is available if impending failure would cause the assets of one party to leave the market if the merger does not occur. Thus to establish a *failing firm* defense, the parties must show that the failing firm cannot (1) meet its financial obligations, (2) reorganize in bankruptcy, and (3) find another buyer whose purchase of the firm would pose lesser anticompetitive risks. The parties must further show that (4) without the merger, the failing firm's assets will exit the market." Ernest Gellhorn & William E. Kovacic, *Antitrust Law and Economics in a Nutshell* 398–99 (4th ed. 1994).

fail position. A situation existing when, after all transactions in a security have been netted out, a broker owes another broker more securities than it has coming in from other firms.

failure. 1. Deficiency; lack; want. **2.** An omission of an expected action, occurrence, or performance. See LAPSE (2).

failure of a condition. A situation in which an event required in a contract is not satisfied, as a result of which the adversely affected party is discharged from performing. • This situation does not void the contract; the parties are still bound, but one party does not have to perform because of the failure of the condition.

failure of consideration. See FAILURE OF CONSIDERATION.

failure of good behavior. A civil servant's act that is ground for removal.

failure of issue. See FAILURE OF ISSUE.

failure of justice. See MISCARRIAGE OF JUSTICE.

failure of proof. A party's not having produced evidence establishing a fact essential to a claim or defense.

failure of title. A seller's inability to establish a good claim to the property contracted for sale. Cf. *clear title* under TITLE.

failure of trust. The lapse of a trust because the instrument creating it has a defect or because of its illegality or other legal impediment.

failure otherwise than on the merits. The defeat of a plaintiff's claim by a procedural device without a decision on the existence of the claim's elements.

failure to bargain collectively. An employer's refusal to discuss labor issues with a union.

failure to make delivery. Nondelivery or misdelivery.

failure to meet obligations. See BANKRUPTCY (2); INSOLVENCY.

failure to perform. A party's not meeting its obligations under a contract. See CONTRACT (4).

failure to state a cause of action. A plaintiff's not having alleged facts in the complaint sufficient to maintain a claim. • This failure warrants dismissal of the complaint.

failure to testify. A party's — esp. a criminal defendant's — decision not to testify. • Under the Fifth Amendment, the prosecutor and the judge cannot comment to the jury on a criminal defendant's failure to testify. But comments on the failure are usu. permissible in a civil case.

failure of consideration. A situation in which a contract's basis or inducement ceases to exist or becomes worthless. • This term, unlike *consideration* per se, relates not to the formation of a contract but to its performance. See CONSIDERATION. Cf. WANT OF CONSIDERATION.

> "An illustration will help indicate how the term is used. If C promises to build a structure for O and O promises to make payment when the work is completed, it is clear that there is consideration on both sides of this contract and that therefore a contract was formed upon the exchange of promises. If C fails to perform, the result is sometimes described as a 'failure of consideration.' 'Failure of consideration' simply means a failure to perform and as used covers both a material breach of constructive conditions and a failure to perform an express condition. The use of the term 'failure of consideration' in this sense appears to be an unnecessary invitation to confusion because the word consideration is being used in two different senses. Fortunately, the use of this phrase has gradually fallen into disuse. It is, however, still sufficiently widespread to be mentioned here. This volume nowhere utilizes 'failure of consideration' as an operative concept." John D. Calamari & Joseph M. Perillo, *The Law of Contracts* § 11–21, at 474–75 (3d ed. 1987).

partial failure of consideration. A situation in which the contract consists of separable items of consideration and separable parts of the agreement, so that if part of the consideration fails, the appropriate part of the agreement can be apportioned to it. • The several parts of the contract are in effect treated as separate contracts, and the contract is voided only to the extent that the consideration for one part fails.

total failure of consideration. A situation in which the contract is indivisible so that a complete lack of consideration voids the contract.

> "The concept of total failure of consideration is a somewhat technical one. In particular there may be a total failure of consideration even though the defendant has actually done some work or expended some money in the performance of the contract, provided that what he has done has not enured to the benefit of the other party. For example, if a person orders machinery to be specially constructed for him, there will be a total failure of consideration if none of the machinery is delivered to him although work may have been commenced and money expended on it. On the other hand, if some benefit has been received under the contract, no matter how trifling, there is no total failure of consideration. In this case, just as there is generally no right to part payment for part performance, so also there is generally no right to part recovery for partial failure of consideration." P.S. Atiyah, *An Introduction to the Law of Contract* 306–07 (3d ed. 1981).

failure of good behavior. See FAILURE.

failure of issue. The fact of dying without children, esp. if they would have inherited the decedent's estate. — Also termed *dying without issue*. See ISSUE (3).

> "There has been considerable litigation during the past several centuries over the meaning of a gift to 'A and his

heirs, but if A shall die without issue, to B and his heirs.' First of all, what does 'die without issue' mean? The answer appears simple — you look to the time of A's death to determine whether or not he has any children or grandchildren. But that is not the way the English courts originally construed this language. The English adopted the so-called 'indefinite failure of issue' construction — if at any time in the future A's line of descent should come to an end, then there was a gift over to B and his heirs. The effect of this was a fee tail in A and a remainder in B. This seems a distortion of the language, and particularly unsuited to American circumstances since the fee tail never found a real home here. Most of our jurisdictions, by judicial decision or statute, adopted the so-called 'definite failure of issue' construction — you look to the date of A's death to determine whether he has issue, and to that time alone. If A has issue at that time, then the gift over to B fails. This seems to be the literal meaning of the words, and it is the only sensible conclusion in a system where the fee tail is virtually a dead letter. The English also struck down the constructional preference for indefinite failure by statute in the nineteenth century." Thomas F. Bergin & Paul G. Haskell, *Preface to Estates in Land and Future Interests* 236–37 (2d ed. 1984).

indefinite failure of issue. A failure of issue whenever it happens, without any certain period within which it must happen.

failure of justice. See MISCARRIAGE OF JUSTICE.

failure of proof. See FAILURE.

failure of title. See FAILURE.

failure of trust. See FAILURE.

failure otherwise than on the merits. See FAILURE.

failure to bargain collectively. See FAILURE.

failure to make delivery. See FAILURE.

failure to meet obligations. See BANKRUPTCY (2); INSOLVENCY.

failure to perform. See FAILURE.

failure-to-perform exclusion. See EXCLUSION (3).

failure to state a cause of action. See FAILURE.

failure to testify. See FAILURE.

failure to thrive. A medical and psychological condition in which a child's height, weight, and motor development fall significantly below average growth rates. • Failure to thrive is sometimes asserted as a ground for terminating parental rights.

faint action. See FEIGNED ACTION.

faint pleader. A false, fraudulent, or collusive manner of pleading.

fair, *adj.* **1.** Impartial; just; equitable; disinterested <everyone thought that Judge Jones was fair>. **2.** Free of bias or prejudice <in jury selection, the lawyers tried to select a fair and impartial jury>.

fair, *n. Hist.* A privileged market for the buying and selling of goods. • A fair was an incorporeal hereditament granted to a town by royal patent or franchise or established by prescription. The franchise to hold a fair conferred important privileges, and a fair, as a legally recognized institution, possessed distinctive legal characteristics, most of which are now obsolete. Cf. *market overt* under MARKET.

fair-and-equitable requirement. *Bankruptcy.* A Bankruptcy Code standard requiring a forced, nonconsensual Chapter 11 plan (a "cramdown" plan) to provide adequately for each class of interests that has not accepted the plan. • In determining whether a cramdown plan is fair and equitable and thus can be confirmed, a bankruptcy court must apply the Code's detailed statutory criteria, consider the plan as a whole, and weigh all the circumstances surrounding the treatment of each impaired class of interests. In addition to the fair-and-equitable requirement, the Chapter 11 cramdown plan must (1) be accepted by at least one impaired class of claims, and (2) not discriminate unfairly among impaired classes that have not accepted the plan. 11 USCA § 1129(b). See CRAMDOWN.

fair and impartial jury. See *impartial jury* under JURY.

fair and impartial trial. See FAIR TRIAL.

fair and proper legal assessment. See EQUALIZATION.

fair and reasonable value. See *fair market value* under VALUE.

fair and valuable consideration. See *fair consideration* under CONSIDERATION.

fair averaging. The process of assessing taxes by using the average of the amount and price of goods acquired over a 12–month period rather than the amount and price at a particular time of the year.

fair cash market value. See *fair market value* under VALUE.

fair cash value. See *fair market value* under VALUE.

fair comment. A statement based on the writer's or speaker's honest opinion about a matter of public concern. • Fair comment is a defense to libel or slander.

fair competition. See COMPETITION.

fair consideration. See CONSIDERATION.

Fair Credit Billing Act. A federal law that facilitates the correction of billing errors by credit-card companies and makes those companies more responsible for the quality of goods purchased by cardholders. 15 USCA §§ 1666–1666j.

fair-credit-reporting act. A federal or state law that regulates the keeping of credit reports and ensures the right of consumers to get and correct their credit reports. • The federal Fair Credit Reporting Act was enacted in 1970. 15 USCA §§ 1681–1681u.

fair-cross-section requirement. *Constitutional law.* The principle that a person's right to an impartial jury, guaranteed by the Sixth Amendment, includes a requirement that the pool of potential jurors fairly represent the composition of the jurisdiction's population. • The pool of potential jurors need not precisely match the composition of the jurisdiction. But the representation of each group must be fair, and there must not be a systematic exclusion or underrepresentation of any group. A minimal disparity in a particular group's representation, such as an absolute disparity of 10%, will not ordinarily violate this principle unless some aggravating factor exists. See DUREN TEST; ABSOLUTE DISPARITY; COMPARATIVE DISPARITY; STATISTICAL-DECISION THEORY.

fair dealing, *n.* **1.** The conduct of business with full disclosure, usu. by a corporate officer with the corporation. **2.** A fiduciary's transacting of business so that, although the fiduciary might derive a personal benefit, all interested persons are fully apprised of that potential and of all other material information about the transaction. Cf. SELF-DEALING.

fair hearing. See HEARING.

Fair Labor Standards Act. A federal law, enacted in 1938, that regulates minimum wages, overtime pay, and the employment of minors. 29 USCA §§ 201–219. — Abbr. FLSA.

fairly-debatable rule. **1.** *Insurance.* In some states, a test that requires an insurer to have a plausible basis for denying a claim to avoid bad-faith liability. **2.** *Zoning.* A doctrine that bars a court from interfering with a zoning decision that is supported by substantial evidence, although it is one on which reasonable minds can differ. • A court will not interfere with a decision supported by substantial evidence.

fair market price. See *fair market value* under VALUE.

fair market value. See VALUE.

fairness doctrine. A federal law, based on an FCC rule, requiring the broadcast media to furnish a reasonable opportunity for the discussion of conflicting views on issues of public importance. • The FCC abandoned the fairness doctrine in 1987. — Also termed *equal-time doctrine.*

fair notice. See NOTICE.

fair on its face. (Of a document) having the appearance of being regular or legal and not capable of being shown to be defective without extraneous evidence.

fair play. Equity, candor, and fidelity in dealings with another.

fair play and substantial justice. The fairness requirement that a court must meet in its assertion of personal jurisdiction over a nonresident defendant to comport with due process. *International Shoe Co. v. Washington,* 326 U.S. 310, 66 S.Ct. 154 (1945). See MINIMUM CONTACTS.

fair preponderance of the evidence. See PREPONDERANCE OF THE EVIDENCE.

fair rate of return. See RATE OF RETURN.

fair-report privilege. A defense to liability for publishing defamatory matter from a report of an official or judicial proceeding, when the report is a full, fair, and accurate account of the proceeding.

fair representation. *Labor law.* Union representation that adequately covers all union members in collective bargaining and in the lodging of grievances.

fair return on investment. See RETURN.

fair sale. See SALE.

fair trade, *n.* Commerce conducted under a fair-trade agreement.

fair-trade agreement. A commercial agreement that a seller will sell all of a producer's goods at or above a specified minimum price. • Fair-trade agreements were valid until 1975, when the Consumer Goods Pricing Act made them illegal. 15 USCA §§ 1, 45.

fair trial. A trial by an impartial and disinterested tribunal in accordance with regular procedures; esp., a criminal trial in which the defendant's constitutional and legal rights are respected. — Also termed *fair and impartial trial.*

fair use. *Copyright.* A reasonable and limited use of a copyrighted work without the author's permission, such as quoting from a book in a book review or using parts of it in a parody. • Fair use is a defense to an infringement claim, depending on the following statutory factors: (1) the purpose and character of the use, (2) the nature of the copyrighted work, (3) the amount of the work used, and (4) the economic impact of the use. 17 USCA § 107.

> "[Fair use is] the most troublesome [problem] in the whole law of copyright." *Dellar v. Samuel Goldwyn, Inc.*, 104 F.2d 661, 662 (2d Cir. 1939) (per curiam).

> "Fair use is a judicial safety valve, empowering courts to excuse certain quotations or copies of copyrighted material even though the literal terms of the Copyright Act prohibit them." Paul Goldstein, *Copyright's Highway* 84 (1994).

fair value. See *fair market value* under VALUE.

fair-value accounting method. See ACCOUNTING METHOD.

fair-value law. A statute allowing a credit against a deficiency for the amount that the fair market value of land exceeds the price at foreclosure. — Also termed *fair-value legislation.*

fair warning. *Criminal law.* The requirement that a criminal statute define an offense with enough precision so that a reasonable person can know what conduct is prohibited and so that a reasonably skilled lawyer can predict what conduct falls within the statute's scope. — Also termed *fair notice.*

fair wear and tear. See WEAR AND TEAR.

fait (fay *or* fe). [Law French fr. Latin *factum*] Anything done; an act or deed. • The term *fait accompli* (fay *or* fe tə-kom-**plee**), meaning "a deed accomplished," which is not merely legal, is related to this word.

fait enrolle (fay *or* fe to*n*-**rohl**). [Law French] *Hist.* An enrolled deed of a sale of a freehold estate.

faith and trust. See FLIM FLAM.

Faithfully Executed Clause. The clause of the U.S. Constitution providing that the President must take care that the laws are carried out faithfully. U.S. Const. art. II, § 3.

fake, *n.* Something that is not what it purports to be. See FORGERY (2); IMPOSTOR.

fake, *vb.* To make or construct falsely. See COUNTERFEIT.

Falcidian law (fal-**sid**-ee-ən). *Roman law.* A law prescribing that no one could give more than three-fourths of one's property in legacies and that the heirs should receive at least one-fourth (the Falcidian portion). • If the testator violated this law, the heir had the right to deduct proportionally from each legatee as necessary. The law, proposed by the Roman tribune Falcidius, was enacted in 40 B.C. — Also termed *lex falcidia.* See LEGITIME.

> "A large number of small legacies might [either] leave nothing for the heir . . . [or] make his part so small as to seem valueless in his eyes. But a Falcidian law, passed in the year 40 B.C., put an end to the whole difficulty. This law secured to the heir a quarter of the net value of the estate; the legatees could obtain only three-quarters: if the legatees named in the will amounted to more than this, they were diminished by proportional reductions. . . . Few measures have accomplished their purpose more satisfactorily than the Falcidian law, which remained in force through the history of the empire, and holds an important place in the system of Justinian." James Hadley, *Introduction to Roman Law* 321–22 (1881).

Falcidian portion. *Roman law.* The one-fourth part of an estate that one or more instituted heirs are entitled to retain. • The Falcidian portion has been abolished in Louisiana, but a legitime heir is entitled to a portion by law. — Also termed *quarta falcidia.* See *forced heir* under HEIR; LEGITIME.

***Falconer* error.** A trial court's failure to instruct the jury that a guilty finding on a manslaughter charge requires acquittal on a murder charge. *Falconer v. Lane*, 905 F.2d 1129 (7th Cir. 1990).

falsa causa. See CAUSA (2).

falsa demonstratio (**fal**-sə *or* **fawl**-sə dem-ən-**stray**-shee-oh). *Roman law.* A false designation; an erroneous description of a person or thing in a legal instrument. • Generally, a simple error in description, grammar, or spelling will not void an instrument or even a single provision in it (such as a bequest by will). — Also termed *false demonstration.*

falsa moneta (**fal**-sə *or* **fawl**-sə mə-**nee**-tə). *Roman law.* Counterfeit money.

falsare (fal-**sair**-ee *or* fawl-), *vb.* [Law Latin] *Hist.* To counterfeit; to falsify.

falsarius (fal-**sair**-ee-əs *or* fawl-). [Law Latin] *Hist.* A counterfeiter. — Also spelled *falcarious.* — Also termed *falsonarius.*

false, *adj.* **1.** Untrue <a false statement>. **2.** Deceitful; lying <a false witness>. **3.** Not genuine; inauthentic <false coinage>. • What is false can be so by intent, by accident, or by mistake.

false action. See FEIGNED ACTION.

false advertising, *n.* The tortious and sometimes criminal act of distributing an advertisement that is untrue, deceptive, or misleading. — Also termed *deceptive advertising.*

false answer. A sham answer in a pleading. See *sham pleading* under PLEADING.

false arrest. See ARREST.

false character. *Hist.* The crime of impersonating a servant's master or mistress. See IMPOSTOR.

false check. See *bad check* under CHECK.

false claim. An assertion or statement that is untrue; esp., overbilling.

False Claims Act. A federal statute establishing civil and criminal penalties against persons who bill the government falsely, deliver less to the government than represented, or use a fake record to decrease an obligation to the government. 18 USCA §§ 286–287; 31 USCA §§ 3729–3733. • The Act may be enforced either by the attorney general or by a private person in a qui tam action.

false conflict of laws. See CONFLICT OF LAWS.

false demonstration. See FALSA DEMONSTRATIO.

false evidence. See *false testimony* under TESTIMONY.

falsehood. A lie. See LIE; PERJURY.

false impersonation. See IMPERSONATION.

false-implication libel. See LIBEL.

false imprisonment. A restraint of a person in a bounded area without justification or consent. • False imprisonment is a common-law misdemeanor and a tort. It applies to private as well as governmental detention. Cf. *false arrest* under ARREST.

> "[In the phrase *false imprisonment*,] false is . . . used not in the ordinary sense of mendacious or fallacious, but in the less common though well-established sense of erroneous or wrong; as in the phrases false quantity, false step, false taste, etc." R.F.V. Heuston, *Salmond on the Law of Torts* 123 n.38 (17th ed. 1977).

> "False imprisonment was a misdemeanor at common law and is recognized by some states today. It differs from kidnapping in that asportation is not required. If the imprisonment is secret, some jurisdictions treat it as kidnapping." Arnold H. Loewy, *Criminal Law in a Nutshell* 65 (2d ed. 1987).

> "Some courts have described false arrest and false imprisonment as causes of action which are distinguishable only in terminology. The two have been called virtually indistinguishable, and identical. However, the difference between them lies in the manner in which they arise. In order to commit false imprisonment, it is not necessary either to intend to make an arrest or actually to make an arrest. By contrast, a person who is falsely arrested is at the same time falsely imprisoned." 32 Am. Jur. 2d *False Imprisonment* § 3 (1995).

false judgment. *Hist.* A writ filed to obtain review of a judgment of a court not of record.

> "After judgment given, a writ also of *false judgment* lies to the courts at Westminster to rehear and review the

cause, and not a writ of *error*; for this is not a court of record...." 3 William Blackstone, *Commentaries on the Laws of England* 34 (1768).

false light. 1. *Torts.* In an invasion-of-privacy action, a plaintiff's allegation that the defendant attributed to the plaintiff views that he or she does not hold and placed the plaintiff before the public in a highly offensive and untrue manner. • If the matter involves the public interest, the plaintiff must prove the defendant's malice. See INVASION OF PRIVACY. **2.** (*usu. pl.*) *Maritime law.* A signal displayed intentionally to lure a vessel into danger. 18 USCA § 1658(b). — Also termed *false light or signal.*

false making. See FORGERY.

false misrepresentation. See MISREPRESENTATION. • This phrase is redundant — *misrepresentation* includes the idea of falsity.

false news. *Hist.* The misdemeanor of spreading false information that causes discord between the monarch and the people or between important people in the realm. 3 Edw. I, ch. 34.

false oath. See PERJURY.

false personation. See *false impersonation* under IMPERSONATION.

false plea. See *sham pleading* under PLEADING (1).

false pretenses. The crime of knowingly obtaining title to another's personal property by misrepresenting a fact with the intent to defraud. • Although unknown to English common law, false pretenses became a misdemeanor under a statute old enough to make it common law in the United States. Modern American statutes make it either a felony or a misdemeanor, depending on how valuable the property is. — Also termed *obtaining property by false pretenses*; *fraudulent pretenses*. Cf. *larceny by trick* under LARCENY; EMBEZZLEMENT.

false promise. See PROMISE.

false report. The criminal offense of informing law enforcement about a crime that did not occur.

false representation. See MISREPRESENTATION.

false return. 1. A process server's or other court official's recorded misrepresentation that process was served, that some other action was taken, or that something is true. **2.** A tax return on which taxable income is incorrectly reported or the tax is incorrectly computed. See TAX RETURN.

false statement. 1. An untrue statement knowingly made with the intent to mislead. See PERJURY. **2.** Any one of three distinct federal offenses: (1) falsifying or concealing a material fact by trick, scheme, or device; (2) making a false, fictitious, or fraudulent representation; and (3) making or using a false document or writing. 18 USCA § 1001.

false swearing. See PERJURY.

false testimony. See TESTIMONY.

false verdict. See VERDICT.

false weight. (*usu. pl.*) A weight or measure that does not comply with governmentally prescribed standards or with the prevailing custom in the place and business in which the weight or measure is used.

falsi crimen. See CRIMEN FALSI.

falsify, *vb.* **1.** To make something false; to counterfeit or forge <the chiropractor falsified his records to help the plaintiff>. See COUNTERFEIT; FORGERY. **2.** *Rare.* To prove something to be false or erroneous <their goal in the appeal was to falsify the jury's verdict>.

falsifying a record. The crime of making false entries or otherwise tampering with a public record with the intent to deceive or injure, or to conceal wrongdoing. 18 USCA §§ 1506, 2071, 2073; Model Penal Code § 224.4.

falsity, *n.* **1.** Something (such as a statement) that is false. See LIE. **2.** The quality of being false. See FALSE.

falsonarius. See FALSARIUS.

falso retorno brevium (**fal**-soh [*or* **fawl**-soh] ri-**tor**-noh **bree**-vee-əm). [Law Latin] *Hist.* A writ against a sheriff for falsely returning a writ.

falsum (**fal**-səm *or* **fawl**-səm), *n.* [Latin] *Roman law.* **1.** A false statement. **2.** A crime involving forgery or falsification.

***falsus in uno* doctrine** (**fal**-səs [*or* **fawl**-səs] in **yoo**-noh). [fr. Latin *falsus in uno, falsus in omnibus* "false in one thing, false in all"] The principle that if the jury believes that a witness's testimony on a material issue is intentionally deceitful, the jury may disregard all of that witness's testimony.

"[T]here is an old maxim 'falsus in uno, falsus in omnibus' (false in one thing, false in all), which is often much overemphasized by counsel, though it is recognized by many courts in their charges to the jury. But this is only primitive psychology, and should be completely discarded." John H. Wigmore, *A Students' Textbook of the Law of Evidence* 181 (1935).

fama publica (**fay**-mə **pəb**-li-kə). [Latin "public repute"] *Hist.* A person's reputation in the community. • A person's *fama publica* could be used against him or her in a criminal proceeding. Cf. ILL FAME.

"Now in the thirteenth century we find in the sheriff's turn a procedure by way of double presentment, and we may see it often, though not always, when a coroner is holding an inquest over the body of a dead man. The *fama publica* is twice distilled. The representatives of the vills make presentments to a jury of twelve freeholders which represents the hundred, and then such of these presentments as the twelve jurors are willing to 'avow,' or make their own, are presented by them to the sheriff. . . . From the very first the legal forefathers of our grand jurors are not in the majority of cases supposed to be reporting crimes that they have witnessed, or even to be the originators of the *fama publica*. We should be guilty of an anachronism if we spoke of them as 'endorsing a bill' that is 'preferred' to them; but still they are handing on and 'avowing' as their own a rumour that has been reported to them by others." 2 Frederick Pollock & Frederic W. Maitland, *The History of English Law Before the Time of Edward I* 643 (2d ed. 1899).

familia (fə-**mil**-ee-ə). [Latin] *Roman law.* **1.** All the persons in the power of the head of a family. See PATERFAMILIAS. **2.** One's legal relations through and with one's family, including all property, ancestral privileges, and duties.

"The testator conveyed to him outright his whole 'familia,' that is, all the rights he enjoyed over and through the family; his property, his slaves, and all his ancestral privileges, together, on the other hand, with all his duties and obligations." Henry S. Maine, *Ancient Law* 170 (17th ed. 1901).

3. A family, including household servants.

"Familia. . . . A family or household, including servants, that is, hired persons (*mercenarii* or *conductitii*,) as well as bondsmen, and all who were under the authority of one master, (*dominus*.) Bracton uses the word in the original sense, as denoting servants or domestics." 1 Alexander M. Burrill, *A Law Dictionary and Glossary* 603–04 (2d ed. 1867).

familiae emptor (fə-**mil**-ee-ee **emp**-tor). [Latin "estate purchaser"] *Roman law.* A trustee who received an inheritance by a fictitious purchase and distributed it as the testator instructed. — Also termed *emptor familiae*. See HERES; TWELVE TABLES.

"At some date, probably long before the XII Tables, men on the point of death, unable to make a true will because there was no imminent sitting of the *Comitia*, adopted the practice of conveying all their property . . . to a person who is described as the *familiae emptor*, and who is said by Gaius to be *in loco heredis*. Instructions were no doubt given to him as to the disposal of the property or part of it, but it is not clear that these were enforceable. . . ." W.W. Buckland, *A Manual of Roman Private Law* 175 (2d ed. 1953).

familiae erciscundae (fə-**mil**-ee-ee ər-sis-**kən**-dee). See ACTIO FAMILIAE ERCISCUNDAE.

familiares regis (fə-mil-ee-**air**-eez **ree**-jis). [Law Latin] *Hist.* **1.** Persons of the king's household. **2.** The ancient title of the six clerks of chancery in England.

family, *n.* **1.** A group consisting of parents and their children. — Also termed *immediate family*. **2.** A group of persons connected by blood, by affinity, or by law. **3.** A group of persons, usu. relatives, who live together. — **familial,** *adj.* See RELATIVE.

extended family. The immediate family together with the collateral relatives who make up a clan; GENS.

immediate family. A person's parents, spouse, children, and siblings.

family allowance. See ALLOWANCE (1).

family arrangement. An informal agreement among family members, usu. to distribute property in a manner other than what the law provides for. — Also termed *family settlement*.

family-automobile doctrine. See FAMILY-PURPOSE RULE.

family-car doctrine. See FAMILY-PURPOSE RULE.

family court. See COURT.

family disturbance. See DOMESTIC DISPUTE.

Family Division. *English law.* A section of the High Court that has jurisdiction over family matters such as divorce and custody and over uncontested probate matters.

family-expense statute. 1. A state law that permits a charge against the property of a spouse for family debts such as rent, food, clothing, and tuition. **2.** A federal tax-code provision providing that a person may not deduct expenses incurred for family, living, or personal purposes. IRC (26 USCA) § 262.

family farmer. See FARMER.

family-farmer bankruptcy. See CHAPTER 12.

family-income insurance. See INSURANCE.

family law. The body of law dealing with marriage, divorce, adoption, child custody and support, and other domestic-relations issues. — Also termed *domestic relations*; *domestic-relations law*.

family leave. An unpaid leave of absence from work taken to have or care for a baby or to care for a sick family member.

family meeting. *Civil law.* **1.** An advisory jury called to aid the court in a family-law matter. **2.** A council of relatives of a minor assembled to advise the minor in his or her affairs and to help administer the minor's property.

family of nations. *Int'l law.* The community of countries to which international law applies. • This term is now obsolescent. It is increasingly rejected as Eurocentric.

> " 'The family of nations' is an aggregate of States which, as the result of their historical antecedents, have inherited a common civilisation, and are at a similar level of moral and political opinion." Thomas E. Holland, *The Elements of Jurisprudence* 396 (13th ed. 1924).

family partnership. A partnership that includes family members. IRC (26 USCA) § 704(e). See FAMILY-PARTNERSHIP RULES.

family-partnership rules. Laws designed to prevent the shifting of income among partners, esp. family members, who may not be dealing at arm's length.

family-purpose rule. *Torts.* The principle that a vehicle's owner is liable for injuries or damage caused by a family member's negligent driving. • Many states have abolished this rule. — Also termed *family-purpose doctrine*; *family-automobile doctrine*; *family-car doctrine*. Cf. GUEST STATUTE.

> "A number of jurisdictions have adopted the so-called 'family purpose' doctrine, under which the owner of a motor vehicle purchased or maintained for the pleasure of his family is liable for injuries inflicted by the negligent operation of the vehicle while it is being used by members of the family for their own pleasure, on the theory that the vehicle is being used for the purpose or business for which it was kept, and that the person operating it is therefore acting as the owner's agent or servant in using it." 8 Am. Jur. 2d *Automobiles and Highway Traffic* § 715, at 296 (1997).

family settlement. See FAMILY ARRANGEMENT.

famosus (fə-**moh**-səs), *adj.* [Latin] *Hist.* **1.** (Of a statement) having a defamatory character. **2.** (Of an action) involving infamy if the defendant lost the case.

famosus libellus (fə-**moh**-səs li-**bel**-əs), *n.* [Latin] *Roman law.* **1.** A libelous writing, esp. a letter to the emperor that attacked someone's character. **2.** The species of injury that is caused by libel.

fanciful mark. See *fanciful trademark* under TRADEMARK.

fanciful term. See *fanciful trademark* under TRADEMARK.

fanciful trademark. See TRADEMARK.

Fannie Mae (**fan**-ee **may**). See FEDERAL NATIONAL MORTGAGE ASSOCIATION.

FAR. (*often pl.*) *abbr.* FEDERAL AVIATION REGULATION <the pilot violated several FARs before the crash>.

farley (**fahr**-lee). *Hist.* Money paid by a tenant in lieu of a chattel (or *heriot*). • The term invariably referred to a tenant in the west of England. See HERIOT.

farm, *n.* **1.** Land and connected buildings used for agricultural purposes. **2.** *Hist.* Rent. • By extension, the term came to mean the land for which the rent was paid. — Also termed and spelled *ferm*; *fearm*; *firme*.

farm, *vb.* **1.** To cultivate land; to conduct the business of farming. **2.** To lease. See FARM OUT.

Farm Credit Administration. The federal agency responsible for supervising the federal farm-credit system. — Abbr. FCA. See FEDERAL FARM CREDIT SYSTEM.

farmee. See FARMOUTEE.

farmer. A person engaged in the business of farming.

family farmer. A person or entity whose income and debts primarily arise from a family-owned and-operated farm; esp., person who received more than 80% of gross income from a farm in the taxable year immediately preceding a Chapter 12 filing. • Only a family farmer can file for Chapter 12 bankruptcy. 11 USCA § 101(18). See CHAPTER 12.

farmer bankruptcy. See CHAPTER 12.

Farmers Home Administration. A division of the U.S. Department of Agriculture that makes mortgage loans to farmers, issues home-mortgage insurance, and funds public-works programs in rural areas and small towns. — Abbr. FmHA; FHA.

farminee. See FARMOUTEE.

farming operation. *Bankruptcy.* A business engaged in farming, tillage of soil, dairy farming, ranching, raising of crops, poultry, or livestock, and production of poultry or livestock products in an unmanufactured state. 11 USCA § 101(21). See CHAPTER 12.

farminor. See FARMOUTOR.

farm let, *vb. Hist.* To lease; to let land for rent. • *To farm let* is a phrasal verb that commonly appeared in real-property leases; it corresponds with its Latin root, *ad firmam tradidi.*

> "A lease is properly a conveyance of any lands or tenements, (usually in consideration of rent or other annual recompense) made for life, for years, or at will, but always for a *less* time than the lessor hath in the premises: for if it be for the *whole* interest, it is more properly an assignment than a lease. The usual words of operation in it are, 'demise, grant, and to farm let; *dimisi, concessi, et ad firmam tradidi.*' " 2 William Blackstone, *Commentaries on the Laws of England* 317–18 (1766).

farmor. See FARMOUTOR.

farm out, *vb.* **1.** To turn over something (such as an oil-and-gas lease) for performance by another. • The term evolved from the Roman practice of transferring the right to collect taxes to a third party for a fee. It was later practiced in England, Scotland, and France but has been long abolished because the practice led to abuses. **2.** *Hist.* To lease for a term. **3.** To exhaust farmland, esp. by continuously raising a single crop.

farmout agreement, *n. Oil & gas.* A transaction in which the owner of an oil-and-gas lease (the farmoutor) assigns the lease to another (the farmoutee), who agrees to drill a well on the lease. • The farmoutor usu. retains an overriding royalty interest in the lease. — Often shortened to *farmout.* — Also written *farm out agreement*; *farm-out agreement.* See ASSIGNMENT.

farmoutee (fahrm-ow-**tee**). An oil-and-gas sublessee to whom the lease is assigned for purposes of drilling a well. — Also termed *farmee*; *farminee.*

farmoutor (**fahrm**-ow-tor *or* -tər). An oil-and-gas lessee who assigns the lease to another, who agrees to drill a well. — Also spelled *farmouter.* — Also termed *farmor*; *farminor.*

farm products. Crops, livestock, and supplies used or produced in farming or products of crops or livestock in their unmanufactured states, if they are in the possession of a debtor engaged in farming. UCC § 9–109(3). Cf. *growing crops* under CROPS.

farthing of land (**fahr**-thing). *Hist.* An area of land measured as one-quarter of a larger area (much as a farthing was one-quarter of a penny). • A farthing of land ranged from a quarter of a hide to a quarter of an acre.

farvand (**fahr**-vənd). *Hist. Maritime law.* Voyage or passage by water under a charterparty.

F.A.S. *abbr.* FREE ALONGSIDE SHIP.

fas (fas), *n.* [Latin] *Roman law.* **1.** Moral law of divine origin; divine law. • *Jus*, by contrast, is created by man. See JUS.

> "The first element to be noted in the Roman composite existing in primitive times, when religion and law were not distinguished, is *fas* — the will of the gods, embodied in rules that regulated not only ceremonials but the conduct of all men as such." Hannis Taylor, *The Science of Jurisprudence* 65 (1908).

> "It is true that the two spheres of *ius* and *fas* overlapped.... All this, however, concerned merely the question of where to draw the line between *ius* and *fas*; it did not blur the distinction between the two. From the standpoint of the history of Roman law, this distinction, consciously made from very early times, was of great importance, since it enabled the Romans to delimit the scope and the contents of strictly legal rules. This attitude may occasionally have caused a certain cold aloofness from purely human problems, but it undoubtedly contributed to the clarity of the legal system." Hans Julius Wolff, *Roman Law: An Historical Introduction* 51–52 (1951).

2. What is right, proper, lawful, and permitted.

FASB (**faz**-bee). *abbr.* FINANCIAL ACCOUNTING STANDARDS BOARD.

FASB statement. An official pronouncement from the Financial Accounting Standards Board establishing a given financial-accounting practice as acceptable.

fast estate. See *real property* under PROPERTY.

fasti (**fas**-tI). [Latin] *Roman law.* **1.** The days on which court can be held. • In this sense, *fasti* is a shortened form of *dies fasti*. **2.** A calendar of days on which court can be held. See *dies fasti* under DIES.

fast land. See LAND.

fast-tracking, *n.* A court's method of accelerating the disposition of cases in an effort to clear its docket. • For example, a judge might order that all discovery must be finished within 90 days, and that trial is set for 30 days later. — **fast-track,** *vb.* See ROCKET DOCKET.

fatal, *adj.* **1.** Of or relating to death <the decision had fatal consequences>. **2.** Providing grounds for legal invalidity <a fatal defect in the contract>.

fatal defect. See DEFECT.

fatal error. See ERROR.

fatal variance. See VARIANCE (1).

father. The male parent. See PARENT.

adoptive father. See *adoptive parent* under PARENT.

biological father. See *natural father*.

foster father. See *foster parent* under PARENT.

legal father. The man recognized by law as the male parent of a child. • A man is the legal father of a child if he was married to the child's natural mother when the child was born, if he has recognized or acknowledged the child, or if he has been declared the child's natural father in a paternity action.

natural father. The man who impregnated the child's natural mother. — Also termed *biological father*.

presumed father. The man presumed to be the father of a child for any of several reasons: (1) because he was married to the child's natural mother when the child was conceived or born, (2) because the child was conceived or born during an invalid marriage, (3) because the man married the mother after the child's birth and agreed either to have his name on the birth certificate or to support the child, or (4) because the man welcomed the child into his home and held out the child as his own.

putative father (**pyoo**-tə-tiv). The alleged biological father of a child born out of wedlock.

stepfather. See STEPFATHER.

Fatico **hearing** (**fat**-ə-koh). *Criminal procedure.* A sentencing hearing at which the prosecution and the defense may present evidence about what the defendant's sentence should be. *United States v. Fatico*, 603 F.2d 1053 (2d Cir. 1979).

fatuum judicium (**fach**-oo-əm joo-**dish**-ee-əm). [Latin] A foolish judgment or verdict.

fault. An error or defect of judgment or of conduct; any deviation from prudence or duty resulting from inattention, incapacity, perversity, bad faith, or mismanagement. See NEGLIGENCE. Cf. LIABILITY.

fault-first method. A means by which to apply a settlement credit to a jury verdict, by first reducing the amount of the verdict by the percentage of the plaintiff's comparative fault, then subtracting from the remainder the amount of any settlements the plaintiff has received on the claim. See SETTLEMENT CREDIT. Cf. SETTLEMENT-FIRST METHOD.

fault of omission. Negligence resulting from a negative act. See *negative act* under ACT (2).

Fauntleroy **doctrine.** The principle that a state must give full faith and credit to another state's judgment, if the other state had proper jurisdiction, even though the judgment is based on a claim that is illegal in the state in which enforcement is sought. *Fauntleroy v. Lum*, 210 U.S. 230, 28 S.Ct. 641 (1908).

fautor (**faw**-tər). *Hist.* **1.** An abettor or supporter; an active partisan. **2.** A person who encourages resistance to execution of process.

faux (foh), *adj.* [Law French] *Hist.* False or counterfeit.

faux (foh), *n.* [French "false"] *Civil law.* The fraudulent alteration of the truth. See CRIMEN FALSI.

faux action. A false action. See PLEADING.

faux money. Counterfeit money.

faux peys (foh **pay**). False weights. See FALSE WEIGHT.

faux serement (foh ser-**mah*n***). A false oath.

favor, *n.* See BIAS.

favored beneficiary. *Wills & estates.* A beneficiary who receives more willed property than others having equal claims to the property, raising a presumption of the beneficiary's undue influence over the testator. See UNDUE INFLUENCE.

favored nation. See MOST FAVORED NATION.

favored-nation clause. See MOST-FAVORED-NATION CLAUSE.

favorite of the law. A person or status entitled to generous and preferential treatment in legal doctrine.

> "It has long been said that the surety is a favorite of the law and his contract strictissimi-juris." Laurence P. Simpson, *Handbook on the Law of Suretyship* 94 (1950).

favoritism. Preference or selection, usu. invidious, based on factors other than merit. See NEPOTISM; PATRONAGE. Cf. DISCRIMINATION (2).

favor legitimationis (**fay**-vər lə-jit-ə-may-shee-**oh**-nis). [Latin "(in) favor of legitimacy"] The principle that a court should attempt to uphold a child's legitimacy.

favor matrimonii (**fay**-vər ma-trə-**moh**-nee-ɪ). [Latin "(in) favor of marriage"] The principle that a court should attempt to uphold the validity of a marriage.

favor negotii (**fay**-vər ni-**goh**-shee-ɪ). [Latin "(in) favor of business"] The principle that favors upholding a contract against a construction that would render the contract illegal or unenforceable.

favor paternitatis (**fay**-vər pə-tər-nə-**tay**-tis). [Latin "(in) favor of paternity"] The principle that facts will be interpreted so as to uphold the paternity of a child.

favor solutionis (**fay**-vər sə-loo-shee-**oh**-nis). [Latin "(in) favor of payment"] *Conflict of laws.* The principle that a contract should be interpreted according to the applicable law governing performance.

favor testamenti (**fay**-vər tes-tə-**men**-tɪ). [Latin "(in) favor of the testament"] The principle that a court should attempt to uphold a will's validity.

fax, *n.* **1.** A method of transmitting over telephone lines an exact copy of a printing. **2.** A machine used for such transmission. — Also termed *telecopier.* **3.** The communication sent or received by such a machine. — Also termed *facsimile*; (in senses 1 & 3) *facsimile transmission.* — **fax,** *vb.*

FBI. *abbr.* FEDERAL BUREAU OF INVESTIGATION.

FCA. *abbr.* FARM CREDIT ADMINISTRATION.

F. Cas. *abbr.* Federal Cases, a series of reported decisions (1789–1880) predating the Federal Reporter.

FCC. *abbr.* FEDERAL COMMUNICATIONS COMMISSION.

FCJ. *abbr.* A failure to comply with a judgment imposed for a traffic violation. • The defendant's driver's license is suspended until the FCJ is remedied and the fines and fees are paid.

FCPV. *abbr.* A failure to comply with parking-violation tickets. • If a person has a certain number of unpaid parking tickets (often six) within a jurisdiction, the secretary of state will prohibit that person's obtaining or renewing a driver's license.

FDA. *abbr.* FOOD AND DRUG ADMINISTRATION.

f/d/b/a. *abbr.* Formerly doing business as.

FDIC. *abbr.* FEDERAL DEPOSIT INSURANCE CORPORATION.

feal (**fee**-əl), *adj. Archaic.* Faithful; truthful. — Also termed *fele.*

fealty (**feel**-tee *or* **fee**-əl-tee). *Hist.* In feudal law, the allegiance that a tenant or vassal owes to a lord. — Also termed *feodality.*

"*Fealty* was the oath by which he swore faithfully to perform the feudal obligations to his lord." Peter Butt, *Land Law* 47 (2d ed. 1988).

fearm. See FARM.

feasance (**fee**-zənts), *n.* The doing or execution of an act, condition, or obligation. — **feasor,** *n.* Cf. MALFEASANCE; MISFEASANCE; NONFEASANCE.

feasant (**fez**-ənt *or* **fee**-zənt). *Archaic.* Doing or causing. See DAMAGE FEASANT.

feasibility standard. *Bankruptcy.* The requirement that, to obtain bankruptcy-court approval, a Chapter 11 reorganization plan must be workable and have a reasonable likelihood of success.

feasor (**fee**-zər), *n.* An actor; a person who commits an act. See TORTFEASOR.

feast, *n.* **1.** *Roman law.* An established holiday or festival in the ecclesiastical calendar, used as the date of a legal instrument. **2.** *Hist.* One of four principal days (feasts) of the year: March 25, the annunciation of the Virgin Mary; June 24, the birth of John the Baptist; September 28, the feast of St. Michael the Archangel; and December 21, the feast of St. Thomas the Apostle. • The four feast days were used as fixed dates (called "quarter-days") for paying rent; before 1875, they were used as a reference point to set terms of courts. — Also termed *feast day*; *feast-day*.

featherbedding. A union practice designed to increase employment and guarantee job security by requiring employers to hire or retain more employees than are needed. • The practice stems from employees' desire for job security in the face of technological improvement. Featherbedding is restricted by federal law but is an unfair labor practice only if, for example, a union exacts pay from an employer for services not performed or not to be performed.

FECA. *abbr.* FEDERAL EMPLOYEES' COMPENSATION ACT.

feciales, *n.* See FETIALES.

fecial law. See FETIAL LAW.

Fed. *abbr.* **1.** FEDERAL. **2.** FEDERAL RESERVE SYSTEM.

Fed. Cir. *abbr.* UNITED STATES COURT OF APPEALS FOR THE FEDERAL CIRCUIT.

federal, *adj.* Of or relating to a system of associated governments with a vertical division of governments into national and regional components having different responsibilities; esp., of or relating to the national government of the United States. — Abbr. Fed.

Federal Acquisition Regulation. (*usu. pl.*) A federal regulation that governs contracting methods, requirements, and procedures with the federal government. 48 CFR ch. 1. — Also termed *Federal Procurement Regulation.*

federal act. A statute enacted by the U.S. Congress. See FEDERAL LAW.

federal agency. See AGENCY (3).

Federal Aviation Act. A federal law establishing the Federal Aviation Agency (FAA) to be responsible for regulation of aircraft and air travel, including aircraft safety, certification of aircraft personnel, and airport development. 49 USCA §§ 44720 et seq.

Federal Aviation Administration. The federal agency charged with regulating air commerce, advancing aviation safety, promoting civil aviation and a national system of airports, achieving efficient use of navigable airspace, developing and operating a common system of air-traffic control and air navigation, and developing and implementing programs and regulations relating to environmental effects of civil aviation. • It became a part of the Department of Transportation in 1967. — Abbr. FAA. — Formerly also termed *Federal Aviation Agency.*

Federal Aviation Regulation. (*usu. pl.*) A federal regulation governing the safety, maintenance, and piloting of civil aircraft. 14 CFR ch. 1. — Abbr. FAR.

Federal Bureau of Investigation. A division of the U.S. Department of Justice charged with investigating all violations of federal laws except those specifically assigned to another federal agency. — Abbr. FBI.

federal census. See CENSUS.

Federal Circuit. See COURT OF APPEALS FOR THE FEDERAL CIRCUIT.

federal citizen. See CITIZEN.

Federal Claims, U.S. Court of. See UNITED STATES COURT OF FEDERAL CLAIMS.

federal-comity doctrine. The principle requiring federal district courts to refrain from interfering in each other's affairs.

federal common law. The body of decisional law derived from federal courts adjudicating federal questions and other matters of federal concern, such as the law applying to disputes between two states, as well as federal foreign-relations law.

> "Notwithstanding *Erie*, the federal common law still lives in a number of areas. In some, such as admiralty . . . the power to create common law has been inferred from a constitutional or statutory grant of jurisdiction, where a federal common law has appeared necessary to accomplish the purposes of the grant. In other cases, on more or less persuasive evidence, the [Supreme] Court has inferred implicit damage remedies on behalf of injured parties from federal statutes imposing duties for their protection, or has found an implicit congressional delegation of authority to make common law, as in actions on collective-bargaining agreements affecting commerce under the Taft–Hartley Act, § 301." David P. Currie, *Federal Jurisdiction in a Nutshell* 226 (3d ed. 1990).

Federal Communications Commission. The federal agency that regulates interstate and foreign communications by radio, television, telephone, and telegraph, and oversees radio and television broadcasting standards, cable-television operations, two-way-radio operators, and satellite communications. — Abbr. FCC.

federal court. See COURT.

federal crime. A criminal offense under a federal statute. • Most federal crimes are codified in Title 18 of the U.S. Code.

Federal Deposit Insurance Corporation. An independent governmental agency that insures bank deposits up to a statutory amount per depositor at each participating bank. • The insurance fund is financed by a premium paid by the participating banks. — Abbr. FDIC.

Federal Employees' Compensation Act. A workers'-compensation law for federal employees. 5 USCA §§ 8101–8152 — Abbr. FECA. See WORKERS' COMPENSATION.

Federal Employers' Liability Act. A workers'-compensation law that provides death and disability benefits for employees of railroads engaged in interstate and foreign commerce. 45 USCA §§ 51–60 — Abbr. FELA.

federal enclave. Territory or land that a state has ceded to the United States. • Examples of federal enclaves are military bases, national parks, federally administered highways, and federal Indian reservations. The U.S. government has exclusive authority and jurisdiction over federal enclaves.

Federal Energy Regulatory Commission. The agency responsible for administering the Natural Gas Act and the Natural Gas Policy Act. • The commission regulates, among other things, interstate oil-and-gas pipelines and some intrastate oil-and-gas operations. — Abbr. FERC. — Also formerly termed *Federal Power Commission*.

federal farm credit bank. One of a system of federally chartered institutions created to provide credit to farm-related activities. • The banks resulted from a merger of federal land banks and federal intermediate credit banks and are supervised by the Farm Credit Administration.

Federal Farm Credit Banks Funding Corporation. A federal corporation that manages the sale of federal farm-credit-system securities in the money and capital markets and also provides advisory services to banks in the federal farm credit system.

federal farm credit system. The national cooperative system of banks and associations providing credit to farmers, agricultural concerns, and related businesses. • The system consists of the banks for cooperatives, the farm credit banks, and the Federal Farm Credit Banks Funding Corporation. It is supervised by the Farm Credit Administration and was originally capitalized by the federal government. The system is now self-funding and owned by its member-borrowers.

federal government. See GOVERNMENT.

federal grand jury. See GRAND JURY.

Federal Home Loan Bank. One of a system (the federal home loan bank system) of 11 regional banks created in 1932 to supply credit for home mortgage lending by savings-and-loan institutions and to provide funds for low- to moderate-income housing programs. • The banks are supervised by the Federal Housing Finance Board. — Abbr. FHLB. — Sometimes shortened to *home loan bank*.

Federal Home Loan Bank Board. A federal agency responsible for regulating federal savings-and-loan associations and the federal home loan bank system. • It was abolished in 1989, when the Office of Thrift Supervision and the Federal Housing Finance Board assumed its functions. — Abbr. FHLBB.

Federal Home Loan Mortgage Corporation. A corporation that purchases both conventional and federally insured first mortgages from members of the Federal Reserve System and other approved banks. — Abbr. FHLMC. — Also termed *Freddie Mac*.

Federal Housing Administration. The HUD division that encourages mortgage lending by insuring mortgage loans on homes meeting the agency's standards. — Abbr. FHA. See HUD.

Federal Housing Finance Board. An independent agency that supervises the federal home-loan-bank system. • It is the successor agency to the Federal Home Loan Bank Board.

federal instrumentality, *n.* **1.** A means or agency used by the national government. **2.** A national agency immune from state control.

Federal Insurance Contributions Act. The federal act imposing the social-security tax on employers and employees. IRC (26 USCA) §§ 3101–3127. — Abbr. FICA.

federal intermediate credit bank. One of a system of twelve regional banks created in 1923 to discount obligations of agricultural credit corporations and similar institutions making short-term loans to farmers and ranchers. • The system is now merged with federal land banks to create the federal farm-credit system.

federalism. The relationship and distribution of power between the national and regional governments within a federal system of government. See OUR FEDERALISM.

Federalist Papers. A series of 85 essays written by Alexander Hamilton, John Jay, and James Madison (under the pseudonym Publius) expounding on and advocating the adoption of the U.S. Constitution. • Most of the essays were published in 1787 and 1788. — Also termed *The Federalist*.

Federalist Society. A national association of lawyers, law students, and others committed to conservative and libertarian viewpoints on political and social matters. • The group is based in Washington, D.C. Cf. NATIONAL LAWYERS GUILD.

Federal Judicial Code. The portion (Title 28) of the U.S. Code dealing with the organization, jurisdiction, venue, and procedures of the federal court system, as well as court officers, personnel, and the Department of Justice.

federal jurisdiction. See JURISDICTION.

Federal Kidnapping Act. A federal law punishing kidnapping for ransom or reward when the victim is transported interstate or internationally. • The law presumes that a victim has been transported in violation of the law if the victim is not released within 24 hours. 18 USCA § 1201. — Also termed *Lindbergh Act*.

> "The Federal Kidnapping Act was passed in 1932 to close a dangerous loophole between state and federal law. At that time, marauding bands of kidnappers were preying upon the wealthy with ruthless abandon, seizing their victims for ransom while operating outside the reach of existing state laws. Knowing that authorities in the victim's home state were powerless once a hostage was transported across state lines, the criminals would kidnap their target in one state, then move quickly to the next. In response, Congress made kidnapping a federal crime when the victim was moved from one state to another, and comprehensive language was used to cover every possible variety of kidnapping followed by interstate transportation." 1 Am. Jur. 2d *Abduction and Kidnapping* § 14, at 185 (1994).

federal labor union. See UNION.

federal land bank. One of a system of twelve regional banks created in 1916 to provide mortgage loans to farmers. • The system is now merged with federal intermediate credit banks to create the federal farm-credit system.

federal law. The body of law consisting of the U.S. Constitution, federal statutes and regulations, U.S. treaties, and federal common law. Cf. STATE LAW.

federal magistrate. See UNITED STATES MAGISTRATE JUDGE.

Federal Maritime Commission. A federal agency that regulates the waterborne foreign and domestic commerce of the United States. — Abbr. FMC.

Federal Mediation and Conciliation Service. *Labor law.* An independent agency whose purpose is to prevent disruptions in the flow of interstate commerce caused by labor disputes through the use of mediation, conciliation, and voluntary arbitration. — Abbr. FMCS.

Federal National Mortgage Association. A corporation that is chartered by the U.S. government but privately owned and managed, and that provides a secondary mortgage market for the purchase and sale of mortgages guaranteed by the Veterans Administration and those insured under the Federal Housing Administration. — Abbr. FNMA. — Also termed *Fannie Mae*.

Federal Power Commission. See FEDERAL ENERGY REGULATORY COMMISSION.

federal preemption. See PREEMPTION (5).

Federal Procurement Regulation. See FEDERAL ACQUISITION REGULATION.

federal question. A legal issue involving the interpretation and application of the U.S. Constitution, an act of Congress, or a treaty. • Jurisdiction over federal questions rests with the federal courts. 28 USCA § 1331.

federal-question jurisdiction. See JURISDICTION.

Federal Register. A daily publication in which U.S. administrative agencies publish their regulations, including proposed regulations for public comment. — Abbr. Fed. Reg.

federal regulations. See CODE OF FEDERAL REGULATIONS.

Federal Reporter. See F. (1).

Federal Reporter Second Series. See F.2D.

Federal Reporter Third Series. See F.3D.

Federal Reserve Board of Governors. The board that supervises the Federal Reserve System and sets national monetary and credit policy. • The Board consists of seven members appointed by the President and confirmed by the Senate for 14–year terms. — Abbr. FRB.

federal reserve note. The paper currency in circulation in the United States. • The notes are issued by the Federal Reserve Banks, are effectively non-interest-bearing promissory notes payable to bearer on demand, and are issued in denominations of $1, $5, $10, $20, $50, $100, $500, $1,000, $5,000, and $10,000.

Federal Reserve System. A network of 12 central banks supervised by the Board of Governors, who are appointed by the President and confirmed by the Senate and who set the reserve requirements for the member banks, review the discount-rate actions of the regional Federal Reserve banks, and set ceilings on the interest rates that member banks may pay. — Abbr. Fed.

> "The Federal Reserve System of 1913 evolved out of a search for consensus among bankers, politicians, and some academic experts. It was a move toward 'central bank' regulation in the European sense .... [The System] seemed to resolve the outstanding problems in money and banking. Federal Reserve banknotes could grow with expanding commercial paper and economic prosperity, and assure a more adequate, reliable monetary growth." William A. Lovett, *Banking and Financial Institutions Law in a Nutshell* 14–15 (1997).

Federal Rules Act. A 1934 statute granting the U.S. Supreme Court the authority to adopt rules of civil procedure for federal courts. • For the rulemaking power of federal courts today, see 28 USCA §§ 2071, 2072.

Federal Rules Decisions. See F.R.D.

Federal Rules of Appellate Procedure. The rules governing appeals to the U.S. courts of appeals from lower courts, some federal-agency proceedings, and applications for writs. — Abbr. Fed. R. App. P.; FRAP.

Federal Rules of Bankruptcy Procedure. The rules governing proceedings instituted under the Bankruptcy Code. — Abbr. Fed. R. Bankr. P.

Federal Rules of Civil Procedure. The rules governing civil actions in the U.S. district courts. — Abbr. Fed. R. Civ. P.; FRCP.

Federal Rules of Criminal Procedure. The rules governing criminal proceedings in the U.S. district courts. — Abbr. Fed. R. Crim. P.

Federal Rules of Evidence. The rules governing the admissibility of evidence at trials in federal courts. — Abbr. Fed. R. Evid.; FRE.

Federal Savings and Loan Insurance Corporation. A federal agency created in 1934 to insure deposits in savings-and-loan associations and savings banks. • When this agency became insolvent in 1989, its assets and liabilities were transferred to an insurance fund managed by the FDIC. — Abbr. FSLIC. See RESOLUTION TRUST CORPORATION.

federal state. See STATE (1).

federal statute. See FEDERAL ACT.

Federal Supplement. See F.SUPP.

Federal Supplement 2d. See F.SUPP.2D.

Federal Tort Claims Act. A statute that limits federal sovereign immunity and allows recovery in federal court for tort damages caused by federal employees, but only if the law of the state where the injury occurred would hold a private person liable for the injury. 28 USCA §§ 2671–2680 — Abbr. FTCA. See *sovereign immunity* under IMMUNITY.

> "Although it has been suggested that the maxim, 'the King can do no wrong' never had an existence in the United States, it has also been declared that in enacting the Federal Tort Claims Act, Congress recognized the manifold injustice that springs from the delimiting effect of the rule represented by that maxim. And it is said that in passing the Act, Congress intended to compensate the victims of negligence in the conduct of governmental activities in circumstances in which a private person would be liable, rather than leave just treatment to the caprice and legislative burden of individual private laws, and to eliminate the burden on Congress of investigating and passing on private bills seeking individual relief." 35 Am. Jur. 2d *Federal Tort Claims Act* § 1, at 296 (1967).

Federal Trade Commission. The independent regulatory agency created in 1914 to enforce the antitrust laws and other prohibitions against false, deceptive, and unfair advertising or trade practices. — Abbr. FTC.

federal transfer. The federal district court's right to move a civil action filed there to any other district or division where the plaintiff could have brought the action originally. 28 USCA § 1404(a). See CHANGE OF VENUE.

federation. A league or union of states, groups, or peoples arranged with a strong central authority and limited regional sovereignties — though the individual states, groups, or peoples may retain rights of varying degrees. Cf. CONFEDERATION.

Fed. R. App. P. *abbr.* FEDERAL RULES OF APPELLATE PROCEDURE.

Fed. R. Bankr. P. *abbr.* FEDERAL RULES OF BANKRUPTCY PROCEDURE.

Fed. R. Civ. P. *abbr.* FEDERAL RULES OF CIVIL PROCEDURE.

Fed. R. Crim. P. *abbr.* FEDERAL RULES OF CRIMINAL PROCEDURE.

Fed. Reg. *abbr.* FEDERAL REGISTER.

Fed. R. Evid. *abbr.* FEDERAL RULES OF EVIDENCE.

fee. 1. A charge for labor or services, esp. professional services.

attorney's fees. See ATTORNEY'S FEES.

contingent fee. See CONTINGENT FEE.

docket fee. A fee charged by a court for filing a claim.

expert-witness fee. A fee paid for the professional services of an expert witness.

***franchise fee.* 1.** A fee paid by a franchisee to a franchisor for franchise rights. • Franchise fees are regulated by state laws. **2.** A fee paid to the government for a government grant of a franchise, such as the one required for operating a radio or television station.

jury fee. A fee, usu. a minimal one, that a party must pay the court clerk to be entitled to a jury trial.

maintenance fee. A fee to pay for the service of reinvesting earnings and dividends in mutual funds.

management fee. A fee charged by an investment manager for supervisory services.

origination fee. A fee charged by a lender for preparing and processing a loan.

***witness fee.* 1.** A statutory fee that must be tendered with a subpoena for the subpoena to be binding. **2.** A fee paid by a party to a witness as reimbursement for reasonable expenses (such as travel, meals, lodging, and loss of time) incurred as a result of the witness's having to attend trial and testify. • Any other payment to a witness is considered unethical.

2. An inheritable interest in land, constituting maximal legal ownership; esp., a fee simple absolute. — Also termed *fee estate*; *feod*; *feodum*; *feud*; *feudum*; *fief*. See FEE SIMPLE.

> "To *enfeoff* someone was to transfer to him an interest in land called a *fief* — or, if you prefer, a *feoff*, *feod*, or *feud*. Our modern word *fee*, a direct lineal descendant of *fief*, implies the characteristic of potentially infinite duration when used to describe an interest in land today; but in the earliest part of the feudal period, a *fief* might have been as small as a life interest. We shall see later that feoffment was *not* used to transfer interests 'smaller' than life interests — e.g., so-called *terms for years* — but for our purposes now we may simply note that transfers of interests for life or 'larger' were accomplished by livery of seisin." Thomas F. Bergin & Paul G. Haskell,

Preface to Estates in Land and Future Interests 11 (2d ed. 1984).

arriere fee (**ar**-ee-air *or* **ar**-ee-ər). *Hist.* A fee dependent on a superior one; a subfief. — Also termed *arriere fief.*

base fee. A fee that has some qualification connected to it and that terminates whenever the qualification terminates. • An example of the words creating a base fee are "to A and his heirs, tenants of the manor of Tinsleydale," which would terminate when A or his heirs are no longer tenants of the manor of Tinsleydale. Among the base fees at common law are the fee simple subject to a condition subsequent and the conditional fee. — Also termed *determinable fee*; *qualified fee*; *limited fee*. See *fee simple determinable* under FEE SIMPLE.

fee expectant. *Rare.* A fee tail created when land is given to a man and wife and the heirs of their bodies. See FRANKMARRIAGE.

fee simple. See FEE SIMPLE.

fee tail. See FEE TAIL.

great fee. *Hist.* In feudal law, a fee held directly from the Crown.

knight's fee. See KNIGHT'S FEE.

lay fee. *Hist.* A fee estate in land held by ordinary feudal tenure, such as socage, rather than by ecclesiastical tenure through frankalmoin. See FRANKALMOIN; SOCAGE.

plowman's fee. *Hist.* A species of tenure for peasants or small farmers by which the land descended in equal shares to all the tenant's sons.

quasi-fee. *Hist.* An estate in fee acquired wrongfully.

fee damages. See DAMAGES.

feeder organization. *Tax.* An entity that conducts a business or trade for the benefit of a tax-exempt organization. • The feeder organization is not tax-exempt. IRC (26 USCA) § 502.

fee estate. See FEE (2).

fee farm. *Hist.* A species of tenure in which land is held in perpetuity at a yearly rent (fee-farm rent), without fealty, homage, or other services than those in the feoffment. — Also termed *feodi firma*; *firma feodi*. See EMPHYTEUSIS.

"Now to all appearance the term *socage*, a term not found in Normandy, has been extending itself upwards; a name appropriate to a class of cultivating peasants has begun to include the baron or prelate who holds land at a rent but is not burdened with military service.... He is sometimes said to have *feodum censuale*; far more commonly he is said to hold 'in fee farm.' This term has difficulties of its own, for it appears in many different guises; a feoffee is to hold *in feofirma, in feufirmam, in fedfirmam, in feudo firmam, in feudo firma, ad firmam feodalem*, but most commonly, *in feodi firma*. The Old English language had both of the words of which this term is compounded, both *feoh* (property) and *feorm* (rent); but so had the language of France, and in Norman documents the term may be found in various shapes, *firmam fedium, feudifirmam*. But, whatever may be the precise history of the phrase, to hold in fee farm means to hold heritably, perpetually, at a rent; the fee, the inheritance, is let to farm." 2 Frederick Pollock & Frederic W. Maitland, *The History of English Law Before the Time of Edward I* 293 (2d ed. 1899).

fee-farm rent. 1. The rent reserved, usu. one-fourth or one-third of the land's value, on granting a fee farm. **2.** A rent charge issuing out of a fee estate. **3.** A perpetual rent on a conveyance in fee simple.

fee interest. See FEE; FEE SIMPLE; FEE TAIL.

feemail (**fee**-mayl). *Slang.* **1.** An attorney's fee extorted by intimidation, threats, or pressure. **2.** The act or process of extorting such a fee. Cf. BLACKMAIL; GRAYMAIL; GREENMAIL.

fee sharing. See FEE SPLITTING.

fee simple. An interest in land that, being the broadest property interest allowed by law, endures until the current holder dies without heirs; esp., a fee simple absolute. — Often shortened to *fee*. — Also termed *estate in fee simple*; *fee-simple title*.

"[*Fee simple*] is a term not likely to be found in modern conversation between laymen, who would in all probability find it quite unintelligible. Yet to a layman of the 14th century the term would have been perfectly intelligible, for it refers to the elementary social relationship of feudalism with which he was fully familiar: the words 'fee' and 'feudal' are closely related.... The estate in fee simple is the largest estate known to the law, ownership of such an estate being the nearest approach to ownership of the land itself which is consonant with the feudal principle of tenure. It is 'the most comprehensive estate in land which the law recognises'; it is the 'most extensive in quantum, and the most absolute in respect to the rights which it confers, of all estates known to the law'. Traditionally, the fee simple has two distinguishing features: first, the owner ('tenant' in fee simple) has the power to dispose of the fee simple, either inter vivos or by will; second, on intestacy the fee simple descends, in the absence of lineal heirs, to collateral heirs — to a brother, for example, if there is no issue." Peter Butt, *Land Law* 35 (2d ed. 1988).

fee simple absolute. An estate of indefinite or potentially infinite duration (e.g., "to Albert and his heirs"). — Often shortened to *fee simple* or *fee*.

"Although it is probably good practice to use the word 'absolute' whenever one is referring to an estate in fee simple that is free of special limitation, condition subsequent, or executory limitation, lawyers frequently refer to such an estate as a 'fee simple' or even as a 'fee.'" Thomas F. Bergin & Paul G. Haskell, *Preface to Estates in Land and Future Interests* 24 (2d ed. 1984).

fee simple conditional. An estate restricted to some specified heirs, exclusive of others (e.g., "to Albert and his female heirs"). • The fee simple conditional is obsolete except in Iowa, Oregon, and South Carolina. — Also termed *general fee conditional*.

"The reader should be careful not to confuse this estate with estates having similar labels, such as the 'estate in fee simple subject to a condition subsequent' ...." Thomas F. Bergin & Paul G. Haskell, *Preface to Estates in Land and Future Interests* 29 n.19 (2d ed. 1984).

fee simple defeasible (di-**fee**-zə-bəl). An estate that ends either because there are no more heirs of the person to whom it is granted or because a special limitation, condition subsequent, or executory limitation takes effect before the line of heirs runs out. — Also termed *qualified fee*.

fee simple determinable. An estate that will automatically end and revert to the grantor if some specified event occurs (e.g., "to Albert and his heirs while the property is used for charitable purposes"). • The future interest retained by the grantor is called a *possibility of reverter*. — Also termed *determinable fee*; *qualified fee*; *fee simple subject to common-law limitation*; *fee simple subject to special limitation*; *fee simple subject to special interest*; *base fee*; *estate on limitation*.

fee simple subject to a condition subsequent. An estate subject to the grantor's power to end the estate if some specified event happens (e.g., "to Albert and his heirs, upon condition that no alcohol is sold on the premises"). • The future interest retained by the grantor is called a *power of termination* (or a *right of entry*). — Also termed *fee simple on a condition subsequent*; *fee simple subject to a power of termination*; *fee simple upon condition*.

fee simple subject to an executory limitation. A fee simple defeasible that is subject to divestment in favor of someone other than the grantor if a specified event happens (e.g., "to Albert and his heirs, but if the property is ever used as a parking lot, then to Bob"). — Also termed *fee simple subject to an executory interest*.

fee simple subject to a power of termination. See *fee simple subject to a condition subsequent*.

fee simple subject to common-law limitation. See *fee simple determinable*.

fee simple subject to special interest. See *fee simple determinable*.

fee simple subject to special limitation. See *fee simple determinable*.

fee simple upon condition. See *fee simple subject to a condition subsequent*.

fee-splitting. 1. The division of attorney's fees between the lawyer who handles a matter and the lawyer who referred the matter. • Some states consider this practice unethical. **2.** The division of attorney's fees between two or more lawyers who represent a client jointly but are not in the same firm. • An attorney is prohibited from splitting a fee with a nonlawyer. — Also termed *fee sharing*.

fee statement. A lawyer's bill for services either already rendered or to be rendered, usu. including itemized expenses.

fee tail. An estate that is inheritable only by specified descendants of the original grantee, and that endures until its current holder dies without issue (e.g., "to Albert and the heirs of his body"). • Most jurisdictions — except Delaware, Maine, Massachusetts, and Rhode Island — have abolished the fee tail. — Also termed *entailed estate*; *estate tail*; *tenancy in tail*; *entail*; *feodum talliatum*. See ENTAIL; TAIL.

"The name fee tail comes from the French *tailler* (to carve) and probably meant that the grantor was able to carve a fee to his exact prescription. This carving could be carried to great lengths and the land could be limited to male descendants generally — fee tail male general; to female issue — fee tail female; or to issue of a specific wife — fee tail special. In the latter case, if the specified wife died, the holder of the estate was said to have a fee tail with possibility of issue extinct — a type of life estate." John E. Cribbet, *Principles of the Law of Property* 47 (2d ed. 1975).

"If we cannot resist the temptation to say that *De Donis* permitted the creation of tailor-made estates, we can at least argue that it is not a pun. Our word 'tailor' and the word 'tail,' as used in 'fee tail,' come from the same source — the French *tailler*, to cut. The word 'tail' in 'fee tail' has nothing to do with that which wags the dog. The estate in fee tail was a *cut* estate — either cut in the sense that the collateral heirs were cut out, or cut in the sense that the estate was carved into a series of discrete life-possession periods to be enjoyed successively by A and his lineal heirs.... We know of no state in the United States that recognizes the estate in fee tail in its strict 1285–1472 form. Wherever it is recognized, the tenant in tail in possession may disentail it by simple deed. In a number of states, the estate in fee tail has been abolished." Thomas F. Bergin & Paul G. Haskell, *Preface to Estates in Land and Future Interests* 30, 32 (2d ed. 1984).

feign (fayn), *vb.* To make up or fabricate; to make a false show of <he feigned an illness>.

feigned, *adj.* Pretended; simulated; fictitious.

feigned accomplice. See INFORMANT.

feigned action. *Hist.* An action brought for an illegal purpose on a pretended right. — Also termed *faint action*; *false action*.

feigned issue. *Hist.* A proceeding in which the parties, by consent, have an issue tried by a jury without actually bringing a formal action. • The proceeding was done when a court either lacked jurisdiction or was unwilling to decide the issue. — Also termed *fictitious issue*.

"The chancellor's decree is either *interlocutory* or *final*. It very seldom happens that the first decree can be final, or conclude the cause; for, if any matter of fact is strongly controverted, this court is so sensible of the deficiency of trial by written depositions, that it will not bind the parties thereby, but usually directs the matter to be tried by jury.... But, as no jury can be summoned to attend this court, the fact is usually directed to be tried at the bar of the court of king's bench or at the assises, upon a *feigned issue*. For, (in order to bring it there, and have the point in dispute, and that only, put in issue) an action is feigned to be brought, wherein the pretended plaintiff declares that he laid a wager of 5*l*. with the defendant that A was heir at law to B; and then avers that he is so; and therefore demands the 5*l*. The defendant allows the wager, but avers that A is not the heir to B; and thereupon the issue is joined.... These feigned issues seem borrowed from the *sponsio judicialis* of the Romans: and are also frequently used in the courts of law, by consent of the parties, to determine some disputed rights without the formality of pleading...." 3 William Blackstone, *Commentaries on the Laws of England* 452 (1768).

feigned recovery. See COMMON RECOVERY.

FELA (**fee**-lə). *abbr.* FEDERAL EMPLOYERS' LIABILITY ACT.

fele (feel). [Law French] See FEAL.

fellow, *n.* **1.** One joined with another in some legal status or relation. **2.** A member of a college, board, corporate body, or other organization.

fellow-officer rule. *Criminal procedure.* The principle that an arrest is valid if the arresting law-enforcement officer lacks personal knowledge to establish probable cause for the arrest but acts upon the knowledge of another officer and the collective knowledge of the law-enforcement office. • This knowledge, which may constitute probable cause, is imputed to the arresting officer. — Also termed *Whiteley rule*.

fellow servant. A coworker; a person who works for the same employer.

superior fellow servant. A worker that has the power of control or direction over a coworker.

fellow-servant rule. A common-law doctrine holding that an employer is not liable for an employee's injuries caused by a negligent coworker. • This doctrine has generally been abrogated by workers'-compensation statutes. In some jurisdictions, employees were considered fellow servants when they were working with one aim or result in view. In others, the relation of fellow servant was tested by the "doctrine of vice principal," meaning that an employer is liable for injuries to an employee if they result from the negligence of another employee who is given power of control or direction over the injured employee. — Also termed *common-employment doctrine*.

"[T]here are numerous orthodox instances in history of the judge making a legal principle; for the bulk of the common law was 'made' by them, and the fellow-servant rule in employer's liability is a typical modern instance." John Henry Wigmore, *Problems of Law* 66 (1920).

felo de se (**fee**-loh *or* **fel**-oh dee **see**), *n.* See SUICIDE (2).

" '*Felo de se*,' or felon of himself is freely spoken of by the early writers as self-murder. Hence one who killed himself before he arrived at the age of discretion or while he was *non compos mentis*, was not a *felo de se*, or suicide .... [B]y the early common law suicide was a felony and was punished by ignominious burial and forfeiture of goods and chattels to the king." Rollin M. Perkins & Ronald N. Boyce, *Criminal Law* 120 (3d ed. 1982).

felon, *n.* A person who has been convicted of a felony.

felonia (fə-**loh**-nee-ə). [Latin "felony"] *Hist.* An offense that results in a vassal's forfeiting his fee.

"The attempt to derive *felonia* from *fel* 'poison' is merely a folk etymology which came into vogue when 'felony' meant a serious crime, and differed from treason. The word was well established in Feudal Law as the characteristic offense against the Feudal relationship. It will hardly do, therefore, to try to determine its meaning merely by reference to English usage...." Max Radin,

Handbook of Anglo-American Legal History 148 n.7 (1936).

felonious (fə-**loh**-nee-əs), *adj*. **1.** Of, relating to, or involving a felony. **2.** Constituting or having the character of a felony. **3.** Proceeding from an evil heart or purpose; malicious; villainous.

felonious assault. See ASSAULT.

felonious homicide. See HOMICIDE.

felony, *n*. A serious crime usu. punishable by imprisonment for more than one year or by death. • Examples include murder, rape, arson, and burglary. At common law, a felony was an offense for which conviction involved the forfeiture of the defendant's lands or goods, or both, to the Crown. Treason was traditionally included in the term *felony*. — Also termed *major crime*; *serious crime*. Cf. MISDEMEANOR.

> "Felony, in the general acceptation of our English law, comprizes every species of crime, which occasioned at common law the forfeiture of lands or goods." 4 William Blackstone, *Commentaries on the Laws of England* 94 (1769).

> "Amongst indictable crimes, the common law singled out some as being so conspicuously heinous that a man adjudged guilty of any of them incurred — not as any express part of his sentence but as a consequence that necessarily ensued upon it — a forfeiture of property, whether of his lands or of his goods or of both (in the case of treason). Such crimes came to be called 'felonies.' The other, and lesser, crimes were known as 'transgressions' or 'trespasses,' and did not obtain their present name of misdemeanours until a much later date. A felony is, therefore, a crime which either involved by common law such a forfeiture, or else has been placed by statute on the footing of those crimes which did involve it." J.W. Cecil Turner, *Kenny's Outlines of Criminal Law* 93 (16th ed. 1952).

treason felony. See TREASON FELONY.

felony de se. See SUICIDE.

felony murder. See MURDER.

felony-murder rule. The doctrine holding that any death resulting from the commission or attempted commission of a felony is murder. • Most states restrict this rule to inherently dangerous felonies such as rape, arson, robbery, and burglary. Cf. MISDEMEANOR-MANSLAUGHTER RULE.

> "[I]t seems fair to suggest that the future of felony murder is uncertain. England, where the doctrine originated, has abolished it. The Model Penal Code recommends its abolition except for the purpose of creating a rebuttable presumption of malice for killings perpetrated during the course of a felony. Although most states have not yet adopted this position, many of the judicial limitations on felony murder discussed above seem to insure that in many states it will be an unusual case in which one is convicted of felony murder, who absent this doctrine, would not have been convicted of murder." Arnold H. Loewy, *Criminal Law in a Nutshell* 46 (2d ed. 1987).

fem-crit. See CRIT.

feme (fem). [Law French] *Archaic*. **1.** A woman. **2.** A wife. — Also spelled *femme*.

feme covert (fem **kəv**-ərt). [Law French] *Archaic*. A married woman. See COVERTURE.

feme sole (fem **sohl**). [Law French] *Archaic*. **1.** An unmarried woman. **2.** A married woman handling the affairs of her separate estate. — Also termed *feme sole trader*.

femicide (**fem**-ə-sɪd). **1.** The killing of a woman. **2.** One who kills a woman.

feminist jurisprudence. See JURISPRUDENCE.

fence, *n*. **1.** A person who receives stolen goods.

> "The receivers of stolen goods almost never 'know' that they have been stolen, in the sense that they could testify to it in a courtroom. The business could not be so conducted, for those who sell the goods — the 'fences' — must keep up a more respectable front than is generally possible for the thieves." *United States v. Werner*, 160 F.2d 438, 441–42 (2d Cir. 1947).

> "The typical 'fence' takes over the stolen property and pays the thief a price. He purports to 'buy' the goods from the thief." Rollin M. Perkins & Ronald N. Boyce, *Criminal Law* 395 (3d ed. 1982).

2. A place where stolen goods are sold. See RECEIVING STOLEN PROPERTY. **3.** LAWFUL FENCE.

fence, *vb*. To sell stolen property to a fence.

fence-month. *Hist*. The summer fawning season when it was unlawful to hunt deer. — Also termed *defense-month*.

fencing patent. See PATENT (3).

feneration (fen-ə-**ray**-shən). *Hist*. **1.** The act or practice of lending money with interest. **2.** USURY.

feod (fyood). See FEE; FEUD.

feodal (**fyoo**-dəl). See FEUDAL.

feodal action. See FEUDAL ACTION.

feodality (fyoo-**dal**-ə-tee). See FEALTY.

feodal system. See FEUDALISM.

feodarum consuetudines (fee-ə-**dair**-əm [*or* fyoo-**dair**-əm] kon-swə-**t**[**y**]**oo**-də-neez). See FEUDARAM CONSUETUDINES.

feodary (**fyoo**-də-ree). *Hist.* An officer of the Court of Wards who traveled with the escheator from county to county in order to receive royal rents and estimate the value of land tenures for the Crown. See COURT OF WARDS AND LIVERIES.

feodatory (**fyoo**-də-tor-ee). See FEUDATORY.

feodi firma (**fee**-ə-dI *or* **fyoo**-dI **fər**-mə). See FEE FARM.

feodi firmarius (**fee**-ə-dI *or* **fyoo**-dI fər-**mair**-ee-əs). *Hist.* The tenant of a fee farm.

feodum (**fee**-ə-dəm *or* **fyoo**-dəm). [Law Latin] *Hist.* **1.** A fee; an inheritable estate.

> "Feodum . . . A fee; the same as *feudum*. This is the word uniformly employed by Glanville and Bracton to denote an estate of inheritance, and an estate held of another by service, instead of *feudum*, which is invariably used by the continental feudists." 1 Alexander M. Burrill, *A Law Dictionary and Glossary* 615 (2d ed. 1867).

2. Part of a lord's estate held by a tenant (i.e., a seigniory). See SEIGNIORY (2). **3.** A payment for services rendered.

feodum antiquum. See *feudum antiquum* under FEUDUM.

feodum apertum. See *feudum apertum* under FEUDUM.

feodum laicum. See *feudum laicum* under FEUDUM.

feodum militis (**fee**-ə-dəm *or* **fyoo**-dəm **mil**-ə-tis). *Hist.* A knight's fee. — Also termed *feodum militare.*

feodum nobile (**fee**-ə-dəm *or* **fyoo**-dəm **noh**-bə-lee). See *feudum nobile* under FEUDUM.

feodum novum (**fee**-ə-dəm *or* **fyoo**-dəm **noh**-vəm). See *feudum novum* under FEUDUM.

feodum simplex (**fee**-ə-dəm *or* **fyoo**-dəm **sim**-pleks). A fee simple.

feodum talliatum (**fee**-ə-dəm *or* **fyoo**-dəm tal-ee-**ay**-təm). A fee tail. — Also spelled *feudum talliatum.*

feoff (**fef** *or* **feef**), *vb.* See ENFEOFF.

feoffamentum (fee-[ə]-fə-**men**-təm). [Law Latin] *Hist.* See FEOFFMENT.

feoffare (fee-[ə]-**fair**-ee), *vb.* [Law Latin] *Hist.* See ENFEOFF.

feoffator (fee-[ə]-**fay**-tər). [Law Latin] *Hist.* See FEOFFOR.

feoffatus (fee-[ə]-**fay**-təs). [Law Latin] *Hist.* See FEOFFEE.

feoffee (fef-**ee** *or* feef-**ee**). The transferee of an estate in fee simple; the recipient of a fief.

feoffee to uses. *Hist.* A person to whom land is conveyed for the use of a third party (called a *cestui que use*); one who holds legal title to land for the benefit of another. Cf. TRUSTEE. See CESTUI QUE USE; GRANT TO USES.

feoffment (**fef**-mənt *or* **feef**-mənt). *Hist.* **1.** The act of conveying a freehold estate; a grant of land in fee simple. — Also termed *feoffment with livery of seisin.*

feoffment to uses. An enfeoffment of land to one person for the use of a third party. • The feoffee was bound in conscience to hold the land according to the prescribed use and could derive no benefit from the holding.

> "Conveyances of freehold land could originally be made only by a feoffment with livery of seisin. This was a solemn ceremony carried out by the parties entering on the land, and the feoffor, in the presence of witnesses, delivering the seisin to the feoffee either by some symbolic act, such as handing him a twig or sod of earth, or by uttering some words such as 'Enter into this land and God give you joy' and leaving him in possession of the land." Robert E. Megarry & H.W.R. Wade, *The Law of Real Property* 47 (5th ed. 1984).

2. The land so granted. **3.** The charter that transfers the land. — Also termed *deed of feoffment.*

feoffment with livery of seisin. See FEOFFMENT (1).

feoffor (**fef**- *or* **feef**-ər *or* -or). The transferor of an estate in fee simple. — Also spelled *feoffer.*

feorme (fərm). *Hist.* A portion of the land's produce owed by the grantee to the lord according to the terms of a charter.

ferae bestiae (**feer**-ee **bes**-tee-ee), *n.* (*pl.*) [Latin] Wild beasts. • Under Roman law, since a wild animal belonged to no one (*res nullius*), it was owned by its captor. See RULE OF CAPTURE (2).

ferae naturae (**feer**-ee nə-**tyoor**-ee). [Latin "of a wild nature"] **1.** *adj.* (Of animals) wild; untamed; undomesticated. **2.** *n.* Wild animals. See RULE OF CAPTURE (2).

FERC (fərk). *abbr.* FEDERAL ENERGY REGULATORY COMMISSION.

ferdella terrae (fər-**del**-ə **ter**-ee). [Latin] *Hist.* **1.** Ten acres of land. **2.** A yard-land (twenty acres).

ferdfare (**fərd**-fair), *n.* [fr. Saxon *fird* "military service" + *fare* "a going"] *Hist.* **1.** A summons to military service. **2.** An exemption from military service. — Also spelled *firdfare*; *fyrdfare*.

ferdingus (**fər**-ding-gəs). *Hist.* A freeman of the lowest class.

***Feres* doctrine** (**feer**-is *or* **feer**-eez or **fer**-ez). *Torts.* The rule that a member of the military is barred from recovering damages from the United States on a claim brought under the Federal Tort Claims Act for injuries sustained in military service. *Feres v. United States*, 340 U.S. 135, 71 S.Ct. 153 (1950). — Also termed *Feres rule*. See ACTIVITY INCIDENT TO SERVICE.

feria (**feer**-ee-ə), *n.* [Law Latin] *Hist.* **1.** A weekday. **2.** A holiday. **3.** See *ferial day* under DAY. **4.** A fair. **5.** A ferry.

feriae (**feer**-ee-ɪ), *n. pl.* [Latin] *Roman law.* Religious and public holidays on which Romans suspended politics and lawsuits, and on which slaves enjoyed a partial break from labor.

ferial day. See DAY.

ferlingum. See FURLONG.

ferlingus. See FURLONG.

ferm. See FARM.

fermer. [Law French] *Hist.* **1.** A lessee, esp. one who holds lands for agricultural purposes. **2.** One who holds something (such as land or an incorporeal right) by the term.

ferriage (**fer**-ee-ij). *Hist.* The toll or fare paid for the transportation of persons or property on a ferry.

ferry, *n.* **1.** A boat or vessel used to carry persons or property across water, usu. with fixed terminals and short distances. **2.** The commercial transportation of persons or property across water. **3.** The place where a ferry passes across water, including the continuation of the highway on both sides of the water. **4.** The right, usu. exclusive, given by government franchise, to carry persons or property across water for a fee. — Also termed *ferry franchise*.

ferry, *vb.* To carry persons or property, usu. across water, for a fee.

ferry franchise. See FERRY (4).

fertile-octogenarian rule. The legal fiction, assumed under the rule against perpetuities, that a woman can become pregnant as long as she is alive. • The case that gave rise to this fiction was *Jee v. Audley*, 1 Cox 324, 29 Eng. Rep. 1186 (ch. 1787). See W. Barton Leach, *Perpetuities: New Hampshire Defertilizes Octogenarians*, 77 Harv. L. Rev. 729 (1963). — Also termed *presumption-of-fertility rule*.

> "Suppose testator bequeaths in trust to pay the income to A for her life, then to pay the income to the children of A for their lives, and upon the death of the survivor of such children, to pay the principal to the grandchildren of A. At the time of the testator's death A is 79 years old, and she has two children. Believe it or not, it has been held that the remainder to the grandchildren of A is violative of the rule against perpetuities and invalid. The law adopted the conclusive presumption that every person is capable of having children until the day he or she dies, as far as the rule against perpetuities is concerned. Consequently, A could have an additional child who would not be a life in being at the testator's death, and that child could have a child who would be born beyond the permissible period. The result of this hypothesis is to invalidate the remainder to the grandchildren. This situation is sometimes referred to as the case of the 'fertile octogenarian.' Remember that the class gift is invalid if it is possible that the interest of any one member of the class can violate the rule." Thomas F. Bergin & Paul G. Haskell, *Preface to Estates in Land and Future Interests* 188 (2d ed. 1984).

festing-man. *Hist.* A bondsman; a surety. See FRANKPLEDGE.

festing-penny. *Hist.* Earnest, or payment, given to a servant when hired.

festinum remedium (fes-**tɪ**-nəm ri-**mee**-dee-əm). [Latin] *Hist.* A speedy remedy. • It was used in cases, such as actions for dower or assize, where the redress of injury was given without unnecessary delay.

festuca (fes-**tyoo**-kə). *Hist.* A rod, staff, or stick used as a pledge (or *gage*) of good faith by a party to a contract or as a token of conveyance of land. — Also termed *fistuca*. See LIVERY OF SEISIN.

"The *wed* or gage, however, was capable of becoming a symbol; an object which intrinsically was of trifling value might be given and might serve to bind a contract. Among the Franks, whom we must regard as being for many purposes our ancestors in law, it took the shape of the *festuca*. Whether this transition from the 'real' to the 'formal' can be accomplished without the intervention of sacral ceremonies seems doubtful. There are some who regard the *festuca* as a stout staff which has taken the place of a spear and is a symbol of physical power. Others see in it a little bit of stick on which imprecatory runes have been cut. It is hard to decide such questions, for, especially under the influence of a new religion, symbols lose their old meanings and are mixed up. Popular etymology confounds confusion." 2 Frederick Pollock & Frederic W. Maitland, *The History of English Law Before the Time of Edward I* 186 (2d ed. 1899).

festum (**fes**-təm). [Latin] A feast-day, holiday, or festival.

fetiales (fee-shee-**ay**-leez), *n. Roman law.* The order of priests whose duties concerned international relations and treaties, including the declaration of war and peace. — Also spelled *feciales*.

fetial law (**fee**-shəl). *Roman law.* A branch of law concerned with matters (such as treaties, embassies, and war declarations) affecting relations between peoples or nations. — Also spelled *fecial law*. — Also termed *jus fetiale*.

feticide (**fee**-tə-sɪd). The act or an instance of killing a fetus, usu. by assaulting and battering the mother; an intentionally induced miscarriage. — Also termed *child destruction*. Cf. INFANTICIDE (1).

fetter, *n.* (*usu. pl.*) A chain or shackle for the feet. — **fetter,** *vb.*

feud, *n. Hist.* **1.** An inheritable estate in land conveyed from a feudal superior to a grantee or tenant, held on the condition of rendering services to the superior.

"It is believed that the forms *feud* and *fief* appear in England but late in the day under the influence of foreign books; they never became terms of our law. It is noticeable also that *feodum* was constantly used in the sense that our *fee* has when we speak of a lawyer's or doctor's fee; payments due for services rendered, at least if they are permanent periodic payments, are *feoda*; the judges, for example, receive *feoda*, not salaries. The etymological problem presented by the English *fee* seems no easy one, because at the Conquest the would-be Latin *feodum* or *feudum* (the *d* in which has puzzled philologists and does not always appear in Domesday Book) is introduced among a people which already has *feoh* as a word for property in general and cattle in particular." 2 Frederick Pollock & Frederic W. Maitland, *The History of English Law Before the Time of Edward I* 236 n.2 (2d ed. 1899).

impartible feud. An indivisible feud; a feud not subject to partition. See FEUDUM INDIVIDUUM.

improper feud. A nonmilitary feud; a feud that is base or servile in nature.

"These were the principal, and very simple, qualities of the genuine or original feuds; being then all of a military nature, and in the hands of military persons: though the feudatories, being under frequent incapacities of cultivating and manuring their own lands, soon found it necessary to commit part of them to inferior tenants.... But this at the same time demolished the ancient simplicity of feuds; and an inroad being once made upon their constitution, it subjected them, in a course of time, to great varieties and innovations. Feuds came to be bought and sold, and deviations were made from the old fundamental rules of tenure and succession; which were held no longer sacred, when the feuds themselves no longer continued to be purely military. Hence these tenures began now to be divided into *feoda propria et impropria*, proper and improper feuds...." 2 William Blackstone, *Commentaries on the Laws of England* 57–58 (1766).

proper feud. A feud based on military service.

2. The interest of the tenant in the land conveyed. **3.** The land itself conveyed. — Also termed (in senses 1, 2 & 3) *fee*; *fief*; *feod*; *feude*; *feudum*. **4.** An enmity or private war existing between families or clans, esp. as a result of a murder.

feudal, *adj.* **1.** Of, relating to, or growing out of feudalism <feudal law>. **2.** Of or relating to a feud <feudal tenure>. Cf. ALLODIAL.

feudal action. *Hist.* A real action; an action that concerned only real property.

feudalism (**fyood**-əl-iz-əm). **1.** A landholding system, particularly applying to medieval Europe, in which all are bound by their status in a hierarchy of reciprocal obligations of service and defense. • The lord was obligated to give the vassal (1) some land, (2) protection, and (3) justice. The lord guaranteed the quiet occupation of the land by the vassal and guaranteed to do right if the vassal became involved in a dispute. In return, the vassal owed the lord some type of service, called "tenure" (literally "means of holding"), because the different types of service were the methods by which the vassals held the property. **2.** The social, political, and economic system of medieval Europe. — Also termed *feudal system*; *feodal system*.

"Modern historical research has taught us that, while it is a mistake to speak of a feudal *system*, the word 'feudalism' is a convenient way of referring to certain fundamental similarities which, in spite of large local variations, can be discerned in the social development of all the peoples of western Europe from about the ninth to the thirteenth centuries." J.L. Brierly, *The Law of Nations* 2 (5th ed. 1955).

feudal law. *Hist.* The real-property law of land tenures that prevailed in England, esp. after the Norman Conquest. See FEUDARUM CONSUETUDINES.

feudal system. See FEUDALISM.

feudarum consuetudines (fee-ə-**dair**-əm [or fyoo-**dair**-əm] kon-swə-**t**[**y**]**oo**-də-neez). [Latin] The customs of feuds. • This was the name of a compilation of feudal laws and customs made in 12th-century Milan. • It is regarded as an authoritative work in continental Europe. — Also spelled *feodarum consuetudines*.

feudary. See FEUDATORY.

feudatory, *adj. Hist.* (Of a vassal) owing feudal allegiance to a lord.

feudatory, *n. Hist.* The grantee of a feud; the vassal or tenant who held an estate by feudal service. — Also termed *feudary*; *feodatory*.

"Every receiver of lands, or feudatory, was therefore bound, when called upon by his benefactor, or immediate lord of his feud or fee, to do all in his power to defend him." 2 William Blackstone, *Commentaries on the Laws of England* 46 (1766).

feude. See FEUD.

feudist. A writer on feuds (for example, Cujacius, Spelman, Craig).

Feudorum Libri (fyoo-**dor**-əm **lɪ**-brɪ). [Latin "the books of the feuds"] *Hist.* The Books of Feuds, a five-book compilation of Lombardic feudal law published in Milan around 1152, during the reign of Henry III. • This unofficial compilation was the main source of tenure law among the nations in Europe. It was widely used in medieval law schools and courts in Italy, France, and Germany. The *Feudorum Libri* were probably known in England but had little effect other than influencing English lawyers to study their own tenure system more critically. — Also termed *Consuetudines Feudorum*; *Usus Feudorum*.

feudum (**fyoo**-dəm). [Law Latin] A fief or feud; a feodum. — Also termed *feodum*; *feum*. Pl. ***feuda*** (**fyoo**-də). See FEUD (1); FIEF; FEE (2).

"The Latin equivalent of *feodum* or *feudum* is the root of the words 'feudal' and 'subinfeudation'. The French form *fief* is favoured by some English historians, but it was not used in law-French." J.H. Baker, *An Introduction to English Legal History* 256 n.4 (3d ed. 1990).

feudum antiquum (**fyoo**-dəm an-**tɪ**-kwəm), *n.* [Law Latin "ancient feud"] *Hist.* **1.** A feud that passed to a vassal from an intestate ancestor. **2.** A feud that ancestors had possessed for more than four generations. **3.** An ancient feud. Pl. ***feuda antiqua*** (**fyoo**-də an-**tɪ**-kwə). — Also termed *feodum antiquum* (**fee**-ə-dəm *or* **fyoo**-dəm). See FEUD (1).

feudum apertum (**fyoo**-dəm ə-**pər**-təm). *Hist.* A feud that reverted to the lord because of a tenant's failure of issue, a crime by the tenant, or some other legal cause. — Also termed *feodum apertum*.

feudum francum (**fyoo**-dəm **frangk**-əm). *Hist.* A free feud; a feud or fee that was noble and free from talliage and subsidies that vulgar feuds (*plebeia feuda*) were subject to.

feudum hauberticum (**fyoo**-dəm haw-**bər**-tə-kəm). *Hist.* A feud that was held on the military service of appearing fully armed when summoned by the lord. See ARRIERBAN.

feudum improprium (**fyoo**-dəm im-**proh**-pree-əm). *Hist.* A feud that was improper or derivative.

feudum individuum (**fyoo**-dəm in-də-**vij**-oo-əm). *Hist.* A feud that was indivisible and descendible only to the eldest son.

feudum laicum (**fyoo**-dəm **lay**-ə-kəm). *Hist.* A lay feud. — Also termed *feodum laicum*.

feudum ligium (**fyoo**-dəm **lij**-ee-əm). *Hist.* **1.** A liege feud; a feud held immediately of the sovereign. **2.** A feud for which the vassal owed fealty to his lord against all other persons.

feudum maternum (**fyoo**-dəm mə-**tər**-nəm). *Hist.* A feud that descended to the feudatory from the maternal side.

feudum militare (**fyoo**-dəm mil-ə-**tair**-ee). *Hist.* A knight's feud. • It was held by knight service and esteemed the most honorable species of tenure. — Also termed *feodum militis*; (in Norman law) *fief d'haubert* or *fief d'hauberk*.

feudum nobile (**fyoo**-dəm **noh**-bə-lee). *Hist.* A feud for which the tenant did guard and owed fealty and homage. — Also termed *feodum nobile.*

feudum novum (**fyoo**-dəm **noh**-vəm). *Hist.* **1.** A new feud. **2.** A feud beginning in the person of the feudatory rather than by succession. — Also spelled *feodum novum.*

feudum novum ut antiquum (**fyoo**-dəm **noh**-vəm ət an-**tI**-kwəm). *Hist.* A new feud held with the qualities of an ancient feud.

feudum paternum (**fyoo**-dəm pə-**tər**-nəm). *Hist.* **1.** A feud that the tenant's paternal ancestors had held for four generations. **2.** A feud descendible only to the heirs on the paternal side. **3.** A feud that could be held only by males.

feudum proprium (**fyoo**-dəm **proh**-pree-əm). *Hist.* An original feud that is military in nature and held by military service.

feudum talliatum (**fyoo**-dəm tal-ee-**ay**-təm). See FEE TAIL.

feu holding (fyoo). *Hist.* A tenancy held by rendering produce or money instead of military service.

feum. See FEUDUM.

ff. *abbr.* **1.** And the pages following. **2.** (*often cap.*) FRAGMENTA.

FGA. *abbr.* **1.** Free from general average. **2.** Foreign general average.

> "*F.G.A.* means Foreign General Average, and implies that, if goods become liable to general average, the rules to be applied will be those of the port of destination or refuge, i.e., the law of the place where the adjustment is made." 2 E.W. Chance, *Principles of Mercantile Law* 128 (P.W. French ed., 10th ed. 1951).

FHA. *abbr.* **1.** FARMERS HOME ADMINISTRATION. **2.** FEDERAL HOUSING ADMINISTRATION.

FHA mortgage. See MORTGAGE.

FHLB. *abbr.* FEDERAL HOME LOAN BANK.

FHLBB. *abbr.* FEDERAL HOME LOAN BANK BOARD.

FHLMC. *abbr.* FEDERAL HOME LOAN MORTGAGE CORPORATION.

fiancer (fyah*n*-**say**), *vb.* [Law French] To pledge one's faith.

fiat (**fee**-aht *or* **fee**-at *or* **fI**-at *or* **fI**-ət), *n.* [Latin "let it be done"] **1.** An order or decree, esp. an arbitrary one <judicial fiat>. **2.** A court decree, esp. one relating to a routine matter such as scheduling <the court requires all motions to contain a fiat — to be filled in by the court — setting the hearing date>. — Also termed *fiaunt.*

fiat justitia (**fI**-at jəs-**tish**-ee-ə). [Latin] *Hist.* Let justice be done. • This phrase signaled the Crown's commission to the House of Lords to hear an appeal.

> "*Fiat Justitia, ruat coelum*, says another maxim, as full of extravagance as it is of harmony: Go heaven to wreck — so justice be but done: — and what is the ruin of kingdoms, in comparison of the wreck of heaven?" Jeremy Bentham, *An Introduction to the Principles of Morals and Legislation* 13–14 n.1 (1823).

fiat money. See MONEY.

fiat ut petitur (**fI**-at ət **pet**-ə-tər). [Latin] Let it be done as it is asked. • An order granting a petition.

fiaunt. See FIAT.

FICA (**fI**-kə). *abbr.* FEDERAL INSURANCE CONTRIBUTIONS ACT.

fictio (**fik**-shee-oh), *n.* [Latin fr. *fingare* "to feign"] *Roman law.* A legal assumption or supposition (such as that the plaintiff was a citizen) necessary to cause certain legal consequences that otherwise would not occur. • Legal fictions allowed Roman magistrates (*praetors*) to expand the law beyond what was strictly allowed by prior law. This practice also occurred in English law — for example, the action of *common recovery*, which allowed a landowner to convey land that by law could not be alienated (such as land held in fee tail). Pl. ***fictiones.***

fictio juris. See LEGAL FICTION.

fiction. See LEGAL FICTION.

fictional action. See *collusive action* under ACTION.

fiction of law. See LEGAL FICTION.

fictitious, *adj.* Of or relating to a fiction, esp. a legal fiction

fictitious action. See ACTION.

fictitious issue. See FEIGNED ISSUE.

fictitious name. See ASSUMED NAME; ALIAS.

fictitious-payee rule. *Commercial law.* The principle that if a drawer or maker issues commercial paper to a payee whom the drawer or maker does not actually intend to have any interest in the instrument, an ensuing forgery of the payee's name will be effective to pass good title to later transferees. — Also termed *padded-payroll rule.*

fictitious person. See *artificial person* under PERSON.

fictitious promise. See *implied promise* under PROMISE.

fide commissary (fɪ-dee **kom**-ə-ser-ee). See CESTUI QUE TRUST.

fide-committee. A beneficiary; CESTUI QUE TRUST. — Also termed *fidei-commissarius.*

> "In a particular case, a *cestuy que trust* is called by the Roman law, *fidei-commissarius.* In imitation of this, I have seen him somewhere or other called in English a *fide-committee.* This term, however, seems not very expressive. A fide-committee, or, as it should have been, a *fidei*-committee, seems, literally speaking, to mean one who is committed to the good faith of another." Jeremy Bentham, *An Introduction to the Principles of Morals and Legislation* 226 n.1 (1823).

fidei-commissarius. See CESTUI QUE TRUST.

fideicommissary (fɪ-dee-ɪ-**kom**-ə-ser-ee), *adj.* *Roman & civil law.* Of or relating to a fideicommissum.

fideicommissary substitution. 1. SUBSTITUTION (5). **2.** SUBSTITUTION (6).

fideicommissum (fɪ-dee-ɪ-kə-**mis**-əm), *n. Roman & civil law.* An arrangement similar to a trust by which a testator gave property to a person for the benefit of another who could not, by law, inherit property. • Over time, this device was used to tie up property for generations, and most civil jurisdictions now prohibit or limit it. — Sometimes spelled *fidei-commissum.* Pl. **fideicommissa.**

> "The many formalities with regard to the institution of heirs and the bequest of legacies, coupled with the fact that many persons, *e.g. peregrini,* were incapable of being instituted heirs, or of being given a legacy, led, in the late Republic, to testators leaving directions to their heirs in favour of given individuals, which, though not binding at law, they hoped their heirs would, in honour, feel bound to carry out. The beginning of *fideicommissa,* therefore, was very like the early practice with regard to trusts in English law, and, as in the case of trusts, a time came when trusts were made binding legally as well as morally.... For brevity, the *fideicommissum* will here be called 'the trust', the person upon whom it was imposed (*fiduciarius*) 'the trustee', and the person in whose favour it was imposed (*fideicommissarius*) 'the beneficiary'." R.W. Leage, *Roman Private Law* 252 (C.H. Ziegler ed., 2d ed. 1930).

fidejubere (fɪ-dee-yə-**beer**-ee). [Latin] *Roman law.* To become a surety. • Forms of this word were spoken by the parties to a *stipulatio* that bound one party to become a surety for the other; the first party asked, "Do you pledge yourself?" (*"fidejubesne?"*), and the second responded, "I do pledge myself" (*"fidejubeo"*). — Sometimes spelled *fideiubere.* See STIPULATIO.

fidejussion (fɪ-di-**jəsh**-ən). *Roman law.* An act by which a person becomes an additional security for another. • The act does not remove the principal's liability but only adds to the surety's security. Fidejussion was one of the five types of adpromission. — Also spelled *fidejussio; fideiussio.* See ADPROMISSION.

fidejussor (fɪ-di-**jəs**-or). **1.** *Roman law.* A guarantor; a person who becomes bound to pay another's debt. **2.** *Hist. Maritime law.* A person who acts as bail for a defendant in the Court of Admiralty. — Also spelled *fideiussor.*

> "The proceedings of the court of admiralty bear much resemblance to those of the civil law, but are not entirely founded thereon; and they likewise adopt and make use of other laws, as occasion requires; such as the Rhodian law, and the laws of Oleron. For the law of England, as has frequently been observed, doth not acknowledge or pay any deference to the civil law considered as such; but merely permits its use in such cases where it judged its determinations equitable, and therefore blends it, in the present instance, with other marine laws.... The first process in these courts is frequently by arrest of the defendant's person; and they also take recognizances or stipulation of certain fidejussors in the nature of bail, and in case of default may imprison both them and their principal." 3 William Blackstone, *Commentaries on the Laws of England* 108–09 (1768).

fidelitas (fi-**del**-ə-tas). [Latin "fidelity"] See FEALTY.

fidelity and guaranty insurance. See *fidelity insurance* under INSURANCE.

fidelity bond. See BOND (2).

fidelity guaranty insurance. See *fidelity insurance* under INSURANCE.

fidelity insurance. See INSURANCE.

fidem mentiri (**fɪ**-dəm men-**tɪ**-rɪ). [Latin] *Hist.* To betray faith or fealty. • The term refers to a feudal tenant who did not keep the fealty sworn to the lord.

fidepromission (**fɪ**-dee-proh-**mish**-ən), *n.* [Latin "faith-promise"] *Roman law.* A contract of guaranty by stipulation. • Fidepromission was one of the five types of adpromission. — **fidepromissor,** *n.* See ADPROMISSION; STIPULATION.

fides (**fɪ**-deez). [Latin] Faith.

fides facta (**fɪ**-deez **fak**-tə). [Latin] *Hist.* Faith-making; faith-pledging. • Among the Franks and Lombards, undertakings were guaranteed by symbolic, formal acts — making one's faith — such as the giving of a rod when property was transferred. See FESTUCA.

fiducia (fi-**d[y]oo**-shee-ə). *Roman law.* An early form of mortgage or pledge in which the debtor passed the title to property to the creditor by a formal act of sale, yet with an express or implied agreement that the creditor would reconvey the property once the debt was paid. • The creditor's ownership in the property was vested without foreclosure or right of redemption.

> "The Roman mortgage (*fiducia*) fell wholly out of use before the time of Justinian, having been displaced by the superior simplicity and convenience of the *hypotheca*; and in this respect modern Continental law has followed the Roman." John Salmond, *Jurisprudence* 443 (Glanville L. Williams ed., 10th ed. 1947).

fiduciarius heres (fi-d[y]oo-shee-**air**-ee-əs **heer**-eez). [Latin "fiduciary heir"] *Roman law.* A person formally named an heir in a testament, but in a fiduciary capacity, and charged to deliver the succession to the person designated by the testament.

fiduciarius tutor (fi-d[y]oo-shee-**air**-ee-əs **t[y]oo**-tər). *Roman law.* A fiduciary guardian; a person who by fulfilling a trust to free someone in power became his or her guardian.

fiduciary (fi-**d[y]oo**-shee-er-ee), *n.* **1.** One who owes to another the duties of good faith, trust, confidence, and candor <the corporate officer is a fiduciary to the shareholders>. **2.** One who must exercise a high standard of care in managing another's money or property <the beneficiary sued the fiduciary for investing in speculative securities>. — **fiduciary,** *adj.*

> "'Fiduciary' is a vague term, and it has been pressed into service for a number of ends.... My view is that the term 'fiduciary' is so vague that plaintiffs have been able to claim that fiduciary obligations have been breached when in fact the particular defendant was not a fiduciary *stricto sensu* but simply had withheld property from the plaintiff in an unconscionable manner." D.W.M. Waters, *The Constructive Trust* 4 (1964).

dilatory fiduciary (**dil**-ə-tor-ee). A trustee or other fiduciary who causes undue delays in administering an estate.

successor fiduciary. A fiduciary who is appointed to succeed or replace a prior one.

temporary fiduciary. An interim fiduciary appointed by the court until a regular fiduciary can be appointed.

fiduciary bond. See BOND (2).

fiduciary contract. *Hist.* An agreement by which one party delivers something to another on condition that the second party will return the thing to the first.

fiduciary debt. A debt founded on or arising from a fiduciary relationship, rather than from a contractual relationship.

fiduciary duty. See DUTY (2).

fiduciary relationship. A relationship in which one person is under a duty to act for the benefit of the other on matters within the scope of the relationship. • Fiduciary relationships — such as trustee-beneficiary, guardian-ward, agent-principal, and attorney-client — require the highest duty of care. Fiduciary relationships usu. arise in one of four situations: (1) when one person places trust in the faithful integrity of another, who as a result gains superiority or influence over the first, (2) when one person assumes control and responsibility over another, (3) when one person has a duty to act for or give advice to another on matters falling within the scope of the relationship, or (4) when there is a specific relationship that has traditionally been recognized as involving fiduciary duties, as with a lawyer and a client or a stockbroker and a customer. — Also termed *fiduciary relation*; *confidential relationship*. Cf. SPECIAL RELATIONSHIP.

fiduciary-shield doctrine. *Corporations.* The principle that a corporate officer's act cannot be the basis for jurisdiction over the officer in an individual capacity.

fief (feef), *n.* See FEE; FEUD. • Metaphorically, the term refers to an area of dominion, esp. in a corporate or governmental bureaucracy.

fief d'hauberk (**feef** doh-**bairk**). See *feudum militare* under FEUDUM.

fief d'haubert. See *feudum militare* under FEUDUM.

fief-tenant. *Hist.* The holder of a fief or fee; a feeholder or freeholder.

field audit. See AUDIT.

field book. A log or book containing a surveyor's notes that are made on-site and that describe by course and distance the running of the property lines and the establishment of the corners.

Field Code. The New York Code of Procedure of 1848, which was the first comprehensive Anglo–American code of civil procedure and served as a model for the Federal Rules of Civil Procedure. • It was drafted by David Dudley Field (1805–1894), a major law-reformer. See *code pleading* under PLEADING (2).

field notes. The notes in a surveyor's field book.

field sobriety test. See SOBRIETY TEST.

field-warehouse financing agreement. The loan agreement in a field-warehousing arrangement.

field warehousing. An inventory-financing method by which a merchant pledges its inventory, which is in the possession of a third person (a warehouser). • This is a method of financing an inventory that cannot economically be delivered to the creditor or third party. The borrower segregates part of the inventory and places it under the nominal control of a lender or third party, so that the lender has a possessory interest. Cf. *floor-plan financing* under FINANCING; PLEDGE.

> "Field warehousing is a way of bringing about the security relationship of a pledge. It is an arrangement for allowing the pledgor a more convenient access to the pledged goods, while the goods are actually in the custody and control of a third person on the pledgor's premises." *Business Factors, Inc. v. Taylor–Edwards Warehouse & Transfer Co.*, 585 P.2d 825, 828 (Wash. Ct. App. 1978).

> "Field warehousing is . . . an arrangement whereby a wholesaler, manufacturer, or merchant finances his business through the pledge of goods remaining on his premises. The arrangement is valid and effective where there is an actual delivery to the warehouseman by the bailor who has hired the warehouseman and given him exclusive possession of the warehouse goods." *In re Covington Grain Co.*, 638 F.2d 1362, 1365 (5th Cir. 1981).

fierding court (**fyər**-ding *or* **feer**-ding). *Hist.* An ancient court of inferior jurisdiction. • Four courts were in each district or hundred.

fieri (**fɪ**-ə-rɪ). [Latin] To be made; to be done. • *Fieri* usu. appears as part of the phrase *in fieri*. See IN FIERI.

fieri facias (**fɪ**-ə-rɪ **fay**-shee-əs). [Latin "that you cause to be done"] A writ of execution that directs a marshal or sheriff to seize and sell a defendant's property to satisfy a money judgment. — Abbr. *fi. fa.*; *Fi. Fa.* Cf. LEVARI FACIAS.

> "It receives its name from the Latin words in the writ (*quod fieri facias de bonis et catallis*, that you cause to be made of the goods and chattels). It is the form of execution in common use in levying upon the judgment-debtor's personal property." John Bouvier, *Bouvier's Law Dictionary* (8th ed. 1914).

> "The writ of 'fieri facias' (commonly called a writ of 'fi fa'), which commanded literally 'that you cause to be made,' was an early common-law means of enforcing payment on a judgment; it was, in effect, an order to the sheriff of the court to enforce a judgment against the debtor by levy, seizure, and sale of his personalty to the extent needed to satisfy a judgment." 30 Am. Jur. 2d *Executions and Enforcement of Judgments* § 14, at 50–51 (1994).

fieri facias de bonis ecclesiasticis (**fɪ**-ə-rɪ **fay**-shee-əs dee **boh**-nis e-klee-z[h]ee-**as**-tə-sis). [Latin "that you cause to be made of the ecclesiastical goods"] *Hist.* A writ of execution — used when the defendant was a beneficed clerk who had no lay fee — that commanded the bishop to satisfy the judgment from the ecclesiastical goods and chattels of the defendant within the diocese. • This was accomplished by issuing a sequestration to levy the debt out of the defendant's benefice. This writ was issued after a *fieri facias* had been returned *nulla bona*.

fieri facias de bonis propriis (**fɪ**-ə-rɪ **fay**-shee-əs dee **boh**-nis **proh**-pree-is). [Latin "that you cause to be made of his own goods"] *Hist.* A writ that executes on an executor's property when a writ *fieri facias de bonis testatoris* is returned by the sheriff nulla bona or devastavit (a wasting of the testator's goods by the executor).

fieri facias de bonis testatoris (**fɪ**-ə-rɪ **fay**-shee-əs dee **boh**-nis tes-tə-**tor**-is). [Latin "that you cause to be made of the testator's goods"] *Hist.* A writ of execution served on an executor for a debt incurred by the testator.

fieri feci (**fɪ**-ə-rɪ **fee**-sɪ). [Latin "I have caused to be made"] *Hist.* A sheriff's return on a *fieri facias* where the sheriff has collected, in whole or in part, the sum to be levied on. • The return is usu. expressed by the word "satisfied."

fi. fa. (*sometimes cap.*) *abbr.* FIERI FACIAS.

FIFO (**fɪ**-foh). *abbr.* FIRST-IN, FIRST-OUT.

FIFRA. *abbr.* Federal Insecticide, Fungicide, and Rodenticide Act. 7 USCA §§ 136–136y.

fifteenth. *Hist.* A tax of one-fifteenth of all the personal property of every subject. • The tax was levied at intervals by act of Parliament. Under Edward III, the value of the fifteenth was assessed and fixed at a specific sum and did not increase as the wealth of the kingdom increased — thus the tax ceased to actually be one-fifteenth. See QUOD PERSONA NEC PREBENDARII.

Fifteenth Amendment. The constitutional amendment, ratified in 1870, guaranteeing all citizens the right to vote regardless of race, color, or prior condition of servitude.

Fifth Amendment. The constitutional amendment, ratified with the Bill of Rights in 1791, providing that a person cannot be (1) required to answer for a capital or otherwise infamous offense unless a grand jury issues an indictment or presentment, (2) subjected to double jeopardy, (3) compelled to engage in self-incrimination on a criminal matter, (4) deprived of life, liberty, or property without due process of law, and (5) deprived of private property for public use without just compensation.

Fifth Amendment, pleading the. See PLEADING THE FIFTH.

Fifty Decisions. Justinian's rulings that settled controversies and eliminated obsolete rules in the law. • The decisions were made in preparation for *Justinian's Digest*. — Also termed (in Latin) *Quinquaginta Decisiones*.

50–percent rule. The principle that liability for negligence is apportioned in accordance with the percentage of fault that the fact-finder assigns to each party, that the plaintiff's recovery will be reduced by the percentage of negligence assigned to the plaintiff, and that the plaintiff's recovery is barred if the plaintiff's percentage of fault is 50% or more. — Also termed *modified-comparative-negligence doctrine*. Cf. PURE-COMPARATIVE-NEGLIGENCE DOCTRINE. See *comparative negligence* under NEGLIGENCE; APPORTIONMENT OF LIABILITY.

fighting age. See AGE.

fighting words. 1. Inflammatory speech that might not be protected by the First Amendment's free-speech guarantee because it might incite a violent response. **2.** Inflammatory speech that is pleadable in mitigation — but not in defense — of a suit for assault.

filacer (**fil**-ə-sər). *Hist.* An officer of the Westminster superior courts who filed the writs on which process was made. • The office was abolished in 1837.

filacium. See FILUM.

filare (fi-**lair**-ee), *vb.* [Law Latin] *Hist.* To file.

file, *n.* **1.** A court's complete and official record of a case <the law clerk went to the courthouse to verify that the motion is in the file>. **2.** A lawyer's complete record of a case <the paralegal stored the file in three drawers in her office>. **3.** A portion or section of a lawyer's case record <the janitor found the correspondence file behind the copy machine>. **4.** A case <Jonah was assigned the Watson file after Amy left the firm>.

file, *vb.* **1.** To deliver a legal document to the court clerk or record custodian for placement into the official record <Tuesday is the deadline for filing a reply brief> <they perfected the security interest by filing>. **2.** To commence a lawsuit <the seller threatened to file against the buyer>. **3.** To record or deposit something in an organized retention system or container for preservation and future reference <please file my notes under the heading "research">.

filed-rate doctrine. A common-law rule forbidding a regulated entity, usu. a common carrier, to charge a rate other than the one on file with the appropriate federal regulatory authority, such as (formerly) the Interstate Commerce Commission. — Also termed *filed-tariff doctrine*. See TARIFF (3).

file wrapper. See PROSECUTION HISTORY.

file-wrapper estoppel. See PROSECUTION-HISTORY ESTOPPEL.

filia (**fil**-ee-ə), *n.* [Latin] A daughter. Pl. ***filiae.***

filial consortium. See CONSORTIUM.

filiation (fil-ee-**ay**-shən). **1.** The fact or condition of being a son or daughter; relationship of a child to a parent.

> "In English we have no word that will serve to express with propriety the person who bears the relation opposed to that of parent. The word *child* is ambiguous, being employed in another sense, perhaps more frequently than in this: more frequently in opposition to *a person of full age*, an *adult*, than in correlation to a *parent*. For the condition itself we have no other word than filiation: an ill-contrived term, not analogous to *paternity* and *maternity*: the proper term would have been *filiality*: the word filiation is as frequently, perhaps, and more consistently, put for the act of establishing a person in the possession of the condition of filiality." Jeremy Bentham, *An Introduction to the Principles of Morals and Legislation* 276 n.2 (1823).

2. Judicial determination of paternity. See PATERNITY SUIT.

filibuster (**fil**-ə-bəs-tər), *n.* **1.** A dilatory tactic, esp. prolonged and often irrelevant speechmaking, employed in an attempt to obstruct legislative action. • The filibuster is common in the U.S. Senate, where the right to debate is unlimited. **2.** In a deliberative body, a member in the minority who resorts to obstructive tactics to prevent the adoption of a measure or procedure that is favored by the majority. — Also termed *filibusterer*. **3.** *Hist.* A person who, together with others, works to invade and revolutionize a foreign state in disregard of international law. — **filibuster,** *vb.* See CLOTURE.

filing, *n.* A particular document (such as a pleading) in the file of a court clerk or record custodian <the lawyer argued that the plaintiff's most recent filing was not germane to the issue before the court>.

filing fee. A sum of money required to be paid to the court clerk before a proceeding can start.

filing status. *Tax.* One of the four categories under which a person files an income tax return. • Under federal law, the four categories are: (1) single; (2) head of household; (3) married filing a joint return; and (4) married filing separate returns.

filiolus (fil-ee-**oh**-ləs). [Latin] *Hist.* A godson. — Also spelled (in old records) *filious*.

filius (**fil**-ee-əs), *n.* [Latin] **1.** A son. **2.** (*pl.*) Descendants. Pl. **filii.** Cf. HERES.

filiusfamilias (**fil**-ee-əs-fə-**mil**-ee-as). [Latin "the son of a family"] *Roman law.* An unemancipated son or daughter, grandson or granddaughter. — Also termed *homo alieni juris*.

> "Every Roman citizen is either a paterfamilias or a filiusfamilias, according as he is free from paternal power (homo sui juris) or not (homo alieni juris). Paterfamilias is the generic name for a homo sui juris, whether child or adult, married or unmarried. Filiusfamilias is the generic name for a homo alieni juris, whether son or daughter, grandson or granddaughter, and so on." Rudolph Sohm, *The Institutes: A Textbook of the History and System of Roman Private Law* 177 (James Crawford Ledlie trans., 3d ed. 1907).

filius mulieratus (**fil**-ee-əs myoo-lee-ə-**ray**-təs). [Law Latin] *Hist.* The eldest legitimate son of a woman who previously had an illegitimate son by the same father; a legitimate son, whose older brother is illegitimate; MULIER PUISNE. Cf. *bastard eisne* under EISNE.

filius nullius (**fil**-ee-əs nə-**lɪ**-əs). [Latin "son of nobody"] *Hist.* An illegitimate child. — Also termed *filius populi*.

> "I proceed next to the rights and incapacities which appertain to a bastard. The rights are very few, being only such as he can *acquire*; for he can *inherit* nothing, being looked upon as the son of nobody; and sometimes called *filius nullius*, sometimes *filius populi*." 1 William Blackstone, *Commentaries on the Laws of England* 447 (1765).

filius populi (**fil**-ee-əs **pop**-yə-lɪ). [Latin "son of the people"] *Hist.* An illegitimate child.

fill-or-kill order. See ORDER (4).

filum (**fɪ**-ləm). [Latin "thread"] *Hist.* **1.** A thread or wire that holds (esp. legal) papers together to form a file. • This was the ancient method of filing legal papers. **2.** An imaginary thread or line passing through the middle of a stream or road. — Also termed (in sense 1) *filacium*.

filum aquae (**fɪ**-ləm **ay**-kwee). [Latin "thread of water"] A line of water; the middle line of a stream of water, supposedly dividing it into two equal parts and usu. constituting the boundary between the riparian owners on each side. — Also termed *medium filum*.

filum forestae (**fɪ**-ləm **for**-ə-stee). [Latin] The border of a forest.

filum viae (**fɪ**-ləm **vɪ**-ee). [Latin] **1.** The middle line of a road. **2.** The boundary between landowners on each side of a road.

final appealable judgment. See *final judgment* under JUDGMENT.

final appealable order. See *final judgment* under JUDGMENT.

final argument. See CLOSING ARGUMENT.

final concord. See CONCORD.

final decision. See *final judgment* under JUDGMENT.

final-decision rule. See FINAL-JUDGMENT RULE.

final decree. See *final judgment* under JUDGMENT.

final injunction. See *permanent injunction* under INJUNCTION.

finalis concordia (fi-**nay**-lis kən-**kor**-dee-ə). [Latin] A final or conclusive agreement. See *final concord* under CONCORD; FINE (1).

finality doctrine. The rule that a court will not judicially review an administrative agency's action until it is final. — Also termed *final-order doctrine*; *doctrine of finality*; *principle of finality*. Cf. FINAL-JUDGMENT RULE.

finality rule. See FINAL-JUDGMENT RULE.

final judgment. See JUDGMENT.

final-judgment rule. The principle that a party may appeal only from a district court's final decision that ends the litigation on the merits. • Under this rule, a party must raise all claims of error in a single appeal. — Also termed *final-decision rule*; *finality rule*. 28 USCA § 1291. Cf. FINALITY DOCTRINE; INTERLOCUTORY APPEALS ACT.

final-offer arbitration. See ARBITRATION.

final order. See ORDER (2).

final-order doctrine. See FINALITY DOCTRINE.

final peace. See *final concord* under CONCORD.

final process. See PROCESS.

final receiver's receipt. The government's acknowledgment that it has received full payment from a person for public land, that it holds the legal title in trust for the person, and that it will in due course issue the person a land patent.

final settlement. See SETTLEMENT.

finance, *n.* **1.** The system in business concerned with the management of money, credit, banking, and investments <after a brief career in finance, Andrea decided to go to law school>. **2.** The science or study of the management of money, etc. <Bill sought a degree in finance because he wanted to be an investment banker>.

finance, *vb.* To raise or provide funds.

finance bill. See BILL (6).

finance charge. An additional payment, usu. in the form of interest, paid by a retail buyer for the privilege of purchasing goods or services in installments. • This phrase is increasingly used as a euphemism for *interest*. See INTEREST (3).

finance company. A nonbank company that deals in loans either by making them or by purchasing notes from another company that makes the loans directly to borrowers.

commercial finance company. A finance company that makes loans to manufacturers and wholesalers. — Also termed *commercial credit company*.

consumer finance company. A finance company that deals directly with consumers in extending credit. — Also termed *small-loan company*.

sales finance company. A finance company that does not deal directly with consumers but instead purchases consumer installment paper arising from the sale of consumer durables "on time." — Also termed *acceptance company*.

finance lease. See LEASE.

financial accounting. See ACCOUNTING (1).

Financial Accounting Standards Board. The independent body of accountants responsible for establishing, interpreting, and improving standards for financial accounting and reporting. — Abbr. FASB.

financial contract. See CONTRACT.

financial futures. See FUTURES (1).

financial institution. A business, organization, or other entity that manages money, credit, or capital, such as a bank, credit union, savings-

and-loan association, securities broker or dealer, pawnbroker, or investment company.

financial intermediary. A financial entity — usu. a commercial bank — that advances the transfer of funds between borrowers and lenders, buyers and sellers, and investors and savers.

financial planner. A person whose business is advising clients about personal finances and investments. • Upon completing a certification program, such a person is called a *certified financial planner*. — Abbr. CFP.

financial report. See FINANCIAL STATEMENT.

financial-responsibility act. A state statute conditioning license and registration of motor vehicles on proof of insurance or other financial accountability.

financial-responsibility clause. A provision in an automobile insurance policy stating that the insured has at least the minimum amount of liability insurance coverage required by a state's financial-responsibility law.

financial statement. A balance sheet, income statement, or annual report that summarizes an individual's or organization's financial condition on a specified date or for a specified period by reporting assets and liabilities. — Also termed *financial report*. Cf. FINANCING STATEMENT.

certified financial statement. A financial statement examined and reported by an independent public or certified public accountant. SEC Rule 12b–2 (17 CFR § 240.12b–2).

consolidated financial statement. The financial report of a company and all its subsidiaries combined as if they were a single entity.

financing, *n.* **1.** The act or process of raising or providing funds. **2.** Funds that are raised or provided. — **finance,** *vb.*

asset-based financing. A method of lending in which lenders and investors look principally to the cash flow from a particular asset for repayment.

construction financing. See *interim financing*.

debt financing. The raising of funds by issuing bonds or notes or by borrowing from a financial institution.

equity financing. **1.** The raising of funds by issuing capital securities (shares in the business) rather than making loans or selling bonds. **2.** The capital so raised.

floor-plan financing. A loan that is secured by merchandise and paid off as the goods are sold. • Usu. such a loan is given by a manufacturer to a retailer or other dealer (as a car dealer). — Also termed *floor planning*. Cf. FIELD WAREHOUSING.

gap financing. Interim financing used to fund the difference between a current loan and a loan to be received in the future, esp. between two long-term loans. See *bridge loan* under LOAN.

interim financing. A short-term loan secured to cover certain major expenditures, such as construction costs, until permanent financing is obtained. — Also termed *construction financing*.

internal financing. A funding method using funds generated through the company's operations rather than from stock issues or bank loans.

link financing. The obtaining of credit by depositing funds in another's bank account to aid the other in obtaining a loan.

outside financing. The raising of funds by selling stocks (equity financing) or bonds (debt financing).

permanent financing. A long-term loan obtained to repay an interim loan, such as a mortgage loan that is used to repay a construction loan.

project financing. A method of funding in which the lender looks primarily to the money generated by a single project as security for the loan. • This type of financing is usu. used for large, complex, and expensive single-purpose projects such as power plants, chemical-processing plants, mines, and toll roads. The lender is usu. paid solely or almost exclusively out of the money generated by the contracts for the facility's output (sometimes paid by customers directly into an account maintained by the lender), such as the electricity sold by a power plant. The lender usu. requires the facility to be developed and owned by a special-purpose entity (sometimes called a bankruptcy-remote entity), which can be a corporation, limited partnership, or other legal entity, that is permitted to perform no function other than developing, owning, and operating the facility. See SINGLE-PURPOSE PROJECT; SPECIAL-PURPOSE ENTITY; BANKRUPTCY-REMOTE ENTITY.

financing agency. See AGENCY (1).

financing statement. A document filed in the public records to notify third parties, usu. prospective buyers and lenders, of a secured party's security interest in goods. Cf. FINANCIAL STATEMENT.

finder. 1. An intermediary who brings together parties for a business opportunity, such as two companies for a merger, a borrower and a financial institution, or an issuer and an underwriter of securities. • A finder differs from a broker-dealer because the finder merely brings two parties together to make their own contract, while a broker-dealer usu. participates in the negotiations. See INTERMEDIARY. **2.** A person who discovers an object, often a lost or mislaid chattel.

finder of fact. See FACT-FINDER.

finder's fee. The amount charged by one who brings together parties for a business opportunity.

finder's-fee contract. An agreement between a finder and one of the parties to a business opportunity.

finding of fact. A determination by a judge, jury, or administrative agency of a fact supported by the evidence in the record, usu. presented at the trial or hearing <he agreed with the jury's finding of fact that the driver did not stop before proceeding into the intersection>. — Often shortened to *finding*. Cf. CONCLUSION OF FACT; CONCLUSION OF LAW.

concurrent finding. (*usu. pl.*) Identical factual findings by two different courts on a specific issue of fact.

essential finding. *Military law.* A military judge's determination of a collateral pretrial motion.

general finding. An undifferentiated finding in favor of one party.

***special finding.* 1.** (*usu. pl.*) A finding of the necessary and ultimate facts to support a judgment in favor of one party. **2.** *Military law.* A military judge's finding that directly relates to the determination of guilt or innocence.

fine, *n.* **1.** An amicable final agreement or compromise of a fictitious or actual suit to determine the true possessor of land. • The fine was formerly used as a form of conveyance to disentail an estate. — Also termed *final concord*; *finalis concordia*. See FOOT OF THE FINE.

> "A peculiar and persistent use of the writ [of covenant] was in levying a fine. A fine — *finalis concordia* — was the compromise of a suit, settled upon terms approved by the court. The dispute, while it might be a reality, was more often fictitious, and was chiefly used as a means of conveying land. . . . Soon after [Glanvill's] book was written, an innovation was made in the procedure which endured until 1833. The terms of the compromise, agreed by the parties and approved by the judges, were entered upon a threefold indenture, one of the parts being given to each of the litigants and the third — the 'foot' or bottom of the document — being kept among the records of the court. The parties thus obtained incontestable evidence and abundant security, and either could sue the other if the agreement were not implemented." C.H.S. Fifoot, *History and Sources of the Common Law: Tort and Contract* 256 (1949).

> "The fine that survived into the nineteenth century was a conveyancing mechanism that had worked in much the same way at the end of the twelfth. It took the form of a compromised law-suit. . . . The terms of the agreement were written out three times on a single piece of parchment which was then cut into three, one part remaining with each party and one, across the bottom and known as the 'foot', with the court. . . . This power to do more than the parties could do by their own act is not a trick harnessing the force of a judicial decision, and it comes from a time when judicial decision was not seen as the only business of courts." S.F.C. Milsom, *Historical Foundations of the Common Law* 151 (1969).

> "Unlike the recovery, which was a *real* action, the fine was a compromised fictitious *personal* action, originally designed as a method of ensuring security in conveyancing and only later being employed for the purpose of barring estates tail. In outline, it operated in the following manner. The intending purchaser brought an action, begun by writ of covenant, against the intending vendor. The parties then applied to the court to compromise the action; by the terms of the compromise (*finis*) the intending vendor admitted that the land belonged to the intending purchaser because he had given it to him, and the terms of the compromise were recorded in the court records. The fine owed its popularity as a means of conveyancing to two factors, neither of which was present in the standard method of conveyance by means of feoffment. First, the enrolling in the court records provided evidence of the transaction which was both permanent and free from the danger of forgery. Secondly, the effect of the fine was to set running a short period of limitation at the expiration of which all claims to the land were barred. It was this second aspect which made the device attractive as a means of 'barring' fees tail." Peter Butt, *Land Law* 102–03 (2d ed. 1988).

executed fine. *Hist.* A fine made on acknowledgment of the right of the grantee to land given to him as a gift from the grantor. • This was abolished in 1833. 3 & 4 Will. 4, ch. 74.

2. FINE FOR ALIENATION. **3.** A fee paid by a tenant to the landlord at the commencement of the tenancy to reduce the rent payments. **4.**

Hist. A money payment from a tenant to the tenant's lord.

common fine. A sum of money due from a tenant to a lord to defray the cost of a court leet or to allow the litigants to try the action closer to home. — Also termed *head-silver.*

5. A pecuniary criminal punishment or civil penalty payable to the public treasury. — **fine,** *vb.*

excessive fine. **1.** *Criminal law.* A fine that is unreasonably high and disproportionate to the offense committed. • The Eighth Amendment proscribes excessive fines. An example of an excessive fine is a civil forfeiture in which the property was not an instrumentality of the crime and the worth of the property was not proportional to the owner's culpability. **2.** A fine or penalty that seriously impairs one's earning capacity, esp. from a business.

fresh fine. *Hist.* A fine levied within the past year.

Fine and Recovery Act. *Hist.* A statute, enacted in 1833, that abolished the use of fines as a method of conveying title to land. See FINE (1). 3 & 4 Will. 4, ch. 74.

fine annullando levato de tenemento quod fuit de antiquo dominico (**fɪ**-nee a-nə-**lan**-doh lə-**vay**-to dee ten-ə-**men**-toh kwod **fyoo**-it dee an-**tɪ**-kwoh də-**min**-ə-koh). [Latin "a fine to be annulled levied from a tenant which was of ancient demesne"] *Hist.* A writ for disannulling a conveyance of land in ancient demesne to the lord's prejudice.

fine capiendo pro terris (**fɪ**-nee kap-ee-**en**-doh proh **ter**-is). [Latin "a fine to be taken for lands"] *Hist.* A writ that an imprisoned felon could use in some circumstances to obtain release from jail and to recover lands and goods taken during imprisonment.

fine for alienation. *Hist.* A fee paid by a tenant to the lord upon the alienation of a feudal estate and substitution of a new tenant. • It was payable by all tenants holding by knight's service or tenants *in capite* by socage tenure. — Often shortened to *fine.*

fine for endowment. *Hist.* A fee paid by a widow of a tenant to the tenant's lord. • If not paid, the widow could not be endowed of her husband's land.

finem facere (**fɪ**-nəm **fay**-sə-ree). [Latin] *Hist.* **1.** To make a composition or compromise; to relinquish a claim in exchange for consideration.

> "In the thirteenth century the king's justices wield a wide and a 'common law' power of ordering that an offender be kept in custody. They have an equally wide power of discharging him upon his 'making fine with the king.' We must observe the language of the time. In strictness they have no power to 'impose a fine.' No tribunal of this period, unless we are mistaken, is ever said to impose a fine. To order the offender to pay so much money to the king — this the judge may not do. If he did it, he would be breaking or evading the Great Charter, for an amercement should be affeered, not by royal justices, but by neighbours of the wrong-doer. What the judges can do is this: — they can pronounce a sentence of imprisonment and then allow the culprit to 'make fine,' that is to make an end (*finem facere*) of the matter by paying or finding security for a certain sum of money. In theory the fine is a bilateral transaction, a bargain; it is not 'imposed,' it is 'made.'" 2 Frederick Pollock & Frederic W. Maitland, *The History of English Law Before the Time of Edward I* 517 (2d ed. 1899).

2. To make a settlement of a penalty. • Magna Carta (ch. 55) specifically limited "[a]ll fines which were made with us unjustly and contrary to the law of the land. . . ." ([*o*]*mnes fines qui injuste et contra legem terrae facti sunt nobiscum*).

fine non capiendo pro pulchre placitando (**fɪ**-nee non kap-ee-**en**-doh proh **pəl**-kree plas-ə-**tan**-doh). [Latin "a fine not to be taken for pleading fairly"] *Hist.* A writ prohibiting court officers from taking fines for fair pleading (i.e., *beaupleader*).

fine print. The part of an agreement or document — usu. in small, light print that is not easily noticeable — referring to disclaimers, restrictions, or limitations.

fine pro redisseisina capiendo (**fɪ**-nee proh re-dis-**see**-zin-ə kap-ee-**en**-doh). [Law Latin "a fine to be taken for again disseising"] *Hist.* A writ that entitled a person imprisoned for twice dispossessing someone (*redisseisin*) to release upon payment of a reasonable fine.

fines le roy (**fɪnz** lə **roy**). [Law French] *Hist.* The king's fines. • A fine or fee that was paid to the monarch for an offense or contempt.

fine sur cognizance de droit, comme ceo que il ad de son done (**fɪn** sər **kon**-ə-zənts də **droyt**, kom **say**-oh kweel **ad** də **sawn dawn**). [Law French "a fine upon acknowledgment of the right, as that which he has of his gift"] *Hist.* The most common fine of conveyance, by which the defendant (also called the *deforciant*) acknowledged in court that he had already conveyed the property to the cognizee. • This form of conveyance took the place of an actual livery of seisin. See FINE (1).

"But, in general, the first species of fine, '*sur cognizance de droit come ceo, etc.*,' is the most used, as it conveys a clean and absolute freehold, and gives the cognizee a seisin in law, without an actual livery; and is therefore called a fine executed, whereas the others are but executory." 2 William Blackstone, *Commentaries on the Laws of England* 353 (1766).

fine sur cognizance de droit tantum (**fīn** sər **kon**-ə-zənts də **droyt tan**-təm). [Law French "fine upon acknowledgment of the right merely"] *Hist.* A fine of conveyance that does not acknowledge a prior conveyance of land. • This type of fine was used to convey reversionary interests — that is, interests that did not require acknowledgment of an earlier livery of seisin. See FINE (1).

fine sur concessit (**fīn** sər kən-**ses**-it). [Law French] *Hist.* A species of conveyance in which the cognizor does not acknowledge the cognizee's preceding right in land but grants the cognizee an estate de novo, usu. for life or years, by way of supposed composition. See FINE (1).

fine sur done, grant et render (**fīn** sər **dawn**, **grant** ay **ren**-dər). [Law French "fine upon gift, grant and render"] *Hist.* A double conveyance, consisting of a *fine sur cognizance de droit come ceo que il ad de son done* and a *fine sur concessit*, used to convey particular limitations of estates. • For example, after acknowledgment of the cognizee's right in the land, the cognizee would grant back to the cognizor or a third party some other estate in the land. See FINE (1).

finger, *vb. Slang.* To identify (a person) as a perpetrator, usu. of a crime <in his grand-jury testimony, Vitale fingered Benson as the gunman>.

fingerprint, *n.* **1.** The distinctive pattern of lines on a human fingertip <no two fingerprints are identical>. **2.** The impression of a fingertip made on any surface <the detective found several fingerprints on the knife>. **3.** An ink impression of the pattern of lines on a fingertip, usu. taken during the booking procedure after an arrest <after Dick had his fingerprints taken, he was put in the drunk tank>. — Also termed *print*; *thumbprint*. — **fingerprint,** *vb.* — **fingerprinting,** *n.* Cf. DNA IDENTIFICATION.

finire (fi-**nī**-ree), *vb.* [Law Latin] *Hist.* **1.** To fine; to pay a fine. **2.** To end or finish a matter.

finis (**fī**-nis *or* **fin**-is). [Latin] *Hist.* **1.** Boundary or limit. **2.** The compromise of a fine of conveyance. See FINE (1).

"The parties then applied to the court to compromise the action; by the terms of the compromise (*finis*) the intending vendor admitted that the land belonged to the intending purchaser because he had given it to him, and the terms of the compromise were recorded in the court records." Peter Butt, *Land Law* 102 (2d ed. 1988).

3. A fine, or payment of money made to satisfy a claim of criminal penalty.

finitio (fi-**nish**-ee-oh). [Law Latin] *Hist.* An ending; death.

finium regundorum actio (**fī**-nee-əm ri-gən-**dor**-əm **ak**-shee-oh). [Latin "action for regulating boundaries"] *Roman law.* An action for settling a boundary dispute.

FIO. *abbr.* Free in and out. • This bill-of-lading term means that the shipper supervises and pays for loading and unloading of cargo.

FIOS. *abbr.* Free in and out stowage. • This shipping term means that the vessel does not pay for the costs of loading, unloading, or stowing.

firdfare. See FERDFARE.

fire, *vb.* To discharge or dismiss a person from employment; to terminate as an employee.

firearm. A weapon that expels a projectile (such as a bullet or pellets) by the combustion of gunpowder or other explosive.

fire-bote. See *housebote* under BOTE (1).

firebug. See INCENDIARY (1).

firefighter's rule. A doctrine holding that a fireman, police officer, or other emergency professional may not hold a person, usu. a property owner, liable for unintentional injuries suffered by the professional in responding to the situation created or caused by the person. — Also termed *fireman's rule*.

fire insurance. See INSURANCE.

fireman's rule. See FIREFIGHTER'S RULE.

fire ordeal. See ORDEAL.

fire sale. See SALE.

firing squad. 1. A group of persons assembled to carry out a capital-punishment sentence by shooting the prisoner with high-powered rifles at the same time from a short distance. **2.** A military detachment that fires a salute, usu. at the burial of the person honored.

firm, *n.* **1.** The title under which one or more persons conduct business jointly. **2.** The association by which persons are united for business purposes. • Traditionally, this term referred to a partnership, as opposed to a company. But today it is frequently used in reference to a company. See LAW FIRM.

firma burgi (**fər**-mə **bər**-jɪ). [Law Latin] *Hist.* A person's right to take the profits of a borough. • The monarch or the borough's lord granted this right to a person upon payment of a fixed sum.

firma feodi. See FEE FARM.

firma noctis. See NOCTEM DE FIRMA.

firmaratio (fər-mə-**ray**-shee-oh). [Law Latin] *Hist.* A tenant's right to the lands and tenements leased to him.

firmarius (fər-**mair**-ee-əs). [Law Latin] A person entitled to take rent or profits. Cf. FERMER (2).

firm bid. See BID (2).

firm-commitment underwriting. See UNDERWRITING.

firme. See FARM.

firmitas (**fər**-mə-tas). [Law Latin] *Hist.* An assurance of some privilege by deed or charter.

firm offer. See *irrevocable offer* under OFFER.

firm-opportunity doctrine. See CORPORATE-OPPORTUNITY DOCTRINE.

First Amendment. The constitutional amendment, ratified with the Bill of Rights in 1791, guaranteeing the freedoms of speech, religion, press, assembly, and petition.

first-blush rule. The principle that allows a court to set aside a verdict as excessive because the verdict causes the mind to immediately conclude that it resulted from passion or prejudice on the part of the jury.

first chair, *n. Slang.* The lead attorney in court for a given case <despite having worked at the firm for six years, the associate had yet to be first chair in a jury trial>. — **first-chair,** *vb.*

first cousin. see COUSIN (1).

first-degree, *adj.* See DEGREE (2).

first-degree murder. See MURDER.

first devisee. See DEVISEE.

first-filing rule. See FIRST-TO-FILE RULE.

first fruits. 1. *Hist.* One year's profits from the land of a tenant *in capite,* payable to the Crown after the tenant's death. — Also termed *primer seisin.* **2.** *Hist. Eccles. law.* The first year's whole profits of a clergyman's benefice, paid by the incumbent to the Pope, or (after the break with Rome) to the Crown. • This revenue was later termed "Queen Anne's Bounty" when it was converted to a fund to benefit the poor. — Sometimes spelled *firstfruits.* — Also termed *primitiae.*

firsthand knowledge. See *personal knowledge* under KNOWLEDGE.

first impression, case of. See CASE.

first-in, first-out. An accounting method that assumes that goods are sold in the order in which they were purchased — that is, the oldest items are sold first. — Abbr. FIFO. Cf. LAST-IN, FIRST-OUT; NEXT-IN, FIRST-OUT.

first instance, court of. See *trial court* under COURT.

first lien. See LIEN.

First Lord of the Admiralty. *Hist.* In Britain, a minister and one of the lord commissioners who presided over the navy. • The First Lord was assisted by other lords, called Sea Lords, and various secretaries.

First Lord of the Treasury. *English law.* The chief officer in charge of the treasury. • Today, this position is held by the Prime Minister.

first magistrate. See MAGISTRATE (1).

first meeting. *Archaic. Criminal law.* The first contact between a killer and a victim after the killer has been informed of the victim's insulting words or conduct that provoked the killing. • If the killing occurred during the first meeting, a murder charge could be reduced to manslaughter. See HEAT OF PASSION.

first mortgage. See MORTGAGE.

first-mortgage bond. See BOND (3).

first of exchange. *Archaic.* The first in a series of drafts (bills of exchange) drawn in duplicate or triplicate for safety in their delivery, the intention being that the acceptance and payment of any one of them, usu. the first to arrive, cancels the others in the set.

first offender. See OFFENDER.

first option to buy. See RIGHT OF PREEMPTION.

first-party insurance. See INSURANCE.

first policy year. *Insurance.* The first year of a life-insurance policy that is annually renewed. • This statutory phrase prohibits an insurer from using the policy's suicide exclusion as a defense — and refusing payment on the policy — when an insured commits suicide after the first year of the policy. The insurer can invoke the suicide exclusion as a defense to payment only if the insured commits suicide in the first policy year.

first purchaser. See PURCHASER (2).

first refusal, right of. See RIGHT OF FIRST REFUSAL.

first-sale doctrine. *Copyright.* The rule that a copyright owner, after conveying the title to a particular copy of the protected work, loses the exclusive right to sell that copy and therefore cannot interfere with later sales or distributions by the new owner.

first taker. See TAKER.

first-to-file rule. *Civil procedure.* **1.** The principle that, when two suits are brought by the same parties, regarding the same issues, in two courts of proper jurisdiction, the court that first acquires jurisdiction usu. retains the suit, to the exclusion of the other court. • The court with the second-filed suit ordinarily stays proceedings or abstains. But an exception exists if the first-filed suit is brought merely in anticipation of the true plaintiff's suit — as an improper attempt at forum-shopping. See ANTICIPATORY FILING. **2.** The doctrine allowing a party to a previously filed lawsuit to enjoin another from pursuing a later-filed action. — Also termed *first-filing rule*; *priority-jurisdiction rule*.

fisc (fisk), *n.* [Latin *fiscus*] The public treasury.

fiscal (**fis**-kəl), *adj.* **1.** Of or relating to financial matters <fiscal year>. **2.** Of or relating to public finances or taxation <the city's sound fiscal policy>.

fiscal agent. See AGENT.

fiscal officer. 1. The person (such as a state or county treasurer) charged with the collection and distribution of public money. **2.** The person (such as a chief financial officer) whose duties are to oversee the financial matters of a corporation or business.

fiscal year. An accounting period of 12 consecutive months <the company's fiscal year is October 1 to September 30>. • A fiscal year is often different from the calendar year, esp. for tax purposes. — Also termed *fiscal period*.

fiscus (**fis**-kəs). [Latin "the basket" *or* "moneybag"] **1.** *Roman law.* The emperor's treasury. • In later Roman times, the term also included the treasury of the state. See AERARIUM. **2.** *Hist.* The treasury of a monarch (as the repository of forfeited property), a noble, or any private person. **3.** The treasury or property of the state as distinguished from the private property of the monarch. Cf. HANAPER.

fishery. 1. A right or liberty of taking fish. • Fishery was an incorporeal hereditament under old English law. — Also termed *piscary*.

free fishery. An exclusive right of fishery, existing by grant or prescription from the monarch, to take fish in public water such as a river or an arm of the sea. — Also termed *libera piscaria*.

right of fishery. The right of persons to fish in public waters, subject to federal and state restrictions and regulations, such as fishing seasons, licensing, and catch limits.

several fishery. A right to fish in waters that are neither on one's own land nor on the land of a person who granted the right to fish.

2. A fishing ground.

common fishery. A fishing ground where all persons have a right to take fish. Cf. *common of piscary* under COMMON.

fishing expedition. An attempt, through broad discovery requests or random questions, to elicit information from another party in the hope that something relevant might be found; esp., such an attempt that exceeds the scope of discovery allowed by procedural rules. — Also termed *fishing trip.*

> "No longer can the time-honored cry of 'fishing expedition' serve to preclude a party from inquiring into the facts underlying his opponent's case." *Hickman v. Taylor*, 329 U.S. 495, 507, 67 S.Ct. 385, 392 (1947).

fish royal. *Hist.* Whales, sturgeon, and porpoises that, when thrown ashore or caught near the English coast, become Crown property.

fistuca. See FESTUCA.

fithwite. See FUTHWITE.

fitness for a particular purpose. See *implied warranty of fitness for a particular purpose* under WARRANTY (2).

Five Mile Act. *Hist.* A 1665 act prohibiting Puritan ministers from teaching or coming within five miles of any town where they had held office if they refused to pledge that they would not seek to overturn the Church of England. • The Act was repealed in 1689.

501(c)(3) organization. See CHARITABLE ORGANIZATION.

fix, *n.* **1.** A dose of an illegal drug <the defendant testified that he robbed the store because he needed to buy a fix>. **2.** A navigational reading.

fix, *vb.* **1.** To announce (an exchange price, interest rate, etc.) <interest was fixed at 6%>. **2.** To agree with another to establish (a price for goods or services), often illegally <representatives of Acme and Widget secretly met to fix prices for their companies' products>. See PRICE-FIXING. **2.** To influence (an action or outcome, esp. a sports event) by improper or illegal means <after losing the election, the challenger claimed that the incumbent had fixed the election>.

fixation. *Copyright.* The process or result of recording a work of authorship in tangible form so that it can be copyrighted under federal law. • Fixation occurs, for instance, when a live television broadcast is transmitted and simultaneously recorded on videotape.

fix bail, *vb.* To set the amount and terms of bail <after hearing the officer's testimony, the judge fixed bail for the defendant at $100,000>. See BAIL.

fixed annuity. See ANNUITY.

fixed asset. See *capital asset* (1) under ASSET.

fixed-benefit plan. See *defined pension plan* under PENSION PLAN.

fixed capital. See CAPITAL.

fixed charge. See *fixed cost* under COST.

fixed cost. See COST (1).

fixed debt. See DEBT.

fixed-dollar investment. See INVESTMENT.

fixed expense. See *fixed cost* under COST.

fixed fee. 1. A fee that will not vary according to the amount of work done or other factor. **2.** In a construction contract, a predetermined amount that is added to costs for calculating payments due under the contract.

fixed income. See INCOME.

fixed-income investment. See INVESTMENT.

fixed-income security. See SECURITY.

fixed liability. See *fixed debt* under DEBT.

fixed opinion. A bias or prejudice that disqualifies a potential juror.

fixed price. See PRICE.

fixed-price contract. See CONTRACT.

fixed-rate mortgage. See MORTGAGE.

fixed-return dividend. See DIVIDEND.

fixed sentence. See SENTENCE.

fixed trust. See TRUST.

fixing a jury. See JURY-FIXING.

fixture. Personal property that is attached to land or a building and that is regarded as an irremovable part of the real property, such as a fireplace built into a home. — Also termed *permanent fixture*. Cf. IMPROVEMENT.

> "A fixture can best be defined as a thing which, although originally a movable chattel, is by reason of its annexation to, or association in use with land, regarded as a part of the land.... The law of fixtures concerns those situations where the chattel annexed still retains a separate identity in spite of annexation, for example a furnace or a light fixture. Where the chattel annexed loses such identity, as in the case of nails, boards, etc., the problem becomes one of accession." Ray Andrews Brown, *The Law of Personal Property* § 137, at 698 & n.1 (2d ed. 1955).

> "Broadly, goods can be classified for the purposes of [UCC §] 9–313 into three categories: those that remain 'pure goods,' those so substantially integrated into real estate as to become real estate themselves, 'pure realty,' and those in the gray area that would pass in a deed to the real estate but that retain separate status as personal property. These last are fixtures." 4 James J. White & Robert S. Summers, *Uniform Commercial Code* § 33–8, at 338 (4th ed. 1995).

tenant's fixture. Removable personal property that a tenant affixes to the leased property but that the tenant can detach and take away.

trade fixture. Removable personal property that a tenant attaches to leased land for business purposes, such as a display counter. • Despite its name, a trade fixture is not usu. treated as a fixture — that is, as irremovable.

fixture filing. The act or an instance of recording, in public real-estate records, a security interest in personal property that is intended to become a fixture. • The creditor files a financing statement in the real-property records of the county where a mortgage on the real estate would be filed. A fixture-filing financing statement must contain a description of the real estate.

FKA. *abbr.* Formerly known as. — Also spelled *F/K/A*; *fka*; *f/k/a*.

flag, *n.* **1.** A usu. rectangular piece of cloth, bunting, or other material decorated with a distinctive design and used as a symbol or signal. **2.** Something symbolized by the display of a flag, such as a ship or nationality. See DUTY OF THE FLAG; LAW OF THE FLAG.

flag of convenience. *Int'l law.* A national flag flown by a ship not because the ship or its crew has an affiliation with the nation, but because the lax controls and modest fees and taxes imposed by that nation have attracted the owner to register it there. • After World War II, shipowners began registering their ships in countries such as Panama, Liberia, and Honduras to avoid expensive and restrictive national regulation of labor, safety, and other matters. Since the late 1950s, there has been increasing international pressure to require a "genuine link" between a ship and its flag state, but this reform has been slow in coming. — Abbr. FOC.

flag of truce. *Int'l law.* A white flag used as a signal when one belligerent wishes to communicate with the other in the field. • The bearers of such a flag may not be fired on, injured, or taken prisoner, as long as they carry out their mission in good faith.

flag desecration. The act of mutilating, defacing, burning, or flagrantly misusing a flag. • Flag desecration is constitutionally protected as a form of free speech. *United States v. Eichman*, 496 U.S. 310, 110 S.Ct. 2404 (1990).

flagrans bellum (**flay**-granz **bel**-əm). [Latin "raging war"] A war currently being waged.

flagrans crimen (**flay**-granz **crI**-mən). [Latin] A crime in the very act of its commission or of recent occurrence; a fresh crime.

flagrante bello (flə-**gran**-tee **bel**-oh). [Latin] During an actual state of war.

flagrante delicto. See IN FLAGRANTE DELICTO.

flag state. The state under whose flag a ship sails. • A ship may fly the flag of one state only.

flash-of-genius rule. *Patents.* The now-defunct principle that a device is not patentable if it was invented as the result of trial and error rather than as a "flash of creative genius." • The rule, which takes its name from language in *Cuno Engineering Corp. v. Automatic Devices Corp.*, 314 U.S. 84, 91, 62 S.Ct. 37, 41 (1941), was legislatively overturned in 1952. 35 USCA § 103.

flat, *adv.* Without an allowance or charge for accrued interest <the stock was sold flat>.

flat, *n.* A house in a larger block; an apartment.

flat bond. See BOND (3).

flat cancellation. See CANCELLATION.

flat money. See *fiat money* under MONEY.

flat reinsurance. See REINSURANCE.

flat sentence. See *determinate sentence* under SENTENCE.

flat tax. See TAX.

flat time. See TIME.

fledwite (**fled**-wɪt). *Hist.* **1.** A discharge from an amercement (a fine) for a fugitive who turns himself or herself in to the monarch. **2.** The fine set on a fugitive as the price for obtaining freedom. **3.** The right to hold court and take an amercement for the offenses of beating and striking. — Also spelled *fleduite.* — Also termed *flighwite.*

flee from justice. See FLIGHT.

fleet insurance. See INSURANCE.

Fleet marriage. See MARRIAGE (1).

fleme (fleem). *Hist.* An outlaw; a fugitive bondman or villein. — Also spelled *flem.* — Also termed *flyma.*

flemene frit (**flee**-mən **frit**). *Hist.* The harboring or aiding of a fleme (a fugitive). — Also termed and spelled *flemenes frinthe*; *flemensfirth*; *flyman frynth*; *flymena frynthe.*

flemeswite (**fleemz**-wɪt). *Hist.* The privilege to possess, or the actual possession of, the goods and fines of a fleme (a fugitive).

Fleta seu Commentarius Juris Anglicani (**flee**-tə syoo kom-ən-**tair**-ee-əs **joor**-is ang-glə-**kay**-nɪ). *Hist.* The title of an ancient treatise on English law, composed in the 13th century and first printed in 1647. • The work is largely derivative, being based on Bracton's *De Legibus et Consuetudinibus.* The unknown author may have been a judge or lawyer who wrote the treatise while in London's Fleet prison. — Often shortened to *Fleta.*

flexdollars. Money that an employer pays an employee, who can apply it to a choice of employee benefits.

flexible constitution. See CONSTITUTION.

flexible-rate mortgage. See *adjustable-rate mortgage* under MORTGAGE.

flextime. A work schedule that employees may change within their discretion, allowing them to work differing hours as long as they work their required number of hours over a specified period (usu. a week).

flexweek. A four-day workweek, usu. consisting of four 10-hour days.

flight. The act or an instance of fleeing, esp. to evade arrest or prosecution <the judge denied bail because the defendant is a flight risk>. — Also termed *flight from prosecution*; *flee from justice.*

flight easement. See *avigational easement* under EASEMENT.

flight from prosecution. See FLIGHT.

flighwite. See FLEDWITE.

flim flam. A scheme by which another is tricked for money; CONFIDENCE GAME. — Also termed *faith and trust.*

flip, *vb. Slang.* **1.** To buy and then immediately resell securities or real estate in an attempt to turn a profit. **2.** To refinance consumer loans. **3.** To turn state's evidence.

flip mortgage. See MORTGAGE.

float, *n.* **1.** The sum of money represented by outstanding or uncollected checks. **2.** The delay between a transaction and the withdrawal of funds to cover the transaction. **3.** The amount of a corporation's shares that are available for trading on the securities market.

float, *vb.* **1.** (Of a currency) to attain a value in the international exchange market solely on the basis of supply and demand <the IMF allowed the peso to float>. **2.** To issue (a security) for sale on the market <PDQ Corp. floated a new series of preferred shares>. **3.** To arrange or negotiate (a loan) <the bank floated a car loan to Alice despite her poor credit history>.

floatage. See FLOTSAM.

floater. See *floating-rate note* under NOTE (1).

floater insurance. See INSURANCE.

floating, *adj.* Not fixed or settled; fluctuating; variable.

floating capital. See CAPITAL.

floating charge. See *floating lien* under LIEN.

floating debt. See DEBT.

floating easement. See EASEMENT.

floating-interest bond. See BOND (3).

floating lien. See LIEN.

floating policy. See INSURANCE POLICY.

floating rate. See INTEREST RATE.

floating-rate note. See NOTE (1).

floating stock. See STOCK.

floating zoning. See ZONING.

floodgate. (*usu. pl.*) A restraint that prevents a release of a usu. undesirable result <the new law opened the floodgates of litigation>.

flood insurance. See INSURANCE.

floodplain. Land that is subject to floodwaters because of its level topography and proximity to a river or arroyo; esp., level land that, extending from a riverbank, is inundated when the flow of water exceeds the channel's capacity.

floodwater. See WATER.

floor. 1. A legislature's central meeting place where the members sit and conduct business, as distinguished from the galleries, corridors, or lobbies <the floor of the Texas Senate>. **2.** The trading area where stocks and commodities are bought and sold on an exchange <the broker placed his buy order with the trader on the floor of the NYSE>. **3.** The lowest limit <the floor for that position is $25,000 per year>.

floor debate. The legislative process of debating a proposed bill before an entire chamber rather than before a committee.

floor-plan financing. See FINANCING.

floor planning. See *floor-plan financing* under FINANCING.

floor-plan rule. The principle by which a vehicle owner who has placed for sale a vehicle in a retail dealer's showroom is estopped to deny the title of an innocent purchaser from the dealer in the ordinary course of retail dealing.

floor price. See PRICE.

floor tax. See TAX.

flotage. See FLOTSAM.

flotation cost. See COST (1).

floterial district. See DISTRICT.

flotsam (**flot**-səm). Goods that float on the water's surface after being abandoned at sea. — Also termed *floatage*; *flotage*. Cf. JETSAM; LAGAN; WAVESON.

flowage. The natural movement of water from a dominant estate to a servient estate. • It is a privilege or easement of the owner of the upper estate and a servitude of the lower estate.

flowage easement. See EASEMENT.

flower bond. See BOND (3).

FLSA. *abbr.* FAIR LABOR STANDARDS ACT.

fluctuating clause. See ESCALATOR CLAUSE.

fly for it. *Hist.* To flee after allegedly committing a crime. • The ancient custom in criminal trials was to ask the jury after its verdict — even a not-guilty verdict — "Did he fly for it?" The purpose was to enable the jury to find whether the defendant had fled from justice. A defendant who had fled would forfeit personal property, even though found not guilty on the underlying charge.

flyma. See FLEME.

flyman frynth. See FLEMENE FRIT.

flymena frynthe. See FLEMENE FRIT.

fly-power assignment. See ASSIGNMENT (2).

flyspeck, *n. Insurance.* A potential trivial defect in title to real property, as a result of which a title-insurance company is likely to exclude any risk from that defect before issuing a policy. — **flyspeck,** *vb.*

FMC. *abbr.* FEDERAL MARITIME COMMISSION.

FMCS. *abbr.* FEDERAL MEDIATION AND CONCILIATION SERVICE.

FmHA. *abbr.* FARMERS HOME ADMINISTRATION.

FMV. See *fair market value* under VALUE.

FNMA. *abbr.* FEDERAL NATIONAL MORTGAGE ASSOCIATION.

FOB. *abbr.* FREE ON BOARD.

FOB destination. See FREE ON BOARD.

FOB shipping. See FREE ON BOARD.

FOC. See *flag of convenience* under FLAG.

foedus (**fee**-dəs). [Latin "league"] *Hist. Int'l law.* A treaty; league; compact.

foenus nauticum (**fee**-nəs **naw**-tə-kəm). [Latin] *Civil law.* Nautical or maritime interest; esp., an extraordinary rate of interest charged to underwrite a hazardous voyage. — Also termed *usura maritima.*

foesting-men. See HABENTES HOMINES.

FOIA (**foy**-ə). *abbr.* FREEDOM OF INFORMATION ACT.

foiable (**foy**-ə-bəl), *adj. Slang.* (Of documents) subject to disclosure under the Freedom of Information Act (FOIA).

folcland. See FOLKLAND.

folio (**foh**-lee-oh). [fr. Latin *folium* "leaf"] **1.** *Hist.* A leaf of a paper or parchment, numbered only on the front. • A folio includes both sides of the leaf, or two pages, with the letters "a" and "b" (or "r" and "v," signifying *recto* and *verso*) added to show which of the two pages was intended. **2.** *Hist.* A certain number of words in a legal document, used as a method of measurement. • In England, 72 or 90 words formed a folio; in the United States, 100 words.

> "Folio ... [a] certain number of words; in conveyances, etc., and proceedings in the High Court amounting to seventy-two, and in parliamentary proceedings to ninety." Ivan Horniman, *Wharton's Law Lexicon* 368 (13th ed. 1925).

3. A page number on a printed book. **4.** A large book the pages of which are formed by folding a sheet of paper only once in the binding to form two leaves, making available four pages (both sides of each leaf).

folkland. *Hist.* Land held by customary law, without written title. — Also spelled *folcland.* Cf. BOOKLAND.

folk laws. See LEGES BARBARORUM.

follow, *vb.* To conform to or comply with; to accept as authority <the lawyer assumed that the Supreme Court would follow its own precedent>.

follow-the-fortunes doctrine. *Insurance.* The principle that a reinsurer must reimburse the reinsured for its payment of settled claims as long as the reinsured's payments were reasonable and in good faith. • This rule prevents a reinsurer from second-guessing a reinsured's good-faith decision to pay a claim arguably not covered under the original insurance policy. — Often shortened to *follow the fortunes.*

follow-the-settlements doctrine. *Insurance.* The principle that an indemnitor must accede to the actions of the indemnitee in adjusting and settling claims; esp., the principle that a reinsurer must follow the actions of the reinsured.

fons juris. See SOURCE OF LAW.

Food and Drug Administration. The federal agency within the Department of Health and Human Services established to determine safety and quality standards for foods, drugs, medical devices, cosmetics, and other household products. — Abbr. FDA.

Food, Drug, and Cosmetic Act. A 1938 federal law prohibiting the transportation in interstate commerce of adulterated or misbranded food, drugs, or cosmetics.

foot acre. A one-foot-deep layer of coal spread over one acre. • This measurement method is used to value coal land for tax purposes.

foot-frontage rule. *Tax.* In property-tax assessment, a principle that confines the lot boundary to the actual frontage on the line of improvement. • The depth of the lot and the number and character of improvements or their value is immaterial if this formula is used.

footgeld (**fuut**-geld). *Hist.* In forest law, a fine imposed for not making a dog incapable of hunting by either cutting out the ball of its paw or cutting off its claws. • The cutting was known as "expeditating" the dog. To be "free" or "quit" of footgeld was to be relieved of the duty to expedite one's dog.

foot of the fine. *Hist.* At common law, the fifth and last part of a fine of conveyance. • This part included the entire matter, reciting the names of the parties and the date, place, and before whom it was acknowledged or levied. See FINE (1).

footprint. 1. *Evidence.* The impression made on a surface of soil, snow, etc., by a human foot or a shoe, boot, or any other foot covering. **2.** *Real estate.* The shape of a building's base.

for account of. A form of indorsement on a note or draft introducing the name of the person entitled to receive the proceeds.

Foraker Act (**for**-ə-kər). The original (1900) federal law providing Puerto Rico with a civil government, but keeping it outside the U.S. customs area. See 48 USCA §§ 731–752.

foraneous (fə-**ray**-nee-əs), *adj.* [fr. Latin *forum* "marketplace"] Of or relating to a court or marketplace.

foraneus (fə-**ray**-nee-əs), *n.* [fr. Latin *foris* "without"] *Hist.* A foreigner; an alien; a stranger.

forathe (**for**-ayth). *Hist.* In forest law, one who can make an oath or bear witness for another.

forbannitus (for-**ban**-ə-təs). [Law Latin] *Hist.* **1.** A pirate; an outlaw. **2.** One who was banished. — Also termed *forisbanitus.*

forbarre (for-**bahr**), *vb.* [Law French] *Hist.* To preclude; to bar out; to estop.

forbatudus (for-bə-**t[y]oo**-dəs). [Law Latin] *Hist.* A person who provokes — and dies in — a fight.

forbearance, *n.* **1.** The act of refraining from enforcing a right, obligation, or debt. • Strictly speaking, *forbearance* denotes an intentional negative act, while *omission* or *neglect* is an unintentional negative act. **2.** The act of tolerating or abstaining. — **forbear,** *vb.*

forbidden degree. See *prohibited degree* under DEGREE (5).

forbidden departure. An impermissible deviation from the federal sentencing guidelines based on race, sex, national origin, creed, religion, or socioeconomic status.

for cause. For a legal reason or ground. • The phrase expresses a common standard governing the removal of a civil servant or an employee under contract. — **for-cause,** *adj.*

force, *n.* Power, violence, or pressure directed against a person or thing.

actual force. Force consisting in a physical act, esp. a violent act directed against a robbery victim. — Also termed *physical force.*

constructive force. Threats and intimidation to gain control or prevent resistance; esp., threatening words or gestures directed against a robbery victim.

deadly force. Violent action known to create a substantial risk of causing death or serious bodily harm. • A person may use deadly force in self-defense only if retaliating against another's deadly force. — Also termed *extreme force.* Cf. *nondeadly force.*

> "Under the common law the use of deadly force is never permitted for the sole purpose of stopping one fleeing from arrest on a misdemeanor charge . . . ." Rollin M. Perkins & Ronald N. Boyce, *Criminal Law* 1098 (3d ed. 1982).

excessive force. Unreasonable or unnecessary force under the circumstances.

irresistible force. Force that cannot be foreseen or controlled, esp. that which prevents the performance of a contractual obligation; FORCE MAJEURE.

legal force. See *reasonable force.*

nondeadly force. **1.** Force that is neither intended nor likely to cause death or serious bodily harm; force intended to cause only minor bodily harm. **2.** A threat of deadly force, such as displaying a knife. — Also termed *moderate force.* Cf. *deadly force.*

physical force. See *actual force.*

reasonable force. Force that is not excessive and that is appropriate for protecting oneself or one's property. • The use of reasonable force will not render a person criminally or tortiously liable. — Also termed *legal force.*

"One does not use jeweller's scales to measure reasonable force." *Reed v. Wastie*, [1972] Crim. L.R. 221 (per Lane, J.) (as quoted in Glanville Williams, *Textbook of Criminal Law* 451 (1978)).

unlawful force. Action constituting an offense or actionable tort directed against a person without that person's consent.

force, *vb.* To compel by physical means or by legal requirement <Barnes used a gun to force Ms. Jillson to use her ATM card> <under the malpractice policy, the insurance company was forced to defend the doctor>.

force and arms. *Hist.* Violence. • The phrase was used in common-law pleading in declarations of trespass and in indictments to denote that the offending act was committed violently. See VI ET ARMIS.

force and effect, *n.* Legal efficacy <mailing the brief had the force and effect of filing it with the clerk>. • The term is now generally regarded as a redundant legalism.

forced conversion. See CONVERSION (1).

forced exile. See EXILE.

forced heir. See HEIR.

forced labor. *Int'l law.* Work exacted from a person under threat of penalty; work for which a person has not offered himself or herself voluntarily. • Under the U.N. Convention on Civil and Political Rights (article 8), exemptions from this definition include (1) penalties imposed by a court, (2) compulsory military service, (3) action taken in an emergency, (4) normal civil obligations, and (5) minor communal services. — Also termed *compulsory labor.*

forced portion. See LEGITIME.

forced resettlement. *Int'l law.* The involuntary transfer of individuals or groups within the jurisdiction of a country whether inside its own territory or into or out of occupied territory.

forced respite. See RESPITE.

forced sale. See SALE.

forced share. See ELECTIVE SHARE.

force majeure (**fors** ma-**zhər**). [Law French "a superior force"] An event or effect that can be neither anticipated nor controlled. • The term includes both acts of nature (e.g., floods and hurricanes) and acts of people (e.g., riots, strikes, and wars). — Also termed *force majesture*; *vis major*; *superior force.* Cf. ACT OF GOD; VIS MAJOR.

force-majeure clause. A contractual provision allocating the risk if performance becomes impossible or impracticable as a result of an event or effect that the parties could not have anticipated or controlled.

forcible, *adj.* Effected by force or threat of force against opposition or resistance.

"[In the law of trespass, the] term 'forcible' is used in a wide and somewhat unnatural sense to include any act of physical interference with the person or property of another. To lay one's finger on another person without lawful justification is as much a forcible injury in the eye of the law, and therefore a trespass, as to beat him with a stick. To walk peacefully across another man's land is a forcible injury and a trespass, no less than to break into his house *vi et armis*. So also it is probably a trespass deliberately to put matter where natural forces will take it on to the plaintiff's land." R.F.V. Heuston, *Salmond on the Law of Torts* 5 (17th ed. 1977).

forcible detainer. 1. The wrongful retention of possession of property by one originally in lawful possession, often with threats or actual use of violence. **2.** FORCIBLE ENTRY AND DETAINER.

forcible entry. At common law, the act or an instance of violently and unlawfully taking possession of lands and tenements against the will of those entitled to possession.

forcible entry and detainer. 1. The act of violently taking and keeping possession of lands and tenements without legal authority.

"To walk across another's land, or to enter his building, without privilege, is a trespass, but this in itself, while a civil wrong, is not a crime. However, if an entry upon real estate is accomplished by violence or intimidation, or if such methods are employed for detention after a peaceable entry, there is a crime according to English law, known as forcible entry and detainer. This was a common-law offense in England, although supplemented by English statutes that are old enough to be common law in this country. . . . It has sometimes been said that there are two separate offenses — (1) forcible entry and (2) forcible detainer. This may be true under the peculiar wording of some particular statute, but in general it seems to be one offense which may be committed in two different ways." Rollin M. Perkins & Ronald N. Boyce, *Criminal Law* 487–88 (3d ed. 1982).

2. A quick and simple legal proceeding for regaining possession of real property from someone who has wrongfully taken, or refused to surrender, possession. — Also termed *forcible detainer*. See EVICTION; EJECTIMENT.

> "Forcible entry and detainer is a remedy given by statute for the recovery of possession of land and of damages for its detention. It is entirely regulated by statute, and the statutes vary materially in the different states." Benjamin J. Shipman, *Handbook of Common-Law Pleading* § 74, at 188 (Henry Winthrop Ballantine ed., 3d ed. 1923).

foreclose, *vb.* To terminate a mortgagor's interest in property; to subject (property) to foreclosure proceedings.

> "Should the mortgagor default in his obligations under the mortgage, the mortgagee will seek to 'foreclose', — i.e., 'end' or 'close' the mortgagor's rights in the security. After taking the appropriate statutory steps, the mortgagee will sell the mortgaged property. If the sale is to someone other than the mortgagor or the mortgagee (a 'third party' sale) the proceeds will go: first, to pay the costs of the foreclosure proceedings; second, to pay off the principal indebtedness and accrued interest; third, if there is anything left over (i.e., any 'equity' existed) this is paid to the mortgagor." Edward H. Rabin, *Fundamentals of Modern Real Property Law* 1087 (1974).

foreclosure (for-**kloh**-zhər). A legal proceeding to terminate a mortgagor's interest in property, instituted by the lender (the mortgagee) either to gain title or to force a sale in order to satisfy the unpaid debt secured by the property. Cf. REPOSSESSION.

equitable foreclosure. A foreclosure method in which the court orders the property sold, and the proceeds are applied first to pay the costs of the suit and sale and then to the mortgage debt. • Any surplus is paid to the mortgagor.

judicial foreclosure. A costly and time-consuming foreclosure method by which the mortgaged property is sold through a court proceeding requiring many standard legal steps such as the filing of a complaint, service of process, notice, and a hearing. • Judicial foreclosure is available in all jurisdictions and is the exclusive or most common method of foreclosure in at least 20 states.

mortgage foreclosure. A foreclosure of the mortgaged property upon the mortgagor's default.

nonjudicial foreclosure. **1.** See *power-of-sale foreclosure*. **2.** A foreclosure method that does not require court involvement.

power-of-sale foreclosure. A foreclosure process by which, according to the mortgage instrument and a state statute, the mortgaged property is sold at a nonjudicial public sale by a public official, the mortgagee, or a trustee, without the stringent notice requirements, burdens, or delays of a judicial foreclosure. • Power-of-sale foreclosure is authorized and used in more than half the states. — Also termed *nonjudicial foreclosure*; *statutory foreclosure*.

strict foreclosure. A rare procedure that gives the mortgagee title to the mortgaged property — without first conducting a sale — after a defaulting mortgagor fails to pay the mortgage debt within a court-specified period. • The use of strict foreclosure is limited to special situations except in those few states that permit this remedy generally.

tax foreclosure. A public authority's seizure and sale of property for nonpayment of taxes.

foreclosure decree. 1. Generally, a decree ordering a judicial foreclosure sale. **2.** A decree ordering the strict foreclosure of a mortgage.

foreclosure sale. See SALE.

foregift. *Hist.* A premium paid for a lease in addition to rent; forehand rent. See FOREHAND RENT (1).

foregoer (for-**goh**-ər). *Hist.* A royal purveyor; a person who buys provisions for the Crown at an appraised (that is, reduced) price while the royal household travels about the country.

forehand rent. *Hist.* **1.** A premium paid by the tenant on the making of a lease, esp. on the renewal of a lease by an ecclesiastical corporation. **2.** Generally, rent payable before a lease begins.

foreign, *adj.* **1.** Of or relating to another country <foreign affairs>. **2.** Of or relating to another jurisdiction <the Arizona court gave full faith and credit to the foreign judgment from Mississippi>. — **foreigner,** *n.*

foreign administration. See *ancillary administration* under ADMINISTRATION.

foreign administrator. See ADMINISTRATOR (1).

foreign agent. See AGENT.

foreign apposer (ə-**pohz**-ər). *Hist.* An Exchequer officer responsible for examining the sheriff's estreat (book of fines), comparing the entries with those in court records, and apposing (interrogating) the sheriff on each sum in the estreat. — Also termed *apposer*.

foreign assignment. See ASSIGNMENT (2).

foreign bill. See BILL (6).

foreign bill of exchange. See *foreign draft* under DRAFT.

foreign bond. See BOND (3).

foreign consulate. See CONSULATE.

foreign corporation. See CORPORATION.

foreign county. See COUNTY.

foreign court. See COURT.

foreign creditor. See CREDITOR.

foreign divorce. See DIVORCE.

foreign document. See DOCUMENT.

foreign domicile. See DOMICILE.

foreign dominion. *Hist.* A country that at one time was a foreign state but that by conquest or cession has come under the British Crown.

foreign draft. See DRAFT.

foreign-earned-income exclusion. The Internal Revenue Code provision that excludes from taxation a limited amount of income earned by nonresident taxpayers outside the United States. • The taxpayer must elect between this exclusion and the foreign tax credit. IRC (26 USCA) § 911(a), (b). See *foreign tax credit* under TAX CREDIT.

foreigner. **1.** *Hist.* A person not an inhabitant of a particular city under discussion. **2.** A citizen of another country.

foreign exchange. **1.** The process of making international monetary transactions; esp., the conversion of one currency to that of a different country. **2.** Foreign currency or negotiable instruments payable in foreign currency, such as traveler's checks.

foreign-exchange rate. The rate at which the currency of one country is exchanged for the currency of another country.

foreign guardian. See GUARDIAN.

foreign immunity. See IMMUNITY (1).

foreign judgment. See JUDGMENT.

foreign jurisdiction. See JURISDICTION.

foreign jury. See JURY.

foreign law. **1.** Generally, the law of another country. **2.** *Conflict of laws.* The law of another state or of a foreign country.

foreign minister. See MINISTER.

foreign object. An item that appears where it does not belong; esp., an item introduced into a living body, such as a sponge that is left in a patient's body during surgery. • The discovery rule usu. tolls the statute of limitations for a medical-malpractice claim based on a foreign object. — Also termed *foreign substance.* See FOREIGN SUBSTANCE.

foreign port. See PORT

foreign-relations law. See INTERNATIONAL LAW.

foreign service. **1.** United States Foreign Service. **2.** FORINSEC SERVICE. **3.** *Hist.* A feudal service performed by a tenant outside of the fee.

foreign situs trust. See TRUST.

Foreign Sovereign Immunities Act. A federal statute providing individuals with a right of action against foreign governments, under certain circumstances, to the extent the claim arises from the private, as opposed to the public, acts of the foreign state. 28 USCA §§ 1602–1611. — Abbr. FSIA. See RESTRICTIVE PRINCIPLE OF SOVEREIGN IMMUNITY.

> "The Foreign Sovereign Immunities Act (FSIA) of 1976 was designed to provide a set of comprehensive regulations governing access to federal and state courts in this country for plaintiffs asserting claims against foreign states and instrumentalities thereof. The enactment of this legislation responded to the reality that increased contacts between American citizens and companies on the one hand, and foreign states and entities owned by foreign states on the other, as well as a constantly expanding range of government activities, had created the need for judicial fora in this country to resolve disputes arising out of these activities." 14A Charles Alan Wright et al., *Federal Practice and Procedure* § 3662, at 160–61 (2d ed. 1998).

foreign state. **1.** A foreign country. **2.** An American state different from the one under discussion.

foreign substance. A substance found in a body, organism, or thing where it is not supposed to be found <the plaintiff sued because she thought she saw — and later confirmed that she had found — a foreign substance (namely, mercury) in her hamburger>.

foreign support order. See SUPPORT ORDER.

foreign tax credit. See TAX CREDIT.

foreign trade zone. See FREE-TRADE ZONE.

foreign trust. See TRUST.

foreign vessel. See VESSEL.

foreign voyage. See VOYAGE.

foreign water. See WATER.

forejudge, *vb.* **1.** To prejudge; to judge beforehand. **2.** Loosely, FORJUDGE.

foreman. **1.** See *presiding juror* under JUROR. **2.** A person who directs the work of employees; an overseer, crew chief, or superintendent.

forematron. *Archaic.* The presiding juror in an all-woman jury.

forensic (fə-**ren**-sik *also*-zik), *adj.* **1.** Used in or suitable to courts of law or public debate <forensic psychiatry>. **2.** Rhetorical; argumentative <Spence's considerable forensic skills>. **3.** *Hist.* Exterior; foreign.

forensic engineering. The use of engineering principles or analysis in a lawsuit, usu. through an expert witness's testimony.

forensic evidence. See EVIDENCE.

forensic linguistics. The science or technique that evaluates the linguistic characteristics of written or oral communications, usu. to determine identity or authorship.

forensic medicine. The branch of medicine that establishes or interprets evidence using scientific or technical facts, such as ballistics. — Also termed *medical jurisprudence.*

forensic pathology. The specific branch of medicine that establishes or interprets evidence dealing with diseases and disorders of the body, esp. those that cause death.

forensics (fə-**ren**-siks *also*-ziks). **1.** The art of argumentative discourse. **2.** The branch of law enforcement dealing with legal evidence relating to firearms and ballistics.

forensic services. *Hist.* In feudal law, the payment of extraordinary aids or the rendition of extraordinary military services.

forensis (fə-**ren**-sis), *adj.* [fr. Latin *forum* "court"] *Roman law.* Of or relating to a court of law. • An advocate, for example, was sometimes known as a *homo forensis.*

foreperson. See *presiding juror* under JUROR.

foreseeability, *n.* The quality of being reasonably anticipatable. • Foreseeability, along with actual causation, is an element of proximate cause in tort law. — **foreseeable,** *adj.*

foreseeable damages. See DAMAGES.

forest, *n. Hist.* A tract of land, not necessarily wooded, reserved to the king or a grantee, for hunting deer and other game.

forestall (for-**stawl**), *vb.* **1.** To prevent (an event, result, etc.). **2.** *Hist.* To intercept or obstruct (a person on a royal highway). **3.** *Hist.* To prevent (a tenant) from coming on the premises. **4.** *Hist.* To intercept (a deer reentering a forest). — Also spelled *forstall.*

forestaller, *n. Hist.* A person who forestalls; one guilty of the offense of forestalling.

forestalling the market. *Hist.* **1.** The taking possession of commodities on their way to the market. **2.** The purchase of goods on their way to the market, with the intention of reselling them at a higher price. **3.** The dissuasion of sellers from taking their goods to the market, or the persuasion of sellers to increase the price of their goods at the market. • At common law, forestalling the market was a criminal offense.

forestry right. A land interest under which a person has the right to enter the land, establish and maintain a crop of trees, harvest them, and construct works for that purpose.

forfeiture (**for**-fi-chər), *n.* **1.** The divestiture of property without compensation. **2.** The loss of a right, a privilege, or property because of a crime, breach of obligation, or neglect of duty. ● Title is simultaneously transferred to another, such as the government, a corporation, or a private person. **3.** Something (esp. money or property) lost or confiscated by this process; a penalty. — **forfeit,** *vb.* — **forfeitable,** *adj.*

civil forfeiture. An in rem proceeding brought by the government against property that either facilitated a crime or was acquired as a result of criminal activity.

criminal forfeiture. A governmental proceeding brought against a person as punishment for the person's criminal behavior.

forfeiture of marriage. Hist. A penalty exacted by a lord from a ward who married without the lord's consent. ● The penalty was a money payment double the value that the marriage would otherwise have been worth to the lord.

forfeiture of pay. Military law. A punishment depriving the guilty party of all or part of his or her military pay.

4. A destruction or deprivation of some estate or right because of the failure to perform some obligation or condition contained in a contract.

forfeiture clause. A contractual provision stating that, under certain circumstances, one party must forfeit something to the other. ● Forfeiture clauses are often held to be void, although they are similar to conditions and other qualifications of estates in land.

forgavel (for-**gav**-əl). *Hist.* A small reserved rent in money; quit-rent.

forgery, *n.* **1.** The act of fraudulently making a false document or altering a real one to be used as if genuine <the contract was void because of the seller's forgery>. — Also termed *false making.* ● Though forgery was a misdemeanor at common law, modern statutes typically make it a felony. **2.** A false or altered document made to look genuine by someone with the intent to deceive <he was not the true property owner because the deed of trust was a forgery>. — Also termed *fake.* — **forge,** *vb.* — **forger,** *n.*

> "While it is true that there is a distinction between fraud and forgery, and forgery contains some elements that are not included in fraud, forgeries are a species of fraud. In essence, the crime of forgery involves the making, altering, or completing of an instrument by someone other than the ostensible maker or drawer or an agent of the ostensible maker or drawer." 37 C.J.S. *Forgery* § 2, at 66 (1997).

double forgery. A draft having a forged payor signature and a forged indorsement.

fori disputationes (**for**-I dis-pyoo-tay-shee-**oh**-neez). [Latin "arguments of the court"] *Roman law.* Arguments or discussions before a court.

forinsec service (fə-**rin**-sik). *Hist.* The feudal services owed by a mesne (i.e., intermediate) lord, esp. those of a military nature. — Also termed *foreign service*; *forinsecum servitium.* Cf. INTRINSEC SERVICE.

> "The terminology of Bracton's day and of yet earlier times neatly expresses the distinction between the service which the tenant owes to his immediate lord by reason of the bargain which exists between them, and the service which was incumbent on the tenement whilst it was in the lord's hand. The former is intrinsec service, the latter forinsec service; the former is the service which is created by, which (as it were) arises within, the bargain between the two persons, *A* and *B*, whose rights and duties we are discussing; the latter arises outside that bargain, is 'foreign' to that bargain.... [T]he term is a relative one; what is 'intrinsec' between *A* and *B* is 'forinsec' as regards *C*." 1 Frederick Pollock & Frederic W. Maitland, *The History of English Law Before the Time of Edward I* 238, 239 n.2 (2d ed. 1898).

forinsecus (fə-**rin**-sə-kəs), *adv.* [fr. Latin *foris* "without"] *Hist.* On the outside.

forinsecus (fə-**rin**-sə-kəs), *n.* [Latin] *Hist.* A foreigner; someone from another jurisdiction.

foris (**for**-is), *adj.* [Latin] Abroad; outdoors; without.

forisbanitus (for-is-**ban**-ə-təs). See FORBANNITUS.

forisfacere (for-is-**fay**-sə-ree), *vb.* [fr. Latin *foris* "without" + *facere* "to make"] *Hist.* **1.** To forfeit (an estate or other property). ● Literally, this means to make the property foreign to oneself. **2.** To violate the law; to do a thing against or without the law.

forisfactum (for-is-**fak**-təm), *adj.* [Law Latin] *Hist.* (Of property) forfeited.

forisfactus (for-is-**fak**-təs). [Law Latin] *Hist.* A criminal; esp., one who has forfeited his or her life by committing a capital offense.

forisfactus servus (for-is-**fak**-təs **sər**-vəs). [Law Latin] *Hist.* A freed slave who has forfeited his or her freedom by committing a crime.

forisfamiliate (for-is-fə-**mil**-ee-ayt), *vb.* [fr. Latin *foris* "outside" + *familia* "family"] *Hist.* To emancipate (a son) from paternal authority by a gift of land. • This act usu. rendered the son ineligible to inherit more property. — Also termed (archaically) *forisfamiliare.*

forisfamiliated (for-is-fə-**mil**-ee-ay-tid), *adj. Hist.* (Of a son) emancipated from paternal authority and in possession of a portion of family land in lieu of inheritance.

> "If our English law at any time knew an enduring *patria potestas* which could be likened to the Roman, that time had passed away long before the days of Bracton.... Bracton, it is true, has copied about this matter some sentences from the Institutes which he ought not to have copied; but he soon forgets them, and we easily see that they belong to an alien system. Our law knows no such thing as 'emancipation,' it merely knows an attainment of full age.... In old times a forisfamiliated son, that is, one whom his father had enfeoffed, was excluded from the inheritance. This is already antiquated, yet Bracton can find nothing else to serve instead of an *emancipatio.*" 2 Frederick Pollock & Frederic W. Maitland, *The History of English Law Before the Time of Edward I* 438, 438 n.3 (2d ed. 1899).

forisfamiliation (for-is-fə-mil-ee-**ay**-shən), *n.* [Law Latin] *Hist.* The act of forisfamiliating a son.

forisjudicatio. See FOREJUDGER.

forisjudicatus. See FOREJUDGER.

forisjurare (for-is-jə-**rair**-ee), *vb.* [Law Latin] *Hist.* To forswear; to renounce under oath. — Also termed *forjurer.*

forisjurare parentilam (for-is-jə-**rair**-ee pə-**ren**-tə-ləm), *vb.* [Law Latin] *Hist.* To renounce parental authority. • One who did so lost all rights of heirship.

forisjurare provinciam (for-is-jə-**rair**-ee prə-**vin**-shee-əm), *vb.* [Law Latin] *Hist.* To renounce under oath one's allegiance to a country.

forjudge, *vb.* **1.** *Hist.* To expel a person, esp. an officer or attorney, from court for some offense or misconduct. **2.** To deprive (a person) of a thing by a judgment; to condemn (a person) to lose a thing. — Also spelled (loosely) *forejudge.*

forjudger (for-**jəj**-ər), *n. Hist.* **1.** A judgment that deprives a person of a thing. **2.** A judgment of expulsion or banishment. — Also termed *forisjudicatio*; *forisjudicatus.*

forjurer. See FORISJURARE.

forjurer royalme (for-zhə-**ray** roy-**ohm**), *vb.* [Law French] *Hist.* To renounce the kingdom under oath; to abjure the realm.

form, *n.* **1.** The outer shape or structure of something, as distinguished from its substance or matter <courts are generally less concerned about defects in form than defects in substance>. **2.** Established behavior or procedure, usu. according to custom or rule <the prosecutor followed the established form in her closing argument>. **3.** A model; a sample; an example <attorneys often draft pleadings by using a form instead of starting from scratch>. **4.** The customary method of drafting legal documents, usu. with fixed words, phrases, and sentences <Jones prepared the contract merely by following the state bar's form>. **5.** A legal document with blank spaces to be filled in by the drafter <the divorce lawyer used printed forms that a secretary could fill in>.

Form 8–K. See 8–K.

Form 10–K. See 10–K.

Form 10–Q. See 10–Q.

forma (**for**-mə). [Latin "form"] *Hist.* The prescribed form of judicial proceedings.

forma et figura judicii (**for**-mə et **fig**-yər-ə joo-**dish**-ee-I). [Latin] *Hist.* The form and shape of judgment. • A form prescribed by statute.

formal, *adj.* **1.** Pertaining to or following established procedural rules, customs, and practices. **2.** Ceremonial. — **formality,** *n.*

formal agreement. See AGREEMENT.

formal contract. See CONTRACT.

formalities. 1. Small points of practice that, though seemingly unimportant, must be observed to achieve a particular legal result. **2.** *Hist.* Robes worn by magistrates on solemn occasions.

formal law. Procedural law.

> "Procedure is by many German writers inappropriately called 'formal law.'" Thomas E. Holland, *The Elements of Jurisprudence* 358 n.2 (13th ed. 1924).

formal party. See *nominal party* under PARTY (2).

formal rulemaking. See RULEMAKING.

forma pauperis. See IN FORMA PAUPERIS.

formata (for-**may**-tə). [Law Latin] *Eccles. law.* Canonical letters.

formata brevia. See BREVIA FORMATA.

formbook. A book that contains sample legal documents, esp. transaction-related documents such as contracts, deeds, leases, wills, trusts, and securities disclosure documents.

formed design. See DESIGN.

formedon (**for**-mə-don). [fr. Latin *forma doni* "form of the gift"] *Hist.* A writ of right for claiming entailed property held by another. • A writ of formedon was the highest remedy available to a tenant in tail. — Also termed *writ of formedon.*

> "Called *formedon*, because the writ comprehended the *form of the gift*. It was of three kinds, in the *descender*, in the *remainder*, and in the *reverter*." 1 Alexander M. Burrill, *A Law Dictionary and Glossary* 650 (2d ed. 1867).

formedon in the descender. A writ of formedon brought by the issue in tail to recover possession of the land.

formedon in the remainder. A writ of formedon brought by a remainderman under a grant or gift in tail to recover possession of the land.

formedon in the reverter. A writ of formedon brought by a reversioner or donor of the grant or gift in tail to recover possession of the land.

former acquittal. See *autrefois acquit* under AUTREFOIS.

former adjudication. An adjudication in a prior action that resulted in a final determination of the rights of the parties or essential fact questions, the result of which bars relitigation. • Collateral estoppel and res judicata are the two types of former adjudication. See COLLATERAL ESTOPPEL; RES JUDICATA.

former jeopardy. The fact of having previously been prosecuted for the same offense. • A defendant enters a plea of former jeopardy to inform the court that he or she should not be prosecuted again. Cf. DOUBLE JEOPARDY.

former punishment. *Military law.* The rule that nonjudicial punishment for a minor offense may bar trial by court-martial for the same offense.

form of action. The common-law legal and procedural device associated with a particular writ, each of which had specific forms of process, pleading, trial, and judgment. • The 11 common-law forms of action were trespass, trespass on the case, trover, ejectment, detinue, replevin, debt, covenant, account, special assumpsit, and general assumpsit.

> "Forms of action are usually regarded as different methods of procedure adapted to cases of different kinds, but in fact the choice between forms of action is primarily a choice between different theories of substantive liability, and the scope of the actions measures the existence and extent of liability at common law.... The development and extension of the different forms of action is the history of the recognition of rights and liability in the law of torts, contracts, and property, and the essentials of rights of action." Benjamin J. Shipman, *Handbook of Common-Law Pleading* §§ 27, 30 at 54, 60 (Henry Winthrop Ballantine ed., 3d ed. 1923).

Form S–1. See S–1.

formula. 1. *Roman law.* A written document, prepared by a praetor and forwarded to a judex, identifying the issue to be tried and the judgment to be given by the judex. • The four parts of a formula were (1) the *demonstratio*, in which the plaintiff stated the facts of the claim; (2) the *intentio*, in which the plaintiff specified the relief sought against the defendant; (3) in certain cases involving property disputes, the *adjudicatio*, in which the judex divided the property between the parties; and (4) the *condemnatio*, in which the judex condemned (usu. to pay the plaintiff a sum) or acquitted the defendant.

> "The Roman judges were not, as with us, the presiding officers in the administration of law and justice. This was the position of the magistrate, the praetor. When a suit at law was commenced, the parties appeared before the praetor, who made a preliminary examination, not to ascertain the merits of the case, but to find the precise points in controversy. He heard the statements of the plaintiff and the counter-statements of the defendant, and from the two he constructed a *formula* (as it was called), a brief technical expression of the disputed issues. He then appointed a *judex* ... instructing him to investigate the matter, and if he found the facts to be so and so, as recited in the formula, then to condemn the accused party, but, if he did not find them so, to acquit him." James Hadley, *Introduction to Roman Law* 59–60 (1881). [This quotation describes only the period of formulary procedure, ca. 150 B.C.–A.D. 25. — Ed.]

2. *Common-law pleading.* A set form of words (such as those appearing in writs) used in judicial proceedings.

formula deal. An agreement between a movie distributor and an independent or affiliated circuit to exhibit a feature movie in all theaters at a specified percentage of the national gross receipts realized by the theaters.

formula instruction. See JURY INSTRUCTION.

formulary. *Hist.* A collection of the forms of proceedings (*formulae*) used in litigation, such as the writ forms kept by the Chancery. See WRIT SYSTEM.

formulary procedure. *Hist.* The common-law method of pleading and practice, which required formulaic compliance with the accepted forms of action even if through elaborate fictions. • In the 19th century, this type of procedure was replaced both in the United States and in England. See *code pleading* under PLEADING (2).

fornication, *n.* Voluntary sexual intercourse between two unmarried persons. • Fornication is a crime in some states, such as Virginia. — **fornicate,** *vb.* Cf. ADULTERY.

> "Fornication was not a common-law crime but was made punishable by statute in a few states as a misdemeanor." Rollin M. Perkins & Ronald N. Boyce, *Criminal Law* 455 (3d ed. 1982).

fornix (**for**-niks). [Latin] *Hist.* **1.** A brothel. **2.** Fornication.

forprise (for-**prīz**). *Hist.* **1.** An exception or reservation. • The term was frequently used in leases and conveyances.

> "Forprise ... [a]n exception or reservation.... We still use it in Conveyances and Leases, wherein *Excepted* and *Forprised* is an usual expression." Thomas Blount, *Nomo-Lexicon: A Law-Dictionary* (1670).

2. An exaction.

for-profit corporation. See CORPORATION.

forschel (**for**-shəl). *Hist.* A strip of land next to a highway. — Also termed *forschet.*

forspeca (for-**spee**-kə). **1.** PROLOCUTOR. **2.** PARANYMPHUS.

forswearing (for-**swair**-ing), *n.* **1.** The act of repudiating or renouncing under oath. **2.** PERJURY. — **forswear,** *vb.*

fortaxed (for-**takst**). *Hist.* Wrongly or extortionately taxed.

forthcoming bond. See BOND (2).

forthwith, *adv.* **1.** Immediately; without delay. **2.** Directly; promptly; within a reasonable time under the circumstances.

fortia (**for**-shə). [Law Latin] *Hist.* **1.** Force. • *Fortia* refers to force used by an accessory to allow the principal to commit the crime. **2.** Power, dominion, or jurisdiction.

fortia frisca (**for**-shə **fris**-kə). [Law Latin] *Hist.* See FRESH FORCE.

fortior (**for**-shee-ər *or* -or), *adj.* [Latin "stronger"] *Hist.* (Of evidence) involving a presumption that, because of the strength of a party's evidence, shifts the burden of proof to the opposing party.

fortuitous (for-**t[y]oo**-ə-təs), *adj.* Occurring by chance. • A fortuitous event may be highly unfortunate. Literally, the term is neutral, despite its common misuse as a synonym for *fortunate.*

fortuitous collision. See COLLISION.

fortuitous event. A happening that, because it occurs only by chance or accident, the parties could not have reasonably foreseen. See FORCE MAJEURE; UNAVOIDABLE-ACCIDENT DOCTRINE.

Fortune 500. An annual compilation of the 500 largest U.S. corporations. • It is published in, and gets its name from, *Fortune* magazine.

forty, *n. Archaic.* Forty acres of land in the form of a square <the south forty>. • To determine a forty, a section of land (640 acres) was quartered, and one of those quarters was again quartered.

forty-days court. See COURT OF ATTACHMENTS.

forum, *n.* **1.** A public place, esp. one devoted to assembly or debate. **2.** A court or other judicial body; a place of jurisdiction. Pl. **forums, fora.**

forum actus (**for**-əm **ak**-təs). [Latin "the forum of the act"] *Hist.* The place where an act was done.

forum conscientiae (**for**-əm kon-shee-**en**-shee-ee). [Latin "the forum of conscience"] *Hist.*

The tribunal or court of conscience. • This court was usu. a court of equity. See COURT OF CONSCIENCE.

forum contentiosum (**for**-əm kən-ten-shee-**oh**-səm). [Latin "the forum of contention"] *Hist.* A court of justice; a place for litigation.

forum contractus (**for**-əm kən-**trak**-təs). [Latin "the forum of the contract"] *Hist.* **1.** The place where a contract was made, and thus the place of jurisdiction. **2.** The court of the place where a contract was made.

forum conveniens (**for**-əm kən-**vee**-nee-enz). [Latin "a suitable forum"] The court in which an action is most appropriately brought, considering the best interests and convenience of the parties and witnesses. Cf. FORUM NON CONVENIENS.

forum domesticum (**for**-əm də-**mes**-ti-kəm). [Latin] *Hist.* A domestic court. • This type of court decides matters (such as professional discipline) arising within the organization that created it.

forum domicilii (**for**-əm dom-ə-**sil**-ee-I). [Latin] *Hist.* The forum or court of the domicile, usu. of the defendant.

forum ecclesiasticum (**for**-əm e-klee-z[h]ee-**as**-ti-kəm). [Latin] *Hist.* An ecclesiastical court. — Also termed *judicium ecclesiasticum*.

forum externum (**for**-əm ek-**stər**-nəm), *n.* [Latin "external tribunal"] *Eccles. law.* A court dealing with legal cases pertaining to or affecting the corporate life of the church.

forum inconveniens. See FORUM NON CONVENIENS.

forum internum (**for**-əm in-**tər**-nəm), *n.* [Latin "internal tribunal"] *Eccles. law.* A court of conscience; a court for matters of conscience.

forum ligeantiae rei (**for**-əm lij-ee-**an**-shee-ee **ree**-I). [Latin] *Hist.* The forum of the defendant's allegiance; the court or jurisdiction of the country to which the defendant owes allegiance.

forum non conveniens (**for**-əm non kən-**vee**-nee-enz). [Latin "an unsuitable court"] *Civil procedure.* The doctrine that an appropriate forum — even though competent under the law — may divest itself of jurisdiction if, for the convenience of the litigants and the witnesses, it appears that the action should proceed in another forum in which the action might originally have been brought. — Also termed *forum inconveniens*.

> "Forum non conveniens allows a court to exercise its discretion to avoid the oppression or vexation that might result from automatically honoring plaintiff's forum choice. However, dismissal on the basis of forum non conveniens also requires that there be an alternative forum in which the suit can be prosecuted. It must appear that jurisdiction over all parties can be secured and that complete relief can be obtained in the supposedly more convenient court. Further, in at least some states, it has been held that the doctrine cannot be successfully invoked when the plaintiff is resident of the forum state since, effectively, one of the functions of the state courts is to provide a tribunal in which their residents can obtain an adjudication of their grievances. But in most instances a balancing of the convenience to all the parties will be considered and no one factor will preclude a forum non coveniens dismissal, as long as another forum is available." Jack H. Friedenthal et al., *Civil Procedure* § 2.17, at 87–88 (2d ed. 1993).

forum originis (**for**-əm ə-**rij**-ə-nis). [Latin] *Hist.* The forum or place of a person's birth, considered as a place of jurisdiction.

forum regium (**for**-əm **ree**-jee-əm). [Latin] *Hist.* The king's court.

forum rei (**for**-əm **ree**-I). [Latin] *Hist.* **1.** The forum of the defendant, i.e., the place where the defendant is domiciled or resides. **2.** FORUM REI SITAE.

forum rei gestae (**for**-əm **ree**-I **jes**-tee). [Latin] *Hist.* The forum or court of a *res gesta* (thing done); the place where an act was done, considered as a place of jurisdiction.

forum rei sitae (**for**-əm **ree**-I **SI**-tee). [Latin] *Hist.* The court where the thing or subject-matter in controversy is situated, considered as a place of jurisdiction. — Often shortened to *forum rei*.

forum seculare (**for**-əm sek-yə-**lair**-ee). [Latin] *Hist.* A secular court. — Also spelled *forum saeculare*.

forum-selection clause. A contractual provision in which the parties establish the place (such as the country, state, or type of court) for specified litigation between them. — Also termed *forum-shopping clause*. Cf. CHOICE-OF-LAW CLAUSE.

forum-shopping. The practice of choosing the most favorable jurisdiction or court in which a claim might be heard. • A plaintiff might engage in forum-shopping, for example, by filing suit in a jurisdiction with a reputation for high jury awards or by filing several similar suits and keeping the one with the preferred judge. Cf. JUDGE-SHOPPING.

forum-shopping clause. See FORUM-SELECTION CLAUSE.

forum state. *Conflict of laws.* The state in which a suit is filed.

for use. For the benefit or advantage of another. See USE.

forward agreement. See FORWARD CONTRACT.

forward and backward at sea. *Marine insurance.* From port to port in the course of a voyage, and not merely from one terminus to the other and back.

forward contract. An agreement to buy or sell a particular nonstandardized asset (usu. currencies) at a fixed price on a future date. • Unlike a futures contract, a forward contract is not traded on a formal exchange. — Also termed *forward agreement.* Cf. FUTURES CONTRACT.

forwarding agent. See AGENT.

forward market. See *futures market* under MARKET.

forward triangular merger. See *triangular merger* under MERGER.

fossa (**fahs**-ə). [Latin "a ditch"] *Hist.* A ditch or pit of water in which a woman who had committed a felony was drowned. See FURCA ET FOSSA.

foster, *adj.* **1.** (Of a relationship) involving parental care given by someone not related by blood <foster home>. **2.** (Of a person) giving or receiving parental care to or from someone not related by blood <foster parent> <foster child>.

foster, *vb.* To give care to (something or someone); esp., to give parental care to (a child who is not one's natural child).

fosterage, *n.* **1.** The act of caring for another's child. **2.** The entrusting of a child to another. **3.** The condition of being in the care of another. **4.** The act of encouraging or promoting.

foster care. **1.** A program for parental care for children in lieu of the parental relationship with biological or adoptive parents. **2.** The area of social services concerned with meeting the needs of children who participate in these types of programs.

foster-care placement. The (usu. temporary) act of placing a child in a home with a person or persons who provide parental care for the child.

foster-care review board. A board that reviews the permanent plans of foster-care placement of neglected and abused children.

foster child. See CHILD.

foster home. A household in which foster care is provided to a child who has been removed from his or her natural parents, usu. for abuse or neglect. • A foster home is usu. an individual home, but it can also be a group home.

fosterlean (**fos**-tər-leen). *Hist.* **1.** Remuneration for rearing a foster child. **2.** JOINTURE.

fosterling. See *foster child* under CHILD.

foster parent. See PARENT.

foul bill of lading. See BILL OF LADING.

foundation. **1.** The basis on which something is supported; esp., evidence or testimony that establishes the admissibility of other evidence <laying the foundation>. **2.** A fund established for charitable, educational, religious, research, or other benevolent purposes; an endowment <the Foundation for the Arts>.

private foundation. A foundation that is supported privately rather than publicly, and that exists to advance charitable or educational projects. • A private foundation is generally exempt from taxation. IRC (26 USCA) § 509.

foundational fact. See *predicate fact* under FACT.

founded on, *adj.* Having as a basis <the suit was founded on the defendant's breach of contract>.

founder, *n.* A person who founds or establishes; esp., a person who supplies funds for an institution's future needs.

founder's share. (*usu. pl.*) In England, a share issued to the founder of a company as a part of the consideration for the business. • Now rare, a founder's share participates in profits only if the dividend on ordinary shares has been paid to a specified amount.

founding father. A prominent figure in the founding of an institution or esp. a country; specif., one who played a leading role in founding the United States of America, esp. in the Revolutionary War and the making of the U.S. Constitution.

foundling. A deserted or abandoned infant.

foundling hospital. A charitable institution, found esp. in Europe, the purpose of which is to care for abandoned children.

four, rule of. See RULE OF FOUR.

four corners. The face of a written instrument. • The phrase derives from the ancient custom of putting all instruments (such as contracts) on a single sheet of parchment, as opposed to multiple pages, no matter how long the sheet might be. At common law, this custom prevented people from fraudulently inserting materials into a fully signed agreement. The requirement was that every contract could have only four corners.

four-corners rule. 1. The principle that a document's meaning is to be gathered from the entire document and not from its isolated parts. **2.** The principle that no extraneous evidence should be used to interpret an unambiguous document. Cf. PAROL-EVIDENCE RULE.

401(k) plan. See EMPLOYEE BENEFIT PLAN.

403(b) plan. See EMPLOYEE BENEFIT PLAN.

Fourteenth Amendment. The constitutional amendment, ratified in 1868, whose primary provisions effectively apply the Bill of Rights to the states by forbidding states from denying due process and equal protection and from abridging the privileges and immunities of U.S. citizenship. • The amendment also gives Congress the power to enforce these provisions, leading to legislation such as the Civil Rights Acts.

Fourth Amendment. The constitutional amendment, ratified with the Bill of Rights in 1791, prohibiting unreasonable searches and seizures and the issuance of warrants without probable cause. See PROBABLE CAUSE.

fourth estate. The journalistic profession; the media. • The term comes from the British Parliament's reporters' gallery, whose influence was said to equal Parliament's three traditional estates: the Lords Spiritual, the Lords Temporal, and the Commons. (In France, the three estates were the clergy, the nobility, and the commons.)

fourth-sentence remand. See REMAND.

four unities. The four qualities needed to create a joint tenancy at common law — namely interest, possession, time, and title. See UNITY (2).

Fox's Libel Act. *Hist.* A 1792 statute that gave the jury in a libel prosecution the right of pronouncing a guilty or not-guilty verdict on the whole matter in issue. • The jury was no longer bound to find the defendant guilty if it found that the defendant had in fact published the allegedly libelous statement. The Act empowered juries to decide whether the defendant's statement conformed to the legal standard for libel.

foy (foy *or* fwah). [Law French] Faith; allegiance.

FPA. *abbr.* Free from particular average.

> "*F.P.A.* means Free from Particular Average; that is to say, the insured can recover only where the loss is total or is due to a general average sacrifice. The claims under the Sue and Labour clause are not affected by this stipulation." 2 E.W. Chance, *Principles of Mercantile Law* 128 (P.W. French ed., 10th ed. 1951).

Fr. *abbr.* **1.** French. **2.** FRAGMENTA.

fractional, *adj.* (Of a tract of land) covering an area less than the acreage reflected on a survey; pertaining to any irregular division of land containing either more or less than the conventional amount of acreage.

fractional currency. See CURRENCY.

Fragmenta (frag-**men**-tə). [Latin "fragments"] *Roman law.* Passages drawn from the writings of Roman jurists and compiled in Justinian's *Digest.* — Abbr. Fr.; Ff.

fragmented literal similarity. See SUBSTANTIAL SIMILARITY.

frame, *vb.* **1.** To plan, shape, or construct; esp., to draft or otherwise draw up (a document). **2.** To incriminate (an innocent person) with false evidence, esp. fabricated. — **framable, frameable,** *adj.*

frame-up, *n.* A plot to make an innocent person appear guilty.

francbordus. See FREE-BORD.

franchise (**fran**-chIz), *n.* **1.** The right to vote. — Also termed *elective franchise.* **2.** The right conferred by the government to engage in a specific business or to exercise corporate powers. — Also termed *corporate franchise*; *general franchise.*

> "When referring to government grants (other than patents, trademarks, and copyrights), the term 'franchise' is often used to connote more substantial rights, whereas the term 'license' connotes lesser rights. Thus, the rights necessary for public utility companies to carry on their operations are generally designated as franchise rights. On the other hand, the rights to construct or to repair, the rights to practice certain professions, and the rights to use or to operate automobiles are generally referred to as licenses." 1 *Eckstrom's Licensing in Foreign and Domestic Operations* § 1.02[3], at 1–10 to 1–11 (David M. Epstein ed., 1998).

> "In a violent conceptual collision, some franchisors maintain that a franchise is merely an embellished license and therefore revocable at will. Franchisees contend that a franchise is a license coupled with an interest, not subject to unlimited control by franchisors. As a result of this disagreement, legislative draftsmen have had difficulty defining 'franchise.'" 1 Harold Brown, *Franchising Realities and Remedies* § 1.03[1], at 1–17 (1998).

franchise appurtenant to land. *Rare.* A franchise that is used in connection with real property and thus is sometimes characterized as real property.

general franchise. A corporation's charter.

special franchise. A right conferred by the government, esp. to a public utility, to use property for a public use but for private profit.

3. The sole right granted by the owner of a trademark or tradename to engage in business or to sell a good or service in a certain area. **4.** The business or territory controlled by the person or entity that has been granted such a right.

commercial franchise. A franchise using local capital and management by contracting with third parties to operate a facility identified as offering a particular brand of goods or services.

sports franchise. A franchise granted by a professional sports league to field a team in that league; the team itself.

trial franchise. A franchise having an initial term of limited duration, such as one year.

franchise, *vb.* To grant (to another) the sole right of engaging in a certain business or in a business using a particular trademark in a certain area.

franchise agreement. The contract between a franchisor and franchisee establishing the terms and conditions of the franchise relationship. • State and federal laws regulate franchise agreements.

franchise appurtenant to land. See FRANCHISE (2).

franchise clause. *Insurance.* A provision in a casualty insurance policy stating that the insurer will pay a claim only if it is more than a stated amount, and that the insured is responsible for all damages if the claim is under that amount. • Unlike a deductible, which the insured always has to pay, with a franchise clause, once the claim exceeds the stated amount, the insurer pays the entire claim.

franchise court. *Hist.* A privately held court that (usu.) exists by virtue of a royal grant, with jurisdiction over a variety of matters, depending on the grant and whatever powers the court acquires over time. • In 1274, Edward I abolished many of these feudal courts by forcing the nobility to demonstrate by what authority (*quo warranto*) they held court. If a lord could not produce a charter reflecting the franchise, the court was abolished. — Also termed *courts of the franchise.*

> "Dispensing justice was profitable. Much revenue could come from the fees and dues, fines and amercements. This explains the growth of the second class of feudal courts, the *Franchise Courts.* They too were private courts held by feudal lords. Sometimes their claim to jurisdiction was based on old pre-Conquest grants.... But many of them were, in reality, only wrongful usurpations of private jurisdiction by powerful lords. These were put down after the famous *Quo Warranto* enquiry in the reign of Edward I." W.J.V. Windeyer, *Lectures on Legal History* 56–57 (2d ed. 1949).

franchisee. One who is granted a franchise.

franchise fee. See FEE (1).

franchiser. One who grants a franchise. — Also spelled *franchisor*.

franchise tax. See TAX.

francigena (fran-sə-**jee**-nə). [Law Latin *francus* "french" + Latin *genitus* "born"] *Hist.* **1.** A person born in France. **2.** Any alien in England; a foreigner. See FRENCHMAN.

francus (**frangk**-əs). [fr. French *franc* "free"] *Hist.* A freeman.

francus bancus. See FREE BENCH.

francus homo (**frangk**-əs **hoh**-moh). *Hist.* A free man.

francus tenens. See FRANK-TENANT.

frank, *adj.* [Law French] *Hist.* Free. — Also spelled *fraunc*; *fraunche*; *fraunke*.

frank, *n.* **1.** (*cap.*) A member of the Germanic people who conquered Gaul in the 6th century. • France received its name from the Franks. **2.** A signature, stamp, or mark affixed to mail as a substitute for postage. **3.** The privilege of sending certain mail free of charge, accorded to members of Congress. — Also termed (in sense 3) *franking privilege*. — **frank,** *vb.*

frankalmoin (**frangk**-al-moyn). [Law French "free alms"] *Hist.* A spiritual tenure by which a religious institution held land, usu. in return for a nonenforceable duty to pray for the donor. • This tenure differed from the tenure by *divine service*, which required the performance of certain divine services. — Also spelled *frankalmoign*; *frankalmoigne*. — Also termed *almoign*; *almoin*; *free alms*; *libera eleemosyna*. See *spiritual tenure* under TENURE.

> "Frankalmoin, or free alms, was a survival of Anglo-Saxon law, and implied simply an indefinite promise to pray for the soul of the donor; but since it was deemed a tenure by which the land was held, the general doctrine of 'services' was applied. On the other hand, in the case of Divine Service, which was much less frequently met with, the tenant promised a definite number of prayers, a duty which might be enforced in the King's courts." A.K.R. Kiralfy, *Potter's Outlines of English Legal History* 210 (5th ed. 1958).

frank bank. See FREE BENCH.

frank-chase. *Hist.* Free chase; a person's liberty or right to hunt or log within a certain area. • Others holding land within the frank-chase area were forbidden from hunting or logging in it. See CHASE.

frank-fee. *Hist.* Freehold land — land that one held to oneself and one's heirs — exempted from all services except homage; land held other than by ancient demesne or copyhold.

frank ferm. *Hist.* An estate in land held in socage, the nature of the fee having been changed from knight's service by enfeoffment for certain yearly services. — Also spelled *frank-ferme*.

franking privilege. See FRANK (3).

frank-law. *Hist.* The rights and privileges of a citizen or freeman; specif., the condition of being legally capable of giving an oath (esp. as a juror or witness). See LEGALIS HOMO.

> "Frank law . . . may be understood from Bracton's description of the consequences of losing it, among which the principal one was, that the parties incurred perpetual infamy, so that they were never afterwards to be admitted to oath, because they were not deemed to be *othesworth*, (that is, not worthy of making oath,) nor allowed to give testimony." 1 Alexander M. Burrill, *A Law Dictionary and Glossary* 657–58 (2d ed. 1867).

franklin (**frangk**-lin). *Hist.* A freeman; a freeholder; a gentleman. — Also spelled *francling*; *frankleyn*; *frankleyne*.

frankmarriage. *Hist.* An entailed estate in which the donor retains control of the land by refusing to accept feudal services from the donee (usu. the donor's daughter) for three generations. • If the donee's issue fail in that time, the land returns to the donor. A donor who accepted homage (and the corresponding services arising from it) from the donee risked losing control of the land to a collateral heir. After three generations — a time considered sufficient to demonstrate that the line was well established — the donee's heir could insist on paying homage; doing so transformed the estate into a fee simple. — Also termed *liberum maritagium*. See MARITAGIUM.

> "Only when homage has been done are we to apply the rule which excludes the lord from the inheritance. This is at the bottom of one of the peculiarities of the 'estate in frankmarriage.' When a father makes a provision for a daughter, he intends that if the daughter has no issue or if her issue fails — at all events if this failure occurs in the course of a few generations — the land shall come back to him or to his heir. Therefore no homage is done for the estate in frankmarriage until the daughter's third heir has entered, for were homage once done, there would be a danger that the land would never come back to the father or to his heir." 2 Frederick Pollock &

Frederic W. Maitland, *The History of English Law Before the Time of Edward I* 291 (2d ed. 1899).

frankpledge. *Hist.* A promise given to the sovereign by a group of ten freeholders (a *tithing*) ensuring the group's good conduct. • The frankpledge was of Saxon origin, but continued after the Norman Conquest. The members of the group were not liable for an injury caused by an offending member, but they did act as bail to ensure that the culprit would appear in court. They were bound to produce a wrongdoer for trial. — Also termed *laughe*. See VIEW OF FRANKPLEDGE. Cf. DECENARY.

"Since there was no elaborate group of royal officials, the policing of the country had to be arranged for in a special way. The commonest way was to hold each household responsible for the offenses of any member of it. A further step was taken when, in the time of Cnut, a group of ten men was formed who were responsible for each other, in the sense that every one was security, *borh*, for the good behavior of the others. This group was called *fri-borh*, frankpledge, and remained for a long time one of the chief police methods of England." Max Radin, *Handbook of Anglo-American Legal History* 33–34 (1936).

Franks hearing. A hearing to determine whether a police officer's affidavit used to obtain a search warrant that yields incriminating evidence was based on false statements by the police officer. *Franks v. Delaware*, 438 U.S. 154, 98 S.Ct. 2674 (1978).

frank-tenant. *Hist.* A freeholder. — Also termed *francus tenens*.

frank-tenement. *Hist.* A free tenement; a freehold. • This term described both the tenure and the estate.

FRAP (frap). *abbr.* FEDERAL RULES OF APPELLATE PROCEDURE.

frater (**fray**-tər). [Latin] *Roman law.* A brother.

frater consanguineus (**fray**-tər kon-sang-**gwin**-ee-əs). A brother or half-brother having the same father.

frater nutricius (**fray**-tər n[y]oo-**trish**-ee-əs). A bastard brother.

frater uterinus (**fray**-tər yoo-tə-**rI**-nəs). A brother or half-brother having the same mother.

fraternal, *adj.* **1.** Of or relating to the relationship of brothers. **2.** Of or relating to a fraternity or a fraternal benefit association.

fraternal benefit association. A voluntary organization or society created for its members' mutual aid and benefit rather than for profit, and whose members have a common and worthy cause, objective, or interest. • These associations usu. have a lodge system, a governing body, rituals, and a benefits system for their members. — Also termed *fraternal benefit society*; *fraternity*; *fraternal lodge*; *fraternal order*. Cf. FRIENDLY SOCIETY.

fraternal insurance. See INSURANCE.

fraternal lodge. See FRATERNAL BENEFIT ASSOCIATION.

fraternal order. See FRATERNAL BENEFIT ASSOCIATION.

fraternal society. See *benevolent association* under ASSOCIATION.

fraternity. See FRATERNAL BENEFIT ASSOCIATION.

frater nutricius. See FRATER.

frater uterinus. See FRATER.

fratres conjurati (**fray**-treez kon-jə-**ray**-tI). [Latin "sworn brothers"] *Hist.* Sworn brothers or companions for the defense of their sovereign or for other purposes.

fratriage (**fra**-tree-ij *or* **fray**-). *Hist.* **1.** A younger brother's portion of his father's estate, received as an inheritance. • Under feudal law, even though the land was from the father's estate, the younger brother was bound to pay homage to the older brother. **2.** A portion of an inheritance given to coheirs. — Also termed *fratriagium*.

fratricide (**fra**-trə-sId *or* **fray**-). **1.** One who has killed one's brother or sister. **2.** The killing of one's brother or sister.

fraud, *n.* **1.** A knowing misrepresentation of the truth or concealment of a material fact to induce another to act to his or her detriment. • Fraud is usu. a tort, but in some cases (esp. when the conduct is willful) it may be a crime. **2.** A misrepresentation made recklessly without belief in its truth to induce another person to act. **3.** A tort arising from a knowing misrepresentation, concealment of material fact, or reckless misrepresentation made to induce another to act to his or her detriment. **4.** Unconscionable dealing; esp., in contract law, the unconscientious use of the power arising out of the parties' relative positions and resulting in an unconscionable bargain. — **fraudulent,** *adj*.

"[T]he use of the term fraud has been wider and less precise in the chancery than in the common-law courts. This followed necessarily from the remedies which they respectively administered. Common law gave damages for a wrong, and was compelled to define with care the wrong which furnished a cause of action. Equity refused specific performance of a contract, or set aside a transaction, or gave compensation where one party had acted unfairly by the other. Thus 'fraud' at common law is a false statement . . . : fraud in equity has often been used as meaning unconscientious dealing — 'although, I think, unfortunately,' a great equity lawyer has said." William R. Anson, *Principles of the Law of Contract* 263 (Arthur L. Corbin ed., 3d Am. ed. 1919).

actual fraud. A concealment or false representation through a statement or conduct that injures another who relies on it in acting. — Also termed *fraud in fact*; *positive fraud*; *moral fraud*.

civil fraud. **1.** FRAUD (3). **2.** *Tax*. An intentional — but not willful — evasion of taxes. • The distinction between an intentional (i.e., *civil*) and willful (i.e., *criminal*) fraud is not always clear, but *civil fraud* carries only a monetary, noncriminal penalty. Cf. *criminal fraud*; TAX EVASION.

common-law fraud. See *promissory fraud*.

constructive fraud. **1.** Unintentional deception or misrepresentation that causes injury to another. — Also termed *legal fraud*; *fraud in contemplation of law*; *equitable fraud*. **2.** See *fraud in law*.

"The layman would probably rather be found guilty of fraud, for he can then say the court was wrong, than be found guilty of 'constructive fraud,' for he does not know what that means and he may doubt whether the court does either." Lon L. Fuller, *Anatomy of the Law* 12 (1968).

criminal fraud. **1.** *Tax*. The willful evasion of taxes accomplished by filing a fraudulent tax return. • *Criminal fraud* subjects the offender to criminal penalties such as fines and imprisonment. Cf. *civil fraud*; TAX EVASION. **2.** *Larceny by trick* under LARCENY.

election fraud. See ELECTION FRAUD.

extrinsic fraud. **1.** Deception that is collateral to the issues being considered in the case; intentional misrepresentation or deceptive behavior outside the transaction itself (whether a contract or a lawsuit), depriving one party of informed consent or full participation. • For example, a person might engage in extrinsic fraud by convincing a litigant not to hire counsel or answer by dishonestly saying the matter will not be pursued. — Also termed *collateral fraud*. **2.** Deception that prevents a person from knowing about or asserting certain rights.

fraud in contemplation of law. See *constructive fraud*.

fraud in fact. See *actual fraud*.

fraud in law. Fraud that is presumed under the circumstances, as when a debtor transfers assets and thereby impairs creditors' efforts to collect sums due. — Also termed *constructive fraud*.

fraud in the factum. Fraud occurring when a legal instrument as actually executed differs from the one intended for execution by the person who executes it, or when the instrument may have had no legal existence. • Compared to fraud in the inducement, fraud in the factum occurs only rarely, as when a blind person signs a mortgage when misleadingly told that it's just a letter. — Also termed *fraud in the execution*; *fraud in the making*. Cf. *fraud in the inducement*.

fraud in the inducement. Fraud occurring when a misrepresentation leads another to enter into a transaction with a false impression of the risks, duties, or obligations involved; an intentional misrepresentation of a material risk or duty reasonably relied on, thereby injuring the other party without vitiating the contract itself, esp. about a fact relating to value. Cf. *fraud in the factum*.

fraud in the making. See *fraud in the factum*.

fraud on the court. A lawyer's or party's misconduct in a judicial proceeding so serious that it undermines or is intended to undermine the integrity of the proceeding. • Examples are bribery of a juror and introduction of fabricated evidence.

fraud on the market. **1.** Fraud occurring when an issuer of securities gives out misinformation that affects the market price of stock, the result being that people who buy or sell are effectively misled even though they did not rely on the statement itself or anything derived from it other than the market price. **2.** The securities-law claim based on such fraud. See FRAUD-ON-THE-MARKET PRINCIPLE.

insurance fraud. Fraud committed against an insurer, as when an insured lies on a policy application or fabricates a claim.

intrinsic fraud. Deception that pertains to an issue involved in an original action. • Examples include the use of fabricated evidence, a false return of service, perjured testimony, and false receipts or other commercial documents.

legal fraud. See *constructive fraud.*

mail fraud. An act of fraud using the U.S. Postal Service, as in making false representations through the mail to obtain an economic advantage. 18 USCA §§ 1341–1347.

moral fraud. See *actual fraud.*

positive fraud. See *actual fraud.*

promissory fraud. A promise to perform made when the promisor had no intention of performing the promise. — Also termed *common-law fraud.*

tax fraud. See TAX EVASION.

wire fraud. An act of fraud using electronic communications, as by making false representations on the telephone to obtain money. • The federal Wire Fraud Act provides that any artifice to defraud by means of wire or other electronic communications (such as radio or television) in foreign or interstate commerce is a crime. 18 USCA § 1343.

fraud, badge of. See BADGE OF FRAUD.

fraudare (fraw-**dair**-ee), *vb.* [Latin] *Roman law.* To defraud.

fraude (frawd). [French] *Civil law.* Fraud committed in performing a contract. Cf. DOL.

fraudfeasor (**frawd**-fee-zər). A person who has committed fraud. — Also termed *defrauder.*

fraud in contemplation of law. See *constructive fraud* under FRAUD.

fraud in fact. See *actual fraud* under FRAUD.

fraud in law. See FRAUD.

fraud in the execution. See *fraud in the factum* under FRAUD.

fraud in the factum. See FRAUD.

fraud in the inducement. See FRAUD.

fraud in the making. See *fraud in the factum* under FRAUD.

fraud on creditors. See FRAUDULENT CONVEYANCE (1).

fraud on the court. See FRAUD.

fraud on the market. See FRAUD.

fraud-on-the-market principle. *Securities.* The doctrine that, in a claim under the antifraud provisions of the federal securities laws, a plaintiff may presumptively establish reliance on a misstatement about a security's value — without proving actual knowledge of the fraudulent statement — if the stock is purchased in an open and developed securities market. • This doctrine recognizes that the market price of an issuer's stock reflects all available public information. The presumption is rebuttable. — Also termed *fraud-on-the-market theory.*

frauds, statute of. See STATUTE OF FRAUDS.

fraudulent act. Conduct involving bad faith, dishonesty, a lack of integrity, or moral turpitude. — Also termed *dishonest act*; *fraudulent or dishonest act.*

fraudulent alienation. 1. The transfer of property with an intent to defraud others, esp. creditors and lienholders. **2.** The transfer of an estate asset by the estate's administrator for little or no consideration.

fraudulent alienee. See ALIENEE.

fraudulent banking. The receipt of a deposit by a banker who knew that the bank was insolvent at the time of the deposit.

fraudulent claim. A false insurance claim. See FRAUD.

fraudulent concealment. See CONCEALMENT.

fraudulent-concealment rule. See CONCEALMENT RULE.

fraudulent conversion. See CONVERSION (2).

fraudulent conveyance. 1. A transfer of property for little or no consideration, made for the purpose of hindering or delaying a creditor by putting the property beyond the creditor's reach; a transaction by which the owner of real or personal property seeks to place the property beyond the reach of creditors. — Also termed *fraud on creditors.*

> "With respect to the general power which is exercisable by deed, it seems that the principle that the donee's creditors can reach the property subject to the exercised general power will have application only to the so-called fraudulent conveyance. That is to say, if the owned assets of the donee after the donative inter vivos exercise

are sufficient to satisfy the creditors, then the exercise of the power will not subject the appointive property to the claims of the creditors; if, on the other hand, the owned assets of the donee are inadequate to satisfy creditors' claims after the exercise of the power, then the transfer resulting from the exercise is likely to fall into the category of the fraudulent conveyance and the creditors will be able to reach the appointive property in the hands of the appointee." Thomas F. Bergin & Paul G. Haskell, *Preface to Estates in Land and Future Interests* 173 (2d ed. 1984).

2. *Bankruptcy.* A prebankruptcy transfer or obligation made or incurred by a debtor for little or no consideration or with the actual intent to hinder, delay, or defraud a creditor. • A bankruptcy trustee may recover such a conveyance from the transferee if the requirements of 11 USCA § 548 are met. — Also termed *fraudulent transfer.* Cf. PREFERENTIAL TRANSFER.

fraudulent debt. See DEBT.

fraudulent joinder. See JOINDER.

fraudulent misrepresentation. See MISREPRESENTATION.

fraudulent or dishonest act. See FRAUDULENT ACT.

fraudulent pretenses. See FALSE PRETENSES.

fraudulent representation. See *fraudulent misrepresentation* under MISREPRESENTATION.

fraudulent sale. See SALE.

fraudulent transfer. See FRAUDULENT CONVEYANCE.

fraus (fraws). [Latin] Deceit; cheating. • For example, a debtor who conveyed property with the specific intent (*fraus*) of defrauding a creditor risked having the conveyance rescinded.

fraus legis (fraws **lee**-jis). [Latin "fraud on the law"] *Roman law.* Evasion of the law; specif., doing something that is not expressly forbidden by statute, but that the law does not want done.

fray. See AFFRAY.

FRB. *abbr.* FEDERAL RESERVE BOARD OF GOVERNORS.

FRCP. *abbr.* FEDERAL RULES OF CIVIL PROCEDURE.

F.R.D. *abbr.* Federal Rules Decisions; a series of reported federal court decisions (beginning in 1938) that construe or apply the Federal Rules of Civil, Criminal, or Appellate Procedure, or the Federal Rules of Evidence. • Also included are rule changes, ceremonial proceedings of federal courts, and articles on federal court practice and procedure. — Often written *FRD.*

FRE. *abbr.* FEDERAL RULES OF EVIDENCE.

Freddie Mac. See FEDERAL HOME LOAN MORTGAGE CORPORATION.

free, *adj.* **1.** Having legal and political rights; enjoying political and civil liberty <a free citizen> <a free populace>. **2.** Not subject to the constraint or domination of another; enjoying personal freedom; emancipated <a free person>. **3.** Characterized by choice, rather than by compulsion or constraint <free will>. **4.** Unburdened <the land was free of any encumbrances>. **5.** Not confined by force or restraint <free from prison>. **6.** Unrestricted and unregulated <free trade>. **7.** Costing nothing; gratuitous <free tickets to the game>. — **freely,** *adv.*

free, *vb.* **1.** To liberate. **2.** To remove (a person or animal) from a constraint or burden.

free agency, *n.* A professional athlete's ability to negotiate an employment contract with any team in the league, rather than being confined to the league's collective system. • Free agency is usu. granted to veteran players who have been in the league for a certain number of years. — **free agent,** *n.* Cf. RESERVE CLAUSE.

free alms. See FRANKALMOIN.

free alongside ship. A mercantile term designating that the seller is responsible for delivering the goods to the dock and for paying the costs of delivery there. • When the seller delivers the goods to the specified dock, the risk of loss passes to the buyer. The abbreviation F.A.S. is more common than the full phrase; it is sometimes erroneously thought to stand for *free along side* as opposed to *free alongside ship.* Cf. FREE ON BOARD; COST, INSURANCE, AND FREIGHT.

free and clear, *adj.* Unencumbered by any liens; marketable <free and clear title>.

free and common socage. See *free socage* under SOCAGE.

free and equal, *adj.* (Of an election) conducted so that the electorate has a reasonable opportunity to vote, with each vote given the same effect.

free bench. *Hist.* A widow's (and occasionally a widower's) interest in the deceased spouse's estate. • *Free bench* gave the surviving spouse a half interest in the estate until death or remarriage. — Also termed *francus bancus*; *frank bank*; *liber bancus*.

> "The bench in question was, we may guess . . . a bench at the fireside. The surviving spouse has in time past been allowed to remain in the house along with the children. In the days when families kept together, the right of the widower or widow to remain at the fireside may have borne a somewhat indefinite character. . . . By way of 'free bench' the surviving spouse now has the enjoyment of one-half of the land until death or second marriage, whether there has ever been a child of the marriage or no." 2 Frederick Pollock & Frederic W. Maitland, *The History of English Law Before the Time of Edward I* 419 (2d ed. 1899).

free-bord. *Hist.* **1.** A small strip of land (usu. 2½ feet wide and lying just outside a fence) that the owner of the fenced property was allowed to claim and use. **2.** The right of claiming that quantity of land. — Also spelled *freebord*; *free bord*; *free-board*. — Also termed *francbordus*.

free chapel. *Hist. Eccles. law.* A church founded by the Crown (or by a person under royal grant) and not subject to the bishop's jurisdiction.

> "[T]hose onely are *Free-chappels*, which are of the King's Foundation, and by him exempted from the Jurisdiction of the Ordinary; but the King may licence a Subject to found such a Chappel, and by his Charter exempt it from the Ordinaries Visitation also. . . . [I]t is called *free*, in respect of its exemption from the Jurisdiction of the Diocesan. . . ." Thomas Blount, *Nomo-Lexicon: A Law–Dictionary* (1670).

free city. *Int'l law.* A country-like political and territorial entity that, although independent in principle, does not have the full capacity to act according to general international law but is nevertheless a subject of international law.

freedman (**freed**-mən). *Hist.* An emancipated slave.

freedom. 1. The state of being free or liberated. **2.** A political right.

freedom of assembly. See RIGHT OF ASSEMBLY.

freedom of association. The right to join with others in a common undertaking that would be lawful if pursued individually. • This right is protected by the First Amendment to the U.S. Constitution. The government may not prohibit outsiders from joining an association, but the insiders do not necessarily have a right to exclude others. Cf. RIGHT OF ASSEMBLY.

freedom of choice. 1. The liberty embodied in the exercise of one's rights. **2.** The parents' opportunity to select a school for their child in a unitary, integrated school system that is devoid of de jure segregation. **3.** The liberty to exercise one's right of privacy, esp. the right to have an abortion. — Also termed *right to choose*.

freedom of contract. The doctrine that people have the right to bind themselves legally; a judicial concept that contracts are based on mutual agreement and free choice, and thus should not be hampered by external control such as governmental interference. • This is the principle that people are able to fashion their relations by private agreements, esp. as opposed to the assigned roles of the feudal system. As Maine famously said, "[T]he movement of progressive societies has been a movement from *Status* to *Contract*." Henry Sumner Maine, *Ancient Law* 165 (1864). — Also termed *liberty of contract*.

> "Like most shibboleths, that of 'freedom of contract' rarely, if ever, received the close examination which its importance deserved, and even today it is by no means easy to say what exactly the nineteenth-century judges meant when they used this phrase. At least it may be said that the idea of freedom of contract embraced two closely connected, but none the less distinct, concepts. In the first place it indicated that contracts were based on mutual agreement, while in the second place it emphasized that the creation of a contract was the result of a free choice unhampered by external control such as government or legislative interference." P.S. Atiyah, *An Introduction to the Law of Contract* 5 (3d ed. 1981).

freedom of expression. The freedom of speech, press, assembly, or religion as guaranteed by the First Amendment; the prohibition of governmental interference with those freedoms.

Freedom of Information Act. The federal statute that establishes guidelines for public disclosure of documents and materials created and held by federal agencies. 5 USCA § 552. — Abbr. FOIA.

freedom of petition. See RIGHT TO PETITION.

freedom of religion. The right to adhere to any form of religion or none, to practice or abstain from practicing religious beliefs, and to be free from governmental interference with or promotion of religion, as guaranteed by the First Amendment and Article VI, § 3 of the U.S. Constitution.

freedom of speech. The right to express one's thoughts and opinions without governmental restriction, as guaranteed by the First Amendment. — Also termed *liberty of speech*.

freedom of the city. *Hist.* An immunity or privilege from some burden, esp. from county jurisdiction and its privilege of municipal taxation and self-government, held under a royal charter.

freedom of the press. The right to print and publish materials without governmental intervention, as guaranteed by the First Amendment. — Also termed *liberty of the press*.

freedom of the seas. *Int'l law.* The principle that the seas beyond territorial waters are not subject to any country's control. • Ships on the high seas are subject only to the jurisdiction of the country whose flag they fly, except in cases of piracy, hijacking, hot pursuit from territorial waters, slave trading, and certain rights of approach by warships. — Also termed *mare liberum*.

free election. See ELECTION.

free enterprise. A private and consensual system of production and distribution, usu. conducted for a profit in a competitive environment that is relatively free of governmental interference. See CAPITALISM.

free entry, egress, and regress (**ee**-gres / **ree**-gres). *Hist.* A person's right to go on land as often as reasonably necessary. • A tenant could go on land to gather crops still growing after the tenancy expired.

Free Exercise Clause. The constitutional provision (U.S. Const. amend. I) prohibiting the government from interfering in people's religious practices or forms of worship. — Also termed *Exercise Clause*. Cf. ESTABLISHMENT CLAUSE.

free fishery. See FISHERY (1).

freehold, *n.* **1.** An estate in land held in fee simple, in fee tail, or for term of life. • At common law, these estates were all created by enfeoffment with livery of seisin. **2.** The tenure by which such an estate is held. — Also termed *freehold estate*; *freehold interest*; *franktenement*; *liberum tenementum*. Cf. LEASEHOLD.

perpetual freehold. An estate given to a grantee for life, and then successively to the grantee's heirs for life. • The effect of this type of freehold was to keep land within a family in perpetuity, much like a fee tail.

> "It took the form of a grant 'to A for life, remainder to A's son for life, remainder to that son's son for life', and so on ad infinitum. Such a limitation, if valid, would have been an effective substitute for the fee tail. The courts, however, set their face against this 'perpetual freehold' (as it was sometimes termed), and in *Lovelace v. Lovelace* (1585) it was held that remainders which did not vest before the determination of the first life estate would fail ex post facto. Subsequently a number of other, not entirely convincing, reasons were found for invalidating perpetual freeholds, ultimately culminating in what is sometimes termed the 'old' rule against perpetuities, but, more commonly, the rule in *Whitby v. Mitchell*, taking its name from the case which marked its emphatic reiteration." Peter Butt, *Land Law* 136 (2d ed. 1988).

freeholder. *Hist.* One who possesses a freehold.

freeholder's court baron. See COURT BARON.

freehold estate. See FREEHOLD.

freehold interest. See FREEHOLD.

freehold land society. (*usu. pl.*) *Hist.* A society in England created to enable mechanics, artisans, and other workers to buy at the lowest possible price freehold land with a sufficient yearly value to entitle the owner to the right to vote in the county in which the land was located.

free ice. *Hist.* Ice in navigable streams that does not belong to the adjacent riparian owner or to another with the right to appropriate it, but that belongs to the person who first appropriates it.

free law. *Hist.* The civil rights enjoyed by a freeman (as opposed to a serf). • Free law could be forfeited if the freeman was convicted of treason or an infamous crime.

freeman. 1. A person who possesses and enjoys all the civil and political rights belonging to the people under a free government. **2.** A person who is not a slave. **3.** *Hist.* A member of a municipal corporation (a city or borough) who possesses full civic rights, esp. the right to vote. **4.** *Hist.* A freeholder. Cf. VILLEIN. **5.** *Hist.* An allodial landowner. Cf. VASSAL. — Also spelled *free man*.

free market. See *open market* under MARKET.

free of all average. *Maritime law.* Insurance that covers a total loss only. — Abbr. FAA.

free on board. A mercantile term denoting that the seller is responsible for delivering goods on board a ship or other conveyance for carriage to the consignee at a specified location <FOB Indianapolis plant>. • The seller must deliver the goods to the vessel named and has the risk of loss until the goods reach that location. — Abbr. FOB. Cf. FREE ALONGSIDE SHIP; COST, INSURANCE, AND FREIGHT.

> "In an *F.O.B.* ('free on board') contract, the goods must be delivered on board by the seller, free of expense to the purchaser, and they are not at the latter's risk until actually delivered on board, when the property in them passes to him. The seller must also give the buyer sufficient notice to enable him to insure against loss during the sea transit. The buyer, on the other hand, must name a ship or authorize the seller to select one. The seller cannot sue for the price until the goods are loaded, and if his inability to load was caused by the buyer's failure to name an effective ship, his only remedy lies in damages. Similarly, *F.O.R.* means 'free on rail.'" 2 E.W. Chance, *Principles of Mercantile Law* 86–87 (P.W. French ed., 10th ed. 1951).

FOB destination. A mercantile term denoting that the seller is required to pay the freight charges as far as the buyer's named destination.

FOB shipping. A mercantile term denoting that the seller is required to bear the risk of placing the goods on a carrier.

free port. A port located outside a country's customs frontier, so that goods may be delivered usu. free of import duties or taxes, without being subjected to customs-control procedures; FREE-TRADE ZONE.

free rider. One who obtains an economic benefit at another's expense without contributing to it. — Also spelled *freerider.*

free socage. See SOCAGE.

free trade, *n.* The open and unrestricted import and export of goods without barriers, such as quotas or tariffs, other than those charged only as a revenue source, as opposed to those designed to protect domestic businesses. Cf. *protective tariff* under TARIFF (2).

free-trade zone. A duty-free area within a country to promote commerce, esp. transshipment and processing, without entering into the country's market. — Also termed *foreign trade zone*; *free port.*

free warren. See WARREN.

freeze, *n.* **1.** A period when the government restricts or immobilizes certain commercial activity.

credit freeze. A period when the government restricts bank-lending.

wage-and-price freeze. A period when the government forbids the increase of wages and prices.

2. A recapitalization of a closed corporation so that the value of its existing capital is concentrated primarily in preferred stock rather than in common stock. • By freezing capital, the owner can transfer the common stock to heirs without taxation while continuing to enjoy preferred-stock income during the owner's lifetime, while the common stock grows.

freeze, *vb.* **1.** To cause to become fixed and unable to increase <to freeze interest rates> <to freeze prices>. **2.** To make immobile by government mandate or banking action <to freeze assets>. **3.** To cease physical movement, esp. when ordered by a law enforcement officer <the police officer shouted at the suspect to freeze>.

freezee, *n.* A person or entity subjected to a freeze-out.

freeze-out, *n. Corporations.* The process, usu. in a closely held corporation, by which the majority shareholders or the board of directors oppresses minority shareholders in an effort to compel them to liquidate their investment on terms favorable to the controlling shareholders. Cf. SQUEEZE-OUT.

> "A 'freeze-out' is usually accomplished by the merger of a corporation into its parent corporation, where the parent corporation owns a large percentage of the shares of the subsidiary, and the minority shareholders are entitled to minimal distributions of cash or securities. A 'freeze-out' may also be used to connote the situation where so large a number of equity shares are issued to the acquiring corporation that the public shareholders own less than 10 percent of the outstanding equity securities and, therefore, have no control over the corporation or any of its decisions. In such event, a short-form merger could later be used to eliminate the minority shareholders." 69A Am. Jur. 2d *Securities Regulation — State* § 245, at 971 n.60 (1993).

freeze out, *vb.* **1.** To subject one to a freeze-out. **2.** To exclude a business competitor <freezing out the competition>.

freeze-out merger. See *cash merger* under MERGER.

freight. 1. Goods transported by water, land, or air. **2.** The compensation paid to a carrier for transporting goods.

dead freight. The amount paid by a shipper to a shipowner for the ship's unused cargo space.

freight absorption. See ABSORPTION (5).

freight forwarder. See *forwarding agent* under AGENT.

freighting voyage. See VOYAGE.

freight rate. See RATE.

frenchman. *Hist.* A stranger; a foreigner. • In early English law, this term was applied to all foreigners, even those not from France.

F reorganization. See REORGANIZATION (2).

fresh, *adj.* Recent; not stale; characterized by newness without any material interval.

fresh complaint. A reasonably prompt lodging of a grievance; esp., a victim's prompt report of a sexual assault to someone trustworthy.

fresh-complaint rule. The theory that the credibility of a sexual-assault victim is bolstered if the victim reports the assault soon after it occurs. • Most courts no longer recognize this theory.

fresh disseisin. See DISSEISIN.

fresh fine. See FINE (5).

fresh force. *Hist.* Force, such as disseisin or deforcement, newly done. • This term refers to force used in a town, and for which a remedy (the Assize of Fresh Force) existed. See *assize of fresh force* under ASSIZE (8).

fresh pursuit. 1. The right of a police officer to make a warrantless search of a fleeing suspect or to cross jurisdictional lines to arrest a fleeing suspect. **2.** The right of a person to use reasonable force to retake property that has just been taken. — Also termed *hot pursuit.*

fresh start. *Bankruptcy.* The favorable financial status obtained by a debtor who receives a release from personal liability on prepetition debts or who reorganizes debt obligations through the confirmation and completion of a bankruptcy plan.

Friday market. See MARKET.

friendly fire. 1. A fire burning where it is intended to burn, yet capable of causing unintended damage. **2.** Military or police gunfire that injures one's own side.

friendly society. In Britain, a voluntary association, supported by subscriptions or contributions, for the purpose of providing financial relief to ill members and to their widows and children upon death. • Friendly societies are regulated by statute. Cf. FRATERNAL BENEFIT ASSOCIATION.

friendly suit. A lawsuit in which all the parties have agreed beforehand to allow a court to resolve the issues. • Friendly suits are often filed by settling parties who wish to have a judgment entered.

friendly suitor. See WHITE KNIGHT.

friendly takeover. See TAKEOVER.

friend of the court. 1. AMICUS CURIAE. **2.** In some jurisdictions, an official who investigates and advises the circuit court in domestic-relations cases involving minors. • The friend of the court may also help enforce court orders in those cases.

fringe benefit. See BENEFIT.

frisk, *n.* A pat-down search to discover a concealed weapon. See STOP AND FRISK. Cf. SEARCH. — Also termed *pat-down.*

frivolous, *adj.* Lacking a legal basis or legal merit; not serious; not reasonably purposeful <a frivolous claim>.

frivolous appeal. An appeal having no legal basis, usu. filed for delay to induce a judgment-creditor to settle or to avoid payment of a judgment. • Federal Rule of Appellate Procedure 38 provides for the award of damages and costs if the appellate court determines that an appeal is frivolous. Fed. R. App. P. 38.

frivolous defense. See DEFENSE (1).

frivolous suit. A lawsuit having no legal basis, often filed to harass or extort money from the defendant.

FRM. See *fixed-rate mortgage* under MORTGAGE.

frolic (**frol**-ik), *n. Torts.* An employee's significant deviation from the employer's business for personal reasons. • A frolic is outside the scope of employment, and thus the employer is not vicariously liable for the employee's actions. Cf. DETOUR.

front, *n.* **1.** The side or part of a building or lot that is open to view, that is the principal entrance, or that faces out to the open (as to a lake or ocean); the foremost part of something <the property's front was its most valuable attribute>. **2.** A person or group that serves to conceal the true identity or activity of the person or group in control <the political party was a front for the terrorist group>. **3.** A political association similar to a party <popular front>.

frontage (**frən**-tij). **1.** The part of land abutting a street or highway or lying between a building's front and a street or highway <the property's value was so low because of its narrow frontage>. **2.** The linear distance of a frontage <the lot's frontage was 90 feet>.

frontage assessment. A municipal fee charged to a property owner for local improvements that abut a street or highway, such as sidewalks, pavements, or sewage lines.

frontager (**frən**-tij-ər), *n.* A person owning or occupying land that abuts a highway, river, seashore, or the like.

front-end money. See SEED MONEY.

front foot. A measurement used to calculate a frontage assessment. — Also termed *abutting foot.*

front-foot rule. The principle that an improvement cost is to be apportioned among several properties in proportion to their frontage, without regard to the benefits conferred on each property. — Also termed *front-foot plan.*

front money. See SEED MONEY.

front wages. See WAGE.

frozen account. See *blocked account* under ACCOUNT.

frozen asset. See ASSET.

frozen deposit. See DEPOSIT (2).

fructuarius (frək-choo-**air**-ee-əs). [Latin "(one) entitled to fruits"] **1.** *Roman & civil law.* One having the usufruct of a thing (as of land and animals). **2.** *Hist.* A lessee.

fructus (**frək**-təs). [Latin "fruits"] **1.** *Roman & civil law.* The natural produce of land and animals; the profit or increase from land and animals. **2.** USUFRUCT.

fructus civiles (**frək**-təs sə-**vI**-leez). [Latin "civil fruits"] Income (such as rent or interest) that one receives from another for the use or enjoyment of a thing, esp. real property or loaned money.

fructus fundi (**frək**-təs **fən**-dI). [Latin "land fruits"] The fruits or produce of land.

fructus industriales (**frək**-təs in-dəs-tree-**ay**-leez). [Latin "industrial fruits"] See EMBLEMENTS.

fructus legis (**frək**-təs **lee**-jis). [Latin "fruits of the law"] The proceeds of judgment or execution.

fructus naturales (**frək**-təs nach-ə-**ray**-leez). [Latin "natural fruits"] The natural produce of land or plants and the offspring of animals. • *Fructus naturales* are considered part of the real property.

fructus pecudum (**frək**-təs **pek**-yə-dəm). [Latin "fruits of the herd"] The produce or increase of flocks or herds.

fructus pendentes (**frək**-təs pen-**den**-teez). [Latin "hanging fruits"] Fruits not yet severed or gathered; fruits united with that which produces them.

fructus percepti (**frək**-təs pər-**sep**-tI). [Latin "gathered fruits"] *Roman & civil law.* Fruits that have been gathered.

fructus rei alienae (**frək**-təs **ree**-I ay-lee-**ee**-nee *or* al-ee-). [Latin "fruits of another's property"] The fruits of another's property; fruits taken from another's estate.

fructus separati (**frək**-təs sep-ə-**ray**-tI). [Latin "separated fruits"] *Roman & civil law.* The produce of a thing after being separated from it, and so becoming in law "fruits."

fructus stantes (**frək**-təs **stan**-teez). [Latin "standing fruits"] Fruits that have not yet been severed from the stalk or stem.

fructuum perceptio (**frək**-choo-əm pər-**sep**-shee-oh). [Latin] *Roman & civil law.* The rightful taking of the produce of property by a person who does not own the property.

fruges (**froo**-jeez). [Latin "fruits" or "crops"] *Roman & civil law.* Edible produce or crops; esculents.

fruit. 1. The produce or product of something (as of land or property). **2.** *Civil law.* Income or goods derived or produced from property without a diminution of the property's value.

civil fruit. *Civil law.* Revenue received from property, such as interest income or a lease payment. See FRUCTUS CIVILES.

natural fruit. *Civil law.* A product of the land or of animals, whether edible or otherwise useful. • Examples are crops and eggs. See FRUCTUS NATURALES.

3. Something (such as evidence) obtained during an activity or operation <the fruit of the officer's search>. See FRUIT-OF-THE-POISONOUS-TREE DOCTRINE.

fruit-and-the-tree doctrine. *Tax.* The rule that an individual who earns income cannot assign that income to another person to avoid taxation.

fruit-of-the-poisonous-tree doctrine. *Criminal procedure.* The rule that evidence derived from an illegal search, arrest, or interrogation is inadmissible because the evidence (the "fruit") was tainted by the illegality (the "poisonous tree"). • Under this doctrine, for example, a murder weapon is inadmissible if the map showing its location and used to find it was seized during an illegal search. — Also termed *fruits doctrine.* See EXCLUSIONARY RULE; ATTENUATION DOCTRINE; INDEPENDENT-SOURCE RULE; INEVITABLE-DISCOVERY RULE.

fruits of a crime. The proceeds acquired through criminal acts.

frustra (**frəs**-trə). [Latin] *Hist.* In vain; to no purpose.

frustration, *n.* **1.** The prevention or hindering of the attainment of a goal, such as contractual performance.

commercial frustration. An excuse for a party's nonperformance because of some unforeseeable and uncontrollable circumstance. — Also termed *economic frustration.*

self-induced frustration. A breach of contract caused by one party's action that prevents the performance. • The phrase is something of a misnomer, since *self-induced frustration* is not really a type of frustration at all but is instead a breach of contract.

temporary frustration. An occurrence that prevents performance and legally suspends the duty to perform for the duration of the event. • If the burden or circumstance is substantially different after the event, then the duty may be discharged.

2. *Contracts.* The doctrine that, if the entire performance of a contract becomes fundamentally changed without any fault by either party, the contract is considered terminated. — Also termed *frustration of purpose.* — **frustrate,** *vb.* Cf. IMPOSSIBILITY (4); IMPRACTICABILITY; MISTAKE.

> "Where the entire performance of a contract becomes substantially impossible without any fault on either side, the contract is prima facie dissolved by the doctrine of frustration. For instance, where a person contracted to let a hall to the plaintiff for use for some concerts, and the hall was accidentally destroyed by fire before the date of the first concert, it was held that the contract was dissolved." P.S. Atiyah, *An Introduction to the Law of Contract* 200–01 (3d ed. 1981).

frustrum terrae (**frəs**-trəm **ter**-ee). [Latin] *Hist.* A piece of land. • This usu. referred to a fragment of land remaining after a survey.

***Frye* test.** The defunct federal common-law rule of evidence on the admissibility of scientific evidence. • It required that the tests or procedures must have gained general acceptance in their particular field. In *Daubert v. Merrell Dow Pharmaceuticals,* 509 U.S. 579, 113 S.Ct. 2786 (1993), the Supreme Court held that scientific evidence must meet the requirements of the Federal Rules of Evidence, not the *Frye* test, to be admissible. *Frye v. United States,* 293 F. 1013 (D.C. Cir. 1923).

FSIA. *abbr.* FOREIGN SOVEREIGN IMMUNITIES ACT.

FSLIC. *abbr.* FEDERAL SAVINGS AND LOAN INSURANCE CORPORATION.

FST. See *field sobriety test* under SOBRIETY TEST.

F.Supp. *abbr.* Federal Supplement, a series of reported decisions of the federal district courts (from 1932 to 1998), the U.S. Court of Claims (1932 to 1960), and the U.S. Customs Court (from 1949 to 1998, but renamed the Court of International Trade in 1980). • It is the first of the Federal Supplement series.

F.Supp.2d. *abbr.* The second series of the Federal Supplement, which includes decisions of federal district courts and the Court of International Trade from 1997 to the present. • Some of the F.Supp. volumes contain cases from 1998 and some of the F.Supp.2d volumes contain cases decided in 1997.

FTC. *abbr.* FEDERAL TRADE COMMISSION.

FTCA. *abbr.* FEDERAL TORT CLAIMS ACT.

fuer (**fyoo**-ər). [Law French "to flee"] Flight from the law. — Also termed *fugere.*

fuer in fait (**fyoo**-ər in **fay**). [Law French "flight in fact"] Actual flight from the law. — Also termed *fugere in facta.*

fuer in ley (**fyoo**-ər in **lay**). [Law French "flight in law"] Legal flight from the law. • If the accused failed to appear, the law treated that failure as flight. — Also termed *fugere in lege.*

fugam fecit (**fyoo**-gəm **fee**-sit). [Law Latin] *Hist.* He fled; he has made flight. • When a jury made this finding in a felony or treason trial, the defendant's property was subject to forfeiture.

fugere. See FUER.

fugere in facta. See *fuer in fait* under FUER.

fugere in lege. See *fuer in ley* under FUER.

fugitation (fyoo-jə-**tay**-shən). *Hist.* A sentence or declaration of fugitive status that was pronounced against an accused person for failing to answer a citation and appear. • The effect was that the person forfeited his or her goods and chattels.

fugitive. **1.** A person who flees or escapes; a refugee. **2.** A criminal suspect who flees, evades, or escapes arrest, prosecution, or imprisonment, esp. by fleeing the jurisdiction or by hiding. — Also termed (in sense 2) *fugitive from justice.*

fugitive-disentitlement doctrine. An equitable rule that allows a trial or appellate court to limit a fugitive's access to civil and criminal courts in the United States.

fugitive-dismissal rule. The principle that an appellate court may dismiss a criminal defendant's appeal if the defendant is a fugitive.

Fugitive Felon Act. A federal statute that makes it a felony to flee across state lines to avoid state-felony prosecution or confinement, or to avoid giving testimony in a state-felony case. 18 USCA § 1073.

fugitive from justice. See FUGITIVE.

fugitive's goods. *Hist.* The goods that a person forfeited as a result of fleeing.

fugitive-slave laws. *Hist.* Federal statutes passed in 1793 and 1850 providing for the surrender and return of slaves who had escaped and fled to a free territory or a free state.

fugitive warrant. See WARRANT (1).

fugitivus (fyoo-jə-**tɪ**-vəs). [Latin] *Roman law.* A fugitive; a runaway slave.

fugue (fyoog). An abnormal state of consciousness in which one appears to function normally but on recovery has no memory of what one did while in that condition.

full age. The age of legal majority; legal age.

full bench. See *full court* under COURT.

full blood. See BLOOD.

full cash value. See VALUE.

full copy. *Equity practice.* A complete transcript of a bill or other pleading, with all indorsements and a copy of all exhibits.

full court. See COURT.

full cousin. See COUSIN (1).

full-covenant-and-warranty deed. See *warranty deed* under DEED.

full coverage. See COVERAGE.

full-crew law. A law that regulates the number of railroad employees required to operate a train.

full defense. See DEFENSE (1).

full disclosure. See DISCLOSURE.

full faith and credit. A state's enforcement of another jurisdiction's laws or judicial decisions.

full-faith-and-credit bond. See *general-obligation bond* under BOND (3).

Full Faith and Credit Clause. U.S. Const. art. IV, § 1, which requires states to give effect to the legislative acts, public records, and judicial decisions of other states.

full hearing. See HEARING.

full indorsement. See *irregular indorsement* under INDORSEMENT.

full interdiction. See INTERDICTION (2).

full name. See NAME.

full-paid stock. See STOCK.

full pardon. See *absolute pardon* under PARDON.

full partner. See *general partner* under PARTNER.

full payout lease. See *finance lease* under LEASE.

full performance. See PERFORMANCE.

full powers. *Int'l law.* An official document designating a person to represent a country for (1) negotiating, adopting, or authenticating the text of a treaty, (2) expressing the consent of the country to be bound by a treaty, or (3) accomplishing any act with respect to the treaty.

full proof. See PROOF.

full-reporting clause. 1. An insurance-policy clause that requires the insured to reveal values and that penalizes the insured if the insured revealed less than required in the policy application. — Also termed *honesty clause.* **2.** An insurance-policy clause providing that the indemnity will not exceed the proportion of the loss that the last reported value bears to the actual value.

full right. The union of good title with actual possession.

full-service lease. See LEASE.

full settlement. See SETTLEMENT.

full value. See *fair market value* under VALUE.

full warranty. See WARRANTY (2).

fully administered. A plea by an executor or administrator that he or she has completely and legally disposed of all the assets of the estate and that the estate has no remaining assets from which a new claim could be satisfied.

fully diluted earnings per share. See EARNINGS PER SHARE.

fully funded, *adj.* **1.** Having sufficient financial resources to meet current payments, even upon bankruptcy <the company's pension plan was fully funded>. **2.** Having completely satisfied a funding requirement; paid <the construction loan was fully funded>. — Also termed *funded.*

fully managed fund. See MUTUAL FUND.

fully paid face-amount certificate. See *face-amount certificate* under CERTIFICATE.

function, *n.* **1.** Activity that is appropriate to a particular business or profession <a court's function is to administer justice>. **2.** Office; duty; the occupation of an office <presidential function>.

functional depreciation. See DEPRECIATION.

functional discount. See DISCOUNT.

functional disease. See DISEASE.

functional feature. *Trademarks.* A design element that, in an engineering sense, is necessary to construct an article, or that, in a commercial sense, is necessary to manufacture a salable product; a product's attribute that is essential to its use, is necessary for its proper and successful operation, and is utilitarian in every detail, without containing any ornamental features. • A functional feature is not eligible for trademark protection.

functionality. *Trademarks.* A shape, configuration, design, or color that is so superior to available alternatives that giving the first user exclusive trademark rights would hinder competition.

aesthetic functionality. A doctrine that denies protection to the design of a product or its container when the design is necessary to enable the product to function as intended.

functional obsolescence. See OBSOLESCENCE.

functionary. A public officer or employee.

functus officio (**fəngk**-təs ə-**fish**-ee-oh). [Latin "having performed his or her office"] (Of an officer or official body) without further authority or legal competence because the duties and functions of the original commission have been fully accomplished. • The term is sometimes abbreviated to *functus* <the court was *functus*>.

fund, *n.* **1.** A sum of money or other liquid assets established for a specific purpose <a fund reserved for unanticipated expenses>.

blended fund. A fund created by income from more than one source, usu. from the sale of a testator's real and personal property.

changing fund. A fund, esp. a trust fund, that changes its form periodically as it is invested and reinvested.

client-security fund. A fund established usu. by a state or a state bar association to compensate persons for losses that they suffered because of their attorneys' misappropriation of funds or other misconduct.

contingent fund. **1.** A fund created by a municipality for expenses that will necessarily arise during the year but that cannot be appropriately classified under any of the specific purposes for which taxes are collected. **2.** A fund segregated by a business to pay unknown costs that may arise in the future. — Also termed *contingency reserve.*

executor fund. A fund established for an executor to pay an estate's final expenses.

fund in court. **1.** Contested money deposited with the court. See INTERPLEADER. **2.** Money deposited to pay a contingent liability.

general fund. **1.** A government's primary operating fund; a state's assets furnishing the means for the support of government and for defraying the legislature's discretionary appropriations. • A general fund is distinguished from assets of a special character, such as trust, escrow, and special-purpose funds. **2.** A nonprofit entity's assets that are not earmarked for a specific purpose.

general revenue fund. The fund out of which a municipality pays its ordinary and incidental expenses.

guaranty fund. A private deposit-insurance fund, raised primarily by assessments on banks, and used to pay the depositors of an insolvent bank. • Guaranty funds preceded the FDIC's federal-deposit insurance, which began in 1933, though many funds continued until the savings-and-loan crisis in the 1980s. Massachusetts has a guaranty fund for uninsured deposits (deposits above $100,000) that are not covered by federal-deposit insurance.

imprest fund (**im**-prest). A fund used by a business for small, routine expenses.

joint-welfare fund. A fund that is established in collective bargaining to provide health and welfare benefits to union employees. • The fund is jointly managed by labor and management representatives. — Also termed *Taft-Hartley fund.*

paid-in fund. A reserve cash fund established by a mutual insurance company to pay unforeseen losses. • The fund is in lieu of a capital stock account.

public fund. (*usu. pl.*) **1.** The revenue or money of a governmental body. **2.** The securities of the national government or a state government.

revolving fund. A fund whose moneys are continually expended and then replenished, such as a petty-cash fund.

sinking fund. A fund consisting of regular deposits that are accumulated with interest to pay off a long-term corporate or public debt. — Abbr. SF.

strike fund. See STRIKE FUND.

Taft-Hartley fund. See *joint-welfare fund.*

trust fund. See TRUST FUND.

unsatisfied-judgment fund. A fund established by a state to compensate persons for losses stemming from an automobile accident caused by an uninsured or underinsured motorist.

2. (*usu. pl.*) Money or other assets, such as stocks, bonds, or working capital, available to pay debts, expenses, and the like <Sue invested her funds in her sister's business>.

current funds. Assets that can be readily converted into cash.

3. A pool of investments owned in common and managed for a fee; MUTUAL FUND <a diverse portfolio of funds>.

fund, *vb.* **1.** To furnish money to (an individual, entity, or venture), esp. to finance a particular project. **2.** To use resources in a manner that produces interest. **3.** To convert (a debt, esp. an open account) into a long-term debt that bears interest at a fixed rate.

fundamental error. See *plain error* under ERROR.

fundamental-fairness doctrine. The rule that applies the principles of due process to a judicial proceeding. • The term is commonly considered synonymous with *due process*.

fundamental interest. See FUNDAMENTAL RIGHT.

fundamental law. The organic law that establishes the governing principles of a nation or state; esp., CONSTITUTIONAL LAW. — Also termed *organic law*. Cf. NATURAL LAW.

fundamental-miscarriage-of-justice exception. The doctrine allowing a federal court in a habeas corpus proceeding to address a claim of constitutional error that, although ordinarily unreviewable, is subject to review because of a state-court procedural default that rendered the proceedings basically unfair. • For the exception to apply, among other things, the petitioner must show by a preponderance of the evidence that constitutional error resulted in the conviction of one who is probably innocent. If the defaulted claim applies only to sentencing, the exception permits review of the claim if the petitioner shows by clear and convincing evidence that, but for the constitutional error, no reasonable jury would have found the petitioner legally eligible for the sentence received.

fundamental right. 1. A right derived from natural or fundamental law. **2.** *Constitutional law.* A significant component of liberty, encroachments of which are rigorously tested by courts to ascertain the soundness of purported governmental justifications. • A fundamental right triggers strict scrutiny to determine whether the law violates the Due Process Clause or the Equal Protection Clause of the 14th Amendment. As enunciated by the Supreme Court, fundamental rights include voting, interstate travel, and various aspects of privacy (such as marriage and contraception rights). — Also termed *fundamental interest*. See STRICT SCRUTINY. Cf. SUSPECT CLASSIFICATION.

fundamental term. See TERM (2).

fundamental trend. See *major trend* under TREND.

fundatio (fən-**day**-shee-oh). [Latin "founding" or "foundation"] *Hist.* The founding of a corporation, particularly an eleemosynary corporation.

fundatio incipiens (fən-**day**-shee-oh in-**sip**-ee-enz). [Latin "incipient foundation"] The incorporation or grant of corporate powers.

fundatio perficiens (fən-**day**-shee-oh pər-**fish**-ee-enz). [Latin "perfecting foundation"] The endowment or gift of funds to a corporation.

funded. See FULLY FUNDED.

funded debt. See DEBT.

fund in court. See FUND (1).

funding, *n.* **1.** The process of financing capital expenditures by issuing long-term debt obligations or by converting short-term obligations into long-term obligations to finance current expenses; the process of creating a funded debt. **2.** The refinancing of a debt before its maturity. — Also termed *refunding*. **3.** The provision or allocation of money for a specific purpose, such as for a pension plan, by putting the money into a reserve fund or investments. **4.** The provision of financial resources to finance a particular activity or project, such as a research study.

fundi publici (**fən**-dɪ **pəb**-lə-sɪ). [Latin] *Hist.* Public lands.

funds transfer. A payment of money from one person or entity to another; esp., the process by which payment is made through a series of transactions between computerized banking systems, beginning with an originator's payment order and ending when a final payment order is received by the beneficiary's bank. • Commercial or wholesale funds transfers are governed by Article 4A of the UCC. Consumer funds transfers are regulated by the federal Electronic Funds Transfer Act (15 USCA

§§ 1693 et seq.). — Also termed (specif.) *electronic funds transfer* (EFT).

fundus (**fən**-dəs). [Latin "land"] *Hist.* **1.** Land or ground in general, without consideration of its specific use. **2.** A farm.

fundus patrimonialis (**fən**-dəs pa-trə-moh-nee-**ay**-lis). [Latin] *Roman law.* Land belonging to the *patrimonium principis* (that is, property belonging to the emperor as such).

funeral expense. See EXPENSE.

fungibiles res (fən-**jib**-ə-leez **reez**). [Latin] *Civil law.* Fungible things.

fungible (**fən**-jə-bəl), *adj.* Regarded as commercially interchangeable with other property of the same kind <corn and wheat are fungible goods, whereas land is not>. — **fungible,** *n.*

fungible goods. See GOODS.

fur (fər). [Latin] *Roman law.* A thief.

furandi animus (fyuu-**ran**-dɪ **an**-ə-məs). See *animus furandi* under ANIMUS.

furca (**fər**-kə). [Latin "fork"] *Roman law.* An instrument of punishment with two prongs to which the arms are tied. • In England, *furca* became another name for *gallows.*

furca et flagellum (**fər**-kə et flə-**jel**-əm). [Law Latin] *Hist.* Gallows and whip. • This referred to the basest of servile tenures — the tenant was completely at the mercy of the lord.

furca et fossa (**fər**-kə et **fahs**-ə). [Law Latin] *Hist.* Gallows and pit. • This phrase was used in ancient grants of criminal jurisdiction for punishing felons: hanging for men and drowning for women.

Furian Caninian law. See LEX FURIA CANINIA.

furigeldum (fyər-ə-**jel**-dəm). [Law Latin *fur* "theft" + *geldum* "payment"] *Hist.* A fine paid for theft.

furlong (**fər**-lawng). One-eighth of a mile, or forty poles. — Also termed *ferlingus*; *ferlingum.*

furlough (**fər**-loh). **1.** A leave of absence from military or other employment duty. **2.** A brief release from prison. See STUDY RELEASE.

fur manifestus (**fər** man-ə-**fes**-təs). [Latin "manifest thief"] *Roman law.* A thief caught in the act of stealing.

furor brevis. See HEAT OF PASSION.

furta (**fər**-tə). *Hist.* A right or privilege from the monarch to try, condemn, and execute criminals within a jurisdiction.

further advance. 1. A second or later loan to a mortgagor by a mortgagee, either on the same security as the original loan or on an additional security. **2.** *Equity practice.* The agreed conversion of arrears of interest on a mortgage security into principal.

further assurance. See ASSURANCE.

further instruction. See *additional instruction* under JURY INSTRUCTION.

furtum (**fər**-təm). [fr. Latin *furvus* "black"] *Hist.* **1.** A theft of movable property. • Under Roman law, *furtum* included not only the taking of another's property, but any handling of the property done with the intent of profiting by it. *Furtum* was a private crime (*delictum*) prosecuted by the person suffering the loss.

> "The word furtum is derived from furvus, a word which means black, because theft is committed secretly and stealthily and usually by night . . . ." R.W. Lee, *The Elements of Roman Law* 385 (4th ed. 1956).

2. The thing stolen.

furtum conceptum (**fər**-təm kən-**sep**-təm). [Latin] *Roman law.* A theft in which the thief is discovered in possession of stolen property after a search with witnesses.

furtum grave (**fər**-təm **gray**-vee *or* **grah**-vay). *Hist. Scots law.* An aggravated degree of theft that, in ancient times, was punishable by death.

furtum manifestum (**fər**-təm man-ə-**fes**-təm). [Latin "open theft"] *Roman law.* A theft in which the thief is caught in the act of theft. See IN FLAGRANTE DELICTO.

furtum oblatum (**fər**-təm ə-**blay**-təm). [Latin "offered theft"] *Roman law.* A theft in which the thief offers stolen property to a person who is then found with the goods; the planting of stolen goods.

Fusian Caninian law. See LEX FURIA CANINIA.

fustigation (fəs-ti-**gay**-shən), *n.* **1.** The beating of someone with a stick or club. **2.** Harsh criticism. — **fustigate,** *vb.*

fustis (**fəs**-tis). *Hist.* **1.** A staff used in making livery of seisin. **2.** A baton or club.

futhwite (**footh**-wIt). *Hist.* A fine for fighting or breaking the peace. — Also termed *fithwite.*

future-acquired property. See AFTER-ACQUIRED PROPERTY (1).

future advance. Money secured by an original security agreement even though it is lent after the security interest has attached.

future-advance clause. A contractual term in a security agreement covering additional loaned amounts on present collateral or collateral to be acquired in the future, regardless of whether the secured party is obliged to make the advances; esp., a provision in an open-end mortgage or deed of trust allowing the borrower to borrow additional sums in the future, secured under the same instrument and by the same security. • This type of clause makes a new security agreement unnecessary when the secured creditor makes a future loan to the debtor.

future-advances mortgage. See MORTGAGE.

future consideration. See CONSIDERATION.

future covenant. See COVENANT (4).

future damages. See DAMAGES.

future earnings. See *lost earnings* under EARNINGS.

future estate. See FUTURE INTEREST.

future goods. See GOODS.

future interest. A property interest in which the privilege of possession or of other enjoyment is future and not present. • A future interest can exist in either the grantor (as with a reversion) or the grantee (as with a remainder or executory interest). Today, most future interests are equitable interests in stocks and debt securities, with power of sale in a trustee. — Also termed *future estate*; *estate in expectancy.* Cf. *present interest* under INTEREST (2).

> "[T]he interest is an existing interest from the time of its creation, and is looked upon as a part of the total ownership of the land or other thing [that] is its subject matter. In that sense, future interest is somewhat misleading, and it is applied only to indicate that the possession or enjoyment of the subject matter is to take place in the future." Lewis M. Simes & Allan F. Smith, *The Law of Future Interests* § 1, at 2–3 (2d ed. 1956).

> "When O transfers today 'to A for five years,' we can say *either* that O has a future interest *or* that he has a 'present' estate subject to a term for years in A. Similarly, when O transfers today his entire estate in fee simple absolute by a conveyance 'to A for five years, then to B and his heirs,' we can say *either* that B has a future interest *or* that he has a 'present' estate subject to a term for years in A. Unhappily, the fact that we have two locutions available to us can be a source of confusion .... To own a future interest *now* means not only to be entitled now to judicial protection of one's possible future possession, but also (in most cases) to be able to make transfers now of that right of possible future possession." Thomas F. Bergin & Paul G. Haskell, *Preface to Estates in Land and Future Interests* 42, 56 (2d ed. 1984).

future performance. See PERFORMANCE.

futures, *n.* **1.** Standardized assets (such as commodities, stocks, or foreign currencies) bought or sold for future acceptance or delivery. — Also termed *financial futures.* **2.** FUTURES CONTRACT. **3.** Future claimants, esp. those who would become members of a class of persons injured by a defendant and thus included in a class action.

futures contract. An agreement to buy or sell a standardized asset (such as a commodity, stock, or foreign currency) at a fixed price at a future time, usu. during a particular time of a month. • Futures contracts are traded on exchanges such as the Chicago Board of Trade or the Chicago Mercantile Exchange. — Often shortened to *futures.* — Also termed *futures agreement*; *time-bargain.* Cf. FORWARD CONTRACT; LEVERAGE CONTRACT; OPTION.

futures market. See MARKET.

futures option. See OPTION.

futures trading. The buying and selling of futures contracts, usu. on formal exchanges.

future use. See *contingent use* under USE (4).

future value. See VALUE.

fyrdfare. See FERDFARE.

G

GA. See *general average* under AVERAGE.

GAAP (gap). *abbr.* GENERALLY ACCEPTED ACCOUNTING PRINCIPLES.

GAAS (gas). *abbr.* GENERALLY ACCEPTED AUDITING STANDARDS.

gabel (gə-**bel**). *Hist.* **1.** A tax or duty on movables. **2.** GAVEL (1). — Also spelled *gabelle.* See LAND-GAVEL.

gabella (gə-**bel**-ə). *Hist.* **1.** A tax or duty on merchandise. **2.** A peasant villager, esp. one who pays rent or tribute. See GAVEL (1). — Also spelled *gavella.*

gage (gayj), *n.* A pledge, pawn, or other thing deposited as security for performance. • An archaic use of this word corresponded to the way *wage* was formerly used in legal contexts: a *gager del ley*, for example, was an earlier form of *wager of law*, while *gager de deliverance* had the same meaning as *wager of deliverance.* Cf. WAGE (2).

> "A single root has sent out many branches which overshadow large fields of law. Gage, engagement, wage, wages, wager, wed, wedding, the Scottish wadset, all spring from one root. In particular we must notice that the word 'gage,' in Latin *vadium*, is applied indiscriminately to movables and immovables, to transactions in which a gage is given and to those in which a gage is taken. When a lord has seized his tenant's goods in distress they are in his hands a gage for the payment of the rent that is in arrear, and the sheriff is always taking gages from those who have no mind to give them. The notion expressed by the word seems to be that expressed by our 'security'...." 2 Frederick Pollock & Frederic W. Maitland, *The History of English Law Before the Time of Edward I* 117–18 (2d ed. 1899).

gage, *vb.* To pawn or pledge; to give as security for. • *Gage* is an older form of *wage*, and often appeared as a phrase, *gager deliverance.*

> "Though the word *Gage* be retained, as it is a Substantive, yet as it is a verb, use hath turned the *Gage* into *Wage* so as it is oftener written *Wage*; as to *Wage Deliverance*, to give security, that a thing shall be delivered: For, if he that distrained, being sued, have not delivered the Cattle that were distrained, then he shall not onely avow the Distress, but *Gager Deliverance*, put in surety, that he will deliver them." Thomas Blount, *Nomo Lexicon: A Law–Dictionary* (1670).

gager del ley. See WAGER OF LAW.

gag order. 1. A judge's order directing parties, attorneys, witnesses, or journalists to refrain from publicly discussing the facts of a case. • When directed to the press, such an order is generally unconstitutional under the First Amendment. **2.** A judge's order that an unruly defendant be bound and gagged during trial to prevent further interruptions.

gain, *n.* **1.** An increase in amount, degree, or value.

pecuniary gain. **1.** A gain of money or of something having monetary value. **2.** *Criminal law.* Any monetary or economic gain that serves as an impetus for the commission of an offense. • In most states, an offense and its punishment are aggravated if the offense was committed for pecuniary gain. Murder, for example, is often aggravated to capital murder if the murderer is paid to commit the crime. See SOLICITATION (2).

2. Excess of receipts over expenditures or of sale price over cost. See PROFIT. **3.** *Tax.* The excess of the amount realized from a sale or other disposition of property over the property's adjusted value. IRC (26 USCA) § 1001. — Also termed *realized gain.*

capital gain. See CAPITAL GAIN.

extraordinary gain. A gain that is both unusual and infrequent, such as the gain realized from selling a large segment of a business.

ordinary gain. A gain from the sale or exchange of a noncapital asset. Cf. CAPITAL GAIN.

recognized gain. The portion of a gain that is subject to income taxation. IRC (26 USCA) § 1001(c). See BOOT (1).

4. (*pl.*) *Civil law.* A type of community property that reflects the increase in property value brought about by the spouses' common skill or labor. See COMMUNITY PROPERTY. Cf. ACQUETS.

gainful employment. See EMPLOYMENT.

gainor. See SOCMAN.

gains, *n.* See GAIN.

gale (gayl). *Hist.* **1.** A periodic payment of rent. See GAVEL (2). **2.** Rent paid by a free miner (the *galee*) for the right to mine a plot of land. **3.** A license to mine a plot of land. • A gale could be conveyed or devised.

***Gallagher* agreement.** A contract that gives one codefendant the right to settle with the plaintiff for a fixed sum at any time during trial and that guarantees payment of the sum regardless of the trial's outcome. *City of Tucson v. Gallagher*, 493 P.2d 1197 (Ariz. 1972). Cf. MARY CARTER AGREEMENT.

gallows. A wooden frame consisting of two upright posts and a crossbeam, from which condemned criminals are hanged by a rope.

gamalis (gə-**may**-lis). [Law Latin] *Hist.* **1.** A child born in lawful wedlock. **2.** A child born to betrothed but unmarried parents.

gambling, *n.* The act of risking something of value, esp. money, for a chance to win a prize. • Gambling is regulated by state and federal law. 18 USCA §§ 1081 et seq. — Also termed *gaming*.

gambling contract. See CONTRACT.

gambling device. Any thing, such as cards, dice, or an electronic or mechanical contrivance, that allows a person to play a game of chance in which money may be won or lost. • Gambling devices are regulated by law, and the use or possession of a gambling device can be illegal. — Also termed *gaming device*.

gambling place. Any location where gambling occurs. 18 USCA § 1081. — Also termed *gaming house*; *gaming room*.

gambling policy. See *wager policy* under INSURANCE POLICY.

gambling verdict. See *chance verdict* under VERDICT.

game, *n.* Wild animals and birds considered as objects of pursuit, for food or sport; esp., animals for which one must have a license to hunt.

game, *vb.* To gamble; to play for a stake.

game law. A federal or state law that regulates the hunting of game, esp. one that forbids the capturing or killing of specified game either entirely or seasonally, describes the means for killing or capturing game in season, or restricts the number and type of game that may be killed or captured in season. 16 USCA §§ 661–667; 18 USCA §§ 41–47.

game of chance. A game whose outcome is determined by luck rather than skill. Cf. GAMBLING DEVICE.

gaming. See GAMBLING.

gaming contract. See *gambling contract* under CONTRACT.

gaming device. See GAMBLING DEVICE.

gaming house. See GAMBLING PLACE.

gaming room. See GAMBLING PLACE.

ganancial (gə-**nan**-shəl), *adj.* Of, relating to, or consisting of community property <a spouse's ganancial rights>. See COMMUNITY PROPERTY.

> "The Spanish [more correctly, the Castilian] form of community property, called the 'ganancial' system, is found today in the nine states of the United States, the Spanish–American republics of Central and South America, the Commonwealth of Puerto Rico and the Philippine Republic." Robert L. Menell & Thomas M. Boykoff, *Community Property in a Nutshell* 10 (2d ed. 1988).

G & A. See *general administrative expense* under EXPENSE.

gang. A group of persons who go about together or act in concert, esp. for antisocial or criminal purposes. • Many gangs (esp. those made up of adolescents) have common identifying signs and symbols, such as hand signals and distinctive colors. — Also termed *street gang*.

gangland. The world of criminal gangs and organized crime.

gangster. A member of a criminal gang or an organized-crime syndicate.

Ganser's syndrome (**gahn**-zər *or* **gan**-sər). An abnormality characterized by the giving of irrelevant and nonsensical answers to questions. • Prisoners sometimes feign this syndrome in an attempt to obtain leniency.

gantlet (**gawnt**-lit). [fr. Swedish *gata* "lane" + *lopp* "course"] **1.** *Hist.* A former military punishment in which the offender was stripped to the waist and forced to run between two rows of soldiers who gave him lashes as he passed. **2.** A series of severe troubles or difficulties; an ordeal. — Also spelled *gauntlet*; (archaically) *gantlope*.

GAO. *abbr.* GENERAL ACCOUNTING OFFICE.

gaol. See JAIL.

gaol delivery. See JAIL DELIVERY.

gaoler. See JAILER.

gaol liberties. See JAIL LIBERTIES.

gap creditor. See CREDITOR.

gap-filler. A rule that supplies a contractual term that the parties failed to include in the contract. • For example, if the contract does not contain a sales price, UCC § 2–305(1) establishes the price as being a reasonable one at the time of delivery.

> "Contracts often have gaps in them, intentional or inadvertent. Gaps arise, too, out of the 'battle of the forms' under sections 2–204 and 2–207. Some gaps are more or less complete, others only partial. Article 2 of the Code includes numerous gap filler provisions which taken together constitute a kind of standardized statutory contract." 1 James J. White & Robert S. Summers, *Uniform Commercial Code* § 3–4 (4th ed. 1995).

gap financing. See FINANCING.

gap period. *Bankruptcy.* The duration of time between the filing of an involuntary bankruptcy petition and the entry of the order for relief. — Often shortened to *gap*.

gap report. In the making of federal court rules, a report that explains any changes made by an advisory committee in the language of a proposed amendment to a procedural rule after its publication for comment. • Before advisory committees began issuing gap reports in the early 1980s, there were complaints that the public record did not show why changes were made after the public-comment period. The five advisory committees — for appellate, bankruptcy, civil, criminal, and evidence rules — therefore began filing the reports to fill in the "gaps" in the record. Although the phrase is sometimes written in capital letters (*GAP report*), it is not an acronym.

gap theory. *Insurance.* The principle that a tortfeasor will be considered underinsured if his or her liability-insurance coverage — although legally adequate — is less than the injured party's underinsured-motorist coverage. • This principle allows an injured party to invoke underinsured-motorist coverage. Cf. EXCESS THEORY.

garandia (gə-**ran**-dee-ə). [Law Latin] *Hist.* A warranty. — Also spelled *garantia* (gə-**ran**-shee-ə).

garauntor (**gar**-ən-tər). [Law French] *Hist.* A warrantor of land. • A *garauntor* was obligated to defend the title and seisin of the alienee. If the alienee was evicted, the *garauntor* had to provide the alienee with other land of equal value.

***Garcia* hearing** (gahr-**see**-ə). *Criminal procedure.* A hearing held to ensure that a defendant who is one of two or more defendants represented by the same attorney understands (1) the risk of a conflict of interest inherent in this type of representation, and (2) that he or she is entitled to the services of an attorney who does not represent anyone else in the defendant's case. *United States v. Garcia*, 517 F.2d 272 (5th Cir. 1975). See CONFLICT OF INTEREST (2).

gard (gahrd). [Law French] *Hist.* **1.** Wardship or custody (of a person). **2.** A precinct (or *ward*) of a city. — Also spelled *garde*; *gardia*.

garde (gahrd). [French] *Civil law.* A relationship that gives rise to liability for a person when an injury is caused by a thing (such as a consumer product) that is considered by law to be that person's responsibility or to be in that person's custody.

gardein (gahr-**deen**). [Law French] *Hist.* A guardian or keeper. — Also spelled *gardian*; *gardien*; *gardeyn*.

gardia (**gahr**-dee-ə). [Law French] *Hist.* Wardship, care, or custody of someone.

gardianus (gahr-dee-**ay**-nəs). [Law Latin] *Hist.* A guardian, defender, or protector; a warden. — Also spelled *guardianus*.

gardianus ecclesiae (gahr-dee-**ay**-nəs e-**klee**-z[h]ee-ee). A churchwarden.

garene (gə-**reen**). [Law French] See WARREN.

***Garmon* doctrine.** See *Garmon preemption* under PREEMPTION.

***Garmon* preemption.** See PREEMPTION.

***Garner* doctrine.** The rule that allows shareholder plaintiffs in a corporate derivative action to discover confidential communications between a corporate officer and the corporation's attorney. • The *Garner* doctrine does not apply to attorney work product, and the movant must show good cause. *Garner v. Wolfinbarger*, 430 F.2d 1093 (5th Cir. 1970). See DERIVATIVE ACTION (1).

garnish, *n. Hist.* Money exacted from a new prisoner by other prisoners or as a jailer's fee. • This practice was banned in England in 1815.

garnish, *vb.* [Old French *garnir* "to warn" "to prepare"] **1.** *Hist.* To serve an heir with notice (i.e., to *warn*) of certain debts that must be paid before the person is entitled to receive property as an heir. **2.** To subject (property) to garnishment; to attach (property held by a third party) in order to satisfy a debt. — Also termed *garnishee.* — **garnishable,** *adj.*

garnishee (gahr-ni-**shee**), *n.* A person or institution (such as a bank) that is indebted to or is bailee for another whose property has been subjected to garnishment. — Also termed *garnishee-defendant* (as opposed to the "principal defendant," i.e., the primary debtor).

garnishee (gahr-ni-**shee**), *vb.* See GARNISH.

garnisher. A creditor who initiates a garnishment action to reach the debtor's property that is thought to be held or owed by a third party (the *garnishee*). — Also spelled *garnishor.*

garnishment, *n.* **1.** A judicial proceeding in which a creditor (or potential creditor) asks the court to order a third party who is indebted to or is bailee for the debtor to turn over to the creditor any of the debtor's property (such as wages or bank accounts) held by that third party. • A plaintiff initiates a garnishment action as a means of either prejudgment seizure or postjudgment collection.

> "Garnishment is a[n] . . . inquisitorial proceeding, affording a harsh and extraordinary remedy. It is an anomaly, a statutory invention sui generis, with no affinity to any action known to the common law. . . . It is a method of seizure; but it is not a 'levy' in the usual acceptation of that term. It is a proceeding by which a diligent creditor may legally obtain preference over other creditors; and it is in the nature of a creditor's bill, or a sequestration of the effects of a debtor in the hands of his debtor." 38 C.J.S. *Garnishment* § 3, at 248–50 (1996).

wrongful garnishment. **1.** An improper or tortious garnishment. **2.** A cause of action against a garnisher for improperly or tortiously filing a garnishment proceeding.

2. The judicial order by which such a turnover is effected. Cf. ATTACHMENT (1); SEQUESTRATION (1).

garnishment lien. See LIEN.

garnishor. See GARNISHER.

***Garrity* statement** (**gar**-ə-tee). A public employee's oral or written report (as of an incident) obtained under a threat of termination of employment. • A public employee usu. makes a *Garrity* statement in the course of an internal investigation (as by a police department). Because a *Garrity* statement is coerced, the statement and any evidence obtained as a result of it cannot be used in a later criminal prosecution against the public employee. The statement and evidence may be used only to evaluate the employee's performance. *Garrity v. New Jersey*, 385 U.S. 493, 87 S.Ct. 616 (1967).

gas-balancing agreement. *Oil & gas.* A contract between owners of a producing gas well setting forth how production will be apportioned among them if one owner sells more gas than the other owners.

> "Gas balancing agreements address the problem of imbalances in production from a gas well or field. Co-owners frequently sell their share of production to different purchasers. . . . Even when co-owners sell to the same purchaser, their contracts are likely to be signed at different times and to have different price and take provisions. Thus, imbalances are inevitable." John S. Lowe, *Oil and Gas Law in a Nutshell* 385 (3d ed. 1995).

gas chamber. A small, sealed room in which capital punishments are carried out by strapping the prisoner into a chair and releasing poisonous fumes.

gas sold. *Oil & gas.* Natural gas that is actually sold but not necessarily all that a well produces. • The term is used in natural-gas leases.

gas used. *Oil & gas.* Natural gas that is consumed while a well is in operation but that is not necessarily sold.

GATT (gat). *abbr.* GENERAL AGREEMENT ON TARIFFS AND TRADE.

gauger (**gay**-jər). A surveying officer who examines containers of liquids to give them a mark of allowance, as containing the lawful measure.

gavel (**gav**-əl). **1.** *Hist.* A tribute, toll, or custom paid to a superior. **2.** *Hist.* An annual payment of rent or revenue, esp. payment in kind, such as gavel-corn, gavel-malt, or oat-gavel. — Sometimes spelled *gabel.* **3.** A mallet used by a presiding officer, often a judge, to bring a meeting or court to order.

gavelbred (**gav**-əl-bred). *Hist.* Rent payable in bread, corn, or some other provision; rent payable in kind.

gavelet (**gav**-əl-it). *Hist.* A writ used in Kent and London to recover rent from land held in gavelkind. See CESSAVIT.

gavelgeld (**gav**-əl-geld). *Hist.* **1.** Property that yields a profit or a toll. **2.** The tribute or toll itself.

gavelherte (**gav**-əl-hərt). *Hist.* A service of plowing performed by a customary tenant.

gaveling man (**gav**-əl-ing man *or* mən). *Hist.* See GAVELMAN.

gavelkind (**gav**-əl-kīnd). *Hist.* **1.** A species of socage tenure arising in land that has descended equally to the decedent's sons. • It was widespread before 1066, when it was mainly superseded by primogeniture. This property-division technique was then largely limited to Kent. The person holding land in this manner enjoyed several advantages not available under the common law: the land could be disposed of by will, did not escheat for felony other than treason or for want of heirs, and was alienable by an heir at age 15. Gavelkind was abolished in 1925. **2.** Land that yields gavel service.

> "Archbishop Hubert Walter, who presided in the king's court . . . obtained from King John a charter empowering him and his successors to convert into military fees the tenements that were holden of their church in gavelkind. The archbishop's main object may have been to get money in the form of rents and scutages, instead of provender and boonworks, 'gavel-corn' and 'gavel-swine,' 'gavel-erth' and 'gavel-rip'. . . ." 2 Frederick Pollock & Frederic W. Maitland, *The History of English Law Before the Time of Edward I* 273 (2d ed. 1899).

gavelman (**gav**-əl-mən). *Hist.* A tenant who is liable for money rent in addition to a customary service to the lord. • A gavelman was formerly a villein who had been released from villenage in consideration of money rent. — Also termed *gaveling man.*

gavelmed (**gav**-əl-meed). *Hist.* A tenant's customary service of mowing the lord's meadowland or grass for hay. — Also spelled *gavelmead.*

gavelrep (**gav**-əl-reep). *Hist.* A tenant's duty to reap the lord's fields at the lord's command; bederepe. — Also spelled *gavelrip.*

gavelwerk (**gav**-əl-wərk). *Hist.* Customary service, either by the tenant's own hands or with the aid of the tenant's carts or carriages.

Gazette (gə-**zet**). An official newspaper of the British government in which acts of State, Crown appointments, notices of bankruptcy, and other legal matters are reported. • Although the *London Gazette* is the most famous, there are also publications called the *Edinburgh Gazette* and the *Belfast Gazette* with similar purposes.

gazumping (gə-**zəmp**-ing). *Slang.* The improper sale of a house, usu. by raising the price after accepting an offer. • Gazumping can take different forms, the usu. one being when a seller raises the price after accepting the buyer's offer. But it may also occur when a competing buyer makes a higher bid than the one already accepted, thus encouraging the seller to back out of the earlier contract.

> "[R]apidly rising house prices led sellers to believe that they have sometimes agreed to sell their property at too low a figure; they may therefore breach their agreement with the first buyer and make a second agreement to sell at a higher price, or they may inform the first buyer that they are not prepared to proceed unless he agrees to raise his price. This process (known for some obscure reason as 'gazumping') can cause some irritation and disappointment to buyers. It may also sometimes cause financial loss, because a buyer may spend money on a survey, or an application for a mortgage which then becomes so much money thrown away if the sale does not proceed." P.S. Atiyah, *An Introduction to the Law of Contract* 137 (3d ed. 1981).

g.b.h. See *grievous bodily harm* under HARM.

GBMI. *abbr.* GUILTY BUT MENTALLY ILL.

gdn. *abbr.* GUARDIAN.

geld, *n. Hist.* A tax paid to the Crown under Anglo-Saxon and Norman kings.

geldable (**geld**-ə-bəl), *adj. Hist.* (Of property) subject to tax or tribute. — Also spelled *gildable.*

GEM. See *growing-equity mortgage* under MORTGAGE.

gender discrimination. See *sex discrimination* under DISCRIMINATION.

General Accounting Office. The federal agency that provides legal and accounting assistance to Congress, audits and investigates federal programs, and settles certain contract claims against the United States. — Abbr. GAO.

general administration. See ADMINISTRATION.

general administrative expense. See EXPENSE.

general administrator. See ADMINISTRATOR (1).

general agency. See AGENCY (1).

general agent. See AGENT; INSURANCE AGENT.

General Agreement on Tariffs and Trade. A multiparty international agreement — signed originally in 1948 — that promotes international trade by lowering import duties and providing equal access to markets. • More than 130 nations are parties to the agreement. — Abbr. GATT.

general appearance. See APPEARANCE.

general assembly. 1. The name of the legislative body in many states. **2.** (*cap.*) The deliberative body of the United Nations.

general assignment. See ASSIGNMENT (2).

general assumpsit. See ASSUMPSIT.

general authority. See AUTHORITY (1).

general average. See AVERAGE.

general-average bond. See BOND (2).

general-average contribution. See *general average* under AVERAGE.

general average loss. See LOSS (3).

general-average statement. *Maritime law.* A statement containing an exact calculation of the general average and each party's contributory share. See AVERAGE (3).

general benefit. See BENEFIT.

general bequest. See BEQUEST.

general challenge. See *challenge for cause* under CHALLENGE (2).

general compromis. See COMPROMIS.

general contractor. See CONTRACTOR.

general counsel. See COUNSEL.

General Counsel's Memorandum. *Tax law.* **1.** A written discussion, issued by the office of the Chief Counsel of the IRS, on the merits of a legal issue involving tax law. **2.** A written explanation, issued by the office of the Chief Counsel of the IRS, explaining the IRS's positions in revenue rulings and technical advice memorandums.

general count. See COUNT.

General Court. The name of the legislatures of Massachusetts and New Hampshire. • "General Court" was a common colonial-era term for a body that exercised judicial and legislative functions. Cf. COURT OF ASSISTANTS.

general court-martial. See COURT-MARTIAL.

general covenant against encumbrances. See *covenant against encumbrances* under COVENANT (4).

general creditor. See *unsecured creditor* under CREDITOR.

general custom. See CUSTOM.

general damages. See DAMAGES.

general debt. See DEBT.

general demurrer. See *general exception* under EXCEPTION.

general denial. See DENIAL.

general deposit. See DEPOSIT (2).

general deputy. See DEPUTY.

general deterrence. See DETERRENCE.

general devise. See DEVISE.

general disability insurance. See INSURANCE.

general discharge. See DISCHARGE (8).

general election. See ELECTION.

general employer. See EMPLOYER.

general exception. See EXCEPTION (1).

general execution. See EXECUTION (4).

general executor. See EXECUTOR.

general expense. See *general administrative expense* under EXPENSE.

general fee conditional. See *fee simple conditional* under FEE SIMPLE.

general finding. See FINDING OF FACT.

general franchise. See FRANCHISE (2).

general fund. See FUND (1).

general guaranty. See GUARANTY.

general guardian. See GUARDIAN.

generalia specialibus non derogant (jen-ə-**ray**-lee-ə spesh-ee-**ay**-lə-bəs non **der**-ə-gənt). [Latin "general things do not derogate from specific things"] The doctrine holding that general words in a later statute do not repeal an earlier statutory provision dealing with a special subject. • This principle illustrates the cautious approach that some courts have adopted in interpreting broad provisions, but there are many exceptions.

general imparlance. See IMPARLANCE.

general improvement. See IMPROVEMENT.

general indorsement. See *blank indorsement* under INDORSEMENT.

general intangible. See INTANGIBLE.

general intent. See INTENT (1).

general issue. See ISSUE (1).

general jail delivery. See JAIL DELIVERY.

general jurisdiction. See JURISDICTION.

general jurisprudence. See JURISPRUDENCE.

General Land Office. A former U.S. Interior Department division that exercised executive power relating to the public lands, including their survey, patenting, and sale or other disposition. • The General Land Office and the U.S. Grazing Service were consolidated into the Bureau of Land Management in 1946. See BUREAU OF LAND MANAGEMENT.

general law. See LAW.

general ledger. See LEDGER (1).

general legacy. See LEGACY.

general legal principle. See GENERAL PRINCIPLE OF LAW.

general legislation. See LEGISLATION.

general letter of credit. See LETTER OF CREDIT.

general liability policy. See *comprehensive general liability policy* under INSURANCE POLICY.

general lien. See LIEN.

general listing. See *open listing* under LISTING (1).

generally accepted accounting principles. The conventions, rules, and procedures that define approved accounting practices at a particular time. • These principles are issued by the Financial Accounting Standards Board for use by accountants in preparing financial statements. The principles include not only broad guidelines of general application but also detailed practices and procedures. — Abbr. GAAP. — Also termed *generally accepted accountancy principles*.

generally accepted auditing standards. The guidelines issued by the American Institute of Certified Public Accountants establishing an auditor's professional qualities and the criteria for the auditor's examination and required reports. — Abbr. GAAS.

general manager. See MANAGER.

general mortgage. See MORTGAGE.

general-mortgage bond. See BOND (3).

general-obligation bond. See BOND (3).

general occupant. See OCCUPANT.

general officer. See OFFICER (2).

general owner. See OWNER.

general pardon. See AMNESTY.

general partner. See PARTNER.

general partnership. See PARTNERSHIP.

general plea. See *general denial* under DENIAL.

general plea in bar. See PLEA IN BAR.

general power. See POWER (4).

general power of appointment. See POWER OF APPOINTMENT.

general power of attorney. See POWER OF ATTORNEY.

general prayer. See PRAYER FOR RELIEF.

general principle of law. **1.** A principle widely recognized by peoples whose legal order has attained a certain level of sophistication. **2.** *Int'l law.* A principle that gives rise to international legal obligations.

> "[T]he adjective 'general' does not refer to several or many orders [i.e., legal systems] as do the general principles of national law, but indicates principles which are applied generally in all cases of the same kind which arise in international law (e.g. the principle of nonintervention)." Hermann Mosler, "General Principles of Law," in 2 *Encyclopedia of Public International Law* 512, 512 (1995).

3. A principle recognized in all kinds of legal relations, regardless of the legal system to which it belongs (state law, federal law, international law, etc.). — Also termed *general legal principle.*

general property. See PROPERTY.

general publication. See PUBLICATION.

general reference. See REFERENCE.

general replication. See REPLICATION.

general reprisal. See REPRISAL.

general retainer. See RETAINER.

general revenue. See REVENUE.

general revenue fund. See FUND (1).

general rule. See RULE.

general sentence. See SENTENCE.

General Services Administration. The independent federal agency that manages the federal government's property and records. • The General Services Administration supervises the construction and operation of buildings, procures and distributes supplies, disposes of surplus property, operates traffic and communications facilities, stores strategic and critical materials, manages automatic data processing systems, and supervises government document- and information-security programs. — Abbr. GSA.

general ship. See SHIP.

general special imparlance. See IMPARLANCE.

general statute. See STATUTE.

general strike. See STRIKE.

general synod. See SYNOD.

general tail. See *tail general* under TAIL.

general tax. See TAX.

general tenancy. See TENANCY.

general term. See TERM (5).

general traverse. See TRAVERSE.

general usage. See USAGE.

general verdict. See VERDICT.

general-verdict rule. The principle that when a general verdict is returned on multiple causes of action (or theories of recovery), it is presumed on appeal that the jury found in the prevailing party's favor on each cause of action.

general verdict subject to a special case. See VERDICT.

general verdict with interrogatories. See VERDICT.

general warrant. See WARRANT (1).

general warranty. See WARRANTY (1).

general warranty deed. See *warranty deed* under DEED.

general welfare. See WELFARE.

General Welfare Clause. U.S. Const. art. I, § 8, cl. 1, which empowers Congress to levy taxes and pay debts in order to provide for the country's general welfare. • The Supreme Court has broadly interpreted this clause to allow Congress to create, for example, the social-security system. — Also termed *Welfare Clause*.

general words. Language used in deeds to convey not only the specific property described in the conveyance but also all easements, privileges, and appurtenances that may belong to the property.

generation. 1. A single degree or stage in the succession of persons in natural descent. **2.** The average time span between the birth of parents and the birth of their children.

generation-skipping tax. See TAX.

generation-skipping transfer. A conveyance of assets to a person more than one generation removed from the transferor, that is, a skip person. • For example, a conveyance either directly or in trust from a grandparent to a grandchild is a generation-skipping transfer subject to a generation-skipping transfer tax. IRC (26 USCA) §§ 2601–2663. See *generation-skipping transfer tax* under TAX; *generation-skipping trust* under TRUST; SKIP PERSON.

generation-skipping transfer tax. See TAX.

generation-skipping trust. See TRUST.

generic, *adj.* **1.** Common or descriptive, and thus not eligible for trademark protection; nonproprietary <a generic name>. **2.** Not having a trademark or brand name <generic drugs>.

genericalness. See GENERICNESS.

generic drug. See DRUG.

generic-drug law. A statute that allows pharmacists to substitute a generic drug for a brand-name drug under specified conditions. • Most states have enacted generic-drug laws to ensure that less-expensive generic drugs are available to consumers.

genericide (jə-**ner**-ə-sɪd). *Trademarks.* The loss or cancellation of a trademark that no longer distinguishes the owner's product from others' products. • Genericide occurs when a trademark becomes such a household name that the consuming public begins to think of the mark not as a brand name but as a synonym for the product itself. Examples of trademarks that have been "killed" by genericide include *aspirin* and *escalator*.

genericism (jə-**ner**-ə-siz-əm). See GENERICNESS.

generic name. *Trademarks.* A term that describes something generally without designating the thing's source or creator, such as the word "car" or "sink." • Generic names cannot be protected as trademarks. — Also termed *generic term*; *generic mark*; *common descriptive name*.

genericness, *n.* The state or condition of being generic <an affirmative defense of genericness in a trademark suit>. — Also termed *genericalness*; *genericism*.

generic term. See GENERIC NAME.

genetic fingerprinting. See DNA IDENTIFICATION.

Geneva Convention (jə-**nee**-və). An international agreement establishing the proper treatment of prisoners of war and of persons injured or killed in battle. • Drafted in 1864, the Convention has since been adopted in revised form by most nations.

genocide (**jen**-ə-sɪd). *Int'l law.* An act committed with the intent to destroy, in whole or part, a national, ethnic, racial, or religious group. • Under the terms of the Geneva Convention of

1948, genocide is a crime (whether committed during war or peace) subject to prosecution either in the nation where the act was committed or by an international tribunal having jurisdiction elsewhere.

> "The draft Convention on the Prevention and Punishment of the Crime of Genocide was adopted by the General Assembly on December 9, 1948 and unanimously recommended for adherence to the members of the United Nations. It came into force in October, 1950 between twenty-four states. The term 'genocide' was first proposed by Dr. Lemkin in the course of the war and incorporated on his suggestion into the Indictment of the Major German War Criminals. The Assembly Resolution on Genocide of December 11, 1946, and the Convention of 1948, are also the result of a remarkable one-man campaign." Georg Schwarzenberger, *Power Politics: A Study of International Society* 634 (2d ed. 1951).

Genoese lottery (jen-oh-**eez** *or* -**ees**). See LOTTERY.

gens (jenz), *n.* [Latin] *Roman law.* A clan or group of families who share the same name and (supposedly) a common ancestor; EXTENDED FAMILY. • Members of a *gens* are freeborn and possess full civic rights. Pl. ***gentes.*** See JUS GENTIUM.

> "A wider group still is the *gens*, of great importance in early law though its importance was gone in classical times. This consisted of all who bore the same *nomen*, the gentile name." W.W. Buckland, *A Manual of Roman Private Law* 61 (2d ed. 1953).

gentes (**jen**-teez). [Latin] *Roman law.* The peoples or nations of the world.

gentile (**jen**-tɪl). [Latin] *Roman law.* A member of a *gens*. See GENS.

gentleman. *Hist.* **1.** A man of noble or gentle birth or rank; a man above the rank of yeoman. **2.** A man belonging to the landed gentry. • Today the term has no precise legal meaning.

gentleman's agreement. See GENTLEMEN'S AGREEMENT.

Gentleman Usher of the Black Rod. An officer of the House of Lords who has various ceremonial duties, including the summoning of the members of the House of Commons to the House of Lords when a bill is to receive royal approval. • The office dates from the 14th century.

gentlemen's agreement. An unwritten agreement that, while not legally enforceable, is secured by the good faith and honor of the parties. — Also spelled *gentleman's agreement.*

gentrification, *n.* The restoration and upgrading of a deteriorated or aging urban neighborhood by middle-class or affluent persons, resulting in increased property values and often in displacement of lower-income residents. — **gentrify,** *vb.*

genuine, *adj.* **1.** (Of a thing) authentic or real; something that has the quality of what it is purported to be or to have <the plaintiff failed to question whether the exhibits were genuine>. **2.** (Of an instrument) free of forgery or counterfeiting <the bank teller could not determine whether the signature on the check was genuine>. UCC § 1–201(18).

genuine issue of material fact. *Civil procedure.* In the law of summary judgments, a triable, substantial, or real question of fact supported by substantial evidence. • An issue of this kind precludes entry of summary judgment.

genus (**jee**-nəs). A general class comprising several species or divisions. • For example, patent law is a species within the genus of intellectual property; burglary is a species within the genus of crime. In the law of sales, *genus* referred to fungibles, while *species* referred to specific, individual items.

geodetic-survey system (jee-ə-**det**-ik). A federally created land-description method consisting of nationwide marks (or *benches*) made at longitude and latitude points. • The geodetic-survey system integrates most of the real property in the United States into one unified form of measurement.

geographically descriptive trademark. See TRADEMARK.

geographic market. See MARKET.

german (**jər**-mən), *adj.* Having the same parents or grandparents; closely related.

brother-german. A full brother; a child of both of one's own parents.

cousin-german. A first cousin; a child of a full sibling of one's mother or father.

germane (jər-**mayn**), *adj.* Relevant; pertinent <the caselaw cited in the brief was not germane to the legal issue pending before the court>.

germanus (jər-**may**-nəs). [Latin] *Roman law.* **1.** *adj.* Having the same father and mother. **2.** *n.*

A whole brother; a child of both of one's own parents.

gerrymandering (**jer**-ee-man-dər-ing *or* **ger**-ee-), *n.* **1.** The practice of dividing a geographical area into electoral districts, often of highly irregular shape, to give one political party an unfair advantage by diluting the opposition's voting strength. — Also termed *political gerrymandering*. **2.** The practice of dividing any geographical or jurisdictional area into political units (such as school districts) to give some group a special advantage. — Also termed *jurisdictional gerrymandering*. — **gerrymander,** *vb.* Cf. REAPPORTIONMENT.

gersum (**gər**-səm). *Hist.* **1.** Money paid for a thing; specif., compensation paid by a tenant to a superior on entering a holding. **2.** A penalty or amercement paid for an offense. — Also spelled *garsumme*; *gersuma*; *gersume*.

gersumarius (jər-s[y]ə-**mair**-ee-əs). *Hist.* Finable; liable to be fined at the discretion of a feudal superior. • A villein who gave his daughter in marriage was *gersumarius* — he was liable to pay a fine to the lord.

gestio (**jes**-chee-oh). [Latin] *Roman law.* **1.** Behavior or conduct. See GESTIO PRO HAEREDE. **2.** The management of a thing, esp. a transaction.

negotiorum gestio (ni-goh-shee-**or**-əm **jes**-chee-oh). See NEGOTIORUM GESTIO.

gestio pro haerede (**jes**-chee-oh proh **her**-ə-dee). [Latin "behavior as heir"] *Roman & Hist. Scots law.* An appointed heir's conduct (such as selling or leasing the decedent's property) that indicates the heir's intent to receive the inheritance and thereby take on the estate's debts.

gestor (**jes**-tor). [Latin] *Roman law.* **1.** One who carries on a business. **2.** NEGOTIORUM GESTOR.

gestu et fama (**jes**-t[y]oo et **fay**-mə). [Latin "demeanor and reputation"] *Hist.* A writ used by a person who had been imprisoned because of a poor reputation in the community to gain release from jail pending the arrival of justices with commissions of gaol delivery. See COMMISSION OF GAOL DELIVERY.

gestum (**jes**-təm). [Latin] *Roman law.* A deed or an act; a thing done. • *Gestum* is synonymous with *factum*. See FACTUM (2).

gesture. A motion of the body calculated to express a thought or emphasize a certain point <the prosecutor was known for her dramatic gestures during closing argument>.

gibbet (**jib**-it), *n. Hist.* A post with one arm extending from the top, from which criminals are either executed by hanging or suspended after death as a warning to other potential offenders; a type of gallows.

double gibbet. A gibbet with two arms extending from its top so that it resembles a capital "T."

gibbet law. See HALIFAX LAW.

GIC. See *guaranteed investment contract* under INVESTMENT CONTRACT.

gift, *n.* **1.** The act of voluntarily transferring property to another without compensation. **2.** A thing so transferred. — **gift,** *vb.*

absolute gift. See *inter vivos gift*.

anatomical gift. A testamentary donation of a bodily organ or organs, esp. for transplant or for medical research.

antenuptial gift. See *prenuptial gift*.

class gift. A gift to a group of persons, uncertain in number at the time of the gift but to be ascertained at a future time, who are all to take in definite proportions, the share of each being dependent on the ultimate number in the group.

> "The typical class gift is to 'children,' 'issue,' 'heirs,' 'brothers and sisters,' 'nieces and nephews,' 'grandchildren.' A class gift is one in which the donor intends to benefit a group or a class of persons, as distinguished from specific individuals; the class gift donor is said to be 'group-minded.' The class gift is one in which the donor intends that the number of donees, from the time of the delivery of the instrument of gift in the case of the inter vivos gift, or from the time of the execution of the will in the case of the testamentary gift, is subject to fluctuation by way of increase or decrease, or by way of increase only, or by way of decrease only, depending on the circumstances of the gift." Thomas F. Bergin & Paul G. Haskell, *Preface to Estates in Land and Future Interests* 136 (2d ed. 1984).

completed gift. A gift that is no longer in the donor's possession and control. • Only a completed gift is taxable under the gift tax.

gift causa mortis (**kaw**-zə **mor**-tis). A gift made in contemplation of the donor's imminent death. • The three essentials are that (1) the gift must be made with a view to the donor's present illness or peril, (2) the donor must actually die from that illness or peril, without ever recovering, and (3) there must be a delivery. Even though *causa mortis* is the more usual word order in modern law, the correct Latin phrasing is *mortis causa* — hence *gift mortis causa*. — Also termed *donatio causa mortis*; *donatio mortis causa*; *gift in contemplation of death*; *transfer in contemplation of death*.

> "A 'gift causa mortis' ... is testamentary, and it is similar to testamentary disposition in the respect that there remains with the donor the power to revoke the gift until his death. In some respects, a gift causa mortis may be said to resemble a contract, for mutual consent and the concurrent will of both parties are necessary to the validity of the transfer." 38A C.J.S. *Gifts* § 85, at 276–77 (1996).

gift inter vivos. See *inter vivos gift*.

gift in trust. A gift of legal title to property that is to be used to benefit the cestui que trust (i.e., the beneficiary).

gift over. A property gift (esp. by will) that takes effect after the expiration of a preceding estate in the property (such as a life estate or fee simple determinable) <to Sarah for life, with gift over to Don in fee>.

gift splitting. See *split gift*.

gratuitous gift. A gift made without consideration, as most gifts are. • Strictly speaking, the term looks redundant, but it answers to the *donum gratuitum* of Roman law.

inter vivos gift (**in**-tər **vI**-vohs *or* -**vee**-vohs). A gift made during the donor's lifetime and delivered with the intention of irrevocably surrendering control over the property. — Also termed *gift inter vivos*; *lifetime gift*; *absolute gift*.

manual gift. *Civil law.* A gift of movable, tangible property, made by delivery without any formalities.

onerous gift (**ohn**-ə-rəs *or* **on**-ə-rəs). A gift made subject to certain conditions imposed on the recipient.

prenuptial gift (pree-**nəp**-shəl). A gift of property from one spouse to another before marriage. • In community-property states, prenuptial gifts are often made to preserve the property's classification as separate property. — Also termed *antenuptial gift*.

split gift. *Tax.* A gift that is made by one spouse to a third person and that, for gift-tax purposes, both spouses treat as being made one-half by each spouse; a gift in which the spouses combine their annual gift-tax exclusions. • A split gift, for example, is eligible for two annual exclusions of $10,000 each, or a total of $20,000 for one gift. See *annual exclusion* under EXCLUSION (1). — Also termed *gift splitting*; *gift-splitting election*.

substitute gift. A testamentary gift to one person in place of another who is unable to take under the will for some reason. — Also termed *substitutional gift*.

taxable gift. A gift that, after adjusting for the annual exclusion and applicable deductions, is subject to the federal unified transfer tax. IRC (26 USCA) § 2503.

testamentary gift (tes-tə-**men**-tə-ree *or* -tree). A gift made in a will.

vested gift. An absolute gift, being neither conditional nor contingent, though its use or enjoyment might not occur until sometime in the future.

gift deed. See DEED.

gift enterprise. 1. A scheme for the distribution of items by chance among those who have purchased shares in the scheme. **2.** A merchant's scheme to induce sales for market value by giving buyers tickets that carry a chance to win a prize. • Gift enterprises are regulated by state law. See LOTTERY.

gift in contemplation of death. See *gift causa mortis* under GIFT.

gift inter vivos. See *inter vivos gift* under GIFT.

gift in trust. See GIFT.

gift over. See GIFT.

gift splitting. See *split gift* under GIFT.

gift-splitting election. See *split gift* under GIFT.

Gifts to Minors Act. See UNIFORM TRANSFERS TO MINORS ACT.

gift tax. See TAX.

gilda mercatoria (**gil**-də mər-kə-**tor**-ee-ə). [Law Latin] *Hist.* A merchant guild; an incorporated society of merchants having exclusive trading rights within a town.

gilour (**gI**-lər). [Law French] *Hist.* A guiler; a person who cheats or deceives. • *Gilour* referred to a person who sold false goods, such as a person who sold pewter as silver.

gilt-edged, *adj.* (Of a security) having the highest rating for safety of investment; exceptionally safe as an investment.

Ginnie Mae (**jin**-ee **may**). See GOVERNMENT NATIONAL MORTGAGE ASSOCIATION.

girth (gərth). [Old English] **1.** A measure of length, equal to a yard. • This term, which was used in Saxon and early English law, was taken from the circumference of a man's body. **2.** The area surrounding a church. **3.** A place of sanctuary. **4.** A band or strap that encircles the body of an animal to fasten something (usu. a saddle) to its back.

gisement (**jIs**- *or* **jIz**-mənt). [Law French] *Archaic.* See AGISTMENT.

giser (**jI**-sər), *vb.* [Law French] *Hist.* (Of an action) to lie; to be capable of being brought as a suit in court. • This verb, in its inflected form *gist*, appeared in such phrases as *ou assise ne gist point* ("when an assise does not lie"), *le action bien gist* ("the action well lies"), and *gist en le bouche* ("it lies in the mouth"), and *cest action gist* ("this action lies").

gisetaker (**jIs**- *or* **jIz**-tay-kər). *Archaic.* See AGISTER.

gist (jist). **1.** The ground or essence (of a legal action) <the gist of the crime>. **2.** The main point <she skimmed the brief to get the gist of it>. • This noun derives from the Law French verb *giser* "to lie." See GISER.

give, *vb.* **1.** To voluntarily transfer (property) to another without compensation <Jack gave his daughter a car on her birthday>. **2.** To confer by a formal act <the First Amendment gives all citizens the right to free speech>. **3.** To present for another to consider <the witness gave compelling testimony before the jury>. **4.** (Of a jury) to impose or award by verdict <the jury gave the defendant the death penalty> <the jury gave the plaintiff $1,000 in damages>.

give bail, *vb.* To post security for one's appearance in court <the court ordered the accused to give bail in the amount of $10,000>. — Also termed *post bail.*

give color, *vb. Hist.* To admit, either expressly or impliedly by silence, an apparent right in an opponent's allegations. • In common-law pleading, a defendant's plea of confession and avoidance had to give color to the plaintiff's allegations in the complaint or the plea would be fatally defective. See COLOR (2).

give, devise, and bequeath, *vb.* To transfer property by will <I give, devise, and bequeath all the rest, residue, and remainder of my estate to my beloved daughter Sarah>. See BEQUEST.

give way, *vb. Maritime law.* (Of a vessel) to deviate from a course, or slow down, in accordance with navigation rules, to allow a second vessel to pass without altering its course.

giving in payment. *Civil law.* The act of discharging a debt by giving something to the creditor (with the creditor's consent) other than what was originally called for. • The phrase is a translation of the French *dation en paiement* and derives from the Roman *datio in solutum.* See DATION EN PAIEMENT. Cf. ACCORD AND SATISFACTION.

gladius (**glay**-dee-əs). [Latin "sword"] *Roman law.* The emblem of the emperor's power, esp. the power to punish criminals. See JUS GLADII.

glaive (glayv). *Hist.* A sword, lance, or horseman's staff. • The glaive was one of the weapons allowed in a trial by combat.

glamour stock. See STOCK.

glass ceiling. An actual or supposed upper limit of professional advancement, esp. for women, as a result of discriminatory practices.

Glass-Steagall Act. A federal statute that protects bank depositors by restricting the securities-related business of commercial banks, specif. by prohibiting banks from owning brokerage firms or engaging in the brokerage business. 12 USCA § 378. — Also termed *Banking Act of 1933.*

glebae ascriptitii. See ADSCRIPTI GLEBAE.

glebe (gleeb). [Latin "clod of earth"] **1.** *Roman law.* The soil of an inheritance; an agrarian estate. • *Servi addicti glebae* ("slaves bound to the land") were serfs attached to and passing with the estate. **2.** *Eccles. law.* Land possessed as part of the endowment or revenue of a church or ecclesiastical benefice.

Globe **election.** *Labor law.* The procedure by which a group of employees is given the opportunity to decide whether to be represented as a distinct group or to be represented as a part of a larger, existing unit. *Globe Machine & Stamping Co.*, 3 NLRB 294 (1937). — Also termed *self-determination election.*

gloss, *n.* **1.** A note inserted between the lines or in the margin of a text to explain a difficult or obscure word in the text <this edition of Shakespeare's works is bolstered by its many glosses on Elizabethan English>. **2.** A collection of explanations; a glossary <the hornbook's copious gloss>. **3.** Pronouncements considered collectively, usu. by courts; interpretation <the statute and its judicial gloss>.

glossators (glah-**say**-tərz). (*usu. cap.*) A group of Italian jurisconsults who, from the 11th to the 13th centuries, were primarily responsible for the revival of the study of Roman law. • They originally worked by glossing (that is, explaining in the margin) difficult or unclear passages, and gradually their writings blossomed into full-blown commentaries and discussions. See POSTGLOSSATORS.

Gloucester, Statute of (**glos**-tər). *Hist.* A statute that allowed a successful plaintiff to recover costs in addition to damages. • The statute was enacted in Gloucester. 6 Edw. I, ch. 1 (1278).

glove silver. *Hist.* Money given as an incentive or reward to a court officer, esp. money given by a sheriff to an assize official when no prisoners were left by the assize for execution. • The name derives from the practice of giving money to servants, ostensibly to buy gloves with.

GMI. *abbr.* GUILTY BUT MENTALLY ILL.

GNMA. *abbr.* GOVERNMENT NATIONAL MORTGAGE ASSOCIATION.

GNP. *abbr.* GROSS NATIONAL PRODUCT.

go bail, *vb. Archaic.* To act as a surety on a bail bond.

God-bote. See BOTE (2).

God-gild. *Hist.* Money paid or something offered for the service of God; esp., a payment of money or a gift (for example, land) to a church. See FRANKALMOIN.

God's penny. *Hist.* Earnest money; a small sum paid on the striking of a bargain. — Also termed *denarius Dei*; *godpenny.*

> "It is among the merchants that the giving of earnest first . . . becomes a form which binds both buyer and seller in a contract of sale. To all appearances this change was not accomplished without the intermediation of a religious idea. All over western Europe the earnest becomes known as the God's penny or Holy Ghost's penny (*denarius Dei*) . . . ." 2 Frederick Pollock & Frederic W. Maitland, *The History of English Law Before the Time of Edward I* 208 (2d ed. 1899).

go forward, *vb.* To commence or carry on with the presentation of a case in court <after the lunch recess, the judge instructed the plaintiff to go forward with its case>.

go hence without day. (Of a defendant to a lawsuit) to be finished with legal proceedings without any further settings on the court's calendar. • Thus, a defendant who "goes hence without day" succeeds in getting a case finally resolved, usu. by dismissal. The phrase derives from the Law French phrase *aller sans jour*, and over time defendants came to use it to request that the case against them be dismissed without the necessity of a day in court. — Sometimes shortened to *go without day*; *without day*. See SINE DIE.

going-and-coming rule. **1.** The principle that torts committed by an employee while commuting to or from work are generally outside the scope of employment. **2.** The principle that denies workers'-compensation benefits to an employee injured while commuting to or from work.

going concern. A commercial enterprise actively engaging in business with the expectation of indefinite continuance.

going-concern value. See VALUE.

going price, *n.* The prevailing or current market value of something. See *fair market value* under VALUE.

going private. The process of changing a public corporation into a close corporation by terminating the corporation's status with the SEC as a publicly held corporation and by having its outstanding publicly held shares acquired by a single shareholder or a small group.

going public. The process of a company's selling stock to the investing public for the first time (after filing a registration statement under applicable securities laws), thereby becoming a public corporation.

going through the bar. *Hist.* A daily process in which the court would ask all barristers present whether they had motions to present. • This practice, which ended in 1873, was conducted according to seniority, except for the last day of a term, when the junior barristers were asked first.

going to the country. *Hist.* The act of requesting a jury trial. • A defendant was said to be "going to the country" by concluding a pleading with the phrase "and of this he puts himself upon the country." Similarly, a plaintiff would conclude a pleading with the phrase "and this the plaintiff prays may be enquired of by the country." — Also termed *go to the country*. Cf. CONCLUSION TO THE COUNTRY.

going value. See *going-concern value* under VALUE.

going witness. See WITNESS.

gold bond. See BOND (3).

gold clause. A provision calling for payment in gold. • Gold clauses, which are now void, were once used in contracts, bonds, and mortgages.

golden handcuffs. Remuneration set at such a high level that the employee earning it cannot leave the firm or company and receive commensurate pay elsewhere. • As a result, the employee often stays in the position even if it is otherwise unrewarding or unpleasant.

golden handshake. An employee dismissal that includes generous compensation.

golden parachute. An employment-contract provision that grants an upper-level executive lucrative severance benefits — including long-term salary guarantees or bonuses — if control of the company changes hands (as by a merger). Cf. TIN PARACHUTE.

> "Key executives may be provided with significant employment contract clauses that are triggered only by a change in the firm's control through a sale, merger, acquisition, or takeover. These contract clauses are commonly termed *golden parachutes*, and they generally provide that if control over the employer's business occurs and the new management terminates the executive, additional compensation will be received.... Golden parachutes are useful in providing long-term incentives for executives to enter industries in which takeover chances are above average. Generally, golden parachutes do not violate public policy." Kurt H. Decker & H. Thomas Felix II, *Drafting and Revising Employment Contracts* § 3.33, at 84 (1991).

golden rule. The principle that, in construing written instruments, a court should adhere to the grammatical and ordinary sense of the words unless that adherence would lead to some manifest absurdity; esp., in statutory construction, the principle that if a statute's literal meaning would lead to an absurd or unjust result, or even to an inconsistency within the statute itself, the statute should be interpreted in a way that avoids such a result or inconsistency. — Also termed *Baron Parke's rule*. Cf. MISCHIEF RULE; PLAIN-MEANING RULE; EQUITY-OF-THE-STATUTE RULE.

> "[T]he 'golden' rule ... allows for a departure from the literal rule when the application of the statutory words in the ordinary sense would be repugnant to or inconsistent with some other provision in the statute or even when it would lead to what the court considers to be an absurdity. The usual consequence of applying the golden rule is that words which are in the statute are ignored or words which are not there are read in. The scope of the golden rule is debatable, particularly so far as the meaning of an 'absurdity' is concerned." Rupert Cross, *Statutory Interpretation* 14 (1976).

golden-rule argument. A jury argument in which a lawyer asks the jurors to reach a verdict by imagining themselves or someone they care about in the place of the injured plaintiff or crime victim. • Because golden-rule arguments ask the jurors to become advocates for the plaintiff or victim and to ignore their obligation to exercise calm and reasonable judgment, these arguments are widely condemned and are considered improper in most states.

goldsmiths' notes. *Hist.* Bankers' cash notes; promissory notes given by bankers to customers as acknowledgments of the receipt of money. • This term derives from the London banking business, which originally was transacted by goldsmiths.

gold standard. A monetary system in which currency is convertible into its legal equivalent in gold or gold coin. • The United States adopted the gold standard in 1900 and abandoned it in 1934. Cf. PAPER STANDARD.

good, *adj.* **1.** Sound or reliable <a good investment>. **2.** Valid, effectual, and enforceable; sufficient under the law <good title>.

good, *n.* See GOODS.

good and lawful fence. See LAWFUL FENCE.

good and merchantable abstract of title. See ABSTRACT OF TITLE.

good and valuable consideration. See *valuable consideration* under CONSIDERATION.

good and workmanlike. (Of a product or service) characterized by quality craftsmanship; constructed or performed in a skillful way or method <the house was built in a good and workmanlike manner>.

good behavior. 1. A standard by which judges are considered fit to continue their tenure. **2.** Orderly conduct, which in the context of penal law allows a prisoner to reduce the time spent in prison. Cf. GOOD TIME.

good cause. See CAUSE (2).

good cause shown. See *good cause* under CAUSE (2).

good consideration. See CONSIDERATION.

good delivery. See DELIVERY.

good faith, *n.* A state of mind consisting in (1) honesty in belief or purpose, (2) faithfulness to one's duty or obligation, (3) observance of reasonable commercial standards of fair dealing in a given trade or business, or (4) absence of intent to defraud or to seek unconscionable advantage. — Also termed *bona fides.* — **good-faith,** *adj*. Cf. BAD FAITH.

> "The phrase 'good faith' is used in a variety of contexts, and its meaning varies somewhat with the context. Good faith performance or enforcement of a contract emphasizes faithfulness to an agreed common purpose and consistency with the justified expectations of the other party; it excludes a variety of types of conduct characterized as involving 'bad faith' because they violate community standards of decency, fairness or reasonableness. The appropriate remedy for a breach of the duty of good faith also varies with the circumstances." Restatement (Second) of Contracts § 205 cmt. a (1981).

good-faith bargaining. *Labor law.* Negotiations between an employer and a representative of employees, usu. a union, in which both parties meet and confer at reasonable times with open minds and with a view to reaching an agreement. • The National Labor Relations Act requires good-faith bargaining, and failure to bargain in good faith is considered an unfair labor practice. 29 USCA §§ 151–169. See UNFAIR LABOR PRACTICE.

good-faith exception. *Criminal procedure.* An exception to the exclusionary rule whereby evidence obtained under a warrant later found to be unsupported by probable cause is nonetheless admissible if the police reasonably relied on the notion that the warrant was valid. • The good-faith exception was adopted by the Supreme Court in *United States v. Leon*, 468 U.S. 897, 104 S.Ct. 3405 (1984).

good-faith margin. See MARGIN.

good-faith purchaser. See *bona fide purchaser* under PURCHASER.

good health. *Insurance.* A state of reasonable healthiness; a state of health free from serious disease. • Good health, a phrase often appearing in life-insurance policies, does not mean perfect health. — Also termed *sound health.*

> "As used in policies of insurance, there is no material difference between the terms 'sound health' and 'good health,' and generally it appears that the two terms are considered to be synonymous. Such expressions are comparative terms, and the rule followed generally is that the term 'good health' or 'sound health,' when used in an insurance contract, means that the applicant has no grave, important, or serious disease, and is free from any ailment that seriously affects the general soundness or healthfulness of his system." 43 Am. Jur. 2d *Insurance* § 1061, at 1069 (1982).

good jury. See *special jury* under JURY.

good moral character, *n.* **1.** A pattern of behavior that is consistent with the community's current ethical standards and that shows an absence of deceit or morally reprehensible conduct. • An alien seeking to be naturalized must show good moral character in the five years preceding the petition for naturalization. **2.** A pattern of behavior conforming to a profession's ethical standards and showing an absence of moral turpitude. • Good moral character is usu. a requirement of persons applying to practice a profession such as law or medicine.

good offices. *Int'l law.* The involvement of one or more countries or an international organization in a dispute between other countries with the aim of contributing to its settlement or at least easing relations between the disputing countries.

Goodright. *Hist.* A name sometimes used as a fictitious plaintiff in an ejectment action. • "John Doe" was used more frequently. — Also termed *Goodtitle*. Cf. JOHN DOE.

goods. 1. Tangible or movable personal property other than money; esp., articles of trade or items of merchandise <goods and services>. • The sale of goods is governed by Article 2 of the UCC. **2.** Things that have value, whether tangible or not <the importance of social goods varies from society to society>.

> " 'Goods' means all things, including specially manufactured goods, that are movable at the time of identification to a contract for sale and future goods. The term includes the unborn young of animals, growing crops,

and other identified things to be severed from real property .... The term does not include money in which the price is to be paid, the subject matter of foreign exchange transactions, documents, letters of credit, letter-of-credit rights, instruments, investment property, accounts, chattel paper, deposit accounts, or general intangibles." UCC § 2-102(a)(24).

capital goods. Goods (such as equipment and machinery) used for the production of other goods or services. — Also termed *industrial goods*.

consumer goods. Goods bought or used primarily for personal, family, or household purposes, and not for resale or for producing other goods. UCC § 9–109(1).

customers' goods. *Insurance*. Goods belonging to the customers of a fire-insurance policyholder; goods held by a policyholder as a bailee.

distressed goods. Goods sold at unusually low prices or at a loss.

durable goods. Consumer goods that are designed to be used repeatedly over a long period, such as automobiles or personal computers. — Also termed *durables*; *hard goods*.

fungible goods (**fən**-jə-bəl). Goods that are interchangeable with one another; goods that, by nature or trade usage, are the equivalent of any other like unit, such as coffee or grain. UCC § 1–201(17).

future goods. Goods that will come into being, such as those yet to be manufactured; goods that are not both existing and identified. • A purported present sale of future goods or any interest in them operates as a contract to sell. UCC § 2–105(2).

hard goods. See *durable goods*.

household goods. Goods that are used in connection with a home. • This term usu. arises when a warehouser claims a lien on what he or she asserts are "household" goods. According to the UCC, a warehouser may claim a lien on a depositor's furniture, furnishings, and personal effects that are used in a dwelling. UCC § 7–209(3)(b).

industrial goods. See *capital goods*.

mobile goods. Goods that are normally used in more than one jurisdiction (such as shipping containers and road-construction machinery) and that are held by the debtor as equipment or leased by the debtor to others. • Under the Uniform Commercial Code, the procedure for perfecting a security interest in mobile goods is generally defined by the law of the state where the debtor is located. UCC § 9–103(3).

nonconforming goods. Goods that fail to meet contractual specifications, allowing the buyer to reject the tender of the goods or to revoke their acceptance. UCC §§ 2–601, 2–608. See PERFECT-TENDER RULE.

ordinary goods. Goods that are anything other than mobile goods, minerals, or goods covered by a certificate of title. UCC § 9–103(1)(a).

prize goods. Goods captured at sea during wartime.

soft goods. Consumer goods (such as clothing) that are not durable goods.

Good Samaritan doctrine (sə-**mar**-i-tən). *Torts*. The principle that a person who is injured while attempting to aid another in imminent danger, and who then sues the one whose negligence created the danger, will not be charged with contributory negligence unless the rescue attempt is an unreasonable one or the rescuer acts unreasonably in performing the attempted rescue. Cf. EMERGENCY DOCTRINE; RESCUE DOCTRINE; LOST-CHANCE DOCTRINE.

good-samaritan law. A statute that exempts from liability a person (such as an off-duty physician) who voluntarily renders aid to another in imminent danger but negligently causes injury while rendering the aid. • Some form of good-samaritan legislation has been enacted in all 50 states and in the District of Columbia. — Also written *Good Samaritan law*. — Also termed *good-samaritan statute*. Cf. GOOD SAMARITAN DOCTRINE.

"The so-called 'Good Samaritan Statutes' ... do not require aid to be given. They merely encourage doctors to stop and give aid to strangers in emergency situations by providing that no physician who *in good faith* renders such aid shall be liable in civil damages as a result of acts or omissions in rendering such aid. Some states have enacted statutes that require a person who is able to do so with no danger or peril to himself to come to the aid of another who is exposed to grave physical harm." Rollin M. Perkins & Ronald N. Boyce, *Criminal Law* 661 (3d ed. 1982).

goods and chattels (**chat**-əlz), *n*. Loosely, personal property of any kind; occasionally, tangible personal property only.

good time. The credit awarded to a prisoner for good conduct, which can reduce the duration of the prisoner's sentence. Cf. GOOD BEHAVIOR; EARNED TIME.

good title. See TITLE (2).

goodwill. A business's reputation, patronage, and other intangible assets that are considered when appraising the business, esp. for purchase; the ability to earn income in excess of the income that would be expected from the business viewed as a mere collection of assets. — Also written *good will*. Cf. *going-concern value* under VALUE.

> "Good will is to be distinguished from that element of value referred to variously as going-concern value, going value, or going business. Although some courts have stated that the difference is merely technical and that it is unimportant to attempt to separate these intangibles, it is generally held that going-concern value is that which inheres in a plant of an established business." 38 Am. Jur. 2d *Good Will* § 2, at 913 (1968).

goose case. See WHITEHORSE CASE.

gore (gor), *n.* **1.** *Hist.* A small, narrow slip of land. **2.** A small (often triangular) piece of land, such as may be left between surveys that do not close. **3.** In some New England states (such as Maine and Vermont), a county's subdivision that has little population and thus is not organized as a town.

Gothland sea laws. See LAWS OF WISBY.

go to protest. (Of commercial paper) to be dishonored by nonpayment or nonacceptance <the draft will go to protest>. See DISHONOR (1); PROTEST (2).

go to the country. See GOING TO THE COUNTRY.

govern, *vb.* (Of a precedent) to control a point in issue <the *Smith* case will govern the outcome of the appeal>.

governing body. 1. GOVERNMENT (2). **2.** A group of (esp. corporate) officers or persons having ultimate control <the board of directors is the governing body of XYZ, Inc.>.

government. 1. The structure of principles and rules determining how a state or organization is regulated. **2.** The sovereign power in a nation or state. **3.** An organization through which a body of people exercise political authority; the machinery by which sovereign power is expressed <the Canadian government>. • In this sense, the term refers collectively to the political organs of a country regardless of their function or level, and regardless of the subject matter they deal with. Cf. NATION; STATE.

central government. See *federal government* (1).

de facto government (di **fak**-toh). **1.** A government that has taken over the regular government and exercises sovereignty over a nation. **2.** An independent government established and exercised by a group of a country's inhabitants who have separated themselves from the parent state.

***federal government.* 1.** A national government that exercises some degree of control over smaller political units that have surrendered some degree of power in exchange for the right to participate in national political matters. — Also termed (in federal states) *central government.* **2.** The U.S. government. — Also termed *national government.*

local government. The government of a particular locality, such as a city or county; a governing body at a lower level than the state government. • The term includes a school district, fire district, transportation authority, and any other special-purpose district or authority. — Also termed *municipal government.*

mixed government. A government containing a blend of forms, as in democracy and monarchy.

municipal government. See *local government.*

national government. See NATIONAL GOVERNMENT, *federal government* (2).

proprietary government. *Hist.* A government granted by the Crown to an individual, in the nature of a feudatory principality, with powers of legislation formerly belonging to the owner of a county palatine. Cf. COUNTY PALATINE.

provisional government. A government temporarily established to govern until a permanent one is organized to replace it.

state government. The government of a state of the United States.

4. The executive branch of the U.S. government. **5.** The prosecutors in a given criminal case <the government has objected to the introduction of that evidence>. **6.** An academic course devoted to the study of government; political science <Bridges is enrolled in Government 101>.

government agency. See AGENCY (3).

government-agency security. See *government security* under SECURITY.

government agent. See AGENT.

governmental act. See GOVERNMENTAL FUNCTION.

governmental activity. See GOVERNMENTAL FUNCTION.

governmental employee benefit plan. See *governmental plan* under EMPLOYEE BENEFIT PLAN.

governmental enterprise. See ENTERPRISE.

governmental function. *Torts.* A government agency's conduct that is expressly or impliedly mandated or authorized by constitution, statute, or other law and that is carried out for the benefit of the general public. • Generally, a governmental entity is immune from tort liability for governmental acts. — Also termed *governmental act*; *governmental activity*. See PUBLIC-FUNCTION DOCTRINE. Cf. PROPRIETARY FUNCTION.

> "[A]ctivities of police or firefighters, though tortious, are usually considered governmental in the sense that they involve the kind of power expected of the government, even if its exercise in the specific case is wrongful. The city is immune as to such activities for this reason. On the other hand, if the city operates a local electric or water company for which fees are charged, this looks very much like private enterprise and is usually considered proprietary.... The difficult distinction between governmental and proprietary functions is even more troubling where the city's conduct combines both kinds of function at once. For example, operation of a sanitary sewer may be deemed governmental, but operation of a storm sewer may be deemed proprietary." *Prosser and Keeton on the Law of Torts* § 131, at 1053–54 (W. Page Keeton ed., 5th ed. 1984).

governmental-function theory. *Constitutional law.* A principle by which private conduct is characterized as state action, esp. for due-process and equal-protection purposes, when a private party is exercising a public function. • Under this theory, for example, a political party (which is a private entity) cannot exclude voters from primary elections on the basis of race. — Also termed *public-function rationale*.

governmental immunity. See *sovereign immunity* under IMMUNITY (1).

governmental instrumentality. A constitutionally or legislatively created agency that is immune from certain kinds of liability, as for taxes or punitive damages.

governmental-interest-analysis technique under INTEREST-ANALYSIS TECHNIQUE.

governmental plan. See EMPLOYEE BENEFIT PLAN.

governmental secret. Information belonging to the government and of a military or diplomatic nature, the disclosure of which would be contrary to the public interest. • Governmental secrets are privileged from disclosure. — Also termed *government secret*. See *executive privilege* under PRIVILEGE (3).

governmental trust. See TRUST.

governmental unit. A subdivision, agency, department, county, parish, municipality, or other unit of the government of a country or a state. • The term includes an organization with a separate corporate existence only if the organization can legally issue debt obligations on which interest is exempt from income taxation under national law. UCC § 9–102(a)(31).

government-annuity society. *Hist.* One of several organizations formed in England to enable the working class to provide for themselves by purchasing, on advantageous terms, a government annuity for life or for a term of years.

government bond. See BOND (3).

government contract. See *procurement contract* under CONTRACT.

government-contract defense. A theory allowing a supplier of goods to the federal government to escape civil liability under state law when the supplier has conformed to reasonably precise specifications established or approved by the government, when two conditions are satisfied: (1) if the supplier has warned the government about any dangers from the goods about which the supplier has knowledge but the government does not, and (2) if the government itself is immune from liability under the *Feres* doctrine. See FERES DOCTRINE.

government-controlled corporation. See *quasi-governmental agency* under AGENCY (3).

government corporation. See *public corporation* (3) under CORPORATION.

government enterprise. See ENTERPRISE.

government-in-exile. An individual or group of individuals residing in a foreign country while (1) claiming supreme authority over a country, (2) being recognized by the hosting country as the supreme authority over that other country, and (3) being organized to perform and actually performing some acts of state on behalf of the home country.

government insurance. See INSURANCE.

Government National Mortgage Association. A federally owned corporation that purchases, on the secondary market, residential mortgages originated by local lenders and that issues federally insured securities backed by these mortgages. — Abbr. GNMA. — Also termed *Ginnie Mae*.

government of laws. The doctrine that government must operate according to established, consistent legal principles and not according to the interests of those who happen to be in power at a given time; esp., the doctrine that judicial decisions must be based on the law, regardless of the character of the litigants or the personal predilections of the judge.

government plan. See *governmental plan* under PLAN.

Government Printing Office. A U.S. government office that prints and publishes federal laws, regulations, forms, and other federal-government documents. — Abbr. GPO.

government secret. See GOVERNMENTAL SECRET.

government-securities interdealer broker. See BROKER.

government security. See SECURITY.

government survey. See SURVEY.

government-survey system. A land-description method that divides the United States into checks or tracts of ground, which are further broken down into smaller descriptions, such as metes and bounds.

government tort. See TORT.

governor. The chief executive official of a U.S. state. • Governors are elected and usu. serve a two- or four-year term.

GPARM. See *graduated-payment adjustable-rate mortgage* under MORTGAGE.

GPO. *abbr.* GOVERNMENT PRINTING OFFICE.

grab law. The various means of debt collection involving remedies outside the scope of federal bankruptcy law, such as attachment and garnishment; aggressive collection practices.

grace period. A period of extra time allowed for taking some required action (such as making payment) without incurring the usual penalty for being late. • Insurance policies typically provide for a grace period of 30 days beyond the premium's due date, during which the premium may be paid without the policy being canceled. And Article 9 of the UCC provides for a 10–day grace period, after the collateral is received, during which a purchase-money security interest must be perfected to have priority over any conflicting security interests. — Also termed *days of grace*; *grace days*.

gradatim (grə-**day**-təm), *adv.* [Latin] *Roman law.* Gradually; by successive degrees. • *Gradatim* refers to the step-by-step admission of successors when there is no heir next in line. See GRADUS.

grade, *n. Criminal law.* An incremental step in the scale of punishments for offenses, based on a particular offense's seriousness <several grades of murder>. See DEGREE (2).

graded offense. See OFFENSE (1).

graduated lease. See LEASE.

graduated-payment adjustable-rate mortgage. See MORTGAGE.

graduated-payment mortgage. See MORTGAGE.

graduated tax. See *progressive tax* under TAX.

gradus (**gray**-dəs). [Latin "step"] **1.** *Roman law.* A step or degree in the familial relationship. • The term identified a position in the order of succession under a will. **2.** *Hist.* A degree, rank, or grade; specif., the rank of a master-in-chancery or a serjeant-at-law.

graffer (**graf**-ər). *Hist.* A notary or scrivener. — Also termed *graffarius*.

graffium (**graf**-ee-əm). *Hist.* A register or cartulary of deeds and other documents establishing title to property, esp. real property. — Also spelled *grafium*.

grafio (**gray**-fee-oh). [Law Latin] *Hist.* **1.** A baron; a viscount. • A grafio was inferior to a count. **2.** A fiscal judge, responsible for collecting taxes and fines. • The term was chiefly used among early European nations.

graft, *n.* **1.** The act of taking advantage of a position of trust to gain money or property dishonestly; esp., a public official's fraudulent acquisition of public funds. **2.** Money or property gained illegally or unfairly.

grainage. *Hist.* A duty consisting of one-twentieth of the salt imported by an alien into London.

grammatical interpretation. See INTERPRETATION.

granatarius (gran-ə-**tair**-ee-əs). [Law Latin] *Hist.* An officer in charge of a granary, esp. one in charge of a religious house's granary.

grand, *adj.* Of or relating to a crime involving the theft of money or property valued more than a statutorily established amount, and therefore considered more serious than those involving a lesser amount <grand theft>. See *grand larceny* under LARCENY. Cf. PETTY.

grand assize. See ASSIZE (5).

grand bill of sale. See BILL (7).

grand cape. See *cape magnum* under CAPE.

grand coutumier de pays et duché de Normandie (gron koo-t[y]oo-**myay** də **pay** ay də-**shay** də nor-man-**dee**). [French] *Hist.* A collection of the common or customary laws of the Duchy of Normandy. • The code was probably compiled in the 13th century, and it still remains the law of Jersey, except to the extent that it has been modified by later legislation and judicial decisions. See CLAMEUR DE HARO.

Grand Day. *English law.* **1.** *Hist.* One of four holy days on which the courts are not in session. • Each of the four court terms had a Grand Day. The four Grand Days were Candlemas Day (February 2), Ascension Day (March 25), St. John the Baptist Day (June 24), and All Saints' Day (November 1). The Inns of Court and of Chancery ceremoniously observed each Grand Day. **2.** A day in each term on which the Benchers of the Inns of Court host ceremonial dinners in their halls. See BENCHER. Cf. TERM (6).

grand distress. See DISTRESS.

grandfather, *vb.* To cover (a person) with the benefits of a grandfather clause <the statute sets the drinking age at 21 but grandfathers those who are 18 or older on the statute's effective date>.

grandfather clause. 1. *Hist.* A clause in the constitutions of some Southern states exempting from suffrage restrictions the descendants of men who voted before the Civil War. **2.** A statutory or regulatory clause that exempts a class of persons or transactions because of circumstances existing before the new rule or regulation takes effect.

grand inquest. See INQUEST.

grand juror. See JUROR.

grand jury. A body of (often 23) people who are chosen to sit permanently for at least a month — and sometimes a year — and who, in ex parte proceedings, decide whether to issue indictments. • If the grand jury decides that evidence is strong enough to hold a suspect for trial, it returns a bill of indictment (a *true bill*) charging the suspect with a specific crime. — Also termed *accusing jury*; *presenting jury*; *jury of indictment*. Cf. *petit jury* under JURY.

investigative grand jury. A grand jury whose primary function is to examine possible crimes and develop evidence not currently available to the prosecution.

screening grand jury. A grand jury whose primary function is to decide whether to issue an indictment.

special grand jury. A grand jury specially summoned, usu. when the regular grand jury either has already been discharged or has not been drawn; a grand jury with limited authority. — Also termed *additional grand jury*; *extraordinary grand jury*.

Grand Jury Clause. The clause of the Fifth Amendment to the U.S. Constitution requiring an indictment by a grand jury before a person can be tried for serious offenses.

grand-jury witness. See WITNESS.

grand larceny. See LARCENY.

Grand Remonstrance (ri-**mon**-strənts). *Hist.* A protest document issued by the House of Commons in 1641, setting forth numerous political grievances against Charles I. • The document demanded three primary remedial measures: (1) improvements in the administration of justice, (2) appointment of trustworthy ministers, and (3) enforcement of the laws against Roman Catholics. It was the first major split between the Royalist and Parliamentary parties, and it led Charles to seek the arrest of the five members who pushed the document through Commons.

grand serjeanty. See SERJEANTY.

Grand Survey. See *grand inquest* (2) under INQUEST.

grange (graynj). *Hist.* A farm furnished with all the necessities for husbandry, such as a barn, granary, and stables; esp., an outlying farm that belonged to a religious establishment or a feudal lord.

Granger Cases (**grayn**-jər). Six U.S. Supreme Court decisions that affirmed the government's right to regulate fees charged by common carriers, warehouses, and grain elevators. • The cases, decided in 1876, arose out of grangers' (i.e., farmers') frustration with the inflated prices they were paying to store and transport their agricultural products. Several state legislatures passed statutes regulating the rates. The affected businesses sued to have the statutes overturned on grounds that they violated the Commerce Clause and the Due Process Clause of the 14th Amendment. The Court rejected these claims, holding that the activities involved affected the public interest and were therefore subject to the government's regulatory authority.

grant, *n.* **1.** An agreement that creates a right of any description other than the one held by the grantor. • Examples include leases, easements, charges, patents, franchises, powers, and licenses. **2.** The formal transfer of real property. **3.** The document by which a transfer is effected; esp., DEED. **4.** The property or property right so transferred.

office grant. A grant made by a legal officer because the owner is either unwilling or unable to execute a deed to pass title, as in the case of a tax deed. See *tax deed* under DEED.

grant, *vb.* **1.** To give or confer (something), with or without compensation <the parents granted the car to their daughter on her 16th birthday>. **2.** To formally transfer (real property) by deed or other writing <the Lewisons granted the townhouse to the Bufords>. **3.** To permit or agree to <the press secretary granted the reporter access to the Oval Office>. **4.** To approve, warrant, or order (a request, motion, etc.) <the court granted the continuance>.

grantback, *n.* A license-agreement provision requiring the licensee to assign or license back to the licensor any improvements that the licensee might make to a patent or other proprietary right.

grant deed. See DEED.

grantee. One to whom property is conveyed.

grantee-grantor index. See INDEX (1).

grant-in-aid. 1. A sum of money given by a governmental agency to a person or institution for a specific purpose; esp., federal funding for a state public program. **2.** *Hist.* AID (1).

granting clause. The words that transfer an interest in a deed or other instrument, esp. an oil-and-gas lease. • In an oil-and-gas lease, the granting clause typically specifies the rights transferred, the uses permitted, and the substances covered by the lease.

grantor. 1. One who conveys property to another. **2.** SETTLOR (1).

grantor-grantee index. See INDEX (1).

grantor's lien. See *vendor's lien* under LIEN.

grantor trust. See TRUST.

grant to uses. *Hist.* A conveyance of legal title to real property to one person for the benefit of another. • If, for example, A conveyed land to B and his heirs to the use of C and his heirs, B — the feoffee to uses — acquired seisin in and had possession of the land and was considered the legal owner. C — the cestui que use — was considered the equitable owner of the land and was entitled to the land's rents, profits, and benefits. Because the cestui que use did not have seisin in the land, he was not subject to feudal payments. From the 13th century forward, the grant to uses was an increasingly popular mode of conveyance. See CESTUI QUE USE; STATUTE OF USES; USE (4).

grass hearth. *Hist.* A tenant's customary service, consisting of the tenant's bringing his plow to the lord's land and plowing it for one day.

gratia curiae (**gray**-shee-ə **kyoor**-ee-ee *or* -I). [Latin] Favor of the court. Cf. RIGOR JURIS.

gratification. *Archaic.* A voluntarily given reward or recompense for a service or benefit; a gratuity.

gratis (**grat**-is *or* **gray**-tis), *adj.* Free; without compensation.

gratis dictum. See DICTUM.

gratuitous (grə-**tyoo**-ə-təs), *adj.* **1.** Done or performed without obligation to do so; given without consideration <gratuitous promise>. Cf. ONEROUS (3). **2.** Done unnecessarily <gratuitous obscenities>. — **gratuity,** *n.*

gratuitous allowance. See ALLOWANCE (1).

gratuitous assignment. See ASSIGNMENT (2).

gratuitous bailment. See BAILMENT.

gratuitous consideration. See CONSIDERATION.

gratuitous contract. See CONTRACT.

gratuitous deed. See *deed of gift* under DEED.

gratuitous deposit. See *gratuitous bailment* under BAILMENT.

gratuitous gift. See GIFT.

gratuitous promise. See PROMISE.

gratuitous surety. See SURETY.

gravamen (grə-**vay**-mən). The substantial point or essence of a claim, grievance, or complaint.

gravatio (grə-**vay**-shee-oh). [Law Latin] *Hist.* An accusation or impeachment.

graymail. A criminal defendant's threat to reveal classified information during the trial in the hope of forcing the government to drop the criminal charge. Cf. BLACKMAIL; GREENMAIL; FEEMAIL.

gray market. See MARKET.

gray-market goods. See PARALLEL IMPORTS.

gray mule case. See WHITEHORSE CASE.

great bodily injury. See *grievous bodily harm* under HARM.

great care. See CARE.

great diligence. See DILIGENCE.

great fee. See FEE (2).

Great Inquest. See *grand inquest* (2) under INQUEST.

Great Lakes rule. *Maritime law.* The principle that an admiralty litigant is entitled to a jury trial in a contract or tort action if the lawsuit arises on waters that span more than one state. See 28 USCA § 1873.

> "The most important distinction between the law and admiralty 'sides' of federal court is that trial by jury is guaranteed for law claims through the Seventh Amendment, but where the case is maintained as an admiralty claim the litigant has neither constitutional nor statutory right to a jury trial. The one exception is the 'Great Lakes Rule' ...." Frank L. Maraist, *Admiralty in a Nutshell* 338 (2d ed. 1988).

Great Law, The. *Hist.* The first code of laws established in Pennsylvania. • The Great Law was passed by an assembly in 1682.

great pond. In Maine and Massachusetts, a body of water larger than ten acres, and thus subject to public ownership. — Also termed *public pond.*

Great Rolls of the Exchequer. See PIPE ROLLS.

great seal. See SEAL.

Great Survey. See *grand inquest* (2) under INQUEST.

great tithe. See TITHE.

Great Waters Program. A scheme created by Congress in 1990 to make the Environmental Protection Agency more directly responsible for protecting large bodies of fresh water and coastal waters from environmental harm caused by air pollution. Clean Air Act Amendments of 1990, 42 USCA § 7412(m).

Great Writ. See HABEAS CORPUS.

gree (gree), *n.* [Law French] *Hist.* A satisfaction received by a party for an offense or injury against the party. See SATISFACTION (1).

"Gree comes of the French word *gree*, good liking: and it signifies in our law, contentment or satisfaction; as in the statute of 1 R. 2, c. 15, to make gree to the parties is to give them contentment or satisfaction for an offence done unto them." *Termes de la Ley* 247 (1st Am. ed. 1812).

green card. A registration card evidencing a resident alien's status as a permanent U.S. resident.

green-card marriage. See *sham marriage* under MARRIAGE (1).

Green Cloth. See BOARD OF GREEN CLOTH.

greenmail. 1. The act of buying enough stock in a company to threaten a hostile takeover and then selling the stock back to the corporation at an inflated price. **2.** The money paid for stock in the corporation's buyback. Cf. BLACKMAIL; FEEMAIL; GRAYMAIL. **3.** A shareholder's act of filing or threatening to file a derivative action and then seeking a disproportionate settlement.

Green River ordinance. A local licensing law that protects residents from unwanted peddlers and salespersons, typically by prohibiting door-to-door solicitations without prior consent. • The ordinance takes its name from Green River, Wyoming, which enacted the first such law in the early 20th century before others came into vogue during the 1930s and 1940s throughout the United States.

green wax. (*pl.*) *Hist.* An Exchequer order (an *estreat*) directing a sheriff to collect the fines and amercements listed in the order. • The name derives from the color of the wax the Exchequer used on the estreat to certify its authenticity. See ESTREAT.

greffier (**gref**-ee-ər *or* gref-**yay**), *n.* [Law French] *Hist.* A registrar, esp. of a court; the court recordkeeper.

Gregorian calendar. See NEW STYLE.

Gregorian Code. See CODEX GREGORIANUS.

gremio juris, in. See IN GREMIO JURIS.

gremio legis, in. See IN GREMIO LEGIS.

Grenville Act. *Hist.* A statute that transferred jurisdiction of parliamentary election petitions from the whole House of Commons to select committees. • The Act was passed in 1770 and repealed in 1828.

G reorganization. See REORGANIZATION (2).

Gresham's law. The principle that inferior products or practices tend to displace superior ones. • This economic principle is popularly attributed to Sir Thomas Gresham (1519–1579), even though earlier writers such as Oresme and Copernicus discussed it earlier.

gressume (**gres**-əm). *Hist.* A fine paid by a copyhold tenant upon the transfer of a copyhold estate, esp. upon the death of the lord. — Also spelled *grasson*; *grassum*; *grossome*; *gersum*.

Gretna-Green marriage. See MARRIAGE (1).

grievance, *n.* **1.** An injury, injustice, or wrong that gives ground for a complaint <a petition for a redress of grievances>. **2.** The complaint itself <the client filed a grievance with the state-bar committee>. **3.** *Labor law.* A complaint that is filed by an employee or the employee's union representative and that usu. concerns working conditions, esp. an alleged violation of a collective-bargaining agreement. See *grievance arbitration* under ARBITRATION; GRIEVANCE PROCEDURE.

grievance arbitration. See ARBITRATION.

grievance procedure. *Labor law.* A process, consisting of several steps, for the resolution of an employee's complaint. • The first step usu. occurs at the shop level and is handled by a supervisor. If the grievance is not resolved at the first step, the grievance is appealed in successive steps that vary among collective-bargaining agreements. The final step of the procedure is grievance arbitration. See *grievance arbitration* under ARBITRATION; GRIEVANCE (3).

grievant, *n. Labor law.* An employee who files a grievance and submits it to the grievance procedure outlined in a collective-bargaining agreement.

grieve, *vb.* To contest under a grievance procedure <the union urged the employee to grieve the suspension>. — **grievable,** *adj.*

grievous bodily harm. See HARM.

GRM. *abbr.* GROSS-RENT MULTIPLIER.

grog-shop. See DRAM SHOP.

gross, easement in. See *easement in gross* under EASEMENT.

gross adventure. See ADVENTURE.

gross average. See *general average* under AVERAGE.

gross charter. See CHARTER (4).

gross earnings. See *gross income* under INCOME.

gross estate. See ESTATE.

gross income. See INCOME.

gross-income multiplier. See GROSS-RENT MULTIPLIER.

gross-income tax. See TAX.

gross interest. See INTEREST (3).

gross lease. See LEASE.

gross misdemeanor. See MISDEMEANOR.

gross national product. The market value of all goods and services produced in a country within a year, used to measure a country's economic development and wealth. — Abbr. GNP.

gross neglect of duty. See DESERTION.

gross negligence. See NEGLIGENCE.

grossome. *Hist.* See GRESSUME.

gross premium. See PREMIUM (1).

gross profit. See PROFIT.

gross receipts. *Tax.* The total amount of money or other consideration received by a business taxpayer for goods sold or services performed in a year, before deductions. IRC (26 USCA) § 448.

gross-receipts tax. See *gross-income tax* under TAX.

gross-rent multiplier. The ratio between the market value of rent-producing property and its annual gross rental income. • The gross-rent multiplier is used as a method to estimate a property's market value. — Abbr. GRM. — Also termed *gross-income multiplier*.

gross sales. See SALE.

gross spread. See SPREAD.

gross up, *vb. Slang. Tax.* To add back to a decedent's gross estate the gift taxes paid by the decedent or the decedent's estate on gifts made by the decedent or the decedent's spouse during the three-year period preceding the decedent's death. IRC (26 USCA) § 2035.

gross weight. See WEIGHT.

ground, *n.* The reason or point that something (as a legal claim or argument) relies on for validity <grounds for divorce> <several grounds for appeal>.

ground, *vb.* **1.** To provide a basis for (something, e.g., a legal claim or argument) <the decision was grounded on public policy>. **2.** To base (something, e.g., a legal principle or judicial decision) on <the court grounded the decision on common law> <strict liability is grounded on public policy>.

groundage (**grown**-dij), *n. Hist. Maritime law.* A tax or toll levied on a vessel lying in port; the tax or toll so paid.

ground landlord. *Hist.* The grantor of an estate on which ground rent is reserved. See *ground rent* under RENT (1).

ground lease. See LEASE.

groundless, *adj.* (Of a legal claim or argument) lacking reason or validity <groundless cause of action>. See FRIVOLOUS.

ground of action. See CAUSE OF ACTION.

ground rent. See RENT (1).

ground-rent lease. See *ground lease* under LEASE.

ground writ. See WRIT.

group annuity. See ANNUITY.

group boycott. See BOYCOTT.

grouping-of-contacts theory. See CENTER-OF-GRAVITY DOCTRINE.

group insurance. See INSURANCE.

group libel. See LIBEL.

group litigation. A set of lawsuits on behalf of or against numerous persons recognized as one litigating entity, such as a civil-rights group.

group policy. See *master policy* under INSURANCE POLICY.

growing crop. See CROP.

growing-equity mortgage. See MORTGAGE.

growth. The gain, increase, or expansion in value of securities or of a business.

growth company. See COMPANY.

growth fund. See MUTUAL FUND.

growth industry. An industry or business segment that demonstrates steadily rising sales and earnings.

growth management. *Land-use planning.* The regulation of a community's rate of growth through ordinances that restrict the issuance of residential building permits. See ZONING.

growth stock. See STOCK.

gruarii (groo-**air**-ee-I), *n. pl. Hist.* The principal officers of a forest. See FOREST.

grubstake contract. See CONTRACT.

grubstaking contract. See *grubstake contract* under CONTRACT.

grundnorm. See *basic norm* under NORM.

GSA. *abbr.* GENERAL SERVICES ADMINISTRATION.

guarantee, *n.* **1.** The assurance that a contract or legal act will be duly carried out. **2.** GUARANTY (1). **3.** Something given or existing as security, such as to fulfill a future engagement or a condition subsequent. **4.** One to whom a guaranty is made. — Also spelled *guaranty.* — **guarantee,** *vb.*

guarantee clause. 1. A provision in a contract, deed, or mortgage by which one person promises to pay the obligation of another. **2.** (*cap.*) U.S. Const. art. IV, § 4, under which the federal government ensures for the states both a republican form of government and protection from invasion or domestic violence.

guaranteed annual wage plan. *Labor law.* A wage-payment method in which the employer agrees either to pay employees a predetermined minimum sum each year or to provide a minimum number of hours of employment each year. • A wide variety of guaranteed annual wage plans are used. For example, an employer may agree to pay employees wages for each week in the year, even though work may not be available at certain times of the year. The purpose of such a plan is to provide a stable labor force year-round.

guaranteed bond. See BOND (3).

guaranteed investment contract. See INVESTMENT CONTRACT.

guaranteed-purchase contract. See *guaranteed-sale contract* under CONTRACT.

guaranteed-sale contract. See CONTRACT.

guaranteed stock. See STOCK.

guarantee stock. See STOCK.

guarantor. One who makes a guaranty or gives security for a debt. • While a surety's liability begins with that of the principal, a guarantor's liability does not begin until the principal debtor is in default. Cf. SURETY.

guarantor of collectibility. One who guarantees a debtor's solvency and is under a duty to pay only if the creditor is unable to collect from the principal debtor after exhausting all legal remedies, including demand, suit, judgment, and any supplementary proceedings.

guarantor of payment. One who guarantees payment of a negotiable instrument when it is due without the holder first seeking payment from another party. • A guarantor of payment is liable only if "payment guaranteed" or equivalent words are added to the guarantor's indorsement.

guarantor trust. See TRUST.

guaranty (**gar**-ən-tee), *n.* **1.** A promise to answer for the payment of some debt, or the performance of some duty, in case of the failure of another who is liable in the first instance. • The term is most common in finance and banking contexts. While a warranty relates to things (not persons), is not collateral, and need not be in writing, a guaranty is an undertaking that a person will pay or do some act, is collateral to the duty of the primary obligor, and must be in writing.

> "Both guaranty and warranty are undertakings by one party to another to indemnify the party assured against some possible default or defect. But a guaranty relates to the future, as a collateral promise designed to protect the promisee from loss in case another fails to perform his duty. A warranty relates to the present or past, and is an independent promise designed to protect the promisee from loss in the event that the facts warranted are not as the promisor states them to be when the contract is made. A warranty is broken as soon as it is made if the facts are not as represented, and is enforceable though oral; whereas a guaranty is not breached until a future default occurs, and is unenforceable unless in writing." Laurence P. Simpson, *Handbook on the Law of Suretyship* 23 (1950).

> "A transaction of guaranty involves at least three parties: a promisor, a creditor (the person to whom the promise is made), and a debtor — although at the time the promise is made, the person denominated the 'creditor' need not have extended the credit to the person denominated as the 'debtor.' The usual guaranty situation arises when the promisor makes a promise to the creditor either as to the solvency of the debtor or as to the payment of the debt." 38 Am. Jur. 2d *Guaranty* § 1, at 996 (1968).

absolute guaranty. An unqualified promise that the principal will pay or perform.

conditional guaranty. A guaranty that requires the performance of some condition by the creditor before the guarantor will become liable.

contingent guaranty. A guaranty in which the guarantor will not be liable unless a specified event occurs.

continuing guaranty. A guaranty that governs a course of dealing for an indefinite time or by a succession of credits. — Also termed *open guaranty*.

general guaranty. **1.** A guaranty addressed to no specific person, so that anyone who acts on it can enforce it. **2.** A guaranty for the principal's default on obligations that the principal undertakes with anyone.

guaranty of collection. A guaranty that is conditioned on the creditor's having first exhausted legal remedies against the principal debtor before suing the guarantor.

guaranty of payment. A guaranty that is not conditioned on the creditor's exhausting legal remedies against the principal debtor before suing the guarantor.

irrevocable guaranty (i-**rev**-ə-kə-bəl). A guaranty that cannot be terminated unless the other parties consent.

limited guaranty. An agreement to answer for a debt arising from a single transaction. — Also termed *noncontinuing guaranty*.

revocable guaranty. A guaranty that the guarantor may terminate without any other party's consent.

special guaranty. **1.** A guaranty addressed to a particular person or group of persons, who are the only ones who can enforce it. **2.** A guaranty that names a definite person as obligee and that can be accepted only by the person named.

specific guaranty. A guaranty of a single debt or obligation.

2. GUARANTEE (1).

guaranty bond. See BOND (2).

guaranty company. See *surety company* under COMPANY.

guaranty fund. See FUND (1).

guaranty insurance. See INSURANCE.

guaranty letter of credit. See *standby letter of credit* under LETTER OF CREDIT.

guaranty of collection. See GUARANTY.

guaranty of payment. See PAYMENT.

guaranty stock. See STOCK.

guaranty treaty. See TREATY.

guardage. *Hist.* **1.** WARDSHIP. **2.** GUARDIANSHIP.

guardhouse lawyer. See JAILHOUSE LAWYER.

guardian, *n.* **1.** One who has the legal authority and duty to care for another's person or property, esp. because of the other's infancy, incapacity, or disability. • A guardian may be appointed either for all purposes or for specific purposes. — Abbr. gdn. — Also termed *custodian*. — **guardianship,** *n.*

chancery guardian (**chan**-sər-ee). A guardian appointed by a court of chancery to manage both the person and the estate of the ward.

domestic guardian. A guardian appointed in the state in which the ward is domiciled.

foreign guardian. A guardian appointed by a court in a state other than the one in which the ward is domiciled. • A foreign guardian cares for the ward's property that is located in the state of appointment.

general guardian. A guardian who has general care and control of the ward's person and estate.

guardian ad litem (ad **lɪ**-təm). A guardian, usu. a lawyer, appointed by the court to appear in a lawsuit on behalf of an incompetent or minor party. — Also termed *special guardian*. Cf. NEXT FRIEND.

guardian by election. A guardian chosen by a child when he or she would otherwise be without one.

guardian by estoppel. See *quasi guardian*.

guardian by nature. *Hist.* The parental guardian of an heir apparent who has not yet reached the age of 21. • Although the common law made the father the guardian by nature and the mother only after the father's death, most states have given both parents equal rights of guardianship over their children (see, e.g., N.Y. Dom. Rel. Law § 81). — Also termed *natural guardian*.

guardian by nurture. *Hist.* The parental guardian of a child who is not the heir apparent, lasting until the child reaches the age of 14. — Also termed *guardian for nurture*.

> "There are also guardians *for nurture*, which are, of course, the father or mother, till the infant attains the age of fourteen years and, in default of father or mother, the ordinary usually assigns some discreet persons to take care of the infant's personal estate, and to provide for his maintenance and education." 1 William Blackstone, *Commentaries on the Laws of England* 449 (1765).

guardian by statute. See *statutory guardian*.

guardian de son tort. See *quasi guardian*.

guardian in chivalry. *Hist.* A guardian who, by virtue of knight's service, had custody of the body and lands of a male heir under 21 or a female heir under 14. • This type of guardian had no accountability for profits.

guardian in socage. *Hist.* A guardian for a child under 14 who has acquired lands by descent. • Such a guardian is usu. a relative who could not possibly inherit from the child. This type of guardianship applied to both the person and the property of the child and lasted only until the child was 14, when the child was allowed to select a guardian. See SOCAGE.

natural guardian. **1.** *Hist.* The eldest son's father, until the son turned 21. **2.** In the absence of statute, the father of a legitimate child until the child reaches the age of 21. • A father of illegitimate children may be appointed as their guardian upon the mother's death. **3.** Most commonly and by statute, either the father or the mother of a minor child — each bearing the title simultaneously. • If one parent dies, the other is the natural guardian.

partial guardian. A guardian whose rights, duties, and powers are strictly limited to those specified in a court order.

quasi-guardian. A guardian who assumes that role without any authority. • Such a person may be made to account as guardian. — Also termed *guardian by estoppel*; *guardian de son tort*.

special guardian. A guardian who has special or limited powers over the ward's person or estate. • Examples are guardians who have custody of the estate but not of the person, those who have custody of the person but not of the estate, and guardians ad litem.

statutory guardian. A guardian appointed by a court having special statutory jurisdiction. — Also termed *guardian by statute*.

testamentary guardian. A guardian appointed by a parent's will for the person and property of a child until the latter reaches the age of majority.

2. *Hist.* A mesne lord who was entitled to treat an infant heir's lands for all practical purposes as the lord's own, enjoying fully their use and whatever profits they yielded. • At the end of the guardianship, when the heir reached majority, no accounting was owed by the mesne lord.

guardian of the poor. *Hist.* A person in charge of the relief and maintenance of the poor in a parish. • Guardians of the poor administered poor-relief funds raised under the Poor Relief Act of 1601. • The function is now performed by local authorities.

guardian of the spiritualities. *Eccles. law.* A person who exercises the spiritual and ecclesiastical jurisdiction of a diocese during a vacancy in the see or the absence of the bishop.

guardian of the temporalities. *Eccles. law.* The person to whom custody of the secular possessions of a vacant see or abbey is committed by the Crown. • Temporalities (secular possessions) are the land, revenue, and tenements that archbishops and bishops have had annexed to their sees.

gubernator navis (g[y]oo-bər-**nay**-tər **nay**-vis). [Latin "ship helmsman"] *Roman law.* The pilot or steersman of a ship. • The *gubernator navis* could be sued for damages if he negligently caused a collision.

guerrilla warfare. See WARFARE.

guest. 1. A person who is entertained or to whom hospitality is extended. **2.** A person who pays for services at an establishment, esp. a hotel or restaurant. **3.** A nonpaying passenger in a motor vehicle.

business guest. *Torts.* See INVITEE.

social guest. *Torts.* See LICENSEE (2).

guest statute. A law that bars a nonpaying passenger in a noncommercial vehicle from suing the host-driver for damages resulting from the driver's ordinary negligence. • Though once common, guest statutes remain in force in only a few states. — Also termed *automobile guest statute.* Cf. FAMILY-PURPOSE RULE.

guidage. *Hist.* **1.** A toll or fee for guiding a traveler through strange or dangerous territory. **2.** The act of guiding a traveler through strange or dangerous territory.

guild. 1. *Hist.* A voluntary society or fraternity of persons employed in the same trade or craft, formed for the mutual benefit and protection of its members, who pay a fee (a *geld* or *gild*) for its general expenses. **2.** *Hist.* A company or corporation. **3.** A group of persons sharing a common vocation who unite to regulate the affairs of their trade in order to protect and promote their common vocation.

guildhall. *Hist.* **1.** The meeting place of a guild. — Also spelled *gildhall.* **2.** The chief hall of a city, used for holding court and the meetings of the municipal corporation.

guild rent. See RENT (1).

guilt, *n.* The fact or state of having committed a wrong, esp. a crime <the state's burden was to prove guilt beyond a reasonable doubt>. Cf. INNOCENCE.

guiltless, *adj.* **1.** Free from guilt; not having committed a wrong <guiltless of the crime>. **2.** Having the quality or appearance of innocence <even though she confessed, the defendant looked guiltless>.

guilty, *adj.* **1.** Having committed a crime; responsible for a crime <guilty of armed robbery>. **2.** Responsible for a civil wrong, such as a tort or breach of contract <guilty of fraudulent misrepresentation>. — **guiltily,** *adv.*

guilty, *n.* **1.** A plea of a criminal defendant who does not contest the charges. **2.** A jury verdict convicting the defendant of the crime charged.

guilty but mentally ill. A form of verdict in a criminal case whereby the jury rejects the defendant's insanity defense but still recommends psychiatric treatment because the defendant is mentally ill. — Abbr. GBMI; GMI. — Also termed *guilty but insane*; *guilty of the act, but so insane as not to be responsible.* See INSANITY DEFENSE.

guilty mind. See MENS REA.

guilty plea. See PLEA (1).

guilty verdict. See VERDICT.

gun-control law. A statute or ordinance that regulates the sale, possession, or use of firearms. • Gun-control laws vary widely among the states, and many cities have gun-control ordinances. Federal law prohibits the illegal sale, possession, and use of firearms. 18 USCA §§ 921–930. See BRADY ACT.

gun-jumping. *Slang.* The act of unlawfully soliciting the public's purchase of securities before the SEC approves a registration statement; the making of offers after the filing of a registration statement, but before its effective date, when such offers violate the Securities Act. — Also termed *conditioning the market.* See REGISTRATION STATEMENT.

gwalstow (**gwawl**-stoh). [fr. Old English *gwal* "gallows" + *stow* "place"] *Hist.* A place where criminals were executed.

gynecocracy (gɪ-nə-**kok**-rə-see *also* jin-ə *or* jɪ-nə-). Government by women; a political state in which women are legally capable of the highest office. — Also spelled *gynaecocracy.*

gyve (jɪv). (*usu. pl.*) *Hist.* A shackle for the leg.

H. *abbr.* **1.** HOUSE OF REPRESENTATIVES. **2.** House report. **3.** HOUSE BILL. **4.** In the citation of English statutes, a king named Henry. **5.** In the Year Books, the Hilary term. See YEAR BOOKS. **6.** In tax assessments and other such official reports, a house.

habe (**hay**-bee). [Law Latin] A form of the salutatory expression *ave* ("hail"). — Also termed *have* (**hay**-vee).

habeas corpora juratorum (**hay**-bee-əs **kor**-pər-ə juur-ə-**tor**-əm). [Law Latin "that you have the bodies of the jurors"] *Hist.* A writ commanding the sheriff to bring in jurors and, if necessary, to take their lands and goods as security to ensure their attendance in court for a trial setting. • This writ issued from the Court of Common Pleas and served the same purpose as a *distringas juratores* in the King's Bench. The writ was abolished in 1852.

habeas corpus (**hay**-bee-əs **kor**-pəs). [Law Latin "that you have the body"] A writ employed to bring a person before a court, most frequently to ensure that the party's imprisonment or detention is not illegal (*habeas corpus ad subjiciendum*). • In addition to being used to test the legality of an arrest or commitment, the writ may be used to obtain review of (1) the regularity of extradition process, (2) the right to or amount of bail, or (3) the jurisdiction of a court that has imposed a criminal sentence. — Abbr. H.C. — Sometimes shortened to *habeas*. — Also termed *writ of habeas corpus*; *Great Writ*.

> "The writ of habeas corpus, by which the legal authority under which a person may be detained can be challenged, is of immemorial antiquity. After a checkered career in which it was involved in the struggles between the common-law courts and the Courts of Chancery and the Star Chamber, as well as in the conflicts between Parliament and the crown, the protection of the writ was firmly written into English law by the Habeas Corpus Act of 1679. Today it is said to be 'perhaps the most important writ known to the constitutional law of England . . . .' " Charles Alan Wright, *The Law of Federal Courts* § 53, at 350 (5th ed. 1994) (quoting *Secretary of State for Home Affairs v. O'Brien*, [1923] A.C. 603, 609).

habeas corpus ad deliberandum et recipiendum (**hay**-bee-əs **kor**-pəs ad di-lib-ə-**ran**-dəm et ri-sip-ee-**en**-dəm). [Law Latin "that you have the body to consider and receive"] *Hist.* A writ used to remove a person for trial from one county to the county where the person allegedly committed the offense. Cf. EXTRADITION.

habeas corpus ad faciendum et recipiendum (**hay**-bee-əs **kor**-pəs ad fay-shee-**en**-dəm et ri-sip-ee-**en**-dəm). [Law Latin "that you have the body to do and receive"] *Hist.* A writ used in civil cases to remove the case, and also the body of the defendant, from an inferior court to a superior court. — Also termed *habeas corpus cum causa*. See CERTIORARI.

habeas corpus ad prosequendum (**hay**-bee-əs **kor**-pəs ad prahs-ə-**kwen**-dəm). [Law Latin "that you have the body to prosecute"] *Hist.* A writ used in criminal cases to bring before a court a prisoner to be tried on charges other than those for which the prisoner is currently being confined.

habeas corpus ad respondendum (**hay**-bee-əs **kor**-pəs ad ree-spon-**den**-dəm). [Law Latin "that you have the body to respond"] *Hist.* A writ used in civil cases to remove a person from one court's custody into that of another court, in which the person may then be sued.

habeas corpus ad satisfaciendum (**hay**-bee-əs **kor**-pəs ad sat-is-fay-shee-**en**-dəm). [Law Latin "that you have the body to make amends"] In England, a writ used to bring a prisoner against whom a judgment has been entered to some superior court so that the plaintiff can proceed to execute that judgment.

habeas corpus ad subjiciendum (**hay**-bee-əs **kor**-pəs ad səb-jish-ee-**en**-dəm). [Law Latin "that you have the body to submit to"] A writ directed to someone detaining another person and commanding that the detainee be brought to court. — Usu. shortened to *habeas corpus*.

habeas corpus ad testificandum (**hay**-bee-əs **kor**-pəs ad tes-ti-fi-**kan**-dəm). [Law Latin "that you have the body to testify"] *Hist.* A writ used in civil and criminal cases to bring a prisoner to court to testify.

habeas corpus cum causa. See *habeas corpus ad faciendum et recipiendum*.

Habeas Corpus Act. 1. One of the four great charters of English liberty (31 Car. 2, 1679), securing to English subjects speedy relief from all unlawful imprisonments. • The other three great charters are Magna Carta, the Petition of Right (3 Car. 1, 1628), and the Bill of Rights (1 Wm. & M. 1689). The Habeas Corpus Act does not apply in Scotland. **2.** A statute deriving ultimately from the English statute and enacted in the United States as a constitutional guarantee of personal liberty.

habeas corpus cum causa. See *habeas corpus ad faciendum et recipiendum* under HABEAS CORPUS.

habendum clause (hə-**ben**-dəm). **1.** The part of a deed that defines the extent of the interest being granted and any conditions affecting the grant. • The introductory words to the clause are ordinarily *to have and to hold.* — Also termed *to-have-and-to-hold clause.* **2.** An oil-and-gas lease provision that defines the lease's primary term and that usu. extends the lease for a secondary term of indefinite duration as long as oil, gas, or other minerals are being produced. • Most jurisdictions require production of paying quantities to keep the lease in effect.

habendum et tenendum (hə-**ben**-dəm et tə-**nen**-dəm). [Law Latin] *Hist.* To have and to hold. • This formal phrase appeared in land deeds and defined the estate or interest being transferred. See HABENDUM CLAUSE; TO HAVE AND TO HOLD.

habentes homines (hə-**ben**-teez **hom**-ə-neez), *n.* [Law Latin "men who have"] *Hist.* Rich men. — Also termed *foesting-men.*

habere (hə-**beer**-ee), *vb.* [Latin "to have"] *Roman law.* To have (the right to) something. • This term was sometimes distinguished from *tenere* (to hold) and *possidere* (to possess), with *habere* referring to the right, *tenere* to the fact, and *possidere* to both.

> " 'Habere' has two meanings; for we say that the owner of a thing 'has' it and also that a nonowner who holds the thing 'has' it. Lastly, we use the word in relation to property deposited with us." *Digest of Justinian* 45.1.38.9 (Ulpian, Ad Sabinum 49).

habere facias possessionem (hə-**beer**-ee **fay**-shee-əs pə-zes[h]-ee-**oh**-nəm), *n.* [Law Latin "that you cause to have possession"] *Hist.* A writ giving a successful ejectment-action plaintiff the possession of the recovered land. — Often shortened to *habere facias* or *hab. fa.*

habere facias seisinam (hə-**beer**-ee **fay**-shee-əs **see**-zi-nəm), *n.* [Law Latin "that you cause to have seisin"] *Hist.* A writ of execution commanding the sheriff to give the applicant seisin of the recovered land. • This writ was the proper process for giving seisin of a freehold, as distinguished from giving only a chattel interest in land. See SEISIN.

habere facias visum (hə-**beer**-ee **fay**-shee-əs **vI**-səm *or* -zəm), *n.* [Law Latin "that you cause to have a view"] *Hist.* A writ allowing a litigant to inspect the lands in controversy.

habere licere (hə-**beer**-ee li-**seer**-ee), *vb.* [Latin "to allow to have"] *Roman law.* To allow a purchaser to possess and enjoy property undisturbed. • The term denoted a seller's duty; if the duty was breached, the purchaser could maintain an *actio ex empto.*

hab. fa. *abbr.* HABERE FACIAS POSSESSIONEM.

habitability. The condition of a building in which inhabitants can live free of serious defects that might harm health and safety <lack of running water adversely affects the apartment's habitability>.

habitability, implied warranty of. See *implied warranty of habitability* under WARRANTY (2).

habitancy (**hab**-ə-tən-see). **1.** DOMICILE. **2.** RESIDENCE.

habitant (a-bee-**ton**), *n.* [French] **1.** *Hist. French law.* A person holding land in feudal tenure from a seignior. **2.** A native of Canada of French descent, esp. one from the farming class.

habitatio (hab-ə-**tay**-shee-oh), *n.* [Latin "dwelling"] *Roman law.* The right to dwell (in a place); the right of free residence in another's house. • This right was usu. given by will.

habitation. 1. The act of inhabiting; occupancy. **2.** A dwelling place; a domicile. **3.** *Civil law.* A right to dwell in the property of another. See RESIDENCE; DOMICILE. Cf. USUFRUCT.

habit evidence. See EVIDENCE.

habitual criminal. See RECIDIVIST.

habitual offender. See RECIDIVIST.

hable (**ab**-əl), *n.* [Law French] *Hist.* A port or harbor; a station for ships.

hacienda particular (ah-**syen**-dah [*or* hah-see-**en**-də] pahr-tee-koo-**lahr**), *n. Spanish law.* Private property.

hacienda pública (ah-**syen**-dah [*or* hah-see-**en**-də] **poo**-blee-kah), *n. Spanish law.* **1.** Public revenue or assets. **2.** A government treasury.

hacienda social (ah-**syen**-dah [*or* hah-see-**en**-də] soh-**syahl**), *n. Spanish law.* Property belonging to a corporation or partnership.

had. Commenced or begun, as used in a statute providing that no legal proceeding may be *had* (usu. followed by the words *or maintained*) <no action for foreclosure may be had or maintained until the debtor has been given at least 30 days' notice>.

hadgonel (**had**-gə-nel), *n. Hist.* A tax or mulct.

***Hadley v. Baxendale* rule.** *Contracts.* The principle that consequential damages will be awarded for breach of contract only if, at the time of contracting, the parties contemplated that this type of damage would result from the breach. *Hadley v. Baxendale*, 9 Exch. 341 (1854). • *Hadley v. Baxendale* is best known for its impact on a nonbreaching party's ability to recover consequential damages, but the case also confirmed the principle that the nonbreaching party may recover damages that arise naturally from the breach. See DAMAGES.

> "The rationale of the decision appears in Baron Alderson's noted statement of what came to be known as the two rules of *Hadley v. Baxendale*. The first rule was that the injured party may recover damages for loss that 'may fairly and reasonably be considered [as] arising naturally, i.e., according to the usual course of things. . . .' The second and more significant rule went to recovery of what have come to be known as 'consequential' damages. . . . By introducing this requirement of 'contemplation' for the recovery of consequential damages, the court imposed an important new limitation on the scope of recovery that juries could allow for breach of contract. The result was to impose a more severe limitation on the recovery of damages for breach of contract than that applicable to actions in tort or for breach of warranty, in which substantial or proximate cause is the test." E. Allan Farnsworth, *Contracts* § 12.14, at 874–75 (1982).

had-not test. See BUT-FOR TEST.

haec est conventio (**heek** est kən-**ven**-shee-oh). [Law Latin] *Hist.* This is the agreement. • These formal words commonly prefaced written agreements.

haec est finalis concordia (**heek** est fi-**nay**-lis kən-**kor**-dee-ə). [Law Latin] *Hist.* This is the final agreement. • The words that began a fine, a fictitious judicial proceeding formerly in use as a mode of conveying land. See FOOT OF THE FINE; FINE.

haec verba. See IN HAEC VERBA.

haereditas. See HEREDITAS.

haeres. See HERES.

haeretico comburendo. See DE HAERETICO COMBURENDO.

hafne (**hay**-vən), *n.* [Old English] A haven or port.

hafne court. *Hist.* Haven courts; one of several courts anciently held in certain ports in England.

Hague Academy of International Law (hayg). A center for advanced studies in international law, both public and private, aimed at facilitating the comprehensive and impartial examination of problems of international legal relations. • It was founded in 1923 on the initiative of the Carnegie Endowment for International Peace and the Institut de Droit International. — Also termed *Académie de Droit International de La Haye.*

Hague Convention. One of a number of international conventions that address different legal issues and attempt to standardize procedures between nations.

Hague Convention on the Civil Aspects of International Child Abduction. An international convention (established in 1980) that seeks to counteract child-snatching by noncustodial parents. • The Hague Convention is a private legal mechanism available to parents seeking the return of, or access to, their children. More than 46 countries are parties to the Convention, including the United States, which became a signatory on July 1, 1988.

Hague Convention on the Service Abroad of Judicial and Extrajudicial Documents. An international convention, convened on November 15, 1965, that dictates the formal and usu. complicated procedures for effecting service of process in a foreign country. • More than 35 countries are parties to the convention, including the United States, which became a signatory on February 10, 1969.

Hague Convention on the Taking of Evidence Abroad in Civil or Commercial Matters. An international convention, convened on October 26, 1968, that provides the formal procedures for obtaining evidence in a foreign country, such as taking a deposition abroad. • More than 27 countries are parties, including the United States, which became a signatory on October 7, 1972.

Hague Tribunal. *Int'l law.* A permanent court of arbitration established by the Hague Peace Conference of 1899 to facilitate immediate recourse to arbitration to settle international differences. • The court was given jurisdiction over all arbitration cases, unless the parties agreed to institute a special tribunal. An international bureau was likewise established to serve as a registry for the court and to issue communications about the court's meetings. The court is "permanent" only in the sense that there is a permanent list of members from whom arbitrators in a given case are selected. Apart from making minor changes in the court, the Second Hague Conference of 1907 provided that, of the two arbitrators appointed by each party, only one should be a national of the appointing state.

haircut. *Securities.* The discount required by the National Association of Securities Dealers on the value of stock that a brokerage firm holds in its own account at the time of filing a monthly report about the firm's net capital condition.

haircut reorganization. See REORGANIZATION (1).

half, *n.* One of two equal parts into which a thing can be divided; MOIETY.

half blood. See BLOOD.

half brother. A male sibling with whom one shares the same father or the same mother, but not both; a brother by one parent only.

halfendeal (**hahv**-ən-deel), *n.* [fr. Law Latin *halfendele*] *Archaic.* Half a thing; a moiety. — Also spelled *half endeal*; *half-endeal*.

half nephew. The son of one's half brother or half sister.

half niece. The daughter of one's half brother or half sister.

half orphan. See ORPHAN (2).

half-pilotage. See PILOTAGE.

half-proof. *Civil law.* **1.** Proof established by one witness, or by a private instrument. See UNUS NULLUS RULE. **2.** Prima facie proof that is nonetheless insufficient to support a sentence or decree.

half-seal. *Hist.* A seal used in the Court of Chancery to seal commissions to the Court of Delegates on the appeal of an ecclesiastical or maritime case. • The use of the seal ended when the Court of Delegates was abolished in 1832. See COURT OF DELEGATES.

half section. See SECTION.

half sister. A female sibling with whom one shares the same father or the same mother, but not both; a sister by one parent only.

half-timer. *Hist.* In England, a child excused from full-time attendance at school under the Factory and Workshop Act of 1908 so that the child could work part-time in a factory or workshop. • The Factory and Workshop Acts from 1901 to 1911 were repealed by the Factory and Workshop (Cotton Cloth Factories) Act of 1929 and the Factories Act of 1937.

half-tongue. *Hist.* In England, a jury empaneled to try an alien, and composed half of one nationality and half of another. • The use of this type of jury ended in 1914 with the passage of the Status of Aliens Act.

halfway house. A transitional housing facility designed to rehabilitate people who have recently left a prison or medical-care facility, or who otherwise need help in adjusting to a normal life. — Also termed *residential community treatment center*.

half-year. See YEAR.

Halifax law. **1.** LYNCH LAW; more broadly, an irrevocable punishment carried out after a summary trial. **2.** The summary and unauthorized trial and execution (usu. by decapitation) of a person accused of a crime. • This term comes from the parish of Halifax, in England, where — according to custom in the forest of Hardwick — this form of private justice was anciently practiced by the free burghers against people accused of stealing. Thieves could be condemned to death by beheading on market day. The last such case is said to have occurred in 1650. — Also termed *gibbet law*; *Halifax inquest*.

haligemot. See HALLMOOT.

hall. 1. A building or room of considerable size, used for meetings of bodies such as public assemblies, conventions, and courts. **2.** *Hist.* A manor house or chief mansion house. • It was called a *hall* because the magistrate's court was typically held there.

hallage (**hawl**-ij), *n. Hist.* A fee or toll due for goods or merchandise sold in a hall used as a market; a toll payable to the lord of a fair or market for commodities sold in the common hall.

hallazgo (ah-**yahs**-goh), *n.* [Spanish] *Spanish law.* **1.** The finding and taking possession of ownerless property. **2.** The first occupant recognized by law.

halle-gemot (**hawl**-gə-moht), *n.* See HALLMOOT.

hallmark. 1. An official stamp affixed by goldsmiths and silversmiths on articles made of gold or silver to show genuineness. **2.** A mark of genuineness.

hallmoot (**hawl**-moot), *n. Hist.* **1.** A court baron; esp., a court held to settle differences between feudal tenants. • Wealthy abbeys commonly held hallmoot courts for lesser tenants, and a central court (the *libera curia*) for greater freehold tenants. **2.** A convention of citizens in their public hall. — Also spelled *hallmote*; *halle-gemot*; *haligemot*; (in sense 2 only) *folkmote*. See COURT BARON.

halymote (**hal**-ə-moht), *n. Hist.* An ecclesiastical court said to have been anciently held on the Sunday before St. Thomas's Day. • Although this definition is standard, the *Oxford English Dictionary* calls it erroneous. In fact, the term appears to be a variant spelling of *hallmoot*. — Also spelled (prob. through false etymology) *holymote*.

ham (ham *or* am). **1.** A place of dwelling; a village. • This word now usu. appears in compound form at the end of place names, such as *Buckingham*. **2.** A small (esp. enclosed) pasture; a piece of land. — Also spelled *hamm*. Cf. HAMLET.

hamel. See HAMLET.

hameleta. See HAMLET.

hamesucken (**haym**-sək-ən), *n. Hist.* The crime of housebreaking or burglary accompanied by violence. — Also spelled *hamesecken*; *hamesoken*.

> "Burglary, or nocturnal housebreaking, *burgi latrocinium*, which by our ancient law was called *hamesecken*, as it is in Scotland to this day, has always been looked upon as a very heinous offence. . . ." 4 William Blackstone, *Commentaries on the Laws of England* 223 (1769).

hamlet. A small village; a part or member of a vill. • A hamlet in a rural community might consist of no more than a store, a church, and a few residences. — Also termed *hamel*; *hameleta*; *hamleta*. See VILL. Cf. HAM.

hamleta. See HAMLET.

hammer, *n. Slang.* A forced sale; a sale at public auction <her jewelry was brought to the hammer>. See *forced sale* under SALE.

Hammurabi, Code of. See CODE OF HAMMURABI.

hanaper (**han**-ə-pər), *n.* [Law Latin *hanaperium* "hamper"] *Hist.* **1.** A basket or hamper used by the Chancery to store writs and returns. **2.** The treasury of the Chancery, funded from the fees charged for writs. Cf. FISCUS.

Hanaper Office. *Hist.* An office formerly belonging to the common-law jurisdiction of the Chancery Court. • The term derives from the storage of writs in a hamper (*in hanaperio*). Crown writs, on the other hand, were stored in the Petty Bag Office. The Hanaper Office was abolished in 1842. See BAGA.

hand, *n.* **1.** A person's handwriting <a holographic will must be in the testator's hand>. **2.** An instrumental part <he had a hand in the crime>. **3.** One who performs some work or labor <Hickory was one of the Gales' hired hands>. **4.** (*usu. pl.*) Possession <the cocaine was now in the hands of the police>. **5.** Assistance <the carpenter lent a hand to the project>. **6.** A measure of length equal to four inches, used in measuring the height of horses <the pony stood ten hands tall>. **7.** *Hist.* An oath <he gave his hand on the matter>. **8.** One or two sides or aspects of an issue or argument <on the one hand we can argue for imprisonment, on the other for leniency>.

hand, *vb.* To give; to deliver <he handed over the documents>.

handbill. A written or printed notice displayed, handed out, or posted, usu. to inform interested people of an event or of something to be done. • Posting and distribution of handbills is regulated by ordinance or statute in most localities.

hand down, *vb.* To announce or file an opinion in a case. • The term was originally used in connection with an appellate-court opinion sent to the court below; it was later expanded to include any decision by a court on a case or point under consideration.

hand-fasting. *Hist.* A betrothal; marrying by clasping another's hand and agreeing to live together as husband and wife.

Hand formula. A balancing test for determining whether conduct has created an unreasonable risk of harm, first formulated by Judge Learned Hand in *United States v. Carroll Towing Co.*, 159 F.2d 169 (2d Cir. 1947). • Under this test, an actor is negligent if the burden of taking adequate precautions against the harm is outweighed by the probable gravity of the harm multiplied by the probability that the harm will occur.

> "The legal standard applicable to most unintentional tort cases is that of negligence, defined by Judge Learned Hand as follows: the defendant is guilty of negligence if the loss caused by the accident, multiplied by the probability of the accident's occurring, exceeds the burden of the precautions that the defendant might have taken to avert it. This is an economic test. . . . Although the Hand formula is of relatively recent origin, the method that it capsulizes has been the basic one used to determine negligence ever since negligence was first adopted as the standard to govern accident cases." Richard A. Posner, *Economic Analysis of Law* § 6.2, at 122–23 (2d ed. 1977).

handhabend (**hand**-hab-ənd), *adj. Hist.* (Of a thief) caught in possession of a stolen item.

handhabend, *n.* [fr. Old English *aet haebbendre handa* "at or with a having hand"] *Hist.* **1.** The bearing of stolen goods in hand or about the person. Cf. BACKBEREND. **2.** A thief or another person caught carrying stolen goods. **3.** Jurisdiction to try a person caught carrying stolen goods. — Also spelled *hand-habende.*

hand money. Money paid in hand to bind a bargain; earnest money paid in cash. See EARNEST MONEY.

hand note. See NOTE (1).

handsale. *Hist.* A sale memorialized by shaking hands. • Over time, *handsale* also came to refer to the earnest money given immediately after the handshake. In some northern European countries, shaking hands was necessary to bind a bargain. This custom sometimes persists for oral contracts. The Latin phrase for *handsale* was *venditio per mutuam manuum complexionem* ("a sale by the mutual joining of hands"). — Also spelled *handsel.*

hands-off agreement. A noncompete contractual provision between an employer and a former employee prohibiting the employee from using information learned during his or her employment to divert or to steal customers from the former employer.

hand up, *vb.* (Of a grand jury) to deliver an indictment to a criminal court.

handwriting. *Evidence.* **1.** A person's chirography; the cast or form of writing peculiar to a person, including the size, shape, and style of letters, and whatever gives individuality to one's writing. **2.** Something written by hand; a writing specimen. • Nonexpert opinion about the genuineness of handwriting, based on familiarity not acquired for litigation purposes, can authenticate a document. Fed. R. Evid. 901(b)(2).

hang, *vb.* (Of a jury) to be unable to reach a verdict <the jury was hung after 12 hours of continuous deliberation>. See *hung jury* under JURY.

hanged, drawn, and quartered. *Hist.* An ancient sentence for high treason, consisting of the prisoner's being drawn on a hurdle to the place of execution, hanged by the neck (but not until dead), disemboweled, and beheaded, and the body then divided into four pieces for the king's disposal. • The sentence was abolished in England in 1870. See TREASON.

hanging, *n.* The act of carrying out an execution by suspending the person above the ground by a rope around the person's neck. • Death is caused by asphyxiation (by being hoisted from the ground) or by a sudden breaking of the cervical vertebrae (by being dropped from a height).

hanging in chains. *Hist.* In England, in atrocious cases, the practice of suspending an executed murderer's body by chains near where the crime was committed. • Hanging in chains was abolished in 1834.

hanging judge. See JUDGE.

hangman. An executioner, esp. one who executes condemned criminals by hanging.

Hansard (**han**-sərd). The official reports of debates in the British Parliament. • The name derives from Luke Hansard, printer of the *Journal of the House of Commons* from 1774 to 1828. The name has varied at different times. In 1892 it became the *Authorised Edition*; in 1909 the title was changed to the *Official Report*; and since 1943 the name *Hansard* has been added to *Official Report*. — Also termed *Hansard Official Report*; *Hansard's Debates*.

hanse (hans), *n.* [German] *Hist.* **1.** A merchant guild, esp. one engaging in trade abroad. **2.** A fee for entrance to the guild; an impost levied on merchants not belonging to the guild.

hanseatic (han-see-**at**-ik), *adj. Hist.* **1.** Of or relating to the union of the Hanse Towns, usu. referred to as the *Hanseatic League*. **2.** Of or relating to a hanse or commercial alliance.

Hanse Towns (hans). *Hist.* The collective name of certain German cities — including Lübeck, Hamburg, and Bremen — that allied in the 12th century to protect and further their mutual commercial interests. • This alliance was usu. called the *Hanseatic League*. The League framed and promulgated a code of maritime law known as the *Laws of the Hanse Towns*, or *Jus Hanseaticum Maritimum*. The League's power peaked in the 14th century, then gradually declined until 1669, when the last general assembly was held.

Hanse Towns, laws of the. *Hist.* The laws of the Hanseatic towns, esp. that of Lübeck, published in German at Lübeck in 1597 and revised and enlarged in 1614.

happiness, right to pursue. The constitutional right to pursue any lawful business or activity — in any manner not inconsistent with the equal rights of others — that might yield the highest enjoyment, increase one's prosperity, or allow the development of one's faculties.

harassment (**har**-əs-mənt *or* hə-**ras**-mənt). Words, conduct, or action (usu. repeated or persistent) that, being directed at a specific person, annoys, alarms, or causes substantial emotional distress in that person and serves no legitimate purpose. • Harassment is actionable in some circumstances, as when a creditor uses threatening or abusive tactics to collect a debt. — **harass** (**har**-əs *or* hə-**ras**), *vb.*

same-sex harassment. Sexual harassment by a supervisor of an employee of the same sex.

sexual harassment. See SEXUAL HARASSMENT.

harbinger (**hahr**-bin-jər), *n.* **1.** *Hist.* In England, a royal officer who went ahead and was responsible for securing lodging for troops or for a traveling royal entourage. **2.** A person or thing that predicts what is to come <a harbinger of bad news>.

harbor, safe. See SAFE HARBOR.

harboring, *n.* The act of affording lodging, shelter, or refuge to a person, esp. a criminal or illegal alien.

harbor line. A line marking the boundary of a certain part of public water that is reserved for a harbor; esp., the line beyond which wharves and other structures may not extend.

hard case. A lawsuit involving equities that tempt a judge to stretch or even disregard a principle of law at issue — hence the expression, "Hard cases make bad law."

hard currency. See CURRENCY.

hard dollars. 1. Cash proceeds given to a seller. **2.** The part of an equity investment that is not deductible in the first year. Cf. SOFT DOLLARS.

hard goods. See *durable goods* under GOODS.

hard labor. Work imposed on prisoners as additional punishment, usu. for misconduct while in prison. • Several states (such as Louisiana, Maine, and New Jersey) impose hard labor as a sentence for a variety of crimes. Hard labor is also imposed in military sentencing.

hard-look doctrine. *Administrative law.* The principle that a court should carefully review an administrative-agency decision to ensure that the decision did not result from expediency, pressure, or whim.

hard money. See MONEY.

hard sell. A sales practice characterized by slogans, aggression, intimidation, and urgent decision-making. Cf. SOFT SELL.

hardship. 1. Privation; suffering or adversity. **2.** *Zoning.* A ground for a variance under some zoning statutes if the zoning ordinance as applied to a particular property is unduly oppressive, arbitrary, or confiscatory. **3.** The severity with which a proposed construction of law would bear on a particular case, sometimes forming a basis (also known as an argument *ab inconvenienti*) against the construction. See AB INCONVENIENTI; HARD CASE.

harm, *n.* Injury, loss, or detriment.

bodily harm. Physical pain, illness, or impairment of the body.

grievous bodily harm. *Criminal and tort law.* Serious physical impairment of the human body. • Typically, the fact-finder must decide in any given case whether the injury meets this general standard. — Abbr. g.b.h. — Also termed *great bodily injury.*

physical harm. Any physical impairment of land, chattels, or the human body.

social harm. An adverse effect on any social interest that is protected by the criminal law.

> "If the phrase 'social harm' is used to include every invasion of any social interest which has been placed under the protection of a criminal sanction (whether by common law or by statute), every crime may be said to involve, in addition to other requirements, (1) the happening of social harm and (2) the fact that the act of some person was the cause of this harm." Rollin M. Perkins & Ronald N. Boyce, *Criminal Law* 830 (3d ed. 1982).

harmful error. See *reversible error* under ERROR.

harmless error. See ERROR (2).

harmonic plane. An arbitrarily selected zero chosen by the U.S. Coast and Geodetic Survey to serve as the base for its tidal tables, charts, and maps.

harmony. Agreement or accord; conformity <the decision in *Jones* is in harmony with earlier Supreme Court precedent>. — **harmonize,** *vb.*

harrow (**har**-oh *or* hə-**roh**), *n.* [fr. Old French *haro*] *Hist.* In Norman and early English law, an outcry (or hue and cry) after felons and malefactors. — Also termed *haro.* See HUE AND CRY. Cf. CLAMEUR DE HARO.

Harter Act. *Maritime law.* An 1893 federal statute that allocates the risks of damage to cargo at sea by relieving a carrier of liability for certain events (such as negligent navigation) provided that the carrier has exercised due diligence in sending the ship out in a seaworthy condition. 46 USCA app. §§ 190–196. See CARRIAGE OF GOODS BY SEA ACT.

> "During the eighteenth century, common carriers began limiting this liability by inserting clauses in bills of lading relieving them from some of the risks of the voyage. Because of their superior bargaining power, the carriers, through such clauses, eventually were able to exculpate themselves from all liability to the shipper or his consignee, even that for damages caused by the negligence of the master and crew during the voyage. American courts refused to honor these exculpatory clauses, holding them invalid because of the inequality of bargaining power between shippers and common carriers. However, courts of other maritime nations upheld such clauses. As a result, American merchant vessels were at a disadvantage in the world market. To lessen this disadvantage, Congress passed the Harter Act. . . ." Frank L. Maraist, *Admiralty in a Nutshell* 58–59 (2d ed. 1988).

Hart–Scott–Rodino Antitrust Improvement Act. A federal statute, enacted in 1976, that generally strengthens the Justice Department's antitrust enforcement powers, esp. by requiring firms to give notice to the Federal Trade Commission and the Justice Department of an intent to merge if one of the firms has annual revenues or assets exceeding $100 million, and the acquisition price or value of the acquired firm exceeds $15 million.

haspa (**has**-pə), *n.* [Law Latin] *Hist.* The hasp of a door. • Livery of seisin was often made in the doorway of a structure located on the property being transferred.

hasta (**has**-tə), *n.* [Latin "spear"] **1.** *Roman law.* A sale by auction, indicated by a spear placed into the ground. • The phrase *hastae subicere* ("to put under the spear") meant to put up for sale at auction. **2.** *Hist.* A symbol used to invest a fief.

Hatch Act. A federal statute, enacted in 1939, that restricts political-campaign activities by federal employees and limits contributions by individuals to political campaigns. 5 USCA §§ 1501–1508. • Senator Carl Hatch sponsored the Act following disclosures that Works Progress Administration officials were using their positions to campaign for the Democratic Party.

hate crime. See CRIME.

hate speech. See SPEECH.

hat money. *Maritime law.* A small gratuity traditionally paid to the master (and sometimes the crew) of a ship for the care of the cargo; PRIMAGE. — Also termed *pocket money.*

hauber ([**h**]**aw**-bər), *n.* [Old French] *Hist.* A high lord; a great baron.

haulage royalty. See ROYALTY (2).

haustus (**haws**-təs), *n.* [Latin "a drawing"] *Roman law.* A species of servitude consisting in the right to draw water from a well or spring on another's property — the term being common esp. in the form *aquaehaustus.* • A right-of-way (*iter*) to the well was implied in the easement.

have. See HABE.

have and hold. See TO HAVE AND TO HOLD.

hawker. An itinerant or traveling salesperson who sells goods in a public street, esp. one who, in a loud voice, cries out the benefits of the items offered for sale; a peddler. • A hawker is usu. required to have a license.

hawking. The act of offering, by outcry, goods for sale from door to door or on a public street.

haybote (**hay**-boht), *n.* [fr. French *haye* "a hedge" + Saxon *bote* "an allowance"] *Hist.* The right or privilege of a tenant for life or years to have material to repair the hedges or fences, or to make farming implements. — Also termed *hedgebote.* See BOTE.

hayward. *Hist.* **1.** An officer of a town or manor responsible for maintaining fences and hedges, esp. to prevent cattle from breaking through to an enclosed pasture. **2.** A cattle herdsman.

Hazantown agreement (**hay**-zən-town). A type of collective-bargaining agreement used in the garment industry, governing the relationship between a jobber and the contractors that produce the jobber's garments. • The agreement does not govern the relationship between the jobber and its own employees. It governs the relationship between the jobber and the contractors that manufacture the garments that the jobber sells, including agreements that the jobber will use only unionized contractors, will ensure that salaries and bonuses are appropriately paid, and will contribute to employee-benefit funds maintained on behalf of the contractor's employees. This term gets its name from Hazantown, Inc., the jobber involved in *Danielson v. Joint Bd. of Coat, Suit & Allied Garment Workers' Union,* 494 F.2d 1230 (2d Cir. 1974). — Also termed *jobber's agreement.*

hazard, *n.* **1.** Danger; peril.

extraordinary hazard. *Workers' compensation.* An unusual occupational danger that is increased by the acts of employees other than the injured worker.

imminent hazard. An immediate danger; esp., in environmental law, a situation in which the continued use of a pesticide will probably result in unreasonable adverse effects on the environment or will involve an unreasonable danger to the survival of an endangered species. 7 USCA § 136(1).

2. The risk or probability of loss or injury, esp. a loss or injury covered by an insurance policy.

moral hazard. **1.** The risk that an insured will destroy property or allow it to be destroyed (usu. by burning) in order to collect the insurance proceeds. **2.** The insured's potential interest, if any, in the burning of the property.

3. *Hist.* An unlawful dice game in which the chances of winning are complicated by arbitrary rules.

hazarder (**haz**-ər-dər), *n. Hist.* A player in an unlawful game of dice. — Also spelled *hazardor.*

hazardous contract. See *aleatory contract* under CONTRACT.

hazardous employment. See EMPLOYMENT.

hazardous negligence. See NEGLIGENCE.

hazardous substance. 1. A toxic pollutant; an imminently dangerous chemical or mixture. **2.** See *hazardous waste* under WASTE (2).

hazardous waste. See WASTE (2).

hazard pay. Special compensation for work done under unpleasant or unsafe conditions.

H.B. See *house bill* under BILL (3).

H.C. *abbr.* **1.** HOUSE OF COMMONS. 2. HABEAS CORPUS.

HDC. *abbr.* HOLDER IN DUE COURSE.

he. A pronoun of the masculine gender, traditionally used and construed in statutes to include both sexes, as well as corporations. • It may also be read as *they*. Because of the trend toward nonsexist language, careful drafters avoid using the generic pronouns *he*, *him*, and *his* unless the reference is only to a male person.

headborough. See BORSHOLDER.

headlease. A primary lease under which a sublease has been granted. — Also spelled *head lease*. — Also termed *primary lease*; *chief lease*.

headlessor. A lessor on a lease of property that has been subleased.

head money. 1. A tax on people who fit within a designated class; a poll tax. See *capitation tax* and *poll tax* under TAX. **2.** A bounty offered by a government for a prisoner taken at sea during a naval engagement. • This bounty is divided among the officers and crew in the same manner as prize money. See PRIZE MONEY. **3.** A tax or duty on shipowners, imposed by an 1882 federal statute, for every immigrant brought into the United States. — Also termed *head tax*. **4.** *Hist.* A bounty or reward paid to a person who killed a bandit or outlaw and produced the head as evidence. See BOUNTY; REWARD.

headnote. A case summary that appears before the printed judicial opinion in a law report, addresses a point of law, and usu. includes the relevant facts bearing on that point of law. — Also termed *syllabus*; *synopsis*; *reporter's syllabus*.

> "The syllabus or headnote is a brief statement of the propositions of law decided in the case, being in the nature of a table of contents of the case. The modern method is to number each proposition in the syllabus, and to indicate, by corresponding figures, the exact place in the decision where the point mentioned in the syllabus can be found. Sometimes, especially in the older reports, the syllabus is inaccurate or misleading, and it is not safe to rely on it without first verifying it from the decision." Frank Hall Childs, *Where and How to Find the Law* 22 (1922).

headnote lawyer. See LAWYER.

head of household. 1. The primary income-provider within a family. **2.** For income-tax purposes, an unmarried or separated person (other than a surviving spouse) who provides a home for dependents for more than one-half of the taxable year. • A head of a household is taxed at a lower rate than a single person who is not head of a household. Cf. HOUSEHOLDER.

headright. In American Indian law, a tribemember's right to a pro rata portion of income from a tribal trust fund set up under the Allotment Act of 1906. • This type of trust fund is funded largely by mineral royalties arising from land held or once held by the tribemember's tribe.

headright certificate. *Hist.* A certificate issued under authority of a Republic of Texas law of 1839 providing that a person was entitled to a grant of 640 acres if the person (1) had immigrated to the Republic between 1 October 1837 and 1 January 1840, (2) was a head of household, and (3) actually resided within the Republic with his or her family. • The grant was to be held under the certificate for three years and then conveyed by absolute deed to the settler.

head shop. A retail establishment that sells items intended for use with illegal drugs.

head-silver. See *common fine* under FINE (4).

head-start injunction. An injunction prohibiting the defendant from using a trade secret for a period equal to the time between the date of the secret's theft and the date when the secret became public, since that period equals the "head start" that the defendant unfairly obtained over the rest of the industry.

headstream. The source of a river.

head tax. 1. See *poll tax* under TAX. **2.** HEAD MONEY (3).

headwater. 1. (*usu. pl.*) The part of a river or stream that is closest to its source. **2.** HEADSTREAM.

health. 1. The state of being sound or whole in body, mind, or soul. **2.** Freedom from pain or sickness.

public health. **1.** The health of the community at large. **2.** The healthful or sanitary condition of the general body of people or the community en masse; esp., the methods of maintaining the health of the community, as by preventive medicine and organized care for the sick. • Many cities have a "public health department" or other agency responsible for maintaining the public health; federal laws dealing with health are administered by the Department of Health and Human Services.

sound health. Insurance. A policy applicant's good condition; a state of health characterized by a lack of grave impairment or disease, or of any ailment that seriously affects the applicant's health.

healthcare-insurance receivable. An interest in or claim under an insurance policy, being a right to payment of a monetary obligation for healthcare goods or services provided. UCC § 9–104(c).

health insurance. See INSURANCE.

health law. A statute, ordinance, or code that prescribes sanitary standards and regulations for the purpose of promoting and preserving the community's health.

health-maintenance organization. A group of participating healthcare providers that furnish medical services to enrolled members of a group health-insurance plan. — Abbr. HMO. Cf. PREFERRED-PROVIDER ORGANIZATION.

health officer. A government official charged with executing and enforcing health laws. • The powers of a health officer (such as the Surgeon General) are regulated by law.

hearing. 1. A judicial session, usu. open to the public, held for the purpose of deciding issues of fact or of law, sometimes with witnesses testifying <the court held a hearing on the admissibility of DNA evidence in the murder case>. **2.** *Administrative law.* Any setting in which an affected person presents arguments to an agency decision-maker <a hearing on zoning variations>. **3.** In legislative practice, any proceeding in which legislators or their designees receive testimony about legislation that might be enacted <the shooting victim spoke at the Senate's hearing on gun control>. See PRELIMINARY HEARING. **4.** *Equity practice.* A trial.

adjudicatory hearing (ə-**joo**-di-kə-tor-ee). **1.** A hearing held by a juvenile court to determine whether a juvenile has engaged in delinquent conduct; a trial of a youth accused of a delinquency. See JUVENILE DELINQUENCY. Cf. *detention hearing*; *disposition hearing*. **2.** *Administrative law.* An agency proceeding in which the rights and duties of a particular person are decided after notice and an opportunity to be heard. — Also termed *adjudicatory proceeding*.

conformity hearing. See CONFORMITY HEARING.

Daubert hearing. See DAUBERT HEARING.

detention hearing. A hearing held by a juvenile court to determine whether a juvenile accused of delinquent conduct should be detained, continued in confinement, or released pending an adjudicatory hearing. Cf. *adjudicatory hearing*; *disposition hearing*.

discharge hearing. See DISCHARGE HEARING.

disposition hearing. A hearing held to determine the most appropriate form of custody or treatment for a juvenile who has been found at an adjudicatory hearing to be a juvenile delinquent or a status offender. Cf. *adjudicatory hearing*; *detention hearing*.

evidentiary hearing. **1.** A hearing at which evidence is presented, as opposed to a hearing at which only legal argument is presented. **2.** See ADMINISTRATIVE PROCEEDING.

exclusionary hearing. A pretrial hearing conducted to review and determine the admissibility of alleged illegally obtained evidence.

fair hearing. A judicial or administrative hearing conducted in accordance with due process.

Fatico hearing. See FATICO HEARING.

Franks hearing. See FRANKS HEARING.

full hearing. **1.** A hearing at which the parties are allowed notice of each other's claims and are given ample opportunity to present their positions with evidence and argument. **2.** See ADMINISTRATIVE PROCEEDING.

hearing de novo (dee *or* di **noh**-voh). **1.** A reviewing court's decision of a matter anew, giving no deference to a lower court's findings. **2.** A new hearing of a matter, conducted as if the original hearing had not taken place.

Jackson–Denno hearing. See JACKSON–DENNO HEARING.

Mapp hearing. See MAPP HEARING.

omnibus hearing. A hearing at which many items are discussed and considered.

public hearing. A hearing that, within reasonable limits, is open to anyone who wishes to observe. • Such a hearing is often characterized by the right to appear and present evidence in a case before an impartial tribunal.

reaffirmation hearing. See REAFFIRMATION HEARING.

revocation hearing. Criminal procedure. A hearing held to determine whether a parolee should be returned to prison for violating the terms of parole.

suppression hearing. A pretrial hearing in which a criminal defendant seeks to prevent the introduction of evidence alleged to have been seized illegally.

trial-type hearing. See ADMINISTRATIVE PROCEEDING.

unfair hearing. A hearing that is not conducted in accordance with due process, as when the defendant is denied the opportunity to prepare or consult with counsel.

Wade hearing. See WADE HEARING.

hearing examiner. See ADMINISTRATIVE-LAW JUDGE.

hearing officer. See ADMINISTRATIVE-LAW JUDGE.

hearsay. 1. Traditionally, testimony that is given by a witness who relates not what he or she knows personally, but what others have said, and that is therefore dependent on the credibility of someone other than the witness. • Such testimony is generally inadmissible under the rules of evidence. **2.** In federal law, a statement (either a verbal assertion or nonverbal assertive conduct), other than one made by the declarant while testifying at the trial or hearing, offered in evidence to prove the truth of the matter asserted. Fed. R. Evid. 801(c). — Also termed *hearsay evidence*; *secondhand evidence*.

double hearsay. A hearsay statement that contains further hearsay statements within it, none of which is admissible unless exceptions to the rule against hearsay can be applied to each level <the double hearsay was the investigation's report stating that Amy admitted to running the red light>. Fed. R. Evid. 805. — Also termed *multiple hearsay*; *hearsay within hearsay*.

hearsay rule. The rule that no assertion offered as testimony can be received unless it is or has been open to test by cross-examination or an opportunity for cross-examination, except as provided otherwise by the rules of evidence, by court rules, or by statute. • The chief reasons for the rule are that out-of-court statements amounting to hearsay are not made under oath and are not subject to cross-examination. Fed. R. Evid. 802. Rule 803 provides 23 explicit exceptions to the hearsay rule, regardless of whether the out-of-court declarant is available to testify, and Rule 804 provides 5 more exceptions for situations in which the declarant is unavailable to testify.

> "[T]he great hearsay rule ... is a fundamental rule of safety, but one overenforced and abused, — the spoiled child of the family, — proudest scion of our jury-trial rules of evidence, but so petted and indulged that it has become a nuisance and an obstruction to speedy and efficient trials." John H. Wigmore, *A Students' Textbook of the Law of Evidence* 238 (1935).

hearsay within hearsay. See *double hearsay* under HEARSAY.

heartbalm statute. A state law that abolishes the rights of action for alienation of affections, breach of promise to marry, criminal conversation, and seduction of a person over the legal age of consent.

hearth money. *Hist.* **1.** A tax of two shillings levied on every fireplace in England (14 Car. 2, ch. 10). • This extremely unpopular tax was enacted in 1662 during the reign of Charles II and abolished in 1688. **2.** PETER-PENCE. — Also termed (in sense 1) *chimney money*.

heat of passion. Rage, terror, or furious hatred suddenly aroused by some immediate provocation, usu. another person's words or actions. • At common law, the heat of passion could serve, in a murder defense, as a mitigating circumstance that would reduce the charge to manslaughter. — Also termed *sudden heat of passion*; *sudden heat*; *sudden passion*; *hot blood*; *furor brevis*. Cf. COLD BLOOD; COOL BLOOD.

> "To constitute the *heat of passion* included in this requirement it is not necessary for the passion to be so extreme that the slayer does not know what he is doing at the time; but it must be so extreme that for the moment his action is being directed by passion rather than by reason." Rollin M. Perkins & Ronald N. Boyce, *Criminal Law* 99 (3d ed. 1982).

heavy work. See WORK.

hebote. See HEREBOTE.

hedagium (hə-**day**-jee-əm), *n.* [Law Latin] *Hist.* A toll or custom due at a wharf for landing goods. • The Crown exempted particular persons and societies from this toll.

hedge, *vb.* To make advance arrangements to safeguard oneself from loss on an investment, speculation, or bet, as when a buyer of commodities insures against unfavorable price changes by buying in advance at a fixed rate for later delivery. — **hedging,** *n.*

hedgebote. See HAYBOTE.

hedge fund. A specialized investment group — usu. organized as a limited partnership or offshore investment company — that offers the possibility of high returns through risky techniques such as selling short or buying derivatives. • Most hedge funds are not registered with the SEC and are therefore restricted in marketing their services to the public.

hedonic damages. See DAMAGES.

hedonistic utilitarianism. See UTILITARIANISM.

heeding presumption. See PRESUMPTION.

heedlessness, *n.* The quality of being thoughtless and inconsiderate; esp., conduct whereby the actor disregards the rights or safety of others. • Heedlessness is often construed to involve the same degree of fault as recklessness. — **heedless,** *adj.* See RECKLESSNESS.

hegemonism (hi-**jem**-ə-niz-əm). **1.** A philosophical position advocating hegemony. **2.** All forms of political extension by means of hegemony.

hegemony (hi-**jem**-ə-nee), *n.* **1.** Influence, authority, or supremacy over others <the hegemony of capitalism>. **2.** The striving for leadership or predominant authority of one state of a confederacy or union over the others; political domination <the former Soviet Union's hegemony over Eastern Europe>. — **hegemonic** (hej-ə-**mon**-ik), *adj.*

heightened scrutiny. See INTERMEDIATE SCRUTINY.

heinous (**hay**-nəs), *adj.* (Of a crime or its perpetrator) that is shockingly atrocious or odious. — **heinousness,** *n.*

heir (air). **1.** A person who, under the laws of intestacy, is entitled to receive an intestate decedent's property, esp. real property. — Also termed *legal heir*; *heir at law*; *lawful heir*; *heir general.*

> "Laymen — and sometimes first-year law students taking exams — wrongly assume that one who receives real property by will is an heir. Technically, the word 'heir' is reserved for one who receives real property by action of the laws of intestacy, which operate today only in the absence of a valid will." Thomas F. Bergin & Paul G. Haskell, *Preface to Estates in Land and Future Interests* 14 n.32 (2d ed. 1984).

2. Loosely, a person who inherits real or personal property, whether by will or by intestate succession.

after-born heir. One born after the death of an intestate from whom the heir is entitled to inherit.

and his heirs. A term of art formerly required to create a fee simple absolute in transferring real property by will <A conveys Blackacre to B and his heirs>. • This phrasing originated in the translation of a Law French phrase used in medieval grants (*a lui et a ses heritiers pour toujours* "to him and his heirs forever"). See FEE SIMPLE.

> "The development reached its culmination when the words 'and his heirs' in a transfer were thought to give full durational ownership to the immediate transferee and no ownership whatever to his heirs. This notion was expressed in the statement that the words 'and his heirs' are words of limitation and not words of purchase. They indicate the durational character of an estate, not its taker." Thomas F. Bergin & Paul G. Haskell, *Preface to Estates in Land and Future Interests* 93–94 (2d ed. 1984).

apparent heir. See *heir apparent.*

beneficiary heir (ben-ə-**fish**-ee-er-ee). *Civil law.* An heir who accepts an inheritance but files a benefit of inventory to limit his or her liability for estate debts to the value of the inheritance. — Also termed *heir beneficiary.* See BENEFIT OF INVENTORY. Cf. *unconditional heir.*

collateral heir. One who is neither a direct descendant nor an ancestor of the decedent, but whose kinship is through a collateral line, such as a brother, sister, uncle, aunt, nephew, niece, or cousin. Cf. *lineal heir.*

expectant heir. An heir who has a reversionary or remainder interest in property, or a chance of succeeding to it. — Also termed *heir expectant.* See REVERSION; REMAINDER. Cf. *prospective heir.*

> "The reader should be aware that one never has an 'heir' until one is dead; one merely has an 'heir expectant' .... Thus, to say that an heir 'owns' anything is conceptually difficult. But ... some unborn heirs may be entitled to the protection of the courts, and thus be said to have estates." Thomas F. Bergin & Paul G. Haskell, *Preface to Estates in Land and Future Interests* 26 n.13 (2d ed. 1984).

forced heir. A person whom the testator or donor cannot disinherit because the law reserves part of the estate for that person.

heir apparent. An heir who is certain to inherit unless he or she dies first or is excluded by a valid will. — Also termed *apparent heir.* Cf. *heir presumptive.*

> "Heirs *apparent* are such, whose right of inheritance is indefeasible, provided they outlive the ancestor; as the eldest son or his issue, who must by the course of the common law be heirs to the father whenever he happens to die." 2 William Blackstone, *Commentaries on the Laws of England* 208 (1766).

heir beneficiary. See *beneficiary heir.*

heir by adoption. A person who has been adopted by (and thus has become an heir to) the deceased. • By statute in most jurisdictions, an adopted child has the same right of succession to intestate property as a biological child unless the deceased clearly expresses a contrary intention. Jurisdictions differ on whether an adopted child may in addition inherit from his or her natural parents or family.

heir by custom. *Hist.* In England, a person whose right of inheritance depends on a particular and local custom, such as gavelkind and borough English. See GAVELKIND; BOROUGH ENGLISH.

heir by devise. One to whom lands are given by will.

heir conventional. *Civil law.* One who takes a succession because of a contract or settlement entitling him or her to it.

heir expectant. See *expectant heir.*

heir in tail. See *heir special.*

heir male. *Hist.* The nearest male blood-relation of a decedent.

heir of the blood. An heir who succeeds to an estate because of consanguinity with the decedent, either in the ascending or descending line.

heir of the body. A lineal descendant of the decedent, excluding a surviving spouse, adopted children, and collateral relations. • The term of art *heirs of the body* was formerly used to create a fee tail <A conveys Blackacre to B and the heirs of his body>. — Also termed *bodily heir.*

heir presumptive. An heir who will inherit if the potential intestate dies immediately, but who may be excluded if another more closely related heir is born. — Also termed *presumptive heir.* Cf. *heir apparent.*

heirs and assigns. A term of art formerly required to create a fee simple <A conveys Blackacre to B and his heirs and assigns>.

heir special. *Hist.* An heir who receives property according to the nature of the estate held in fee tail. • Heirs special were said to receive property *per formam doni* ("by the form of the gift"). — Also termed *heir in tail.*

joint heir. **1.** A coheir. **2.** A person who is or will be an heir to both of two designated persons at the death of the survivor of them, the word *joint* being here applied to the ancestors rather than the heirs.

known heir. An heir who is present to claim an inheritance, the extent of which depends on there being no closer relative.

laughing heir. An heir distant enough to feel no grief when a relative dies and leaves a windfall to the heir.

lineal heir. A person who is either an ancestor or a descendant of the decedent, such as a parent or child. Cf. *collateral heir.*

natural heir. An heir by consanguinity as distinguished from a collateral heir, an heir by adoption, or a statutory heir (such as a person's spouse).

presumptive heir. See *heir presumptive.*

pretermitted heir (pree-tər-**mit**-id). A child or spouse who has been omitted from a will, as when a testator makes a will naming his or her two children and then, sometime later, has two more children who are not mentioned in the will. • Most states have so-called "pretermitted-heir statutes" under which an omitted child or spouse receives the same share of the estate as if the testator had died intestate, unless the omission was intentional. — Also termed (more specifically) *pretermitted child*; *pretermitted spouse.* See PRETERMITTED-HEIR STATUTE.

prospective heir. An heir who may inherit but may be excluded; an heir apparent or an heir presumptive. Cf. *expectant heir.*

right heir. **1.** *Hist.* The preferred heir to an estate tail, as distinguished from a general heir. • An estate tail would pass to a general heir only on the failure of the preferred heir and his line. **2.** HEIR (1).

testamentary heir (tes-tə-**men**-tə-ree *or* -tree). *Civil law.* A person who is appointed heir in the decedent's will.

unconditional heir. *Civil law.* A person who chooses — expressly or tacitly — to inherit without any reservation or without making an inventory. Cf. *beneficiary heir.*

heir apparent. See HEIR.

heir by adoption. See HEIR.

heir by custom. See HEIR.

heir by devise. See HEIR.

heir conventional. See HEIR.

heirdom. The state of being an heir; succession by inheritance.

heir expectant. See *expectant heir* under HEIR.

heir general. See HEIR.

heir-hunter. A person whose business is to track down missing heirs.

heir in tail. See *heir special* under HEIR.

heirless estate. See ESTATE.

heirloom. 1. An item of personal property that by local custom, contrary to the usual legal rule, descends to the heir along with the inheritance, instead of passing to the executor or administrator of the last owner; traditional examples are an ancestor's coat of armor, family portraits, title deeds, and keys. • Blackstone gave a false etymology that many have copied: "The termination, *loom*, is of Saxon origin; in which language it signifies a limb or member; so that an heirloom is nothing else, but a limb or member of the inheritance." 2 William Blackstone, *Commentaries on the Law of England* 427 (1766). In fact, *loom* derives from Old English *geloma* "utensil," and *loom* meant "implement, tool." **2.** Popularly, a valued possession of great sentimental value passed down through generations within a family.

> "Heir-looms, strictly so called, are now very seldom to be met with. They may be defined to be such personal chattels as go, by force of a *special custom*, to the heir, along with the inheritance, and not to the executor or administrator of the last owner. The owner of an heir-loom cannot by his will bequeath the heir-loom, if he leave the land to descend to his heir; for in such a case the force of custom will prevail over the bequest, which, not coming into operation until after the decease of the owner, is too late to supersede the custom.... In popular language the term 'heir-loom' is generally applied to plate, pictures or articles of property which have been assigned by deed of settlement or bequeathed by will to trustees, in trust to permit the same to be used and enjoyed by the persons for the time being in possession, under the settlement or will, of the mansion-house in which the articles may be placed." Joshua Williams, *Principles of the Law of Personal Property* 13–14 (11th ed. 1881).

heir male. See HEIR.

heir of the blood. See HEIR.

heir of the body. See HEIR.

heir presumptive. See HEIR.

heirs and assigns. See HEIR.

heirship. 1. The quality or condition of being an heir. **2.** The relation between an ancestor and an heir.

heir special. See HEIR.

hell-or-high-water clause. A clause in a personal-property lease requiring the lessee to continue to make full rent payments to the lessor even if the thing leased is unsuitable, defective, or destroyed.

hell-or-high-water rule. 1. The principle that a personal-property lessee must pay the full rent due, regardless of any claim against the lessor, unless the lessee proves unequal bargaining power or unconscionability. **2.** *Insurance.* The principle that an insured's automobile-liability policy will cover the insured while using a vehicle owned by another if the insured uses the vehicle in a manner within the scope of the permission granted.

henceforth, *adv.* From now on <the newly enacted rule will apply henceforth>.

Henricus Vetus (hen-**rI**-kəs **vee**-təs). [Law Latin] Henry the Old (or *Elder*). • This term was used in early English charters to distinguish King Henry I from later kings of the same name.

heordpenny (**hərd**-pen-ee), *n.* See PETER-PENCE.

Hepburn Act. A 1906 federal statute that amended the Interstate Commerce Act to (1) increase the (now defunct) Interstate Commerce Commission's jurisdiction to include pipelines, (2) prohibit free passes except to employees, (3) prohibit common carriers from transporting any products (except timber) in which they had an interest, and (4) require joint tariffs and a uniform system of accounts.

heptarchy (**hep**-tahr-kee). **1.** A government by seven rulers. **2.** A nation divided into seven governments, specif. the seven Anglo–Saxon kingdoms of Kent, Sussex, Essex, Wessex, East Anglia, Mercia, and Northumbria existing before the Norman Conquest.

herald, *n.* **1.** In England and Scotland, one of several officers responsible for keeping genealogical lists and tables, adjusting armorial bearings, and regulating the ceremonies at royal coronations and funerals. • There are six in England and three in Scotland. **2.** *Hist.* A messenger who announces royal or state proclamations, and who carries diplomatic messages (esp. proclamations of war, peace, or truce) between kings or countries.

Heralds' College. A royal corporation responsible in England for granting and recording armorial insignia and genealogies, and for dealing with matters of precedence. • The College was founded by Richard III in 1484, is governed by the Earl Marshal, and consists of three kings of arms, six heralds, and four pursuivants. The heralds' books, based on family-lineage inquiries made throughout England, are considered good evidence of pedigrees. The heralds' office is still allowed to make grants of arms and to grant name changes. • Also termed *College of Arms.*

herbage (**ər**-bij). In England, an easement or liberty of pasturage on another's land.

herdwerch (**hərd**-wərk), *n. Hist.* Herdsmen's work, or customary labor, done by shepherds and inferior tenants at the lord's will. — Also spelled *heordwerch.*

hereafter, *adv.* **1.** From now on; henceforth <because of the highway construction, she will hereafter take the bus to work>. **2.** At some future time <the court will hereafter issue a ruling on the gun's admissibility>. **3.** HEREINAFTER <the exhibits hereafter referred to as Exhibit A and Exhibit B>.

here and there. See VALUE DATE.

herebannum (her-ə-**ban**-əm), *n.* [Law Latin fr. Old English *here* "army" + *bann* "proclamation"] *Hist.* **1.** A proclamation summoning the army into the field. **2.** A mulct or fine for not joining that army when summoned. **3.** A tax or tribute for the support of that army.

herebote (**her**-ə-boht), *n.* [fr. Old English *here* "army" + *bod* "command"] *Hist.* In England, a royal edict summoning the people to the battlefield; an edict commanding subjects into battle. — Also spelled *herebode*; *hebote.*

hereby, *adv.* By this document; by these very words <I hereby declare my intention to run for public office>.

heredad (e-re-**dahth**), *n. Spanish law.* **1.** A piece of land under cultivation; a cultivated farm. **2.** An inheritance or heirship.

heredad yacente (e-re-**dath** yah-**sen**-te). An inheritance not yet accepted. See *hereditas jacens* under HEREDITAS.

heredero (e-re-**ther**-oh), *n. Spanish law.* **1.** An owner of a cultivated farm. **2.** An heir.

heredes. See HERES.

heredes proximi (hə-**ree**-deez **prok**-sə-mɪ), *n.* [Latin] Nearest or next heirs.

heredes remotiores (hə-**ree**-deez ri-moh-shee-**or**-eez), *n.* [Latin] Heirs more remote; relatives other than children or descendants.

heredipeta (he-rə-**dip**-ə-tə), *n.* [Law Latin] *Hist.* A legacy-hunter; the seeker of an inheritance.

heredis instituto (hə-**ree**-dis in-sti-**t[y]oo**-toh), *n.* [Latin] *Roman law.* The designation in a will of a person as the testator's heir. • A testator's failure to appoint an heir could destroy the validity of the will.

hereditament (her-ə-**dit**-ə-mənt *or* hə-**red**-i-tə-mənt). **1.** Any property that can be inherited; anything that passes by intestacy. **2.** Real property; land.

corporeal hereditament (kor-**por**-ee-əl). A tangible item of property, such as land, a building, or a fixture.

incorporeal hereditament (in-kor-**por**-ee-əl). An intangible right in land, such as an easement. • The various types at common law were advowsons, annuities, commons, dignities, franchises, offices, pensions, rents, tithes, and ways.

hereditary, *adj.* Of or relating to inheritance; that descends from an ancestor to an heir.

hereditary succession. See SUCCESSION (2).

hereditas (hə-**red**-i-tas), *n.* [Latin] **1.** *Roman law.* An inheritance by universal succession to a decedent. • This succession applied whether the decedent died testate or intestate, and whether in trust (*ex fideicommisso*) for another or not. The comparable right under Praetorian law was *bonorum possessio*, possession of an inheritance that could be the basis of a right to succeed. **2.** *Hist.* An estate transmissible by descent; an inheritance. — Also spelled *haereditas.*

hereditas damnosa (hə-**red**-i-tas dam-**noh**-sə). A burdensome inheritance; an inheritance whose debts exceed its assets.

hereditas jacens (hə-**red**-i-tas **jay**-senz). [Latin *iaceo* "to lie"] **1.** Property belonging to an estate before an heir accepts it. • This term had a similar meaning at common law. See ABEYANCE (2).

> "Hereditas jacens is the term applied to an inheritance which has not yet vested, an inheritance, that is to say, which has been 'delata' to a heres extraneus (i.e. voluntarius), but has not yet been acquired by him." Rudolph Sohm, *The Institutes: A Textbook of the History and System of Roman Private Law* 512 (James Crawford Ledlie trans., 3d ed. 1907).

2. *Hist.* A decedent's estate that has no heir or legatee to take it; an escheated estate. — Also termed *caduca*. See ESCHEAT. **3.** *Hist.* An inheritance without legal owner and thus open to the first occupant. — Also spelled *hereditas iacens*.

hereditas legitima (hə-**red**-i-tas lə-**jit**-i-mə). A succession or inheritance devolving by operation of law rather than by will. See INTESTACY.

hereditas luctuosa (hə-**red**-i-tas lək-choo-**oh**-sə). A sad or mournful inheritance; one that disturbs the natural order of mortality (*turbato ordine mortalitatis*), as that of a parent inheriting a child's estate. • This term is more literary than legal. — Also termed *tristis successio*.

hereditas testamentaria (hə-**red**-i-tas tes-tə-men-**tair**-ee-ə). Testamentary inheritance; succession to an estate under a decedent's will.

heredity. 1. *Archaic.* Hereditary succession; an inheritance. **2.** The hereditary transmission of characteristics from a parent to a child; the biological law by which a living being tends to repeat itself in its descendants.

herein, *adv.* In this thing (such as a document, section, or matter) <the due-process arguments stated herein should convince the court to reverse the judgment>.

hereinafter, *adv.* Later in this document <the buyer agrees to purchase the property described hereinafter>. — Also loosely termed *hereafter*.

herenach (**her**-ə-nak), *n.* [fr. Old Irish *airchinnich* "chief man"] An archdeacon. — Also spelled *erenach*.

hereof, *adv.* Of this thing (such as a provision or document) <the conditions hereof are stated in section 3>.

heres (**heer**-eez), *n.* [Latin] *Roman law.* A successor to the rights and liabilities of a deceased person; an heir. • Because the *heres* succeeded to both the rights and the debts of the decedent, the office was more similar to a modern executor than an heir at law. The institution of the *heres* was the essential characteristic of a testament; if this was not done, the instrument was called a *codicillus*. — Also spelled (in Law Latin) *haeres*. Pl. ***heredes*** (hə-**ree**-deez) or (for *haeres*) ***haeredes***.

heres astrarius (as-**trair**-ee-əs). [Law Latin "heir of the hearth"] An heir who has received, by conveyance, an ancestor's estate during the ancestor's lifetime.

heres de facto (di **fak**-toh). [Law Latin "heir from fact"] *Hist.* **1.** An heir whose status arises from the disseisin or other wrongful act of the heir's ancestor. See DISSEISIN. **2.** An heir in fact, as distinguished from an heir by law (*de jure*).

heres ex asse (**as**-ee). [Latin "sole heir"] *Roman law.* An heir to the whole estate.

heres ex testamento. See *heres factus*.

heres extraneus (ek-**stray**-nee-əs). [Latin "extraneous heir"] *Roman law.* An external heir; one not subject to the testator's power (*potestas*) and hence not bound to accept the inheritance.

heres factus (**fak**-təs). [Latin "made heir"] An heir appointed by will; a testamentary heir. — Also termed *heres ex testamento*; *heres institutus*. Cf. *heres natus*.

heres fideicommissarius (**fI**-dee-I-kom-ə-**sair**-ee-əs). [Latin] *Roman law.* The person for whose benefit an estate was given by will to a fiduciary heir. • This office corresponds closely with the *cestui qui trust* of the common law. Cf. *heres fiduciarius*.

heres fiduciarius (fi-d[y]oo-shee-**air**-ee-əs). [Latin "fiduciary heir"] *Roman law.* A person made heir by will, in trust for the benefit of another; an heir subject to a trust. Cf. *heres fideicommissarius*.

heres institutus. See *heres factus*.

heres legitimus (lə-**jit**-i-məs). [Latin "lawful heir"] *Roman law.* An heir entitled to succeed (on intestacy) by statute.

heres natus (**nay**-təs). [Latin "heir by birth"] An heir by reason of birth; an heir at law or by intestacy. Cf. *heres factus*.

heres necessarius (nes-ə-**sair**-ee-əs). [Latin "necessary heir"] *Roman law.* A person compelled to serve as heir, usu. either a slave freed on the testator's death or a free person in the testator's power.

heres rectus (**rek**-təs). [Law Latin] *Hist.* A right or proper heir.

heres suus (**s**[**y**]**oo**-əs). [Latin "one's own heir"] **1.** A decedent's proper or natural heir; a lineal descendant of the deceased. **2.** *Roman law.* A free person who was subject to the testator's power (*potestas*) but who could exercise full legal rights upon the testator's death.

heres suus et necessarius (**s**[**y**]**oo**-əs et nes-ə-**sair**-ee-əs). [Latin "one's own and necessary heir"] A free person subject to the decedent's *potestas*. • These heirs were called *necessary* because they became heirs by law, not by the decedent's choice. But since this was also true of slaves, when named heirs in a will, the former class was designated *suus et necessarius* by way of distinction, the word *suus* denoting that the necessity arose from the relationship to the decedent.

ultimas heres (**əl**-ti-məs). The last or remote heir; the lord.

heresy (**her**-ə-see), *n.* **1.** Opinion or doctrine contrary to (usu. Catholic) church dogma. **2.** *Hist.* In England, an offense against religion, consisting not in totally denying Christianity, but in publicly denying some of its essential doctrines; an opinion on divine subjects devised solely by human reason, openly taught, and obstinately maintained. • This offense is now subject only to ecclesiastical correction and is no longer punishable by the secular law.

hereto, *adv.* To this document <the exhibits are attached hereto>.

heretofore, *adv.* Up to now; before this time <a question that has not heretofore been decided>.

hereunder, *adv.* **1.** Later in this document <review the provisions hereunder before signing the consent form>. **2.** In accordance with this document <notice hereunder must be provided within 30 days after the loss>.

herewith, *adv.* With or in this document <enclosed herewith are three copies>.

heriot (**her**-ee-ət), *n.* [fr. Old English *here* "army" + *geatwa* "trappings"] *Hist.* A customary tribute of goods and chattels, payable to the lord of the fee on the tenant's death. • *Heriot* derives from an earlier feudal service consisting of military equipment returned to the lord on the tenant's death; over time it came to refer only to the chattel payment due at the tenant's death.

> "We are told that the ancient heriot (*heregeatu*, military apparel) had at one time consisted of the horses and arms lent by the lord to his man which on the man's death were returned to the lord.... Turning to manorial surveys, we find it among the commonest of customs that when a tenant in villeinage dies, the lord shall have the best beast; sometimes a similar due is taken from the goods of the dead freeholder, and it is to these customary dues that the name 'heriot' permanently attaches itself." 1 Frederick Pollock & Frederic W. Maitland, *The History of English Law Before the Time of Edward I* 312, 317 (2d ed. 1898).

heriot custom. A heriot due by custom. • This term is used primarily to distinguish a *heriot service* from an ordinary heriot.

heriot service. A tribute arising from special reservation in a grant or lease of lands, and thus amounting to little more than rent.

herislit (**her**-ə-sleet *or* **hair**-), *n.* [Old English] *Hist.* **1.** The act of surrendering; laying down of arms. **2.** The crime of deserting from an army.

heritable (**her**-i-tə-bəl), *adj.* INHERITABLE.

heritable bond. See BOND (2).

heritable obligation. See *inheritable obligation* under OBLIGATION.

heritable security. See SECURITY.

heritage (**her**-i-tij), *n. Scots law.* Land, together with all property connected to it (such as a house).

Her Majesty's Stationery Office. See STATIONERY OFFICE.

hermeneutics (hər-mə-**n**[**y**]**oo**-tiks), *n.* The art of interpreting texts, esp. as a technique used in critical legal studies. — **hermeneutical, hermeneutic,** *adj.*

Hermogenian Code. See CODEX HERMOGENIANUS.

hesia (**hee**-zhee-ə *or* **hee**-shee-ə), *n.* [Law Latin] An easement.

hetaerarcha (het-ər-**ahr**-kə), *n.* [Greek, then Latin] *Roman law.* The head of a society, corporation, or college.

hetaeria (hə-**teer**-ee-ə), *n.* [Latin] *Roman law.* A society, guild, or college; a fraternity. — Also termed *hetaery*.

heuristic (hyuu-**ris**-tik), *adj*. Of or relating to a method of learning or problem-solving by using trial-and-error and other experimental techniques <heuristic discovery methods>.

HEW. *abbr*. The Department of Health, Education, and Welfare, a former agency of the U.S. government created in 1953. • When the Department of Education was created in 1979, the name HEW was changed to the Department of Health and Human Services (HHS).

Heydon's case, rule in. See MISCHIEF RULE.

HGN test. *abbr*. HORIZONTAL-GAZE NYSTAGMUS TEST.

HHS. *abbr*. The Department of Health and Human Services, a federal agency that administers health, welfare, and income-security policies and programs, the largest of which is social security.

hidage (**hīd**-ij), *n*. *Hist*. A tax, payable to the Crown, based on every hide of land. — Also spelled *hydage*. See HIDE.

> "Of the same nature with scutages upon knights'-fees were the assessments of hydage upon all other lands, and of talliage upon cities and burghs. But they all gradually fell into disuse, upon the introduction of subsidies, about the time of king Richard II and king Henry IV." 1 William Blackstone, *Commentaries on the Laws of England* 300 (1765).

hidalgo (hi-**dal**-goh *or* ee-**thahl**-goh), *n*. [fr. Spanish *hijo* "son" + *algo* "property"] In Spain, a man belonging to the lower nobility; a gentleman of property.

hidalguia (ee-thahl-**gee**-yə), *n*. [Spanish] In Spain, nobility by descent or lineage.

HIDC. *abbr*. HOLDER IN DUE COURSE.

hidden asset. See ASSET.

hidden defect. See DEFECT.

hidden tax. See TAX.

hide, *n*. *Hist*. **1.** In England, a measure of land consisting in as much as could be worked with one plow, variously estimated at from 30 to 120 acres but probably determined by local usage. • A hide was anciently employed as a unit of taxation. Cf. CARUCATE. **2.** As much land as would support one family or the dwellers in a mansion-house. **3.** A house; a dwelling-house.

hidegild (**hīd**-gild), *n*. [Old English] *Hist*. A sum of money paid by a villein or servant to avoid a whipping. — Also spelled *hidgild*; *hydegeld*; *hudegeld*.

hidel (**hīd**-əl *or* **hid**-əl), *n*. [Old English] *Hist*. A hiding-place; a place of protection or sanctuary.

high bailiff. See BAILIFF.

High Commission Court. See COURT OF HIGH COMMISSION.

High Court. See HIGH COURT OF JUSTICE.

High Court of Admiralty. In England, a court exercising jurisdiction in matters relating to shipping, collision, and salvage cases. • The court dates from the 14th century, and much of its early history concerns prize and piracy cases. Its jurisdiction varied through the centuries, sometimes extending into criminal matters and other areas of law not related directly to maritime issues. The Judicature Acts of 1873–1875 merged the Court into the High Court as part of the Probate, Divorce, and Admiralty Division. The Administration of Justice Act of 1970 established a new Admiralty Court as part of the Queen's Bench Division of the High Court. It is regulated by the Supreme Court Act of 1981. — Also termed *Court of the Lord High Admiral*; *Court of Admiralty*. Cf. ADMIRALTY (1).

> "To the office of the Lord High Admiral (originally a naval official concerned with the command of the fleet and the suppression of piracy and wrecking) there was annexed a court which acquired a jurisdiction over civil cases of a maritime nature. Just how and when this happened is too cloudy and controversial for simple or even accurate summary, but by the time of Richard II (1377–1400) the admiral and vice-admiral were transacting enough judicial business to move Parliament to limit their jurisdiction by statute to 'a thing done upon the sea,' and in Tudor times the court was well established as a court of record, doing a large civil business. It slowly but surely took away most of their business from the local maritime courts in the port towns, and attracted the easily aroused jealousy of the common law courts, as well as the dislike of those who feared it as a prerogative court.... These factors resulted in the rather anticlimactic eclipse of the court for almost two centuries." Grant Gilmore & Charles L. Black, Jr., *The Law of Admiralty* § 1–4, at 9–10 (2d ed. 1975).

High Court of Chivalry. *Hist*. A court of honor having jurisdiction over matters relating to deeds of arms and war, armorial insignia, and precedence. — Also termed *Court of Chivalry*; *Court of Earl Marshal*. See COURT OF HONOR.

> "This *Curia Marescalli*, or High Court of Chivalry, was revived by James I as a court of honour, which not only

tried the right to distinctions of honour and coat armour but also redressed affronts to honour such as slander. The slander jurisdiction was later denied, leaving it with a jurisdiction probably confined to disputes over armorial bearings, which are determined according to the law of arms. The court, which has only sat once since 1737, is the last English court to use the procedure of the civil law." J.H. Baker, *An Introduction to English Legal History* 142 (3d ed. 1990).

High Court of Delegates. See COURT OF DELEGATES.

High Court of Errors and Appeals. See COURT OF ERRORS AND APPEALS.

High Court of Justice. The superior civil court of England and Wales. — Often shortened to *High Court.*

High Court of Justiciary (jə-**stish**-ee-er-ee). The superior criminal court of Scotland, acting both as a trial court and as a court of criminal appeal.

high crime. See CRIME.

high diligence. See *great diligence* under DILIGENCE.

higher court. See *court above* under COURT.

higher scale. See SCALE.

highest and best use. See USE (1).

highest court. The court of last resort in a particular jurisdiction; a court whose decision is final and cannot be appealed because no higher court exists to consider the matter. • The U.S. Supreme Court, for example, is the highest federal court.

highest degree of care. See DEGREE OF CARE.

highest proved value. See VALUE.

high flier. *Slang.* A security that has strongly attracted public interest so that investors pay an unusually high price.

highgrade, *vb.* **1.** To steal rich ore, as from a mine by a miner. **2.** To mine only esp. valuable ore (such as gold).

high-grade security. See SECURITY.

high justice. See JUSTICE (3).

high-low agreement. A settlement in which a defendant agrees to pay the plaintiff a minimum recovery in return for the plaintiff's agreement to accept a maximum amount regardless of the outcome of the trial. — Also termed *hilo settlement.*

high-managerial agent. See AGENT.

high-probability rule. *Marine insurance.* The principle that an insured may abandon a vessel if it appears extremely likely that a total loss is imminent.

high seas. See SEA.

high-test marriage. See *covenant marriage* under MARRIAGE (1).

high treason. See TREASON.

high-water line. See *high-water mark* under WATER MARK.

high-water mark. See WATER MARK.

highway. 1. Broadly, any main route on land, on water, or in the air. **2.** A free and public roadway or street that every person may use. **3.** The main public road connecting towns or cities. **4.** The entire width between boundaries of every publicly maintained way when part is open to public use for purposes of vehicular traffic.

common highway. A highway for use by the public for any purpose of transit or traffic.

public highway. A highway controlled and maintained by governmental authorities for general use.

highway act. (*usu. pl.*) One of a body of statutes governing the laying out, construction, repair, and use of highways. — Also termed *highway law.*

highwayman. A highway robber; a person who robs on a public road.

highway rate. *Hist.* In England, a tax for the maintenance and repair of highways.

highway robbery. See ROBBERY.

highway tax. See TAX.

higuela (ee-**gay**-lah), *n. Spanish law.* A receipt given by a decedent's heir, setting forth what property the heir has received from the estate.

hijack, *vb.* **1.** To commandeer (a vehicle or airplane), esp. at gunpoint. **2.** To steal or rob from (a vehicle or airplane in transit).

Hilary Rules. *Hist.* A collection of English pleading rules designed to ease the strict pleading requirements of the special-pleading system, esp. by limiting the scope of the general issue in the formed actions and by forcing the defendant to set up affirmatively all matters other than a denial of the breach of duty or of the wrongful act. • Promulgated in England in the 1834 Hilary Term, these rules followed an 1828 initiative to examine procedural laws and other subjects and to report to Parliament changes that might be enacted. The rules had the unintended effect of extending the reach of strict-pleading requirements into new areas of law. Widespread dissatisfaction with the Hilary Rules led to the liberalization of the pleading system under the 1873–1875 Judicature Acts. — Formerly also termed *New Rules.*

> "The failure of the Hilary Rules ... lay in their insistence on special pleading as it was understood late in the eighteenth century. That parties should plead precisely, and clarify as far as possible the issue between them, is one thing; that their endeavours to do so should be judged by the extremely artificial standards of the old system, was quite another." Theodore F.T. Plucknett, *A Concise History of the Common Law* 416 (5th ed. 1956).

Hilary sittings. In England, a term of court beginning on January 11 of each year and ending on the Wednesday before Easter. • The Hilary sittings were known as *Hilary term* until 1875. Cf. EASTER SITTINGS; MICHAELMAS SITTING.

hilo settlement. See HIGH-LOW AGREEMENT.

***Hilton* doctrine.** *Civil procedure.* The rule that in a dispute between parties to an oil-and-gas lease, royalty owners who would lose their rights if the defendant's lease were terminated are regarded as indispensable parties to a proceeding challenging the lease. *Hilton v. Atlantic Refining Co.*, 327 F.2d 217 (5th Cir. 1964).

Himalaya clause. *Maritime law.* A provision in a bill of lading extending the carrier's liability limitations under the Carriage of Goods by Sea Act to the carrier's agents and independent contractors. • This type of clause is usu. strictly construed. See CARRIAGE OF GOODS BY SEA ACT.

> "An exculpatory or other beneficial clause which seeks to extend to noncarriers, partial immunity or other protections afforded to the carrier by the bill of lading is popularly known to the admiralty bar as a Himalaya clause. This misnomer derives from an earlier British case involving the vessel *Himalaya*, Adler v. Dickson...." Nicholas J. Healy, *Carriage of Goods by Sea: Application of the "Himalaya Clause" to Subdelegees of the Carrier*, 2 Mar. Law. 91, 111 (1977).

hine (hɪn), *n. Hist.* In England, a husbandry servant. — Also spelled *hind.*

hinefare (**hɪn**-fair), *n. Hist.* In England, the loss or departure of a servant from the master.

hinegeld (**hɪn**-geld), *n. Hist.* A ransom for an offense committed by a servant.

hipoteca (ee-poh-**tek**-ah), *n. Spanish law.* A mortgage of real property. See HYPOTHECATION.

hire, *vb.* **1.** To engage the labor or services of another for wages or other payment. **2.** To procure the temporary use of property, usu. at a set price. **3.** To grant the temporary use of services <hire themselves out>.

hired gun. *Slang.* **1.** An expert witness who testifies favorably for the party paying his or her fee, often because of that financial relationship rather than because of the facts. **2.** A lawyer who stops at nothing to accomplish the client's goals, regardless of moral consequences.

hireling, *n.* a person who is hired or serves for wages, esp. one who works only for the sake of payments.

hire-purchase agreement. See LEASE-PURCHASE AGREEMENT.

hiring. See LOCATIO.

hiring at will. See *employment at will* under EMPLOYMENT.

his. Properly a possessive pronoun of the masculine gender, but traditionally used and construed to include both sexes. • Because of the trend toward nonsexist language, careful drafters now generally avoid using *his* (and the personal pronouns *he* and *him*) unless the reference is only to a male person.

His Honor; Her Honor. **1.** A title customarily given to a judge. **2.** A title customarily given to the mayor of a city. **3.** A title given by the Massachusetts Constitution to the lieutenant governor of the commonwealth. Cf. YOUR HONOR.

his testibus (his **tes**-tə-bəs). [Law Latin] *Hist.* These being witnesses. • The concluding clause of deeds and charters typically opened with these words, which stated the names of the witnesses to the instrument. This clause appeared in deeds and charters until the 16th century. — Also spelled *hijs testibus*; *hiis testibus*.

historical cost. See *acquisition cost* under COST (1).

historical jurisprudence. See JURISPRUDENCE.

historic bay. See BAY.

historic-preservation law. An ordinance prohibiting the demolition or exterior alteration of certain historic buildings or of all buildings in a historic district.

historic site. A building, structure, area, or property that is significant in the history, architecture, archeology, or culture of a country, state, or city, and has been so designated by statute. • A historic site usu. cannot be altered without the permission of the appropriate authorities.

hit-and-run statute. A law requiring a motorist involved in an accident to remain at the scene and to give certain information to the police and others involved.

hitherto, *adv.* Until now; heretofore.

H.L. *abbr.* HOUSE OF LORDS.

HLA test. *abbr.* A human-leukocyte-antigen test that uses a tissue-typing process to determine the probability of fatherhood. See PATERNITY TEST. Cf. DNA IDENTIFICATION.

HMO. *abbr.* HEALTH-MAINTENANCE ORGANIZATION.

hoard, *vb.* To acquire and hold (goods) beyond one's reasonable needs, usu. because of an actual or anticipated shortage or price increase <hoarding food and medical supplies during wartime>.

hobbler. *Hist.* In England, a light horseman or bowman; a tenant bound by his tenure to maintain a small light horse for military service.

Hobbs Act. A federal anti-racketeering act making it a crime to interfere with interstate commerce by extortion, robbery, or physical violence. 18 USCA § 1951. See RACKETEER INFLUENCED AND CORRUPT ORGANIZATIONS ACT.

hobby loss. See LOSS.

hodgepodge. 1. HOTCHPOT (1). **2.** An unorganized mixture.

hodgepodge act. A statute that deals with incongruous subjects.

> "*Hodge-Podge Act* .... Such acts, besides being evident proofs of the ignorance of the makers of them, or of their want of good faith, are calculated to create a confusion which is highly prejudicial to the interests of justice .... In many states bills, except general appropriation bills, can contain but one subject, which must be expressed in the title." 1 John Bouvier, *Bouvier's Law Dictionary* 1444 (8th ed. 1914).

hold, *n. Archaic.* In England, tenure. • This word occurs most often in conjunction with others — for example, *freehold, leasehold* — and rarely in its separate form. See HOLDING (4).

hold, *vb.* **1.** To possess by a lawful title <Sarah holds the account as her separate property>. **2.** (Of a court) to adjudge or decide <this court thus holds the statute to be unconstitutional>. **3.** To direct and bring about officially; to conduct according to law <we must hold an election every two years>. **4.** To keep in custody or under an obligation <I will ask the judge to hold you accountable>. **5.** To take or have an estate from another; to have an estate on condition of paying rent or performing service <James holds Hungerstream Manor under lease>. **6.** To conduct or preside at; to convoke, open, and direct the operations of <Judge Brown holds court four days a week>. **7.** To possess or occupy; to be in possession and administration of <Wendy holds the office of treasurer>.

holder. 1. A person who has legal possession of a negotiable instrument and is entitled to receive payment on it. **2.** A person with legal possession of a document of title or an investment security. **3.** A person who possesses or uses property.

holder for value. A person who has given value in exchange for a negotiable instrument. • Under the UCC, examples of "giving value" include acquiring a security interest in the instrument or accepting the instrument in payment of an antecedent claim. UCC

§ 3–303(a). — Also termed *bona fide holder for value*.

holder in due course. A person who in good faith has given value for a negotiable instrument that is complete and regular on its face, is not overdue, and, to the possessor's knowledge, has not been dishonored. • Under UCC § 3–305, a holder in due course takes the instrument free of all claims and personal defenses, but subject to real defenses. — Abbr. HDC; HIDC. — Also termed *due-course holder*.

holder in good faith. One who takes property or an instrument without knowledge of any defect in its title.

holder of record. See STOCKHOLDER OF RECORD.

hold harmless, *vb.* To absolve (another party) from any responsibility for damage or other liability arising from the transaction; INDEMNIFY. — Also termed *save harmless*.

hold-harmless agreement. A contract in which one party agrees to indemnify the other. — Also termed *save-harmless agreement*. See INDEMNITY.

hold-harmless clause. See INDEMNITY CLAUSE.

holding, *n.* **1.** A court's determination of a matter of law pivotal to its decision; a principle drawn from such a decision. Cf. OBITER DICTUM. **2.** A ruling on evidence or other questions presented at trial. **3.** (*usu. pl.*) Legally owned property, esp. land or securities. **4.** *Hist.* In feudal law, tenure.

holding cell. See JAIL.

holding charge. A criminal charge of some minor offense filed to keep the accused in custody while prosecutors take time to build a bigger case and prepare more serious charges.

holding company. See COMPANY.

holding-company tax. See TAX.

holding over. A tenant's action in continuing to occupy the leased premises after the lease term has expired. • Holding over creates a tenancy at sufferance, with the tenant being referred to as a *holdover*. See *tenancy at sufferance* under TENANCY.

holding period. *Tax.* The time during which a capital asset must be held to determine whether gain or loss from its sale or exchange is long-term or short-term.

holding zone. See ZONE.

hold order. A notation in a prisoner's file stating that another jurisdiction has charges pending against the prisoner and instructing prison officials to alert authorities in that other jurisdiction instead of releasing the prisoner.

hold out, *vb.* **1.** To represent (oneself or another) as having a certain legal status, as by claiming to be an agent or partner with authority to enter into transactions <even though he was only a promoter, Schwartz held himself out as the principal>. **2.** To refuse to yield or submit; to stand firm <Womack held out for a higher salary and better benefits>.

holdover tenancy. See *tenancy at sufferance* under TENANCY.

holdover tenant. See TENANT.

holdup. See STICKUP.

holograph (**hol**-ə-graf), *n.* A document (such as a will or deed) that is entirely handwritten by its author. — Also termed *olograph*. Cf. ONOMASTIC; SYMBOLIC. — **holographic,** *adj*.

holographic will. See WILL.

homage (**hom**-ij). In feudal times, a ceremony that a new tenant performed for the lord to acknowledge the tenure. • This was the most honorable service that a free tenant might do for a lord. In the ceremony, kneeling before the lord, the tenant placed his hands between the lord's hands while saying, "I become your man from this day forward, of life and limb and earthly honor, and to you will be faithful and loyal, and bear you faith, for the tenements that I claim to hold of you, saving the faith that I owe unto our sovereign lord the king, so help me God."

> "Homage is an oath of fidelity, acknowledging himself to be the lord's man: wherein the tenant must be ungirt, uncovered, kneel upon both knees, and hold both his hands together between the lord's hands sitting before him. This is to be done only to the lord himself." Sir Henry Finch, *Law, or a Discourse Thereof* 143 (1759).

homage ancestral (**hom**-ij an-**ses**-trəl). [Law French] A type of homage in which a tenant and the tenant's ancestors have held immemorially of another by the service of homage. • This long-standing relationship bound the lord to warrant the title and to hold the tenant clear of all services to superior lords. — Also spelled *homage auncestral* (aw-**mahzh** *on*-se-**stral**).

homage liege (**hom**-ij **leej**). Homage due the sovereign alone as supreme lord, done without any saving or exception of the rights of other lords. — Also termed *homagium ligium* (hə-**may**-jee-əm **lI**-jee-əm).

homage jury. See JURY.

homagio respectuando (hə-**may**-jee-oh ri-spek-choo-**an**-doh), *n.* [Law Latin "homage to the respected"] *Hist.* A writ to the escheator commanding the delivery of seisin of lands to the heir of the king's tenant, even though the heir had not performed homage.

homagium (hə-**may**-jee-əm), *n.* [Law Latin] See HOMAGE.

homagium ligium. See *homage liege* under HOMAGAE.

homagium planum (**play**-nəm), *n.* [Law Latin "plain homage"] *Hist.* A type of homage binding the homager to nothing more than fidelity, without obligation either of military service or of attendance in the superior's courts.

homagium reddere (**red**-ə-ree), *n.* [Law Latin "to renounce homage"] *Hist.* The process, prescribed in feudal law by a set form and method, by which a vassal disowns and defies the lord.

homagium simplex (**sim**-pleks), *n.* [Law Latin "simple homage"] *Hist.* A type of homage that acknowledges tenure, while reserving the rights of other lords.

hombre bueno (**awm**-bray **bway**-noh), *n. Spanish law.* **1.** A judge. **2.** An arbitrator chosen by the parties to a suit. **3.** A man in good standing; one who is competent to testify in a suit.

home equity loan. See LOAN.

home office. 1. A corporation's principal office or headquarters. **2.** (*cap.*) In England, the Department of State, responsible for overseeing the internal affairs of the country.

homeowners' association. See ASSOCIATION.

homeowner's equity loan. See LOAN.

homeowner's insurance. See INSURANCE.

homeowner's policy. See INSURANCE POLICY.

Home Owners Warranty. A warranty and insurance program that, among other coverage, insures a new home for ten years against major structural defects. • The program was developed by the Home Owners Warranty Corporation, a subsidiary of the National Association of Home Builders. Builders often provide this type of coverage, and many states provide similar warranty protection by statute. — Abbr. HOW. — Also spelled *Home Owners' Warranty.*

home port. See PORT.

home-port doctrine. *Maritime law.* The rule mandating that a vessel engaged in interstate and foreign commerce is taxable only at its home port, usu. where the vessel is registered.

home rule. A state legislative provision or action allocating a measure of autonomy to a local government, conditional on its acceptance of certain terms. Cf. LOCAL OPTION.

> "Home rule in the United States was sometimes envisioned in its early days as giving the cities to whom such rule was granted full-fledged sovereignty over local affairs, thus bringing about dual state and local sovereignty along the national plan of federal and state governments. But such local sovereignty has never developed, nor have any clear-cut distinctions between state and local power." Osborne M. Reynolds, Jr., *Handbook of Local Government Law* § 35, at 96 (1982).

home-rule charter. See CHARTER (3).

homestead. The house, outbuildings, and adjoining land owned and occupied by a person or family as a residence. • As long as the homestead does not exceed in area or value the limits fixed by law, in most states it is exempt from forced sale for collection of a debt. — Also termed *homestead estate.*

business homestead. The premises on which a family's business is located. • In some states, business homesteads are exempt from execution or judicial sale for most kinds of debt.

constitutional homestead. A homestead, along with its exemption from forced sale, conferred on the head of a household by a state constitution.

homesteader. One who acquires or occupies a homestead.

homestead law. A statute exempting a homestead from execution or judicial sale for debt, unless all owners, usu. a husband and wife, have jointly mortgaged the property or otherwise subjected it to creditors' claims.

"Almost all states also have legislative provisions, commonly referred to as homestead laws, designed to protect the family home from the reach of certain classes of creditors.... The protection afforded by an exemption statute is not absolute. A federal tax claim may be satisfied from 'exempt property.' A number of states make similar exceptions for state taxes, claims for alimony and child support, materialmen and mechanics' liens. By statute in most states, case law in others, purchase money mortgages and security interests are generally not affected by an exemption statute." David G. Epstein & Steve H. Nickles, *Consumer Law in a Nutshell* 384–85 (2d ed. 1981).

homicide (**hom**-ə-sɪd), *n.* The killing of one person by another. — **homicidal,** *adj.*

"The legal term for killing a man, whether lawfully or unlawfully, is 'homicide.' There is no *crime* of 'homicide.' Unlawful homicide at common law comprises the two crimes of murder and manslaughter. Other forms of unlawful homicide have been created by statute: certain new forms of manslaughter (homicide with diminished responsibility, and suicide pacts), infanticide, and causing death by dangerous driving." Glanville Williams, *Textbook of Criminal Law* 204 (1978).

criminal homicide. **1.** Homicide prohibited and punishable by law, such as murder or manslaughter. **2.** The act of purposely, knowingly, recklessly, or negligently causing the death of another human being. Model Penal Code § 210.1.

criminally negligent homicide. See *negligent homicide.*

excusable homicide. **1.** Homicide resulting from a person's lawful act, committed without intention to harm another. **2.** See *justifiable homicide* (1).

felonious homicide. Homicide committed unlawfully, without legal justification or excuse. • This is the category into which murder and manslaughter fall.

homicide by misadventure. See ACCIDENTAL KILLING.

homicide per infortunium (pər in-for-**t**[**y**]**oo**-nee-əm). [Latin "homicide by misfortune"] The unintentional killing of another while engaged in a lawful act; ACCIDENTAL KILLING. See PER INFORTUNIUM.

innocent homicide. Homicide that does not involve criminal guilt.

justifiable homicide. **1.** The killing of another in self-defense when faced with the danger of death or serious bodily injury. — Also termed *excusable homicide.* See SELF-DEFENSE. **2.** A killing mandated or permitted by the law, such as execution for a capital crime or killing to prevent a crime or a criminal's escape.

"It should be noted that a justifiable homicide is not criminal, since it is a killing which the law has either commanded or permitted: the *actus* in such a case is not legally punishable, and therefore we may perhaps say that it is an *actus* of killing which is not *reus.* As we shall see in most cases of justifiable homicide the killing is intentional, and therefore the mental element of criminal responsibility is clearly present: but there is no crime committed since there is no *actus reus.*" J.W. Cecil Turner, *Kenny's Outlines of Criminal Law* 109 (16th ed. 1952).

"English lawyers once distinguished between 'excusable' homicide (e.g. accidental non-negligent killing) and 'justifiable' homicide (e.g. killing in self-defence or in the arrest of a felon) and different legal consequences once attached to these two forms of homicide. To the modern lawyer this distinction has no longer any legal importance: he would simply consider both kinds of homicide to be cases where some element, negative or positive, required in the full definition of criminal homicide (murder or manslaughter) was lacking. But the distinction between these two different ways in which actions may fail to constitute a criminal offence is still of great moral importance. Killing in self-defence is an exception to a general rule making killing punishable; it is admitted because the policy or aims which in general justify the punishment of killing (e.g. protection of human life) do not include cases such as this. In the case of 'justification' what is done is regarded as something which the law does not condemn, or even welcomes." H.L.A. Hart, "Prolegomenon to the Principles of Punishment," in *Punishment and Responsibility* 1, 13 (1968).

negligent homicide. Homicide resulting from the careless performance of a legal or illegal act in which the danger of death is apparent; the killing of a human being by criminal negligence. — Also termed *criminally negligent homicide.* See *criminal negligence* under NEGLIGENCE.

"There is no common-law offense known as 'negligent homicide.' As a matter of the common law of crimes any killing below the grade of manslaughter is innocent homicide. Some of the new penal codes have a classification scheme which (omitting degrees or other variations) divides criminal homicide into murder, manslaughter and criminally negligent homicide — or simply negligent homicide. For the most part, however, this has been achieved by removing from manslaughter the offense of homicide by criminal negligence and using this to constitute the newly named offense. Thus, though there are a few exceptions, most states will have no homicide offense which would be below common-law manslaughter." Rollin M. Perkins & Ronald N. Boyce, *Criminal Law* 116–17 (3d ed. 1982).

reckless homicide. The unlawful killing of another person with conscious indifference toward that person's life. Cf. MANSLAUGHTER.

vehicular homicide. The killing of another person by one's unlawful or negligent operation of a motor vehicle.

homicidium (hom-ə-**sI**-dee-əm), *n.* [Latin] Homicide.

homicidium ex casu (eks **kay**-s[y]oo). Homicide by accident. See ACCIDENTAL KILLING.

homicidium ex justitia (eks jəs-**tish**-ee-ə). Homicide in the administration of justice, or in the carrying out of a legal sentence. See *justifiable homicide* (2) under HOMICIDE.

homicidium ex necessitate (eks nə-ses-i-**tay**-tee). Homicide from inevitable necessity, such as for the protection of one's person or property. See *justifiable homicide* (1) under HOMICIDE.

homicidium ex voluntate (eks vol-ən-**tay**-tee). Voluntary or willful homicide. See *criminal homicide* under HOMICIDE.

hominatio (hom-ə-**nay**-shee-oh), *n.* [Law Latin] *Hist.* Homage; the act of performing homage.

homine capto in withernamium (**hom**-ə-nee **kap**-toh in wi<u>th</u>-ər-**nay**-mee-əm). [Law Latin "for taking a man in withernam"] *Hist.* A writ for the arrest of a person who had taken a bondman out of the country to prevent a replevy. See WITHERNAM.

homine replegiando (**hom**-ə-nee ri-plee-jee-**an**-doh). [Law Latin "for replevying a man"] *Hist.* A writ to replevy a man out of prison, or out of the custody of a private person.

homines (**hom**-ə-neez), *n.* [Latin "men"] *Hist.* Feudal tenants entitled to have their causes and other matters tried only in their lord's court. See HOMO.

homines ligii (**lI**-jee-I). [Latin] *Hist.* Liege men; feudal tenants or vassals, esp. those who held immediately of the sovereign.

homiplagium (hom-ə-**play**-jee-əm), *n.* [Law Latin] *Hist.* The act of maiming a man.

hommes de fief (awm də **feef**), *n.* [French "men of the fief"] *Hist.* Feudal tenants; peers in the lords' courts. — Also termed *hommes feodaux.*

homo (**hoh**-moh), *n.* [Latin] *Hist.* **1.** A male human. **2.** A member of humankind; a human being of either sex. **3.** A slave. **4.** A vassal; a feudal tenant. **5.** A retainer, dependent, or servant. Pl. ***homines.*** See HOMINES.

homo alieni juris (ay-lee- *or* al-ee-**ee**-nI **joor**-is). See FILIUSFAMILIAS.

homo chartularius (kahr-chə-**lair**-ee-əs). A slave manumitted by charter.

homo commendatus (kom-ən-**day**-təs). A man who commends himself into another's power for protection or support.

homo ecclesiasticus (e-klee-z[h]ee-**as**-ti-kəs). A church vassal; one bound to serve a church, esp. in an agricultural capacity.

homo exercitalis (eg-zər-shə-**tay**-lis). A man of the army; a soldier.

homo feodalis (fyoo-**day**-lis). A fee man; a vassal or tenant who holds a fee.

homo fiscalis (fis-**kay**-lis). A servant or vassal belonging to the treasury (*fiscus*). — Also termed *homo fiscalinus.*

homo francus (**frangk**-əs). **1.** *Hist.* In England, a freeman. **2.** A Frenchman.

homo ingenuus (in-**jen**-yoo-əs). A free and lawful man; a yeoman.

homo liber (**lI**-bər). **1.** A free man. **2.** A freeman lawfully competent to be a juror. **3.** An allodial proprietor, as distinguished from a feudal tenant. See ALLODIAL.

homo ligius (**lI**-jee-əs). A liege man, esp. the vassal of a king.

homo novus (**noh**-vəs). **1.** A new tenant or vassal; one invested with a new fee. **2.** A tenant pardoned after being convicted of a crime.

homo pertinens (**pər**-tə-nenz). A feudal bondman or vassal; one belonging to the soil.

homo regius (**ree**-jee-əs). A king's vassal.

homo Romanus (rə-**may**-nəs). A Roman. • A term used in Germanic law codes to describe the Roman inhabitants of Gaul and other former Roman provinces.

homo sui juris (**s[y]oo**-I **joor**-is). See PATERFAMILIAS.

homo trium litterarum (**trI**-əm lit-ə-**rair**-əm). ["a man of three letters"] A thief. • The "three letters" refers to *f, u,* and *r,* for the Latin word *fur* ("thief").

homologación. See HOMOLOGATION.

homologare (hom-ə-lə-**gair**-ee), *vb.* [Law Latin] *Civil law.* **1.** To confirm or approve; to consent or assent. **2.** To confess.

homologate (hə-**mol**-ə-gayt), *vb. Civil law.* To approve or confirm officially <the court homologated the sale>.

homologation (hə-mol-ə-**gay**-shən). *Civil law.* **1.** Confirmation, esp. of a court granting its approval to some action. **2.** The consent inferred by law from parties' failure, for a ten-day period, to complain of an arbitrator's sentence, of an appointment of a syndic (or assignee) of an insolvent, or of a settlement of successions. **3.** The approval given by a judge of certain acts and agreements, to render them more binding and executory. — Also termed (in Spanish law) *homologación* ([h]oh-moh-loh-gas-**yohn**). See *judgment homologating the tableau* under JUDGMENT.

Hon. *abbr.* HONORABLE.

honeste vivere ([h]ə-**nes**-tee **vɪ**-və-ree). [Latin] *Roman law.* To live honestly. • This was one of the three general precepts in which Justinian expressed the requirements of the law. Cf. ALTERUM NON LAEDERE; SUUM CUIQUE TRIBUERE.

honesty clause. See FULL-REPORTING CLAUSE (1).

honor, *n.* **1.** In the United States, a courtesy title given to judges and certain other public officials. **2.** (*usu. pl.*) In England, those dignities or privileges, degrees of nobility, knighthood, and other titles that flow from the Crown. **3.** *Hist.* In England, a seigniory of several manors held under one baron or lord paramount.

honor, *vb.* **1.** To accept or pay (a negotiable instrument) when presented. **2.** To recognize, salute, or praise.

Honorable. A title of respect given to judges, members of the U.S. Congress, ambassadors, and the like <The Honorable Ruth Bader Ginsburg>. — Abbr. Hon.

honorable discharge. See DISCHARGE (8).

honorable-engagement clause. *Reinsurance.* An arbitration provision in a reinsurance contract allowing the arbitrators to view the reinsurance arrangement reasonably — in line with the agreement's general purposes — rather than strictly according to the rules of law or an overly technical interpretation of contract language.

honorarium (on-ə-**rair**-ee-əm), *n.* **1.** A payment of money or anything of value made to a person for services rendered for which fees cannot legally be or are not traditionally paid. • Federal law restricts the payment of honoraria to members of Congress. **2.** A voluntary reward for that for which no remuneration could be collected by law; a voluntary donation in consideration of services that admit of no compensation in money. **3.** *Roman law.* A gratuitous payment, esp. for professional services, as distinguished from compensation for physical labor. Pl. **honoraria.** Cf. MERCES.

honorary canon. See CANON (5).

honorary feud. *Hist.* In England, a title of nobility descending to the eldest son only. See FEUD.

honorary services. *Hist.* Special services rendered to the king by a person holding tenure of grand serjeanty. • The services usu. consisted of carrying the royal banner or sword, or serving at the king's coronation as a butler, as a champion, or in some other capacity.

honorary trust. See TRUST.

horae juridicae (**hor**-ee juu-**rid**-i-see), *n. pl.* [Latin] *Hist.* Juridical hours. • The time during which judges sat in court to attend to judicial business. — Also termed *horae judicii* (hor-ee joo-**dish**-ee-ee).

horca (**or**-kah), *n. Spanish law.* **1.** A gallows. **2.** A stick for administering corporal punishment. **3.** A designated place for administering corporal punishment.

hordera (hor-**deer**-ə), *n.* [Law Latin] *Hist.* In England, a treasurer. — Also termed *hordarius* (hor-**dair**-ee-əs).

horderium (hor-**deer**-ee-əm), *n.* [Law Latin] *Hist.* In England, a hoard, treasury, or repository.

horizontal agreement. See *horizontal restraint* under RESTRAINT OF TRADE.

horizontal competition. See COMPETITION.

horizontal-gaze nystagmus test. *Criminal law.* A test for intoxication, commonly performed on persons suspected of driving under the influence of alcohol, in which the suspect's eyes are observed to detect involuntary jerking movements as they follow horizontal motion. — Abbr. HGN test. See NYSTAGMUS.

horizontal integration. See *horizontal merger* under MERGER.

horizontal merger. See MERGER.

horizontal nonprivity. See NONPRIVITY.

horizontal price-fixing. See PRICE-FIXING.

horizontal privity. See PRIVITY.

horizontal-property act. A statute dealing with cooperatives and condominiums.

horizontal restraint. See RESTRAINT OF TRADE.

horizontal union. See *craft union* under UNION.

hornbook. 1. A book explaining the basics of a given subject. **2.** A textbook containing the rudimentary principles of an area of law. Cf. CASEBOOK.

> "*Hornbook* ... The first book of children, covered with horn to keep it unsoiled." Samuel Johnson, *A Dictionary of the English Language* (1755).

hornbook law. See BLACKLETTER LAW.

hornbook method. A method of legal instruction characterized by a straightforward presentation of legal doctrine, occasionally interspersed with questions. • The hornbook method predominates in civil-law countries, and in certain fields of law, such as procedure and evidence. — Also termed *lecture method*. Cf. CASEBOOK METHOD; SOCRATIC METHOD.

horn tenure. See CORNAGE.

hors (or). [French] **1.** Out or out of. **2.** Outside or outside of.

hors de son fee (**or** də son **fee**), *n.* [French "out of his fee"] *Hist.* A defensive plea in an action for rent or services by which the defendant alleged that the land in question was outside the plaintiff's fee.

horse case. See WHITEHORSE CASE.

horseshedding, *n.* The instruction of a witness favorable to one's case (esp. a client) about the proper method of responding to questions while giving testimony. — Also termed *woodshedding*. — **horseshed,** *vb.* Cf. SANDPAPERING.

hospitalaria. See HOSTILARIA.

Hospitallers (**hos**-pi-təl-ərz). A military and religious order founded by the Catholic Church in the 12th century and so called because it built a hospital at Jerusalem to care for pilgrims. • The Crown seized all its lands and goods in England under the Grantees of Reversions Act (1540). The Hospitallers still functions in several countries as a humanitarian society.

hospitator (**hos**-pə-tay-tər), *n.* [Law Latin] A host or entertainer.

hospitator communis (kə-**myoo**-nis). A common innkeeper.

hospitator magnus (**mag**-nəs). The marshal of a camp.

hospitia (hah-**spish**-ee-ə), *n.* [Latin] Inns.

hospitia cancellariae (kan-sə-**lair**-ee-I). Inns of chancery.

hospitia communia (kə-**myoo**-nee-ə). Common inns.

hospitia curiae (**kyoor**-ee-I). Inns of court.

hospiticide (hah-**spit**-ə-sId), *n.* A host who murders a guest.

hospitium (hah-**spish**-ee-əm), *n.* [Latin] An inn; a household.

hostage. 1. An innocent person held captive by another who threatens to kill or harm that person if one or more demands are not met. • Hostage-taking is a federal crime. 18 USCA § 1203. Cf. KIDNAPPING. **2.** *Int'l law.* A person who is given into an enemy's possession, in time of war, with his or her freedom or life to stand as security for the performance of some agreement made to the enemy by the belligerent power giving the hostage.

hostelagium (hos-tə-**lay**-jee-əm), *n.* [Law Latin] *Hist.* A right to receive lodging and entertainment, anciently reserved by lords in their tenants' houses.

hosteler (**hos**-tə-lər). **1.** A person who stays in a youth hostel. **2.** A stableman. **3.** *Archaic.* A person who receives and entertains guests, esp. at a monastery. **4.** *Archaic.* An innkeeper. See HOSTLER.

hostes (**hos**-teez), *n. pl.* [Latin] Enemies. Sing. ***hostis*** (**hos**-tis).

hostes humani generis (hyoo-**may**-nI **jen**-ə-ris). Enemies of the human race; specif., pirates.

hosticide (**hos**-tə-sɪd), *n.* **1.** A person who kills an enemy. **2.** The killing of an enemy.

hostilaria (hos-tə-**lair**-ee-ə), *n.* [Latin] A place or room in a religious house used to receive guests and strangers. — Also termed *hospitalaria* (hos-pə-tə-**ler**-[ee-]ə).

hostile amendment. See AMENDMENT (1).

hostile bidder. See CORPORATE RAIDER.

hostile embargo. See EMBARGO (1).

hostile-environment sexual harassment. See SEXUAL HARASSMENT.

hostile possession. See POSSESSION.

hostile takeover. See TAKEOVER.

hostile witness. See WITNESS.

hostility. 1. A state of enmity between individuals or nations. **2.** An act or series of acts displaying antagonism. **3.** *Usu. pl.* Acts of war.

hostler ([**h**]**os**-lər). [fr. *hosteler*] *Archaic.* **1.** A stableman; an ostler. **2.** An innkeeper. • By the 16th century, this term had lost its "innkeeper" sense, and referred exclusively to a stableman.

hot blood. See HEAT OF PASSION.

hot cargo. *Labor law.* Goods produced or handled by an employer with whom a union has a dispute.

hot-cargo agreement. *Labor law.* A voluntary agreement between a union and a neutral employer by which the latter agrees to exert pressure on another employer with whom the union has a dispute, as by ceasing or refraining from handling, using, selling, transporting, or otherwise dealing in any of the products of an employer that the union has labeled as unfair. • Most agreements of this type were prohibited by the Landrum–Griffin Act of 1959. See LANDRUM-GRIFFIN ACT.

hot check. See *bad check* under CHECK.

hotchpot (**hoch**-pot), *n.* **1.** The blending of items of property to secure equality of division, esp. as practiced in cases in which advancements of an intestate's property must be made up to the estate by a contribution or by an accounting. — Also termed *hotchpotch*; *hodgepodge*. **2.** In community-property states, the property that falls within the community estate.

hot court. See COURT.

hot document. See DOCUMENT.

hotel divorce. See DIVORCE.

hotelkeeper's lien. See LIEN.

hot issue. See ISSUE (2).

hot pursuit. 1. FRESH PURSUIT. **2.** *Int'l law.* The legitimate chase of a foreign vessel on the high seas just after that vessel has violated the law of the pursuing state while within that state's jurisdiction.

hot stock. See *hot issue* under ISSUE (2).

hot-water ordeal. See ORDEAL.

house. 1. A home, dwelling, or residence.

ancient house. *Hist.* In England, a house that has stood long enough to acquire an easement of support against the adjoining land or building.

bawdy house. See DISORDERLY HOUSE.

house of correction. **1.** A reformatory. **2.** A place for the confinement of juvenile offenders or those who have committed crimes of lesser magnitude. — Also termed *house of refuge*.

house of prostitution. See DISORDERLY HOUSE.

house of refuge. See *house of correction*.

house of worship. A building or place set apart for and devoted to the holding of religious services or exercises or public worship; a church or chapel, or a place similarly used.

public house. **1.** *Archaic.* An inn. **2.** A tavern where alcoholic beverages may be bought and consumed on the premises. • The British term *pub* is an abbreviation of *public house*. — Also termed (in sense 2) *tippling house*.

2. A branch of a legislature or a quorum of such a branch; esp., the lower chamber of a bicameral legislature. **3.** HOUSE OF REPRESENTATIVES.

houseage (**howz**-ij). A fee paid for housing goods, as by a carrier or at a wharf.

house arrest. The confinement of a person who is accused or convicted of a crime to his or her home usu. by attaching an electronically monitored bracelet to the criminal offender. • Most house-arrest programs require the offender to work and permit leaving the home only for reasons such as work, medical needs, or community-service obligations.

house bill. See BILL (3).

house-bote. See BOTE (1).

housebreaking. The crime of breaking into a dwelling or other secured building, with the intent to commit a felony inside; BURGLARY. • *Burglary* is now used more than *housebreaking*. In England, for example, *housebreaking* was replaced in 1968 with statutory burglary, though the term is still used in Scots law.

> "The oldest term for this purpose [i.e., of distinguishing between common-law burglary and its statutory enlargements], still encountered at times, is 'housebreaking'; a more recent suggestion is 'breaking and entering,' and peace officers sometimes speak of a 'breakin.' " Rollin M. Perkins & Ronald N. Boyce, *Criminal Law* 270 (3d ed. 1982).

houseburning. The common-law misdemeanor of intentionally burning one's own house that is within city limits or that is close enough to other houses that they might be in danger of catching fire (although no actual damage to them results). — Also termed *combustio domorum*. Cf. ARSON.

house counsel. See *in-house counsel* under COUNSEL.

house-duty. *Hist. English law.* A tax first imposed in 1851 on inhabited houses. 14 & 15 Vict., ch. 36 (repealed 1924). • This tax replaced the window tax, which levied a duty on houses with more than six windows. See *window tax* under TAX.

household, *adj.* Belonging to the house and family; domestic.

household, *n.* **1.** A family living together. **2.** A group of people who dwell under the same roof. Cf. FAMILY.

householder. 1. A person who keeps house with his or her family; the head or master of a family. **2.** A person who has a household. **3.** An occupier of a house. Cf. HEAD OF HOUSEHOLD.

household goods. See GOODS.

house law. *Hist.* A regulatory code promulgated by the head of a royal or noble family, or of a prominent private family, governing intrafamily relationships and acts concerning events such as marriage, disposition of property, and inheritance. • Such a code had no legal authority but was enforced within the family by personal and economic sanctions.

House of Commons. The lower chamber of the British and Canadian parliaments. — Abbr. H.C.

house of correction. See HOUSE.

House of Delegates. 1. The body vested with the control and administration of the American Bar Association. **2.** The lower chamber of the state legislature in Maryland, Virginia, and West Virginia.

house of ill fame. See DISORDERLY HOUSE.

House of Lords. The upper chamber of the British Parliament, of which the 11-member judicial committee provides judges who serve as the final court of appeal in most civil cases. • In practice, the Lords sit as committees, usu. of five but occasionally of seven. Two committees may sit simultaneously. — Abbr. H.L. — Also termed *Lords*.

> " 'House of Lords' is an ambigous expression. It refers (1) to all the peers who choose to sit as the Upper House of the legislature (Parliament), and also (2) to a court consisting of the highest level of the judiciary." Glanville Williams, *Learning the Law* 8 (11th ed. 1982).

house of prostitution. See DISORDERLY HOUSE.

house of refuge. See *house of correction* under HOUSE.

House of Representatives. 1. The lower chamber of the U.S. Congress, composed of 435 members — apportioned among the states on the basis of population — who are elected to two-year terms. **2.** The lower house of a state legislature. — Abbr. H.R. — Often shortened to *House*.

house of worship. See HOUSE.

housing codes. See BUILDING CODES.

housing court. See COURT.

hovering act. *Int'l law.* A statute applying to a coastal country's criminal jurisdiction over ships, and persons aboard those ships, when the ships are outside the country's territory.

> "The notion of hovering acts evolved long before that of a belt of uniform width in the form of territorial waters. Great Britain's first anti-smuggling legislation to operate at a stated distance seaward was in 1719, applying to the master of any ship 'found at anchor or hovering within two leagues from the shore.' Later enactments extended this limit to three, then four, then eight leagues. A statute of 1794 gave power to seize and confiscate customable goods in vessels 'found at anchor, or hovering' inside specific straight lines drawn between lines on the British coasts, thus resembling the 'King's Chambers' of the Stuart era. In 1805 the British Parliament extended the seizure limit to 100 leagues (300 miles) from the coasts of Great Britain and Ireland in respect of vessels 'belonging wholly or in part to His Majesty's subjects, or whereof one-half of the persons on board shall be subjects of His Majesty.' Foreign-flag vessels could have fallen within this category. In the case of *Le Louis* (1817) 165 E.R. 1464, the British Admiralty judge Lord Stowell described these statutes as being permitted by 'the common courtesy of nations for their convenience.'" Geoffrey Marston, "Hovering Acts," in 2 *Encyclopedia of Public International Law* 884–85 (1995).

HOW. *abbr.* HOME OWNERS WARRANTY.

howsoever, *adv.* In whatever way; however.

H.R. *abbr.* HOUSE OF REPRESENTATIVES.

H.R. 10 plan. See KEOGH PLAN.

hub-and-spoke conspiracy. See *wheel conspiracy* under CONSPIRACY.

huc usque (hək əs-kwee), *adv.* [Latin] *Hist.* Hitherto. • This term commonly appeared in pleadings. — Also spelled *hucusque.*

HUD. *abbr.* The Department of Housing and Urban Development, a federal agency responsible for programs and policies that address the country's housing needs and that develop and improve neighborhoods.

hudegeld. See HYDEGELD.

hue and cry. *Hist.* **1.** The public uproar that, at common law, a citizen was expected to initiate after discovering a crime. — Also termed *vociferatio.*

> "Hue and Cry is the old Common Law mode of pursuing, 'with horn and voice,' persons suspected of felony, or having inflicted a wound from which death is likely to ensue." 1 Joseph Chitty, *A Practical Treatise on the Criminal Law* 26 (2d ed. 1826).

> "All were obliged to pursue the criminal when the hue and cry was raised. Neglect of these duties entailed an amercement of the individual, the township or the hundred. The sheriffs and the constables were under special obligations, as conservatores pacis, to fulfil these duties." 1 William Holdsworth, *A History of English Law* 294 (7th ed. 1956).

2. The pursuit of a felon accompanying such an uproar. **3.** A written proclamation for the capture of a felon.

hui (**hoo**-ee), *n.* Under Hawaiian law, an association of persons who own land together, usu. as tenants in common.

huissier (wee-**syay**), *n.* [French fr. *huis* "door"] **1.** *French law.* An usher of a court; an officer (such as a marshal) who serves process. **2.** *Hist.* In England, a ministerial officer attached to a court, responsible for service of process, issuing executions, and maintaining order during court sessions.

hulk, *n. Hist.* In England, a dismantled ship used as a prison. • Living conditions in hulks were notoriously poor, and their use as prisons ended as part of the broad prison-reform movements of the mid–19th century.

humanitarian doctrine. See LAST-CLEAR-CHANCE DOCTRINE.

humanitarian law. *Int'l law.* Law dealing with such matters as the use of weapons and other means of warfare, the treatment of war victims by the enemy, and generally the direct impact of war on human life and liberty.

human rights. The freedoms, immunities, and benefits that, according to modern values (esp. at an international level), all human beings should be able to claim as a matter of right in the society in which they live. See UNIVERSAL DECLARATION OF HUMAN RIGHTS.

hundred. *Hist.* **1.** A county subdivision, formerly having its own local court.

> "*The hundred* was a group of adjoining townships. It may have consisted of an area taxed at one hundred hides. Other explanations of the term 'hundred' are that the unit may have consisted of one hundred households, or the area had to supply one hundred fighting men for the national defence." L.B. Curzon, *English Legal History* 7 (2d ed. 1979).

2. The populace of such a subdivision. **3.** See *hundred court* under COURT. **4.** In the United States, a political division derived from the

English county division. • Hundreds existed in colonial Delaware, Maryland, Pennsylvania, and Virginia. Today, they exist only in Delaware. — **hundredal** (**hun**-dri-dəl), *adj*.

hundredarius (hən-dri-**dair**-ee-əs), *n*. [Law Latin] *Hist*. **1.** HUNDREDARY. **2.** HUNDREDOR (1).

hundredary (**hən**-dri-der-ee), *n*. [Law Latin] *Hist*. The chief or presiding officer of a hundred. — Also termed *hundredarius*.

hundred court. See COURT.

hundredes earldor (**hən**-dridz **ərl**-dər), *n*. [Latinized Old English] *Hist*. The presiding officer in a hundred court. — Also termed *hundredes man*.

hundred moot. See *hundred court* under COURT.

hundredor (**hən**-dri-dər), *n*. *Hist*. **1.** A freeholder of a hundred who can sue in, or act as judge of, a hundred court. **2.** A person who has been empaneled (or is fit to be empaneled) on a hundred-court jury, and who dwells within the hundred where the cause of action arose. **3.** An officer who has jurisdiction of a hundred and who holds the hundred court. **4.** The bailiff of a hundred.

hundred penny. *Hist*. In England, a tax collected from the hundred by the sheriff or lord of the hundred.

hundred rolls. *Hist*. Records that list the various feudal tenancies and feudal obligations existing among English lords and tenants. • The *hundred rolls* were compiled in 1274–75 by royal commissioners from inquiries put to hundred-court juries in order to alert the Crown to the existence of feudal relationships that infringed on royal prerogatives (and thereby royal revenue).

hung jury. See JURY.

hurto (**oor**-toh), *n*. *Spanish law*. Theft.

husband. A married man; a man who has a lawful wife living. • Etymologically, the word signified the *house bond*, the man who, according to Saxon ideas and institutions, held around him the family, for which he was legally responsible.

husbandman. *Archaic*. A farmer.

husbandria (həz-bən-**dree**-ə), *n*. [Law Latin] *Hist*. HUSBANDRY.

husbandry. 1. Agriculture or farming; cultivation of the soil for food. • In some states, tools and equipment used in farming are exempt from forced sale for collection of a debt. **2.** Generally, care of a household; careful management of resources.

husband-wife immunity. See IMMUNITY (2).

husband-wife privilege. See *marital privilege* under PRIVILEGE (3).

huscarle (**hoos**-kahrl), *n*. [Old English] *Hist*. **1.** A house servant or domestic; a man of the household. **2.** A king's vassal, thane, or baron; an earl's man or vassal.

husfastne (**hoos**-fas[t]-ən), *n*. [Old English] *Hist*. A person who holds house and land; a man bound to a frankpledge.

husgablum (**hoos**-gab-ləm), *n*. [Old English] *Hist*. A tax or tribute levied upon a house; house rent.

hush money. *Slang*. A bribe to suppress the dissemination of certain information; a payment to secure silence.

husting. (*usu. pl.*) [Old English] **1.** *Hist*. A deliberative assembly, esp. one called by the king or other leader. **2.** *Hist*. COURT OF HUSTINGS. **3.** *Hist*. The raised platform used by officials of the Court of Hustings. **4.** *Hist*. The raised platform used to nominate candidates for Parliament. • This practice ended after passage of the Ballot Act in 1872. **5.** Any place where political campaign speeches are made.

hutesium et clamor (h[y]oo-**tee**-z[h]ee-əm et **klam**-ər). [Law Latin] HUE AND CRY.

hybrid action. *Labor law*. A lawsuit in which a union member asserts claims against the employer for breach of a collective bargaining agreement, and against the union for breach of the duty of fair representation.

hybrid class action. See CLASS ACTION.

hybrid security. See SECURITY.

hydegeld (**hɪd**-geld), *n*. *Hist*. **1.** In England, a discharge for an assault on a trespassing servant. **2.** HIDEGILD. — Also spelled *hudegeld*.

***Hydraflow* test.** A principle for deciding when an inadvertent disclosure of a privileged document is a waiver of the attorney-client privilege, whereby the court considers the reasonableness of the precautions taken to prevent the inadvertent disclosure, the number of disclosures involved, the extent of the disclosure, the promptness of any efforts to remedy the disclosure, and whether justice would be best served by permitting the disclosing party to retrieve the document. *Hydraflow, Inc. v. Enidine, Inc.*, 145 F.R.D. 626 (W.D.N.Y. 1993). — Also termed *middle-of-the-road test*. Cf. *lenient test*; *strict test*.

hypobolum (hi-**pob**-ə-ləm), *n.* [Latin fr. Greek] *Civil law.* A legacy given to a wife, in addition to her dowry, on the death of her husband.

hypothec (hɪ-**poth**-ek *or* hi-). *Civil law.* A mortgage given to a creditor on property to secure a debt; HYPOTHECA.

hypotheca (hɪ-pə-**thee**-kə *or* hip-ə-), *n.* [Latin] *Roman law.* A mortgage of property in which the debtor was allowed to keep, but not alienate, the property.

> "Yet another mode of creating a security is possible, by which not merely the ownership of a thing but its possession also remains with the debtor. This is called by the Roman lawyers and their modern followers 'hypotheca.' Hypothecs may arise by the direct application of a rule of law, by judicial decision, or by agreement." Thomas E. Holland, *The Elements of Jurisprudence* 235 (13th ed. 1924).

hypothecaria actio (hɪ-poth-ə-**kair**-ee-ə **ak**-shee-oh), *n.* [Latin] *Roman law.* A hypothecary action; an action to enforce a mortgage or to obtain the surrender of the thing mortgaged.

hypothecarii creditores (hɪ-poth-ə-**kair**-ee-ɪ kred-ə-**tor**-eez), *n.* [Latin] *Roman law.* Hypothecary creditors; those who lent money on the security of a hypotheca.

hypothecary (hɪ-**poth**-ə-ker-ee), *adj.* Of, relating to, or involving a hypothec or hypothecation.

hypothecary action. *Civil law.* A lawsuit to enforce a creditor's claims under a hypothec or hypothecation.

hypothecary debt. See DEBT.

hypothecate (hɪ-**poth**-ə-kayt), *vb.* To pledge (property) as security or collateral for a debt, without delivery of title or possession.

hypothecation (hɪ-poth-ə-**kay**-shən), *n.* The pledging of something as security without delivery of title or possession. — **hypothecator** (hɪ-**poth**-ə-kay-tər), *n.*

tacit hypothecation. **1.** *Civil law.* A type of lien or mortgage that is created by operation of law and without the parties' express agreement. — Also termed *tacit mortgage*. **2.** See *maritime lien* under LIEN.

hypothecation bond. See BOND (2).

hypothèque (ee-poh-**tek**), *n.* *French law.* Hypothecation; the right vested in a creditor by the assignment to the creditor of real estate as security for a debt, whether or not accompanied by possession. • *Hypothèque* may be *légale*, as the charge that the state has over the lands of its accountants, or that a married woman has over the lands of her husband; *judiciaire*, when it is the result of a judgment of a court of justice; or *conventionelle*, when it is the result of the parties' agreement.

hypothetical creditor. See CREDITOR.

hypothetical lien creditor. See *hypothetical creditor* under CREDITOR.

hypothetical question. A trial device that solicits an expert witness's opinion based on assumptions treated as facts established by evidence. — Also termed *abstract question*.

hypothetical tenant. *Hist.* A fictional person used for assessing property taxes, which are based on what the person would pay to lease the property.

I

IABA. *abbr.* INTER-AMERICAN BAR ASSOCIATION.

ibid. (**ib**-id). *abbr.* [Latin *ibidem*] In the same place. • This abbreviation, used in citations (mostly outside law), denotes that the reference is to a work cited immediately before, and that the cited matter appears on the same page of the same book (unless a different page is specified). — Also termed *ib*. Cf. ID.

ICC. *abbr.* **1.** INTERNATIONAL COMMERCE COMMISSION. **2.** INTERNATIONAL CRIMINAL COURT.

ICJ. *abbr.* INTERNATIONAL COURT OF JUSTICE.

id. (id). *abbr.* [Latin *idem*] The same. • *Id.* is used in a legal citation to refer to the authority cited immediately before <*id.* at 55>. Cf. IBID.

idem per idem (**I**-dem pər **I**-dem). [Latin] The same for the same. • This phrase refers to an illustration that adds nothing to a matter under consideration.

idem sonans (**I**-dem **soh**-nanz), *adj.* [Latin] (Of words or names) sounding the same, regardless of spelling <the names Jon and John are *idem sonans*>.

> "The names of parties should be correctly spelled, but misspelling which does not change the sound works no harm; it matters not how incorrectly names are spelled, if they are *idem sonans* (the same sound)." Edwin E. Bryant, *The Law of Pleading Under the Codes of Civil Procedure* 186 (2d ed. 1899).

idem sonans (**I**-dem **soh**-nanz), *n.* [Latin] A legal doctrine preventing a variant spelling of a name in a document from voiding the document if the misspelling is pronounced the same way as the true spelling.

identification of goods. A process that enables a buyer to obtain an identifiable (and therefore insurable) interest in goods before taking possession from the seller. • The goods are identified in any manner agreed to by the parties. UCC § 2–501.

identification parade. See LINEUP.

identify, *vb.* **1.** To prove the identity of (a person or thing) <the witness identified the weapon>. **2.** To look upon as being associated (*with*) <the plaintiff was identified with the environmental movement>. **3.** To specify (certain goods) as the object of a contract <identify the appliances to the contract>. See IDENTIFICATION OF GOODS.

identitate nominis (**I**-den-ti-**tay**-tee **nom**-ə-nis). See DE IDENTITATE NOMINIS.

identity. 1. The identical nature of two or more things; esp., in patent law, the sameness in two devices of the function performed, the way it is performed, and the result achieved. • Under the doctrine of equivalents, infringement may be found even if the accused device is not identical to the claimed invention. See DOCTRINE OF EQUIVALENTS. **2.** *Evidence.* The authenticity of a person or thing.

identity of interests. *Civil procedure.* A relationship between two parties who are so close that suing one serves as notice to the other, so that the other may be joined in the suit. Fed. R. Civ. P. 15(c)(3).

identity of parties. *Civil procedure.* A relationship between two parties who are so close that a judgment against one prevents later action against the other because of res judicata.

ideo (**I**-dee-oh), *adv.* [Latin] Therefore; for that reason.

ideo consideratum est (**I**-dee-oh kən-sid-ə-**ray**-təm est). [Latin] *Hist.* Therefore it is considered. • These words often prefaced a judgment at common law, and came to refer to the judgment itself. Cf. CONSIDERATUM EST PER CURIAM.

idiochira (id-ee-oh-**kI**-rə). [Greek "one's own hand"] *Hist.* An instrument executed privately, rather than before a public officer; esp., a deed written in one's own hand.

idiocy. *Archaic.* The condition of a person who, from birth, has never had any glimmering of reasoning or intellectual faculties. — Also termed *idiopathic insanity*.

idiot. A person afflicted with profound mental retardation. • This term has largely fallen out of use in modern legal and medical contexts. Cf. IMBECILE.

idiota (id-ee-**oh**-tə). [Latin] *Civil law.* **1.** An unlearned, simple person. **2.** A private person; one not in public office.

idiota inquirendo (id-ee-**oh**-tə in-kwI-**ren**-doh *or* in-kwə-**ren**-doh). See DE IDIOTA INQUIRENDO.

idoneitas (I-doh-**nee**-ə-tas). [fr. Latin *idoneus* "suitable"] *Hist.* A person's ability or fitness. — Also termed *idoneity*.

idoneum se facere; idoneare se (I-**doh**-nee-əm see **fay**-sə-ree; I-doh-nee-**air**-ee see). [Law Latin "to make oneself sufficient; to clear oneself"] *Hist.* To purge oneself, by oath, of a crime that one is accused of committing.

idoneus (I-**doh**-nee-əs), *adj.* [Latin] *Roman law.* (Of a person or thing) appropriate or suitable. • A responsible or solvent man, for example, was known as an *idoneus homo*, while a pledge of sufficient security was termed *idonea cautio*. — Also spelled *idoneous*.

i.e. *abbr.* [Latin *id est*] That is <the federal government's highest judicial body, i.e., the Supreme Court>. Cf. E.G.

i.f.p. *abbr.* IN FORMA PAUPERIS.

IFP affidavit. See *poverty affidavit* under AFFIDAVIT.

ignis judicium (**ig**-nis joo-**dish**-ee-əm). [Latin] *Hist.* Trial by fire. See *fire ordeal* under ORDEAL.

ignominy (**ig**-nə-min-ee). Public disgrace or dishonor. — **ignominious,** *adj.*

ignoramus (ig-nə-**ray**-məs). [Law Latin] *Hist.* We do not know. • This notation, when written on a bill of indictment, indicated the grand jury's rejection of the bill. See NOT FOUND; NO BILL. Cf. TRUE BILL.

> "When the grand jury have heard the evidence, if they think it a groundless accusation, they used formerly to endorse on the back of the bill, '*ignoramus*;' or, we know nothing of it; intimating, that, though the facts might possibly be true, that truth did not appear to them: but now they assert in English, more absolutely, 'not a true bill;' and then the party is discharged without farther answer." 4 William Blackstone, *Commentaries on the Laws of England* 301 (1769).

ignorantia (ig-nə-**ran**-shee-ə). [Latin] Ignorance; esp., ignorance of the law.

> "*Ignorantia* .... Divided in the civil law, into *ignorantia facti* (ignorance of fact) and *ignorantia juris* (ignorance of law). Lord Coke accepts this division ...." 2 Alexander M. Burrill, *A Law Dictionary and Glossary* 40 (2d ed. 1867).

ignorantia facti (ig-nə-**ran**-shee-ə **fak**-tI). [Latin] Ignorance of fact.

ignorantia facti excusat (ig-nə-**ran**-shee-ə **fak**-tI ek-**skyoo**-sat *or* -zat). [Latin] Ignorance of fact is an excuse; whatever is done under a mistaken impression of a material fact is excused or provides grounds for relief. • This maxim refers to the principle that acts done and contracts made under mistake or ignorance of a material fact are voidable.

> "'*Ignorantia facti excusat*,' however, is obviously too sweeping even for a general statement of law, because it is clear (to mention only one point for the moment) that if a certain deed would constitute exactly the same crime under either of two factual situations, it will be no excuse that one was mistaken for the other." Rollin M. Perkins & Ronald N. Boyce, *Criminal Law* 1044 (3d ed. 1982).

ignorantia juris (ig-nə-**ran**-shee-ə **joor**-is). [Latin] Ignorance of law. • Under Roman law, this type of ignorance (unlike *ignorantia facti*) did not excuse mistaken conduct, except in the case of minors and those under disability.

ignorantia juris non excusat (ig-nə-**ran**-shee-ə **joor**-is non ek-**skyoo**-sat *or* -zat). [Latin] Lack of knowledge about a legal requirement or prohibition is never an excuse to a criminal charge. • In English, the idea is commonly rendered *ignorance of the law is no excuse*. — Often shortened to *ignorantia juris*. — Also termed *ignorantia juris neminem excusat* (ignorance of the law excuses no one); *ignorantia legis non excusat*; *ignorantia juris haud excusat*.

> "Almost the only knowledge of law possessed by many people is that ignorance of it is no excuse (*ignorantia juris non excusat*). This maxim was originally formulated at a time when the list of crimes, broadly speaking, represented current morality (*mala in se*), but we now have many other crimes that are the result of administrative or social regulation (*mala prohibita*), which are equally governed by the maxim. The rule is, then, that whereas ignorance of fact can excuse, to the extent that it negatives *mens rea* or fault, ignorance of the law

generally does not." Glanville Williams, *Textbook of Criminal Law* 405 (1978).

ignoratio elenchi (ig-nə-**ray**-shee-oh e-**leng**-kI *or* ig-nə-**rah**-tee-oh i-**leng**-kee). [Law Latin "ignorance of the conclusion to be proved"] An advocate's misunderstanding of an opponent's position, manifested by an argument that fails to address the opponent's point; the overlooking of an opponent's counterargument. • This fallacy of logic often involves an advocate's trying to prove something that is immaterial to the point to be decided.

ignore, *vb.* **1.** To refuse to notice, recognize, or consider. **2.** (Of a grand jury) to reject (an indictment) as groundless; to no-bill (a charge).

ill, *adj.* (Of a pleading) defective, bad, or null.

illation (i-**lay**-shən). **1.** The act or process of inferring. **2.** An inference; that which is inferred.

illegal, *adj.* Forbidden by law; unlawful <illegal dumping> <an illegal drug>.

illegal alien. See ALIEN.

illegal consideration. See CONSIDERATION.

illegal contract. See CONTRACT.

illegal entry. 1. *Criminal law.* The unlawful act of going into a building with the intent to commit a crime. • In some jurisdictions, illegal entry is a lesser included offense of burglary. **2.** *Immigration.* The unauthorized entrance of an alien into the United States by arriving at the wrong time or place, by evading inspection, or by fraud.

illegality. 1. An act that is not authorized by law. **2.** The state of not being legally authorized.

> "A contract made *ultra vires* is void; but not [strictly speaking] on the ground of illegality. Lord Cairns ... takes exception to the use of the term 'illegality,' pointing out that it is not the *object* of the contracting parties, but the *incapacity* of one of them, that avoids the contract." William R. Anson, *Principles of the Law of Contract* 190 (Arthur L. Corbin ed., 3d Am. ed. 1919).

> "It must not be thought that illegality in the law of contract is co-terminous with illegality in the criminal law, for a contract may be illegal without involving any breach of the criminal law at all." P.S. Atiyah, *An Introduction to the Law of Contract* 257 (3d ed. 1981).

3. The state or condition of being unlawful. • The affirmative defense of illegality must be expressly set forth in the response to the opponent's pleading. Fed. R. Civ. P. 8(c).

illegally obtained evidence. See EVIDENCE.

illegal per se. Unlawful in and of itself.

illegal rate. See INTEREST RATE.

illegal search. See *unreasonable search* under SEARCH.

illegal strike. See STRIKE.

illegal tax. See *erroneous tax* under TAX.

illegitimacy. The state or condition of a child born outside a lawful marriage. — Also termed *bastardy.*

illegitimate, *adj.* **1.** (Of a child) born out of wedlock <illegitimate son>. **2.** Against the law; unlawful <illegitimate contract for the sale of contraband>. **3.** Improper <illegitimate conduct>. **4.** Incorrectly inferred <illegitimate conclusion>.

illegitimate child. See CHILD.

ill fame. Evil repute; notorious bad character. Cf. FAMA PUBLICA.

illicenciatus (il-lI-sen-shee-**ay**-təs). [Law Latin] Without license.

illicit (i[l]-**lis**-ət), *adj.* Illegal or improper <illicit relations>.

illicit cohabitation. See COHABITATION.

illicitum collegium (i-**lis**-ə-təm kə-**lee**-jee-əm). [Law Latin] *Roman law.* An illegal association; a *collegium* engaging in illegal activity. • Members of an *illicitum collegium* were subject to prosecution.

Illinois land trust. See *land trust* under TRUST.

illiquid asset. See ASSET.

illusory (i-**loo**-sə-ree), *adj.* Deceptive; based on a false impression.

illusory appointment. See APPOINTMENT (3).

Illusory Appointment Act. An 1839 English statute providing that no appointment of property is to be declared invalid on grounds that it is illusory. • This statute was repealed and reissued in 1925 as part of the Law of Property Act.

illusory contract. See CONTRACT.

illusory promise. See PROMISE.

illusory tenant. See TENANT.

illusory trust. See TRUST.

illustrative evidence. See *demonstrative evidence* under EVIDENCE.

imaginary damages. See *punitive damages* under DAMAGES.

imagining. See COMPASSING.

imbargo. *Archaic.* See EMBARGO (1).

imbecile (**im**-bə-səl *or* -sil). A person afflicted with severe mental retardation. Cf. IDIOT.

imbezzle. *Archaic.* See EMBEZZLE.

imbracery. See EMBRACERY.

IMF. *abbr.* INTERNATIONAL MONETARY FUND.

imitation. *Trademarks.* An item that so resembles a trademarked item as to be likely to induce the belief that it is genuine.

immaterial, *adj.* (Of evidence) tending to prove some fact that is not properly at issue; lacking any logical connection with the consequential facts. — **immateriality,** *n.* Cf. IRRELEVANT.

> "The rules of substantive law and of pleading are what determine immateriality; and if the probandum is immaterial, of course no evidence to prove it is wanted." John H. Wigmore, *A Students' Textbook of the Law of Evidence* 37 (1935).

immaterial averment. See AVERMENT.

immaterial breach. See *partial breach* under BREACH OF CONTRACT.

immaterial evidence. See EVIDENCE.

immaterial fact. See FACT.

immaterial issue. See ISSUE (1).

immaterial variance. See VARIANCE (1).

immediate, *adj.* **1.** Occurring without delay; instant <an immediate acceptance>. **2.** Not separated by other persons or things <her immediate neighbor>. **3.** Having a direct impact; without an intervening agency <the immediate cause of the accident>. — **immediacy, immediateness,** *n.*

immediate annuity. See ANNUITY.

immediate breach. See BREACH OF CONTRACT.

immediate cause. See CAUSE (1).

immediate control. 1. *Criminal procedure.* The area within an arrestee's reach. • A police officer may conduct a warrantless search of this area to ensure the officer's safety and to prevent the arrestee from destroying evidence. **2.** Vehicular control that is close enough to allow the driver to instantly govern the vehicle's movements. • A driver's failure to maintain immediate control over the vehicle could be evidence of negligence.

imminent danger. See DANGER.

immediate death. See DEATH.

immediate descent. See DESCENT.

immediate family. See FAMILY.

immediate intent. See INTENT (1).

immediately-apparent requirement. *Criminal procedure.* The principle that a police officer must have probable cause to believe that an item is contraband before seizing it. • This plain-view exception to the warrant requirement was first announced in *Coolidge v. New Hampshire*, 403 U.S. 443, 91 S.Ct. 2022 (1971).

> "An object may not be seized from a car merely because the police plain view of it was lawfully acquired; there must be probable cause that the object is a fruit, instrumentality or evidence of crime. And under the 'immediately apparent' requirement of *Coolidge v. New Hampshire*, this probable cause must be determined without examination of the object other than is justified by the purpose underlying police entry of the vehicle." Wayne R. LaFave & Jerold H. Israel, *Criminal Procedure* § 3.7, at 201 (2d ed. 1992).

immediate notice. See NOTICE.

immediate-notice clause. *Insurance.* A provision in many insurance policies obligating the insured to notify the insurer as soon as possible after a claim arises. • A requirement in a policy for "prompt" or "immediate" notice — or that notice must be given "immediately," "at once," "forthwith," "as soon as practicable," or "as soon as possible" — generally means that the notice must be given within a reasonable time under the circumstances.

immediate possession. See POSSESSION (3).

immemorial (im-ə-**mor**-ee-əl), *adj.* Beyond memory or record; very old. See TIME IMMEMORIAL.

immemorial usage. See USAGE.

immigrant. A person who arrives in a country to settle there permanently; a person who immigrates.

alien immigrant. An immigrant who has not yet been naturalized.

immigration, *n.* The act of entering a country with the intention of settling there permanently. — **immigrate,** *vb.* — **immigrant,** *n.* Cf. EMIGRATION.

Immigration and Nationality Act. A comprehensive federal law regulating immigration, naturalization, and the exclusion of aliens. 8 USCA §§ 1101–1537. — Also termed *Nationality Act.*

Immigration and Naturalization Service. A U.S. Department of Justice agency that administers the Immigration and Nationality Act and operates the U.S. Border Patrol. — Abbr. INS.

Immigration Appeals Board. See BOARD OF IMMIGRATION APPEALS.

imminent danger. See DANGER (1).

imminent hazard. See HAZARD (1).

imminently dangerous. (Of a person, behavior, or thing) reasonably certain to place life and limb in peril. • This term is relevant in several legal contexts. For example, if a mental condition renders a person imminently dangerous to self or others, he or she may be committed to a mental hospital. And the imminently dangerous behavior of pointing a gun at someone's head could subject the actor to criminal and tort liability. Further, the manufacturer of an imminently dangerous product may be held to a strict-liability standard in tort.

imminent-peril doctrine. See EMERGENCY DOCTRINE (1).

immiscere (i-**mis**-ə-ree), *vb.* [Latin] *Roman law.* To mix or mingle with; to meddle with. • This term took on the figurative sense of meddling in another's affairs (e.g., acting as if one were an heir), for which a person could be prosecuted.

immobilia (im-ə-**bil**-ee-ə). Immovables. — Also termed *res immobiles* (**reez** i-**moh**-bə-leez).

immobilia situm sequuntur (im-ə-**bil**-ee-ə **sI**-təm sə-**kwən**-tər). [Latin] Immovable things follow their site. • This principle means that immovables are governed by the law of the place where they are fixed. — Sometimes shortened to *immobilia situm.*

immobilis, *adj.* (i-**moh**-bə-lis). [Latin] Immovable.

immobilize, *vb.* To make immobile; esp., to turn (movable property) into immovable property or to turn (circulating capital) into fixed capital.

immoral consideration. See CONSIDERATION.

immoral contract. See CONTRACT.

immovable, *n.* (*usu. pl.*) Property that cannot be moved; an object so firmly attached to land that it is regarded as part of the land. — **immovable,** *adj.* See FIXTURE. Cf. MOVABLE.

> "Considered in its legal aspect, an immovable, that is to say, a piece of land, includes the following elements: — 1. A determinate portion of the earth's surface. 2. The ground beneath the surface down to the centre of the world. All the pieces of land in England meet together in one terminable point at the earth's centre. 3. Possibly the column of space above the surface *ad infinitum.*" John Salmond, *Jurisprudence* 428 (Glanville L. Williams ed., 10th ed. 1947).

immune, *adj.* Having immunity; exempt from a duty or liability.

immunity. 1. Any exemption from a duty, liability, or service of process; esp., such an exemption granted to a public official.

> "An *immunity* is a defense to tort liability which is conferred upon an entire group or class of persons or entities under circumstances where considerations of public policy are thought to require special protection for the person, activity or entity in question at the expense

of those injured by its tortious act. Historically, tort litigation against units of government, public officers, and charities, and between spouses, parents and children, has been limited or prohibited on this basis." Edward J. Kionka, *Torts in a Nutshell* 341 (2d ed. 1992).

absolute immunity. A complete exemption from civil liability, usu. afforded to officials while performing particularly important functions, such as a representative enacting legislation and a judge presiding over a lawsuit. Cf. *qualified immunity.*

congressional immunity. Either of two special immunities given to members of Congress: (1) the exemption from arrest while attending a session of the body to which the member belongs, excluding an arrest for treason, breach of the peace, or a felony, or (2) the exemption from arrest or questioning for any speech or debate entered into during a legislative session. U.S. Const. art. I, § 6, cl. 1. See SPEECH AND DEBATE CLAUSE.

constitutional immunity. Immunity created by a constitution.

diplomatic immunity. The general exemption of diplomatic ministers from the operation of local law, the exception being that a minister who is plotting against the security of the host nation may be arrested and sent out of the country. • A minister's family shares in diplomatic immunity to a great, though ill-defined, degree.

discretionary immunity. A qualified immunity for a public official's acts, granted when the act in question required the exercise of judgment in carrying out official duties (such as planning and policy-making). 28 USCA § 2680(a).

"Probably no one test will control the decision on discretionary immunity. Although the fact that the government has omitted to act is not in itself a defense, the discretionary immunity is frequently emphasized in nonfeasance cases. On the other hand, where the government's activity is affirmative, specific, and in violation of a statute, regulation, or constitutional provision imposing a duty upon government, courts are often willing to say there is no room for discretion." *Prosser and Keeton on the Law of Torts* § 131, at 1041–42 (W. Page Keeton ed., 5th ed. 1984).

executive immunity. **1.** The absolute immunity of the U.S. President or a state governor from civil damages for actions that are within the scope of official responsibilities. **2.** The qualified immunity from civil claims against lesser executive officials, who are liable only if their conduct violates clearly established constitutional or statutory rights. • Executive immunity generally protects an official while carrying out clearly established responsibilities about which a reasonable person would know. Cf. *executive privilege* under PRIVILEGE (1).

foreign immunity. The immunity of a foreign sovereign, its agents, and its instrumentalities from litigation in U.S. courts.

government immunity. See *sovereign immunity.*

intergovernmental immunity. The immunity between the federal and state governments based on their independent sovereignty. See INTERGOVERNMENTAL-IMMUNITY DOCTRINE.

judicial immunity. The immunity of a judge from civil liability arising from the performance of judicial duties.

legislative immunity. The immunity of a legislator from civil liability arising from the performance of legislative duties. See *congressional immunity.*

qualified immunity. Immunity from civil liability for a public official who is performing a discretionary function, as long as the conduct does not violate clearly established constitutional or statutory rights. — Also termed *prima facie privilege.* Cf. *absolute immunity.*

sovereign immunity. **1.** A government's immunity from being sued in its own courts without its consent. • Congress has waived most of the federal government's sovereign immunity. See FEDERAL TORT CLAIMS ACT. **2.** A state's immunity from being sued in federal court by the state's own citizens. — Also termed *governmental immunity.*

work-product immunity. See WORK-PRODUCT RULE.

2. *Torts.* A doctrine providing a complete defense to a tort action. • Unlike a privilege, immunity does not negate the tort, and it must be raised affirmatively or it will be waived. Cf. PRIVILEGE (2).

charitable immunity. The immunity of a charitable organization from tort liability. • This immunity has been eliminated or restricted in most states. — Also termed *eleemosynary defense.*

corporate immunity. A corporate officer's immunity from personal liability for a tortious act committed while acting in good faith and within the course of corporate duties.

husband-wife immunity. The immunity of one spouse from a tort action by the other spouse for personal injury. • This immunity has been abolished in most states. — Also termed *interspousal immunity*; *marital immunity*.

judgmental immunity. See ERROR-OF-JUDGMENT RULE.

marital immunity. See *husband-wife immunity*.

parental immunity. **1.** The principle that an unemancipated minor child is prohibited from suing a parent for damages allegedly caused by parental negligence. • This immunity has been retained by most states but is not applied in intentional-tort cases or in auto-accident cases covered by insurance. — Also termed *parent-child immunity*. **2.** The principle that parents are not liable for damages caused by the ordinary negligence of their minor child.

3. *Criminal law.* Freedom from prosecution granted by the government in exchange for the person's testimony. • By granting immunity, the government can compel testimony — despite the Fifth Amendment right against self-incrimination — because that testimony can no longer incriminate the witness.

pocket immunity. Immunity that results from the prosecutor's decision not to prosecute, instead of from a formal grant of immunity. — Also termed *informal immunity*.

testimonial immunity. Immunity from the use of the compelled testimony against the witness. • Any information derived from that testimony, however, is generally admissible against the witness.

transactional immunity. Immunity from prosecution for any event or transaction described in the compelled testimony. • This is the broadest form of immunity.

use immunity. Immunity from the use of the compelled testimony (or any information derived from that testimony) in a future prosecution against the witness. • After granting use immunity, the government can still prosecute if it shows that its evidence comes from a legitimate independent source. — Also termed *use/derivative-use immunity*.

immunize, *vb.* To grant immunity to <the new legislation immunized the police officers from liability>.

impacted area. A region that is affected by some event; esp., a region in which the school population increases due to an influx of federal employees who are working on a federal project or activity, but the tax revenue declines due to the U.S. government's immunity from local taxes.

impact rule. *Torts.* The common-law requirement that physical contact must have occurred to allow damages for negligent infliction of emotional distress. • This rule has been abandoned in most jurisdictions. — Also termed *physical-impact rule*.

impair, *vb.* To diminish the value of (property or a property right). • This term is commonly used in reference to diminishing the value of a contractual obligation to the point that the contract becomes invalid or a party loses the benefit of the contract. See CONTRACTS CLAUSE.

impaired capital. See CAPITAL.

impairing the morals of a minor. The offense of an adult's engaging in sex-related acts, short of intercourse, with a minor. • Examples of this conduct are fondling, taking obscene photographs, and showing pornographic materials. Cf. CONTRIBUTING TO THE DELINQUENCY OF A MINOR.

impairment, *n.* The fact or state of being damaged, weakened, or diminished <impairment of collateral>. — **impair,** *vb.*

impalement, *n. Hist.* An ancient mode of inflicting punishment by thrusting a sharp pole through the body. — Formerly also spelled *empalement*. — **impale,** *vb.*

impanel, *vb.* See EMPANEL.

imparcare (im-pahr-**kair**-ee), *vb.* [Law Latin "to enclose"] *Hist.* To impound; to confine in prison. See CARCER.

imparl (im-**pahrl**), *vb.* **1.** *Hist.* To request or obtain an imparlance. **2.** To confer with the opposing party in an effort to settle a dispute amicably; to discuss settlement.

imparlance (im-**pahr**-lənts). *Hist.* **1.** A continuance granted for the purpose of giving the requesting party (usu. the defendant) further time to answer the adversary's last pleading (esp. the plaintiff's writ, bill, or count), often so that the parties will have time to settle the dispute. • Imparlances were abolished in England in 1853. **2.** A petition for such a continuance. **3.** The permission granting such a continuance. — Formerly also spelled *emparlance*. — Also termed *licentia loquendi*.

> "After defence made, the defendant must put in his *plea*. But, before he pleads, he is entitled to demand one *imparlance*, or *licentia loquendi*, and may have more granted by consent of the plaintiff; to see if he can end

the matter amicably without farther suit, by talking with the plaintiff. . . ." 3 William Blackstone, *Commentaries on the Laws of England* 298 (1768).

"An imparlance is the time allowed by the court to either party, upon request, to answer the pleading of his opponent. Imparlance, from the French 'parler' — to speak — in its most common signification, means time to plead. Formerly the parties, in the course of oral pleadings, were allowed time to speak or confer with one another, so that they might endeavor to settle the matters in dispute, and later, when the pleadings came to be in writing, the court permitted a certain time for each to plead to or answer the pleading of his opponent. In modern practice the term is rarely used . . . ." Benjamin J. Shipman, *Handbook of Common-Law Pleading* § 234, at 405 (Henry Winthrop Ballantine ed., 3d ed. 1923).

general imparlance. The allowance of time until the court's next term, without reserving to the defendant the benefit of any exception. • With this type of imparlance, the requesting defendant cannot later object to the jurisdiction of the court or plead any matter in abatement.

general special imparlance. The allowance of time with a saving of all exceptions, so that a defendant might later plead not only in abatement but also to the jurisdiction.

special imparlance. The allowance of time with a saving only of exceptions to the writ, bill, or count, but not to the court's jurisdiction.

impartial, *adj.* Unbiased; disinterested.

impartial chair. 1. ARBITRATOR. **2.** MEDIATOR. — Also termed *impartial chairman*.

impartial expert. See EXPERT.

impartial jury. See JURY.

impartible (im-**pahr**-tə-bəl), *adj.* Indivisible <an impartible estate>.

impartible feud. See FEUD.

impasse (**im**-pas). A point in labor negotiations at which agreement cannot be reached. • A neutral third party (such as a mediator) is often called in to help resolve an impasse.

"Not only is the employer free after impasse to implement changes already offered to the union, but either party is free after impasse to decline to negotiate further. Since impasse signifies that the parties have exhausted (at least temporarily) the avenues of bargaining, termination of bargaining at that point cannot be thought to demonstrate a cast of mind against reaching agreement." Robert A. Gorman, *Basic Text on Labor Law: Unionization and Collective Bargaining* 447 (1976).

impeach, *vb.* **1.** To charge with a crime or misconduct; esp., to formally charge (a public official) with a violation of the public trust. • Impeaching a federal official, such as the President, the Vice President, or a judge, requires that a majority of the U.S. House of Representatives vote to return at least one article of impeachment to the U.S. Senate, itemizing the charges and explaining their factual grounds. Even if an official is impeached, removal from office does not occur unless two-thirds of the senators vote for conviction. <President Nixon resigned from office to avoid being impeached>. **2.** To discredit the veracity of (a witness) <the lawyer hoped that her star witness wouldn't be impeached on cross-examination>. **3.** To challenge the accuracy or authenticity of (a document) <the handwriting expert impeached the holographic will>.

impeachable offense. An offense for which a public official may legally be impeached, during the first step in a two-step process that may, depending on the vote in the U.S. Senate, lead to the official's removal from office. • The U.S. Constitution states that "[t]he President, Vice President and all civil Officers of the United States, shall be removed from Office on Impeachment for, and Conviction of, Treason, Bribery, or other high Crimes and Misdemeanors." The meaning of this language was much debated during the impeachment and trial of President Bill Clinton, against whom two articles of impeachment were returned by the House of Representatives. The question arose what type of misdemeanor will suffice, and whether the *high* in *high crimes* modifies *misdemeanors* as well. No definitive answer resulted from the proceedings.

impeachment. 1. The act (by a legislature) of calling for the removal from office of a public official, accomplished by presenting a written charge of the official's alleged misconduct; esp., the initiation of a proceeding in the U.S. House of Representatives against a federal official, such as the President or a judge. • Congress's authority to remove a federal official stems from Article II, Section 4 of the Constitution, which authorizes the removal of an official for "Treason, Bribery, or other high Crimes and Misdemeanors." The grounds upon which an official can be removed do not, however, have to be criminal in nature. They usu. involve some type of abuse of power or breach of the public trust. Articles of impeachment — which can be approved by a simple majority in the House — serve as the charging instrument for the later trial in the Senate. If the President is impeached, the Chief Justice of the Supreme

Court presides over the Senate trial. The defendant can be removed from office by a two-thirds majority of the senators who are present. In the United Kingdom, impeachment is by the House of Commons and trial by the House of Lords. But no case has arisen there since 1801, and many British scholars consider impeachment obsolete. **2.** The act of discrediting a witness, as by catching the witness in a lie or by demonstrating that the witness has been convicted of a criminal offense. **3.** The act of challenging the accuracy or authenticity of evidence.

impeachment court. See COURT FOR THE TRIALS OF IMPEACHMENT.

impeachment evidence. See EVIDENCE.

impeachment of verdict. A party's attack on a verdict, alleging impropriety by a member of the jury.

impeachment of waste. *Hist.* An action for waste against the tenant of the harmed property.

> "[F]or above five hundred years past, all tenants for life or for any less estate, have been punishable or liable to be impeached for waste, both voluntary and permissive; unless their leases be made, as sometimes they are, without impeachment of waste...." 2 William Blackstone, *Commentaries on the Laws of England* 283 (1766).

impechiare (im-pee-chee-**air**-ee), *vb.* [fr. Law French *empescher* "to impeach"] *Hist.* To impeach; to accuse.

impediens (im-**pee**-dee-enz). [Law Latin] *Hist.* A person who hinders. • The defendant (or *deforciant*) in a fine of conveyance was sometimes so called. See FINE (1).

impediment (im-**ped**-ə-mənt). A hindrance or obstruction; esp., some fact (such as legal minority) that bars a marriage, if known, but that does not void the marriage if discovered after the ceremony.

impeditor (im-**ped**-ə-tər). [Law Latin] *Hist.* A person who interferes with a patron's right of advowson, i.e., the right to appoint a clerk to a benefice. — Also termed *disturber*. See DE CLERICO ADMITTENDO.

impensae (im-**pen**-see). [Latin] *Roman law.* Expenditures made on a thing.

impensae necessariae (im-**pen**-see nes-ə-**sair**-ee-ee). Expenditures necessary to prevent deterioration, destruction, or loss of a thing — such as money expended for building repair or maintenance.

impensae utiles (im-**pen**-see **yoo**-tə-leez). Useful expenditures that improve something and increase its selling value.

impensae voluptariae (im-**pen**-see vol-əp-**tair**-ee-ee). Expenditures made on a thing for ornamental purposes only.

imperative authority. See AUTHORITY (4).

imperative law. See LAW.

imperative theory of law. The theory that law consists of the general commands issued by a country or other political community to its subjects and enforced by courts with the sanction of physical force. • Imperative theorists believe that if there are rules predating or independent of the country, those rules may closely resemble law or even substitute for it, but they are not law. See POSITIVE LAW. Cf. NATURAL LAW.

imperfect duty. See DUTY (1).

imperfect justification. See JUSTIFICATION.

imperfect right. See RIGHT.

imperfect self-defense. See SELF-DEFENSE.

imperfect statute. See STATUTE.

imperfect title. See TITLE (2).

imperfect trust. See *executory trust* under TRUST.

imperfect usufruct. See *quasi-usufruct* under USUFRUCT.

imperfect war. See WAR.

imperial state. See STATE (1).

imperitia (im-pə-**rish**-ee-ə). [Latin] *Roman law.* Lack of skill or competence; inexperience. • The Romans considered *imperitia* to be a type of *culpa* that gave rise to liability in tort or liability under a contract calling for the rendering of services (such as a *locatio conductio operis*). *Imperitus* denoted an incompetent judge.

imperium (im-**peer**-ee-əm). [Latin] *Roman law.* Power or dominion; esp., the legal authority wielded by superior magistrates under the Republic, and later by the emperor under the Empire. • *Imperium* applied to different types of authority under Roman law, and thus had different meanings. For example, *imperium domesticum* described the power of the head of a household.

impersonal. See IN REM.

impersonation. The act of impersonating someone. — Also termed *personation.*

false impersonation. The crime of falsely representing oneself as another person, usu. a law-enforcement officer, for the purpose of deceiving someone. — Also termed *false personation.* See IMPOSTOR.

impertinent matter. *Procedure.* In pleading, matter that is not relevant to the action or defense. • A federal court may strike any impertinent matter from a pleading. Fed. R. Civ. P. 12(f). Cf. SCANDALOUS MATTER.

"The court will not strike out the matter unless its impertinence clearly appears; for if erroneously stricken out, the error is irremediable; if left to stand, the court may set the matter right in taxing the costs. Matter which is scandalous is also impertinent." William C. Anderson, *A Dictionary of Law* 526 (1889).

impescare (im-pə-**skair**-ee), *vb.* [fr. Law French *empescher* "to impeach"] *Hist.* To impeach; to accuse.

impetitio vasti (im-pə-**tish**-ee-oh **vas**-tI). See IMPEACHMENT OF WASTE.

impetrare (im-pə-**trair**-ee), *vb.* [Latin] *Roman law.* To obtain by request. • This word often appeared in petitions requesting a *formula* for an action from a praetor. It performed a similar function under English law for those seeking a writ from Chancery. The English word *impetrate* derives from this Latinism. Cf. FORMULA.

impetration (im-pə-**tray**-shən). **1.** *Hist.* The act of petitioning for a writ. **2.** *Hist. Eccles. law.* The act of obtaining a papal benefice for the disposal of the king or other lay patron. — **impetrate,** *vb.*

impignorata (im-pig-nə-**ray**-tə). [Law Latin] *Hist.* Given in pledge; pledged or mortgaged.

impignoration (im-pig-nə-**ray**-shən), *n. Hist.* The act of pawning or putting to pledge. — **impignorate,** *vb.*

impinge, *vb.* To encroach or infringe (*on* or *upon*) <impinge on the defendant's rights>.

implacitare (im-plas-ə-**tair**-ee), *vb.* [fr. Latin *placitum* "plea"] *Hist.* To implead; to sue.

implead, *vb.* **1.** To bring (someone) into a lawsuit; esp., to bring (a new party) into the action. Cf. INTERPLEAD. **2.** *Hist.* To bring an action against; to accuse. — Formerly also spelled *emplead*; *empleet.*

impleader, *n.* A procedure by which a third party is brought into a lawsuit, esp. by a defendant who seeks to shift liability to someone not sued by the plaintiff. Fed. R. Civ. P. 14. — Also termed *third-party practice*; *vouching-in.* Cf. INTERPLEADER; INTERVENTION (1).

implementation plan. *Environmental law.* A detailed outline of steps needed to meet environmental-quality standards by an established time.

implicate, *vb.* **1.** To show (a person) to be involved in (a crime, misfeasance, etc.) <when he turned state's evidence, he implicated three other suspects>. **2.** To be involved or affected <three judges were implicated in the bribery>.

implication. 1. The act of showing involvement in something, esp. a crime or misfeasance <the implication of the judges in the bribery scheme>. **2.** An inference drawn from something said or observed <the implication was that the scheme involved several persons>.

necessary implication. An implication so strong in its probability that anything to the contrary would be unreasonable.

implicit cost. See *opportunity cost* under COST.

implied, *adj.* Not directly expressed; recognized by law as existing inferentially <implied agreement>. See IMPLY (1). Cf. EXPRESS.

implied acceptance. See ACCEPTANCE (4).

implied acquittal. See ACQUITTAL.

implied actual knowledge. See *actual knowledge* (2) under KNOWLEDGE.

implied admission. See ADMISSION (1).

implied agency. See AGENCY (1).

implied amnesty. See AMNESTY.

implied assent. See ASSENT.

implied assertion. See *assertive conduct* under CONDUCT.

implied assumption. See ASSUMPTION.

implied authority. See AUTHORITY (1).

implied color. See COLOR.

implied condition. See CONDITION (2).

implied confession. See CONFESSION.

implied consent. See CONSENT.

implied consideration. See CONSIDERATION.

implied contract. See CONTRACT.

implied covenant. See COVENANT (1).

implied covenant of good faith and fair dealing. See COVENANT (1).

implied dedication. See DEDICATION.

implied duty of cooperation. See DUTY (1).

implied easement. See EASEMENT.

implied in fact, *adj.* Inferable from the facts of the case.

implied-in-fact condition. See CONDITION (2).

implied-in-fact contract. See CONTRACT.

implied in law, *n.* Imposed by operation of law and not because of any inferences that can be drawn from the facts of the case.

implied-in-law condition. See *constructive condition* under CONDITION (2).

implied-in-law contract. See CONTRACT.

implied intent. See INTENT (1).

implied malice. See MALICE.

implied negative covenant. See COVENANT (1).

implied notice. See NOTICE.

implied partnership. See *partnership by estoppel* under PARTNERSHIP.

implied power. See POWER (4), (5).

implied promise. See PROMISE.

implied reciprocal covenant. See COVENANT (4).

implied reciprocal servitude. See *implied reciprocal covenant* under COVENANT (4).

implied repeal. See REPEAL.

implied reservation. See RESERVATION.

implied-reservation-of-water doctrine. A legal doctrine permitting the federal government to use and control, for public purposes, water appurtenant to federal lands. See EMINENT DOMAIN.

implied term. See TERM (2).

implied trust. See *resulting trust* under TRUST.

implied waiver. See WAIVER (1).

implied warranty. See WARRANTY (2).

implied warranty of fitness for a particular purpose. See WARRANTY (2).

implied warranty of habitability. See WARRANTY (2).

implied warranty of merchantability. See WARRANTY (2).

imply, *vb.* **1.** To express or involve indirectly; to suggest <the opinion implies that the court has adopted a stricter standard for upholding punitive-damages awards>. **2.** (Of a court) to impute or impose on equitable or legal grounds <the court implied a contract between the parties>. **3.** To read into (a document) <citing grounds of fairness, the court implied a condition that the parties had not expressed>. See *implied term* under TERM (2). — **implication,** *n.*

"Sometimes, when a Court implies a term it is merely reading in what is already logically implicit in the language of the contract. Sometimes a Court is adding something to the contract which the parties probably had in mind but did not actually express. Sometimes, again, the Court is adding terms which the parties would probably have expressed if the matter had been brought to their attention. In yet other cases a Court adds terms to a contract which it thinks the parties ought in fairness and justice to have included, even though they might not have done so if the matter had been brought to their attention. In the first type of case the phrase 'implied term' is unobjectionable. In the last type of case, on the other hand, it seems clear that the Court is merely applying a rule of law, albeit a rule which can be excluded by express agreement. But in the intermediate positions it is difficult to dogmatize about which approach is more accurate, particularly as the different cases tend to shade off into each other. The theory still is that the Courts have no power to add to the contract but may only read in what is implicit in it. This theory, however, is becoming more and more difficult to reconcile with the facts." P.S. Atiyah, *An Introduction to the Law of Contract* 178 (3d ed. 1981).

import, *n.* **1.** A product brought into a country from a foreign country where it originated <imports declined in the third quarter>. See PARALLEL IMPORTS. **2.** The process of bringing foreign goods into a country <the import of products affects the domestic economy in significant ways>. **3.** The meaning; esp., the implied meaning <the court must decide the import of that obscure provision>. **4.** Importance; significance <time will tell the relative import of Judge Posner's decisions in American law>.

importation. The bringing of goods into a country from another country.

import duty. See DUTY (4).

imported litigation. One or more lawsuits brought in a state that has no interest in the dispute.

importer. A person or entity that brings goods into a country from a foreign country and pays customs duties.

Import–Export Clause. U.S. Const. art. I, § 10, cl. 2, which prohibits states from taxing imports or exports. • The Supreme Court has liberally interpreted this clause, allowing states to tax imports as long as the tax does not discriminate in favor of domestic goods. — Also termed *Export Clause.*

import letter of credit. See LETTER OF CREDIT.

import quota. See QUOTA.

importune (im-por-**t[y]oon**), *vb.* To solicit forcefully; to request persistently, and sometimes irksomely.

impose, *vb.* To levy or exact (a tax or duty).

imposition. An impost or tax.

impositive fact. See FACT.

impossibility. 1. The fact or condition of not being able to occur, exist, or be done. **2.** A fact or circumstance that cannot occur, exist, or be done. **3.** *Contracts.* A fact or circumstance that excuses performance because (1) the subject or means of performance has deteriorated, has been destroyed, or is no longer available, (2) the method of delivery or payment has failed, (3) a law now prevents performance, or (4) death or illness prevents performance. • Increased or unexpected difficulty and expense do not usu. qualify as an impossibility and thus do not excuse performance. — Also termed *impossibility of performance.*

"The doctrines of Impossibility, Commercial Impracticability or as the Uniform Commercial Code knows it, Excuse by Failure of Presupposed Conditions, comprise unclimbed peaks of contract doctrine. Clearly, all of the famous early and mid-twentieth century mountaineers, Corbin, Williston, Farnsworth and many lesser men have made attempts on this topic but none has succeeded in conquering the very summit.... In spite of attempts by all of the contract buffs and even in the face of eloquent and persuasive general statements, it remains impossible to predict with accuracy how the law will apply to a variety of relatively common cases. Both the cases and the Code commentary are full of weasel words such as 'severe' shortage, 'marked' increase, 'basic' assumptions, and 'force majeure.' " James J. White & Robert S. Summers, *Uniform Commercial Code* § 3–9, at 155 (3d ed. 1988).

4. The doctrine by which such a fact or circumstance excuses contractual performance. Cf. FRUSTRATION; IMPRACTICABILITY. **5.** *Criminal law.* A fact or circumstance preventing the commission of a crime.

factual impossibility. Impossibility due to the fact that the illegal act cannot physically be accomplished, such as trying to pick an empty pocket. • Factual impossibility is not a defense to the crime of attempt. — Also termed *physical impossibility.*

legal impossibility. Impossibility due to the fact that what the defendant intended to do is not illegal, such as hunting while erroneously believing that it is not hunting season. • Legal impossibility is a defense to the crime of attempt.

impossibility-of-performance doctrine. The principle that a party may be released from a contract on the ground that uncontrollable circumstances have rendered performance impossible. Cf. FRUSTRATION; IMPRACTICABILITY.

impossible consideration. See CONSIDERATION.

impossible contract. See CONTRACT.

impost (**im**-pohst). A tax or duty, esp. a customs duty <the impost was assessed when the ship reached the mainland>. See DUTY (4).

impostor (im-**pos**-tər). One who pretends to be someone else to deceive others, esp. to receive the benefits of a negotiable instrument. — Also spelled *imposter*.

impostor rule. *Commercial law.* The principle that an impostor's indorsement of a negotiable instrument is not a forgery, and that the drawer or maker who issues the instrument to the imposter is negligent and therefore liable to the holder for payment. • If a drawer or maker issues an instrument to an impostor, any resulting forgery of the payee's name will be effective in favor of a person paying on the instrument in good faith or taking it for value or collection. UCC § 3–404.

impotence (**im**-pə-tənts). A man's inability to achieve an erection and therefore to have sexual intercourse. • Because an impotent husband cannot consummate a marriage, impotence has often been cited as a ground for annulment. — Also termed *impotency*; *physical incapacity*.

impound, *vb.* **1.** To place (something, such as a car or other personal property) in the custody of the police or the court, often with the understanding that it will be returned intact at the end of the proceeding. **2.** To take and retain possession of (something, such as a forged document to be produced as evidence) in preparation for a criminal prosecution.

impound account. See ACCOUNT.

impoundment. 1. The action of impounding; the state of being impounded. See IMPOUND. **2.** *Constitutional law.* The President's refusal to spend funds appropriated by Congress. • Although not authorized by the Constitution and seldom used, the impoundment power effectively gives the executive branch a line-item veto over legislative spending.

impracticability (im-prak-ti-kə-**bil**-ə-tee). *Contracts.* **1.** A fact or circumstance that excuses a party from performing an act, esp. a contractual duty, because (though possible) it would cause extreme and unreasonable difficulty. • For performance to be truly impracticable, the duty must become much more difficult or much more expensive to perform, and this difficulty or expense must have been unanticipated. **2.** The doctrine by which such a fact or circumstance excuses performance. Cf. FRUSTRATION; IMPOSSIBILITY.

commercial impracticability. The occurrence of a contingency whose nonoccurrence was an assumption in the contract, as a result of which one party cannot perform.

imprescriptible (im-prə-**skrip**-tə-bəl), *adj.* Not subject to prescription; not capable of being acquired by prescription.

imprescriptible right. See RIGHT.

impressment (im-**pres**-mənt), *n.* **1.** The act of forcibly taking (something) for public service. **2.** A court's imposition of a constructive trust on equitable grounds. See *constructive trust* under TRUST. **3.** *Archaic.* The method by which armed forces were formerly expanded, when so-called press-gangs seized men off the streets and forced them to join the army or navy. Cf. CRIMPING. — **impress,** *vb.*

imprest fund. See FUND (1).

imprest money (**im**-prest). A payment made to a soldier or sailor upon enlistment or impressment.

imprimatur (im-pri-**may**-tər *or* -**mah**-tər). [Latin "let it be printed"] **1.** A license required to publish a book. • Once required in England, the imprimatur is now encountered only rarely in countries that censor the press. **2.** A general grant of approval; commendatory license or sanction.

imprimis (im-**prI**-mis), *adv.* [fr. Latin *in primis* "in the first"] In the first place. — Also termed *in primis*.

imprison, *vb.* To confine (a person) in prison.

imprisonment, *n.* **1.** The act of confining a person, esp. in a prison <the imprisonment of Jackson was entirely justified>. **2.** The state of being confined; a period of confinement <Jack-

son's imprisonment lasted 14 years>. See FALSE IMPRISONMENT.

> "Imprisonment, by whatever name it is called, is a harsh thing, and the discipline that must be exercised over human beings in close confinement can never be wholly agreeable to those subject to it. When an attempt is made to hide the harsh realities of criminal justice behind euphemistic descriptions, a corrupting irony may be introduced into ordinary speech that is fully as frightening as Orwell's 'Newspeak.' " Lon L. Fuller, *Anatomy of the Law* 57 (1968).

improper, *adj.* **1.** Incorrect; unsuitable or irregular. **2.** Fraudulent or otherwise wrongful.

improper cumulation of actions. *Hist.* Under the common-law pleading system, the joining of inconsistent causes of action in one proceeding. • This is permitted under most modern pleading systems.

improper feud. See FEUD.

improper influence. See UNDUE INFLUENCE.

impropriate rector. See RECTOR (1).

impropriation (im-proh-pree-**ay**-shən). *Eccles. law.* The annexing of an ecclesiastical benefice to the use of a lay person, whether individual or corporate.

improve, *vb.* **1.** To increase the value or enhance the appearance of something. **2.** To develop (land), whether or not the development results in an increase or a decrease in value.

improved land. Real property that has been developed. • The improvements may or may not enhance the value of the land.

improved value. *Real estate.* In the appraisal of property, the value of the land plus the value of any improvements.

improvement. An addition to real property, whether permanent or not; esp., one that increases its value or utility or that enhances its appearance. — Also termed *land improvement.* Cf. FIXTURE.

general improvement. An improvement whose primary purpose or effect is to benefit the public generally, though it may incidentally benefit property owners in its vicinity.

local improvement. A real-property improvement, such as a sewer or sidewalk, financed by special assessment, and specially benefiting adjacent property.

necessary improvement. An improvement made to prevent the deterioration of property.

valuable improvement. An improvement that adds permanent value to the freehold. • Because of its nature, a valuable improvement would not typically be made by anyone other than the owner. A valuable improvement may be slight and of small value, as long as it is both permanent and beneficial to the property.

improvement bond. See *revenue bond* under BOND (3).

improvidence (im-**prahv**-ə-dənts). A lack of foresight and care in the management of property, esp. as grounds for removing an estate administrator.

improvident (im-**prahv**-ə-dənt), *adj.* **1.** Lacking foresight and care in the management of property. **2.** Of or relating to a judgment arrived at by using misleading information or a mistaken assumption.

impruiare (im-proo-ee-**air**-ee), *vb.* [Law Latin] *Hist.* To improve land.

impubes (im-**pyoo**-beez). [Latin] *Roman law.* A child under the age of puberty. • Under Roman law, this term referred to a male under 14 and a female under 12. Cf. INFANS.

impugn (im-**pyoon**), *vb.* To challenge or call into question (a person's character, the truth of a statement, etc.). — **impugnment,** *n.*

impulse, *n.* A sudden urge or inclination that prompts an unplanned action.

uncontrollable impulse. An impulse that is so overwhelming that it cannot be resisted. • In some jurisdictions, an uncontrollable impulse serves as a defense to criminal conduct committed while in the grip of the impulse. See IRRESISTIBLE-IMPULSE TEST.

impunity (im-**pyoo**-nə-tee). An exemption or protection from punishment <because she was a foreign diplomat, she was able to disregard the parking tickets with impunity>. See IMMUNITY.

imputation, *n.* The act or an instance of imputing something, esp. fault or crime, to a person; an accusation or charge <an imputation of negligence>.

imputation of payment. *Civil law.* The act of applying or directing payment to principal or interest.

impute (im-**pyoot**), *vb.* To ascribe or attribute; to regard (usu. something undesirable) as being done, caused, or possessed by <the court imputed malice to the defamatory statement>. — **imputation,** *n.* — **imputable,** *adj.*

> "The word 'impute' comes from im (in) and putare (reckon). It means to bring into the reckoning, to attribute or to ascribe. It is sometimes used to attribute vicariously, — to ascribe as derived from another. This is included properly within the general import of the term but it is not its primary meaning. It may be used in many senses. Thus we may impute (ascribe) intent, knowledge, guilt, and so forth. Here it is used in the basic sense of imputing (ascribing) the fact itself. Harm has been done. Did the defendant do it? Usually such an inquiry is purely factual. What really happened? At times, however, when all the facts are known we have to ask: Will the law impute (attribute or ascribe) what happened to the defendant? That is what is meant here by 'imputability.'" Rollin M. Perkins & Ronald N. Boyce, *Criminal Law* 605 (3d ed. 1982).

imputed disqualification. See *vicarious disqualification* under DISQUALIFICATION.

imputed income. See INCOME.

imputed interest. See INTEREST (3).

imputed knowledge. See KNOWLEDGE.

imputed negligence. See NEGLIGENCE.

imputed notice. See NOTICE.

in, *prep.* Under or based on the law of <to bring an action in contract>.

in absentia (in ab-**sen**-shee-ə *or* ab-**sen**-shə). [Latin] In the absence of (someone); in (someone's) absence <tried in absentia>.

in action. (Of property) attainable or recoverable through litigation. See CHOSE IN ACTION.

inactive case. See CASE.

inactive stock. See STOCK.

inadequate consideration. See CONSIDERATION.

inadequate damages. See DAMAGES.

inadequate remedy at law. A remedy (such as money damages) that does not sufficiently correct the wrong, as a result of which an injunction may be available to the disadvantaged party. See IRREPARABLE-INJURY RULE.

inadmissible, *adj.* **1.** (Of a thing) not allowable or worthy of being admitted. **2.** (Of evidence) excludable by some rule of evidence.

in adversum (in ad-**vər**-səm). [Law Latin] Against an adverse party.

> "Where a decree is obtained against one who resists, it is termed 'a decree not by consent but *in adversum.*'" 1 John Bouvier, *Bouvier's Law Dictionary* 1518 (8th ed. 1914).

inadvertence, *n.* An accidental oversight; a result of carelessness.

inadvertent discovery. *Criminal procedure.* A law-enforcement officer's unexpected finding of incriminating evidence in plain view. • Even though this type of evidence is obtained without a warrant, it can be used against the accused under the plain-view exception to the warrant requirement.

inadvertent negligence. See NEGLIGENCE.

inaedificatio (in-ee-di-fi-**kay**-shee-oh). [Latin] *Roman law.* The act of building on another's land with one's own materials, or on one's own land with another's materials. • Regardless of the source of the materials, the building became the property of the landowner.

in aequali jure (in ee-**kway**-lɪ **joor**-ee). [Law Latin] In equal right.

in aequali manu (in ee-**kway**-lɪ **man**-yoo). [Law Latin] In equal hand. • This phrase refers to property held indifferently between two parties, as when the parties to an instrument deposit it in the hands of a neutral third person. — Also termed *in aequa manu.*

inalienable, *adj.* Not transferable or assignable <inalienable property interests>. — Also termed *unalienable.*

inalienable interest. See INTEREST (2).

inalienable right. See RIGHT.

in alieno solo (in ay-lee- *or* al-ee-**ee**-noh **soh**-loh). [fr. Law French *en auter soile*] In another's land.

in alio loco (in **al**-ee-oh **loh**-koh). [Latin] In another's place. See CEPIT IN ALIO LOCO.

in ambiguo (in am-**big**-yoo-oh). [Law Latin] In doubt.

in apicibus juris (in ə-**pis**-ə-bəs **joor**-is). [Latin] Among the extremes (or most subtle doctrines) of the law.

inarbitrable, *adj.* **1.** (Of a dispute) not capable of being arbitrated; not subject to arbitration. **2.** Not subject to being decided.

in arbitrio alieno (in ahr-**bi**-tree-oh ay-lee-**ee**-noh *or* al-ee-). [Law Latin] According to the judgment of another. ● This term refers to property bequeathed to a trustee for the benefit of others, to be used in the trustee's discretion.

in arbitrium judicis (in ahr-**bi**-tree-əm **joo**-di-sis). [Latin] At the decision or discretion of the judge.

in arcta et salva custodia (in **ahrk**-tə et **sal**-və kə-**stoh**-dee-ə). [Latin] In close and safe custody.

in arrears (in ə-**reerz**). *adj. or adv.* **1.** Behind in the discharging of a debt or other obligation <the tenants were in arrears with the rent>. **2.** At the end of a term or period instead of the beginning <the interests, fees, and costs are payable in arrears>.

in articulo mortis (in ahr-**tik**-yə-loh **mor**-tis). [Law Latin] At the point of death. Cf. IN EXTREMIS.

inaudita altera parte (in-**aw**-di-tə *or* in-aw-**dɪ**-tə **al**-tə-rə **pahr**-tee). [Latin "without hearing the other party"] Ex parte. ● The term is sometimes used in decisions of the European Court of Justice. See EX PARTE.

inauguration (i-naw-gyə-**ray**-shən), *n.* **1.** A formal ceremony inducting someone into office. **2.** A formal ceremony introducing something into public use. **3.** The formal commencement of a period of time or course of action. — **inaugurate** (i-**naw**-gyə-rayt), *vb.* — **inauguratory** (i-**naw**-gyə-rə-tor-ee), *adj.* — **inaugurator** (i-**naw**-gyə-ray-tər), *n.*

in autre droit (in **oh**-trə droyt). [Law French] See EN AUTRE DROIT.

in banc. See EN BANC.

in banco. See EN BANC.

in bank. See EN BANC.

in being. Existing in life <life in being plus 21 years>. ● In property law, this includes children conceived but not yet born. See LIFE IN BEING.

> "The intentional killing of one not 'in being,' i.e. an unborn child, was until 1929 punishable neither as murder nor as infanticide. There can be no murder nor manslaughter of a child which dies before being born or even whilst being born, only of one that has been born and, moreover, been born alive." J.W. Cecil Turner, *Kenny's Outlines of Criminal Law* 104 (16th ed. 1952).

in blank. (Of an indorsement) not restricted to a particular indorsee. See *blank indorsement* under INDORSEMENT.

inboard, *adj. Maritime law.* (Of cargo) stowed between the boards (i.e., sides) of the vessel; esp., stowed inside or near the vessel's centerline.

in bonis esse (in **boh**-nis **es**-ee *or* **es**-ay). [Latin "to be among the goods"] *Roman law.* **1.** To be someone's property. **2.** (Of property) held in possession without benefit of a solemn act (such as *mancipatio*) required to transfer ownership, until ownership might be acquired by the passage of time. See *bonitarian ownership* under OWNERSHIP.

Inc. *abbr.* Incorporated.

in cahoots. See CAHOOTS.

in camera (in **kam**-ə-rə), *adv. & adj.* [Law Latin "in a chamber"] **1.** In the judge's private chambers. **2.** In the courtroom with all spectators excluded. **3.** (Of a judicial action) taken when court is not in session. — Also termed (in reference to the opinion of one judge) *in chambers*.

in camera inspection. A trial judge's private consideration of evidence.

in camera proceeding. See PROCEEDING.

in camera sitting. See SITTING.

incapacitated person. A person who is impaired by an intoxicant, by mental illness or deficiency, or by physical illness or disability to the extent that personal decision-making is impossible.

incapacitation, *n.* **1.** The action of disabling or depriving of legal capacity. **2.** The state of being disabled or lacking legal capacity. — **incapacitate,** *vb.*

incapacity. 1. Lack of physical or mental capabilities. **2.** Lack of ability to have certain legal consequences attach to one's actions. • For example, a five-year-old has an incapacity to make a binding contract. **3.** DISABILITY (1). **4.** DISABILITY (2). Cf. INCOMPETENCY.

testimonial incapacity. The lack of capacity to testify.

incapax doli (in-**kay**-paks **doh**-lI). See CAPAX DOLI.

in capita. Individually. See PER CAPITA.

in capite (in **kap**-ə-tee). [Law Latin "in chief"] *Hist.* A type of tenure in which a person held land directly of the Crown. — Also termed *tenure in capite.*

incarceration, *n.* The act or process of confining someone; IMPRISONMENT. — **incarcerate,** *vb.* — **incarcerator,** *n.*

shock incarceration. Incarceration in a military-type setting, usu. for three to six months, during which the offender is subjected to strict discipline, physical exercise, and hard labor. • After successfully completing the program, the offender is placed on probation. — Also termed *boot camp.* Cf. *shock probation* under PROBATION (1).

in casu proviso (in **kay**-s[y]oo prə-**vI**-zoh). See CASU PROVISO.

incendiary (in-**sen**-dee-er-ee), *n.* **1.** One who deliberately and unlawfully sets fire to property. — Also termed *arsonist*; *firebug.* **2.** An instrument (such as a bomb) or chemical agent designed to start a fire. — **incendiary,** *adj.*

incentive pay plan. A compensation plan in which increased productivity is rewarded with higher pay.

incentive stock option. See STOCK OPTION (2).

incentive zoning. See ZONING.

incerta persona (in-**sər**-tə pər-**soh**-nə). [Latin "uncertain person"] *Roman law.* A person (or corporate body) that could not inherit property, such as a person whose existence was uncertain or whom the testator could not identify by name (such as the first person to appear at the testator's funeral). Pl. ***incertae personae.***

"A legacy could only be given to a person with whom the testator had *testamentifactio*, and in the time of Gaius could not be made in favour of an *incerta persona, e.g.* 'whoever shall come to my funeral'; among *incertae personae* were reckoned *postumi alieni, i.e.* all *postumi* except persons who on birth become *sui heredes* of the testator, *e.g.* a grandchild begotten to a son who has been emancipated would be a *postumus alienus* in this sense." R.W. Leage, *Roman Private Law* 244–45 (C.H. Ziegler ed., 2d ed. 1930).

"Another change under Justinian was of much greater importance. Gifts of all kinds could now be made to *incertae personae* . . . ." W.W. Buckland, *A Textbook of Roman Law: From Augustus to Justinian* 363 (3d ed. 1963).

incest, *n.* Sexual relations between family members or close relatives, including children related by adoption. • Incest was not a crime under English common law but was punished as an ecclesiastical offense. Modern statutes make it a felony. — **incestuous,** *adj.*

incestuosi (in-ses-choo-**oh**-sI). [Law Latin] *Hist.* Children begotten incestuously. Cf. ADULTERINI.

incestuous adultery. See ADULTERY.

in chambers. See IN CAMERA (1).

inchartare (in-kahr-**tair**-ee), *vb.* [Law Latin "to put in charter"] *Hist.* To grant by written instrument.

in chief. 1. Principal, as opposed to collateral or incidental. **2.** Denoting the part of a trial in which the main body of evidence is presented. See CASE-IN-CHIEF.

Inchmaree clause (**inch**-mə-ree). (*often cap.*) *Maritime law.* An insurance-policy provision that protects against risks not caused by nature, such as a sailor's negligence or a latent defect in machinery. • This term is taken from a British ship, the *Inchmaree*, whose sinking in 1884 gave rise to litigation that led to the clause bearing its name.

"The most celebrated decision of recent times under the 'general' clause was doubtless Thames & Mersey Marine Ins. Co. v. Hamilton, Fraser & Co., 12 App.Cas. 484 (1887). A pump, insured as part of the machinery of a vessel, clogged through valve failure and was damaged. The House of Lords held this accident arose neither through a 'peril of the sea' nor through a cause ejusdem generis with the enumerated perils. . . . This was a disquieting decision, for it more than suggested that many costly accidents that might be suffered by the expensive machinery on steam vessels were not covered by the standard marine policy. The result was the inclusion of the celebrated 'Inchmaree' clause in hull policies, extending special coverage not only to machinery breakage but to many other classes of loss not covered by the standard perils clause as restrictively construed." Grant Gilmore & Charles L. Black, Jr., *The Law of Admiralty* § 4–8, at 74 n.90 (2d ed. 1975).

inchoate (in-**koh**-it), *adj.* Partially completed or imperfectly formed; just begun. — **inchoateness,** *n.* Cf. CHOATE.

"The word 'inchoate,' not much used in ordinary discourse, means 'just begun,' 'undeveloped.' The common law has given birth to three general offences which are usually termed 'inchoate' or 'preliminary' crimes — attempt, conspiracy, and incitement. A principal feature of these crimes is that they are committed even though the substantive offence is not successfully consummated. An attempt fails, a conspiracy comes to nothing, words of incitement are ignored — in all these instances, there may be liability for the inchoate crime." Andrew Ashworth, *Principles of Criminal Law* 395 (1991).

inchoate crime. See *inchoate offense* under OFFENSE (1).

inchoate dower. See DOWER.

inchoate instrument. See INSTRUMENT.

inchoate interest. See INTEREST.

inchoate lien. See LIEN.

inchoate offense. See OFFENSE (1).

inchoate right. 1. A right that has not fully developed, matured, or vested. **2.** *Patents.* An inventor's right that has not yet vested into a property right because the patent application is pending.

incident, *adj.* Dependent upon, subordinate to, arising out of, or otherwise connected with (something else, usu. of greater importance) <the utility easement is incident to the ownership of the tract>. — **incident,** *n.*

incident, *n.* **1.** A discrete occurrence or happening <an incident of copyright infringement> **2.** A dependent, subordinate, or consequential part (of something else) <child support is a typical incident of divorce>.

incidental, *adj.* Subordinate to something of greater importance; having a minor role <the FAA determined that the wind played only an incidental part in the plane crash>.

incidental admission. See ADMISSION (1).

incidental authority. See AUTHORITY (1).

incidental beneficiary. See BENEFICIARY.

incidental damages. See DAMAGES.

incidental demand. See DEMAND (1).

incidental power. See *incident power* under POWER.

incidental use. See USE (1).

incident of ownership. (*usu. pl.*) Any right of control that may be exercised over a transferred life-insurance policy so that the policy's proceeds will be included in a decedent's gross estate for estate-tax purposes <because Douglas still retained the incidents of ownership after giving his life-insurance policy to his daughter, the policy proceeds were taxed against his estate>. • The incidents of ownership include the rights to change the policy's beneficiaries and to borrow against, assign, and cancel the policy.

incident power. See POWER.

incident to employment. *Workers' compensation.* A risk that is related to or connected with a worker's job duties.

incidere (in-**sid**-ə-ree), *vb.* [Latin "fall into or on"] *Roman law.* To come within the scope of a law or to fall into a legal category; esp. to become involved in a situation that entangles a person in a legal action. • This term had a similar meaning under English law. For example, a person might become liable to (or "fall into") amercement (*incidere in misericordiam*). See AMERCEMENT.

incipitur (in-**sip**-i-tər). [Law Latin] *Hist.* It is begun. • This refers to the practice of entering the commencement of a pleading on the court roll.

incite, *vb.* To provoke or stir up (someone to commit a criminal act, or the criminal act itself). Cf. ABET.

incitee. A person who has been incited, esp. to commit a crime.

inciteful, *adj.* Tending to incite <inciteful speech>.

incitement, *n.* **1.** The act or an instance of provoking, urging on, or stirring up. **2.** *Criminal law.* The act of persuading another person to commit a crime; SOLICITATION (2). — **inciteful,** *adj.*

> "An inciter is one who counsels, commands or advises the commission of a crime. It will be observed that this definition is much the same as that of an accessory before the fact. What, then, is the difference between the two? It is that in incitement the crime has not (or has not necessarily) been committed, whereas a party cannot be an accessory in crime unless the crime has been committed. An accessory before the fact is party to consummated mischief; an inciter is guilty only of an inchoate crime." Glanville Williams, *Criminal Law* 612 (2d ed. 1961).

> "Emphasis upon the theory of one offense with guilt attaching to several is quite appropriate because it is still part of the groundwork of our legal philosophy, so far as perpetrators, abettors and inciters are concerned, despite the fact that some of the statutes require lipservice to the notion of a separate substantive offense, in the effort to avoid certain procedural difficulties. It explains how one may be guilty of a crime he could not perpetrate, by having caused or procured it as a result of his abetment or incitement." Rollin M. Perkins & Ronald N. Boyce, *Criminal Law* 732–33 (3d ed. 1982).

inciter. A person who incites another to commit a crime; an aider or abettor.

incivile (in-**siv**-ə-lee), *adj.* [Law Latin] Irregular; out of the due course of law.

incivism (**in**-si-viz-əm). Unfriendliness toward one's own country or its government; lack of good citizenship.

inclausa (in-**klaw**-zə). [Law Latin] *Hist.* An enclosure near a house; a home close. See CLOSE.

inclose, *vb.* See ENCLOSE.

inclosure. See ENCLOSURE.

include, *vb.* To contain as a part of something. • The participle *including* typically indicates a partial list <the plaintiff asserted five tort claims, including slander and libel>. But some drafters use phrases such as *including without limitation* and *including but not limited to* — which mean the same thing. Cf. NAMELY.

included offense. See *lesser included offense* under OFFENSE.

inclusionary-approach rule. The principle that evidence of a prior crime, wrong, or act is admissible for any purpose other than to show a defendant's criminal propensity as long as it is relevant to some disputed issue and its probative value outweighs its prejudicial effect.

inclusio unius est exclusio alterius. See EXPRESSIO UNIUS EST EXCLUSIO ALTERIUS.

incognito (in-kog-**nee**-toh *or* in-**kog**-ni-toh), *adj.* Without making one's name or identity known <Binkley flew incognito to France>.

incola (**in**-kə-lə). [Latin "an inhabitant"] *Roman law.* A foreign resident without full civil rights. — Also termed *incolant.*

income. The money or other form of payment that one receives, usu. periodically, from employment, business, investments, royalties, gifts, and the like. See EARNINGS. Cf. PROFIT.

accrued income. Money earned but not yet received.

accumulated income. Income that is retained in an account; esp., income that a trust has generated, but that has not yet been reinvested or distributed by the trustee.

accumulated taxable income. The income of a corporation as adjusted for certain items (such as excess charitable contributions), less the dividends-paid deduction and the accumulated-earnings credit. • It serves as the base upon which the accumulated-earnings tax is imposed. See *accumulated-earnings tax* under TAX.

active income. **1.** Wages; salary. **2.** Income from a trade or business.

adjusted gross income. Gross income minus allowable deductions specified in the tax code. — Abbr. AGI.

adjusted ordinary gross income. A corporation's gross income less capital gains and certain expenses. • The IRS uses this calculation to determine whether a corporation is a personal holding company. If 60% or more of a corporation's AOGI consists of certain passive investment income, the company has met the test for personal-holding-company classification. IRC (26 USCA) § 543(b). — Abbr. AOGI. See *personal holding company* under COMPANY.

aggregate income. The combined income of a husband and wife who file a joint tax return.

blocked income. Money earned by a foreign taxpayer but not subject to U.S. taxation because the foreign country prohibits changing the income into dollars.

current income. Income that is due within the present accounting period. — Also termed *current revenue.*

deferred income. Money received at a time later than when it was earned, such as a check received in January for commissions earned in November.

disposable income. Income that may be spent or invested after payment of taxes and other primary obligations. — Also termed *disposable earnings.*

dividend income. The income resulting from a dividend distribution and subject to tax.

earned income. Money derived from one's own labor or active participation; earnings from services. Cf. *unearned income* (2).

exempt income. Income that is not subject to income tax.

fixed income. Money received at a constant rate, such as a payment from a pension or annuity.

gross income. Total income from all sources before deductions, exemptions, or other tax reductions. — Also termed *gross earnings.*

imputed income. The benefit one receives from the use of one's own property, the performance of one's services, or the consumption of self-produced goods and services.

income in respect of a decedent. Income earned by a person, but not collected before death. • This income is included in the decedent's gross estate for estate-tax purposes. For income-tax purposes, it is taxed to the estate or, if the estate does not collect the income, it is taxed to the eventual recipient. — Abbr. I.R.D.

> "If a decedent has earned income that he or she had not received before death and was not *entitled* to receive before death, such income is known — for Federal Income Tax purposes — as 'income in respect of a decedent' (I.R.D.). For example, if the decedent earned fees or salary or wages for work done before death but not payable until later, and if decedent was a cash method taxpayer (versus an accrual method taxpayer), that earned but unpaid income would not properly be shown on the final income tax return filed for the decedent, for that taxable period ends with the date of death. Rather it is I.R.D. that becomes taxable to the estate of the decedent." John K. McNulty, *Federal Estate and Gift Taxation in a Nutshell* 89 (5th ed. 1994).

investment income. See *unearned income.*

net income. Total income from all sources minus deductions, exemptions, and other tax reductions. • Income tax is computed on net income. — Also termed *net earnings.*

net operating income. Income derived from operating a business, after subtracting operating costs.

nonoperating income. Business income derived from investments rather than operations.

ordinary income. **1.** For business-tax purposes, earnings from the normal operations or activities of a business. — Also termed *operating income.* **2.** For individual income-tax purposes, income that is derived from sources such as wages, commissions, and interest (as opposed to income from capital gains).

other income. Income not derived from an entity's principal business, such as earnings from dividends and interest.

passive income. Income derived from a business activity over which the earner does not participate directly or have immediate control, such as copyright royalties. See PASSIVE ACTIVITY.

passive investment income. Investment income that does not involve or require active participation, such as gross receipts from royalties, rental income, dividends, interest, annuities, and gains from the sale or exchange of securities. IRC (26 USCA) § 1362(d).

personal income. The total income received by an individual from all sources.

portfolio income. Income from interest, dividends, rentals, royalties, capital gains, or other investment sources. • Portfolio income is not considered passive income; therefore, net passive losses cannot be used to offset net portfolio income.

prepaid income. Income received but not yet earned. — Also termed *deferred revenue.*

previously taxed income. An S corporation's undistributed taxable income taxed to the shareholders as of the last day of the corporation's tax year. • This income could usu. be withdrawn later by the shareholders without tax consequences. PTI has been replaced by the accumulated adjustments account. — Abbr. PTI.

real income. Income adjusted to allow for inflation or deflation so that it reflects true purchasing power.

regular income. Income that is received at fixed or specified intervals.

split income. An equal division between spouses of earnings reported on a joint tax return, allowing for equal tax treatment in community-property and common-law states.

taxable income. Gross income minus all allowable deductions and exemptions. • Taxable income is multiplied by the applicable tax rate to compute one's tax liability.

unearned income. **1.** Earnings from investments rather than labor. — Also termed *investment income.* **2.** Income received but not yet earned; money paid in advance. Cf. *earned income.*

unrelated business income. Taxable income generated by a tax-exempt organization from a trade or business unrelated to its exempt purpose or activity.

income approach. A method of appraising real property based on capitalization of the income that the property is expected to generate. Cf. MARKET APPROACH; COST APPROACH.

income averaging. *Tax.* A method of computing tax by averaging a person's current income with that of preceding years.

> "A distinct departure from the strict annual system of taxing income is the concept of averaging income, allowed until repeal by the 1986 T.R.A.... [T]he *rate* at which the item was taxed was made to depend not only on the rates and level of income for that year, but upon the taxpayer's experience over the past four years. The item was (sometimes) taxed *as if* it had been received over a four-year period. Especially for authors, actors, athletes, and other taxpayers who have fluctuating or bunched income and face graduated tax rates that apply on an annual basis, income averaging was most important." John K. McNulty, *Federal Income Taxation of Individuals in a Nutshell* 353 (5th ed. 1995).

income-based plan. See CHAPTER 13.

income-basis method. A method of computing the rate of return on a security using the interest and price paid rather than the face value.

income beneficiary. See BENEFICIARY.

income bond. See BOND (3).

income exclusion. See EXCLUSION.

income fund. See MUTUAL FUND.

income in respect of a decedent. See INCOME.

income property. See PROPERTY.

income-shifting. The practice of transferring income to a taxpayer in a lower tax bracket, such as a child, to reduce tax liability. See *kiddie tax* under TAX.

income statement. A statement of all the revenues, expenses, gains, and losses that a business incurred during a given period. — Also termed *statement of income*; *profit-and-loss statement*; *earnings report.* Cf. BALANCE SHEET.

income stock. See STOCK.

income tax. See TAX.

income-tax deficiency. See DEFICIENCY.

income-tax return. See TAX RETURN.

income-tax withholding. See WITHHOLDING.

income-withholding order. A court order providing for the withholding of a person's income, usu. to enforce a child-support order.

income yield. See CAPITALIZATION RATE.

in common. Shared equally with others, without division into separate ownership parts. See *tenancy in common* under TENANCY.

in communi (in kə-**myoo**-nɪ). [Law Latin] In common.

incommunicado (in-kə-myoo-ni-**kah**-doh), *adj.* [Spanish] **1.** Without any means of communication. **2.** (Of a prisoner) having the right to communicate only with a few designated people.

incommutable (in-kə-**myoot**-ə-bəl), *adj.* (Of an offense) not capable of being commuted.

incompatibility, *n.* The quality or state of being incompatible; irreconcilability. • Incompatibility is recognized as a no-fault ground for divorce in many states. See *no-fault divorce* under DIVORCE.

incompetence, *n.* **1.** The state or fact of being unable or unqualified to do something <the dispute was over her alleged incompetence as a legal assistant>. **2.** INCOMPETENCY <the court held that the affidavit was inadmissible because of the affiant's incompetence>.

incompetency, *n.* Lack of legal ability in some respect, esp. to stand trial or to testify <once the defense lawyer established her client's in-

competency, the client did not have to stand trial>. — Also termed *incompetence*; *mental incompetence*. — **incompetent,** *adj*. Cf. INCAPACITY.

incompetency hearing. See PATE HEARING.

incompetent, *adj*. **1.** (Of a witness) unqualified to testify. **2.** (Of evidence) inadmissible. • This sense is often criticized, as in the quotation below.

> "[*Incompetent*] is constantly used loosely as equivalent to 'inadmissible' on any ground. This use should be avoided." John H. Wigmore, *A Students' Textbook of the Law of Evidence* 36 (1935).

incompetent evidence. See EVIDENCE.

incomplete instrument. See INSTRUMENT.

incomplete transfer. See TRANSFER.

inconclusive, *adj*. (Of evidence) not leading to a conclusion or definite result.

in consideratione inde (in kən-sid-ə-ray-shee-**oh**-nee **in**-dee). [Law Latin] In consideration thereof.

in consideratione legis (in kən-sid-ə-ray-shee-**oh**-nee **lee**-jis). [Law Latin] **1.** In consideration or contemplation of law. **2.** In abeyance.

in consideratione praemissorum (in kən-sid-ə-ray-shee-**oh**-nee pree-mi-**sor**-əm). [Law Latin] In consideration of the premises.

in consimili casu (in kən-**sim**-ə-lɪ **kay**-s[y]oo). See CONSIMILI CASU.

inconsistent, *adj*. Lacking consistency; not compatible with another fact or claim <inconsistent statements>.

inconsistent defense. See DEFENSE (1).

inconsistent presumption. See *conflicting presumption* under PRESUMPTION.

inconsistent statement. See PRIOR INCONSISTENT STATEMENT.

in conspectu ejus (in kən-**spek**-t[y]oo **ee**-jəs). [Law Latin] In his sight or view.

in contemplation of death. See CONTEMPLATION OF DEATH.

incontestability clause. An insurance-policy provision (esp. found in a life-insurance policy) that prevents the insurer, after a specified period (usu. one or two years), from disputing the policy's validity on the basis of fraud or mistake; a clause that bars all defenses except those reserved (usu. conditions and the payment of premiums). • Most states require that a life-insurance policy contain a clause making the policy incontestable after it has been in effect for a specified period, unless the insured does not pay premiums or violates policy conditions relating to military service. Some states also require similar provisions in accident and sickness policies. — Also termed *noncontestability clause*; *incontestable clause*; *uncontestable clause*. Cf. CONTESTABILITY CLAUSE.

incontestable policy. See INSURANCE POLICY.

incontinenti (in-kon-ti-**nen**-tɪ), *adv*. [Law Latin] Immediately; without any interval or intermission. — Also spelled *in continenti*.

incontrovertible-physical-facts doctrine. See PHYSICAL-FACTS RULE.

inconvenient forum. See FORUM NON CONVENIENS.

incorporamus (in-kor-pə-**ray**-məs). [Law Latin] *Hist*. We incorporate. • This word indicated an intent to incorporate.

> "All the other methods therefore whereby corporations exist, by common law, by prescription, and by act of parliament, are for the most part reducible to this of the king's letters patent, or charter of incorporation. The king's creation may be performed by the words '*creamus, erigimus, fundamus, incorporamus*,' or the like." 1 William Blackstone, *Commentaries on the Laws of England* 461 (1765).

incorporate, *vb*. **1.** To form a legal corporation <she incorporated the family business>. **2.** To combine with something else <incorporate the exhibits into the agreement>. **3.** To make the terms of another (esp. earlier) document part of a document by specific reference <the codicil incorporated the terms of the will>; esp., to apply the provisions of the Bill of Rights to the states by interpreting the 14th Amendment's Due Process Clause as encompassing those provisions.

incorporation, *n*. **1.** The formation of a legal corporation. See ARTICLES OF INCORPORATION. **2.** *Constitutional law*. The process of applying the provisions of the Bill of Rights to the states by interpreting the 14th Amendment's Due Process Clause as encompassing those provisions. • In a variety of opinions since 1897, the Supreme Court has incorporated all of the Bill of Rights except the following provisions: (1) the Second Amendment right to bear arms, (2) the Third Amendment prohibition of quartering soldiers, (3) the Fifth Amendment right to grand-jury indictment, (4) the Seventh Amendment right to a jury trial in a civil case, and (5) the Eighth Amendment prohibition of excessive bail and fines.

> ***selective incorporation.*** Incorporation of certain provisions of the Bill of Rights. • Justice Benjamin Cardozo, who served from 1932 to 1938, first advocated this approach.
>
> ***total incorporation.*** Incorporation of all of the Bill of Rights. • Justice Hugo Black, who served from 1937 to 1971, first advocated this approach.

3. INCORPORATION BY REFERENCE. — **incorporate,** *vb.*

incorporation by reference. A method of making a secondary document part of a primary document by including in the primary document a statement that the secondary document should be treated as if it were contained within the primary one. — Often shortened to *incorporation.* — Also termed *adoption by reference.*

incorporator. A person who takes part in the formation of a corporation, usu. by executing the articles of incorporation. — Also termed *corporator.*

> "An 'incorporator' must be sharply distinguished from a 'subscriber.' The latter agrees to buy shares in the corporation; in other words, a subscriber is an investor and participant in the venture. An 'incorporator' on the other hand serves the largely ceremonial or ministerial functions described in this section. At one time many states required that an incorporator also be a subscriber of shares; however, such requirement appears to have disappeared in all states." Robert W. Hamilton, *The Law of Corporations in a Nutshell* 34 (3d ed. 1991).

in corpore (in **kor**-pə-ree). [Latin] In body or substance; in a material thing or object.

incorporeal (in-kor-**por**-ee-əl), *adj.* Having a conceptual existence but no physical existence; intangible <copyrights and patents are incorporeal property>. — **incorporeality,** *n.* Cf. CORPOREAL.

incorporeal chattel. See *incorporeal property* under PROPERTY.

incorporeal hereditament. See HEREDITAMENT.

incorporeal ownership. See OWNERSHIP.

incorporeal possession. See POSSESSION (3).

incorporeal property. See PROPERTY.

incorporeal right. See RIGHT.

incorporeal thing. See THING.

incorrigibility (in-kor-ə-jə-**bil**-ə-tee *or* in-kahr-). Serious or persistent misbehavior by a child, making reformation by parental control impossible or unlikely. Cf. JUVENILE DELINQUENCY.

incorrigible (in-**kor**-ə-jə-bəl *or* in-**kahr**-), *adj.* Incapable of being reformed; delinquent.

incorrigible child. See CHILD.

Incoterm (**in**[**g**]-koh-tərm). A standardized shipping term, defined by the International Chamber of Commerce, that apportions the costs and liabilities of international shipping between buyers and sellers. See C.I.F.; F.O.B.

increase (**in**-krees), *n.* **1.** The extent of growth or enlargement. **2.** *Archaic.* The produce of land or the offspring of human beings or animals. — **increase** (in-**krees**), *vb.*

increase, costs of. See COSTS OF INCREASE.

increased-risk-of-harm doctrine. See LOSS-OF-CHANCE DOCTRINE.

increment (**in**[**g**]-krə-mənt), *n.* A unit of increase in quantity or value. — **incremental,** *adj.*

> ***unearned increment.*** An increase in the value of real property due to population growth.

incremental cash flow. See CASH FLOW.

incrementum (in-krə-**men**-təm). [Latin] *Hist.* Increase. • This term appeared in various phrases, such as *costs de incremento* ("costs of increase"). See COSTS OF INCREASE.

increscitur (in-**kres**-i-tər). See ADDITUR.

incriminate (in-**krim**-ə-nayt), *vb.* **1.** To charge (someone) with a crime <the witness incriminated the murder suspect>. **2.** To identify (oneself or another) as being involved in the commission of a crime or other wrongdoing <the defendant incriminated an accomplice>. — Also termed *criminate.* — **incriminatory,** *adj.*

incriminating, *adj.* Demonstrating or indicating involvement in criminal activity <incriminating evidence>.

incriminating admission. See ADMISSION (1).

incriminating circumstance. A situation or fact showing either that a crime was committed or that a particular person committed it.

incriminating evidence. See EVIDENCE.

incriminating statement. See STATEMENT.

incrimination. 1. The act of charging someone with a crime. **2.** The act of involving someone in a crime. — Also termed *crimination.* See SELF-INCRIMINATION.

incroach, *vb. Archaic.* See ENCROACH.

incroachment. *Archaic.* See ENCROACHMENT.

in cujus rei testimonium (in **kyoo**-jəs **ree**-ɪ tes-tə-**moh**-nee-əm). [Law Latin] *Hist.* In witness whereof. • These words were used to conclude deeds. The modern phrasing of the testimonium clause in deeds and other instruments — beginning with *in witness whereof* — is a loan translation of the Latin.

inculpatae tutelae moderatio. See MIDERAMEN INCULPATAE TUTELAE.

inculpate (in-**kəl**-payt *or* **in**-kəl-payt), *vb.* **1.** To accuse. **2.** To implicate (oneself or another) in a crime or other wrongdoing; INCRIMINATE. — **inculpation,** *n.* — **inculpatory** (in-**kəl**-pə-tor-ee), *adj.*

inculpatory evidence. See EVIDENCE.

incumbent (in-**kəm**-bənt), *n.* One who holds an official post, esp. a political one. — **incumbency,** *n.* — **incumbent,** *adj.*

incumbrance. See ENCUMBRANCE.

incur, *vb.* To suffer or bring on oneself (a liability or expense). — **incurrence,** *n.* — **incurrable,** *adj.*

incurramentum (in-kə-rə-**men**-təm). [fr. Latin *in* "upon" + *currere* "to run"] *Hist.* The incurring of a fine or penalty.

in custodia legis (in kə-**stoh**-dee-ə **lee**-jis). [Latin] In the custody of the law <the debtor's automobile was *in custodia legis* after being seized by the sheriff>. • The phrase is traditionally used in reference to property taken into the court's charge during pending litigation over it.

inde (**in**-dee), *adv.* [Latin] *Hist.* Thence; thereof. • This word appeared in several Latin phrases, such as *quod eat inde sine die* ("that he go thence without date").

indebitatus (in-deb-i-**tay**-təs), *p.pl.* [Law Latin] Indebted. See NUNQUAM INDEBITATUS.

indebitatus assumpsit (in-deb-i-**tay**-təs ə-**səm**[**p**]-sit). See ASSUMPSIT.

indebiti solutio (in-**deb**-i-tɪ sə-**l**[**y**]**oo**-shee-oh). [Latin] *Roman & Scots law.* Payment of what is not owed. • Money paid under the mistaken belief that it was owed could be recovered by *condictio indebiti.* See *condictio indebiti* under CONDICTIO.

> "*Indebiti Solutio* — When a person has paid in error what he was not bound to pay the law lays upon the person who has received payment a duty of restitution. . . . Payment (solutio) includes any performance whereby one person has been enriched at the expense of another. Usually it will be the handing over of money or of some other thing, but it may also consist in undertaking a new liability or in discharging an existing liability." R.W. Lee, *The Elements of Roman Law* 373–74 (4th ed. 1956).

indebitum (in-**deb**-i-təm). *Roman law.* A debt that in fact is not owed. • Money paid for a nonexistent debt could be recovered by the action *condictio indebiti.* Cf. DEBITUM.

> "A conditional debt if paid could be recovered as an *indebitum,* so long as the condition was outstanding." W.W. Buckland, *A Manual of Roman Private Law* 255 (2d ed. 1953).

indebtedness (in-**det**-id-nis). **1.** The condition or state of owing money. **2.** Something owed; a debt.

indecency, *n.* The condition or state of being outrageously offensive, esp. in a vulgar or sexual way. • Unlike obscene material, indecent speech is protected under the First Amendment. — **indecent,** *adj.* Cf. OBSCENITY.

> "*Obscenity* is that which is offensive to chastity. *Indecency* is often used with the same meaning, but may also include anything which is outrageously disgusting. These were not the names of common-law crimes, but were words used in describing or identifying certain deeds which were." Rollin M. Perkins & Ronald N. Boyce, *Criminal Law* 471 (3d ed. 1982).

indecent assault. See *sexual assault* (2) under ASSAULT.

indecent exhibition. The act of publicly displaying or offering for sale something (such as a photograph or book) that is outrageously offensive, esp. in a vulgar or sexual way.

indecent exposure. An offensive display of one's body in public, esp. of the genitals. Cf. LEWDNESS; OBSCENITY.

> "*Indecent exposure* of the person to public view is also a common-law misdemeanor. Blackstone did not deal with it separately. 'The last offense which I shall mention,' he said, 'more immediately against religion and morality, and cognizable by the temporal courts, is that of open and notorious *lewdness*; either by frequenting houses of ill fame, which is an indictable offense; or by some grossly scandalous and public indecency, for which the punishment is by fine and imprisonment.' In other words private indecency was exclusively under the jurisdiction of the ecclesiastical court but public indecency of an extreme nature was indictable." Rollin M. Perkins & Ronald N. Boyce, *Criminal Law* 473 (3d ed. 1982) (quoting 4 William Blackstone, *Commentaries on the Laws of England* 64 (1769)).

indecent liberties. Improper behavior toward a child, esp. of a sexual nature.

indecimable (in-**des**-ə-mə-bəl), *adj. Hist.* Not titheable; not liable for tithes.

indefeasible (in-də-**feez**-ə-bəl), *adj.* (Of a claim or right) that cannot be defeated, revoked, or lost <an indefeasible estate>.

indefeasible remainder. See REMAINDER.

indefeasibly vested remainder. See *indefeasible remainder* under REMAINDER.

indefensus (in-də-**fen**-səs). [Latin "undefended"] *Roman law.* A person who fails to make a defense or plea to an action. • The term later acquired a similar meaning in English law.

indefinite detainee. See NONREMOVABLE INMATE.

indefinite failure of issue. See FAILURE OF ISSUE.

indefinite sentence. See *indeterminate sentence* under SENTENCE.

indefinite sentencing. See INDETERMINATE SENTENCING.

in Dei nomine (in **dee**-I **nahm**-ə-nee). [Latin] *Hist.* In the name of God. • The opening phrase of certain writs.

in delicto (in də-**lik**-toh). [Latin] In fault. Cf. EX DELICTO.

indemnification (in-dem-nə-fi-**kay**-shən), *n.* **1.** The action of compensating for loss or damage sustained. **2.** The compensation so made. — **indemnificatory,** *adj.*

indemnifier. See INDEMNITOR.

indemnify (in-**dem**-nə-fI), *vb.* **1.** To reimburse (another) for a loss suffered because of a third party's act or default. **2.** To promise to reimburse (another) for such a loss. **3.** To give (another) security against such a loss.

indemnis (in-**dem**-nis), *adj.* [Latin] *Hist.* Free from loss or damage; harmless.

indemnitee (in-dem-nə-**tee**). One who receives indemnity from another.

indemnitor (in-**dem**-nə-tər *or* -tor). One who indemnifies another. — Also termed *indemnifier.*

indemnity (in-**dem**-nə-tee), *n.* **1.** A duty to make good any loss, damage, or liability incurred by another. **2.** The right of an injured party to claim reimbursement for its loss, damage, or liability from a person who has such a duty. **3.** Reimbursement or compensation for loss, damage, or liability in tort; esp., the right of a party who is secondarily liable to recover from the party who is primarily liable for reimbursement of expenditures paid to a third party for injuries resulting from a violation of a common-law duty. — **indemnitory,** *adj.* Cf. CONTRIBUTION.

double indemnity. The payment of twice the basic benefit in the event of a specified loss, esp. as in an insurance contract requiring the insurer to pay twice the policy's face amount in the case of accidental death.

indemnity against liability. A right to indemnity that arises on the indemnitor's default, regardless of whether the indemnitee has suffered a loss.

"*Indemnity against Liability* — Where the indemnity is against liability, the cause of action is complete and the indemnitee may recover on the contract as soon as his liability has become fixed and established, even though he has sustained no actual loss or damage at the time he seeks to recover. Thus, under such a contract, a cause of action accrues to the indemnitee on the recovery of a judgment against him, and he may recover from the indemnitor without proof of payment of the judgment." 42 C.J.S. *Indemnity* § 22 (1991).

indemnity bond. See BOND (2).

indemnity clause. A contractual provision in which one party agrees to answer for any specified or unspecified liability or harm that the other party might incur. — Also termed *hold-harmless clause*; *save-harmless clause*. Cf. EXEMPTION CLAUSE.

indemnity insurance. See *first-party insurance* under INSURANCE.

indemnity land. 1. Public land granted to a railroad company to help defray the cost of constructing a right-of-way. • This land indemnifies a railroad company for land given in a previous grant but since rendered unavailable for railroad use by a disposition or reservation made after the original grant. **2.** Federally owned land granted to a state to replace previously granted land that has since been rendered unavailable for the state's use. — Also termed *place land*.

indemnity principle. *Insurance.* The doctrine that an insurance policy should not confer a benefit greater in value than the loss suffered by the insured.

indent, *n. Hist.* An indented certificate of indebtedness issued by the U.S. government or a state government in the late 18th or early 19th century.

indent (in-**dent**), *vb. Hist.* **1.** To cut in a serrated or wavy line; esp., to sever (an instrument) along a serrated line to create multiple copies, each fitting into the angles of the other. See CHIROGRAPH; INDENTURE (1).

"If a deed be made by more parties than one, there ought to be regularly as many copies of it as there are parties, and each should be cut or indented (formerly in acute angles *instar dentium*, but at present in a waving line) on the top or side, to tally or correspond with the other; which deed, so made, is called an indenture.... Deeds thus made were denominated *syngrapha* by the canonists; and with us *chirographa*, or hand-writings; the word *cirographum* or *cyrographum* being usually that which is divided in making the indenture...." 2 William Blackstone, *Commentaries on the Laws of England* 295–96 (1766).

2. To agree by contract; to bind oneself. **3.** To bind (a person) by contract.

indenture (in-**den**-chər), *n.* **1.** A formal written instrument made by two or more parties with different interests, traditionally having the edges serrated, or indented, in a zigzag fashion to reduce the possibility of forgery and to distinguish it from a deed poll. Cf. *deed poll* under DEED. **2.** A deed or elaborate contract signed by two or more parties.

"The distinction between a *deed poll* and an *indenture* is no longer important since 8 & 9 Vict. c. 106, § 5. Formerly a deed made by one party had a polled or smooth-cut edge, a deed made between two or more parties was copied for each on the same parchment, and the copies cut apart with indented edges, so as to enable them to be identified by fitting the parts together. Such deeds were called indentures. An indented edge is not now necessary to give the effect of an indenture to a deed purporting to be such." William R. Anson, *Principles of the Law of Contract* 84 (Arthur L. Corbin ed., 3d Am. ed. 1919).

corporate indenture. A document containing the terms and conditions governing the issuance of debt securities, such as bonds or debentures.

debenture indenture. See DEBENTURE INDENTURE.

trust indenture. **1.** A document containing the terms and conditions governing a trustee's conduct and the trust beneficiaries' rights. — Also termed *indenture of trust*. **2.** See *deed of trust* under DEED.

indenture of a fine. *Hist.* A document engrossed by the chirographer of fines to reflect penalties assessed by the court. • The chirographer prepared indentures in duplicate on the same piece of parchment, then split the parchment along an indented line through a word, sentence, or drawing placed on the parchment to help ensure its authenticity. See CHIROGRAPHER OF FINES.

indenture of trust. See *trust indenture* under INDENTURE.

indenture trustee. See TRUSTEE (1).

independence, *n.* The state or quality of being independent; esp., a country's freedom to manage all its affairs, whether external or internal, without control by other countries.

independent, *adj.* **1.** Not subject to the control or influence of another <independent investigation>. **2.** Not associated with another (often larger) entity <an independent subsidiary>. **3.** Not dependent or contingent on something else <an independent person>.

independent adjuster. See ADJUSTER.

independent advice. Counsel that is impartial and not given to further the interests of the person giving it. • Whether a testator or donor received independent advice before making a disposition is often an important issue in an undue-influence challenge to the property disposition. — Also termed *proper independent advice.*

independent agency. See AGENCY (3).

independent agent. See AGENT.

independent audit. See AUDIT.

independent contract. See CONTRACT.

independent contractor. One who is hired to undertake a specific project but who is left free to do the assigned work and to choose the method for accomplishing it. • Unlike an employee, an independent contractor who commits a wrong while carrying out the work does not create liability for the one who did the hiring. Cf. EMPLOYEE.

independent counsel. See COUNSEL.

independent covenant. See COVENANT (1).

independent executor. See EXECUTOR.

independent intervening cause. See *intervening cause* under CAUSE (1).

independent investigation committee. See SPECIAL LITIGATION COMMITTEE.

independent personal representative. See *personal representative* under REPRESENTATIVE.

independent probate. See *informal probate* under PROBATE.

independent promise. See *unconditional promise* under PROMISE.

independent regulatory agency. See *independent agency* under AGENCY (3).

independent regulatory commission. See *independent agency* under AGENCY (3).

independent-significance doctrine. The principle that effect will be given to a testator's disposition that is not done solely to avoid the requirements of a will.

independent-source rule. *Criminal procedure.* The rule providing — as an exception to the fruit-of-the-poisonous-tree doctrine — that evidence obtained by illegal means may nonetheless be admissible if that evidence is also obtained by legal means unrelated to the original illegal conduct. See FRUIT-OF-THE-POISONOUS-TREE DOCTRINE. Cf. INEVITABLE-DISCOVERY RULE.

independent state. See SOVEREIGN STATE.

independent union. See UNION.

indestructible trust. See TRUST.

indeterminate, *adj.* Not definite; not distinct or precise.

indeterminate bond. See BOND (3).

indeterminate conditional release. A type of release from prison granted upon the fulfillment of certain conditions. • The release remains revocable if additional conditions are breached.

indeterminate sentence. See SENTENCE.

indeterminate sentencing. The practice of not imposing a definite term of confinement, but instead prescribing a range for the minimum and maximum term, leaving the precise term to be fixed in some other way, usu. based on the prisoner's conduct and apparent rehabilitation while incarcerated. — Also termed *indefinite sentencing.* See *indeterminate sentence* under SENTENCE.

index, *n.* **1.** An alphabetized listing of the topics or other items included in a single book or document, or in a series of volumes, usu. found at the end of the book, document, or series <index of authorities>.

grantee-grantor index. An index, usu. kept in the county recorder's office, alphabetically listing by grantee the volume and page number of the grantee's recorded property transactions. • In some jurisdictions, the grantee-grantor index is combined with the grantor-grantee index.

grantor-grantee index. An index, usu. kept in the county recorder's office, alphabetically listing by grantor the volume and page number of the grantor's recorded property transactions.

tract index. An index, usu. kept in the county recorder's office, listing, by location of each parcel of land, the volume and page number of the recorded property transactions affecting the parcel.

2. A number, usu. expressed in the form of a percentage or ratio, that indicates or measures a series of observations, esp. those involving a market or the economy <cost-of-living index> <stock index>.

advance-decline index. A stock-market indicator showing the cumulative net difference between stock-price advances and declines.

index animi sermo (**in**-deks **an**-ə-mɪ **sər**-moh). [Latin] Speech is the index of the mind. • This maxim supports the concept that the language of a statute or instrument is the best guide to the drafter's intent.

indexation. See INDEXING.

index crime. See *index offense* under OFFENSE (1).

index fund. See MUTUAL FUND.

indexing. 1. The practice or method of adjusting of wages, pension benefits, insurance, or other types of payments to compensate for inflation. **2.** The practice of investing funds to track or mirror an index of securities. — Also termed *indexation*.

index lease. See LEASE.

index of authorities. An alphabetical list of authorities cited in a brief, usu. with subcategories for cases, statutes, and treatises. — Also termed *table of authorities*.

index offense. See OFFENSE (1).

Indian Claims Commission. A federal agency — dissolved in 1978 — that adjudicated claims brought by American Indians, a tribe, or another identifiable group of Indians against the United States. • The U.S. Court of Federal Claims currently hears these claims.

Indian country. 1. The land within the borders of all Indian reservations, the land occupied by an Indian community (whether or not located within a recognized reservation), and any land held in trust by the United States but beneficially owned by an Indian or tribe. **2.** *Hist.* Any region (esp. during the U.S. westward migration) where a person was likely to encounter Indians.

Indian land. Land owned by the United States but held in trust for and used by American Indians. — Also termed *Indian tribal property*. Cf. TRIBAL LAND.

Indian reservation. An area that the federal government has designated for use by an American Indian tribe, where the tribe generally settles and establishes a tribal government.

Indian Territory. A former U.S. territory — now a part of the state of Oklahoma — to which the Cherokee, Choctaw, Chickasaw, Creek, and Seminole tribes were forcibly removed between 1830 and 1843. • In the late 19th century, most of this territory was ceded to the United States, and in 1907 the greater part of it became the State of Oklahoma.

Indian title. A right of occupancy that the federal government grants to an American Indian tribe based on the tribe's immemorial possession of the area. — Also termed *aboriginal title*.

Indian tribal property. See INDIAN LAND.

Indian tribe. A group, band, nation, or other organized group of indigenous American people, including any Alaskan native village, that is recognized as eligible for the special programs and services provided by the U.S. government because of Indian status (42 USCA § 9601(36)); esp., any such group having a federally recognized governing body that carries out substantial governmental duties and powers over an area (42 USCA § 300f(14); 40 CFR § 146.3). • A tribe may be identified in various ways, esp. by past dealings with other tribes or with the federal, state, or local government, or by recognition in historical records.

> "The Indian tribe is the fundamental unit of Indian Law; in its absence there is no occasion for the law to operate. Yet there is no all-purpose definition of an Indian tribe. A group of Indians may qualify as a tribe

for the purpose of one statute or federal program, but fail to qualify for others. Definitions must accordingly be used with extreme caution." William C. Canby, Jr., *American Indian Law in a Nutshell* 3–4 (2d ed. 1988).

indicare (in-di-**kair**-ee), *vb.* [Latin] **1.** *Roman law.* To accuse (someone) of a crime. **2.** *Civil law.* To show or discover. **3.** *Civil law.* To fix or tell the price of a thing. See INDICIUM.

indicator. *Securities.* An average or index that shows enough of a correlation to market trends or economic conditions that it can help analyze market performance.

coincident indicator. An economic or market-activity index or indicator that shows changing trends near the same time that overall conditions begin to change.

economic indicator. See ECONOMIC INDICATOR.

lagging indicator. **1.** An index that indicates a major stock-market change sometime after the change occurs. **2.** See *lagging economic indicator* under ECONOMIC INDICATOR.

leading indicator. **1.** A quantifiable index that predicts a major stock-market change. **2.** See *leading economic indicator* under ECONOMIC INDICATOR.

indicavit (in-di-**kay**-vit). [Law Latin "he has indicated"] *Hist.* A writ of prohibition by which a church patron removes to a common-law court an ecclesiastical-court action between two clerics who dispute each other's right to a benefice. • The writ was long available — nominally up to the 20th century — under the statute *De Conjunctim Feoffatis* (1306). Actions concerning clerics' rights to a benefice were usu. tried in ecclesiastical courts, but they could be removed to a common-law court if the action involved a church patron in some way, as when one cleric was appointed by a certain patron and the other cleric was appointed by another patron. Cf. ADVOWSON.

indicia (in-**dish**-ee-ə), *n.* **1.** *Roman law.* Evidence. **2.** (*pl.*) Signs; indications <the purchase receipts are indicia of ownership>.

indicia of title. A document that evidences ownership of personal or real property.

indicium (in-**dish**-ee-əm). [Latin] *Roman law.* **1.** The act of accusing someone of a crime. **2.** The act of promising recompense for a certain service. **3.** A sign or mark; esp., something used as a type of proof. See INDICARE.

indict (in-**dIt**), *vb.* To charge (a person) with a crime by formal legal process, esp. by grand-jury presentation. — Also formerly spelled *endite; indite.*

indictable offense (in-**dIt**-ə-bəl ə-**fents**). See OFFENSE (1).

indictee (in-dI-**tee**). A person who has been indicted; one officially charged with a crime.

indictio (in-**dik**-shee-oh). [Latin] **1.** *Roman law.* An imperial proclamation establishing a 15–year period for the reassessment of property values for tax purposes. • *Indictio* also referred to the 15–year cycle itself. **2.** A declaration or proclamation, such as a declaration of war (*indictio belli*). **3.** An indictment.

indictment (in-**dIt**-mənt), *n.* **1.** The formal written accusation of a crime, made by a grand jury and presented to a court for prosecution against the accused person. **2.** The act or process of preparing or bringing forward such a formal written accusation. Cf. INFORMATION; PRESENTMENT (2).

barebones indictment. An indictment that cites only the language of the statute allegedly violated; an indictment that does not provide a factual statement.

"What has been called 'a bare bones indictment using only statutory language' is quite common, and entirely permissible so long as the statute sets forth fully, directly, and expressly all essential elements of the crime intended to be punished." 1 Charles Alan Wright, *Federal Practice and Procedure* § 125, at 558–59 (3d ed. 1999).

duplicitous indictment (d[y]oo-**plis**-ə-təs). The joining of two or more offenses in the same count of an indictment. — Also termed *duplicitous information.*

joint indictment. An indictment that charges two or more people with an offense.

indictor (in-**dIt**-ər *or* in-**dI**-tor). A person who causes another to be indicted.

in diem (in **dI**-əm *or* **dee**-əm). [Latin] For each day; per day. Cf. PER DIEM.

indigena (in-**dij**-ə-nə). [Latin "native"] *Hist.* A subject born within the English realm or naturalized by act of Parliament. Cf. ALIENIGENA.

indigent (**in**-di-jənt), *n.* A poor person. — **indigency, indigence,** *n.* — **indigent,** *adj.* See PAUPER.

indigent defendant. A person who is too poor to hire a lawyer and who, upon indictment, becomes eligible to receive aid from a court-appointed attorney and a waiver of court costs. See IN FORMA PAUPERIS.

indignity. *Family law.* A ground for divorce consisting in one spouse's pattern of behavior calculated to humiliate the other.

indirect attack. See COLLATERAL ATTACK.

indirect confession. See CONFESSION.

indirect contempt. See *constructive contempt* under CONTEMPT.

indirect cost. See COST (1).

indirect evidence. See *circumstantial evidence* under EVIDENCE.

indirect loss. See *consequential loss* under LOSS.

indirect notice. See *implied notice* under NOTICE.

indirect possession. See *mediate possession* under POSSESSION.

indirect-purchaser doctrine. *Antitrust.* The principle that in litigation for price discrimination, the court will ignore sham middle parties in determining whether different prices were paid by different customers for the same goods. • This doctrine gives standing to bring an antitrust action to a party who is not an immediate purchaser of a product. Thus, if a manufacturer sells a product to a retailer, but dictates the terms by which the retailer must sell the product to a consumer, a court will ignore the retailer and treat the consumer as the direct purchaser of the product.

indirect tax. See TAX.

indiscriminate attack. *Int'l law.* An aggressive act that (1) is not carried out for a specific military objective, (2) employs a means of combat not directed at a specific military objective, or (3) employs a means of combat the effects of which cannot be limited in accordance with an international protocol such as the Geneva Convention of 1949.

indispensable-element test. *Criminal law.* A common-law test for the crime of attempt, based on whether the defendant acquires control over the thing that is essential to the crime. • Under this test, for example, a person commits a crime by buying the explosives with which to detonate a bomb. See ATTEMPT (2).

indispensable evidence. See EVIDENCE.

indispensable party. See PARTY (2).

indistanter (in-di-**stan**-tər), *adv.* [Law Latin "immediately"] Forthwith; without delay.

individual, *adj.* **1.** Existing as an indivisible entity. **2.** Of or relating to a single person or thing, as opposed to a group.

individual account plan. See *defined-contribution plan* under EMPLOYEE BENEFIT PLAN.

individual asset. See ASSET.

individual debt. See DEBT.

individual liberty. See *personal liberty* under LIBERTY.

individual property. See SEPARATE PROPERTY (1).

individual proprietorship. See SOLE PROPRIETORSHIP.

individual retirement account. A savings or brokerage account to which a person may contribute up to a specified amount of earned income each year ($2,000 under current law). • The contributions, along with any interest earned in the account, are not taxed until the money is withdrawn after a participant reaches 59½ (or before then, if a 10% penalty is paid). — Abbr. IRA.

> ***Roth IRA.*** An IRA in which contributions are nondeductible when they are made. • No further taxes are assessed on the contributions (or accrued interest) when the money is withdrawn (if all applicable rules are followed). This term takes its name from Senator William Roth, who sponsored the legislation creating this type of IRA.

indivisible, *adj.* Not separable into parts <an indivisible debt>.

indivision. *Civil law.* Undivided ownership of property; the condition of being owned by coowners each having an undivided interest in the property.

indivisum (in-di-VI-səm *or* -zəm), *adj.* [Latin] *Roman law.* (Of property) held in common; not divided.

indorsee (in-dor-**see**). A person to whom a negotiable instrument is transferred by indorsement. — Also spelled *endorsee.*

indorsee in due course. An indorsee who, in the ordinary course of business, acquires a negotiable instrument in good faith for value, before its maturity, and without knowledge of its dishonor.

indorsement, *n.* **1.** The placing of a signature, sometimes with an additional notation, on the back of a negotiable instrument to transfer or guarantee the instrument or to acknowledge payment. **2.** The signature or notation itself. — Also spelled *endorsement.* — **indorse,** *vb.*

"The clever indorser can subscribe his or her name under a variety of magic phrases. The Code specifies the legal effect of some of these phrases. Qualified indorsements ('without recourse') limit the liability of the indorser if the instrument is dishonored. Restrictive indorsements such as 'for deposit only,' 'pay any bank,' and the like set the terms for further negotiation of the instrument. Their main purpose is to prevent thieves and embezzlers from cashing checks." 2 James J. White & Robert S. Summers, *Uniform Commercial Code* § 16–7, at 92–93 (4th ed. 1995).

accommodation indorsement. An indorsement to an instrument by a third party who acts as surety for another party who remains primarily liable. See ACCOMMODATION PAPER.

anomalous indorsement. See *irregular indorsement.*

blank indorsement. An indorsement that names no specific payee, thus making the instrument payable to the bearer and negotiable by delivery only. UCC § 3–205(b). — Also termed *indorsement in blank*; *general indorsement.*

collection indorsement. See *restrictive indorsement.*

conditional indorsement. An indorsement that restricts the instrument in some way, as by limiting how the instrument can be paid or transferred; an indorsement giving possession of the instrument to the indorsee, but retaining title until the occurrence of some condition named in the indorsement. • Wordings that indicate this type of indorsement are "Pay to Brad Jones when he becomes 18 years of age" and "Pay to Brigitte Turner, or order, unless before payment I give you notice to the contrary." Cf. *special indorsement.*

full indorsement. See *special indorsement.*

general indorsement. See *blank indorsement.*

indorsement in blank. See *blank indorsement.*

indorsement in full. See *special indorsement.*

indorsement without recourse. See *qualified indorsement.*

irregular indorsement. An indorsement by a person who signs outside the chain of title and who therefore is neither a holder nor a transferor of the instrument. • An irregular indorser is generally treated as an accommodation party. See ACCOMMODATION PARTY. — Also termed *anomalous indorsement*; *full indorsement.*

qualified indorsement. An indorsement that passes title to the instrument but limits the indorser's liability to later holders if the instrument is later dishonored. • Typically, a qualified indorsement is made by writing "without recourse" or "sans recourse" over the signature. — Also termed *indorsement without recourse.* UCC § 3–415(b). See WITHOUT RECOURSE.

restrictive indorsement. An indorsement that includes a condition (e.g., "pay Josefina Cardoza only if she has worked 8 full hours on April 13") or any other language restricting further negotiation (e.g., "for deposit only"). — Also termed *collection indorsement.*

special indorsement. An indorsement that specifies the person to receive payment or to whom the goods named by the document must be delivered. UCC § 3–205(a). — Also termed *indorsement in full*; *full indorsement.* Cf. *conditional indorsement.*

trust indorsement. An indorsement stating that the payee becomes a trustee for a third person (e.g., "pay Erin Ray in trust for Kaitlin Ray"); a restrictive indorsement that limits the instrument to the use of the indorser or another person.

unauthorized indorsement. An indorsement made without authority, such as a forged indorsement.

unqualified indorsement. An indorsement that does not limit the indorser's liability on the paper. • It does not, for example, include the phrase "without recourse."

unrestrictive indorsement. An indorsement that includes no condition or language restricting negotiation. — Also termed *unrestricted indorsement.*

indorser. A person who transfers a negotiable instrument by indorsement. — Also spelled *endorser*.

accommodation indorser. An indorser who acts as surety for another person.

in dubio (in **d**[**y**]**oo**-bee-oh), *adv.* & *adj.* [Latin] In doubt.

inducement, *n.* **1.** The act or process of enticing or persuading another person to take a certain course of action. See *fraud in the inducement* under FRAUD.

active inducement. The act of intentionally causing a third party to infringe a valid patent. • Active inducement requires proof of an actual intent to cause the patent infringement.

2. *Contracts.* The benefit or advantage that causes a promisor to enter into a contract. **3.** *Criminal law.* An enticement or urging of another person to commit a crime. **4.** The preliminary statement in a pleading; esp., in an action for defamation, the plaintiff's allegation that extrinsic facts gave a defamatory meaning to a statement that is not defamatory on its face, or, in a criminal indictment, a statement of preliminary facts necessary to show the criminal character of the alleged offense. Cf. INNUENDO (2); COLLOQUIUM. — **induce,** *vb.*

inducement of breach of contract. See TORTIOUS INTERFERENCE WITH CONTRACTUAL RELATIONS.

inducie legales (in-**d**[**y**]**oo**-shee-ee lə-**gay**-leez). [Latin] *Civil & Scots law.* The days allowed after summons for a defendant to appear in court.

inducing infringement. See *infringement in the inducement* under INFRINGEMENT.

induct, *vb.* **1.** To put into possession of (something, such as an office or benefice). **2.** To admit as a member. **3.** To enroll for military service.

inductio (in-**dək**-shee-oh). [Latin] *Roman law.* The act of erasing a writing or part of it, as when a testator struck a legacy from a will.

induction. **1.** The act or process of initiating <the induction of three new members into the legal fraternity>. **2.** The act or process of reasoning from specific instances to general propositions <after looking at several examples, the group reasoned by induction that it is a very poor practice to begin a new paragraph by abruptly bringing up a new case>. Cf. DEDUCTION (3).

indult (in-**dəlt**). *Eccles. law.* A dispensation granted by the Pope to do or obtain something contrary to canon law. — Also termed *indulto.*

indulto (in-**dəl**-toh). [Spanish] **1.** A pardon or amnesty. **2.** *Hist.* A duty paid on imported goods to the Spanish or Portuguese Crown.

in duplo (in **d**[**y**]**oo**-ploh), *adv.* & *adj.* [Law Latin] *Hist.* In double. • This term appeared in phrases such as *damna in duplo* ("double damages"). — Also termed (in Roman law) *in duplum.*

industrial-development bond. See BOND (3).

industrial disease. See OCCUPATIONAL DISEASE.

industrial espionage. See ESPIONAGE.

industrial goods. See *capital goods* under GOODS.

industrial life insurance. See INSURANCE.

industrial relations. All dealings and relationships between an employer and its employees, including collective bargaining about issues such as safety and benefits.

industrial-revenue bond. See *industrial-development bond* under BOND (3).

industrial union. See UNION.

industry. **1.** Diligence in the performance of a task. **2.** Systematic labor for some useful purpose; esp., work in manufacturing or production. **3.** A particular form or branch of productive labor; an aggregate of enterprises employing similar production and marketing facilities to produce items having markedly similar characteristics.

industry-wide liability. See *enterprise liability* under LIABILITY.

indutiae (in-**d**[**y**]**oo**-shee-ee). [Latin] **1.** *Roman & int'l law.* A truce or cessation of hostilities; an armistice. — Also spelled (in Roman law) *indutiae*. **2.** *Roman & civil law.* A delay allowed for performing an obligation. **3.** *Maritime law.* A period of 20 days in which a bottomry-bond debtor may unload the ship's cargo and pay the bond. — Also spelled *induciae*.

in eadem causa (in ee-**ay**-dəm **kaw**-zə), *adv.* [Latin] *Hist.* In the same cause; in the same state or condition.

inebriate (in-**ee**-bree-ət), *n. Archaic.* An intoxicated person; esp., a habitual drunkard.

inebriated (in-**ee**-bree-ay-tid), *adj.* Drunk; besotted.

ineffective assistance of counsel. See ASSISTANCE OF COUNSEL.

ineligible, *adj.* (Of a person) legally disqualified to serve in office. — **ineligibility,** *n.*

in emulationem vicini (in em-yə-lay-shee-**oh**-nəm vi-**SI**-nI), *adj.* [Latin "in envy or hatred of a neighbor"] *Hist.* (Of a cause of action) brought for an act done solely to hurt or distress another, such as raising a high fence.

inequitable (in-**ek**-wi-tə-bəl), *adj.* Not fair; opposed to principles of equity <an inequitable ruling>.

in equity. In a chancery court rather than a court of law; before a court exercising equitable jurisdiction.

inequity (in-**ek**-wi-tee), *n.* **1.** Unfairness; a lack of equity. **2.** An instance of injustice.

inescapable peril. A danger that one cannot avoid without another's help. See LAST-CLEAR-CHANCE DOCTRINE.

in esse (in **es**-ee *also* **es**-ay). [Latin "in being"] In actual existence; IN BEING <the court was concerned only with the rights of the children *in esse*>. Cf. IN POSSE.

inessential mistake. See *unessential mistake* under MISTAKE.

in est de jure (in **est** dee **joor**-ee). [Latin] It is implied as of right or by law.

in evidence. Having been admitted into evidence <the photograph was already in evidence when the defense first raised an objection to it>.

inevitable accident. See *unavoidable accident* under ACCIDENT.

inevitable-accident doctrine. See UNAVOIDABLE-ACCIDENT DOCTRINE.

inevitable-discovery rule. *Criminal procedure.* The rule providing — as an exception to the fruit-of-the-poisonous-tree doctrine — that evidence obtained by illegal means may nonetheless be admissible if the prosecution can show that the evidence would eventually have been legally obtained anyway. See FRUIT-OF-THE-POISONOUS-TREE DOCTRINE. Cf. INDEPENDENT-SOURCE RULE.

in excambio (in eks-**kam**-bee-oh), *adv.* [Law Latin] *Hist.* In exchange. • This phrase appeared in deeds of exchange.

inexcusable neglect. See NEGLECT.

in exitu (in **eks**-ə-t[y]oo *or* **eg**-zə-t[y]oo), *adv.* & *adj.* [Law Latin] *Hist.* In issue. • These words sometimes appeared in phrases such as *de materia in exitu* ("of the matter in issue").

in extenso (in ek-**sten**-soh). [Latin] In full; unabridged <set forth *in extenso*>.

in extremis (in ek-**stree**-mis). [Latin "in extremity"] **1.** In extreme circumstances. **2.** Near the point of death; on one's deathbed. • Unlike *in articulo mortis*, the phrase *in extremis* does not always mean at the point of death. Cf. *in articulo mortis*.

in facie curiae (in **fay**-shee-ee **kyoor**-ee-ee), *adv.* & *adj.* [Law Latin "in the face of the court"] *Hist.* In the presence of the court.

in facie ecclesiae (in **fay**-shee-ee e-**klee**-z[h]ee-ee), *adv.* & *adj.* [Law Latin "in the face of the church"] *Hist.* In the presence of the church. • A marriage solemnized in a parish church or public chapel was said to be *in facie ecclesiae*.

in faciendo (in fay-shee-**en**-doh), *adv.* & *adj.* [Law Latin] In the performance of an act; in feasance.

in fact. Actual or real; resulting from the acts of parties rather than by operation of law. Cf. IN LAW.

in facto (in **fak**-toh), *adv.* [Latin] *Hist.* In fact; in deed.

infamia (in-**fay**-mee-ə), *n.* [Latin] *Roman law.* **1.** Bad reputation; ill-fame. **2.** Loss of honor as a citizen.

infamia facti (in-**fay**-mee-ə **fak**-tI). Infamy in fact, though not yet judicially proved.

infamia juris (in-**fay**-mee-ə **joor**-is). Infamy established by judicial verdict.

infamis (in-**fay**-mis), *adj.* [Latin] *Roman law.* (Of a person or action) of ill-repute. • A person was automatically *infamis* if held liable for certain torts or breaches of fiduciary duty. This type of condemnation carried with it certain disabilities, such as disqualification from office.

infamous (**in**-fə-məs), *adj.* **1.** (Of a person) having a bad reputation. **2.** (Of conduct) that is punishable by imprisonment.

infamous crime. See CRIME.

infamous punishment. See PUNISHMENT.

infamy (**in**-fə-mee), *n.* **1.** Disgraceful repute. **2.** The loss of reputation or position resulting from a person's being convicted of an infamous crime. See *infamous crime* under CRIME.

infancy. 1. MINORITY (1). **2.** Early childhood.

natural infancy. At common law, the period ending at age seven, during which a child was presumed to be without criminal capacity.

3. The beginning stages of anything.

infangthief (**in**-fang-theef). [fr. Old English *in* "in" + *fangen* "taken" + *theof* "thief"] *Hist.* A privilege held by a lord of a manor to try a thief captured on the property. Cf. UTFANGTHIEF.

infans (**in**-fanz). [Latin] *Roman law.* A child under seven years old. • On turning seven years old, an *infans* became known as an *impubes*. An *infans* had no capacity in the law. Cf. IMPUBES.

infant, *n.* **1.** A newborn baby. **2.** MINOR.

> "An infant in the eyes of the law is a person under the age of twenty-one years, and at that period (which is the same in the French and generally in the American law) he or she is said to attain majority; and for his torts and crimes an infant may be liable; but for his contracts, as a general rule, he is not liable, unless the contract is for necessaries." John Indermaur, *Principles of the Common Law* 195 (Edmund H. Bennett ed., 1st Am. ed. 1878).

infantia (in-**fan**-shee-ə). [Latin] *Roman law.* The period of a person's life from birth to seven years; early childhood.

infanticide (in-**fant**-ə-sId). **1.** The act of killing a newborn child, esp. by the parents or with their consent. • In archaic usage, the word referred also to the killing of an unborn child. — Also termed *child destruction*; *neonaticide*. Cf. FETICIDE. **2.** The practice of killing newborn children. **3.** One who kills a newborn child.

in favorem libertatis (in fə-**vor**-əm lib-ər-**tay**-tis). [Law Latin] In favor of liberty.

in favorem vitae (in fə-**vor**-əm **vI**-tee), *adv.* [Law Latin] In favor of life.

infect, *vb.* **1.** To contaminate <the virus infected the entire network>. **2.** To taint with crime <one part of the city has long been infected with illegal drug-dealing>. **3.** To make (a ship or cargo) liable in the seizure of contraband, which is only a part of its cargo <claiming that the single package of marijuana had infected the ship, the Coast Guard seized the entire vessel>. — **infection,** *n.* — **infectious,** *adj.*

infection, doctrine of. *Int'l law.* The principle that any goods belonging to an owner of contraband and carried on the same ship as the contraband may be seized or otherwise treated in the same manner as the contraband itself.

infeft, *p.pl. Scots law.* Enfeoffed. See ENFEOFF.

in feodo simpliciter (in **fee**-ə-doh *or* **fyoo**-doh sim-**plis**-i-tər). [Law Latin] In fee simple. See FEE SIMPLE.

infeoff, *vb.* See ENFEOFF.

infeoffment. See ENFEOFFMENT.

infer, *vb.* To conclude from facts or from factual reasoning; to draw as a conclusion or inference.

inference (**in**-fər-ənts), *n.* **1.** A conclusion reached by considering other facts and deducing a logical consequence from them. **2.** The process by which such a conclusion is reached; the process of thought by which one moves from evidence to proof. — **infer,** *vb.* — **inferential,** *adj.* — **inferrer,** *n.*

inference-on-inference rule. The principle that a presumption based on another presumption cannot serve as a basis for determining an ultimate fact.

inferential fact. See FACT.

inferior court. See COURT.

inferred authority. See *incidental authority* under AUTHORITY (1).

infeudate. See ENFEOFF.

infeudation (in-fyoo-**day**-shən), *n.* Under the feudal system of landholding, the process of giving a person legal possession of land; ENFEOFFMENT (1). — **infeudate,** *vb.* Cf. SUBINFEUDATION.

> "So thorough was the process by which the land of England became subject to fixed obligations to the king — the process generally referred to today as the *infeudation* of England — that by the time of the famous Domesday survey, a scant twenty years after Hastings, it was possible to assign to almost every rock and stone of English soil its precise duty to the Crown." Thomas F. Bergin & Paul G. Haskell, *Preface to Estates in Land and Future Interests* 3 (2d ed. 1984).

inficiari. See INFITIARI.

inficiatio. See INFITIATIO.

infidel (**in**-fə-dəl). **1.** A person who does not believe in something specified, esp. a particular religion. **2.** *Hist.* A person who violates a feudal oath of fealty.

infidelis (in-fi-**dee**-lis *or* -**del**-is). [Latin] *Hist.* **1.** INFIDEL (1). **2.** INFIDEL (2).

infidelitas (in-fi-**dee**-lə-tas *or* -**del**-ə-tas), *n.* [Latin] *Hist.* Infidelity; faithlessness to one's feudal oath.

> "Many of the smaller misdeeds were regarded as exhibitions of an *infidelitas*, which, however, did not amount to a *felonia*." 2 Frederick Pollock & Frederic W. Maitland, *The History of English Law Before the Time of Edward I* 513–14 (2d ed. 1899).

infidelity. Unfaithfulness to an obligation; esp., marital unfaithfulness. Cf. ADULTERY.

infiduciare (in-fi-**d[y]oo**-shee-air-ee), *vb.* [Law Latin] *Hist.* To pledge property.

in fieri (in **fɪ**-ə-rɪ), *adj.* [fr. Latin *in* "in" + *fieri* "to be done"] (Of a legal proceeding) that is pending or in the course of being completed.

in fine (in **fɪ**-nee *or* **fɪn**), *adv.* [Latin] **1.** In short; in summary. **2.** At the end (of a book, chapter, section, etc.).

infirmative, *adj. Rare.* (Of evidence) tending to weaken or invalidate a criminal accusation <an infirmative fact>. Cf. CRIMINATIVE.

infirmative hypothesis. *Criminal law.* An approach to a criminal case in which the defendant's innocence is assumed, and incriminating evidence is explained in a manner consistent with that assumption.

infirmity (in-**fər**-mə-tee), *n.* Physical weakness caused by age or disease; esp., in insurance law, an applicant's ill health that is poor enough to deter an insurance company from insuring the applicant. — **infirm,** *adj.*

infitiari (in-fish-ee-**air**-ɪ), *vb.* [Latin "to deny"] *Roman law.* To deny a plaintiff's allegation; esp., to deny liability on a debt. — Also spelled *inficiari.*

infitiatio (in-fish-ee-**ay**-shee-oh), *n.* [Latin] *Roman law.* The denial of a debt or liability; the denial of a plaintiff's allegation. — Also spelled *inficiatio.*

in flagrante delicto (in flə-**gran**-tee də-**lik**-toh). [Latin "while the crime is ablaze"] In the very act of committing a crime or other wrong; red-handed <the sheriff caught them *in flagrante delicto*>.

inflammatory (in-**flam**-ə-tor-ee), *adj.* Tending to cause strong feelings of anger, indignation, or other type of upset; tending to stir the passions. • Evidence can be excluded if its inflammatory nature outweighs its probative value.

inflation, *n.* A general increase in prices coinciding with a fall in the real value of money. — **inflationary,** *adj.* Cf. DEFLATION.

cost-push inflation. Inflation caused by a rise in production costs.

demand-pull inflation. Inflation caused by an excess of demand over supply.

inflation rate. The pace of change in the prices of goods and services in a particular period. • The primary indexes for measuring the rate are the Consumer Price Index and the Producer Price Index.

infliction of emotional distress. See INTENTIONAL INFLICTION OF EMOTIONAL DISTRESS; NEGLIGENT INFLICTION OF EMOTIONAL DISTRESS.

influence district. A voting district in which a racial or ethnic minority group does not constitute a majority of the voters, but does make up a sufficient proportion of the voters to constitute an influential minority, thus being able to elect its preferred candidate with a reasonable number of crossover votes from other groups. Cf. MAJORITY-MINORITY DISTRICT.

informal, *adj*. Not done or performed in accordance with normal forms or procedures <an informal proceeding>.

informal agency action. Administrative-agency activity other than adjudication or rulemaking, such as investigation, publicity, or supervision. Cf. RULEMAKING.

informal contract. See *parol contract* (2) under CONTRACT.

informal dividend. See DIVIDEND.

informal immunity. See *pocket immunity* under IMMUNITY (3).

informal marriage. See *common-law marriage* under MARRIAGE (1).

informal probate. See PROBATE.

informal proceeding. See PROCEEDING.

informal proof of claim. See PROOF OF CLAIM.

informal rulemaking. See RULEMAKING.

informant. One who informs against another; esp., one who confidentially supplies information to the police about a crime, sometimes in exchange for a reward or special treatment. — Also termed *informer*; *feigned accomplice*.

informant's privilege. See PRIVILEGE (3).

in forma pauperis (in **for**-mə **paw**-pə-ris). [Latin "in the manner of a pauper"] In the manner of an indigent who is permitted to disregard filing fees and court costs <when suing, a poor person is generally entitled to proceed *in forma pauperis*>. — Abbr. *i.f.p.*

***in forma pauperis* affidavit.** See *poverty affidavit* under AFFIDAVIT.

information. A formal criminal charge made by a prosecutor without a grand-jury indictment. • The information is used to prosecute misdemeanors in most states. About half the states allow its use in felony prosecutions as well. Cf. INDICTMENT.

informational picketing. See PICKETING.

information and belief, on. (Of an allegation or assertion) based on secondhand information that the declarant believes to be true. • For the historical precursor to this phrase, see INSINUATIO.

information letter. A written statement issued by the Department of Labor — in particular, by the Pension and Welfare Benefits Administration — that calls attention to a well-established interpretation or principle of ERISA, without applying it to a specific factual situation.

information return. See TAX RETURN.

informative advertising. See ADVERTISING.

informed consent. See CONSENT.

informed intermediary. See INTERMEDIARY.

informer. 1. INFORMANT. **2.** A private citizen who brings a penal action to recover a penalty. • Under some statutes, a private citizen is required to sue the offender for a penalty before any criminal liability can attach. — Also termed *common informer*. See COMMON INFORMER.

informer's privilege. See *informant's privilege* under PRIVILEGE (3).

in foro (in **for**-oh), *adv*. [Latin] In a forum, court, or tribunal; in the forum.

in foro conscientiae (in **for**-oh kon-shee-**en**-shee-ee), *adv*. [Latin "in the forum of conscience"] Privately or morally rather than legally <this moral problem cannot be dealt with by this court, but only *in foro conscientiae*>.

in foro contentioso (in **for**-oh kən-ten-shee-**oh**-soh), *adv*. [Latin] In the forum of contention or litigation.

in foro ecclesiastico (in **for**-oh e-klee-z[h]ee-**as**-ti-koh), *adv.* [Law Latin] In an ecclesiastical court.

in foro externo (in **for**-oh ek-**stər**-noh), *adv.* [Latin "in an external forum"] *Eccles. law.* In a court that is handling a case pertaining to or affecting the corporate life of the church. See FORUM EXTERNUM.

in foro humano (in **for**-oh hyoo-**may**-noh), *adv.* In a human as opposed to a spiritual forum.

> "[T]his may be murder or manslaughter in the sight of God, yet *in foro humano* it cannot come under the judgment of felony. . . ." 1 Hale P.C. 429.

in foro interno (in **for**-oh in-**tər**-noh), *adv.* [Latin "in an internal forum"] *Eccles. law.* In a court of conscience; in a court for matters of conscience. See FORUM INTERNUM.

in foro saeculari (in **for**-oh sek-yə-**lair**-I), *adv.* [Law Latin] In a secular court.

infra (**in**-frə), *adv. & adj.* [Latin "below"] Later in this text. • *Infra* is used as a citational signal to refer to a later-cited authority. In medieval Latin, *infra* also acquired the sense "within." Cf. INTRA; SUPRA.

infra aetatem (**in**-frə ee-**tay**-təm), *adj.* [Latin] Underage. — Also spelled *infra etatem.*

infra annos nubiles (**in**-frə **an**-ohs **n[y]oo**-bə-leez), *adj.* [Law Latin] *Hist.* Under marriageable years; i.e., not old enough to wed.

infra annum (**in**-frə **an**-əm), *adv.* [Law Latin] Under a year; within a year.

infra annum luctus (**in**-frə **an**-əm **lək**-təs), *adv.* [Latin] *Hist.* Within the year of mourning. • The referred to the one-year period of mourning during which a widow was prohibited from remarrying.

infra civitatem (**in**-frə siv-i-**tay**-təm), *adv.* [Law Latin] Within the state.

infra corpus comitatus (**in**-frə **kor**-pəs kom-ə-**tay**-təs), *adv. & adj.* [Law Latin] *Hist.* Within the body of a county. • In English law, this phrase referred to a body of water that was completely enclosed by land, and therefore exempt from admiralty jurisdiction.

infraction, *n.* A violation, usu. of a rule or local ordinance and usu. not punishable by incarceration. — **infract,** *vb.*

civil infraction. An act or omission that, though not a crime, is prohibited by law and is punishable. • In some states, many traffic violations are classified as civil infractions.

infra dignitatem curiae (**in**-frə dig-ni-**tay**-təm **kyoor**-ee-ee), *adj.* [Law Latin "beneath the dignity of the court"] (Of a case) too trifling in amount or character to be entertained by a court.

infra furorem (**in**-frə fyə-**ror**-əm), *adv.* [Law Latin] During madness; while in a state of insanity.

infra hospitium (**in**-frə hah-**spish**-ee-əm). [Law Latin "within the inn"] The doctrine that an innkeeper is liable for goods deposited by a guest.

infra jurisdictionem (**in**-frə joor-is-dik-shee-**oh**-nəm), *adv. & adj.* [Law Latin] Within the jurisdiction.

infra praesidia (**in**-frə prə-**sid**-ee-ə). [Latin "within the defenses"] *Hist.* The international-law doctrine that someone who captures goods will be considered the owner of the goods if they are brought completely within the captor's power. • This term is a corruption of the Roman-law term *intra praesidia,* which referred to goods or persons taken by an enemy during war. Under the principle of *postliminium,* the captured person's rights or goods were restored to prewar status when the captured person returned. See POSTLIMINIUM.

> "In war, when those who are our enemies have captured someone on our side and have taken him into their own lines [*intra praesidia*]; for if during the same war he returns he has *postliminium,* that is, all his rights are restored to him just as if he had not been captured by the enemy." *Digest of Justinian* 49.15.5.1 (Pomponius, Quintus Mucius 37).

infrastructure. The underlying framework of a system; esp., public services and facilities (such as highways, schools, bridges, sewers, and water systems) needed to support commerce as well as economic and residential development.

in fraudem creditorum (in **fraw**-dəm kre-di-**tor**-əm), *adv.* [Latin] In fraud of creditors.

in fraudem legis (in **fraw**-dəm **lee**-jis), *adv.* [Latin] In fraud of the law. • With an intent to evade the law.

infringement, *n. Intellectual property.* An act that interferes with one of the exclusive rights of a patent, copyright, or trademark owner. — **infringe,** *vb.* See INTELLECTUAL PROPERTY. Cf. PLAGIARISM.

contributory infringement. **1.** The act of participating in, or contributing to, the infringing acts of another person. • For contributory infringement, the law imposes vicarious liability. **2.** *Patents.* The act of aiding or abetting another person's patent infringement by knowingly selling a nonstaple item that has no substantial noninfringing use and is especially adapted for use in a patented combination or process. • In the patent context, contributory infringement is statutorily defined in the Patent Act. 35 USCA § 271(c). **3.** *Copyright.* The act of either (1) actively inducing, causing, or materially contributing to the infringing conduct of another person, or (2) providing the goods or means necessary to help another person infringe (as by making facilities available for an infringing performance). • In the copyright context, contributory infringement is a common-law doctrine. **4.** *Trademarks.* A manufacturer's or distributor's conduct in knowingly supplying, for resale, goods bearing an infringing mark.

copyright infringement. The act of violating any of a copyright owner's exclusive rights granted by the federal Copyright Act, 17 USCA §§ 106, 602. • A copyright owner has several exclusive rights in copyrighted works, including the rights (1) to reproduce the work, (2) to prepare derivative works based on the work, (3) to distribute copies of the work, (4) for certain kinds of works, to perform the work publicly, (5) for certain kinds of works, to display the work publicly, (6) for sound recordings, to perform the work publicly, and (7) to import into the United States copies acquired elsewhere.

criminal infringement. The statutory criminal offense of either (1) willfully infringing a copyright to obtain a commercial advantage or financial gain (17 USCA § 506; 18 USCA § 2319), or (2) trafficking in goods or services that bear a counterfeit mark (18 USCA § 2320). • Under the second category, the statute imposes criminal penalties if the counterfeit mark is (1) identical with, or substantially indistinguishable from, a mark registered on the Principal Register of the U.S. Patent and Trademark Office, and (2) likely to confuse or deceive the public.

direct infringement. *Patents.* The act of making, using, selling, offering for sale, or importing into the United States, without the patent owner's permission, a product that is covered by the claims of a valid patent. 35 USCA § 271(a). Cf. *contributory infringement*; *infringement in the inducement.*

domain-name infringement. Infringement of another's trademark or servicemark by the use of a confusingly similar Internet domain name.

infringement in the inducement. *Patents.* The act of actively and knowingly aiding and abetting direct infringement by another person. • While the term is occasionally used in copyright and trademark law to mean contributory infringement, it is usu. reserved for the patent context. — Also termed *inducing infringement.*

innocent infringement. The act of violating an intellectual-property right without knowledge or awareness that the act constitutes infringement. • An innocent infringer may, in limited circumstances, escape liability for some or all of the damages. In the copyright context, damages may be limited if (1) the infringer was misled by the lack of a copyright notice on an authorized copy of the copyrighted work, distributed under the owner's authority before March 1989 (the effective date of the Berne Convention Implementation Act of 1988), and (2) the infringing act occurred before the infringer received actual notice of the copyright. 17 USCA § 405(b). In the trademark context, publishers and distributors of paid advertisements who innocently infringe a mark have no liability for damages. 15 USCA § 1114. In both contexts, the innocent infringer is immunized only from an award of monetary damages, not from injunctive relief.

literal infringement. *Patents.* Infringement in which every element and every limitation of a patent claim is present, exactly, in the accused product or process. Cf. DOCTRINE OF EQUIVALENTS.

nonliteral infringement. See DOCTRINE OF EQUIVALENTS.

patent infringement. The unauthorized making, using, offering to sell, selling, or importing into the United States any patented invention. 35 USCA § 271(a).

> "In determining whether an accused device or composition infringes a valid patent, resort must be had in the first instance to the words of the claim. If accused matter falls clearly within the claim, infringement is made out and that is the end of it." *Graver Tank & Mfg. Co. v. Linde Air Prods. Co.*, 339 U.S. 605, 607, 70 S.Ct. 854, 855 (1950) (Jackson, J.).

trademark infringement. The unauthorized use of a trademark — or of a confusingly similar name, word, symbol, or any combination of these — in connection with the same or related goods or services and in a manner that is likely to cause confusion, deception, or mistake about the source of the goods or services. See LIKELIHOOD-OF-CONFUSION TEST.

vicarious infringement. A person's liability for an infringing act of someone else, even though the person has not directly committed an act of infringement. • For example, a concert theater can be vicariously liable for an infringing performance of a hired band.

willful infringement. An intentional and deliberate infringement of another person's intellectual property.

infringer. A person who interferes with one of the exclusive rights of a patent, copyright, or trademark owner. See INFRINGEMENT.

in full. Relating to the whole or complete amount <payment in full>.

in full life. (Of a person) alive in fact and in law; neither naturally nor civilly dead.

in futuro (in fyə-**tyoor**-oh), *adv.* [Latin] In the future. Cf. IN PRAESENTI.

in generali passagio (in jen-ə-**ray**-lI pə-**say**-jee-oh), *adv.* [Law Latin] *Hist.* In the general passage (to the holy land with a company of Crusaders). • This type of pilgrimage excused an absence from court during the Crusades. Cf. SIMPLEX PASSAGIUM.

in genere (in **jen**-ər-ee). [Latin "in kind"] Belonging to the same class, but not identical.

ingenuitas (in-jə-**n[y]oo**-ə-tas). [Latin] *Roman law.* The condition or status of a free-born person.

ingenuitas regni (in-jə-**n[y]oo**-ə-tas **reg**-nI). [Law Latin] *Hist.* The freemen, yeomanry, or commonalty of the kingdom. • This term was occasionally applied to the nobility.

ingenuus (in-**jen**-yoo-əs). [Latin] *Roman law.* A free-born person. • There were no distinctions among *ingenui*, as there were among *libertini* (persons born into slavery but later freed). Cf. LATINI JUNIANI; SERVUS.

in globo (in **gloh**-boh), *adv.* [Latin "in a mass"] As an undivided whole rather than separately <settlement paid *in globo* to the three defendants>.

ingratitude, *n. Civil law.* Lack of appreciation for a generous or kind act, esp. for a gift received. • Under Louisiana law, a gift may be reclaimed on grounds of ingratitude if the recipient mistreats the giver by, for example, attempting to murder the giver or refusing to provide the giver with needed food.

ingratus (in-**gray**-təs), *adj.* [Latin] *Roman law.* (Of a person) ungrateful; (of conduct) marked by ingratitude. • Ungrateful acts or words (such as spiteful comments from a freedman toward a former master) could form the basis for a return to a prior inferior status.

in gremio juris (in **gree**-mee-oh **joor**-is), *adv. & adj.* [Law Latin] *Civil & Scots law.* In the bosom of the right. • This phrase describes a clause formerly inserted in an instrument to bind holders to its terms.

in gremio legis (in **gree**-mee-oh **lee**-jis), *adv. & adj.* [Law Latin] In the bosom of the law. • This is a figurative expression for something that is under the protection of the law, such as a land title that is in abeyance.

ingress (**in**-gres). **1.** The act of entering. **2.** The right or ability to enter; access. Cf. EGRESS.

ingress, egress, and regress. The right of a lessee to enter, leave, and reenter the land in question.

ingressus (in-**gres**-əs). [Latin "ingress, entry"] *Hist.* The fee paid by an heir to a feudal lord to enter the estate of a decedent.

in gross. Undivided; still in one large mass. See *easement in gross* under EASEMENT.

ingross, *vb.* See ENGROSS.

ingrossator (in-groh-**say**-tər). [Law Latin] *Hist.* An engrosser; a clerk who writes records or instruments on parchment. • The Engrosser of the Great Roll, for example, was known as the *Ingrossator Magni Rotuli.* See CLERK OF THE PIPE.

inhabit, *vb.* To dwell in; to occupy permanently or habitually as a residence.

in hac parte (in hak **pahr**-tee). [Latin] On this part or side.

in haec verba (in heek **vər**-bə). [Latin] In these same words; verbatim.

inhere (in-**heer**), *vb.* To exist as a permanent, inseparable, or essential attribute or quality of a thing; to be intrinsic to something.

inherent authority. See AUTHORITY (1).

inherent condition. See CONDITION (2).

inherent covenant. See COVENANT (1).

inherent defect. See *hidden defect* under DEFECT.

inherently dangerous. Requiring special precautions at all times to avoid injury; dangerous per se. See DANGEROUS INSTRUMENTALITY.

inherent power. See POWER.

inherent right. See *inalienable right* under RIGHT.

inherit, *vb.* **1.** To receive (property) from an ancestor under the laws of intestate succession upon the ancestor's death. **2.** To receive (property) as a bequest or devise. — **inheritor,** *n.*

inheritable, *adj.* **1.** (Of property) capable of being inherited. **2.** (Of a person) capable of inheriting. — Also termed *heritable.*

inheritable blood. See BLOOD.

inheritable obligation. See OBLIGATION.

inheritance. 1. Property received from an ancestor under the laws of intestacy. **2.** Property that a person receives by bequest or devise.

several inheritance. An inheritance that descends to two persons severally, as by moieties.

inheritance tax. See TAX.

inheritor. A person who inherits; an heir.

inheritrix. *Archaic.* A female heir; an heiress.

inhibition. 1. *Eccles. law.* A writ issued by a superior ecclesiastical court, forbidding a judge from proceeding in a pending case. • This writ served a function similar to the common-law writ of prohibition. **2.** *Eccles. law.* A writ issuing from an ecclesiastical court, prohibiting a member of the clergy from taking office. **3.** *Hist.* WRIT OF PROHIBITION. **4.** *Scots law.* A writ issued to prohibit a debtor from encumbering the debtor's inheritable property to the prejudice of a creditor.

in hoc (in **hok**), *adv.* [Latin] In this; in respect to this.

inhonestus (in-hə-**nes**-təs), *adj.* [Latin] *Roman law.* **1.** (Of a person) of ill repute. **2.** (Of conduct) morally shameful.

in-house counsel. See COUNSEL.

inhuman treatment. *Family law.* Physical or mental cruelty so severe that it endangers life or health. • Inhuman treatment is usu. grounds for divorce. See CRUELTY.

in iisdem terminis (in ee-**IS**-dem **tər**-mə-nis), *adv.* [Law Latin] In the same terms.

in individuo (in in-di-**vid**-yoo-oh), *adv.* [Law Latin] In the distinct, identical, or individual form. See IN SPECIE.

in infinitum (in in-fə-**NI**-təm). [Latin "in infinity"] To infinity. • This phrase was in reference to a line of succession that is indefinite.

in initio (in i-**nish**-ee-oh). [Latin "in the beginning"] At the beginning or outset. Cf. AB INITIO.

in invitum (in in-**VI**-təm). [Latin] Against an unwilling person <the nonparty appealed after being compelled to participate in the proceedings *in invitum*>.

initial appearance. See APPEARANCE.

initial determination. See DETERMINATION (1).

initial disclosure. *Civil procedure.* In federal practice, the requirement that parties make available to each other the following information without first receiving a discovery request: (1) the names, addresses, and telephone numbers of persons likely to have relevant, discoverable information, (2) a copy or description of all relevant documents, data compilations, and tangible items in the party's possession, custody, or control, (3) a damages computation, and (4) any relevant insurance agreements. Fed. R. Civ. P. 26(a)(1)(A)–(D).

initial margin requirement. See MARGIN REQUIREMENT.

initial protest. See PROTEST (2).

initial public offering. See OFFERING.

initial surplus. See SURPLUS.

initiation of charges. *Military law.* The first report to the proper military authority of an alleged commission of an offense by a person subject to the Uniform Code of Military Justice. Cf. PREFERRING OF CHARGES.

initiative (i-**nish**-ee-ə-tiv *or* i-**nish**-ə-tiv). An electoral process by which a percentage of voters can propose legislation and compel a vote on it by the legislature or by the full electorate. • Recognized in some state constitutions, the initiative is one of the few methods of direct democracy in an otherwise representative system. Cf. REFERENDUM.

in itinere (in I-**tin**-ər-ee), *adv.* [Latin] *Hist.* On a journey; on the way. • This term referred to the justices in eyre (justices *in itinere*) and to goods en route to a buyer. See EYRE; IN TRANSITU.

injoin, *vb. Archaic.* See ENJOIN.

in judicio (in joo-**dish**-ee-oh), *adv.* & *adj.* [Latin] *Roman law.* Before the judge. • *In judicio* refers to the second stage of a Roman trial, held before a private judge known as a *judex.* — Also spelled *in iudicio.* — Also termed *apud iudicem.* See FORMULA (1). Cf. IN JURE (2).

injunction (in-**jəngk**-shən), *n.* A court order commanding or preventing an action. • To get an injunction, the complainant must show that there is no plain, adequate, and complete remedy at law and that an irreparable injury will result unless the relief is granted. See IRREPARABLE-INJURY RULE. — Also termed *writ of injunction.*

> "In a general sense, every order of a court which commands or forbids is an injunction; but in its accepted legal sense, an injunction is a judicial process or mandate operating *in personam* by which, upon certain established principles of equity, a party is required to do or refrain from doing a particular thing. An injunction has also been defined as a writ framed according to the circumstances of the case, commanding an act which the court regards as essential to justice, or restraining an act which it esteems contrary to equity and good conscience; as a remedial writ which courts issue for the purpose of enforcing their equity jurisdiction; and as a writ issuing by the order and under the seal of a court of equity." 1 Howard C. Joyce, *A Treatise on the Law Relating to Injunctions* § 1, at 2–3 (1909).

affirmative injunction. See *mandatory injunction.*

ex parte injunction. A preliminary injunction issued after the court has heard from only the moving party.

final injunction. See *permanent injunction.*

interlocutory injunction. See *preliminary injunction.*

mandatory injunction. An injunction that orders an affirmative act or mandates a specified course of conduct. — Also termed *affirmative injunction.* Cf. *prohibitory injunction.*

permanent injunction. An injunction granted after a final hearing on the merits. • Despite its name, a permanent injunction does not necessarily last forever. — Also termed *perpetual injunction*; *final injunction.*

perpetual injunction. See *permanent injunction.*

preliminary injunction. A temporary injunction issued before or during trial to prevent an irreparable injury from occurring before the court has a chance to decide the case. • A preliminary injunction will be issued only after the defendant receives notice and an opportunity to be heard. — Also termed *interlocutory injunction*; *temporary injunction*; *provisional injunction.* Cf. TEMPORARY RESTRAINING ORDER.

preventive injunction. An injunction designed to prevent a loss or injury in the future. Cf. *reparative injunction.*

prohibitory injunction. An injunction that forbids or restrains an act. • This is the most common type of injunction. Cf. *mandatory injunction.*

provisional injunction. See *preliminary injunction.*

quia-timet injunction (**kwI**-ə **tI**-mət *or* **kwee**-ə **tim**-et). [Latin "because he fears"] An injunction granted to prevent an action that has been threatened but has not yet violated the plaintiff's rights. See QUIA TIMET.

reparative injunction (ri-**par**-ə-tiv). An injunction requiring the defendant to restore the plaintiff to the position that the plaintiff occupied before the defendant committed the wrong. Cf. *preventive injunction.*

special injunction. *Hist.* An injunction in which the prohibition of an act is the only relief ultimately sought, as in prevention of waste or nuisance.

temporary injunction. See *preliminary injunction.*

injunction bond. See BOND (2).

injunctive, *adj.* That has the quality of directing or ordering; of or relating to an injunction. — Also termed *injunctional.*

in jure (in **joor**-ee). [Latin "in law"] **1.** According to the law. **2.** *Roman law.* Before the praetor or other magistrate. ● *In jure* referred to the first stage of a Roman trial, held before the praetor for the purpose of establishing the legal issues present in the action. Evidence was taken in the second stage, which was held before a *judex.* — Also spelled *in iure.* See FORMULA (1). Cf. IN JUDICIO.

in jure alterius (in **joor**-ee al-**teer**-ee-əs), *adv.* [Latin] In another's right.

in jure cessio (in **joor**-ee **sesh**-ee-oh). [Latin "a surrender in law"] *Roman law.* A fictitious trial held to transfer ownership of property. ● At trial, the transferee appeared before a praetor and asserted ownership of the property. The actual owner also appeared, but did not contest the assertion, and so allowed the transfer of the property to the plaintiff. — Also spelled *in iure cessio.*

in jure proprio (in **joor**-ee **proh**-pree-oh), *adv.* [Latin] In one's own right.

injuria (in-**joor**-ee-ə). [Latin] See INJURY (1); WRONG. Pl. ***injuriae*** (in-**joor**-ee-ee).

> "By *injuria* (or outrage), as the fourth ground of delict obligation, is meant some affronting wrong, calculated to wound the self-respect and touch the honor of the person injured, to humiliate or degrade him in the view of others." James Hadley, *Introduction to Roman Law* 243 (N.Y., D. Appleton & Co. 1881).

> "The term *injuria* [is best] used in its original and proper sense of *wrong* (*in jus,* contrary to law). The modern use of 'injury' as a synonym for damage is unfortunate but inveterate." R.F.V. Heuston, *Salmond on the Law of Torts* 13 nn.51–52 (17th ed. 1977).

injuria absque damno (in-**joor**-ee-ə **abs**-kwee **dam**-noh). [Latin "injury without damage"] A legal wrong that will not sustain a lawsuit because no harm resulted from it. — Also termed *injuria sine damno.* Cf. DAMNUM SINE INJURIA.

> "Just as there are cases in which damage is not actionable as a tort (*damnum sine injuria*), so conversely there are cases in which behaviour is actionable as a tort, although it has been the cause of no damage at all (*injuria sine damno*). Torts are of two kinds — namely, those which are actionable *per se,* and those which are actionable only on proof of actual damage resulting from them. Thus the act of trespassing upon another's land is actionable even though it has done the plaintiff not the slightest harm. Similarly, a libel is actionable *per se,* while slander (that is to say, oral as opposed to written defamation) is in most cases not actionable without proof of actual damage." R.F.V. Heuston, *Salmond on the Law of Torts* 14 (17th ed. 1977).

injurious, *adj.* Harmful; tending to injure.

injurious exposure. *Workers' compensation.* Contact with a substance that would cause injury if the person were repeatedly exposed to it over time. ● An employer may be found liable for harm resulting from injurious exposure.

injurious falsehood. See DISPARAGEMENT.

injury, *n.* **1.** The violation of another's legal right, for which the law provides a remedy; a wrong or injustice. See WRONG. **2.** Harm or damage. — **injure,** *vb.* — **injurious,** *adj.*

accidental injury. An injury resulting from external, violent, and unanticipated causes; esp., a bodily injury caused by some external force or agency operating contrary to a person's intentions, unexpectedly, and not according to the usual order of events.

bodily injury. Physical damage to a person's body. — Also termed *physical injury.* Cf. *grievous bodily harm* under HARM.

civil injury. Physical harm or property damage caused by breach of a contract or by a criminal offense redressable through a civil action.

compensable injury (kəm-**pen**-sə-bəl). *Workers' compensation.* An injury caused by an accident arising from the employment and in the course of the employee's work, and for which the employee is statutorily entitled to receive compensation.

continual injury. An injury that recurs at repeated intervals. — Also termed (but improperly) *continuous injury.*

continuing injury. An injury that is still in the process of being committed. ● An example is the constant smoke or noise of a factory.

direct injury. **1.** An injury resulting directly from violation of a legal right. **2.** An injury resulting directly from a particular cause, without any intervening causes.

injury in fact. An actual or imminent invasion of a legally protected interest, in contrast to an invasion that is conjectural or hypothetical. ● An injury in fact gives the victim standing to bring an action for damages.

irreparable injury (i-**rep**-ər-ə-bəl). An injury that cannot be adequately measured or compensated by money and is therefore often considered remediable by injunction. — Also termed *irreparable harm*. See IRREPARABLE-INJURY RULE.

> "The term 'irreparable injury,' however, is not to be taken in its strict literal sense. The rule does not require that the threatened injury should be one not physically capable of being repaired. If the threatened injury would be substantial and serious — one not easily to be estimated, or repaired by money — and if the loss or inconvenience to the plaintiff if the injunction should be refused (his title proving good) would be much greater than any which can be suffered by the defendant through the granting of the injunction, although his title ultimately prevails, the case is one of such probable great or 'irreparable' damage as will justify a preliminary injunction." Elias Merwin, *Principles of Equity and Equity Pleading* 426–27 (H.C. Merwin ed., 1896).

legal injury. Violation of a legal right.

malicious injury. **1.** An injury resulting from a willful act committed with knowledge that it is likely to injure another or with reckless disregard of the consequences. **2.** MALICIOUS MISCHIEF.

permanent injury. **1.** A completed wrong whose consequences cannot be remedied for an indefinite period. **2.** An injury to land the consequences of which will endure until the reversioner takes possession, as a result of which the reversioner has a present right of possession.

personal injury. *Torts.* **1.** In a negligence action, any harm caused to a person, such as a broken bone, a cut, or a bruise; bodily injury. **2.** Any invasion of a personal right, including mental suffering and false imprisonment. **3.** For purposes of workers' compensation, any harm (including a worsened preexisting condition) that arises in the scope of employment.

physical injury. See *bodily injury*.

reparable injury (**rep**-ər-ə-bəl). An injury that can be adequately compensated by money.

scheduled injury. A partially disabling injury for which a predetermined amount of compensation is allowed under a workers'-compensation statute.

injury in fact. See INJURY.

injury-in-fact trigger. See ACTUAL-INJURY TRIGGER.

injustice. **1.** An unjust state of affairs; unfairness. **2.** An unjust act.

in jus vocare (in **jəs** voh-**kair**-ee), *vb.* [Latin] *Roman law.* To summon a defendant to court.

in kind, *adv.* **1.** In goods or services rather than money <payment in cash or in kind>. **2.** In a similar way; with an equivalent of what has been offered or received <returned the favor in kind>. — **in-kind,** *adj.* <in-kind repayment>.

inlagare (in-lə-**gair**-ee), *vb.* [Law Latin] *Hist.* To restore (an outlaw) to the protection of the law. Cf. UTLAGARE.

inlagation (in-lə-**gay**-shən), *n.* [Law Latin] *Hist.* The act of restoring an outlaw to the protection of the law; inlawry. Cf. UTLAGATION.

inlagh (**in**-law). *Hist.* A person within the protection of the law, in contrast to an outlaw. Cf. UTLAGH.

inland. **1.** The interior part of a country or region, away from the coast or border. **2.** *Hist.* The portion of a feudal estate lying closest to the lord's manor and dedicated to the support of the lord's family. — Also termed (in sense 2) *inlantal*. Cf. UTLAND.

inland bill of exchange. See *domestic bill* (2) under BILL (6).

inland draft. See DRAFT.

inland marine insurance. See INSURANCE.

inland revenue. See INTERNAL REVENUE.

inland trade. See TRADE.

inland waters. See INTERNAL WATERS.

inlantal (**in**-lan-təl). *Hist.* See INLAND (2). — Also spelled *inlantale*.

in law. Existing in law or by force of law; in the contemplation of the law. Cf. IN FACT.

in-law, *n.* A relative by marriage.

inlaw, *vb. Archaic.* To place (an offender) under the protection of the law. Cf. OUTLAW (1).

> "If the king inlaws him, he comes back into the world like a new-born babe, *quasi modo genitus*, capable indeed of acquiring new rights, but unable to assert any of those that he had before his outlawry." 1 Frederick Pollock & Frederic W. Maitland, *The History of English Law Before the Time of Edward I* 477 (2d ed. 1898).

in lecto mortali (in **lek**-toh mor-**tay**-lɪ), *adv.* & *adj.* [Latin] On the deathbed.

in liberam elemosinam (in **lib**-ər-əm el-ə-mə-**sɪ**-nəm). [Latin "in free alms"] *Hist.* Land given away for a charitable purpose; land given away to be held in frankalmoin. — Also spelled *in liberam eleemosinam.* — Also termed *in libera elemosina.* See FRANKALMOIN.

in libero sochagio (in **lib**-ər-oh sə-**kay**-jee-oh), *adv.* [Law Latin] In free socage. See SOCAGE.

in lieu of. Instead of or in place of; in exchange or return for <the creditor took a note in lieu of cash> <the defendant was released in lieu of $5,000 bond>.

in limine (in **lim**-ə-nee), *adv.* [Latin "at the outset"] Preliminarily; presented to only the judge, before or during trial <a question to be decided in limine>. See MOTION IN LIMINE.

in-limine, *adj.* (Of a motion or order) raised preliminarily, esp. because of an issue about the admissibility of evidence believed by the movant to be prejudicial <in-limine motion>.

in litem (in **lɪ**-tem *or* -təm), *adv.* [Latin] For a suit; to the suit. See AD LITEM.

in loco (in **loh**-koh). [Latin] In the place of.

in loco parentis (in **loh**-koh pə-**ren**-tis), *adv.* & *adj.* [Latin "in the place of a parent"] Acting as a temporary guardian of a child.

in loco parentis, *n.* Supervision of a young adult by an administrative body such as a university.

in majorem cautelam (in mə-**jor**-əm kaw-**tee**-ləm), *adv.* [Latin] For a greater security.

in manu mortua. See IN MORTUA MANU.

inmate. 1. A person confined in a prison, hospital, or other institution. **2.** *Archaic.* A person living inside a place; one who lives with others in a dwelling.

in medias res (in **mee**-dee-əs **reez** *or* in **me**-dee-ahs **rays**), *adv.* [Latin] Into the middle of things; without preface or introduction.

in mercy, *adv.* At a judge's discretion concerning punishment. • A judgment formerly noted (by the Law Latin phrase *in misericordia*) which litigant lost by stating that the unsuccessful party was in the court's mercy. A plaintiff held in mercy for a false claim, for example, was said to be *in misericordia pro falso clamore suo.*

in misericordia (in miz-ə-ri-**kor**-dee-ə). [Law Latin] See IN MERCY.

in mitiori sensu (in mish-ee-**or**-ɪ **sens**-[y]oo), *adv.* [Law Latin] In a milder or more favorable sense. • This phrase appeared as part of the former rule applied in slander actions. A word capable of two meanings would be given the one more favorable to the defendant.

> "Within half a century of its first appearance, the action for words had become part of the everyday business of the common-law courts, in particular the King's Bench. In the early days there were often more slander cases in the rolls than *assumpsit* .... The judges apparently came to regret this aspect of their increased jurisdiction, especially since juries frequently awarded sums of money quite disproportionate to the harm and to the ability of the wrongdoer to pay .... [T]he principal effect of the judicial reaction was that a spirit of repression began to manifest itself .... The ... most effective attack was launched in the 1570s, when the courts began the policy of construing ambiguous or doubtful words in the milder sense (*in mitiori sensu*) so that they would not be actionable." J.H. Baker, *An Introduction to English Legal History* 500–01 (3d ed. 1990).

in modum assisae (in **moh**-dəm ə-**sɪ**-zee), *adv.* [Law Latin] In the manner or form of an assize. See ASSIZE.

in modum juratae (in **moh**-dəm juu-**ray**-tee), *adv.* [Law Latin] In the manner or form of a jury.

in mora (in **mor**-ə), *adv.* & *adj.* [Latin] *Roman law.* In delay; in default. • This was said of a debtor who delayed performance or failed to perform.

in mortua manu (in **mor**-choo-ə **man**-yoo), *adv.* [Law Latin] *Hist.* In a dead hand. • Land held by a religious society was described this way because the church could hold property perpetually without rendering feudal service. — Also termed *in manu mortua.* See MORTMAIN; DEADHAND CONTROL.

innavigable (in-**nav**-i-gə-bəl), *adj.* **1.** (Of a body of water) not capable of, or unsuitable for, navigation. **2.** *Marine insurance.* (Of a vessel) unfit for service. — Also termed *unnavigable.*

inner bar. *English law.* The group of senior barristers, called the Queen's Counsel or King's Counsel, who are admitted to plead within the bar of the court. Cf. OUTER BAR.

inner barrister. See BARRISTER.

inner cabinet. See CABINET.

inning. (*pl.*) Land reclaimed from the sea.

innkeeper. A person who, for compensation, keeps open a public house for the lodging and entertainment of travelers. • A keeper of a boarding house is usually not considered an innkeeper.

innocence, *n.* The absence of guilt; esp., freedom from guilt for a particular offense. Cf. GUILT.

actual innocence. *Criminal law.* The absence of facts that are prerequisites for the sentence given to a defendant. • In death-penalty cases, actual innocence is an exception to the cause-and-prejudice rule, and can result in a successful challenge to the death sentence on the basis of a defense that was not presented to the trial court. The prisoner must show by clear and convincing evidence that, but for constitutional error in the trial court, no reasonable juror would find the defendant eligible for the death penalty. See *Sawyer v. Whitley*, 505 U.S. 333, 112 S.Ct. 2514 (1992). Cf. CAUSE-AND-PREJUDICE RULE.

legal innocence. *Criminal law.* The absence of one or more procedural or legal bases to support the sentence given to a defendant. • In the context of a petition for writ of habeas corpus or other attack on the sentence, legal innocence is often contrasted with actual innocence. Actual innocence, which focuses on the facts underlying the sentence, can sometimes be used to obtain relief from the death penalty based on trial-court errors that were not objected to at trial, even if the petitioner cannot meet the elements of the cause-and-prejudice rule. But legal innocence, which focuses on the applicable law and procedure, is not as readily available. Inadvertence or a poor trial strategy resulting in the defendant's failure to assert an established legal principle will not ordinarily be sufficient to satisfy the cause-and-prejudice rule or to establish the right to an exception from that rule. See CAUSE-AND-PREJUDICE RULE.

innocent, *adj.* Free from guilt; free from legal fault. Cf. NOT GUILTY (2).

innocent agent. *Criminal law.* A person whose action on behalf of a principal is unlawful but does not merit prosecution because the agent had no knowledge of the principal's illegal purpose.

innocent-construction rule. The doctrine that an allegedly libelous statement will be given an innocuous interpretation if the statement is either ambiguous or harmless.

innocent conveyance. See CONVEYANCE.

innocent homicide. See HOMICIDE.

innocent infringement. See INFRINGEMENT.

innocent junior user. *Trademarks.* A person who, without any actual or constructive knowledge, uses a trademark that has been previously used in a geographically distant market, and who may continue to use the trademark in a limited geographic area as long as the senior user does not use the mark there.

innocent misrepresentation. See MISREPRESENTATION.

innocent party. See PARTY (2).

innocent passage. *Int'l law.* The right of a foreign ship to pass through a country's territorial waters, esp. waters connecting two open seas; the right of a foreign vessel to travel through a country's maritime belt without paying a toll. • Passage is considered innocent as long as it is not prejudicial to the peace, good order, and security of the coastal country. — Also termed *right of innocent passage*. Cf. TRANSIT PASSAGE.

> "The term 'innocent passage' accurately denotes the nature of the right as well as its limitations. In the first place it is a right of 'passage,' that is to say, a right to use the waters as a thoroughfare between two points outside them; a ship proceeding through the maritime belt to a port of the coastal state would not be exercising a right of passage. In the second place the passage must be 'innocent'; a ship exercising the right must respect the local regulations as to navigation, pilotage, and the like, and, of course, it must not do any act which might disturb the tranquillity of the coastal state. That state therefore must be entitled to exercise *some* jurisdiction over ships in passage, but the extent of this is not altogether certain, and in particular there is some doubt how far the coastal state may enforce its own criminal or civil laws against persons on board a ship in passage." J.L. Brierly, *The Law of Nations* 188–89 (5th ed. 1955).

innocent purchaser. See *bona fide purchaser* under PURCHASER.

innocent purchaser for value. See *bona fide purchaser for value* under PURCHASER.

innocent spouse. *Tax.* A spouse who may be relieved of liability for taxes on income that the other spouse did not include on a joint tax return. • The innocent spouse must prove that the other spouse omitted the income, that the innocent spouse did not know and had no reason to know of the omission, and that it would be unfair under the circumstances to hold the innocent spouse liable.

innocent trespass. See TRESPASS.

innocent trespasser. See TRESPASSER.

Inn of Chancery. *Hist.* Any of nine collegiate houses where students studied either to gain entry into an Inn of Court or to learn how to frame writs in order to serve in the chancery courts. • Over time, the Inns — Clement's, Clifford's, Lyon's, Furnival's, Thavies', Symond's, Barnard's, Staples', and the New Inn — became little more than dining clubs, and never exercised control over their members as the Inns of Court did. The Inns of Chancery were all dissolved in the 19th century. Cf. INN OF COURT.

Inn of Court. 1. Any of four autonomous institutions, one or more of which English barristers must join to receive their training and of which they remain members for life: The Honourable Societies of Lincoln's Inn, the Middle Temple, the Inner Temple, and Gray's Inn. • These powerful bodies examine candidates for the Bar, "call" them to the Bar, and award the degree of barrister. **2.** (*pl.*) In the United States, an organization (formally named the *American Inns of Court Foundation*) with more than 100 local chapters, whose members include judges, practicing attorneys, law professors, and law students. • Through monthly meetings, the chapters emphasize practice skills, professionalism, and ethics, and provide mentors to train students and young lawyers in the finer points of good legal practice.

innominate (i-**nom**-ə-nit), *adj. Civil law.* Unclassified; having no special name or designation. See *innominate contract* under CONTRACT.

innominate contract. See CONTRACT.

innominate obligations. Obligations having no specific classification or name because they are not strictly contractual, delictual, or quasi-contractual. • An example is the obligation of a trustee to a beneficiary. — Also termed *obligationes innominati.*

innominate real contract. See *innominate contract* under CONTRACT.

in nomine Dei, Amen (in **nahm**-ə-nee **dee**-I, ay-**men**). [Latin] *Hist.* In the name of God, Amen. • This phrase formerly appeared at the beginning of a will or other instrument.

innotescimus (in-oh-**tes**-ə-məs). [Law Latin "we make known"] *Hist.* A certification, in the form of letters patent, of a charter of feoffment or other instrument not filed of record. • This term derives from the word of emphasis appearing at the end of the document. Cf. EXEMPLIFICATION.

innoxiare (i-nok-shee-**air**-ee), *vb.* [Law Latin] *Hist.* To purge (a person) of fault.

in nubibus (in **n[y]oo**-bi-bəs), *adv.* & *adj.* [Law Latin] In the clouds. • An expression for something that is under the protection of the law.

innuendo (in-yoo-**en**-doh). [Latin "by hinting"] **1.** An oblique remark or indirect suggestion, usu. of a derogatory nature. **2.** An explanatory word or passage inserted parenthetically into a legal document. • In criminal law, an innuendo takes the form of a statement in an indictment showing the application or meaning of matter previously expressed, the meaning of which would not otherwise be clear. In the law of defamation, an innuendo is the plaintiff's explanation of a statement's defamatory meaning when that meaning is not apparent from the statement's face. For example, the innuendo of the statement "David burned down his house" can be shown by pleading that the statement was understood to mean that David was defrauding his insurance company (the fact that he had insured his house is pleaded and proved by *inducement*). Cf. INDUCEMENT (4); COLLOQUIUM.

> "Innuendo (from *innuo*, to nod or beckon with the head) is a word used in declarations and law pleadings, to ascertain a person or thing which was named before.... If a man say, that such a one had the pox, innuendo the French pox, this will not be admitted, because the French pox was not mentioned before, and the words shall be construed in a more favourable sense. But, if in discourse of the French pox, one say, that such a one had the pox, innuendo the French pox, this will be admitted to render that certain which was uncertain before." 2 Richard Burn, *A New Law Dictionary* 24 (1792).

> "It is not a true innuendo to repeat the obvious meaning of defamatory words in other language, or in an embroidered or exaggerated way. Otherwise an ingenious pleader could perplex the judge and jury and harry the defendant by ringing the changes on the same words, creating numerous different causes of action, each requiring a

separate verdict. A true innuendo relies on a conjunction of the words used and some extrinsic fact. Thus it is defamatory in itself to say that a man's affairs are being investigated by the Fraud Squad: but the statement does not support the innuendo that those affairs are being carried on fraudulently. Conversely, the statement 'X is a good advertiser' is innocent in itself, but carries a libellous innuendo if published to persons who know the extrinsic fact that X is an eminent member of the Bar." R.F.V. Heuston, *Salmond on the Law of Torts* 149 (17th ed. 1977). [The example about lawyers' advertising no longer has relevance to American law. — Eds.]

in nullius bonis (in nə-**lɪ**-əs **boh**-nis). See NULLIUS IN BONIS.

in nullo est erratum (in **nəl**-oh est i-**ray**-təm), *adj.* [Law Latin "in nothing is there error"] *Hist.* Of or relating to a demurrer that denies any error and at once refers a question of law to the court.

inofficiosus (in-ə-fish-ee-**oh**-səs), *adj.* [Latin "inofficious"] *Roman law.* Contrary to a natural duty of affection, used esp. of a will that unjustly disinherits a child or close relative.

inofficious testament. See TESTAMENT.

inofficious will. See *inofficious testament* under TESTAMENT.

in omnibus (in **ahm**-ni-bəs). [Latin] In all things; on all points <a case parallel *in omnibus*>.

inoperative, *adj.* Having no force or effect; not operative <an inoperative statute>.

inops consilii (**in**-ahps kən-**sil**-ee-ɪ), *adj.* [Latin] Destitute of counsel; without legal counsel. • This term described actions taken without benefit of legal advice, as when a testator drafts a will without the help of an attorney.

"[T]hat in devises by last will and testament, (which, being often drawn up when the party is *inops consilii*, and are always more favoured in construction than formal deeds, which are presumed to be made with great caution, fore-thought, and advice) in these devises, I say, remainders may be created in some measure contrary to the rules before laid down. . . ." 2 William Blackstone, *Commentaries on the Laws of England* 172 (1766).

inordinatus (in-or-də-**nay**-təs), *n.* [Latin "disorderly; unordained"] *Hist.* See INTESTATE.

in pacato solo (in pə-**kay**-toh **soh**-loh), *adv.* [Latin] In a country that is at peace.

in pace Dei et regis (in **pay**-see **dee**-ɪ et **ree**-jis), *adv.* [Law Latin] *Hist.* In the peace of God and the king. • This phrase was used in an appeal from a murder conviction.

in pais (in **pay** *or* **pays**). [Law French "in the country"] Outside court or legal proceedings. See *estoppel in pais* under ESTOPPEL.

in paper. *Hist.* Of a proceeding that is within the jurisdiction of the trial court; that is, before the record is prepared for an appeal.

"Formerly, the suitors were much perplexed by writs of error brought upon very slight and trivial grounds, as misspellings and other mistakes of the clerks, all which might be amended at the common law, while all the proceedings were in *paper*, for they were then considered in *fieri*, and therefore subject to the control of the courts." 3 William Blackstone, *Commentaries on the Laws of England* 407 (1768).

in pari causa (in **par**-ɪ **kaw**-zə), *adv.* [Latin "in an equal case"] In a case affecting two parties equally or in which they have equal rights <*in pari causa*, the possessor ordinarily defeats the nonpossessory claimant>.

in pari delicto (in **par**-ɪ də-**lik**-toh), *adv.* [Latin "in equal fault"] Equally at fault <the court denied relief because both parties stood *in pari delicto*>.

***in pari delicto* doctrine,** *n.* [Latin] The principle that a plaintiff who has participated in wrongdoing may not recover damages resulting from the wrongdoing.

in pari materia (in **par**-ɪ mə-**teer**-ee-ə). [Latin "in the same matter"] **1.** *adj.* On the same subject; relating to the same matter. • It is a canon of construction that statutes that are *in pari materia* may be construed together, so that inconsistencies in one statute may be resolved by looking at another statute on the same subject.

"[I]t seems that the present position is that, when an earlier statute is *in pari materia* with a later one, it is simply part of its context to be considered by the judge in deciding whether the meaning of a provision in the later statute is plain." Rupert Cross, *Statutory Interpretation* 128 (1976).

2. *adv.* Loosely, in conjunction with <the Maryland constitutional provision is construed *in pari materia* with the Fourth Amendment>.

in patiendo (in pash-ee-**en**-doh), *adv.* & *adj.* [fr. Latin *patior* "suffer"] In suffering or permitting.

in pectore judicis (in **pek**-tə-ree **joo**-di-sis), *adv. & adj.* [Latin] In the breast of the court.

in pejorem partem (in pə-**jor**-əm **pahr**-təm), *adv.* [Law Latin] In the worst part; on the worst side.

inpenny and outpenny. *Hist.* A customary payment of a penny on entering into and going out of a tenancy.

in perpetuam rei memoriam (in pər-**pech**-oo-əm [*or* pər-**pe**-tyoo-əm] **ree**-ɪ mə-**mor**-ee-əm), *adv.* [Latin] In perpetual memory of a matter. • This phrase refers to a deposition taken to preserve the deponent's testimony.

in perpetuity (in pər-pə-**t[y]oo**-ə-tee). Forever. See PERPETUITY.

in perpetuum (in pər-**pech**-oo-əm *or* pər-**pe**-tyoo-əm), *adv.* [Latin] Forever; perpetually. — Sometimes spelled *imperpetuum*.

in perpetuum rei testimonium (in pər-**pech**-oo-əm [*or* pər-**pe**-tyoo-əm] **ree**-ɪ tes-ti-**moh**-nee-əm), *adv.* [Law Latin] In perpetual testimony of a matter. • This phrase refers to a statute that confirms existing common law.

> "Statutes also are either *declaratory* of the common law, or *remedial* of some defects therein. Declaratory, where the old custom of the kingdom is almost fallen into disuse, or become disputable; in which case the parliament has thought proper, *in perpetuum rei testimonium*, and for avoiding all doubts and difficulties, to declare what the common law is and ever hath been." 1 William Blackstone, *Commentaries on the Laws of England* 86 (1765).

in personam (in pər-**soh**-nəm), *adj.* [Latin "against a person"] Involving or determining the personal rights and interests of the parties. — Also termed *personal.* — **in personam,** *adv.* See *action in personam* under ACTION. Cf. IN REM.

> "An action is said to be *in personam* when its object is to determine the rights and interests of the parties themselves in the subject-matter of the action, however the action may arise, and the effect of a judgment in such an action is merely to bind the parties to it. A normal action brought by one person against another for breach of contract is a common example of an action *in personam*." R.H. Graveson, *Conflict of Laws* 98 (7th ed. 1974).

in personam judgment. See *personal judgment* under JUDGMENT.

in personam jurisdiction. See *personal jurisdiction* under JURISDICTION.

in pios usus (in **pɪ**-əs **yoo**-səs), *adv.* [Law Latin] *Hist.* For pious uses; for religious purposes. • This phrase referred to property used by, or claimed by, the church, such as the property of an intestate who had no known heirs.

in plena vita (in **plee**-nə **vɪ**-tə), *adv. & adj.* [Law Latin] In full life.

in pleno comitatu (in **plee**-noh kahm-i-**tay**-t[y]oo), *adv. & adj.* [Law Latin] In full county court.

in pleno lumine (in **plee**-noh **loo**-mə-nee), *adv. & adj.* In the light of day; in common knowledge; in public.

in point. See ON POINT.

in posse (in **pos**-ee). [Latin] Not currently existing, but ready to come into existence under certain conditions in the future; potential <the will contemplated both living children and children *in posse*>. Cf. IN ESSE.

in potestate parentis (in poh-tes-**tay**-tee pə-**ren**-tis), *adv. & adj.* [Latin] *Hist.* In the power of a parent. See PATRIA POTESTAS.

in praemissorum fidem (in pree-mə-**sor**-əm [*or* prem-ə-] **fɪ**-dəm), *adv. & adj.* [Law Latin] *Hist.* In confirmation or attestation of the premises. • This phrase commonly appeared in notarized documents.

in praesenti (in pri-**zen**-tɪ *or* pree-). [Latin] At present; right now. Cf. IN FUTURO.

in prender (in **pren**-dər), *adj.* [Law French "in taking"] *Hist.* (Of a right) consisting in property taken to fulfill a claim to it, such as an incorporeal hereditament (as a *heriot custom*) that a lord had to seize in order to exercise the right to it. Cf. IN RENDER.

in-presence rule. The principle that a police officer may make a warrantless arrest of a person who commits a misdemeanor offense not in the officer's actual presence but within the officer's immediate vicinity.

> "The common law rule with respect to misdemeanors was quite different; a warrant was required except when a breach of the peace occurred in the presence of the arresting officer. . . . Though the 'in presence' rule might be construed as requiring that the misdemeanor *in fact* have occurred in the officer's presence, the modern view is that the officer may arrest if he has probable cause to believe the offense is being committed in his presence."

Wayne R. LaFave & Jerold H. Israel, *Criminal Procedure* § 3.5, at 169–70 (2d ed. 1992).

in primis (in **prI**-mis). See IMPRIMIS.

in principio (in prin-**sip**-ee-oh), *adv.* [Latin] At the beginning.

in promptu (in **promp**-t[y]oo), *adv.* & *adj.* [Latin "at hand"] *Archaic.* Impromptu.

in propria persona (in **proh**-pree-ə pər-**soh**-nə). [Latin "in one's own person"] See PRO SE.

inquest. 1. An inquiry by a coroner or medical examiner, sometimes with the aid of a jury, into the manner of death of a person who has died under suspicious circumstances, or who has died in prison. — Also termed *coroner's inquest*; *inquisition after death.* **2.** An inquiry into a certain matter by a jury empaneled for that purpose. **3.** The finding of such a specially empaneled jury. **4.** A proceeding, usu. ex parte, to determine, after the defendant has defaulted, the amount of the plaintiff's damages. Cf. INQUISITION.

***grand inquest.* 1.** An impeachment proceeding. **2.** *Hist.* (*cap.*) The survey of the lands of England in 1085–1086, by order of William the Conqueror, and resulting in the Domesday Book — Also termed *Great Inquest*; *Grand Survey*; *Great Survey*; See DOMESDAY BOOK. **3.** *Hist.* Grand jury.

inquest of office. *Hist.* An inquest conducted by a coroner, sheriff, or other royal officer into the Crown's right to property by reason of escheat, treason, or other ground of forfeiture.

5. WARDMOTE.

inquest jury. See JURY.

inquest of office. See INQUEST.

inquilinus (in-kwə-**lI**-nəs). [Latin] *Roman law.* A person who leases or lives in another's house; esp., an urban tenant.

inquirendo (in-kwə-**ren**-doh). [Latin] *Hist.* An inquiry or investigation; esp., an inquiry into a matter concerning the Crown's interests, such as lands that are forfeited to the Crown.

inquiry. 1. *Int'l law.* FACT-FINDING (2). **2.** *Hist.* A writ to assess damages by the sheriff or sheriff's deputies.

inquiry notice. See NOTICE.

inquisitio (in-kwə-**zish**-ee-oh). [Latin] Inquisition or inquest. See INQUISITION (1).

inquisitio post mortem (in-kwə-**zish**-ee-oh pohst **mor**-təm). [Latin] See *inquest of office* under INQUEST.

inquisition. 1. The record of the finding of the jury sworn by the coroner to inquire into a person's death. **2.** A judicial inquiry, esp. in a derogatory sense. **3.** A persistent, grueling examination conducted without regard for the examinee's dignity or civil rights. Cf. INQUEST.

inquisition after death. See INQUEST (1).

inquisitor. 1. An officer who examines and inquires, such as a coroner or sheriff. **2.** A person who inquires; esp., one who examines another in a harsh or hostile manner. **3.** *Hist. Eccles. law.* An officer authorized to inquire into heresies; esp., an officer of the Spanish Inquisition.

inquisitorial court. A court in which the inquisitorial system prevails.

> "We should remember that in the 'inquisitorial court' the roles of prosecutor, defender, and judge are combined in one person or group of persons. It is no accident that such a court commonly holds its sessions in secret. The usual explanation for this is that the methods by which it extracts confessions cannot stand public scrutiny. But the reason runs deeper. The methods employed by an inquisitorial court, even if open to the public, could scarcely be a secret of meaningful observation by an outsider. It is only when the roles of prosecutor, defender, and judge are separated that a process of decision can take on an order and coherence that will make it understandable to an outside audience and convince that audience that all sides of the controversy have been considered." Lon L. Fuller, *Anatomy of the Law* 35–36 (1968).

inquisitorial system. A system of proof-taking used in civil law, whereby the judge conducts the trial, determines what questions to ask, and defines the scope and the extent of the inquiry. • This system prevails in most of continental Europe, in Japan, and in Central and South America. Cf. ADVERSARY SYSTEM.

in re (in **ree** *or* **ray**). [Latin "in the matter of"] (Of a judicial proceeding) not formally including adverse parties, but rather involving something (such as an estate). • The term is often used in case citations, esp. in uncontested proceedings <*In re Butler's Estate*>. — Also termed *matter of* <*Matter of Butler's Estate*>.

in rebus (in **ree**-bəs), *adv.* [Latin] In things, cases, or matters.

in rem (in **rem**), *adj.* [Latin "against a thing"] Involving or determining the status of a thing, and therefore the rights of persons generally with respect to that thing. — Also termed (archaically) *impersonal.* — **in rem,** *adv.* See *action in rem* under ACTION. Cf. IN PERSONAM.

> "An action *in rem* is one in which the judgment of the court determines the title to property and the rights of the parties, not merely as between themselves, but also as against all persons at any time dealing with them or with the property upon which the court had adjudicated." R.H. Graveson, *Conflict of Laws* 98 (7th ed. 1974).

quasi in rem (**kway**-sI in **rem** *or* **kway**-zI). [Latin "as if against a thing"] Involving or determining the rights of a person having an interest in property located within the court's jurisdiction. See *action quasi in rem* under ACTION.

in rem judgment. See *judgment in rem* under JUDGMENT.

in rem jurisdiction. See JURISDICTION.

in render (in **ren**-dər), *adj.* [Law French "in yielding or paying"] *Hist.* (Of property) required to be given or rendered. Cf. IN PRENDER.

in rerum natura (in **reer**-əm nə-**tyuur**-ə), *adv.* & *adj.* [Law Latin] *Hist.* In the nature of things; in existence. • This phrase was used in a dilatory plea alleging that the plaintiff was a fictitious person, and therefore not capable of bringing the action.

inroll, *vb.* See ENROLL (1).

inrollment. See ENROLLMENT.

INS. *abbr.* IMMIGRATION AND NATURALIZATION SERVICE.

insane, *adj.* Mentally deranged; suffering from one or more delusions or false beliefs that (1) have no foundation in reason or reality, (2) are not credible to any reasonable person of sound mind, and (3) cannot be overcome in a sufferer's mind by any amount of evidence or argument. See INSANITY.

insane asylum. See ASYLUM (3).

insane delusion. An irrational, persistent belief in an imaginary state of facts that deprives a person of the capacity to undertake acts of legal consequence, such as making a will.

insanity, *n.* Any mental disorder severe enough that it prevents a person from having legal capacity and excuses the person from criminal or civil responsibility. • Insanity is a legal, not a medical, standard. — Also termed *legal insanity*; *lunacy.* Cf. *diminished capacity* under CAPACITY.

> "The lawyers refer to 'insanity.' This is a legal term only, and one that is not used by the psychiatrist; the latter prefers to speak of mental disorder, mental illness, or of psychosis or neurosis." Winfred Overholser, *Psychiatry and the Law*, 38 Mental Hygiene 243, 244 (1954).

> "The word 'insanity' is commonly used in discussions of this problem although some other term would seem to be preferable such as 'mental disease or defect,' — which may be shortened to 'mental disorder' in general discussions if this is clearly understood to include disease of the mind, congenital lack, and damage resulting from traumatic injury, but to exclude excitement or stupefaction resulting from liquor or drugs. Apart from its uses in the law 'insanity' is usually employed to indicate mental disorder resulting from deterioration or damage as distinguished from congenital deficiency. Criminal incapacity may result as readily from one as from the other, but while the earlier authorities spoke of the 'idiot' and the 'madman,' . . . the more recent tendency in the law has been to include both under the 'insanity' label." Rollin M. Perkins & Ronald N. Boyce, *Criminal Law* 952 (3d ed. 1982).

> "Another objection to the word 'insanity' is the unwarranted assumption that it refers to a very definite mental condition, seldom put into words but apparent in many discussions of the problem." *Id.*

emotional insanity. Insanity produced by a violent excitement of the emotions or passions, although reasoning faculties may remain unimpaired; a passion that for a period creates complete derangement of intellect. • Emotional insanity is sometimes described as an irresistible impulse to do an act. See IRRESISTIBLE-IMPULSE TEST.

temporary insanity. Insanity that exists only at the time of a criminal act.

insanity defense. *Criminal law.* An affirmative defense alleging that a mental disorder caused the accused to commit the crime. • Unlike other defenses, a successful insanity defense results not in acquittal but instead in a special verdict ("not guilty by reason of insanity") that usu. leads to the defendant's commitment to a mental institution. — Also termed *insanity plea.* See MCNAGHTEN RULES; SUBSTANTIAL-CAPACITY TEST; IRRESISTIBLE-IMPULSE TEST; DURHAM RULE; APPRECIATION TEST.

black-rage insanity defense. An insanity defense based on an African-American defendant's hatred of white people. • This defense was first used in the mid-1990s.

Insanity Defense Reform Act of 1984 test. See APPRECIATION TEST.

insanity plea. See INSANITY DEFENSE.

inscriptio (in-**skrip**-shee-oh), *n.* [Latin] *Roman law.* A written accusation detailed in an official register. • The accuser was liable to punishment if the accused was acquitted. — ***inscribere,*** *vb.* See INSCRIPTION (3).

inscription, *n.* **1.** The act of entering a fact or name on a list, register, or other record. **2.** An entry so recorded. **3.** *Civil law.* An agreement whereby an accuser must, if the accusation is false, receive the same punishment that the accused would have been given if found guilty. — **inscribe,** *vb.* — **inscriptive,** *adj.*

inscriptiones (in-skrip-shee-**oh**-neez). [Latin] *Hist.* Title deeds; written instruments by which rights or interests are granted.

insecure, *adj.* Having a good-faith belief that the possibility of receiving payment or performance from another party to a contract is unlikely.

insecurity clause. A loan-agreement provision that allows the creditor to demand immediate and full payment of the loan balance if the creditor has reason to believe that the debtor is about to default, as when the debtor suddenly loses a significant source of income. Cf. ACCELERATION CLAUSE.

in separali (in sep-ə-**ray**-lI), *adv.* & *adj.* [Law Latin] In several; in severalty.

inside director. See DIRECTOR.

inside information. Information about a company's financial or market situation obtained not from public disclosure, but from a source within the company or a source that owes the company a duty to keep the information confidential. — Also termed *insider information.* See INSIDER TRADING.

insider. 1. *Securities.* A person who has knowledge of facts not available to the general public.

temporary insider. A person or firm that receives inside information in the course of performing professional duties for a client. • Generally, that person or firm is subject to the same proscriptions as an insider.

2. One who takes part in the control of a corporation, such as an officer or director, or one who owns 10% or more of the corporation's stock. **3.** *Bankruptcy.* An entity or person who is so closely related to a debtor that any deal between them will not be considered an arm's-length transaction and will be subject to close scrutiny.

insider dealing. See INSIDER TRADING.

insider information. See INSIDE INFORMATION.

insider preference. See PREFERENCE.

insider report. See REPORT (1).

insider trading. The use of material, nonpublic information in trading the shares of a company by a corporate insider or other person who owes a fiduciary duty to the company. • This is the classic definition. The Supreme Court has also approved a broader definition, known as the "misappropriation theory": the deceitful acquisition and misuse of information that properly belongs to persons to whom one owes a duty. Thus, under the misappropriation theory, it is insider trading for a lawyer to trade in the stock of XYZ Corp. after learning that a client of the lawyer's firm is planning a takeover of XYZ. But under the classic definition, that is not insider trading because the lawyer owed no duty to XYZ itself. — Also termed *insider dealing.*

> "'What is insider trading?' The term is probably best defined, to the extent any definition is adequate, as 'the purchase or sale of securities on the basis of material, non-public information.' What counts as 'non-public information'? What non-public information can be deemed 'material'? When is a trader who is in possession of material, non-public information trading 'on the basis of' that information? Must the information be about the company whose securities are being purchased or sold? What characteristics establish 'insider' status sufficient to warrant legal proscriptions of trading? These are all questions that are derived from the definition of insider trading just offered . . . ." C. Edward Fletcher, *Materials on the Law of Insider Trading* 3 (1991).

> "A number of different parties may be subject to a variety of monetary penalties under the federal securities laws for engaging in illegal insider trading. These parties may include actual traders, their tippers, as well as broker-dealers and investment advisors (when they fail to take appropriate steps to prevent the insider trading violation(s) or fail to maintain and enforce policies and procedures reasonably designed to prevent the occurrence of such trading). Measures that may be ordered include (1) requiring the subject party to 'disgorge' the ill-gotten profits (or loss avoided) in an SEC enforcement action, (2) subjecting individuals to a maximum criminal fine of $1 million and 10 years imprisonment, and (3) in

an SEC enforcement action, within a court's discretion, ordering the subject party to pay into the U.S. Treasury a treble damage penalty amounting to three times the profit gained or loss avoided." Marc I. Steinberg, *Understanding Securities Law* 277–78 (2d ed. 1996).

insidiatio viarum (in-sid-ee-**ay**-shee-oh vI-**air**-əm). [Latin "ambush on the highway"] *Hist.* The crime of waylaying someone along the roadway. See LATROCINATION; HIGHWAYMAN.

insilium (in-**sil**-ee-əm). [Law Latin] *Hist.* Pernicious advice or counsel.

in simili materia (in **sim**-ə-lI mə-**teer**-ee-ə), *adv.* & *adj.* [Law Latin] Of the same or a similar subject matter.

insimul (in-**sim**-əl *or* **in**-si-məl), *adv.* [Latin] Together, jointly.

insimul computassent (in-**sim**-əl *or* **in**-si-məl kahm-pyoo-**tas**-ənt). [Law Latin "they accounted together"] *Hist.* A count in an assumpsit action asserting that the parties had reviewed their accounts and that the defendant voluntarily agreed to pay the amount sought by the plaintiff. • This term derives from the initial words of the count.

insimul tenuit (in-**sim**-əl *or* **in**-si-məl **ten**-yoo-it). [Law Latin "he held together"] *Hist.* A writ brought by a coparcener to recover a fee tail alienated by an earlier tenant; a type of *formedon in the descender*. See *formedon in the descender* under FORMEDON.

insinuare (in-sin-yoo-**air**-ee), *vb.* [Latin] *Roman & civil law.* To register; to deposit (an instrument) with a public registry.

insinuatio (in-sin-yoo-**ay**-shee-oh). [Law Latin] *Hist.* Information or suggestion. • This term sometimes appeared in the phrase *ex insinuatione* ("on the information"), which is the precursor to the modern *on information and belief*. See INFORMATION AND BELIEF.

insinuation (in-sin-yoo-**ay**-shən). *Civil law.* **1.** The act of depositing (an instrument) with a public registry for recording. **2.** A document that evidences a donation of property.

insinuation of a will. *Civil law.* The first production of a will for probate.

in solido (in **sol**-ə-doh). [Latin "as a whole"] (Of an obligation) creating joint and several liability. • The term is used in civil-law jurisdictions such as Louisiana. — Also termed *in solidum*. See SOLIDARY.

in solidum (in **sol**-ə-dəm). See IN SOLIDO.

in solo (in **soh**-loh), *adv.* & *adj.* [Latin] In the soil or ground.

in solo alieno (in **soh**-loh ay-lee-**ee**-noh *or* al-ee-), *adv.* & *adj.* [Latin] In another's ground.

in solo proprio (in **soh**-loh **proh**-pree-oh), *adv.* & *adj.* [Latin] In one's own ground.

insolvency, *n.* **1.** The condition of being unable to pay debts as they fall due or in the usual course of business. **2.** The inability to pay debts as they mature. — Also termed *failure to meet obligations*. See BANKRUPTCY (2). Cf. SOLVENCY.

balance-sheet insolvency. Insolvency created when the debtor's liabilities exceed its assets. • Under some state laws, balance-sheet insolvency prevents a corporation from making a distribution to its shareholders.

equity insolvency. Insolvency created when the debtor cannot meet its obligations as they fall due. • Under most state laws, equity insolvency prevents a corporation from making a distribution to its shareholders.

insolvency proceeding. *Archaic.* A bankruptcy proceeding to liquidate or rehabilitate an estate. See BANKRUPTCY (1).

insolvent, *adj.* (Of a debtor) having liabilities that exceed the value of assets; having stopped paying debts in the ordinary course of business or being unable to pay them as they fall due. — **insolvent,** *n.*

in specie (in **spee**-shee-ee *or* **spee**-shee). [Latin "in kind"] In the same or like form; IN KIND <the partners were prepared to return the borrowed items *in specie*>.

inspectator. *Archaic.* A prosecutor, adversary, or inspector.

inspection. A careful examination of something, such as goods (to determine their fitness for purchase) or items produced in response to a discovery request (to determine their relevance to a lawsuit).

inspection right. The legal entitlement in certain circumstances to examine articles or documents, such as a consumer's right to inspect goods before paying for them.

inspection search. See *administrative search* under SEARCH.

inspector. **1.** A person authorized to inspect something. **2.** A police officer who ranks below a superintendent or deputy superintendent, and who is in charge of several precincts.

inspector general. (*often cap.*) **1.** One of several federal officials charged with supervising a particular agency's audits or investigations. **2.** A governor-appointed state official who oversees internal review within executive agencies to ensure that there is no waste or abuse of resources.

inspeximus (in-**spek**-si-məs), *vb.* [Latin "we have inspected"] *Hist.* A charter in which the grantor confirms an earlier charter. • *Inspeximus* was the opening word of the charter. — Also termed *vidimus.*

install, *vb.* To induct (a person) into an office or a rank <the newly elected governor was soon installed in office>.

installment, *n.* A periodic partial payment of a debt.

installment accounting method. See ACCOUNTING METHOD.

installment contract. See CONTRACT.

installment credit. See CREDIT (4).

installment debt. See DEBT.

installment land contract. See *contract for deed* under CONTRACT.

installment loan. See LOAN.

installment note. See NOTE (1).

installment plan. See INSTALLMENT SALE.

installment sale. A conditional sale in which the buyer makes a down payment followed by periodic payments and the seller retains title or a security interest until all payments have been received. — Also termed *installment plan; retail installment sale.*

disguised installment sale. *Bankruptcy.* A debtor's leasing ploy to try to keep property outside the bankruptcy estate, whereby a lease either presents the lessee-debtor with a bargain purchase option or transfers title to the lessee-debtor at the end of the lease term. • When such a lease is discovered, the property is treated as part of the bankruptcy estate, meaning that to defeat competing creditors, the lessor must have perfected a security interest.

instance, *n.* **1.** An example or occurrence <there were 55 instances of reported auto theft in this small community last year>. **2.** The act of instituting legal proceedings <court of first instance>. **3.** Urgent solicitation or insistence <she applied for the job at the instance of her friend>.

instance, *vb.* To illustrate by example; to cite <counsel instanced three cases for the court to consider>.

instance court. See COURT.

instant, *adj.* This; the present (case, judgment, order, etc.); now being discussed <the instant order is not appealable>.

instantaneous crime. See CRIME.

instantaneous death. See DEATH.

instant case. See *case at bar* under CASE.

instanter (in-**stan**-tər), *adv.* Instantly; at once <the defendant was ordered to file its motion instanter>.

instar (**in**-stahr). [Latin] *Hist.* Likeness; the equivalent of a thing. • This term appeared in phrases such as *instar omnium* ("equivalent or tantamount to all").

in statu quo (in **stay**-t[y]oo **kwoh**). [Latin "in the state in which"] In the same condition as previously <Johnson, as a minor, can recover the whole of what he paid if he puts the other party *in statu quo* by returning all the value received>. — Also termed *in statu quo ante.* See STATUS QUO.

instigate, *vb.* To goad or incite (someone) to take some action or course.

instinct, *adj. Archaic.* Imbued or charged <the contract is instinct with an obligation of good faith>.

in stirpes (in **stər**-peez). See PER STIRPES.

institor (**in**-sti-tor *or* -tər). [Latin] *Roman law.* A person to whom the transaction of any particular business is committed; esp., a shopkeeper or other person in charge of a commercial business. See *actio institoria* under ACTIO.

institorial power. See POWER (4).

institute, *n.* **1.** A legal treatise or commentary, such as Coke's *Institutes* in four volumes (published in 1628). **2.** (*cap.* & *pl.*) An elementary treatise on Roman law in four books. • This treatise is one of the four component parts of the *Corpus Juris Civilis.* — Also termed *Institutes of Justinian*; *Justinian's Institutes.* See CORPUS JURIS CIVILIS. **3.** (*cap.* & *pl.*) An elementary treatise written by the Roman jurist Gaius. • The *Institutes,* written in the second century A.D., served as a foundation for the *Institutes of Justinian.* — Also termed *Institutes of Gaius.* **4.** (*cap.* & *pl.*) A paraphrase of Justinian's *Institutes* written in Greek by Theophilus, a law professor at Constantinople who helped prepare the *Institutes of Justinian.* • This work was prepared in the sixth century A.D. — Also termed *Paraphrase of Theophilus*; *Institutes of Theophilus.* **5.** *Civil law.* A person named in a will as heir, but under directions to pass the estate on to some other specified person (called the *substitute*). **6.** An organization devoted to the study and improvement of the law. See AMERICAN LAW INSTITUTE.

institute, *vb.* To begin or start; commence <institute legal proceedings against the manufacturer>.

Institutes of Gaius. See INSTITUTE.

Institutes of Justinian. See INSTITUTE.

Institutes of Theophilus. See INSTITUTE.

institution. 1. The commencement of something, such as a civil or criminal action. **2.** An elementary rule, principle, or practice. **3.** An established organization, esp. one of a public character, such as a facility for the treatment of mentally disabled persons. — Also termed *public institution.* **4.** *Civil law.* A testator's appointment of an heir; the designation of an institute. See INSTITUTE (5). **5.** *Eccles. law.* The investiture of a benefice, by which a cleric becomes responsible for the spiritual needs of the members of a parish. Cf. PRESENTATION; ADVOWSON.

institutional broker. See BROKER.

institutional investor. One who trades large volumes of securities, usu. by investing other people's money into large managed funds. • Institutional investors are often pension funds, investment companies, trust managers, or insurance companies. See MUTUAL FUND.

institutionalize, *vb.* **1.** To place (a person) in an institution. **2.** To give (a rule or practice) official sanction.

institutional lender. A business, esp. a bank, that routinely makes loans to the general public.

institutional litigant. An organized group that brings lawsuits not merely to win but also to bring about a change in the law or to defend an existing law.

> "Our second observation relates to what has been called the 'institutional litigant.' There are organized groups, such as labour unions or trade associations, that have a continuing interest in the development of the common law. A group of this sort may take a case to litigation, not so much for the sake of a determination of the case itself, but for the purpose of bringing about a change in the law or of defending an existing rule against a change sought by some other group. When such groups are involved, the usual arguments against prospective changes in the law through judicial decisions lose much of their force. Indeed, when the litigants have this sort of long-term interest, a judicial proceeding may take on, with the assent of all involved, something of the nature of a legislative hearing." Lon L. Fuller, *Anatomy of the Law* 163 (1968).

institutional market. See MARKET.

institutiones (in-sti-t[y]oo-shee-**oh**-neez). [Latin] *Roman law.* Elementary works of law; institutes. See INSTITUTE.

instruct, *vb.* See CHARGE (3).

instructed verdict. See *directed verdict* under VERDICT.

instruction. See JURY INSTRUCTION.

instrument. 1. A written legal document that defines rights, duties, entitlements, or liabilities, such as a contract, will, promissory note, or share certificate. **2.** *Commercial law.* An unconditional promise or order to pay a fixed amount of money, with or without interest or other fixed charges described in the promise or order. • Under the UCC, a promise or order must meet several other, specifically listed requirements to qualify as an instrument. UCC § 3–104(a). See NEGOTIABLE INSTRUMENT. **3.** A means by which something is achieved, performed, or furthered <an instrument of social equality>.

inchoate instrument. An unrecorded instrument that must, by law, be recorded to serve as effective notice to third parties. • Until the instrument is recorded, it is effective only between the parties to the instrument.

incomplete instrument. A paper that, although intended to be a negotiable instrument, lacks an essential element. • An incomplete instrument may be enforced if it is subsequently completed. UCC § 3–115.

perfect instrument. An instrument (such as a deed or mortgage) that is executed and filed with a public registry.

instrumentality, *n.* **1.** A thing used to achieve an end or purpose. **2.** A means or agency through which a function of another entity is accomplished, such as a branch of a governing body.

instrumentality rule. The principle that a corporation is treated as a subsidiary if it is controlled to a great extent by another corporation.

instrument of appeal. *Hist. English law.* A document used to appeal a judgment of divorce rendered by a trial judge of the Probate, Divorce and Admiralty Division to the full panel of the court. • The use of the instrument of appeal ended in 1881, when appeals were taken to the Court of Appeal rather than the full panel of the Probate, Divorce and Admiralty Division.

instrumentum (in-stroo-**men**-təm). [Latin] *Hist.* A document, deed, or instrument; esp., a document that is not under seal, such as a court roll.

insubordination. 1. A willful disregard of an employer's instructions, esp. behavior that gives the employer cause to terminate a worker's employment. **2.** An act of disobedience to proper authority; esp., a refusal to obey an order that a superior officer is authorized to give.

insufficient evidence. See EVIDENCE.

insufficient funds. See NOT SUFFICIENT FUNDS.

insula (**in**-s[y]ə-lə). [Latin] *Roman law.* **1.** An island. **2.** A detached house or block of apartments leased to tenants.

insular court. See COURT.

insular possession. See POSSESSION (4).

insurable, *adj.* Able to be insured <an insurable risk>. — **insurability,** *n.*

insurable interest. See INTEREST (2).

insurable value. The worth of the subject of an insurance contract, usu. expressed as a monetary amount.

insurance (in-**shuur**-ənts), *n.* **1.** An agreement by which one party (the *insurer*) commits to do something of value for another party (the *insured*) upon the occurrence of some specified contingency; esp., an agreement by which one party assumes a risk faced by another party in return for a premium payment. **2.** The amount for which someone or something is covered by such an agreement. — **insure,** *vb.*

> "Insurance, or as it is sometimes called, assurance, is a contract by which one party, for a consideration, which is usually paid in money either in one sum or at different times during the continuance of the risk, promises to make a certain payment of money upon the destruction or injury of something in which the other party has an interest. In fire insurance and in marine insurance the thing insured is property; in life or accident insurance it is the life or health of the person." 1 George J. Couch, *Couch on Insurance* § 1.2, at 4–5 (2d ed. 1984).

accident and health insurance. See *health insurance.*

accident insurance. An agreement to indemnify against expense, loss of time, suffering, or death resulting from an accident. Cf. *casualty insurance.*

accounts-receivable insurance. Insurance against losses resulting from the insured's inability to collect outstanding accounts receivable because of damage to or destruction of records.

additional insurance. Insurance added to an existing policy.

all-risk insurance. Insurance that covers every kind of insurable loss except what is specifically excluded.

annuity insurance. An agreement to pay the insured (or *annuitant*) for a stated period or for life.

assessable insurance. Insurance in which the insured is liable for additional premiums if a loss is unusually large.

assessment insurance. A type of mutual insurance in which the policyholders are assessed as losses are incurred; a policy in which payments to an insured are not unalterably fixed, but are dependent on the collection of assessments necessary to pay the amount insured.

automobile insurance. An agreement to indemnify against one or more kinds of loss associated with the use of an automobile, including damage to a vehicle and liability for personal injury.

aviation insurance. Insurance that protects the insured against a loss connected with the use of an aircraft. • This type of insurance can be written to cover a variety of risks, including bodily injury, property damage, and hangarkeepers' liability.

broad-form insurance. Comprehensive insurance. • This type of insurance usu. takes the form of an endorsement to a liability or property policy, broadening the coverage that is typically available.

bumbershoot insurance. **1.** Marine insurance that provides broad coverage for ocean marine risks. **2.** See *umbrella insurance*. • This term derives from the British slang term for *umbrella*. The term applies esp. to a policy insured through the London insurance market. See *umbrella policy* under INSURANCE POLICY.

burial insurance. Insurance that pays for the holder's burial and funeral expenses.

business-interruption insurance. An agreement to protect against one or more kinds of loss from the interruption of an ongoing business, such as a loss of profits while the business is shut down to repair fire damage.

captive insurance. **1.** Insurance that provides coverage for the group or business that established it. **2.** Insurance that a subsidiary provides to its parent company, usu. so that the parent company can deduct the premiums set aside as loss reserves.

cargo insurance. An agreement to pay for damage to freight damaged in transit.

casualty insurance. An agreement to indemnify against any loss resulting from a broad group of causes such as legal liability, theft, accident, property damage, and workers' compensation. • The meaning of casualty insurance has become blurred because of the rapid increase in different types of insurance coverage. Cf. *accident insurance*.

coinsurance. **1.** Insurance provided jointly by two or more insurers. **2.** Property insurance that requires the insured to bear a portion of any loss if the property is not covered up to a certain percentage of its full value. • A coinsurance clause sets a minimum for which property must be insured, and anything below that amount requires the insured to share proportionally in any loss.

collision insurance. Automobile insurance that covers damage to the insured's vehicle, but does not cover a personal injury resulting from an accident.

commercial insurance. An indemnity agreement in the form of a deed or bond to protect against a loss caused by a party's breach of contract.

> "Commercial insurance is a popular and very elastic term, having reference to indemnity agreements issued in the form of an insurance bond or policy, whereby parties to commercial contracts are, to a designated extent, guaranteed against loss by reason of a breach of contractual obligations on the part of the other contracting party. To this class belong policies of 'contract,' 'credit,' and 'title' insurances." Thomas Gold Frost, *A Treatise on Guaranty Insurance* § 3, at 14 (2d ed. 1909).

comprehensive insurance. Insurance that combines coverage against many kinds of losses that may also be insured separately. • This is commonly used, for example, in an automobile-insurance policy.

compulsory insurance. Statutorily required insurance; esp., motor-vehicle liability insurance that a state requires as a condition to registration of the vehicle.

convertible collision insurance. Collision insurance that carries a low premium until a claim is made against the policy.

convertible insurance. Insurance that can be changed to another form without further evidence of insurability, usu. referring to a term-life-insurance policy that can be changed to permanent insurance without a medical examination.

credit insurance. An agreement to indemnify against loss that may result from the death, disability, or insolvency of someone to whom credit is extended. • A debtor typically purchases this type of insurance to ensure the repayment of the loan.

credit life insurance. Life insurance on a borrower, usu. in a consumer installment loan, in which the amount due is paid if the borrower dies.

crime insurance. Insurance covering losses occasioned by a crime committed by someone other than the insured.

crop insurance. Insurance that protects against loss to growing crops from natural perils such as hail and fire.

decreasing term insurance. Insurance that declines in value during the term; esp., life insurance that lessens in value to zero by the end of the term.

deposit insurance. A federally sponsored indemnification program to protect depositors against the loss of their money, up to a specified maximum, if the bank or savings-and-loan association fails or defaults.

directors' and officers' liability insurance. An agreement to indemnify corporate directors and officers against judgments, settlements, and fines arising from negligence suits, shareholder actions, and other business-related suits. — Often shortened to *D & O liability insurance*; *D & O insurance.*

disability insurance. Coverage purchased to protect a person from a loss of income during a period of incapacity for work.

double insurance. Insurance coverage by more than one insurer for the same interest and for the same insured. • The insured is entitled to only a single indemnity from a loss, and to recover this, the insured may either (1) sue each insurer for its share of the loss, or (2) sue one or more of the insurers for the entire amount, leaving any paying insurers to recover from the others their respective shares of the loss.

dread-disease insurance. Health insurance that covers medical expenses arising from the treatment of any of several specified diseases.

employers'-liability insurance. **1.** An agreement to indemnify an employer against an employee's claim not covered under the workers'-compensation system. **2.** An agreement to indemnify against liability imposed on an employer for an employee's negligence that injures a third party.

employment-practices liability insurance. Insurance that provides coverage for claims arising from an insured's injury-causing employment practice, such as discrimination, defamation, or sexual harassment. — Abbr. *EPL insurance.*

endowment insurance. A type of life insurance that is payable either to the insured at the end of the policy period or to the insured's beneficiary if the insured dies before the period ends.

errors-and-omissions insurance. An agreement to indemnify for loss sustained because of a mistake or oversight by the insured — though not for loss due to the insured's intentional wrongdoing. • For example, lawyers often carry this insurance as part of their malpractice coverage to protect them in suits for damages resulting from inadvertent mistakes (such as missing a procedural deadline). While this insurance does not cover the insured's intentional wrongdoing, it may cover an employee's intentional, but unauthorized, wrongdoing. — Often shortened to *E & O insurance.*

excess insurance. An agreement to indemnify against any loss that exceeds the amount of coverage under another policy. Cf. *primary insurance.* See EXCESS CLAUSE.

excess lines insurance. See *surplus lines insurance.*

extended insurance. Insurance that continues in force beyond the date that the last premium was paid by drawing on its cash value.

extended-term insurance. Insurance that remains in effect after a default in paying premiums, as long as the policy has cash value to pay premiums. • Many life-insurance policies provide this feature to protect against forfeiture of the policy if the insured falls behind in premium payments.

family-income insurance. An agreement to pay benefits for a stated period following the death of the insured. • At the end of the payment period, the face value is paid to the designated beneficiary.

fidelity insurance. An agreement to indemnify an employer against a loss arising from the lack of integrity or honesty of an employee or of a person holding a position of trust, such as a loss from embezzlement. — Also termed *fidelity guaranty insurance*; *fidelity and guaranty insurance*; *surety and fidelity insurance.*

fire insurance. An agreement to indemnify against property damage caused by fire, wind, rain, or other similar disaster.

first-party insurance. A policy that applies to oneself or one's own property, such as life insurance, health insurance, disability insurance, and fire insurance. — Also termed *indemnity insurance.*

fleet insurance. Insurance that covers a number of vehicles owned by the same entity.

floater insurance. An agreement to indemnify against a loss sustained to movable property, wherever its location within the territorial limit set by the policy.

flood insurance. Insurance that indemnifies against a loss caused by a flood. • This type of insurance is often sold privately but subsidized by the federal government.

fraternal insurance. Life or health insurance issued by a fraternal benefit society to its members.

general-disability insurance. Disability insurance that provides benefits to a person who cannot perform any job that the person is qualified for. — Also termed *total-disability insurance.*

government insurance. Life insurance underwritten by the federal government to military personnel, veterans, and government employees.

group insurance. A form of insurance offered to a member of a group, such as the employees of a business, as long as that person remains a member of the group. • Group insurance is typically health or life (usu. term life) insurance issued under a master policy between the insurer and the employer, who usu. pays all or part of the premium for the insured person. Other groups, such as unions and associations, often offer group insurance to their members.

> " 'Group Insurance' refers to a method of marketing standard forms of insurance, such as life insurance, whereby a master policy is issued to the party negotiating the contract with the insurer (frequently an employer), and certificates of participation are issued to the individual insured members of the group (frequently employees)." John F. Dobbyn, *Insurance Law in a Nutshell* 13 (2d ed. 1989).

guaranty insurance (**gar**-ən-tee). An agreement to cover a loss resulting from another's default, insolvency, or specified misconduct. — Also termed *surety insurance.*

> "The term 'guaranty insurance' is generic in its scope and signification, and embraces within it those subsidiary species of insurance contracts known as 'fidelity,' 'commercial,' and 'judicial' insurances .... In legal acceptation guaranty insurance is an agreement whereby one party (called the 'insurer') for a valuable consideration (termed the 'premium') agrees to indemnify another (called the 'insured') in a stipulated amount against loss or damage arising through dishonesty, fraud, unfaithful performance of duty or breach of contract on the part of a third person ... sustaining a contractual relationship to the party thus indemnified." Thomas Gold Frost, *A Treatise on Guaranty Insurance* § 1, at 11 (2d ed. 1909).

health insurance. Insurance covering medical expenses resulting from sickness or injury. — Also termed *accident and health insurance; sickness and accident insurance.*

homeowner's insurance. Insurance that covers both damage to the insured's residence and liability claims made against the insured (esp. those arising from the insured's negligence).

indemnity insurance. See *first-party insurance.*

industrial life insurance. Life insurance characterized by (1) a small death benefit (usu. $2,000 or less), (2) premium payments that are due weekly, biweekly, or monthly and that are collected at home by the insurer's representative, and (3) no required medical examination of the insured.

inland marine insurance. An agreement to indemnify against losses arising from the transport of goods on domestic waters (i.e., rivers, canals, and lakes). Cf. *ocean marine insurance.*

insurance of the person. Insurance intended to protect the person, such as life, accident, and disability insurance.

interinsurance. See *reciprocal insurance.*

joint life insurance. Life insurance on two or more persons, payable to the survivor or survivors when one of the policyholders dies.

judicial insurance. Insurance intended to protect litigants and others involved in the court system.

> "By judicial insurance reference is had to insurance bonds or policies issued, in connection with the regular course of judicial or administrative procedure, for the purpose of securing the faithful performance of duty on the part of court appointees, to guarantee due compliance with the terms of undertakings entered into by parties litigant before the courts, and to secure proper administration of statute law." Thomas Gold Frost, *A Treatise on Guaranty Insurance* § 3, at 14 (2d ed. 1909).

key-employee insurance. Life insurance taken out by a company on an essential or valuable employee, with the company as beneficiary. — Also termed *key-man insurance; key-person insurance; key-executive insurance.*

last-survivor insurance. Life insurance on two or more persons, payable on the death of all the insureds.

lease insurance. An agreement to indemnify a leaseholder for the loss of a favorable lease terminated by damage to the property from a peril covered by the policy. • The amount payable is the difference between the rent and the actual rental value of the property, multiplied by the remaining term of the lease.

level-premium insurance. Insurance whose premiums remain constant throughout the life of the agreement. • Most whole life policies are set up this way.

liability insurance. An agreement to cover a loss resulting from one's liability to a third party, such as a loss incurred by a driver who injures a pedestrian. • The insured's claim under the policy arises once the insured's liability to a third party has been asserted. — Also termed *third-party insurance*; *public-liability insurance*.

life insurance. An agreement between an insurance company and the policyholder to pay a specified amount to a designated beneficiary on the insured's death. — Also termed (in Britain) *assurance*.

> "Life and accident insurance has been defined as a contract whereby one party, for a stipulated consideration, agrees to indemnify another against injury by accident or death from any cause not expected in the contract. Strictly speaking, however, a contract of life insurance is not one of indemnity, but is an absolute engagement to pay a certain sum at the end of a definite or indefinite time." 43 Am. Jur. 2d *Insurance* § 3 (1982).

limited-payment life insurance. Life insurance that requires premium payments for less than the life of the agreement.

limited-policy insurance. Insurance that covers only specified perils; esp., health insurance that covers a specific type of illness (such as dread-disease insurance) or a risk relating to a stated activity (such as travel-accident insurance).

Lloyd's insurance. Insurance provided by insurers as individuals, rather than as a corporation. • The insurers' liability is several but not joint. Most states either prohibit or strictly regulate this type of insurance. See LLOYD'S OF LONDON.

loss insurance. Insurance purchased by a person who may suffer a loss at the hands of another. • This is the converse of *liability insurance*, which is purchased by potential defendants. — Also termed *first-party insurance*; *self-insurance*.

malpractice insurance (mal-**prak**-tis). An agreement to indemnify a professional person, such as a doctor or lawyer, against negligence claims. See *errors-and-omissions insurance*.

manual-rating insurance. A type of insurance whereby the premium is set using a book that classifies certain risks on a general basis, rather than evaluating each individual case.

marine insurance. An agreement to indemnify against injury to a ship, cargo, or profits involved in a certain voyage or for a specific vessel during a fixed period.

mortgage insurance. **1.** An agreement to pay off a mortgage if the insured dies or becomes disabled. **2.** An agreement to provide money to the lender if the mortgagor defaults on the mortgage payments. — Also termed *private mortgage insurance* (abbr. PMI).

mutual insurance. A system of insurance (esp. life insurance) whereby the policyholders become members of the insurance company, each paying premiums into a common fund from which each can draw in the event of a loss.

national-service life insurance. See NATIONAL-SERVICE LIFE INSURANCE.

no-fault auto insurance. An agreement to indemnify for a loss due to personal injury or property damage arising from the use of an automobile, regardless of who caused the accident.

nonassessable insurance. Insurance in which the premium is set and the insurer is barred from demanding additional payments from the insured.

occupational-disability insurance. Disability insurance that provides benefits to a person who cannot perform his or her regular job.

ocean marine insurance. Insurance that covers risks arising from the transport of goods by sea. Cf. *inland marine insurance*.

old-age and survivors insurance. See OLD-AGE AND SURVIVORS INSURANCE.

ordinary insurance. Life insurance having an interest-sensitive cash value, such as whole life insurance or universal life insurance. • Ordinary insurance is one of three main categories of life insurance. Cf. *group insurance*; *industrial life insurance*.

ordinary life insurance. See *whole life insurance*.

overinsurance. See OVERINSURANCE.

paid-up insurance. Insurance that remains in effect even though no more premiums are due.

participating insurance. A type of insurance that allows a policyholder to receive dividends. • This insurance is invariably issued by a mutual company.

partnership insurance. **1.** Life insurance on the life of a partner, purchased to ensure the remaining partners' ability to buy out a deceased partner's interest. **2.** Health insurance for a partner, payable to the partnership to allow it to continue to operate while the partner is unable to work due to illness or injury.

patent insurance (**pat**-ənt). **1.** Insurance against loss from an infringement of the insured's patent. **2.** Insurance against a claim that the insured has infringed another's patent. **3.** Insurance that funds a claim against a third party for infringing the insured's patent.

port-risk insurance. Insurance on a vessel lying in port. Cf. *time insurance*; *voyage insurance*.

primary insurance. Insurance that attaches immediately on the happening of a loss; insurance that is not contingent on the exhaustion of an underlying policy. Cf. *excess insurance*.

private mortgage insurance. See *mortgage insurance*.

products-liability insurance. An agreement to indemnify a manufacturer, supplier, or retailer for a loss arising from the insured's liability to a user who is harmed by any product manufactured or sold by the insured.

profit insurance. Insurance that reimburses the insured for profits lost because of a specified peril.

property insurance. An agreement to indemnify against property damage or destruction. — Also termed *property-damage insurance*.

public-liability insurance. See *liability insurance*.

reciprocal insurance. A system whereby several individuals or businesses act through an agent to underwrite one another's risks, making each insured an insurer of the other members of the group. — Also termed *interinsurance*.

reinsurance. See REINSURANCE.

renewable term insurance. Insurance that the insured may continue at the end of a term, but generally at a higher premium. • The insured usu. has the right to renew for additional terms without a medical examination.

replacement insurance. Insurance under which the value of the loss is measured by the current cost of replacing the insured property. See *replacement cost* under COST.

retirement-income insurance. An agreement whereby the insurance company agrees to pay an annuity beginning at a certain age if the insured survives beyond that age, or the value of the policy if the insured dies before reaching that age.

self-insurance. A plan under which a business sets aside money to cover any loss. — Also termed *first-party insurance*.

sickness and accident insurance. See *health insurance*.

single-premium insurance. Life insurance that is paid for in one payment rather than a series of premiums over time.

social insurance. Insurance provided by a government to persons facing particular perils (such as unemployment or disability) or to persons who have a certain status (such as the elderly or the blind). • Social insurance — such as that created by the Social Security Act of 1935 — is usu. part of a government's broader social policy. See WELFARE STATE.

split-dollar insurance. An arrangement between two people (often an employer and employee) in which life insurance is written on the life of one, though both share the premium payments. • On the insured's death or other event terminating the plan, the noninsured person receives the cash value of the insurance as reimbursement, and the beneficiary named by the insured is entitled to the remainder.

step-rate-premium insurance. Insurance whose premiums increase at times specified in the policy.

stop-loss insurance. Insurance that protects a self-insured employer from catastrophic losses or unusually large health costs of covered employees. • Stop-loss insurance essentially provides excess coverage for a self-insured employer. The employer and the insurance carrier agree to the amount the employer will cover, and the stop-loss insurance will cover claims exceeding that amount.

straight life insurance. See *whole life insurance*.

surety and fidelity insurance. See *fidelity insurance*.

surety insurance. See *guaranty insurance*.

surplus-lines insurance. Insurance with an insurer that is not licensed to transact business within the state where the risk is located. — Also termed *excess-lines insurance*.

term life insurance. Life insurance that covers the insured for only a specified period. Cf. *whole life insurance*.

third-party insurance. See *liability insurance.*

time insurance. *Marine insurance.* Insurance covering the insured for a specified period. Cf. *voyage insurance.*

title insurance. An agreement to indemnify against damage or loss arising from a defect in title to real property, usu. issued to the buyer of the property by the title company that conducted the title search.

> "Title insurance is normally written by specialized companies that maintain tract indexes: companies involved in writing life or casualty usually are not involved in title insurance. Title insurance is an unusual type of insurance in a few respects. For one thing, it is not a recurring policy: There is only a single premium, and a title insurance policy written on behalf of an owner theoretically remains outstanding forever to protect him or her from claims asserted by others. It is more similar to an indemnification agreement than to an insurance policy. For another, title insurance companies generally do not take risks that they know about. If the title search shows that a risk exists, the company will exclude that risk from the coverage of the policy." Robert W. Hamilton, *Fundamentals of Modern Business* 84 (1989).

total-disability insurance. See *general-disability insurance.*

travel-accident insurance. Health insurance limited to injuries sustained while traveling.

umbrella insurance. Insurance that is supplemental, providing coverage that exceeds the basic or usual limits of liability. — Also termed *bumbershoot insurance.*

underinsurance. See UNDERINSURANCE.

unemployment insurance. A type of social insurance that pays money to workers who are unemployed for reasons unrelated to job performance. • Individual states administer unemployment insurance, which is funded by payroll taxes. — Also termed *unemployment compensation.*

universal life insurance. A form of term life insurance in which the premiums are paid from the insured's earnings from a money-market fund.

variable life insurance. A form of life insurance in which the premiums are invested in securities and whose death benefits thus depend on the securities' performance, though there is a minimum guaranteed death benefit.

voyage insurance. *Marine insurance.* Insurance covering the insured between destinations. Cf. *time insurance.*

war-risk insurance. **1.** Insurance covering damage caused by war. • Ocean marine policies are often written to cover this type of risk. **2.** Life and accident insurance provided by the federal government to members of the armed forces. • This type of insurance is offered because the hazardous nature of military service often prevents military personnel from obtaining private insurance.

whole life insurance. Life insurance that covers an insured for life, during which the insured pays fixed premiums, accumulates savings from an invested portion of the premiums, and receives a guaranteed benefit upon death. — Also termed *ordinary life insurance*; *straight life insurance.* Cf. *term life insurance.*

insurance adjuster. A person who determines the value of a loss to the insured and settles the claim against the insurer. See ADJUSTER.

insurance agent. A person authorized by an insurance company to sell its insurance policies. — Also termed *producer*; (in property insurance) *recording agent*; *record agent.*

general agent. An agent with the general power of making insurance contracts on behalf of an insurer.

special agent. An agent whose powers are usu. confined to soliciting applications for insurance, taking initial premiums, and delivering policies when issued. — Also termed *local agent*; *solicitor.*

insurance broker. One who sells insurance policies without an exclusive affiliation with a particular insurance company. See BROKER.

insurance certificate. **1.** A document issued by an insurer as evidence of insurance or membership in an insurance or pension plan. **2.** A document issued by an insurer to a shipper as evidence that a shipment of goods is covered by a marine insurance policy.

insurance commissioner. A public official who supervises the insurance business conducted in a state.

insurance company. A corporation or association that issues insurance policies.

captive insurance company. A company that insures the liabilities of its owner. • The insured is usu. the sole shareholder and the only customer of the captive insurer. — Also termed *captive insurer.*

mixed insurance company. An insurance company having characteristics of both stock and mutual companies in that it distributes part of the profits to stockholders and also makes distributions to the insureds.

mutual insurance company. An insurance company whose policyholders are both insurers and insureds because they pay premiums into a common fund, from which claims are paid. — Often shortened to *mutual company.*

> "Mutual insurance companies are organized by a number of persons for the purpose of transacting some particular insurance business .... A company is a mutual one when the persons constituting the company contribute either cash or assessable premium notes, or both, to a common fund, out of which each is entitled to indemnity in case of loss. The distinguishing feature is mutuality, evidenced by the co-operation of members, uniting for that purpose, each taking a proportionate part in the management of its affairs and being at once insurer and insured, contributing to a fund from which all losses are paid .... Democratic ownership and control is a fundamental characteristic of a mutual insurance company." 18 John Alan Appleman, *Insurance Law and Practice* § 10041, at 79–80 (1945).

stock insurance company. An insurance company operated as a private corporation and owned by stockholders who share in the company's profits and losses.

stock life-insurance company. A stock insurance company that does life-insurance business.

insurance fraud. See FRAUD.

insurance of the person. See INSURANCE.

insurance policy. 1. A contract of insurance. **2.** A document detailing such a contract. — Often shortened to *policy.* — Also termed *policy of insurance*; *contract of insurance.*

accident policy. A type of business or personal policy that insures against loss resulting directly from bodily injuries sustained during the policy term solely by accidental means.

assessable policy. A policy under which a policyholder may be held liable for losses of the insurance company beyond its reserves.

bailee policy. A floating policy that covers goods in a bailee's possession but does not particularly describe the covered goods.

basic-form policy. A policy that offers limited coverage against loss. • A basic-form policy generally covers damages from fire, windstorm, explosion, riot, aircraft, vehicles, theft, or vandalism. — Also termed *limited policy.*

blanket policy. An agreement to indemnify all property, regardless of location.

block policy. An all-risk policy that covers groups of property (such as property held in bailment or a business's merchandise) against most perils. See *all-risk insurance* under INSURANCE.

broad-form policy. A policy that offers broad protection with few limitations. • This policy offers greater coverage than a basic-form policy, but less than an open-perils policy.

claims-made policy. An agreement to indemnify against all claims made during a specified period, regardless of when the incidents that gave rise to the claims occurred. — Also termed *discovery policy.*

closed policy. An insurance policy whose terms cannot be changed. • A fraternal benefit society is not permitted to write closed policies. — Also termed *closed insurance contract.*

commercial general liability policy. See *comprehensive general liability policy.*

completed-operations policy. A policy usu. purchased by a building contractor to cover accidents arising out of a job or an operation that the contractor has completed.

comprehensive general liability policy. An insurance policy, usu. obtained by a business, that covers damages that the insured becomes legally obligated to pay to a third party because of bodily injury or property damage. — Often shortened to *CGL policy*; *general liability policy.* — Also termed *commercial general liability policy.*

concurrent policy. One of two or more insurance policies that cover the same risk. • Concurrent insurance policies are stated in almost identical terms so that liability can be apportioned between the insurers.

corrected policy. A policy issued after a redetermination of risk to correct a misstatement in the original policy.

discovery policy. See *claims-made policy.*

endowment policy. A life-insurance policy payable at the end of a specified period, even if the insured survives that period, or upon the insured's death if death occurs before the end of the period.

extended policy. A policy that remains in effect beyond the time when premiums are no longer paid.

floating policy. An insurance policy covering property that frequently changes in quantity or location, such as jewelry. — Also termed *running policy*; *blanket policy.*

following-form policy. An insurance policy that adopts the terms and conditions of another insurance policy.

gambling policy. See *wager policy.*

group policy. See *master policy.*

homeowner's policy. A multiperil policy providing coverage for a variety of risks, including loss by fire, water, burglary, and the homeowner's negligent conduct.

incontestable policy. A policy containing a provision that prohibits the insurer from contesting or canceling the policy on the basis of statements made in the application.

interest policy. A policy whose terms indicate that the insured has an interest in the subject matter of the insurance. Cf. *wager policy.*

joint life policy. A life-insurance policy that matures and becomes due upon the death of any of those jointly insured.

lapsed policy. **1.** An insurance policy on which there has been a default in premium payments. **2.** An insurance policy that, because of statutory provisions, remains in force after a default in premium payments. • Statutes normally provide a 30- or 31-day grace period after nonpayment of premiums.

level-rate legal-reserve policy. A policy that seeks to build a reserve equal to the policy's face value by the end of the insured's life.

life policy. A life-insurance policy that requires lifetime annual fixed premiums and that becomes payable only on the death of the insured. — Also termed *regular life policy.*

limited policy. **1.** An insurance policy that specifically excludes certain classes or types of loss. **2.** See *basic-form policy.*

manuscript policy. An insurance policy containing nonstandard provisions that have been negotiated between the insurer and the insured.

master policy. An insurance policy that covers those under a group-insurance plan. — Also termed *group policy.* See *group insurance* under INSURANCE.

mixed policy. *Marine insurance.* A policy combining aspects of both a voyage policy and a time policy.

multiperil policy. An insurance policy that covers several types of losses, such as a homeowner's policy that covers losses from fire, theft, and personal injury. — Also termed *named-perils policy.*

nonmedical policy. An insurance policy issued without a prior medical examination of the applicant.

occurrence policy. An agreement to indemnify for any loss from an event that occurs within the policy period, regardless of when the claim is made.

open-perils policy. A property insurance policy covering all risks against loss except those specifically excluded from coverage.

open policy. See *unvalued policy.*

paid-up policy. A policy that remains in effect after premiums are no longer due.

participating policy. A policy that allows the holder a right to dividends or rebates from future premiums. • This type of policy is issued by a mutual company.

regular life policy. See *life policy.*

running policy. See *floating policy.*

standard policy. **1.** An insurance policy providing insurance that is recommended or required by state law, usu. regulated by a state agency. **2.** An insurance policy that contains standard terms used for similar insurance policies nationwide, usu. drafted by an insurance industrial association such as Insurance Services Office.

survivorship policy. A joint life policy that is payable upon the death of the last survivor named in the policy.

term policy. A life-insurance policy that gives protection for a specified period, but that does not have a cash value or reserve value.

time policy. An insurance policy that is effective only during a specified period.

tontine policy (**tahn**-teen *or* tahn-**teen**). An insurance policy in which a group of participants share advantages so that upon the default or death of any participant, his or her advantages are distributed among the remaining participants until only one remains, whereupon the whole goes to that sole participant. • Under the tontine plan of insurance, no accumulation or earnings are credited to the policy unless it remains in force for the tontine period of a specified number of years. Thus, those who survive the period and keep their policies in force share in the accumulated funds, and those who die or permit their policies to lapse during the period do not. This type of policy takes its name from Lorenzo Tonti, an Italian who invented it in the 17th century. Today, newer and more ingenious forms of insurance have largely made tontine policies defunct. See TONTINE.

umbrella policy. An insurance policy covering losses that exceed the basic or usual limits of liability provided by other policies. See *umbrella insurance* under INSURANCE.

unvalued policy. A policy that does not state a value of the insured property but that, upon loss, requires proof of the property's worth. — Also termed *open policy*.

valued policy. An insurance policy in which the sum to be paid when a loss occurs is fixed by the terms of the contract. • The value agreed on is conclusive for a total loss and provides a basis for determining recovery in cases of partial loss. This value is in the nature of liquidated damages.

voyage policy. A marine-insurance policy that insures a vessel or its cargo during a specified voyage.

wager policy. An insurance policy issued to a person who is shown to have no insurable interest in the person or property covered by the policy. • Wager policies are illegal in most states. — Also termed *gambling policy*. See *insurable interest* under INTEREST (2). Cf. *interest policy*.

insurance pool. A group of several insurers that, to spread the risk, combine and share premiums and losses.

insurance premium. See PREMIUM (1).

insurance rating. The process by which an insurer arrives at a policy premium for a particular risk. — Often shortened to *rating*.

insurance trust. See TRUST.

insurance underwriter. 1. INSURER. **2.** An insurance-company employee who is responsible for determining whether to issue a policy and the amount to charge for the coverage provided.

insure, *vb.* **1.** To secure, by payment of a premium, the payment of a sum of money in the event of a loss. **2.** To issue or procure an insurance policy on or for.

insured, *n.* A person who is covered or protected by an insurance policy. — Also termed *assured*.

additional insured. A person who is covered by an insurance policy but who is not the primary insured. • An additional insured may, or may not, be specifically named in the policy.

class-one insured. In a motor-vehicle policy, the named insured and any relative residing with the named insured.

class-two insured. In a motor-vehicle policy, a person lawfully occupying a vehicle at the time of an accident.

named insured. A person designated in an insurance policy as the one covered by the policy.

insurer. One who agrees, by contract, to assume the risk of another's loss and to compensate for that loss. — Also termed *underwriter*; *insurance underwriter*; *carrier*; *assurer* (for life insurance).

quasi-insurer. A service provider who is held to strict liability in the provision of services, such as an innkeeper or a common carrier.

insurgent, *n.* A person who, for political purposes, engages in armed hostility against an established government. — **insurgent,** *adj.* — **insurgency,** *n.*

insuring agreement. See INSURING CLAUSE.

insuring clause. A provision in an insurance policy or bond reciting the risk assumed by the insurer or establishing the scope of the coverage. — Also termed *insuring agreement*.

insurrection. A violent revolt against an oppressive authority, usu. a government.

in tail. See TAIL.

intake. *Hist. English law.* A piece of land temporarily taken from a common or moorland by a tenant to raise a crop.

intake day. The day on which new cases are assigned to the courts.

intangible, *adj.* Not capable of being touched; impalpable.

intangible, *n.* Something that is not tangible; esp., an asset that is not corporeal, such as intellectual property.

general intangible. Any personal property other than goods, accounts, chattel paper, documents, instruments, investment property, rights to proceeds of written letters of credit, and money. • Some examples are goodwill, things in action, and literary rights.

UCC § 9–103(b). See *intangible property* under PROPERTY.

payment intangible. A general intangible under which the account debtor's principal obligation is a monetary obligation. UCC § 9–103(d).

intangible asset. See ASSET.

intangible drilling costs. *Oil & gas.* Expenses incurred in drilling, testing, and completing an oil or gas well. • These costs are deductible in the year they are incurred. — Also termed *intangible drilling and development costs.* IRC (26 USCA) § 263.

intangible movable. See MOVABLE.

intangible property. See PROPERTY.

intangible tax. See TAX.

integer (**in**-tə-jər), *adj.* [Latin] *Archaic.* Whole; untouched. See RES NOVA.

integrated agreement. See INTEGRATED CONTRACT.

integrated bar. See BAR.

integrated contract. One or more writings constituting a final expression of one or more terms of an agreement. — Also termed *integrated agreement*; *integrated writing.* See INTEGRATION (2).

completely integrated contract. An integrated agreement adopted by the parties as a full and exclusive statement of the terms of the agreement. • The parties are therefore prohibited from varying or supplementing the contractual terms through parol (extrinsic) evidence.

partially integrated contract. An integrated agreement other than a completely integrated agreement.

integrated property settlement. A contract, incorporated into a divorce decree, that divides up the assets of divorcing spouses.

integrated writing. See *integrated contract* under CONTRACT.

integration. 1. The process of making whole or combining into one. **2.** *Contracts.* The full expression of the parties' agreement, so that all earlier agreements are superseded, the effect being that neither party may later contradict or add to the contractual terms. — Also termed *merger.* See PAROL-EVIDENCE RULE.

complete integration. The fact or state of fully expressing the intent of the parties.

partial integration. The fact or state of not fully expressing the parties' intent, so that the contract can be changed by the admission of parol (extrinsic) evidence.

3. The incorporation of different races into existing institutions (such as public schools) for the purpose of reversing the historical effects of racial discrimination. Cf. DESEGREGATION. **4.** *Antitrust.* A firm's performance of a function that it could have obtained on the open market. • A firm can achieve integration by entering a new market on its own, by acquiring a firm that operates in a secondary market, or by entering into a contract with a firm that operates in a secondary market. — Also termed *vertical integration.* See *vertical merger* under MERGER.

backward integration. A firm's acquisition of ownership of facilities that produce raw materials or parts for the firm's products.

5. *Securities.* The requirement that all security offerings over a given period are to be considered a single offering for purposes of determining an exemption from registration. • The Securities and Exchange Commission and the courts apply five criteria to determine whether two or more transactions are part of the same offering of securities: (1) whether the offerings are part of a single plan of financing, (2) whether the offerings involve issuance of the same class of securities, (3) whether the offerings are made at or about the same time, (4) whether the same type of consideration is received, and (5) whether the offerings are made for the same general purpose. 17 CFR § 230.502.

integration clause. A contractual provision stating that the contract represents the parties' complete and final agreement and supersedes all informal understandings and oral agreements relating to the subject matter of the contract. — Also termed *merger clause*; *entire-contract clause.* See INTEGRATION (2); PAROL-EVIDENCE RULE.

integration rule. The rule that if the parties to a contract have embodied their agreement in a final document, any other action or statement is without effect and is immaterial in determining the terms of the contract.

integrity right. See MORAL RIGHT.

intellectual property. 1. A category of intangible rights protecting commercially valuable products of the human intellect. • The category comprises primarily trademark, copyright, and patent rights, but also includes trade-secret rights, publicity rights, moral rights, and rights against unfair competition. **2.** A commercially valuable product of the human intellect, in a concrete or abstract form, such as a copyrightable work, a protectable trademark, a patentable invention, or a trade secret. — Abbr. IP.

intemperance. A lack of moderation or temperance; esp., habitual or excessive drinking of alcoholic beverages.

intend, *vb.* **1.** To have in mind a fixed purpose to reach a desired objective; to have as one's purpose <Daniel intended to become a lawyer>. **2.** To contemplate that the usual consequences of one's act will probably or necessarily follow from the act, whether or not those consequences are desired for their own sake <although he activated the theater's fire alarm only on a dare, the jury found that Wilbur intended to cause a panic>. **3.** To signify or mean <the parties intended for the writing to supersede their earlier handshake deal>.

intendant (in-**ten**-dənt). A director of a government agency, esp. (as used in 17th- and 18th-century France) a royal official charged with the administration of justice or finance.

intended beneficiary. See BENEFICIARY.

intended to be recorded. (Of a deed or other instrument) not yet filed with a public registry, but forming a link in a chain of title.

intended-use doctrine. *Products liability.* The rule imposing a duty on a manufacturer to develop a product so that it is reasonably safe for its intended or foreseeable users. • In determining the scope of responsibility, the court considers the defendant's marketing scheme and the foreseeability of the harm.

intendment (in-**tend**-mənt). **1.** The sense in which the law understands something <the intendment of a contract is that the contract is legally enforceable>. — Also termed *intendment of law.* **2.** A decision-maker's inference about the true meaning or intention of a legal instrument <there is no need for intendment, the court reasoned, when the text of the statute is clear>. — Formerly also spelled *entendment.*

common intendment. The natural or common meaning in legal interpretation.

3. A person's expectations when interacting with others within the legal sphere.

> "Our institutions and our formalized interactions with one another are accompanied by certain interlocking expectations that may be called intendments, even though there is seldom occasion to bring these underlying expectations across the threshold of consciousness. In a very real sense when I cast my vote in an election my conduct is directed and conditioned by an anticipation that my ballot will be counted in favor of the candidate I actually vote for. This is true even though the possibility that my ballot will be thrown in the wastebasket, or counted for the wrong man, may never enter my mind as an object of conscious attention. In this sense the institution of elections may be said to contain an intendment that the votes cast will be faithfully tallied, though I might hesitate to say, except in a mood of rhetoric, that the election authorities had entered a contract with me to count my vote as I had cast it." Lon L. Fuller, *The Morality of Law* 217 (rev. ed. 1969).

intent. 1. The state of mind accompanying an act, esp. a forbidden act. • While motive is the inducement to do some act, intent is the mental resolution or determination to do it. When the intent to do an act that violates the law exists, motive becomes immaterial. Cf. MOTIVE; SCIENTER.

> "The phrase 'with intent to,' or its equivalents, may mean any one of at least four different things: — (1) That the intent referred to must be the sole or exclusive intent; (2) that it is sufficient if it is one of several concurrent intents; (3) that it must be the chief or dominant intent, any others being subordinate or incidental; (4) that it must be a determining intent, that is to say, an intent in the absence of which the act would not have been done, the remaining purposes being insufficient motives by themselves. It is a question of construction which of those meanings is the true one in the particular case." John Salmond, *Jurisprudence* 383–84 (Glanville L. Williams ed., 10th ed. 1947).

constructive intent. A legal principle that actual intent will be presumed when an act leading to the result could have been reasonably expected to cause that result.

> "Constructive intent is a fiction which permits lip service to the notion that intention is essential to criminality, while recognizing that unintended consequences of an act may sometimes be sufficient for guilt of some offenses." Rollin M. Perkins & Ronald N. Boyce, *Criminal Law* 835 (3d ed. 1982).

general intent. The state of mind required for the commission of certain common-law crimes not requiring a specific intent or not imposing strict liability. • General intent usu. takes the form of recklessness (involving actual awareness of a risk and the culpable taking of that risk) or negligence (involving blameworthy inadvertence).

immediate intent. The intent relating to a wrongful act; the part of the total intent coincident with the wrongful act itself.

implied intent. A person's state of mind that can be inferred from speech or conduct, or from language used in an instrument to which the person is a party.

intent to kill. An intent to cause the death of another; esp., a state of mind that, if found to exist during an assault, can serve as the basis for an aggravated-assault charge.

manifest intent. Intent that is apparent or obvious based on the available circumstantial evidence, even if direct evidence of intent is not available. • For example, some fidelity bonds cover an employer's losses caused by an employee's dishonest or fraudulent acts committed with a manifest intent to cause a loss to the employer and to obtain a benefit for the employee. Establishing manifest intent sufficient to trigger coverage does not require direct evidence that the employee intended the employer's loss. Even if the employee did not actively want that result, but the result was substantially certain to follow from the employee's conduct, the requisite intent will be inferred.

predatory intent. Antitrust. A business's intent to injure a competitor by unfair means, esp. by sacrificing revenues to drive a competitor out of business.

specific intent. The intent to accomplish the precise criminal act that one is later charged with. • At common law, the specific-intent crimes were robbery, assault, larceny, burglary, forgery, false pretenses, embezzlement, attempt, solicitation, and conspiracy.

testamentary intent. A testator's intent that a particular instrument function as his or her last will and testament. • Testamentary intent is required for a will to be valid.

transferred intent. Intent that has been shifted from the originally intended wrongful act to the wrongful act actually committed. • For example, if a person intends to kill one person but kills another, the intent may be transferred to the actual act. See TRANSFERRED-INTENT DOCTRINE.

ulterior intent. The intent that passes beyond a wrongful act and relates to the objective for the sake of which the act is done; MOTIVE. • For example, a thief's immediate intent may be to steal another's money, but the ulterior intent may be to buy food with that money.

2. A lawmaker's state of mind and purpose in drafting or voting for a measure.

legislative intent. See LEGISLATIVE INTENT.

original intent. The mental state of the drafters or enactors of the U.S. Constitution, a statute, or another document.

intentio (in-**ten**-shee-oh). [Latin] **1.** *Roman law.* The part of a formula in which the plaintiff's claim against the defendant is stated. See FORMULA (1). **2.** *Hist.* A count or declaration in a real action. • *Intentio* was an earlier name for *narratio*. See NARRATIO.

intention, *n.* The willingness to bring about something planned or foreseen; the state of being set to do something. — **intentional,** *adj.*

> "Intention is the purpose or design with which an act is done. It is the foreknowledge of the act, coupled with the desire of it, such foreknowledge and desire being the cause of the act, inasmuch as they fulfil themselves through the operation of the will. An act is intentional if, and in so far as, it exists in idea before it exists in fact, the idea realising itself in the fact because of the desire by which it is accompanied." John Salmond, *Jurisprudence* 378 (Glanville L. Williams ed., 10th ed. 1947).

intentional, *adj.* Done with the aim of carrying out the act.

intentional act. See ACT (2).

intentional infliction of emotional distress. The tort of intentionally or recklessly causing another person severe emotional distress through one's extreme or outrageous acts. • In a few jurisdictions, a physical manifestation of the mental suffering is required for the plaintiff to recover. — Also termed (in some states) *outrage*. See EMOTIONAL DISTRESS. Cf. NEGLIGENT INFLICTION OF EMOTIONAL DISTRESS.

intentional-injury exclusion. See *expected/intended exclusion* under EXCLUSION (3).

intentional manslaughter. See *voluntary manslaughter* under MANSLAUGHTER.

intentional tort. See TORT.

intentional wrong. See WRONG.

intent of the legislature. See LEGISLATIVE INTENT.

intent to kill. See INTENT (1).

intent-to-use application. *Trademarks.* An application filed with the U.S. Patent and Trademark Office to register a trademark or servicemark on the principal register based on a bona fide intention to use the mark. • Trademark rights have traditionally been established by actual use in commerce. In 1988, the Federal Trademark Act (the Lanham Act) was amended to permit applications to be filed based on merely the intent to use the mark. 15 USCA § 1051(b).

inter (**in**-tər), *prep.* [Latin] Among.

inter alia (**in**-tər **ay**-lee-ə *or* **ah**-lee-ə), *adv.* [Latin] Among other things.

inter alios (**in**-tər **ay**-lee-əs *or* **ah**-lee-əs), *adv.* [Latin] Among other persons.

Inter-American Bar Association. An organization of lawyers from North America, Central America, and South America whose purpose is to promote education, cooperation, and professional exchanges among lawyers from different American countries. — Abbr. IABA.

inter apices juris (**in**-tər **ay**-pə-seez [*or* **ap**-ə-seez] **joor**-is), *adv.* [Law Latin] Among the subtleties of the law. See APEX JURIS.

intercalare (in-tər-kə-**lair**-ee), *vb.* [Latin] *Civil law.* To introduce or insert among others; esp., to introduce a day or month into the calendar. • From this Latin term derives the rare English word *intercalate*, roughly synonymous with *interpolate*.

intercedere (in-tər-**see**-də-ree), *vb.* [Latin] *Roman law.* To assume another's debt; esp., to act as surety for another.

intercept, *vb.* To covertly receive or listen to (a communication). • The term usu. refers to covert reception by a law-enforcement agency. See WIRETAPPING.

interchangeable bond. See BOND (3).

inter conjuges (**in**-tər **kahn**-jə-geez), *adv.* & *adj.* [Law Latin] Between husband and wife.

intercourse. 1. Dealings or communications, esp. between businesses, governmental entities, or the like. **2.** Physical sexual contact, esp. involving the penetration of the vagina by the penis.

interdependence. *Int'l law.* The reliance of countries on each other to ensure their mutual subsistence and advancement.

interdict (**in**-tər-dikt), *n. Roman & civil law.* **1.** An injunction or other prohibitory decree.

decretal interdict (di-**kreet**-əl). An interdict that signified the praetor's order or decree by applying the remedy in a pending case.

edictal interdict (ee-**dik**-təl). An interdict that declared the praetor's intention to give a remedy in certain cases, usu. in a way that preserves or restores possession.

exhibitory interdict. An interdict by which a praetor compelled a person or thing to be produced.

possessory interdict. An interdict that protected a tenant who had been ejected or threatened with disturbance. • Possessory interdicts were summary processes of Roman law.

prohibitory interdict. An interdict by which a praetor forbade something to be done.

restitutory interdict (ri-**stich**-ə-tor-ee *or* res-ti-**t**[**y**]**oo**-tə-ree). An interdict by which a praetor directed something to be restored to someone who had been dispossessed of it.

2. *Eccles. law.* An order prohibiting a person from attending divine services or barring their being conducted at a particular place. **3.** *Civil law.* One who is subject to interdiction.

limited interdict. A person whose right to care for himself or herself has been partially removed because of mental incapacity; a person subject to limited interdiction.

interdict (in-tər-**dikt**), *vb.* **1.** To forbid or restrain. **2.** *Civil law.* To remove a person's right to handle personal affairs because of mental incapacity.

interdiction. 1. The act of prohibiting.

interdiction of commercial intercourse. *Int'l law.* A governmental prohibition of commercial trade.

2. *Civil law.* The act of depriving a person of the right to care for his or her affairs because of mental incapacity.

full interdiction. The complete removal of one's right to care for oneself and one's affairs or estate because of mental incapacity. — Also termed *complete interdiction.*

limited interdiction. The partial removal of one's right to care for one's affairs or estate because of mental incapacity.

interdictory (in-tər-**dik**-tər-ee), *adj.* **1.** Of or relating to an interdiction. **2.** Having the power to interdict. — Also termed *interdictive.*

interdictum quod vi aut clam (in-tər-**dik**-təm kwod **vI** awt **klam**). [Latin "interdict because of force or stealth"] *Roman law.* An interdict issued against a person who forcibly (*vi*) or secretly (*clam*) altered the claimant's property. • The interdict required the defendant to restore the property to its previous condition.

interesse (in-tər-**es**-ee). [Latin] **1.** Monetary interest. **2.** A legal interest in property.

interessee (in-tə-re-**see**). See *real party in interest* under PARTY (2).

interesse termini (in-tər-**es**-ee **tər**-mə-nI). [Latin "interest of term or end"] *Archaic.* A lessee's right of entry onto the leased property; esp., a lessee's interest in real property before taking possession. • An *interesse termini* is not an estate; it is an interest for the term. It gives the lessee a claim against any person who prevents the lessee from entering or accepting delivery of the property.

interest, *n.* **1.** Advantage or profit, esp. of a financial nature <conflict of interest>. **2.** A legal share in something; all or part of a legal or equitable claim to or right in property <right, title, and interest>.

absolute interest. An interest that is not subject to any condition.

contingent interest. An interest that the holder may enjoy only upon the occurrence of a condition precedent.

controlling interest. Sufficient ownership of stock in a company to control policy and management; esp., a greater-than–50% ownership interest in an enterprise.

direct interest. A certain, absolute interest <the juror was disqualified because she had a direct interest in the lawsuit>.

entire interest. A whole interest or right, without diminution. See FEE SIMPLE.

equitable interest. An interest held by virtue of an equitable title or claimed on equitable grounds, such as the interest held by a trust beneficiary.

expectation interest. The interest of a nonbreaching party in receiving a benefit that would have resulted if the contract had been performed. See *expectation damages* under DAMAGES; BENEFIT-OF-THE-BARGAIN RULE.

future interest. See FUTURE INTEREST.

inalienable interest. An interest that cannot be sold or traded.

inchoate interest. A property interest that has not yet vested.

insurable interest. A legal interest in another person's life or health or in the protection of property from injury, loss, destruction, or pecuniary damage. • To take out an insurance policy, a potential insured must have an insurable interest. If a policy does not have an insurable interest as its basis, it will usu. be considered a form of wagering and thus be held unenforceable. See *wager policy* under INSURANCE POLICY.

junior interest. An interest that is subordinate to a senior interest.

legal interest. An interest recognized by law, such as legal title.

possessory interest. See POSSESSORY INTEREST.

present interest. A property interest in which the privilege of possession or enjoyment is present and not merely future; an interest entitling the holder to immediate possession. — Also termed *present estate.* Cf. FUTURE INTEREST.

proprietary interest. The interest held by a property owner together with all appurtenant rights, such as a stockholder's right to vote the shares.

reliance interest. The interest a nonbreaching party has in recovering costs stemming from that party's reliance on the performance of the contract.

senior interest. An interest that takes precedence over others; esp., a debt security or preferred share that has a higher claim on a corporation's assets and earnings than that of a junior obligation or common share.

terminable interest. See TERMINABLE INTEREST.

vested interest. An interest the right to the enjoyment of which, either present or future, is not subject to the happening of a condition precedent.

3. The compensation fixed by agreement or allowed by law for the use or detention of money, or for the loss of money by one who is entitled to its use; esp., the amount owed to a lender in return for the use of borrowed money. — Also termed *finance charge.* See USURY.

accrued interest. Interest that is earned but not yet paid, such as interest that accrues on real estate and that will be paid when the property is sold if, in the meantime, the rental income does not cover the mortgage payments.

add-on interest. Interest that is computed on the original face amount of a loan and that remains the same even as the principal declines. • A $10,000 loan with add-on interest at 8% payable over three years would require equal annual interest payments of $800 for three years, regardless of the unpaid principal amount. With add-on interest, the effective rate of interest is typically about twice the stated add-on interest rate. In the example just cited, then, the effective rate of interest would be about 16%. — Also termed *block interest*. See *add-on loan* under LOAN.

Boston interest. Interest computed by using a 30-day month rather than the exact number of days in the month. — Also termed *New York interest*.

compound interest. Interest paid on both the principal and the previously accumulated interest. Cf. *simple interest*.

conventional interest. Interest at a rate agreed to by the parties themselves, as distinguished from that prescribed by law. Cf. *interest as damages*.

discount interest. The interest that accrues on a discounted investment instrument (such as a government bond) as it matures. • The investor receives the interest when the instrument is redeemed.

gross interest. A borrower's interest payment that includes administrative, service, and insurance charges.

imputed interest. Interest income that the IRS attributes to a lender regardless of whether the lender actually receives interest from the borrower. • This is common esp. in loans between family members.

interest as damages. Interest allowed by law in the absence of a promise to pay it, as compensation for a delay in paying a fixed sum or a delay in assessing and paying damages. Cf. *conventional interest*.

New York interest. See *Boston interest*.

prepaid interest. Interest paid before it is earned.

qualified residence interest. *Tax.* Interest paid on debt that is secured by one's home and that was incurred to purchase, build, improve, or refinance the home. • This type of interest is deductible from adjusted gross income.

simple interest. Interest paid on the principal only and not on accumulated interest. • Interest accrues only on the principal balance regardless of how often interest is paid. — Also termed *straight-line interest*. Cf. *compound interest*.

straight-line interest. See *simple interest*.

unearned interest. Interest received by a financial institution before it is earned.

interest-analysis technique. *Conflict of laws.* A method of resolving choice-of-law questions by reviewing a state's laws and the state's interests in enforcing those laws to determine whether that state's laws or those of another state should apply. — Also termed *governmental-interest-analysis technique*.

> "Professor Brainerd Currie gets the major credit for developing the interest analysis, or governmental interest analysis, technique. Interest analysis requires an examination into competing laws to determine their underlying policies and the strength of the relative interests the competing sovereigns have in the application of their respective laws in the particular situation. The facts will vary and the strength of the relevant policies will wax and wane accordingly." David D. Siegel, *Conflicts in a Nutshell* 237 (2d ed. 1994).

interest arbitration. See ARBITRATION.

interest as damages. See INTEREST (3).

interest bond. See BOND (3).

interest-coverage ratio. The ratio between a company's pretax earnings and the annual interest payable on bonds and loans.

interested party. See PARTY (2).

interested person. See PERSON.

interested witness. See WITNESS.

interest-equalization tax. See TAX.

interest factor. *Insurance.* In life-insurance ratemaking, an estimate of the interest or rate of return that the insurer will earn on premium payments over the life of a policy. • The interest factor is one element that a life insurer uses to calculate premium rates. See PREMIUM RATE; *gross premium* (1) under PREMIUM (1). Cf. MORTALITY FACTOR; RISK FACTOR.

interest-free loan. See LOAN.

Interest on Lawyers' Trust Accounts. A program that allows a lawyer or law firm to deposit a client's retained funds into an interest-bearing account that designates the interest payments to charitable, law-related purposes, such as providing legal aid to the poor. • Almost all states have either a voluntary or mandatory IOLTA program. — Abbr. IOLTA.

interest-only mortgage. See MORTGAGE.

interest policy. See INSURANCE POLICY.

interest rate. The percentage that a borrower of money must pay to the lender in return for the use of the money, usu. expressed as a percentage of the principal payable for a one-year period. — Often shortened to *rate.* — Also termed *rate of interest.*

annual percentage rate. The actual cost of borrowing money, expressed in the form of an annualized interest rate. — Abbr. APR.

bank rate. The rate of interest at which the Federal Reserve lends funds to member banks.

contract rate. The interest rate printed on the face of a bond certificate.

coupon rate. The specific interest rate for a coupon bond. — Also termed *coupon interest rate.* See *coupon bond* under BOND (1).

discount rate. **1.** The interest rate at which a member bank may borrow money from the Federal Reserve. • This rate controls the supply of money available to banks for lending. Cf. *rediscount rate.* **2.** The percentage of a commercial paper's face value paid by an issuer who sells the instrument to a financial institution. **3.** The interest rate used in calculating present value.

effective rate. The actual annual interest rate, which incorporates compounding when calculating interest, rather than the stated rate or coupon rate.

face rate. See *nominal rate.*

floating rate. A varying interest rate that is tied to a financial index such as the prime rate.

illegal rate. An interest rate higher than the rate allowed by law. See USURY.

legal rate. **1.** The interest rate imposed as a matter of law when none is provided by contract. **2.** The maximum interest rate, set by statute, that may be charged on a loan. See USURY.

lock rate. A mortgage-application interest rate that is established and guaranteed for a specified period. — Also termed *locked-in rate.*

nominal rate. The interest rate stated in a loan agreement or on a bond, with no adjustment made for inflation. — Also termed *coupon rate*; *face rate*; *stated rate.*

prime rate. The interest rate that a commercial bank holds out as its lowest rate for a short-term loan to its most creditworthy borrowers, usu. large corporations. • This rate, which can vary slightly from bank to bank, often dictates other interest rates for various personal and commercial loans. — Often shortened to *prime.* — Also termed *prime lending rate.*

real rate. An interest rate that has been adjusted for inflation over time.

rediscount rate. The interest rate at which a member bank may borrow from the Federal Reserve on a loan secured by commercial paper that has already been resold by the bank.

stated rate. See *nominal rate.*

variable rate. An interest rate that varies at preset intervals in relation to the current market rate (usu. the prime rate).

interest-rate swap. An agreement to exchange interest receipts or interest-payment obligations, usu. to adjust one's risk exposure, to speculate on interest-rate changes, or to convert an instrument or obligation from a fixed to a floating rate — or from a floating to a fixed rate. • The parties to such an agreement are termed "counterparties."

plain-vanilla swap. A typical interest-rate swap that involves one counterparty's paying a fixed interest rate while the other assumes a floating interest rate based on the amount of the principal of the underlying debt. • The underlying debt, called the "notional" amount of the swap, does not change hands — only the interest payments are exchanged.

interest unity. See *unity of interest* under UNITY.

interest warrant. See WARRANT (2).

interference, *n.* **1.** The act of meddling in another's affairs. **2.** An obstruction or hindrance. **3.** *Patents.* An administrative proceeding in the U.S. Patent and Trademark Office to determine which applicant is entitled to the patent when two or more applicants claim the same invention. • This proceeding occurs when the same invention is claimed (1) in two pending applications, or (2) in one pending application and a patent issued within a year of the pending application's filing date. — **interfere,** *vb.*

interference with a business relationship. See TORTIOUS INTERFERENCE WITH PROSPECTIVE ADVANTAGE.

interference with a contractual relationship. See TORTIOUS INTERFERENCE WITH CONTRACTUAL RELATIONS.

intergovernmental immunity. See IMMUNITY (1).

intergovernmental-immunity doctrine. *Constitutional law.* The principle that both the federal government and the states are independent sovereigns, and that neither sovereign may intrude on the other in certain political spheres. Cf. PREEMPTION.

interim, *adj.* Done, made, or occurring for an intervening time; temporary or provisional <an interim director>.

interim bond. See BOND (2).

interim committitur (**in**-tə-rim kə-**mit**-ə-tər). [Latin "in the meantime, let him be committed"] A court order directing that a defendant be incarcerated pending further action.

interim curator. See CURATOR (2).

interim financing. See FINANCING.

interim measure of protection. *Int'l law.* An international tribunal's act to prevent a litigant from prejudicing the final outcome of a lawsuit by arbitrary action before a judgment has been reached.

interim-occupancy agreement. A contract governing an arrangement (called a *leaseback*) whereby the seller rents back property from the buyer. See LEASEBACK.

interim order. See ORDER (2).

interim receipt. The written acknowledgment of a premium paid on an insurance policy that is pending final approval.

interim relief. See RELIEF.

interim statement. *Accounting.* A periodic financial report issued during the fiscal year (usu. quarterly) that indicates the company's current performance. • The SEC requires the company to file such a statement if it is distributed to the company's shareholders. — Also termed *interim report.*

interim trustee. See TRUSTEE (2).

interim zoning. See ZONING.

interinsurance. See *reciprocal insurance* under INSURANCE.

interinsurance exchange. See RECIPROCAL EXCHANGE.

Interior Department. See DEPARTMENT OF THE INTERIOR.

interlineation (in-tər-lin-ee-**ay**-shən), *n.* **1.** The act of writing something between the lines of an earlier writing. **2.** Something written between the lines of an earlier writing. — **interline,** *vb.* Cf. INTERPOLATION.

interlining. A carrier's practice of transferring a shipment to another carrier to reach a destination not served by the transferring carrier.

interlocking confessions. See CONFESSION.

interlocking director. See DIRECTOR.

interlocutor (in-tər-**lok**-yə-tər). *Scots law.* A nonfinal judicial order disposing of any part of a case.

interlocutory (in-tər-**lok**-yə-tor-ee), *adj.* (Of an order, judgment, appeal, etc.) interim or temporary, not constituting a final resolution of the whole controversy.

interlocutory appeal. See APPEAL.

Interlocutory Appeals Act. A federal statute, enacted in 1958, that grants discretion to a U.S. court of appeals to review an interlocutory order in a civil case if the trial judge states in writing that the order involves a controlling question of law on which there is substantial ground for difference of opinion, and that an immediate appeal from the order may materially advance the termination of the litigation. 28 USCA § 1292(b).

interlocutory decision. See *interlocutory order* under ORDER (2).

interlocutory decree. See *interlocutory judgment* under JUDGMENT.

interlocutory injunction. See *preliminary injunction* under INJUNCTION.

interlocutory judgment. See JUDGMENT.

interlocutory order. See ORDER (2).

interloper, *n.* **1.** One who interferes without justification. **2.** One who trades illegally. — **interlope,** *vb.*

intermeddler. See OFFICIOUS INTERMEDDLER.

intermediary (in-tər-**mee**-dee-er-ee), *n.* A mediator or go-between; a third-party negotiator. — **intermediate** (in-tər-**mee**-dee-ayt), *vb.* Cf. FINDER.

> ***informed intermediary.*** *Products liability.* A person who is in the chain of distribution from the manufacturer to the consumer and who knows the risks of the product. — Also termed *learned intermediary.*

intermediary bank. See BANK.

intermediate account. See ACCOUNT.

intermediate court. See COURT.

intermediate order. See *interlocutory order* under ORDER (2).

intermediate scrutiny. *Constitutional law.* A standard lying between the extremes of rational-basis review and strict scrutiny. • Under the standard, if a statute contains a quasi-suspect classification (such as gender or legitimacy), the classification must be substantially related to the achievement of an important governmental objective. — Also termed *middle-level scrutiny*; *mid-level scrutiny*; *heightened scrutiny.* Cf. STRICT SCRUTINY; RATIONAL-BASIS TEST.

intermediation. 1. Any process involving an intermediary. **2.** The placing of funds with a financial intermediary that reinvests the funds, such as a bank that lends the funds to others or a mutual fund that invests the funds in stocks, bonds, or other instruments.

in terminis terminantibus (in **tər**-mə-nis tər-mə-**nan**-ti-bəs), *adv.* & *adj.* [Law Latin] In terms of determination; in express or determinate terms.

intermittent easement. See EASEMENT.

intermittent sentence. See SENTENCE.

intermixture of goods. See CONFUSION OF GOODS.

intern, *n.* An advanced student or recent graduate who is apprenticing to gain practical experience before entering a specific profession. — **internship,** *n.* See CLERK (4).

intern, *vb.* **1.** To segregate and confine a person or group, esp. those suspected of hostile sympathies in time of war. See INTERNMENT. **2.** To work in an internship.

internal act. See ACT (2).

internal-affairs doctrine. *Conflict of laws.* The rule that in disputes involving a corporation and its relationships with its shareholders, directors, officers, or agents, the law to be applied is the law of the state of incorporation.

internal affairs of a foreign corporation. *Conflict of laws.* Matters that involve only the inner workings of a corporation, such as dividend declarations and the selection of officers.

> "The old statement that a court will not hear cases involving the internal affairs of a foreign corporation has been practically dropped from the law today, and the result when appropriate is achieved under the forum non conveniens rule. Modern courts recognize their jurisdiction to entertain such suits, and insist only upon a discretionary power to refuse to exercise the existent jurisdiction when the facts make it both feasible and more desirable for the case to be heard by a court of the state of incorporation." Robert A. Leflar, *American Conflicts Law* § 255, at 512–13 (3d ed. 1977).

internal audit. See AUDIT.

internal financing. See FINANCING.

internal law. See LAW.

internal rate of return. See RATE OF RETURN.

internal revenue. Governmental revenue derived from domestic taxes rather than from customs or import duties. — Also termed (outside the United States) *inland revenue.*

Internal Revenue Code. Title 26 of the U.S. Code, containing all current federal tax laws. — Abbr. IRC. — Also termed *tax law.*

Internal Revenue Service. The branch of the U.S. Treasury Department responsible for administering the Internal Revenue Code and providing taxpayer education. — Abbr. IRS.

internal security. The field of law dealing with measures taken to protect a country from subversive activities.

internal-security act. A statute illegalizing and controlling subversive activities of organizations whose purpose is believed to be to overthrow or disrupt the government. • In the United States, many provisions in such statutes have been declared unconstitutional. One such law was repealed in 1993. See 50 USCA § 781.

internal sovereignty. See SOVEREIGNTY.

internal waters. Any natural or artificial body or stream of water within the territorial limits of a country, such as a bay, gulf, river mouth, creek, harbor, port, lake, or canal.

> "Waters on the landward side of the baseline of the territorial sea form part of the internal waters of a State." Geneva Convention on the Territorial Sea and the Contiguous Zone, Apr. 29, 1958, art. 5, ¶ 1.

international administrative law. See ADMINISTRATIVE LAW.

international agreement. A treaty or other contract between different countries, such as GATT or NAFTA. See GENERAL AGREEMENT ON TARIFFS AND TRADE; NORTH AMERICAN FREE TRADE AGREEMENT.

> "Though international agreements are known by a variety of titles, such as treaties, conventions, pacts, acts, declarations, protocols, accords, arrangements, concordats, and *modi vivendi*, none of these terms has an absolutely fixed meaning. The more formal political agreements, however, are usually called *treaties* or *conventions*." Oscar Svarlien, *An Introduction to the Law of Nations* 261 (1955).

International Bank for Reconstruction and Development. See WORLD BANK.

international bill of exchange. See *foreign draft* under DRAFT.

international control. *Int'l law.* The supervision over countries and their subdivisions for the purpose of ensuring the conformity of their conduct with international law.

> "[S]upervision is exercised increasingly not only over the conduct of governmental and intergovernmental institutions, but also over the acts and omissions of individuals to establish their conformity with requirements of public international law. Yet even where supranational entities, notably the European Communities, exercise international control over the conduct of individuals and corporate bodies, generally the supervision is destined to verify or secure conformity of governmental measures with relevant rules of law." Hugo J. Hahn, "International Controls," in 2 *Encyclopedia of Public International Law* 1079–80 (1995).

International Court of Justice. The 15-member U.N. tribunal that sits primarily at The Hague, Netherlands, to adjudicate disputes between countries that voluntarily submit cases for decision. • Appeal from the court lies only with the U.N. Security Council. — Abbr. ICJ. — Also termed *World Court.*

international crime. *Int'l law.* A crime against international law, occurring when three conditions are satisfied: (1) the criminal norm must derive either from a treaty concluded under international law or from customary international law, and must have direct binding force on individuals without intermediate provisions of municipal law, (2) the provision must be made for the prosecution of acts penalized by international law in accordance with the principle of universal jurisdiction, so that the international character of the crime might show in the mode of prosecution itself (e.g., before the International Criminal Court), and (3) a treaty establishing liability for the act must bind the great majority of countries.

International Criminal Court. A court that was established by the U.N. Security Council to adjudicate international crimes such as terrorism. • The court was repeatedly proposed and discussed throughout the 20th century, but was established only in 1998. In the absence of any international criminal code, the court applies general principles of international criminal law. — Abbr. ICC.

International Criminal Police Organization. An international law-enforcement group founded in 1923 and headquartered in Lyons, France. • The organization gathers and shares information on transnational criminals with more than 180 member nations. — Also termed *Interpol.*

international economic law. International law relating to investment, economic relations, economic development, economic institutions, and regional economic integration.

international enclave. See ENCLAVE.

international extradition. See EXTRADITION.

internationalization. The act or process of bringing a territory of one country under the protection or control of another or of several countries.

> "[T]he concept of internationalization is characterized by three elements: the abolition or limitation of the sovereignty of a specific State; the serving of community interests or at least the interests of a group of States; and the establishment of an international institutional framework, not necessarily involving an international organization." Rüdiger Wolfrum, "Internationalization," in 2 *Encyclopedia of Public International Law* 1395 (1995).

international jurisdiction. See JURISDICTION.

international law. The legal principles governing the relationships between nations; more modernly, the law of international relations, embracing not only nations but also such participants as international organizations, multinational corporations, nongovernmental organizations, and even individuals (such as those who invoke their human rights or commit war crimes). — Also termed *public international law*; *law of nations*; *law of nature and nations*; *jus gentium*; *jus gentium publicum*; *jus inter gentes*; *foreign-relations law*; *interstate law*; *law between states* (the word *state*, in the latter two phrases, being equivalent to *nation* or *country*). Cf. TRANSNATIONAL LAW.

> "Convenient ... as is on many accounts the phrase 'International Law,' to express those rules of conduct in accordance with which, either in consequence of their express consent, or in pursuance of the usage of the civilised world, nations are expected to act, it is impossible to regard these rules as being in reality anything more than the moral code of nations.... 'International law,' so far as its doctrines have been generally received, is decisive of all questions which arise between one State and another." Thomas E. Holland, *The Elements of Jurisprudence* 134–35, 392–93 (13th ed. 1924).

> "[I]nternational law or the law of nations must be defined as law applicable to states in their mutual relations and to individuals in their relations with states. International law may also, under this hypothesis, be applicable to certain interrelationships of individuals themselves, where such interrelationships involve matters of international concern." Philip C. Jessup, *A Modern Law of Nations* 17 (1949).

customary international law. International law that derives from customary law and serves to supplement codified norms.

private international law. International conflict of laws. • Legal scholars frequently lament the name "private international law" because it misleadingly suggests a body of law somehow parallel to public international law, when in fact it is merely a part of each legal system's private law. — Also termed *international private law*; *jus gentium privatum*. See CONFLICT OF LAWS (2).

> " 'International Private law,' 'Internationales Privatrecht,' though a dangerously ambiguous term, is not incapable of being understood to denote the mode in which rules of private law are borrowed by the Courts of one State from those of another." Thomas E. Holland, *The Elements of Jurisprudence* 422 (13th ed. 1924).

International Law Commission. A body created in 1948 by the United Nations for the purpose of codifying international law. • The Commission is composed of experts in international law. It sits at the European Office of the United Nations in Geneva, though its annual meetings are sometimes held elsewhere.

international legal community. 1. The collective body of countries whose mutual legal relations are based on sovereign equality. **2.** More broadly, all organized entities having the capacity to take part in international legal relations. **3.** An integrated organization on which a group of countries, by international treaty, confer part of their powers for amalgamated enterprise. • In this sense, the European Community is a prime example.

international legislation. *Int'l law.* **1.** Lawmaking among countries or intergovernmental organizations, displaying structural and procedural characteristics that are the same as national legislation. **2.** The product of any concerted effort to change international law by statute. **3.** The process of trying to change international law by statute. **4.** Loosely, the making of customary international law by a majority with the effect that a dissenter either is bound by the revised text or ceases to be a party to it. **5.** Loosely, the adoption by international bodies of binding decisions, other than judicial and arbitral decisions, concerning specific situations or disputes.

International Monetary Fund. A U.N. agency established to stabilize international exchange rates and promote balanced trade. — Abbr. IMF.

international organization. *Int'l law.* An association of countries, established by and operated according to multilateral treaty, whose purpose is to pursue the common aims of those countries. • Examples include the World Health Organization, the International Civil Aviation Organization, and the Organization of Petroleum Exporting Countries.

international person. *Int'l law.* An actor that has a legal personality in international law; one who, being a subject of international law, enjoys rights, duties, and powers established in international law and has the ability to act on the international plane.

international private law. See *private international law* under INTERNATIONAL LAW; CONFLICT OF LAWS.

international regime. See REGIME.

international relations. **1.** World politics. **2.** Global political interaction primarily among sovereign nations. **3.** The academic discipline devoted to studying world politics, embracing international law, international economics, and the history and art of diplomacy.

international river. *Int'l law.* A river that flows through or between two or more countries. • An international river raises the question whether each riparian state has full control of its own part of the river, or whether control is limited because the river is useful or even necessary to other states.

international seabed. The seabed and ocean floor, as well as the subsoil, lying beyond the territorial limits of nations. — Also termed *international seabed area.*

International Trade Court. See COURT OF INTERNATIONAL TRADE.

international union. See UNION.

international will. See WILL.

internecine (in-tər-**nee**-sin *or* in-tər-**nee**-sɪn *or* in-tər-**nes**-een), *adj.* **1.** Deadly; characterized by mass slaughter. **2.** Mutually deadly; destructive of both parties <an internecine civil war>. **3.** Loosely, of or relating to conflict within a group <internecine faculty politics>.

internment (in-**tərn**-mənt), *n.* The government-ordered detention of people suspected of disloyalty to the government, such as the confinement of Japanese Americans during World War II. — **intern,** *vb.*

internuncio (in-tər-**nən**-shee-oh), *n.* [fr. Latin *internuntius*] **1.** A messenger between two parties. **2.** A broker who serves as agent of both parties to a transaction. — Also termed *internuncius.* **3.** A papal representative at a foreign court, ranking below a nuncio. Cf. NUNCIO. — **internuncial,** *adj.*

inter pares (**in**-tər **pair**-eez), *adv.* & *adj.* [Latin] Between peers; between people in an equal position.

inter partes (in-tər **pahr**-teez), *adv.* [Latin "between parties"] Between two or more parties; with two or more parties in a transaction. — ***inter partes,*** *adj.* Cf. EX PARTE.

interpellate (in-tər-**pel**-ayt), *vb.* **1.** (Of a judge) to interrupt, with a question, a lawyer's argument. **2.** (Of a legislator) to interrupt a legislature's calendar by bringing into question a ministerial policy, esp. in the legislature of France, Italy, or Germany.

interplea. A pleading by which a stakeholder places the disputed property into the court's registry; the plea made by an interpleader. See INTERPLEADER.

interplead, *vb.* **1.** (Of a claimant) to assert one's own claim regarding property or an issue already before the court. **2.** (Of a stakeholder) to institute an interpleader action, usu. by depositing disputed property into the court's registry to abide the court's decision about who is entitled to the property. Cf. IMPLEAD.

interpleader, *n.* **1.** A suit to determine a right to property held by a usu. disinterested third party (called a *stakeholder*) who is in doubt about ownership and who therefore deposits the property with the court to permit interested parties to litigate ownership. • Typically, a stakeholder initiates an interpleader both to determine who should receive the property and to avoid multiple liability. Fed. R. Civ. P. 22. See STAKEHOLDER (1). Cf. IMPLEADER; INTERVENTION (1). **2.** Loosely, a party who interpleads.

> "Interpleader is a form of joinder open to one who does not know to which of several claimants he or she is liable, if liable at all. It permits him or her to bring the claimants into a single action, and to require them to litigate among themselves to determine which, if any, has a valid claim. Although the earliest records of a procedure similar to interpleader were at common law, it soon became an equitable rather than a legal procedure." Charles Alan Wright, *The Law of Federal Courts* § 74, at 531 (4th ed. 1983).

Interpol (**in**-tər-pohl). See INTERNATIONAL CRIMINAL POLICE ORGANIZATION.

interpolation (in-tər-pə-**lay**-shən), *n.* The act of inserting words into a document to change or clarify the meaning. • In a negative sense, interpolation can refer to putting extraneous or false words into a document to change its meaning. — **interpolate,** *vb.* — **interpolative,** *adj.* — **interpolator,** *n.* Cf. INTERLINEATION.

interposition, *n.* **1.** The act of submitting something (such as a pleading or motion) as a defense to an opponent's claim. **2.** *Archaic.* The action of a state, while exercising its sovereignty, in rejecting a federal mandate that it believes is unconstitutional or overreaching. • The Supreme Court has declared that interposition is an illegal defiance of constitutional authority. — **interpose,** *vb.*

interpretatio (in-tər-pri-**tay**-shee-oh). [Latin] *Roman law.* An opinion of a Roman jurist (an interpreter of the law, not an advocate) who did not usu. appear in court. • Such an opinion was not originally binding, but by the Law of Citations (A.D. 426), the opinions of five jurists acquired binding force. See CITATIONS, LAW OF.

interpretation, *n.* **1.** The process of determining what something, esp. the law or a legal document, means; the ascertainment of meaning.

> "Interpretation, as applied to written law, is the art or process of discovering and expounding the intended signification of the language used, that is, the meaning which the authors of the law designed it to convey to others." Henry Campbell Black, *Handbook on the Construction and Interpretation of the Laws* 1 (1896).

> "There is more to interpretation in general than the discovery of the meaning attached by the author to his words. Even if, in a particular case, that meaning is discoverable with a high degree of certitude from external sources, the question whether it has been adequately expressed remains." Rupert Cross, *Statutory Interpretation* 149 (1976).

administrative interpretation. An interpretation given to a law or regulation by an administrative agency.

authentic interpretation. Interpretation arrived at by asking the drafter or drafting body what the intended meaning was.

> "The procedure of referring the doubtful statute to its author has acquired a name in the literature of jurisprudence. It is called 'authentic interpretation.' ... [Although] this device has been tried in ... recent times in certain European countries, ... [it] has always failed, and no thoughtful adviser would recommend it to any government today." Lon L. Fuller, *Anatomy of the Law* 29–30 (1968).

customary interpretation. Interpretation based on earlier rulings on the same subject.

extensive interpretation. A liberal interpretation that applies a statutory provision to a case not falling within its literal words.

grammatical interpretation. Interpretation that is based exclusively on the words themselves.

liberal interpretation. Interpretation according to what the reader believes the author reasonably intended, even if, through inadvertence, the author failed to think of it.

limited interpretation. See *restrictive interpretation.*

logical interpretation. Interpretation that departs from the literal words on the ground that there may be other, more satisfactory evidence of the author's true intention.

restrictive interpretation. An interpretation that is bound by a principle or principles existing outside the interpreted text. — Also termed *restricted interpretation*; *limited interpretation*; *interpretatio limitata.* Cf. *unrestrictive interpretation.*

strict interpretation. Interpretation according to what the reader believes the author must have been thinking at the time of the writing, and no more. • Typically, this type of reading gives a text a narrow meaning.

unrestrictive interpretation. Interpretation in good faith, without reference to any specific principle. Cf. *restrictive interpretation.*

2. The understanding one has about the meaning of something. **3.** A translation, esp. oral, from one language to another. **4.** CHARACTERIZATION. — **interpret,** *vb.* — **interpretative, interpretive,** *adj.* See CONSTRUCTION (2).

interpretation clause. A legislative or contractual provision giving the meaning of words frequently used or explaining how the document as a whole is to be construed.

interpretative rule. *Administrative law.* **1.** The requirement that an administrative agency explain the statutes under which it operates. **2.** An administrative rule explaining an agency's interpretation of a statute. — Also termed *interpretive rule.* Cf. LEGISLATIVE RULE.

interpreted testimony. See TESTIMONY.

interpreter. A person who translates, esp. orally, from one language to another; esp., a person who is sworn at a trial to accurately translate the testimony of a witness who is deaf or who speaks a foreign language.

interpretive rule. See INTERPRETATIVE RULE.

interpretivism. A doctrine of constitutional interpretation holding that judges must follow norms or values expressly stated or implied in the language of the Constitution. Cf. NONINTERPRETIVISM; ORIGINALISM.

"A long-standing dispute in constitutional theory has gone under different names at different times, but today's terminology seems as helpful as any. Today we are likely to call the contending sides 'interpretivism' and 'noninterpretivism' — the former indicating that judges deciding constitutional issues should confine themselves to enforcing norms that are stated or clearly implicit in the written Constitution, the latter the contrary view that courts should go beyond that set of references and enforce norms that cannot be discovered within the four corners of the instrument." John Hart Ely, *Democracy and Distrust* 1 (1980).

inter quattuor parietes (**in**-tər **kwah**-too-ər pə-**rI**-ə-teez), *adv.* & *adj.* [Law Latin] Within the four walls.

inter regalia (**in**-tər ri-**gay**-lee-ə), *adj.* [Latin] Included in the royal powers or prerogatives; among other things belonging to the sovereign. See REGALIA.

interregnum (in-tə-**reg**-nəm). **1.** An interval between reigns; the time when a throne is vacant between the reign of a sovereign and the accession of a successor. **2.** *Archaic.* Authority exercised during a temporary vacancy of the throne or a suspension of the regular government. **3.** A break or pause in a continuous event.

interrogatee (in-ter-ə-gə-**tee**). A person who is interrogated. — Also termed *interrogee* (in-ter-ə-**gee**).

interrogation, *n.* The formal or systematic questioning of a person; esp., intensive questioning by the police, usu. of a person arrested for or suspected of committing a crime. — **interrogate,** *vb.* — **interrogative,** *adj.*

custodial interrogation. Intense police questioning of a detained person.

investigatory interrogation. Routine, nonaccusatory questioning by the police of a person who is not in custody.

interrogative question. *Civil law.* In a criminal trial, a question asked of a witness to elicit inadmissible evidence relating to the crime at issue in the case. Cf. ASSERTIVE QUESTION.

interrogator (in-**ter**-ə-gay-tər). One who poses questions to another.

interrogatory (in-tə-**rog**-ə-tor-ee), *n.* A written question (usu. in a set of questions) submitted to an opposing party in a lawsuit as part of discovery.

cross-interrogatory. An interrogatory from a party who has received a set of interrogatories.

special interrogatory. A written jury question whose answer is required to supplement a general verdict. • This term is not properly used in federal practice, which authorizes interrogatories and special verdicts, but not special interrogatories. Fed. R. Civ. P. 49. The term is properly used, however, in the courts of some states. — Also termed *special issue.*

interrogee. See INTERROGATEE.

in terrorem (in te-**ror**-əm), *adv.* & *adj.* [Latin "in order to frighten"] By way of threat; as a warning <the demand letter was sent *in terrorem*; the client has no intention of actually suing>.

in terrorem **clause.** A provision designed to threaten one into action or inaction; esp., a testamentary provision that threatens to dispossess any beneficiary who challenges the terms of the will. See NO-CONTEST CLAUSE.

in terrorem populi (in te-**ror**-əm **pop**-yə-lI), *adv.* [Latin] *Hist.* To the terror of the people. • This phrase was necessary in an indictment for riot.

interruptio (in-tər-**rəp**-shee-oh). [Latin] Interruption. • This word refers to a break in the possession of land that ends a prescriptive claim.

inter rusticos (**in**-tər **rəs**-ti-kohs), *adv.* [Latin] Among the unlearned.

inter se (**in**-tər **see** *or* **say**). [Latin "between or among themselves"] (Of a right or duty) owed between the parties rather than to others. — Also termed *inter sese* (**in**-tər **see**-see).

"[T]he law of nations is, or at least includes, a branch of natural law, namely, the rules of natural justice as applicable to the relations of states *inter se*." John Salmond, *Jurisprudence* 32 (Glanville L. Williams ed., 10th ed. 1947).

intersection. A place where two roads meet or form a junction.

inter se **doctrine.** *Int'l law.* The now-defunct doctrine that relations between members of the

British Commonwealth were in no circumstances international and were incapable of giving rights and duties under international law.

inter sese. See INTER SE.

interspousal, *adj*. Between husband and wife.

interspousal immunity. See *husband-wife immunity* under IMMUNITY (2).

interstate, *adj*. Between two or more states or residents of different states.

interstate agreement. An agreement between states. Cf. *interstate compact* under COMPACT.

interstate commerce. See COMMERCE.

Interstate Commerce Commission. The now-defunct federal agency established by the Interstate Commerce Act in 1887 to regulate surface transportation between states by certifying carriers and pipelines and by monitoring quality and pricing. • In December 1995, when Congress eliminated this agency, the Surface Transportation Board (STB) — a three-member board that is a division of the Department of Transportation — assumed most of the agency's duties. — Abbr. ICC.

interstate compact. See COMPACT.

interstate extradition. See EXTRADITION.

interstate income-withholding order. A court order entered to enforce a support order of a court of another state by withholding income of the defaulting person.

interstate law. 1. INTERNATIONAL LAW. **2.** The rules and principles used to determine controversies between residents of different states.

interstate rendition. See RENDITION.

intersubjective zap. In critical legal studies, a so-called spontaneous moment of shared intuition. — Also termed *zap*.

intervening act. See *intervening cause* under CAUSE (1).

intervening agency. See *intervening cause* under CAUSE (1).

intervening cause. See CAUSE (1).

intervening force. See *intervening cause* under CAUSE (1).

intervenor. One who voluntarily enters a pending lawsuit because of a personal stake in it. — Also spelled *intervener*.

intervention, *n*. **1.** The entry into a lawsuit by a third party who, despite not being named a party to the action, has a personal stake in the outcome. • The intervenor sometimes joins the plaintiff in claiming what is sought, sometimes joins the defendant in resisting what is sought, and sometimes takes a position adverse to both the plaintiff and the defendant. Cf. IMPLEADER; INTERPLEADER. **2.** The legal procedure by which such a third party is allowed to become a party to the litigation. **3.** *Int'l law*. One nation's interference by force, or threat of force, in another nation's internal affairs or in questions arising between other nations. — **intervene,** *vb*.

> "Intervention may or may not involve the use of force. It is frequently possible for a powerful state to impair the political independence of another weaker state without actually utilizing its armed forces. This result may be accomplished by lending open approval, as by the relaxation of an arms embargo, to a revolutionary group headed by individuals ready to accept the political or economic dominance of the intervening state. It may be accomplished by the withholding of recognition of a new government, combined with various forms of economic and financial pressure until the will of the stronger state prevails through the resignation or overthrow of the government disapproved." Philip C. Jessup, *A Modern Law of Nations* 172–73 (1949).

humanitarian intervention. An intervention by the international community to curb abuses of human rights within a country, even if the intervention infringes the country's sovereignty.

intervention duty. *Maritime law*. A shipowner's obligation to remedy hazardous working conditions for longshore workers, even though the shipowner did not create the condition, when the shipowner knows of a nonobvious condition arising in an area that cannot be avoided by the longshore workers in performing their duties. Cf. ACTIVE-OPERATIONS DUTY; TURNOVER DUTY.

inter virum et uxorem (**in**-tər **vI**-rəm et ək-**sor**-əm), *adv*. & *adj*. [Latin] Between husband and wife.

inter vivos (in-tər **vI**-vohs *or* **vee**-vohs), *adj*. [Latin "between the living"] Of or relating to property conveyed not by will or in contemplation of an imminent death, but during the conveyor's lifetime. — ***inter vivos***, *adv.*

***inter vivos* gift.** See GIFT.

***inter vivos* transfer.** See TRANSFER.

***inter vivos* trust.** See TRUST.

intestabilis (in-tes-**tay**-bə-lis), *adj.* [Latin] *Hist.* Disqualified from being a witness.

intestacy (in-**tes**-tə-see). The state or condition of a person's having died without a valid will. Cf. TESTACY.

intestate (in-**tes**-tayt), *adj.* **1.** Of or relating to a person who has died without a valid will <having revoked her will without making a new one, she was intestate when she died>. **2.** Of or relating to the property owned by a person who died without a valid will <an intestate estate>. **3.** Of or relating to intestacy <a spouse's intestate share>. Cf. TESTATE. **4.** *Archaic.* (Of a person) not qualified to testify <the witness could not testify after being found intestate>.

intestate, *n.* One who has died without a valid will. Cf. TESTATOR.

intestate law. The relevant statute governing succession to estates of those who die without a valid will.

intestate succession. The method used to distribute property owned by a person who dies without a valid will. — Also termed *hereditary succession*. Cf. TESTATE SUCCESSION.

intestato (in-tes-**tay**-toh), *adv.* [Latin] *Roman law.* (Of a succession) without a will.

intestatus (in-tes-**tay**-təs). [Latin] *Roman law.* An intestate; a person who dies without a will. • This term had the same meaning in early English law.

in testimonium (in tes-tə-**moh**-nee-əm), *adv.* & *adj.* [Latin] In witness; in evidence of which. • This phrase sometimes opens attestation clauses.

in the course of employment. *Workers' compensation.* (Of an accident) having happened to an on-the-job employee within the scope of employment.

intimidation, *n.* Unlawful coercion; extortion. • In England, intimidation was established as a tort in the 1964 case of *Rookes v. Barnard*, 1964 App. Cos. 1129 (P.C. 1964) (appeal taken from B.C.). — **intimidate,** *vb.* — **intimidatory,** *adj.* — **intimidator,** *n.*

> "The wrong of intimidation includes all those cases in which harm is inflicted by the use of unlawful threats whereby the lawful liberty of others to do as they please is interfered with. This wrong is of two distinct kinds, for the liberty of action so interfered with may be either that of the plaintiff himself, or that of other persons with resulting damage to the plaintiff." R.F.V. Heuston, *Salmond on the Law of Torts* 364 (17th ed. 1977).

intitle, *vb. Archaic.* See ENTITLE.

in toto (in **toh**-toh), *adv.* [Latin "in whole"] Completely; as a whole <the company rejected the offer *in toto*>.

intoxicant, *n.* A substance (esp. liquor) that deprives a person of the ordinary use of the senses or of reason.

intoxication, *n.* A diminished ability to act with full mental and physical capabilities because of alcohol or drug consumption; drunkenness. — **intoxicate,** *vb.*

culpable intoxication. See *voluntary intoxication.*

involuntary intoxication. The ingestion of alcohol or drugs against one's will or without one's knowledge. • Involuntary intoxication is an affirmative defense to a criminal or negligence charge.

pathological intoxication. An extremely exaggerated response to an intoxicant. • This may be treated as involuntary intoxication if it is unforeseeable.

public intoxication. The appearance of a person who is under the influence of drugs or alcohol in a place open to the general public. • In most American jurisdictions, public intoxication is considered a misdemeanor, and in some states, alcoholism is a defense if the offender agrees to attend a treatment program.

self-induced intoxication. See *voluntary intoxication.*

voluntary intoxication. A willing ingestion of alcohol or drugs to the point of impairment done with the knowledge that one's physical and mental capabilities would be impaired. • Voluntary intoxication is not a defense to a general-intent crime, but may be admitted to refute the existence of a particular state of mind for a specific-intent crime. — Also termed *culpable intoxication*; *self-induced intoxication*.

intoxilyzer (in-**tok**-si-lɪ-zər). See BREATHALYZER.

intoximeter (in-tok-**sim**-ə-tər). See BREATHALYZER.

intra (**in**-trə), *adv.* & *adj.* [Latin] Within. Cf. INFRA.

> "The use of *infra* (below) in the sense and place of *intra* (within) is a corruption of very ancient date.... The expression 'under age' (the correct literal translation of *infra aetatem*) indeed, is of more common occurrence than 'within age.' But the use of *infra* in the sense of *intra*, as expressive of *place*, is an undoubted barbarism." 2 Alexander M. Burrill, *A Law Dictionary and Glossary* 75 (2d ed. 1867).

intra anni spatium (**in**-trə **an**-ɪ **spay**-shee-əm), *adv.* & *adj.* [Latin] Within the space of a year.

intraday (**in**-trə-day), *adj.* Occurring within a single day.

intra-enterprise conspiracy. See CONSPIRACY.

intra fidem (**in**-trə **fɪ**-dəm), *adj.* [Latin] Within belief; credible.

intragovernmental, *adj.* Within a government; between a single government's departments or officials.

intraliminal right (in-trə-**lim**-ə-nəl). *Mining law.* The privilege to mine ore in areas within the boundaries of a mineral claim. • In contrast to an extralateral right, an intraliminal right does not give the holder the right to mine a vein of ore outside the lease even if the vein lies mostly within the lease. Cf. APEX RULE.

intra luctus tempus (**in**-trə **lək**-təs **tem**-pəs), *adv.* & *adj.* [Latin] Within the time of mourning.

intra maenia (**in**-trə **mee**-nee-ə), *adv.* & *adj.* [Latin] *Hist.* Within the walls (of a house). • This term was used most commonly in reference to domestic servants.

intransitive covenant. See COVENANT (1).

in transitu (in **tran**-si-t[y]oo *or* **tranz**-i-t[y]oo). [Latin "in transit; on the journey"] *Archaic.* Being conveyed from one place to another.

intra parietes (**in**-trə pə-**rɪ**-ə-teez), *adv.* [Latin] Within one's own walls (i.e., in private). • This phrase was formerly used most commonly in reference to matters settled out of court.

intra quattuor maria (**in**-tər **kwah**-too-ər **mar**-ee-ə), *adv.* & *adj.* [Latin] Within the four seas.

intrastate commerce. See COMMERCE.

intra trajectum (**in**-trə trə-**jek**-təm), *adv.* & *adj.* [Latin] In the passage over; on the voyage over. — Also spelled *in traiectu*.

intra vires (**in**-trə **vɪ**-reez), *adj.* [Latin "within the powers (of)"] Of or referring to an action taken within a corporation's or person's scope of authority <calling a shareholders' meeting is an *intra vires* function of the board of directors>. — **intra vires,** *adv.* Cf. ULTRA VIRES.

intrinsec service (in-**trin**-zik *or* -sik). *Hist.* The feudal services owed by a tenant to an immediate lord; the services arising from an agreement between the tenant and the lord. — Also termed *intrinsecum servitium* (in-**trin**-si-kəm sər-**vish**-ee-əm).

intrinsic (in-**trin**-zik *or* -sik), *adj.* Belonging to a thing by its very nature; not dependent on external circumstances; inherent; essential.

intrinsic ambiguity. See *patent ambiguity* under AMBIGUITY.

intrinsic evidence. See EVIDENCE.

intrinsic fraud. See FRAUD.

intrinsic value. See VALUE.

introduce into evidence. To have (a fact or object) admitted into the trial record, allowing it to be considered in the jury's or the court's decision.

introducta (in-trə-**dək**-tə). [Latin] *Roman law.* Personal property brought into a leased apartment by the tenant. • The lessor held a tacit mortgage over *introducta* to ensure payment of rent. Cf. INVECTA ET ILLATA.

introductory clause. The first paragraph of a contract, which typically begins with words such as "This Agreement is made on [date] between [parties' names]." — Also termed *commencement*; *exordium*.

intromission (in-trə-**mish**-ən). **1.** The transactions of an employee or agent with funds provided by an employer or principal; loosely, dealing in the funds of another. **2.** *Scots law.* An intermeddling with the affairs or property of another; the possession of another's property, with or without legal authority.

legal intromission. An authorized intromission, such as a creditor's enforcement of a debt.

necessary intromission. The intromission occurring when a spouse continues in possession of the deceased spouse's goods, for preservation.

vitious intromission (**vish**-əs). An heir's unauthorized dealing with the personal property of a deceased person. — Also spelled *vicious intromission.*

> "The effect of vitious intromission is to render the heir who is guilty of it liable, under the passive title of vitious intromission, for the debts of the ancestor universally — the severity of this passive title being intended to prevent the carrying off of moveables, which are, from their nature, so liable to embezzlement." William Bell, *Bell's Dictionary and Digest of the Law of Scotland* 521 (George Watson ed., 1882).

3. Penile penetration into the vagina.

intrusion, *n.* **1.** A person's entering without permission. See TRESPASS. **2.** In an action for invasion of privacy, a highly offensive invasion of another person's seclusion or private life. — **intrude,** *vb.* — **intrusive,** *adj.* — **intruder,** *n.*

intrust, *vb. Archaic.* See ENTRUST.

inundate. To overflow or overwhelm; esp., to flood with water.

inure (in-**yoor**), *vb.* **1.** To take effect; to come into use <the settlement proceeds must inure to the benefit of the widow and children>. **2.** To make accustomed to something unpleasant; to habituate <abused children become inured to violence>. — Also spelled *enure.* — **inurement,** *n.*

inurement. A benefit; something that is useful or beneficial <a taxable inurement to the benefit of a private person>.

in utero (in **yoo**-tə-roh). [Latin "in the uterus"] In the womb; during gestation or before birth <child *in utero*>.

in utroque jure (in yuu-**troh**-kwee **joor**-ee), *adv.* & *adj.* [Latin] In both laws — that is, civil law and canon law.

invadiare (in-vay-dee-**air**-ee), *vb.* [Law Latin] *Hist.* To pledge or mortgage land.

invadiatio (in-vay-dee-**ay**-shee-oh). [Law Latin] *Hist.* A pledge or mortgage. Cf. VADIATIO.

invadiatus (in-vay-dee-**ay**-təs). [Law Latin] *Hist.* A person who is under a pledge.

invalid (in-**val**-id), *adj.* **1.** Not legally binding <an invalid contract>. **2.** Without basis in fact <invalid allegations>.

invalid (**in**-və-lid), *n.* A person who, because of serious illness or other disability, lacks the physical or mental capability of managing one's day-to-day life.

invalid agreement. See *invalid contract* under CONTRACT.

invalid contract. See CONTRACT.

invalid will. See WILL.

invasion. 1. A hostile or forcible encroachment on the rights of another. **2.** The incursion of an army for conquest or plunder. **3.** *Trusts.* A withdrawal from principal. • In the third sense, the term is used as a metaphor.

invasion of privacy. An unjustified exploitation of one's personality or intrusion into one's personal activity, actionable under tort law and sometimes under constitutional law. • The four types of invasion of privacy in tort are (1) an appropriation, for one's benefit, of another's name or likeness, (2) an offensive, intentional interference with a person's seclusion or private affairs, (3) the public disclosure, of an objectionable nature, of private information about another, and (4) the use of publicity to place another in a false light in the public eye. See RIGHT OF PRIVACY.

invecta et illata (in-**vek**-tə et i-**lay**-tə). [Latin "(things) carried in and (things) brought in"] *Roman law.* Goods brought onto a rural or urban leasehold by the lessee. • The lessor held a tacit mortgage over the goods to ensure payment of rent. Cf. INTRODUCTA.

inveigle (in-**vay**-gəl), *vb.* To lure or entice through deceit or insincerity <she blamed her friend for inveigling her into the investment>. — **inveiglement,** *n.*

invent, *vb.* To create (something) for the first time.

invented consideration. See CONSIDERATION.

inventio (in-**ven**-shee-oh). [Latin] **1.** *Roman law.* A thing found; a finding. • The finder of treasure either acquired title to the property or shared it with the landowner on whose land it was found. **2.** TREASURE TROVE. Pl. ***inventiones.***

invention, *n.* **1.** A patentable device or process created through independent effort and characterized by an extraordinary degree of skill or ingenuity; a newly discovered art or operation. • *Invention* embraces the concept of nonobviousness. **2.** The act or process of creating such a device or process. **3.** Generally, anything that is created or devised. — **invent,** *vb.*

> "An 'invention' is any art, machine, manufacture, design, or composition of matter, or any new and useful improvement thereof, or any variety of plant, which is or may be patentable under the patent laws. [37 CFR § 501.3(d).]" 60 Am. Jur. 2d *Patents* § 894, at 601 n.98 (1987).

inventory, *n.* **1.** A detailed list of assets <make an inventory of the estate>. **2.** *Accounting.* The portion of a financial statement reflecting the value of a business's raw materials, works-in-progress, and finished products <the company's reported inventory was suspiciously low>. **3.** Raw materials or goods in stock <the dealership held a sale to clear out its October inventory>. **4.** *Bankruptcy.* Personal property leased or furnished, held for sale or lease, or to be furnished under a contract for service; raw materials, work in process, or materials used or consumed in a business, including farm products such as crops or livestock <the debtor was found to have inventory that was valued at $300,000>. — **inventory,** *vb.*

> "Section 547 itself defines 'inventory' and 'receivable.' Do not use the U.C.C. definitions of these terms, or the definitions of them learned in business law classes. It is especially important to note that, for purposes of section 547, 'inventory' includes 'farm products such as crops or livestock ....' " David G. Epstein et al., *Bankruptcy* § 6–35, at 351 (1993).

inventory fee. A probate court's fee for services rendered to a decedent's estate.

inventory search. See SEARCH.

inventory-turnover ratio. *Accounting.* The result of dividing the cost of goods by the average inventory. • This calculation is used to determine the effectiveness of the company's inventory-management policy.

in ventre sa mere (in **ven**-tree sa **mer**). See EN VENTRE SA MERE.

inventus (in-**ven**-təs), *p.pl.* [Latin] Found. • This word appears in various phrases, such as *thesaurus inventus* ("treasure trove") and *non est inventus* ("he is not found").

inveritare (in-ve-rə-**tair**-ee), *vb.* [Law Latin] To make proof of a thing.

inverse condemnation. See CONDEMNATION.

inverse floater. See *inverse-floating-rate note* under NOTE.

inverse-floating-rate note. See NOTE (1).

inverse-order-of-alienation doctrine. The principle that if one has not collected on the mortgage or lien on a property sold off in successive parcels, one may collect first from the parcel still held by the original owner, then from the parcel sold last, then next to last, and so on until the amount has been satisfied. — Also termed *rule of marshaling liens.*

inverse zoning. See ZONING.

inverted market. See BACKWARDATION.

invest, *vb.* **1.** To supply with authority or power <the U.S. Constitution invests the President with the power to conduct foreign affairs>. **2.** To apply (money) for profit <Jillson invested her entire savings in the mutual fund>. **3.** To make an outlay of money for profit <Baird invested in stocks>. — **investor,** *n.*

investigate, *vb.* **1.** To inquire into (a matter) systematically; to make (a suspect) the subject of a criminal inquiry <the police investigated the suspect's involvement in the murder>. **2.** To make an official inquiry <after the judge dismissed the case, the police refused to investigate further>.

investigating bureau. See CREDIT-REPORTING BUREAU.

investigating magistrate. See MAGISTRATE.

investigative detention. See DETENTION.

investigative grand jury. See GRAND JURY.

investigatory interrogation. See INTERROGATION.

investigatory power. See POWER (4).

investigatory stop. See STOP AND FRISK.

investitive fact. See FACT.

investiture (in-**ves**-tə-chuur). **1.** The act of formally installing a person in a ceremony in which the person is clothed in the insignia of the office's position or rank; esp., the installation of a cleric in office. **2.** LIVERY OF SEISIN.

investment. 1. An expenditure to acquire property or assets to produce revenue; a capital outlay.

fixed-dollar investment. An investment whose value is the same when sold as it was when purchased. • Examples are bonds held to maturity, certain government securities, and savings accounts.

fixed-income investment. An investment (including preferred stock) that pays a fixed dividend throughout its life and is not redeemable unless the corporation makes a special call.

net investment. **1.** The net cash required to start a new project. **2.** The gross investment in capital goods less capital consumption, including depreciation.

2. The asset acquired or the sum invested. **3.** INVESTITURE (1). **4.** LIVERY OF SEISIN.

investment adviser. A person who, for pay, advises others, either directly or through publications or writings, about the value of securities or the advisability of investing in, purchasing, or selling securities, or who is in the business of issuing reports on securities. • The term generally excludes an employee of an investment adviser; a depository institution, such as a bank; lawyers, accountants, engineers, and teachers whose investment advice is solely incidental to the practice of their profession; a broker-dealer whose advice is incidental to the conduct of business and who receives no special compensation for that advice; and publishers of bona fide newspapers, newsmagazines, or business or financial publications of general, regular, or paid circulation.

Investment Advisors Act. A federal statute — administered by the Securities and Exchange Commission — that regulates investment advisers. 15 USCA §§ 80b–1 et seq.

investment bank. See BANK.

investment banker. A person or institution that underwrites, sells, or assists in raising capital for businesses, esp. for new issues of stocks or bonds; a trader at an investment bank. See *investment bank* under BANK.

investment banking. The business of underwriting or selling securities; esp., the marketing of new stocks or bonds.

investment bill. See BILL (6).

investment company. See COMPANY.

Investment Company Act. A 1940 federal statute enacted to curb financial malpractices and abuses by regulating investment-company activities and transactions — specifically, by requiring registration of investment companies and prohibiting transactions by unregistered companies; by making certain persons ineligible as affiliated persons or underwriters; by regulating affiliations of directors, officers, and employees; by barring changes in investment policy without shareholder approval; and by regulating contracts of advisers and underwriters. 15 USCA §§ 80a–1 et seq.

investment contract. 1. A contract in which money is invested in a common enterprise with profits to come solely from the efforts of others; an agreement or transaction in which a party invests money in expectation of profits derived from the efforts of a promoter or other third party. **2.** A transaction in which an investor furnishes initial value or risk capital to an enterprise, a portion of that amount being subjected to the risks of the enterprise. • In such an arrangement, the investor typically does not receive the right to exercise control over the managerial decisions of the enterprise.

> "[A]n investment contract for purposes of the Securities Act means a contract, transaction or scheme whereby a person invests his money in a common enterprise and is led to expect profits solely from the efforts of the promoter or a third party.... It embodies a flexible rather than a static principle, one that is capable of adaptation to meet the countless and variable schemes devised by those who seek the use of the money of others on the promise of profits." *SEC v. Howey Co.*, 328 U.S. 293, 298–99, 66 S.Ct. 1100, 1103 (1946).

guaranteed investment contract. An investment contract under which an institutional investor invests a lump sum (such as a pension fund) with an insurer that promises to return the principal (the lump sum) and a certain amount of interest at the contract's end. — Abbr. GIC.

investment discretion. The ability of a person to (1) determine what will be purchased or sold by or for an account, (2) decide what will be purchased or sold by or for the account even though another may have the responsibility, or (3) influence the purchase or sale of securities or property in a way that, according to an administrative agency such as the Securities and Exchange Commission, should be subject to the agency's governing rules and regulations.

investment-grade bond. See BOND (3).

investment-grade rating. Any of the top four symbols (AAA, AA, A, or BAA) given to a bond after an appraisal of its quality by a securities-evaluation agency such as Moody's. • The rating indicates the degree of risk in an investment in the bond.

investment income. See *unearned income* (1) under INCOME.

investment indebtedness. *Tax.* Debt incurred by a taxpayer to acquire or carry assets that may produce income. • The Internal Revenue Code limits the amount of deductible interest on this type of debt.

investment property. Any asset purchased to produce a profit, whether from income or resale.

investment security. See SECURITY.

investment tax credit. See TAX CREDIT.

investment trust. See *investment company* under COMPANY.

investor. 1. A buyer of a security or other property who seeks to profit from it without exhausting the principal. **2.** Broadly, a person who spends money with an expectation of earning a profit.

invidious discrimination (in-**vid**-ee-əs di-skrim-ə-**nay**-shən). See DISCRIMINATION.

in vinculis (in **ving**-kyə-lis). [Latin "in chains"] In actual custody.

> "The engagement of a magistrate to an accomplice, that if he will give his evidence, he will experience favor, is merely in the nature of a recommendation to mercy, for no authority is given to a justice of the peace to pardon an offender, and to tell him that he shall be a witness against others. He is not therefore assured of his pardon, but gives his evidence *in vinculis*, in custody: and it depends on his behaviour, whether he shall or shall not be admitted to mercy." 1 Joseph Chitty, *A Practical Treatise on the Criminal Law* 82–83 (2d ed. 1826).

inviolability (in-vɪ-ə-lə-**bil**-ə-tee), *n.* The quality or fact of being safe from violation.

inviolable (in-**vɪ**-ə-lə-bəl), *adj.* Safe from violation; incapable of being violated. — **inviolability,** *n.*

inviolate (in-**vɪ**-ə-lit), *adj.* Free from violation; not broken, infringed, or impaired.

in viridi observantia (in **vir**-ə-dɪ ob-zər-**van**-shee-ə), *adj.* [Latin "in fresh observance"] Present to the minds of people, and in full force and operation.

invisible, *adj.* *Accounting.* Not reported in a financial statement <invisible earnings>.

invitation, *n.* *Torts.* In the law of negligence, the enticement of others to enter, remain on, or use property or its structures. — **invite,** *vb.*

invitation to negotiate. A solicitation for one or more offers, usu. as a preliminary step to forming a contract. — Also termed *invitation seeking offers*; *invitation to bid*; *invitation to treat*; *solicitation for bids*; *preliminary letter.* Cf. OFFER.

invited error. See ERROR (2).

invitee (in-vɪ-**tee**). A person who has an express or implied invitation to enter or use another's premises, such as a business visitor or a member of the public to whom the premises are held open. • The occupier has a duty to inspect the premises and to warn the invitee of dangerous conditions. — Also termed *business guest*; *licensee with an interest.* Cf. LICENSEE (2); TRESPASSER.

public invitee. An invitee who is invited to enter and remain on property for a purpose for which the property is held open to the public.

inviter. One who expressly or impliedly invites another onto the premises for business purposes. — Also spelled *invitor.* Cf. INVITEE.

invitor. See INVITER.

invocation. **1.** The act of calling upon for authority or justification. **2.** The act of enforcing or using a legal right <an invocation of the contract clause>.

invoice, *n.* An itemized list of goods or services furnished by a seller to a buyer, usu. specifying the price and terms of sale; a bill of costs. — **invoice,** *vb.*

consular invoice. An invoice used to hasten the entry of goods into a country by bearing the signature of the country's consul as assurance that the shipment's contents have been preverified for quantity and value.

sales invoice. A document showing details of a purchase or sale, including price and quantity of merchandise.

invoice book. A journal into which invoices are copied.

involuntary, *adj.* Not resulting from a free and unrestrained choice; not subject to control by the will. — **involuntariness,** *n.*

> "[T]he law, like everyday thought, usually confines the notion of *involuntary* to that subclass of cases which involve purely physical, physiological, or psychological movements of our limbs, like reflexes and convulsions, movements in sleep, during sleepwalking, or under hypnosis, or due to some disease of the brain, lunacy, or automatism." Alan R. White, *Grounds of Liability* 60–61 (1985).

involuntary alienation. See ALIENATION.

involuntary bailment. See BAILMENT.

involuntary bankruptcy. See BANKRUPTCY.

involuntary confession. See CONFESSION.

involuntary conversion. See CONVERSION (2).

involuntary conveyance. See *involuntary alienation* under ALIENATION.

involuntary deposit. See DEPOSIT (6).

involuntary dismissal. See DISMISSAL (1).

involuntary dissolution. See DISSOLUTION.

involuntary euthanasia. See EUTHANASIA.

involuntary gap claim. See CLAIM (5).

involuntary intoxication. See INTOXICATION.

involuntary lien. See LIEN.

involuntary manslaughter. See MANSLAUGHTER.

involuntary payment. See PAYMENT.

involuntary petition. See PETITION.

involuntary servitude. See SERVITUDE (3).

involuntary stranding. See *accidental stranding* under STRANDING.

involuntary suretyship. See SURETYSHIP.

involuntary trust. See *constructive trust* under TRUST.

in witness whereof. The traditional beginning of the concluding clause (termed the *testimonium clause*) of a will or deed. See TESTIMONIUM CLAUSE.

IOLTA (I-**ohl**-tə). *abbr.* INTEREST ON LAWYERS' TRUST ACCOUNTS.

IOU (I-oh-**yoo**). [abbr. "I owe you"] **1.** A memorandum acknowledging a debt. **2.** The debt itself. — Also termed *due-bill.*

IP. *abbr.* INTELLECTUAL PROPERTY.

IPO. See *initial public offering* under OFFERING.

ipse (**ip**-see). [Latin "he himself"] The same; the very person.

ipse dixit (**ip**-see **dik**-sit). [Latin "he himself said it"] Something asserted but not proved <his testimony that she was a liar was nothing more than an *ipse dixit*>.

ipsissima verba (ip-**sis**-ə-mə **vər**-bə). [Latin "the very (same) words"] The exact words used by somebody being quoted <on its face, the *ipsissima verba* of the statute supports the plaintiff's position on the ownership issue>.

ipso facto (**ip**-soh **fak**-toh). [Latin "by the fact itself"] By the very nature of the situation <if 25% of all contractual litigation is caused by faulty drafting, then, *ipso facto*, the profession needs to improve its drafting skills>.

ipso facto clause. A contract clause that specifies the consequences of a party's bankruptcy. — Also termed *bankruptcy clause.*

ipso jure (**ip**-soh **joor**-ee). [Latin "by the law itself"] By the operation of the law itself <despite the parties' actions, the property will revert to the state, *ipso jure*, on May 1>.

IRA (I-ahr-**ay** *or* I-rə). *abbr.* INDIVIDUAL RETIREMENT ACCOUNT.

IRAC (I-rak). A mnemonic acronym used mostly by law students and their writing instructors, esp. as a method of answering essay questions on law exams. • The acronym is commonly said to stand for either (1) issue, rule, application, conclusion, or (2) issue, rule, analysis, conclusion.

ira motus (I-rə **moh**-təs), *adj.* [Latin] Moved or excited by anger or passion. • This term was formerly used in the plea of *son assault demesne.*

IRC. *abbr.* INTERNAL REVENUE CODE.

I.R.D. See *income in respect of a decedent* under INCOME.

ire ad largum (I-ree ad **lahr**-gəm), *vb.* [Latin] To go at large; i.e., to be released from judicial restraint.

iron-safe clause. A provision in a fire-insurance policy requiring the insured to preserve the books and inventory records of a business in a fireproof safe.

IRR. See *internal rate of return* under RATE OF RETURN.

irrational, *adj.* Not guided by reason or by a fair consideration of the facts <an irrational ruling>. See ARBITRARY.

irrebuttable presumption. See *conclusive presumption* under PRESUMPTION.

irreconcilable differences. Persistent and unresolvable disagreements between spouses. • These differences may be cited — without specifics — as grounds for no-fault divorce. Cf. IRRETRIEVABLE BREAKDOWN OF THE MARRIAGE.

irrecusable, *adj.* (Of an obligation) that cannot be avoided, although made without one's consent, as the obligation to not strike another without some lawful excuse. Cf. RECUSABLE.

irredeemable bond. See *annuity bond* under BOND (3).

irrefragable (i-**ref**-rə-gə-bəl), *adj.* Unanswerable; not to be controverted; impossible to refute <the defense feebly responded to the prosecution's irrefragable arguments>.

irregular, *adj.* Not in accordance with law, method, or usage; not regular.

irregular indorsement. See INDORSEMENT.

irregularity. 1. Something irregular; esp., an act or practice that varies from the normal conduct of an action. **2.** *Eccles. law.* An impediment to clerical office.

irregular judgment. See JUDGMENT.

irregular process. See PROCESS (2).

irregular succession. See SUCCESSION (2).

irrelevance, *n.* **1.** The quality or state of being inapplicable to a matter under consideration. — Also termed *irrelevancy.* **2.** IRRELEVANCY.

irrelevancy, *n.* **1.** Something not relevant. — Also termed *irrelevance.* **2.** IRRELEVANCE.

irrelevant (i-**rel**-ə-vənt), *adj.* (Of evidence) having no probative value; not tending to prove or disprove a matter in issue. — **irrelevance,** *n.* Cf. IMMATERIAL.

irremediable breakdown of the marriage. See IRRETRIEVABLE BREAKDOWN OF THE MARRIAGE.

irreparable damages. See DAMAGES.

irreparable harm. See *irreparable injury* under INJURY.

irreparable injury. See INJURY.

irreparable-injury rule (i-**rep**-ə-rə-bəl). The principle that equitable relief (such as an injunction) is available only when no adequate legal remedy (such as monetary damages) exists. • Although this rule is one that courts continue to cite, the courts do not usu. follow it literally in practice. — Also termed *adequacy test*.

"The irreparable injury rule has received considerable scholarly attention. In 1978, Owen Fiss examined the possible reasons for the rule and found them wanting. A vigorous debate over the economic wisdom of applying the rule to specific performance of contracts began about the same time, and soon came to center on the transaction costs of administering the two remedies. Both Fiss and Dan Dobbs have noted that the rule does not seem to be taken very seriously, and in a review of Fiss's book, I argued that the definition of adequacy pulls most of the rule's teeth. The Restatement (Second) of Torts dropped the rule from the blackletter and condemned it as misleading, but replaced it only with a long and unstructured list of factors to be considered.... [M]any sophisticated lawyers believe that the rule continues to reflect a serious preference for legal over equitable remedies." Douglas Laycock, *The Death of the Irreparable Injury Rule* 9 (1991).

irrepleviable (i-rə-**plev**-ee-ə-bəl), *adj.* (Of property) not capable of being replevied. — Formerly also spelled *irreplevisable*. Cf. REPLEVIABLE.

irresistible force. See FORCE.

irresistible-impulse test. *Criminal law.* A test for insanity, holding that a person is not criminally responsible for an act if mental disease prevented that person from controlling potentially criminal conduct. • The few jurisdictions that have adopted this test have combined it with the *McNaghten* rules. — Also termed *control test*; *volitional test*. See INSANITY DEFENSE; MCNAGHTEN RULES.

"The first reaction of the legal profession to the irresistible impulse defense, when it was introduced to the law many years ago, was inclined to be favorable. Then a change set in and for many years the prevailing view was strongly against its recognition. Present indications are that the tide is changing again. There seems to be a growing belief to the effect that ignoring the possibility of such a defense fails to give full recognition to the fundamental concept of mens rea." Rollin M. Perkins & Ronald N. Boyce, *Criminal Law* 975 (3d ed. 1982).

irretrievable breakdown of the marriage. A ground for divorce that is based on incompatibility between marriage partners and that is used in many states as the sole ground of no-fault divorce. — Also termed *irretrievable breakdown*; *irremediable breakdown of the marriage*. Cf. IRRECONCILABLE DIFFERENCES.

irrevocable (i-**rev**-ə-kə-bəl), *adj.* Unalterable; committed beyond recall. — **irrevocability,** *n.*

irrevocable guaranty. See GUARANTY.

irrevocable letter of credit. See LETTER OF CREDIT.

irrevocable offer. See OFFER.

irrevocable power of attorney. See POWER OF ATTORNEY.

irrevocable trust. See TRUST.

irrogare (i-rə-**gair**-ee), *vb.* [Latin] *Civil law.* To inflict a penalty; to make or ordain, as a law.

irrotulatio (i-rah-chə-**lay**-shee-oh). [Law Latin] An enrollment; an entry on a record.

IRS. *abbr.* INTERNAL REVENUE SERVICE.

island. A tract of land surrounded by water but smaller than a continent; esp., land that is continually surrounded by water and not submerged except during abnormal circumstances.

ISO. *abbr.* Incentive stock option. See STOCK OPTION (2).

isolated sale. See SALE.

is qui cognoscit (is kwI cog-**nos**-it). [Latin "he who recognizes"] The cognizor in a fine. See COGNIZOR.

is qui cognoscitur (is kwI cog-**nos**-ə-tər). [Latin "he who is recognized"] A cognizee in a fine. See COGNIZEE.

issuable, *adj.* **1.** Capable of being issued <an issuable writ>. **2.** Open to dispute or contention <an issuable argument>. **3.** Possible as an outcome <an award as high as $5 million is issuable in this case>.

issuable defense. See DEFENSE (1).

issuable plea. See PLEA (3).

issue, *n.* **1.** A point in dispute between two or more parties.

"In federal civil procedure, an issue is a single, certain, and material point arising out of the allegations and contentions of the parties; it is matter affirmed on one side and denied on the other, and when a fact is alleged in the complaint and denied in the answer, the matter is then put in issue between the parties." 35A C.J.S. *Federal Civil Procedure* § 357, at 541 (1960).

collateral issue. A question or issue not directly connected with the matter in dispute.

deep issue. The fundamental issue to be decided by a court in ruling on a point of law.

> "Essentially, a deep issue is the ultimate, concrete question that a court needs to answer to decide a point your way. *Deep* refers to the deep structure of the case — not to deep thinking. The deep issue is the final question you pose when you can no longer usefully ask the follow-up question, 'And what does *that* turn on?'" Bryan A. Garner, *The Winning Brief* 49 (1999).

general issue. **1.** A plea (often a general denial) by which a party denies the truth of every material allegation in an opposing party's pleading. **2.** The issue arising from such a plea.

> "The general issue is a denial of the legal conclusion sought to be drawn from the declaration. It denies by a general form of expression the defendant's liability, and enables the defendant to contest, without specific averments of the defense to be asserted, most of the allegations which the plaintiff may be required to prove to sustain his action, and in some actions to raise also various affirmative defenses. It fails to perform the functions of pleading, either in giving notice or in reducing the case to specific issues." Benjamin J. Shipman, *Handbook of Common-Law Pleading* § 169, at 304 (Henry Winthrop Ballantine ed., 3d ed. 1923).

immaterial issue. An issue not necessary to decide the point of law.

issue of fact. A point supported by one party's evidence and controverted by another's.

issue of law. A point on which the evidence is undisputed, the outcome depending on the court's interpretation of the law.

legal issue. A legal question, usu. at the foundation of a case and requiring a court's decision.

special issue. **1.** At common law, an issue arising from a specific allegation in a pleading. • Special issues are no longer used in most jurisdictions. **2.** See *special interrogatory* under INTERROGATORY.

ultimate issue. A not-yet-decided point that is sufficient either in itself or in connection with other points to resolve the entire case.

2. A class or series of securities that are simultaneously offered for sale. See OFFERING.

hot issue. A security that, after an initial or secondary offering, is traded in the open market at a substantially higher price. — Also termed *hot stock*.

new issue. A stock or bond sold by a corporation for the first time, often to raise working capital. See BLUE-SKY LAW.

original issue. The first issue of securities of a particular type or series.

shelf issue. An issue of securities that were previously registered but not released at the time of registration.

3. *Wills & estates.* Lineal descendants; offspring.

lawful issue. Descendants, including descendants more remote than children. • At common law, the term included only those who were children of legally recognized subsisting marriages. See DESCENDENT; HEIR.

4. *Commercial law.* The first delivery of a negotiable instrument by its maker or holder.

issue, *vb.* **1.** To accrue <rents issuing from land> **2.** To be put forth officially <without probable cause, the search warrant will not issue> **3.** To send out or distribute officially <issue process> <issue stock>.

issued stock. See STOCK.

issue estoppel. See COLLATERAL ESTOPPEL.

issue of fact. See ISSUE (1).

issue of law. See ISSUE (1).

issue pleading. See PLEADING (2).

issue preclusion. See COLLATERAL ESTOPPEL.

issuer. **1.** A person or entity (such as a corporation or bank) that issues securities, negotiable instruments, or letters of credit. **2.** A bailee that issues negotiable or nonnegotiable documents of title.

nonreporting issuer. An issuer not subject to the reporting requirements of the Exchange Act because it (1) has not voluntarily become subject to the reporting requirements, (2) has not had an effective registration statement under the Securities Act within the fiscal year, and (3) did not, at the end of its last fiscal year, meet the shareholder or asset tests under the Exchange Act registration requirements.

issue roll. *Hist. English law.* A court record on which the issues in contested matters are briefly noted. • This practice was abolished in 1834. See INCIPITUR.

ita lex scripta est (I-tə leks **skrip**-tə est). [Latin] So the law is written. • This expression means that the law must be obeyed despite the apparent rigor of its application. The idea is that we must be content with the law as it stands, without inquiring into its reasons. — Sometimes shortened to *ita scripta est* ["so it is written"].

> "If practice be the whole he is taught, practice must also be the whole he will ever know: if he be uninstructed in the elements and first principles upon which the rule of practice is founded, the least variation from established precedents will totally distract and bewilder him: *ita lex scripta est* is the utmost his knowledge will arrive at; he must never aspire to form, and seldom expect to comprehend, any arguments drawn *a priori*, from the spirit of the laws and the natural foundations of justice." 1 William Blackstone, *Commentaries on the Laws of England* 32 (1765).

ita te Deus adjuvet (I-tə tee **dee**-əs **aj**-ə-vet). [Latin] So help you God. • An old form of administering an oath in England, usu. in connection with other words, such as: *Ita te Deus adjuvet, et sacrosancta Dei Evangelia* ("So help you God, and God's holy gospels"), and *Ita te Deus adjuvet et omnes sancti* ("So help you God and all the saints").

item. 1. A piece of a whole, not necessarily separated. **2.** *Commercial law.* A negotiable instrument or a promise or order to pay money handled by a bank for collection or payment. • The term does not include a payment order governed by division 11 of the UCC or a credit- or debit-card slip. UCC 4–104(a)(9).

par item. An item that a drawee bank will remit to another bank without charge.

3. In drafting, a subpart of text that is the next smaller unit than a subparagraph. • In federal drafting, for example, "(4)" is the item in the following citation: Rule 19(a)(1)(B)(4). — Also termed (in sense 3) *clause.*

itemize, *vb.* To list in detail; to state by items <an itemized bill>.

itemized deduction. See DEDUCTION.

item veto. See *line-item veto* under VETO.

iter (I-tər *or* **it**-ər). [Latin] **1.** *Roman law.* A servitude that allows the holder to walk or ride on horseback (but not drive a draft animal) through another's land. Cf. ACTUS (3); VIA (2). **2.** *Hist.* A journey; esp., a circuit made by an eyre justice. See EYRE.

itinerate (I-**tin**-ə-rayt), *vb.* (Of a judge) to travel on a circuit for the purpose of holding court. — **itineration,** *n.* — **itinerant,** *adj.* & *n.* See CIRCUIT.

itinerate vendor. See VENDOR.

iudex (**yoo**-deks). [Latin] See JUDEX.

ius (yəs *or* yoos). [Latin "law, right"] See JUS.

ius praetorium. See LEX PRAETORIUM.

ius primae noctis. See MARCHETUM.

iustae nuptiae. See JUSTAE NUPTIAE.

J

J. *abbr.* **1.** JUDGE. **2.** JUSTICE (2). **3.** JUDGMENT. **4.** JUS. **5.** JOURNAL.

JA. *abbr.* **1.** JUDGE ADVOCATE. **2.** See *joint account* under ACCOUNT.

Jac. *abbr.* Jacobus — the Latin form of the name *James*, used principally in citing statutes enacted during the reigns of English kings of that name (e.g., "St. 1, Jac. 2").

jacens (**jay**-senz). [Latin] Lying; fallen; in abeyance. See *hereditas jacens* under HEREDITAS.

Jackson–Denno **hearing.** A court proceeding held outside the jury's presence to determine whether the defendant's confession was voluntary and therefore admissible as evidence. *Jackson v. Denno*, 378 U.S. 368, 84 S.Ct. 1774 (1964). — Also termed *Jackson v. Denno hearing*.

Jackson **standard.** *Criminal law.* The principle that the standard of review on appeal — when a criminal defendant claims that there is insufficient evidence to support the conviction — is to determine whether, after considering the evidence in the light most favorable to the prosecution, any rational trier of fact could have found the essential elements of the crime beyond a reasonable doubt. *Jackson v. Virginia*, 443 U.S. 307, 99 S.Ct. 2781 (1979).

Jackson v. Denno **hearing.** See JACKSON–DENNO HEARING.

jactitation (jak-ti-**tay**-shən). **1.** A false boasting or claim that causes injury to another. **2.** *Civil law.* SLANDER OF TITLE.

jactitation of marriage. *Hist.* **1.** False and actionable boasting or claiming that one is married to another. **2.** An action against a person who falsely boasts of being married to the complainant.

> "Jactitation of marriage is a cause of action which arises when a person falsely alleges that he or she is married to the petitioner, and the remedy sought is a perpetual injunction against the respondent to cease making such allegations. The cause is now uncommon in English municipal law and almost unknown in the conflict of laws." R.H. Graveson, *Conflict of Laws* 349 (7th ed. 1974).

jactura (jak-**t**[**y**]**oor**-ə), *n.* [Latin] *Civil law.* **1.** A throwing of goods overboard to lighten or save a vessel; JETTISON. **2.** A loss incurred from this; general average. See *general average* under AVERAGE. — Also termed *jactus*.

JAG. *abbr.* JUDGE ADVOCATE GENERAL.

JAG Manual. See MANUAL OF THE JUDGE ADVOCATE GENERAL.

jail, *n.* A place where persons awaiting trial or those convicted of misdemeanors are confined. — Also spelled (esp. in BrE) *gaol.* — Also termed *holding cell*; *lockup*; *jailhouse.* — **jail,** *vb.* Cf. PRISON.

jail credit. Time spent by a criminal defendant in confinement awaiting trial. • This time is usu. deducted from the defendant's final sentence (if convicted).

jail delivery. **1.** An escape by several prisoners from a jail. **2.** *Hist.* A clearing procedure by which all prisoners at a given jail are tried for the offenses that they are accused of having committed. **3.** *Hist.* The commission issued to judges of assize, directing them to clear a jail by trying — and either acquitting or condemning — all the inmates. **4.** *Archaic.* The court charged with the trial of all ordinary criminal cases. See COMMISSION OF GAOL DELIVERY.

general jail delivery. Collectively, acquittals in high numbers as a result of either lax or reckless administration of the law or defects in the law.

jailer. A keeper, guard, or warden of a prison or jail. — Also spelled (esp. in BrE) *gaoler.*

jailhouse. See JAIL.

jailhouse lawyer. A prison inmate who seeks release through legal procedures or who gives legal advice to other inmates. — Also termed *guardhouse lawyer.*

jail liberties. Bounds within which a jail or prison lies and throughout which certain prisoners are allowed to move freely, usu. after giving bond for the liberties. • The bounds are considered an extension of the prison walls. Historically, jail liberties were given in England to those imprisoned for debt. The prisoners were allowed to move freely within the city in which the prison was located. — Also spelled *gaol liberties*. — Also termed *jail limits*.

> "[S]tatutes were from time to time passed enlarging the gaol liberties, in order to mitigate the hardships of imprisonment: thus, the whole city of Boston was held the 'gaol liberties' of its county gaol. And so with a large part of New York City.... The prisoner, while within the limits, is considered as within the walls of the prison." 1 John Bouvier, *Bouvier's Law Dictionary* 1333–34 (8th ed. 1914).

Jamaican switch. An illegal scheme whereby one conspirator convinces the victim of a need for help in handling a large sum of money, usu. by claiming to have found the money or by claiming to be an unsophisticated foreigner, and promises to share part of the money with the victim or asks the victim for help in finding a suitable charity to donate to, at which time the other conspirator appears and promises to assist if both the victim and first conspirator provide good-faith money, the intent being for the two conspirators to leave with all the money, including the victim's.

***James* hearing.** A court proceeding held to determine whether the out-of-court statements of a coconspirator should be admitted into evidence, by analyzing whether there was a conspiracy, whether the declarant and the defendant were part of the conspiracy, and whether the statement was made in furtherance of the conspiracy. *United States v. James*, 590 F.2d 575 (5th Cir. 1979); Fed. R. Evid. 801(d)(2)(E).

Jane Doe. A fictitious name for a female party to a legal proceeding, used because the party's true identity is unknown or because her real name is being withheld. — Also termed *Jane Roe*; *Mary Major*. Cf. JOHN DOE.

Janus-faced (**jay**-nəs-fayst), *adj*. Having two contrasting or contradictory aspects; two-faced <a Janus-faced plea>.

***Jason* clause.** *Maritime law*. A bill-of-lading clause requiring contribution in general average even when the loss is the result of the carrier's negligence, for which the carrier is otherwise exempt from liability by statute. • The clause is named after the Supreme Court case that upheld its enforceability, *The Jason*, 225 U.S. 32, 32 S.Ct. 560 (1912). See *general average* under AVERAGE.

jaywalking, *n*. The act or instance of crossing a street without heeding traffic regulations, as by crossing between intersections or at a place other than a crosswalk. — **jaywalk,** *vb*.

JCP. *abbr*. Justice of the Common Pleas. See COURT OF COMMON PLEAS.

J.D. *abbr*. JURIS DOCTOR.

Jedburgh justice (**jed**-bər-ə). See JUSTICE (1).

Jeddart justice (**jed**-ərt). See *Jedburgh justice* under JUSTICE (1).

jedge and warrant (jej). *Scots law*. The authority given by the Dean of Guild to rebuild or repair a dilapidated tenement.

Jedwood justice (**jed**-wəd). See *Jedburgh justice* under JUSTICE (1).

***Jencks* material.** *Criminal procedure*. A prosecution witness's written or recorded pretrial statement that a criminal defendant, upon filing a motion after the witness has testified, is entitled to have in preparing to cross-examine the witness. • The defense may use a statement of this kind for impeachment purposes. *Jencks v. United States*, 353 U.S. 657, 77 S.Ct. 1007 (1957); Jencks Act, 18 USCA § 3500. Cf. BRADY MATERIAL.

***Jensen* doctrine.** The principle that the states may not apply their workers'-compensation statutes to maritime workers injured on navigable waters while performing traditional maritime duties. *Southern Pac. Co. v. Jensen*, 244 U.S. 205, 37 S.Ct. 524 (1917).

jeofail (**jef**-ayl), *n*. [fr. French *j'ay faillé*] *Archaic*. **1.** An error or oversight in pleading. **2.** The acknowledgment of such an error. — Also spelled *jeofaile*.

jeopardy. The risk of conviction and punishment that a criminal defendant faces at trial. • Jeopardy attaches in a jury trial when the jury is empaneled, and in a bench trial when the first witness is sworn. — Also termed *legal jeopardy*. See DOUBLE JEOPARDY.

jeopardy assessment. See ASSESSMENT.

jetsam (**jet**-səm). Goods that, after being abandoned at sea, sink and remain underwater. Cf. FLOTSAM; LAGAN; WAVESON.

jettison (**jet**-ə-sən), *n. Maritime law.* The act of voluntarily throwing cargo overboard to lighten or stabilize a ship that is in immediate danger. — Also termed *jactura.* — **jettison,** *vb.* See *general average* under AVERAGE.

jeux de bourse (**zhoo** də **bərs**), *n.* [French "games of the stock exchange"] Speculation in stocks or bonds, as by dealing in options or futures.

***Jewell* instruction** (**joo**-wəl). *Criminal procedure.* A court's instruction to the jury that the defendant can be found to have the requisite criminal mental state despite being deliberately ignorant of some of the facts surrounding the crime. • If a defendant claims ignorance of some fact essential to the crime, such as not knowing that a particular bag contained drugs, but the surrounding circumstances would put a reasonable person on notice that there was a high probability of illegality, as when the defendant has taken the bag from a known drug-dealer and has noticed the smell of marijuana coming from the bag, then the court may instruct the jury that it is entitled to infer the defendant's guilty knowledge if the defendant deliberately avoided knowledge of the critical facts. *United States v. Jewell*, 532 F.2d 697 (9th Cir. 1976). — Also termed *deliberate-indifference instruction.*

Jim Crow law. *Hist.* A law enacted or purposely interpreted to discriminate against blacks, such as a law requiring separate restrooms for blacks and whites. • Jim Crow laws are unconstitutional under the 14th Amendment.

jingle rule. See DUAL-PRIORITIES RULE.

JJ. *abbr.* **1.** Judges. **2.** Justices.

J.N. *abbr.* JOHN-A-NOKES.

JNOV. *abbr.* Judgment *non obstante veredicto.* See *judgment notwithstanding the verdict* under JUDGMENT.

job action. *Labor law.* A concerted, temporary action by employees (such as a sickout or work slowdown), intended to pressure management to concede to the employees' demands without resorting to a strike. See STRIKE.

jobber, *n.* **1.** One who buys from a manufacturer and sells to a retailer; a wholesaler or middleman. **2.** A middleman in the exchange of securities among brokers. — Also termed *stockjobber; stock-jobber.* **3.** One who works by the job; a contractor. — **job,** *vb.*

jobber's agreement. See HAZANTOWN AGREEMENT.

jobbery, *n.* The practice or act of perverting a public service in a way that serves private ends; unfair means to serve private interests.

job security. Protection of an employee's job, often through a union contract.

job-targeting program. An initiative by a labor union to maintain or improve its share of the labor in a particular market by financing or backing contractors who bid on targeted projects. — Also termed *market-recovery program.*

jocus partitus (**joh**-kəs pahr-**tɪ**-təs), *n.* [Law Latin "divided game"] *Hist.* A gambling arrangement made by the parties on a lawsuit's outcome.

John-a-Nokes. *Archaic.* A fictitious name for an unknown party to a legal proceeding, esp. the first party. • The name is short for "John who dwells at the oak." — Abbr. J.N. — Also spelled *John-a-Noakes.*

John-a-Stiles. *Archaic.* A fictitious name for an unknown party to a legal proceeding, esp. the second party. • The name is short for "John who dwells at the stile." — Abbr. J.S. — Also spelled *John-a-Styles.*

John Doe. A fictitious name used in a legal proceeding to designate a person whose identity is unknown, to protect a person's known identity, or to indicate that a true defendant does not exist. Cf. JANE DOE; RICHARD ROE.

> "Sheriffs in time growing remiss in their duty, allowed of any persons as *pledges*, sometimes returning the names of fictitious persons as *pledges*, at others, neglecting to require or return any at all.... And the legislature, to supply the want of real persons as *pledges*, and recompense the defendant where he has been unjustly or vexatiously sued, has by various statutes, either given him the costs he has incurred in making his defence; or else deprived the plaintiff of recovering those costs he is entitled to by law, in cases of obtaining a verdict, by leaving it to the judge at the trial to certify on the record, that he had little or no cause of action. Since these statutes for allowing the defendant his costs, where the plaintiff fails, or is nonsuited, the writ to the coroner to affeer the *pledges* has fallen into disuse, and two good-

natured personages, *John Doe* and *Richard Roe*, from their universal acquaintance and peculiar longevity, have become the ready and common *pledges* of every suitor." 1 George Crompton, *Rules and Cases of Practice in the Courts of King's Bench and Common Pleas* xlvii (3d ed. 1787).

"The fictitious names *John Doe* and *Richard Roe* regularly appeared in actions of ejectment ... at common law. *Doe* was the nominal plaintiff, who by a fiction was said to have entered land under a valid lease; *Roe* was said to have ejected *Doe*, and the lawsuit took the title *Doe v. Roe*. These fictional allegations disappeared upon the enactment of the Common Law Procedure Act of 1852.... Beyond actions of ejectment, and esp. in the U.S., *John Doe*, *Jane Doe*, *Richard Roe*, *Jane Roe*, and *Peter Poe* have come to identify a party to a lawsuit whose true name is either unknown or purposely shielded." Bryan A. Garner, *A Dictionary of Modern Legal Usage* 290–91 (2d ed. 1995).

John Doe summons. See SUMMONS.

joinder, *n.* The uniting of parties or claims in a single lawsuit. — **join,** *vb.* Cf. CONSOLIDATION (4).

collusive joinder. Joinder of a defendant, usu. a nonresident, in order to have a case removed to federal court. See *manufactured diversity* under DIVERSITY OF CITIZENSHIP.

compulsory joinder. The necessary joinder of a party if either of the following is true: (1) in that party's absence, those already involved in the lawsuit cannot receive complete relief; or (2) the absence of such a party, claiming an interest in the subject of an action, might either impair the protection of that interest or leave some other party subject to multiple or inconsistent obligations. Fed. R. Civ. P. 19(a). — Also termed *mandatory joinder.*

fraudulent joinder. The bad-faith joinder of a party, usu. a resident of the state, to prevent removal of a case to federal court.

joinder in demurrer. *Common-law pleading.* A set form of words by which either party accepts or joins in a legal issue; esp., the plaintiff's acceptance of the defendant's issue of law.

joinder in issue. See *joinder of issue.*

joinder in pleading. *Common-law pleading.* One party's acceptance of the opposing party's proposed issue and mode of trial.

joinder of error. A written denial of the errors alleged in an assignment of errors in a criminal case.

joinder of issue. **1.** The submission of an issue jointly for decision. **2.** The acceptance or adoption of a disputed point as the basis of argument in a controversy. — Also termed *joinder in issue.* **3.** The taking up of the opposite side of a case, or of the contrary view on a question.

joinder of offenses. The charging of an accused with two or more crimes as multiple counts in a single indictment or information. • Unless later severed, joined offenses are tried together at a single trial. Fed. R. Crim. P. 8(a).

joinder of remedies. The joinder of alternative claims, such as breach of contract and quantum meruit, or of one claim with another prospective claim, such as a creditor's claim against a debtor to recover on a loan and the creditor's claim against a third party to set aside the transfer of the loan's collateral.

mandatory joinder. See *compulsory joinder.*

misjoinder. See MISJOINDER.

nonjoinder. See NONJOINDER.

permissive joinder. The optional joinder of parties if (1) their claims or the claims asserted against them are asserted jointly, severally, or in respect of the same transaction or occurrence, and (2) any legal or factual question common to all of them will arise. Fed. R. Civ. P. 20.

joinder in demurrer. See JOINDER.

joinder in issue. See *joinder of issue* (2) under JOINDER.

joinder in pleading. See JOINDER.

joinder of error. See JOINDER.

joinder of issue. See JOINDER.

joinder of offenses. See JOINDER.

joinder of remedies. See JOINDER.

joint, *adj.* **1.** (Of a thing) common to or shared by two or more persons or entities <joint bank account>. **2.** (Of a person or entity) combined, united, or sharing with another <joint heirs>.

joint account. See ACCOUNT.

joint action. See ACTION.

joint activity. See JOINT PARTICIPATION.

joint administration. *Bankruptcy.* The management of two or more bankruptcy estates, usu. involving related debtors, under one docket for purposes of handling various administrative matters, including notices to creditors, to conclude the cases more efficiently. • A bankruptcy court can order a joint administration when there are two or more cases pending involving a husband and wife, a partnership and at least one partner, two or more business partners, or a business and an affiliate. The intent should be to increase the administrative efficiency of administering the two cases; the substantive rights of creditors should not ordinarily be affected. Fed. R. Bankr. P. 1015. — Also termed *procedural consolidation.* Cf. *substantive consolidation* under CONSOLIDATION.

joint adventure. See JOINT VENTURE.

joint and mutual will. See WILL.

joint and reciprocal will. See *joint and mutual will* under WILL.

joint and several, *adj.* (Of liability, responsibility, etc.) apportionable either among two or more parties or to only one or a few select members of the group, at the adversary's discretion; together and in separation.

joint and several bond. See BOND (3).

joint and several liability. See LIABILITY.

joint and several note. See NOTE (1).

joint-and-survivorship account. See *joint account* under ACCOUNT.

joint annuity. See ANNUITY.

joint authors. *Copyright.* Two or more authors who collaborate in producing a copyrightable work, each author intending to merge his or her respective contributions into a single work, and each being able to exploit the work as desired while remaining accountable for a pro rata share of the profits to the coauthor or coauthors.

joint ballot. See BALLOT (3).

joint board. *Labor law.* A committee — usu. made up of an equal number of representatives from management and the union — established to conduct grievance proceedings or resolve grievances.

joint bond. See BOND (3).

joint-check rule. The principle that, when an owner or general contractor issues a check that is made jointly payable to a subcontractor and the subcontractor's materialman, the materialman's indorsement on the check certifies that it has been paid all amounts due to it, up to the amount of the check. • This rule protects the owner or general contractor from lien foreclosure by a materialman who was not paid by the subcontractor. By issuing a joint check, the owner or general contractor is not left merely to hope that the subcontractor pays all the materialmen. And the materialman is protected because it can refuse to indorse the check until it is satisfied that the subcontractor will pay it the appropriate amount.

joint committee. See COMMITTEE.

joint contract. See CONTRACT.

joint covenant. See COVENANT (1).

joint creditor. See CREDITOR.

joint custody. See CUSTODY (2).

joint debtor. See DEBTOR.

joint defendant. See CODEFENDANT.

joint-defense privilege. See PRIVILEGE (3).

joint demise. See DEMISE.

joint employment. See EMPLOYMENT.

joint enterprise. 1. *Criminal law.* An undertaking by two or more persons who set out to commit an offense they have conspired to commit. See CONSPIRACY. **2.** *Torts.* An undertaking by two or more persons with an equal right to direct and benefit from the endeavor, as a result of which one participant's negligence may be imputed to the others. — Also termed (in senses 1 and 2) *common enterprise.* **3.** JOINT VENTURE. **4.** A joint venture for noncommercial purposes.

> "A business relationship is needed for a joint venture but not for a joint enterprise. Thus, a joint enterprise may be defined as a non-commercial joint venture." 46 Am. Jur. 2d *Joint Ventures* § 6, at 27 (1994).

joint estate. See ESTATE.

joint executor. See EXECUTOR.

joint heir. See HEIR.

joint indictment. See INDICTMENT.

joint liability. See LIABILITY.

joint life insurance. See INSURANCE.

joint life policy. See INSURANCE POLICY.

joint mortgage. See MORTGAGE.

joint negligence. See NEGLIGENCE.

joint note. See NOTE (1).

joint obligation. See OBLIGATION.

joint offense. See OFFENSE (1).

joint ownership. See OWNERSHIP.

joint participation. *Civil-rights law.* A pursuit undertaken by a private person in concert with a governmental entity or state official, resulting in the private person's performing public functions and thereby being subject to claims under the civil-rights laws. — Also termed *joint activity.* See SYMBIOTIC-RELATIONSHIP TEST; NEXUS TEST.

joint rate. See RATE.

joint resolution. See RESOLUTION (1).

jointress. *Hist.* A woman who has a jointure. — Also termed *jointuress.* See JOINTURE (1).

joint return. See TAX RETURN.

joint session. See SESSION.

joint-stock association. See *joint-stock company* under COMPANY.

joint-stock company. See COMPANY.

joint tariff. See TARIFF (4).

joint tenancy. See TENANCY.

joint tortfeasors. See TORTFEASOR.

joint trespass. See TRESPASS.

joint trial. See TRIAL.

joint trustee. See COTRUSTEE.

jointure (**joyn**-chər). **1.** A woman's freehold life estate in land, made in consideration of marriage in lieu of dower and to be enjoyed by her only after her husband's death; a settlement under which a wife receives such an estate. • The four essential elements are that (1) the jointure must take effect immediately upon the husband's death, (2) it must be for the wife's own life, and not for another's life or for a term of years, (3) it must be held by her in her own right and not in trust for her, and (4) it must be in lieu of her entire dower. See DOWER. **2.** An estate in lands given jointly to a husband and wife before they marry. See JOINTRESS.

jointuress. See JOINTRESS.

joint venture. A business undertaking by two or more persons engaged in a single defined project. • The necessary elements are: (1) an express or implied agreement; (2) a common purpose that the group intends to carry out; (3) shared profits and losses; and (4) each member's equal voice in controlling the project. — Also termed *joint adventure*; *joint enterprise.* Cf. PARTNERSHIP; STRATEGIC ALLIANCE.

> "There is some difficulty in determining when the legal relationship of joint venture exists, with authorities disagreeing as to the essential elements.... The joint venture is not as much of an entity as is a partnership." Henry G. Henn & John R. Alexander, *Laws of Corporations* § 49, at 106 (3d ed. 1983).

joint-venture corporation. See CORPORATION.

joint verdict. See VERDICT.

joint welfare fund. See FUND (1).

joint will. See WILL.

joker. **1.** An ambiguous clause inserted in a legislative bill to render it inoperative or uncertain in some respect without arousing opposition at the time of passage. **2.** A rider or amendment that is extraneous to the subject of the bill.

Jones Act. *Maritime law.* A federal statute that allows a seaman injured during the course of employment to recover damages for the injuries in a negligence action against the employer. • If a seaman dies from such injuries, the seaman's personal representative may maintain an action against the employer. 46 USCA app. § 688.

Jones Act vessel. See VESSEL.

jour (zhoor), *n.* [French] Day <*jour en banc*>.

journal. 1. A book or record kept usu. daily, as of the proceedings of a legislature or the events of a ship's voyage. **2.** *Accounting.* In double-entry bookkeeping, a book in which original entries are recorded before being transferred to a ledger. **3.** A periodical or magazine, esp. one published for a scholarly or professional group. — Abbr. J.

journal entry. See ENTRY (2).

journalist's privilege. See PRIVILEGE (3).

journal of notarial acts (noh-**tair**-ee-əl). The notary public's sequential record of notarial transactions, usu. a bound book listing the date, time, and type of each official act, the type of instrument acknowledged or verified before the notary, the signature of each person whose signature is notarized, the type of information used to verify the identity of parties whose signatures are notarized, and the fee charged. • This journal, required by law in most states, provides a record that may be used as evidence in court. — Also termed *notarial record*; *notarial register*; *notary record book*; *sequential journal*.

journeys accounts. *Hist.* The number of days (usu. 15) after the abatement of a writ within which a new writ could be obtained. • This number was based on how many days it took for the plaintiff to travel (or *journey*) to the court.

joyriding, *n.* The illegal driving of someone else's automobile without permission, but with no intent to deprive the owner of it permanently. — Also termed *unauthorized use of a vehicle*. — **joyride,** *vb.* — **joyrider,** *n.*

> "When the automobile began to appear and was limited to the possession of a few of the more fortunate members of the community, many persons who ordinarily respected the property rights of others, yielded to the temptation to drive one of these new contrivances without the consent of the owner. This became so common that the term 'joyrider' was coined to refer to the person who indulged in such unpermitted use of another's car. For the most part it was a relatively harmless type of trespass . . . ." Rollin M. Perkins & Ronald N. Boyce, *Criminal Law* 333 (3d ed. 1982).

J.P. *abbr.* JUSTICE OF THE PEACE.

J.P. court. See *justice court* under COURT.

J.S. *abbr.* JOHN-A-STILES.

J.S.D. [Law Latin *juris scientiae doctor*] *abbr.* DOCTOR OF JURIDICAL SCIENCE.

jubere (juu-**beer**-ee), *vb.* [Latin] *Civil law.* **1.** To order, direct, or command. **2.** To assure or promise.

J.U.D. [Law Latin *juris utriusque doctor* "doctor of both laws"] A title given to a doctor of both civil and canon law.

judex (**joo**-deks), *n.* [Latin] **1.** *Roman law.* A private person appointed by a praetor or other magistrate to hear and decide a case. • The Roman judex was originally drawn from a panel of qualified persons of standing but was later himself a magistrate. **2.** *Roman & civil law.* A judge. **3.** *Hist.* A juror. — Also spelled *iudex*. Pl. **judices** (**joo**-di-seez).

judex ad quem (ad **kwem**). *Civil law.* A judge to whom an appeal is taken.

judex a quo (ay **kwoh**). *Civil law.* A judge from whom an appeal is taken.

judex datus (**day**-təs). *Roman law.* A judex assigned by a magistrate or provincial governor to try a case.

judex delegatus (del-ə-**gay**-təs). *Civil law.* A delegated judge; a special judge.

judex fiscalis (fis-**kay**-lis). *Roman law.* A judex having jurisdiction of matters relating to the *fiscus*. See FISCUS (1).

judex ordinarius (or-də-**nair**-ee-əs). *Civil law.* A judge having jurisdiction in his own right rather than by delegated authority.

judex pedaneus (pə-**day**-nee-əs). *Roman law.* A judex to whom petty cases are delegated; an inferior or deputy judge. — Also termed *judex specialis*.

judex quaestionis (kwes-chee-**oh**-nis *or* kwes-tee-). *Roman law.* The chairman of the jury in a criminal case, normally a magistrate of lower rank than praetor.

judex selectus (sə-**lek**-təs). *Civil law.* A judge selected to hear the facts in a criminal case.

judex specialis (spesh-ee-**ay**-lis). *Roman law.* See *judex pedaneus*.

judge, *n.* A public official appointed or elected to hear and decide legal matters in court. — Abbr. J. (and, in plural, JJ.).

associate judge. An appellate judge who is neither a chief judge nor a presiding judge. — Also termed *puisne judge.*

chief judge. The judge who presides over the sessions and deliberations of a court, while also overseeing the administration of the court. — Abbr. C.J.

circuit judge. **1.** A judge who sits on a circuit court; esp., a federal judge who sits on a U.S. court of appeals. **2.** *Hist.* A special judge added to a court for the purpose of holding trials, but without being a regular member of the court. — Abbr. C.J.

city judge. See *municipal judge.*

continuing part-time judge. A judge who serves repeatedly on a part-time basis by election or under a continuing appointment.

county judge. A local judge having criminal or civil jurisdiction, or sometimes both, within a county.

de facto judge (di **fak**-toh). A judge operating under color of law but whose authority is procedurally defective, such as a judge appointed under an unconstitutional statute.

district judge. A judge in a federal or state judicial district. — Abbr. D.J.

hanging judge. A judge who is harsh with defendants, esp. those accused of capital crimes, and sometimes corruptly so.

judge of probate. See *probate judge.*

judge ordinary. *Hist.* The judge of the English Court for Divorce and Matrimonial Causes from 1857–1875.

judge pro tempore. See *visiting judge.*

lay judge. A judge who is not a lawyer.

municipal judge. A local judge having criminal or civil jurisdiction, or sometimes both, within a city. — Also termed *city judge.*

presiding judge. **1.** A judge in charge of a particular court or judicial district; esp., the senior active judge on a three-member panel that hears and decides cases. **2.** A chief judge. — Abbr. P.J. — Also termed *president judge.*

probate judge. A judge having jurisdiction over probate, inheritance, guardianships, and the like. — Also termed *judge of probate*; *surrogate*; *register.*

puisne judge (**pyoo**-nee). [Law French *puisné* "later born"] **1.** A junior judge; a judge without distinction or title. • This was the title formerly used in English common-law courts for a judge other than the chief judge. Today *puisne judge* refers to any judge of the English High Court, apart from the Chief Justice. **2.** See *associate judge.*

senior judge. **1.** The judge who has served for the longest time on a given court. **2.** A federal judge who qualifies for senior status and chooses this status over retirement.

side judge. *Archaic.* A judge — or one of two judges — of inferior rank, associated with a judge of a higher rank for the purpose of constituting a court.

special judge. A judge appointed or selected to sit — usu. in a specific case — in the absence or disqualification of the regular judge or otherwise as provided by statute.

> "Many, if not all, jurisdictions have made provision for the selection of a substitute or special judge to serve in place of the regular judge in the event of disqualification, voluntary recusal, disability, or other absence of the regular judge. The circumstances under which a special or substitute judge may act in place of the regular judge, and the manner in which such a judge may be chosen, are matters of purely local regulation, entirely dependent on local constitutions and statutes." 46 Am. Jur. 2d *Judges* § 248, at 331 (1994).

temporary judge. See *visiting judge.*

trial judge. The judge before whom a case is tried. • This term is used most commonly on appeal from the judge's rulings.

visiting judge. A judge appointed by the presiding judge of an administrative region to sit temporarily on a given court, usu. in the regular judge's absence. — Also termed *temporary judge*; *judge pro tempore.*

judge advocate. *Military law.* **1.** A legal adviser on a military commander's staff. **2.** Any officer in the Judge Advocate General's Corps or in a department of a U.S. military branch. — Abbr. JA.

staff judge advocate. A certified military lawyer with the staff of a convening or supervisory authority that exercises general court-martial jurisdiction.

Judge Advocate General. The senior legal officer and chief legal adviser of the Army, Navy, or Air Force. — Abbr. JAG.

judge-made law. **1.** The law established by judicial precedent rather than by statute. See COMMON LAW. **2.** The law that results when judges construe statutes contrary to legislative intent. See JUDICIAL ACTIVISM. — Also termed (in sense 2) *judicial legislation*; *bench legislation.*

judgement. See JUDGMENT.

judge of probate. See *probate judge* under JUDGE.

judge ordinary. See JUDGE.

judge *pro tempore* (proh **tem**-pə-ree). See *visiting judge* under JUDGE.

judge's chamber. See CHAMBER.

judgeship. 1. The office or authority of a judge. **2.** The period of a judge's incumbency.

judge-shopping. The practice of filing several lawsuits asserting the same claims — in a court or a district with multiple judges — with the hope of having one of the lawsuits assigned to a favorable judge and to nonsuit or voluntarily dismiss the others. Cf. FORUM-SHOPPING.

judge trial. See *bench trial* under TRIAL.

judgment. 1. A court's final determination of the rights and obligations of the parties in a case. • The term *judgment* includes a decree and any order from which an appeal lies. Fed. R. Civ. P. 54. — Also spelled (esp. in BrE) *judgement*. — Abbr. J. Cf. RULING; OPINION (1). **2.** *English law*. An opinion delivered by a member of the appellate committee of the House of Lords; a Law Lord's judicial opinion.

> "An action is instituted for the enforcement of a right or the redress of an injury. Hence a judgment, as the culmination of the action declares the existence of the right, recognizes the commission of the injury, or negatives the allegation of one or the other. But as no right can exist without a correlative duty, nor any invasion of it without a corresponding obligation to make amends, the judgment necessarily affirms, or else denies, that such a duty or such a liability rests upon the person against whom the aid of the law is invoked." 1 Henry Campbell Black, *A Treatise on the Law of Judgments* § 1, at 2 (2d ed. 1902).

accumulative judgment. A second or additional judgment against a person who has already been convicted, the execution of which is postponed until the completion of any prior sentence.

agreed judgment. A settlement that becomes a court judgment when the judge sanctions it. — Also termed *consent judgment*; *stipulated judgment*.

alternative judgment. A determination that gives the losing party options for satisfying that party's duties.

cognovit judgment (kog-**noh**-vit). A debtor's confession of judgment; judgment entered in accordance with a cognovit. See CONFESSION OF JUDGMENT; COGNOVIT.

confession of judgment. See CONFESSION OF JUDGMENT.

consent judgment. See *agreed judgment*.

declaratory judgment. A binding adjudication that establishes the rights and other legal relations of the parties without providing for or ordering enforcement. • Declaratory judgments are often sought, for example, by insurance companies in determining whether a policy covers a given insured or peril. — Also termed *declaratory decree*; *declaration*.

default judgment. See DEFAULT JUDGMENT.

deferred judgment. A judgment placing a convicted defendant on probation, the successful completion of which will prevent entry of the underlying judgment of conviction. • This type of probation is common with minor traffic offenses. — Also termed *deferred adjudication*; *deferred-adjudication probation*; *deferred prosecution*; *probation before judgment*; *probation without judgment*; *pretrial intervention*.

deficiency judgment. A judgment against a debtor for the unpaid balance of the debt if a foreclosure sale or a sale of repossessed personal property fails to yield the full amount of the debt due. — Also termed *deficiency decree*.

definitive judgment. See *final judgment*.

determinative judgment. See *final judgment*.

domestic judgment. A judgment rendered by the courts of the state or country where the judgment or its effect is at issue.

dormant judgment. A judgment that has not been executed or enforced within the statutory time limit. • As a result, any judgment lien may have been lost and execution cannot be issued unless the judgment creditor first revives the judgment. See REVIVAL (1).

erroneous judgment. A judgment issued by a court with jurisdiction to issue it, but containing an improper application of law. • This type of judgment is not void, but can be corrected by a trial court while the court retains plenary jurisdiction, or in a direct appeal. See ERROR (2).

excess judgment. A judgment that exceeds all of the defendant's insurance coverage.

executory judgment (eg-**zek**-yə-tor-ee). A judgment that has not been carried out, such as a yet-to-be fulfilled order for the defendant to pay the plaintiff.

final judgment. A court's last action that settles the rights of the parties and disposes of all issues in controversy, except for the award of costs (and, sometimes, attorney's fees) and enforcement of the judgment. — Also termed *final appealable judgment*; *final decision*; *final decree*; *definitive judgment*; *determinative judgment*; *final appealable order*.

foreign judgment. A judgment rendered by a court of a state or country different from that where the judgment or its effect is at issue.

in personam judgment. See *personal judgment*.

in rem judgment. See *judgment in rem*.

interlocutory judgment (in-tər-**lok**-yə-tor-ee). An intermediate judgment that determines a preliminary or subordinate point or plea but does not finally decide the case. — Also termed *interlocutory decree*.

irregular judgment. A judgment that may be set aside because of some irregularity in the way it was rendered, such as a clerk's failure to send a defendant notice that a default judgment has been rendered.

judgment as a matter of law. A judgment rendered during a jury trial — either before or after the jury's verdict — against a party on a given issue when there is no legally sufficient basis for a jury to find for that party on that issue. • In federal practice, the term *judgment as a matter of law* has replaced both the directed verdict and the judgment notwithstanding the verdict. Fed. R. Civ. P. 50. Cf. SUMMARY JUDGMENT.

judgment by default. See DEFAULT JUDGMENT.

judgment homologating the tableau (hə-**mahl**-ə-gay-ting / ta-**bloh** *or* **tab**-loh). *Civil law.* A judgment approving a plan for distributing property of a decedent's estate. • The distribution plan is known as the tableau of distribution. La. Code Civ. Proc. art. 3307. See HOMOLOGATION.

judgment in personam. See *personal judgment*.

judgment in rem (in **rem**). A judgment that determines the status or condition of property and that operates directly on the property itself. — Also termed *in rem judgment*.

judgment in retraxit. See *judgment of retraxit*.

judgment inter partes. See *personal judgment*.

judgment nil capiat per billa (nil **kap**-ee-ət pər **bil**-ə). Judgment that the plaintiff take nothing by the bill; a take-nothing judgment in a case instituted by a bill.

judgment nil capiat per breve (nil **kap**-ee-ət pər **breev** *or* **bree**-vee). Judgment that the plaintiff take nothing by the writ; a take-nothing judgment in a case instituted by a writ.

judgment nisi (**nI**-sI). A provisional judgment that, while not final or absolute, may become final on a party's motion. See NISI.

judgment notwithstanding the verdict. A judgment entered for one party even though a jury verdict has been rendered for the opposing party. — Also termed *judgment non obstante veredicto* (non ahb-**stan**-tee ver-ə-**dik**-toh). — Abbr. JNOV. See *judgment as a matter of law*.

judgment of acquittal. A judgment, rendered on the defendant's motion or court's own motion, that acquits the defendant of the offense charged when the evidence is insufficient. See *directed verdict* under VERDICT.

judgment of blood. See *death sentence* under SENTENCE.

judgment of conviction. The written record of a criminal judgment, consisting of the plea, the verdict or findings, the adjudication, and the sentence. Fed. R. Crim. P. 32(d)(1).

judgment of dismissal. A final determination of a case without a trial on its merits. See DISMISSAL.

judgment of nolle prosequi (**nahl**-ee **prahs**-ə-kwI). A judgment entered against a plaintiff who, after appearance but before judgment on the merits, has decided to abandon prosecution of the lawsuit. See NOLLE PROSEQUI.

judgment of nonsuit. **1.** *Hist.* The judgment given against a plaintiff who fails to be present in court to hear the jury render its verdict or who, after issue is joined, fails to bring the issue to be tried in due time. • This judgment does not prevent the plaintiff from filing the same case again. **2.** NONSUIT (2).

judgment of repleader. See REPLEADER.

judgment of retraxit (ri-**trak**-sit). *Hist.* A judgment against a plaintiff who has voluntarily retracted the claim. • Such a judgment bars the plaintiff from relitigating the claim. — Also termed *judgment in retraxit*. See RETRAXIT.

judgment on the merits. A judgment based on the evidence rather than on technical or procedural grounds. — Also termed *decision on the merits.*

judgment on the pleadings. A judgment based solely on the allegations and information contained in the pleadings, and not on any outside matters. Fed. R. Civ. P. 12(c). Cf. SUMMARY JUDGMENT.

judgment on the verdict. A judgment for the party receiving a favorable jury verdict.

judgment quasi in rem (**kway**-sI [*or* -zI] in **rem**). A judgment based on the court's jurisdiction over the defendant's interest in property rather than on its jurisdiction over the defendant or the property.

judgment quod billa cassetur (kwod **bil**-ə kə-**see**-tər). Judgment that the bill be quashed. • This is a judgment for the defendant.

judgment quod breve cassetur (kwod **breev** *or* **bree**-vee kə-**see**-tər). Judgment that the writ be quashed. • This is a judgment for the defendant.

judgment quod computet. See QUOD COMPUTET.

judgment quod recuperet (kwod ri-**kyoo**-pər-it). Judgment that the plaintiff recover.

judgment respondeat ouster (ri-**spon**-dee-at **ows**-tər). *Hist.* An interlocutory judgment requiring the defendant who has made a dilatory plea to give a more substantial defense.

money judgment. A judgment for damages subject to immediate execution, as distinguished from equitable or injunctive relief.

nunc pro tunc judgment (**nəngk** proh **təngk**). A procedural device by which the record of a judgment is amended to accord with what the judge actually said and did, so that the record will be accurate. • This device is often used to correct defects in real-estate titles.

personal judgment. **1.** A judgment that imposes personal liability on a defendant and that may therefore be satisfied out of any of the defendant's property within judicial reach. **2.** A judgment resulting from an action in which a court has personal jurisdiction over the parties. **3.** A judgment against a person as distinguished from a judgment against a thing, right, or status. — Also termed *judgment in personam* (in pər-**soh**-nəm); *in personam judgment*; *judgment inter partes* (**in**-tər **pahr**-teez).

simulated judgment. *Civil law.* A judgment that, although founded on an actual debt and intended for collection by the usual legal processes, is actually entered into by the parties to give one of them an undeserving advantage or to defraud third parties.

stipulated judgment. See *agreed judgment.*

summary judgment. See SUMMARY JUDGMENT.

take-nothing judgment. A judgment for the defendant providing that the plaintiff recover nothing in damages or other relief. — Also termed (in some states) *no cause of action.*

voidable judgment. A judgment that, although seemingly valid, is defective in some material way; esp., a judgment that, although rendered by a court having jurisdiction, is irregular or erroneous.

void judgment. A judgment that has no legal force or effect, the invalidity of which may be asserted by any party whose rights are affected at any time and any place, whether directly or collaterally. • From its inception, a void judgment continues to be absolutely null. It is incapable of being confirmed, ratified, or enforced in any manner or to any degree. One source of a void judgment is the lack of subject-matter jurisdiction.

judgmental immunity. See ERROR-OF-JUDGMENT RULE.

judgment as a matter of law. See JUDGMENT.

judgment book. See *judgment docket* under DOCKET.

judgment by default. See DEFAULT JUDGMENT.

judgment creditor. A person having a legal right to enforce execution of a judgment for a specific sum of money.

bona fide judgment creditor. One who recovers a judgment without engaging in fraud or collusion.

judgment debt. See DEBT.

judgment debtor. A person against whom a money judgment has been entered but not yet satisfied.

judgment docket. See DOCKET (1).

judgment execution. EXECUTION.

judgment file. See *judgment docket* under DOCKET.

judgment homologating the tableau. See JUDGMENT.

judgment in personam. See *personal judgment* under JUDGMENT.

judgment in rem. See JUDGMENT.

judgment in retraxit. See *judgment of retraxit* under JUDGMENT.

judgment *inter partes*. See *personal judgment* under JUDGMENT.

judgment lien. See LIEN.

judgment *nil capiat per billa*. See JUDGMENT.

judgment *nil capiat per breve*. See JUDGMENT.

judgment nisi. See JUDGMENT.

judgment *non obstante veredicto*. See *judgment notwithstanding the verdict* under JUDGMENT.

judgment note. **1.** A nonnegotiable promissory note, illegal in most states, containing a power of attorney to appear and confess judgment for a specified sum. **2.** COGNOVIT NOTE.

judgment notwithstanding the verdict. See JUDGMENT.

judgment n.o.v. See *judgment notwithstanding the verdict* under JUDGMENT.

judgment of acquittal. See JUDGMENT.

judgment of blood. See *death sentence* under SENTENCE.

judgment of dismissal. See JUDGMENT.

judgment of nolle prosequi. See JUDGMENT.

judgment of nonsuit. See JUDGMENT.

judgment of repleader. See REPLEADER.

judgment of retraxit. See JUDGMENT.

judgment on the merits. See JUDGMENT.

judgment on the pleadings. See JUDGMENT.

judgment on the verdict. See JUDGMENT.

judgment-proof, *adj.* (Of an actual or potential judgment debtor) unable to satisfy a judgment for money damages because the person has no property, does not own enough property within the court's jurisdiction to satisfy the judgment, or claims the benefit of statutorily exempt property. — Also termed *execution-proof.*

judgment quasi in rem. See JUDGMENT.

judgment *quod billa cassetur*. See JUDGMENT.

judgment *quod breve cassetur*. See JUDGMENT.

judgment *quod computet*. See QUOD COMPUTET.

judgment *quod recuperet*. See JUDGMENT.

judgment record. See *judgment docket* under DOCKET.

judgment respondeat ouster. See JUDGMENT.

judgment roll. See *judgment docket* under DOCKET.

> "As the pleadings constitute part of the record, it is indispensable that they be filed. In some of the codes they must be filed at the institution of the action; in others, by or before the first day of the term; in others, at or before the trial. They must be used in making the 'judgment roll,' and in the practice of each State (not here considered) procedure is provided to procure filing." Edwin E. Bryant, *The Law of Pleading Under the Codes of Civil Procedure* 179 (2d ed. 1899).

judgment sale. See *execution sale* under SALE.

judicable (**joo**-di-kə-bəl), *adj. Rare.* Capable of being adjudicated; triable; justiciable.

judicare (joo-di-**kair**-ee), *vb.* [Latin] *Civil law.* To judge; to decide or determine judicially; to give judgment or sentence.

judicative (**joo**-di-kay-tiv *or* -kə-tiv), *adj. Rare.* See ADJUDICATIVE.

judicator (**joo**-di-kay-tər), *n.* A person authorized to act or serve as a judge.

judicatory (**joo**-di-kə-tor-ee), *adj.* **1.** Of or relating to judgment. **2.** By which a judgment may be made; giving a decisive indication.

judicatory (**joo**-di-kə-tor-ee), *n.* **1.** A court; any tribunal with judicial authority <a church judicatory>. **2.** The administration of justice <working toward a more efficient judicatory>.

judicature (**joo**-di-kə-chər). **1.** The action of judging or of administering justice through duly constituted courts. **2.** JUDICIARY (3). **3.** A judge's office, function, or authority.

Judicature Acts. A series of statutes that reorganized the superior courts of England in 1875. • The Judicature Acts were superseded by the Supreme Court Act of 1981.

judices (**joo**-di-seez). [Latin] *pl.* JUDEX.

judicia (joo-**dish**-ee-ə). [Latin] *pl.* JUDICIUM.

judicial (joo-**dish**-əl), *adj.* **1.** Of, relating to, or by the court <judicial duty>. **2.** In court <the witness's judicial confession>. **3.** Legal <the Attorney General took no judicial action>. **4.** Of or relating to a judgment <an award of judicial interest at the legal rate>. Cf. JUDICIOUS.

quasi-judicial. See QUASI-JUDICIAL.

judicial act. See ACT (2)

judicial activism, *n.* A philosophy of judicial decision-making whereby judges allow their personal views about public policy, among other factors, to guide their decisions, usu. with the suggestion that adherents of this philosophy tend to find constitutional violations and are willing to ignore precedent. — **judicial activist,** *n.* Cf. JUDICIAL RESTRAINT (3).

> "[I]f to resolve the dispute the court must create a new rule or modify an old one, that is law creation. Judges defending themselves from accusations of judicial activism sometimes say they do not make law, they only apply it. It is true that in our system judges are not supposed to and generally do not make new law with the same freedom that legislatures can and do; they are, in Oliver Wendell Holmes's phrase, 'confined from molar to molecular motions.' The qualification is important, but the fact remains that judges make, and do not just find and apply, law." Richard A. Posner, *The Federal Courts: Crisis and Reform* 3 (1985).

judicial activity report. A regular report, usu. monthly or quarterly, on caseload and caseflow within a given court or court system.

judicial administration. The process of doing justice through a system of courts.

judicial admission. See ADMISSION (1).

judicial arbitration. See ARBITRATION.

Judicial Article. Article III of the U.S. Constitution, which creates the Supreme Court, vests in Congress the right to create inferior courts, provides for life tenure for federal judges, and specifies the powers and jurisdiction of the federal courts.

judicial assize. See ASSIZE (6).

judicial bias. See BIAS.

judicial bond. See BOND (2).

judicial branch. The branch of government consisting of the courts, whose function is to interpret, apply, and generally administer and enforce the laws; JUDICIARY (1). Cf. LEGISLATIVE BRANCH; EXECUTIVE BRANCH.

judicial bypass. A procedure permitting a person to obtain a court's approval for an act that would ordinarily require the approval of someone else, such as a law that requires a minor to notify a parent before obtaining an abortion but allows an appropriately qualified minor to obtain a court order permitting the abortion without parental notice.

judicial cognizance. See JUDICIAL NOTICE.

judicial combat. See TRIAL BY COMBAT.

judicial comity. See COMITY.

Judicial Committee of the Privy Council. A tribunal created in 1833 with jurisdiction to hear certain admiralty and ecclesiastical appeals, and certain appeals from the Commonwealth. • Its decisions are not treated as binding precedent in the United Kingdom, but they are influential because of the overlapping composition of members of the Council and the House of Lords in its judicial capacity.

judicial compensation. **1.** The remuneration that judges receive for their work. **2.** *Civil law.* A court's judgment finding that two parties are mutually obligated to one another and crafting the amount of the judgment in accordance with the amount that each party owes. • A claim for compensation is usu. contained in a reconventional demand. La. Code Civ. Proc. 1062. See *reconventional demand* under DEMAND (1).

judicial confession. See CONFESSION.

judicial control. *Civil law.* A doctrine by which a court can deny cancellation of a lease if the lessee's breach is of minor importance, is not caused by the lessee, or is based on a good-faith mistake of fact.

judicial council. A regularly assembled group of judges whose mission is to increase the efficiency and effectiveness of the courts on which they sit; esp., a semiannual assembly of a federal circuit's judges called by the circuit's chief judge. 28 USCA § 332.

judicial day. See *juridical day* under DAY.

judicial dictum. See DICTUM.

judicial discretion. See DISCRETION.

judicial economy. Efficiency in the operation of the courts and the judicial system; esp., the efficient management of litigation so as to minimize duplication of effort and to avoid wasting the judiciary's time and resources. • A court can enter a variety of orders based on judicial economy. For instance, a court may consolidate two cases for trial to save the court and the parties from having two trials, or it may order a separate trial on certain issues if doing so would provide the opportunity to avoid a later trial that would be more complex and time-consuming.

judicial-economy exception. An exemption from the final-judgment rule, by which a party may seek immediate appellate review of a nonfinal order if doing so might establish a final or nearly final disposition of the entire suit. See FINAL-JUDGMENT RULE.

judicial estoppel. See ESTOPPEL.

judicial evidence. See EVIDENCE.

judicial fact. See FACT.

judicial foreclosure. See FORECLOSURE.

judicial immunity. See IMMUNITY (1).

judicial insurance. See INSURANCE.

judicialize, *vb.* **1.** To pattern (procedures, etc.) after a court of law <these administrative hearings have been judicialized>. **2.** To bring (something not traditionally within the judicial system) into the judicial system <political questions are gradually becoming judicialized>. — **judicialization,** *n.*

judicial jurisdiction. See JURISDICTION.

judicial knowledge. See JUDICIAL NOTICE.

judicial legislation. See JUDGE-MADE LAW (2); LEGISLATION.

judicial lien. See LIEN.

judicial mortgage. See MORTGAGE.

judicial notice. A court's acceptance, for purposes of convenience and without requiring a party's proof, of a well-known and indisputable fact; the court's power to accept such a fact <the trial court took judicial notice of the fact that water freezes at 32 degrees Fahrenheit>. Fed R. Evid. 201. — Also termed *judicial cognizance*; *judicial knowledge*.

judicial oath. See OATH.

judicial officer. **1.** A judge or magistrate. **2.** Any officer of the court, such as a bailiff or court reporter.

judicial opinion. See OPINION (1).

judicial order. See ORDER (2).

judicial power. **1.** The authority vested in courts and judges to hear and decide cases and to make binding judgments on them; the power to construe and apply the law when controversies arise over what has been done or not done under it. • Under federal law, this power is vested in the U.S. Supreme Court and in whatever inferior courts Congress establishes. The other two great powers of government are the legislative power and the executive power. **2.** A power conferred on a public officer involving the exercise of judgment and discretion in deciding questions of right in specific cases affecting personal and proprietary interests. • In this sense, the phrase is contrasted with *ministerial power*.

judicial privilege. See PRIVILEGE (3).

judicial proceeding. See PROCEEDING.

judicial process. See PROCESS.

judicial question. A question that is proper for determination by the courts, as opposed to a moot question or one properly decided by the executive or legislative branch. Cf. POLITICAL QUESTION.

judicial record. See DOCKET (1).

judicial remedy. See REMEDY.

judicial restraint. **1.** A restraint imposed by a court, as by a restraining order, injunction, or judgment. **2.** The principle that, when a court can resolve a case based on a particular issue, it should do so, without reaching unnecessary issues. **3.** A philosophy of judicial decision-making whereby judges avoid indulging their personal beliefs about the public good and instead try merely to interpret the law as legislated and according to precedent. — Also termed (in senses 2 & 3) *judicial self-restraint*. Cf. JUDICIAL ACTIVISM.

judicial review. **1.** A court's power to review the actions of other branches or levels of government; esp., the courts' power to invalidate legislative and executive actions as being unconstitutional. **2.** The constitutional doctrine providing for this power. **3.** A court's review of a lower court's or an administrative body's factual or legal findings.

de novo judicial review. A court's nondeferential review of an administrative decision, usu. through a review of the administrative record plus any additional evidence the parties present.

judicial sale. See SALE.

judicial self-restraint. See JUDICIAL RESTRAINT.

judicial separation. See SEPARATION (1).

judicial sequestration. See SEQUESTRATION.

judicial settlement. See SETTLEMENT.

judicial stacking. See STACKING.

judicial-tenure commission. A commission that reviews complaints against judges, investigates those complaints, and makes recommendations about appropriate measures to the highest court in the jurisdiction.

judicial trustee. See TRUSTEE (1).

judicial writ. See WRIT.

judicia publica. See JUDICIUM.

judiciary (joo-**dish**-ee-er-ee *or* joo-**dish**-ə-ree), *n.* **1.** The branch of government responsible for interpreting the laws and administering justice. Cf. EXECUTIVE (1); LEGISLATURE. **2.** A system of courts. **3.** A body of judges. — Also termed (in sense 3) *judicature*. — **judiciary,** *adj.*

judicious (joo-**dish**-əs), *adj.* Well-considered; discreet; wisely circumspect <the court's judicious application of the rules of evidence>. — **judiciousness,** *n.* Cf. JUDICIAL.

judicium (joo-**dish**-ee-əm), *n.* [Latin] *Hist.* **1.** A judgment. **2.** A judicial proceeding; a trial. **3.** A court or tribunal. Pl. ***judicia.***

judicium capitale (kap-i-**tay**-lee). [Latin] *Hist.* A judgment of death; a capital sentence.

judicium parium (**par**-ee-əm). [Latin] *Hist.* A judgment of one's peers; a jury trial or verdict.

judicium publicum (joo-**dish**-ee-əm **pəb**-li-kəm). [Latin "public trials"] A criminal proceeding under a public statute. • The term derived from the Roman rule allowing any member of the public to initiate a prosecution. See COMITIA.

judicium Dei (joo-**dish**-ee-əm **dee**-I). *Hist.* God's supposed judgment on the merits of the case, made manifest by the outcome of an observable event. • Examples dating from Norman times were the trial by combat and the ordeal. See ORDEAL; TRIAL BY COMBAT.

judicium ecclesiasticum. See FORUM ECCLESIASTICUM.

judicium parium. See JUDICIUM.

judicium publica. See JUDICIUM.

juge (zhoozh), *n.* [French] *French law.* A judge.

juge de paix (**zhoozh** də **pe** *or* **pay**). An inferior judge; esp., a police magistrate.

juge d'instruction (**zhoozh** da*n*-strook-**syawn**). A magistrate who conducts preliminary criminal proceedings, as by taking complaints, interrogating parties and witnesses, and formulating charges.

juicio (**hwee**-syoh). *Spanish law.* A trial or suit.

Julian calendar. See OLD STYLE.

jumbo certificate. A certificate of deposit of $100,000 or more. — Also termed *jumbo.*

jumbo mortgage. See MORTGAGE.

jump bail, *vb.* (Of an accused) to fail to appear in court at the appointed time, even after posting a bail bond and promising to appear. — Also termed *skip bail.* See BAIL-JUMPING.

jump citation. See *pinpoint citation* under CITATION.

jumping a claim. *Hist.* The act of taking possession of public land to which another has previously acquired a claim. • The first occupant has the right to the land both under squatter law and custom and under preemption laws of the United States.

junior, *adj.* Lower in rank or standing; subordinate <a junior interest>.

junior bond. See BOND (3).

junior counsel. See COUNSEL.

junior creditor. See CREDITOR.

junior execution. See EXECUTION.

junior interest. See INTEREST (2).

junior lien. See LIEN.

junior mortgage. See MORTGAGE.

junior partner. See PARTNER.

junior security. See SECURITY.

junior writ. See WRIT.

junk bond. See BOND (3).

jura (**joor**-ə), *n. pl.* [Latin] JUS.

jura fiscalia (fis-**kay**-lee-ə). *Hist.* Fiscal rights; rights of the Exchequer.

jura majestatis (maj-ə-**stay**-tis). *Hist.* Rights of sovereignty or majesty.

jura mixti dominii (**miks**-tɪ də-**min**-ee-ɪ). *Hist.* Rights of mixed dominion; the king's or queen's right or power of jurisdiction.

jura personarum (pər-sə-**nair**-əm). Rights of persons. See JUS PERSONARUM.

jura praediorum (pree-dee-**or**-əm). *Hist.* The rights of estates.

jura regalia (ri-**gay**-lee-ə). *Hist.* Royal rights; the prerogatives of the Crown. See REGALIA.

jura rerum (**reer**-əm). Rights of things. See JUS RERUM.

jura summi imperii (**səm**-ɪ im-**peer**-ee-ɪ). *Hist.* Rights of supreme dominion; rights of sovereignty.

jural (**joor**-əl), *adj.* **1.** Of or relating to law or jurisprudence; legal <jural and equitable rules>. **2.** Of or relating to rights and obligations <jural relations>.

jural act. See ACT (2).

jural activity. See *jural act* under ACT (2).

jural agent. An official — someone who has the appropriate authoritative status in society to enforce or affect the society's legal system — who engages in a jural act. • Common examples include judges, legislators, and police officers acting in their official capacities. See *jural act* under ACT (2).

jural cause. See *proximate cause* under CAUSE (1).

jura majestatis. See JURA.

juramentum (joor-ə-**men**-təm), *n.* [Latin] *Civil law.* An oath. Pl. **juramenta** (joor-ə-**men**-tə).

juramentum calumniae (kə-**ləm**-nee-ee). An oath of calumny. See *oath of calumny* under OATH.

juramentum corporalis (kor-pə-**ray**-lis). A corporal oath. See *corporal oath* under OATH.

juramentum in litem (in **lɪ**-tem *or* -təm). An oath in litem. See *oath in litem* under OATH.

juramentum judiciale (joo-dish-ee-**ay**-lee). An oath by which the judge defers the decision of the case to either of the parties

juramentum necessarium (nes-ə-**sair**-ee-əm). A necessary or compulsory oath.

juramentum voluntarium (vol-ən-**tair**-ee-əm). A voluntary oath.

jura mixti dominii. See JURA.

jurant (**joor**-ənt), *n. Archaic.* One who takes an oath. — **jurant,** *n.*

jura personarum. See JURA.

jura praediroum. See JURA.

jura regalia. See JURA.

jura rerum. See JURA.

jura summi imperii. See JURA.

jurat (**joor**-at). **1.** [fr. Latin *jurare* "to swear"] A certification added to an affidavit or deposition stating when and before what authority the affidavit or deposition was made. • A jurat typically says "Subscribed and sworn to before me this ____ day of [month], [year]," and the officer (usu. a notary public) thereby certifies three things: (1) that the person signing the document did so in the officer's presence, (2) that the signer appeared before the officer on the date indicated, and (3) that the officer administered an oath or affirmation to the signer, who swore to or affirmed the contents of the document. — Also termed *jurata.* Cf. VERIFICATION.

witness jurat. A subscribing witness's acknowledgment certificate. • Even though this certificate is technically an acknowledgment and not a true jurat, the phrase *witness jurat* is commonly used. See ACKNOWLEDGMENT.

2. [fr. Latin *juratus* "one sworn"] In France and the Channel Islands, a municipal officer or magistrate.

jurata (juu-**ray**-tə), *n.* **1.** *Hist.* A jury of 12 persons; esp., a jury existing at common law. **2.** JURAT (1).

juration (juu-**ray**-shən). *Archaic.* **1.** The act of administering an oath. **2.** The act of swearing on oath.

jurative. See JURATORY.

jurator (juu-**ray**-tər). *Archaic.* See JUROR.

juratory (**joor**-ə-tor-ee), *adj.* Of, relating to, or containing an oath. — Also termed *jurative.*

jure (**joor**-ee), *adv.* [Latin] **1.** By right; in right. **2.** By law. See DE JURE.

jure belli (**bel**-I). By the right or law of war.

jure civili (sə-**vI**-lI). By the civil law.

jure coronae (kə-**roh**-nee). In right of the Crown.

jure divino (di-**vI**-noh). By divine right.

jure ecclesiae (e-**klee**-z[h]ee-ee). In right of the church.

jure gentium (**jen**-shee-əm). By the law of nations.

jure repraesentationis (rep-rə-zen-tay-shee-**oh**-nis). By right of representation; in the right of another person.

jure uxoris (ək-**sor**-is). In right of a wife.

jure gestionis (**joor**-ee jes-chee-**oh**-nis), *n.* [Latin "by way of doing business"] A nation's acts that are essentially commercial or private, in contrast to its public acts. • Under the Foreign Sovereign Immunities Act, a foreign country's immunity is limited to claims involving its public acts. The Act's immunity does not extend to claims arising from the private or commercial acts of a foreign state. 28 USCA § 1605. Cf. JURE IMPERII. See COMMERCIAL-ACTIVITY EXCEPTION; RESTRICTIVE PRINCIPLE OF SOVEREIGN IMMUNITY.

jure imperii (**joor**-ee im-**peer**-ee-I), *n.* [Latin "by right of sovereignty"] The public acts that a nation undertakes as a sovereign state, for which the sovereign is usu. immune from suit or liability. Cf. JURE GESTIONIS; COMMERCIAL-ACTIVITY EXCEPTION. See RESTRICTIVE PRINCIPLE OF SOVEREIGN IMMUNITY.

juridical (juu-**rid**-i-kəl), *adj.* **1.** Of or relating to judicial proceedings or to the administration of justice. **2.** Of or relating to law; legal. — Also termed *juridic.* Cf. NONJURIDICAL.

juridical day. See DAY.

juridical link. A legal relationship between members of a potential class action, sufficient to make a single suit more efficient or effective than multiple suits, as when all members of the class have been similarly affected by an allegedly illegal regulation. — Also termed *juridical relationship.*

jurimetrics (joor-ə-**me**-triks), *n.* The use of scientific or empirical methods, including measurement, in the study or analysis of legal matters. — **jurimetrician** (joor-ə-me-**trish**-ən), **jurimetricist** (joor-ə-**me**-trə-sist), *n.*

juris (**joor**-is). [Latin] **1.** Of law. **2.** Of right.

juris privati (pri-**vay**-tI). Of private right; relating to private property or private law.

juris publici (**pəb**-li-sI). Of public right; relating to common or public use, or to public law.

juriscenter (**joor**-ə-sen-tər *or* joor-ə-**sen**-tər), *n. Conflict of laws.* The jurisdiction that is most appropriately considered a couple's domestic center of gravity for matrimonial purposes.

jurisconsult (joor-is-**kon**-səlt *or* -kən-**səlt**). One who is learned in the law, esp. in civil or international law; JURIST.

jurisdiction, *n.* **1.** A government's general power to exercise authority over all persons and things within its territory <New Jersey's jurisdiction>. **2.** A court's power to decide a case or issue a decree <the constitutional grant of federal-question jurisdiction>. **3.** A geographic area within which political or judicial authority may be exercised <the accused fled to another jurisdiction>. **4.** A political or judicial subdivision within such an area <other jurisdictions have decided the issue differently>. — **jurisdictional,** *adj.* Cf. VENUE.

ancillary jurisdiction. A court's jurisdiction to adjudicate claims and proceedings that arise out of a claim that is properly before the court. • For example, if a plaintiff brings a lawsuit in federal court based on a federal question (such as a claim under Title VII), the defendant may assert a counterclaim that the court would not otherwise have jurisdiction over (such as a state-law claim of stealing company property). The concept of ancillary jurisdiction has now been codified, along with the concept of pendent jurisdiction, in the supplemental-jurisdiction statute. 28 USCA § 1367. See *supplemental jurisdiction.* Cf. *pendent jurisdiction.*

anomalous jurisdiction. **1.** Jurisdiction that is not granted to a court by statute, but that is inherent in the court's authority to govern lawyers and other officers of the court, such as the power to issue a preindictment order suppressing illegally seized property. **2.** An appellate court's provisional jurisdiction to review the denial of a motion to intervene in a case, so that if the court finds that the denial was correct, then its jurisdiction disappears — and it must dismiss the appeal for want of jurisdiction — because an order denying a motion to intervene is not a final, appealable order. See ANOMALOUS-JURISDICTION RULE.

appellate jurisdiction. The power of a court to review and revise a lower court's decision. • For example, U.S. Const. art. III, § 2 vests appellate jurisdiction in the Supreme Court, while 28 USCA §§ 1291–1295 grant appellate jurisdiction to lower federal courts of appeals. Cf. *original jurisdiction.*

arising-in jurisdiction. A bankruptcy court's jurisdiction over issues relating to the administration of the bankruptcy estate, and matters that occur only in a bankruptcy case. 28 USCA §§ 157, 1334.

common-law jurisdiction. **1.** A place where the legal system derives ultimately from the English common-law system <England, the United States, Australia, and other common-law jurisdictions>. **2.** A court's jurisdiction to try such cases as were cognizable under the English common law <in the absence of a controlling statute, the court exercised common-law jurisdiction over those claims>.

concurrent jurisdiction. **1.** Jurisdiction exercised simultaneously by more than one court over the same subject matter and within the same territory, with the litigant having the right to choose the court in which to file the action. **2.** Jurisdiction shared by two or more states, esp. over the physical boundaries (such as rivers or other bodies of water) between them. — Also termed *coordinate jurisdiction*; *overlapping jurisdiction.* Cf. *exclusive jurisdiction.*

> "In several cases, two States divided by a river exercise concurrent jurisdiction over the river, no matter where the inter-state boundary may be; in some cases by the Ordinance of 1787 for organizing Territories northwest of the Ohio River, in some cases by Acts of Congress organizing Territories or admitting States, and in some cases by agreements between the States concerned." 1 Joseph H. Beale, *A Treatise on the Conflict of Laws* § 44.3, at 279 (1935).

consent jurisdiction. Jurisdiction that parties have agreed to, either by agreement, by contract, or by general appearance. • Parties may not, by agreement, confer subject-matter jurisdiction on a federal court that would not otherwise have it.

contentious jurisdiction. **1.** A court's jurisdiction exercised over disputed matters. **2.** *Eccles. law.* The branch of ecclesiastical-court jurisdiction that deals with contested proceedings.

continuing jurisdiction. A court's power to retain jurisdiction over a matter after entering a judgment, allowing the court to modify its previous rulings or orders. See CONTINUING-JURISDICTION DOCTRINE.

coordinate jurisdiction. See *concurrent jurisdiction.*

criminal jurisdiction. A court's power to hear criminal cases.

diversity jurisdiction. A federal court's exercise of authority over a case involving parties from different states and an amount in controversy greater than a statutory minimum (now $75,000). 28 USCA § 1332. See DIVERSITY OF CITIZENSHIP; AMOUNT IN CONTROVERSY.

equity jurisdiction. At common law, the power to hear certain civil actions according to the procedure of the court of chancery, and to resolve them according to equitable rules.

"[T]he term equity jurisdiction does not refer to jurisdiction in the sense of the power conferred by the sovereign on the court over specified subject-matters or to jurisdiction over the res or the persons of the parties in a particular proceeding but refers rather to the merits. The want of equity jurisdiction does not mean that the court has no power to act but that it should not act, as on the ground, for example, that there is an adequate remedy at law." William Q. de Funiak, *Handbook of Modern Equity* 38 (2d ed. 1956).

exclusive jurisdiction. A court's power to adjudicate an action or class of actions to the exclusion of all other courts <federal district courts have exclusive jurisdiction over actions brought under the Securities Exchange Act>. Cf. *concurrent jurisdiction.*

extraterritorial jurisdiction. A court's ability to exercise power beyond its territorial limits. See LONG-ARM STATUTE.

federal jurisdiction. **1.** The exercise of federal-court authority. **2.** The area of study dealing with the jurisdiction of federal courts.

federal-question jurisdiction. The exercise of federal-court power over claims arising under the U.S. Constitution, an act of Congress, or a treaty. 28 USCA § 1331.

foreign jurisdiction. **1.** The powers of a court of a sister state or foreign country. **2.** Extraterritorial process, such as long-arm service of process.

general jurisdiction. **1.** A court's authority to hear a wide range of cases, civil or criminal, that arise within its geographic area. **2.** A court's authority to hear all claims against a defendant, at the place of the defendant's domicile or the place of service, without any showing that a connection exists between the claims and the forum state. Cf. *limited jurisdiction*; *specific jurisdiction.*

in personam jurisdiction. See *personal jurisdiction.*

in rem jurisdiction (in **rem**). A court's power to adjudicate the rights to a given piece of property, including the power to seize and hold it. — Also termed *jurisdiction in rem.* See IN REM. Cf. *personal jurisdiction.*

international jurisdiction. A court's power to hear and determine matters between different countries or persons of different countries.

judicial jurisdiction. The legal power and authority of a court to make a decision that binds the parties to any matter properly brought before it.

jurisdiction in personam. See *personal jurisdiction.*

jurisdiction in rem. See *in rem jurisdiction.*

jurisdiction of the person. See *personal jurisdiction.*

jurisdiction of the subject matter. See *subject-matter jurisdiction.*

jurisdiction over the person. See *personal jurisdiction.*

jurisdiction quasi in rem. See *quasi-in-rem jurisdiction.*

legislative jurisdiction. A legislature's general sphere of authority to enact laws and conduct all business related to that authority, such as holding hearings.

limited jurisdiction. Jurisdiction that is confined to a particular type of case or that may be exercised only under statutory limits and prescriptions. — Also termed *special jurisdiction.* Cf. *general jurisdiction.*

"It is a principle of first importance that the federal courts are courts of limited jurisdiction. ... The federal courts ... cannot be courts of general jurisdiction. They are empowered to hear only such cases as are within the judicial power of the United States, as defined in the Constitution, and have been entrusted to them by a jurisdictional grant by Congress." Charles Alan Wright, *The Law of Federal Courts* § 7, at 27 (5th ed. 1994).

original jurisdiction. A court's power to hear and decide a matter before any other court can review the matter. Cf. *appellate jurisdiction.*

overlapping jurisdiction. See *concurrent jurisdiction.*

pendent jurisdiction (**pen**-dənt). A court's jurisdiction to hear and determine a claim over which it would not otherwise have jurisdiction, because the claim arises from the same transaction or occurrence as another claim that is properly before the court. • For example, if a plaintiff brings suit in federal court claiming that the defendant, in one transaction, violated both a federal and a state law, the federal court has jurisdiction over the federal claim (under federal-question jurisdiction) and also has jurisdiction over the state claim that is pendent to the federal claim. Pendent jurisdiction has now been codified as supplemental jurisdiction. 28 USCA § 1367. — Also termed *pendent-claim jurisdiction*. See *supplemental jurisdiction*. Cf. *ancillary jurisdiction*.

pendent-party jurisdiction. A court's jurisdiction to adjudicate a claim against a party who is not otherwise subject to the court's jurisdiction, because the claim by or against that party arises from the same transaction or occurrence as another claim that is properly before the court. • Pendent-party jurisdiction has been a hotly debated subject, and was severely limited by the U.S. Supreme Court in *Finley v. United States*, 490 U.S. 545, 109 S.Ct. 2003 (1990). The concept is now codified in the supplemental-jurisdiction statute, and it applies to federal-question cases but not to diversity-jurisdiction cases. 28 USCA § 1367. Neither pendent-party jurisdiction nor supplemental jurisdiction may be used to circumvent the complete-diversity requirement in cases founded on diversity jurisdiction. See *supplemental jurisdiction*.

personal jurisdiction. A court's power to bring a person into its adjudicative process; jurisdiction over a defendant's personal rights, rather than merely over property interests. — Also termed *in personam jurisdiction*; *jurisdiction in personam*; *jurisdiction of the person*; *jurisdiction over the person*. See IN PERSONAM. Cf. *in rem jurisdiction*.

plenary jurisdiction (**plee**-nə-ree *or* **plen**-ə-ree). A court's full and absolute power over the subject matter and the parties in a case.

probate jurisdiction. Jurisdiction over matters relating to wills, settlement of decedents' estates, and (in some states) guardianship and the adoption of minors.

quasi-in-rem jurisdiction (**kway**-sI in **rem** *or* **kway**-zI). Jurisdiction over a person but based on that person's interest in property located within the court's territory. — Also termed *jurisdiction quasi in rem*. See *quasi in rem* under IN REM.

special jurisdiction. See *limited jurisdiction*.

specific jurisdiction. Jurisdiction that stems from the defendant's having certain minimum contacts with the forum state so that the court may hear a case whose issues arise from those minimum contacts. Cf. *general jurisdiction*.

subject-matter jurisdiction. Jurisdiction over the nature of the case and the type of relief sought; the extent to which a court can rule on the conduct of persons or the status of things. — Also termed *jurisdiction of the subject matter*.

summary jurisdiction. **1.** A court's jurisdiction in a summary proceeding. **2.** The court's authority to issue a judgment or order (such as a finding of contempt) without the necessity of a trial or other process. **3.** *English law*. A court's power to make an order immediately, without obtaining authority or referral, as in a magistrate's power to dispose of a criminal case without referring it to the Crown Court for a formal trial or without drawing a jury.

supplemental jurisdiction. Jurisdiction over a claim that is part of the same case or controversy as another claim over which the court has original jurisdiction. • Since 1990, federal district courts have had supplemental jurisdiction which includes jurisdiction over both ancillary and pendent claims. 28 USCA § 1367. See *ancillary jurisdiction*; *pendent jurisdiction*.

territorial jurisdiction. **1.** Jurisdiction over cases arising in or involving persons residing within a defined territory. **2.** Territory over which a government, one of its courts, or one of its subdivisions has jurisdiction.

transient jurisdiction (**tran**-shənt). Personal jurisdiction over a defendant who is served with process while in the forum state only temporarily (such as during travel).

voluntary jurisdiction. **1.** Jurisdiction exercised over unopposed matters. **2.** *Eccles. law*. Jurisdiction in cases in which contentious litigation is not allowed.

jurisdictional amount. See AMOUNT IN CONTROVERSY.

jurisdictional fact. See FACT.

jurisdictional-fact doctrine. *Administrative law*. The principle that if evidence is presented challenging the factual findings that triggered an agency's action, then a court will review the facts to determine whether the agency had authority to act in the first place. • This doctrine is generally no longer applied. Cf. CONSTITUTIONAL-FACT DOCTRINE.

jurisdictional gerrymandering. See GERRYMANDERING (2).

jurisdictional limits. The geographic boundaries or the constitutional or statutory limits within which a court's authority may be exercised.

jurisdictional plea. See PLEA (3).

jurisdictional statement. See JURISDICTION CLAUSE.

jurisdictional strike. See STRIKE.

jurisdiction clause. 1. At law, a statement in a pleading that sets forth the court's jurisdiction to act in the case. — Also termed *jurisdictional statement*. **2.** *Equity practice*. The part of the bill intended to show that the court has jurisdiction, usu. by an averment that adequate relief is unavailable outside equitable channels.

jurisdiction in personam. See *personal jurisdiction* under JURISDICTION.

jurisdiction in rem. See *in rem jurisdiction* under JURISDICTION.

jurisdiction of the person. See *personal jurisdiction* under JURISDICTION.

jurisdiction of the subject matter. See *subject-matter jurisdiction* under JURISDICTION.

jurisdiction over the person. See *personal jurisdiction* under JURISDICTION.

jurisdiction quasi in rem. See *quasi-in-rem jurisdiction* under JURISDICTION.

Juris Doctor (**joor**-is **dok**-tər). Doctor of law — the law degree most commonly conferred by an American law school. — Abbr. J.D. — Also termed *Doctor of Jurisprudence*; *Doctor of Law*. Cf. MASTER OF LAWS; LL.B.; LL.D.

juris et de jure (**joor**-is et dee **joor**-ee). [Latin] Of law and of right <a presumption *juris et de jure* cannot be rebutted>.

jurisinceptor (joor-is-in-**sep**-tər). [Latin] *Hist.* A student of the civil law.

jurisperitus (joor-is-pə-**rɪ**-təs), *adj.* [Latin] (Of a person) skilled or learned in law. See LEGISPERITUS.

juris privati. [Latin] See JURIS.

jurisprude (**joor**-is-prood), *n.* **1.** A person who makes a pretentious display of legal knowledge or who is overzealous about the importance of legal doctrine. **2.** JURISPRUDENT.

jurisprudence (joor-is-**prood**-ənts), *n.* **1.** Originally (in the 18th century), the study of the first principles of the law of nature, the civil law, and the law of nations. — Also termed *jurisprudentia naturalis* (joor-is-proo-**den**-shee-ə nach-ə-**ray**-lis). **2.** More modernly, the study of the general or fundamental elements of a particular legal system, as opposed to its practical and concrete details. **3.** The study of legal systems in general. **4.** Judicial precedents considered collectively. **5.** In German literature, the whole of legal knowledge. **6.** A system, body, or division of law. **7.** CASELAW.

> "Jurisprudence addresses the questions about law that an intelligent layperson of speculative bent — not a lawyer — might think particularly interesting. What is law? ... Where does law come from? ... Is law an autonomous discipline? ... What is the purpose of law? ... Is law a science, a humanity, or neither? ... A practicing lawyer or a judge is apt to think questions of this sort at best irrelevant to what he does, at worst naive, impractical, even childlike (how high is up?)." Richard A. Posner, *The Problems of Jurisprudence* 1 (1990).

analytical jurisprudence. A method of legal study that concentrates on the logical structure of law, the meanings and uses of its concepts, and the terms and the modes of its operation.

censorial jurisprudence. See LAW REFORM.

comparative jurisprudence. The scholarly study of the similarities and differences between the legal systems of different jurisdictions, such as between civil-law and common-law countries. — Also termed *comparative law*. Cf. INTERNATIONAL LAW.

> "What is known as comparative jurisprudence — namely, the study of the resemblances and differences between different legal systems — is not a separate branch of jurisprudence co-ordinate with the analytical, historical, and ethical, but is merely a particular method of that science in all its branches. We compare English law with Roman law either for the purpose of analytical jurisprudence, in order the better to comprehend the conceptions and principles of each of those systems; or for the purpose of historical jurisprudence, in order that we may better understand the course of development of each system; or for the purpose of ethical jurisprudence, in order that we may better judge the practical merits and demerits of each of them. Apart from such purposes the comparative study of law would be merely futile." John Salmond, *Jurisprudence* 7–8 n.(c) (Glanville L. Williams ed., 10th ed. 1947).

equity jurisprudence. **1.** The legal science treating the rules, principles, and maxims that govern the decisions of a court of equity. **2.** The cases and controversies that are considered proper subjects of equity. **3.** The nature and form of the remedies that equity grants.

ethical jurisprudence. The branch of legal philosophy concerned with the law from the viewpoint of its ethical significance and adequacy. • This area of study brings together moral and legal philosophy. — Also termed (in German) *Rechtsphilosophie*; (in French) *philosophie du droit*.

expository jurisprudence. The scholarly exposition of the contents of an actual legal system as it now exists or once existed. — Also termed *systematic jurisprudence*.

feminist jurisprudence. A branch of jurisprudence that examines the relationship between women and law, including the history of legal and social biases against women, the elimination of those biases in modern law, and the enhancement of women's legal rights and recognition in society.

> "The first published use of the phrase 'feminist jurisprudence' occurred in 1978 when Professor Ann Scales published an article called *Toward a Feminist Jurisprudence*. Feminist legal theory is diverse, and anything but monolithic. Many feminists believe that it is difficult to generalize about feminist jurisprudence. It is, however, possible to understand feminist legal theory as a reaction to the jurisprudence of modern legal scholars (primarily male scholars) who tend to see law as a process for interpreting and perpetuating a universal, gender-neutral public morality. Feminist legal scholars, despite their differences, appear united in claiming that 'masculine' jurisprudence of 'all stripes' fails to acknowledge, let alone respond to, the interests, values, fears, and harms experienced by women." Gary Minda, *Postmodern Legal Movements* 129–30 (1995).

***general jurisprudence.* 1.** The scholarly study of the fundamental elements of a given legal system. — Also termed *jurisprudentia generalis*.

> "The term 'general jurisprudence' involves the misleading suggestion that this branch of legal science is that which relates not to any single system of law, but to those conceptions and principles that are to be found in all developed legal systems, and which are therefore in this sense general. It is true that a great part of the matter with which it is concerned is common to all mature systems of law. All of these have the same essential nature and purposes, and therefore agree to a large extent in their first principles. But it is not because of universal reception that any principles pertain to the theory or philosophy of law. For this purpose such reception is neither sufficient nor necessary. Even if no system in the world save that of England recognised the legislative efficacy of judicial precedents, the theory of case-law would none the less be a fit and proper subject of general jurisprudence. *Jurisprudentia generalis* is not the study of legal systems in general, but the study of the general or fundamental elements of a particular legal system." John Salmond, *Jurisprudence* 3 n.(b) (Glanville L. Williams ed., 10th ed. 1947).

2. The scholarly study of the law, legal theory, and legal systems generally. — Also termed *jurisprudentia universalis*; *philosophy of law*; *legal philosophy*.

> "According to Austin (1790–1859), general jurisprudence is the study of the 'principles, notions and distinctions' common to the maturer systems of law." Rupert Cross & J.W. Harris, *Precedent in English Law* 2 (4th ed. 1991).

historical jurisprudence. The branch of legal philosophy concerned with the history of the first principles and conceptions of a legal system, dealing with (1) the general principles governing the origin and development of law, and (2) the origin and development of the legal system's first principles.

> "Historical jurisprudence was a passive restraining mode of thought on legal subjects by way of reaction from the active creative thought of the era of philosophy. It was a reaction, too, from the confident disregard of traditional legal institutions and conditions of time and place which characterized the French Revolution. We were not ready for it in the fore part of the last century. But we accepted it eagerly toward the end of that century when it was already moribund in Europe." Roscoe Pound, *The Formative Era of American Law* 113 (1938).

jurisprudence constante (kən-**stan**-tee). *Civil law.* The doctrine that a court should give great weight to a rule of law that is accepted and applied in a long line of cases, and should not overrule or modify its own decisions unless clear error is shown and injustice will arise from continuation of a particular rule of law. • Civil-law courts are not bound by the common-law doctrine of stare decisis. But they do recognize the doctrine of *jurisprudence constante*, which is similar to stare decisis, one exception being that *jurisprudence constante* does not command strict adherence to a legal principle applied on one occasion in the past. Cf. STARE DECISIS.

jurisprudence of conceptions. The extension of a maxim or definition, usu. to a logical extreme, with relentless disregard for the consequences. • The phrase appears to have been invented by Roscoe Pound. See *Mechanical Jurisprudence*, 8 Colum. L. Rev. 605, 608 (1908).

normative jurisprudence. See NATURAL LAW (2).

particular jurisprudence. The scholarly study of the legal system within a particular jurisdiction, the focus being on the fundamental assumptions of that system only.

positivist jurisprudence. A theory that denies validity to any law that is not derived from or sanctioned by a sovereign or some other determinate source. — Also termed *positivist jurisprudence*.

sociological jurisprudence. A philosophical approach to law stressing the actual social effects of legal institutions, doctrines, and practices. • This influential approach was started by Roscoe Pound in 1906 and became a precursor to legal realism. — Also termed *sociology of law*. See LEGAL REALISM.

systematic jurisprudence. See *expository jurisprudence*.

jurisprudent, *n*. A person learned in the law; a specialist in jurisprudence. — Also termed *jurisprude*.

jurisprudentia generalis. See *general jurisprudence* (1) under JURISPRUDENCE.

jurisprudential (joor-is-proo-**den**-shəl), *adj*. Of or relating to jurisprudence.

jurisprudentia naturalis. See JURISPRUDENCE (1).

jurisprudentia universalis. See *general jurisprudence* (2) under JURISPRUDENCE.

juris publici. See JURIS.

jurist. 1. One who has thorough knowledge of the law; esp., a judge or an eminent legal scholar. — Also termed *legist*. **2.** JURISPRUDENT.

juristic, *adj*. **1.** Of or relating to a jurist <juristic literature>. **2.** Of or relating to law <a corporation is a typical example of a juristic person>.

juristic act. See *act in the law* under ACT (2).

juristic person. See *artificial person* under PERSON.

Juris utriusque Doctor. See J.U.D.

juror (**joor**-ər *also* **joor**-or). A person serving on a jury panel. — Also formerly termed *layperson*.

grand juror. A person serving on a grand jury.

petit juror (**pet**-ee). A trial juror, as opposed to a grand juror.

presiding juror. The juror who chairs the jury during deliberations and speaks for the jury in court by announcing the verdict. • The presiding juror is usu. elected by the jury at the start of deliberations. — Also termed *foreman*; *foreperson*.

tales-juror (**tay**-leez- *or* **taylz**-joor-ər). See TALESMAN.

juror misconduct. See MISCONDUCT.

jury, *n*. A group of persons selected according to law and given the power to decide questions of fact and return a verdict in the case submitted to them.

advisory jury. A jury empaneled to hear a case when the parties have no right to a jury trial. • The judge may accept or reject the advisory jury's verdict.

blue-ribbon jury. A jury consisting of jurors who are the most highly educated on a given panel, sometimes used in a complex civil case (usu. by stipulation of the parties) and sometimes also for a grand jury (esp. those investigating governmental corruption). • An even more elite group of jurors, involving specialists in a technical field, is called a *blue-blue-ribbon jury*.

common jury. See *petit jury*.

coroner's jury. A jury summoned by a coroner to investigate the cause of death.

deadlocked jury. See *hung jury*.

death-qualified jury. *Criminal law*. A jury that is fit to decide a case involving the death penalty because the jurors have no absolute ideological bias against capital punishment. Cf. *life-qualified jury*.

fair and impartial jury. See *impartial jury*.

foreign jury. A jury obtained from a jurisdiction other than that in which the case is brought.

good jury. See *special jury*.

grand jury. See GRAND JURY.

homage jury. *Hist*. A jury in a court baron, consisting of tenants who made homage to the lord. See COURT BARON.

hung jury. A jury that cannot reach a verdict by the required voting margin. — Also termed *deadlocked jury*.

impartial jury. A jury that has no opinion about the case at the start of the trial and that bases its verdict on competent legal evidence. — Also termed *fair and impartial jury*.

inquest jury. A jury summoned from a particular district to appear before a sheriff, coroner, or other ministerial officer and inquire about the facts concerning a death. See INQUEST.

jury de medietate linguae (dee mee-dee-ə-**tay**-tee **ling**-gwee). [Latin "jury of halfness of language"] *Hist.* A jury made up of half natives and half aliens, allowed when one of the parties is an alien.

jury of indictment. See GRAND JURY.

jury of matrons. *Hist.* A jury of "discreet and lawful women" impaneled to try a question of pregnancy, as when a woman sentenced to death pleads, in stay of execution, that she is pregnant.

jury of the vicinage (**vis**-ə-nij). **1.** At common law, a jury from the county where the crime occurred. **2.** A jury from the county where the court is held. See VICINAGE.

life-qualified jury. *Criminal law.* In a case involving a capital crime, a jury selected from a venire from which the judge has excluded anyone unable or unwilling to consider a sentence of life imprisonment, instead of the death penalty, if the defendant is found guilty. Cf. *death-qualified jury.*

mixed jury. **1.** DEMY-SANGUE. **2.** A jury composed of both men and women or persons of different races.

petit jury (**pet**-ee). A jury (usu. consisting of 6 or 12 persons) summoned and empaneled in the trial of a specific case. — Also termed *petty jury*; *trial jury*; *common jury*; *traverse jury*. Cf. GRAND JURY.

shadow jury. A group of mock jurors paid to observe a trial and report their reactions to a jury consultant hired by one of the litigants. ● The shadow jurors, who are matched as closely as possible to the real jurors, provide counsel with information about the jury's likely reactions to the trial. — Also termed *phantom jury.*

sheriff's jury. *Hist.* A jury selected and summoned by a sheriff to hold inquests for various purposes, such as assessing damages in an action in which the defendant makes no defense or ascertaining the mental condition of an alleged lunatic.

special jury. **1.** A jury chosen from a panel that is drawn specifically for that case. ● Such a jury is usu. empaneled at a party's request in an unusually important or complicated case. — Also termed *struck jury*. See STRIKING A JURY. **2.** At common law, a jury composed of persons above the rank of ordinary freeholders, usu. summoned to try more important questions than those heard by ordinary juries. — Also termed *good jury.*

struck jury. A jury selected by allowing the parties to alternate in striking from a list any person whom a given party does not wish to have on the jury, until the number is reduced to the appropriate number (traditionally 12).

traverse jury. See *petit jury.*

trial jury. See *petit jury.*

jury box. The enclosed part of a courtroom where the jury sits. — Also spelled *jury-box.*

jury challenge. See CHALLENGE (2).

jury charge. 1. See JURY INSTRUCTION. **2.** A set of jury instructions. — Often shortened to *charge.*

jury commissioner. An officer responsible for choosing the panels of potential jurors in a given county.

jury *de medietate linguae.* See JURY.

jury direction. See JURY INSTRUCTION.

jury duty. 1. The obligation to serve on a jury. **2.** Actual service on a jury. — Also termed *jury service.*

jury fee. See FEE (1).

jury-fixing. The act or an instance of illegally procuring the cooperation of one or more jurors who actually influence the outcome of the trial. — Also termed *fixing a jury*. Cf. EMBRACERY; JURY-PACKING.

jury instruction. (*usu. pl.*) A direction or guideline that a judge gives a jury concerning the law of the case. — Often shortened to *instruction.* — Also termed *jury charge*; *charge*; *jury direction*; *direction.*

additional instruction. A jury charge, beyond the original instructions, that is usu. given in response to the jury's question about the evidence or some point of law. — Also termed *further instruction.*

affirmative converse instruction. An instruction presenting a hypothetical that, if true, commands a verdict in favor of the defendant. ● An affirmative converse instruction usu. begins with language such as "your verdict must be for the defendant if you believe. . . ."

affirmative instruction. An instruction that removes an issue from the jury's consideration, such as an instruction that whatever the evidence, the defendant cannot be convicted under the indictment count to which the charge is directed. — Also termed *affirmative charge*.

argumentative instruction. An instruction that assumes facts not in evidence, that singles out or unduly emphasizes a particular issue, theory, or defense, or that otherwise invades the jury's province regarding the weight, probative value, or sufficiency of the evidence.

binding instruction. See *mandatory instruction*.

cautionary instruction. **1.** A judge's instruction to the jurors to disregard certain evidence or consider it for specific purposes only. **2.** A judge's instruction for the jury not to be influenced by outside factors and not to talk to anyone about the case while the trial is in progress.

curative instruction. A judge's instruction that is intended to correct an erroneous instruction.

formula instruction. A jury charge intended to be the complete statement of the law on which the jury must base its verdict.

further instruction. See *additional instruction*.

mandatory instruction. An instruction requiring a jury to find for one party and against the other if the jury determines that, based on a preponderance of the evidence, a given set of facts exists. — Also termed *binding instruction*.

model jury instruction. A form jury charge usu. approved by a state bar association or similar group regarding matters arising in a typical case. • Courts usu. accept model jury instructions as authoritative. — Also termed *pattern jury instruction*; *pattern jury charge*; *model jury charge*.

ostrich instruction. *Criminal procedure*. An instruction stating that a defendant who deliberately avoided acquiring actual knowledge can be found to have acted knowingly.

pattern jury charge. See *model jury instruction*.

pattern jury instruction. See *model jury instruction*.

peremptory instruction. A court's explicit direction that a jury must obey, such as an instruction to return a verdict for a particular party. See *directed verdict* under VERDICT.

single-juror instruction. An instruction stating that if any juror is not reasonably satisfied with the plaintiff's evidence, then the jury cannot render a verdict for the plaintiff.

special instruction. An instruction on some particular point or question involved in the case, usu. in response to counsel's request for such an instruction.

standard instruction. A jury instruction that has been regularly used in a given jurisdiction.

jury list. A list of persons who may be summoned to serve as jurors.

juryman. *Archaic*. See JUROR.

jury nullification. A jury's knowing and deliberate rejection of the evidence or refusal to apply the law either because the jury wants to send a message about some social issue that is larger than the case itself or because the result dictated by law is contrary to the jury's sense of justice, morality, or fairness.

jury of indictment. See GRAND JURY.

jury of matrons. See JURY.

jury of the vicinage. See JURY.

jury-packing. The act or an instance of contriving to have a jury composed of persons who are predisposed toward one side or the other. — Also termed *packing a jury*. Cf. EMBRACERY; JURY-FIXING.

jury panel. See VENIRE (1).

jury pardon. A rule that permits a jury to convict a defendant of a lesser offense than the offense charged if sufficient evidence exists to convict the defendant of either offense.

jury pool. See VENIRE (1).

jury process. **1.** The procedure by which jurors are summoned and their attendance is enforced. **2.** The papers served on or mailed to potential jurors to compel their attendance.

jury question. **1.** An issue of fact that a jury decides. See QUESTION OF FACT. **2.** A special question that a court may ask a jury that will deliver a special verdict. See *special interrogatory* under INTERROGATORY.

jury sequestration. See SEQUESTRATION (7).

jury service. See JURY DUTY.

jury summation. See CLOSING ARGUMENT.

jury-tampering. See EMBRACERY.

jury trial. See TRIAL.

jury wheel. A physical device or electronic system used for storing and randomly selecting names of potential jurors.

jurywoman. *Archaic.* A female juror; esp., a member of a jury of matrons. See *jury of matrons* under JURY.

jus (jəs *also* joos *or* yoos), *n.* [Latin "law, right"] **1.** Law in the abstract. **2.** A system of law. **3.** A legal right, power, or principle. — Abbr. J. — Also spelled *ius*. Pl. ***jura*** (**joor**-ə *also* **yoor**-ə). Cf. LEX.

jus abstinendi (jəs ab-stə-**nen**-dɪ), *n.* [Law Latin "right of abstaining"] *Roman & civil law.* The right of an heir to renounce or decline an inheritance, as when it would require taking on debt.

jus abutendi (jəs ab-yə-**ten**-dɪ), *n.* [Latin "right of abusing"] *Roman & civil law.* The right to make full use of property, even to the extent of wasting or destroying it. Cf. JUS UTENDI.

jus accrescendi (jəs ak-rə-**sen**-dɪ), *n.* [Latin "right of accretion"] A right of accrual; esp., the right of survivorship that a joint tenant enjoys. See RIGHT OF SURVIVORSHIP.

jus actus (jəs **ak**-təs), *n.* [Latin] *Roman law.* A rural servitude giving a person the right of passage for a carriage or cattle.

jus ad rem (jəs ad rem), *n.* [Law Latin "right to a thing"] A right in specific property arising from another person's duty and valid only against that person; an inchoate or incomplete right to a thing. Cf. JUS IN RE.

jus aedilium (jəs ee-**dil**-ee-əm), *n.* [Latin "law of the aediles"] *Roman law.* The body of law developed through the edicts and adjudications of aediles. — Also termed *jus aedilicium* (jəs ee-dɪ-**lish**-ee-əm). See AEDILE; JUS HONORARIUM.

Jus Aelianum (jəs ee-lee-**ay**-nəm), *n.* [Latin] *Roman law.* A manual of laws drawn up in the second century B.C. by the consul Sextus Aelius, consisting of three parts: (1) the laws of the Twelve Tables; (2) a commentary on them; and (3) the forms of procedure. See TWELVE TABLES.

jus aequum (jəs **ee**-kwəm), *n.* [Latin "law that is equal or fair"] *Roman law.* Law characterized by equity, flexibility, and adaptation to the circumstances of a particular case. Cf. JUS STRICTUM.

jus aesneciae (jəs ees-**neesh**-ee-ee), *n.* [Latin] *Roman law.* The right of primogeniture.

jus albanagii (jəs al-bə-**nay**-jee-ɪ), *n.* [Law Latin "confiscating the goods of aliens"] See DROIT D'AUBAINE.

jus albinatus (jəs al-bi-**nay**-təs), *n.* [Law Latin "right of alien confiscation"] See DROIT D'AUBAINE.

jus angariae (jəs ang-**gair**-ee-ee), *n.* [Latin "right of angary"] See ANGARY.

jus aquaeductus (jəs ak-wə-**dək**-təs), *n.* [Latin] *Roman & civil law.* A servitude that gives a landowner the right to conduct water from another's land through pipes or channels.

jus aquaehaustus (jəs **ak**-wee **haws**-təs), *n.* [Latin] *Roman law.* A servitude that grants a right to water one's cattle on another's field or to draw water from another's well.

jus banci (jəs **ban**-sɪ), *n.* [Law Latin "right of bench"] *Hist.* The right or privilege of having an elevated and separate seat of judgment, formerly allowed only to the king's judges, who administered what was from then on called "high justice."

jus belli (jəs **bel**-ɪ), *n.* [Latin "law of war"] The law of nations as applied during wartime, defining in particular the rights and duties of the belligerent powers and of neutral nations.

jus bellum dicendi (jəs **bel**-əm di-**sen**-dɪ), *n.* [Latin] The right of proclaiming war.

jus canonicum (jəs kə-**non**-i-kəm), *n.* [Law Latin] See CANON LAW (1).

jus civile (jəs si-**vɪ**-lee). [Latin] See CIVIL LAW (1).

jus civitatis (jəs siv-i-**tay**-təs), *n.* [Latin] *Roman law.* The right of citizenship; the right of a Roman citizen.

jus cloacae (jəs kloh-**ay**-see), *n.* [Latin "right of sewer or drain"] *Civil law.* An easement consisting in the right of having a sewer or conducting surface water over or through the land of one's neighbor.

jus cogens (jəs **koh**-jenz), *n.* [Latin "compelling law"] A mandatory norm of general international law from which no two or more nations may exempt themselves or release one another. Cf. JUS DISPOSITIVUM.

> "Viewed from the perspective of international law as understood in the first part of the 20th century, *jus cogens* seemed hardly conceivable, since at that time the will of States was taken as paramount: States could, between themselves, abrogate any of the rules of customary international law.... [Yet] [a]fter World War II the international community became conscious of the necessity for any legal order to be based on some consensus concerning fundamental values which were not at the disposal of the subjects of this legal order. As H. Mosler rightly stresses, there is a close connection between *jus cogens* and the recognition of a 'public order of the international community' (The International Society as a Legal Community (rev. ed. 1980 p. 19). Without expressly using the notion of *jus cogens*, the [International Court of Justice] implied its existence when it referred to obligations *erga omnes* in its judgment of February 5, 1970 in the Barcelona Traction Case. The Court spoke of the 'obligations of a State towards the international community as a whole' where were 'the concern of all States' and for whose protection all States could be held to have a 'legal interest' (ICJ Reports (1970) p. 3, at 32). These obligations are seen as fundamentally different from those existing *vis-á-vis* another State in the field of diplomatic protection." Jochen Abr. Frowein, in 3 *Encyclopedia of Public International Law* 66 (1997).

jus commercii (jəs kə-**mər**-shee-ɪ), *n.* [Latin "right of commerce"] *Roman & civil law.* The right to make contracts, acquire and transfer property, and conduct business transactions.

jus commune (jəs kə-**myoo**-nee), *n.* **1.** *Roman & civil law.* The common or public law or right, as opposed to a law or right established for special purposes. Cf. JUS SINGULARE. **2.** The common law of England. See COMMON LAW (3).

jus compascuum (jəs kəm-**pas**-kyoo-əm), *n.* [Latin "the right to feed together"] *Hist.* The right of common pasture. Cf. COMMON (1).

jus connubii (jəs kə-**n[y]oo**-bee-ɪ), *n.* [Latin "right of marriage"] See CONNUBIUM.

jus coronae (jəs kə-**roh**-nee), *n.* [Latin "right of the Crown"] The right of succession to the English throne.

jus cudendae monetae (jəs kyoo-**den**-dee mə-**nee**-tee), *n.* [Law Latin] *Hist.* The right of coining money.

jus curialitatis (jəs kyoor-ee-al-ə-**tay**-tis), *n.* [Law Latin] *Hist.* The right of curtesy.

jus dare (jəs **dair**-ee), *vb.* [Latin] To give or make the law. • This is the function and prerogative of the legislature. Cf. JUS DICERE.

jus deliberandi (jəs di-lib-ə-**ran**-dɪ), *n.* [Latin "right of deliberating"] *Roman & civil law.* A right granted to an heir to take time to consider whether to accept or reject an inheritance.

jus de non appellando (jəs dee non ap-ə-**lan**-doh). [Latin] The supreme judicial power.

jus dicere (jəs **dɪ**-sər-ee), *vb.* [Latin] To declare or decide the law. • This is the function and prerogative of the judiciary. Cf. JUS DARE.

jus disponendi (jəs dis-pə-**nen**-dɪ), *n.* [Latin "right of disposing"] The right to dispose of property; the power of alienation.

jus dispositivum (jəs dis-poz-ə-**tɪ**-vəm), *n.* [Latin "law subject to the disposition of the parties"] *Int'l law.* A norm that is created by the consent of participating nations, as by an international agreement, and is binding only on the nations that agree to be bound by it. Cf. JUS COGENS.

jus distrahendi (jəs dis-trə-**hen**-dɪ), *n.* [Latin "right of distraining"] The right to sell pledged goods upon default.

jus dividendi (jəs div-i-**den**-dɪ), *n.* [Latin "right of dividing"] The right to dispose of real property by will.

jus divinum (jəs di-**vɪ**-nəm). See DIVINE LAW; NATURAL LAW (1).

jus duplicatum (jəs d[y]oo-pli-**kay**-təm). See DROIT-DROIT.

jus ecclesiasticum (jəs e-klee-z[h]ee-**as**-ti-kəm). [Law Latin] See ECCLESIASTICAL LAW.

jus edicendi (jəs ed-i-**sen**-dɪ *or* ee-di-), *n.* [Latin "right of decreeing"] *Roman law.* The right (esp. of the praetors) to issue edicts. See JUS PRAETORIUM.

jus ex non scripto (jəs eks non **skrip**-toh). See UNWRITTEN LAW.

jus falcandi (jəs fal-**kan**-dɪ), *n.* [Latin] *Hist.* The right of mowing or cutting.

jus fetiale (jəs fee-shee-**ay**-lee), *n.* [Latin] **1.** FETIAL LAW. **2.** The law of negotiation and diplomacy. • This phrase captured the classical notion of international law. — Also spelled *jus feciale.*

jus fiduciarium (jəs fi-d[y]oo-shee-**air**-əm), *n.* [Latin] *Civil law.* A right in trust. Cf. JUS LEGITIMUM.

jus fluminum (jəs **floo**-mə-nəm), *n.* [Latin] *Civil law.* The right to use rivers.

jus fodiendi (jəs foh-dee-**en**-dɪ), *n.* [Latin] *Civil law.* The right to dig on another's land.

jus fruendi (jəs froo-**en**-dɪ), *n.* [Latin "right of enjoying"] *Roman & civil law.* The right to use and enjoy another's property without damaging or diminishing it. See USUFRUCT.

jus futurum (jəs fyoo-**t[y]oor**-əm), *n.* [Latin "future right"] *Civil law.* A right that has not fully vested; an inchoate or expectant right.

jus gentium (jəs **jen**-shee-əm), *n.* [Latin "law of nations"] **1.** INTERNATIONAL LAW. **2.** *Roman law.* The body of law, taken to be common to different peoples, and applied in dealing with the relations between Roman citizens and foreigners. — Also termed *jus inter gentes.*

> "The early Roman law (the *jus civile*) applied only to Roman citizens. It was formalistic and hard and reflected the status of a small, unsophisticated society rooted in the soil. It was totally unable to provide a relevant background for an expanding, developing nation. This need was served by the creation and progressive augmentation of the *jus gentium.* This provided simplified rules to govern the relations between foreigners, and between foreigners and citizens.... The progressive rules of the *jus gentium* gradually overrode the narrow *jus civile* until the latter system ceased to exist. Thus, the *jus gentium* became the common law of the Roman Empire and was deemed to be of universal application." Malcolm N. Shaw, *International Law* 15 (4th ed. 1997).

jus gentium privatum (jəs **jen**-shee-əm pri-**vay**-təm). See *private international law* under INTERNATIONAL LAW.

jus gentium publicum (jəs **jen**-shee-əm **pəb**-li-kəm). See INTERNATIONAL LAW.

jus gladii (jəs **glad**-ee-ɪ), *n.* [Latin "right of the sword"] *Roman law.* The executory power of the law; the power or right to inflict the death penalty. • This term took on a similar meaning under English law.

> "And the prosecution of these offences is always at the suit and in the name of the king, in whom, by the texture of our constitution, the *jus gladii,* or executory power of the law, entirely resides." 4 William Blackstone, *Commentaries on the Laws of England* 177 (1765).

jus habendi (jəs hə-**ben**-dɪ), *n.* [Latin] *Civil law.* The right to have a thing; the right to be put in actual possession of property.

jus haereditatis (jəs hə-red-ə-**tay**-tis), *n.* [Latin] *Civil law.* The right of inheritance.

jus hauriendi (jəs haw-ree-**en**-dɪ), *n.* [Latin] *Civil law.* The right of drawing water.

jus honorarium (jəs [h]on-ə-**rair**-ee-əm), *n.* [Latin "magisterial law"] *Roman law.* The body of law established by the edicts of the supreme magistrates, including the praetors (*jus praetorium*) and the aediles (*jus aedilium*).

jus honorum (jəs [h]ə-**nor**-əm), *n.* [Latin] *Roman law.* The right of a citizen to hold public office. Cf. JUS SUFFRAGII.

jus imaginis (jəs ə-**maj**-ə-nis), *n.* [Latin] *Roman law.* The right to use or display pictures or statues of ancestors.

jus immunitatis (jəs i-myoo-nə-**tay**-tis), *n.* [Latin "law of immunity"] *Civil law.* Exemption from the burden of public office.

jus incognitum (jəs in-**kog**-nə-təm), *n.* [Latin] *Civil law.* An unknown or obsolete law.

jus individuum (jəs in-də-**vij**-oo-əm), *n.* [Latin] An individual or indivisible right; a right that cannot be divided.

jus in personam (jəs in pər-**soh**-nəm), *n.* [Latin "right against a person"] A right of action against a particular person to enforce that person's obligation. See *right in personam* under RIGHT.

jus in re (jəs in ree), *n.* [Law Latin "right in or over a thing"] A right in property valid against anyone in the world; a complete and perfect right to a thing. — Also termed *jus in rem.* Cf. JUS AD REM.

jus in re aliena (jəs in ree ay-lee-**ee**-nə *or* al-ee-), *n.* [Latin] An easement or right in or over another's property; ENCUMBRANCE. — Also termed *right in re aliena.*

jus in rem (jəs in rem), *n.* [Latin "right against a thing"] See JUS IN RE.

jus in re propria (jəs in ree **proh**-pree-ə), *n.* [Latin] The right of enjoyment that is incident to full ownership of property; full ownership itself. — Also termed *right in re propria.*

jus inter gentes (jəs **in**-tər **jen**-teez), *n.* [Latin "law among nations"] See JUS GENTIUM.

jus Italicum (jəs I-**tal**-ə-kəm), *n.* [Latin] *Roman law.* The right, law, and liberties of certain Roman colonies, including quiritarian ownership and exemption from property taxes imposed by the republic.

jus itineris (jəs I-**tin**-ə-ris), *n.* [Latin] *Roman law.* A rural servitude granting the right to pass over an adjoining field on foot or horseback.

jusjurandum (jəs-juu-**ran**-dəm), *n.* [Latin] An oath. See JURAMENTUM.

jus Latii (jəs **lay**-shee-I), *n.* [Latin] *Roman law.* The right of a person who is not a Roman citizen to have certain privileges of citizenship. — Also termed *jus Latium.*

jus legitimum (jəs lə-**jit**-ə-məm), *n.* [Latin] *Civil law.* A right enforceable in law. Cf. JUS FIDUCIARIUM.

jus liberorum (jəs lib-ə-**ror**-əm), *n.* [Latin "right of children"] *Roman law.* A privilege conferred on a parent who has several children; esp., a right of inheritance given to a woman with three or more children. — Also termed *jus trium liberorum.*

jus mariti (jəs mə-**rI**-tI), *n.* [Latin] The right of a husband; esp., the husband's right to his wife's movable estate by virtue of the marriage.

jus merum (jəs **meer**-əm). See MERE RIGHT.

jus moribus constitutum (jəs **mor**-ə-bəs kon-stə-**t[y]oo**-təm). [Latin] See UNWRITTEN LAW.

jus naturae (jəs nə-**t[y]oor**-ee). [Latin] See NATURAL LAW.

jus naturale (jəs nach-ə-**ray**-lee). [Latin] See NATURAL LAW.

jus navigandi (jəs nav-ə-**gan**-dI), *n.* [Latin] *Civil law.* The right of navigation; the right of commerce by sea.

jus necessitatis (jəs nə-ses-i-**tay**-tis), *n.* [Latin] A person's right to do what is required for which no threat of legal punishment is a dissuasion. • This idea implicates the proverb that necessity knows no law (*necessitas non habet legem*), so that an act that would be objectively understood as necessary is not wrongful even if done with full and deliberate intention.

jus non sacrum (jəs non **say**-krəm), *n.* [Latin "nonsacred law"] *Roman law.* The body of law regulating the duties of a civil magistrate in preserving the public order. Cf. JUS SACRUM.

jus non scriptum (jəs non **skrip**-təm). See UNWRITTEN LAW.

jus offerendi (jəs ahf- *or* awf-ə-**ren**-dI), *n.* [Latin] *Roman law.* The right of subrogation; the right to succeed to a senior creditor's lien and priority upon tendering the amount due to that creditor.

jus oneris ferendi (jəs **on**-ə-ris fə-**ren**-dI), *n.* [Latin] *Roman law.* An urban servitude granting the right to support and build on another's house wall.

jus pascendi (jəs pə-**sen**-dI). See *servitus pascendi* under SERVITUS.

jus patronatus (jəs pa-trə-**nay**-təs), *n.* [Latin] *Eccles. law.* The right of patronage; the right to present a clerk to a benefice.

jus personarum (jəs pər-sə-**nair**-əm), *n.* [Latin "law of persons"] *Civil law.* The law governing the rights of persons having special relations with one another (such as parents and children or guardians and wards) or having limited rights (such as aliens or incompetent persons). See LAW OF PERSONS. Cf. JUS RERUM.

jus poenitendi (jəs pen-i-**ten**-dI), *n.* [Latin] The right to rescind or revoke an executory contract when the other party defaults.

jus portus (jəs **por**-təs), *n.* [Latin] *Civil & maritime law.* The right of port or harbor.

jus positivum. See POSITIVE LAW.

jus possessionis (jəs pə-zes[h]-ee-**oh**-nis), *n.* [Latin] *Civil law.* A right of which possession is the source or title; a possessor's right to continue in possession. Cf. JUS PROPRIETATIS.

jus possidendi (jəs pos-ə-**den**-dɪ), *n.* [Latin] *Civil law.* A person's right to acquire or to retain possession; an owner's right to possess.

jus postliminii (jəs pohst-lə-**min**-ee-ɪ). [Latin] See POSTLIMINIUM.

jus praesens (jəs **pree**-senz *or* -zenz), *n.* [Latin "present right"] *Civil law.* A right that has been completely acquired; a vested right.

jus praetorium (jəs pri-**tor**-ee-əm), *n.* [Latin "law of the praetors"] *Roman law.* The body of law developed through the edicts and adjudications of praetors. See PRAETOR; JUS HONORARIUM.

jus precarium (jəs pri-**kair**-ee-əm), *n.* [Latin] *Civil law.* A right to a thing held for another, for which there was no remedy by legal action but only by entreaty or request.

jus presentationis (jəs prez-ən-tay-shee-**oh**-nis), *n.* [Latin] *Civil law.* The right to present a clerk to a church.

jus primae noctis (jəs **prɪ**-mee **nok**-tis). [Latin "right of first night"] See DROIT DU SEIGNEUR.

jus privatum (jəs pri-**vay**-təm), *n.* [Latin "private law"] **1.** *Roman & civil law.* The law governing the relations and transactions between individuals. **2.** The right, title, or dominion of private ownership. See PRIVATE LAW. Cf. JUS PUBLICUM.

jus projiciendi (jəs prə-jish-ee-**en**-dɪ), *n.* [Latin] *Civil law.* A servitude granting the right to build a projection (such as a balcony) from one's house in the open space belonging to a neighbor.

jus proprietatis (jəs prə-prɪ-ə-**tay**-tis), *n.* [Latin] *Civil law.* A right in property based on ownership rather than actual possession. Cf. JUS POSSESSIONIS.

jus protegendi (jəs proh-tə-**jen**-dɪ), *n.* [Latin] *Civil law.* A servitude granting the right to make the roof or tiling of one's house extend over a neighbor's house.

jus publicum (jəs **pəb**-li-kəm), *n.* [Latin "public law"] **1.** *Roman & civil law.* The public law of crimes, of officers, of the priesthood, and of the status of persons. **2.** The right, title, or dominion of public ownership; esp., the government's right to own real property in trust for the public benefit. See PUBLIC LAW. Cf. JUS PRIVATUM.

jus quaesitum (jəs kwi-**sɪ**-təm *or* -**zɪ**-təm), *n.* [Latin] *Civil law.* **1.** A right to ask or recover, as from one who is under an obligation. **2.** An acquired right.

jus quiritium (jəs kwi-**rɪ**-shee-əm), *n.* [Latin] *Roman law.* The ancient, primitive law of the Romans before the development of the *jus praetorium* and the *jus gentium.*

jus recuperandi (jəs ri-k[y]oo-pə-**ran**-dɪ), *n.* [Latin] *Civil law.* The right of recovering, esp. lands.

jus regendi (jəs ri-**jen**-dɪ), *n.* [Law Latin] A proprietary right vested in a sovereign.

jus relictae (jəs ri-**lik**-tee), *n.* [Law Latin "right of a widow"] *Civil & Scots law.* A widow's claim to her share of her deceased husband's movable estate. • If the widow has children, her share is one-third; if not, her share is one-half.

jus relicti (jəs ri-**lik**-tɪ), *n.* [Law Latin "right of a widower"] *Civil & Scots law.* A widower's right in his deceased wife's separate movable estate, historically two-thirds if there were surviving children, and otherwise one-half. Under the Married Women's Property Act of 1881, the amount became one-third in the case of surviving children, and otherwise one-half.

jus repraesentationis (jəs rep-ri-zen-tay-shee-**oh**-nis), *n.* [Latin] *Civil law.* The right to represent or be represented by another.

jus rerum (jəs **reer**-əm), *n.* [Latin "law of things"] *Civil law.* The law regulating the rights and powers of persons over things, as how property is acquired, enjoyed, and transferred. See LAW OF THINGS. Cf. JUS PERSONARUM.

jus respondendi (jəs ree-spon-**den**-dɪ), *n.* [Latin "the right of responding"] *Roman law.* The authority conferred on certain jurists of delivering legal opinions that became binding law.

jus retentionis (jəs ri-ten-shee-**oh**-nis), *n.* [Latin] *Civil law.* The right of retaining something.

jus retractus (jəs ri-**trak**-təs), *n.* [Latin "the right of retraction"] *Civil law.* **1.** The right of certain relatives of one who has sold immovable property to repurchase it. **2.** A debtor's right, upon sale of the debt by the creditor, to have a third person redeem it within a year for the price paid by the purchaser.

jus sacrum (jəs **say**-krəm), *n.* [Latin "sacred law"] *Roman law.* The body of law regulating matters of public worship, such as sacrifices and the appointment of priests. Cf. JUS NON SACRUM.

jus sanguinis (jəs **sang**-gwə-nis), *n.* [Latin "right of blood"] The rule that a child's citizenship is determined by the parents' citizenship. • Most nations follow this rule. Cf. JUS SOLI.

jus scriptum (jəs **skrip**-təm). [Latin] See WRITTEN LAW.

jus singulare (jəs sing-gyə-**lair**-ee), *n.* [Latin "individual law"] *Roman & civil law.* A law or right established for special purposes, as opposed to the common or public law or right. Cf. JUS COMMUNE (1).

jus soli (jəs **soh**-lI), *n.* [Latin "right of the soil"] The rule that a child's citizenship is determined by place of birth. • This is the U.S. rule, as affirmed by the 14th Amendment to the Constitution. Cf. JUS SANGUINIS.

jus spatiandi (jəs spay-shee-**an**-dI), *n.* [Latin "right of walking about"] *Civil law.* The public's right-of-way over specific land for purposes of recreation and instruction.

jus stapulae (jəs **stay**-pyə-lee), *n.* [Law Latin "right of staple"] *Civil law.* A town's right or privilege of stopping imported merchandise and forcing it to be offered for sale in its own market. See STAPLE.

jus strictum (jəs **strik**-təm), *n.* [Latin "strict law"] *Roman law.* Law rigorously interpreted without modification. — Also termed *strictum jus.* See STRICTI JURIS. Cf. JUS AEQUUM.

jus suffragii (jəs sə-**fray**-jee-I), *n.* [Latin] *Roman law.* The right of a citizen to vote. Cf. JUS HONORUM.

just, *adj.* Legally right; lawful; equitable.

justa causa (**jəs**-tə **kaw**-zə), *n.* [Latin] *Civil law.* A just cause; a lawful ground. See *good cause* under CAUSE (2).

justae nuptiae (**jəs**-tee **nəp**-shee-ee), *n.* [Latin "legal marriage"] *Roman law.* A marriage between two persons who had the legal capacity to wed. • *Justae nuptiae* was the only union that created the familial relationship known as *patria potestas.* — Also spelled *iustae nuptiae.* See *patria potestas* under POTESTAS. Cf. CONCUBINATUS.

> "*Iustae nuptiae* is such a marriage as satisfies all the rules of civil law. Any marriage between two persons who had the capacity of civil marriage with each other (*conubium*) was necessarily *iustae nuptiae,* for if the union was defective in any other respect it was no marriage at all. On the other hand, if there was no *conubium* between the parties it might still be actually a marriage (*nuptiae, nuptiae non iustae*), the wife being *uxor non iusta,* the children *liberi non iusti.* Such a marriage, in which one party at least would not be a *civis,* did not produce *patria potestas* over children. . . ." W.W. Buckland, *A Manual of Roman Private Law* 63–64 (2d ed. 1953).

jus talionis. See LEX TALIONIS.

just-as-probable rule. *Workers' compensation.* A doctrine whereby a workers'-compensation claim will be denied if it is equally likely that the injury resulted from a non-work-related cause as from a work-related cause.

just cause. See *good cause* under CAUSE (2).

just compensation. See COMPENSATION.

just deserts (di-**zərts**). What one really deserves; esp., the punishment that a person deserves for having committed a crime. — Also termed *deserts.*

jus tertii (jəs **tər**-shee-I), *n.* [Latin] **1.** The right of a third party.

> "[N]o defendant in an action of trespass can plead the *jus tertii* — the right of possession outstanding in some third person — as against the fact of possession in the plaintiff." R.F.V. Heuston, *Salmond on the Law of Torts* 46 (17th ed. 1977).

2. The doctrine that, particularly in constitutional law, courts do not decide what they do not need to decide.

> "Jus tertii . . . says nothing about the nature of legal argument on the merits of a case once formed, but as a symbol for the separability of cases is a useful term of art. Translated, however, it reads 'right of a third person.' It may once have been associated with a presumption of common-law jurisprudence that one cannot be harmed by an action that achieves its effect through

effects upon others, cannot be 'indirectly' harmed." Joseph Vining, *Legal Identity* 120 (1978).

justice. 1. The fair and proper administration of laws.

commutative justice (kə-**myoo**-tə-tiv *or* **kom**-yə-tay-tiv). Justice concerned with the relations between persons and esp. with fairness in the exchange of goods and the fulfillment of contractual obligations.

distributive justice. Justice owed by a community to its members, including the fair disbursement of common advantages and sharing of common burdens.

Jedburgh justice (**jed**-bər-ə). A brand of justice involving punishment (esp. execution) first and trial afterwards. • The term alludes to Jedburgh, a Scottish border town where in the 17th century raiders were said to have been hanged without the formality of a trial. Jedburgh justice differs from lynch law in that the former was administered by an established court (albeit after the fact). — Also termed *Jeddart justice*; *Jedwood justice*. Cf. LIDFORD LAW; LYNCH LAW.

justice in personam. See *personal justice*.

justice in rem. See *social justice*.

natural justice. Justice as defined in a moral, as opposed to a legal, sense. — Also termed *justitia naturalis*. Cf. NATURAL LAW.

personal justice. Justice between parties to a dispute, regardless of any larger principles that might be involved. — Also termed *justice in personam*.

popular justice. Demotic justice, which is usu. considered less than fully fair and proper even though it satisfies prevailing public opinion in a particular case. Cf. *social justice*.

"Nothing is more treacherous than popular justice in many of its manifestations, subject as it is to passion, to fallacy, and to the inability to grasp general notions or to distinguish the essential from the inessential." Carleton K. Allen, *Law in the Making* 387 (7th ed. 1964).

positive justice. Justice as it is conceived, recognized, and incompletely expressed by the civil law or some other form of human law. Cf. POSITIVE LAW.

social justice. Justice that conforms to a moral principle, such as that all people are equal. — Also termed *justice in rem*. Cf. *personal justice*.

substantial justice. Justice fairly administered according to rules of substantive law, regardless of any procedural errors not affecting the litigant's substantive rights; a fair trial on the merits.

2. A judge, esp. of an appellate court or a court of last resort. — Abbr. J. (and, in plural, JJ.).

associate justice. An appellate-court justice other than the chief justice.

chief justice. The presiding justice of an appellate court, usu. the highest appellate court in a jurisdiction and esp. the U.S. Supreme Court. — Abbr. C.J.

circuit justice. **1.** A justice who sits on a circuit court. **2.** A U.S. Supreme Court justice who has jurisdiction over one or more of the federal circuits, with power to issue injunctions, grant bail, or stay execution in those circuits.

circuit-riding justice. *Hist.* A U.S. Supreme Court justice who, under the Judiciary Act of 1789, was required to travel within a circuit to preside over trials. • In each of three circuits that then existed, two justices sat with one district judge. See CIRCUIT-RIDING.

3. *Hist.* Judicial cognizance of causes or offenses; jurisdiction.

high justice. *Hist.* Jurisdiction over crimes of every kind, including high crimes.

low justice. *Hist.* Jurisdiction over petty offenses.

justice-broker. *Archaic.* A judge who sells judicial decisions.

justice court. See COURT.

justice ejectment. See EJECTMENT.

justice in eyre (air). *Hist.* One of the itinerant judges who, in medieval times, investigated allegations of wrongdoing, tried cases, and levied fines. — Also termed *justicia errante*; *justiciar in itinere*. See EYRE.

justice in personam. See *personal justice* under JUSTICE (1).

justice in rem. See *social justice* under JUSTICE (1).

justicement. *Archaic.* **1.** The administration of justice. **2.** (*pl.*) All things relating to justice.

justice of the peace. A local judicial officer having jurisdiction over minor criminal offenses and minor civil disputes, and authority to perform routine civil functions (such as administering oaths and performing marriage ceremonies). — Abbr. J.P. Cf. MAGISTRATE.

justice-of-the-peace court. See *justice court* under COURT.

justice of the quorum. *Hist.* A distinction conferred on a justice of the peace by directing — in the commission authorizing the holding of quarter sessions — that from among those holding court must be two or more specially so named. • The distinction was conferred on some, or occasionally all, of the justices of the peace of a county in England.

justicer, *n. Archaic.* One who administers justice; a judge.

justiceship. 1. The office or authority of a justice. **2.** The period of a justice's incumbency.

justice's warrant. See *peace warrant* under WARRANT (1).

justiciability (jə-stish-ee-ə-**bil**-ə-tee), *n.* The quality or state of being appropriate or suitable for review by a court. See MOOTNESS DOCTRINE; RIPENESS. Cf. STANDING.

> "Concepts of justiciability have been developed to identify appropriate occasions for judicial action.... The central concepts often are elaborated into more specific categories of justiciability — advisory opinions, feigned and collusive cases, standing, ripeness, mootness, political questions, and administrative questions." 13 Charles Alan Wright et al., *Federal Practice and Procedure* § 3529, at 278–79 (2d ed. 1984).

justiciable (jə-**stish**-ee-ə-bəl *or* jəs-**tish**-ə-bəl), *adj.* (Of a case or dispute) properly brought before a court of justice; capable of being disposed of judicially <a justiciable controversy>.

justicia errante. See JUSTICE IN EYRE.

justiciar (jə-**stish**-ee-ər), *n.* **1.** *Hist.* A royal judicial officer in medieval England; esp., a justice presiding over a superior court. **2.** JUSTICIARY (2). — Also spelled *justicier.*

justiciarii itinerantes (jəs-tish-ee-**air**-ee-ɪ ɪ-tin-ə-**ran**-teez), *n.* [Latin "itinerant justices"] Justices in eyre. See JUSTICE IN EYRE.

justiciarii residentes (jəs-tish-ee-**air**-ee-ɪ rez-i-**den**-teez), *n.* [Latin "resident justices"] *Hist.* Justices who usu. held court in Westminster, as opposed to traveling with the eyre. Cf. EYRE.

justiciar in itinere. See JUSTICE IN EYRE.

justiciary (jə-**stish**-ee-er-ee), *adj.* Of or relating to the administration of justice; pertaining to the law.

justiciary (jə-**stish**-ee-er-ee), *n.* **1.** A justice or judge. **2.** *Hist.* The chief administrator of both government and justice. • From the time of the Norman Conquest in 1066 until the reign of Henry III (1216–1272), the justiciary presided in the King's Court and in the Exchequer, supervising all governmental departments and serving as regent in the king's absence. These functions were later divided among several officials such as the lord chancellor, the chief justice, and the lord high treasurer. — Also termed *justiciar*; *chief justiciar*; *capitalis justiciarius.* **3.** *Scots law.* The administration of justice, esp. of criminal law.

justicier. See JUSTICIAR.

justicies (jə-**stish**-ee-eez). *Hist.* A writ empowering the sheriff to allow certain debt cases in a county court. • The writ was so called because of the significant word in the writ's opening clause, which stated in Latin, "We command you that you do justice to [a person named]."

justicing room. *Hist.* A room in which cases are heard and justice is administered; esp., such a room in the house of a justice of the peace.

justifiable, *adj.* Capable of being legally or morally justified; excusable; defensible.

justifiable homicide. See HOMICIDE.

justification, *n.* **1.** A lawful or sufficient reason for one's acts or omissions. **2.** A showing, in court, of a sufficient reason why a defendant did what the plaintiff or prosecution charges the defendant to answer for. — Also termed *justification defense*; *necessity defense.* **3.** A surety's proof of having enough money or credit to provide security for the party for whom it is required. — **justify,** *vb.* — **justificatory** (jəs-**ti**-fi-kə-tor-ee), *adj.*

> "A little bit of history: the term 'justification' was formerly used for cases where the aim of the law was not frustrated, while 'excuse' was used for cases where it was not thought proper to punish. Killing a dangerous criminal who had tried to avoid arrest was *justified*, since the law (if one may personify) wished this to happen, whereas killing in self-defence was merely *excused*. The distinction was important because justification was a defence to the criminal charge while an excuse was not, being merely the occasion for a royal pardon. By the end of the middle ages (it is difficult to assign a fixed date) even excuses were recognised by the courts, since when there has been no reason to distinguish between justification

and excuse." Glanville Williams, *Textbook of Criminal Law* 39 (1978).

imperfect justification. A reason or cause that is insufficient to completely justify a defendant's behavior but that can be used to mitigate criminal punishment.

justification defense. *Criminal & tort law.* A defense that arises when the defendant has acted in a way that the law does not seek to prevent. • Traditionally, the following defenses were justifications: consent, self-defense, defense of others, defense of property, necessity (choice of evils), the use of force to make an arrest, and the use of force by public authority. — Sometimes shortened to *justification*. Cf. EXCUSE (2).

justificator (**jəs**-tə-fi-kay-tər). *Hist.* **1.** A compurgator who testifies under oath in defense of an accused person. **2.** A juror.

Justinian Code (jəs-**tin**-ee-ən). *Roman law.* A collection of imperial constitutions drawn up by a commission of ten persons appointed by Justinian, and published in A.D. 529. • The Code replaced all prior imperial law, but was in force only until A.D. 534, when it was supplanted by the *Codex Repetitae Praelectionis*. — Also termed *Justinianean Code* (jəs-tin-ee-**an**-ee-ən); *Code of Justinian*; *Codex Justinianeus* (**koh**-deks-jəs-tin-ee-**ay**-n(ee)əs); *Codex Vetus* ("Old Code").

Justinianist (jə-**stin**-ee-ə-nist), *n.* **1.** One who is knowledgeable about the codification of Justinian. **2.** One who has been trained in civil law.

Justinian's Institutes. See INSTITUTE.

justitia (jəs-**tish**-ee-ə), *n.* [Latin] Justice.

justitia denegata (jəs-**tish**-ee-ə dee-nə-**gay**-tə). See DENIAL OF JUSTICE.

justitia naturalis (jəs-**tish**-ee-ə nach-ə-**ray**-lis). See *natural justice* under JUSTICE (1).

justitium (jəs-**tish**-ee-əm), *n.* [Latin] *Civil law.* A suspension or intermission of the administration of justice in the courts, as for vacation time.

jus tripertitum (jəs trɪ-pər-**tɪ**-təm), *n.* [Latin "law in three parts"] *Roman law.* The law of wills in the time of Justinian, deriving from the praetorian edicts, from the civil law, and from the imperial constitutions.

jus trium liberorum (jəs **trɪ**-əm lib-ə-**ror**-əm). [Latin] See JUS LIBERORUM.

just title. See TITLE (2).

just value. See *fair market value* under VALUE.

just war. See BELLUM JUSTUM.

jus utendi (jəs yoo-**ten**-dɪ), *n.* [Latin "right of using"] *Roman & civil law.* The right to use another's property without consuming it or destroying its substance. See USUFRUCT. Cf. JUS ABUTENDI.

jus vitae necisque (jəs **vɪ**-tee ni-**sis**-kwee), *n.* [Latin "right of life and death"] *Roman law.* The power held by the head of the household over persons under his paternal power and over his slaves. • This right was abolished under later Roman law. See PATRIA POTESTAS.

juvenile (**joo**-və-nəl *or* -nɪl), *n.* A person who has not reached the age (usu. 18) at which one should be treated as an adult by the criminal-justice system; MINOR. — **juvenile,** *adj.* — **juvenility** (joo-və-**nil**-ə-tee), *n.*

juvenile court. See COURT.

juvenile delinquency. Antisocial behavior by a minor; esp., behavior that would be criminally punishable if the actor were an adult, but instead is usu. punished by special laws pertaining only to minors. — Also termed *delinquent minor*. Cf. INCORRIGIBILITY.

"'Juvenile delinquency,' when employed as a technical term rather than merely a descriptive phrase, is entirely a legislative product . . . ." Rollin M. Perkins & Ronald N. Boyce, *Criminal Law* 940 (3d ed. 1982).

juvenile delinquent. A minor guilty of criminal behavior, which is usu. punished by special laws not pertaining to adults. — Also termed *juvenile offender*; *youthful offender*; *delinquent minor*. See OFFENDER.

juvenile officer. A juvenile-court employee who works with the judge to direct and develop the court's child-welfare work. — Also termed *county agent*.

juvenile parole. See PAROLE.

juvenile petition. See PETITION.

juxta (**jəks**-tə). [Latin] Near; following; according to.

juxta conventionem (**jəks**-tə kən-ven-shee-**oh**-nəm). [Latin] According to the covenant.

juxta formam statuti (**jəks**-tə **for**-məm stə-**t**[**y**]**oo**-tɪ). [Latin] According to the form of the statute.

juxtaposition (jəks-tə-pə-**zish**-ən), *n.* **1.** The act or an instance of placing two or more things side by side or near one another. **2.** *Patents.* See AGGREGATION. — **juxtapose** (jəks-tə-**pohz**), *vb.* — **juxtapositional,** *adj.*

juxta ratam (**jəks**-tə **ray**-təm). [Latin] At or after the rate.

juxta tenorem sequentem (**jəks**-tə tə-**nor**-əm sə-**kwen**-təm). [Latin] According to the tenor following.

juzgado (hoos-**gah**-thoh). [Spanish "court"] The judiciary; the judges who concur in a decision.

K. *abbr.* Contract.

k/a. *abbr.* Known as.

Kaldor-Hicks efficiency. See WEALTH MAXIMIZATION.

kalendar. *Archaic.* See CALENDAR.

kalendarium (kal-ən-**dair**-ee-əm). *Roman law.* **1.** A book of accounts in which a moneylender recorded the names of debtors and the principal and interest due. **2.** A written register of births, recorded daily.

kalends. See CALENDS.

kangaroo court. See COURT.

K.B. *abbr.* KING'S BENCH.

K.C. *abbr.* KING'S COUNSEL.

keelage (**keel**-ij). *Hist.* **1.** The right to the demand payment of a toll by a ship entering or anchoring in a harbor. **2.** The toll so paid.

keelhaul (**keel**-hawl), *vb.* **1.** *Hist.* To drag (a person) through the water under the bottom of a ship as punishment or torture. **2.** To rebuke or reprimand harshly.

keeper. One who has the care, custody, or management of something and who usu. is legally responsible for it <a dog's keeper> <a keeper of lost property>.

Keeper of the Briefs. See CUSTOS BREVIUM.

Keeper of the Broad Seal. See KEEPER OF THE GREAT SEAL.

Keeper of the Great Seal. In England and Scotland, an officer who has custody of the Great Seal and who authenticates state documents of the highest importance. • In England, the duties of the Keeper of the Great Seal are now discharged by the Lord Chancellor. — Also termed *Lord Keeper of the Great Seal*; *Lord Keeper*; *Keeper of the Broad Seal*; *Custos Sigilli*.

Keeper of the King's Conscience. See LORD CHANCELLOR.

Keeper of the Privy Seal (**priv**-ee). **1.** LORD PRIVY SEAL. **2.** In Scotland and Cornwall, an officer similar to the English Lord Privy Seal.

Keeper of the Rolls. See CUSTOS ROTULORUM.

Keogh plan (**kee**-oh). A tax-deferred retirement program developed for the self-employed. • This plan is also known as a *H.R. 10 plan*, after the House of Representatives bill that established the plan. — Also termed *self-employed retirement plan*. See INDIVIDUAL RETIREMENT ACCOUNT.

KeyCite, *vb.* To determine the subsequent history of (a case, statute, etc.) by using the online citator of the same name to establish that the point being researched is still good law. — **KeyCiting,** *n.*

key-employee insurance. See INSURANCE.

key-executive insurance. See *key-employee insurance* under INSURANCE.

key man. See KEY PERSON.

key-man insurance. See *key-employee insurance* under INSURANCE.

key money. **1.** Payment (as rent or security) required from a new tenant in exchange for a key to the leased property. **2.** Payment made (usu. secretly) by a prospective tenant to a landlord or current tenant to increase the chance of obtaining a lease in an area where there is a housing shortage. • Key money in the first sense is a legal transaction; key money in the second sense is usu. an illegal bribe that violates housing laws.

key-number system. A legal-research indexing system developed by West Publishing Company (now the West Group) to catalogue American caselaw with headnotes. • In this system, a number designates a point of law, allowing a researcher to find all reported cases addressing a particular point by referring to its number.

key person. An important officer or employee; a person primarily responsible for a business's success. — Also termed *key man*.

key-person insurance. See *key-employee insurance* under INSURANCE.

kickback, *n.* A return of a portion of a monetary sum received, esp. as a result of coercion or a secret agreement <the contractor paid the city official a 5% kickback on the government contract>. — Also termed *payoff*. Cf. BRIBERY.

kicker. 1. An extra charge or penalty, esp. a charge added to a loan in addition to interest. **2.** An equity participation that a lender seeks as a condition for lending money, so that the lender may participate in rentals, profits, or extra interest.

kickout clause. A contractual provision allowing a party to end or modify the contract if a specified event occurs <under the kick-out clause, the company could refuse to sell the land if it were unable to complete its acquisition of the new headquarters>.

kiddie tax. See TAX.

kidnap, *vb.* To seize and take away (a person) by force or fraud, often with a demand for ransom.

kidnapping. The crime of seizing and taking away a person by force or fraud, often with a demand for ransom. — Also termed (archaically) *manstealing*.

> "At early common law, kidnapping required a forcible asportation of the victim to another country. Under modern statutes, the asportation need not be this extensive." Arnold H. Loewy, *Criminal Law in a Nutshell* 64 (2d ed. 1987).

aggravated kidnapping. Kidnapping accompanied by some aggravating factor (such as a demand for ransom or injury of the victim).

child-kidnapping. The kidnapping of a child, often without the element of force or fraud (as when someone walks off with another's baby stroller). — Also termed *child-stealing*; *baby-snatching*.

parental kidnapping. The kidnapping of a child by one parent in violation of the other parent's custody or visitation rights.

simple kidnapping. Kidnapping not accompanied by an aggravating factor.

killer amendment. See AMENDMENT (1).

killing by misadventure. See ACCIDENTAL KILLING.

kin, *n.* **1.** One's relatives; family. — Also termed *kindred*. **2.** A relative by blood, marriage, or adoption, though usu. by blood only; a kinsman or kinswoman.

kind arbitrage. See ARBITRAGE.

kindred, *n.* **1.** One's relatives; KIN (1). **2.** Family relationship; KINSHIP.

King. *English law.* The British government; the Crown.

> "In modern times it has become usual to speak of the Crown rather than of the King, when we refer to the King in his public capacity as a body politic. We speak of the property of the Crown, when we mean the property which the King holds in right of his Crown. So we speak of the debts due by the Crown, of legal proceedings by and against the Crown, and so on. The usage is one of great convenience, because it avoids a difficulty which is inherent in all speech and thought concerning corporations sole, the difficulty, namely, of distinguishing adequately between the body politic and the human being by whom it is represented and whose name it bears." John Salmond, *Jurisprudence* 341–42 (Glanville L. Williams ed., 10th ed. 1947).

King's advocate. See LORD ADVOCATE.

King's Bench. Historically, the highest common-law court in England, so called during the reign of a king. • In 1873, the court's jurisdiction was transferred to the Queen's Bench Division of the High Court of Justice. — Abbr. K.B. — Also termed *Court of King's Bench*; *Coram Rege Court*. Cf. QUEEN'S BENCH; QUEEN'S BENCH DIVISION.

> "The court of *King's Bench* is the highest court of ordinary justice in criminal cases within the realm, and paramount to the authority of justices of gaol delivery, and commissions of oyer and terminer. It has jurisdiction over all criminal causes, from high treason down to the most trivial misdemeanor or breach of the peace." 1 Joseph Chitty, *A Practical Treatise on the Criminal Law* 156 (2d ed. 1826).

King's Chambers. In the United Kingdom, waters lying within an imaginary line drawn from headland to headland around the coast of Great Britain.

King's Counsel. In the United Kingdom, Canada, and territories that have retained the rank, an elite, senior-level barrister or advocate appointed to serve as counsel to the king. — Also termed *senior counsel.* — Abbr. K.C. Cf. QUEEN'S COUNSEL.

King's Court. See CURIA REGIS.

King's evidence. See *Queen's evidence* under EVIDENCE.

King's Great Sessions in Wales. See COURT OF GREAT SESSIONS IN WALES.

King's peace. *Hist.* A royal subject's right to be free from crime (to "have peace") in certain areas subject to the king's immediate control, such as the king's palace or highway. • A breach of the peace in one of these areas subjected the offender to punishment in the king's court. Over time, the area subject to the king's peace grew, which in turn increased the jurisdiction of the royal courts. — Also written *King's Peace.* Cf. AGAINST THE PEACE AND DIGNITY OF THE STATE.

> "A breach of the King's Peace was at one time the most comprehensive of all offences against the Crown; it indeed included, and still includes, all the more serious crimes. At one time, in fact, every indictment charged the accused with an offence 'against the peace of our Sovereign Lord the King'; and, though this form is no longer employed, that is mainly because the imperative duty of not disturbing the King's Peace has by now evolved into an elaborate system of Criminal Law." Edward Jenks, *The Book of English Law* 134 (P.B. Fairest ed., 6th ed. 1967).

King's proctor. See QUEEN'S PROCTOR.

King's silver. *Hist.* Money paid in the Court of Common Pleas for a license to levy a feudal fine; an amount due on granting a *congé d'accorder* in levying a fine of lands. • It amounted to three-twentieths of the supposed annual value of the land, or ten shillings for every five marks of land. — Also termed *post-fine.* See CONGÉ D'ACCORDER; FINE (1).

kinship. Relationship by blood, marriage, or adoption. — Also termed *kindred.*

kintal. See QUINTAL.

kissing the Book. *Hist.* The practice of touching one's lips to a copy of the Bible (esp. the New Testament) after taking an oath in court. • This practice — formerly used in England — was replaced by the practice of placing one's hand on the Bible while swearing.

kitchen cabinet. See CABINET.

kiting. See CHECK-KITING.

***Klaxon* doctrine** (**klak**-sən). *Conflict of laws.* The principle that a federal court exercising diversity jurisdiction must apply the choice-of-law rules of the state where the court sits. • In *Klaxon Co. v. Stentor Elec. Mfg. Co.*, the Supreme Court extended the rule of *Erie v. Tompkins* to choice-of-law issues. 313 U.S. 487, 61 S.Ct. 1020 (1941). — Also termed *Erie/Klaxon doctrine.* See ERIE DOCTRINE.

kleptomania (klep-tə-**may**-nee-ə), *n.* A compulsive urge to steal, esp. without economic motive. — **kleptomaniac,** *n.* & *adj.*

knight. **1.** *Hist.* In the Middle Ages, a person of noble birth who, having been trained in arms and chivalry, was bound to follow an earl, baron, or other superior lord into battle. **2.** In modern Britain, a man upon whom the monarch has bestowed an honorary dignity (knighthood) as a reward for personal merit of some kind. • The status of knighthood no longer relates to birth or possessions and does not involve military service.

knight bachelor. See BACHELOR (3).

knight service. *Hist.* A type of tenure in which a knight held land of another person or the Crown in exchange for a pledge of military service. — Also termed *knight's service.* Cf. BASE SERVICE; SOCAGE; VILLEINAGE.

> "By far the greater part of England is held of the king by knight's service (*per servitium militare*): it is comparatively rare for the king's tenants in chief to hold by any of the other tenures. In order to understand this tenure we must form the conception of a unit of military service. That unit seems to be the service of one knight or fully armed horseman (*servitium unius militis*) to be done to the king in his army for forty days in the year, if it be called for." 1 Frederick Pollock & Frederic W. Maitland, *The History of English Law Before the Time of Edward I* 254 (2d ed. 1898).

knight's fee. *Hist.* The amount of land that gave rise to the obligation of knight service. • The amount varied from less than a hide to more than six hides. See HIDE.

knight's service. See KNIGHT SERVICE.

knock-and-announce rule. *Criminal procedure.* The requirement that the police knock at the door and announce their identity, authority, and purpose before entering a residence to execute an arrest or search warrant.

knock-for-knock agreement. An arrangement between insurers whereby each will pay the claim of its insured without claiming against the other party's insurance.

knockoff, *n.* An unauthorized copy or imitation of another's product, usu. for sale at a substantially lower price than the original.

knock off, *vb.* **1.** To make an unauthorized copy of (another's product), usu. for sale at a substantially lower price than the original <the infringer knocked off popular dress designs>. **2.** *Slang.* To murder <the gang leader was knocked off by one of his lieutenants>. **3.** *Slang.* To rob or burglarize <the thieves knocked off the jewelry store in broad daylight>.

know all men by these presents. Take note. • This archaic form of address — a loan translation of the Latin *noverint universi per praesentes* — was traditionally used to begin certain legal documents such as bonds and powers of attorney, but in modern drafting style the phrase is generally considered deadwood. See NOVERINT UNIVERSI PER PRAESENTES. Cf. PATEAT UNIVERSIS PER PRAESENTES.

know-how. The information, practical knowledge, techniques, and skill required to achieve some practical end, esp. in industry or technology. • Know-how is considered intangible property in which rights may be bought and sold. See TRADE SECRET.

knowing, *adj.* **1.** Having or showing awareness or understanding; well-informed <a knowing waiver of the right to counsel>. **2.** Deliberate; conscious <a knowing attempt to commit fraud>. — **knowingly,** *adv.*

knowledge. 1. An awareness or understanding of a fact or circumstance. Cf. INTENT (1); NOTICE; SCIENTER.

> "It is necessary ... to distinguish between producing a result intentionally and producing it knowingly. Intention and knowledge commonly go together, for he who intends a result usually knows that it will follow, and he who knows the consequences of his act usually intends them. But there may be intention without knowledge, the consequence being desired but not foreknown as certain or even probable. Conversely, there may be knowledge without intention, the consequence being foreknown as the inevitable concomitant of that which is desired, but being itself an object of repugnance rather than desire, and therefore not intended. When King David ordered Uriah the Hittite to be set in the forefront of the hottest battle, he intended the death of Uriah only, yet he knew for a certainty that many others of his men would fall at the same time and place." John Salmond, *Jurisprudence* 380–81 (Glanville L. Williams ed., 10th ed. 1947).

> " 'Knowingly' or 'knowledge' has a broad sweep when used in connection with the element of a crime, and an untrue representation has been 'knowingly' made if by one who knows it is untrue, believes it is untrue or is quite aware that he has not the slightest notion whether it is true or not." Rollin M. Perkins & Ronald N. Boyce, *Criminal Law* 379 (3d ed. 1982).

> "[B]ecause there are several areas of the criminal law in which there may be good reason for distinguishing between one's objectives and [one's] knowledge, the modern approach is to define separately the mental states of knowledge and intent .... This is the approach taken in the Model Penal Code [§ 2.02(2)(a) & (b)]." Wayne R. LaFave & Austin W. Scott, Jr., *Criminal Law* 218 (2d ed. 1986).

***actual knowledge.* 1.** Direct and clear knowledge, as distinguished from constructive knowledge <the employer, having witnessed the accident, had actual knowledge of the worker's injury>. — Also termed *express actual knowledge.* **2.** Knowledge of such information as would lead a reasonable person to inquire further <under the discovery rule, the limitations period begins to run once the plaintiff has actual knowledge of the injury>. — Also termed (in sense 2) *implied actual knowledge.*

> "The third issue in section 523(a)(3) is the meaning of 'notice or actual knowledge.' Under the Uniform Commercial Code knowledge means actually knowing something; notice means having received information from which one could infer the existence of the relevant fact. What the adjective 'actual' adds to the idea of 'knowledge' is unclear." David G. Epstein et al., *Bankruptcy* § 7-27, at 516 (1993).

common knowledge. See COMMON KNOWLEDGE.

constructive knowledge. Knowledge that one using reasonable care or diligence should have, and therefore that is attributed by law to a given person <the court held that the partners had constructive knowledge of the partnership agreement even though none of them had read it>.

express actual knowledge. See *actual knowledge* (1).

firsthand knowledge. See *personal knowledge.*

implied actual knowledge. See *actual knowledge* (2).

imputed knowledge. Knowledge attributed to a given person, esp. because of the person's legal responsibility for another's conduct <the principal's imputed knowledge of its agent's dealings>.

personal knowledge. Knowledge gained through firsthand observation or experience, as distinguished from a belief based on what someone else has said. • Rule 602 of the Federal Rules of Evidence requires lay witnesses to have personal knowledge of the matters they testify about. An affidavit must also be based on personal knowledge, unless the affiant makes clear that a statement relies on "information and belief." — Also termed *firsthand knowledge*.

reckless knowledge. A defendant's belief that there is a risk that a prohibited circumstance exists, regardless of which the defendant goes on to take the risk.

scientific knowledge. *Evidence.* Knowledge that is grounded on scientific methods that have been supported by adequate validation. • Four primary factors are used to determine whether evidence amounts to scientific knowledge: (1) whether it has been tested; (2) whether it has been subject to peer review and publication; (3) the known or potential rate of error; and (4) the degree of acceptance within the scientific community. See DAUBERT TEST; SCIENTIFIC METHOD.

superior knowledge. Knowledge greater than that had by another person, esp. so as to adversely affect that person <in its fraud claim, the subcontractor alleged that the general contractor had superior knowledge of the equipment shortage>.

2. *Archaic.* CARNAL KNOWLEDGE.

knowledge-of-falsity exclusion. See EXCLUSION (3).

known creditor. See CREDITOR.

known heir. See HEIR.

known-loss doctrine. *Insurance.* A principle denying insurance coverage when the insured knows before the policy takes effect that a specific loss has already happened or is substantially certain to happen. — Also termed *known-risk doctrine*.

koop (kohp), *n.* [Dutch] *Dutch law.* Purchase; bargain.

koopbrief (**kohp**-breef). [Dutch] *Dutch law.* A deed of sale.

L

L. *abbr.* **1.** LAW (5). **2.** LORD (1). **3.** LOCUS. **4.** LATIN.

L. A measure of the money supply, including M3 items plus banker's acceptances, T-bills, and similar long-term investments. See M3.

label, *n.* **1.** An informative logo, title, or similar marking affixed to a manufactured product. **2.** Any writing (such as a codicil) attached to a larger writing. **3.** A narrow slip of paper or parchment attached to a deed or writ in order to hold a seal.

label-and-significant-characteristics test. *Securities.* The rule that an instrument will be governed by the securities laws if it is labeled a stock and has the significant characteristics typically associated with shares of stock.

labeling. Under the Federal Food, Drug, and Cosmetic Act, any label or other written, printed, or graphic matter that is on a product or its container, or that accompanies the product. • To come within the Act, the labeling does not need to accompany the product. It may be sent before or after delivery of the product, as long as delivery of the product and the written material are part of the same distribution program.

labina (lə-**bI**-nə), *n.* *Archaic.* Land covered by water; swampland.

la bomba (lə **bom**-bə). (*sometimes cap.*) An incendiary device consisting of a plastic bag filled with fuel and placed inside a paper bag stuffed with tissue and rigged with a fuse. • A person who uses such a device to start a fire violates the federal arson statute. 18 USCA § 844(j).

labor, *n.* **1.** Work of any type, including mental exertion <the fruits of one's labor>. • The term usu. refers to work for wages as opposed to profits. **2.** Workers considered as an economic unit or a political element <a dispute between management and labor over retirement benefits>. **3.** A Spanish land measure equal to 177 $^1/_7$ acres. • This measure has been used in Mexico and was once used in Texas.

labor, *vb.* **1.** To work, esp. with great exertion <David labored long and hard to finish the brief on time>. **2.** *Archaic.* To tamper with or improperly attempt to influence (a jury). • This sense derives from the idea that the tamperer "endeavors" to influence the jury's verdict. See EMBRACERY. — **laborer,** *n.*

labor agreement. An agreement between an employer and a union governing working conditions, wages, benefits, and grievances. — Also termed *labor contract*; *union contract.*

laborariis (lay-bə-**rair**-ee-is), *n.* [Latin "about laborers"] *Hist.* An ancient writ against a person who had no other means of support but refused to work throughout the year.

laboratory conditions. *Labor law.* The ideal conditions for a union election, in which the employees may exercise free choice without interference from the employer, the union, or anyone else.

labor contract. See LABOR AGREEMENT.

labor dispute. A controversy between an employer and its employees concerning the terms or conditions of employment, or concerning the association or representation of those who negotiate or seek to negotiate the terms or conditions of employment.

Labor Disputes Act. See NORRIS–LAGUARDIA ACT.

laborer. **1.** A person who makes a living by physical labor. **2.** WORKER.

laborer's lien. See *mechanic's lien* under LIEN.

laboring a jury. See EMBRACERY.

labor–management relations. The broad spectrum of activities concerning the relationship between employers and employees, both union and nonunion. See FAIR LABOR STANDARDS ACT; NATIONAL LABOR RELATIONS ACT; NATIONAL LABOR RELATIONS BOARD.

Labor–Management Relations Act. A federal statute, enacted in 1947, that regulates certain union activities, permits suits against unions for proscribed acts, prohibits certain strikes and boycotts, and provides steps for settling strikes involving national emergencies. 29 USCA §§ 141 et seq. — Also termed *Taft-Hartley Act.* See NATIONAL LABOR RELATIONS BOARD.

labor organization. See UNION.

labor-relations act. A statute regulating relations between employers and employees. • Although the Labor–Management Relations Act is the chief federal labor-relations act, various states have enacted these statutes as well.

Labor Relations Board. See NATIONAL LABOR RELATIONS BOARD.

labor union. See UNION.

lacca. See LACTA.

Lacey Act. A federal law, originally enacted in 1900, that permits states to enforce their own game laws against animals imported from other states or countries. 16 USCA §§ 661 et seq. See GAME LAW.

la chambre des esteilles (lə **shahm**-brə də zes-**tay**), *n.* [French] *Hist.* The Star Chamber. See STAR CHAMBER, COURT OF.

laches (**lach**-iz). [Law French "remissness; slackness"] **1.** Unreasonable delay or negligence in pursuing a right or claim — almost always an equitable one — in a way that prejudices the party against whom relief is sought.

> "Early in its history, Chancery developed the doctrine that where the plaintiff in equity delayed beyond the period of the statute applicable at law, relief would be refused on the ground of laches even though no specific prejudice to the defendant was shown. Today, in most states, there are statutes of limitations applying to suits in equity. Despite these, however, the doctrine still holds that even if the delay is for a shorter period of time than that of the statute, it may still bar equitable relief if it is unreasonable and prejudicial to the defendant." John F. O'Connell, *Remedies in a Nutshell* 16 (2d ed. 1985).

2. The equitable doctrine by which a court denies relief to a claimant who has unreasonably delayed or been negligent in asserting the claim, when that delay or negligence has prejudiced the party against whom relief is sought. Cf. LIMITATION (3).

> "The doctrine of laches ... is an instance of the exercise of the reserved power of equity to withhold relief otherwise regularly given where in the particular case the granting of such relief would be unfair or unjust." William F. Walsh, *A Treatise on Equity* 472 (1930).

laches, estoppel by. See *estoppel by laches* under ESTOPPEL.

***Lackey* claim.** A prisoner's assertion that incarceration on death row for a protracted period is cruel and unusual punishment. *Lackey v. Texas*, 514 U.S. 1045, 115 S.Ct. 1421 (1995) (denying cert.).

lack of jurisdiction. See WANT OF JURISDICTION.

lack of prosecution. See WANT OF PROSECUTION.

lacta (**lak**-tə), *n.* [Law Latin] *Hist.* Lack of or defect in the weight of money. — Also termed *lacca.*

l'acte de l'état civil. See ACTE (1).

lada (**lay**-də), *n.* [Law Latin] **1.** *Hist.* A court of justice. **2.** A canal for draining marshy ground; a watercourse; a lade.

lade (layd), *n. Hist.* The mouth of a river. — Also spelled *lode.*

laden in bulk, *adj. Maritime law.* (Of a vessel) freighted with a cargo that lies loose in the hold, protected from water and moisture by mats and dunnage, instead of cargo packed in containers. • Cargoes of corn, salt, and similar items are usu. shipped in bulk.

lading, bill of. See BILL OF LADING.

lady. In Britain, a title belonging to the wife of a peer, (by courtesy) the wife of a baronet or knight, or any single or married woman whose father was a nobleman carrying a rank of earl or higher.

lady-court. *Hist.* The court of a lady of the manor.

lady's friend. *Hist.* The title of an officer in the English House of Commons, whose duty was to secure a suitable provision for a wife when her husband sought a parliamentary divorce. • In 1857, parliamentary divorces and the office of lady's friend were abolished by statute.

laenland. See LOANLAND.

laesae majestatis (**lee**-zee maj-ə-**stay**-tis). See LESE MAJESTY.

laesa majestas (**lee**-zə mə-**jes**-tas). See LESE MAJESTY.

laesio enormis (**lee**-shee-oh i-**nor**-mis), *n.* [Latin "loss beyond half or great"] *Civil law.* **1.** The sale of a thing for which the buyer paid less than half of its real value. • The seller could rescind the sale, but the buyer could keep the item purchased by paying the full value. **2.** The principle by which a seller may rescind a contract if a sale yields less than half the true value of the thing sold. — Also termed *lesion.*

> "Lesion (*laesio enormis*) was the rule, established very late, that a seller could rescind a contract if he had received less than half its real value .... [I]n spite of its imperfections, lesion not only was adopted in all modern civilian systems (French Code Civil 1674–1683), but became the means of testing the validity of contracts generally by their fairness, a principle embodied in the German Civil Code (section 138) and the Swiss Code of Obligations (section 21). Such a test is no more difficult to apply in law than in equity, where it has long been established in our system. As the Romans applied it, it was a clumsy and inadequate way of reaching this result. In modern courts, in civil-law countries, it invests judges with a discretion not very likely to be abused, but sufficient to act as a deterrent to the grosser forms of economic exploitation." Max Radin, *Handbook of Roman Law* 233–34 (1927).

laesio ultra dimidium vel enormis (**lee**-shee-oh **əl**-trə di-**mid**-ee-əm vel i-**nor**-mis), *n.* [Latin] *Roman law.* The injury sustained by one party to an onerous contract when the overreaching party receives twice the value of that party's money or property, such as a purchaser who pays less than half of the value of the property sold, or a seller who receives more than double the property's value. See *adhesion contract* under CONTRACT.

laesiwerp (**lee**-zə-wərp), *n.* [Saxon fr. *laisus* "bosom" + *werpire* "to surrender"] *Hist.* A thing surrendered to another's hands or power; a thing given or delivered.

laet (layt), *n. Hist.* A person of a class between servile and free.

laga. See LAGE.

lagan (**lag**-ən), *n.* Goods that are abandoned at sea but attached to a buoy so that they may be recovered. — Also termed *lagend*; *lagon*; *ligan*; *ligen*; *logan.* Cf. FLOTSAM; JETSAM; WAVESON.

lage (law *or* lay), *n.* [fr. Saxon *lag* "law"] *Hist.* **1.** Law. **2.** The territory in which certain law was in force, such as danelage, mercenlage, and West–Saxon lage. • This term is essentially an obsolete form of the word *law.* — Also termed *lagh*; *laga*; *lagu.* See DANELAW; MERCENLAGE; WEST-SAXON LAW.

lage day (**law** day). A law day; a juridical day; a day of open court. — Also termed *lagh day.*

lageman (**law**-mən *or* **lay**-mən). See LEGALIS HOMO.

lagend (**lag**-ənd). See LAGAN.

lagging economic indicator. See ECONOMIC INDICATOR.

lagging indicator. See INDICATOR.

lagh day. See LAGE DAY.

lagon (**lag**-ən). See LAGAN.

lagu. See LAGE.

lahman (**law**-mən *or* **lay**-mən), *n.* [Saxon fr. *lah* "law"] *Archaic.* A lawyer. — Also termed *lagemannus.*

laicus (**lay**-ə-kəs), *n.* [Law Latin] *Hist.* A layman; one who is not in the ministry.

***Laidlaw* vacancy.** Under the National Labor Relations Act, a genuine opening in an employer's workforce, resulting from the employer's expanding its workforce or discharging a particular employee, or from an employee's resigning or otherwise leaving the employment. • The opening is required to be offered to striking workers, in order of seniority, after a strike has been resolved. *Laidlaw Corp. v. NLRB*, 414 F.2d 99 (7th Cir. 1969).

lairwite (**lair**-wɪt), *n.* [fr. Saxon *lagan* "to lie" + *wite* "a fine"] *Hist.* A fine for adultery or fornication paid to the lord of the manor; specif., a lord's privilege of receiving a fine for fornication with the lord's female villeins. — Also termed *lairesite*; *lecherwite*; *legerwite*; *leyerwite.*

lais gents (**lay** zho*n*[ts]), *n. pl.* [Law French] *Hist.* Laymen; a jury.

laissez-faire (les-ay-**fair**), *n.* [French "let (people) do (as they choose)"] **1.** Governmental abstention from interfering in economic or commercial affairs. **2.** The doctrine favoring such abstention. — **laissez-faire,** *adj.*

laity (**lay**-ə-tee). Collectively, persons who are not members of the clergy.

lake, *n.* **1.** A large body of standing water in a depression of land or basin supplied from the drainage of an extended area. **2.** A widened or expanded part of a river.

Lambeth degree (**lam**-bəth). *Hist.* A degree conferred by the Archbishop of Canterbury, rather than by a university, as authorized under the Ecclesiastical Licenses Act of 1533 (25 Hen. 8, ch. 21).

***Lamb-Weston* rule.** *Insurance.* The doctrine that, when two insurance policies provide coverage for a loss, and each of them contains an other-insurance clause — creating a conflict in the order or apportionment of coverage — both of the other-insurance clauses will be disregarded and liability will be prorated between the insurers. *Lamb-Weston, Inc. v. Oregon Auto. Ins. Co.*, 341 P.2d 110 (Or. 1959).

lame duck. An elected official who is serving out a term after someone else has been elected as a successor.

lame-duck amendment. See TWENTIETH AMENDMENT.

lame-duck session. See SESSION.

lammas land. See LAND.

land, *n.* **1.** An immovable and indestructible three-dimensional area consisting of a portion of the earth's surface, the space above and below the surface, and everything growing on or permanently affixed to it. **2.** An estate or interest in real property.

"In its legal significance, 'land' is not restricted to the earth's surface, but extends below and above the surface. Nor is it confined to solids, but may encompass within its bounds such things as gases and liquids. A definition of 'land' along the lines of 'a mass of physical matter occupying space' also is not sufficient, for an owner of land may remove part or all of that physical matter, as by digging up and carrying away the soil, but would nevertheless retain as part of his 'land' the space that remains. Ultimately, as a juristic concept, 'land' is simply an area of three-dimensional space, its position being identified by natural or imaginary points located by reference to the earth's surface. 'Land' is not the fixed contents of that space, although, as we shall see, the owner of that space may well own those fixed contents. Land is immoveable, as distinct from chattels, which are moveable; it is also, in its legal significance, indestructible. The contents of the space may be physically severed, destroyed or consumed, but the space itself, and so the 'land', remains immutable." Peter Butt, *Land Law* 9 (2d ed. 1988).

accommodation land. Land that is bought by a builder or speculator, who erects houses or improvements on it and then leases it at an increased rent.

arable land (**ar**-ə-bəl). Land that is fit for cultivation, as distinguished from swampland. — Formerly also termed *araturia.*

bounty land. A portion of public land given or donated as a reward, esp. for military services.

certificate land. Land in the western part of Pennsylvania set apart after the American Revolution to be bought with certificates the soldiers received in lieu of pay.

Crown land. Demesne land of the Crown; esp., in England and Canada, land belonging to the sovereign personally, or to the government, as distinguished from land held under private ownership. — Also termed *demesne land of the Crown.* See *demesne land.*

demesne land (di-**mayn** *or* di-**meen**). *Hist.* Land reserved by a lord for personal use.

donation land. Land granted from the public domain to an individual as a gift, usu. as a reward for services or to encourage settlement in a remote area. • The term was initially used in Pennsylvania to reward Revolutionary War soldiers.

enclosed land. Land that is actually enclosed and surrounded with fences.

fabric land. *Hist.* Land given toward the maintenance, repair, or rebuilding of a cathedral or other church. • This term derives from funds given *ad fabricam ecclesiae reparandam* ("to repair the fabric of the church").

"Fabrick-Lands are lands given towards the maintenance, rebuilding, or repair of Cathedrals or other churches.... In antient time almost every one gave by his Will more or less to the *Fabrick* of the Cathedral or Parish-Church where he liv'd." Thomas Blount, *Nomo-Lexicon: A Law-Dictionary* (1670).

fast land. (*often pl.*) Land that is above the high-water mark and that, when flooded by a government project, is subjected to a governmental taking. • Owners of fast lands are entitled to just compensation for the taking. See TAKING.

indemnity land. See INDEMNITY LAND.

lammas land (**lam**-əs). *Hist.* Land over which persons other than the owner have the right of pasturage during winter, from lammas (reaping time) until sowing time.

lieu land (loo). Public land within indemnity limits granted in lieu of those lost within place limits.

life land. *Hist.* Land leased for a term measured by the life of one or more persons. — Also termed *life-hold.*

mineral land. Land that contains deposits of valuable minerals in quantities justifying the costs of extraction and using the land for mining, rather than agricultural or other purposes.

place land. See INDEMNITY LAND.

public land. Unappropriated land belonging to the federal or a state government; the general public domain. Cf. INDEMNITY LAND.

school land. Public real estate set apart for sale by a state to establish and fund public schools.

seated land. Land that is occupied, cultivated, improved, reclaimed, farmed, or used as a place of residence, with or without cultivation.

swamp and overflowed land. Land that, because of its boggy, marshy, fenlike character, is unfit for cultivation, requiring drainage or reclamation to render it available for beneficial use. • Such lands were granted out of the U.S. public domain to the littoral states by acts of Congress in 1850 and thereafter. 43 USCA §§ 981 et seq.

tideland. See TIDELAND.

land, law of. See LAW OF THE LAND.

land agent. See LAND MANAGER.

land bank. 1. A bank created under the Federal Farm Loan Act to make loans at low interest rates secured by farmland. **2.** A program in which land is retired from agricultural production for conservation or tree-cultivation purposes. — Also termed *soil bank.* See FEDERAL HOME LOAN BANK.

land boundary. The limit of a landholding, usu. described by linear measurements of the borders, by points of the compass, or by stationary markers. See BOUNDARY; FORTY; LEGAL DESCRIPTION.

land certificate. A document entitling a person to receive from the government a certain amount of land by following prescribed legal steps. • It contains an official description of the land, as well as the name and address of the person receiving the entitlement, and is prima facie evidence of the truth of the matters it contains. — Also termed *land warrant.*

landcheap. *Hist.* A customary fine paid in money or cattle when any real property within a manor or borough was transferred.

land contract. See *contract for deed* under CONTRACT.

land cop. *Hist.* The sale of land evidenced by the transfer in court of a rod or festuca as a symbol of possession. • The seller handed the rod to the reeve and the reeve handed it to the purchaser. The conveyance occurred in court to provide better evidence of the transfer and to bar the claims of expected heirs.

land court. See COURT.

land damages. See *just compensation* under COMPENSATION.

land department. A federal or state bureau that determines factual matters regarding the control and transfer of public land. • The federal land department includes the General Land Office headed by the Secretary of the Interior. See DEPARTMENT OF THE INTERIOR.

land description. See LEGAL DESCRIPTION.

land district. See DISTRICT.

landed, *adj.* **1.** (Of a person) having an estate in land. **2.** (Of an estate, etc.) consisting of land.

landed estate. See ESTATE.

landed-estates court. See COURT.

landed property. See *landed estate* under ESTATE.

landed security. See SECURITY.

landed servitude. See *servitude appurtenant* under SERVITUDE (1).

landefricus (lan-də-**frɪ**-kəs). *Hist.* A landlord or lord of the soil.

landegandman (lan-də-**gand**-mən *or* **lan**-də-gənd-mən). *Hist.* A customary or inferior tenant of a manor.

land flip. *Real estate.* A transaction in which a piece of property is purchased for one price and immediately sold, usu. to a fictitious entity, for a much higher price, to dupe a lender or later purchaser into thinking that the property is more valuable than it actually is.

land-gavel (**land**-gav-əl). *Hist.* A tax or rent issuing from land. — Also spelled *landgable*; *land-gabel*; *land-gafol*. See GAVEL.

land grant. A donation of public land to an individual, a corporation, or a subordinate government.

private land grant. A land grant to a natural person. See *land patent* under PATENT (1).

landhlaford (**land**-[h]lav-ərd). *Hist.* A proprietor of land; a lord of the soil.

landholder. One who possesses or owns land.

land improvement. See IMPROVEMENT.

landing. 1. A place on a river or other navigable water for loading and unloading goods, or receiving and delivering passengers and pleasure boats. **2.** The termination point on a river or other navigable water for these purposes. **3.** The act or process of coming back to land after a voyage or flight.

landing law. A law prohibiting the possession or sale of fish or game that have been taken illegally.

land lease. See *ground lease* under LEASE.

landlocked, *adj.* Surrounded by land, often with the suggestion that there is little or no way to get in or out without crossing the land of another <the owner of the landlocked property purchased an access easement from the adjoining landowner>.

landlord. 1. At common law, the feudal lord who retained the fee of the land. **2.** One who leases real property to another. — Also termed (in sense 2) *lessor*.

absentee landlord. A landlord who does not live on the leased premises — and usu. who lives far away. — Also termed *absentee management*.

landlord-and-tenant relationship. See LANDLORD–TENANT RELATIONSHIP.

landlord's lien. See LIEN.

landlord's warrant. See WARRANT (1).

landlord–tenant relationship. The familiar legal relationship existing between the lessor and lessee of real estate. • The relationship is contractual, created by a lease (or agreement for lease) for a term of years, from year to year, for life, or at will, and exists when one person occupies the premises of another with the lessor's permission or consent, subordinated to the lessor's title or rights. There must be a landlord's reversion, a tenant's estate, transfer of possession and control of the premises, and (generally) an express or implied contract. — Also termed *landlord-and-tenant relationship*. See LEASE.

land manager. *Oil & gas.* A person who, usu. on behalf of an oil company, contracts with landowners for the mineral rights to their land. — Also termed *exploration manager*; *land agent*; *landman*.

landmark. 1. A feature of land (such as a natural object, or a monument or marker) that demarcates the boundary of the land <according to the 1891 survey, the crooked oak tree is the correct landmark at the property's northeast corner>. **2.** A historically significant building or site <the schoolhouse built in 1898 is the county's most famous landmark>. See MONUMENT.

landmark decision. A judicial decision that significantly changes existing law. • Examples are *Brown v. Board of Educ.*, 347 U.S. 483, 74 S.Ct. 686 (1954) (holding that segregation in public schools violates the Equal Protection Clause), and *Palsgraf v. Long Island R.R.*, 162 N.E. 99 (N.Y. 1928) (establishing that a defendant's duty in a negligence action is limited to plaintiffs within the apparent zone of danger — that is, plaintiffs to whom damage could be reasonably foreseen). — Also termed *landmark case*. Cf. LEADING CASE.

land office. A government office in which sales of public land are recorded.

landowner. One who owns land.

land patent. See PATENT (2).

land-poor, *adj.* (Of a person) owning a substantial amount of unprofitable or encumbered land, but lacking the money to improve or maintain the land or to pay the charges due on it.

landreeve. *Hist.* A person charged with (1) overseeing certain parts of a farm or estate, (2) attending to the timber, fences, gates, buildings, private roads, and watercourses, (3) stocking the commons, (4) watching for encroachments of all kinds, (5) preventing and detecting waste and spoliation by tenants and others, and (6) reporting on findings to the manager or land steward.

land revenue. See REVENUE.

Landrum–Griffin Act. A federal law, originally enacted in 1959 as the Labor–Management Reporting and Disclosure Act, designed to (1) curb corruption in union leadership and undemocratic conduct in internal union affairs, (2) outlaw certain types of secondary boycotts, and (3) prevent so-called hot-cargo provisions in collective-bargaining agreements. See HOT CARGO.

lands, *n. pl.* **1.** At common law, property less extensive than either tenements or hereditaments. **2.** By statute in some states, land including tenements and hereditaments. See HEREDITAMENTS; TENEMENTS.

land sales contract. See *contract for deed* under CONTRACT.

land scrip. A negotiable instrument entitling the holder, usu. a person or company engaged in public service, to possess specified areas of public land.

lands, tenements, and hereditaments. Real property. • The term was traditionally used in wills, deeds, and other instruments.

land tax. See *property tax* under TAX.

land-tenant. See TERRE-TENANT.

Land Titles and Transfer Act. *Hist.* An 1875 statute establishing a registry for titles to real property, and providing for the transfer of lands and recording of those transfers. 38 & 39 Vict., ch. 87. • The act is analogous in some respects to American recording laws, such as those providing for a registry of deeds. A system of title registration superseded this registry system in 1925.

land trust. See TRUST.

land trust certificate. An instrument granting the holder a share of the benefits of property ownership, while the trustee retains legal title. See *land trust* under TRUST.

land-use planning. The deliberate, systematic development of real estate through methods such as zoning, environmental-impact studies, and the like. — Also termed *urban planning.*

land-use regulation. An ordinance or other legislative enactment intended to govern the development of real estate.

> "Public regulation of the use and development of land comes in a variety of forms which generally focus on four aspects of land use: (1) the type of use, such as whether it will be used for agricultural, commercial, industrial, or residential purposes; (2) the density of use, manifested in concerns over the height, width, bulk, or environmental impact of the physical structures on the land; (3) the aesthetic impact of the use, which may include the design and placement of structures on the land; and (4) the effect of the particular use of the land on the cultural and social values of the community, illustrated by community conflicts over adult entertainment, housing for service-dependent groups such as low-income families and developmentally disabled persons, and whether the term *family* should be defined in land use regulations to include persons who are not related by blood or marriage." Peter W. Salsich, Jr., *Land Use Regulation* 1 (1991).

land waiter. *English law.* A customhouse officer with the responsibility of examining, tasting, weighing, measuring, and accounting for merchandise landing at any port.

land warfare. See WARFARE.

land warrant. See LAND CERTIFICATE.

Langdell system. See CASEBOOK METHOD.

langeman (**lan**-jə-mən), *n. Hist.* A lord of a manor. Pl. **langemanni** (lan-jə-**man**-I).

language. 1. Any means of conveying or communicating ideas, esp. by human speech, written characters, or sign language <what language did they speak?>. **2.** The letter or grammatical import of a document or instrument, as distinguished from its spirit <the language of the statute>.

languidus (**lang**-gwi-dəs), *n.* [Law Latin "sick"] *Hist.* At common law, a return of process made by the sheriff when a defendant whom the sheriff had taken into custody was too sick to be removed.

Lanham Act (**lan**-əm). A federal trademark statute, enacted in 1946, that provides for a national system of trademark registration and protects the owner of a federally registered mark against the use of similar marks if any confusion might result. • The Lanham Act's scope is independent of and concurrent with state common law. 15 USCA §§ 1051 et seq.

lapidation (lap-ə-**day**-shən). An execution by stoning a person to death. — **lapidate** (**lap**-ə-dayt), *vb*.

lappage (**lap**-ij). Interference; lap and overlap; conflict. • Lappage applies when two different owners claim under deeds or grants that, in part, cover the same land.

lapping. An embezzlement technique by which an employee takes funds from one customer's accounts receivable and covers it by using a second customer's payment to pay the first account, then a third customer's payment to pay the second account, and so on.

lapse, *n*. **1.** The termination of a right or privilege because of a failure to exercise it within some time limit or because a contingency has occurred or not occurred. **2.** *Wills & estates*. The failure of a testamentary gift, esp. when the beneficiary dies before the testator dies. See ANTILAPSE STATUTE. Cf. ADEMPTION.

lapse, *vb*. **1.** (Of an estate or right) to pass away or revert to someone else because conditions have not been fulfilled or because a person entitled to possession has failed in some duty. See *lapsed policy* under INSURANCE POLICY. **2.** (Of a devise, grant, etc.) to become void.

lapsed devise. See DEVISE.

lapsed legacy. See LEGACY.

lapsed policy. See INSURANCE POLICY.

lapse patent. See PATENT (2).

lapse statute. See ANTILAPSE STATUTE.

larcenable (**lahr**-sə-nə-bəl), *adj*. Subject to larceny <because it cannot be carried away, real estate is not larcenable>.

larcenist. One who commits larceny. See LARCENY.

larcenous (**lahr**-sə-nəs), *adj*. **1.** Of, relating to, or characterized by larceny <a larcenous taking>. **2.** (Of a person) contemplating or tainted with larceny; thievish <a larcenous purpose>.

larcenous intent. A state of mind existing when a person (1) knowingly takes away the goods of another without any claim or pretense of a right to do so, and (2) intends to deprive the owner of them or to convert the goods to personal use. See LARCENY.

larceny (**lahr**-sə-nee), *n*. The unlawful taking and carrying away of someone else's personal property with the intent to deprive the possessor of it permanently. • Common-law larceny has been broadened by some statutes to include embezzlement and false pretenses, all three of which are often subsumed under the statutory crime of "theft."

> "[T]he distinctions between larceny, embezzlement and false pretenses serve no useful purpose in the criminal law but are useless handicaps from the standpoint of the administration of criminal justice. One solution has been to combine all three in one section of the code under the name of 'larceny.' This has one disadvantage, however, because it frequently becomes necessary to add a modifier to make clear whether the reference is to common-law larceny or to statutory larceny." Rollin M. Perkins & Ronald N. Boyce, *Criminal Law* 389 (3d ed. 1982).

aggravated larceny. Larceny accompanied by some aggravating factor (as when the theft is from a person).

complicated larceny. See *mixed larceny*.

compound larceny. See *mixed larceny*.

constructive larceny. Larceny in which the perpetrator's felonious intent to appropriate the goods is construed from the defendant's conduct at the time of asportation, although a felonious intent was not present before that time.

grand larceny. Larceny of property worth more than a statutory cutoff amount, usu. $100. Cf. *petit larceny*.

> "The English law, as the result of an early statute [the Statute of Westminster I, ch. 15 (1275)], classified this offense [larceny] as either (1) grand larceny or (2) petit larceny (now frequently written petty larceny), the former being a capital offense and the latter punishable by forfeiture of goods and whipping, but not death. Both, as mentioned earlier, were felonies. The offense was grand larceny if the value of the property stolen exceeded twelve pence and petit larceny if it did not. Modern statutes very generally retain this same classification (sometimes without using these labels) but with different penalties and different values set as the dividing line." Rollin M. Perkins & Ronald N. Boyce, *Criminal Law* 335 (3d ed. 1982).

larceny by bailee. Larceny committed by a bailee who converts the property to personal use or to the use of a third party.

larceny by extortion. Larceny in which the perpetrator obtains property by threatening to (1) inflict bodily harm on anyone or commit any other criminal offense, (2) accuse anyone of a criminal offense, (3) expose any secret tending to subject any person to hatred, contempt, or ridicule, or impair one's credit or business reputation, (4) take or withhold action as an official, or cause an official to take or withhold action, (5) bring about or continue a strike, boycott, or other collective unofficial action, if the property is not demanded or received for the benefit of the group in whose interest the actor purports to act, (6) testify or provide information or withhold testimony or information with respect to another's legal claim or defense, or (7) inflict any other harm that would not benefit the actor. Model Penal Code § 223.4. See EXTORTION.

larceny by trick. Larceny in which the taker misleads the rightful possessor, by misrepresentation of fact, into giving up possession of (but not title to) the goods. — Also termed *larceny by trick and deception*; *larceny by trick and device*; *larceny by fraud and deception*. Cf. FALSE PRETENSES; *cheating by false pretenses* under CHEATING.

larceny from the person. Larceny in which the goods are taken directly from the person, but without violence or intimidation, the victim usu. being unaware of the taking. • Pickpocketing is a typical example. This offense is similar to robbery except that violence or intimidation is not involved. Cf. ROBBERY.

larceny of property lost, mislaid, or delivered by mistake. Larceny in which one obtains control of property the person knows to be lost, mislaid, or delivered by mistake (esp. in the amount of property or identity of recipient) and fails to take reasonable measures to restore the property to the rightful owner. Model Penal Code § 223.5.

mixed larceny. **1.** Larceny accompanied by aggravation or violence to the person. Cf. *simple larceny*. **2.** Larceny involving a taking from a house. — Also termed *compound larceny*; *complicated larceny*.

petit larceny. Larceny of property worth less than a statutory cutoff amount, usu. $100. — Also spelled *petty larceny*. Cf. *grand larceny*.

simple larceny. Larceny unaccompanied by aggravating factors; larceny of personal goods unattended by an act of violence. Cf. *mixed larceny* (1).

larger parcel. *Eminent domain.* A portion of land that is not a complete parcel, but is the greater part of an even bigger tract, entitling the owner both to damages for the parcel taken and for severance from the larger tract. • To grant both kinds of damages, a court generally requires the owner to show unity of ownership, unity of use, and contiguity of the land. But some states and the federal courts do not require contiguity when there is strong evidence of unity of use.

laron (**lar**-ən), *n.* [Law French] *Hist.* A thief.

***Larrison* rule** (**lar**-ə-sən). *Criminal law.* The doctrine that a defendant may be entitled to a new trial on the basis of newly discovered evidence of false testimony by a government witness if the jury might have reached a different conclusion without the evidence and it unfairly surprised the defendant at trial. *Larrison v. United States*, 24 F.2d 82 (7th Cir. 1928).

> "The most usual rule in cases in which it is claimed that there was false testimony at the trial or that the witness has since recanted is the 'Larrison rule,' taking its name from the Seventh Circuit case in which it was announced. This is that three requirements must be met before a new trial will be granted on this ground: '(a) [That the] the court is reasonably well satisfied that the testimony given by a material witness [was] false. (b) That without it the jury *might* have reached a different conclusion. (c) That the party seeking the new trial was taken by surprise when the false testimony was given and was unable to meet it for it did not know of its falsity until after the trial.' " 3 Charles Alan Wright, *Federal Practice and Procedure* § 557.1, at 343 (2d ed. 1982) (quoting *Larrison*, 24 F.2d at 87–88).

lascivious (lə-**siv**-ee-əs), *adj.* (Of conduct) tending to excite lust; lewd; indecent; obscene.

lascivious cohabitation. The offense committed by two persons not married to each other who live together as husband and wife and engage in sexual intercourse. • This offense, where it still exists, is seldom prosecuted.

last, *n. Hist.* **1.** A burden. **2.** A measure of weight used for bulky commodities.

last antecedent, rule of the. See RULE OF THE LAST ANTECEDENT.

last-clear-chance doctrine. *Torts.* The rule that a plaintiff who was contributorily negligent may nonetheless recover from the defendant if the defendant had the last opportunity to prevent the harm but failed to use reasonable care to do so (in other words, if the defendant's negligence is later in time than the plaintiff's). • This doctrine allows the plaintiff to rebut the contributory-negligence defense in the few jurisdictions where contributory negligence completely bars recovery. — Also termed *discovered-peril doctrine*; *humanitarian doctrine*; *last-opportunity doctrine*; *subsequent-negligence doctrine*; *supervening-negligence doctrine*.

last-employer rule. The doctrine that liability for an occupational injury or illness falls to the employer who exposed the worker to the injurious substance just before the first onset of the disease or injury. — Also termed *last-injurious-exposure rule*.

last heir. *Hist.* The person — either the lord of the manor or the sovereign — to whom lands come by escheat when there is no lawful heir.

last illness. The sickness ending in the person's death. — Also termed *last sickness*.

last-in, first-out. An accounting method that assumes that the most recent purchases are sold or used first, matching current costs against current revenues. — Abbr. LIFO. Cf. FIRST-IN, FIRST-OUT; NEXT-IN, FIRST-OUT.

last-injurious-exposure rule. See LAST-EMPLOYER RULE.

last-link doctrine. The rule that an attorney need not divulge nonprivileged information if doing so would reveal information protected by the attorney-client privilege, particularly if the information would provide essential evidence to support indicting or convicting the client of a crime. • This doctrine is often relied on as an exception to the rule that a client's identity is not privileged. For example, if divulging the client's name would supply the last link of evidence to indict or convict the client of a crime, the name need not be disclosed.

last-opportunity doctrine. See LAST-CLEAR-CHANCE DOCTRINE.

last-proximate-act test. *Criminal law.* A common-law test for the crime of attempt, based on whether the defendant does the final act necessary to commit an offense (such as pulling the trigger of a gun, not merely aiming it). • This test has been rejected by most courts as too lenient. See ATTEMPT (2).

last resort, court of. See *court of last resort* under COURT.

last sickness. See LAST ILLNESS.

last-straw doctrine. *Employment law.* The rule that the termination of employment may be justified by a series of incidents of poor performance, not one of which alone would justify termination, followed by a final incident showing a blatant disregard for the employer's interests.

last-survivor insurance. See INSURANCE.

last-treatment rule. The doctrine that, for an ongoing physician–patient relationship, the statute of limitations on a medical-malpractice claim begins to run when the treatment stops or the relationship ends.

last will. See WILL.

last will and testament. A person's final will. See WILL.

lata culpa. See CULPA.

lata negligentia (**lay**-tə neg-lə-**jen**-shee-ə). See NEGLIGENTIA.

latching. A survey of a mine; an underground survey.

late, *adj.* **1.** Tardy; coming after an appointed or expected time <a late filing>. **2.** (Of a person) only recently having died <the late Secretary of State>.

latens (**lay**-tenz), *adj.* [Latin] Hidden or unapparent.

latent (**lay**-tənt), *adj.* Concealed; dormant <a latent defect>. Cf. PATENT.

latent ambiguity. See AMBIGUITY.

latent deed. See DEED.

latent defect. See *hidden defect* under DEFECT.

latent equity. See EQUITY.

latent intent. See *dormant legislative intent* under LEGISLATIVE INTENT.

latent intention. See *dormant legislative intent* under LEGISLATIVE INTENT.

lateral departure. See DEPARTURE.

lateral sentencing. See *lateral departure* under DEPARTURE.

lateral support. See SUPPORT.

laterare (lat-ə-**rair**-ee). [Law Latin] *Hist.* To lie sideways, rather than endways. • This term was formerly used in land descriptions.

latifundium (lat-ə-**fən**-dee-əm), *n.* [Latin fr. *latus* "broad" + *fundus* "land"] *Roman law.* A large private estate, usu. made up of smaller ones, common in the last few centuries of the Republic.

Latin. The language of the ancient Romans and a primary language of the civil, canon, and (formerly) common law.

> "The value of the Latin has always consisted in its peculiar expressiveness as a language of law terms, in its superior conciseness which has made it the appropriate language of law maxims, and in its almost unlimited capacity of condensation by means of abbreviations and contractions, many of which are retained in popular use at the present day." 2 Alexander M. Burrill, *A Law Dictionary and Glossary* 131 (2d ed. 1867).

> "The Latin maxims have largely disappeared from arguments and opinions. In their original phraseology they convey no idea that cannot be well expressed in modern English." William C. Anderson, *Law Dictionaries*, 28 Am. L. Rev. 531, 532 (1894).

latinarius (lat-ə-**nair**-ee-əs), *n.* [Latin] *Hist.* An interpreter of Latin.

latini juniani (lə-**tɪ**-nɪ joo-nee-**ay**-nɪ), *n.* [Latin] *Roman law.* A class of former slaves who, although they were freed, did not acquire full rights of citizenship. — Also spelled *latini iuniani.* — Also termed *libertini.* See LEX JUNIA NORBANA. Cf. INGENUUS; SERVUS.

> "Upon all these persons . . . a new and definite status was conferred; they were henceforth to be known as *Latini Juniani*, their position being based upon *Latinitas*, a status which had been enjoyed by certain Latin colonists. A *Latinus Junianus* had no public rights . . . . But he had part of the *commercium, i.e.* he could acquire proprietary and other rights *inter vivos*, but not *mortis causâ*. A *Latinus Junianus*, therefore, could neither take under a will . . . nor could he make one . . . . But, subject to these disabilities, a *Latinus Junianus* was a free man, and his children, though not, like the children of citizens, under his *potestas*, were free-born citizens." R.W. Leage, *Roman Private Law* 68–69 (C.H. Ziegler ed., 2d ed. 1930).

latitat (**lat**-ə-tat), *n.* [Law Latin "he lurks"] *Hist.* A writ issued in a personal action after the sheriff returned a bill of Middlesex with the notation that the defendant could not be found. • The writ was called *latitat* because of its fictitious recital that the defendant lurks about in the county. It was abolished by the Process in Courts of Law at Westminster Act of 1832 (St. 2, Will. 4, ch. 39). See BILL OF MIDDLESEX; TESTATUM.

> "Latitat is a writ by which all men in personal actions are originally called in the king's bench to answer. And it is called latitat, because it is supposed by the writ that the defendant cannot be found in the county of Middlesex, as it appears by the return of the sheriff of that county, but that he lurks in another county: and therefore to the sheriff of that county is this writ directed to apprehend him." *Termes de la Ley* 277 (1st Am. ed. 1812).

latitatio (lat-ə-**tay**-shee-oh), *n.* [Law Latin] *Civil law.* A lurking; a hiding; a concealment, esp. to avoid a trial.

Latium maius (**lay**-shee-əm **may**-əs), *n.* [Latin] *Roman law.* The greater rights conferred on the inhabitants of Latium and, later, colonies outside Italy, including a widespread right of Roman citizenship. — Also spelled *Latium majus* (**may**-jəs). — Also termed *maius Latium.* Cf. LATIUM MINUS.

> "Under the Principate there is a distinction between *Latium maius* and *Latium minus*. The former referred to the rights granted to colonies founded as a *coloniae Latinae* outside Italy, combined with the concession of Roman citizenship to a larger group of individuals than *Latium minus*, in which only the municipal magistrates and members of the municipal council . . . were rewarded with Roman citizenship." Adolf Berger, *Encyclopedic Dictionary of Roman Law* 537–38 (1953).

Latium minus (**lay**-shee-əm **mɪ**-nəs), *n.* [Latin] *Roman law.* Certain limited rights conferred on colonies founded outside Italy. — Also termed *minus Latium.* Cf. LATIUM MAIUS.

lator (**lay**-tər), *n.* [Latin "a bearer, proposer"] *Civil law.* **1.** A bearer; a messenger. **2.** A maker or giver of laws.

latro (**la**-troh), *n.* [Latin] *Roman law.* A robber; a thief.

latrocination (la-trə-sə-**nay**-shən). [fr. Latin *latrocinium* "highway robbery"] *Archaic.* The act of robbing; a depredation; a theft. — Also termed *latrociny*; *latrocinium.* See LARCENY; THEFT.

latrocinium (la-trə-**sin**-ee-əm), *n.* [Latin fr. *latro* "a robber"] *Hist.* **1.** LATROCINATION. **2.** Something stolen. **3.** The right to judge and execute thieves.

latrociny (**la**-trə-sə-nee). See LATROCINATION.

laudamentum (law-də-**men**-təm), *n. Hist.* A jury award.

laudare (law-**dair**-ee), *vb.* [Latin] **1.** *Civil law.* To name; to cite or quote as authority. **2.** *Hist.* To determine or pass upon (a case, etc.) judicially.

laudatio (law-**day**-shee-oh), *n.* [Latin] *Roman law.* Court testimony concerning an accused person's good behavior and integrity of life. • This testimony resembles the practice in modern criminal trials of calling persons to speak favorably about a defendant's character.

laudator (law-**day**-tər), *n.* [Latin] **1.** *Roman law.* A character witness in a criminal trial. **2.** *Hist.* An arbitrator. Pl. ***laudatores*** (law-də-**tor**-eez).

laudemium (law-**dee**-mee-əm), *n.* [Law Latin] *Roman law.* A sum paid to a landowner by a person succeeding to a particular form of land contract by gift, devise, exchange, or sale; HERIOT. • The payment equaled 2% of the purchase money, and was paid to the landowner for acceptance of the successor. — Also termed (in old English law) *acknowledgment money.* See EMPHYTEUSIS.

laudere auctorem (law-**deer**-ee awk-**tor**-əm). See NOMINATIO AUCTORIS.

laudum (**law**-dəm), *n.* [Law Latin] *Hist.* An arbitrament. See ARBITRAMENT.

laughe, *n.* See FRANKPLEDGE.

laughing heir. See HEIR.

launch, *n.* **1.** The movement of a vessel from the land into the water, esp. by sliding along ways from the stocks on which the vessel was built. **2.** A large open boat used in any service; LIGHTER.

laundering, *n.* The federal crime of transferring illegally obtained money through legitimate persons or accounts so that its original source cannot be traced. 18 USCA § 1956. — Also termed *money-laundering.* — **launder,** *vb.*

laundry list. *Slang.* An enumeration of items, as in a statute or court opinion <Texas's consumer-protection law contains a laundry list of deceptive trade practices>.

laureate (**lor**-ee-it), *n.* **1.** *Hist.* An officer of the sovereign's household, who composed odes annually on the sovereign's birthday, on the new year, and occasionally on the occurrence of a remarkable victory. **2.** A person honored for great achievement in the arts and sciences, and esp. in poetry.

laus Deo (**laws dee**-oh *or* **lows day**-oh). [Latin] *Archaic.* Praise be to God. • This was a heading to a bill of exchange.

law. 1. The regime that orders human activities and relations through systematic application of the force of politically organized society, or through social pressure, backed by force, in such a society; the legal system <respect and obey the law>. **2.** The aggregate of legislation, judicial precedents, and accepted legal principles; the body of authoritative grounds of judicial and administrative action <the law of the land>. **3.** The set of rules or principles dealing with a specific area of a legal system <copyright law>. **4.** The judicial and administrative process; legal action and proceedings <when settlement negotiations failed, they submitted their dispute to the law>. **5.** A statute <Congress passed a law>. — Abbr. L. **6.** COMMON LAW <law but not equity>. **7.** The legal profession <she spent her entire career in law>.

> "Some twenty years ago I pointed out two ideas running through definitions of law: one an imperative idea, an idea of a rule laid down by the lawmaking organ of a politically organized society, deriving its force from the authority of the sovereign; and the other a rational or ethical idea, an idea of a rule of right and justice deriving its authority from its intrinsic reasonableness or conformity to ideals of right and merely recognized, not made, by the sovereign." Roscoe Pound, "More About the Nature of Law," in *Legal Essays in Tribute to Orrin Kip McMurray* at 513, 515 (1935).

> "All law is the law of a group of individuals or of groups made up of individuals. No one can make a law purely for himself. He may form a resolution, frame an ambition, or adopt a rule, but these are private prescriptions, not laws." Tony Honoré, *Making Law Bind: Essays Legal and Philosophical* 33 (1987).

> "It will help to distinguish three senses of the word 'law.' The first is law as a distinctive social institution; that is the sense invoked when we ask whether primitive law is really law. The second is law as a collection of sets of propositions — the sets we refer to as antitrust law, the law of torts, the Statute of Frauds, and so on. The third is law as a source of rights, duties, and powers, as in the sentence 'The law forbids the murdering heir to inherit.'" Richard A. Posner, *The Problems of Jurisprudence* 220–21 (1990).

adjective law. See ADJECTIVE LAW.

canon law. See CANON LAW.

caselaw. See CASELAW.

civil law. See CIVIL LAW.

common law. See COMMON LAW.

consuetudinary law (kon-swə-**t[y]oo**-də-ner-ee). [fr. Latin *consuetudo* "custom"] *Hist.* Ancient customary law that is based on an oral tradition.

conventional law. See CONVENTIONAL LAW.

customary law. See CUSTOMARY LAW.

divine law. See DIVINE LAW.

enacted law. Law that has its source in legislation; WRITTEN LAW.

federal law. See FEDERAL LAW.

general law. **1.** Law that is neither local nor confined in application to particular persons. • Even if there is only one person or entity to which a given law applies when enacted, it is general law if it purports to apply to all persons or places of a specified class throughout the jurisdiction. — Also termed *general statute*; *law of a general nature*. Cf. *special law*. **2.** A statute that relates to a subject of a broad nature.

imperative law. A rule in the form of a command; a rule of action imposed on people by some authority that enforces obedience.

> "Strictly speaking, it is not possible to say that imperative law is a command in the ordinary sense of the word. A 'command' in the ordinary meaning of the word is an expression of a wish by a person or body as to the conduct of another person, communicated to that other person. But (1) in the case of the law there is no determinate person who as a matter of psychological fact commands all the law. We are all born into a community in which law already exists, and at no time in our lives do any of us command the whole law. The most that we do is to play our part in enforcing or altering particular portions of it. (2) Ignorance of the law is no excuse; thus a rule of law is binding even though not communicated to the subject of the law." John Salmond, *Jurisprudence* 21 n.(c) (Glanville L. Williams ed., 10th ed. 1947).

internal law. **1.** Law that regulates the domestic affairs of a country. Cf. INTERNATIONAL LAW. **2.** LOCAL LAW (3).

local law. See LOCAL LAW.

natural law. See NATURAL LAW.

permanent law. A statute that continues in force for an indefinite time.

positive law. See POSITIVE LAW.

procedural law. See PROCEDURAL LAW.

special law. A law that pertains to and affects a particular case, person, place, or thing, as opposed to the general public. — Also termed *special act*; *private law*. Cf. *general law* (1).

state law. See STATE LAW.

sumptuary law. See SUMPTUARY LAW.

tacit law. A law that derives its authority from the people's consent, without a positive enactment.

unenacted law. Law that does not have its source in legislation; UNWRITTEN LAW (1).

law and economics. (*often cap.*) **1.** A discipline advocating the economic analysis of the law, whereby legal rules are subjected to a cost-benefit analysis to determine whether a change from one legal rule to another will increase or decrease allocative efficiency and social wealth. • Originally developed as an approach to antitrust policy, law and economics is today used by its proponents to explain and interpret a variety of legal subjects. **2.** The field or movement in which scholars devote themselves to this discipline. **3.** The body of work produced by these scholars.

law and literature. (*often cap.*) **1.** Traditionally, the study of how lawyers and legal institutions are depicted in literature; esp., the examination of law-related fiction as sociological evidence of how a given culture, at a given time, views law. — Also termed *law in literature*. **2.** More modernly, the application of literary theory to legal texts, focusing esp. on lawyers' rhetoric, logic, and style, as well as legal syntax and semantics. — Also termed *law as literature*. **3.** The field or movement in which scholars devote themselves to this study or application. **4.** The body of work produced by these scholars.

law arbitrary. A law not found in the nature of things, but imposed by the legislature's mere will; a bill not immutable.

law as literature. See LAW AND LITERATURE.

law between states. See INTERNATIONAL LAW.

lawbook. A book, usu. a technical one, about the law; esp., a primary legal text such as a statute book or book that reports caselaw. — Also spelled *law book*.

lawbreaker, *n.* A person who violates or has violated the law.

lawburrows (**law**-bər-ohz). *Scots law.* Security guaranteeing the peaceable behavior of a party; security to keep the peace.

law clerk. See CLERK (4).

law commission. (*often cap.*) An official or quasi-official body of people formed to propose legal reforms intended to improve the administration of justice. • Such a body is often charged with the task of reviewing the law with an eye toward systematic development and reform, esp. through codification.

law court. See COURT (1), (2). — Also spelled *lawcourt.*

law court of appeals. *Hist.* An appellate tribunal, formerly existing in South Carolina, for hearing appeals from the courts of law.

law-craft, *n.* The practice of law.

> "This quest for ever-broader empirical understanding must, of course, be kept under reasonable control in practical law-craft, lest it delay necessary decisions in a continually expanding and pointlessly expensive fact-finding spiral." Bruce A. Ackerman, *Reconstructing American Law* 30 (1984).

law day. 1. *Archaic.* The yearly or twice-yearly meeting of one of the early common-law courts. **2.** *Archaic.* The day appointed for a debtor to discharge a mortgage or else forfeit the property to the lender. **3.** (*cap.*) A day on which American schools, public assemblies, and courts draw attention to the importance of law in modern society. • Since 1958, the ABA has sponsored Law Day on May 1 of each year.

law department. A branch of a corporation, government agency, university, or the like charged with handling the entity's legal affairs.

law enforcement. 1. The detection and punishment of violations of the law. • This term is not limited to the enforcement of criminal laws. For example, the Freedom of Information Act contains an exemption from disclosure for information compiled for law-enforcement purposes and furnished in confidence. That exemption is valid for the enforcement of a variety of noncriminal laws (such as national-security laws) as well as criminal laws. See 5 USCA § 552(b)(7). **2.** CRIMINAL JUSTICE (2). **3.** Police officers and other members of the executive branch of government charged with carrying out and enforcing the criminal law.

Law Enforcement Assistance Administration. A federal agency (part of the Department of Justice) responsible for administering law-enforcement grants under the Omnibus Crime Control and Safe Streets Act of 1968. — Abbr. LEAA.

Law Enforcement Information Network. A computerized communications system used in some states to document drivers' license records, automobile registrations, wanted persons' files, etc. — Abbr. LEIN.

law-enforcement officer. A person whose duty is to enforce the laws and preserve the peace. See PEACE OFFICER; SHERIFF.

law-enforcement system. See CRIMINAL-JUSTICE SYSTEM.

law firm. An association of lawyers who practice law together, usu. sharing clients and profits, in a business traditionally organized as a partnership but often today as either a professional corporation or a limited-liability company. • Many law firms have a hierarchical structure in which the partners (or shareholders) supervise junior lawyers known as "associates," who are usu. employed on a track to partnership.

Law French. The corrupted form of the Norman French language that arose in England in the centuries after William the Conqueror invaded England in 1066 and that was used for several centuries as the primary language of the English legal system; the Anglo–French used in medieval England in judicial proceedings, pleadings, and lawbooks. — Also written *law French.* — Abbr. L.F. See NORMAN FRENCH.

> "To the linguist, law French is a corrupt dialect by definition. Anglo–French was in steady decline after 1300. Lawyers such as Fortescue, on the other hand, were probably serious in maintaining that it was the vernacular of France which was deteriorating by comparison with the pristine Norman of the English courts. That Fortescue could make such a claim, while living in France, is in itself a clear demonstration that by the middle of the fifteenth century there was a marked difference between the French of English lawyers and the French of France." J.H. Baker, *A Manual of Law French* 11 (1979).

> "Law French refers to the Anglo–Norman patois used in legal documents and all judicial proceedings from the 1260s to the reign of Edward III (1327–1377), and used with frequency in legal literature up to the early 18th century. When first introduced into England, this brand of French was the standard language used in Normandy; by the 1300s, through linguistic isolation, it became a corrupted language — by French standards, at any rate." Bryan A. Garner, *A Dictionary of Modern Legal Usage* 504–05 (2d ed. 1995).

> "That Law French was barbarous in its decrepitude does not in the least diminish the value of it to our law when it was full of vitality. It helped to make English law one of the four indigenous systems of the civilized world, for it exactly expressed legal ideas in a technical language which had no precise equivalent." Percy H. Winfield, *The Chief Sources of English Legal History* 14 (1925).

lawful, *adj*. Not contrary to law; permitted by law <the police officer conducted a lawful search of the premises>. See LEGAL.

lawful admission. *Immigration*. Legal entry into the country, including under a valid immigrant visa. • Lawful admission is one of the requirements for an immigrant to receive a naturalization order and certificate. 8 USCA §§ 1101(a)(20), 1427(a)(1).

lawful age. See AGE.

lawful arrest. See ARREST.

lawful authorities. Those persons (such as the police) with the right to exercise public power, to require obedience to their lawful commands, and to command or act in the public name.

lawful cause. See *good cause* under CAUSE (2).

lawful condition. See CONDITION (2).

lawful damages. See DAMAGES.

lawful dependent. See DEPENDENT.

lawful entry. See ENTRY (1).

lawful fence. A strong, substantial, and well-suited barrier that is sufficient to prevent animals from escaping property and to protect the property from trespassers. — Also termed *legal fence*; *good and lawful fence*.

lawful goods. Property that one may legally hold, sell, or export; property that is not contraband.

lawful heir. See HEIR.

lawful issue. See ISSUE (3).

lawful man. See LEGALIS HOMO.

lawful money. See MONEY.

lawful representative. See REPRESENTATIVE.

lawgiver. 1. A legislator, esp. one who promulgates an entire code of laws. **2.** A judge with the power to interpret law. — **lawgiving,** *adj*. & *n*.

> "John Chipman Gray in his *The Nature and Sources of the Law* (1921) repeats a number of times a quotation from Bishop Hoadley [1676–1761]: 'Whoever hath an *absolute authority to interpret* any written or spoken laws, it is *he* who is truly the *Law-giver* to all intents and purposes, and not the person who first wrote or spoke them.' " Lon L. Fuller, *Anatomy of the Law* 23–24 (1968).

law-hand. *Hist*. An outmoded rococo method of handwriting once used by scribes in preparing legal documents.

law in literature. See LAW AND LITERATURE.

Law Latin. A corrupted form of Latin formerly used in law and legal documents, including judicial writs, royal charters, and private deeds. • It primarily consists of a mixture of Latin, French, and English words used in English sentence structures. — Abbr. L.L.; L. Lat. — Also written *law Latin*.

> "LAW LATIN. A technical kind of Latin, in which the pleadings and proceedings of the English courts were enrolled and recorded from a very early period to the reign of George II .... The principal peculiarities of this language consist first, in its construction, which is adapted so closely to the English idiom as to answer to it sometimes word for word; and, secondly, in the use of numerous words 'not allowed by grammarians nor having any countenance of Latin,' but framed from the English by merely adding a Latin termination, as *murdrum* from murder ...." 2 Alexander M. Burrill, *A Law Dictionary and Glossary* 135 (2d ed. 1867).

> "Law Latin, sometimes formerly called 'dog Latin,' is the bastardized or debased Latin formerly used in law and legal documents. For the most part, we have escaped its clutches. In 1730, Parliament abolished Law Latin in legal proceedings, but two years later found it necessary to allow Latin phrases that had previously been in common use, such as *fieri facias*, *habeas corpus*, *ne exeat*, and *nisi prius*. As Blackstone would later say, some Latinisms were 'not ... capable of an English dress with any degree of seriousness.' 3 William Blackstone, *Commentaries* 323 (1768)." Bryan A. Garner, *A Dictionary of Modern Legal Usage* 505 (2d ed. 1995).

law list. 1. A publication compiling the names and addresses of practicing lawyers and other information of interest to the profession, such as court calendars, lawyers with specialized practices, stenographers, and the like. **2.** A legal directory such as Martindale–Hubbell. • Many states and large cities also have law lists or directories. See MARTINDALE-HUBBELL LAW DIRECTORY.

Law Lord. A member of the appellate committee of the House of Lords, consisting of the Lord Chancellor, the salaried Lords of Appeal in Ordinary, and any peer who holds or has held high judicial office. — Also written *law lord*.

lawmaker. See LEGISLATOR.

lawmaking. See LEGISLATION (1).

law martial. See MARTIAL LAW.

law merchant. A system of customary law that developed in Europe during the Middle Ages and regulated the dealings of mariners and merchants in all the commercial countries of the world until the 17th century. • Many of the law merchant's principles came to be incorporated into the common law, which in turn formed the basis of the Uniform Commercial Code. — Also termed *commercial law*; *lex mercatoria*.

lawnote. See NOTE (2).

law of a general nature. See *general law* under LAW.

law of arms. See ARMS, LAW OF.

law of capture. See RULE OF CAPTURE.

law of Citations. See CITATIONS, LAW OF.

law of competence. A law establishing and defining the powers of a government official, including the circumstances under which the official's pronouncements constitute laws. — Also termed *power-delegating law*. See *jural act* under ACT (2); JURAL AGENT.

law of evidence. See EVIDENCE (4).

law of marque (mahrk). A rule of reprisal allowing one who has been wronged but cannot obtain justice to take the goods of the wrongdoer found within the wronged person's precinct, in satisfaction of the wrong.

law of nations. See INTERNATIONAL LAW.

law of nature. See NATURAL LAW.

law of nature and nations. See INTERNATIONAL LAW.

law of obligations. The category of law dealing with proprietary rights in personam. • It is one of the three departments into which civil law is divided. See IN PERSONAM. Cf. LAW OF PROPERTY; LAW OF STATUS.

law of persons. The law relating to persons; the law that pertains to the different statuses of persons. • This is also commonly known as the *jus personarum*, a shortened form of *jus quod ad personas pertinet* ("the law that pertains to persons"). See JUS PERSONARUM.

law of property. The category of law dealing with proprietary rights in rem. • It is one of the three departments into which civil law is divided. See IN REM. Cf. LAW OF OBLIGATIONS; LAW OF STATUS.

law of shipping. The part of maritime law relating to the building, equipping, registering, owning, inspecting, transporting, and employing of ships, along with the laws applicable to shipmasters, agents, crews, and cargoes; the maritime law relating to ships. — Also termed *shipping law*. See MARITIME LAW; JONES ACT.

law of status. The category of law dealing with personal or nonproprietary rights, whether in rem or in personam. • It is one of the three departments into which civil law is divided. Cf. LAW OF OBLIGATIONS; LAW OF PROPERTY.

law of the apex. *Mining law.* The principle that title to a given tract of mineral land, with defined mining rights, goes to the person who locates the surface covering the outcrop or apex.

law of the case. **1.** The doctrine holding that a decision rendered in a former appeal of a case is binding in a later appeal. **2.** An earlier decision giving rise to the application of this doctrine. Cf. LAW OF THE TRIAL; RES JUDICATA; STARE DECISIS.

law of the circuit. **1.** The law as announced and followed by a U.S. Circuit Court of Appeals. **2.** The rule that one panel of judges on a U.S. Circuit Court of Appeals should not overrule a decision of another panel of judges on the same court. **3.** The rule that an opinion of one U.S. Circuit Court of Appeals is not binding on another circuit but may be considered persuasive.

law of the flag. *Maritime law.* The law of the nation whose flag is flown by a particular vessel. • A shipowner who sends a vessel into a foreign port gives notice by the flag to all potential contracting parties of the owner's intent for that law to regulate all contracts made involving the ship or its cargo.

law of the land. 1. The law in effect in a country and applicable to its members, whether the law is statutory, administrative, or case-made. **2.** Due process of law. See DUE PROCESS. — Also termed *lex terrae*; *ley de terre*.

law of the partnership. The rule that the parties' agreement controls the features of a partnership.

law of the place. Under the Federal Tort Claims Act, the state law applicable to the place where the injury occurred. • Under the Act, the federal government waives its sovereign immunity for specified injuries, including certain wrongful acts or omissions of a government employee causing injury that the United States, if it were a private person, would be liable for under the law of the state where the incident occurred. 28 USCA § 1346(b).

law of the sea. The body of international law governing how nations use and control the sea and its resources. Cf. MARITIME LAW.

law of the staple. *Hist.* The law administered in the court of the mayor of the staple; the law merchant. See STAPLE.

law of the trial. A legal theory or court ruling that is not objected to and is used or relied on in a trial <neither party objected to the court's jury instruction, so it became the law of the trial>. Cf. LAW OF THE CASE.

law of things. The law pertaining to things; the law that is determined by changes in the nature of things. • This is also commonly known as the *jus rerum*, a shortened form of *jus quod ad res pertinet* ("the law that pertains to things"). See JUS RERUM.

law practice. An attorney's professional business, including the relationships that the attorney has with clients and the goodwill associated with those relationships. Cf. PRACTICE OF LAW.

law question. See QUESTION OF LAW.

law reform. The process of, or a movement dedicated to, streamlining, modernizing, or otherwise improving a nation's laws generally or the code governing a particular branch of the law; specif., the investigation and discussion of the law on a topic (e.g., bankruptcy), usu. by a commission or expert committee, with the goal of formulating proposals for change to improve the operation of the law. — Also termed *science of legislation*; *censorial jurisprudence*.

law report. See REPORT (3).

law reporter. See REPORT (3).

law review. 1. A journal containing scholarly articles, essays, and other commentary on legal topics by professors, judges, law students, and practitioners. • Law reviews are usu. published at law schools and edited by law students <law reviews are often grossly overburdened with substantive footnotes>. **2.** The law-student staff and editorial board of such a journal <she made law review>.

law Salique (sə-**leek**). See SALIC LAW.

law school. An institution for formal legal education and training. • Graduates who complete the standard program, usu. three years in length, receive a Juris Doctor (or, formerly, a Bachelor of Laws).

accredited law school. A law school approved by the state and the Association of American Law Schools, or by the state and the American Bar Association. • In all states except California, only graduates of an accredited law school may take the bar examination.

Law School Admissions Test. A standardized examination purporting to measure the likelihood of success in law school. • Most American law schools use the results of this examination in admissions decisions. — Abbr. LSAT.

Law Society. A professional organization in England, chartered in 1845, governing the education, practice, and conduct of articled clerks and solicitors. • A clerk or solicitor must be enrolled with the Law Society to be admitted to the legal profession.

Law Society of Scotland. A professional organization established by statute in 1949, governing the admission, conduct, and practice of solicitors enrolled to practice in Scotland.

Laws of Amalfi (ah-**mahl**-fee). See AMALPHITAN CODE.

laws of Oléron (**oh**-lə-ron *or* aw-lay-**ron**). The oldest collection of modern maritime laws, thought to be a code existing at Oléron (an island off the coast of France) during the 12th century. • It was introduced into England, with certain additions, in the reign of Richard I (1189–99).

laws of the several states. State statutes and state-court decisions on questions of general law.

laws of war. *Int'l law.* The body of rules and principles observed by civilized nations for the regulation of matters inherent or incidental to the conduct of a public war, such as the relations of neutrals and belligerents, blockades, captures, prizes, truces and armistices, capitulations, prisoners, and declarations of war and peace. See GENEVA CONVENTION.

laws of Wisby (**wiz**-bee). A code of maritime customs and decisions adopted on the island of Gothland (in the Baltic Sea), where Wisby was the principal port. • Most scholars believe that this code postdates the laws of Oléron. The code was influential throughout northern Europe. — Also spelled *laws of Wisbuy*. — Also termed *Gothland sea laws*.

law spiritual. See ECCLESIASTICAL LAW.

lawsuit, *n.* See SUIT.

lawsuit, *vb. Archaic.* To proceed against (an adversary) in a lawsuit; to sue.

law-talk, *n.* **1.** LEGALESE. **2.** Discussion that is heavily laced with lawyers' concerns and legal references.

law-worthy, *adj. Hist.* Entitled to or deserving the benefit and protection of the law. — Also termed *law-worth*. See LIBERAM LEGEM AMITTERE; LEGALIS HOMO; LIBERA LEX.

law writer. A person who writes on legal subjects, usu. from a technical, nonpopular point of view.

lawyer, *n.* One who is licensed to practice law. — **lawyerly, lawyerlike,** *adj.* — **lawyerdom,** *n.* Cf. ATTORNEY; COUNSEL.

certified military lawyer. A person qualified to act as counsel in a general court-martial. • To be qualified, the person must be (1) a judge advocate of the Army, Navy, Air Force, or Marine Corps, or a law specialist of the Coast Guard, (2) a graduate of an accredited law school, or a member of a federal-court bar or the bar of the highest court of a state, and (3) certified as competent to perform such duties by the Judge Advocate General of the armed force that the person is a member of.

criminal lawyer. A lawyer whose primary work is to represent criminal defendants. • This term is rarely if ever applied to prosecutors despite their integral involvement in the criminal-justice system.

headnote lawyer. *Slang.* A lawyer who relies on the headnotes of judicial opinions rather than taking the time to read the opinions themselves.

jailhouse lawyer. See JAILHOUSE LAWYER.

transactional lawyer. A lawyer who works primarily on transactions such as licensing agreements, mergers, acquisitions, joint ventures, and the like.

lawyer, *vb.* **1.** To practice as a lawyer <Mike spends his days and nights lawyering, with little time for recreation>. **2.** To supply with lawyers <the large law-school class will certainly help lawyer the state>. — **lawyering,** *n.*

lawyer-client privilege. See *attorney-client privilege* under PRIVILEGE (3).

lawyer-witness rule. The principle that an attorney who will likely be called as a fact witness at trial may not participate as an advocate in the case, unless the testimony will be about an uncontested matter or the amount of attorney's fees in the case, or if disqualifying the attorney would create a substantial hardship for the client. • The rule permits an attorney actively participating in the case to be a witness on merely formal matters but discourages testimony on other matters on behalf of a client. *Model Rules of Professional Conduct* Rule 3.7 (1987). — Also termed *advocate-witness rule*; *attorney-witness rule*.

lay, *adj.* **1.** Not ecclesiastical; nonclerical. **2.** Not expert, esp. with reference to law or medicine; nonprofessional.

lay, *n. Maritime law.* A share of the profits of a fishing or whaling trip, akin to wages, allotted to the officers and seamen.

lay, *vb.* To allege or assert.

> "**The Laying of Damages.** — At common law the declaration must 'lay damages.' " Edwin E. Bryant, *The Law of Pleading Under the Codes of Civil Procedure* 209 (2d ed. 1899).

layaway. An agreement between a retail seller and a consumer to hold goods for future sale. • The seller sets the goods aside and agrees to sell them to the consumer at an agreed price in the future. The consumer deposits with the seller some portion of the price of the goods, and may agree to other conditions with the seller, such as progress payments. The consumer receives the goods once the full purchase price has been paid.

lay corporation. See CORPORATION.

lay damages, *vb.* To allege damages, esp. in the complaint. See AD DAMNUM CLAUSE.

lay day. See DAY.

lay fee. See FEE (2).

lay impropriator (im-**proh**-pree-ay-tər). *Eccles. law.* A layperson holding a spiritual appropriation.

laying a foundation. *Evidence.* Introducing evidence of certain facts needed to render later evidence relevant, material, or competent. • For example, propounding a hypothetical question to an expert is necessary before the expert may render an opinion.

laying of the venue. A statement in a complaint naming the district or county in which the plaintiff proposes that any trial of the matter should occur. See VENUE.

lay investiture. *Eccles. law.* The ceremony of placing a bishop in possession of lands, money revenues, and other diocesan temporalities.

lay judge. See JUDGE.

layman. 1. A person who is not a member of the clergy. **2.** A person who is not a member of a profession or an expert on a particular subject. — Also termed *layperson.*

layoff. The termination of employment at the employer's instigation; esp., the termination — either temporary or permanent — of a large number of employees in a short time. — **lay off,** *vb.*

mass layoff. *Labor law.* Under the Worker Adjustment and Retraining Notification Act, a reduction in force that results in the loss of work at a single site, of 30 days or more, for at least 500 full-time employees, or 50 or more full-time employees if they make up at least 33 percent of the employees at that site. 29 USCA § 2101(a)(3). See WORKER ADJUSTMENT AND RETRAINING NOTIFICATION ACT.

layoff bet. See BET.

layoff bettor. A bookmaker who accepts layoff bets from other bookmakers. See *layoff bet* under BET.

lay opinion testimony. See TESTIMONY.

layperson. 1. See LAYMAN. **2.** *Hist.* See JUROR.

lay system. *Maritime law.* A system in which a fishing vessel's catch is sold at auction, and then the proceeds are provided first to the provider of supplies and then to the master and crew.

lay tenure. See TENURE.

laytime. The period permitted for the unloading of a chartered vessel. • If more time is used to unload the vessel, the vessel's owner is entitled to compensation for the delay.

lay witness. See WITNESS.

LBO. See *leveraged buyout* under BUYOUT.

LC. *abbr.* **1.** LETTER OF CREDIT. **2.** LETTER OF CREDENCE. — Also written L/C.

L-Claim proceeding. Under the Racketeer Influenced and Corrupt Organizations Act, a hearing that is connected with a criminal proceeding, and that is intended to ensure that property ordered to be forfeited belongs to the defendant. • A petition for an L–Claim proceeding is filed by someone other than the defendant who claims an interest in property that has been ordered to be forfeited. The proceeding's purpose is not to divide the defendant's estate among competing claimants, and general creditors of the defendant should not be allowed to maintain an L–Claim petition. To succeed, an L–Claim petitioner must be able to show an interest in a specific asset that has been ordered forfeited. The proceeding is referred to as an L–Claim proceeding because its legal basis is subsection *l* of RICO's penalty provision. 18 USCA § 1963(*l*)(2).

LEAA. *abbr.* LAW ENFORCEMENT ASSISTANCE ADMINISTRATION.

leaching (**leech**-ing). The process by which moving fluid separates the soluble components of a material. • Under CERCLA, leaching is considered a release of contaminants. The term is sometimes used to describe the migration of contaminating materials, by rain or groundwater, from a fixed source, such as a landfill. 42 USCA § 9601(22).

lead counsel. See COUNSEL.

leading case. 1. A judicial decision that first definitively settled an important legal rule or principle and that has since been often and consistently followed. • An example is *Miranda v. Arizona*, 384 U.S. 436, 86 S.Ct. 1602 (1966) (creating the exclusionary rule for evidence improperly obtained from a suspect being interrogated while in police custody). Cf. LANDMARK DECISION. **2.** An important, often the most important, judicial precedent on a particular legal issue. **3.** Loosely, a reported case that is cited as the dispositive authority on an issue being litigated. — Also termed (in sense 3) *ruling case*.

leading counsel. See *lead counsel* under COUNSEL.

leading economic indicator. See ECONOMIC INDICATOR.

leading indicator. See INDICATOR.

leading-object rule. See MAIN-PURPOSE RULE.

leading of a use. *Hist.* In a deed, the specification, before the levy of a fine of land, of the person to whose use the fine will inure. • If the deed is executed after the fine, it "declares" the use.

> "As if A., tenant in tail, with reversion to himself in fee, would settle his estate on B. for life, remainder to C. in tail, remainder to D. in fee .... He therefore usually, after making the settlement proposed, covenants to levy a fine ... and directs that the same shall enure to the uses in such settlement mentioned. This is now a deed to *lead* the uses of the fine or recovery, and the fine when levied, or recovery when suffered, shall enure to the uses so specified, and no other." 2 William Blackstone, *Commentaries on the Laws of England* 363 (1766).

leading question. A question that suggests the answer to the person being interrogated; esp., a question that may be answered by a mere "yes" or "no." • Leading questions are generally allowed only in cross-examination. — Also termed *categorical question*; *suggestive question*; *suggestive interrogation*.

lead-lag study. A survey used to determine the amount of working capital that a utility company must reserve and include in its rate base, by comparing the time the company has to pay its bills and the time taken by its customers to pay for service. • Lead time is the average number of days between the company's receipt and payment of invoices it receives. Lag time is the average number of days between the company's billing of its customers and its receipt of payment. By analyzing the difference in timing between inward cash flow and outward cash flow, the amount of necessary reserves can be calculated.

leads doctrine. *Tax.* In a tax-evasion case, the rule that the government is obligated to investigate all the taxpayer's leads that are reasonably accessible and that, if true, would establish the taxpayer's innocence, or the government risks having the trial judge presume that any leads not investigated are true and exonerating.

league. 1. A covenant made by nations, groups, or individuals for promoting common interests or ensuring mutual protection. **2.** An alliance or association of nations, groups, or individuals formed by such a covenant. **3.** A unit of distance, usu. measuring about three miles.

League of Nations. An organization of nations formed in 1919 to promote international cooperation and peace. • President Woodrow Wilson endorsed the League in an address to Congress, but the United States never joined. The League dissolved in 1946 and turned its assets over to the United Nations.

leakage. 1. The waste of a liquid caused by its leaking from a storage container. **2.** An allowance against duties granted by customs to an importer of liquids for losses sustained by this waste. **3.** *Intellectual property.* Loss in value of a piece of intellectual property because of unauthorized copying. • The types of intellectual property most susceptible to leakage are recordable media such as compact discs and videotapes.

leal (leel), *adj.* [Law French] *Hist.* Loyal.

lean, *vb.* **1.** To incline or tend in opinion or preference. • A court is sometimes said to "lean against" the position of one of the advocates before it, meaning that the court regards the advocate's position disfavorably. **2.** To yield; to submit.

leapfrog development. An improvement of land that requires the extension of public facilities from their current stopping point, through undeveloped land that may be scheduled for future development, to the site of the improvement.

leap year. See YEAR.

learned (**lər**-nid), *adj.* **1.** Having a great deal of learning; erudite. • A lawyer might refer to an adversary as a "learned colleague" or "learned opponent," which may be, depending on tone of voice, either a genuine compliment or a subtle slight. **2.** Well-versed in the law and its history. • Statutes sometimes require that judges be "learned in the law," a phrase commonly construed as meaning that they must have received a regular legal education.

learned intermediary. See *informed intermediary* under INTERMEDIARY.

learned-intermediary doctrine. The principle that a prescription-drug manufacturer fulfills its duty to warn of a drug's potentially harmful effects by informing the prescribing physician, rather than the end-user, of those effects.

learned-treatise rule. *Evidence.* An exception to the hearsay rule, by which a published text may be established as authoritative, either by expert testimony or by judicial notice. • Under the Federal Rules of Evidence, a statement contained in a published treatise, periodical, or pamphlet on sciences or arts (such as history and medicine) can be established as authoritative — and thereby admitted into evidence for the purpose of examining or cross-examining an expert witness — by expert testimony or by the court taking judicial notice of the authoritative nature or reliability of the text. If the statement is admitted into evidence, it may be read into the trial record, but it may not be received as an exhibit. Fed. R. Evid. 803(18).

learning, *n.* **1.** *Hist.* Legal doctrine. **2.** The act of acquiring knowledge.

lease, *n.* **1.** A contract by which a rightful possessor of real property conveys the right to use and occupy that property in exchange for consideration, usu. rent. • The lease term can be for life, for a fixed period, or for a period terminable at will. **2.** Such a conveyance plus all covenants attached to it. **3.** The written instrument memorializing such a conveyance and its covenants. — Also termed *lease agreement*; *lease contract*. **4.** The piece of real property so conveyed. **5.** A contract by which the rightful possessor of personal property conveys the right to use that property in exchange for consideration.

assignable lease. A lease that can be transferred by a lessee. See SUBLEASE.

capital lease. See LEASE-PURCHASE AGREEMENT.

commercial lease. A lease for business purposes.

community lease. A lease in which a number of lessors owning interests in separate tracts execute a lease in favor of a single lessee.

concurrent lease. A lease that begins before a previous lease ends, entitling the new lessee to be paid all rents that accrue on the previous lease after the new lease begins, and to appropriate remedies against the holding tenant.

> "A landlord who has granted a lease may nevertheless grant another lease of the same land for all or some of the period of the first lease. The second lease does not deprive the lessee under the first lease of the right to possession of the property, but is, in reality, a lease of the reversion. Because the two leases operate concurrently during at least some part of their respective durations, they are known as 'concurrent leases'." Peter Butt, *Land Law* 233 (2d ed. 1988).

consumer lease. **1.** A lease of goods by a person who is in the business of selling or leasing a product to someone who leases it primarily for personal or household use. UCC § 2A–103(1)(e). **2.** A residential — rather than commercial — lease.

durable lease. A lease that reserves a rent payable annually, usu. with a right of reentry for nonpayment.

edge lease. *Oil & gas.* A lease located on the edge of a field.

finance lease. A fixed-term lease used by a business to finance capital equipment. • The lessor's service is usu. limited to financing the asset, and the lessee pays maintenance costs and taxes and has the option of purchasing the asset at lease-end for a nominal price. Finance leases strongly resemble security agreements and are written almost exclusively by financial institutions as a way to help a commercial customer obtain an expensive capital item that the customer might not otherwise be able to afford. UCC § 2A–103(1)(g). — Also termed *full payout lease*.

> "By carving out the 'finance lease' for special treatment, the drafters of Article 2A have recognized a distinct species of lease that is written almost exclusively by financial institutions and — although treated as a true lease — does not normally carry with it certain of the responsibilities that the typical lessor bears under Article 2A." 2 James J. White & Robert S. Summers, *Uniform Commercial Code* § 13–3, at 4 (4th ed. 1995).

> "A finance lease is the product of a three-party transaction. The supplier manufactures or supplies the goods

pursuant to the lessee's specification, perhaps even pursuant to a purchase order, sales agreement, or lease agreement between the supplier and the lessee. After the prospective finance lease is negotiated, a purchase order, sales agreement, or lease agreement is entered into by the lessor (as buyer or prime lessee) or an existing order, agreement, or lease is assigned by the lessee to the lessor, and the lessor and the lessee then enter into a lease or sublease of the goods. Due to the limited function usually performed by the lessor, the lessee looks almost entirely to the supplier for representations, covenants, and warranties. If a manufacturer's warranty carries through, the lessee may also look to that. Yet, this definition does not restrict the lessor's function solely to the supply of funds; if the lessor undertakes or performs other functions, express warranties, covenants, and the common law will protect the lessee." UCC § 2A-102 cmt. at 14–15 (Proposed Final Draft, 30 Apr. 1999).

full-service lease. A lease in which the lessor agrees to pay all maintenance expenses, insurance premiums, and property taxes.

graduated lease. A lease in which rent varies depending on future contingencies, such as operating expenses or gross income.

gross lease. A lease in which the lessee pays a flat amount for rent, out of which the lessor pays all the expenses (such as gas, water, and electricity).

ground lease. A long-term (usu. 99–year) lease of land only. • Such a lease typically involves commercial property, and any improvements built by the lessee usu. revert to the lessor. — Also termed *ground-rent lease*; *land lease*.

headlease. See HEADLEASE.

index lease. A lease that provides for increases in rent according to the increases in the consumer price index.

land lease. See *ground lease*.

leveraged lease. A lease that is collateral for the loan through which the lessor acquired the leased asset, and that provides the lender's only recourse for nonpayment of the debt; a lease in which a creditor provides nonrecourse financing to the lessor (who has substantial leverage in the property) and in which the lessor's net investment in the lease, apart from nonrecourse financing, declines during the early years and increases in later years. — Also termed *third-party equity lease*; *tax lease*.

master lease. A lease that controls later leases or subleases.

mineral lease. A lease in which the lessee has the right to explore for and extract oil, gas, or other minerals. • The rent usu. is based on the amount or value of the minerals extracted.

mining lease. A lease of a mine or mining claim, in which the lessee has the right to work the mine or claim, usu. with conditions on the amount and type of work to be done. • The lessor is compensated in the form of either fixed rent or royalties based on the amount of ore mined.

month-to-month lease. A tenancy with no written contract. • Rent is paid monthly, and usu. one month's notice by the landlord or tenant is required to terminate the tenancy. See *periodic tenancy* under TENANCY.

net lease. A lease in which the lessee pays rent plus property expenses (such as taxes and insurance).

net-net-net lease. A lease in which the lessee pays all the expenses, including mortgage interest and amortization, leaving the lessor with an amount free of all claims. — Also termed *triple net lease*.

oil-and-gas lease. A lease granting the right to extract oil and gas from a specified piece of land. • Although called a "lease," this interest is typically considered a determinable fee in the minerals rather than a grant of possession for a term of years.

operating lease. A lease of property (esp. equipment) for a term that is shorter than the property's useful life. • Under an operating lease, the lessor is responsible for paying taxes and other expenses on the property. Cf. *capital lease*; LEASE-PURCHASE AGREEMENT.

parol lease (pə-**rohl** *or* **par**-əl). A lease based on an oral agreement; an unwritten lease.

percentage lease. A lease in which the rent is based on a percentage of gross (or net) sales or profits, with a set minimum rent.

perpetual lease. **1.** An ongoing lease not limited in duration. **2.** A grant of lands in fee with a reservation of a rent in fee; a fee farm.

proprietary lease. A lease between a cooperative apartment association and a tenant.

sandwich lease. A lease in which the lessee subleases the property to a third party, esp. for more rent than under the original lease.

short lease. A lease of brief duration, often less than six months.

sublease. See SUBLEASE.

synthetic lease. A method for financing the purchase of real estate, whereby the lender creates a special-purpose entity that buys the property and then leases it to the ultimate user (usu. a corporation). • A synthetic lease is treated as a loan for tax purposes and as an operating lease for accounting purposes, so that the "lessee" can deduct the property's depreciation and the loan's interest yet keep both the asset and the debt off its balance sheet.

tax lease. **1.** The instrument or estate given to the purchaser of land at a tax sale when the law does not permit the sale of an estate in fee for nonpayment of taxes but instead directs the sale of an estate for years. **2.** See *leveraged lease.*

third-party equity lease. See *leveraged lease.*

timber lease. A real-property lease that contemplates that the lessee will cut timber on the leased premises.

top lease. A lease granted on property already subject to a mineral lease, and taking effect only if the existing lease expires or terminates.

unless lease. *Oil & gas.* A lease that terminates automatically unless the lessee begins drilling operations or begins making delay-rental payments.

lease, *vb.* **1.** To grant the possession and use of (land, buildings, rooms, movable property, etc.) to another in return for rent or other consideration <the city leased the stadium to the football team>. **2.** To take a lease of; to hold by a lease <Carol leased the townhouse from her uncle>.

lease agreement. See LEASE (3).

lease and release. *Hist.* A method of transferring seisin without livery, whereby the owner and the transferee would enter into a lease for a term of years, to take effect only when the transferee entered the property, whereupon the owner would release all interest in the property to the transferee by written instrument. • Once the transferee owned both the term and the freehold interest, the two interests would merge to form one estate in fee simple. This lease-and-release procedure was fully acceptable to the courts, on the theory that livery of seisin to one already occupying the land was unnecessary.

leaseback, *n.* The sale of property on the understanding, or with the express option, that the seller may lease the property from the buyer immediately upon the sale. — Also termed *sale and leaseback.*

lease contract. See LEASE (3).

lease for years. See *tenancy for a term* under TENANCY.

leasehold, *n.* A tenant's possessory estate in land or premises, the four types being the tenancy for years, the periodic tenancy, the tenancy at will, and the tenancy at sufferance. • Although a leasehold has some of the characteristics of real property, it has historically been classified as a chattel real. — Also termed *leasehold estate*; *leasehold interest.* See TENANCY. Cf. FREEHOLD.

leasehold improvements. Beneficial changes to leased property (such as a parking lot or driveway) made by or for the benefit of the lessee. • The phrase is used in a condemnation proceeding to determine the share of compensation to be allocated to the lessee.

leasehold interest. **1.** LEASEHOLD; esp., for purposes of eminent domain, the lessee's interest in the lease itself, measured by the difference between the total remaining rent and the rent the lessee would pay for similar space for the same period. **2.** A lessor's or lessee's interest under a lease contract. UCC § 2A–103. **3.** WORKING INTEREST.

leasehold mortgage. See MORTGAGE.

leasehold mortgage bond. See BOND (3).

leasehold value. The value of a leasehold interest. • This term usu. applies to a long-term lease when the rent paid under the lease is lower than current market rates. Some states permit the lessee to claim the leasehold interest from the landlord in a condemnation proceeding, unless the lease prohibits such a claim. Other states prohibit these claims by statute. See LEASEHOLD INTEREST; NO-BONUS CLAUSE.

lease insurance. See INSURANCE.

lease-lend. See LEND-LEASE.

lease-purchase agreement. A rent-to-own purchase plan under which the buyer takes possession of the goods with the first payment and takes ownership with the final payment; a lease of property (esp. equipment) by which ownership of the property is transferred to the lessee at the end of the lease term. • Such a lease is usu. treated as an installment sale. Under a capital lease, the lessee is responsible for paying taxes and other expenses on the property. — Also termed *lease-to-purchase agreement*; *hire-purchase agreement*; *capital lease*. Cf. *operating lease* under LEASE.

least-intrusive-means doctrine. A doctrine requiring the government to exhaust all other investigatory means before seeking sensitive testimony, as by compelling an attorney to testify before a grand jury on matters that may be protected by the attorney-client privilege.

least-intrusive-remedy doctrine. The rule that a legal remedy should provide the damaged party with appropriate relief, without unduly penalizing the opposing party or the jurisdiction's legal system, as by striking only the unconstitutional portion of a challenged statute while leaving the rest of the statute intact.

least-restrictive educational environment. See LEAST-RESTRICTIVE ENVIRONMENT.

least-restrictive environment. Under the Individuals with Disabilities Education Act, the school setting that, to the greatest extent appropriate, educates a disabled child together with children who are not disabled. 20 USCA § 1412(5). — Also termed *least-restrictive-educational environment*. Cf. MAINSTREAMING.

least-restrictive-means test. The rule that a law or governmental regulation, even when based on a legitimate governmental interest, should be crafted in a way that will protect individual civil liberties as much as possible, and should be only as restrictive as is necessary to accomplish a legitimate governmental purpose.

leaute (**low**-tay), *n.* [Law French "legality"] *Hist.* Legality; the condition of a lawful man (*legalis homo*). See LEGALIS HOMO.

leave, *vb.* **1.** To give by will; to bequeath or devise <she left her ranch to her stepson>. **2.** To depart willfully with the intent not to return <Nelson left Texas and became a resident of Massachusetts>. **3.** To depart.

leave and license. *Hist.* In an action for trespass to land, the defense that the plaintiff consented to the defendant's presence.

leave no issue, *vb.* To die without a surviving child, children, or descendants. • The spouse of a deceased child is usu. not issue.

leave of absence. A worker's temporary absence from employment or duty with the intention to return. • Salary and seniority normally are unaffected by a leave of absence.

leave of court. Judicial permission to follow a nonroutine procedure <the defense sought leave of court to allow the defendant to exit the courtroom when the autopsy photographs are shown>. — Often shortened to *leave*.

LEC. *abbr.* LOCAL-EXCHANGE CARRIER.

leccator (lə-**kay**-tər). [Latin] *Archaic.* A debauched person; a lecher. — Also termed *lecator*.

lecherwite (**lech**-ər-wIt). See LAIRWITE.

lecture method. See HORNBOOK METHOD.

ledger (**lej**-ər). **1.** A book or series of books used for recording financial transactions in the form of debits and credits. — Also termed *general ledger*. **2.** *Archaic.* A resident ambassador or agent. — Also termed (in sense 2) *leger*; *lieger*.

ledo (**lee**-doh), *n.* [Latin] *Hist.* The rising water of the sea; neap tide. See *neap tide* under TIDE.

leet (leet). *Hist.* A criminal court. • The last remaining leets were abolished in England in 1977.

> "Leet is a court derived out of the sheriff's turn, and inquires of all offences under the degree of high treason that are committed against the crown and dignity of the king. But those offences which are to be punished with loss of life or member, are only inquirable there, and to be certified over to the justices of assise. See stat. 1 E. 3, c. 17." *Termes de la Ley* 278–79 (1st Am. ed. 1812).

left-handed marriage. See *morganatic marriage* under MARRIAGE.

legabilis (lə-**gay**-bə-lis), *n.* [Latin] *Hist.* Property or goods that may be given by will. • As an adjective, the term also meant "bequeathable."

legacy (**leg**-ə-see), *n.* A gift by will, esp. of personal property and often of money. Cf. BEQUEST; DEVISE.

absolute legacy. A legacy given without condition and intended to vest immediately.

accumulated legacy. A legacy that has not yet been paid to a legatee.

accumulative legacy. **1.** Another legacy given to a legatee, but by a different will. **2.** See *additional legacy.*

additional legacy. Another legacy given to a legatee in the same will (or in a codicil to the same will) that gave the first legacy. — Also termed *accumulative legacy.*

alternate legacy. A legacy by which the testator gives the legatee a choice of one of two or more items.

conditional legacy. A legacy that will take effect or be defeated subject to the occurrence or nonoccurrence of an event.

contingent legacy. A legacy that depends on an uncertain event and thus has not vested. • An example is a legacy given to one's granddaughter "if or when she attains the age of 21."

cumulative legacies. Two or more legacies that, being given in the same will to the same person (often in similar language), are considered additional to one another and not merely a repeated expression of the same gift.

demonstrative legacy (di-**mon**-strə-tiv). A legacy paid from a particular source if that source has enough money. • If it does not, the amount of the legacy not paid from that source is taken from the estate's general assets.

general legacy. A gift of personal property that the testator intends to come from the general assets of the estate, payable in money or items indistinguishable from each other, such as shares of stock.

lapsed legacy. A legacy to a legatee who dies either before the testator dies or before the legacy is payable. • It falls into the residual estate unless the jurisdiction has an antilapse statute. See ANTILAPSE STATUTE.

modal legacy (**moh**-dəl). A legacy accompanied by directions about the manner in which it will be applied to the legatee's benefit <a modal legacy for the purchase of a business>.

pecuniary legacy (pi-**kyoo**-nee-er-ee). A legacy of a sum of money.

residuary legacy (ri-**zij**-oo-er-ee). A legacy of the estate remaining after the satisfaction of all claims and all specific, general, and demonstrative legacies.

specific legacy. A legacy of property that can be distinguished from the other property forming the testator's estate. — Also termed *special legacy.*

substitutional legacy. A legacy that replaces a different legacy already given to a legatee.

trust legacy. A legacy of personal property to trustees to be held in trust, with the income usu. paid to a specified beneficiary.

vested legacy. A legacy given in such a way that the legatee has a fixed, indefeasible right to its payment. • A legacy is said to be vested when the testator's words making the bequest convey a transmissible interest, whether present or future, to the legatee. Thus, a legacy to be paid when the legatee reaches the age of 21 is a vested legacy because it is given unconditionally and absolutely. Although the legacy is vested, the legatee's enjoyment of it is deferred.

void legacy. A legacy that never had any legal existence. • The subject matter of such a legacy is treated as a part of the estate and passes under the residuary clause of a will or (in the absence of a residuary clause) under the rules for intestate succession.

legacy duty. 1. A tax on a legacy, often with the provision that the rate increases as the relationship of the legatee becomes more remote from the testator. — Also termed *collateral inheritance tax.* **2.** *Hist.* A tax imposed on personal property (other than a leasehold) passing by will or through intestacy.

legacy tax. See TAX.

legal, *adj.* **1.** Of or relating to law; falling within the province of law <pro bono legal services>. **2.** Established, required, or permitted by law; LAWFUL <it is legal to carry a concealed handgun in some states>. **3.** Of or relating to law as opposed to equity.

legal act. 1. Any act not condemned as illegal. • For example, a surgeon's incision is a legal act, while stabbing is an illegal one. **2.** An action or undertaking that creates a legally recognized obligation; an act that binds a person in some way.

> "A lunatic, though capable of holding property, was in Roman law incapable of any legal act." Thomas E. Holland, *The Elements of Jurisprudence* 354 (13th ed. 1924).

3. See *act in the law* under ACT (2). **4.** See *act of the law* under ACT (2).

legal-acumen doctrine (**lee**-gəl-ə-**kyoo**-mən). The principle that if a defect in, or the invalidity of, a claim to land cannot be discovered without legal expertise, then equity may be invoked to remove the cloud created by the defect or invalidity.

legal-advice exception. **1.** The rule that an attorney may withhold as privileged the client's identity and information regarding fees, if there is a strong probability that disclosing the information would implicate the client in the criminal activity for which the attorney was consulted. **2.** An exemption contained in open-meetings legislation, permitting a governmental body to meet in closed session to consult with its attorney about certain matters.

legal age. See *age of capacity* under AGE.

legal aid. Free or inexpensive legal services provided to those who cannot afford to pay full price. • Legal aid is usu. administered locally by a specially established organization. See LEGAL SERVICES CORPORATION.

legal analyst. See PARALEGAL.

legal asset. See ASSET.

legal assistant. **1.** PARALEGAL. **2.** A legal secretary.

legal brief. See BRIEF.

legal capital. See CAPITAL.

legal cause. See *proximate cause* under CAUSE (1).

legal centralism. The theory suggesting that state-constructed legal entities form the center of legal life and control lesser normative systems (such as the family or business networks) that define appropriate behavior and social relationships. — Also termed *legal centrism*; *legocentrism* (lee-goh-**sen**-triz-əm).

legal-certainty test. *Civil procedure.* A test designed to establish whether the jurisdictional amount has been met. • The amount claimed in the complaint will control unless there is a "legal certainty" that the claim is actually less than the minimum amount necessary to establish jurisdiction. See AMOUNT IN CONTROVERSY.

legal citology (sɪ-**tol**-ə-jee). The study of citations (esp. in footnotes) and their effect on legal scholarship. — Often shortened to *citology*. — **legal citologist** (sɪ-**tol**-ə-jist), *n.*

Legal Code. See CODE (2).

legal conclusion. A statement that expresses a legal duty or result but omits the facts creating or supporting the duty or result. Cf. CONCLUSION OF LAW; CONCLUSION OF FACT; FINDING OF FACT.

legal consideration. See *valuable consideration* under CONSIDERATION.

legal cruelty. See CRUELTY.

legal custody. See CUSTODY (2), (3).

legal custom. See CUSTOM.

legal death. **1.** See *brain death* under DEATH. **2.** CIVIL DEATH.

legal debt. See DEBT.

legal defense. See DEFENSE (1).

legal demand. See DEMAND (1).

legal dependent. See DEPENDENT.

legal description. A formal description of real property, including a description of any part subject to an easement or reservation, complete enough that a particular piece of land can be located and identified. • The description can be made by reference to a government survey, metes and bounds, or lot numbers of a recorded plat. — Also termed *land description*.

legal discretion. See *judicial discretion* under DISCRETION.

legal distributee. See DISTRIBUTEE.

legal duty. See DUTY (1).

legal-elements test. *Criminal law.* A method of determining whether one crime is a lesser-included offense in relation to another crime, by examining the components of the greater crime to analyze whether a person who commits the greater crime necessarily commits the lesser one too. — Also termed *same-elements test*.

legal entity. A body, other than a natural person, that can function legally, sue or be sued, and make decisions through agents. • A typical example is a corporation. Cf. LEGAL PERSON.

legalese (lee-gə-**leez**). The jargon characteristically used by lawyers, esp. in legal documents <the partner chided the associate about the rampant legalese in the draft sublease>. Cf. PLAIN-LANGUAGE MOVEMENT.

legal estate. See ESTATE.

legal estoppel. See ESTOPPEL.

legal ethics. 1. The standards of minimally acceptable conduct within the legal profession, involving the duties that its members owe one another, their clients, and the courts. — Also termed *etiquette of the profession*. **2.** The study or observance of those duties. **3.** The written regulations governing those duties. See MODEL RULES OF PROFESSIONAL CONDUCT.

legal evidence. See EVIDENCE.

legal excuse. See EXCUSE.

legal fact. See FACT.

legal father. See FATHER.

legal fence. See LAWFUL FENCE.

legal fiction. An assumption that something is true even though it may be untrue, made esp. in judicial reasoning to alter how a legal rule operates. • The constructive trust is an example of a legal fiction. — Also termed *fiction of law*; *fictio juris*.

> "I ... employ the expression 'Legal Fiction' to signify any assumption which conceals, or affects to conceal, the fact that a rule of law has undergone alteration, its letter remaining unchanged, its operation being modified.... It is not difficult to understand why fictions in all their forms are particularly congenial to the infancy of society. They satisfy the desire for improvement, which is not quite wanting, at the same time that they do not offend the superstitious disrelish for change which is always present." Henry S. Maine, *Ancient Law* 21–22 (17th ed. 1901).

> "Legal fiction is the mask that progress must wear to pass the faithful but blear-eyed watchers of our ancient legal treasures. But though legal fictions are useful in thus mitigating or absorbing the shock of innovation, they work havoc in the form of intellectual confusion." Morris R. Cohen, *Law and the Social Order* 126 (1933).

legal force. See *reasonable force* under FORCE.

legal formalism, *n.* The theory that law is a set of rules and principles independent of other political and social institutions. • Legal formalism was espoused by such scholars as Christopher Columbus Langdell and Lon Fuller. — **legal formalist,** *n.* Cf. LEGAL REALISM.

legal fraud. See *constructive fraud* (1) under FRAUD.

legal heir. See HEIR (1).

legal holiday. A day designated by law as exempt from court proceedings, issuance of process, and the like. • Legal holidays vary from state to state. — Sometimes shortened to *holiday*. — Also termed *nonjudicial day*.

legal impossibility. See IMPOSSIBILITY.

legal inconsistency. See *legally inconsistent verdict* under VERDICT.

legal injury. See INJURY.

legal-injury rule. The doctrine that the statute of limitations on a claim does not begin to run until the claimant has sustained some legally actionable damage. • Under this rule, the limitations period is tolled until the plaintiff has actually been injured. — Also termed *damage rule*.

legal innocence. See INNOCENCE.

legal insanity. See INSANITY.

legal interest. See INTEREST (2).

legal intromission. See INTROMISSION.

legal investments. See LEGAL LIST.

legalis homo (lə-**gay**-lis **hoh**-moh). [Latin "lawful man"] *Hist.* A person who has full legal capacity and full legal rights; one who has not been deprived of any rights in court by outlawry, excommunication, or infamy. • A *legalis homo* was said to stand *rectus in curia* ("right in court"). A lawful man was able to serve as a juror and to swear an oath. Pl. ***legales homines*** (lə-**gay**-leez **hom**-ə-neez). — Also termed *legal man*; *lawful man*; *lageman*; *liber et legalis homo*. See RECTUS IN CURIA.

legalism, *n.* **1.** Formalism carried almost to the point of meaninglessness; an inclination to exalt the importance of law or formulated rules in any area of action.

> "What is legalism? It is the ethical attitude that holds moral conduct to be a matter of rule following, and

moral relationships to consist of duties and rights determined by rules." Judith N. Shklar, *Legalism: Law, Morals, and Political Trials* 1 (1964).

"If ... the law and the lawyer are to make a socially valuable contribution to the operation of the social security system, there must be abandoned old-established habits of thought as to the nature of law and the whole gamut of practices summed up in the layman's word of deadly insult, 'legalism' — his word for rigid attachment to legal precedent, the substitution of legal rule for policy, the fettering of discretion, the adversary style, the taking of technical points, formality." Leslie Scarman, *English Law — The New Dimension* 43 (1974).

2. A mode of expression characteristic of lawyers; a jargonistic phrase characteristic of lawyers, such as "pursuant to."

legalis moneta Angliae (lə-**gay**-lis mə-**nee**-tə **ang**-glee-ee), *n.* [Latin] Lawful money of England.

legal issue. See ISSUE (1).

legalist, *n.* A person who views things from a legal or formalistic standpoint; esp., one who believes in strict adherence to the letter of the law rather than its spirit.

legalistic, *adj.* Characterized by legalism; exalting the importance of law or formulated rules in any area of action <a legalistic argument>.

legality. 1. Strict adherence to law, prescription, or doctrine; the quality of being legal. **2.** The principle that a person may not be prosecuted under a criminal law that has not been previously published. — Also termed (in sense 2) *principle of legality*.

legalize, *vb.* **1.** To make lawful; to authorize or justify by legal sanction <the bill to legalize marijuana never made it to the Senate floor>. **2.** To imbue with the spirit of the law; to make legalistic <legalized conceptions of religion>. — **legalization,** *n.*

legalized nuisance. See NUISANCE.

legal jeopardy. See JEOPARDY.

legal liability. See LIABILITY.

legal life estate. See *life estate* under ESTATE.

legal life tenant. See LIFE TENANT.

legal list. A group of investments in which institutions and fiduciaries (such as banks and insurance companies) may legally invest according to state statutes. • States usu. restrict the legal list to high-quality securities meeting certain specifications. — Also termed *approved list*; *legal investments*.

legally, *adv.* In a lawful way; in a manner that accords with the law.

legally determined, *adj.* (Of a claim, issue, etc.) decided by legal process <liability for the accident was legally determined>.

legally incapacitated person. A person, other than a minor, who is permanently or temporarily impaired by mental illness, mental deficiency, physical illness or disability, or use of drugs or alcohol to the extent that the person lacks sufficient understanding to make or communicate responsible personal decisions or to enter into contracts. — Abbr. LIP. — Also termed *legally incompetent person*; *incompetent*, n.

legally inconsistent verdict. See VERDICT.

legally liable. See LIABLE.

legally sufficient consideration. See *sufficient consideration* under CONSIDERATION.

legal malice. See *implied malice* under MALICE.

legal malpractice. See MALPRACTICE.

legal man. See LEGALIS HOMO.

legal maxim. See MAXIM.

legal memory. The period during which a legal right or custom can be determined or established. • Traditionally, common-law legal memory began in the year 1189, but in 1540 it became a steadily moving period of 60 years. Cf. TIME IMMEMORIAL (1).

"Because of the importance to feudal landholders of seisin and of real property in general, the writ of right has been called 'the most solemn of all actions.' Nevertheless, it was believed that the time within which such a complainant would be allowed to prove an ancestor to have been seised of the estate in question must be limited. At first this was done by selecting an arbitrary date in the past, before which 'legal memory' would not run. The date initially was Dec. 1, 1135 (the death of Henry I); in 1236 it was changed by statute to Dec. 19, 1154 (the coronation of Henry II); and in 1275 it became Sept. 3, 1189 (the coronation of Richard I). Finally, in 1540, an arbitrary period of sixty years was set as the period of 'legal memory.' The latter change was probably made because it was felt that a 350-year statute of limitations was somewhat awkward." Thomas F. Bergin & Paul G. Haskell, *Preface to Estates in Land and Future Interests* 45 n.65 (2d ed. 1984).

legal mind. The intellect, legal capacities, and attitudes of a well-trained lawyer — often used as a personified being <although this distinction occurs naturally to the legal mind, it is too technical to be satisfactory>.

legal monopoly. See MONOPOLY.

legal moralism. The theory that a government or legal system may prohibit conduct that is considered immoral.

legal mortgage. See MORTGAGE.

legal name. See NAME.

legal negligence. See *negligence per se* under NEGLIGENCE.

legal newspaper. See NEWSPAPER.

legal notice. See NOTICE.

legal obligation. See OBLIGATION.

legal officer. See OFFICER (2).

legal opinion. See OPINION (2).

legal order. 1. Traditionally, a set of regulations governing a society and those responsible for enforcing them. **2.** Modernly, such regulations and officials plus the processes involved in creating, interpreting, and applying the regulations.

legal owner. See OWNER.

legal paternalism. The theory that a government or legal system is justified in controlling the individual affairs of the citizens. • This theory is often associated with legal positivists. See PATERNALISM; LEGAL POSITIVISM.

legal person. See *artificial person* under PERSON. Cf. LEGAL ENTITY.

legal personality. See PERSONALITY.

legal-personal representative. See REPRESENTATIVE.

legal philosophy. See *general jurisprudence* under JURISPRUDENCE.

legal portion. See LEGITIME.

legal positivism, *n.* The theory that legal rules are valid only because they are enacted by an existing political authority or accepted as binding in a given society, not because they are grounded in morality or in natural law. • Legal positivism has been espoused by such scholars as H.L.A. Hart. — **legal positivist,** *n.* See POSITIVE LAW. Cf. LOGICAL POSITIVISM.

"[I]t will be helpful to offer some comparisons between legal positivism and its counterpart in science. Scientific positivism condemns any inquiry projecting itself beyond observable phenomena; it abjures metaphysics, it renounces in advance any explanation in terms of ultimate causes. Its program of research is to chart the regularities discernible in the phenomena of nature at the point where they become open to human observation, without asking — as it were — how they got there. In the setting of limits to inquiry there is an obvious parallel between scientific and legal positivism. The legal positivist concentrates his attention on law at the point where it emerges from the institutional processes that brought it into being. It is the finally made law itself that furnishes the subject of his inquiries. How it was made and what directions of human effort went into its creation are for him irrelevancies." Lon L. Fuller, *Anatomy of the Law* 177–78 (1968).

legal possessor. One with the legal right to possess property, such as a buyer under a conditional sales contract, as contrasted with the legal owner who holds legal title. See *legal owner* under OWNER.

legal practice. See PRACTICE OF LAW.

legal practitioner. A lawyer.

"Legal practitioners may be either barristers, special pleaders not at the bar, certified conveyancers, or solicitors. The three latter may recover their fees, but the first may not, their acting being deemed of a voluntary nature, and their fees merely in the light of honorary payments; and it follows from this, that no action lies against them for negligence or unskilfulness." John Indermaur, *Principles of the Common Law* 169 (Edmund H. Bennett ed., 1st Am. ed. 1878).

legal prejudice. See PREJUDICE.

legal presumption. See *presumption of law* under PRESUMPTION.

legal proceeding. Any proceeding authorized by law and instituted in a court or tribunal to acquire a right or to enforce a remedy.

legal process. See PROCESS.

legal question. See QUESTION OF LAW.

legal rate. See INTEREST RATE.

legal realism, *n.* The theory that law is based, not on formal rules or principles, but instead on judicial decisions that should derive from social interests and public policy. • American legal realism — which flourished in the early 20th century — was espoused by such scholars as John Chipman Gray, Oliver Wendell Holmes, and Karl Llewellyn. — **legal realist,** *n.* Cf. LEGAL FORMALISM.

legal regime. See REGIME.

legal relation. The connection in law between one person or entity and another; VINCULUM JURIS.

legal remedy. See REMEDY.

legal representative. See *personal representative* under REPRESENTATIVE.

legal rescission. See RESCISSION.

legal research. 1. The finding and assembling of authorities that bear on a question of law. **2.** The field of study concerned with the effective marshaling of authorities that bear on a question of law.

legal reserve. See RESERVE.

legal residence. See DOMICILE (2).

legal right. See RIGHT.

legal ruling. See RULING.

legal science. The field of study that, as one of the social sciences, deals with the institutions and principles that particular societies have developed (1) for defining the claims and liabilities of persons against one another in various circumstances, and (2) for peaceably resolving disputes and controversies in accordance with principles accepted as fair and right in the particular community at a given time.

legal secretary. An employee in a law office whose responsibilities include typing legal documents and correspondence, keeping records and files, and performing other duties supportive of the employer's law practice. • Legal secretaries usu. are more highly skilled, and therefore more highly compensated, than secretaries in general business.

legal seisin. See *seisin in law* under SEISIN.

legal separation. See SEPARATION (1).

Legal Services Corporation. A corporation established by the Legal Services Corporation Act of 1974 (42 USCA § 2996) to provide legal help to clients who cannot afford legal services.

legal servitude. See SERVITUDE (1).

legal signature. See SIGNATURE.

legal subdivision. See SUBDIVISION.

legal subrogation. See SUBROGATION.

legal succession. See SUCCESSION (2); DESCENT.

legal tender. The money (bills and coins) approved in a country for the payment of debts, the purchase of goods, and other exchanges for value. See TENDER (4).

legal theory. 1. See *general jurisprudence* under JURISPRUDENCE. **2.** The principle under which a litigant proceeds, or on which a litigant bases its claims or defenses in a case.

legal title. See TITLE (2).

legal usufruct. See USUFRUCT.

legal voter. See VOTER (2).

legal willfulness. See WILLFULNESS.

legal wrong. See WRONG.

legantine. See LEGATINE.

legare (lə-**gair**-ee), *vb.* [Latin] *Roman law.* To bequeath or give (property) by will.

legatarius (leg-ə-**tair**-ee-əs), *n.* [Latin] **1.** *Roman law.* The person to whom property is bequeathed. **2.** *Hist.* A legate; a messenger or envoy. See LEGATE.

legatary (**leg**-ə-ter-ee). *Archaic.* See LEGATEE.

legate (**leg**-it). [fr. Latin *legare* "to send as deputy"] **1.** *Roman law.* An official undertaking a special mission for the emperor, such as assisting in a judicial function or conducting a census. **2.** *Roman law.* A senator or other official chosen to assist the emperor, a governor, or a general in a military or administrative activity. **3.** A papal representative who may or may not have both diplomatic and ecclesiastical status; a diplomatic agent of the Vatican.

legate a latere (ay **lat**-ə-ree). See LEGATUS.

legate missus (**mis**-əs). See LEGATUS.

legate natus (**nay**-təs). See LEGATUS.

4. A representative of a state or the highest authority in a state; an ambassador; a person commissioned to represent a country in a foreign country. — Also termed *legatus*. — **legatine,** *adj*.

legate (lə-**gayt**), *vb*. To give or leave as a legacy; BEQUEATH.

legatee (leg-ə-**tee**). **1.** One who is named in a will to take personal property; one who has received a legacy or bequest. **2.** Loosely, one to whom a devise of real property is given. — Also termed (archaically) *legatary*.

residuary legatee (ri-**zij**-oo-er-ee). A person designated to receive the residue of a decedent's estate. See *residuary estate* under ESTATE.

specific legatee. The recipient, under a will, of designated property that is transferred by the owner's death.

legatine (**leg**-ə-tin *or* -tɪn), *adj*. Of or relating to a legate. — Also termed (erroneously) *legantine*.

legatine constitution. *Hist. Eccles. law.* A code of ecclesiastical laws enacted in English national synods in 1220 and 1268. • The synods were held under papal legates during the reign of Henry III.

legatine court. A court held by a papal legate and having ecclesiastical jurisdiction.

legation (lə-**gay**-shən). **1.** The act or practice of sending a diplomat to another country; a diplomatic mission. **2.** A body of diplomats sent to a foreign country and headed by an envoy extraordinary or a minister plenipotentiary. **3.** The official residence of a diplomatic minister in a foreign country. Cf. EMBASSY.

legator (lə-**gay**-tər *or* leg-ə-**tor**). One who bequeaths a legacy; TESTATOR.

legatory (**leg**-ə-tor-ee), *n. Hist.* The one-third portion of a freeman's estate in land that he could dispose of by will. • The other two portions of the estate were subject to claims of the wife and children.

legatum (lə-**gay**-təm), *n*. [Latin fr. *legare* "to bequeath"] **1.** *Roman law.* A legacy; a gift left by a deceased person to be paid from the estate by the heir. **2.** *Hist.* A legacy to the church or burial place.

legatum optionis (lə-**gay**-təm op-shee-**oh**-nis), *n*. [Latin] *Roman law.* A legacy of one of several items that the designated beneficiary chooses from the testator's estate. • Originally, if the heir died after the testator but before making the selection, the heir's representative was unable to make the choice and the legacy failed. Justinian later changed the law to make selection by the representative under these circumstances valid.

legatus (lə-**gay**-təs). A legate. Pl. ***legati*** (lə-**gay**-tɪ) See LEGATE.

legatus a latere (ay **lat**-ə-ree). [Latin "legate from the (Pope's) side"] A papal legate (esp. a cardinal) appointed for a special diplomatic mission and not as a permanent representative. • This is a type of *legatus missus*. — Also termed *legate a latere*. Cf. NUNCIO.

legatus missus (**mis**-əs). [Latin "legate sent"] A legate sent on a special mission. — Also termed *legate missus*; *legatus datus* (**day**-təs).

legatus natus (**nay**-təs). [Latin "legate born"] A bishop or archbishop who claims to be a legate by virtue of office in an important see, such as Canterbury. — Also termed *legate natus*.

legem amittere (**lee**-jəm ə-**mit**-ə-ree), *vb*. [Latin "to lose one's law"] *Hist.* To lose the privilege of taking an oath, usu. because of a criminal conviction.

legem facere (**lee**-jəm **fay**-sə-ree), *vb*. [Law Latin] *Hist.* To make an oath; to wage law.

legem ferre (**lee**-jəm **fer**-ee), *vb*. [Latin "to carry the proposal"] *Roman law.* To propose a law to the public.

legem habere (**lee**-jəm hə-**beer**-ee), *vb*. [Latin] *Hist.* To be able to testify under oath. • Witnesses with criminal convictions were unable to testify until the 19th century, by the Evidence Act of 1843 (6 & 7 Vict., ch. 85).

legem jubere (**lee**-jəm jə-**beer**-ee), *vb.* [Latin] *Roman law.* To pass a proposed law.

legem ponere (**lee**-jəm **poh**-nə-ree), *vb.* [Latin] *Hist.* **1.** To propound a law. **2.** To pay in cash.

legem sciscere (**lee**-jəm **sis**-ə-ree), *vb.* [Latin] *Roman law.* (Of the people) to consent to a proposed law.

legem vadiare (**lee**-jəm vad-ee-**air**-ee), *vb.* [Latin] *Hist.* To wage law; to offer to make a sworn defense to an action for debt, accompanied by 11 neighbors as character witnesses. See COMPURGATION.

legenita (lə-**jen**-ə-tə), *n. Hist.* A fine for the seduction of another man's wife. — Also termed *legruita* (lə-**groo**-ə-tə).

leger, *n. Archaic.* See LEDGER (2).

legerwite. See LAIRWITE.

leges (**lee**-jeez), *n.pl.* [Latin] See LEX.

leges Angliae (**lee**-jeez **ang**-glee-ee), *n.* [Latin] *Hist.* The laws of England, as distinguished from the civil law and other legal systems.

leges barbarorum (**lee**-jeez bahr-bə-**ror**-əm), *n.* [Latin "laws of the barbarians"] *Hist.* The customary laws of medieval European law; esp., the customary laws of Germanic tribes during the Middle Ages. — Also termed *folk laws.* See SALIC LAW.

leges Edwardi Confessoris (**lee**-jeez ed-**wahr**-dɪ kon-fə-**sor**-is), *n.* [Latin "Laws of Edward the Confessor"] *Hist.* A legal treatise written between 1130 and 1135, of dubious authority, compiling English law as it stood at the end of the reign of Henry I.

> "[W]e have a book [*leges Edwardi Confessoris*] written in Latin which expressly purports to give us the law of Edward as it was stated to the Conqueror in the fourth year of his reign by juries representing the various parts of England .... It is a private work of a bad and untrustworthy kind. It has about it something of the political pamphlet and is adorned with pious legends. The author, perhaps a secular clerk of French parentage, writes in the interest of the churches, and, it is to be feared, tells lies for them." 1 Frederick Pollock & Frederic W. Maitland, *The History of English Law Before the Time of Edward I* 103 (2d ed. 1898).

leges et consuetudines regni (**lee**-jeez et kon-swə-**t[y]oo**-də-neez **reg**-nɪ), *n.* [Latin "laws and customs of the kingdom"] *Hist.* The common law. • This was the accepted term for the common law since at least the late 12th century.

leges Henrici (**lee**-jeez hen-**rɪ**-sɪ), *n.* [Latin] *Hist.* A book anonymously written between 1114 and 1118 containing Anglo–Saxon and Norman law. • The book lends insight to the period before the full development of Norman law in England. — Also termed *leges Henrici Primi.*

> "Closely connected with the *Quadripartitus* is a far more important book, the so-called *Leges Henrici*. It seems to have been compiled shortly before the year 1118. After a brief preface, it gives us Henry's coronation charter (this accounts for the name which has unfortunately been given in modern days to the whole book), and then the author makes a gallant, if forlorn, attempt to state the law of England. At first sight the outcome seems to be a mere jumble of fragments .... But the more closely we examine the book, the more thoroughly convinced we shall be that its author has undertaken a serious task in a serious spirit; he means to state the existing law of the land ...." 1 Frederick Pollock & Frederic W. Maitland, *The History of English Law Before the Time of Edward I* 99 (2d ed. 1898).

leges imperii (**lee**-jeez im-**peer**-ee-ɪ). [Latin] The laws of the government.

leges Juliae (**lee**-jeez **joo**-lee-ee), *n.* [Latin] *Roman law.* Laws enacted during the reign of Augustus or of Julius Caesar. • Together with the *lex Aebutia,* the *leges Juliae* effectively abolished the *legis actiones,* the ancient form of Roman civil procedure using prescribed oral forms.

leges non scriptae (**lee**-jeez non **skrip**-tee), *n.* [Latin] *Hist.* Unwritten or customary laws, including ancient acts of Parliament. Cf. LEGES SCRIPTAE.

leges publicae (**lee**-jeez **pəb**-lə-see). [Latin] *Roman law.* Statutes passed by the vote of the Roman people in popular assemblies. • Most *leges publicae* were of temporary political interest. — Often shortened to *leges.*

Leges Regiae (**lee**-jeez **ree**-ji-ee). *Roman law.* Fragments of customary law relating mostly to religious rites and traditionally attributed to Roman kings.

leges sacratae (**lee**-jeez sə-**kray**-tee), *n.* [Latin] *Roman law.* Laws whose violation was punished by devoting the offender to the infernal gods.

leges scriptae (**lee**-jeez **skrip**-tee), *n.* [Latin] *Hist.* Written laws; esp., statutory laws or acts of Parliament that are reduced to writing before becoming binding. Cf. LEGES NON SCRIPTAE.

leges sub graviori lege (**lee**-jeez səb grav-ee-**or**-I **lee**-jee), *n.* [Latin] Laws under a weightier law.

leges tabellariae (**lee**-jeez tab-ə-**lair**-ee-ee), *n.* [Latin] *Roman law.* Laws that regulated voting by ballot.

legibus solutus (**lee**-jə-bəs sə-**loo**-təs), *adj.* [Latin "released from the laws"] *Roman law.* (Of the emperor or other designated person) not bound by the law.

legiosus (lee-jee-**oh**-səs), *adj.* [Law Latin] *Hist.* Litigious.

legislate, *vb.* **1.** To make or enact laws <the role of our lawmakers is to legislate, not to adjudicate>. **2.** To bring (something) into or out of existence by making laws; to attempt to control (something) by legislation <virtually every attempt to legislate morality has failed>.

legislation. 1. The process of making or enacting a positive law in written form, according to some type of formal procedure, by a branch of government constituted to perform this process. — Also termed *lawmaking*; *statute-making.* **2.** The law so enacted. **3.** The whole body of enacted laws.

ancillary legislation. Legislation that is auxiliary to principal legislation.

antideficiency legislation. **1.** Legislation enacted to provide revenue to cover a budget deficiency. **2.** Legislation enacted to limit the rights of secured creditors to recover in excess of the security.

class legislation. See *local and special legislation.*

general legislation. Legislation that applies to the community at large.

judicial legislation. The making of new legal rules by judges; JUDGE-MADE LAW (2).

"It has been said to be 'merely misleading' to speak of judicial legislation, and it must be admitted that to do so is to use highly metaphorical language. There is no equivalent to the authoritative text of a statute, and, even when they are not bound by a statute or indistinguishable precedent, the judges' power to innovate is limited by what they cannot consider as well as by what they must consider. They cannot conduct those extensive examinations of empirical data and considerations of social policy which precede, or should precede, much legislation." Rupert Cross & J.W. Harris, *Precedent in English Law* 34 (4th ed. 1991).

local and special legislation. Legislation that affects only a specific geographic area or a particular class of persons. • Such legislation is unconstitutional if it arbitrarily or capriciously distinguishes between members of the same class. — Also termed *class legislation.*

pork-barrel legislation. Legislation that favors a particular local district by allocating funds or resources to projects (such as constructing a highway or a post office) of economic value to the district and of political advantage to the district's legislator.

subordinate legislation. **1.** Legislation that derives from any authority other than the sovereign power in a state and that therefore depends for its continued existence and validity on some superior or supreme authority. **2.** REGULATION (2).

supreme legislation. Legislation that derives directly from the supreme or sovereign power in a state and is therefore incapable of being repealed, annulled, or controlled by any other legislative authority.

4. A proposed law being considered by a legislature <gun-control legislation was debated in the House>. **5.** The field of study concentrating on statutes.

legislative, *adj.* Of or relating to lawmaking or to the power to enact laws.

legislative apportionment. See APPORTIONMENT.

legislative branch. The branch of government responsible for enacting laws; LEGISLATURE. Cf. EXECUTIVE BRANCH; JUDICIAL BRANCH.

legislative committee. See COMMITTEE.

legislative council. 1. A state agency that studies legislative problems and plans legislative strategy between regular legislative sessions. **2.** In some English-speaking jurisdictions, the upper house of a legislature (corresponding to an American senate). **3.** In some English-speaking jurisdictions, the lower house of a legislature (corresponding to an American House of Representatives).

legislative counsel. A person or group charged with helping legislators fulfill their legislative duties, as by performing research, drafting bills, and the like.

legislative court. See COURT.

legislative district. See DISTRICT.

legislative districting. The process of dividing a state into territorial districts to be represented in the state or federal legislature. See APPORTIONMENT; GERRYMANDERING; REAPPORTIONMENT.

legislative divorce. See DIVORCE.

legislative-equivalency doctrine. The rule that a law should be amended or repealed only by the same procedures that were used to enact it.

legislative fact. See FACT.

legislative function. **1.** The duty to determine legislative policy. **2.** The duty to form and determine future rights and duties. See LEGISLATIVE POWER.

legislative history. The background and events leading to the enactment of a statute, including hearings, committee reports, and floor debates. • Legislative history is sometimes recorded so that it can later be used to aid in interpreting the statute.

legislative immunity. See IMMUNITY (1).

legislative intent. The design or plan that the legislature had at the time of enacting a statute. — Also termed *intention of the legislature*; *intent of the legislature*; *congressional intent*; *parliamentary intent*.

> "The intention of the legislature is a common but very slippery phrase, which, popularly understood, may signify anything from intention embodied in positive enactment to speculative opinion as to what the legislature probably would have meant, although there has been an omission to enact it. In a court of law or equity, what the legislature intended to be done or not to be done can only be legitimately ascertained from that which it has chosen to enact, either in express words or by reasonable and necessary implication." *Saloman v. Saloman & Co.*, [1897] A.C. 22, at 38 (as quoted in Rupert Cross, *Statutory Interpretation* 36–37 (1976)).

dormant legislative intent. The intent that the legislature would have had if a given ambiguity, inconsistency, or omission had been called to the legislators' minds. — Sometimes shortened to *dormant intent*. — Also termed *latent intent*; *latent intention*.

legislative investigation. A formal inquiry conducted by a legislative body incident to its legislative authority. • A legislature has many of the same powers as a court to support a legislative inquiry, including the power to subpoena and cross-examine a witness and to hold a witness in contempt.

legislative jurisdiction. See JURISDICTION.

legislative law. See STATUTORY LAW.

legislative officer. See OFFICER (1).

legislative power. *Constitutional law.* The power to make laws and to alter them at discretion; a legislative body's exclusive authority to make, amend, and repeal laws. • Under federal law, this power is vested in Congress, consisting of the House of Representatives and the Senate. A legislative body may delegate a portion of its lawmaking authority to agencies within the executive branch for purposes of rulemaking and regulation. But a legislative body may not delegate its authority to the judicial branch, and the judicial branch may not encroach on legislative duties.

legislative privilege. See PRIVILEGE (3).

legislative rule. An administrative rule created by an agency's exercise of delegated quasi-legislative authority. • A legislative rule has the force of law. — Also termed *substantive rule*. Cf. INTERPRETATIVE RULE.

legislative veto. See VETO.

legislator, *n.* One who makes laws within a given jurisdiction; a member of a legislative body. — **legislatorial** (lej-is-lə-**tor**-ee-əl), *adj.*

legislature. The branch of government responsible for making statutory laws. • The federal government and most states have bicameral legislatures, usu. consisting of a house of representatives and a senate. Cf. EXECUTIVE (1); JUDICIARY (1).

legisperitus (lee-jis-**per**-ə-təs), *n.* [Law Latin] *Hist.* A lawyer or advocate; one skilled in the law. Cf. JURISPERITUS.

legisprudence (lee-jis-**proo**-dənts). The systematic analysis of statutes within the framework of jurisprudential philosophies about the role and nature of law.

legist (**lee**-jist). **1.** One learned or skilled in the law; a lawyer. **2.** JURIST. — Formerly also termed *legister*.

legitimacy. 1. Lawfulness. **2.** The status of a person who is born within a lawful marriage or who acquires that status by later action of the parents. Cf. ILLEGITIMACY.

legitima gubernatio (lə-**jit**-ə-mə g[y]oo-bər-**nay**-shee-oh). [Latin "lawful government"] See RECTA GUBERNATIO.

legitimate, *adj.* **1.** Complying with the law; lawful <a legitimate business>. **2.** Born of legally married parents <a legitimate child>. **3.** Genuine; valid <a legitimate complaint>. — **legitimacy,** *n.*

legitimate child. See CHILD.

legitimate portion. See LEGITIME.

legitimation, *n.* **1.** The act of making something lawful; authorization. **2.** The act or process of authoritatively declaring a person legitimate. **3.** *Hist.* Proof of a person's identity and of legal permission to reside in a certain place or engage in a certain occupation. — **legitimate,** *vb.*

legitimatio per subsequens matrimonium (lə-jit-ə-**may**-shee-oh pər səb-**see**-kwenz ma-trə-**moh**-nee-əm), *n.* [Latin] The legitimation of a child born outside wedlock by the later marriage of the parents.

legitime (**lej**-ə-tim). *Civil law.* The part of a testator's free movable property that his or her children (and occasionally other heirs) are legally entitled to regardless of the will's terms. • The legitime cannot be denied the children without legal cause. In Roman law, the amount of the legitime was one-fourth of the claimant's share on intestacy. — Also spelled (esp. in Scotland) *legitim*. — Also termed *legal portion*; *legitimate portion*; *forced portion*. See *forced heir* under HEIR.

legitimi heredes (lə-**jit**-ə-mɪ hə-**ree**-deez), *n. pl.* [Latin] *Roman law.* Heirs on intestacy, as determined by the Twelve Tables. • They might include paternal relatives of the deceased. — Also spelled *legitimi haeredes*. See TWELVE TABLES.

legitimus (lə-**jit**-ə-məs), *adj.* [Latin] *Roman law.* (Of a person) legitimate; lawful.

legit vel non (**lee**-jit vel **non**). [Latin] *Eccles. law.* Does he read or not. • This was the formal question propounded by a court to an ordinary (an ecclesiastical official) when an accused person claimed exemption from the death penalty by benefit of clergy. If the ordinary found that the accused was entitled to exemption, he responded "*legit ut clericus*," or, "he reads like a clerk." See BENEFIT OF CLERGY.

lego (**lee**-goh). [Latin] *Roman law.* I bequeath. • This was a common term in a will.

legocentrism. See LEGAL CENTRALISM.

lego-literary (lee-goh-**lit**-ər-er-ee), *adj. Rare.* Of or relating to law and literature. See LAW AND LITERATURE.

legruita. See LEGENITA.

leguleian (leg-yə-**lee**-ən), *n. Rare.* A pettifogging lawyer. — Also termed *leguleius* (leg-yoo-**lee**-əs). — **leguleian,** *adj.*

LEIN. *abbr.* LAW ENFORCEMENT INFORMATION NETWORK.

leipa (**lɪ**-pə), *n.* [Law Latin] *Hist.* A runaway or fugitive.

lemon law. 1. A statute designed to protect a consumer who buys a substandard automobile, usu. by requiring the manufacturer or dealer either to replace the vehicle or to refund the full purchase price. • Almost all states have lemon laws in effect. — Also termed *lemon protection*. **2.** By extension, a statute designed to protect a consumer who buys any products of inferior quality. — Also termed (in sense 2) *quality-of-products legislation*.

le mort saisit le vif **doctrine** (lə **mor** se-**zee** lə **veef**). [French "the dead seizes the living"] The principle requiring that there be no gap in the possession of a freehold estate in land, so that legal title vests immediately in the heirs upon the death of the person through whom they claim title. • The doctrine does not exclude unknown heirs or heirs absent at the date of death.

lend, *vb.* **1.** To allow the temporary use of (something), sometimes in exchange for compensation, on condition that the thing or its equivalent be returned. **2.** To provide (money) temporarily on condition of repayment, usu. with interest.

lender. A person or entity from which something (esp. money) is borrowed.

lend-lease. A mutually beneficial exchange made between friendly parties; esp., an arrangement made in 1941, under the Lend–Lease Act, whereby U.S. destroyers were lent to Great Britain in exchange for Britain's leasing of land to the United States for military bases. — Also termed *lease-lend.*

lenient, *adj.* Tolerant; mild; merciful <lenient sentence>.

lenient test. The principle that the attorney-client privilege applicable to a document will be waived only by a knowing or intentional disclosure, and will not usu. be waived by an inadvertent disclosure. Cf. *strict test*; *Hydraflow test.*

lenity (**len**-ə-tee). The quality or condition of being lenient; mercy or clemency. See RULE OF LENITY.

lenity rule. See RULE OF LENITY.

leodes (lee-**oh**-deez), *n.* [Law Latin] *Hist.* **1.** A vassal. **2.** Service to be provided to another. **3.** Compensation to be paid by one who killed or seriously injured a vassal, divided among the sovereign, the vassal's lord, and the vassal's next of kin; WERGILD.

leonina societas (lee-ə-**nI**-nə sə-**sI**-ə-tas). See SOCIETAS LEONINA.

leonine contract (**lee**-ə-nIn). See *adhesion contract* under CONTRACT.

leproso amovendo (lep-**roh**-soh ay-moh-**ven**-doh), *n.* [Latin "for removing a leper"] *Hist.* A writ to remove a leper who participated in public gatherings, such as church or meetings.

le roy (lər **wah** *or* lə **roy**), *n.* [Law French] The king. — Also spelled *le roi.*

le roy le veut (lər **wah** lə **voo**). [Law French] *Hist.* The king (or the queen) wills it. • This is the form of the king's or queen's approval to a public bill passed by Parliament. For a queen, the sentence is *la reine le veut.*

> "If the king consents to a public bill, the clerk usually declares, '*le roy le veut*, the king wills it so to be:' if to a private bill, '*soit fait comme il est desiré*, be it as it is desired.' If the king refuses his assent, it is in the gentle language of '*le roy s'avisera*, the king will advise upon it.' " 1 William Blackstone, *Commentaries on the Laws of England* 184 (1765).

le roy remercie ses loyal sujets, accepte leur benevolence, et ainsi le veut (lər **wah** ruu-mair-**see** say lwI-**ahl** soo-**zhay**, ak-**sept** luu[r] bay-nay-voh-**lawns**, ay *an*-**see** lə **vuu**). [Law French] *Hist.* The king thanks his loyal subjects, accepts their benevolence, and therefore wills it to be so. • This is a form of the royal assent to a bill of supply, authorizing money for public purposes. For a queen, the sentence was *la reine remercie ses loyal sujets . . . .*

le roy s'avisera (lər **wah** sa-veez-**rah**). [Law French] The king will advise upon it. • This is a form of the refusal of royal assent to a public bill in Parliament (not exercised since 1713). It corresponds to the judicial phrase *curia advisari vult.* For a queen, the sentence was *la reine s'avisera.* See CURIA ADVISARI VULT.

lese majesty (leez **maj**-əs-tee). [Law French "injured majesty"] **1.** A crime against the state, esp. against the ruler. See *high treason* under TREASON. **2.** An attack on a custom or traditional belief. — Also spelled *lèse-majesté*; *lèse majesty*; *leze majesty.* — Also termed *laesa majestas*; *crimen laesae majestatis.*

lesion (**lee**-zhən). **1.** An injury or wound; esp., an area of wounded tissue. **2.** *Civil law.* Loss from another's failure to perform a contract; the injury suffered by one who did not receive the equivalent value of what was bargained for. — Also spelled (in sense 2) *lésion.* **3.** See LAESIO ENORMIS.

> "The concept of *lésion*, unknown as such to the common law, may be defined as a detriment to one of the parties to a contract which results from an imbalance or disparity between the performance promised on the two sides. Down through the ages, civilians have differed over whether it gave the injured party a right of avoidance or rescission. Classical Roman law, designed for a society whose members were strong enough to protect their own interests, denied the right, but by the time of the French Revolution the right had come to be recognized, particularly by the canonists and Pothier. But the Revolution, both because of its emphasis on individual will and because of economic reasons, was hostile to the concept of *lésion* and the Civil Code provided that it did not affect the validity of a contract except in certain prescribed instances, most notably the case of the vendor of real property. The number of exceptions was enlarged both by subsequent legislation and, at least indirectly, by judicial decision, and this raised a question of the reversal of the general principle that rejected the concept." Allan Farnsworth, "The Development of the Civil Law of Obligations in New States: Senegal, Madagascar, and

Ethiopia," in *Essays on the Civil Law of Obligations* 64 (Joseph Dainow ed., 1969).

less developed country. See DEVELOPING COUNTRY.

lessee (le-**see**). One who has a possessory interest in real or personal property under a lease; TENANT.

lessee in the ordinary course of business. A person that, in good faith and without knowledge that the lease is in violation of a third party's ownership rights, security interest, or leasehold interest, leases in the ordinary course from a person in the business of selling or leasing goods of that kind. UCC § 2A–102(a)(26). • The UCC specifically excludes pawnbrokers from the definition.

merchant lessee. A lessee who is a merchant of goods similar to those being leased. UCC § 2A–102(a)(31).

lessee's interest. The appraised value of leased property from the lessee's perspective for purposes of assignment or sale. • The value is usu. the property's market value minus the lessor's interest. Cf. LESSOR'S INTEREST.

lesser included offense. See OFFENSE (1).

lessor (**les**-or *or* le-**sor**). One who conveys real or personal property by lease; LANDLORD.

lessor of the plaintiff. *Hist.* The true party in interest prosecuting an action for ejectment. • At common law, an ejectment action theoretically was only for the recovery of the unexpired term of the lease. Conventions of pleadings at the time required the true plaintiff to grant a fictitious lease, thereby becoming a lessor, to an equally fictitious plaintiff in whose name the action would be prosecuted.

lessor's interest. The present value of the future income under a lease, plus the present value of the property after the lease expires. Cf. LESSEE'S INTEREST.

let, *n.* An impediment or obstruction <free to act without let or hindrance>.

let, *vb.* **1.** To allow or permit <the court, refusing to issue an injunction, let the nuisance continue>. **2.** To offer (property) for lease; to rent out <the hospital let office space to several doctors>. **3.** To award (a contract), esp. after bids have been submitted <the federal agency let the project to the lowest bidder>.

lethal, *adj.* Deadly; fatal <a lethal drug>.

lethal injection. An injection of a deadly substance into a prisoner, done to carry out a sentence of capital punishment.

lethal weapon. See *deadly weapon* under WEAPON.

letter. 1. A written communication that is usu. enclosed in an envelope, sealed, stamped, and delivered; esp., an official written communication <an opinion letter>. **2.** (*usu. pl.*) A written instrument containing or affirming a grant of some power or right <letters testamentary>. **3.** Strict or literal meaning <the letter of the law>. • This sense is based on the sense of a letter of the alphabet. Cf. SPIRIT OF THE LAW.

letter-book. A merchant's book for holding correspondence.

letter contract. See CONTRACT.

letter missive. 1. *Hist.* A letter from the king (or queen) to the dean and chapter of a cathedral, containing the name of the person whom the king wants elected as bishop. **2.** *Hist.* After a lawsuit is filed against a peer, peeress, or lord of Parliament, a request sent to the defendant to appear and answer the suit. **3.** *Civil law.* The appellate record sent by a lower court to a superior court. — Also termed *letter dimissory.*

letter of advice. A notice that a draft has been sent by the drawer to the drawee. UCC § 3–701.

letter of attorney. See POWER OF ATTORNEY (1).

letter of attornment. A grantor's letter to a tenant, stating that the leased property has been sold and directing the tenant to pay rent to the new owner. See ATTORNMENT (1).

letter of comment. See DEFICIENCY LETTER.

letter of credence. A document that accredits a diplomat to the government of the country to which he or she is sent. — Abbr. LC; L/C. — Also termed *letters of credence.*

letter of credit. An instrument under which the issuer (usu. a bank), at a customer's request, agrees to honor a draft or other demand for payment made by a third party (the *beneficiary*), as long as the draft or demand complies with specified conditions, and regardless of whether any underlying agreement between the customer and the beneficiary is satisfied. • Letters of credit are governed by Article 5 of the UCC. — Abbr. LC; L/C. — Often shortened to *credit.* — Also termed *circular letter of credit*; *circular note*; *bill of credit.*

> "There is some confusion over the exact nature of credits. They resemble a number of commercial devices that are not credits. Often, there is confusion between letters of credit and guaranties, and occasionally between letters of credit and lines of credit. In the credit transaction itself, it is important to distinguish the credit from other contracts and from the acceptance. Generally, the broad credit transaction consists of three separate relationships. These include those that are (1) between the issuer and the beneficiary; (2) between the beneficiary and the account party; and (3) between the account party and the issuer. The first is the letter-of-credit engagement. The second is usually called the underlying contract, and the third is called the application agreement." John F. Dolan, *The Law of Letters of Credit* ¶ 2.01, at 2–2 (1984).

> "A credit is an original undertaking by one party (the issuer) to substitute his financial strength for that of another (the account party), with that undertaking to be triggered by the presentation of a draft or demand for payment and, often, other documents. The credit arises in a number of situations, but generally the account party seeks the strength of the issuer's financial integrity or reputation so that a third party (the beneficiary of the credit) will give value to the account party." John F. Dolan, *The Law of Letters of Credit* ¶ 2.02, at 2–3 (1984).

> "A seller hesitates to give up possession of its goods before it is paid. But a buyer wishes to have control of the goods before parting with its money. To relieve this simple tension, merchants developed the device known as the 'letter of credit' or simply the 'credit' or the 'letter.' Today, letters of credit come in two broad varieties. The 'commercial' letter dates back at least 700 years. It is a mode of payment in the purchase of goods, mostly in international sales. The 'standby' letter of credit is a much more recent mutant. It 'backs up' obligations in a myriad of settings. In the most common standby a bank promises to pay a creditor upon documentary certification of the applicant's default." 3 James J. White & Robert S. Summers, *Uniform Commercial Code* § 26–1, at 105 (4th ed. 1995).

clean letter of credit. A letter of credit that is payable on its presentation. • No document needs to be presented along with it. — Also termed *suicide letter of credit.* Cf. *documentary letter of credit.*

commercial letter of credit. A letter of credit used as a method of payment in a sale of goods (esp. in an international transaction), with the buyer being the issuer's customer and the seller being the beneficiary, so that the seller can obtain payment directly from the issuer instead of from the buyer.

confirmed letter of credit. A letter of credit that directly obligates a financing agency (such as a bank) doing business in the seller's financial market to a contract of sale. UCC § 2–325(3).

documentary letter of credit. A letter of credit that is payable when presented with another document, such as a certificate of title or invoice. — Abbr. DL/C. Cf. *clean letter of credit.*

export letter of credit. A commercial letter of credit issued by a foreign bank, at a foreign buyer's request, in favor of a domestic exporter.

general letter of credit. A letter of credit addressed to any and all persons without naming anyone in particular. Cf. *special letter of credit.*

guaranty letter of credit. See *standby letter of credit.*

import letter of credit. A commercial letter of credit issued by a domestic bank, at an importer's request, in favor of a foreign seller.

irrevocable letter of credit (i-**rev**-ə-kə-bəl). A letter of credit in which the issuing bank guarantees that it will not withdraw the credit or cancel the letter before the expiration date; a letter of credit that cannot be modified or revoked without the customer's consent.

negotiation letter of credit. A letter of credit in which the issuer's engagement runs to drawers and indorsers under a standard negotiation clause.

> "Letter-of-credit law has long distinguished the straight credit from the negotiation credit. The engagement of the former runs to the beneficiary; the engagement of the latter runs to 'drawers, endorsers, and bona fide holders.' This quoted phrase is the traditional negotiation clause. The significance of it is that it obviously extends the credit engagement to parties other than the person with whom the account party is doing business." John F. Dolan, *The Law of Letters of Credit* ¶ 8.02[6], at 8–11 (1984).

open letter of credit. A letter of credit that can be paid on a simple draft without the need for documentary title.

revocable letter of credit (**rev**-ə-kə-bəl). A letter of credit in which the issuing bank reserves the right to cancel and withdraw from the transaction upon appropriate notice. • The letter cannot be revoked if the credit has already been paid by a third party.

revolving letter of credit. A letter of credit that self-renews by providing for a continuing line of credit that the beneficiary periodically draws on and the customer periodically repays. • A revolving letter of credit is used when there will be multiple drafts under a single transaction or multiple transactions under a single credit. — Abbr. RL/C.

special letter of credit. A letter of credit addressed to a particular individual, firm, or corporation. Cf. *general letter of credit.*

standby letter of credit. A letter of credit used to guarantee either a monetary or a nonmonetary obligation (such as the performance of construction work), whereby the issuer agrees to pay the beneficiary if the customer defaults on its obligation. — Abbr. SL/C. — Also termed *guaranty letter of credit.*

straight letter of credit. A letter of credit requiring that drafts drawn under it be presented to a specified party.

suicide letter of credit. See *clean letter of credit.*

time letter of credit. A letter of credit that is duly honored by the issuer accepting drafts drawn under it. — Also termed *acceptance credit; usance credit.*

transferable letter of credit. A letter of credit that authorizes the beneficiary to assign the right to draw under it.

traveler's letter of credit. **1.** A letter of credit addressed to a correspondent bank, from which one can draw credit by identifying oneself as the person in whose favor the credit is drawn. **2.** A letter of credit used by a person traveling abroad, by which the issuing bank authorizes payment of funds to the holder in the local currency by a local bank. • The holder signs a check on the issuing bank, and the local bank forwards it to the issuing bank for its credit.

letter of exchange. See DRAFT (1).

letter of intent. A written statement detailing the preliminary understanding of parties who plan to enter into a contract or some other agreement; a noncommittal writing preliminary to a contract. • A letter of intent is not meant to be binding and does not hinder the parties from bargaining with a third party. Business people typically mean not to be bound by a letter of intent, and courts ordinarily do not enforce one; but courts occasionally find that a commitment has been made. — Abbr. LOI. — Also termed *memorandum of intent.* Cf. *precontract* under CONTRACT.

letter of license. *English law.* An agreement signed by all the creditors of a financially troubled business that does the following: (1) grants the debtor more time to pay debts, (2) permits the debtor to continue business in the hope of overcoming its financial distress, and (3) protects the debtor from arrest, lawsuit, or other interference while the letter is in effect. See ARRANGEMENT WITH CREDITORS.

letter of recall. **1.** A document sent from one nation's executive to that of another, stating that the former executive is summoning a minister back to his or her own country. **2.** A manufacturer's letter to a buyer of a particular product, asking the buyer to bring the product back to the dealer for repair or replacement.

letter of recredentials. A formal letter from the diplomatic secretary of state of a host country to a foreign minister or ambassador who has been recalled. • The letter officially accredits the foreign minister back to his or her home country.

letter of request. A document issued by one court to a foreign court, requesting that the foreign court (1) take evidence from a specific person within the foreign jurisdiction or serve process on an individual or corporation within the foreign jurisdiction and (2) return the testimony or proof of service for use in a pending case. See Fed. R. Civ. P. 28. Pl. **letters of request.** — Also termed *letter rogatory* (**rog**-ə-tor-ee); *rogatory letter; requisitory letter* (ri-**kwiz**-ə-tor-ee).

letter of the law. The strictly literal meaning of the law, rather than the intention or policy behind it. — Also termed *litera legis.* Cf. SPIRIT OF THE LAW.

letter of undertaking. An agreement by which a shipowner — to avoid having creditors seize the ship and release it on bond — agrees to post security on the ship, and to enter an appearance, acknowledge ownership, and pay any final decree entered against the vessel whether it is lost or not.

> "Such informal or extra-legal agreements save court costs and the marshal's fees, avoid the annoyance of having the vessel even temporarily arrested and may well be cheaper than the usual surety bond.... In *Continental Grain Co. v. Federal Barge Lines, Inc.*, [268 F.2d 240 (5th Cir. 1959), *aff'd*, 364 U.S. 19, 80 S.Ct. 1470 (1960)], Judge Brown commented that a letter of undertaking given by a shipowner would be treated 'as though, upon the libel being filed, the vessel had actually been seized, a claim filed, a stipulation to abide decrees with sureties executed and filed by claimant, and the vessel formally released. Any other course would imperil the desirable avoidance of needless cost, time and inconvenience to litigants, counsel, ships, clerks, marshals, keepers and court personnel through the ready acceptance of such letters of undertakings.' [268 F.2d at 243]. If, as Judge Brown suggests, the informal agreement is treated

as having the same effect as a formal release under bond or stipulation, few questions relating to their use will ever have to be litigated." Grant Gilmore & Charles L. Black, Jr., *The Law of Admiralty* § 9–89, at 800–01 (2d ed. 1975).

letter rogatory. See LETTER OF REQUEST.

letter ruling. *Tax.* A written statement issued by the IRS to an inquiring taxpayer, explaining the tax implications of a particular transaction. — Also termed *private letter ruling.*

letters. *Wills & estates.* Letters of administration, letters of conservatorship, letters of guardianship, and letters testamentary, collectively. Uniform Probate Code § 1–201(23). See LETTER (2).

letters *ad colligendum bona defuncti* (ad kol-ə-**jen**-dəm **boh**-nə di-**fungk**-tI), *n.* [Law Latin] *Hist.* An authorization from a judicial officer to an approved person to collect and maintain the goods of a person who died intestate. • These letters were issued only if no representative or creditor existed to exercise this function.

letters close. See LETTERS SECRET.

letter security. See *restricted security* under SECURITY.

letters of absolution. *Hist.* Letters issued by an abbot releasing a member of his order from his vows of obedience to that order, thus permitting entry into another order.

letters of administration. A formal document issued by a probate court to appoint the administrator of an estate. • Letters of administration originated in the Probate of Testaments Act of 1357 (31 Edw. 3, ch. 4), which provided that in case of intestacy the ordinary (a high-ranking ecclesiastical official within a territory) should depute the decedent's closest friends to administer the estate; a later statute, the Executors Act of 1529 (21 Hen. 8, ch. 4), authorized the ordinary to grant administration either to the surviving spouse or to next of kin, or to both of them jointly. — Also termed *administration letters.* See ADMINISTRATION (4). Cf. LETTERS TESTAMENTARY.

letters of administration c.t.a. Letters of administration appointing an administrator *cum testamento annexo* (with the will annexed) either because the will does not name an executor or because the named executor does not qualify. See *administration cum testamento annexo* under ADMINISTRATION.

letters of administration d.b.n. Letters of administration appointing an administrator *de bonis non* (concerning goods not yet administered) because the named executor failed to complete the estate's probate. See *administration de bonis non* under ADMINISTRATION.

letters of credence. See LETTER OF CREDENCE.

letters of guardianship. A document issued by a court appointing a guardian to care for a minor's or an incapacitated adult's well-being, property, and affairs. • It defines the scope of the guardian's rights and duties, including the extent of control over the ward's education and medical issues. See GUARDIAN.

letters of marque (mahrk). A license authorizing a private citizen to engage in reprisals against citizens or vessels of another nation. • Congress has the exclusive power to grant letters of marque (U.S. Const. art. I, § 8, cl. 11), but it has not done so since the 19th century. — Also termed *letters of marque and reprisal.*

"[F]ormerly it was not uncommon for a state to issue 'letters of marque' to one of its own subjects, who had met with a denial of justice in another state, authorizing him to redress the wrong for himself by forcible action, such as the seizure of the property of subjects of the delinquent state." J.L. Brierly, *The Law of Nations* 321 (5th ed. 1955).

letters of safe conduct. *Hist.* Formal written permission from the English sovereign to a citizen of a nation at war with England, permitting that person to travel and ship goods, to England or on the high seas, without risk of seizure. • Passports or licenses from foreign ambassadors now may serve the same purpose. See SAFE CONDUCT.

letters of slains. *Hist.* Letters to the Crown from the relatives of a slain person concurring with the offender's application for a royal pardon. • A pardon could not be granted without the family's concurrence. — Also spelled *letters of slanes.*

letters patent. 1. *Hist.* A document granting some right or privilege, issued under governmental seal but open to public inspection. — Also termed *literae patentes* (**lit**-ər-ee pə-**ten**-teez). Cf. LETTERS SECRET. **2.** A governmental grant of the exclusive right to use an invention or design. See PATENT (2).

letters rogatory. See LETTER OF REQUEST.

letters secret. *Hist.* A governmental document that is issued to a private person, closed and sealed, and thus not made available for public inspection. — Also termed *letters close*. Cf. LETTERS PATENT (1).

letters testamentary. The instrument by which a probate court approves the appointment of an executor under a will and authorizes the executor to administer the estate. Cf. LETTERS OF ADMINISTRATION.

letter stock. See *restricted security* under SECURITY.

lettre (**le**-trə), *n.* [French "letter"] *Hist.* A formal instrument granting some authority.

lettre de cachet (**le**-trə də ka-**shay**). [French "letter with a seal"] A royal warrant issued for the imprisonment of a person without trial.

leuca (**loo**-kə), *n.* [Law Latin] *Hist.* **1.** *French law.* A league, consisting of 1,500 paces. **2.** A league, consisting of 1,000 paces. **3.** A privileged space of one mile around a monastery.

levance and couchance (**lev**-ənts / **kow**-chənts). *Hist.* The state or condition of being levant and couchant. See LEVANT AND COUCHANT.

levandae navis causa (lə-**van**-dee **nay**-vis **kaw**-zə), *n.* [Latin "for the sake of lightening the ship"] *Maritime law.* The practice of throwing goods overboard to avoid total loss, entitling the owner to compensation from other participants in the maritime venture. See JETTISON; *general average* under AVERAGE.

levant and couchant (**lev**-ənt / **kow**-chənt), *adj.* [Law French *couchant et levant* "lying down and rising up"] *Hist.* (Of cattle and other beasts) trespassing on land for a period long enough to have lain down to rest and risen to feed (usu. at least one night and one day). • This period was the minimum required as grounds for distraint. — Also termed *couchant and levant.*

levari facias (lə-**vair**-ɪ **fay**-shee-əs). [Law Latin "that you cause to be levied"] A writ of execution ordering a sheriff to seize a judgment debtor's goods and income from lands until the judgment debt is satisfied. • This writ is now used chiefly in Delaware. Cf. FIERI FACIAS.

levari facias damna de disseisitoribus (lə-**vair**-ɪ **fay**-shee-əs **dam**-nə dee dis-see-zə-**tor**-ə-bəs), *n.* [Law Latin "that you cause to be levied the rest of the debt"] *Hist.* A writ directing the sheriff to levy property to pay damages owed to one wrongfully dispossessed of a freehold estate. See DISSEISIN.

levari facias quando vicecomes returnavit quod non habuit emptores (lə-**vair**-ɪ **fay**-shee-əs **kwon**-doh vɪ-see-**koh**-meez ree-tər-**nay**-vit kwod non **hay**-byoo-it emp-**tor**-eez), *n.* [Law Latin "that you cause to be levied the damages from the disseisors"] *Hist.* A writ directing a sheriff, who had already seized some of the debtor's property and found it unsalable, to sell as much additional property as necessary to pay the entire debt.

levari facias residuum debiti (lə-**vair**-ɪ **fay**-shee-əs ri-**zij**-oo-əm **deb**-ə-tɪ), *n.* [Law Latin "that you cause to be levied when the sheriff has returned that it had no buyers"] *Hist.* A writ directing the sheriff to levy upon a debtor's lands or goods to pay the remainder of a partially satisfied debt.

levato velo (lə-**vay**-toh **vee**-loh), *n.* [Latin "with the curtain raised"] *Roman law.* The principle, applied to cases of wreck and salvage, and later to all maritime matters, that cases should be heard promptly. • Although commentators disagree about the origin of the expression, it probably refers to the place where causes were heard. A sail was spread before the door, and when the cases were heard, the sail was raised, allowing suitors to come into court and have their causes immediately heard.

levee (**lev**-ee), *n.* **1.** An embankment constructed along the edge of a river to prevent flooding. **2.** A landing place on a body of navigable water for loading and unloading goods or receiving and delivering passengers and boats.

levee district. A local or regional political subdivision organized to construct and maintain levees within its territory at public expense.

levée en masse. See LEVY EN MASSE.

level-premium insurance. See INSURANCE.

level-rate legal-reserve policy. See INSURANCE POLICY.

leverage, *n.* **1.** Positional advantage; effectiveness. **2.** The use of credit or borrowed funds (such as buying on margin) to improve one's speculative ability and to increase an investment's rate of return. **3.** The advantage obtained from using credit or borrowed funds rather than equity capital. **4.** The ratio between a corporation's debt and its equity capital. — Also termed *leverage ratio*. **5.** The effect of this ratio on common-stock prices.

leverage, *vb.* **1.** To provide (a borrower or investor) with credit or funds to improve speculative ability and to seek a high rate of return. **2.** To supplement (available capital) with credit or outside funds. **3.** To fund (a company) with debt as well as shareholder equity. **4.** *Antitrust.* To use power in one market to gain an unfair advantage in another market. **5.** *Insurance.* To manipulate two coverages, as by an insurer withholding settlement of one claim to influence a claim arising under another source of coverage.

leverage contract. An agreement for the purchase or sale of a contract for the future delivery of a specified commodity, usu. silver, gold, or another precious metal, in a standard unit and quantity, for a particular price, with no right to a particular lot of the commodity. • A leverage contract operates much like a futures contract, except that there is no designated contract market for leverage contracts. The market sets the uniform terms of a futures contract. But in a leverage contract, the individual merchant sets the terms, does not guarantee a repurchase market, and does not guarantee to continue serving or acting as the broker for the purchaser. Leverage contracts are generally forbidden for agricultural commodities. 7 USCA § 23(a). Cf. FUTURES CONTRACT.

leveraged buyout. See BUYOUT.

leveraged lease. See LEASE.

leveraged recapitalization. See RECAPITALIZATION.

leverage fund. See *dual fund* under MUTUAL FUND.

leverage ratio. See LEVERAGE (4).

leveraging up. See *leveraged recapitalization* under RECAPITALIZATION.

leviable (**lev**-ee-ə-bəl), *adj.* **1.** Able to be levied; assessable <the fine is leviable on each offense>. **2.** Able to be levied upon; seizable in execution of a judgment <leviable goods>.

levir (**lee**-vər), *n.* [Latin] *Roman law.* **1.** A husband's brother. **2.** A wife's brother-in-law.

levis (**lee**-vis), *adj.* [Latin] *Hist.* Light; trifling.

levis culpa. See CULPA.

levis nota (**lee**-vis **noh**-tə), *n.* [Latin] *Hist.* Slight mark or brand.

levissima culpa. See CULPA.

levy (**lev**-ee), *n.* **1.** The imposition of a fine or tax; the fine or tax so imposed. — Also termed *tax levy*. **2.** The enlistment of soldiers into the military; the soldiers so enlisted. **3.** The legally sanctioned seizure and sale of property; the money obtained from such a sale. — Also termed (in sense 3) *levy of execution*.

wrongful levy. A levy on a third party's property that is not subject to a writ of execution.

levy, *vb.* **1.** To impose or assess (a fine or a tax) by legal authority <levy a tax on gasoline>. **2.** To enlist for service in the military <the troops were quickly levied>. **3.** To declare or wage (a war) <the rival clans levied war against each other>. **4.** To take or seize property in execution of a judgment <the judgment creditor may levy on the debtor's assets>.

levy court. See COURT.

levy en masse. A large conscription or mobilization of troops, esp. in response to a threatened invasion. — Also spelled *levée en masse*; *levy in mass*.

levy of execution. See LEVY (3).

lewd, *adj.* Obscene or indecent; tending to moral impurity or wantonness <lewd behavior>.

lewd and lascivious cohabitation. See *illicit cohabitation* under COHABITATION.

lewd house. See DISORDERLY HOUSE (2).

lewdness. Gross, wanton, and public indecency that is outlawed by many state statutes; a sexual act that the actor knows will likely be observed by someone who will be affronted or alarmed by it. Model Penal Code § 251.1. Cf. INDECENT EXPOSURE; OBSCENITY.

lex (leks), *n.* [Latin "law"] **1.** Law, esp. statutory law. **2.** Positive law, as opposed to natural law. • Strictly speaking, *lex* is a statute, whereas *jus* is law in general (as well as a right). **3.** A system or body of laws, written or unwritten, that are peculiar to a jurisdiction or to a field of human activity. **4.** A collection of uncodified laws within a jurisdiction. **5.** LEX PUBLICA. **6.** LEX PRIVATA. **7.** *Civil law.* A legislative bill. Pl. ***leges*** (**lee**-jeez). Cf. JUS.

lex actus (**leks ak**-təs). See LEX LOCI ACTUS.

lex Aebutia (**leks** i-**byoo**-shee-ə), *n.* [Latin] *Roman law.* A statute that introduced simplified forms of pleading and procedure.

lex aeterna (**leks** ee-**tər**-nə). [Latin] Eternal law. See NATURAL LAW (1).

lex anastasiana (**leks** an-ə-stay-shee-**ay**-nə), *n.* [Latin] *Roman law.* **1.** A law establishing that emancipated brothers and sisters receive an intestate inheritance equal to those not emancipated. **2.** A law providing that a person purchasing a debt from the original creditor for less than its nominal value was not entitled to recover from the debtor more than the amount paid with lawful interest. See AGNATI.

lex Angliae (**leks ang**-glee-ee), *n.* [Latin] *Hist.* The law of England; the common law.

lex apparens (**leks** ə-**par**-enz), *n.* [Law Latin "apparent law"] *Hist.* The legal processes of trial by ordeal or wager of battle. • The plaintiff could not summon the defendant for trial by these processes before establishing a clear or apparent right through testimony. See ORDEAL.

lex Apuleja (**leks** ap-yə-**lee**-jə), *n.* [Latin] *Roman law.* A law giving a co-guarantor, who had paid more than the proper share of debt, an action of reimbursement against the remaining guarantors. — Also spelled *lex Apuleia.*

lex Aquilia (**leks** ə-**kwil**-ee-ə), *n.* [Latin "Aquilian law"] *Roman law.* A celebrated law generally regulating damages done to property, including compensation to be paid for injury to another's slave or livestock. • The law superseded the earlier provisions of the Twelve Tables. — Also termed *Aquilian law.*

lex Atilia (**leks** ə-**til**-ee-ə). [Latin] *Roman law.* A law granting to magistrates the right to appoint guardians. • The law is named after the person who proposed it, perhaps the tribune L. Atilius Regulus. — Also termed *Atilian law.*

lex Atinia (**leks** ə-**tin**-ee-ə). [Latin] *Roman law.* A law declaring that a prescriptive right cannot be acquired in stolen property. — Also termed *Atinian law.*

lex Baiuvariorum (**leks** bay-ə-vair-ee-**or**-əm). [Latin] *Hist.* The law of Bavaria, a barbarian nation in the Early Middle Ages, first collected (together with the law of the Franks and Alemanni) by Theodoric (ca. 454–526), and finally completed and promulgated by Dagobert (ca. 612–639). — Also termed *lex Baioriorum*; *lex Boiorum.*

lex barbara (**leks bahr**-bə-rə), *n.* [Latin] *Roman law.* The law of barbarian nations, i.e., those that were not subject to the Roman Empire.

lex Boiorum. See LEX BAIUVARIORUM.

lex Brehonia (**leks** bri-**hoh**-nee-ə), *n.* [Law Latin] *Hist.* The Brehon or Irish law.

lex Bretoisa (**leks** bre-**toy**-sə), *n.* [Latin] *Hist.* The law of ancient Britons; the law of Marches of Wales.

lex Burgundionum (**leks** bər-gən-dee-**oh**-nəm), *n.* [Law Latin] *Hist.* The law of the Burgundians, first published about A.D. 495.

lex Calpurnia (**leks** kal-**pər**-nee-ə), *n.* [Latin] *Roman law.* A law extending the *lex Silia* by establishing procedures to recover goods other than money. See LEX SILIA.

lex Canuleia (**leks** kan-yoo-**lee**-ə), *n.* [Latin] *Roman law.* A law granting plebeians the right to marry patricians.

lex causae (**leks kaw**-zee). [Latin] The applicable law.

lex Cincia (**leks sin**-shee-ə), *n.* [Latin] *Roman law.* A law prohibiting certain types of gifts and all gifts or donations of property beyond a certain measure, except to a near relative.

lex Claudia (**leks klaw**-dee-ə), *n.* [Latin] *Roman law.* A law that abolished the ancient guardianship of adult women by their male agnate relatives.

lex comitatus (**leks** kom-ə-**tay**-təs), *n.* [Law Latin] *Hist.* The law of the county; the law administered in the county court before the earl and his deputies.

lex commercii (**leks** kə-**mər**-shee-I), *n.* [Latin] The law of business or commerce; commercial law. — Also termed *lex commissoria* (**leks** kom-ə-**sor**-ee-ə).

lex communis (**leks** kə-**myoo**-nis), *n.* [Latin] The common law. See JUS COMMUNE.

lex contractus (**leks** kən-**trak**-təs). See LEX LOCI CONTRACTUS.

lex Cornelia (**leks** kor-**nee**-lee-ə *or* kor-**neel**-yə), *n.* [Latin] *Roman law.* One of several laws passed by the dictator L. Cornelius Sulla. — Also termed *Cornelian law.*

lex Cornelia de aedictis (**leks** kor-**nee**-lee-ə dee ee-**dik**-tis), *n.* [Latin] *Roman law.* The law forbidding a praetor from departing, during his term of office, from the edict he had promulgated at the term's commencement.

lex Cornelia de falso (**leks** kor-**nee**-lee-ə dee **fal**-soh *or* **fawl**-soh), *n.* [Latin] *Roman law.* The Cornelian law, passed by the dictator Sulla, providing that the same penalty should attach to forgery of a testament by one in captivity as to forgery of a testament made in one's own country. — Also termed *lex Cornelia de falsis.*

lex Cornelia de injuriis (**leks** kor-**nee**-lee-ə dee in-**joor**-ee-is), *n.* [Latin] *Roman law.* The Cornelian law providing a civil action for the recovery of a penalty in certain cases of bodily injury and violent invasion of property. — Also spelled *lex Cornelia de iniuriis.*

> "Lex Cornelia de iniuriis .... Punished three kinds of injury committed by violence: *pulsare* (beating), *verberare* (striking, causing pains) and *domum introire* (forcible invasion of another's domicile)." Adolf Berger, *Encyclopedic Dictionary of Roman Law* 549 (1953).

lex Cornelia de sicariis et veneficis (**leks** kor-**nee**-lee-ə dee si-**kair**-ee-is et və-**nee**-fə-sis), *n.* [Latin] *Roman law.* The Cornelian law, passed by the dictator Sulla, addressing assassins and poisoners and containing provisions making the killing of another's slave punishable by death or exile. • The act was extended by Emperor Antoninus Pius to include a master who killed his own slave.

lex Cornelia de sponsu (**leks** kor-**nee**-lee-ə dee **spon**-s[y]oo), *n.* [Latin] *Roman law.* A law prohibiting one from acting as surety for the same debtor to the same creditor in the same year for more than a specified amount.

lex Danorum (**leks** dan-**or**-əm). See DANELAW.

lex delicti (**leks** də-**lik**-tI). See LEX LOCI DELICTI.

lex deraisnia (**leks** də-**rayn**-ee-ə), *n.* [Law Latin] *Hist.* A law by which a party denies an accusation, showing it to be against reason or probability.

lex de responsis prudentium (**leks** dee ri-**spon**-sis proo-**den**-shee-əm). [Latin "law on the replies of the jurisprudents"] See CITATIONS, LAW OF.

lex domicilii (**leks** dom-ə-**sil**-ee-I). [Latin] **1.** The law of the country where a person is domiciled. **2.** The determination of a person's rights by establishing where, in law, that person is domiciled. See Restatement (Second) of Conflict of Laws §§ 11 et seq. (1971).

Lex Duodecim Tabularum (**leks** d[y]oo-ə-**des**-əm tab-yə-**lair**-əm). See TWELVE TABLES.

lex et consuetudo parliamenti (**leks** et kon-swə-**t[y]oo**-doh parl-[y]ə-**men**-tI), *n.* [Latin] *Hist.* The law and custom (or usage) of Parliament.

lex et consuetudo regni (**leks** et kon-swə-**t[y]oo**-do **reg**-nI), *n.* [Latin] *Hist.* The law and custom of the realm; the common law.

lex Fabia de plagiariis (**leks** **fay**-bee-ə dee plaj-ee-**air**-ee-əs), *n.* [Latin] *Hist.* A law directed against kidnapping and harboring of slaves.

lex Falcidia (**leks** fal-**sid**-ee-ə). See FALCIDIAN LAW.

lex fori (**leks** **for**-I). [Latin] The law of the forum; the law of the jurisdiction where the case is pending <the *lex fori* governs whether the death penalty is a possible punishment for a first-degree-murder conviction>. — Also termed *lex ordinandi*. Cf. LEX LOCI (1).

lex Francorum (**leks** frang-**kor**-əm), *n.* [Law Latin] The law of the Franks, promulgated by Theodoric I, son of Clovis I, at the same time as the law of Alemanni and Bavaria.

lex Frisionum (**leks** frizh-ee-**oh**-nəm), *n.* [Law Latin] The law of the Frisians, promulgated in the middle of the eighth century.

lex Furia Caninia (**leks** **fyoor**-ee-ə kə-**nI**-nee-ə), *n.* [Latin] *Roman law.* A law prohibiting masters from freeing by will more than a certain number or proportion of their slaves. • Justinian later abrogated this law. — Also termed *lex Fusia Caninia*; *Furian Caninian law*; *Fusian Caninian law*.

lex Furia testamentaria (**leks fyoor**-ee-ə tes-tə-men-**tair**-ee-ə), *n.* [Latin] *Roman law.* A law prohibiting a testator from bequeathing more than 1,000 pounds of copper in weight or the equivalent. • This was the first law restricting legacies.

lex Fusia Caninia. See LEX FURIA CANINIA.

lex Gabinia (**leks** gə-**bin**-ee-ə), *n.* [Latin] *Roman law.* A law introducing election by ballot. — Also termed *lex Gabinia tabellaria* (**leks** gə-**bin**-ee-ə tab-ə-**lair**-ee-ə).

lex generalis (**leks** jen-ə-**ray**-lis). A law of general application, as opposed to one that affects only a particular person or a small group of people.

lex Genucia (**leks** jə-**n[y]oo**-shee-ə), *n.* [Latin] *Roman law.* A law, often and easily evaded, prohibiting the charging of interest on loans between Roman citizens.

lex Gothica (**leks goth**-ik-ə), *n.* [Law Latin] *Hist.* The law of the Goths. • It was first promulgated in writing in A.D. 466.

lex Horatia Valeria (**leks** hə-**ray**-shee-ə və-**leer**-ee-ə), *n.* [Latin] *Roman law.* A law making enactments by the assembly of the people in tribes binding on all citizens.

lex Hortensia (**leks** hor-**ten**-s[h]ee-ə), *n.* [Latin] *Roman law.* A law extending to the plebeians full participation in public laws of government and worship; specif., an important constitutional law that made laws passed by the assemblies of the common people (the plebeians) binding on all citizens. • Previously, plebeian assemblies could not bind the patrician classes. See JUS PUBLICUM; JUS SACRUM.

lex Hostilia de furtis (**leks** hos-**til**-ee-ə dee **fər**-tis), *n.* [Latin] *Roman law.* A law providing that the state could prosecute a person for theft without the owner's participation, as when the owner was busy on an official mission.

lexical definition. See DEFINITION.

lex imperatoria (**leks** im-pər-ə-**tor**-ee-ə), *n.* [Latin] Imperial law; Roman law.

Lexis (**lek**-sis). An online computer service that provides access to databases of legal information, including federal and state caselaw, statutes, and secondary materials.

lex judicialis (**leks** joo-dish-ee-**ay**-lis), *n.* [Latin "judicial law"] An ordeal. See ORDEAL.

lex Julia (**leks joo**-lee-ə), *n.* [Latin] *Roman law.* One of several Roman statutes dating from the reign of Augustus (27 B.C.–A.D. 14) and distinguished by additional words describing the particular subject matter, as in *lex Julia de adulteriis*.

lex Julia de adulteriis (**leks joo**-lee-ə dee ə-**dəl**-tər-ee-is), *n.* [Latin] *Roman law.* A law regulating marriage, discouraging celibacy, and encouraging marriage portions.

lex Julia de ambitu (**leks joo**-lee-ə dee **am**-bi-t[y]oo), *n.* [Latin] *Roman law.* A law discouraging illegal means of office-seeking.

lex Julia de annona (**leks joo**-lee-ə dee ə-**noh**-nə), *n.* [Latin] *Roman law.* A law discouraging business combinations that raise the prices of basic goods, esp. food.

lex Julia de cessione bonorum (**leks joo**-lee-ə dee ses[h]-ee-**oh**-nee bə-**nor**-əm), *n.* [Latin] *Roman law.* A law governing bankruptcies.

lex Julia de majestate (**leks joo**-lee-ə dee maj-ə-**stay**-tee), *n.* [Latin] *Roman law.* A law imposing capital punishment on a person acting against the emperor or state.

lex Julia de maritandis ordinibus (**leks joo**-lee-ə dee mar-ə-**tan**-dis or-**din**-ə-bəs), *n.* [Latin] *Roman law.* A law regulating marriages, as by forbidding senators and their children from intermarrying with freedmen and outlaws, and freedmen from intermarrying with outlaws. • This statute is usu. considered as one law with the *lex Papia Poppea*, which exempted women with three children or more from being placed under guardianship.

lex Julia de peculatu (**leks joo**-lee-ə dee pek-yə-**lay**-t[y]oo), *n.* [Latin] *Roman law.* A law punishing a person who steals public money, public property, or sacred objects. • Punishment consisted of death or deportation.

lex Julia de residuis (**leks joo**-lee-ə dee ri-**zij**-oo-is), *n.* [Latin] *Roman law.* A law punishing persons who could not account for public money in their charge.

lex Junia Norbana (**leks joo**-nee-ə nor-**bay**-nə), *n.* [Latin] *Roman law.* A law granting certain freedom status to improperly manumitted slaves but not full rights of citizenship; a law granting rights of *latini Juniani*. See LATINI JUNIANI.

> "After the *lex Junia Norbana*, we find the following classes of persons, under the division of the law of persons into free men or slaves: 1. *Ingenui*, or persons born free. 2. *Libertini* . . . ex-slaves who, on gaining their freedom, became *cives*. 3. *Latini Juniani* . . . ex-slaves who, on manumission and by reason of some defect therein, became something short of full citizens. 4. *Dediticii* . . . . 5. Slaves proper." R.W. Leage, *Roman Private Law* 70 (C.H. Ziegler ed., 2d ed. 1930).

lex Junia Velleja (**leks joo**-nee-ə və-**lee**-yə), *n.* [Latin] *Roman law.* A law providing that certain kinds of descendants must be treated as posthumously born children of a decedent for purposes of heirship.

lex Kantiae (**leks kan**-shee-ee), *n.* [Law Latin] *Hist.* A body of customs, mainly concerning land tenure, prevailing in Kent during the time of Edward I.

lex ligeantiae (**leks** lij-ee-**an**-shee-ee). The law of the country to which a person owes national allegiance. • Some jurists have thought that this law ought to decide many of the questions that have usu. been determined by the *lex domicilii*.

lex loci (**leks loh**-sɪ). [Latin] **1.** The law of the place; local law. Cf. LEX FORI. **2.** LEX LOCI CONTRACTUS.

lex loci actus (**leks loh**-sɪ **ak**-təs), *n.* [Law Latin] The law of the place where an act is done or a transaction is completed. — Often shortened to *lex actus*.

lex loci celebrationis (**leks loh**-sɪ sel-ə-bray-shee-**oh**-nis), *n.* [Latin "law of the place of the ceremony"] The law of the place where a contract, esp. of marriage, is made. • This law usu. governs when the validity of a marriage is at issue. Restatement (Second) of Conflict of Laws § 283(2) (1971).

lex loci contractus (**leks loh**-sɪ kən-**trak**-təs). [Latin] The law of the place where a contract is executed or to be performed. • *Lex loci contractus* is often the proper law by which to decide contractual disputes. — Often shortened to *lex loci*; *lex contractus*.

lex loci delicti (**leks loh**-sɪ də-**lik**-tɪ). [Latin] The law of the place where the tort was committed. — Often shortened to *lex delicti*. — Also termed *lex loci delictus*; *lex loci delicti commissi*; *place-of-wrong rule*; *place-of-wrong law*.

lex loci rei sitae (**leks loh**-sɪ **ree**-ɪ **sɪ**-tee). [Latin] LEX SITUS.

lex loci solutionis (**leks loh**-sɪ sə-loo-shee-**oh**-nis), *n.* [Latin "law of the place of solution"] The law of the place where a contract is to be performed (esp. by payment). — Often shortened to *lex solutionis*.

lex Longobardorum (**leks** long-goh-bahr-**dor**-əm), *n.* [Latin "law of the Lombards"] *Hist.* An ancient legal code developed between the fifth and eighth centuries, in force until the reign of Charlemagne.

lex manifesta (**leks** man-ə-**fes**-tə). [Law Latin] *Hist.* **1.** Open law; manifest law. **2.** Trial by duel or ordeal. — Also termed *manifest law*.

lex mercatoria (**leks** mər-kə-**tor**-ee-ə), *n.* [Latin "mercantile law"] See LAW MERCHANT.

lex merciorum (**leks** mər-shee-**or**-əm). See MERCENLAGE.

lex monetae (**leks** mə-**nee**-tee). [Latin] The law of the country whose money is in question.

lex naturae (**leks** nə-**tyoor**-ee). See NATURAL LAW.

lex naturale (**leks** nach-ə-**ray**-lee). See NATURAL LAW.

lex non scripta (**leks** non **skrip**-tə), *n.* [Latin "unwritten law"] Common law, including customs and local laws, as distinguished from statutory law; UNWRITTEN LAW. Cf. LEX SCRIPTA.

lex ordinandi (**leks** or-də-**nan**-dɪ). See LEX FORI.

lex Papia Poppea (**leks pay**-pee-ə pah-**pee**-ə), *n.* [Latin] *Roman law.* A law proposed by the consuls Papius and Poppeus at the request of Augustus. • It is usu. considered with the *lex Julia de maritandis ordinibus* as one law. — Also termed *Papian law*; *Poppean law*. See *lex Julia de maritandis ordinibus* under LEX JULIA.

lex patriae (**leks pay**-tree-ee *or* **pa**-tree-ee), *n.* [Latin] National law; the law of one's country.

lex Petronia (**leks** pə-**troh**-nee-ə), *n.* [Latin] *Roman law.* A law forbidding masters from placing their slaves with wild beasts in a sporting contest, without appropriate permission from a magistrate.

lex Plaetoria (**leks** pli- *or* plee-**tor**-ee-ə), *n.* [Latin] *Roman law.* A law protecting minors against frauds and permitting them to apply for a guardian.

lex Poetelia (**leks** poh-ə-**tee**-lee-ə), *n.* [Latin] *Roman law.* A law abolishing a creditor's right to treat his debtor inhumanely, as by beating or fettering the debtor.

lex Pompeia de parricidiis (**leks** pom-**pee**-ə dee par-ə-**SI**-dee-is), *n.* [Latin] *Roman law.* A law punishing a person for causing the death of his or her own parent, child, or other specified relative. • The offender was killed by being sewn up in a sack with a dog, a rooster, a poisonous snake, and a monkey, and then thrown into the ocean or a river.

lex posterior derogat priori (**leks** pah-**steer**-ee-ər **der**-ə-gat prI-**or**-I), *n.* [Latin "a later law prevails over an earlier one"] The principle that a later statute negates the effect of a prior one if the later statute expressly repeals, or is obviously repugnant to, the earlier law.

lex praetoria (**leks** pri- *or* pree-**tor**-ee-ə), *n.* [Latin "praetorian law"] **1.** *Roman law.* A law requiring that every freedman with a will must leave a patron half the property. — Also termed *ius praetorium.* **2.** *Hist.* The applicable rules in a court of equity.

lex privata (**leks** prI-**vay**-tə), *n.* [Latin "private law"] *Roman law.* A clause in a private contract. — Sometimes shortened to *lex.*

lex publica (**leks pəb**-li-kə), *n.* [Latin "public law"] *Roman law.* **1.** A law passed by a popular assembly and binding on all people. **2.** A written law. — Sometimes shortened to *lex.*

lex Publilia (**leks** p[y]oo-**blil**-ee-ə), *n.* [Latin "Publilian law"] *Roman law.* A law dispensing with senatorial approval for the enactments of the *plebs* (common citizens).

lex regia (**leks ree**-jee-ə), *n.* [Latin "royal law"] *Roman law.* A law ostensibly enacted by the Roman people granting wide legislative and executive powers to the emperor, such as providing that the emperor was a source of law, the emperor had full legislative powers, and the emperor's will or pleasure had the full force of law.

lex Rhodia (**leks roh**-dee-ə), *n.* [Latin] *Roman law.* The Rhodian law, esp. on the subject of jettison, preserved in the Pandects. See RHODIAN LAW.

lex Romana (**leks** rə-**may**-nə), *n.* [Latin] ROMAN LAW.

Lex Romana Visigothorum (**leks** rə-**may**-nə viz-ə-gah-**thor**-əm). See BREVIARUM ALARICIANUM.

lex Salica (**leks sal**-ə-kə), *n.* [Latin] See SALIC LAW.

lex Scribonia (**leks** skri-**boh**-nee-ə), *n.* [Latin] *Roman law.* A law abolishing the acquisition of certain interests in land through prescription.

lex scripta (**leks skrip**-tə), *n.* [Latin "written law"] Law authorized or created by statute rather than custom or usage; WRITTEN LAW. Cf. LEX NON SCRIPTA.

lex Sempronia (**leks** sem-**proh**-nee-ə), *n.* [Latin] *Hist.* A law preventing senators from being judges, and allowing knights to so serve.

lex Silia (**leks sil**-ee-ə), *n.* [Latin] *Roman law.* A law providing for personal actions for a fixed sum of money.

lex situs (**leks sI**-təs), *n.* [Law Latin] The law of the place where property is located. — Also termed *lex loci rei sitae.* See Restatement (Second) of Conflict of Laws §§ 222 et seq. (1971).

lex solutionis. See LEX LOCI SOLUTIONIS.

lex talionis (**leks** tal-ee-**oh**-nis), *n.* [Law Latin] The law of retaliation, under which punishment should be in kind — an eye for an eye, a tooth for a tooth, and so on. — Also termed *eye for an eye*; *jus talionis*; *principle of retribution.*

> "Kant, for example, expresses the opinion that punishment cannot rightly be inflicted for the sake of any benefit to be derived from it either by the criminal himself or by society, and that the sole and sufficient reason and justification of it lies in the fact that evil has been done by him who suffers it. Consistently with this view, he derives the measure of punishment, not from any elaborate considerations as to the amount needed for

the repression of crime, but from the simple principle of *lex talionis*: 'Thine eye shall not pity; but life shall go for life, eye for eye, tooth for tooth, hand for hand, foot for foot' [*Deuteronomy*, xix 21]. No such principle, indeed, is capable of literal interpretation; but subject to metaphorical and symbolical applications it is in Kant's view the guiding rule of the ideal scheme of criminal justice." John Salmond, *Jurisprudence* 118 (Glanville L. Williams ed., 10th ed. 1947).

"But if the old form of the *lex talionis*, an eye for an eye or a tooth for a tooth, sounds too barbaric today, may we not reformulate the retributive theory and put it thus: Everyone is to be punished alike in proportion to the gravity of his offense or to the extent to which he has made others suffer?" Morris R. Cohen, *Reason and Law* 53 (1961).

lex terrae (**leks ter**-ee). [Law Latin] See LAW OF THE LAND.

lex Theodosiana. See BREVIARUM ALARICIANUM.

lex validitatis (**leks** val-ə-**day**-tis), *n.* [Latin] *Conflict of laws.* The presumption of validity given to marriages, contracts, and other matters.

lex Visigothorum (**leks** viz-ə-gah-**thor**-əm), *n.* [Latin "law of the Visigoths"] The law of a division of the Goths (a Germanic tribe) known as the Visigoths, who conquered Spain in the 5th century. • In the late 7th century, Kings Recceswinth and Erwig imposed a Visigothic common law, and it is to this law that the phrase *lex Visigothorum* usu. applies. — Also termed *liber iudiciorum*. — Also spelled *lex Wisigothorum*.

lex Voconia (**leks** və-**koh**-nee-ə), *n.* [Latin] *Roman law.* A law regulating inheritance, esp. by women. — Also termed *Voconian law*.

"Lex Voconia .... Contained several provisions concerned with the law of succession: (1) No woman could be heir ... to an estate having a value greater than a fixed amount .... (2) Admitted among female agnates only the sisters of the deceased to intestate succession. (3) No one person — male or female — could receive by legacy more than the heir (or all heirs together) instituted in the last will." Adolf Berger, *Encyclopedic Dictionary of Roman Law* 561 (1953).

lex Wallensica (**leks** wawl-**en**-zə-kə), *n.* [Latin] Welsh law.

ley civile (**lay** see- *or* sə-**veel**), *n.* [Law French] *Hist.* **1.** The civil law. **2.** The Roman law. — Also termed *ley escripte*.

ley de terre (**lay** də **tair**). [Law French] See LAW OF THE LAND.

ley escripte (**lay es**-kript). See LEY CIVILE.

ley gager (**lay gay**-jər), *n.* [Law French] *Hist.* Wager of law; the defendant's giving of security to make law on a particular day. See WAGER OF LAW.

leze majesty. See LESE MAJESTY.

L.F. *abbr.* LAW FRENCH.

LHWCA. *abbr.* LONGSHORE AND HARBOR WORKERS' COMPENSATION ACT.

liability, *n.* **1.** The quality or state of being legally obligated or accountable; legal responsibility to another or to society, enforceable by civil remedy or criminal punishment <liability for injuries caused by negligence>. — Also termed *legal liability*. **2.** (*often pl.*) A financial or pecuniary obligation; DEBT <tax liability> <assets and liabilities>.

"The term 'liability' is one of at least double signification. In one sense it is the synonym of *duty*, the correlative of *right*; in this sense it is the opposite of *privilege* or *liberty*. If a duty rests upon a party, society is now commanding performance by him and threatening penalties. In a second sense, the term 'liability' is the correlative of *power* and the opposite of *immunity*. In this case society is not yet commanding performance, but it will so command if the possessor of the power does some operative act. If one has a power, the other has a liability. It would be wise to adopt the second sense exclusively. Accurate legal thinking is difficult when the fundamental terms have shifting senses." William R. Anson, *Principles of the Law of Contract* 9 (Arthur L. Corbin ed., 3d Am. ed. 1919).

"Liability or responsibility is the bond of necessity that exists between the wrongdoer and the remedy of the wrong. This *vinculum juris* is not one of mere duty or obligation; it pertains not to the sphere of *ought* but to that of *must*." John Salmond, *Jurisprudence* 364 (Glanville L. Williams ed., 10th ed. 1947).

absolute liability. See *strict liability*.

accomplice liability. Criminal responsibility of one who acts with another before, during, or after a crime. See 18 USCA § 2.

accrued liability. A debt or obligation that is properly chargeable in a given accounting period but that is not yet paid.

alternative liability. Liability arising from the tortious acts of two or more parties — when the plaintiff proves that one of the defendants has caused harm but cannot prove which one caused it — resulting in a shifting of the burden of proof to each defendant. Restatement (Second) of Torts § 433B(3) (1965).

civil liability. **1.** Liability imposed under the civil, as opposed to the criminal, law. **2.** The state of being legally obligated for civil damages.

contingent liability. A liability that will occur only if a specific event happens; a liability that depends on the occurrence of a future and uncertain event. • In financial statements, contingent liabilities are usu. stated in footnotes.

current liability. A business liability that will be paid or otherwise discharged with current assets or by creating other current liabilities within the next year (or operating cycle).

derivative liability. Liability for a wrong that a person other than the one wronged has a right to redress. • Examples include liability to a widow in a wrongful-death action and liability to a corporation in a shareholder's derivative suit.

enterprise liability. Liability imposed on each member of an industry responsible for manufacturing a harmful or defective product, allotted by each manufacturer's market share of the industry. — Also termed *industry-wide liability.* See *market-share liability.*

joint and several liability. Liability that may be apportioned either among two or more parties or to only one or a few select members of the group, at the adversary's discretion. • Thus, each liable party is individually responsible for the entire obligation, but a paying party may have a right of contribution and indemnity from nonpaying parties. See *solidary liability.*

joint liability. Liability shared by two or more parties.

liability in solido. See *solidary liability.*

liability without fault. See *strict liability.*

limited liability. Liability restricted by law or contract; esp., the liability of a company's owners for nothing more than the capital they have invested in the business.

market-share liability. Liability that is imposed, usu. severally, on each member of an industry, based on each member's share of the market, or respective percentage of the product that is placed on the market. • This theory of liability usu. applies only in the situation in which a plaintiff cannot trace the harmful exposure to a particular product, as when several products contain a fungible substance. For example, it is sometimes applied to a claim that the plaintiff was harmed by exposure to asbestos. See *enterprise liability.*

penal liability. Liability arising from a proceeding intended at least partly to penalize a wrongdoer. Cf. *remedial liability.*

personal liability. Liability for which one is personally accountable and for which a wronged party can seek satisfaction out of the wrongdoer's personal assets.

premises liability. See PREMISES LIABILITY.

primary liability. Liability for which one is directly responsible, as opposed to secondary liability.

products liability. See PRODUCTS LIABILITY.

remedial liability. Liability arising from a proceeding whose object contains no penal element. • The two types of proceedings giving rise to this liability are specific enforcement and restitution. Cf. *penal liability.*

secondary liability. Liability that does not arise unless the primarily liable party fails to honor its obligation.

several liability. Liability that is separate and distinct from another's liability, so that the plaintiff may bring a separate action against one defendant without joining the other liable parties.

shareholder's liability. **1.** The statutory, added, or double liability of a shareholder for a corporation's debts, despite full payment for the stock. **2.** The liability of a shareholder for any unpaid stock listed as fully owned on the stock certificate, usu. occurring either when the shareholder agrees to pay full par value for the stock and obtains the certificate before the stock is paid for, or when partially paid-for stock is intentionally issued by a corporation as fully paid, the consideration for it being entirely fictitious. — Also termed *stockholder's liability.*

solidary liability (**sol**-ə-der-ee). *Civil law.* The liability of any one debtor among two or more joint debtors to pay the entire debt if the creditor so chooses. • This is equivalent to joint and several liability in the common law. — Also termed *liability in solido.* See *joint and several liability.*

stockholder's liability. See *shareholder's liability.*

strict liability. Liability that does not depend on actual negligence or intent to harm, but that is based on the breach of an absolute duty to make something safe. • Strict liability most often applies either to ultrahazardous activities or in products-liability cases. — Also termed *absolute liability*; *liability without fault.*

vicarious liability (vI-**kair**-ee-əs). Liability that a supervisory party (such as an employer) bears for the actionable conduct of a subordinate or associate (such as an employee) because of the relationship between the two parties. See RESPONDEAT SUPERIOR.

liability bond. See BOND (2).

liability dividend. See *scrip dividend* under DIVIDEND.

liability in solido. See *solidary liability* under LIABILITY.

liability insurance. See INSURANCE.

liability limit. The maximum amount of coverage that an insurance company will provide on a single claim under an insurance policy. — Also termed *limit of liability*; *policy limits*.

liability without fault. See *strict liability* under LIABILITY.

liable (**lI**-ə-bəl *also* **lI**-bəl), *adj.* **1.** Responsible or answerable in law; legally obligated. **2.** (Of a person) subject to or likely to incur (a fine, penalty, etc.). — Also termed *legally liable*. See LIABILITY.

libel (**lI**-bəl), *n.* **1.** A defamatory statement expressed in a fixed medium, esp. writing but also a picture, sign, or electronic broadcast. • Libel is classified as both a crime and a tort but is no longer prosecuted as a crime. — Also termed *defamatory libel*. See DEFAMATION. Cf. SLANDER.

> "Libel is written or visual defamation; slander is oral or aural defamation." Robert D. Sack & Sandra S. Baron, *Libel, Slander, and Related Problems* § 2.3, at 67 (2d ed. 1994).

> "The distinction itself between libel and slander is not free from difficulty and uncertainty. As it took form in the seventeenth century, it was one between written and oral words. But later on libel was extended to include pictures, signs, statues, motion pictures, and even conduct carrying a defamatory imputation, such as hanging the plaintiff in effigy, erecting a gallows before his door, dishonoring his valid check drawn upon the defendant's bank, or even ... following him over a considerable period in a conspicuous manner. From this it has been concluded that libel is that which is communicated by the sense of sight, or perhaps also by touch or smell, while slander is that which is conveyed by the sense of hearing." W. Page Keeton et al., *The Law of Torts* § 112, at 786 (5th ed. 1984).

criminal libel. At common law, a malicious libel that is designed to expose a person to hatred, contempt, or ridicule and that may subject the author to criminal sanctions. • Because of constitutional protections of free speech, libel is no longer criminally prosecuted.

false-implication libel. Libel of a public figure in a news article that creates a false implication or impression even though each statement in the article, taken separately, is true. See FALSE LIGHT; INVASION OF PRIVACY.

group libel. Libel that defames a class of persons, esp. because of their race, sex, national origin, religious belief, or the like. • Civil liability for group libel is rare because the plaintiff must prove that the statement applied particularly to him or her. Cf. *hate speech* under SPEECH.

libel per quod (pər **kwod**). **1.** Libel that is actionable only on allegation and proof of special damages. • Most jurisdictions do not recognize libel per quod, holding instead that general damages from libel are presumed. **2.** Libel in which the defamatory meaning is not apparent from the statement on its face but rather must be proved from extrinsic circumstances. See INNUENDO (2).

libel per se (pər **say**). **1.** Libel that is actionable in itself, requiring no proof of special damages. • Most jurisdictions do not distinguish between libel per se and libel per quod, holding instead that general damages from libel are presumed. **2.** Libel that is defamatory on its face, such as the statement "Frank is a thief."

obscene libel. *Hist.* **1.** The common-law crime of publishing, with the intent to corrupt, material (esp. sexual words or pictures) that tends to deprave or corrupt those whose minds are open to immoral influences. **2.** A writing, book, picture, or print that is so obscene that it shocks the public sense of decency.

seditious libel. Libel made with the intent of inciting sedition. • Like other forms of criminal libel, seditious libel is no longer prosecuted. See SEDITION.

trade libel. See TRADE LIBEL.

2. The act of making such a statement. **3.** The complaint or initial pleading in an admiralty or ecclesiastical case.

libel, *vb.* **1.** To defame (someone) in a permanent medium, esp. in writing. **2.** To sue in admiralty or ecclesiastical court.

libelant (**lI**-bəl-ənt). **1.** The party who institutes a suit in admiralty or ecclesiastical court by filing a libel. **2.** LIBELER. — Also spelled *libellant*.

libelee (lɪ-bəl-**ee**). The party against whom a libel has been filed in admiralty or ecclesiastical court. — Also spelled *libellee*.

libeler. One who publishes a written defamatory statement. — Also spelled *libeller*. — Also termed *libelant*.

libellary procedure (**lɪ**-bəl-er-ee). *Roman law*. A procedure in which the parties submitted their claims to the magistrate without formally making an issue and with only a short statement (a *libellus*) of the basis for the lawsuit.

libellos agere (lə-**bel**-əs **aj**-ə-ree), *vb*. [Latin] *Roman law*. To assist the emperor in responding to petitions. — Also termed *libellum agere*.

libellous, *adj*. See LIBELOUS.

libellus (lə-**bel**-əs), *n*. [Latin] **1.** *Roman law*. A small book; a writing; a petition. **2.** *Hist*. An instrument conveying all or part of land. **3.** Any one of a number of legal petitions or documents, such as a bill of complaint.

libellus accusatorius (lə-**bel**-əs ə-kyoo-zə-**tor**-ee-əs), *n*. [Latin] *Roman law*. A formal criminal accusation.

libellus appellatorius (lə-**bel**-əs ə-pel-ə-**tor**-ee-əs), *n*. [Latin] *Roman law*. An appeal.

libellus consultatorius (lə-**bel**-əs kon-səl-**tor**-ee-əs), *n*. [Latin] *Roman law*. A petition to the emperor from a judge or official asking for guidance.

libellus conventionis (lə-**bel**-əs kən-ven-shee-**oh**-nis), *n*. [Latin] *Roman law*. The statement of a plaintiff's claim in a petition sent to the magistrate, who directs its delivery to the defendant.

> "The *libellus conventionis* was very like the *intentio* of the formulary system, and the modern statement of claim, since it set forth in a succinct manner the nature of the plaintiff's right and the circumstances attending its alleged violation." R.W. Leage, *Roman Private Law* 417 (C.H. Ziegler ed., 2d ed. 1930).

libellus divortii (lə-**bel**-əs di-**vor**-shee-ɪ), *n*. [Latin] *Roman law*. A bill of divorce.

libellus famosus (lə-**bel**-əs fə-**moh**-səs), *n*. [Latin] *Roman law*. A defamatory publication.

> "Libellus famosus . . . . According to the *Lex Cornelia de iniuriis* punishment was inflicted on the person who wrote (*scripserit*), composed (*composuerit*) or edited (*ediderit*) such a lampoon, even if the publication was made under another name or anonymously (*sine nomine*)." Adolf Berger, *Encyclopedic Dictionary of Roman Law* 562 (1953).

libellus rerum (lə-**bel**-əs **reer**-əm), *n*. [Latin] *Hist*. An inventory.

libellus supplex (lə-**bel**-əs **səp**-leks), *n*. [Latin] *Roman law*. A petition, esp. to the emperor. • All petitions to the emperor had to be in writing.

libel of review. *Maritime law*. A new proceeding attacking a final decree after the right to appeal has expired. See LIBEL (3).

libelous, *adj*. Constituting or involving libel; defamatory <a libelous newspaper story>. — Also spelled *libellous*.

libel per quod. See LIBEL.

libel per se. See LIBEL.

liber (**lɪ**-bər), *adj*. [Latin "free"] **1.** (Of courts, public places, etc.) open and accessible. **2.** (Of a person) having the state or condition of a freeman. **3.** (Of a person) free from another's service or authority.

liber (**lɪ**-bər), *n*. [Latin "book"] **1.** A book of records, esp. of deeds. **2.** A main division of a literary or professional work.

libera batella (**lib**-ər-ə bə-**tel**-ə), *n*. [Latin "free boat"] *Hist*. The right to have a boat fish in certain waters; free fishery.

libera chasea habenda (**lib**-ər-ə **chay**-see-ə hə-**ben**-də), *n*. [Law Latin] *Hist*. A judicial writ granting a person the right to a free chase belonging to the person's manor, after the jury's verdict granting that right. See CHASE.

libera eleemosyna (**lib**-ər-ə el-ə-**mos**-ə-nə). See FRANKALMOIN.

libera falda (**lib**-ər-ə **fal**-də *or* **fawl**-də). See DE LIBERA FALDA.

liberal, *adj*. **1.** (Of a condition, state, opinion, etc.) not restricted; expansive; tolerant <liberal policy>. **2.** (Of a person or entity) opposed to conservatism; advocating expansive freedoms and individual expression <liberal party>. **3.** (Of an act, etc.) generous <a liberal gift>. **4.** (Of an interpretation, construction, etc.) not strict or literal; loose <a liberal reading of the statute>.

liberal construction. See CONSTRUCTION.

libera lex (**lib**-ər-ə **leks**), *n.* [Latin "free law"] *Hist.* Free law; the law of the land. • This phrase referred to the law enjoyed by free and lawful men, as opposed to men who had lost the benefit and protection of the law as a result of committing crimes. See LIBERAM LEGEM AMITTERE.

liberal interpretation. See INTERPRETATION.

liberam legem amittere (**lib**-ər-əm **lee**-jəm ə-**mit**-ə-ree). [Latin] *Hist.* To lose one's free law. • This phrase refers to falling, by crime or infamy, from the status of *libera lex.* By what was known as a "villenous judgment," a person would be discredited as juror and witness, would forfeit goods and chattels and lands for life, would have his houses razed and trees uprooted, and would go to prison. This was the ancient punishment of a conspirator and of a party involved in a wager of battle who cried "craven." — Also termed *amittere liberam legem; amittere legem terrae* ("to lose the law of the land"). See VILLENOUS JUDGMENT.

libera piscaria (**lib**-ər-ə pis-**kair**-ee-ə). See *free fishery* under FISHERY (1).

liberare (lib-ə-**rair**-ee), *vb.* **1.** *Civil law.* To set (a person) free. **2.** *Hist.* To deliver or transfer (a writ, etc.).

liber assisarum (**lI**-bər as-I-**zair**-əm), *n.* [Law Latin "Book of Assizes"] *Hist.* A collection of cases arising in assizes and other country trials. • It was the fourth volume of the reports of the reign of Edward III.

liberate (lib-ə-**ray**-tee), *n.* [Law Latin] *Hist.* **1.** A chancery writ to the Exchequer ordering the payment of an annual pension or other sum. **2.** A writ to the sheriff authorizing delivery of any property given as bond and then taken when a defendant forfeited a recognizance. **3.** A writ to a jailer ordering delivery of a prisoner who had paid bail. **4.** A writ to a sheriff commanding him to deliver to the plaintiff lands or goods pledged as part of a commercial trade loan arrangement (a statute staple) available in certain merchant towns in England. • If a debtor defaulted on this obligation, the creditor could obtain a writ of extent, which directed the sheriff to take an inventory and entitled the creditor to keep the debtor's property for a time until the rentals on the property equaled the amount due. The writ of *liberate* was issued after the inventory had been performed under the writ of extent. See EXTENT; STAPLE.

liberate, *vb.* To set (a person) free, as from slavery, bondage, or enemy control.

liberatio (lib-ə-**ray**-shee-oh), *n.* [Law Latin] *Hist.* Money paid for the delivery or use of a thing; a payment.

liberation. 1. The act or an instance of freeing someone or something. **2.** *Civil law.* Final payment under a contract, thereby extinguishing the debt.

liberation movement. *Int'l law.* An organized effort to achieve the political independence of a particular nation or people.

liberative, *adj.* Serving or tending to free or release.

liberative prescription. See PRESCRIPTION (1).

Liber Authenticorum (**lI**-bər aw-then-tə-**kor**-əm), *n.* [Latin] *Roman law.* The authentic collection of Justinian's Greek novels, as distinguished from another similar work, the *Epitome Juliani* (ə-**pit**-ə-mee joo-lee-**ay**-nI).

libera warrena (**lib**-ər-ə wor-**ee**-nə). See *free warren* under WARREN.

liber bancus (**lI**-bər **bang**-kəs). See FREE BENCH.

liber et legalis homo (**lI**-bər et lə-**gay**-lis). See LEGALIS HOMO.

liberi (**lib**-ər-I), *n. pl.* [Latin] *Roman law.* **1.** Children. **2.** Grandchildren. **3.** Descendants.

liber iudiciorum. See LEX VISIGOTHORUM.

liber judicialis of Alfred (**lI**-bər joo-dish-ee-**ay**-lis), *n.* [Law Latin] See DOME BOOK.

liber niger (**lI**-bər **nI**-jər), *n.* [Latin "black book"] *Hist.* An ancient record, such as the register in the Exchequer and the register of charters of abbeys and cathedrals.

Liber Niger Parvus (**lI**-bər **nI**-jər **pahr**-vəs). See BLACK BOOK OF THE EXCHEQUER.

liber ruber scaccarii (lɪ-bər **roo**-bər skə-**kair**-ee-ɪ), *n.* [Law Latin] *Hist.* Red book of the Exchequer. • This was an ancient register of the names of those holding land *per baroniam* during the reign of Henry II.

libertas (li-**bər**-tas *or* **lib**-ər-tas), *n.* [Latin "liberty, freedom"] *Hist.* A privilege or franchise.

libertas ecclesiastica (li-**bər**-tas e-klee-z[h]ee-**as**-ti-kə), *n.* [Law Latin "church liberty"] *Hist.* Immunity from secular law, enjoyed by religious houses that are subject to ecclesiastical law.

libertatibus allocandis (lib-ər-**tay**-tə-bəs al-ə-**kan**-dis). See DE LIBERTATIBUS ALLOCANDIS.

libertatibus exigendis in itinere (lib-ər-**tay**-tə-bəs ek-sə-**jen**-dis in ɪ-**tin**-ə-ree), *n.* [Latin] *Hist.* A writ from the king to one of a panel of itinerant judges (the justices in eyre) ordering them to admit an attorney to represent a criminal defendant. See EYRE.

liberti (li-**bər**-tɪ), *n. pl.* [Latin] *Roman law.* Manumitted slaves, considered in their relation with their former masters, who were known as *patrons.*

liberticide (lə-**bər**-tə-sɪd), *n.* **1.** The destruction of liberty. **2.** A destroyer of liberty.

liberties. *Hist.* **1.** Privileged districts exempt from the sheriff's jurisdiction. **2.** In American colonial times, laws. **3.** Political subdivisions of Philadelphia.

libertini (lib-ər-**tɪ**-nɪ). Manumitted slaves, considered apart from their relation to their patrons. See LIBERTI.

liberty. 1. Freedom from arbitrary or undue external restraint, esp. by a government <give me liberty or give me death>. **2.** A right, privilege, or immunity enjoyed by prescription or by grant; the absence of a legal duty imposed on a person <the liberties protected by the Constitution>.

> "[Liberty] denotes not merely freedom from bodily restraint but also the right of the individual to contract, to engage in any of the common occupations of life, to acquire useful knowledge, to marry, establish a home and bring up children, to worship God according to the dictates of his own conscience, and generally to enjoy those privileges long recognized at common law as essential to the orderly pursuit of happiness by free men." *Meyer v. Nebraska,* 262 U.S. 390, 399, 43 S.Ct. 625, 626 (1923).

> "The sphere of my legal liberty is that sphere of activity within which the law is content to leave me alone." John Salmond, *Jurisprudence* 239 (Glanville L. Williams ed., 10th ed. 1947).

> "The word *liberty* has become a symbol around which have clung some of the most generous human emotions. We have been brought up to thrill with admiration at the men who say, Give me liberty or give me death. But the philosopher asks whether all those who are devoted to liberty mean the same thing. Does liberty or freedom, for instance, involve free trade? Does it involve freedom to preach race hatred or the overthrow of all that we regard as sacred? Many who believe in liberty characterize the freedom which they are not willing to grant, as license, and they do it so often that one may be inclined to think that what we really need is less liberty and more license. Moreover, there is a confusion between the absence of legal restraint and the presence of real freedom as positive power to do what we want. The legal freedom to earn a million dollars is not worth a cent to one who has no real opportunity. It is fashionable to assert that men want freedom above all other things, but a strong case may be made out for the direct contrary. Absolute freedom is just what people do not want . . . ." Morris R. Cohen, *Reason and Law* 101–02 (1961).

civil liberty. See CIVIL LIBERTY.

individual liberty. See *personal liberty.*

natural liberty. The power to act as one wishes, without any restraint or control, unless by nature.

> "This natural liberty . . . being a right inherent in us by birth . . . . But every man, when he enters into society, gives up a part of his natural liberty, as the price of so valuable a purchase; and, in consideration of receiving the advantages of mutual commerce, obliges himself to conform to those laws, which the community has thought proper to establish." 1 William Blackstone, *Commentaries on the Laws of England* 121 (1765).

personal liberty. One's freedom to do as one pleases, limited only by the government's right to regulate the public health, safety, and welfare. — Also termed *individual liberty.*

political liberty. A person's freedom to participate in the operation of government, esp. in the making and administration of laws.

religious liberty. Freedom — as guaranteed by the First Amendment — to express, without external control other than one's own conscience, any or no system of religious opinion and to engage in or refrain from any form of religious observance or public or private religious worship, as long as it is consistent with the peace and order of society.

Liberty Clause. The Due Process Clause in the 14th Amendment to the U.S. Constitution. See DUE PROCESS CLAUSE.

liberty interest. An interest protected by the due-process clauses of state and federal constitutions. See FUNDAMENTAL RIGHT (2).

liberty not. See NO-DUTY.

liberty of a port. *Marine insurance.* A license incorporated in a marine policy allowing the vessel to dock and trade at a designated port other than the principal port of destination.

liberty of contract. See FREEDOM OF CONTRACT.

liberty of speech. See FREEDOM OF SPEECH.

liberty of the globe. *Marine insurance.* A license incorporated in a marine policy authorizing the vessel to go to any part of the world, rather than be confined to a particular port of destination.

liberty of the press. See FREEDOM OF THE PRESS.

liberum maritagium (**lib**-ər-əm mar-ə-**tay**-jee-əm). See FRANKMARRIAGE.

liberum servitium (**lib**-ər-əm sər-**vish**-ee-əm), *n.* [Law Latin] See SERVITIUM LIBERUM.

liberum socagium (**lib**-ər-əm sok-**ay**-jee-əm), *n.* [Law Latin] See *free socage* under SOCAGE.

liberum tenementum (**lib**-ər-əm ten-ə-**men**-təm), *n.* [Law Latin] *Hist.* **1.** A plea of freehold; a defensive common-law pleading in an action for trespass to lands. • The defendant pleaded either ownership of the land in question or authorization from the freehold owner. **2.** FREEHOLD.

liberum veto. See VETO.

libra (**lɪ**-brə), *n.* [Latin] *Hist.* An English pound; a sum of money equal to a pound sterling. Pl. ***librae.***

libra arsa (**lɪ**-brə **ahr**-sə), *n.* [Law Latin] *Hist.* A pound melted to test its purity.

libra numerata (**lɪ**-brə n[y]oo-mə-**ray**-tə), *n.* [Law Latin] *Hist.* A pound of money that has been counted.

libra pensa (**lɪ**-brə **pen**-sə), *n.* [Law Latin] *Hist.* A pound of money by weight.

libripens (**lib**-rə-penz), *n.* [Latin] *Roman law.* A person who holds a bronze balance during actual or ritual sales, such as the ceremonies of emancipating a son from his father or conveying real property. • The purchaser strikes the balance with a piece of bronze to symbolize completion of the sale. The seller then receives the bronze as a sign of the purchase money. See EMANCIPATION.

license, *n.* **1.** A revocable permission to commit some act that would otherwise be unlawful; esp., an agreement (not amounting to a lease or profit à prendre) that it will be lawful for the licensee to enter the licensor's land to do some act that would otherwise be illegal, such as hunting game. See SERVITUDE. **2.** The certificate or document evidencing such permission. — **license,** *vb.*

bare license. A license in which no property interest passes to the licensee, who is merely not a trespasser. • It is revocable at will. — Also termed *naked license*; *mere license.*

box-top license. See *shrink-wrap license.*

compulsory license. *Copyright.* A statutorily created license that allows certain parties to use copyrighted material without the explicit permission of the copyright owner in exchange for a specified royalty.

exclusive license. A license that gives the licensee the exclusive right to perform the licensed act and that prohibits the licensor from granting the right to anyone else; esp., such a license of a copyright, patent, or trademark right.

license coupled with an interest. An irrevocable license conveyed with an interest in land or a chattel interest. • An injunction may be obtained to prevent the wrongful revocation of such a license. — Also termed *license coupled with the grant of an interest.*

mere license. See *bare license.*

naked license. **1.** A license allowing a licensee to use a trademark on any goods and services the licensee chooses. **2.** See *bare license.*

shrink-wrap license. A printed license that is displayed on the outside of a software package and that advises the buyer that by opening the package, the buyer becomes legally obligated to abide by the terms of the license. • Shrink-wrap licenses usu. seek to (1) prohibit users from making unauthorized copies of the software, (2) prohibit modifications to the software, (3) limit use of the software to one computer, (4) limit the manufacturer's liability, and (5) disclaim warranties. — Also written *shrinkwrap license.* — Also termed *box-top license*; *tear-me-open license.*

license bond. See BOND (2).

license coupled with the grant of an interest. See *license coupled with an interest* under LICENSE.

licensee. 1. One to whom a license is granted. **2.** One who has permission to enter or use another's premises, but only for one's own purposes and not for the occupier's benefit. • The occupier has a duty to warn the licensee of any dangerous conditions known to the occupier but unknown to the licensee. An example of a licensee is a social guest. Cf. INVITEE; TRESPASSER.

bare licensee. A licensee whose presence on the premises the occupier tolerates but does not necessarily approve, such as one who takes a shortcut across another's land. — Also termed *naked licensee*; *mere licensee.*

licensee by invitation. One who is expressly or impliedly permitted to enter another's premises to transact business with the owner or occupant or to perform an act benefiting the owner or occupant.

licensee by permission. One who has the owner's permission or passive consent to enter the owner's premises for one's own convenience, curiosity, or entertainment.

licensee with an interest. See INVITEE.

mere licensee. See *bare licensee.*

naked licensee. See *bare licensee.*

license fee. 1. A monetary charge imposed by a governmental authority for the privilege of pursuing a particular occupation, business, or activity. — Also termed *license tax.* **2.** A charge of this type accompanied by a requirement that the licensee take some action, or be subjected to regulations or restrictions.

license in amortization. *Hist.* A license authorizing the conveyance of property otherwise invalid under the statutes of mortmain. See MORTMAIN.

license tax. See LICENSE FEE (1).

licensing. 1. The sale of a license authorizing another to use something (such as computer software) protected by copyright, patent, or trademark. **2.** A governmental body's process of issuing a license.

licensor. One who grants a license to another. — Also spelled *licenser.*

licentia (li-**sen**-shee-ə), *n.* [fr. Latin *licere* "to be lawful"] *Hist.* License; permission.

licentia concordandi (li-**sen**-shee-ə kon-kor-**dan**-dɪ), *n.* [Law Latin "license to agree"] *Hist.* One of the proceedings on levying a fine of lands. See CONGÉ D'ACCORDER.

> "The *licentia concordandi,* or leave to agree the suit. For, as soon as the action is brought, the defendant knowing himself to be in the wrong, is supposed to make overtures of peace and accommodation to the plaintiff. Who, accepting them, but having, upon suing out the writ, given pledges to prosecute his suit, which he endangers if he now deserts it without license, he therefore applies to the court for leave to make the matter up." 2 William Blackstone, *Commentaries on the Laws of England* 350 (1766).

licentia loquendi (li-**sen**-shee-ə loh-**kwen**-dɪ). [Latin "license to speak"] See IMPARLANCE.

licentia surgendi (li-**sen**-shee-ə sər-**jen**-dɪ), *n.* [Law Latin "license to arise"] *Hist.* Permission or writ from the court to a tenant in a real action to get out of bed and appear in court, following the tenant's earlier plea of inability to appear because of illness that confined the tenant to bed. • The tenant could lose the case by default for falsely claiming illness. See DE MALO; ESSOIN.

licentiate (lɪ-**sen**-shee-ət), *n.* One who has obtained a license or authoritative permission to exercise some function, esp. to practice a profession <a licentiate in law should be held to high ethical standards>.

licentious (lɪ-**sen**-shəs), *adj.* Lacking or ignoring moral or legal restraint, esp. in sexual activity; lewd; lascivious. — **licentiousness,** *n.*

licere (li-**seer**-ee), *vb.* [Latin] *Roman law.* **1.** To be allowed by law. **2.** To bid for an item, as at an auction.

licet (**lɪ**-set *or* **lis**-ət). [Latin] *Hist.* **1.** It is permitted; it is lawful. **2.** It is conceded; it is granted.

licit (**lis**-it), *adj.* Not forbidden by law; permitted; legal. — **licitly,** *adv.*

licitari (lis-ə-**tair**-ee), *vb.* [Latin] *Roman law.* To bid for an item, esp. repeatedly during the same sale.

licitation (lis-ə-**tay**-shən). **1.** The offering for sale or bidding for purchase at an auction; esp., in civil law, an auction held to partition property held in common. **2.** CANT.

licitator (lis-ə-**tay**-tər), *n.* [Latin] *Roman law.* The bidder at a sale.

Lidford law (**lid**-fərd). *Hist.* A form of lynch law permitting a person to be punished first and tried later. • The term took its name from the town of Lidford (now Lydford) where this type of action supposedly took place. Cf. *Jedburgh justice* under JUSTICE.

lie, *vb.* **1.** To tell an untruth; to speak or write falsely <she lied on the witness stand>. See PERJURY. **2.** To have foundation in the law; to be legally supportable, sustainable, or proper <in such a situation, an action lies in tort>. **3.** To exist; to reside <final appeal lies with the Supreme Court>.

lie detector. See POLYGRAPH.

liege (leej), *adj. Hist.* **1.** Entitled to feudal allegiance and service. **2.** Bound by feudal tenure to a lord paramount; owing allegiance and service. **3.** Loyal; faithful. — Also termed *ligius.*

liege, *n. Hist.* **1.** A vassal bound to feudal allegiance. — Also termed *liege man*; *liege woman.* **2.** A loyal subject of a monarch or other sovereign. **3.** A feudal lord entitled to allegiance and service; a sovereign or superior lord. — Also termed (in sense 3) *liege lord.*

liege homage, *n. Hist.* Homage paid by one sovereign to another, including pledges of loyalty and services.

liege lord, *n. Hist.* See LIEGE (3).

liege man, *n. Hist.* See LIEGE (1).

lieger, *n. Archaic.* See LEDGER (2).

liege woman, *n. Hist.* See LIEGE (1).

lie in franchise, *vb. Hist.* (Of wrecks, waifs, strays, etc.) to be seizable without judicial action.

lie in grant, *vb. Hist.* (Of incorporeal hereditaments) to be passable by deed or charter without the ceremony of livery of seisin.

lie in livery, *vb. Hist.* (Of corporeal hereditaments) to be passable by livery of seisin rather than by deed.

lien (leen *or* **lee**-ən), *n.* A legal right or interest that a creditor has in another's property, lasting usu. until a debt or duty that it secures is satisfied. • Typically, the creditor does not take possession of the property on which the lien has been obtained. — **lien,** *vb.* — **lienable, liened,** *adj.* Cf. PLEDGE (1).

accountant's lien. The right of an accountant to retain a client's papers until the accountant's fees have been paid.

agent's lien. A lien against property of the estate, in favor of an agent, to secure the agent's compensation as well as all necessary expenses incurred under the agent's power.

agister's lien (ə-**jis**-tərz). A lien on the animals under an agister's care, to secure payment of the agister's fee. See AGISTER; AGISTMENT.

agricultural lien. **1.** A statutory lien that protects a seller of farming equipment by giving the seller a lien on crops grown with the equipment. **2.** *Secured transactions.* An interest (other than a security interest) in farm products having three characteristics: (1) it must secure payment or performance of an obligation for goods or services furnished in connection with a debtor's farming operation, or of an obligation for rent on real property leased by a debtor in connection with farming; (2) it must be created by statute in favor of a person either who in the ordinary course of business furnished goods or services to a debtor in connection with the debtor's farming, or who leased real property to a debtor in connection with the debtor's farming; and (3) the effectiveness of the interest must not depend on the person's possession of the personal property. UCC § 9–102(a)(3).

architect's lien. A statutory lien on real property in favor of an architect who has drawn the plans for and supervised the construction of improvements on the property.

artisan's lien. See *mechanic's lien.*

attachment lien. A lien on property seized by prejudgment attachment. • Such a lien is initially inchoate but becomes final and perfected upon entry of a judgment for the attaching creditor and relates back to the date when the lien first arose. — Also termed *lien of attachment.* See ATTACHMENT.

attorney's lien. The right of an attorney to hold or retain a client's money or property (a *retaining lien*) or to encumber money payable to the client and possessed by the court (a *charging lien*) until the attorney's fees have been properly determined and paid.

banker's lien. The right of a bank to satisfy a customer's matured debt by seizing the customer's money or property in the bank's possession.

blanket lien. A lien that gives a creditor the entitlement to take possession of any or all of the debtor's real property to cover a delinquent loan.

carrier's lien. A carrier's right to retain possession of cargo until the owner of the cargo pays its shipping costs.

charging lien. **1.** An attorney's lien on a judgment that the attorney has helped the client obtain. **2.** A lien on specified property in the debtor's possession.

chattel lien. See *mechanic's lien.*

choate lien (**koh**-it). A lien in which the lienholder, the property, and the monetary amount are established so that the lien is perfected and nothing else needs to be done to make it enforceable.

common-law lien. **1.** A lien granted by the common law, rather than by statute, equity, or agreement by the parties. **2.** The right of one person to retain possession of property belonging to another until certain demands of the possessing party are met. • This type of lien, unlike an equitable lien, cannot exist without possession.

concurrent lien. One of two or more liens of equal priority attaching to the same property.

construction lien. See *mechanic's lien.*

consummate lien (kən-**səm**-it). A judgment lien arising after the denial of a motion for a new trial. Cf. *inchoate lien.*

conventional lien. A lien that is created by the express agreement of the parties, in circumstances in which the law would not create a lien.

deferred lien. A lien effective at a future date, as distinguished from a present lien that is currently possessory.

demurrage lien (di-**mər**-ij). A carrier's lien on goods for any unpaid demurrage charges. See DEMURRAGE.

dragnet lien. A lien that is enlarged to cover any additional credit extended to the debtor by the same creditor.

equitable lien. A right, enforceable only in equity, to have a demand satisfied from a particular fund or specific property, without having possession of the fund or property. • It arises mainly in four circumstances: (1) when an occupant of land, believing in good faith to be the owner of that land, makes improvements, repairs, or other expenditures that permanently increase the land's value, (2) when one of two or more joint owners makes expenditures of that kind, (3) when a tenant for life completes permanent and beneficial improvements to the estate begun earlier by the testator, and (4) when land or other property is transferred subject to the payment of debts, legacies, portions, or annuities to third persons.

execution lien. A lien on property seized by a levy of execution. • Such a lien gives the execution creditor priority over later transferees of the property and over prior unrecorded conveyances of interests in the property. See EXECUTION.

factor's lien. A lien, usu. statutory, on property held on consignment by a factor. • It allows the factor to keep possession of the property until the account has been settled. See UCC § 9–102(2). See FACTOR (2).

first lien. A lien that takes priority over all other charges or encumbrances on the same property and that must be satisfied before other charges may share in proceeds from the property's sale.

floating lien. **1.** A lien that is expanded to cover any additional property obtained by the debtor while the debt is outstanding. **2.** A lien that continues to exist even when the collateral changes in character, classification, or location. — Also termed *floating charge.*

garnishment lien. A lien on a debtor's property held by a garnishee. • Such a lien attaches in favor of the garnishing creditor when a garnishment summons is served and also impounds any credits the garnishee owes the debtor so that they must be paid to the garnishing creditor. — Also termed *lien of garnishment.* See GARNISHMENT.

general lien. A possessory lien by which the lienholder may retain any of the debtor's goods in the lienholder's possession until any debt due from the debtor, whether in connection with the retained goods or otherwise, has been paid. • Factors, insurance brokers, packers, stockbrokers, and bankers have a general lien over the property of their clients or customers. Cf. *particular lien.*

grantor's lien. See *vendor's lien.*

hotelkeeper's lien. A possessory or statutory lien allowing an innkeeper to hold, as security for payment, personal property that a guest brought into the hotel.

inchoate lien (in-**koh**-it). A judgment lien that may be defeated if the judgment is vacated or a motion for new trial is granted. Cf. *consummate lien.*

involuntary lien. A lien arising without the debtor's consent.

judgment lien. A lien imposed on a judgment debtor's nonexempt property. • This lien gives the judgment creditor the right to attach the judgment debtor's property. — Also termed *lien of judgment.* See EXEMPT PROPERTY.

judicial lien. A lien obtained by judgment, levy, sequestration, or other legal or equitable process or proceeding. • If a debtor is adjudged to owe money to a creditor and the judgment has not been satisfied, the creditor can ask the court to impose a lien on specific property owned and possessed by the debtor. After the court imposes the lien, it usu. issues a writ directing the local sheriff to seize the property, sell it, and turn over the proceeds to the creditor.

junior lien. A lien that is subordinate to one or more other liens on the same property.

laborer's lien. See *mechanic's lien.*

landlord's lien. **1.** At common law, a lien that gave a landlord the right to seize a tenant's property and sell it publicly to satisfy overdue rent. See DISTRESS. **2.** Generally, a statutory lien on a tenant's personal property at the leased premises in favor of a landlord who receives preferred-creditor status on that property. • Such a lien usu. secures the payment of overdue rent or compensation for damage to the premises.

lien of attachment. See *attachment lien.*

lien of factor at common law. *Hist.* A lien not created by statute; a common-law lien.

lien of garnishment. See *garnishment lien.*

lien of judgment. See *judgment lien.*

maritime lien. A lien on a vessel, given to secure the claim of a creditor who provided maritime services to the vessel or who suffered an injury from the vessel's use. — Also termed *tacit hypothecation.*

mechanic's lien. A statutory lien that secures payment for labor or materials supplied in improving, repairing, or maintaining real or personal property, such as a building, an automobile, or the like. — Also termed *artisan's lien*; *chattel lien* (for personal property); *construction lien* (for labor); *garageman's lien* (for repaired vehicles); *laborer's lien* (for labor); *materialman's lien* (for materials).

mortgage lien. A lien on the mortgagor's property securing the mortgage.

municipal lien. A lien by a municipal corporation against a property owner for the owner's proportionate share of a public improvement that specially and individually benefits the owner.

particular lien. A possessory lien by which the possessor of goods has the right to retain specific goods until a debt incurred in connection with those goods has been paid. — Also termed *special lien.* Cf. *general lien.*

possessory garageman's lien. A lien on a vehicle in the amount of the repairs performed by the garage.

possessory lien. A lien allowing the creditor to keep possession of the encumbered property until the debt is satisfied. • A power of sale may or may not be combined with this right of possession. Examples include pledges of chattels, the liens of innkeepers, garageman's liens, and vendor's liens. See PLEDGE.

prior lien. A lien that is superior to one or more other liens on the same property, usu. because it was perfected first. — Also termed *priority lien.*

retaining lien. An attorney's right to retain a client's papers in the attorney's possession until the client has paid for the attorney's services. • The attorney's retaining lien is barred by law in some states.

second lien. A lien that is next in rank after a first lien on the same property and therefore is next entitled to satisfaction out of the proceeds from the property's sale.

secret lien. A lien not appearing of record and unknown to purchasers; a lien reserved by the vendor and kept hidden from third parties, to secure the payment of goods after delivery.

senior lien. A lien that has priority over other liens on the same property.

special lien. See *particular lien.*

specific lien. A lien secured on a particular thing by a contract or by a judgment, execution, attachment, or other legal proceeding.

statutory lien. **1.** A lien arising solely by force of statute, not by agreement of the parties. • Examples are federal tax liens and mechanic's liens. **2.** *Bankruptcy.* Either of two types of liens: (1) a lien arising solely by force of a statute on specified circumstances or conditions, or (2) a lien of distress for rent, whether or not statutory. • For bankruptcy purposes, a statutory lien does not include a security interest or judicial lien, whether or not the interest or lien arises from or is made effective by a statute.

tax lien. **1.** A lien placed on property and all rights to property by the federal government for unpaid federal taxes. **2.** A lien on real estate in favor of a state or local government that may be foreclosed for nonpayment of taxes. • A majority of states have adopted the Uniform Federal Tax Lien Registration Act.

vendee's lien. *Real estate.* A buyer's lien on the purchased land as security for repayment of purchase money paid in, enforceable if the seller does not or cannot convey good title.

vendor's lien. **1.** *Real estate.* A seller's lien on land as security for the purchase price. • This lien may be foreclosed in the same way as a mortgage: the buyer usu. has a redemption period within which to pay the full purchase price. — Also termed *grantor's lien.* **2.** A lien held by a seller of goods, who retains possession of the goods until the buyer has paid in full.

voluntary lien. A lien created with the debtor's consent.

warehouser's lien. A lien covering storage charges for goods stored with a bailee. — Also termed *warehouseman's lien.*

lienable, *adj.* (Of property) legally amenable to a lien; capable of being subject to a lien.

lien account. See ACCOUNT.

lien avoidance. *Bankruptcy.* A debtor's depriving a creditor of a security interest in an asset of the bankruptcy estate. 11 USCA §§ 506(d), 522(f).

lien creditor. See CREDITOR.

lienee (leen-**ee** *or* lee-ən-**ee**). **1.** One whose property is subject to a lien. **2.** An encumbrancer who holds a lien; LIENHOLDER.

> "[A] mortgagee is the owner of the property, while a pledgee or other lienee is merely an encumbrancer of it." John Salmond, *Jurisprudence* 440 (Glanville L. Williams ed., 10th ed. 1947).

lienholder. A person having or owning a lien. — Also termed *lienor; lienee.*

lien of a covenant. The beginning portion of a covenant, stating the names of the parties and the character of the covenant.

lien of attachment. See *attachment lien* under LIEN.

lien of factor at common law. See LIEN.

lien of garnishment. See *garnishment lien* under LIEN.

lien of judgment. See *judgment lien* under LIEN.

lienor. See LIENHOLDER.

lien-stripping. *Bankruptcy.* The practice of splitting a mortgagee's secured claim into secured and unsecured components and reducing the claim to the market value of the debtor's residence, thereby allowing the debtor to modify the terms of the mortgage and reduce the amount of the debt. • The U.S. Supreme Court has prohibited lien-stripping in all Chapter 7 cases (*Nobelman v. American Savs. Bank,* 508 U.S. 324, 113 S.Ct. 2106 (1993)) and in Chapter 13 cases involving a debtor's principal residence (*Dewsnup v. Timm,* 502 U.S. 410, 112 S.Ct. 773 (1992)), and the Bankruptcy Reform Act of 1994 modified the Bankruptcy Code to prohibit lien-stripping in Chapter 11 cases involving an individual's principal residence.

lien theory. The idea that a mortgage resembles a lien, so that the mortgagee acquires only a lien on the property and the mortgagor retains both legal and equitable title unless a valid foreclosure occurs. • Most American states — commonly called *lien states, lien jurisdictions,* or *lien-theory jurisdictions* — have adopted this theory. Cf. TITLE THEORY.

lien waiver. See WAIVER (2).

lieu conus (l[y]oo **kon**-yoo), *n.* [Law French] *Hist.* A place generally known and noticed by those about it, such as a castle or manor.

lieu land. See LAND.

lieu tax. See TAX.

lieutenancy. The rank, office, or commission of a lieutenant. See COMMISSION OF LIEUTENANCY.

lieutenant. **1.** A deputy of or substitute for another; one acting by vicarious authority <he sent his chief lieutenant to the meeting>. **2.** A composite part of the title of many government and military officials who are subordinate to others, esp. when the duties of the higher official may devolve to the subordinate <lieutenant governor>. **3.** In the U.S. Army, a commissioned officer next below captain. **4.** In the U.S. Navy, an officer next below lieutenant commander.

lieutenant colonel. In the U.S. military, an officer next below colonel and above major.

lieutenant commander. In the U.S. Navy, an officer next below commander and above lieutenant.

lieutenant general. In the U.S. Army, an officer next below four-star general and above major general.

lieutenant governor. A deputy or subordinate governor, sometimes charged with such duties as presiding over the state legislature, but esp. important as the governor's successor if the governor dies, resigns, or becomes disabled.

life annuity. See ANNUITY.

life beneficiary. One who receives payments or other benefits from a trust for life.

life-care contract. An agreement in which one party is assured of care and maintenance for life in exchange for transferring property to the other party.

life estate. See ESTATE.

life estate pur autre vie. See ESTATE.

life expectancy. 1. The period for which a person of a given age and sex is expected to live, according to actuarial tables. **2.** The period for which a given person is expected to live, taking into account individualized characteristics like heredity, past and present diseases, and other relevant medical data. See ACTUARIAL TABLE; LIFE TABLE.

life-hold. See *life land* under LAND.

life in being. Under the rule against perpetuities, anyone alive when a future interest is created, whether or not the person has an interest in the estate. Cf. MEASURING LIFE.

life-income period-certain annuity. See ANNUITY.

life insurance. See INSURANCE.

life-insurance trust. See TRUST.

life interest. An interest in real or personal property measured by the duration of the holder's or another named person's life. See *life estate* under ESTATE.

life land. See LAND.

lifelode. See LIVELODE.

life of a writ. The effective period during which a writ may be levied. • That period usu. ends on the day that the law or the writ itself provides that it must be returned to court.

life-owner. See LIFE TENANT.

life peerage. *English law.* The grant of the noble title of baron to a person for life, offered through letters patent. • The Life Peerages Act of 1958 first allowed this and removed the disqualifications of women from serving in the House of Lords. See PEER.

life policy. See INSURANCE POLICY.

life-qualified jury. See JURY.

lifer. See NONREMOVABLE INMATE.

life-rent. *Scots law.* See USUFRUCT.

life sentence. See SENTENCE.

life-sustaining procedure. A medical procedure that uses mechanical or artificial means to sustain, restore, or substitute for a vital function and that serves only or mainly to postpone death.

life table. An actuarial table that gives the probable proportions of people who will live to different ages. Cf. ACTUARIAL TABLE.

life tenancy. See *life estate* under ESTATE.

life tenant. A person who, until death, is beneficially entitled to land; the holder of a life estate. — Also termed *tenant for life*; *life-owner*. See *life estate* under ESTATE.

equitable life tenant. A life tenant not automatically entitled to possession but who makes an election allowed by law to a person of that status — such as a spouse — and to whom a court will normally grant possession if security or an undertaking is given.

legal life tenant. A life tenant who is automatically entitled to possession by virtue of a legal estate.

lifetime gift. See *inter vivos gift* under GIFT.

LIFO (lI-foh). *abbr.* LAST-IN, FIRST-OUT.

lift, *vb.* **1.** To stop or put an end to; to revoke or rescind <lift the stay>. **2.** To discharge or pay off (a debt or obligation) <lift a mortgage>. **3.** *Slang.* To steal <lift a purse>.

lifting costs. *Oil & gas.* The cost of producing oil and gas after drilling is complete but before the oil and gas is removed from the property, including transportation costs, labor, costs of supervision, supplies, costs of operating the pumps, electricity, repairs, depreciation, certain royalties payable to the lessor, gross-production taxes, and other incidental expenses.

liga (**lee**-gə), *n.* [Law Latin] *Hist.* A league or confederation.

ligan (lI-gən), *n.* See LAGAN.

ligare (lə-**gair**-ee), *vb.* [Latin] *Hist.* **1.** To tie or bind. **2.** To enter into a treaty or league.

ligea (**lee**-jee-ə), *n.* [Law Latin] *Hist.* A female subject; a liege woman. See LIEGE (1).

ligeance (lI-jənts *or* **lee**-jənts). *Hist.* **1.** The obedience of a citizen to the citizen's sovereign or government; allegiance. **2.** The territory of a state or sovereign. — Also spelled *liegeance.* See LIEGE.

> "Liegeance is a true and faithful obedience of the subject due to his sovereign; and this liegeance, which is an incident inseparable to every subject, is in four manners; the first is natural, the second acquired, the third local, and the fourth legal." *Termes de la Ley* 280 (1st Am. ed. 1812).

ligen, *n.* See LAGAN.

ligeus (**lee**-jee-əs), *n.* [Law Latin] *Hist.* A male subject; a liege man. See LIEGE (1).

light-and-air easement. See EASEMENT.

lighterage (lI-tər-ij). **1.** The loading and unloading of goods between a ship and a lighter. **2.** The compensation paid for this service. **3.** The loading and unloading of freight between a railroad car and a ship's side.

light most favorable. The standard of scrutinizing or interpreting a verdict by accepting as true all evidence and inferences that support it and disregarding all contrary evidence and inferences <in reviewing the defendant's motion for judgment notwithstanding the verdict, the court reviewed the evidence in the light most favorable to the verdict>. — Also termed *most favorable light.*

lights, ancient. See ANCIENT-LIGHTS DOCTRINE.

light work. See WORK.

ligius (**lee**-jee-əs), *n.* [Law Latin] *Hist.* A person bound to another by solemn relationship, as between subject and sovereign. See LIEGE.

lignagium (lig-**nay**-jee-əm), *n.* [Law Latin] *Hist.* **1.** A right to cut firewood. **2.** The payment for this right.

ligula (**lig**-yə-lə), *n.* [Law Latin] *Hist.* A copy or transcript of a court roll or deed.

like, *adj.* **1.** Equal in quantity, quality, or degree; corresponding exactly <like copies>. **2.** Similar or substantially similar <like character>.

like-kind exchange. An exchange of trade, business, or investment property (except inventory or securities) for property of the same kind, class, or character. • Such an exchange is not taxable unless cash or other property is received. IRC (26 USCA) § 1031.

like-kind property. *Tax.* Property that is of such a similar kind, class, or character to other property that a gain from an exchange of the property is not recognized for federal income-tax purposes. See LIKE-KIND EXCHANGE.

likelihood-of-confusion test. *Trademark.* The test for infringement, based on the probability that a substantial number of ordinarily prudent buyers will be misled or confused about the source of a product when its trademark allegedly infringes on that of an earlier product.

likelihood-of-success-on-the-merits test. *Civil procedure.* The rule that a litigant who seeks a preliminary injunction, or seeks to forestall the effects of a judgment during appeal, must show a reasonable probability of success in the litigation or appeal.

limbo time. The period when an employee is neither on duty nor off duty, as a railroad worker awaiting transportation from a duty assignment to the place of final release. 49 USCA § 21103(b)(4); *Brotherhood of Locomo-*

tive Eng'rs v. Atchison, Topeka & Santa Fe R.R., 516 U.S. 152, 116 S.Ct. 595 (1996).

limenarcha (lim-ən-**ahr**-kə), *n.* [Latin] *Roman law.* An officer in charge of a harbor or port.

limine. See IN LIMINE.

limine out (**lim**-ə-nee), *vb.* (Of a court) to exclude (evidence) by granting a motion in limine <the trial judge limined out most of the plaintiff's medical records>.

limit, *n.* **1.** A restriction or restraint. **2.** A boundary or defining line. **3.** The extent of power, right, or authority. — **limit,** *vb.* — **limited,** *adj.*

limitation. 1. The act of limiting; the state of being limited. **2.** A restriction. **3.** A statutory period after which a lawsuit or prosecution cannot be brought in court. — Also termed *limitations period*; *limitation period.* See STATUTE OF LIMITATIONS. Cf. LACHES. **4.** *Property.* The restriction of the extent of an estate; the creation by deed or devise of a lesser estate out of a fee simple. See WORDS OF LIMITATION.

collateral limitation. *Hist.* A limitation that makes the duration of an estate dependent on another event (other than the life of the grantee), such as an estate to A until B turns 21.

conditional limitation. **1.** See *executory limitation.* **2.** A lease provision that automatically terminates the lease if a specified event occurs, such as if the lessee defaults.

executory limitation. A restriction that causes an estate to automatically end and revest in a third party upon the happening of a specified event. • This type of limitation, which was not recognized at common law, can be created only as a shifting use or executory devise. It is just simply a condition subsequent in favor of someone other than the transferor. — Also termed *conditional limitation.* See *fee simple subject to an executory limitation* under FEE SIMPLE.

"When a condition subsequent is created in favor of someone other than the transferor, the *Restatement of Property* calls the condition subsequent an *executory limitation.* It calls A's estate an *estate in fee simple subject to an executory limitation.*" Thomas F. Bergin & Paul G. Haskell, *Preface to Estates in Land and Future Interests* 52 (2d ed. 1984).

limitation over. An additional estate created or contemplated in a conveyance, to be enjoyed after the first estate expires or is exhausted. • An example of language giving rise to a limitation over is "to A for life, remainder to B."

special limitation. A restriction that causes an estate to end automatically and revert to the grantor upon the happening of a specified event. See *fee simple determinable* under FEE SIMPLE.

"[I]f a deed or will uses such words as 'for so long as,' 'while,' 'during,' or 'until' to introduce the circumstances under which an estate may end prior to its running its maximum course, it is generally assumed that a special limitation was intended." Thomas F. Bergin & Paul G. Haskell, *Preface to Estates in Land and Future Interests* 50 (2d ed. 1984).

limitation of assize. *Hist.* A period prescribed by statute within which a person is required to allege that the person was properly seised of lands sued for under a writ of assize.

limitation-of-damages clause. A contractual provision by which the parties agree on a maximum amount of damages recoverable for a future breach of the agreement. — Also termed *liquidated-damages clause.*

limitation-of-liability act. A federal or state law that limits the type of damages that may be recovered, the liability of particular persons or groups, or the time during which an action may be brought. See FEDERAL TORT CLAIMS ACT; *sovereign immunity* under IMMUNITY (1).

limitation-of-remedies clause. A contractual provision that restricts the remedies available to the parties if a party defaults. • Under the UCC, such a clause is valid unless it fails of its essential purpose or it unconscionably limits consequential damages. UCC § 2–719. Cf. LIQUIDATED-DAMAGES CLAUSE; PENALTY CLAUSE.

limitation on indebtedness. See DEBT LIMITATION.

limitation over. See LIMITATION.

limitation period. See LIMITATION (3).

limitations, statute of. See STATUTE OF LIMITATIONS.

limitations period. See LIMITATION (3).

limited administration. See ADMINISTRATION.

limited admissibility. See ADMISSIBILITY.

limited appeal. See APPEAL.

limited appearance. See *special appearance* under APPEARANCE.

limited-capacity well. See WELL.

limited company. See COMPANY.

limited court. See COURT.

limited defense. See *personal defense* under DEFENSE (4).

limited divorce. See DIVORCE.

limited executor. See EXECUTOR.

limited fee. See *base fee* under FEE (2).

limited guaranty. See GUARANTY.

limited interdiction. See INTERDICTION (2).

limited interpretation. See *restrictive interpretation* under INTERPRETATION.

limited jurisdiction. See JURISDICTION.

limited liability. See LIABILITY.

limited-liability company. See COMPANY.

limited-liability corporation. See *limited-liability company* under COMPANY.

limited-liability partnership. See PARTNERSHIP.

limited monarchy. See MONARCHY.

limited owner. See OWNER.

limited partner. See PARTNER.

limited partnership. See PARTNERSHIP.

limited partnership association. See PARTNERSHIP ASSOCIATION.

limited-payment life insurance. See INSURANCE.

limited policy. See INSURANCE POLICY.

limited policy insurance. See INSURANCE.

limited power of appointment. See POWER OF APPOINTMENT.

limited publication. See PUBLICATION.

limited public forum. See *designated public forum* under PUBLIC FORUM.

limited-purpose public figure. See PUBLIC FIGURE.

limited trust. See TRUST.

limited veto. See *qualified veto* under VETO.

limited warranty. See WARRANTY (2).

limit of liability. See LIABILITY LIMIT.

limit order. See ORDER (4).

Lincoln's Inn. One of the Inns of Court. See INN OF COURT (1).

Lindbergh Act. See FEDERAL KIDNAPPING ACT.

line, *n.* **1.** A demarcation, border, or limit <the line between right and wrong>. **2.** A person's occupation or business <what line of business is Watson in?>. **3.** The ancestry of a person; lineage <the Fergusons came from a long line of wheat farmers>.

> ***collateral line.*** A line of descent connecting persons who are not directly related to each other as ascendants or descendants, but whose relationship consists in common descent from the same ancestor.
>
> ***direct line.*** A line of descent traced through only those persons who are related to each other directly as ascendants or descendants.
>
> ***maternal line.*** A person's ancestry or relationship with another traced through the mother.
>
> ***paternal line.*** A person's ancestry or relationship with another traced through the father.

4. In manufacturing, a series of closely related products.

linea (**lin**-ee-ə), *n.* [Latin "line"] *Hist.* A line of descent.

> ***linea directa*** (**lin**-ee-ə də-**rek**-tə), *n.* [Latin "direct line"] *Roman law.* The relationship among persons in the direct line of ascent and descent, such as grandfather, father, and son.

linea transversa (**lin**-ee-ə trans-**vər**-sə), *n.* [Latin "transverse line"] *Roman law.* The relationship between persons in the collateral line of descent, such as uncle and nephew. — Also termed *linea obliqua.*

lineage (**lin**-ee-əj). Ancestry and progeny; family, ascending or descending.

lineal (**lin**-ee-əl), *adj.* Derived from or relating to common ancestors, esp. in a direct line; hereditary. Cf. COLLATERAL (1).

lineal, *n.* A lineal descendant; a direct blood relative.

lineal consanguinity. See CONSANGUINITY.

lineal descent. See DESCENT.

lineal heir. See HEIR.

lineal warranty. See WARRANTY (1).

linea obliqua. See *linea transversa* under LINEA.

linea reta. See LINEA.

linea transversalis. See LINEA.

line-item veto. See VETO.

line of credit. The maximum amount of borrowing power extended to a borrower by a given lender, to be drawn upon by the borrower as needed. — Also termed *credit line.*

line of demarcation. See DEMARCATION LINE.

line of title. CHAIN OF TITLE.

lines and corners. See METES AND BOUNDS.

lineup. A police identification procedure in which a criminal suspect and other physically similar persons are shown to the victim or a witness to determine whether the suspect can be identified as the perpetrator of the crime. — Also termed (in BrE) *identification parade.* Cf. SHOWUP.

Lingle **test.** *Labor law.* The principle that a union member's state-law claim against the employer is not preempted by the Labor–Management Relations Act if resolution of the state-law claim does not require an interpretation of the collective-bargaining agreement. *Lingle v. Norge Division of Magic Chef, Inc.,* 486 U.S. 399, 108 S.Ct. 1877 (1988). See MARCUS MODEL; WHITE MODEL.

link, *n.* **1.** A unit in a connected series; something that binds separate things <link in the chain of title>. **2.** A unit of land measurement <one link equals 7.92 inches>.

link financing. See FINANCING.

link-in-chain principle. *Criminal procedure.* The principle that a criminal defendant's Fifth Amendment privilege against self-incrimination protects the defendant from not only answering directly incriminating questions but also giving answers that might connect the defendant to criminal activity in the chain of evidence.

LIP. *abbr.* LEGALLY INCAPACITATED PERSON.

liquere (li-**kweer**-ee), *vb.* [Latin] *Roman law.* To be clear, evident, or apparent. • When a judex appointed to try a civil case swore under oath *sibi non liquere* ("that it was not clear to him"), he would be discharged from deciding the case. See NON LIQUET.

liquid, *adj.* **1.** (Of an asset) capable of being readily converted into cash. **2.** (Of a person or entity) possessing assets that can be readily converted into cash.

liquid asset. See *current asset* under ASSET.

liquidate, *vb.* **1.** To determine by litigation or agreement the amount of (damages or indebtedness). **2.** To settle (an obligation) by payment or other adjustment. **3.** To ascertain the liabilities and distribute the assets of (an entity), esp. in bankruptcy or dissolution. **4.** To convert (a nonliquid asset) into cash. **5.** To liquidate something, such as a debt or corporation. **6.** *Slang.* To get rid of (a person), esp. by killing.

liquidated, *adj.* **1.** (Of an amount or debt) settled or determined, esp. by agreement. **2.** (Of an asset or assets) converted into cash.

liquidated amount. A figure readily computed, based on an agreement's terms.

liquidated claim. See CLAIM (3).

liquidated damages. See DAMAGES.

liquidated-damages clause. A contractual provision that determines in advance the measure of damages if a party breaches the agreement. • Traditionally, courts have upheld such a clause unless the agreed-on sum is deemed a penalty for one of the following reasons: (1) the sum grossly exceeds the probable damages on breach, (2) the same sum is made payable for any variety of different breaches (some major, some minor), or (3) a mere delay in payment has been listed among the events of default. Cf. LIMITATION-OF-REMEDIES CLAUSE; PENALTY CLAUSE.

liquidated debt. See DEBT.

liquidated demand. See *liquidated claim* under CLAIM (2).

liquidating distribution. See DISTRIBUTION.

liquidating dividend. See *liquidation dividend* under DIVIDEND.

liquidating partner. See PARTNER.

liquidating price. See *redemption price* under PRICE.

liquidating trust. See TRUST.

liquidation, *n.* **1.** The act of determining by agreement or by litigation the exact amount of something (as a debt or damages) that before was uncertain. **2.** The act of settling a debt by payment or other satisfaction. **3.** The act or process of converting assets into cash, esp. to settle debts.

one-month liquidation. A special election, available to certain shareholders, that determines how the distributions received in liquidation by electing shareholders will be treated for federal income-tax purposes. • To qualify for the election, the corporation must be completely liquidated within one month. IRC § 333 (26 USCA § 333).

partial liquidation. A liquidation that does not completely dispose of a company's assets; esp., a liquidation occurring when some corporate assets are distributed to shareholders (usu. on a pro rata basis) and the corporation continues to operate in a restricted form.

twelve-month liquidation. A liquidation occurring within 12 months from adoption of the liquidation plan to complete liquidation, subject to a tax law prohibiting the company from recognizing any gains or losses on property sold within that time frame. • Generally, inventory will not be included unless a bulk sale occurs. IRC (26 USCA) § 337.

4. *Bankruptcy.* The process — under Chapter 7 of the Bankruptcy Code — of collecting a debtor's nonexempt property, converting that property to cash, and distributing the cash to the various creditors. • Upon liquidation, the debtor hopes to obtain a discharge, which releases the debtor from any further personal liability for prebankruptcy debts. Cf. REHABILITATION (3).

liquidation dividend. See DIVIDEND.

liquidation preference. See PREFERENCE.

liquidation price. See PRICE.

liquidation value. See VALUE.

liquidator. A person appointed to wind up a business's affairs, esp. by selling off its assets. See LIQUIDATION (3), (4). Cf. RECEIVER.

liquid debt. See DEBT.

liquidity. 1. The quality or state of being readily convertible to cash. **2.** *Securities.* The characteristic of having enough units in the market that large transactions can occur without substantial price variations. • Most stocks traded on the New York Stock Exchange, for example, have liquidity.

liquidity ratio. The ratio between a person's or entity's assets that are held in cash or liquid form and the amount of the person's or entity's current liabilities, indicating the ability to pay current debts as they come due.

liquor offense. See OFFENSE (1).

lis (lis). [Latin] A piece of litigation; a controversy or dispute.

lis alibi pendens (lis **al**-ə-bɪ **pen**-dənz). [Latin] A lawsuit pending elsewhere.

lis mota (lis **moh**-tə), *n.* [Latin "a lawsuit moved"] *Hist.* A dispute that has begun and later forms the basis of a lawsuit.

lis pendens (lis **pen**-dənz). [Latin "a pending lawsuit"] **1.** A pending lawsuit. **2.** The jurisdiction, power, or control acquired by a court over property while a legal action is pending. **3.** A notice, recorded in the chain of title to real property, required or permitted in some jurisdictions to warn all persons that certain property is the subject matter of litigation, and that any interests acquired during the pendency of the suit are subject to its outcome. — Also termed (in sense 3) *notice of lis pendens*; *notice of pendency*. Cf. PENDENTE LITE.

list, *n.* **1.** A roll or register, as of names. **2.** A docket of cases ready for hearing or trial. See CALENDAR (2); DOCKET.

list, *vb.* **1.** To set down or enter (information) in a list. **2.** To register (a security) on an exchange so that it may be publicly traded. **3.** To place (property) for sale under an agreement with a real-estate agent or broker.

listed security. See SECURITY.

listed security exchange. An organized secondary security market operating at a designated location, such as the New York Stock Exchange.

listed stock. See *listed security* under SECURITY.

lister. A person authorized to compile lists of taxable property for assessment and appraisal; an assessor.

listing. 1. *Real estate.* An agreement between a property owner and an agent, whereby the agent agrees to try to secure a buyer or tenant for a specific property at a certain price and terms in return for a fee or commission. — Also termed *listing agreement*.

exclusive-agency listing. A listing providing that one agent has the right to be the only person, other than the owner, to sell the property during a specified period. — Also termed *exclusive-authorization-to-sell listing*.

general listing. See *open listing*.

multiple listing. A listing providing that the agent will allow other agents to try to sell the property. • Under this agreement, the original agent gives the selling agent a percentage of the commission or some other stipulated amount.

net listing. A listing providing that the agent agrees to sell the owner's property for a set minimum price, any amount over the minimum being retained by the agent as commission. — Also termed *net sale contract*.

open listing. A listing that allows selling rights to be given to more than one agent at a time, obligates the owner to pay a commission when a specified broker makes a sale, and reserves the owner's right to personally sell the property without paying a commission. — Also termed *nonexclusive listing*; *general listing*; *simple listing*.

2. *Securities.* The contract between a firm and a stock exchange by which the trading of the firm's securities on the exchange is handled. See *listed security* under SECURITY.

dual listing. The listing of a security on more than one exchange.

3. *Tax.* The creation of a schedule or inventory of a person's taxable property; the list of a person's taxable property.

listing agent. The real-estate broker's representative who obtains a listing agreement with the owner. Cf. SELLING AGENT.

listing agreement. See LISTING (1).

list of creditors. A schedule giving the names and addresses of creditors, along with amounts owed them. • This list is required in a bankruptcy proceeding.

list price. See PRICE.

litem (**lI**-tem *or* -təm). See AD LITEM.

litem denuntiare (**lI**-tem də-nən-shee-**air**-ee). [Latin "to announce a suit"] *Roman law.* **1.** The summoning of a defendant by a magistrate in the late classical period. **2.** The notification by a buyer to the seller of a claim by a third party to the things sold. — Also spelled *litem denunciare*. Cf. LITIS DENUNTIATIO.

litem suam facere (**lI**-tem **s[y]oo**-əm **fay**-sə-ree), *vb.* [Latin "to make a suit one's own"] *Roman law.* (Of a judex) to show partiality to one side in a dispute or otherwise neglect official duties.

lite pendente (**lI**-tee pen-**den**-tee). [Latin] See PENDENTE LITE.

litera (**lit**-ər-ə), *n.* [Latin "letter"] *Hist.* **1.** A letter. **2.** The letter of a law, as distinguished from its spirit. Pl. ***literae.*** — Also spelled *litterae*. See LETTER (3).

literacy test. A test of one's ability to read and write, formerly required in some states as a condition for registering to vote. • Congress banned this use of literacy tests in 1975.

literae mortuae (**lit**-ər-ee **mor**-choo-ee), *n.* [Latin] *Hist.* Dead letters; filler words in a statute.

literae patentes (**lit**-ər-ee pə-**ten**-teez), *n.* [Law Latin "open letters"] See LETTERS PATENT (1).

literae procuratoriae (**lit**-ər-ee prok-yə-rə-**tor**-ee-ee), *n.* [Law Latin] *Hist.* Letters of procuration; letters of attorney; power of attorney. See POWER OF ATTORNEY.

literae recognitionis (**lit**-ər-ee rek-əg-nish-ee-**oh**-nis), *n.* [Latin] *Hist.* A bill of lading. See BILL OF LADING.

literae scriptae manent (**lit**-ər-ee **skrip**-tee **man**-ent), *n.* [Latin] *Hist.* Written words last.

literae sigillatae (**lit**-ər-ee sij-ə-**lay**-tee), *n.* [Latin] *Hist.* Sealed letters. • A sheriff's return on a writ was often called *literae sigillatae*.

literal, *adj.* According to expressed language. • Literal performance of a condition requires exact compliance with its terms.

literal canon. See STRICT CONSTRUCTIONISM.

literal construction. See *strict construction* under CONSTRUCTION.

literal contract. See CONTRACT.

litera legis. See LETTER OF THE LAW.

literal infringement. See INFRINGEMENT.

literal interpretation. See *strict construction* under CONSTRUCTION.

literal proof. See PROOF.

literal rule. See STRICT CONSTRUCTIONISM.

literary, *adj.* Of or relating to literature, books, or writings.

literary composition. An original expression of mental effort in written words arranged in an intelligent and purposeful order. See LITERARY WORK.

literary property. 1. The physical property in which an intellectual production is embodied, such as a book, screenplay, or lecture. **2.** An owner's exclusive right to possess, use, and dispose of such a production. See COPYRIGHT; INTELLECTUAL PROPERTY.

literary work. A work, other than an audiovisual work, that is expressed in words, numbers, or other symbols, regardless of the medium that embodies it. 17 USCA § 101.

> "Copyright protection extends to literary works which are defined as works, other than audiovisual works, expressed in words, numbers, or other verbal or numerical symbols or indicia, regardless of the nature of the material objects, such as books, periodicals, manuscripts, phonorecords, film, tapes, disks, or cards in which they are embodied. The term 'literary work' does not connote any criterion of literary merit or qualitative value and includes catalogs and directories; similar factual, reference or instructional works; compilations of data; computer data bases, and computer programs." 18 Am. Jur. 2d *Copyright and Literary Property* § 25, at 360 (1985).

literate, *adj.* **1.** Able to read and write a language. **2.** Knowledgeable and educated. — **literacy,** *n.*

literatura (lit-ər-ə-**t[y]uur**-ə), *n.* [Latin fr. *litera* "a letter"] *Hist.* Education. • *Ad literaturam ponere* means the right to educate one's children, esp. male children. During feudal times, servile tenants could not educate their children without the lord's consent.

litigable (**lit**-ə-gə-bəl), *adj.* Able to be contested or disputed in court <litigable claims>. — **litigability,** *n.*

litigant. A party to a lawsuit.

litigation, *n.* **1.** The process of carrying on a lawsuit <the attorney advised his client to make a generous settlement offer in order to avoid litigation>. **2.** A lawsuit itself <several litigations pending before the court>. — **litigate,** *vb.* — **litigatory, litigational,** *adj.*

litigation costs. See COST (3).

litigation privilege. See PRIVILEGE (1).

litigator. 1. *Archaic.* A party to a lawsuit; a litigant. **2.** A trial lawyer. **3.** A lawyer who prepares cases for trial, as by conducting discovery and pretrial motions, trying cases, and handling appeals.

litigious (li-**tij**-əs), *adj.* **1.** Fond of legal disputes; contentious <our litigious society>. **2.** *Archaic.* Of or relating to the subject of a lawsuit <the litigious property>. **3.** *Archaic.* Of or relating to lawsuits; litigatory <they

couldn't settle the litigious dispute>. — **litigiousness, litigiosity** (li-tij-ee-**os**-ə-tee), *n.*

litigious right. *Civil law.* A right that cannot be exercised without first being determined in a lawsuit. • If the right is sold, it must be in litigation at the time of sale to be considered a litigious right.

litis aestimatio (**lI**-tis es-tə-**may**-shee-oh), *n.* [Latin] *Roman law.* The measure of damages.

litis contestatio (**lI**-tis kon-tes-**tay**-shee-oh), *n.* [Latin] **1.** *Roman law.* The final agreement of the parties to a suit on the issue to be decided. **2.** The contested issue itself. **3.** *Eccles. law.* The defendant's general denial. See CONTESTATIO LITIS.

litis denuntiatio (**lI**-tis də-nən-s[h]ee-**ay**-shee-oh), *n.* [Latin] *Civil law.* The process by which a land purchaser, sued for possession of the land by a third party, notified the land seller and demanded aid in defending the suit under the seller's warranty of title. — Also spelled *litis denunciatio.* Cf. LITEM DENUNTIARE.

litis dominium (**lI**-tis də-**min**-ee-əm), *n.* [Latin] See DOMINUS LITIS.

litispendence (lI-tis-**pen**-dənts). *Archaic.* The time during which a lawsuit is pending.

litteris obligatio (**lit**-ər-is ob-lə-**gay**-shee-oh), *n.* [Latin] *Roman law.* An obligation arising from written entries in account books; an obligation arising from a literal contract. See *literal contract* under CONTRACT.

littoral (**lit**-ər-əl), *adj.* Of or relating to the coast or shore of an ocean, sea, or lake <the littoral right to limit others' consumption of the water>. Cf. RIPARIAN.

litura (li-**t[y]oor**-ə), *n.* [Latin] *Roman law.* A blot or obliteration in a will or other instrument.

livelihood. A means of supporting one's existence, esp. financially.

livelode. *Archaic.* Livelihood; maintenance. — Also termed *lifelode.*

livery (**liv**-ə-ree *or* **liv**-ree). The delivery of the possession of real property. Cf. DELIVERY.

livery in chivalry. *Hist.* The delivery of possession of real property from a guardian to a ward in chivalry when the ward reached majority.

livery office. An office designated for the delivery of lands.

livery of seisin. *Hist.* The ceremony by which a grantor conveyed land to a grantee. • Livery of seisin involved either (1) going on the land and having the grantor symbolically deliver possession of the land to the grantee by handing over a twig, a clod of dirt, or a piece of turf (called *livery in deed*) or (2) going within sight of the land and having the grantor tell the grantee that possession was being given, followed by the grantee's entering the land (called *livery in law*). See SEISIN.

> "[W]e may now pause to wonder how transfer of these potentially infinite interests was accomplished. Without a modern system of land records, it would be desirable that the transfer be effected with sufficient ceremony not only to mark itself indelibly in the memories of the participants, but also to give notice to interested persons such as the mesne lord above the transferor. The central idea was to make ritual *livery* (meaning 'delivery,' from the Old French *livrer*) of *seisin* (meaning, roughly, 'possession,' from the Old French *saisir* or *seisir*). The transferor and transferee would go to the land to be transferred, and the transferor would then hand to the transferee a lump of soil or a twig from a tree — all the while intoning the appropriate words of grant, together with the magical words 'and his heirs' if the interest transferred was to be a potentially infinite one." Thomas F. Bergin & Paul G. Haskell, *Preface to Estates in Land and Future Interests* 10–11 (2d ed. 1984).

lives in being. See LIFE IN BEING.

live storage. The storage of cars in active daily use, rather than cars put away for an extended period. • A garage owner's responsibility sometimes depends on whether a car is in live or dead storage. Cf. DEAD STORAGE.

live thalweg. See THALWEG.

living, *n.* One's source of monetary support or resources; esp., one's employment.

living separate and apart. (Of spouses) residing in different places and having no intention of resuming marital relations. • One basis for no-fault divorce in many states exists if the spouses have lived apart for a specified period.

living trust. See *inter vivos trust* under TRUST.

living will. An instrument, signed with the formalities necessary for a will, by which a person states the intention to refuse medical treatment and to release healthcare providers from all liability if the person becomes both terminally ill and unable to communicate such a refusal. — Also termed *declaration of a desire for a natural death*; *directive to physicians*. Cf. ADVANCE DIRECTIVE.

L.J. *abbr.* **1.** Law Judge. **2.** Law Journal. **3.** Lord Justice.

L.JJ. *abbr.* Lords justices.

L.L. *abbr.* LAW LATIN.

L.Lat. *abbr.* LAW LATIN.

LL.B. *abbr.* Bachelor of Laws. • This was formerly the law degree ordinarily conferred by American law schools. It is still the normal degree in British law schools. Cf. JURIS DOCTOR.

L.L.C. See *limited-liability company* under COMPANY.

LL.D. *abbr.* Doctor of Laws — commonly an honorary law degree.

LL.J. *abbr.* Lords justices.

LL.M. *abbr.* MASTER OF LAWS.

Lloyd's. See LLOYD'S OF LONDON.

Lloyd's association. See LLOYD'S UNDERWRITERS.

Lloyd's bond. See BOND (3).

Lloyd's insurance. See INSURANCE.

Lloyd's of London. **1.** A London insurance mart where individual underwriters gather to quote rates and write insurance on a wide variety of risks. **2.** A voluntary association of merchants, shipowners, underwriters, and brokers formed not to write policies but instead to issue a notice of an endeavor to members who may individually underwrite a policy by assuming shares of the total risk of insuring a client. • The names of the bound underwriters and the attorney-in-fact appear on the policy. — Also termed *Lloyd's*; *London Lloyd's*.

Lloyd's underwriters. An unincorporated association of underwriters who, under a common name, engage in the insurance business through an attorney-in-fact having authority to obligate the underwriters severally, within specified limits, on insurance contracts that the attorney makes or issues in the common name. — Also termed *Lloyd's association*; *American Lloyd's*.

L.L.P. See *limited-liability partnership* under PARTNERSHIP.

load, *n.* An amount added to a security's price or to an insurance premium in order to cover the sales commission and expenses <the mutual fund had a high front-end load>. — Also termed *sales load*; *acquisition cost*.

load factor. **1.** The ratio of a utility customer's usage levels during a given period compared to the customer's demand during peak periods. **2.** An analysis of the number of passengers on an airplane or other common carrier compared to available capacity.

load fund. See MUTUAL FUND.

loading. *Insurance.* An amount added to a life-insurance premium to cover the insurer's business expenses and contingencies. — Also termed *expense loading*. See *gross premium* (1) under PREMIUM (1).

load line. *Maritime law.* **1.** The depth to which a safely loaded ship will sink in salt water. **2.** One of a set of graduated marks on the side of a ship, indicating the depth to which the ship can be loaded in varying waters (such as salt water or freshwater) and weather conditions. • Load lines must, by law in most maritime countries, be cut and painted amidships. — Also termed (in sense 2) *load-line marks*; *Plimsoll marks*.

> "The interest of shipowners led them, in early times, to load vessels to a point beyond safety; the greater the weight of the vessel's load, of course, the lower she rides in the water, and the more vulnerable she is to heavy seas. Many seamen consequently lost their lives. Britain led the way in establishing standards of depth in the water believed to be safe; Samuel Plimsoll, M.P., was the moving spirit, and gave his name to the Plimsoll mark, now seen on the side of all large vessels, which marks the limits of safety for different seas and seasons. Since 1929, the United States has made mandatory the placing of and compliance with loadline marks. . . ." Grant Gilmore & Charles L. Black, Jr., *The Law of Admiralty* § 11–12, at 987 (2d ed. 1975).

loadmanage. The fee paid to loadsmen, who sail in small vessels acting as pilots for larger ships.

loan, *n.* **1.** An act of lending; a grant of something for temporary use <Trina gave him the laptop as a loan, not a gift>. **2.** A thing lent for the borrower's temporary use; esp., a sum of money lent at interest <Larry applied for a car loan>.

accommodation loan. A loan for which the lender receives no consideration in return. See ACCOMMODATION.

add-on loan. A loan in which the interest is calculated at the stated rate for the loan agreement's full term for the full principal amount, and then the interest is added to the principal before installment payments are calculated, resulting in an interest amount higher than if it were calculated on the monthly unpaid balance. • Consumer loans are typically add-on loans. — Also termed *contract loan.* See *add-on interest* under INTEREST (3).

amortized loan. A loan calling for periodic payments that are applied first to interest and then to principal, as provided by the terms of the note. See AMORTIZATION (1).

back-to-back loan. A loan arrangement by which two firms lend each other funds denominated in different currencies for a specified period.

below-market loan. See *interest-free loan.*

bridge loan. A short-term loan that is used to cover costs until more permanent financing is arranged. — Also termed *swing loan.*

broker call loan. See *call loan.*

building loan. A type of bridge loan used primarily for erecting a building. • The loan is typically advanced in parts as work progresses and is used to pay the contractor, subcontractors, and material suppliers. See *interim financing* under FINANCING.

call loan. A loan for which the lender can demand payment at any time, usu. with 24 hours' notice, because there is no fixed maturity date. — Also termed *broker call loan; demand loan.* Cf. *term loan.*

character loan. A loan made in reliance on the borrower's character and stable earnings. • Character loans are usu. secured by a mortgage or by other property, but sometimes they are unsecured.

clearing loan. A loan made to a bond dealer pending the sale of a bond issue.

collateral loan. See *secured loan.*

commercial loan. A loan that a financial institution gives to a business, generally for 30 to 90 days.

commodity loan. A loan secured by a commodity (such as cotton or wool) in the form of a warehouse receipt or other negotiable instrument.

consolidation loan. A loan whose proceeds are used to pay off other individual loans, thereby creating a more manageable debt.

consumer loan. A loan that is given to an individual for family, household, personal, or agricultural purposes and that is generally governed by truth-in-lending statutes and regulations.

contract loan. See *add-on loan.*

Crown loan. *Tax.* An interest-free demand loan, usu. from parent to child, in which the borrowed funds are invested and the income from the investment is taxed at the child's rate. • This type of loan is named for one Harry Crown of Chicago, reputedly one of the first persons to use it. See *kiddie tax* under TAX.

day loan. A short-term loan to a broker to finance daily transactions.

demand loan. See *call loan.*

discount loan. A loan in which interest is deducted in advance, at the time the loan is made.

home equity loan. A line of bank credit given to a homeowner, using as collateral the homeowner's equity in the home. — Often shortened to *equity loan.* See EQUITY (7).

installment loan. A loan that is to be repaid in usu. equal portions over a specified period.

interest-free loan. Money loaned to a borrower at no charge or, under the Internal Revenue Code, with a charge that is lower than the market rate. IRC (26 USCA) § 7872. — Also termed (in the IRC) *below-market loan.*

maritime loan. A loan providing that a lender will not be repaid if the cargo is damaged or lost because of a navigational peril, but that the lender will be repaid plus interest if the cargo arrives safely or is damaged because of the carrier's negligence.

mortgage loan. A loan secured by a mortgage or deed of trust on real property.

nonperforming loan. An outstanding loan that is not being repaid.

nonrecourse loan. A secured loan that allows the lender to attach only the collateral, not the borrower's personal assets, if the loan is not repaid.

participation loan. A loan issued by two or more lenders. See LOAN PARTICIPATION.

policy loan. An insurer's loan to an insured, secured by the policy's cash reserve.

precarious loan. **1.** A loan that may be recalled at any time. **2.** A loan in danger of not being repaid.

premium loan. A loan made to an insured by the insurer to enable the insured to pay further premiums. • The reserve value of the policy serves as collateral.

recourse loan. A loan that allows the lender, if the borrower defaults, not only to attach the collateral but also to seek judgment against the borrower's (or guarantor's) personal assets.

revolver loan. A single loan that a debtor takes out in lieu of several lines of credit or other loans from various creditors, and that is subject to review and approval at certain intervals. • A revolver loan is usu. taken out in an attempt to resolve problems with creditors. Cf. *revolving credit* under CREDIT (4).

revolving loan. A loan that is renewed at maturity.

secured loan. A loan that is secured by property or securities. — Also termed *collateral loan*.

short-term loan. A loan with a due date of less than one year, usu. evidenced by a note.

signature loan. An unsecured loan based solely on the borrower's promise or signature. • To obtain such a loan, the borrower must usu. be highly creditworthy.

swing loan. See *bridge loan*.

term loan. A loan with a specified due date, usu. of more than one year. • Such a loan typically cannot be repaid before maturity without incurring a penalty. — Also termed *time loan*. Cf. *call loan*.

loan, *vb.* To lend, esp. money.

loan-amortization schedule. A schedule that divides each loan payment into an interest component and a principal component. • Typically, the interest component begins as the largest part of each payment and declines over time. See AMORTIZATION (1).

loan association. See SAVINGS-AND-LOAN ASSOCIATION.

loan broker. See BROKER.

loan-brokerage fee. See MORTGAGE DISCOUNT.

loan certificate. A certificate that a clearinghouse issues to a borrowing bank in an amount equal to a specified percentage of the value of the borrowing bank's collateral on deposit with the clearinghouse's loan committee.

loan commitment. A lender's binding promise to a borrower to lend a specified amount of money at a certain interest rate, usu. within a specified period and for a specified purpose (such as buying real estate). See MORTGAGE COMMITMENT.

loaned employee. See *borrowed employee* under EMPLOYEE.

loaned servant. See *borrowed employee* under EMPLOYEE.

loan for consumption. An agreement by which a lender delivers goods to a borrower who consumes them and who is obligated to return goods of the same quantity, type, and quality.

loan for exchange. A contract by which a lender delivers personal property to a borrower who agrees to return similar property, usu. without compensation for its use.

loan for use. An agreement by which a lender delivers an asset to a borrower who must use it according to its normal function or according to the agreement, and who must return it when finished using it. • No interest is charged.

loanland. *Hist.* A tenancy involving the loan of land by one person to another. — Also spelled *laenland*. Cf. BOOKLAND; FOLKLAND.

loan participation. The coming together of multiple lenders to issue a large loan (called a *participation loan*) to one borrower, thereby reducing each lender's individual risk.

loan ratio. See LOAN-TO-VALUE RATIO.

loan-receipt agreement. *Torts.* A settlement agreement by which the defendant lends money to the plaintiff interest-free, the plaintiff not being obligated to repay the loan unless he or she recovers money from other tortfeasors responsible for the same injury.

loansharking, *n.* The practice of lending money at excessive and esp. usurious rates, and often threatening or using extortion to enforce repayment. — Also termed *extortionate credit transaction*. — **loan-shark,** *vb.* — **loan shark,** *n.*

loan society. *English law.* A club organized to collect deposits from and make loans to industrial workers. • The loan societies were forerunners of the American savings-and-loan associations.

loan-to-value ratio. The ratio, usu. expressed as a percentage, between the amount of a mortgage loan and the value of the property pledged as security for the mortgage. • For example, an $80,000 loan on property worth $100,000 results in a loan-to-value ratio of 80% — which is usu. the highest ratio that lenders will agree to without requiring the debtor to buy mortgage insurance. — Often shortened to *LTV ratio*. — Also termed *loan ratio*.

loan value. 1. The maximum amount that may be lent safely on property or life insurance without jeopardizing the lender's need for protection from the borrower's default. **2.** The amount of money an insured can borrow against the cash value of his or her life-insurance policy.

lobby, *vb.* **1.** To talk with a legislator, sometimes in a luxurious setting, in an attempt to influence the legislator's vote <she routinely lobbies for tort reform in the state legislature>. **2.** To support or oppose (a measure) by working to influence a legislator's vote <the organization lobbied the bill through the Senate>. **3.** To try to influence (a decision-maker) <the lawyer lobbied the judge for a favorable ruling>. — **lobbying,** *n.* — **lobbyist,** *n.*

lobbying act. A federal or state law governing the conduct of lobbyists, usu. by requiring them to register and file reports. • An example is the Federal Regulation of Lobbying Act, 12 USCA § 261.

local act. See LOCAL LAW.

local action. See ACTION.

local agent. See AGENT.

local allegiance. See *actual allegiance* under ALLEGIANCE.

local and special legislation. See LEGISLATION.

local assessment. See ASSESSMENT.

local chattel. Personal property that is affixed to land; FIXTURE.

local concern. An activity conducted by a municipality in its proprietary capacity.

local court. See COURT.

local custom. See CUSTOM.

local-exchange carrier. *Telecommunications law.* An entity that provides telephone service, usu. on a local basis, through a local-exchange network. 47 USCA § 153(26). — Abbr. LEC. See LOCAL-EXCHANGE NETWORK.

local-exchange network. *Telecommunications law.* A system for providing telephone service on a local basis. • A local-exchange network usu. consists of such elements as switches, local loops, and transport trunks, and capabilities such as billing databases and operator services. Switches are pieces of equipment that direct calls to the appropriate destination. Local loops are the wires that connect telephones to the switches. Transport trunks are the wires that carry calls from switch to switch. All the elements of a local-exchange network are often referred to as a bundle, and there are federal requirements that a local-exchange carrier who controls a local-exchange network permit competition by selling some access, including unbundled access, to its local-exchange network. 47 USCA § 251(c). See LOCAL-EXCHANGE CARRIER; UNBUNDLING RULES.

local government. See GOVERNMENT.

local improvement. See IMPROVEMENT.

local-improvement assessment. See *local assessment* under ASSESSMENT.

locality, *n.* A definite region; vicinity; neighborhood; community.

locality of a lawsuit. The place where a court may exercise judicial authority.

locality-plus test. *Maritime law.* The rule that, for a federal court to exercise admiralty jurisdiction, not only must the alleged wrong occur on navigable waters, it must also relate to a traditional maritime activity. — Also termed *maritime-connection doctrine*.

locality rule. 1. The doctrine that, in a professional-malpractice suit, the standard of care to be applied to the professional's conduct is the reasonable care exercised by similar professionals in the same vicinity and professional community.

> "With respect to medical doctors (and sometimes dentists and others), the standard of care has been further limited by the so-called 'locality rule.' A physician historically was required only to possess and apply the knowledge and use the skill and care that is ordinarily used by reasonably well-qualified physicians *in the locality in which he practices*, or, usually, in 'similar localities.' This frequently made it difficult or impossible for a plaintiff to prove the applicable standard since other doctors in the same locality are notoriously reluctant to testify against their professional colleagues. However, with the advent of improved communication and continuing medical education, the reason for the rule has abated, and today the trend is toward its abolition." Edward J. Kionka, *Torts in a Nutshell* 270–71 (2d ed. 1992).

2. The doctrine that, in determining the appropriate amount of attorney's fees to be awarded in a suit, the proper basis is the rate charged by similar attorneys for similar work in the vicinity.

localization doctrine. The doctrine that a foreign corporation, by doing sufficient business in a state, will subject itself to that state's laws.

local law. 1. A statute that relates to or operates in a particular locality rather than the entire state. **2.** A statute that applies to particular persons or things rather than an entire class of persons or things. — Also termed (in senses 1 & 2) *local act*; *local statute*. **3.** The law of a particular jurisdiction, as opposed to the law of a foreign state. — Also termed *internal law*. **4.** *Conflict of laws*. The body of standards, principles, and rules — excluding conflict-of-laws rules — that the state courts apply to controversies before them. Restatement (Second) of Conflict of Laws § 4(1) (1971).

local option. An option that allows a municipality or other governmental unit to determine a particular course of action without the specific approval of state officials. — Also termed *local veto*. Cf. HOME RULE.

local rule. 1. A rule based on the physical conditions of a state and the character, customs, and beliefs of its people. **2.** A rule by which an individual court supplements the procedural rules applying generally to all courts within the jurisdiction. • Local rules deal with a variety of matters, such as requiring extra copies of motions to be filed with the court or prohibiting the reading of newspapers in the courtroom. Fed. R. Civ. P. 83.

local statute. See LOCAL LAW.

local union. See UNION.

local usage. A practice or method regularly observed in a particular place, sometimes considered by a court in interpreting a document. UCC § 1–205(2)(3). See CUSTOM AND USAGE.

local veto. See LOCAL OPTION.

locare (lə-**kair**-ee), *vb.* [Latin] *Roman law.* To let or hire out.

locarium (lə-**kair**-ee-əm), *n.* [Law Latin] *Hist.* Rent.

locatarius (loh-kə-**tair**-ee-əs), *n.* [Latin] *Hist.* A person with whom something is deposited; a depositee.

locatio (lə-**kay**-shee-oh), *n.* [Latin] *Roman & civil law.* Any contract by which the use of the thing bailed, or the use of the labor or services, is stipulated to be given for a compensation. • This type of contract benefits both parties. — Also termed *lease*; *hiring*.

locatio conductio (lə-**kay**-shee-oh kən-**duk**-shee-oh), *n.* [Latin] A letting for hire. • This is one of three types of contract for permissive use, the other two being *commodatum* and *mutuum*.

locatio custodiae (lə-**kay**-shee-oh kəs-**toh**-dee-ee), *n.* [Latin] The hiring of care or service, as when the bailee is to protect the thing bailed.

locatio operarum (lə-**kay**-shee-oh op-ə-**rair**-əm), *n.* [Latin] A contract in which an employer hires a worker to perform labor or services on material supplied by the employer for a specified price. — Also termed *locatio operis faciendi*. Cf. REDEMPTIO OPERIS.

locatio operis faciendi (lə-**kay**-shee-oh **op**-ə-ris fay-shee-**en**-dɪ), *n.* [Latin "the letting of a job to be done"] See *locatio operarum*.

locatio operis mercium vehendarum (lə-**kay**-shee-oh **op**-ə-ris **mər**-shee-əm vee-hən-**dair**-əm), *n.* [Latin "the letting of the job of carrying goods"] A bailment in which goods are delivered to the bailee for transport elsewhere.

locatio rei (lə-**kay**-shee-oh **ree**-ɪ), *n.* [Latin "letting of a thing"] The hiring of a thing for use, by which the hirer gains the temporary use of the thing; a bailment or lease in which the bailee or lessee may use the item for a fee.

location. 1. The specific place or position of a person or thing. **2.** The act or process of locating. **3.** *Real estate.* The designation of the boundaries of a particular piece of land, either on the record or on the land itself. **4.** *Mining law.* The act of appropriating a mining claim. — Also termed *mining location.* See MINING CLAIM. **5.** The claim so appropriated. **6.** *Civil law.* A contract for the temporary use of something for hire; a leasing for hire. See LOCATIO.

locative calls (**lok**-ə-tiv). *Property.* In land descriptions, specific descriptions that fix the boundaries of the land. • Locative calls may be marks of location, landmarks, or other physical objects. If calls in a description conflict, locative calls control over those indicating a general area of a boundary. See CALL (5); DIRECTORY CALLS.

locator (loh-**kay**-tər), *n.* [Latin] **1.** *Roman & civil law.* One who lets for hire; the bailor or lessor in a *locatio.* **2.** One who is entitled to locate land or set the boundaries of a mining claim.

locatum (lə-**kay**-təm), *n.* [Latin] *Hist.* A hiring. See BAILMENT.

Lochnerize (**lok**-nər-ɪz), *vb.* To examine and strike down economic legislation under the guise of enforcing the Due Process Clause, esp. in the manner of the U.S. Supreme Court during the early 20th century. • The term takes its name from the decision in *Lochner v. New York*, 198 U.S. 45, 25 S.Ct. 539 (1905), in which the Court invalidated New York's maximum-hours law for bakers. — **Lochnerization,** *n.*

lockbox. 1. A secure box, such as a post-office box, strongbox, or safe-deposit box. **2.** A facility offered by a financial institution for quickly collecting and consolidating checks and other funds from a party's customers.

lockdown. The temporary confinement of prisoners in their cells during a state of heightened alert caused by an escape, riot, or other emergency.

locked in, *adj.* **1.** (Of a person) unable to sell appreciated securities and realize the gain because of liability for capital gains taxes <my accountant advised me not to sell the stock because I am locked in>. **2.** (Of a price, rate, etc.) staying the same for a given period <the 7% mortgage rate is locked in for 30 days>.

locked-in rate. See *lock rate* under INTEREST RATE.

lockout. 1. An employer's withholding of work and closing of a business because of a labor dispute. **2.** Loosely, an employee's refusal to work because the employer unreasonably refuses to abide by an expired employment contract while a new one is being negotiated. Cf. STRIKE; BOYCOTT; PICKETING.

lock rate. See INTEREST RATE.

lockup, *n.* **1.** JAIL. **2.** LOCKUP OPTION.

lockup option. A defense against a corporate takeover, in which a friendly party is entitled to buy parts of a corporation for a set price when a person or group acquires a certain percentage of the corporation's shares. • An agreement of this kind may be illegal, to the extent it is not undertaken to serve the best interests of the shareholders. — Often shortened to *lockup.*

loco parentis. See IN LOCO PARENTIS.

locum tenens (**loh**-kəm **tee**-nenz *or* **ten**-ənz), *n.* [Law Latin "holding the place"] *Hist.* A deputy; a substitute; a representative.

locuples (**lok**-yə-pleez), *adj.* [Latin] *Civil law.* Having the means to pay any amount that the plaintiff might recover. — Also termed *locuplete.*

locus (**loh**-kəs). [Latin "place"] The place or position where something is done or exists. — Abbr. L. See SITUS.

locus actus (**loh**-kəs **ak**-təs). [Latin "place of the act"] The place where an act is done; the place of performance.

locus contractus (**loh**-kəs kən-**trak**-təs). [Latin "place of the contract"] The place where a contract is made. Cf. LEX LOCI CONTRACTUS.

locus criminis (**loh**-kəs **krim**-ə-nis), *n.* [Latin] The place where a crime is committed.

locus delicti (**loh**-kəs də-**lik**-tɪ). [Latin "place of the wrong"] The place where an offense is committed; the place where the last event necessary to make the actor liable occurs. Cf. LEX LOCI DELICTI.

> "When a statute does not indicate where Congress considered the place of committing the crime to be, the site

or *locus delicti* must be determined from the nature of the crime and the location of the acts or omissions constituting the offense." *United States v. Clinton*, 574 F.2d 464, 465 (9th Cir. 1978).

locus in quo (**loh**-kəs in **kwoh**). [Latin "place in which"] The place where something is alleged to have occurred.

locus partitus (**loh**-kəs pahr-**tI**-təs), *n.* [Latin "a place divided"] *Hist.* The act of dividing two towns or counties to determine which of them contains the land or place in question.

locus poenitentiae (**loh**-kəs pen-ə-**ten**-shee-ee). [Latin "place of repentance"] **1.** A point at which it is not too late for one to change one's legal position; the possibility of withdrawing from a contemplated course of action, esp. a wrong, before being committed to it.

> "The requirement of an overt act before conspirators can be prosecuted and punished exists ... to provide a *locus poenitentiae* an opportunity for the conspirators to reconsider, terminate the agreement, and thereby avoid punishment." *People v. Zamora*, 557 P.2d 75, 82 (Cal. 1976).

2. The opportunity to withdraw from a negotiation before finally concluding the contract.

locus publicus (**loh**-kəs **pəb**-li-kəs), *n.* [Latin] *Roman law.* A public place.

> "Locus publicus .... A parcel of public land. It is property of the Roman people and is protected by various interdicts ... against violation by private individuals who might endanger its public character or its use by the people." Adolf Berger, *Encyclopedic Dictionary of Roman Law* 568 (1953).

locus regit actum (**loh**-kəs **ree**-jit **ak**-təm), *n.* [Latin "the place rules the act"] *Int'l law.* The rule that a transaction complying with the legal formalities of the country where it is created will be considered valid in the country where it is to be effective, even if that country requires additional formalities.

locus rei sitae (**loh**-kəs **ree**-I **sI**-tee), *n.* [Latin "place where a thing is situated"] *Civil law.* The rule that the place where the land is located is the proper forum in a case involving real estate.

locus sigilli (**loh**-kəs si-**jil**-I), *n.* [Latin] The place of the seal. • Today this phrase is almost always abbreviated "L.S." These are the traditional letters appearing on many notarial certificates to indicate where the notary public's embossed seal should be placed. If a rubber-stamp seal is used, it should be placed near but not over this abbreviation. See NOTARY SEAL.

> "For some period in history seals were required to consist of wax affixed to the parchment or paper on which the terms of the instrument were written. The wax was required to have an identifiable impression made upon it. Usually this was made by a signet ring. In time when ordinary people, who did not have signet rings, learned to read and write, it was to be expected that substitutes for the traditional seal would be accepted by the law. Thus, today it would be generally accurate to say that a seal may consist of wax, a gummed wafer, an impression on the paper, the word 'seal,' the letters 'L.S.' (locus sigilli) or even a pen scratch." John D. Calamari & Joseph M. Perillo, *The Law of Contracts* § 7-3, at 296 (3d ed. 1987).

locus standi (**loh**-kəs **stan**-dI *or* -dee). [Latin "place of standing"] The right to bring an action or to be heard in a given forum; STANDING.

lode, *n.* **1.** MINERAL LODE. **2.** LADE.

lode claim. See MINING CLAIM.

lodemanage, *n. Hist.* The hiring of a pilot to guide a vessel. — Also termed *loadmanage.*

lodestar. 1. A guiding star; an inspiration or model. **2.** A reasonable amount of attorney's fees in a given case, usu. calculated by multiplying a reasonable number of hours worked by the prevailing hourly rate in the community for similar work, and often considering such additional factors as the degree of skill and difficulty involved in the case, the degree of its urgency, its novelty, and the like. • Most statutes that authorize an award of attorney's fees use the lodestar method for computing the award.

lodger. 1. A person who rents and occupies a room in another's house. **2.** A person who occupies a designated area in another's house but acquires no property interest in that area, which remains in the owner's legal possession.

logan. See LAGAN.

logbook. 1. A ship's or aircraft's journal containing an account of each trip, often with a history of events during the voyage. **2.** Any journal or record of events.

logia (**loj**-ee-ə), *n.* [Latin] *Hist.* A small house or cottage.

logical-cause doctrine. The principle that, if the plaintiff proves that an injury occurred and proves a logical cause of it, a party desiring to defeat the claim cannot succeed merely by showing that there is another imaginable cause, but must also show that the alternative cause is more probable than the cause shown by the plaintiff.

logical interpretation. See INTERPRETATION.

logical positivism. A philosophical system or movement requiring that meaningful statements be in principle verifiable. Cf. LEGAL POSITIVISM.

logical-relationship standard. *Civil procedure.* A test applied to determine whether a defendant's counterclaim is compulsory, by examining whether both claims are based on the same operative facts or whether those facts activate additional rights, otherwise dormant, for the defendant. • One of the most important factors considered is whether hearing the claims together would promote judicial economy and efficiency. Fed. R. Civ. P. 13(a).

> "[U]nder the fourth test — frequently referred to as the 'logical relationship' standard — the principal consideration in determining whether a counterclaim is compulsory rests on the efficiency or economy of trying the counterclaim in the same litigation as the main claim. As a result, the convenience of the court, rather than solely the counterclaim's relationship to the facts or issues of the opposing claim, is controlling. The hallmark of this approach is flexibility. Although the fourth test has been criticized for being overly broad in scope and uncertain in application, it has by far the widest acceptance among the courts." Jack H. Friedenthal et al., *Civil Procedure* § 6.7, at 352 (2d ed. 1993).

logium (**loj**-ee-əm), *n.* [Latin] *Hist.* A lodge, hovel, or outhouse.

logographus (log-ə-**graf**-əs), *n.* [Latin] *Roman law.* A bookkeeper or public clerk.

logrolling, *n.* **1.** The exchanging of political favors; esp., the trading of votes among legislators to gain support of measures that are beneficial to each legislator's constituency. **2.** The legislative practice of including several propositions in one measure or proposed constitutional amendment so that the legislature or voters will pass all of them, even though these propositions might not have passed if they had been submitted separately. • Many state constitutions have single-subject clauses that prohibit this practice. — **logroll,** *vb.*

LOI. *abbr.* LETTER OF INTENT.

loitering, *n.* The criminal offense of remaining in a certain place (such as a public street) for no apparent reason. • Loitering statutes are generally held to be unconstitutionally vague. — **loiter,** *vb.* Cf. VAGRANCY.

lollipop syndrome. A situation in which one parent in a custody battle provides the child with fun, gifts, and good times, and leaves all matters of discipline to the other parent.

London commodity option. An agreement to buy or sell a futures contract for a commodity traded on the London markets, for a particular price and within a particular time.

London Lloyd's. See LLOYD'S OF LONDON.

Lone Pine **order.** A case-management order in a toxic-tort lawsuit involving many plaintiffs, establishing procedures and deadlines for discovery, including requiring the plaintiffs to timely produce evidence and expert opinions to substantiate each plaintiff's exposure to the hazardous substance, the injury suffered, and the cause of the injury. *Lore v. Lone Pine Corp.*, No. L-33606-85 (N.J. Super. Ct. Nov. 18, 1986). • Although the *Lone Pine* opinion is unreported, it has become famous for the kind of case-management order involved, in part because the plaintiffs' claims were dismissed for failure to timely provide expert opinions.

long, *adj.* **1.** Holding a security or commodity in anticipation of a rise in price <a buyer long on pharmaceutical stock>. **2.** Of or relating to a purchase of securities or commodities in anticipation of rising prices <a long position>. Cf. SHORT.

long, *adv.* By a long purchase; into or in a long position <bought the wheat long>.

long account. See ACCOUNT.

long-arm, *adj.* Relating to or arising from a long-arm statute <long-arm jurisdiction>.

long-arm statute. A statute providing for jurisdiction over a nonresident defendant who has had contacts with the territory where the statute is in effect. • Most state long-arm statutes extend this jurisdiction to its constitutional limits. — Also termed *single-act statute.*

Long Parliament. *Hist.* **1.** The English Parliament of Charles I meeting between 1640 and 1653, dissolved by Oliver Cromwell in 1653, then recalled and finally dissolved in 1660. **2.** The English Parliament that met between 1661 and 1678, after the restoration of the monarchy. • This Parliament is sometimes called the "Long Parliament of Charles II" to distinguish it from that of sense 1.

long robe. *Hist.* The legal profession <gentlemen of the long robe>. See ROBE.

long-run incremental cost. *Antitrust.* A cost threshold for determining whether predatory pricing has occurred, consisting of all costs that, over a several-year period, would not be incurred if the product in question were not offered. • It differs from average variable cost because it includes some costs that do not vary in the short run but that do vary over a longer period, depending on whether a particular product is offered. — Abbr. LRIC. Cf. AVERAGE VARIABLE COST.

Longshore and Harbor Workers' Compensation Act. A federal law designed to provide workers'-compensation benefits to persons, other than seamen, who work in maritime occupations, esp. stevedoring and ship service. 33 USCA § 901. — Abbr. LHWCA.

> "Employees who are engaged in maritime-related activities but who do not qualify as 'seamen' may be classified as 'maritime workers' entitled to the benefits provided by the Longshore and Harbor Workers' Compensation Act .... Persons covered by the act, which has the attributes of the usual workers' compensation law, include (1) employees injured on the Outer Continental Shelf in the course of mineral exploration and production activities, and (2) employees within American territorial waters who fall within the Congressional definition of a 'maritime worker,' and who are injured on 'navigable waters'." Frank L. Maraist, *Admiralty in a Nutshell* 44 (2d ed. 1988).

longshoreman. A maritime laborer, such as a stevedore, who works on the wharves in a port; a person who loads and unloads ships.

long-term capital gain. See CAPITAL GAIN.

long-term capital loss. See LOSS.

long-term debt. See DEBT.

long-term security. See SECURITY.

long title. See TITLE (3).

long ton. See TON.

look-and-feel protection. Copyright protection of the images generated or revealed when one activates a computer program.

lookout, *n.* A careful, vigilant watching <the motorist's statutory duty of proper lookout>.

look-through principle. A doctrine for allocating transfer-gains taxes on real estate by looking beyond the entity possessing legal title to identify the beneficial owners of the property.

loophole. An ambiguity, omission, or exception (as in a law or other legal document) that provides a way to avoid a rule without violating its literal requirements; esp., a tax-code provision that allows a taxpayer to legally avoid or reduce income taxes.

loopification, *n.* In critical legal studies, the collapse of a legal distinction resulting when the two ends of a continuum become so similar that they become indistinguishable <it may be impossible to distinguish "public" from "private" because of loopification>. — **loopify,** *vb.*

loose construction. See *liberal construction* under CONSTRUCTION.

looseleaf service. A type of lawbook having pages that are periodically replaced with updated pages, designed to cope with constant change and increasing bulk.

> "The first loose leaf service covered the federal income tax, and was published in 1913 shortly after the Federal Income Tax Law of 1913 went into effect. It was followed in 1914 by a service reporting on the activities of the Federal Trade Commission, which had just been established. The loose leaf method was, therefore, first used as a means of reporting new tax and business laws which were to be subject to administrative interpretation .... These first loose leaf services were designed ... not to reprint just the bare text of the revenue and commission acts, but to follow up and report each new development on these new laws as it occurred." Arthur Sydney Beardsley, *Legal Bibliography and the Use of Law Books* § 185, at 313–14 (1937).

loquela (lə-**kwee**-lə), *n.* [Law Latin "talk"] *Hist.* **1.** The oral discussions between the parties to a lawsuit leading to the issue, now called the pleadings. **2.** Settlement discussions.

loquela sine die (lə-**kwee**-lə **sI**-nee **dI**-ee *or* **sin**-ay **dee**-ay), *n.* [Law Latin] *Hist.* Indefinite postponement of an action.

lord. 1. A title of honor or nobility belonging properly to a baron but applied also to anyone who attains the rank of a peer. — Abbr. L. **2.** (*cap.* & *pl.*) HOUSE OF LORDS. **3.** A property owner whose land is in a tenant's possession; LANDLORD (1).

temporal lord (**tem**-pə-rəl). One of the English peers (other than ecclesiastical) who sit in Parliament.

Lord Advocate. *Scots law.* An important political functionary in Scottish affairs who acts as the principal Crown counsel in civil cases, the chief public prosecutor of crimes, and legal adviser to the government on matters of Scots law. — Formerly also termed *King's advocate.*

Lord Campbell's Act. 1. The 1846 English statute that created a wrongful-death claim for the relatives of a decedent when the decedent would have had a claim if he or she had been merely injured and not killed. • Technically known as the Fatal Accidents Act of 1846, this statute changed the earlier rule, under which a tortfeasor who would have been liable to another escaped liability if the victim died. Cf. WRONGFUL-DEATH ACTION.

> "The common law not only denied a tort recovery for injury once the tort victim had died, it also refused to recognize any new and independent cause of action in the victim's dependents or heirs for their own loss at his death.... The result was that it was cheaper for the defendant to kill the plaintiff than to injure him, and that the most grievous of all injuries left the bereaved family of the victim, who frequently were destitute, without a remedy. Since this was intolerable, it was changed in England by the passage of the Fatal Accidents Act of 1846, otherwise known as Lord Campbell's Act, which has become a generic name for similar statutes." *Prosser and Keeton on the Law of Torts* § 127, at 945 (W. Page Keeton ed., 5th ed. 1984).

2. An American state's wrongful-death statute patterned after the original English act.

Lord Chamberlain. The second officer of the royal household in England, who serves as a peer, a privy councilor, and a member of the ruling government. — Also termed *lord chamberlain of the household.*

Lord Chancellor. The highest judicial officer in England. • The Lord Chancellor sits as speaker of the House of Lords, is a member of the Cabinet, and presides at appellate judicial proceedings. — Also termed *Lord High Chancellor*; *Keeper of the King's Conscience.*

Lord Chief Justice of England. The chief judge of the Queen's Bench Division of the High Court of Justice. • The Lord Chief Justice also serves on the Court of Appeal, and ranks second only to the Lord Chancellor in the English judicial hierarchy. — Formerly termed *Chief Justice of England.* Cf. CHIEF JUSTICE OF THE COMMON PLEAS.

Lord Denman's Act. See DENMAN'S ACT.

Lord High Chancellor. See LORD CHANCELLOR.

Lord High Steward. *Hist.* The speaker *pro tempore* and presiding officer in the House of Lords during a criminal trial of a peer for a felony or for treason. • The privilege of peerage in criminal proceedings was abolished in 1948.

Lord High Treasurer. *Hist.* An officer in charge of the royal revenues and customs duties, and of leasing the Crown lands. • The functions of the Lord High Treasurer are now vested in the lords commissioners of the treasury.

lord in gross. *Hist.* A lord holding the title not by virtue of a manor; a lord without a manor.

Lord Justice Clerk. The second judicial officer in Scotland, with special responsibility for criminal law.

Lord Justice General. The highest judicial officer in Scotland, and head of the High Court of Justiciary. • The Lord Justice General also holds the office of Lord President of the Court of Session.

Lord Justice of Appeal. A judge of the English Court of Appeal. — Often shortened to *lord justice.* — Abbr. L.J. (or, in pl., either LL.J. or L.JJ.).

Lord Keeper. See KEEPER OF THE GREAT SEAL.

Lord Keeper of the Great Seal. See KEEPER OF THE GREAT SEAL.

Lord Keeper of the Privy Seal. See LORD PRIVY SEAL.

Lord Langdale's Act. See WILLS ACT (2).

Lord Lieutenant. 1. An honorary officeholder who is the Queen's representative in a county and the principal military officer there, originally appointed to muster the inhabitants to defend the country. **2. Hist.** The former viceroy of the Crown in Ireland.

Lord Lyndhurst's Act. See LYNDHURST'S ACT.

Lord Mansfield's rule. The principle that neither spouse may testify about whether the husband had access to the wife at the time of a child's conception. • In effect, this rule —

which has been abandoned by many states — made it impossible to bastardize a child born during a marriage.

lord mayor. **1.** *Hist.* The chief officer of the corporation of the city of London, so called because the fourth charter of Edward III conferred on that officer the honor of having maces carried before him by the sergeants. **2.** The title of the principal magistrate of a city, the office of which has been conferred by letters patent.

lord mayor's court. See COURT.

Lord of Appeal. A member of the House of Lords, of whom at least three must be present for the hearing and determination of appeals, and including the Lord Chancellor, the Lords of Appeal in Ordinary, and the peers that have held high judicial offices, such as ex-chancellors and judges of the superior court in Great Britain and Ireland.

Lord of Appeal in Ordinary. A person appointed and salaried to aid the House of Lords in the hearing of appeals. • These lords rank as barons for life, and sit and vote in the House of Lords even after retirement.

Lord of Parliament. A member of the House of Lords.

Lord President. The highest judicial officer in Scotland, and head of the Court of Session. • The Lord President also holds the office of Lord Justice General of Scotland.

Lord Privy Seal (**priv**-ee). *English law.* An officer who has custody of the privy seal and who authenticates either a state document before it passes to receive the Great Seal or a document that does not require the Great Seal because of its minor importance. • The Lord Privy Seal has nominal official duties but is often made a member of the British cabinet. — Also termed *Keeper of the Privy Seal*; *Lord Keeper of the Privy Seal*; *Privy Seal*.

Lords. See HOUSE OF LORDS.

Lord's Day Act. See BLUE LAW.

lordship. **1.** Dominion. **2.** An honorary title used for a nobleman other than a duke. **3.** A customary title for a judge or some other public official.

Lords Marchers. See MARCHERS.

lord spiritual. An archbishop or bishop who is a member of the House of Lords.

lord temporal. A House of Lords member who is not an ecclesiastic.

Lord Tenterden's rule. See EJUSDEM GENERIS.

loser-pays rule. See ENGLISH RULE.

loss. **1.** The failure to keep possession of something. **2.** A decrease in value; the amount by which a thing's original cost exceeds its later selling price. **3.** The amount of financial detriment caused by an insured person's death or an insured property's damage, for which the insurer becomes liable. **4.** *Tax.* The excess of a property's adjusted value over the amount realized from its sale or other disposition. IRC (26 USCA) § 1001. — Also termed (in sense 4) *realized loss*.

actual loss. A loss resulting from the real and substantial destruction of insured property.

actual total loss. **1.** See *total loss*. **2.** *Marine insurance.* The total loss of a vessel covered by an insurance policy (1) by its real and substantive destruction, (2) by injuries that destroy its existence as a distinct individual of a particular class, (3) by its being reduced to a wreck irretrievably beyond repair, or (4) by its being placed beyond the insured's control and beyond the insured's power of recovery.

capital loss. The loss realized upon selling or exchanging a capital asset. Cf. CAPITAL GAIN.

casualty loss. For tax purposes, the total or partial destruction of an asset resulting from an unexpected or unusual event, such as an automobile accident or a tornado.

consequential loss. A loss arising from the results of damage rather than from the damage itself. • A consequential loss is proximate when the natural and probable effect of the wrongful conduct, under the circumstances, is to set in operation the intervening cause from which the loss directly results. When the loss is not the natural and probable effect of the wrongful conduct, the loss is remote. — Also termed *indirect loss*. Cf. *direct loss*.

constructive total loss. **1.** Such serious damage to the insured property that the cost of repairs would exceed the value of the thing repaired. — Also termed *constructive loss*. **2.** *Marine underwriting.* According to the traditional American rule, such serious damage to the insured property that the cost of repairs would exceed half the value of the thing repaired. See *total loss.*

direct loss. A loss that results immediately and proximately from an event. Cf. *consequential loss.*

disaster loss. A casualty loss sustained in a geographic area that the President designates as a disaster area. • It may be treated as having occurred during the previous tax year so that a victim may receive immediate tax benefits.

economic loss. See ECONOMIC LOSS.

extraordinary loss. A loss that is both unusual and infrequent, such as a loss resulting from a natural disaster.

general average loss. *Marine underwriting.* A loss at sea usu. incurred when cargo is thrown overboard to save the ship; a loss due to the voluntary and intentional sacrifice of part of a venture (usu. cargo) to save the rest of the venture from imminent peril. • Such a loss is borne equally by all the interests concerned in the venture. See AVERAGE (3).

hobby loss. A nondeductible loss arising from a personal hobby, as contrasted with an activity engaged in for profit. • The law generally presumes that an activity is engaged in for profit if profits are earned during at least three of the last five years. IRC (26 USCA) § 183.

indirect loss. See *consequential loss.*

long-term capital loss. A loss on a capital asset held for an extended period, usu. at least 12 months.

net loss. The excess of all expenses and losses over all revenues and gains.

net operating loss. The excess of operating expenses over revenues, the amount of which can be deducted from gross income if other deductions do not exceed gross income. — Abbr. NOL.

ordinary loss. *Tax.* A loss incurred from the sale or exchange of an item that is used in a trade or business. • The loss is deductible from ordinary income, and thus is more beneficial to the taxpayer than a capital loss.

out-of-pocket loss. The difference between the value of what the buyer paid and the market value of what was received in return. • In breach-of-contract cases, out-of-pocket loss is used to measure restitution damages.

paper loss. A loss that is realized only by selling something (such as a security) that has decreased in market value. — Also termed *unrealized loss.*

partial loss. A loss of part of the insured property; damage not amounting to a total loss. Cf. *total loss.*

particular average loss. *Marine underwriting.* A loss suffered by and borne alone by particular interests in a maritime venture. • Such a loss is usu. a partial loss.

passive loss. A loss, with limited tax deductibility, from an activity in which the taxpayer does not materially participate, from a rental activity, or from a tax-shelter activity.

pecuniary loss. A loss of money or of something having monetary value.

recognized loss. *Tax.* The portion of a loss that is subject to income taxation. IRC (26 USCA) § 1001(c).

salvage loss. **1.** Generally, a loss that presumptively would have been a total loss if certain services had not been rendered. **2.** *Marine underwriting.* The difference between the salvage value, less the salvage charges, and the original value of the insured property.

total loss. The complete destruction of insured property so that nothing of value remains and the subject matter no longer exists in its original form. • Generally, a loss is total if, after the damage occurs, no substantial remnant remains standing that a reasonably prudent uninsured owner, desiring to rebuild, would use as a basis to restore the property to its original condition. — Also termed *actual total loss.* Cf. *partial loss*; *constructive total loss.*

unrealized loss. See *paper loss.*

loss carryback. See CARRYBACK.

loss carryforward. See CARRYOVER.

loss carryover. See CARRYOVER.

loss insurance. See INSURANCE.

loss leader. A good or commodity sold at a very low price, usu. below cost, to attract customers to buy other items. — Sometimes shortened to *leader.* See BAIT AND SWITCH.

loss-of-bargain damages. See *expectation damages* under DAMAGES.

loss-of-bargain rule. The doctrine that damages for a breach of a contract should put the injured party in the position it would have been in if both parties had performed their contractual duties.

loss-of-chance doctrine. A rule in some states providing a claim against a doctor who has engaged in medical malpractice that, although it does not result in a particular injury, decreases or eliminates the chance of surviving or recovering from the preexisting condition for which the doctor was consulted. — Also termed *lost-chance doctrine*; *increased-risk-of-harm doctrine*.

loss of consortium (kən-**sor**-shee-əm). A loss of the benefits that one spouse is entitled to receive from the other, including companionship, cooperation, aid, affection, and sexual relations. • Loss of consortium can be recoverable as damages in a personal-injury or wrongful-death action.

loss-of-use exclusion. See *failure-to-perform exclusion* under EXCLUSION (3).

loss-payable clause. An insurance-policy provision that authorizes the payment of proceeds to someone other than the named insured, esp. to someone who has a security interest in the insured property. • Typically, a loss-payable clause either designates the person as a beneficiary of the proceeds or assigns to the person a claim against the insurer, but the clause usu. does not treat the person as an additional insured. See MORTGAGE CLAUSE.

loss payee. A person or entity named in an insurance policy (under a loss-payable clause) to be paid if the insured property suffers a loss.

loss ratio. 1. *Insurance*. The ratio between premiums paid and losses incurred during a given period. **2.** A bank's loan losses compared to its loan assets; a business's receivable losses compared to its receivables.

loss reserve. See RESERVE.

lost, *adj*. **1.** (Of property) beyond the possession and custody of its owner and not locatable by diligent search <lost at sea> <lost papers>. **2.** (Of a person) missing <lost child>.

lost-chance doctrine. 1. LOSS-OF-CHANCE DOCTRINE. **2.** A rule permitting a claim, in limited circumstances, against someone who fails to come to the aid of a person who is in imminent danger of being injured or killed. Cf. GOOD SAMARITAN DOCTRINE.

lost corner. See CORNER.

lost earning capacity. A person's diminished earning power resulting from an injury. • This impairment is recoverable as an element of damages in a tort action. Cf. *lost earnings* under EARNINGS.

> "To some extent the phrases 'loss of earnings' and 'loss of earning capacity' are used interchangeably. But the preferred view is that they are different concepts. The former covers real loss which can be proved at the trial; the latter covers loss of the chances of getting equivalent work in the future." R.F.V. Heuston, *Salmond on the Law of Torts* 572 (17th ed. 1977).

lost earnings. See EARNINGS.

lost-expectation damages. See *expectation damages* under DAMAGES.

lost or not lost. *Marine insurance*. A policy provision fixing the effective date of the policy to a time preceding the policy date, even if the insured ship has already been lost when the policy is executed, as long as neither party then knows, or has means of knowing, that the ship has been lost.

lost profits. A measure of damages that allows a seller to collect the profit that would have been made on the sale if the buyer had not breached. UCC § 2–708(2).

lost property. See PROPERTY.

lost-volume seller. A seller of goods who, after a buyer has breached a sales contract, resells the goods to a different buyer who would have bought identical goods from the seller's inventory even if the original buyer had not breached. • Such a seller is entitled to lost profits, rather than contract price less market price, as damages from the original buyer's breach. UCC § 2–708(2).

lost will. See WILL.

lot. 1. A tract of land, esp. one having specific boundaries or being used for a given purpose.

minimum lot. A lot that has the least amount of square footage allowed by a local zoning law.

nonconforming lot. A previously lawful lot that now violates a newly adopted, or amended zoning ordinance.

2. An article that is the subject of a separate sale, lease, or delivery, whether or not it is sufficient to perform the contract. UCC

§§ 2–105(5); 2A–103(1)(s). **3.** A specified number of shares or a specific quantity of a commodity designated for trading.

odd lot. A number of shares of stock or the value of a bond that is less than a round lot.

round lot. The established unit of trading for stocks and bonds. • A round lot of stock is usu. 100 shares, and a round lot of bonds is usu. $1,000 or $5,000 par value. — Also termed *even lot*; *board lot*.

lot and scot. *Hist.* A collection of duties paid by voters before voting in certain cities and boroughs.

lot line. A land boundary that separates one tract from another <from the street to the alley, the lot line is 150 feet>.

lottery. A method of raising revenues, esp. state-government revenues, by selling tickets and giving prizes (usu. large cash prizes) to those who hold tickets with winning numbers that are drawn at random. — Also termed *lotto*.

Dutch lottery. A lottery in which tickets are drawn from classes, and the number and value of prizes are fixed and increasing with each class. • This type of lottery originated in Holland in the 16th century. — Also termed *class lottery*.

Genoese lottery (jen-oh-**eez** *or* -**ees**). A lottery in which, out of 90 consecutive numbers, five are drawn by lot, each player wagering that one or more of the numbers they have chosen will be drawn. • This type of lottery originated in Genoa in about 1530. — Also termed *number lottery*; *numerical lottery*.

love day. See DAY.

lowbote (**loh**-boht). *Hist.* Compensation paid for the death of one killed in a disturbance.

low diligence. See *slight diligence* under DILIGENCE.

lower chamber. See CHAMBER.

lower court. **1.** See *court below* under COURT. **2.** See *inferior court* under COURT.

lower estate. See *servient estate* under ESTATE.

lower-of-cost-or-market method. A means of pricing or costing inventory by which inventory value is set at either acquisition cost or market cost, whichever is lower.

lower scale. See SCALE.

lowest responsible bidder. A bidder who has the lowest price conforming to the contract specifications and who is financially able and competent to complete the work, as shown by the bidder's prior performance.

low-grade security. See SECURITY.

low justice. See JUSTICE (3).

low-water mark. See WATER MARK.

loyalty, *n.* Faithfulness or allegiance to a person, cause, duty, or government. — **loyal,** *adj.*

loyalty oath. See *oath of allegiance* under OATH.

L.P. See *limited partnership* under PARTNERSHIP.

L.R. *abbr.* Law Reports.

LRIC. *abbr.* LONG-RUN INCREMENTAL COST.

L.S. *abbr.* LOCUS SIGILLI.

LSAT. *abbr.* LAW SCHOOL ADMISSIONS TEST.

Ltd. *abbr.* Limited — used in company names to indicate limited liability.

LTV ratio. See LOAN-TO-VALUE RATIO.

lucid, *adj.* **1.** Understandable. **2.** Rational. **3.** Sane.

lucid interval. **1.** A brief period during which an insane person regains sanity sufficient to regain the legal capacity to contract and act on his or her own behalf. **2.** A period during which a person has enough mental capacity to understand the concept of marriage and the duties and obligations it imposes.

lucra nuptialia (**loo**-krə nəp-shee-**ay**-lə). [Latin] *Roman law.* The property that one spouse receives from another, whether by gift, marriage-gift, dos, or testamentary disposition. See POENAE SECUNDARUM NUPTIARUM.

lucrativa causa (loo-krə-**tI**-və **kaw**-zə), *n.* [Latin] *Roman law.* A cause of enrichment for which the acquirer pays nothing (e.g., a bequest).

lucrativa usucapio (loo-krə-**tI**-və yoo-z[y]oo-**kay**-pee-oh *or* -**kap**-ee-oh), *n.* [Latin] *Roman law.* A means of acquiring title to land by possession and the exclusion of the rightful heirs for one year after the death of the landowner. See USUCAPIO.

lucrative (**loo**-krə-tiv), *adj.* **1.** Profitable; remunerative <a lucrative business>. **2.** *Civil law.* Acquired or held without accepting burdensome conditions or giving consideration <lucrative ownership>.

lucrative bailment. See *bailment for hire* under BAILMENT.

lucrative office. See OFFICE.

lucrative title. See TITLE (2).

lucre (**loo**-kər), *n.* Monetary gain; profit.

lucri causa (**loo**-krI **kaw**-zə). [Latin] For the sake of gain. • *Lucri causa* was formerly an essential element of larceny, but today the thief's intent to deprive the possessor of property is generally sufficient. See LARCENY.

> " '*Lucri causa*' literally means for the sake of gain. On rare occasions the suggestion has been made that no taking is with intent to steal unless the thief is motivated by some purpose of gain or advantage. Even those advancing this suggestion have not insisted upon an intent to gain a *pecuniary* advantage. An intent to take away property and destroy it for the purpose of destroying evidence has been held to be sufficient even by those who have been inclined to insist upon *lucri causa* as essential to an intent to steal. The generally accepted view does not include this element at all. It regards intent to deprive the owner of his property permanently, or an intent to deal with another's property unlawfully in such a manner as to create an obviously unreasonable risk of permanent deprivation, as all that is required to constitute the *animus furandi* — or intent to steal." Rollin M. Perkins & Ronald N. Boyce, *Criminal Law* 332–33 (3d ed. 1982).

lucrum (**loo**-krəm), *n.* [Latin] **1.** *Roman law.* Gain; profit. **2.** *Hist.* A small parcel of land.

lucrum cessans (**loo**-krəm **ses**-anz), *n.* [Latin "ceasing gain"] *Roman law.* Interest or damages awarded for an expected future loss (such as anticipated loss of profits) as opposed to an actual realizable loss. — Also termed *lucrum interceptum.* See DAMNUM EMERGENS.

lucrum interceptum (**loo**-krəm in-tər-**sep**-təm). See LUCRUM CESSANS.

luctuosa hereditas (lək-choo-**oh**-sə hə-**red**-i-tas), *n.* [Latin "mournful inheritance"] See *hereditas luctuosa* under HEREDITAS.

luctus (**lək**-təs), *n.* [Latin] *Roman law.* Mourning.

luminar (loo-mə-**nair**-ee), *n.* [Latin "lamp"] *Hist.* A small lamp or candle set burning on a church altar, the maintenance of which was provided by lands and rents. Pl. ***luminaria.***

lumping sale. See SALE.

lump-sum agreement. *Int'l law.* A payment made to a country's citizens who have been injured in some manner by another country. • This method of settling claims has become increasingly common in the last 40 years as an alternative to submitting the claims to an international tribunal.

lump-sum alimony. See *alimony in gross* under ALIMONY.

lump-sum payment. See PAYMENT.

lunacy. See INSANITY.

lunar month. See MONTH (3).

lunch-hour rule. The doctrine that an employer is not responsible for injuries suffered or caused by an employee who takes a lunch break off work premises and, during the break, is not performing tasks in the course of the employment.

luxury tax. See TAX.

lying by. The act or fact of being present at a transaction affecting one's interests but remaining silent. • Courts often treat a person who was "lying by" at a transaction as having agreed to it and as being prevented from objecting to it.

lying in wait. *Criminal law.* The series of acts involved in watching, waiting, and hiding from someone, with the intent of killing or inflicting serious bodily injury on that person. • Because lying in wait shows premeditation and deliberation, it can result in an increased sentence.

lynch, *vb.* To hang (a person) by mob action without legal authority.

lynch law. The administration of summary punishment, esp. death, for an alleged crime, without legal authority.

Lyndhurst's Act. *Hist.* The statute rendering marriages within certain degrees of kinship null and void. Marriage Act of 1835, 5 & 6 Will. 4, ch. 54. — Also termed *Lord Lyndhurst's Act.*

lytae (**lI**-tee), *n.* [Latin, fr. Greek] *Roman law.* Civil-law students in their fourth year of study.

M

M. 1. *abbr.* MORTGAGE. **2.** *Hist.* A letter engraved on a treasury note to show that the note bears interest at the rate of one mill per centum. **3.** *Hist.* A brand placed on the left thumb of a person convicted of manslaughter who claimed the benefit of clergy.

M1. A measure of the money supply including cash, checking accounts, and travelers' checks.

M2. A measure of the money supply including M1 items, plus savings and time deposits, money-market accounts, and overnight-repurchase agreements.

M3. A measure of the money supply including M2 items, plus large time deposits and money-market funds held by institutions.

mace. 1. *Hist.* A weapon used in warfare, consisting of a staff topped by a heavy head, usu. of metal. **2.** A scepter; an ornamental form of weapon used as an emblem of the dignity of an office, as in Parliament and the U.S. House of Representatives. • In the House of Commons, it is laid on the table when the Speaker is in the chair. In the U.S. House of Representatives, it is usu. placed to the right of the Speaker and is borne upright by the sergeant-at-arms on extraordinary occasions, as when necessary to quell a disturbance or bring refractory members to order. **3.** A chemical liquid that can be sprayed in a person's face to cause dizziness and temporary immobilization.

Macedonian Decree. See SENATUS CONSULTUM MACEDONIAUM.

mace-greff (**mays**-gref). *Hist.* A purchaser of stolen goods; esp., a person who knowingly buys stolen food. — Also spelled *mace-griefe*.

mace-proof, *vb.* To exempt from an arrest; to secure against an arrest.

machination (mak-ə-**nay**-shən). **1.** An act of planning a scheme, esp. for an evil purpose. **2.** The scheme so planned.

machine. *Patents.* A device or apparatus consisting of fixed and moving parts that work together to perform some function. • Machines are one of the statutory categories of inventions that can be patented. Cf. MANUFACTURE; PROCESS (3).

***Machinists* preemption.** See PREEMPTION.

MACRS. *abbr.* Modified Accelerated Cost Recovery System. See ACCELERATED COST RECOVERY SYSTEM.

mactator (mak-**tay**-tər), *n.* [Law Latin "slaughterer"] *Hist.* A murderer.

maculare (mak-yə-**lair**-ee), *vb.* [Law Latin] *Hist.* To wound (a person).

made law. See POSITIVE LAW.

Mad Parliament. *Hist.* A commission of 24 men summoned to Oxford in 1258 by Henry III and his barons to carry out certain reforms and settle differences between the king and the barons. • The assembly was called the Mad Parliament because of the character and violence of the proceedings. The commission produced the Provisions of Oxford. — Also termed *parliamentum insanum*. See PROVISIONS OF OXFORD.

magister (mə-**jis**-tər), *n.* [fr. Latin *magis* "more"] *Roman law.* **1.** A master; a superior, esp. by office or position. **2.** A teacher; esp. one who has obtained eminence in a particular field of learning.

magister ad facultates (mə-**jis**-tər ad fak-əl-**tay**-teez), *n.* [Latin "master for permissions"] *Eccles. law.* **1.** An officer who grants dispensations, as to marry or to eat meat on prohibited days. **2.** MASTER OF THE FACULTIES.

magister bonorum vendendorum (mə-**jis**-tər bə-**nor**-əm ven-den-**dor**-əm), *n.* [Law Latin "master for sale of goods"] *Roman law.* A master appointed by the creditors of an insolvent debtor to direct the sale of the debtor's property.

magister cancellariae (mə-**jis**-tər kan-sə-**lair**-ee-ee), *n.* [Law Latin "master in chancery"] *Hist.* A master in chancery — so called because the officer was a priest.

magisterial (maj-ə-**steer**-ee-əl), *adj.* Of or relating to the character, office, powers, or duties of a magistrate. — Also termed *magistral*; *magistratic.*

magisterial precinct. A county subdivision that defines the territorial jurisdiction of a magistrate, constable, or justice of the peace. — Also termed *magisterial district.*

magister libellorum (mə-**jis**-tər lɪ-bə-**lor**-əm), *n.* [Latin "master of written petitions"] *Roman law.* The chief of the imperial chancery bureau that handled petitions to the emperor.

magister litis (mə-**jis**-tər **lɪ**-tis), *n.* [Latin "master of a lawsuit"] *Roman law.* A person who directs or controls a lawsuit.

magister navis (mə-**jis**-tər **nay**-vis), *n.* [Latin "master of a ship"] *Roman law.* The master of a trading vessel.

magister palatii (mə-**jis**-tər pə-**lay**-shee-ɪ), *n.* [Latin "master of the palace"] *Civil law.* A master of the palace, similar to the English Lord Chamberlain.

magister societatis (mə-**jis**-tər sə-sɪ-ə-**tay**-tis), *n.* [Latin "master of partnership"] *Roman law.* A person appointed to administer a partnership's business; a managing partner.

magistracy (**maj**-ə-strə-see). **1.** The office, district, or power of a magistrate. **2.** A body of magistrates.

magistral, *adj.* **1.** Of or relating to a master or masters <an absolutely magistral work>. **2.** Formulated by a physician <a magistral ointment>. **3.** MAGISTERIAL.

magistralia brevia (maj-ə-**stray**-lee-ə **bree**-vee-ə), *n.* [Law Latin "magisterial writs"] *Hist.* Magisterial writs, which were drafted by clerks of the chancery for use in special matters.

magistrate (**maj**-ə-strayt), *n.* **1.** The highest-ranking official in a government, such as the king in a monarchy, the president in a republic, or the governor in a state. — Also termed *chief magistrate*; *first magistrate.* **2.** A local official who possesses whatever power is specified in the appointment or statutory grant of authority. **3.** A judicial officer with strictly limited jurisdiction and authority, often on the local level and often restricted to criminal cases. Cf. JUSTICE OF THE PEACE. — **magisterial** (maj-ə-**stir**-ee-əl), *adj.*

committing magistrate. A judicial officer who conducts preliminary criminal hearings and may order that a defendant be released for lack of evidence, sent to jail to await trial, or released on bail. See *examining court* under COURT.

district-court magistrate. In some states, a quasi-judicial officer given the power to set bail, accept bond, accept guilty pleas, impose sentences for traffic violations and similar offenses, and conduct informal hearings on civil infractions.

investigating magistrate. A quasi-judicial officer responsible for examining and sometimes ruling on certain aspects of a criminal proceeding before it comes before a judge.

> "The institution of the *investigating magistrate* is another measure for preserving the integrity of the law at the level of enforcement. In this case the measure is directed not toward curing the evils of a lax or sporadic enforcement, but toward the evils of an opposite nature, those resulting from an excess of zeal on the part of the prosecutor. Under the system in question, before a criminal charge may be brought before the regular courts it must be investigated by a special official and, in effect, certified as deserving trial in court. The investigating magistrate is thus a kind of quasi-judge standing halfway between the prosecutor and the regular court. The danger of the institution lies precisely in this twilight zone of function which it occupies. The certification of a case for trial inevitably tends to confirm the criminal charge against the suspect, thus creating what may amount in practice to a strong presumption of guilt. The element of prejudgment involved constitutes a threat to the integrity of the trial in open court; the accused has, in effect, had a kind of half-trial in advance of the real trial, and this half-trial is conducted, not *before* but *by* a kind of half-judge who acts essentially as an inquisitorial court. In those countries where it is a part of the legal system, the role of the investigating magistrate continues to be a subject of some debate, and even where it is generally accepted, there is always some lingering concern lest it become the subject of inconspicuous abuse." Lon L. Fuller, *Anatomy of the Law* 38–39 (1968).

metropolitan stipendiary magistrate (stɪ-**pen**-dee-er-ee). *English law.* A stipendiary magistrate with jurisdiction in inner London areas. See *stipendiary magistrate.*

police magistrate. A judicial officer who has jurisdiction to try minor criminal offenses, breaches of police regulations, and similar violations. — Also termed *police justice.*

stipendiary magistrate (stɪ-**pen**-dee-er-ee). *English law.* A salaried magistrate that performs either in the place of or along with Justices of the Peace, and is appointed from barristers and solicitors of seven years standing.

U.S. Magistrate. See UNITED STATES MAGISTRATE JUDGE.

Magistrate Judge, U.S. See UNITED STATES MAGISTRATE JUDGE.

magistrate's court. See COURT.

magistratic, *adj*. See MAGISTERIAL.

magistratus (maj-ə-**stray**-təs), *n*. [fr. Latin *magister* "a master"] *Roman law*. **1.** A magistrate. **2.** A magistrate's office.

> "Magistratus. Denotes both the public office and the official himself. Magistracy was a Republican institution; under the Principate some *magistratus* continued to exist but with gradually diminishing importance; in the post-Diocletian Empire some former magistracies still exist but reduced nearly completely to an honorific title .... The most characteristic features of the Republican magistracy were the limited duration (one year) and colleagueship since each magistracy was covered by at least two persons ... with equal power .... Magistrates were elected by the people .... During his year of service a *magistratus* could not be removed. Misdemeanor in office could be prosecuted only after the term, hence the tenure of an office for two consecutive years was prohibited .... The tenure of a public office was considered an honor; for that reason the magistrates did not receive any compensation. Their political influence was, however, of greatest importance ...." Adolf Berger, *Encyclopedic Dictionary of Roman Law* 571–72 (1953).

magna assisa (**mag**-nə ə-**sI**-zə), *n*. [Law Latin] *Hist*. The grand assize. See *grand assize* under ASSIZE (5).

magna assisa eligenda (**mag**-nə ə-**sI**-zə el-ə-**jen**-də). See DE MAGNA ASSISA ELIGENDA.

Magna Carta (**mag**-nə **kahr**-tə). [Latin "great charter"] The English charter that King John granted to the barons in 1215 and that Henry III and Edward I later confirmed. • It is generally regarded as one of the great common-law documents and as the foundation of constitutional liberties. The other three great charters of English liberty are the Petition of Right (3 Car. (1628)), the Habeas Corpus Act (31 Car. 2 (1679)), and the Bill of Rights (1 Will. & M. (1689)). — Also spelled *Magna Charta*.

> "The history of Magna Carta is the history not only of a document but also of an argument. The history of the document is a history of repeated re-interpretation. But the history of the argument is a history of a continuous element of political thinking. In this light there is no inherent reason why an assertion of law originally conceived in aristocratic interests should not be applied on a wider scale." J.C. Holt, *Magna Carta* 16 (1965).

magna centum (**mag**-nə **sen**-təm), *n*. [Law Latin "great hundred"] Six score, or 120.

magna culpa (**mag**-nə **kəl**-pə). [Latin "great fault"] *Roman law*. Gross fault. • This is sometimes equivalent to *dolus*. See DOLUS.

magna negligentia. See NEGLIGENTIA.

Magnuson–Moss Warranty Act (**mag**-nə-sən–**maws** *or*–**mos**). A federal statute requiring that a written warranty of a consumer product fully and conspicuously disclose, in plain language, the terms and conditions of the warranty, including whether the warranty is full or limited, according to standards given in the statute. 15 USCA §§ 2301–2312.

magnus rotulus statutorum (**mag**-nəs **roch**-ə-ləs stach-ə-**tor**-əm). [Law Latin "the great statute roll"] The first of the English statute rolls, beginning with Magna Carta and ending with Edward III.

maiden. 1. A young unmarried woman. **2.** *Scots law*. An instrument used to behead criminals. • It was the prototype of the guillotine. Hence, "*to kiss the maiden* was to be put to death." H. Percy Smith, *Glossary of Terms and Phrases* 307 (1883).

maiden assize. See ASSIZE (1).

maiden rent. See MARCHET.

maiestas (mə-**yes**-tas). See MAJESTAS.

maihem. See MAIM.

maihematus (may-hə-**may**-təs), *p.pl.* [Law Latin] Maimed; wounded.

maihemium. See MAIM.

mail, *n*. **1.** One or more items that have been properly addressed, stamped with postage, and deposited for delivery in the postal system. **2.** An official system for delivering such items; the postal system. **3.** One or more written or oral messages sent electronically (e.g., through e-mail or voicemail).

certified mail. Mail for which the sender requests proof of delivery in the form of a receipt signed by the addressee. • The receipt (a green card, which is usu. referred to as such) must be signed before the mail will be delivered. — Also termed *certified mail, return receipt requested.*

registered mail. Mail that the U.S. Postal Service records at the time of mailing and at each point on its route so as to guarantee safe delivery.

mail, *vb.* **1.** To deposit (a letter, package, etc.) with the U.S. Postal Service; to ensure that a letter, package, etc. is properly addressed, stamped, and placed into a receptacle for mail pickup. **2.** To deliver (a letter, package, etc.) to a private courier service that undertakes delivery to a third person, often within a specified time.

mailable, *adj.* (Of a letter or package) lawful to send through a postal service.

mailbox rule. 1. *Contracts.* The principle that an acceptance becomes effective — and binds the offeror — once it has been properly mailed. • The mailbox rule does not apply, however, if the offer provides that an acceptance is not effective until received. **2.** The principle that when a pleading or other document is filed or served by mail, filing or service is deemed to have occurred on the date of mailing. • The mailbox rule varies from jurisdiction to jurisdiction. For example, it sometimes applies only to certain types of filings, and it may apply when a party uses an overnight courier instead of U.S. mail.

mail cover. A process by which the U.S. Postal Service provides a government agency with information on the face of an envelope or package (such as a postmark) for the agency's use in locating a fugitive, identifying a coconspirator, or obtaining other evidence necessary to solve a crime.

mail fraud. See FRAUD.

mail-order divorce. See DIVORCE.

maim, *n. Archaic.* The type of injury required for the commission of mayhem; esp., serious injury to part of a person's body that is necessary for fighting. — Also termed *maihem; maihemium.* — **maim,** *vb.* See MAYHEM.

> "Maihem or maim is where by the wrongful act of another any member is hurt or taken away, whereby the party is made unperfect to fight: as if a bone be taken out of the hand .... But the cutting of an ear or nose, or breaking of the hinder teeth, or such like, is no maihem, because it is rather a deformity of body than diminishing of strength; and that is commonly tried by the justices beholding the party. And if the justices stand in doubt whether the hurt be a maihem or not, they use and will of their own discretion take the help and opinion of some skilful chirurgeon, to consider thereof, before they determine upon the cause." *Termes de la Ley* 283–84 (1st Am. ed. 1812).

> " 'Maim' is the modern equivalent of the old word 'mayhem,' and some have long been inclined to abandon the earlier word entirely. There is a tendency, on the other hand, to retain 'mayhem' for the offense and to use 'maim' for the type of injury originally required for such a crime. This usage has a distinct advantage because statutory enlargements have included another type of injury within the scope of this offense, and today mayhem (the offense) may involve something other than *maim* (the injury)." Rollin M. Perkins & Ronald N. Boyce, *Criminal Law* 239 (3d ed. 1982).

mainad (**may**-nəd). [fr. Saxon *manath* "a deceitful oath"] *Hist.* Perjury.

main-a-main (may-nah-**mayn**), *adv.* [Law French] *Hist.* Immediately.

main channel. See CHANNEL.

main demand. See DEMAND (1).

maine-port. *Hist.* A small tribute (such as loaves of bread) that parishioners pay to the rector in lieu of tithes.

main opinion. See *majority opinion* under OPINION (1).

mainour (**may**-nər), *n.* [fr. Law French *manier* "to handle"] *Hist.* A stolen article found in the hands of a thief. • At common law, the thief could be arraigned and tried without an indictment. — Also spelled *manour; meinour.* — Also termed *mannopus; manuopus.*

mainovre (mə-**noo**-vər), *n.* [fr. Law French *main* "hand" + *oeuvre* "work"] *Hist.* **1.** A trespass committed by hand. **2.** Manual labor. — Also spelled *mainoeuvre.*

mainpernable (**mayn**-pər-nə-bəl), *adj.* Capable of being bailed; bailable.

mainpernor (**mayn**-pər-nər), *n.* [Law French, fr. O.F. *main* "hand" + *pernor* "taker"] *Hist.* **1.** A surety for a prisoner's appearance; one who gives mainprise for another.

> "Mainpernors differ from bail, in that a man's bail may imprison or surrender him up before the stipulated day of appearance; mainpernors can do neither, but are barely sureties for his appearance at the day: bail are only sureties, that the party be answerable for the special

matter for which they stipulate; mainpernors are bound to produce him to answer all charges whatsoever." 3 William Blackstone, *Commentaries on the Laws of England* 128 (1768).

2. A form of bail taken under a writ of mainprise. — Also termed *manucaptor* (man-yoo-**kap**-tər). See MAINPRISE.

main pot. *Tax.* A step in evaluating tax liability in which qualified transactions are compared to determine whether a net gain or loss has occurred. IRC (26 USCA) § 1231. — Also termed *big pot*; *hotchpot*; *hodgepodge*. Cf. CASUALTY POT.

mainprise (**mayn**-prīz), *n.* [Law French, fr. Old French *main* "hand" + *prise* "taking"] *Hist.* **1.** Delivery of a prisoner to the mainpernor. **2.** A suretyship undertaking that makes the surety responsible for a prisoner's appearance in court on a specified date and time. **3.** A writ ordering the sheriff to release a prisoner after taking security for the prisoner's appearance. — Also spelled *mainprize*. — Also termed *writ of mainprise*; *manucaption* (man-yoo-**kap**-shən). See DE HOMINE REPLEGIANDO.

mainprise, *vb. Hist.* To release (a prisoner) on the surety of a mainpernor.

main-purpose rule. *Contracts.* The doctrine that if a promise to guarantee another's debt is made primarily for the promisor's own benefit, then the statute of frauds does not apply and the promise does not have to be in writing. — Also termed *main-purpose doctrine*; *leading-object rule*.

main-relief rule. A doctrine by which venue for a lawsuit may be founded on the primary relief sought by the plaintiff, even if other claims, which alone would not support venue, are included in the suit.

main-rent. See VASSALAGE.

main sea. See SEA.

mainstreaming. The practice of educating a disabled student in a class with students who are not disabled, in a regular-education setting, as opposed to a special-education one. Cf. LEAST-RESTRICTIVE ENVIRONMENT.

mainsworn (**mayn**-sworn), *p.pl. Hist.* Forsworn, by making a false oath with a hand on a book. • This was used primarily in north England.

maintain, *vb.* **1.** To continue (something). **2.** To continue in possession of (property, etc.). **3.** To assert (a position or opinion); to uphold (a position or opinion) in argument. **4.** To care for (property) for purposes of operation productivity or appearance; to engage in general repair and upkeep. **5.** To support (someone) financially; esp., to pay alimony to. **6.** (Of a third party to a lawsuit) to assist a litigant in prosecuting or defending a lawsuit; to meddle in someone else's litigation.

maintainor. *Criminal law.* A person who meddles in someone else's litigation by providing money or other assistance; a person who is guilty of maintenance. — Also spelled *maintainer*. See MAINTENANCE (6).

maintenance, *n.* **1.** The continuation of something, such as a lawsuit. **2.** The continuing possession of something, such as property. **3.** The assertion of a position or opinion; the act of upholding a position in argument. **4.** The care and work put into property to keep it operating and productive; general repair and upkeep. **5.** Financial support given by one person to another; esp., ALIMONY. See MAINTENANCE IN GROSS.

separate maintenance. Money paid by one married person to another for support if they are no longer living as husband and wife. • This type of maintenance is often mandated by a court order. — Also termed *separate support*.

6. Assistance in prosecuting or defending a lawsuit given to a litigant by someone who has no bona fide interest in the case; meddling in someone else's litigation. Cf. CHAMPERTY.

maintenance and cure. *Maritime law.* Compensation provided to a sailor who becomes sick or injured while a member of a vessel's crew.

maintenance assessment. See ASSESSMENT.

maintenance bond. See BOND (2).

maintenance call. See *margin call* under CALL.

maintenance fee. See *maintenance assessment* under ASSESSMENT; FEE (1).

maintenance in gross. *Family law.* A fixed amount of money to be paid upon divorce by one former spouse to the other, in a lump sum or in installments. • The total amount is not supposed to be modified regardless of any change in either spouse's circumstances.

maintenance margin requirement. See MARGIN REQUIREMENT.

maior (**may**-ər). [Latin] **1.** *Roman law.* An older person, esp. one older than 25 and hence of full age. **2.** *Roman law.* An ascendant; an ancestor. **3.** *Hist.* A mayor.

maister (**may**-stər). *Archaic.* A master.

maître (**may**-trə *or* **mayt**-ər), *n.* [French] *French law.* A master, esp. of a vessel.

maius Latium. See LATIUM MAIUS.

majestas (mə-**jes**-tas), *n.* [Latin "supreme power"] *Roman law.* **1.** The majesty, sovereign authority, or supreme prerogative of the state or sovereign; supreme power of the people, esp. as represented by their highest representatives. **2.** CRIMEN MAIESTATIS. — Also spelled *majestas.*

> "*Majestas* .... From being an attribute of the *princeps,* the word 'majesty' came to be an honorific title confined, at first, to the Roman emperors of the West but later extended to all kings. From the time of Henry II, it has been used in England, the full form being 'Her Most Gracious Majesty'. The usual form is 'Her Majesty'." David M. Walker, *The Oxford Companion to Law* 798 (1980).

major, *n.* See ADULT.

major action. *Environmental law.* An undertaking that has had or will have a significant impact on the environment, for which an environmental-impact statement usu. must be filed under some state laws and under the National Environmental Policy Act. Cf. MAJOR-FEDERAL ACTION.

major-and-minor fault rule. See MAJOR-MINOR FAULT RULE.

major annus (**may**-jər **an**-əs). [Latin "the greater year"] A leap year, made up of 366 days.

majora regalia (mə-**jor**-ee ri-**gay**-lee-ə). See *regalia majora* under REGALIA.

major crime. See FELONY.

major disaster. A hurricane, tornado, storm, flood, earthquake, drought, fire, or other catastrophe that, when it occurs within the United States, the President determines to be a sufficiently severe threat to warrant disaster assistance by the federal government. • When the President declares a major disaster, the federal government supplements the efforts and available resources of states and local governments and relief organizations in alleviating the damage, loss, hardship, and suffering caused by the catastrophe. 40 CFR § 109.2.

major dispute. See DISPUTE.

majores (mə-**jor**-eez), *n.* [Latin "greater persons"] **1.** *Roman law.* Ancestors; forebears. — Also spelled *maiores.* **2.** *Hist.* Greater persons; persons of a higher status.

major federal action. *Environmental law.* An undertaking by a federal agency that will have a significant impact on the environment, such as constructing an aqueduct or dam, constructing a highway through wetlands, or adopting certain agency regulations. • Under the National Environmental Policy Act, a federal agency that plans to take a major federal action that may significantly affect the environment is required to prepare and file an environmental-impact statement, along with any public comments, with the Environmental Protection Agency. 40 CFR §§ 1506.9, 1508.18

majority. 1. The status of one who has attained the age of majority (usu. 18). See AGE OF MAJORITY. Cf. MINORITY (1). **2.** A number that is more than half of a total; a group of more than 50 percent <the candidate received 50.4 percent of the votes — barely a majority>. Cf. PLURALITY; MINORITY (2).

absolute majority. A majority of all those who are entitled to vote in a particular election, whether or not they actually cast ballots. See QUORUM.

simple majority. A majority of those who actually vote in a particular election.

supermajority. A majority substantially greater than 50 percent. • Such a majority is needed for certain extraordinary actions, such as ratifying a constitutional amendment or approving a fundamental corporate change. — Also termed *extraordinary majority.*

majority-consent procedure. *Corporations.* A statutory provision allowing shareholders to avoid a shareholders' meeting and to act instead by written consent of the holders of a majority of shares. • Delaware and a few other states have enacted such procedures.

majority-minority district. A voting district in which a racial or ethnic minority group makes up a majority of the voting citizens. Cf. INFLUENCE DISTRICT.

majority opinion. See OPINION (1).

majority rule. 1. A political principle that a majority of a group has the power to make decisions that bind the group. • It is governance by the majority of those who actually participate, regardless of the number entitled to participate. **2.** *Corporations.* The common-law principle that a director or officer owes no fiduciary duty to a shareholder with respect to a stock transaction. • This rule has been restricted by both federal insider-trading rules and state-law doctrine. Cf. SPECIAL-FACTS RULE.

majority shareholder. See SHAREHOLDER.

majority voting. See VOTING.

major life activity. Any activity that an average person in the general population can perform with little or no difficulty, such as seeing, hearing, sleeping, eating, walking, traveling, and working. • A person who is substantially limited in a major life activity is protected from discrimination under a variety of disability laws, most significantly the Americans with Disabilities Act and the Rehabilitation Act. 42 USCA § 12102(2); 29 USCA § 705(9)(B). See AMERICANS WITH DISABILITIES ACT.

major-minor fault rule. *Maritime law.* The principle that if the fault of one vessel in a collision is uncontradicted and sufficient to account for the accident, then the other vessel is presumed not to have been at fault and therefore not to have contributed to the accident. — Also termed *major-and-minor fault rule.*

major trend. See TREND.

majus jus (**may**-jəs **jəs**). [Law Latin "a greater right"] *Hist.* A greater right. • This was a plea in a real action.

make, *vb.* **1.** To cause (something) to exist <to make a record>. **2.** To enact (something) <to make law>. **3.** To acquire (something) <to make money on execution>. **4.** To legally perform, as by executing, signing, or delivering (a document) <to make a contract>.

make law. 1. To legislate. **2.** To issue a legal precedent, esp. a judicial decision, that establishes a new rule of law on a particular subject. **3.** *Hist.* To deny a plaintiff's charge under oath, in open court, with compurgators.

maker. 1. One who frames, promulgates, or ordains (as in *lawmaker*). **2.** A person who signs a promissory note. See NOTE (1). Cf. CO-MAKER. **3.** DRAWER.

accommodation maker. One who signs a note as a surety. See ACCOMMODATION (2); *accommodation indorser* under INDORSER.

prime maker. The person who is primarily liable on a note or other negotiable instrument.

makeup gas. *Oil & gas.* Natural gas that has been paid for by the purchaser, usu. under a take-or-pay contract, but that is to be delivered in the years following payment. See *take-or-pay contract* under CONTRACT.

make-whole doctrine. *Insurance.* The principle that, unless the insurance policy provides otherwise, an insurer will not receive any of the proceeds from the settlement of a claim, except to the extent that the settlement funds exceed the amount necessary to fully compensate the insured for the loss suffered.

mal (mal), *adj.* [Law French "bad; wrong; against"] Bad; wrong. • In Law French, *mal* was a separable word, equivalent to the Latin *male* ("badly"). In its modern uses, *mal-* is a prefix in terms such as *maladministration* and *malpractice.*

mala antiqua (**mal**-ə an-**tɪ**-kwə). Old crimes; offenses that date back to antiquity.

maladministration. Poor management or regulation, esp. in an official capacity. — Also termed *misadministration.*

mala fides (**mal**-ə **fɪ**-deez), *n.* See BAD FAITH.

mala in se (**mal**-ə in **say** *or* **see**). See MALUM IN SE.

malandrinus (mal-ən-**drɪ**-nəs), *n.* [Law Latin "brigand"] *Hist.* A thief; a pirate.

malapportionment, *n.* The improper or unconstitutional apportionment of a legislative district. — **malapportion,** *vb.* See APPORTIONMENT; GERRYMANDERING.

mala praxis (**mal**-ə **prak**-sis). [Law Latin] *Hist.* Malpractice; unskilled treatment, esp. by a doctor.

> "Injuries, affecting a man's *health*, are where by any unwholesome practices of another a man sustains any apparent damage in his vigor or constitution. As by selling him bad provisions or wine . . . or by the neglect or unskilful management of his physician, surgeon, or apothecary. For it hath been solemnly resolved . . . that *mala praxis* is a great misdemeanor and offence at common law, whether it be for curiosity and experiment, or by neglect; because it breaks the trust which the party had placed in his physician, and tends to the patient's destruction." 3 William Blackstone, *Commentaries on the Laws of England* 122 (1768).

mala prohibita (**mal**-ə proh-**hib**-i-tə). See MALUM PROHIBITUM.

malconduct in office. See *official misconduct* under MISCONDUCT.

male creditus (**mal**-ee **kred**-ə-təs). [Law Latin] *Hist.* (Of a person) in bad repute; untrusted.

malediction (mal-ə-**dik**-shən). *Hist.* A curse connected with the donation of property to a church and applicable against anyone attempting to violate the church's rights.

malefaction (mal-ə-**fak**-shən), *n.* [Latin *malefacere* "to do evil"] *Archaic.* An evil deed; a crime or offense. — Also termed *maleficium.* — **malefactory,** *adj.*

malefactor (**mal**-ə-fak-tər), *n.* [Latin] *Hist.* A wrongdoer; a criminal.

maleficium (mal-ə-**fish**-ee-əm), *n.* [Latin "a misdeed"] *Roman law.* See MALEFACTION.

malesworn (**mayl**-sworn), *p.pl.* Forsworn. — Also spelled *malsworn.*

malfeasance (mal-**fee**-zənts), *n.* A wrongful or unlawful act; esp., wrongdoing or misconduct by a public official; MISFEASANCE IN PUBLIC OFFICE. — **malfeasant** (mal-**fee**-zənt), *adj.* — **malfeasor** (mal-**fee**-zər), *n.* Cf. MISFEASANCE; NONFEASANCE.

malfunction theory. *Products-liability law.* A principle permitting a products-liability plaintiff to prove that a product was defective by proving that the product malfunctioned, instead of requiring the plaintiff to prove a specific defect. • A plaintiff relying on the malfunction theory usu. must also prove that the product was not misused, and must disprove all reasonable explanations for the occurrence other than a defect.

mal gree (mal **gree**). [Law French "against the will"] *Hist.* Against the will; without consent.

malice, *n.* **1.** The intent, without justification or excuse, to commit a wrongful act. **2.** Reckless disregard of the law or of a person's legal rights. **3.** Ill will; wickedness of heart. • This sense is most typical in nonlegal contexts. — **malicious,** *adj.*

> "Malice means in law wrongful intention. It includes any intent which the law deems wrongful, and which therefore serves as a ground of liability. Any act done with such an intent is, in the language of the law, malicious, and this legal usage has etymology in its favour. The Latin *malitia* means badness, physical or moral — wickedness in disposition or in conduct — not specifically or exclusively ill-will or malevolence; hence the malice of English law, including all forms of evil purpose, design, intent, or motive. [But] intent is of two kinds, being either immediate or ulterior, the ulterior intent being commonly distinguished as the motive. The term malice is applied in law to both these forms of intent, and the result is a somewhat puzzling ambiguity which requires careful notice. When we say that an act is done maliciously, we mean one of two distinct things. We mean either that it is done intentionally, or that it is done with some wrongful motive." John Salmond, *Jurisprudence* 384 (Glanville L. Williams ed., 10th ed. 1947).

> "[M]alice in the legal sense imports (1) the absence of all elements of justification, excuse or recognized mitigation, and (2) the presence of either (a) an actual intent to cause the particular harm which is produced or harm of the same general nature, or (b) the wanton and wilful doing of an act with awareness of a plain and strong likelihood that such harm may result. . . . The Model Penal Code does not use 'malice' because those who formulated the Code had a blind prejudice against the word. This is very regrettable because it represents a useful concept despite some unfortunate language employed at times in the effort to express it." Rollin M. Perkins & Ronald N. Boyce, *Criminal Law* 860 (3d ed. 1982).

actual malice. **1.** The deliberate intent to commit an injury, as evidenced by external circumstances. — Also termed *express malice*; *malice in fact.* Cf. *implied malice.* **2.** *Defamation.* Knowledge (by the person who utters or publishes a defamatory statement) that a statement is false, or reckless disregard about whether the statement is true. • To recover for defamation, a plaintiff who is a public official or public figure must overcome the defendant's qualified privilege by proving the defendant's actual malice. And for certain other types of claims, a plaintiff must prove actual malice to recover presumed or punitive damages. — Also termed *New York Times malice*; *constitutional malice.*

common-law malice. See *actual malice* (2).

constructive malice. See *implied malice.*

express malice. **1.** *Criminal law.* The intent to kill or seriously injure arising from a deliberate, rational mind. **2.** See *actual malice* (1). **3.** *Defamation.* The bad-faith publication of defamatory material.

implied malice. Malice inferred from a person's conduct. — Also termed *constructive malice*; *legal malice*; *malice in law.* Cf. *actual malice* (1).

malice in fact. See *actual malice.*

particular malice. Malice that is directed at a particular person. — Also termed *special malice.*

transferred malice. Malice directed to one person or object but instead harming another in the way intended for the first.

> "[I]f A shoots at B intending to kill him, but the shot actually kills C, this is held to be murder of C. So also if A throws a stone at one window and breaks another, it is held to be malicious damage to the window actually broken. This doctrine, which is known as the doctrine of transferred malice, applies only where the harm intended and the harm done are of the same kind. If A throws a stone at a human being and unintentionally breaks a window, he cannot be convicted of malicious damage to the window." John Salmond, *Jurisprudence* 382 (Glanville L. Williams ed., 10th ed. 1947).

universal malice. The state of mind of a person who determines to take a life on slight provocation, without knowing or caring who may be the victim.

malice aforethought. The requisite mental state for common-law murder, encompassing any one of the following: (1) the intent to kill, (2) the intent to inflict grievous bodily harm, (3) extremely reckless indifference to the value of human life (the so-called "abandoned and malignant heart"), or (4) the intent to commit a felony (which leads to culpability under the felony-murder rule). — Also termed *premeditated malice*; *preconceived malice*; *malice prepense*; *malitia praecogitata.*

> "Malice aforethought is the term which came into use during medieval times to indicate the mental element necessary in the felony of murder. It has been the subject of voluminous jurisprudential enquiry . . . ." J.W. Cecil Turner, *Kenny's Outlines of Criminal Law* 27 (16th ed. 1952).

> "Every intentional killing is with malice aforethought unless under circumstances sufficient to constitute (1) justification, (2) excuse, or (3) mitigation." Rollin M. Perkins & Ronald N. Boyce, *Criminal Law* 58 (3d ed. 1982).

malice exception. A limitation on a public official's qualified immunity, by which the official can face civil liability for willfully exercising discretion in a way that violates a known or well-established right. See *qualified immunity* under IMMUNITY (1).

malice in fact. See *actual malice* (1) under MALICE.

malice in law. See *implied malice* under MALICE.

malice prepense. See MALICE AFORETHOUGHT.

malicious, *adj.* **1.** Substantially certain to cause injury. **2.** Without just cause or excuse.

malicious abandonment. See ABANDONMENT.

malicious abuse of legal process. See ABUSE OF PROCESS.

malicious abuse of process. See ABUSE OF PROCESS.

malicious accusation. See ACCUSATION.

malicious act. An intentional, wrongful act performed against another without legal justification or excuse.

malicious arrest. See ARREST.

malicious assault with a deadly weapon. See ASSAULT.

malicious bankruptcy. An abuse of process by which a person wrongfully petitions to have another person adjudicated a bankrupt or to have a company wound up as insolvent.

malicious damage. See MALICIOUS MISCHIEF.

malicious execution. See EXECUTION.

malicious injury. See INJURY.

malicious killing. An intentional killing without legal justification or excuse.

maliciously damaging the property of another. See MALICIOUS MISCHIEF.

malicious mischief. The common-law misdemeanor of intentionally destroying or damaging another's property. • Although modern statutes predominantly make this offense a misdemeanor, a few make it a felony (depending on the nature of the property or its value). — Also termed *malicious mischief and trespass*; *malicious injury*; *malicious trespass*; *malicious damage*; *maliciously damaging the property of another*; (in the Model Penal Code) *criminal mischief*.

> "Such phrases as 'malicious mischief and trespass,' 'malicious injury,' and 'maliciously damaging the property of another,' are merely additional labels used at times to indicate the same offense. It was a misdemeanor according to the common law of England, although some confusion has resulted from Blackstone's statement that it was 'only a trespass at common law.' Before the word 'misdemeanor' became well established the old writers tended to use the word 'trespass' to indicate an offense below the grade of felony. And it was used at times by Blackstone for this purpose, as in the phrase 'treason, felony, or trespass.'" Rollin M. Perkins & Ronald N. Boyce, *Criminal Law* 405 (3d ed. 1982).

malicious motive. See MOTIVE.

malicious prosecution. 1. The institution of a criminal or civil proceeding for an improper purpose and without probable cause. **2.** The cause of action resulting from the institution of such a proceeding. • Once a wrongful prosecution has ended in the defendant's favor, he or she may sue for tort damages. — Also termed (in the context of civil proceedings) *malicious use of process*. Cf. ABUSE OF PROCESS; VEXATIOUS SUIT.

> "The distinction between an action for malicious prosecution and an action for abuse of process is that a malicious prosecution consists in maliciously causing process to be issued, whereas an abuse of process is the employment of legal process for some purpose other than that which it was intended by the law to effect — the improper use of a regularly issued process. For instance, the initiation of vexatious civil proceedings known to be groundless is not abuse of process, but is governed by substantially the same rules as the malicious prosecution of criminal proceedings." 52 Am. Jur. 2d *Malicious Prosecution* § 2, at 187 (1970).

malicious trespass. See MALICIOUS MISCHIEF.

malicious use of process. See MALICIOUS PROSECUTION.

malignare (mal-əg-**nair**-ee), *vb*. [Latin] *Hist*. **1.** To malign; to slander. **2.** To maim.

malinger, *vb*. To feign illness or disability, esp. in an attempt to avoid an obligation or to continue receiving disability benefits.

malison (**mal**-ə-zən *or* -sən). [fr. Latin *malum* "evil" + *sonus* "a sound"] *Hist*. A curse. — Also spelled *maleson*.

malitia (mə-**lish**-ee-ə). [Latin "malice"] *Hist*. An actual evil design; express malice. • *Malitia* originally signified general wrongdoing, and did not describe a wrongdoer's state of mind; *malitia praecogitata*, for example, indicated only the seriousness of the offense, though it was eventually rendered *malice aforethought*.

malitia praecogitata (pree-koj-ə-**tay**-tə). See MALICE AFORETHOUGHT. — Also termed *malitia excogitata* (eks-koj-ə-**tay**-tə).

> "[T]he word *felony* is often coupled with what will in the future be another troublesome term of art, to wit, *malice aforethought* or *malice prepense* (*malitia excogitata, praecogitata*).... When it first came into use, it hardly signified a state of mind; some qualifying adjective such as *praemeditata* or *excogitata* was needed if much note was to be taken of intention or of any other psychical fact. When we first meet with *malice prepense* it seems to mean little more than intentional wrong-doing; but the somewhat weighty adjectives which are coupled with *malitia* in its commonest context — adjectives such as *excogitata* — are, if we mistake not, traces of the time when *forsteal*, *guetapens*, waylaying, the setting of ambush, was (what few crimes were) a specially reserved plea of the crown to be emended, if indeed it was emendable, by a heavy *wite*." 2 Frederick Pollock & Frederic W. Maitland, *The History of English Law Before the Time of Edward I* 468–69 (2d ed. 1899).

malleable, *adj*. **1.** (Of an object) capable of extension by hammering <the metal was malleable>. **2.** (Of a person) capable of being influenced <the young student was malleable>.

Malleus Maleficarum (**mal**-ee-əs mal-ə-fi-**kair**-əm). [Latin "Hammer of Witches"] *Hist*. An encyclopedic work of demonology and witchcraft, prepared in 1486 by two Dominican friars (Heinrich Kraemer and Johann Sprenger) as part of their efforts to eradicate witchcraft in Germany. • The *Malleus Maleficarum* was based largely on folk beliefs, but it was relied on as an authoritative source on how to detect, extract confessions from, and prosecute witches for several centuries after it first appeared.

***Mallory* rule.** See MCNABB–MALLORY RULE.

mallum (**mal**-əm), *n*. [Law Latin] *Hist*. **1.** A superior court; a high court that handles important business. **2.** A public national assembly.

malo animo (**mal**-oh **an**-ə-moh), *adv*. [Latin] With evil intent; with malice.

malo grato (**mal**-oh **gray**-toh), *adv*. [Latin] Unwillingly.

Maloney Act. A 1938 amendment to the Securities Exchange Act of 1934, providing for broker registration in over-the-counter markets.

malpractice (mal-**prak**-tis). An instance of negligence or incompetence on the part of a professional. • To succeed in a malpractice claim, a plaintiff must also prove proximate cause and damages. — Also termed *professional negligence*.

legal malpractice. A lawyer's failure to render professional services with the skill, prudence, and diligence that an ordinary and reasonable lawyer would use under similar circumstances. — Also termed *attorney malpractice*.

medical malpractice. A doctor's failure to exercise the degree of care and skill that a physician or surgeon of the same medical specialty would use under similar circumstances. — Often shortened to *med. mal.*

malpractice insurance. See INSURANCE.

maltreatment. Bad treatment (esp. improper treatment by a surgeon) resulting from ignorance, neglect, or willfulness. See MALPRACTICE.

malum (**mal**-əm *also* **may**-ləm), *n.* [Latin] Something bad or evil. Pl. ***mala.***

malum in se (**mal**-əm in **say** *or* **see**), *n.* [Latin "evil in itself"] A crime or an act that is inherently immoral, such as murder, arson, or rape. — Also termed *malum per se*. Pl. ***mala in se.*** — ***malum in se,*** *adj.* Cf. MALUM PROHIBITUM.

"The basis for the distinction between *mala in se* and *mala prohibita*, between what one might call a crime and an offence — or between what one might call a felony and a misdemeanour, if one could modernize those terms so that the latter was given its natural meaning — is that crime means to the ordinary man something that is sinful or immoral, and an offence at worst a piece of misbehaviour." Patrick Devlin, *The Enforcement of Morals* 33 (1968).

"The distinction between offenses *mala in se* and offenses *mala prohibita* was recognized at least as early as the fifteenth century. It has been criticized repeatedly. About a century and a half ago the distinction was said to be one 'not founded upon any sound principle' and which had 'long since been exploded.' [Quoting *Bensley v. Bignold*, 5 B. & A. 335, 341, 106 Eng. Rep. 1214, 1216 (1822); other citations omitted.] The Supreme Court, however, has shown that it is just as firmly entrenched today as it was in 1495." Rollin M. Perkins & Ronald N. Boyce, *Criminal Law* 880 (3d ed. 1982).

malum prohibitum (**mal**-əm proh-**hib**-i-təm), *n.* [Latin "prohibited evil"] An act that is a crime merely because it is prohibited by statute, although the act itself is not necessarily immoral. • Misdemeanors such as jaywalking and running a stoplight are *mala prohibita*, as are many regulatory violations. Pl. ***mala prohibita.*** — ***malum prohibitum,*** *adj.* Cf. MALUM IN SE.

"Much of the criminal law that is regulatory in character — the part of it that deals with *malum prohibitum* rather than *malum in se* — is based upon the ... principle ... that the choice of the individual must give way to the convenience of the many." Patrick Devlin, *The Enforcement of Morals* 16 (1968).

"As customarily used these phrases are mutually exclusive. An offense *malum prohibitum* is not a wrong which is prohibited, but something which is wrong *only* in the sense that it is against the law. This is emphasized at times by such phrases as '*malum prohibitum* only' or 'but *malum prohibitum*,' although it is understood without any such qualification. A failure to understand this usage of the terms has led some to assume that all statutory additions to the common law of crimes are *mala prohibita*. One writer emphasized his confusion by speaking of embezzlement as *malum prohibitum*. This assumption is utterly without foundation. An act may be *malum in se* although no punishment is provided by law. If this defect is corrected by appropriate legislation, what previously was *malum in se* does not cease to be so by reason of having been defined and made punishable by law." Rollin M. Perkins & Ronald N. Boyce, *Criminal Law* 884–85 (3d ed. 1982).

malveilles (mal-**vay** *also* mal-**vayls**), *n.* [French "misdemeanors"] *Hist.* **1.** Ill will. **2.** Crimes; misdemeanors; malicious acts.

malveis procurors (**mal**-vay prə-**kyoor**-ərz). [Law French "defective procurers"] *Hist.* Persons who pack juries, as by nomination or other practice.

malversation (mal-vər-**say**-shən), *n.* [French "ill behavior"] Official corruption; a misbehavior, esp. by someone exercising an office.

man. 1. An adult male. **2.** Humankind. — Also termed *mankind*. **3.** A human being. **4.** *Hist.* A vassal; a feudal tenant.

manacle (**man**-ə-kəl). A shackle; a handcuff.

managed care. A system of comprehensive healthcare provided by a health-maintenance organization, a preferred-provider organization, or a similar group.

management. The people in a company who are responsible for its operation.

middle management. People who manage operations within a company and execute top management's directives.

top management. The highest level of a company's management, at which major policy decisions and long-term business plans are made. — Also termed *upper management*.

management buyout. See BUYOUT.

management fee. See FEE (1).

manager. 1. A person who administers or supervises the affairs of a business, office, or other organization.

general manager. A manager who has overall control of a business, office, or other organization, including authority over other managers. • A general manager is usu. equivalent to a president or chief executive officer of a corporation.

2. A legislator appointed by either legislative house to serve on a conference committee, esp. a joint committee that tries to reconcile differences in a bill passed by both houses in different versions. — Also termed *conferee*; *manager of a conference*. **3.** A representative appointed by the House of Representatives to prosecute an impeachment before the Senate.

manager of a conference. See MANAGER (2).

managing agent. See AGENT.

managing conservator. See CONSERVATOR.

managing conservatorship. See CUSTODY (2).

managium (mə-**nay**-jee-əm), *n.* [Law Latin fr. Law French *manage* "a dwelling"] *Hist.* A dwelling; a mansion house. — Also termed *mensa* (**men**-sə).

***Manahan*-type carried interest.** *Oil & gas.* A transaction in which the owner of a lease assigns all the working interest to someone else — who takes on specified costs of drilling and development — and the assignor retains a reversionary interest in part of the working interest, which reverts to the assignor once the assignee has recovered the specified costs during the payout period. *Manahan Oil Co. v. Commissioner*, 8 T.C. 1159 (1947).

man-bote. See BOTE (2).

manceps (**man**-seps), *n.* [Latin "an agent"] **1.** *Roman law.* A purchaser of something at a state auction, esp. a right or advantage, as in the right to farm taxes. **2.** *Roman law.* A state postmaster.

> "Manceps. One who at a public auction, conducted by a magistrate, through the highest bid obtained the right to collect taxes (a tax farmer) or custom duties, the lease of public land (*ager publicus*) or other advantages (a monopoly). — In postal organization *manceps* was a post-station master." Adolf Berger, *Encyclopedic Dictionary of Roman Law* 573 (1953).

3. A person who undertakes to perform a task and gives security for the performance.

manche-present (mahnsh-pray-**zon**). [Law French "a gift from the giver's sleeve"] A bribe.

mancipare (man-sə-**pair**-ee), *vb.* [fr. Latin *manus* "hand" + *capere* "to take"] *Roman law.* **1.** To alienate (a thing) by real or fictitious sale. **2.** To sell (a person), esp. fictitiously as part of the emancipation process. See MANCIPATION.

mancipatio (man-sə-**pay**-shee-oh), *n.* [Latin] See MANCIPATION.

mancipation. [fr. Latin *mancipatio* "hand-grasp"] **1.** *Roman law.* A legal formality for acquiring property by either an actual or a simulated purchase. • The formality consisted in laying hold of a thing and asserting title to it before five witnesses, followed by weighing the real or pretended purchase money on scales. This form of sale was abolished by Justinian.

> "Mancipatio is the solemn sale per aes et libram. In the presence of five witnesses (cives Romani puberes) a skilled weighmaster (libripens) weighs out to the vendor a certain amount of uncoined copper (aes, raudus, rauduscululum) which is the purchase-money, and the purchaser, with solemn words, takes possession with his hand — hence the description of the act as 'hand-grasp' — of the thing purchased as being his property." Rudolph Sohm, *The Institutes: A Textbook of the History and System of Roman Private Law* 48 (James Crawford Ledlie trans., 3d ed. 1907).

2. A similar form used for making a will, adoption, emancipation of slaves, etc. — Also termed *mancipatio*. Cf. EMANCIPATION.

mancipi res (**man**-sə-pI **reez**). See RES MANCIPI.

mancipium (man-**sip**-ee-əm), *n.* [Latin "a slave"] *Roman law.* **1.** A slave, esp. by virtue of being captured by an enemy in war. **2.** A temporary quasi-slave status often occurring in an emancipation, as when a son is emancipated from his father. See MANCIPATION.

> "But if the *patria potestas* could be created, it could also be terminated, by an artificial process .... The father could not by a simple act of his own will release the son from his control. For this purpose he must sell him out of his own hands into that state of *mancipium* or qualified slavery of which we have spoken. Even then the father's power was not destroyed: it was suspended during the existence of the *mancipium*; but if the *mancipium* ceased, if the son was set free by the person who held him in that condition, the father's right revived .... It was not until he had sold him three times over, that he used up his right of control beyond the possibility of a revival. This, then, was the form by which the son was liberated from the *patria potestas*." James Hadley, *Introduction to Roman Law* 126–27 (1881).

M & A. *abbr.* Mergers and acquisitions. See MERGER.

mandamus (man-**day**-məs), *n.* [Latin "we command"] A writ issued by a superior court to compel a lower court or a government officer to perform mandatory or purely ministerial duties correctly. — Also termed *writ of mandamus.* Pl. **mandamuses.** — **mandamus,** *vb.*

alternative mandamus. A mandamus issued upon the first application for relief, commanding the defendant either to perform the act demanded or to appear before the court at a specified time to show cause for not performing it.

peremptory mandamus. An absolute and unqualified command to the defendant to do the act in question. • It is issued when the defendant defaults on, or fails to show sufficient cause in answer to, an alternative mandamus.

mandans (**man**-danz). *Roman law.* The principal for whom an agent deals with third parties. See MANDATOR.

mandant (**man**-dənt), *n.* [French] *French & Scots law.* A principal in a contract of mandate, such as a bailor in a bailment. See MANDATOR.

mandatary (**man**-də-ter-ee), *n.* **1.** A person to whom a mandate is given. See MANDATE (5). **2.** An agent, esp. one who acts gratuitously but is entitled to be indemnified for expenses incurred in carrying out the mandate. — Also termed (in Roman law) *mandatarius.* — **mandatary,** *adj.*

mandate, *n.* **1.** An order from an appellate court directing a lower court to take a specified action. **2.** A judicial command directed to an officer of the court to enforce a court order. **3.** In politics, the electorate's overwhelming show of approval for a given political platform. **4.** *Civil law.* A written command given by a principal to an agent. **5.** *Civil law.* A commission or contract by which one person (the *mandator*) requests someone (the *mandatary*) to perform some service gratuitously, the commission becoming effective when the mandatary agrees. • In this type of contract, no liability is created until the service requested has begun. The mandatary is bound to use reasonable care in performance, while the mandator is bound to indemnify against loss incurred in performing the service. — Also termed *mandatum.* **6.** *Int'l law.* An authority given by the League of Nations and, later, the United Nations to certain governments to take over the administration and development of certain territories. Cf. TRUSTEESHIP (2). — **mandate,** *vb.* — **mandatory,** *adj.*

mandate rule. The doctrine that, after an appellate court has remanded a case to a lower court, the lower court must follow the decision that the appellate court has made in the case, unless new evidence or an intervening change in the law dictates a different result.

mandator (man-**day**-tər *or* **man**-day-tər). **1.** A person who delegates the performance of a mandate to another. **2.** *Civil law.* The person who employs another (called a *mandatary* or *mandatarius*) in a gratuitous agency. — Also termed *mandant.* **3.** BAILOR (1).

mandatory, *adj.* Of, relating to, or constituting a command; required; preemptory.

mandatory injunction. See INJUNCTION.

mandatory instruction. See JURY INSTRUCTION.

mandatory joinder. See *compulsory joinder* under JOINDER.

mandatory penalty. See *mandatory sentence* under SENTENCE.

mandatory presumption. See *conclusive presumption* under PRESUMPTION.

mandatory punishment. See *mandatory sentence* under SENTENCE.

mandatory sentence. See SENTENCE.

mandatory statute. See STATUTE.

mandatory subject of bargaining. *Labor law.* A topic that is required by the National Labor

Relations Act to be discussed in good faith by the parties during labor negotiations; an essential employment matter, including wages, hours, and other terms and conditions of employment, about which management and the union are required to negotiate in good faith, and that can lawfully form the basis of a collective-bargaining impasse. 29 USCA § 158(d). — Often shortened to *mandatory subject*. Cf. PERMISSIVE SUBJECT OF BARGAINING.

mandatum (man-**day**-təm). A bailment in which the bailee will, without recompense, perform some service relating to the goods; MANDATE (5). • This type of bailment is for the sole benefit of the bailor.

mandavi ballivo (man-**day**-vɪ bə-**lɪ**-voh). [Law Latin "I have commanded the bailiff"] *Hist.* A sheriff's return stating that the sheriff ordered a bailiff to execute a writ.

man-endangering state of mind. See PERSON-ENDANGERING STATE OF MIND.

manerium (mə-**neer**-ee-əm), *n.* [Law Latin, fr. Latin *manere* "to remain"] *Hist.* A manor.

> "The term *manerium* seems to have come in with the Conqueror, though other derivatives from the Latin verb *manere*, in particular *mansa*, *mansio*, *mansiuncula* had been freely employed by the scribes of the land-books. But these had as a rule been used as representatives of the English *hide*, and just for this reason they were incapable of expressing the notion that the Normans desired to express by the word *manerium*. In its origin that word is but one more name for a house. Throughout the Exeter Domesday the word *mansio* is used instead of the *manerium* of the Exchequer record, and even in the Exchequer record we may find these two terms used interchangeably ...." Frederic W. Maitland, *Domesday Book and Beyond* 108–09 (1921).

mangonare (mang-gə-**nair**-ee), *vb.* [fr. Latin *mango* "a dealer"] To buy in a market; to deal.

manhood. 1. A male person's majority. **2.** *Hist.* A ceremony of a vassal paying homage to the vassal's lord. — Also termed *homagium*.

> "Besides an oath of *fealty*, or profession of faith to the lord, which was the parent of our oath of allegiance, the vassal or tenant upon investiture did usually *homage* to his lord; openly and humbly kneeling, being ungirt, uncovered, and holding up his hands both together between those of the lord, who sate before him; and there professing that 'he did become his *man*, from that day forth, of life and limb and earthly honour:' and then he received a kiss from his lord. Which ceremony was denominated *homagium*, or *manhood*, by the feudists." 2 William Blackstone, *Commentaries on the Laws of England* 53 (1766).

manifest, *n.* A document listing the cargo or passengers carried on a ship, airplane, or other vehicle.

manifestation of intention. *Wills & estates.* The external expression of the testator's intention, as distinguished from an undisclosed intention. — Also termed *manifestation of intent*.

manifestation theory. *Insurance.* The doctrine that coverage for an injury or disease falls to the policy in effect when the symptoms of the covered injury or disease first appear. Cf. EXPOSURE THEORY; ACTUAL-INJURY TRIGGER; TRIPLE TRIGGER.

> "Some injuries do not manifest themselves until a period of time has elapsed between the occurrence of the event that produces the harm and the time when it becomes apparent. Particularly when these claims result from what often were not recognized as dangerous products or chemicals when the exposure occurred, such as asbestos or dioxin, the consequences are referred to as 'delayed manifestation' injuries .... [Under the] '[m]anifestation' theory ... [some] courts have concluded that coverage is provided by the insurance policy in place at the time the injury becomes apparent, that is, when the injury is manifested." Robert E. Keeton & Alan I. Widiss, *Insurance Law: A Guide to Fundamental Principles, Legal Doctrines, and Commercial Practices* § 5.10(d)(3), at 598 (1988).

manifest constitutional error. See ERROR (2).

manifest-disregard doctrine. The principle that an arbitration award will be vacated if the arbitrator knows the applicable law and deliberately chooses to disregard it, but will not be vacated for a mere error or misunderstanding of the law.

manifest error. See ERROR (2).

manifest-error-or-clearly-wrong rule. In some jurisdictions, the doctrine that an appellate court cannot set aside a trial court's finding of fact unless a review of the entire record reveals that the finding has no reasonable basis.

manifest injustice. An error in the trial court that is direct, obvious, and observable, such as a defendant's guilty plea that is involuntary or that is based on a plea agreement that the prosecution rescinds.

manifest intent. See INTENT (1).

manifest law. See LEX MANIFESTA.

manifest necessity. *Criminal procedure.* A sudden and overwhelming emergency, beyond the court's and parties' control, that makes conducting a trial or reaching a fair result impossible and that therefore authorizes the granting of a mistrial. • The standard of manifest necessity must be met to preclude a defendant from successfully raising a plea of former jeopardy after a mistrial.

manifesto. A written statement publicly declaring the issuer's principles, policies, or intentions; esp., a formal document explaining why a state or nation declared war or took some other significant international action.

manifest weight of the evidence. A deferential standard of review under which a verdict will be reversed or disregarded only if another outcome is obviously correct and the verdict is clearly unsupported by the evidence. Cf. WEIGHT OF THE EVIDENCE.

manipulation. *Securities.* The illegal practice of raising or lowering a security's price by creating the appearance of active trading. • Manipulation is prohibited by section 10(b) of the Securities Exchange Act of 1934. 15 USCA § 78j(b). — Also termed *market manipulation*; *stock manipulation*.

mankind. See MAN (2).

Mann Act. A federal law, enacted originally in 1948, that criminalizes the transportation of any person in interstate or foreign commerce for prostitution or similar sexual activities. 18 USCA § 2421. — Also termed *White Slave Traffic Act*.

manner and form. See ***modo et forma***.

mannire (mə-**nı**-ree), *vb.* [Law Latin] *Hist.* To summon (an adverse party) to court; to prosecute (a case).

mannopus (man-**oh**-pəs). [fr. Latin *manus* "hand" + *opus* "work"] *Hist.* **1.** Manual labor. **2.** A day's work. **3.** MAINOUR.

manor. **1.** A feudal estate, usu. granted by the king to a lord or other high person and cultivated as a unit. • In more ancient times, the lord's manor included a village community, usu. comprised of serfs.

> "[T]o ask for a definition of a manor is to ask for what can not be given. We may however draw a picture of a typical manor, and, this done, we may discuss the deviations from this type .... [W]e may regard the typical manor (1) as being, *qua* vill, a unit of public law, of police and fiscal law, (2) as being a unit in the system of agriculture, (3) as being a unit in the management of property, (4) as being a jurisdictional unit. But we ... see that hardly one of these traits can be considered as absolutely essential. The most important is the connection between the manor and the vill ...." 1 Frederick Pollock & Frederic W. Maitland, *The History of English Law Before the Time of Edward I* 596–97 (2d ed. 1898).

> "The term [*manor*] applied, after the Norman conquest, to estates organized under knights, ecclesiastical corporations, or otherwise, and managed and cultivated as units. By the end of the 11th century, the main element was the feudal lord, and soon he came to be regarded as the owner of the manor, and to have authority over the tenants, and the right to hold a court for them .... In the thirteenth and fourteenth centuries, a manor also implied a right of jurisdiction exercised through a court baron, attended by both freeholders and villein tenants .... In the eighteenth century the manorial court decayed rapidly, cases being generally brought in the King's courts, the only surviving business being copyhold conveyancing." David M. Walker, *The Oxford Companion to Law* 803 (1980).

reputed manor. A manor in which the demesne lands and services become absolutely separated. • The manor is no longer a manor in actuality, only in reputation. — Also termed *seigniory in gross*.

2. A jurisdictional right over tenants of an estate, usu. exercised through a court baron. **3.** *Hist.* In the United States, a tract of land occupied by tenants who pay rent to a proprietor. **4.** A mansion on an estate.

manorial extent. *Hist.* A survey of a manor by a jury of tenants, giving the numbers and names of tenants, the size of their holdings, the kind of tenure, and the kind and amount of the tenants' services.

manorial system. The medieval system of land ownership in which serfs and some freemen cultivated the soil of a manor in return for a lord's protection. See MANOR.

manse (mans), *n.* [Law Latin] *Hist.* **1.** A portion of land large enough to maintain one family; a sufficient amount of land to be worked by a yoke of oxen for a year. **2.** A house without land; MESSUAGE. **3.** In Scotland, a clergyman's dwelling. — Also termed *mansus*.

manser (**man**-sər), *n.* [Law Latin] *Hist.* A bastard.

Mansfield rule. The doctrine that a juror's testimony or affidavit about juror misconduct may not be used to challenge the verdict. • This Mansfield rule is intended to ensure that jurors are heard through their verdict, not through their postverdict testimony. In practice, the rule lessens the possibility that losing parties will seek to penetrate the secrets of the jury room. The rule was first announced in *Vaise v. Delaval*, 99 Eng. Rep. 944 (K.B. 1785), in an opinion by William Murray, first Earl of Mansfield, the Lord Chief Justice of the Court of King's Bench.

mansio (**man**-shee-oh), *n.* [Law Latin] *Hist.* **1.** An inn. **2.** A house.

mansion-house. 1. *Hist.* The residence of the lord of a manor. **2.** DWELLING-HOUSE.

mansion-house rule. The doctrine that a tract of land lying in two counties will be assessed, for property-tax purposes, in the county in which the house is located.

manslaughter, *n.* The unlawful killing of a human being without malice aforethought. — **manslaughter,** *vb.* Cf. MURDER.

involuntary manslaughter. Homicide in which there is no intention to kill or do grievous bodily harm, but that is committed with criminal negligence or during the commission of a crime not included within the felony-murder rule. — Also termed *negligent manslaughter*. Cf. ACCIDENTAL KILLING.

"Involuntary manslaughter is a 'catch-all' concept. It includes all manslaughter not characterized as voluntary." Rollin M. Perkins & Ronald N. Boyce, *Criminal Law* 104 (3d ed. 1982).

"The only differences between the legal use and the everyday use of 'voluntary,' 'not voluntary,' and 'involuntary' seem to be (a) a more frequent use of 'involuntary' as a synonym of 'not voluntary' and (b) a technical use of 'involuntary' in the crime of 'involuntary manslaughter,' where it seems to have the meaning of 'unintentional.' Thus, as contrasted with 'voluntary manslaughter,' there is no suggestion that death, as contrasted with harm, was intended or foreseen. Though it is often confined to cases of assault and battery where death results, for example either from the withholding of food or from excessive chastisement of a child, some jurists say that it can be due to any unlawful and dangerous action causing death." Alan R. White, *Grounds of Liability* 61–62 (1985).

voluntary manslaughter. An act of murder reduced to manslaughter because of extenuating circumstances such as adequate provocation (arousing the "heat of passion") or diminished capacity. — Also termed *intentional manslaughter*.

manstealing. See KIDNAPPING.

mansuetae naturae (man-**swee**-tee nə-**tyoor**-ee). [Latin "of a tamable nature"] *Civil law.* **1.** *adj.* (Of animals) tame or tamable. **2.** *n.* Tame animals; animals accustomed to come to the hand.

mansuetus (man-**swee**-təs), *adj.* [Latin] *Roman law.* Tame; tamed.

mansus. See MANSE.

manticulate (man-**tik**-yə-layt), *vb.* To pick pockets.

mantle children. *Hist.* Children born out of wedlock and later legitimized when their parents married, by standing under a cloak with the parents during the marriage ceremony.

"Our law ... has no need to distinguish between various sorts of illegitimate children. A child is either a legitimate child or a bastard .... In the sharp controversy over this principle ... the champion of what we may call the high-church party alleged that old English custom was in accord with the law of the church as defined by Alexander III. Probably there was some truth in this assertion. It is not unlikely that old custom, though it would not have held that the marriage in itself had any retroactive effect, allowed the parents on the occasion of their marriage to legitimate the already existing offspring of their union. The children were placed under the cloak which was spread over their parents during the marriage ceremony, and became 'mantle children.' We hear of this practice in Germany and France and Normandy; but we have here rather an act of adoption than a true legitimation ... and it would not have fully satisfied the church." 2 Frederick Pollock & Frederic W. Maitland, *The History of English Law Before the Time of Edward I* 397–98 (2d ed. 1899).

manual, *adj.* Used or performed by hand <manual labor>.

manual delivery. Delivery of personal property by actual and corporeal change in possession.

Manual for Courts–Martial. A manual that implements the Uniform Code of Military Justice. • It was adopted in 1969 by presidential executive order.

manual gift. See GIFT.

manualis obedientia (man-yoo-**ay**-lis ə-bee-dee-**en**-shee-ə). [Latin "obedience by (taking or kissing) hand"] Sworn obedience upon an oath.

manual labor. Work performed chiefly through muscular exertion, with or without tools or machinery.

Manual of the Judge Advocate General. The Secretary of the Navy's directive on military justice, with minor variations between rules applicable to the Navy and those applicable to the Marine Corps. — Also termed *JAG Manual*.

manual-rating insurance. See INSURANCE.

manu brevi (**man**-yoo **bree**-vI). [Latin "with a short hand"] *Roman & civil law.* Directly; by the shortest route. • This described the transfer of ownership to a person already in physical possession. Cf. MANU LONGA.

manucaptio (man-yə-**kap**-shee-oh), *n.* [Law Latin] *Hist.* **1.** Surety; security; bail. **2.** A writ allowing a person to be admitted to bail, when the person had been arrested for a felony but could not be admitted to bail by the sheriff. See MAINPRISE.

manucaption. See MAINPRISE.

manucaptor. See MAINPERNOR.

manufacture, *n. Patents.* A thing that is made or built by a human being (or by a machine), as distinguished from something that is a product of nature. • Manufactures are one of the statutory categories of inventions that can be patented. Examples of manufactures are chairs and tires. — Also termed *article of manufacture*. Cf. MACHINE; PROCESS (3).

> "A manufacture must have a definable structure that is claimed as its patentable characteristic. Manufactures are, after all, a category of product patents, and therefore must be 'things,' as opposed to ways or means. In summary, a patentable manufacture is any *human-made structure* that has inventive characteristics." Arthur R. Miller & Michael H. Davis, *Intellectual Property in a Nutshell* 30 (2d ed. 1990).

manufactured diversity. See DIVERSITY OF CITIZENSHIP.

manufactured home. *Secured transactions.* A structure, transportable in one or more sections, that when traveling is 8 body feet or more in width or 40 body feet or more in length, or, when erected on site, is 320 or more square feet, and that is built on a permanent chassis and designed to be used as a dwelling with or without a permanent foundation when connected to the required utilities, and that has within it plumbing, heating, air-conditioning, and electrical systems. UCC § 9–102(a)(36).

manufacturer. A person or entity engaged in producing or assembling new products. • A federal law has broadened the definition to include those who act for (or are controlled by) any such person or entity in the distribution of new products, as well as those who import new products for resale. 42 USCA § 4902(6).

manufacturer's liability. See PRODUCTS LIABILITY.

manufacturing cost. See COST (1).

manufacturing defect. See DEFECT.

manu forti (**man**-yoo **for**-tI). [Latin] With strong hand. • This term was used in old writs of trespass to allege forcible entry, as in *manu forti et cum multitudine gentium* ("with strong hand and multitude of people").

manu longa (**man**-yoo **long**-gə). [Latin "with a long hand"] *Roman & civil law.* Indirectly; by the longest route. • This described the transfer of ownership by pointing out the limits of the land transferred. Cf. MANU BREVI.

manumission (man-yə-**mish**-ən). [Latin *manumissio* "I send out of hand"] *Roman law.* The granting of liberty to a slave or bondman; the freeing of one from the power of another; emancipation. • Manumission was so called because the slaves were sent out of the hand of their masters.

> "Manumission is a kind of new birth. The master (patronus) therefore stands to his freedman in a relation analogous to the relation between father and son. The patron, as such, is entitled, as against his libertus, to a father's rights of succession and guardianship. He has the right of moderate chastisement (levis coercitio). He has the same claim to be treated with respect as he has against his son. He can claim to be supported by the libertus, if he falls into poverty. He is, lastly, entitled to certain services on the part of the freedman, which he can, if necessary, enforce by action, provided only the freedman had promised them after his manumission and in a manner not derogatory to his liberty." Rudolph Sohm, *The Institutes: A Textbook of the History and System of Roman Private Law* 170 (James Crawford Ledlie trans., 3d ed. 1907).

manumit (man-yə-**mit**), *vb.* To free (a slave).

manung (**man**-əng). *Hist.* An official's jurisdictional district. — Also spelled *monung*.

manuopus (man-yoo-**oh**-pəs). See MAINOUR.

manupes (**man**-yə-peez), *n.* [Law Latin] *Hist.* A full 12-inch foot as a legal measure.

manupretium (man-yə-**pree**-shee-əm). [Latin] *Roman law.* Compensation for performed labor or services.

manurable (mə-**n[y]oor**-ə-bəl), *adj.* [Law French fr. Old French *main* "hand"] *Hist.* (Of a thing) capable of being held in hand; capable of being touched.

manure (mə-**nyoor**), *vb.* [Law French fr. Old French *main* "hand"] *Hist.* To use (something) manually; to perform manual labor on (something).

manus (**man**-əs *also* **may**-nəs). [Latin "hand"] **1.** *Roman law.* The power exercised by the head of a family over all its members and slaves; esp., a husband's power over his wife. **2.** *Hist.* A compurgator, or the oath taken. • This usage of *manus* may stem from the affiant's placing a hand on the Bible while taking the oath. See COMPURGATOR.

manuscript. An unpublished writing; an author's typescript or written work product that is proposed for publication.

manus mortua (**man**-əs **mor**-choo-ə). [Latin "dead hand"] See MORTMAIN.

manutenentia (man-yə-tə-**nen**-shee-ə), *n.* [Law Latin] *Hist.* The old writ of maintenance. See MAINTENANCE.

manworth. *Hist.* The value of a person's life.

Mapp **hearing.** *Criminal procedure.* A hearing held to determine whether evidence implicating the accused was obtained as the result of an illegal search and seizure, and should therefore be suppressed. *Mapp v. Ohio*, 367 U.S. 643, 81 S.Ct. 1684 (1961).

mara (**mair**-ə), *n.* [Law Latin] *Hist.* A lake; a pool; a body of water that cannot be drained.

maraud (mə-**rawd**), *vb.* To rove about to pillage or plunder; to loot.

marcatus (mahr-**kay**-təs), *n.* [Law Latin] *Hist.* The yearly rent of a tract of land.

Marchers. *Hist.* Lords who lived on the borders of Scotland and Wales, and operated, with the permission of the English sovereigns, under their own private laws. • The laws were eventually abolished by the statute 27 Hen. 8, ch. 26. — Also termed *Lords Marchers.*

> "Thus the Lords Marchers were practically independent potentates of a kind very unusual in England. From this two consequences flowed. In the first place there grew up in their jurisdictions a mixture of Welsh custom and English law known as the custom of the Marches. In the second place, although they held of the king, their allegiance sat so lightly upon them that it was necessary to declare in 1354 that 'all the Lords of the Marches of Wales shall be perpetually attending and annexed to the crown of England, and not to the principality of Wales, in whose hands so ever the same principality be.'" 1 William Holdsworth, *A History of English Law* 121 (7th ed. 1956).

marches (**mahr**-chəz). *Hist.* Boundaries between countries or territories, specif. the borders between England and Wales, and England and Scotland.

marchet (**mahr**-chet). *Hist.* A fee paid by a feudal tenant to the lord so that the tenant's daughter could marry someone outside the lord's jurisdiction or so that the lord would waive the *droit du seigneur.* — Also termed *marcheta*; *marchetum*; *merchet*; *mercheta*; *merchetum*; *maiden rent.* See DROIT DU SEIGNEUR.

> "Any service which stamps the tenant as an unfree man, stamps his tenure as unfree; and in common opinion such services there are, notably the *merchetum.* Now among the thousands of entries in English documents relating to this payment, it would we believe be utterly impossible to find one which gave any sanction to the tales of a *ius primae noctis.* The context in which this duty is usually mentioned explains at least one of the reasons which underlie it. The tenant may not give his daughter (in some cases his son or daughter) in marriage — at least not outside the manor .... No doubt a subjection to this restraint was regarded as very base, and sometimes it is described in vigourous words which express a free man's loathing for servility: — 'he must buy, he must make ransom for, his flesh and blood.'" 1 Frederick Pollock & Frederic W. Maitland, *The History of English Law Before the Time of Edward I* 372 (2d ed. 1898).

march-in rights. *Patents.* The government's right to step in and grant a new license or revoke an existing license if the owner of a federally funded invention (or the owner's licensee) has not adequately developed or applied the invention within a reasonable time. 35 USCA § 203.

marchioness (**mahr**-shə-nis *or* mahr-shə-**nes**), *n.* [fr. Law Latin *marchionissa*, the feminine counterpart to *marchio* "marquess"] A female dignity, equivalent to a marquis, conferred by creation or by marriage with a marquis. See MARQUIS.

Marcus model. *Labor law.* A method for determining whether a union member's state-law claim against the employer is preempted by federal law, by focusing on whether the state-law claim can be maintained independently of an interpretation of the collective-bargaining agreement. • In *Lingle v. Norge Div. of Magic Chef, Inc.*, 486 U.S. 399, 108 S.Ct. 1877 (1988), the Supreme Court held that a union member's state-law retaliatory-discharge claim was not preempted by the Labor–Management Relations Act because the claim could be resolved without interpreting the collective-bargaining agreement. There are at least two models for applying the *Lingle* test: the White model, which focuses on whether the claim is negotiable or nonnegotiable (that is, whether state law allows the claim to be waived by a private contract), and the Marcus model, which focuses on the independence of the claim in relation to the collective-bargaining agreement. Under the Marcus model, if the claim can be maintained separately from an interpretation of the collective-bargaining agreement, it is not preempted regardless of whether the claim is generally waivable in contract. The Marcus model is named for the author of the law-review note in which it was proposed. Stephanie R. Marcus, Note, *The Need for a New Approach to Federal Preemption of Union Members' State Law Claims*, 99 Yale L.J. 209 (1989). Cf. WHITE MODEL. See LINGLE TEST.

mare (**mair**-ee *or* **mahr**-ee), *n. Hist.* [Latin] The sea. See SEA.

mare clausum (**mair**-ee *or* **mahr**-ee **klaw**-zəm). [Latin "closed sea"] A sea or other body of navigable water that is under the jurisdiction of a particular nation and is closed to other nations.

mare liberum (**mair**-ee *or* **mahr**-ee **lib**-ər-əm *or* **lɪ**-bər-əm). [Latin "free sea"] **1.** A sea or other body of navigable water that is open to all nations. **2.** FREEDOM OF THE SEAS.

marescallus (mar-ə-**skal**-əs), *n.* [Law Latin] **1.** A marshal; a high royal officer. — Also termed *mareschal*. **2.** A master of the stables. **3.** A military officer, similar to a constable, who acted as quartermaster. **4.** An officer of the Court of Exchequer. **5.** A state officer. **6.** An officer of a manor.

marettum (mə-**ret**-əm), *n.* [fr. Latin *mare* "the sea" + *tegere* "to cover"] *Hist.* Marshy ground flooded by the sea.

margin, *n.* **1.** A boundary or edge. **2.** A measure or degree of difference. **3.** PROFIT MARGIN. **4.** The difference between a loan's face value and the market value of the collateral that secures the loan. **5.** Cash or collateral required to be paid to a securities broker by an investor to protect the broker against losses from securities bought on credit. **6.** The amount of an investor's equity in securities bought on credit through the broker. — **margin,** *vb.* — **marginal, margined,** *adj.*

good-faith margin. The amount of margin that a creditor exercising good judgment would customarily require for a specified security position. • This amount is established without regard to the customer's other assets or securities positions held with respect to unrelated transactions.

marginable security. See SECURITY.

margin account. See ACCOUNT.

marginal cost. See COST (1).

marginal note. A brief notation, in the nature of a subheading, placed in the margin of a printed statute for ease of reference. • Many jurisdictions hold that notes of this kind cannot be used as the basis for an argument about the interpretation of a statute. — Also termed *side-note*.

marginal revenue. See REVENUE.

marginal tax rate. See TAX RATE.

margin call. See CALL.

margin deficiency. *Securities.* The extent to which the amount of the required margin exceeds the equity in a margin account.

margined security. See SECURITY.

margin list. A Federal Reserve Board list limiting the loan value of a particular bank's stock to a certain percentage (e.g., 50%) of its market value. • When a bank is not on the list, no limit is placed on the loan value of stock used as collateral.

margin requirement. *Securities.* The percentage of the purchase price that a buyer must deposit with a broker to buy a security on margin. • This percentage of the purchase price is set and adjusted by the Federal Reserve Board.

> "Margin requirements are the statutory and administrative restrictions placed upon the percentage of the value

of securities that may be borrowed for the purpose of the purchase of such securities, the term 'margin' referring to the percentage of the value that must be paid in cash by the purchaser. Such requirements have been implemented for the purposes of preventing the excessive use of credit for the purchase or carrying of securities, and of reducing the aggregate amount of the national credit resources, which are directed by speculation into the stock market, and of achieving a more balanced use of such resources." 69 Am. Jur. 2d *Securities Regulation — Federal* § 481 (1993).

initial margin requirement. The minimum percentage of the purchase price that a buyer must deposit with a broker. • The Federal Reserve Board establishes minimum margin requirements to prevent excessive speculation and price volatility.

maintenance margin requirement. The minimum equity that a buyer must keep in a margin account, expressed as a percentage of the account value.

margin stock. See *marginable security* under SECURITY.

margin transaction. A securities or commodities transaction made through a broker on a margin account. — Also termed *buying on margin*. See MARGIN (5).

mariage de convenance. See *marriage of convenience* under MARRIAGE (1).

marinarius (mar-ə-**nair**-ee-əs), *n.* [Law Latin] *Hist.* A seaman; a mariner. • *Marinarius capitaneus* (kap-ə-**tay**-nee-əs) was the admiral or warden of the ports.

marine, *adj.* **1.** Of or relating to the sea <marine life>. **2.** Of or relating to sea navigation or commerce <marine insurance> <marine interest>.

marine belt. See *territorial waters* under WATER.

marine carrier. See CARRIER.

marine contract. See CONTRACT.

Marine Court in the City of New York. The New York City court, originally created to resolve seamen's disputes, that was the predecessor of the City Court of New York.

marine insurance. See INSURANCE.

marine interest. See MARITIME INTEREST.

marine league. A geographical measure of distance equal to one-twentieth part of a degree of latitude, or three nautical miles.

marine peril. See PERIL OF THE SEA.

marine protest. A writing attested by a justice of the peace, a notary public, or a consul, made or verified by the master of a vessel, stating that the vessel has suffered a severe voyage and that the master has engaged in neither misconduct nor negligence. See PROTEST.

mariner. A person employed on a vessel in sea navigation; SEAMAN.

marine-rescue doctrine. The rule that when a person on a ship goes overboard, the ship must use all reasonable means to retrieve the person from the water if the person can be seen, and, if the person cannot be seen, must search for the person as long as it is reasonably possible that the person is still alive.

marine risk. See PERIL OF THE SEA.

mariner's will. See *soldier's will* under WILL.

marine rule. The doctrine that if the cost of restoring damaged property would exceed one-half the value of the property before the damage, then the property is deemed to be totally destroyed. • The marine rule developed in the context of applying marine insurance to damaged ships, but it has also been applied to other property, including buildings.

maritagium (mar-ə-**tay**-jee-əm), *n.* [Law Latin] *Hist.* **1.** A lord's right to arrange a marriage for his infant ward. **2.** DOWER. **3.** Dowry; a marriage gift. See DOS.

"[W]hile to the common lawyer *dos* meant dower, in other systems it meant dowry: a gift to the wife, or to husband and wife, by the bride's parents or other relatives. In England this was called the 'marriage-gift' or *maritagium*. Marriage-gifts were commonly made either to establish a cadet branch of a family or to assist a daughter who was not an heiress to make a good match." J.H. Baker, *An Introduction to English Legal History* 310 (3d ed. 1990).

maritagium habere (mar-ə-**tay**-jee-əm hə-**beer**-ee). [Law Latin] To have the right of arranging a woman's marriage. • This was a privilege granted by the Crown to favored subjects. See MARITAGIUM.

marital, *adj.* Of or relating to the marriage relationship <marital property>.

marital agreement. Any agreement between spouses concerning the division and ownership of marital property; esp., a premarital contract or separation agreement that is primarily concerned with dividing marital property in the event of divorce. — Also termed *marriage settlement*; *property settlement*. See PRENUPTIAL AGREEMENT; POSTNUPTIAL AGREEMENT.

marital-communications privilege. See *marital privilege* (1) under PRIVILEGE (3).

marital deduction. See DEDUCTION.

marital-deduction trust. See TRUST.

marital dissolution. See DIVORCE.

marital immunity. See *husband-wife immunity* under IMMUNITY (2).

marital portion. *Civil law.* The portion of a deceased spouse's estate to which the surviving spouse is entitled.

marital privilege. See PRIVILEGE (3).

marital property. See PROPERTY.

marital rape. See RAPE.

marital rights. Rights and incidents (such as property or cohabitation rights) arising from the marriage contract.

maritare (mar-ə-**tair**-ee), *vb. Hist.* To marry.

maritima Angliae (mə-**rit**-ə-mə **ang**-glee-ee). [Law Latin] *Hist.* **1.** The seacoast. **2.** The Crown's sea revenue, as from wreckage and from whales or sturgeons cast ashore. • The revenue was formerly collected by sheriffs and later by the Lord High Admiral.

maritima incrementa (mə-**rit**-ə-mə in-krə-**men**-tə). [Latin "marine increases"] *Hist.* Alluvion caused by the sea; land gained from the sea.

maritime (**mar**-i-tɪm), *adj.* **1.** Connected with or situated near the ocean. **2.** Of or relating to sea navigation or commerce.

> "The word 'maritime' has in the Constitution its appropriate meaning, *i.e.*, relating to the sea, and 'sea' is a word of wide extension and application .... Its classical and scriptural equivalents are applied to all sorts of navigable waters. It is not restricted, even in common speech, to waters where the tide ebbs and flows, for the Baltic Sea, the Black Sea, the Sea of Azof, the Sea of Marmora, the Mediterranean Sea, the great scenes of early maritime enterprise, have no visible tide." 1 Steven F. Friedell, *Benedict on Admiralty* § 103, at 7–5 (7th ed. 1996).

Maritime Administration. A federal agency that promotes and regulates the activities of the U.S. merchant marine, esp. by directing emergency operations, establishing specifications for shipbuilding and design, and determining navigation routes. • The Maritime Act of 1981 transferred the Maritime Administration from the Department of Commerce to the Department of Transportation.

maritime belt. See *territorial waters* under WATER.

Maritime Commission. A federal agency that regulates the waterborne foreign and domestic commerce of the United States by: (1) ensuring that U.S. international trade is open to all countries on fair and equitable terms, (2) guarding against unauthorized monopolies in U.S. waterborne commerce, and (3) ensuring that financial responsibility is maintained to clean up oil spills and indemnify injured passengers.

maritime-connection doctrine. See LOCALITY-PLUS TEST.

maritime contract. See CONTRACT.

maritime court. See ADMIRALTY (1).

maritime employment. Under the Longshoremen's and Harbor Workers' Compensation Act, a job that is related to the loading, unloading, construction, or repair of a vessel. 33 USCA § 902(3).

maritime flavor. The relation of a given case to shipping concerns. • This is a factor used in determining federal admiralty jurisdiction over a particular matter by analyzing whether the matter sufficiently relates to marine and shipping concerns and whether there is need for a federal response.

> "There is perhaps no more elusive concept in the law of admiralty than 'maritime flavor.' ... While 'maritime flavor' is incapable of precise definition, certain observations may be helpful. Generally, courts find 'maritime flavor' in those events and transactions which are major concerns of the shipping industry. This is tempered by the realization that exercise of federal control will not necessarily promote maritime shipping with the same vigor as control by a coastal or predominantly maritime state. Since federal law will not necessarily be more

favorable, courts may find 'maritime flavor' only when there is a perceived need for a uniform national rule, which can only be provided by the federal sovereign." Frank L. Maraist, *Admiralty in a Nutshell* 23 (2d ed. 1988).

maritime interest. Interest charged on a loan secured by a sea vessel or its cargo, or both. • Because of the lender's considerable risk, the interest rate may be extraordinarily high. — Also termed *marine interest.*

maritime jurisdiction. The exercise of authority over maritime cases by the U.S. district courts sitting in admiralty. See 28 USCA § 1333. • Cases falling within this jurisdiction are governed by the Supplemental Rules for Certain Admiralty and Maritime Claims — a supplement to the Federal Rules of Civil Procedure. See ADMIRALTY (1).

maritime law. The body of law governing marine commerce and navigation, the transportation at sea of persons and property, and marine affairs in general; the rules governing contract, tort, and workers'-compensation claims arising out of commerce on or over water. — Also termed *admiralty*; *admiralty law*. Cf. LAW OF THE SEA.

maritime lien. See LIEN.

maritime loan. See LOAN.

maritime service. *Maritime law.* Work performed in connection with a ship or commerce on navigable waters, such as service to preserve a ship's crew, cargo, or equipment.

maritime state. *Hist.* The collective officers and mariners of the British navy.

maritime tort. See TORT.

maritus (mə-**rɪ**-təs), *n.* [Latin] A husband; a married man.

mark, *n.* **1.** A symbol, impression, or feature on something, usu. to identify it or distinguish it from something else. **2.** TRADEMARK (1). **3.** SERVICEMARK.

benchmark. See BENCHMARK.

certification mark. See CERTIFICATION MARK.

collective mark. See COLLECTIVE MARK.

demimark. See DEMIMARK.

markdown. A reduction in a selling price.

marked money. Money that bears a telltale mark so that the money can be traced, usu. to a perpetrator of a crime, as when marked money is given to a kidnapper as ransom.

market, *n.* **1.** A place of commercial activity in which goods or services are bought and sold <the farmers' market>. — Also termed *mart.* **2.** A geographic area or demographic segment considered as a place of demand for particular goods or services <the foreign market for microchips>. **3.** The opportunity for buying and selling goods or services; the extent of economic demand <a strong job market for accountants>. **4.** A securities or commodities exchange <the stock market closed early because of the blizzard>. **5.** The business of such an exchange; the enterprise of buying and selling securities or commodities <the stock market is approaching an all-time high>. **6.** The price at which the buyer and seller of a security or commodity agree <the market for oil is $16 per barrel>.

advancing market. See *bull market.*

aftermarket. See *secondary market.*

auction market. A market (such as the New York Stock Exchange) in which securities are bought and sold by competitive bidding through brokers. Cf. *negotiated market.*

bear market. A securities market characterized by falling prices over a prolonged period. — Also termed *down market*; *receding market.*

black market. An illegal market for goods that are controlled or prohibited by the government, such as the underground market for prescription drugs.

bull market. A securities market characterized by rising prices over a prolonged period. — Also termed *advancing market*; *strong market.*

buyer's market. A market in which supply significantly exceeds demand, resulting in lower prices.

capital market. A securities market in which stocks and bonds with long-term maturities are traded.

common market. An economic association formed by several nations to reduce trade barriers among them; esp. (*usu. cap.*), EUROPEAN UNION.

discount market. The portion of the money market in which banks and other financial institutions trade commercial paper.

down market. See *bear market.*

forward market. See *futures market.*

free market. See *open market.*

Friday market. The normal tendency for stock-prices to decline on Fridays. • The tendency occurs because many investors balance their accounts before the weekend to avoid any adverse changes in market prices over the weekend.

futures market. A commodity exchange in which futures contracts are traded; a market for a trade (e.g., commodities futures contracts and stock options) that is negotiated at the current price but calls for delivery at a future time. — Also termed *forward market.* See FUTURES CONTRACT.

geographic market. *Antitrust.* The part of a relevant market that identifies the regions in which a firm might compete. • If a firm can raise prices or cut production without causing a quick influx of supply to the area from outside sources, that firm is operating in a distinct geographic market.

> "For purposes of [the Sherman Act], the relevant geographic market comprises the area in which the defendant effectively competes with other individuals or businesses for distribution of the relevant product. Stated differently, the relevant geographic market consists of the area from which the sellers of a particular product derive their customers, and the area within which the purchasers of the product can practically seek the product." 54 Am. Jur. 2d *Monopolies, Restraints of Trade, and Unfair Trade Practices* § 57, at 119–20 (1996).

gray market. A market in which legal but perhaps unethical methods are used to avoid a manufacturer's distribution chain and thereby sell goods (esp. imported goods) at prices lower than those envisioned by the manufacturer. See PARALLEL IMPORTS.

> "One of the most controversial areas of customs law concerns 'gray market goods,' goods produced abroad with authorization and payment but which are imported into unauthorized markets. Trade in gray market goods has increased dramatically in recent years, in part because fluctuating currency exchange rates create opportunities to import and sell such goods at a discount rate from local price levels." Ralph H. Folsom & Michael W. Gordon, *International Business Transactions* § 20.8 (1995).

institutional market. The demand among large investors and corporations for short-term funds and commercial paper.

market overt. An open, legally regulated public market where buyers, with some exceptions, acquire good title to products regardless of any defects in the seller's title. Cf. FAIR.

money market. The financial market for dealing in short-term negotiable instruments such as commercial paper, certificates of deposit, banker's acceptances, and U.S. Treasury securities.

negotiated market. A market (such as an over-the-counter securities market) in which buyers and sellers seek each other out and negotiate prices. Cf. *auction market.*

open market. A market in which any buyer or seller may trade and in which prices and product availability are determined by free competition. — Also termed *free market.*

original market. See *primary market.*

over-the-counter market. See OVER-THE-COUNTER MARKET.

primary market. The market for goods or services that are newly available for buying and selling; esp., the securities market in which new securities are issued by corporations to raise capital. — Also termed *original market.*

product market. *Antitrust.* The part of a relevant market that applies to a firm's particular product by identifying all reasonable substitutes for the product and by determining whether these substitutes limit the firm's ability to affect prices.

> "For purposes of an antitrust claim under ... the Sherman Act, the relevant product market includes those services or commodities which are reasonably interchangeable by consumers for the same purposes. In order to establish the relevant product market, therefore, a plaintiff must sufficiently identify what types of products are reasonably interchangeable substitutes for the defendant's product within the appropriate area of competition." 54 Am. Jur. 2d *Monopolies, Restraints of Trade, and Unfair Trade Practices* § 58, at 121 (1996).

public market. A market open to both purchasers and sellers.

receding market. See *bear market.*

recognized market. A market where the items bought and sold are numerous and similar, where competitive bidding and bartering are not prevalent, and where prices paid in sales of comparable items are publicly quoted. • Examples of recognized markets include stock and commodities exchanges. Under the UCC, a secured creditor may, upon the debtor's default, sell the collateral in a recognized market without notifying the debtor. Such a sale is presumed to be commercially reasonable.

relevant market. *Antitrust.* A market that is capable of being monopolized — that is, a market in which a firm can raise prices above the competitive level without losing so many sales that the price increase would be unprofitable. • The relevant market includes both the *product market* and the *geographic market*.

secondary market. The market for goods or services that have previously been available for buying and selling; esp., the securities market in which previously issued securities are traded among investors. — Also termed *aftermarket*.

seller's market. A market in which demand exceeds (or approaches) supply, resulting in raised prices.

soft market. A market (esp. a stock market) characterized by falling or drifting prices and low volume.

spot market. A market (esp. in commodities) in which payment or delivery is immediate <the spot market in oil>.

strong market. See *bull market*.

thin market. A market in which the number of bids or offerings is relatively low.

marketability. Salability; the probability of selling property, goods, securities, or services at specified times, prices, and terms.

marketability test. *Mining law.* The principle that, for someone to obtain a patent on a mining claim on federal land, there must be a showing that a reasonably prudent person could extract and market the claimed mineral at a profit, and that at the time of discovery, a large enough market for the mineral existed to attract the efforts of a reasonably prudent person.

marketable, *adj.* Of commercially acceptable quality; fit for sale and in demand by buyers. — Also termed *merchantable*.

marketable security. See SECURITY.

marketable title. See TITLE (2).

marketable-title act. A state statute providing that a person can establish good title to land by searching the public records only back to a specified time (such as 40 years ago). See *marketable title* under TITLE (2).

market activity. See MARKET VOLUME.

market approach. A method of appraising real property, by surveying the market and comparing the property to similar pieces of property that have been recently sold, and making appropriate adjustments for differences between the properties, including location, size of the property, and the dates of sale. — Also termed *comparative-sales approach*; *market-comparison approach*; *market-data approach*. Cf. COST APPROACH; INCOME APPROACH.

market average. A price level for a specific group of stocks.

market-comparison approach. See MARKET APPROACH.

market correction. See DOWN REVERSAL.

market-data approach. See MARKET APPROACH.

market equity. The percentage of the total market value that a particular company's securities account for, represented by each class of security. Cf. BOOK EQUITY.

marketing, *n.* **1.** The act or process of promoting and selling products or services. **2.** The part of a business concerned with meeting customers' needs. **3.** The area of study concerned with the promotion and selling of products or services.

marketing contract. See CONTRACT.

marketing defect. See DEFECT.

market intermediary. *Securities.* A person whose business is to enter into transactions on both sides of the market. Investment Company Act, 15 USCA § 80a–3(c)(2)(B)(i).

market-maker. *Securities.* One who helps establish a market for securities by reporting bid-and-asked quotations. • A market-maker is typically a specialist permitted to act as a dealer, a dealer acting in the capacity of block positioner, or a dealer who, with respect to a security, routinely enters quotations in an interdealer communication system or otherwise and is willing to buy and sell securities for the dealer's own account.

market-making, *n.* The practice of establishing prices for over-the-counter securities by reporting bid-and-asked quotations. • A broker-dealer engaged in this practice, which is regulated by both the NASD and the SEC, buys and sells securities as a principal for its own account, and thus accepts two-way bids (both to buy and to sell). See BID AND ASKED.

market manipulation. See MANIPULATION.

market order. See ORDER (4).

market-out clause. *Oil & gas.* A contract provision permitting a pipeline-purchaser of natural gas to lower the purchase price if market conditions make it uneconomical to continue buying at the contract price, and permitting the well owner to respond by accepting the lower price or by rejecting it and canceling the contract.

market overt. See MARKET.

market-participant doctrine. The principle that, under the Commerce Clause, a state does not discriminate against interstate commerce by acting as a buyer or seller in the market, by operating a proprietary enterprise, or by subsidizing private business. • Under the Dormant Commerce Clause principle, the Commerce Clause — art. I, § 8, cl. 3 of the U.S. Constitution — disallows most state regulation of, or discrimination against, interstate commerce. But if the state is participating in the market instead of regulating it, the Dormant Commerce Clause analysis does not apply, and the state activity will generally stand. See *Dormant Commerce Clause* under COMMERCE CLAUSE.

marketplace of ideas. A forum in which expressions of opinion can freely compete for acceptance without governmental restraint. • Although Justice Oliver Wendell Holmes was the first jurist to discuss the concept as a metaphor for explaining freedom of speech, the phrase *marketplace of ideas* dates in American caselaw only from 1954.

market portfolio. See PORTFOLIO.

market power. The ability to reduce output and raise prices above the competitive level — specifically, above marginal cost — for a sustained period, and to make a profit by doing so. • In antitrust law, a large amount of market power may constitute monopoly power. See MONOPOLIZATION. Cf. MARKET SHARE.

> "In economic terms, market power is the ability to raise prices without a total loss of sales; without market power, consumers shop around to find a rival offering a better deal." 54 Am. Jur. 2d *Monopolies, Restraints of Trade, and Unfair Trade Practices* § 49, at 110 n.87 (1996).

market price. See PRICE.

market quotation. The most current price at which a security or commodity trades.

market-recovery program. See JOB-TARGETING PROGRAM.

market share. The percentage of the market for a product that a firm supplies, usu. calculated by dividing the firm's output by the total market output. • In antitrust law, market share is used to measure a firm's market power, and if the share is high enough — generally 70% or more — then the firm may be guilty of monopolization. See MONOPOLIZATION. Cf. MARKET POWER.

market-share liability. See LIABILITY.

market-share theory. *Antitrust.* A method of determining damages for lost profits by calculating the impact of the defendant's violation on the plaintiff's output or market share. Cf. BEFORE-AND-AFTER THEORY; YARDSTICK THEORY.

market structure. The broad organizational characteristics of a particular market, including seller concentration, product differentiation, and barriers to entry.

market trend. See TREND.

market value. See *fair market value* under VALUE.

market value at the well. *Oil & gas.* The value of oil or gas at the place where it is sold, minus the reasonable cost of transporting it and processing it to make it marketable.

market volume. 1. The total number of shares traded on one day on a stock exchange. **2.** The total number of shares of one stock traded on one day. — Also termed *market activity*.

***Mark Hopkins* doctrine.** The principle that when an employee leaves a job because of a labor dispute, any later employment the employee has must be bona fide and intended as permanent for the employee to avoid a labor-dispute disqualification from unemployment benefits if the employee leaves the later job. *Mark Hopkins, Inc. v. Employment Comm'n*, 151 P.2d 229 (Cal. 1944).

marking estoppel. See ESTOPPEL.

markon. An amount (usu. expressed as a percentage) initially added to a product's cost to obtain the list price. • Further increases or decreases in price are called *markups* or *markdowns*, respectively.

marksman. **1.** A person who, not being able to write, signs documents with some kind of character or symbol. **2.** A highly skilled shooter.

***Marks* rule.** The doctrine that, when the U.S. Supreme Court issues a fractured, plurality opinion, the opinion of the Justices concurring in the judgment on the narrowest grounds — that is, the legal standard with which a majority of the Court would agree — is considered the Court's holding. *Marks v. United States*, 430 U.S. 188, 97 S.Ct. 990 (1977).

mark up, *vb.* **1.** To increase (the price of goods, etc.) **2.** To revise or amend (a legislative bill, a rule, etc.). **3.** To place (a case) on the trial calendar.

markup, *n.* **1.** An amount added to an item's cost to determine its selling price. See PROFIT MARGIN. **2.** A session of a congressional committee during which a bill is revised and put into final form before it is reported to the appropriate house.

***Markush* doctrine** (**mahr**-kəsh). *Patents.* An exception to the policy against use of alternative language in claims, by which in certain claims (esp. those involving chemical components) a claimant can use an alternative, subgeneric phrase when there is no applicable, commonly accepted generic expression. *Ex parte Markush*, 1925 Dec. Comm'r Pat. 126.

> "The Patent Office early adopted a policy against use of alternative language in claims. Thus, a claimant could not use the specific alternative phrase 'glass or plastic' but could use a generic phrase (such as 'impervious transparent material') that would cover effectively the desired alternatives. The *Markush* doctrine developed as an exception .... With chemical compounds there may be no suitable phrase to cover the alternatives. Under limited circumstances a claimant could use an artificial or coined subgeneric group in the form of 'material selected from the group consisting of X, Y, and Z.' " 2 Donald S. Chisum, *Patents* § 8.06[2], at 8–119 to 8–120 (1992).

marque (mahrk). *Archaic.* Reprisal. See LETTERS OF MARQUE.

marque, law of. *Archaic.* A reprisal entitling one who has been wronged and is unable to receive ordinary justice to take the goods of the wrongdoer (if they can be found within one's own precinct) in satisfaction for the wrong. See LETTERS OF MARQUE.

marquis (**mahr**-kwis *or* mahr-**kee**). An English nobleman below and next in order to a duke. — Also termed *marquess*.

marquisate (**mahr**-kwi-sit *or* -zit), *n.* [Law Latin] *Hist.* The seigniory of a marquis.

marriage, *n.* **1.** The legal union of a man and woman as husband and wife. • Although the common law regarded marriage as a civil contract, it is more properly the civil status or relationship existing between a man and a woman who agree to and do live together as spouses. The essentials of a valid marriage are (1) parties legally capable of contracting marriage, (2) mutual consent or agreement, and (3) an actual contracting in the form prescribed by law.

> "It has frequently been said by courts, and even by Legislatures, that marriage is a 'civil contract.' But to conclude from these statements that marriage ... has all, or even many, of the incidents of an ordinary private contract, would be a grave error. In fact, these statements to the effect that marriage is a 'civil contract' will be found, upon examination, to have been used only for the purpose of expressing the idea that marriage, in the American states, is a civil, and not a religious institution, or that ... in some states mutual consent alone without formal celebration is sufficient to constitute a valid marriage known as a common law marriage, or that, as is true in all states, the mutual consent of the parties is essential, even in the case of a ceremonial marriage." Joseph W. Madden, *Handbook of the Law of Persons and Domestic Relations* § 1–3, at 2–3 (1931).

clandestine marriage (klan-**des**-tin). **1.** A marriage that rests merely on the agreement of the parties. **2.** A marriage entered into in a secret way, as one solemnized by an unauthorized person or without all required formalities. See *Fleet marriage*.

common-law marriage. A marriage that takes legal effect, without license or ceremony, when a couple live together as husband and wife, intend to be married, and hold themselves out to others as a married couple. • Common-law marriages are permitted in 14 states and in the District of Columbia. — Also termed *informal marriage*.

consensual marriage. Marriage by consent alone, without any formal process. See *common-law marriage*.

consular marriage. A marriage solemnized in a foreign country by a consul or diplomatic official of the United States. • Consular marriages are recognized in some jurisdictions.

covenant marriage. A marriage that is entered into under a law establishing certain requirements for marriage and divorce in a state that otherwise allows for no-fault divorce. • In the late 1990s, several states (beginning with Louisiana) passed laws providing for covenant marriages. The requirements vary, but most of these laws require couples who opt for a covenant marriage to undergo premarital counseling. A divorce will be granted only after the couple has undergone marital counseling and has been separated for a specified period (usu. at least 18 months). The divorce prerequisites typically can be waived with proof that a spouse has committed adultery, been convicted of a felony, abandoned the family for at least one year, or physically or sexually abused the other spouse or a child. — Also termed *high-test marriage.*

cross-marriage. A marriage by a brother and sister to two people who are also brother and sister.

de facto marriage (di **fak**-toh). A marriage that, despite the parties' living under color of law as man and wife, is defective for some reason.

Fleet marriage. *Hist.* A clandestine marriage performed in the 17th or 18th century in the Fleet prison in London by a chaplain who had been imprisoned for debt. • Parliament attempted to stop the practice, but it was not until the statute of 26 George 2, ch. 33, declaring marriages performed outside public chapels or churches to be void and punishable as a felony, that the practice ceased.

green-card marriage. See *sham marriage.*

Gretna-Green marriage. A marriage entered into in a jurisdiction other than where the parties reside to avoid some legal impediment that exists where they live; a runaway marriage. • Gretna Green is a Scottish village close to the English border that served as a convenient place for eloping English couples to wed.

> "A 'Gretna–Green marriage' was a marriage solemnized in Scotland by parties who went there to avoid the delay and formalities required in England.... In the United States, the term describes marriages celebrated between residents of a State who go to a place beyond and yet near to the boundary line of an adjoining State, on account of some advantage afforded by the law of that State." William C. Anderson, *A Dictionary of Law* 496 (1889).

high-test marriage. See *covenant marriage.*

informal marriage. See *common-law marriage.*

left-handed marriage. See *morganatic marriage.*

marriage in jest. A voidable marriage in which the parties lack the requisite intent to marry.

marriage of convenience. **1.** A marriage contracted for social or financial advantages rather than out of mutual love. — Also termed *mariage de convenance.* **2.** Loosely, an ill-considered marriage that, at the time, is convenient to the parties involved.

mixed marriage. See MISCEGENATION.

morganatic marriage (mor-gə-**nat**-ik). *Hist.* A marriage between a man of superior status to a woman of inferior status, with the stipulation that the wife and her children cannot participate in the title or possessions of the husband. • By extension, the term later referred to the marriage of a woman of superior status to a man of inferior status. — Also termed *left-handed marriage.*

plural marriage. A marriage in which one spouse is already married to someone else; a bigamous or polygamous union.

putative marriage (**pyoo**-tə-tiv). A marriage in which the husband and wife believe in good faith that they are married, but for some technical reason are not formally married (as when the ceremonial official was not authorized to perform a marriage). • Putative marriages are usu. treated as valid and do not need to be formalized.

Scotch marriage. A marriage by consensual contract, without the necessity of a formal ceremony, so called because this kind of marriage was until 1940 recognized as valid under Scots law.

sham marriage. A marriage in which a U.S. citizen marries a foreign citizen for the sole purpose of allowing the foreign citizen to become a permanent U.S. resident. • Sham marriages are illegal if made with an intent to circumvent immigration law. — Also termed *green-card marriage.*

voidable marriage. A marriage that is initially invalid but that remains in effect unless terminated by court order. • For example, a marriage is voidable if either party is underage or otherwise legally incompetent, or if one party used fraud, duress, or force to induce the other party to enter the marriage. The legal imperfection in such a marriage can be inquired into only during the lives of both spouses, in a proceeding to obtain a judgment declaring it void.

void marriage. A marriage that is invalid from its inception, that cannot be made valid, and that can be terminated by either party without obtaining a divorce or annulment. • For example, a marriage is void if the parties are too closely related or if either party is already married.

2. The act or ceremony so uniting them; a wedding. — **marital,** *adj.*

ceremonial marriage. A wedding that follows all the statutory requirements and that has been solemnized before a religious or civil official.

civil marriage. A wedding ceremony conducted by an official, such as a judge, or by some other authorized person — as distinguished from one solemnized by a member of the clergy.

proxy marriage. A wedding in which someone stands in for an absent bride or groom, as when one party is stationed overseas in the military. • Proxy marriages are prohibited in most states.

marriage article. A premarital stipulation between spouses who intend to incorporate the stipulation in a postnuptial agreement.

marriage broker. One who arranges a marriage in exchange for consideration. • A marriage broker may be subject to criminal liability for public-policy reasons.

marriage ceremony. The religious or civil proceeding that solemnizes a marriage. — Also termed *wedding*.

marriage certificate. A document that is executed by the religious or civil official presiding at a marriage ceremony and filed with a public authority (usu. the county clerk) as evidence of the marriage.

marriage in jest. See MARRIAGE (1).

marriage license. A document, issued by a public authority, that grants a couple permission to marry. • Most states require the couple to take blood tests before obtaining the license.

marriage-notice book. An English registry of marriage applications and licenses.

marriage of convenience. See MARRIAGE (1).

marriage portion. See DOWRY.

marriage promise. See PROMISE.

marriage records. Government or church records containing information on prospective couples (such as a woman's maiden name and address) and on wedding services performed.

marriage settlement. See MARITAL AGREEMENT, PRENUPTIAL AGREEMENT.

marshal, *n.* **1.** A law-enforcement officer with duties similar to those of a sheriff. **2.** A judicial officer who provides court security, executes process, and performs other tasks for the court. — **marshalship,** *n.*

United States Marshal. A federal official who carries out the orders of a federal court. • U.S. Marshals are employees of the executive branch of government.

marshal, *vb.* To arrange or rank in order <the brief effectively marshaled the appellant's arguments>.

marshaling assets, rule of. See RULE OF MARSHALING ASSETS.

marshaling doctrine. The principle that, when a senior creditor has recourse to two or more funds to satisfy its debt, and a junior creditor has recourse to only one fund to satisfy its debt, the senior creditor must satisfy its debt out of the funds in which the junior creditor has no interest.

marshaling the evidence. 1. Arranging all of a party's evidence in the order that it will be presented at trial. **2.** The practice of formulating a jury charge so that it arranges the evidence to give more credence to a particular interpretation.

Marshal of the Queen's Bench. *Hist.* A custodial officer of the Queen's Bench prison. • The position was abolished by the Queen's Prison Act of 1842 (St. 5 & 6 Vict., ch. 22).

Marshalsea (**mahr**-shəl-see), *n.* [fr. Law Latin *marescallia*] *Hist.* **1.** The court or seat of the marshal of the royal household. **2.** A debtor's prison in London under the jurisdiction of the Court of Marshalsea. See COURT OF MARSHALSEA.

mart. See MARKET (1).

marte suo decurrere (**mahr**-tee **s[y]oo**-oh də-**kər**-ər-ee). [Latin] *Hist.* To run its course by its own force. • In the civil law, this term was applied to a suit that ran its course without obstruction.

martial law (**mahr**-shəl). **1.** The law by which during wartime the army, instead of civil authority, governs the country because of a perceived need for military security or public safety. • The military assumes control purportedly until civil authority can be restored. **2.** A body of firm, strictly enforced rules that are imposed because of a perception by the country's rulers that civil government has failed, or might fail, to function. • Martial law is usu. imposed when the rulers foresee an invasion, insurrection, economic collapse, or other breakdown of the rulers' desired social order.

> "Martial law is the public law of necessity. Necessity calls it forth, necessity justifies its exercise, and necessity measures the extent and degree to which it may be employed. That necessity is no formal, artificial, legalistic concept but an actual and factual one: it is the necessity of taking action to safeguard the state against insurrection, riot, disorder, or public calamity. What constitutes necessity is a question of fact in each case." Frederick B. Wiener, *A Practical Manual of Martial Law* 16 (1940).

> "[M]artial law is nothing more and nothing less than an application of the common law doctrine that force, to whatever degree necessary, may be used to repress illegal force. Martial law is the public right of self-defense against a danger threatening the order or the existence of the state. Where the ordinary civil authorities — the police — are unable to resist or subdue a disturbance, additional force, military in nature, may be applied. The extent of military force used depends in each instance upon the extent of the disturbance." *Id.* at 16–17.

absolute martial law. The carrying on of government functions entirely by military agencies, as a result of which the authority of civil agencies is superseded.

qualified martial law. The carrying on of government functions partly by military agencies, as a result of which the authority of some civil agencies is superseded.

3. The law by which the army in wartime governs foreign territory that it occupies. **4.** Loosely, MILITARY LAW.

Martindale-Hubbell Law Directory. A series of books, published annually, containing a roster of lawyers and law firms in most cities of the United States, corporate legal departments, government lawyers, foreign lawyers, and lawyer-support providers, as well as a digest of the laws of the states, the District of Columbia, and territories of the United States, and a digest of the laws of many foreign jurisdictions, including Canada and its provinces.

***Martinez* report.** A report that courts sometimes require a pro se party to file in order to clarify a vague or incomprehensible complaint. *Martinez v. Aaron*, 570 F.2d 317 (10th Cir. 1978).

Mary Carter agreement. A contract (usu. a secret one) by which one or more, but not all, codefendants settle with the plaintiff and obtain a release, along with a provision granting them a portion of any recovery from the nonparticipating codefendants. • In a Mary Carter agreement, the participating codefendants agree to remain parties to the lawsuit and, if no recovery is awarded against the nonparticipating codefendants, to pay the plaintiff a settled amount. Such an agreement is void as against public policy in some states but is valid in others if disclosed to the jury. *Booth v. Mary Carter Paint Co.*, 202 So. 2d 8 (Fla. Dist. Ct. App. 1967). Cf. GALLAGHER AGREEMENT.

Mary Major. See JANE DOE.

masking, *n.* In critical legal studies, the act or an instance of concealing something's true nature <being a crit, Max contends that the legal system is merely an elaborate masking of social injustices>. — **mask,** *vb.*

massa (**mas**-ə), *n.* [Latin] *Roman law.* A mass or lump of metal, esp. of gold and silver before it is made into a cup or other useful or ornamental object.

Massachusetts ballot. See BALLOT (4).

Massachusetts trust. See *business trust* under TRUST.

mass-action theory. The principle that, as long as a labor union is functioning, it is vicariously liable for the joint acts of its members.

mass-appraisal method. A technique for valuing large areas of land by studying market data to determine the price that similar property would sell for, without engaging in a parcel-by-parcel analysis.

mass asset. See ASSET.

mass layoff. See LAYOFF.

mass murderer. A person who commits a series of separate but related homicides, whether committed over a short or an extended period.

mass tort. See TORT.

master, *n.* **1.** One who has personal authority over another's services; EMPLOYER <the law of master and servant>. **2.** A parajudicial officer (such as a referee, an auditor, an examiner, or an assessor) specially appointed to help a court with its proceedings. • A master may take testimony, hear and rule on discovery disputes and other pretrial matters, compute interest, value annuities, investigate encumbrances on land titles, and the like — usu. with a written report to the court. Fed. R. Civ. P. 53.

special master. A master appointed to assist the court with a particular matter or case.

standing master. A master appointed to assist the court on an ongoing basis.

master agreement. *Labor law.* An agreement between a union and industry leaders, the terms of which serve as a model for agreements between the union and individual companies within the industry.

master and servant. The relation between two persons, one of whom (the master) has authority over the other (the servant), with the power to direct the time, manner, and place of the services. • This relationship is similar to that of principal and agent, but that terminology applies to employments in which the employee has some discretion, while the servant is almost completely under the control of the master. Also, an agent usu. acts for the principal in business relations with third parties, while a servant does not.

Master at Common Law. An officer of an English superior court of common law, appointed to record court proceedings, supervise the issuance of writs, and receive and account for fees paid into the court.

Master-General of the Ordnance. See MASTER OF THE ORDNANCE.

Master in Chancery. A senior official or clerk of a court of chancery who assists the Chancellor in various duties such as inquiring into matters referred by the court, examining cases, taking oaths and affidavits, hearing testimony, and computing damages. • There were many Masters in Chancery at the same time. The office was abolished in 1897 and was replaced by the office of Master of the Supreme Court. — Also termed *master of the chancery.* See MASTER OF THE SUPREME COURT.

Master in Lunacy. *Hist.* A judicial officer appointed by the Lord Chancellor to conduct inquiries into the state of mind of people alleged to be lunatics incapable of handling their own affairs and to ensure in each case that the lunatic's property is properly managed for his or her benefit.

master lease. See LEASE.

master limited partnership. See PARTNERSHIP.

master of a ship. *Maritime law.* A commander of a merchant vessel; a captain of a ship. • The master is responsible for the vessel's navigation and the safety and care of the crew and cargo. — Also termed *shipmaster.*

Master of Laws. A law degree conferred on those completing graduate-level legal study, beyond the J.D. degree. — Abbr. LL.M. Cf. JURIS DOCTOR.

Master of Requests. *Hist.* A judge of the Court of Requests.

master of the chancery. See MASTER IN CHANCERY.

Master of the Crown Office. *English law.* A Supreme Court officer who is appointed by the Lord Chief Justice. • Formerly, the Master was the Queen's Coroner and attorney, who was originally appointed by the Lord Chancellor to prosecute criminal cases in the name of the Crown.

Master of the Faculties. *Eccles. law.* An officer in the archdiocese of Canterbury who heads the Court of Faculties, grants licenses, and admits or removes notaries public. — Also termed *magister ad facultates.* See COURT OF FACULTIES.

Master of the Horse. *English law.* A peer who as third officer of the royal household, next to the lord steward and lord chamberlain, attends the sovereign on state occasions. • The official was originally in charge of the royal stables, but that duty is now entrusted to the Crown Equerry.

Master of the Mint. *Hist.* A salaried warden who supervised all activities of the royal mint. • The office was abolished under the Coinage Act of 1870 and replaced with Master Worker and Warden of Her Majesty's Royal Mint.

Master of the Ordnance. *Hist.* Beginning with the reign of Henry VIII, a superior officer responsible for the royal artillery and weapons. • The more modern representative is the Master-General of the Ordnance, a military officer and member of the Army Council. — Also termed *Master-General of the Ordnance.*

Master of the Pells. See CLERK OF THE PELLS.

Master of the Rolls. The president of the Court of Appeal in England. • Formerly, the Master of the Rolls was an assistant judge to a court of chancery, responsible for keeping the rolls and chancery records. In recent times, the most famous Master of the Rolls was Lord Denning (who lived from 1899 to 1999).

> "Since 1875, the Master of the Rolls has been president of the Court of Appeal. Until 1958 he had the general responsibility for the public records (a responsibility then transferred to the Lord Chancellor) and is still responsible for the records of the Chancery of England. He admits persons as solicitors of the Supreme Court." David M. Walker, *The Oxford Companion to Law* 816 (1980).

Master of the Supreme Court. An official of the Queen's Bench and Chancery Divisions of the Supreme Court who fills the several positions of master in the common-law courts, the Queen's Coroner and Attorney, the Master of the Crown Office, record and writ clerks, and associates.

master plan. *Land-use planning.* A municipal plan for housing, industry, and recreation facilities, including their projected environmental impact. See PLANNED-UNIT DEVELOPMENT.

master policy. See INSURANCE POLICY.

master-servant rule. See RESPONDEAT SUPERIOR.

master's report. A master's formal report to a court, usu. containing a recommended decision in a case as well as findings of fact and conclusions of law.

mast selling. *Hist.* The practice of selling the goods of a dead seaman at the mast.

matched order. See ORDER (4).

matching principle. *Tax.* A method for handling expense deductions, by which the depreciation in a given year is matched by the associated tax benefit.

mate. 1. A spouse. **2.** A second-in-command officer on a merchant vessel. **3.** A petty officer who assists a warrant officer. **4.** A friend or companion.

materfamilias (may-tər-fə-**mil**-ee-əs), *n.* [Latin] *Roman law.* **1.** The wife of a *paterfamilias,* or the mistress of a family. **2.** A respectable woman of a household, either married or single.

materia (mə-**teer**-ee-ə), *n.* [Latin] **1.** *Roman law.* Materials, esp. for building, as distinguished from the form given to something by the exercise of labor or skill. **2.** Matter; substance.

material, *adj.* **1.** Of or relating to matter; physical <material goods>. **2.** Having some logical connection with the consequential facts <material evidence>. **3.** Of such a nature that knowledge of the item would affect a person's decision-making process; significant; essential <material alteration of the document>. — **materiality,** *n.* Cf. RELEVANT.

material allegation. See ALLEGATION.

material alteration. See ALTERATION.

material breach. See BREACH OF CONTRACT.

material change in circumstances. *Family law.* An involuntary occurrence that, if it had been known at the time of the divorce decree, would have resulted in the court's issuing a different decree, as when an involuntary job loss creates a need to modify the decree to provide for reduced child-support payments.

material evidence. See EVIDENCE.

material fact. See FACT.

material information. *Securities.* Information that would be important to a reasonable investor in making an investment decision. • In the context of an "efficient" market, materiality translates into information that alters the price of a firm's stock. Securities Exchange Act of 1934 § 10(b), 15 USCA § 78j(b); 17 CFR § 240.10b–5.

materialman. A person who supplies materials used in constructing or repairing a structure or vehicle.

materialman's lien. See *mechanic's lien* under LIEN.

material misrepresentation. See MISREPRESENTATION.

material representation. See REPRESENTATION.

material terms. Contractual provisions dealing with significant issues such as subject matter, price, payment terms, quantity, quality, duration, or the work to be done.

material witness. See WITNESS.

maternal, *adj.* Of, relating to, or coming from one's mother <maternal property>. Cf. PATERNAL.

maternal line. See LINE.

maternal-line descent. See DESCENT.

maternal property. See PROPERTY.

matertera magna (mə-**tər**-tər-ə **mag**-nə), *n.* [Latin] *Roman law.* A great-aunt; the sister of one's grandmother.

matertera major (mə-**tər**-tər-ə **may**-jər), *n.* [Latin] *Roman law.* A greater aunt; the sister of one's great-grandmother.

matertera maxima (mə-**tər**-tər-ə **maks**-ə-mə), *n.* [Latin] *Roman law.* A greatest aunt; the sister of one's great-great-grandmother. — Also termed *abmatertera.*

mathematical evidence. See EVIDENCE.

***Mathews v. Eldridge* test.** *Constitutional law.* The principle for determining whether an administrative procedure provides due-process protection, by analyzing (1) the nature of the private interest that will be affected by the governmental action, (2) the risk of an erroneous deprivation through the procedure used, (3) the probable value of additional or substitute procedural safeguards, (4) the governmental function involved, and (5) the administrative burden and expense that would be created by requiring additional or substitute procedural safeguards. *Mathews v. Eldridge,* 424 U.S. 319, 96 S.Ct. 893 (1976).

matima (**mat**-i-mə), *n.* [Law Latin] *Roman law.* A godmother.

matricide (**ma**-trə-sɪd), *n.* **1.** The act of killing one's own mother. **2.** One who kills his or her mother. — **matricidal,** *adj.*

matricula (mə-**trik**-yə-lə), *n.* [Latin] **1.** *Roman law.* A register of public officials. **2.** *Hist.* A register or certificate of enrollment in any organized group or society.

matriculate, *vb.* To enroll or register (in a university, college, etc.).

matrimonial action. See ACTION.

matrimonial cohabitation. See COHABITATION.

matrimonial domicile. See DOMICILE.

matrimonial home. See *matrimonial domicile* under DOMICILE.

matrimonial res. The marriage state. See RES.

matrimonium (ma-trə-**moh**-nee-əm), *n.* [Latin] *Roman law.* Marriage. — Also termed *nuptiae* (**nəp**-shee-ee).

matrimony, *n.* The act or state of being married; MARRIAGE. — **matrimonial,** *adj.*

matrix (**may**-triks), *n.* [Latin] **1.** *Hist.* Mother. **2.** *Civil law.* The original legal instrument, from which all copies must be made. **3.**

A list of the parties to a lawsuit, including the addresses at which pleadings and notices can be served. • A matrix is commonly used to list the names and addresses of creditors and other parties in a bankruptcy case. Many bankruptcy courts have specific rules on how to prepare the matrix.

matrix ecclesia (**may**-triks e-**klee**-z[h]ee-ə). [Latin] A mother church; a cathedral church in relation to parochial churches in the same diocese.

matter, *n.* **1.** A subject under consideration, esp. involving a dispute or litigation; CASE (1) <this is the only matter on the court's docket today>. **2.** Something that is to be tried or proved; an allegation forming the basis of a claim or defense <the matters raised in the plaintiff's complaint are not actionable under state law>.

matter in deed. **1.** A matter that can be proved by a writing under seal. **2.** See *matter of fact.*

matter in pais (in **pay**). A matter of fact that has not been recorded in writing and that must therefore be proved by parol evidence.

matter of fact. A matter involving a judicial inquiry into the truth of alleged facts. — Also termed *matter in deed.*

matter of form. A matter concerned only with formalities or noncritical characteristics <the objection that the motion was incorrectly titled related to a matter of form>. Cf. *matter of substance.*

matter of law. A matter involving a judicial inquiry into the applicable law.

matter of record. A matter that has been entered on a judicial or other public record and therefore can be proved by producing that record.

matter of substance. A matter concerning the merits or critical elements, rather than mere formalities <the party objected because the motion was based on a repealed statute that related to a matter of substance>. Cf. *matter of form.*

new matter. A matter not previously raised by either party in the pleadings, usu. involving new issues with new facts to be proved.

special matter. *Common-law pleading.* Out-of-the-ordinary evidence that a defendant is allowed to enter, after notice to the plaintiff, under a plea of the general issue.

matter in controversy. See AMOUNT IN CONTROVERSY.

matter of. See IN RE.

matter of course. Something done as a part of a routine process or procedure.

mature, *vb.* (Of a debt or obligation) to become due <the bond matures in ten years>. — **maturity,** *n.* — **mature,** *adj.*

matured claim. See CLAIM (3).

maturity date. See *date of maturity* under DATE.

maturity value. The amount that is due and payable on an obligation's maturity date.

maugre (**maw**-gər), *prep. Archaic.* Despite <the witness may testify maugre counsel's objection>.

maxim (**mak**-sim). A traditional legal principle that has been frozen into a concise expression. • Examples are "possession is nine-tenths of the law" and *caveat emptor* ("let the buyer beware"). — Also termed *legal maxim.*

maximalist retributivism. See RETRIBUTIVISM.

maximum cure. *Maritime law.* The point at which a seaman who is injured or sick has stabilized, and no additional medical treatment will improve the seaman's condition. • A shipowner's obligation to provide maintenance and cure to a sick or injured seaman usu. continues until the seaman has reached maximum cure. See MAINTENANCE AND CURE.

maximum medical improvement. The point at which an injured person's condition stabilizes, and no further recovery or improvement is expected, even with additional medical intervention. • This term is most often used in the context of a workers'-compensation claim. An injured employee usu. receives temporary benefits until reaching maximum medical improvement, at which time a determination can be made about any permanent disability the employee has suffered and any corresponding benefits the employee should receive. — Abbr. MMI.

maximum sentence. See SENTENCE.

may, *vb.* **1.** Is permitted to <the plaintiff may close>. • This is the primary legal sense — usu. termed the "permissive" or "discretionary" sense. **2.** Has a possibility (to); might <the defendant may win on appeal>. Cf. CAN. **3.** Loosely, is required to; shall; must <if two or more defendants are jointly indicted, any defendant who so requests may be tried separately>. • In dozens of cases, courts have held *may* to be synonymous with *shall* or *must,* usu. in an effort to effectuate legislative intent.

mayhem (**may**-hem), *n.* **1.** The crime of maliciously injuring a person's body, esp. to impair or destroy the victim's capacity for self-defense. • Modern statutes usu. treat this as a form of aggravated battery. — Also termed *grievous bodily harm.* See BATTERY.

> "Mayhem, according to the English common law, is maliciously depriving another of the use of such of his members as may render him less able, in fighting, either to defend himself or to annoy his adversary. It is a felony." Rollin M. Perkins & Ronald N. Boyce, *Criminal Law* 239 (3d ed. 1982).

2. Violent destruction. **3.** Rowdy confusion or disruption. — **maim** (for sense 1), *vb.*

May it please the court. An introductory phrase that lawyers use when first addressing a court, esp. when presenting oral argument to an appellate court.

mayn (mayn), *n.* [Law French] *Hist.* A hand; handwriting.

maynover (mə-**noo**-vər *or* may-**noh**-vər), *n.* [Law French] *Hist.* A work by hand; something produced by manual labor.

mayor, *n.* An official who is elected or appointed as the chief executive of a city, town, or other municipality. — **mayoral** (**may**-ər-əl), *adj.*

mayoralty (**may**-ər-əl-tee). The office or dignity of a mayor. — Also termed *mayorship.*

mayor of the staple. *Hist.* A person appointed to take recognizances of debt between staple merchants, and to hear disputes arising between merchants. See STAPLE.

mayor's court. See COURT.

mayorship. See MAYORALTY.

MBE. See *Multistate Bar Examination* under BAR EXAMINATION.

MBO. See *management buyout* under BUYOUT.

MC. *abbr.* MEMBER OF CONGRESS.

McCarran Act. A federal law requiring, among other things, members of the Communist party to register with the Attorney General and requiring Communist organizations to provide the government with a list of its members. • The Act was passed during the Cold War but was later repealed in response to a U.S. Supreme Court decision declaring portions of the Act unconstitutional. — Also termed *McCarran Internal Security Act*; *Subversive Activities Control Act of 1950.*

McCarran–Ferguson Act. A federal law allowing a state to regulate insurance companies doing business in that state, and also to levy a tax on them. 15 USCA §§ 1011–1015.

McCarran Internal Security Act. See MCCARRAN ACT.

***McClanahan* presumption.** The presumption that the states do not have jurisdiction to tax members of a Native American tribe who live or work on tribal land. • The presumption is not limited to tribal members who live or work on a formal reservation. Instead, it includes those who live or work on informal reservations, in dependent tribal communities, and on tribal allotments. *McClanahan v. Arizona Tax Comm'n,* 411 U.S. 164, 93 S.Ct. 1257 (1973).

***McDonnell Douglas* test.** *Employment law.* The principle for applying a shifting burden of proof in employment-discrimination cases, essentially requiring the plaintiff to come forward with evidence of discrimination and the defendant to come forward with evidence showing that the employment action complained of was taken for nondiscriminatory reasons. • Under this test, the plaintiff is first required to establish a prima facie case of discrimination, as by showing that the plaintiff is a member of a protected group and suffered an adverse employment action. If the plaintiff satisfies that burden, then the defendant must articulate a legitimate, nondiscriminatory reason for the employment action complained of. If the defendant satisfies that burden, then the plaintiff must prove that the defendant's stated reason is just a pretext for discrimination and that discrimination was the real reason for the employment action. *McDonnell Douglas Corp. v. Green,* 411 U.S. 792, 93 S.Ct. 1817 (1973).

***McNabb–Mallory* rule.** *Criminal procedure.* The doctrine that a confession is inadmissible if obtained during an unreasonably long detention period between arrest and a preliminary hearing. • Because of the broader protections afforded under the *Miranda* rule, the *McNabb–Mallory* rule is rarely applied in modern cases. *McNabb v. United States,* 318 U.S. 332, 63 S.Ct. 608 (1943); *Mallory v. United States,* 354 U.S. 449, 77 S.Ct. 1356 (1957). — Often shortened to *Mallory rule.*

***McNaghten* rules** (mik-**nawt**-ən). *Criminal law.* The doctrine that a person is not criminally responsible for an act when a mental disability prevented the person from knowing either (1) the nature and quality of the act, or (2) whether the act was right or wrong. • The federal courts and most states have adopted this test in some form. *McNaghten's Case,* 8 Eng. Rep. 718 (H.L. 1843). — Also spelled *McNaughten rules*; *M'Naghten rules*; *M'Naughten rules.* — Also termed *right-and-wrong test*; *right-wrong test.* See INSANITY DEFENSE.

> "Four points stand out and should be understood whenever reference to M'Naghten is made other than in regard to procedure. (1) It applies only in case of 'a defect of reason, from disease of the mind' and without this the following do not apply except that 'disease' as so used will be interpreted to include congenital defect or traumatic injury. (2) If, because of this 'defect of reason,' the defendant did not know what he was doing he is not guilty of crime. (3) Even if the defendant knew what he was doing he is not guilty of crime if, because of this 'defect of reason,' he did not know he was doing wrong. (4) If the defendant acted under an insane delusion, and was not otherwise insane, his accountability to the crimi-

nal law is the same as if the facts were as they seemed to him to be." Rollin M. Perkins & Ronald N. Boyce, *Criminal Law* 959–60 (3d ed. 1982).

***McNary* comity.** The principle that a U.S. district court should not hear a taxpayer's civil-rights challenge to the administration of a state's tax system. *Fair Assessment in Real Estate Ass'n v. McNary*, 454 U.S. 100, 102 S.Ct. 177 (1981).

M.D. *abbr.* **1.** Middle District, usu. in reference to U.S. judicial districts. **2.** Doctor of medicine.

MDL. *abbr.* MULTIDISTRICT LITIGATION.

MDV. *abbr.* MOTION FOR DIRECTED VERDICT.

mean, *adj.* **1.** Of or relating to an intermediate point between two points or extremes <a mean position>. **2.** Medium in size <a mean height>. **3.** (Of a value, etc.) average <a mean score>.

meander line (mee-**an**-dər). A survey line (not a boundary line) on a portion of land, usu. following the course of a river or stream.

mean high tide. See TIDE.

meaning. The sense of anything, but esp. of words; that which is conveyed (or intended to be conveyed) by a written or oral statement or other communicative act.

objective meaning. The meaning that would be attributed to an unambiguous document (or portion of a document) by a disinterested reasonable person who is familiar with the surrounding circumstances. • Parties to a contract are often held to its objective meaning, which they are deemed to have had reason to know, even if they subjectively understood or intended something else.

plain meaning. The meaning attributed to a document (usu. by a court) based on a commonsense reading of the words, giving them their ordinary sense and without reference to extrinsic indications of the author's intent. — Also termed *ordinary meaning*. See PLAIN-MEANING RULE.

subjective meaning. The meaning that one party to a legal document attributes to it when the document is written, executed, or otherwise adopted.

mean lower low tide. See TIDE.

mean low tide. See TIDE.

mean reserve. See RESERVE.

means, *n.* **1.** Available resources, esp. for the payment of debt; income. **2.** Something that helps to attain an end; an instrument; a cause.

means-plus-function clause. *Patent law.* An element in a patent claim, usu. in a claim for a combination patent, asserting that the design is a way to perform a given function or is a step in the process of performing a given function. • The claim will be interpreted as including the structure or means stated in the patent, and reasonable equivalents, but not all possible means of achieving the same function. 35 USCA § 112. See *combination patent* under PATENT.

mean trading price. See PRICE.

measure of damages. The basis for calculating damages to be awarded to someone who has suffered an injury. • For example, the measure of damages in an action on a penal bond is compensation for the actual loss, not exceeding the established penalty.

measuring life. Under the rule against perpetuities, the last beneficiary to die who was alive at the testator's death and who usu. holds a preceding interest. • A measuring life is used to determine whether an interest will vest under the rule against perpetuities. Cf. LIFE IN BEING.

measuring money. *Hist.* An extra duty collected on cloth. • It was abolished during the reign of Henry IV.

mechanic's lien. See LIEN.

medfee (**med**-fee). *Hist.* A bribe or reward; compensation given for things exchanged of unequal value.

media concludendi (**mee**-dee-ə kon-kloo-**den**-dɪ). [Latin] *Hist.* The steps of an argument.

media nox (**mee**-dee-ə **noks**), *n.* [Latin] *Hist.* Midnight.

medianus homo (mee-dee-**ay**-nəs **hoh**-moh). [Latin] *Hist.* A man of middle fortune.

mediate datum (mee-dee-**ay**-tee **day**-təm). [Latin] An intermediate fact whose existence implies the existence of ultimate facts.

mediate descent. See DESCENT.

mediate evidence. See *secondary evidence* under EVIDENCE.

mediate possession. See POSSESSION (3).

mediate powers (**mee**-dee-it). Subordinate powers incidental to primary powers, esp. as given by a principal to an agent; powers necessary to accomplish the principal task <adjusting debt is a mediate power to collecting debt>. Cf. PRIMARY POWERS.

mediate testimony. See *secondary evidence* under EVIDENCE.

mediation (mee-dee-**ay**-shən), *n.* **1.** A method of nonbinding dispute resolution involving a neutral third party who tries to help the disputing parties reach a mutually agreeable solution. — Also termed *conciliation.* Cf. ARBITRATION. **2.** *Int'l law.* A neutral country's interference in the controversies of other countries to maintain international stability. — **mediate** (**mee**-dee-ayt), *vb.* — **mediatory** (**mee**-dee-ə-tor-ee), *adj.* — **mediator** (**mee**-dee-ay-tər), *n.*

> "The distinction between *mediation* and *conciliation* is widely debated among those interested in ADR, arbitration, and international diplomacy. Some suggest that *conciliation* is 'a nonbinding arbitration,' whereas *mediation* is merely 'assisted negotiation.' Others put it this way: *conciliation* involves a third party's trying to bring together disputing parties to help them reconcile their differences, whereas *mediation* goes further by allowing the third party to suggest terms on which the dispute might be resolved. Still others reject these attempts at differentiation and contend that there is no consensus about what the two words mean — that they are generally interchangeable. Though a distinction would be convenient, those who argue that usage indicates a broad synonymy are most accurate." Bryan A. Garner, *A Dictionary of Modern Legal Usage* 554 (2d ed. 1995).

Mediation and Conciliation Service. A federal agency that tries to prevent the interruption of commerce resulting from labor disputes, by assisting parties in settling their disputes through mediation and conciliation. • The agency can intervene on its own motion or on the motion of a party to the dispute. — Also termed *Federal Mediation and Conciliation Service.* 29 USCA §§ 172, 173.

mediators of questions. *Hist.* Six persons authorized by 27 Edw. 3, St. 2, ch. 24 to settle disputes between merchants.

Medicaid. A government program that provides medical aid to those who cannot afford private medical services. • Medicaid is jointly funded by the federal and state governments.

Medicaid-qualifying trust. See TRUST.

medical directive. See ADVANCE DIRECTIVE.

medical-emergency exception. *Criminal law.* The principle that a police officer does not need a warrant to enter a person's home if the entrance is made to render aid to someone whom the officer reasonably believes to be in need of immediate assistance.

medical evidence. See EVIDENCE.

medical examiner. A public official who investigates deaths, conducts autopsies, and helps the state prosecute homicide cases. • Medical examiners have replaced coroners in many states. — Sometimes shortened to *examiner.*

medical expense. See EXPENSE.

medical jurisprudence. See FORENSIC MEDICINE.

medical malpractice. See MALPRACTICE.

medical probability. See REASONABLE MEDICAL PROBABILITY.

medicals. See *medical expense* (2) under EXPENSE.

Medicare. A federal program — established under the Social Security Act — that provides health insurance for the elderly and the disabled.

medicolegal (med-i-koh-**lee**-gəl), *adj.* Involving the application of medical science to law <the coroner's medicolegal functions>. See FORENSIC MEDICINE.

medietas linguae (mi-**dɪ**-ə-tas **ling**-gwee), *n.* [Law Latin] *Hist.* Half-tongue. • The term was applied to a jury equally divided between natives and aliens. See DE MEDIETATE LINGUAE.

medio. See DE MEDIO.

medium filum. See *filum aquae* under FILUM.

medium of exchange. Any commodity generally accepted as payment in a transaction and recognized as a standard of value <money is a medium of exchange>. See LEGAL TENDER.

medium tempus (**mee**-dee-əm **tem**-pəs). [Latin "intermediate period"] *Hist.* See *mesne profits* under PROFIT.

medium work. See WORK.

medletum (med-**lee**-təm), *n.* [Law Latin fr. French *mesler* "to mingle"] *Hist.* **1.** A mixing together of something. **2.** An affray or sudden encounter; a melee. **3.** Interference in a business matter.

medley (**med**-lee). An affray; sudden or casual fighting. Cf. CHANCE-MEDLEY.

med. mal. See *medical malpractice* under MALPRACTICE.

meer dreit (meer drayt *or* dreet). See MERE RIGHT.

meeting, *n.* An assembly of persons, esp. to discuss and act on matters in which they have a common interest. — **meet,** *vb.*

annual meeting. *Corporations.* A yearly meeting of shareholders for the purpose of electing directors and conducting other routine business. • The time and place of such a meeting are usu. specified in the corporation's articles or bylaws. — Also termed *regular meeting*; *stated meeting.*

called meeting. See *special meeting.*

creditors' meeting. *Bankruptcy.* The first meeting of a debtor's creditors and equity security holders, presided over by the U.S. Trustee and at which a bankruptcy trustee may be elected and the debtor may be examined under oath. 11 USCA § 341. — Also termed *meeting of creditors*; *341 meeting.*

organizational meeting. *Corporations.* An initial meeting of a new corporation's directors to adopt bylaws, elect officers, and conduct other business.

regular meeting. See *annual meeting.*

special meeting. *Corporations.* A meeting called by the board of directors, an officer, or a group of shareholders for some extraordinary purpose, such as to vote on a merger. — Also termed *called meeting.*

stated meeting. See *annual meeting.*

341 meeting. See *creditors' meeting.*

meeting-competition defense. *Antitrust.* A defense to a charge of price discrimination whereby the defendant shows that the lower price was a good-faith attempt to match what it believed to be a competitor's equally low offer.

meeting of creditors. — See *creditors' meeting* under MEETING.

meeting of the minds. *Contracts.* Actual assent by both parties to the formation of a contract. • This was required under the traditional subjective theory of assent, but modern contract doctrine requires only objective manifestations of assent. — Also termed *mutuality of assent*; *aggregatio mentium.* See MUTUAL ASSENT.

megalopolis (meg-ə-**lop**-ə-lis). A heavily populated, continuous urban area that includes many cities.

Megan's law (**meg**-ən *or* **may**-gən). A statute requiring local authorities to notify a community of any resident who is a convicted sex offender released from prison. • Although many of these statutes were enacted in the late 1980s, they took their popular name from Megan Kanka of New Jersey, a seven-year-old who in 1994 was raped and murdered by a twice-convicted sex offender who lived across the street from her house. All states have these laws, but only some require community notification (as by publishing offenders' pictures in local newspapers); in others, people must call a state hotline or submit names of persons they suspect.

meigne (mayn), *n.* [Law French] *Hist.* See MEINY.

meindre age (**min**-dər **ayj** *or* **azh**), *n.* [Law French] *Hist.* Lesser age; minority. See MINORITY (1).

meiny (**may**-nee), *n.* [Law French] *Hist.* A family, esp. a royal household. — Also spelled *meine*; *meinie*; *meigne.*

melior (**mee**-lee-ər), *adj.* [Latin] Better; the better, as in *melior res* ("the better thing or chattel").

meliorations (meel-yə-**ray**-shənz). **1.** *Scots law.* Improvements — other than repairs — on an estate. **2.** Lasting improvements.

melioribus damnis. See DE MELIORIBUS DAMNIS.

melius inquirendum (**mee**-lee-əs in-kwə-**ren**-dəm), *n.* [Law Latin "to be better inquired into"] *Hist.* A writ ordering the escheator to investigate a matter further, as by inquiring who is the next heir of a party who died seised of lands.

member. *Military law.* A person assigned to a court-martial to determine guilt and punishment.

member bank. See BANK.

member firm. *Securities.* A brokerage firm with at least one director, officer, or general partner who holds a seat in an organized securities exchange. — Also termed (if organized as a corporation) *member corporation*.

member of a crew. *Maritime law.* Under the Jones Act, a person who is attached to a navigating vessel and assists or aids in navigation; SEAMAN.

member of Congress. An elected official who sits in either the U.S. Senate or the House of Representatives. • The official may be appointed to fill an unexpired term. — Abbr. MC.

member of Parliament. A person with the right to sit in one of the two houses of Parliament. — Abbr. MP.

membrana (mem-**bray**-nə), *n.* [Latin "parchment"] *Hist.* **1.** A skin of parchment. **2.** A notebook of leaves of parchment. • The English rolls were made of several types of parchment and the term *membrana* was used in referring to them.

membrum (**mem**-brəm), *n.* [Latin "limb"] A division of something, esp. a slip or small piece of land.

memorandum. 1. An informal written note or record outlining the terms of a transaction or contract <the memorandum indicated the developer's intent to buy the property at its appraised value>. • To satisfy the statute of frauds, a memorandum can be written in any form, but it must (1) identify the parties to the contract, (2) indicate the contract's subject matter, (3) contain the contract's essential terms, and (4) contain the signature of the party against whom enforcement is sought. — Also termed *memorial*; *note*. See STATUTE OF FRAUDS. **2.** An informal written communication used esp. in offices <the firm sent a memorandum reminding all lawyers to turn in their timesheets>. — Often shortened to *memo*. **3.** A party's written statement of its legal arguments presented to the court, usu. in the form of a brief <memorandum of law>. Pl. **memoranda, memorandums.**

memorandum articles. *Marine insurance.* Goods described in the memorandum clause. See MEMORANDUM CLAUSE.

memorandum check. See CHECK.

memorandum clause. A marine-insurance clause protecting underwriters from liability for injury to goods that are particularly perishable, or for minor damages.

memorandum decision. See *memorandum opinion* under OPINION (1).

memorandum in error. A document alleging a factual error, usu. accompanied by an affidavit of proof.

memorandum of alteration. *English law.* A patentee's disclaimer of certain rights — such as rights to part of an invention that is not new and useful — to avoid losing the whole patent. • Under former law, if a patent was granted to two inventions, one of which was not new and useful, the entire patent would be defective.

memorandum of association. *English law.* A legal document setting up a corporation — either with or without limited liability — and including the company's name, purpose, and duration. See ARTICLES OF INCORPORATION.

memorandum of intent. See LETTER OF INTENT.

memorandum of understanding. See LETTER OF INTENT.

memorandum opinion. See OPINION (1).

memorandum sale. See SALE.

memorial, *n.* **1.** An abstract of a legal record, esp. a deed; MEMORANDUM (1). **2.** A written statement of facts presented to a legislature or executive as a petition.

memoriter (mə-**mor**-ə-tər), *adv.* [Latin "with an accurate memory"] From memory; by recollection. • *Memoriter* proof of a written instrument is furnished by the recollection of a witness who knew the instrument.

menacing, *n.* An attempt to commit common-law assault. • The term is used esp. in jurisdictions that have defined assault to include battery. See ASSAULT.

mendacity (men-**das**-ə-tee), *n.* **1.** The quality of being untruthful. **2.** A lie; falsehood. — **mendacious** (men-**day**-shəs), *adj.*

men of straw. *Hist.* False witnesses who wandered around courts and were paid to give untrue testimony. • They stuffed straw into their shoes so that advocates could recognize them. See STRAW MAN.

mens (menz), *n.* [Latin] Mind; intention; will.

mensa. See MANAGIUM.

mensa et thoro (**men**-sə et **thor**-oh). [Latin] From bed and board. See *divorce a mensa et thoro* under DIVORCE.

mensalia (men-**say**-lee-ə), *n.* [fr. Latin *mensa* "a table"] Parsonages; spiritual livings. — Also termed *mensal benefices.*

mensis (**men**-sis), *n.* [Latin] *Roman law.* A month.

mens legis (**menz lee**-jis). [Latin "the mind of the law"] The spirit or purpose of a law.

mens legislatoris (**menz** lej-is-lə-**tor**-is). [Latin "the intention of the lawmaker"] Legislative intent.

mensor (**men**-sor), *n.* [fr. Latin *metiri* "to measure"] *Roman law.* A measurer of land; a surveyor.

mens rea (**menz ree**-ə). [Law Latin "guilty mind"] The state of mind that the prosecution, to secure a conviction, must prove that a defendant had when committing a crime; criminal intent or recklessness <the *mens rea* for theft is the intent to deprive the rightful owner of the property>. • *Mens rea* is the second of two essential elements of every crime at common law, the other being the *actus reus.* — Also termed *mental element*; *criminal intent*; *guilty mind.* Pl. ***mentes reae*** (**men**-teez **ree**-ee). Cf. ACTUS REUS.

> "There are only two states of mind which constitute *mens rea*, and they are *intention*, and *recklessness*." J.W. Cecil Turner, *Kenny's Outlines of Criminal Law* 29–30 (16th ed. 1952).

> "Most English lawyers would however now agree with Sir James Fitzjames Stephen that the expression *mens rea* is unfortunate, though too firmly established to be expelled, just because it misleadingly suggests that, in general, moral culpability is essential to a crime, and they would assent to the criticism expressed by a later judge that the true translation of *mens rea* is 'an intention to do the act which is made penal by statute or by the common law.' [*Allard v. Selfridge,* (1925) 1 K.B. at 137 (per Shearman, J.)]." H.L.A. Hart, "Legal Responsibility and Excuses," in *Punishment and Responsibility* 28, 36 (1968).

> "Some years ago the mens-rea doctrine was criticized on the ground that the Latin phrase is 'misleading.' If the words 'mens rea' were to be regarded as self-explanatory they would be open to this objection, but they are to be considered merely as a convenient label which may be attached to any psychical fact sufficient for criminal guilt (in connection with socially-harmful conduct). This includes a field too complex for any brief self-explanatory phrase, and since it is important to have some sort of dialectic shorthand to express the idea, this time-honored label will do as well as any." Rollin M. Perkins & Ronald N. Boyce, *Criminal Law* 826–27 (3d ed. 1982).

mensularius (men-sə-**lair**-ee-əs), *n.* [fr. Latin *mensa* "a table"] *Roman law.* A dealer in money; a moneychanger; a banker.

mensura (men-**s[y]oor**-ə), *n.* [Latin] *Hist.* A measure.

mensura domini regis (men-**s[y]oor**-ə **dom**-ə-nI **ree**-jis). [Law Latin "the measure of our lord the king"] *Hist.* The standard weights and measures established under Richard I, in his Parliament at Westminster in 1197.

> "Thus, under king Richard I, in his parliament holden at Westminster, A.D. 1197, it was ordained that there shall be only one weight and one measure throughout the kingdom, and that the custody of the assise or standard of weights and measures shall be committed to certain persons in every city and borough .... In king John's time this ordinance of king Richard was frequently dispensed with for money which occasioned a provision to be made for enforcing it .... These original standards were called *pondus regis*, and *mensura domini regis*; and are directed by a variety of subsequent statutes to be kept in the exchequer, and all weights and measures to be made conformable thereto." 1 William Blackstone, *Commentaries on the Laws of England* 265–66 (1765).

mental anguish. See EMOTIONAL DISTRESS.

mental capacity. See CAPACITY (3).

mental cruelty. See CRUELTY.

mental distress. See EMOTIONAL DISTRESS.

mental element. See MENS REA.

mental illness. 1. A disorder in thought or mood so substantial that it impairs judgment, behavior, perceptions of reality, or the ability to cope with the ordinary demands of life. **2.** Mental disease that is severe enough to necessitate care and treatment for the afflicted person's own welfare or the welfare of others in the community.

mental incompetence. See INCOMPETENCY.

mental reservation. One party's silent understanding or exception to the meaning of a contractual provision.

mental shock. See SHOCK.

mental suffering. See EMOTIONAL DISTRESS.

mente captus (**men**-tee **kap**-təs). [Latin "captured in mind"] Persons who are habitually insane.

mentes reae (**men**-teez **ree**-ee). *pl.* MENS REA.

mentiri (men-**tɪ**-rɪ), *vb.* [Latin] To lie.

mentition (men-**tish**-ən), *n.* [fr. Latin *mentitio* "lying"] The act of lying.

mera noctis (**meer**-ə **nok**-tis), *n.* [Latin "middle of the night"] Midnight.

mercantile (**mər**-kən-teel *or* -tɪl *or* -til), *adj.* Of or relating to merchants or trading; commercial <the mercantile system>.

mercantile agent. See AGENT.

mercantile law. See COMMERCIAL LAW (1).

Mercantile Law Amendment Acts. The Mercantile Law Amendment Act of 1856 (19 & 20 Vict., chs. 60, 97) and the Mercantile Law Amendment Act (Scotland) of 1856, passed primarily to reconcile parts of the mercantile laws of England, Scotland, and Ireland.

mercantile paper. See *commercial paper* (1) under PAPER.

mercative (mər-**kay**-tiv), *adj.* [fr. Latin *mercatum* "a market"] *Scots law.* Belonging to trade.

mercatum (mər-**kay**-təm), *n.* [Law Latin] A market; a contract of sale; a bargain.

mercedary (**mər**-sə-der-ee), *n.* [Latin] An employer; one who hires.

mercenarius (mər-sə-**nair**-ee-əs), *n.* [Latin] **1.** An employee; a servant. **2.** A soldier of fortune. — Also spelled *mercennarius.*

mercenary (**mər**-sə-ner-ee). *Int'l law.* A professional soldier hired by someone other than his or her own government to fight in a foreign country.

mercenlage (**mər**-sən-law). [fr. Saxon *myrcnalag*] The law of the Mercians. • This was one of the three principal legal systems prevailing in England at the beginning of the 11th century. It was observed in many midland counties and those bordering on Wales. — Also spelled *merchenlage* (**mər**-shən-law). — Also termed *lex merciorum* (**leks** mər-shee-**or**-əm); *Mercian law* (**mər**-shee-ən *or* **mər**-shən). See DANELAW; WEST SAXON LAW.

> "[A]bout the beginning of the eleventh century there were three principal systems of laws prevailing in different districts .... The *Mercen-Lage*, or Mercian laws, which were observed in many of the midland counties, and those bordering on the principality of Wales; the retreat of the ancient Britons; and therefore very probably intermixed with the British or Druidical customs." 1 William Blackstone, *Commentaries on the Laws of England* 65 (1765).

merces (**mər**-seez), *n.* [Latin] *Roman law.* **1.** An agreed payment for services specifically contracted for.

> "There must be consent, a thing let, and an agreed payment (*merces*) .... The *merces* must be certain and Justinian's texts say that, as in sale, it must be money. But there is not the same difficulty here, and Gaius does not state such a rule. It is possible that it did not exist in classical law and, even under Justinian, some cases cannot be reconciled with the rule. The rent of land might be in produce and even a fraction of the crop. This last conflicts with the rule of Gaius that it must be certain: it is held by some writers that the text is interpolated, by others that the relation was not really *locatio conductio*, but *societas* (partnership). The *merces* was not usually a lump sum: more often it was a series of periodical payments." W.W. Buckland, *A Manual of Roman Private Law* 289–90 (2d ed. 1953).

2. A reward, esp. for a gratuitous service. Cf. HONORARIUM.

> "A recompense paid for any kind of services, without a preceding agreement (e.g., for saving one's life) is also called *merces*." Adolf Berger, *Encyclopedic Dictionary of Roman Law* 581 (1953).

merchandise (**mər**-chən-dɪz *also* -dɪs). Goods that are bought and sold in business; commercial wares.

merchandise broker. See BROKER.

Merchandise Marks Acts. *Hist.* An 1887 English statute (50 & 51 Vict., ch. 28) making it a misdemeanor to fraudulently mark merchandise for sale or to sell merchandise so marked. • The statute was repealed in 1968.

merchant. One whose business is buying and selling goods for profit; esp., a person or entity that holds itself out as having expertise peculiar to the goods in which it deals and is therefore held by the law to a higher standard of expertise than a nonmerchant is held. • Because the term relates solely to goods, a supplier of services is not considered a merchant.

> "The definition of 'merchant' in [UCC] Section 2-104(1) identifies two separate but often interrelated criteria: Does the seller 'deal in goods' of that kind, or does the seller 'otherwise by his occupation' hold himself out as having special knowledge with respect to the goods? It should be emphasized that the drafters have placed these two criteria in the alternative by use of the word 'or.' Thus, the definition clearly catches all those who regularly sell inventory even though they may have no expertise regarding the particular product. This would include distributors, wholesalers, and retail dealers. Dealers who sell prepackaged goods containing a defect over which they have no control might be surprised to learn that they have given an implied warranty of merchantability with respect to the goods, but such is the law." Barkley Clark & Christopher Smith, *The Law of Product Warranties* § 5.02[1], at 5-25 (1984).

merchantable (**mər**-chənt-ə-bəl), *adj.* Fit for sale in the usual course of trade at the usual selling prices; MARKETABLE. — Also termed *salable.* — **merchantability,** *n.* See *implied warranty of merchantability* under WARRANTY (2).

merchantable title. See *marketable title* under TITLE (2).

merchant exception. *Contracts.* An exemption from the statute of frauds making a contract between merchants enforceable if, within a reasonable time after they reach an oral agreement, a written confirmation of the terms is sent, to which the recipient does not object within ten days of receiving it. • The only effect of failing to object to the written confirmation is that the recipient will be precluded from relying on the statute of frauds — or the lack of a formal, written agreement — as a defense to a breach-of-contract claim. The party seeking to enforce an agreement must still prove that an agreement was reached. UCC § 2-201(2).

merchantman. *Archaic.* A vessel employed in foreign or interstate commerce or in the merchant service.

merchant's accounts. Current, mutual accounts between merchants showing debits and credits for merchandise.

merchant's defense. The principle that a store owner will not be held liable for reasonably detaining a suspected shoplifter, to facilitate an investigation by a law-enforcement officer, if probable cause exists to suspect the detained person of wrongfully removing merchandise from the store.

merchant seaman. See SEAMAN.

merchant's firm offer. See *irrevocable offer* under OFFER.

Merchant Shipping Acts. English statutes to improve shipping conditions by, among other things, vesting the superintendence of merchant shipping in the board of trade.

merchet (**mər**-chet). See MARCHET.

mercheta. See MARCHET.

merchetum. See MARCHET.

merciament (**mər**-see-ə-mənt). *Archaic.* See AMERCEMENT.

Mercian law. See MERCENLAGE.

Mercimoniatus Angliae (mər-sə-moh-nee-**ay**-təs **ang**-glee-ee). [Law Latin] *Hist.* English customs duties on merchandise brought into the country.

mercy. Compassionate treatment, as of criminal offenders or of those in distress; esp., imprisonment, rather than death, imposed as punishment for capital murder. See CLEMENCY.

mercy killing. See EUTHANASIA.

mere (mair *or* mer), *n.* [Law French] Mother, as in the phrase *en ventre sa mere* ("in its mother's womb").

mere-continuation doctrine. A principle under which a successor corporation will be held liable for the acts of a predecessor corporation, if only one corporation remains after the transfer of assets, and both corporations share an identity of stock, shareholders, and directors. — Also termed *continuity-of-entity doctrine.* Cf. SUBSTANTIAL-CONTINUITY DOCTRINE.

mere-evidence rule. *Criminal procedure.* The former doctrine that a search warrant allows seizure of the instrumentalities of the crime (such as a murder weapon) or the fruits of the crime (such as stolen goods), but does not permit the seizure of items that have evidentiary value only (such as incriminating documents). • The Supreme Court has abolished this rule, and today warrants may be issued to search for and seize all evidence of a crime. *Warden v. Hayden*, 387 U.S. 294, 87 S.Ct. 1642 (1967); Fed. R. Crim. P. 41(b).

mere license. See *bare license* under LICENSE.

mere licensee. See *bare licensee* under LICENSEE.

mere motu. See EX MERE MOTU.

mere right. An abstract right in property, without possession or even the right of possession. — Also termed *jus merum*; *merum jus*; *meer dreit.*

> "The mere *right of property*, the *jus proprietatis*, without either possession or even the right of possession. This is frequently spoken of in our books under the name of the *mere right, jus merum*; and the estate of the owner is in such cases said to be totally devested, and *put to a right*. A person in this situation may have the true ultimate property of the lands in himself: but by the intervention of certain circumstances, either by his own negligence, the solemn act of his ancestor, or the determination of a court of justice, the presumptive evidence of that right is strongly in favour of his antagonist; who has thereby obtained the absolute right of possession .... The heir therefore in this case has only a *mere right*, and must be strictly held to the proof of it, in order to recover the lands." 2 William Blackstone, *Commentaries on the Laws of England* 197–98 (1766).

merestone (**meer**-stohn). *Archaic.* A stone that marks land boundaries. — Also spelled *mearstone.*

meretricious (mer-ə-**trish**-əs), *adj.* **1.** Involving prostitution; of an unlawful sexual nature <a meretricious encounter>. **2.** (Of a romantic relationship) involving either unlawful sexual connection or lack of capacity on the part of one party <a meretricious marriage>. **3.** Superficially attractive but fake nonetheless; alluring by false show <meretricious advertising claims>.

mergee (mər-**jee**). A participant in a corporate merger.

merger. 1. The act or an instance of combining or uniting. **2.** *Contracts.* The substitution of a superior form of contract for an inferior form, as when a written contract supersedes all oral agreements and prior understandings.

> "Where two parties have made a simple contract for any purpose, and afterwards have entered into an identical engagement by deed, the simple contract is *merged* in the deed and becomes extinct. This extinction of a lesser in a higher security, like the extinction of a lesser in a greater interest in lands, is called *merger*." William R. Anson, *Principles of the Law of Contract* 85 (Arthur L. Corbin ed., 3d Am. ed. 1919).

3. *Property.* The absorption of a lesser estate into a greater estate when both become the same person's property. **4.** *Criminal law.* The absorption of a lesser included offense into a more serious offense when a person is charged with both crimes, so that the person is not subject to double jeopardy. • For example, a defendant cannot be convicted of both attempt (or solicitation) and the completed crime — though merger does not apply to conspiracy and the completed crime. — Also termed *merger of offenses.* **5.** *Civil procedure.* The effect of a judgment for the plaintiff, which absorbs any claim that was the subject of the lawsuit into the judgment, so that the plaintiff's rights are confined to enforcing the judgment. Cf. BAR (5). **6.** The joining of the procedural aspects of law and equity. **7.** The absorption of one company (esp. a corporation) that ceases to exist into another that retains its own name and identity and acquires the assets and liabilities of the former. • Corporate mergers must conform to statutory formalities and usu. must be approved by a majority of the outstanding shares. Cf. CONSOLIDATION (2); BUYOUT.

bust-up merger. A merger in which the acquiring corporation sells off lines of business owned by the target corporation to repay the loans used in the acquisition.

cash merger. A merger in which shareholders of the target company must accept cash for their shares. — Also termed *cash-out merger*; *freeze-out merger.*

conglomerate merger. A merger between unrelated businesses that are neither competitors nor customers or suppliers of each other.

> "A merger which is neither vertical nor horizontal is a conglomerate merger. A pure conglomerate merger is one in which there are no economic relationships between the acquiring and the acquired firm. Mixed conglomerate mergers involve horizontal or vertical relationships, such as the acquisition of a firm producing the same product as the acquirer but selling it in a different geographical market, which is not a horizontal merger because the merging companies are not competitors ...." 54 Am. Jur. 2d *Monopolies, Restraints of Trade, and Unfair Trade Practices* § 169, at 226 (1996).

de facto merger (di **fak**-toh). A transaction that has the economic effect of a statutory merger but that is cast in the form of an acquisition or sale of assets or voting stock. • Although such a transaction does not meet the statutory requirements for a merger, a court will generally treat it as a statutory merger for purposes of the appraisal remedy.

downstream merger. A merger of a parent corporation into its subsidiary.

forward triangular merger. See *triangular merger*.

freeze-out merger. See *cash merger*.

horizontal merger. A merger between two or more businesses that are on the same market level because they manufacture similar products in the same geographic region; a merger of direct competitors. — Also termed *horizontal integration*.

product-extension merger. A merger in which the products of the acquired company are complementary to those of the acquiring company and may be produced with similar facilities, marketed through the same channels, and advertised by the same media.

reverse triangular merger. A merger in which the acquiring corporation's subsidiary is absorbed into the target corporation, which becomes a new subsidiary of the acquiring corporation. — Also termed *reverse subsidiary merger*.

short-form merger. A merger that is less expensive and time-consuming than an ordinary statutory merger, usu. permitted when a subsidiary merges into a parent that already owns most of the subsidiary's shares. • Such a merger is generally accomplished when the parent adopts a merger resolution, mails a copy of the plan to the subsidiary's record shareholders, and files the executed articles of merger with the secretary of state, who issues a certificate of merger.

statutory merger. A merger provided by and conducted according to statutory requirements.

stock merger. A merger involving one company's purchase of another company's capital stock.

triangular merger. A merger in which the target corporation is absorbed into the acquiring corporation's subsidiary, with the target's shareholders receiving stock in the parent corporation. — Also termed *subsidiary merger*; *forward triangular merger*.

upstream merger. A merger of a subsidiary corporation into its parent.

vertical merger. A merger between businesses occupying different levels of operation for the same product, such as between a manufacturer and a retailer; a merger of buyer and seller.

8. The blending of the rights of a creditor and debtor, resulting in the extinguishment of the creditor's right to collect the debt. • As originally developed in Roman law, a merger resulted from the marriage of a debtor and creditor, or when a debtor became the creditor's heir. — Also termed *confusion*; *confusion of debts*; *confusion of rights*. Cf. CONFUSION OF TITLES.

merger clause. See INTEGRATION CLAUSE.

merger of offenses. See MERGER (4).

meritorious (mer-ə-**tor**-ee-əs), *adj.* **1.** (Of an act, etc.) meriting esteem or reward <meritorious trial performance>. **2.** (Of a case, etc.) meriting a legal victory; having legal worth <meritorious claim>.

meritorious consideration. See *good consideration* under CONSIDERATION.

meritorious defense. See DEFENSE (1).

merit regulation. Under state blue-sky laws, the practice of requiring securities offerings not only to be accompanied by a full and adequate disclosure but also to be substantively fair, just, and equitable.

merits. 1. The elements or grounds of a claim or defense; the substantive considerations to be taken into account in deciding a case, as opposed to extraneous or technical points, esp. of procedure <trial on the merits>. **2.** EQUITY (3) <on questions of euthanasia, the Supreme Court has begun to concern itself with the merits as well as the law>.

merit system. The practice of hiring and promoting employees, esp. government employees, based on their competence rather than political favoritism. Cf. SPOILS SYSTEM.

Merit Systems Protection Board. A federal agency with jurisdiction to review civil-service-employee appeals and related matters, such as actions brought by the Office of Special Counsel. • The Board succeeded to certain functions of the Civil Service Commission.

***Merrill* doctrine.** The principle that the government cannot be estopped from disavowing an agent's unauthorized act. *Federal Crop Ins. Corp. v. Merrill*, 332 U.S. 380, 68 S.Ct. 1 (1947).

merum (**meer**-əm). [Latin] *Hist.* Mere; naked.

merum jus (**meer**-əm **jəs**). See MERE RIGHT.

merx (mərks). [Latin] *Hist.* Trade articles; merchandise.

mescreaunt (mes-kree-**awnt** *or* **mis**-kree-ənt). [Law French] *Hist.* MISCREANT. — Also termed *mescroyant.*

mese (meez *or* mees), *n.* [Law French] *Hist.* A house. — Also spelled *mees*; *meas.*

mesnalty (**meen**-əl-tee), *n.* [fr. Law French and English mesne "middle"] *Hist.* **1.** The estate or manor held by a mesne lord. **2.** The right of the mesne; the tenure of the mesne lord. — Also spelled *mesnality.* See MESNE LORD.

mesne (meen), *adj.* Occupying a middle position; intermediate or intervening <the mesne encumbrance has priority over the third mortgage, but is subordinate to the first mortgage>.

mesne, writ of. See DE MEDIO.

mesne assignment. See ASSIGNMENT (2).

mesne conveyance. See CONVEYANCE.

mesne encumbrance. See ENCUMBRANCE.

mesne lord. *Hist.* A feudal lord who stood between a tenant and the chief lord, and held land from a superior lord. See LORD (3).

mesne process. See PROCESS.

mesne profits. See PROFIT.

mesonomic (mes-ə-**nom**-ik *also* mee-zə-), *adj.* Of, relating to, or involving an act that, although it does not affect a person's physical freedom, has legal consequences in its evolution. • This term was coined by the philosopher Albert Kocourek in his book *Jural Relations* (1927). Cf. ZYGNOMIC.

message. A written or oral communication, often sent through a messenger or other agent, or electronically (e.g., through e-mail or voicemail).

annual message. A message from the President or a governor given at the opening of an annual legislative session.

Presidential message. A communication from the President to the U.S. Congress on matters pertaining to the state of the union, esp. of matters requiring legislative consideration. U.S. Const. art. II, § 3. — Also termed *State of the Union.*

special message. A message from the President or a governor relating to a particular matter.

veto message. See VETO MESSAGE.

message from the Crown. An official communication from the sovereign to Parliament.

messarius (mə-**sair**-ee-əs), *n.* [fr. Latin *messis*] *Hist.* A chief servant; a bailiff; an overseer of the harvest.

messenger. 1. One who conveys a communication; esp., one employed to deliver telegrams or other communications. **2.** *Hist.* An officer who performs certain ministerial duties, such as taking temporary charge of assets of an insolvent estate.

messuage (**mes**-wij). A dwelling house together with the curtilage, including any outbuildings. See CURTILAGE.

meta (**mee**-tə). [Latin] **1.** *Roman law.* The mark where a racecourse ends or around which chariots turn; by extension, a limit in space or time. **2.** *Hist.* A boundary; a border.

metalaw (**met**-ə-law). A hypothetical set of legal principles based on the rules of existing legal systems and designed to provide a framework of agreement for these different systems.

> "[T]he Constitution controls the deployment of governmental power and defines the rules for how such power may be structured and applied. The Constitution, therefore, is not a body of rules about ordinary private actions, but a collection of rules about the rules and uses of law: in a word, *metalaw.*" Laurence H. Tribe, *Constitutional Choices* 246 (1985).

metallum (mə-**tal**-əm), *n.* *Roman law.* **1.** Metal; a mine. **2.** Labor in mines as punishment for a crime. • This was one of the most severe punishments short of death.

metatus (mə-**tay**-təs), *n.* [Law Latin] *Hist.* A dwelling; quarters; a seat.

metayer system (me-**tay**-yər *or* met-ə-**yay**). An agricultural system in which land is divided into small farms among single families who pay a landlord a fixed portion — usu. half — of the produce and the landlord provides the stock. • The system was formerly prevalent in parts of France and Italy, and in the southern part of the United States. — Also written *métayer system*.

metecorn (**meet**-korn). *Archaic.* A portion of corn a lord pays a tenant for labor.

metegavel (**meet**-gav-əl). *Archaic.* A rent or tribute paid in supplies of food.

metelotage (me-te-loh-**tahzh**). [French] **1.** *French law.* The leasing of a ship. **2.** A seaman's wages.

mete out, *vb.* To dispense or measure out (justice, punishment, etc.) <shortly after the jury returned its verdict, the judge meted out an appropriate punishment>.

meter. 1. A metric unit of length equal to 39.368 inches. **2.** An instrument of measurement used to measure use or consumption, esp. used by a utility company to measure utility consumption <a gas meter> <a water meter> <a parking meter>.

meter rate. A rate that a utility company applies to determine a charge for service <meter rate based on kilowatt-hours of electricity>.

metes and bounds (meets). The territorial limits of real property as measured by distances and angles from designated landmarks and in relation to adjoining properties. • Metes and bounds are usu. described in deeds and surveys to establish the boundary lines of land. — Also termed *butts and bounds*; *lines and corners*.

metewand (**meet**-wahnd). *Archaic.* A measuring staff of varying lengths.

meteyard (**meet**-yahrd). *Archaic.* A metewand that is one yard long.

method. A mode of organizing, operating, or performing something, esp. to achieve a goal <method of election> <method of performing a job>.

metric system. A decimal system for measuring length, weight, area, or volume, based on the meter as a unit length and the kilogram as a unit mass.

metropolitan, *adj.* Of or relating to a city or metropolis.

metropolitan, *n. Eccles. law.* An archbishop; the head of a province <the Archbishop of Canterbury is a metropolitan>.

metropolitan council. An official or quasi-official body appointed or elected by voters of a metropolitan area to provide for the unified administration of services (such as sewage disposal or public transportation) to the cities and towns within the metropolitan area.

metropolitan district. See DISTRICT.

metteshep (**meet**-shəp). *Hist.* **1.** An acknowledgment paid in a measure of corn. **2.** A penalty imposed on a tenant for neglect of duty, such as failing to cut the lord's corn. — Also spelled *mettenschep*.

metus (**mee**-təs). [Latin] *Roman law.* **1.** Fear of imminent danger; apprehension of serious danger, esp. in the form of duress to force a person to do something.

> "Fear (metus) had the same effect as fraud as regards the avoidance of the contract. It might be set up by way of defence (exceptio metus) or be the ground of restitutio in integrum, or give rise to an action (actio metus) .... It was not any kind of fear which grounded this action. The evil threatened must be of a serious character ...." R.W. Lee, *The Elements of Roman Law* 352 (4th ed. 1956).

2. A threat by which damage is done to another's property.

meubles (**muu**-bəl *or* **myoo**-blə), *n.* [Law French] Movables, such as household utensils. See MOVABLES.

Mexican divorce. See DIVORCE.

MFN. *abbr.* MOST FAVORED NATION.

Michaelmas sitting (**mik**-əl-məs). *Hist.* A term of English common-law courts, running from November 2 to November 25.

miche (mich), *vb. Hist.* To hide; to sneak; to play truant. — Also spelled *mitch*.

michery (**mich**-ər-ee). *Hist.* Theft; cheating.

***Midcal* test.** *Antitrust.* The doctrine that the anticompetitive acts of a private party will be considered state acts — and thereby protected from liability under the antitrust laws — if the acts are within a clearly articulated and affirmatively expressed policy of the state, and if the conduct is actively supervised by the state. *California Retail Liquor Dealers Ass'n v. Midcal Aluminum, Inc.*, 445 U.S. 97, 100 S.Ct. 937 (1980). See STATE-ACTION DOCTRINE; ACTIVE SUPERVISION.

mid-channel. See MIDDLE LINE OF MAIN CHANNEL.

middle burden of proof. A level of required persuasion, between the preponderance-of-the-evidence standard and the beyond-a-reasonable-doubt standard, by which a party is required to prove a fact by clear and convincing evidence. See *clear and convincing evidence* under EVIDENCE.

middle-level scrutiny. See INTERMEDIATE SCRUTINY.

middle line of main channel. The equidistant point in the main channel of the river between the well-defined banks on either shore; the middle thread of a river's current. — Also termed *mid-channel*; *middle of the river*.

middleman. An intermediary or agent between two parties; esp., a dealer (such as a wholesaler) who buys from producers and sells to retailers or consumers.

middle management. See MANAGEMENT.

middle of the river. See MIDDLE LINE OF MAIN CHANNEL.

middle-of-the-road test. See HYDRAFLOW TEST.

middle thread. The center line of something; esp., an imaginary line drawn lengthwise through the middle of a stream's current.

mid-level scrutiny. See INTERMEDIATE SCRUTINY.

midnight deadline. A time limit for doing something, ending at midnight on a particular day. • For a bank, the midnight deadline is midnight on the next banking day following the day on which the bank receives the relevant item or from which the time for taking action begins to run, whichever is later. UCC § 4–104(a)(10).

midshipman. A naval cadet; a student at the U.S. Naval Academy.

midsummer-day. The summer solstice, usu. occurring about June 22. • It was formerly one of the four quarter-days for the payment of rents.

midway. See THALWEG.

***Midwest Piping* rule.** *Labor law.* The doctrine that an employer may not recognize multiple unions during a period in which there are conflicting claims of representation. *Midwest Piping & Supply Co.*, 63 NLRB Dec. (CCH) 1060 (1945).

migrant worker. *Int'l law.* A person who works seasonally as an agricultural laborer in a foreign country.

migration. Movement (of people or animals) from one country or region to another.

migratory corporation. See CORPORATION.

migratory divorce. See DIVORCE.

***Mike O'Connor* rule.** *Labor law.* The doctrine that unilateral changes that an employer makes after a union victory in an initial-representation election — but before the employer's objections have been resolved — are automatic violations of the National Labor Relations Act if the employer's objections are rejected. • If the employer's objections are sustained, any failure-to-bargain charge will be dismissed because the employer had no duty to bargain. But if the employer's objections are rejected, the employer is considered to have been under a duty to bargain as of the date of the election, which is why the unilateral changes are automatic violations of the Act. *Mike O'Connor Chevrolet–Buick–GMC Co.*, 209 NLRB Dec. (CCH) 701 (1974).

mild exigency. A circumstance that justifies a law-enforcement officer's departure from the knock-and-announce rule, such as the likelihood that the building's occupants will try to escape, resist arrest, or destroy evidence. See KNOCK-AND-ANNOUNCE RULE.

mile. **1.** A measure of distance equal to 5,280 feet. — Also termed *statute mile*. **2.** NAUTICAL MILE.

mileage. **1.** The distance in miles between two points. **2.** The distance a vehicle has traveled as reflected by an odometer. **3.** An allowance paid for travel expenses, as of a witness or public employee.

miles (**mI**-leez), *n.* [Latin] **1.** *Roman law.* A soldier. **2.** *Hist.* A knight.

militare (mil-ə-**tair**-ee), *vb.* [Latin] **1.** *Roman law.* To serve as a soldier. • This verb later referred to serving in public office, civil or military. **2.** *Hist.* To be knighted.

military, *adj.* **1.** Of or relating the armed forces <military base>. **2.** Of or relating to war <military action>.

military, *n.* The armed forces.

military board. A group of persons appointed to act as a fact-finding agency or as an advisory body to the appointing military authority.

military bounty land. Land offered to members of the military as a reward for services. See *donation land* under LAND.

military commission. A court, usu. composed of both civilians and military officers, that is modeled after a court-martial and that tries and decides cases concerning martial-law violations. See COURT-MARTIAL.

military-contractor defense. The principle that a manufacturer who produces equipment for the military is immune from tort liability, to the same extent as the federal government, if the manufacturer did not design the equipment, participated minimally in the design, or received government authorization to proceed with a design after warning the government of the possible dangers of the design and of possible alternative designs.

military court. A court that has jurisdiction over members of the armed forces and that enforces the Code of Military Justice. See CODE OF MILITARY JUSTICE.

military court of inquiry. A military court that has special and limited jurisdiction and that is convened to investigate specific matters and, traditionally, to determine whether further procedures are warranted. 10 USCA § 935.

military government. *Int'l law.* The control of all or most public functions within a country, or the assumption and exercise of governmental functions, by military forces or individual members of those forces; government exercised by a military commander under the direction of the executive or sovereign, either externally during a foreign war or internally during a civil war. • A military government's actions supersede all local law. See MARTIAL LAW.

military judge. A commissioned officer of the armed forces who is on active duty and is a member of a bar of a federal court or of the highest court of a state. • The Judge Advocate General of the particular service must certify a military judge as qualified for duty. A military judge of a general court-martial must also be a member of an independent judiciary. A military judge is detailed to every general court-martial and usu. to a special court-martial.

military jurisdiction. The three types of governmental power given the military by the U.S. Constitution — specif., jurisdiction under military law, jurisdiction under military government, and jurisdiction under martial law.

military justice. A structure of punitive measures designed to foster order, morale, and discipline within the military.

military law. The branch of public law governing military discipline and other rules regarding service in the armed forces. • It is exercised both in peacetime and in war, is recognized by civil courts, and includes rules far broader than for the punishment of offenders. — Also termed *military justice.* — Sometimes loosely termed *martial law.* Cf. MARTIAL LAW.

> "Military Law . . . is largely, but not exclusively, statutory in character, and prescribes the rights of, and imposes duties and obligations upon, the several classes of persons composing its military establishment; it creates military tribunals, endows them with appropriate jurisdiction and regulates their procedure; it also defines military offenses and, by the imposition of adequate penalties, endeavors to prevent their occurrence." George B. Davis, *A Treatise on the Military Law of the United States* 1 (3d ed. 1915).

military leave. A policy contained in employment policies or collective-bargaining agreements allowing a long-term leave of absence — without an accompanying loss of benefits — for a person in active service in the U.S. armed forces.

military necessity. *Int'l law.* A principle of warfare that permits enough coercive force to achieve a desired end, as long as the force used is not more than is called for by the situation. •

This principle dates from the Hague Convention on Laws and Customs of War on Land of October 18, 1907, which prohibits the destruction or seizure of enemy property "unless such destruction of seizure be imperatively demanded by the necessities of war."

military objective. *Int'l law.* An object that by its nature, location, or use contributes to military action, and is thus susceptible to attack. • Under Geneva Convention Protocol 1 (1977), only military — rather than civilian — objects are proper targets.

military offense. An offense, such as desertion, that lies within the jurisdiction of a military court. See COURT-MARTIAL.

military officer. A person who has command in the armed forces.

Military Rules of Evidence. The rules of evidence applicable to military law and courts-martial. — Abbr. MRE.

military tenure. See TENURE.

military testament. See *soldier's will* under WILL.

militate (**mil**-ə-tayt), *vb.* To exert a strong influence <the evidence of police impropriety militates against a conviction>. Cf. MITIGATE.

milites (**mil**-ə-teez), *n.* **1.** *Roman law.* Members of the military. **2.** *Hist.* Knights who are part of the royal army, by virtue of feudal tenure.

> "[Knights] are also called in our law *milites*, because they formed a part of the royal army, in virtue of their feudal tenures; one condition of which was, that every one who held a knight's fee immediately under the crown ... was obliged to be knighted and attend the king in his wars, or fine for his non-compliance." 1 William Blackstone, *Commentaries on the Laws of England* 404 (1765).

3. *Scots law.* Freeholders holding estates from barons.

militia (mə-**lish**-ə). **1.** A body of citizens armed and trained, esp. by a state, for military service apart from the regular armed forces. • The Constitution recognizes a state's right to form a "well-regulated militia" but also grants Congress the power to activate, organize, and govern a federal militia. U.S. Const. amend. II; U.S. Const. art. I, § 8, cl. 15–16. See NATIONAL GUARD. **2.** *Roman law.* Military service.

Militia Clause. One of two clauses of the U.S. Constitution giving Congress the power to call forth, arm, and maintain a military force to enforce compliance with its laws, suppress insurrections, and repel invasions. U.S. Const. art. I, § 8, cls. 15 and 16.

mill. 1. A machine that grinds corn, grain, or other substances, esp. using a wheel and circular motion. • The substance ground in a mill is sometimes called grist, esp. when it is a grain. Courts sometimes refer to the grinding process as a metaphor for the judicial process <suits to collect on promissory notes are grist for the summary-judgment mill because the material facts in such cases are often undisputed>. **2.** The building in which the grinding is performed, along with the site, dam, or other items connected with the mill. **3.** The tenth part of a cent.

millage rate. See MILL RATE.

Miller Act. A federal law requiring the posting of performance and payment bonds before an award is made for a contract for construction, alteration, or repair of a public work or building. 40 USCA §§ 270a–270d–1.

Miller–Tydings Act. A federal law, enacted in 1937 as an amendment to the Sherman Act, exempting fair-trade laws from the application of the Sherman Act and legalizing resale-price-maintenance agreements between producers and retailers of products. • The Act was repealed by the Consumer Goods Pricing Act of 1975.

***Miller v. Shugart* agreement.** A settlement in which an insured consents to a judgment in favor of the plaintiff, on the condition that the plaintiff will satisfy the judgment only out of proceeds from the insured's policy, and will not seek recovery against the insured personally. • Although the phrase takes its name from a Minnesota case, it is used in other jurisdictions as well. *Miller v. Shugart*, 316 N.W.2d 729 (Minn. 1982).

milling in transit. An arrangement in which a shipment is temporarily detained at an intermediate point, usu. for the application of some manufacturing process, with or without an increase of a freight charge by the carrier.

mill power. A unit of water power used in defining quantities and weights of water available to a lessee.

mill privilege. The right of a mill-site owner to construct a mill and to use power from the stream to operate the mill, with due regard to the rights of other owners along the stream's path.

mill rate. A tax applied to real property whereby each mill represents $1 of tax assessment per $1,000 of the property's assessed value <the mill rate for taxes in this county is 10 mills, so for a home valued at $100,000, the owner will pay $1,000 in property taxes>. — Also termed *millage rate*.

mill site. 1. A small tract of land on or contiguous to a watercourse, suitable for the erection and operation of a mill. **2.** *Mining law*. A small parcel of nonmineral public land (not exceeding five acres) claimed and occupied by an owner of a mining claim because the extra space is needed for mining or ore-reduction operations. 30 USCA § 42.

***Mimms* order.** A police officer's command for a motorist to get out of the vehicle. • A *Mimms* order need not be independently justified if the initial stop was lawful. *Pennsylvania v. Mimms*, 434 U.S. 106, 98 S.Ct. 330 (1977).

mina (**mI**-nə), *n*. [Law Latin] *Hist*. A measure of grain or corn.

minage (**mI**-nij), *n*. [Law French] *Hist*. A toll for selling grain or corn by the *mina*.

minare (mi-**nair**-ee), *vb*. [Law Latin] *Hist*. To mine.

mind. 1. The source of thought and intellect; the seat of mental faculties. **2.** The ability to will, direct, or assent. **3.** Memory.

mind and memory. *Archaic*. A testator's mental capacity to make a will <she argued that her uncle was not of sound mind and memory when executing the will because he had Alzheimer's disease>. • This phrase was generally used as part of the phrase *of sound mind and memory*, referring to the capacity of a testator to make a will. See BONA MEMORIA; CAPACITY.

mine. 1. An underground excavation used to obtain minerals, ores, or other substances. **2.** A mineral deposit; a place containing a mineral deposit.

mineral, *n*. Any natural inorganic matter that has a definite chemical composition and specific physical properties that give it value <most minerals are crystalline solids>.

mineral deed. See DEED.

mineral district. A particular region of the country where valuable minerals are typically found and mined.

mineral entry. The right of entry on public land to mine valuable mineral deposits.

> "It is the policy of the United States, as expressed in Acts of Congress, to make public lands available to the people for the purpose of mining valuable mineral deposits, and to encourage exploration for, and development of, mineral resources on public lands. Accordingly, the United States has reserved all lands 'valuable for minerals' . . . from disposition under the nonmineral statutes, and has made them open to entry for mining purposes, under regulations prescribed by law . . . . In other words . . . where statute authorizes the Federal Government to acquire lands, without indicating that lands are to be acquired for a particular purpose, lands so acquired are public lands subject to mineral entry." 53A Am. Jur. 2d *Mines and Minerals* § 23, at 274 (1996).

mineral interest. See MINERAL RIGHT.

mineral land. See LAND.

mineral lease. See LEASE.

mineral lode. A mineral bed of rock with definite boundaries in a general mass of a mountain; any belt of mineralized rock lying within boundaries that clearly separate it from neighboring rock. — Also termed *lode*.

> "Typically, a lode is a concentration of valuable mineral with boundaries sufficiently distinct to import such a definite trend, continuity, and apartness to the formation that it can be traced through the enclosing mass of rock." 1 *American Law of Mining* § 32.02(2), at 32–7 (2d ed. 1998).

mineral right. The right to search for, develop, and remove minerals from land or to receive a royalty based on the production of minerals. • Such a right is usu. granted by a mineral lease. — Also termed *mineral interest*. See SUBSURFACE RIGHT. Cf. SURFACE RIGHT.

mineral royalty. See ROYALTY (2).

mineral servitude. See SERVITUDE (1).

minerator (**min**-ər-ay-tər). [Law Latin] A miner.

miner's inch. A measurement of water discharge, equaling nine-gallons per minute from a one-inch square pipe. • The precise measurement of a miner's inch varies in different localities.

minimal contacts. See MINIMUM CONTACTS.

minimalist retributivism. See RETRIBUTIVISM.

minimal participant. *Criminal law.* Under the federal sentencing guidelines, a defendant who is among the least culpable of a group of criminal actors, as when the defendant does not understand the scope or structure of the criminal enterprise or the actions of the other members of the group. • The offense level for a crime of a minimal participant can be decreased by four levels. U.S. Sentencing Guidelines Manual § 3B1.2(a). Cf. MINOR PARTICIPANT.

minimal scrutiny. See RATIONAL-BASIS TEST.

mini-maxi, *n.* An underwriting arrangement for a securities transaction, whereby a broker is required to sell the minimum number of securities on an all-or-none basis and the balance on a best-efforts basis. See UNDERWRITING (2).

miniment (min-ə-mənt). See MUNIMENT.

minimization requirement. *Criminal law.* The mandate that police officers acting under an eavesdropping warrant must use the wiretap in a way that will intercept the fewest possible conversations that are not subject to the warrant.

minimum, *adj.* Of, relating to, or constituting the smallest acceptable or possible quantity in a given case <minimum charge to a customer of a public utility>.

minimum contacts. A nonresident defendant's forum-state connections, such as business activity or actions foreseeably leading to business activity, that are substantial enough to bring the defendant within the forum-state court's personal jurisdiction without offending traditional notions of fair play and substantial justice. *International Shoe Co. v. Washington*, 326 U.S. 310, 66 S.Ct. 154 (1945). — Also termed *minimal contacts.*

minimum-fee schedule. *Hist.* A list of the lowest fees that a lawyer may charge, set by a state bar association. • The courts held that minimum-fee schedules, now defunct, violated antitrust laws.

minimum lot. See LOT (1).

minimum-royalty clause. *Patents.* A royalty-agreement provision that prescribes a fixed payment by the licensee to the patent owner, regardless of whether the invention is used or not.

minimum sale. See EXHIBITION VALUE.

minimum scrutiny. See RATIONAL-BASIS TEST.

minimum sentence. See SENTENCE.

minimum tax. See *alternative minimum tax* under TAX.

minimum wage. See WAGE.

mining. The process of extracting ore or minerals from the ground; the working of a mine. • This term also encompasses oil and gas drilling.

mining claim. A parcel of land that contains precious metal in its soil or rock and that is appropriated by a person according to established rules and customs known as the process of *location*. See LOCATION (4).

lode claim. A mining claim (on public land) to a well-defined vein embedded in rock; a mining claim to a mineral lode.

placer claim. A mining claim that is not a lode claim; a claim where the minerals are not located in veins or lodes within rock, but are usu. in softer ground near the earth's surface.

> "It has long been recognized that the distinction between lode and placer claims must be tempered by scientific findings as to the nature of the mineral deposits under consideration, and the practicalities of modern mining methods, which may permit the use of surface mining methods to remove certain lodes or veins of minerals previously only reached by underground methods." 53A Am. Jur. 2d *Mines and Minerals* § 21, at 273 (1996).

mining lease. See LEASE.

mining location. See LOCATION (4), (5).

mining partnership. An association of persons to jointly share a mining business, including the profits, expenses, and losses. • The partnership has features of both a tenancy in common and an ordinary commercial partnership.

"It has generally been held that the law governing ordinary commercial or trading partnerships applies, with a few exceptions, to mining partnerships. The principal exception and the main distinction between mining partnerships and commercial partnerships generally is based on the fact that the principle of delectus personae, meaning the right of a partner to exercise choice and preference as to the admission of any new members to the firm, and as to the persons to be so admitted, does not apply to mining partnerships . . . ." 58 C.J.S. *Mines and Minerals* § 387, at 380 (1998).

mining rent. Consideration given for a mining lease, whether the lease creates a tenancy, conveys a fee, or grants a mere license or incorporeal right.

minister, *n.* **1.** A person acting under another's authority; an agent. **2.** A prominent government officer appointed to manage an executive or administrative department. **3.** A diplomatic representative, esp. one ranking below an ambassador.

foreign minister. **1.** A minister of foreign affairs, who in many countries is equivalent to the U.S. Secretary of State. **2.** An ambassador, minister, or envoy from a foreign government.

minister plenipotentiary (plen-ə-pə-**ten**-shee-er-ee). A minister ranking below an ambassador but possessing full power and authority as a governmental representative, esp. as an envoy of a sovereign ruler. • This officer is often regarded as the personal representative of a head of state.

public minister. A high diplomatic representative such as an ambassador, envoy, or resident, but not including a commercial representative such as a consul.

4. A person authorized by a Christian church to perform religious functions.

ministerial, *adj.* Of or relating to an act that involves obedience to instructions or laws instead of discretion, judgment, or skill <the court clerk's ministerial duties include recording judgments on the docket>.

ministerial-function test. The principle that the First Amendment disallows judicial resolution of an employment-discrimination claim under Title VII, if the employee's responsibilities are religious in nature, as in acting as a liaison between a religion and its adherents, spreading faith, participating in church governance, supervising a religious order, and supervising participation in religious ritual and worship. 42 USCA § 2000e–1(a). See TITLE VII OF THE CIVIL RIGHTS ACT OF 1964.

ministerial officer. See OFFICER (1).

ministerial trust. See *passive trust* under TRUST.

minister plenipotentiary. See MINISTER.

ministrant (**min**-ə-strənt). **1.** One who ministers; a dispenser. **2.** *Hist. Eccles. law.* A party who cross-examines a witness.

ministri regis (mi-**nis**-trɪ **ree**-jis). [Latin] *Hist.* Ministers of the king. • This term was applied to judges and ministerial officers.

minitrial. A private, voluntary, and informal form of dispute resolution in which each party's attorney presents an abbreviated version of its case to a neutral third party and to the opponent's representatives, who have settlement authority. • The third party may render an advisory opinion on the anticipated outcome of litigation. Cf. *summary jury trial* under TRIAL.

minor, *n.* A person who has not reached full legal age; a child or juvenile. — Also termed *infant.*

emancipated minor. A minor who is self-supporting and independent of parental control, usu. as a result of a court order. See EMANCIPATION.

minor aetas (**mɪ**-nər **ee**-tas). [Latin] *Hist.* Lesser age; minority; infancy.

minora regalia (mi-**nor**-ə ri-**gay**-lee-ə). See *reglia minora* under REGALIA.

minor crime. See MISDEMEANOR.

minor dispute. See DISPUTE.

minor fact. See FACT.

minority. 1. The state or condition of being under legal age. — Also termed *infancy*; *nonage.* Cf. MAJORITY (1). **2.** A group having fewer than a controlling number of votes. Cf. MAJORITY (2). **3.** A group that is different in some respect (such as race or religious belief) from the majority and that is sometimes treated differently as a result; a member of such a group. • Some courts have held that the term *minority*, in this sense, is not limited to a group that is outnumbered. It may also be applied to a group that has been traditionally discriminated against or socially suppressed, even if its members are in the numerical majority in an area.

minority discount. A reduction in the value of a closely held business's shares that are owned by someone who has only a minority interest in the business. • The concept underlying a minority discount is recognition that controlling shares — those owned by someone who can control the business — are worth more in the market than noncontrolling shares. But when dissenting shareholders object to a corporate act, such as a merger, and become entitled to have their shares appraised and bought by the corporation, many courts hold that incorporating a minority discount into the valuation of the dissenters' shares is inequitable and is not permitted. See APPRAISAL REMEDY.

minority opinion. See *dissenting opinion* under OPINION (1).

minority shareholder. See SHAREHOLDER.

minor participant. *Criminal law.* Under the federal sentencing guidelines, a defendant who is less culpable for a crime than the other members of the group committing the crime, but who has more culpability than a minimal participant. • A defendant who is a minor participant can have the offense level for the crime decreased by two levels. U.S. Sentencing Guidelines Manual § 3B1.2(b). Cf. MINIMAL PARTICIPANT.

minor's estate. See ESTATE.

mint, *n.* **1.** A government-authorized place for coining money. **2.** A large supply, esp. of money.

mintage. 1. The mint's charge for coining money. **2.** The product of minting; money.

mint-mark. An authorized mark on a coin showing where it was minted.

minus (**mɪ**-nəs). [Latin] *Roman law.* Less; less than; not at all. • A debt remaining wholly unpaid was called *minus solutum.*

minus Latium. See LATIUM MINUS.

minute book. 1. A book in which a court clerk enters minutes of court proceedings. **2.** A record of the subjects discussed and actions taken at a corporate directors' or shareholders' meeting. — Also termed *minutes book.*

minute entry. See *minute order* (1) under ORDER (2).

minute order. See ORDER (2).

minutes. 1. Memoranda or notes of a transaction or proceeding. **2.** *Scots law.* Written forms for preserving evidence.

> "When it is necessary to preserve evidence of any incidental judicial act or statement, this is done in the Court of Session, and also in the inferior courts, by a minute. Thus, where the pursuer restricts his libel, or makes a reference to the defender's oath ... this is done by a minute. Strictly speaking, those minutes ought to be prepared by the clerk of court, as their form imports. They commence with the name of the counsel ... and purport to be a statement made by him ...." William Bell, *Bell's Dictionary and Digest of the Law of Scotland* 721 (George Watson ed., 7th ed. 1890).

minutes book. See MINUTE BOOK.

minutio (mi-**n**[**y**]**oo**-shee-oh). [Latin] *Roman law.* A lessening or reduction. See DEMINUTIO.

***Miranda* hearing** (mə-**ran**-də). A pretrial proceeding held to determine whether the *Miranda* rule has been followed and thus whether the prosecutor may introduce into evidence the defendant's statements to the police made after arrest. See MIRANDA RULE.

***Miranda* rule.** The doctrine that a criminal suspect in police custody must be informed of certain constitutional rights before being interrogated. • The suspect must be advised of the right to remain silent, the right to have an attorney present during questioning, and the right to have an attorney appointed if the suspect cannot afford one. If the suspect is not advised of these rights or does not validly waive them, any evidence obtained during the interrogation cannot be used against the suspect at trial. *Miranda v. Arizona*, 384 U.S. 436, 86 S.Ct. 1602 (1966).

Mirandize (mə-**ran**-dɪz), *vb. Slang.* To read (an arrestee) rights under the *Miranda* rule <the defendant was arrested, Mirandized, and interrogated>. See MIRANDA RULE.

mirror-image rule. *Contracts.* The doctrine that the acceptance of a contractual offer must be positive, unconditional, unequivocal, and unambiguous, and must not change, add to, or qualify the terms of the offer; the common-law principle that for a contract to be formed, the terms of an acceptance must correspond exactly with those of the offer. • In modern commercial contexts, the mirror-image rule has been replaced by UCC § 2-207, which allows parties to enforce their agreement despite minor discrepancies between the offer and the acceptance. — Also termed *ribbon-matching rule*. See BATTLE OF THE FORMS.

> "If an offeree purports to accept an offer but in doing so adds various conditions and qualifications of his own, is the acceptance binding on the offeror, at least in part? Generally speaking, the answer is no: the common law rule, reflected in Restatement Section 59, is that a statement of acceptance is effective only if it is a mirror image of the offer and expresses unconditional assent to all of the terms and conditions imposed by the offeror." Marvin A. Chirelstein, *Concepts and Case Analysis in the Law of Contracts* 54 (1990).

misa (**mI**-zə). [Law Latin] *Hist.* **1.** The issue in a writ of right; a mise. **2.** An agreement; a compromise.

misadministration. See MALADMINISTRATION.

misadventure. 1. A mishap or misfortune. **2.** Homicide committed accidentally by a person doing a lawful act and having no intent to injure; ACCIDENTAL KILLING.

misallege, *vb.* To erroneously assert (a fact, a claim, etc.).

misapplication, *n.* The improper or illegal use of funds or property lawfully held. — **misapply,** *vb.*

misappropriation, *n.* The application of another's property or money dishonestly to one's own use. — **misappropriate,** *vb.* See EMBEZZLEMENT. Cf. APPROPRIATION; EXPROPRIATION.

misappropriation theory. *Securities.* The doctrine that a person who wrongfully uses confidential information to buy or sell securities in violation of a duty owed to the one who is the information source is guilty of securities fraud.

misbehavior in office. See *official misconduct* under MISCONDUCT.

misbranding, *n.* The act or an instance of labeling one's product falsely or in a misleading way. • Misbranding is prohibited by federal and state law. — **misbrand,** *vb.*

miscarriage of justice. A grossly unfair outcome in a judicial proceeding, as when a defendant is convicted despite a lack of evidence on an essential element of the crime. — Also termed *failure of justice*.

miscegenation (mi-sej-ə-**nay**-shən). A marriage between persons of different races, formerly considered illegal in some jurisdictions. • In 1967, the U.S. Supreme Court held that laws banning interracial marriages are unconstitutional. *Loving v. Virginia*, 388 U.S. 1, 87 S.Ct. 1817 (1967). But for years, such laws technically remained on the books in some states. The last remaining state-law ban on interracial marriages was a provision in the state constitution of Alabama. The Alabama legislature voted to repeal the ban, subject to a vote of the state's citizens, in 1999. — Also termed *mixed marriage, interracial marriage*.

miscellaneous itemized deduction. See DEDUCTION.

mischarge. An erroneous jury instruction that may be grounds for reversing a verdict. — Also termed *misdirection*.

mischief (**mis**-chəf). **1.** A condition in which a person suffers a wrong or is under some hardship, esp. one that a statute seeks to remove or for which equity provides a remedy <this legislation seeks to eliminate the mischief of racially restrictive deed covenants>. **2.** Injury or damage caused by a specific person or thing <the vandals were convicted of criminal mischief>. **3.** The act causing such injury or damage <their mischief damaged the abbey>.

mischief rule. In statutory construction, the doctrine that a statute should be interpreted by first identifying the problem (or "mischief") that the statute was designed to remedy and then adopting a construction that will suppress the problem and advance the remedy. — Also termed *rule in Heydon's Case*; *purpose approach*. Cf. GOLDEN RULE; PLAIN-MEANING RULE; EQUITY-OF-THE-STATUTE RULE.

misconduct (mis-**kon**-dəkt). **1.** A dereliction of duty; unlawful or improper behavior.

***affirmative misconduct.* 1.** An affirmative act of misrepresentation or concealment of a material fact; intentional wrongful behavior. • Some courts hold that there must be an ongoing pattern of misrepresentation or false promises, as opposed to an isolated act of providing misinformation. **2.** With respect to a claim of estoppel against the federal government, a misrepresentation or concealment of a material fact by a government employee — beyond a merely innocent or negligent misrepresentation.

juror misconduct. A juror's violation of the court's charge or the law, committed either during trial or in deliberations after trial, such as (1) communicating with outsiders, witnesses, attorneys, bailiffs, or judges about the case, (2) bringing into the jury room information about the case but not in evidence, and (3) conducting experiments regarding theories of the case outside the court's presence.

official misconduct. A public officer's corrupt violation of assigned duties by malfeasance, misfeasance, or nonfeasance. — Also termed *misconduct in office*; *misbehavior in office*; *malconduct in office*; *misdemeanor in office*; *corruption in office*; *official corruption*.

wanton misconduct. An act, or a failure to act when there is a duty to do so, in reckless disregard of another's rights, coupled with the knowledge that injury will probably result. — Also termed *wanton and reckless misconduct*.

willful misconduct. Misconduct committed voluntarily and intentionally.

"This term of art [*willful misconduct*] has defied definition, but it is clear that it means something more than negligence. Two classic examples of misconduct which will defeat the seaman's claim are intoxication and venereal disease." Frank L. Maraist, *Admiralty in a Nutshell* 185–86 (3d ed. 1996).

2. An attorney's dishonesty or attempt to persuade a court or jury by using deceptive or reprehensible methods.

miscontinuance. A continuance erroneously ordered by a court.

miscreant (**mis**-kree-ənt). An apostate; an unbeliever.

misdate. To erroneously date (a document, etc.).

misdelivery. Delivery not according to the contractual specifications.

misdemeanant (mis-də-**mee**-nənt), *n.* A person who has been convicted of a misdemeanor.

misdemeanor (mis-di-**mee**-nər). **1.** A crime that is less serious than a felony and is usu. punishable by fine, penalty, forfeiture, or confinement (usu. for a brief term) in a place other than prison (such as a county jail). — Also termed *minor crime*; *summary offense*. Cf. FELONY.

"'Misdemeanor' was the label ultimately adopted to apply to all offenses other than treason or felony. The term included a wide variety of wrongs and misprisions. Many of the substantive legal principles and procedures applicable to felonies were not applied in the case of misdemeanors. The difference in treatment between felonies and misdemeanors has carried over from common law to current practice, and today misdemeanors are often treated differently than felonies [in] the procedures employed in trying such cases as well as [in] the consequences of a conviction. The traditional distinction between felonies and misdemeanors has been abolished in England." Rollin M. Perkins & Ronald N. Boyce, *Criminal Law* 15 (3d ed. 1982).

gross misdemeanor. A serious misdemeanor, though not a felony.

treasonable misdemeanor. See TREASONABLE MISDEMEANOR.

2. *Archaic.* Any crime, including a felony.

"A crime, or misdemeanor, is an act committed, or omitted, in violation of a public law, either forbidding or commanding it. This general definition comprehends both crimes and misdemeanors; which, properly speaking, are mere synonymous terms: though, in common usage, the word, 'crimes,' is made to denote such offences as are of a deeper and more atrocious dye; while smaller faults, and omissions of less consequence, are comprised under the gentler names of 'misdemeanors' only." 4 William Blackstone, *Commentaries on the Laws of England* 5 (1769).

misdemeanor in office. See *official misconduct* under MISCONDUCT.

misdemeanor-manslaughter rule. The doctrine that a death occurring during the commission of a misdemeanor (or sometimes a nondangerous felony) is involuntary manslaughter. • Many states and the Model Penal Code have abolished this rule. Cf. FELONY-MURDER RULE.

"Companion to the felony-murder rule is the so-called misdemeanor-manslaughter rule[:] ... Homicide resulting from the perpetration or attempted perpetration of an unlawful act, less than a dangerous felony, is manslaughter if the unlawful act is malum in se." Rollin M. Perkins & Ronald N. Boyce, *Criminal Law* 108 (3d ed. 1982).

misdescription. **1.** A contractual error or falsity that deceives, injures, or materially misleads one of the contracting parties. **2.** A bailee's inaccurate identification, in a document of title, of goods received from the bailor. **3.** An inaccurate legal description of land in a deed.

misdirection. See MISCHARGE.

mise (meez *or* mɪz), *n.* [Law French] *Hist.* **1.** Expenses incurred in litigation. **2.** The general issue in a writ of right. • When a tenant pleads superior title to the plaintiff, the tenant is said to join the *mise* on the mere right. **3.** A settlement; a compromise, as in the *Mise of Lewes* between Henry III and the rebelling barons.

***mise* money.** *Hist.* Money paid by contract to purchase a privilege.

miserabile depositum (miz-ə-**ray**-bə-lee di-**poz**-ə-təm). [Law Latin "a pitiful deposit"] *Civil law.* A deposit or bailment made in an emergency, as in a shipwreck, fire, or insurrection.

miserere (miz-ə-**reer**-ee). [Latin] *Hist.* Have mercy. • This is the first phrase of the 51st psalm, used to test a person claiming benefit of clergy. See NECK VERSE.

misericordia (miz-ə-ri-**kor**-dee-ə). [Law Latin] *Hist.* **1.** Mercy. **2.** An arbitrary fine as a punishment. **3.** An exemption from a fine.

misericordia communis (miz-ə-ri-**kor**-dee-ə kə-**myoo**-nis). [Law Latin] *Hist.* A fine levied on a whole county.

misfeasance (mis-**fee**-zənts), *n.* **1.** A lawful act performed in a wrongful manner. **2.** More broadly, a transgression or trespass; MALFEASANCE. — **misfeasant,** *adj.* — **misfeasor,** *n.* Cf. NONFEASANCE.

misfeasance in public office. The tort of excessive or malicious or negligent exercise of statutory powers by a public officer. — Also termed *malfeasance.*

mishering. See MISKERING.

misjoinder (mis-**joyn**-dər). **1.** The improper union of parties in a civil case. See JOINDER. Cf. DISJOINDER; NONJOINDER. **2.** The improper union of offenses in a criminal case.

miskenning (mis-**ken**-ing). [fr. French *misw* "wrong" + Saxon *cennan* "to declare"] **1.** A wrongful summons. **2.** A pleading mistake or irregularity.

> "But every defeated plaintiff could be amerced 'for a false claim.' Incidentally too any falsehood . . . that is, any fraudulent misuse of the machinery of the law, would be punished by imprisonment. Then again every default in appearance brought an amercement on the defaulter and his pledges. Every mistake in pleading, every *miskenning* . . . brought an amercement on the pleader if the mistake was to be retrieved. A litigant who hoped to get to the end of his suit without an amercement must have been a sanguine man; for he was playing a game of forfeits." 2 Frederick Pollock & Frederic W. Maitland, *The History of English Law Before the Time of Edward I* 519 (2d ed. 1899).

miskering (**mis**-kər-ing). *Hist.* Freedom or immunity from amercement. — Also termed *abishering; abishersing; mishering; mishersing.*

mislaid property. See PROPERTY.

mislay, *vb.* To deposit (property, etc.) in a place not afterwards recollected; to lose (property, etc.) by forgetting where it was placed. See *mislaid property* under PROPERTY.

misleading, *adj.* (Of an instruction, direction, etc.) delusive; calculated to be misunderstood.

misnomer (mis-**noh**-mər). A mistake in naming a person, place, or thing, esp. in a legal instrument. • In federal pleading — as well as in most states — misnomer of a party can be corrected by an amendment, which will relate back to the date of the original pleading. Fed. R. Civ. P. 15(c)(3).

misperformance. A faulty attempt to discharge an obligation (esp. a contractual one). Cf. PERFORMANCE; NONPERFORMANCE.

mispleading. Pleading incorrectly. • A party who realizes that its pleading is incorrect can usu. amend the pleading, as a matter of right, within a certain period, and can thereafter amend with the court's permission.

misprision (mis-**prizh**-ən). **1.** Concealment or nondisclosure of a serious crime by one who did not participate in the crime.

clerical misprision. A court clerk's mistake or fraud that is apparent from the record.

misprision of felony. Concealment or nondisclosure of someone else's felony.

> "In fact, whatever the law may be, it is not the general custom to prosecute for misprision of felony, even where a person who knows of a felony is questioned by the police and refuses to make a statement. Indeed, Stephen, writing in the nineteenth century, regarded the offence as 'practically obsolete'; and American courts have refused to recognise it as subsisting. But there have been four successful prosecutions in England during the last quarter-century . . . ." Glanville Williams, *Criminal Law* 424 (2d ed. 1961).

misprision of treason. Concealment or nondisclosure of someone else's treason.

negative misprision. The wrongful concealment of something that should be revealed <misprision of treason>.

positive misprision. The active commission of a wrongful act <seditious conduct against the government is positive misprision>.

2. Seditious conduct against the government. **3.** An official's failure to perform the duties of public office. **4.** Misunderstanding; mistake.

"The word 'misprision' has been employed with different meanings. While Blackstone thought of it as referring to a grave misdemeanor, it seems to have been used earlier to indicate the entire field of crime below the grade of treason or felony before the word 'misdemeanor' became the generally accepted label for this purpose. More recently it has been said: 'Misprision is nothing more than a word used to describe a misdemeanor which does not possess a specific name.' [*United States v. Perlstein*, 126 F.2d 789, 798 (3d Cir. 1942).] It has been associated with two specific offenses, and only these, from the earliest times. They are misprision of treason and misprision of felony, which consist of the criminal default of one in regard to the crime of another." Rollin M. Perkins & Ronald N. Boyce, *Criminal Law* 572 (3d ed. 1982).

misprisor (mis-**prI**-zər). One who commits misprision of felony.

misreading. An act of fraud in which a person incorrectly reads the contents of an instrument to an illiterate or blind person with the intent to deceitfully obtain that person's signature.

misrecital. An incorrect statement of a factual matter in a contract, deed, pleading, or other instrument.

misrepresentation, *n.* **1.** The act of making a false or misleading statement about something, usu. with the intent to deceive. **2.** The statement so made; an assertion that does not accord with the facts. — Also termed *false representation*; (redundantly) *false misrepresentation*. — **misrepresent,** *vb.* Cf. REPRESENTATION.

"A misrepresentation, being a false assertion of fact, commonly takes the form of spoken or written words. Whether a statement is false depends on the meaning of the words in all the circumstances, including what may fairly be inferred from them. An assertion may also be inferred from conduct other than words. Concealment or even non-disclosure may have the effect of a misrepresentation .... [A]n assertion need not be fraudulent to be a misrepresentation. Thus a statement intended to be truthful may be a misrepresentation because of ignorance or carelessness, as when the word 'not' is inadvertently omitted or when inaccurate language is used. But a misrepresentation that is not fraudulent has no consequences ... unless it is material." Restatement (Second) of Contracts § 159 cmt. a (1981).

fraudulent misrepresentation. A false statement that is known to be false or is made recklessly — without knowing or caring whether it is true or false — and that is intended to induce a party to detrimentally rely on it. — Also termed *fraudulent representation*; *deceit.*

"A misrepresentation is fraudulent if the maker intends his assertion to induce a party to manifest his assent and the maker (a) knows or believes that the assertion is not in accord with the facts, or (b) does not have the confidence that he states or implies in the truth of the assertion, or (c) knows that he does not have the basis that he states or implies for the assertion." Restatement (Second) of Contracts § 162(1) (1981).

innocent misrepresentation. A false statement not known to be false; a misrepresentation that, though false, was not made fraudulently.

material misrepresentation. **1.** *Contracts.* A false statement that is likely to induce a reasonable person to assent or that the maker knows is likely to induce the recipient to assent. **2.** *Torts.* A false statement to which a reasonable person would attach importance in deciding how to act in the transaction in question or to which the maker knows or has reason to know that the recipient attaches some importance. See Restatement (Second) of Torts § 538 (1979).

"The materiality of a misrepresentation is determined from the viewpoint of the maker, while the justification of reliance is determined from the viewpoint of the recipient.... The requirement of materiality may be met in either of two ways. First, a misrepresentation is material if it would be likely to induce a reasonable person to manifest his assent. Second, it is material if the maker knows that for some special reason it is likely to induce the particular recipient to manifest his assent. There may be personal considerations that the recipient regards as important even though they would not be expected to affect others in his situation, and if the maker is aware of this the misrepresentation may be material even though it would not be expected to induce a reasonable person to make the proposed contract. One who preys upon another's known idiosyncrasies cannot complain if the contract is held voidable when he succeeds in what he is endeavoring to accomplish.... Although a nonfraudulent misrepresentation that is not material does not make the contract voidable under the rules stated in this Chapter, the recipient may have a claim to relief under other rules, such as those relating to breach of warranty." Restatement (Second) of Contracts § 162 cmt. c (1979).

negligent misrepresentation. A careless or inadvertent false statement in circumstances where care should have been taken.

misrepresentee. A person to whom a fact has been misrepresented.

misrepresenter. A person who misrepresents a fact to another. — Also spelled *misrepresentor*.

missilia (mi-**sI**-lee-ə). [fr. Latin *mittere* "to throw"] *Roman law.* Money that the praetors, consuls, or wealthy individuals throw as gifts to people on the street.

missing-evidence rule. The doctrine that, when a party fails to present evidence at trial that the party controls and that would have been proper to present, the jury is entitled to infer that the evidence would have been unfavorable to that party.

missing person. **1.** Someone whose whereabouts are unknown and, after a reasonable time, seem to be unascertainable. **2.** Someone whose continuous and unexplained absence entitles the heirs to petition a court to declare the person dead and to divide up the person's property. See SEVEN-YEARS'-ABSENCE RULE. Cf. DISAPPEARED PERSON.

missing ship. *Maritime law.* A vessel that has been gone for an unreasonably long time, leading to the presumption that it is lost at sea; esp., a vessel that has been gone longer than the average time it takes a vessel to make a similar voyage in the same season.

missing-witness rule. The doctrine that, when a party fails to present a witness at trial who is available only to that party and whose testimony would have been admissible, the jury is entitled to infer that the witness's testimony would have been unfavorable to that party.

mistake, *n.* **1.** An error, misconception, or misunderstanding; an erroneous belief. **2.** *Contracts.* The situation in which the parties to a contract did not mean the same thing — or when one or both, while meaning the same thing, formed untrue conclusions about the subject matter of the contract — as a result of which the contract may be rendered void. Cf. FRUSTRATION.

> "The word *mistake* is generally used in the law of contracts to refer to an erroneous belief — 'a belief that is not in accord with the facts.' To avoid confusion, it should not be used, as it sometimes is in common speech, to refer to an improvident act, such as the making of a contract, that results from such an erroneous belief. Nor should it be used, as it sometimes is by courts and writers, to refer to what is more properly called a misunderstanding, a situation in which two parties attach different meanings to their language." E. Allan Farnsworth, *Contracts* § 9.2, at 649 (1982) (quoting Restatement (Second) of Contracts § 151 (1981)).

> "In this Restatement the word 'mistake' is used to refer to an erroneous belief. A party's erroneous belief is therefore said to be a 'mistake' of that party. The belief need not be an articulated one, and a party may have a belief as to a fact when he merely makes an assumption with respect to it, without being aware of alternatives. The word 'mistake' is not used here, as it is sometimes used in common speech, to refer to an improvident act, including the making of a contract, that is the result of such an erroneous belief. This usage is avoided here for the sake of clarity and consistency. Furthermore, the erroneous belief must relate to the facts as they exist at the time of the making of the contract. A party's prediction or judgment as to events to occur in the future, even if erroneous, is not a 'mistake' as that word is defined here. An erroneous belief as to the contents or effect of a writing that expresses the agreement is, however, a mistake. Mistake alone, in the sense in which the word is used here, has no legal consequences. The legal consequences of mistake in connection with the creation of contractual liability are determined by [substantive rules]." Restatement (Second) of Contracts § 151 cmt. a (1981).

bilateral mistake. See *mutual mistake* (1).

common mistake. See *mutual mistake* (2).

essential mistake. *Contracts.* A mistake serious enough that no real consent could have existed, so that there was no real agreement.

inessential mistake. See *unessential mistake.*

mistake of fact. A mistake about a fact that is material to a transaction. — Also termed *error in fact*; *error of fact.*

mistake of law. A mistake about the legal effect of a known fact or situation. — Also termed *error in law*; *error of law.*

mutual mistake. **1.** A mistake in which each party misunderstands the other's intent. — Also termed *bilateral mistake.* **2.** A mistake that is shared and relied on by both parties to a contract. • A court will often revise or nullify a contract based on a mutual mistake about a material term. — Also termed (in sense 2) *common mistake.*

> "The term 'common mistake' is more usually, but less grammatically, referred to as 'mutual mistake'. Cheshire and Fifoot on *Contract* have made a heroic effort to introduce and establish the more correct term, and it does seem to be gaining ground. However, the beginner is warned that the term 'mutual mistake' is nearly always used by the Courts to mean what we here call 'common mistake'." P.S. Atiyah, *An Introduction to the Law of Contract* 190 n.7 (3d ed. 1981).

nonessential mistake. See *unessential mistake.*

unessential mistake. *Contracts.* A mistake that does not relate to the nature of the contents of an agreement, but only to some external circumstance, so that the mistake has no effect on the validity of the agreement. — Also termed *inessential mistake*; *nonessential mistake*; *collateral mistake.*

unilateral mistake. A mistake by only one party to a contract. • A unilateral mistake is usu. not grounds to rescind the contract.

mistery (**mis**-tər-ee). *Hist.* A business; a trade. — Also spelled *mystery.*

mistrial. **1.** A trial that the judge brings to an end, without a determination on the merits, because of a procedural error or serious misconduct occurring during the proceedings. **2.** A trial that ends inconclusively because the jury cannot agree on a verdict.

misuse, *n.* **1.** *Products liability.* A defense alleging that the plaintiff used the product in an improper, unintended, or unforeseeable manner. **2.** *Patents.* The use of a patent either to improperly extend the granted monopoly to nonpatented goods or to violate antitrust laws.

misuser. An abuse of a right or office, as a result of which the person having the right might lose it <it is an act of misuser to accept a bribe>. Cf. USER.

mitigate (**mit**-ə-gayt), *vb.* To make less severe or intense <the fired employee mitigated her damages for wrongful termination by accepting a new job>. — **mitigation,** *n.* — **mitigatory** (**mit**-ə-gə-tor-ee), *adj.* Cf. MILITATE.

mitigating circumstance. See CIRCUMSTANCE.

mitigation-of-damages doctrine. The principle requiring a plaintiff, after an injury or breach of contract, to use ordinary care to alleviate the effects of the injury or breach. • If the defendant can show that the plaintiff failed to mitigate damages, the plaintiff's recovery may be reduced. — Also termed *avoidable-consequences doctrine.*

mitigation of punishment. *Criminal law.* A reduction in punishment due to mitigating circumstances that reduce the criminal's level of culpability, such as the existence of no prior convictions. See *mitigating circumstances* under CIRCUMSTANCE.

mitiori sensu. See IN MITIORI SENSU.

mitter avant (**mit**-ər ə-**vant**), *vb.* [Law French] *Hist.* To present or produce (evidence, etc.) to a court.

mittimus (**mit**-ə-məs). [Law Latin "we send"] *Hist.* **1.** A court order or warrant directing a jailer to detain a person until ordered otherwise; COMMITMENT (4). **2.** A certified transcript of a prisoner's conviction or sentencing proceedings. **3.** A writ directing the transfer of records from one court to another. Pl. **mittimuses.**

mixed action. See ACTION.

mixed blood. See BLOOD.

mixed cognation. See COGNATION.

mixed condition. See CONDITION (2).

mixed contract. See CONTRACT.

mixed cost. See COST (1).

mixed government. See GOVERNMENT.

mixed insurance company. See INSURANCE COMPANY.

mixed jury. See JURY.

mixed larceny. See LARCENY.

mixed law. A law concerning both persons and property.

mixed marriage. See MISCEGENATION.

mixed-motive doctrine. *Employment law.* The principle that, when the evidence in an employment-discrimination case shows that the complained-of employment action was based in part on a nondiscriminatory reason and in part on a discriminatory reason, the plaintiff must show that discrimination was a motivating factor for the employment action and, if the plaintiff makes that showing, then the defendant must show that it would have taken the same action without regard to the discriminatory reason.

mixed nuisance. See NUISANCE.

mixed policy. See INSURANCE POLICY.

mixed presumption. See PRESUMPTION.

mixed property. See PROPERTY.

mixed question. **1.** MIXED QUESTION OF LAW AND FACT. **2.** An issue involving conflicts of foreign and domestic law.

mixed question of law and fact. An issue that is neither a pure question of fact nor a pure question of law. • Mixed questions of law and fact are typically resolved by juries. — Also termed *mixed question of fact and law.* — Often shortened to *mixed question.*

"Many issues in a lawsuit involve elements of both law and fact. Whether these be referred to as mixed questions of law and fact, or legal inferences from the facts, or the application of law to the facts, there is substantial authority that they are not protected by the 'clearly erroneous' rule and are freely reviewable. This principle has been applied to antitrust violations, bankruptcy, contracts, copyright, taxation, and to other areas of the law." 9A Charles Alan Wright & Arthur R. Miller, *Federal Practice and Procedure* § 2589, at 608–11 (2d ed. 1995).

mixed tithes. See TITHE.

mixed trust. See TRUST.

mixed war. See WAR.

mixtion (**miks**-chən). *Archaic.* **1.** The process of mixing products together so that they can no longer be separated. **2.** The product of mixing.

mixtum imperium (**miks**-təm im-**peer**-ee-əm). [Latin] *Hist.* Mixed authority; mixed jurisdiction. • This term refers to the power of subordinate civil magistrates.

MLA. *abbr.* MOTION FOR LEAVE TO APPEAL.

MMI. *abbr.* MAXIMUM MEDICAL IMPROVEMENT.

***M'Naghten* rules.** See MCNAGHTEN RULES.

***M'Naughten* rules.** See MCNAGHTEN RULES.

M.O. *abbr.* MODUS OPERANDI.

mobile goods. See GOODS.

***Mobile–Sierra* doctrine.** The principle that the Federal Energy Regulatory Commission may not grant a rate increase to a natural-gas producer unless the producer's contract authorizes a rate increase, or unless the existing rate is so low that it may adversely affect the public interest (as by threatening the continued viability of the public utility to continue its service). *United Gas Pipe Line Co. v. Mobile Gas Serv. Corp.*, 350 U.S. 332, 76 S.Ct. 373 (1956); *Federal Power Comm'n v. Sierra Pac. Power Co.*, 350 U.S. 348, 76 S.Ct. 368 (1956). — Also termed *Sierra–Mobile doctrine*.

mobilia (moh-**bil**-ee-ə), *n.* [Latin "movables"] *Roman law.* Movable things. • The term primarily refers to inanimate objects but sometimes also refers to animals.

mobilia sequuntur personam (moh-**bil**-ee-ə si-**kwən**-tər pər-**soh**-nəm). [Latin] *Int'l law.* Movables follow the person — i.e., the law of the person. • This is the general principle that rights of ownership and transfer of movable property are determined by the law of the owner's domicile.

"The maxim *mobilia sequuntur personam* is the exception rather than the rule, and is probably to be confined to certain special classes of general assignments such as marriage settlements and devolutions on death and bankruptcy." *Handel v. Slatford*, 1953 Q.B. 248, 257 (Eng. C.A.).

"Under the influence of Savigny many Continental systems in the mid-nineteenth century led the way for Anglo-American law in limiting the operation of the doctrine of *mobilia sequuntur personam* to universal assignments of movables, adopting for particular assignments the single principle of the *lex situs* of the movable." R.H. Graveson, *Conflict of Laws* 457 (7th ed. 1974).

mock trial. **1.** A fictitious trial organized to allow law students, or sometimes lawyers, to practice the techniques of trial advocacy. **2.** A fictitious trial, arranged by a litigant's attorney, to assess trial strategy, to estimate the case's value or risk, and to evaluate the case's strengths and weaknesses. • In this procedure, people from the relevant jury pool are hired to sit as mock jurors who, after a condensed presentation of both sides, deliberate and reach a verdict (often while being observed by the participants behind a one-way glass). The jurors may later be asked specific questions about various arguments, techniques, and other issues. Because the mock jurors usu. do not know which side has hired them, their candid views are thought to be helpful in formulating trial strategies. Cf. MOOT COURT.

modal legacy. See LEGACY.

mode. A manner of doing something <mode of proceeding> <mode of process>.

model act. A statute drafted by the National Conference of Commissioners on Uniform State Laws and proposed as guideline legislation for the states to borrow from or adapt to suit their individual needs. • Examples of model acts include the Model Employment Termination Act and the Model Punitive Damages Act. Cf. UNIFORM ACT.

Model Code of Professional Responsibility. A set of ethical guidelines for lawyers, organized in the form of canons, disciplinary rules, and ethical considerations. • Published by the ABA in 1969, this code has been replaced in most states by the Model Rules of Professional Conduct.

model jury charge. See *model jury instruction* under JURY INSTRUCTION.

model jury instruction. See JURY INSTRUCTION.

Model Penal Code. A proposed criminal code drafted by the American Law Institute and used as the basis for criminal-law revision by many states. — Abbr. MPC.

Model Penal Code test. See SUBSTANTIAL-CAPACITY TEST.

Model Rules of Professional Conduct. A set of ethical guidelines for lawyers, organized in the form of 52 rules — some mandatory, some discretionary — together with explanatory comments. • Published by the ABA in 1983, these rules have generally replaced the Model Code of Professional Responsibility and have been adopted as law by many states.

moderamen inculpatae tutelae (moh-də-**ray**-mən in-kəl-**pay**-tee t[y]oo-**tee**-lee). [Latin] *Roman law.* The remedy or plea of justifiable defense. • This phrase refers to the degree of force justified in self-defense. — Also termed *inculpatae tutelae moderatio* (mod-ə-**ray**-shee-oh).

moderate castigavit (mod-ə-**ray**-tee kas-tə-**gay**-vit). [Latin "he moderately chastised"] *Hist.* A plea justifying a trespass because it is really a chastisement that the defendant is legally entitled to inflict on the plaintiff because of their relationship.

moderate force. See *nondeadly force* under FORCE.

moderator. A presider at a meeting or assembly.

modiatio (moh-dee-**ay**-shee-oh), *n.* [Latin] *Hist.* A duty paid for every tierce of wine. See PRISAGE.

modification. 1. A change to something; an alteration <a contract modification>. **2.** A qualification or limitation of something <a modification of drinking habits>.

Modified Accelerated Cost Recovery System. See ACCELERATED COST RECOVERY SYSTEM.

modified-comparative-negligence doctrine. See 50-PERCENT RULE.

modius (**moh**-dee-əs), *n.* [Latin "a measure"] *Hist.* **1.** A bushel. **2.** An uncertain measure, as of land.

modo et forma (**moh**-doh et **for**-mə). [Latin] In manner and form. • In common-law pleading, this phrase began the conclusion of a traverse. Its object was to put the burden on the party whose pleading was being traversed not only to prove the allegations of fact but also to establish as correct the manner and form of the pleading. — Also termed *manner and form.*

modus (**moh**-dəs). [Latin "mode"] **1.** *Criminal procedure.* The part of a charging instrument describing the manner in which an offense was committed. **2.** *Roman & civil law.* Mode; manner; consideration, esp. the manner in which a gift, bequest, servitude, etc. is to be employed. **3.** *Eccles. law.* DE MODO DECIMANDI. See MODUS OPERANDI.

modus decimandi (**moh**-dəs des-ə-**man**-dɪ). See DE MODO DECIMANDI.

modus de non decimando (**moh**-dəs dee non des-ə-**man**-doh). See DE NON DECIMANDO.

modus habilis (**moh**-dəs **hab**-ə-lis). [Latin] A valid manner (in proving a debt, etc.).

modus operandi (**moh**-dəs op-ə-**ran**-dɪ *or* -dee). [Latin "a manner of operating"] A method of operating or a manner of procedure; esp., a pattern of criminal behavior so distinctive that investigators attribute it to the work of the same person <staging a fight at the train station was part of the pickpocket's modus operandi>. — Abbr. M.O. Pl. **modi operandi.**

modus tenendi (**moh**-dəs tə-**nen**-dɪ). [Latin] *Hist.* The manner of holding. • This phrase referred to the different types of tenures by which estates were held.

Modus Tenendi Parliamentum (**moh**-dəs tə-**nen**-dɪ pahr-lə-**men**-təm). [Law Latin "the manner of holding Parliament"] *Hist.* A 14th-century writing on the powers of Parliament, translated in the 17th century and edited by T.D. Hardy in 1846.

modus transferrendi (**moh**-dəs trans-fər-**en**-dɪ). [Law Latin] *Hist.* The manner of transferring.

modus vacandi (**moh**-dəs və-**kan**-dɪ). [Law Latin] *Hist.* The manner of vacating. • This term was often used in determining the circumstances under which a vassal surrendered an estate to a lord.

modus vivendi (**moh**-dəs vi-**ven**-dɪ *or* -dee). [Latin "means of living (together)"] *Int'l law.* A temporary, provisional arrangement concluded between subjects of international law and giving rise to binding obligations on the parties.

> "[Modus vivendi] is an instrument of toleration looking towards a settlement, by preparing for or laying down the basis of a method of living together with a problem or by bridging over some difficulty pending a permanent settlement. Normally it is used for provisional and interim arrangements which ultimately are to be replaced by a formal agreement of a more permanent and detailed character. There is no clear distinction of a *modus vivendi* from other treaties. The most distinguishing feature is its provisional character; nevertheless a *modus vivendi* may be exercised for an indefinite period of time if it is prolonged *sine die* or if a definitive solution to the problem cannot be reached by treaty. Some 'temporary' arrangements have actually turned out to be quite durable." Walter Rudolf, "Modus Vivendi," in 3 *Encyclopedia of Public International Law* 443 (1997).

moeble (**myoo**-bəl), *adj.* [Law French] *Hist.* Movable, as in the phrase *biens moebles* ("movable goods").

moiety (**moy**-ə-tee). **1.** A half of something (such as an estate). **2.** A portion less than half; a small segment. **3.** In customs law, a payment made to an informant who assists in the seizure of contraband.

moiety act. *Criminal law.* A law providing that half of an imposed fine will inure to the benefit of the informant.

mole. A person who uses a long affiliation with an organization to gain access to and betray confidential information.

molestation. 1. The persecution or harassment of someone, as in the molestation of a witness. **2.** The act of making unwanted and indecent advances to or on someone, esp. for sexual gratification. — **molest,** *vb.* — **molester,** *n.*

child molestation. Any indecent or sexual activity on, involving, or surrounding a child, usu. under the age of 14. See Fed. R. Evid. 414(d).

molliter manus imposuit (**mol**-ə-tər **man**-əs im-**poz**-[y]ə-wit). [Latin] *Hist.* He gently laid hands upon. • This phrase was used in actions of trespass and assault to justify a defendant's use of force as reasonable, as when it was necessary to keep the peace.

monarchy. A government in which a single person rules, with powers varying from absolute dictatorship to the merely ceremonial.

limited monarchy. A monarchical form of government in which the monarch's power is subject to constitutional or other restraints. — Also termed *constitutional monarchy.*

moneta (mə-**nee**-tə), *n.* [Latin] Money.

monetagium (mon-ə-**tay**-jee-əm), *n.* [Law Latin "mintage"] *Hist.* **1.** The right to coin money; mintage. **2.** A tribute paid by s tenant to persuade a lord not to change coinage.

monetarism (**mon**-i-tə-riz-əm). An economic theory claiming that the money supply is the basic influence on the economy. • The theory was originated by Milton Friedman in the late 1960s.

monetary, *adj.* **1.** Of or relating to money <monetary value> <monetary damages>. **2.** Financial <monetary services> <monetary investments>.

monetary bequest. See *pecuniary bequest* under BEQUEST.

money. 1. The medium of exchange authorized or adopted by a government as part of its currency <coins and currency are money>. UCC § 1–201(24). **2.** Assets that can be easily converted to cash <demand deposits are money>. **3.** Capital that is invested or traded as a commodity <the money market> **4.** (*pl.*) Funds; sums of money <investment moneys>. — Also spelled (in sense 4) *monies.* See MEDIUM OF EXCHANGE; LEGAL TENDER.

current money. Money that circulates throughout a country; currency.

fiat money. Paper currency not backed by gold or silver. — Also termed *flat money.*

hard money. **1.** Coined money, in contrast to paper currency. **2.** Cash.

lawful money. Money that is legal tender for the payment of debts.

paper money. Paper documents that circulate as currency; bills drawn by a government against its own credit.

real money. **1.** Money that has metallic or other intrinsic value, as distinguished from paper currency, checks, and drafts. **2.** Current cash, as opposed to money on account.

money bequest. See *pecuniary bequest* under BEQUEST.

money bill. See *revenue bill* under BILL (3).

money broker. See BROKER.

money changer. One whose primary business is exchanging currencies.

money claim. *Hist.* Under the English Judicature Act of 1875, money claimed as damages, as for breaches of contract and rent arrearages.

money count. See COUNT.

money demand. A claim for a fixed, liquidated sum, as opposed to a damage claim that must be assessed by a jury.

moneyed capital. See CAPITAL.

moneyed corporation. See CORPORATION.

money had and received. See *action for money had and received* under ACTION.

money judgment. See JUDGMENT.

money land. Money held in a trust providing for its conversion into land.

money-laundering. See LAUNDERING.

money made. A sheriff's return on a writ of execution signifying that the sum stated on the writ was collected.

money market. See MARKET.

money-market account. An interest-bearing account at a bank or other financial institution. • Such an account usu. pays interest competitive with money-market funds but allows a limited number of transactions per month. See *money market* under MARKET.

money-market fund. See MUTUAL FUND.

money order. A negotiable draft issued by an authorized entity (such as a bank, telegraph company, post office, etc.) to a purchaser, in lieu of a check to be used to pay a debt or otherwise transmit funds upon the credit of the issuer.

money paid. See *action for money paid* under ACTION.

money-purchase plan. See EMPLOYEE BENEFIT PLAN.

money scrivener. See SCRIVENER.

money supply. The total amount of money in circulation in the economy. See M1; M2; M3.

monger (**məng**-gər). *Archaic.* A seller of goods; a dealer <moneymonger>.

monier (moh-**nyair** *or* **mən**-ee-ər), *n.* [fr. Law Latin *monetarius* "a moneyer"] *Hist.* **1.** A minister of the mint. **2.** A banker; a dealer in money. — Also spelled *moneyer.*

monies. See MONEY (4).

moniment. *Archaic.* A memorial; a monument.

monition (mə-**nish**-ən), *n.* **1.** Generally, a warning or caution; ADMONITION. **2.** *Civil & maritime law.* A summons to appear in court as a defendant or to answer contempt charges. **3.** *Eccles. law.* A formal notice from a bishop demanding that an offense within the clergy be corrected. — **monish** (**mon**-ish), *vb.* — **monitory** (**mon**-ə-tor-ee), *adj.*

monitory letter. *Eccles. law.* Admonitory communications sent from an ecclesiastical judge to staff members in response to reported abuses or scandals.

monocracy (mə-**nok**-rə-see). A government by one person.

monocrat (**mon**-ə-krat). A monarch who governs alone.

monogamy (mə-**nog**-ə-mee), *n.* **1.** The custom prevalent in most modern cultures restricting a person to one spouse at a time. **2.** The fact of being married to only one spouse. — **monogamous,** *adj.* — **monogamist,** *n.* Cf. BIGAMY; POLYGAMY.

monomachy (mə-**nom**-ə-kee). *Hist.* See DUEL (2).

monomania (mon-ə-**may**-nee-ə). Insanity about some particular subject or class of subjects, usu. manifested by a single insane delusion. • A will made by someone suffering from this condition is usu. held valid unless the evidence shows that particular provisions in the will were influenced by the insane delusion. — **monomaniacal,** adj. — **monomaniac,** n.

monopolium (mon-ə-**poh**-lee-əm). [Latin fr. Greek *monopolion* "a selling alone"] *Hist.* The sole power of sale; a monopoly.

monopolization, *n.* The act or process of obtaining a monopoly. • In federal antitrust law, monopolization is an offense with two elements: (1) the possession of monopoly power — that is, the power to fix prices and exclude competitors — within the relevant market, and (2) the willful acquisition or maintenance of that power, as distinguished from growth or development as a consequence of a superior product, business acumen, or historical accident. *United States v. Grinnell Corp.*, 384 U.S. 563, 86 S.Ct. 1698 (1966). — **monopolize,** *vb.* — **monopolistic,** *adj.* — **monopolist,** *n.*

attempted monopolization. The effort to monopolize any part of interstate or foreign commerce, consisting in (1) a specific intent to control prices or destroy competition in the relevant market, (2) predatory or anticompetitive conduct, and (3) a "dangerous probability" of success in achieving monopoly in the relevant market.

monopoly, *n.* **1.** Control or advantage obtained by one supplier or producer over the commercial market within a given region. **2.** The market condition existing when only one economic entity produces a particular product or provides a particular service. • The term is now commonly applied also to situations that approach but do not strictly meet this definition.

> "[Ninety per cent] is enough to constitute a monopoly; it is doubtful whether sixty or sixty-four per cent is enough; and certainly thirty-three per cent is not." *United States v. Aluminum Co. of Am.*, 148 F.2d 416, 424 (2d Cir. 1945) (Hand, J.).

> "In the modern sense, a monopoly exists when all, or so nearly all, of an article of trade or commerce within a community or district, is brought within the hands of one person or set of persons, as practically to bring the handling or production of the commodity or thing within such single control to the exclusion of competition or free traffic therein. A monopoly is created when, as the result of efforts to that end, previously competing businesses are so concentrated in the hands of a single person or corporation, or a few persons or corporations acting together, that they have power, for all practical purposes, to control the prices of a commodity and thus to suppress competition. In brief, a monopoly is the practical suppression of effective business competition which thereby creates a power to control prices to the public harm." 54A Am. Jur. 2d *Monopolies, Restraints of Trade, and Unfair Trade Practices* § 781, at 107 (1996).

bilateral monopoly. A hypothetical market condition in which there is only one buyer and one seller, resulting in transactional delays because either party can hold out for a better deal without fearing that the other party will turn to a third party.

legal monopoly. The exclusive right granted by government to business to provide utility services that are, in turn, regulated by the government.

natural monopoly. A monopoly resulting from a circumstance over which the monopolist has no power, as when the market is so limited for a product that only one plant is needed to meet demand.

3. *Patents.* The exclusive right to make, use, and sell an invention.

monopoly leveraging. A theory of liability holding that a party violates the antitrust laws when it exploits its monopoly power in one market to gain a competitive advantage in another market.

monopoly power. The power to control prices or to exclude competition. • The size of the market share is a primary determinant of whether monopoly power exists.

monopsony (mə-**nop**-sə-nee), *n.* A market situation in which one buyer controls the market. — **monopsonistic,** *adj.*

Monroe Doctrine. The principle that the United States will allow no intervention or domination by any non-American nation in the Western Hemisphere. • This principle, which has some recognition in international law (though not as a formal doctrine), was first announced by President James Monroe in 1823.

> "The Monroe doctrine is a policy which the United States has followed in her own interest more or less consistently for more than a century, and in itself is not contrary to international law, though possible applications of it might easily be so. But it certainly is not a *rule* of international law. It is comparable to policies such as the 'balance of power' in Europe, or the British policies of maintaining the independence of Belgium or the security of our sea-routes to the East, or the former Japanese claim to something like a paramount influence over developments in the Far East. Apart from other objections, it is impossible to regard as a rule of law a doctrine which the United States claims the sole right to interpret, which she interprets in different senses at different times, and which she applies only as and when she chooses. Nor is the doctrine, as Article 21 of the Covenant described it, a 'regional understanding', for the

other states of the region concerned, that is to say, the Continent of America, have never been parties to it and indeed have often resented it." J.L. Brierly, *The Law of Nations* 314 (5th ed. 1955).

monstrans de droit (**mon**-strənz də **droyt**). [Law French] *Hist.* A manifestation of right as a method of obtaining restitution from the Crown. • It was replaced by the writ of right. Currently, restitution is obtained by an ordinary action against the government.

monstrans de faits (**mon**-strənz də **fay**[**ts**]). [Law French] *Hist.* A showing of deeds; a profert.

monstraverunt (mon-strə-**veer**-ənt). [Latin "they have showed"] *Hist.* A writ of relief for tenants of ancient demesne who were distrained by their lord to do more than the tenure required.

"The little writ serves the turn of a man who claims land according to the custom of the manor; but the tenants of whom we are speaking are protected, and protected collectively, against any increase of their services. This is very plain when the manor is in the hands of a mesne lord. If he attempts to increase the customary services, some of the tenants, acting on behalf of all, will go to the royal chancery and obtain a writ against him. Such a writ begins with the word *Monstraverunt*. The king addresses the lord: — 'A,B and C, men of your manor of X, which is of the ancient demesne of the crown of England, have shown us that you exact from them other customs and services than those which they owe, and which their ancestors did in the time when that manor was in the hands of our predecessors, kings of England; therefore we command you to cease from such exactions, otherwise we shall order our sheriff to interfere.' " 1 Frederick Pollock & Frederic W. Maitland, *The History of English Law Before the Time of Edward I* 388 (2d ed. 1898).

montes pietatis (**mon**-teez pI-ə-**tay**-tis). [Latin "mountains of piety"] *Hist.* Institutions established to lend money upon pledges of goods.

month. 1. One of the twelve periods of time in which the calendar is divided <the month of March>. — Also termed *calendar month*; *civil month*. **2.** Any time period approximating 30 days <due one month from today>. **3.** At common law, a period of 28 days; the period of one revolution of the moon <a lunar month>. — Also termed *lunar month*. **4.** One-twelfth of a tropical year; the time it takes the sun to pass through one sign of the zodiac, usu. approximating 30 days <a solar month> — Also termed *solar month*.

month-to-month lease. See LEASE.

month-to-month tenancy. See *periodic tenancy* under TENANCY.

Montreal Agreement. A private agreement, signed by most international airlines, waiving both the Warsaw Convention's limitation on liability for death and personal-injury cases (currently about $20,000) and the airline's due-care defenses, raising the liability limit per passenger to $75,000, and providing for absolute liability on the part of the carrier (in the absence of passenger negligence) for all flights originating, stopping, or terminating in the United States. • The Montreal Agreement was the result of negotiations in 1965 and 1966 following the United States' denunciation of the Warsaw Convention, based primarily on its low liability limits. — Also termed *Agreement Relating to Liability Limitation of the Warsaw Convention and the Hague Protocol*.

monument, *n.* **1.** A written document or record, esp. a legal one. **2.** Any natural or artificial object that is fixed permanently in land and referred to in a legal description of the land. — **monumental,** *adj.*

natural monument. A nonartificial permanent thing on land, such as a tree, river, or beach. — Also termed *natural object*.

Moody's Investor's Service. An investment analysis and advisory service. — Often shortened to *Moody's*.

moonlighting. The fact or practice of working at a second job after the hours of a regular job. — Also termed *dual employment*; *multiple job-holding*.

moonshine. *Slang.* A distilled alcoholic beverage, esp. whiskey, that is illegally manufactured.

moorage. 1. An act of mooring a vessel at a wharf. **2.** A mooring charge.

moot, *adj.* **1.** *Archaic.* Open to argument; debatable. **2.** Having no practical significance; hypothetical or academic <the question on appeal became moot once the parties settled their case>. — **mootness,** *n.*

moot, *vb.* **1.** *Archaic.* To raise or bring forward (a point or question) for discussion. **2.** To render (a question) moot or of no practical significance.

moot court. **1.** A fictitious court held usu. in law schools to argue moot or hypothetical cases, esp. at the appellate level. **2.** A practice session for an appellate argument in which a lawyer presents the argument to other lawyers, who first act as judges by asking questions and who later provide criticism on the argument. — Also termed *practice court*. Cf. MOCK TRIAL.

moot man. *Hist.* A person who argued cases in the Inns of Court.

mootness doctrine. The principle that American courts will not decide moot cases — that is, cases in which there is no longer any actual controversy. Cf. RIPENESS.

mop. See STATUTE FAIR.

mora (**mor**-ə), *n.* [Latin] *Roman law.* Willful delay or default in fulfilling a legal obligation.

> "*Mora.* This was wrongful failure to discharge a legal obligation on demand made at a fitting time and place. It must be wilful: failure to appear, by mistake, or in a *bona fide* belief that there was no *obligatio*, or doubt about it, or by mishap, did not suffice to put a debtor *in mora*." W.W. Buckland, *A Manual of Roman Private Law* 338 (2d ed. 1953).

mora (**mor**-ə), *n.* [Law Latin] *Hist.* A moor; unprofitable ground.

moral absolutism. The view that a person's action can always properly be seen as right or wrong, regardless of the situation or the consequences. — Also termed *ethical absolutism*; *objective ethics*. Cf. MORAL RELATIVISM.

moral certainty. Absolute certainty. • Moral certainty is not required to sustain a criminal conviction. See REASONABLE DOUBT.

moral consideration. See *good consideration* under CONSIDERATION.

moral depravity. See MORAL TURPITUDE.

moral duress. See DURESS (2).

moral duty. See DUTY (1).

moral evidence. See EVIDENCE.

moral fraud. See *actual fraud* under FRAUD.

moral hazard. See HAZARD (2).

morality. **1.** Conformity with recognized rules of correct conduct. **2.** The character of being virtuous, esp. in sexual matters.

> "[T]he terms 'morality' and 'immorality' . . . are understood to have a sexual connotation. In fact, the terms 'ethics' and 'morals' are no longer interchangeable in everyday speech. A governmental official arraigned on a 'morals charge' will be accused of something quite different from one accused of an 'ethics violation.' " William P. Golding, *Philosophy of Law* 55 (1975).

3. A system of duties; ethics.

private morality. A person's ideals, character, and private conduct, which are not valid governmental concerns if the individual is to be considered sovereign over body and mind and if the need to protect the individual's physical or moral well-being is insufficient to justify governmental intrusion. • In his essay *On Liberty* (1859), John Stuart Mill distinguished between conduct or ideals that affect only the individual from conduct that may do harm to others. Mill argued that governmental intrusion is justified only to prevent harm to others, not to influence a person's private morality.

public morality. **1.** The ideals or general moral beliefs of a society. **2.** The ideals or actions of an individual to the extent that they affect others.

moral law. A collection of principles defining right and wrong conduct; a standard to which an action must conform to be right or virtuous.

> "It quite often happens that the moral law disapproves of something which the secular permits as a concession to human frailty." Patrick Devlin, *The Enforcement of Morals* 78 (1968).

moral necessity. See NECESSITY.

moral obligation. A duty that is based only on one's conscience and that is not legally enforceable. • In contract law, moral obligation may support a promise in the absence of traditional consideration, but only if the promisor has previously received some actual benefit from the promisee.

moral person. See *artificial person* under PERSON.

moral relativism. The view that there are no absolute or constant standards of right and wrong. — Also termed *ethical relativism*; *subjective ethics*. Cf. MORAL ABSOLUTISM.

moral right. (*usu. pl.*) *Copyright.* A right protecting a visual artist's work beyond the ordinary protections of copyright. • Moral rights include both *integrity rights*, which protect the work from changes that damage the artist's or the work's reputation, and *attribution rights*, which allow the artist to claim authorship of the work and to prevent the unlawful use of the author's name in reference to a modified version of the work. Visual Artists Rights Act of 1990 (17 USCA §§ 106A, 113).

moral suasion. The act or effort of persuading by appeal to principles of morality.

moral turpitude. 1. Conduct that is contrary to justice, honesty, or morality. • In the area of legal ethics, offenses involving moral turpitude — such as fraud or breach of trust — traditionally make a person unfit to practice law. — Also termed *moral depravity*. **2.** *Military law*. Any conduct for which the applicable punishment is a dishonorable discharge or confinement not less than one year.

> "Moral turpitude means, in general, shameful wickedness — so extreme a departure from ordinary standards of honest, good morals, justice, or ethics as to be shocking to the moral sense of the community. It has also been defined as an act of baseness, vileness, or depravity in the private and social duties which one person owes to another, or to society in general, contrary to the accepted and customary rule of right and duty between people." 50 Am. Jur. 2d *Libel and Slander* § 165, at 454 (1995).

moral wrong. See WRONG.

moratorium (mor-ə-**tor**-ee-əm). **1.** An authorized postponement, usu. a lengthy one, in the deadline for paying a debt or performing an obligation. **2.** The period of this delay. **3.** The suspension of a specific activity. Pl. **moratoriums, moratoria.**

moratory (**mor**-ə-tor-ee), *adj*. Of or relating to a delay; esp., of or relating to a moratorium.

moratory damages. See DAMAGES.

morganatic marriage. See MARRIAGE (1).

morgangiva (mor-**gan**-jə-və), *n*. [Law Latin "moving gift"] *Hist*. A gift made to the bride on the morning after the wedding; a type of dowry. — Also spelled *morgangina*.

Morgan presumption. A presumption that shifts the burden of proof by requiring the person against whom it operates to produce sufficient evidence to outweigh the evidence that supports the presumed fact, as in requiring a criminal defendant who was arrested while in possession of an illegal substance — and is thereby presumed to have knowingly possessed it — to produce sufficient evidence to entitle the jury to find that the defendant's evidence outweighs the evidence of knowing possession. See Edmund M. Morgan, *Instructing the Jury Upon Presumptions and Burdens of Proof*, 47 Harv. L. Rev. 59, 82–83 (1933). Cf. THAYER PRESUMPTION.

mors (morz), *n*. [Latin] Death.

morsellum terrae (mor-**sel**-əm **ter**-ee). [Law Latin "a morsel of earth"] *Hist*. A small parcel of land.

mors naturalis (**morz** nach-ə-**ray**-lis). See *natural death* under DEATH.

mortality factor. *Insurance*. In life-insurance ratemaking, an estimate of the average number of deaths that will occur each year at each specific age, calculated by using an actuarial table. • The mortality factor is one element that a life insurer uses to calculate premium rates. See ACTUARIAL TABLE; PREMIUM RATE. Cf. INTEREST FACTOR; RISK FACTOR.

mortality table. See ACTUARIAL TABLE.

mort civile (mor[t] see-**veel**). [Law French] See CIVIL DEATH (1).

mort d'ancestor (mor[t] **dan**-ses-tər). [Law French "death of an ancestor"] *Hist*. An assize founded on the death of an ancestor.

> "Another of the petty assizes was that of mort d'ancestor, founded on the Assize of Northhampton 1176. The question in this assize was whether the plaintiff's father (or other close ancestor) had been seised in fee — that is, of an inheritable estate — on the day he died, and whether the plaintiff was his next heir; if both questions were answered in the affirmative, the plaintiff was entitled to be put in seisin." J.H. Baker, *An Introduction to English Legal History* 267–68 (3d ed. 1990).

mortgage (**mor**-gij), *n*. **1.** A conveyance of title to property that is given as security for the payment of a debt or the performance of a duty and that will become void upon payment or performance according to the stipulated terms. **2.** A lien against property that is granted to secure an obligation (such as a debt) and that is extinguished upon payment or performance according to stipulated terms. **3.** An instrument (such as a deed or contract) specifying the terms of such a transaction. **4.** Loosely, the loan on which such a transaction is based. **5.** The mortgagee's rights conferred by such a transaction. **6.** Loosely, any real-property security transaction, including a deed of trust. — Abbr. M. — **mortgage,** *vb.*

> "The chief distinction between a mortgage and a pledge is that by a mortgage the general title is transferred to the mortgagee, subject to be revested by performance of the condition; while by a pledge the pledgor retains the general title in himself, and parts with the possession for a special purpose. By a mortgage the title is transferred; by a pledge, the possession." Leonard A. Jones, *A Treatise on the Law of Mortgages* § 4, at 5–6 (5th ed. 1908).

adjustable-rate mortgage. A mortgage in which the lender can periodically adjust the mortgage's interest rate in accordance with fluctuations in some external market index. — Abbr. ARM. — Also termed *variable-rate mortgage*; *flexible-rate mortgage*.

all-inclusive mortgage. See *wraparound mortgage*.

amortized mortgage. A mortgage in which the mortgagor pays the interest as well as a portion of the principal in the periodic payment. • At maturity, the periodic payments will have completely repaid the loan. — Also termed *self-liquidating mortgage*. See AMORTIZATION. Cf. *straight mortgage*.

balloon-payment mortgage. A mortgage requiring periodic payments for a specified time and a lump-sum payment of the outstanding balance at maturity.

blanket mortgage. A mortgage covering two or more properties that are pledged to support a debt.

bulk mortgage. **1.** A mortgage of personal property in bulk; a pledge of an aggregate of goods in one location. **2.** A mortgage of more than one real-estate parcel.

chattel mortgage (**chat**-əl). A mortgage on goods purchased on installment, whereby the seller transfers title to the buyer but retains a lien securing the unpaid balance. • Chattel mortgages have generally been replaced by security agreements, which are governed by Article 9 of the UCC. Cf. *retail installment contract* under CONTRACT.

closed-end mortgage. A mortgage that does not permit either prepayment or additional borrowing against the collateral. Cf. *open-end mortgage*.

closed mortgage. A mortgage that cannot be paid in full before maturity without the lender's consent.

collateral mortgage. *Civil law.* A mortgage securing a promissory note pledged as collateral security for a principal obligation.

consolidated mortgage. A mortgage created by combining two or more mortgages.

construction mortgage. A mortgage used to finance a construction project.

contingent-interest mortgage. A mortgage whose interest rate is directly related to the economic performance of the pledged property.

conventional mortgage. A mortgage, not backed by government insurance, by which the borrower transfers a lien or title to the lending bank or other financial institution. • These mortgages, which feature a fixed periodic payment of principal and interest throughout the mortgage term, are typically used for home financing. — Also termed *conventional loan*.

direct-reduction mortgage. An amortized mortgage in which the principal and interest payments are paid at the same time — usu. monthly in equal amounts — with interest being computed on the remaining balance. — Abbr. DRM.

dry mortgage. A mortgage that creates a lien on property but does not impose on the mortgagor any personal liability for any amount that exceeds the value of the premises.

equitable mortgage. A transaction that has the intent but not the form of a mortgage, and that a court of equity will treat as a mortgage. Cf. *technical mortgage*.

> "Courts of equity are not governed by the same principles as courts of law in determining whether a mortgage has been created, and generally, whenever a transaction resolves itself into a security, or an offer or attempt to pledge land as security for a debtor liability, equity will treat it as a mortgage, without regard to the form it may assume, or the name the parties may choose to give it. The threshold issue in an action seeking imposition of an equitable mortgage is whether the plaintiff has an adequate remedy at law. In applying the doctrine of equitable mortgages doubts are resolved in favor of the transaction being a mortgage." 59 C.J.S. *Mortgages* § 12, at 62 (1998).

extended first mortgage. See *wraparound mortgage*.

FHA mortgage. A mortgage that is insured fully or partially by the Federal Housing Administration.

first mortgage. A mortgage that is senior to all other mortgages on the same property.

fixed-rate mortgage. A mortgage with an interest rate that remains the same over the life of the mortgage regardless of market conditions. — Abbr. FRM.

flexible-rate mortgage. **1.** See *adjustable-rate mortgage.* **2.** See *renegotiable-rate mortgage.*

flip mortgage. A graduated-payment mortgage allowing the borrower to place all or some of the down payment in a savings account and to use the principal and interest to supplement lower mortgage payments in the loan's early years.

future-advances mortgage. A mortgage in which part of the loan proceeds will not be paid until a future date.

general mortgage. *Civil law.* A blanket mortgage against all the mortgagor's present and future property. La. Civ. Code art. 3285.

graduated-payment adjustable-rate mortgage. A mortgage combining features of the graduated-payment mortgage and the adjustable-rate mortgage. — Abbr. GPARM.

graduated-payment mortgage. A mortgage whose initial payments are lower than its later payments. • The payments are intended to gradually increase, as the borrower's income increases over time.

growing-equity mortgage. A mortgage that is fully amortized over a significantly shorter term than the traditional 25– to 30–year mortgage, with increasing payments each year. — Abbr. GEM.

interest-only mortgage. A balloon-payment mortgage on which the borrower must at first make only interest payments, but must make a lump-sum payment of the full principal at maturity. — Also termed *standing mortgage*; *straight-term mortgage.*

joint mortgage. A mortgage given to two or more mortgagees jointly.

judicial mortgage. *Civil law.* A judgment lien created by a recorded legal judgment.

jumbo mortgage. A mortgage loan in a principal amount that exceeds the dollar limits for a government guarantee.

junior mortgage. A mortgage that is subordinate to another mortgage on the same property. — Also termed *puisne mortgage.*

leasehold mortgage. A mortgage secured by a lessee's leasehold interest.

legal mortgage. *Civil law.* A creditor's mortgage arising by operation of law on the debtor's property. — Also termed *tacit mortgage.*

open-end mortgage. A mortgage that allows the mortgagor to borrow additional funds against the same property. Cf. *closed-end mortgage.*

package mortgage. A mortgage that includes both real and incidental personal property, such as a refrigerator or stove.

participation mortgage. **1.** A mortgage that permits the lender to receive profits of the venture in addition to the normal interest payments. **2.** A mortgage held by more than one lender.

price-level-adjusted mortgage. A mortgage with a fixed interest rate but the principal balance of which is adjusted to reflect inflation. — Abbr. PLAM.

puisne mortgage. See *junior mortgage.*

purchase-money mortgage. A mortgage that a buyer gives the seller, when the property is conveyed, to secure the unpaid balance of the purchase price. — Abbr. PMM. See SECURITY AGREEMENT.

renegotiable-rate mortgage. A government-sponsored mortgage that requires the mortgagee to renegotiate its terms every three to five years, based on market conditions. — Also termed *flexible-rate mortgage*; *rollover mortgage.*

reverse annuity mortgage. A mortgage in which the lender disburses money over a long period to provide regular income to the (usu. elderly) borrower, and in which the loan is repaid in a lump sum when the borrower dies or when the property is sold. — Abbr. RAM. — Also termed *reverse mortgage.*

rollover mortgage. See *renegotiable-rate mortgage.*

second mortgage. A mortgage that is junior to a first mortgage on the same property, but that is senior to any later mortgage.

> "A landowner who already holds land subject to a mortgage may wish to hypothecate his equity. He does this by taking out a '*second mortgage.*' Should the mortgagor default in his obligation on the first mortgage, the first mortgagee may foreclose. If there is a deficiency upon sale, the second mortgagee loses his security in the equity because there is no equity. If the mortgagee does not default on the first mortgage, but does on the second, the second mortgagee can foreclose on the mortgagor's equity. Such a foreclosure would not affect the first mortgagee's rights." Edward H. Rabin, *Fundamentals of Modern Real Property Law* 1087 (1974).

self-liquidating mortgage. See *amortized mortgage.*

senior mortgage. A mortgage that has priority over another mortgage (a junior mortgage) on the same property.

shared-appreciation mortgage. A mortgage giving the lender the right to recover (as contingent interest) an agreed percentage of the property's appreciation in value when it is sold or at some other specified, future date. — Abbr. SAM.

shared-equity mortgage. A mortgage in which the lender shares in the profits from the property's resale. • The lender must usu. first purchase a portion of the property's equity by providing a portion of the down payment.

special mortgage. *Civil law.* A mortgage burdening only particular, specified property of the mortgagor. La. Civ. Code art. 3285.

standing mortgage. See *interest-only mortgage.*

straight mortgage. A mortgage in which the mortgagor is obligated to pay interest during the mortgage term along with a final payment of principal at the end of the term. Cf. *amortized mortgage.*

straight-term mortgage. See *interest-only mortgage.*

submortgage. See SUBMORTGAGE.

tacit mortgage. See *legal mortgage.*

technical mortgage. A traditional, formal mortgage, as distinguished from an instrument having the character of an equitable mortgage. Cf. *equitable mortgage.*

VA mortgage. A veteran's mortgage that is guaranteed by the Veterans Administration.

variable-rate mortgage. See *adjustable-rate mortgage.*

Welsh mortgage. A type of mortgage, formerly common in Wales and Ireland, by which the mortgagor, without promising to pay the debt, transfers title and possession of the property to the mortgagee, who takes the rents and profits and applies them to the interest, often with a stipulation that any surplus will reduce the principal. • The mortgagee cannot compel the mortgagor to redeem, and cannot foreclose the right to redeem, because no time is fixed for payment. The mortgagor is never in default, but may redeem at any time.

wraparound mortgage. A second mortgage issued when a lender assumes the payments on the borrower's low-interest first mortgage (usu. issued through a different lender) and lends additional funds. • Such a mortgage covers both the outstanding balance of the first mortgage and the additional funds loaned. 12 CFR § 226.17 cmt. 6. — Also termed *extended first mortgage*; *all-inclusive mortgage.*

zero-rate mortgage. A mortgage with a large down payment but no interest payments, with the balance paid in equal installments.

mortgage-backed security. See SECURITY.

mortgage banker. An individual or organization that originates real-estate loans for a fee, resells them to other parties, and services the monthly payments.

mortgage bond. See BOND (3).

mortgage broker. See BROKER.

mortgage certificate. A document evidencing part ownership of a mortgage.

mortgage clause. An insurance-policy provision that protects the rights of a mortgagee when the insured property is subject to a mortgage. • Such a clause usu. provides that any insurance proceeds must be allocated between the named insured and the mortgagee "as their interests may appear." — Also termed *mortgagee clause.* See LOSS-PAYABLE CLAUSE; ATIMA.

open mortgage clause. A mortgage clause that does not protect the mortgagee if the insured mortgagor does something to invalidate the policy (such as committing fraud). • This type of clause has been largely superseded by the mortgage-loss clause, which affords the mortgagee more protection. — Also termed *simple mortgage clause.* Cf. MORTGAGE-LOSS CLAUSE.

standard mortgage clause. A mortgage clause that protects the mortgagee's interest even if the insured mortgagor does something to invalidate the policy. • In effect, this clause creates a separate contract between the insurer and the mortgagee. — Also termed *union mortgage clause.*

mortgage commitment. A lender's written agreement with a borrower stating the terms on which it will lend money for the purchase of specified real property, usu. with a time limitation.

mortgage company. A company that makes mortgage loans and then sells or assigns them to investors.

mortgage-contingency clause. A real-estate-sale provision that conditions the buyer's performance on obtaining a mortgage loan.

mortgage deed. See DEED.

mortgage discount. The difference between the mortgage principal and the amount the mortgage actually sells for; the up-front charge by a lender at a real-estate closing for the costs of financing. • Although usu. paid by the buyer, the discount is sometimes paid by the seller when required by law, as with a VA mortgage. — Also termed *point*; *mortgage point*; *loan-brokerage fee*; *new-loan fee*.

mortgagee (mor-gə-**jee**). One to whom property is mortgaged; the mortgage-creditor, or lender. — Also termed *mortgage-holder*.

mortgagee in possession. A mortgagee who takes control of mortgaged land by agreement with the mortgagor, usu. upon default of the loan secured by the mortgage.

mortgagee clause. See MORTGAGE CLAUSE.

mortgagee policy. A title-insurance policy that covers only the mortgagee's title and not the owner's title. Cf. OWNER'S POLICY.

mortgage foreclosure. See FORECLOSURE.

mortgage-guarantee insurance. Insurance provided by the Mortgage Guarantee Insurance Company to mortgage lenders that grant mortgages to parties having less than a 20% down payment. • The cost of the insurance is included in the closing costs.

mortgage-holder. See MORTGAGEE.

mortgage insurance. See INSURANCE.

mortgage lien. See LIEN.

mortgage loan. See LOAN.

mortgage-loss clause. A mortgage clause providing that title insurance will not be invalidated by the mortgagor's acts. • Thus, even if the mortgagor does an act that would otherwise make the policy void, the act merely voids the policy as against the mortgagor, but it remains in full force for the benefit of the mortgagee. — Also termed *New York standard clause*; *union-loss clause*. Cf. *open mortgage clause* under MORTGAGE CLAUSE.

mortgage market. The conditions that provide the demand for new mortgage loans and the later resale of those loans in the secondary mortgage market.

primary mortgage market. The national market in which mortgages are originated.

secondary mortgage market. The national market in which existing mortgages are bought and sold, usu. on a package basis.

mortgage note. See NOTE (1).

mortgage point. See POINT (2); MORTGAGE DISCOUNT.

mortgage servicing. The administration of a mortgage loan, including the collection of payments, release of liens, and payment of property insurance and taxes. • Servicing is usu. performed by the lender or the lender's agent, for a fee.

mortgage warehousing. An arrangement in which a mortgage company holds loans for later resale at a discount.

mortgaging out. The purchase of real property by financing 100% of the purchase price.

mortgagor (mor-gə-**jor** *or* **mor**-gə-jər). One who mortgages property; the mortgage-debtor, or borrower. — Also spelled *mortgager*; *mortgageor*.

mortis causa (**mor**-tis **kaw**-zə). See *gift causa mortis* under GIFT.

mortmain (**mort**-mayn). [French "deadhand"] The condition of lands or tenements held inalienably by an ecclesiastical or other corporation. See AMORTIZE; DEADHAND CONTROL.

mortmain statute. A law that limits gifts or other dispositions of land to corporations (esp. charitable ones) and that prohibits corporations from holding land in perpetuity. • In England, laws such as the Provisions of Westminster and Magna Carta essentially required the Crown's authorization before land could vest in a corporation. The object was to prevent lands from being held by religious corporations in perpetuity. Although this type of restriction was not generally part of the common law in the United States, it influenced the enactment of certain state laws restricting the amount of property a corporation can hold for religious or charitable purposes. — Also termed *mortmain act*; *statute of mortmain*.

mortuary. 1. A place where cadavers are prepared for burial; a place where dead bodies are held before burial. **2.** A burial place. **3.** *Hist.* A customary gift left by a deceased to a parish church for past tithes owed.

mortuary table. See ACTUARIAL TABLE.

mortuum vadium (**mor**-choo-əm **vay**-dee-əm). See *vadium mortuum* under VADIUM.

mortuus (**mor**-choo-əs), *adj*. [Latin] *Hist.* **1.** Dead. **2.** A sheriff's return that the named party is dead.

mortuus civiliter (**mor**-choo-əs sə-**vil**-ə-tər). [Latin "civilly dead"] A person civilly dead, deprived of civil rights. See CIVIL DEATH.

mortuus sine prole (**mor**-choo-əs **sI**-nee **proh**-lee). [Latin] Dead without issue. — Abbr. *m.s.p.*

most favorable light. See LIGHT MOST FAVORABLE.

most favored nation. A treaty status granted to a nation, usu. in international trade, allowing it to enjoy the privileges accorded to the other nations that are parties to the treaty. • The primary effect of most-favored-nation status is lower trade tariffs. — Also termed *most-favored-nation status*. — Abbr. MFN.

most-favored-nation clause. **1.** A clause in an agreement between two nations providing that each will treat the other as well as it treats any other nation that is given preferential treatment. **2.** By extension, such a clause in any contract, but esp. an oil-and-gas contract. — Often shortened to *favored-nation clause*; *MFN clause*. — Also termed *most-favored-nations clause*. Cf. *preferential tariff* under TARIFF.

most-favored-nation status. See MOST FAVORED NATION.

most-favored-tenant clause. A commercial-lease provision ensuring that the tenant will be given the benefit of any negotiating concessions given to other tenants.

most-significant-relationship test. *Conflict of laws*. The doctrine that, to determine the state law to apply to a dispute, the court should determine which state has the most substantial connection to the occurrence and the parties. • For example, in a tort case, the court should consider where the injury occurred, where the conduct that caused the injury occurred, the residence, place of business, or place of incorporation of the parties, and the place where the relationship between the parties, if any, is centered. Restatement (Second) of Conflict of Laws § 145 (1971). In a case involving a contract, the court should consider where the contract was made, where the contract was negotiated, where the contract was to be performed, and the domicile, place of business, or place of incorporation of the parties. *Id.* § 188.

most suitable use. See *highest and best use* under USE (1).

most-suitable-use value. See *optimal-use value* under VALUE.

moteer (**moh**-teer). *Hist.* A customary payment or service made at the lord's court.

mother. A woman who has given birth to or legally adopted a child. • The term is sometimes interpreted as including a pregnant woman who has not yet given birth.

adoptive mother. See *adoptive parent* under PARENT.

foster mother. See *foster parent* under PARENT.

mother country. A colonizing nation; a colonial power. Cf. COLONY.

Mother Hubbard clause. **1.** A clause stating that a mortgage secures all the debts that the mortgagor may at any time owe to the mortgagee. — Also termed *anaconda clause*; *dragnet clause*. **2.** *Oil & gas*. A provision in an oil-and-gas lease or a mineral or royalty deed conveying small strips of land or irregularly shaped acreage outside the area described in the lease or deed. • Such a provision is usu. included to override any inaccuracies in the description of the land. — Also termed *cover-all clause*. **3.** A court's written declaration that any relief not expressly granted in a specific ruling or judgment is denied.

mother-in-law. The mother of a person's spouse.

motion. **1.** A written or oral application requesting a court to make a specified ruling or order. **2.** A proposal made under formal parliamentary procedure.

calendar motion. A motion relating to the time of court appearances. • Examples include motions to continue, motions to advance, and motions to reset.

contradictory motion. *Civil law.* A motion that is likely to be contested or that the nonmoving side should have an opportunity to contest.

dilatory motion (**dil**-ə-tor-ee). **1.** A motion made solely for the purpose of delay. **2.** A motion that has the effect of delaying the proceedings.

ex parte motion (eks **pahr**-tee). A motion made to the court without notice to the adverse party; a motion that a court considers and rules on after hearing from fewer than all sides.

omnibus motion. A motion that makes several requests or asks for multiple forms of relief.

posttrial motion. A motion made after judgment is entered, such as a motion for new trial.

speaking motion. A motion that addresses matters not raised in the pleadings.

special motion. A motion specifically requiring the court's discretion upon hearing, as distinguished from one granted as a matter of course.

motion for a more definite statement. See MOTION FOR MORE DEFINITE STATEMENT.

motion for a new trial. See MOTION FOR NEW TRIAL.

motion for a protective order. See MOTION FOR PROTECTIVE ORDER.

motion for a repleader. *Common-law pleading.* An unsuccessful party's posttrial motion asking that the pleadings begin anew because the issue was joined on an immaterial point. • The court never awards a repleader to the party who tendered the immaterial issue.

motion for directed verdict. A party's request that the court enter judgment in its favor before submitting the case to the jury because there is no legally sufficient evidentiary foundation on which a reasonable jury could find for the other party. • Under the Federal Rules of Civil Procedure, the equivalent court paper is known as a motion for judgment as a matter of law. — Also termed *motion for a directed verdict.* — Abbr. MDV. See MOTION FOR JUDGMENT AS A MATTER OF LAW; *directed verdict* under VERDICT.

motion for j.n.o.v. See MOTION FOR JUDGMENT NOTWITHSTANDING THE VERDICT.

motion for judgment as a matter of law. A party's request that the court enter a judgment in its favor before the case is submitted to the jury, or after a contrary jury verdict, because there is no legally sufficient evidentiary basis on which a jury could find for the other party. • Under the Federal Rules of Civil Procedure, a party may move for judgment as a matter of law anytime before the case has been submitted to the jury. This kind of motion was formerly known as a *motion for directed verdict* (and still is in many jurisdictions). If the motion is denied and the case is submitted to the jury, resulting in an unfavorable verdict, the motion may be renewed within ten days after entry of the judgment. This aspect of the motion replaces the court paper formerly known as a *motion for judgment notwithstanding the verdict.* Fed. R. Civ. P. 50.

motion for judgment notwithstanding the verdict. A party's request that the court enter a judgment in its favor despite the jury's contrary verdict because there is no legally sufficient evidentiary basis for a jury to find for the other party. • Under the Federal Rules of Civil Procedure, this procedure has been replaced by the provision for a motion for judgment as a matter of law, which must be presented before the case has been submitted to the jury but can be reasserted if it is denied and the jury returns an unfavorable verdict. Fed. R. Civ. P. 50. — Also termed *motion for j.n.o.v.* See MOTION FOR JUDGMENT AS A MATTER OF LAW.

motion for judgment of acquittal. A criminal defendant's request, at the close of the government's case or the close of all evidence, to be acquitted because there is no legally sufficient evidentiary basis on which a reasonable jury could return a guilty verdict. • If the motion is granted, the government has no right of appeal. — Abbr. MJOA.

motion for judgment on the pleadings. A party's request that the court rule in its favor based on the pleadings on file, without accepting evidence, as when the outcome of the case rests on the court's interpretation of the law. Fed. R. Civ. P. 12(c).

motion for leave to appeal. A request that an appellate court review an interlocutory order that meets the standards of the collateral-order doctrine. — Abbr. MLA. See COLLATERAL-ORDER DOCTRINE.

motion for more definite statement. A party's request that the court require an opponent to amend a vague or ambiguous pleading to which the party cannot reasonably be required to respond. Fed. R. Civ. P. 12(e). — Also termed *motion for a more definite statement.*

> "Another disfavored motion is the motion for a more definite statement. By a 1948 amendment to the rules, the old bill of particulars was abolished. The motion for more definite statement, which serves much the same function, is to be granted only where a pleading to which a responsive pleading is permitted is so vague or ambiguous that the party cannot reasonably be required to frame a responsive pleading. If the pleading is sufficiently definite that the opponent can reply to it, the motion for more definite statement should be denied and any particulars that the opponent needs to prepare for trial obtained by depositions, interrogatories, and similar discovery procedures. The motion is never proper where no responsive pleading is permitted, nor should it be used to force the plaintiff to include additional particulars that may make the complaint vulnerable to a motion to dismiss." Charles Alan Wright, *The Law of Federal Courts* § 66, at 461–62 (5th ed. 1994).

motion for new trial. A party's postjudgment request that the court vacate the judgment and order a new trial for such reasons as factually insufficient evidence, newly discovered evidence, or jury misconduct. • In many jurisdictions, this motion is required before a party can raise such matters on appeal. — Also termed *motion for a new trial.*

motion for protective order. A party's request that the court protect it from potentially abusive action by the other party, usu. relating to discovery, as when one party seeks discovery of the other party's trade secrets. • A court will sometimes craft a protective order to protect one party's trade secrets by ordering that any secret information exchanged in discovery be used only for purposes of the pending suit and not be publicized. — Also termed *motion for a protective order.*

motion for relief from stay. See MOTION TO LIFT THE STAY.

motion for relief from the judgment. A party's request that the court correct a clerical mistake in the judgment — that is, a mistake that results in the judgment's incorrectly reflecting the court's intentions — or to relieve the party from the judgment because of such matters as (1) inadvertence, surprise, or excusable neglect, (2) newly discovered evidence that could not have been discovered through diligence in time for a motion for new trial, (3) the judgment's being the result of fraud, misrepresentation, or misconduct by the other party, or (4) the judgment's being void or having been satisfied or released. Fed. R. Civ. P. 60. Cf. MOTION TO ALTER OR AMEND THE JUDGMENT.

motion for summary judgment. A request that the court enter judgment without a trial because there is no genuine issue of material fact to be decided by a fact-finder — that is, because the evidence is legally insufficient to support a verdict in the nonmovant's favor. • In federal court and in most state courts, the movant-defendant must point out in its motion the absence of evidence on an essential element of the plaintiff's claim, after which the burden shifts to the nonmovant-plaintiff to produce evidence raising a genuine fact issue. But if a party moves for summary judgment on its own claim or defense, then it must establish each element of the claim or defense as a matter of law. Fed. R. Civ. 56. — Abbr. MSJ. — Also termed *summary-judgment motion*; *motion for summary disposition.* See SUMMARY JUDGMENT.

motion in arrest of judgment. 1. A defendant's motion claiming that a substantial error appearing on the face of the record vitiates the whole proceeding and the judgment. **2.** A postjudgment motion in a criminal case claiming that the indictment is insufficient to sustain a judgment or the verdict is somehow insufficient.

motion in limine (in **lim**-ə-nee). A pretrial request that certain inadmissible evidence not be referred to or offered at trial. • Typically, a party makes this motion when it believes that mere mention of the evidence during trial would be highly prejudicial and could not be remedied by an instruction to disregard. If, after the motion is granted, the opposing party mentions or attempts to offer the evidence in the jury's presence, a mistrial may be ordered. A ruling on a motion in limine does not preserve evidentiary error for appellate purposes. Instead, to raise such an error on appeal, a party must have formally objected when the evidence was actually admitted or excluded during trial.

motion to alter or amend the judgment. A party's request that the court correct a substantive error in the judgment, such as a manifest error of law or fact. • Under the Federal Rules of Civil Procedure, a motion to alter or amend the judgment must be filed within ten days after the judgment is entered. It should not ordinarily be used to correct clerical errors in a judgment. Those types of errors — that is, errors that result in the judgment not reflecting the court's intention — may be brought in a motion for relief from the judgment, which does not have the ten-day deadline. A motion to alter or amend the judgment is usu. directed to substantive issues regarding the judgment, such as an intervening change in the law or newly discovered evidence that was not available at trial. Fed. R. Civ. P. 59(e). Cf. MOTION FOR RELIEF FROM THE JUDGMENT.

motion to compel discovery. A party's request that the court force the party's opponent to respond to the party's discovery request (as to answer interrogatories or produce documents). Fed. R. Civ. P. 37(a). — Often shortened to *motion to compel*. — Also termed *motion to enforce discovery*.

motion to dismiss. A request that the court dismiss the case because of settlement, voluntary withdrawal, or a procedural defect. • Under the Federal Rules of Civil Procedure, a plaintiff may voluntarily dismiss the case (under Rule 41(a)) or the defendant may ask the court to dismiss the case, usu. based on one of the defenses listed in Rule 12(b). These defense include lack of personal or subject-matter jurisdiction, improper venue, insufficiency of process, the plaintiff's failure to state a claim on which relief can be granted, and the failure to join an indispensable party. A defendant will frequently file a motion to dismiss for failure to state a claim, which is governed by Rule 12(b)(6), claiming that even if all the plaintiff's allegations are true, they would not be legally sufficient to state a claim on which relief might be granted. — Abbr. MTD.

motion to enforce discovery. See MOTION TO COMPEL DISCOVERY.

motion to lift the stay. *Bankruptcy*. A party's request that the bankruptcy court alter the automatic bankruptcy stay to allow the movant to act against the debtor or the debtor's property, as when a creditor seeks permission to foreclose on a lien because its security interest is not adequately protected. — Also termed *motion for relief from stay*; *motion to modify the stay*.

motion to modify the stay. See MOTION TO LIFT THE STAY.

motion to quash (kwahsh). A party's request that the court nullify process or an act instituted by the other party, as in seeking to nullify a subpoena.

motion to remand. In a case that has been removed from state court to federal court, a party's request that the federal court return the case to state court, usu. because the federal court lacks jurisdiction or because the procedures for removal were not properly followed. 28 USCA § 1447(c).

motion to strike. **1.** *Civil procedure*. A party's request that the court delete insufficient defenses or immaterial, redundant, impertinent, or scandalous statements from an opponent's pleading. Fed. R. Civ. P. 12(f). **2.** *Evidence*. A request that inadmissible evidence be deleted from the record and that the jury be instructed to disregard it.

motion to suppress. A request that the court prohibit the introduction of illegally obtained evidence at a criminal trial.

motion to transfer venue. A request that the court transfer the case to another district or county, usu. because the original venue is improper under the applicable venue rules or because of local prejudice. See VENUE; CHANGE OF VENUE.

motive. Something, esp. willful desire, that leads one to act. — Also termed *ulterior intent*. Cf. INTENT.

> "The term 'motive' is unfortunately ambiguous. That feeling which internally urges or pushes a person to do or refrain from doing an act is an emotion, and is of course evidential towards his doing or not doing the act. But when that evidential fact comes in turn to be evidenced, we must rely on two sorts of data, (a) the person's own expressions of that emotion, e.g., 'I hate M,' or 'I wish I owned that necklace'; and (b) external circumstances likely in human experience to arouse the emotion, e.g., a slander on D may be evidence that D became angry; a purse of money left in sight of D may be evidence that D's desire to have it was aroused. Now this second sort of evidential circumstance (b) is loosely referred to as 'motive,' — though in reality it is only evidential of the emotion, which itself is evidential of the act." John H. Wigmore, *A Students' Textbook of the Law of Evidence* 76 (1935).

bad motive. A person's knowledge that an act is wrongful while the person commits the act.

malicious motive. A motive for bringing a prosecution, other than to do justice.

Motor Carrier Act. A federal statute, originally enacted in 1935 (49 USCA §§ 502–507), subjecting commercial motor carriers of freight and passengers in interstate commerce to the regulations of the Interstate Commerce Commission, now the U.S. Department of Transportation. • The Act was repealed in the 1980s.

movable, *n.* (*usu. pl.*) **1.** Property that can be moved or displaced, such as personal goods.

"Movables and immovables. The main distinction drawn in later Roman law and modern systems based thereon between kinds of things subject to ownership and possession. While basically the distinction corresponds to everyday conceptions, assigning animals and vehicles to the former and land and buildings to the latter category, particular things may be assigned to one category rather than the other for reasons of convenience. Thus, in French law, farm implements and animals are immovables. The distinction is also important in international private law, more so than that between real and personal . . . Thus, land held on lease is personal property by English law for historical reason, but in international private law it is a right in immovable property." David M. Walker, *The Oxford Companion to Law* 858 (1980).

intangible movable. A physical thing that can be moved but that cannot be touched in the usual sense. • Examples are light and electricity.

" 'Intangible movables' is a term of art in the common law which has been applied more widely than its meaning literally justifies, which is merely to those things that have physical existence and can be moved, though cannot be touched in the normal sense, such as light, electricity and radioactive waves. In English law the term has been generally applied to interests created by law which have only a legal, not a physical existence, and are accordingly capable only of legal, not physical, movement. It is convenient, however, to retain a term which is generally accepted and understood in this special legal meaning." R.H. Graveson, *Conflict of Laws* 470 (7th ed. 1974).

2. *Scots law.* A nonheritable right. — Also spelled *moveable.* — **movable,** *adj.* Cf. IMMOVABLE.

"Moveables are, in the phraseology of the law of Scotland, opposed to heritage; so that every species of property, and every right a person can hold, is by that law either heritable or moveable. Hence, moveables are not merely corporeal subjects capable of being moved, but every species of property, corporeal or incorporeal, which does not descend to the heir in heritage." William Bell, *Bell's Dictionary and Digest of the Law of Scotland* 662 (George Watson ed., 1882).

movable estate. See *personal property* under PROPERTY.

movable freehold. The land a seashore owner acquires or loses as water recedes or approaches.

movant (**moov**-ənt). One who makes a motion to the court. — Formerly also spelled *movent.*

move, *vb.* **1.** To make an application (to a court) for a ruling, order, or some other judicial action <the appellant moved the court for a new trial>. **2.** To propose under formal parliamentary procedure <the senator moved that a vote be taken>.

movent. See MOVANT.

mover, *n. Slang.* A stock that experiences spectacular market price changes; a very unstable stock.

moving expense. See EXPENSE.

moving papers. The papers that constitute or support a motion in a court proceeding. — Also termed *motion papers.*

moving violation. An infraction of a traffic law while the vehicle is in motion.

MP. *abbr.* Member of Parliament. See PARLIAMENT.

MPC. *abbr.* MODEL PENAL CODE.

MPC test. See SUBSTANTIAL-CAPACITY TEST.

Mr. Denman's Act. See DENMAN'S ACT.

MRE. *abbr.* MILITARY RULES OF EVIDENCE.

MSJ. *abbr.* MOTION FOR SUMMARY JUDGMENT.

m.s.p. *abbr.* MORTUUS SINE PROLE.

MTD. *abbr.* MOTION TO DISMISS.

MUD. See *municipal utility district* under DISTRICT.

mug book. A collection of mug shots of criminal suspects maintained by law-enforcement agencies (such as the FBI and police departments) to be used in identifying criminal offenders.

mug shot. A photograph of a person's face taken after the person has been arrested and booked.

mulct (məlkt), *n.* A fine or penalty.

mulct, *vb.* **1.** To punish by a fine. **2.** To deprive or divest of, esp. fraudulently.

mulier (**myoo**-lee-ər), *n.* [Latin] **1.** *Roman law.* A woman. • This term at various times referred to a marriageable virgin, a woman not a virgin, a wife, and a mother. **2.** *Hist. & Scots law.* A legitimate son; the son of a *mulier* ("lawful wife"). — Also termed *mulieratus.*

mulier puisne (**myoo**-lee-ər **pyoo**-nee). [Law Latin] *Hist.* The younger lawful son, usu. distinguished from the *bastard eigné* ("the elder bastard son").

> "The common law developed one exception to its harsh doctrine of bastardy. Where the eldest son was born out of wedlock (the *bastard eigné*) and the next son was born to the same parents after the marriage (the *mulier puisné*), and upon the ancestor's death the *bastard eigné* entered as heir and remained in undisturbed possession until his own death, the *bastard eigné* was treated as if he had been legitimate with respect to the inheritance of that land. The reason given by Littleton was that a person who was legitimate by the Canon law could not be bastardised posthumously, when he no longer had the opportunity to contest the issue." J.H. Baker, *An Introduction to English Legal History* 559 (3d ed. 1990).

mulierty (**myoo**-lee-ər-tee). *Hist.* The condition of a legitimate child, as distinguished from a bastard.

multa (**məl**-tə), *n.* [Latin "a fine"] *Hist. Eccles. law.* A fine the bishops paid to the king so that they could make and probate wills and administer estates. — Also termed *multura episcopi* (məl-**t[y]oor**-ə i-**pis**-kə-pɪ).

multicraft union. See UNION.

multidistrict litigation. *Civil procedure.* Federal-court litigation in which civil actions pending in different districts and involving common fact questions are transferred to a single district for coordinated pretrial proceedings, after which the actions are returned to their original districts for trial. • Multidistrict litigation is governed by the Judicial Panel on Multidistrict Litigation, which is composed of seven circuit and district judges appointed by the Chief Justice of the United States. 28 USCA § 1407. — Abbr. MDL.

multifarious (məl-tə-**fair**-ee-əs), *adj.* **1.** (Of a single pleading) improperly joining distinct matters or causes of action, and thereby confounding them. **2.** Improperly joining parties in a lawsuit. **3.** Diverse; many and various. — **multifariousness,** *n.*

multilateral, *adj.* Involving more than two parties <a multilateral agreement>.

multilevel-distribution program. See PYRAMID SCHEME.

multimaturity bond. See *put bond* under BOND (3).

multinational corporation. See CORPORATION.

multipartite, *adj.* (Of a document, etc.) divided into many parts.

multiperil policy. See INSURANCE POLICY.

multiple access. See ACCESS.

multiple admissibility. See ADMISSIBILITY.

multiple counts. See COUNT.

multiple damages. See DAMAGES.

multiple dependent claim. See CLAIM (6).

multiple evidence. See EVIDENCE.

multiple hearsay. See *double hearsay* under HEARSAY.

multiple job-holding. See MOONLIGHTING.

multiple listing. See LISTING (1).

multiple offense. See OFFENSE (1).

multiple-party account. See ACCOUNT.

multiple sentences. See SENTENCE.

multiplicity (məl-tə-**plis**-i-tee), *n. Criminal procedure.* The improper charging of the same offense in several counts of the indictment or information. • Multiplicity violates the Fifth Amendment protection against double jeopardy. — **multiplicitous** (məl-tə-**plis**-i-təs), *adj.*

multiplicity of actions. The existence of two or more lawsuits litigating the same issue against the same defendant. — Also termed *multiplicity of suits*; *multiplicity of proceedings.* See PIECEMEAL LITIGATION.

multiplied damages. See *multiple damages* under DAMAGES.

Multistate Bar Examination. See BAR EXAMINATION.

multistate corporation. See CORPORATION.

multital (**məl**-ti-təl), *adj.* **1.** Of or relating to legal relations that exist among three or more people, esp. a multitude of people. Cf. UNITAL.

> "Tort and breach of contract are alike breaches of *duty*, but in the case of tort the pre-existing duty of the wrong-

doer was one that was shared by every other member of society; and the injured party whose right was violated had not merely one right, he had a multitude of rights. His rights and the correlative duties of others were 'multital.' The secondary right and duty, however, arising from the tort, are relations that exist between the two persons only. They are 'unital.' In the case of a breach of contract, both the primary right and duty and the secondary right and duty are 'unital.'" William R. Anson, *Principles of the Law of Contract* 11 (Arthur L. Corbin ed., 3d Am. ed. 1919).

2. *Rare*. See IN REM.

multura episcopi. See MULTA.

mund (mənd *or* muund). [Old English "hand"] *Hist.* A right to protection or guardianship; a guardian. Cf. MANUS (1).

"Once more we see prerogatival rights growing, while feudal claims fall into the background; and in the case of lunacy we see a guardianship, a *mund*, which is not profitable to the guardian, and this at present is a novel and noteworthy thing." 1 Frederick Pollock & Frederic W. Maitland, *The History of English Law Before the Time of Edward I* 481 (2d ed. 1898).

munera (**myoo**-nər-ə), *n.* [Law Latin "graces"] *Hist.* Tenancies at will; tenancies made at the grantor's pleasure.

muni (**myoo**-nee), *n.* See *municipal bond* under BOND (3).

municeps (**myoo**-nə-seps). [fr. Latin *munus* "office" + *capere* "to take"] *Roman law.* **1.** A citizen of a municipality (*municipium*). **2.** A member of the council of a *municipium*.

municipal, *adj.* **1.** Of or relating to a city, town, or local governmental unit. **2.** Of or relating to the internal government of a state or nation (as contrasted with *international*).

municipal, *n.* See *municipal bond* under BOND (3).

municipal action. Any authorized exercise of governmental power by a municipal officer, board, agency, or other municipal body.

municipal affairs. The matters relating to the local government of a municipality.

municipal aid. Financial or other assistance provided by a municipality to a private business, usu. to encourage it to relocate to the municipality.

municipal attorney. See CITY ATTORNEY.

municipal bond. See BOND (3).

municipal charter. A written document making the persons residing within a fixed boundary, along with their successors, a corporation and body politic for and within that boundary, and prescribing the powers, privileges, and duties of the corporation.

municipal corporation. A city, town, or other local political entity formed by charter from the state and having the autonomous authority to administer the state's local affairs. — Also termed *municipality*. Cf. *quasi-corporation* under CORPORATION.

municipal corporation de facto. A corporation recognized to exist, although it has not fully complied with statutory requirements, when there is (1) a valid law authorizing its incorporation, (2) a colorable and bona fide attempt to organize under that law, and (3) an assumption of powers conferred under that law.

municipal court. See COURT.

municipal domicile. See DOMICILE.

municipal election. See ELECTION.

municipal function. The duties and responsibilities that a municipality owes its members.

municipal government. See *local government* under GOVERNMENT.

municipality. **1.** MUNICIPAL CORPORATION. **2.** The governing body of a municipal corporation.

municipal judge. See JUDGE.

municipal law. **1.** The ordinances and other laws applicable within a city, town, or other local governmental entity. **2.** The internal law of a nation, as opposed to international law.

municipal lien. See LIEN.

municipal officer. A person who occupies a municipal office — usu. mandated by statute or charter — and who may be required to take an oath and exercise sovereign authority in carrying out public duties, with compensation incident to the office irrespective of the actual services rendered.

municipal ordinance. See ORDINANCE.

municipal security. See *municipal bond* under BOND (3).

municipal utility district. See DISTRICT.

municipal warrant. See WARRANT (2).

municipium (myoo-nə-**sip**-ee-əm). [fr. Latin *munus* "honor" + *capere* "to take"] *Roman law*. A self-governing town; specif., any community allied with or conquered by Rome and allowed to maintain certain privileges (such as maintaining separate laws called *leges municipales*) and to exchange certain rights with Rome, such as intermarriage with Roman citizens.

muniment (**myoo**-nə-mənt). A document (such as a deed or charter) evidencing the rights or privileges of a person, family, or corporation. — Also termed (archaically) *miniment*.

muniment house. *Hist.* A place (such as a room in a castle or cathedral) where titles, deeds, and other evidences of title are stored.

muniment of title. Documentary evidence of title, such as a deed or a judgment regarding the ownership of property. — Also termed *common assurance*. See CHAIN OF TITLE.

murder, *n.* The killing of a human being with malice aforethought. • At common law, the crime of murder was not subdivided, but many state statutes have adopted the degree structure outlined below (though the Model Penal Code has not). — **murder,** *vb.* — **murderous,** *adj.* See MALICE AFORETHOUGHT. Cf. MANSLAUGHTER.

> "The word 'murder' has . . . had a devious history. Its original sense is the particularly heinous crime of secret slaying. After the conquest it was observed that Normans were frequently found dead under mysterious circumstances, and so William I enacted that if anyone were found slain and the slayer were not caught, then the hundred should pay a fine; this fine is a *murdrum*. The practice soon grew up to taking inquests and if it were presented that the dead man was English, then the fine was not due. In 1267 it was enacted that accidental deaths should not give rise to *murdrum*, and finally in 1340 presentment of Englishry and *murdrum* were abolished. Henceforth the word slowly tends to get linked up with 'malice aforethought' and so we get the classical formulae describing the crime of murder." Theodore F.T. Plucknett, *A Concise History of the Common Law* 445 (5th ed. 1956).

depraved-heart murder. A murder resulting from an act so reckless and careless of the safety of others that it demonstrates the perpetrator's complete lack of regard for human life.

felony murder. Murder that occurs during the commission of a felony (esp. a serious one). — Also termed (in English law) *constructive murder*. See FELONY-MURDER RULE.

first-degree murder. Murder that is willful, deliberate, or premeditated, or that is committed during the course of another serious felony (often limited to rape, kidnapping, robbery, burglary, or arson). • All murder perpetrated by poisoning or by lying in wait is considered first-degree murder. All types of murder not involving willful, deliberate, and premeditated killing are usu. considered second-degree murder. — Also termed *murder of the first degree*; *murder one*.

murder by torture. A murder preceded by the intentional infliction of pain and suffering on the victim.

> "In some jurisdictions, a murder by torture may constitute murder in the first degree. It occurs when a defendant intentionally inflicts pain and suffering upon his victim for the purpose of revenge, extortion, or persuasion." 2 Charles E. Torcia, *Wharton's Criminal Law* § 144, at 281 (15th ed. 1994).

murder of the first degree. See *first-degree murder*.

murder one. See *first-degree murder*.

second-degree murder. Murder that is not aggravated by any of the circumstances of first-degree murder. — Also termed *murder of the second degree*; *murder two*.

serial murder. A murder pattern in which one criminal selects several victims at random or because the victims share similar characteristics.

third-degree murder. A wrong that did not constitute murder at common law. • Only a few states have added to their murder statutes a third degree of murder. The other states classify all murders in two degrees. Manslaughter is not a degree of the crime of murder, but instead is a distinct offense.

willful murder. The unlawful and intentional killing of another without excuse or mitigating circumstances.

murdrum (**mər**-drəm). [Law Latin] *Hist.* **1.** The secret killing of someone. **2.** A fine against the tithing where the secret and unsolved homicide took place.

> "The readiness with which the Norman administrators seized on this Anglo–Saxon system was probably due to its effectiveness in collecting the *murdrum*, the murder fine. In ordinary cases of homicide, the whole district — except the kin of the suspect — would be zealous to

> bring the malefactor to justice. But we can readily see that, if the person killed was a Norman, every effort would be made to shield the murderer. The Norman rulers had recourse to the device . . . of imposing a group responsibility. The tithing within which the murdered Norman was found was compelled to pay a fine or to discover and surrender the homicide. The word *murdrum* is a word of uncertain etymology, and has given us our term for willful homicide." Max Radin, *Handbook of Anglo-American Legal History* 175–76 (1936).

3. Murder; specif., murder with malice aforethought. See MALICE AFORETHOUGHT.

murorum operatio (myuur-**or**-əm op-ə-**ray**-shee-oh). [Latin] *Hist.* Repair work to the fortifications of buildings, cities, or castles, performed by their inhabitants.

muster, *vb. Military law.* **1.** To assemble together (troops) for inspection or service. **2.** To assemble together (potential troops) for enlistment.

muster roll. *Maritime law.* A shipmaster's account listing the name, age, national character, and quality of every employee on the ship. • In wartime, it is used in ascertaining a ship's neutrality.

mutation, *n.* A significant and basic alteration; esp., in property law, the alteration of a thing's status, such as from separate property to community property. — **mutate,** *vb.* — **mutational,** *adj.*

mutatio nominis (myoo-**tay**-shee-oh **nom**-ə-nis). [Latin] *Roman law.* Change of name. • It was allowed provided that no prejudice was thereby caused to others. The related phrase *mutato nomine* (myoo-**tay**-toh **nom**-ə-nee) means "the name having been changed."

mutatis mutandis (myoo-**tay**-tis myoo-**tan**-dis). [Latin] All necessary changes having been made; with the necessary changes <what was said regarding the first contract applies *mutatis mutandis* to all later ones>.

mute, *n.* **1.** A person who cannot speak. **2.** A person (esp. a prisoner) who stands silent when required to answer or plead. • Formerly, if a prisoner stood mute, a jury was empaneled to determine whether the prisoner was intentionally mute or mute by an act of God. By the Criminal Law Act of 1827 (7 & 8 Geo. 4, ch. 28), if a prisoner was mute by malice, the officer automatically entered a plea of not guilty and the trial proceeded. If adjudicated to be insane, the prisoner was kept in custody until the Crown determined what should be done.

mutilation, *n.* **1.** The act or an instance of rendering a document legally ineffective by subtracting or altering — but not completely destroying — an essential part through cutting, tearing, burning, or erasing. **2.** *Criminal law.* The act of cutting off or permanently damaging a body part, esp. an essential one. — **mutilate,** *vb.* — **mutilator,** *n.* See MAYHEM.

mutiny (**myoo**-tə-nee), *n.* **1.** An insubordination or insurrection of armed forces, esp. sailors, against the authority of their commanders; a forcible revolt by members of the military against constituted authority, usu. their commanding officers.

> "Both mutiny and failure to prevent, suppress, or report a mutiny are capital offenses. . . . The elements of mutiny are (1) creation of any violence or disturbance or acting in concert with others to refuse to obey orders (2) with the intent to usurp or override lawful military authority. One fails to prevent, suppress, or report mutiny when he does not take all reasonable means to overcome or report mutiny. Concert of action is not required for mutiny when the accused creates violence or disturbance." Charles A. Shanor & L. Lynn Hogue, *Military Law in a Nutshell* 197–98 (2d ed. 1996).

2. Loosely, any uprising against authority. — **mutinous,** *adj.*

Mutiny Act. *Hist.* An English statute enacted annually from 1689 to 1879 to provide for a standing army and to punish mutiny, desertion, and other military offenses. • It was merged into the Army Discipline and Regulation Act of 1879 (ch. 33).

mutual, *adj.* **1.** Generally, directed by each toward the other or others; reciprocal. **2.** (Of a condition, credit covenant, promise, etc.) reciprocally given, received, or exchanged. **3.** (Of a right, etc.) belonging to two parties; common. — **mutuality,** *n.*

mutual account. See ACCOUNT.

mutual affray. See MUTUAL COMBAT.

mutual-agreement program. A prisoner-rehabilitation plan in which the prisoner agrees to take part in certain self-improvement activities to receive a definite parole date.

mutual assent. Agreement by both parties to a contract, usu. in the form of offer and acceptance. • In modern contract law, mutual assent is determined by an objective standard — that is, by the apparent intention of the parties as manifested by their actions. Cf. MEETING OF THE MINDS.

mutual association. A mutually owned, cooperative savings and loan association, with the deposits being shares of the association. • A mutual association is not allowed to issue stock and is usu. regulated by the Office of Thrift Supervision, an agency of the U.S. Treasury Department. — See SAVINGS-AND-LOAN ASSOCIATION.

mutual-benefit association. A fraternal or social organization that provides benefits for its members, usu. on an assessment basis.

> "In the absence of ... statutory definition, the question of the extent to which mutual benefit, fraternal beneficiary, and like associations or societies, are within the meaning of the insurance laws must depend upon the terms of the different statutes, and the various circumstances of each particular case .... Broadly speaking, when a company, society, or association, either voluntary or incorporated, and whether known as a relief, benevolent, or benefit society, or by some similar name, contracts for a consideration to pay a sum of money upon the happening of a certain contingency, and the prevalent purpose and nature of the organization is that of insurance, it will be regarded as an insurance company and its contracts as insurance contracts ...." 2A George J. Couch, *Couch on Insurance* § 20:2, at 11 (rev. 2d ed. 1984).

mutual-benefit insurance. Benefits provided by a mutual-benefit association upon the occurrence of a loss.

mutual combat. A consensual fight on equal terms — arising from a moment of passion but not in self-defense — between two persons armed with deadly weapons. • A murder charge may be reduced to voluntary manslaughter if death occurred by mutual combat. — Also termed *mutual affray*. Cf. DUEL.

mutual company. See COMPANY.

mutual contract. See *bilateral contract* under CONTRACT.

mutual debts. See DEBT.

mutual demands. Countering demands between two parties at the same time <a claim and counterclaim in a lawsuit are mutual demands>.

mutual fund. 1. An investment company that invests its shareholders' money in a usu. diversified selection of securities. — Often shortened to *fund*. **2.** Loosely, a share in such a company.

balanced fund. A mutual fund that maintains a balanced investment in stocks and bonds, investing a certain percentage in senior securities.

bond fund. A mutual fund that invests primarily in specialized corporate bonds or municipal bonds.

closed-end fund. A mutual fund having a fixed number of shares that are traded on a major securities exchange or an over-the-counter market.

common-stock fund. A mutual fund that invests only in common stock.

dual fund. A closed-end mutual fund that invests in two classes of stock — stock that pays dividends and stock that increases in investment value without dividends. • A dual fund combines characteristics of an income fund and a growth fund. — Also termed *dual-purpose fund*; *leverage fund*; *split fund*.

fully managed fund. A mutual fund whose policy allows reasonable discretion in trading securities in combination or quantity.

growth fund. A mutual fund that typically invests in well-established companies whose earnings are expected to increase. • Growth funds usu. pay small dividends but offer the potential for large share-price increases.

hedge fund. See HEDGE FUND.

income fund. A mutual fund that typically invests in securities that consistently produce a steady income, such as bonds or dividend-paying stocks.

index fund. A mutual fund that invests in the stock of companies constituting a specific market index, such as Standard & Poor's 500 stocks, and thereby tracks the stock average.

leverage fund. See *dual fund*.

load fund. A mutual fund that charges a commission, usu. ranging from 4 to 9%, either when shares are purchased (a *front-end load*) or when they are redeemed (a *back-end load*).

money-market fund. A mutual fund that invests in low-risk government securities and short-term notes.

no-load fund. A mutual fund that does not charge any sales commission (although it may charge fees to cover operating costs).

open-end fund. A mutual fund that continually offers new shares and buys back existing shares on demand. • An open-end fund will continue to grow as more shareholders invest because it does not have a fixed number of shares outstanding.

performance fund. A mutual fund characterized by an aggressive purchase of stocks expected to show near-term growth.

split fund. See *dual fund*.

utility fund. A mutual fund that invests only in public-utility securities.

value fund. A mutual fund that invests in stocks that its manager believes to be priced below their true market value.

vulture fund. An investment company that purchases bankrupt or insolvent companies to reorganize them in hopes of reselling them at a profit.

mutual insurance. See INSURANCE.

mutual insurance company. An insurer whose policyholders are its owners, as opposed to a stock insurance company owned by outside shareholders. Cf. STOCK INSURANCE COMPANY.

mutuality. The state of sharing or exchanging something; a reciprocation; an interchange <mutuality of obligation>.

mutuality doctrine. The collateral-estoppel requirement that, to bar a party from relitigating an issue determined against that party in an earlier action, both parties must have been in privity with one another in the earlier proceeding.

mutuality of assent. See MEETINGS OF THE MINDS.

mutuality of contract. See MUTUALITY OF OBLIGATION.

mutuality of debts. *Bankruptcy.* For purposes of setoff, the condition in which debts are owed between parties acting in the same capacity, even though the debts are not of the same character and did not arise out of the same transaction.

mutuality of estoppel. The collateral-estoppel principle that a judgment is not conclusively in favor of someone unless the opposite decision would also be conclusively against that person.

mutuality of obligation. The agreement of both parties to a contract to be bound in some way. — Also termed *mutuality of contract*. See MUTUAL ASSENT.

> "The doctrine of mutuality of obligation is commonly expressed in the phrase that in a bilateral contract 'both parties must be bound or neither is bound.' But this phrase is over-generalization because the doctrine is not one of mutuality of obligation but rather one of mutuality of consideration. Phrasing the rule in terms of mutuality of obligation rather than in terms of consideration has led to so-called exceptions and judicial circumventions.... It has been suggested that the term 'mutuality of obligation' should be abandoned and we must agree in the light of the confusion that this term has engendered." John D. Calamari & Joseph M. Perillo, *The Law of Contracts* § 4–12, at 226 (3d ed. 1987).

mutuality of remedy. The availability of a remedy, esp. equitable relief, to both parties to a transaction, usu. required before either party can be granted specific performance. See SPECIFIC PERFORMANCE.

mutual mistake. See MISTAKE.

mutual promises. See PROMISE.

mutual rescission. See RESCISSION (2).

mutual savings bank. See BANK.

mutual testaments. See *mutual wills* under WILL.

mutual will. See WILL.

mutuant (**myoo**-choo-ənt). The provider of property in a mutuum. See MUTUUM.

mutuari (myoo-choo-**air**-I), *vb.* [Latin] To borrow.

mutuary (**myoo**-choo-er-ee). The recipient of property in a mutuum. See MUTUUM.

mutuatus (myoo-choo-**ay**-təs), *n.* [Latin] A borrowing; a loan of money.

mutus et surdus (**myoo**-təs et **sər**-dəs). [Latin] Deaf and dumb.

mutuum (**myoo**-choo-əm). **1.** A transaction (sometimes referred to as a bailment) in which goods are delivered, but instead of being returned, are replaced by other goods of the same kind. • At common law such a transaction is regarded as a sale or exchange, and not as a bailment, because the particular goods are not returned. **2.** *Roman law.* A loan in which the borrower is entitled to consume the goods lent and return an equivalent amount. • This was one of three types of contract for permissive use, the other two being *commodatum* (kom-ə-**day**-təm) and *locatio conductio* (loh-**kay**-shee-oh kən-**dək**-shee-oh).

mysterious disappearance. A loss of property under unknown or baffling circumstances that are difficult to understand or explain. • The term is used in insurance policies covering theft.

> "Under a policy insuring against loss of property by 'mysterious disappearance' recovery is generally allowed where the article disappears from the place the insured left it, while recovery is ordinarily disallowed where the insured has no recollection of when he last had possession of the article and cannot say when or from what place it disappeared. Thus the addition of the words 'mysterious disappearance' to a theft policy does not transform it to an 'all loss' policy covering lost or mislaid articles, but it remains a theft policy." 43 Am. Jur. 2d *Insurance* § 501, at 575–76 (1982).

mystic testament. See *mystic will* under WILL.

mystic will. See WILL.

N

n.a. *abbr.* **1.** (*cap.*) National Association. See *national bank* under BANK. **2.** Not applicable. **3.** Not available. **4.** Not allowed.

NAFTA (**naf**-tə). *abbr.* NORTH AMERICAN FREE TRADE AGREEMENT.

naked, *adj.* (Of a legal act or instrument) lacking confirmation or validation <naked ownership of property>.

naked authority. See AUTHORITY (1).

naked bailment. See *gratuitous bailment* under BAILMENT.

naked confession. See CONFESSION.

naked contract. See NUDUM PACTUM.

naked debenture. See DEBENTURE (3).

naked deposit. See *gratuitous bailment* under BAILMENT, DEPOSIT (5).

naked expectancy. See *naked possibility* under POSSIBILITY.

naked land trust. See *land trust* under TRUST.

naked license. See LICENSE.

naked licensee. See *bare licensee* under LICENSEE.

naked option. See OPTION.

naked owner. See OWNER.

naked possession. See POSSESSION.

naked possibility. See POSSIBILITY.

naked power. See POWER.

naked promise. See *gratuitous promise* under PROMISE.

naked trust. See *passive trust* under TRUST.

nam (nam), *n.* [Old English *naam*] *Hist.* The act of distraining property.

nam (nam *or* nahm), *prep.* [Latin] For.

> "Nam .... This particle is frequently used as introductory to the quotation of a maxim, and sometimes erroneously treated as a part of the maxim quoted." 2 Alexander M. Burrill, *A Law Dictionary and Glossary* 219 (2d ed. 1867).

namare (nə-**mair**-ee), *vb.* [Law Latin] *Hist.* To distrain property.

namation (nə-**may**-shən), *n.* [fr. Old English *nam*] *Hist.* **1.** The act of distraining property. **2.** *Scots law.* The impounding of property. — Also termed *namatio.*

name, *n.* A word or phrase identifying or designating a person or thing and distinguishing that person or thing from others.

alias. See ALIAS.

assumed name. See ASSUMED NAME.

corporate name. The registered name under which a corporation conducts legal affairs such as suing, being sued, and paying taxes; the name that a corporation files with a state authority (usu. the secretary of state) as the name under which the corporation will conduct its affairs. • A corporate name usu. includes, and in many states is required to include, the word "corporation," "incorporated," or "company," or an abbreviation of one of those words. Cf. ASSUMED NAME.

distinctive name. A name, esp. a tradename, that clearly distinguishes one thing from another. • To maintain an action for tradename infringement, the plaintiff must prove, among other things, that it owns a distinctive name.

fictitious name. See ASSUMED NAME; ALIAS.

full name. A person's first name, middle name (or middle initial), and surname.

generic name. See GENERIC NAME.

legal name. A person's full name as recognized in law, consisting of a first name (usu.

given at birth or at a baptism or christening) and a last name (usu. a family name).

nickname. See NICKNAME.

street name. See STREET NAME.

tradename. See TRADENAME.

name-and-arms clause. *Hist.* A clause (usu. in a will or settlement transferring property) providing that the property's recipient must assume and continue using the testator's or settlor's surname and coat-of-arms, or else the property will pass to another person.

named insured. See INSURED.

named-insured exclusion. See EXCLUSION (3).

named partner. See *name partner* under PARTNER.

named-perils policy. See *multiperil policy* under INSURANCE POLICY.

named plaintiff. See *class representative* under REPRESENTATIVE.

namely, *adv.* By name or particular mention; that is to say <the plaintiff asserted two claims, namely wrongful termination and slander>. • The term indicates what is to be included by name. By contrast, *including* implies a partial list and indicates that something is not listed. See INCLUDE.

name partner. See PARTNER.

namium (**nay**-mee-əm), *n.* [Law Latin] *Hist.* The act of distraining property.

namium vetitum (**nay**-mee-əm **vet**-ə-təm), *n.* [Law Latin "taking prohibited"] *Hist.* A refused or prohibited taking or redelivery. • This term is most often associated with the circumstance in which a lord's bailiff distrained animals or goods, and was ordered by the lord to take them to an unknown place or otherwise not to redeliver them when the sheriff came to replevy them. — Also termed *vetitum namium.*

nanny tax. See TAX.

nantissement (non-tis-**mahn**), *n.* [French] *French law.* A security or pledge. • If it involves movable property, it is called "gage." If it involves immovable property such as real estate, it is called "antichrèse."

Napoleonic Code. 1. (*usu. pl.*) The codification of French law commissioned by Napoleon in the 19th century, including the *Code civil* (1804), the *Code de procédure civil* (1806), the *Code de commerce* (1807), the *Code pénal* (1810), and the *Code d'instruction crimenelle* (1811). — Also termed *Code Napoléon* (abbr. CN). **2.** Loosely, CIVIL CODE (2).

NAR. *abbr.* NATIONAL ASSOCIATION OF REALTORS.

narcoanalysis (nahr-koh-ə-**nal**-ə-sis). The process of injecting a "truth-serum" drug into a patient to induce semiconsciousness, and then interrogating the patient. • This process has been utilized to enhance the memory of a witness.

narcotic, *n.* **1.** An addictive drug, esp. an opiate, that dulls the senses and induces sleep. **2.** (*usu. pl.*) A drug that is controlled or prohibited by law. — **narcotic,** *adj.*

narr. *abbr.* NARRATIO.

narr-and-cognovit law (nahr-and-kahg-**noh**-vit). [Latin *narratio* "declaration" and *cognovit* "the person has conceded"] *Hist.* A law providing that a plaintiff will be granted judgment on a note through an attorney's confession that the amount shown on the note, together with interest and costs, constitutes a legal and just claim. Cf. COGNOVIT JUDGMENT; *confession of judgment* under JUDGMENT.

narratio (nə-**ray**-shee-oh), *n.* [Latin "narrative"] *Hist.* A declaration, complaint, or petition in which the plaintiff sets out the facts of a case; an oral narrative by the plaintiff of the facts and legal arguments on which the claim is based. • The term has also been called the "conte" or "tale." — Abbr. *narr.*

> "[T]he making of the count, in Latin the *narratio*, was the very centre of the legal process. We do not know how it came about that the litigant was allowed to speak through the mouth of another, though it has been suggested that it was not to prevent mistakes being made but to prevent them being fatal. Certainly the litigant could disavow what was said on his behalf; and perhaps it was only 'said' by him when he formally adopted it. If this is right, our modern barrister began as one who could harmlessly blunder." S.F.C. Milsom, *Historical Foundations of the Common Law* 28 (1969).

narrative evidence. See EVIDENCE.

narrator (na-**ray**-tor *or* na-**ray**-tər), *n.* [Law Latin] *Hist.* A pleader or counter; a person who prepares pleadings (i.e., *narrs*). • For example, a serjeant-at-law was also known as *serviens narrator*. Pl. **narratores** (na-rə-**tor**-eez).

> "The Latin *narrator* and its French equivalent *contour* became technical terms. If an English term was in use, it was perhaps *forspeaker*." 1 Frederick Pollock & Frederic W. Maitland, *The History of English Law Before the Time of Edward I* 215 n.1 (2d ed. 1898).

narrow-channel rule. The navigational requirement that a vessel traveling down a slim fairway must keep as near to the fairway wall on the vessel's starboard side as is safe and practicable. 33 USCA § 2009(a)(i).

narrowly tailored, *adj.* (Of a content-neutral restriction on the time, place, or manner of speech in a designated public forum) being only as broad as is reasonably necessary to promote a substantial governmental interest that would be achieved less effectively without the restriction; no broader than absolutely necessary. See *designated public forum* under PUBLIC FORUM.

narrow sea. (*often pl.*) A sea running between two coasts that are close to each another. • The English Channel, for example, is a narrow sea.

nasciturus (nas-ə-**t[y]oor**-əs *or* -**t[y]ər**-əs), *n.* [fr. Latin *nascor* "to be born"] *Roman law.* An unborn child.

NASD. *abbr.* NATIONAL ASSOCIATION OF SECURITIES DEALERS.

NASDAQ (**naz**-dak). *abbr.* NATIONAL ASSOCIATION OF SECURITIES DEALERS AUTOMATED QUOTATION SYSTEM.

natale (nə-**tay**-lee), *n.* [Latin "of or belonging to birth"] *Hist.* The status a person acquires by birth. • For example, if one or both parents of a child were serfs, the child was generally regarded as a serf, and a child born free rarely became a serf. See NATIVUS.

nati et nascituri (**nay**-tI et nas-ə-**t[y]oor**-I *or* -**t[y]ər**-I), *n. pl.* [Latin "born and to be born"] *Hist.* A person's heirs, near and remote.

natio (**nay**-shee-oh), *n.* [Latin] *Hist.* **1.** A nation. **2.** A group of students. **3.** A native place.

nation, *n.* **1.** A large group of people having a common origin, language, and tradition and usu. constituting a political entity. • When a nation is coincident with a state, the term *nation-state* is often used. — Also termed *nationality.*

> "The nearest we can get to a definition is to say that a nation is a group of people bound together by common history, common sentiment and traditions, and, usually (though not always, as, for example, Belgium or Switzerland) by common heritage. A state, on the other hand, is a society of men united under one government. These two forms of society are not necessarily coincident. A single nation may be divided into several states, and conversely a single state may comprise several nations or parts of nations." John Salmond, *Jurisprudence* 136 (Glanville L. Williams ed., 10th ed. 1947).

2. A community of people inhabiting a defined territory and organized under an independent government; a sovereign political state. Cf. STATE.

national, *adj.* **1.** Of or relating to a nation <national anthem>. **2.** Nationwide in scope <national emergency>.

national, *n.* **1.** A member of a nation. **2.** A person owing permanent allegiance to and under the protection of a state. 8 USCA § 1101(a)(21).

national of the United States. A citizen of the United States or a noncitizen who owes permanent allegiance to the United States. 8 USCA § 1101(a)(22). — Also termed *U.S. national*; *U.S. citizen.*

National Aeronautics and Space Act. A 1958 federal statute that created the National Aeronautics and Space Administration (NASA), a civilian agency of the federal government whose functions include conducting space research, improving aeronautical travel, building manned and unmanned space vehicles, developing operational space programs, and engaging in other space activities devoted to peaceful purposes for the benefit of all humankind. 42 USCA §§ 2451–2484.

national association. See *national bank* under BANK.

National Association of Realtors. An association of real-estate brokers and agents promoting education, professional standards, and modernization in areas of real estate such as brokerage, appraisal, and property management. — Abbr. NAR.

National Association of Securities Dealers. A group of brokers and dealers empowered by the SEC to regulate the over-the-counter securities market. — Abbr. NASD.

National Association of Securities Dealers Automated Quotation system. A computerized system for recording transactions and displaying price quotations for a group of actively traded securities on the over-the-counter market. — Abbr. NASDAQ.

national bank. See BANK.

National Bar Association. An organization comprised primarily of African–American members of the legal profession, which was founded in 1925 and which seeks to promote education, professionalism, and the protection of civil rights. — Abbr. NBA.

National Conference of Commissioners on Uniform State Laws. An organization that drafts and proposes statutes for adoption by individual states, with the goal of making the laws on various subjects uniform among the states. • Founded in 1892 and composed of representatives from all 50 states, the Conference has drafted more than 200 uniform laws, including the Uniform Commercial Code. — Abbr. NCCUSL. — Also termed *Uniform Law Commissioners*. See UNIFORM ACT; MODEL ACT.

national currency. Money (both notes and coins) approved by a national government and placed in circulation as a medium of exchange. See LEGAL TENDER.

National Daily Quotation Service. See PINK SHEET.

national debt. The total financial obligation of the federal government, including such instruments as Treasury bills, notes, and bonds, as well as foreign debt.

national defense. 1. All measures taken by a nation to protect itself against its enemies. • A nation's protection of its collective ideals and values is included in the concept of national defense. **2.** A nation's military establishment.

national domicile. See DOMICILE.

national emergency. A state of national crisis or a situation requiring immediate and extraordinary national action.

National Environmental Policy Act. A 1969 federal statute establishing U.S. environmental policy. • The statute requires federal agencies to submit an environmental-impact statement with every proposal for a program or law that would affect the environment. 42 USCA §§ 4321–4347 — Abbr. NEPA. See ENVIRONMENTAL-IMPACT STATEMENT.

national government. The government of an entire country, as distinguished from that of a province, state, subdivision, or territory of the country and as distinguished from an international organization.

National Guard. The U.S. militia, which is maintained as a reserve for the U.S. Army and Air Force. • Its members are volunteers, recruited and trained on a statewide basis and equipped by the federal government. A state may request the National Guard's assistance in quelling disturbances, and the federal government may order the National Guard into active service in times of war or other national emergency. See MILITIA.

nationality. 1. NATION (1). **2.** The relationship between a citizen of a nation and the nation itself, customarily involving allegiance by the citizen and protection by the state; membership in a nation. **3.** The formal relationship between a ship and the nation under whose flag the ship sails. See FLAG STATE.

> " 'Nationality' is a term which has long been used to define the legal relationship between a state and a ship which is authorized by the state to fly its flag.... Discussions in the International Law Commission in 1951 reflected concern that the use of the term 'nationality' in reference to ships was misleading as it implied similarity to the term's use in defining the legal relationship between a state and its citizen. Nonetheless, the term has continued to be the one most often employed in describing the relationship between a ship and its flag state. It is important to realize, however, that in spite of their common names, the legal relationship ascribed to the nationality of ships does differ from that arising from the nationality of natural or juridical persons." Louis B. Sohn & Kristen Gustafson, *The Law of the Sea in a Nutshell* 1–2 (1984).

Nationality Act. See IMMIGRATION AND NATIONALITY ACT.

nationalization, *n.* **1.** The act of bringing an industry under governmental control or ownership. **2.** The act of giving a person the status of a citizen. See NATURALIZATION.

nationalize, *vb.* **1.** To bring (an industry) under governmental control or ownership. **2.** To give (a person) the status of a citizen; NATURALIZE.

National Labor Relations Act. A federal statute regulating the relations between employers and employees and establishing the National Labor Relations Board. 29 USCA §§ 151–169. •

The statute is also known as the Wagner Act of 1935. It was amended by the Taft–Hartley Act of 1947 and the Landrum–Griffin Act of 1959. — Also termed *Wagner Act*. — Abbr. NLRA.

National Labor Relations Board. A federal agency (created by the National Labor Relations Act) that regulates employer-employee relations by establishing collective bargaining, conducting union elections, and prohibiting unfair labor practices. 29 USCA § 153. — Abbr. NLRB. — Often shortened to *Labor Relations Board*.

National Lawyers Guild. An association of lawyers, law students, and legal workers dedicated to promoting a left-wing political and social agenda. • Founded in 1937, it now comprises some 4,000 members. Cf. FEDERALIST SOCIETY.

National Mediation Board. A federal agency that, among other things, mediates disputes between rail and air carriers and their employees over wages and working conditions. • It was created by the Railway Labor Act. 45 USCA §§ 154–163. — Abbr. NMB.

National Motor Vehicle Theft Act. See DYER ACT.

national origin. The country in which a person was born, or from which the person's ancestors came. • This term is used in several antidiscrimination statutes, including Title VII of the Civil Rights Act of 1964, which prohibits discrimination because of an individual's "race, color, religion, sex, or national origin." 42 USCA § 2000e–2.

National Priorities List. *Environmental law.* The Environmental Protection Agency's list of the most serious uncontrolled or abandoned hazardous-waste sites that are identified for possible long-term remediation as Superfund sites. 40 CFR § 35.6015. — Abbr. NPL.

National Quotation Bureau. A company that publishes daily price quotations (*pink sheets*) of over-the-counter securities.

National Reporter System. A series of lawbooks, published by the West Group, containing every published decision of the federal and state courts in the United States. • For federal courts, the system includes the *Supreme Court Reporter*, *Federal Reporter*, *Federal Claims Reporter*, *Federal Supplement*, *Federal Rules Decisions*, *Bankruptcy Reporter*, *Military Justice Reporter*, and *Veterans Appeals Reporter*. For state courts, the system includes the *Atlantic Reporter*, *New York Supplement*, *North Eastern Reporter*, *North Western Reporter*, *Pacific Reporter*, *South Eastern Reporter*, *Southern Reporter*, and *South Western Reporter*.

National Response Center. *Environmental law.* A nationwide communication center located in Washington, D.C., responsible for receiving, and relaying to appropriate federal officials, all notices of oil discharges and other releases of hazardous substances. 40 CFR § 310.11.

national-security privilege. See *state-secrets privilege* under PRIVILEGE (3).

national-service life insurance. A policy, issuable to a person in active U.S. military service on or after October 8, 1940, that provides life insurance at favorable rates. • This insurance was established by the National Service Life Insurance Act of 1940, and is regulated by the Administrator of Veterans Affairs. 38 USCA §§ 1901–1929.

national synod. See SYNOD.

National Transportation Safety Board. An independent government agency that investigates some transportation accidents, conducts safety studies, hears and rules on licensing appeals, and proposes safety guidelines and improved safety standards for the transportation industry. 49 USCA §§ 1101–1155. — Abbr. NTSB.

national-treatment clause. A provision contained in some treaties, usu. commercial ones, according foreigners the same rights, in certain respects, as those accorded to nationals.

national union. See UNION.

nations, law of. See INTERNATIONAL LAW.

native, *n.* **1.** A person who is a citizen of a particular place, region, or nation by virtue of having been born there. **2.** A person whose national origin derives from having been born within a particular place. **3.** Loosely, a person born abroad whose parents are citizens of the nation and are not permanently residing abroad. **4.** Loosely, a person or thing belonging to a group indigenous to a particular place. • The term *Native American* is sometimes shortened to *native*.

native-born, *adj.* Born in the nation specified <a native-born Canadian>. • This term is sometimes considered redundant. See NATIVE.

nativi conventionarii (nə-**tI**-vI kən-ven-shee-ə-**nair**-ee-I), *n. pl.* [Law Latin] *Hist.* Villeins by contract.

nativi de stipite (nə-**tI**-vI dee **stip**-ə-tee), *n. pl.* [Law Latin] *Hist.* Villeins by birth. See NATIVUS; NATALE.

nativitas (nə-**tiv**-ə-tas), *n.* [Law Latin] *Hist.* The servitude or bondage of serfs.

nativo habendo (nə-**tI**-voh hə-**ben**-doh), *n.* DE NATIVO HABENDO.

nativus (nə-**tI**-vəs), *n.* [Law Latin] *Hist.* A person who is born a villein or serf.

> "Having seen what serfdom means, we may ask how men become serfs. The answer is that almost always the serf is a born serf; *nativus* and *villanus* were commonly used as interchangeable terms . . . ." 1 Frederick Pollock & Frederic W. Maitland, *The History of English Law Before the Time of Edward I* 422 (2d ed. 1898).

natural, *adj.* **1.** In accord with the regular course of things in the universe and without accidental or purposeful interference <a natural death as opposed to murder>. **2.** Normal; proceeding from the regular character of a person or thing <it is natural for a duck to fly south in the winter>. **3.** Brought about by nature as opposed to artificial means <a natural lake>. **4.** Inherent; not acquired or assumed <natural talent>. **5.** Indigenous; native <the original or natural inhabitants of a country>. **6.** Of or relating to birth <natural child as distinguished from adopted child>. **7.** Untouched by civilization; wild <only a small part of the forest remains in its natural state>. — **naturally,** *adv.*

natural, *n.* **1.** A person who is native to a place. See NATIVE; NATURAL-BORN CITIZEN. **2.** A person or thing especially suited for a particular endeavor.

natural-accumulation doctrine. The rule that a governmental entity or other landowner is not required to remove naturally occurring ice or snow from public property, such as a highway, unless the entity has, by taking some affirmative action (such as highway construction), increased the travel hazard to the public.

natural affection. The love naturally existing between close relatives, such as parent and child. • Natural affection may be valid consideration for a completed contract but insufficient to support an unperformed contract. See CONSIDERATION; *executory contract* under CONTRACT.

natural allegiance. See ALLEGIANCE.

natural and probable consequence. See NATURAL CONSEQUENCE.

natural-born citizen. See CITIZEN.

Natural Born Citizen Clause. The clause of the U.S. Constitution barring persons not born in the United States from the presidency. U.S. Const. art. II, § 1, cl. 5.

natural-born subject. See SUBJECT.

natural boundary. See BOUNDARY.

natural channel. See CHANNEL.

natural child. See CHILD.

natural cognation. See COGNATION.

natural consequence. Something that predictably occurs as the result of an act <plaintiff's injuries were the natural consequence of the car wreck>. — Also termed *natural and probable consequence.*

natural day. See DAY.

natural death. See DEATH.

natural-death act. A statute that allows a person to issue a written directive instructing a physician to withhold life-sustaining procedures if the person should become terminally ill.

natural domicile. See *domicile of origin* under DOMICILE.

natural duty. See *moral duty* under DUTY (1).

natural equity. See EQUITY (3).

natural father. See FATHER.

natural flood channel. See CHANNEL.

natural fruit. See FRUIT.

natural guardian. See GUARDIAN.

natural heir. See HEIR.

natural infancy. See INFANCY.

naturalis possessio (nach-ə-**ray**-lis pə-**zes**[**h**]-ee-oh). Mere detention of an object. • This type of possession exists when the possessor's holding of the object is limited by a recognition of another person's outstanding right. The holder may be a usufructuary, a bailee, or a servant.

naturalization. The granting of citizenship to a foreign-born person under statutory authority.

Naturalization Clause. The constitutional provision stating that every person born or naturalized in the United States is a citizen of the United States and of the state of residence. U.S. Const. amend. XIV, § 1. See JUS SOLI.

naturalization court. A court having jurisdiction to hear and decide naturalization petitions. • Naturalization courts were abolished as a result of the Immigration Act of 1990. Under current U.S. law, the Attorney General has the sole authority to naturalize citizens. But after a hearing before an immigration officer, an applicant may seek review of the denial of an application for naturalization in the federal district court for the district in which the applicant resides. If an applicant is certified to be eligible for naturalization, the oath of allegiance may be administered by the Attorney General, a federal district court, or a state court of record. See *oath of allegiance* under OATH.

naturalize, *vb.* To grant citizenship to (a foreign-born person) under statutory authority. — **naturalization,** *n.*

naturalized citizen. See CITIZEN.

natural justice. See JUSTICE (1).

natural law. **1.** A physical law of nature <gravitation is a natural law>. **2.** A philosophical system of legal and moral principles purportedly deriving from a universalized conception of human nature or divine justice rather than from legislative or judicial action; moral law embodied in principles of right and wrong <many ethical teachings are based on natural law>. — Also termed *law of nature*; *natural justice*; *lex aeterna*; *eternal law*; *lex naturae*; *divine law*; *jus divinum*; *jus naturale*; *jus naturae*; *normative jurisprudence*. Cf. FUNDAMENTAL LAW; POSITIVE LAW.

> "Natural law, as it is revived today, seeks to organize the ideal element in law, to furnish a critique of old received ideals and give a basis for formulating new ones, and to yield a reasoned canon of values and a technique of applying it. I should prefer to call it philosophical jurisprudence. But one can well sympathize with those who would salvage the good will of the old name as an asset of the science of law." Roscoe Pound, *The Formative Era of American Law* 29 (1938).

> "It is true that when medieval writers spoke of natural law as being discoverable by reason, they meant that the best human reasoning could discover it, and not, of course, that the results to which any and every individual's reasoning led him was natural law. The foolish criticism of Jeremy Bentham: 'a great multitude of people are continually talking of the law of nature; and then they go on giving you their sentiments about what is right and what is wrong; and these sentiments, you are to understand, are so many chapters and sections of the law of nature', merely showed a contempt for a great conception which Bentham had not taken the trouble to understand." J.L. Brierly, *The Law of Nations* 20–21 (5th ed. 1955).

> "[N]atural law is often an idealization of the opposite to that which prevails. Where inequality or privilege exists, natural law demands its abolition." Morris R. Cohen, *Reason and Law* 96 (1961).

natural liberty. See LIBERTY.

natural life. A person's physical life span.

natural monopoly. See MONOPOLY.

natural monument. See MONUMENT.

natural object. **1.** A person likely to receive a portion of another person's estate based on the nature and circumstances of their relationship. — Also termed *natural object of bounty*; *natural object of one's bounty*; *natural object of testator's bounty*. **2.** NATURAL BOUNDARY. **3.** NATURAL MONUMENT.

natural obligation. See OBLIGATION.

natural person. See PERSON.

natural possession. See POSSESSION.

natural premium. See PREMIUM (1).

natural presumption. See PRESUMPTION.

natural resource. **1.** Any material from nature having potential economic value or providing for the sustenance of life, such as timber, minerals, oil, water, and wildlife. **2.** Environmental features that serve a community's well-being or recreational interests, such as parks.

natural right. See RIGHT.

natural servitude. See SERVITUDE (1).

natural succession. See SUCCESSION (2).

natural watercourse. See WATERCOURSE.

natural wear and tear. See WEAR AND TEAR.

natural wrong. See *moral wrong* under WRONG.

natural year. See YEAR.

nature. **1.** A fundamental quality that distinguishes one thing from another; the essence of something. **2.** A wild condition, untouched by civilization. **3.** A disposition or personality of someone or something. **4.** Something pure or true as distinguished from something artificial or contrived. **5.** The basic instincts or impulses of someone or something. **6.** The elements of the universe, such as mountains, plants, planets, and stars.

natus (**nay**-təs), *adj.* [Latin] Born; (of a child) alive.

nauclerus (naw-**kleer**-əs), *n.* [Latin fr. Greek *naus* "ship" + *klros* "allotment"] *Roman law.* A shipmaster.

naulage (**naw**-lij), *n.* [Old French fr. Law Latin *naulagium* "passage money"] The fare for passengers or goods traveling by ship. See NAULUM.

naulum (**naw**-ləm), *n.* [Latin fr. Greek *naus* "ship"] *Roman law.* Fare; freights; a shipowner's fee for carrying people or goods from one place to another. • The term derives from the mythological reference to money placed in the mouths of the dead as a toll so that Charon would lead them across the river Styx to the underworld.

nauta (**naw**-tə), *n.* [Latin fr. Greek *naus* "ship"] *Roman law.* A sailor.

nautical, *adj.* Of or relating to ships or shipping, carriage by sea, or navigation.

nautical assessor. A person skilled in maritime matters who is summoned in an admiralty case to assist the judge on points requiring special expertise.

nautical mile. A measure of distance for air and sea navigation, equal to one minute of arc of a great circle of the earth. • Different measures have been used by different countries because the earth is not a perfect sphere. Since 1959, however, the United States has used an international measure for a nautical mile, set by the Hydrographic Bureau, equal to 6,076.11549 feet, or 1,852 meters.

nauticum fenus (**naw**-ti-kəm **fee**-nəs), *n.* [Greek *nautikum* "nautical" + Latin *fenus* "interest"] *Roman & civil law.* A loan on bottomry made to a transporter of merchandise by ship. • The loan is subject to an extremely high rate of interest because it does not have to be repaid unless the ship safely reaches its destination. The *nauticum fenus* is both a loan and marine insurance. The rate, originally unlimited because of the risks of sea travel, was eventually fixed at 12%. The money loaned is *pecunia trajecticia* (money conveyed overseas). — Also spelled *nauticum foenus.* — Also termed *nautica pecunia; foenus nauticum.*

NAV. *abbr.* NET ASSET VALUE.

navagium (na-**vay**-jee-əm), *n.* [Latin "ship; voyage"] *Hist.* A tenant's duty to transport the lord's goods by ship.

naval, *adj.* **1.** Of or relating to ships or shipping. **2.** Of or relating to a navy. See NAVY.

naval law. A system of regulations governing naval forces. See CODE OF MILITARY JUSTICE.

navarch (**nay**-vahrk), *n.* [fr. Greek *naus* "ship" + *archos* "chief"] *Hist.* A master of an armed ship. — Also termed *navarchus.* Cf. NAVICULARIUS.

navicularius (nə-vik-yə-**lair**-ee-əs), *n.* [Latin "shipowner"] *Hist.* A person engaged in the shipping business.

navigable (**nav**-i-gə-bəl), *adj.* **1.** Capable of allowing vessels or vehicles to pass, and thereby usable for travel or commerce <the channel was barely navigable because it was so narrow>.

navigable in fact, *adj.* Naturally usable for travel or commerce. • A stream is navigable in fact if, in its natural and ordinary state, it can be used for travel or commerce.

2. Capable of being steered <navigable aircraft>. See NAVIGABLE WATER.

navigable airspace. The area above the legally established minimum flight altitudes, including the area needed to ensure safe takeoffs and landings of aircraft. 49 USCA § 40102(a)(30).

navigable sea. *Int'l law.* The ocean waters divided into three zones of control among nations: (1) the inland waters, which are near a nation's shores and over which a nation has complete sovereignty; (2) territorial waters, which are measured from the seaward edge of the inland waters, over which a nation has extensive control but over which innocent parties must be allowed to travel to other nations; and (3) the high seas, which are international waters not subject to the domain of any single nation.

navigable water. 1. At early common law, any body of water affected by the ebb and flow of the tide. • This test was first adopted in England because most of England's in-fact navigable waters are influenced by the tide, unlike the large inland rivers that are capable of supporting commerce in the United States.

> "[N]avigable waters in English admiralty law generally were defined as those waters subject to the ebb and flow of the tide. This limitation was acceptable for an American nation composed of states along the Atlantic coast, where inland streams generally were not used for commerce beyond the reach of tidal fluctuations. However, the expansion of the American nation westward resulted in the use for water-borne commerce of a number of important streams — most notably the Mississippi River — to carry goods and people far beyond the effect of tide waters." Frank L. Maraist, *Admiralty in a Nutshell* 18 (2d ed. 1988).

2. (*usu. pl.*) A body of water that is used, or typically can be used, as a highway for commerce with ordinary modes of trade and travel on water. • Under the Commerce Clause, Congress has broad jurisdiction over all navigable waters in the United States.

navigable water of the United States. Navigable water that alone — or in combination with other waters — forms a continuous highway for commerce with other states or foreign countries.

navigate, *vb.* **1.** To travel or sail in a vessel on water <to navigate from New York to Bermuda>. **2.** To steer <to navigate the plane>. **3.** To make way through, on, or about something <the plaintiff was unable to navigate the stairs in the dark>.

navigation. 1. The act of sailing vessels on water. **2.** The process and business of directing the course of a vessel from one place to another. See RULES OF NAVIGATION.

navigation servitude. 1. An easement allowing the federal government to regulate commerce on navigable water without having to pay compensation for interference with private ownership rights. See NAVIGABLE WATER.

> "The navigation servitude, because of its link to navigable waters and the protection of navigation, is often confused with the public trust doctrine. The navigation servitude, however, is a paramount federal servitude on navigable waters based on the commerce power rather than on ownership or trust responsibilities." Donna R. Christie, *Coastal and Ocean Management Law in a Nutshell* 34 (1994).

2. An easement, based on the state police power or public trust doctrine, that allows a state to regulate commerce on navigable water and provide limited compensation for interference with private ownership rights. • The state servitude is inferior to the federal servitude.

navis (**nay**-vis), *n.* [Latin] A ship; a vessel.

navy. 1. A fleet of ships. **2.** The military sea force of a country, including its collective ships and its corps of officers and enlisted personnel; esp. (*usu. cap.*), the division of the U.S. armed services responsible primarily for seagoing forces. • The U.S. Constitution gives Congress the power to establish a navy and make laws governing the naval forces. U.S. Const. art. I, § 8, cl. 13–14.

Navy Department. A division of the Department of Defense that oversees the operation and efficiency of the Navy, including the Marine Corps component (and the U.S. Coast Guard when operating as a naval service). • Established in 1798, the Department is headed by the Secretary of the Navy, who is appointed by the President and reports to the Secretary of Defense.

nazeranna (naz-ə-**ran**-ə). *Hist.* The amount that a person pays to the government as an acknowledgment for public office or a grant of public lands.

N.B. *abbr.* [Latin *nota bene*] Note well; take notice — used in documents to call attention to something important.

NBA. *abbr.* NATIONAL BAR ASSOCIATION.

NCCUSL (nə-**k**[**y**]**oo**-səl). *abbr.* NATIONAL CONFERENCE OF COMMISSIONERS ON UNIFORM STATE LAWS.

n.c.d. *abbr.* NEMINE CONTRA DICENTE.

N.D. *abbr.* Northern District, in reference to U.S. judicial districts.

ne admittas (nee ad-**mit**-əs), *n.* [Latin "that you admit not"] *Eccles. law.* A writ prohibiting a bishop, usu. in a *quare impedit* action, from admitting the other party's clerk to be a parson of a church. • After a party institutes a *quare impedit* action to enforce a right to propose a clerk to the position of parson of a vacant church (right of advowson), that party can resort to the *ne admittas* writ if it is believed that the bishop will admit another person's proposed clerk before the *quare impedit* action concludes. See QUARE IMPEDIT.

neap tide. See TIDE.

near, *adv.* **1.** Close to; not far away, as a measure of distance <the neighbors' houses are near one another>. **2.** Almost; close in degree <a near miss>. **3.** Closely tied by blood <my brother is a near relative>. **4.** Familiar; intimate <a near friend>.

near money. See *current asset* under ASSET.

neat, *adj.* **1.** Clean; pure. **2.** Free from extraneous matter.

neat weight. See *net weight* under WEIGHT.

ne baila pas (nə **bay**-lə **pah**), *n.* [Law French "he or she did not deliver"] In an action for detinue, a defendant's plea denying the receipt of the property in question.

necation (ni-**kay**-shən), *n.* [fr. Latin *necare* "to kill"] *Hist.* The act of killing.

necessaries. 1. Things that are indispensable to living <an infant's necessaries include food, shelter, and clothing>. — Also termed *necessities of life.* **2.** Things that are essential to maintaining the lifestyle to which one is accustomed <a multimillionaire's necessaries may include a chauffeured limousine and a private chef>. • The term includes whatever is reasonably needed for subsistence, health, comfort, and education, considering the person's age, station in life, and medical condition, but it excludes (1) anything purely ornamental, (2) anything solely for pleasure, (3) what the person is already supplied with, (4) anything that concerns someone's estate or business as opposed to personal needs, and (5) borrowed money.

> "Things may be of a useful character, but the quality or quantity supplied may take them out of the character of necessaries. Elementary textbooks might be a necessary to a student of law, but not a rare edition of 'Littleton's Tenures,' or eight or ten copies of 'Stephen's Commentaries.' Necessaries also vary according to the station in life of the infant or his peculiar circumstances at the time. The quality of clothing suitable to an Eton boy would be unnecessary for a telegraph clerk; the medical attendance and diet required by an invalid would be unnecessary to one in ordinary health. It does not follow therefore that because a thing is of a useful class, a judge is bound to allow a jury to say whether or no it is a necessary." William R. Anson, *Principles of the Law of Contract* 172 (Arthur L. Corbin ed., 3d Am. ed. 1919).

necessarily included offense. See *lesser included offense* under OFFENSE (1).

necessarius (ne-sə-**sair**-ee-əs), *adj.* [Latin] **1.** Necessary; essential. **2.** Unavoidable; obligatory; compelling.

necessary and proper, *adj.* Being appropriate and well adapted to fulfilling an objective.

Necessary and Proper Clause. The clause of the U.S. Constitution permitting Congress to make laws "necessary and proper" for the execution of its enumerated powers. U.S. Const. art. I, § 8, cl. 18. • The Supreme Court has broadly interpreted this clause to grant Congress the implied power to enact any law reasonably designed to achieve an express constitutional power. *McCulloch v. Maryland,* 17 U.S. (4 Wheat.) 316 (1819). — Also termed *Basket Clause*; *Coefficient Clause*; *Elastic Clause*; *Sweeping Clause.*

necessary damages. See *general damages* under DAMAGES.

necessary deposit. See DEPOSIT (5).

necessary diligence. See DILIGENCE.

necessary domicile. See DOMICILE.

necessary implication. See IMPLICATION.

necessary improvement. See IMPROVEMENT.

necessary inference. A conclusion that is unavoidable if the premise on which it is based is taken to be true.

necessary intromission. See INTROMISSION.

necessary party. See PARTY (2).

necessary repair. An improvement to property that is both needed to prevent deterioration and proper under the circumstances.

necessary way. See *easement by necessity* under EASEMENT.

necessitas (nə-**ses**-i-tas), *n.* [Latin] *Roman law.* **1.** Necessity. **2.** A force or influence that compels an unwilling person to act. • The term refers to a lack of free will to do a legal act, as opposed to *libera voluntas* ("free will").

necessitas culpabilis (nə-**ses**-i-tas kəl-**pay**-bə-lis). [Latin "culpable necessity"] *Hist.* An unfortunate necessity that, while essentially excusing the act done under its compulsion, does not necessarily relieve the actor from blame.

> "And as to the necessity which excuses a man who kills another *se defendendo* lord Bacon entitles it *necessitas culpabilis* .... For the law intends that the quarrel or assault arose from some unknown wrong ... and since in quarrels both parties may be, and usually are, in some fault; and it scarce can be tried who was originally in the wrong; the law will not hold the survivor entirely guiltless. But it is clear, in the other case, that where I kill a thief that breaks into my house, the original default can never be upon my side." 4 William Blackstone, *Commentaries on the Laws of England* 186–87 (1769).

necessities. 1. Indispensable things of any kind. **2.** NECESSARIES.

necessities of life. See NECESSARIES (1).

necessitous, *adj.* Living in a state of extreme want; hard up.

necessitous circumstances. The situation of one who is very poor; extreme want.

necessitudo (nə-ses-i-**t[y]oo**-doh), *n.* [Latin "need"] *Hist.* **1.** An obligation. **2.** A close connection or relationship between persons, such as a family relationship.

necessity. 1. *Criminal law.* A justification defense for a person who acts in an emergency that he or she did not create and who commits a harm that is less severe than the harm that would have occurred but for the person's actions. • For example, a mountain climber lost in a blizzard can assert necessity as a defense to theft of food and blankets from another's cabin. — Also termed *choice of evils*; *duress of circumstances.* **2.** *Torts.* A privilege that may relieve a person from liability for trespass or conversion if that person, having no alternative, harms another's property in an effort to protect life or health.

> "In some cases even damage intentionally done may not involve the defendant in liability when he is acting under necessity to prevent a greater evil. The precise limits of the defence are not clear, for it has affinities with certain other defences, such as act of God, self-help, duress, or inevitable accident. It is distinguishable from self-defence on the ground that this presupposes that the plaintiff is prima facie a wrongdoer: the defence of necessity contemplates the infliction of harm on an innocent plaintiff. The defence, if it exists, enables a defendant to escape liability for the intentional interference with the security of another's person or property on the ground that the acts complained of were necessary to prevent greater damage to the commonwealth or to another or to the defendant himself, or to their or his property. The use of the term necessity serves to conceal the fact that the defendant always has a choice between two evils. This is what distinguishes the defence of necessity from that of impossibility." R.F.V. Heuston, *Salmond on the Law of Torts* 493 (17th ed. 1977).

moral necessity. A necessity arising from a duty incumbent on a person to act in a particular way.

physical necessity. A necessity involving an actual, tangible force that compels a person to act in a particular way.

private necessity. *Torts.* A necessity that involves only the defendant's personal interest and thus provides only a limited privilege. • For example, if the defendant harms the plaintiff's dock by keeping a boat moored to the dock during a hurricane, the defendant can assert private necessity but must compensate the plaintiff for the dock's damage.

public necessity. *Torts.* A necessity that involves the public interest and thus completely excuses the defendant's liability. • For example, if the defendant destroys the plaintiff's house to stop the spread of a fire that threatens the town, the defendant can assert public necessity.

necessity defense. See JUSTIFICATION (2).

neck verse. *Hist.* A verse, usu. consisting of the opening verse of Psalm 51 (*Miserere mei, Deus* "Have mercy on me, O God"), which was used as a literacy test for an accused who claimed benefit of clergy. • An accused who read the passage satisfactorily would not receive the maximum sentence (the person's neck would be saved). Although judges could assign any passage, they usu. chose Psalm 51, so that for many years criminals memorized this verse and pretended to read it. Still, the records show that many accused persons failed the test. The reading of the neck verse was abolished in 1707. See BENEFIT OF CLERGY.

> "During the fourteenth and fifteenth centuries the judges' attitudes to benefit of clergy changed completely, and they came to see it as a regular means of escape from the mandatory death penalty. Physical appearance was disregarded, and reading became the sole test of clerical status. When a man was convicted of a felony, he would fall on his knees and'pray the book'; he would then be tendered a passage from the psalter, known as the neck-verse, and if he could read or recite it satisfactorily his clergy was taken to be proved .... Strictly speaking, the decision whether the convict read'as a clerk' was for the ordinary; but he was subject to the control of the judges, and could be fined for refusing to accept someone. By the end of the sixteenth century as many as half of all men convicted of felony were recorded as having successfully claimed benefit of clergy." J.H. Baker, *An Introduction to English Legal History* 587 (3d ed. 1990).

necropsy (**nek**-rop-see). See AUTOPSY (1).

ne disturba pas (nə di-**stər**-bə **pah**), *n.* [Law French "did not disturb"] *Eccles. law.* A defendant's general denial (plea of the general issue) in a *quare impedit* action. See QUARE IMPEDIT.

ne dona pas (nə **doh**-nə **pah**), *n.* [Law French "did not give"] *Hist.* A defendant's general denial (plea of the general issue) in a formedon action, alleging that the plaintiff was given the right to land under a gift of tail. — Also termed *non dedit.* See FORMEDON.

nee (nay), *adj.* [French] (Of a woman) born. • This term is sometimes used after a married woman's name to indicate her maiden name <Mrs. Robert Jones nee Thatcher>. — Also spelled *née.*

need, *n.* **1.** The lack of something important; a requirement. **2.** Indigence. — **need,** *vb.*

needy, *adj.* **1.** Needful; necessary. **2.** Indigent; very poor. • *Needy* implies a more permanent and less urgent condition than *necessitous.* See NECESSITOUS.

ne exeat republica (nee **ek**-see-ət [*or* **ek**-see-at] ri-**pəb**-li-kəh), *n.* [Latin "let him not go out of the republic"] **1.** A writ restraining a person from leaving the republic. **2.** A chancery writ ordering the person to whom it is addressed not to leave the jurisdiction of the court or the state. • *Ne exeat* writs — no longer widely used — are usu. issued to ensure the satisfaction of a claim against the defendant. — Often shortened to *ne exeat.* — Also termed *writ of ne exeat; ne exeat regno.*

> "The district courts of the United States ... shall have such jurisdiction to make and issue in civil actions, writs and orders of injunction, and of *ne exeat republica,* orders appointing receivers, and such other orders and processes ... as may be necessary or appropriate for the enforcement of the internal revenue laws." IRC (26 USCA) § 7402(a).

> "Such a writ [*ne exeat*] might be issued upon the commencement of the suit for equitable relief, during the pendency of the suit, or upon issuance of the final decree to secure its enforcement. But such writ related primarily to the person of the defendant and issued only upon satisfactory proof that he planned or intended to remove himself beyond the court's jurisdiction so that he might escape obedience to such command as might be or had been laid upon him. The writ has been frequently termed an equitable bail. It involves taking and keeping the defendant in custody until he gives bail or bond in a designated amount, conditioned upon his keeping himself amenable to the effective processes of the court." William Q. de Funiak, *Handbook of Modern Equity* 21 (2d ed. 1956).

nefas (**nee**-fas), *n.* [Latin *ne* "not" + *fas* "right"] **1.** *Roman law.* Something that the gods forbid. **2.** *Roman law.* Something against the law or custom. **3.** *Hist.* Something that is wicked.

nefastus (ni-**fas**-təs), *n.* [Latin *ne* "not" + *fastus* "lawful for public business"] *Roman law.* A day when it is unlawful to open the courts, administer justice, or hold public assemblies. • The priests in charge of supervising the laws and religious observances established an official calendar, on which certain days, marked "*nefasti,*" were to be devoted to religious or public ceremonies. — Also termed *dies nefasti.* Cf. *dies fasti* under DIES.

negate, *vb.* **1.** To deny. **2.** To nullify; to render ineffective.

negative, *adj.* **1.** Of or relating to something bad; not positive <a negative attitude>. **2.** Of or relating to refusal of consent; not affirmative <a negative answer>.

negative, *n.* **1.** A word or phrase of denial or refusal <"no" and "not" are negatives>. **2.** A word expressing the opposite of the positive <two negatives and one positive>. **3.** The original plate of a photograph, on which light and shadows are the opposite of the positive images later created and printed <not only the pictures, but also the negatives, were required to

be returned>. **4.** *Archaic.* The power of veto <the king's negative has eroded>.

negative, *vb.* To negate; to deny, nullify, or render ineffective <the jury negatived fraud>.

negative act. See ACT (2).

negative amortization. See AMORTIZATION.

negative averment. See AVERMENT.

negative cash flow. See CASH FLOW.

negative causation. See CAUSATION.

Negative Commerce Clause. See COMMERCE CLAUSE.

negative condition. See CONDITION (2).

negative contingent fee. See *reverse contingent fee* under CONTINGENT FEE.

negative covenant. See COVENANT (1).

negative duty. See DUTY (1).

negative easement. See EASEMENT.

negative evidence. See EVIDENCE.

negative externality. See EXTERNALITY.

negative misprision. See MISPRISION.

negative plea. See PLEA (3).

negative-pledge clause. 1. A provision requiring a borrower, who borrows funds without giving security, to refrain from giving future lenders any security without the consent of the first lender. **2.** A provision, usu. in a bond indenture, stating that the issuing entity will not pledge its assets if it will result in less security to the bondholders under the indenture agreement.

negative pregnant. A denial implying its affirmative opposite by seeming to deny only a qualification of the allegation and not the allegation itself. • An example is the statement, "I didn't steal the money last Tuesday," the implication being that the theft might have happened on another day. — Also termed *negative pregnant with an affirmative.* Cf. AFFIRMATIVE PREGNANT.

negative prescription. See PRESCRIPTION (3).

negative proof. See PROOF.

negative reprisal. See REPRISAL.

negative right. See RIGHT.

negative servitude. See SERVITUDE (1).

negative statute. See STATUTE.

negative testimony. See *negative evidence* under EVIDENCE.

negative veto. See *qualified veto* under VETO.

neglect, *n.* The omission of proper attention to a person or thing, whether inadvertent, negligent, or willful; the act or condition of disregarding. — **neglect,** *vb.* — **neglectful,** *adj.*

> " 'Neglect' is not the same thing as 'negligence'. In the present connection the word 'neglect' indicates, as a purely objective fact, that a person has not done that which it was his duty to do; it does not indicate the *reason* for this failure. 'Negligence,' on the other hand, is a subjective state of mind, and it indicates a particular reason why the man has failed to do his duty, namely because he has not kept the performance of the duty in his mind as he ought to have done. A man can 'neglect' his duty either intentionally or negligently." J.W. Cecil Turner, *Kenny's Outlines of Criminal Law* 108 n.1 (16th ed. 1952).

child neglect. See CHILD NEGLECT.

culpable neglect. Censurable or blameworthy neglect; neglect that is less than gross carelessness but more than the failure to use ordinary care.

excusable neglect. A failure — which the law will excuse — to take some proper step at the proper time (esp. in neglecting to answer a lawsuit) not because of the party's own carelessness, inattention, or willful disregard of the court's process, but because of some unexpected or unavoidable hindrance or accident or because of reliance on the care and vigilance of the party's counsel or on a promise made by the adverse party.

inexcusable neglect. Unjustifiable neglect; neglect that implies more than unintentional inadvertence. • A finding of inexcusable neglect in, for example, failing to file an answer to a complaint will prevent the setting aside of a default judgment.

willful neglect. Intentional neglect; deliberate neglect.

neglected child. See CHILD.

neglect hearing. A judicial hearing involving alleged child abuse or some other situation in which a child has not been properly cared for. • Depending on the jurisdiction, this type of hearing might take place in various types of courts, such as a family court, a juvenile court, a probate court, or a district court.

negligence, *n.* **1.** The failure to exercise the standard of care that a reasonably prudent person would have exercised in a similar situation; any conduct that falls below the legal standard established to protect others against unreasonable risk of harm, except for conduct that is intentionally, wantonly, or willfully disregardful of others' rights. • The term denotes culpable carelessness. The Roman-law equivalents are *culpa* and *negligentia*, as contrasted with *dolus* (wrongful intention). — Also termed *actionable negligence*; *ordinary negligence*; *simple negligence*. **2.** A tort grounded in this failure, usu. expressed in terms of the following elements: duty, breach of duty, causation, and damages.

> "Negligence in law ranges from inadvertence that is hardly more than accidental to sinful disregard of the safety of others." Patrick Devlin, *The Enforcement of Morals* 36 (1968).

> "During the first half of the nineteenth century, negligence began to gain recognition as a separate and independent basis of tort liability. Its rise coincided in a marked degree with the Industrial Revolution; and it very probably was stimulated by the rapid increase in the number of accidents caused by industrial machinery, and in particular by the invention of railways. It was greatly encouraged by the disintegration of the old forms of action, and the disappearance of the distinction between direct and indirect injuries, found in trespass and case .... Intentional injuries, whether direct or indirect, began to be grouped as a distinct field of liability, and negligence remained as the main basis for unintended torts. Negligence thus developed into the dominant cause of action for accidental injury in this nation today." W. Page Keeton et al., *The Law of Torts* § 28, at 161 (W. Page Keeton ed., 5th ed. 1984).

> "Negligence is a matter or risk — that is to say, of recognizable danger of injury .... In most instances, it is caused by heedlessness or inadvertence, by which the negligent party is unaware of the results which may follow from his act. But is may also arise where the negligent party has considered the possible consequences carefully, and has exercised his own best judgment. The almost universal use of the phrase 'due care' to describe conduct which is not negligent should not obscure the fact that the essence of negligence is not necessarily the absence of solicitude for those who may be adversely affected by one's actions but is instead behavior which should be recognized as involving unreasonable danger to others." W. Page Keeton et al., *The Law of Torts* § 31, at 169 (5th ed. 1984).

active negligence. Negligence resulting from an affirmative or positive act, such as driving through a barrier. Cf. *passive negligence*.

advertent negligence. Negligence in which the actor is aware of the unreasonable risk that he or she is creating; RECKLESSNESS. — Also termed *willful negligence*.

collateral negligence. An independent contractor's negligence, for which the employer is generally not liable. See COLLATERAL-NEGLIGENCE DOCTRINE.

comparative negligence. A plaintiff's own negligence that proportionally reduces the damages recoverable from a defendant. — Also termed *comparative fault*. See COMPARATIVE-NEGLIGENCE DOCTRINE.

concurrent negligence. The negligence of two or more parties acting independently but causing the same damage. Cf. *joint negligence*.

contributory negligence. **1.** A plaintiff's own negligence that played a part in causing the plaintiff's injury and that is significant enough (in a few jurisdictions) to bar the plaintiff from recovering damages. • In most jurisdictions, this defense has been superseded by comparative negligence. See CONTRIBUTORY-NEGLIGENCE DOCTRINE. **2.** *Rare.* The negligence of a third party — neither the plaintiff nor the defendant — whose act or omission played a part in causing the plaintiff's injury.

> "The contributory negligence of a third party is no excuse for the negligence of the defendant." Thomas E. Holland, *The Elements of Jurisprudence* 154 (13th ed. 1924).

criminal negligence. Gross negligence so extreme that it is punishable as a crime. • For example, involuntary manslaughter or other negligent homicide can be based on criminal negligence, as when an extremely careless automobile driver kills someone. — Also termed *culpable negligence*; *gross negligence*.

> "Though the legislatures and the courts have often made it clear that criminal liability generally requires more fault than the ordinary negligence which will do for tort liability, they have not so often made it plain just what is required in addition to tort negligence — greater risk, subjective awareness of the risk, or both. Statutes are sometimes worded in terms of 'gross negligence' or 'culpable negligence' or 'criminal negligence,' without any further definition of these terms.... The courts thus have had to do their best with little guidance from the legislature, with varying results." Wayne R. LaFave & Austin W. Scott, Jr., *Criminal Law* § 3.7, at 235–37 (2d ed. 1986).

culpable negligence. Negligent conduct that, while not intentional, involves a disregard of the consequences likely to result from one's actions.

> " 'Culpable negligence,' while variously defined, has been held incapable of exact definition; it means something more than negligence .... In connection with negligence, the word 'culpable' is sometimes used in the sense of 'blamable,' and it has been regarded as expressing the thought of a breach of a duty or the commission of a fault; but culpable negligence has been held to amount to more than 'blameworthy' conduct .... It does not involve the element of intent .... On the other hand, it has been said to be intentional conduct which the actor may not intend to be harmful but which an ordinary and reasonably prudent man would recognize as involving a strong probability of injury to others." 65 C.J.S. *Negligence* § 1(13) (1966).

gross negligence. **1.** A lack of slight diligence or care. **2.** A conscious, voluntary act or omission in reckless disregard of a legal duty and of the consequences to another party, who may typically recover exemplary damages. — Also termed *reckless negligence*; *wanton negligence*; *willful negligence*; *willful and wanton negligence*; *hazardous negligence*. **3.** See *criminal negligence*.

> "Negligence is gross if the precautions to be taken against harm are very simple, such as persons who are but poorly endowed with physical and mental capacities can easily take." H.L.A. Hart, "Negligence, *Mens Rea* and Criminal Responsibility," in *Punishment and Responsibility* 136, 149 (1968).

> "*Gross Negligence.* As it originally appeared, this was very great negligence, or the want of even slight or scant care. It has been described as a failure to exercise even that care which a careless person would use. Several courts, however, dissatisfied with a term so nebulous ... have construed gross negligence as requiring willful, wanton, or reckless misconduct, or such utter lack of all care as will be evidence thereof .... But it is still true that most courts consider that 'gross negligence' falls short of a reckless disregard of the consequences, and differs from ordinary negligence only in degree, and not in kind." *Prosser and Keeton on the Law of Torts* § 34, at 211–12 (W. Page Keeton ed., 5th ed. 1984).

hazardous negligence. **1.** Careless or reckless conduct that exposes someone to extreme danger of injury or to imminent peril. **2.** See *gross negligence*.

imputed negligence. Negligence of one person charged to another; negligence resulting from a party's special relationship with another party who is originally negligent — so that, for example, a parent might be held responsible for some acts of a child.

inadvertent negligence. Negligence in which the actor is not aware of the unreasonable risk that he or she is creating, but should have foreseen and avoided it. — Also termed *simple negligence*.

joint negligence. The negligence of two or more persons acting together to cause an accident. Cf. *concurrent negligence*.

legal negligence. See *negligence per se*.

negligence in law. Failure to observe a duty imposed by law. See *negligence per se*; *legal negligence*.

negligence per se. Negligence established as a matter of law, so that breach of the duty is not a jury question. • Negligence per se usu. arises from a statutory violation. — Also termed *legal negligence*.

ordinary negligence. Lack of ordinary diligence; the failure to use ordinary care. • The term is most commonly used to differentiate between *negligence* and *gross negligence*.

passive negligence. Negligence resulting from a person's failure or omission in acting, such as failing to remove hazardous conditions from public property. Cf. *active negligence*.

professional negligence. See MALPRACTICE.

reckless negligence. See *gross negligence*.

simple negligence. See *inadvertent negligence*.

slight negligence. The failure to exercise the great care of an extraordinarily prudent person, resulting in liability in special circumstances (esp. those involving bailments or carriers) in which lack of ordinary care would not result in liability; lack of great diligence.

subsequent negligence. The negligence of the defendant when, after the defendant's initial negligence and the plaintiff's contributory negligence, the defendant discovers — or should have discovered — that the plaintiff was in a position of danger and fails to exercise due care in preventing the plaintiff's injuries. — Also termed *supervening negligence*. See LAST-CLEAR-CHANCE DOCTRINE.

tax negligence. Negligence arising out of the disregard of tax-payment laws, for which the Internal Revenue Service may impose a penalty — 5% of the amount underpaid. IRC (26 USCA) § 6651(a).

wanton negligence. See *gross negligence*.

willful and wanton negligence. See *gross negligence*.

willful negligence. See *advertent negligence*.

negligence rule. *Commercial law.* The principle that if a party's negligence contributes to an unauthorized signing or a material alteration in a negotiable instrument, that party is estopped from raising this issue against later parties who transfer or pay the instrument in good faith. • Examples of negligence include leaving blanks or spaces on the amount line of the instrument, erroneously mailing the instrument to a person with the same name as the payee, and failing to follow internal procedures designed to prevent forgeries.

negligent, *adj.* Characterized by a person's failure to exercise the degree of care that someone of ordinary prudence would have exercised in the same circumstance <the negligent driver went through the stop sign> <negligent construction caused the bridge to collapse>. **negligently,** *adv.*

"[A] careful consideration is needed of the differences between the meaning of expressions like 'inadvertently' and 'while his mind was a blank' on the one hand, and 'negligently' on the other. In ordinary English, and also in lawyers' English, when harm has resulted from someone's negligence, if we say of that person that he has acted negligently we are not thereby *merely* describing the frame of mind in which he acted. 'He negligently broke a saucer' is not the same *kind* of expression as 'he inadvertently broke a saucer'. The point of the adverb 'inadvertently' *is* merely to inform us of the agent's psychological state, whereas if we say 'He broke it negligently' we are not merely adding to this an element of blame or reproach, but something quite specific, viz. we are referring to the fact that the agent failed to comply with a standard of conduct with which any ordinary reasonable man *could* and *would* have complied: a standard requiring him to take precautions against harm. The word 'negligently', both in legal and in non-legal contexts, makes an essential reference to an omission to do what is thus required: it is not a flatly descriptive psychological expression like 'his mind was a blank'." H.L.A. Hart, "Negligence, *Mens Rea* and Criminal Responsibility," in *Punishment and Responsibility* 136, 147–48 (1968).

negligent entrustment. The act of leaving a dangerous article (such as a gun or car) with a person who the lender knows, or should know, is likely to use it in an unreasonably risky manner.

negligent escape. See ESCAPE (3).

negligent homicide. See HOMICIDE.

negligentia (neg-li-**jen**-shee-ə), *n.* [Latin] *Roman law.* Carelessness; inattentive omission. • *Negligentia* can be of varying degrees, which may or may not result in actionable liability. See CULPA. Cf. DILIGENTIA.

"In the sources *negligentia* is tantamount to *culpa*, and similarly graduated (*magna, lata negligentia*). Precision in terminology is no more to be found here than in the field of *culpa*. One text declares ... 'gross negligence (*magna negligentia*) is *culpa*, *magna culpa* is *dolus*'; another says: 'gross negligence (*dissoluta negligentia*) is near to *dolus* (*prope dolum*).' In the saying '*lata culpa* is exorbitant (extreme) negligence, i.e., not to understand (*intelligere*) what all understand' ... *negligentia* is identified with ignorance." Adolf Berger, *Encyclopedic Dictionary of Roman Law* 593 (1953).

lata negligentia (**lay**-tə neg-li-**jen**-shee-ə). Extreme negligence resulting from an unawareness of something that the actor should have known.

magna negligentia (**mag**-nə neg-li-**jen**-shee-ə). See *gross negligence* under NEGLIGENCE.

negligent infliction of emotional distress. The tort of causing another severe emotional distress through one's negligent conduct. • Most courts will allow a plaintiff to recover damages for emotional distress if the defendant's conduct results in physical contact with the plaintiff, or, when no contact occurs, if the plaintiff is in the zone of danger. See EMOTIONAL DISTRESS; ZONE-OF-DANGER RULE. Cf. INTENTIONAL INFLICTION OF EMOTIONAL DISTRESS.

negligent manslaughter. See *involuntary manslaughter* under MANSLAUGHTER.

negligent misrepresentation. See MISREPRESENTATION.

negligent offense. See OFFENSE (1).

négoce (ni-**gohs**), *n.* [French] Trade; business.

negotiability. The capability of commercial paper to have its title transferred by indorsement and delivery, or by delivery alone, so that the transferee has a rightful claim on it. • Negotiability (which pertains to commercial paper) differs from assignability (which pertains to contracts in general) because an assignee traditionally takes title subject to all equities, and an assignment is not complete without notice to the debtor, whereas an indorsee takes free of all equities and without any notice to the debtor.

negotiable, *adj.* **1.** (Of a written instrument) capable of being transferred by delivery or indorsement when the transferee takes the instrument for value, in good faith, and without notice of conflicting title claims or defenses. **2.** (Of a deal, agreement, etc.) capable of being accomplished. **3.** (Of a price or deal) subject to further bargaining and possible change. Cf. NONNEGOTIABLE; ASSIGNABLE.

"The term 'negotiable,' in its enlarged signification, is used to describe any written security which may be transferred by indorsement and delivery, or by delivery merely, so as to vest in the indorsee the legal title, and thus enable him to bring a suit thereon in his own name. But in a strictly commercial classification, and as the term is technically used, it applies only to those instruments which, like bills of exchange, not only carry the legal title with them by indorsement, or delivery, but carry as well, when transferred before maturity, the right of the transferee to demand the full amounts which their faces call for. 'Assignable' is the more appropriate term to describe bonds, and ordinary notes, or notes of hand as they are most commonly called; as 'negotiable' is the more fitting term to describe the peculiar instruments of commerce." 1 John W. Daniel, *A Treatise on the Law of Negotiable Instruments* § 2, at 3 (Thomas H. Calvert ed., 7th ed. 1933).

negotiable bill of lading. See BILL OF LADING.

negotiable bond. See BOND (2).

negotiable certificate of deposit. A security issued by a financial institution as a short-term source of funds, usu. with a fixed interest rate and maturity of one year or less.

negotiable document of title. See DOCUMENT OF TITLE.

negotiable instrument. A written instrument that (1) is signed by the maker or drawer, (2) includes an unconditional promise or order to pay a specified sum of money, (3) is payable on demand or at a definite time, and (4) is payable to order or to bearer. UCC § 3–104(a). — Also termed *negotiable paper*; *negotiable note*. • Among the various types of negotiable instruments are bills of exchange, promissory notes, bank checks, certificates of deposit, and other negotiable securities.

"What are called 'negotiable instruments,' or 'paper to bearer,' such as bills of exchange, or promissory notes, do really pass from hand to hand, either by delivery or indorsement, giving to each successive recipient a right against the debtor, to which no notice to the debtor is essential, and which, if the paper is held bona fide and for value, is unaffected by flaws in the title of intermediate assignors." Thomas E. Holland, *The Elements of Jurisprudence* 315–16 (13th ed. 1924).

"One must first understand that a negotiable instrument is a peculiar animal and that many animals calling for the payment of money and others loosely called 'commercial paper' are not negotiable instruments and not subject to the rules of Article 3." James J. White & Robert S. Summers, 2 *Uniform Commercial Code* § 16–1, at 70 (4th ed. 1995).

negotiable note. See NEGOTIABLE INSTRUMENT.

negotiable order of withdrawal. A negotiable instrument (such as a check) payable on demand and issued against funds deposited with a financial institution. — Abbr. NOW.

negotiable-order-of-withdrawal account. See *NOW account* under ACCOUNT.

negotiable paper. See NEGOTIABLE INSTRUMENT.

negotiable words. The terms and phrases that make a document a negotiable instrument. — Also termed *words of negotiability*. See NEGOTIABLE INSTRUMENT.

negotiate, *vb.* **1.** To communicate with another party for the purpose of reaching an understanding <they negotiated with their counterparts for weeks on end>. **2.** To bring about by discussion or bargaining <she negotiated a software license agreement>. **3.** To transfer (an instrument) by delivery or indorsement, whereby the transferee takes the instrument for value, in good faith, and without notice of conflicting title claims or defenses <Jones negotiated the check at the neighborhood bank>.

negotiated market. See MARKET.

negotiated offering. See OFFERING.

negotiated plea. See PLEA (1).

negotiating bank. A financial institution that discounts or purchases drafts drawn under a letter of credit issued by another bank.

negotiation, *n.* **1.** A consensual bargaining process in which the parties attempt to reach agreement on a disputed or potentially disputed matter. • Negotiation usu. involves complete autonomy for the parties involved, without the intervention of third parties.

"Negotiation, we may say, ought strictly to be viewed simply as a means to an end; it is the road the parties must travel to arrive at their goal of mutually satisfactory settlement. But like other means, negotiation is easily converted into an end in itself; it readily becomes a game played for its own sake and a game played with so little reserve by those taken up with it that they will sacrifice their own ultimate interests in order to win it." Lon L. Fuller, *Anatomy of the Law* 128 (1968).

2. (*usu. pl.*) Dealings conducted between two or more parties for the purpose of reaching an understanding. **3.** The transfer of an instrument by delivery or indorsement whereby the transferee takes it for value, in good faith, and without notice of conflicting title claims or defenses. — **negotiate,** *vb.* — **negotiable,**

adj. — **negotiability,** *n.* See HOLDER IN DUE COURSE.

due negotiation. The transfer of a negotiable document of title so that the transferee takes it free of certain claims enforceable against the transferor. • This is the good-faith-purchase exception to the doctrine of derivative title. UCC §§ 7–501(4); 7–502(1).

negotiation letter of credit. See LETTER OF CREDIT.

negotiorum gestio (ni-goh-shee-**or**-əm **jes**-chee-oh), *n.* [Latin "management of affairs"] *Roman & civil law.* A quasi-contractual situation in which an actor (*negotiorum gestor*) manages or interferes in the business transaction of another person (*dominus negotii*) in that person's absence, done without authority but out of concern or friendship. • By such conduct, the actor was bound to conduct the matter to a conclusion and to deliver the transaction's proceeds to the person, who likewise was bound to reimburse the actor for any expenses incurred. A *negotiorum gestio* did not exist if the *gestor* acted self-interestedly or if the owner expressly forbade the *gestor* from acting on the owner's behalf.

negotiorum gestor (ni-goh-shee-**or**-əm **jes**-tor), *n.* [Latin "a manager of affairs"] *Roman & civil law.* A person who volunteers to render some necessary service to property, or to a business, in the absence of its owner. • This person has a claim to be compensated by the owner for the trouble taken, and the owner has a claim for any loss that results from the *negotiorum gestor*'s fault. — Sometimes shortened to *gestor.* See NEGOTIORUM GESTIO.

negotium (ni-**goh**-shee-əm), *n.* [Latin] *Roman law.* **1.** A matter; an affair, as in *negotium absentis*, a matter concerning an absent person. **2.** A transaction; an agreement. **3.** A trade; a business. **4.** A civil or criminal trial. Pl. ***negotia.***

n.e.i. *abbr.* NON EST INVENTUS.

neife (neef), *n.* [Law French] *Hist.* A person born into bondage or serfdom; specif., a female serf. — Also spelled *naif*; *neif*; *niefe.*

> "For the children of villeins were also in the same state of bondage with their parents; whence they were called in Latin, *nativi*, which gave rise to the female appellation of a villein, who was called a *neife.*" 2 William Blackstone, *Commentaries on the Laws of England* 93–94 (1766).

neighbor, *n.* **1.** A person who lives near another <Jensen's neighbor spotted the fire>. **2.** A person or thing situated near something <Canada is the United States' neighbor to the north>. **3.** A person in relation to humankind <love thy neighbor>.

neighborhood. 1. The immediate vicinity; the area near or next to a specified place. **2.** People living in a particular vicinity, usu. forming a community within a larger group and having similar economic statuses and social interests. **3.** The condition of being close together.

neighborhood effect. See EXTERNALITY.

neighboring rights. *Copyright.* The intellectual-property rights of performers, producers of sound recordings, and broadcasters. • Each of these right-holders creates something deserving of copyright protection, but these rights are less central to copyright law than such highly creative productions as novels and sculptures.

neighbor principle. The doctrine that one must take reasonable care to avoid acts or omissions that one can reasonably foresee will be likely to injure one's neighbor. • According to this principle, *neighbor* includes all persons who are so closely and directly affected by the act that the actor should reasonably think of them when engaging in the act or omission in question.

ne injuste vexes (nee in-**jəs**-tee **vek**-seez), *n.* [Law Latin "do not trouble unjustly"] *Hist.* A writ prohibiting a lord from demanding more services from a tenant than the tenure allowed.

> "The writ of *ne injuste vexes* ... which prohibits distresses for greater services than are really due to the lord; being itself of the prohibitory kind, and yet in the nature of a writ of right. It lies, where the tenant in fee-simple and his ancestors have held of the lord by certain services; and the lord hath obtained seisin of more or greater services, by the inadvertent payment or performance of them by the tenant himself. Here the tenant cannot ... avoid the lord's possessory right, because of the seisin given by his own hands; but is driven to this writ, to devest the lord's possession, and establish the mere right of property, by ascertaining the services, and reducing them to their proper standard." 3 William Blackstone, *Commentaries on the Laws of England* 234 (1768).

neither party. A docket entry reflecting the parties' agreement not to continue to appear to prosecute and defend a lawsuit. • This entry is equivalent to a dismissal.

ne luminibus officiatur (nee loo-**min**-i-bəs ə-fish-ee-**ay**-tər), *n.* [Latin "not impede light"] *Roman law.* A servitude restraining a home-owner from constructing anything that blocks light to an adjoining house.

nemine contradicente (**nem**-i-nee kahn-trə-di-**sen**-tee). [fr. Latin *nemo* "nobody" + *contradicere* "contradict"] Without opposition or dissent. • This phrase expresses the lack of opposition by members of a court, legislative body, or other group to a resolution or vote <the motion passed *nemine contradicente*>. It is used in the English House of Commons. — Abbr. *nem. con.*; *n.c.d.* — Also termed *nemine dissentiente.*

nemine dissentiente (**nem**-i-nee di-sen-shee-**en**-tee). [fr. Latin *nemo* "nobody" + *dissentio* "dissents"] NEMINE CONTRADICENTE. • This phrase is used in the House of Lords. — Abbr. *nem dis.*; *n.d.*

nemo (**nee**-moh), *n.* [Latin] No one; no man. • This term is the first word of many Latin maxims, such as *nemo est supra leges* ("no one is above the law").

neonaticide. See INFANTICIDE.

NEPA (**nee**-pə). *abbr.* NATIONAL ENVIRONMENTAL POLICY ACT.

nephew. 1. The son of a person's brother or sister; sometimes understood to include the son of a person's brother-in-law or sister-in-law. • This term is extended in some wills to include a grandnephew. **2.** *Hist.* A grandchild. **3.** *Hist.* A descendant.

> "*[N]ephew* . . . a son's or daughter's son, a grandson (also . . . a granddaughter), later also a brother's or sister's son, a nephew, in general a descendant . . . . The application, as with all other terms denoting relationship beyond the first degree, formerly varied ('grandson,' 'nephew,' 'cousin,' 'kinsman,' etc.); its final exclusive use for 'nephew' instead of 'grandson' is prob. due in part to the fact that, by reason of the great difference in age, a person has comparatively little to do with his grandsons, if he has any, while nephews are proverbially present and attentive, if their uncle is of any importance." 5 *The Century Dictionary and Cyclopedia* 3968 (1895).

nepos (**nep**-ohs), *n.* [Latin] **1.** *Roman law.* A grandson. **2.** *Hist.* A nephew. • The term *nepos* later became *neveu* and then "nephew." See NEPHEW.

nepotism (**nep**-ə-tiz-əm), *n.* Bestowal of official favors (esp. in hiring) on one's relatives. — **nepotistic,** *adj.*

neptis (**nep**-tis), *n.* [Latin] *Hist.* **1.** A granddaughter. **2.** A female descendant.

ne relessa pas (nə rə-**les**-ə **pah**), *n.* [Law French "did not release"] A plaintiff's reply to a defendant's plea of release as a defense to liability in a case.

nerve-center test. A method courts sometimes use to determine the location of a company's principal place of business, by which the principal place of business is determined to be the location where the corporate officers, directors, and (sometimes) shareholders reside, and where they direct and control the corporation's activities.

net, *n.* **1.** An amount of money remaining after a sale, minus any deductions for expenses, commissions, and taxes. **2.** The gain or loss from a sale of stock. **3.** See *net weight* under WEIGHT.

net assets. See NET WORTH.

net asset value. The market value of a share in a mutual fund, computed by deducting any liabilities of the fund from its total assets and dividing the difference by the number of outstanding fund shares. — Abbr. NAV. — Also termed *asset value.* See MUTUAL FUND.

net balance. See *net proceeds* under PROCEEDS.

net book value. An asset's value as that value appears on an organization's books, less the asset's depreciation since the last valuation.

net-capital rules. *Securities.* Basic financial-responsibility standards adopted by the Securities and Exchange Commission under the Securities Exchange Act of 1934. • Under these rules, securities brokers are required to maintain a minimum level of capitalization and to maintain aggregate indebtedness at a level less than a specified multiple of the broker's net capital. 15 USCA § 78o(c)(3); SEC Rule 15c3–1 (17 CFR § 240.15c3–1).

net cash flow. See CASH FLOW.

net cost. See COST (1).

net earnings. See *net income* under INCOME.

net estate. See ESTATE.

nether house of Parliament. *Hist.* The lower house of Parliament; the English House of

Commons. • This name was given to the House of Commons at the time of Henry VIII.

net income. See INCOME.

net investment. See INVESTMENT.

net lease. See LEASE.

net level annual premium. See PREMIUM (1).

net listing. See LISTING (1).

net loss. See LOSS.

net national product. The total value of goods and services produced in a country during a specific period, after deducting capital replacement costs.

net-net-net lease. See LEASE.

net operating asset. See ASSET.

net operating income. See INCOME.

net operating loss. See LOSS.

net position. 1. The difference between long and short contracts held by a securities or commodities trader. **2.** The amount gained or lost because of a change in the value of a stock or commodity.

net premium. See PREMIUM (1).

net present value. See PRESENT VALUE.

net price. See PRICE.

net proceeds. See PROCEEDS.

net profit. See PROFIT.

net quick assets. See ASSET; QUICK-ASSET RATIO.

net realizable value. 1. For a receivable, the amount of cash expected from the collection of present customer balances. **2.** For inventory, the selling price less the completion and disposal costs. **3.** An accounting method requiring the value of scrap or by-products to be treated as a reduction in the cost of the primary products.

net rent. See RENT (1).

net return. See RETURN.

net revenue. See *net profit* under PROFIT.

net sale. See SALE.

net sale contract. See *net listing* under LISTING.

net single premium. See PREMIUM (1).

net valuation premium. See *net premium* under PREMIUM (1).

net value. See VALUE.

net weight. See WEIGHT.

network element. *Telecommunications*. A facility or piece of equipment used to provide telecommunications service, as by a local-exchange network, and each feature, function, or capability of the service. 47 USCA § 153(29).

net worth. A measure of one's wealth, usu. calculated as the excess of total assets over total liabilities. — Also termed *net assets*.

net-worth method. The procedure the Internal Revenue Service uses to determine the taxable income of a taxpayer who doesn't keep adequate records. • The change in net worth for the year determines the taxpayer's gross income, after taking into account nontaxable receipts and nondeductible expenses.

net yield. See YIELD.

ne unques (nee **əng**-kweez). [Law French] Never.

ne unques accouple (nee **əng**-kweez ə-**kəp**-əl), *n.* [Law French "never married"] In a dower action by a widow to recover the estate of her deceased husband, a tenant's plea denying the woman's marriage to the decedent. See DOWER.

ne unques executor (nee **əng**-kweez ig-**zek**-yə-tər), *n.* [Law French "never executor"] A plea that the defendant or plaintiff is not an executor as alleged.

ne unques seise que dower (nee **əng**-kweez **see**-zee kə **dow**-ər), *n.* [Law French "never seised of a dowable estate"] *Hist.* In a dower action, the tenant's general denial (plea of general issue) that the widow's husband was never seised of a dowable estate of inheritance.

ne unques son receiver (nee **əng**-kweez sawn ri-**see**-vər), *n.* [Law French "never a receiver"] In an action for an accounting, the defendant's plea denying the receipt of anything from the plaintiff.

neutral, *adj.* **1.** Indifferent. **2.** (Of a judge, mediator, arbitrator, or actor in international law) refraining from taking sides in a dispute.

neutral, *n.* **1.** A person or country taking no side in a dispute. Cf. BELLIGERENT. **2.** A nonpartisan arbitrator typically selected by two other arbitrators — one of whom has been selected by each side in the dispute.

neutrality, *n.* The condition of a nation that in time of war takes no part in the dispute but continues peaceful dealings with the belligerents. — **neutral,** *adj.*

armed neutrality. A condition of neutrality that the neutral state is willing to maintain by military force.

neutrality law. *Int'l law.* An act that prohibits a nation from militarily aiding either of two or more belligerent powers with which the nation is at peace; esp., a federal statute forbidding acts — such as the equipping of armed vessels or the enlisting of troops — designed to assist either of two belligerents that are at peace with the United States. 22 USCA §§ 441–457.

neutrality proclamation. *Int'l law.* At the outbreak of a war between two nations, an announcement by the President that the United States is neutral and that its citizens may not violate the neutrality laws, as in the Neutrality Proclamation of 1793, issued during the war between France and Great Britain.

neutralization. 1. The act of making something ineffective. **2.** The process by which a country's integrity has been permanently guaranteed by international treaty, conditionally on its maintaining a perpetual neutrality except in its own defense. • Switzerland is the only remaining example, having been neutralized by the Treaty of Vienna in 1815 — a provision reaffirmed by the Treaty of Versailles in 1919. **3.** The act of declaring certain persons or property neutral and safe from capture. See NEUTRAL PROPERTY. **4.** *Evidence.* The cancellation of unexpected harmful testimony from a witness by showing, usu. by cross-examination, that the witness has made conflicting statements. • For example, a prosecutor may attempt to neutralize testimony of a state witness who offers unexpected adverse testimony. See IMPEACHMENT.

neutral principles. *Constitutional law.* Rules grounded in law, as opposed to rules based on personal interests or beliefs. • In this context, the phrase was popularized by Herbert Wechsler. See *Toward Neutral Principles of Constitutional Law*, 73 Harv. L. Rev. 1 (1959).

neutral property. Things belonging to citizens of a country that is not a party to a war, as long as the things are properly used and labeled. • For example, harmless neutral property aboard a captured belligerent ship would not normally be subject to seizure. But the hiding of explosives in otherwise neutral property could allow the property to be seized as contraband.

ne varietur (nee vair-ee-**ee**-tər), *n.* [Latin "it must not be altered"] A notation of identity that a person, usu. a notary, places on documents or translations of documents. • In Louisiana, this notation is typically placed on a collateral mortgage note to bind and identify the note with the collateral mortgage.

never indebted, plea of. A common-law traverse — or denial — by which the defendant in an action on a contract debt denies that an express or implied contract existed. See TRAVERSE.

new, *adj.* **1.** (Of a person, animal or thing) recently come into being <the new car was shipped from the factory this morning>. **2.** (Of any thing) recently discovered <a new cure for cancer>. **3.** (Of a person or condition) changed from the former state <she has a new state of mind>. **4.** Unfamiliar; unaccustomed <she asked for directions because she was new to the area>. **5.** Beginning afresh <a new day in court>.

new acquisition. See ACQUISITION.

new and useful. *Patents.* Two of the requirements for an invention to be patentable — namely, that the invention be novel and that it have practical utility. 35 USCA § 101. See PATENT (3).

new asset. See ASSET.

new assignment. See ASSIGNMENT (5).

new-business rule. The principle precluding an award of damages for lost profits to a business with no recent record of profitability, because the damages would be too speculative.

new cause of action. See CAUSE OF ACTION.

new-contract dispute. See *major dispute* under DISPUTE.

new debtor. See DEBTOR.

new-debtor syndrome. Conduct showing a debtor's bad faith in filing for bankruptcy, as a result of which the court may dismiss the bankruptcy petition. • An example is the debtor's formation of a corporation, immediately before the bankruptcy filing, solely to take advantage of the bankruptcy laws.

new drug. See DRUG.

new-for-old. 1. *Marine insurance.* In adjusting a partial marine-insurance loss, the principle that old materials apply toward payment of the new, so that the old material's value is deducted from the total repair expenses, and then from that balance one-third of the cost of repairs (one-third of the new materials for the old on the balance) is deducted and charged against the insured shipowner. — Also termed *deduction for new.* **2.** The principle that a party whose property has been damaged is entitled to recover only the amount necessary to restore the property to the condition it was in before the damage, instead of acquiring a new item to replace one that was old and depreciated.

New Inn. *Hist. English law.* One of the Inns of Chancery (collegiate houses) in which law students were placed before entering the Inns of Court. • This practice continued until approximately 1650, when the buildings began to be used only by attorneys and solicitors. See INNS OF CHANCERY. Cf. INNS OF COURT.

new issue. See ISSUE (2).

new-loan fee. See MORTGAGE DISCOUNT.

newly discovered evidence. See EVIDENCE.

new matter. See MATTER.

new promise. See PROMISE.

new-rule principle. *Criminal procedure.* A doctrine barring federal courts from granting habeas corpus relief to a state prisoner because of a rule, not dictated by existing precedent, announced after the prisoner's conviction and sentence became final. — Also termed *nonretroactivity principle.* See HABEAS CORPUS.

new ruling. *Criminal procedure.* A Supreme Court ruling not dictated by precedent existing when the defendant's conviction became final and thus not applicable retroactively to habeas cases. • For example, when the Court in *Ford v. Wainwright*, 477 U.S. 399, 106 S.Ct. 2595 (1986), ruled that the Eighth Amendment prohibits execution of insane prisoners, this new ruling was nonretroactive because it departed so widely from prior doctrine. *Teague v. Lane*, 489 U.S. 288, 109 S.Ct. 1060 (1989). See HABEAS CORPUS.

new series. See N.S.

newsman's privilege. See *journalist's privilege* (1) under PRIVILEGE (3).

newspaper. A publication for general circulation, usu. in sheet form, appearing at regular intervals, usu. daily or weekly, and containing matters of general public interest, such as current events.

> ***daily newspaper.*** A newspaper customarily published five to seven days every week. — Often shortened to *daily.*
>
> ***legal newspaper.*** A newspaper containing matters of legal interest including summaries of cases, legal advertisements, legislative or regulatory changes, and local bankruptcy notices.
>
> ***newspaper of general circulation.*** A newspaper that contains news and information of interest to the general public, rather than to a particular segment, and that is available to the public within a certain geographic area. • Legal notices (such as a class-action notice) are often required by law to be published in a newspaper of general circulation.
>
> ***official newspaper.*** A newspaper designated to contain all the public notices, resolves, acts, and advertisements of a state or municipal legislative body.

newspaper prospectus. See PROSPECTUS.

new style. The modern system for ordering time according to the Gregorian method, introduced by Pope Gregory XIII in 1582 and adopted in England and the American colonies in 1752. • Because the Julian calendar was slightly longer than the astronomical year, the vernal equinox was displaced by ten days. Pope Gregory reformed the calendar by announcing that October 5, 1582 would be called October 15. And, while generally retaining a leap year for years divisible by 4, he skipped leap years in years divisible by 100 (such as 1800 and 1900), but retained leap years for years divisible by 400 (such as 2000). Thus, the years 2000, 2004, 2008, etc. are leap years, but 2100 is not. — Abbr. n.s. — Also termed *Gregorian calendar*. Cf. OLD STYLE.

new trial. A postjudgment retrial or reexamination of some or all of the issues determined in an earlier judgment. • The trial court may order a new trial, either by motion of a party or on the court's own initiative. Also, an appellate court, in reversing the trial court's judgment, may remand the case to the trial court for a new trial on some or all of the issues on which the reversal is based. Fed. R. Civ. P. 59. See MOTION FOR NEW TRIAL; REMAND.

new value. See VALUE.

new works. See WORKS.

New York interest. See *Boston interest* under INTEREST (3).

New York standard clause. See MORTGAGE-LOSS CLAUSE.

New York Stock Exchange. An unincorporated association of member firms that handle the purchase and sale of securities both for themselves and for customers. • This exchange, the dominant one in the United States, trades in only large companies having at least one million outstanding shares. — Abbr. NYSE.

New York Supplement. A set of regional lawbooks that, being part of the West Group's National Reporter System, contain every published decision from intermediate and lower courts of record in New York, from 1888 to date. • The first series ran from 1888 to 1937; the second series is the current one. — Abbr. N.Y.S.; N.Y.S.2d.

***New York Times* rule.** A commonsense rule of ethical conduct holding that one should not do anything arguably newsworthy — in public or in private — that one would mind having reported on the front page of a major newspaper. • In various communities, a local newspaper is substituted for the *Times*. — Also termed *New York Times test*; *New York Times v. Sullivan rule*. See *actual malice* under MALICE.

nexi (**nek**-sI), *n. pl.* [Latin] *Roman law*. Debtors given in bondage to creditors until their debts have been paid. See NEXUM.

next devisee. See DEVISEE.

next eventual estate. See ESTATE.

next friend. A person who appears in a lawsuit to act for the benefit of an incompetent or minor plaintiff, but who is not a party to the lawsuit and is not appointed as a guardian. — Also termed *prochein ami*. Cf. *guardian ad litem* under GUARDIAN.

next-in, first-out. A method of inventory valuation (but not a generally accepted accounting principle) whereby the cost of goods is based on their replacement cost rather than their actual cost. — Abbr. NIFO. Cf. FIRST-IN, FIRST-OUT; LAST-IN, FIRST-OUT.

next of kin. 1. The person or persons most closely related by blood to a decedent. **2.** The person or persons entitled to inherit personal property from a decedent who has not left a will. See HEIR.

next presentation. *Hist. Eccles law*. In the law of advowsons, the right to present to the bishop a clerk to fill the first vacancy in a local parsonage. See ADVOWSON.

nexum (**nek**-səm), *n.* [Latin] *Roman law*. A transaction or practice under which a debtor, upon a failure to repay the debt, could be seized and held in bondage until the debt was repaid.

> "*Nexum*. This highly controversial matter will be briefly dealt with as *nexum* had long been obsolete in classical law. Little is really known of it: it has been doubted whether there ever was such an institution. No text tells us that there was a contract called nexum .... But we have texts which speak of *nexum* as creative of obligation ... and many literary texts dealing with debtors who were *nexi*, so that it may be taken as certain that there was such a transaction ... which in some way reduced debtors to a sort of slavery, that great hardships resulted and that a *l. Poetelia* ... practically ended this state of things, presumably by requiring an actual judgment before seizure. The effect was not to abolish *nexum*, but, by depriving it of its chief value, the power of seizure ... to leave it with no advantages to counterbalance its clumsiness, so that it went out of use." W.W. Buckland, *A Textbook of Roman Law: From Augustus to Justinian* 429–30 (Peter Stein ed., 3d ed. 1963).

nexus. A connection or link, often a causal one <cigarette packages must inform consumers of the nexus between smoking and lung cancer>. Pl. **nexuses; nexus.**

nexus test. The standard by which a private person's act is considered state action — and may give rise to liability for violating someone's constitutional rights — if the conduct is so closely related to the government's conduct that the choice to undertake it may fairly be said to be that of the state. • While similar to the symbiotic-relationship test, the nexus test focuses on the particular act complained of, instead of on the overall relationship of the parties. Still, some courts use the terms and analyses interchangeably. — Also termed *close-nexus test.* Cf. SYMBIOTIC-RELATIONSHIP TEST. See JOINT PARTICIPATION; STATE-COMPULSION TEST.

> "The complaining party must ... show that there is a sufficiently close nexus between the State and the challenged action of the regulated entity so that the action of the latter may be fairly treated as that of the State itself. The purpose of this requirement is to assure that constitutional standards are invoked only when it can be said that the State is responsible for the specific conduct of which the plaintiff complains.... [O]ur precedents indicate that a State normally can be held responsible for a private decision only when it has exercised coercive power or has provided such significant encouragement, either overt or covert, that the choice must in law be deemed to be that of the State." *Blum v. Yaretsky*, 457 U.S. 991, 1004, 102 S.Ct. 2777, 2786 (1982).

NGO. *abbr.* NONGOVERNMENTAL ORGANIZATION.

NGRI. See *not guilty by reason of insanity* under NOT GUILTY.

nichil (**nich**-əl), *n.* [Old French *nichil* fr. Latin *nihil* "nothing"] *Hist. English law.* A debt owed to the Exchequer's office but nihiled by sheriffs as nonleviable. • Once a year, an officer of the Clerk of Nichils enrolled these amounts and sent them to the treasurer's remembrancer's office from which process was issued for their recovery. Both offices were abolished in 1833. — Also spelled *nichill*; *nichel.*

nichil, *vb.* (Of a sheriff) to make return that a debt is worthless, because the debtor either cannot be found or is unable to pay.

nickname, *n.* **1.** A shortened version of a person's name <"Bill" is William's nickname>. **2.** A descriptive or alternative name, in addition to or instead of the actual name <David Smith's nickname is "Red">.

niece. 1. The daughter of a person's brother or sister; sometimes understood to include the daughter of a person's brother-in-law or sister-in-law. • This term is extended in some wills to include a grandniece. See NEPHEW.

nient (nee-**ent**). [Law French] Not; nothing.

nient culpable (nee-**ent kəl**-pə-bəl), *n.* [Law French] *Hist.* A general plea of "not guilty" in a tort or criminal action.

> "When the prisoner hath thus pleaded not guilty, *non culpabilis*, or *nient culpable*; which was formerly used to be abbreviated upon the minutes, thus, '*non* (or *nient*) *cul.*' the clerk of the assise, or clerk of the arraigns, on behalf of the crown replies, that the prisoner is guilty, and that he is ready to prove him so." 4 William Blackstone, *Commentaries on the Laws of England* 333 (1769).

nient dedire (nee-**ent** də-**deer**), *vb.* [Law French] *Hist.* To deny nothing; to be subject to a default judgment.

nient le fait (nee-**ent** lə **fay**). [Law French] *Hist.* Not the deed. • This term was the earlier version of *non est factum.* See NON EST FACTUM.

nient seisi (nee-**ent see**-zee), *n.* [Law French "not seised"] *Hist.* The general denial in a writ to recover an annuity.

NIFO (**nɪ**-foh). *abbr.* NEXT-IN, FIRST-OUT.

night. 1. The time from sunset to sunrise. **2.** Darkness; the time when a person's face is not discernible. • This definition was used in the common-law definition of certain offenses, such as burglary.

> "The definition of a burglar, as given by Sir Edward Coke, is, 'he that by night breaketh and entereth into a mansion-house, with intent to commit a felony.' ... The *time* must be by night, and not by day; for in the daytime there is no burglary .... As to what is reckoned night, and what day, for this purpose anciently the day was accounted to begin only at sunrising, and to end immediately upon sunset; but the better opinion seems to be, that if there be daylight ... enough, begun or left, to discern a man's face withal, it is no burglary. But this does not extend to moonlight; for then many midnight burglaries would go unpunished: and besides, the malignity of the offence does not so properly arise from its being done in the dark, as at the dead of night when all the creation, except beasts of prey, are at rest; when sleep has disarmed the owner, and rendered his castle defenceless." 4 William Blackstone, *Commentaries on the Laws of England* 224 (1769).

3. Thirty minutes after sunset and thirty minutes before sunrise, or a similar definition as set forth by statute, as in a statute requiring specific authorization for night searches. **4.** Evening. — Also termed *nighttime*. Cf. DAY.

nightwalker. 1. *Hist.* A person who suspiciously wanders about at night and who might disturb the peace. • Nightwalking was an example of a "common" offense requiring no specific facts to be asserted in the indictment. **2.** A sleepwalker. **3.** A prostitute who walks the streets at night; streetwalker.

nihil. See NIHIL EST.

nihil capiat per breve (**nɪ**-hil **kap**-ee-ət pər **bree**-vee *or* breev), *n.* [Latin "Let him take nothing by his writ"] A judgment against the plaintiff in an action at bar or in abatement. — Also termed *nihil capiat per billam* ("let him take nothing by his bill").

nihil dicit (**nɪ**-hil **dɪ**-sit), *n.* [Latin "he says nothing"] **1.** The failure of a defendant to answer a lawsuit. **2.** See *nil-dicit default judgment* under DEFAULT JUDGMENT.

***nihil-dicit* default judgment.** See DEFAULT JUDGMENT.

nihil est (**nɪ**-hil est). [Latin "there is nothing"] A form of return by a sheriff or constable who was unable to serve a writ because nothing was found to levy on. — Often shortened to *nihil*. Cf. NULLA BONA.

nihil habet (**nɪ**-hil **hay**-bət). [Latin "he has nothing"] A form of return by a sheriff or constable who was unable to serve a *scire facias* or other writ on the defendant. See SCIRE FACIAS.

nihilism (**nɪ**-əl-iz-əm). **1.** A doctrine maintaining that there is no rational justification for moral principles and that there is no objective truth. **2.** The view that traditional beliefs are unfounded and that life is meaningless and useless. **3.** A theory that the existing economic, social, or political institutions should be destroyed, regardless of the result, because of the basic undesirability of those institutions. • This theory, featured by Ivan Turgenev in his 1861 novel *Fathers and Sons*, was popular among Russian extremists until the collapse of the czarist government.

nihilist, *n.* A person who advocates nihilism. See NIHILISM.

nil (nil). [Latin] Nothing. • This word is a contracted form of *nihil*. See NIHIL EST.

nil debet (nil **deb**-ət). [Latin "he owes nothing"] *Hist.* A general denial in a debt action on a simple contract.

> "The proper general issue in debt on simple contracts and statutes is 'nil debet,' which is a formal denial of the debt. It denies not only the existence of any contract, but under it any matters in excuse or in discharge may also be shown." Benjamin J. Shipman, *Handbook of Common–Law Pleading* § 184, at 327 (Henry Winthrop Ballantine ed., 3d ed. 1923).

***nil-dicit* default judgment.** See DEFAULT JUDGMENT.

nil habuit in tenementis (nil **hab**-yoo-it in ten-ə-**men**-tis), *n.* [Law Latin "he has nothing in the tenements"] *Hist.* In an action to recover rent on a lease, the defendant's plea that the landlord has no title or interest in the property at issue.

nil ligatum (nil li-**gay**-təm). [Latin "nothing is bound"] No obligation has been incurred.

nimble dividend. See DIVIDEND.

nimmer. A petty thief; pilferer; pickpocket.

Nineteenth Amendment. The constitutional amendment, ratified in 1920, providing that a citizen's right to vote cannot be denied or abridged by the United States, or by any state within it, on the basis of sex. — Also termed *Women's Suffrage Amendment*.

1933 Act. See SECURITIES ACT OF 1933.

1934 Act. See SECURITIES EXCHANGE ACT OF 1934.

ninety-day letter. Statutory notice of a tax deficiency sent by the IRS to a taxpayer. • During the 90 days after receiving the notice, the taxpayer must pay the taxes (and, if desired, seek a refund) or challenge the deficiency in tax court. IRC (26 USCA) §§ 6212, 6213. — Also written *90–day letter*. — Also termed *notice of deficiency*; *deficiency notice*; *tax-deficiency notice*. Cf. THIRTY-DAY LETTER.

Ninth Amendment. The constitutional amendment, ratified with the Bill of Rights in 1791, providing that rights listed in the Constitution must not be construed in a way that denies or disparages unlisted rights, which are retained by the people.

nisi (**nI**-sI), *adj.* [Latin "unless"] (Of a court's ex parte ruling or grant of relief) having validity unless the adversely affected party appears and shows cause why it should be withdrawn <a decree *nisi*>. See *decree nisi* under DECREE.

nisi decree. See *decree nisi* under DECREE.

nisi feceris (**nI**-sI **fee**-sə-ris), *n.* [Law Latin "unless you have done so"] *Hist.* A clause in a manorial writ providing that the king's court or officer will do justice if the lords fail. • This provision allowed royal courts to usurp the jurisdiction of manorial courts.

nisi prius (**nI**-sI **prI**-əs). [Latin "unless before then"] A civil trial court in which, unlike in an appellate court, issues are tried before a jury. • The term is obsolete in the United States except in New York and Oklahoma. — Abbr. n.p.

nisi prius clause. An entry to the record authorizing a jury trial in the designated county. See NISI PRIUS.

nisi prius roll. The transcript of a case at nisi prius. — Also termed *nisi prius record.*

nitroglycerine charge. See ALLEN CHARGE.

n.l. *abbr.* NON LIQUET.

NLRA. *abbr.* NATIONAL LABOR RELATIONS ACT.

NLRB. *abbr.* NATIONAL LABOR RELATIONS BOARD.

NMB. *abbr.* NATIONAL MEDIATION BOARD.

NMI. *abbr.* No middle initial.

no-action clause. An insurance-policy provision that bars suit against the insurer until the liability of the insured has been determined by a judgment.

no-action letter. A letter from the staff of a governmental agency stating that if the facts are as represented in a person's request for an agency ruling, the staff will advise the agency not to take action against the person. • Typically, a no-action letter is requested from the SEC on such matters as shareholder proposals, resales of stock, and marketing techniques.

no actus reus (noh **ak**-təs **ree**-əs). A plea in which a criminal defendant either denies involvement with a crime or asserts that the harm suffered is too remote from the criminal act to be imputable to the defendant.

no-answer default judgment. See DEFAULT JUDGMENT.

no arrival, no sale. A delivery term, included in some sales contracts, by which the seller assumes the duty to deliver the goods to a specified place, and assumes the risk of loss for the goods while they are in transit. • If the goods arrive damaged or late, the buyer can either avoid the contract or accept the goods at a discount.

no award. In an action to enforce an award, the defendant's plea denying that an award was made.

nobile officium (**noh**-bə-lee ə-**fish**-ee-əm), *n.* [Latin "noble office or privilege"] *Scots law.* The power of a superior court to give equitable relief when none is possible under law.

nobility, *n. pl.* **1.** Persons of social or political preeminence, usu. derived by inheritance or from the sovereign. • In English law, there are various degrees of nobility, or peerage, such as dukes, marquises, earls, viscounts, and barons, and their female counterparts. Nobility is generally created either by a writ of summons to sit in Parliament or by a royal grant through letters patent, and was once usu. accompanied by a large land grant. Nobility by writ descended to a person's bodily heirs. The modern practice is to grant nobility by letters patent, which provide limitations as to future heirs. The U.S. Constitution prohibits granting a title of nobility. U.S. Const. art. I, § 9, cl. 8.

> "In England nobility is apt to be confounded with the peculiar institution of the British peerage. Yet nobility, in some shape or another, has existed in most places and times or the world's history, while the British peerage is an institution purely local, and one which has actually hindered the existence of a nobility in the sense which the word bears in most other countries.... Nobility, then, in the strict sense of the word, is the hereditary handing on from generation to generation of some acknowledged pre-eminence, a pre-eminence founded on hereditary succession, and on nothing else.... The preeminence so handed on may be of any kind, from substantial political power to mere social respect and precedence." 17 *Encyclopaedia Britannica* 538 (9th ed. 1907).

2. Persons of high or noble character. **3.** The collective body of persons making up the noble class.

no bill, *n.* A grand jury's notation that insufficient evidence exists for an indictment on a criminal charge <the grand jury returned a no

bill instead of the indictment the prosecutors expected>. — **no-bill,** *vb.* <the grand jury no-billed three of the charges>. Cf. TRUE BILL.

no-bonus clause. *Landlord-tenant law.* A lease provision that takes effect upon governmental condemnation, limiting the lessee's damages to the value of any improvements to the property and preventing the lessee from recovering the difference between the lease's fixed rent and the property's market rental value. See CONDEMNATION.

no cause of action. See *take-nothing judgement* under JUDGMENT.

nocent (**noh**-sənt), *adj.* [fr. Latin *nocere* "harm"] *Archaic* **1.** Injurious; harmful. **2.** Guilty; criminal. • This word is the little-used antonym of *innocent.*

nocent (**noh**-sənt), *n.* [fr. Latin *nocere* "harm"] *Hist.* A person who is guilty.

no-claim, *n.* The lack of a claim. • Legal philosophers devised this term to denote the opposite of a claim. As one jurisprudent has said apologetically, "there is no word in English which expresses the lack of a claim and therefore the rather barbarous 'no-claim' has been suggested." George Whitecross Paton, *A Textbook of Jurisprudence* 291 (G.W. Paton & David P. Derham eds., 4th ed. 1972).

no-confidence vote. The formal legal method by which a legislative body, by a majority vote, forces the resignation of a cabinet or ministry. — Also termed *vote of no confidence.*

no contest. A criminal defendant's plea that, while not admitting guilt, the defendant will not dispute the charge. • This plea is often preferable to a guilty plea, which can be used against the defendant in a later civil lawsuit. — Also termed *nolo contendere*; *non vult contendere.*

no-contest clause. A testamentary provision conditioning a gift or legacy on the beneficiary's not challenging the will.

noctanter (nok-**tan**-tər), *n.* [Latin "by night"] *Hist.* A chancery writ issued to a sheriff as a first step in the recovery of damages for destroying a ditch or hedge. • The neighboring villagers (vills) were held liable for the damages unless they indicted the offender.

noctem de firma (**nok**-təm dee **fər**-mə), *n.* [Law Latin "night of duty (payable)"] *Hist.* The duty or custom of providing entertainment or provisions for a night. • At the time of the Norman Conquest, this was the duty or custom of entertaining the king for one night. — Also termed *noctes*; *firma noctis.*

nocumentum (nok-yə-**men**-təm). [fr. Latin *nocere* "to harm"] *Hist.* A nuisance. • There was no remedy at law for a nuisance causing only property damage, but there was a remedy for a nuisance causing injury.

no-duty, *n.* Liberty not to do an act. — Also termed *liberty not.*

no-duty doctrine. **1.** *Torts.* The rule that a defendant who owes no duty to the plaintiff is not liable for the plaintiff's injury. **2.** The rule that the owner or possessor of property has no duty to warn or protect an invitee from known or obvious hazards.

***Noerr-Pennington* doctrine.** The principle that the First Amendment shields from liability (esp. under antitrust laws) companies that join together to lobby the government. • The doctrine derives from a line of Supreme Court cases beginning with *Eastern R.R. Presidents Conference v. Noerr Motor Freight, Inc.*, 365 U.S. 127, 81 S.Ct. 523 (1961), and *United Mine Workers v. Pennington*, 381 U.S. 657, 85 S.Ct. 1585 (1965).

no evidence. **1.** The lack of a legally sufficient evidentiary basis for a reasonable fact-finder to rule in favor of the party who bears the burden of proof <there is no evidence in the record about his whereabouts at midnight>. • Under the Federal Rules of Civil Procedure, a party can move for judgment as a matter of law to claim that the other party — who bears the burden of proof — has been fully heard and has not offered sufficient evidence to prove one or more essential elements of the suit or defense. Fed. R. Civ. P. 50. Though such a contention is usu. referred to as a no-evidence motion, the issue is not whether there was actually no evidence, but rather whether the evidence was sufficient for the fact-finder to be able to reasonably rule in favor of the other party.

> "Since judgment as a matter of law deprives the party opposing the motion of a determination of the facts by a jury, it should be granted cautiously and sparingly. Nevertheless, the federal courts do not follow the rule that a scintilla of evidence is enough to create an issue for the jury. The question is not whether there is literally no evidence upon which the jury properly could find a verdict for that party." 9A Charles Alan Wright & Ar-

thur Miller, *Federal Practice and Procedure* § 2524, at 252–54 (2d ed. 1995).

2. Evidence that has no value in an attempt to prove a matter in issue <that testimony is no evidence of an alibi>.

no-eyewitness rule. *Torts.* The largely defunct principle holding that if no direct evidence shows what a dead person did to avoid an accident, the jury may infer that the person acted with ordinary care for his or her own safety. • In a jurisdiction where the rule persists, a plaintiff in a survival or wrongful-death action can assert the rule to counter a defense of contributory negligence.

no-fault, *adj.* Of or relating to a claim that is adjudicated without any determination that a party is blameworthy <no-fault divorce>.

no-fault auto insurance. See INSURANCE.

no-fault divorce. See DIVORCE.

no funds. An indorsement marked on a check when there are insufficient funds in the account to cover the check.

no goods. See NULLA BONA.

n.o.i.b.n. *abbr.* NOT OTHERWISE INDEXED BY NAME.

no-knock search. See SEARCH.

no-knock search warrant. See SEARCH WARRANT.

NOL. See *net operating loss* under LOSS.

nolens volens (**noh**-lenz **voh**-lenz), *adv.* & *adj.* [Latin] Willing or unwilling <*nolens volens*, the school district must comply with the court's injunction>.

no-limit order. See ORDER (4).

nolissement (nə-lis-**mahn**), *n.* [French] *French law.* The chartering of a ship; AFFREIGHTMENT.

nolition (noh-**lish**-ən). The absence of volition; unwillingness.

nolle prosequi (**nahl**-ee **prahs**-ə-kwɪ), *n.* [Latin "not to wish to prosecute"] **1.** A legal notice that a lawsuit has been abandoned. **2.** A docket entry showing that the plaintiff or the prosecution has abandoned the action. — Often shortened to *nolle.*

"In America the term [*nolle prosequi*] bears the same meaning as in England, with one exception. The attorney-general has not the same discretion with which English law invests him. Although in some States the prosecuting officer may enter a *nolle prosequi* at his discretion, in others the leave of the court must be obtained." 17 *Encyclopaedia Britannica* 546 (9th ed. 1907).

"Nolle prosequi is a formal entry on the record by the prosecuting officer by which he declares that he will not prosecute the case further, either as to some of the counts of the indictment, or as to part of a divisible count, or as to some of the persons accused, or altogether. It is a judicial determination in favor of accused and against his conviction, but it is not an acquittal, nor is it equivalent to a pardon." 22A C.J.S. *Criminal Law* § 419, at 1 (1989).

nolle prosequi (**nahl**-ee **prahs**-ə-kwɪ), *vb.* To abandon (a suit or prosecution); to have (a case) dismissed by a *nolle prosequi* <the state *nolle prosequied* the charges against Johnson>. — Often shortened to *nolle pros*; *nol-pros*; *nol-pro.*

no-load fund. See MUTUAL FUND.

nolo contendere (**noh**-loh kən-**ten**-də-ree). [Latin "I do not wish to contend"] NO CONTEST. — Often shortened to *nolo.*

no man's land. *Labor law.* The lack of clear jurisdiction between a state government and the federal government over labor disputes. • This term was common in the 1950s, but its use has declined as later laws have clarified jurisdictional issues.

NOM clause. *abbr.* NO-ORAL-MODIFICATION CLAUSE.

nomen (**noh**-men *or* -mən), *n.* [Latin] **1.** *Roman law.* A personal name. • A Roman citizen generally had three names: a *praenomen* ("first name"), a *nomen* ("the name of the family group"), and *cognomen* ("a surname"). **2.** *Roman law.* A claim; an obligation. **3.** *Hist.* A person's first name. **4.** More broadly, any name. See AGNOMEN.

nomen collectivum (**noh**-men kol-ək-**tɪ**-vəm), *n.* [Latin] A collective name; a name of a class of things.

nomen generale (**noh**-men jen-ə-**ray**-lee), *n.* [Latin] A general name; a *genus.*

nomen generalissimum (**noh**-men jen-ə-rə-**lis**-i-məm), *n.* [Law Latin] A name with the most general meaning.

> "*Nomen generalissimum*. A very general name: a comprehensive term. Such are the terms crime, demand, draft, estate, goods, grant, heir, house, instrument, interest, land, merchandise, obligation, offense." William C. Anderson, *A Dictionary of Law* 711 (1889).

nomen juris (**noh**-men **joor**-is), *n*. [Latin] A legal name or designation.

nomen transcripticium (**noh**-men tran-skrip-**tish**-ee-əm), *n*. [Latin "entry (in an account transferred)"] *Roman law*. A creditor's entry of a money debt into a new account (*expensilatio*) after closing another account, thereby creating, with the debtor's permission, a literal contract from an existing obligation, which may or may not have been enforceable. Pl. ***nomina transcripticia***.

> "The subject will, perhaps, become clearer by examples: ... A has in the past had dealings by way of sale, exchange, etc., with B, of which an account appears in his *codex* showing a balance against B for 500 *aurei*. A, with B's consent, closes this account by a statement on the opposite page (contrary to fact) that B has paid the *aurei* ... and opens a new account with the statement (contrary to strict fact) that he has advanced to B the sum of 500 *aurei*. Hence the *expensilatio* represents a *nomen transcripticium*; a *nomen* (debt) has been transferred from one account to another .... In effect the old contracts between A and B have been novated, *i.e.* extinguished, one single obligation having been substituted in their place; obviously a course which offered many advantages to both parties, as it simplified the accounts, and saved disputes about the previous transactions." R.W. Leage, *Roman Private Law* 317–18 (C.H. Ziegler ed., 2d ed. 1930).

no-merit brief. See ANDERS BRIEF.

nominal (**nahm**-ə-nəl), *adj*. **1.** Existing in name only <the king was a nominal figurehead as he had no power>. **2.** (Of a price or amount) trifling, esp. as compared to what would be expected <the lamp sold for a nominal price of ten cents>. **3.** Of or relating to a name or term <a nominal definition>. — **nominally,** *adv*.

nominal account. See ACCOUNT.

nominal asset. See ASSET.

nominal capital. See CAPITAL.

nominal consideration. See CONSIDERATION.

nominal damages. See DAMAGES.

nominal partner. See PARTNER.

nominal party. See PARTY (2).

nominal-payee rule. *Commercial law*. The rule that validates any person's indorsement of an instrument (such as a check) when the instrument's drawer intended for the payee to have no interest in the instrument. UCC § 3–404(b).

nominal rate. See INTEREST RATE.

nominal sentence. See SENTENCE.

nominal trust. See *passive trust* under TRUST.

nominal value. See PAR VALUE.

nominal yield. See YIELD.

nominate, *vb*. **1.** To propose (a person) for election or appointment <Steven nominated Jane for president>. **2.** To name or designate (a person) for a position <the testator nominated an executor, who later withdrew because he couldn't perform his duties>.

nominate contract. See CONTRACT.

nominatim (nah-mi-**nay**-təm), *adv*. [fr. Latin *nomen* "name"] *Roman law*. By name. • This term refers to mentioning someone or something expressly or specifically by name, so that (for example) to disinherit persons *nominatim* means that there is no doubt who is meant to be excluded.

nominating and reducing. *Hist*. A method used, esp. in London, to obtain special jurors from which to select a jury panel. • Under this method, a number representing each person on a sheriff's list is drawn from a box until 48 unchallenged people have been nominated. Each party then strikes 12 people and the remaining 24 constitute the panel.

nominatio auctoris (nah-mi-**nay**-shee-oh awk-**tor**-is), *n*. [Latin "naming of the originator (or seller)"] **1.** In an action for the recovery of something, such as real estate, the defendant's plea that the property is actually owned by another party. • The true owner is then required to defend the action. **2.** *Roman law*. In an action alleging ownership of an item, the defendant's plea naming the seller, who then must assist in the defense of the action against the plaintiff. — Also termed *laudare auctorem*.

nomination. **1.** The act of proposing a person for election or appointment. **2.** The act of naming or designating a person for a position.

nomination paper. (*usu. pl.*) A document filed by an independent political group — usu. one not qualifying as a political party or able to hold primary elections — to place one or more nominees on a general-election ballot.

nomination to a living. *Eccles. law.* A right to offer a clerk to the owner of an advowson for presentation to the bishop of the diocese. • The owner of an advowson can grant the right to another but is then bound to present whomever the grantee chooses.

nominativus pendens (nahm-ə-nə-**tI**-vəs **pen**-denz), *n.* [Latin "nominative hanging"] In a sentence, a nominative phrase that is not grammatically connected with the rest of the sentence. — Also termed *nominative absolute.*

> "Nominativus pendens .... The opening words in the form of a deed *inter partes* ('This deed,' etc., down to 'whereas'), though an intelligible and convenient part of the deed, having regard to the predicate 'witnesseth' or 'nor this deed witnesseth,' are sometimes of this kind." William A. Jowitt, *The Dictionary of English Law* 1230 (1959).

nomina villarum (**nahm**-ə-nə vi-**lair**-əm), *n.* [Latin "names of the villages"] *Hist.* In the reign of Edward II, a list compiled by sheriffs of the names of the villages and possessors in their respective counties.

nomine (**nahm**-ə-nee). [fr. Latin *nomen* "name"] *Roman law.* **1.** By name; under the name of, as in *sine nomine edere librum* ("to publish [a book] anonymously"). **2.** On behalf of, as in *proprio (suo) nomine* ("on one's own behalf").

nominee. 1. A person who is proposed for an office, position, or duty. **2.** A person designated to act in place of another, usu. in a very limited way. **3.** A party who holds bare legal title for the benefit of others or who receives and distributes funds for the benefit of others.

nominee trust. See TRUST.

nomine poenae (**nahm**-ə-nee **pee**-nee), *n.* [Latin "in the name of penalty"] **1.** *Civil law.* A clause in a testament requiring the heir to do something by way of penalty. **2.** At common law, a penalty for nonperformance, such as additional rent to be paid by a tenant to a landlord for failing to perform certain conditions in a lease.

nomocanon (nə-**mok**-ə-non *or* noh-mə-**kan**-ən). **1.** A collection of canon and imperial laws applicable to ecclesiastical matters in the orthodox churches. • The first nomocanon is falsely ascribed to Johannes Scholasticus, patriarch of Constantinople, in 553. Later canons consist primarily of the canons of the Quinisext and the ecclesiastical laws of Justinian. **2.** A collection of the ancient canons of the apostles, councils, and fathers, without regard to imperial constitutions.

nomographer (nə-**mog**-rə-fər). **1.** A person who drafts laws. **2.** A person skilled in nomography.

nomography (nə-**mog**-rə-fee). **1.** The art of drafting laws. **2.** A treatise on the drafting of laws.

nomothete (**noh**-mə-theet), *n.* [fr. Greek *nomos* "law" + *thetes* "a person who prescribes"] *Hist.* A lawgiver. — Also spelled *nomotheta.*

> "It was [in ancient Greek law] provided that all motions to repeal or amend an existing law should be brought before the ecclesia or general meeting of citizens, at the beginning of the year. They might be then and there rejected; but if a motion was received favorably, the ecclesia appointed a body of nomothetes, sometimes as many as a thousand in number, before whom the proposal was put on trial according to the regular forms of Athenian judicial procedure. A majority vote of the nomothetes was decisive for acceptance or rejection." 5 *Century Dictionary and Cyclopedia* 4011 (1895).

non (non). [Latin] Not; no. • This term negates, sometimes as a separate word and sometimes as a prefix.

nonability. 1. The lack of legal capacity, esp. to sue on one's own behalf. **2.** A plea or exception raising a lack of legal capacity.

nonacceptance. 1. The refusal or rejection of something, such as a contract offer. See REJECTION. **2.** A buyer's rejection of goods because they fail to conform to contractual specifications. See UCC § 2–601(a). **3.** A drawee's failure or refusal to receive and pay a negotiable instrument.

non acceptavit (non ak-sep-**tay**-vit). [Latin "he did not accept"] In an assumpsit action against the acceptor of a bill of exchange, the defendant's plea denying acceptance of the bill.

nonaccess. *Family law.* Absence of opportunity for sexual intercourse. • Nonaccess is often used as a defense by the alleged father in paternity cases.

non accrevit infra sex annos (non ə-**kree**-vit **in**-frə **seks an**-ohs), *n.* [Latin "it did not accrue in six years"] *Hist.* The general pleading form for the statute-of-limitations defense.

nonacquiescence (non-ak-wee-**es**-ənts). *Administrative law.* An agency's policy of declining to be bound by lower-court precedent that is contrary to the agency's interpretation of its organic statute, but only until the Supreme Court has ruled on the issue.

> "Too much nonacquiescence, however, would interfere with the courts' ability to prevent an agency from violating its statutory mandate. The practice is generally upheld, but is considered questionable when an agency adheres to its legal position in a case that could only be reviewed in a circuit that has already rejected the agency's stance. When the Social Security Administration made frequent use of the latter kind of nonacquiescence in the administration of its disability benefits program in the 1980's, it was widely criticized." Ernest Gellhorn & Ronald M. Levin, *Administrative Law and Process in a Nutshell* 98 n.2 (4th ed. 1997).

nonactuarially sound retirement system. A retirement plan that uses current contributions and assets to pay current benefit obligations, instead of investing contributions to pay future benefits. Cf. ACTUARIALLY SOUND RETIREMENT SYSTEM.

nonadmission. 1. The failure to acknowledge something. **2.** The refusal to allow something, such as evidence in a legal proceeding.

nonadmitted asset. See ASSET.

nonae et decimae (**noh**-nee et **des**-ə-mee), *n. pl.* [Law Latin "ninths and tenths"] *Hist.* Two payments that church-farm tenants make to the church, the first being rent for the land and the second being a tithe.

nonage (**non**-ij). **1.** MINORITY (1). **2.** NONAGIUM.

nonaggression pact. *Int'l law.* A treaty in which two or more countries agree not to engage in aggressive military operations against one another. — Also termed *nonaggression treaty.*

nonagium (noh-**nay**-jee-əm). [Latin "a ninth"] *Hist.* The ninth part of a decedent's personal property, sometimes payable to the parish clergy for pious uses. — Also termed *nonage.*

nonaligned state. *Int'l law.* A (usu. less developed) country that has banded together with other similarly situated countries to enhance its political and economic position in the world. • The movement of nonaligned states formally began at a summit in 1961, and during the Cold War these countries declared their independence from both the western and the Soviet blocs.

nonancestral estate. See ESTATE.

nonapparent easement. See *discontinuous easement* under EASEMENT.

nonapparent servitude. See SERVITUDE (1).

nonappearance. The failure to appear in court, esp. to prosecute or defend a lawsuit. See DEFAULT; NONSUIT.

nonassertive conduct. See CONDUCT.

nonassessable insurance. See INSURANCE.

nonassessable stock. See STOCK.

non assumpsit (non ə-**səm**[**p**]-sit). [Latin "he did not undertake"] *Hist.* A general denial in an action of assumpsit. See ASSUMPSIT.

> " 'Non assumpsit' is the general issue in assumpsit, whether special or general, and is in effect a formal denial of liability on the promise or contract alleged. It denies not only the inducement or statement of the plaintiff's right, but also the breach, and allows any defense tending to show that there was no debt or cause of action at the time of commencing suit." Benjamin J. Shipman, *Handbook of Common-Law Pleading* § 182, at 322 (Henry Winthrop Ballantine ed., 3d ed. 1923).

non assumpsit infra sex annos (non ə-**səm**[**p**]-sit **in**-frə **seks an**-ohs), *n.* [Latin "he did not undertake within six years"] *Hist.* The specific pleading form for the statute-of-limitations defense in an action of assumpsit.

nonbailable, *adj.* **1.** (Of a person) not entitled to bail <the defendant was nonbailable because of a charge of first-degree murder>. **2.** (Of an offense) not admitting of bail <murder is a nonbailable offense>.

nonbank, *adj.* Of, relating to, or being an entity other than a bank <a nonbank depositor> <a nonbank creditor>.

nonbank bank. See BANK.

nonbillable time. An attorney's or paralegal's time that is not chargeable to a client. Cf. BILLABLE HOUR.

noncallable bond. See BOND (3).

noncallable security. See SECURITY.

noncancelability clause. An insurance-policy provision that prevents the insurer from canceling the policy after an insured's loss, as long as the premium has been paid.

noncapital, *adj.* (Of a crime) not involving or deserving of the death penalty <noncapital murder>.

noncareer vice-consul. See VICE-CONSUL.

noncash charge. See CHARGE.

non cepit (non **see**-pit). [Latin "he did not take"] *Hist.* A general denial in a replevin action that puts at issue both the taking and the place of taking. See REPLEVIN.

> "'Non cepit' is the general issue in replevin, and is a formal denial both of the fact and the place of the alleged taking. It denies the taking only, and not the plaintiff's right of possession. Where replevin may be and is brought for goods lawfully obtained, but unlawfully detained, the general issue is 'non detinet,' which is a denial of the detention. It denies the detention only, and not the plaintiff's right." Benjamin J. Shipman, *Handbook of Common-Law Pleading* § 178, at 318 (Henry Winthrop Ballantine ed., 3d ed. 1923).

noncitizen. A person who is not a citizen of a particular place. See ALIEN.

nonclaim. A person's failure to pursue a right within the legal time limit, resulting in that person's being barred from asserting the right. See STATUTE OF LIMITATIONS.

nonclaim statute. See STATUTE.

noncode state. *Hist.* A state that, at a given time, had not procedurally merged law and equity, so that equity was still administered as a separate system. • The term was current primarily in the early to mid–20th century. — Also termed *common-law state.* Cf. CODE STATE.

noncombatant, *adj.* **1.** Not serving in a fighting capacity <noncombatant personnel>. **2.** Not designed for combat <noncombatant vehicle>.

noncombatant, *n.* **1.** An armed-service member who serves in a non-fighting capacity. **2.** A civilian in wartime.

noncommercial partnership. See *nontrading partnership* under PARTNERSHIP.

noncommissioned officer. See OFFICER (2).

noncompete covenant. See *noncompetition covenant* under COVENANT (1).

noncompetition covenant. See COVENANT (1).

non compos mentis (non **kom**-pəs **men**-tis), *adj.* [Latin "not master of one's mind"] **1.** Insane. **2.** Incompetent. Cf. COMPOS MENTIS.

non concessit (non kən-**ses**-it), *n.* [Law Latin "he did not grant"] *Hist.* **1.** *English law.* The plea by which the defendant denies that certain rights were given by letters patent to the plaintiff. • For example, if a plaintiff sues for the infringement of a patent right, the defendant can deny that the Crown granted the plaintiff that right as alleged in the plaintiff's declaration. **2.** A plea by a stranger to a deed, by which the title and operation of the deed are placed in issue.

nonconforming goods. See GOODS.

nonconforming lot. See LOT (1).

nonconforming use. See USE (1).

nonconformist. A person who refuses to follow established customs, practices, beliefs, or ideas; esp., a person who refuses to adhere to specific religious doctrines or church requirements.

nonconformity. The failure to comply with something, as in a contract specification.

nonconsensual, *adj.* Not occurring by mutual consent <nonconsensual sexual relations>.

nonconsent. 1. Lack of voluntary agreement. **2.** *Criminal law.* In the law of rape, the refusal to engage willingly in sexual intercourse. See CONSENT.

non constat (non **kon**-stat). [Latin "it is not settled"] It is not certain or agreed. • The phrase is generally used to state that some conclusion does not necessarily follow although it might appear on its face to follow. Cf. NON SEQUITUR.

> "Non Constat .... Words frequently used, particularly in argument, to express dissatisfaction with the conclusions of the other party: as, it was moved in arrest of judgment that the declaration was not good, because *non*

constat whether AB was seventeen years of age when the action was commenced." 3 John Bouvier, *Bouvier's Law Dictionary* 2355 (8th ed. 1914).

nonconstitutional, *adj.* Of or relating to some legal basis or principle other than those of the U.S. Constitution or a state constitution <the appellate court refused — on nonconstitutional procedural grounds — to hear the defendant's argument about cruel and unusual punishment>. Cf. UNCONSTITUTIONAL.

nonconsumable, *n.* A thing (such as land, a vehicle, or a share of stock) that can be enjoyed without any change to its substance other than a natural diminishment over time. Cf. CONSUMABLE.

noncontestability clause. See INCONTESTABILITY CLAUSE.

noncontinuing guaranty. See *limited guaranty* under GUARANTY.

noncontinuous easement. See *discontinuous easement* under EASEMENT.

noncontract, *adj.* See NONCONTRACTUAL.

noncontract demurrage. See DEMURRAGE.

noncontractual, *adj.* Not relating to or arising from a contract <a noncontractual obligation>. — Also termed *noncontract.*

noncontractual duty. See DUTY (1).

noncontribution clause. A fire-insurance-policy provision stating that only the interests of the property owner and the first mortgagee are protected under the policy.

noncontributory, *adj.* **1.** Not involved in something. **2.** (Of an employee benefit plan) funded solely by the employer.

noncontributory pension plan. See PENSION PLAN.

noncore proceeding. See RELATED PROCEEDING.

noncovered wages. See WAGE.

non culpabilis (non kəl-**pay**-bə-ləs). [Latin] Not guilty. — Abbr. *non cul.*

noncumulative dividend. See DIVIDEND.

noncumulative preferred stock. See STOCK.

noncumulative stock. See *noncumulative preferred stock* under STOCK.

noncumulative voting. See VOTING.

noncustodial, *adj.* **1.** (Of an interrogation, etc.) not taking place while a person is in custody. **2.** Of or relating to someone, esp. a parent, who does not have sole or primary custody.

noncustodial sentence. See SENTENCE.

non damnificatus (non dam-nə-fə-**kay**-təs). [Latin "he is not damaged"] In an action of debt on a bond that holds the plaintiff harmless, the defendant's plea that the plaintiff has not been damaged.

nondeadly force. See FORCE.

non decimando (non des-ə-**man**-doh). See DE NON DECIMANDO.

non dedit (non **dee**-dit), *n.* [Latin "he did not grant"] NE DONA PAS.

nondelegable (non-**del**-ə-gə-bəl), *adj.* (Of a power, function, etc.) not capable of being entrusted to another's care <the duty to maintain the premises is a nondelegable duty>.

nondelegable duty. See DUTY (1).

nondelegation doctrine. See DELEGATION DOCTRINE.

nondelivery. A failure to transfer or convey something, such as goods. Cf. DELIVERY.

non demiset (non də-**mI**-zit). [Latin "he did not demise"] *Hist.* **1.** A defensive plea in an action for rent when the plaintiff failed to plead that the demise was by indenture. • It could not be used if the plaintiff alleged an indenture. **2.** In a replevin action, a plea in bar to an avowry for arrears of rent.

non detinet (non **det**-i-net *or* **det**-ə-nət). [Latin "he does not detain"] *Hist.* **1.** The pleading form of a general denial in a detinue action for recovery of goods detained by the defendant. • A *non detinet* denies both the detention and the plaintiff's right of possession or property in the goods claimed. See DETINUE. **2.** Loosely, NON CEPIT.

nondirection. The failure of a judge to properly instruct a jury on a necessary point of law.

nondischargeable debt. A debt (such as one for delinquent taxes) that is not released through bankruptcy.

nondisclosure. The failure or refusal to reveal something that either might be or is required to be revealed.

nondiscretionary trust. See *fixed trust* under TRUST.

non distringendo (non di-strin-**jen**-doh). [Law Latin "not to be distrained"] A writ to prevent the distraint of something.

nondiverse, *adj.* **1.** Of or relating to similar types <the attorney's practice is nondiverse: she handles only criminal matters>. **2.** (Of a person or entity) having the same citizenship as the party or parties on the other side of a lawsuit <the parties are nondiverse because both plaintiff and defendant are California citizens>. See *diversity jurisdiction* under JURISDICTION.

nones (nohnz), *n.* [fr. Latin *nonus* "ninth"] **1.** *Roman law.* In the Roman calendar, the ninth day before the ides, being the 7th of March, May, July, and October, and the 5th of the other months. **2.** *Eccles. law.* In religious houses, such as the Roman Catholic church, one of the seven daily canonical hours (about 3:00 p.m.) for prayer and devotion. **3.** *Archaic.* The ninth hour after sunrise, usu. about 3:00 p.m. Cf. CALENDS.

nonessential mistake. See *unessential mistake* under MISTAKE.

nonessential term. See *nonfundamental term* under TERM (2).

non est factum (non est **fak**-təm). [Latin "it is not his deed"] *Hist.* A denial of the execution of an instrument sued on.

> "The general issue in covenant is 'non est factum,' which is a formal denial that the deed is the deed of the defendant." Benjamin J. Shipman, *Handbook of Common-Law Pleading* § 187, at 331 (Henry Winthrop Ballantine ed., 3d ed. 1923).

non est inventus (non est in-**ven**-təs). [Latin "he is not found"] *Hist.* A statement in a sheriff's return indicating that the person ordered arrested could not be found in the sheriff's jurisdiction. — Abbr. *n.e.i.*

> "If *non est inventus* was returned to the bill, and the plaintiff had reason to think that the defendant was still in the same county, he might have another *bill*, and after that a third, and so on till the defendant was caught ...." 1 George Crompton, *Practice Common-Placed: Rules and Cases of Practice in the Courts of King's Bench and Common Pleas* xxxv (3d ed. 1787).

nonexclusive easement. See *common easement* under EASEMENT.

nonexclusive listing. See *open listing* under LISTING (1).

nonexempt property. See EXEMPT PROPERTY.

nonfeasance (non-**feez**-ənts), *n.* The failure to act when a duty to act existed. — **nonfeasant,** *adj.* — **nonfeasor,** *n.* Cf. MALFEASANCE; MISFEASANCE; FEASANCE.

> "Hence there arose very early a difference, still deeply rooted in the law of negligence, between 'misfeasance' and 'nonfeasance' — that is to say, between active misconduct working positive injury to others and passive inaction or a failure to take steps to protect them from harm." W. Page Keeton et al., *The Law of Torts* § 56, at 374 (5th ed. 1984).

non fecit (non **fee**-sit). [Latin "he did not make it"] A denial in an assumpsit action on a promissory note.

non fecit vastum contra prohibitionem (non **fee**-sit **vas**-təm **kahn**-trə proh-[h]ə-bish-ee-**oh**-nəm). [Latin "he did not commit waste against the prohibition"] In an estrepement action, a tenant's denial of any destruction to lands after an adverse judgment but before the sheriff has delivered possession of the lands to the plaintiff.

nonforfeitable, *adj.* Not subject to forfeiture. See FORFEITURE.

nonforfeiture option. See OPTION.

nonfreehold estate. See ESTATE.

nonfunctional, *n. Trademarks.* A feature of a good that, although it might identify or distinguish the good from others, is unrelated to the product's use.

nonfundamental term. See TERM (2).

nongovernmental organization. *Int'l law.* Any scientific, professional, business, or public-interest organization that is neither affiliated with nor under the direction of a government;

an international organization that is not the creation of an agreement among countries, but rather is composed of private individuals or organizations. • Examples of these organizations, which are often granted consultative status with the United Nations, include OPEC, Greenpeace, and the Red Cross. — Abbr. NGO.

> "This term should not be taken to refer to the membership of the organization: governments or branches of governments are members of many non-governmental organizations. The notion 'non-governmental' refers to the *function* of the international organization. Non-governmental organizations are not endowed with government powers. They operate under rules of private and not of public law." Henry G. Schermers, *International Institutional Law* 12 (1972).

non impedivit (non im-pə-**dɪ**-vit), *n.* [Latin "he did not impede"] The defendant's general denial in a *quare impedit* action. • This is the Latin form equivalent to *ne disturba pas*. See NE DISTURBA PAS; QUARE IMPEDIT.

non implacitando aliquem de libero tenemento sine brevi (non im-plas-ə-**tan**-doh **al**-ə-kwem dee **lib**-ər-oh ten-ə-**men**-toh **sɪ**-nee **bree**-vɪ) [Latin "not impleading anyone of his free tenement without a breve"] *Hist.* A writ that, without a writ from the king, prohibited bailiffs or others from distraining anyone from touching their freehold estates.

noninfamous crime. See CRIME.

non infregit conventionem (non in-**free**-jit kən-ven-shee-**oh**-nəm). [Latin "he committed no breach of covenant"] *Hist.* A defensive plea in an action for breach of covenant.

noninstallment credit. See CREDIT (4).

noninsurable risk. See RISK.

nonintercourse. 1. The refusal of one country to deal commercially with another. • For example, the Non–Intercourse Act of 1809, a congressional act, prohibited the importation of British or French goods. **2.** The lack of access, communication, or sexual relations between husband and wife.

non-interest-bearing bond. See *discount bond* under BOND (3).

non interfui (non in-**tər**-fyoo-ɪ). [Latin "I was not present"] A reporter's note.

noninterpretivism, *n.* In constitutional interpretation, the doctrine holding that judges are not confined to the Constitution's text or preratification history but may instead look to evolving social norms and values as the basis for constitutional judgments. — **noninterpretivist,** *n.* Cf. INTERPRETIVISM; ORIGINALISM.

nonintervention. *Int'l law.* The principle that a country should not interfere in the internal affairs of another country. • The U.N. Charter binds it from intervening "in matters which are essentially within the domestic jurisdiction of any state...." U.N. Charter art. 2(7). — Also termed *principle of nonintervention*.

nonintervention executor. See *independent executor* under EXECUTOR.

nonintervention will. See WILL.

non intromittendo, quando breve praecipe in capite subdole impetratur (non in-troh-mi-**ten**-doh, **kwon**-doh **bree**-vee **pree**-sə-pee [*or* **pres**-ə-pee] in **kap**-ə-tee **səb**-də-lee im-pə-**tray**-tər), *n.* [Latin "not interfering, when the writ praecipe in capite was obtained by deceit"] *Hist.* A writ issued to the King's Bench or Eyre, commanding them not to aid a person who obtained a praecipe in capite for lands from the king because that person likely obtained the writ deceitfully, and ordering them to put that person to the writ of right.

nonintromittent clause (non-in-troh-**mit**-ənt). *English law.* A clause in the charter of a borough exempting it from the jurisdiction of the justices of the peace appointed for the borough's county.

nonissuable plea. See PLEA (3).

nonjoinder. The failure to bring a person who is a necessary party into a lawsuit. Fed. R. Civ. P. 12(b)(7), 19. Cf. JOINDER; MISJOINDER; DISJOINDER.

nonjudicial day. See DAY.

nonjudicial foreclosure. See FORECLOSURE.

nonjudicial punishment. See PUNISHMENT.

nonjuridical (non-juu-**rid**-i-kəl), *adj.* **1.** Not of or relating to judicial proceedings or to the administration of justice <the dispute was nonjuridical>. **2.** Not of or relating to the law; not legal <a natural person is a nonjuridical entity>. Cf. JURIDICAL.

non juridicus (non juu-**rid**-i-kəs), *adj.* [Latin "not judicial"] Of or relating to a day when courts do not sit or when legal proceedings cannot be conducted, such as a Sunday.

nonjuror. 1. Someone who is not serving as a juror. **2.** *Hist.* A person who refuses to pledge allegiance to the sovereign; specif., in England and Scotland, a clergyman who refused to break the oath to James II and his heirs and successors, and recognize William of Orange as king. • In Scotland, a nonjuror was also recognized by the Presbyterian Church as a clergyman who refused to renounce the Episcopal Church when it was disestablished in favor of Presbyterianism.

nonjury, *adj.* Of or relating to a matter determined by a judicial officer, such as a judge, rather than a jury <the plaintiff asked for a nonjury trial>.

nonjury trial. See *bench trial* under TRIAL.

nonjusticiable (non-jəs-**tish**-ee-ə-bəl), *adj.* Not proper for judicial determination <the controversy was nonjusticiable because none of the parties had suffered any harm>.

nonjusticiable question. See POLITICAL QUESTION.

nonlapse statute. See ANTILAPSE STATUTE.

nonleviable (non-**lev**-ee-ə-bəl), *adj.* (Of property or assets) exempt from execution, seizure, forfeiture, or sale, as in bankruptcy. See HOMESTEAD LAW.

non liquet (non **lI**-kwet *or* **li**-kwet). [Latin "it is not clear"] **1.** *Civil law.* The principle that a decision-maker may decline to decide a dispute on the ground that the matter is unclear. • Even British judges formerly sometimes said *Non liquet* and found for the defendant. **2.** *Int'l law.* A tribunal's nondecision resulting from the unclarity of the law applicable to the dispute at hand. • In modern usage, the phrase appears almost always in passages stating what a court must not do: tribunals are routinely disallowed from declaring a *non liquet.* — Abbr. *n.l.*

nonliquidating distribution. See DISTRIBUTION.

nonliteral infringement. See DOCTRINE OF EQUIVALENTS.

nonmailable, *adj.* Of or relating to a letter or parcel that cannot be transported by mail for a particular reason such as the package's size, contents, or obscene label.

nonmarital child. See *illegitimate child* under CHILD.

nonmarketable security. See SECURITY.

nonmedical policy. See INSURANCE POLICY.

nonmember bank. See BANK.

non merchandizanda victualia (non mər-chən-di-**zan**-də vik-choo-**ay**-lee-ə), *n.* [Law Latin "not to merchandise victuals"] *Hist.* A writ directing justices of assize to investigate and punish town magistrates who retailed victuals while in office.

nonmerchantable title. See *unmarketable title* under TITLE (2).

non molestando (non moh-lə-**stan**-doh), *n.* [Law Latin "by not molesting"] *Hist.* A writ available to a person whose possession of land has been disturbed, contrary to the Crown's protection.

nonmonetary item. An asset or liability whose price fluctuates over time (such as land, equipment, inventory, and warranty obligations).

nonmovant (non-**moov**-ənt). A litigating party other than the one that has filed the motion currently under consideration <the court, in ruling on the plaintiff's motion for summary judgment, properly resolved all doubts in the nonmovant's favor>.

nonnavigable, *adj.* **1.** (Of a body of water) unaffected by the tide. **2.** (Of a body of water) incapable of allowing vessels to pass for travel or commerce. **3.** (Of any vessel) incapable of being steered.

nonnegotiable, *adj.* **1.** (Of an agreement or term) not subject to change <the kidnapper's demands were nonnegotiable>. **2.** (Of an instrument or note) incapable of transferring by indorsement or delivery. Cf. NEGOTIABLE INSTRUMENT.

nonnegotiable bill of lading. See *straight bill of lading* under BILL OF LADING.

nonnegotiable document of title. See DOCUMENT OF TITLE.

non obstante (non ahb-**stan**-tee *or* əb-**stan**-tee), *n.* [Latin "notwithstanding"]. **1.** *Hist.* A doctrine used by the Crown of England to give effect to certain documents, such as grants or letters patent, despite any laws to the contrary. • This doctrine was abolished by the Bill of Rights. **2.** A phrase used in documents to preclude any interpretation contrary to the stated object or purpose. **3.** NON OBSTANTE VEREDICTO.

non obstante veredicto (non ahb-**stan**-tee [*or* əb-**stan**-tee] ver-ə-**dik**-toh). [Latin] Notwithstanding the verdict. — Often shortened to *non obstante*. — Abbr. n.o.v.; NOV. See *judgment notwithstanding the verdict* under JUDGMENT.

nonobviousness. *Patents.* **1.** (Of an invention) the quality of being sufficiently different from the prior art that, at the time the invention was made, it would not have been obvious to a person having ordinary skill in the art relevant to the invention. **2.** The requirement that this quality must be demonstrated for an invention to be patentable. • Nonobviousness may be demonstrated with evidence concerning prior art or with other objective evidence, such as commercial success or professional approval. 35 USCA § 103. Cf. NOVELTY.

nonoccupant visitor. *Criminal procedure.* A person who owns, coowns, is employed by, or is a patron of a business enterprise where a search is being conducted in accordance with a search warrant.

nonoccupational, *adj.* **1.** Not relating to one's job. **2.** Of or relating to a general-disability policy providing benefits to an individual whose disability prevents that individual from working at any occupation.

nonoccupier. One who does not occupy a particular piece of land; esp., an entrant on land who is either an invitee or a licensee. See INVITEE; LICENSEE (2).

non omittas propter liberatem (non ə-**mit**-əs **prop**-tər lib-ə-**ray**-təm). [Latin "do not omit because of any liberty"] *Hist.* A clause, usu. contained in writs of execution, directing the sheriff to execute the writ regardless of whether the sheriff had been granted the requisite special authority from a franchise (liberty) or district.

nonoperating income. See INCOME.

nonoperative performance bond. See PERFORMANCE BOND.

nonoriginal bill. See BILL (2).

nonparticipating, *adj.* Of or relating to not taking part in something; specif., not sharing or having the right to share in profits or surpluses. — Often shortened to *nonpar.*

nonparticipating preferred stock. See STOCK.

nonpayment. Failure to deliver money or other valuables, esp. when due, in discharge of an obligation. Cf. PAYMENT (1).

nonperformance. Failure to discharge an obligation (esp. a contractual one). Cf. PERFORMANCE; MISPERFORMANCE.

nonperforming loan. See LOAN.

nonpersonal action. See ACTION.

non plevin (non **plev**-in). [Latin] *Hist.* The failure to timely replevy land after it is taken by the Crown on a default.

non ponendis in assisis et juratis (non pə-**nen**-dis in ə-**sI**-zis et juu-**ray**-tis), *n.* [Law Latin "not to be put in assizes and juries"] *Hist.* A writ discharging a person from jury duty.

nonprivity (non-**priv**-ə-tee). The fact or state of not being in privity of contract with another; lack of privity. See PRIVITY.

horizontal nonprivity. The lack of privity occurring when the plaintiff is not a buyer within the distributive chain, but one who consumes, uses, or is otherwise affected by the goods. • For example, a houseguest who becomes ill after eating meat that her host bought from the local deli is in horizontal nonprivity with the deli.

vertical nonprivity. The lack of privity occurring when the plaintiff is a buyer within the distributive chain who did not buy directly from the defendant. • For example, someone who buys a drill from a local hardware store and later sues the drill's manufacturer is in vertical nonprivity with the manufacturer.

nonprobate, *adj.* **1.** Of or relating to some method of estate disposition apart from wills <nonprobate distribution>. **2.** Of or relating to the property so disposed <nonprobate assets>.

non procedendo ad assisam (non proh-sə-**den**-doh ad ə-**sɪ**-zəm). See DE NON PROCEDENDO AD ASSISAM.

non procedendo ad assisam rege inconsulto (non proh-sə-**den**-doh ad ə-**sɪ**-zəm **ree**-jee in-kən-**səl**-toh). [Latin] *Hist.* A writ to put a stop to the trial of a case (pertaining to one who is in the king's service, etc.) when the king has not been consulted.

nonprofit association. A group organized for a purpose other than to generate income or profit, such as a scientific, religious, or educational organization.

nonprofit corporation. See CORPORATION.

nonproliferation treaty. See TREATY.

non pros (**non** prahs). *abbr.* NON PROSEQUITUR.

non prosequitur (non prə-**sek**-wə-tər *or* proh-). [Latin "he does not prosecute"] The judgment rendered against a plaintiff who has not pursued the case. — Often shortened to *non pros*.

nonpublic forum. *Constitutional law.* Public property that is not designated or traditionally considered an arena for public communication, such as a jail or a military base. • The government's means of regulating a nonpublic forum need only be reasonable and viewpoint-neutral to be constitutional. Cf. PUBLIC FORUM.

non-purchase-money, *adj.* Not pertaining to or being an obligation secured by property obtained by a loan <non-purchase-money mortgage>. Cf. *purchase-money mortgage* under MORTGAGE.

nonqualified deferred-compensation plan. See EMPLOYEE BENEFIT PLAN.

nonqualified pension plan. See PENSION PLAN.

nonqualified stock option. See STOCK OPTION.

non quieta movere (non kwɪ-**ee**-tə moh-**veer**-ee), *n.* [Latin "not to disturb what is settled"] Stare decisis. • *Non quieta movere* expresses the same principle as *stare decisis*. It is part of the longer phrase *stare decisis et non quieta movere* ("to adhere to precedents, and not to unsettle things that are established"). See STARE DECISIS.

nonrecognition. *Int'l law.* The refusal of one government to recognize the legitimacy of another government.

nonrecognition provision. *Tax.* A statutory rule that allows all or part of a realized gain or loss not to be recognized for tax purposes. • Generally, this type of provision only postpones the recognition of the gain or loss. See RECOGNITION (3).

nonrecourse, *adj.* Of or relating to an obligation that can be satisfied only out of the collateral securing the obligation and not out of the debtor's other assets.

nonrecourse loan. See LOAN.

nonrecourse note. See NOTE (1).

nonrecurring dividend. See *extraordinary dividend* under DIVIDEND.

nonrefoulement (non-ri-**fowl**-mənt). [French] A refugee's right of not being expelled from one state to another, esp. to one where his or her life or liberty would be threatened. Cf. REFOULEMENT.

nonrefund annuity. See ANNUITY.

nonremovable inmate. An otherwise deportable alien who cannot be deported because the United States does not maintain diplomatic ties with the alien's country of origin. — Also termed *indefinite detainee*; *lifer*.

nonrenewal. A failure to renew something, such as a lease or an insurance policy.

nonreporting issuer. See ISSUER.

nonresidence, *n.* **1.** *Eccles. law.* The absence of a spiritual person from the rectory (benefice). • This was normally an offense punishable by sequestering the benefice and forfeiting part of its income. **2.** The status of living outside the limits of a particular place.

nonresident, *n.* One who does not live within the jurisdiction in question. — Abbr. n.r. — **nonresident,** *adj.*

nonresident alien. See ALIEN.

nonresident decedent. See DECEDENT.

non residentia clerici regis (non rez-i-**den**-shee-ə **kler**-ə-sI **ree**-jis). See DE NON RESIDENTIA CLERICI REGIS.

non residentio pro clerico regis (non rez-i-**den**-shee-oh proh **kler**-ə-koh **ree**-jis). [Latin "by nonresidence for a royal clerk"] *Hist.* A writ ordering a bishop not to harass a clerk who, being employed in the royal service, has become a nonresident.

nonresident-motorist statute. A state law governing the liabilities and obligations of nonresidents who use the state's highways.

nonretroactivity principle. See NEW-RULE PRINCIPLE.

non sanae mentis (non **say**-nee **men**-tis), *adj.* [Latin] Not of sound mind.

non-self-governing territory. See TERRITORY.

non sequitur (non **sek**-wə-tər). [Latin "it does not follow"] **1.** An inference or conclusion that does not logically follow from the premises. **2.** A remark or response that does not logically follow from what was previously said. Cf. NON CONSTAT.

nonservice. The failure to serve a summons, warrant, or other process in a civil or criminal case.

nonshareholder constituency. A group of nonstockholders, such as employees or the public, who have an interest in the corporation's business — an interest that the corporation may legally consider, in addition to shareholders' interests, in making major policy decisions. — Also termed *alternative constituency.*

nonskip person. *Tax.* A person who is not a skip person for purposes of the generation-skipping transfer tax. IRC (26 USCA) § 2613(b). See SKIP PERSON.

non solvendo pecuniam ad quam clericus mulctatur pro non-residentia (non sol-**ven**-doh pi-**kyoo**-nee-əm ad kwam **kler**-ə-kəs məlk-**tay**-tər proh non-rez-ə-**den**-shee-ə). [Latin] *Hist.* A writ prohibiting an ordinary from taking a pecuniary mulct imposed on a clerk of the sovereign for nonresidence.

nonsovereign state. See STATE (1).

nonstatutory bond. See *voluntary bond* under BOND (3).

nonstock corporation. See CORPORATION.

non submissit (non səb-**mis**-it). [Latin "he did not submit"] In a debt action on a bond to perform an arbitration award, a defendant's denial that he or she submitted to the arbitration.

non sui juris (non **s[y]oo**-I *or* **soo**-ee **joor**-is), *adj.* [Latin "not of one's own right"] Lacking legal age or capacity. Cf. SUI JURIS.

nonsuit, *n.* **1.** A plaintiff's voluntary dismissal of a case or of a defendant, without a decision on the merits. • Under the Federal Rules of Civil procedure, a voluntary dismissal is equivalent to a nonsuit. Fed. R. Civ. P. 41(a). — Also termed *voluntary discontinuance.* **2.** A court's dismissal of a case or of a defendant because the plaintiff has failed to make out a legal case or to bring forward sufficient evidence. See *judgment of nonsuit* under JUDGMENT. — **nonsuit,** *vb.*

> "It did not follow [in the 15th–18th centuries], of course, that the issue in a trial at *nisi prius* would ever get to the jury at all, for it might be that the plaintiff would be 'non-suited' on the ground that he had failed to prove something which was essential to his case or that the case which he had proved was different from that which he had pleaded." Geoffrey Radcliffe & Geoffrey Cross, *The English Legal System* 184 (G.J. Hand & D.J. Bentley eds., 6th ed. 1977).

> "Nonsuit . . . is equivalent to a demurrer to the evidence in that, even if all facts that plaintiff presents are true, the evidence is not, as a matter of law, sufficient to entitle plaintiff to a judgment. However, a voluntary nonsuit, unlike a demurrer or a directed verdict which resolves the action on its merits, may result in another trial of the cause." 75A Am. Jur. 2d *Trial* § 853 (1991).

compulsory nonsuit. An involuntary nonsuit.

non sum informatus (non səm in-fər-**may**-təs), *n.* [Latin "I am not informed"] *Hist.* A type of default judgment based on a defense attorney's statement that the client gave no instructions to answer the lawsuit.

nonsupport. The failure to support a person that one is legally obliged to provide for, such as a child, spouse, or other dependent. • Nonsupport is a crime in most states, where it is often termed *criminal nonsupport.*

non tenent insimul (non **ten**-ənt **in**-sim-əl), *n.* [Latin "they do not hold together"] *Hist.* In a partition action, the defendant's plea denying a joint tenancy with the plaintiff in the estate at issue.

non tenuit (non **ten**-yuu-wit). [Latin] In an action of replevin, the plaintiff's plea in bar to the defendant's assertion of a rightful taking of property (avowry), whereby the plaintiff denies holding the property in the manner and form alleged.

nontenure (non **ten**-yər). *Hist.* A general denial in a real action, whereby the defendant denies holding some or all of the land in question.

nonterm. See NON TERMINUS.

non terminus (non **ter**-mi-nəs), *n.* [Law Latin "not the end"] *Hist.* The vacation between two terms of a court. • In England, it was also called "the time of days of the king's peace." — Also termed *nonterm*; *non term*.

nontestifying expert. See *consulting expert* under EXPERT.

nontrading partnership. See PARTNERSHIP.

nontraditional public forum. See *designated public forum* under PUBLIC FORUM.

nonunion, *adj.* **1.** (Of a person or thing) not belonging to or affiliated with a labor union <a nonunion worker> <a nonunion contract>. **2.** (Of a position or belief) not favoring labor unions <she will not alter her nonunion stance>. **3.** (Of a product) not made by labor-union members <the equipment was of nonunion manufacture>.

nonuse. 1. The failure to exercise a right <nonuse of the easement>. **2.** The condition of not being utilized <the equipment was in nonuse>.

nonuser. The failure to exercise a right (such as a franchise or easement), as a result of which the person having the right might lose it <the government may not revoke a citizen's voting right because of nonuser>. Cf. USER (1).

non usurpavit (non yoo-sər-**pay**-vit). [Latin "he has not usurped"] A defendant's denial of an alleged usurpation of an office or franchise.

non valentia agere (non və-**len**-shee-ə **aj**-ə-ree). [Latin] Inability to sue. See NONABILITY.

nonverbal testimony. See TESTIMONY.

nonvital term. See *nonfundamental term* under TERM (2).

nonvoluntary euthanasia. See EUTHANASIA.

nonvoting stock. See STOCK.

non vult contendere (non vəlt kən-**ten**-də-ree). [Latin "he will not contest it"] NO CONTEST.

nonwaiver agreement. *Insurance.* A contract (supplementing a liability-insurance policy) in which the insured acknowledges that the insurer's investigation or defense of a claim against the insured does not waive the insurer's right to contest coverage later. — Also termed *reservation of rights*.

nook of land. *Hist.* A variable quantity of land, often 12.5 acres.

no-oral-modification clause. A contractual provision stating that the parties cannot make any oral modifications or alterations to the agreement. — Abbr. NOM clause. See INTEGRATION CLAUSE.

no par. See *no-par stock* under STOCK.

no-par stock. See STOCK.

no-par-value stock. See *no-par stock* under STOCK.

no-pass, no-play rule. A state law requiring public-school students who participate in extracurricular activities (such as sports or band) to maintain a minimum grade-point average or else lose the right to participate.

no progress. See WANT OF PROSECUTION.

no recourse. 1. The lack of means by which to obtain reimbursement from, or a judgment against, a person or entity <the bank had no recourse against the individual executive for collection of the corporation's debts>. **2.** A notation indicating that such means are lacking <the bill was indorsed "no recourse">. See *nonrecourse loan* under LOAN; WITHOUT RECOURSE.

no-retreat rule. *Criminal law.* The doctrine that the victim of a murderous assault may use deadly force in self-defense if there is no reasonable alternative to avoid the assailant's threatened harm. • A majority of American jurisdictions have adopted this rule. Cf. RETREAT RULE.

no-right, *n.* The absence of right against another in some particular respect. • A no-right is the correlative of a privilege. — Also termed *liability.*

"A says to B, 'If you will agree to pay me $100 for this horse you may have him and you may indicate your agreement by taking him.' This is a physical fact, called an offer, consisting of certain muscular acts of A having certain physical results in B. The legal relations immediately following are (in part) as follows: B now has the *privilege* of taking the horse and A has *no-right* that he shall not . . . ." William R. Anson, *Principles of the Law of Contract* 321 (Arthur L. Corbin ed., 3d Am. ed. 1919).

" 'No-right' is sometimes derided as being a purely negative concept. If a no-right is something that is not a right, the class of no-rights must, it is said, include elephants. The answer is that negative terms are often useful as alternative ways of stating propositions involving negatives. For instance, the terms 'alien,' 'cold,' and 'dark' are all negative or privative, because their meaning includes the idea of the absence of something else. The proposition that A is an alien means that A is not a British subject; in the one mode of statement the negative is incorporated in the noun, whereas in the other it is expressed as a separate word. Similarly the word 'liberty' is negative, and critics who attack the concept of no-right should logically attack the concept of liberty also. . . . [L]iberty means 'no-duty not.' . . . [F]or the sake of clear thinking it is necessary to give each of the four meanings [of right] a separate name. Words like 'no-right' and 'no-duty' may seem uncouth at first sight, but it is surely a clear and useful statement to say that 'right' sometimes means 'no-duty not.' " John Salmond, *Jurisprudence* 240–41 n.(u) (Glanville L. Williams ed., 10th ed. 1947).

norm. 1. A model or standard accepted (voluntarily or involuntarily) by society or other large group, against which society judges someone or something. • An example of a norm is the standard for right or wrong behavior. **2.** An actual or set standard determined by the typical or most frequent behavior of a group.

basic norm. In the legal theory of Hans Kelsen, the law from which all the other laws in a society derive. • Kelsen's "pure theory of law" maintains that laws are norms. Therefore, a society's legal system is made up of its norms, and each legal norm derives its validity from other legal norms. Ultimately, the validity of all laws is tested against the "basic norm," which may be as simple as the concept that all pronouncements of the monarch are to be obeyed. Or it may be an elaborate system of lawmaking, such as a constitution. — Also termed *grundnorm.* See PURE THEORY.

normal, *adj.* **1.** According to a regular pattern; natural <it is normal to be nervous in court>. **2.** According to an established rule or norm <it is not normal to deface statues>. **3.** Setting a standard or norm <a normal curriculum was established in the schools>.

normal balance. A type of debit or credit balance that is usu. found in ledger accounts. • For example, assets usu. have debit balances and liabilities usu. have credit balances.

normal college. See NORMAL SCHOOL.

normal law. The law as it applies to persons who are free from legal disabilities.

normal market. See CONTANGO.

normal mind. A mental capacity that is similar to that of the majority of people who can handle life's ordinary responsibilities.

normal school. A training school for public-school teachers. • Normal schools first appeared in the United States in the 1800s and were two-year post-high-school training programs for elementary-school teachers. At the turn of the century, normal schools expanded into four-year teaching colleges. Most of these institutions have developed into liberal arts colleges offering a wider variety of education and teaching programs. — Also termed *normal college.*

Norman French. A language that was spoken by the Normans and became the official language of English courts after the Norman Conquest in 1066. • The language deteriorated into Law French and continued to be used until the late 17th century. English became the official language of the courts in 1731.

normative, *adj.* Establishing or conforming to a norm or standard <Rawls's theory describes normative principles of justice>.

normative jurisprudence. See NATURAL LAW.

Norris–La Guardia Act (**nor**-is lə **gwahr**-dee-ə). A 1932 federal law that forbids federal courts from ruling on labor policy and that severely limits their power to issue injunctions in labor disputes. • The statute was passed to curb federal-court abuses of the injunctive process, to declare the government's neutrality on labor policy, to curtail employers' widespread use of injunctions to thwart union activity, and to promote the use of collective bargaining to resolve disputes. 29 USCA §§ 101–115. — Also termed *Labor Disputes Act*.

Norroy (**nor**-oy). *English law*. The third of the three Kings at Arms (and the chief herald), whose province lies on the north side of the river Trent. • The Norroy's duties have included the supervision of weddings and funerals of nobility. See HERALD.

North American Free Trade Agreement. A trilateral treaty — entered into on January 1, 1994 between the United States, Canada, and Mexico — that phases out all tariffs and eliminates many nontariff barriers (such as quotas) inhibiting the free trade of goods between the participating nations. — Abbr. NAFTA.

North Eastern Reporter. A set of regional lawbooks that, being part of the West Group's National Reporter System, contain every published decision from Illinois, Indiana, Massachusetts, New York, and Ohio, from 1885 to date. • The first series ran from 1885 to 1936; the second series is the current one. — Abbr. N.E.; N.E.2d.

North Western Reporter. A set of regional lawbooks that, being part of the West Group's National Reporter System, contain every published decision from Iowa, Michigan, Minnesota, Nebraska, North Dakota, South Dakota, and Wisconsin, from 1879 to date. • The first series ran from 1879 to 1941; the second series is the current one. — Abbr. N.W.; N.W.2d.

Northwest Territory. *Hist.* The first possession of the United States, being the geographical region south of the Great Lakes, north of the Ohio River, and east of the Mississippi River, as designated by the Continental Congress in the late 1700s. • This area includes the present states of Ohio, Indiana, Illinois, Michigan, Wisconsin, and the eastern part of Minnesota.

noscitur a sociis (**nos**-ə-tər ay [*or* ah] **soh**-shee-is). [Latin "it is known by its associates"] A canon of construction holding that the meaning of an unclear word or phrase should be determined by the words immediately surrounding it. Cf. EJUSDEM GENERIS; EXPRESSIO UNIUS EST EXCLUSIO ALTERIUS; RULE OF RANK.

> "The *ejusdem generis* rule is an example of a broader linguistic rule or practice to which reference is made by the Latin tag *noscitur a sociis*. Words, even if they are not general words like 'whatsoever' or 'otherwise' preceded by specific words, are liable to be affected by other words with which they are associated." Rupert Cross, *Statutory Interpretation* 118 (1976).

no-setoff certificate. See WAIVER OF DEFENSES.

no-shop provision. A stipulation prohibiting one or more parties to a commercial contract from pursuing or entering into a more favorable agreement with a third party.

nosocomus (nos-ə-**koh**-məs), *n.* [Greek "an attendant on the side"] *Hist.* A person who manages a hospital that cares for paupers.

no-strike clause. A labor-agreement provision that prohibits employees from striking for any reason and establishes instead an arbitration system for resolving labor disputes.

nota (**noh**-tə), *n.* [Latin "mark"] *Hist.* **1.** A promissory note. **2.** A brand placed on a person by law.

nota bene (**noh**-tə **ben**-ee *or* **bee**-nee *or* **ben**-ay). See N.B.

notae (**noh**-tee), *n. pl.* [Latin] *Hist.* Shorthand characters. See NOTARIUS.

notarial, *adj.* Of or relating to the official acts of a notary public <a notarial seal>. See NOTARY PUBLIC.

notarial act. An official function of a notary public, such as placing a seal on an affidavit. See NOTARY PUBLIC.

notarial protest certificate. See PROTEST CERTIFICATE.

notarial record. See JOURNAL OF NOTARIAL ACTS.

notarial register. See JOURNAL OF NOTARIAL ACTS.

notarial seal. See NOTARY SEAL.

notarial will. See WILL.

notarius (noh-**tair**-ee-əs), *n.* [fr. Latin *nota* "a character or mark"] **1.** *Roman law.* A writer (sometimes a slave) who takes dictation or records proceedings by shorthand. • A *notarius* was later also called a *scriba*. **2.** *Roman law.* An officer who takes a magistrate's dictation by shorthand. **3.** *Hist.* An officer who prepares deeds and other contracts. **4.** A notary or a scribe.

notary public (**noh**-tə-ree), *n.* A person authorized by a state to administer oaths, certify documents, attest to the authenticity of signatures, and perform official acts in commercial matters, such as protesting negotiable instruments. — Often shortened to *notary*. — Abbr. n.p. Pl. **notaries public.** — **notarize,** *vb.* — **notarial,** *adj.*

> "A notary public is an officer long known to the civil law, and designated as *registrarius*, *actuarius*, or *scrivarius*." John Proffatt, *A Treatise on the Law Relating to the Office and Duties of Notaries Public* § 1, at 1 (John F. Tyler & John J. Stephens eds., 2d ed. 1892).

> "The notary public, or notary, is an official known in nearly all civilized countries. The office is of ancient origin. In Rome, during the republic, it existed, the title being *tabelliones forenses*, or *personae publicae*; and there are records of the appointment of notaries by the Frankish kings and the Popes as early as the ninth century. They were chiefly employed in drawing up legal documents; as scribes or scriveners they took minutes and made short drafts of writings, either of a public or a private nature. In modern times their more characteristic duty is to attest the genuineness of any deeds or writings, in order to render the same available as evidence of the facts therein contained." Benjamin F. Rex, *The Notaries' Manual* § 1, at 1–2 (J.H. McMillan ed., 6th ed. 1913).

notary record book. See JOURNAL OF NOTARIAL ACTS.

notary seal. 1. The imprint or embossment made by a notary public's seal. **2.** A device, usu. a stamp or embosser, that makes an imprint on a notarized document. — Also termed *notarial seal.*

embossed seal. **1.** A notary seal that is impressed onto a document, raising the impression above the surface. • An embossed seal clearly identifies the original document because the seal is only faintly reproducible. For this reason, this type of seal is required in some states and on some documents notarized for federal purposes. **2.** The embossment made by this seal.

rubber-stamp seal. **1.** In most states, a notary public's official seal, which is inkstamped onto documents and is therefore photographically reproducible. • It typically includes the notary's name, the state seal, the words "Notary Public," the name of the county where the notary's bond is filed, and the expiration date of the notary's commission. **2.** The imprint made by this seal.

notation credit. A letter of credit specifying that anyone purchasing or paying a draft or demand for payment made under it must note the amount of the draft or demand on the letter. See LETTER OF CREDIT.

note, *n.* **1.** A written promise by one party (the *maker*) to pay money to another party (the *payee*) or to bearer. • A note is a two-party negotiable instrument, unlike a draft (which is a three-party instrument). — Also termed *promissory note*. Cf. DRAFT (1).

accommodation note. A note that an accommodating party has signed and thereby assumed secondary liability for; ACCOMMODATION PAPER.

approved indorsed note. A note indorsed by a person other than the maker to provide additional security.

balloon note. A note requiring small periodic payments but a very large final payment. • The periodic payments usu. cover only interest, while the final payment (the balloon payment) represents the entire principal.

banknote. See BANKNOTE.

blue note. A note that maintains a life-insurance policy in effect until the note becomes due.

bought note. A written memorandum of a sale delivered to the buyer by the broker responsible for the sale.

circular note. See LETTER OF CREDIT.

coal note. *Hist.* A promissory note written according to a statute that required payment for coal out of any vessel in the port of London to be in cash or by promissory note containing the words "value received in coal." • Noncompliance with the statute resulted in a fine of £100.

cognovit note. See COGNOVIT NOTE.

collateral note. See *secured note.*

coupon note. A note with attached interest coupons that the holder may present for payment as each coupon matures.

demand note. A note payable whenever the creditor wants to be paid. See *call loan* under LOAN.

executed note. A note that has been signed and delivered.

floating-rate note. A note carrying a variable interest rate that is periodically adjusted within a predetermined range, usu. every six months, in relation to an index, such as Treasury bill rates. — Also termed *floater.*

hand note. A note that is secured by a collateral note.

installment note. A note payable at regular intervals. — Also termed *serial note.*

inverse-floating-rate note. A note structured in such a way that its interest rate moves in the opposite direction from the underlying index (such as the London Interbank Offer Rate). • Many such notes are risky investments because if interest rates rise, the securities lose their value and their coupon earnings fall. — Also termed *inverse floater.*

joint and several note. A note for which multiple makers are jointly and severally liable for repayment, meaning that the payee may legally look to all the makers, or any one of them, for payment of the entire debt. See *joint and several liability* under LIABILITY.

joint note. A note for which multiple makers are jointly, but not severally, liable for repayment, meaning that the payee must legally look to all the makers together for payment of the debt. See *joint liability* under LIABILITY.

mortgage note. A note evidencing a loan for which real property has been offered as security.

negotiable note. See NEGOTIABLE INSTRUMENT.

nonrecourse note. A note that may be satisfied upon default only by means of the collateral securing the note, not by the debtor's other assets. Cf. *recourse note.*

note of hand. See *promissory note.*

premium note. A promissory note given by an insured to an insurance company for part or all of the premium.

promissory note. An unconditional written promise, signed by the maker, to pay absolutely and in any event a certain sum of money either to, or to the order of, the bearer or a designated person. — Also termed *note of hand.*

recourse note. A note that may be satisfied upon default by pursuing the debtor's other assets in addition to the collateral securing the note. Cf. *nonrecourse note.*

reissuable note. A note that may again be put into circulation after having once been paid.

renewal note. A note that continues an obligation that was due under a prior note.

sale note. A broker's memorandum on the terms of a sale, given to the buyer and seller.

savings note. A short-term, interest-bearing paper issued by a bank or the U.S. government.

secured note. A note backed by a pledge of real or personal property as collateral. — Also termed *collateral note.*

sold note. A written memorandum of sale delivered to the seller by the broker responsible for the sale, and usu. outlining the terms of the sale. See CONFIRMATION SLIP.

stock note. A note that is secured by securities, such as stocks or bonds.

tax-anticipation note. A short-term obligation issued by state or local governments to finance current expenditures and that usu. matures once the local government receives individual and corporate tax payments. — Abbr. TAN.

time note. A note payable only at a specified time and not on demand.

treasury note. See TREASURY NOTE.

unsecured note. A note not backed by collateral.

2. A scholarly legal essay shorter than an article and restricted in scope, explaining or criticizing a particular set of cases or a general area of the law, and usu. written by a law student for publication in a law review. — Also termed *comment*; *lawnote.* Cf. ANNOTATION. **3.** A minute or memorandum intended for later reference; MEMORANDUM (1).

note, *vb.* **1.** To notice carefully or with particularity <the defendant noted that the plaintiff seemed nervous>. **2.** To put down in writing <the court reporter noted the objection in the record>. **3.** *Archaic.* To brand <as punishment, the criminal was noted>. See NOTA.

note broker. See BROKER.

note of a fine. *Hist. English law.* A step in the judicial process for conveying land, consisting of a chirographer's brief of the proceedings before the documents of conveyance are engrossed. — Also termed *abstract of a fine.* See FINE.

note of allowance. *English law.* A master's note, upon receiving a party's memorandum of an error of law in a case, allowing error to be asserted.

note of hand. See *promissory note* under NOTE (1). Pl. **notes of hand.**

note of protest. A notary's preliminary memo, to be formalized at a later time, stating that a negotiable instrument was neither paid nor accepted upon presentment. See PROTEST.

note payable. See *account payable* under ACCOUNT.

note receivable. See *account receivable* under ACCOUNT.

note verbal (noht **vər**-bəl). *Int'l law.* An unsigned diplomatic note, usu. written in the third person, that sometimes accompanies a diplomatic message or note of protest to further explain the country's position or to request certain action. — Also spelled *note verbale* (vair-**bahl**).

not-for-profit corporation. See *nonprofit corporation* under CORPORATION.

not found. Words placed on a bill of indictment, meaning that the grand jury has insufficient evidence to support a true bill. See IGNORAMUS; NO BILL. Cf. TRUE BILL.

not guilty. 1. *Criminal law.* A defendant's plea denying the crime charged. **2.** A jury verdict acquitting the defendant because the prosecution failed to prove the defendant's guilt beyond a reasonable doubt.

***not guilty by reason of insanity.* 1.** A not-guilty verdict, based on mental illness, that usu. does not release the defendant but instead results in commitment to a mental institution. **2.** A criminal defendant's plea of not guilty that is based on the insanity defense. — Abbr. NGRI. — Also termed *not guilty on the ground of insanity.* See INSANITY DEFENSE.

3. *Common-law pleading.* A defendant's plea denying both an act of trespass alleged in a plaintiff's declaration and the plaintiff's right to possess the property at issue.

> "In trespass, whether to person or property, the general issue is 'not guilty.' It operates in the first place as a denial that the defendant committed the act of trespass alleged, to wit, the application of force to the plaintiff's person, the entry on his land, or the taking or damages of his goods. It also denies the plaintiff's possession, title, or right of possession of the land or goods." Benjamin J. Shipman, *Handbook of Common-Law Pleading* § 170, at 307–08 (Henry Winthrop Ballantine ed., 3d ed. 1923).

not guilty by statute. *Hist.* Under certain acts of Parliament, the pleading form for a defendant's general denial in a civil action. • This pleading form allowed a public officer to indicate action under a statute. The officer had to write the words "by statute" in the margin along with the year, chapter, and section of the applicable statute, and the defendant could not file any other defense without leave of court. The right to plead "not guilty by statute" was essentially removed by the Public Authorities Protection Act of 1893.

4. A general denial in an ejectment action.

> "The general issue in ejectment is not guilty. This plea operates as follows: (1) As a denial of the unlawfulness of the withholding; i.e., of the plaintiff's title and right of possession. (2) All defenses in excuse or discharge, including the statute of limitations, are available under the general issue in ejectment." Benjamin J. Shipman, *Handbook of Common-Law Pleading* § 188, at 333 (Henry Winthrop Ballantine ed., 3d ed. 1923).

not-guilty plea. See PLEA (1).

nothous (**noh**-thəs), *adj. Archaic.* Spurious; illegitimate.

nothus (**noh**-thəs), *n.* [fr. Greek *nothos* "false"] *Roman law.* An illegitimate child; one of base birth. • If the child's mother was a Roman citizen, the child was also a Roman citizen. — Also termed *spurius.*

notice, *n.* **1.** Legal notification required by law or agreement, or imparted by operation of law as a result of some fact (such as the recording of an instrument); definite legal cognizance, actual or constructive, of an existing right or title <under the lease, the tenant must give the landlord written notice 30 days before vacating the premises>. • A person has notice of a fact or condition if that person (1) has actual knowledge of it; (2) has received a notice of it; (3) has reason to know about it; (4) knows about a related fact; or (5) is considered as having been able to ascertain it by checking an official filing or recording. **2.** The condition of being so notified, whether or not actual awareness exists <all prospective buyers were on notice of the judgment lien>. **3.** A written or printed announcement <the notice of sale was posted on the courthouse bulletin board>. Cf. KNOWLEDGE.

actual notice. Notice given directly to, or received personally by, a party.

adequate notice. See *due notice.*

commercial-law notice. Under the UCC, notice of a fact arising either as a result of actual knowledge or notification of the fact, or as a result of circumstances under which a person would have reason to know of the fact. UCC § 1–201(25).

constructive notice. Notice arising by presumption of law from the existence of facts and circumstances that a party had a duty to take notice of, such as a registered deed or a pending lawsuit; notice presumed by law to have been acquired by a person and thus imputed to that person. — Also termed *legal notice*.

direct notice. Actual notice of a fact that is brought directly to a party's attention. — Also termed *positive notice*.

due notice. Sufficient and proper notice that is intended to and likely to reach a particular person or the public; notice that is legally adequate given the particular circumstance. — Also termed *adequate notice*; *legal notice*.

express notice. Actual knowledge or notice given to a party directly, not arising from any inference, duty, or inquiry.

fair notice. **1.** Sufficient notice apprising a litigant of the opposing party's claim. **2.** The requirement that a pleading adequately apprise the opposing party of a claim. • A pleading must be drafted so that an opposing attorney of reasonable competence would be able to ascertain the nature and basic issues of the controversy and the evidence probably relevant to those issues. **3.** FAIR WARNING.

immediate notice. **1.** Notice given as soon as possible. **2.** More commonly, and esp. on notice of an insurance claim, notice that is reasonable under the circumstances.

implied notice. Notice that is inferred from facts that a person had a means of knowing and that is thus imputed to that person; actual notice of facts or circumstances that, if properly followed up, would have led to a knowledge of the particular fact in question. — Also termed *indirect notice*; *presumptive notice*.

imputed notice. Information attributed to a person whose agent, having received actual notice of the information, has a duty to disclose it to that person. • For example, notice of a hearing may be imputed to a witness because it was actually disclosed to that witness's attorney of record.

indirect notice. See *implied notice*.

inquiry notice. Notice attributed to a person when the information would lead an ordinarily prudent person to investigate the matter further; esp., the time at which the victim of an alleged securities fraud became aware of facts that would have prompted a reasonable person to investigate.

judicial notice. See JUDICIAL NOTICE.

legal notice. **1.** See *constructive notice*. **2.** See *due notice*.

notice by publication. See *public notice*.

personal notice. Oral or written notice, according to the circumstances, given directly to the affected person.

positive notice. See *direct notice*.

presumptive notice. See *implied notice*.

public notice. Notice given to the public or persons affected, usu. by publishing in a newspaper of general circulation. • This notice is usu. required, for example, in matters of public concern. — Also termed *notice by publication*.

reasonable notice. Notice that is fairly to be expected or required under the particular circumstances.

record notice. Constructive notice of the contents of an instrument, such as a deed or mortgage, that has been properly recorded.

notice, *vb.* **1.** To give legal notice to or of <the plaintiff's lawyer noticed depositions of all the experts that the defendant listed>. **2.** To realize or give attention to <the lawyer noticed that the witness was leaving>.

notice act. See NOTICE STATUTE.

notice-and-comment period. *Administrative law.* The statutory time frame during which an administrative agency publishes a proposed regulation and receives public comment on the regulation. • The regulation cannot take effect until after this period expires. — Often shortened to *comment period*.

notice-and-comment rulemaking. See *informal rulemaking* under RULEMAKING.

notice by publication. See *public notice* under NOTICE.

notice doctrine. The equitable doctrine that when a new owner takes an estate with notice that someone else had a claim on it at the time of the transfer, that claim may still be asserted against the new owner even if it might have been disregarded at law. — Also termed *doctrine of notice*.

notice filing. The perfection of a security interest under Article 9 of the UCC by filing only a financing statement, as opposed to a copy or abstract of the security agreement. • The financing statement must contain (1) the debtor's signature, (2) the secured party's name and address, (3) the debtor's name and mailing address, and (4) a description of the types of, or items of, collateral.

notice of appeal. A document filed with a court and served on the other parties, stating an intention to appeal a trial court's judgment or order. • In most jurisdictions, filing a notice of appeal is the act by which the appeal is perfected. For instance, the Federal Rules of Appellate Procedure provide that an appeal is taken by filing a notice of appeal with the clerk of the district court from which the appeal is taken, and that the clerk is to send copies of the notice to all the other parties' attorneys, as well as the court of appeals. Fed. R. App. P. 3(a), (d). — Also termed *claim of appeal*. See APPEAL.

notice of appearance. 1. *Procedure.* A party's written notice filed with the court or oral announcement on the record informing the court and the other parties that the party wants to participate in the case. **2.** *Bankruptcy.* A written notice filed with the court or oral announcement in open court by a person who wants to receive all pleadings in a particular case. • This notice is usu. filed by an attorney for a creditor who wants to be added to the official service list. **3.** A pleading filed by an attorney to notify the court and the other parties that he or she represents one or more parties in the lawsuit.

notice of deficiency. See NINETY-DAY LETTER.

notice of dishonor. Notice to the indorser of an instrument that acceptance or payment has been refused. • This notice — along with presentment and actual dishonor — is a condition of an indorser's secondary liability. UCC § 3–503(a).

notice of lis pendens. See LIS PENDENS (3).

notice of motion. Written certification that a party to a lawsuit has filed a motion or that a motion will be heard or considered by the court at a particular time. • Under the Federal Rules of Civil Procedure, the requirement that a motion be made in writing is fulfilled if the motion is stated in a written notice of the hearing on the motion. Also, the courts in most jurisdictions require all motions to include a certificate, usu. referred to as a certificate of service, indicating that the other parties to the suit have been given notice of the motion's filing. Notice of any hearing or other submission of the motion must usu. be provided to all parties by the party requesting the hearing or submission. Fed. R. Civ. P. 5(d), 7(b)(1); Fed. R. Civ. P. Form 19.

notice of orders or judgments. Written notice of the entry of an order or judgment, provided by the court clerk or one of the parties. • Notice of a judgment is usu. provided by the clerk of the court in which the judgment was entered. If the court does not provide notice, a party is usu. required to provide it. Under the Federal Rules of Civil Procedure and the Federal Rules of Criminal Procedure, the clerk is required to provide immediate notice of any order or judgment to any party to the case who is not in default. Fed. R. Civ. P. 77(d); Fed. R. Crim. P. 49(c).

notice of pendency. See LIS PENDENS (3).

notice of protest. 1. A statement, given usu. by a notary public to a drawer or indorser of a negotiable instrument, that the instrument was neither paid nor accepted; information provided to the drawer or indorser that protest was made for nonacceptance or nonpayment of a note or bill. See PROTEST (2). **2.** A shipowner's or crew's declaration under oath that damages to their vessel or cargo were the result of perils of the sea and that the shipowner is not liable for the damages. See PERIL OF THE SEA.

notice of removal. The pleading by which the defendant removes a case from state court to federal court. • A notice of removal is filed in the federal district court in the district and division in which the suit is pending. The notice must contain a short and plain statement of the grounds for removal and must include a copy of all process, pleadings, and orders that have been served on the removing party while the case has been pending. The removing party must also notify the state court and other parties to the suit that the notice of removal has been filed. A notice of removal must be filed, if at all, within 30 days after the defendant is served with process in the suit. 28 USCA § 1446; *Murphy Bros., Inc. v. Michetti Pipe Stringing, Inc.*, 119 S.Ct. 1322 (1999).

notice of trial. A document issued by a court informing the parties of the date on which the lawsuit is set for trial. • While the court typically provides the notice to all parties, it may instead instruct one party to send the notice to all the others.

notice pleading. See PLEADING (2).

notice-prejudice rule. A doctrine barring an insurer from using late notice as a reason to deny an insured's claim unless the insurer can show that it was prejudiced by the untimely notice.

notice-race statute. See RACE-NOTICE STATUTE.

notice statute. A recording act providing that the person with the most recent valid claim, and who purchased without notice of an earlier, unrecorded claim, has priority. • About half the states have notice statutes. — Also termed *notice act*. Cf. RACE STATUTE; RACE-NOTICE STATUTE.

notice to appear. A summons or writ by which a person is cited to appear in court. • This is an informal phrase sometimes used to refer to the summons or other initial process by which a person is notified of a lawsuit. The Federal Rules of Civil Procedure require the summons to state that the defendant must appear and defend within a given time and that failure to do so will result in a default judgment. Fed. R. Civ. P. 4(a). See PROCESS; SUMMONS; DEFAULT JUDGMENT; NOTICE TO PLEAD.

notice to creditors. *Bankruptcy.* A formal notice to creditors that a creditors' meeting will be held, that proofs of claim must be filed, or that an order for relief has been granted.

notice to plead. A warning to a defendant, stating that failure to file a responsive pleading within a prescribed time will result in a default judgment. • The Federal Rules of Civil Procedure require the summons to notify the defendant that failure to appear and defend within a prescribed time will result in a default judgment. Fed. R. Civ. P. 4(a). See PROCESS; SUMMONS; DEFAULT JUDGMENT; NOTICE TO APPEAR.

notice to produce. See REQUEST FOR PRODUCTION.

notice to quit. **1.** A landlord's written notice demanding that a tenant surrender and vacate the leased property, thereby terminating the tenancy. **2.** A landlord's notice to a tenant to pay any back rent within a specified period (often seven days) or else vacate the leased premises.

notification. **1.** *Int'l law.* A formal announcement of a legally relevant fact, action, or intent, such as notice of an intent to withdraw from a treaty. **2.** NOTICE.

notify, *vb.* **1.** To inform (a person or group) in writing or by any method that is understood <I notified the court of the change in address>. **2.** *Archaic.* To give notice of; to make known <to notify the lawsuit to all the defendants>. See NOTICE.

noting protest. See PROTEST (2).

notio (**noh**-shee-oh), *n.* [fr. Latin *noscere* "to know"] **1.** *Roman law.* An investigation of a case. **2.** *Hist.* The authority of a judge to try a case.

notitia (noh-**tish**-ee-ə), *n.* [Latin "knowledge"] **1.** *Roman law.* Knowledge; information. • This term carried over for a time into English practice. **2.** *Roman law.* A list; register; catalogue. • The *notitia dignitatum* (dig-ni-**tay**-təm) was a list of the high offices in the Eastern and Western parts of the empire. **3.** *Hist.* Notice. **4.** A list of ecclesiastical sees.

not law. A judicial decision regarded as wrong by the legal profession.

> "Even when it is not possible to point out any decision that affects the point in question in any one of the ways enumerated, it sometimes happens that the profession has grown to ignore the old decision as wrong or obsolete; and though this does not happen often, when it does happen, the old decision is very likely not to be followed in case the point is squarely raised again. This is one of the instances in which lawyers rather mystically, though soundly, say that a decision is 'not law.'" William M. Lile et al., *Brief Making and the Use of Law Books* 329 (3d ed. 1914).

notoriety. **1.** The state of being generally, and often unfavorably, known and spoken of <the company executive achieved notoriety when she fled the country to avoid paying taxes>. **2.** A person in such a state <the notoriety gave a rare interview>.

notorious, *adj.* **1.** Generally known and spoken of. **2.** (Of the possession of property) so conspicuous as to impute notice to the true owner. — Also termed (in sense 2) *open and notorious.* See ADVERSE POSSESSION.

notorious cohabitation. See COHABITATION.

notorious insolvency. *Scots law.* A bankruptcy; the stage of insolvency in which the debtor has publicly acknowledged insolvency under the statute. • This stage is usu. followed by sequestration, which is notorious insolvency coupled with the appointment of a trustee for creditors. — Also termed *notour bankruptcy.*

"Bankruptcy, according to the law of Scotland, is public or notorious insolvency. When a debtor in an obligation cannot fulfil his obligation as undertaken . . . a position which constitutes insolvency — and makes public acknowledgment, in manner determined by statute, of his inability, the status or condition of bankruptcy has arisen, and the insolvent debtor is, in the language of the statutes, a 'notour' bankrupt . . . . The law of notour bankruptcy is mainly statutory. Legislation has fixed the circumstances which constitute the status, and determined all the most important results." George Watson, *Bell's Dictionary and Digest of the Law of Scotland* 78 (3d ed. 1882).

notorious possession. See POSSESSION.

not otherwise indexed by name. A phrase used in shipping and tariff construction, usu. to show a classification of something generally rather than specifically. • For example, a shipment of aircraft and boat engines merely labeled "other articles" is *not otherwise indexed by name*. — Abbr. n.o.i.b.n.

notour bankruptcy. See NOTORIOUS INSOLVENCY.

not possessed. *Common-law pleading.* In an action in trover, the defendant's plea denying possession of the articles allegedly converted. See TROVER.

not proven. An archaic jury verdict — now used only in Scots criminal law — equivalent in result to not guilty, but carrying with it a strong suspicion of wrongdoing. — Also termed *Scotch verdict*.

not satisfied. A form of return by a sheriff or constable, on a writ of execution, indicating only that the amount due on a judgment was not paid. • A general return of this type is usu. viewed as technically deficient because it does not state why the writ was not satisfied. Cf. NULLA BONA.

not sufficient funds. The notation of dishonor (of a check) indicating that the drawer's account does not contain enough money to cover payment. — Abbr. NSF. — Also termed *insufficient funds*.

notwithstanding, *prep.* Despite; in spite of <notwithstanding the conditions listed above, the landlord can terminate the lease if the tenant defaults>.

n.o.v. *abbr.* NON OBSTANTE VEREDICTO.

nova causa interveniens. See *intervening cause* under CAUSE (1).

nova custuma (**noh**-və **kəs**-t[y]ə-mə), *n.* [Law Latin "new custom"] *Hist.* A tax; an imposition. Cf. ANTIQUA CUSTUMA.

novae narrationes (**noh**-vee nə-ray-shee-**oh**-neez), *n.* [Law Latin "new counts or tales"] *Hist.* A collection of pleading forms published during the reign of Edward III.

nova statuta (**noh**-və stə-**t[y]oo**-tə), *n. pl.* [Law Latin] *Hist.* New statutes. • This term refers to the statutes passed beginning with the reign of Edward III. Cf. VETERA STATUTA.

novation (noh-**vay**-shən), *n.* The act of substituting for an old obligation a new one that either replaces an existing obligation with a new obligation or replaces an original party with a new party. • A novation may substitute (1) a new obligation between the same parties, (2) a new debtor, or (3) a new creditor. — Also termed *substituted agreement*; (Roman law) *novatio* (noh-**vay**-shee-oh). — **novate** (noh-**vayt** *or* **noh**-vayt), *vb.* — **novatory** (**noh**-və-tor-ee), *adj.* See *substituted contract* under CONTRACT; ACCORD (2).

"The only way in which it is possible to transfer contractual duties to a third party is by the process of novation, which requires the consent of the other party to the contract. In fact novation really amounts to the extinction of the old obligation, and the creation of a new one, rather than to the transfer of the obligation from one person to another. Thus if B owes A £100, and C owes B the same amount, B cannot transfer to C the legal duty of paying his debt to A without A's consent. But if A agrees to accept C as a debtor in place of B, and if C agrees to accept A as his creditor in place of B, the three parties may make a tripartite agreement to this effect, known as novation. The effect of this is to extinguish B's liability to A and create a new liability on the part of C." P.S. Atiyah, *An Introduction to the Law of Contract* 283 (3d ed. 1981).

"The word 'novation' is used in a variety of senses. Courts frequently use it as synonymous with 'substituted contract.' Most academic writers and both contracts restatements, however, restrict its use to describe a substituted contract involving at least one obligor or obligee who was not a party to the original contract. . . . The development of a separate category under the rubric 'novation' is doubtless traceable to problems of consideration formerly thought to be present in such contracts because of the former common law rule that consideration must be supplied by the promisee. This rule has long been laid to rest almost everywhere." John D. Calamari & Joseph M. Perillo, *The Law of Contracts* § 11-8, at 444-45 (3d ed. 1987).

objective novation. *Civil law.* A novation involving the substitution of a new obligation for an old one.

subjective novation. *Civil law.* A novation involving the substitution of a new obligor for a previous obligor who has been discharged by the obligee.

novel assignment. See *new assignment* under ASSIGNMENT (5).

novel disseisin (**nov**-əl dis-**see**-zin), *n.* A recent disseisin. See DISSEISIN; ASSISE OF NOVEL DISSEISIN.

Novellae (nə-**vel**-ee). See NOVELS.

Novellae Constitutiones. See NOVELS.

Novellae Leonis (nə-**vel**-ee lee-**oh**-nis), *n.* [Latin "novels of Leo"] A collection of 113 ordinances issued by Emperor Leo from A.D. 887–893.

Novels. A collection of 168 constitutions issued by the Roman emperor Justinian and his immediate successors. • Taken together, the Novels make up one of four component parts of the *Corpus Juris Civilis.* — Also termed *Novellae*; *Novellae Constitutiones.* See CORPUS JURIS CIVILIS.

novelty. *Patents.* **1.** The fact that an invention is new in form and in function or performance. **2.** The requirement that this fact must be demonstrated for an invention to be patentable. • If the invention has been previously patented, described in a publication, or known or used by others, it is not novel. 35 USCA § 102. Cf. NONOBVIOUSNESS.

noverca (nə-**vər**-kə), *n.* [Latin] A stepmother.

noverint universi per praesentes (**noh**-və-rənt yoo-ni-**vər**-sı pər pri-**zen**-teez). [Latin] Know all men by these presents. • This is a formal phrase once found at the beginning of deeds of release. In translation, they still sometimes appear on various types of legal documents. See KNOW ALL MEN BY THESE PRESENTS; PATEAT UNIVERSIS PER PRAESENTES.

novigild (**noh**-və-gild), *n.* [fr. Latin *novem* "nine" + Anglo–Saxon *gid* or *geld* "a payment"] *Hist.* The money a person must pay for damaging another person's property, the amount equaling nine times the purchase price of the property damaged.

novi operis nuntiatio (**noh**-vı **ahp**-ə-ris nən-shee-**ay**-shee-oh), *n.* [Latin "new work protest"] *Roman law.* A protest or prohibition against an *opus novum* ("new work"). • A person whose rights were impaired by the building or tearing of down a structure could protest at the worksite and forbid further activity. — Also termed *(edictum) de novi operis nuntiatione.*

noviter perventa (**noh**-və-tər pər-**ven**-tə), *n. pl.* [Law Latin "newly known"] *Eccles. law.* Newly discovered facts, which are usu. allowed to be introduced in a case even after the pleadings are closed.

novus actus interveniens (**noh**-vəs **ak**-təs in-tər-**vee**-nee-ənz). See *intervening cause* under CAUSE (1).

novus homo (**noh**-vəs **hoh**-moh), *n.* [Latin "new man"] *Hist.* A man who has been pardoned for a crime.

NOW. *abbr.* **1.** NEGOTIABLE ORDER OF WITHDRAWAL. **2.** National Organization for Women.

NOW account. See ACCOUNT.

now comes. See COMES NOW.

noxa (**nok**-sə), *n.* [Latin "injury"] *Hist.* **1.** *Roman law.* An offense such as injury to a person or property, esp. one committed by a slave or son. **2.** *Roman law.* The obligation to pay for damage committed by a son, slave, or animal. • The father or master generally had to pay for the damages or else surrender the offender to the injured party. **3.** An offense, generally. **4.** The punishment for an offense. **5.** Something that exerts a harmful effect on the body.

noxal (**nok**-səl), *adj. Archaic.* Of or relating to a claim against a father or owner for damage done by a son, a slave, or an animal.

noxal action. [fr. Latin *actio noxalis* "injurious action"] **1.** *Roman law.* The claim against a master or father for a tort committed by a son, a slave, or an animal. • The head of the family could be sued either to pay a penalty due or to surrender the tortfeasor to the victim. Roman law also provided for the surrender of animals that caused damage under *actio de pauperie.* **2.** *Hist.* A person's claim to recover for damages committed by a person's son, slave, or animal.

noxious (**nok**-shəs), *adj.* **1.** Harmful to health; injurious. **2.** Unwholesome; corruptive. **3.** *Archaic.* Guilty.

n.p. *abbr.* **1.** NISI PRIUS. **2.** NOTARY PUBLIC.

NPL. *abbr.* NATIONAL PRIORITIES LIST.

NPV. See *net present value* under PRESENT VALUE.

n.r. *abbr.* **1.** New reports. **2.** Not reported. **3.** NONRESIDENT.

n.s. *abbr.* **1.** New series. • This citation form indicates that a periodical has been renumbered in a new series. **2.** NEW STYLE.

NSF. *abbr.* NOT SUFFICIENT FUNDS.

NTSB. *abbr.* NATIONAL TRANSPORTATION SAFETY BOARD.

nubilis (**n**[**y**]**oo**-bə-lis), *n.* [Latin "marriageable"] *Civil law.* A person, esp. a girl, who is old enough to be married.

nuclear-nonproliferation treaty. See *nonproliferation treaty* under TREATY.

nuda detentio (**n**[**y**]**oo**-də di-**ten**-shee-oh). [Latin] See *possessio naturalis* under POSSESSIO.

nuda patientia (**n**[**y**]**oo**-də pash-ee-**en**-shee-ə). [Latin] Mere sufferance.

nuda possessio (**n**[**y**]**oo**-də pə-**zes**[**h**]-ee-oh). [Latin] Mere possession.

nude, *adj.* **1.** Naked; unclothed. **2.** Lacking in consideration or in some essential particular. See NUDUM PACTUM. **3.** Mere; lacking in description.

nude contract. See NUDUM PACTUM.

nude matter. A mere allegation.

> "[N]ude matter is not of so high nature, as either a mater of Record or a speciality, otherwise there called mater in deede; which maketh mee to thinke, that nude mater is a naked allegation of a thing done, to be proved only by witnesses, and not either by Record, or other speciality in writing vnder seale." John Cowell, *The Interpreter* (1607).

nude pact. See NUDUM PACTUM.

nudum pactum (**n**[**y**]**oo**-dəm **pak**-təm). [Latin "bare agreement"] **1.** *Roman law.* An informal agreement that is not legally enforceable, because it does not fall within the specific classes of agreements that can support a legal action. • But a *pactum* could create an exception to or modification of an existing obligation. **2.** An agreement that is unenforceable as a contract because it is not "clothed" with consideration. — Also termed *naked contract*; *nude contract*; *nude pact.*

nugatory (**n**[**y**]**oo**-gə-tor-ee), *adj.* Of no force or effect; useless; invalid <the Supreme Court rendered the statute nugatory by declaring it unconstitutional>.

nuisance. 1. A condition or situation (such as a loud noise or foul odor) that interferes with the use or enjoyment of property. • Liability might or might not arise from the condition or situation. — Formerly also termed *annoyance.*

> "A nuisance may be merely a right thing in the wrong place, like a pig in the parlor instead of the barnyard." *Village of Euclid v. Amber Realty Co.*, 272 U.S. 365, 388, 47 S.Ct. 114, 118 (1926).

> "A 'nuisance' is a state of affairs. To conduct a nuisance is a tort. In torts, the word 'nuisance' has had an extremely elastic meaning; sometimes it is little more than a pejorative term, a weasel word used as a substitute for reasoning.... The general distinction between a nuisance and a trespass is that the trespass flows from a physical invasion and the nuisance does not." Roger A. Cunningham et al., *The Law of Property* § 7.2, at 417 (2d ed. 1993).

2. Loosely, an act or failure to act resulting in an interference with the use or enjoyment of property. • In this sense, the term denotes the action causing the interference, rather than the resulting condition <the Slocums' playing electric guitars in their yard constituted a nuisance to their neighbors>.

> "There is perhaps no more impenetrable jungle in the entire law than that which surrounds the word 'nuisance.' It has meant all things to all people, and has been applied indiscriminately to everything from an alarming advertisement to a cockroach baked in a pie." *Prosser and Keeton on the Law of Torts* § 86, at 616 (W. Page Keeton ed., 5th ed. 1984).

3. The class of torts arising from such conditions, acts, or failures to act when they occur unreasonably. — Also termed *actionable nuisance.*

> "Nuisance is really a field of tortious liability rather than a single type of tortious conduct: the feature which gives it unity is the interest invaded — that of the use and enjoyment of land. The tort emphasises the harm to the plaintiff rather than the conduct of the defendant." R.F.V. Heuston, *Salmond on the Law of Torts* 50–51 (17th ed. 1977).

abatable nuisance. A nuisance so easily removable that the aggrieved party may lawfully cure the problem without notice to the liable party, such as overhanging tree branches.

absolute nuisance. **1.** Interference with a property right that a court considers fixed or invariable, such as a riparian owner's right to use a stream in its natural condition. **2.** See *nuisance per se.* **3.** Interference in a place where it does not reasonably belong, even if the interfering party is careful. **4.** Interference for which a defendant is held strictly liable for resulting harm, esp. in the nature of pollution. Cf. *qualified nuisance.*

Sense (4) has been disapproved: "[T]he use of the term 'nuisance' to describe the tort liability that sometimes results from accidental invasions produces too much confusion." *Prosser and Keeton on the Law of Torts* § 89, at 637 (W. Page Keeton ed., 5th ed. 1984).

anticipatory nuisance. A condition that, although not yet at the level of a nuisance, is very likely to become one, so that a party may obtain an injunction prohibiting the condition. — Also termed *prospective nuisance.*

attractive nuisance. A dangerous condition that may attract children onto land, thereby causing a risk to their safety. See ATTRACTIVE-NUISANCE DOCTRINE.

"[T]he doctrine acquired the unfortunate misnomer 'attractive nuisance,' a label which persists to this day. It cannot be taken literally, since the courts have now largely rejected the notion that the child must be attracted by that which injures him, and whether or not the condition is in fact a 'nuisance' has nothing at all to do with defendant's liability to the child." Edward J. Kionka, *Torts in a Nutshell* 89 (2d ed. 1992).

cognate nuisance. *Rare.* Interference with an easement.

"The term nuisance is applied to torts of two distinct groups, first, acts of wrongful user by an owner or possessor of land resulting in an unreasonable interference with the rights of enjoyment of the owner or possessor of neighboring land, and, second, wrongful interferences with easements or other incorporeal rights." William F. Walsh, *A Treatise on Equity* 170 (1930).

"When an easement was interfered with, an action on the case lay as a matter of course.... Such an interference is sometimes called 'cognate nuisance' to distinguish it from interferences with the personal enjoyment of the incidents of occupying the land." J.H. Baker, *An Introduction to English Legal History* 486 (3d ed. 1990).

common nuisance. See *public nuisance.*

continuing nuisance. A nuisance that is either uninterrupted or frequently recurring. • It need not be constant or unceasing, but it must occur often enough that it is almost continuous.

legalized nuisance. A nuisance sanctioned by legislative, executive, or other official action and therefore immune from liability, such as a city park.

mixed nuisance. A condition that is both a private nuisance and a public nuisance, so that it is dangerous to the community at large but also causes particular harm to private individuals.

nuisance at law. See *nuisance per se.*

nuisance dependent on negligence. See *qualified nuisance.*

nuisance in fact. A nuisance existing because of the circumstances of the use or the particular location. • For example, a machine emitting high-frequency sound may be a nuisance only if a person's dog lives near enough to the noise to be disturbed by it. — Also termed *nuisance per accidens.*

nuisance per se (pər **say**). Interference so severe that it would constitute a nuisance under any circumstances; a nuisance regardless of location or circumstances of use, such as a leaky nuclear-waste storage facility. — Also termed *nuisance at law; absolute nuisance.*

permanent nuisance. A nuisance that cannot readily be abated at reasonable expense. Cf. *temporary nuisance.*

private nuisance. A condition that interferes with a person's enjoyment of property, but does not involve a trespass. • The condition constitutes a tort for which the adversely affected person may recover damages or obtain an injunction.

"Trespass and private nuisance are alike in that each is a field of tort liability rather than a single type of tortious conduct. In each, liability may arise from an intentional or an unintentional invasion. For an intentional trespass, there is liability without harm; for a private nuisance, there is no liability without significant harm.... In private nuisance an intentional interference with the plaintiff's use or enjoyment is not of itself a tort, and unreasonableness of the interference is necessary for liability." Restatement (Second) of Torts § 821D cmt. d (1979).

"The different ways and combinations of ways in which the interest in the use or enjoyment of land may be invaded are infinitely variable. A private nuisance may consist of an interference with the physical condition of the land itself, as by vibration or blasting which damages a house, the destruction of crops, flooding, raising the water table, or the pollution of a stream or of an underground water supply." *Prosser and Keeton on the Law of Torts* § 87, at 619 (W. Page Keeton ed., 5th ed. 1984).

prospective nuisance. See *anticipatory nuisance.*

public nuisance. An unreasonable interference with a right common to the general public, such as a condition dangerous to health, offensive to community moral standards, or unlawfully obstructing the public in the free use of public property. • Such a nuisance may lead to a civil injunction or criminal prosecution. — Also termed *common nuisance.*

> "Public and private nuisances are not in reality two species of the same genus at all. There is no generic conception which includes the crime of keeping a common gaming-house and the tort of allowing one's trees to overhang the land of a neighbour. A public nuisance falls within the law of torts only in so far as it may in the particular case constitute some form of tort also. Thus the obstruction of a highway is a public nuisance; but if it causes any special and peculiar damage to an individual, it is also a tort actionable at his suit." R.F.V. Heuston, *Salmond on the Law of Torts* 49–50 (17th ed. 1977).

> "[P]ublic nuisance ... is an amorphous and unsatisfactory area of the law covering an ill-assorted collection of wrongs, some of which have little or no association with tort and only appear to fill a gap in criminal law. Others cover what could be generally described as 'noisome trade,' which could be dealt with under some form of statutory nuisance. Yet a third group deals with what we would generally describe as 'abuses of the highway' ...." R.W.M. Dias & B.S. Markesinis, *Tort Law* 254 (1984).

qualified nuisance. A condition that, though lawful in itself, is so negligently permitted to exist that it creates an unreasonable risk of harm and, in due course, actually results in injury to another. • It involves neither an intentional act nor a hazardous activity. — Also termed *nuisance dependent on negligence.* Cf. *absolute nuisance.*

temporary nuisance. A nuisance that can be corrected by a reasonable expenditure of money or labor. Cf. *permanent nuisance.*

nuisance in fact. See NUISANCE.

nuisance money. See *nuisance settlement* under SETTLEMENT.

nuisance per accidens. See *nuisance in fact* under NUISANCE.

nuisance per se. See NUISANCE.

nuisance settlement. See SETTLEMENT.

nul (nəl). [Law French] No; none. • This negative particle begins many phrases, such as *nul tiel.*

nul agard (**nəl** ə-**gahrd**), *n.* [Law French "no award"] In an action to enforce an arbitration award on an arbitration bond, a plea denying the existence of the award. Cf. AGARD.

nul disseisin (**nəl** dis-**see**-zin). [Law French "no disseisin"] In a real action, a defendant's plea that the plaintiff was not deprived of the possession of any land and tenements. See DISSEISIN.

nul fait agard (nəl **fay** ə-**gahrd**). [Law French] No award was made. Cf. AGARD.

null, *adj.* Having no legal effect; without binding force; VOID <the contract was declared null and void>. • The phrase *null and void* is a common redundancy.

nulla bona (**nəl**-ə **boh**-nə). [Latin "no goods"] A form of return by a sheriff or constable upon an execution when the judgment debtor has no seizable property within the jurisdiction. Cf. NIHIL EST.

nulla poena sine lege (**nəl**-ə **pee**-nə **sI**-nee **lee**-jee *or* **sin**-ay **lay**-gay). [Latin] No punishment without a law authorizing it.

nullification (nəl-i-fi-**kay**-shən), *n.* **1.** The act of making something void; specif., the action of a state in abrogating a federal law, on the basis of state sovereignty. **2.** The state or condition of being void. See JURY NULLIFICATION.

nullification doctrine. The theory — espoused by southern states before the Civil War — advocating a state's right to declare a federal law unconstitutional and therefore void.

nullify, *vb.* To make void; to render invalid.

nullity (**nəl**-ə-tee). **1.** Something that is legally void <the forged commercial transfer is a nullity>. **2.** The fact of being legally void <she filed a petition for nullity of marriage>.

absolute nullity. *Civil law.* **1.** An act that is void because it is against public policy, law, or order. **2.** The state of such a nullity. See NULLITY OF MARRIAGE.

relative nullity. *Civil law.* **1.** A legal nullity that can be cured by confirmation because the object of the nullity is valid. **2.** The state of such a nullity.

nullity of marriage. 1. The invalidity of a presumed or supposed marriage because it is void on its face or has been voided by court order. • A void marriage, as in an incestuous marriage, is invalid on its face and requires no formality to end. A voidable marriage, such as a marriage lacking requisite parental consent, requires a court order to invalidate.

"The declaration of nullity is appropriate if the marriage is relatively null or absolutely null yet one or both spouses were in good faith. If the marriage is relatively null, civil effects flow until the declaration of nullity. On the other hand, the marriage that is absolutely null generally produces civil effects only if one or both of the spouses were in good faith and only so long as good faith lasts." 16 Katherine S. Spaht & W. Lee Hargrave, *Louisiana Civil Law Treatise: Matrimonial Regimes* § 7.6, at 348 (2d ed. 1997).

2. A suit brought to nullify a marriage. See ANNULMENT.

nullius filius (nə-**lI**-əs **fil**-ee-əs), *n.* [Latin "son of no one"] An illegitimate child.

nullius in bonis (nə-**lI**-əs in **boh**-nis), *adj.* [Latin "among the property of no person"] *Hist.* Belonging to no one. • Wild animals were considered to be *nullius in bonis*. — Also termed *in nullius bonis*.

nullius juris (nə-**lI**-əs **joor**-is). [Latin] *Hist.* Of no legal force.

nullum arbitrium (**nəl**-əm ahr-**bi**-tree-əm), *n.* [Law Latin "no decision"] *Hist.* In an action to enforce an arbitration bond, a plea denying the existence of an arbitration award.

nullum est erratum (**nəl**-əm est ə-**ray**-təm), *n.* [Latin "there is no error in the record"] In response to an assignment of error, the common plea that there is no error in the record. • The effect of the plea is essentially to admit well-pleaded facts.

nullum fecerunt arbitrium (**nəl**-əm fə-**see**-rənt ahr-**bi**-tree-əm). [Latin "they never submitted to arbitration"] *Hist.* In an action to enforce an arbitration award, the defendant's plea denying that there had been an arbitration.

Nullum Tempus Act (**nəl**-əm **tem**-pəs akt), *n.* [Latin] *Hist. English law.* The Crown Suits Act of 1769 (amended in 1862) that limited the Crown's time to sue, in land and other specified matters, to 60 years. • The statute altered the common-law rule of *nullum tempus aut locus occurrit regi* ("no time or place affects the Crown"), which was based on the idea that the Crown was too busy with governmental affairs to timely attend to its legal affairs.

nullum tempus occurrit reipublicae (**nəl**-əm **tem**-pəs ə-**kər**-it ree-I-**pəb**-lə-see), *n.* [Latin "no time runs against the state"] The principle that a statute of limitations does not apply to a commonwealth or state unless a statute specifically provides that it does. • The purpose of the rule is to fully protect public rights and property from injury.

nul tiel (nəl teel). [Law Latin] No such. • This phrase typically denotes a plea that denies the existence of something.

nul tiel corporation, *n.* [Law French "no such corporation exists"] A plea denying the existence of an alleged corporation. • The defense of *nul tiel corporation* must usu. be affirmatively pleaded by a defendant before a plaintiff is required to prove its corporate existence.

nul tiel record, *n.* [Law French "no such record"] A plea denying the existence of the record on which the plaintiff bases a claim. • Evidence may generally be introduced to invalidate the record only, not the statements in the record. See *trial by record* under TRIAL.

"The proper general issue in debt on judgments is 'nul tiel record,' which denies the existence of the record alleged. Nul tiel record sets up: (1) the defense either that there is no record at all in existence; or (2) one different from that which the defendant has declared of; or (3) that the judgment is void on the face of the record." Benjamin J. Shipman, *Handbook of Common-Law Pleading* § 186, at 330 (Henry Winthrop Ballantine ed., 3d ed. 1923).

nul tort (nəl tort), *n.* [Law French "no wrong"] *Hist.* A type of general denial in an action to recover lands and tenements, by which the defendant claims that no wrong was done. See NUL DISSEISIN.

"The *general* issue, or general plea, is what traverses, thwarts, and denies at once the whole declaration; without offering any special matter whereby to evade it .... [I]n real actions, *nul tort*, no wrong done; *nul disseisin*, no disseisin; and in a writ of right, that the tenant has more right to hold than the demandant has to demand. These pleas are called the general issue, because, by importing an absolute and general denial of what is alleged in the declaration, they amount at once to an issue; by which we mean a fact affirmed on one side and denied on the other." 3 William Blackstone, *Commentaries on the Laws of England* 305 (1768).

nul waste (nəl wayst), *n.* [Law French "no waste"] *Hist.* The defendant's general denial in an action to recover damages for the destruction of lands and tenements. See NUL TORT.

number lottery. See *Genoese lottery* under LOTTERY.

numbers game. A type of lottery in which a person bets that on a given day a certain series of numbers will appear from some arbitrarily chosen source, such as stock-market indexes or the U.S. Treasury balance. • The game creates a fund from which the winner's share is drawn and is subject to regulation as a lottery.

numerata pecunia (n[y]oo-mə-**ray**-tə pi-**kyoo**-nee-ə), *n.* [Latin] *Hist.* Money counted or paid.

numerical lottery. See *Genoese lottery* under LOTTERY.

numerosity (n[y]oo-mər-**ahs**-ə-tee). The requirement in U.S. district courts that, for a case to be certified as a class action, the party applying for certification must show, among other things, that the class of potential plaintiffs is so large that the joinder of all of them into the suit is impracticable. See CLASS ACTION.

nummata (nə-**may**-tə), *n.* [Law Latin "money"] The monetary price of something.

nummata terrae (nə-**may**-tə **ter**-ee), *n.* [Law Latin] *Hist.* An acre of land.

nunciato (nən-shee-**ay**-toh). See NUNTIATIO.

nuncio (**nən**-shee-oh), *n.* [Italian, fr. Latin *nunciare* "to announce"] **1.** A papal ambassador to a foreign court or government; a representative of the Vatican in a country that maintains diplomatic relations with it. — Also termed *nuncius*; *nuntio*. Cf. INTERNUNCIO; LEGATE. **2.** *Archaic.* A messenger.

nunc pro tunc (**nəngk** proh **təngk** *or* **nuungk** proh **tuungk**). [Latin "now for then"] Having retroactive legal effect through a court's inherent power <the court entered a *nunc pro tunc* order to correct a clerical error in the record>.

> "When an order is signed 'nunc pro tunc' as of a specified date, it means that a thing is now done which should have been done on the specified date." 35A C.J.S. *Federal Civil Procedure* § 370, at 556 (1960).

***nunc pro tunc* amendment.** See AMENDMENT (3).

***nunc pro tunc* judgment.** See JUDGMENT.

nuncupare (nəng-kyuu-**pair**-ee), *vb.* [Latin "call by name"] *Hist.* To name or pronounce orally. • *Nuncupare heredem* means to name an heir before public witnesses.

nuncupate (**nəng**-kyə-payt), *vb.* [fr. Latin *nuncupare* "call by name"] **1.** *Hist.* To designate or name. **2.** To vow or declare publicly and solemnly. **3.** To declare orally, as a will. **4.** To dedicate or inscribe (a work).

nuncupative (**nəng**-kyə-pay-tiv *or* nəng-**kyoo**-pə-tiv), *adj.* [fr. Latin *nuncupare* "to name"] Stated by spoken word; declared orally.

nuncupative will. See WILL.

nundinae (**nən**-də-nee), *n.* [fr. Latin *novem* "nine" + *dies* "day"] **1.** *Roman law.* A fair or market. **2.** *Roman law.* The period between two consecutive markets (usu. eight days). • This period was often fixed for the payment of debts.

nundination (nən-di-**nay**-shən), *n.* [fr. Latin *nundinatio* "the holding of a market or fair"] *Hist.* The act of buying or selling at a fair.

nunquam indebitatus (**nən**[g]-kwam in-deb-i-**tay**-təs), *n.* [Latin "never indebted"] *Hist.* A defensive plea in a debt action, by which the defendant denies any indebtedness to the plaintiff. Cf. CONCESSIT SOLVERE.

nuntiatio (nən-shee-**ay**-shee-oh), *n.* [Latin "a declaration"] *Hist.* A formal declaration or protest. • A *nuntiatio novi operiis* was an injunction placed on the construction of a new building by the person protesting the construction. — Also spelled *nunciato*.

nuntio. See NUNCIO.

nuntius (**nən**-shee-əs), *n.* [Latin "bearer of news"] **1.** *Roman law.* A messenger. • Declarations through a messenger were usu. as valid as those by letter. **2.** *Hist.* A messenger sent to make an excuse for a party's absence in court. **3.** *Hist.* An officer of the court. — Also termed *summoner*; *beadle*. **4.** *Eccles. law.* NUNCIO (1).

nuper obiit (**n**[**y**]**oo**-pər **oh**-bee-it), *n.* [Latin "lately died"] *Hist.* A writ available to an heir to establish the equal division of land when, on the death of an ancestor who held the estate in fee simple, a coheir took the land and prevented the other heirs from possessing it. The writ was abolished in 1833. See COPARCENER.

nuptiae (**nəp**-shee-ee). See MATRIMONIUM.

nuptiae secundae (**nəp**-shee-ee sə-**kən**-dee), *n.* [Latin] *Eccles. law.* A second or subsequent marriage. • In canon law, second or subsequent marriages were frowned upon, and priests would not attend those ceremonies.

nuptial (**nəp**-shəl), *adj.* Of or relating to marriage.

Nuremberg defense (**n**[**y**]**ər**-əm-bərg). The defense asserted by a member of the military who has been charged with the crime of failing to obey an order and who claims that the order was illegal, esp. that the order would result in a violation of international law. • The term is sometimes used more broadly to describe situations in which citizens accused of committing domestic crimes, such as degradation of government property, claim that their crimes were justified or mandated by international law.

nurture, *vb.* **1.** To supply with nourishment. **2.** To train, educate, or develop.

nurus (**n**[**y**]**oor**-əs), *n.* [Latin] A daughter-in-law.

nychthemeron (nik-**thee**-mər-ahn), *n.* [Greek] An entire day and night; a 24-hour period.

NYSE. *abbr.* NEW YORK STOCK EXCHANGE.

nystagmus (ni-**stag**-məs). A rapid, involuntary jerking or twitching of the eyes, sometimes caused by ingesting drugs or alcohol. • The "horizontal gaze nystagmus test" is one of the field-sobriety tests given to people suspected of being intoxicated. In the procedure, the suspect is told to focus on an object, such as a pencil, and to track its movement, usu. from side to side, by moving only the eyes. Intoxication is indicated if the eyes jerk or twitch while tracking the object.

OASDHI. *abbr.* Old Age, Survivors, Disability, and Health Insurance. See OLD-AGE AND SURVIVORS' INSURANCE.

OASDI. *abbr.* Old Age, Survivors, and Disability Insurance. See OLD-AGE AND SURVIVORS' INSURANCE.

OASI. *abbr.* OLD-AGE AND SURVIVORS' INSURANCE.

oath. 1. A solemn declaration, accompanied by a swearing to God or a revered person or thing, that one's statement is true or that one will be bound to a promise. • The person making the oath implicitly invites punishment if the statement is untrue or the promise is broken. The legal effect of an oath is to subject the person to penalties for perjury if the testimony is false. **2.** A statement or promise made by such a declaration. **3.** A form of words used for such a declaration. **4.** A formal declaration made solemn without a swearing to God or a revered person or thing; AFFIRMATION.

> "The word 'oath' (apart from its use to indicate a profane expression) has two very different meanings: (1) a solemn appeal to God in attestation of the truth of a statement or the binding character of such a promise; (2) a statement or promise made under the sanction of such an appeal." Rollin M. Perkins & Ronald N. Boyce, *Criminal Law* 515 (3d ed. 1982).

assertory oath (ə-**sər**-tə-ree). An oath by which one attests to some factual matter, rather than making a promise about one's future conduct. • A courtroom witness typically takes such an oath.

corporal oath (**kor**-pər-əl). An oath made solemn by touching a sacred object, esp. the Bible.

> "*Oath* (*Juramentum*) Is a calling Almighty God to witness that the Testimony is true; therefore it is aptly termed *Sacramentum*, a Holy Band, a Sacred Tye, or Godly Vow. And it is called a *Corporal Oath*, because the party when he swears, toucheth with his right hand the *Holy Evangelists* or Book of the *New Testament*." Thomas Blount, *Nomo-Lexicon: A Law–Dictionary* (1670).

decisive oath. *Civil law.* An oath by a party in a lawsuit, used to decide the case because the party's adversary, not being able to furnish adequate proof, offered to refer the decision of the case to the party. — Also termed *decisory oath*.

extrajudicial oath. An oath that, although formally sworn, is taken outside a legal proceeding or outside the authority of law.

judicial oath. An oath taken in the course of a judicial proceeding, esp. in open court.

loyalty oath. See *oath of allegiance*.

oath ex officio (eks ə-**fish**-ee-oh). At common law, an oath under which a member of the clergy who was accused of a crime could swear innocence before an ecclesiastical court.

oath in litem (**lɪ**-tem *or* -təm). *Civil law.* An oath taken by a plaintiff in testifying to the value of the thing in dispute when there is no evidence of value or when the defendant has fraudulently suppressed evidence of value.

oath of allegiance. An oath by which one promises to maintain fidelity to a particular sovereign or government. • This oath is most often administered to a high public officer, to a soldier or sailor, or to an alien applying for naturalization. — Also termed *loyalty oath*; *test oath*.

oath of calumny (**kal**-əm-nee). An oath, taken by a plaintiff or defendant, that attests to the party's good faith and to the party's belief that there is a bona fide cause of action. See CALUMNY.

oath of office. An oath taken by a person about to enter into the duties of public office, by which the person promises to perform the duties of that office in good faith.

oath of supremacy. *Hist. English law.* An oath required of those taking office, along with the oaths of allegiance and abjuration, declaring that the sovereign is superior to the church in ecclesiastical matters.

oath purgatory. See *purgatory oath*.

oath suppletory. See *suppletory oath*.

pauper's oath. An affidavit or verification of poverty by a person requesting public funds or services. See *poverty affidavit* under AFFIDAVIT; IN FORMA PAUPERIS.

promissory oath. An oath that binds the party to observe a specified course of conduct in the future. • Both the oath of office and the oath of allegiance are types of promissory oaths.

purgatory oath. An oath taken to clear oneself of a charge or suspicion. — Also termed *oath purgatory*.

suppletory oath (**səp**-lə-tor-ee). **1.** *Civil law.* An oath administered to a party, rather than a witness, in a case in which a fact has been proved by only one witness. • In a civil-law case, two witnesses are needed to constitute full proof. See HALF-PROOF. **2.** An oath administered to a party to authenticate or support some piece of documentary evidence offered by the party. — Also termed *oath suppletory*.

test oath. See *oath of allegiance*.

oath against an oath. See SWEARING CONTEST.

oath ex officio. See OATH.

oath-helper. See COMPURGATOR.

oath in litem. See OATH.

oath of abjuration. See ABJURATION.

oath of allegiance. See OATH.

oath of calumny. See OATH.

oath of office. See OATH.

oath of supremacy. See OATH.

Oath or Affirmation Clause. The clause of the U.S. Constitution requiring members of Congress and the state legislatures, and all member of the executive or judicial branches — state or local — to pledge by oath or affirmation to support the Constitution. U.S. Const. art. VI, cl. 3.

oath purgatory. See *purgatory oath* under OATH.

oath-rite. The form or ceremony used when taking an oath.

oath suppletory. See *suppletory oath* under OATH.

oathworthy, *adj.* Legally capable of making an oath.

obaeratus (oh-bə-**ray**-təs). [Latin] *Roman law.* A debtor obliged to serve the creditor until the debt is discharged.

ob continentiam delicti (ob kon-tə-**nen**-shee-əm də-**lik**-tɪ). [Latin] On account of contiguity to the offense; being contaminated by association with something illegal.

ob contingentiam (ob kon-tin-**jen**-shee-əm). [Latin] On account of connection; in case of contingency.

obedience. Compliance with a law, command, or authority.

obediential obligation. See OBLIGATION.

ob favorem mercatorum (ob fə-**vor**-əm mər-kə-**tor**-əm). [Latin] In favor of merchants.

obiit (**oh**-bee-it). [Latin] He died; she died.

obiit sine prole (**oh**-bee-it **sɪ**-nee **proh**-lee *also* **sin**-ay **prohl**). [Latin] He died without issue. — Abbr. *o.s.p.*

obit. 1. *Archaic.* A memorial service on the anniversary of a person's death. **2.** A record or notice of a person's death; an obituary.

obiter (**oh**-bid-ər), *adv.* [Latin "by the way"] Incidentally; in passing <the judge said, obiter, that a nominal sentence would be inappropriate>.

obiter, *n.* See OBITER DICTUM.

obiter dictum (**ob**-i-tər **dik**-təm). [Latin "something said in passing"] A judicial comment made during the course of delivering a judicial opinion, but one that is unnecessary to the decision in the case and therefore not precedential (though it may be considered persuasive). — Often shortened to *dictum* or, less commonly, *obiter*. Pl. **obiter dicta.** See DICTUM. Cf. HOLDING (1); RATIO DECIDENDI.

> "Strictly speaking an 'obiter dictum' is a remark made or opinion expressed by a judge, in his decision upon a cause, 'by the way' — that is, incidentally or collaterally, and not directly upon the question before the court; or it is any statement of law enunciated by the judge or court merely by way of illustration, argument, analogy, or suggestion.... In the common speech of lawyers, all such extrajudicial expressions of legal opinion are referred to as 'dicta,' or 'obiter dicta,' these two terms being used interchangeably." William M. Lile et al., *Brief Making and the Use of Law Books* 304 (3d ed. 1914).

obiter ex post facto (**ob**-i-tər eks post **fak**-toh). A court's holding that, according to a later court, was expressed in unnecessarily broad terms. • Some authorities suggest that this is not, properly speaking, a type of obiter dictum at all.

object (**ob**-jekt), *n.* **1.** A person or thing to which thought, feeling, or action is directed <the natural object of one's bounty>. See NATURAL OBJECT. **2.** Something sought to be attained or accomplished; an end, goal, or purpose <the financial objects of the joint venture>.

object (əb-**jekt**), *vb.* **1.** To state in opposition; to put forward as an objection <the plaintiff objected that the defendant's discovery requests were overbroad>. **2.** To state or put forward an objection, esp. to something in a judicial proceeding <the defense objected to the testimony on the ground that it was privileged>. — **objector,** *n.*

objectant. See CONTESTANT.

objection, *n.* A formal statement opposing something that has occurred, or is about to occur, in court and seeking the judge's immediate ruling on the point. • The party objecting must usu. state the basis for the objection to preserve the right to appeal an adverse ruling.

continuing objection. A single objection to all the questions in a given line of questioning. • A judge may allow a lawyer to make a continuing objection when the judge has overruled an objection applicable to many questions, and the lawyer wants to preserve the objection for the appellate record. — Also termed *running objection.*

general objection. An objection made without specifying any grounds in support of the objection. • A general objection preserves only the issue of relevancy. — Also termed *broadside objection.*

speaking objection. An objection that contains more information (often in the form of argument) than needed by the judge to sustain or overrule it. • Many judges prohibit lawyers from using speaking objections, and sometimes even from stating the grounds for objections, because of the potential for influencing the jury.

specific objection. An objection that is accompanied by a statement of one or more grounds in support of the objection.

objection in point of law. A defensive pleading by which the defendant admits the facts alleged by the plaintiff but objects that they do not make out a legal claim.

objective, *adj.* **1.** Of, relating to, or based on externally verifiable phenomena, as opposed to an individual's perceptions, feelings, or intentions <the objective facts>. **2.** Without bias or prejudice; disinterested <because her son was involved, she felt she could not be objective>. Cf. SUBJECTIVE.

objective ethics. See MORAL ABSOLUTISM.

objective meaning. See MEANING.

objective novation. See NOVATION.

objective standard. See STANDARD.

objective theory of contract. The doctrine that a contract is not an agreement in the sense of a subjective meeting of the minds but is instead a series of external acts giving the objective semblance of agreement. — Often shortened to *objective theory.* Cf. SUBJECTIVE THEORY OF CONTRACT; MEETING OF THE MINDS.

object of a right. The thing in respect of which a right exists; the subject matter of a right. — Also termed *subject of a right.* See SUBJECT OF A RIGHT.

object offense. See OFFENSE (1).

object of the power. See *permissible appointee* under APPOINTEE.

object of the power of appointment. See *permissible appointee* under APPOINTEE.

objurgatrix (ob-jər-**gay**-triks). *Hist.* A common scold. See SCOLD.

oblatio (ah-**blay**-shee-oh). [Latin] *Roman law.* A tender of payment (as of a debt).

oblation (ah-**blay**-shən). An offering or sacrifice, esp. one in a religious or ritualistic ceremony.

obligate, *vb.* **1.** To bind by legal or moral duty. **2.** To commit (funds, property, etc.) to meet or secure an obligation.

obligatio (ah-blə-**gay**-shee-oh). [Latin] *Roman law.* An obligation; a legal bond. Pl. ***obligationes*** (ah-blə-gay-shee-**oh**-neez).

obligatio civilis (ah-blə-**gay**-shee-oh sə-**VI**-lis). [Latin "civil obligation"] **1.** An obligation recognized under *jus civile* as opposed to one recognized only under *jus honorarium.* — Also termed *obligatio praetoria* (ah-blə-**gay**-shee-oh pri-**tor**-ee-ə); *obligatio honoraria* (ah-blə-**gay**-shee-oh [h]on-ə-**rair**-ee-ə). **2.** A legally enforceable obligation, such as one by contract.

obligatio ex contractu (ah-blə-**gay**-shee-oh eks kən-**trak**-t[y]oo). [Latin "contractual obligation"] A contractual obligation.

obligatio ex delicto (ah-blə-**gay**-shee-oh eks də-**lik**-toh). [Latin "tortious obligation"] An obligation arising from a wrongdoing against the person or property of another; an obligation enforceable in tort. — Also termed *obligatio ex maleficio* (mal-ə-**fish**-ee-oh).

obligatio naturalis (ah-blə-**gay**-shee-oh nach-ə-**ray**-lis). [Latin "natural obligation"] An obligation that is not legally enforceable; an obligation deriving only from the law of nature.

obligatio quasi ex contractu (ah-blə-**gay**-shee-oh **kway**-sI [*or* -zI] eks kən-**trak**-t[y]oo). [Latin "obligation from quasi-contract"] An obligation arising between two persons who have not contracted with each other but have formed a relationship similar to a contractual one; a quasi-contractual obligation. See *implied-in-law contract* under CONTRACT.

obligatio quasi ex delicto (ah-blə-**gay**-shee-oh **kway**-sI [*or* -zI] eks də-**lik**-toh). [Latin "obligation from something resembling a tort"] An obligation arising from a wrong that is not covered by an *obligatio ex delicto* but that nonetheless creates liability. — Also termed *obligatio quasi ex maleficio* (mal-ə-**fish**-ee-oh).

obligation, *n.* **1.** A legal or moral duty to do or not do something. **2.** A formal, binding agreement or acknowledgment of a liability to pay a certain amount or to do a certain thing for a particular person or set of persons. — Also termed *legal obligation.* See DUTY; LIABILITY.

"[I]n English-speaking countries an unfortunate habit has arisen of using 'obligation' in a lax manner as co-extensive with duties of every kind." Frederick Pollock, *A First Book of Jurisprudence* 82 (1896).

"A man cannot be obliged or bound to the entire community: his duties to the political society of which he is a member are matters of public, or criminal law. Nor can the whole community be under an obligation to him: the rights on his part correlative to the duties owed to him would be rights *in rem*, would be in the nature of property as opposed to obligation. The word *obligation* has been unfortunately used in this sense by Austin and Bentham as including the general duty, which the law imposes on all, to respect such rights as the law sanctions. Whether the rights are to personal freedom or security, to character, or to those more material objects which we commonly call property, they impose corresponding duties on all to forbear from molesting the right. Such rights are rights *in rem*. But it is of the essence of obligation that the duties which it imposes are imposed on definite persons, and are themselves definite: the rights which it creates are rights *in personam*." William R. Anson, *Principles of the Law of Contract* 9 (Arthur L. Corbin ed., 3d Am. ed. 1919).

"Obligation in its popular sense is merely a synonym for duty. Its legal sense, derived from Roman law, differs from this in several respects. In the first place, obligations are merely one class of duties, namely, those which are the correlatives of rights *in personam*. An obligation is the *vinculum juris*, or bond of legal necessity, which binds together two or more determinate individuals.... Secondly, the term obligatio is in law the name, not merely of the duty, but also of the correlative right. It denotes the legal relation or *vinculum juris* in its entirety, including the right of the one party, no less than the liability of the other. Looked at from the point of view of the person entitled, an obligation is a right; looked at from the point of view of the person bound, it is a duty.... An obligation, therefore, may be defined as a proprietary right *in personam* or a duty which corresponds to such a right." John Salmond, *Jurisprudence* 460 (Glanville L. Williams ed., 10th ed. 1947).

absolute obligation. An obligation requiring strict fulfillment according to the terms of the engagement, without any alternatives to the obligor.

accessory obligation. An obligation that is incidental to another obligation. • For example, a mortgage to secure payment of a bond is an accessory obligation. The primary obligation is to pay the bond itself. Cf. *primary obligation* (1).

alternative obligation. An obligation that can be satisfied in two different ways, at the choice of the obligor.

bifactoral obligation (bI-**fak**-tər-əl). An obligation created by two parties.

conditional obligation. An obligation that depends on an uncertain event.

conventional obligation. An obligation that results from actual agreement of the parties; a contractual obligation. Cf. *obediential obligation.*

correal obligation (**kor**-ee-əl *or* kə-**ree**-əl). *Roman law.* A joint obligation.

"A correal obligation means a plurality of obligations based on a community of obligation: a joint liability in respect of the whole of the same debt or a joint right in respect of the whole of the same claim." Rudolph Sohm, *The Institutes: A Textbook of the History and System of*

Roman Private Law 361 (James Crawford Ledlie trans., 3d ed. 1907).

current obligation. An obligation that is presently enforceable, but not past due.

inheritable obligation. An obligation that may be enforced by a successor of the creditor or against a successor of the debtor. — Also termed *heritable obligation.*

joint obligation. **1.** An obligation that binds two or more debtors to a single performance for one creditor. **2.** An obligation that binds one debtor to a single performance for two or more creditors.

natural obligation. *Civil law.* A moral duty that is not enforceable by judicial action. ● Natural obligations are recognized in civil-law jurisdictions. While they are not enforceable by judicial action, something that has been performed under a natural obligation may not be reclaimed. For example, if an indigent patient in a hospital has no legal obligation to pay for the treatment but does so anyway, that person cannot later reclaim the payments voluntarily made. — Also termed *obligatio naturalis.*

obediential obligation (ə-bee-dee-**en**-shəl). An obligation incumbent on the parties as a result of their situation or relationship, such as an obligation of parents to care for their children. Cf. *conventional obligation.*

primary obligation. **1.** An obligation that arises from the essential purpose of the transaction between the parties. Cf. *accessory obligation.* **2.** A fundamental contractual term imposing a requirement on a contracting party from which other obligations may arise.

pure obligation. *Scots law.* An absolute obligation already due and immediately enforceable.

secondary obligation. A duty, promise, or undertaking that is incident to a primary obligation; esp., a duty to make reparation upon a breach of contract. — Also termed *accessory obligation.*

several obligation. **1.** An obligation that binds two or more debtors to separate performances for one creditor. **2.** An obligation that binds one debtor to separate performances for two or more creditors.

simple obligation. An obligation that does not depend on an outside event; an unconditional obligation.

single obligation. An obligation with no penalty attached for nonperformance, as when one party simply promises to pay 20 dollars to another.

solidary obligation (**sol**-ə-der-ee). *Roman & civil law.* An obligation that binds each of two or more debtors for the entire performance. ● Solidary obligations are analogous to common-law joint and several obligations.

> "A solidary obligation means the *separate* liability of several persons in respect of one and the same object. The normal case of a solidary obligation is a joint delict, as when two or more persons, acting jointly, do damage to property or commit a theft. So far as the obligation creates a duty to pay damages, it is solidary. Each of the co-delinquents is liable to make good the whole of the same damage." Rudolph Sohm, *The Institutes: A Textbook of the History and System of Roman Private Law* 361–62 (James Crawford Ledlie trans., 3d ed. 1907).

statutory obligation. An obligation — whether to pay money, perform certain acts, or discharge duties — that is created by or arises out of a statute, rather than based on an independent contractual or legal relationship.

unifactoral obligation (yoo-nə-**fak**-tər-əl). An obligation created by one party.

obligation, mutuality of. See MUTUALITY OF OBLIGATION.

obligational. See OBLIGATORY.

obligatio naturalis. See OBLIGATIO.

obligation bond. See *general obligation bond* under BOND (3).

obligationes innominati. See INNOMINATE OBLIGATIONS.

Obligation of Contracts Clause. See CONTRACTS CLAUSE.

obligations, law of. See LAW OF OBLIGATIONS.

obligatio praetoria. See *obligatio civilis* (1) under OBLIGATIO.

obligatio quasi ex contractu. See OBLIGATIO.

obligatio quasi ex delicto. See OBLIGATIO.

obligatio quasi ex maleficio. See *obligatio quasi ex delicto* under OBLIGATIO.

obligatory (ə-**blig**-ə-tor-ee), *adj.* **1.** Legally or morally binding <an obligatory promise>. **2.** Required; mandatory <attendance is not obligatory>. **3.** Creating or recording an obligation <a writing obligatory>. — Also termed (rarely) *obligational.*

oblige (ə-**blɪj**), *vb.* **1.** To bind by legal or moral duty; obligate. **2.** To bind by doing a favor or service.

obligee (ob-lə-**jee**). **1.** One to whom an obligation is owed; a promisee or creditor. **2.** *Archaic.* One who is obliged to do something; OBLIGOR (1).

> "Several dictionaries, such as *The Random House College Dictionary* (rev. ed. 1988) and *Webster's New World Dictionary* (1979), define *obligee* in its etymological sense ['obliged'], as if it were synonymous with *obligor*. *Random House*, for example, defines *obligee* as 'a person who is under obligation,' but that meaning ought to be reserved for *obligor*. An *obligee*, in modern usage, is one to whom an obligation is owed." Bryan A. Garner, *A Dictionary of Modern Legal Usage* 609 (2d ed. 1995).

obligor (ob-lə-**gor** *or* **ob**-lə-gor). **1.** One who has undertaken an obligation; a promisor or debtor. **2.** *Archaic.* One who obliges another to do something; OBLIGEE (1).

oblique (ə-**bleek**), *adj.* **1.** Not direct in descent; collateral <an oblique heir>. **2.** Indirect; circumstantial <oblique evidence>.

oblique evidence. See *circumstantial evidence* under EVIDENCE.

obliquus (ob-**lɪ**-kwəs). [Latin "oblique"] *Hist.* (Of a line of descent) collateral; indirect. Cf. RECTUS.

obliterate, *vb.* **1.** To wipe out, rub off, or erase (a writing or other markings). **2.** To remove from existence; to destroy all traces of. — **obliteration,** *n.*

obliterated corner. See CORNER.

oblivion. 1. The act or fact of forgetting or having forgotten <the oblivion of sleep>. **2.** The state of being completely forgotten or unknown <a once-famous politician now in oblivion>. **3.** An official disregard of an offense; pardon; amnesty <an act of oblivion by Parliament>.

obloquy (**ob**-lə-kwee). **1.** Abusive or defamatory language; CALUMNY. **2.** The state or condition of being ill spoken of; disgrace or bad repute.

obnoxious, *adj.* **1.** Offensive; objectionable <obnoxious behavior>. **2.** Contrary; opposed <a practice obnoxious to the principle of equal protection under the law>. **3.** *Archaic.* Exposed to harm; liable to something undesirable <actions obnoxious to criticism>.

obreption (ob-**rep**-shən). The obtaining of a gift or dispensation from a sovereign or ecclesiastical authority by fraud. Cf. SUBREPTION.

obrogate (**ob**-rə-gayt), *vb. Civil law.* To modify or repeal (a law) in whole or in part by passing a new law. — **obrogation,** *n.* Cf. ABROGATE.

obscene, *adj.* Extremely offensive under contemporary community standards of morality and decency; grossly repugnant to the generally accepted notions of what is appropriate. • Under the Supreme Court's three-part test, material is legally obscene — and therefore not protected under the First Amendment — if, taken as a whole, the material (1) appeals to the prurient interest in sex, as determined by the average person applying contemporary community standards; (2) portrays sexual conduct, as specifically defined by the applicable state law, in a patently offensive way; and (3) lacks serious literary, artistic, political, or scientific value. *Miller v. California*, 413 U.S. 15, 93 S.Ct. 2607 (1973).

> "If there be no abstract definition, ... should not the word 'obscene' be allowed to indicate the present critical point in the compromise between candor and shame at which the community may have arrived here and now?" *United States v. Kennerley*, 209 F. 119, 121 (S.D.N.Y. 1913) (per Hand, J.).

obscene libel. See LIBEL.

obscenity, *n.* **1.** The quality or state of being morally abhorrent or socially taboo, esp. as a result of referring to or depicting sexual or excretory functions. **2.** Something (such as an expression or act) that has this quality. See CONTEMPORARY COMMUNITY STANDARD. Cf. INDECENCY.

> "Obscenity is not deemed to be protected by the First Amendment, and the operative legal tests for obscenity are spongy and leave much to the vagaries of juries asked to evaluate expert testimony on literary merit, offensiveness, and other unmeasurables." Richard A. Posner, *Law and Literature: A Misunderstood Relation* 329 (1988).

observe, *vb.* To adhere to or abide by (a law, rule, or custom) <a traffic citation for failing to observe the speed limit>.

observer. *Int'l law.* A representative of a country or international organization who attends meetings of an international body (such as the United Nations) to which the observer's country does not belong. • Observers do not vote or sign documents, but they are sometimes allowed to participate in discussions.

obses (**ob**-seez), *n.* [Latin] A hostage in wartime. Pl. ***obsides.***

obsignare (ob-sig-**nair**-ee), *vb.* [Latin] *Civil law.* To seal up, as with money that has been tendered and refused.

obsignation, *n.* A formal ratification or confirmation, esp. by an official seal. — **obsignatory** (ob-**sig**-nə-tor-ee), *adj.*

obsolescence (ob-sə-**les**-ənts). **1.** The process or state of falling into disuse or becoming obsolete. **2.** A diminution in the value or usefulness of property, esp. as a result of technological advances. • For tax purposes, obsolescence is usu. distinguished from physical deterioration. Cf. DEPRECIATION.

economic obsolescence. Obsolescence that results from external economic factors, such as decreased demand or changed governmental regulations.

functional obsolescence. Obsolescence that results either from inherent deficiencies in the property, such as inadequate equipment or design, or from improvements in the property since its use began.

planned obsolescence. A system or policy of deliberately producing consumer goods that will wear out or become outdated after limited use, thus inducing consumers to buy new items more frequently. — Also termed *built-in obsolescence.*

obsolescent, *adj.* Going out of use; becoming obsolete.

obsolete, *adj.* No longer in general use; out-of-date.

obstante (ob-**stan**-tee *or* əb-). [Latin] Withstanding; hindering. See NON OBSTANTE VEREDICTO.

obsta principiis (**ob**-stə prin-**sip**-ee-is). [Latin] Withstand beginnings; resist the first approaches or encroachments.

obstinate desertion. See DESERTION.

obstrict (əb-**strikt**), vb. To coerce. — **obstrictive,** *adj.* — **obstrictiveness,** *n.*

> "*The element of coercion or obstrictiveness.* The contrast here is between voluntary and obstricted (or coerced) conduct. The coercion need not be actual (objective), but may be merely potential (subjective) by fear of the possible force; as, when the faithful canine, Towser, susceptible to the sight of a feline enemy, is tempted to pursue, but upon his owner's stern voice and a shake of the stick, Towser turns humbly back and crushes his impulse." John Henry Wigmore, *Problems of Law* 7–8 (1920).

obstriction. *Archaic.* Obligation; bond.

obstruction of justice. Interference with the orderly administration of law and justice, as by giving false information to or withholding evidence from a police officer or prosecutor, or by harming or intimidating a witness or juror. • Obstruction of justice is a crime in most jurisdictions. — Also termed *obstructing justice*; *obstructing public justice.*

> "The goal, — to proscribe every wilful act of corruption, intimidation or force which tends in any way to distort or impede the administration of law either civil or criminal — has been very largely attained, partly by aid of legislation. And any punishable misdeed of such a nature which is not recognized as a distinct crime, is usually called 'obstruction of justice,' or 'obstructing justice,' — a common-law misdemeanor." Rollin M. Perkins & Ronald N. Boyce, *Criminal Law* 552 (3d ed. 1982).

obtaining property by false pretenses. See FALSE PRETENSES.

obtest (ob- *or* əb-**test**), *vb.* **1.** To call to or invoke as a witness. **2.** To ask for earnestly; beseech; implore. **3.** To protest.

obtulit se (**ob**-t[y]ə-lit **see**). [Latin] Offered himself. • In old English practice, these words were entered on the record when one party appeared ("offered himself") in court against an opposing party who did not appear.

ob turpem causam (ob **tər**-pəm **kaw**-zəm). [Latin] For an immoral consideration.

obvention (ob- *or* əb-**ven**-shən). *Eccles. law.* An incoming fee or revenue, esp. one that comes occasionally or incidentally.

obviate (**ob**-vee-ayt), *vb.* **1.** To dispose of or do away with (a thing); to anticipate and prevent from arising <they obviated the growing problem through legislation>. **2.** To make unnecessary <the movant obviated the all-night drafting session by getting the opponent to agree to an extension>. — **obviation,** *n.* — **obviator,** *n.*

obviousness, *n. Patents.* The quality or state of being easily apparent to a person with ordinary skill in a given art, considering the scope and content of the prior art, so that the person could reasonably believe that, at the time it was conceived, the invention was to be expected. • An invention that is determined to be obvious cannot be patented. — **obvious,** *adj.* Cf. NONOBVIOUSNESS.

obviousness double patenting. See DOUBLE PATENTING.

o.c. *abbr.* **1.** OPE CONSILIO. **2.** Orphan's court. See *probate court* under COURT.

occasio (ə-**kay**-zhee-oh). [Law Latin] *Hist.* **1.** A tax that a lord imposed on his vassals or tenants for his necessity. **2.** Hindrance or trouble; esp., vexatious litigation.

occupancy. 1. The act, state, or condition of holding, possessing, or residing in or on something; actual possession, residence, or tenancy, esp. of a dwelling or land. **2.** The act of taking possession of something that has no owner (such as abandoned property) so as to acquire legal ownership. See ADVERSE POSSESSION. **3.** The period or term during which one owns, rents, or otherwise occupies property. **4.** The state or condition of being occupied. **5.** The use to which property is put.

occupant. 1. One who has possessory rights in, or control over, certain property or premises. **2.** One who acquires title by occupancy.

general occupant. A person who occupies land in the interim arising after the death of a *pur autre vie* tenant but before the death of the person who serves as the measuring life for the estate. • A general occupancy can arise when the grant to the *pur autre vie* tenant does not state who may occupy the land after the death of the first tenant. Because no heir is named, the land can be occupied by the first possessor of the land. — Also termed *common occupant.* Cf. CESTUI QUE VIE.

special occupant. A *pur autre vie* tenant's heir who occupies land in the interim between the death of the tenant and the death of the person who serves as the measuring life for the estate. • A special occupancy can arise when the grant to the *pur autre vie* tenant provides that possession is for the life of the tenant, then to the tenant's heirs.

occupare (ok-yə-**pair**-ee), *vb.* [Latin] *Civil law.* To seize or take possession of (property); to enter (land) upon a vacant possession.

occupatile (**ok**-yə-pə-tɪl). *Hist.* Property that has been left by its rightful owner and is now possessed by another.

occupatio (ok-yə-**pay**-shee-oh). *Roman law.* A mode of acquisition by which a person obtains absolute title by first possessing a thing that previously belonged to no one, such as a fish in the sea or a wild bird.

occupation. 1. An activity or pursuit in which a person is engaged; esp., a person's usual or principal work or business. **2.** The possession, control, or use of real property; OCCUPANCY. **3.** The seizure and control of a territory by military force; the condition of territory that has been placed under the authority of a hostile army. **4.** The period during which territory seized by military force is held.

occupational-disability insurance. See INSURANCE.

occupational disease. A disease that is contracted as a result of exposure to debilitating conditions or substances in the course of employment. • Employees who suffer from occupational diseases are eligible for workers' compensation. Courts have construed the term to include a variety of ailments, including lung conditions (such as asbestosis or black lung), hearing loss, and carpal tunnel syndrome. — Also termed *industrial disease.*

> "Certain diseases and infirmities which develop gradually and imperceptibly as a result of engaging in particular employments and which are generally known and understood to be usual incidents or hazards thereof, are distinguished from those having a traumatic origin, or otherwise developing suddenly and unexpectedly, by the terms 'occupational,' and 'industrial.'" 82 Am. Jur. 2d *Workers' Compensation* § 326 (1992).

occupational hazard. A danger or risk that is peculiar to a particular calling or occupation. • Occupational hazards include both accidental injuries and occupational diseases.

Occupational Safety and Health Act of 1970. A 1970 federal statute that requires employers to (1) keep the workplace free from recognized hazards that cause or are likely to cause death or serious physical harm to employees, and (2) comply with standards promulgated by the Secretary of Labor. — Abbr. OSHA (**oh**-shə).

> "Although OSHA has been one of the most controversial pieces of protective legislation ever enacted, Congress has not passed any substantive amendments to the Act. There have been, however, some limitations on OSHA enforcement activity attached to appropriations bills. In addition, OSHA has been affected by newer laws such as the Criminal Fine Enforcement Act, the Equal Access to Justice Act, and the Surface Transportation Assistance Act.... The Act covers employment in every state, the

District of Columbia, Puerto Rico, and all American territories, an estimated 5 million workplaces and 75 million employees." Mark A. Rothstein, *Occupational Safety and Health Law* 7 (1990).

Occupational Safety and Health Administration. A federal agency that establishes and enforces health and safety standards in various industries. • This agency, created in 1970 as part of the Labor Department, routinely conducts inspections of businesses and issues citations for noncompliance with its standards. — Abbr. OSHA.

occupational tax. See *occupation tax* under TAX.

occupation tax. See TAX.

occupavit (ok-yə-**pay**-vit). [Law Latin] *Hist.* A writ to regain possession to land or a tenement from which one was ejected in time of war.

occupying claimant. A person who claims the right under a statute to recover for the cost of improvements done to land that is later found not to belong to the person.

occupying-claimant act. See BETTERMENT ACT.

occurrence. Something that happens or takes place; specif., an accident, event, or continuing condition that results in personal injury or property damage that is neither expected nor intended from the standpoint of an insured party. • This specific sense is the standard definition of the term under most liability policies.

occurrence policy. See INSURANCE POLICY.

occurrence rule. *Civil procedure.* The rule that a limitations period begins to run when the alleged wrongful act or omission occurs, rather than when the plaintiff discovers the injury. • This rule applies, for example, to most breach-of-contract claims. See STATUTE OF LIMITATIONS. Cf. DISCOVERY RULE.

ocean. 1. The continuous body of salt water that covers more than 70% of the earth's surface; the high seas; the open sea. See SEA. **2.** Any of the principal geographic divisions of this body. • There are generally considered to be five oceans: Atlantic, Pacific, Indian, Arctic, and Antarctic.

ocean bill of lading. See BILL OF LADING.

ocean marine insurance. See INSURANCE.

octo tales (**ok**-toh **tay**-leez *or* **taylz**). [Latin "eight such"] **1.** A supply of eight additional jurors for a trial. **2.** A writ commanding a sheriff to summon eight more jurors for a trial. See TALES.

octroi (**ok**-troy *or* ahk-**trwah**), *n.* [French] **1.** *Hist.* A grant or privilege of a charter by a sovereign. **2.** A local tax levied on certain goods that are brought into a city (esp. in some European countries). **3.** The place where such a tax is collected. **4.** The agency for collecting such a tax.

octroy (**ok**-troy), *vb.* (Of a sovereign) to grant or concede as a privilege.

o/d. *abbr.* OVERDRAFT (2).

OD. *abbr.* **1.** Overdose. **2.** OVERDRAFT (2). **3.** See *ordinary seaman* under SEAMAN.

odal (**oh**-dəl), *n. Hist.* Land not subject to feudal duties or burdens; ALLODIUM. — Also termed *odel*; *odhal*; *odhall*. — **odal,** *adj.* <an odal right>.

odd lot. See LOT (3).

odd-lot, *adj.* Of, relating to, or designating a worker who is so substantially disabled as to be unable to find stable employment in the ordinary labor market, and thus is considered totally disabled and entitled to workers'-compensation benefits under the odd-lot doctrine <an odd-lot worker who could find only sporadic employment>.

odd-lot doctrine. *Workers' compensation.* The doctrine that permits a finding of total disability for an injured claimant who, though able to work sporadically, cannot obtain regular employment and steady income and is thus considered an "odd lot" in the labor market.

odel. See ODAL.

odhal. See ODAL.

odhall. See ODAL.

odio et atia. See DE ODIO ET ATIA.

odium (**oh**-dee-əm). **1.** The state or fact of being hated. **2.** A state of disgrace, usu. resulting from detestable conduct. **3.** Hatred or strong aversion accompanied by loathing or contempt. — **odious,** *adj.*

oeconomicus (ee-kə-**nom**-ə-kəs). [Law Latin] *Hist.* An executor of a will.

oeconomus (ee-**kon**-ə-məs). [Latin] *Civil law.* A manager or administrator.

of counsel. See COUNSEL.

of course. 1. Following the ordinary procedure <the writ was issued as a matter of course>. **2.** Naturally; obviously; clearly <we'll appeal that ruling, of course>.

off-board, *adj.* Outside a major exchange; over-the-counter or between private parties <an off-board securities transaction>. — Also termed *off-the-board.* See OVER-THE-COUNTER.

offender. A person who has committed a crime.

adult offender. **1.** A person who has committed a crime after reaching the age of majority. **2.** A person who, having committed a crime while a minor, has been convicted after reaching the age of majority. **3.** A juvenile who has committed a crime and is tried as an adult rather than as a juvenile.

first offender. A person who authorities believe has committed a crime but who has never before been convicted of a crime. • Such a person is often treated leniently at sentencing or in plea negotiations.

repeat offender. A person who has been convicted of a crime more than once; RECIDIVIST.

status offender. A youth who engages in conduct that — though not criminal by adult standards — is considered inappropriate enough to bring a charge against the youth in juvenile court; a juvenile who commits a status offense. Cf. *youthful offender;* JUVENILE DELINQUENT.

youthful offender. **1.** A person in late adolescence or early adulthood who has been convicted of a crime. • A youthful offender is often eligible for special programs not available to older offenders, including community supervision, the successful completion of which may lead to erasing the conviction from the offender's record. **2.** JUVENILE DELINQUENT. — Also termed *young offender; youth offender.* Cf. *status offender.*

offense (ə-**fents**). **1.** A violation of the law; a crime, often a minor one. See CRIME.

acquisitive offense. An offense characterized by the unlawful appropriation of another's property. • This is a generic term that refers to a variety of crimes (such as larceny) rather than a particular one.

anticipatory offense. See *inchoate offense.*

arrestable offense. *English law.* An offense for which the punishment is fixed by law or for which a statute authorizes imprisonment for five years, or an attempt to commit such an offense. • This statutory category, created in 1967, abolished the traditional distinction between felonies and misdemeanors. — Also spelled (esp. in BrE) *arrestable offence.*

capital offense. A crime for which the death penalty may be imposed. — Also termed *capital crime.*

civil offense. See *public tort* under TORT.

cognate offense. A lesser offense that is related to the greater offense because it shares several of the elements of the greater offense and is of the same class or category. • For example, shoplifting is a cognate offense of larceny because both crimes require the element of taking property with the intent to deprive the rightful owner of that property. Cf. *lesser included offense.*

continuing offense. A crime that is committed over a period of time, such as a conspiracy, so that the last act of the crime controls for the commencement of the statute of limitations.

cumulative offense. An offense committed by repeating the same act at different times.

divisible offense. A crime that includes one or more crimes of lesser grade. • For example, murder is a divisible offense comprising assault, battery, and assault with intent to kill.

extraneous offense. An offense beyond or unrelated to the offense for which a defendant is on trial.

graded offense. A crime that is divided into various degrees of severity with corresponding levels of punishment, such as murder (first-degree and second-degree) or assault (simple and aggravated). See DEGREE (2).

impeachable offense. See IMPEACHABLE OFFENSE.

inchoate offense. A step toward the commission of another crime, the step in itself being serious enough to merit punishment. • In criminal law, the three inchoate offenses are attempt, conspiracy, and solicitation. The term is sometimes criticized (see quot. below). — Also termed *anticipatory offense*; *inchoate crime*; *preliminary crime*.

"These preliminary crimes have sometimes been erroneously described as 'inchoate' offences. This is misleading because the word 'inchoate' connotes something which is not yet completed, and it is therefore not accurately used to denote something which is itself complete, even though it be a link in a chain of events leading to some object which is not yet attained. The offence of incitement is fully performed even though the person incited immediately repudiates the suggested deed, a conspiracy is committed although the conspirators have not yet moved to execute their purposed crime, and the performance of a criminal attempt must always have been reached before the end is gained. In all these instances it is the ultimate crime which is inchoate and not the preliminary crime, the position indeed being just the same as in the example imagined above of a man who stole a revolver and committed other crimes in order to effect his purpose of murder. There the murder was inchoate, but the larceny and other crimes (including the attempt) were completed." J.W. Cecil Turner, *Kenny's Outlines of Criminal Law* 77 (16th ed. 1952).

included offense. See *lesser included offense*.

index offense. One of eight classes of crimes reported annually by the FBI in the Uniform Crime Report. • The eight classes are murder (and nonnegligent homicide), rape, robbery, aggravated assault, burglary, larceny-theft, arson, and auto theft. — Also termed *index crime*.

indictable offense. A crime that can be prosecuted only by indictment. • In federal court, such an offense is one punishable by death or by imprisonment for more than one year or at hard labor. Fed. R. Crim. P. 7(a). See INDICTMENT.

joint offense. An offense (such as conspiracy) committed by the participation of two or more persons.

lesser included offense. A crime that is composed of some, but not all, of the elements of a more serious crime and that is necessarily committed in carrying out the greater crime <battery is a lesser included offense of murder>. • For double-jeopardy purposes, a lesser included offense is considered the "same offense" as the greater offense, so that acquittal or conviction of either offense precludes a separate trial for the other. — Also termed *included offense*; *necessarily included offense*. Cf. *cognate offense*.

liquor offense. Any crime involving the inappropriate use or sale of intoxicating liquor. See DRAM-SHOP LIABILITY; DRIVING WHILE INTOXICATED.

multiple offense. An offense that violates more than one law but that may require different proof so that an acquittal or conviction under one statute does not exempt the defendant from prosecution under another.

necessarily included offense. See *lesser included offense*.

negligent offense. A violation of law arising from a defective discharge of duty or from criminal negligence. See *criminal negligence* under NEGLIGENCE.

object offense. The crime that is the object of the defendant's attempt, solicitation, conspiracy, or complicity. • For example, murder is the object offense in a charge of attempted murder. — Also termed *target offense*.

offense against property. A crime against another's personal property. • The common-law offenses against property were larceny, embezzlement, cheating, cheating by false pretenses, robbery, receiving stolen goods, malicious mischief, forgery, and uttering forged instruments. Although the term *crimes against property*, a common term in modern usage, includes crimes against real property, the term *offense against property* is traditionally restricted to personal property. Cf. CRIMES AGAINST PROPERTY.

offense against public justice and authority. A crime that impairs the administration of justice. • The common-law offenses of this type were obstruction of justice, barratry, maintenance, champerty, embracery, escape, prison breach, rescue, misprision of felony, compounding a crime, subornation of perjury, bribery, and misconduct in office.

offense against the habitation. A crime against another's house — traditionally either arson or burglary.

offense against the person. A crime against the body of another human being. • The common-law offenses against the person were murder, manslaughter, mayhem, rape, assault, battery, robbery, false imprisonment, abortion, seduction, kidnapping, and abduction. Cf. CRIMES AGAINST PERSONS.

offense against the public health, safety, comfort, and morals. A crime traditionally viewed as endangering the whole of society. • The common-law offenses of this type were nuisance, bigamy, adultery, fornication, lewdness, illicit cohabitation, incest, miscegenation, sodomy, bestiality, buggery, abortion, and seduction.

offense against the public peace. A crime that tends to disturb the peace. • The common-law offenses of this type were riot, unlawful assembly, dueling, rout, affray, forcible entry and detainer, and libel on a private person.

petty offense. A minor or insignificant crime.

"[W]e find ... an apparent implication that a 'petty offense' is not a 'crime.' Much could be said for such a position but it is not the law at the present time. In the federal penal code, for example, it is provided that any misdemeanor 'the penalty for which does not exceed imprisonment for a period of six months or a fine of not more than $500, or both, is a petty offense.' " Rollin M. Perkins & Ronald N. Boyce, *Criminal Law* 22 (3d ed. 1982) (quoting 18 USCA § 1(3)).

political offense. See POLITICAL OFFENSE.

public offense. An act or omission forbidden by law.

public-welfare offense. A minor offense that involves no moral delinquency, being intended only to secure the effective regulation of conduct in the interest of the community. • An example is driving a car with one brake-light missing. — Also termed *regulatory offense*; *contravention*.

regulatory offense. **1.** A statutory crime, as opposed to a common-law crime. **2.** See *public-welfare offense*.

same offense. **1.** For double-jeopardy purposes, the same criminal act, omission, or transaction for which the person has already stood trial. See DOUBLE JEOPARDY. **2.** For sentencing and enhancement-of-punishment purposes, an offense that is quite similar to a previous one.

second offense. An offense committed after conviction for a first offense. • The previous conviction, not the indictment, forms the basis of the charge of a second offense.

separate offense. **1.** An offense arising out of the same event as another offense but containing some differences in elements of proof. • A person may be tried, convicted, and sentenced for each separate offense. **2.** An offense arising out of a different event entirely from another offense under consideration.

serious offense. An offense not classified as a petty offense and usu. carrying at least a six-month sentence. — Also termed *serious crime*. Cf. *petty offense*.

sexual offense. An offense involving unlawful sexual conduct, such as prostitution, indecent exposure, incest, pederasty, and bestiality.

status offense. **1.** See *status crime* under CRIME. **2.** A minor's violation of the juvenile code by doing some act that would not be considered illegal if an adult did it, but that indicates that the minor is beyond parental control. • Examples include running away from home, truancy, and incorrigibility. See JUVENILE DELINQUENCY.

substantive offense (**səb**-stən-tiv). A crime that is complete in itself and is not dependent on another crime for one of its elements. — Also termed *substantive crime*.

summary offense. An offense (such as a petty misdemeanor) that can be prosecuted without an indictment. Cf. *indictable offense*.

target offense. See *object offense*.

unnatural offense. See SODOMY.

unrelated offense. A crime that is independent from the charged offense.

2. *Civil law.* An intentional unlawful act that causes injury or loss to another and that gives rise to a claim for damages. • This sense of *offense* is essentially the same as the common-law intentional tort.

quasi-offense. *Civil law.* A negligent unlawful act that causes injury or loss to another and that gives rise to a claim for damages. • This is equivalent to the common-law tort of negligence. — Also termed *quasi-delict*.

offense against property. See OFFENSE (1).

offense against public justice and authority. See OFFENSE (1).

offense against the habitation. See OFFENSE (1).

offense against the person. See OFFENSE (1).

offense against the public health, safety, comfort, and morals. See OFFENSE (1).

offense against the public peace. See OFFENSE (1).

offensive (ə-**fen**-siv), *adj.* **1.** Of or for attack <an offensive weapon>. **2.** Unpleasant or disagreeable to the senses; obnoxious <an offensive odor>. **3.** Causing displeasure, anger, or resentment; esp., repugnant to the prevailing sense of what is decent or moral <patently offensive language and photographs>. See OBSCENE.

offensive and defensive league. *Int'l law.* A league binding the parties not only to aid one another when attacked but also to support one another when attacking in offensive warfare.

offensive collateral estoppel. See COLLATERAL ESTOPPEL.

offensive strike. See STRIKE.

offensive-use waiver. An exemption from the attorney-client privilege, whereby a litigant is considered to have waived the privilege by seeking affirmative relief, if the claim relies on privileged information that would be outcome-determinative and that the opposing party has no other way to obtain. Cf. AT-ISSUE WAIVER.

offer, *n.* **1.** The act or an instance of presenting something for acceptance <the prosecutor's offer of immunity>. **2.** A promise to do or refrain from doing some specified thing in the future; a display of willingness to enter into a contract on specified terms, made in a way that would lead a reasonable person to understand that an acceptance, having been sought, will result in a binding contract <she accepted the $750 offer on the Victorian armoire>. Cf. ACCEPTANCE.

> "[A]n offer is, in effect, a promise by the offeror to do or abstain from doing something, provided that the offeree will accept the offer and pay or promise to pay the 'price' of the offer. The price, of course, need not be a monetary one. In fact, in bilateral contracts, as we explained earlier, the mere promise of payment of the price suffices to conclude the contract, while in a unilateral contract it is the actual payment of the price which is required." P.S. Atiyah, *An Introduction to the Law of Contract* 44 (3d ed. 1981).

irrevocable offer (i-rev-ə-kə-bəl). An offer that includes a promise to keep it open for a specified period, during which the offer cannot be withdrawn without the offeror's becoming subject to liability for breach of contract. • Traditionally, this type of promise must be supported by consideration to be enforceable, but under UCC § 2–205, a merchant's signed, written offer giving assurances that it will be held open — but lacking consideration — is nonetheless irrevocable for the stated period (or, if not stated, for a reasonable time not exceeding three months). — Also termed (in the UCC) *firm offer*; (specif.) *merchant's firm offer*.

> "It has sometimes been asserted that an irrevocable offer is 'a legal impossibility.' See Langdell, Summary of the Law of Contracts, § 178, also § 4; Wormser, 'The True Conception of Unilateral Contracts,' 26 *Yale Law Journal*, 137, note; Lee, Title Contracts, in Jenks' Dig. of Eng. Civ. Law, § 195; Ashley, Contracts, § 13. A close analysis shows that there is nothing impossible either in the conception itself or in its application. If we define 'offer' as an *act* on the part of the offeror . . . , then no offer can ever be revoked, for it is of yesterday — it is indeed *factum*. But if we mean by 'offer' the legal relation that results from the offeror's act, the *power* then given to the offeree of creating contractual relations by doing certain voluntary acts on his part, then the offer may be either revocable or irrevocable according to the circumstances. The idea of an irrevocable power is not at all an unfamiliar one." William R. Anson, *Principles of the Law of Contract* 53–54 n.3 (Arthur L. Corbin ed., 3d Am. ed. 1919).

offer to all the world. An offer, by way of advertisement, of a reward for the rendering of specified services, addressed to the public at large. • As soon as someone renders the services, a contract is made.

public-exchange offer. A takeover attempt in which the bidder corporation offers to exchange some of its securities for a specified number of the target corporation's voting shares. Cf. TENDER OFFER.

standing offer. An offer that is in effect a whole series of offers, each of which is capable of being converted into a contract by a distinct acceptance.

two-tier offer. See TWO-TIER OFFER.

3. A price at which one is ready to buy or sell; BID <she lowered her offer to $200>. **4.** ATTEMPT (2) <an offer to commit battery>. — **offer,** *vb.* — **offeror,** *n.* — **offeree,** *n.*

> "Where criminal assault has been given this dual scope, a definition in terms of 'an attempt or offer' to commit a battery is assumed to represent both grounds. The word 'offer,' it is said, signifies a threat that places the other in reasonable apprehension of receiving an immediate battery. It would be a mistake, however, to assume that the word carried any such significance when it first appeared in the definition of this offense. In one of its meanings, 'offer' is a synonym of 'attempt.'" Rollin M. Perkins & Ronald N. Boyce, *Criminal Law* 163 (3d ed. 1982).

offer in compromise. See OFFER OF COMPROMISE.

offering, *n.* **1.** The act of making an offer; something offered for sale. **2.** The sale of an issue of securities. See ISSUE (2).

all-or-none offering. An offering that allows the issuer to terminate the distribution if the entire block of offered securities is not sold.

initial public offering. A company's first public sale of stock; the first offering of an issuer's equity securities to the public through a registration statement. — Abbr. IPO.

negotiated offering. A securities offering in which the terms (including the underwriters' compensation) have been negotiated between the issuer and the underwriters.

primary offering. An offering of newly issued securities.

private offering. An offering made only to a small group of interested buyers. — Also termed *private placement*.

public offering. An offering made to the general public.

registered offering. A public offering of securities registered with the SEC and with appropriate state securities commissions. — Also termed *registered public offering*.

rights offering. An issue of stock-purchase rights allowing shareholders to buy newly issued stock at a fixed price, usu. below market value, and in proportion to the number of shares they already own. — Also termed *privileged subscription*. Cf. PREEMPTIVE RIGHT.

secondary offering. **1.** Any offering by an issuer of securities after its initial public offering. **2.** An offering of previously issued securities by persons other than the issuer. See *secondary distribution* (1) under DISTRIBUTION.

special offering. An offering of a large block of stock that, because of its size and the market in the particular issue, is specially handled on the floor of the stock exchange.

undigested offering. A public offering of securities that remain unsold because there is insufficient demand at the offered price.

offering circular. A document, similar to a prospectus, that provides information about a private securities offering. — Also termed *offering statement*.

offering price. See *asking price* under PRICE.

offering statement. See OFFERING CIRCULAR.

offer of compromise. An offer by one party to settle a dispute amicably (usu. by paying money) to avoid or end a lawsuit or other legal action. • An offer of compromise is usu. not admissible at trial as evidence of the offering party's liability. — Also termed *offer in compromise*; *offer of settlement*.

offer of judgment. A settlement offer by one party to allow a specified judgment to be taken against the party. • In federal procedure (and in many states), if the adverse party rejects the offer, and if a judgment finally obtained by that party is not more favorable than the offer, then that party must pay the costs incurred after the offer was made. Fed. R. Civ. P. 68.

offer of performance. *Contracts.* One party's reasonable assurance to the other, through words or conduct, of a present ability to fulfill contractual obligations. • When performances are to be exchanged simultaneously, each party is entitled to refuse to proceed with the exchange until the other party makes an appropriate offer of performance.

> "The requirement of an offer of performance is to be applied in the light of what is reasonably to be expected by the parties in view of the practical difficulties of absolute simultaneity and is subject to the agreement of the parties, as supplemented or qualified by usage and course of dealing." Restatement (Second) of Contracts § 238 cmt. b (1981).

offer of proof. *Procedure.* A presentation of evidence for the record (but outside the jury's presence) usu. made after the judge has sustained an objection to the admissibility of that evidence, so that the evidence can be preserved on the record for an appeal of the judge's ruling. • An offer of proof, which may also be used to persuade the court to admit the evidence, consists of three parts: (1) the evidence itself, (2) an explanation of the purpose for which it is offered (its relevance), and (3) an argument supporting admissibility. Such an offer may include tangible evidence or testimony (through questions and answers, a lawyer's narrative description, or an affidavit). Fed. R. Evid. 103(a)(2). — Also termed *avowal*.

offer of settlement. See OFFER OF COMPROMISE.

offer to all the world. See OFFER.

office. 1. A position of duty, trust, or authority, esp. one conferred by a governmental authority for a public purpose <the office of attorney general>. **2.** (*often cap.*) A division of the U.S. government ranking immediately below a department <the Patent and Trademark Office>. **3.** A place where business is conducted or services are performed <a law office>.

alienation office. *English law.* An office for the recovery of fines levied upon writs of covenant and entries.

lucrative office. **1.** A position that produces fee revenue or a salary to the office holder. **2.** A position that yields a salary adequate to the services rendered and exceeding incidental expenses; a position whose pay is tied to the performance of the office's duties.

office audit. See AUDIT.

office-block ballot. See BALLOT (4).

office expense. See OVERHEAD.

office grant. See GRANT.

office hours. See *nonjudicial punishment* under PUNISHMENT.

office lawyer. See OFFICE PRACTITIONER.

office of honor. An uncompensated public position of considerable dignity and importance to which public trusts or interests are confided.

office practice. A law practice that primarily involves handling matters outside of court, such as negotiating and drafting contracts, preparing wills and trusts, setting up corporations and partnerships, and advising on tax or employment issues.

office practitioner. A lawyer who does not litigate; an attorney whose work is accomplished primarily in the office, without court appearances. — Also termed *office lawyer*.

officer. 1. A person who holds an office of trust, authority, or command. • In public affairs, the term refers esp. to a person holding public office under a national, state, or local government, and authorized by that government to exercise some specific function. In corporate law, the term refers esp. to a person elected or appointed by the board of directors to manage the daily operations of a corporation, such as a CEO, president, secretary, or treasurer. Cf. DIRECTOR (2).

acting officer. One performing the duties of an office — usu. temporarily — but who has no claim of title to the office.

administrative officer. **1.** An officer of the executive department of government, usu. of inferior rank. **2.** A ministerial or executive officer, as distinguished from a judicial officer.

corporate officer. An officer of a corporation, such as a CEO, president, secretary, or treasurer.

county officer. An officer whose authority and jurisdiction are confined to the limits of the county served.

de facto officer. See *officer de facto*.

de jure officer. See *officer de jure*.

legislative officer. **1.** A member of a federal, state, or municipal legislative body. **2.** A government official whose duties relate primarily to the enactment of laws, such as a federal or state congressman. • State and federal constitutions generally restrict legislative officers' duties to the enactment of legislation. But legislative officers occasionally exercise judicial functions, such as presenting or hearing cases of impeachment of other government officers.

ministerial officer. An officer who primarily executes mandates issued by the officer's superiors. • One who performs specified legal duties when the appropriate conditions have been met, but who does not exercise personal judgment or discretion in performing those duties.

officer de facto (di **fak**-toh). **1.** An officer who exercises the duties of an office under color of an appointment or election, but who has failed to qualify for office for any one of various reasons, as by being under the required age, having failed to take the oath, having not furnished a required bond, or having taken office under a statute later declared unconstitutional. **2.** *Corporations*. One who is acting under color of right and with apparent authority, but who is not legally a corporate officer. • The corporation is bound by all acts and contracts of an officer de facto in the same way as it is with those of an officer de jure. — Also termed *de facto officer*.

officer de jure (di **juur**-ee). **1.** An officer who exercises the duties of an office for which the holder has fulfilled all the qualifications. **2.** A duly authorized corporate officer. — Also termed *de jure officer*.

state officer. **1.** A person whose authority or jurisdiction extends to the general public or state as a whole, as distinguished from an officer whose authority and jurisdiction is confined to the limits of a particular political subdivision. **2.** An officer exercising authority under a state — rather than the federal — government.

subordinate officer. **1.** An officer ranking below and performing under the direction of another officer. **2.** An independent officer subject only to statutory direction.

United States officer. An officer appointed under the authority of the federal government; specif., an officer appointed in the manner described in Article II, section 2, of the U.S. Constitution.

2. *Military law*. One who holds a commission in the armed services, or a military post higher than that of the lowest ranks.

brevet officer (brə-**vet** *or* **brev**-it). A military officer who holds a nominal rank above that for which the person is paid.

commissioned officer. An officer in the armed forces who holds grade and office under a presidential commission.

general officer. A military officer whose command extends to a body of forces composed of several regiments. • Examples are generals, lieutenant-generals, major-generals, and brigadiers.

legal officer. **1.** The officer responsible for handling military justice within a command. **2.** The adviser and assistant to a commanding officer on military-law matters. **3.** Any commissioned officer of the Navy, Marine Corps, or Coast Guard who has been designated to perform legal duties for a command.

noncommissioned officer. An enlisted person in the Army, Air Force, or Marine Corps in certain pay grades above the lowest pay grade. • Examples are sergeants and corporals.

officer of the day. An officer who has charge, for the time being, of the guard, prisoners, and police of a military force or camp. — Also termed *orderly officer*.

officer of the guard. A commissioned officer whose detail is to command the guard of a military force or camp. • The officer of the guard is under the command of the officer of the day.

orderly officer. See *officer of the day*.

petty officer. An enlisted person in the Navy or Coast Guard with a pay-grade of E–4 or higher.

presiding officer. **1.** The president of the court in a special court-martial that does not have a military judge. **2.** In a court-martial with a military judge, the military judge.

superior commissioned officer. A commissioned officer who is superior in command or rank.

warrant officer. A person who holds a commission or warrant in a warrant-officer grade. • A warrant officer's rank is below a second lieutenant or ensign but above cadets, midshipmen, and enlisted personnel.

officer de facto. See OFFICER (1).

officer de jure. See OFFICER (1).

officer of the court. A person who is charged with upholding the law and administering the judicial system. • Typically, *officer of the court* refers to a judge, clerk, bailiff, sheriff, or the like, but the term also applies to a lawyer, who is obliged to obey court rules and who owes a duty of candor to the court. — Also termed *court officer*.

officer of the day. See OFFICER (2).

officer of the guard. See OFFICER (2).

officer of the peace. See PEACE OFFICER.

official (ə-**fish**-əl), *adj.* **1.** Of or relating to an office or position of trust or authority <official duties>. **2.** Authorized or approved by a proper authority <a company's official policy>.

official, *n.* **1.** One who holds or is invested with a public office. **2.** One authorized to act for a corporation or organization, esp. in a subordinate capacity. **3.** (*usu. cap.*) OFFICIAL PRINCIPAL.

official bond. See BOND (2).

official corruption. See *official misconduct* under MISCONDUCT.

official misconduct. See MISCONDUCT.

official newspaper. See NEWSPAPER.

official principal. (*usu. cap.*) *Eccles. law.* A person appointed by an archbishop, bishop, or deacon to exercise jurisdiction in and preside over an ecclesiastical court. — Sometimes shortened to *official*.

official privilege. See PRIVILEGE (3).

official report. See REPORT (2).

official use. See USE (4).

officina brevium (aw-fə-**sI**-nə **bree**-vee-əm). [Latin "workshop of writs"] *Hist.* OFFICINA JUSTITIAE.

officina justitiae (aw-fə-**sI**-nə jəs-**tish**-ee-ee). [Latin "workshop of justice"] *Hist.* The court of chancery, where the king's writs were issued. — Also termed *officina brevium*. See CHANCERY.

officio. See EX OFFICIO.

officious intermeddler (ə-**fish**-əs). A person who confers a benefit on another without being requested or having a legal duty to do so, and who therefore has no legal grounds to demand restitution for the benefit conferred. — Sometimes shortened to *intermeddler*.

officious testament. See TESTAMENT.

officious will. See *officious testament* under TESTAMENT.

off point. Not discussing the precise issue at hand; irrelevant. Cf. ON POINT.

offset, *n.* Something (such as an amount or claim) that balances or compensates for something else; SETOFF.

offset, *vb.* To balance or calculate against; to compensate for <the gains offset the losses>.

offset account. See ACCOUNT.

offspring. Children; issue; progeny.

off-the-board, *adj.* See OFF-BOARD.

off-year election. See ELECTION.

of record. 1. Recorded in the appropriate records <counsel of record>. See ATTORNEY OF RECORD. **2.** (Of a court) that has proceedings taken down stenographically or otherwise documented <court of record>. See *court of record* under COURT.

of the essence. (Of a contractual requirement) so important that if the requirement is not met, the promisor will be held to have breached the contract and a rescission by the promisee will be justified <time is of the essence>.

OID. *abbr.* ORIGINAL-ISSUE DISCOUNT.

oil-and-gas lease. See LEASE.

Oireachtas (**air**-ək-thəs *or* **eer**-ək-təs). The Parliament of the Republic of Ireland.

old-age and survivors' insurance. (*usu. cap.*) A system of insurance, subsidized by the federal government, that provides retirement benefits for persons who turn 65 and payments to survivors upon the death of the insured. • This was the original name for the retirement and death benefits established by the Social Security Act of 1935. As the scope of these benefits expanded, the name changed to Old Age, Survivors, and Disability Insurance (OASDI), and then to Old Age, Survivors, Disability, and Health Insurance (OASDHI). Today, the system is most often referred to as *social security*. — Abbr. OASI. See SOCIAL SECURITY.

Old *Natura Brevium* (nə-**t**[y]**oor**-ə **bree**-vee-əm). *Hist.* A treatise on the writs in use during the reign of Edward III. — Abbr. O.N.B. See BREVE.

old style. The system of ordering time according to the Julian method, introduced by Julius Caesar in 46 B.C., by which all years have 365 days except the years divisible by 4, which have 366 days. • This differs from the modern calendar in that it assumes that there are exactly 365.25 days in a year. But there are actually slightly less than 365.25 days in a year, so the old-style calendar adds too many days over time. The Julian calendar was reformed by Pope Gregory XIII in 1582. — Abbr. o.s. — Also termed *Julian calendar*. Cf. NEW STYLE.

Oléron, laws of (**oh**-lə-ron *or* aw-lay-**ron**). See LAWS OF OLÉRON.

oligarchy (**ol**-ə-gahr-kee), *n.* A government in which a small group of persons exercises control; the persons who constitute such a government. — **oligarchic, oligarchical,** *adj.*

oligopoly (ol-ə-**gop**-ə-lee), *n.* Control or domination of a market by a few large sellers, creating high prices and low output similar to those found in a monopoly. — **oligopolistic,** *adj.* — **oligopolist,** *n.* See MONOPOLY.

oligopsony (ol-ə-**gop**-sə-nee), *n.* Control or domination of a market by a few large buyers or customers. — **oligopsonistic,** *adj.* — **oligopsonist,** *n.*

olograph, *n.* HOLOGRAPH. — **olographic,** *adj.*

olographic will. See *holographic will* under WILL.

ombudsman (**om**-bədz-mən). **1.** An official appointed to receive, investigate, and report on private citizens' complaints about the government. **2.** A similar appointee in a nongovernmental organization (such as a company or university). — Often shortened to *ombuds*.

> "An ombudsman serves as an alternative to the adversary system for resolving disputes, especially between citizens and government agencies .... An ombudsman is ... (1) an independent and nonpartisan officer of the legislature who supervises the administration; (2) one who deals with specific complaints from the public against administrative injustice and maladministration; and (3) one who has the power to investigate, criticize and publicize, but not to reverse administration action." 4 Am. Jur. 2d *Alternative Dispute Resolution* § 23 (1995).

omission, *n.* **1.** A failure to do something; esp., a neglect of duty <the complaint alleged that the driver had committed various negligent acts and omissions>. **2.** The act of leaving something out <the contractor's omission of the sales price rendered the contract void>. **3.** The state of having been left out or of not having been done <his omission from the roster caused no harm>. **4.** Something that is left out, left undone, or otherwise neglected <the many omissions from the list were unintentional>. — Formerly also termed *omittance.* — **omit,** *vb.* — **omissive, omissible,** *adj.*

omittance. *Archaic.* OMISSION.

omnibus (**om**-ni-bəs), *adj.* Relating to or dealing with numerous objects or items at once; including many things or having various purposes.

omnibus bill. See BILL (3).

omnibus clause. 1. A provision in an automobile-insurance policy that extends coverage to all drivers operating the insured vehicle with the owner's permission. **2.** RESIDUARY CLAUSE.

omnibus count. See COUNT.

omnibus hearing. See HEARING.

omnibus motion. See MOTION.

omnium (**om**-nee-əm). The total amount or value of the items in a combined fund or stock. • The term is used primarily in mercantile law and in Great Britain.

OMVI. *abbr.* Operating a motor vehicle while intoxicated. See DRIVING UNDER THE INFLUENCE.

OMVUI. *abbr.* Operating a motor vehicle under the influence. See DRIVING UNDER THE INFLUENCE.

on all fours. (Of a law case) squarely on point (with a precedent) on both facts and law; nearly identical in all material ways <our client's case is on all fours with the Supreme Court's most recent opinion>. Cf. WHITEHORSE CASE.

> "The courts, nowadays, are governed largely by precedent, and this imposes on the advocate the necessity of supporting his client's cause by concrete authorities — cases 'on all fours' with, or at least analogous to, the case at bar." William M. Lile et al., *Brief Making and the Use of Law Books* 98 (3d ed. 1914).

O.N.B. *abbr.* OLD NATURA BREVIUM.

on board bill of lading. See BILL OF LADING.

on demand. When presented or upon request for payment <this note is payable on demand>. — Also termed *on call.* See PAYABLE.

one-action rule. In debtor-creditor law, the principle that when a debt is secured by real property, the creditor must foreclose on the collateral before proceeding against the debtor's unsecured assets.

one-court-of-justice doctrine. A principle in some states holding that there is but a single court in the state and that this court is composed of several divisions, such as the supreme court, the courts of appeals, and district courts, probate courts, and any other legislatively created courts. • Michigan, for example, has embodied this doctrine in its constitution (art. VI, § 1). — Also termed *one court of justice.*

one-day, one-trial method. A system of summoning and using jurors whereby a person answers a jury summons and participates in the venire for one day only, unless the person is actually impaneled for a trial, in which event the juror's service lasts for the entire length of the trial. • This system, which is used in several states, reduces the average term of service and expands the number of individual jurors called.

180–day rule. 1. A rule that, in some jurisdictions, allows a person charged with a felony to be released on personal recognizance if the person has been in jail for 180 days without being brought to trial, and if the delay has not resulted from the defendant's own actions. **2.** A rule requiring all pending charges against a prison inmate to be brought to trial in 180 days or to be dismissed with prejudice.

one-month liquidation. See LIQUIDATION.

one-person, one-vote rule. *Constitutional law.* The principle that the Equal Protection Clause requires legislative voting districts to have about the same population. *Reynolds v. Sims,* 377 U.S. 533, 84 S.Ct. 1362 (1964). — Also termed *one-man, one-vote rule.* See APPORTIONMENT.

onerando pro rata portione. See DE ONERANDO PRO RATA PORTIONE.

onerare (on-ə-**rair**-ee), *vb.* [Latin] *Hist.* To burden or load.

onerari non (on-ə-**rair**-I non). [Law Latin] *Hist.* Ought not to be charged. • In pleading, these words were used by a defendant to begin a plea in a debt action. Cf. ACTIO NON.

oneratio (on-ə-**ray**-shee-oh). [Law Latin] *Hist.* A cargo or lading.

onerous (**oh**-nər-əs *or* **on**-ər-əs), *adj.* **1.** Excessively burdensome or troublesome; causing hardship <onerous discovery requests>. **2.** Having or involving obligations that outweigh the advantages <onerous property>. **3.** *Civil law.* Done or given in return for something of equivalent value; supported by consideration <an onerous contract>. — **onerousness,** *n.* Cf. GRATUITOUS.

onerous contract. See CONTRACT.

onerous gift. See GIFT.

onerous title. See TITLE (2).

one-satisfaction rule. The principle that a plaintiff is only entitled to one recovery for a particular harm, and that the plaintiff must elect a single remedy if the jury has awarded more than one. • This rule is, for example, one of the foundations of a defendant's right to have a jury verdict reduced by the amount of any settlements the plaintiff has received from other entities for the same injury. — Also termed *single-recovery rule.*

one-subject rule. The principle that a statute should embrace only one topic, which should be stated in its title.

onomastic (on-ə-**mas**-tik), *adj.* **1.** Of or relating to names or nomenclature. **2.** (Of a signature on an instrument) in a handwriting different from that of the body of the document; esp., designating an autograph signature alone, as distinguished from the main text in a different hand or in typewriting. Cf. HOLOGRAPH; SYMBOLIC. — **onomastics** (for sense 1), *n.*

on or about. Approximately; at or around the time specified. • This language is used in pleading to prevent a variance between the pleading and the proof, usu. when there is any uncertainty about the exact date of a pivotal event. When used in nonpleading contexts, the phrase is mere jargon.

on pain of. Followed by punishment inflicted if one does not comply with a command or condition <ordered to cease operations on pain of a $2,000 fine>.

on point. Discussing the precise issue now at hand; apposite <this opinion is not on point as authority in our case>. — Also termed *in point.* Cf. OFF POINT.

on-sale bar. *Patents.* A statutory bar prohibiting patent eligibility if an invention was sold or offered for sale more than one year before the filing of a patent application.

on the brief. (Of a lawyer) having participated in preparing a given brief. • The names of all the lawyers on the brief are typically listed on the front cover.

on the merits. (Of a judgment) delivered after the court has heard and evaluated the evidence and the parties' substantive arguments.

on the pleadings. (Of a judgment) rendered for reasons that are apparent from the faces of the complaint and answer, without hearing or evaluating the evidence or the substantive arguments. See SUMMARY JUDGMENT.

onus (**oh**-nəs). **1.** A burden; a load. **2.** A disagreeable responsibility; an obligation. **3.** ONUS PROBANDI.

onus probandi (**oh**-nəs prə-**ban**-dI). [Latin] BURDEN OF PROOF. — Often shortened to *onus.*

op. *abbr.* (*often cap.*) **1.** OPINION (1). **2.** Opinions.

OPEC (**oh**-pek). *abbr.* Organization of Petroleum Exporting Countries.

ope consilio (**oh**-pee kən-**sil**-ee-oh). [Latin] *Civil law.* By aid and counsel. • The term is usu. applied to accessories to crimes. It is analogous to the common-law concept of aiding and abetting. — Abbr. o.c. Also spelled *ope et consilio.*

open, *adj.* **1.** Manifest; apparent; notorious. **2.** Visible; exposed to public view; not clandestine. **3.** Not closed, settled, fixed, or terminated.

open account. See ACCOUNT.

open and notorious. **1.** NOTORIOUS (2). **2.** (Of adultery) known and recognized by the public and flouting the accepted standards of morality in the community.

open and notorious adultery. See ADULTERY.

open and notorious possession. See *notorious possession* under POSSESSION.

open bid. See BID (2).

open court. 1. A court that is in session, presided over by a judge, attended by the parties and their attorneys, and engaged in judicial business. • *Open court* usu. refers to a proceeding in which formal entries are made on the record. The term is distinguished from a court that is hearing evidence in camera or from a judge that is exercising merely magisterial powers. **2.** A court session that the public is free to attend. • Most state constitutions have open-court provisions guaranteeing the public's right to attend trials.

open credit. See *revolving credit* under CREDIT (4).

open diplomacy. See DIPLOMACY.

open-door law. See SUNSHINE LAW.

open-end, *adj.* **1.** Allowing for future changes or additions <open-end credit plan>. **2.** Continuously issuing or redeeming shares on demand at the current net asset value <open-end investment company>. — Also termed *open-ended.*

open-end fund. See MUTUAL FUND.

open-end mortgage. See MORTGAGE.

open-end mortgage bond. See BOND (3).

open entry. See ENTRY (1).

open-fields doctrine. *Criminal procedure.* The rule permitting a warrantless search of the area outside a property owner's curtilage, which includes the home and any adjoining land (such as a yard) that is within an enclosure or otherwise protected from public scrutiny. — Also termed *open-field doctrine*; *open-fields rule.* Cf. PLAIN-VIEW DOCTRINE.

open guaranty. See *continuing guaranty* under GUARANTY.

opening statement. At the outset of a trial, an advocate's statement giving the fact-finder a preview of the case and of the evidence to be presented, but not containing argument. — Also termed (incorrectly) *opening argument.*

open letter of credit. See LETTER OF CREDIT.

open listing. See LISTING (1).

open market. See MARKET.

open-meeting law. See SUNSHINE LAW.

open mortgage clause. See MORTGAGE CLAUSE.

open order. See ORDER (4).

open-perils policy. See INSURANCE POLICY.

open policy. See *unvalued policy* under INSURANCE POLICY.

open possession. See *notorious possession* under POSSESSION.

open price. See PRICE.

open sea. See HIGH SEAS.

open season. A specific time of year when it is legal to hunt or catch game or fish.

open session. See SESSION.

open shop. See SHOP.

open-shop–closed-shop operation. See DOUBLE-BREASTED OPERATION.

open town. *Int'l law.* An undefended city in a combat zone that is laid open to the grasp of the attacking forces.

open union. See UNION.

open verdict. See VERDICT.

operating a motor vehicle under the influence. See DRIVING UNDER THE INFLUENCE.

operating a motor vehicle while intoxicated. See DRIVING UNDER THE INFLUENCE.

operating-cost ratio. The ratio between the net sales of a business and its operating costs.

operating expense. See EXPENSE.

operating income. See *ordinary income* under INCOME.

operating interest. See WORKING INTEREST.

operating lease. See LEASE.

operating profit. See PROFIT.

operating under the influence. See DRIVING UNDER THE INFLUENCE.

operating while intoxicated. See DRIVING UNDER THE INFLUENCE.

operational, *adj.* **1.** Engaged in operation; able to function. **2.** Ministerial.

operation of law. The means by which a right or a liability is created for a party regardless of the party's actual intent <because the court didn't rule on the motion for rehearing within 30 days, it was overruled by operation of law>.

operative, *adj.* **1.** Being in or having force or effect; esp., designating the part of a legal instrument that gives effect to the transaction involved <the operative provision of the contract>. **2.** Having principal relevance; essential to the meaning of the whole <*may* is the operative word of the statute>.

operative fact. See FACT.

operative performance bond. See PERFORMANCE BOND.

operis novi nuntiatio (**op**-ər-is **noh**-vI nən-shee-**ay**-shee-oh). [Latin "declaration of a new work"] *Civil law.* A protest or warning against a new work undertaken by another to one's detriment.

OPIC. *abbr.* OVERSEAS PRIVATE INVESTMENT CORPORATION.

opinio juris sive necessitatis (ə-**pin**-ee-oh **joor**-is **sI**-vee nə-ses-i-**tay**-tis). [Latin "opinion that an act is necessary by rule of law"] *Int'l law.* The principle that for a country's conduct to rise to the level of international customary law, it must be shown that the conduct stems from the country's belief that international law (rather than moral obligation) mandates the conduct. — Also termed *opinio juris.*

opinion. 1. A court's written statement explaining its decision in a given case, usu. including the statement of facts, points of law, rationale, and dicta. — Abbr. op. — Also termed *judicial opinion.* See DECISION. Cf. JUDGMENT; RULING.

***advisory opinion.* 1.** A nonbinding statement by a court of its interpretation of the law on a matter submitted for that purpose. • Federal courts are constitutionally prohibited from issuing advisory opinions by the case-or-controversy requirement, but other courts, such as the International Court of Justice, render them routinely. See CASE-OR-CONTROVERSY REQUIREMENT. **2.** A written statement, issued only by an administrator of an employee benefit plan, that interprets ERISA and applies it to a specific factual situation. • Only the parties named in the request for the opinion can rely on it, and its reliability depends on the accuracy and completeness of all material facts.

concurring opinion. See CONCURRENCE (3).

dissenting opinion. An opinion by one or more judges who disagree with the decision reached by the majority. — Often shortened to *dissent.* — Also termed *minority opinion.*

majority opinion. An opinion joined in by more than half of the judges considering a given case. — Also termed *main opinion.*

memorandum opinion. A unanimous opinion stating the decision of the court; an opinion that briefly reports the court's conclusion, usu. without elaboration because the decision follows a well-established legal principle or does not relate to any point of law. — Also termed *memorandum decision.*

minority opinion. See *dissenting opinion.*

per curiam opinion (pər **kyoor**-ee-əm). An opinion handed down by an appellate court without identifying the individual judge who wrote the opinion. — Sometimes shortened to *per curiam.*

plurality opinion. An opinion lacking enough judges' votes to constitute a majority, but receiving more votes than any other opinion.

seriatim opinions (seer-ee-**ay**-tim). A series of opinions written individually by each judge on the bench, as opposed to a single opinion speaking for the court as a whole.

***slip opinion.* 1.** A court opinion that is published individually after being rendered and then collectively in advance sheets before being released for publication in a reporter. • Unlike an unpublished opinion, a slip opinion can usu. be cited as authority. Cf. ADVANCE SHEETS. **2.** *Archaic.* A preliminary draft of a court opinion not yet ready for publication. — Also termed *slip decision.* Cf. *unpublished opinion.*

unpublished opinion. An opinion that the court has specifically designated as not for publication. • Court rules usu. prohibit citing an unpublished opinion as authority. Such an opinion is considered binding on only the parties to the particular case in which it is issued. Cf. *slip opinion*.

2. A formal expression of judgment or advice based on an expert's special knowledge; esp., a document, usu. prepared at a client's request, containing a lawyer's understanding of the law that applies to a particular case. — Also termed *opinion letter*.

> "The essence of a lawyer's job is to obtain the facts and the law with due diligence and then to give advice. But, strangely, no controlling definition has evolved for what is an 'opinion.' The lack of a definition is not crucial for some purposes. On the other hand, a definition is vital in other areas; for example, to determine within a law firm when peer review is necessary ...." 8 Arnold S. Jacobs, *Opinion Letters in Securities Matters* § 3, at Intro–12 (1998).

adverse opinion. An outside auditor's opinion that a company's financial statements do not conform with generally accepted accounting principles or do not accurately reflect the company's financial position.

audit opinion. A certified public accountant's opinion regarding the audited financial statements of an entity.

coverage opinion. A lawyer's opinion on whether a particular event is covered by a given insurance policy.

legal opinion. A written document in which an attorney provides his or her understanding of the law as applied to assumed facts. • The attorney may be a private attorney or attorney representing the state or other governmental entity. Private attorneys frequently render legal opinions on the ownership of real estate or minerals, insurance coverage, and corporate transactions. A party may be entitled to rely on a legal opinion, depending on factors such as the identity of the parties to whom the opinion was addressed and the law governing these opinions. See *coverage opinion*.

title opinion. A lawyer's or title company's opinion on the state of title for a given piece of real property, usu. describing whether the title is clear and marketable or whether it is encumbered. See TITLE SEARCH.

unqualified opinion. An audit opinion given by an accountant who is satisfied that the financial statements reviewed were fairly presented and consistent with the previous year, and that the audit was performed in accordance with generally accepted auditing standards.

3. A witness's thoughts, beliefs, or inferences about facts in dispute, as opposed to personal knowledge of the facts themselves. — Also termed (in sense 3) *conclusion*. See *opinion evidence* under EVIDENCE.

opinion evidence. See EVIDENCE.

opinion letter. See OPINION (2).

opinion rule. *Evidence.* The principle that a witness should testify to facts, not opinions, and that a witness's opinions are often excludable from evidence. • Traditionally, this principle is regarded as one of the important exclusionary rules in evidence law. It is based on the idea that a witness who has observed data should provide the most factual evidence possible, leaving the jury to draw inferences and conclusions from the evidence. Under this system, the witness's opinion is unnecessary.

> "This rule [the opinion rule] is an historical blunder, for the early cases excluding 'opinion' meant a belief by a person who had personally seen and known nothing, and was therefore not qualified to speak; whereas the modern rule applies it to witnesses who have had personal observation as a basis for their inference. Moreover, it is a senseless rule, for not once in a thousand times can the observed data be exactly and fully reproduced in words. Still further, no harm could be done by letting the witness offer his inference, except perhaps the waste of a moment's time, whereas the application of the rule wastes vastly more time. And finally the rule is so pedantically applied by most courts that it excludes the most valuable testimony, such as would be used in all affairs of life outside a court room." John H. Wigmore, *A Students' Textbook of the Law of Evidence* 156 (1935).

> "The [opinion] rule in its stark simplicity might be interpreted as excluding all value judgments, that is to say all statements not being factual propositions susceptible of some sort of empirical proof or disproof. The rule, if it is to be given any purely logical meaning at all, must be interpreted as excluding at least all inferences drawn from perceived data. Even if value judgments are saved by construing the rule as having application only to factual propositions, the rule would seem to purport to exclude all such propositions in the formulation of which inference by the witness has played some part." Zelman Cowen, *Essays on the Law of Evidence* 162 (1956).

opinion testimony. See TESTIMONY.

oppignorate (ə-**pig**-nə-rayt), *vb. Archaic.* To pawn or pledge. — Also spelled *oppignerate*. Cf. PIGNORATE.

opponent. 1. An adverse party in a contested matter. **2.** A party that is challenging the admissibility of evidence — opposed to *proponent*.

opportunity. The fact that the alleged doer of an act was present at the time and place of the act.

opportunity cost. See COST (1).

opportunity to be heard. The chance to appear in a court or other tribunal and present evidence and argument before being deprived of a right by governmental authority. • The opportunity to be heard is a fundamental requirement of procedural due process. It ordinarily includes the right to receive fair notice of the hearing, to secure the assistance of counsel, and to cross-examine adverse witnesses. See *procedural due process* under DUE PROCESS.

opposer. 1. *Intellectual property.* One who formally seeks to prevent the grant of a patent or the registration of a trademark. **2.** *Hist.* APPOSER.

oppression. 1. The act or an instance of unjustly exercising authority or power. **2.** An offense consisting in the abuse of discretionary authority by a public officer who has an improper motive, as a result of which a person is injured. • This offense does not include extortion, which is typically a more serious crime. **3.** *Contracts.* Coercion to enter into an illegal contract. • Oppression is grounds for the recovery of money paid or property transferred under an illegal contract. See DURESS; UNCONSCIONABILITY. **4.** *Corporations.* Unfair treatment of minority shareholders (esp. in a close corporation) by the directors or those in control of the corporation. See FREEZE-OUT. — Also termed (in sense 4) *shareholder oppression.* — **oppress,** *vb.* — **oppressive,** *adj.*

oppressor. A public official who unlawfully or wrongfully exercises power under color of authority in a way that causes a person harm; one who commits oppression.

OPRA. *abbr.* OPTIONS PRICE REPORTING AUTHORITY.

optimal-use value. See VALUE.

opt in, *vb.* To choose to participate in (something) <when the choice of settling or not settling came, the Joneses opted in, hoping to avoid a lengthy trial>.

option, *n.* **1.** The right or power to choose; something that may be chosen <the lawyer was running out of options for settlement>. **2.** A contract made to keep an offer open for a specified period, so that the offeror cannot revoke the offer during that period <the option is valid because it is supported by consideration>. — Also termed *option contract.* See *irrevocable offer* under OFFER. **3.** The right conveyed by such a contract <Phil declined to exercise his first option to buy the house>. **4.** The right (but not the obligation) to buy or sell a given quantity of securities, commodities, or other assets at a fixed price within a specified time <trading stock options is a speculative business>. Cf. FUTURES CONTRACT.

call option. An option to buy something (esp. securities) at a fixed price even if the market rises; the right to require another to sell. — Often shortened to *call.*

cash-value option. The right of a life-insurance policyholder to surrender the policy for its cash value at a specified time or at any time.

commodity option. An option to buy or sell a commodity.

futures option. An option to buy or sell a futures contract.

naked option. A call option that grants another the right to buy stock even though the option-giver does not own the stock to back up that commitment. — Also termed *uncovered option.*

nonforfeiture option. A policyholder's option, upon the lapse of premium payments, to continue an insurance policy for a shorter period than the original term, to surrender the policy for its cash value, to continue the policy for a reduced amount, or to take some other action rather than forfeit the policy.

option to purchase real property. A contract by which an owner of realty enters an agreement with another allowing the latter to buy the property at a specified price within a specified time, or within a reasonable time in the future, but without imposing an obligation to purchase upon the person to whom it is given.

put option. An option to sell something (esp. securities) at a fixed price even if the market declines; the right to require another to buy. — Often shortened to *put.*

seller's option. A special stock-exchange transaction that gives the seller the right to deliver the security within a specified period, usu. 5 to 60 days.

settlement option. *Insurance.* A life-insurance-policy clause providing choices in the method of paying benefits to a beneficiary, as by lump-sum payment or periodic installments.

stock option. See STOCK OPTION.

uncovered option. See *naked option*.

option, *vb.* To grant or take an option on (something) <Ward optioned his first screenplay to the studio for $50,000>.

option agreement. *Corporations.* A share-transfer restriction that commits the shareholder to sell, but not the corporation or other shareholders to buy, the shareholder's shares at a fixed price when a specified event occurs. Cf. BUY-SELL AGREEMENT (2); OPTION (2).

optional bond. See BOND (3).

optional completeness, rule of. See RULE OF OPTIONAL COMPLETENESS.

optional-completeness doctrine. See RULE OF OPTIONAL COMPLETENESS.

optional writ. See WRIT.

option contract. See OPTION (2).

optionee (op-shə-**nee**). One who receives an option from another. — Also termed *option-holder*.

optionor (**op**-shə-nər *or* op-shə-**nor**). One who grants an option to another. — Also spelled *optioner*. — Also termed *option-giver*.

option premium. See PREMIUM (4).

option spread. *Securities.* The difference between the option price and the fair market value of the underlying stock when the option is exercised. See SPREAD.

Options Price Reporting Authority. A national market-system plan approved by the SEC for collecting and disseminating last-sale and quotation information on options traded on a five-member exchange consisting of the American Stock Exchange, the Chicago Board of Options Exchange, the New York Stock Exchange, the Pacific Stock Exchange, and the Philadelphia Stock Exchange. — Abbr. OPRA.

option tender bond. See *put bond* under BOND (3).

option to purchase real property. See OPTION.

opt out, *vb.* To choose not to participate in (something) <with so many plaintiffs opting out of the class, the defendant braced itself for multiplicitous lawsuits>.

opus (**oh**-pəs), *n.* [Latin "work"] A product of work or labor; esp., an artistic, literary, or musical work or composition. Pl. **opuses, opera** (**ah**-pə-rə *or* **oh**-pə-rə).

opus novum (**oh**-pəs **noh**-vəm). [Latin "new work"] *Civil law.* A structure newly built on land. See NOVI OPERIS NUNTIATIO.

O.R. *abbr.* Own recognizance; on one's own recognizance <the prosecutor agreed not to object to releasing the suspect O.R.>. See RECOGNIZANCE.

oraculum (ə-**rak**-yə-ləm). [Latin "a prophetic declaration"] *Roman law.* A response or sentence delivered by the emperor.

oral, *adj.* Spoken or uttered; not expressed in writing. Cf. PAROL.

oral argument. An advocate's spoken presentation before a court (esp. an appellate court) supporting or opposing the legal relief at issue.

> "[T]he oral argument is the one chance for *you* (not for some chance-assigned mere judge) to answer any questions you can stir any member of the court into being bothered about and into bothering with, and the one chance to sew up each such question into a remembered point in favor.... In any but freak situations, oral argument is a must." Karl N. Llewellyn, *The Common Law Tradition: Deciding Appeals* 240 (1960).

oral confession. See CONFESSION.

oral contract. See *parol contract* (1) under CONTRACT.

oral deposition. See DEPOSITION.

oral trust. See TRUST.

oral will. See WILL.

oratio consultoria (or-**ay**-shee-oh kon-səl-**tor**-ee-ə). See LIBELLUS CONSULTORIA.

orator (**or**-ə-tər). **1.** *Roman law.* An advocate or pleader. **2.** *Hist.* A plaintiff or petitioner in an action in chancery.

oratrix (**or**-ə-triks). *Hist.* A female orator.

orbation (or-**bay**-shən). *Hist.* Bereavement or deprivation of one's parents or children.

ordeal. *Hist.* A primitive form of trial in which an accused person was subjected to a dangerous or painful physical test, the result being considered a divine revelation of the person's guilt or innocence. • The participants believed that God would reveal a person's culpability by protecting an innocent person from the torture. The ordeal was commonly used in Europe as late as the 13th century, and was sporadically used even later. — Also termed *trial by ordeal*; *judicium Dei* ("judgment of God"); *vulgaris purgatio*. Cf. CANFARA.

> "Ordeals involved an appeal to God to reveal the truth in human disputes, and they required priestly participation to achieve this rapport with the Deity. Several forms of ordeal were recognised by the early Christian Church, but in England they usually took the form of fire or water. In the former, a piece of iron was put into a fire and then in the party's hand; the hand was bound, and inspected a few days later: if the burn had festered, God was taken to have decided against the party. The ordeal of cold water required the party to be trussed and lowered into a pond; if he sank, the water was deemed to have 'received him' with God's blessing, and so he was quickly fished out.... In 1215, the Lateran Council ... took the decisive step of forbidding clergy to participate any more in ordeals. This led in England to the introduction of the criminal trial jury." J.H. Baker, *An Introduction to English Legal History* 5–6 (3d ed. 1990).

ordeal by fire. An ordeal in which the accused person was forced to hold a piece of hot metal or to walk barefoot across a hot surface, the judgment of guilt or innocence depending on how quickly the person's hands or feet healed. — Also termed *fire ordeal*.

ordeal by water. **1.** An ordeal in which guilt or innocence depended on whether the accused person floated or sank after being submerged in cold water. • Those who sank were declared innocent, while those who floated were adjudged guilty because floating revealed the water's (and therefore God's) rejection of the accused. This type of ordeal was used esp. in witchcraft trials. — Also termed *ordeal by cold water*. **2.** An ordeal in which guilt or innocence was determined by how quickly the accused person's arm healed after being placed in boiling water. — Also termed (in sense 2) *ordeal by hot water*; (in both senses) *water ordeal*.

ordelf (**or**-delf). See OREDELF.

ordels (or-**deelz**). *Hist. English law.* The right to conduct trials by ordeal within a given jurisdiction.

order, *n.* **1.** A command, direction, or instruction. **2.** A written direction or command delivered by a court or judge. — Also termed *court order*; *judicial order*.

> "An order is the mandate or determination of the court upon some subsidiary or collateral matter arising in an action, not disposing of the merits, but adjudicating a preliminary point or directing some step in the proceedings." 1 Henry Campbell Black, *A Treatise on the Law of Judgments* § 1, at 5 (2d ed. 1902).

administrative order. **1.** An order issued by a government agency after an adjudicatory hearing. **2.** An agency regulation that interprets or applies a statutory provision.

decretal order (di-**kree**-təl). A court of chancery's interlocutory order that is issued on motion of a party and has the effect of a final decree. See *decree nisi* under DECREE.

ex parte order (eks **pahr**-tee). An order made by the court upon the application of one party to an action without notice to the other.

final order. An order that is dispositive of the entire case. See *final judgment* under JUDGMENT.

interim order. **1.** A temporary court decree that takes effect until something else occurs. **2.** See *interlocutory order*.

interlocutory order (in-tər-**lok**-yə-tor-ee). An order that relates to some intermediate matter in the case; any order other than a final order. • Most interlocutory orders are not appealable until the case is fully resolved. But by rule or statute, most jurisdictions allow some types of interlocutory orders (such as preliminary injunctions and class-certification orders) to be immediately appealed. — Also termed *interlocutory decision*; *interim order*; *intermediate order*. See *appealable decision* under DECISION; COLLATERAL-ORDER DOCTRINE.

minute order. **1.** An order recorded in the minutes of the court rather than directly on a case docket. • Although practice varies, traditionally when a trial judge is sitting officially, with or without a court reporter, a clerk or deputy clerk keeps minutes. When the judge makes an oral order, the only record of that order may be in the minutes. It is therefore referred to as a minute order. — Also termed *minute entry*. **2.** A court order not directly relating to a case, such as an order adopting a local rule of court. • In this sense, the court is not a single judge acting in an adjudicatory capacity, but a chief judge, or a group of two or more judges, acting for a court in an administrative or some other nonadjudicatory capacity.

preclusion order. An order barring a litigant from presenting or opposing certain claims or defenses for failing to comply with a discovery order.

show-cause order. An order directing a party to appear in court and explain why the party took (or failed to take) some action or why the court should or should not grant some relief. — Also termed *order to show cause.*

standing order. A forward-looking order that applies to all cases pending before a court. • Some individual judges issue a standing order on a subject when there is no local rule bearing on it, often because a rule would not be acceptable to other judges on the court. Standing orders are frequently criticized because they undermine uniformity of procedural rules, esp. at the local level.

turnover order. An order by which the court commands a judgment debtor to surrender certain property to a judgment creditor, or to the sheriff or constable on the creditor's behalf. • Such an order is usu. directed to property that is difficult to acquire by the ordinary judgment-collection process, such as share certificates and accounts receivable.

3. The words in a draft (such as a check) directing one person to pay money to or deliver something to a designated person. • An order should appear to be the demand of a right as opposed to the request for a favor. See *order paper* under PAPER. **4.** *Securities.* A customer's instructions to a broker about how and when to buy or sell securities.

all-or-none order. An order to buy a security to be executed either in its entirety or not at all.

alternative order. An order to buy a security by either of two alternatives (e.g., buy a stock at a limited price or buy on a stop order). — Also termed *either-or order.*

buy order. An investor's instruction to purchase stock.

day order. An order to buy or sell on one particular day only. Cf. *open order.*

discretionary order. An order to buy or sell at any price acceptable to the broker.

either-or order. See *alternative order.*

fill-or-kill order. An order that must be executed as soon as it reaches the trading floor. • If the order is not filled immediately, it is canceled.

limit order. An order to buy or sell at a specified price, regardless of market price. Cf. *no-limit order.*

market order. An order to buy or sell at the best price immediately available on the market. — Also termed *order at the market.*

matched order. An order to buy and sell the same security, at about the same time, in about the same quantity, and at about the same price.

no-limit order. An order to buy or sell securities with no limits on price. Cf. *limit order.*

open order. An order that remains in effect until filled by the broker or canceled by the customer. Cf. *day order.*

order at the market. See *market order.*

percentage order. An order to buy or sell a stated amount of a certain stock after a fixed number of shares of the stock have traded.

scale order. An order to buy or sell a security at varying price ranges.

sell order. An investor's instruction to sell stock.

split order. An order directing a broker to sell some stock at one price and some stock at another price.

stop order. An order to buy or sell when the security's price reaches a specified level (the *stop price*) on the market. • By fixing the price beforehand, the investor is cushioned against stock fluctuations. — Also termed *stop-loss order.*

time order. An order that becomes a market or limited-price order at a specified time.

order absolute. See *decree absolute* under DECREE.

order assigning residue. A probate court's order naming the persons entitled to receive parts of an estate and allotting that share to each.

order at the market. See *market order* under ORDER (4).

order bill of lading. See BILL OF LADING.

order document. See *order paper* under PAPER.

ordered, adjudged, and decreed. Judicially mandated; required by court order.

"The usual style of a decree is 'it is ordered, adjudged, and decreed'; and of an order or rule, 'it is ordered,' etc." 1 Henry Campbell Black, *A Treatise on the Law of Judgments* § 2, at 6–7 (2d ed. 1902).

order instrument. See *order paper* under PAPER.

orderly officer. See *officer of the day* under OFFICER (2).

order nisi. See *decree nisi* under DECREE.

Order of the Coif (koyf). **1.** Formerly, the order of serjeants-at-law, the highest order of counsel at the English Bar. • The last serjeant was appointed to the Order in 1875. **2.** An honorary legal fraternity composed of a select few law students with the highest grades. See COIF.

order paper. See PAPER.

order to show cause. See *show-cause order* under ORDER (2).

ordinance (**or**-də-nənts). An authoritative law or decree; esp., a municipal regulation. • Municipal governments can pass ordinances on matters that the state government allows to be regulated at the local level. — Also termed *bylaw*; *municipal ordinance*.

"An ordinance ... may be purely administrative in nature, establishing offices, prescribing duties, or setting salaries; it may have to do with the routine or procedure of the governing body. Or it may be a governmental exercise of the power to control the conduct of the public — establishing rules which must be complied with, or prohibiting certain actions or conduct. In any event it is the determination of the sovereign power of the state as delegated to the municipality. It is a legislative enactment, within its sphere, as much as an act of the state legislature." 1 Judith O'Gallagher, *Municipal Ordinances* § 1A.01, at 3 (2d ed. 1998).

ordinandi lex (or-də-**nan**-dɪ **leks**). [Latin] The law of procedure, as distinguished from substantive law.

ordinarily prudent person. See REASONABLE PERSON.

ordinary, *adj.* **1.** Occurring in the regular course of events; normal; usual. Cf. EXTRAORDINARY. **2.** (Of a judge) having jurisdiction by right of office rather than by delegation. **3.** (Of jurisdiction) original or immediate, as opposed to delegated.

ordinary, *n.* **1.** *Eccles. law.* A high-ranking official who has immediate jurisdiction over a specified territory, such as an archbishop over a province or a bishop over a diocese. **2.** *Civil law.* A judge having jurisdiction by right of office rather than by delegation. **3.** A probate judge. • The term is used in this sense only in some U.S. states.

ordinary and necessary business expense. See *ordinary and necessary expense* under EXPENSE.

ordinary and necessary expense. See EXPENSE.

ordinary annuity. See ANNUITY.

ordinary care. See *reasonable care* under CARE.

ordinary course of business. See COURSE OF BUSINESS.

ordinary diligence. See DILIGENCE.

ordinary gain. See GAIN (3).

ordinary goods. See GOODS.

ordinary high tide. See *mean high tide* under TIDE.

ordinary income. See INCOME.

ordinary insurance. See INSURANCE.

ordinary law. See STATUTORY LAW.

ordinary life insurance. See *whole life insurance* under INSURANCE.

ordinary loss. See LOSS.

ordinary meaning. See *plain meaning* under MEANING.

ordinary-meaning rule. See PLAIN-MEANING RULE.

ordinary negligence. See NEGLIGENCE.

ordinary's court. A probate court. • This term is used only in some parts of the United States. — Also termed *court of ordinary*.

ordinary seaman. See SEAMAN.

ordinary shares. See *common stock* under STOCK.

ordinatio forestae (or-di-**nay**-shee-oh for-**es**-tee), *n.* See ASSISA DE FORESTA.

ordinatum est (or-də-**nay**-təm est). [Law Latin] *Hist.* It is ordered. • These were the usual first words of a court order entered in Latin.

ordinis beneficium (**or**-də-nis ben-ə-**fish**-ee-əm). [Latin "the benefit of order"] *Civil law.* The privilege of a surety by which the creditor must exhaust the principal debtor's property before having recourse against the surety. See DISCUSSION.

ordo attachiamentorum (**or**-doh ə-tach-ee-ə-men-**tor**-əm). [Law Latin] *Hist.* The order of attachments.

ordo judicorum (**or**-doh joo-di-**kor**-əm). [Latin] *Eccles. law.* The order of judgments; the rule by which the course of hearing each case was prescribed.

ordonnance (**or**-də-nənts *or* or-doh-**nahns**). [French] **1.** A law, decree, or ordinance. **2.** A compilation of a body of law on a particular subject, esp. prizes and captures at sea.

oredelf (**or**-delf). *Hist.* The right to dig for mineral ore on one's own land. — Also spelled *oredelfe*; *ordelf*.

ore tenus (**or**-ee **tee**-nəs *or* **ten**-əs), *adv.* & *adj.* [Latin "by word of mouth"] **1.** Orally <pleading carried on ore tenus>. **2.** Made or presented orally <ore tenus evidence>.

ore tenus rule. The presumption that a trial court's findings of fact are correct and should not be disturbed unless clearly wrong or unjust.

organic act. See *organic statute* under STATUTE.

organic disease. See DISEASE.

organic law. 1. The body of laws (as in a constitution) that define and establish a government; FUNDAMENTAL LAW. **2.** *Civil law.* Decisional law; CASELAW.

organic statute. See STATUTE.

organization. 1. A body of persons (such as a union or corporation) formed for a common purpose. **2.** See UNION.

organizational expense. See EXPENSE.

organizational meeting. See MEETING.

organizational picketing. See PICKETING.

organizational strike. See *recognition strike* under STRIKE.

organized crime. 1. Widespread criminal activities that are coordinated and controlled through a central syndicate. See RACKETEERING. **2.** Persons involved in these criminal activities; a syndicate of criminals who rely on their unlawful activities for income. See SYNDICATE.

organized labor. 1. Workers who are affiliated by membership in a union. **2.** A union, or unions collectively, considered as a political force.

original acquisition. See ACQUISITION.

original bill. See BILL (2).

original contractor. See *general contractor* under CONTRACTOR.

original conveyance. See *primary conveyance* under CONVEYANCE.

original cost. See *acquisition cost* under COST (1).

original-document rule. See BEST-EVIDENCE RULE.

original estate. See ESTATE.

original evidence. See EVIDENCE.

originalia (ə-rij-ə-**nay**-lee-ə *or* -**nayl**-yə). *Hist.* Records compiled in the Chancery and transmitted to the Remembrancer's office in the Exchequer. • These records were kept from 1236 to 1837. Cf. RECORDA.

original intent. See INTENT (2).

originalism. *Constitutional law.* The theory that the U.S. Constitution should be interpreted according to the intent of those who drafted and adopted it. Cf. INTERPRETIVISM; NONINTERPRETIVISM.

original issue. See ISSUE (2).

original-issue discount. The amount by which a bond is sold below its par value when it is first issued. — Abbr. OID.

originality. *Copyright.* **1.** The quality or state of being the product of independent creation and having a minimum degree of creativity. • Originality is a requirement for copyright protection. But this is a lesser standard than that of novelty in patent law: to be original, a work does not have to be novel or unique. Cf. NOVELTY. **2.** The degree to which a product claimed for copyright is the result of an author's independent efforts. Cf. CREATIVITY.

> " 'Original' in reference to a copyrighted work means that the particular work 'owes its origin' to the 'author.' No large measure of novelty is necessary." *Alfred Bell & Co. v. Catalda Fine Arts, Inc.*, 191 F.2d 99, 102 (2d Cir. 1951) (Frank, J.).

original jurisdiction. See JURISDICTION.

original market. See *primary market* under MARKET.

original-package doctrine. *Constitutional law.* The principle that imported goods are exempt from state taxation as long as they are unsold and remain in the original packaging. • The Supreme Court abolished this doctrine in 1976, holding that states can tax imported goods if the tax is nondiscriminatory. See IMPORT-EXPORT CLAUSE.

original precedent. See PRECEDENT.

original process. See PROCESS.

original promise. See PROMISE.

original title. See TITLE (2).

original writ. See WRIT.

original-writing rule. See BEST-EVIDENCE RULE.

origination clause. (*often cap.*) **1.** The constitutional provision that all bills for increasing taxes and raising revenue must originate in the House of Representatives, not the Senate (U.S. Const. art. I, § 7, cl. 1). • The Senate may, however, amend revenue bills. **2.** A provision in a state constitution requiring that revenue bills originate in the lower house of the state legislature.

origination fee. See FEE (1).

originator. The entity that initiates a funds transfer subject to UCC article 4A. UCC § 4A–104(c).

ornest. *Hist.* See TRIAL BY COMBAT.

ORP. *abbr.* Ordinary, reasonable, and prudent — the standard on which negligence cases are based.

orphan, *n.* **1.** A child whose parents are dead. **2.** A child with one dead parent and one living parent. — More properly termed *half orphan.* **3.** A child who has been deprived of parental care and has not been legally adopted; a child without a parent or guardian.

orphan drug. See DRUG.

orphan's court. See *probate court* under COURT.

OS. See *ordinary seaman* under SEAMAN.

o.s. *abbr.* OLD STYLE.

OSHA (**oh**-shə). *abbr.* **1.** OCCUPATIONAL SAFETY AND HEALTH ACT OF 1970. **2.** OCCUPATIONAL SAFETY AND HEALTH ADMINISTRATION.

o.s.p. *abbr.* OBIIT SINE PROLE.

ostendit vobis (os-**ten**-dit **voh**-bis). [Latin] *Hist.* Shows to you. • In old pleading, these words were used by a demandant to begin a count.

ostensible (ah-**sten**-sə-bəl), *adj.* Open to view; declared or professed; apparent.

ostensible agency. See *agency by estoppel* under AGENCY (1).

ostensible agent. See *apparent agent* under AGENT.

ostensible authority. See *apparent authority* under AUTHORITY (1).

ostensible partner. See *nominal partner* under PARTNER.

ostrich defense. A criminal defendant's claim not to have known of the criminal activities of an associate.

ostrich instruction. See JURY INSTRUCTION.

OTC. *abbr.* OVER-THE-COUNTER.

OTC market. *abbr.* OVER-THE-COUNTER MARKET.

other consideration. See CONSIDERATION.

other income. See INCOME.

other-insurance clause. An insurance-policy provision that attempts to limit coverage if the insured has other coverage for the same loss. • The three major other-insurance clauses are the pro rata clause, the excess clause, and the escape clause. See ESCAPE CLAUSE; EXCESS CLAUSE; PRO RATA CLAUSE.

OUI. *abbr.* Operating under the influence. See DRIVING UNDER THE INFLUENCE.

our federalism. (*often cap.*) The doctrine holding that a federal court must refrain from hearing a constitutional challenge to state action if federal adjudication would be considered an improper intrusion into the state's right to enforce its own laws in its own courts. See ABSTENTION. Cf. FEDERALISM.

oust, *vb.* To put out of possession; to deprive of a right or inheritance.

ouster. 1. The wrongful dispossession or exclusion of someone (esp. a cotenant) from property (esp. real property). **2.** The removal of a public or corporate officer from office. Cf. EJECTMENT.

ouster le main (**ow**-stər lə **mayn**). [Law French "remove the hand"] *Hist.* **1.** A delivery of land out of the monarch's hands because the monarch has no right or title to hold it. **2.** A judgment or writ granting such a delivery. **3.** A delivery of land from a guardian to a ward once the ward attains legal age. — Also written *ouster-le-main.*

outbuilding. A detached building (such as a shed or garage) within the grounds of a main building.

outcome-determinative test. *Civil procedure.* A test used to determine whether an issue is substantive for purposes of the *Erie* doctrine by examining the issue's potential effect on the outcome of the litigation. See ERIE DOCTRINE.

outer bar. *English law.* A group of junior barristers who sit outside the dividing bar in the court. • These barristers rank below the King's Counsel or Queen's Counsel. — Also termed *utter bar.* Cf. INNER BAR.

outer barrister. See BARRISTER.

outfangthief (**owt**-fang-theef). [fr. Old English *ut* "out" + *fangen* "taken" + *theof* "thief"] *Hist.* The right of a lord of a manor to pursue a thief outside the manor's jurisdiction and to bring the thief back for trial and punishment. — Also spelled *utfangthief.* Cf. INFANGTHIEF.

outlaw, *n.* **1.** A person who has been deprived of the benefit and protection of the law; a person under a sentence of outlawry. **2.** A lawless person or habitual criminal; esp., a fugitive from the law. **3.** *Int'l law.* A person, organization, or nation under a ban or restriction because it is considered to be in violation of international law or custom.

outlaw, *vb.* **1.** To deprive (someone) of the benefit and protection of the law; to declare an outlaw <outlaw the fugitive>. **2.** To make illegal <outlaw fireworks within city limits>. **3.** To remove from legal jurisdiction or enforcement; to deprive of legal force <outlaw a claim under the statute>.

outlawry. 1. *Hist.* The act or process of depriving someone of the benefit and protection of the law. **2.** The state or condition of being outlawed; the status of an outlaw. **3.** Disregard or disobedience of the law. See SACER; CONSECRATIO CAPITIS.

outlaw strike. See *wildcat strike* under STRIKE.

out-of-court, *adj.* Not done or made as part of a judicial proceeding <an out-of-court settlement> <an out-of-court statement that was not under oath>. See EXTRAJUDICIAL.

out-of-court settlement. See SETTLEMENT.

out-of-pocket expense. See EXPENSE.

out-of-pocket loss. See LOSS.

out-of-pocket rule. The principle that a defrauded buyer may recover from the seller as damages the difference between the amount paid for the property and the actual value received. Cf. BENEFIT-OF-THE-BARGAIN RULE (2).

out of the state. See BEYOND SEAS.

output contract. See CONTRACT.

outrage, *n.* See INTENTIONAL INFLICTION OF EMOTIONAL DISTRESS.

outrageous conduct. See CONDUCT.

outside director. See DIRECTOR.

outside financing. See FINANCING.

outside party. See THIRD PARTY.

outsourcing agreement. An agreement to handle substantially all of a party's business requirements, esp. in the areas of data processing and information management.

outstanding, *adj.* **1.** Unpaid; uncollected <outstanding debts>. **2.** Publicly issued and sold <outstanding shares>.

outstanding capital stock. See *outstanding stock* under STOCK.

outstanding security. See SECURITY.

outstanding stock. See STOCK.

outstanding warrant. See WARRANT (1).

over, *adj.* (Of a property interest) intended to take effect after the failure or termination of a prior estate; preceded by some other possessory interest <a limitation over> <a gift over>.

overage, *n.* **1.** An excess or surplus, esp. of goods or merchandise. **2.** A percentage of retail sales paid to a store's landlord in addition to fixed rent.

overbreadth doctrine. *Constitutional law.* The doctrine holding that if a statute is so broadly written that it deters free expression, then it can be struck down on its face because of its chilling effect — even if it also prohibits acts that may legitimately be forbidden. • The Supreme Court has used this doctrine to invalidate a number of laws, including those that would disallow peaceful picketing or require loyalty oaths. Cf. VAGUENESS DOCTRINE.

overdraft. **1.** A withdrawal of money from a bank in excess of the balance on deposit. **2.** The amount of money so withdrawn. — Abbr. OD; o/d. **3.** A line of credit extended by a bank to a customer (esp. an established or institutional customer) who might overdraw on an account.

overdraw, *vb.* To draw on (an account) in excess of the balance on deposit; to make an overdraft.

overhead, *n.* Business expenses (such as rent, utilities, or support-staff salaries) that cannot be allocated to a particular product or service; fixed or ordinary operating costs. — Also termed *administrative expense*; *office expense*.

overheated economy. See ECONOMY.

overinclusive, *adj.* (Of legislation) extending beyond the class of persons intended to be protected or regulated; burdening more persons than necessary to cure the problem <an overinclusive classification>.

overinsurance. **1.** Insurance (esp. from the purchase of multiple policies) that exceeds the value of the thing insured. **2.** Excessive or needlessly duplicative insurance.

overissue, *n.* An issue of securities beyond the authorized amount of capital or credit.

overlapping jurisdiction. See *concurrent jurisdiction* under JURISDICTION.

overplus. See SURPLUS.

overreaching, *n.* **1.** The act or an instance of taking unfair commercial advantage of another, esp. by fraudulent means. **2.** The act or an instance of defeating one's own purpose by going too far. — **overreach,** *vb.*

overridden veto. See VETO.

override (oh-vər-**rɪd**), *vb.* To prevail over; to nullify or set aside <Congress mustered enough votes to override the President's veto>.

override (**oh**-vər-rɪd), *n.* **1.** A commission paid to a manager on a sale made by a subordinate. **2.** A commission paid to a real-estate broker who listed a property when, within a reasonable amount of time after the expiration of the listing, the owner sells that property directly to a buyer with whom the broker had negotiated during the term of the listing. **3.** ROYALTY (2).

overriding royalty. See ROYALTY (2).

overrule, *vb.* **1.** To rule against; to reject <the judge overruled all of the defendant's objections>. **2.** (Of a court) to overturn or set aside (a precedent) by expressly deciding that it should no longer be controlling law <in *Brown*

v. Board of Education, the Supreme Court overruled *Plessy v. Ferguson*>. Cf. VACATE (1).

> "If a decision is not a recent one, and especially if it seems to be very poor, it should not be relied upon without ascertaining whether it may not have been expressly or impliedly overruled by some subsequent one; that is, whether the court may not have laid down a contrary principle in a later case." Frank Hall Childs, *Where and How to Find the Law* 94 (1922).

> "Overruling is an act of superior jurisdiction. A precedent overruled is definitely and formally deprived of all authority. It becomes null and void, like a repealed statute, and a new principle is authoritatively substituted for the old." John Salmond, *Jurisprudence* 189 (Glanville L. Williams ed., 10th ed. 1947).

overseas bill of lading. See BILL OF LADING.

Overseas Private Investment Corporation. A corporation created by the federal government to finance and insure overseas investments by U.S. companies. • Chartered in 1969, the corporation is a for-profit entity that is not federally funded, but its insurance commitments are backed by the full faith and credit of the federal government. — Abbr. OPIC.

oversubscription. A situation in which there are more subscribers to a new issue of securities than there are securities available for purchase.

overt, *adj.* Open and observable; not concealed or secret <the conspirators' overt acts>.

overt act. *Criminal law.* **1.** An act that indicates an intent to kill or seriously harm another person and thus gives that person a justification to use self-defense. **2.** An outward act, however innocent in itself, done in furtherance of a conspiracy, treason, or criminal attempt. • An overt act is usu. a required element of these crimes. **3.** See ACTUS REUS. — Also termed *positive act.*

over-the-counter, *adj.* **1.** Not listed or traded on an organized securities exchange; traded between buyers and sellers who negotiate directly <over-the-counter stocks>. **2.** (Of drugs) sold legally without a doctor's prescription <over-the-counter cough medicine>. — Abbr. OTC.

over-the-counter market. The market for securities that are not traded on an organized exchange. • Over-the-counter (OTC) trading usu. occurs through telephone or computer negotiations between buyers and sellers. Many of the more actively traded OTC stocks are listed on NASDAQ. — Abbr. OTC market.

overtime. **1.** The hours worked by an employee in excess of a standard day or week. • Under the Fair Labor Standards Act, employers must pay extra wages (usu. 1½ times the regular hourly rate) to certain employees (usu. nonsalaried ones) for each hour worked in excess of 40 hours per week. **2.** The extra wages paid for excess hours worked.

overtry, *vb.* (Of a trial lawyer) to try a lawsuit by expending excessive time, effort, and other resources to explore minutiae, esp. to present more evidence than the fact-trier can assimilate, the result often being that the adversary gains arguing points by disputing the minutiae.

overturn, *vb.* To overrule or reverse <the court overturned a long-established precedent>.

owelty (**oh**-əl-tee). **1.** Equality as achieved by a compensatory sum of money given after an exchange of parcels of land having different values or after an unequal partition of real property. **2.** The sum of money so paid.

OWI. *abbr.* Operating while intoxicated. See DRIVING UNDER THE INFLUENCE.

owing, *adj.* That is yet to be paid; owed; due <a balance of $5,000 is still owing>.

owling. *Hist.* The smuggling of wool or sheep out of England. • The term usu. refers to nighttime smuggling.

own, *vb.* To have or possess as property; to have legal title to.

owned-property exclusion. See EXCLUSION (3).

owner. One who has the right to possess, use, and convey something; a proprietor. See OWNERSHIP.

adjoining owner. A person who owns land abutting another's; ABUTTER.

beneficial owner. **1.** One recognized in equity as the owner of something because use and title belong to that person, even though legal title may belong to someone else; esp., one for whom property is held in trust. — Also termed *equitable owner.* **2.** A corporate shareholder who has the power to buy or sell the shares, but who is not registered on the corporation's books as the owner.

equitable owner. See *beneficial owner* (1).

general owner. One who has the primary or residuary title to property; one who has the ultimate ownership of property. Cf. *special owner*.

legal owner. One recognized by law as the owner of something; esp., one who holds legal title to property for the benefit of another. See TRUSTEE.

limited owner. A tenant for life; the owner of a life estate. See *life estate* under ESTATE.

naked owner. *Civil law.* A person whose property is burdened by a usufruct. See USUFRUCT.

owner of record. See STOCKHOLDER OF RECORD.

owner pro hac vice (proh hahk **vee**-chay). See *demise charter* under CHARTER (4).

record owner. **1.** A property owner in whose name the title appears in the public records. **2.** STOCKHOLDER OF RECORD.

sole and unconditional owner. *Insurance.* The owner who has full equitable title to, and exclusive interest in, the insured property.

special owner. One (such as a bailee) with a qualified interest in property. Cf. *general owner*.

owners' association. The basic governing entity for a condominium or planned unit developments. • It is usu. an unincorporated association or a nonprofit corporation.

owners' equity. The aggregate of the owners' financial interests in the assets of a business entity; the capital contributed by the owners plus any retained earnings. — Also termed (in a corporation) *shareholders' equity*; *stockholders' equity*.

"Owner's equity is the residual claim of the owners of the business on its assets after recognition of the liabilities of the business. Owner's equity represents the amounts contributed by the owners to the business, plus the accumulated income of the business since its formation, less any amounts that have been distributed to the owners." Charles H. Meyer, *Accounting and Finance for Lawyers in a Nutshell* 4 (1995).

ownership. The collection of rights allowing one to use and enjoy property, including the right to convey it to others. • Ownership implies the right to possess a thing, regardless of any actual or constructive control. Ownership rights are general, permanent, and inheritable. Cf. POSSESSION; TITLE (1).

"Possession is the *de facto* exercise of a claim; ownership is the *de jure* recognition of one. A thing is owned by me when my claim to it is maintained by the will of the state as expressed in the law; it is possessed by me, when my claim to it is maintained by my own self-assertive will. Ownership is the guarantee of the law; possession is the guarantee of the facts. It is well to have both forms if possible; and indeed they normally co-exist." John Salmond, *Jurisprudence* 311 (Glanville L. Williams ed., 10th ed. 1947).

"Ownership does not always mean absolute dominion. The more an owner, for his advantage, opens up his property for use by the public in general, the more do his rights become circumscribed by the statutory and constitutional powers of those who use it." *Marsh v. Alabama*, 326 U.S. 501, 506, 66 S.Ct. 276, 278 (1946) (Black, J.).

bare ownership. See *trust ownership*.

beneficial ownership. A beneficiary's interest in trust property.

bonitarian ownership (bahn-ə-**tair**-ee-in). *Roman law.* A type of equitable ownership recognized by a praetor when the property was conveyed by an informal transfer, or by a formal transfer by one not the true owner.

contingent ownership. Ownership in which title is imperfect but is capable of becoming perfect on the fulfillment of some condition; conditional ownership.

corporeal ownership. The actual ownership of land or chattels.

incorporeal ownership. The ownership of rights in land or chattels.

joint ownership. Ownership shared by two or more persons whose interests, at death, pass to the survivor or survivors by virtue of the right of survivorship.

ownership in common. Ownership shared by two or more persons whose interests, at death, pass to the dead owner's heirs or successors.

qualified ownership. Ownership that is shared, restricted to a particular use, or limited in the extent of its enjoyment.

trust ownership. A trustee's interest in trust property. — Also termed *bare ownership*.

vested ownership. Ownership in which title is perfect; absolute ownership.

owner's policy. *Real estate.* A title-insurance policy covering the owner's title as well as the mortgagee's interest. Cf. MORTGAGEE POLICY.

own-product exclusion. See EXCLUSION (3).

own-work exclusion. See EXCLUSION (3).

oxfild (**oks**-fild). *Hist.* A restitution made by a county or hundred for a wrong done by someone within that region.

oxgang (**oks**-gang). *Hist.* An amount of land equal to what an ox plows in one year, usu. 12 to 15 acres. • An oxgang, equaling one-eighth of a carucate, was used to assess land for tax purposes. — Also termed *oxgate*; *bovata terrae*. Cf. CARUCATE.

oyer (**oy**-ər *or* **oh**-yər). [fr. Old French *oïr* "to hear"] *Hist.* **1.** A criminal trial held under a commission of oyer and terminer. See COMMISSION OF OYER AND TERMINER. **2.** The reading in open court of a document (esp. a deed) that is demanded by one party and read by the other. **3.** *Common-law pleading.* A prayer to the court by a party opposing a profert, asking to have the instrument on which the opponent relies read aloud. • Oyer can be demanded only when a profert has been properly made, but it is disallowed for a private writing under seal.

> "A party having a right to demand oyer is yet not obliged, in all cases, to exercise that right; nor is he obliged, in all cases, after demanding it, to notice it in the pleading he afterwards files or delivers. Sometimes, however, he is obliged to do both, namely, where he has occasion to found his answer upon any matter contained in the deed of which profert is made, and not set forth by his adversary. In these cases the only admissible method of making such matter appear to the court is to demand oyer, and, from the copy given, set forth the whole deed verbatim in his pleading." Benjamin J. Shipman, *Handbook of Common-Law Pleading* § 289, at 483 (Henry Winthrop Ballantine ed., 3d ed. 1923).

oyer, demand of. See DEMAND OF OYER.

oyer and terminer (**oy**-ər an[d] **tər**-mə-nər). [Law French *oyer et terminer* "to hear and determine"] **1.** See COMMISSION OF OYER AND TERMINER. **2.** COURT OF OYER AND TERMINER (2).

oyez (**oh**-yes *or* **oh**-yez *or* **oh**-yay). [Law French] Hear ye; the utterance *oyez, oyez, oyez* is usu. used in court by the public crier to call the courtroom to order when a session begins or when a proclamation is about to be made.

P

P.A. *abbr.* See *professional association* under ASSOCIATION.

paage (**pay**-ij). See PEDAGE.

PAC (pak). *abbr.* POLITICAL-ACTION COMMITTEE.

pacare (pə-**kair**-ee), *vb.* [Law Latin] *Hist.* To pay.

PACER. *abbr.* PUBLIC ACCESS TO COURT ELECTRONIC RECORDS.

pacification (pas-ə-fi-**kay**-shən), *n. Int'l law.* The act of making peace between two belligerent nations. — **pacify** (**pas**-ə-fī), *vb.*

pacificist. See PACIFIST.

Pacific Reporter. A set of regional lawbooks that, being part of the West Group's National Reporter System, contain every published decision from Alaska, Arizona, California, Colorado, Hawaii, Idaho, Kansas, Montana, Nevada, New Mexico, Oklahoma, Oregon, Utah, Washington, and Wyoming, from 1883 to date. • The first series ran from 1883 to 1931. — Abbr. P.; P.2d.

pacifism (**pas**-ə-fiz-əm). *Int'l law.* The advocacy of peaceful methods rather than war as a means of solving disputes.

pacifist (**pas**-ə-fist), *n.* A person who is opposed to war; a person who believes in pacifism. — Also termed *pacificist.* Cf. CONSCIENTIOUS OBJECTOR.

pack, *vb.* To choose or arrange (a tribunal, jurors, etc.) to accomplish a desired result <pack a jury>.

package mortgage. See MORTGAGE.

packing, *n.* A gerrymandering technique in which a dominant political or racial group minimizes minority representation by concentrating the minority into as few districts as possible. Cf. CRACKING; STACKING (2).

packing a jury. See JURY-PACKING.

Pac-Man defense (**pak**-man). An aggressive antitakeover defense by which the target company attempts to take over the bidder company by making a cash tender offer for the bidder company's shares. • The name derives from a video game popular in the 1980s, the object of which was to gobble up the enemy. This defense is seldom used today.

pact. An agreement between two or more parties; esp., an agreement (such as a treaty) between two or more nations or governmental entities.

pacta sunt servanda (**pak**-tə sənt sər-**van**-də). [Latin "agreements must be kept"] The rule that agreements and stipulations, esp. those contained in treaties, must be observed <the Quebec courts have been faithful to the *pacta sunt servanda* principle>.

pact de non alienando (**pakt** dee **non** ay-lee-ə-**nan**-doh). [Latin] *Civil law.* An agreement not to alienate encumbered (esp. mortgaged) property. • This stipulation will not void a sale to a third party, but it does allow the mortgagee to proceed directly against the mortgaged property without notice to the purchaser.

pactio (**pak**-shee-oh). [Latin] *Civil law.* **1.** The negotiating process that results in a *pactum.* **2.** The *pactum* arrived at; an agreement.

paction (**pak**-shən). **1.** PACTIO. **2.** *Int'l law.* An agreement between two nations to be performed by a single act.

pactional, *adj.* Relating to or generating an agreement. — **pactionally,** *adv.*

pactum (**pak**-təm). [Latin] *Roman & civil law.* An agreement or convention; a pact. — Also termed *pactum conventum.*

pactum constitutae pecuniae (**pak**-təm kon-stə-**t[y]oo**-tee pi-**kyoo**-nee-ee). [Latin "agreement for a fixed sum of money"] An agreement in which someone promises to pay an existing debt of his own or another on a certain date.

pactum de constituto (**pak**-təm dee kon-sti-**t[y]oo**-toh). [Latin "an agreement from a contract or compact"] An agreement under which one person will pay another's debt in exchange for which the second person agrees not to sue the first on some claim that has arisen. • The *pactum de constituto* was one of the five types of adpromission in Roman law. See ADPROMISSION.

pactum de non petendo (**pak**-təm dee non pə-**ten**-doh). [Latin "agreement not to sue"] An agreement in which a creditor promises to not enforce the debt.

pactum de quota litis (**pak**-təm dee **kwoh**-tə **lI**-tis). [Latin "agreement about a portion of the amount in issue"] An agreement in which a creditor promises to pay a portion of a difficult-to-collect debt to a person attempting to collect it; an agreement to share the proceeds of a litigation.

pad, *vb. Slang.* (Of a lawyer, paralegal, etc.) to overstate the number of (billable hours worked). — **padding,** *n.* See BILLABLE HOUR.

padded-payroll rule. See FICTITIOUS-PAYEE RULE.

paid-in capital. See CAPITAL.

paid-in fund. See FUND (1).

paid-in surplus. See SURPLUS.

paid-up insurance. See INSURANCE.

paid-up policy. See INSURANCE POLICY.

paid-up stock. See *full-paid stock* under STOCK.

pain and suffering. Physical discomfort or emotional distress compensable as an element of damages in torts. See DAMAGES.

pain of, on. See ON PAIN OF.

pains and penalties, bill of. See BILL OF PAINS AND PENALTIES.

pairing-off. In legislative practice, an agreement between two legislators who are on opposite sides of an issue to abstain from voting on the issue, usu. done when one of the legislators cannot attend the session. • The pairing-off is usu. announced and made a matter of record.

pais (pay *or* pays). See IN PAIS.

Palace Court. *Hist.* A court having jurisdiction over all personal actions arising within 12 miles of Whitehall. • This court was created by James I in response to complaints about the inconvenience of using the itinerant Court of the Marshalsea; its jurisdiction was similar, but the court remained in Whitehall. It was abolished along with the Court of the Marshalsea in 1849. See COURT OF THE MARSHALSEA.

> "The court of the *marshalsea*, and the *palace court* at Westminster, though two distinct courts, are frequently confounded together. The former was originally holden before the steward and marshal of the king's house, and was instituted to administer justice between the king's domestic servants, that they might not be drawn into other courts, and thereby the king lose their service.... But this court being ambulatory, and obliged to follow the king in all his progresses, so that by the removal of the household, actions were frequently discontinued, and doubts having arisen as to the extent of its jurisdiction ... [the king] erected a new court of record, called the *curia palatii*, or *palace-court*, to be held before the steward of the household and knight marshal, and the steward of the court, or his deputy; with jurisdiction to hold plea of all manner of personal actions whatsoever, which shall arise between any parties within twelve miles of his majesty's palace at Whitehall." 3 William Blackstone, *Commentaries on the Laws of England* 76 (1768).

palimony (**pal**-ə-moh-nee). A court-ordered allowance paid by one member to the other of a couple that, though unmarried, formerly cohabited. Cf. ALIMONY.

pallio cooperire (**pal**-ee-oh koh-op-ə-**rI**-ree). [Latin "to cover with a pallium"] *Hist.* A marriage of persons who have already had a child together. • The pallium was a veil or cover over the bride, which was extended to cover the bastard child. Its removal at the wedding was deemed to legitimate the child.

Palmer's Act. An English statute, enacted in 1856, giving a person accused of a crime falling outside the jurisdiction of the Central Criminal Court the right to have the case tried in that court. St. 19 & 20 Vict., ch. 16. — Also termed *Central Criminal Court Act.* See CENTRAL CRIMINAL COURT.

palming off. See PASSING OFF.

***Palsgraf* rule** (**pawlz**-graf). *Torts.* The principle that negligent conduct resulting in injury will lead to liability only if the actor could have reasonably foreseen that the conduct would injure the victim. • In *Palsgraf v. Long Island R.R.*, 248 N.Y. 339, 162 N.E. 99 (1928), two railroad attendants negligently dislodged a package of fireworks from a man they were helping board a train. The package exploded on impact and knocked over some scales that fell on Mrs. Palsgraf. The New York Court of Appeals, in a 4–3 majority opinion written by Chief Justice Benjamin Cardozo, held that the attendants could not have foreseen the possibility of injury to Palsgraf and therefore did not breach any duty to her. In the dissenting opinion, Justice William S. Andrews asserted that the duty to exercise care is owed to all, and thus a negligent act will subject the actor to liability to all persons proximately harmed by it, whether foreseeable or not. Both opinions have been widely cited to support the two views expressed in them.

pandect (**pan**-dekt). **1.** A complete legal code, esp. of a nation or a system of law, together with commentary. **2.** (*cap.* & *pl.*) The 50 books constituting Justinian's *Digest* (one of the four works making up the *Corpus Juris Civilis*), first published in A.D. 533. — Also termed (in sense 2) *Digest*. — Also spelled (in reference to German law) *pandekt*. Pl. **pandects, pandectae.** See CORPUS JURIS CIVILIS.

pander, *n.* One who engages in pandering. — Also termed *panderer*. See PIMP.

pandering (**pan**-dər-ing), *n.* **1.** The act or offense of recruiting a prostitute, finding a place of business for a prostitute, or soliciting customers for a prostitute. — Also termed *promoting prostitution*. **2.** The act or offense of selling or distributing textual or visual material (such as magazines or videotapes) openly advertised to appeal to the recipient's sexual interest. • Although the concept of pandering was invoked by the U.S. Supreme Court in *Ginzburg v. United States*, 383 U.S. 463, 86 S.Ct. 942 (1966), it has seldom been discussed by the Court since then. — **pander,** *vb.*

P & L. *abbr.* Profit and loss. See INCOME STATEMENT.

panel. 1. A list of persons summoned as potential jurors. **2.** A group of persons selected for jury duty; VENIRE. **3.** A set of judges selected from a complete court to decide a specific case; esp., a group of three judges designated to sit for an appellate court.

panelation (pan-əl-**ay**-shən). The act of empaneling a jury. — Also spelled *panellation*.

panel-shopping. The practice of choosing the most favorable group of judges to hear an appeal.

papal law (**pay**-pəl). See CANON LAW.

paper. 1. Any written or printed document or instrument. **2.** A negotiable document or instrument evidencing a debt; esp., commercial documents or negotiable instruments considered as a group. See NEGOTIABLE INSTRUMENT. **3.** (*pl.*) COURT PAPERS.

accommodation paper. See ACCOMMODATION PAPER.

bankable paper. Notes, checks, bank bills, drafts, and other instruments received as cash by banks.

bearer paper. An instrument payable to the person who holds it rather than to the order of a specific person. • Bearer paper is negotiated simply by delivering the instrument to a transferee. — Also termed *bearer document*; *bearer instrument*.

chattel paper (**chat**-əl). See CHATTEL PAPER.

commercial paper. **1.** An instrument, other than cash, for the payment of money. • Commercial paper — typically existing in the form of a draft (such as a check) or a note (such as a certificate of deposit) — is governed by Article 3 of the UCC. But even though the UCC uses the term *commercial paper* when referring to negotiable instruments of a particular kind (drafts, checks, certificates of deposit, and notes as defined by Article 3), the term long predates the UCC as a business and legal term in common use. Before the UCC, it was generally viewed as synonymous with *negotiable paper* or *bills and notes*. It was sometimes applied even to nonnegotiable instruments. — Also termed *mercantile paper*. See NEGOTIABLE INSTRUMENT.

> " 'Commercial paper' is rather a popular than a technical expression, often used, however, both in statutes and in decisions of courts, to designate those simple forms of contract long recognized in the world's commerce and governed by the law merchant." 1 Joseph F. Randolph, *A Treatise on the Law of Commercial Paper* § 1, at 1 (2d ed. 1899).

> "Defined most broadly, commercial paper refers to any writing embodying rights that are customarily conveyed by transferring the writing. A large subset of commercial paper consists of such writings that are negotiable, which means that the law enables a transferee to acquire the embodied rights free of claims and defenses against the transferor." Richard E. Speidel, *Negotiable Instruments and Check Collection in a Nutshell* 1 (4th ed. 1993).

2. Such instruments collectively. — Also termed *bills and notes*. 3. Loosely, a short-term unsecured promissory note, usu. issued and sold by one company to meet another company's immediate cash needs.

commodity paper. An instrument representing a loan secured by a bill of lading or warehouse receipt.

order paper. An instrument payable to a specific payee or to any person that the payee designates. — Also termed *order document*; *order instrument*.

paper loss. See LOSS.

paper money. See MONEY.

paper patent. See PATENT (3).

paper profit. See PROFIT.

paper standard. A monetary system based entirely on paper; a system of currency that is not convertible into gold or other precious metal. Cf. GOLD STANDARD.

paper street. A thoroughfare that appears on plats, subdivision maps, and other publicly filed documents, but that has not been completed or opened for public use.

paper title. See TITLE (2).

Papian law. See LEX PAPIA POPPEA.

par. See PAR VALUE.

parage (**par**-ij), *n.* [Law French] *Hist.* Equality of condition, blood, or dignity; esp., the equal tenure in land existing among the nobility who inherit from a common ancestor. — Also termed *paragium*. Cf. DISPARAGARE (2).

paragium (pə-**ray**-jee-əm). [Law Latin] PARAGE.

parajudge. See UNITED STATES MAGISTRATE JUDGE.

paralegal, *n.* A person who assists a lawyer in duties related to the practice of law but who is not a licensed attorney. — Also termed *legal assistant*; *legal analyst*. — **paralegal,** *adj.*

paralegalize, *vb. Slang.* To proofread, cite-check, and otherwise double-check the details in (a legal document).

parallel citation. See CITATION.

parallel imports. Goods bearing valid trademarks that are manufactured abroad and imported into the United States to compete with domestically manufactured goods bearing the same valid trademarks. • Domestic parties commonly complain that parallel imports compete unfairly in the U.S. market. But U.S. trademark law does not prohibit the sale of most parallel imports. — Also termed *gray-market goods*. See *gray market* under MARKET.

paramount title. See TITLE (2).

paraph (**par**-əf), *n.* 1. *Hist.* A flourish that follows a signature, intended as a safeguard against forgery. 2. *Civil law.* A signature itself; esp., a notary public's signature on a document, followed by the date, names of the parties, and seal.

paraph (**par**-əf), *vb. Civil law.* To add a paraph to <paraphed the contract>.

parapherna (par-ə-**fər**-nə). [Greek "things brought on the side"] *Roman law.* Property of a wife not forming part of her dowry. See DOS (1).

paraphernalia (par-ə-fər-**nay**-lee-ə). *Hist.* Property that a wife was allowed to keep, in addition to her dowry, on the death of her husband.

> "[I]n one particular instance the wife may acquire a property in some of her husband's goods: which shall remain to her after his death and not go to the executors. These are called her *paraphernalia*, which is a term borrowed from the civil law ... signifying something over and above her dower." 2 William Blackstone, *Commentaries on the Laws of England* 435–36 (1765).

paraphernal property. See EXTRADOTAL PROPERTY.

Paraphrase of Theophilus. See INSTITUTE (4).

paratitla (par-ə-**tɪt**-lə), *n. pl.* [Law Latin] *Roman & civil law.* Notes or abstracts prefixed to titles of law, giving a summary of their contents.

paratum habeo (pə-**ray**-təm **hay**-bee-oh). [Law Latin "I have him in readiness"] *Hist.* A sheriff's return of a *capias ad respondendum*, signifying that the defendant is ready to be brought to court.

paratus est verificare (pə-**ray**-təs est ver-ə-fi-**kair**-ee). [Law Latin] He is ready to verify. •

This phrase formerly concluded a verified pleading.

paravail (par-ə-**vayl** *or* **par**-ə-vayl), *adj.* [Law French "at the bottom"] *Hist.* (Of a tenant) holding of another tenant.

parcel, *n.* **1.** A small package or bundle. **2.** A tract of land.

parcel, *vb.* To divide and distribute (goods, land, etc.) <Alex parceled out the inheritance>.

parcenary (**pahr**-sə-ner-ee). See COPARCENARY.

parcener (**pahr**-sə-nər). See COPARCENER.

parco fracto (**pahr**-koh **frak**-toh). See DE PARCO FRACTO.

par delictum (pahr di-**lik**-təm). [Latin] Equal guilt; equal wrong.

pardon, *n.* The act or an instance of officially nullifying punishment or other legal consequences of a crime. • A pardon is usu. granted by the chief executive of a government <the President has the sole power to issue pardons for federal offenses, while state governors have the power to issue pardons for state crimes>. — Also termed *executive pardon.* — **pardon,** *vb.* See CLEMENCY. Cf. COMMUTATION (2); REPRIEVE.

absolute pardon. A pardon that releases the wrongdoer from punishment and restores the offender's civil rights without qualification. — Also termed *full pardon*; *unconditional pardon.*

conditional pardon. A pardon that does not become effective until the wrongdoer satisfies a prerequisite or that will be revoked upon the occurrence of some specified act.

general pardon. See AMNESTY.

partial pardon. A pardon that exonerates the offender from some but not all of the punishment or legal consequences of a crime.

pardon attorney. A Justice Department lawyer who considers applications for federal pardons and forwards those of promising candidates for review by the President.

parens binubus (**par**-enz bɪ-**n[y]oo**-bəs). [Latin "twice-married parent"] *Roman law.* A parent who has remarried.

parens patriae (**par**-enz **pay**-tree-ee *or* **pa**-tree-ɪ). [Latin "parent of his or her country"] **1.** The state regarded as a sovereign; the state in its capacity as provider of protection to those unable to care for themselves <the attorney general acted as *parens patriae* in the administrative hearing>. **2.** A doctrine by which a government has standing to prosecute a lawsuit on behalf of a citizen, esp. on behalf of someone who is under a legal disability to prosecute the suit <*parens patriae* allowed the state to institute proceedings>. • The state ordinarily has no standing to sue on behalf of its citizens, unless a separate, sovereign interest will be served by the suit. — Also termed *doctrine of parens patriae.*

parent. 1. The lawful father or mother of someone. • In ordinary usage, the term denotes more than responsibility for conception and birth. The term commonly includes (1) either the natural father or the natural mother of a child, (2) the adoptive father or adoptive mother of a child, (3) a child's putative blood parent who has expressly acknowledged paternity, and (4) an individual or agency whose status as guardian has been established by judicial decree. In law, parental status based on any criterion may be terminated by judicial decree.

adoptive parent. A parent by virtue of legal adoption. See ADOPTION (1).

foster parent. An adult who, though without blood ties or legal ties, cares for and rears a child, esp. an orphaned or neglected child that might otherwise be deprived of nurture. • Foster parents sometimes give care and support temporarily until a child is legally adopted by others.

2. See *parent corporation* under CORPORATION.

parentage (**pair**-ən-tij *or* **par**-). The state or condition of being a parent; kindred in the direct ascending line.

parentage action. See PATERNITY SUIT.

parental consortium. See CONSORTIUM.

parental immunity. See IMMUNITY (2).

parental kidnapping. See KIDNAPPING.

Parental Kidnapping Prevention Act. A federal law, enacted in 1980, providing a penalty for child-kidnapping by a noncustodial parent and requiring a state to recognize and enforce a child-custody order rendered by a court of another state. 28 USCA § 1738A; 42 USCA

§§ 654, 655, 663. — Abbr. PKPA. Cf. UNIFORM CHILD CUSTODY JURISDICTION ACT.

parental-liability law. A statute obliging parents to pay damages for torts (esp. intentional ones) committed by their minor children. • All states have these laws, but most limit the parents' liability to about $3,000 per tort.

parental-preference doctrine. The principle that a fit parent, who is willing and able to care for a minor child, should be granted custody instead of someone who is not the child's parent. — Also termed *parental-presumption rule.*

parental-responsibility statute. A law imposing criminal sanctions (such as fines) on parents whose minor children commit crimes as a result of the parents' failure to exercise sufficient control over them. — Also termed *control-your-kid law.*

parental rights. A parent's rights concerning his or her child, including the right to educate and discipline the child and the right to control the child's earnings and property.

parent-child immunity. See *parental immunity* under IMMUNITY (2).

parent company. See *parent corporation* under CORPORATION.

parent corporation. See CORPORATION.

parentela (par-ən-**tee**-lə), *n. pl.* [Law Latin] Persons who can trace descent from a common ancestor.

parentelic method (par-ən-**tee**-lik *or* **-tel**-ik). A scheme of computation used to determine the paternal or maternal collaterals entitled to inherit.

parenticide (pə-**ren**-tə-sɪd). **1.** The act of murdering one's parent. **2.** A person who murders his or her parent.

pares curiae (**par**-eez **kyoor**-ee-ee). [Law Latin "peers of the court"] *Hist.* A lord's tenants who sat in judgment of a fellow tenant.

pares regni (**par**-eez **reg**-nɪ). [Law Latin] *Hist.* Peers of the realm.

Pareto optimality (pə-**ray**-toh *or* pə-**ret**-oh), *n.* An economic situation in which no person can be made better off without making someone else worse off. • The term derives from the work of Vilfredo Pareto (1848–1923), an Italian economist and sociologist. — **Pareto-optimal,** *adj.*

Pareto superiority, *n.* An economic situation in which an exchange can be made that benefits someone and injures no one. • When such an exchange can no longer be made, the situation becomes one of Pareto optimality. — **Pareto-superior,** *adj.*

pari causa, in. See IN PARI CAUSA.

pari delicto, in. See IN PARI DELICTO.

paries communis (**pair**-ee-eez kə-**myoo**-nis). [Latin] A common wall; a party wall.

pari materia, in. See IN PARI MATERIA.

parimutuel betting (par-i-**myoo**-choo-əl). A system of gambling in which bets placed on a race are pooled and then paid (less a management fee and taxes) to those holding winning tickets.

pari passu (**pahr**-ee **pahs**-oo *or* **pair**-ɪ, **pair**-ee, *or* **par**-ee **pas**-[y]oo). [Latin "by equal step"] Proportionally; at an equal pace; without preference <creditors of a bankrupt estate will receive distributions *pari passu*>.

pari ratione (**pair**-ɪ ray-shee-**oh**-nee *or* rash-ee-**oh**-nee). [Latin] *Roman & civil law.* For the like reason; by like mode of reasoning.

parish. 1. In Louisiana, a governmental subdivision analogous to a county in other U.S. states. **2.** *Eccles. law.* A division of a town or district, subject to the ministry of one pastor.

district parish. *Eccles. law.* A geographical division of an English parish made by the Crown's commissioners for the building of new churches for worship, celebration of marriages, christenings, and burials.

parish court. See *county court* under COURT.

par item. See ITEM.

parium judicium (**pair**-ee-əm joo-**dish**-ee-əm). [Law Latin] The judgment of peers; trial by a jury of one's peers or equals.

Parker **doctrine.** See STATE-ACTION DOCTRINE.

parking. **1.** The sale of securities subject to an agreement that the seller will buy them back at a later time for a similar price. • Parking is illegal if done to circumvent securities regulations or tax laws. It is often a method of evading the net-capital requirements of the National Association of Securities Dealers (NASD), which requires a brokerage firm to discount the value of any stock it holds in its own account when it files its monthly report about its net-capital condition. To reach technical compliance with the NASD's net-capital requirements, a brokerage firm "sells" stock from its own account to a customer at market price, thereby avoiding the discount for reporting purposes. Having filed its report, it can then "buy" the shares back from the customer, usu. at the same price at which it "sold" the stock, plus interest. **2.** The placement of assets in a safe, short-term investment while other investment opportunities are being considered. — Also termed (in sense 1) *stock-parking*.

parking-lot rule. The principle that workers'-compensation insurance covers the injuries suffered by an employee on the employer's premises when the employee is arriving at or leaving work. — Also termed *premises rule*.

parliament. The supreme legislative body of some nations; esp. (*cap.*), in the United Kingdom, the national legislature consisting of the monarch, the House of Lords, and the House of Commons.

parliamentary diplomacy. See DIPLOMACY.

parliamentary divorce. See DIVORCE.

parliamentary intent. See LEGISLATIVE INTENT.

parliamentary law. The body of rules and precedents governing the proceedings of legislative and deliberative assemblies.

parliamentary privilege. See PRIVILEGE (1); *legislative privilege* under PRIVILEGE (3).

parliamentum insanum. See MAD PARLIAMENT.

par of exchange. The equality of a given sum of one country's currency and the like sum of money of a foreign country into which it is to be exchanged.

parol (pə-**rohl** *or* **par**-əl), *adj.* **1.** Oral; unwritten <parol evidence>. **2.** Not under seal <parol contract>.

parol (pə-**rohl** *or* **par**-əl), *n.* **1.** An oral statement or declaration. **2.** *Hist.* The oral pleadings in a case.

> "Anciently pleadings were conducted in court orally, and the whole pleadings were called the parol; but for centuries the pleadings in civil actions have been required to be in writing." Edwin E. Bryant, *The Law of Pleading Under the Codes of Civil Procedure* 178–79 (2d ed. 1899).

parol agreement. See *parol contract* (1) under CONTRACT.

parol arrest. See ARREST.

parol contract. See CONTRACT.

parol demurrer. See DEMURRER.

parole (pə-**rohl**), *n.* The release of a prisoner from imprisonment before the full sentence has been served. • Although not available under some sentences, parole is usu. granted for good behavior on the condition that the parolee regularly report to a supervising officer for a specified period. — **parole,** *vb.* Cf. PARDON; PROBATION (1).

> "The essence of parole is release from prison, before completion of the sentence, on condition that the prisoner abide by certain rules during the balance of the sentence. Parole is not freedom." 59 Am. Jur. 2d *Pardon and Parole* § 6 (1987).

juvenile parole. The conditional release of a juvenile offender from confinement. — Also termed *aftercare*.

parole board. A governmental body that decides whether prisoners may be released from prison before completing their sentences. — Also termed *board of parole*; *parole commission*.

parolee (pə-roh-**lee**). A prisoner who is released on parole.

parole revocation. The administrative act of returning a parolee to prison because of the parolee's failure to abide by the conditions of parole (as by committing a new offense).

parol evidence. See EVIDENCE.

parol-evidence rule. *Contracts.* The principle that a writing intended by the parties to be a final embodiment of their agreement cannot be modified by evidence that adds to, varies, or contradicts the writing. • This rule usu. operates to prevent a party from introducing extrinsic evidence of negotiations that occurred before or while the agreement was being reduced to its final written form. See INTEGRATION (2); MERGER (2). Cf. FOUR-CORNERS RULE.

> "The basic principle is often called the 'parol evidence rule', and according to this rule evidence is not admissible to contradict or qualify a complete written contract. The rule is usually stated in the form of a rule of evidence, but it is probably best regarded as a rule of substantive law. The question is not really whether evidence can be admitted which might vary the written document, but whether, if the evidence is admitted, it will have the legal effect of varying the document." P.S. Atiyah, *An Introduction to the Law of Contract* 161–62 (3d ed. 1981).

> "The parol evidence rule assumes that the formal writing reflects the parties' minds at a point of maximum resolution and, hence, that duties and restrictions that do not appear in the written document, even though apparently accepted at an earlier stage, were not intended by the parties to survive. In addition, and quite apart from the survival of matters discarded in the course of negotiations, there is the obvious danger of outright fraud." Marvin A. Chirelstein, *Concepts and Case Analysis in the Law of Contracts* 82–83 (1990).

parol lease. See LEASE.

parols de ley (pə-**rohlz** də **lay**). [Law French] Words of law; technical words.

parol trust. See *oral trust* under TRUST.

***Parratt–Hudson* doctrine.** The principle that a state actor's random, unauthorized deprivation of someone's property does not amount to a due-process violation if the state provides an adequate postdeprivation remedy. *Parratt v. Taylor*, 451 U.S. 527, 101 S.Ct. 1908 (1984); *Hudson v. Palmer*, 468 U.S. 517, 104 S.Ct. 3194 (1984).

parricide (**par**-ə-sɪd), *n.* **1.** The act of killing a close relative, esp. a parent. **2.** One who kills such a relative. — **parricidal,** *adj.* Cf. PATRICIDE.

pars (pahrz). [Latin] *Hist.* A party to an action.

pars enitia (**pahrz** i-**ni**-shee-ə). [Law Latin "oldest's part"] *Hist.* An oldest child's portion of lands divided by lot.

parson. See RECTOR (1).

pars rea (**pahrz ree**-ə). A party defendant.

parte inaudita (**pahr**-tee in-aw-**dy**-tə *or* in-**aw**-di-tə). [Latin "one side being unheard"] Of or relating to action taken ex parte.

parte non comparente (**pahr**-tee non kom-pə-**ren**-tee). [Latin] The party not having appeared.

partes finis nihil habuerunt (**pahr**-teez **fɪ**-nis **nɪ**-hil hab-yoo-**eer**-ənt). [Law Latin "the parties to the fine had nothing"] *Hist.* A plea to set aside a conveyance of land on grounds that the transferor did not have a sufficient ownership interest in the property to alienate it.

> "Yet where a *stranger* ... officiously interferes in an estate which in nowise belongs to him, his fine is of no effect; and may at any time be set aside ... by pleading that '*partes finis nihil habuerunt.*'" 2 William Blackstone, *Commentaries on the Laws of England* 356–57 (1765).

partial account. A preliminary accounting of an executor's or administrator's dealings with an estate.

partial assignment. See ASSIGNMENT (2).

partial average. See *particular average* under AVERAGE.

partial breach. See BREACH OF CONTRACT.

partial defense. See DEFENSE (1).

partial dependent. See DEPENDENT.

partial disability. See DISABILITY (1).

partial eviction. See EVICTION.

partial evidence. See EVIDENCE.

partial failure of consideration. See FAILURE OF CONSIDERATION.

partial guardian. See GUARDIAN.

partial integration. See INTEGRATION (2).

partial limitation. *Insurance.* A policy provision in which the insurer agrees to pay a total loss if the actual loss exceeds a specified amount.

partial liquidation. See LIQUIDATION.

partial loss. See LOSS.

partially disclosed principal. See PRINCIPAL (1).

partially integrated contract. See INTEGRATED CONTRACT.

partial pardon. See PARDON.

partial release. See RELEASE.

partial summary judgment. See SUMMARY JUDGMENT.

partial verdict. See VERDICT.

partial zoning. See ZONING.

partiarius (pahr-shee-**air**-ee-əs), *n.* [Latin] *Roman law.* **1.** A legatee entitled to a portion of an inheritance along with the appointed heirs. **2.** A tenant who is bound to hand over a portion of the crop in lieu of rent.

particeps (**pahr**-tə-seps), *n.* [Latin] **1.** A participant. **2.** A part owner.

particeps criminis (**pahr**-tə-seps **krim**-ə-nis), *n.* [Latin "partner in crime"] **1.** An accomplice or accessory. Pl. ***participes criminis*** (pahr-**tis**-ə-peez). See ACCESSORY.

> "Even in felonies but little practical importance now attaches to the distinctions between the first three of these four classes of 'accomplices' — a term which the law applies to all the *participes criminis*, whatever their degree of 'complicity' in the offence, though popular use generally limits it to those who take only a minor part. For the maximum punishment prescribed for any given crime is the same in the case of all three classes." J.W. Cecil Turner, *Kenny's Outlines of Criminal Law* 90 (16th ed. 1952).

2. The doctrine that one participant in an unlawful activity cannot recover in a civil action against another participant in the activity. • This is a civil doctrine only, having nothing to do with criminal responsibility.

participating bond. See BOND (3).

participating insurance. See INSURANCE.

participating policy. See INSURANCE POLICY.

participating preferred stock. See STOCK.

participation, *n.* **1.** The act of taking part in something, such as a partnership. **2.** The right of employees to receive part of a business's profits; profit-sharing. — **participate,** *vb.*

participation loan. See LOAN.

participation mortgage. See MORTGAGE.

participation stock. See STOCK.

particular average. See AVERAGE.

particular average loss. See LOSS.

particular custom. See *local custom* under CUSTOM.

particular damages. See *special damages* under DAMAGES.

particular estate. See ESTATE.

particular jurisprudence. See JURISPRUDENCE.

particular lien. See LIEN.

particular malice. See MALICE.

particular partnership. See PARTNERSHIP.

particulars, bill of. See BILL OF PARTICULARS.

particulars of sale. A document that describes the various features of a thing (such as a house) that is for sale.

particular successor. See SUCCESSOR.

particular tenant. See TENANT.

particular title. See TITLE (2).

partitio (pahr-**tish**-ee-oh), *n.* [Latin] *Roman law.* Division; partition.

partitio legata (pahr-**tish**-ee-oh lə-**gay**-tə). [Latin] A directive from a testator to an heir to divide the inheritance and deliver a designated portion to a named legatee; a testamentary partition.

partition, *n.* **1.** Something that separates one part of a space from another. **2.** The act of dividing; esp., the division of real property held jointly or in common by two or more persons into individually owned interests. — **partition,** *vb.* — **partible,** *adj.*

definitive partition. A partition that is irrevocable.

provisional partition. A temporary partition, often made before the remainder of the property can be divided.

partner. **1.** One who shares or takes part with another, esp. in a venture with shared benefits and shared risks; an associate or colleague <partners in crime>. **2.** One of two or more persons who jointly own and carry on a business for profit <the firm and its partners were sued for malpractice>. See PARTNERSHIP. **3.** One of two persons who are married or who live together; a spouse or companion <my partner in life>.

dormant partner. See *silent partner.*

general partner. A partner who ordinarily takes part in the daily operations of the business, shares in the profits and losses, and is personally responsible for the partnership's debts and liabilities. — Also termed *full partner.*

junior partner. A partner whose participation is limited with respect to both profits and management.

limited partner. A partner who receives profits from the business but does not take part in managing the business and is not liable for any amount greater than his or her original investment. — Also termed *special partner*; (in civil law) *partner in commendam.* See *limited partnership* under PARTNERSHIP.

liquidating partner. The partner appointed to settle the accounts, collect the assets, adjust the claims, and pay the debts of a dissolving or insolvent firm.

name partner. A partner whose name appears in the name of the partnership <Mr. Tibbs is a name partner in the accounting firm of Gibbs & Tibbs>. — Also termed *named partner*; *title member.*

nominal partner. A person who is held out as a partner in a firm or business but who has no actual interest in the partnership. — Also termed *ostensible partner*; *partner by estoppel.*

partner in commendam (in kə-**men**-dəm). See *limited partner.*

quasi-partner. A person who joins others in an enterprise that appears to be, but is not, a partnership. • A joint adventurer, for example, is a quasi-partner.

secret partner. A partner whose connection with the firm is concealed from the public. — Also termed *sleeping partner.*

senior partner. A high-ranking partner, as in a law firm.

silent partner. A partner who shares in the profits but who has no active voice in management of the firm and whose existence is often not publicly disclosed. — Also termed *dormant partner.*

sleeping partner. See *secret partner.*

special partner. See *limited partner.*

surviving partner. The partner who, upon the partnership's dissolution because of another partner's death, serves as a trustee to administer the firm's remaining affairs.

partner in commendam. See *limited partner* under PARTNER.

partnership. A voluntary association of two or more persons who jointly own and carry on a business for profit. • Under the Uniform Partnership Act, a partnership is presumed to exist if the persons agree to share proportionally the business's profits or losses. Cf. JOINT VENTURE; STRATEGIC ALLIANCE.

collapsible partnership. *Tax.* A partnership formed by partners who intend to dissolve it before they realize any income. • Any partner's gain resulting from unrealized receivables or inventory that has increased substantially in value will be treated by the IRS as ordinary income rather than as capital gain. IRC (26 USCA) § 751. Cf. *collapsible corporation* under CORPORATION.

commercial partnership. See *trading partnership.*

family partnership. See FAMILY PARTNERSHIP.

general partnership. A partnership in which all partners participate fully in running the business and share equally in profits and losses (though the partners' monetary contributions may vary).

implied partnership. See *partnership by estoppel.*

limited-liability partnership. A partnership in which a partner is not liable for a negligent act committed by another partner or by an employee not under the partner's supervision. • All states have enacted statutes that allow a business (typically a law firm or accounting firm) to register as this type of partnership. — Abbr. L.L.P.

limited partnership. A partnership composed of one or more persons who control the business and are personally liable for the partnership's debts (called *general partners*), and one or more persons who contribute capital and share profits but who cannot manage the business and are liable only for the amount of their contribution (called *limited partners*). • The chief purpose of a limited partnership is to enable persons to invest their money in a business without taking an active part in managing the business, and without risking more than the sum originally contributed, while securing the cooperation of others who have ability and integrity but insufficient money. — Abbr. L.P. — Also termed *special partnership*; (in civil law) *partnership in commendam*.

"Unknown at common law, the limited partnership was derived from the *commenda* or *societe en commandite* of continental Europe to permit a person to invest and share in the profits of a partnership business and yet limit one's liability to one's investment. It was first recognized in the United States by a New York statute of 1822. It is now recognized by statute in all American jurisdictions." Henry G. Henn & John R. Alexander, *Laws of Corporations* § 28, at 86 (3d ed. 1983).

"[T]he two primary characteristics of a limited partnership [are] liability of limited partners only for their agreed contributions, and a hierarchical structure with management in one or more general partners and very little power or authority in the limited partners. Thus, limited partners are typically — although not necessarily — passive contributors of capital.... In this respect they resemble shareholders in a corporation, but, depending on the details of the organizational documents, they may have greater or lesser rights." 3 Alan R. Bromberg & Larry E. Ribstein, *Bromberg and Ribstein on Partnerships* § 12.01, at 12:5–12:6 (1999).

master limited partnership. A limited partnership whose interests or shares are publicly traded. See *publicly traded partnership*.

nontrading partnership. A partnership that does not buy and sell but instead is a partnership of employment or occupation. — Also termed *noncommercial partnership*.

particular partnership. A partnership in which the members unite to share the benefits of a single transaction or enterprise.

partnership at will. A partnership that any partner may dissolve at any time without thereby incurring liability. Cf. *partnership for a term*.

partnership by estoppel. A partnership implied by law when one or more persons represent themselves as partners to a third party who relies on that representation. • A person who is deemed a partner by estoppel becomes liable for any credit extended to the partnership by the third party. — Also termed *implied partnership*.

partnership for a term. A partnership that exists for a specified duration or until a specified event occurs. • Such a partnership can be prematurely dissolved by any partner, but that partner may be held liable for breach of the partnership agreement. Cf. *partnership at will*.

partnership in commendam. See *limited partnership*.

publicly traded partnership. A partnership whose interests are traded either over-the-counter or on a securities exchange. • These partnerships are treated as corporations for income-tax purposes. — Abbr. PTP.

special partnership. **1.** See *limited partnership*. **2.** A partnership formed only for a single venture.

subpartnership. An arrangement between a firm's partner and a nonpartner to share the partner's profits and losses in the firm's business, but without forming a legal partnership between the partner and the nonpartner.

tiered partnership. An ownership arrangement consisting of one parent partnership that is a partner in one or more subsidiary partnerships.

trading partnership. A partnership whose usual business involves buying and selling. — Also termed *commercial partnership*.

umbrella limited partnership. A limited partnership used by a real-estate investment trust to acquire investment properties in exchange for shares in the partnership. See *umbrella partnership real-estate investment trust* under REAL-ESTATE INVESTMENT TRUST.

universal partnership. A partnership formed by persons who agree to contribute all their individually owned property — and to devote all their skill, labor, and services — to the partnership.

partnership agreement. A contract defining the partners' rights and duties toward one another — not the partners' relationship with third parties. — Also termed *articles of partnership*.

partnership association. A business organization that combines the features of a limited partnership and a close corporation. • Partnership associations are statutorily recognized in only a few states. — Also termed *statutory partnership association*; *limited partnership association*.

partnership at will. See PARTNERSHIP.

partnership by estoppel. See PARTNERSHIP.

partnership certificate. A document that evidences the participation of the partners in a partnership. • The certificate is often furnished to financial institutions when the partnership borrows money.

partnership distribution. See DISTRIBUTION.

partnership for a term. See PARTNERSHIP.

partnership in commendam. See *limited partnership* under PARTNERSHIP.

partnership insurance. See INSURANCE.

partner's lien. A partner's right to have the partnership property applied in payment of the partnership's debts and to have whatever is due the firm from fellow partners deducted from what would otherwise be payable to them for their shares.

part payment. A buyer's delivery of money or other thing of value to the seller, and its acceptance by the seller, when the money or the value of the thing does not equal the full sum owed.

part performance. **1.** The accomplishment of some but not all of one's contractual obligations. **2.** A party's execution, in reliance on an opposing party's oral promise, of enough of an oral contract's requirements that a court may hold the statute of frauds not to apply. **3.** PART-PERFORMANCE DOCTRINE.

part-performance doctrine. The equitable principle by which a failure to comply with the statute of frauds is overcome by a party's execution, in reliance on an opposing party's oral promise, of an oral contract's requirements. — Sometimes shortened to *part performance*.

> "Part performance is not an accurate designation of such acts as taking possession and making improvements when the contract does not provide for such acts, but such acts regularly bring the doctrine into play. The doctrine is contrary to the words of the Statute of Frauds, but it was established by English courts of equity soon after the enactment of the Statute. Payment of purchase-money, without more, was once thought sufficient to justify specific enforcement, but a contrary view now prevails, since in such cases restitution is an adequate remedy. English decisions treated a transfer of possession of the land as sufficient, if unequivocally referable to the oral agreement, apparently on the ground that the promise to transfer had been executed by a common-law conveyance. Such decisions are not generally followed in the United States. Enforcement has instead been justified on the ground that repudiation after 'part performance' amounts to a 'virtual fraud.' A more accurate statement is that courts with equitable powers are vested by tradition with what in substance is a dispensing power based on the promisee's reliance, a discretion to be exercised with caution in the light of all the circumstances." Restatement (Second) of Contracts § 129 cmt. a (1981).

part-sovereign state. See SOVEREIGN STATE.

party. **1.** One who takes part in a transaction <a party to the contract>.

> "Note, that if an Indenture be made between two as Parties thereto in the Beginning, and in the Deed one of them grants or lets a Thing to another who is not named in the Beginning, he is not Party to the Deed, nor shall take any Thing thereby." John Rastell, *Les Termes de la Ley* 471 (26th ed. 1721).

> "A person who takes part in a legal transaction or proceeding is said to be a party to it. Thus, if an agreement, conveyance, lease, or the like, is entered into between A. and B., they are said to be parties to it; and the same expression is often, though not very correctly, applied to the persons named as the grantors or releasors in a deed-poll." 2 Stewart Rapalje & Robert L. Lawrence, *A Dictionary of American and English Law* 930 (1883).

party of the first part. *Archaic.* The party named first in a contract; esp., the owner or seller.

party of the second part. *Archaic.* The party named second in a contract; esp., the buyer.

2. One by or against whom a lawsuit is brought <a party to the lawsuit>.

adverse party. A party whose interests are opposed to the interests of another party to the action.

aggrieved party. A party whose personal, pecuniary, or property rights have been adversely affected by another person's actions or by a court's decree or judgment. — Also termed *party aggrieved*; *person aggrieved*.

formal party. See *nominal party*.

indispensable party. A party who, having interests that would inevitably be affected by a court's judgment, must be included in the case. • If such a party is not included, the case must be dismissed. Fed. R. Civ. P. 19(b). Cf. *necessary party*.

innocent party. A party who did not consciously or intentionally participate in an event or transaction.

interested party. A party who has a recognizable stake (and therefore standing) in a matter.

necessary party. A party who, being closely connected to a lawsuit, should be included in the case if feasible, but whose absence will not require dismissal of the proceedings. See *compulsory joinder* under JOINDER. Cf. *indispensable party*.

nominal party. A party who, having some interest in the subject matter of a lawsuit, will not be affected by any judgment but is nonetheless joined in the lawsuit to avoid procedural defects. • An example is the disinterested stakeholder in a garnishment action. — Also termed *formal party*. Cf. *real party in interest*.

party aggrieved. See *aggrieved party*.

party in interest. See *real party in interest*.

party opponent. An adversary in a legal proceeding. — Sometimes written *party-opponent*.

party to be charged. A defendant in an action to enforce a contract falling within the statute of frauds.

prevailing party. A party in whose favor a judgment is rendered, regardless of the amount of damages awarded <in certain cases, the court will award attorney's fees to the prevailing party>. — Also termed *successful party*.

proper party. A party who may be joined in a case for reasons of judicial economy but whose presence is not essential to the proceeding. See *permissive joinder* under JOINDER.

real party in interest. A person entitled under the substantive law to enforce the right sued upon and who generally, but not necessarily, benefits from the action's final outcome. — Also termed *party in interest*; (archaically) *interessee*. Cf. *nominal party*.

> "[T]he 'real party in interest' is the party who, by the substantive law, possesses the right sought to be enforced, and not necessarily the person who will ultimately benefit from the recovery.... The concept of real party in interest should not be confused with the concept of standing. The standing question arises in the realm of public law, when governmental action is attacked on the ground that it violates private rights or some constitutional principle.... Unfortunately, ... confusion between standing on the one hand and real party in interest or capacity on the other has been increasing." Charles Alan Wright, *The Law of Federal Courts* § 70, at 490 & n.2 (5th ed. 1994).

successful party. See *prevailing party*.

third party. See THIRD PARTY.

party-column ballot. See BALLOT (4).

party in interest. See *real party in interest* under PARTY (2).

party of the first part. See PARTY (1).

party of the second part. See PARTY (1).

party opponent. See PARTY (2).

party to be charged. See PARTY (2).

party wall. See WALL.

parum cavisse videtur (**par**-əm kə-**vis**-ee vi-**dee**-tər). [Latin] *Hist.* He seems to have taken too little care; he seems to have been incautious. • This expression was used by a judge when pronouncing a death sentence.

par value. The value of an instrument or security as shown on its face; esp., the arbitrary dollar amount assigned to a stock share by the corporate charter, or the principal of a bond. — Often shortened to *par*. — Also termed *face value*; *nominal value*; *stated value*.

> "At one time par value had considerable importance because it was widely viewed as the amount for which the shares would be issued: shares with a par value of one hundred dollars could be subscribed for at one hundred dollars per share with confidence that all other identical shares would also be issued for $100. This practice, however, long ago fell into disuse. Today, par value serves only a minor function and is in no way an indication of the price at which the shares are issued, with this one exception: The one basic rule about setting the price for shares of common stock with a par value is that the price must be equal to or greater than par value." Robert W. Hamilton, *The Law of Corporations in a Nutshell* 109 (3d ed. 1991).

par-value stock. See STOCK.

pass, *vb.* **1.** To pronounce or render an opinion, ruling, sentence, or judgment <the court refused to pass on the constitutional issue, deciding the case instead on procedural grounds>. **2.** To transfer or be transferred <the woman's will passes title to the house to her nephew, much to her husband's surprise> <title passed when the nephew received the deed>. **3.** To enact (a legislative bill or resolution) <Congress has debated whether to pass a balanced-budget amendment to the Constitution>. **4.** To approve or certify (something) as meeting specified requirements <the mechanic informed her that the car had passed inspection>. **5.** To publish, transfer, or circulate (a thing, often a forgery) <he was found guilty of passing counterfeit bills>. **6.** To forgo or proceed beyond <the case was passed on the court's trial docket because the judge was presiding over a criminal trial>.

passage, *n.* **1.** The passing of a legislative measure into law. **2.** A right, privilege, or permission to pass over land or water; an easement to travel through another's property.

pass-along, *adj.* See PASS-THROUGH.

passbook. A depositor's book in which a bank records all the transactions on an account. — Also termed *bankbook*.

passed dividend. See DIVIDEND.

passim (**pas**-im), *adv.* [Latin] Here and there; throughout (the cited work). • In modern legal writing, the citation signal *see generally* is preferred to *passim* as a general reference, although *passim* can be useful in a brief's index of authorities to show that a given authority is cited throughout the brief.

passing off, *n.* The act or an instance of falsely representing one's own product as that of another in an attempt to deceive potential buyers. • Passing off is actionable in tort under the law of unfair competition. — Also termed *palming off*. — **pass off,** *vb.* Cf. MISAPPROPRIATION.

passive, *adj.* Not involving active participation; esp., of or relating to a business enterprise in which an investor does not have immediate control over the activity that produces income.

passive activity. *Tax.* A business activity in which the taxpayer does not materially participate and therefore does not have immediate control over the income. • A typical example is the ownership and rental of real property by someone not in the real-property business.

passive bond. See BOND (3).

passive breach of contract. See BREACH OF CONTRACT.

passive concealment. See CONCEALMENT.

passive debt. See DEBT.

passive duty. See *negative duty* under DUTY (1).

passive euthanasia. See EUTHANASIA.

passive income. See INCOME.

passive investment income. See INCOME.

passive loss. See LOSS.

passive negligence. See NEGLIGENCE.

passive trust. See TRUST.

passport. 1. A formal document certifying a person's identity and citizenship so that the person may travel to and from a foreign country. **2.** See SEA LETTER.

pass the witness. See TAKE THE WITNESS.

pass-through, *adj.* (Of a seller's or lessor's costs) chargeable to the buyer or lessee. — Also termed *pass-along*.

pass-through security. See SECURITY.

pass-through taxation. See TAXATION.

past consideration. See CONSIDERATION.

past recollection recorded. *Evidence.* A document concerning events that a witness once knew about but can no longer remember. • The document itself is evidence and, despite being hearsay, may be admitted (or read into the record) if it was prepared or adopted by the witness when the events were fresh in the witness's memory. Fed. R. Evid. 803(5). — Also termed *recorded recollection*; *past recorded recollection*. Cf. PRESENT RECOLLECTION REFRESHED.

***Pasula–Robinette* test.** The principle that if a miner establishes a prima facie case of retaliation for filing a claim under the Mine Safety and Health Act, the mine operator can still prevail by proving, as an affirmative defense, that (1) the miner did not engage in a protected activity, (2) the adverse action was based on the miner's unprotected activity, and (3) the mine operator would have taken the same action based solely on the unprotected activity. • To establish a prima facie case of retaliation, the evidence must show that the miner engaged in a protected activity and that an adverse employment action occurred based at least in part on that activity. 30 USCA § 815(c); *Secretary ex rel. Pasula v. Consolidation Coal Co.*, 2 FMSHRC 2786 (1980); *Secretary ex rel. Robinette v. United Coal Co.*, 3 FMSHRC 802 (1981).

pat-down, *n.* See FRISK.

pateat universis per praesentes (**pat**-ee-at yoo-nə-**vər**-sis pər pri-**zen**-teez). [Law Latin] Let it be open to all men by these presents. Cf.

KNOW ALL MEN BY THESE PRESENTS; NOVERINT UNIVERSI PER PRAESENTES.

***Pate* hearing.** A proceeding in which the trial court seeks to determine whether a criminal defendant is competent to stand trial. *Pate v. Robinson*, 383 U.S. 375, 86 S.Ct. 836 (1966); 18 USCA § 4241. — Also termed *competency hearing*; *incompetency hearing*.

patent (**pay**-tənt), *adj*. Obvious; apparent <a patent ambiguity>. Cf. LATENT.

patent (**pat**-ənt), *n*. **1.** The governmental grant of a right, privilege, or authority. **2.** The official document so granting. — Also termed *public grant*. See LETTERS PATENT.

call patent. A land patent in which the corners have been staked but the boundary lines have not been run out at the time of the grant.

land patent. An instrument by which the government conveys a grant of public land to a private person.

lapse patent. A land patent substituting for an earlier patent to the same land that lapsed because the previous patentee did not claim it.

3. The exclusive right to make, use, or sell an invention for a specified period (usu. 17 years), granted by the federal government to the inventor if the device or process is novel, useful, and nonobvious. 35 USCA §§ 101–103.

> "What, exactly, is a patent and how does it operate to foster the 'progress of the useful arts'? In its simplest terms a patent is an agreement between an inventor and the public, represented by the federal government: in return for a full public disclosure of the invention the inventor is granted the right for a fixed period of time to exclude others from making, using, or selling the defined invention in the United States. It is a limited monopoly, designed not primarily to reward the inventor (this may or may not follow), but to encourage a public disclosure of inventions so that after the monopoly expires, the public is free to take unrestricted advantage of the invention." Earl W. Kintner & Jack L. Lahr, *An Intellectual Property Law Primer* 7–11 (2d ed. 1982).

basic patent. A patent granted to an invention recognized by industry or the scientific community as pioneering, unexpected, and unprecedented. — Also termed *pioneer patent*.

combination patent. A patent granted for an invention that unites existing components in a novel way.

design patent. A patent granted for a new, original, and ornamental design for an article of manufacture; a patent that protects a product's appearance or nonfunctional aspects. • Design patents — which, unlike utility patents, have a term of only 14 years — are similar to copyrights.

fencing patent. A patent procured in an effort to broaden the scope of the invention beyond the article or process that is actually intended to be manufactured or licensed. Cf. DOUBLE PATENTING.

paper patent. A patent granted for a discovery or invention that has never been used commercially. • A paper patent receives less protection under the law than a patent granted for a device that is actually used in industry.

pioneer patent. See *basic patent*.

plant patent. A patent granted for the invention or discovery of a new and distinct variety of asexually reproducing plant.

process patent. A patent for a method of treating specified materials to produce a certain result; a patent outlining a means of producing a physical result independently of the producing mechanism. • The result might be brought about by chemical action, by applying some element or power of nature, by mixing certain substances together, or by heating a substance to a certain temperature.

reissue patent. A patent that is issued to correct one or more errors in an original patent, as to revise the specification or to fix an invalid claim. • A reissue patent replaces the original patent and lasts for the rest of the original patent's term. 35 USCA § 251. — Sometimes shortened to *reissue*.

> "[R]eissue patents are relatively rare, because the push and pull of the patent prosecution process tends to make the claims both accurate and as broad as the U.S. Patent and Trademark Office will allow." Stephen Elias, *Patent, Copyright and Trademark* 278 (1996).

utility patent. A patent granted for one of the following types of inventions: a process, a machine, a manufacture, or a composition of matter (such as a new chemical). • Utility patents are the most commonly issued patents. 35 USCA § 101.

patentable, *adj*. Capable of being patented <patentable processes>.

patent ambiguity. See AMBIGUITY.

Patent and Copyright Clause. The constitutional provision granting Congress the authority to promote the advancement of science and the arts by establishing a national system for patents and copyrights. U.S. Const. art. I, § 8, cl. 8.

Patent and Trademark Office. The Department of Commerce agency that examines patent and trademark applications, issues patents, registers trademarks, and furnishes patent and trademark information and services to the public. — Abbr. PTO.

patent defect. See DEFECT.

patent disclaimer. See DISCLAIMER.

patentee (pat-ən-**tee**). One who has been granted a patent.

patent infringement. See INFRINGEMENT.

patent insurance. See INSURANCE.

patent medicine. A packaged drug that is protected by trademark and is available without prescription.

patent of precedence. *Hist.* A royal grant to barristers that the Crown wished to honor by conferring such rank and preaudience as assigned in the grant.

patentor (**pat**-ən-tər *or* pat-ən-**tor**). One who grants a patent.

patent pending. The designation given to an invention while the Patent and Trademark Office is processing the patent application. • No protection against infringement exists, however, unless an actual patent is granted. — Abbr. pat. pend.

patent pooling. The cross-licensing of patents among patentholders. • Patent pooling does not violate antitrust laws unless it is done to suppress competition or control an industry.

patent right. See RIGHT.

patent-right dealer. A person who sells or brokers the sale of patent rights.

patent writ. See WRIT.

pater (**pay**-tər), *n.* [Latin] Father.

paterfamilias (pay-tər-fə-**mil**-ee-əs *or* pah-tər-), *n.* [Latin] *Roman law.* The male head of a family or household; esp., one invested with *potestas* (power) over another. — Also termed *homo sui juris.* See *patria potestas* under POTESTAS.

paternal, *adj.* Of, relating to, or coming from one's father <paternal property>. Cf. MATERNAL.

paternalism, *n.* A government's policy or practice of taking responsibility for the individual affairs of its citizens, esp. by supplying their needs or regulating their conduct in a heavy-handed manner. — **paternalistic,** *adj.*

paternal line. See LINE.

paternal-line descent. See DESCENT.

paternal property. See PROPERTY.

paternity (pə-**tər**-ni-tee). The state or condition of being a father, esp. a biological one; fatherhood.

paternity suit. A court proceeding to determine whether a person is the father of a child (esp. one born out of wedlock), usu. initiated by the mother in an effort to obtain child support. — Also termed *paternity action*; *parentage action*; *bastardy proceeding.*

paternity test. A test, usu. involving DNA identification or tissue-typing, for determining whether a given man is the biological father of a particular child. See DNA IDENTIFICATION; HLA TEST.

pater patriae (**pay**-tər **pay**-tree-ee *or* **pa**-tree-ee). [Latin] Father of the country. See PARENS PATRIAE.

pathological intoxication. See INTOXICATION.

pathology (pə-**thol**-ə-jee), *n.* The branch of medical study that examines the origins, symptoms, and nature of diseases. — **pathological** (path-ə-**loj**-i-kəl), *adj.* — **pathologist** (pə-**thol**-ə-jist), *n.*

patiens (**pay**-shee-enz), *n.* [Latin] A person who suffers or permits; the passive party in a transaction. Cf. AGENS (1).

patient, *n.* A person under medical or psychiatric care.

patient-litigant exception. An exemption from the doctor-patient privilege, whereby the privilege is lost when the patient sues the doctor for malpractice.

patient-physician privilege. See *doctor-patient privilege* under PRIVILEGE (3).

patient's bill of rights. A general statement of patient rights voluntarily adopted by a health-care provider or mandated by statute, covering such matters as access to care, patient dignity and confidentiality, personal safety, consent to treatment, and explanation of charges.

pat. pend. *abbr.* PATENT PENDING.

patria (**pay**-tree-ə *or* **pa**-tree-ə), *n.* [Latin] **1.** *Roman law.* The fatherland; a person's home area. **2.** *Hist.* The country or the area within it, such as a county or neighborhood. **3.** *Hist.* A jury, as when a defendant "puts himself upon the country" (*ponit se super patriam*). See CONCLUSION TO THE COUNTRY; GOING TO THE COUNTRY; PAYS.

> "Though our Latin uses *patria*, our French uses *pays*, which descends from Latin *pagus*. The 'country' of this formula is not our father-land but 'the country-side.' " 2 Frederick Pollock & Frederic W. Maitland, *The History of English Law Before the Time of Edward I* 624 n.1 (2d ed. 1899).

patria potestas. See POTESTAS.

patricide (**pa**-trə-sId), *n.* **1.** The act of killing one's own father. **2.** One who kills his or her father. — **patricidal,** *adj.* Cf. PARRICIDE.

patrimonial (pa-trə-**moh**-nee-əl), *adj.* Of or relating to an inheritance, esp. from a male ancestor.

patrimonium (pa-trə-**moh**-nee-əm), *n.* [Latin] *Roman law.* Property that is capable of being inherited; private property.

patrimony (**pa**-trə-moh-nee). **1.** An estate inherited from one's father or other ancestor; legacy or heritage. **2.** *Civil law.* All of a person's assets and liabilities that are capable of monetary valuation and subject to execution for a creditor's benefit.

patron. **1.** A regular customer or client of a business. **2.** A person who protects or supports some person or thing.

patronage (**pay**-trə-nij). **1.** The giving of support, sponsorship, or protection. **2.** All the customers of a business; clientele. **3.** The power to appoint persons to governmental positions or to confer other political favors. — Also termed (in sense 3) *political patronage.* See SPOILS SYSTEM.

patruus (**pa**-troo-əs), *n.* [Latin] *Roman & civil law.* A father's brother; a paternal uncle.

patruus magnus (**pa**-troo-əs **mag**-nəs), *n.* [Latin] *Roman & civil law.* A grandfather's brother; a great-uncle.

patruus maximus (**pa**-troo-əs **mak**-sə-məs). See ABPATRUUS.

pattern, *n.* A mode of behavior or series of acts that are recognizably consistent <a pattern of racial discrimination>.

pattern jury charge. See *model jury instruction* under JURY INSTRUCTION.

pattern jury instruction. See *model jury instruction* under JURY INSTRUCTION.

pattern of racketeering activity. Two or more related criminal acts that amount to, or pose a threat of, continued criminal activity. • This phrase derives from the federal Racketeer Influenced and Corrupt Organizations Act. See RACKETEERING.

pattern similarity. See *comprehensive nonliteral similarity* under SUBSTANTIAL SIMILARITY.

paucital (**paw**-si-təl), *adj. Rare.* See IN PERSONAM.

pauper. A very poor person, esp. one who receives aid from charity or public funds; an indigent. See IN FORMA PAUPERIS.

pauperies (**paw**-pər-eez), *n.* [Latin "impoverishment"] *Roman law.* Damage done by a four-footed animal. • The animal's owner was liable for the damage.

pauper's affidavit. See *poverty affidavit* under AFFIDAVIT.

pauper's oath. See OATH.

pawn, *n.* **1.** An item of personal property deposited as security for a debt; a pledge or guarantee. **2.** The act of depositing personal property in this manner. **3.** The condition of being held on deposit as a pledge. — **pawn,** *vb.* Cf. BAILMENT.

pawnbroker, *n.* One who lends money, usu. at a high interest rate, in exchange for personal property that is deposited as security by the borrower. — **pawnbroking,** *n.*

pawnee. One who receives a deposit of personal property as security for a debt.

pawnor. One who deposits an item of personal property as security for a debt. — Also spelled *pawner*.

pax regis (**paks ree**-jis), *n.* [Latin "the king's peace"] *Hist.* **1.** The government's guarantee of peace and security of life and property to all within the law's protection. **2.** VERGE (1).

payable, *adj.* (Of a sum of money or a negotiable instrument) that is to be paid. • An amount may be payable without being due. Debts are commonly payable long before they fall due.

payable after sight. Payable after acceptance or protest of nonacceptance. See *sight draft* under DRAFT.

payable on demand. Payable when presented or upon request for payment; payable at any time.

payable to bearer. Payable to anyone holding the instrument.

payable to order. Payable only to a specified payee.

payable, *n.* See *account payable* under ACCOUNT.

payable date. See DATE.

pay any bank. A draft indorsement that permits only banks to acquire the rights of a holder until the draft is either returned to the customer initiating collection or specially indorsed by a bank to a person who is not a bank. UCC § 4–201(b).

payback method. An accounting procedure that measures the time required to recover a venture's initial cash investment.

payback period. The length of time required to recover a venture's initial cash investment, without accounting for the time value of money.

paydown. A loan payment in an amount less than the total loan principal.

payee. One to whom money is paid or payable; esp., a party named in commercial paper as the recipient of the payment.

payer. See PAYOR.

paying quantities. *Oil & gas.* An amount earned from oil and gas production after paying the well's drilling, equipping, and operating costs <production in paying quantities>.

payment. 1. Performance of an obligation, usu. by the delivery of money. • Performance may occur by delivery and acceptance of things other than money, but there is a payment only if money or other valuable things are given and accepted in partial or full discharge of an obligation. **2.** The money or other valuable thing so delivered in satisfaction of an obligation.

advance payment. A payment made in anticipation of a contingent or fixed future liability or obligation.

balloon payment. A final loan payment that is usu. much larger than the preceding regular payments and that discharges the principal balance of the loan. See *balloon note* under NOTE (1).

conditional payment. Payment of an obligation only on condition that something be done. • Generally, the payor reserves the right to demand the payment back if the condition is not met.

constructive payment. A payment made by the payor but not yet credited by the payee. • For example, a rent check mailed on the first of the month is a constructive payment even though the landlord does not deposit the check until ten days later.

***direct payment.* 1.** A payment made directly to the payee, without using an intermediary. **2.** A payment that is absolute and unconditional on the amount, the due date, and the payee.

down payment. The portion of a purchase price paid in cash (or its equivalent) at the time the sale agreement is executed. Cf. BINDER (2); EARNEST MONEY.

involuntary payment. A payment obtained by fraud or duress.

lump-sum payment. A payment of a large amount all at once, as opposed to smaller payments over time.

payment bond. See BOND (2).

payment date. See DATE.

payment in due course. A payment to the holder of a negotiable instrument at or after its maturity date, made by the payor in good faith and without notice of any defect in the holder's title. See HOLDER IN DUE COURSE.

payment intangible. See INTANGIBLE.

payment into court. A party's money or property deposited with a court for distribution after a proceeding according to the parties' settlement or the court's order. See INTERPLEADER.

payoff. See KICKBACK.

payola (pay-**oh**-lə). An indirect and secret payment for a favor, esp. one relating to business; a bribe.

payor. One who pays; esp., a person responsible for paying a negotiable instrument. — Also spelled *payer*. See DRAWEE.

payor bank. See BANK.

payout period. The time required for an asset to produce enough revenue to pay back the initial investment; esp., in oil-and-gas law, the time required for a well to produce a sufficient amount of oil or gas to pay back the investment in the well.

payout ratio. The ratio between a corporation's dividends per share and its earnings per share. Cf. COMMON-STOCK RATIO.

payroll. 1. A list of employees to be paid and the amount due to each of them. **2.** The total compensation payable to a company's employees for one pay period.

payroll tax. See TAX.

pays (pay *or* pays), *n.* [Law French] The country; a jury. See PATRIA.

PBGC. *abbr.* PENSION BENEFIT GUARANTY CORPORATION.

P.C. *abbr.* **1.** See *professional corporation* under CORPORATION. **2.** POLITICAL CORRECTNESS. **3.** PRIVY COUNCILLOR.

PCR action. See POSTCONVICTION-RELIEF PROCEEDING.

P.D. *abbr.* PUBLIC DEFENDER.

peace, *n.* A state of public tranquility; freedom from civil disturbance or hostility <breach of the peace>. — **peaceable,** *adj.* — **peaceful,** *adj.*

armed peace. A situation in which two or more nations, while at peace, are actually armed for possible or probable hostilities.

peace, justice of. See JUSTICE OF THE PEACE.

peaceable possession. See POSSESSION.

peace bond. See BOND (2).

peace officer. A civil officer (such as a sheriff or police officer) appointed to maintain public tranquility and order. • This term may also include a judge who hears criminal cases or another public official (such as a mayor) who may be statutorily designated as a peace officer for limited purposes. — Also termed *officer of the peace*; *conservator of the peace*.

Peace of God and the church. *Hist.* The cessation of litigation between terms and on Sundays and holidays.

peacetime. A period in which a country has declared neither a war nor a national emergency, even if the country is involved in a conflict or quasi-conflict.

peace treaty. See TREATY.

peace warrant. See WARRANT (1).

peak demand. The point (during some specified period) at which customer use results in the highest level of demand for a utility.

peccavi (pe-**kay**-vɪ *or* pe-**kah**-vee), *n.* [Latin "I have sinned"] An acknowledgment or confession of guilt.

peculation (pek-yə-**lay**-shən), *n.* Embezzlement, esp. by a public official. — **peculate** (**pek**-yə-layt), *vb.* — **peculative** (**pek**-yə-lə-tiv), *adj.* — **peculator** (**pek**-yə-lay-tər), *n.* Cf. DEPECULATION.

peculatus (pek-yə-**lay**-təs), *n.* [Latin] *Roman law.* The offense of stealing or embezzling public funds; peculation.

peculiar-risk doctrine. The principle that an employer will be liable for injury caused by an independent contractor if the employer failed to take precautions against a risk that is peculiar to the contractor's work and that the employer should have recognized. — Also termed *peculiar-risk exception*.

peculium (pi-**kyoo**-lee-əm), *n.* [Latin] *Roman law.* Property given by the head of a household to a son or slave, to be used at that person's discretion for business transactions.

pecunia (pi-**kyoo**-nee-ə), *n.* [Latin] *Hist.* **1.** Money. **2.** Real or personal property.

pecunia constituta (pi-**kyoo**-nee-ə kon-sti-**t[y]oo**-tə). [Latin "fixed sum of money"] *Roman law.* A debt reaffirmed by a promise to pay (i.e., a *constitutum*).

pecunia non numerata (pi-**kyoo**-nee-ə non n[y]oo-mə-**ray**-tə). [Latin] *Roman law.* Money not paid.

pecunia numerata (pi-**kyoo**-nee-ə n[y]oo-mə-**ray**-tə). [Latin] *Hist.* Money numbered or counted out; money given to pay a debt.

pecuniary (pi-**kyoo**-nee-er-ee), *adj.* Of or relating to money; monetary <a pecuniary interest in the lawsuit>.

pecuniary benefit. See BENEFIT.

pecuniary bequest. See BEQUEST.

pecuniary cause. *Eccles. law.* A lawsuit maintainable in an ecclesiastical court to redress an injury relating to the church, such as a parishioner's failure to pay a tithe to a parson.

pecuniary damages. See DAMAGES.

pecuniary gain. See GAIN (1).

pecuniary legacy. See LEGACY.

pecuniary loss. See LOSS.

pecunia trajectitia (pi-**kyoo**-nee-ə traj-ek-**tish**-ee-ə). [Latin "money conveyed overseas"] *Roman law.* Money loaned in connection with the transport of goods by ship. See NAUTICUM FENUS.

pedage (**ped**-ij). *Hist.* Money paid as a toll to travel through another's land. — Also termed *paage*; *pedagium*.

pedagium (pi-**day**-jee-əm). [Law Latin] See PEDAGE.

pedal possession. See POSSESSION.

pedaneus (pi-**day**-nee-əs), *n.* [Latin] *Roman law.* A judge who sat at the foot of the tribunal (i.e., in the lowest seat) ready to try minor cases at the command of the magistrate; an assistant judge.

pederasty (**ped**-ər-as-tee), *n.* Anal intercourse between a man and a boy. • Pederasty is illegal in all states. — **pederast** (**ped**-ə-rast), *n.* Cf. SODOMY.

pedigree. A history of family succession; ancestry or lineage.

pedis abscissio (**pee**-dis *or* **ped**-is ab-**sish**-ee-oh). [Latin "cutting off a foot"] *Hist.* Punishment by cutting off the offender's foot.

pedis positio (**pee**-dis *or* **ped**-is pə-**zish**-ee-oh). [Latin "the placement of the foot"] *Hist.* A putting or placing of the foot. • This term denoted possession of land by actual entry.

pedis possessio. See POSSESSIO.

***pedis possessio* doctrine** (**pee**-dis *or* **ped**-is pə-**zes[h]**-ee-o). [Latin "possession-of-a-foot doctrine"] The principle that a prospector working on land in the public domain is entitled to freedom from fraudulent or forcible intrusions while actually working on the site.

Peeping Tom. A person who spies on another (as through a window), usu. to gain sexual pleasure; VOYEUR.

peer, *n.* **1.** A person who is of equal status, rank, or character with another.

> "The commonalty, like the nobility, are divided into several degrees; and, as the lords, though different in rank, yet all of them are peers in respect of their nobility, so the commoners, though some are greatly superior to others, yet all are in law peers, in respect of their want of nobility . . . ." 1 William Blackstone, *Commentaries on the Laws of England* 391 (1765).

2. A member of the British nobility (such as a duchess, marquis, earl, viscount, or baroness). — **peerage** (**peer**-ij), *n.*

> "The Crown has power to create any number of peers and of any degree. In modern practice the power is exercised on the advice of the Prime Minister and the honour is most commonly a reward for political services. Peerages can be, and have been, conferred for party political reasons; 12 were created in 1712 to save the government, and 16 to help pass the Reform Bill in 1832. In 1832 and 1911 the Opposition of the House of Lords was overcome by the threat to create enough peers to secure a majority. . . . The main privilege of a peer is to

sit and vote in the House of Lords." David M. Walker, *The Oxford Companion to Law* 942 (1980).

peer-reviewed journal. A publication whose practice is to forward submitted articles to disinterested experts who screen them for scholarly or scientific reliability, the idea being that articles actually published have already withstood expert scrutiny and comment.

peer-review organization. A government agency that monitors health-regulation compliance by private hospitals requesting public funds (such as Medicare payments). — Abbr. PRO.

peer-review privilege. See PRIVILEGE (3).

peers of fees. *Hist.* Vassals or tenants of the same lord who judged disputes arising out of fees.

peine forte et dure (**pen for** tay **door** *or* **payn fort** ay **dyoor**). [French "strong and hard punishment"] *Hist.* The punishment of an alleged felon who refused to plead, consisting of pressing or crushing the person's body under heavy weights until the accused either pleaded or died.

> "In all other felonies, however, the punishment of *peine forte et dure* was, until lately, denounced as the consequence of an obstinate silence. The greatest caution and deliberation were indeed to be exercised before it was resorted to; and the prisoner was not only to have '*trina admonitio*,' but a respite of a few hours, and the sentence was to be distinctly read to him, that he might be fully aware of the penalty he was incurring." 1 Joseph Chitty, *A Practical Treatise on the Criminal Law* 425–26 (2d ed. 1826).

> "In old English law, a person charged with felony who, refusing to accept jury trial, was pressed to death (*peine forte et dure*), was not regarded as committing suicide, so that he did not forfeit his property." Glanville Williams, *The Sanctity of Life and the Criminal Law* 270 n.4 (1957).

pell. See CLERK OF THE PELLS.

pellex (**pel**-eks), *n.* [Latin] *Roman law.* A concubine.

penal (**pee**-nəl), *adj.* Of, relating to, or being a penalty or punishment, esp. for a crime.

> "The general rule is that penal statutes are to be construed strictly. By the word 'penal' in this connection is meant not only such statutes as in terms impose a fine, or corporal punishment, or forfeiture as a consequence of violating laws, but also all acts which impose by way of punishment damages beyond compensation for the benefit of the injured party, or which impose any special burden, or take away or impair any privilege or right." William M. Lile et al., *Brief Making and the Use of Law Books* 344 (3d ed. 1914).

> "The word *penal* connotes some form of punishment imposed on an individual by the authority of the state. Where the primary purpose of a statute is expressly enforceable by fine, imprisonment, or similar punishment the statute is always construed as penal." 3 Norman J. Singer, *Sutherland Statutes and Statutory Construction* § 59.01, at 1 (4th ed. 1986).

penal action. See ACTION.

penal bill. See *penal bond* under BOND (2).

penal bond. See BOND (2).

penal clause. See PENALTY CLAUSE.

penal code. A compilation of criminal laws, usu. defining and categorizing the offenses and setting forth their respective punishments. — Also termed *criminal code*. See MODEL PENAL CODE.

penal custody. See CUSTODY (1).

penal institution. See PRISON.

penal law. 1. See *penal statute* under STATUTE. **2.** CRIMINAL LAW.

penal liability. See LIABILITY.

penal redress. See REDRESS.

penal sanction. See *criminal sanction* under SANCTION.

penal statute. See STATUTE.

penal sum. The monetary amount specified as a penalty in a penal bond. See *penal bond* under BOND (2).

penalty. 1. Punishment imposed on a wrongdoer, esp. in the form of imprisonment or fine. • Though usu. for crimes, penalties are also sometimes imposed for civil wrongs. **2.** Excessive liquidated damages that a contract purports to impose on a party that breaches. • If the damages are excessive enough to be considered a penalty, a court will usu. not enforce that particular provision of the contract. Some contracts specify that a given sum of damages is intended "as liquidated damages and not as a penalty" — but even that language is not foolproof.

"A *penalty* is a sum which a party ... agrees to pay or forfeit in the event of a breach, but which is fixed, not as a pre-estimate of probable actual damages, but as a *punishment*, the threat of which is designed to prevent the breach, or as *security*, where the sum is deposited or the covenant to pay is joined in by one or more sureties, to insure that the person injured shall collect his actual damages. Penalties ... are not recoverable or retainable as such by the person in whose favor they are framed ...." Charles T. McCormick, *Handbook on the Law of Damages* § 146, at 600 (1935).

civil penalty. A fine assessed for a violation of a statute or regulation <the EPA levied a civil penalty of $10,000 on the manufacturer for exceeding its pollution limits>.

statutory penalty. A penalty imposed for a statutory violation; esp., a penalty imposing automatic liability on a wrongdoer for violation of a statute's terms without reference to any actual damages suffered.

penalty clause. A contractual provision that assesses an excessive monetary charge against a defaulting party. • Penalty clauses are generally unenforceable. — Often shortened to *penalty*. — Also termed *penal clause*. Cf. LIQUIDATED-DAMAGES CLAUSE; LIMITATION-OF-REMEDIES CLAUSE.

"It not infrequently happens that contracts provide for what is to happen in the event of a breach by the parties, or by one of them. Such provisions may be perfectly simple attempts to avoid future disputes, and to quantify the probable amount of any loss. That is unobjectionable. But sometimes clauses of this kind are not designed to quantify the amount of the probable loss, but are designed to terrorize, or frighten, the party into performance. For example, a contract may provide that the promisor is to pay £5 on a certain event, but if he fails to do so, he must then pay £500. Now a clause of that kind is called a penalty clause by lawyers, and for several hundred years it has been the law that such promises cannot be enforced. The standard justification for the law here is that it is unfair and unconscionable to enforce clauses which are designed to act *in terrorem*." P.S. Atiyah, *Promises, Morals, and Law* 57–58 (1981).

penance. *Eccles. law.* A punishment assessed by an ecclesiastical court for some spiritual offense.

pend, *vb.* (Of a lawsuit) to be awaiting decision or settlement.

pendency (**pen**-dən-see), *n.* The state or condition of being pending or continuing undecided.

pendens. See LIS PENDENS.

pendent (**pen**-dənt), *adj.* **1.** Not yet decided; pending <a pendent action>. **2.** Of or relating to pendent jurisdiction or pendent-party jurisdiction <pendent parties>. **3.** Contingent; dependent <pendent upon a different claim>.

pendent-claim jurisdiction. See *pendent jurisdiction* under JURISDICTION.

pendente lite (pen-**den**-tee **lɪ**-tee), *adv.* [Latin "while the action is pending"] During the proceeding or litigation; contingent on the outcome of litigation. — Also termed *lite pendente*. Cf. LIS PENDENS.

***pendente lite* administration.** See ADMINISTRATION.

pendent jurisdiction. See JURISDICTION.

pendent-party jurisdiction. See JURISDICTION.

pending, *adj.* Remaining undecided; awaiting decision <a pending case>.

pending, *prep.* **1.** Throughout the continuance of; during <in escrow pending arbitration>. **2.** While awaiting; until <the injunction was in force pending trial>.

pending-ordinance doctrine. The principle that a municipality may properly deny an application for a property use that, although it would satisfy existing law, would violate a law that is pending when the application is made. • This doctrine was judicially created, mainly to short-circuit landowners' attempts to circumvent a new ordinance by applying for a nonconforming use on the eve of its approval.

penetration pricing. Pricing of a new product below its anticipated market price to enter a market, discourage competition, and recover the initial investment.

penitentiary (pen-ə-**ten**-shə-ree), *n.* A correctional facility or other place of long-term confinement for convicted criminals; PRISON. — **penitentiary,** *adj.*

***Pennoyer* rule** (pə-**noy**-ər). The principle that a court may not issue a personal judgment against a defendant over which it has no personal jurisdiction. *Pennoyer v. Neff*, 95 U.S. 714 (1877).

Pennsylvania rule. *Torts.* The principle that a tortfeasor who violates a statute in the process of causing an injury has the burden of showing that the violation did not cause the injury.

penny stock. See STOCK.

penology (pee-**nol**-ə-jee), *n.* The study of penal institutions, crime prevention, and the punishment and rehabilitation of criminals, including the art of fitting the right treatment to an offender. — **penological** (pee-nə-**loj**-i-kəl), *adj.* — **penologist** (pee-**nol**-ə-jist), *n.* Cf. CRIMINOLOGY.

pen register. A mechanical device that logs dialed telephone numbers, without overhearing the telephone conversation, by monitoring electrical impulses. Cf. WIRETAPPING.

pensio (**pen**-shee-oh), *n.* [Latin] *Roman & civil law.* A payment for the use of a thing, such as rent for the use of another's house.

pension. A fixed sum paid regularly to a person (or to the person's beneficiaries), esp. by an employer as a retirement benefit. Cf. ANNUITY.

vested pension. A pension in which an employee (or employee's estate) has rights to benefits purchased with the employer's contributions to the plan, even if the employee is no longer employed by this employer at the time of retirement. • The vesting of qualified pension plans is governed by ERISA. See EMPLOYEE RETIREMENT INCOME SECURITY ACT.

Pension Benefit Guaranty Corporation. The federal agency that guarantees the payment of retirement benefits covered by private pension plans that lack sufficient assets to pay the promised benefits. — Abbr. PBGC.

pensioner. A recipient or beneficiary of a pension plan.

pension plan. An employer's plan established to pay long-term retirement benefits to employees or their beneficiaries; a plan providing systematically for the payment of definitely determinable benefits to employees over a period of years, usu. for life, after retirement. • Retirement benefits are typically determined by such factors as years of the employee's service and compensation received. ERISA governs the administration of many pension plans. See EMPLOYEE RETIREMENT INCOME SECURITY ACT. Cf. EMPLOYEE BENEFIT PLAN.

contributory pension plan. A pension plan in which both the employer and the employee contribute.

defined-contribution plan. See EMPLOYEE BENEFIT PLAN.

defined pension plan. A pension plan in which the employer promises specific benefits to each employee. — Also termed *fixed-benefit plan.*

noncontributory pension plan. A pension plan contributed to only by the employer.

nonqualified pension plan. A deferred-compensation plan in which an executive increases retirement benefits by annual additional contributions to the company's basic plan.

qualified pension plan. A pension plan that complies with federal law (ERISA) and thus allows the employee to receive tax benefits for contributions and tax-deferred investment growth.

top-hat plan. An unfunded pension plan that is maintained by an employer primarily for the purpose of providing deferred compensation for a select group of managers or highly paid employees. • Top-hat plans are generally not subject to the broad remedial provisions of ERISA because Congress recognized that certain individuals, by virtue of their position or compensation level, can substantially influence the design or operation of their deferred-compensation plan.

pension trust. See TRUST.

penumbra (pi-**nəm**-brə), *n.* A surrounding area or periphery of uncertain extent. • In constitutional law, the Supreme Court has ruled that the specific guarantees in the Bill of Rights have penumbras containing implied rights, esp. the right of privacy. Pl. **penumbras, penumbrae** (pi-**nəm**-bree). — **penumbral** (pi-**nəm**-brəl), *adj.*

> "Problems of fringe meaning are sometimes spoken of as 'problems of the penumbra', the point being that, in the case of a great many words, there is no doubt about the hard core of their meanings, but different views may well be taken on the question whether the words are applicable to things or situations outside that hard core." Rupert Cross, *Statutory Interpretation* 57 (1976).

peonage (**pee**-ə-nij), *n.* Illegal and involuntary servitude in satisfaction of a debt. — **peon,** *n.*

> "Peonage, which is a term descriptive of a condition that existed in Spanish America, and especially in Mexico, and in the territory of New Mexico, and which may be defined as the status or condition of compulsory service based upon the indebtedness of the peon to the master, the basic fact being the indebtedness, is abolished and prohibited by an act of Congress which further declares that any statute, resolution, regulation, ordinance, or usage of any territory or state designed or operating to establish, maintain, or enforce, directly or indirectly, the voluntary or involuntary service or labor of any persons

as peons, in liquidation of any debt or obligation, or otherwise, shall be null and void [42 USCA § 1994]." 45 Am. Jur. 2d *Involuntary Servitude and Peonage* § 10, at 935–36 (1969).

people. (*usu. cap.*) The citizens of a state as represented by the prosecution in a criminal case <*People v. Snyder*>.

people's court. 1. A court in which ordinary people can resolve small disputes. See *small-claims court* under COURT. **2.** In totalitarian countries, a group of nonlawyer citizens, often illiterate commoners, convened at the scene of a crime to pass judgment or impose punishment on the accused criminal. **3.** (*cap.*) In Nazi Germany, a tribunal that dealt with political offenses.

peppercorn. A small or insignificant thing or amount; nominal consideration <the contract was upheld despite involving mere peppercorn>. See *nominal consideration* under CONSIDERATION.

per (pər), *prep.* **1.** Through; by <the dissent, per Justice Thomas>. **2.** For each; for every <55 miles per hour>. **3.** In accordance with the terms of; according to <per the contract>.

perambulation. The act or custom of walking around the boundaries of a piece of land, either to confirm the boundaries or to preserve evidence of them.

perambulatione facienda. See DE PERAMBULATIONE FACIENDA.

per annum (pər **an**-əm), *adv.* [Latin] By, for, or in each year; annually <interest of eight percent per annum>.

P/E ratio. *abbr.* PRICE-EARNINGS RATIO.

per autre vie. See PUR AUTRE VIE.

per aversionem (pər ə-vər-zhee-**oh**-nəm). [Latin "for a lump sum"] *Roman & civil law.* Of a sale in which goods are taken in bulk or land is bought by estimation of the number of acres. • This type of sale is so called because the buyer "turns away" from a careful scrutiny of the things purchased.

per bouche (pər **boosh**). [Law French] By the mouth; orally.

per capita (pər **kap**-i-tə), *adj.* [Latin "by the head"] **1.** Divided equally among all individuals, usu. in the same class <the court will distribute the property to the descendants on a per capita basis>. Cf. PER STIRPES.

"*Per capita* means taking as an individual and not as a representative of an ancestor. Suppose the testator ... with three living children and three grandchildren who are the issue of a deceased son, had desired and had so stated in his will that his own children and the children of his deceased son should share equally in the estate. In that event the estate would be divided into six parts and each of the three children and each of the three grandchildren would receive an equal portion of the total estate — namely, one-sixth." Gilbert Thomas Stephenson, *Wills* 30 (1934).

per capita with representation. Divided equally among all members of a class of takers, including those who have predeceased the testator, so that no family stocks are cut off by the prior death of a taker. • For example, if T (the testator) has three children — A, B, and C — and C has two children but predeceases T, C's children would still take C's share when T's estate is distributed.

2. Allocated to each person; possessed by each individual <the average annual per capita income has increased over the last two years>. — **per capita,** *adv.*

per capita tax. See *poll tax* under TAX.

percentage lease. See LEASE.

percentage-of-completion method. See ACCOUNTING METHOD.

percentage order. See ORDER (4).

perception. *Civil law.* The act of taking into possession (as rents, profits, etc.).

percolating water. See WATER.

per consequens (pər **kon**-sə-kwenz). [Latin] By consequence; consequently.

per considerationem curiae (pər kən-sid-ə-ray-shee-**oh**-nəm **kyoor**-ee-ee). [Law Latin] By the consideration of the court.

per contra (pər **kon**-trə). [Latin] On the other hand; to the contrary; by contrast.

per curiam (pər **kyoor**-ee-əm), *adv. & adj.* [Latin] By the court as a whole.

per curiam, *n.* See *per curiam opinion* under OPINION (1).

per curiam opinion. See OPINION (1).

per diem (pər **dɪ**-əm *or* **dee**-əm), *adv.* [Latin] By the day; for each day. Cf. IN DIEM.

per diem, *adj.* Based on or calculated by the day <per diem interest>.

per diem, *n.* **1.** A monetary daily allowance, usu. to cover expenses. **2.** A daily fee.

perdonatio utlagariae (pər-də-**nay**-shee-oh ət-lə-**gair**-ee-ee). [Law Latin "pardon of outlawry"] *Hist.* A pardon given to a person outlawed for failing to obey a court's summons. • A person who voluntarily surrendered was eligible for this type of pardon.

perduellio (pər-d[y]oo-**el**-ee-oh). [Latin "treason"] *Roman law.* Treasonous conduct, such as joining the enemy or deserting the battlefield. • *Perduellio* was later absorbed into a broader category of crimes against the state, the *crimen laesae majestatis.* — Also termed *perduellion* (pər-d[y]oo-**el**-yən). See CRIMEN LAESAE MAJESTATIS.

perdurable (pər-**d[y]uur**-ə-bəl), *adj.* (Of an estate in land) lasting or enduring; durable; permanent.

perempt (pər-**empt**), *vb.* **1.** *Civil law.* To quash, do away with, or extinguish. **2.** *Slang.* To exercise a peremptory challenge.

peremption. *Civil law.* The period during which a legal right exists. • If the right is not exercised during this period, it is destroyed. Whereas prescription simply bars a specific remedy, peremption bars the action itself. Cf. PRESCRIPTION (1). See STATUTE OF REPOSE.

peremptory (pər-**emp**-tə-ree), *adj.* **1.** Final; absolute; conclusive; incontrovertible <the king's peremptory order>. **2.** Not requiring any shown cause; arbitrary <peremptory challenges>.

peremptory, *n.* See *peremptory challenge* under CHALLENGE (2).

peremptory challenge. See CHALLENGE (2).

peremptory day. See DAY.

peremptory defense. See DEFENSE (1).

peremptory exception. See EXCEPTION (1).

peremptory instruction. See JURY INSTRUCTION.

peremptory mandamus. See MANDAMUS.

peremptory plea. See PLEA (3).

peremptory strike. See *peremptory challenge* under CHALLENGE (2).

peremptory writ. See WRIT.

per eundem (pər ee-**ən**-dəm). [Latin] By the same. • This term often appears in the phrase *per eundem in eadem* ("by the same judge in the same case").

perfect (pər-**fekt**), *vb.* To take all legal steps needed to complete, secure, or record (a claim, right, or interest); to put in final conformity with the law <perfect a security interest> <perfect the title>.

perfect attestation clause. A provision in a testamentary instrument asserting that all actions required to make a valid testamentary disposition have been performed.

perfect competition. See COMPETITION.

perfect duty. See DUTY (1).

perfected security interest. See SECURITY INTEREST.

perfect equity. See EQUITY.

perfecting amendment. See AMENDMENT (1).

perfect instrument. See INSTRUMENT.

perfection. Validation of a security interest as against other creditors, usu. by filing a statement with some public office or by taking possession of the collateral. Cf. ATTACHMENT (4).

automatic perfection. The self-operative perfection of a purchase-money security interest without filing or without possession of the collateral. • The security interest is perfected simply by the attachment of the security interest, without any additional steps. See *purchase-money security interest* under SECURITY INTEREST.

temporary perfection. The continuous perfection of a security interest for a limited period. • For example, a security interest in proceeds from the original collateral is perfected for ten days after the debtor receives the proceeds; the interest will become unperfected after this ten-day period unless certain statutory requirements are met. On most instruments, a secured party who advances new value under a written security agreement obtains a 21-day perfection period, even if the secured party does not file a financing statement and the collateral remains with the debtor. UCC § 9–304(4).

perfect right. See RIGHT.

perfect self-defense. See SELF-DEFENSE.

perfect tender. See TENDER (2).

perfect-tender rule. *Commercial law.* The principle that a buyer may reject a seller's goods if the quality, quantity, or delivery of the goods fails to conform precisely to the contract. • Although the perfect-tender rule was adopted by the UCC (§ 2–601), other Code provisions — such as the seller's right to cure after rejection — have softened the rule's impact. Cf. SUBSTANTIAL-PERFORMANCE DOCTRINE.

> "At common law, a buyer of goods possessed a legal right to insist upon 'perfect tender' by the seller. If the goods failed to conform exactly to the description in the contract — whether as to quality, quantity or manner of delivery — the buyer could reject the goods and rescind the contract, which meant that the parties would be returned to the positions they occupied before the contract was entered into." Marvin A. Chirelstein, *Concepts and Case Analysis in the Law of Contracts* 112 (1990).

perfect title. See TITLE (2).

perfect usufruct. See USUFRUCT.

perfect war. See WAR.

per feloniam (pər fə-**loh**-nee-əm). [Latin] *Hist.* With criminal intent.

perfidy (**pər**-fə-dee). *Int'l law.* A combatant's conduct that creates the impression that an adversary is entitled to, or is obliged to accord, protection under international law, when in fact the conduct is a ruse to gain an advantage. • Acts of perfidy include feigning an intent to negotiate under a flag of truce, or feigning protected status by using signs, emblems, or uniforms of the United Nations or of a neutral country.

per formam doni (pər **for**-məm **doh**-nɪ). [Law Latin] By the form of the gift; by the designation of the giver rather than by operation of law.

performance, *n.* **1.** The successful completion of a contractual duty, usu. resulting in the performer's release from any past or future liability; EXECUTION (2). — Also termed *full performance.* — **perform,** *vb.* Cf. NONPERFORMANCE.

defective performance. A performance that, whether partial or complete, does not completely comply with the contract. • One example is late performance.

future performance. Performance in the future of an obligation that will become due under a contract.

misperformance. See MISPERFORMANCE.

nonperformance. See NONPERFORMANCE.

part performance. See PART PERFORMANCE.

specific performance. See SPECIFIC PERFORMANCE.

substantial performance. Performance of the primary, necessary terms of an agreement. See SUBSTANTIAL-PERFORMANCE DOCTRINE.

2. The equitable doctrine by which acts consistent with an intention to fulfill an obligation are construed to be in fulfillment of that obligation, even if the party was silent on the point. **3.** A company's earnings. **4.** The ability of a corporation to maintain or increase earnings.

performance bond. 1. A bond given by a surety to ensure the timely performance of a contract. • In major international agreements, performance bonds are typically issued by banks, but sometimes also by insurance companies. The face amount of the bond is typically 2% of the value of performance, but occasionally as much as 5%. **2.** A third party's agreement to guarantee the completion of a construction contract upon the default of the general contractor. — Also termed *completion bond*; *surety bond*; *contract bond.* Cf. *common-law bond* under BOND (2).

nonoperative performance bond. A performance bond that is not currently in effect but is activated upon the issuance of the buyer's letter of credit or other approved financing.

operative performance bond. A performance bond that has been activated by the issuance of the buyer's letter of credit or other approved financing.

revolving performance bond. A performance bond that is in effect on a continuing basis for the duration of the contract, usu. plus an additional number of days (often 45).

up-front performance bond. A performance bond given before the issuance of the buyer's letter of credit or other financing.

performance fund. See MUTUAL FUND.

performance plan. A bonus compensation plan in which executives are paid according to the company's growth.

performance right. A copyright holder's exclusive right to recite, play, act, show, or otherwise render the protected work publicly, whether directly or by technological means (as by broadcasting the work on television).

performance shares. Stock given to an executive when the corporation meets a performance objective.

performance stock. See *glamour stock* under STOCK.

per fraudem (pər **fraw**-dəm), *adv.* [Latin] By fraud; fraudulently.

periculosus (pər-ik-yə-**loh**-səs), *adj.* [Latin] Dangerous; perilous.

periculum (pə-**rik**-yə-ləm), *n.* [Latin] *Civil law.* Peril; danger; risk.

peril. 1. Exposure to the risk of injury, damage, or loss <the perils of litigation>. **2.** *Insurance.* The cause of a loss to person or property <insured against all perils>. Cf. RISK (3).

peril of the sea. An action of the elements at sea of such force as to overcome the strength of a well-founded ship and the normal precautions of good marine practice. • A peril of the sea may relieve a carrier from liability for the resulting losses. — Also termed *danger of navigation*; *danger of river*; *marine peril*; *marine risk*; (in regard to the Great Lakes) *perils of the lakes*.

> "Of the marine perils, by far the most important are those 'of the seas'. What is covered is not any loss that may happen *on* the sea, but fortuitous losses occurring through extraordinary action of the elements at sea, or any accident or mishap in navigation. By far the greatest number of claims for marine loss, and of the insurance problems connected with other topics treated in this book arise under this clause. Extraordinary action of the wind and waves is a sea peril. Collision, foundering, stranding, striking on rocks and icebergs, are all covered under these words. Even a swell from a passing ship may be a 'peril of the sea'. On the other hand, ordinary wear and tear are not included under the coverage of this or any other phrase in the clause, nor are losses which are anticipatable as regular incidents of sea carriage in general or of navigation in a particular part of the world." Grant Gilmore & Charles L. Black, Jr., *The Law of Admiralty* § 2–9, at 72–73 (2d ed. 1975).

per incuriam (pər in-**kyoor**-ee-əm), *adj.* (Of a judicial decision) wrongly decided, usu. because the judge or judges were ill-informed about the applicable law.

> "As a general rule the only cases in which decisions should be held to have been given *per incuriam* are those of decisions given in ignorance or forgetfulness of some inconsistent statutory provision or of some authority binding on the court concerned, so that in such cases some features of the decision or some step in the reasoning on which it is based is found on that account to be demonstrably wrong. This definition is not necessarily exhaustive, but cases not strictly within it which can properly be held to have been decided *per incuriam*, must in our judgment, consistently with the *stare decisis* rule which is an essential part of our law, be of the rarest occurrence." Rupert Cross & J.W. Harris, *Precedent in English Law* 149 (4th ed. 1991).

per infortunium (pər in-for-**t[y]oo**-nee-əm), *adj. or adv.* [Latin] By misadventure. • At common law, when one person killed another *per infortunium*, a conviction and royal pardon were necessary even when there was no fault. See *homicide per infortunium* under HOMICIDE.

> "It may seem strange to modern minds that for centuries it was a rule of our law that a man who killed another either by misadventure (*per infortunium*) or in reasonable self-defence (against an attack not itself felonious), although he did not commit a felony, must yet be held guilty of unlawful homicide and require the King's pardon if he were to escape punishment, and even if granted pardon would still be liable to suffer forfeiture of his property; and that he was exposed to claims for compensation from the family of the deceased." J.W. Cecil Turner, *Kenny's Outlines of Criminal Law* 113 (16th ed. 1952).

periodic alimony. See *permanent alimony* under ALIMONY.

periodic estate. See ESTATE.

periodic-payment-plan certificate. See CERTIFICATE.

periodic tenancy. See TENANCY.

peripheral right. See RIGHT.

periphrasis (pə-**rif**-rə-sis), *n.* A roundabout way of writing or speaking; circumlocution. — **periphrastic** (per-ə-**fras**-tik), *adj.*

perjury (**pər**-jər-ee), *n.* The act or an instance of a person's deliberately making material false or misleading statements while under oath. — Also termed *false swearing*; *false oath*; (archaically) *forswearing*. — **perjure** (**pər**-jər), *vb.* — **perjured** (**pər**-jərd), **perjurious** (pər-**juur**-ee-əs), *adj.* — **perjuror** (**pər**-jər-ər), *n.*

perjury-trap doctrine. The principle that a perjury indictment against a person must be dismissed if the prosecution secures it by calling that person as a grand-jury witness in an effort to obtain evidence for a perjury charge, esp. when the person's testimony does not relate to issues material to the ongoing grand-jury investigation.

perk, *n.* See PERQUISITE.

per legem terrae (pər **lee**-jəm **ter**-ee). [Law Latin] By the law of the land; by due process of law.

permanent abode. See DOMICILE (1).

permanent alimony. See ALIMONY.

permanent allegiance. See ALLEGIANCE.

permanent chargé d'affaires. See CHARGÉ D'AFFAIRES.

permanent committee. See *standing committee* under COMMITTEE.

permanent disability. See DISABILITY (1).

permanent employment. See EMPLOYMENT.

permanent financing. See FINANCING.

permanent fixture. See FIXTURE.

permanent injunction. See INJUNCTION.

permanent injury. See INJURY.

permanent law. See LAW.

permanent nuisance. See NUISANCE.

permanent trespass. See TRESPASS.

permanent ward. See WARD.

per metas et bundas (pər **mee**-təs et **bən**-dəs). [Law Latin] By metes and bounds.

per minas. See *duress per minas* under DURESS.

permissible appointee. See APPOINTEE.

permission. 1. The act of permitting. **2.** A license or liberty to do something; authorization.

permissive abstention. See ABSTENTION.

permissive counterclaim. See COUNTERCLAIM.

permissive inference. See *permissive presumption* under PRESUMPTION.

permissive joinder. See JOINDER.

permissive presumption. See PRESUMPTION.

permissive subject of bargaining. *Labor law.* An employment or collective-bargaining issue, other than a basic employment issue, that is not required to be the subject of collective bargaining but that cannot be implemented by management without union approval. • For example, altering the scope of the bargaining unit does not affect a term or condition of employment, so it is a permissive, instead of mandatory, subject of bargaining. Disagreement on a permissive subject of bargaining cannot be used as the basis for an impasse in negotiating a collective-bargaining agreement, unlike a mandatory subject of bargaining. — Often shortened to *permissive subject.* Cf. MANDATORY SUBJECT.

permissive use. See USE (4).

permissive waste. See WASTE (1).

permit (**pər**-mit), *n.* A certificate evidencing permission; a license <a gun permit>.

permit (pər-**mit**), *vb.* **1.** To consent to formally <permit the inspection to be carried out>. **2.** To give opportunity for <lax security permitted the escape>. **3.** To allow or admit of <if the law so permits>.

permit bond. See *license bond* under BOND (2).

permit card. *Labor law.* A document issued by a union to a nonunion member to allow the person to work on a job covered by a union contract.

per mitter le droit (pər **mit**-ər lə **droyt**). [Law French] *Hist.* By passing the right. • This described how releases became effective, as when a person disseised of land released the estate to the disseisor, at which time the right and possession combined to give the disseisor the entire estate.

per mitter l'estate (pər **mit**-ər lə-**stayt**). [Law French] *Hist.* By passing the estate. • This described the manner in which a joint tenant's right to an entire estate arose when the tenant received the remaining estate from the other joint tenant.

permutatio (pər-myoo-**tay**-shee-oh), *n.* [Latin] *Roman law.* An agreement for barter or exchange.

per my et per tout (pər **mee** ay pər **too[t]**). [Law French] By the half and by the whole. • This phrase described the estate held by joint tenants: *by the half* for purposes of survivorship, *by the whole* for purposes of alienation. Cf. PER TOUT ET NON PER MY.

pernancy (**pər**-nən-see). *Hist.* A taking or reception, as of the profits of an estate.

pernor of profits (**pər**-nər *or* -nor). *Hist.* A person who receives the profits of property; one who has the pernancy of the profits.

perp (pərp), *n. Slang.* Perpetrator <the police brought in the perp for questioning>. See PERPETRATOR.

perpars (**pər**-pahrz). [Law Latin, fr. Latin *per partes* "by parts"] See PURPART.

perpetrate, *vb.* To commit or carry out (an act, esp. a crime) <find whoever perpetrated this heinous deed>. — **perpetration,** *n.*

perpetrator. A person who commits a crime or offense.

perpetua (pər-**pech**-oo-ə). See *exceptio peremptoria* under EXCEPTIO.

perpetual bond. See *annuity bond* under BOND (3).

perpetual edict. See EDICT.

perpetual freehold. See FREEHOLD.

perpetual injunction. See *permanent injunction* under INJUNCTION.

perpetual lease. See LEASE.

perpetual statute. See STATUTE.

perpetual succession. See SUCCESSION (4).

perpetual trust. See TRUST.

perpetuating testimony. The means or procedure for preserving for future use witness testimony that might otherwise be unavailable at trial.

perpetuities, rule against. See RULE AGAINST PERPETUITIES.

perpetuity (pər-pə-**t[y]oo**-ə-tee). **1.** The state of continuing forever. **2.** *Hist.* An unbarrable entail. **3.** *Hist.* An inalienable interest. **4.** An interest that does not take effect or vest within the period prescribed by law. • In reference to the rule against perpetuities, only sense 4 is now current. See RULE AGAINST PERPETUITIES.

> "A perpetuity is a thing odious in law, and destructive of the Commonwealth; it would put a stop to commerce and prevent the circulation of the riches of the Kingdom, and therefore is not to be countenanced in equity. If in equity you could come nearer to a perpetuity than the rules of Common Law would admit, all men being desirous to continue their estates in their families, would settle their estates by way of trust; which might indeed make well for the jurisdiction of the court, but would be destructive of the commonwealth." (1683) 1 Vern. 163 (per Lord North) (as quoted in George W. Keeton, *English Law: The Judicial Contribution* 118 (1974)).

perpetuity of the king *or* **queen.** A fiction of English law that for political purposes the king or queen is immortal; that is, a monarch dies, but the office is never vacant.

per procurationem (pər prok-yə-ray-shee-**oh**-nəm). [Latin] By proxy. — Abbr. *per pro.*; *p. proc.*; *p. pro.*; *p.p.* — Also termed *per procuration.*

per quae servitia (pər **kwee** sər-**vish**-ee-ə). [Latin "by which services"] *Hist.* A real action by which the grantee of a landed estate could compel the tenants of the grantor to attorn to him. • This action was abolished in the 19th century.

perquisite (**pər**-kwi-zit). A privilege or benefit given in addition to one's salary or regular wages. — Often shortened to *perk*.

perquisitor (pər-**kwiz**-ə-tər). [Latin "a seeker out"] *Hist.* A purchaser; esp., one who first acquires an estate by sale or gift.

per quod (pər **kwod**), *adv.* & *adj.* [Latin "whereby"] Requiring reference to additional facts; (of libel or slander) actionable only on allegation and proof of special damages. See *libel per quod* under LIBEL; *slander per quod* under SLANDER.

per quod consortium amisit (pər **kwod** kən-**sor**-shee-əm ə-**mI**-zit). [Law Latin] *Hist.* Whereby he lost the company (of his wife). • This phrase was used in a trespass declaration to describe the loss suffered by a husband whose wife had been beaten or otherwise abused.

per quod servitium amisit (pər **kwod** sər-**vish**-ee-əm ə-**mI**-zit). [Law Latin] *Hist.* Whereby he lost the services (of his servant). • This phrase was used in a trespass declaration to describe the loss suffered by a master whose servant had been injured by another.

per se (pər **say**), *adv.* & *adj.* [Latin] **1.** Of, in, or by itself; standing alone, without reference to additional facts. See *libel per se* under LIBEL. **2.** As a matter of law.

persecutio (pər-sə-**kyoo**-shee-oh), *n.* [Latin] *Roman law.* A lawsuit or civil claim.

per se deadly weapon. See *deadly weapon per se* under WEAPON.

persequi (**pər**-sə-kwI), *vb.* [Latin] *Roman law.* To claim through a judicial proceeding.

per se rule. *Antitrust.* The judicial principle that a trade practice violates the Sherman Act simply if the practice is a restraint of trade, regardless of whether it actually harms anyone. See SHERMAN ANTITRUST ACT. Cf. RULE OF REASON.

per se violation. *Antitrust.* A trade practice (such as price-fixing) that is considered inherently anticompetitive and injurious to the public without any need to determine whether it has actually injured market competition.

persistent price discrimination. See PRICE DISCRIMINATION.

person. 1. A human being. **2.** An entity (such as a corporation) that is recognized by law as having the rights and duties of a human being. **3.** The living body of a human being <contraband found on the smuggler's person>.

> "So far as legal theory is concerned, a person is any being whom the law regards as capable of rights and duties. Any being that is so capable is a person, whether a human being or not, and no being that is not so capable is a person, even though he be a man. Persons are the substances of which rights and duties are the attributes. It is only in this respect that persons possess juridical significance, and this is the exclusive point of view from which personality receives legal recognition." John Salmond, *Jurisprudence* 318 (Glanville L. Williams ed., 10th ed. 1947).

artificial person. An entity, such as a corporation, created by law and given certain legal rights and duties of a human being; a being, real or imaginary, who for the purpose of legal reasoning is treated more or less as a human being. — Also termed *fictitious person*; *juristic person*; *legal person*; *moral person*.

disabled person. A person who has a disability. See DISABILITY.

fictitious person. See *artificial person*.

interested person. A person having a property right in or claim against a thing, such as a trust or decedent's estate.

juristic person. See *artificial person*.

legal person. See *artificial person*.

moral person. See *artificial person*.

natural person. A human being, as distinguished from an artificial person created by law.

person in loco parentis (in **loh**-koh pə-**ren**-tis). A person acting in the place of a parent; a person who has assumed the obligations of a parent without formally adopting the child.

person of incidence. The person against whom a right is enforceable; a person who owes a legal duty.

person of inherence (in-**heer**-ənts). The person in whom a legal right is vested; the owner of a right.

private person. **1.** A person who does not hold public office or serve in the military. **2.** *Civil law.* An entity such as a corporation or partnership that is governed by private law.

protected person. **1.** A person for whom a conservator has been appointed or other protective order has been made. **2.** *Int'l law.* A person who is protected by a rule of international law; esp., one who is in the hands of an occupying force during a conflict. • Protected persons are entitled to a standard of treatment (including a prohibition on coercion and corporal punishment) by the Geneva Convention Relative to the Protection of Civilian Persons in Time of War (1949). **3.** *English law.* An inhabitant of a protectorate of the United Kingdom. • Though not a British subject, such a person is given diplomatic protection by the Crown.

persona (pər-**soh**-nə), *n.* [Latin] *Roman law.* A person; an individual human being.

personable, *adj.* Having the status of a legal person (and thus the right to plead in court, enter into contracts, etc.) <a personable entity>.

persona designata (pər-**soh**-nə dez-ig-**nay**-tə). [Latin] A person considered as an individual (esp. in a legal action) rather than as a member of a class.

persona ficta (pər-**soh**-nə **fik**-tə). [Latin "false mask"] *Hist.* A fictional person, such as a corporation.

> "But units other than individual men can be thought of as capable of acts, or of rights and liabilities: such are Corporations and even *Hereditates Iacentes*. Accordingly the way is clear to apply the name of person to these also. The mediaeval lawyers did so, but as they regarded Corporations as endowed with personality by a sort of creative act of the State, and received from the Roman lawyers the conception of the *hereditas iacens* as representing the *persona* of the deceased rather than as itself being a person, they called these things *Personae Fictae*, an expression not used by the Romans." W.W. Buckland, *Elementary Principles of the Roman Private Law* 16 (1912).

person aggrieved. See *aggrieved party* under PARTY (2).

persona grata (pər-**soh**-nə **gray**-tə *or* **grah**-tə *or* **grat**-ə), *n.* [Latin] An acceptable person; esp., a diplomat who is acceptable to a host country. Pl. **personae gratae** (pər-**soh**-nee **gray**-tee *or* **grah**-tee *or* **grat**-ee). Cf. PERSONA NON GRATA.

personal, *adj.* **1.** Of or affecting a person <personal injury>. **2.** Of or constituting personal property <personal belongings>. See IN PERSONAM.

personal action. See ACTION.

personal asset. See ASSET.

personal bond. See BOND (2).

personal chattel. See CHATTEL.

personal check. See CHECK.

personal defense. See DEFENSE (4).

personal demand. See DEMAND (2).

personal effects. Items of a personal character; esp., personal property owned by a decedent at the time of death.

personal estate. See *personal property* under PROPERTY.

personal evidence. See TESTIMONY.

personal exemption. See EXEMPTION.

personal holding company. See COMPANY.

personal-holding-company tax. See *holding-company tax* under TAX.

personal income. See INCOME.

personal injury. See INJURY.

personalis actio (pər-sə-**nay**-lis **ak**-shee-oh). [Latin] *Hist.* A personal action; an action *in personam*.

personaliter (pər-sə-**nay**-lə-tər), *adv.* [Latin] Personally; in person.

personality. The legal status of one regarded by the law as a person; the legal conception by which the law regards a human being or an artificial entity as a person. — Also termed *legal personality.*

> "Legal personality . . . refers to the particular device by which the law creates or recognizes units to which it ascribes certain powers and capacities." George Whitecross Paton, *A Textbook of Jurisprudence* 393 (G.W. Paton & David P. Derham eds., 4th ed. 1972).

personal judgment. See JUDGMENT.

personal jurisdiction. See JURISDICTION.

personal justice. See JUSTICE (1).

personal knowledge. See KNOWLEDGE.

personal law. The law that governs a person's family matters, usu. regardless of where the person goes. • In common-law systems, personal law refers to the law of the person's domicile. In civil-law systems, it refers to the law of the individual's nationality (and so is sometimes called *lex patriae*). Cf. TERRITORIAL LAW.

> "The idea of the personal law is based on the conception of man as a social being, so that those transactions of his daily life which affect him most closely in a personal sense, such as marriage, divorce, legitimacy, many kinds of capacity, and succession, may be governed universally by that system of law deemed most suitable and adequate for the purpose .... [A]lthough the law of the domicile is the chief criterion adopted by English courts for the personal law, it lies within the power of any man of full age and capacity to establish his domicile in any country he chooses, and thereby automatically to make the law of that country his personal law." R.H. Graveson, *Conflict of Laws* 188 (7th ed. 1974).

personal liability. See LIABILITY.

personal liberty. See LIBERTY.

personal notice. See NOTICE.

personal property. See PROPERTY.

personal-property tax. See TAX.

personal recognizance. See RECOGNIZANCE.

personal replevin. See REPLEVIN.

personal representative. See REPRESENTATIVE.

personal right. See RIGHT.

personal security. See SECURITY.

personal service. 1. Actual delivery of the notice or process to the person to whom it is directed. — Also termed *actual service*. **2.** An act done personally by an individual. • In this sense, a personal service is an economic service involving either the intellectual or manual personal effort of an individual, as opposed to the salable product of the person's skill.

personal servitude. See SERVITUDE (1).

personal statute. See STATUTE.

personal suretyship. See SURETYSHIP.

personal tort. See TORT.

personal trust. See *private trust* under TRUST.

personalty (**pərs**-ən-əl-tee). Personal property as distinguished from real property. See *personal property* (1) under PROPERTY.

quasi-personalty. Things that are considered movable by the law, though fixed to real property either actually (as with a fixture) or fictitiously (as with a lease for years).

personal warranty. See WARRANTY (2).

personam. See IN PERSONAM.

persona non grata (pər-**sohn**-ə non **grah**-də), *n.* [Latin] An unwanted person; esp., a diplomat who is not acceptable to a host country. Pl. **personae non gratae.** Cf. PERSONA GRATA.

persona standi in judicio (pər-**soh**-nə **stan**-dɪ in joo-**dish**-ee-oh). [Law Latin] Capacity of standing in judgment; the right to appear in court.

personation. See IMPERSONATION.

person-endangering state of mind. An intent to kill, inflict great bodily injury, act in wanton disregard of an unreasonable risk, or perpetrate a dangerous felony. — Also termed *man-endangering state of mind*.

person in loco parentis. See PERSON.

person of incidence. See PERSON.

person of inherence. See PERSON.

person of opposite sex sharing living quarters. See POSSLQ.

per stirpes (pər **stər**-peez), *adv.* & *adj.* [Latin "by roots or stocks"] Proportionally divided between beneficiaries according to their deceased ancestor's share. — Also termed *in stirpes*. Cf. PER CAPITA.

persuade, *vb.* To induce (another) to do something <Steve persuaded his neighbor to sign the release after the accident>.

persuasion. The act of influencing or attempting to influence others by reasoned argument; the act of persuading.

persuasion burden. See BURDEN OF PERSUASION.

persuasive authority. See AUTHORITY (4).

persuasive precedent. See PRECEDENT.

pertain, *vb.* To relate to; to concern.

pertinent, *adj.* Pertaining to the issue at hand; relevant <pertinent testimony>.

pertinent art. See *analogous art* under ART.

per totam curiam (pər **toh**-təm **kyoor**-ee-əm). [Law Latin] By the whole court.

per tout et non per my (pər **too**[**t**] ay **non** pər **mee**). [Law French] By the whole and not by the half. • This phrase described the estate given to a husband and wife — both are seised of the entire estate. Cf. PER MY ET PER TOUT.

perturbator (**pər**-tər-bay-tər). [Law Latin] *Hist.* A man who disturbs the peace.

perturbatrix (pər-tər-**bay**-triks), *n.* [Law Latin] *Hist.* A woman who disturbs the peace.

per universitatem (pər yoo-nə-vər-sə-**tay**-təm). [Latin] *Civil law.* By an aggregate or whole; as an entirety. • This term describes the acquisition of an entire estate, esp. of an entire inheritance by universal succession.

perverse verdict. See VERDICT.

per vivam vocem (pər **vI**-vəm **voh**-səm). [Law Latin] By the living voice.

petens (**pet**-enz). [Latin] *Hist.* A demandant; a plaintiff in a real action.

peter-pence. *Hist.* A tax levied on each house in England and paid to the Pope, so called because it was collected on St. Peter's Day. — Also termed *hearth money.*

petit (**pet**-ee *or* **pet**-it), *adj.* [Law French "minor, small"] See PETTY.

petit cape. See *cape parvum* under CAPE.

petite assize. See ASSIZE (5).

***Petite* policy.** The Department of Justice rule forbidding a federal prosecution after a previous state or federal prosecution based on the same acts unless (1) the prosecution has been approved by the Assistant Attorney General, (2) there is a substantial federal interest supporting the prosecution, (3) the previous prosecution failed to vindicate the federal interest, and (4) there is sufficient evidence to sustain a conviction. *Petite v. United States*, 361 U.S. 529, 80 S.Ct. 450 (1960).

> "('Petite Policy') .... The purpose of this policy is to vindicate substantial federal interests through appropriate federal prosecutions, to protect persons charged with criminal conduct from the burdens associated with multiple prosecutions and punishments for substantially the same act(s) or transaction(s), to promote efficient utilization of Department resources, and to promote coordination and cooperation between federal and state prosecutors." *United States Attorneys' Manual* § 9–2.031 (Sept. 1997).

> "In response to the Court's continuing sensitivity to the fairness implications of the multiple prosecution power, the Justice Department adopted the policy of refusing to bring a federal prosecution following a state prosecution except when necessary to advance compelling interests of federal law enforcement. The *Petite* policy was designed to limit the exercise of the power to bring successive prosecutions for the same offense to situations comporting with the rationale for the existence of that power. Although not constitutionally mandated, this Executive policy serves to protect interests which, but for the 'dual sovereignty' principle inherent in our federal system, would be embraced by the Double Jeopardy Clause. In light of the parallel purposes of the Government's *Petite* policy and the fundamental constitutional guarantee against double jeopardy, the federal courts should be receptive, not circumspect, when the Government seeks leave to implement that policy." *Rinaldi v. United States*, 434 U.S. 22, 28–29, 98 S.Ct. 81, 85 (1977) (citation omitted).

petitio (pə-**tish**-ee-oh), *n.* [Latin] **1.** *Civil law.* A plaintiff's suit, esp. in an action in rem. **2.** *Hist.* A petition or demand; esp., a count in a real action.

petition, *n.* **1.** A formal written request presented to a court or other official body.

> ***involuntary petition.*** A petition filed in a bankruptcy court by a creditor seeking to declare a debtor bankrupt. • This type of petition may be filed only under Chapter 7 or Chapter 11 of the Bankruptcy Code.

> ***juvenile petition.*** A petition filed in a juvenile court, alleging delinquent conduct by the accused. • The accusations made in a juvenile petition are tried in an adjudicatory hearing. See *adjudicatory hearing* under HEARING.

> ***voluntary petition.*** A petition filed with a bankruptcy court by a debtor seeking protection from creditors.

2. In some states, a lawsuit's first pleading; COMPLAINT. — **petition,** *vb.*

petition de droit. See PETITION OF RIGHT.

petitioner. A party who presents a petition to a court or other official body, esp. when seeking relief on appeal. Cf. RESPONDENT (2).

petition in bankruptcy. A formal written request, presented to a bankruptcy court, seeking protection for an insolvent debtor. • The debtor (in a voluntary bankruptcy) or the debtor's creditors (in an involuntary bankruptcy) can file such a petition to initiate a bankruptcy proceeding.

petition of right. 1. (*cap.*) One of the four great charters of English liberty (3 Car. (1628)), establishing that "no man be compelled to make or yield any gift, loan, benevolence, tax, or such like charge, without common consent by act of parliament." • The other three great charters are Magna Carta, the Habeas Corpus Act (31 Car. 2 (1679)), and the Bill of Rights (1 W. & M. (1689)). **2.** *Hist.* A proceeding in chancery by which a subject claims that a debt is owed by the Crown or that the Crown has broken a contract or wrongfully detained the subject's property. • Although the petition is addressed directly to the Crown, the courts adjudicate the claim just as in an action between private parties. — Also termed *petition de droit.*

petit juror. See JUROR.

petit jury. See JURY.

petit larceny. See LARCENY.

petitor (**pet**-ə-tər), *n.* [Latin] *Roman law.* A plaintiff in a civil action.

petitorium (pet-ə-**tor**-ee-əm). See *petitory action* under ACTION.

petitory action. See ACTION.

petit serjeanty. See SERJEANTY.

pettifogger (**pet**-i-fog-ər), *n.* **1.** A lawyer lacking in education, ability, sound judgment, or common sense. **2.** A lawyer who clouds an issue with insignificant details. — **pettifoggery** (pet-i-**fog**-ər-ee), *n.*

petty, *adj.* Relatively insignificant or minor <a petty crime>. Cf. GRAND.

petty assize. See ASSIZE (6).

petty cash. See CASH.

petty jury. See *petit jury* under JURY.

petty larceny. See *petit larceny* under LARCENY.

petty offense. See OFFENSE (1).

petty officer. See OFFICER (2).

petty sessions. *Hist. English law.* Sessions of justice-of-the-peace court held to try minor misdemeanors summarily (i.e., without a jury).

petty treason. See TREASON.

p.fat. *abbr.* PRAEFATUS.

phantom jury. See *shadow jury* under JURY.

phantom stock. See STOCK.

phantom stock plan. A long-term benefit plan under which a corporate employee is given units having the same characteristics as the employer's stock shares. • It is termed a "phantom" plan because the employee doesn't actually hold any shares but instead holds the right to the value of those shares. — Also termed *shadow stock plan.*

Philadelphia lawyer. A shrewd and learned lawyer. • This term can have positive or negative connotations today, but when it first appeared (in colonial times), it carried only a positive sense deriving from Philadelphia's position as America's center of learning and culture.

philosophie du droit. See *ethical jurisprudence* under JURISPRUDENCE.

philosophy of law. See *general jurisprudence* (2) under JURISPRUDENCE.

phonorecord (**foh**-noh-rek-ərd). A physical object (such as a phonographic record, cassette tape, or compact disc) from which fixed sounds can be perceived, reproduced, or otherwise communicated directly or with a machine's aid. • The term is fairly common in copyright contexts since it is defined in the U.S. Copyright Act of 1976 (17 USCA § 101).

p.h.v. *abbr.* PRO HAC VICE.

phylacist (**fɪ**-lə-sist), *n. Archaic.* A jailer. — Also spelled *phylasist.*

physical cruelty. See CRUELTY.

physical custody. See CUSTODY (1), (2).

physical diagnosis. See DIAGNOSIS.

physical disability. See DISABILITY (1).

physical fact. See FACT.

physical-facts rule. *Evidence.* The principle that oral testimony may be disregarded when it is inconsistent or irreconcilable with the physical evidence in the case. — Also termed *doctrine of incontrovertible physical facts*; *incontrovertible-physical-facts doctrine.*

physical force. See *actual force* under FORCE.

physical harm. See HARM.

physical-impact rule. See IMPACT RULE.

physical impossibility. See *factual impossibility* under IMPOSSIBILITY.

physical incapacity. See IMPOTENCE.

physical injury. See *bodily injury* under INJURY.

physical-inventory accounting method. See ACCOUNTING METHOD.

physical necessity. See NECESSITY.

physical-proximity test. *Criminal law.* A common-law test for the crime of attempt, focusing on how much more the defendant would have needed to do to complete the offense. See ATTEMPT (2).

physical shock. See SHOCK.

physician-client privilege. See *doctor-patient privilege* under PRIVILEGE (3).

physician's directive. See ADVANCE DIRECTIVE.

P.I. *abbr.* **1.** Personal injury. **2.** Private investigator.

piacle (**pɪ**-ə-kəl), *n. Archaic.* A serious crime.

pia fraus (**pɪ**-ə **fraws**). [Latin "pious fraud"] A subterfuge or evasion considered morally justifiable; esp., evasion or disregard of the law in the interests of a religious institution, such as the church's circumventing the mortmain statutes.

picaroon (pik-ə-**roon**). A robber or plunderer.

picketing. The demonstration by one or more persons outside a business or organization to protest the entity's activities or policies and to pressure the entity to meet the protesters' demands; esp., an employees' demonstration aimed at publicizing a labor dispute and influencing the public to withhold business from the employer. Cf. BOYCOTT; STRIKE.

common-situs picketing. The illegal picketing by union workers of a construction site, stemming from a dispute with one of the subcontractors.

informational picketing. Picketing to inform the public about a matter of concern to the union.

organizational picketing. Picketing by a union in an effort to persuade the employer to accept the union as the collective-bargaining agent of the employees; esp., picketing by members of one union when the employer has already recognized another union as the bargaining agent for the company's employees.

secondary picketing. The picketing of an establishment with which the picketing party has no direct dispute in order to pressure the party with which there is a dispute. See *secondary boycott* under BOYCOTT; *secondary strike* under STRIKE.

unlawful picketing. Picketing carried on in violation of law, as when the picketers use threats or violence to dissuade other employees from returning to work.

pickpocket. A thief who steals money or property from the person of another, usu. by stealth but sometimes by physical diversion such as bumping into or pushing the victim.

piecemeal zoning. See *partial zoning* under ZONING.

piecework. Work done or paid for by the piece or job.

piepowder court (**pɪ**-pow-dər). *Hist.* In medieval England, a court having jurisdiction over a fair or market and presided over by the organizer's steward. • The name is a corruption of two French words (*pied* and *poudre*) meaning "dusty feet." — Also termed *court of piepowder*. — Also spelled *piepoudre*; *piedpoudre*; *pipowder*; *py-powder*.

piercing the corporate veil. The judicial act of imposing personal liability on otherwise immune corporate officers, directors, and shareholders for the corporation's wrongful acts. — Also termed *disregarding the corporate entity*. See CORPORATE VEIL.

pignorate (**pig**-nə-rayt), *vb.* **1.** To give over as a pledge; to pawn. **2.** To take in pawn. — **pignorative,** *adj*. Cf. OPPIGNORATE.

pignoratio (pig-nə-**ray**-shee-oh), *n.* [Latin] **1.** *Roman law.* The act of handing something over to a creditor as security; the act of depositing as a pledge. **2.** *Civil law.* The impounding of another's cattle that have damaged property until the cattle's owner pays for the damage.

pignoratitia actio (pig-nə-rə-**tish**-ee-ə **ak**-shee-oh). [Latin] *Roman law.* An action founded on a pledge, either by the debtor (an action *directa*) or by a creditor (an action *contraria*). Cf. *cautio pignoratitia* under CAUTIO.

pignorative contract. See CONTRACT.

pignoris capio (**pig**-nə-ris **kap**-ee-oh). [Latin "taking a pledge"] *Roman law.* A form of extrajudicial execution by which a creditor took a pledge from a debtor's property.

pignus (**pig**-nəs), *n.* [Latin "pledge"] A bailment in which goods are delivered to secure the payment of a debt or performance of an engagement, accompanied by a power of sale in case of default. • This type of bailment is for the benefit of both parties. — Also termed *pawn*; *pledge*.

pignus judiciale (**pig**-nəs joo-dish-ee-**ay**-lee). [Latin] *Civil law.* The lien that a judgment creditor has on the property of the judgment debtor.

pignus legale (**pig**-nəs lə-**gay**-lee). [Latin] *Civil law.* A lien arising by operation of law, such as a landlord's lien on the tenant's property.

pilferage (**pil**-fər-ij), *n.* **1.** The act or an instance of stealing. **2.** The items stolen. — **pilfer** (**pil**-fər), *vb.* See LARCENY; THEFT.

pillage (**pil**-ij), *n.* **1.** The forcible seizure of another's property, esp. in war; esp., the wartime plundering of a city or territory. **2.** The property so seized or plundered; BOOTY. — **pillage,** *vb.* — Also termed *plunder*.

pillory (**pil**-ə-ree), *n. Hist.* A wooden framework with holes through which an offender's head and hands are placed. • A person put in a pillory usu. had to stand rather than sit (as with the stocks). Cf. STOCKS.

pilot. See COMPULSORY PILOT; VOLUNTARY PILOT.

pilotage (**pɪ**-lə-tij). **1.** The navigating of vessels; the business of navigating vessels. **2.** Compensation that a pilot receives for navigating a vessel, esp. into and out of harbor or through a channel or passage.

compulsory pilotage. A requirement, imposed by law in some jurisdictions, that vessels approaching or leaving a harbor must take on a licensed pilot to guide the vessel into or out of the harbor.

half-pilotage. Compensation equaling half the value of services that a pilot has offered to perform. • Shipowners can avoid compulsory pilotage in some jurisdictions by payment of half-pilotage.

pimp, *n.* A person who solicits customers for a prostitute, usu. in return for a share of the prostitute's earnings. — **pimp,** *vb.* See PANDERING (1). Cf. BAWD.

pincite. See *pinpoint citation* under CITATION.

Pinkerton **rule.** *Criminal law.* The doctrine imposing liability on a conspirator for all offenses committed in furtherance of the conspiracy, even if those offenses are actually performed by coconspirators. *Pinkerton v. United States*, 328 U.S. 640, 66 S.Ct. 1180 (1946).

pink sheet. A daily publication listing over-the-counter stocks, their market-makers, and their prices. • Printed on pink paper, pink sheets are published by the National Quotation Bureau, a private company. — Also termed *National Daily Quotation Service*.

pink slip. *Slang.* A notice of employment termination given to an employee by an employer.

pinpoint citation. See CITATION.

pioneer drug. See DRUG.

pioneer patent. See *basic patent* under PATENT (3).

Pipe Rolls. *Hist.* The Exchequer's records of royal revenue, including revenue from feudal holdings, judicial fees, and tax revenue collected by the sheriffs. • The Pipe Rolls comprise 676 rolls, covering the years 1131 and 1156 to 1833 (except for gaps in 1216 and 1403). — Also termed *Great Rolls of the Exchequer.*

> "The Pipe rolls (so called possibly because of their pipe-like appearance when rolled up and stacked) were the rolls of the Exchequer and consist of parchment skins sewn together. Roger of Salisbury, Henry I's Treasurer, had established a rudimentary national financial system and the Pipe roll recording financial details at the end of Henry's reign is in existence .... The rolls contain much information concerning royal debtors, administration, and personnel of the King's government." L.B. Curzon, *English Legal History* 64–65 (2d ed. 1979).

piracy, *n.* **1.** Robbery, kidnapping, or other criminal violence committed at sea. **2.** A similar crime committed aboard a plane or other vehicle; hijacking.

air piracy. The crime of using force or threat to seize control of an aircraft; the hijacking of an aircraft, esp. one in flight. — Also termed *aircraft piracy.*

3. The unauthorized and illegal reproduction or distribution of materials protected by copyright, patent, or trademark law. See INFRINGEMENT. — **pirate,** *vb.* — **piratical** (pI-**rat**-ə-kəl), *adj.* — **pirate,** *n.*

> "[T]he test of piracy [is] not whether the identical language, the same words, are used, but whether the substance of the production is unlawfully appropriated." Eaton S. Drone, *A Treatise on the Law of Property in Intellectual Productions* 97 (1879).

piscary. 1. See FISHERY. **2.** See *common of piscary* under COMMON (1).

PITI. *abbr.* Principal, interest, taxes, and insurance — the components of a monthly mortgage payment.

P.J. See *presiding judge* under JUDGE.

PKPA. *abbr.* PARENTAL KIDNAPPING PREVENTION ACT.

pl. *abbr.* PLACITUM (8).

P.L. *abbr.* PUBLIC LAW.

placard (**plak**-ahrd *or* **plak**-ərd). **1.** *Hist.* An official document, such as a license or permit. **2.** An advertisement posted in a public place.

place land. See LAND.

placement. 1. The act of selling a new issue of securities or arranging a loan or mortgage. **2.** The act of finding employment for a person, esp. as done by an employment agency.

place of abode. A person's residence or domicile. See RESIDENCE; DOMICILE.

place of business. A location at which one carries on a business. Cf. DOMICILE (2).

place of contracting. The country or state in which a contract is entered into.

place of delivery. The place where goods sold are to be sent by the seller. • If no place is specified in the contract, the seller's place of business is usu. the place of delivery. UCC § 2–308.

place of employment. The location at which work done in connection with a business is carried out; the place where some process or operation related to the business is conducted.

place-of-wrong law. See LEX LOCI DELICTI.

place-of-wrong rule. See LEX LOCI DELICTI.

placer claim. See MINING CLAIM.

placita (**plas**-ə-tə), *n.* [Latin] *pl.* PLACITUM.

placitabile (plas-ə-**tay**-bə-lee), *adj.* [Law Latin] That may be pleaded; pleadable.

placita communia (**plas**-ə-tə kə-**myoo**-nee-ə). [Latin] Common pleas; civil actions between subject and subject.

placita coronae (**plas**-ə-tə kə-**roh**-nee). [Latin] Pleas of the Crown; criminal actions.

placita juris (**plas**-ə-tə **joor**-is). [Law Latin "pleas of law"] *Hist.* Positive statements or guiding principles of the law, in contrast to legal conclusions or maxims.

placitare (plas-ə-**tair**-ee), *vb.* [Law Latin] To plead; to bring an action in a court of law.

placitory (**plas**-ə-tor-ee), *adj.* [Law Latin] Of or relating to pleas or pleading.

placitum (**plas**-ə-təm), *n.* [Latin] *Hist.* **1.** *Roman law.* An agreement between parties. **2.** *Roman law.* An imperial constitution. **3.** A judicial decision. **4.** A court; a judicial tribunal. **5.** A judicial proceeding; a trial. **6.** A fine, mulct, or pecuniary punishment. **7.** A pleading or plea. **8.** A paragraph or section of a title or page where the point decided in a case is set forth separately. — Abbr. (in sense 8) pl. Pl. ***placita.***

placitum fractum (**plas**-ə-təm **frak**-təm). [Law Latin] *Hist.* A day past or lost to the defendant.

placitum nominatum (**plas**-ə-təm nom-ə-**nay**-təm). [Law Latin] *Hist.* The day appointed for a defendant to appear and plead.

plagiarism (**play**-jə-riz-əm), *n.* The act or an instance of copying or stealing another's words or ideas and attributing them as one's own. — **plagiarize** (**play**-jə-rɪz), *vb.* — **plagiarist** (**play**-jə-rist), *n.* Cf. INFRINGEMENT.

> "Plagiarism, which many people commonly think has to do with copyright, is not in fact a legal doctrine. True plagiarism is an ethical, not a legal, offense and is enforceable by academic authorities, not courts. Plagiarism occurs when someone — a hurried student, a neglectful professor, an unscrupulous writer — falsely claims someone else's words, whether copyrighted or not, as his own. Of course, if the plagiarized work is protected by copyright, the unauthorized reproduction is also a copyright infringement." Paul Goldstein, *Copyright's Highway* 12 (1994).

> "That the supporting evidence for the accusation of plagiarism may on occasion be elusive, insufficient, or uncertain, is not the same as thinking that the definition of plagiarism is uncertain. The gray areas may remain resistant to adjudication without being resistant to definition. It may be perfectly clear what constitutes plagiarism ('using the work of another *with an intent to deceive*') without its being clear that what faces us is truly a case of this." Christopher Ricks, "Plagiarism," 97 *Proceedings of the British Academy* 149, 151 (1998).

plagiarius (play-jee-**air**-ee-əs), *n.* [Latin] *Roman law.* A kidnapper.

plagium (**play**-jee-əm), *n.* [Latin] *Roman law.* The act of kidnapping, which included harboring another's slave.

plaideur (play- *or* ple-**dər**), *n.* [Law French "pleader"] *Archaic.* An attorney at law; an advocate.

plaidoyer (ple-dwah-**yay**), *n.* [French] *Hist.* An advocate's plea.

plain bond. See DEBENTURE.

plain error. See ERROR (2).

plain-feel doctrine. *Criminal procedure.* The principle that a police officer, while conducting a legal pat-down search, may seize any contraband that the officer can clearly identify, by touch, as being illegal or incriminating. — Also termed *plain-touch doctrine.*

plain-language law. Legislation requiring nontechnical, readily comprehensible language in consumer contracts such as residential leases or insurance policies. • Many of these laws have genuinely simplified the needlessly obscure language in which consumer contracts have traditionally been couched.

plain-language movement. **1.** The loosely organized campaign to encourage legal writers and business writers to write clearly and concisely — without legalese — while preserving accuracy and precision. **2.** The body of persons involved in this campaign.

plain meaning. See MEANING.

plain-meaning rule. The rule that if a writing, or a provision in a writing, appears to be unambiguous on its face, its meaning must be determined from the writing itself without resort to any extrinsic evidence. • Though often applied, this rule is often condemned as simplistic because the meaning of words varies with the verbal context and the surrounding circumstances, not to mention the linguistic ability of the users and readers (including judges). — Also termed *ordinary-meaning rule.* Cf. GOLDEN RULE; MISCHIEF RULE; EQUITY-OF-THE STATUTE RULE.

> "On its positive side, the plain meaning rule states a tautology: Words should be read as saying what they say. The rule tells us to respect meaning but it does so without disclosing what the specific meaning is. At best, it reaffirms the preeminence of the statute over materials extrinsic to it. In its negative aspect, on the other hand, the rule has sometimes been used to read ineptly expressed language out of its proper context, in violation of established principles of meaning and communication. To this extent it is an impediment to interpretation." Reed Dickerson, *The Interpretation and Application of Statutes* 229 (1975).

plain-sight rule. See PLAIN-VIEW DOCTRINE.

plaint. **1.** *Archaic.* A complaint, esp. one filed in a replevin action. See COMPLAINT (1). **2.** *Civil law.* A complaint or petition, esp. one intended to set aside an allegedly invalid testament.

plaintiff. The party who brings a civil suit in a court of law. — Abbr. pltf. Cf. DEFENDANT.

plaintiff in error. *Archaic.* See APPELLANT; PETITIONER.

plaintiff's-viewpoint rule. The principle that courts should measure the amount in controversy in a case by analyzing only the amount of damages claimed by the plaintiff.

plain-touch doctrine. See PLAIN-FEEL DOCTRINE.

plain-vanilla swap. See INTEREST-RATE SWAP.

plain-view doctrine. *Criminal procedure.* The rule permitting a police officer's warrantless seizure and use as evidence of an item observed in plain view from a lawful position or during a legal search when the officer has probable cause to believe that the item is evidence of a crime. — Also termed *clear-view doctrine*; *plain-sight rule*. Cf. OPEN-FIELDS DOCTRINE.

PLAM. See *price-level-adjusted mortgage* under MORTGAGE.

plan, *n.* **1.** BANKRUPTCY PLAN. **2.** EMPLOYEE BENEFIT PLAN.

planned obsolescence. See OBSOLESCENCE.

planned-unit development. A land area zoned for a single-community subdivision with flexible restrictions on residential, commercial, and public uses. — Abbr. PUD. Cf. RESIDENTIAL CLUSTER.

planning board. A local government body responsible for approving or rejecting proposed building projects. • In most jurisdictions, the planning board's decisions are subject to the review of the city council. — Also termed *planning commission*.

plan of rehabilitation. See BANKRUPTCY PLAN.

plan of reorganization. See BANKRUPTCY PLAN.

plan-of-the-convention doctrine. The principle that each U.S. state, by ratifying the U.S. Constitution, has consented to the possibility of being sued by each of the other states, and has no immunity from such a suit under the 11th Amendment.

plant patent. See PATENT (3).

plat. 1. A small piece of land; PLOT (1). **2.** A map describing a piece of land and its features, such as boundaries, lots, roads, and easements.

platform. A statement of principles and policies adopted by a political party as the basis of the party's appeal for public support.

plat map. A document that gives the legal descriptions of pieces of real property by lot, street, and block number. • A plat map is usu. drawn after the property has been described by some other means, such as a government survey. Once a plat map is prepared, property descriptions are defined by referring to the appropriate map.

plea, *n.* **1.** An accused person's formal response of "guilty," "not guilty," or "no contest" to a criminal charge.

blind plea. A guilty plea made without the promise of a concession from either the judge or the prosecutor. Cf. *negotiated plea*.

guilty plea. An accused person's formal admission in court of having committed the charged offense. • A guilty plea is usu. part of a plea bargain. It must be made voluntarily, and only after the accused has been informed of and understands his or her rights. A guilty plea ordinarily has the same effect as a guilty verdict and conviction after a trial on the merits.

insanity plea. See INSANITY DEFENSE.

negotiated plea. The plea agreed to by a criminal defendant and the prosecutor in a plea bargain. See PLEA BARGAIN. Cf. *blind plea*.

not-guilty plea. An accused person's formal denial in court of having committed the charged offense. • The prosecution must then prove all elements of the charged offense beyond a reasonable doubt if the defendant is to be convicted.

2. At common law, the defendant's responsive pleading in a civil action. Cf. DECLARATION (7). **3.** A factual allegation offered in a case; a pleading. Cf. DEMURRER.

affirmative plea. See *pure plea*.

anomalous plea. An equitable plea consisting in both affirmative and negative matter. • That is, it is partly confession and avoidance and partly traverse. The plea is appropriate when the plaintiff, in the bill, has anticipated the plea, and the defendant then traverses the anticipatory matters. — Also termed *plea not pure*. Cf. *pure plea*.

common plea. **1.** A common-law plea in a civil action as opposed to a criminal prosecution. — Also termed *common cause*; *common suit*. **2.** *Hist.* A plea made by a commoner.

"By 'common pleas' Magna Carta meant no more than ordinary pleas between commoners." Alan Harding, *A Social History of English Law* 51 (1966).

dilatory plea (**dil**-ə-tor-ee). A plea that does not challenge the merits of a case but that seeks to delay or defeat the action on procedural grounds.

"Dilatory pleas are those which do not answer the general right of the plaintiff, either by denial or in confession and avoidance, but assert matter tending to defeat the particular action by resisting the plaintiff's present right of recovery. They may be divided into two main classes: (1) Pleas to the jurisdiction and venue. (2) Pleas in abatement. A minor class, sometimes recognized, is pleas in suspension of the action." Benjamin J. Shipman, *Handbook of Common-Law Pleading* § 220, at 382 (Henry Winthrop Ballantine ed., 3d ed. 1923).

double plea. A plea consisting in two or more distinct grounds of complaint or defense for the same issue. Cf. *alternative pleading* under PLEADING (2); DUPLICITY (2).

issuable plea. A plea on the merits presenting a complaint to the court. Cf. *issuable defense* under DEFENSE (1).

jurisdictional plea. A plea asserting that the court lacks jurisdiction either over the defendant or over the subject matter of the case. — Also termed *plea to the jurisdiction*.

negative plea. A plea that traverses some material fact or facts stated in the bill.

nonissuable plea. A plea on which a court ruling will not decide the case on the merits, such as a plea in abatement.

peremptory plea. A plea that responds to the merits of the plaintiff's claim.

plea in abatement. A plea that objects to the place, time, or method of asserting the plaintiff's claim but does not dispute the claim's merits. • A defendant who successfully asserts a plea in abatement leaves the claim open for continuation in the current action or reassertion in a later action if the defect is cured.

plea in bar. See PLEA IN BAR.

plea in confession and avoidance. See CONFESSION AND AVOIDANCE.

plea in discharge. A plea alleging that the defendant has previously satisfied and discharged the plaintiff's claim.

plea in equity. A special defense relying on one or more reasons why the suit should be dismissed, delayed, or barred. • The various kinds are (1) pleas to the jurisdiction, (2) pleas to the person, (3) pleas to the form of the bill, and (4) pleas in bar of the bill. • Pleas in equity generally fall into two classes: *pure pleas* and *anomalous pleas*.

plea in estoppel. *Common-law pleading.* A plea that neither confesses nor avoids but pleads a previous inconsistent act, allegation, or denial on the part of the adverse party to preclude that party from maintaining an action or defense.

plea in reconvention. *Civil law.* A plea that sets up a new matter, not as a defense, but as a cross-complaint, setoff, or counterclaim.

plea in suspension. A plea that shows some ground for not proceeding in the suit at the present time and prays that the proceedings be stayed until that ground is removed, such as a party's being a minor or the plaintiff's being an alien enemy.

plea not pure. See *anomalous plea*.

plea of confession and avoidance. See CONFESSION AND AVOIDANCE.

plea of privilege. A plea that raises an objection to the venue of an action. See CHANGE OF VENUE (1).

plea of release. A plea that admits the claim but sets forth a written discharge executed by a party authorized to release the claim. See RELEASE (2).

plea puis darrein continuance (**pwis dar**-ayn kən-**tin**-yoo-ənts). [Law French "plea since the last continuance"] A plea that alleges new defensive matter that has arisen during a continuance of the case and that did not exist at the time of the defendant's last pleading.

plea to further maintenance to the action. *Hist.* A defensive plea asserting that events occurring after the commencement of the action necessitate its dismissal. • The plea is obsolete because of the pleading requirements in federal and state rules of civil procedure.

plea to the declaration. A plea in abatement that objects to the declaration and applies immediately to it. — Also termed *plea to the count*.

plea to the jurisdiction. See *jurisdictional plea*.

plea to the person of the defendant. A plea in abatement alleging that the defendant has a legal disability to be sued.

plea to the person of the plaintiff. A plea in abatement alleging that the plaintiff has a legal disability to sue.

plea to the writ. A plea in abatement that objects to the writ (summons) and applies (1) to the form of the writ for a matter either apparent on the writ's face or outside the writ, or (2) to the way in which the writ was executed or acted on.

pure plea. An equitable plea that affirmatively alleges new matters that are outside the bill. • If proved, the effect is to end the controversy by dismissing, delaying, or barring the suit. A pure plea must track the allegations of the bill, not evade it or mistake its purpose. Originally, this was the only plea known in equity. — Also termed *affirmative plea*. Cf. *anomalous plea*.

rolled-up plea. *Defamation.* A defendant's plea claiming that the statements complained of are factual and that, to the extent that they consist of comment, they are fair comment on a matter of public interest. See FAIR COMMENT.

special plea. A plea alleging one or more new facts rather than merely disputing the legal grounds of the action or charge. • All pleas other than general issues are special pleas. See *general issue* under ISSUE (1).

plea bargain, *n.* A negotiated agreement between a prosecutor and a criminal defendant whereby the defendant pleads guilty to a lesser offense or to one of multiple charges in exchange for some concession by the prosecutor, usu. a more lenient sentence or a dismissal of the other charges. — Also termed *plea agreement*; *negotiated plea*. — **plea-bargain,** *vb.* — **plea-bargaining,** *n.*

plead, *vb.* **1.** To make a specific plea, esp. in response to a criminal charge <he pleaded not guilty>. **2.** To assert or allege in a pleading <fraud claims must be pleaded with particularity>. **3.** To file or deliver a pleading <the plaintiff hasn't pleaded yet>.

pleader. 1. A party who asserts a particular pleading. **2.** A person who pleads in court on behalf of another. **3.** *Hist.* At common law, a person who (though not an attorney) specialized in preparing pleadings for others. — Also termed *special pleader*. **4.** *Hist.* NARRATOR.

pleading, *n.* **1.** A formal document in which a party to a legal proceeding (esp. a civil lawsuit) sets forth or responds to allegations, claims, denials, or defenses. • In federal civil procedure, the main pleadings are the plaintiff's complaint and the defendant's answer.

accusatory pleading. An indictment, information, or complaint by which the government begins a criminal prosecution.

amended pleading. A pleading that replaces an earlier pleading and that contains matters omitted from or not known at the time of the earlier pleading.

> "An amendment is the correction of an error or the supplying of an omission in the process or pleadings. An amended pleading differs from a supplemental pleading in that the true function of the latter is to spread upon the record matter material to the issue which has arisen *subsequent* to the filing of a pleading, while matter of amendment purely is matter that might *well have been pleaded at the time the pleading sought to be amended was filed*, but which through error or inadvertence was omitted or misstated. It has been declared that the allowance of amendments is incidental to the exercise of all judicial power and is indispensable to the ends of justice." Eugene A. Jones, *Manual of Equity Pleading and Practice* 68 (1916).

anomalous pleading. A pleading that is partly affirmative and partly negative in its allegations.

articulated pleading. A pleading that states each allegation in a separately numbered paragraph.

defective pleading. A pleading that fails to meet minimum standards of sufficiency or accuracy in form or substance.

responsive pleading. A pleading that replies to an opponent's earlier pleading. See ANSWER.

sham pleading. An obviously frivolous or absurd pleading that is made only for purposes of vexation or delay. — Also termed *sham plea*; *false plea*.

shotgun pleading. A pleading that encompasses a wide range of contentions, usu. supported by vague factual allegations.

supplemental pleading. A pleading that either corrects a defect in an earlier pleading or addresses facts arising since the earlier pleading was filed. • Unlike an amended pleading, a supplemental pleading merely adds to the earlier pleading and does not replace it.

2. A system of defining and narrowing the issues in a lawsuit whereby the parties file formal documents alleging their respective positions.

alternative pleading. A form of pleading whereby the pleader alleges two or more independent claims or defenses that are not necessarily consistent with each other, such as alleging both intentional infliction of emotional distress and negligent infliction of emotional distress based on the same conduct. Fed. R. Civ. P. 8(e)(2). Cf. DUPLICITY (2); *double plea* under PLEA (3).

artful pleading. A plaintiff's disguised phrasing of a federal claim as solely a state-law claim in order to prevent a defendant from removing the case from state court to federal court.

code pleading. A procedural system requiring that the pleader allege merely the facts of the case giving rise to the claim, not the legal conclusions necessary to sustain the claim. — Also termed *fact pleading*. Cf. *issue pleading*.

common-law pleading. The system of pleading historically used in the three common-law courts of England (the King's Bench, the Common Pleas, and the Exchequer) up to 1873.

equity pleading. The system of pleading used in courts of equity. • In most jurisdictions, rules unique to equity practice have been largely supplanted by rules of court, esp. where law courts and equity courts have merged.

issue pleading. The common-law method of pleading, the main purpose of which was to frame an issue. Cf. *code pleading*.

notice pleading. A procedural system requiring that the pleader give only a short and plain statement of the claim showing that the pleader is entitled to relief, and not a complete detailing of all the facts. Fed. R. Civ. P. 8(a).

special pleading. See SPECIAL PLEADING.

3. The legal rules regulating the statement of the plaintiff's claims and the defendant's defenses <today, pleading is a much simpler subject than it was in former years>.

pleading the baby act. See BABY ACT, PLEADING THE.

pleading the Fifth. The act or an instance of asserting one's right against self-incrimination under the Fifth Amendment. — Also termed *taking the Fifth*. See RIGHT AGAINST SELF-INCRIMINATION.

plead over, *vb.* **1.** To fail to notice a defective allegation in an opponent's pleading. **2.** *Hist.* To plead the general issue after a defendant has had a dilatory plea overruled. See AIDER BY PLEADING OVER.

plea in abatement. See PLEA (3).

plea in bar. A plea that seeks to defeat the plaintiff's or prosecutor's action completely and permanently.

general plea in bar. A criminal defendant's plea of not guilty by which the defendant denies every fact and circumstance necessary to be convicted of the crime charged.

special plea in bar. A plea that, rather than addressing the merits and denying the facts alleged, sets up some extrinsic fact to show why a criminal defendant cannot be tried for the offense charged. • Examples include the plea of *autrefois acquit* and the plea of pardon.

plea in confession and avoidance. See CONFESSION AND AVOIDANCE.

plea in discharge. See PLEA (3).

plea in equity. See PLEA (3).

plea in reconvention. See PLEA (3).

plea in suspension. See PLEA (3).

plea not pure. See *anomalous plea* under PLEA (3).

plea of confession and avoidance. See CONFESSION AND AVOIDANCE.

plea of pregnancy. *Hist.* A plea of a woman convicted of a capital crime to stay her execution until she gives birth. See *jury of matrons* under JURY.

plea of privilege. See PLEA (3).

plea of release. See PLEA (3).

plea of sanctuary. See DECLINATORY PLEA.

plea of tender. At common law, a pleading asserting that the defendant has consistently been willing to pay the debt demanded, has offered it to the plaintiff, and has brought the money into court ready to pay the plaintiff. See TENDER.

plea puis darrein continuance. See PLEA (3).

pleasure appointment. The assignment of someone to employment that can be taken away at any time, with no requirement for notice or a hearing.

plea to further maintenance to the action. See PLEA (3).

plea to the count. See *plea to the declaration* under PLEA (3).

plea to the declaration. See PLEA (3).

plea to the jurisdiction. See *jurisdictional plea* under PLEA (3).

plea to the person of the defendant. See PLEA (3).

plea to the person of the plaintiff. See PLEA (3).

plea to the writ. See PLEA (3).

plebiscite (**pleb**-ə-sIt *or* **pleb**-ə-sit), *n.* **1.** A binding or nonbinding referendum on a proposed law, constitutional amendment, or significant public issue. **2.** *Int'l law.* A direct vote of a country's electorate to decide a question of public importance, such as union with another country or a proposed change to the constitution. — **plebiscitary** (plə-**bi**-sə-ter-ee), *adj.*

plebiscitum (pleb-ə-**sI**-təm), *n.* [Latin] *Roman law.* An enactment passed at the request of a tribune by the assembly of the common people (the *concilium plebis*). Pl. ***plebiscita.*** See CONCILIUM PLEBIS.

plebs (plebz), *n.* [Latin] *Roman law.* The common people in ancient Rome; the general body of citizens. Pl. **plebes** (**plee**-beez).

pledge, *n.* **1.** A bailment or other deposit of personal property to a creditor as security for a debt or obligation; PAWN (2). Cf. LIEN. **2.** The item of personal property so deposited; PAWN (1). **3.** Broadly, the act of providing something as security for a debt or obligation. **4.** The thing so provided. **5.** *Hist.* A person who acts as a surety for the prosecution of a lawsuit. • In early practice, pledges were listed at the end of the declaration. Over time the listing of pledges became a formality, and fictitious names (such as "John Doe" or "Richard Roe") were allowed. — **pledge,** *vb.* — **pledgeable,** *adj.*

> "A pledge is something more than a mere lien and something less than a mortgage." Leonard A. Jones, *A Treatise on the Law of Collateral Securities and Pledges* § 2, at 4 (Edward M. White rev., 3d ed. 1912).

> "A pledge is a bailment of personal property to secure an obligation of the bailor. If the purpose of the transaction is to transfer property for security only, then the courts will hold the transaction a pledge, even though in form it may be a sale or other out-and-out transfer." Ray Andrews Brown, *The Law of Personal Property* § 128, at 622 (2d ed. 1936).

> "The pledge is as old as recorded history and is still in use, as the presence of pawnbrokers attests. In this transaction the debtor borrows money by physically transferring to a secured party the possession of the property to be used as security, and the property will be returned if the debt is repaid. Since the debtor does not retain the use of pledged goods, this security device has obvious disadvantages from the debtor's point of view." Ray D. Henson, *Secured Transactions* § 3-1, at 17 (3d ed. 1983).

pledged account. See ACCOUNT.

pledgee. One with whom a pledge is deposited.

pledgery. *Archaic.* See SURETYSHIP (1).

pledgor. One who gives a pledge to another. — Also spelled *pledger.*

plegiis acquietandis. See DE PLEGIIS ACQUIETANDIS.

plena aetas (**plee**-nə **ee**-tas). [Latin] Full age. See AGE OF MAJORITY.

plena forisfactura (**plee**-nə for-is-**fak**-chər-ə). [Latin "complete forfeiture"] A forfeiture of all that one possesses.

plena probatio. See *probatio plena* under PROBATIO.

plenarty (**plee**-nər-tee *or* **plen**-ər-tee), *n. Hist.* The condition of being full or occupied; esp., the state of a benefice that is occupied by an incumbent.

plenary (**plee**-nə-ree *or* **plen**-ə-ree), *adj.* **1.** Full; complete; entire <plenary authority>. **2.** (Of an assembly) to be attended by all members or participants <plenary session>.

plenary action. See ACTION.

plenary confession. See CONFESSION.

plenary jurisdiction. See JURISDICTION.

plenary power. See POWER.

plenary session. See SESSION.

plenary suit. See SUIT.

plene (**plee**-nee), *adv.* [Latin] Fully; completely; sufficiently.

plene administravit (**plee**-nee ad-min-ə-**stray**-vit). [Law Latin "he has fully administered"] *Hist.* A defensive plea in which an executor or administrator asserts that no assets remain in the estate to satisfy the plaintiff's demand.

plene administravit praeter (**plee**-nee ad-min-ə-**stray**-vit **pree**-tər). [Law Latin "he has fully administered, except"] *Hist.* A defensive plea in which an executor or administrator asserts that no assets remain in the estate, except a stated few that are insufficient to satisfy the plaintiff's demand.

plene computavit (**plee**-nee kom-pyoo-**tay**-vit). [Law Latin "he has fully accounted"] *Hist.* A plea in an action of account render, alleging that the defendant has fully accounted. See ACCOUNTING (3).

plenipotentiary (plen-ə-pə-**ten**-shee-er-ee). A person who has full power to do a thing; a person fully commissioned to act for another. See *minister plenipotentiary* under MINISTER.

plenum dominium. See *dominium plenum* under DOMINIUM (1).

plevin (**plev**-in), *n. Archaic.* An assurance or warrant; a pledge.

Plimsoll marks. See LOAD LINE.

plot, *n.* **1.** A measured piece of land; LOT (1). **2.** A plan forming the basis of a conspiracy.

plot plan. A plan that shows a proposed or present use of a plot of land, esp. of a residential area.

plottage. The increase in value achieved by combining small, undeveloped tracts of land into larger tracts of land.

plow back, *vb.* To reinvest earnings and profits into a business instead of paying them out as dividends or withdrawals.

plowbote. See BOTE (1).

plowland. See CARUCATE.

plowman's fee. See FEE (2).

pltf. *abbr.* PLAINTIFF.

plunder. See PILLAGE.

plunderage. *Maritime law.* The embezzling of goods on a ship.

plurality. A large number or quantity that does not constitute a majority; a number greater than another, regardless of the margin <a four-member plurality of the Supreme Court agreed with this view, which gets more votes than any other>. Cf. MAJORITY (2).

plurality opinion. See OPINION (1).

plural marriage. See MARRIAGE (1).

pluries (**pluur**-ee-eez), *n.* [Latin "many times"] A third or subsequent writ issued when the previous writs have been ineffective; a writ issued after an alias writ. — Also termed *pluries writ.*

plurinational administrative institution. *Int'l law.* An entity designed to perform transnational administrative activities when politically oriented international organizations and traditional international agreements are unsuitable. • These institutions usu. arise in fields where transnational arrangements are necessary (such as natural-resource management, transportation, or utilities), and they are often organized as international corporations, national agencies, or private corporations.

plus petitio (**pləs** pə-**tish**-ee-oh). [Latin] *Roman law.* The mistake of claiming more in one's pleadings than is due. • This was fatal to the action under classical law. Under Justinian, however, a claimant could continue the action, but could be liable for treble damages to any person injured by the overstated claim.

p.m. *abbr.* POST MERIDIEM.

PM. *abbr.* **1.** POSTMASTER. **2.** PRIME MINISTER.

PMI. *abbr.* Private mortgage insurance. See *mortgage insurance* under INSURANCE.

PMM. See *purchase-money mortgage* under MORTGAGE.

PMRT. See *purchase-money resulting trust* under TRUST.

PMSI. See *purchase-money security interest* under SECURITY INTEREST.

P.O. *abbr.* Post office.

poaching, *n.* The illegal taking or killing of fish or game on another's land. — **poach,** *vb.*

pocket immunity. See IMMUNITY (3).

pocket money. See HAT MONEY.

pocket part. A supplemental pamphlet inserted usu. into the back inside cover of a lawbook, esp. a treatise or code, to update the material in the main text until the publisher issues a new edition of the entire work. • Legal publishers frequently leave a little extra room inside their hardcover books so that pocket parts may later be added.

pocket veto. See VETO.

P.O.D. *abbr.* Pay on delivery.

poena (**pee**-nə). [Latin] Punishment; penalty.

poena corporalis (**pee**-nə kor-pə-**ray**-lis). [Latin] Corporal punishment.

poenae secundarum nuptiarum (**pee**-nee sek-ən-**dair**-əm nəp-shee-**air**-əm), *n.* [Latin "penalties of second marriages"] *Roman law.* Disabilities that, for the protection of children of a first marriage, are imposed on a parent who remarries. See PARENS BINUBUS.

> "If either parent re-married, the interests of the children of the first marriage were protected (in the later Roman Empire) by a number of legal rules the effect of which was to confer certain benefits on the children and to impose certain disabilities — the so-called poenae secundarum nuptiarum — on the parens binubus. The most important of these rules was that which declared that all the property which the parens binubus had acquired gratuitously from his or her deceased spouse, whether by way of gift, dos, donatio propter nuptias, or testamentary disposition — the so-called lucra nuptialia — should become ipso jure the property of the children of the first marriage at the moment of the conclusion of the second marriage, and that only a usufruct should be reserved for the parens binubus." Rudolph Sohm, *The Institutes: A Textbook of the History and System of Roman Private Law* 477 (James Crawford Ledlie trans., 3d ed. 1907).

poenalis (pi-**nay**-lis), *adj.* [Latin] *Roman law.* Imposing a penalty; penal.

poena pilloralis (**pee**-nə pil-ə-**ray**-lis). [Latin] *Hist.* Punishment of the pillory.

poenitentia (pee-nə-**ten**-shee-ə *or* pen-ə). [Latin] *Roman law.* Reconsideration; changing one's mind.

poinding (**pin**-ding). *Scots law.* A judgment creditor's seizing of a debtor's property to satisfy the debt.

point, *n.* **1.** A pertinent and distinct legal proposition, issue, or argument <point of error>. **2.** One percent of the face value of a loan (esp. a mortgage loan), paid up front to the lender as a service charge or placement fee <the borrower hoped for only a two-point fee on the mortgage>. — Also termed *mortgage point.* See MORTGAGE DISCOUNT. **3.** A unit used for quoting stock, bond, or commodity prices <the stock closed up a few points today>.

point-and-click agreement. An electronic version of a shrink-wrap license in which a computer user agrees to the terms of an electronically displayed agreement by pointing the mouse to a particular location on the screen and then clicking. See *shrink-wrap license* under LICENSE.

point of error. An alleged mistake by a lower court asserted as a ground for appeal. See ERROR (2); WRIT OF ERROR.

point of law. A discrete legal proposition at issue in a case.

reserved point of law. An important or difficult point of law that arises during trial but that the judge sets aside for future argument or decision so that testimony can continue.

point system. *Criminal law.* A system that assigns incremental units to traffic violations, the accumulation of a certain number within a year resulting in the automatic suspension of a person's driving privileges.

poisonous-tree doctrine. See FRUIT-OF-THE-POISONOUS-TREE DOCTRINE.

poison pill. A corporation's defense against an unwanted takeover bid whereby shareholders are granted the right to acquire equity or debt securities at a favorable price to increase the bidder's acquisition costs. See SHARK REPELLENT. Cf. PORCUPINE PROVISION.

> "Another recent tactic is the 'poison pill' which is a conditional stock right that is triggered by a hostile takeover and makes the takeover prohibitively expensive. The poison pill is a variation of the scorched earth

defense...." Thomas Lee Hazen, *The Law of Securities Regulation* § 11.20, at 575 (2d ed. 1990).

police, *n.* **1.** The governmental department charged with the preservation of public order, the promotion of public safety, and the prevention and detection of crime. **2.** The officers or members of this department.

police blotter. See ARREST RECORD.

police court. See *magistrate's court* (1) under COURT.

police jury. *Civil law.* The governing body of a parish.

police justice. See *police magistrate* under MAGISTRATE.

police magistrate. See MAGISTRATE.

police officer. A peace officer responsible for preserving public order, promoting public safety, and preventing and detecting crime. Cf. PEACE OFFICER.

police power. 1. The inherent and plenary power of a sovereign to make all laws necessary and proper to preserve the public security, order, health, morality, and justice. • It is a fundamental power essential to government, and it cannot be surrendered by the legislature or irrevocably transferred away from government.

"[I]t is possible to evolve at least two main attributes or characteristics which differentiate the police power: it aims directly to secure and promote the public welfare, and it does so by restraint or compulsion." Ernst Freund, *The Police Power* § 3, at 3 (1904).

2. A state's Tenth Amendment right, subject to due-process and other limitations, to establish and enforce laws protecting the public's health, safety, and general welfare, or to delegate this right to local governments. **3.** Loosely, the power of the government to intervene in the use of privately owned property, as by subjecting it to eminent domain. See EMINENT DOMAIN.

police science. See CRIMINAL JUSTICE.

police state. See STATE (1).

policy. 1. The general principles by which a government is guided in its management of public affairs. See PUBLIC POLICY. **2.** A document containing a contract of insurance; INSURANCE POLICY. **3.** A type of lottery in which bettors select numbers to bet on and place the bet with a "policy writer."

policyholder. One who owns an insurance policy, regardless of whether that person is the insured party. — Also termed *policyowner*.

policy limits. See LIABILITY LIMIT.

policy loan. See LOAN.

policy of insurance. See INSURANCE POLICY.

policy of the law. See PUBLIC POLICY.

policyowner. See POLICYHOLDER.

policy proof of interest. *Insurance.* Evidence — shown by possession of a policy — that a person making a claim has an insurable interest in the loss. — Abbr. PPI.

policy reserve. See RESERVE.

policy stacking. See STACKING.

policy value. *Insurance.* The amount of cash available to a policyholder on the surrender or cancellation of the insurance policy.

policy year. *Insurance.* The year beginning on the date that a policy becomes effective. Cf. ANNIVERSARY DATE.

political, *adj.* Pertaining to politics; of or relating to the conduct of government.

political-action committee. An organization formed by a special-interest group to raise and contribute money to the campaigns of political candidates who the group believes will promote its interests. — Abbr. PAC.

political assessment. See ASSESSMENT.

political asylum. See ASYLUM (2).

political corporation. See *public corporation* (2) under CORPORATION.

political correctness, *n.* **1.** The doctrine favoring the elimination of language and practices that might offend political sensibilities, esp. in racial or sexual matters. **2.** An instance in which a person conforms to this doctrine. — Abbr. P.C. — **politically correct,** *adj.*

political crime. See CRIME.

political economy. See ECONOMY.

political gerrymandering. See GERRYMANDERING (1).

political law. See POLITICAL SCIENCE.

political liberty. See LIBERTY.

political offense. A crime directed against the security or governmental system of a nation, such as treason, sedition, or espionage. • Under principles of international law, the perpetrator of such an offense cannot be extradited.

political party. An organization of voters formed to influence the government's conduct and policies by nominating and electing candidates to public office. • The United States has traditionally maintained a two-party system, which today comprises the Democratic and Republican parties.

political patronage. See PATRONAGE (3).

political power. The power vested in a person or body of persons exercising any function of the state; the capacity to influence the activities of the body politic. — Also termed *civil power*.

sovereign political power. Power that is absolute and uncontrolled within its own sphere. • Within its designated limits, its exercise and effective operation do not depend on, and are not subject to, the power of any other person and cannot be prevented or annulled by any other power recognized within the constitutional system. — Often shortened to *sovereign power*. — Also termed *supreme power*.

subordinate political power. Power that, within its own sphere of operation, is subject in some degree to external control because there exists some superior constitutional power that can prevent, restrict, direct, or annul its operation. — Often shortened to *subordinate power*.

political question. A question that a court will not consider because it involves the exercise of discretionary power by the executive or legislative branch of government. — Also termed *nonjusticiable question*. Cf. JUDICIAL QUESTION.

political-question doctrine. The judicial principle that a court should refuse to decide an issue involving the exercise of discretionary power by the executive or legislative branch of government.

political right. See RIGHT.

political science. The branch of learning concerned with the study of the principles and conduct of government. — Also termed *political law*.

political society. See STATE (1).

political subdivision. A division of a state that exists primarily to discharge some function of local government.

political trial. See TRIAL.

politics. 1. The science of the organization and administration of the state. **2.** The activity or profession of engaging in political affairs.

polity (**pol**-ə-tee). **1.** The total governmental organization as based on its goals and policies. **2.** A politically organized body or community.

polity approach. A method of resolving church-property disputes by which a court examines the structure of the church to determine whether the church is independent or hierarchical, and then resolves the dispute in accordance with the decision of the proper church-governing body.

poll, *n.* **1.** A sampling of opinions on a given topic, conducted randomly or obtained from a specified group. **2.** The act or process of voting at an election. **3.** The result of the counting of votes. **4.** (*usu. pl.*) The place where votes are cast.

poll, *vb.* **1.** To ask how each member of (a group) individually voted <after the verdict was read, the judge polled the jury>. **2.** To question (people) so as to elicit votes, opinions, or preferences <the committee polled 500 citizens about their views>. **3.** To receive (a given number of votes) in an election <the third-party candidate polled only 250 votes in the county>.

pollicitation. *Contracts.* The offer of a promise.

> "By a *promise* we mean an accepted offer as opposed to an offer of a promise, or, as Austin called it, a *pollicitation*." William R. Anson, *Principles of the Law of Contract* 6 (Arthur L. Corbin ed., 3d Am. ed. 1919).

poll tax. See TAX.

pollute, *vb.* To corrupt or defile; esp., to contaminate the soil, air, or water with noxious substances. — **pollution,** *n.* — **polluter,** *n.*

pollution exclusion. See EXCLUSION (3).

po. lo. suo. *abbr.* PONIT LOCO SUO.

polyandry (**pol**-ee-an-dree). The condition or practice of having more than one husband. Cf. POLYGYNY.

polyarchy (**pol**-ee-ahr-kee). Government by many persons. — Also termed *polygarchy* (**pol**-ə-gahr-kee).

polygamy (pə-**lig**-ə-mee), *n.* The state of being simultaneously married to more than one spouse; multiple marriages. — **polygamous,** *adj.* — **polygamist,** *n.* Cf. BIGAMY; MONOGAMY.

> "Polygamy (many marriages) is employed at times as a synonym of bigamy and at other times to indicate the simultaneous marriage of two or more spouses." Rollin M. Perkins & Ronald N. Boyce, *Criminal Law* 458 (3d ed. 1982).

polygarchy. See POLYARCHY.

polygraph, *n.* A device used to evaluate veracity by measuring and recording involuntary physiological changes in the human body during interrogation. • Polygraph results are inadmissible as evidence in most states. — Also termed *lie detector.* — **polygraphic,** *adj.* — **polygraphy,** *n.*

polygyny (pə-**lij**-ə-nee). The condition or practice of having more than one wife. Cf. POLYANDRY.

pone (**poh**-nee). [Latin "put"] *Hist.* An original writ used to remove an action from an inferior court (such as a manorial court or county court) to a superior court. • The writ was so called from the initial words of its mandate, which required the recipient to "put" the matter before the court issuing the writ.

ponendis in assisis (pə-**nen**-dis in ə-**sI**-zis). [Latin "to be placed in assizes"] *Hist.* A writ directing the sheriff to empanel a jury for an assize or real action.

ponendo sigillum ad exceptionem. See DE PONENDO SIGILLUM AD EXCEPTIONEM.

ponendum in ballium (pə-**nen**-dəm in **bal**-ee-θm). [Latin "to be placed in bail"] *Hist.* A writ commanding that a prisoner be bailed in a bailable matter.

pone per vadium (**poh**-nee pər **vay**-dee-əm). [Latin] *Hist.* A writ commanding the sheriff to summon a defendant who has failed to appear in response to an initial writ by attaching some of the defendant's property and requiring the defendant to find sureties. • It was so called from the words of the writ, *pone per vadium et salvos plegios* ("put by gage and safe pledges").

ponit loco suo (**poh**-nit **loh**-ko **s[y]oo**-oh). [Latin] Puts in his place. • This phrase was formerly used in a power of attorney. — Abbr. *po. lo. suo.*

ponit se super patriam (**poh**-nit see **s[y]oo**-pər **pay**-tree-əm *or* **pa**-tree-əm). [Latin "he puts himself upon the country"] *Hist.* A defendant's plea of not guilty in a criminal action. — Abbr. *po. se.* See GOING TO THE COUNTRY; PATRIA (3).

pontiff. 1. *Roman law.* A member of the council of priests in ancient Rome. — Also termed *pontifex.*

> "The specialists who interpreted the Twelve Tables and the unwritten part of the law were called *pontiffs.* At first they dealt with both sacred law (how to appease the gods) and secular law (how to secure peace among men). Some of them later confined themselves to secular law. As an example of how they interpreted the law, the Twelve Tables said that if a father sells his son three times (into bondage, to pay off debts) the son is to be free from his father's power. The Twelve Tables said nothing about a daughter. The pontiffs held that if a father sold his daughter once, she was free." Tony Honoré, *About Law* 13 (1995).

2. The leader of the Catholic Church; the Pope.

Ponzi scheme (**pon**-zee). A fraudulent investment scheme in which money contributed by later investors generates artificially high dividends for the original investors, whose example attracts even larger investments. • Money from the new investors is used directly to repay or pay interest to old investors, usu. without any operation or revenue-producing activity other than the continual raising of new funds. This scheme takes its name from Charles Ponzi, who in the late 1920s was convicted for fraudulent schemes he conducted in Boston. Cf. PYRAMID SCHEME.

pool, *n.* **1.** An association of individuals or entities who share resources and funds to promote their joint undertaking; esp., an association of persons engaged in buying or selling commodities. • If such an association is formed to eliminate competition throughout a single industry, it is a restraint of trade that violates federal antitrust laws. **2.** A gambling scheme in which numerous persons contribute stakes for betting on a particular event (such as a sporting event).

pooling. See COMMUNITIZATION.

pooling agreement. A contractual arrangement by which corporate shareholders agree that their shares will be voted as a unit. — Also termed *voting agreement*; *shareholder voting agreement*; *shareholder-control agreement*.

pooling of interests. A method of accounting used in mergers, whereby the acquired company's assets are recorded on the acquiring company's books at their cost when originally acquired. • No goodwill account is created under the pooling method.

pop, *n. Telecommunications.* A calculation of the potential customer base for a mobile-phone-service provider, calculated by the number of people living in the area multiplied by the company's percentage ownership of the area's cellular service.

Poppean law. See LEX PAPIA POPPEA.

popular action. See QUI TAM ACTION.

popular election. See ELECTION.

popular justice. See JUSTICE (1).

populus (**pop**-yə-ləs). [Latin] *Roman law.* The people; the whole body of Roman citizens, patricians, and plebeians.

porcupine provision. A clause in a corporation's charter or bylaws designed to prevent a takeover without the consent of the board of directors. Cf. SHARK REPELLENT; POISON PILL.

pork-barrel legislation. See LEGISLATION.

pornography, *n.* Material (such as writings, photographs, or movies) depicting sexual activity or erotic behavior in a way that is designed to arouse sexual excitement. • Pornography is protected speech under the First Amendment unless it is determined to be legally obscene. — **pornographic,** *adj.* See OBSCENITY.

child pornography. Material depicting a person under the age of 18 engaged in sexual activity. • Child pornography is not protected by the First Amendment — even if it falls short of the legal standard for obscenity — and those directly involved in its distribution can be criminally punished.

port. 1. A harbor where ships load and unload cargo. **2.** Any place where persons and cargo are allowed to enter a country and where customs officials are stationed. — Also termed (in sense 2) *port of entry*.

foreign port. **1.** One exclusively within the jurisdiction of another country or state. **2.** A port other than a home port.

home port. The port that is either where a vessel is registered or where its owner resides.

port of call. A port at which a ship stops during a voyage.

port of delivery. The port that is the terminus of any particular voyage and where the ship unloads its cargo.

port of departure. The port from which a vessel departs on the start of a voyage.

port of destination. The port at which a voyage is to end. • This term generally includes any stopping places at which the ship receives or unloads cargo.

port of discharge. The place where a substantial part of the cargo is discharged.

portable business. A law practice that an attorney can take from one firm or geographic location to another, with little loss in client relationships. — Also termed *portable practice*.

port authority. A state or federal agency that regulates traffic through a port or that establishes and maintains airports, bridges, tollways, and public transportation.

portfolio. The various securities or other investments held by an investor at any given time. • An investor will often hold several different types of investments in a portfolio for the purpose of diversifying risk.

market portfolio. A value-weighted portfolio of every asset in a particular market.

portfolio income. See INCOME.

portio legitima (**por**-shee-oh lə-**jit**-ə-mə). [Latin "lawful portion"] *Civil law.* The portion of an inheritance that a given heir is entitled to, and of which the heir cannot be deprived by the testator without special cause.

portion. A share or allotted part (as of an estate).

port of call. See PORT.

port of delivery. See PORT.

port of departure. See PORT.

port of destination. See PORT.

port of discharge. See PORT.

port of entry. See PORT.

portorium (por-**tohr**-ee-əm). [Law Latin] *Hist.* **1.** A tax or toll levied at a port or at the gates of a city. **2.** A toll for passing over a bridge.

port-risk insurance. See INSURANCE.

portsale. *Hist.* A public sale of goods to the highest bidder; an auction.

port toll. A duty paid for bringing goods into a port.

portwarden. An official responsible for the administration of a port.

po. se. *abbr.* PONIT SE SUPER PATRIAM.

position. The extent of a person's investment in a particular security or market.

position of the United States. The legal position of the federal government in a case involving the Equal Access to Justice Act. • The position's reasonableness in light of precedent determines whether the government will be liable for the opposing party's attorney's fees.

positive act. See OVERT ACT.

positive condition. See CONDITION (2).

positive covenant. See COVENANT (1).

positive duty. See DUTY (1).

positive easement. See *affirmative easement* under EASEMENT.

positive evidence. See *direct evidence* (1) under EVIDENCE.

positive externality. See EXTERNALITY.

positive fraud. See *actual fraud* under FRAUD.

positive justice. See JUSTICE (1).

positive law. A system of law promulgated and implemented within a particular political community by political superiors, as distinct from moral law or law existing in an ideal community or in some nonpolitical community. • Positive law typically consists of enacted law — the codes, statutes, and regulations that are applied and enforced in the courts. The term derives from the medieval use of *positum* (Latin "established"), so that the phrase *positive law* literally means law established by human authority. — Also termed *jus positivum*; *made law*. Cf. NATURAL LAW.

> "A judge is tethered to the positive law but should not be shackled to it." Patrick Devlin, *The Enforcement of Morals* 94 (1968).

positive misprision. See MISPRISION.

positive notice. See *direct notice* under NOTICE.

positive prescription. See PRESCRIPTION (2).

positive proof. See PROOF.

positive reprisal. See REPRISAL.

positive right. See RIGHT.

positive servitude. See SERVITUDE (1).

positive testimony. See *affirmative testimony* under TESTIMONY.

positive wrong. See WRONG.

positivi juris (poz-ə-**tɪ**-vɪ **joor**-is). [Law Latin] Of positive law. See POSITIVE LAW.

positivism. The doctrine that all true knowledge is derived from observable phenomena, rather than speculation or reasoning. See LEGAL POSITIVISM; LOGICAL POSITIVISM; *positivist jurisprudence* under JURISPRUDENCE.

positivistic, *adj.* Of or relating to legal positivism. See LEGAL POSITIVISM.

positivistic jurisprudence. See *positivist jurisprudence* under JURISPRUDENCE.

posse (**pos**-ee). [Latin] **1.** A possibility. See IN POSSE. Cf. IN ESSE. **2.** Power; ability.

posse comitatus (**pos**-ee kom-ə-**tay**-təs), *n.* [Latin "power of the county"] A group of citizens who are called together to assist the sheriff in keeping the peace. — Often shortened to *posse.*

possess, *vb.* To have in one's actual control; to have possession of. — **possessor,** *n.*

possessio (pə-**zes**[**h**]-ee-oh). [Latin] The de facto relation between the holder of a thing and the thing itself.

pedis possessio (**pee**-dis *or* **ped**-is pə-**zes**[**h**]-ee-oh). [Latin] A foothold; an actual possession of real property, implying either actual occupancy or enclosure or use. See PEDIS POSSESSIO DOCTRINE.

possessio bona fide (pə-**zes**[**h**]-ee-oh **boh**-nə **fI**-dee). [Latin] Possession in good faith. Cf. *possessio mala fide.*

possessio bonorum (pə-**zes**[**h**]-ee-oh bə-**nor**-əm). [Latin] *Roman law.* Possession of goods.

possessio civilis (pə-**zes**[**h**]-ee-oh sə-**vI**-lis). [Latin] *Roman law.* Legal possession; that is, possession accompanied with an intent to become the owner. • *Possessio civilis* served as the basis for acquiring property by prescription (*usucapio*). Cf. *possessio naturalis.*

possessio fratris (pə-**zes**[**h**]-ee-oh **fray**-tris *or* **fra**-tris). [Latin] *Hist.* The possession or seisin of a brother; that is, a possession of an estate by a brother that would entitle his full sister to succeed him as heir, to the exclusion of a half-brother.

possessio mala fide (pə-**zes**[**h**]-ee-oh **mal**-ə **fI**-dee). [Latin] Possession in bad faith. Cf. *possessio bona fide.*

possessio naturalis (pə-**zes**[**h**]-ee-oh nach-ə-**ray**-lis). [Latin "natural possession"] *Roman law.* The simple holding of a thing, with no intent of keeping it permanently. — Also termed *nuda detentio.* See *natural possession* under POSSESSION. Cf. *possessio civilis.*

possession. 1. The fact of having or holding property in one's power; the exercise of dominion over property. **2.** The right under which one may exercise control over something to the exclusion of all others; the continuing exercise of a claim to the exclusive use of a material object. **3.** (*usu. pl.*) Something that a person owns or controls; PROPERTY (2). **4.** A territorial dominion of a state or nation. Cf. OWNERSHIP; TITLE (1).

"[A]s the name of Possession is . . . one of the most important in our books, so it is one of the most ambiguous. Its legal senses (for they are several) overlap the popular sense, and even the popular sense includes the assumption of matters of fact which are not always easy to verify. In common speech a man is said to possess or to be in possession of anything of which he has the apparent control, or from the use of which he has the apparent power of excluding others. . . . [A]ny of the usual outward marks of ownership may suffice, in the absence of manifest power in some one else, to denote as having possession the person to whom they attach. Law takes this popular conception as a provisional groundwork, and builds up on it the notion of possession in a technical sense, as a definite legal relation to something capable of having an owner, which relation is distinct and separable both from real and from apparent ownership, though often concurrent with one or both of them." Frederick Pollock & Robert Samuel Wright, *An Essay on Possession in the Common Law* 1–2 (1888).

"In the whole range of legal theory there is no conception more difficult than that of possession. The Roman lawyers brought their usual acumen to the analysis of it, and since their day the problem has formed the subject of a voluminous literature, while it still continues to tax the ingenuity of jurists. Nor is the question one of mere curiosity or scientific interest, for its practical importance is not less than its difficulty. The legal consequences which flow from the acquisition and loss of possession are many and serious. Possession, for example, is evidence of ownership; the possessor of a thing is presumed to be the owner of it, and may put all other claimants to proof of their title." John Salmond, *Jurisprudence* 285 (Glanville L. Williams ed., 10th ed. 1947).

actual possession. Physical occupancy or control over property. Cf. *constructive possession.*

adverse possession. See ADVERSE POSSESSION.

bona fide possession. Possession of property by a person who in good faith does not know that the property's ownership is disputed.

civil possession. *Civil law.* Possession existing by virtue of a person's intent to own a property even though the person no longer occupies or has physical control of it.

constructive possession. Control or dominion over a property without actual possession or custody of it. — Also termed *effective possession*; *possessio fictitia.* Cf. *actual possession.*

corporeal possession. Possession of a material object, such as a farm or a coin. — Also termed *natural possession*; *possessio corporis*; (Ger.) *Sachenbesitz.*

derivative possession. Lawful possession by one (such as a tenant) who does not hold title.

direct possession. See *immediate possession.*

effective possession. See *constructive possession.*

exclusive possession. The exercise of exclusive dominion over property, including the use and benefit of the property.

hostile possession. Possession asserted against the claims of all others, including the record owner. See ADVERSE POSSESSION.

immediate possession. Possession that is acquired or retained directly or personally. — Also termed *direct possession.*

incorporeal possession. Possession of something other than a material object, such as an easement over a neighbor's land, or the access of light to the windows of a house. — Also termed *possessio juris*; *quasi-possession.*

> "It is a question much debated whether incorporeal possession is in reality true possession at all. Some are of opinion that all genuine possession is corporeal, and that the other is related to it by way of analogy merely. They maintain that there is no single generic conception which includes *possessio corporis* and *possessio juris* as its two specific forms. The Roman lawyers speak with hesitation and even inconsistency on the point. They sometimes include both forms under the title of *possessio*, while at other times they are careful to qualify incorporeal possession as *quasi possessio* — something which is not true possession, but is analogous to it. The question is one of no little difficulty, but the opinion here accepted is that the two forms do in truth belong to a single genus. The true idea of possession is wider than that of corporeal possession, just as the true idea of ownership is wider than that of corporeal ownership." John Salmond, *Jurisprudence* 288–89 (Glanville L. Williams ed., 10th ed. 1947).

indirect possession. See *mediate possession.*

insular possession. An island territory of the United States, such as Puerto Rico.

mediate possession (**mee**-dee-it). Possession of a thing through someone else, such as an agent. • In every instance of mediate possession, there is a direct possessor (such as an agent) as well as a mediate possessor (the principal). — Also termed *indirect possession.*

> "If I go myself to purchase a book, I acquire direct possession of it; but if I send my servant to buy it for me, I acquire mediate possession of it through him, until he has brought it to me, when my possession becomes immediate." John Salmond, *Jurisprudence* 300 (Glanville L. Williams ed., 10th ed. 1947).

naked possession. The mere possession of something, esp. real estate, without any apparent right or colorable title to it.

natural possession. *Civil law.* The exercise of physical detention or control over a thing, as by occupying a building or cultivating farmland. • Natural possession may be had without title, and may give rise to a claim of unlawful possession or a claim of ownership by acquisitive prescription. The term "natural possession" has been replaced by the term "corporeal possession" in the Louisiana Civil Code, by virtue of a 1982 revision. The change was nonsubstantive. La. Civ. Code Ann. art. 3425 (West 1994). See *corporeal possession*; PRESCRIPTION (2).

notorious possession. Possession or control that is evident to others; possession of property that, because it is generally known by people in the area where the property is located, gives rise to a presumption that the actual owner has notice of it. • Notorious possession is one element of adverse possession. — Also termed *open possession*; *open and notorious possession.* See ADVERSE POSSESSION.

peaceable possession. Possession (as of real property) not disturbed by another's hostile or legal attempts to recover possession. Cf. ADVERSE POSSESSION.

pedal possession. Actual possession, as by living on the land or by improving it. • This term usu. appears in adverse-possession contexts.

possession in fact. Actual possession that may or may not be recognized by law. • For example, an employee's possession of an employer's property is for some purposes not legally considered possession, the term *detention* or *custody* being used instead. — Also termed *possessio naturalis.*

possession in law. **1.** Possession that is recognized by the law either because it is a specific type of possession in fact or because the law for some special reason attributes the advantages and results of possession to someone who does not in fact possess. **2.** See *constructive possession.* — Also termed *possessio civilis.*

> "There is no conception which will include all that amounts to possession in law, and will include nothing else, and it is impossible to frame any definition from which the concrete law of possession can be logically deduced." John Salmond, *Jurisprudence* 287 (Glanville L. Williams ed., 10th ed. 1947).

possession of a right. The de facto relation of continuing exercise and enjoyment of a right, as opposed to the de jure relation of ownership. — Also termed *possessio juris*; (Ger.) *Rechtsbesitz.*

precarious possession. *Civil law.* Possession of property by someone other than the owner on behalf of or with permission of the owner. • A lessee may have precarious possession of the leased property.

quasi possession. See *incorporeal possession.*

scrambling possession. Possession that is uncertain because it is in dispute. • With scrambling possession, the dispute is over who actually has possession — not over whether a party's possession is lawful.

possession unity. See *unity of possession* under UNITY.

possessor. One who has possession. — **possessorial** (pos-ə-**sor**-ee-əl), *adj.*

possessor bona fide (**boh**-nə **fɪ**-dee). A possessor who believes that no other person has a better right to the possession.

possessor mala fide (**mal**-ə **fɪ**-dee). A possessor who knows that someone else has a better right to the possession.

possessorium (pos-ə-**sor**-ee-əm). See *possessory action* under ACTION.

possessory (pə-**zes**-ə-ree), *adj.* Of, relating to, or having possession.

possessory action. See ACTION.

possessory claim. The title of a claimant to public land who has filed a declaratory statement but has not paid for the land.

possessory conservator. See CONSERVATOR.

possessory garageman's lien. See LIEN.

possessory interest. 1. The present right to control property, including the right to exclude others, by a person who is not necessarily the owner. **2.** A present or future right to the exclusive use and possession of property.

> "We shall use the term 'possessory interest' to include both present and future interests, and to exclude such interests as easements and profits. The reader should note that the Restatement of Property uses the term 'possessory' to refer only to interests that entitle the owner to *present* possession. See Restatement, Property §§ 7, 9, 153 (1936)." Thomas F. Bergin & Paul G. Haskell, *Preface to Estates in Land and Future Interests* 19–20 n.1 (2d ed. 1984).

possessory lien. See LIEN.

possessory warrant. A process similar to a search warrant used by a civil plaintiff to search for and recover property wrongfully taken.

possibilitas (pos-ə-**bil**-ə-tas). [Latin] Possibility; a possibility.

possibility. 1. An event that may or may not happen. **2.** A contingent interest in real or personal property.

naked possibility. A mere chance or expectation that a person will acquire future property. • A conveyance of a naked possibility is usu. void for lack of subject matter, as in a deed conveying all rights to a future estate not yet in existence. — Also termed *bare possibility*; *naked expectancy*.

possibility coupled with an interest. An expectation recognized in law as an estate or interest, as occurs in an executory devise or in a shifting or springing use. • This type of possibility may be sold or assigned.

remote possibility. A limitation dependent on two or more facts or events that are contingent and uncertain; a double possibility. — Also termed *possibility on a possibility*.

possibility of reverter. A future interest retained by a grantor after conveying a fee simple determinable, so that the grantee's estate terminates automatically and reverts to the grantor if the terminating event ever occurs. • In this type of interest, the grantor transfers an estate whose maximum potential duration equals that of the grantor's own estate and attaches a special limitation that operates in the grantor's favor. — Often shortened to *reverter*. See *fee simple determinable* under FEE SIMPLE. Cf. POWER OF TERMINATION.

> "Most treatise-writers define the possibility of reverter as the interest a transferor keeps when he transfers a fee simple determinable or a fee simple conditional. See, e.g., 1 American Law of Property § 4.12; Simes & Smith § 281. Although this definition is all right as far as it goes, it fails to provide for interests less than the fee simple that are granted on special limitation.... Although we call the possibility of reverter an 'estate,' the courts of an earlier era would probably have called it a 'possibility of becoming an estate.'" Thomas F. Bergin & Paul G. Haskell, *Preface to Estates in Land and Future Interests* 58 n.5 (2d ed. 1984).

possibility on a possibility. See *remote possibility* under POSSIBILITY.

POSSLQ (**pahs**-əl-kyoo). *abbr.* A person of opposite sex sharing living quarters. • Although this term is intended to include only a person's roommate of the opposite sex to whom the person is not married, the phrase literally includes those who are married. This overbreadth has occasionally been criticized. See CUPOS.

> "In the 1980 census, the United States Census Bureau — recognizing a societal change with numerous persons living together without being 'officially' married — counted not only persons who were 'Single' and

'Married,' but also 'Persons of the Opposite Sex Sharing Living Quarters.' The acronym is *POSSLQ* — and, of course, is pronounced *possle-kew*. It has been suggested that, although the source was stunningly unlikely, it was the Very Word that society has been looking for to describe these relationships: POSSLQ. Precise, business-like, nonjudgmental. And, in its own way, sort of poetic, too ...." *Fischer v. Dallas Federal Savings and Loan Ass'n*, 106 F.R.D. 465 (N.D. Tex. 1985).

post. [Latin] After. Cf. ANTE.

post, *vb.* **1.** To publicize or announce by affixing a notice in a public place <foreclosure notice was posted at the county courthouse>. **2.** To transfer (accounting entries) from an original record to a ledger <post debits and credits>. **3.** To place in the mail <post a letter>. **4.** To make a payment or deposit; to put up <post bail>.

postal currency. See CURRENCY.

post-answer default judgment. See DEFAULT JUDGMENT.

post audit. See AUDIT.

post bail, *vb.* See GIVE BAIL.

postconviction-relief proceeding. A state or federal procedure for a prisoner to request a court to vacate or correct a conviction or sentence. — Also termed *postconviction-remedy proceeding*; *PCR action*; *postconviction proceeding*.

postdate, *vb.* To put a date on (an instrument, such as a check) that is later than the actual date. Cf. ANTEDATE; BACKDATE.

postdated check. See CHECK.

post diem (pohst **dɪ**-əm). [Latin] After the day. • A plea of payment *post diem* is made after the day when the money becomes due.

post disseisina. See DE POST DISSEISINA.

postea (**poh**-stee-ə), *n.* [Latin "afterwards"] *Hist.* A formal statement, endorsed on a *nisi prius* record, giving an account of the proceedings at the trial of the action.

"With the verdict of the jury [in the 15th–18th centuries] ... the proceedings at *nisi prius* closed, and the case was sent back to the court at Westminster from which it issued for judgment, after a statement of the holding of the trial and of the verdict had been added to the record. This statement, from the fact that it began with the Latin word 'postea,' or 'afterwards,' was known as the 'postea' and was in fact drafted by the party in whose favour the verdict had gone, whence the phrase 'postea to the plaintiff' or 'the defendant,' which is found in the old reports." Geoffrey Radcliffe & Geoffrey Cross, *The English Legal System* 185 (G.J. Hand & D.J. Bentley eds., 6th ed. 1977).

posted water. See WATER.

posteriores (pah-steer-ee-**or**-eez). [Latin] *Roman law.* Descendants in a direct line beyond the sixth degree.

posteriority (pah-steer-ee-**or**-ə-tee). The condition or state of being subsequent. • This word was formerly used to describe the relationships existing between a tenant and the two or more lords the tenant held of; the tenant held the older tenancy "by priority" and the more recent one "by posteriority."

posterity, *n.* **1.** Future generations collectively. **2.** All the descendants of a person to the furthest generation.

post facto (pohst **fak**-toh). [Latin] After the fact. See EX POST FACTO.

post-factum (pohst-**fak**-təm). [Latin] An after-act; an act done afterwards. — Also termed *postfactum*.

post-fine. See KING'S SILVER.

postglossators (pohst-glah-**say**-tərz). *(often cap.)* A group of Italian jurisconsults who were active during the 14th and 15th centuries writing commentaries and treatises that related Roman law to feudal and Germanic law, canon law, and other contemporary bodies of law. • The postglossators constituted the second wave of Roman-law study after its revival in the 11th century, the first being that of the glossators. — Also termed *commentators*. See GLOSSATORS.

post hoc (pohst hok). [Latin fr. *post hoc, ergo propter hoc* "after this, therefore because of this"] **1.** *adv.* After this; consequently. **2.** *adj.* Of or relating to the fallacy of assuming causality from temporal sequence; confusing sequence with consequence.

posthumous (**pos**-chə-məs), *adj.* Occurring or existing after death; esp., (of a child) born after the father's death.

posthumous child. See CHILD.

posthumous work. *Copyright.* The product of an author who died before publication.

posting. 1. *Accounting.* The act of transferring an original entry to a ledger. **2.** The act of mailing a letter. **3.** A method of substituted service of process by displaying the process in a prominent place (such as the courthouse door) when other forms of service have failed. See SERVICE (1). **4.** A publication method, as by displaying municipal ordinances in designated localities. **5.** The act of providing legal notice, as by affixing notices of judicial sales at or on the courthouse door. **6.** The procedure for processing a check, including one or more of the following steps: (1) verifying any signature, (2) ascertaining that sufficient funds are available, (3) affixing a "paid" or other stamp, (4) entering a charge or entry to a customer's account, and (5) correcting or reversing an entry or erroneous action concerning the check.

postjudgment discovery. See DISCOVERY.

postliminium (pohst-lə-**min**-ee-əm), *n.* [fr. Latin *post* "after" + *limen* "threshold"] **1.** *Roman & civil law.* The doctrine that a restoration of a person's lost rights or status relates back to the time of the original loss or deprivation, esp. in regard to the restoration of the status of a prisoner of war.

> "[A] person who is taken captive and comes back within the limits of the Empire is correctly described as returning by postliminium. By 'limen' (threshold) we mean the frontier of a house, and the old lawyers applied the word to the frontier of the Roman State; so that the word postliminium conveys the idea of recrossing the frontier. If a prisoner is recovered from a beaten foe he is deemed to have come back by postliminium." R.W. Lee, *The Elements of Roman Law* 85–86 (4th ed. 1956).

2. *Int'l law.* The act of invalidating all an occupying force's illegal acts, and the post-occupation revival of all illegitimately modified legal relations to their former condition, esp. the restoration of property to its rightful owner. — Also termed *postliminy.*

post litem motam (pohst **lɪ**-təm **moh**-təm). [Law Latin] After suit commenced. • Depositions held after litigation had begun were formerly sometimes so called.

postman. *Hist.* A barrister in the Court of Exchequer who had precedence in motions. • The postman was so called because of the post he stood next to when making motions.

postmark. An official mark put by the post office on an item of mail to cancel the stamp and to indicate the place and date of sending or receipt.

postmaster. A U.S. Postal Service official responsible for a local branch of the post office. — Abbr. PM.

Postmaster General. The head of the U.S. Postal Service.

post meridiem (pohst mə-**rid**-ee-əm). [Latin] After noon. — Abbr. p.m.; PM.

postmortem, *adj.* Done or occurring after death <a postmortem examination>.

postmortem, *n.* See AUTOPSY.

post natus (pohst **nay**-təs). [Latin] A person born after a certain political event that affected the person's political rights; esp., a person born after the Declaration of Independence. Cf. ANTE NATUS.

post-note. A banknote payable at a future time rather than on demand.

postnuptial (pohst-**nəp**-shəl), *adj.* Made or occurring after marriage <a postnuptial contract>.

postnuptial agreement (pohst-**nəp**-shəl). An agreement entered into after marriage defining each spouse's property rights in the event of death or divorce. — Also termed *postnuptial settlement.* Cf. PRENUPTIAL AGREEMENT.

post-obit bond. See BOND (3).

postpone, *vb.* **1.** To put off to a later time. **2.** To place lower in precedence or importance; esp., to subordinate (a lien) to a later one. — **postponement,** *n.*

post prolem suscitatam (pohst **proh**-ləm səs-ə-**tay**-təm). [Law Latin] After issue born.

post-terminal sitting. A court session held after the normal term.

post terminum (pohst **tər**-mə-nəm). [Law Latin] After term, as a writ returned after the ending of a judicial term.

posttrial discovery. See *postjudgment discovery* under DISCOVERY.

posttrial motion. See MOTION.

postulatio (pos-chə-**lay**-shee-oh). [Latin] *Hist. Eccles. law.* A petition requesting the transfer of a bishop.

postulatio actionis (pos-chə-**lay**-shee-oh ak-shee-**oh**-nis). [Latin] *Roman law.* A request or petition to a magistrate having jurisdiction for permission to bring an action to redress a wrong. • This was similar to the former practice of applying for a writ.

potentate (**poh**-tən-tayt). A ruler who possesses great power or sway; a monarch.

potentia (pə-**ten**-shee-ə). [Latin] Possibility; power.

potential, *adj.* Capable of coming into being; possible <things having a potential existence may be the subject of mortgage, assignment, or sale>.

potential Pareto superiority. See WEALTH MAXIMIZATION.

potentia propinqua (pə-**ten**-shee-ə prə-**ping**-kwə). [Latin] Common possibility.

potestas (pə-**tes**-təs). [Latin "power"] *Roman law.* Authority or power, such as the power of a magistrate to enforce the law, or the authority of a master over a slave.

patria potestas (**pay**-tree-ə *or* **pa**-tree-ə pə-**tes**-təs). [Latin "paternal power"] The authority held by the male head of a family over his children and further descendants in the male line, unless emancipated. • Initially, the father had extensive powers over the family, including the power of life and death. Over time, the broad nature of the *patria potestas* gradually became more in the nature of a responsibility to support and maintain family members.

> "The power of the father continued ordinarily to the close of his life, and included not only his own children, but also the children of his sons, and those of his sons' sons, if any such were born during his lifetime.... Originally and for a long time the *patria potestas* had a terribly despotic character. Not only was the father entitled to all the service and all the acquisitions of his child, as much as to those of a slave, but he had the same absolute control over his person. He could inflict upon him any punishment however severe.... Consider now that the *patria potestas* had this character and extent down to the Christian era: that, in general, every citizen of the republic who had a living father was in this condition, unable to hold property, unable to acquire any thing for himself, wholly dependent on his father in property and person ... without help or vindication from the law.... The reason which caused the Romans to accept and uphold the *patria potestas*, to maintain it with singular tenacity against the influence of other systems with which they came in contact, must have been the profound impression of family unity, the conviction that every family was, and of right ought to be, one body, with one will and one executive." James Hadley, *Introduction to Roman Law* 119–21 (1881).

potestative condition. See CONDITION (2).

pound, *n.* **1.** A place where impounded property is held until redeemed. **2.** A place for the detention of stray animals. **3.** A measure of weight equal to 16 avoirdupois ounces or 7,000 grains. **4.** The basic monetary unit of the United Kingdom, equal to 100 pence. — Also termed (in sense 4) *pound sterling.*

poundage fee. A percentage commission awarded to a sheriff for moneys recovered under judicial process, such as execution or attachment.

pound-breach. *Hist.* The offense of breaking a pound for the purpose of taking out something that has been impounded.

pound of land. An uncertain quantity of land, usu. thought to be about 52 acres.

pound sterling. See POUND.

pour acquit (**poor** a-**kee**), *n.* [French "for acquittance"] *French law.* The formula that a creditor adds when signing a receipt.

pour appuyer (**poor** a-poo-**yay**). [Law French] For the support of; in the support of.

pour autrui (**poor** oh-troo-**ee**). [Law French] For others.

pour faire **proclaimer** (**poor fair** prə-**klay**-mər), *n.* [Law French "for making a proclamation"] *Hist.* A writ addressed to the mayor or bailiff of a city or town, requiring that official to make a proclamation about some matter, such as a nuisance.

pour out, *vb. Slang.* To deny (a claimant) damages or relief in a lawsuit <the plaintiff was poured out of court by the jury's verdict of no liability>.

pourover trust. See TRUST.

pourover will. See WILL.

pourparty (**poor**-pahr-tee). [Law French] See PURPARTY.

pourpresture (poor-**pres**-chər). [Law French] See PURPRESTURE.

pour seisir terres (poor **sI**-zər **ter**-eez). [Law French "for seizing the lands"] *Hist.* A writ by which the Crown could seize land that the wife of its deceased tenant, who held *in capite*, had for her dower if she married without leave.

poverty. 1. The condition of being indigent; the scarcity of the means of subsistence <war on poverty>. **2.** Dearth of something desirable <a poverty of ideas>.

poverty affidavit. See AFFIDAVIT.

***Powell* doctrine.** See CORRUPT-MOTIVE DOCTRINE.

power. 1. The ability to act or not act. **2.** Dominance, control, or influence over another. **3.** The legal right or authorization to act or not act; the ability conferred on a person by the law to alter, by an act of will, the rights, duties, liabilities, or other legal relations either of that person or of another. **4.** A document granting legal authorization. See AUTHORITY. **5.** An authority to affect an estate in land by (1) creating some estate independently of any estate that the holder of the authority possesses, (2) imposing a charge on the estate, or (3) revoking an existing estate. See POWER OF APPOINTMENT.

appendant power (ə-**pen**-dənt). **1.** A power that gives the donee a right to appoint estates that attach to the donee's own interest. **2.** A power held by a donee who owns the property interest in the assets subject to the power, and whose interest can be divested by the exercise of the power. • The power appendant is generally viewed as adding nothing to the ownership and thus is not now generally recognized as a true power. — Also termed *power appendant*.

beneficial power. A power that is executed for the benefit of the power's donee, as distinguished from a *trust power*, which is executed for the benefit of someone other than the power's donee (i.e., a trust beneficiary).

collateral power. A power created when the donee has no estate in the land, but simply the authority to appoint.

concurrent power. A political power independently exercisable by both federal and state governments in the same field of legislation.

congressional power. The authority vested in the U.S. Senate and House of Representatives to enact laws and take other constitutionally permitted actions. U.S. Const. art. I.

enumerated power. A political power specifically delegated to a governmental branch by a constitution. — Also termed *express power*.

general power. Power that can be exercised in anyone's favor, including the agent, to affect another's interest in property; a power that authorizes the alienation of a fee to any alienee.

implied power. A political power that is not enumerated but that nonetheless exists because it is needed to carry out an express power.

incident power. A power that, although not expressly granted, must exist because it is necessary to the accomplishment of an express purpose. — Also termed *incidental power*.

inherent power. A power that necessarily derives from an office, position, or status.

institorial power (in-stə-**tor**-ee-əl). *Civil law.* The power given by a business owner to an agent to act in the owner's behalf.

investigatory power (in-**ves**-tə-gə-tor-ee). (*usu. pl.*) The authority conferred on a governmental agency to inspect and compel disclosure of facts germane to an investigation.

judicial power. See JUDICIAL POWER.

naked power. The power to exercise rights over something (such as a trust) without having a corresponding interest in that thing. Cf. *power coupled with an interest*.

plenary power (**plee**-nə-ree *or* **plen**-ə-ree). Power that is broadly construed; esp., a court's power to dispose of any matter properly before it.

police power. See POLICE POWER.

power appendant. See *appendant power*.

power coupled with an interest. A power to do some act, conveyed along with an interest in the subject matter of the power. • A power coupled with an interest is not held for the benefit of the principal, and it is irrevocable due to the agent's interest in the subject property. For this reason, some authorities assert that it is not a true agency power. — Also termed *power given as security*; *proprietary power*. Cf. *naked power*.

"[S]uppose that the principal borrows money from the agent and by way of security authorizes the agent to sell Blackacre if the loan is not repaid and pay himself out of the proceeds. In such case there is no more reason why the principal should be permitted to revoke than if he had formally conveyed or mortgaged Blackacre to the agent. Hence it would be highly unfair to the agent to allow his principal to revoke. The reason why such a case is not properly governed by the considerations usually making an agency revocable is that this is in reality not a case of agency at all. In a normal agency case the power is conferred upon the agent to enable him to do something for the principal while here it is given to him to enable him to do something for himself. Coupled with an interest means that the agent must have a present interest in the property upon which the power is to operate." Harold Gill Reuschlein & William A. Gregory, *The Law of Agency and Partnership* § 47, at 99 (1990).

power in gross. A power held by a donee who has an interest in the assets subject to the power but whose interest cannot be affected by the exercise of the power. • An example is a life tenant with a power over the remainder.

power of acceptance. An offeree's power to bind an offeror to a contract by accepting the offer.

power of revocation (rev-ə-**kay**-shən). A power that a person reserves in an instrument (such as a trust) to revoke the legal relationship that the person has created.

power of sale. A power granted to sell the property that the power relates to.

power over oneself. See CAPACITY (2).

power over other persons. See AUTHORITY (1).

private power. A power vested in a person to be exercised for personal ends and not as an agent for the state.

proprietary power. See *power coupled with an interest.*

public power. A power vested in a person as an agent or instrument of the functions of the state. • Public powers comprise the various forms of legislative, judicial, and executive authority.

quasi-judicial power. An administrative agency's power to adjudicate the rights of those who appear before it.

quasi-legislative power. An administrative agency's power to engage in rulemaking. 5 USCA § 553.

relative power. A power that relates directly to land, as distinguished from a collateral power.

reserved power. A political power that is not enumerated or prohibited by a constitution, but instead is reserved by the constitution for a specified political authority, such as a state government. See TENTH AMENDMENT.

resulting power. A political power derived from the aggregate powers expressly or impliedly granted by a constitution.

special power. **1.** A power that either does not allow the entire estate to be conveyed or restricts to whom the estate may be conveyed. **2.** An agent's limited authority to perform only specific acts or to perform under specific restrictions.

spending power. The power granted to a governmental body to spend public funds; esp., the congressional power to spend money for the payment of debt and provision of the common defense and general welfare of the United States. U.S. Const. art. I, § 8, cl. 1.

taxing power. The power granted to a governmental body to levy a tax; esp., the congressional power to levy and collect taxes as a means of effectuating Congress's delegated powers. U.S. Const. art. I, § 8, cl. 1. See SIXTEENTH AMENDMENT.

power appendant. See POWER.

power coupled with an interest. See POWER.

power-delegating law. See LAW OF COMPETENCE.

power given as security. See *power coupled with an interest* under POWER.

power in gross. See POWER.

power of acceptance. See POWER.

power of alienation. The capacity to sell, transfer, assign, or otherwise dispose of property.

power of appointment. A power conferred on a donee by will or deed to select and nominate one or more recipients of the donor's estate or income. — Also termed *enabling power.*

general power of appointment. A power of appointment by which the donee can appoint — that is, dispose of the donor's property — in favor of anyone the donee chooses.

limited power of appointment. A power of appointment by which the donee can appoint to only the person or class specified in the instrument creating the power. — Also termed *special power of appointment.*

testamentary power of appointment (tes-tə-**men**-tə-ree *or* -tree). A power of appointment created by a will.

power-of-appointment trust. See TRUST.

power of attorney. 1. An instrument granting someone authority to act as agent or attorney-in-fact for the grantor. — Also termed *letter of attorney*. **2.** The authority so granted. Pl. **powers of attorney.** See ATTORNEY (1).

durable power of attorney. A power of attorney that remains in effect during the grantor's incompetency. • Such instruments commonly allow an agent to make healthcare decisions for a patient who has become incompetent.

general power of attorney. A power of attorney that authorizes an agent to transact business for the principal.

irrevocable power of attorney (i-**rev**-ə-kə-bəl). A power of attorney that the principal cannot revoke. — Also termed *power of attorney coupled with an interest*. See *power coupled with an interest* under POWER.

power of attorney coupled with an interest. See *irrevocable power of attorney*.

special power of attorney. A power of attorney that limits the agent's authority to only a specified matter.

power of revocation (rev-ə-**kay**-shən). See POWER.

power of sale. See POWER.

power-of-sale clause. A provision in a mortgage or deed of trust permitting the mortgagee or trustee to sell the property without court authority if the payments are not made.

power-of-sale foreclosure. See FORECLOSURE.

power of termination. A future interest retained by a grantor after conveying a fee simple subject to a condition subsequent, so that the grantee's estate terminates (upon breach of the condition) only if the grantor exercises the right to retake it. — Also termed *right of entry*; *right of reentry*; *right of entry for breach of condition*; *right of entry for condition broken*. See *fee simple subject to a condition subsequent* under FEE SIMPLE. Cf. POSSIBILITY OF REVERTER.

power over oneself. See CAPACITY (2).

power over other persons. See AUTHORITY (1).

power politics. *Int'l law.* An approach to foreign policy that encourages a nation to use its economic and military strength to enlarge its own power as an end in itself; a system in which a country is willing to bring its economic and (esp.) military strength to bear in an effort to increase its own power.

p.p. *abbr.* **1.** PER PROCURATIONEM. **2.** PROPRIA PERSONA.

PPI. *abbr.* POLICY PROOF OF INTEREST.

PPO. *abbr.* PREFERRED-PROVIDER ORGANIZATION.

p. pro. *abbr.* PER PROCURATIONEM.

p. proc. *abbr.* PER PROCURATIONEM.

PR. *abbr.* PUBLIC RELATIONS.

practicable, *adj.* (Of a thing) reasonably capable of being accomplished; feasible.

practicably irrigable acreage. Land that is susceptible to prolonged irrigation, at reasonable cost.

practice, *n.* **1.** The procedural methods and rules used in a court of law <local practice requires that an extra copy of each motion be filed with the clerk>. **2.** PRACTICE OF LAW <where is your practice?>.

practice act. A statute governing practice and procedure in courts. • Practice acts are usu. supplemented with court rules such as the Federal Rules of Civil Procedure.

practice book. A volume devoted to the procedures in a particular court or category of courts, usu. including court rules, court forms, and practice directions.

practice court. 1. MOOT COURT. **2.** (*cap.*) BAIL COURT.

practice of law. The professional work of a duly licensed lawyer, encompassing a broad range of services such as conducting cases in court, preparing papers necessary to bring about various transactions from conveying land to effecting corporate mergers, preparing legal opinions on various points of law, drafting wills and other estate-planning documents, and advising clients on countless types of legal questions. • The term also includes activities that comparatively few lawyers engage in but that require legal expertise, such as drafting legislation and court rules. — Also termed *legal practice*. Cf. LAW PRACTICE.

unauthorized practice of law. The practice of law by a person, typically a nonlawyer, who has not been licensed or admitted to practice law in a given jurisdiction. — Abbr. UPL.

"The definitions and tests employed by courts to delineate unauthorized practice by non-lawyers have been vague or conclusory, while jurisdictions have differed significantly in describing what constitutes unauthorized practice in particular areas.

"Certain activities, such as the representation of another person in litigation, are generally proscribed. Even in that area, many jurisdictions recognize exceptions for such matters as small-claims and landlord-tenant tribunals and certain proceedings in administrative agencies. Moreover, many jurisdictions have authorized law students and others not locally admitted to represent indigent persons or others as part of clinical legal education programs.

"Controversy has surrounded many out-of-court activities such as advising on estate planning by bank trust officers, advising on estate planning by insurance agents, stock brokers, or benefit-plan and similar consultants, filling out or providing guidance on forms for property transactions by real estate agents, title companies, and closing-service companies, and selling books or individual forms containing instructions on self-help legal services accompanied by personal, non-lawyer assistance on filling them out in connection with legal procedures such as obtaining a marriage dissolution. The position of bar associations has traditionally been that non-lawyer provisions of such services denies the person served the benefit of such legal measures as the attorney-client privilege, the benefits of such extraordinary duties as that of confidentiality of client information and the protection against conflicts of interest, and the protection of such measures as those regulating lawyer trust accounts and requiring lawyers to supervise non-lawyer personnel. Several jurisdictions recognize that many such services can be provided by non-lawyers without significant risk of incompetent service, that actual experience in several states with extensive non-lawyer provision of traditional legal services indicates no significant risk of harm to consumers of such services, that persons in need of legal services may be significantly aided in obtaining assistance at a much lower price than would be entailed by segregating out a portion of a transaction to be handled by a lawyer for a fee, and that many persons can ill afford, and most persons are at least inconvenienced by, the typically higher cost of lawyer services." Restatement (Third) of the Law Governing Lawyers § 4 cmt. c (1998).

practick (**prak**-tik). *Scots law.* A precedent that is not necessarily binding.

practitioner. A person engaged in the practice of a profession, esp. law or medicine.

praeceptores (pree-sep-**tor**-eez). [Law Latin "masters"] *Hist.* The chief clerks of Chancery, responsible for preparing remedial writs.

praecipe (**pree**-sə-pee *or* **pres**-ə-pee), *n.* [Latin "command"] **1.** At common law, a writ ordering a defendant to do some act or to explain why inaction is appropriate. — Also termed *writ of praecipe*. **2.** A written motion or request seeking some court action, esp. a trial setting or an entry of judgment. — Also spelled *precipe*. — **praecipe,** *vb.*

praecipe quod reddat (**pree**-sə-pee or **pres**-ə-pee kwod **red**-at). [Latin "command that he render"] *Hist.* A writ directing the defendant to return certain property. • An action for common recovery was often begun with this writ. When the writ was brought to recover land, it was termed *ingressu*. See COMMON RECOVERY.

"The *praecipe quod reddat* was the proper writ when the plaintiff's action was for a specifick thing; as for the recovery of a debt certain, or for the restoration of such a chattel, or for giving up such a house, or so much land, specifying the nature and quantity of it. By this writ the sheriff was commanded to summon the tenant or defendant to appear at *Westminster*, at such a day in term." 1 George Crompton, *Rules and Cases of Practice in the Courts of King's Bench and Common Pleas* xxxix (3d ed. 1787).

praecipitium (pree-sə-**pish**-ee-əm *or* pres-ə-). [Latin] *Roman law.* The punishment of casting a criminal from the Tarpeian rock.

praeco (**pree**-koh). [Latin] *Roman law.* A herald or crier.

praedia (**pree**-dee-ə), *n.* [Latin] *pl.* PRAEDIUM.

praedial (**pree**-dee-əl), *adj.* See PREDIAL.

praedictus (pri-**dik**-təs). [Law Latin] *Hist.* Aforesaid. • In pleading, *praedictus* usu. referred to a defendant, a town, or lands, *idem* to a plaintiff, and *praefatus* to a person other than a party. Cf. PRAEFATUS.

praedium (**pree**-dee-əm), *n.* [Latin] *Roman law.* Land; an estate. Pl. ***praedia.***

praedia bellica (**pree**-dee-ə **bel**-ə-kə). [Latin] Property seized in war; booty.

praedia stipendiaria (**pree**-dee-ə stI-pen-dee-**air**-ee-ə). [Latin] Provincial lands belonging to the public.

praedia tributaria (**pree**-dee-ə trib-yoo-**tair**-ee-ə). [Latin] Provincial lands belonging to the emperor.

praedium dominans (**pree**-dee-əm **dom**-ə-nanz). [Latin] A dominant estate.

praedium rusticum (**pree**-dee-əm **rəs**-ti-kəm). [Latin] An estate used for agricultural purposes.

praedium serviens (**pree**-dee-əm **sər**-vee-enz). [Latin] An estate burdened by a servitude; a servient estate.

praedium urbanum (**pree**-dee-əm ər-**bay**-nəm). [Latin] An estate used for business or for dwelling; any estate other than a *praedium rusticum*.

praedo (**pree**-doh), *n.* [Latin] *Roman law.* A robber.

praefatus (pri-**fay**-təs). [Latin] Aforesaid. — Abbr. *praefat; p. fat.* Cf. PRAEDICTUS.

praefectura (pri-**fek**-chər-ə), *n.* [Latin] *Roman law.* **1.** The office of prefect. **2.** A town or territory administered by a prefect.

praefectus vigilium (pri-**fek**-təs vi-**jil**-ee-əm), *n.* [Latin "prefect of the watch"] *Roman law.* An officer with police and fire-prevention duties. • This officer had the authority to punish offenses relating to the public peace.

praefectus villae (pri-**fek**-təs **vil**-ee), *n.* [Latin] *Hist.* The mayor of a town.

praefine. See PRIMER FINE.

praejuramentum (pree-juur-ə-**men**-təm), *n.* [Law Latin] *Hist.* A preparatory oath.

praelegatum (pree-lə-**gay**-təm), *n.* [Latin] *Roman law.* A legacy given in advance of the whole or part of the share that a given heir would be entitled to receive out of an inheritance. • This was similar to an advancement.

praemium emancipationis (**pree**-mee-əm i-man-sə-pay-shee-**oh**-nis), *n.* [Latin "reward for emancipation"] *Roman law.* A compensation allowed by Constantine to a father on the emancipation of his child, consisting of one-third of the property that came to the child from his mother's side. • Justinian replaced this with the usufruct of half the child's separate property.

praemium pudicitiae (**pree**-mee-əm pyoo-də-**sish**-ee-ee), *n.* [Latin "the price of chastity"] *Hist.* Compensation paid by a man who seduced a chaste woman. — Also termed *praemium pudoris.*

praemunire (pree-myoo-**nI**-ree), *n.* [Latin *praemoneri* "to be forewarned"] *Hist.* The criminal offense of obeying an authority other than the king. • *Praemunire* stems from the efforts of Edward I (1272–1307) to counter papal influence in England, and takes its name from the writ's initial words: *praemunire facias* ("that you cause to be forewarned"). *Praemunire* offenses included an archbishop's refusal to elect a royal nominee as bishop, and an assertion that Parliament had legislative authority without the sovereign.

praenomen (pree-**noh**-mən), *n.* [Latin] *Roman law.* The first of a person's three names, given to distinguish the person from family members.

praepositus (pree-**poz**-ə-təs), *n.* [Latin] *Hist.* **1.** An officer next in authority to the alderman of a hundred. **2.** A steward or bailiff of an estate.

praepositus villae (pree-**poz**-ə-təs **vil**-ee), *n.* [Latin] *Hist.* A constable of a town; a petty constable.

praerogativa regis (pree-rog-ə-**tI**-və **ree**-jis), *n.* [Law Latin "of the Crown's prerogative"] *Hist.* A declaration made at the time of Edward I (1272–1307) defining certain feudal and political rights of the Crown, including the right to wardship of an idiot's lands to protect the idiot's heirs from disinheritance or alienation. — Also termed *de praerogativa regis* (dee pree-rog-ə-**tI**-və **ree**-jis).

> "The king's right is distinctly stated in the document known as *praerogativa Regis*, which we believe to come from the early years of Edward I. The same document seems to be the oldest that gives us any clear information about a wardship of lunatics. The king is to provide that the lunatic and his family are properly maintained out of the income of his estate, and the residue is to be handed over to him upon his restoration to sanity, or, should he die without having recovered his wits, is to be administered by the ordinary for the good of his soul; but the king is to take nothing to his own use." 1 Frederick Pollock & Frederic W. Maitland, *The History of English Law Before the Time of Edward I* 481 (2d ed. 1898).

praescriptio (pri-**skrip**-shee-oh), *n.* [Latin] *Roman law.* **1.** A preliminary portion of a *formula* that defines the scope of action or states an exception or objection to the action. **2.** A defensive plea in an action to recover land by which the defendant asserts ownership based on continuous possession for a prescribed time. — Also termed (in sense 2) *praescriptio longi temporis.*

praeses (**pree**-seez), *n.* [Latin] **1.** *Roman law.* A governor of a province. **2.** The president of a college or university.

praestare (pree-**stair**-ee), *vb.* [Latin] *Roman law.* **1.** To perform an obligation. **2.** To undertake liability.

praesumitur pro negante (pri-**zyoo**-mə-tər proh ni-**gan**-tee). [Latin] It is presumed for the negative. • This is the rule of the House of Lords when the votes are equal on a motion.

praesumptio (pri-**zəmp**-shee-oh). [Latin] A presumption.

praesumptio fortior (pri-**zəmp**-shee-oh **for**-shee-ər *or* -or). [Latin] A strong presumption (of fact); a presumption strong enough to shift the burden of proof to the opposing party.

praesumptio hominis (pri-**zəmp**-shee-oh **hom**-ə-nis). [Latin] The presumption of an individual; that is, a natural presumption unfettered by rules.

praesumptio juris (pri-**zəmp**-shee-oh **joor**-is). [Latin] A presumption of law; that is, one in which the law assumes the existence of something until it is disproved. See *presumption of law* under PRESUMPTION.

praesumptio Muciana (pri-**zəmp**-shee-oh myoo-shee-**ay**-nə). [Latin] *Roman law.* The rebuttable presumption that in case of doubt a thing possessed by a married woman had been given to her by her husband. • The presumption was named after the jurist Quintus Mucius.

praeteritio (pree-tə- *or* pret-ə-**rish**-ee-oh). [Latin] A testator's exclusion of an heir by passing the heir over.

praetor (**pree**-tər). [Latin] *Roman law.* A magistrate responsible for identifying and framing the legal issues in a case and ordering a lay judge (*judex*) to hear evidence and decide the case in accordance with the statement of the issues.

praetor fidei-commissarius (**pree**-tər **fi**-dee-ɪ-kom-ə-**sair**-ee-əs). A special praetor having jurisdiction of cases involving trusts.

praetorian edict. See EDICT.

praevaricator (pree-var-ə-**kay**-tər). See PREVARICATOR.

pratique (pra-**teek** *or* **prat**-ik). *Maritime law.* A license allowing a vessel to trade in a particular country or port after complying with quarantine requirements or presenting a clean bill of health.

praxis (**prak**-sis). [Greek "doing; action"] In critical legal studies, practical action; the practice of living the ethical life in conjunction and in cooperation with others.

prayer for relief. A request addressed to the court and appearing at the end of a pleading; esp., a request for specific relief or damages. — Often shortened to *prayer.* — Also termed *demand for relief.*

"*The prayer for relief.* The plaintiff prays in his bill for the relief to which he supposes himself entitled on the case made out in the bill. This is called the *special* prayer. He then prays for general relief, usually in these words: 'And the plaintiff (*or* your orator) prays for such further or other relief as the nature of the case may require, and as may be agreeable to equity and good conscience.' Both prayers are generally inserted in the bill, — the special prayer first, the general following." Edwin E. Bryant, *The Law of Pleading Under the Codes of Civil Procedure* 69 (2d ed. 1899).

general prayer. A prayer for additional unspecified relief, traditionally using language such as, "Plaintiff additionally prays for such other and further relief to which she may show herself to be justly entitled." • The general prayer typically follows a special prayer.

special prayer. A prayer for the particular relief to which a plaintiff claims to be entitled.

prayer in aid. See AID PRAYER.

prayer of process. A conclusion in a bill in equity requesting the issuance of a subpoena if the defendant fails to answer the bill.

preamble (**pree**-am-bəl), *n.* An introductory statement in a constitution, statute, or other document explaining the document's basis and objective; esp., a statutory recital of the inconveniences for which the statute is designed to provide a remedy. — **preambulary** (pree-**am**-byə-ler-ee), **preambular** (pree-**am**-byə-lər), *adj.*

preappointed evidence. See EVIDENCE.

preaudience. *English law.* The right of a senior barrister to be heard in court before other barristers.

prebankruptcy, *adj.* Occurring before the filing of a bankruptcy petition <prebankruptcy transactions>.

prebend (**preb**-ənd), *n.* **1.** A stipend granted in a cathedral church for the support of the members of the chapter. **2.** The property from which the stipend comes.

prebendary (**preb**-ən-der-ee). A person serving on the staff of a cathedral who receives a stipend from the cathedral's endowment.

precariae (pri-**kair**-ee-ee). [Law Latin "favors"] *Hist.* Day labor that tenants of certain manors were bound to give their lords at harvest time. — Also termed *preces.*

precarious, *adj.* Dependent on the will or pleasure of another; uncertain.

precarious loan. See LOAN.

precarious possession. See POSSESSION.

precarious right. See RIGHT.

precarious trade. See TRADE.

precarium (pri-**kair**-ee-əm). [Latin] **1.** *Roman law.* Property granted or lent, to be returned at the will of the grantor. **2.** *Hist.* An estate or tenure arising from a precarious grant, and usu. characterized by uncertainty or arduous conditions of tenure.

precatory (**prek**-ə-tor-ee), *adj.* (Of words) requesting, recommending, or expressing a desire for action, but usu. in a nonbinding way. • An example of precatory language is "it is my wish and desire to . . . ."

precatory trust. See TRUST.

precedence (**pres**-ə-dənts *or* prə-**seed**-ənts), *n.* **1.** The act or state of going before; esp., the order or priority in place or time observed by or for persons of different statuses (such as political dignitaries) on the basis of rank during ceremonial events. **2.** The order in which persons may claim the right to administer an intestate's estate. • The traditional order is (1) surviving spouse, (2) next of kin, (3) creditors, and (4) public administrator.

precedent (prə-**seed**-ənt *also* **pres**-ə-dənt), *adj.* Preceding in time or order <condition precedent>.

precedent (**pres**-ə-dənt), *n.* **1.** The making of law by a court in recognizing and applying new rules while administering justice. **2.** A decided case that furnishes a basis for determining later cases involving similar facts or issues. — **precedential,** *adj.* See STARE DECISIS.

> "In law a precedent is an adjudged case or decision of a court of justice, considered as furnishing a rule or authority for the determination of an identical or similar case afterwards arising, or of a similar question of law. The only theory on which it is possible for one decision to be an authority for another is that the facts are alike, or, if the facts are different, that the principle which governed the first case is applicable to the variant facts." William M. Lile et al., *Brief Making and the Use of Law Books* 288 (3d ed. 1914).

> "A precedent . . . is a judicial decision which contains in itself a principle. The underlying principle which thus forms its authoritative element is often termed the *ratio decidendi*. The concrete decision is binding between the parties to it, but it is the abstract *ratio decidendi* which alone has the force of law as regards the world at large." John Salmond, *Jurisprudence* 191 (Glanville L. Williams ed., 10th ed. 1947).

> "One may say, roughly, that a case becomes a precedent only for such a general rule as is necessary to the actual decision reached, when shorn of unessential circumstances." 1 James Parker Hall, Introduction, *American Law and Procedure* xlviii (1952).

> "One may often accord respect to a precedent not by embracing it with a frozen logic but by drawing from its thought the elements of a new pattern of decision." Lon L. Fuller, *Anatomy of the Law* 151 (1968).

binding precedent. A precedent that a court must follow. • For example, a lower court is bound by an applicable holding of a higher court in the same jurisdiction. — Also termed *authoritative precedent*; *binding authority.* Cf. *imperative authority* under AUTHORITY (4).

declaratory precedent. A precedent that is merely the application of an already existing legal rule.

original precedent. A precedent that creates and applies a new legal rule.

persuasive precedent. A precedent that a court may either follow or reject, but that is entitled to respect and careful consideration. • For example, if the case was decided in a neighboring jurisdiction, the court might evaluate the earlier court's reasoning without being bound to decide the same way.

precedent sub silentio (səb sə-**len**-shee-oh). A legal question that was neither argued nor considered in a judicial decision that is or might be treated as a precedent.

3. DOCTRINE OF PRECEDENT. **4.** A form of pleading or property-conveyancing instrument. • Precedents are often compiled in book form and used by lawyers as guides for preparing similar documents.

> "Collections of Precedents have existed from very early times. In this connection precedents must not be confused with judicial precedents or case law. We refer here simply to common-form instruments compiled for use in practice, whereby the lawyer can be more or less certain that he is using the correct phraseology for the particular case before him. They were used both in conveyancing and litigation.... It is interesting to note that these precedents were apparently among the first legal works to be published after printing was introduced. Collections of conveyancing precedents continued to be brought up to date or new volumes issued...." A.K.R. Kiralfy, *Potter's Outlines of English Legal History* 42–43 (5th ed. 1958).

prece partium (**pree**-see **pahr**-shee-əm). [Law Latin] On the prayer of the parties.

precept (**pree**-sept). **1.** A standard or rule of conduct; a command or principle <several legal precepts govern here>. **2.** A writ or warrant issued by an authorized person demanding another's action, such as a judge's order to an officer to bring a party before the court <the sheriff executed the precept immediately>.

preces (**pree**-seez). [Latin "prayers"] *Roman law.* A petition addressed to the emperor by a private person. Cf. RESCRIPT (3).

preces primariae (**pree**-seez prɪ-**mair**-ee-ee). [Latin] *Hist.* The right of the sovereign to appoint a person to fill a vacant prebendary office after the sovereign's accession. • This right was exercised during the reign of Edward I. — Also termed *primae preces.* See PREBENDARY.

precinct. A geographical unit of government, such as an election district, a police district, or a judicial district.

precipe (**pre**-sə-pee). See PRAECIPE.

précis (pray-**see** *or* **pray**-see), *n.* [French] A concise summary of a text's essential points; an abstract. Pl. **précis** (pray-**seez** *or* **pray**-seez).

precludi non debet (pri-**kloo**-dɪ non **dee**-bet *or* **deb**-et). [Latin "he ought not to be barred"] *Hist.* The beginning of a plaintiff's reply to a plea in bar in which the plaintiff objects to being barred from maintaining the action.

preclusion order. See ORDER (2).

precompounded prescription drug. See DRUG.

preconceived malice. See MALICE AFORETHOUGHT.

precontract. See CONTRACT.

predate, *vb.* See ANTEDATE.

predatory intent. See INTENT (1).

predatory pricing. Unlawful below-cost pricing intended to eliminate specific competitors and reduce overall competition; pricing below an appropriate measure of cost for the purpose of eliminating competitors in the short run and reducing competition in the long run. See ANTITRUST.

predecease, *vb.* To die before (another) <she predeceased her husband>.

predecessor. 1. One who precedes another in an office or position. **2.** An ancestor.

predecisional, *adj.* Of, relating to, or occurring during the time before a decision.

predial (**pree**-dee-əl), *adj.* Of, consisting of, relating to, or attached to land <predial servitude>. — Also spelled *praedial.*

predial servitude. See *servitude appurtenant* under SERVITUDE.

predicate act. In the law of RICO, one of two or more related acts of racketeering necessary to establish a pattern. See RACKETEER INFLUENCED AND CORRUPT ORGANIZATIONS ACT.

predicate fact. See FACT.

prediction theory. See BAD-MAN THEORY; PREDICTIVE THEORY OF LAW.

predictive theory of law. The view that the law is nothing more than a set of predictions about what the courts will decide in given circumstances. • This theory is embodied in Holmes's famous pronouncement, "The prophecies of what the courts will do in fact, and nothing more pretentious, are what I mean by the law." Oliver Wendell Holmes, Jr., *The Path of the Law,* 10 Harv. L. Rev. 457, 460–61 (1897). — Also termed *prediction theory.* Cf. BAD-MAN THEORY.

predisposition. A person's inclination to engage in a particular activity; esp., an inclination that vitiates a criminal defendant's claim of entrapment.

preemption (pree-**emp**-shən), *n.* **1.** The right to buy before others. See RIGHT OF PREEMPTION. **2.** The purchase of something under this right. **3.** An earlier seizure or appropriation. **4.** The occupation of public land so as to establish a preemptive title. **5.** *Constitutional law.* The principle (derived from the Supremacy Clause) that a federal law can supersede or supplant any inconsistent state law or regulation. — Also termed (in sense 5) *federal preemption.* — **preempt,** *vb.* — **preemptive,** *adj.* See COMPLETE-PREEMPTION DOCTRINE.

Garmon preemption. *Labor law.* A doctrine prohibiting state and local regulation of activities that are actually or arguably (1) protected by the National Labor Relations Act's rules relating to the right of employees to organize and bargain collectively, or (2) prohibited by the National Labor Relations Act's provision that governs unfair labor practices. *San Diego Bldg. Trades Council v. Garmon,* 359 U.S. 236, 79 S.Ct. 773 (1959). — Also termed *Garmon doctrine.* See COLLECTIVE BARGAINING; UNFAIR LABOR PRACTICE.

Machinists preemption. *Labor law.* The doctrine prohibiting state regulation of an area of labor activity or management-union relations that Congress has intentionally left unregulated. *Lodge 76, Int'l Ass'n of Machinists v. Wisconsin Employment Relations Comm'n,* 427 U.S. 132, 96 S.Ct. 2548 (1976).

preemption claimant. One who has settled on land subject to preemption, intending in good faith to acquire title to it.

preemption right. The privilege to take priority over others in claiming land subject to preemption. • The privilege arises from the holder's actual settlement of the land.

preemptive right. A shareholder's privilege to purchase newly issued stock — before the shares are offered to the public — in an amount proportionate to the shareholder's current holdings in order to prevent dilution of the shareholder's ownership interest. • This right must be exercised within a fixed period, usu. 30 to 60 days. — Also termed *subscription privilege.* See SUBSCRIPTION RIGHT. Cf. *rights offering* under OFFERING.

preexisting condition. See CONDITION (2).

preexisting duty. See DUTY (1).

preexisting-duty rule. *Contracts.* The rule that if a party does or promises to do what the party is already legally obligated to do — or refrains or promises to refrain from doing what the party is already legally obligated to refrain from doing — the party has not incurred detriment. • This rule's result is that the promise does not constitute adequate consideration for contractual purposes. For example, if a builder agrees to construct a building for a specified price but later threatens to walk off the job unless the owner promises to pay an additional sum, the owner's new promise is not enforceable because, under the preexisting-duty rule, there is no consideration for that promise. — Also termed *preexisting-legal-duty rule.*

prefect (**pree**-fekt), *n.* **1.** A high official or magistrate put in charge of a particular command, department, or region. **2.** In New Mexico, a probate judge.

prefer, *vb.* **1.** To put forward or present for consideration; esp. (of a grand jury), to bring (a charge or indictment) against a criminal suspect <the defendant claimed he was innocent of the charges preferred against him>. **2.** To give priority to, such as to one creditor over another <the statute prefers creditors who are first to file their claims>.

preference. **1.** The act of favoring one person or thing over another; the person or thing so favored. **2.** Priority of payment given to one or more creditors by a debtor; a creditor's right to receive such priority. **3.** *Bankruptcy.* PREFERENTIAL TRANSFER.

insider preference. A transfer of property by a bankruptcy debtor to an insider more than 90 days before but within one year after the filing of the bankruptcy petition.

liquidation preference. A preferred shareholder's right, once the corporation is liquidated, to receive a specified distribution before common shareholders receive anything.

voidable preference. See PREFERENTIAL TRANSFER.

preference shares. See *preferred stock* under STOCK.

preferential assignment. See PREFERENTIAL TRANSFER.

preferential debt. See DEBT.

preferential rule. *Evidence.* A rule that prefers one kind of evidence to another. • It may work provisionally, as when a tribunal refuses to consider one kind of evidence until another kind (presumably better) is shown to be unavailable, or it may work absolutely, as when the tribunal refuses to consider anything but the better kind of evidence.

> "There are only three or four . . . sets of [preferential] rules. There is a rule preferring the production of the *original of a document*, in preference to a copy. There is a rule requiring the *attesting witness* to a will to be summoned to evidence its execution. And there is a rule preferring the magistrate's *official report* of testimony taken before him. Then there are a few miscellaneous rules, such as the officially certified enrollment of a statute, etc." John H. Wigmore, *A Students' Textbook of the Law of Evidence* 219 (1935).

preferential shop. See SHOP.

preferential tariff. See TARIFF (2).

preferential transfer. *Bankruptcy.* A prebankruptcy transfer made by an insolvent debtor to or for the benefit of a creditor, thereby allowing the creditor to receive more than its proportionate share of the debtor's assets; specif., an insolvent debtor's transfer of a property interest for the benefit of a creditor who is owed on an earlier debt, when the transfer occurs no more than 90 days before the date when the bankruptcy petition is filed or (if the creditor is an insider) within one year of the filing, so that the creditor receives more than it would otherwise receive through the distribution of the bankruptcy estate. • Under the circumstances described in 11 USCA § 547, the bankruptcy trustee may recover — for the estate's benefit — a preferential transfer from the transferee. — Also termed *preference*; *voidable preference*; *voidable transfer*; *preferential assignment*. Cf. FRAUDULENT CONVEYANCE (2).

preferred, *adj.* Possessing or accorded a priority or privilege <a preferred claim>.

preferred creditor. See CREDITOR.

preferred dividend. See DIVIDEND.

preferred docket. See DOCKET (2).

preferred-provider organization. A group of healthcare providers (such as doctors, hospitals, and pharmacies) that agree to provide medical services at a discounted cost to covered persons in a given geographic area. — Abbr. PPO. Cf. HEALTH-MAINTENANCE ORGANIZATION.

preferred stock. See STOCK.

preferring of charges. *Military law.* The formal completion of a charge sheet, which includes signing and swearing to the charges and specifications. • Only a person subject to the Uniform Code of Military Justice can prefer charges. Cf. INITIATION OF CHARGES.

prehearing conference. An optional conference for the discussion of procedural and substantive matters on appeal, usu. held in complex civil, criminal, tax, and agency cases. • Those attending are typically the attorneys involved in the case as well as a court representative such as a judge, staff attorney, or deputy clerk. Fed. R. App. P. 33.

> "The prehearing conference, if held, generally is scheduled after the time for appeal and cross-appeal has passed, and as soon as it becomes apparent that the case is complex due to the legal issues, the length of the record, or the number of parties. In a complex or multiparty case, the conference provides a forum in which to discuss briefing responsibilities, timing, and handling the record and joint appendix. There may be some discussion of the amount of oral argument the parties desire and how that argument will be divided . . . ." Michael E. Tigar, *Federal Appeals: Jurisdiction and Practice* § 8.06, at 309–10 (2d ed. 1993).

prejudice, *n.* **1.** Damage or detriment to one's legal rights or claims. See *dismissal with/without prejudice* under DISMISSAL.

legal prejudice. A condition that, if shown by a party, will usu. defeat the opposing party's action; esp., a condition that, if shown by the defendant, will defeat a plaintiff's motion to dismiss a case without prejudice. • The defendant may show that dismissal will deprive the defendant of a substantive property right or preclude the defendant from raising a defense that will be unavailable or endangered in a second suit.

undue prejudice. The harm resulting from a fact-trier's being exposed to evidence that is persuasive but inadmissible (such as evidence of prior criminal conduct) or that so arouses the emotions that calm and logical reasoning is abandoned.

2. A preconceived judgment formed without a factual basis; a strong bias. — **prejudice,** *vb.* — **prejudicial,** *adj.*

prejudicial error. See *reversible error* under ERROR (2).

prejudicial publicity. Extensive media attention devoted to an upcoming civil or criminal trial. • Under the Due Process Clause, extensive coverage of a criminal trial may deprive the defendant of a fair trial.

preliminary, *adj*. Coming before and usu. leading up to the main part of something <preliminary negotiations>.

preliminary complaint. See COMPLAINT.

preliminary crime. See *inchoate offense* under OFFENSE (1).

preliminary evidence. See EVIDENCE.

preliminary hearing. A criminal hearing (usu. conducted by a magistrate) to determine whether there is sufficient evidence to prosecute an accused person. • If sufficient evidence exists, the case will be set for trial or bound over for grand-jury review, or an information will be filed in the trial court. — Also termed *preliminary examination*; *probable-cause hearing*; *bindover hearing*; *examining trial*. Cf. ARRAIGNMENT.

preliminary injunction. See INJUNCTION.

preliminary inquiry. *Military law*. The initial investigation of a reported or suspected violation of the Uniform Code of Military Justice. Cf. PRETRIAL INVESTIGATION.

preliminary-inquiry officer. *Military law*. The person, usu. an officer, who conducts a preliminary inquiry.

preliminary letter. See INVITATION TO NEGOTIATE.

preliminary objection. *Int'l law*. In a case before an international tribunal, an objection that, if upheld, would render further proceedings before the tribunal impossible or unnecessary. • An objection to the court's jurisdiction is an example of a preliminary objection.

preliminary proof. See PROOF.

preliminary prospectus. See PROSPECTUS.

preliminary statement. The introductory part of a brief or memorandum in support of a motion, in which the advocate summarizes the essence of what follows. • In at least two jurisdictions, New York and New Jersey, the preliminary statement is a standard part of court papers. In many other jurisdictions, advocates do not routinely include it. But preliminary statements are typically allowed, even welcomed, though not required.

preliminary warrant. See WARRANT (1).

premarital agreement. See PRENUPTIAL AGREEMENT.

prematurity. 1. The circumstance existing when the facts underlying a plaintiff's complaint do not yet create a live claim. Cf. RIPENESS. **2.** The affirmative defense based on this circumstance.

premeditated, *adj*. Done with willful deliberation and planning; consciously considered beforehand <a premeditated killing>.

premeditated malice. See MALICE AFORETHOUGHT.

premeditation, *n*. Conscious consideration and planning that precedes some act (such as committing a crime). — **premeditate,** *vb*.

premier serjeant. See SERJEANT-AT-LAW.

premise (**prem**-is), *n*. A previous statement or contention from which a conclusion is deduced. — Also spelled (in BrE) *premiss*. — **premise** (**prem**-is *or* pri-**mIz**), *vb*.

premises (**prem**-ə-siz). **1.** Matters (usu. preliminary facts or statements) previously referred to in the same instrument <wherefore, premises considered, the plaintiff prays for the following relief>. **2.** A house or building, along with its grounds <smoking is not allowed on these premises>.

premises liability. A landowner's or landholder's tort liability for conditions or activities on the premises.

premises rule. See PARKING-LOT RULE.

premium, *n*. **1.** The periodic payment required to keep an insurance policy in effect. — Also termed *insurance premium*.

advance premium. A payment made before the start of the period covered by the insurance policy.

earned premium. The portion of an insurance premium applicable to the coverage period that has already expired. • For example, if the total premium for a one-year insurance policy is $1,200, the earned premium after three months is $300.

gross premium. **1.** The net premium plus expenses (i.e., the loading), less the interest factor. See LOADING; INTEREST FACTOR. **2.** The premium for participating life insurance. See *participating insurance* under INSURANCE.

natural premium. The actual cost of life insurance based solely on mortality rates. • This amount will be less than a net premium. See *net premium*.

net level annual premium. A net premium that stays the same each year.

net premium. **1.** Generally, the premium amount for an insurance policy less agent commissions. **2.** The portion of the premium that covers the estimated cost of claims. **3.** The money needed to provide benefits under an insurance policy. • The net premium in a life-insurance policy is calculated by using an assumed interest and mortality-table rate; it does not include additional expense amounts that will be charged to the policyholder. — Also termed *net valuation premium*.

net single premium. The money that must be collected from a policyholder at one time to guarantee enough money to pay claims made on an insurance policy. • This amount assumes that interest accrues at an expected rate and is based on a prediction of the likelihood of certain claims.

net valuation premium. See *net premium*.

unearned premium. The portion of an insurance premium applicable to the coverage period that has not yet occurred. • In the same example as above under *earned premium*, the unearned premium after three months is $900.

2. A sum of money paid in addition to a regular price, salary, or other amount; a bonus. **3.** The amount by which a security's market value exceeds its face value. — Also termed (specif.) *bond premium*. Cf. DISCOUNT (3).

control premium. A premium paid for shares carrying the power to control a corporation. • The control premium is often computed by comparing the aggregate value of the controlling block of shares with the cost that would be incurred if the shares could be acquired at the going market price per share.

4. The amount paid to buy a securities option. — Also termed (in sense 4) *option premium*.

premium bond. See BOND (3).

premium loan. See LOAN.

premium note. See NOTE (1).

premium on capital stock. See *paid-in surplus* under SURPLUS.

premium rate. *Insurance.* The price per unit of life insurance. • It is usu. expressed as a cost per thousands of dollars of coverage. Life insurers use three factors — the interest factor, the mortality factor, and the risk factor — to calculate premium rates. — Sometimes shortened to *rate*. See INTEREST FACTOR; MORTALITY FACTOR; RISK FACTOR.

premium stock. See STOCK.

premium tax. See TAX.

prenatal tort. See TORT.

prender de baron (**pren**-dər də **bar**-ən). [Law French "a taking of husband"] *Hist.* A plea asserting that the former wife of a murder victim should not be allowed to appeal a murder case against the alleged killer because she has since remarried.

prenup, *n.* See PRENUPTIAL AGREEMENT.

prenuptial (pree-**nəp**-shəl), *adj.* Made or occurring before marriage; premarital. — Also termed *antenuptial* (an-tee-**nəp**-shəl).

prenuptial agreement. An agreement made before marriage usu. to resolve issues of support and property division if the marriage ends in divorce or by the death of a spouse. — Also termed *antenuptial agreement*; *antenuptial contract*; *premarital agreement*; *premarital contract*; *marriage settlement*. — Sometimes shortened to *prenup*. See SETTLEMENT (2). Cf. POSTNUPTIAL AGREEMENT.

prenuptial gift. See GIFT.

prenuptial will. See WILL.

prepaid expense. See EXPENSE.

prepaid income. See INCOME.

prepaid interest. See INTEREST (3).

prepaid legal services. An arrangement — usu. serving as an employee benefit — that enables a person to make advance payments for future legal services.

preparation. *Criminal law.* The act or process of devising the means necessary to commit a crime. Cf. ATTEMPT.

prepayment clause. A loan-document provision that permits a borrower to satisfy a debt before its due date, usu. without paying a penalty.

prepayment penalty. A charge assessed against a borrower who elects to pay off a loan before it is due.

prepetition (pree-pə-**tish**-ən), *adj.* Occurring before the filing of a petition (esp. in bankruptcy) <prepetition debts>.

preponderance (pri-**pon**-dər-ənts), *n.* Superiority in weight, importance, or influence. — **preponderate** (pri-**pon**-dər-ayt), *vb.* — **preponderant** (pri-**pon**-dər-ənt), *adj.*

preponderance of the evidence. The greater weight of the evidence; superior evidentiary weight that, though not sufficient to free the mind wholly from all reasonable doubt, is still sufficient to incline a fair and impartial mind to one side of the issue rather than the other. • This is the burden of proof in a civil trial, in which the jury is instructed to find for the party that, on the whole, has the stronger evidence, however slight the edge may be. — Also termed *preponderance of proof*; *balance of probability.* Cf. *clear and convincing evidence* under EVIDENCE.

prerogative (pri-**rog**-ə-tiv), *n.* An exclusive right, power, privilege, or immunity, usu. acquired by virtue of office. — **prerogative,** *adj.*

prerogative court. In New Jersey, a probate court.

prerogative writ. See *extraordinary writ* under WRIT.

pres (pray). [Law French] Near. See CY PRES.

presale. The sale of real property (such as condominium units) before construction has begun.

prescribable (pri-**skrɪb**-ə-bəl), *adj.* (Of a right) that can be acquired by prescription.

prescription, *n.* **1.** The effect of the lapse of time in creating and destroying rights.

liberative prescription. *Civil law.* A bar to a lawsuit resulting from its untimely filing. • This term is essentially the civil-law equivalent to a statute of limitations. See STATUTE OF LIMITATIONS.

2. The acquisition of title to a thing (esp. an intangible thing such as the use of real property) by open and continuous possession over a statutory period. — Also termed *positive prescription*; *acquisitive prescription.* Cf. ADVERSE POSSESSION.

prescription in a que estate (ah **kee**). [Law French "prescription in whose estate"] A claim of prescription based on the immemorial enjoyment of the right by the claimant and the former owners whose estate the claimant has succeeded to.

3. The extinction of a title or right by failure to claim or exercise it over a long period. — Also termed *negative prescription*; *extinctive prescription.* **4.** The act of establishing authoritative rules; a rule so established. **5.** *Int'l law.* The acquisition of a territory through a continuous and undisputed exercise of sovereignty over it. — **prescribe,** *vb.* Cf. PROSCRIPTION.

prescriptive easement. See EASEMENT.

prescriptive right. A right obtained by prescription <after a nuisance has been continuously in existence for 20 years, a prescriptive right to continue it is acquired as an easement appurtenant to the land on which it exists>.

presence-of-defendant rule. The principle that a felony defendant is entitled to be present at every major stage of the criminal proceeding. Fed. R. Crim. P. 43.

presence of the court. The company or proximity of the judge or other courtroom official. • For purposes of contempt, an action is in the presence of the court if it is committed within the view of the judge or other person in court and is intended to disrupt the court's business.

> "Some decisions indicate that the term 'in the presence of the court' is to be given a liberal interpretation, that 'the court' consists not of the judge, the courtroom, the jury, or the jury room individually, but of all of these combined, and that the court is present wherever any of its constituent parts is engaged in the prosecution of the business of the court according to law." 17 Am. Jur. 2d *Contempt* § 19 (1990).

presence-of-the-testator rule. The principle that a testator must be aware (through sight or other sense) that the witnesses are signing the will. • Many jurisdictions interpret this requirement liberally, and the Uniform Probate Code has dispensed with it.

present, *adj.* **1.** Now existing; at hand <a present right to the property>. **2.** Being the one under consideration <the present appeal does not deal with that issue>. **3.** In attendance; not elsewhere <all present voted for him>.

present ability. See ABILITY.

presentation. 1. The delivery of a document to an issuer or named person for the purpose of initiating action under a letter of credit; PRESENTMENT (3). **2.** *Hist. Eccles. law.* A benefice patron's recommendation of a person to fill a vacant benefice. • If the benefice's bishop rejected the appointee, the patron could enforce the right to fill the vacancy by writ of *quare impedit* in the Court of Common Pleas. See QUARE IMPEDIT. Cf. ADVOWSON; INSTITUTION.

present case. See *case at bar* under CASE.

present conveyance. See CONVEYANCE.

present covenant. See COVENANT (4).

presentence hearing. A proceeding at which a judge or jury receives and examines all relevant information regarding a convicted criminal and the related offense before passing sentence. — Also termed *sentencing hearing*.

presentence investigation report. A probation officer's detailed account of a convicted defendant's educational, criminal, family, and social background, conducted at the court's request as an aid in passing sentence. — Abbr. PSI. — Often shortened to *presentence report*.

present enjoyment. See ENJOYMENT.

presenter. *Commercial law.* Any person presenting a document (such as a draft) to an issuer for honor. UCC § 5-102.

present estate. See ESTATE.

presenting bank. See BANK.

presenting jury. See GRAND JURY.

present interest. See INTEREST (2).

presentment (pri-**zent**-mənt). **1.** The act of presenting or laying before a court or other tribunal a formal statement about a matter to be dealt with legally. **2.** A formal written accusation returned by a grand jury on its own initiative, without a prosecutor's previous indictment request.

> "A grand jury has only two functions, either to indict or to return a 'no bill.' The Constitution speaks also of a 'presentment,' but this is a term with a distinct historical meaning now not well understood. Historically presentment was the process by which a grand jury initiated an independent investigation and asked that a charge be drawn to cover the facts should they constitute a crime. With United States attorneys now always available to advise grand juries, proceeding by presentment is an outmoded practice." 1 Charles Alan Wright, *Federal Practice and Procedure* § 110, at 459 (3d ed. 1999).

3. The formal production of a negotiable instrument for acceptance or payment.

> "Presentment and dishonor occur, for instance, when the holder of a check attempts to cash it at the drawee bank, but payment is refused because the drawer lacks sufficient funds on deposit. The demand for payment is presentment. The bank's refusal to pay is dishonor." 2 James J. White & Robert S. Summers, *Uniform Commercial Code* § 16-8, at 100 (4th ed. 1995).

presentment for acceptance. Production of an instrument to the drawee, acceptor, or maker for acceptance. • This type of presentment may be made anytime before maturity, except that with bills payable at sight, after demand, or after sight, presentment must be made within a reasonable time.

presentment for payment. Production of an instrument to the drawee, acceptor, or maker for payment. • This type of presentment must be made on the date when the instrument is due.

presentment of Englishry. *Hist.* The offering of proof that a slain person was English rather than (before the Conquest) a Dane or (after the Conquest) a Norman. • This requirement was issued first by the conquering Danes and then by the Normans to protect these groups from the English by the threat of a village- or hundred-wide amercement if the inhabitants failed to prove that a dead person found among them was English.

presentment warranty. See WARRANTY (2).

present recollection refreshed. *Evidence.* A witness's memory that has been enhanced by showing the witness a document that describes the relevant events. • The document itself is merely a memory stimulus and is not admitted in evidence. Fed. R. Evid. 612. — Also termed *refreshing recollection*; *present recollection revived*. Cf. PAST RECOLLECTION RECORDED.

presents, *n. pl. Archaic*. The instrument under consideration. • This is usu. part of the phrase *these presents*, which is part of the longer phrase *know all men by these presents* (itself a loan translation from the Latin *noverint universi per praesentes*). See KNOW ALL MEN BY THESE PRESENTS.

present sale. See SALE.

present sense impression. *Evidence*. One's perception of an event or condition, formed during or immediately after the fact. • A statement containing a present sense impression is admissible even if it is hearsay. Fed. R. Evid. 803(1). Cf. EXCITED UTTERANCE.

present use. See USE (4).

present value. The sum of money that, with compound interest, would amount to a specified sum at a specified future date; future value discounted to its value today. — Also termed *present worth*.

adjusted present value. An asset's value determined by adding together its present value and the value added by capital-structure effects. — Abbr. APV.

net present value. The present value of net cash flow from a project, discounted by the cost of capital. • This value is used to evaluate the project's investment potential. — Abbr. NPV.

preside, *vb*. **1.** To occupy the place of authority, esp. as a judge during a hearing or trial <preside over the proceedings>. **2.** To exercise management or control <preside over the estate>.

president, *n*. **1.** The chief political executive of a government; the head of state. **2.** The chief executive officer of a corporation or other organization. — **presidential,** *adj*.

presidential elector. See ELECTOR.

Presidential message. See MESSAGE.

president judge. See *presiding judge* under JUDGE.

president of a court-martial. *Military law*. The senior member in rank present at a court-martial trial.

President of the United States. The highest executive officer of the federal government of the United States. • The President is elected to a four-year term by a majority of the presidential electors chosen by popular vote from the states. The President must be a natural citizen, must be at least 35 years old, and must have been a resident for 14 years within the United States. U.S. Const. art. II, § 1.

presiding judge. See JUDGE.

presiding juror. See JUROR.

presiding officer. See OFFICER (2).

press, *n*. **1.** The news media; print and broadcast news organizations collectively. **2.** *Hist*. A piece of parchment, as one sewed together to make up a roll or record of judicial proceedings.

prest (prest). *Hist*. A duty to be paid by the sheriff upon his account in the Exchequer or for money remaining in his custody.

prestation (pre-**stay**-shən). *Hist*. **1.** A payment (or *presting*) of money. **2.** The rendering of a service.

prest money. *Hist*. A monetary payment made to a soldier or sailor on enlistment.

presume, *vb*. To assume beforehand; to suppose to be true in the absence of proof.

presumed father. See FATHER.

presumed-seller test. A method of imposing product liability on a manufacturer if the manufacturer, having full knowledge of the product's dangerous propensities, would be negligent in placing the product on the market.

presumption. A legal inference or assumption that a fact exists, based on the known or proven existence of some other fact or group of facts. • Most presumptions are rules of evidence calling for a certain result in a given case unless the adversely affected party overcomes it with other evidence. A presumption shifts the burden of production or persuasion to the opposing party, who can then attempt to overcome the presumption. See BURDEN OF PRODUCTION.

> "A presumption may be defined to be an inference as to the existence of one fact from the existence of some other fact founded upon a previous experience of their connec-

tion." William P. Richardson, *The Law of Evidence* § 53, at 25 (3d ed. 1928).

absolute presumption. See *conclusive presumption.*

artificial presumption. See *presumption of law.*

conclusive presumption. A presumption that cannot be overcome by any additional evidence or argument <it is a conclusive presumption that a child under the age of seven is incapable of committing a felony>. — Also termed *absolute presumption*; *irrebuttable presumption*; *mandatory presumption*; *presumption juris et de jure*. Cf. *rebuttable presumption.*

"'Conclusive presumptions' or 'irrebuttable presumptions' are usually mere fictions, to disguise a rule of substantive law (e.g., the conclusive presumption of malice from an unexcused defamation); and when they are not fictions, they are usually repudiated by modern courts." John H. Wigmore, *A Students' Textbook of the Law of Evidence* 454 (1935).

"Conclusive presumptions, sometimes called irrebuttable presumptions of law, are really rules of law. Thus it is said that a child under the age of fourteen years is conclusively presumed to be incapable of committing rape. This is only another way of saying that such a child cannot be found guilty of rape." Richard Eggleston, *Evidence, Proof and Probability* 92 (1978).

conditional presumption. See *rebuttable presumption.*

conflicting presumption. One of two or more presumptions that would lead to opposite results. — Also termed *inconsistent presumption.*

"'Conflicting presumptions' are simply two ordinary presumptions that would give opposite results; usually they are really successive presumptions. E.g., where A proves himself to be the son of N, wife of M, but M and N were already separated, and later M married P, and had a son B, the later marriage of M might presume a prior divorce from N before separation to make it valid, and yet the birth of A from a married mother might be presumed legitimate, and thus the question whether A or B was the legitimate son would be attended by opposing presumptions. But in this aspect the doctrine of presumptions is clouded with difficulties and leads to much vain speculation and logical unrealism." John H. Wigmore, *A Students' Textbook of the Law of Evidence* 454 (1935).

disputable presumption. See *rebuttable presumption.*

factual presumption. See *presumption of fact.*

heeding presumption. A rebuttable presumption that an injured product user would have followed a warning label had the product manufacturer provided one.

inconsistent presumption. See *conflicting presumption.*

irrebuttable presumption. See *conclusive presumption.*

legal presumption. See *presumption of law.*

mandatory presumption. See *conclusive presumption.*

McClanahan presumption. See MCCLANAHAN PRESUMPTION.

mixed presumption. A presumption containing elements of both law and fact.

Morgan presumption. See MORGAN PRESUMPTION.

natural presumption. A deduction of one fact from another, based on common experience.

permissive presumption. A presumption that a trier of fact is free to accept or reject from a given set of facts. — Also termed *permissive inference.*

presumption juris et de jure. See *conclusive presumption.*

presumption of fact. A type of rebuttable presumption that may be, but as a matter of law need not be, drawn from another established fact or group of facts <the possessor of recently stolen goods is, by presumption of fact, considered the thief>. — Also termed *factual presumption.*

presumption of general application. A presumption that applies across the board to all legislation, as a result of which lawmakers need not list each such presumption in all bills.

"One function of the word 'presumption' in the context of statutory interpretation is to state the result of this legislative reliance (real or assumed) on firmly established legal principles. There is a 'presumption' that *mens rea* is required in the case of statutory crimes, and a 'presumption' that statutory powers must be exercised reasonably. These presumptions apply although there is no question of linguistic ambiguity in the statutory wording under construction, and they may be described as 'presumptions of general application.' At the level of interpretation, their function is the promotion of brevity on the part of the draftsman. Statutes make dreary enough reading as it is, and it would be ridiculous to insist in each instance upon an enumeration of the general principles taken for granted." Rupert Cross, *Statutory Interpretation* 142–43 (1976).

presumption of intent. A permissive presumption that a criminal defendant who intended to commit an act did so.

presumption of law. A legal assumption that a court is required to make if certain facts are established and no contradictory evidence is produced <by presumption of law, a criminal defendant is considered innocent until proven guilty beyond a reasonable doubt>. — Also termed *legal presumption*; *artificial presumption*; *praesumptio juris*.

prima facie presumption. See *rebuttable presumption*.

procedural presumption. A presumption that may be rebutted by credible evidence.

rebuttable presumption. An inference drawn from certain facts that establish a prima facie case, which may be overcome by the introduction of contrary evidence. — Also termed *prima facie presumption*; *disputable presumption*; *conditional presumption*; *presumptio juris*. Cf. *conclusive presumption*.

statutory presumption. A rebuttable or conclusive presumption that is created by statute.

Thayer presumption. See THAYER PRESUMPTION.

presumption of death. A presumption that arises on the unexpected disappearance and continued absence of a person for an extended period, commonly seven years.

presumption of fact. See PRESUMPTION.

presumption-of-fertility rule. See FERTILE-OCTOGENARIAN RULE.

presumption of general application. See PRESUMPTION.

presumption-of-identity rule. The common-law rule that unless there is a specific, applicable statute in another state, a court will presume that the common law has developed elsewhere identically with how it has developed in the court's own state, so that the court may apply its own state's law. • Today this rule applies primarily in Georgia. See *Shorewood Packaging Corp. v. Commercial Union Ins.*, 865 F. Supp. 1577 (N.D. Ga. 1994).

presumption of innocence. The fundamental criminal-law principle that a person may not be convicted of a crime unless the government proves guilt beyond a reasonable doubt, without any burden placed on the accused to prove innocence.

presumption of intent. See PRESUMPTION.

presumption of law. See PRESUMPTION.

presumption of legitimacy. The presumption that the husband of a woman who gives birth is the father of the child.

presumption of natural and probable consequences. *Criminal law.* The presumption that *mens rea* may be derived from proof of the defendant's conduct.

presumption of survivorship. The presumption that one of two or more victims of a common disaster survived the others, based on the supposed survivor's youth, good health, or other reason rendering survivorship likely.

presumption of validity. *Patents.* The assumption that the holder of a patent is entitled to a statutory presumption of validity.

presumptive (pri-**zəmp**-tiv), *adj.* **1.** Giving reasonable grounds for belief or presumption. **2.** Based on a presumption. — **presumptively,** *adv.*

presumptive authority. See *implied authority* under AUTHORITY (1).

presumptive damages. See *punitive damages* under DAMAGES.

presumptive death. See DEATH.

presumptive evidence. See EVIDENCE.

presumptive heir. See *heir presumptive* under HEIR.

presumptive notice. See *implied notice* under NOTICE.

presumptive proof. See *conditional proof* under PROOF.

presumptive sentence. See SENTENCE.

presumptive title. See TITLE (2).

presumptive trust. See *resulting trust* under TRUST.

pretax, *adj.* Existing or occurring before the assessment or deduction of taxes <pretax income>.

pretax earnings. See EARNINGS.

prête-nom (pret-**nohm**). [French] One who lends his name.

preterlegal (pree-tər-**lee**-gəl), *adj. Rare.* Beyond the range of what is legal; not according to law <preterlegal customs>.

pretermission (pree-tər-**mish**-ən). **1.** The condition of one who is pretermitted, as an heir of a testator. **2.** The act of omitting an heir from a will.

pretermission statute. See PRETERMITTED-HEIR STATUTE.

pretermit (pree-tər-**mit**), *vb.* **1.** To ignore or disregard purposely <the court pretermitted the constitutional question by deciding the case on procedural grounds>. **2.** To neglect or overlook accidentally <the third child was pretermitted in the will>.

pretermitted child. See *pretermitted heir* under HEIR.

pretermitted defense. See DEFENSE (1).

pretermitted heir. See HEIR.

pretermitted-heir statute. A state law that grants a pretermitted heir the right to inherit a share of the testator's estate, usu. by treating the heir as though the testator had died intestate. — Also termed *pretermission statute.*

pretermitted spouse. See *pretermitted heir* under HEIR.

pretext (**pree**-tekst), *n.* A false or weak reason or motive advanced to hide the actual or strong reason or motive. — **pretextual** (pree-**teks**-choo-əl), *adj.*

pretextual arrest. See ARREST.

pretextus (pree-**teks**-təs). [Latin] A pretext.

pretium (**pree**-shee-əm). [Latin] Price; value; worth.

pretium affectionis (**pree**-shee-əm ə-fek-shee-**oh**-nis). An enhanced value placed on a thing by the fancy of its owner, growing out of an attachment for the specific article and its associations; sentimental value. • This value is not taken as a basis for measuring damages.

pretium periculi (**pree**-shee-əm pə-**rik**-yə-lɪ). The price of the risk, such as the premium paid on an insurance policy.

pretorial court (pri-**tor**-ee-əl). See COURT.

pretrial conference. An informal meeting at which opposing attorneys confer, usu. with the judge, to work toward the disposition of the case by discussing matters of evidence and narrowing the issues that will be tried. • The conference takes place shortly before trial and ordinarily results in a pretrial order. — Often shortened to *pretrial.* — Also termed *pretrial hearing.*

pretrial detention. See DETENTION.

pretrial discovery. See DISCOVERY.

pretrial diversion. See DIVERSION PROGRAM.

pretrial hearing. See PRETRIAL CONFERENCE.

pretrial intervention. **1.** DIVERSION PROGRAM. **2.** See *deferred judgment* under JUDGMENT.

pretrial investigation. *Military law.* An investigation to decide whether a case should be recommended for forwarding to a general court-martial.

pretrial order. A court order setting out the claims and defenses to be tried, the stipulations of the parties, and the case's procedural rules, as agreed to by the parties or mandated by the court at a pretrial conference.

prevail, *vb.* **1.** To obtain the relief sought in an action; to win a lawsuit <the plaintiff prevailed in the Supreme Court>. **2.** To be commonly accepted or predominant <it's unclear which line of precedent will prevail>.

prevailing party. See PARTY (2).

prevarication (pri-var-ə-**kay**-shən), *n.* The act or an instance of lying or avoiding the truth; equivocation. — **prevaricate** (pri-**var**-ə-kayt), *vb.*

prevaricator (pri-**var**-ə-kay-tər). [Latin] **1.** A liar; an equivocator. **2.** *Roman law.* One who betrays another's trust, such as an advocate who aids the opposing party by betraying the client. — Also spelled (in sense 2) *praevaricator.*

prevent, *vb.* To hinder or impede <a gag order to prevent further leaks to the press>.

preventative custody. See CUSTODY (1).

prevention. *Civil law.* The right of one of several judges having concurrent jurisdiction to exercise that jurisdiction over a case that the judge is first to hear.

prevention doctrine. *Contracts.* The principle that each contracting party has an implied duty to not do anything that prevents the other party from performing its obligation. — Also termed *prevention-of-performance doctrine.*

preventive custody. See CUSTODY (1).

preventive detention. See DETENTION.

preventive injunction. See INJUNCTION.

preventive punishment. See PUNISHMENT.

previously taxed income. See INCOME.

price. The amount of money or other consideration asked for or given in exchange for something else; the cost at which something is bought or sold.

agreed price. The price for a sale, esp. of goods, arrived at by mutual agreement. Cf. *open price.*

asked price. The lowest price at which a seller is willing to sell a security at a given time. See SPREAD (2).

asking price. The price at which a seller lists property for sale, often implying a willingness to sell for less. — Also termed *ask price*; *offering price.*

at-the-market price. A retail price that store owners in the same vicinity generally charge.

bid price. The highest price that a prospective buyer is willing to pay for a security at a given time. See SPREAD (2).

call price. **1.** The price at which a bond may be retired before its maturity. **2.** See *strike price.*

ceiling price. **1.** The highest price at which a buyer is willing to buy. **2.** The highest price allowed by a government agency or by some other regulatory institution.

closing price. The price of a security at the end of a given trading day. — Also termed *close.*

exercise price. See *strike price.*

ex-works price. The price of goods as they leave the factory. See EX WORKS.

fixed price. A price that is agreed upon by a wholesaler and a retailer for the later sale or resale of an item. • Agreements to fix prices are generally prohibited by state and federal statutes.

floor price. The lowest price at which a seller is willing to sell.

liquidation price. A price that is paid for property sold to liquidate a debt. • Liquidation price is usu. below market price. — Also termed *liquidation value.*

list price. A published or advertised price of goods; retail price.

market price. The prevailing price at which something is sold in a specific market. See *fair market value* under VALUE.

mean trading price. *Securities.* The average of the daily trading price of a security determined at the close of the market each day during a 90–day period.

net price. The price of something, after deducting cash discounts.

offering price. See *asking price.*

open price. The price for a sale, esp. of goods, that has not been settled at the time of a sale's conclusion. UCC § 2–305. Cf. *agreed price.*

put price. See *strike price.*

redemption price. **1.** The price of a bond that has not reached maturity, purchased at the issuer's option. **2.** The price of shares when a mutual-fund shareholder sells shares back to the fund. — Also termed *liquidating price*; *repurchase price.*

reserve price. The price announced at an auction as the lowest that will be entertained. See WITH RESERVE; WITHOUT RESERVE.

sales price. The total amount for which property is sold, often including the costs of any services that are a part of the sale. • Under sales-tax statutes, the amount is typically valued in money even if the value is not received in money. — Also termed *selling price.*

spot price. The amount for which a commodity is sold in a spot market. See SPOT TRADING.

strike price. *Securities.* The price for which a security will be bought or sold under an option contract if the option is exercised. — Also termed *striking price*; *exercise price*; *call price*; *put price*. See OPTION.

subscription price. See SUBSCRIPTION PRICE.

suggested retail price. The sales price recommended to a retailer by a manufacturer of the product.

support price. A minimum price set by the federal government for a particular agricultural commodity.

target price. A price set by the federal government for particular agricultural commodities. • If the market price falls below the target price, farmers receive a subsidy from the government for the difference.

transfer price. The charge assigned to an exchange of goods or services between a corporation's organizational units.

unit price. A price of a food product expressed in a well-known measure such as ounces or pounds.

upset price. The lowest amount that a seller is willing to accept for property or goods sold at auction.

wholesale price. The price that a retailer pays for goods purchased (usu. in bulk) from a wholesaler for resale to consumers at a higher price.

price amendment. *Securities.* A change in a registration statement, prospectus, or prospectus supplement affecting the offering price, the underwriting and selling discounts or commissions, the amount of proceeds, the conversion rates, the call prices, or some other matter relating to the offering price.

price/cost analysis. A technique of determining, for antitrust purposes, whether predatory pricing has occurred by examining the relationship between a defendant's prices and either its average variable cost or its average total cost.

price discrimination. The practice of offering identical or similar goods to different buyers at different prices when the costs of producing the goods are the same. • Price discrimination can violate antitrust laws if it reduces competition. It may be either direct, as when a seller charges different prices to different buyers, or indirect, as when a seller offers special concessions (such as favorable credit terms) to some but not all buyers.

persistent price discrimination. A monopolist's systematic policy of obtaining different rates of return from different sales groupings.

price-earnings ratio. The ratio between a stock's current share price and the corporation's earnings per share for the last year. • Some investors avoid stocks with high price-earnings ratios because those stocks may be overpriced. — Abbr. P/E ratio. Cf. *earnings yield* under YIELD.

price expectancy. See EXHIBITION VALUE.

price-fixing. The artificial setting or maintenance of prices at a certain level, contrary to the workings of the free market. • Price-fixing is usu. illegal per se under antitrust law.

> "Price-fixing agreements may or may not be aimed at complete elimination of price competition. The group making those agreements may or may not have the power to control the market. But the fact that the group cannot control the market prices does not necessarily mean that the agreement as to prices has no utility to the members of the combination. The effectiveness of price-fixing agreements is dependent on many factors, such as competitive tactics, position in the industry, the formula underlying price policies. Whatever economic justification particular price-fixing agreements may be thought to have, the law does not permit an inquiry into their reasonableness. They are all banned because of their actual or potential threat to the central nervous system of the economy." *United States v. Socony–Vacuum Oil Co.*, 310 U.S. 150, 225–26 n.59, 60 S.Ct. 811, 845 n.59 (1940).

horizontal price-fixing. Price-fixing among competitors on the same level, such as retailers throughout an industry.

vertical price-fixing. Price-fixing among parties in the same chain of distribution, such as manufacturers and retailers attempting to control an item's resale price.

price index. An index of average prices as a percentage of the average prevailing at some other time (such as a base year). See CONSUMER PRICE INDEX; PRODUCER PRICE INDEX.

price leadership. A market condition in which an industry leader establishes a price that others in the field adopt as their own. • Price leadership alone does not violate antitrust laws without other evidence of an intent to create a monopoly.

price-level-adjusted mortgage. See MORTGAGE.

price memorandum. *Securities.* A document created by an underwriter to explain how securities are priced for a public offering and, typically, to show estimates and appraisals that are not allowed as part of the offering documents.

price support. The artificial maintenance of prices (as of a particular commodity) at a certain level, esp. by governmental action (as by subsidy).

price war. A period of sustained or repeated price-cutting in an industry (esp. among retailers), designed to undersell competitors or force them out of business.

priest-penitent privilege. See PRIVILEGE (3).

primae impressionis (**prI**-mee im-pres[h]-ee-**oh**-nis). [Law Latin] Of the first impression. See *case of first impression* under CASE.

primae preces. See PRECES PRIMARIAE.

prima facie (**prI**-mə **fay**-shə *or* **fay**-shee), *adv.* [Latin] At first sight; on first appearance but subject to further evidence or information <the deed is prima facie valid>.

prima facie, *adj.* Sufficient to establish a fact or raise a presumption unless disproved or rebutted <a prima facie showing>.

prima facie case. 1. The establishment of a legally required rebuttable presumption. **2.** A party's production of enough evidence to allow the fact-trier to infer the fact at issue and rule in the party's favor.

prima facie evidence. See EVIDENCE.

prima facie presumption. See *rebuttable presumption* under PRESUMPTION.

prima facie privilege. See *qualified immunity* under IMMUNITY (1).

prima facie tort. See TORT.

primage (**prI**-mij). See HAT MONEY.

primary, *n.* See *primary election* under ELECTION.

primary activity. *Labor law.* Concerted action (such as a strike or picketing) directed against an employer with which a union has a dispute. Cf. SECONDARY ACTIVITY.

primary allegation. See ALLEGATION.

primary authority. See AUTHORITY (4).

primary beneficiary. See BENEFICIARY.

primary boycott. See BOYCOTT.

primary cause. See *proximate cause* under CAUSE (1).

primary committee. *Bankruptcy.* A group of creditors organized to help the debtor draw up a reorganization plan.

primary conveyance. See CONVEYANCE.

primary election. See ELECTION.

primary evidence. See *best evidence* under EVIDENCE.

primary fact. See FACT.

primary insurance. See INSURANCE.

primary-jurisdiction doctrine. A judicial doctrine whereby a court tends to favor allowing an agency an initial opportunity to decide an issue in a case in which the court and the agency have concurrent jurisdiction.

primary lease. See HEADLEASE.

primary liability. See LIABILITY.

primary-line competition. See *horizontal competition* under COMPETITION.

primary-line injury. *Antitrust.* Under the price-discrimination provisions of the Robinson–Patman Act, the practice of charging below-cost, predatory prices in an attempt to eliminate the seller's competition in the market. 15 USCA § 13(a). • A primary-line injury, which hinders or seeks to hinder competition among the seller's competitors, is distinguishable from a secondary-line injury, which refers to discriminatory pricing that hinders or seeks to hinder competition among the seller's customers, by favoring one customer over another in the prices the seller charges. Cf. SECONDARY-LINE INJURY.

> "Liggett contends that Brown & Williamson's discriminatory volume rebates to wholesalers threatened substantial competitive injury by furthering a predatory pricing scheme designed to purge competition from the economy segment of the cigarette market. This type of injury, which harms direct competitors of the discriminating seller, is known as a primary-line injury." *Brooke Group Ltd. v. Brown & Williamson Tobacco Corp.*, 509 U.S. 209, 220, 113 S.Ct. 2578, 2586 (1993).

primary market. See MARKET.

primary mortgage market. See MORTGAGE MARKET.

primary obligation. See OBLIGATION.

primary offering. See OFFERING.

primary plea. See *primary allegation* under ALLEGATION.

primary powers. The chief powers given by a principal to an agent to accomplish the agent's tasks. Cf. MEDIATE POWERS.

primary reserve ratio. See RESERVE RATIO.

primary right. See RIGHT.

primate (**prɪ**-mit). A chief ecclesiastic; an archbishop or bishop having jurisdiction over other bishops within a province.

prime, *n*. See *prime rate* under INTEREST RATE.

prime, *vb*. To take priority over <Watson's preferred mortgage primed Moriarty's lien>.

prime contractor. See *general contractor* under CONTRACTOR.

prime cost. See COST (1).

prime lending rate. See *prime rate* under INTEREST RATE.

prime maker. See MAKER.

prime minister. (*often cap.*) The chief executive of a parliamentary government; the head of a cabinet. — Abbr. PM.

primer (**prim**-ər *or* **prɪ**-mər). [Law French] First; primary <primer seisin>.

prime rate. See INTEREST RATE.

primer election. A first choice; esp., the eldest coparcener's pick of land on division of the estate. See ELECTION.

primer fine (**prim**-ər *or* **prɪ**-mər **fɪn**). [Latin] *Hist*. A fee payable to the Crown on the suing out of a writ of praecipe to begin a conveyance by fine. See FINE (1). — Also termed *praefine*.

primer seisin. See SEISIN.

prime serjeant. See *premier serjeant* under SERJEANT-AT-LAW.

prime tenant. See TENANT.

primitiae (pri-**mish**-ee-ee). [fr. Latin *primus* "first"] See FIRST FRUITS. — **primitial** (pri-**mish**-əl), *adj*.

primogeniture (prɪ-mə-**jen**-ə-chər). **1.** The state of being the firstborn child among siblings. **2.** The common-law right of the firstborn son to inherit his ancestor's estate, usu. to the exclusion of his younger siblings. — Also termed (in sense 2) *primogenitureship*. See BOROUGH ENGLISH.

> "We might note here, parenthetically, that the English preference for single-file male descent — that is, the system of descent known as *primogeniture* — was never cordially received in this country. Our statutes of descent and distribution uniformly provide for sons' and daughters' sharing the inheritance equally. Although this seems a fairer method than primogeniture, which was finally abolished in Britain with the 1925 reforms, the descent of property to an ever-expanding group of heirs can seriously complicate the clearing of old titles." Thomas F. Bergin & Paul G. Haskell, *Preface to Estates in Land and Future Interests* 9 (2d ed. 1984).

primo venienti (**prɪ**-moh ven-ee-**en**-tɪ). [Latin] To the one first coming. • This refers to the former practice by estate executors of paying debts as they were presented without regard to whether the estate had enough assets to pay all the debts.

primum decretum (**prɪ**-məm di-**kree**-təm). [Latin "first decree"] **1.** *Hist. Eccles. law*. A preliminary decree granted in favor of the plaintiff on the nonappearance of a defendant. **2.** *Maritime law*. A provisional decree.

princeps (**prin**-seps). [Latin] *Roman law*. A leading person, esp. the emperor.

principal, *adj*. Chief; primary; most important.

principal, *n*. **1.** One who authorizes another to act on his or her behalf as an agent. Cf. AGENT (1).

disclosed principal. A principal whose identity is revealed by the agent to a third party. • A disclosed principal is always liable on a contract entered into by the agent with the principal's authority, but the agent is usu. not liable.

partially disclosed principal. A principal whose existence — but not actual identity — is revealed by the agent to a third party.

undisclosed principal. A principal whose identity is kept secret by the agent. • An undisclosed principal and the agent are both liable on a contract entered into by the agent with the principal's authority.

2. One who commits or participates in a crime. Cf. ACCESSORY (2); ACCOMPLICE (2).

> "The student should notice that in criminal law the word 'principal' suggests the very converse of the idea which it represents in mercantile law. In the former, as we have seen, an accessory proposes an act, and the 'principal' carries it out. But in the law of contract, and in that of tort, the 'principal' only authorizes an act, and the 'agent' carries it out. Where the same transaction is both a tort and a crime, this double use of the word may cause confusion. For example, if, by an innkeeper's directions, his chamber-maid steals jewels out of a guest's portmanteau, the maid is the 'principal' in a *crime*, wherein her master is an accessory before the fact; whilst she is also the agent in a *tort*, wherein her master is the 'principal'." J.W. Cecil Turner, *Kenny's Outlines of Criminal Law* 89 (16th ed. 1952).

principal in the first degree. The perpetrator of a crime.

> "By a principal in the first degree, we mean the actual offender — the man in whose guilty mind lay the latest blamable mental cause of the criminal act. Almost always, of course, he will be the man by whom this act itself was done. But occasionally this will not be so; for the felony may have been committed by the hand of an innocent agent who, having no blamable intentions in what he did, incurred no criminal liability by doing it. In such a case the man who instigates this agent is the real offender; his was the last *mens rea* that preceded the crime, though it did not cause it immediately but mediately." J.W. Cecil Turner, *Kenny's Outlines of Criminal Law* 85–86 (16th ed. 1952).

principal in the second degree. One who helped the perpetrator at the time of the crime. — Also termed *accessory at the fact*. See ABETTOR.

> "The distinction between principals in the first and second degrees is a distinction without a difference except in those rare instances in which some unusual statute has provided a different penalty for one of these than for the other. A principal in the first degree is the immediate perpetrator of the crime while a principal in the second degree is one who did not commit the crime with his own hands but was present and abetting the principal. It may be added, in the words of Mr. Justice Miller, that one may perpetrate a crime, not only with his own hands, but 'through the agency of mechanical or chemical means, as by instruments, poison or powder, or by an animal, child, or other innocent agent' acting under his direction." Rollin M. Perkins & Ronald N. Boyce, *Criminal Law* 736 (3d ed. 1982) (quoting *Beausoliel v. United States*, 107 F.2d 292, 297 (D.C. Cir. 1939)).

3. One who has primary responsibility on an obligation, as opposed to a surety or indorser. **4.** The corpus of an estate or trust. **5.** The amount of a debt, investment, or other fund, not including interest, earnings, or profits.

principal action. See *main demand* under DEMAND (1).

principal contract. See CONTRACT.

principal covenant. See COVENANT (1).

principal creditor. See CREDITOR.

principal demand. See *main demand* under DEMAND (1).

principal fact. See FACT.

principal in the first degree. See PRINCIPAL (2).

principal in the second degree. See PRINCIPAL (2).

principalis (prin-sə-**pay**-lis), *adj.* [Latin] Principal, as in *principalis debitor* ("principal debtor").

principal place of business. The place of a corporation's chief executive offices, which is typically viewed as the "nerve center."

principal right. See RIGHT.

principle, *n.* A basic rule, law, or doctrine.

principle of finality. See FINALITY DOCTRINE.

principle of legality. See LEGALITY (2).

principle of nonintervention. See NONINTERVENTION.

principle of retribution. See LEX TALIONIS.

print, *n.* See FINGERPRINT.

Printers Ink Statute. A model statute drafted in 1911 and adopted in a number of states making it a misdemeanor to print an advertisement that contains a false or deceptive statement.

prior, *adj.* **1.** Preceding in time or order <under this court's prior order>. **2.** Taking precedence <a prior lien>.

prior, *n. Criminal law. Slang.* A previous conviction <because the defendant had two priors, the judge automatically enhanced his sentence>.

prior-appropriation doctrine. The rule that, among the persons whose properties border on a waterway, the earliest users of the water have the right to take all they can use before anyone else has a right to it. Cf. RIPARIAN-RIGHTS DOCTRINE.

prior art. See ART.

prior-claim rule. The principle that before suing for a tax refund or abatement, a taxpayer must first assert the claim to the Internal Revenue Service.

prior consistent statement. A witness's earlier statement that is consistent with the witness's trial testimony. • A prior consistent statement is not hearsay if it is offered to rebut a charge that the testimony was improperly influenced or fabricated. Fed. R. Evid. 801(d)(1)(B).

prior creditor. See CREDITOR.

prior inconsistent statement. A witness's earlier statement that conflicts with the witness's testimony at trial. • In federal practice, extrinsic evidence of an unsworn prior inconsistent statement is admissible — if the witness is given an opportunity to explain or deny the statement — for impeachment purposes only. Fed. R. Evid. 613(b), 801(d)(1)(A).

priori petenti (prɪ-**or**-ɪ pə-**ten**-tɪ). [Latin "to the first person applying"] *Wills & estates.* The principle that when two or more persons are equally entitled to administer an estate, the court will appoint the person who applies first.

priority. 1. The status of being earlier in time or higher in degree or rank; precedence. **2.** An established right to such precedence; esp., a creditor's right to have a claim paid before other creditors of the same debtor receive payment. **3.** The doctrine that, as between two courts, jurisdiction should be accorded the court in which proceedings are first begun.

priority claim. See CLAIM (5).

priority-jurisdiction rule. See FIRST-TO-FILE RULE.

priority lien. See *prior lien* under LIEN.

priority of invention. The determination that one among several patent applications, for substantially the same invention, should receive the patent when the Patent and Trademark Office has declared interference. • This determination depends on the date of conception, the date of reduction to practice, and diligence.

priority of liens. The ranking of liens in the order in which they are perfected.

prior lien. See LIEN.

prior petens (**prɪ**-ər **pet**-enz). [Latin] The person first applying.

prior preferred stock. See STOCK.

prior restraint. A governmental restriction on speech or publication before its actual expression. • Prior restraints violate the First Amendment unless the speech is obscene, is defamatory, or creates a clear and present danger to society.

> "The legal doctrine of prior restraint (or formal censorship before publication) is probably the oldest form of press control. Certainly it is one of the most efficient, since one censor, working in the watershed, can create a drought of information and ideas long before they reach the fertile plain of people's minds. In the United States, the doctrine of prior restraint has been firmly opposed by the First Amendment to the Constitution, and by the Supreme Court, perhaps most notably in the case of *Near v. Minnesota*, decided in 1931. But the philosophy behind that doctrine lives zestfully on, and shows no signs of infirmities of age." David G. Clark & Earl R. Hutchinson, *Mass Media and the Law* 11 (1970).

prior-use bar. See PUBLIC-USE BAR.

prior-use doctrine. The principle that, without legislative authorization, a government agency may not appropriate property already devoted to a public use.

prisage (**prɪ**-zij). *Hist.* A royal duty on wine imported into England. • Prisage was replaced by butlerage in the reign of Edward I. Cf. BUTLERAGE.

prisel en auter lieu (**prɪ**-zəl awn **oh**-tayl-**yoo**). [Law French "a taking in another place"] A plea in abatement in a replevin action.

prison. A state or federal facility of confinement for convicted criminals, esp. felons. — Also termed *penitentiary*; *penal institution*; *adult correctional institution*. Cf. JAIL.

prison breach. A prisoner's forcible breaking and departure from a place of lawful confinement; the offense of escaping from confinement in a prison or jail. • *Prison breach* has traditionally been distinguished from *escape* by the presence of force; this distinction has been abandoned in some jurisdictions. — Also termed *prison breaking*. Cf. ESCAPE (2).

> "Breach of prison by the offender himself, when committed for *any* cause, was felony at the common law: or even conspiring to break it. But this severity is mitigated by the statute *de frangentibus prisonam*, I Edw. II, which enacts that no person shall have judgment of life or member, for breaking prison, unless committed for some capital offence. So that to break prison, when lawfully committed for any treason or felony, remains still a felony as at the common law; and to break prison, when lawfully confined upon any other inferior charge, is still punishable as a high misdemeanor by fine and imprisonment." 4 William Blackstone, *Commentaries on the Laws of England* 130–31 (1769).

prison camp. A usu. minimum-security camp for the detention of trustworthy prisoners who are often employed on government projects.

prisoner. 1. A person who is serving time in prison. **2.** A person who has been apprehended by a law-enforcement officer and is in custody, regardless of whether the person has yet been put in prison.

> "While breach of prison, or prison breach, means breaking out of or away from prison, it is important to have clearly in mind the meaning of the word 'prison.' If an officer arrests an offender and takes him to jail the layman does not think of the offender as being 'in prison' until he is safely behind locked doors, but no one hesitates to speak of him as a 'prisoner' from the moment of apprehension. He is a prisoner because he is 'in prison . . . whether he were actually in the walls of a prison, or only in the stocks, or in the custody of any person who had lawfully arrested him. . . .' " Rollin M. Perkins & Ronald N. Boyce, *Criminal Law* 566 (3d ed. 1982) (quoting 2 Hark. P.C. ch. 18, § 1 (6th ed. 1788)).

prisoner at the bar. An accused person who is on trial.

prisoner of conscience. *Int'l law.* A person who, not having used or advocated the use of violence, has been imprisoned by reason of a political, religious, or other conscientiously held belief or by reason of ethnic origin, sex, color, or language.

prisoner's dilemma. A logic problem — often used by law-and-economics scholars to illustrate the effect of cooperative behavior — involving two prisoners who are being separately questioned about their participation in a crime: (1) if both confess, they will each receive a 5-year sentence; (2) if neither confesses, they will each receive a 3-year sentence; and (3) if one confesses but the other does not, the confessing prisoner will receive a 1-year sentence while the silent prisoner will receive a 10-year sentence. See EXTERNALITY.

prist (prist). [Law French] *Hist.* Ready. • In oral pleading, this term was used to express a joinder of issue.

privacy, invasion of. See INVASION OF PRIVACY.

privacy, right of. See RIGHT OF PRIVACY.

privacy law. A federal or state statute that protects a person's right to be left alone or restricts public access to personal information such as tax returns and medical records. — Also termed *privacy act*.

private, *adj.* **1.** Relating or belonging to an individual, as opposed to the public or the government. **2.** (Of a company) not having shares that are freely available on an open market. **3.** Confidential; secret.

private agent. See AGENT.

private annuity. See ANNUITY.

private attorney. See ATTORNEY (1).

private-attorney-general doctrine. The equitable principle that allows the recovery of attorney's fees to a party who brings a lawsuit that benefits a significant number of people, requires private enforcement, and is important to society as a whole.

private bank. See BANK.

private bill. See BILL (3).

private boundary. See BOUNDARY.

private carrier. See CARRIER.

private corporation. See CORPORATION.

private delict. See DELICT.

private easement. See EASEMENT.

privateer (prI-və-**teer**), *n.* **1.** A vessel owned and operated by private persons, but authorized by a nation on certain conditions to damage the commerce of the enemy by acts of piracy. **2.** A sailor on such a vessel.

privateering, *n. Int'l law.* The practice of arming privately owned merchant ships for the purpose of attacking enemy trading ships. • Before the practice was outlawed, governments commissioned privateers by issuing letters of marque to their merchant fleets. Privateering was prohibited by the Declaration of Paris Concerning Naval Warfare of 1856, which has been observed by nearly all nations since that time. — **privateer,** *vb.*

private fact. See FACT.

private foundation. See FOUNDATION.

private international law. See INTERNATIONAL LAW.

private judging. A type of alternative dispute resolution whereby the parties hire a private individual to hear and decide a case. • This process may occur as a matter of contract between the parties or in connection with a statute authorizing such a process. — Also termed *rent-a-judging.*

private land grant. See LAND GRANT.

private law. **1.** The body of law dealing with private persons and their property and relationships. Cf. PUBLIC LAW (1). **2.** SPECIAL LAW.

private letter ruling. See LETTER RULING.

private morality. See MORALITY.

private mortgage insurance. See *mortgage insurance* under INSURANCE.

private necessity. See NECESSITY.

private nuisance. See NUISANCE.

private offering. See OFFERING.

private person. See PERSON.

private placement. **1.** The placement of a child for adoption by a parent, lawyer, doctor, or private agency, but not by a government agency. — Also termed *direct placement.* **2.** See *private offering* under OFFERING.

private power. See POWER.

private property. See PROPERTY.

private prosecutor. See PROSECUTOR (2).

private publication. See *limited publication* under PUBLICATION.

private reprimand. See REPRIMAND.

private right. See RIGHT.

private sale. See SALE.

private school. See SCHOOL.

private seal. See SEAL.

private search. See SEARCH.

private sector. The part of the economy or an industry that is free from direct governmental control. Cf. PUBLIC SECTOR.

private servitude. See SERVITUDE (1).

private signature. See SIGNATURE.

private statute. See *special statute* under STATUTE.

private stream. See STREAM.

private trust. See TRUST.

private war. See WAR.

private water. See WATER.

private way. See WAY.

private wharf. See WHARF.

private wrong. See WRONG.

privation (prI-**vay**-shən). **1.** The act of taking away or withdrawing. **2.** The condition of being deprived.

privatization (prI-və-tə-**zay**-shən), *n.* The act or process of converting a business or industry from governmental ownership or control to private enterprise. — **privatize,** *vb.*

privatum (prI-**vay**-təm). [Latin] Private. ● This term appeared in phrases such as *jus privatum* ("private law").

privies (**priv**-eez). See PRIVY.

privigna (prI-**vig**-nə), *n.* [Latin] *Roman & civil law.* A daughter of one's husband or wife by a previous marriage; a stepdaughter.

privignus (prI-**vig**-nəs). [Latin] *Roman & civil law.* A son of one's husband or wife by a previous marriage; a stepson.

privilege. 1. A special legal right, exemption, or immunity granted to a person or class of persons; an exception to a duty.

absolute privilege. A privilege that immunizes an actor from suit, no matter how wrongful the action might be, and even though it is done with an improper motive. Cf. *qualified privilege.*

conditional privilege. See *qualified privilege.*

deliberative-process privilege. A privilege permitting the government to withhold documents relating to policy formulation to encourage open and independent discussion among those who develop government policy.

litigation privilege. A privilege protecting the attorneys and parties in a lawsuit from defamation claims arising from statements made in the course of the suit.

parliamentary privilege. The right of a particular question, motion, or statement to take precedence over all other business before the legislative body.

privilege from arrest. An exemption from arrest, as that enjoyed by members of Congress during legislative sessions. U.S. Const. art. I, § 6.

qualified privilege. A privilege that immunizes an actor from suit only when the privilege is properly exercised in the performance of a legal or moral duty. — Also termed *conditional privilege.* Cf. *absolute privilege.*

> "Qualified privilege . . . is an intermediate case between total absence of privilege and the presence of absolute privilege." R.F.V. Heuston, *Salmond on the Law of Torts* 165 (17th ed. 1977).

special privilege. A privilege granted to a person or class of persons to the exclusion of others and in derogation of the common right.

testimonial privilege. A right not to testify based on a claim of privilege; a privilege that overrides a witness's duty to disclose matters within the witness's knowledge, whether at trial or by deposition.

viatorial privilege (vI-ə-**tor**-ee-əl). A privilege that overrides a person's duty to attend court in person and to testify.

work-product privilege. See WORK-PRODUCT RULE.

2. An affirmative defense by which a defendant acknowledges at least part of the conduct complained of but asserts that the defendant's conduct was authorized or sanctioned by law; esp., in tort law, a circumstance justifying or excusing an intentional tort. See JUSTIFICATION (2). Cf. IMMUNITY (2). **3.** An evidentiary rule that gives a witness the option to not disclose the fact asked for, even though it might be relevant; the right to prevent disclosure of certain information in court, esp. when the information was originally communicated in a professional or confidential relationship.

accountant-client privilege. The protection afforded to a client from an accountant's unauthorized disclosure of materials submitted to or prepared by the accountant.

antimarital-facts privilege. See *marital privilege* (2).

attorney-client privilege. The client's right to refuse to disclose and to prevent any other person from disclosing confidential communications between the client and the attorney. — Also termed *lawyer-client privilege*; *client's privilege.*

> "There are a number of ways to organize the essential elements of the attorney-client privilege to provide for an orderly analysis. One of the most popular is Wigmore's schema: '(1) Where legal advice of any kind is sought (2) from a professional legal adviser in his capacity as such, (3) the communications relating to that purpose (4) made in confidence (5) by the client (6) are at his instance permanently protected (7) from disclosure by himself or by the legal adviser, (8) except the privilege be waived.' Though this organization has its virtues, there is some question as to whether it completely states the modern privilege." 24 Charles Alan Wright & Kenneth W. Graham, Jr., *Federal Practice and Procedure* § 5473, at 103–04 (1986) (quoting 8 John Henry Wigmore, *Evidence* § 2292, at 554 (John T. McNaughton rev., 1961)).

> "At the present time it seems most realistic to portray the attorney-client privilege as supported in part by its traditional utilitarian justification, and in part by the integral role it is perceived to play in the adversary system itself. Our system of litigation casts the lawyer in the role of fighter for the party whom he represents. A strong tradition of loyalty attaches to the relationship of

attorney and client, and this tradition would be outraged by routine examination of the lawyer as to the client's confidential disclosures regarding professional business. To the extent that the evidentiary privilege, then, is integrally related to an entire code of professional conduct, it is futile to envision drastic curtailment of the privilege without substantial modification of the underlying ethical system to which the privilege is merely ancillary." John W. Strong, *McCormick on Evidence* § 87, at 121–22 (4th ed. 1992).

clergyman-penitent privilege. See *priest-penitent privilege.*

doctor-patient privilege. The right to exclude from evidence in a legal proceeding any confidential communication that a patient makes to a physician for the purpose of diagnosis or treatment, unless the patient consents to the disclosure. — Also termed *physician-client privilege*; *patient-physician privilege.*

editorial privilege. See *journalist's privilege* (2).

executive privilege. A privilege, based on the constitutional doctrine of separation of powers, that exempts the executive branch of the federal government from usual disclosure requirements when the matter to be disclosed involves national security or foreign policy. Cf. *executive immunity* under IMMUNITY (1).

husband-wife privilege. See *marital privilege.*

informant's privilege. The qualified privilege that a government can invoke to prevent disclosure of the identity and communications of its informants. • In exercising its power to formulate evidentiary rules for federal criminal cases, the U.S. Supreme Court has consistently declined to hold that the government must disclose the identity of informants in a preliminary hearing or in a criminal trial. *McCray v. Illinois*, 386 U.S. 300, 312, 87 S.Ct. 1056, 1063 (1967). A party can usu. overcome the privilege if it can demonstrate that the need for the information outweighs the public interest in maintaining the privilege. — Also termed *informer's privilege.*

joint-defense privilege. The rule that a defendant can assert the attorney-client privilege to protect a confidential communication made to a codefendant's lawyer if the communication was related to the defense of both defendants. — Also termed *common-interest doctrine.*

journalist's privilege. **1.** A reporter's protection, under constitutional or statutory law, from being compelled to testify about confidential information or sources. — Also termed *reporter's privilege*; *newsman's privilege.* See SHIELD LAW (1). **2.** A publisher's protection against defamation lawsuits when the publication makes fair comment on the actions of public officials in matters of public concern. — Also termed *editorial privilege.* See FAIR COMMENT.

judicial privilege. *Defamation.* The privilege protecting any statement made in the course of and with reference to a judicial proceeding by any judge, juror, party, witness, or advocate.

legislative privilege. *Defamation.* The privilege protecting (1) any statement made in a legislature by one of its members, and (2) any paper published as part of legislative business. — Also termed (in a parliamentary system) *parliamentary privilege.*

marital privilege. **1.** The privilege allowing a spouse not to testify, and to prevent another from testifying, about confidential communications with the other spouse during the marriage. — Also termed *marital-communications privilege.* **2.** The privilege allowing a spouse not to testify in a criminal case as an adverse witness against the other spouse, regardless of the subject matter of the testimony. — Also termed (in sense 2) *privilege against adverse spousal testimony*; *antimarital-facts privilege.* **3.** The privilege immunizing from a defamation lawsuit any statement made between husband and wife. — Also termed (in all senses) *spousal privilege*; *husband-wife privilege.*

national-security privilege. See *state-secrets privilege.*

newsman's privilege. See *journalist's privilege* (1).

official privilege. The privilege immunizing from a defamation lawsuit any statement made by one state officer to another in the course of official duty.

parliamentary privilege. See *legislative privilege.*

patient-physician privilege. See *doctor-patient privilege.*

peer-review privilege. A privilege that protects from disclosure the proceedings and reports of a medical facility's peer-review committee, which reviews and oversees the patient care and medical services provided by the staff.

physician-client privilege. See *doctor-patient privilege.*

priest-penitent privilege. The privilege barring a clergy member from testifying about a confessor's communications. — Also termed *clergyman-penitent privilege*.

privilege against adverse spousal testimony. See *marital privilege* (2).

psychotherapist-patient privilege. A privilege that a person can invoke to prevent the disclosure of a confidential communication made in the course of diagnosis or treatment of a mental or emotional condition by or at the direction of a psychotherapist. • The privilege can be overcome under certain conditions, as when the examination is ordered by a court. — Also termed *psychotherapist-client privilege*.

reporter's privilege. See *journalist's privilege* (1).

self-critical-analysis privilege. A privilege protecting individuals and entities from divulging the results of candid assessments of their compliance with laws and regulations, to the extent that the assessments are internal, the results were intended from the outset to be confidential, and the information is of a type that would be curtailed if it were forced to be disclosed. • This privilege is founded on the public policy that it is beneficial to permit individuals and entities to confidentially evaluate their compliance with the law, so that they will monitor and improve their compliance with it. — Also termed *self-policing privilege*.

spousal privilege. See *marital privilege*.

state-secrets privilege. A privilege that the government may invoke against the discovery of a material that, if divulged, could compromise national security. — Also termed *national-security privilege*.

4. *Civil law.* A creditor's right, arising from the nature of the debt, to priority over the debtor's other creditors. **5.** HAT MONEY.

privilege against self-incrimination. See RIGHT AGAINST SELF-INCRIMINATION.

privileged, *adj.* Not subject to the usual rules or liabilities; esp., not subject to disclosure during the course of a lawsuit <a privileged document>.

privileged communication. See COMMUNICATION.

privileged debt. See DEBT.

privileged evidence. See EVIDENCE.

privileged subscription. See RIGHTS OFFERING.

privileged villeinage. See VILLEINAGE.

privilege from arrest. See PRIVILEGE (1).

Privileges and Immunities Clause. The constitutional provision (U.S. Const. art. IV, § 2, cl. 1) prohibiting a state from favoring its own citizens by discriminating against other states' citizens who come within its borders.

Privileges or Immunities Clause. The constitutional provision (U.S. Const. amend. XIV, § 1) prohibiting state laws that abridge the privileges or immunities of U.S. citizens. • The clause was effectively nullified by the Supreme Court in the *Slaughter-House Cases*, 83 U.S. (16 Wall.) 36 (1873). Cf. DUE PROCESS CLAUSE; EQUAL PROTECTION CLAUSE.

privilege tax. See TAX.

privilegium (priv-ə-**lee**-jee-əm). [Latin] **1.** *Roman law.* A law passed against or in favor of a specific individual. **2.** *Roman law.* A special right, esp. one giving priority to a creditor. **3.** *Civil law.* Every right or favor that is granted by the law but is contrary to the usual rule.

privilegium clericale (priv-ə-**lee**-jee-əm kler-ə-**kay**-lee). [Law Latin] See BENEFIT OF CLERGY.

privity (**priv**-ə-tee). **1.** The connection or relationship between two parties, each having a legally recognized interest in the same subject matter (such as a transaction, proceeding, or piece of property); mutuality of interest <privity of contract>.

horizontal privity. *Commercial law.* The legal relationship between a party and a nonparty who is related to the party (such as a buyer and a member of the buyer's family).

privity of blood. **1.** Privity between an heir and an ancestor. **2.** Privity between coparceners.

privity of contract. The relationship between the parties to a contract, allowing them to sue each other but preventing a third party from doing so. • The requirement of privity has been relaxed under modern laws and doctrines of implied warranty and strict liability, which allow a third-party beneficiary or other foreseeable user to sue the seller of a defective product.

"To many students and practitioners of the common law *privity of contract* became a fetish. As such, it operated to deprive many a claimant of a remedy in cases where according to the *mores* of the time the claim was just. It has made many learned men believe that a *chose* in action *could not* be assigned. Even now, it is gravely asserted that a man cannot be made the debtor of another against his will. But the common law was gradually influenced by equity and by the law merchant, so that by assignment a debtor could become bound to pay a perfect stranger to himself, although until the legislature stepped in, the common-law courts characteristically made use of a fiction and pretended that they were not doing that which they really were doing." William R. Anson, *Principles of the Law of Contract* 335 (Arthur L. Corbin ed., 3d Am. ed. 1919).

"It is an elementary principle of English law — known as the doctrine of 'Privity of Contract' — that contractual rights and duties only affect the parties to a contract, and this principle is the distinguishing feature between the law of contract and the law of property. True proprietary rights are 'binding on the world' in the lawyer's traditional phrase. Contractual rights, on the other hand, are only binding on, and enforceable by, the immediate parties to the contract. But this distinction, fundamental though it be, wears a little thin at times. On the one hand, there has been a constant tendency for contractual rights to be extended in their scope so as to affect more and more persons who cannot be regarded as parties to the transaction. On the other hand, few proprietary rights are literally 'binding on the world'." P.S. Atiyah, *An Introduction to the Law of Contract* 265 (3d ed. 1981).

"The doctrine of privity means that a person cannot acquire rights or be subject to liabilities *arising under* a contract to which he is not a party. It does not mean that a contract between A and B cannot affect the legal rights of C indirectly." G.H. Treitel, *The Law of Contract* 538 (8th ed. 1991).

privity of estate. A mutual or successive relationship to the same right in property, as between grantor and grantee or landlord and tenant.

privity of possession. Privity between parties in successive possession of real property. • The existence of this type of privity is often at issue in adverse-possession claims.

vertical privity. **1.** *Commercial law.* The legal relationship between parties in a product's chain of distribution (such as a manufacturer and a seller). **2.** Privity between one who signs a contract containing a restrictive covenant and one who acquires the property burdened by it.

2. Joint knowledge or awareness of something private or secret, esp. as implying concurrence or consent <privity to a crime>.

privy (**priv**-ee), *n. pl.* A person having a legal interest of privity in any action, matter, or property; a person who is in privity with another. • Traditionally, there were six types of privies: (1) *privies in blood,* such as an heir and an ancestor; (2) *privies in representation,* such as an executor and a testator or an administrator and an intestate person; (3) *privies in estate,* such as grantor and grantee or lessor and lessee; (4) *privies in respect to a contract* — the parties to a contract; (5) *privies in respect of estate and contract,* such as a lessor and lessee where the lessee assigns an interest, but the contract between lessor and lessee continues because the lessor does not accept the assignee; and (6) *privies in law,* such as husband and wife. Pl. **privies.**

Privy Council. In Britain, the principal council of the sovereign, composed of the cabinet ministers and other persons chosen by royal appointment to serve as privy councillors. • The functions of the Privy Council are now mostly ceremonial. See JUDICIAL COMMITTEE OF THE PRIVY COUNCIL.

Privy Councillor. A member of the Privy Council.

privy purse. *English law.* The income set apart for the sovereign's personal use.

privy seal. **1.** A seal used in making out grants or letters patent before they are passed under the great seal. **2.** (*cap.*) LORD PRIVY SEAL.

privy signet. *Hist.* The signet or seal used by the sovereign in making out grants and private letters.

privy verdict. See VERDICT.

prize. **1.** Something of value awarded in recognition of a person's achievement. **2.** A vessel or cargo captured at sea or seized in port by the forces of a nation at war, and therefore liable to being condemned or appropriated as enemy property.

prize court. See COURT.

prize fighting. Fighting for a reward or prize; esp., professional boxing.

"Prize fighting . . . was not looked upon with favor by the common law as was a friendly boxing match or wrestling match. On the other hand it was not punishable by the common law unless it was fought in a public place, or for some other reason constituted a breach of the peace." Rollin M. Perkins & Ronald N. Boyce, *Criminal Law* 480 (3d ed. 1982).

prize goods. See GOODS.

prize law. The system of laws applicable to the capture of prize at sea, dealing with such matters as the rights of captors and the distribution of the proceeds.

prize money. 1. A dividend from the proceeds of a captured vessel, paid to the captors. **2.** Money offered as an award.

PRO. *abbr.* PEER-REVIEW ORGANIZATION.

pro (proh). [Latin] For.

proamita (proh-**am**-ə-tə). [Latin] *Roman & civil law.* A great-great aunt; the sister of one's great-grandfather.

proamita magna (proh-**am**-ə-tə **mag**-nə). [Latin] *Civil law.* A great-great-great-aunt.

proavia (proh-**ay**-vee-ə). [Latin] *Roman & civil law.* A great-grandmother.

proavunculus (proh-ə-**vəngk**-yə-ləs). [Latin] *Civil law.* A great-grandmother's brother.

probabilis causa (prə-**bay**-bə-lis **kaw**-zə). [Latin] Probable cause.

probable cause. A reasonable ground to suspect that a person has committed or is committing a crime or that a place contains specific items connected with a crime. • Under the Fourth Amendment, probable cause — which amounts to more than a bare suspicion but less than evidence that would justify a conviction — must be shown before an arrest warrant or search warrant may be issued. — Also termed *reasonable cause*; *sufficient cause*; *reasonable grounds*. Cf. REASONABLE SUSPICION.

> "Probable cause may not be established simply by showing that the officer who made the challenged arrest or search subjectively believed he had grounds for his action. As emphasized in *Beck v. Ohio* [379 U.S. 89, 85 S.Ct. 223 (1964)]: 'If subjective good faith alone were the test, the protection of the Fourth Amendment would evaporate, and the people would be "secure in their persons, houses, papers, and effects" only in the discretion of the police.' The probable cause test, then, is an objective one; for there to be probable cause, the facts must be such as would warrant a belief by a reasonable man." Wayne R. LaFave & Jerold H. Israel, *Criminal Procedure* § 3.3, at 140 (2d ed. 1992).

probable-cause hearing. See PRELIMINARY HEARING.

probable consequence. An effect or result that is more likely to follow its supposed cause than not to follow it.

probable-desistance test. *Criminal law.* A common-law test for the crime of attempt, focusing on whether the defendant has exhibited dangerous behavior indicating a likelihood of committing the crime. See ATTEMPT (2).

probable evidence. See *presumptive evidence* under EVIDENCE.

probandum (proh-**ban**-dəm), *n.* A fact to be proved. Pl. **probanda.** See *fact in issue* under FACT.

probata (proh-**bay**-tə). [Latin] *pl.* PROBATUM.

probate (**proh**-bayt), *n.* **1.** The judicial procedure by which a testamentary document is established to be a valid will; the proving of a will to the satisfaction of the court. • Unless set aside, the probate of a will is conclusive upon the parties to the proceedings (and others who had notice of them) on all questions of testamentary capacity, the absence of fraud or undue influence, and due execution of the will. But probate does not preclude inquiry into the validity of the will's provisions or on their proper construction or legal effect. — Also termed *proof of will*.

informal probate. Probate designed to operate with minimal involvement of the probate court. • Most modern probate codes encourage this type of administration, with an independent personal representative. — Also termed *independent probate*.

probate in common form. *Hist.* Probate granted in the registry, without any formal procedure in court, on the executor's ex parte application. • This type of probate is revocable.

probate in solemn form. *Hist.* Probate granted in open court, as a final decree, when all interested parties have been given notice. • This type of probate is irrevocable for all parties who have had notice of the proceeding, unless a later will is discovered.

small-estate probate. An informal procedure for administering small estates, less structured than the normal process and usu. not requiring the assistance of an attorney.

2. Loosely, a personal representative's actions in handling a decedent's estate. **3.** Loosely, all the subjects over which probate courts have jurisdiction. **4.** *Archaic.* A nonresident plaintiff's proof of a debt by swearing before a notary public or other officer that the debt is correct, just, and due, and by having the notary attach a jurat.

probate, *vb.* **1.** To admit (a will) to proof. **2.** To administer (a decedent's estate). **3.** To grant probation to (a criminal); to reduce (a sentence) by means of probation.

probate asset. See *legal asset* under ASSET.

probate bond. See BOND (2).

probate code. A collection of statutes setting forth the law (substantive and procedural) of decedents' estates and trusts.

probate court. See COURT.

probate distribution. See DISTRIBUTION.

probate duty. See DUTY (4).

probate estate. A decedent's property subject to administration by a personal representative. See *decedent's estate* under ESTATE.

probate homestead. A homestead, exempt from creditors' claims, set apart for use by a decedent's surviving spouse and minor children. See HOMESTEAD.

probate in common form. See PROBATE.

probate in solemn form. See PROBATE.

probate judge. See JUDGE.

probate jurisdiction. See JURISDICTION.

probate register. See REGISTER.

probatio (prə-**bay**-shee-oh). [Latin] *Roman & civil law.* Proof.

plena probatio. See *probatio plena.*

probatio mortua (prə-**bay**-shee-oh **mor**-choo-ə). [Latin] Dead proof; proof by an inanimate object such as a deed or other instrument.

probatio plena (prə-**bay**-shee-oh **plee**-nə). [Latin] *Civil law.* Full proof; proof by two witnesses or a public instrument. — Also termed *plena probatio.*

probatio semi-plena (prə-**bay**-shee-oh sem-I-**plee**-nə). [Latin] *Civil law.* Half-full proof; half-proof; proof by one witness or a private instrument.

probatio viva (prə-**bay**-shee-oh **vI**-və). [Latin] Living proof; that is, proof by the mouth of a witness.

probation. 1. A court-imposed criminal sentence that, subject to stated conditions, releases a convicted person into the community instead of sending the criminal to jail or prison. Cf. PAROLE.

shock probation. Probation that is granted after a brief stay in jail or prison. • Shock probation is intended to awaken the defendant to the reality of confinement for failure to abide by the conditions of probation. This type of probation is discretionary with the sentencing judge and is usu. granted within 180 days of the original sentence. Cf. *shock incarceration* under INCARCERATION.

2. The act of judicially proving a will. See PROBATE.

probation before judgment. See *deferred judgment* under JUDGMENT.

probationer. A convicted criminal who is on probation.

probation officer. A government officer who supervises the conduct of a probationer.

probation without judgment. See *deferred judgment* under JUDGMENT.

probatio plena. See PROBATIO.

probatio semi-plena. See PROBATIO.

probatio viva. See PROBATIO.

probative (**proh**-bə-tiv), *adj.* Tending to prove or disprove. • Courts can exclude relevant evidence if its probative value is substantially outweighed by the danger of unfair prejudice. Fed. R. Evid. 403. — **probativeness,** *n.*

probative evidence. See EVIDENCE.

probative fact. See FACT.

probator (proh-**bay**-tər), *n. Hist.* An accused person who confesses to a crime but asserts that another also participated in the crime. • The probator had to undertake to prove the supposed accomplice's guilt.

probatum (proh-**bay**-təm), *n.* [Latin] Something conclusively established or proved; proof. Pl. ***probata.*** Cf. ALLEGATUM.

pro bono (proh **boh**-noh), *adv. & adj.* [Latin *pro bono publico* "for the public good"] Being or involving uncompensated legal services performed esp. for the public good <took the case pro bono> <50 hours of pro bono work each year>.

pro bono et malo (proh **boh**-noh et **mal**-oh). [Latin] For good and ill. See DE BONO ET MALO.

probus et legalis homo (**proh**-bəs et lə-**gay**-lis **hoh**-moh). [Law Latin] A good and lawful man. • This phrase referred to a juror who was legally competent to serve on a jury. Pl. ***probi et legales homines.***

procedendo (proh-sə-**den**-doh). [Latin] A higher court's order directing a lower court to determine and enter a judgment in a previously removed case.

procedendo ad judicium. See DE PROCEDENDO AD JUDICIUM.

procedural consolidation. See JOINT ADMINISTRATION.

procedural-default doctrine. The principle that a federal court lacks jurisdiction to review the merits of a habeas corpus petition if a state court has refused to review the complaint because the petitioner failed to follow reasonable state-court procedures.

procedural due process. See DUE PROCESS.

procedural law. The rules that prescribe the steps for having a right or duty judicially enforced, as opposed to the law that defines the specific rights or duties themselves. — Also termed *adjective law*. Cf. SUBSTANTIVE LAW.

procedural presumption. See PRESUMPTION.

procedural right. See RIGHT.

procedural unconscionability. See UNCONSCIONABILITY.

procedure. 1. A specific method or course of action. **2.** The judicial rule or manner for carrying on a civil lawsuit or criminal prosecution. See CIVIL PROCEDURE; CRIMINAL PROCEDURE.

proceeding. 1. The regular and orderly progression of a lawsuit, including all acts and events between the time of commencement and the entry of judgment. **2.** Any procedural means for seeking redress from a tribunal or agency. **3.** An act or step that is part of a larger action. **4.** The business conducted by a court or other official body; a hearing. **5.** *Bankruptcy.* A particular dispute or matter arising within a pending case — as opposed to the case as a whole.

> "'Proceeding' is a word much used to express the business done in courts. A proceeding in court is an act done by the authority or direction of the court, express or implied. It is more comprehensive than the word 'action,' but it may include in its general sense all the steps taken or measures adopted in the prosecution or defense of an action, including the pleadings and judgment. As applied to actions, the term 'proceeding' may include — (1) the institution of the action; (2) the appearance of the defendant; (3) all ancillary or provisional steps, such as arrest, attachment of property, garnishment, injunction, writ of *ne exeat*; (4) the pleadings; (5) the taking of testimony before trial; (6) all motions made in the action; (7) the trial; (8) the judgment; (9) the execution; (10) proceedings supplementary to execution, in code practice; (11) the taking of the appeal or writ of error; (12) the *remittitur*, or sending back of the record to the lower court from the appellate or reviewing court; (13) the enforcement of the judgment, or a new trial, as may be directed by the court of last resort." Edwin E. Bryant, *The Law of Pleading Under the Codes of Civil Procedure* 3–4 (2d ed. 1899).

adjudicatory proceeding. See *adjudicatory hearing* under HEARING.

administrative proceeding. See ADMINISTRATIVE PROCEEDING.

collateral proceeding. A proceeding brought to address an issue incidental to the principal proceeding.

competency proceeding. A proceeding to assess a person's mental capacity. • A competency hearing may be held either in a criminal context to determine a defendant's competency to stand trial or as a civil proceeding to assess whether a person should be committed to a mental-health facility.

contempt proceeding. A judicial or quasi-judicial hearing conducted to determine whether a person has committed contempt.

core proceeding. See CORE PROCEEDING.

criminal proceeding. A proceeding instituted to determine a person's guilt or innocence or to set a convicted person's punishment; a criminal hearing or trial.

ex parte proceeding (eks **pahr**-tee). A proceeding in which not all parties are present or given the opportunity to be heard. — Also termed *ex parte hearing*.

in camera proceeding (in **kam**-ə-rə). A proceeding held in a judge's chambers or other private place.

informal proceeding. A trial conducted in a more relaxed manner than a typical court trial, such as an administrative hearing or a trial in small-claims court.

judicial proceeding. Any court proceeding.

non-core proceeding. See RELATED PROCEEDING.

related proceeding. See RELATED PROCEEDING.

special proceeding. **1.** A proceeding that can be commenced independently of a pending action and from which a final order may be appealed immediately. **2.** A proceeding involving statutory or civil remedies or rules rather than the rules or remedies ordinarily available under rules of procedure; a proceeding providing extraordinary relief.

summary proceeding. A nonjury proceeding that settles a controversy or disposes of a case in a relatively prompt and simple manner. — Also termed *summary trial*. Cf. *plenary action* under ACTION.

"Summary proceedings were such as were directed by Act of Parliament, there was no jury, and the person accused was acquitted or sentenced only by such person as statute had appointed for his judge. The common law was wholly a stranger to summary proceedings." A.H. Manchester, *Modern Legal History of England and Wales, 1750–1950* 160 (1980).

supplementary proceeding. **1.** A proceeding held in connection with the enforcement of a judgment, for the purpose of identifying and locating the debtor's assets available to satisfy the judgment. **2.** A proceeding that in some way supplements another.

proceeds (**proh**-seedz), *n.* **1.** The value of land, goods, or investments when converted into money; the amount of money received from a sale <the proceeds are subject to attachment>. **2.** Something received upon selling, exchanging, collecting, or otherwise disposing of collateral. UCC § 9–306(1). • Proceeds differ from other types of collateral because they constitute any collateral that has changed in form. For example, if a farmer borrows money and gives the creditor a security interest in the harvest, the harvested wheat is collateral. If the farmer then exchanges the harvest for a tractor, the tractor becomes the proceeds of the wheat.

net proceeds. The amount received in a transaction minus the costs of the transaction (such as expenses and commissions). — Also termed *net balance*.

proceres (**pros**-ə-reez). [Latin] Nobles; lords. See DOMUS PROCERUM.

process, *n.* **1.** The proceedings in any action or prosecution <due process of law>. **2.** A summons or writ, esp. to appear or respond in court <service of process>. — Also termed *judicial process*; *legal process*.

"*Process* is so denominated because it *proceeds* or issues forth in order to bring the defendant into court, to answer the charge preferred against him, and signifies the writs or judicial means by which he is brought to answer." 1 Joseph Chitty, *A Practical Treatise on the Criminal Law* 338 (2d ed. 1826).

bailable process. A process instructing an officer to take bail after arresting a defendant. • The defendant's discharge is required by law after the tender of suitable security.

civil process. A process that issues in a civil lawsuit.

compulsory process. A process, with a warrant to arrest or attach included, that compels a person to appear in court as a witness.

criminal process. A process (such as an arrest warrant) that issues to compel a person to answer for a crime.

final process. A process issued at the conclusion of a judicial proceeding; esp., a writ of execution.

irregular process. A process not issued in accordance with prescribed practice. • Whether the process is void or merely voidable depends on the type of irregularity. Cf. *regular process*.

mesne process (meen). **1.** A process issued between the commencement of a lawsuit and the final judgment or determination. **2.** The procedure by which a contumacious defendant is compelled to plead.

original process. A process issued at the beginning of a judicial proceeding.

"Original process is any writ or notice by which a defendant is called upon to appear and answer the plaintiff's declaration. The commencement of the suit at common law was formerly by original writ. Judicial process was by summons, attachment, arrest and outlawry." Benjamin J. Shipman, *Handbook of Common-Law Pleading* § 3, at 17 (Henry Winthrop Ballantine ed., 3d ed. 1923).

regular process. A process that issues lawfully according to prescribed practice. Cf. *irregular process*.

summary process. **1.** An immediate process, issuing and taking effect without intermediate applications or delays. **2.** A legal procedure used to resolve a controversy more efficiently and expeditiously than ordinary methods. **3.** The legal documents achieving such a result. **4.** A procedure for repossessing real property from a tenant upon default. See *summary eviction* under EVICTION. **5.** See SHOW-CAUSE PROCEEDING.

trust process. In some states (particularly in New England), garnishment or foreign attachment.

void process. Legal process that, in some material way, does not comply with the required form.

3. *Patents.* A method, operation, or series of actions intended to achieve some end or result. Cf. MACHINE; MANUFACTURE.

> "A process is a way of doing something. If it is a patentable process, it must be a new, useful, and nonobvious way of doing something. If the process is patentable, the result of that process — the something getting done — need not of itself be new, useful, or nonobvious. In other words, the result of an inventive process need not be an invention itself." Arthur R. Miller & Michael H. Davis, *Intellectual Property in a Nutshell* 24 (2d ed. 1990).

process, abuse of. See MALICIOUS ABUSE OF PROCESS.

process agent. See AGENT.

process by foreign attachment. See FACTORIZING PROCESS.

processioning. The survey and inspection of land boundaries, performed esp. in the former English colonies along the southeastern seaboard, and analogous to the English *perambulation.*

process patent. See PATENT (3).

process server. A person authorized by law or by a court to formally deliver process to a defendant or respondent. See SERVICE (1).

processum continuando (prə-**ses**-əm kən-tin-yoo-**an**-doh). [Latin "for continuing process"] *Hist.* A writ for the continuation of process after the death of a justice authorized to review cases by a commission of oyer and terminer.

procès-verbal (proh-**say**-vair-**bahl**). [French "official record of oral proceedings"] *Civil & int'l law.* A detailed, authenticated written report of a proceeding, esp. of an international conference; PROTOCOL (3). ● A *procès-verbal* may be cast in various forms, according to the style a country prefers.

prochein ami (**proh**-shen ə-**mee**). [Law French] See NEXT FRIEND.

proclaim, *vb.* To declare formally or officially.

proclamation. A formal public announcement made by the government.

proclamation by lord of manor. *Hist.* A proclamation (repeated three times) made by the lord of a manor requiring an heir or devisee of a deceased copyholder to pay a fine and be admitted to the estate, failing which the lord could seize the lands provisionally.

proclamation of exigents (**eks**-ə-jənts). *Hist.* Repeated proclamations by the sheriff of an imminent outlawing of a person in the county where the person lived. See EXIGENT.

proclamation of rebellion. *Hist.* A proclamation made by the sheriff, warning a person who failed to obey a Chancery subpoena or attachment that a commission of rebellion would issue if the person continued to resist the Chancery process. See COMMISSION OF REBELLION.

proclamation of recusants (**rek**-yə-zənts). *Hist.* A proclamation by which persons who willfully absented themselves from church could be convicted on nonappearance at the assizes.

proclamator (**prok**-lə-may-tər). *Hist.* An official at the English Court of Common Pleas responsible for making proclamations.

pro-con divorce. See DIVORCE.

pro consilio impendendo (proh kən-**sil**-ee-oh im-pen-**den**-doh). [Law Latin] For counsel to be given. ● Advice given could formerly serve as consideration for the grant of an annuity.

proconsul (proh-**kon**-səl). [Latin] *Roman law.* **1.** An ex-consul who continued to exercise the powers of a consul after leaving office. **2.** The governor of certain senatorial provinces.

pro corpore regni (proh **kor**-pə-ree **reg**-nɪ). [Latin] In behalf of the body of the realm.

proctor. 1. One appointed to manage the affairs of another. **2.** PROCURATOR (4).

procuracy (**prok**-yə-rə-see). The document that grants power to an attorney-in-fact; a letter of agency.

procurare (prok-yə-**rair**-ee), *vb.* [Latin] To take care of another's affairs.

procuratio (prok-yə-**ray**-shee-oh). [Latin] Management of another's affairs; agency.

procuration (prok-yə-**ray**-shən). **1.** The act of appointing someone as an agent or attorney-in-fact. **2.** The authority vested in a person so appointed; the function of an attorney. **3.** PROCUREMENT.

procuration fee. *English law.* A commission or brokerage allowed to a solicitor for obtaining a loan. — Also termed *procuration money.*

procurator (**prok**-yə-ray-tər). **1.** *Roman law.* A person informally appointed to represent another in a judicial proceeding. Cf. COGNITOR. **2.** *Roman law.* A government official, usu. subordinate in authority to a provincial governor. **3.** *Hist. English law.* An agent, attorney, or servant. **4.** *Eccles. law.* An advocate of a religious house; one who represents a religious society in its legal matters. — Also termed *proctor.* **5.** An agent or attorney-in-fact. **6.** *Scots law.* A solicitor who represents clients in the lower courts.

procuratores ecclesiae parochialis (prok-yə-rə-**tor**-eez e-**klee**-z[h]ee-ee pə-roh-kee-**ay**-lis). [Latin] *Hist.* A churchwarden; a representative of a parish church.

procurator fiscal. *Scots law.* The representative of the Lord Advocate in inferior courts, responsible for investigating crimes and prosecuting in court.

procurator in rem suam (prok-yə-**ray**-tər in rem **s[y]oo**-əm). [Latin] **1.** *Roman law.* An assignee of a right of action. **2.** *Scots law.* Procurator in his own affair. • This phrase refers to a situation in which a person acts under a power of attorney with reference to property that the person has acquired.

procuratorium (prok-yə-rə-**tor**-ee-əm). [Law Latin] *Hist.* The instrument by which a person appointed a procurator as the person's representative in litigation.

procurator litis (prok-yə-**ray**-tər **lI**-tis). [Latin] *Roman law.* A person who represents another in a lawsuit. Cf. DEFENSOR (1).

procurator negotiorum (prok-yə-**ray**-tər ni-goh-shee-**or**-əm). [Latin] *Civil law.* An attorney-in-fact; a manager of business affairs for another.

procurator provinciae (prok-yə-**ray**-tər prə-**vin**-shee-ee). [Latin] *Roman law.* A provincial officer responsible for overseeing revenue matters. • This officer also exercised some judicial powers over revenue-related issues.

procuratrix (prok-yə-**ray**-triks). [Latin] *Hist.* A female agent or attorney-in-fact.

procurement (proh-**kyoor**-mənt), *n.* **1.** The act of getting or obtaining something. — Also termed *procuration.* **2.** The act of persuading or inviting another, esp. a woman or child, to have illicit sexual intercourse. — **procure,** *vb.*

procurement contract. See CONTRACT.

procurement of breach of contract. See TORTIOUS INTERFERENCE WITH CONTRACTUAL RELATIONS.

procurer. One who induces or prevails upon another to do something, esp. to engage in an illicit sexual act. See PIMP.

procuring an abortion. See ABORTION.

procuring cause. See CAUSE (1).

pro. def. *abbr.* PRO DEFENDENTE.

pro defectu emptorum (proh di-**fek**-t[y]oo emp-**tor**-əm). [Latin] For want of purchasers.

pro defectu exitus (proh di-**fek**-t[y]oo **eks**-ə-təs). [Latin] For, or in case of, default of issue.

pro defectu haeredis (proh di-**fek**-t[y]oo hə-**ree**-dis). [Latin] For want of an heir.

pro defectu justitiae (proh di-**fek**-t[y]oo jəs-**tish**-ee-ee). [Latin] For defect or want of justice.

pro defendente (proh def-ən-**den**-tee). [Latin] For the defendant. — Abbr. *pro. def.* Cf. PRO QUERENTE.

pro derelicto (proh der-ə-**lik**-toh). [Latin] As derelict or abandoned. • This refers to property subject to usucaption. See USUCAPIO.

prodigal (**prod**-ə-gəl), *n. Civil law.* A person whose affairs are managed by a curator because of the person's wasteful spending or other bad conduct.

pro dignitate regali (proh dig-nə-**tay**-tee ri-**gay**-lɪ). [Latin] In consideration of the royal dignity.

prodigus (**prod**-ə-gəs). [Latin] *Roman law.* See PRODIGAL.

prodition (prə-**dish**-ən). *Archaic.* Treason; treachery.

proditor (**prod**-ə-tər). *Archaic.* A traitor.

proditorie (proh-di-**tor**-ee-ee), *adv.* [Latin] Treasonably. • This word formerly appeared in a treason indictment.

pro diviso (proh di-**vɪ**-zoh). [Latin] As divided; i.e., in severalty.

pro domino (proh **dom**-ə-noh). [Latin] As master or owner; in the character of a master.

pro donatione (proh də-**nay**-shee-oh-nee). [Latin] *Roman & civil law.* As a gift; as in case of gift. • This is a ground of usucaption. See USUCAPIO.

pro dote (proh **doh**-tee). [Latin] *Civil law.* As a dowry; by title of dowry. • This is a ground of usucaption. See USUCAPIO.

produce (**proh**-doos), *n.* The product of natural growth, labor, or capital; esp., agricultural products.

produce (prə-**doos**), *vb.* **1.** To bring into existence; to create. **2.** To provide (a document, witness, etc.) in response to subpoena or discovery request. **3.** To yield (as revenue). **4.** To bring (oil, etc.) to the surface of the earth.

producent (prə-**d[y]oo**-sənt), *n. Hist. Eccles. law.* The party calling a witness.

producer. See INSURANCE AGENT.

producer price index. An index of wholesale price changes, issued monthly by the U.S. Bureau of Labor Statistics. — Formerly also termed *wholesale price index.* Cf. CONSUMER PRICE INDEX.

producing cause. See *proximate cause* under CAUSE (1).

product. Something that is distributed commercially for use or consumption and that is usu. (1) tangible personal property, (2) the result of fabrication or processing, and (3) an item that has passed through a chain of commercial distribution before ultimate use or consumption. See PRODUCTS LIABILITY.

defective product. A product that is unreasonably dangerous for normal use, as when it is not fit for its intended purpose, inadequate instructions are provided for its use, or it is inherently dangerous in its design or manufacture.

product defect. See DEFECT.

product-extension merger. See MERGER.

production burden. See BURDEN OF PRODUCTION.

production for commerce. The production of goods that an employer intends for interstate commerce. • This is one criterion by which an employer may be subject to the Fair Labor Standards Act.

production of suit. *Common-law pleading.* The plaintiff's burden to produce evidence to confirm the allegations made in the declaration.

productio sectae (prə-**dək**-shee-oh **sek**-tee). [Latin] See PRODUCTION OF SUIT.

product liability. See PRODUCTS LIABILITY.

product market. See MARKET.

products liability, *n.* **1.** A manufacturer's or seller's tort liability for any damages or injuries suffered by a buyer, user, or bystander as a result of a defective product. • Products liability can be based on a theory of negligence, strict liability, or breach of warranty. **2.** The legal theory by which liability is imposed on the manufacturer or seller of a defective product. **3.** The field of law dealing with this theory. — Also termed *product liability*; (specif.) *manufacturer's liability.* — **product-liability,** *adj.* See LIABILITY.

"The law of products liability is that body of common and statutory law permitting money reparation for substandard conduct of others resulting in product-related injury to the injured party's person or property. Resistance to the description of products liability as a doctrine having receded, there is today a guiding tenet in the law of product-related injury that is the distillate of seventy years of decisional law. The birth of the doctrine can be dated at 1916, the publication of the immensely influential decision in *MacPherson v. Buick Motor Co.*, [217 N.Y. 382, 111 N.E. 1050 (1916)], in which the New York Court of Appeals held that the manufacturer of any product capable of serious harm if incautiously made owed a duty of care in the design, inspection, and fabrication of the product, a duty owed not only to the immediate purchaser but to all persons who might foreseeably come into contact with the product. Following MacPherson, the doctrine as formed by decisions of the ensuing decades is that a buyer, user, consumer or bystander in proximity to an unreasonably dangerous product, and who is injured in person or in property by its dangerous propensities, may recover in damages from the manufacturer or intermediate seller." 1 M. Stuart Madden, *Products Liability* § 1.1, at 1–2 (2d ed. 1988).

strict products liability. Products liability arising when the buyer proves that the goods were unreasonably dangerous and that (1) the seller was in the business of selling goods, (2) the goods were defective when they were in the seller's hands, (3) the defect caused the plaintiff's injury, and (4) the product was expected to and did reach the consumer without substantial change in condition.

products-liability action. A lawsuit brought against a manufacturer, seller, or lessor of a product — regardless of the substantive legal theory or theories upon which the lawsuit is brought — for personal injury, death, or property damage caused by the manufacture, construction, design, formulation, installation, preparation, or assembly of a product. — Also termed *product-liability action*.

products-liability insurance. See INSURANCE.

product test. See DURHAM RULE.

pro emptore (proh emp-**tor**-ee). [Latin] *Civil law*. As a purchaser; by the title of a purchaser. See USUCAPIO.

pro facto (proh **fak**-toh). [Latin] For the fact; considered or held as fact.

pro falso clamore suo (proh **fal**-soh [*or* **fawl**-soh] klə-**mor**-ee **s[y]oo**-oh). [Latin "for his false claim"] A nominal amercement of a plaintiff for a false allegation, inserted in a judgment for the defendant.

profane, *adj*. (Of speech or conduct) irreverent to something held sacred.

profectitius (proh-fek-**tish**-ee-əs). [Latin] That which descends from an ancestor.

profer (**proh**-fər). *Hist*. **1.** An offer or proffer. **2.** A return made by a sheriff of an account into the Exchequer.

proferens (proh-**fer**-enz). [Latin] The party that proposes a contract or a condition in a contract. Pl. ***proferentes*** (proh-fə-**ren**-teez).

profert (**proh**-fərt). *Common-law pleading*. A declaration on the record stating that a party produces in court the deed or other instrument relied on in the pleading.

profert in curia (**proh**-fərt in **kyoor**-ee-ə). [Law Latin] He produces in court. • In common-law pleading, this phrase was used in a declaration asserting that the plaintiff was ready to produce, or had produced, the deed or other instrument on which the action was founded.

profess, *vb*. To declare openly and freely; to confess.

professio juris (prə-**fes[h]**-ee-oh **joor**-is). [Latin] A recognition of the right of a contracting party to stipulate the law that will govern the contract.

profession. 1. A vocation requiring advanced education and training. **2.** Collectively, the members of such a vocation.

professional, *n*. A person who belongs to a learned profession or whose occupation requires a high level of training and proficiency.

professional association. See ASSOCIATION.

professional corporation. See CORPORATION.

professional negligence. See MALPRACTICE.

proffer (**prof**-ər), *vb*. To offer or tender (something, esp. evidence) for immediate acceptance. — **proffer,** *n*.

proffered evidence. See EVIDENCE.

proficua (prə-**fik**-yoo-ə). [Law Latin] *Hist*. Profits; esp., the profits of an estate in land.

profit, *n*. **1.** The excess of revenues over expenditures in a business transaction; GAIN (2). Cf. EARNINGS; INCOME.

accumulated profit. Profit that has accrued but not yet been distributed; earned surplus. — Also termed *undivided profit.* See *retained earnings* under EARNINGS.

gross profit. Total sales revenue less the cost of the goods sold, no adjustment being made for additional expenses and taxes. Cf. *net profit.*

mesne profits. The profits of an estate received by a tenant in wrongful possession between two dates. — Also termed (archaically) *medium tempus.*

net profit. Total sales revenue less the cost of the goods sold and all additional expenses. — Also termed *net revenue.* Cf. *gross profit.*

operating profit. Total sales revenue less all operating expenses, no adjustment being made for any nonoperating income and expenses, such as interest payments.

paper profit. A profit that is anticipated but not yet realized. • Gains from stock holdings, for example, are paper profits until the stock is actually sold at a price higher than its original purchase price. — Also termed *unrealized profit.*

surplus profit. *Corporations.* The excess of revenue over expenditures. • Some jurisdictions prohibit the declaration of a dividend from sources other than surplus profit.

undistributed profit. See *retained earnings* under EARNINGS.

undivided profit. See *accumulated profit.*

unrealized profit. See *paper profit.*

2. A servitude that gives the right to pasture cattle, dig for minerals, or otherwise take away some part of the soil; PROFIT À PRENDRE. • A profit may be either appurtenant or in gross. See SERVITUDE.

profit-and-loss account. See ACCOUNT.

profit-and-loss statement. See INCOME STATEMENT.

profit à prendre (a **prawn**-drə *or* ah **prahn**-dər). [Law French "profit to take"] (*usu. pl.*) A right or privilege to go on another's land and take away something of value from its soil or from the products of its soil (as by mining, logging, or hunting). — Also termed *right of common.* Pl. **profits à prendre.** Cf. EASEMENT.

profiteering, *n.* The taking advantage of unusual or exceptional circumstances to make excessive profits, as in the selling of scarce goods at inflated prices during war. — **profiteer,** *vb.*

profit insurance. See INSURANCE.

profit margin. 1. The difference between the cost of something and the price for which it is sold. **2.** The ratio, expressed as a percentage, between this difference and the selling price. • For example, a widget costing a retailer $10 and selling for $15 has a profit margin of 33% ($5 difference divided by $15 selling price). — Often shortened to *margin.*

profit-sharing plan. An employer's benefit plan that allows an employee to share in the company's profits. • ERISA governs the administration of many profit-sharing plans. See EMPLOYEE RETIREMENT INCOME SECURITY ACT.

qualified profit-sharing plan. A plan in which an employer's contributions are not taxed to the employee until distribution. • The employer is allowed to deduct the contributions. IRC (26 USCA) § 401.

pro forma (proh **for**-mə), *adj.* [Latin "for form"] **1.** Made or done as a formality. **2.** (Of an invoice or financial statement) provided in advance to describe items, predict results, or secure approval.

progener (proh-**jee**-nər). [Latin] A grandson-in-law.

progeny (**proj**-ə-nee), *n. pl.* **1.** Children or descendants; offspring <only one of their progeny attended law school>. **2.** A group of successors; esp., a line of opinions succeeding a leading case <*Erie* and its progeny>.

prognosis (prog-**noh**-sis). **1.** The process of forecasting the probable outcome of a present medical condition (such as a disease). **2.** The forecast of such an outcome. Cf. DIAGNOSIS.

program trading. A form of computerized securities trading that usu. involves buying or selling large amounts of stocks while simultaneously selling or buying index futures in offsetting amounts.

progressive tax. See TAX.

pro hac vice (proh hahk **vee**-chay *or* hak **vɪ**-see *also* hahk **vees**). [Latin] For this occasion or particular purpose. • The phrase usu. refers to a lawyer who has not been admitted to practice in a particular jurisdiction but who is admitted there temporarily for the purpose of conducting a particular case. — Abbr. *p.h.v.* See *admission* *pro hac vice* under ADMISSION (2). For *owner pro hac vice*, see *demise charter* under CHARTER (4).

prohibit, *vb.* **1.** To forbid by law. **2.** To prevent or hinder.

prohibited degree. See DEGREE.

prohibitio de vasto, directa parti (proh-hə-**bish**-ee-oh dee **vas**-toh, di-**rek**-tə **pahr**-tɪ). [Latin "prohibition of waste, directed to the party"] *Hist.* A writ issued during litigation prohibiting a tenant from committing waste.

prohibition. 1. A law or order that forbids a certain action. **2.** An extraordinary writ issued by an appellate court to prevent a lower court from exceeding its jurisdiction or to prevent a nonjudicial officer or entity from exercising a power. — Also termed (in sense 2) *writ of prohibition.*

> "Prohibition is a kind of common-law injunction to prevent an unlawful assumption of jurisdiction.... It is a common-law injunction against governmental usurpation, as where one is called coram non judice (before a judge unauthorized to take cognizance of the affair), to answer in a tribunal that has no legal cognizance of the cause. It arrests the proceedings of any tribunal, board, or person exercising judicial functions in a manner or by means not within its jurisdiction or discretion." Benjamin J. Shipman, *Handbook of Common-Law Pleading* § 341, at 542 (Henry Winthrop Ballantine ed., 3d ed. 1923).

3. (*cap.*) The period from 1920 to 1933, when the manufacture, transport, and sale of alcoholic beverages in the United States was forbidden by the 18th Amendment to the Constitution. • The 18th Amendment was repealed by the 21st Amendment.

prohibitory injunction. See INJUNCTION.

prohibitory interdict. See INTERDICT (1).

pro illa vice (proh **il**-ə **vɪ**-see). [Latin] For that turn.

pro indefenso (proh in-də-**fen**-soh). [Latin] As undefended; as making no defense.

pro indiviso (proh in-də-**vɪ**-zoh), *adj.* [Latin "as undivided"] (Of property) owned or possessed by several persons at the same time, without partition.

pro interesse suo (proh in-tər-**es**-ee **s[y]oo**-oh). [Latin] According to his interest; to the extent of his interest. • A third party, for example, may be allowed to intervene *pro interesse suo.*

project financing. See FINANCING.

projectio (prə-**jek**-shee-oh). [Latin] Alluvion created by the sea. See ALLUVION.

projector. See PROMOTER.

projet (proh-**zhay**). [French] A draft of a proposed measure, treaty, or convention.

pro laesione fidei (proh lee-zhee-**oh**-nee **fɪ**-dee-ɪ). [Latin] For breach of faith.

pro legato (proh lə-**gay**-toh). [Latin] As a legacy; by the title of a legacy. • This is a ground of usucaption. See USUCAPIO.

proles (**proh**-leez). [Latin] Offspring; esp., the issue of a lawful marriage.

proletariat (proh-lə-**tair**-ee-ət). The working class; those without capital who sell their labor to survive.

proletarius (proh-lə-**tair**-ee-əs). [Latin] *Roman law.* One of the common people; a member of a lower class who owned little or no property.

prolicide (**proh**-lə-sɪd). The killing of offspring; esp., the crime of killing a child shortly before or after birth.

prolixity (proh-**lik**-sə-tee). The unnecessary and superfluous stating of facts in pleading or evidence.

prolocutor (proh-**lok**-yə-tər). **1.** *Eccles. law.* The president or chair of a convocation. **2.** *Hist.* The speaker of the British House of Lords. • This office now belongs to the Lord Chancellor.

pro majori cautela (proh mə-**jor**-ɪ kaw-**tee**-lə). [Latin] For greater caution; by way of additional security. • This phrase usu. applies to an act done or to a clause put in an instrument as a precaution.

promatertera (proh-mə-**tər**-tər-ə). [Latin] *Roman & civil law.* A great-great-aunt; the sister of one's great-grandmother.

promatertera magna (proh-mə-**tər**-tər-ə **mag**-nə). [Latin] *Civil law.* A great-great-great-aunt.

promise, *n.* **1.** The manifestation of an intention to act or refrain from acting in a specified manner, conveyed in such a way that another is justified in understanding that a commitment has been made; a person's assurance that the person will or will not do something. • A binding promise — one that the law will enforce — is the essence of a contract.

"By common usage, a promise is an expression leading another person justifiably to expect certain conduct on the part of the promisor. Such an expression is a promise, whether enforceable at law or not. It is indeed an essential element in every contract. Society does not guarantee the fulfillment of all expectations so induced." William R. Anson, *Principles of the Law of Contract* 6 n.3 (Arthur L. Corbin ed., 3d Am. ed. 1919).

"[*Promise*] means not only the physical manifestations of assurance by words or conduct, but also the moral duty to make good the assurance by performance. If by reason of other operative facts the promise is recognized as creating a legal duty, the promise is a contract." Samuel Williston, *A Treatise on the Law of Contracts* § 1A, at 4 (Walter H.E. Jaeger ed., 3d ed. 1957).

"It is well to make clear two points at the outset .... The first is that I do not believe that all promises are morally binding; accordingly, I use the term 'promise' without prejudging the question whether the promise creates an obligation. The second is that, where a promise does create an obligation, the reason for that may depend upon whether the promise was explicit or implied. There is thus, in my view, a fundamental distinction between explicit and implied promises, and when I use the word 'promise' without qualification, I normally mean an explicit promise." P.S. Atiyah, *Promises, Morals, and Law* 8 (1981).

2. The words in a promissory note expressing the maker's intention to pay a debt. • A mere written acknowledgment that a debt is due is insufficient to constitute a promise. — **promise,** *vb.*

aleatory promise (**ay**-lee-ə-tor-ee). A promise conditional on the happening of a fortuitous event, or on an event that the parties believe is fortuitous.

alternative promise. A contractual promise to do one of two or more things, any one of which must satisfy the promisee for the promise to qualify as consideration.

"A promise in the alternative may be made because each of the alternative performances is the object of desire to the promisee. Or the promisee may desire one performance only, but the promisor may reserve an alternative which he may deem advantageous. In either type of case the promise is consideration if it cannot be kept without some action or forbearance which would be consideration if it alone were bargained for. But if the promisor has an unfettered choice of alternatives, and one alternative would not have been consideration if separately bargained for, the promise in the alternative is not consideration." Restatement (Second) of Contracts § 77 cmt. b (1981).

bare promise. See *naked promise.*

collateral promise. A promise to guarantee the debt of another, made primarily without benefit to the party making the promise. • Unlike an original promise, a collateral promise must be in writing to be enforceable. See MAIN-PURPOSE RULE.

conditional promise. A promise that is conditioned on the occurrence of an event <she made a conditional promise to sell the gold on April 2 unless the price fell below $300 an ounce before that time>. • A conditional promise is not illusory as long as the condition is not entirely within the promisor's control.

dependent promise. A promise to be performed by a party only when another obligation has first been performed by another party.

divisible promises. Promises that are capable of being divided into independent parts.

false promise. A promise made with no intention of carrying it out.

fictitious promise. See *implied promise.*

gratuitous promise. A promise made in exchange for nothing; a promise not supported by consideration. • A gratuitous promise is not ordinarily legally enforceable. — Also termed *bare promise*; *naked promise.*

illusory promise. A promise that appears on its face to be so insubstantial as to impose no obligation on the promisor; an expression cloaked in promissory terms but actually containing no commitment by the promisor. • For example, if a guarantor promises to make good on the principal debtor's obligation "as long as I think it's in my commercial interests," the promisor is not really bound.

"An apparent promise which, according to its terms, makes performance optional with the promisor no matter what may happen, or no matter what course of conduct in other respects he may pursue, is in fact no promise. Such an expression is often called an illusory promise." Samuel Williston, *A Treatise on the Law of Contracts* § 1A, at 5 (Walter H.E. Jaeger ed., 3d ed. 1957).

implied promise. A promise created by law to render a person liable on a contract so as to avoid fraud or unjust enrichment. — Also termed *fictitious promise.*

"Under some circumstances the promise inferred is called an implied promise and in others it is referred to as a constructive promise. But whichever conclusion is reached, the result is the same. In other words an implied promise and a constructive promise are not treated differently. The theoretical difference between the two is that a promise implied from the conduct of the parties arises by construction of law, only when justice requires it under the circumstances." John D. Calamari & Joseph M. Perillo, *The Law of Contracts* § 4–12, at 234–35 (3d ed. 1987).

independent promise. See *unconditional promise.*

marriage promise. A betrothal; an engagement to be married.

mutual promises. Promises given simultaneously by two parties, each promise serving as consideration for the other.

new promise. A previously unenforceable promise that a promisor revives and agrees to fulfill, as when a debtor agrees to pay a creditor an amount discharged in the debtor's bankruptcy.

original promise. A promise to guarantee the debt of another, made primarily for the benefit of the party making the promise. • An original promise need not be in writing to be enforceable. See MAIN-PURPOSE RULE.

promise implied in fact. A promise existing by inference from the circumstances or actions of the parties. See *implied promise.*

promise in consideration of marriage. A promise for which the actual performance of the marriage is the consideration, as when a man agrees to transfer property to a woman if she will marry him. • A promise to marry, however, is not considered a promise in consideration of marriage.

promise in restraint of trade. A promise whose performance would limit competition in any business or restrict the promisor in the exercise of a gainful occupation. • Such a promise is usu. unenforceable.

remedial promise. A seller's promise to repair or replace goods, or the like, or to refund the price if the goods (1) do not conform to the contract or to a representation at the time of the delivery of the goods, (2) conform at the time of delivery but later fail to perform as agreed, or (3) contain a defect. UCC § 2–102(a)(31).

unconditional promise. A promise that either is unqualified or requires nothing but the lapse of time to make the promise presently enforceable. • A party who makes an unconditional promise must perform that promise even though the other party has not performed according to the bargain. — Also termed *independent promise.*

voidable promise. A promise that one party may, under the law, declare void by reason of that party's incapacity or mistake, or by reason of the fraud, breach, or other fault of the other party.

promisee (prom-is-**ee**). One to whom a promise is made.

promise implied in fact. See PROMISE.

promise in consideration of marriage. See PROMISE.

promise in restraint of trade. See PROMISE.

promise not to compete. See *noncompetition covenant* under COVENANT (1).

promisor (prom-is-**or**). One who makes a promise; esp., one who undertakes a contractual obligation.

promissor (**prom**-is-ər). [Latin] *Civil law.* A promisor; specif., a party who undertakes to do a thing in response to the interrogation of the other party (the *stipulator*).

promissory, *adj.* Containing or consisting of a promise <the agreement's promissory terms>.

promissory condition. See CONDITION (2).

promissory estoppel. See ESTOPPEL.

promissory fraud. See FRAUD.

promissory note. See NOTE (1).

promissory oath. See OATH.

promissory representation. See REPRESENTATION.

promissory warranty. See WARRANTY (3).

promoter. 1. A person who encourages or incites. **2.** A founder or organizer of a corporation or business venture; one who takes the entrepreneurial initiative in founding or organizing a business or enterprise. — Formerly also termed *projector.*

> "The complete judicial acceptance of the term 'promoter' is a matter of comparatively recent date. In some of the early cases, persons engaged in the formation of a corporation are spoken of as 'projectors.' Other cases of about the same period, though recognizing the obligations flowing therefrom, do not give any name to the relation in which such persons stand to the contemplated company. The word *promoter*, while undoubtedly employed in common parlance before that time, does not seem to have been used in any reported decision until after it had been used, and for the purposes of the act defined, in the Joint Stock Companies Act of 1844.... [A] person may be said to be a promoter of a corporation if before its organization, he directly or indirectly solicits subscriptions to its stock, or assumes to act in its behalf in the purchase of property, or in the securing of its charter, or otherwise

assists in its organization." Manfred W. Ehrich, *The Law of Promoters* § 1, at 2–3; § 13, at 15 (1916).

"A promoter is a person who takes the initiative in developing and organizing a new business venture. A promoter may act either alone or with co-promoters. The term 'promoter' is not one of opprobrium; indeed, the promoter is often an aggressive, imaginative entrepreneur who fulfills the essential economic function of taking an idea and creating a profitable business to capitalize on the idea." Robert W. Hamilton, *The Law of Corporations in a Nutshell* 64 (3d ed. 1991).

promoting prostitution. See PANDERING.

promulgare (proh-məl-**gair**-ee), *vb.* [Latin] *Roman law.* To promulgate; to make (a law) publicly known after its enactment.

promulgate (prə-**məl**-gayt *or* **prom**-əl-gayt), *vb.* **1.** To declare or announce publicly; to proclaim. **2.** To put (a law or decree) into force or effect.

promulgation (prom-əl-**gay**-shən *or* proh-məl-). The official publication of a new law or regulation, by which it is put into effect.

promutuum (proh-**myoo**-choo-əm). [Latin "as if lent"] *Civil law.* A quasi-contract in which a person who received money or property in error agrees to return what was received to the person who paid it.

pronepos (proh-**nep**-ohs). [Latin] *Roman & civil law.* A great-grandson.

proneptis (proh-**nep**-tis). [Latin] *Roman & civil law.* A great-granddaughter.

pro non scripto (**proh** non **skrip**-toh). [Latin] As not written; as though it had not been written.

pronotary (proh-**noh**-tə-ree), *n.* First notary.

pronounce, *vb.* To announce formally <pronounce judgment>.

pronunciation (prə-nən-see-**ay**-shən). *Archaic.* A sentence or decree.

pronurus (**proh**-nə-rəs). [Latin] *Civil law.* The wife of a grandson or great-grandson.

proof, *n.* **1.** The establishment or refutation of an alleged fact by evidence; the persuasive effect of evidence in the mind of a fact-finder. **2.** Evidence that determines the judgment of a court. **3.** An attested document that constitutes legal evidence.

affirmative proof. Evidence establishing the fact in dispute by a preponderance of the evidence.

conditional proof. A fact that amounts to proof as long as there is no other fact amounting to disproof. — Also termed *presumptive proof.*

double proof. **1.** *Bankruptcy.* Proof of claims by two or more creditors against the same debt. • This violates the general rule that there can be only one claim with respect to a single debt. **2.** *Evidence.* Corroborating government evidence (usu. by two witnesses) required to sustain certain convictions.

full proof. **1.** *Civil law.* Proof by two witnesses or by public instrument. **2.** Evidence that satisfies the minds of the jury of the truth of the fact in dispute beyond a reasonable doubt.

literal proof. *Civil law.* Written evidence. Cf. *testimonial proof.*

negative proof. Proof that establishes a fact by showing that its opposite is not or cannot be true. Cf. *positive proof.*

positive proof. Direct or affirmative proof. Cf. *negative proof.*

preliminary proof. *Insurance.* The first proof offered of a loss occurring under a policy, usu. sent in to the underwriters with a notification of the claim.

presumptive proof. See *conditional proof.*

proof beyond a reasonable doubt. Proof that precludes every reasonable hypothesis except that which it tends to support.

testimonial proof. *Civil law.* Proof by the evidence of witnesses, rather than proof by written instrument. Cf. *literal proof.*

proof, burden of. See BURDEN OF PROOF.

proof brief. See BRIEF.

proof of acknowledgment. An authorized officer's certification — based on a third party's testimony — that the signature of a person (who usu. does not appear before the notary) is genuine and was freely made. — Also termed *certificate of proof.*

proof of claim. *Bankruptcy.* A creditor's written statement that is submitted to show the basis and amount of the creditor's claim. Pl. **proofs of claim.**

informal proof of claim. A proof of claim stating a creditor's demand for payment and intent to hold the debtor's bankruptcy estate liable, but that does not comply with the Bankruptcy Code's form for proofs of claim. • A late-filed proof of claim may be given effect if the creditor had timely filed an informal proof of claim.

proof of debt. The establishment by a creditor of a debt in some prescribed manner (as by affidavit) as a first step in recovering the debt from an estate or property; PROOF OF CLAIM.

proof of loss. An insured's formal statement of loss required by an insurance company before it will determine whether the policy covers the loss.

proof of service. A document filed (as by a sheriff) in court as evidence that process has been successfully served on a party. — Also termed *return of service*. See SERVICE (1).

proof of will. See PROBATE (1).

pro opere et labore (proh **op**-ə-ree et lə-**bor**-ee). [Latin] For work and labor.

propaganda. *Int'l law.* **1.** The systematic dissemination of doctrine, rumor, or selected information to promote or injure a particular doctrine, view, or cause. **2.** The ideas or information so disseminated.

> "As early as the Middle Ages, both the Church and worldly powers had realised that public opinion was of importance in their struggles with each other.... [R]ulers thought it necessary to put their case before public opinion in neutral and hostile countries, though they did their best to prevent any 'seditious' material from abroad reaching their own loyal subjects. The position changed with the growth of democracy and of the demand for the popular control of foreign affairs. Then propaganda became an indispensable secondary weapon of power politics both in peace and war." Georg Schwarzenberger, *Power Politics: A Study of International Society* 166–67 (2d ed. 1951).

pro partibus liberandis (proh **pahr**-ti-bəs lib-ə-**ran**-dis). [Latin "to free the portions"] *Hist.* A writ for the partition of lands among coheirs.

propatruus (proh-**pay**-troo-əs *or* -**pa**-troo-əs). [Latin] *Roman & civil law.* A great-grandfather's brother.

propatruus magnus (proh-**pay**-troo-əs [*or* -**pa**-troo-əs] **mag**-nəs). [Latin] *Roman & civil law.* A great-great-great-uncle.

pro per, *adv.* & *adj.* See PRO PERSONA.

pro per, *n.* See PRO SE.

proper care. See *reasonable care* under CARE.

proper evidence. See *admissible evidence* under EVIDENCE.

proper feud. See FEUD.

proper independent advice. See INDEPENDENT ADVICE.

proper law. *Conflict of laws.* The substantive law that, under the principles of conflicts of law, governs a transaction.

proper lookout, *n.* The duty of a vehicle operator to exercise caution to avoid collisions with pedestrians or other vehicles.

proper party. See PARTY (2).

pro persona (proh pər-**soh**-nə), *adv.* & *adj.* [Latin] For one's own person; on one's own behalf <a *pro persona* brief>. — Sometimes shortened to *pro per*. See PRO SE.

property. 1. The right to possess, use, and enjoy a determinate thing (either a tract of land or a chattel); the right of ownership <the institution of private property is protected from undue governmental interference>. **2.** Any external thing over which the rights of possession, use, and enjoyment are exercised <the airport is city property>.

> "In its widest sense, property includes all a person's legal rights, of whatever description. A man's property is all that is *his in law*. This usage, however, is obsolete at the present day, though it is common enough in the older books.... In a second and narrower sense, property includes not all a person's rights, but only his proprietary as opposed to his personal rights. The former constitute his estate or property, while the latter constitute his status or personal condition. In this sense a man's land, chattels, shares, and the debts due to him are his property; but not his life or liberty or reputation.... In a third application, which is that adopted [here], the term includes not even all proprietary rights, but only those which are both proprietary and *in rem*. The law of property is the law of proprietary rights *in rem*, the law of proprietary rights *in personam* being distinguished from it as the law of obligations. According to this usage a freehold or leasehold estate in land, or a patent or copyright, is property; but a debt or the benefit of a contract is not.... Finally, in the narrowest use of the term, it includes nothing more than corporeal property — that is to say, the right of ownership in a material object, or that object itself." John Salmond, *Jurisprudence* 423–24 (Glanville L. Williams ed., 10th ed. 1947).

abandoned property. Property that the owner voluntarily surrenders, relinquishes, or disclaims. Cf. *lost property*; *mislaid property*.

absolute property. Property that one has full and complete title to and control over.

common property. **1.** Property that is held jointly by two or more persons. **2.** See COMMON AREA.

community property. See COMMUNITY PROPERTY.

corporeal property. **1.** The right of ownership in material things. **2.** Property that can be perceived, as opposed to incorporeal property; tangible property.

distressed property. Property that must be sold because of mortgage foreclosure or because it is part of an insolvent estate.

exempt property. See EXEMPT PROPERTY.

general property. Property belonging to a general owner. See *general owner* under OWNER.

income property. Property that produces income, such as rental property.

incorporeal property. **1.** An in rem proprietary right that is not classified as corporeal property. • Incorporeal property is traditionally broken down into two classes: (1) *jura in re aliena* (encumbrances), whether over material or immaterial things, examples being leases, mortgages, and servitudes; and (2) *jura in re propria* (full ownership over an immaterial thing), examples being patents, copyrights, and trademarks. **2.** A legal right in property having no physical existence. • Patent rights, for example, are incorporeal property. — Also termed *incorporeal chattel*; *incorporeal thing*.

intangible property. Property that lacks a physical existence. • Examples include bank accounts, stock options, and business goodwill. Cf. *tangible property*.

intellectual property. See INTELLECTUAL PROPERTY.

literary property. See LITERARY PROPERTY.

lost property. Property that the owner no longer possesses because of accident, negligence, or carelessness, and that cannot be located by an ordinary, diligent search. Cf. *abandoned property*; *mislaid property*.

marital property. Property that is acquired from the time when a marriage begins until one spouse files for divorce (assuming that a divorce decree actually results). • In equitable-distribution states, the phrase *marital property* is the rough equivalent of *community property*. See COMMUNITY PROPERTY; EQUITABLE DISTRIBUTION.

maternal property. Property that comes from the mother of a party, and other ascendants of the maternal stock.

mislaid property. Property that has been voluntarily relinquished by the owner with an intent to recover it later — but that cannot now be found. Cf. *abandoned property*; *lost property*.

> "A distinction is drawn between lost property and mislaid property. An article is 'mislaid' if it is intentionally put in a certain place for a temporary purpose and then inadvertently left there when the owner goes away. A typical case is the package left on the patron's table in a bank lobby by a depositor who put the package there for a moment while he wrote a check and then departed without remembering to take it with him. There is always a 'clue' to the ownership of property which is obviously *mislaid* rather than *lost*, because of the strong probability that the owner will know where to return for his chattel when he realizes he has gone away without it." Rollin M. Perkins & Ronald N. Boyce, *Criminal Law* 310–11 (3d ed. 1982).

mixed property. Property with characteristics of both real property and personal property — such as heirlooms and fixtures.

movable property. See MOVABLE.

neutral property. See NEUTRAL PROPERTY.

paternal property. Property that comes from the father of a party, and other ascendants of the paternal stock.

personal property. **1.** Any movable or intangible thing that is subject to ownership and not classified as real property. — Also termed *personalty*; *personal estate*; *movable estate*; (in plural) *things personal*. Cf. *real property*. **2.** Property not used in a taxpayer's trade or business or held for income production or collection.

private property. Property — protected from public appropriation — over which the owner has exclusive and absolute rights.

public property. State- or community-owned property not restricted to any one individual's use or possession.

qualified property. A temporary or special interest in a thing (such as a right to possess it), subject to being totally extinguished by the occurrence of a specified contingency over which the qualified owner has no control.

qualified-terminable-interest property. Property that passes by a QTIP trust from a deceased spouse to the surviving spouse and that (if the executor so elects) qualifies for the marital deduction provided that the spouse is entitled to receive income in payments made at least annually for life and that no one has the power to appoint the property to anyone other than the surviving spouse. • This property is included in the surviving spouse's estate at death, where it is subject to the federal estate tax. See *QTIP trust* under TRUST.

real property. Land and anything growing on, attached to, or erected on it, excluding anything that may be severed without injury to the land. • Real property can be either corporeal (soil and buildings) or incorporeal (easements). — Also termed *realty*; *real estate*. Cf. *personal property*.

> "Historically, the line between real and personal property stems from the types of assets administered on death respectively, in the king's and in the church's courts. The king's courts, concerned with the preservation of the feudal structure, dealt with fees simple, fees tail and life estates. Estates for years, gradually evolving out of contracts made by feudally unimportant persons, clearly became interests in land but never fully attained the historical dignity of being 'real property.' The early economic unimportance of money, goods and things other than land permitted the church courts to take over the handling of all such assets on the death of the owner. When the development of trade and of capitalism caused assets of these types to assume great, and sometimes paramount, importance we found ourselves with the two important categories of property, namely 'real' and 'personal' property, each with its set of rules evolved from a different matrix. The pressure of modern society has been strongly for assimilation and the resultant elimination of this line, but this movement is far from complete attainment of its goal." 1 Richard R. Powell, *Powell on Real Property* § 5.04, at 5–7 to 5–8 (Patrick J. Rohan ed., rev. ed. 1998).

scheduled property. *Insurance*. Property itemized on a list (usu. attached to an insurance policy) that records property values, which provide the basis for insurance payments in the event of a loss under an insurance policy.

separate property. See SEPARATE PROPERTY.

special property. Property that the holder has only a qualified, temporary, or limited interest in, such as (from a bailee's standpoint) bailed property.

tangible personal property. Corporeal personal property of any kind; personal property that can be seen, weighed, measured, felt, or touched, or is in any way perceptible to the senses.

tangible property. Property that has physical form and characteristics. Cf. *intangible property*.

property, law of. See LAW OF PROPERTY.

property crimes. See CRIMES AGAINST PROPERTY.

property-damage insurance. See *property insurance* under INSURANCE.

property dividend. See *asset dividend* under DIVIDEND.

property insurance. See INSURANCE.

property of the debtor. *Bankruptcy*. Property that is owned or (in some instances) possessed by the debtor, including property that is exempted from the bankruptcy estate. 11 USCA § 541(b).

property of the estate. *Bankruptcy*. The debtor's tangible and intangible property interests (including both legal and equitable interests) that fall under the bankruptcy court's jurisdiction because they were owned or held by the debtor when the bankruptcy petition was filed. 11 USCA § 541.

property right. See RIGHT.

property settlement. 1. A judgment in a divorce case determining the distribution of the marital property between the divorcing parties. **2.** MARITAL AGREEMENT.

property tax. See TAX.

property tort. See TORT.

prophylactic (proh-fə-**lak**-tik), *adj*. Formulated to prevent something <a prophylactic rule>. — **prophylaxis** (proh-fə-**lak**-sis), **prophylactic,** *n*.

propinquity (prə-**ping**-kwə-tee). The state of being near; specif., kindred or parentage <degrees of propinquity>.

propior sobrina (**proh**-pee-ər sə-**brɪ**-nə), *n*. [Latin] *Civil law*. The daughter of a great-uncle or great-aunt, paternal or maternal.

propior sobrino (**proh**-pee-ər sə-**brɪ**-noh), *n*. [Latin] *Civil law*. The son of a great-uncle or great-aunt, paternal or maternal.

propone (prə-**pohn**), *vb*. To put forward for consideration or adjudication <propone a will for probate>.

proponent, *n.* **1.** A person who puts forward a legal instrument for consideration or acceptance; esp., one who offers a will for probate. **2.** A person who puts forward a proposal; one who argues in favor of something <a proponent of gun control>.

proportionality. *Int'l law.* The principle that the use of force should be in proportion to the threat or grievance provoking the use of force.

proportionality review. *Criminal law.* An appellate court's analysis of whether a death sentence is arbitrary or capricious by comparing the case in which it was imposed with similar cases in which the death penalty was approved or disapproved.

proportional representation. An electoral system that allocates legislative seats to each political group in proportion to its popular voting strength.

proportional tax. See *flat tax* under TAX.

proposal. Something offered for consideration or acceptance.

proposed regulation. A draft administrative regulation that is circulated among interested parties for comment. — Abbr. prop. reg.

propositus (proh-**poz**-ə-təs). [Law Latin] *Civil law.* A person from whom descent is to be traced; the person whose rights or obligations are in issue.

pro possessore (proh pos-ə-**sor**-ee). [Latin] As a possessor; by title of a possessor; by virtue of possession alone.

pro posse suo (proh **pos**-ee **s[y]oo**-oh). [Latin] To the extent of one's power or ability.

propound (prə-**pownd**), *vb.* **1.** To offer for consideration or discussion. **2.** To make a proposal. **3.** To put forward (a will) as authentic.

propounder. An executor or administrator who offers a will or other testamentary document for admission to probate; PROPONENT.

prop. reg. *abbr.* PROPOSED REGULATION.

propria persona (**proh**-pree-ə pər-**soh**-nə). [Latin] In his own person; that is, pro se. — Abbr. *p.p.*

proprietary (prə-**prI**-ə-ter-ee), *adj.* **1.** Of or relating to a proprietor <the licensee's proprietary rights>. **2.** Of, relating to, or holding as property <the software designer sought to protect its proprietary data>.

proprietary act. See PROPRIETARY FUNCTION.

proprietary article. See ARTICLE.

proprietary capacity. See CAPACITY (1).

proprietary capital. See CAPITAL.

proprietary drug. See DRUG.

proprietary duty. A duty owed by a municipality while acting in a proprietary, rather than governmental, activity.

proprietary function. *Torts.* A municipality's conduct that is performed for the profit or benefit of the municipality, rather than for the benefit of the general public. • Generally, a municipality is not immune from tort liability for proprietary acts. — Also termed *proprietary act.* Cf. GOVERNMENTAL FUNCTION.

proprietary government. See GOVERNMENT.

proprietary information. Information in which the owner has a protectable interest. See TRADE SECRET.

proprietary interest. See INTEREST (2).

proprietary lease. See LEASE.

proprietary power. See *power coupled with an interest* under POWER.

proprietary right. See RIGHT.

proprietas (prə-**prI**-ə-tas). [Latin] *Hist.* Ownership.

> ***proprietas nuda*** (prə-**prI**-ə-tas **n[y]oo**-də). Naked ownership; the mere title to property, without the usufruct.
>
> ***proprietas plena*** (prə-**prI**-ə-tas **plee**-nə). Full ownership, including both the title and the usufruct.

proprietate probanda (prə-prI-ə-**tay**-tee prə-**ban**-də). See DE PROPRIETATE PROBANDA.

proprietor, *n.* An owner, esp. one who runs a business. — **proprietorship,** *n.* See SOLE PROPRIETORSHIP.

propriety. *Hist.* Privately owned possessions; property.

proprio vigore (**proh**-pree-oh vi-**gor**-ee). [Latin] By its own strength.

propter (**prop**-tər). [Latin] For; on account of.

propter affectum (**prop**-tər ə-**fek**-təm). See *challenge propter affectum* under CHALLENGE (2).

propter defectum (**prop**-tər də-**fek**-təm). See *challenge propter defectum* under CHALLENGE (2).

propter defectum sanguinis (**prop**-tər də-**fek**-təm **sang**-gwi-nis). [Latin] On account of failure of blood.

propter delictum (**prop**-tər də-**lik**-təm). See *challenge propter delictum* under CHALLENGE.

propter honoris respectum (**prop**-tər hə-**nor**-is ri-**spek**-təm). [Latin] On account of respect of honor or rank.

propter impotentiam (**prop**-tər im-pə-**ten**-shee-əm). [Latin] On account of helplessness. • This was formerly given as a ground for gaining a property interest in a wild animal, based on the animal's inability to escape (as where, for example, a young bird could not yet fly away).

propter privilegium (**prop**-tər priv-ə-**lee**-jee-əm). [Latin] On the account of privilege. • This describes a way of acquiring a property interest in a wild animal, based on the claimant's exclusive right to hunt in a particular park or preserve.

pro quer. *abbr.* PRO QUERENTE.

pro querente (proh kwə-**ren**-tee). [Latin] For the plaintiff. — Abbr. *pro quer.* Cf. PRO DEFENDENTE.

pro rata (proh **ray**-tə *or* **rah**-tə *or* **ra**-tə), *adv.* Proportionately; according to an exact rate, measure, or interest <the liability will be assessed pro rata between the defendants>. — **pro rata,** *adj.* See RATABLE.

pro rata clause. An insurance-policy provision — usu. contained in the "other insurance" section of the policy — that limits the insurer's liability to payment of the portion of the loss that the face amount of the policy bears to the total insurance available on the risk. — Also termed *pro rata distribution clause.* Cf. ESCAPE CLAUSE; EXCESS CLAUSE.

prorate (**proh**-rayt *or* proh-**rayt**), *vb.* To divide, assess, or distribute proportionately <prorate taxes between the buyer and the seller>. — **proration,** *n.*

pro re nata (proh ree **nay**-tə). [Latin "in the light of what has arisen"] A law or course of action adopted in response to a pressing exigency, rather than in conformity with established precedent.

> "So far as may be, the state leaves the rule of right to be declared and constituted by the agreement of those concerned with it. So far as possible, it contents itself with executing the rules which its subjects have made for themselves. And in so doing it acts wisely. For, in the first place, the administration of justice is enabled in this manner to escape in a degree not otherwise attainable the disadvantages inherent in the recognition of rigid principles of law. Such principles we must have; but if they are established *pro re nata* by the parties themselves, they will possess a measure of adaptability to individual cases which is unattainable by the more general legislation of the state itself." John Salmond, *Jurisprudence* 352 (Glanville L. Williams ed., 10th ed. 1947).

prorogation (proh-rə-**gay**-shən). The act of putting off to another day; esp., the discontinuance of a legislative session until its next term.

prorogue (proh-**rohg** *or* prə-), *vb.* **1.** To postpone or defer. **2.** To discontinue a session of (a legislative assembly, esp. the British Parliament) without dissolution. **3.** To suspend or discontinue a legislative session.

proscribe, *vb.* **1.** To outlaw or prohibit; to forbid. **2.** *Roman & civil law.* To post or publish the name of (a person) as condemned to death and forfeiture of property.

proscription, *n.* **1.** The act of prohibiting; the state of being prohibited. **2.** A prohibition or restriction. — **proscriptive,** *adj.* Cf. PRESCRIPTION.

pro se (proh **say** *or* **see**), *adv.* & *adj.* [Latin] For oneself; on one's own behalf; without a lawyer <the defendant proceeded pro se> <a pro se defendant>. — Also termed *pro persona*; *in propria persona.*

pro se, *n.* One who represents oneself in a court proceeding without the assistance of a lawyer <the third case on the court's docket involving a pro se>. — Also termed *pro per.*

prosecute, *vb.* **1.** To commence and carry out a legal action <because the plaintiff failed to prosecute its contractual claims, the court dismissed the suit>. **2.** To institute and pursue a criminal action against (a person) <the notorious felon has been prosecuted in seven states>. **3.** To engage in; carry on <the company prosecuted its business for 12 years before going bankrupt>. — **prosecutory,** *adj.*

prosecuting attorney. See DISTRICT ATTORNEY.

prosecuting witness. See WITNESS.

prosecution. 1. The commencement and carrying out of any action or scheme <the prosecution of a long, bloody war>. **2.** A criminal proceeding in which an accused person is tried <the conspiracy trial involved the prosecution of seven defendants>. — Also termed *criminal prosecution.*

sham prosecution. A prosecution that seeks to circumvent a defendant's double-jeopardy protection by appearing to be prosecuted by another sovereignty, when it is in fact controlled by the sovereignty that already prosecuted the defendant for the same crime. • A sham prosecution is, in essence, a misuse of the dual-sovereignty rule. Under that rule, a defendant's protection against double jeopardy does not provide protection against a prosecution by a different sovereignty. For example, if the defendant was first tried in federal court and acquitted, that fact would not forbid the state authorities from prosecuting the defendant in state court. But a sham prosecution — for example, a later state-court prosecution that is completely dominated or manipulated by the federal authorities that already prosecuted the defendant, so that the state-court proceeding is merely a tool of the federal authorities — will not withstand a double-jeopardy challenge. See DUAL-SOVEREIGNTY DOCTRINE.

3. The government attorneys who initiate and maintain a criminal action against an accused defendant <the prosecution rests>.

prosecution history. *Patents.* The complete record of proceedings in the Patent and Trademark Office from the initial application to the issued patent. — Also termed *file wrapper.*

prosecution-history estoppel. *Patents.* The doctrine preventing a patent holder from invoking the doctrine of equivalents if the holder, during the application process, surrendered certain claims or interpretations of the invention. — Also termed *file-wrapper estoppel.* See DOCTRINE OF EQUIVALENTS.

prosecutor, *n.* **1.** A legal officer who represents the government in criminal proceedings. See DISTRICT ATTORNEY; UNITED STATES ATTORNEY; ATTORNEY GENERAL.

public prosecutor. See DISTRICT ATTORNEY.

special prosecutor. A lawyer appointed to investigate and, if justified, seek indictments in a particular case. See *independent counsel* under COUNSEL.

2. A private person who institutes and carries on a legal action, esp. a criminal action. — Also termed (in sense 2) *private prosecutor.* — **prosecutorial,** *adj.*

prosecutorial discretion. See DISCRETION.

prosecutorial misconduct. A prosecutor's improper or illegal act (or failure to act), esp. involving an attempt to persuade the jury to wrongly convict a defendant or assess an unjustified punishment. • If prosecutorial misconduct results in a mistrial, a later prosecution may be barred under the Double Jeopardy Clause.

prosecutrix (pros-ə-**kyoo**-triks). *Archaic.* A female prosecutor.

prosequi (**prahs**-ə-kwɪ), *vb.* [Latin] To follow up or pursue; to sue or prosecute. See NOLLE PROSEQUI.

prosequitur (prə-**sek**-wə-tər *or* proh-). [Latin] He follows or pursues; he prosecutes.

prosocer (**proh**-sə-sər). [Latin] *Civil law.* A father-in-law's father; a spouse's grandfather.

prosocerus (prə-**sos**-ə-rəs). [Latin] *Civil law.* A wife's or husband's grandmother.

pro socio (proh **soh**-shee-oh). [Latin] As a partner. • This was the name of an action on behalf of a partner.

pro solido (proh **sol**-ə-doh). [Latin] For the whole; without division.

prospectant evidence. See EVIDENCE.

prospective, *adj.* **1.** Effective or operative in the future <prospective application of the new statute>. Cf. RETROACTIVE. **2.** Anticipated or expected; likely to come about <prospective clients>.

prospective damages. See DAMAGES.

prospective heir. See HEIR.

prospective nuisance. See *anticipatory nuisance* under NUISANCE.

prospective statute. See STATUTE.

prospective waiver. See WAIVER (1).

prospectus (prə-**spek**-təs). A printed document that describes the main features of an enterprise (esp. a corporation's business) and that is distributed to prospective buyers or investors; esp., a written description of a securities offering. • Under SEC regulations, a publicly traded corporation must provide a prospectus before offering to sell stock in the corporation. Pl. **prospectuses.** See REGISTRATION STATEMENT. Cf. TOMBSTONE.

newspaper prospectus. A summary prospectus that the SEC allows to be disseminated through advertisements in newspapers, magazines, or other periodicals sent through the mails as second-class matter (though not distributed by the advertiser), when the securities involved are issued by a foreign national government with which the United States maintains diplomatic relations.

preliminary prospectus. A prospectus for a stock issue that has been filed but not yet approved by the SEC. • The SEC requires such a prospectus to contain a notice — printed in distinctive red lettering — that the document is not complete or final. That notice, which is usu. stamped or printed in red ink, typically reads as follows: "The information here given is subject to completion or amendment. A registration statement relating to these securities has been filed with the Securities and Exchange Commission. These securities cannot be sold — and offers to buy cannot be accepted — until the registration statement becomes effective. This prospectus does not constitute an offer to buy. And these securities cannot be sold in any state where the offer, solicitation, or sale would be unlawful before registration or qualification under the securities laws of that state." — Also termed *red-herring prospectus*; *red herring.*

prostitution, *n.* **1.** The act or practice of engaging in sexual activity for money or its equivalent; commercialized sex.

> "Prostitution is not itself a crime in England or Scotland, although certain activities of prostitutes and those who profit from prostitution are prohibited, such as soliciting in a public place, procuring, letting premises for the purpose of prostitution and so forth. On the other hand, prostitution was, at least at one time, prohibited in all American jurisdictions." Rollin M. Perkins & Ronald N. Boyce, *Criminal Law* 470 (3d ed. 1982).

2. The act of debasing. — **prostitute,** *vb.* — **prostitute,** *n.*

pro tanto (proh **tan**-toh), *adv.* & *adj.* [Latin] To that extent; for so much; as far as it goes <the debt is pro tanto discharged> <a pro tanto payment>.

protected activity. Conduct that is permitted or encouraged by a statute or constitutional provision, and for which the actor may not legally be retaliated against. • For example, Title VII of the Civil Rights Act prohibits an employer from retaliating against an employee who opposes a discriminatory employment practice or helps in investigating an allegedly discriminatory employment practice. An employee who is retaliated against for engaging in one of those activities has a claim against the employer. 42 USCA § 2000e–3(a).

protected class. See CLASS (1).

protected person. See PERSON.

protecting power. *Int'l law.* A country responsible for protecting another country's citizens during a conflict or a suspension of diplomatic ties between the citizens' country and a third party. • After a protecting power is accepted by both belligerents, it works to ensure the proper treatment of nationals who are in a belligerent's territory, esp. prisoners of war. If the parties cannot agree on a protecting power, the Red Cross is often appointed to this position.

protection, *n.* **1.** The act of protecting. **2.** PROTECTIONISM. **3.** COVERAGE (1). **4.** A document given by a notary public to sailors and other persons who travel abroad, certifying that the bearer is a U.S. citizen. — **protect,** *vb.*

protectionism. The protection of domestic businesses and industries against foreign competition by imposing high tariffs and restricting imports.

protection money. 1. A bribe paid to an officer as an inducement not to interfere with the criminal activities of the briber. • Examples include payments to an officer in exchange for the officer's releasing an arrestee, removing records of traffic violations from a court's files, and refraining from making a proper arrest. **2.** Money extorted from a business owner by one who promises to "protect" the business premises, with the implied threat that if the owner does not pay, the person requesting the payment will harm the owner or damage the premises.

protection order. See RESTRAINING ORDER (1).

protective committee. A group of security holders or preferred stockholders appointed to protect the interests of their group when the corporation is liquidated or reorganized.

protective custody. See CUSTODY (1).

protective order. 1. A court order prohibiting or restricting a party from engaging in a legal procedure (esp. discovery) that unduly annoys or burdens the opposing party or a third-party witness. **2.** RESTRAINING ORDER (1).

protective search. See SEARCH.

protective sweep. A police officer's quick and limited search — conducted after the officer has lawfully entered the premises — based on a reasonable belief that such a search is necessary to protect the officer or others from harm.

protective tariff. See TARIFF (2).

protective trust. See TRUST.

protectorate (prə-**tek**-tə-rət). **1.** *Int'l law.* The relationship between a weaker nation and a stronger one when the weaker nation has transferred the management of its more important international affairs to the stronger nation. **2.** *Int'l law.* The weaker or dependent nation within such a relationship. **3.** (*usu. cap.*) The period in British history — from 1653 to 1659 — during which Oliver Cromwell and Richard Cromwell governed. **4.** The British government in the period from 1653 to 1659.

pro tem. *abbr.* PRO TEMPORE.

pro tempore (proh **tem**-pə-ree), *adv.* & *adj.* [Latin] For the time being; appointed to occupy a position temporarily <a judge pro tempore>. — Abbr. pro tem.

protest, *n.* **1.** A formal statement or action expressing dissent or disapproval. **2.** A notary public's written statement that, upon presentment, a negotiable instrument was neither paid nor accepted. — Also termed *initial protest*; *noting protest.* Cf. NOTICE OF DISHONOR.

> "Noting or initial protest is a memorandum made on [a dishonored] instrument, with the notary's initials, date, and the amount of noting charges, together with a statement of the cause of dishonor, such as 'no effects,' 'not advice,' or 'no account.' This is done to charge the memory of the notary, and should be done on the day of dishonor." Frederick M. Hinch, *John's American Notary and Commission of Deeds Manual* § 442, at 281 (3d ed. 1922).

3. A formal statement, usu. in writing, disputing a debt's legality or validity but agreeing to make payment while reserving the right to recover the amount at a later time. • The disputed debt is described as *under protest.* **4.** *Int'l law.* A formal communication from one subject of international law to another objecting to conduct or a claim by the latter as violating international law. See SUBJECT OF INTERNATIONAL LAW. — **protest,** *vb.*

protestando (proh-tə-**stan**-doh). [Law Latin] Protesting. • This emphatic word was used in a protestation to allege or deny something in an oblique manner.

protestation (prot-ə-**stay**-shən). *Common-law pleading.* A declaration by which a party makes an oblique allegation or denial of some fact, claiming that it does or does not exist or is or is not legally sufficient, while not directly affirming or denying the fact.

> "The practice of protestation of facts not denied arose where the pleader, wishing to avail himself of the right to contest in a future action some traversable fact in the pending action, passes it by without traverse, but at the same time makes a declaration collateral or incidental to his main pleading, importing that the fact so passed over is untrue. The necessity for this arose from the rule that pleadings must not be double, and that every pleading is taken to admit such matters as it does not traverse. Such being its only purpose, it is wholly without effect in the action in which it occurs . . . ." Benjamin J. Shipman, *Handbook of Common-Law Pleading* § 207, at 358 (Henry Winthrop Ballantine ed., 3d ed. 1923).

protest certificate. A notarial certificate declaring (1) that a holder in due course has recruited the notary public to present a previously refused or dishonored negotiable instrument, (2) that the notary has presented the instrument to the person responsible for payment or acceptance (the *drawee*), (3) that the instrument was presented at a given time and place, and (4) that the drawee refused or dishonored the instrument. • In former practice, the notary would issue a protest certificate, which could then be presented to the drawee and any other liable parties as notice that the holder could seek damages for the dishonored negotiable instrument. — Also termed *notarial protest certificate*. See NOTICE OF DISHONOR.

protest fee. A fee charged by a bank or other financial institution when an item (such as a check) is presented but cannot be collected.

prothonotary (prə-**thon**-ə-ter-ee *or* proh-thə-**noh**-tə-ree), *n*. A chief clerk in certain courts of law. — Also termed *protonotary*. — **prothonotarial,** *adj*.

protocol. 1. A summary of a document or treaty. **2.** A treaty amending and supplementing another treaty. **3.** The formal record of the proceedings of a conference or congress. — Also termed *procès-verbal*. **4.** The minutes of a meeting, usu. initialed by all participants after confirming accuracy. **5.** The rules of diplomatic etiquette; the practices that nations observe in the course of their contacts with one another.

protonotary. See PROTHONOTARY.

protutor (proh-**t**[**y**]**oo**-tər). *Civil law*. A person who, though not legally appointed as a guardian, administers another's affairs.

prout patet per recordum (**proh**-ət **pay**-tet pər ri-**kor**-dəm). [Latin] As appears by the record.

provable, *adj*. Capable of being proved.

prove, *vb*. To establish or make certain; to establish the truth of (a fact or hypothesis) by satisfactory evidence.

prover. *Hist*. A person charged with a felony who attempts to obtain a pardon by confessing and naming accomplices.

prove up, *vb*. To present or complete the proof of (something) <deciding not to put a doctor on the stand, the plaintiff attempted to prove up his damages with medical records only>.

prove-up, *n*. The establishment of a prima facie claim. • A prove-up is necessary when a factual assertion is unopposed because even without opposition, the claim must be supported by evidence.

provided, *conj*. On the condition or understanding (*that*) <we will sign the contract provided that you agree to the following conditions>.

province, *n*. **1.** An administrative district into which a country has been divided. **2.** A sphere of activity of a profession such as medicine or law.

provincialis (prə-vin-shee-**ay**-lis). [Latin] One who has a domicile in a province.

provincial synod. See SYNOD.

provision. 1. A clause in a statute, contract, or other legal instrument. **2.** A stipulation made beforehand. See PROVISO.

provisional, *adj*. **1.** Temporary <a provisional injunction>. **2.** Conditional <a provisional government>.

provisional attachment. See ATTACHMENT (1).

provisional court. See COURT.

provisional director. See DIRECTOR.

provisional government. See GOVERNMENT.

provisional injunction. See *preliminary injunction* under INJUNCTION.

provisional partition. See PARTITION.

provisional remedy. See REMEDY.

provisional seizure. See ATTACHMENT (1).

provision of a fine. *Hist*. A proclamation made after the conveying of land by fine, read aloud in court 16 times — four times in the term when the fine was made, and four times in the three succeeding terms.

Provisions of Oxford. *Hist*. During the reign of Henry III, a constitution created by the Mad Parliament and forming the King's advisory council that met with a group of barons several times a year to handle the country's affairs and resolve grievances, esp. those resulting from the King's avoidance of his obligations under Magna Carta. • The Provisions were effective until the baron uprising in 1263 under Simon de Montfort.

proviso (prə-**vɪ**-zoh). **1.** A limitation, condition, or stipulation upon whose compliance a legal or formal document's validity or application may depend. **2.** In drafting, a provision that begins with the words *provided that* and supplies a condition, exception, or addition.

provisor. **1.** *Hist.* A provider of care or sustenance. **2.** *Eccles. law.* A person nominated by the Pope to be the next incumbent of a benefice that is not yet vacant.

provocation, *n.* Something (such as words or actions) that arouses anger or animosity in another, causing that person to respond in the heat of passion. • "Adequate" provocation can reduce a murder charge to voluntary manslaughter. — **provoke,** *vb.* — **provocative,** *adj.* See MANSLAUGHTER.

provost marshal. *Military law.* A staff officer who supervises a command's military police and advises the commander.

proxenete (prok-sə-**nee**-tə). [Latin] *Roman & civil law.* **1.** A person who negotiates or arranges the terms of a contract between parties; a broker. **2.** A person who negotiates marriages; a matchmaker. — Also termed *proxeneta.*

proximate (**prok**-sə-mit), *adj.* **1.** Immediately before or after. **2.** Very near or close in time.

proximate cause. See CAUSE (1).

proximate consequence. A result following an unbroken sequence from some (esp. negligent) event.

proximate damages. See DAMAGES.

proximity. The quality or state of being near in time, place, order, or relation.

proxy, *n.* **1.** One who is authorized to act as a substitute for another; esp., in corporate law, a person who is authorized to vote another's stock shares. **2.** The grant of authority by which a person is so authorized. **3.** The document granting this authority.

proxy contest. A struggle between two corporate factions to obtain the votes of uncommitted shareholders. • A proxy contest usu. occurs when a group of dissident shareholders mounts a battle against the corporation's managers. — Also termed *proxy fight.*

proxy marriage. See MARRIAGE (2).

proxy solicitation. A request that a corporate shareholder authorize another person to cast the shareholder's vote at a corporate meeting.

proxy statement. An informational document that accompanies a proxy solicitation and explains a proposed action (such as a merger) by the corporation.

PRP. *abbr.* Potentially responsible party.

prudent, *adj.* Circumspect or judicious in one's dealings; cautious. — **prudence,** *n.*

prudent-investor rule. *Trusts.* The principle that a fiduciary must invest in only those securities or portfolios of securities that a reasonable person would buy. — Also termed *prudent-person rule.*

prudent person. See REASONABLE PERSON.

prurient (**pruur**-ee-ənt), *adj.* Characterized by or arousing inordinate or unusual sexual desire <films appealing to prurient interests>. — **prurience,** *n.* See OBSCENITY.

p.s. *abbr.* (*usu. cap.*) **1.** Public statute. See PUBLIC LAW (2). **2.** Postscript.

pseudo-foreign-corporation statute. A state law regulating foreign corporations that either derive a specified high percentage of their income from that state or have a high percentage of their stock owned by people living in that state.

pseudograph (**soo**-də-graf). A false writing; a forgery.

pseudo-guarantee treaty. See *guaranty treaty* under TREATY.

pseudonym (**sood**-ə-nim), *n.* A fictitious name or identity. — **pseudonymous** (soo-**don**-ə-məs), *adj.* — **pseudonymity** (sood-ə-**nim**-ə-tee), *n.*

PSI. *abbr.* PRESENTENCE INVESTIGATION REPORT.

psychopath (**sɪ**-kə-path), *n.* **1.** A person with a mental disorder characterized by an extremely antisocial personality that often leads to aggressive, perverted, or criminal behavior. **2.** Loosely, a person who is mentally ill or unstable. — Also termed *sociopath.* — **psychopathy** (sɪ-**kop**-ə-thee), *n.* — **psychopathic** (sɪ-kə-**path**-ik), *adj.*

psychotherapist-client privilege. See *psychotherapist-patient privilege* under PRIVILEGE (3).

psychotherapist-patient privilege. See PRIVILEGE (3).

PTI. See *previously taxed income* under INCOME.

PTO. *abbr.* PATENT AND TRADEMARK OFFICE.

PTP. See *publicly traded partnership* under PARTNERSHIP.

Pub. L. *abbr.* PUBLIC LAW (2).

public, *adj.* **1.** Relating or belonging to an entire community, state, or nation. **2.** Open or available for all to use, share, or enjoy. **3.** (Of a company) having shares that are available on an open market.

public, *n.* **1.** The people of a nation or community as a whole <a crime against the public>. **2.** A place open or visible to the public <in public>.

public access to court electronic records. A computer system by which subscribers can obtain online information from the federal courts, including information from a court's docket sheet about the parties, filing, and orders in a specific case. — Abbr. PACER.

public accommodation. A business establishment that provides lodging, food, entertainment, or other services to the public; esp. (as defined by the Civil Rights Act of 1964), one that affects interstate commerce or is supported by state action.

public administration. See ADMINISTRATION.

public administrator. See ADMINISTRATOR (1).

public advocate. See ADVOCATE.

public agency. See AGENCY (3).

public agent. See AGENT.

publican (**pəb**-li-kən). *Hist.* A person authorized by license to keep a public house for consumption of alcoholic beverages on or off the premises.

publicanus (pəb-li-**kay**-nəs). [Latin] A farmer of the public revenue; that is, a tax collector.

public appointment. See APPOINTMENT (1).

publication, *n.* **1.** Generally, the act of declaring or announcing to the public. **2.** *Copyright.* The distribution of copies of a work to the public. • At common law, publication marked the dividing line between state and federal protection, but the Copyright Act of 1976 superseded most of common-law copyright and thereby diminished the significance of publication.

> "The concept of publication was of immense importance under the 1909 Act. It became a legal word of art, denoting a process much more esoteric than is suggested by the lay definition of the term. That it thus evolved was due largely to the American dichotomy between common law and statutory copyright, wherein the act of publication constituted the dividing line between the two systems of protection [state and federal]." 1 Melville B. Nimmer & David Nimmer, *Nimmer on Copyright* § 4.01, at 4–3 (Supp. 1997).

general publication. A distribution of copies not limited to a selected group, whether or not restrictions are placed on the use of the work. • A general publication was generally held to divest common-law rights in a work.

limited publication. A distribution of copies limited to a selected group at a time when copies are not available to persons not included in the group; a publication that communicates the contents of a work to a definitely selected group and for a limited purpose, without the right of diffusion, reproduction, distribution, or sale. — Also termed *private publication.*

3. *Defamation.* The communication of defamatory words to someone other than the person defamed.

> "Publication means the act of making the defamatory statement known to any person or persons other than the plaintiff himself. It is not necessary that there should be any publication in the popular sense of making the statement public. A private and confidential communication to a single individual is sufficient. Nor need it be published in the sense of being written or printed; for we have seen that actions as well as words may be defamatory. A communication to the person defamed himself, however, is not a sufficient publication on which to found civil proceedings; though it is otherwise in the case of a criminal prosecution, because such a communication may provoke a breach of the peace. Nor does a communi-

cation between husband and wife amount to publication; domestic intercourse of this kind is exempt from the restrictions of the law of libel and slander. But a statement by the defendant to the wife or husband of the plaintiff is a ground of action." R.F.V. Heuston, *Salmond on the Law of Torts* 154 (17th ed. 1977).

"The publication of a libel might be in the form of a book, pamphlet or newspaper, but nothing of that nature is required. A letter sent to a single individual is sufficient." Rollin M. Perkins & Ronald N. Boyce, *Criminal Law* 489 (3d ed. 1982).

4. *Wills.* The formal declaration made by a testator when signing the will that it is the testator's will.

public attorney. See ATTORNEY (2).

public authority. See AUTHORITY (3).

public-benefit corporation. See *public corporation* under CORPORATION.

public bill. See BILL (3).

public boundary. See BOUNDARY.

public building. A building that is accessible to the public; esp., one owned by the government.

public carrier. See *common carrier* under CARRIER.

public character. See PUBLIC FIGURE.

public contract. See CONTRACT.

public controversy. See CONTROVERSY.

public-convenience-and-necessity standard. A common criterion used by a governmental body to assess whether a particular request or project is suitable for the public.

public corporation. See CORPORATION.

public debt. See DEBT.

public defender. A lawyer or staff of lawyers, usu. publicly appointed, whose duty is to represent indigent criminal defendants. — Abbr. P.D.

public delict. See DELICT.

public disclosure of private facts. The public revelation of some aspect of a person's private life without a legitimate public purpose. • The disclosure is actionable in tort if the disclosure would be highly objectionable to a reasonable person. See INVASION OF PRIVACY.

public document. See DOCUMENT.

public domain. **1.** Government-owned land. **2.** The realm of publications, inventions, and processes that are not protected by copyright or patent. • Things in the public domain can be appropriated by anyone without liability for infringement.

"[P]ublic domain is the status of an invention, creative work, commercial symbol, or any other creation that is not protected by any form of intellectual property. Public domain is the rule: intellectual property is the exception." 1 J. Thomas McCarthy, *McCarthy on Trademarks and Unfair Competition* § 1.01[2], at 1–3 (3d ed. 1996).

public-duty doctrine. *Torts.* The rule that a governmental entity (such as a state or municipality) cannot be held liable for an individual plaintiff's injury resulting from a governmental officer's or employee's breach of a duty owed to the general public rather than to the individual plaintiff. — Also termed *public-duty rule.* See SPECIAL-DUTY DOCTRINE.

public easement. See EASEMENT.

public enemy. See ENEMY.

public entity. See ENTITY.

public-exchange offer. See OFFER.

public fact. See FACT.

public figure. A person who has achieved fame or notoriety or who has voluntarily become involved in a public controversy. • A public figure (or public official) suing for defamation must prove that the defendant acted with actual malice. *New York Times Co. v. Sullivan*, 376 U.S. 254, 84 S.Ct. 710 (1964). — Also termed *public character.*

limited-purpose public figure. A person who, having become involved in a particular public issue, has achieved fame or notoriety in relation to that particular issue.

public forum. *Constitutional law.* Public property where people traditionally gather to express ideas and exchange views. • To be constitutional, the government's regulation of a public forum must be narrowly tailored to serve a significant government interest and must usu. be limited to time-place-or-manner restrictions. Cf. NONPUBLIC FORUM.

designated public forum. Public property that has not traditionally been open for public assembly and debate but that the government has opened for use by the public as a place for expressive activity, such as a public-university facility or a publicly owned theater. • Unlike a traditional public forum, the government does not have to retain the open character of a designated public forum. Also, the subject matter of the expression permitted in a designated public forum may be limited to accord with the character of the forum; content-neutral time, place, and manner restrictions are generally permissible. But any prohibition based on the content of the expression must be narrowly drawn to effectuate a compelling state interest, as with a traditional public forum. — Also termed *limited public forum*; *nontraditional public forum*.

traditional public forum. Public property that has by long tradition — as opposed to governmental designation — been used by the public for assembly and expression, such as a public street, public sidewalk, or public park. • To be constitutional, the government's content-neutral restrictions of the time, place, or manner of expression must be narrowly tailored to serve a significant government interest, and leave open ample alternative channels of communication. Any government regulation of expression that is based on the content of the expression must meet the even higher constitutional test of being narrowly tailored to serve a compelling state interest.

public-function doctrine. See PUBLIC-FUNCTION TEST.

public-function rationale. See GOVERNMENTAL-FUNCTION THEORY.

public-function test. In a section 1983 suit, the doctrine that a private person's actions constitute state action if the private person performs functions that are traditionally reserved to the state. — Also termed *public-function doctrine*; *public-function theory*.

public fund. See FUND (1).

public grant. See PATENT (2).

public health. See HEALTH.

public hearing. See HEARING.

public highway. See HIGHWAY.

public house. See HOUSE.

publici juris (**pəb**-li-sɪ **joor**-is). [Latin] Of public right <a tradename may through general use cease to indicate specifically the merchandise of any particular person and may so become merely descriptive and *publici juris*>.

public institution. See INSTITUTION (3).

public interest. 1. The general welfare of the public that warrants recognition and protection. **2.** Something in which the public as a whole has a stake; esp., an interest that justifies governmental regulation.

public-interest exception. The principle that an appellate court may consider and decide a moot case — although such decisions are generally prohibited — if (1) the case involves a question of considerable public importance, (2) the question is likely to arise in the future, and (3) the question has evaded appellate review.

public international law. See INTERNATIONAL LAW.

public intoxication. See INTOXICATION.

public invitee. See INVITEE.

publicist. 1. A public-relations person. **2.** An international-law scholar.

public land. See LAND.

public law. 1. The body of law dealing with the relations between private individuals and the government, and with the structure and operation of the government itself; constitutional law, criminal law, and administrative law taken together. Cf. PRIVATE LAW (1). **2.** A statute affecting the general public. • Federal public laws are first published in *Statutes at Large* and are eventually collected by subject in the U.S. Code. — Abbr. Pub. L.; P.L. — Also termed *public statute* (abbr. p.s.); *general statute*. Cf. *general law* (1) under LAW. **3.** Constitutional law.

public-liability insurance. See *liability insurance* under INSURANCE.

publicly held corporation. See *public corporation* (1) under CORPORATION.

publicly traded partnership. See PARTNERSHIP.

public market. See MARKET.

public-meeting law. See SUNSHINE LAW.

public minister. See MINISTER.

public morality. See MORALITY.

public necessity. See NECESSITY.

public notice. See NOTICE.

public nuisance. See NUISANCE.

public offense. See OFFENSE (1).

public offering. See OFFERING.

public office. A position whose occupant has legal authority to exercise a government's sovereign powers for a fixed period.

public official. A person elected or appointed to carry out some portion of a government's sovereign powers.

public passage. A right held by the public to pass over a body of water, whether the underlying land is publicly or privately owned.

public person. A sovereign government, or a body or person delegated authority under it.

public policy. 1. Broadly, principles and standards regarded by the legislature or by the courts as being of fundamental concern to the state and the whole of society. • Courts sometimes use the term to justify their decisions, as when declaring a contract void because it is "contrary to public policy." — Also termed *policy of the law*.

> "The policy of the law, or public policy, is a phrase of common use in estimating the validity of contracts. Its history is obscure; it is most likely that agreements which tended to restrain trade or to promote litigation were the first to elicit the principle that the courts would look to the interests of the public in giving efficacy to contracts. Wagers, while they continued to be legal, were a frequent provocative of judicial ingenuity on this point, as is sufficiently shown by the case of *Gilbert v. Sykes* [16 East 150 (1812)] . . . : but it does not seem probable that the doctrine of public policy began in the endeavor to elude their binding force. Whatever may have been its origin, it was applied very frequently, and not always with the happiest results, during the latter part of the eighteenth and the commencement of the nineteenth century. Modern decisions, however, while maintaining the duty of the courts to consider the public advantage, have tended more and more to limit the sphere within which this duty may be exercised." William R. Anson, *Principles of the Law of Contract* 286 (Arthur L. Corbin ed., 3d Am. ed. 1919).

2. More narrowly, the principle that a person should not be allowed to do anything that would tend to injure the public at large.

public-policy limitation. *Tax.* A judicially developed principle that a person should not be allowed to deduct expenses related to an activity that is contrary to the public welfare. • This principle is reflected in the Internal Revenue Code's specific disallowance provisions (such as for kickbacks and bribes).

public pond. See GREAT POND.

public power. See POWER.

public property. See PROPERTY.

public prosecutor. See DISTRICT ATTORNEY.

public purpose. An action by or at the direction of a government for the benefit of the community as a whole.

public record. See RECORD.

public relations. 1. The business of creating or maintaining a company's goodwill or good public image. **2.** A company's existing goodwill or public image. — Abbr. PR.

public reprimand. See REPRIMAND.

public right. See RIGHT.

public safety. The welfare and protection of the general public, usu. expressed as a governmental responsibility <Department of Public Safety>.

public sale. See SALE.

public school. See SCHOOL.

public seal. See SEAL.

public sector. The part of the economy or an industry that is controlled by the government. Cf. PRIVATE SECTOR.

public security. See SECURITY.

public service. 1. A service provided or facilitated by the government for the general public's convenience and benefit. **2.** Government employment; work performed for or on behalf of the government.

public-service commission. See COMMISSION (3).

public-service corporation. See CORPORATION.

public servitude. See SERVITUDE (1).

public statute. 1. See *general statute* under STATUTE. **2.** See PUBLIC LAW (2).

public stock. See STOCK.

public store. See STORE.

public tort. See TORT.

public, true, and notorious. *Hist. Eccles. law.* The concluding words of each allegation in a court petition.

public trust. See *charitable trust* under TRUST.

public-trust doctrine. The principle that navigable waters are preserved for the public use, and that the state is responsible for protecting the public's right to the use.

publicum jus (**pəb**-li-kəm **jəs**). [Latin] See JUS PUBLICUM.

public use. See USE (1).

public-use bar. *Patents.* A statutory bar that prevents the granting of a patent for an invention that was publicly used or sold in the United States more than one year before the application date. 35 USCA § 102(b). — Also termed *prior-use bar.*

public utility. See UTILITY.

public utility district. See *municipal utility district* under DISTRICT.

Public Utility Holding Company Act. A federal law enacted in 1935 to protect investors and consumers from the economic disadvantages produced by the small number of holding companies that owned most of the nation's utilities. • The Act also sought to protect the public from deceptive security advertising. 15 USCA §§ 79 et seq. — Abbr. PUHCA.

public verdict. See VERDICT.

public vessel. See VESSEL.

Public Vessels Act. A federal law enacted in 1925 to allow claims against the United States for damages caused by one of its vessels. 46 USCA §§ 781–790.

public war. See WAR.

public water. See WATER.

public welfare. See WELFARE.

public-welfare offense. See OFFENSE (1).

public wharf. See WHARF.

public works. See WORKS.

public worship. See WORSHIP.

public wrong. See WRONG.

publish, *vb.* **1.** To distribute copies (of a work) to the public. **2.** To communicate (defamatory words) to someone other than the person defamed. **3.** To declare (a will) to be the true expression of one's testamentary intent. **4.** To make (evidence) available to a jury during trial. See PUBLICATION.

PUC. *abbr.* Public Utilities Commission.

PUD. *abbr.* **1.** PLANNED-UNIT DEVELOPMENT. **2.** See *municipal utility district* under DISTRICT.

pudzeld. See WOOD-GELD.

pueblo (**pweb**-loh). [Spanish] A town or village, esp. in the southwestern United States.

puer (**pyoo**-ər), *n.* [Latin] *Roman law.* **1.** A child, esp. a boy. **2.** A male slave. Pl. ***pueri*** (**pyoor**-I).

puerility (pyoo-ə-**ril**-ə-tee *or* pyuu-**ril**-ə-tee). *Civil law*. A child's status between infancy and puberty.

pueritia (pyoo-ə-**rish**-ee-ə). [Latin] *Roman law*. Childhood, esp. up to the age of 17, the minimum age for pleading before a magistrate. Cf. AETAS INFANTIAE PROXIMA; AETAS PUBERTATI PROXIMA.

puffer. See BY-BIDDER.

puffing. 1. The expression of an exaggerated opinion — as opposed to a factual representation — with the intent to sell a good or service. • Puffing involves expressing opinions, not asserting something as a fact. Although there is some leeway in puffing goods, a seller may not misrepresent them or say that they have attributes that they do not possess. — Also termed *puffery*; *sales puffery*; *dealer's talk*.

> " 'Dealer's puffing,' so long as it remains in the realm of opinion or belief, will not support a conviction of false pretenses however extravagant the statements." Rollin M. Perkins & Ronald N. Boyce, *Criminal Law* 369 (3d ed. 1982).

2. Secret bidding at an auction by or on behalf of a seller; BY-BIDDING.

PUHCA. *abbr.* PUBLIC UTILITY HOLDING COMPANY ACT.

puis (pwis *or* pwee). [French] Afterwards; since.

puis darrein continuance (**pwis dar**-ayn kən-**tin**-yoo-ənts). [Law French "since the last continuance"] See *plea puis darrein continuance* under PLEA (3).

puisne (**pyoo**-nee), *adj.* [Law French] Junior in rank; subordinate.

puisne judge. See JUDGE.

puisne mortgage. See *junior mortgage* under MORTGAGE.

***Pullman* abstention.** See ABSTENTION.

pulsare (pəl-**sair**-ee), *vb.* [Latin] *Civil law*. To accuse or charge; to proceed against at law.

pulsator (pəl-**say**-tər). *Civil law*. A plaintiff or actor.

punctum temporis (**pəngk**-təm **tem**-pə-ris). [Latin] A point of time; an instant.

punies (**pyoo**-neez). *Slang*. Punitive damages. See DAMAGES.

punishable, *adj.* **1.** (Of a person) subject to a punishment <there is no dispute that Jackson remains punishable for these offenses>. **2.** (Of a crime or tort) giving rise to a specified punishment <a felony punishable by imprisonment for up to 20 years>. — **punishability,** *n.*

punishment, *n.* A sanction — such as a fine, penalty, confinement, or loss of property, right, or privilege — assessed against a person who has violated the law. — **punish,** *vb.* See SENTENCE.

> "Punishment in all its forms is a loss of rights or advantages consequent on a breach of law. When it loses this quality it degenerates into an arbitrary act of violence that can produce nothing but bad social effects." Glanville Williams, *Criminal Law* 575 (2d ed. 1961).

> "In the treatment of offenders there is a clear and unmistakable line of division between the function of the judge and that of the penologist. I should modify that: the law is clear only if it is first made clear in what sense the word 'treatment' is being used. For in this context the word can be used in two senses, one wide and the other narrow. Let me take the wide meaning first. The object of a sentence is to impose punishment. For 'punishment', a word which to many connotes nothing but retribution, the softer word 'treatment' is now frequently substituted; this is the wider meaning. The substitution is made, I suppose, partly as a concession to the school which holds that crime is caused by mental sickness, but more justifiably as a reminder that there are other methods of dealing with criminal tendencies besides making the consequences of crime unpleasant." Patrick Devlin, *The Judge* 32–33 (1979).

capital punishment. See DEATH PENALTY (1).

corporal punishment. Physical punishment; punishment that is inflicted upon the body (including imprisonment).

cruel and unusual punishment. Punishment that is torturous, degrading, inhuman, grossly disproportionate to the crime in question, or otherwise shocking to the moral sense of the community. • Cruel and unusual punishment is prohibited by the Eighth Amendment.

cumulative punishment. Punishment that increases in severity when a person is convicted of the same offense more than once.

deterrent punishment. Punishment the purpose of which is to deter others from committing crimes by making an example of the offender so that like-minded people are warned of the consequences of crime.

excessive punishment. Punishment that is not justified by the gravity of the offense or the defendant's criminal record. See *excessive fine* (1) under FINE (5).

infamous punishment. Punishment by imprisonment, usu. in a penitentiary. See *infamous crime* under CRIME.

nonjudicial punishment. *Military law.* A procedure in which a person subject to the Uniform Code of Military Justice receives official punishment for a minor offense. • In the Navy and Coast Guard, nonjudicial punishment is termed *captain's mast*; in the Marine Corps, it is termed *office hours*; and in the Army and Air Force, it is referred to as *Article 15.* Nonjudicial punishment is not a court-martial.

preventive punishment. Punishment the purpose of which is to prevent a repetition of wrongdoing by disabling the offender.

reformative punishment. Punishment the purpose of which is to change the character of the offender.

retributive punishment. Punishment the purpose of which is to satisfy the community's retaliatory sense of indignation that is provoked by injustice.

"The fact that it is natural to hate a criminal does not prove that retributive punishment is justified." Glanville Williams, *The Sanctity of Life and the Criminal Law* 60 (1957).

punitive, *adj.* Involving or inflicting punishment. — Also termed *punitory.*

punitive articles. *Military law.* Articles 77–134 in the Uniform Code of Military Justice. • These articles list the crimes in the military-justice system.

punitive damages. See DAMAGES.

punitive segregation. See SEGREGATION.

punitive statute. See *penal statute* under STATUTE.

punitory. See PUNITIVE.

punitory damages. See *punitive damages* under DAMAGES.

pupillary substitution (**pyoo**-pə-ler-ee). See SUBSTITUTION (4).

pupillus (pyoo-**pil**-əs). [Latin] *Roman law.* A child under the age of puberty and under the authority of a *tutor.*

pur (pər *or* poor). [Law French] By; for.

pur autre vie (pər **oh**-trə [*or* **oh**-tər] **vee**). [Law French "for another's life"] For or during a period measured by another's life <a life estate *pur autre vie*>. — Also spelled *per autre vie.*

purchase, *n.* **1.** The act or an instance of buying. **2.** The acquisition of real property by one's own or another's act (as by will or gift) rather than by descent or inheritance. — **purchase,** *vb.* Cf. DESCENT (1).

purchase, words of. See WORDS OF PURCHASE.

purchase accounting method. See ACCOUNTING METHOD.

purchase agreement. A sales contract. Cf. REPURCHASE AGREEMENT.

purchase money. The initial payment made on property secured by a mortgage.

purchase-money interest. See *purchase-money security interest* under SECURITY INTEREST.

purchase-money mortgage. See MORTGAGE.

purchase-money resulting trust. See TRUST.

purchase-money security interest. See SECURITY INTEREST.

purchase order. A document authorizing a seller to deliver goods with payment to be made later.

purchaser. 1. One who obtains property for money or other valuable consideration; a buyer.

affiliated purchaser. *Securities.* Any of the following: (1) a person directly or indirectly acting in concert with a distribution participant in connection with the acquisition or distribution of the securities involved; (2) an affiliate who directly or indirectly controls the purchases of those securities by a distribution participant, or whose purchases are controlled by such a participant, or whose purchases are under common control with those of such a participant; (3) an affiliate, who is a broker or a dealer (except a broker-dealer whose business consists solely of effecting transactions in "exempted securities," as defined in the Exchange Act); (4) an affiliate (other than a broker-dealer) who regularly purchases securities through a broker-dealer, or otherwise, for its own account or for the account of others, or recommends or exercises investment discretion in the purchase or sale of securities (with certain specified exceptions). SEC Rule 10b–18(a)(2) (17 CFR § 240.10b–18(a)(2)).

bona fide purchaser. One who buys something for value without notice of another's claim to the item or of any defects in the seller's title; one who has in good faith paid valuable consideration for property without notice of prior adverse claims. — Abbr. BFP. — Also termed *good-faith purchaser*; *purchaser in good faith*; *innocent purchaser*.

bona fide purchaser for value. One who purchases legal title to real property, without actual or constructive notice of any infirmities, claims, or equities against the title. • Generally, a bona fide purchaser for value is not affected by the transferor's fraud against a third party, and has a superior right to the transferred property as against the transferor's creditor to the extent of the consideration that the purchaser has paid. — Also termed *innocent purchaser for value*.

good-faith purchaser. See *bona fide purchaser*.

innocent purchaser. See *bona fide purchaser*.

innocent purchaser for value. See *bona fide purchaser for value*.

purchaser for value. A purchaser who pays consideration for the property bought.

purchaser in good faith. See *bona fide purchaser*.

2. One who acquires real property by means other than descent or inheritance.

first purchaser. An ancestor who first acquired an estate that still belongs to the family.

pure accident. See *unavoidable accident* under ACCIDENT.

pure annuity. See *nonrefund annuity* under ANNUITY.

pure-comparative-negligence doctrine. The principle that liability for negligence is apportioned in accordance with the percentage of fault that the fact-finder assigns to each party and that a plaintiff's percentage of fault reduces the amount of recoverable damages but does not bar recovery. Cf. 50-PERCENT RULE. See *comparative negligence* under NEGLIGENCE; APPORTIONMENT OF LIABILITY.

pure easement. See *easement appurtenant* under EASEMENT.

pure obligation. See OBLIGATION.

pure plea. See PLEA (3).

pure race statute. See RACE STATUTE.

pure risk. See RISK.

pure speech. See SPEECH.

pure theory. The philosophy of Hans Kelsen, in which he contends that a legal system must be "pure" — that is, self-supporting and not dependent on extralegal values. • Kelsen's theory, set out in such works as *General Theory of Law and the State* (1945) and *The Pure Theory of Law* (1934), maintains that laws are norms handed down by the state. Laws are not defined in terms of history, ethics, sociology, or other external factors. Rather, a legal system is an interconnected system of norms, in which coercive techniques are used to secure compliance. The validity of each law, or legal norm, is traced to another legal norm. Ultimately, all laws must find their validity in the society's basic norm (*grundnorm*), which may be as simple as the concept that the constitution was validly enacted. See *basic norm* under NORM.

pure villeinage. See VILLEINAGE.

purgation (pər-**gay**-shən). *Hist.* The act of cleansing or exonerating oneself of a crime or accusation by an oath or ordeal.

canonical purgation. Purgation by 12 oath-helpers in an ecclesiastical court. See COMPURGATION.

vulgar purgation. Purgation by fire, hot irons, battle, or cold water; purgation by means other than by oath-helpers. • Vulgar purgation was so called because at first it was not sanctioned by the church.

purgatory oath. See OATH.

purge, *vb.* To exonerate (oneself or another) of guilt <purged the defendant of contempt>.

purpart (**pər**-pahrt). A share of an estate formerly held in common; a part in a division. — Formerly also termed *purparty*; *perparts*.

purparty (**pər**-pahr-tee). A part of an estate allotted to a coparcener. — Also spelled *pourparty*.

purport (**pər**-port), *n*. The idea or meaning that is conveyed or expressed, esp. by a formal document.

purport (pər-**port**), *vb*. To profess or claim falsely; to seem to be <the document purports to be a will, but it is neither signed nor dated>.

purported, *adj*. Reputed; rumored.

purpose. An objective, goal, or end; specif., the business activity that a corporation is chartered to engage in.

purpose approach. See MISCHIEF RULE.

purpose clause. An introductory clause to a statute explaining its background and stating the reasons for its enactment.

purposeful, *adj*. Done with a specific purpose in mind.

purposive construction. See CONSTRUCTION.

purpresture (pər-**pres**-chər). An encroachment upon public rights and easements by appropriation to private use of that which belongs to the public. — Also spelled *pourpresture*.

purprise (pər-**prɪz**), *vb*. [Law French] *Hist*. To encroach on land illegally; to make a purpresture.

purse, *n*. A sum of money available to the winner of a contest or event; a prize.

purser. A person in charge of accounts and documents on a ship.

pursuant to. 1. In compliance with; in accordance with; under <she filed the motion pursuant to the court's order>. **2.** As authorized by; under <pursuant to Rule 56, the plaintiff moves for summary judgment>. **3.** In carrying out <pursuant to his responsibilities, he ensured that all lights had been turned out>.

pursuit. 1. An occupation or pastime. **2.** The act of chasing to overtake or apprehend. See FRESH PURSUIT.

pursuit of happiness. The principle — announced in the Declaration of Independence — that a person should be allowed to pursue the person's desires (esp. in regard to an occupation) without unjustified interference by the government.

pur tant que (pər tant **kyoo** *or* poor **tahn** kə). [Law French] Forasmuch as; because; to the intent that.

purus idiota (**pyoor**-əs id-ee-**oh**-tə). [Latin] An absolute or congenital idiot. See IDIOT.

purview (**pər**-vyoo). **1.** Scope; area of application. **2.** The body of a statute following the preamble.

> "The word 'purview' appears sometimes to be confined to so much of the body of the statute as would be left by omitting the exceptions, provisos, and savings clauses; and as the word is ambiguous, and not very useful at best, a wise course may be not to use it at all." William M. Lile et al., *Brief Making and the Use of Law Books* 336 (3d ed. 1914).

pusher. A person who sells illicit drugs.

put, *n*. See *put option* under OPTION.

putative (**pyoo**-tə-tiv), *adj*. Reputed; believed; supposed.

putative father. See FATHER.

putative marriage. See MARRIAGE (1).

putative spouse. *Family law*. A spouse who believes in good faith that his or her invalid marriage is legally valid. See *putative marriage* under MARRIAGE (1).

put bond. See BOND (3).

put in, *vb*. To place in due form before a court; to place among the records of a court.

put option. See OPTION.

put price. See *strike price* under PRICE.

puttable (**puut**-ə-bəl), *adj*. (Of a security) capable of being required by the holder to be redeemed by the issuing company.

putting in fear. The threatening of another person with violence to compel the person to hand over property. • These words are part of the common-law definition of robbery.

pyramid distribution plan. See PYRAMID SCHEME.

pyramiding. A speculative method used to finance a large purchase of stock or a controlling interest by pledging an investment's unrealized profit. See LEVERAGE; MARGIN.

pyramiding inferences, rule against. *Evidence.* A rule prohibiting a fact-finder from piling one inference on another to arrive at a conclusion. • Today this rule is followed in only a few jurisdictions. Cf. REASONABLE-INFERENCE RULE.

pyramid scheme. A property-distribution scheme in which a participant pays for the chance to receive compensation for introducing new persons to the scheme, as well as for when those new persons themselves introduce participants. • Pyramid schemes are illegal in most states. — Also termed *endless-chain scheme*; *chain-referral scheme*; *multilevel-distribution program*; *pyramid distribution plan*. Cf. PONZI SCHEME.

Q. *abbr.* QUESTION. • This abbreviation is almost always used in deposition and trial transcripts to denote each question asked by the examining lawyer.

Q-and-A. *abbr.* QUESTION-AND-ANSWER.

Q.B. *abbr.* QUEEN'S BENCH.

Q.B.D. *abbr.* QUEEN'S BENCH DIVISION.

Q.C. *abbr.* QUEEN'S COUNSEL.

q.c.f. *abbr.* QUARE CLAUSUM FREGIT.

Q.D. *abbr.* [Latin *quasi dicat*] As if he should say.

QDRO (**kwah**-droh). *abbr.* QUALIFIED DOMESTIC-RELATIONS ORDER.

Q.E.D. *abbr.* [Latin *quod erat demonstrandum*] Which was to be demonstrated or proved.

Q.E.F. *abbr.* [Latin *quod erat faciendum*] Which was to be done.

Q.E.N. *abbr.* [Latin *quare executionem non*] Why execution should not be issued.

qq.v. See Q.V.

Q.S. See *quarter session* under SESSION.

QTIP trust. See TRUST.

qua (kway *or* kwah). [Latin] In the capacity of; as <the fiduciary, qua fiduciary, is not liable for fraud, but he may be liable as an individual>.

quacumque via data (kway-**kəm**-kwee **vɪ**-ə **day**-tə). [Latin] Whichever way given; whichever way you take it.

quadragesima (kwah-drə-**jes**-i-mə), *n.* [Latin "fortieth"] *Hist.* **1.** Lent — so called because it runs about 40 days. **2.** The first Sunday in Lent — so called because it is about the fortieth day before Easter.

quadragesimals (kwah-drə-**jes**-i-məlz), *n. pl.* [fr. Latin *quadragesima* "the fortieth"] *Hist.* Offerings made on Mid–Lent Sunday by daughter churches to the mother church.

quadriennium (kwah-dree-**en**-ee-əm), *n.* [Latin fr. *quatuor* "four" + *annus* "year"] *Roman law.* The four-year course of study required of law students before they were qualified to study the Code or collection of imperial constitutions.

quadriennium utile (kwah-dree-**en**-ee-əm **yoo**-tə-lee). *Scots law.* A four-year period after the attainment of majority within which the young adult may seek to annul any contract under seal made while the person was a minor.

quadripartite, *adj. Hist.* (Of an indenture, etc.) drawn, divided, or executed in four parts.

quadripartite, *n.* A book or treatise divided into four parts.

quadruplator (kwah-**droo**-plə-tor), *n.* [Latin] *Roman law.* An informer who, by law, could institute criminal proceedings that would result in a fourfold penalty and then receive a reward for doing so. Pl. ***quadruplatores*** (kwah-drə-plə-**tor**-eez).

quadruplicatio (kwah-drə-pli-**kay**-shee-oh), *n.* [fr. Latin *quadruplicatus* "quadrupled"] *Civil law.* A defendant's pleading, following the *triplicatio* and similar to the *rebutter* at common law; the third defensive pleading. — Also termed *quadruplication*; (in old Scots law) *quadruply*.

quae est eadem (kwee est ee-**ay**-dəm). [Law Latin] *Hist.* Which is the same. • This phrase was used by a defendant in a trespass action to show that the trespass the defendant was justified in committing was the same as that alleged in the plaintiff's pleading; that is, the plaintiff gave the defendant permission to enter, and so the defendant entered the property. — Formerly also termed *que est le mesme*.

quae plura (kwee **ploor**-ə). [Law Latin "what more"] *Hist.* A writ ordering the escheator, when it appeared that not all of a decedent's property had been located, to inquire about any additional lands and tenements the decedent held at the time of death.

quaere (**kweer**-ee), *vb.* [Latin] Inquire; query; examine. • This term was often used in the syllabus of a reported case to show that a point was doubtful or open to question.

quaerens (**kweer**-enz), *n.* [Law Latin] *Hist.* One who complains; a plaintiff.

quaerens nihil capiat per billam (**kweer**-enz **nI**-hil **kap**-ee-ət pər **bil**-əm). [Law Latin] *Hist.* Let the plaintiff take nothing by his bill. • This was a form of judgment for the defendant.

quaerens non invenit plegium (**kweer**-enz non in-**vee**-nit **plee**-jee-əm). [Law Latin "the plaintiff did not find a pledge"] *Hist.* A sheriff's return to a writ requiring him to take security from the plaintiff for prosecution of the plaintiff's claim.

quaesta (**kwees**-tə), *n.* [Latin "demands"] Remissions of penance, authorized by the Pope to those who contributed a certain amount to the church. — Also termed *quesita*.

quaestio (**kwes**-chee-oh *or* **kwees**-chee-oh), *n.* [Latin fr. *quaerere* "to inquire"] *Roman law.* **1.** A special committee appointed to hear one or more criminal cases, sometimes with the power to try all cases of a given class arising within a specified period. **2.** An interrogation by inflicting torture. **3.** The torture so inflicted. Pl. ***quaestiones.***

quaestionarius (kwes-chee-ə-**nair**-ee-əs). See QUAESTOR.

quaestiones perpetuae (kwes-chee-**oh**-neez pər-**pech**-oo-ee). [Latin "perpetual inquiries"] *Roman law.* Permanent commissions to hear criminal cases.

quaestio vexata (**kwes**-chee-oh vek-**say**-tə). [Law Latin] See VEXED QUESTION.

quaestor (**kwes**-tər *or* **kwees**-tər). [Latin] **1.** *Roman law.* An officer who maintained and administered the public money, performing tasks such as making necessary payments, receiving revenues, keeping accurate accounts, registering debts and fines, supervising the accommodation of foreign ambassadors, and financing the burials and monuments of distinguished citizens.

> "The office of quaestor goes back at least to the beginning of the Republic. Each year two quaestors were nominated by the consuls, later elected by the comitia tributa, to assist the consuls in matters of finance. This continued to be their principal concern, but they enlarged their functions as their numbers increased." R.W. Lee, *The Elements of Roman Law* 15 (4th ed. 1956).

2. *Hist.* An agent of the Pope who carried *quaesita* from door to door. — Also termed *questionarius*. Pl. ***quaestores.*** See QUAESTA.

quaestores parricidii (kwes-**tor**-eez par-ə-**sI**-dee-I), *n. pl.* [Latin "quaestors of parricide"] *Roman law.* Two officers (usu. appointed annually) who were deputized to search out and try all cases of parricide and other capital offenses.

quaestor sacri palatii (**kwes**-tər **say**-krI pə-**lay**-shee-I). [Latin "quaestor of the sacred palace"] *Roman law.* An officer of the imperial court who acted as legal adviser to the emperor.

> "The *quaestor sacri palatii* was one of the highest civil functionaries in the later Empire, concerned with the preparation of enactments and legal decisions to be issued by the emperor. He was the principal legal adviser of the emperor and he was [often] chosen from among the persons with considerable legal training." Adolf Berger, *Encyclopedic Dictionary of Roman Law* 664 (1953).

quaestus (**kwes**-təs *or* **kwee**-stəs). [Latin] **1.** *Roman law.* Profit, esp. from a business. **2.** *Hist.* Acquisition; purchase. • This term refers to a purchased estate, as distinguished from *haereditas*, referring to an estate obtained by descent.

quale jus (**kway**-lee *or* **kwah**-lee **jəs**). [Latin "what kind of right"] *Hist.* A writ ordering an escheator to inquire into the extent of a religious person's right to a judgment, before its execution, to make sure that the judgment was not collusively made to avoid the mortmain statute.

qualification. 1. The possession of qualities or properties (such as fitness or capacity) inherently or legally necessary to make one eligible for a position or office, or to perform a public duty or function <voter qualification requires one to meet residency, age, and registration requirements>. **2.** A modification or limitation of terms or language; esp., a restriction of terms that would otherwise be interpreted broadly <the contract contained a qualification requiring the lessor's permission before exercising the right to sublet>. **3.** CHARACTERIZATION (1). — **qualify,** *vb.*

qualified, *adj.* **1.** Possessing the necessary qualifications; capable or competent <a qualified medical examiner>. **2.** Limited; restricted <qualified immunity>. — **qualify,** *vb.*

qualified acceptance. See ACCEPTANCE (1).

qualified disclaimer. See DISCLAIMER.

qualified domestic-relations order. A state-court order or judgment that relates to alimony, child support, or some other state domestic-relation matter and that (1) recognizes or provides for an alternate payee's right to receive all or part of any benefits due a participant under a pension, profit-sharing, or other retirement benefit plan, (2) otherwise satisfies the provisions of section 414 of the Internal Revenue Code, and (3) is exempt from the ERISA rule prohibiting the assignment of plan benefits. • Among other things, the QDRO must set out certain facts, including the name and last-known mailing address of the plan participant and alternate payee, the amount or percentage of benefits going to the alternate payee, and the number of payments to which the plan applies. The benefits provided under a QDRO are treated as income to the actual recipient. IRC (26 USCA) § 414(p)(1)(A); 29 USCA § 1056(d)(3)(D)(i). — Abbr. QDRO.

qualified elector. A legal voter; a person who meets the voting requirements for age, residency, and registration and who has the present right to vote in an election. See QUALIFIED VOTER.

qualified estate. See ESTATE.

qualified fee. **1.** See *fee simple defeasible* under FEE SIMPLE. **2.** See *fee simple determinable* under FEE SIMPLE.

qualified general denial. See DENIAL.

qualified immunity. See IMMUNITY (1).

qualified indorsement. See INDORSEMENT.

qualified institutional buyer. See BUYER.

qualifiedly (**kwah**-lə-fīd-lee *or* -fī-əd-lee), *adv.* In a fit or qualified manner <qualifiedly privileged>.

qualified martial law. See MARTIAL LAW.

qualified nuisance. See NUISANCE.

qualified opinion. An audit-report statement containing exceptions or qualifications to certain items in the accompanying financial statement.

qualified ownership. See OWNERSHIP.

qualified pension plan. See PENSION PLAN.

qualified privilege. See PRIVILEGE (1).

qualified profit-sharing plan. See PROFIT-SHARING PLAN.

qualified property. See PROPERTY.

qualified residence interest. See INTEREST (3).

qualified stock option. See STOCK OPTION.

qualified-terminable-interest property. See PROPERTY.

qualified veto. See VETO.

qualified voter. **1.** QUALIFIED ELECTOR. **2.** A qualified elector who exercises the right to vote; a person who votes.

qualified witness. See WITNESS.

qualifying event. Any one of several specified occasions that, but for the continuation-of-coverage provisions under the Consolidated Omnibus Budget Reconciliation Act of 1985 (COBRA), would result in a loss of benefits to a covered employee under a qualified benefit plan. • These occasions include employment termination, a reduction in work hours, the employee's separation or divorce, the employee's death, and the employer's bankruptcy. IRC (26 USCA) § 4980B(f)(3).

qualifying share. A share of common stock purchased by someone in order to become a director of a corporation that requires its directors to be shareholders. See SHARE (2).

quality. **1.** The particular character or properties of a person, thing, or act, often essential for a particular result <she has leadership quality> <greed is a negative quality>. **2.** The character or degree of excellence of a person or substance, esp. in comparison with others <the quality of work performed under the contract>.

quality of estate. **1.** The period when the right of enjoying an estate is conferred upon the owner, whether at present or in the future. **2.** The manner in which the owner's right of enjoyment of an estate is to be exercised, whether solely, jointly, in common, or in coparcenary.

quality-of-products legislation. See LEMON LAW (2).

quamdiu (**kwam**-dee-yoo). [Latin] *Hist.* As long as; so long as. • This was a word of limitation formerly used in conveyances.

quamdiu bene se gesserint (**kwam**-dee-yoo **bee**-nee see **jes**-ər-int). [Law Latin] As long as they shall conduct themselves properly. • This term refers to the holding of an office, specif. the Act of Settlement, 1700, ch. 2, which provided that a judge's tenure was no longer at the king's pleasure, but could continue until death or improper conduct. Cf. GOOD BEHAVIOR; DURANTE BENE PLACITO.

> "But at present, by the long and uniform usage of many ages, our kings have delegated their whole judicial power to the judges of their several courts .... And, in order to maintain both the dignity and independence of the judges in the superior courts, it is enacted by the statute 13 W. III. c.2 that their commissions shall be made (not as formerly, *durante bene placito*, but) *quamdiu bene se gesserint*, and their salaries ascertained and established; but that it may be lawful to remove them on the address of both houses of parliament." 1 William Blackstone, *Commentaries on the Laws of England* 267 (1765).

quango (**kwang**-goh). See QUASI-AUTONOMOUS NONGOVERNMENTAL ORGANIZATION.

quanti minoris (**kwon**-tI mi-**nor**-is). [Latin "how much less"] *Civil law.* An action brought by a purchaser of an article to reduce the purchase price due to the article's defects.

quantitative rule. An evidentiary rule requiring that a given type of evidence is insufficient unless accompanied by additional evidence before the case is closed. • Such a rule exists because of the known danger or weakness of certain types of evidence. — Also termed *synthetic rule.*

quantity discount. See *volume discount* under DISCOUNT.

quantum (**kwon**-təm). [Latin "an amount"] The required, desired, or allowed amount; portion or share <a quantum of evidence>. Pl. **quanta** (**kwon**-tə).

quantum damnificatus (**kwon**-təm dam-nə-fi-**kay**-təs). [Latin "how much damnified"] *Hist.* The issue of damages submitted by a court of equity to the jury.

quantum meruit (**kwon**-təm **mer**-oo-it). [Latin "as much as he has deserved"] **1.** The reasonable value of services; damages awarded in an amount considered reasonable to compensate a person who has rendered services in a quasi-contractual relationship. **2.** A claim or right of action for the reasonable value of services rendered. **3.** At common law, a count in an assumpsit action to recover payment for services rendered to another person. • Quantum meruit is still used today as an equitable remedy to provide restitution for unjust enrichment. It is often pleaded as an alternative claim in a breach-of-contract case so that the plaintiff can recover even if the contract is voided. See *implied-in-law contract* under CONTRACT.

quantum valebant (**kwon**-təm və-**lee**-bant *or* -bənt). [Latin "as much as they were worth"] **1.** The reasonable value of goods and materials. **2.** At common law, a count in an assumpsit action to recover payment for goods sold and delivered to another. • *Quantum valebant* — although less common than *quantum meruit* — is still used today as an equitable remedy to provide restitution for another's unjust enrichment.

quarantina habenda. See DE QUARANTINA HABENDA.

quarantine. **1.** *Hist.* A period of 40 days, esp. for the isolation and detention of ships containing persons or animals suspected of having or carrying a dangerous communicable disease, in order to prevent the spread of the disease.

> "Quarantine .... The name is drawn from the fact that the period was formerly commonly 40 (Ital. *quaranta*) days. In 1423 Venice established a lazaretto or quarantine station on an island to check the growth of disease brought in by ships. In the sixteenth century quarantine became widespread and there developed the system of bills of health, certificates that the last port was free from disease; a clean bill entitled a ship to use the port without subjection to quarantine." David M. Walker, *The Oxford Companion to Law* 1022 (1980).

2. *Hist.* A widow's privilege to remain in her husband's house for 40 days after his death while her dower is being assigned. • This right was enforced by a writ *de quarantina habenda.* See DE QUARANTINA HABENDA. **3.** The isolation of a person or animal afflicted with a communicable disease or the prevention of such a person or animal from coming into a particular area, the purpose being to prevent the spread of disease. • Federal, state, and local authorities are required to cooperate in the enforcement of quarantine laws. 42 USCA § 243(a).

> "Power to make quarantine regulations is one of the most frequent powers conferred on boards of health. Such regulations constitute a proper exercise of the police power, provided they are not in conflict with federal regulations on the subject or that legislation by Congress is absent, and that they do not abridge rights protected by the Fourteenth Amendment." 39 Am. Jur. 2d *Health* § 59, at 529–30 (1999).

4. A place where a quarantine is in force. — Also spelled *quarentine; quarentene.* — **quarantine,** *vb.*

quare (**kwair**-ee). [Latin] Why; for what reason; on what account. • This was used in various common-law writs, esp. writs in trespass.

quare clausum fregit (**kwair**-ee **klaw**-zəm **free**-jit). [Latin] Why he broke the close. — Abbr. *qu. cl. fr.*; *q.c.f.* See TRESPASS QUARE CLAUSUM FREGIT.

quare ejecit infra terminum (**kwair**-ee i-**jee**-sit **in**-frə **tər**-mə-nəm), *n.* [Law Latin "why he ejected within the term"] *Hist.* A writ for a lessee who was prematurely ejected, when the ejector was not actually in possession but one claiming under the ejector was.

> "For this injury the law has provided him with two remedies ... the writ of *ejectione firmae*; ... and the writ of *quare ejecti infra terminum*; which lies not against the wrongdoer or ejector himself, but his feoffee or other person claiming under him. These are mixed actions, somewhat between real and personal; for therein are two things recovered, as well restitution of the term of years, as damages for the ouster or wrong." 3 William Blackstone, *Commentaries on the Laws of England* 199 (1768).

quare impedit (**kwair**-ee **im**-pə-dit). [Latin "why he hinders"] *Hist. Eccles. law.* A writ or action to enforce a patron's right to present a person to fill a vacant benefice. — Also termed *writ of quare impedit.* See PRESENTATION; ADVOWSON.

> "The writ of *quare impedit* commands the disturbers, the bishop, the pseudo-patron, and his clerk, to permit the plaintiff to present a proper person (without specifying the particular clerk) to such a vacant church, which pertains to his patronage; and which the defendants, as he alleges, do obstruct: and unless they so do, then that they appear in court to shew the reason why they hinder him." 3 William Blackstone, *Commentaries on the Laws of England* 248 (1768).

quare incumbravit (**kwair**-ee in-kəm-**bray**-vit), *n.* [Law Latin "why he incumbered"] *Hist.* A writ or action to compel a bishop to explain why he encumbered the church when, within six months after the vacation of a benefice and after a *ne admittas* was received, the bishop conferred the benefice on his clerk while two other clerks were contending for the right of presentation in a *quare impedit* action. • The writ was abolished by the Real Property Limitation Act of 1833, ch. 27.

quare intrusit (**kwair**-ee in-**troo**-sit), *n.* [Law Latin "why he thrust in"] *Hist.* A writ allowing a lord to recover the value of a marriage, when the lord offered a suitable marriage to a ward but the ward rejected it and married someone else. • It was abolished by the Tenures Abolition Act, 1660, ch. 24.

quare non permittit (**kwair**-ee non pər-**mit**-it), *n.* [Law Latin "why he did not permit"] *Hist.* A writ for one who has a right to present to a church, against the proprietor.

quarentena terrae (kwahr-en-**tee**-nə **ter**-ee), *n.* [Law Latin "a quantity of land"] *Hist.* A furlong.

quarentine. See QUARANTINE.

quare obstruxit (**kwair**-ee əb-**strək**-sit), *n.* [Law Latin "why he obstructed"] *Hist.* A writ for one who could not enjoy a privilege to pass through a neighbor's land because the neighbor had obstructed the path.

quarrel. 1. An altercation or angry dispute; an exchange of recriminations, taunts, threats, or accusations between two persons. **2.** *Archaic.* A complaint; a legal action.

> "Quarrels is derived from *querendo*, and extends not only to actions as well real as personal, but also to the causes of actions and suits: so that by the release of all quarrels, not only actions depending in suit, but causes of action and suit also are released; and quarrels, controversies and debates, are words of one sense, and of one and the same signification, Coke, lib. 8, fol. 153." *Termes de la Ley* 330 (1st Am. ed. 1812).

quarta divi Pii (**kwor**-tə **dI**-vI **pI**-I). [Latin "quarter of the deified Pius"] *Roman law.* The quarter portion of a testator's estate required to be left to an adopted child who had been unjustly emancipated or disinherited.

quarta falcidia (**kwor**-tə fal-**sid**-ee-ə). [Latin "Falcidian fourth"] See FALCIDIAN PORTION.

quarter, *n.* In the law of war, the act of showing mercy to a defeated enemy by sparing lives and accepting a surrender <to give no quarter>.

quarter day. See DAY.

quartering, *n. Hist.* **1.** The dividing of a criminal's body into quarters after execution, esp. as part of the punishment for a crime such as high treason. See HANGED, DRAWN, AND QUARTERED. **2.** The furnishing of living quarters to members of the military. • The Third Amendment generally protects U.S. citizens from being forced to use their homes to quarter soldiers. U.S. Const. amend. III. **3.** The dividing of a shield into four parts to show four different coats of arms. — **quarter,** *vb.*

quarterly report. A financial report issued by a corporation (and by most mutual funds and investment managers) every three months.

quarter seal. See SEAL.

quarter section. See SECTION.

quarter session. See SESSION.

Quarter Sessions Court. See COURT OF GENERAL QUARTER SESSIONS OF THE PEACE.

quarters of coverage. The number of quarterly payments made by a person into the social-security fund as a basis for determining the person's entitlement to benefits.

quarto die post (**kwor**-toh **dɪ**-ee **pohst**), *n.* [Law Latin "on the fourth day after"] The defendant's appearance day, being four days (inclusive) from the return of the writ.

quash (kwahsh), *vb.* **1.** To annul or make void; to terminate <quash an indictment> <quash proceedings>. **2.** To suppress or subdue; to crush out <quash a rebellion>.

quashal (**kwahsh**-əl), *n.* The act of quashing something <quashal of the subpoena>.

quasi (**kway**-sɪ *or* **kway**-zɪ *also* **kwah**-zee). [Latin "as if"] Seemingly but not actually; in some sense; resembling; nearly.

> "QUASI. A Latin word frequently used in the civil law, and often prefixed to English words. It is not a very definite word. It marks the resemblance, and supposes a little difference, between two objects, and in legal phraseology the term is used to indicate that one subject resembles another, with which it is compared, in certain characteristics, but that there are also intrinsic and material differences between them. It negatives the idea of identity, but implies a strong superficial analogy, and points out that the conceptions are sufficiently similar for one to be classed as the equal of the other." 74 C.J.S. *Quasi*, at 2 (1951).

quasi-admission. See ADMISSION (1).

quasi-affinity. See AFFINITY.

quasi-autonomous nongovernmental organization. A semipublic administrative body (esp. in the United Kingdom) having some members appointed and financed by, but not answerable to, the government, such as a tourist authority, a university-grants commission, a price-and-wage commission, a prison or parole board, or a medical-health advisory panel. • This term is more commonly written as an acronym, *quango* (**kwang**-goh), without capital letters.

quasi-contract. See *implied-in-law contract* under CONTRACT.

quasi-corporation. See CORPORATION.

quasi-crime. See CRIME.

quasi-delict. See DELICT.

quasi-deposit. See DEPOSIT (5).

quasi-derelict. See DERELICT.

quasi-domicile. See *commercial domicile* under DOMICILE.

quasi-easement. See EASEMENT.

quasi-enclave. See ENCLAVE.

quasi-entail. See ENTAIL.

quasi-estoppel. See ESTOPPEL.

quasi-fee. See FEE (2).

quasi-guarantee treaty. See *guaranty treaty* under TREATY.

quasi-guardian. See GUARDIAN.

quasi in rem. See IN REM.

quasi-in-rem jurisdiction. See JURISDICTION.

quasi-insurer. See INSURER.

quasi-judicial, *adj.* Of, relating to, or involving an executive or administrative official's adjudicative acts. • Quasi-judicial acts, which are valid if there is no abuse of discretion, often determine the fundamental rights of citizens. They are subject to review by courts.

> "Quasi-judicial is a term that is . . . not easily definable. In the United States, the phrase often covers judicial decisions taken by an administrative agency — the test is the nature of the tribunal rather than what it is doing. In England quasi-judicial belongs to the administrative category and is used to cover situations where the administrator is bound by the law to observe certain forms and possibly hold a public hearing but where he is a free agent in reaching the final decision. If the rules are broken, the determination may be set aside, but it is not sufficient to show that the administration is biased in favour of a certain policy, or that the evidence points to a different conclusion." George Whitecross Paton, *A Textbook of Jurisprudence* 336 (G.W. Paton & David P. Derham eds., 4th ed. 1972).

quasi-judicial act. **1.** A judicial act performed by an official who is not a judge. **2.** An act performed by a judge who is not acting entirely in a judicial capacity. See JUDICIAL ACT.

quasi-judicial power. See POWER.

quasi-legislative, *adj.* (Of an act, function, etc.) not purely legislative in nature <the administrative agency's rulemaking, being partly adjudicative, is not entirely legislative — that is, it is quasi-legislative>.

quasi-legislative power. See POWER.

quasi-municipal corporation. See *quasi-corporation* under CORPORATION.

quasi-national domicile. See DOMICILE.

quasi-offense. See OFFENSE (2).

quasi-partner. See PARTNER.

quasi-personalty. See PERSONALTY.

quasi-possession. See *incorporeal possession* under POSSESSION.

quasi-posthumous child. See CHILD.

quasi-public corporation. See CORPORATION.

quasi-pupillary substitution. See SUBSTITUTION (4).

quasi-realty. See REALTY.

quasi-seisin. See SEISIN.

quasi-suspect classification. See SUSPECT CLASSIFICATION.

quasi-tenant. See TENANT.

quasi-tort. See TORT.

quasi traditio (**kway**-sI [*or* -zI] trə-**dish**-ee-oh). [Latin "as if transfer"] *Roman law.* A party's acquisition of a servitude by using it with the informal permission or acquiescence of the owner.

> "According to the civil law again a servitude — that is, a limited right of user in respect of a thing not one's own, e.g. a usufruct or a right of way — could only be created by means of certain definite legal forms. The praetorian law, on the other hand, allowed a servitude to be created by a so-called quasi traditio servitutis; that is, it was satisfied if one party gave the other, without any form, permission to exercise the right of user in question." Rudolph Sohm, *The Institutes: A Textbook of the History and System of Roman Private Law* 82 (James Crawford Ledlie trans., 3d ed. 1907).

quasi-trustee. See TRUSTEE (1).

quasi-usufruct. See USUFRUCT.

quatuor pedibus currit (**kwah**-too-or **ped**-ə-bəs **kər**-it). [Law Latin] It runs upon four feet; it runs upon all fours. • The term commonly described a precedent that was extremely close to a point being decided. See ON ALL FOURS.

qu. cl. fr. *abbr.* QUARE CLAUSUM FREGIT.

queen. **1.** A woman who possesses, in her own right, the sovereignty and royal power in a monarchy. • Among the more famous English queens are Queen Mary, Queen Elizabeth I, Queen Victoria, and Queen Elizabeth II. — Also termed *queen regnant.* **2.** The wife of a reigning king. • She has some royal prerogatives (such as having her own officers), but is in many ways legally no different from the rest of the king's subjects. — Also termed *queen consort.* **3.** A queen who rules in place of the actual sovereign (e.g., if the sovereign is a child). — Also termed *queen regent.* **4.** DOWAGER-QUEEN.

queen dowager. See DOWAGER-QUEEN.

queen mother. See DOWAGER-QUEEN.

Queen's Bench. Historically, the highest common-law court in England, presided over by the reigning monarch. • The jurisdiction of this court now lies with the Queen's Bench Division of the High Court of Justice; when a king begins to reign, the name automatically changes to *King's Bench.* — Abbr. Q.B. — Also termed *Court of Queen's Bench.* Cf. KING'S BENCH.

Queen's Bench Division. The English court, formerly known as the Queen's Bench or King's Bench, that presides over tort and contract actions, applications for judicial review, and some magistrate-court appeals. — Abbr. Q.B.D.

Queen's Counsel. In the United Kingdom, Canada, and territories that have retained the rank, an elite, senior-level barrister or advocate originally appointed to serve as counsel to the queen. — Also termed *senior counsel.* — Abbr. Q.C. Cf. KING'S COUNSEL.

Queen's evidence. See EVIDENCE.

Queen's prison. A prison established in 1842 in Southwark, to be used for debtors and criminals confined under authority of the superior courts at Westminster, the highest court of admiralty, and the bankruptcy laws. • It replaced the Queen's Bench Prison, Fleet Prison, and Marshalsea Prison but was closed in 1862.

Queen's proctor. A solicitor that represents the Crown in domestic-relations, probate, and admiralty cases. • For example, in a suit for divorce or nullity of marriage, the Queen's proctor might intervene to prove collusion between the parties. — Also termed (when a king reigns) *King's proctor.*

que est le mesme (**kyoo** ay lə **mem**). [Law French] See QUAE EST EADEM.

quem redditum reddit (**kwem red**-ə-təm **red**-it), *n.* [Law Latin "which return he made"] *Hist.* A writ for a grantee of a rent (not a rent service) to force the tenant to consent to the transfer.

querela (kwə-**ree**-lə). [Law Latin fr. Latin *queri* "to complain"] *Hist.* **1.** A complaint; the plaintiff's count or declaration. **2.** A cause of action. **3.** *Roman law.* An action.

querela coram rege a concilio discutienda et terminanda (kwə-**ree**-lə **kor**-əm **ree**-jee ay kən-**sil**-ee-oh dis-kə-shee-**en**-də et tər-mə-**nan**-də), *n.* [Law Latin "a dispute to be discussed and resolved by the council in front of the king"] *Hist.* A writ ordering someone to appear before the king to answer to a trespass.

querela inofficiosi testamenti (kwə-**ree**-lə in-ə-fish-ee-**oh**-sI tes-tə-**men**-tI), *n.* [Latin "a dispute of an undutiful will"] *Roman law.* An action allowing a descendant, ascendant, or sibling who was unjustly disinherited or passed over by a parent's will to have the will set aside as undutifully made.

> "By far the most important is due to the *querela inofficiosi testamenti.* By this procedure, though the forms had been complied with, near relatives with obvious claims (the classes of those entitled having been gradually widened) might attack the will as contrary to natural duty (*inofficiosum*) and get it set aside." W.W. Buckland, *A Manual of Roman Private Law* 199 (2d ed. 1953).

querens (**kweer**-enz), *n.* [Latin fr. *queri* "to complain"] *Hist.* A plaintiff; the complaining party.

questa (**kwes**-tə), *n.* [Law Latin] *Hist.* A quest; an inquest or inquiry upon the oaths of an impaneled jury.

question. **1.** A query directed to a witness. — Abbr. Q.

categorical question. **1.** LEADING QUESTION. **2.** (*pl.*) A series of questions, on a particular subject, arranged in systematic or consecutive order.

cross-question. A question asked of a witness during cross-examination. — Abbr. XQ.

direct question. A question asked of a witness during direct examination.

hypothetical question. See HYPOTHETICAL QUESTION.

leading question. See LEADING QUESTION.

2. An issue in controversy; a matter to be determined.

certified question. See CERTIFIED QUESTION.

federal question. See FEDERAL QUESTION.

judicial question. See JUDICIAL QUESTION.

mixed question. See MIXED QUESTION.

mixed question of law and fact. See MIXED QUESTION OF LAW AND FACT.

political question. See POLITICAL QUESTION.

question of fact. See QUESTION OF FACT.

question of law. See QUESTION OF LAW.

question-and-answer. 1. The portion of a deposition or trial transcript in which evidence is developed through a series of questions asked by the lawyer and answered by the witness. — Abbr. Q-and-A. **2.** The method for developing evidence during a deposition or at trial, requiring the witness to answer the examining lawyer's questions, without offering unsolicited information. **3.** The method of instruction used in many law-school classes, in which the professor asks questions of one or more students and then follows up each answer with another question. — Also termed *Socratic method*. See SOCRATIC METHOD.

question of fact. 1. An issue that has not been predetermined and authoritatively answered by the law. • An example is whether a particular criminal defendant is guilty of an offense or whether a contractor has delayed unreasonably in constructing a building. **2.** An issue that does not involve what the law is on a given point. **3.** A disputed issue to be resolved by the jury in a jury trial or by the judge in a bench trial. — Also termed *fact question*. See FACT-FINDER. **4.** An issue capable of being answered by way of demonstration, as opposed to a question of unverifiable opinion.

question of law. 1. An issue to be decided by the judge, concerning the application or interpretation of the law <a jury cannot decide questions of law, which are reserved for the court>. **2.** A question that the law itself has authoritatively answered, so that the court may not answer it as a matter of discretion <under the sentencing guidelines, the punishment for a three-time offender is a question of law>. **3.** An issue about what the law is on a particular point; an issue in which parties argue about, and the court must decide, what the true rule of law is <both parties appealed on the question of law>. **4.** An issue that, although it may turn on a factual point, is reserved for the court and excluded from the jury; an issue that is exclusively within the province of the judge and not the jury <whether a contractual ambiguity exists is a question of law>. — Also termed *legal question*; *law question*.

questman. *Hist.* **1.** An instigator of a lawsuit or prosecution. **2.** A person who was chosen to inquire into abuses, esp. those relating to weights and measures. **3.** A churchwarden; SIDESMAN. — Also termed *questmonger*.

questus est nobis (**kwes**-təs est **noh**-bis), *n.* [Law Latin "hath complained to us"] *Hist.* By 15 Edw., a writ against someone who continued a nuisance that existed before inheritance or purchase. • The former law provided recovery only against the party who had first caused the nuisance.

quia (**kwI**-ə *or* **kwee**-ə). [Latin] *Hist.* Because; whereas. • This term was used to point out the consideration in a conveyance.

Quia Emptores (**kwI**-ə *or* **kwee**-ə emp-**tor**-eez). [Latin "since purchasers"] *Hist.* A statute giving fee-simple tenants (other than those holding directly of the Crown) the power to alienate their land and bind the transferee to perform the same services for the lord as the transferor had been obliged to perform. • The statute, enacted in 1290, tended to concentrate feudal lordships in the Crown by eliminating multiple layers of fealty. 18 Edw., ch. 1. — Also termed *Quia Emptores Terrarum*.

> "Edward I and his lords wished, for political reasons, to prevent the growth of subinfeudation, and in 1290 the Statute *Quia Emptores* was enacted. It took its name from the beginning of its preamble — 'Since purchasers ....' " L.B. Curzon, *English Legal History* 300 (2d ed. 1979).

quia erronice emanavit (**kwI**-ə i-**roh**-nə-see em-ə-**nay**-vit). [Law Latin] *Hist.* Because it issued erroneously.

quia timet (**kwI**-ə **tI**-mət *or* **kwee**-ə **tim**-et). [Latin "because he fears"] A legal doctrine that allows a person to seek equitable relief from future probable harm to a specific right or interest.

> "Quia timet is the right to be protected against anticipated future injury that cannot be prevented by the present action. The doctrine of 'quia timet' permits equitable relief based on a concern over future probable injury to certain rights or interests, where anticipated future injury cannot be prevented by a present action at law, such as where there is a danger that a defense at law might be prejudiced or lost if not tried immediately." 27A Am. Jur. 2d *Equity* § 93, at 581 (1996).

***quia-timet* injunction.** See INJUNCTION.

quick asset. See ASSET.

quick-asset ratio. The ratio between an entity's current or liquid assets (such as cash and accounts receivable) and its current liabilities. — Also termed *quick ratio*; *acid-test ratio*.

quick condemnation. See CONDEMNATION.

quick dispatch. See DISPATCH.

quickening. The first motion felt in the womb by the mother of the fetus, usu. occurring near the middle of the pregnancy.

quickie strike. See *wildcat strike* under STRIKE.

quick ratio. See QUICK-ASSET RATIO.

quidam (**kwɪ**-dəm), *n.* [Latin] Somebody. • This term has esp. been used in French law to designate a person whose name is unknown.

quid pro quo (**kwid** proh **kwoh**), *n.* [Latin "something for something"] A thing that is exchanged for another thing of more or less equal value; a substitute <the discount was given as a quid pro quo for the extra business>. Cf. CONSIDERATION.

quid pro quo sexual harassment. See SEXUAL HARASSMENT.

quiet, *vb.* **1.** To pacify or silence (a person, etc.). **2.** To make (a right, position, title, etc.) secure or unassailable by removing disturbing causes or disputes.

quieta non movere (kwɪ-**ee**-tə non moh-**veer**-ee). [Latin] Not to unsettle things that are established. See STARE DECISIS.

quietare (kwɪ-ə-**tair**-ee), *vb.* [Law Latin] *Hist.* To acquit, discharge, or hold harmless. • This term was used in conveyances.

quiet diplomacy. See *secret diplomacy* under DIPLOMACY.

quiete clamantia (kwɪ-**ee**-tee klə-**man**-shee-ə), *n.* [Law Latin] *Hist.* Quitclaim.

quiete clamare (kwɪ-**ee**-tee klə-**mair**-ee), *vb.* [Law Latin] *Hist.* To quitclaim or renounce all pretensions of right and title.

quiet enjoyment. See ENJOYMENT.

quiet-title action. See *action to quiet title* under ACTION.

quietus (kwɪ-**ee**-təs), *adj.* [Law Latin] **1.** Quit; acquitted; discharged, esp. from a debt or obligation, or from serving as an executor. • In England, this term was formerly used by the Clerk of the Pipe, in a discharge given to an accountant, usu. concluding with *abinde recessit quietus* ("hath gone quit thereof"), called *quietus est.* **2.** *Hist.* The removal of a judge from the bench.

quietus redditus (kwɪ-**ee**-təs **red**-ə-təs). [Law Latin] See QUIT RENT.

qui improvide (**kwɪ** im-**prov**-ə-dee). [Latin "who unforeseeably"] *Hist.* A supersedeas granted when a writ is erroneously sued out or wrongfully awarded.

Quinquaginta Decisiones. See FIFTY DECISIONS.

quinquepartite (kwin[g]-kwə-**pahr**-tɪt). [Latin "in five parts"] *Hist.* Consisting of five parts; divided into five parts.

quintal (**kwin**-təl). *Hist.* A weight of 100 pounds. — Also termed *kintal.*

quinto exactus (**kwin**-toh eg-**zak**-təs). [Latin "exacted the fifth time"] *Hist.* A sheriff's return made after a defendant had been called to five county courts but failed to appear. • The county coroners then ordered that the defendant be deprived of the benefits of the law.

> "And, if a *non est inventus* is returned upon all of them, a writ of *exigent* or *exigi facias* may be sued out, which requires the sheriff to cause the defendant to be proclaimed, required, or exacted, in five county courts successively, to render himself; and, if he does, then to take him, as in a *capias*: but if he does not appear, and is returned *quinto exactus*, he shall then be outlawed by the coroners of the county." 3 William Blackstone, *Commentaries on the Laws of England* 283 (1768).

quiritarian (kwi-rə-**tair**-ee-ən), *adj.* *Roman law.* Legal as opposed to equitable; LEGAL (3). — Also termed *quiritary*. Cf. BONITARIAN.

quit, *adj.* (Of a debt, obligation, or person) acquitted; free; discharged.

quit, *vb.* **1.** To cease (an act, etc.); to stop <he didn't quit stalking the victim until the police intervened>. **2.** To leave or surrender possession of (property) <the tenant received a notice to quit but had no intention of quitting the premises>.

qui tam action (kwɪ tam). [Latin *qui tam pro domino rege quam pro se ipso in hac parte sequitur* "who as well for the king as for himself sues in this matter"] An action brought under a statute that allows a private person to sue for a penalty, part of which the government or some specified public institution will receive. — Also termed *popular action.* — Often shortened to *qui tam* (Q.T.).

quitclaim, *n.* **1.** A formal release of one's claim or right. **2.** See *quitclaim deed* under DEED.

quitclaim, *vb.* **1.** To relinquish or release (a claim or right). **2.** To convey all of one's interest in (property), to whatever extent one has an interest; to execute a quitclaim deed.

quitclaim deed. See DEED.

quit rent. *Hist.* A payment to a feudal lord by a freeholder or copyholder, so called because upon payment the tenant goes "quit and free" (discharged) of all other services. — Also spelled *quitrent.* — Also termed *quietus redditus.*

quittance. 1. A release or discharge from a debt or obligation. **2.** The document serving as evidence of such a release. See ACQUITTANCE.

quoad (**kwoh**-ad). [Latin] As regards; with regard to <with a pledge, the debtor continues to possess *quoad* the world at large>.

quoad hoc (**kwoh**-ad **hok**). [Latin] As to this; with respect to this; so far as this is concerned. • A prohibition *quoad hoc* is a prohibition of certain things among others, such as matters brought in an ecclesiastical court that should have been brought in a temporal court.

quoad sacra (**kwoh**-ad **say**-krə). [Latin] As to sacred things; for religious purposes. • This term often referred to property that was located so far from the parish to which it belonged that it was annexed *quoad sacra* to another parish, allowing the inhabitants to attend the closer parish's services. But the land continued to belong to the original parish for all civil purposes.

quo animo (**kwoh an**-ə-moh), *adv.* [Latin] With what intention or motive. See ANIMUS.

quocumque modo velit, quocumque modo possit (kwoh-**kəm**-kwee **moh**-doh **vel**-it, kwoh-**kəm**-kwee **moh**-doh **pahs**-it). [Latin] In any way he wishes; in any way he can.

quod billa cassetur (kwod **bil**-ə kə-**see**-tər), *n.* [Latin "that the bill be quashed"] The common-law form of a judgment sustaining a plea in abatement that proceeds from a bill instead of an original writ. See CASSETUR BILLA.

quod clerici non eligantur in officio ballivi, etc. (kwod **kler**-ə-sɪ non el-ə-**gan**-tər in ə-**fish**-ee-oh bal-**lɪ**-vɪ), *n.* [Law Latin "that clerks are not chosen in the office of a bailiff, etc."] *Hist.* A writ exempting a clerk, who was to be appointed as a bailiff, beadle, reeve, or other officer, from serving in the office.

quod computet (kwod **kom**-pyə-tet). [Law Latin "that he account"] The first judgment in an action of account, requiring the defendant to give an accounting before auditors. — Also termed *judgment quod computet.*

> "In this action, if the plaintiff succeeds, there are two judgments: the first is, that the defendant do account (*quod computet*) before auditors appointed by the court; and, when such account is finished, then the second judgment is, that he do pay the plaintiff so much as he is found in arrear." 3 William Blackstone, *Commentaries on the Laws of England* 163 (1768).

quod cum (**kwod** kəm). [Law Latin] For that; whereas. • In common-law pleading, this phrase introduced explanations for the claims alleged, as in *assumpsit* actions.

quod ei deforceat (kwod **ee**-ɪ di-**for**-see-ət), *n.* [Law Latin "that he deforces him"] *Hist.* A writ allowed by St. Westm. 2, 13 Edw., ch. 4 for the owners of a particular estate (such as a life estate or fee tail) who had lost land unwittingly by default in a possessory action. • Up to that time, only owners in fee simple could recover property after such a default.

quod erat demonstrandum (kwod **er**-ət dem-ən-**stran**-dəm). See Q.E.D.

quod erat faciendum (kwod **er**-ət fay-shee-**en**-dəm). See Q.E.F.

quod fuit concessum (kwod **f[y]oo**-it kən-**ses**-əm). [Law Latin] Which was granted. • This phrase was used in old reports to indicate that an argument or point made by counsel was approved or allowed by the court.

quod jussu (kwod **jəs**-[y]oo). [Latin "which was done by order"] *Roman law.* An action by one who contracted with a son or slave upon the authorization of the father or master, to compel the father or master to honor the agreement.

quod non fuit negatum (kwod non **f[y]oo**-it ni-**gay**-təm). [Law Latin] *Hist.* Which was not denied. • This phrase usu. signifies that an argument or proposal is not denied or controverted by the court.

quod nota (kwod **noh**-tə). [Latin] *Hist.* Which note; which mark. • This is a reporter's note directing attention to a point or rule.

quod partes replacitent (kwod **pahr**-teez ri-**plas**-i-tənt), *n.* [Law Latin "that the parties do replead"] *Hist.* The judgment ordering repleader when an issue is formed on so immaterial a point that the court does not know for whom to give a judgment. • The parties must then reconstruct their pleadings.

quod partitio fiat (kwod pahr-**tish**-ee-oh **fɪ**-ət). [Latin "that partition be made"] *Hist.* In a partition suit, a judgment granting the partition.

quod permittat (kwod pər-**mit**-it), *n.* [Latin "that he permit"] *Hist.* A writ to prevent an interference in the exercise of a right, such as a writ for the heir of someone disseised of a common of pasture against the heir of the disseisor.

quod permittat prosternere (kwod pər-**mit**-it proh-**stər**-nə-ree), *n.* [Law Latin "that he permit to abate"] *Hist.* A writ to abate a nuisance, similar in nature to a petition of right.

> "This is a writ commanding the defendant to permit the plaintiff to abate, *quod permittat prosternere*, the nuisance complained of; and, unless he so permits, to summon him to appear in court, and shew cause why he will not. And this writ lies as well *for* the alienee of the party first injured, as *against* the alienee of the party first injuring; as hath been determined by all the judges. And the plaintiff shall have judgment herein to abate the nuisance, and to recover damages against the defendant." 3 William Blackstone, *Commentaries on the Laws of England* 222 (1768).

quod recuperet (kwod ri-**k[y]oo**-pər-it), *n.* [Law Latin "that he do recover"] *Hist.* The ordinary judgment for a plaintiff in an action at law. • The judgment might be either final or interlocutory depending on whether damages had been ascertained at the time the judgment was rendered. — Also termed *judgment quod recuperet*.

quod si contingat (kwod **sɪ** kon-**ting**-at). [Law Latin] *Hist.* That if it happen. • These words were used to create a condition in a deed.

quod vide (kwod **vɪ**-dee *or* **vee**-day). See Q.V.

quod voluit non dixit (kwod **vol**-yoo-it non **dik**-sit). [Latin] *Hist.* That he did not say what he intended. • This phrase was sometimes used in an argument concerning the intention of a lawmaker or testator.

quo jure (kwoh **joor**-ee). [Law Latin "by what right"] *Hist.* A writ for someone holding land to which another claimed a common, to compel the latter to prove title.

quominus (**kwoh**-mə-nəs *or* kwoh-**mɪ**-nəs). [Latin *quo minus* "by which the less"] *Hist.* A 14th-century Exchequer writ alleging that the plaintiff had lent the defendant a sum of money and that the plaintiff was unable to repay a debt of similar amount to the Crown because of the debt to the defendant. • In effect, the plaintiff pleaded the fiction that he was a debtor of the king who could not repay that debt because of the defendant's failure to repay him. — Also termed *writ of quominus*.

quorum, *n.* The minimum number of members (usu. a majority) who must be present for a body to transact business or take a vote. Pl. **quorums.**

quota. 1. A proportional share assigned to a person or group; an allotment <the university's admission standards included a quota for in-state residents>. **2.** A quantitative restriction; a minimum or maximum number <Faldo met his sales quota for the month>.

export quota. A restriction on the products that can be sold to foreign countries. • In the United States, export quotas can be established by the federal government for various purposes, including national defense, price support, and economic stability.

import quota. A restriction on the volume of a certain product that can be brought into the country from a foreign country. • In the United States, the President may establish a quota on an item that poses a threat of serious injury to a domestic industry.

quotation. 1. A statement or passage that is reproduced, attributed, and cited. **2.** The amount stated as a stock's or commodity's current price. **3.** A contractor's estimate for a given job. — Sometimes shortened to *quote*.

quotient verdict. See VERDICT.

quousque (kwoh-**əs**-kwee). [Latin] *Hist.* As long as; how long; until; how far. • This term was used in conveyances as a limitation.

quovis modo (**kwoh**-vis **moh**-doh). [Latin] In whatever manner.

quo warranto (kwoh wə-**ran**-toh *also* kwoh **wahr**-ən-toh). [Law Latin "by what authority"] **1.** A common-law writ used to inquire into the authority by which a public office is held or a franchise is claimed. — Also termed *writ of quo warranto.* **2.** An action by which the state seeks to revoke a corporation's charter. • The Federal Rules of Civil Procedure are applicable to proceedings for quo warranto "to the extent that the practice in such proceedings is not set forth in statutes of the United States and has therefore conformed to the practice in civil actions." Fed. R. Civ. P. 81(a)(2).

> "Sometimes the term 'quo warranto' is used to describe not only the proceedings under the common-law writ of quo warranto, but also proceedings under an information in the nature of a writ of quo warranto or similar statutory remedies." 74 C.J.S. *Quo Warranto* § 1(e), at 177 (1951).

q.v. *abbr.* [Latin *quod vide*] Which see — used in non-*Bluebook* citations for cross-referencing. Pl. **qq.v.**

R

R. *abbr.* **1.** REX. **2.** REGINA. **3.** RANGE.

rabbinical divorce. See DIVORCE.

race act. See RACE STATUTE.

race-notice statute. A recording law providing that the person who records first, without notice of prior unrecorded claims, has priority. • About half the states have race-notice statutes. — Also termed *race-notice act*; *notice-race statute*. Cf. RACE STATUTE; NOTICE STATUTE.

race of diligence. *Bankruptcy.* A first-come, first-served disposition of assets.

race statute. A recording act providing that the person who records first, regardless of notice, has priority. • Only Louisiana and North Carolina have race statutes. — Also termed *pure race statute*; *race act*. Cf. NOTICE STATUTE; RACE-NOTICE STATUTE.

race to the courthouse. 1. *Bankruptcy.* The competition among creditors to make claims on assets, usu. motivated by the advantages to be gained by those who act first in preference to other creditors. • Chapter 11 of the Bankruptcy Code, as well as various other provisions, is intended to prevent a race to the courthouse and instead to promote equality among creditors. **2.** *Civil procedure.* The competition between disputing parties, both of whom know that litigation is inevitable, to prepare and file a lawsuit in a favorable or convenient forum before the other side files in one that is less favorable or less convenient. • A race to the courthouse may result after one party informally accuses another of breach of contract or intellectual-property infringement. When informal negotiations break down, both want to resolve the matter quickly, usually to avoid further business disruption. While the accuser races to sue for breach of contract or infringement, the accused seeks a declaratory judgment that no breach or infringement has occurred. See ANTICIPATORY FILING.

rachat (rah-**shah**), *n.* [French] **1.** Repurchase; redemption. **2.** Ransom.

racheter (rah-shə-**tay**), *vb.* [French] **1.** To repurchase or buy back. **2.** To ransom.

racial discrimination. See DISCRIMINATION.

rack, *n. Hist.* An instrument of torture on which a person was slowly stretched, formerly used to interrogate someone charged with a crime.

racket, *n.* **1.** An organized criminal activity; esp., the extortion of money by threat or violence. **2.** A dishonest or fraudulent scheme or business.

racketeer, *n.* A person who engages in racketeering. — **racketeer,** *vb.*

Racketeer Influenced and Corrupt Organizations Act. A law designed to attack organized criminal activity and preserve marketplace integrity by investigating, controlling, and prosecuting persons who participate or conspire to participate in racketeering. • Enacted in 1970, the federal Racketeer Influenced and Corrupt Organizations Act (RICO) applies only to activity involving interstate or foreign commerce. 18 USCA §§ 1961–1968. Since then, many states have adopted laws (sometimes called "little RICO" acts) based on the federal statute. The federal and most state RICO acts provide for enforcement not only by criminal prosecution but also by civil lawsuit, in which the plaintiff can sue for treble damages.

> "Before criminal or civil liability can attach under RICO, it must be shown that the two or more acts of racketeering alleged in the criminal indictment or civil complaint constitute a pattern of racketeering activity on the part of the culpable person. The statutory definition of pattern 'requires at least two' predicate acts occurring within ten years of each other, with one of them occurring after October 15, 1970. More broadly put, the pattern of racketeering activity is a scheme of unlawful conduct with a nexus to both the culpable person and the enterprise." David R. McCormack, *Racketeering Influenced Corrupt Organizations* § 1.04, at 1–20 (1998).

racketeering, *n.* **1.** A system of organized crime traditionally involving the extortion of money from businesses by intimidation, violence, or other illegal methods. **2.** A pattern of illegal activity (such as bribery, extortion, fraud, and murder) carried out as part of an enterprise (such as a crime syndicate) that is owned or controlled by those engaged in the illegal activity. • The modern sense (sense 2) derives from the federal RICO statute, which greatly broadened the term's original sense to include such activities as mail fraud, securities fraud, and the collection of illegal gambling debts.

rack-rent, *n.* Rent equal to or nearly equal to the full annual value of the property; excessively or unreasonably high rent. — **rack-rent,** *vb.*

raffle, *n.* A form of lottery in which each participant buys one or more chances to win a prize.

raid, *n.* **1.** A sudden attack or invasion by law-enforcement officers, usu. to make an arrest or to search for evidence of a crime. **2.** An attempt by a business or union to lure employees or members from a competitor. **3.** An attempt by a group of speculators to cause a sudden fall in stock prices by concerted selling.

raider. See CORPORATE RAIDER.

railroad, *vb.* **1.** To transport by train. **2.** To send (a measure) hastily through a legislature so that there is little time for consideration and debate. **3.** To convict (a person) hastily, esp. by the use of false charges or insufficient evidence.

railroad-aid bond. See BOND (3).

railroad company. See *railroad corporation* under CORPORATION.

railroad corporation. See CORPORATION.

Railway Labor Act. A 1926 federal law giving transportation employees the right to organize without management interference and establishing guidelines for the resolution of labor disputes in the transportation industry. • In 1934, the law was amended to include the airline industry and to establish the National Mediation Board. 45 USCA §§ 151–188. See NATIONAL MEDIATION BOARD.

rainmaker, *n.* A lawyer who generates a large amount of business for a law firm, usu. through wide contacts within the business community <the law firm fell on hard times when the rainmaker left and took his clients with him>. — **rainmaking,** *n.*

raise, *vb.* **1.** To increase in amount or value <the industry raised prices>. **2.** To gather or collect <the county raised property taxes>. **3.** To bring up for discussion or consideration; to introduce or put forward <the party raised the issue in its pleading>. **4.** To create or establish <the person's silence raised an inference of consent>. **5.** To increase the stated amount of (a negotiable instrument) by fraudulent alteration <the indorser raised the check>.

raised check. See CHECK.

raising an instrument. The act of fraudulently altering a negotiable instrument, esp. a check, to increase the sum stated as being payable. See *raised check* under CHECK.

rake-off, *n.* A percentage or share taken, esp. from an illegal transaction; an illegal bribe, payoff, or skimming of profits. — **rake off,** *vb.*

rally, *n.* A sharp rise in price or trading (as of stocks) after a declining market.

RAM. See *reverse annuity mortgage* under MORTGAGE.

Rambo lawyer. A lawyer, esp. a litigator, who uses aggressive, unethical, or illegal tactics in representing a client and who lacks courtesy and professionalism in dealing with other lawyers. — Often shortened to *Rambo*.

R and D. *abbr.* RESEARCH AND DEVELOPMENT.

range, *n.* *Land law.* In U.S. government surveys, a strip of public land running due north to south, consisting of a row of townships, at six-mile intervals. — Abbr. R.

ranger. 1. *Hist.* In England, an officer or keeper of a royal forest, appointed to patrol the forest, drive out stray animals, and prevent trespassing. **2.** An officer or warden who patrols and supervises the care and preservation of a public park or forest. **3.** One of a group of soldiers who patrol a given region; esp., in the U.S. military, a soldier specially trained for surprise raids and close combat. **4.** A member of a special state police force.

rank, *n.* A social or official position or standing, as in the armed forces <the rank of captain>.

rank and file. 1. The enlisted soldiers of an armed force, as distinguished from the officers. **2.** The general membership of a union.

ransom, *n.* **1.** The release of a captured person or property in exchange for payment of a demanded price. **2.** Money or other consideration demanded or paid for the release of a captured person or property. See KIDNAPPING.

ransom, *vb.* **1.** To obtain the release of (a captive) by paying a demanded price. **2.** To release (a captive) upon receiving such a payment. **3.** To hold and demand payment for the release of (a captive).

ransom bill. *Int'l law.* A contract by which a vessel or other property captured at sea during wartime is ransomed in exchange for release and safe conduct to a friendly destination. — Also termed *ransom bond.*

rap, *n. Slang.* **1.** Legal responsibility for a criminal act <he took the rap for his accomplices>. **2.** A criminal charge <a murder rap>. **3.** A criminal conviction; esp., a prison sentence <a 20-year rap for counterfeiting>.

rape, *n.* **1.** At common law, unlawful sexual intercourse committed by a man with a woman not his wife through force and against her will. • The common-law crime of rape required at least a slight penetration of the penis into the vagina. Also at common law, a husband could not be convicted of raping his wife. **2.** Unlawful sexual activity (esp. intercourse) with a person (usu. a female) without consent and usu. by force or threat of injury. • Most modern state statutes have broadened the definition along these lines. Marital status is now usu. irrelevant, and sometimes so is the victim's gender. — Also termed (in some statutes) *unlawful sexual intercourse*; *sexual assault*; *sexual battery*; *sexual abuse*. Cf. *sexual assault* under ASSAULT.

> "[Another] offence, against the female part also of his majesty's subjects, but attended with greater aggravations than that of forcible marriage, is the crime of *rape, raptus mulierum*, or the carnal knowledge of a woman forcibly and against her will." 4 William Blackstone, *Commentaries on the Laws of England* 210 (1769).

> "If force is to be declared an element of the crime [of rape] it becomes necessary to resort to the fiction of 'constructive force' to take care of those cases in which no force is needed beyond what is involved in the very act of intercourse itself. A better analysis is to recognize that the requirement of force is simply a means of demonstrating that the unlawful violation of the woman was without her consent and against her will. Therefore, evidence of serious force need not be shown in many cases. Hence the better view is that 'force' is not truly speaking an element of the crime itself, but if great force was not needed to accomplish the act the necessary *lack of consent* has been *disproved* in other than exceptional situations. The courts today frequently state the position that a woman's resistance need not be 'more than her age, strength, the surrounding facts, and all attending circumstances' make reasonable." Rollin M. Perkins & Ronald N. Boyce, *Criminal Law* 211–12 (3d ed. 1982).

date rape. Rape committed by someone known to the victim, esp. by the victim's social companion. — Also termed *acquaintance rape.*

marital rape. A husband's sexual intercourse with his wife by force or without her consent. • Marital rape was not a crime at common law, but under modern statutes the marital exemption no longer applies, and in most jurisdictions a husband can be convicted of raping his wife.

statutory rape. Unlawful sexual intercourse with a person under the age of consent (as defined by statute), regardless of whether it is against that person's will. • Generally, only an adult may be convicted of this crime. A person under the age of consent cannot be convicted. — Also termed *rape under age.* See AGE OF CONSENT.

> "Carnal knowledge of a child is frequently declared to be rape by statute and where this is true the offense is popularly known as 'statutory rape,' although not so designated in the statute." Rollin M. Perkins & Ronald N. Boyce, *Criminal Law* 198 (3d ed. 1982).

3. *Archaic.* The act of seizing and carrying off a person (esp. a woman) by force; abduction. **4.** The act of plundering or despoiling a place. **5.** *Hist.* One of the six administrative districts into which Sussex, England was divided, being smaller than a shire and larger than a hundred.

rape, *vb.* **1.** To commit rape against. **2.** *Archaic.* To seize and carry off by force; abduct. **3.** To plunder or despoil. — **rapist, raper,** *n.*

rape shield statute. See SHIELD LAW (2).

rape under age. See *statutory rape* under RAPE.

rapina (rə-**pɪ**-nə). [Latin "robbery, pillage"] *Civil law.* The forcible taking of another's movable property with the intent to appropriate it to one's own use.

> "Rapina is the taking away of a thing by violent means. It gives rise to the praetorian actio vi bonorum raptorum . . . ." Rudolph Sohm, *The Institutes: A Textbook of the History and System of Roman Private Law* 419 (James Crawford Ledlie trans., 3d ed. 1907).

rapine (**rap**-in). **1.** Forcible seizure and carrying off of another's property; pillage or plunder. **2.** *Archaic.* Rape.

rapport à succession (ra-**por** ah sook-ses-**syawn**), *n.* [French "return to succession"] *Civil law.* The restoration to an estate of property that an heir received in advance from the decedent, so that an even distribution may be made among all the heirs. Cf. HOTCHPOT.

rapporteur (ra-por-**tuur** *or* **-tər**), *n.* [French] An official who makes a report of committee proceedings for a larger body (esp. a legislature).

rapprochement (ra-prosh-**mah*n***). The establishment or restoration of cordial relations between two or more nations. — Also spelled *rapprochment.*

rap sheet. *Slang.* A person's criminal record.

raptu haeredis (**rap**-t[y]oo hə-**ree**-dis), *n.* [Latin] *Hist.* A writ for taking away an heir held in socage. See SOCAGE.

rapture. *Archaic.* **1.** Forcible seizure and carrying off of another person (esp. a woman); abduction. **2.** RAPE (1).

raptu virginum (**rap**-t[y]oo **vər**-ji-nəm). See DE RAPTU VIRGINUM.

rapuit (**rap**-yoo-it). [Latin] *Hist.* Ravished. • The term was formerly used in indictments for rape. See RAVISHMENT.

RAR. *abbr.* REVENUE AGENT'S REPORT.

rasure (**ray**-zhər). **1.** The scraping or shaving of a document's surface to remove the writing from it; erasure. **2.** Obliteration.

ratable (**ray**-tə-bəl), *adj.* **1.** Proportionate <ratable distribution>. **2.** Capable of being estimated, appraised, or apportioned <because hundreds of angry fans ran onto the field at the same time, blame for the goalpost's destruction is not ratable>. **3.** Taxable <the government assessed the widow's ratable estate>. See PRO RATA.

ratchet theory. *Constitutional law.* The principle that Congress — in exercising its enforcement power under the 14th Amendment — can increase, but cannot dilute, the scope of 14th Amendment guarantees as previously defined by the Supreme Court. • Thus, the enabling clause works in only one direction, like a ratchet.

rate, *n.* **1.** Proportional or relative value; the proportion by which quantity or value is adjusted <rate of inflation>. **2.** An amount paid or charged for a good or service <the rate for a business-class fare is $550>.

class rate. A single rate applying to the transportation of several articles of the same general character.

confiscatory rate. A utility rate so low that the utility company cannot realize a reasonable return on its investment.

freight rate. A rate charged by a carrier for the transportation of cargo, usu. based on the weight, volume, or quantity of goods but sometimes also on the goods' value or the mileage.

joint rate. A single rate charged by two or more carriers to cover a shipment of goods over a single route.

union rate. The wage scale set by a union as a minimum wage to be paid and usu. expressed as an hourly rate or piecework rate.

3. INTEREST RATE <the rate on the loan increases by 2% after five years>. **4.** *English law.* A sum assessed or payable to the local government in the place where a ratepayer dwells or has property. See RATEPAYER. — **rate,** *vb.*

rate base. The investment amount or property value on which a company, esp. a public utility, is allowed to earn a particular rate of return.

rate of interest. See INTEREST RATE.

rate of return. The annual income from an investment, expressed as a percentage of the investment. See RETURN (5).

fair rate of return. The amount of profit that a public utility is permitted to earn, as determined by a public utility commission.

internal rate of return. *Accounting.* A discounted-cash-flow method of evaluating a long-term project, used to determine the actual return on an investment. — Abbr. IRR.

ratepayer. *English law.* A person who pays local taxes; a person liable to pay rates. See RATE (4).

ratification, *n.* **1.** Confirmation and acceptance of a previous act, thereby making the act valid from the moment it was done <the board of directors' ratification of the president's resolution>. **2.** *Contracts.* A person's binding adoption of an act already completed but either not done in a way that originally produced a legal obligation or done by a third party having at the time no authority to act as the person's agent <an adult's ratification of a contract signed during childhood is necessary to make the contract enforceable>.

> "Ratification may take place by express words indicating an intention to confirm the contract. These words may consist of a new express promise, or such words as 'I do ratify and confirm.' A mere acknowledgment that the contract was in fact made and that it has not been performed is not sufficient as a ratification. It is sometimes said that a ratification is ineffective unless made with knowledge of the possession of a legal power to disaffirm, but the cases holding the contrary seem to have the better reason." William R. Anson, *Principles of the Law of Contract* 179–80 (Arthur L. Corbin ed., 3d Am. ed. 1919).

3. *Int'l law.* The final establishment of consent by the parties to a treaty to be bound by it, usu. including the exchange or deposit of instruments of ratification <the ratification of the nuclear-weapons treaty>. — **ratify,** *vb.* Cf. CONFIRMATION.

ratihabitio (rat-ə-hə-**bish**-ee-oh), *n.* [Latin fr. *ratum habere* "to hold ratified"] *Civil law.* Ratification or approval, esp. by a principal of an agent's transaction.

ratiocination (rash-ee-os-ə-**nay**-shən), *n.* The process or an act of reasoning. — **ratiocinate** (rash-ee-**os**-ə-nayt), *vb.* — **ratiocinative** (rash-ee-**os**-ə-nay-tiv), *adj.*

ratio decidendi (**ray**-shee-oh des-ə-**den**-dɪ), *n.* [Latin "the reason for deciding"] **1.** The principle or rule of law on which a court's decision is founded <many poorly written judicial opinions do not contain a clearly ascertainable *ratio decidendi*>. **2.** The rule of law on which a later court thinks that a previous court founded its decision; a general rule without which a case must have been decided otherwise <this opinion recognizes the Supreme Court's *ratio decidendi* in the school desegregation cases>. — Often shortened to *ratio.* Pl. ***rationes decidendi*** (**ray**-shee-oh-neez des-ə-**den**-dɪ). Cf. OBITER DICTUM; HOLDING.

> "The phrase 'the *ratio decidendi* of a case' is slightly ambiguous. It may mean either (1) the rule that the judge who decided the case intended to lay down and apply to the facts, or (2) the rule that a later court concedes him to have had the power to lay down." Glanville Williams, *Learning the Law* 75 (11th ed. 1982).

> "There are . . . two steps involved in the ascertainment of the *ratio decidendi* . . . . First, it is necessary to determine all the facts of the case as seen by the judge; secondly, it is necessary to discover which of those facts were treated as material by the judge." Rupert Cross & J.W. Harris, *Precedent in English Law* 65–66 (4th ed. 1991).

ratio legis (**ray**-shee-oh **lee**-jəs), *n.* [Latin] The reason or purpose for making a law <the Senator argued that the rapid spread of violent crime was a compelling *ratio legis* for the gun-control statute>. — Also termed *ratio juris.*

rationabile estoverium (rash-[ee]-ə-**nay**-bə-lee es-tə-**veer**-ee-əm), *n.* [Law Latin "reasonable necessaries"] *Hist.* Alimony.

rationabilibus divisis. See DE RATIONABILIBUS DIVISIS.

rationabili parte bonorum. See DE RATIONABILI PARTE BONORUM.

rational-basis test. *Constitutional law.* A principle whereby a court will uphold a law as valid under the Equal Protection Clause if it bears a reasonable relationship to the attainment of some legitimate governmental objective. — Also termed *rational-purpose test; rational-relationship test; minimal scrutiny; minimum scrutiny.* Cf. STRICT SCRUTINY; INTERMEDIATE SCRUTINY.

ratione (ray-shee-**oh**-nee *or* rash-ee-**oh**-nee). [Latin] By reason; on account.

ratione domicilii (dom-ə-**sil**-ee-ɪ). By reason of domicile.

ratione impotentiae (im-pə-**ten**-shee-ee). By reason of inability. • This was the basis for a property right in young wild animals that were unable to run or fly. See FERAE NATURAE.

ratione loci (**loh**-sɪ). By reason of place. • This was the basis for a property right in rabbits and hares.

ratione materiae (mə-**teer**-ee-ee). By reason of the matter involved.

ratione personae (pər-**soh**-nee). By reason of the person concerned.

ratione privilegii (priv-ə-**lee**-jee-ɪ). By reason of privilege. • This was the basis for a property right in animals of warren. See WARREN.

ratione rei sitae (**ree**-ɪ **sɪ**-tee). By reason of the situation of a thing.

ratione soli (**soh**-lɪ). By reason of the soil. • This was the basis for a property right in bees.

ratione tenurae (**ten**-yə-ree). By reason of tenure.

rationes (ray-shee-**oh**-neez *or* rash-ee-**oh**-neez), *n.* [Latin "reasons"] *Hist.* The pleadings in a suit.

ratio scripta (**ray**-shee-oh **skrip**-tə), *n.* [Latin] *Roman law.* Written reason.

rattening (**rat**-ning). *Hist.* The practice of taking away tools, destroying machinery, and the like in an attempt either to compel a worker to join a union or to enforce a company's compliance with union rules. • Rattening was formerly a common labor-union tactic in England, and it was a criminal offense.

ravishment, *n. Archaic.* **1.** Forcible seizure and carrying off of another person (esp. a woman); abduction. **2.** RAPE (1). • In this sense the term is widely considered inappropriate for modern usage, given its romantic connotations (in other contexts) of ecstasy and delight. — **ravish,** *vb.*

re (ree *or* ray), *prep.* Regarding; in the matter of; IN RE. • The term is often used as a signal or introductory title announcing the subject of business correspondence.

rea (**ree**-ə), *n.* [Latin] In civil and canon law, a female defendant. Pl. ***reae.***

reacquired stock. See *treasury stock* under STOCK.

readjustment, *n.* Voluntary reorganization of a financially troubled corporation by the shareholders themselves, without a trustee's or a receiver's intervention. — **readjust,** *vb.*

ready, willing, and able. (Of a prospective buyer) legally and financially capable of consummating a purchase.

> " 'READY, WILLING, AND ABLE' — A phrase referring to a prospective buyer of property who is legally capable and financially able to consummate the deal. Traditionally, the broker earns a commission upon procuring a 'ready, willing, and able' buyer on the listing terms, regardless of whether the seller actually goes through with the sale. The 'ready and willing' means, generally, that the broker must in fact produce a buyer who indicates that he or she is prepared to accept the terms of the seller and is willing to enter into a contract for sale. The buyer is not 'ready and willing' when he or she enters into an option with the seller, but the buyer is 'ready and willing' when the option is exercised. The buyer is not 'ready and willing' when the offer is subject to any new conditions, such as making the closing date an unreasonably long period, for example, one year from the offer.... The 'able' requires that the buyer be financially able to comply with the terms of the sale in both initial cash payment and any necessary financing. The broker is not required to show that the purchaser has actual cash or assets to pay off the mortgage. But the broker is required to reveal the identity of the buyer if requested by the seller." John W. Reilly, *The Language of Real Estate* 326 (4th ed. 1993).

reaffirmation, *n.* **1.** Approval of something previously decided or agreed to; renewal <the Supreme Court's reaffirmation of this principle is long overdue>. **2.** *Bankruptcy.* An agreement between the debtor and a creditor by which the debtor promises to repay a prepetition debt that would otherwise be discharged at the conclusion of the bankruptcy <the debtor negotiated a reaffirmation so that he could keep the collateral>. • There are two main requirements for a reaffirmation to be enforceable: (1) the agreement must contain a clear and conspicuous provision stating that the debtor may rescind the reaffirmation agreement anytime before discharge or within 60 days after the agreement is filed with the court; and (2) for a debtor who is not represented by counsel, the court must determine that the reaffirmation is in the debtor's best interest and does not impose an undue hardship. 11 USCA § 524(c). — Also termed (in sense 2) *reaffirmation agreement.* — **reaffirm,** *vb.*

reaffirmation hearing. *Bankruptcy.* A hearing at which the debtor and a creditor present a reaffirmation of a dischargeable debt for the court's approval. • The reaffirmation hearing is usu. held simultaneously with the discharge hearing. See DISCHARGE HEARING.

real, *adj.* **1.** Of or relating to things (such as lands and buildings) that are fixed or immovable <real property> <a real action>. **2.** *Civil law.* Of, relating to, or attached to a thing (whether movable or immovable) rather than a person <a real right>. **3.** Actual; genuine; true <real authority>. **4.** (Of money, income, etc.) measured in terms of purchasing power rather than nominal value; adjusted for inflation <real wages>.

real account. See ACCOUNT.

real action. See ACTION.

real asset. See ASSET.

real authority. See *actual authority* under AUTHORITY (1).

real chattel. See *chattel real* under CHATTEL.

real contract. See CONTRACT.

real covenant. See *covenant running with the land* under COVENANT (4).

real defense. See DEFENSE (4).

real earnings. See EARNINGS.

real estate. See *real property* under PROPERTY.

real-estate agent. See AGENT.

real-estate broker. See BROKER.

real-estate investment trust. A company that invests in and manages a portfolio of real estate, with the majority of the trust's income distributed to its shareholders. • Such a trust may qualify for special income-tax treatment if it distributes 95% of its income to its shareholders. — Abbr. REIT. See *investment company* under COMPANY. Cf. REAL-ESTATE MORTGAGE TRUST.

umbrella-partnership real-estate investment trust. A REIT that controls and holds most of its properties through an umbrella limited partnership, as a result of which the trust can acquire properties in exchange for the limited-partnership interests in the umbrella while triggering no immediate tax obligations for certain sellers. • This is a structure that many REITs now use. — Abbr. UPREIT.

real-estate-mortgage investment conduit. An entity that holds a fixed pool of mortgages or mortgage-backed securities (such as collateralized mortgage obligations), issues interests in itself to investors, and receives favorable tax treatment by passing its income through to those investors. • Real-estate-mortgage investment conduits were created by the Tax Reform Act of 1986. They can be organized as corporations, partnerships, or trusts. To qualify for tax-exempt status, the entity must meet two requirements: (1) almost all of the entity's assets must be real-estate mortgages (though a few other cash-flow-maintaining assets are allowed); and (2) all interests in the entity must be classified as either regular interests (which entitle the holder to principal and interest income through debt or equity) or residual interests (which provide contingent income). — Abbr. REMIC.

real-estate mortgage trust. A real-estate investment trust that buys and sells mortgages rather than real property. — Abbr. REMT. Cf. REAL-ESTATE INVESTMENT TRUST.

real estate owned. Property acquired by a lender, usu. through foreclosure, in satisfaction of a debt. — Abbr. REO.

Real Estate Settlement Procedures Act. A federal law that requires lenders to provide home buyers with information about known or estimated settlement costs. 12 USCA §§ 2601–2617. — Abbr. RESPA. See REGULATION X.

real-estate syndicate. A group of investors who pool their money for the buying and selling of real property. • Most real-estate syndicates operate as limited partnerships or real-estate investment trusts.

real evidence. See EVIDENCE.

realignment (ree-ə-**lin**-mənt), *n.* The process by which a court, usu. in determining diversity jurisdiction, identifies and rearranges the parties as plaintiffs and defendants according to their ultimate interests. — **realign,** *vb.*

real income. See INCOME.

realization, *n.* **1.** Conversion of noncash assets into cash assets. **2.** *Tax.* An event or transaction, such as the sale or exchange of property, that substantially changes a taxpayer's economic position so that income tax may be imposed or a tax allowance granted. Cf. RECOGNITION (3). — **realize,** *vb.*

realized gain. See GAIN (3).

realized loss. See LOSS (4).

real law. 1. The law of real property; real-estate law. **2.** *Civil law.* The law relating to specific things as opposed to persons.

real money. See MONEY.

real party in interest. See PARTY (2).

real property. See PROPERTY.

real rate. See INTEREST RATE.

real right. See RIGHT.

real security. See SECURITY.

real servitude. See *servitude appurtenant* under SERVITUDE (1).

real statute. See STATUTE.

real suretyship. See SURETYSHIP.

real things. Property that is fixed and immovable, such as lands and buildings; real property. — Also termed *things real*. See *real property* under PROPERTY. Cf. *chattel real* under CHATTEL.

realtor (**reel**-tər). **1.** *(cap.) Servicemark.* A member of the National Association of Realtors. **2.** Loosely, any real-estate agent or broker.

realty. See *real property* under PROPERTY.

quasi-realty. *Hist.* Things that the law treats as fixed to realty, but are themselves movable, such as title deeds.

real wages. See WAGE.

real wrong. See WRONG.

reapportionment, *n.* Realignment of a legislative district's boundaries to reflect changes in population. • The U.S. Supreme Court has required federal reapportionment. See U.S. Const. art. I, § 2, cl. 3. — Also termed *redistricting*. — **reapportion,** *vb.* Cf. GERRYMANDERING.

reargument, *n.* The presentation of additional arguments, which often suggest that a controlling legal principle has been overlooked, to a court (usu. an appellate court) that has already heard initial arguments. — **reargue,** *vb.* Cf. REHEARING.

rearrest. See ARREST.

reasonable, *adj.* **1.** Fair, proper, or moderate under the circumstances <reasonable pay>. **2.** According to reason <your argument is reasonable but not convincing>.

> "It is extremely difficult to state what lawyers mean when they speak of 'reasonableness.' In part the expression refers to ordinary ideas of natural law or natural justice, in part to logical thought, working upon the basis of the rules of law." John Salmond, *Jurisprudence* 183 n.(u) (Glanville L. Williams ed., 10th ed. 1947).

> "In one sense the word [*reasonable*] describes the proper use of the reasoning power, and in another it is no more than a word of assessment. Reasoning does not help much in fixing a reasonable or fair price or a reasonable or moderate length of time, or in estimating the size of a doubt. Lawyers say a reasonable doubt, meaning a substantial one; the Court of Appeal has frowned upon the description of a reasonable doubt as one for which reasons could be given." Patrick Devlin, *The Judge* 134 (1979).

3. (Of a person) having the faculty of reason <a reasonable person would have looked both ways before crossing the street>. **4.** *Archaic.* Human <criminal homicide is traditionally called the unlawful killing of a "reasonable person">. — **reasonableness,** *n.*

reasonable accommodation. 1. An action taken to adapt or adjust for a disabled person, done in a way that does not impose an undue hardship on the party taking the action. • Under the Americans with Disabilities Act, an employer must make reasonable accommodations for an employee's disability. Examples of reasonable accommodations that have been approved by the courts include providing additional unpaid leave, modifying the employee's work schedule, and reassigning the employee to a vacant position. **2.** An action taken to adapt or adjust for an employee's religious need or practice, done in a way that does not impose an undue hardship on the employer.

reasonable care. See CARE.

reasonable cause. See PROBABLE CAUSE.

reasonable diligence. See *due diligence* (1) under DILIGENCE.

reasonable doubt. The doubt that prevents one from being firmly convinced of a defendant's guilt, or the belief that there is a real possibility that a defendant is not guilty. • "Beyond a reasonable doubt" is the standard used by a jury to determine whether a criminal defendant is guilty. In deciding whether guilt has been proved beyond a reasonable doubt, the jury must begin with the presumption that the defendant is innocent. See BURDEN OF PERSUASION.

> "Reasonable doubt ... is a term often used, probably pretty well understood, but not easily defined. It is not a mere possible doubt; because every thing relating to human affairs, and depending on moral evidence, is open to some possible or imaginary doubt. It is that state of the case, which, after the entire comparison and consideration of all the evidence, leaves the minds of jurors in that condition that they cannot say they feel an abiding conviction, to a moral certainty, of the truth of the charge." *Commonwealth v. Webster*, 59 Mass. (5 Cush.) 295, 320 (1850) (per Lemuel Shaw, J.).

> "The gravamen of Lord Goddard's objection to the formula of 'reasonable doubt' seems to have been the muddle occasionally created by an impromptu effort to explain to a jury the meaning of this phrase. A simple solution would be to refrain from explaining it, relying on the common sense of the jury. As Barton J. said in an

Australian case, 'one embarks on a dangerous sea if he attempts to define with precision a term which is in ordinary use with reference to this subject-matter, and which is usually stated to a jury without embellishment as a well understood expression.' However, some modes of embellishment seem to be unobjectionable. There is probably no harm in telling the jury, as some judges do, that a reasonable doubt is one for which a sensible reason can be supplied." Glanville Williams, *Criminal Law* 873 (2d ed. 1961).

reasonable-expectation doctrine. *Insurance.* The rule that resolves an insurance-policy ambiguity in favor of the insured's reasonable expectations.

reasonable force. See FORCE.

reasonable grounds. See PROBABLE CAUSE.

reasonable-inference rule. An evidentiary principle providing that a jury, in deciding a case, may properly consider any reasonable inference drawn from the evidence presented at trial.

reasonable man. See REASONABLE PERSON.

reasonable medical probability. In proving the cause of an injury, a standard requiring a showing that the injury was more likely than not caused by a particular stimulus, based on the general consensus of recognized medical thought. — Also termed *reasonable medical certainty*.

reasonable notice. See NOTICE.

reasonable person. 1. A hypothetical person used as a legal standard, esp. to determine whether someone acted with negligence. • The reasonable person acts sensibly, does things without serious delay, and takes proper but not excessive precautions. — Also termed *reasonable man*; *prudent person*; *ordinarily prudent person*; *reasonably prudent person*. See *reasonable care* under CARE.

"The reasonable man connotes a person whose notions and standards of behaviour and responsibility correspond with those generally obtained among ordinary people in our society at the present time, who seldom allows his emotions to overbear his reason and whose habits are moderate and whose disposition is equable. He is not necessarily the same as the average man — a term which implies an amalgamation of counter-balancing extremes." R.F.V. Heuston, *Salmond on the Law of Torts* 56 (17th ed. 1977).

2. *Archaic.* A human being.

"In the antique phraseology which has been repeated since the time of Lord Coke the *actus reus* of murder (and therefore of any criminal homicide) was declared to be unlawfully killing a reasonable person who is in being and under the King's peace, the death following within a year and a day. In this sentence the word 'reasonable' does not mean 'sane', but 'human'. In criminal law, a lunatic is a *persona* for all purposes of protection, even when not so treated for the assessment of liability." J.W. Cecil Turner, *Kenny's Outlines of Criminal Law* 102 (16th ed. 1952).

reasonable royalty. See ROYALTY (1).

reasonable suspicion. A particularized and objective basis, supported by specific and articulable facts, for suspecting a person of criminal activity. • A police officer must have a reasonable suspicion to stop a person in a public place. See STOP AND FRISK. Cf. PROBABLE CAUSE.

reasonable time. 1. *Contracts.* The time needed to do what a contract requires to be done, based on subjective circumstances. • If the contracting parties do not fix a time for performance, the law will usu. presume a reasonable time. **2.** *Commercial law.* The time during which the UCC permits a party to accept an offer, inspect goods, substitute conforming goods for rejected goods, and the like.

reasonable use. See USE (1).

reasonable-use theory. *Property.* The principle that owners of riparian land may make reasonable use of their water if this use does not affect the water available to lower riparian owners.

reasonably prudent person. See REASONABLE PERSON.

reason to know. Information from which a person of ordinary intelligence — or of the superior intelligence that the person may have — would infer that the fact in question exists or that there is a substantial enough chance of its existence that, if the person is exercising reasonable care, the person's action would be based on the assumption of its possible existence.

reassurance. See REINSURANCE.

rebate, *n.* A return of part of a payment, serving as a discount or reduction. — **rebate,** *vb.*

rebellion. 1. Open, organized, and armed resistance to an established government or ruler. **2.** Open resistance or opposition to an authority or tradition. **3.** *Hist.* Disobedience of a legal command or summons.

rebus sic stantibus (**ree**-bəs sik **stan**-tə-bəs). [Law Latin "things standing thus"] *Civil & int'l law.* The principle that all agreements are concluded with the implied condition that they are binding only as long as there are no major changes in the circumstances. See CLAUSA REBUS SIC STANTIBUS.

rebut, *vb.* To refute, oppose, or counteract (something) by evidence, argument, or contrary proof <rebut the opponent's expert testimony> <rebut a presumption of negligence>.

rebuttable presumption. See PRESUMPTION.

rebuttal, *n.* **1.** In-court contradiction of an adverse party's evidence. **2.** The time given to a party to present contradictory evidence or arguments. Cf. CASE-IN-CHIEF.

rebuttal evidence. See EVIDENCE.

rebuttal witness. See WITNESS.

rebutter. 1. *Common-law pleading.* The defendant's answer to a plaintiff's surrejoinder; the pleading that followed the rejoinder and surrejoinder, and that might in turn be answered by the surrebutter. **2.** One who rebuts.

recall, *n.* **1.** Removal of a public official from office by popular vote. **2.** A manufacturer's request to consumers for the return of defective products for repair or replacement. **3.** Revocation of a judgment for factual or legal reasons. — **recall,** *vb.*

recall election. See ELECTION.

recall exclusion. See *sistership exclusion* under EXCLUSION (3).

recant (ri-**kant**), *vb.* **1.** To withdraw or renounce (prior statements or testimony) formally or publicly <the prosecution hoped the eyewitness wouldn't recant her corroborating testimony on the stand>. **2.** To withdraw or renounce prior statements or testimony formally or publicly <under grueling cross-examination, the witness recanted>. — **recantation,** *n.*

recapitalization, *n.* An adjustment or recasting of a corporation's capital structure — that is, its stocks, bonds, or other securities — through amendment of the articles of incorporation or merger with a parent or subsidiary. • An example of recapitalization is the elimination of unpaid preferred dividends and the creation of a new class of senior securities. — **recapitalize,** *vb.* Cf. REORGANIZATION (2).

leveraged recapitalization. Recapitalization whereby the corporation substitutes debt for equity in the capital structure, usu. to make the corporation less attractive as a target for a hostile takeover. — Also termed *leveraging up.*

recaption. 1. At common law, lawful seizure of another's property for a second time to secure the performance of a duty; a second distress. See DISTRESS. **2.** Peaceful retaking, without legal process, of one's own property that has been wrongfully taken.

recapture, *n.* **1.** The act or an instance of retaking or reacquiring; recovery. **2.** The lawful taking by the government of earnings or profits exceeding a specified amount; esp., the government's recovery of a tax benefit (such as a deduction or credit) by taxing income or property that no longer qualifies for the benefit. **3.** *Int'l law.* The retaking of a prize or booty so that the property is legally restored to its original owner. See POSTLIMINIUM (2). — **recapture,** *vb.*

recapture clause. 1. A contract provision that limits prices or allows for the recovery of goods if market conditions greatly differ from what the contract anticipated. **2.** A commercial-lease provision that grants the landlord both a percentage of the tenant's profits above a fixed amount of rent and the right to terminate the lease — and thus recapture the property — if those profits are too low.

receding market. See *bear market* under MARKET.

receipt, *n.* **1.** The act of receiving something <my receipt of the document was delayed by two days>. **2.** A written acknowledgment that something has been received <keep the receipt for the gift>.

accountable receipt. A receipt coupled with an obligation.

warehouse receipt. See WAREHOUSE RECEIPT.

3. (*usu. pl.*) Something received; INCOME <post the daily receipts in the ledger>.

receipt, *vb.* **1.** To acknowledge in writing the receipt of (something, esp. money) <the bill must be receipted>. **2.** To give a receipt for (something, esp. money) <the bookkeeper receipted the payments>.

receiptor (ri-**see**-tər). A person who receives from a sheriff another's property seized in garnishment and agrees to return the property upon demand or execution.

receivable, *adj.* **1.** Capable of being admitted or accepted . **2.** Awaiting receipt of payment <accounts receivable>. **3.** Subject to a call for payment <a note receivable>.

receivable, *n.* See *account receivable* under ACCOUNT.

receiver. A disinterested person appointed by a court, or by a corporation or other person, for the protection or collection of property that is the subject of diverse claims (for example, because it belongs to a bankrupt or is otherwise being litigated). Cf. LIQUIDATOR.

ancillary receiver. One who is appointed as a receiver in a particular area to assist a foreign receiver in collecting the assets of an insolvent corporation or other entity.

> "An ancillary receiver of a corporation or unincorporated association may be appointed (a) by a competent court of a state in which there are assets of the corporation or unincorporated association at the time of the commencement of the action for the appointment of such receiver, or (b) in the case of a corporation, by a competent court of the state of incorporation. . . . The purpose of such an ancillary receivership is to aid the foreign primary receivership in the collection and taking charge of assets of the estate being administered." 66 Am. Jur. 2d *Receivers* § 436, at 239 (1973).

receiver general. A public official in charge of a government's receipts and treasury. Pl. **receivers general.**

receivership. 1. The state or condition of being in the control of a receiver. **2.** The position or function of being a receiver appointed by a court or under a statute. **3.** A proceeding in which a court appoints a receiver.

dry receivership. A receivership in which there is no equity available to pay general creditors.

receiving state. The country to which a diplomatic agent or consul is sent by the country represented by that agent. Cf. SENDING STATE.

receiving stolen property. The criminal offense of acquiring or controlling property known to have been stolen by another person. • Some jurisdictions require the additional element of wrongful intent. In some jurisdictions it is a felony, but in others it is either a felony or a misdemeanor depending on the value of the property. — Also termed *receiving stolen goods*. See FENCE.

recens insecutio (**ree**-senz in-sə-**kyoo**-shee-oh). [Latin "fresh pursuit"] *Hist.* Pursuit of a thief immediately after discovery of the theft. See FRESH PURSUIT.

reception. The adoption in whole or in part of the law of one jurisdiction by another jurisdiction.

receptitious (ree-sep-**tish**-əs), *adj. Roman law.* **1.** (Of property) retained by the wife and not included in the dowry. **2.** (Of a dowry) returnable by agreement to the donor upon the husband's death.

receptus (ri-**sep**-təs). [Latin "(a person) having been received"] *Civil law.* An arbitrator. • The term takes its name from the idea that the arbitrator is "received" by the parties to settle their dispute.

recess (**ree**-ses), *n.* **1.** A brief break in judicial proceedings <the court granted a two-hour recess for lunch>. Cf. CONTINUANCE (3). **2.** An interval between sittings of the same legislative body <Congress took a monthlong recess>. — **recess** (ri-**ses**), *vb.*

recession. A period characterized by a sharp slowdown in economic activity, declining employment, and a decrease in investment and consumer spending. Cf. DEPRESSION.

recessus maris (ri-**ses**-əs **mair**-əs). [Latin] A going back or retreat of the sea. See RELICTION.

Recht (rekt). [German "right"] **1.** Law generally. **2.** A body of law. **3.** A right or claim.

Rechtsphilosophi (**rekts**-fə-los-ə-fee). See *ethical jurisprudence* under JURISPRUDENCE.

recidivate (ri-**sid**-ə-vayt), *vb.* To return to a habit of criminal behavior; to relapse into crime.

recidivation. *Archaic.* See RECIDIVISM.

recidivism (ri-**sid**-ə-viz-əm), *n.* A tendency to relapse into a habit of criminal activity or behavior. — Also termed (archaically) *recidivation.* — **recidivous, recidivist,** *adj.*

recidivist (ri-**sid**-ə-vist), *n.* One who has been convicted of multiple criminal offenses, usu. similar in nature; a repeat offender <proponents of prison reform argue that prisons don't cure the recidivist>. — Also termed *habitual offender*; *habitual criminal*; *repeater*; *career criminal.*

reciprocal (ri-**sip**-rə-kəl), *adj.* **1.** Directed by each toward the other or others; MUTUAL . **2.** BILATERAL <a reciprocal contract>. **3.** Corresponding; equivalent .

reciprocal contract. See *bilateral contract* under CONTRACT.

reciprocal dealing. A business arrangement in which a buyer having greater economic power than a seller agrees to buy something from the seller only if the seller buys something in return. • Reciprocal dealing usu. violates antitrust laws. — Also termed *reciprocal-dealing arrangement.* Cf. TYING ARRANGEMENT.

reciprocal exchange. An association whose members exchange contracts and pay premiums through an attorney-in-fact for the purpose of insuring themselves and each other. • A reciprocal exchange can consist of individuals, partnerships, trustees, or corporations, but the exchange itself is unincorporated. — Also termed *interinsurance exchange*; *reciprocal insurance exchange*; *reciprocal interinsurance exchange.* See *reciprocal insurance* under INSURANCE.

reciprocal insurance. See INSURANCE.

reciprocal insurance exchange. See RECIPROCAL EXCHANGE.

reciprocal interinsurance exchange. See RECIPROCAL EXCHANGE.

reciprocal negative easement. See EASEMENT.

reciprocal trade agreement. An agreement between two countries providing for the exchange of goods between them at lower tariffs and better terms than exist between one of the countries and other countries.

reciprocal trust. See TRUST.

reciprocal will. See *mutual will* under WILL.

reciprocity (res-ə-**pros**-i-tee). **1.** Mutual or bilateral action <the Arthurs stopped receiving social invitations from friends because of their lack of reciprocity>. **2.** The mutual concession of advantages or privileges for purposes of commercial or diplomatic relations <Texas and Louisiana grant reciprocity to each other's citizens in qualifying for in-state tuition rates>.

recision. See RESCISSION.

recission. See RESCISSION.

recital. 1. An account or description of some fact or thing <the recital of the events leading up to the accident>. **2.** A preliminary statement in a contract or deed explaining the background of the transaction or showing the existence of particular facts <the recitals in the settlement agreement should describe the underlying dispute>. — **recite,** *vb.*

> "The parties may wish to begin the agreement with a statement of their intentions. Often they do this through recitals, which were traditionally introduced by 'whereas,' but can simply state the background without this formality." Scott J. Burnham, *Contract Drafting Guidebook* § 8.4, at 158 (2d ed. 1992).

reckless, *adj.* Characterized by the creation of a substantial and unjustifiable risk of harm to others and by a conscious (and sometimes deliberate) disregard for or indifference to that risk; heedless; rash. • Reckless conduct is much more than mere negligence: it is a gross deviation from what a reasonable person would do. — **recklessly,** *adv.* See RECKLESSNESS. Cf. WANTON.

> "Intention cannot exist without foresight, but foresight can exist without intention. For a man may foresee the possible or even probable consequences of his conduct and yet not desire them to occur; none the less if he persists on his course he knowingly runs the risk of bringing about the unwished result. To describe this state of mind the word 'reckless' is the most appropriate. The words 'rash' and 'rashness' have also been used to indicate this same attitude." J.W. Cecil Turner, *Kenny's Outlines of Criminal Law* 28 (16th ed. 1952).

reckless disregard. 1. Conscious indifference to the consequences (of an act). **2.** *Defamation.* Serious indifference to truth or accuracy of a publication. • "Reckless disregard for the truth" is the standard in proving the defendant's actual malice toward the plaintiff in a libel action.

reckless driving. The criminal offense of operating a motor vehicle in a manner that shows conscious indifference to the safety of others.

reckless endangerment. The criminal offense of putting another person at substantial risk of death or serious injury. • This is a statutory, not a common-law, offense.

reckless homicide. See HOMICIDE.

reckless knowledge. See KNOWLEDGE.

reckless negligence. See *gross negligence* under NEGLIGENCE.

recklessness, *n.* **1.** Conduct whereby the actor does not desire harmful consequence but nonetheless foresees the possibility and consciously takes the risk. • Recklessness involves a greater degree of fault than negligence but a lesser degree of fault than intentional wrongdoing. **2.** The state of mind in which a person does not care about the consequences of his or her actions. — Also termed *heedlessness*. Cf. WANTONNESS.

"The ordinary meaning of the word [*recklessness*] is a high degree of carelessness. It is the doing of something which in fact involves a grave risk to others, whether the doer realises it or not. The test is therefore objective and not subjective." R.F.V. Heuston, *Salmond on the Law of Torts* 194 (17th ed. 1977).

"An abiding difficulty in discussing the legal meaning of recklessness is that the term has been given several different shades of meaning by the courts over the years. In the law of manslaughter, 'reckless' was long regarded as the most appropriate adjective to express the degree of negligence needed for a conviction: in this sense, it meant a high degree of carelessness. In the late 1950s the courts adopted a different meaning of recklessness in the context of *mens rea*, referring to D's actual awareness of the risk of the prohibited consequence occurring: we shall call this 'common-law recklessness.' Controversy was introduced into this area in the early 1980s, when the House of Lords purported to broaden the meaning of recklessness so as to include those who failed to give thought to an obvious risk that the consequence would occur ...." Andrew Ashworth, *Principles of Criminal Law* 154 (1991).

reclamation (rek-lə-**may**-shən), *n.* **1.** The act or an instance of improving the value of economically useless land by physically changing the land, such as irrigating a desert. **2.** *Commercial law.* A seller's limited right to retrieve goods delivered to a buyer when the buyer is insolvent. UCC § 2–702(2). **3.** The act or an instance of obtaining valuable materials from waste materials. — **reclaim,** *vb.*

reclusion (ri-**kloo**-zhən). *Civil law.* Incarceration as punishment for a crime; esp., solitary confinement or confinement at hard labor in a penitentiary.

recognition, *n.* **1.** Confirmation that an act done by another person was authorized. See RATIFICATION. **2.** The formal admission that a person, entity, or thing has a particular status; esp., a nation's act in formally acknowledging the existence of another nation or national government. **3.** *Tax.* The act or an instance of accounting for a taxpayer's realized gain or loss for the purpose of income-tax reporting. Cf. NONRECOGNITION PROVISION; REALIZATION (2). **4.** An employer's acknowledgment that a union has the right to act as a bargaining agent for employees. **5.** *Int'l law.* Official action by a country acknowledging, expressly or by implication, *de jure* or *de facto*, the legality of the existence of a government, a country, or a situation such as a change of territorial sovereignty. **6.** See RULE OF RECOGNITION. — **recognize,** *vb.*

recognition clause. *Real estate.* A clause providing that, when a tract of land has been subdivided for development, the ultimate buyers of individual lots are protected if the developer defaults on the mortgage. • Such a clause is typically found in a blanket mortgage or a contract for deed.

recognition picketing. See PICKETING.

recognition strike. See STRIKE.

recognitor (ri-**kog**-nə-tər), *n.* **1.** *Hist.* A member of a jury impaneled on an assize or inquest. See RECOGNITION. **2.** *Rare.* RECOGNIZOR.

recognizance (ri-**kog**-nə-zənts). **1.** A bond or obligation, made in court, by which a person promises to perform some act or observe some condition, such as to appear when called, to pay a debt, or to keep the peace. • Most commonly, a recognizance takes the form of a bail bond that guarantees an unjailed criminal defendant's return for a court date <the defendant was released on his own recognizance>. See RELEASE ON RECOGNIZANCE.

"Recognizances are aptly described as 'contracts made with the Crown in its judicial capacity.' A recognizance is a writing acknowledged by the party to it before a judge or officer having authority for the purpose, and enrolled in a court of record. It usually takes the form of a promise, with penalties for the breach of it, to keep the peace, to be of good behavior, or to appear at the assizes." William R. Anson, *Principles of the Law of Contract* 80–81 (Arthur L. Corbin ed., 3d Am. ed. 1919).

> "A recognizance is an acknowledgment of an obligation in court by the recognizor binding him to make a certain payment subject to the condition that on the performance of a specified act the obligation shall be discharged." 1 Samuel Williston, *A Treatise on the Law of Contracts* § 6, at 18 (Walter H.E. Jaeger ed., 3d ed. 1957).

personal recognizance. The release of a defendant in a criminal case in which the court takes the defendant's word that he or she will appear for a scheduled matter or when told to appear. • This type of release dispenses with the necessity of the person's posting money or having a surety sign a bond with the court.

2. See *bail bond* under BOND (2).

recognized gain. See GAIN (3).

recognized loss. See LOSS.

recognized market. See MARKET.

recognizee (ri-kog-nə-**zee**). A person in whose favor a recognizance is made; one to whom someone is bound by a recognizance.

recognizor (ri-kog-nə-**zor**). A person who is obligated under a recognizance; one who is bound by a recognizance.

> "A recognizance is an acknowledgment upon record of a former debt, and he who so acknowledges such debt to be due is termed the recognizor, and he to whom or for whose benefit he makes such acknowledgment is termed the recognizee." John Indermaur, *Principles of the Common Law* 8 (Edmund H. Bennett ed., 1st Am. ed. 1878).

recollection, *n.* **1.** The action of recalling something to the mind, esp. through conscious effort. **2.** Something recalled to the mind. — **recollect,** *vb.* See PAST RECOLLECTION RECORDED; PRESENT RECOLLECTION REFRESHED.

recompensable. See COMPENSABLE.

recompense (**rek**-əm-pents), *n.* Repayment, compensation, or retribution for something, esp. an injury or loss. — **recompense,** *vb.*

reconciliation (rek-ən-sil-ee-**ay**-shən), *n.* **1.** Restoration of harmony between persons or things that had been in conflict <a reconciliation between the plaintiff and the defendant is unlikely even if the lawsuit settles before trial>. **2.** *Family law.* Voluntary resumption, after a separation, of full marital relations between spouses <the court dismissed the divorce petition after the parties' reconciliation>. **3.** *Accounting.* An adjustment of accounts so that they agree, esp. by allowing for outstanding items . — **reconcile** (**rek**-ən-sɪl), *vb.*

reconciliation statement. An accounting or financial statement in which discrepancies are adjusted.

reconduction, *n.* **1.** *Civil law.* The renewal of a lease. — Also termed *relocation.* Cf. TACIT RELOCATION. **2.** *Int'l law.* The forcible return of aliens (esp. illegal aliens, destitute or diseased aliens, or alien criminals who have served their punishment) to their country of origin. — Also termed (in sense 2) *renvoi.* — **reconduct,** *vb.*

reconsideration. The action of discussing or taking something up again <legislative reconsideration of the measure>.

reconsignment. A change in the terms of a consignment while the goods are in transit. See CONSIGNMENT.

reconstruction. 1. The act or process of rebuilding, re-creating, or reorganizing something <an expert in accident reconstruction>. **2.** *Patents.* A rebuilding of a broken, worn-out, or otherwise inoperative patented article in such a way that a new article is created, thus resulting in an infringement <the replacement of the machine's essential parts was an infringing reconstruction rather than a permissible repair>. **3.** (*cap.*) The process by which the Southern states that had seceded during the Civil War were readmitted into the Union during the years following the war (i.e., from 1865 to 1877) <the 13th, 14th, and 15th Amendments to the U.S. Constitution are a lasting legacy of Reconstruction>.

recontinuance. 1. Resumption or renewal. **2.** The recovery of an incorporeal hereditament that had been wrongfully deprived.

reconvention. *Civil law.* The act or process of making a counterclaim. See COUNTERCLAIM.

reconventional demand. See DEMAND (1).

reconversion. The notional or imaginary process by which an earlier constructive conversion — meaning a change of personal into real property, or real into personal property — is annulled and taken away, and the converted property restored to its original quality. See *equitable conversion* under CONVERSION (1).

reconveyance, *n.* The restoration or return of something (esp. an estate or title) to a former owner or holder. — **reconvey,** *vb.*

record, *n.* **1.** A documentary account of past events, usu. designed to memorialize those events; information that is inscribed on a tangible medium or that, having been stored in an electronic or other medium, is retrievable in perceivable form. UCC § 2A–102(a)(34).

defective record. **1.** A record that fails to conform to requirements of appellate rules. **2.** A flawed real-estate title resulting from a defect on the property's record in the registry of deeds.

public record. A record that a governmental unit is required by law to keep, such as land deeds kept at a county courthouse. • Public records are generally open to view by the public. Cf. *public document* under DOCUMENT.

silent record. *Criminal procedure.* A record that fails to disclose that a defendant voluntarily and knowingly entered a plea, waived a right to counsel, or took any other action affecting his or her rights.

2. The official report of the proceedings in a case, including the filed papers, a verbatim transcript of the trial or hearing (if any), and tangible exhibits. See DOCKET (1).

recorda (ri-**kor**-də). *Hist.* In England, records that contained the judgments and pleadings in actions tried before the barons of the Exchequer. Cf. ORIGINALIA.

record agent. See INSURANCE AGENT.

recordal. See RECORDATION.

recordare (ree-kor-**dair**-ee), *n.* [Law Latin] *Hist.* A writ to bring up on appeal a judgment of a justice of the peace.

recordari facias loquelam (ree-kor-**dair**-I **fay**-shee-əs lə-**kwee**-ləm), *n.* [Law Latin "you cause the plaint to be recorded"] *Hist.* In England, a writ by which a suit or plaint in replevin could be removed from a county court to a superior court (esp. to one of the courts of Westminster Hall). — Abbr. *re. fa. lo.* See PLAINT (1).

recordation (rek-ər-**day**-shən), *n.* The act or process of recording an instrument, such as a deed or mortgage, in a public registry. • Recordation generally perfects a person's interest in the property against later purchasers (including later mortgagees), but the effect of recordation depends on the type of recording act in effect. — Also termed *recordal.*

record date. See DATE.

recorded recollection. See PAST RECOLLECTION RECORDED.

recorder. **1.** *Hist.* A magistrate with criminal jurisdiction in some British cities or boroughs. **2.** A municipal judge with the criminal jurisdiction of a magistrate or a police judge and sometimes also with limited civil jurisdiction. **3.** A municipal or county officer who keeps public records such as deeds, liens, and judgments.

court recorder. A court official who records court activities using electronic recording equipment, usu. for the purpose of preparing a verbatim transcript. Cf. COURT REPORTER (1).

recorder of deeds. See REGISTER OF DEEDS.

recorder's court. A court having jurisdiction over felony cases. • This court exists in only a few jurisdictions, such as Michigan, where the recorder's court hears felony cases arising within the Detroit city limits.

recording act. A law that establishes the requirements for recording a deed or other property interest and the standards for determining priorities between persons claiming interests in the same property (usu. real property). • Recording acts — the three main types of which are the *notice statute*, the *race statute*, and the *race-notice statute* — are designed to protect bona fide purchasers from earlier unrecorded interests. — Also termed *recording statute.* See NOTICE STATUTE; RACE STATUTE; RACE-NOTICE STATUTE.

recording agent. See INSURANCE AGENT.

recording statute. See RECORDING ACT.

record notice. See NOTICE.

recordo et processu mittendis. See DE RECORDO ET PROCESSU MITTENDIS.

record on appeal. The record of a trial-court proceeding as presented to the appellate court for review. — Also termed *appellate record.* See RECORD (2).

record owner. See OWNER.

record title. See TITLE (2).

recordum (ri-**kor**-dəm). [Law Latin] *Hist.* A record, esp. a judicial one.

recoupment (ri-**koop**-mənt), *n.* **1.** The recovery or regaining of something, esp. expenses. **2.** The withholding, for equitable reasons, of all or part of something that is due. See EQUITABLE RECOUPMENT. **3.** Reduction of a plaintiff's damages because of a demand by the defendant arising out of the same transaction. Cf. SETOFF. **4.** The right of a defendant to have the plaintiff's claim reduced or eliminated because of the plaintiff's breach of contract or duty in the same transaction. **5.** An affirmative defense alleging such a breach. **6.** *Archaic.* A counterclaim arising out of the same transaction or occurrence as the one on which the original action is based. • In modern practice, the recoupment has been replaced by the compulsory counterclaim. — **recoup,** *vb.*

recourse (**ree**-kors *or* ri-**kors**). **1.** The act of seeking help or advice. **2.** Enforcement of, or a method for enforcing, a right. **3.** The right of a holder of a negotiable instrument to demand payment from the drawer or indorser if the instrument is dishonored. See WITH RECOURSE; WITHOUT RECOURSE. **4.** The right to repayment of a loan from the borrower's personal assets, not just from the collateral that secured the loan.

recourse loan. See LOAN.

recourse note. See NOTE (1).

recover, *vb.* **1.** To get back or regain in full or in equivalence <the landlord recovered higher operating costs by raising rent>. **2.** To obtain by a judgment or other legal process <the plaintiff recovered punitive damages in the lawsuit>. **3.** To obtain (a judgment) in one's favor <the plaintiff recovered a judgment against the defendant>. **4.** To obtain damages or other relief; to succeed in a lawsuit or other legal proceeding <the defendant argued that the plaintiff should not be allowed to recover for his own negligence>.

recoverable, *adj.* Capable of being recovered, esp. as a matter of law <court costs and attorney's fees are recoverable under the statute>. — **recoverability,** *n.*

recoveree. *Hist.* The party against whom a judgment is obtained in a common recovery. See COMMON RECOVERY.

recoveror. *Hist.* The demandant who obtains a judgment in a common recovery. See COMMON RECOVERY.

recovery. 1. The regaining or restoration of something lost or taken away. **2.** The obtainment of a right to something (esp. damages) by a judgment or decree. **3.** An amount awarded in or collected from a judgment or decree.

double recovery. **1.** A judgment that erroneously awards damages twice for the same loss, based on two different theories of recovery. **2.** Recovery by a party of more than the maximum recoverable loss that the party has sustained.

recrimination (ri-krim-i-**nay**-shən), *n. Archaic.* In a divorce suit, a countercharge that the complainant has been guilty of an offense constituting a ground for divorce. • Recriminations are now virtually obsolete because of the prevalence of no-fault divorce. — **recriminatory,** *adj.*

recross-examination. A second cross-examination, after redirect examination. — Often shortened to *recross.* See CROSS-EXAMINATION.

recta gubernatio (**rek**-tə g[y]oo-bər-**nay**-shee-oh), *n.* [Latin "right government"] A government in which the highest power, however strong and unified, is neither arbitrary nor irresponsible, and derives from a law that is superior to itself. — Also termed *legitima gubernatio.*

rectification (rek-tə-fi-**kay**-shən), *n.* **1.** A court's equitable correction of a contractual term that is misstated; the judicial alteration of a written contract to make it conform to the true intention of the parties when, in its original form, it did not reflect this intention. • As an equitable remedy, the court alters the terms as written so as to express the true intention of the parties. The court might do this when the rent is wrongly recorded in a lease or when the area of land is incorrectly cited in a deed. **2.** A court's slight modification of words of a statute as a means of carrying out what the court is convinced must have been the legislative intent. • For example, courts engage in rectification when they read *and* as *or* or *shall* as *may,* as they frequently must do because of unfastidious drafting. — **rectify,** *vb.* See REFORMATION.

rectification of boundaries. *Hist.* An action to determine or correct the boundaries between two adjoining pieces of land.

rectification of register. *Hist.* A process by which a person whose name was wrongly entered in or omitted from a record can compel the recorder to correct the error.

rectitudo (rek-tə-**t**[**y**]**oo**-doh). [Law Latin] A right or legal due; a tribute or payment.

recto de advocatione. See DE RECTO DE ADVOCATIONE.

recto de rationabili parte. See DE RECTO DE RATIONABILI PARTE.

recto patens. See DE RECTO PATENS.

rector (**rek**-tər). **1.** *Eccles. law.* The spiritual head and presiding officer of a church. — Also termed *parson*. Cf. VICAR.

impropriate rector. A lay rector as opposed to a spiritual rector.

rector sinecure (sɪ-nee-**kyoor**-ee). A rector who does not have the cure of souls.

2. *Roman law.* A governor or ruler.

rector provinciae (prə-**vin**-shee-ee). A governor of a province.

rectum (**rek**-təm). [Latin] **1.** Right. **2.** A trial or accusation.

rectus (**rek**-təs). [Latin "right"] *Hist.* (Of a line of descent) straight; direct. Cf. OBLIQUUS.

rectus in curia (**rek**-təs in **kyoor**-ee-ə), *adj.* [Latin "right in the court"] *Hist.* Free from charge or offense; competent to appear in court and entitled to the benefit of law. See LEGALIS HOMO.

recuperatio (ri-k[y]oo-pə-**ray**-shee-oh), *n.* [Latin "recovery"] *Hist.* Judicial restitution of something that has been wrongfully taken or denied.

recuperatore (ri-k[y]oo-pə-rə-**tor**-ee), *n.* [Latin] *Roman law.* A special judge who was appointed to decide controversies between Roman citizens and strangers in an expedited fashion, but whose jurisdiction was gradually extended to include cases that could be brought before an ordinary judge.

recusable (ri-**kyoo**-zə-bəl), *adj.* **1.** (Of an obligation) arising from a party's voluntary act and that can be avoided. Cf. IRRECUSABLE. **2.** (Of a judge) capable of being disqualified from sitting on a case. **3.** (Of a fact) providing a basis for disqualifying a judge from sitting on a case.

recusal (ri-**kyoo**-zəl), *n.* Removal of oneself as judge or policy-maker in a particular matter, esp. because of a conflict of interest. — Also termed *recusation*; *recusement*. Cf. DISQUALIFICATION.

recusant (**rek**-yə-zənt *or* ri-**kyoo**-zənt), *adj.* Refusing to submit to an authority or comply with a command <a recusant witness>.

recusant (**rek**-yə-zənt *or* ri-**kyoo**-zənt), *n.* **1.** *Eccles. law.* A person (esp. a Roman Catholic) who refuses to attend the services of the established Church of England. **2.** A person who refuses to submit to an authority or comply with a command.

recusation (rek-yə-**zay**-shən). **1.** *Civil law.* An objection, exception, or appeal; esp., an objection alleging a judge's prejudice or conflict of interest. **2.** RECUSAL.

recuse (ri-**kyooz**), *vb.* **1.** To remove (oneself) as a judge in a particular case because of prejudice or conflict of interest <the judge recused himself from the trial>. **2.** To challenge or object to (a judge) as being disqualified from hearing a case because of prejudice or a conflict of interest <the defendant filed a motion to recuse the trial judge>.

recusement. See RECUSAL.

redaction (ri-**dak**-shən), *n.* **1.** The careful editing (of a document), esp. to remove confidential references or offensive material. **2.** A revised or edited document. — **redact,** *vb.* — **redactional,** *adj.*

reddendo (ri-**den**-doh). *Scots law.* **1.** A clause in a charter specifying a duty or service due from a vassal to a superior. **2.** The duty or service specified in this clause.

reddendo singula singulis (ri-**den**-doh **sing**-gyə-lə **sing**-gyə-lis). [Latin "by rendering each to each"] Assigning or distributing separate things to separate persons, or separate words to separate subjects. • This was used as a rule of construction designed to give effect to the intention of the parties who drafted the instrument. — Also termed *referendo singula singulis*.

reddendum (ri-**den**-dəm). A clause in a deed by which the grantor reserves some new thing (esp. rent) out of what had been previously granted.

reddidit se (**red**-ə-dit **see**). [Latin "he has rendered himself"] *Hist.* A person who has personally appeared in order to discharge bail.

reddition (ri-**dish**-ən). *Hist.* An acknowledgment in court that one is not the owner of certain property being demanded, and that it in fact belongs to the demandant.

redditus. See REDITUS.

redeemable bond. See BOND (3).

redeemable security. See SECURITY.

redeemable stock. See STOCK.

redelivery. An act or instance of giving back or returning something; restitution.

redelivery bond. See *replevin bond* under BOND (2).

redemise, *n.* An act or instance of conveying or transferring back (an estate) already demised. — **redemise,** *vb.* See DEMISE.

redemption, *n.* **1.** The act or an instance of reclaiming or regaining possession by paying a specific price. **2.** *Bankruptcy.* A debtor's right to repurchase property from a buyer who obtained the property at a forced sale initiated by a creditor. **3.** *Securities.* The reacquisition of a security by the issuer. ● Redemption usu. refers to the repurchase of a bond before maturity, but it may also refer to the repurchase of stock and mutual-fund shares. — Also termed (in reference to stock) *stock redemption*; *stock repurchase.* **4.** *Property.* The payment of a defaulted mortgage debt by a borrower who does not want to lose the property. — **redeem,** *vb.* — **redeemable, redemptive, redemptional** *adj.*

statutory redemption. The statutory right of a defaulting mortgagor to recover property, within a specified period, after a foreclosure or tax sale, by paying the outstanding debt or charges. ● The purpose is to protect against the sale of property at a price far less than its value. See REDEMPTION PERIOD.

tax redemption. A taxpayer's recovery of property taken for nonpayment of taxes, accomplished by paying the delinquent taxes and any interest, costs, and penalties.

redemptioner. A person who redeems; esp., one who redeems real property under the equity of redemption or the right of redemption. See EQUITY OF REDEMPTION; RIGHT OF REDEMPTION.

redemption period. The statutory period during which a defaulting mortgagor may recover property after a foreclosure or tax sale by paying the outstanding debt or charges.

redemption price. See PRICE.

redemptio operis (ri-**demp**-shee-oh **op**-ə-ris), *n.* [Latin "redemption of work"] *Civil law.* A contract in which a worker agrees to perform labor or services for a specified price. Cf. *locatio operis* under LOCATIO.

redeundo (ree-dee-**ən**-doh). [Latin] Returning; in returning; while returning.

redevance (ruu-də-**vahns**). [French] *Hist.* Dues payable by a tenant to the lord, not necessarily in money.

red herring. 1. An irrelevant legal or factual issue <law students should avoid discussing the red herrings that professors raise in exams>. **2.** See *preliminary prospectus* under PROSPECTUS.

red-herring prospectus. See *preliminary prospectus* under PROSPECTUS.

redhibere (red-hi-**beer**-ee), *vb.* [Latin] *Civil law.* **1.** To return (a defective purchase) to the seller. **2.** (Of a seller) to take back (a defective purchase).

redhibition (red-[h]i-**bish**-ən), *n. Civil law.* The voidance of a sale as the result of an action brought on account of some defect in a thing sold, on grounds that the defect renders the thing either useless or so imperfect that the buyer would not have originally purchased it. — **redhibitory** (red-**hib**-ə-tor-ee), *adj.*

redhibitory action. See ACTION.

redhibitory defect. *Civil law.* A fault or imperfection in something sold, as a result of which the buyer may return the item and demand back the purchase price. — Also termed *redhibitory vice.*

redimere (ri-**dim**-ə-ree), *vb.* [Latin] **1.** To buy back; repurchase. **2.** To obtain the release of by payment; ransom.

redirect examination. A second direct examination, after cross-examination, the scope ordinarily being limited to matters covered during cross-examination. — Often shortened to *redirect.* — Also termed (in England) *reexamination.* See DIRECT EXAMINATION.

rediscount, *n.* **1.** The act or process of discounting a negotiable instrument that has already been discounted, as by a bank. **2.** (*usu. pl.*) A negotiable instrument that has been discounted a second time. — **rediscount,** *vb.* See DISCOUNT.

rediscount rate. See INTEREST RATE.

redisseisin (ree-dis-**see**-zin), *n.* **1.** A disseisin by one who has already dispossessed the same person of the same estate. **2.** A writ to recover an estate that has been dispossessed by redisseisin. — Also spelled *redisseizin.* — **redisseise** (ree-dis-**seez**), *vb.* See DISSEISIN.

redisseisina. See DE REDISSEISINA.

redistribution. The act or process of distributing something again or anew <redistribution of wealth>.

redistrict, *vb.* To organize into new districts, esp. legislative ones; reapportion.

redistricting. See REAPPORTIONMENT.

reditus (**red**-ə-təs), *n.* [Latin "return"] A revenue or return; esp., rent. — Also spelled *redditus.*

reditus albi (**al**-bɪ). [Latin "white return"] Rent payable in silver or other money.

reditus capitales (kap-ə-**tay**-leez). [Latin "capital return"] Chief rent paid by a freeholder to go quit of all other services. See QUIT RENT.

reditus nigri (**nig**-rɪ). [Latin "black return"] Rent payable in goods or labor rather than in money.

reditus quieti (kwɪ-**ee**-tɪ). [Latin "quiet return"] See QUIT RENT.

reditus siccus (**sik**-əs). [Latin "dry return"] Rent seck. See *rent seck* under RENT (2).

redlining, *n.* **1.** Credit discrimination (usu. unlawful discrimination) by a financial institution that refuses to make loans on properties in allegedly bad neighborhoods. **2.** The process of creating a new draft of a document showing suggested revisions explicitly alongside the text of an earlier version. — **redline,** *vb.*

redraft, *n.* A second negotiable instrument offered by the drawer after the first instrument has been dishonored. — **redraft,** *vb.*

redress (ri-**dres** *or* **ree**-dres), *n.* **1.** Relief; remedy <money damages, as opposed to equitable relief, is the only redress available>. **2.** A means of seeking relief or remedy <if the statute of limitations has run, the plaintiff is without redress>. — **redress** (ri-**dres**), *vb.* — **redressable,** *adj.*

penal redress. A form of penal liability requiring full compensation of the injured person as an instrument for punishing the offender; compensation paid to the injured person for the full value of the loss (an amount that may far exceed the wrongdoer's benefit). See RESTITUTION (3).

restitutionary redress. Compensation paid to one who has been injured, the amount being the pecuniary value of the benefit to the wrongdoer. See RESTITUTION (2).

red tape. A bureaucratic procedure required to be followed before official action can be taken; esp., rigid adherence to time-consuming rules and regulations; excessive bureaucracy. • The phrase originally referred to the red ribbons that lawyers and government officials once used to tie their papers together.

reductio ad absurdum (ri-**dək**-shee-oh *or* ri-**dək**-tee-oh ad ab-**sər**-dəm). [Latin "reduction to the absurd"] In logic, disproof of an argument by showing that it leads to a ridiculous conclusion.

reduction to practice. *Patents.* The physical act of producing the desired results by means conceived by an inventor; the physical construction of an inventor's conception into actual working form. • The date of reduction to practice is critical in determining priority between inventors competing for a patent on the same invention. See INVENTION.

actual reduction to practice. The use of an idea or invention — as by testing it — to establish that the idea or invention will perform its intended purpose. *Brunswick Corp. v. United States*, 34 Fed. Cl. 532 (1995).

constructive reduction to practice. Filing a patent application on an invention or design. *Brunswick Corp. v. United States*, 34 Fed. Cl. 532 (1995).

reenactment rule. In statutory construction, the principle that when reenacting a law, the legislature implicitly adopts well-settled judicial or administrative interpretations of the law.

reentry, *n.* **1.** The act or an instance of retaking possession of land by someone who formerly held the land and who reserved the right to retake it when the new holder let it go. **2.** A landlord's resumption of possession of leased premises upon the tenant's default under the lease. — **reenter,** *vb.* See POWER OF TERMINATION.

reeve (reev). *Hist.* **1.** A ministerial officer of high rank having local jurisdiction; the chief magistrate of a hundred. • The reeve executed process, kept the peace, and enforced the law by holding court within the hundred. **2.** A minor officer serving the Crown at the hundred level; a bailiff or deputy-sheriff. **3.** An overseer of a manor, parish, or the like. — Also spelled *reve.* — Also termed *greve.*

> "All the freeholders, unless relieved by special exemption, 'owed suit' at the hundred-moot, and the reeve of the hundred presided over it. In Anglo-Saxon times, the reeve was an independent official, and the hundred-moot was not a preliminary stage to the shire-moot at all.... But after the Conquest the hundred assembly, now called a court as all the others were, lost its importance very quickly. Pleas of land were taken from it, and its criminal jurisdiction limited to one of holding suspects in temporary detention. The reeve of the hundred became the deputy of the sheriff, and the chief purpose of holding the hundred court was to enable the sheriff to hold his *tourn* and to permit a 'view of frankpledge,' i.e., an inspection of the person who ought to belong to the frankpledge system." Max Radin, *Handbook of Anglo-American Legal History* 174–75 (1936).

shire-reeve. The reeve of a shire. • The *shire-reeve* was a forerunner of the sheriff. — Also spelled *shire-reve.* — Also termed *shire-gerefa.*

reexamination, *n.* **1.** REDIRECT EXAMINATION <the attorney focused on the defendant's alibi during reexamination>. **2.** *Patents.* A procedure whereby a party can seek review of a patent on the basis of additional references to prior art not originally considered by the U.S. Patent Office <the alleged infringer, hoping to avoid liability, sought reexamination of the patent to narrow its scope>. — **reexamine,** *vb.*

reexchange, *n.* **1.** A second or new exchange. **2.** The process of recovering the expenses that resulted from the dishonor of a bill of exchange in a foreign country. **3.** The expenses themselves.

reexecution. The equitable remedy by which a lost or destroyed deed or other instrument is restored. • Equity compels the party or parties to execute a new deed or instrument if a claimant properly proves a right under one that has been lost or destroyed.

reexport, *n.* **1.** The act of exporting again something imported. **2.** A good or commodity that is exported again. — **reexport,** *vb.*

reextent. *Hist.* A second extent made upon complaint that the earlier extent was improper. See EXTENT.

re. fa. lo. *abbr.* RECORDARI FACIAS LOQUELAM.

refare (ri-**fair**-ee), *vb.* [Latin] To bereave; rob; take away.

refection. *Civil law.* Repair or restoration, as of a building.

referee. A type of master appointed by a court to assist with certain proceedings. • In some jurisdictions, referees take testimony before reporting to the court. See MASTER (2).

referee in bankruptcy. A federal judicial officer who administers bankruptcy proceedings. • Abolished by the Bankruptcy Reform Act of 1978, these referees were replaced by bankruptcy judges. — Also termed *register in bankruptcy.* See BANKRUPTCY JUDGE.

reference, *n.* **1.** The act of sending or directing to another for information, service, consideration, or decision; specif., the act of sending a case to a master or referee for information or decision.

general reference. A court's reference of a case to a referee, usu. with all parties' consent, to decide all issues of fact and law. • The referee's decision stands as the judgment of the court.

special reference. A court's reference of a case to a referee for decisions on specific questions of fact. • The special referee makes findings and reports them to the trial judge, who treats them as advisory only and not as binding decisions.

2. An order sending a case to a master or referee for information or decision. **3.** Mention or citation of one document or source in another document or source. — **refer,** *vb.*

reference statute. See STATUTE.

referendarius (ref-ə-ren-**dair**-ee-əs). [Law Latin] *Roman law.* An officer who received petitions to the emperor and who delivered answers to the petitioners. See APOCRISARIUS.

referendo singula singulis. See REDDENDO SINGULA SINGULIS.

referendum. 1. The process of referring a state legislative act, a state constitutional amendment, or an important public issue to the people for final approval by popular vote. **2.** A vote taken by this method. Pl. **referendums, referenda.** Cf. INITIATIVE.

referral. The act or an instance of sending or directing to another for information, service, consideration, or decision <referral of the client to an employment-law specialist> <referral of the question to the board of directors>.

referral sales contract. A dual agreement consisting of an agreement by the consumer to purchase goods or services (usu. at an inflated price) and an agreement by the seller to compensate the consumer for each customer (or potential customer) referred to the seller. — Also termed *referral sales agreement.*

> "The problem inherent in a referral sales contract is the problem inherent in a chain letter — the success of the arrangement depends on an inexhaustible supply of customers. For example, if each buyer submits 25 names and each of these 'referrals' becomes a buyer under a similar agreement, the completion of the seventh round of referrals requires 6.1 trillion persons.... Both courts and legislatures have acted against referral sales.... The Uniform Consumer Credit Code prohibits the use of referral sales schemes in which the rebate is conditioned on 'the occurrence of an event after the time the consumer agrees to buy or lease.' In other words, a referral scheme keyed to the consumer merely furnishing names is not affected; a referral scheme keyed to the consumer furnishing names of people who actually become customers is prohibited." David G. Epstein & Steve H. Nickles, *Consumer Law in a Nutshell* 39 (2d ed. 1981).

refinancing, *n.* An exchange of an old debt for a new debt, as by negotiating a different interest rate or term or by repaying the existing loan with money acquired from a new loan. — **refinance,** *vb.*

reformation (ref-ər-**may**-shən), *n.* An equitable remedy by which a court will modify a written agreement to reflect the actual intent of the parties, usu. to correct fraud or mutual mistake, such as an incomplete property description in a deed. • The actual intended agreement usu. must be established by clear and convincing evidence. — **reform,** *vb.* See RECTIFICATION.

reformative punishment. See PUNISHMENT.

reformatory, *n.* A penal institution for young offenders, esp. minors. — Also termed *reform school.*

refoulement (ri-**fowl**-mənt). [French] Expulsion or return of a refugee from one state to another. Cf. NONREFOULEMENT.

refreshing recollection. See PRESENT RECOLLECTION REFRESHED.

refugee. A person who flees or is expelled from a country, esp. because of persecution, and seeks haven in another country.

refund, *n.* **1.** The return of money to a person who overpaid, such as a taxpayer who overestimated tax liability or whose employer withheld too much tax from earnings. **2.** The money returned to a person who overpaid. **3.** The act of refinancing, esp. by replacing outstanding securities with a new issue of securities. — **refund,** *vb.*

refund annuity. See ANNUITY.

refunding. See FUNDING.

refunding bond. See BOND (2).

re-funding bond. See BOND (3).

refusal. 1. The denial or rejection of something offered or demanded <the lawyer's refusal to answer questions was based on the attorney-client privilege>. **2.** An opportunity to accept or reject something before it is offered to others; the right or privilege of having this opportunity <she promised her friend the first refusal on her house>. See RIGHT OF FIRST REFUSAL.

refusal to deal. A company's declination to do business with another company. • A business has the right to refuse to deal only if it is not accompanied by an illegal restraint of trade.

refusal to pay. See VEXATIOUS DELAY.

refus de justice (ruu-**foo** də zhoos-**tees**). See DENIAL OF JUSTICE.

refutantia (ref-yoo-**tan**-shee-ə), *n.* [Law Latin] *Hist.* An acquittance or an acknowledgment renouncing all future claims.

refute, *vb.* **1.** To prove (a statement) to be false. **2.** To prove (a person) to be wrong. Cf. REBUTTAL.

Reg. *abbr.* **1.** REGULATION. **2.** REGISTER.

reg, *n.* (*usu. pl.*) REGULATION (3) <review not only the tax code but also the accompanying regs>.

regale episcoporum (ri-**gay**-lee ə-pis-kə-**por**-əm). *Eccles. law.* The temporal rights and privileges of a bishop.

regalia (ri-**gay**-lee-ə). **1.** *Hist.* Rights held by the Crown under feudal law. • *Regalia* is a shortened form of *jura regalia.*

regalia majora (mə-**jor**-ə). [Latin "greater rights"] The Crown's greater rights; the Crown's dignity, power, and royal prerogatives, as distinguished from the Crown's rights to revenues.

regalia minora (mi-**nor**-ə). [Latin "lesser rights"] The Crown's lesser rights; the Crown's lesser prerogatives (such as the rights of revenue), as distinguished from its royal prerogatives.

2. *Hist.* Feudal rights usu. associated with royalty, but held by the nobility.

> "Counties palatine are so called *a palatio*; because the owners thereof, the earl of Chester, the bishop of Durham, and the duke of Lancaster, had in those counties *jura regalia*, as fully as the king hath in his palace. . . ." 1 William Blackstone, *Commentaries on the Laws of England* 113 (1765).

3. Emblems of royal authority, such as a crown or scepter, given to the monarch at coronation. **4.** Loosely, finery or special dress.

regard, *n.* **1.** Attention, care, or consideration <without regard for the consequences>. **2.** *Hist.* In England, an official inspection of a forest to determine whether any trespasses have been committed. **3.** *Hist.* The office or position of a person appointed to make such an inspection.

regardant (ri-**gahr**-dənt), *adj. Hist.* Attached or annexed to a particular manor <a villein regardant>. See VILLEIN.

regarder. An official who inspects a forest to determine whether any trespasses have been committed. — Also termed *regarder of the forest.*

reg. brev. *abbr.* REGISTRUM BREVIUM.

rege inconsulto (**ree**-jee in-kən-**səl**-toh). [Latin] *Hist.* A writ issued by a sovereign directing one or more judges not to proceed in a case that might prejudice the Crown until advised to do so.

regency. 1. The office or jurisdiction of a regent or body of regents. **2.** A government or authority by regents. **3.** The period during which a regent or body of regents governs.

regent. 1. A person who exercises the ruling power in a kingdom during the minority, absence, or other disability of the sovereign. **2.** A governor or ruler. **3.** A member of the governing board of an academic institution, esp. a state university. **4.** *Eccles. law.* A master or professor of a college.

reg. gen. *abbr.* REGULA GENERALIS.

regicide (**rej**-ə-sɪd). **1.** The killing or murder of a king. **2.** One who kills or murders a king, esp. to whom one is subject.

regime (rə-**zheem** *or* ray-**zheem**). A system of rules, regulations, or government <the community-property regime>. — Also spelled *régime.*

international regime. A set of norms of behavior and rules and policies that cover international issues and that facilitate substantive or procedural arrangements among countries.

legal regime. A set of rules, policies, and norms of behavior that cover any legal issue and that facilitate substantive or procedural arrangements for deciding that issue.

régime dotal (ray-**zheem** doh-**tahl**). *Hist. civil law.* The right and power of a husband to administer his wife's dotal property, the property being returned to the wife when the marriage is dissolved by death or divorce. See DOTAL PROPERTY.

régime en communauté (ray-**zheem** on koh-moo-noh-**tay** *or* kom-yoo-). *Hist. civil law.* The community of property between husband and wife arising automatically upon their marriage, unless excluded by marriage contract.

regina (ri-**jI**-nə). (*usu. cap.*) **1.** A queen. **2.** The official title of a queen. **3.** The prosecution side (as representatives of the queen) in criminal proceedings in a monarchy. — Abbr. R. Cf. REX.

regio assensu (**ree**-jee-oh ə-**sen**-s[y]oo). [Latin] *Eccles. law.* A writ by which a sovereign assents to the election of a bishop.

regional securities exchange. See SECURITIES EXCHANGE.

register, *n.* **1.** A governmental officer who keeps official records <each county employs a register of deeds and wills>. Cf. REGISTRAR.

probate register. One who serves as the clerk of a probate court and, in some jurisdictions, as a quasi-judicial officer in probating estates.

2. PROBATE JUDGE. **3.** A book in which all docket entries are kept for the various cases pending in a court. — Also termed *register of actions.* **4.** An official record or list, such as a corporation's list of the names and addresses of its shareholders. — Abbr. Reg. — Also termed *registry.*

register, *vb.* **1.** To enter in a public registry <register a new car>. **2.** To enroll formally <five voters registered yesterday>. **3.** To make a record of <counsel registered three objections>. **4.** (Of a lawyer, party, or witness) to check in with the clerk of court before a judicial proceeding <please register at the clerk's office before entering the courtroom>. **5.** To file (a new security issue) with the Securities and Exchange Commission or a similar state agency <the company hopes to register its securities before the end of the year>.

registered agent. See AGENT.

registered bond. See BOND (2), (3).

registered broker. See BROKER.

registered check. See CHECK.

registered corporation. See CORPORATION.

registered dealer. See DEALER.

registered mail. See MAIL.

registered offering. See OFFERING.

registered organization. An organization created under state or federal law, for which the state or federal government must maintain a public record showing that the organization has been duly organized. UCC § 9–102(a)(47).

registered public offering. See *registered offering* under OFFERING.

registered representative. See REPRESENTATIVE.

registered security. See SECURITY.

registered stock. See *registered security* under SECURITY.

registered tonnage. See REGISTER TONNAGE.

registered trademark. See TRADEMARK.

registered voter. A person who is qualified to vote and whose name is recorded in the voting district where he or she resides.

register in bankruptcy. See REFEREE IN BANKRUPTCY.

register of actions. See REGISTER.

Register of Copyrights. The federal official who is in charge of the U.S. Copyright Office, which issues regulations and processes applications for copyright registration. — Also termed (erroneously) *Registrar of Copyrights.*

register of deeds. A public official who records deeds, mortgages, and other instruments affecting real property. — Also termed *registrar of deeds*; *recorder of deeds.*

register of land office. *Hist.* A federal officer appointed for each federal land district to take charge of the local records and to administer the sale, preemption, or other disposition of public lands within the district.

register of ships. *Maritime law.* A record kept by a customs collector containing the names and owners of commercial vessels and other key information about the vessels. ● When a ship logs in with customs, it receives a certificate of registry. Cf. REGISTRY (2).

Register of the Treasury. An officer of the U.S. Treasury whose duty is to keep accounts of receipts and expenditures of public money, to record public debts, to preserve adjusted accounts with vouchers and certificates, to record warrants drawn on the Treasury, to sign and issue government securities, and to supervise the registry of vessels under federal law. 31 USCA § 161.

register of wills. A public official who records probated wills, issues letters testamentary and letters of administration, and serves generally as clerk of the probate court. • The register of wills exists only in some states.

register's court. *Hist.* A probate court in Pennsylvania. See *probate court* under COURT.

register tonnage. The volume of a vessel available for commercial use, officially measured and entered in a record for purposes of taxation. — Also termed *registered tonnage*.

registrant. One who registers; esp., one who registers something for the purpose of securing a right or privilege granted by law upon official registration.

registrar. A person who keeps official records; esp., a school official who maintains academic and enrollment records. Cf. REGISTER (1).

registrarii liber (rej-ə-**strair**-ee-I **lI**-bər). [Latin] *Hist.* The register's book in chancery, containing all decrees. — Abbr. *reg. lib.*

registrarius (rej-ə-**strair**-ee-əs). [Latin] *Hist.* A registrar or register; a notary.

Registrar of Copyrights. See REGISTER OF COPYRIGHTS.

registrar of deeds. See REGISTER OF DEEDS.

registration, *n.* **1.** The act of recording or enrolling <the county clerk handles registration of voters>.

criminal registration. The requirement in some communities that any felon who spends any time in the community must register his or her name with the police.

special registration. Voter registration for a particular election only.

2. *Securities.* The complete process of preparing to sell a newly issued security to the public <the security is currently in registration>. — **register,** *vb.*

shelf registration. Registration with the SEC of securities to be sold over time, the purpose being to avoid the delays and market uncertainties of individual registration.

> "It is generally contemplated that the entire allotment of securities covered by a registered offering will be made available for purchase on the effective date. This is not always the case, however. For example, insiders, promoters or underwriters might receive securities directly from the issuer with an intent to resell at a later date. . . . [I]t may be desirable to get a debt offering all ready to go but wait for a propitious moment to release it. These and other delayed offerings have led to what is known as shelf registration. In a shelf registration the registration statement is filed but the securities are put on the shelf until the manner and date of the offering are determined." Thomas Lee Hazen, *The Law of Securities Regulation* § 3.8, at 119 (2d ed. 1994).

registration statement. A document containing detailed information required by the SEC for the public sale of corporate securities. • The statement includes the prospectus to be supplied to prospective buyers. See PROSPECTUS.

registrum brevium (ri-**jis**-trəm **bree**-vee-əm). [Latin] *Hist.* The register of writs. — Abbr. *reg. brev.*

registrum judicale (ri-**jis**-trəm joo-di-**kay**-lee). [Latin] *Hist.* The register of judicial writs. — Abbr. *reg. jud.*

registrum originale (ri-**jis**-trəm ə-rij-ə-**nay**-lee). [Latin] *Hist.* The register of original writs. — Abbr. *reg. orig.*

registry. 1. REGISTER (2). **2.** *Maritime law.* The list or record of ships subject to a particular country's maritime regulations. • A ship is listed under the nationality of the flag it flies. See CERTIFICATE OF REGISTRY. Cf. REGISTER OF SHIPS; *enrollment of vessels* under ENROLLMENT.

reg. jud. *abbr.* REGISTRUM JUDICALE.

reg. lib. *abbr.* REGISTRARII LIBER.

regnal (**reg**-nəl), *adj.* Of or relating to a monarch's reign <Queen Elizabeth II is in her forty-seventh regnal year since her accession to the throne in 1952>.

regnal year. A year of a monarch's reign, marked from the date or anniversary of the monarch's accession. • Before 1962, British statutes were cited by the regnal years in which they were enacted. Since 1962, British statutes have been cited by calendar year rather than regnal year. (A table of British regnal years is listed in Appendix F of this book.)

regnant (**reg**-nənt), *adj*. Exercising rule, authority, or influence; reigning <a queen regnant>.

reg. orig. *abbr*. REGISTRUM ORIGINALE.

reg. pl. *abbr*. REGULA PLACITANDI.

regrant, *n*. The act or an instance of granting something again; the renewal of a grant (as of property). — **regrant,** *vb*.

regrating, *n*. *Hist*. **1.** The purchase of market commodities (esp. necessary provisions) for the purpose of reselling them in or near the same market at a higher price. **2.** The resale of commodities so purchased. • In England, regrating was a criminal offense. — **regrate,** *vb*.

> "Regrating is described by [5 & 6 Edw. 6, ch. 14] to be the buying of corn, or other dead victual, in any market, and selling them again in the same market, or within four miles of the place. For this also enhances the price of the provisions, as every successive seller must have a successive profit." 4 William Blackstone, *Commentaries on the Laws of England* 158 (1769).

regress, *n*. **1.** The act or an instance of going or coming back; return or reentry <free entry, egress, and regress>. **2.** The right or liberty of going back; reentry. Cf. EGRESS; INGRESS. **3.** *Hist*. The right to repayment or compensation; recourse. — **regress** (ri-**gres**), *vb*.

regressive tax. See TAX.

regula (**reg**-yə-lə). [Latin] A rule.

regula catoniana (**reg**-yə-lə kay-toh-nee-**ay**-nə *or* kə-toh-). [Latin "rule of Cato"] *Roman law*. The principle that the lapse of time will not cure something void at the outset. • The *regula catoniana*, named for the Roman legal scholar Cato, was usu. used to set aside a bequest in which the testator did not have the power or capacity to make the bequest.

regula generalis (**reg**-yə-lə jen-ə-**ray**-lis). [Latin] A general rule, esp. of a court. — Abbr. *reg. gen.*; r.g. Pl. ***regulae generales.***

regula placitandi (**reg**-yə-lə plas-ə-**tan**-dɪ). [Latin] *Hist*. A rule of pleading. — Abbr. *reg. pl.*

regular army. See ARMY.

regular course of business. See COURSE OF BUSINESS.

regular election. See *general election* under ELECTION.

regular income. See INCOME.

regular life policy. See *life policy* under INSURANCE POLICY.

regular meeting. See *annual meeting* under MEETING.

regular process. See PROCESS.

regular session. See SESSION.

regular term. See TERM (5).

regular use. See USE (1).

regulation, *n*. **1.** The act or process of controlling by rule or restriction <the federal regulation of the airline industry>. **2.** BYLAW (1) <the CEO referred to the corporate regulation>. **3.** A rule or order, having legal force, issued by an administrative agency or a local government <Treasury regulations explain and interpret the Internal Revenue Code>. — Also termed (in sense 3) *agency regulation*; *subordinate legislation*; *delegated legislation*. — Often shortened to *reg*; *Reg*. — **regulate,** *vb*. — **regulatory, regulable,** *adj*. See MERIT REGULATION.

Regulation A. An SEC regulation that exempts stock offerings of up to $5 million from certain registration requirements.

Regulation D. An SEC regulation that exempts certain stock offerings (such as those offered by private sale) from registration under the Securities Act of 1933.

Regulation J. A Federal Reserve Board regulation that governs the collection of checks by and the transfer of funds through member banks.

Regulation Q. A Federal Reserve Board regulation that sets interest-rate ceilings and regulates advertising of interest on savings accounts. • This regulation, which applies to all commercial banks, was created by the Banking Act of 1933.

Regulation T. A Federal Reserve Board regulation that limits the amount of credit that a securities broker or dealer may extend to a customer, and that sets initial margin requirements and payment rules for securities transactions. • The credit limit and margin rules usu. require the customer to provide between 40 and 60% of the purchase price.

Regulation U. A Federal Reserve Board regulation that limits the amount of credit that a bank may extend to a customer who buys or carries securities on margin.

Regulation X. A HUD regulation that implements the provisions of the Real Estate Settlement Procedures Act. See REAL ESTATE SETTLEMENT PROCEDURES ACT.

Regulation Z. A Federal Reserve Board regulation that implements the provisions of the federal Consumer Credit Protection Act for member banks. See CONSUMER CREDIT PROTECTION ACT.

regulatory agency. See AGENCY (3).

regulatory offense. See OFFENSE (1).

regulatory search. See *administrative search* under SEARCH.

rehabilitation, *n.* **1.** *Criminal law.* The process of seeking to improve a criminal's character and outlook so that he or she can function in society without committing other crimes <rehabilitation is a traditional theory of criminal punishment, along with deterrence and retribution>. Cf. DETERRENCE; RETRIBUTION (1). **2.** *Evidence.* The restoration of a witness's credibility after the witness has been impeached <the inconsistencies were explained away during the prosecution's rehabilitation of the witness>. **3.** *Bankruptcy.* The process of reorganizing a debtor's financial affairs — under Chapter 11, 12, or 13 of the Bankruptcy Code — so that the debtor may continue to exist as a financial entity, with creditors satisfying their claims from the debtor's future earnings <the corporation's rehabilitation was successful>. — Also termed *debtor rehabilitation.* Cf. LIQUIDATION (4). — **rehabilitate,** *vb.* — **rehabilitative,** *adj.*

rehabilitative alimony. See ALIMONY.

rehearing. A second or subsequent hearing of a case or an appeal, usu. held to consider an error or omission in the first hearing <the appellant, dissatisfied with the appellate court's ruling, filed a petition for rehearing>. — Abbr. reh'g. Cf. REARGUMENT.

reh'g. *abbr.* REHEARING.

rei (**ree**-ɪ). *pl.* REUS.

reif (reef). *Scots law.* Robbery.

reification (ree-ə-fi-**kay**-shən), *n.* **1.** Mental conversion of an abstract concept into a material thing. **2.** *Civil procedure.* Identification of the disputed thing in a nonpersonal action and attribution of an in-state situs to it for jurisdictional purposes. **3.** *Commercial law.* Embodiment of a right to payment in a writing (such as a negotiable instrument) so that a transfer of the writing also transfers the right. — **reify** (**ree**-ə-fɪ *or* **ray**-), *vb.*

rei interventus (**ree**-ɪ in-tər-**ven**-təs), *n.* [Latin "things intervening"] Actions or efforts by one party to a contract with the consent of the other party, so that the one party has made a partial performance and the other cannot repudiate without being in breach.

reimbursement, *n.* **1.** Repayment. **2.** Indemnification. — **reimburse,** *vb.*

reimbursement alimony. See ALIMONY.

reinscription, *n.* *Civil law.* A second or renewed recordation of a mortgage or other title document. — **reinscribe,** *vb.*

reinstate, *vb.* To place again in a former state or position; to restore <the judge reinstated the judgment that had been vacated>. — **reinstatement,** *n.*

reinsurance. Insurance of all or part of one insurer's risk by a second insurer, who accepts the risk in exchange for a percentage of the original premium. — Also termed *reassurance.*

> "The term 'reinsurance' has been used by courts, attorneys, and textwriters with so little discrimination that much confusion has arisen as to what that term actually connotes. Thus, it has so often been used in connection with transferred risks, assumed risks, consolidations and mergers, excess insurance, and in other connections that it now lacks a clean-cut field of operation. Reinsurance, to an insurance lawyer, means one thing only — the ceding by one insurance company to another of all or a portion of its risks for a stipulated portion of the premium, in which the liability of the reinsurer is solely to the reinsured, which is the ceding company, and in which contract the ceding company retains all contact with the

original insured, and handles all matters prior to and subsequent to loss." 13A John Alan Appleman & Jean Appleman, *Insurance Law and Practice* § 7681, at 479–80 (1976).

excess reinsurance. Reinsurance in which a reinsurer assumes liability only for an amount of insurance that exceeds a specified sum. See *excess insurance* under INSURANCE.

facultative reinsurance. Reinsurance of an individual risk at the option (the "faculty") of the reinsurer.

flat reinsurance. Reinsurance (esp. of marine insurance) that cannot be canceled or modified.

treaty reinsurance. Reinsurance under a broad agreement of all risks in a given class as soon as they are insured by the direct insurer.

reinsurance treaty. A contract of reinsurance (usu. long-term) covering different classes or lines of business of the reinsured (such as professional liability, property, etc.) and obligating the reinsurer in advance to accept the cession of covered risks. • Rather than receive individual notice of each specific claim covered, the treaty reinsurer will generally receive periodic reports providing basic information on the losses paid. — Also termed *treaty of reinsurance*. See BORDEREAU. Cf. FACULTATIVE CERTIFICATE.

reinsured, *n.* An insurer that transfers all or part of a risk it underwrites to a reinsurer, usu. along with a percentage of the original premium. — Also termed *cedent*; *cedant*.

reinsurer. An insurer that assumes all or part of a risk underwritten by another insurer, usu. in exchange for a percentage of the original premium.

reinvestment. 1. The addition of interest earned on a monetary investment to the principal sum. **2.** A second, additional, or repeated investment; esp., the application of dividends or other distributions toward the purchase of additional shares (as of a stock or a mutual fund).

reissuable note. See NOTE (1).

reissue. 1. An abstractor's certificate certifying to the correctness of an abstract. • A reissue is an important precaution when the abstract comprises an original abstract brought down to a certain date and then several continuations or extensions showing matters that have occurred since the date of the original abstract. **2.** See *reissue patent* under PATENT (3).

reissue patent. See PATENT (3).

REIT (reet). *abbr.* REAL-ESTATE INVESTMENT TRUST.

rejection. 1. A refusal to accept a contractual offer. **2.** A refusal to accept tendered goods as contractual performance. • Under the UCC, a buyer's rejection of nonperforming goods must be made within a reasonable time after tender or delivery, and notice of the rejection must be given to the seller. — **reject,** *vb.* Cf. REPUDIATION; RESCISSION; REVOCATION.

rejoinder, *n. Common-law pleading.* The defendant's answer to the plaintiff's reply (or replication). — **rejoin,** *vb.*

related good. *Trademarks.* A good that infringes a trademark because it appears to come from the same source as the marked good, despite not competing with the marked good. • For example, a cutting tool named "McKnife" might infringe the "McDonald's" trademark as a related good.

related proceeding. *Bankruptcy.* A proceeding that involves a claim that will affect the administration of the debtor's estate (such as a tort action between the debtor and a third party), but that does not arise under bankruptcy law and could be adjudicated in a state court. • A related proceeding must be adjudicated in federal district court unless the parties consent to bankruptcy-court jurisdiction or unless the district court refers the matter to the bankruptcy court or to state court. — Also termed *noncore proceeding*. Cf. CORE PROCEEDING.

relation back, *n.* **1.** The doctrine that an act done at a later time is considered to have occurred at an earlier time. • For example, in federal civil procedure, an amended pleading relates back, for purposes of the statute of limitations, to the time when the original pleading was filed. Fed. R. Civ. P. 15(c). **2.** A judicial application of that doctrine. — **relate back,** *vb.*

relative, *n.* A person connected with another by blood or affinity; a kinsman.

collateral relative. A relative who is not in the direct line of inheritance, such as a cousin.

relative-convenience doctrine. The principle that an injunction or other equitable relief may be denied if it would cause one party great inconvenience but the other party little or no inconvenience.

relative fact. See FACT.

relative nullity. See NULLITY.

relative power. See POWER.

relative right. See RIGHT.

relator. **1.** The real party in interest in whose name a state or an attorney general brings a lawsuit. See EX REL. **2.** The applicant for a writ, esp. a writ of mandamus, prohibition, or quo warranto. **3.** A person who furnishes information on which a civil or criminal case is based; an informer.

relatrix (ri-**lay**-triks). *Archaic.* A female relator.

relaxatio (ree-lak-**say**-shee-oh). [Law Latin] *Hist.* An instrument by which one relinquishes a right or claim to another; a release.

release, *n.* **1.** Liberation from an obligation, duty, or demand; the act of giving up a right or claim to the person against whom it could have been enforced <the employee asked for a release from the noncompete agreement>. — Also termed *discharge*; *surrender*. **2.** The relinquishment or concession of a right, title, or claim. **3.** A written discharge, acquittance, or receipt <Jones signed the release before accepting the cash from Hawkins>. **4.** A written authorization or permission for publication <the newspaper obtained a release from the witness before printing his picture on the front page>. **5.** The act of conveying an estate or right to another, or of legally disposing of it <the release of the easement on February 14>. **6.** A deed or document effecting a conveyance <the legal description in the release was defective>. See *deed of release* under DEED. **7.** The action of freeing or the fact of being freed from restraint or confinement <he became a model citizen after his release from prison>. **8.** A document giving formal discharge from custody <after the sheriff signed the release, the prisoner was free to go>. — **release,** *vb.*

conditional release. **1.** A discharge from an obligation based on some condition, the failure of which defeats the release. **2.** An early discharge of a prison inmate, who is then subject to the rules and regulations of parole.

partial release. A release of a portion of a creditor's claims against property; esp., a mortgagee's release of specified parcels covered by a blanket mortgage.

release clause. *Real estate.* **1.** A blanket-mortgage provision that enables the mortgagor to obtain a partial release of a specific parcel of land from the mortgage upon paying more than the pro rata portion of the loan. • Mortgagees commonly include a clause that disallows a partial release if the mortgagor is in default on any part of the mortgage. **2.** A purchase-agreement provision that allows a seller who has accepted an offer containing a contingency to continue to market the property and accept other offers. • If the seller accepts another buyer's offer, the original buyer typically has a specified time (such as 72 hours) to waive the contingency (such as the sale of the buyer's present house) or to release the seller from the agreement.

releasee. **1.** One who is released, either physically or by contractual discharge. **2.** One to whom an estate is released.

release of mortgage. A written document that discharges a mortgage upon full payment by the borrower and that is publicly recorded to show that the borrower has full equity in the property.

release on recognizance. The pretrial release of an arrested person who promises, usu. in writing but without supplying a surety or posting bond, to appear for trial at a later date. — Also termed *release on own recognizance*. — Abbr. ROR.

release to uses. Conveyance of property, by deed of release, by one party to a second party for the use of the first party or a third party. See *deed of release* under DEED; STATUTE OF USES.

releasor. One who releases property or a claim to another. — Also spelled *releaser*.

relegatio (rel-ə-**gay**-shee-oh), *n.* [fr. Latin *relegare* "to send away"] *Roman law.* Temporary or permanent banishment of a citizen or condemned criminal without the full loss of the person's civil rights or property. Cf. DEPORTATIO.

> "Relegatio. The expulsion of a citizen ordered either by an administrative act of a magistrate or by judgment in a criminal trial. In the latter case the *relegatio* was sometimes combined with additional punishments, such as confiscation of the whole or of a part of the property of the condemned person, loss of Roman citizenship, con-

finement in a certain place. A milder form of *relegatio* was the exclusion of the wrongdoer from residence in a specified territory. Illicit return was punished with the death penalty." Adolf Berger, *Encyclopedic Dictionary of Roman Law* 673 (1953).

relegation, *n.* **1.** Banishment or exile, esp. a temporary one. **2.** Assignment or delegation. — **relegate,** *vb.*

relevance. The fact, quality, or state of being relevant; relation or pertinence to the issue at hand. — Also termed *relevancy.*

relevancy. See RELEVANCE.

relevant, *adj.* Logically connected and tending to prove or disprove a matter in issue; having appreciable probative value — that is, rationally tending to persuade people of the probability or possibility of some alleged fact. Cf. MATERIAL.

"The word 'relevant' means that any two facts to which it is applied are so related to each other that according to the common course of events one either taken by itself or in connection with other facts proves or renders probable the past, present, or future existence or non-existence of the other." James Fitzjames Stephen, *A Digest of the Law of Evidence* 2 (4th ed. 1881).

relevant art. See ART.

relevant evidence. See EVIDENCE.

relevant market. See MARKET.

reliance, *n.* Dependence or trust by a person, esp. when combined with action based on that dependence or trust. — **rely,** *vb.*

detrimental reliance. Reliance by one party on the acts or representations of another, causing a worsening of the first party's position. • Detrimental reliance may serve as a substitute for consideration and thus make a promise enforceable as a contract. See *promissory estoppel* under ESTOPPEL.

reliance damages. See DAMAGES.

reliance interest. See INTEREST (2).

reliance-loss damages. See DAMAGES.

relict (**rel**-ikt). A widow.

relicta verificatione (ri-**lik**-tə ver-ə-fi-kay-shee-**oh**-nee). [Latin "his pleading being abandoned"] *Hist.* A confession of judgment accompanied by a withdrawal of the plea. See COGNOVIT ACTIONEM.

reliction (ri-**lik**-shən). **1.** A process by which a river or stream shifts its location, causing the recession of water from its bank. **2.** The alteration of a boundary line because of the gradual removal of land by a river or stream. See ACCRETION; DERELICTION.

relief. 1. A payment made by an heir of a feudal tenant to the feudal lord for the privilege of succeeding to the ancestor's tenancy.

"A mesne lord could, upon the death of his tenant, accept the tenant's heir as tenant; but he was not required to do so. When he did accept his deceased tenant's heir as tenant, it was typically because the heir had paid the mesne lord a substantial sum (known as a *relief*) for the re-grant of the tenancy." Thomas F. Bergin & Paul G. Haskell, *Preface to Estates in Land and Future Interests* 8 (2d ed. 1984).

2. Aid or assistance given to those in need, esp., financial aid provided by the state. **3.** The redress or benefit, esp. equitable in nature (such as an injunction or specific performance), that a party asks of a court. — Also termed *remedy*. Cf. REMEDY.

affirmative relief. The relief sought by a defendant by raising a counterclaim or cross-claim that could have been maintained independently of the plaintiff's action.

alternative relief. Judicial relief that is mutually exclusive with another form of judicial relief. • In pleading, a party may request alternative relief, as by asking for both specific performance and damages. Fed. R. Civ. P. 8(a). Cf. ELECTION OF REMEDIES.

coercive relief. Active judicial relief, either legal or equitable, that the government will enforce.

interim relief. Relief that is granted on a preliminary basis before an order finally disposing of a request for relief.

therapeutic relief. The relief, esp. in a settlement, that requires the defendant to take remedial measures as opposed to paying damages. • An example is a defendant-corporation (in an employment-discrimination suit) that agrees to undergo sensitivity training. — Often shortened to *therapeutics*.

religion. A system of faith and worship usu. involving belief in a supreme being and usu. containing a moral or ethical code; esp., such a system recognized and practiced by a particular church, sect, or denomination. • In construing the protections under the Establishment Clause and the Free Exercise Clause, courts have interpreted the term *religion* quite broadly to include a wide variety of theistic and nontheistic beliefs.

religion, freedom of. See FREEDOM OF RELIGION.

Religion Clause. In the Bill of Rights, the provision stating that "Congress shall make no law respecting an establishment of religion or prohibiting the free exercise thereof." U.S. Const. amend. I.

religious corporation. See CORPORATION.

religious liberty. See LIBERTY.

relinquishment, *n.* The abandonment of a right or thing. — **relinquish,** *vb.*

reliqua (**rel**-ə-kwə). [Latin] *Civil law.* The remainder of a debt after balancing or liquidating an account; money left unpaid.

relitigate, *vb.* To litigate (a case or matter) again or anew <relitigate the issue in federal court>. — **relitigation,** *n.*

relocatio (ree-loh-**kay**-shee-oh). [Latin] *Civil law.* The renewal of a lease; RECONDUCTION (1).

relocation. 1. Removal and establishment of someone or something in a new place. **2.** *Mining law.* Appropriation of a new tract of land for a mining claim, as by an owner who wishes to change the boundaries of the original tract or by a stranger who wishes to claim an abandoned or forfeited tract. **3.** *Civil law.* RECONDUCTION (1). Cf. TACIT RELOCATION.

rem. See IN REM.

remainder. *Property.* **1.** A future interest arising in a third person — that is, someone other than the creator of the estate or the creator's heirs — who is intended to take after the natural termination of the preceding estate. • For example, if a grant is "to A for life, and then to B," B's future interest is a remainder. Cf. EXECUTORY INTEREST; REVERSION; POSSIBILITY OF REVERTER.

> "Whether a remainder is vested or contingent depends upon the language employed. If the conditional element is incorporated into the description of, or the gift to the remainder-man, then the remainder is contingent; but if, after words giving a vested interest, a clause is added divesting it, the remainder is vested. Thus, on a devise to A. for life, remainder to his children, but if any child dies in the lifetime of A. his share to go to those who survive, the share of each child is vested, subject to be divested by his death. But on a devise to A. for life, remainder to such of his children as survive him, the remainder is contingent." John Chipman Gray, *The Rule Against Perpetuities* 66 (1886).

2. The property in a decedent's estate that is not otherwise specifically devised or bequeathed in a will.

> "Under the names of 'remainders' and 'executory limitations,' various classes of interests in land could be created in expectancy, either at the Common Law or under the Statute of Uses. The differences between the two classes were highly technical; and the learning involved in acquiring a knowledge of the rules of determining them [is] quite out of proportion to the value obtained." Edward Jenks, *The Book of English Law* 263 (P.B. Fairest ed., 6th ed. 1967).

accelerated remainder. A remainder that has passed to the remainderman, as when the gift to the preceding beneficiary fails.

alternative remainder. A remainder in which the disposition of property is to take effect only if another disposition does not take effect.

charitable remainder. A remainder, usu. from a life estate, that is given to a charity; for example, "to Jane for life, and then to the American Red Cross."

contingent remainder. A remainder that is either given to an unascertained person or made subject to a condition precedent. • An example is "to A for life, and then, if B has married before A dies, to B." — Also termed *executory remainder*; *remainder subject to a condition precedent.*

> "Unlike a vested remainder, a contingent remainder is *either* subject to a condition precedent (in addition to the natural expiration of a prior estate), *or* owned by unascertainable persons, *or both.* But the contingent remainder, like the vested remainder, 'waits patiently' for possession. It is so created that it can become a present estate (if ever it does) immediately upon, and no sooner than, the natural expiration of particular estates that stand in front of it and were created simultaneously with it." Thomas F. Bergin & Paul G. Haskell, *Preface to Estates in Land and Future Interests* 73 (2d ed. 1984).

cross-remainder. A future interest that results when particular estates are given to two or more persons in different parcels of land, or in the same land in undivided shares, and the remainders of all the estates are made to vest in the survivor or survivors. • Two examples of devises giving rise to cross-remainders are (1) "to A and B for life, with the remainder to the survivor and her heirs," and (2) "Blackacre to A and Whiteacre to B, with the remainder of A's estate to B on A's failure of issue, and the remainder of B's estate to A on B's failure of issue." • If no tenants or issue survive, the remainder vests in a third party (sometimes known as the *ulterior remainderman*). Each tenant in common has a reciprocal, or *cross*, remainder in the share of the others. This type of remainder could not be created by deed unless expressly stated. It could, however, be implied in a will.

> "By a will also an estate may pass by mere implication, without any express words to direct its course.... So also, where a devise of black-acre to A and of white-acre to B in tail, and if they both die without issue, then to C in fee: here A and B have *cross remainders* by implication, and on the failure of either's issue, the other or his issue shall take the whole; and C's remainder over shall be postponed till the issue of both shall fail." 2 William Blackstone, *Commentaries on the Laws of England* 381 (1766).

defeasible remainder. A vested remainder that will be eliminated if a condition subsequent occurs. • An example is "to A for life, and then to B, but if B ever sells liquor on the land, then to C." — Also termed *remainder subject to divestment.*

executed remainder. See *vested remainder.*

executory remainder. See *contingent remainder.*

indefeasible remainder. A vested remainder that is not subject to a condition subsequent. — Also termed *indefeasibly vested remainder.*

remainder subject to a condition precedent. See *contingent remainder.*

remainder subject to divestment. See *defeasible remainder.*

remainder subject to open. A vested remainder that is given to one person but that may later have to be shared with others. • An example is "to A for life, and then equally to all of B's children." — Also termed *remainder subject to partial divestment.*

vested remainder. A remainder that is given to an ascertained person and that is not subject to a condition precedent. • An example is "to A for life, and then to B." — Also termed *executed remainder.*

remainder bequest. See *residuary bequest* under BEQUEST.

remainderer. See REMAINDERMAN.

remainder interest. The property that passes to a beneficiary after the expiration of an intervening income interest. • For example, if a grantor places real estate in trust with income to A for life and remainder to B upon A's death, then B has a remainder interest.

remainderman. A person who holds or is entitled to receive a remainder. — Also termed *remainderer; remainderperson; remainor.*

remainder subject to a condition precedent. See *contingent remainder* under REMAINDER.

remainder subject to divestment. See *defeasible remainder* under REMAINDER.

remainder subject to open. See REMAINDER.

remainder subject to partial divestment. See *remainder subject to open* under REMAINDER.

remainor. See REMAINDERMAN.

remake rights. *Copyright.* The rights to produce one or more additional movies or screenplays based on what is substantially the same story as is contained in the original movie or screenplay for which the rights have been granted.

remand (ri-**mand** *also* **ree**-mand), *n.* **1.** The act or an instance of sending something (such as a case, claim, or person) back for further action. **2.** An order remanding a case, claim, or person.

fourth-sentence remand. In a claim for social-security benefits, a court's decision affirming, reversing, or modifying the decision of the Commissioner of Social Security. • This type of remand is called a fourth-sentence remand because it is based on the fourth sentence of 42 USCA § 405(g): "The court shall have power to enter, upon the pleadings and transcript of the record, a judgment affirming, modifying, or reversing the decision of the Commissioner of Social Security, with or without remanding the cause for a rehearing." See *Melkonyan v. Sullivan*, 501 U.S. 89, 111 S.Ct. 2157 (1991).

sixth-sentence remand. In a claim for social-security benefits, a court's decision that the claim should be reheard by the Commissioner of Social Security because new evidence is available, which was not available before, that might change the outcome of the proceeding. • This type of remand is called a sixth-sentence remand because it is based on the sixth sentence of 42 USCA § 405(g): "The court may, on motion of the Commissioner of Social Security made for good cause shown before the Commissioner files the Commissioner's answer, remand the case to the Commissioner of Social Security for further action by the Commissioner of Social Security, and it may at any time order additional evidence to be taken before the Commissioner of Social Security, but only upon a showing that there is new evidence which is material and that there is good cause for the failure to incorporate such evidence into the record in a prior proceeding . . . ." See *Melkonyan v. Sullivan*, 501 U.S. 89, 111 S.Ct. 2157 (1991).

remand (ri-**mand**), *vb.* **1.** To send (a case or claim) back to the court or tribunal from which it came for some further action <the appellate court reversed the trial court's opinion and remanded the case for new trial>. Cf. REMOVAL (2). **2.** To recommit (an accused person) to custody after a preliminary examination <the magistrate, after denying bail, remanded the defendant to custody>.

remanentia (rem-ə-**nen**-shee-ə). [Law Latin] *Hist.* A remainder or perpetuity.

remanent pro defectu emptorum (**rem**-ə-nənt proh di-**fek**-t[y]oo emp-**tor**-əm). [Latin] *Hist.* Remains unsold for want of buyers. • This language was used in a return of a writ of execution when the sheriff could not sell the seized property.

remanet (**rem**-ə-net). **1.** A case or proceeding whose hearing has been postponed. **2.** A remainder or remnant.

remargining, *n. Securities.* The act or process of depositing additional cash or collateral with a broker when the equity in a margin account falls to an insufficient level. — **remargin,** *vb.* See *margin account* under ACCOUNT.

remediable, *adj.* Capable of being remedied, esp. by law <remediable wrongs>. — **remediability,** *n.*

remedial, *adj.* **1.** Affording or providing a remedy; providing the means of obtaining redress <a remedial action>. **2.** Intended to correct, remove, or lessen a wrong, fault, or defect <a remedial statute>. **3.** Of or relating to a means of enforcing an existing substantive right; procedural <a remedial right>.

remedial action. *Environmental law.* An action intended to bring about or restore long-term environmental quality; esp., under CERCLA, a measure intended to permanently alleviate pollution when a hazardous substance has been released or might be released into the environment, so as to prevent or minimize any further release of hazardous substances and thereby minimize the risk to public health or to the environment. 42 USCA § 9601(24); 40 CFR § 300.6. — Also termed *remedy*. Cf. CERCLA; REMOVAL ACTION.

remedial enforcement. See *secondary right* under RIGHT.

remedial law. **1.** A law providing a means to enforce rights or redress injuries. **2.** A law passed to correct or modify an existing law; esp., a law that gives a party a new or different remedy when the existing remedy, if any, is inadequate.

remedial liability. See LIABILITY.

remedial promise. See PROMISE.

remedial right. See RIGHT.

remedial statute. See STATUTE.

remedial trust. See *constructive trust* under TRUST.

remedies. The field of law dealing with the means of enforcing rights and redressing wrongs.

remedy, *n.* **1.** The means of enforcing a right or preventing or redressing a wrong; legal or equitable relief. **2.** REMEDIAL ACTION. — **remedy,** *vb.* Cf. RELIEF.

> "A remedy is anything a court can do for a litigant who has been wronged or is about to be wronged. The two most common remedies are judgments that plaintiffs are entitled to collect sums of money from defendants and orders to defendants to refrain from their wrongful conduct or to undo its consequences. The court decides under the substantive law whether the litigant has been wronged; it conducts its inquiry in accordance with the procedural law. The law of remedies falls somewhere between substance and procedure, distinct from both but overlapping with both." Douglas Laycock, *Modern American Remedies* 1 (1985).

adequate remedy at law. A legal remedy (such as an award of damages) that provides sufficient relief to the petitioning party, thus preventing the party from obtaining equitable relief.

administrative remedy. A nonjudicial remedy provided by an administrative agency. • Ordinarily, if an administrative remedy is available, it must be exhausted before a court will hear the case. See EXHAUSTION OF REMEDIES.

concurrent remedy. One of two or more legal actions available to redress a wrong.

cumulative remedy. A remedy available to a party in addition to another remedy that still remains in force.

equitable remedy. A nonmonetary remedy, such as an injunction or specific performance, obtained when monetary damages cannot adequately redress the injury. See IRREPARABLE-INJURY RULE.

extrajudicial remedy. A remedy not obtained from a court, such as repossession. — Also termed *self-help remedy.*

extraordinary remedy. A remedy — such as a writ of mandamus or habeas corpus — not available to a party unless necessary to preserve a right that cannot be protected by a standard legal or equitable remedy.

judicial remedy. A remedy granted by a court; esp., a tort remedy that is either ordinary (as in an action for damages) or extraordinary (as in an equitable suit for an injunction).

legal remedy. A remedy available in a court of law, as distinguished from a remedy available only in equity. • After the merger of law and equity, this distinction became no longer legally relevant.

provisional remedy. **1.** A restraining order or injunctive relief pending the disposition of an action; a temporary remedy, such as attachment, incidental to the primary action and available to a party while the action is pending. **2.** An equitable proceeding before judgment to provide for the postjudgment safety and preservation of property.

remedy over. A remedy that arises from a right of indemnification or subrogation. • For example, if a city is liable for injuries caused by a defect in a street, the city has a "remedy over" against the person whose act or negligence caused the defect.

self-help remedy. See *extrajudicial remedy.*

specific remedy. A remedy for breach of contract whereby the injured party is awarded the very performance that was contractually promised, as when the court orders a defaulting seller of goods to deliver the specified goods to the buyer (as opposed to paying damages).

speedy remedy. A remedy (such as a restraining order) that, under the circumstances, can be pursued expeditiously before the aggrieved party has incurred substantial detriment.

substitutional remedy. A remedy for breach of contract intended to give the promisee something as a replacement for the promised performance, as when the court orders a defaulting seller of goods to pay the buyer damages (as opposed to delivering the goods).

remedy, mutuality of. See MUTUALITY OF REMEDY.

réméré (ray-may-**ray**), *n.* [French] The right of repurchase.

REMIC (**rem**-ik *or* **ree**-mik). *abbr.* REAL-ESTATE-MORTGAGE INVESTMENT CONDUIT.

remise (ri-**mIz**), *vb.* To give up, surrender, or release (a right, interest, etc.) <the quitclaim deed provides that the grantor remises any rights in the property>.

remission. 1. A cancellation or extinguishment of all or part of a financial obligation; a release of a debt or claim.

conventional remission. *Civil law.* A remission expressly granted to a debtor by a creditor having capacity to alienate.

tacit remission. *Civil law.* A remission arising by operation of law, as when a creditor surrenders an original title to the debtor.

2. A pardon granted for an offense. **3.** Relief from a forfeiture or penalty. **4.** A diminution or abatement of the symptoms of a disease.

remit, *vb.* **1.** To pardon or forgive <the wife could not remit her husband's infidelity>. **2.** To abate or slacken; to mitigate <the receipt of money damages remitted the embarrassment of being fired>. **3.** To refer (a matter for decision) to some authority, esp. to send back (a case) to a lower court <the appellate court remitted the case to the trial court for further factual determinations>. See REMAND. **4.** To send or put back to a previous condition or position <a landlord's breach of a lease does not justify the tenant's refusal to pay rent; instead, the tenant is remitted to the right to recover damages>. **5.** To transmit (as money) <upon receiving the demand letter, she promptly remitted the amount due>. — **remissible** (for senses 1–4), *adj.* — **remittable** (for sense 5), *adj.*

remittance. 1. A sum of money sent to another as payment for goods or services. **2.** An instrument (such as a check) used for sending money. **3.** The action or process of sending money to another person or place.

remittance advice. See ADVICE.

remittee. One to whom payment is sent.

remitter. 1. The principle by which a person having two titles to an estate, and entering on it by the later or more defective title, is deemed to hold the estate by the earlier or more valid title. **2.** The act of sending back a case to a lower court. **3.** One who sends payment to someone else. — Also spelled (in sense 3) *remittor.*

remitting bank. See BANK.

remittit damna (ri-**mit**-it **dam**-nə). [Latin] *Hist.* An entry on the record by which a plaintiff declares that he or she remits part of the damages that have been awarded.

remittitur (ri-**mit**-i-tər). **1.** The process by which a court reduces or proposes to reduce the damages awarded in a jury verdict. **2.** A court's order reducing an award of damages <the defendant sought a remittitur of the $100 million judgment>. Cf. ADDITUR.

remittitur of record. The action of sending the transcript of a case back from an appellate court to a trial court; the notice for doing so.

remittor. See REMITTER (3).

remonetization, *n.* The restoration of a precious metal (such as gold or silver) to its former use as legal tender. — **remonetize,** *vb.*

remonstrance (ri-**mon**-strənts), *n.* **1.** A presentation of reasons for opposition or grievance. **2.** A formal document stating reasons for opposition or grievance. **3.** A formal protest against governmental policy, actions, or officials. — **remonstrate** (ri-**mon**-strayt), *vb.*

remote, *adj.* **1.** Far removed or separated in time, space, or relation. **2.** Slight. **3.** *Property.* Beyond the 21 years after some life in being by which a devise must vest. See RULE AGAINST PERPETUITIES.

remote cause. See CAUSE (1).

remote damages. See *speculative damages* under DAMAGES.

remote possibility. See POSSIBILITY.

removal, *n.* **1.** The transfer or moving of a person or thing from one location, position, or residence to another. **2.** The transfer of an action from state to federal court. • In removing a case to federal court, a litigant must timely file the removal papers and must show a valid basis for federal-court jurisdiction. — **remove,** *vb.* Cf. REMAND (1).

civil-rights removal. Removal of a case from state to federal court for any of these reasons: (1) because a person has been denied or cannot enforce a civil right in the state court, (2) because a person is being sued for performing an act under color of authority derived from a law providing for equal rights, or (3) because a person is being sued for refusing to perform an act that would be inconsistent with equal rights.

removal action. *Environmental law.* An action, esp. under CERCLA, intended to bring about the short-term abatement and cleanup of pollution (as by removing and disposing of toxic materials). Cf. CERCLA; REMEDIAL ACTION.

removal bond. See BOND (2).

REMT. *abbr.* REAL-ESTATE MORTGAGE TRUST.

remuneration (ri-myoo-nə-**ray**-shən), *n.* **1.** Payment; compensation. **2.** The act of paying or compensating. — **remunerate,** *vb.* — **remunerative,** *adj.*

rencounter (ren-**kown**-tər). A hostile meeting or contest; a battle or combat. — Also spelled *rencontre* (ren-**kon**-tər).

render, *n. Hist.* **1.** A payment in money, goods, or services made by a feudal tenant to the landlord. **2.** A return conveyance made by the grantee to the grantor in a fine. See FINE (1).

render, *vb.* **1.** To transmit or deliver <render payment>. **2.** (Of a judge) to deliver formally <render a judgment>. **3.** (Of a jury) to agree on and report formally <render a verdict>. **4.** To pay as due <render an account>.

rendezvous, *n.* **1.** A place designated for meeting or assembly, esp. of troops or ships. **2.** The meeting or assembly itself.

rendition, *n.* **1.** The action of making, delivering, or giving out, such as a legal decision. **2.** The return of a fugitive from one state to the state where the fugitive is accused or convicted of a crime. — Also termed *interstate rendition.* Cf. EXTRADITION.

rendition of judgment. The judge's oral or written ruling containing the judgment entered. Cf. ENTRY OF JUDGMENT.

rendition warrant. See WARRANT (1).

renege (ri-**nig** *or* ri-**neg**), *vb.* To fail to keep a promise or commitment; to back out of a deal.

renegotiable-rate mortgage. See MORTGAGE.

renegotiation, *n.* **1.** The act or process of negotiating again or on different terms; a second or further negotiation. **2.** The reexamination and adjustment of a government contract to eliminate or recover excess profits by the contractor. — **renegotiate,** *vb.*

renewable term insurance. See INSURANCE.

renewal, *n.* **1.** The act of restoring or reestablishing. **2.** The re-creation of a legal relationship or the replacement of an old contract with a new contract, as opposed to the mere extension of a previous relationship or contract. — **renew,** *vb.* Cf. EXTENSION (1); REVIVAL (1).

renewal note. See NOTE (1).

renounce, *vb.* **1.** To give up or abandon formally (a right or interest); to disclaim <renounce an inheritance>. **2.** To refuse to follow or obey; to decline to recognize or observe <renounce one's allegiance>.

renovare (ren-ə-**vair**-ee), *vb.* [Latin] *Hist.* To renew.

rent, *n.* **1.** Consideration paid, usu. periodically, for the use or occupancy of property (esp. real property).

ceiling rent. The maximum rent that can be charged under a rent-control regulation.

double rent. Twice the amount of rent agreed to; specif., a penalty of twice the amount of rent against a tenant who holds possession of the leased property after the date provided in the tenant's notice to quit. • The penalty was provided by the Distress for Rent Act, 1737, 11 Geo. 2., ch. 19, § 13.

dry rent. Rent reserved without a distress clause allowing the rent to be collected by distress; rent that can be collected only by an ordinary legal action.

economic rent. See ECONOMIC RENT.

ground rent. **1.** Rent paid by a tenant under a long-term lease for the use of undeveloped land, usu. for the construction of a commercial building. See *ground lease* under LEASE. **2.** An inheritable interest, in rental income from land, reserved by a grantor who conveys the land in fee simple. • This type of ground rent is found primarily in Maryland and Pennsylvania.

guild rent. *Hist.* Rent payable to the Crown by a guild. — Also spelled *gild-rent.*

net rent. The rental price for property after payment of expenses, such as repairs, utilities, and taxes.

rack-rent. See RACK-RENT.

2. *Hist.* A compensation or return made periodically by a tenant or occupant for the possession and use of lands or corporeal hereditaments; money, chattels, or services issuing usu. annually out of lands and tenements as payment for use.

quit rent. See QUIT RENT.

rent charge. The right to receive an annual sum from the income of land, usu. in perpetuity, and to retake possession if the payments are in arrears. — Also spelled *rent-charge*; *rentcharge.* — Also termed *fee-farm rent.*

> "Rent-charge is a rent with liberty to distrain. As when a man seised of land granteth by a deed poll, or by indenture, a yearly rent going out of the same land to another in fee or fee-tail, or for a term of life, etc. with clause of distress, or maketh a feoffment in fee by indenture, reserving to himself a certain yearly rent, with clause of distress." Sir Henry Finch, *Law, or a Discourse Thereof* 155 (1759).

> "A rentcharge is an annual or periodic payment charged upon, and payable by the owner of, land. Unlike a rent service, in the case of a rentcharge there is no tenure or privity of estate between the parties. The owner of a rentcharge has no tenurial relationship with the land upon which it is charged. A rentcharge is a species of incorporeal property, but, unlike an easement, is incorporeal property in gross, being enjoyed by the owner personally and not in the capacity of proprietor of land." Peter Butt, *Land Law* 330 (2d ed. 1988).

rent seck. A rent reserved by deed but without any clause of distress. — Also spelled *rent-seck.* — Also termed *dry rent.*

rent service. A rent with some corporeal service incident to it (as by fealty) and with a right of distress.

3. *Civil law.* A contract by which one party conveys to another party a tract of land or other immovable property, to be held by the other party as owner and in perpetuity, in exchange for payment of an annual sum of money or quantity of fruits. See FRUIT (3). — Also termed *rent of lands*. **4.** The difference between the actual return from a commodity or service and the cost of supplying it; the difference between revenue and opportunity cost. — **rent,** *vb.*

rentage. Rent or rental.

rent-a-judging. See PRIVATE JUDGING.

rental, *n.* **1.** The amount received as rent.

delay rental. *Oil & gas.* A periodic payment made by an oil-and-gas lessee to postpone exploration during the primary lease term. See DRILLING-DELAY-RENTAL CLAUSE.

2. The income received from rent. **3.** A record of payments received from rent. — **rental,** *adj.*

rentcharge. See RENT (2).

rent control. A restriction imposed, usu. by municipal legislation, on the maximum rent that a landlord may charge for rental property, and often on a landlord's power of eviction.

rente (rawnt), *n.* [French "income, rent"] *French law.* **1.** Annual income or rent.

rente foncière (faw*n*-**syair**) [French "ground rent"] A rent that is payable for the use of land and is perpetual.

rente viagère (vee-ah-**zhair**). [French "life rent"] A rent charge or annuity that is payable for life; a life interest or annuity.

2. (*usu. pl.*) Interest paid annually by the French government on the public debt; a government stock, bond, or annuity.

rentee. *Rare.* A tenant.

rente foncière. See RENTE.

rente viagère. See RENTE.

rentier (raw*n*-**tyay**). [French] **1.** A person who owns or holds *rentes*. See RENTE. **2.** A person who makes or lives off an income from property or investment; a stockholder or annuitant.

rent of lands. See RENT (3).

rent seck. See RENT (2).

rent-seeking, *n.* Economic behavior motivated by an incentive to overproduce goods that will yield a return greater than the cost of production. • The term is often used in the field of law and economics. See RENT (4).

rent service. See RENT (2).

rents, issues, and profits. The total income or profit arising from the ownership or possession of property.

rent strike. A refusal by a group of tenants to pay rent until grievances with the landlord are heard or settled.

renunciation (ri-nən-see-**ay**-shən), *n.* **1.** The express or tacit abandonment of a right without transferring it to another. **2.** *Criminal law.* Complete and voluntary abandonment of criminal purpose — sometimes coupled with an attempt to thwart the activity's success — before a crime is committed. • Renunciation can be an affirmative defense to attempt, conspiracy, and the like. Model Penal Code § 5.01(4). — Also termed *withdrawal*; *abandonment*. **3.** *Wills & estates.* The act of waiving a right under a will and claiming instead a statutory share. See RIGHT OF ELECTION. — **renounce,** *vb.* — **renunciative, renunciatory,** *adj.*

renvoi (ren-**voy**), *n.* [French "sending back"] **1.** The doctrine under which a court in resorting to foreign law adopts as well the foreign law's conflict-of-laws principles, which may in turn refer the court back to the law of the forum. **2.** The problem arising when one state's rule on conflict of laws refers a case to the law of another state, and that second state's conflict-of-law rule refers the case either back to the law of the first state or to a third state. See CONFLICT OF LAWS. **3.** RECONDUCTION (2).

REO. *abbr.* REAL ESTATE OWNED.

reo absente (**ree**-oh ab-**sten**-tee). [Latin] The defendant being absent; the absence of the defendant.

reorganization, *n.* **1.** *Bankruptcy.* A financial restructuring of a corporation, esp. in the repayment of debts, under a plan created by a trustee and approved by a court. See CHAPTER 11.

haircut reorganization. A restructuring of the indebtedness that remains after a creditor forgives a portion of the debtor's obligation.

2. *Tax.* A restructuring of a corporation, as by a merger or recapitalization, in order to improve its tax treatment under the Internal Revenue Code. • The Code classifies the various types of reorganizations with different letters. IRC (26 USCA) § 368(a)(1). Cf. RECAPITALIZATION.

A reorganization. A reorganization that involves a merger or consolidation under a specific state statute.

B reorganization. A reorganization in which one corporation exchanges its voting shares for another corporation's voting shares.

C reorganization. A reorganization in which one corporation exchanges its voting shares for substantially all the assets of another corporation.

D reorganization. A reorganization in which the corporation transfers some or all of its assets to another corporation that is controlled by the transferor or its shareholders, and then the stock of the transferee corporation is distributed.

E reorganization. A reorganization that involves a recapitalization.

F reorganization. A reorganization that involves a mere change in the identity, form, or place of organization of a corporation.

G reorganization. A reorganization that involves a transfer of all or part of the corporation's assets to another corporation in a bankruptcy or similar proceeding.

reorganization bond. See *adjustment bond* under BOND (3).

reorganization plan. *Bankruptcy.* A plan of restructuring submitted by a corporation for approval by the court in a Chapter 11 case. See CHAPTER 11.

rep. *abbr.* **1.** REPORT. **2.** REPORTER. **3.** REPRESENTATIVE. **4.** REPUBLIC.

reparable injury. See INJURY.

reparation (rep-ə-**ray**-shən). **1.** The act of making amends for a wrong. **2.** (*usu. pl.*) Compensation for an injury or wrong, esp. for wartime damages or breach of an international obligation.

reparative injunction. See INJUNCTION.

repeal, *n.* Abrogation of an existing law by legislative act. — **repeal,** *vb.*

express repeal. Repeal effected by specific declaration in a new statute.

implied repeal. Repeal effected by irreconcilable conflict between an old law and a new law. — Also termed *repeal by implication.*

repealer. 1. A legislative act abrogating an earlier law. **2.** One who repeals.

repealing clause. A statutory provision that repeals an earlier statute.

repeater. See RECIDIVIST.

repeat offender. See OFFENDER.

repetition. *Civil law.* A demand or action for restitution or repayment. See SOLUTIO INDEBITI.

repetitum namium (ri-**pet**-ə-təm **nay**-mee-əm). [Law Latin] *Hist.* A second, repeated, or reciprocal distress; WITHERNAM.

repetundae (rep-ə-**tən**-dee). [Latin] *Roman law.* **1.** Money or things that can be reclaimed by a person who was forced to give them to a public official as a bribe. **2.** The illegal act of forcing someone to give money or things as a bribe; extortion.

replacement cost. See COST (1).

replacement-cost depreciation method. See DEPRECIATION METHOD.

replacement insurance. See INSURANCE.

replead, *vb.* **1.** To plead again or anew; to file a new pleading, esp. to correct a defect in an earlier pleading. **2.** To make a repleader.

repleader (ree-**plee**-dər). *Common-law pleading.* A court order or judgment — issued on the motion of a party who suffered an adverse verdict — requiring the parties to file new pleadings because of some defect in the original pleadings. — Also termed *judgment of repleader.*

replegiare (ri-plee-jee-**air**-ee), *vb.* [Law Latin] *Hist.* To take back on pledge or surety; to replevy.

repleviable (ri-**plev**-ee-ə-bəl), *adj.* Capable of being replevied; recoverable by replevin <re-

pleviable property>. — Also spelled *replevisable* (ri-**plev**-ə-sə-bəl). Cf. IRREPLEVIABLE.

replevin (ri-**plev**-in), *n.* **1.** An action for the repossession of personal property wrongfully taken or detained by the defendant, whereby the plaintiff gives security for and holds the property until the court decides who owns it. **2.** A writ obtained from a court authorizing the retaking of personal property wrongfully taken or detained. — Also termed (in sense 2) *writ of replevin*. Cf. DETINUE; TROVER.

> "*Replevin* is a remedy ground and granted upon a distress, being a re-deliverance of the thing distrained to remain with the first possessor, on security or pledges given by him to try the right with the distrainer, and to answer him in a course of law." *The Pocket Lawyer and Family Conveyancer* 105 (3d ed. 1833).

> "The action of replevin lies, where specific personal property has been wrongfully taken and is wrongfully detained, to recover possession of the property, together with damages for its detention. To support the action it is necessary: (a) That the property shall be personal. (b) That the plaintiff, at the time of suit, shall be entitled to the immediate possession. (c) That (at common law) the defendant shall have wrongfully taken the property (replevin in the cepit). But, by statute in most states, the action will now also lie where the property is wrongfully detained, though it was lawfully obtained in the first instance (replevin in the detinet). (d) That the property shall be wrongfully detained by the defendant at the time of suit." Benjamin J. Shipman, *Handbook of Common-Law Pleading* § 49, at 120 (Henry Winthrop Ballantine ed., 3d ed. 1923).

personal replevin. At common law, an action to replevy a person out of prison or out of another's custody. • Personal replevin has been largely superseded by the writ of habeas corpus as a means of investigating the legality of an imprisonment. See HABEAS CORPUS.

replevin in cepit (in **see**-pit). An action for the repossession of property that is both wrongfully taken and wrongfully detained.

replevin in detinet (in **det**-i-net). An action for the repossession of property that is rightfully taken but wrongfully detained.

replevin, *vb. Archaic.* REPLEVY.

replevin bond. See BOND (2).

replevisable. See REPLEVIABLE.

replevisor (ri-**plev**-ə-sər). The plaintiff in a replevin action.

replevy (ri-**plev**-ee), *n. Archaic.* REPLEVIN.

replevy, *vb.* **1.** To recover possession of (goods) by a writ of replevin. **2.** To recover (goods) by replevin. **3.** *Archaic.* To bail (a prisoner).

replevy bond. See *replevin bond* under BOND (2).

repliant (ri-**plI**-ənt). A party who makes a replication (i.e., a common-law reply). — Also spelled *replicant*.

replicare (rep-lə-**kair**-ee), *vb.* [Latin] *Hist.* To reply; to answer a defendant's plea.

replicatio (rep-lə-**kay**-shee-oh), *n.* [Latin] *Hist.* The plaintiff's answer to the defendant's exception or plea; a replication.

replication (rep-lə-**kay**-shən). A plaintiff's or complainant's reply to a defendant's plea or answer; REPLY (2).

anticipatory replication. *Equity pleading.* The denial in an original bill of defensive matters that the defendant might rely on. • A defendant who relies on the anticipated defense must traverse the anticipatory matter in addition to setting up the defense.

general replication. *Equity pleading.* A replication that consists of a general denial of the defendant's plea or answer and an assertion of the truth and sufficiency of the bill.

replication de injuria. *Common-law pleading.* A traverse occurring only in the replication whereby the plaintiff is permitted to traverse the whole substance of a plea consisting merely of legal excuse, when the matter does not involve a title or interest in land, authority of law, authority of fact derived from the opposing party, or any matter of record. — Also termed *replication de injuria sua propria, absque tali causa*.

replication per fraudem. *Common-law pleading.* A replication asserting that the discharge pleaded by the defendant was obtained by fraud.

special replication. *Equity pleading.* A replication that puts in issue a new fact to counter a new matter raised in the defendant's plea or answer.

reply, *n.* **1.** *Civil procedure.* In federal practice, the plaintiff's response to the defendant's counterclaim (or, by court order, to the defendant's or a third party's answer). Fed. R. Civ. P. 7(a). **2.** *Common-law pleading.* The plaintiff's response to the defendant's plea or answer. • The reply is the plaintiff's second pleading, and it is followed by the defendant's rejoinder. — Also termed (in sense 2) *replication*. — **reply,** *vb*.

reply brief. See BRIEF.

repo (**ree**-poh). **1.** REPOSSESSION. **2.** REPURCHASE AGREEMENT.

report, *n*. **1.** A formal oral or written presentation of facts <according to the treasurer's report, there is $300 in the bank>.

insider report. A monthly report that must be filed with the SEC when more than 10% of a company's stock is traded.

2. A written account of a court proceeding and judicial decision <the law clerk sent the court's report to counsel for both sides>.

official report. (*usu. pl.*) The governmentally approved set of reported cases within a given jurisdiction.

"[I]t may justly be said that all reports are in a sense 'official,' or that to use the term 'official reports' as referring to any particular series of reports is a misnomer, for it is certainly misleading. The mere fact that each state authorizes or requires publication of reports of its Supreme Court decisions, and, to insure such publication, agrees to purchase a stated number of each volume of the reports, cannot be said to give such a series preeminence as an 'official' publication." William M. Lile et al., *Brief Making and the Use of Law Books* 33 (3d ed. 1914).

3. (*usu. pl.*) A published volume of judicial decisions by a particular court or group of courts <U.S. Reports>. • Generally, these decisions are first printed in temporary paperback volumes, and then printed in hardbound reporter volumes. Law reports may be either official (published by a government entity) or unofficial (published by a private publisher). Court citations frequently include the names of both the official and unofficial reports. — Also termed *reporter*; *law report*; *law reporter*. Cf. ADVANCE SHEETS. **4.** (*usu. pl.*) A collection of administrative decisions by one or more administrative agencies. — Abbr. rep. — **report,** *vb*.

reporter. 1. A person responsible for making and publishing a report; esp., a lawyer-consultant who prepares drafts of official or semiofficial writings such as court rules or Restatements <the reporter to the Advisory Committee on Bankruptcy Rules explained the various amendments>. **2.** REPORTER OF DECISIONS. **3.** REPORT (3) <Supreme Court Reporter>. — Abbr. rep.; rptr.

"It may not come amiss to remark that the National Report System is usually spoken of as the 'Reporters,' and one of the component parts of that system is in like manner spoken of as a 'Reporter.' Wherever, in this or the succeeding chapters of this work, the word is used with a capital, it refers to one or more of the parts of the National Reporter System. When the word 'reporter' is used without capitalization, it refers to the person who reports or edits the cases in any series of reports to which reference is being made." William M. Lile et al., *Brief Making and the Use of Law Books* 37 (3d ed. 1914).

reporter of decisions. The person responsible for publishing a court's opinions. • The reporter of decisions often has duties that include verifying citations, correcting spelling and punctuation, and suggesting minor editorial improvements before judicial opinions are released or published. — Often shortened to *reporter*. — Also termed *court reporter*.

reporter's privilege. See *journalist's privilege* (1) under PRIVILEGE (3).

reporter's record. See TRANSCRIPT.

reporter's syllabus. See HEADNOTE.

reporting company. A company that, because it issues publicly traded securities, must comply with the reporting requirements of the Securities Exchange Act of 1934.

report of proceedings. See TRANSCRIPT.

reports, *n*. See REPORT.

Reports, The. A series of 13 volumes of caselaw published in the 17th century by Sir Edward Coke.

repose (ri-**pohz**), *n*. **1.** Cessation of activity; temporary rest. **2.** A statutory period after which an action cannot be brought in court, even if it expires before the plaintiff suffers any injury. See STATUTE OF REPOSE.

repository (ri-**poz**-ə-tor-ee). A place where something is deposited or stored; a warehouse or storehouse.

repossession, *n*. The act or an instance of retaking property; esp., a seller's retaking of goods sold on credit when the buyer has failed to pay for them. — Often shortened to *repo*. — **repossess,** *vb*. Cf. FORECLOSURE.

representation, *n*. **1.** A presentation of fact — either by words or by conduct — made to induce someone to act, esp. to enter into a contract <the buyer relied on the seller's repre-

sentation that the roof did not leak>. Cf. MISREPRESENTATION.

> "Representation . . . may introduce terms into a contract and affect performance: or it may induce a contract and so affect the intention of one of the parties, and the formation of the contract. . . . At common law, . . . if a representation did not afterwards become a substantive part of the contract, its untruth (save in certain excepted cases and apart always from fraud) was immaterial. But if it did, it might be one of two things: (1) it might be regarded by the parties as a vital term going to the root of the contract (when it is usually called a 'condition'); and in this case its untruth entitles the injured party to repudiate the whole contract; or (2) it might be a term in the nature only of an independent subsidiary promise (when it is usually called a 'warranty'), which is indeed a part of the contract, but does not go to the root of it; in this case its untruth only gives rise to an action *ex contractu* for damages, and does *not* entitle the injured party to repudiate the whole contract." William R. Anson, *Principles of the Law of Contract* 218, 222 (Arthur L. Corbin ed., 3d Am. ed. 1919).

affirmative representation. A representation asserting the existence of certain facts pertaining to a given subject matter.

false representation. See MISREPRESENTATION.

material representation. A representation that relates directly to the matter in issue or that actually causes an event to occur (such as a party's relying on the representation in entering into a contract). • Material representation is a necessary element of an action for fraud.

promissory representation. A representation about what one will do in the future; esp., a representation made by an insured about what will happen during the time of coverage, stated as a matter of expectation and amounting to an enforceable promise.

2. The act or an instance of standing for or acting on behalf of another, esp. by a lawyer on behalf of a client <Clarence Darrow's representation of Mr. Scopes>. **3.** The fact of a litigant's having such a close alignment of interests with another person that the other is considered as having been present in the litigation <the named plaintiff provided adequate representation for the absent class members>. See ADEQUATE REPRESENTATION. **4.** The assumption by an heir of the rights and obligations of his or her predecessor <each child takes a share by representation>. See PER STIRPES. — **represent,** *vb.*

representation, estoppel by. See *estoppel by representation* under ESTOPPEL.

representation election. See ELECTION.

representative, *n.* **1.** One who stands for or acts on behalf of another <the owner was the football team's representative at the labor negotiations>. See AGENT.

accredited representative. A person with designated authority to act on behalf of another person, group, or organization, usu. by being granted that authority by law or by the rules of the group or organization <as an officer of the union, she was the accredited representative of the employees in the wage dispute>.

class representative. A person who sues on behalf of a group of plaintiffs in a class action. — Also termed *named plaintiff.* See CLASS ACTION.

independent personal representative. See *personal representative.*

lawful representative. **1.** A legal heir. **2.** An executor or administrator. **3.** Any other legal representative.

legal-personal representative. **1.** When used by a testator referring to personal property, an executor or administrator. **2.** When used by a testator referring to real property, one to whom the real estate passes immediately upon the testator's death. **3.** When used concerning the death of a seaman, the public administrator, executor, or appointed administrator in the seaman's state of residence.

personal representative. A person who manages the legal affairs of another because of incapacity or death, such as the executor of an estate. — Also termed *independent personal representative*; *legal representative.*

registered representative. A person approved by the SEC and stock exchanges to sell securities to the public. — Also termed *customer's man*; *customer's person.*

2. A member of a legislature, esp. of the lower house <one senator and one representative attended the rally>. — Abbr. rep.

representative action. **1.** CLASS ACTION. **2.** DERIVATIVE ACTION (1).

representative capacity. The position of one standing or acting for another, esp. through delegated authority <an agent acting in a representative capacity for the principal>.

representee. One to whom a representation is made.

> "First, where the representor can show that he was not negligent, he will not be liable under the 1967 Act; and secondly, where the representee wants to claim damages

at the contractual rate, for loss of his bargain, it may be that the Misrepresentation Act will not suffice." P.S. Atiyah, *An Introduction to the Law of Contract* 165 (3d ed. 1981).

representor. One who makes a representation.

"[I]t is arguable that even where a contracting party does not intend to guarantee the accuracy of what he says, the other party is at least entitled to assume that due care has been taken by the representor." P.S. Atiyah, *An Introduction to the Law of Contract* 309 (3d ed. 1981).

repressive tax. See *sin tax* under TAX.

reprieve (ri-**preev**), *n.* Temporary postponement of the execution of a criminal sentence, esp. a death sentence. — **reprieve,** *vb.* Cf. COMMUTATION (2); PARDON.

"The term *reprieve* is derived from *reprendre*, to keep back, and signifies the withdrawing of the sentence for an interval of time, and operates in delay of execution." 1 Joseph Chitty, *A Practical Treatise on the Criminal Law* 757 (2d ed. 1826).

reprimand, *n.* In professional responsibility, a form of disciplinary action — imposed after trial or formal charges — that declares the lawyer's conduct improper but does not limit his or her right to practice law. — **reprimand,** *vb.*

private reprimand. A reprimand that is not published but instead communicated only to the lawyer, or that is published without identifying the lawyer by name.

public reprimand. A reprimand that is published, usu. in a bar journal or legal newspaper.

reprisal (ri-**prɪ**-zəl). **1.** (*often pl.*) *Int'l law.* The use of force, short of war, against another country to redress an injury caused by that country.

" 'Reprisals' is a word with a long history, and modern writers are not agreed on the meaning which should be given to it today. Literally and historically it denotes the seizing of property or persons by way of retaliation .... Reprisals when they are taken today are taken by a state, but some writers would still limit the word to acts of taking or withholding the property of a foreign state or its nationals, for example by an embargo, whilst others would abandon the historical associations and use it to denote any kind of coercive action not amounting to war whereby a state attempts to secure satisfaction from another for some wrong which the latter has committed against it." J.L. Brierly, *The Law of Nations* 321–22 (5th ed. 1955).

general reprisal. A reprisal by which a nation directs all its military officers and citizens to redress an injury caused by another nation. • An example is a command to seize the property of the offending nation wherever it is found.

negative reprisal. A reprisal by which a nation refuses to perform an obligation to another nation, such as the fulfillment of a treaty.

positive reprisal. A reprisal by which a nation forcibly seizes another nation's property or persons.

special reprisal. A reprisal by which a nation authorizes an aggrieved private citizen to redress an injury caused by another nation. • An example is an authorization for a private citizen to seize a particular vessel of the offending nation. See LETTERS OF MARQUE.

2. (*often pl.*) *Int'l law.* An act of forceful retaliation for injury or attack by another country; formerly, in war, the killing of prisoners in response to an enemy's war crimes (now unlawful). Cf. RETORSION. **3.** Any act or instance of retaliation, as by an employer against a complaining employee.

reprise (ri-**prɪz**), *n.* An annual deduction, duty, or payment out of a manor or estate, such as an annuity.

reprobation (rep-rə-**bay**-shən). The act of raising an objection or exception, as to the competency of a witness or the sufficiency of evidence. — **reprobate** (**rep**-rə-bayt), *vb.* — **reprobationary** (rep-rə-**bay**-shə-ner-ee), **reprobative** (**rep**-rə-bay-tiv), *adj.*

reprobator (**rep**-rə-bay-tər). *Scots law. Hist.* A proceeding to disqualify a witness or to invalidate the testimony of an objectionable witness. — Also termed *action of reprobator*.

reproduction right. A copyright holder's exclusive right to make copies or phonorecords of the protected work. • Unauthorized copying constitutes infringement.

reproductive rights. A person's rights relating to the control of his or her procreative activities; specif., the cluster of civil liberties relating to pregnancy, abortion, and sterilization, esp. the personal bodily rights of women in their decision whether to become pregnant or bear a child. • The phrase includes the idea of being able to make reproductive decisions free from discrimination, coercion, or violence. Human-rights scholars increasingly consider reproductive rights to be protected by international human-rights law.

republic, *n.* A system of government in which the people hold sovereign power and elect representatives who exercise that power. • It contrasts on the one hand with a pure democracy, in which the people or community as an organized whole wield the sovereign power of government, and on the other with the rule of one person (such as a king, emperor, czar, or sultan). — Abbr. rep. — **republican,** *adj.* Cf. DEMOCRACY.

republication, *n.* **1.** The act or an instance of publishing again or anew. **2.** *Wills & estates.* Reestablishment of the validity of a previously revoked will by repeating the formalities of execution or by using a codicil. • The result is to make the old will effective from the date of republication. — Also termed (in sense 2) *revalidation.* — **republish,** *vb.* Cf. REVIVAL (2).

repudiate, *vb.* **1.** To reject or renounce (a duty or obligation); esp., to indicate an intention not to perform (a contract). **2.** *Hist.* To divorce or disown (one's wife).

repudiatee (ri-pyoo-dee-ə-**tee**). A party to a contract that has been repudiated by the other party.

repudiation (ri-pyoo-dee-**ay**-shən), *n.* A contracting party's words or actions that indicate an intention not to perform the contract in the future; a threatened breach of contract. — **repudiatory** (ri-**pyoo**-dee-ə-tor-ee), **repudiable** (ri-**pyoo**-dee-ə-bəl), *adj.* Cf. REJECTION; RESCISSION.

> "A repudiation is (a) a statement by the obligor to the obligee indicating that the obligor will commit a breach that would of itself give the obligee a claim for damages for total breach under § 243, or (b) a voluntary affirmative act which renders the obligor unable or apparently unable to perform without such a breach." Restatement (Second) of Contracts § 250 (1981).

> "Unfortunately, the terminology adopted by lawyers in this field has been neither uniform nor consistent, owing primarily to the historical difference between common law and equity, each originating in a different Court. Thus, whereas common lawyers tend to talk of repudiating a contract, equity lawyers talk of rescinding or setting aside a contract. Further inconsistency arises from the special terminology used in relation to certain special contracts. For instance, in a contract of sale of goods, we talk of the buyer rejecting the goods rather than repudiating the contract, although this usually amounts to the same thing. Further confusion arises from the fact that lawyers use the word 'repudiation' indiscriminately to mean rightful and wrongful repudiation, and it may not always be clear, at any rate to the beginner, which they mean. However, the main difficulty is the divergence between common law and equity, and this divergence is so deep-rooted that lawyers still feel that repudiation and rescission are different things. Thus most books on the law of Contract discuss the right to repudiate the contract for breach of condition in a section on Remedies, while they treat of the right to rescind a contract in the section on Misrepresentation. Indeed, so different are repudiation and rescission believed to be, that serious confusion is caused in the law of sale of goods by the fact that the Sale of Goods Act regulates the former but not the latter." P.S. Atiyah, *An Introduction to the Law of Contract* 294 (3d ed. 1981).

anticipatory repudiation. Repudiation of a contractual duty before the time for performance, giving the injured party an immediate right to damages for total breach, as well as discharging the injured party's remaining duties of performance. • This type of repudiation occurs when the promisor unequivocally disavows any intention to perform when the time for performance comes. Once the repudiation occurs, the nonrepudiating party has three options: (1) treat the repudiation as an immediate breach and sue for damages; (2) ignore the repudiation, urge the repudiator to perform, wait for the specified time of performance, and sue if the repudiating party does not perform; and (3) cancel the contract. — Also termed *renunciation.* See *anticipatory breach* under BREACH OF CONTRACT.

> The first Restatement lists three actions that constitute anticipatory repudiation: "(a) a positive statement to the promisee or other person having a right under the contract, indicating that the promisor will not or cannot substantially perform his contractual duties; (b) transferring or contracting to transfer to a third person an interest in specific land, goods, or in any other thing essential for the substantial performance of his contractual duties; (c) any voluntary affirmative act which renders substantial performance of his contractual duties impossible, or apparently impossible." Restatement of Contracts § 318 (1932).

total repudiation. An unconditional refusal by a party to perform the acts required by a contract. • This type of repudiation justifies the other party in refraining from performance.

repudiator (ri-**pyoo**-dee-ay-tər). One who repudiates; esp., a party who repudiates a contract.

repugnancy (ri-**pəg**-nən-see). An inconsistency or contradiction between two or more parts of a legal instrument (such as a contract or statute).

repugnant (ri-**pəg**-nənt), *adj.* Inconsistent or irreconcilable with; contrary or contradictory to <the court's interpretation was repugnant to the express wording of the statute>.

repugnant verdict. See VERDICT.

repurchase, *n.* The act or an instance of buying something back or again; esp., a corporation's buying back of some or all of its stock at market price. — **repurchase,** *vb.* See REDEMPTION.

repurchase agreement. A short-term loan agreement by which one party sells a security to another party but promises to buy back the security on a specified date at a specified price. — Often shortened to *repo.*

repurchase price. See *redemption price* under PRICE.

reputation, *n.* The esteem in which a person is held by others. • Evidence of reputation may be introduced as proof of character whenever character evidence is admissible. Fed. R. Evid. 405. — **reputational,** *adj.*

reputational evidence. See *reputation evidence* under EVIDENCE.

reputation evidence. See EVIDENCE.

reputed manor. See MANOR.

request for admission. *Civil procedure.* In pretrial discovery, a party's written factual statement served on another party who must admit, deny, or object to the substance of the statement. • Ordinarily, many requests for admission appear in one document. The admitted statements — along with any statements not denied or objected to — will be treated by the court as established, and therefore do not have to be proved at trial. Fed. R. Civ. P. 36. — Abbr. RFA. — Also termed *request for admissions*; *request to admit.*

request for instructions. *Procedure.* During trial, a party's written request that the court instruct the jury on the law as set forth in the request. Fed. R. Civ. P. 51. — Abbr. RFI. — Also termed *request to charge.*

request for production. *Procedure.* In pretrial discovery, a party's written request that another party provide specified documents or other tangible things for inspection and copying. Fed. R. Civ. P. 34. — Abbr. RFP. — Also termed *notice to produce*; *demand for document inspection.*

request to admit. See REQUEST FOR ADMISSION.

request to charge. See REQUEST FOR INSTRUCTIONS.

required-records doctrine. The principle that the privilege against self-incrimination does not apply when one is being compelled to produce business records that are kept in accordance with government regulations and that involve public aspects. • Some courts have held that certain medical records and tax forms fall within this doctrine and are thus not protected by the privilege against self-incrimination.

required reserve. See RESERVE.

requirements contract. See CONTRACT.

requisition (rek-wə-**zish**-ən), *n.* **1.** An authoritative, formal demand <a state governor's requisition for another state's surrender of a fugitive>. **2.** A governmental seizure of property <the state's requisition of the shopping center during the weather emergency>. See TAKING. — **requisition,** *vb.*

requisitionist. One who makes a formal demand (as for the performance of an obligation or the return of a fugitive). See REQUISITION (1).

requisitory letter. See LETTER OF REQUEST.

rere-county (**reer**-kown-tee). *Hist.* A subsidiary English county court held by the sheriff on the day after the regular county court. — Also spelled *rere county*; *rier county.*

res (rays *or* reez *or* rez), *n.* [Latin "thing"] **1.** An object, interest, or status, as opposed to a person <jurisdiction of the res — the real property in Colorado>. **2.** The subject matter of a trust; CORPUS (2) <the stock certificate is the res of the trust>. Pl. **res.**

res accessoria (rays ak-ses-**or**-ee-ə). [Latin] *Civil law.* An accessory thing; a thing that is related to a principal thing.

res adjudicata (rays ə-joo-di-**kay**-tə *or* -**kah**-tə). See RES JUDICATA.

resale, *n.* **1.** The act of selling goods or property — previously sold to a buyer who breached the sales contract — to someone else. UCC § 2-706. **2.** A retailer's selling of goods, previously purchased from a manufacturer or wholesaler, to consumers. — **resell,** *vb.*

resale-price maintenance. A form of price-fixing in which a manufacturer forces or persuades several different retailers to sell the manufacturer's product at the same price, thus preventing competition. • Resale-price maintenance is per se illegal under antitrust law. But a manufacturer is permitted to suggest a retail price as long as it does not compel retailers to sell at that price. See *vertical price-fixing* under PRICE-FIXING.

res caduca (rays kə-**d[y]oo**-kə). [Latin] *Civil law*. A fallen thing; an escheat.

resceit (ri-**seet**). *Hist.* The admittance of an interested third party to plead in a case between two others; intervention.

rescind (ri-**sind**), *vb.* **1.** To abrogate or cancel (a contract) unilaterally or by agreement. **2.** To make void; to repeal or annul <rescind the legislation>. — **rescindable,** *adj.*

rescissio (ri-**sis[h]**-ee-oh). [Latin] *Civil law*. Annulment or voidance of something; rescission.

rescission (ri-**sizh**-ən), *n.* **1.** A party's unilateral unmaking of a contract for a legally sufficient reason, such as the other party's material breach. • Rescission is generally available as a remedy or defense for a nondefaulting party and restores the parties to their precontractual positions. **2.** An agreement by contracting parties to discharge all remaining duties of performance and terminate the contract. — Also termed (in sense 2) *agreement of rescission*; *mutual rescission*; *abandonment*. — Also spelled *recision*; *recission*. — **rescissory** (ri-**sis**-ə-ree *or* ri-**siz**-), *adj.* Cf. REJECTION; REPUDIATION.

> "The [UCC] takes cognizance of the fact that the term 'rescission' is often used by lawyers, courts and businessmen in many different senses; for example, termination of a contract by virtue of an option to terminate in the agreement, cancellation for breach and avoidance on the grounds of infancy or fraud. In the interests of clarity of thought — as the consequences of each of these forms of discharge may vary — the Commercial Code carefully distinguishes three circumstances. 'Rescission' is utilized as a term of art to refer to a mutual agreement to discharge contractual duties. 'Termination' refers to the discharge of duties by the exercise of a power granted by the agreement. 'Cancellation' refers to the putting an end to the contract by reason of a breach by the other party. Section 2–720, however, takes into account that the parties do not necessarily use these terms in this way." John D. Calamari & Joseph M. Perillo, *The Law of Contracts* § 21–2, at 864–65 (3d ed. 1987).

equitable rescission. Rescission that is decreed by a court of equity.

legal rescission. Rescission that is effected by the agreement of the parties.

rescissory damages. See DAMAGES.

res communes (rays kə-**myoo**-neez). [Latin "common things"] *Civil law*. Things common to all; things that cannot be owned or appropriated, such as light, air, and the sea.

res controversa (rays kon-trə-**vər**-sə). [Latin] *Civil law*. A matter in controversy; a point in question.

res coronae (rays kə-**roh**-nee). [Latin] *Hist.* Things of the Crown, such as ancient manors, homages of the king, and liberties.

res corporales (rays kor-pə-**ray**-leez). [Latin] *Civil law*. Corporeal things; tangible things that are perceptible to the senses.

rescous (**res**-kəs). **1.** RESCUE (2). **2.** RESCUE (3).

rescript (**ree**-skript), *n.* **1.** A judge's written order to a court clerk explaining how to dispose of a case. **2.** An appellate court's written decision, usu. unsigned, that is sent down to the trial court. **3.** A Roman emperor's or a Pope's written answer to a legal inquiry or petition. Cf. PRECES. **4.** A duplicate or counterpart; a rewriting.

rescue, *n.* **1.** The act or an instance of saving or freeing someone from danger or captivity. **2.** The forcible and unlawful freeing of a person from arrest or imprisonment. — Also termed *rescous*.

> "A *rescue* signifies a forcible setting at liberty, against law, of a person duly arrested. It is necessary, that the rescuer should have knowledge that the person whom he sets at liberty has been apprehended for a criminal offence, if he be in the custody of a private person; but if he be under the care of an officer, then he is to take notice of it at his peril." 1 Joseph Chitty, *A Practical Treatise on the Criminal Law* 62 (2d ed. 1826).

3. The forcible retaking by the owner of goods that have been lawfully distrained. — Also termed *rescous*. Cf. REPOSSESSION. **4.** *Int'l law*. The retaking of a prize by persons captured with it, so that the property is legally restored to its original owner. See POSTLIMINIUM (2). — **rescue,** *vb.*

rescue clause. See SUE-AND-LABOR CLAUSE.

rescue doctrine. *Torts.* The principle that a tortfeasor who negligently endangered a person is liable for injuries to someone who reasonably attempted to rescue the person in danger. • The rationale for this doctrine is that an attempted rescue of someone in danger is always foreseeable. Thus, if the tortfeasor is negligent toward the rescuee, the tortfeasor is also negligent toward the rescuer. Cf. EMERGENCY DOCTRINE; GOOD SAMARITAN DOCTRINE.

rescussu. See DE RESCUSSU.

res derelicta (rays der-ə-**lik**-tə). [Latin] A thing thrown away or forsaken by its owner; abandoned property.

res dominans (rays **dom**-ə-nanz). [Latin] The dominant property entitled to enjoy a servitude. See *dominant estate* under ESTATE.

research and development. An effort (as by a company or business enterprise) to create or improve products or services, esp. by discovering new technology or advancing existing technology. — Abbr. R and D; R & D.

reseiser (ri-**see**-zər). *Hist.* The taking of lands by the monarch in a case in which a general livery or ouster le main was previously misused.

resentencing, *n.* The act or an instance of imposing a new or revised criminal sentence. — **resentence,** *vb.*

reservation. 1. The creation of a new right or interest (such as an easement), by and for the grantor, in real property being granted to another. Cf. EXCEPTION (3).

implied reservation. An implied easement that reserves in a landowner an easement across a portion of sold land, such as a right-of-way over land lying between the seller's home and the only exit. • An implied reservation arises only if the seller could have expressly reserved an easement, but for some reason failed to do so. See *implied easement* under EASEMENT.

> "If the implied easement is in favor of the conveyee and is appurtenant to the tract conveyed, it is called an implied grant; if the implied easement is in favor of the conveyor and is appurtenant to the tract retained, it is called an implied reservation." Ralph E. Boyer et al., *The Law of Property* 311 (4th ed. 1991).

2. The establishment of a limiting condition or qualification; esp., a nation's formal declaration, upon signing or ratifying a treaty, that its willingness to become a party to the treaty is conditioned on certain additional terms that will limit the effect of the treaty in some way. **3.** A tract of public land set aside for a special purpose; esp., a tract of land set aside for use by an American Indian tribe. — Also termed (in sense 3) *reserve.*

reservation of rights. See NONWAIVER AGREEMENT.

reserve, *n.* **1.** Something retained or stored for future use; esp., a fund of money set aside by a bank or an insurance company to cover future liabilities.

amortization reserve. An account created for bookkeeping purposes to extinguish an obligation gradually over time.

bad-debt reserve. A reserve to cover losses on uncollectible accounts receivable.

legal reserve. The minimum amount of liquid assets that a bank or an insurance company must maintain by law to meet depositors' or claimants' demands.

loss reserve. **1.** An insurance company's reserve that represents the estimated value of future payments, as for losses incurred but not yet reported. **2.** A bank's reserve set aside to cover possible losses, as from defaulting loans.

mean reserve. In insurance, the average of the beginning reserve (after the premium has been paid for the policy year) and the ending reserve of the policy year.

policy reserve. An insurance company's reserve that represents the difference between net premiums and expected claims for a given year. • This type of reserve is kept esp. by life-insurance companies.

required reserve. The minimum amount of money, as required by the Federal Reserve Board, that a bank must hold in the form of vault cash and deposits with regional Federal Reserve Banks.

sinking-fund reserve. A reserve used to pay long-term debt. See *sinking fund* under FUND (1).

unearned-premium reserve. An insurance company's reserve that represents premiums that have been received in advance but not yet applied to policy coverage. • If a policyholder cancels coverage before the policy expires but has already paid a premium for the full policy period, the insurance company refunds the policyholder out of this reserve.

2. RESERVATION (3). **3.** See *net value* under VALUE. — **reserve,** *vb.*

reserve account. See *impound account* under ACCOUNT.

reserve bank. See *member bank* under BANK.

Reserve Board. See FEDERAL RESERVE BOARD OF GOVERNORS.

reserve clause. A clause in a professional athlete's contract restricting the athlete's right to change teams, even after the contract expires. • Reserve clauses are uncommon in modern professional sports. Cf. FREE AGENCY.

reserved easement. See EASEMENT.

reserved point of law. See POINT OF LAW.

reserved power. See POWER.

Reserved Power Clause. See TENTH AMENDMENT.

reserved surplus. See *appropriated surplus* under SURPLUS.

reserve price. See PRICE.

reserve ratio. The Federal Reserve Board's measurement of a member bank's required reserves. See *required reserve* under RESERVE.

> ***primary reserve ratio.*** The ratio between a bank's required reserves (cash in vault plus deposits with Federal Reserve Banks) and its demand and time deposits.
>
> ***secondary reserve ratio.*** The ratio between a bank's government securities and its demand and time deposits.

reset, *n. Scots law.* **1.** The act or an instance of receiving stolen goods with the intent of depriving the owner of them. **2.** *Archaic.* The harboring or sheltering of a criminal or outlaw. — **reset,** *vb.*

resettlement, *n.* **1.** The settlement of one or more persons in a new or former place. **2.** The reopening of an order or decree for the purpose of correcting a mistake or adding an omission.

res fungibiles (rays fən-**jib**-ə-leez). [Latin] *Civil law.* Fungible things; things that are commercially interchangeable.

res gestae (rays **jes**-tee *also* **jes**-tɪ), *n. pl.* [Latin "things done"] The events at issue, or other events contemporaneous with them. • In evidence law, words and statements about the res gestae are usu. admissible under a hearsay exception (such as present sense impression or excited utterance). Where the Federal Rules of Evidence or state rules fashioned after them are in effect, the use of *res gestae* is now out of place. See Fed. R. Evid. 803(1), (2). — Also termed *res gesta.*

> "The Latin expression 'res gestae' or 'res gesta,' literally 'things done' or 'thing transacted,' has long served as a catchword .... [T]he phrase has frequently served both to let in utterances which in strictness were not admissible and to exclude utterances which might well have been admitted. And frequently also its indefiniteness has served as a basis for rulings where it was easier for the judge to invoke this imposing catchword than to think through the real question involved. The phrase is antiquated. By modern judges it is being gradually discarded. It is superfluous, and serves only to obscure the logic of the rules. It should be left to oblivion." John H. Wigmore, *A Students' Textbook of the Law of Evidence* 279 (1935).
>
> "The res gestae embraces not only the actual facts of the transaction and the circumstances surrounding it, but the matters immediately antecedent to and having a direct causal connection with it, as well as acts immediately following it and so closely connected with it as to form in reality a part of the occurrence." *State v. Fouquette*, 221 P.2d 404, 416–17 (Nev. 1950).

res gestae witness. See WITNESS.

res habiles (rays **hab**-ə-leez). [Latin] *Civil law.* Things that may be acquired by prescription.

resiance (**rez**-ee-ənts). *Archaic.* Residence; abode.

resiant (**rez**-ee-ənt), *adj. Archaic.* Continually dwelling or abiding in a place; resident.

resiant, *n. Archaic.* A resident.

residence. 1. The act or fact of living in a given place for some time <a year's residence in New Jersey>. **2.** The place where one actually lives, as distinguished from a domicile <she made her residence in Oregon>. • *Residence* usu. just means bodily presence as an inhabitant in a given place; *domicile* usu. requires bodily presence plus an intention to make the place one's home. A person thus may have more than one residence at a time but only one domicile. Sometimes, though, the two terms are used synonymously. Cf. DOMICILE. **3.** The place where a corporation or other enterprise does business or is registered to do business <Pantheon Inc.'s principal residence is in Delaware>. **4.** A house or other fixed abode; a dwelling <a three-story residence>.

residency. **1.** A place of residence, esp. an official one <the diplomat's residency>. **2.** The fact or condition of living in a given place <one year's residency to be eligible for in-state tuition>.

resident, *n.* A person who has a residence in a particular place. • A resident is not necessarily either a citizen or a domiciliary. Cf. CITIZEN; DOMICILIARY.

resident agent. See *registered agent* under AGENT.

resident alien. See ALIEN.

residential cluster. *Land-use planning.* An area of land developed as a unit with group housing and open common space. Cf. PLANNED-UNIT DEVELOPMENT.

residential community treatment center. See HALFWAY HOUSE.

residua (ri-**zij**-oo-ə). *pl.* RESIDUUM.

residual, *adj.* Of, relating to, or constituting a residue; remaining; leftover <a residual claim> <a residual functional disability>.

residual, *n.* **1.** A leftover quantity; a remainder. **2.** (*often pl.*) A disability remaining after an illness, injury, or operation. **3.** (*usu. pl.*) A fee paid to a composer or performer for each repeated broadcast (esp. on television) of a film, program, or commercial.

residual estate. See *residuary estate* under ESTATE.

residual value. See *salvage value* under VALUE.

residuary (ri-**zij**-oo-er-ee), *adj.* Of, relating to, or constituting a residue; residual <a residuary gift>.

residuary, *n.* *Wills & estates.* **1.** See *residuary estate* under ESTATE. **2.** See *residuary legatee* under LEGATEE.

residuary bequest. See BEQUEST.

residuary clause. *Wills & estates.* A testamentary clause that disposes of any estate property remaining after the satisfaction of specific bequests and devises.

residuary devise. See DEVISE.

residuary devisee. See DEVISEE.

residuary estate. See ESTATE.

residuary legacy. See LEGACY.

residuary legatee. See LEGATEE.

residue. **1.** Something that is left over after a part is removed or disposed of; a remainder. **2.** See *residuary estate* under ESTATE.

residuum (ri-**zij**-oo-əm). **1.** That which remains; a residue. **2.** See *residuary estate* under ESTATE. Pl. **residua** (ri-**zij**-oo-ə).

residuum rule. *Administrative law.* The principle that an agency decision based partly on hearsay evidence will be upheld on judicial review only if the decision is founded on at least some competent evidence. • The residuum rule has generally been rejected by federal and state courts.

resignation, *n.* **1.** The act or an instance of surrendering or relinquishing an office, right, or claim. **2.** A formal notification of relinquishing an office or position. — **resign,** *vb.*

res immobiles (rays i-**moh**-bə-leez). [Latin] *Civil law.* Immovable things; chattels real. See IMMOBILIA.

res incorporales (rays in-kor-pə-**ray**-leez). [Latin] *Civil law.* Incorporeal things; intangible things that are not perceptible to the senses. See *incorporeal thing* under THING.

res integra (rays **in**-tə-grə *also* in-**teg**-rə). [Latin "an entire thing"] See RES NOVA.

res inter alios acta (rays **in**-tər **ay**-lee-ohs **ak**-tə). [Latin "a thing done between others"] **1.** *Contracts.* The common-law doctrine holding that a contract cannot unfavorably affect the rights of a person who is not a party to the contract. **2.** *Evidence.* The rule prohibiting the admission of collateral facts into evidence.

res ipsa loquitur (rays **ip**-sə **loh**-kwə-tər). [Latin "the thing speaks for itself"] **1.** *Torts.* The doctrine providing that, in some circumstances, the mere fact of an accident's occurrence raises an inference of negligence so as to establish a prima facie case. — Often shortened to *res ipsa.* — Also termed *resipsy.*

"The phrase 'res ipsa loquitur' is a symbol for the rule that the fact of the occurrence of an injury, taken with the surrounding circumstances, may permit an inference or raise a presumption of negligence, or make out a plaintiff's prima facie case, and present a question of fact for defendant to meet with an explanation. It is merely a short way of saying that the circumstances attendant on the accident are of such a nature as to justify a jury, in light of common sense and past experience, in inferring that the accident was probably the result of the defendant's negligence, in the absence of explanation or other evidence which the jury believes." Stuart M. Speiser, *The Negligence Case: Res Ipsa Loquitur* § 1:2, at 5–6 (1972).

"It is said that *res ipsa loquitur* does not apply if the cause of the harm is known. This is a dark saying. The application of the principle nearly always presupposes that some part of the causal process is known, but what is lacking is evidence of its connection with the defendant's act or omission. When the fact of control is used to justify the inference that defendant's negligence was responsible it must of course be shown that the thing in his control in fact caused the harm. In a sense, therefore, the cause of the harm must be known before the maxim can apply." H.L.A. Hart & Tony Honoré, *Causation in the Law* 419–20 (2d ed. 1985).

"Res ipsa loquitur is an appropriate form of circumstantial evidence enabling the plaintiff in particular cases to establish the defendant's likely negligence. Hence the res ipsa loquitur doctrine, properly applied, does not entail any covert form of strict liability.... The doctrine implies that the court does not know, and cannot find out, what actually happened in the individual case. Instead, the finding of likely negligence is derived from knowledge of the causes of the type or category of accidents involved." Restatement (Third) of Torts § 15 cmt. a (Discussion Draft 1999).

2. *Criminal law.* A test used to determine whether a defendant has gone beyond preparation and committed an attempt, based on whether the defendant's act itself indicated to an observer what the defendant intended to do. — Also termed (in sense 2) *equivocality.*

resisting arrest. The crime of obstructing or opposing a police officer who is making an arrest. — Also termed *resisting lawful arrest.*

resisting unlawful arrest. The act of opposing a police officer who is making an unlawful arrest. • Most jurisdictions have accepted the Model Penal Code position prohibiting the use of force to resist an unlawful arrest when the person arrested knows that a police officer is making the arrest. But some jurisdictions allow an arrestee to use nondeadly force to prevent the arrest.

res judicata (rays joo-di-**kay**-tə *or* -**kah**-tə). [Latin "a thing adjudicated"] **1.** An issue that has been definitively settled by judicial decision. **2.** An affirmative defense barring the same parties from litigating a second lawsuit on the same claim, or any other claim arising from the same transaction or series of transactions and that could have been — but was not — raised in the first suit. • The three essential elements are (1) an earlier decision on the issue, (2) a final judgment on the merits, and (3) the involvement of the same parties, or parties in privity with the original parties. Restatement (Second) of Judgments §§ 17, 24 (1982). — Also termed *res adjudicata*; *claim preclusion*. Cf. COLLATERAL ESTOPPEL.

" 'Res judicata' has been used in this section as a general term referring to all of the ways in which one judgment will have a binding effect on another. That usage is and doubtless will continue to be common, but it lumps under a single name two quite different effects of judgments. The first is the effect of foreclosing any litigation of matters that never have been litigated, because of the determination that they should have been advanced in an earlier suit. The second is the effect of foreclosing relitigation of matters that have once been litigated and decided. The first of these, preclusion of matters that were never litigated, has gone under the name, 'true res judicata,' or the names, 'merger' and 'bar.' The second doctrine, preclusion of matters that have once been decided, has usually been called 'collateral estoppel.' Professor Allan Vestal has long argued for the use of the names 'claim preclusion' and 'issue preclusion' for these two doctrines [Vestal, *Rationale of Preclusion*, 9 St. Louis U. L.J. 29 (1964)], and this usage is increasingly employed by the courts as it is by Restatement Second of Judgments." Charles Alan Wright, *The Law of Federal Courts* § 100A, at 722–23 (5th ed. 1994).

res litigiosae (rays li-tij-ee-**oh**-see). [Latin] *Civil law.* Things that are in litigation; property or rights that are the subject of a pending action.

res mancipi (rays **man**-sə-pɪ). [Latin "things of mancipium"] *Roman law.* Property that can be transferred only by a formal ceremony of mancipation. — Also termed *mancipi res*; *things mancipi*. See MANCIPATION.

res mobiles (rays **moh**-bə-leez). [Latin] *Civil law.* Movable things; chattels personal.

res nec mancipi (rays nek **man**-sə-pɪ). [Latin "things not of mancipium"] *Roman law.* Property that can be transferred without a formal ceremony of mancipation. — Also termed *things nec mancipi.*

res nova (rays **noh**-və). [Latin "new thing"] **1.** An undecided question of law. **2.** A case of first impression. — Also termed *res integra.* See *case of first impression* under CASE.

res nullius (rays nə-**lɪ**-əs). [Latin "thing of no one"] A thing that can belong to no one; an ownerless chattel.

resolution. 1. A formal expression of an opinion, intention, or decision by an official body or assembly (esp. a legislature).

concurrent resolution. A resolution passed by one house and agreed to by the other. • It expresses the legislature's opinion on a subject but does not have the force of law.

joint resolution. A legislative resolution passed by both houses. • It has the force of law and is subject to executive veto.

simple resolution. A resolution passed by one house only. • It expresses the opinion or affects the internal affairs of the passing house, but it does not have the force of law.

2. Formal action by a corporate board of directors or other corporate body authorizing a particular act, transaction, or appointment.

shareholder resolution. A resolution by shareholders, usu. to ratify the actions of the board of directors.

3. A document containing such an expression or authorization.

Resolution Trust Corporation. A federal agency established to act as a receiver for insolvent federal savings-and-loan associations and to transfer or liquidate those associations' assets. • The agency was created when the Federal Savings and Loan Insurance Corporation was abolished in 1989. — Abbr. RTC. See FEDERAL SAVINGS AND LOAN INSURANCE CORPORATION.

resolutive condition. See *resolutory condition* under CONDITION (2).

resolutory (ri-**zahl**-yə-tor-ee), *adj.* Operating or serving to annul, dissolve, or terminate <a resolutory clause>.

resolutory condition. See CONDITION (2).

resort, *n.* Something that one turns to for aid or refuge <the court of last resort>. — **resort,** *vb.*

RESPA (**res**-pə). *abbr.* REAL ESTATE SETTLEMENT PROCEDURES ACT.

respite (**res**-pit), *n.* **1.** A period of temporary delay; an extension of time. **2.** A temporary suspension of a death sentence; a reprieve. **3.** A delay granted to a jury or court for further consideration of a verdict or appeal. **4.** *Civil law.* An agreement between a debtor and several creditors for an extension of time to repay the various debts. — **respite,** *vb.*

forced respite. A respite in which some of the creditors are compelled by a court to give the same extension of time that the other creditors have agreed to.

voluntary respite. A respite in which all the creditors agree to the debtor's proposal for an extension of time.

respondeat ouster (ri-**spon**-dee-at **ow**-stər). [Latin "let him make further answer"] A judgment or order that a party who made a dilatory plea that has been denied must now plead on the merits.

> "In case of felony, if the plea be held bad, the judgment is *respondeat ouster*; or rather, as the defendant generally pleads over to the felony, the jury are charged again, and that at the same time with the issue on the plea of autrefois acquit, to inquire of the second issue, and the trial proceeds as if no plea in bar had been pleaded." 1 Joseph Chitty, *A Practical Treatise on the Criminal Law* 461 (2d ed. 1826).

respondeat superior (ri-**spon**-dee-at soo-**peer**-ee-ər *or* sə-peer-ee-**or**). [Law Latin "let the superior make answer"] *Torts.* The doctrine holding an employer or principal liable for the employee's or agent's wrongful acts committed within the scope of the employment or agency. — Also termed *master-servant rule.* See SCOPE OF EMPLOYMENT.

> "Most courts have made little or no effort to explain the result, and have taken refuge in rather empty phrases, such as 'he who does a thing through another does it himself,' or the endlessly repeated formula of 'respondeat superior,' which in itself means nothing more than 'look to the man higher up.'" W. Page Keeton et al., *The Law of Torts* § 69, at 500 (5th ed. 1984).

respondent. 1. The party against whom an appeal is taken; APPELLEE. **2.** The party against whom a motion or petition is filed. Cf. PETITIONER. **3.** At common law, the defendant in an equity proceeding. **4.** *Civil law.* One who answers for another or acts as another's security.

respondent bank. See BANK.

respondentia (ree-spon-**den**-shee-ə *or* res-pon-). [Law Latin fr. Latin *respondere* "to answer"] A loan secured by the cargo on one's ship rather than the ship itself. Cf. BOTTOMRY.

respondentia bond. See BOND (2).

respondere non debet (ri-**spon**-də-ree non **deb**-ət). [Latin] *Common-law pleading.* The prayer of a plea in which the defendant insists that he or she does not have to answer — because of a privilege, for example.

responsalis (res-pon-**say**-lis). [Law Latin] **1.** *Hist.* One who appears and answers for another. **2.** *Eccles. law.* A proctor. See APOCRISARIUS.

responsa prudentium (ri-**spon**-sə proo-**den**-shee-əm). [Latin "the answers of the learned"] *Hist.* The opinions and judgments of eminent lawyers or jurists on questions of law addressed to them. • The *responsa prudentium* originally constituted part of the early Roman civil law. Roman citizens seeking legal advice, as well as magistrates and judges, often referred legal questions to leading jurists so as to obtain their opinions (*responsa*). The *responsa* of some leading jurists were collected, much in the manner of caselaw digests, and many of them passed into Justinian's Digest. The phrase *responsa prudentium* gradually migrated to the common law, but today it is of primarily historical use. — Also spelled *responsa prudentum.*

> "[T]he *judex*, or as we would now call him, the referee, might have no technical knowledge of law whatever. Under such conditions the unlearned judicial magistrates naturally looked for light and leading to the jurisconsults who instructed them through their *responsa prudentium*, the technical name given to their opinions as experts, which were promptly recorded on tablets by their students or disciples." Hannis Taylor, *The Science of Jurisprudence* 90–91 (1908).

> "In [classical Latin] *responsa prudentium* is the usual form, but most of the legal sources . . . have *prudentum* following the example of Blackstone (1765)." *The Oxford English Dictionary* (2d ed. 1989).

responsibility, *n.* **1.** LIABILITY (1). **2.** *Criminal law.* A person's mental fitness to answer in court for his or her actions. See COMPETENCY. **3.** *Criminal law.* Guilt. — Also termed (in senses 2 & 3) *criminal responsibility.* — **responsible,** *adj.*

> "[As for] the ambiguities of the word 'responsibility,' . . . it is, I think, still important to distinguish two of the very different things this difficult word may mean. To say that someone is legally responsible for something often means only that under legal rules he is liable to be made either to suffer or to pay compensation in certain eventualities. The expression 'he'll pay for it' covers both these things. In this the primary sense of the word, though a man is normally only responsible for his own actions or the harm he has done, he may be also responsible for the actions of other persons if legal rules so provide. Indeed in this sense a baby in arms or a totally insane person might be legally responsible — again, if the rules so provide; for the word simply means liable to be made to account or pay and we might call this sense of the word 'legal accountability'. But the new idea — the programme of eliminating responsibility — is not, as some have feared, meant to eliminate legal accountability: persons who break the law are not just to be left free. What is to be eliminated are enquiries as to whether a person who has done what the law forbids was responsible at the time he did it and responsible in this sense does not refer to the legal status of accountability. It means the capacity, so far as this is a matter of a man's mind or will, which normal people have to control their actions and conform to law. In this sense of responsibility a man's responsibility can be said to be 'impaired'." H.L.A. Hart, "Changing Conceptions of Responsibility," in *Punishment and Responsibility* 186, 196–97 (1968).

responsible broker-dealer. See BROKER.

responsive, *adj.* Giving or constituting a response; answering <the witness's testimony is not responsive to the question>.

responsive pleading. See PLEADING (1).

responsive verdict. See VERDICT.

res privatae (rays pri-**vay**-tee). [Latin "private things"] *Roman & civil law.* Things that can be owned by individuals.

res publicae (rays **pəb**-li-see). [Latin "public things"] *Roman & civil law.* Things that cannot be individually owned because they belong to the public, such as the sea, navigable waters, and highways.

res quotidianae (rays kwoh-tid-ee-**ay**-nee). [Latin] *Civil law.* Everyday matters; familiar points or questions.

res religiosae (rays ri-lij-ee-**oh**-see). [Latin] *Civil law.* Religious things; esp., burial places.

res sanctae (rays **sangk**-tee). [Latin "sacred thing"] *Roman law.* The walls of a city. • The Romans considered maintenance of city walls so important that damage to a city's walls was a capital offense.

res serviens (rays **sər**-vee-enz). [Latin] The servient property subject to a servitude. See *servient estate* under ESTATE.

rest, *vb.* **1.** (Of a litigant) to voluntarily conclude presenting evidence in a trial <after the police officer's testimony, the prosecution rested>. **2.** (Of a litigant) to voluntarily conclude presenting evidence in (a trial) <the defense rested its case after presenting just two witnesses>.

Restatement. One of several influential treatises, published by the American Law Institute, describing the law in a given area and guiding its development. • Although the Restatements are frequently cited in cases and commentary, they are not binding on the courts. Restatements have been published in the following areas of law: Agency, Conflict of Laws, Contracts, Foreign Relations Law of the United States, Judgments, Law Governing Lawyers, Property, Restitution, Security, Suretyship and Guaranty, Torts, Trusts, and Unfair Competition. — Also termed *Restatement of the Law.*

> "We speak of the work which the organization should undertake as a restatement; its object should not only be to help make certain much that is now uncertain and to simplify unnecessary complexities, but also to promote those changes which will tend better to adapt the laws to the needs of life. The character of the restatement which we have in mind can be best described by saying that it should be at once analytical, critical and constructive." Committee on the Establishment of a Permanent Organization for the Improvement of the Law (Elihu Root, chairman), *Report Proposing the Establishment of an American Law Institute*, 1 ALI Proc. 14 (1923).

restater. An author or reporter of a Restatement.

restaur (res-**tor**). **1.** The recourse that insurers (esp. marine underwriters) have against each other according to the date of their insurance. **2.** The recourse that marine insurers have against a ship's master if a loss occurs through the master's fault or negligence. **3.** The recourse that one has against a guarantor or other person under a duty to indemnify. — Also spelled *restor*.

restitutio in integrum (res-tə-**t[y]oo**-shee-oh in **in**-tə-grəm). [Law Latin] *Roman & civil law.* Restoration to the previous condition or the status quo. • In Roman law, a praetor could accomplish this by annulling a contract or transaction that was strictly legally valid but inequitable and by restoring the parties to their previous legal relationship. The phrase is still sometimes used in American law (esp. in Louisiana) when a court annuls a contract and orders restitution on equitable grounds.

restitution, *n.* **1.** Return or restoration of some specific thing to its rightful owner or status. **2.** Compensation for benefits derived from a wrong done to another. **3.** Compensation or reparation for the loss caused to another. • In senses 2 and 3, restitution is available in tort and contract law and is sometimes ordered as a condition of probation in criminal law. — **restitutionary,** *adj.*

> "The term 'restitution' appears in early decisions, but general recognition probably began with the publication of the *Restatement of Restitution* [in 1937]. The term is not wholly apt since it suggests restoration to the successful party of some benefit obtained from him. Usually this will be the case where relief is given, but by no means always. There are cases in which the successful party obtains restitution of something he did not have before, for example a benefit received by the defendant from a third person which justly should go to the plaintiff." 1 George E. Palmer, *The Law of Restitution* § 1.1, at 4 (1978).

> " 'Restitution' is an ambiguous term, sometimes referring to the disgorging of something which has been taken and at times referring to compensation for injury done. Often, the result under either meaning of the term would be the same. If the plaintiff has been defrauded into paying $1,000 to the defendant, his loss and the defendant's gain coincide. Where they do not coincide, as where the plaintiff is out of pocket more than the defendant has gained and the defendant's conduct is tortious, the plaintiff will recover his loss in a quasi-contractual or equitable action for restitution. Unjust impoverishment as well as unjust enrichment is a ground for restitution. If the defendant is guilty of a non-tortious misrepresentation, the measure of recovery is not rigid but, as in other cases of restitution, such factors as relative fault, the agreed upon risks, and the fairness of alternative risk allocations not agreed upon and not attributable to the fault of either party need to be weighed." John D. Calamari & Joseph M. Perillo, *The Law of Contracts* § 9-23, at 376 (3d ed. 1987).

restitutionary redress. See REDRESS.

restitution damages. See DAMAGES.

restitutione extracti ab ecclesia (res-tə-t[y]oo-shee-**oh**-nee ek-**strak**-tɪ ab e-**klee**-z[h]ee-ə). [Latin] *Eccles. law.* A writ restoring someone who had been suspected or accused of a felony to the church.

restitutione temporalium (res-tə-t[y]oo-shee-**oh**-nee tem-pə-**ray**-lee-əm). [Latin] *Eccles. law.* A writ directing the sheriff to restore the temporalities of a diocese to a bishop. See TEMPORALITY (2).

restitutory interdict. See INTERDICT (1).

restor. See RESTAUR.

restraining order. 1. A court order prohibiting or restricting a person from harassing, threatening, and sometimes even contacting or approaching another specified person. • This type of order is issued most commonly in cases of domestic violence. — Also termed *protection order*; *protective order*. **2.** TEMPORARY RESTRAINING ORDER.

restraint, *n.* **1.** Confinement, abridgment, or limitation <a restraint on the freedom of speech>. See PRIOR RESTRAINT. **2.** Prohibition of action; holding back <the victim's family exercised no restraint — they told the suspect exactly what they thought of him>. **3.** RESTRAINT OF TRADE.

restraint of marriage. A condition (esp. in a gift or bequest) that nullifies the grant to which it applies if the grantee marries or remarries. • Restraints of marriage are usu. void if they are general or unlimited in scope.

restraint of princes. *Archaic.* An embargo. • The phrase still occasionally appears in marine-insurance contexts. — Also termed *restraint of princes and rulers*; *restraint of princes, rulers, and people.* See EMBARGO.

restraint of trade. *Antitrust.* An agreement between or combination of businesses intended to eliminate competition, create a monopoly, artificially raise prices, or otherwise adversely affect the free market. • Restraints of trade are usu. illegal, but may be declared reasonable if they are in the best interests of both the parties and the public. — Often shortened to *restraint.* — Also termed *conspiracy in restraint of trade.* See PER SE RULE; RULE OF REASON.

horizontal restraint. A restraint of trade imposed by agreement between competitors at the same level of distribution. • The restraint is horizontal not because it has horizontal effects, but because it is the product of a horizontal agreement. — Also termed *horizontal agreement.*

unreasonable restraint of trade. A restraint of trade that produces a significant anticompetitive effect and thus violates antitrust law.

vertical restraint. A restraint of trade imposed by agreement between firms at different levels of distribution (as between manufacturer and retailer).

restraint on alienation. 1. A restriction, usu. in a deed of conveyance, on a grantee's ability to sell or transfer real property; a provision that conveys an interest and that, even after the interest has become vested, prevents the owner from disposing of it at all or from disposing of it in particular ways or to particular persons. • Restraints on alienation are generally unenforceable as against public policy favoring the free alienability of land. — Also termed *unreasonable restraint on alienation.* **2.** A trust provision that prohibits or penalizes alienation of the trust corpus.

restricted interpretation. See *restrictive interpretation* under INTERPRETATION.

restricted security. See SECURITY.

restricted stock. See *restricted security* under SECURITY.

restricted surplus. See SURPLUS.

restriction. 1. A limitation or qualification. **2.** A limitation (esp. in a deed) placed on the use or enjoyment of property. See *restrictive covenant* under COVENANT (4). **3.** *Military law.* A deprivation of liberty involving moral and legal, rather than physical, restraint. • A military restriction is imposed as punishment either by a commanding officer's nonjudicial punishment or by a summary, special, or general court-martial. Restriction is a lesser restraint because it permits the restricted person to perform full military duties. See *nonjudicial punishment* under PUNISHMENT.

restriction in lieu of arrest. A restriction in which a person is ordered to stay within specific geographical limits, such as a base or a ship, and is permitted to perform full military duties.

restrictive condition. See *negative condition* under CONDITION (2).

restrictive covenant. See COVENANT (4).

restrictive covenant in equity. See *restrictive covenant* under COVENANT (4).

restrictive indorsement. See INDORSEMENT.

restrictive interpretation. See INTERPRETATION.

restrictive principle of sovereign immunity. The doctrine by which a foreign nation's immunity does not apply to claims arising from the nation's private or commercial acts, but protects the nation only from claims arising from its public functions. See COMMERCIAL-ACTIVITY EXCEPTION; JURE GESTIONIS; JURE IMPERII.

> "[T]he [Foreign Sovereign] Immunities Act codified the so-called 'restrictive' principle of sovereign immunity, as recognized in international law. Under this doctrine, the immunity of a foreign state in the courts of the United States is 'restricted' to claims involving the foreign state's public acts and does not extend to suits based on its commercial or private conduct." 14A Charles Alan Wright et al., *Federal Practice and Procedure* § 3662, at 161–62 (3d ed. 1998).

resulting power. See POWER.

resulting trust. See TRUST.

resulting use. See USE (4).

resummons. A second or renewed summons to a party or witness already summoned. See SUMMONS.

resumption. **1.** The taking back of property previously given up or lost. **2.** *Hist.* The retaking by the Crown or other authority of lands or rights previously given to another (as because of false suggestion or other error).

res universitatis (rays yoo-nə-vər-sə-**tay**-tis). [Latin] *Civil law.* Things belonging to a community (such as a municipality) and free to be used by all its members, such as public buildings and streets.

resurrender, *n. Hist.* The return of a copyhold estate to a mortgagor by the mortgagee after the debt has been repaid. See SURRENDER OF COPYHOLD.

retail, *n.* The sale of goods or commodities to ultimate consumers, as opposed to the sale for further distribution or processing. — **retail,** *vb.* — **retail,** *adj.* Cf. WHOLESALE.

retailer, *n.* A person or entity engaged in the business of selling personal property to the public or to consumers, as opposed to selling to those who intend to resell the items.

retail installment contract. See CONTRACT.

retail installment contract and security agreement. See *retail installment contract* under CONTRACT.

retail installment sale. See INSTALLMENT SALE.

retail sales tax. See *sales tax* under TAX.

retainage (ri-**tayn**-ij). A percentage of what a landowner pays a contractor, withheld until the construction has been satisfactorily completed and all mechanic's liens are released or have expired.

retained earnings. See EARNINGS.

retainer, *n.* **1.** A client's authorization for a lawyer to act in a case <the attorney needed an express retainer before making a settlement offer>. **2.** A fee paid to a lawyer to secure legal representation <he requires a $100,000 retainer>. — Also termed *retaining fee.* — **retain,** *vb.* Cf. ATTORNEY'S FEES.

general retainer. A retainer for a specific length of time rather than for a specific project.

special retainer. A retainer for a specific case or project.

retaining fee. See RETAINER (2).

retaining lien. See LIEN.

retaliatory discharge. See DISCHARGE (7).

retaliatory eviction. See EVICTION.

retaliatory law. A state law restraining another state's businesses — as by levying taxes — in response to similar restraints imposed by the second state on the first state's businesses.

retaliatory tariff. See TARIFF (2).

retallia (ri-**tal**-ee-ə). [Law Latin] *Hist.* The sale of goods or commodities in small quantities; retail.

retenementum (ri-ten-ə-**men**-təm). *Hist.* A withholding; restraint or detainment.

retinue. A group of persons who are retained to follow and attend to a sovereign, noble, or other distinguished person.

retired stock. See *treasury stock* under STOCK.

retirement, *n.* **1.** Voluntary termination of one's own employment or career, esp. upon reaching a certain age <she traveled around the world after her retirement>. **2.** Withdrawal from action or for privacy <Carol's retirement to her house by the lake>. **3.** Withdrawal from circulation; payment of a debt <retirement of a series of bonds>. See REDEMPTION. — **retire,** *vb.*

retirement annuity. See ANNUITY.

retirement-income insurance. See INSURANCE.

retirement plan. See EMPLOYEE BENEFIT PLAN.

retorna brevium (ri-**tor**-nə **bree**-vee-əm). [Law Latin] *Hist.* The return of a writ. • This was the indorsement on a writ by a sheriff or other officer, reporting on the writ's execution.

retorno habendo. See DE RETORNO HABENDO.

retorsion (ri-**tor**-shən). *Int'l law.* An act of lawful retaliation in kind for another nation's unfriendly or unfair act. • Examples of retorsion include suspending diplomatic relations, expelling foreign nationals, and restricting travel rights. — Also spelled *retortion.* Cf. REPRISAL (2).

retraction, *n.* **1.** The act of taking or drawing back <retraction of anticipatory repudiation before breach of contract>. **2.** The act of recanting; a statement in recantation <retraction of a defamatory remark>. **3.** *Wills & estates.* A withdrawal of a renunciation <because of her retraction, she took property under her uncle's will>. See RENUNCIATION (3). — **retract,** *vb.*

retraxit (ri-**trak**-sit). [Latin "he has withdrawn"] A plaintiff's voluntary withdrawal of a lawsuit in court so that the plaintiff forfeits the right of action. • In modern practice, retraxit is called *voluntary dismissal* or *dismissal with prejudice.* See *judgment of retraxit* under JUDGMENT.

retreat rule. *Criminal law.* The doctrine holding that the victim of a murderous assault must choose a safe retreat instead of resorting to deadly force in self-defense, unless (1) the victim is at home or in his or her place of business (the so-called *castle doctrine*), or (2) the assailant is a person whom the victim is trying to arrest. • A minority of American jurisdictions have adopted this rule. Cf. NO-RETREAT RULE.

retrial, *n.* A new trial of an action that has already been tried. — **retry,** *vb.* See TRIAL DE NOVO.

retribution, *n.* **1.** *Criminal law.* Punishment imposed as repayment or revenge for the offense committed; requital. Cf. DETERRENCE; REHABILITATION (1). **2.** Something justly deserved; repayment; reward. — **retribute,** *vb.* — **retributive,** *adj.*

retributive danger. See DANGER.

retributive punishment. See PUNISHMENT.

retributivism (ri-**trib**-yə-tə-viz-əm). The legal theory by which criminal punishment is justified, as long as the offender is morally accountable, regardless of whether deterrence or other good consequences would result. • According to retributivism, a criminal is thought to have a debt to pay to society, which is paid by punishment. The punishment is also sometimes said to be society's act of paying back the criminal for the wrong done. Opponents of retributivism sometimes refer to it as "vindictive theory." Cf. *hedonistic utilitarianism* under UTILITARIANISM; UTILITARIAN-DETERRENCE THEORY.

maximalist retributivism. The classical form of retributivism, espoused by scholars such as Immanuel Kant, under which it is argued that society has a duty, not just a right, to punish a criminal who is guilty and culpable, that is, someone who has no justification or excuse for the illegal act.

minimalist retributivism. The more contemporary form of retributivism, which maintains that no one should be punished in the absence of guilt and culpability (that is, unless punishment is deserved), and that a judge may absolve the offender from punishment, wholly or partially, when doing so would further societal goals such as rehabilitation or deterrence.

retroactive, *adj.* (Of a statute, ruling, etc.) extending in scope or effect to matters that have occurred in the past. — Also termed *retrospective.* Cf. PROSPECTIVE (1). — **retroactivity,** *n.*

> "'Retroactivity' is a term often used by lawyers but rarely defined. On analysis it soon becomes apparent, moreover, that it is used to cover at least two distinct concepts. The first, which may be called 'true retroactivity,' consists in the application of a new rule of law to an act or transaction which was completed before the rule was promulgated. The second concept, which will be referred to as 'quasi-retroactivity,' occurs when a new rule of law is applied to an act or transaction in the process of completion.... [T]he foundation of these concepts is the distinction between completed and pending transactions ...." T.C. Hartley, *The Foundations of European Community Law* 129 (1981).

retroactive law. A legislative act that looks backward or contemplates the past, affecting acts or facts that existed before the act came into effect. • A retroactive law is not unconstitutional unless it (1) is in the nature of an ex post facto law or a bill of attainder, (2) impairs the obligation of contracts, (3) divests vested rights, or (4) is constitutionally forbidden. — Also termed *retrospective law.*

retrocession. 1. The act of ceding something back (such as a territory or jurisdiction). **2.** The return of a title or other interest in property back to its former or rightful owner. **3.** The process of transferring all or part of a reinsured risk to another reinsurance company; reinsurance of reinsurance. • Subsequent retrocessions are referred to as *first retrocession*, *second retrocession*, and so on. **4.** The amount of risk that is so transferred.

retrocessionaire. *Reinsurance*. A reinsurer of a reinsurer. See RETROCESSION.

retrocessional agreement. An agreement providing for reinsurance of reinsurance.

retrospectant evidence. See EVIDENCE.

retrospective, *adj*. See RETROACTIVE.

retrospective law. See RETROACTIVE LAW.

retrospective statute. See STATUTE.

return, *n*. **1.** A court officer's bringing back of an instrument to the court that issued it; RETURN OF WRIT <a sheriff's return of citation>. **2.** A court officer's indorsement on an instrument brought back to the court, reporting what the officer did or found <a return of *nulla bona*>. See FALSE RETURN (1). **3.** TAX RETURN <file your return before April 15>. **4.** (*usu. pl.*) An official report of voting results <election returns>. **5.** Yield or profit <return on an investment>. See RATE OF RETURN. — **return,** *vb*.

capital return. *Tax*. Revenue that represents the repayment of cost or capital and thus is not taxable as income.

fair return on investment. The usual or reasonable profit in a business, esp. a public utility.

net return. The profit on an investment after deducting all investment expenses.

return date. See *return day* under DAY.

return day. See DAY.

returning board. An official body or commission that canvasses election returns.

return of service. See PROOF OF SERVICE.

return of writ. The sheriff's bringing back a writ to the court that issued it, with a short written account (usu. on the back) of the manner in which the writ was executed. — Often shortened to *return*. See RETURN (1).

re-up, *vb*. **1.** To reenlist in one of the armed forces <the soldier re-upped the day after being discharged>. **2.** To sign an extension to a contract, esp. an employment agreement <the star athlete re-upped in a three-year deal worth $12 million>.

reus (**ree**-əs). [Latin] *Roman & civil law*. **1.** A defendant. Cf. ACTOR (3). **2.** A party to a suit, whether plaintiff or defendant. **3.** A party to a contract or transaction. Pl. ***rei***.

revalidation. See REPUBLICATION.

revaluation, *n*. An increase in the value of one currency in relation to another currency. — **revalue,** *vb*. Cf. DEVALUATION.

revaluation surplus. See SURPLUS.

rev'd. *abbr*. Reversed.

reve (reev). *Hist*. The bailiff of a franchise or manor.

revendication, *n*. **1.** The recovery or claiming back of something by a formal claim or demand. **2.** *Civil law*. An action to recover rights in and possession of property that is wrongfully held by another. • This is analogous to the common-law replevin. — **revendicate,** *vb*.

revenue. Gross income or receipts.

general revenue. The income stream from which a state or municipality pays its obligations unless a law calls for payment from a special fund. See *general fund* under FUND (1).

land revenue. Revenue derived from lands owned by the Crown in Great Britain. • Crown lands have been so largely granted away to subjects that they are now transferred within very narrow limits. See *Crown land* under LAND.

marginal revenue. The amount of revenue earned from the sale of one additional unit.

revenue agent's report. A report indicating any adjustments made to a tax return as a result of an IRS audit. • After an audit, this report is mailed to the taxpayer along with a 30–day letter. — Abbr. RAR. See 30–DAY LETTER.

revenue bill. See BILL (3).

revenue bond. See BOND (3).

Revenue Procedure. An official statement by the IRS regarding the administration and procedures of the tax laws. — Abbr. Rev. Proc.

Revenue Ruling. An official interpretation by the IRS of the proper application of the tax law to a specific transaction. • Revenue Rulings carry some authoritative weight and may be relied on by the taxpayer who requested the ruling. — Abbr. Rev. Rul.

revenue stamp. A stamp used as evidence that a tax has been paid.

revenue tariff. See TARIFF (2).

reversal, *n.* **1.** An appellate court's overturning of a lower court's decision. **2.** *Securities.* A change in a security's near-term market-price trend. — **reverse,** *vb.*

reverse annuity mortgage. See MORTGAGE.

reverse bonus. See *reverse contingent fee* under CONTINGENT FEE.

reverse-confusion doctrine. *Intellectual property.* The rule that it is unfair competition if the defendant's use of a title that is confusingly similar to the one used by the plaintiff leads the public to believe that the plaintiff's work is the same as the defendant's, or that it is derived from or associated in some manner with the defendant. • Under the conventional passing-off form of unfair competition, similarity of titles leads the public to believe that the defendant's work is the same as the plaintiff's work, or is in some manner derived from the plaintiff. But in reverse confusion, the unfair competition results from the confusion created about the origin of the plaintiff's work.

reverse contingent fee. See CONTINGENT FEE.

reverse discrimination. See DISCRIMINATION.

reverse doctrine of equivalents. See DOCTRINE OF EQUIVALENTS.

reverse FOIA suit (**foy**-ə). A lawsuit by the owner of a trade secret to prevent an agency from releasing that secret to the general public. See FREEDOM OF INFORMATION ACT.

reverse spot zoning. See ZONING.

reverse stock split. See STOCK SPLIT.

reverse subsidiary merger. See *reverse triangular merger* under MERGER.

reverse triangular merger. See MERGER.

reversible error. See ERROR (2).

reversio (ri-**vər**-shee-oh). [Law Latin] *Hist.* The returning of land to the grantor.

reversion, *n.* **1.** A future interest in land arising by operation of law whenever an estate owner grants to another a particular estate, such as a life estate or a term of years, but does not dispose of the entire interest. • A reversion occurs automatically upon termination of the prior estate, as when a life tenant dies. — Also termed *reversionary estate*; *estate in reversion*; *equitable reversion.* **2.** Loosely, REMAINDER. — **revert,** *vb.* — **reversionary,** *adj.* Cf. POSSIBILITY OF REVERTER; REMAINDER.

reversioner. 1. One who possesses the reversion to an estate; the grantor or heir in reversion. **2.** Broadly, one who has a lawful interest in land but not the present possession of it.

reverter. See POSSIBILITY OF REVERTER.

reverter guarantee. *Real estate.* A mortgage clause protecting the mortgagee against a loss occasioned by the occurrence of a terminating event under a possibility of reverter. See POSSIBILITY OF REVERTER.

revest, *vb.* To vest again or anew <revesting of title in the former owner>.

rev'g. *abbr.* Reversing.

review, *n.* Consideration, inspection, or reexamination of a subject or thing. — **review,** *vb.*

administrative review. **1.** Judicial review of an administrative proceeding. **2.** Review of an administrative proceeding within the agency itself.

appellate review. Examination of a lower court's decision by a higher court, which can affirm, reverse, or modify the decision.

discretionary review. The form of appellate review that is not a matter of right but that occurs only with the appellate court's permission. See CERTIORARI.

judicial review. See JUDICIAL REVIEW.

reviewable issue. See *appealable decision* under DECISION.

revised statutes. See STATUTE.

revision, *n.* **1.** A reexamination or careful review for correction or improvement. **2.** *Military law.* The reconvening of a general or special court-martial to revise its action or to correct the record because of an improper or inconsistent action concerning the findings or the sentence. • A revision can occur only if it will not materially prejudice the accused.

revival, *n.* **1.** Restoration to current use or operation; esp., the act of restoring the validity or legal force of an expired contract or dormant judgment. — Also termed (for a dormant judgment) *revival of judgment.* Cf. RENEWAL (2). **2.** *Wills & estates.* The reestablishment of the validity of a revoked will by revoking the will that invalidated the original will. Cf. REPUBLICATION. — **revive,** *vb.*

revival statute. See STATUTE.

revivor. A proceeding to revive an action ended because of either the death of one of the parties or some other circumstance.

revocable (**rev**-ə-kə-bəl), *adj.* Capable of being canceled or withdrawn <a revocable transfer>.

revocable guaranty. See GUARANTY.

revocable letter of credit. See LETTER OF CREDIT.

revocable trust. See TRUST.

revocation (rev-ə-**kay**-shən), *n.* **1.** An annulment, cancellation, or reversal, usu. of an act or power. **2.** *Contracts.* Withdrawal of an offer by the offeror. **3.** *Wills & estates.* Invalidation of a will by the testator, either by destroying the will or by executing a new one. — **revoke,** *vb.* Cf. REPUDIATION; RESCISSION.

revocation hearing. See HEARING.

revocatory action (**rev**-ə-kə-tor-ee *or* ri-**vok**-ə-tor-ee). *Civil law.* An action brought by a creditor to annul a contract that has been entered into by the debtor and that will increase the debtor's insolvency.

revocatur (ree-voh-**kay**-tər). [Latin] *Hist.* It is recalled. • In former English practice, this was used as a notation on a judgment that was set aside because of a factual error (as opposed to being reversed because of legal error).

revolution, *n.* An overthrow of a government, usu. resulting in fundamental political change; a successful rebellion. — **revolt,** *vb.* — **revolutionary,** *adj.* & *n.*

revolver loan. See LOAN.

revolving charge account. See *revolving credit* under CREDIT (4).

revolving credit. See CREDIT (4).

revolving fund. See FUND (1).

revolving letter of credit. See LETTER OF CREDIT.

revolving loan. See LOAN.

revolving performance bond. See PERFORMANCE BOND.

Rev. Proc. *abbr.* REVENUE PROCEDURE.

Rev. Rul. *abbr.* REVENUE RULING.

Rev. Stat. See *revised statutes* under STATUTE.

reward, *n.* Something of value, usu. money, given in return for some service or achievement, such as recovering property or providing information that leads to the capture of a criminal. — **reward,** *vb.*

rex (reks). (*usu. cap.*) **1.** A king. **2.** The official title of a king. **3.** The prosecution side (as representatives of the king) in criminal proceedings in a monarchy. — Abbr. R. Cf. REGINA.

rezone, *vb.* To change the zoning boundaries or restrictions of (an area) <rezone the neighborhood>. See ZONING.

RFA. *abbr.* REQUEST FOR ADMISSION.

RFI. *abbr.* REQUEST FOR INSTRUCTIONS.

RFP. *abbr.* REQUEST FOR PRODUCTION.

r.g. *abbr.* REGULA GENERALIS.

rhadamanthine (rad-ə-**man**-thin), *adj.* (*often cap.*) (Of a judge) rigorous and inflexible <the

judge's rhadamanthine interpretation of procedural requirements makes it essential to study the local rules before appearing in court>.

Rhodian law (**roh**-dee-ən). The earliest known system or code of maritime law, supposedly dating from 900 B.C. • Rhodian law was purportedly developed by the people of the island Rhodes, located in the Aegean Sea and now belonging to Greece. The ancient inhabitants of Rhodes are said to have controlled the seas because of their commercial prosperity and naval superiority. Despite the uncertainties about its history, Rhodian law has often been cited as a source of admiralty and maritime law.

> "A strong tradition says that a maritime code was promulgated by the Island of Rhodes, in the Eastern Mediterranean, at the height of its power; the ridiculously early date of 900 B.C. has even been assigned to this suppositious code — a date accepted uncritically by some legal scholars. But even the existence of such a code has been pretty well cast in doubt, and we know next to nothing of its contents, if it existed. It is interesting to note, however, that the root-principle of the highly distinctive maritime-law system of general average ... is clearly stated in Justinian's Digest, and that the Rhodian Law is invoked as authority." Grant Gilmore & Charles L. Black, Jr., *The Law of Admiralty* § 1–2, at 3–4 (2d ed. 1975).

ribbon-matching rule. See MIRROR-IMAGE RULE.

Richard Roe. A fictitious name for a male party to a legal proceeding, used because the party's true identity is unknown or because his real name is being withheld; esp., the second of two such parties. Cf. JOHN DOE.

RICO (**ree**-koh). *abbr.* RACKETEER INFLUENCED AND CORRUPT ORGANIZATIONS ACT.

rider. An attachment to some document, such as a legislative bill or an insurance policy, that amends or supplements the document.

rien culp (ry*an* kəlp). [Law French "not guilty"] *Hist.* A plea of not guilty.

rien dit (ry*an* dee). [Law French "says nothing"] *Hist.* A plea of *nihil dicit.* See NIHIL DICIT.

rien luy doit (**ry*an*** lwee **dwah**). [Law French "owes him nothing"] *Hist.* A plea of *nil debet.* See NIL DEBET.

riens en arrière (**ry*an*** aw-nah-ree-**air**). [Law French "nothing in arrear"] *Hist.* A plea in a debt action for arrearages of account.

riens passa per le fait (**ry*an*** pah-**sah** pair lə **fay**). [Law French "nothing passed by the deed"] *Hist.* A plea by which a party seeks to avoid the operation of a deed that has been enrolled or acknowledged in court.

riens per descent (**ry*an*** pair day-**sawn**). [Law French "nothing by descent"] *Hist.* The plea of an heir who is sued for the ancestor's debt and who received no land or assets from the ancestor.

rier county. See RERE-COUNTY.

rigging the market. The practice of artificially inflating stock prices, by a series of bids, so that the demand for those stocks appears to be high and investors will therefore be enticed into buying the stocks. See MANIPULATION.

right, *n.* **1.** That which is proper under law, morality, or ethics <know right from wrong>. **2.** Something that is due to a person by just claim, legal guarantee, or moral principle <the right of liberty>. **3.** A power, privilege, or immunity secured to a person by law <the right to dispose of one's estate>. **4.** A legally enforceable claim that another will do or will not do a given act; a recognized and protected interest the violation of which is a wrong <a breach of duty that infringes one's right>. **5.** (*often pl.*) The interest, claim, or ownership that one has in tangible or intangible property <a debtor's rights in collateral> <publishing rights>.

> "Right is a correlative to duty; where there is no duty there can be no right. But the converse is not necessarily true. There may be duties without rights. In order for a duty to create a right, it must be a duty *to act or forbear.* Thus, among those duties which have rights corresponding to them do not come the duties, if such there be, which call for an inward state of mind, as distinguished from external acts or forbearances. It is only to acts and forbearances that others have a right. It may be our duty to love our neighbor, but he has no right to our love." John Chipman Gray, *The Nature and Sources of the Law* 8–9 (2d ed. 1921).

> "[T]he word 'right' is one of the most deceptive of pitfalls; it is so easy to slip from a qualified meaning in the premise to an unqualified one in the conclusion. Most rights are qualified." *American Bank & Trust Co. v. Federal Reserve Bank of Atlanta,* 256 U.S. 350, 358, 41 S.Ct. 499, 500 (1921) (Holmes, J.).

absolute right. A right that belongs to every human being, such as the right of personal liberty; a natural right. Cf. *relative right.*

accessory right. A supplementary right that has been added to the main right that is vested in the same owner. • For example, the right in a security is accessory to the right that is secured; a servitude is accessory to the ownership of the land for whose benefit the servitude exists. Cf. *principal right*.

accrued right. A matured right; a right that is ripe for enforcement (as through litigation).

acquired right. A right that a person does not naturally enjoy, but that is instead procured, such as the right to own property.

civil right. See CIVIL RIGHT.

conditional right. A right that depends on an uncertain event; a right that may or may not exist. • For example, parents have the conditional right to punish their child, the condition being that the punishment must be reasonable.

conjugal rights. See CONJUGAL RIGHTS.

equitable right. A right cognizable within a court of equity. • If a legal right and an equitable right conflict, the legal right ordinarily prevails over and destroys the equitable right even if the legal right arose after the equitable right. With the merger of law and equity in federal and most state courts, the procedural differences between legal and equitable rights have been largely abolished. Cf. *legal right*.

expectant right. A right that depends on the continued existence of present conditions until some future event occurs; a contingent right.

fundamental right. See FUNDAMENTAL RIGHT.

imperfect right. A right that is recognized by the law but is not enforceable. • Examples include time-barred claims and claims exceeding the local limits of a court's jurisdiction.

> "[T]here are certain rights, sometimes called imperfect rights, which the law recognizes but will not enforce directly. Thus a statute-barred debt cannot be recovered in a court of law, but for certain purposes the existence of the debt has legal significance. If the debtor pays the money, he cannot later sue to recover it as money paid without consideration; and the imperfect right has the faculty of becoming perfect if the debtor makes an acknowledgment of the debt from which there can be inferred a promise to pay." George Whitecross Paton, *A Textbook of Jurisprudence* 286 (G.W. Paton & David P. Derham eds., 4th ed. 1972).

imprescriptible right. A right that cannot be lost to prescription.

inalienable right. A right that cannot be transferred or surrendered; esp., a natural right such as the right to own property. — Also termed *inherent right*.

incorporeal right. A right to intangible, rather than tangible, property. • A right to a legal action (a *chose in action*) is an incorporeal right. See CHOSE IN ACTION.

inherent right. See *inalienable right*.

legal right. **1.** A right created or recognized by law. **2.** A right historically recognized by common-law courts. Cf. *equitable right*.

natural right. A right that is conceived as part of natural law and that is therefore thought to exist independently of rights created by government or society, such as the right to life, liberty, and property. See NATURAL LAW.

negative right. A right entitling a person to have another refrain from doing an act that might harm the person entitled.

patent right. A right secured by a patent.

perfect right. A right that is recognized by the law and is fully enforceable.

peripheral right. A right that surrounds or springs from another right.

personal right. **1.** A right that forms part of a person's legal status or personal condition, as opposed to the person's estate. **2.** See *right in personam*.

political right. The right to participate in the establishment or administration of government, such as the right to vote or the right to hold public office. — Also termed *political liberty*.

positive right. A right entitling a person to have another do some act for the benefit of the person entitled.

precarious right. A right enjoyed at the pleasure of another; a right that can be revoked at any time.

primary right. A right prescribed by the substantive law, such as a right not to be defamed or assaulted. • The enforcement of a primary right is termed *specific enforcement*.

principal right. A right to which has been added a supplementary right in the same owner. Cf. *accessory right*.

private right. A personal right, as opposed to a right of the public or the state. Cf. *public right*.

procedural right. A right that derives from legal or administrative procedure; a right that helps in the protection or enforcement of a substantive right. Cf. *substantive right*.

property right. A right to specific property, whether tangible or intangible.

proprietary right. A right that is part of a person's estate, assets, or property, as opposed to a right arising from the person's legal status.

public right. A right belonging to all citizens and usu. vested in and exercised by a public office or political entity. Cf. *private right.*

real right. **1.** *Civil law.* A right that is connected with a thing rather than a person. • Real rights include ownership, use, habitation, usufruct, predial servitude, pledge, and real mortgage.

> "The term 'real rights' (*jura in re*) is an abstraction unknown to classical Roman law. The classical jurists were preoccupied with the availability of remedies rather than the existence of *substantive* rights, and did not have a generic term to include all 'rights' which civilian scholars of following generations classified as 'real.' The expression ('real rights') was first coined by medieval writers elaborating on the *Digest* in an effort to explain ancient procedural forms of action in terms of substantive rights." A.N. Yiannopoulos, *Real Rights in Louisiana and Comparative Law*, 23 La. L. Rev. 161, 163 (1963).

2. JUS IN RE. **3.** See *right in rem.*

relative right. A right that arises from and depends on someone else's right, as distinguished from an absolute right. Cf. *absolute right.*

remedial right. The secondary right to have a remedy that arises when a primary right is broken.

right in personam (in pər-**soh**-nəm). An interest protected solely against specific individuals. — Also termed *personal right*; *jus in personam.* See IN PERSONAM.

right in rem (in **rem**). A right exercisable against the world at large. — Also termed *real right*; *jus in rem.* See IN REM.

> "A right *in rem* need not relate to a tangible *res.* Thus a right that one's reputation should not be unjustifiably attacked is today described as a right *in rem*, since it is a right that avails against persons generally. This shows how far the conception has developed from the Roman notion of *actio in rem*, for one who sues to protect his reputation is not asking for judgment for a specific *res.* It should also be noticed that on breach of a right *in rem*, a right *in personam* arises against the aggressor." George Whitecross Paton, *A Textbook of Jurisprudence* 300 (G.W. Paton & David P. Derham eds., 4th ed. 1972).

secondary right. A right prescribed by procedural law to enforce a substantive right, such as the right to damages for a breach of contract. • The enforcement of a secondary right is variously termed *secondary enforcement*, *remedial enforcement*, or *sanctional enforcement.* — Also termed *remedial right*; *sanctioning right.*

substantial right. An essential right that potentially affects the outcome of a lawsuit and is capable of legal enforcement and protection, as distinguished from a mere technical or procedural right.

substantive right (**səb**-stən-tiv). A right that can be protected or enforced by law; a right of substance rather than form. Cf. *procedural right.*

vested right. A right that so completely and definitely belongs to a person that it cannot be impaired or taken away without the person's consent.

right against self-incrimination. A criminal defendant's or a witness's constitutional right — under the Fifth Amendment, but waivable under certain conditions — guaranteeing that a person cannot be compelled by the government to testify if the testimony might result in the person's being criminally prosecuted. • Although this right is most often asserted during a criminal prosecution, a person can also "plead the Fifth" in a civil, legislative, administrative, or grand-jury proceeding. — Also termed *privilege against self-incrimination*; *right to remain silent.* See SELF-INCRIMINATION.

> "The right against self-incrimination, protected by the Fifth Amendment, is central to the accusatorial system of criminal justice: together with the presumption of innocence, the right against self-incrimination ensures that the state must bear the burden of prosecution.... The right against self-incrimination is personal. It may be claimed only by the person who himself might be at risk for testifying. It may not be claimed on behalf of another ...." Jethro K. Lieberman, *The Evolving Constitution* 481–82 (1992).

right-and-wrong test. See MCNAGHTEN RULES.

rightful, *adj.* **1.** (Of an action) equitable; fair <a rightful dispossession>. **2.** (Of a person) legitimately entitled to a position <a rightful heir>. **3.** (Of an office or piece of property) that one is entitled to <her rightful inheritance>.

right heir. See HEIR.

right in personam. See RIGHT.

right in re aliena. See JUS IN RE ALIENA.

right in rem. See RIGHT.

right in re propria. See JUS IN RE PROPRIA.

right of action. **1.** The right to bring a specific case to court. **2.** A right that can be enforced by legal action; a chose in action. Cf. CAUSE OF ACTION.

right of angary. See ANGARY.

right of approach. *Int'l law.* The right of a warship on the high seas to draw near another vessel to determine its nationality.

right of assembly. The constitutional right — guaranteed by the First Amendment — of the people to gather peacefully for public expression of religion, politics, or grievances. — Also termed *freedom of assembly*; *right to assemble.* Cf. FREEDOM OF ASSOCIATION; *unlawful assembly* under ASSEMBLY.

right of audience. A right to appear and be heard in a given court. • The term is chiefly used in England to denote the right of a certain type of lawyer to appear in a certain type of court.

right of common. See PROFIT A PRENDRE.

right of contribution. See CONTRIBUTION (1).

right of dissent and appraisal. See APPRAISAL REMEDY.

right of election. *Wills & estates.* A spouse's statutory right to choose, upon the other spouse's death, either the share under the deceased spouse's will or a share of the estate as defined in the probate statute, which usu. amounts to what the spouse would have received if the deceased spouse had died intestate. — Also termed *widow's election.* See ELECTION (2).

right of entry. 1. The right of taking or resuming possession of land or other real property in a peaceable manner. **2.** POWER OF TERMINATION. **3.** The right to go into another's real property for a special purpose without committing trespass. • An example is a landlord's right to enter a tenant's property to make repairs. **4.** The right of an alien to go into a jurisdiction for a special purpose. • An example is an exchange student's right to enter another country to attend college.

right of entry for breach of condition. See POWER OF TERMINATION.

right of entry for condition broken. See POWER OF TERMINATION.

right of exoneration. See EQUITY OF EXONERATION.

right of first refusal. A potential buyer's contractual right to meet the terms of a third party's offer if the seller intends to accept that offer. • For example, if Beth has a right of first refusal on the purchase of Sam's house, and if Sam intends to accept Terry's offer to buy the house for $300,000, Beth can match this offer and prevent Terry from buying it. Cf. RIGHT OF PREEMPTION.

right of fishery. See FISHERY (1).

right of innocent passage. See INNOCENT PASSAGE.

right of petition. See RIGHT TO PETITION.

right of possession. The right to hold, use, occupy, or otherwise enjoy a given property; esp., the right to enter real property and eject or evict a wrongful possessor.

right of preemption. A potential buyer's contractual right to have the first opportunity to buy, at a specified price, if the seller chooses to sell. • For example, if Beth has a right of preemption on Sam's house for five years at $100,000, Sam can either keep the house for five years (in which case Beth's right expires) or, if he wishes to sell during those five years, offer the house to Beth, who can either buy it for $100,000 or refuse to buy, but if she refuses, Sam can sell to someone else. — Also termed *first option to buy.* Cf. RIGHT OF FIRST REFUSAL.

right of privacy. 1. The right to personal autonomy. • The U.S. Constitution does not explicitly provide for a right of privacy, but the Supreme Court has repeatedly ruled that this right is implied in the "zones of privacy" created by specific constitutional guarantees. **2.** The right of a person and the person's property to be free from unwarranted public scrutiny or exposure. — Also termed *right to privacy.* See INVASION OF PRIVACY.

right of publicity. The right to control the use of one's own name, picture, or likeness and to prevent another from using it for commercial benefit without one's consent.

right of redemption. See EQUITY OF REDEMPTION.

right of reentry. See POWER OF TERMINATION.

right of rescission. See RIGHT TO RESCIND.

right of revolution. The inherent right of a people to cast out their rulers, change their polity, or effect radical reforms in their system of government or institutions, by force or general uprising, when the legal and constitutional methods of making such changes have proved inadequate or are so obstructed as to be unavailable.

right of search. *Int'l law.* The right to stop, visit, and examine vessels on the high seas to discover whether they or the goods they carry are liable to capture; esp., a belligerent state's right to stop any merchant vessel of a neutral state on the high seas and to search as reasonably necessary to determine whether the ship has become liable to capture under the international law of naval warfare. • This right carries with it no right to destroy without full examination, unless those on a given vessel actively resist. — Also termed *right of visit*; *right of visit and search*; *right of visitation*; *right of visitation and search*. See VISIT.

right of subrogation. See EQUITY OF SUBROGATION.

right of support. *Property.* **1.** A landowner's right to have the land supported by adjacent land and by the underlying earth. **2.** A servitude giving the owner of a house the right to rest timber on the walls of a neighboring house.

right of survivorship. A joint tenant's right to succeed to the whole estate upon the death of the other joint tenant. — Also termed *jus accrescendi*. See SURVIVORSHIP; *joint tenancy* under TENANCY.

right of termination. *English law.* A remedy involving the ending of contractual relations, accorded to a party to a contract when the other party breaches a duty that arises under the contract. • The right of termination is contrasted with a right to rescind, which arises when the other party breaches a duty that arises independently of the contract. — Also termed *right to terminate*.

right of transit passage. See TRANSIT PASSAGE.

right of visit. See RIGHT OF SEARCH.

right of visit and search. See RIGHT OF SEARCH.

right of visitation. **1.** VISITATION RIGHT. **2.** RIGHT OF SEARCH.

right of visitation and search. See RIGHT OF SEARCH.

right-of-way. **1.** A person's legal right, established by usage or by contract, to pass through grounds or property owned by another. Cf. EASEMENT. **2.** The right to build and operate a railway line or a highway on land belonging to another, or the land so used. **3.** The right to take precedence in traffic.

right of wharfing out. *Hist.* A right to the exclusive use of submerged lands, as by establishing a permanent structure or wharf on the land to dock oceangoing vessels.

rights arbitration. See *grievance arbitration* under ARBITRATION.

rights-consciousness. See CLAIMS-CONSCIOUSNESS.

rights off. See EX RIGHTS.

rights offering. See OFFERING.

rights on. See CUM RIGHTS.

right to assemble. See RIGHT OF ASSEMBLY.

right to bear arms. The constitutional right of persons to own firearms.

right to choose. See FREEDOM OF CHOICE.

right-to-convey covenant. See *covenant of seisin* under COVENANT (4).

right to counsel. A criminal defendant's constitutional right, guaranteed by the Sixth Amendment, to representation by a court-appointed lawyer if the defendant cannot afford to hire one. — Also termed *access to counsel*. See ASSISTANCE OF COUNSEL.

right to die. The right of a terminally ill person to refuse life-sustaining treatment. — Also termed *right to refuse treatment*. See ADVANCE DIRECTIVE.

right-to-know act. A federal or state statute requiring businesses (such as chemical manufacturers) that produce hazardous substances to disclose information about the substances both to the community where they are produced or stored and to employees who handle them. — Also termed *right-to-know statute*.

right to petition. The constitutional right — guaranteed by the First Amendment — of the people to make formal requests to the government, as by lobbying or writing letters to public officials. — Also termed *right of petition*; *freedom of petition*.

right to privacy. See RIGHT OF PRIVACY.

right to refuse treatment. See RIGHT TO DIE.

right to remain silent. See RIGHT AGAINST SELF-INCRIMINATION.

right to rescind. *English law.* The remedy accorded to a party to a contract when the other party breaches a duty that arises independently of the contract. • The right to rescind is contrasted with a right of termination, which arises when the other party breaches a duty that arises under the contract. — Also termed *right of rescission*.

right to terminate. See RIGHT OF TERMINATION.

right to travel. A person's constitutional right — guaranteed by the Privileges and Immunities Clause — to travel freely between states.

right to vote. See SUFFRAGE.

right-to-work law. A state law that prevents labor–management agreements requiring a person to join a union as a condition of employment. See SHOP.

right-wrong test. See MCNAGHTEN RULES.

rigid constitution. See CONSTITUTION.

rigor juris (**rig**-ər **joor**-is). [Latin] Strictness of law. Cf. GRATIA CURIAE.

rigor mortis (**rig**-ər **mor**-tis). The temporary stiffening of a body's joints and muscles after death. • The onset of rigor mortis can vary from 15 minutes to several hours after death, depending on the body's condition and on atmospheric factors.

ringing out. See RINGING UP.

ringing the changes. Fraud consisting in the offender's using a large banknote to pay for a small purchase, waiting for the shopkeeper to put change on the counter, and then, by a series of maneuvers involving changes of mind — such as asking for some other article of little value or for smaller change for some of the money on the counter — creating a confused situation in which the offender picks up much more of the money than is really due.

ringing up. A method by which a group of commodities dealers discharge contracts for future delivery in advance by using offsets, cancellations, and price adjustments, thus saving the cost of actual delivery and change of possession. — Also termed *ringing out*.

riot, *n.* An unlawful disturbance of the peace by an assembly of usu. three or more persons acting with a common purpose in a violent or tumultuous manner that threatens or terrorizes the public. — **riot,** *vb.* — **riotous,** *adj.* Cf. *unlawful assembly* under ASSEMBLY; CIVIL COMMOTION; ROUT.

> "A riot is defined as an unlawful assembly (i.e. an assembly come together in pursuance of an unlawful purpose), consisting of at least three persons, which has begun to create a breach of the peace. At Common Law it is an indictable misdemeanour, punishable by a fine and imprisonment. But the statutory form of it, introduced by the Riot Act of 1714, is better known. By that statute, passed to deal with Jacobite disturbances, it was provided that the members of a riotous assembly of twelve or more persons which does not disperse within an hour after the reading by a magistrate of the proclamation contained in the Act, become guilty of felony, which, at the time of the passing of the Act, was a capital offence, and is, even now, punishable with imprisonment for life." Edward Jenks, *The Book of English Law* 136 (P.B. Fairest ed., 6th ed. 1967).

> "A riot is a tumultuous disturbance of the peace by three or more persons acting together (a) in the commission of a crime by open force, or (b) in the execution of some enterprise, lawful or unlawful, in such a violent, turbulent and unauthorized manner as to create likelihood of public terror and alarm.... When they come together for this purpose they are guilty of unlawful assembly. When they start on their way to carry out their common design they are guilty of *rout*. In the actual execution of their design they are guilty of *riot*." Rollin M. Perkins & Ronald N. Boyce, *Criminal Law* 483 (3d ed. 1982).

Riot Act. A 1714 English statute that made it a capital offense for 12 or more rioters to continue together for an hour after a magistrate has officially proclaimed that rioters must disperse. • This statute was not generally accepted in the United States and did not become a part of American common law. It did, however, become a permanent part of the English language in the slang phrase *reading the Riot Act* (meaning "to reprimand vigorously"), which originally referred to the official command for rioters to disperse.

riotous assembly. See ASSEMBLY.

riparian (ri-**pair**-ee-ən *or* rɪ-), *adj.* Of, relating to, or located on the bank of a river or stream (or occasionally another body of water, such as a lake) <riparian land> <a riparian owner>. Cf. LITTORAL.

riparian proprietor. A landowner whose property borders on a stream or river.

riparian right. (*often pl.*) The right of a landowner whose property borders on a body of water or watercourse. • Such a landowner traditionally has the right to make reasonable use of the water. — Also termed *water right.*

riparian-rights doctrine. The rule that owners of land bordering on a waterway have equal rights to use the water passing through or by their property. Cf. PRIOR-APPROPRIATION DOCTRINE.

ripeness, *n.* **1.** The circumstance existing when a case has reached, but has not passed, the point when the facts have developed sufficiently to permit an intelligent and useful decision to be made. **2.** The requirement that this circumstance must exist before a court will decide a controversy. — **ripen,** *vb.* — **ripe,** *adj.* See JUSTICIABILITY. Cf. MOOTNESS DOCTRINE; PREMATURITY (1).

rising of court. *Archaic.* **1.** A court's final adjournment of a term. **2.** A recess or temporary break in a court's business, as at the end of the day.

risk, *n.* **1.** The chance of injury, damage, or loss; danger or hazard <many feel that skydiving is not worth the risk>. See ASSUMPTION OF THE RISK. **2.** Liability for injury, damage, or loss if it occurs <the consumer-protection statute placed the risk on the manufacturer instead of the buyer>. **3.** *Insurance.* The chance or degree of probability of loss to the subject matter of an insurance policy <the insurer undertook the risk in exchange for a premium>. Cf. PERIL (2). **4.** *Insurance.* The amount that an insurer stands to lose <the underwriter took steps to reduce its total risk>. **5.** *Insurance.* A person or thing that an insurer considers a hazard; someone or something that might be covered by an insurance policy <she's a poor risk for health insurance>. **6.** *Insurance.* The type of loss covered by a policy; a hazard from a specified source <this homeowner's policy covers fire risks and flood risks>. — **risk,** *vb.*

absorbable risk. A potential loss that a corporation believes that it can cover either with available capital or with self-insurance.

assigned risk. One who is a poor risk for insurance but whom an insurance company is forced to insure because of state law. • For example, an accident-prone driver is an assigned risk in a state with a compulsory motor-vehicle-insurance statute.

classified risk. In life and health policies, the risk created by a policyholder's substandard health or other peril.

noninsurable risk. A risk for which insurance will not be written because the risk is too uncertain to be the subject of actuarial analysis.

pure risk. A risk that always results in a loss.

speculative risk. A risk that can result in either a loss or a gain.

risk arbitrage. See ARBITRAGE.

risk-averse, *adj.* (Of a person) uncomfortable with volatility or uncertainty; not willing to take risks; very cautious <a risk-averse investor>.

risk-benefit test. See RISK-UTILITY TEST.

risk capital. See CAPITAL.

risk-capital test. *Securities.* A test of whether a transaction constitutes the sale of a security (and is thus subject to securities laws) based on whether the seller is soliciting risk capital with which to develop a business venture. Cf. CAPITAL-RISK TEST.

risk factor. *Insurance.* In life-insurance ratemaking, the estimated cost of present and future claims, based on a mortality table. • The risk factor is one element that a life insurer uses to calculate premium rates. See PREMIUM RATE. Cf. INTEREST FACTOR; MORTALITY FACTOR.

risk management. The procedures or systems used to minimize accidental losses, esp. to a business.

risk of jury doubt. See BURDEN OF PERSUASION.

risk of loss. The danger or possibility that a party will have to bear the costs and expenses for the damage, destruction, or inability to locate goods or other property.

risk of nonpersuasion. See BURDEN OF PERSUASION.

risk-utility test. A method of imposing product liability on a manufacturer if the evidence shows that a reasonable person would conclude that the benefits of a product's particular design versus the feasibility of an alternative safer design did not outweigh the dangers inherent in the original design. — Also termed *danger-utility test*; *risk-benefit test*. Cf. CONSUMER-CONTEMPLATION TEST.

RL/C. See *revolving letter of credit* under LETTER OF CREDIT.

robbery, *n.* The illegal taking of property from the person of another, or in the person's presence, by violence or intimidation; aggravated larceny. — **rob,** *vb.* See LARCENY; THEFT. Cf. BURGLARY.

> "Robbery is larceny from the person by violence or intimidation. It is a felony both at common law and under modern statutes. Under some of the new penal codes robbery does not require an actual taking of property. If force or intimidation is used in the attempt to commit theft this is sufficient." Rollin M. Perkins & Ronald N. Boyce, *Criminal Law* 343 (3d ed. 1982).

aggravated robbery. Robbery committed by a person who either carries a dangerous weapon — often called *armed robbery* — or inflicts bodily harm on someone during the robbery.

armed robbery. Robbery committed by a person carrying a dangerous weapon, regardless of whether the weapon is revealed or used. • Most states punish armed robbery as an aggravated form of robbery rather than as a separate crime.

conjoint robbery (kən-**joynt**). A robbery committed by two or more persons.

highway robbery. **1.** Robbery committed against a traveler on or near a public highway. **2.** Figuratively, a price or fee that is unreasonably high; excessive profit or advantage.

simple robbery. Robbery that does not involve an aggravating factor or circumstance.

robe. (*often cap.*) The legal or judicial profession <eminent members of the robe>.

Robinson–Patman Act. A federal statute (specif., an amendment to the Clayton Act) prohibiting price discrimination that hinders competition or tends to create a monopoly. 15 USCA § 13. See ANTITRUST LAW; CLAYTON ACT.

rocket docket. 1. An accelerated dispute-resolution process. **2.** A court or judicial district known for its speedy disposition of cases. **3.** A similar administrative process, in which disputes must be decided within a specified time (such as 60 days).

rogatory letter (**rog**-ə-tor-ee). See LETTER OF REQUEST.

roll, *n.* **1.** A record of a court's or public office's proceedings. **2.** An official list of the persons and property subject to taxation. — Also termed (in sense 2) *tax roll*; *tax list*; *assessment roll*. Cf. TAXPAYERS' LISTS.

rolled-up plea. See PLEA (3).

rollover, *n.* **1.** The extension or renewal of a short-term loan; the refinancing of a maturing loan or note. **2.** The transfer of funds (such as IRA funds) to a new investment of the same type, esp. so as to defer payment of taxes. — **roll over,** *vb.*

rollover mortgage. See *renegotiable-rate mortgage* under MORTGAGE.

Roman–Dutch law. A system of law in Holland from the mid–15th century to the early 19th century, based on a mixture of Germanic customary law and Roman law as interpreted in medieval lawbooks. • This law forms the basis of modern South African law, the law of several other countries in southern Africa, and the law of Sri Lanka.

Romanesque law. See CIVIL LAW (1).

Romanist, *n.* One who is versed in or practices Roman law; a Roman-law specialist.

Roman law. 1. The legal system of the ancient Romans, forming the basis of the modern civil law. — Also termed *civil law*. **2.** CIVIL LAW (1).

> "The Roman law is the body of rules that governed the social relations of many peoples in Europe, Asia, and Africa for some period between the earliest prehistoric times and 1453 A.D. This date should perhaps be extended to 1900 A.D., or even to the present time, and we might include America in the territory concerned.... Yet the essential fact is that no present-day community ... consciously applies as binding upon its citizens the rules of Roman law in their unmodified form. That law is an historical fact. It would have only a tepid historical interest ... if it were not for the circumstance that, before it became a purely historical fact, it was worked into the foundation and framework of what is called the civil law ...." Max Radin, *Handbook of Roman Law* 1 (1927).

> "Roman law is not only the best-known, the most highly developed, and the most influential of all legal systems of the past; apart from English law, it is also the only one

whose entire and unbroken history can be traced from early and primitive beginnings to a stage of elaborate perfection in the hands of skilled specialists." Hans Julius Wolff, *Roman Law: An Historical Introduction* 5 (1951).

root. *Civil law.* A descendant.

root of title. The recorded land transaction, usu. at least 40 years old, that is used to begin a title search. See CHAIN OF TITLE; TITLE SEARCH.

ROR. *abbr.* RELEASE ON RECOGNIZANCE.

Roth IRA. See INDIVIDUAL RETIREMENT ACCOUNT.

round lot. See LOT (3).

rout (rowt), *n.* The offense that occurs when an unlawful assembly makes some move toward the accomplishment of its participants' common purpose. Cf. RIOT.

"The word 'rout' comes from the same source as the word 'route.' It signifies that three or more who have gathered together in unlawful assembly are 'on their way.' It is not necessary for guilt of this offense that the design be actually carried out, nor that the journey be made in a tumultuous manner." Rollin M. Perkins & Ronald N. Boyce, *Criminal Law* 483 (3d ed. 1982).

Royal Marriages Act. A 1772 statute (12 Geo. 3, ch. 1) forbidding members of the royal family from marrying without the sovereign's permission, except on certain conditions.

"Royal Marriages Act .... An Act occasioned by George III's fear of the effect on the dignity and honour of the royal family of members thereof contracting unsuitable marriages, two of his brothers having done so .... It provided that marriages of descendants of George II, other than the issue of princesses who marry into foreign families, should not be valid unless they had the consent of the King in Council, or, if the parties were aged over 25, they had given 12 months' notice to the Privy Council, unless during that time both Houses of Parliament expressly declare disapproval of the proposed marriage." David M. Walker, *The Oxford Companion to Law* 1091 (1980).

royalty. 1. A payment made to an author or inventor for each copy of a work or article sold under a copyright or patent.

reasonable royalty. A royalty that a licensee would be willing to pay the inventor while still making a reasonable profit from use of the patented invention.

2. A share of the product or profit from real property, reserved by the grantor of a mineral lease, in exchange for the lessee's right to mine or drill on the land. — Also termed (in sense 2) *override.*

haulage royalty. A royalty paid to a landowner for moving coal via a subterranean passageway under the landowner's land from a mine located on an adjacent property. • The payment is calculated at a certain amount per ton of coal.

mineral royalty. A right to a share of income from mineral production.

overriding royalty. A royalty retained by a mineral lessee when the property is subleased.

shut-in royalty. *Oil & gas.* A payment made by an oil-and-gas lessee to the lessor to keep the lease in force when a well capable of producing is not utilized because there is no market for the oil or gas. • Generally, without such a payment, the lease will terminate at the end of the primary term unless actual production has begun.

rptr. *abbr.* REPORTER.

R.S. See *revised statutes* under STATUTE.

RTC. *abbr.* RESOLUTION TRUST CORPORATION.

rubber check. See *bad check* under CHECK.

rubber-stamp seal. See NOTARY SEAL.

rubric (**roo**-brik). **1.** The title of a statute or code <the rubric of the relevant statute is the Civil Rights Act of 1964>. **2.** A category or designation <assignment of rights falls under the rubric of contract law>. **3.** An authoritative rule, esp. for conducting a public worship service <the rubric dictates whether the congregation should stand or kneel>. **4.** An introductory or explanatory note; a preface <a well-known scholar wrote the rubric to the book's fourth edition>. **5.** An established rule, custom, or law <what is the rubric in the Northern District of Texas regarding appearance at docket call?>.

rule, *n.* **1.** Generally, an established and authoritative standard or principle; a general norm mandating or guiding conduct or action in a given type of situation.

general rule. A rule applicable to a class of cases or circumstances.

special rule. A rule applicable to a particular case or circumstance only.

2. A regulation governing a court's or an agency's internal procedures.

rule, *vb.* **1.** To command or require; to exert control <the dictator ruled the country>. **2.** To decide a legal point <the court ruled on the issue of admissibility>.

rule, the. An evidentiary and procedural rule by which all witnesses are excluded from the courtroom while another witness is testifying <invoking "the rule">. • The phrase "the rule" is used chiefly in the American South and Southwest, but it is a universal practice to exclude witnesses before they testify.

Rule 10b–5. The SEC rule that prohibits deceptive or manipulative practices (such as material misrepresentations or omissions) in the buying or selling of securities. — Also termed *antifraud rule.*

Rule 11. *Civil procedure.* **1.** In federal practice, the procedural rule requiring the attorney of record or the party (if not represented by an attorney) to sign all pleadings, motions, and other papers filed with the court and — by this signing — to represent that the paper is filed in good faith after an inquiry that is reasonable under the circumstances. • This rule provides for the imposition of sanctions, upon a party's or the court's own motion, if an attorney or party violates the conditions stated in the rule. Fed. R. Civ. P. 11. **2.** In Texas practice, the procedural rule requiring agreements between attorneys or parties concerning a pending suit to be in writing, signed, and filed in the court's record or made on the record in open court. Tex. R. Civ. P. 11.

rule absolute. See *decree absolute* under DECREE.

rule against accumulations. See ACCUMULATIONS, RULE AGAINST.

rule against perpetuities. *Property.* The rule prohibiting a grant of an estate unless the interest must vest, if at all, no later than 21 years after the death of some person alive when the interest was created. — Sometimes written *Rule Against Perpetuities*; *Rule against Perpetuities.*

> "The true form of the Rule against Perpetuities is believed to be this: — NO INTEREST SUBJECT TO A CONDITION PRECEDENT IS GOOD, UNLESS THE CONDITION MUST BE FULFILLED, IF AT ALL, WITHIN TWENTY-ONE YEARS AFTER SOME LIFE IN BEING AT THE CREATION OF THE INTEREST." John Chipman Gray, *The Rule Against Perpetuities* 144 (1886).

> "Another scholar who spent a substantial part of an academic lifetime attempting to bring order and add sense to the rule [against perpetuities], W. Barton Leach, described the rule as a 'technicality-ridden legal nightmare' and a 'dangerous instrumentality in the hands of most members of the bar.' " Thomas F. Bergin & Paul G. Haskell, *Preface to Estates in Land and Future Interests* 178 (2d ed. 1984) (quoting Leach, *Perpetuities Legislation, Massachusetts Style*, 67 Harv. L. Rev. 1349 (1954)).

> "The Rule Against Perpetuities is a rule against remoteness of vesting. A contingent future interest is invalid under the orthodox rule if, at the time of the creation of the interest, the circumstances are such that the contingency may go unresolved for too long a time. The Rule is not concerned with the duration of interests, that is, the length of time that they endure. It is not a rule against suspension of the power of alienation, nor a rule against restraints on alienation. It is not a rule that directly limits the duration of trusts .... The orthodox rule is satisfied if all contingent future interests are so created that they must vest, if they vest at all, within the perpetuities period." Robert J. Lynn, *The Modern Rule Against Perpetuities* 9 (1966).

> "The common law Rule Against Perpetuities (modified by statute in some states) provides that no interest is valid unless it must vest within 21 years after lives in being when the interest was created. The rule is something of a misnomer. It does not limit the duration of a condition in a bequest, but rather limits the testator's power to earmark gifts for remote descendants." Richard A. Posner, *Economic Analysis of Law* § 18.7, at 394 (2d ed. 1977).

rule in Heydon's case. See MISCHIEF RULE.

Rule in Shelley's Case. *Property.* The rule that if — in a single grant — a freehold estate is given to a person and a remainder is given to the person's heirs, the remainder belongs to the named person and not the heirs, so that the person is held to have a fee simple absolute. • The rule, which dates from the 14th century but draws its name from the famous 16th-century case, has been abolished in most states. *Wolfe v. Shelley*, 76 Eng. Rep. 206 (K.B. 1581).

> "[T]he rule in Shelley's Case, the Don Quixote of the law, which, like the last knight errant of chivalry, has long survived every cause that gave it birth and now wanders aimlessly through the reports, still vigorous, but equally useless and dangerous." *Stamper v. Stamper*, 28 S.E. 20, 22 (N.C. 1897).

Rule in Wild's Case. *Property.* The rule construing a grant to "A and A's children" as a fee tail if A's children do not exist at the effective date of the instrument, and as a joint tenancy if A's children do exist at the effective date. • The rule has been abolished along with the fee tail in most states.

rulemaking, *n.* The process used by an administrative agency to formulate, amend, or repeal a rule or regulation. — Also termed *administrative rulemaking.* — **rulemaking,** *adj.* Cf. ADMINISTRATIVE ADJUDICATION; INFORMAL AGENCY ACTION.

formal rulemaking. Agency rulemaking that, when required by statute or the agency's discretion, must be on the record after an opportunity for an agency hearing, and must comply with certain procedures, such as allowing the submission of evidence and the cross-examination of witnesses. Cf. *informal rulemaking.*

informal rulemaking. Agency rulemaking in which the agency publishes a proposed regulation and receives public comments on the regulation, after which the regulation can take effect without the necessity of a formal hearing on the record. • Informal rulemaking is the most common procedure followed by an agency in issuing its substantive rules. — Also termed *notice-and-comment rulemaking.* See NOTICE-AND-COMMENT PERIOD. Cf. *formal rulemaking.*

rule nisi. See *decree nisi* under DECREE.

rule of capture. 1. The doctrine that if the donee of a general power of appointment manifests an intent to assume control of the property for all purposes and not just for the purpose of appointing it to someone, the donee captures the property and the property goes to the donee's estate. • One common way for the donee to show an intent to assume control for all purposes is to include provisions in his or her will blending the appointing property with the donee's own property. **2.** *Property.* The principle that wild animals belong to the person who captures them, regardless of whether they were originally on another person's land. **3.** *Water law.* The principle that a surface landowner can extract and appropriate all the groundwater beneath the land by drilling or pumping, even if doing so drains away groundwaters to the point of drying up springs and wells from which other landowners benefit. • This doctrine has been widely abolished or limited by legislation. **4.** *Oil & gas.* The principle that the owner of a mineral right covering migratory (sometimes termed "fugacious") substances can extract and appropriate them by drilling or pumping, subject to the prior or contemporaneous capture of the same minerals by another mineral-rights holder into the same subterraneous mineral deposit elsewhere. — Also termed *doctrine of capture*; *law of capture.*

rule of completeness. See RULE OF OPTIONAL COMPLETENESS.

rule of construction. See *canon of construction* under CANON (1).

rule of court. A rule governing the practice or procedure in a given court <federal rules of court>. See LOCAL RULE.

rule of decision. A rule, statute, body of law, or prior decision that provides the basis for deciding or adjudicating a case.

rule of four. The convention that for certiorari to be granted by the U.S. Supreme Court, four justices must vote in favor of the grant. See CERTIORARI.

rule of inconvenience. The principle of statutory interpretation holding that a court should not construe a statute in a way that will jeopardize an important public interest or produce a serious hardship for anyone, unless that interpretation is unavoidable.

rule of interpretation. See *canon of construction* under CANON (1).

rule of justice. A jurisprudential principle that determines the sphere of individual liberty in the pursuit of individual welfare, so as to confine that liberty within limits that are consistent with the general welfare of humankind.

rule of law. 1. A substantive legal principle <under the rule of law known as respondeat superior, the employer is answerable for all wrongs committed by an employee in the course of the employment>. **2.** The supremacy of regular as opposed to arbitrary power <citizens must respect the rule of law>. — Also termed *supremacy of law.* **3.** The doctrine that every person is subject to the ordinary law within the jurisdiction <all persons within the United States are within the American rule of law>. **4.** The doctrine that general constitutional principles are the result of judicial decisions determining the rights of private individuals in the courts <under the rule of law, Supreme Court caselaw makes up the bulk of what we call "constitutional law">. **5.** Loosely, a legal ruling; a ruling on a point of law <the *ratio decidendi* of a case is any rule of law reached by the judge as a necessary step in the decision>.

rule of lenity (**len**-ə-tee). The judicial doctrine holding that a court, in construing an ambiguous criminal statute that sets out multiple or inconsistent punishments, should resolve the ambiguity in favor of the more lenient punishment. — Also termed *lenity rule*.

rule of marshaling assets. An equitable doctrine that requires a senior creditor, having two or more funds to satisfy its debt, to first dispose of the fund not available to a junior creditor. • It prevents the inequity that would result if the senior creditor could choose to satisfy its debt out of the only fund available to the junior creditor and thereby exclude the junior creditor from any satisfaction. — Also termed *rule of marshaling securities*; *rule of marshaling remedies*.

rule of marshaling liens. See INVERSE-ORDER-OF-ALIENATION DOCTRINE.

rule of marshaling remedies. See RULE OF MARSHALING ASSETS.

rule of marshaling securities. See RULE OF MARSHALING ASSETS.

rule of necessity. A rule requiring a judge or other official to hear a case, despite bias or conflict of interest, when disqualification would result in the lack of any competent court or tribunal.

rule of optional completeness. The rule of evidence providing that when a party introduces part of a writing or an utterance at trial, the opposing party may require that the remainder of the passage be read to establish the full context. • The rule has limitations: first, no utterance can be received if it is irrelevant, and second, the remainder of the utterance must explain the first part. In many jurisdictions, the rule applies to conversations, to an opponent's admissions, to confessions, and to all other types of writings — even account books. But the Federal Rules of Evidence limit the rule to writings and recorded statements. Fed. R. Evid. 106. In most jurisdictions, including federal, the remainder is admissible unless its admission would be unfair or misleading. — Also termed *rule of completeness*; *doctrine of completeness*; *doctrine of optional completeness*; *completeness doctrine*; *optional-completeness rule*; *optional-completeness doctrine*.

rule of rank. A doctrine of statutory construction holding that a statute dealing with things or persons of an inferior rank cannot by any general words be extended to things or persons of a superior rank. • Blackstone gives the example of a statute dealing with deans, prebendaries, parsons, vicars, *and others* having spiritual promotion. According to Blackstone, this statute is held not to extend to bishops, even though they have spiritual promotion, because deans are the highest persons named, and bishops are of a higher order. Cf. EJUSDEM GENERIS; EXPRESSIO UNIUS EST EXCLUSIO ALTERIUS; NOSCITUR A SOCIIS.

rule of reason. *Antitrust.* The judicial doctrine holding that a trade practice violates the Sherman Act only if the practice is an unreasonable restraint of trade, based on economic factors. See SHERMAN ANTITRUST ACT; RESTRAINT OF TRADE. Cf. PER SE RULE.

rule of recognition. In the legal theory of H.L.A. Hart, a legal system's fundamental rule, by which all other rules are identified and understood. • In *The Concept of Law* (1961), Hart contends that a society's legal system is centered on rules. There are primary rules of obligation, which prescribe how a person should act in society, and secondary rules, by which the primary rules are created, identified, changed, and understood. A "rule of recognition" is a secondary rule, and serves to instruct citizens on when a pronouncement or societal principle constitutes a rule of obligation. Cf. RULES OF CHANGE; *basic norm* under NORM.

> "This rule [the rule of recognition] may amount to no more than specifying a list of primary rules carved on a public monument. Or it may actually be a complete set of rules . . . ." Martin P. Golding, *Philosophy of Law* 44 (1975).

rule of right. The source of a right; the rule that gives rise to a right.

rule of 72. A method for determining how many years it takes to double money invested at a compound interest rate. • For example, at a compound rate of 6%, it takes 12 years (72 divided by 6) for principal to double.

rule of 78. A method for computing the amount of interest that a borrower saves by paying off a loan early, when the interest payments are higher at the beginning of the loan period. • For example, to determine how much interest is saved by prepaying a 12-month loan after 6 months, divide the sum of the digits for the remaining six payments (21) by the sum of the digits for all twelve payments (78) and multiply that percentage by the total interest. — Also termed *rule of the sum of the digits*.

rule of the last antecedent. An interpretative principle by which a court determines that qualifying words or phrases modify the words or phrases immediately preceding them and not words or phrases more remote, unless the extension is necessary from the context or the spirit of the entire writing. • For example, an application of this rule might mean that, in the phrase *Texas courts, New Mexico courts, and New York courts in the federal system*, the words *in the federal system* might be held to modify only *New York courts* and not *Texas courts* or *New Mexico courts*. — Also termed *doctrine of the last antecedent*; *doctrine of the last preceding antecedent*.

rule of the sum of the digits. See RULE OF 78.

rules of change. In the legal theory of H.L.A. Hart, the fundamental rules by which a legal system's other rules are altered. • In Hart's theory, a legal system's primary rules are subject to identification and change by secondary rules. Among those rules are "rules of change," which prescribe how laws are altered or repealed. Cf. RULE OF RECOGNITION.

rules of court. See COURT RULES.

Rules of Decision Act. A federal statute (28 USCA § 1652) providing that a federal court, when exercising diversity jurisdiction, must apply the substantive law of the state in which the court sits. See *diversity jurisdiction* under JURISDICTION.

rules of navigation. The principles and regulations that govern the steering and sailing of vessels to avoid collisions. • Examples include the new International Rules governing conduct on the high seas and the Inland Rules governing navigation on the inland waters of the United States and U.S. vessels on the Canadian waters of the Great Lakes. 33 USCA §§ 1602–1608, 2001(a).

rule to show cause. See SHOW-CAUSE PROCEEDING.

ruling, *n.* The outcome of a court's decision either on some point of law or on the case as a whole. — Also termed *legal ruling*. — **rule,** *vb.* Cf. JUDGMENT; OPINION (1).

> "A distinction is sometimes made between rules and rulings. Whether or not a formal distinction is declared, in common usage 'legal ruling' (or simply 'ruling') is a term ordinarily used to signify the outcome of applying a legal test when that outcome is one of relatively narrow impact. The immediate effect is to decide an issue in a single case. This meaning contrasts, for example, with the usual meaning of 'legal rule' (or simply 'rule'). The term 'rule' ordinarily refers to a legal proposition of general application. A 'ruling' may have force as precedent, but ordinarily it has that force because the conclusion it expresses (for example, 'objection sustained') explicitly depends upon and implicitly reiterates a 'rule' — a legal proposition of more general application . . . ." Robert E. Keeton, *Judging* 67–68 (1990).

ruling case. See LEADING CASE (3).

ruling letter. See DETERMINATION LETTER.

run, *vb.* **1.** To expire after a prescribed period <the statute of limitations had run, so the plaintiff's lawsuit was barred>. **2.** To accompany a conveyance or assignment of (land) <the covenant runs with the land>. **3.** To apply <the injunction runs against only one of the parties in the dispute>.

runner. 1. A law-office employee who delivers papers between offices and files papers in court. **2.** One who solicits personal-injury cases for a lawyer.

running account. See ACCOUNT.

running days. See LAW DAYS.

running objection. See *continuing objection* under OBJECTION.

running policy. See *floating policy* under INSURANCE POLICY.

S

s. *abbr.* **1.** STATUTE. **2.** SECTION (1). **3.** (*usu. cap.*) SENATE.

S–1. An SEC form that a company usu. must file before listing and trading its securities on a national exchange. • Used primarily by first-time issuers of securities, this form is the basic, full-length registration statement that requires a great deal of information about the issuer and the securities being sold. The SEC has also adopted modified forms for smaller enterprises, such as Forms SB–1 and SB–2. — Also termed *Form S–1.*

Sabbath-breaking. The violation of laws or rules on observing the Sabbath; esp., the violation of a blue law.

Sabbath law. See BLUE LAW.

sabotage (**sab**-ə-tahzh), *n.* **1.** The destruction, damage, or knowingly defective production of materials, premises, or utilities used for national defense or for war. 18 USCA §§ 2151 et seq. **2.** The willful and malicious destruction of an employer's property or interference with an employer's normal operations, esp. during a labor dispute. — **sabotage,** *vb.*

saboteur (sab-ə-**tər**), *n.* A person who commits sabotage.

sacer (**sas**-ər), *adj.* [Latin "sacred; forfeited to a god"] *Roman law.* (Of an outlaw or a wrongdoer) punished by being placed outside the law's protection. See CONSECRATIO CAPITIS; OUTLAWRY.

sachbaro. See SAGIBARO.

Sache (**zahk**-ə). [German] A thing; an article or matter. See THING.

sacramentales (sak-rə-men-**tay**-leez), *n. pl.* [Law Latin fr. Latin *sacramentum* "oath-takers"] *Hist.* Compurgators; people who take an oath swearing to a defendant's innocence. Sing. *sacramentalis.*

sacramentum (sak-rə-**men**-təm), *n.* [Latin "an oath"] *Roman law.* **1.** A procedure for remedying a wrong; one of the *legis actiones* proceedings, used in both *in rem* and *in personam* actions when no other remedy was prescribed.

> "*Sacramentum* .... Where it took the form of an action *in rem*, the proceedings were as follows: the plaintiff secured the presence of the defendant in Court, the XII Tables entitling him, if the defendant refused to come, to bring him by force, and the object in dispute (*e.g.* the slave) had also to be there. The plaintiff then, holding a wand ... in one hand, seized the object with the other and claimed ownership .... Thereupon the defendant went through exactly the same ceremony, and used the same words .... The plaintiff next asked for the defendant's title ... , the defendant's reply being a general assertion of ownership .... Whereupon the plaintiff denied the right, and challenged the defendant to a bet ... and the defendant made a like challenge .... The praetor then — (*a*) Awarded possession of the slave to one of the parties pending the trial ... (*b*) Required the person so given possession to give security ... and (*c*) Required both parties to give security ...." R.W. Leage, *Roman Private Law* 388–90 (C.H. Ziegler ed., 2d ed. 1930).

2. The deposit of money made by both parties to the *sacramentum* and given to the winning party after the cause was determined.

> "[T]he money staked as a wager ... was known as sacramentum. The word evidently has a religious significance. The sum of the wager, forfeited by the party found to be in the wrong, was anciently devoted to religious purposes, later went to the public chest. But there is reason to think that at a still earlier period the word sacramentum meant, not a thing staked as a wager on the result of litigation, but an oath by each party as to the justice of his cause, involving a penalty to be paid to the offended deity if the oath was found to be false." R.W. Lee, *The Elements of Roman Law* 422–23 (4th ed. 1956).

3. An oath of allegiance given by a soldier upon enlistment.

sacramentum decisionis (sak-rə-**men**-təm di-sizh-ee-**oh**-nis). [Latin "the oath of decision"] *Civil law.* The offer by one party to accept the opposing party's oath as decisive of the issues involved in a lawsuit.

> "The defendant or person accused was ... to make oath of his own innocence, and to produce a certain number of compurgators, who swore they believed his oath. Somewhat similar also to this is the *sacramentum decisionis*, or the voluntary and decisive oath of the civil law; where one of the parties to the suit, not being able to prove his

charge, offers to refer the decision of the cause to the oath of his adversary: which the adversary was bound to accept, or tender the same proposal back again; otherwise the whole was taken as confessed by him." 3 William Blackstone, *Commentaries on the Laws of England* 342 (1768).

sacramentum fidelitatis (sak-rə-**men**-təm fi-del-ə-**tay**-tis). [Law Latin] *Hist.* The oath of fidelity, given by a vassal to a lord.

sacrilege (**sak**-rə-lij). **1.** The act or an instance of desecrating or profaning a sacred thing. **2.** *Hist.* Larceny of sacred objects, as from a church.

sacrilegium (sak-rə-**lee**-jee-əm). [Latin fr. *sacer* "sacred" + *legere* "to steal"] *Roman law.* **1.** The theft of a sacred thing, punishable by death. **2.** Violation of an imperial law.

"In the later Empire the conception of *sacrilegium* was somewhat distorted and those 'who through ignorance or negligence confound, violate and offend the sanctity of a divine law' . . . were considered guilty of *sacrilegium*. 'Divine' is here used in the sense of imperial, issued by the emperor . . . . Thus *sacrilegium* and *sacrilegus* became rather general terms applied to the neglect or violation of imperial orders or enactments." Adolf Berger, *Encyclopedic Dictionary of Roman Law* 689 (1953).

sacrilegus (sə-**kril**-ə-gəs). [Latin "sacrilegious"] *Roman law.* (A person) guilty of *sacrilegium*. See SACRILEGIUM.

sacristan (**sak**-ri-stən). [Latin] *Hist.* A caretaker of a church; a sexton of a church.

sacristy (**sak**-ri-stee). See VESTRY (1).

saemend (**see**-mənd). [Old English] *Hist.* An arbitrator; an umpire.

saevitia (si-**vish**-ee-ə). [Latin fr. *saevus* "cruel"] *Hist.* Cruelty in a marriage, as a result of which cohabitation is dangerous enough to justify a decree of separation.

safe, *adj.* Not exposed to danger; not causing danger <driving at a safe limit of speed>.

safe-berth clause. See SAFE-PORT CLAUSE.

safe-conduct. *Int'l law.* **1.** A privilege granted by a belligerent allowing an enemy, a neutral, or some other person to travel within or through a designated area for a specified purpose. **2.** A document conveying this privilege.

"Safe-conduct . . . . The grantee is inviolable so long as he complies with the conditions imposed on him or necessitated by the circumstances of the case. Unless stated, a safe-conduct does not cover goods or luggage. They may be given also for ships and for goods. To be effective under international law the grant must have been arranged between belligerents." David M. Walker, *The Oxford Companion to Law* 1098 (1980).

safe-deposit box. A lockbox stored in a bank's vault to secure a customer's valuables. • It usu. takes two keys (one held by the bank and one held by the customer) to open the box. — Often shortened to *deposit box*. — Also termed *safety-deposit box*.

safe-deposit company. See DEPOSITARY (1).

safe harbor. 1. An area or means of protection. **2.** A provision (as in a statute or regulation) that affords protection from liability or penalty. • SEC regulations, for example, provide a safe harbor for an issuer's business forecasts that are made in good faith.

safekeeping. Under the Securities Investors Protection Act, the holding of a security on behalf of the investor or broker that has paid for it. 15 USCA § 78lll(2).

safe-port clause. A clause in a voyage or time charter expressly providing that the ship must go to a safe port nominated or ordered by the charterer. • The ship can refuse an order to proceed to an unsafe port; compliance with the order exposes the charterer to liability for damage to the vessel resulting from entering an unsafe port. — Also termed *safe-berth clause*.

Safety Appliance Act. A federal law regulating the safety of equipment used by railroads in interstate commerce. 49 USCA §§ 20301 et seq.

safety-deposit box. See SAFE-DEPOSIT BOX.

safety engineering. The inspection and study of potentially dangerous conditions, usu. in an industrial environment, so that precautionary measures can be taken.

safe workplace. A place of employment in which all dangers that should reasonably be removed have been removed; a place of employment that is reasonably safe given the nature of the work performed. See OCCUPATIONAL SAFETY AND HEALTH ADMINISTRATION.

sagibaro (**sag**-ə-bar-oh), *n.* [Old English] *Hist.* A determiner of disputes; a judge. — Also termed *sachbaro* (**sak**-bar-oh).

said, *adj.* Aforesaid; above-mentioned. • The adjective *said* is obsolescent in legal drafting, its last bastion being patent claims. But even in that context the word is giving way to the ordinary word *the*, which if properly used is equally precise. See AFORESAID.

> "The word 'said' is used by many practitioners rather than 'the' to refer back to previously recited elements, sometimes to a previously cited anything. This practice is unobjectionable, although perhaps overly legalistic. If 'saids' or 'thes' are used, one should be consistent in the usage and not alternate between those words in repetitions of the same element or among different elements." Robert C. Faber, *Landis on Mechanics of Patent Claim Drafting* § 23, at 50 (3d ed. 1990).

sailor's will. See *soldier's will* under WILL.

sake and soke (sayk / sohk). *Hist.* A lord's right to hold court and compel attendance. — Also spelled *sak and soc* (sak / sok).

salable (**say**-lə-bəl *or* **sayl**-ə-bəl), *adj.* Fit for sale in the usual course of trade at the usual selling price; MERCHANTABLE. — **salability** (say-lə-**bil**-ə-tee *or* sayl-ə-**bil**-ə-tee), *n.*

salable value. See *fair market value* under VALUE.

salarium (sə-**lair**-ee-əm), *n.* [Latin "salt money"] **1.** *Roman law.* An allowance, esp. for living expenses, given to persons in noble professions (such as teachers or doctors) who were not allowed to sue for fees. **2.** *Roman law.* Wages for persons engaged in military service on an emergency basis. • The regular soldier's pay is a *stipendium*. **3.** *Hist.* The rent or profits of a hall or house.

salary. An agreed compensation for services — esp. professional or semiprofessional services — usu. paid at regular intervals on a yearly basis, as distinguished from an hourly basis. • Salaried positions are usu. exempt from the requirements of the Fair Labor Standards Act (on overtime and the like) but are subject to state regulation. Cf. WAGE.

accrued salary. A salary that has been earned but not yet paid.

sale, *n.* **1.** The transfer of property or title for a price. **2.** The agreement by which such a transfer takes place. • The four elements are (1) parties competent to contract, (2) mutual assent, (3) a thing capable of being transferred, and (4) a price in money paid or promised.

absolute sale. A sale in which possession and title to the property pass to the buyer immediately upon the completion of the bargain. Cf. *conditional sale.*

approval sale. See *sale on approval.*

auction sale. See AUCTION.

average gross sales. The amount of total sales divided by the number of sales transactions in a specific period.

bona fide sale. A sale made by a seller in good faith, for valuable consideration, and without notice of a defect in title or any other reason not to hold the sale.

bootstrap sale. **1.** A sale in which the purchase price is financed by earnings and profits of the thing sold; esp., a leveraged buyout. See BUYOUT. **2.** A seller's tax-saving conversion of a business's ordinary income into a capital gain from the sale of corporate stock.

bulk sale. See BULK TRANSFER.

cash-against-documents sale. See *documentary sale.*

cash sale. **1.** A sale in which cash payment is concurrent with the receipt of the property sold. **2.** A securities transaction on the stock-exchange floor requiring cash payment and same-day delivery.

compulsory sale. The forced sale of real property in accordance with either an eminent-domain order or an order for a judicial sale arising from nonpayment of taxes.

conditional sale. **1.** A sale in which the buyer gains immediate possession but the seller retains title until the buyer performs a condition, esp. payment of the full purchase price. See *conditional sales contract* under CONTRACT. **2.** A sale accompanied by an agreement to resell upon specified terms. Cf. *absolute sale.*

consignment sale. A sale of an owner's property (such as clothing or furniture) by a third party entrusted to make the sale. See CONSIGNMENT.

consumer-credit sale. A sale in which the seller extends credit to the consumer. • A consumer-credit sale includes a lease in which the lessee's rental payments equal or exceed the retail value of the item rented.

credit sale. A sale of goods to a buyer who is allowed to pay for the goods at a later time.

distress sale. **1.** A form of liquidation in which the seller receives less for the goods than what would be received under normal sales conditions; esp., a going-out-of-business sale. **2.** A foreclosure or tax sale.

dock sale. A sale in which a purchaser takes possession of the product at the seller's shipping dock, esp. for transportation outside the state.

documentary sale. A sale in which the buyer pays upon the seller's tender of documents of title covering the goods, plus a sight draft requiring the buyer to pay "at sight." • This type of sale typically occurs before delivery of the goods, which might be en route when the buyer pays. — Also termed *cash-against-documents sale*.

exclusive sale. A sale made by a broker under an exclusive-agency listing. See *exclusive-agency listing* under LISTING.

execution sale. A forced sale of a debtor's property by a government official carrying out a writ of execution. — Also termed *forced sale*; *judgment sale*; *sheriff's sale*. See EXECUTION.

executory sale. A sale agreed upon in principle but with a few minor details remaining.

fair sale. A foreclosure sale or other judicial sale conducted with fairness toward the rights and interests of the affected parties.

fire sale. **1.** A sale of merchandise at reduced prices because of fire or water damage. **2.** Any sale at greatly reduced prices, esp. due to an emergency. • Fire sales are often regulated to protect the public from deceptive sales practices.

forced sale. **1.** See *execution sale*. **2.** A hurried sale by a debtor because of financial hardship or a creditor's action. Cf. *voluntary sale*.

foreclosure sale. The sale of mortgaged property, authorized by a court decree or a power-of-sale clause, to satisfy the debt. See FORECLOSURE.

fraudulent sale. A sale made to defraud the seller's creditors by converting into cash property that should be used to satisfy the creditors' claims.

gross sales. Total sales (esp. in retail) before deductions for returns and allowances. — Also termed *sales in gross*.

installment sale. See INSTALLMENT SALE.

isolated sale. An infrequent or one-time sale that does not carry an implied warranty of merchantability.

judgment sale. See *execution sale*.

judicial sale. A sale conducted under the authority of a judgment or court order, such as an execution sale. — Also termed *sheriff's sale*.

lumping sale. A court-ordered sale in which several distinct pieces of property are sold together for a single sum.

memorandum sale. A conditional sale in which the buyer takes possession but does not accept title until approving the property.

net sale. The amount of money remaining from a sale, after deducting returns, allowances, rebates, discounts, and other expenses.

present sale. Under the UCC, a sale accomplished by the making of a contract. UCC § 2–106(1).

private sale. An unadvertised sale negotiated and concluded directly between the buyer and seller, not through an agent.

public sale. A sale made after public notice, as in an auction or sheriff's sale.

retail installment sale. See INSTALLMENT SALE.

sale and leaseback. See LEASEBACK.

sale and return. See *sale or return*.

sale as is. A sale in which the buyer accepts the property in its existing condition unless the seller has misrepresented its quality. — Also termed *sale with all faults*.

sale by sample. A sale in which the parties understand that the goods exhibited constitute the standard with which the goods not exhibited correspond and to which all deliveries should conform. • Any sample that is made part of the basis of the bargain creates an express warranty that the whole of the goods will conform to the sample or model. — Also termed *sample sale*.

sale in gross. **1.** A sale of a tract of land made with no guarantee about the exact amount or size of the land being sold. **2.** (*pl.*) See *gross sales*.

sale on approval. A sale in which completion hinges on the buyer's satisfaction, regardless of whether the goods conform to the contract. • Title and risk of loss remain with the seller until the buyer approves. UCC § 2–326(1)(a). — Also termed *approval sale*.

sale on credit. A sale accompanied by delivery of possession, but with payment deferred to a later date.

sale or return. A sale in which the buyer may return the goods to the seller, regardless of whether they conform to the contract, if the goods were delivered primarily for resale. • This transaction is a type of consignment in which the seller (usu. a distributor) sells goods to the buyer (often a retailer), who then tries to resell the goods, but a buyer who cannot resell is allowed to return them to the seller. Title and risk of loss are with the buyer until the goods are returned. UCC § 2–326(1)(b). — Also termed *sale and return*.

sale per aversionem (pər ə-vər-zhee-**oh**-nəm). *Civil law*. A conveyance of all immovable property that falls within the boundaries stated in a purchase agreement, as opposed to a specified amount of acreage. • The sales price will not be modified because of a surplus or shortage in the amount of property that is exchanged, because the boundary description is the binding definition of the property conveyed. La. Civ. Code art. 2495.

sales in gross. See *gross sales*.

sale with all faults. See *sale as is*.

sale with right of redemption. A sale in which the seller reserves the right to retake the goods by refunding the purchase price.

sample sale. See *sale by sample*.

sheriff's sale. **1.** See *execution sale*. **2.** See *judicial sale*.

short sale. A sale of a security that the seller does not own or has not contracted for at the time of sale, and that the seller must borrow to make delivery. • Such a sale is usu. made when the seller expects the security's price to drop. If the price does drop, the seller can make a profit on the difference between the price of the shares sold and the lower price of the shares bought to pay back the borrowed shares.

short sale against the box. A short sale of a security by a seller who owns enough shares of the security to cover the sale but borrows shares anyway because the seller wants to keep ownership a secret or because the owned shares are not easily accessible. • Delivery may be made with either the owned or the borrowed shares, so it is less risky than an ordinary short sale. The phrase *against the box* refers to the owned shares that are in safekeeping; formerly, the "box" was a container used to store stock certificates.

similar sales. *Eminent domain*. Sales of like property in the same locality and time frame, admissible in a condemnation action to determine the marketable value of the particular property at issue.

simulated sale. A sale in which no price or other consideration is paid or intended to be paid, and in which there is no intent to actually transfer ownership. • Simulated sales are usu. done in an attempt to put property beyond the reach of creditors. — Also termed *simulated transaction*.

tax sale. A sale of property because of nonpayment of taxes. See *tax deed* under DEED.

voluntary sale. A sale made freely with the seller's consent. Cf. *forced sale*.

wash sale. A sale of securities made at about the same time as a purchase of the same securities (such as within 30 days), resulting in no change in beneficial ownership. • A loss from a wash sale is usu. not tax-deductible. And securities laws prohibit a wash sale made to create the false appearance of market activity. — Also termed *wash transaction*.

sale and leaseback. See LEASEBACK.

sale and return. See *sale or return* under SALE.

sale as is. See SALE.

sale by sample. See SALE.

sale in gross. See SALE.

sale note. See NOTE (1).

sale-of-business doctrine. The outmoded rule holding that the transfer of stock incident to the sale of a business does not constitute a transfer of securities. • This doctrine was rejected by the U.S. Supreme Court in *Landreth Timber Co. v. Landreth*, 471 U.S. 681, 105 S.Ct. 2297 (1985), and its companion case, *Gould v. Ruefenacht*, 471 U.S. 701, 105 S.Ct. 2308 (1985).

sale of land. A transfer of title to real estate from one person to another by a contract of sale. • A transfer of real estate is often referred to as a conveyance rather than a sale.

sale on approval. See SALE.

sale on credit. See SALE.

sale or exchange. **1.** *Tax*. A voluntary transfer of property for value (as distinguished from a gift) resulting in a gain or loss recognized for federal tax purposes. **2.** A transfer of property; esp., a situation in which proceeds of a sale are to be vested in another estate of the same character and use.

sale or return. See SALE.

sale per aversionem. See SALE.

sales agreement. A contract in which ownership of property is presently transferred, or will be transferred in the future, from a seller to a buyer for a fixed sum. UCC § 2–106(1).

sales-assessment-ratio study. A method for calculating the assessment level for taxable property in a jurisdiction, by comparing the assessed value and the actual sales price of a statistically reliable sample of the property in the jurisdiction, to determine the percentage by which the assessed values are above or below the sales prices.

sales finance company. See FINANCE COMPANY.

sales in gross. See *gross sales* under SALE.

sales invoice. See INVOICE.

sales journal. A book used to record sales of merchandise on account.

sales load. See LOAD.

sales mix. The relative combination of individual-product sales to total sales.

sales price. See PRICE.

sales puffery. See PUFFING (1).

sales tax. See TAX.

sale with all faults. See *sale as is* under SALE.

sale with right of redemption. See SALE.

Salic law (**sal**-ik *or* **say**-lik). An influential early medieval Frankish code of law that originated with the Salian Franks and that deals with a variety of civil property and family issues but is primarily a penal code listing the punishments for various crimes. • Salic law is the principal compilation of the early Germanic laws known collectively as *leges barbarorum* ("laws of the barbarians"). Salic law also designated a rule barring females from the line of succession to the throne, as a result of which references to *Salic law* have sometimes referred only to the code provision excluding women from inheriting certain lands (which probably existed only because military duties were connected with the inheritance). In the late 19th century, Oliver Wendell Holmes revived scholarly interest in Salic law by referring to it throughout *The Common Law* (1881). — Also termed *Salique law*; *law Salique* (sə-**leek** *or* **sal**-ik); *lex Salica* (leks **sal**-ə-kə).

salting, *n. Labor law.* A union tactic that involves a paid union employee going to work for a targeted nonunion employer with the intention of organizing the workforce. • The union agent (known as a *salt*) is considered an employee of the nonunion company and is protected by the National Labor Relations Act.

salus (**sal**-əs), *n.* [Latin] Health; prosperity; safety.

salva gardia. See DE SALVA GARDIA.

salvage (**sal**-vij), *n.* **1.** The rescue of imperiled property. **2.** The property saved or remaining after a fire or other loss, sometimes retained by an insurance company that has compensated the owner for the loss. **3.** Compensation allowed to a person who, having a duty to do so, helps save a ship or its cargo. — **salvage,** *vb.*

> "When some special and extraordinary assistance is rendered, whereby a ship, the persons on it, or its cargo, are saved, the persons rendering such successful assistance, who are called salvors, are entitled to a compensation, which is called salvage." John Indermaur, *Principles of the Common Law* 168 (Edmund H. Bennett ed., 1st Am. ed. 1878).

> "Salvage is a reward payable either by the shipowner or by the owners of goods carried in the ship to persons who save the ship or cargo from shipwreck, capture or other loss. The right to salvage is an ancient rule of maritime law and is not based on contractual rights. The actual amount payable is, as a rule, assessed by the Court. Sometimes an express agreement, fixing an amount, is made before the assistance is rendered, but this is not a question of salvage in the strict sense, which always implies service by persons who are under no obligation to render it." 2 E.W. Chance, *Principles of Mercantile Law* 98 (P.W. French ed., 10th ed. 1951).

salvage charges. *Insurance.* Costs necessarily incurred in salvage.

salvage loss. See LOSS.

salvager. See SALVOR.

salvage service. The aid or rescue given, either voluntarily or by contract, to a vessel in need of assistance because of present or apprehended danger. • Although salvage may involve towing, it is distinguished from *towing service,* which is rendered merely to expedite a voyage, not to respond to dangerous circumstances.

salvage value. See VALUE.

salvo (**sal**-voh). [Latin fr. *salvus* "safe"] *Hist.* **1.** Saving; excepting. • This term was used in deeds. **2.** Safely.

salvo conductu. See DE SALVO CONDUCTU.

salvo jure (**sal**-voh **joor**-ee). [Latin "the rule being safe"] Without prejudice to.

salvor (**sal**-vər), *n.* [Law Latin] *Hist.* A person who saves a vessel and its cargo from danger or loss; a person entitled to salvage. — Also termed *salvager.*

> "A 'salvor' is a person who, without any particular relation to a ship in distress, proffers useful service, and gives it as a volunteer adventurer, without any pre-existing covenant that connected him with the duty of employing himself for the preservation of the ship. To be a salvor, one must have the intention and capacity to save the distressed property involved, but need not have an intent to acquire it." 68 Am. Jur. 2d *Salvage* § 2, at 270 (1993).

salvus plegius (**sal**-vəs **plee**-jee-əs). [Law Latin] *Hist.* A safe pledge; a satisfactory pledge. See PLEDGE.

SAM. See *shared-appreciation mortgage* under MORTGAGE.

same, *pron.* The very thing just mentioned or described; it or them <two days after receiving the goods, Mr. Siviglio returned same>.

same-actor inference. *Employment law.* The doctrine that when an employee is hired and fired by the same person, and the termination occurs a reasonably short time after the hiring, the termination will be presumed not to be based on a discriminatory reason.

same-elements test. See LEGAL-ELEMENTS TEST.

same-evidence test. *Criminal law.* A test of whether the facts alleged in a given case are essentially identical to those alleged in a previous case. • If they are the same, the Fifth Amendment's prohibition against double jeopardy will bar the later action, which is essentially a second prosecution for the same offense. This principle was first announced in *Blockburger v. United States*, 284 U.S. 299, 52 S.Ct. 180 (1932). — Also termed *Blockburger test*; *actual-evidence test.* See *same offense* under OFFENSE (1); DOUBLE JEOPARDY.

same invention. *Patents.* **1.** A second invention claiming the identical subject matter as a previous invention. **2.** Within a reissue statute, the invention described in the original patent.

same-invention double patenting. See DOUBLE PATENTING (1).

same offense. See OFFENSE (1).

same-sex harassment. See HARASSMENT.

sample sale. See *sale by sample* under SALE.

sanae mentis (**san**-ee **men**-tis). [Law Latin] *Hist.* Of sound mind; of sane mind.

sanctio (**sangk**-shee-oh). [Latin fr. *sancio* "to ordain, confirm, or forbid under penalty"] *Roman law.* A particular clause in a statute imposing a penalty on any violation of that statute. • Despite its appearance, this term does not derive from the Latin *sanctus*, meaning "holy."

> "Sanctio (legis). A clause in a statute which strengthens its efficacity by fixing a penalty for its violation, by forbidding its derogation through a later enactment, or by releasing from responsibility any one who by acting in accordance with the statute violated another law. The purpose of the sanction clause was to settle the relation between the new statute and former and future legislation. Thus the *sanctio* could also state that a previous statute remained fully or partially in force without being changed by the new one." Adolf Berger, *Encyclopedic Dictionary of Roman Law* 689 (1953).

sanction (**sangk**-shən), *n.* **1.** Official approval or authorization <the committee gave sanction to the proposal>. **2.** A penalty or coercive measure that results from failure to comply with a law, rule, or order <a sanction for discovery abuse>.

> "Without adequate sanctions the procedure for discovery would often be ineffectual. Under Rule 37 [of the Federal Rules of Civil Procedure], ... any party or person who seeks to evade or thwart full and candid discovery incurs the risk of serious consequences, which may involve imprisonment for contempt of court, an order that designated facts be taken to be established, an order refusing the delinquent party the right to support or oppose designated claims or defenses, striking out pleadings or parts of pleadings, rendering judgment by default, dismissal of the action or a claim therein, or assessment of expenses and attorney's fees. Sanctions are intended to prompt a party to respond." 8A Charles Alan Wright et al., *Federal Practice and Procedure* § 2281, at 595–95 (2d ed. 1994).

criminal sanction. A sanction attached to a criminal conviction, such as a fine or restitution. — Also termed *penal sanction.*

> "A criminal sanction ... is a legally authorized post-conviction deprivation suffered by a human being

through governmental action. By using the words 'post-conviction' in that definition, criminal sanctions are thus limited to those imposed upon defendants in criminal proceedings who, by reason or in consequence of a judgment entered upon a verdict of guilty found by a jury, or judge sitting without a jury (the latter having been legally waived), or upon a plea of guilty, or a plea of nolo contendere, stand convicted." *A Treatise on the Law of Crimes* § 2.00, at 66 (Marian Quinn Barnes ed., 7th ed. 1967).

death-penalty sanction. *Civil procedure.* A court's order dismissing the suit or entering a default judgment in favor of the plaintiff because of extreme discovery abuses by a party or because of a party's action or inaction that shows an unwillingness to participate in the case. • Such a sanction is rarely ordered, and is usu. preceded by orders of lesser sanctions that have not been complied with or that have not remedied the problem.

shame sanction. A criminal sanction designed to stigmatize or disgrace a convicted offender, and often to alert the public about the offender's conviction. • A shame sanction usu. publicly associates the offender with the crime that he or she committed. An example is being required to post a sign in one's yard stating, "Convicted Child Molester Lives Here." — Also termed *shame sentence*; *shaming sanction*; *shaming sentence*; *scarlet-letter punishment*; *scarlet-letter sentence*.

3. *Int'l law.* An economic or military coercive measure taken by one or more countries toward another to force it to comply with international law <U.N. sanctions against a renegade nation>.

sanction, *vb.* **1.** To approve, authorize, or support <the court will sanction the trust disposition if it is not against public policy>. **2.** To penalize by imposing a sanction <the court sanctioned the attorney for violating the gag order>.

sanctionable, *adj.* (Of conduct or action) meriting sanctions; likely to be sanctioned.

sanctioning right. See *secondary right* under RIGHT.

sanctions tort. A means of recovery for another party's discovery abuse, whereby the judge orders the abusive party to pay a fine to the injured party for the discovery violation. • This is not a tort in the traditional sense, but rather a form of punishment that results in monetary gain for the injured party.

sanctity of contract. The principle that the parties to a contract, having duly entered into it, must honor their obligations under it.

"[Sanctity of contract] is merely another facet of freedom of contract, but the two concepts cover, to some extent, different grounds. The sanctity of contractual obligations is merely an expression of the principle that once a contract is freely and voluntarily entered into, it should be held sacred, and should be enforced by the Courts if it is broken. No doubt this very sanctity was an outcome of freedom of contract, for the reason why contracts were held sacred was the fact that the parties entered into them of their own choice and volition, and settled the terms by mutual agreement." P.S. Atiyah, *An Introduction to the Law of Contract* 12 (3d ed. 1981).

sanctuary. 1. A safe place, esp. where legal process cannot be executed; asylum.

"In medieval England, as elsewhere in Europe, there were a number of ecclesiastical places where the king's writ did not run. The underlying theory was that consecrated places should not be profaned by the use of force, but the result in practice was that thieves and murderers could take refuge and thereby gain immunity even against the operation of criminal justice. This was the privilege called 'sanctuary.' In the case of parochial churches, the sanctuary lasted for forty days only. Before the expiration of this period, the fugitive had to choose whether to stand trial or 'abjure' the realm .... This was only permitted if he made a written confession to the coroner, which resulted in the forfeiture of his property as on conviction; his life only was spared ...." J.H. Baker, *An Introduction to English Legal History* 585 (3d ed. 1990).

2. A holy area of a religious building; esp., the area in a church where the main altar is located.

sandbagging, *n.* A trial lawyer's remaining cagily silent when a possible error occurs at trial, with the hope of preserving an issue for appeal if the court does not correct the problem. • Such a tactic does not usu. preserve the issue for appeal because objections must be promptly made to alert the trial judge of the possible error.

S & L. *abbr.* SAVINGS-AND-LOAN ASSOCIATION.

sandpapering, *n.* A lawyer's general preparation of a witness before a deposition or trial. Cf. HORSESHEDDING.

sandwich lease. See LEASE.

sane, *adj.* Having a relatively sound and healthy mind; capable of reason and of distinguishing right from wrong.

sanguis (**sang**-gwis), *n.* [Latin] **1.** *Roman law.* Blood relationship. **2.** *Hist.* Consanguinity. **3.** *Hist.* The right of a chief lord to judge cases involving bloodshed.

sanitary code. A set of ordinances regulating the food and healthcare industries.

sanity. The state or condition of having a relatively sound and healthy mind. Cf. INSANITY.

sanity hearing. 1. An inquiry into the mental competency of a person to stand trial. **2.** A proceeding to determine whether a person should be institutionalized.

sans ce que (sanz **see** kə *or* **sawn** sə **kə**). [Law French] See ABSQUE HOC.

sans frais (saw*n* **fray**). [Law French] Without expense.

sans impeachment de wast (sanz im-**peech**-mənt də **wayst**). [Law French] *Hist.* Without impeachment of waste.

sans jour (saw*n* **zhoor** *or* sanz **joor**). [Law French] *Hist.* Without day; SINE DIE. See ALLER SANS JOUR.

sans recours (saw*n* rə-**koor** *or* sanz ri-**kuur**). See WITHOUT RECOURSE.

sap, *n.* A club, a blackjack, a hose containing rocks in the middle, or any other object generally used as a bludgeon.

SAR. *abbr.* **1.** STOCK-APPRECIATION RIGHT. **2.** SUSPICIOUS-ACTIVITY REPORT.

sasine. See SEISIN.

satellite litigation. 1. One or more lawsuits related to a major piece of litigation that is being conducted in another court <the satellite litigation in state court prevented the federal judge from ruling on the issue>. **2.** Peripheral skirmishes involved in the prosecution of a lawsuit <the plaintiffs called the sanctions "satellite litigation," drummed up by the defendants to deflect attention from the main issues in the case>.

satellite state. See CLIENT STATE.

satisdare (sat-is-**dair**-ee), *vb.* [Latin fr. *satis* "sufficient" + *dare* "to give"] *Roman law.* To give security in the form of *satisdatio.* See SATISDATIO.

satisdatio (sat-is-**day**-shee-oh), *n.* [Latin fr. *satisdare*] *Roman law.* Security given by a person, such as a debtor, through a surety.

satisfaction, *n.* **1.** The giving of something with the intention, express or implied, that it is to extinguish some existing legal or moral obligation. • Satisfaction differs from performance because it is always something given as a substitute for or equivalent of something else, while performance is the identical thing promised to be done. — Also termed *satisfaction of debt.* **2.** The fulfillment of an obligation; esp., the payment in full of a debt. **3.** SATISFACTION PIECE. **4.** *Wills & estates.* The payment by a testator, during the testator's lifetime, of a legacy provided for in a will; ADVANCEMENT. **5.** *Wills & estates.* A testamentary gift intended to satisfy a debt owed by the testator to a creditor. — **satisfy,** *vb.* See ACCORD AND SATISFACTION.

satisfaction contract. See CONTRACT.

satisfaction of debt. See SATISFACTION (1).

satisfaction of judgment. 1. The complete discharge of obligations under a judgment. **2.** The document filed and entered on the record indicating that a judgment has been paid.

> "Generally, a satisfaction of a judgment is the final act and end of a proceeding. Satisfaction implies or manifests an expression of finality as to all questions of liability and damages involved in the litigation. Once satisfaction occurs, further alteration or amendment of a final judgment generally is barred. Satisfaction of a judgment, when entered of record by the act of the parties, is prima facie evidence that the creditor has received payment of the amount of the judgment or its equivalent, and operates as an extinguishment of the judgment debt." 47 Am. Jur. 2d *Judgments* § 1006, at 443 (1995).

satisfaction of lien. 1. The fulfillment of all obligations made the subject of a lien. **2.** The document signed by the lienholder releasing the property subject to a lien.

satisfaction of mortgage. 1. The complete payment of a mortgage. **2.** A discharge signed by the mortgagee or mortgage holder indicating that the property subject to the mortgage is released or that the mortgage debt has been paid and the mortgage conditions have been fully satisfied.

satisfaction piece. A written statement that one party (esp. a debtor) has discharged its obligation to another party, who accepts the discharge. — Also termed *certificate of discharge*; *satisfaction*.

satisfactory evidence. See EVIDENCE.

satisfactory proof. See *satisfactory evidence* under EVIDENCE.

satisfied term. See TERM (4).

Saturday-night special. 1. A handgun that is easily obtained and concealed. **2.** *Corporations.* A surprise tender offer typically held open for a limited offering period (such as one week) to maximize pressure on a shareholder to accept. • These tender offers are now effectively prohibited by section 14(e) of the Williams Act. 15 USCA § 78n(e).

saunkefin (saw*n*-kə-**fan**). [fr. Law French *sang quifin*] *Hist.* End of blood; the failure of a line of succession.

sauvagine (soh-və-**zheen**). [Law French] *Hist.* **1.** Wild animal. **2.** Wild nature of an animal.

save, *vb.* **1.** To preserve from danger or loss <save a ship in distress>. **2.** To lay up; to hoard <save money>. **3.** To toll or suspend (the operation, running, etc.) of something <save a statute of limitations>. **4.** To except, reserve, or exempt (a right, etc.) <to save vested rights>. **5.** To lessen or avoid (a cost, resource, etc.) <save labor>.

save harmless. See HOLD HARMLESS.

save-harmless agreement. See HOLD-HARMLESS AGREEMENT.

save-harmless clause. See INDEMNITY CLAUSE.

saver default (**say**-vər di-**fawlt**). [Law French] *Hist.* To excuse a default. — Also spelled *saver de fault*; *saver defaut*.

> "Saver default is the same as to excuse a default. And this is properly when a man having made default in court, comes afterwards, and alleges a good cause why he did it, as imprisonment at the same time, or the like." *Termes de la Ley* 352 (1st Am. ed. 1812).

saving clause. 1. A statutory provision exempting from coverage something that would otherwise be included. • A saving clause is generally used in a repealing act to preserve rights and claims that would otherwise be lost. **2.** SAVING-TO-SUITORS CLAUSE. **3.** SEVERABILITY CLAUSE. — Also termed *savings clause*.

savings account. A savings-bank depositor's account usu. bearing interest or containing conditions (such as advance notice) to the right of withdrawal.

savings-account trust. See *Totten trust* under TRUST.

savings-and-loan association. A financial institution — often organized and chartered like a bank — that primarily makes home-mortgage loans but also usu. maintains checking accounts and provides other banking services. — Often shortened to S & L. — Also termed *loan association*; *thrift institution*; *thrift*. Cf. BUILDING-AND-LOAN ASSOCIATION.

> "The thrift institutions, mutual savings banks, savings and loan associations, and credit unions, originally were created to meet needs for saving, credit and loans of people whose resources and income were modest. Commercial banks, merchants, money lenders, and pawn shops often did not serve this demand for loans or savings as well, or with interest rates as favorable to poor individuals, and families. During the last two centuries, thrift institutions were gradually developed, therefore, by social reformers, philanthropic benefactors, religious and fraternal organizations, trade unions, employers, and thrift entrepreneurs (in most countries of the world) as a collateral type of banking or financial intermediation." William A. Lovett, *Banking and Financial Institutions Law in a Nutshell* 236 (1997).

savings bank. See BANK.

savings-bank trust. See *Totten trust* under TRUST.

savings bond. See BOND (3).

savings clause. See SAVING CLAUSE.

savings note. See NOTE (1).

saving-to-suitors clause. *Maritime law.* A federal statutory provision that allows a party to bring suit in either state or federal court, but requires both courts to apply federal substantive law. — Also termed *saving clause*. 28 USCA § 1333(1).

savor, *vb.* To partake of the character of or bear affinity to (something). • In traditional legal idiom, an interest arising from land is said to "savor of the realty." — Also spelled *savour*.

S.B. See *senate bill* under BILL (3).

SBA. *abbr.* SMALL BUSINESS ADMINISTRATION.

SBIC. *abbr.* SMALL BUSINESS INVESTMENT COMPANY.

sc. *abbr.* SCILICET.

S.C. *abbr.* **1.** SUPREME COURT. **2.** Same case. • In former practice, when put between two citations, the abbreviation indicated that the same case is reported in both places.

scab. A person who works under conditions contrary to a union contract; esp., a worker who crosses a union picket line to replace a union worker during a strike. — Also termed *strikebreaker*.

scabini (skə-**bɪ**-nɪ). [Law Latin] *Hist.* Judges or the judge's assessors in the court held by the count; magistrates. • The term was found in a charter from the wardens of Lynn in Norfolk, during the reign of Henry VIII. But even earlier than that, the title was used in Charlemagne's empire (the French equivalent being *édevins*) and later Germanized as *Schöffen*.

scalam (**skay**-ləm), *n.* [Latin] *Hist.* Scale. • *Ad scalam* was the method of paying money to the Exchequer, in which sixpence was added to each twenty shillings to compensate for a deficiency in weight, although no scales were actually used.

scale, *n.* **1.** A progression of degrees; esp., a range of wage rates. **2.** A wage according to a range of rates. **3.** An instrument for weighing. **4.** *Hist.* In the practice of the English Supreme Court of Judicature, the fee charged by a solicitor for a particular type of case. • Unless the court ordered otherwise, the *lower scale* applied to all causes and matters assigned by the Judicature Acts to the King's Bench, or the Probate, Divorce, and Admiralty divisions; to all actions for debt, contract, or tort; and to almost all causes and matters assigned by the acts to the Chancery division and in which the amount in controversy was less than £1,000. The *higher scale* applied in all other cases, and in actions falling under one of the lower-scale classes if the principal relief sought was injunctive.

scale order. See ORDER (4).

scale tolerance. The nominal variation of the mass or weight of the same goods on different scales.

scaling law. *Hist.* A statute establishing a process for adjusting value differences between depreciated paper money and specie. • Statutes of this type were necessary when paper depreciated after both the American Revolution and the Civil War.

scalping, *n.* **1.** The purchase of a security by an investment adviser before the adviser recommends that a customer buy the same security. • This practice is usu. considered unethical because the customer's purchase will increase the security's price, thus enabling the investment adviser to sell at a profit. **2.** The excessive markup or markdown on a transaction by a market-maker. • This action violates NASD guidelines. **3.** The practice of selling something (esp. a ticket) at a price above face value once it becomes scarce (usu. just before a high-demand event begins). — **scalp,** *vb.*

scandal. 1. Disgraceful, shameful, or degrading acts or conduct. **2.** Slander. See SCANDALOUS MATTER.

> "**Scandal** consists in the allegation of anything which is unbecoming the dignity of the court to hear, or is contrary to decency or good manners, or which charges some person with a crime not necessary to be shown in the cause, to which may be added that any unnecessary allegation, bearing cruelly upon the moral character of an individual, is also scandalous. The matter alleged, however, must be not only offensive, but also *irrelevant* to the cause, for however offensive it be, if it be pertinent and material to the cause the party has a right to plead it. It may often be necessary to charge false representations, fraud and immorality, and the pleading will not be open to the objection of scandal, if the facts justify the charge." Eugene A. Jones, *Manual of Equity Pleading and Practice* 50–51 (1916).

scandalous matter. *Civil procedure.* A matter that is both grossly disgraceful (or defamatory) and irrelevant to the action or defense. • A federal court — upon a party's motion or on its own — can order a scandalous matter struck from a pleading. Fed. R. Civ. P. 12(f). Cf. IMPERTINENT MATTER.

scandalum magnatum (**skan**-də-ləm mag-**nay**-təm). [Law Latin] *Hist.* Actionable slander of powerful people; specif., defamatory comments regarding persons of high rank, such as peers, judges, or state officials.

> "Words spoken in derogation of a peer, a judge, or other great officer of the realm, which are called *scandalum magnatum*, are held to be still more heinous; and,

though they be such as would not be actionable in the case of a common person, yet when spoken in disgrace of such high and respectable characters, they amount to an atrocious injury: which is redressed by an action on the case founded on many ancient statutes; as well on behalf of the crown, to inflict the punishment of imprisonment on the slanderer, as on behalf of the party, to recover damages for the injury sustained." 3 William Blackstone, *Commentaries on the Laws of England* 123–24 (1768).

scarlet-letter punishment. See *shame sanction* under SANCTION.

scatter-point analysis. A method for studying the effect that minority-population changes have on voting patterns, involving a plotting of the percentage of votes that candidates receive to determine whether voting percentages increase or decrease as the percentages of voters of a particular race increase or decrease.

scènes à faire (**sen** ah **fair**). [French "scenes for action"] In copyright law, standard or general themes that are common to a wide variety of works and are therefore not copyrightable.

schedule, *n.* A written list or inventory; esp., a statement that is attached to a document and that gives a detailed showing of the matters referred to in the document <Schedule B to the title policy lists the encumbrances on the property>. — **schedule,** *vb.* — **scheduled,** *adj.*

scheduled injury. See INJURY.

scheduled property. See PROPERTY.

scheme. 1. A systemic plan; a connected or orderly arrangement, esp. of related concepts <legislative scheme>. **2.** An artful plot or plan, usu. to deceive others <a scheme to defraud creditors>.

schism (**siz**-əm *or* **skiz**-əm). **1.** A breach or rupture; a division, esp. among members of a group, as of a union. **2.** A separation of beliefs and doctrines by persons of the same organized religion, religious denomination, or sect.

"It has been held that the civil courts are not concerned with mere schisms stemming from disputations over matters of religious doctrine, not only because such questions are essentially ecclesiastical rather than judicial, but also because of the separation between the church and the state .... However, it has also been held that the situation is different in the case of self-governing congressional churches, for here the courts do not hesitate to assume jurisdiction when a schism affects property rights, for in this form ... each local congregation is independent and autonomous and there is no recourse within the denomination." 66 Am. Jur. 2d *Religious Societies* § 51, at 804 (1973).

school, *n.* **1.** An institution of learning and education, esp. for children.

"Although the word 'school' in its broad sense includes all schools or institutions, whether of high or low degree, the word 'school' frequently has been defined in constitutions and statutes as referring only to the public common schools generally established throughout the United States .... When used in a statute or other contract, 'school' usually does not include universities, business colleges, or other institutions of higher education unless the intent to include such institutions is clearly indicated." 68 Am. Jur. 2d *Schools* § 1, at 355 (1993).

district school. A public school contained in and maintained by a school district. See SCHOOL DISTRICT.

private school. A school maintained by private individuals, religious organizations, or corporations, funded, at least in part, by fees or tuition, and open only to pupils selected and admitted based on religious affiliations or other particular qualifications.

public school. An elementary, middle, or high school established under state law, regulated by the local state authorities in the various political subdivisions, funded and maintained by public taxation, and open and free to all children of the particular district where the school is located. — Also termed *common school.*

2. The collective body of students under instruction in an institution of learning. **3.** A group of people adhering to the same philosophy or system of beliefs.

school board. An administrative body, made up of a number of directors or trustees, responsible for overseeing public schools within a city, county, or district. Cf. BOARD OF EDUCATION.

school bond. See BOND (3).

school district. A political subdivision of a state, created by the legislature and invested with local powers of self-government, to build, maintain, fund, and support the public schools within its territory and to otherwise assist the state in administering its educational responsibilities.

consolidated school district. A public-school district in which two or more existing schools have consolidated into a single district.

school land. See LAND.

science of legislation. See LAW REFORM.

sciendum est (sɪ-**en**-dəm **est**). [Latin] *Roman law.* It is to be known or understood. • This phrase often introduced a particular topic or explanation.

scienter (sɪ-**en**-tər *or* see-), *n.* [Latin "knowingly"] **1.** A degree of knowledge that makes a person legally responsible for the consequences of his or her act or omission; the fact of an act's having been done knowingly, esp. as a ground for civil damages or criminal punishment. See KNOWLEDGE; MENS REA. **2.** A mental state consisting in an intent to deceive, manipulate, or defraud. • In this sense, the term is used most often in the context of securities fraud. The Supreme Court has held that to establish a claim for damages under Rule 10b–5, a plaintiff must prove that the defendant acted with scienter. *Ernst & Ernst v. Hochfelder*, 425 U.S. 185, 96 S.Ct. 1375 (1976).

scientific evidence. See EVIDENCE.

scientific knowledge. See KNOWLEDGE.

scientific method. An analytical technique by which a hypothesis is formulated and then systematically tested through observation and experimentation.

sci. fa. *abbr.* SCIRE FACIAS.

scil. *abbr.* SCILICET.

scilicet (**sil**-ə-set *or* -sit). [fr. Latin *scire licet* "that you may know"] That is to say; namely; VIDELICET. • Like *videlicet*, this word is used in pleadings and other instruments to introduce a more particular statement of matters previously mentioned in general terms. It has never been quite as common, however, as *videlicet*. — Abbr. sc.; scil.; (erroneously) ss.

scintilla (sin-**til**-ə). A spark or trace <the standard is that there must be more than a scintilla of evidence>. Pl. **scintillas** (sin-**til**-əz).

scintilla juris (sin-**til**-ə **joor**-is). [Law Latin "a spark of right"] *Hist.* A fragment of law or right. • This refers to a figurative expression in the law of uses providing a trace of seisin rights to remain in the feoffees sufficient to allow contingent uses to be executed under the Statute of Uses. It was abolished in the Law of Property Amendment Act of 1860. See STATUTE OF USES.

scintilla-of-evidence rule. A common-law doctrine holding that if even the slightest amount of relevant evidence exists on an issue, then a motion for summary judgment or for directed verdict cannot be granted and the issue must go to the jury. • Federal courts do not follow this rule, but some states apply it. — Also termed *scintilla rule.*

scire facias (**sɪ**-ree **fay**-shee-əs). [Law Latin "you are to make known, show cause"] A writ requiring the person against whom it is issued to appear and show cause why some matter of record should not be annulled or vacated, or why a dormant judgment against that person should not be revived. — Abbr. *sci. fa.*

amicable scire facias to revive a judgment. A written agreement in which a person against whom a revival of an action is sought agrees to the entry of an adverse judgment.

scire facias ad audiendum errores (**sɪ**-ree **fay**-shee-əs ad aw-dee-**en**-dəm e-**ror**-eez). [Law Latin "that you cause to know to hear errors"] *Hist.* A common-law writ allowing a party who had assigned error to compel the opposing party to plead. • It was abolished in 1875.

scire facias ad disprobandum debitum (**sɪ**-ree **fay**-shee-əs ad dis-proh-**ban**-dəm **deb**-ə-təm). [Law Latin "that you cause to know to disprove the debt"] *Hist.* A writ allowing a defendant in a foreign attachment against the plaintiff to disprove or avoid the debt recovered by the plaintiff, within a year and a day from the time of payment.

scire facias ad rehabendam terram (**sɪ**-ree **fay**-shee-əs ad re-hə-**ben**-dəm **ter**-əm), *n.* [Law Latin "that you cause to know to recover the land"] *Hist.* A writ allowing a judgment debtor to recover lands taken in execution after the debtor has satisfied the judgment.

scire facias quare restitutionem non (**sɪ**-ree **fay**-shee-əs **kwair**-ee res-tə-t[y]oo-shee-**oh**-nəm non), *n.* [Law Latin "that you cause to know why restitution not"] *Hist.* A writ for restitution after an execution on a judgment is levied but not paid and the judgment is later reversed on appeal.

scire facias sur mortgage (**sɪ**-ree **fay**-shee-əs sər **mor**-gij), *n.* [Law Latin "that you cause to know on mortgage"] *Hist.* A writ ordering a defaulting mortgagor to show cause why the mortgage should not be foreclosed and the property sold in execution.

scire facias sur municipal claim (**sɪ**-ree **fay**-shee-əs sər myoo-**nis**-ə-pəl **klaym**), *n.*

[Law Latin "that you cause to know on municipal claim"] *Hist.* A writ compelling the payment of a municipal claim out of the property to which a municipal lien is attached.

scire feci (**sI**-ree **fee**-sI). [Latin "I have caused to know"] *Hist.* The sheriff's return to a writ of scire facias, indicating that notice was given to the parties against whom the writ was issued.

***scire fieri* inquiry** (**sI**-ree **fI**-ə-rI), *n.* [Law Latin] *Hist.* A writ to ascertain the location of a testator's property from an executor, when the sheriff returned nulla bona to a writ of execution *fieri facias de bonis testatoris*. See FIERI FACIAS.

scite (sIt). [fr. Latin *situs*] *Archaic.* **1.** A location; a site. **2.** The site of a capital messuage. **3.** A municipal ordinance. — Also termed *site*.

scofflaw (**skof**-law). A person who treats the law with contempt; esp., one who avoids various laws that are not easily enforced <some scofflaws carry mannequins in their cars in order to drive in the carpool lane>.

scold, *n. Hist.* A person who regularly breaks the peace by scolding people, increasing discord, and generally being a public nuisance to the neighborhood. • This behavior was formerly punishable in various ways, including having an iron bridle fitted to the person's mouth. — Also termed *common scold*; *objurgatrix*. See BRANKS.

scolding bridle. See BRANKS.

scope note. In a digest, a precis appearing after a title and showing concisely what subject matter is included and what is excluded.

> "In the Century and Decennial Digests, though not in the various digests of the Key-Number Series, there is printed immediately following each topic title a couple of paragraphs which are called the Scope-Note. The first paragraph of this scope-note shows very briefly the character of the subject-matter included under the title. The second paragraph shows the 'Exclusions' — i.e., what related matter has been excluded in order to conform to the plan of the Digest — and directs the reader to the proper title under which such related matter may be found. Consequently a little study of the scope-note will ofttimes repay the searcher for a few moments' time consumed in so doing." William M. Lile et al., *Brief Making and the Use of Law Books* 116 (3d ed. 1914).

scope of a patent. *Patents.* The invention limits protected under a patent, determined by methods based on established principles of patent law.

scope of authority. *Agency.* The reasonable power that an agent has been delegated or might foreseeably be delegated in carrying out the principal's business. See SCOPE OF EMPLOYMENT; RESPONDEAT SUPERIOR.

scope of employment. The range of reasonable and foreseeable activities that an employee engages in while carrying out the employer's business. See RESPONDEAT SUPERIOR. Cf. ZONE OF EMPLOYMENT.

scorched-earth defense. *Corporations.* An antitakeover tactic by which a target corporation sells its most valuable assets or divisions in order to reduce its value after acquisition and thus try to defeat a hostile bidder's tender offer. See CROWN JEWEL.

S corporation. See CORPORATION.

scot. *Hist.* A payment; esp., a customary tax.

scotal (**skot**-əl). *Hist.* An extortionary practice by which forest officers forced people to patronize the officers' alehouses, often in exchange for the officers' ignoring forest offenses. • This practice was prohibited in 1217 by the Charter of the Forest, ch. 7. — Also spelled *scotale* (**skot**-ayl).

scot and lot. *Hist.* **1.** The customary payment of a share of taxes based on one's ability. **2.** A municipal tax on the right to vote.

Scotch marriage. See MARRIAGE (1).

Scotch verdict. See NOT PROVEN.

scottare (skə-**tair**-ee), *vb.* [Law Latin] *Hist.* To pay a tax.

scrambling possession. See POSSESSION.

scrap value. See *salvage value* under VALUE.

scratching the ticket. A party member's rejection of a candidate on a regular party ticket by canceling the candidate's name or by voting for one or more nominees of the opposing political party.

scrawl. See SCROLL (3).

screening grand jury. See GRAND JURY.

screening mechanism. See ETHICAL WALL.

scriba (**skri**-bə), *n.* [Latin] *Roman law.* A court or office clerk; a scribe; a secretary. • In England, the *scriba regis* was the king's secretary.

scribere est agere (**skri**-bə-ree est **aj**-ə-ree). [Latin] *Hist.* To write is to act.

> "But now it seems clearly to be agreed, that, by the common law and the statute of Edward III, words spoken amount only to a high misdemeanor, and no treason. For they may be spoken in heat, without any intention .... If the words be set down in writing, it argues more deliberate intention; and it has been held that writing is an overt act of treason; for *scribere est agere*. But even in this case the bare words are not the treason, but the deliberate act of writing them." 4 William Blackstone, *Commentaries on the Laws of England* 80 (1769).

scrip. 1. A document that entitles the holder to receive something of value. **2.** Paper money issued for temporary use.

scrip dividend. See DIVIDEND.

script. 1. An original or principal writing. **2.** Handwriting.

scriptum indentatum (**skrip**-təm in-den-**tay**-təm). [Law Latin "indented writing"] *Hist.* An indenture.

scrivener (**skriv**-[ə]-nər). A writer; esp., a professional drafter of contracts or other documents.

money scrivener. A money broker; one who obtains money for mortgages or other loans.

scrivener's error. See *clerical error* under ERROR (2).

scrivener's exception. An exemption from the attorney-client privilege whereby the privilege does not attach if the attorney is retained solely to perform a ministerial task for the client, such as preparing a statutory-form deed.

scroll, *n.* **1.** A roll of paper; a list. **2.** A draft or outline to be completed at a later time. **3.** A written mark; esp., a character affixed to a signature in place of a seal. — Also termed *scrawl.*

scruet-roll (**skroo**-ət-**rohl**). *Hist.* The record of bail accepted in a habeas corpus case.

scrutator (skroo-**tay**-tər), *n.* [Latin fr. *scrutari* "to search"] *Hist.* A bailiff or officer who enforces the king's water rights, as by supervising wreckage, flotsam, and jetsam; a customs officer.

S.Ct. *abbr.* **1.** SUPREME COURT. **2.** Supreme Court Reporter.

scutage (**skyoo**-tij), *n.* [fr. Latin *scutum* "a shield"] *Hist.* **1.** A monetary payment levied by the king on barons as a substitute for some or all of the knights to be supplied to the king by each baron. • This payment seems to date from the 12th century, Henry II (1154–1189) having levied five scutages in the first 11 years of his reign. **2.** A fee paid by a tenant-in-chief by knight-service in lieu of serving in a war. **3.** A tax on a knight's estate to help furnish the army. — Also termed *escuage.*

> "Scutage .... Shield-money, in mediaeval feudal law, a payment in lieu of military service, paid by a tenant-in-chief in respect of the service of knights which he owed to the Crown. His personal obligation to serve could not be discharged by scutage but only by fine. Payment of scutage, though known in France and Germany, was most highly developed in England where it became a general tax on knights' estates at rates which by the thirteenth century were standardized. King John demanded frequent and heavy scutages and Magna Carta forbade the levying of scutage without the consent of a general council. Scutage was divided between the King and the tenants-in-chief who gave personal service in the campaign. It became obsolete by the fourteenth century." David M. Walker, *The Oxford Companion to Law* 1121 (1980).

scutagio habendo. See DE SCUTAGIO HABENDO.

scyra (**shy**-rə), *n.* [Law Latin "shire"] *Hist.* **1.** A county; shire. **2.** A county's inhabitants.

S.D. *abbr.* Southern District, in reference to U.S. judicial districts.

s/d b/l. *abbr.* Sight draft with bill of lading attached. See *sight draft* under DRAFT.

sea. 1. The ocean <on the sea>. **2.** A large landlocked part of the ocean; a large body of salt water smaller than a regular ocean <the Mediterranean Sea>. **3.** The ocean swell <a rough sea>. **4.** An extremely large or extended quantity <a sea of documents>.

high seas. The seas or oceans beyond the jurisdiction of any country. • Under international law, the high seas traditionally began three miles from the coast, but under the 1982 U.N. Convention on the Law of the Sea, coastal shores now have a 200–mile exclusive economic zone. — Also termed *open seas; main sea.*

"Outside territorial waters the law of no one country applies, since the high seas are free." R.H. Graveson, *Conflict of Laws* 584 (7th ed. 1974).

main sea. *Archaic.* The open ocean; high seas.

navigable sea. See NAVIGABLE SEA.

territorial sea. See *territorial waters* under WATER.

seabed. The sea floor; the ground underlying the ocean, over which nations may assert sovereignty, esp. if underlying their territorial waters.

sea brief. See SEA LETTER.

seagoing vessel. See VESSEL.

seal, *n.* **1.** An impression or sign that has legal consequence when applied to an instrument. **2.** A fastening that must be broken before access can be obtained.

"The use of the seal in England seems to have begun after the Norman Conquest, spreading from royalty and a few of the nobility to those of lesser rank. Originally a seal often consisted of wax bearing the imprint of an individualized signet ring, and in the seventeenth century Lord Coke said that wax without impression was not a seal. But in the United States the courts have not required either wax or impression. Impressions directly on the paper were recognized early and are still common for notarial and corporate seals, and gummed wafers have been widely used. In the absence of statute decisions have divided on the effectiveness of the written or printed word 'seal,' the printed initials 'L.S.' (locus sigilli, meaning place of the seal), a scrawl made with a pen (often called a 'scroll') and a recital of sealing. Most states in which the seal is still recognized now have statutes giving effect to one or more such devices." Restatement (Second) of Contracts § 96 cmt. a (1981).

"The time-honoured form of seal was a blob of wax at the foot of the document, bearing an imprint of some kind, often a crest or motto. The use of wax was not, however, necessary for a seal, and any mark or impression on the paper was sufficient as long as it was made with the intention of affixing a seal. Recent English cases have been willing to find the necessary intention in circumstances where courts in the past would almost certainly have declined; so much so that it may now be the common law that a document purporting to be executed as a deed but lacking actual sealing will be regarded as sealed as long as it contains a printed or written indication of where the mark or impression constituting the seal should be placed if it were to be affixed." Peter Butt, *Land Law* 481–82 (2d ed. 1988).

corporate seal. A seal adopted by a corporation for executing and authenticating its corporate and legal instruments.

great seal. **1.** The official seal of the United States, of which the Secretary of State is the custodian. — Also termed *seal of the United States*. **2.** The official seal of a particular state. — Also termed *seal of the state*; *state seal*. **3.** The official seal of Great Britain, of which the Lord Chancellor is the custodian.

notary seal. See NOTARY SEAL.

private seal. A corporate or individual seal, as distinguished from a public seal.

public seal. A seal used to certify documents belonging to a public authority or government bureau.

quarter seal. A seal (originally a quarter section of the great seal) maintained in the Scotch chancery to be used on particular grants from the Crown. See *great seal* (3).

seal of the state. See *great seal* (2).

seal of the United States. See *great seal* (1).

state seal. See *great seal* (2).

seal, *vb.* **1.** To authenticate or execute (a document) by use of a seal. **2.** To close (an envelope, etc.) tightly; to prevent access to (a document, record, etc.).

sea law. See MARITIME LAW.

sealed bid. See BID (2).

sealed-container rule. *Products liability.* The principle that a seller is not liable for a defective product if it receives the product from the manufacturer and sells it without knowing of the defect or having a reasonable opportunity to inspect the product.

sealed contract. See *contract under seal* under CONTRACT.

sealed instrument. At common law and under some statutes, an instrument to which the bound party has affixed a personal seal, usu. recognized as providing indisputable evidence of the validity of the underlying obligations. • The common-law distinction between sealed and unsealed instruments has been abolished by many states, and the UCC provides that the laws applicable to sealed instruments do not apply to contracts for the sale of goods or negotiable instruments. UCC § 2–203. See *contract under seal* under CONTRACT; SPECIALTY.

"At common law, the seal served to render documents indisputable as to the terms of the underlying obligation, thereby dispensing with the necessity of witnesses; the sealed instrument was considered such reliable evidence that it actually became the contract itself — called a 'specialty' — the loss of which meant loss of all rights of the obligee against the obligor. The seal also had many "other consequences at common law, some of which have been retained in jurisdictions which still recognize the seal .... In states where the seal is still recognized, its primary legal significance is often the application of a longer statute of limitations to actions on sealed instruments." 69 Am. Jur. 2d *Seals* § 2, at 617–18 (1993).

sealed testament. See *mystic will* under WILL.

sealed verdict. See VERDICT.

sealed will. See *mystic will* under WILL.

sea letter. *Hist.* A manifest issued during a war by authorities of a port where a neutral vessel is fitted, certifying the vessel's nationality, specifying the nature of and destination of the vessel's cargo, and allowing the vessel to sail under the neutral flag of its owner. • The last sea letter was issued at the Port of New York in 1806, and the use of sea letters was discontinued by proclamation of President James Madison. — Also termed *sea brief*; *sea pass*; *passport*.

sealing records. The act or practice of officially preventing access to particular (esp. juvenile-criminal) records, in the absence of a court order. See EXPUNGEMENT.

seal of the state. See *great seal* (2) under SEAL.

seal of the United States. See *great seal* (1) under SEAL.

seaman. *Maritime law.* A person who assists in the navigation and operation of a vessel at sea; a sailor or mariner, esp. one below the rank of officer. • Seamen's injuries are covered under the Jones Act. — Also termed *mariner*. See JONES ACT. Cf. STEVEDORE.

"The Jones Act plaintiff must be a 'seaman' who is injured (or killed) 'in the course of his employment.' The 'course of ... employment' requirement at least excluded passengers, guests, trespassers, pirates (unless of course the pirate was suing his own employer) and so on. Who else might be excluded (or included) was, as a matter of initial construction, impossible to say. After a half-century of litigation the answer to the riddle is not apparent. The Supreme Court has alternated between giving the term 'seaman' an exceedingly broad construction and giving it a much narrower one. Consequently defendants have been encouraged to argue, in all but the most obvious cases, that plaintiff is not a Jones Act seaman and that the action must be dismissed. Thus there has always been, there continues to be, and presumably there will go on being a substantial volume of depressing litigation of this type." Grant Gilmore & Charles L. Black, Jr., *The Law of Admiralty* § 6–21, at 328 (2d ed. 1975).

"The traditional seaman is a member of the crew of a merchant vessel .... However, vessels are not limited in their functions to the transportation of goods over water. The performance by a vessel of some other mission, such as operating as a cruise ship, necessitates the presence aboard ship of employees who do not 'man, reef and steer' the vessel .... Exploration for oil and gas on navigable waters has led to further expansion of the concept of a 'seaman.' In 1959, in the celebrated case of *Offshore Oil Co. v. Robinson*, 266 F.2d 769 (5th Cir. 1959), the Fifth Circuit held that floating drilling structures are 'vessels' and that the amphibious oil workers aboard them are entitled to the seaman's remedies against their employers and the operators of the 'vessels' on which they are employed." Frank L. Maraist, *Admiralty in a Nutshell* 178–80 (2d ed. 1988).

able-bodied seaman. An experienced seaman who is qualified for all seaman's duties and certified by an inspecting authority. — Abbr. AB; ABS. — Also termed *able seaman*; *bluewater seaman*.

merchant seaman. A sailor employed by a private vessel, as distinguished from one employed in public or military service.

ordinary seaman. A seaman who has some experience but who is not proficient enough to be classified as an able-bodied seaman. — Abbr. OS; OD.

seaman's will. See *soldier's will* under WILL.

sea pass. See SEA LETTER.

search, *n.* **1.** An examination of a person's body, property, or other area that the person would reasonably be expected to consider as private, conducted by a law-enforcement officer for the purpose of finding evidence of a crime. • Because the Fourth Amendment prohibits unreasonable searches (as well as seizures), a search cannot ordinarily be conducted without probable cause. — **search,** *vb.*

"It must be recognized that whenever a police officer accosts an individual and restrains his freedom to walk away, he has 'seized' that person. And it is nothing less than sheer torture of the English language to suggest that a careful exploration of the outer surfaces of a person's clothing all over his or her body in an attempt to find weapons is not a 'search.'" *Terry v. Ohio*, 392 U.S. 1, 16, 88 S.Ct. 1868, 1877 (1968) (Warren, J.).

administrative search. A search of public or commercial premises carried out by a regulatory authority for the purpose of enforcing compliance with health, safety, or security regulations. • The probable cause required for an administrative search is less stringent than that required for a search incident to a criminal investigation. — Also termed *regulatory search*; *inspection search*.

border search. A search conducted by immigration or customs officials at the border of a country to detect and prevent illegal entries of people or things. • A border search requires no warrant.

checkpoint search. A search anywhere on a military installation.

consent search. A warrantless search conducted after the person who is to be searched or who has authority over the property to be searched voluntarily gives consent.

"The voluntariness of a consent to search is 'to be determined from the totality of all the circumstances.' [*Schneckloth v. Bustamonte*, 412 U.S. 218, 93 S.Ct. 2041 (1973).] Among the factors to be considered in determining the effectiveness of an alleged consent to search are whether the defendant (1) has minimal schooling or was of low intelligence; (2) was mentally ill or intoxicated; (3) was under arrest at the time the consent was given; (4) was overpowered by officers, handcuffed, or similarly subject to physical restriction; (5) has seized from him by the police the keys to the premises thereafter searched; (6) employed evasive conduct or attempted to mislead the police; (7) denied guilt or the presence of any incriminatory objects in his premises; (8) earlier gave a valid confession or otherwise cooperated, as by instigating the search, or at least the investigation leading to the search; or (10) was refused his request to consult with counsel. The presence of some of these factors is not controlling, however, as each case must stand or fall on its own special facts." Jerold H. Israel & Wayne R. LaFave, *Criminal Procedure in a Nutshell* 141–42 (5th ed. 1993).

constructive search. A subpoena of a corporation's records.

"[I]t is settled that the so-called 'constructive search' involved in an administrative subpoena of corporate books or records constitutes a 'search' or 'seizure' within the meaning of the Fourth Amendment." 68 Am. Jur. 2d *Searches and Seizures* § 44, at 674 (1993).

exigent search (**eks**-ə-jənt). A warrantless search carried out in response to a sudden emergency. • This type of search is often performed to preserve evidence or to ensure the safety of the arresting officers.

illegal search. See *unreasonable search*.

inventory search. A complete search of an arrestee's person before being booked into jail. • All possessions found are typically held in police custody.

no-knock search. A search of property by the police without knocking and announcing their presence and purpose before entry. • A no-knock search warrant may be issued under limited circumstances, as when a prior announcement would lead to the destruction of the objects searched for, or would endanger the safety of the police officer or another person.

private search. A search conducted by a private person rather than by a law-enforcement officer. • Items found during a private search are generally admissible in evidence if the person conducting the search was not acting at the direction of a law-enforcement officer.

protective search. A search of a detained suspect and the area within the suspect's immediate control, conducted to protect the arresting officer's safety (as from a concealed weapon) and often to preserve evidence. • A protective search can be conducted without a warrant. *Chimel v. California*, 395 U.S. 752, 89 S.Ct. 2034 (1969). — Also termed *search incident to arrest*; *Chimel search* (shə-**mel**).

regulatory search. See *administrative search*.

shakedown search. A usu. random and warrantless search for illicit or contraband material (such as weapons or drugs) in a prisoner's cell. — Often shortened to *shakedown*.

strip search. A search of a person conducted after that person's clothes have been removed, the purpose usu. being to find any contraband the person might be hiding.

unreasonable search. A search conducted without probable cause or other considerations that would make it legally permissible. — Also termed *illegal search*.

voluntary search. A search in which no duress or coercion was applied to obtain the defendant's consent. See *consent search*.

zone search. A search of a crime scene (such as the scene of a fire or explosion) by dividing it up into specific sectors.

2. An examination of public documents or records for information; esp., TITLE SEARCH. **3.** *Int'l law.* The wartime process of boarding and examining the contents of a merchant vessel for contraband. • A number of treaties regulate the manner in which the search must be conducted. See RIGHT OF SEARCH.

search-and-seizure warrant. See SEARCH WARRANT.

search book. A lawbook that contains no statements of the law but instead consists of lists or tables of cases, statutes, and the like, used simply to help a researcher find the law. • Most indexes, other than index-digests, are search books.

search incident to arrest. See *protective search* under SEARCH (1).

search warrant. A judge's written order authorizing a law-enforcement officer to conduct a search of a specified place and to seize evidence. — Also termed *search-and-seizure warrant*. See WARRANT (1).

anticipatory search warrant. A search warrant based on an affidavit showing probable cause that evidence of a certain crime (such as illegal drugs) will be located at a specific place in the future.

blanket search warrant. **1.** A single search warrant that authorizes the search of more than one area. **2.** An unconstitutional warrant that authorizes the seizure of everything found at a given location, without specifying which items may be seized.

no-knock search warrant. A search warrant that authorizes the police to enter premises without knocking and announcing their presence and purpose before entry because a prior announcement would lead to the destruction of the objects searched for or would endanger the safety of the police or another person. See *no-knock search* under SEARCH.

sea reeve (**see** reev). *Hist.* An officer appointed to watch the shore and enforce a lord's maritime rights, including the right to wreckage.

sea rover. **1.** A person who roves the sea for plunder; a pirate. **2.** A pirate vessel.

seasonable, *adj.* Within the time agreed on; within a reasonable time <seasonable performance of the contract>.

seasonal employment. See EMPLOYMENT.

seat, *n.* **1.** Membership and privileges in an organization; esp., membership on a securities or commodities exchange <her seat at the exchange dates back to 1998>. **2.** The center of some activity <the seat of government>.

seated land. See LAND.

seat of government. The nation's capital, a state capital, a county seat, or other location where the principal offices of the national, state, and local governments are located.

seaward. See CUSTOS MARIS.

seaworthy, *adj.* (Of a vessel) properly equipped and sufficiently strong and tight to resist the perils reasonably incident to the voyage for which the vessel is insured. • An implied condition of marine-insurance policies, unless otherwise stated, is that the vessel will be seaworthy. — **seaworthiness,** *n.*

seaworthy vessel. See VESSEL.

SEC. *abbr.* SECURITIES AND EXCHANGE COMMISSION.

secession. The process or act of withdrawing, esp. from a religious or political association <the secession from the established church> <the secession of 11 states at the time of the Civil War>.

seck (sek), *adj. Hist.* **1.** Lacking the right or remedy of distress. **2.** Lacking profits, usu. due to a reversion without rent or other service. See RENT SECK.

Second Amendment. The constitutional amendment, ratified with the Bill of Rights in 1791, guaranteeing the right to keep and bear arms as necessary for securing freedom through a well-regulated militia.

secondary, *adj.* (Of a position, status, use, etc.) subordinate or subsequent.

secondary, *n. Hist.* An officer of the courts of the King's Bench and common pleas, so called because he was next to the chief officer. • By the Superior Courts (Officers) Act (1837), the secondary office was abolished. St. 7 Will. 4; 1 Vict., ch. 30.

secondary activity. *Labor law.* A union's picketing or boycotting a secondary or neutral party, with the goal of placing economic pressure on that party so that it will stop doing business with the employer that is the primary subject of the labor dispute. • Secondary activities are forbidden by the Labor–Management Relations Act. 29 USCA § 158(b)(4). See *secondary boycott* under BOYCOTT; *secondary picketing* under PICKETING. Cf. PRIMARY ACTIVITY.

secondary affinity. See AFFINITY.

secondary authority. See AUTHORITY (4).

secondary beneficiary. See *contingent beneficiary* under BENEFICIARY.

secondary boycott. See BOYCOTT.

secondary conveyance. See CONVEYANCE.

secondary creditor. See CREDITOR.

secondary distribution. See DISTRIBUTION.

secondary easement. See EASEMENT.

secondary evidence. See EVIDENCE.

secondary invention. *Patents.* An invention that uses or incorporates established elements or combinations to achieve a new and useful result.

secondary lender. A wholesale mortgage buyer who purchases first mortgages from banks and savings-and-loan associations, enabling them to restock their money supply and loan more money.

secondary liability. See LIABILITY.

secondary-line competition. See *vertical competition* under COMPETITION.

secondary-line injury. *Antitrust.* Under the price-discrimination provisions of the Robinson–Patman Act, the act of hindering or seeking to hinder competition among a seller's customers by selling substantially the same products at favorable prices to one customer, or a select group of customers, to the detriment of others. 15 USCA § 13(a). • A secondary-line injury, which refers to competition among the seller's customers, is distinguishable from a primary-line injury, which refers to the anticompetitive effects that predatory pricing has on the direct competitors of the seller. Cf. PRIMARY-LINE INJURY.

secondary market. See MARKET.

secondary meaning. *Intellectual property.* A special sense that a trademark or tradename for a business, goods, or services has acquired even though the trademark or tradename was not originally protectable. — Also termed *special meaning*; *trade meaning*.

secondary mortgage market. See MORTGAGE MARKET.

secondary obligation. See OBLIGATION.

secondary offering. See OFFERING.

secondary party. *Commercial law.* **1.** A party not primarily liable under an instrument, such as a guarantor. **2.** The drawer or indorser of a negotiable instrument.

secondary picketing. See PICKETING.

secondary reserve ratio. See RESERVE RATIO.

secondary right. See RIGHT.

secondary strike. See STRIKE.

secondary trading. See TRADING.

secondary use. See *shifting use* under USE (4).

second chair, *n.* A lawyer who helps the lead attorney in court, usu. by examining some of the witnesses, arguing some of the points of law, and handling parts of the voir dire, opening statement, and closing argument <the young associate was second chair for the fraud case>. — **second-chair,** *vb.*

second-collision doctrine. See CRASHWORTHINESS DOCTRINE.

second cousin. See COUSIN.

second-degree murder. See MURDER.

second deliverance. See DELIVERANCE.

second delivery. See DELIVERY.

second distress. See DISTRESS.

secondhand evidence. See HEARSAY.

second-impact doctrine. See CRASHWORTHINESS DOCTRINE.

second lien. See LIEN.

second-look doctrine. **1.** WAIT-AND-SEE PRINCIPLE. **2.** An approach that courts use to monitor the continuing effectiveness or validity of an earlier order. • For example, a family court may reconsider a waiver of alimony, and a federal court may reconsider a law that Congress has passed a second time after the first law was struck down as unconstitutional.

second mortgage. See MORTGAGE.

second offense. See OFFENSE (1).

second-permittee doctrine. *Insurance.* The principle that, when a third person is allowed to use an insured's car by permission granted by someone else to whom the insured gave permission to use the car, the third person's use of the car will be a permissive use, under the insured's automobile-liability-insurance policy, as long as that use falls within the scope of the permission originally given by the insured.

second surcharge. See SURCHARGE (vb).

secrecy. The state or quality of being concealed, esp. from those who would be affected by the concealment; hidden.

secret, *n.* **1.** Something that is kept from the knowledge of others or shared only with those concerned. See TRADE SECRET. **2.** Information that cannot be disclosed without a breach of trust; specif., information that is acquired in the attorney-client relationship and that either (1) the client has requested be kept private or (2) the attorney believes would be embarrassing or likely to be detrimental to the client if disclosed. • Under the ABA Code of Professional Responsibility, a lawyer cannot reveal a client's secret unless the client consents after full disclosure. DR 4–101. Cf. CONFIDENCE (3).

secretarius (sek-rə-**tair**-ee-əs), *n.* [Law Latin] See APOCRISARIUS.

secretary. A corporate officer in charge of official correspondence, minutes of board meetings, and records of stock ownership and transfer. — Also termed *clerk of the corporation.*

Secretary General. The chief administrative officer of the United Nations, nominated by the Security Council and elected by the General Assembly.

secretary of embassy. A diplomatic officer appointed as secretary or assistant, usu. to an ambassador or minister plenipotentiary.

secretary of legation. An officer employed to attend a foreign mission and perform certain clerical duties.

secretary of state. 1. (*usu. cap.*) The cabinet member who heads the State Department and directs foreign policy. • The Secretary of State is fourth in line of succession to the presidency after the Vice President, the Speaker of the House, and the President pro tempore of the Senate. **2.** A state government official who is responsible for the licensing and incorporation of businesses, the administration of elections, and other formal duties. • The secretary of state is elected in some states and appointed in others.

secret ballot. See BALLOT (3).

secret diplomacy. See DIPLOMACY.

secrete (si-**kreet**), *vb.* To conceal or secretly transfer (property, etc.), esp. to hinder or prevent officials or creditors from finding it.

secret equity. See *latent equity* under EQUITY.

secret lien. See LIEN.

secret partner. See PARTNER.

Secret Service. A federal law-enforcement agency — organized as a division of the Treasury Department — primarily responsible for preventing counterfeiting and protecting the President and other public officials.

secret testament. See *mystic will* under WILL.

secret trust. See TRUST.

secret will. See *mystic will* under WILL.

secta (**sek**-tə), *n.* [Latin "suit"] **1.** *Roman law.* A group of followers, as of a particular religion or school of philosophy, law, etc.; a religious sect. **2.** *Hist.* People whom a plaintiff must bring to court to support the plaintiff's case. **3.** *Hist.* A lawsuit.

secta ad molendinum. See DE SECTA AD MOLENDINUM.

secta curiae (**sek**-tə **kyoor**-ee-ee). [Latin "suit of court"] *Hist.* Attendance at court, esp. by feudal tenants, who are obligated to attend the lord's court as jurors or parties.

secta facienda per illam quae habet eniciam partem (**sek**-tə fay-shee-**en**-də pər **il**-əm kwee **hay**-bət i-**nish**-ee-əm **pahr**-təm), *n.* [Law Latin "suit to be performed by her who has the eldest part"] *Hist.* A writ ordering the eldest heir or coparcener to perform suit and services for all the coheirs or coparceners.

secta regalis (**sek**-tə ri-**gay**-lis). [Latin "king's suit"] *Hist.* An obligation to attend the sheriff's court twice a year, so called because it had the same functions and jurisdiction as the king's court.

sectarian, *adj.* Of or relating to a particular religious sect <sectarian college>.

sectatores (sek-tə-**tor**-eez), *n.* [Latin] *Roman law.* Supporters of candidates for office, who accompany a candidate during a campaign, primarily to impress voters.

secta unica tantum facienda pro pluribus haereditatibus (**sek**-tə **yoo**-nə-kə **tan**-təm fay-shee-**en**-də proh **ploor**-ə-bəs hə-red-ə-**tay**-tə-bəs), *n.* [Law Latin "one suit alone to be performed for several inheritances"] *Hist.* A writ exempting the eldest heir, distrained by a lord to perform several services for the coheirs, from performing all services but one.

section. 1. A distinct part or division of a writing, esp. a legal instrument. — Abbr. § ; sec.; s. **2.** *Real estate.* A piece of land containing 640 acres, or one square mile. • Traditionally, public lands in the United States were divided into 640–acre squares, each one called a "section." — Also termed *section of land.*

half section. A piece of land containing 320 acres, laid off either by a north-and-south or by an east-and-west line; half a section of land.

quarter section. A piece of land containing 160 acres, laid off by a north-south or east-west line; one quarter of a section of land, formerly the amount usu. granted to a homesteader. — Often shortened to *quarter.*

section 8(f) agreement. *Labor law.* A labor contract that is negotiated between an employer in the construction business and a union that cannot demonstrate that it represents a majority of the employees at the time the contract is executed. 29 USCA § 158(f). • This is an exception to the general rule that an employer need only negotiate with a union that can demonstrate majority status. It was enacted in part because of the nature of the construction industry, in which the employers may have several different jobs in different parts of the country, the jobs are typically completed in a relatively short time, and the workforce is often transient. Since the workforce often does not have sufficient ties to a particular employer to petition for a certification election, section 8(f) agreements are directed toward providing a certain level of protection in recognition of that fact. But section 8(f) agreements are not equivalent to collective-bargaining agreements. For example, the employer can legally repudiate the agreement at any time, and the employees may not legally picket to enforce the agreement. The main protection such an agreement provides is a monetary obligation, which can be enforced, if necessary, in federal court. And if the union achieves majority status, the section 8(f) agreement will essentially become a fully enforceable collective-bargaining agreement.

section of land. See SECTION.

sectis non faciendis (**sek**-tis non fay-shee-**en**-dis). See DE SECTIS NON FACIENDIS.

sectores (sek-**tor**-eez), *n.* [Latin] *Roman law.* Successful bidders at public auctions.

secular, *adj.* Worldly, as distinguished from spiritual <secular business>.

secular clergy. 1. Clergy who have no particular religious affiliation or do not belong to a particular religious denomination. **2.** Clergy who live in their parishes and minister there, as contrasted with regular clergy who live in monasteries.

secundum (si-**kən**-dəm). [Latin] *Roman law.* According to; in favor of, as in *secundum actorem* ("in favor of the plaintiff").

secundum aequum et bonum (si-**kən**-dəm **ee**-kwəm et **boh**-nəm). [Latin] *Hist.* According to what is just and good.

secundum allegata et probata (si-**kən**-dəm al-ə-**gay**-tə et prə-**bay**-tə). [Latin] *Hist.* According to what is alleged and proved.

secundum artem (si-**kən**-dəm **ahr**-təm). [Latin] *Hist.* According to the art or trade.

secundum bonos mores (si-**kən**-dəm **boh**-nohs **mor**-eez). [Latin] *Hist.* According to good usages; customary.

secundum consuetudinem manerii (si-**kən**-dəm kon-swə-**t[y]oo**-də-nəm mə-**neer**-ee-I). [Law Latin] *Hist.* According to the custom of the manor.

secundum formam chartae (si-**kən**-dəm **for**-məm **kahr**-tee). [Law Latin] *Hist.* According to the form of the charter.

secundum formam doni (si-**kən**-dəm **for**-məm **doh**-nI). [Latin] *Hist.* According to the form of the gift or grant.

secundum formam statuti (si-**kən**-dəm **for**-məm stə-**t[y]oo**-tI). [Law Latin] *Hist.* According to the form of the statute.

secundum legem communem (si-**kən**-dəm **lee**-jəm kə-**myoo**-nəm). [Law Latin] *Hist.* According to the common law.

secundum normam legis (si-**kən**-dəm **nor**-məm **lee**-jis). [Latin] *Hist.* According to the rule of law; by rule of law.

secundum regulam (si-**kən**-dəm **reg**-yə-ləm). [Latin] *Hist.* According to the rule; by rule.

secundum subjectam materiam (si-**kən**-dəm səb-**jek**-təm mə-**teer**-ee-əm). [Law Latin] *Hist.* According to the subject matter.

secured, *adj.* **1.** (Of debt or obligation) supported or backed by security or collateral. **2.** (Of a creditor) protected by a pledge, mortgage, or other encumbrance of property that helps ensure financial soundness and confidence. See SECURITY.

secured bond. See BOND (3).

secured claim. See CLAIM (5).

secured creditor. See CREDITOR.

secured debt. See DEBT.

secured loan. See LOAN.

secured note. See NOTE (1).

secured party. See *secured creditor* under CREDITOR.

secured transaction. A business arrangement by which a buyer or borrower gives collateral to the seller or lender to guarantee payment of an obligation. • Article 9 of the UCC deals with secured transactions. See SECURITY AGREEMENT.

securitas (si-**kyoor**-i-tas), *n.* [Latin] **1.** *Roman law.* Security; freedom from liability. **2.** *Civil law.* A release.

securitatem inveniendi (si-kyoor-i-**tay**-təm in-vee-nee-**en**-dI), *n.* [Law Latin] *Hist.* A writ from the Crown requiring subjects to find security to ensure that they would not leave the kingdom without the Crown's permission. • It was replaced by *ne exeat regno.* See NE EXEAT REPUBLICA.

securitate pacis (si-kyoor-i-**tay**-tee **pay**-sis), *n.* [Law Latin "of security of the peace"] *Hist.* A writ for someone fearing bodily harm from another, as when the person has been threatened with violence. — Also termed *securitatis pacis*; *writ of threats.*

securities act. A federal or state law protecting the public by regulating the registration, offering, and trading of securities. See SECURITIES ACT OF 1933; SECURITIES EXCHANGE ACT OF 1934; BLUE-SKY LAW.

Securities Act of 1933. The federal law regulating the registration and initial public offering of securities, with an emphasis on full public disclosure of financial and other information. 15 USCA §§ 77a–77aa. — Also termed *Securities Act*; *1933 Act.*

Securities and Exchange Commission. The federal agency that regulates the issuance and trading of securities in an effort to protect investors against fraudulent or unfair practices. • The Commission was established by the Securities Exchange Act of 1934. — Abbr. SEC.

securities broker. See BROKER.

securities exchange. 1. A marketplace or facility for the organized purchase and sale of securities, esp. stocks. **2.** A group of people who organize themselves to create such a marketplace. — Often shortened to *exchange.* — Also termed *stock exchange.*

regional securities exchange. A securities exchange that focuses on stocks and bonds of local interest, such as the Boston, Philadelphia, and Midwest stock exchanges.

Securities Exchange Act of 1934. The federal law regulating the public trading of securities. • This law provides for the registration and supervision of securities exchanges and brokers, and regulates proxy solicitations. The Act also established the SEC. 15 USCA §§ 78a et seq. — Also termed *Exchange Act*; *1934 Act.*

Securities Investor Protection Act. A 1970 federal law establishing the Securities Investor Protection Corporation that, although not a governmental agency, is designed to protect investors and help brokers and dealers in financial trouble. — Abbr. SIPA. 15 USCA §§ 78aaa et seq.

Securities Investor Protection Corporation. A corporation established under the Securities Investor Protection Act to protect investors and help brokers and dealers in financial trouble. — Abbr. SIPC. See SECURITIES INVESTOR PROTECTION ACT.

securities-offering distribution. See DISTRIBUTION.

securitize, *vb.* To convert (assets) into negotiable securities for resale in the financial market, allowing the issuing financial institution to remove assets from its books, to improve its capital ratio and liquidity while making new loans with the security proceeds. — **securitized,** *adj.* — **securitization,** *n.*

security, *n.* **1.** Collateral given or pledged to guarantee the fulfillment of an obligation; esp., the assurance that a creditor will be repaid (usu. with interest) any money or credit extended to a debtor. **2.** A person who is bound by some type of guaranty; SURETY. **3.** The state of being secure, esp. from danger or attack. **4.** An instrument that evidences the holder's ownership rights in a firm (e.g., a stock), the holder's creditor relationship with a firm or government (e.g., a bond), or the holder's other rights (e.g., an option). • A security indicates an interest based on an investment in a common enterprise rather than direct participation in the enterprise. Under an important statutory definition, a security is any interest or instrument relating to finances, including a note, stock, treasury stock, bond, debenture, evidence of indebtedness, certificate of interest or participation in a profit-sharing agreement, collateral trust certificate, preorganization certificate or subscription, transferable share, investment contract, voting trust certificate, certificate of deposit for a security, fractional undivided interest in oil, gas, or other mineral rights, or certificate of interest or participation in, temporary or interim certificate for, receipt for, guarantee of, or warrant or right to subscribe to or purchase any of these things. A security also includes any put, call, straddle, option, or privilege on any security, certificate of deposit, group or index of securities, or any such device entered into on a national securities exchange, relating to foreign currency. 15 USCA § 77b(1). Cf. SHARE (2); STOCK (4).

> "Securities differ from most other commodities in which people deal. They have no intrinsic value in themselves — they represent rights in something else. The value of a bond, note or other promise to pay depends on the financial condition of the promisor. The value of a share of stock depends on the profitability or future prospects of the corporation or other entity which issued it; its market price depends on how much other people are willing to pay for it, based on their evaluation of those prospects." David L. Ratner, *Securities Regulation in a Nutshell* 1 (4th ed. 1992).

> "What do the following have in common: scotch whiskey, self-improvement courses, cosmetics, earthworms, beavers, muskrats, rabbits, chinchillas, fishing boats, vacuum cleaners, cemetery lots, cattle embryos, master recording contracts, animal feeding programs, pooled litigation funds, and fruit trees? The answer is that they have all been held to be securities within the meaning of federal or state securities statutes. The vast range of such unconventional investments that have fallen within the ambit of the securities laws' coverage is due to the broad statutory definition of a 'security' ...." 1 Thomas Lee Hazen, *Treatise on the Law of Securities Regulation* § 1.5, at 28–29 (3d ed. 1995).

adjustment security. A stock or bond that is issued during a corporate reorganization. • The security holders' relative interests are readjusted during this process.

assessable security. A security on which a charge or assessment covering the obligations of the issuing company is made. • Bank and insurance-company stock may be assessable.

asset-backed security. A debt security (such as a bond) that is secured by assets that have been pooled and secured by the assets from the pool.

bearer security. An unregistered security payable to the holder. Cf. *bearer bond* under BOND (3).

certificated security. A security that is a recognized investment vehicle, belongs to or is divisible into a class or series of shares, and is represented on an instrument payable to the bearer or a named person.

collateral security. A security, subordinate to and given in addition to a primary security, that is intended to guarantee the validity or convertibility of the primary security.

consolidated security. (*usu. pl.*) A security issued in large enough numbers to provide the funds to retire two or more outstanding issues of debt securities.

conversion security. The security into which a convertible security may be converted, usu. common stock.

convertible security. A security (usu. a bond or preferred stock) that may be exchanged by the owner for another security, esp. common stock from the same company, and usu. at a fixed price on a specified date. — Also termed (specif.) *convertible debt*; *convertible stock*.

coupon security. A security with detachable interest coupons that the holder must present for payment as they mature. • Coupon securities are usu. in denominations of $1,000, and they are negotiable.

debt security. A security representing funds borrowed by the corporation from the holder of the debt obligation; esp., a bond, note, or debenture. • Generally, a debt security is any security that is not an equity security. See BOND (3).

divisional security. A special type of security issued to finance a particular project.

equity security. A security representing an ownership interest in a corporation, such as a share of stock, rather than a debt interest, such as a bond; any stock or similar security, or any security that is convertible into stock or similar security or carrying a warrant or right to subscribe to or purchase stock or a similar security, and any such warrant or right.

exempt security. A security that need not be registered under the provisions of the Securities Act of 1933 and is exempt from the margin requirements of the Securities Exchange Act of 1934.

fixed-income security. A security that pays a fixed rate of return, such as a bond with a fixed interest rate or a preferred stock with a fixed dividend.

government security. A security issued by a government, a government agency, or a government corporation; esp., a security (such as a Treasury bill) issued by a U.S. government agency, with the implied backing of Congress. — Also termed *government-agency security*; *agency security*.

heritable security. *Scots law.* A debt instrument secured by a charge on heritable property. See *heritable bond* under BOND (2).

high-grade security. A security issued by a company of sound financial condition and having the ability to maintain good earnings (e.g., a utility company security).

hybrid security. A security with features of both a debt instrument (such as a bond) and an equity interest (such as a share of stock). • An example of a hybrid security is a convertible bond, which can be exchanged for shares in the issuing corporation and is subject to stock-price fluctuations.

investment security. An instrument issued in bearer or registered form as a type commonly recognized as a medium for investment and evidencing a share or other interest in the property or enterprise of the issuer.

junior security. A security that is subordinate to a senior security.

landed security. A mortgage or other encumbrance affecting land.

letter security. See *restricted security*.

listed security. A security accepted for trading on a securities exchange. • The issuing company must have met the SEC's registration requirements and complied with the rules of the particular exchange. — Also termed *listed stock*. See DELISTING.

long-term security. **1.** A new securities issue with an initial maturity of ten years or more. **2.** On a balance sheet, a security with a remaining maturity of one year or more.

low-grade security. A security with low investment quality. • Low-grade securities usu. offer higher yields to attract capital. See *junk bond* under BOND (3).

marginable security. A security that can be bought on margin. — Also termed *margin stock*. See MARGIN.

margined security. A security that is bought on margin and that serves as collateral in a margin account. See MARGIN.

marketable security. A security that the holder can readily sell on a stock exchange or an over-the-counter market.

mortgage-backed security. A security (esp. a pass-through security) backed by mortgages.

municipal security. See *municipal bond* under BOND (3).

noncallable security. A security that cannot be redeemed, or bought back, at the issuer's option. — Also termed (specif.) *noncallable bond*.

nonmarketable security. **1.** A security that cannot be sold on the market (such as government bonds) and can be redeemed only by the holder. **2.** A security that is not of investment quality.

outstanding security. A security that is held by an investor and has not been redeemed by the issuing corporation.

pass-through security. A security that passes through payments from debtors to investors. • Pass-through securities are usu. assembled and sold in packages to investors by private lenders who deduct a service fee before passing the principal and interest payments through to the investors.

personal security. **1.** An obligation for the repayment of a debt, evidenced by a pledge or note binding a natural person, as distinguished from property. **2.** A person's legal right to enjoy life, health, and reputation.

public security. A negotiable or transferable security that is evidence of government debt.

real security. The security of mortgages or other liens or encumbrances upon land. See COLLATERAL.

redeemable security. Any security, other than a short-term note, that, when presented to the issuer, entitles the holder to receive a share of the issuer's assets or the cash equivalent. — Also termed *callable security*.

registered security. **1.** A security whose owner is recorded in the issuer's books. • The issuer keeps a record of the current owners for purposes of sending dividends, proxies, and the like. **2.** A security that is to be offered for sale and for which a registration statement has been submitted. — Also termed (specif.) *registered stock*.

restricted security. A security that is not registered with the SEC and therefore may not be sold publicly unless specified conditions are met. • A restricted security is usu. acquired in a nonpublic transaction in which the buyer gives the seller a letter stating the buyer's intent to hold the stock as an investment rather than resell it. — Also termed *restricted stock*; *letter security*; *letter stock*; *unregistered security*.

senior security. A security of a class having priority over another class as to the distribution of assets or the payment of dividends. 15 USCA § 77r(d)(4).

shelf security. A security that is set aside for shelf registration.

short-term security. A bond or note that matures and is payable within a brief period (often one year).

speculative security. A security that, as an investment, involves a risk of loss greater than would usu. be involved; esp., a security whose value depends on proposed or promised future promotion or development, rather than on present tangible assets or conditions.

structured security. (*usu. pl.*) A security whose cash-flow characteristics depend on one or more indexes, or that has an embedded forward or option, or a security for which an investor's investment return and the issuer's payment obligations are contingent on, or highly sensitive to, changes in the value of the underlying assets, indices, interest rates, or cash flows. SEC Rule 434(h) (17 CFR § 230.434(h)).

treasury security. See *treasury stock* under STOCK.

uncertificated security. A share or other interest in property or an enterprise, or an obligation of the issuer that is not represented by an instrument but is registered on the issuer's books. UCC § 8–102(a)(18). • This term was called *uncertified security* in previous versions of the UCC.

unlisted security. An over-the-counter security that is not registered with a stock exchange. — Also termed *unlisted stock*.

unregistered security. See *restricted security*.

voting security. See *voting stock* under STOCK.

when-issued security. A security that can be traded even though it has not yet been issued. • Any transaction that takes place does not become final until the security is issued.

worthless security. A security that has lost its value, for which a loss (usu. capital) is allowed for tax purposes. IRC (26 USCA) § 165.

zero-coupon security. A security (esp. a bond) that is issued at a large discount but pays no interest.

security agreement. An agreement that creates or provides for an interest in specified real or personal property to guarantee the performance of an obligation.

Security Council. A body of the United Nations, consisting of five permanent members (China, France, Russia, the United Kingdom, and the United States) and ten additional members elected at stated intervals, charged with the responsibility of maintaining international peace and security, and esp. of preventing or halting wars by diplomatic, economic, or military action.

security deposit. See DEPOSIT (3).

security for costs. Money, property, or a bond given to a court by a plaintiff or an appellant to secure the payment of court costs if that party loses.

security grade. See SECURITY RATING.

security grading. See SECURITY RATING.

security interest. A property interest created by agreement or by operation of law to secure performance of an obligation (esp. repayment of a debt). • Although the UCC limits the creation of a security interest to personal property, the Bankruptcy Code defines the term to mean "a lien created by an agreement." 11 USCA § 101(51).

perfected security interest. A security interest that has completed the statutory requirements for achieving priority over other security interests that are subject to the same requirements.

purchase-money security interest. A security interest that is created when a buyer uses the lender's money to make the purchase and immediately gives the lender security (UCC § 9–107); a security interest that is either (1) taken or retained by the seller of the collateral to secure all or part of its price or (2) taken by a person who by making advances or incurring an obligation gives value to enable the debtor to acquire rights in or the use of collateral if that value is in fact so used. • If a buyer's purchase of a boat, for example, is financed by a bank that loans the amount of the purchase price, the bank's security interest in the boat that secures the loan is a purchase-money security interest. — Abbr. PMSI. — Also termed *purchase-money interest*.

unperfected security interest. A security interest held by a creditor who has not established priority over any other creditor. • The only priority is over the debtor.

security rating. 1. The system for grading or classifying a security by financial strength, stability, or risk. • Firms such as *Standard and Poor's* and *Moody's* grade securities. — Also termed *security grade*; *security grading*; *security rate*. **2.** The classification that a given security is assigned to under this system.

secus (**see**-kəs). [Latin] Otherwise; to the contrary.

sedato animo (si-**day**-toh **an**-ə-moh). [Latin] With stated or settled purpose.

se defendendo (**see** def-en-**den**-doh), *adv.* [Law Latin] In self-defense; in defending oneself <homicide *se defendendo*>.

> "Homicide *se defendendo* is of two kinds. (1) Such, as tho it excuseth from death, yet it excuseth not the forfeiture of goods, ... (2) Such as wholly acquits from all kinds of forfeiture." 1 Hale P.C. 478.

sedentary work. See WORK.

sedente curia (si-**den**-tee **kyoor**-ee-ə). [Latin] The court sitting; during the court sitting.

sede plena (**see**-dee **plee**-nə). [Latin] *Hist.* The see being filled. • This term indicated that a bishop's see was not vacant.

sedes (**see**-deez), *n.* [Latin "a seat"] **1.** *Roman law.* A private residence. **2.** *Roman law.* Judicial office; the bench. **3.** *Hist.* A see; a bishop's dignity.

sedge flat. A tract of land below the high-water mark.

sedition, *n.* An agreement, communication, or other preliminary activity aimed at inciting treason or some lesser commotion against public authority; advocacy aimed at inciting or producing — and likely to incite or produce — imminent lawless action. • At common law, sedition included defaming a member of the royal family or the government. The difference between *sedition* and *treason* is that the former is committed by preliminary steps, while the latter entails some overt act for carrying out the plan. But of course, if the plan is merely for some small commotion, even accomplishing the plan does not amount to treason. — **seditious,** *adj.* Cf. TREASON.

> "*Sedition* — This, perhaps the very vaguest of all offences known to the Criminal Law, is defined as the speaking or writing of words calculated to excite disaffection against the Constitution as by law established, to procure the alteration of it by other than lawful means, or to incite any person to commit a crime to the disturbance of the peace, or to raise discontent or disaffection, or to promote ill-feeling between different classes of the community. A charge of sedition is, historically, one of the chief means by which Government, especially at the end of the eighteenth and the beginning of the nineteenth century, strove to put down hostile critics. It is evident that the vagueness of the charge is a danger to the liberty of the subject, especially if the Courts of Justice can be induced to take a view favourable to the Government." Edward Jenks, *The Book of English Law* 136 (P.B. Fairest ed., 6th ed. 1967).

seditious conspiracy. See CONSPIRACY.

seditious libel. See LIBEL.

seditious speech. See SPEECH.

sed non allocatur (sed non al-ə-**kay**-tər). [Law Latin] *Hist.* But it is not allowed or upheld. • This phrase was formerly used to indicate the court's disagreement with the arguments of counsel.

sed per curiam (sed pər **kyoor**-ee-əm). [Latin] But by the court. • This phrase is used to introduce: (1) a statement made by the court disagreeing with counsel's arguments; or (2) the opinion of the whole court when different from the opinion of the single judge immediately before quoted.

sed quaere (sed **kweer**-ee). [Latin] But inquire; examine this further. • This remark indicates that the correctness of a particular statement is challenged.

seduction. The offense that occurs when a man entices a woman of previously chaste character to have unlawful intercourse with him by means of persuasion, solicitation, promises, or bribes, or other means not involving force. • Many states have abolished this offense for persons over the age of legal consent. Traditionally, the parent has an action to recover damages for the loss of the child's services. But in measuring damages, the jury may consider not just the loss of services but also the distress and anxiety that the parent has suffered in being deprived of the child's comfort and companionship. Though seduction was not a crime at common law, many American states made it a statutory crime until the late 20th century.

sed vide (sed **vɪ**-dee). [Latin] But see. • This remark, followed by a citation, directs the reader's attention to an authority or a statement that conflicts with or contradicts the statement or principle just given. — Also termed *but see.*

see, *n.* The area or district of a bishop's jurisdiction <the see of Canterbury>.

seed money. Start-up money for a business venture. — Also termed *front money*; *front-end money.*

segregation, *n.* **1.** The act or process of separating. **2.** The unconstitutional policy of separating people on the basis of color, nationality, religion, or the like. — **segregate,** *vb.* — **segregative,** *adj.*

de facto segregation. Segregation that occurs without state authority, usu. on the basis of socioeconomic factors.

de jure segregation. Segregation that is permitted by law.

punitive segregation. The act of removing a prisoner from the prison population for placement in separate or solitary confinement, usu. for disciplinary reasons.

seignior (**seen**-yər), *n.* [Law French] *Hist.* An owner of something; a lord of a fee or manor. — Also spelled *seigneur* (seen- *or* sayn-**yər**); *seignor.* See SEIGNIORY.

seignior in gross (**seen**-yər in **grohs**), *n.* A lord having no manor but enjoying the other rights of lordship.

seigniorage (**seen**-yər-ij), *n.* [Law French] **1.** *Hist.* The tenure existing between lord and vassal. **2.** *Hist.* A prerogative of the Crown; specif., the charge for coining bullion into money; mintage. **3.** A royalty. **4.** A profit.

seignioress (**seen**-yər-es *or* -is), *n.* [Law French] *Hist.* A female superior; a lady.

seigniory (**seen**-yər-ee), *n.* [Law French] *Hist.* **1.** The rights and powers of a lord; esp., a grantor's retained right to have the grantee perform services in exchange for the transfer of land. **2.** A lord's dominions; a feudal or manor lordship; esp., land held subject to such a retained right in the grantor. — Also spelled *seignory.*

seigniory in gross (**seen**-yər-ee in **grohs**). See *reputed manor* under MANOR.

seignory. See SEIGNIORY.

seise (seez), *vb.* To invest with seisin or establish as a holder in fee simple; to put in possession <he became seised of half a section of farmland near Tulia>.

seisin (**see**-zin), *n.* Possession of a freehold estate in land; ownership. — Also spelled *seizin.* — Also termed *vesture*; *seisina*; (in Scots law) *sasine.*

> "Originally, seisin meant simply possession and the word was applicable to both land and chattels. Prior to the fourteenth century it was proper to speak of a man as being seised of land or seised of a horse. Gradually, seisin and possession became distinct concepts. A man could be said to be in possession of chattels, or of lands wherein he had an estate for years, but he could not be said to be seised of them. Seisin came finally to mean, in relation to land, possession under claim of a freehold estate therein. The tenant for years had possession but not seisin; seisin was in the reversioner who had the fee. And although the word 'seisin' appears in modern statutes with a fair degree of frequency, it is usually treated as synonymous

with ownership." Cornelius J. Moynihan, *Introduction to the Law of Real Property* 98–99 (2d ed. 1988).

actual seisin. See *seisin in deed.*

constructive seisin. See *seisin in law.*

covenant of seisin. See COVENANT (4).

customary seisin. See *quasi seisin.*

equitable seisin. See *seisin in law.*

legal seisin. See *seisin in law.*

livery of seisin. See LIVERY OF SEISIN.

primer seisin (**prim**-ər *or* **prɪ**-mər **see**-zin). *Hist.* A right of the Crown to receive, from the heir of a tenant who died in possession of a knight's fee, one year's profits of the inherited estate (or half a year's profits if the estate was in reversion); FIRST FRUITS (1).

quasi-seisin. A copyholder's possession of lands, the freehold possession being in the lord. — Also termed *customary seisin.*

seisin in deed. Actual possession of a freehold estate in land, by oneself or by one's tenant or agent, as distinguished from legal possession. — Also termed *seisin in fact*; *actual seisin.*

seisin in fact. See *actual seisin.*

seisin in law. The right to immediate possession of a freehold estate in land, as when an heir inherits land but has not yet entered it. — Also termed *legal seisin*; *constructive seisin*; *equitable seisin.*

seisina (**see**-zin-ə), *n.* [Law Latin] *Hist.* Seisin.

seisina habenda (**see**-zin-ə hə-**ben**-də). See DE SEISINA HABENDA.

seisin in fact. See *actual seisin* under SEISIN.

seize, *vb.* **1.** To forcibly take possession (of a person or property). **2.** To place (someone) in possession. **3.** To be in possession (of property). See SEISIN; SEIZURE.

seizure, *n.* The act or an instance of taking possession of a person or property by legal right or process; esp., in constitutional law, a confiscation or arrest that may interfere with a person's reasonable expectation of privacy.

select committee. See *special committee* under COMMITTEE.

select council. See COUNCIL.

selecti judices (si-**lek**-tɪ **joo**-di-seez). [Latin] *Roman law.* Jurors on the official panel prepared by the praetor, who for a specific trial were drawn by lot subject to challenge and sworn to office in a similar manner to modern juries.

selective disclosure. The act of divulging part of a privileged communication, or one of several privileged communications, usu. because the divulged portion is helpful to the party giving the information, while harmful portions of the communication are withheld. • Such a disclosure can result in a limited waiver of the privilege for all communications on the same subject matter as the divulged portion.

selective enforcement. The practice of law-enforcement officers who use wide or even unfettered discretion about when and where to carry out certain laws; esp., the practice of singling a person out for prosecution or punishment under a statute or regulation because the person is a member of a protected group or because the person has exercised or is planning to exercise a constitutionally protected right. — Also termed *selective prosecution.* Cf. VINDICTIVE PROSECUTION.

"The chief of police of a New England town once declared to the press that he believed in a strict curfew law, 'selectively enforced.' 'Selective enforcement' in this case means that the policeman decides for himself who ought to be sent home from the street; legislative candour would suggest that if this is the intention it ought to be expressed in the law itself, instead of being concealed behind words that are 'strict' and categorical." Lon L. Fuller, *Anatomy of the Law* 42 (1968).

selective incorporation. See INCORPORATION.

selective prosecution. See SELECTIVE ENFORCEMENT.

selective prospectivity. A court's decision to apply a new rule of law in the particular case in which the new rule is announced, but to apply the old rule in all other cases pending at the time the new rule is announced or in which the facts predate the new rule's announcement.

Selective Service System. An executive agency charged with maintaining records of all persons eligible for military service. — Abbr. SSS.

selectman. A municipal officer elected annually in some New England towns to transact business and perform some executive functions.

self-applying, *adj.* (Of a statute, ordinance, etc.) requiring no more for interpretation than a familiarity with the ordinary meanings of words.

self-authentication. See AUTHENTICATION.

self-crimination. See SELF-INCRIMINATION.

self-critical-analysis privilege. See PRIVILEGE (3).

self-dealing, *n.* Participation in a transaction that benefits oneself instead of another who is owed a fiduciary duty. • For example, a corporate director might engage in self-dealing by participating in a competing business to the corporation's detriment. — **self-deal,** *vb.* Cf. FAIR DEALING.

self-defense, *n.* **1.** The use of force to protect oneself, one's family, or one's property from a real or threatened attack. • Generally, a person is justified in using a reasonable amount of force in self-defense if he or she believes that the danger of bodily harm is imminent and that force is necessary to avoid this danger. — Also termed *defense of self.* Cf. ADEQUATE PROVOCATION.

"The law of self-defence, as it is applied by the courts, turns on two requirements: the force must have been necessary, and it must have been reasonable." Andrew Ashworth, *Principles of Criminal Law* 114 (1991).

imperfect self-defense. The use of force by one who makes an honest but unreasonable mistake that force is necessary to repel an attack. • In some jurisdictions, such a self-defender will be charged with a lesser offense than the one committed.

perfect self-defense. The use of force by one who accurately appraises the necessity and the amount of force to repel an attack.

2. *Int'l law.* The right of a state to defend itself against a real or threatened attack. — Also spelled (esp. in BrE) *self-defence.* — **self-defender,** *n.*

"Self-defence, properly understood, is a legal right, and as with other legal rights the question whether a specific state of facts warrants its exercise is a legal question. It is not a question on which a state is entitled, in any special sense, to be a judge in its own cause." J.L. Brierly, *The Law of Nations* 319 (5th ed. 1955).

self-destruction. See SUICIDE.

self-determination contract. See CONTRACT.

self-determination election. See GLOBE ELECTION.

self-employed retirement plan. See KEOGH PLAN.

self-employment tax. See TAX.

self-executing, *adj.* (Of an instrument) effective immediately without the need of any type of implementing action <the wills had self-executing affidavits attached>. • Legal instruments may be self-executing according to various standards. For example, treaties are self-executing under the Supremacy Clause of the U.S. Constitution (Article VI, § 2) if textually capable of judicial enforcement and intended to be enforced in that manner.

self-help, *n.* An attempt to redress a perceived wrong by one's own action rather than through the normal legal process. • The UCC and other statutes provide for particular self-help remedies (such as repossession) if the remedy can be executed without breaching the peace. UCC § 9–503. — Also termed *self-redress*; *extrajudicial enforcement.*

"Notice to the debtor is generally not required prior to self-help repossession of collateral by the creditor upon default, although the provision for self-help repossession has been held to violate due process requirements in some instances, and states under the Uniform Consumer Credit Code require particular notice requirements. Furthermore, while the UCC generally does not require notice to the debtor upon self-help repossession of the collateral upon the debtor's default, the agreement between the parties may require such notice prior to repossession." 68A Am. Jur. 2d *Secured Transactions* § 608, at 466 (1993).

self-help remedy. See *extrajudicial remedy* under REMEDY.

self-incrimination. The act of indicating one's own involvement in a crime or exposing oneself to prosecution, esp. by making a statement. — Also termed *self-crimination*; *self-inculpation.* See RIGHT AGAINST SELF-INCRIMINATION.

Self-Incrimination Clause. The clause of the Fifth Amendment to the U.S. Constitution barring the government from compelling criminal defendants to testify against themselves.

self-induced frustration. See FRUSTRATION.

self-induced intoxication. See *voluntary intoxication* under INTOXICATION.

self-insurance. See INSURANCE.

self-insured retention. *Insurance.* The amount of an otherwise-covered loss that is not covered by an insurance policy and that usu. must be paid before the insurer will pay benefits <the defendant had a $1 million CGL policy to cover the loss, but had to pay a self-insured retention of $100,000, which it had agreed to so that the policy premium would be lower>. — Abbr. SIR. Cf. DEDUCTIBLE.

self-killing. See SUICIDE.

self-liquidating mortgage. See *amortized mortgage* under MORTGAGE.

self-murder. See SUICIDE.

self-policing privilege. See *self-critical-analysis privilege* under PRIVILEGE (3).

self-proved will. See WILL.

self-proving affidavit. See AFFIDAVIT.

self-redress. See SELF-HELP.

self-serving declaration. See DECLARATION (6).

self-settled trust. See TRUST.

self-slaughter. See SUICIDE.

self-stultification. The act or an instance of testifying about one's own deficiencies. See STULTIFY.

sell, *vb.* To transfer (property) by sale.

seller. 1. A person who sells or contracts to sell goods; a vendor. UCC § 2–103(1)(d). **2.** Generally, a person who sells anything; the transferor of property in a contract of sale.

seller's market. See MARKET.

seller's option. See OPTION.

selling agent. The real-estate broker's representative who sells the property, as opposed to the agent who lists the property for sale. Cf. LISTING AGENT.

selling price. See *sales price* under PRICE.

sell-off, *n.* A period when heavy pressure to sell causes falling stock-market prices.

sell order. See ORDER (4).

semble (**sem**-bəl). [Law French] It seems; it would appear <semble that the parties' intention was to create a binding agreement>. • This term is used chiefly to indicate an obiter dictum in a court opinion or to introduce an uncertain thought or interpretation. — Abbr. sem.; semb.

semestria (si-**mes**-tree-ə), *n.* [Latin "half-yearly matters"] *Roman law.* The collected decisions of Roman emperors, issued every six months. — Also spelled *semenstria.*

semi-matrimonium (**sem**-I ma-trə-**moh**-nee-əm), *n.* [Latin] A half-marriage.

seminary. 1. An educational institution, such as a college, academy, or other school. **2.** The building in which the institution performs its functions.

seminaufragium (sem-I-naw-**fray**-jee-əm), *n.* [Latin] *Hist.* A half-shipwreck, as when goods are cast overboard in a storm or when a damaged ship's repair costs are more than the ship's worth.

semi-plena probatio (sem-I-**plee**-nə proh-**bay**-shee-oh), *n.* [Latin] Half-proof.

semi-skilled work. See WORK.

semper (**sem**-pər). [Latin] Always. • This term introduces several Latin maxims, such as *semper in dubiis benigniora praeferenda sunt* ("in doubtful cases, the more favorable constructions are always to be preferred").

senage (**see**-nij). [French] Money paid for synodals; tribute-money. See SYNODAL.

senate. 1. The upper chamber of a bicameral legislature. **2.** (*cap.*) The upper house of the U.S. Congress, composed of 100 members — two from each state — who are elected to six-year terms. — Abbr. S.

senate bill. See BILL (3).

senator. A person who is a member of a senate.

senatores (sen-ə-**tor**-eez), *n. pl.* [Latin] *Roman law.* **1.** Members of the Roman senate. **2.** Members of the municipal councils.

senatorial courtesy. 1. The tradition that the President should take care in filling a high-level federal post (such as a judgeship) with a person agreeable to the senators from the nominee's home state, lest the senators defeat confirmation.

> "The risk of a deadlock is minimized by [the President's] consulting informally with the Senators from the State in which the office lies, if they are members of his own political party. Actually this amounts in most instances to his taking the advice of these two Senators as to a selection. A nomination approved by them is practically certain of final confirmation by the Senate as a whole. The arrangement is a 'log-rolling' one, which has been dignified by the name of 'Senatorial courtesy.' 'If you will help me to get the appointments I want in my State, I will help you get the appointments you want in your State.' " Herbert W. Horwill, *The Usages of the American Constitution* 129 (1925).

2. Loosely, civility among senators <a decline of senatorial courtesy>.

senatus (si-**nay**-təs), *n.* [Latin] *Roman law.* **1.** The senate; the great national council of Roman statesmen and dignitaries. **2.** The meeting place for the Roman senate.

senatus consulta (si-**nay**-təs kən-**səl**-tə). [Latin] *Roman law.* Advice from the Roman Senate, which had no legal weight (though it was usu. followed) until the end of the second century A.D., when it became the official expression of the imperial will.

> "*Senatus consulta.* — In the regal and republican periods the Senate enjoyed no legislative power. It was an advisory body, nominated by the King, and at first purely patrician. Later it . . . included patricians and plebeians . . . its chief duty still being to tender advice to the magistrates . . . . The theory still was, till the time of Hadrian, that *senatus consulta* were directions to the magistrates, who were now in fact, if not in name, bound to give effect to them, till by a process of gradual usurpation *senatus consulta* came to be direct legislation." R.W. Leage, *Roman Private Law* 12–13 (C.H. Ziegler ed., 2d ed. 1930).

Senatus consulto (si-**nay**-təs kən-**səl**-toh). [Latin] *Roman law.* By the decree of the Senate.

senatus consultum (si-**nay**-təs kən-**səl**-təm). [Latin] *Roman law.* A decree of the Roman Senate. — Also termed *senatus consult.*

senatus consultum Macedonianum (si-**nay**-təs kən-**səl**-təm mas-ə-doh-nee-**ay**-nəm), *n.* [Latin "Macedo's Decree"] *Roman law.* A senate decree, first given under Claudius and renewed by Vespasian, to protect children from making unconscionable loans with creditors in expectation of their father's death, by making actions to recover such loans unlawful. — Also termed *Macedonian Decree.*

> "In the principate of Vespasian, 69–79 A.D., a *senatus consultum* was passed which forbade loans to a *filius-familias*. It was called the *senatus consultum — Macedonianum*, after one Macedo, a usurer who had made such a loan and thereby instigated a hard-pressed debtor to kill his father in order to enter into his inheritance. To prevent tragic possibilities like these, the *senatus consultum* declared that no action would lie to recover money lent to a *filius-familias*." Max Radin, *Handbook of Roman Law* 188–89 (1927).

> "The *senatus consultum Macedonianum* reads as follows: 'Whereas Macedo's borrowings gave him an added incentive to commit a crime to which he was naturally predisposed and whereas those who lend money on terms which are dubious, to say the least, often provide evil men with the means of wrongdoing, it has been decided, in order to teach pernicious moneylenders that a son's debt cannot be made good by waiting for his father's death, that a person who has lent money to a son-in-power is to have no claim or action even after the death of the person in whose power he was.' " *Digest of Justinian* 14.6.1 (Ulpian, Ad Sabinum 49).

senatus consultum ultimae necessitatis (si-**nay**-təs kən-**səl**-təm **əl**-tə-mee nə-ses-i-**tay**-tis). [Latin] *Roman law.* A decree of the senate of the last necessity. • This decree usu. preceded the nomination of a leader with absolute power in a time of emergency. — Also termed *senatus consultum ultimum.*

senatus consultum Velleianum (si-**nay**-təs kən-**səl**-təm vel-ee-**ay**-nəm). [Latin "Velleian Decree"] *Roman law.* A senate decree, probably of A.D. 46, to protect women from making unconscionable guarantees, suretyship undertakings, or debt assumptions for their husbands and for others generally, by making actions to enforce such undertakings unlawful.

senatus decreta (si-**nay**-təs di-**kree**-tə), *n.* [Latin] *Roman law.* The senate's decisions.

sending state. The country from which a diplomatic agent or consul is sent abroad. Cf. RECEIVING STATE.

senescallus (sen-əs-**kal**-əs), *n.* [Law Latin] See SENESCHAL.

seneschal (**sen**-ə-shəl), *n.* [Law French] *Hist.* **1.** A French title of office, equivalent to a steward in England. • A seneschal was originally a duke's lieutenant or a lieutenant to other dignities of the kingdom. **2.** The steward of a manor. — Also termed *senescallus.*

senility. Mental feebleness or impairment caused by old age. • A senile person (in the legal, as opposed to the popular, sense) is incompetent to enter into a binding contract or to execute a will. — Also termed *senile dementia* (**see**-nɪl di-**men**-shee-ə).

senior, *adj.* **1.** (Of a debt, etc.) first; preferred, as over junior obligations. **2.** (Of a person) older than someone else. **3.** (Of a person) higher in rank or service. **4.** (Of a man) elder, as distinguished from the man's son who has the same name.

senior counsel. 1. See *lead counsel* under COUNSEL. **2.** See KING'S COUNSEL; QUEEN'S COUNSEL.

senior interest. See INTEREST (2).

seniority. 1. The preferential status, privileges, or rights given an employee based on the employee's length of service with an employer. • Employees with seniority may receive additional or enhanced benefit packages and obtain competitive advantages over fellow employees in layoff and promotional decisions. **2.** The status of being older or senior.

seniority system. *Employment law.* Any arrangement that recognizes length of service in making decisions about job layoffs and promotions or other advancements.

senior judge. See JUDGE.

senior lien. See LIEN.

senior mortgage. See MORTGAGE.

senior partner. See PARTNER.

senior security. See SECURITY.

senior status. The employment condition of a judge who, having taken semiretirement, continues to perform certain judicial duties that the judge is willing and able to undertake.

sensitivity training. Instructional sessions for management and employees designed to counteract the callous treatment of others, esp. women and minorities, in the workplace.

sensus (**sen**-səs). [Latin] *Hist.* Sense; meaning; signification. • The word appears in its inflected form in phrases such as *malo sensu* ("an evil sense"), *mitiori sensu* ("in a milder sense"), and *sensu honesto* ("in an honest sense").

sentence, *n.* The judgment that a court formally pronounces after finding a criminal defendant guilty; the punishment imposed on a criminal wrongdoer <a sentence of 20 years in prison>. — **sentence,** *vb.*

accumulative sentences. See *consecutive sentences.*

aggregate sentence. A sentence that arises from a conviction on multiple counts in an indictment.

concurrent sentences. Two or more sentences of jail time to be served simultaneously. • For example, if a defendant receives concurrent sentences of 5 years and 15 years, the total amount of jail time is 15 years.

conditional sentence. A sentence of confinement if the defendant fails to perform the conditions of probation.

consecutive sentences. Two or more sentences of jail time to be served in sequence. • For example, if a defendant receives consecutive sentences of 20 years and 5 years, the total amount of jail time is 25 years. — Also termed *cumulative sentences*; *accumulative sentences.*

death sentence. A sentence that imposes the death penalty. — Also termed *judgment of blood.* See DEATH PENALTY.

deferred sentence. A sentence that will not be carried out if the defendant meets certain requirements, such as complying with conditions of probation.

determinate sentence. A sentence for a fixed length of time rather than for an unspecified duration. — Also termed *definite sentence*; *definitive sentence*; *fixed sentence*; *flat sentence*; *straight sentence.*

fixed sentence. **1.** See *determinate sentence.* **2.** See *mandatory sentence.*

flat sentence. See *determinate sentence.*

general sentence. An undivided, aggregate sentence in a multicount case; a sentence that does not specify the punishment imposed for each count. • General sentences are prohibited.

indeterminate sentence. **1.** A sentence of an unspecified duration, such as one for a term of 10 to 20 years. **2.** A maximum prison term that the parole board can reduce, through statutory authorization, after the inmate has served the minimum time required by law. — Also termed *indefinite sentence.* See INDETERMINATE SENTENCING.

intermittent sentence. A sentence consisting of periods of confinement interrupted by periods of freedom. — Also termed (when served on weekends) *weekend sentence*.

life sentence. A sentence that imprisons the convicted criminal for life — though in some jurisdictions the prisoner may become eligible for release on good behavior, rehabilitation, or the like.

mandatory sentence. A sentence set by law with no discretion for the judge to individualize punishment. — Also termed *mandatory penalty*; *mandatory punishment*; *fixed sentence*.

maximum sentence. The highest level of punishment provided by law for a particular crime.

minimum sentence. The least amount of time that a defendant must serve in prison before becoming eligible for parole.

multiple sentences. Concurrent or consecutive sentences, if a defendant is found guilty of more than one offense.

nominal sentence. A criminal sentence in name only; an exceedingly light sentence.

noncustodial sentence. A criminal sentence (such as probation) not requiring prison time.

presumptive sentence. An average sentence for a particular crime (esp. provided under sentencing guidelines) that can be raised or lowered based on the presence of mitigating or aggravating circumstances.

split sentence. A sentence in which part of the time is served in confinement — to expose the offender to the unpleasantness of prison — and the rest on probation.

straight sentence. See *determinate sentence*.

suspended sentence. A sentence postponed so that the defendant is not required to serve time unless he or she commits another crime or violates some other court-imposed condition. • A suspended sentence, in effect, is a form of probation. — Also termed *withheld sentence*.

weekend sentence. See *intermittent sentence*.

sentence cap. *Military law.* A pretrial plea agreement in a court-martial proceeding, by which a ceiling is placed on the maximum penalty that can be imposed.

sentence-factor manipulation. See *sentencing entrapment* under ENTRAPMENT.

sentence-package rule. *Criminal procedure.* The principle that a defendant can be resentenced on an aggregate sentence — that is, one arising from a conviction on multiple counts in an indictment — when the defendant successfully challenges part of the conviction, as by successfully challenging some but not all of the counts.

sentencing council. A panel of three or more judges who confer to determine a criminal sentence. • Sentencing by a council occurs less frequently than sentencing by a single trial judge.

sentencing entrapment. See ENTRAPMENT.

sentencing guidelines. A set of standards for determining the punishment that a convicted criminal should receive, based on the nature of the crime and the offender's criminal history. • The federal government and several states have adopted sentencing guidelines in an effort to make judicial sentencing more consistent.

sentencing hearing. See PRESENTENCE HEARING.

sententia (sen-**ten**-shee-ə), *n.* [Latin] *Roman law.* **1.** Sense; meaning. **2.** An opinion, esp. a legal opinion. **3.** A judicial decision.

SEP (sep). See *simplified employee pension plan* under EMPLOYEE BENEFIT PLAN.

separability clause. See SEVERABILITY CLAUSE.

separable, *adj.* Capable of being separated or divided <a separable controversy>.

separable controversy. A claim that is separate and independent from the other claims being asserted in a suit. • This term is most often associated with the statute that permits an entire case to be removed to federal court if one of the claims, being separate and independent from the others, presents a federal question that is within the jurisdiction of the federal courts. 28 USCA § 1441(c).

separaliter (sep-ə-**ray**-lə-tər). [Latin] *Hist.* Separately. • This term was formerly used in an indictment to emphasize that multiple defendants were being charged with separate offenses, when it appeared from the general language of the indictment that the defendants were jointly charged.

separate, *adj.* (Of liability, cause of action, etc.) individual; distinct; particular; disconnected.

separate action. See ACTION.

separate and apart. (Of a husband and wife) living away from each other, along with at least one spouse's intent to dissolve the marriage.

separate-but-equal doctrine. The now-defunct doctrine that African–Americans could be segregated if they were provided with equal opportunities and facilities in education, public transportation, and jobs. • This rule was established in *Plessy v. Ferguson*, 163 U.S. 537, 16 S.Ct. 1138 (1896), and overturned in *Brown v. Board of Education*, 347 U.S. 483, 74 S.Ct. 686 (1954).

separate caucus. See CAUCUS.

separate count. See COUNT.

separate covenant. See *several covenant* under COVENANT (1).

separate demise. See DEMISE.

separate estate. See ESTATE.

separate examination. **1.** The private interrogation of a witness, apart from the other witnesses in the same case. **2.** The interrogation of a wife outside the presence of her husband by a court clerk or notary for the purpose of acknowledging a deed or other instrument. • This was done to ensure that the wife signed without being coerced to do so by her husband.

separate maintenance. See MAINTENANCE.

separate offense. See OFFENSE (1).

separate property. **1.** In a community-property state, property that a spouse owned before marriage or acquired during marriage by inheritance or by gift from a third party, or property acquired during marriage but after the spouses have entered into a separation agreement and have begun living apart. — Also termed *individual property*. Cf. COMMUNITY PROPERTY; *marital property* under PROPERTY. **2.** In some common-law states, property titled to one spouse or acquired by one spouse individually during marriage.

separate return. See TAX RETURN.

separate-sovereigns rule. *Criminal procedure.* The principle that a person may be tried twice for the same offense — despite the Double Jeopardy Clause — if the prosecutions are conducted by separate sovereigns, as by the federal government and a state government or by two different states. See DOUBLE JEOPARDY.

separate support. See *separate maintenance* under MAINTENANCE.

separate trading of registered interest and principal of securities. A treasury security by which the owner receives either principal or interest, but usu. not both. — Abbr. STRIP.

separate trial. See TRIAL.

separatim (sep-ə-**ray**-tim). [Latin] *Hist.* Severally. • This term referred to the formation of several covenants in a deed.

separation. **1.** An arrangement whereby a husband and wife live apart from each other while remaining married, either by mutual consent or by judicial decree; the act of carrying out such an arrangement. — Also termed *legal separation*; *judicial separation*. **2.** The status of a husband and wife having begun such an arrangement, or the judgment or contract that brought the arrangement about. **3.** Cessation of a contractual relationship, esp. in an employment situation. — **separate,** *vb.*

separation agreement. An agreement between spouses in the process of a divorce or legal separation concerning alimony, property division, child custody and support, and the like. — Also termed *separation order* (if approved or sanctioned judicially).

separation a mensa et thoro. See *divorce a mensa et thoro* under DIVORCE.

separation from bed and board. See *divorce a mensa et thoro* under DIVORCE.

separation of patrimony. *Civil law.* The act of providing creditors of a succession the right to collect against the class of estate property from which the creditors should be paid, by separating certain succession property from property rights belonging to the heirs.

separation of powers. The division of governmental authority into three branches of government — legislative, executive, and judicial — each with specified duties on which neither of the other branches can encroach; the constitutional doctrine of checks and balances by which the people are protected against tyranny. Cf. DIVISION OF POWERS.

> "[T]he doctrine of the separation of powers was adopted by the convention of 1787 not to promote efficiency but to preclude the exercise of arbitrary power. The purpose was not to avoid friction, but, by means of the inevitable friction incident to the distribution of the governmental powers among three departments, to save the people from autocracy." Justice Louis Brandeis (as quoted in Roscoe Pound, *The Development of Constitutional Guarantees of Liberty* 94 (1957)).

> "Although in political theory much has been made of the vital importance of the separation of powers, it is extraordinarily difficult to define precisely each particular power. In an ideal state we might imagine a legislature which had supreme and exclusive power to lay down general rules for the future without reference to particular cases; courts whose sole function was to make binding orders to settle disputes between individuals which were brought before them by applying these rules to the facts which were found to exist; an administrative body which carried on the business of government by issuing particular orders or making decisions of policy within the narrow confines of rules of law that it could not change. The legislature makes, the executive executes, and the judiciary construes the law." George Whitecross Paton, *A Textbook of Jurisprudence* 330 (G.W. Paton & David P. Derham eds., 4th ed. 1972).

separation of witnesses. The exclusion of witnesses (other than the plaintiff and defendant) from the courtroom to prevent them from hearing the testimony of others.

separation order. See SEPARATION AGREEMENT.

separation pay. See SEVERANCE PAY.

sequatur sub suo periculo (si-**kway**-tər səb **s[y]oo**-oh pə-**rik**-[y]ə-loh), *n.* [Law Latin "let him follow at his peril"] *Hist.* A writ available when a sheriff returned nihil to several summonses; specif., a writ issued after the sheriff returned nihil to a warrant *ad warrantizandum* and following an *alias* and a *pluries* writ. See SICUT ALIAS.

sequela (si-**kwee**-lə), *n.* [Latin "that which follows"] *Hist.* Suit; process, as in *sequela curiae* ("a suit of court") and *sequela causae* ("the process of a cause"). Pl. ***sequelae*** (si-**kwee**-lee).

sequela villanorum (si-**kwee**-lə vil-ə-**nor**-əm). [Law Latin] *Hist.* The family and appurtenances to a villein's goods, which were at the lord's disposal.

sequential journal. See JOURNAL OF NOTARIAL ACTS.

sequester (si-**kwes**-tər), *n.* **1.** An across-the-board cut in government spending. **2.** A person with whom litigants deposit property being contested until the case has concluded; a sequestrator.

sequester, *vb.* **1.** To seize (property) by a writ of sequestration. **2.** To segregate or isolate (a jury or witness) during trial. — Also termed *sequestrate.*

sequestered account. See ACCOUNT.

sequesterer. See SEQUESTRATOR.

sequestrari facias (see-kwes-**trair**-I **fay**-shee-əs), *n.* [Law Latin "you are to cause to be sequestered"] *Hist. Eccles. law.* A process to enforce a judgment against a clergyman in a benefice, by which the bishop was ordered to sequester a church's rents, tithes, or other profits until the debt was paid.

sequestrate, *vb.* See SEQUESTER.

sequestratio (see-kwes-**tray**-shee-oh), *n.* [Latin] *Roman law.* The depositing of an object in dispute with a holder either voluntarily or by court order.

sequestration (see-kwes-**tray**-shən), *n.* **1.** The process by which property is removed from the possessor pending the outcome of a dispute in which two or more parties contend for it. Cf. ATTACHMENT (1); GARNISHMENT.

conventional sequestration. The parties' voluntary deposit of the property at issue in a lawsuit.

judicial sequestration. The court-ordered deposit of the property at issue in a lawsuit.

2. The setting apart of a decedent's personal property when no one has been willing to act as a personal representative for the estate. **3.** A judicial writ commanding the sheriff or other officer to seize the goods of a person named in the writ. • This writ is sometimes issued against a civil defendant who has defaulted or has acted in contempt of court. **4.** The court-ordered seizure of a bankrupt's estate for the benefit of creditors. **5.** *Int'l law.* The seizure by a belligerent power of enemy assets. **6.** The freezing of a government agency's funds; SEQUESTER (1). **7.** Custodial isolation of a trial jury to prevent tampering and exposure to publicity, or of witnesses to prevent them from hearing the testimony of others. — Also termed (in sense 7) *jury sequestration.*

sequestrator (**see**-kwes-tray-tər). **1.** An officer appointed to execute a writ of sequestration. **2.** A person who holds property in sequestration. — Also termed *sequesterer*.

sequestro habendo (si-**kwes**-troh hə-**ben**-doh), *n.* [Law Latin] *Hist. Eccles. law.* A writ from the sovereign to the bishop ordering the discharge of the sequestration of a benefice's profits.

serendipity doctrine. *Criminal procedure.* The principle that all evidence discovered during a lawful search is eligible to be admitted into evidence at trial.

serf. *Hist.* A person in a condition of feudal servitude, bound to labor at the will of a lord; a villein. • Serfs differed from slaves in that they were bound to the native soil rather than being the absolute property of a master.

> "As the categories became indistinct, the more abject varieties of slavery disappeared and in the twelfth century the word 'villein' became the general term for unfree peasants. 'Serf' did not become a legal term of art, and in so far as it remained in use it did not connote a status lower than that of villein. The merger was to the detriment of the *villani*, but it ensured that full slavery was not received as part of the common law." J.H. Baker, *An Introduction to English Legal History* 532 (3d ed. 1990).

sergeant. **1.** *Hist.* A person who is not a knight but holds lands by tenure of military service. **2.** *Hist.* A municipal officer performing duties for the Crown. **3.** *Hist.* A bailiff. **4.** SERGEANT-AT-ARMS. **5.** A noncommissioned officer in the armed forces ranking a grade above a corporal. **6.** An officer in the police force ranking below a captain or lieutenant. — Also spelled *serjeant*.

sergeant-at-arms. **1.** *Hist.* An armed officer attending a sovereign. **2.** An officer the Crown assigns to attend a session of Parliament. **3.** A court-appointed officer to attend a legislative body, as by serving process and maintaining order during a legislative session. — Also spelled *serjeant-at-arms*.

Sergeant Schultz defense. An assertion by a criminal or civil defendant who claims that he or she was not an active participant in an alleged scheme or conspiracy, and that he or she knew nothing, saw nothing, and heard nothing. • This defense is named after a character from the television series *Hogan's Heroes*, in which Sergeant Schultz, a German guard in charge of prisoners of war during World War II, would avoid controversy over the prisoners' schemes by proclaiming that he saw nothing and knew nothing.

serial bond. See BOND (3).

serial murder. See MURDER.

serial note. See *installment note* under NOTE.

serial right. The right of publication; esp., a right reserved in a publishing contract giving the author or publisher the right to publish the manuscript in installments (as in a magazine) before or after the publication of the book.

serial violation. *Civil-rights law.* The practice by an employer of committing a series of discriminatory acts against an employee, all of which arise out of the same discriminatory intent or animus. • Such a series of discriminatory acts will usu. be considered a continuing violation. For a claim on the violation to be timely, at least one of the discriminatory acts must fall within the time permitted to assert the claim (e.g., 300 days for a Title VII claim). Cf. SYSTEMATIC VIOLATION.

seriatim (seer-ee-**ay**-tim), *adv.* [Latin] One after another; in a series; successively <the court disposed of the issues seriatim>. — Also termed *seriately* (**seer**-ee-ət-lee).

seriatim, *adj.* Occurring in a series.

seriatim opinions. See OPINION (1).

series bonds. See BOND (3).

serious, *adj.* **1.** (Of conduct, opinions, etc.) weighty; important <serious violation of rules>. **2.** (Of an injury, illness, accident, etc.) dangerous; potentially resulting in death or other severe consequences <serious bodily harm>.

serious and willful misconduct. *Workers' compensation.* An intentional act performed with the knowledge that it is likely to result in serious injury or with a wanton and reckless disregard of its probable consequences.

serious crime. **1.** See *serious offense* under OFFENSE (1). **2.** See FELONY.

serious illness. *Insurance.* A disorder that permanently or materially impairs, or is likely to permanently or materially impair, the health of the insured or an insurance applicant.

serious offense. See OFFENSE (1).

serjeant. See SERGEANT.

serjeant-at-arms. See SERGEANT-AT-ARMS.

serjeant-at-law. *Hist. English law.* A barrister of superior grade; one who had achieved the highest degree of the legal profession, having (until 1846) the exclusive privilege of practicing in the Court of Common Pleas. • Every judge of the common-law courts was required to be a serjeant-at-law until the Judicature Act of 1873. The rank was gradually superseded by that of Queen's Counsel. — Often shortened to *serjeant*. — Also termed *serviens narrator*.

premier serjeant. The serjeant given the primary right of preaudience by royal letters patent. — Also termed *prime serjeant*. See PREAUDIENCE.

serjeanty (**sahr**-jən-tee). *Hist.* A feudal tenure by knight service due only to the king. — Also spelled *sergeanty*.

grand serjeanty. *Hist.* Serjeanty requiring the tenant to personally perform a service to the king, as by carrying the king's banner or sword or officiating at the king's coronation.

petit serjeanty (**pet**-ee). *Hist.* Serjeanty that either did not have to be performed personally by the tenant or was not personal in nature, such as an annual payment of rent by a bow, sword, arrow, or other war implement.

serment (**sər**-mənt). *Hist.* An oath.

serological test (seer-ə-**loj**-ə-kəl). A state-ordered blood test to determine the presence of venereal disease in a couple applying for a marriage license.

serva aliena. See SERVUS.

servage (**sər**-vij). *Hist.* A feudal service consisting of (in addition to paying rent) furnishing one or more workers for the lord.

servant. A person who is employed by another to do work under the control and directions of the employer. See EMPLOYEE.

> "A servant, strictly speaking, is a person who, by contract or operation of law, is for a limited period subject to the authority or control of another person in a particular trade, business or occupation .... The word *servant*, in our legal *nomenclature*, has a broad significance, and embraces all persons of whatever rank or position who are in the employ, and subject to the direction or control of another in any department of labor or business. Indeed it may, in most cases, be said to be synonymous with employee." H.G. Wood, *A Treatise on the Law of Master and Servant* § 1, at 2 (2d ed. 1886).

serve, *vb.* **1.** To make legal delivery of (a notice or process) <a copy of the pleading was served on all interested parties>. **2.** To present (a person) with a notice or process as required by law <the defendant was served with process>.

service, *n.* **1.** The formal delivery of a writ, summons, or other legal process <after three attempts, service still had not been accomplished>. — Also termed *service of process*. **2.** The formal delivery of some other legal notice, such as a pleading <be sure that a certificate of service is attached to the motion>.

constructive service. **1.** See *substituted service*. **2.** Service accomplished by a method or circumstance that does not give actual notice.

personal service. See PERSONAL SERVICE (1).

service by publication. The service of process on an absent or nonresident defendant by publishing a notice in a newspaper or other public medium.

sewer service. The fraudulent service of process on a debtor by a creditor seeking to obtain a default judgment.

substituted service. Any method of service allowed by law in place of personal service, such as service by mail. — Also termed *constructive service*.

3. The act of doing something useful for a person or company for a fee <your services were no longer required>.

personal service. See PERSONAL SERVICE (2).

4. A person or company whose business is to do useful things for others <a linen service>.

civil service. See CIVIL SERVICE.

salvage service. See SALVAGE SERVICE.

5. An intangible commodity in the form of human effort, such as labor, skill, or advice <contract for services>.

service, *vb.* To provide service for; specif., to make interest payments on (a debt) <service the deficit>.

service by publication. See SERVICE (2).

service charge. **1.** A charge assessed for the performing of a service, such as the charge assessed by a bank against the expenses of maintaining or servicing a customer's checking account. **2.** The sum of (1) all charges payable by the buyer and imposed by the seller as an incident to the extension of credit and (2) charges incurred for investigating the collateral or creditworthiness of the buyer or for commissions for obtaining the credit. UCCC § 2.109. — Also termed (in sense 2) *credit service charge*.

service contract. See CONTRACT.

service establishment. Under the Fair Labor Standards Act, an establishment that, although having the characteristics of a retail store, primarily furnishes services to the public, such as a barber shop, laundry, or automobile-repair shop.

service life. The period of the expected usefulness of an asset. • It may or may not coincide with the asset's depreciable life for income-tax purposes.

servicemark. A name, phrase, or other device used to identify and distinguish the services of a certain provider. • Servicemarks identify and afford protection to intangible things such as services, as distinguished from the protection already provided for marks affixed to tangible things such as goods and products. — Often shortened to *mark*. — Also spelled *service mark*; *service-mark*. Cf. TRADEMARK (1).

service-occupation tax. See TAX.

service of process. See SERVICE (1).

serviens narrator (**sər**-vee-enz nə-**ray**-tər). See SERJEANT-AT-LAW.

servient (**sər**-vee-ənt), *adj.* (Of an estate) subject to a servitude or easement. See *servient estate* under ESTATE.

servient estate. See ESTATE.

servient property. See *servient estate* under ESTATE.

servient tenant. See TENANT.

servient tenement. See *servient estate* under ESTATE.

servitiis acquietandis (sər-**vish**-ee-is ə-kwɪ-ə-**tan**-dis), *n.* [Law Latin "for being quit of service"] *Hist.* A writ exempting a person from performing certain services, either because they are not due or because they are due someone other than the distrainor.

servitium (sər-**vish**-ee-əm), *n.* [Latin "service"] *Hist.* The duty of service; esp., a duty of performance and obedience of a tenant to the lord.

servitium feodale et praediale (sər-**vish**-ee-əm fee-ə-**day**-lee [*or* fyoo-**day**-lee] et pree-dee-**ay**-lee), *n.* [Law Latin] *Hist.* A personal service due only by reason of lands held in fee.

servitium forinsecum (sər-**vish**-ee-əm fə-**rin**-si-kəm), *n.* [Law Latin] *Hist.* A service due the king rather than a lord.

servitium intrinsecum (sər-**vish**-ee-əm in-**trin**-si-kəm), *n.* [Law Latin] *Hist.* The ordinary service due from a tenant to the chief lord.

servitium liberum (sər-**vish**-ee-əm **lib**-ər-əm), *n.* [Law Latin] *Hist.* The service by a free tenant (not a vassal) to the lord, as by attending the lord's court or accompanying the lord into military service. — Also termed *liberum servitium*; *servitium liberum armorum*.

servitium regale (sər-**vish**-ee-əm ri-**gay**-lee). [Latin "royal service"] *Hist.* The right of a lord of a royal manor to settle disputes, make assessments, mint money, and the like.

servitium scuti (sər-**vish**-ee-əm **sk**[**y**]**oo**-tɪ). [Latin "service of the shield"] *Hist.* Knight service.

servitium socae (sər-**vish**-ee-əm **soh**-see). [Latin "service of the plow"] *Hist.* Socage.

servitor of bills (**sər**-vi-tər). *Hist.* A messenger of the marshal of the King's Bench, sent out to summon people to court. — Also termed *tipstave*.

servitude. 1. An encumbrance consisting in a right to the limited use of a piece of land without the possession of it; a charge or burden on an estate for another's benefit <the easement by necessity is an equitable servitude>. • The three types of servitudes are easements, licenses, and profits. See EASEMENT; LICENSE; PROFIT (2).

acquired servitude. A servitude that requires a special mode of acquisition before it comes into existence.

additional servitude. A servitude imposed on land taken under an eminent-domain proceeding for a different type of servitude, as when a highway is constructed on land condemned for a public sidewalk. • A landowner whose land is burdened by an additional servitude is entitled to further compensation.

apparent servitude. *Civil law.* A predial servitude that is manifested by exterior signs or constructions, such as a roadway. Cf. *nonapparent servitude.*

landed servitude. See *servitude appurtenant.*

legal servitude. A servitude arising from a legal limitation on a property's use.

mineral servitude. A servitude granting the right to enter another's property to explore for and extract minerals.

natural servitude. A servitude naturally appurtenant to land, requiring no special mode of acquisition. • An example is the right of land, unencumbered by buildings, to the support of the adjoining land.

navigation servitude. See NAVIGATION SERVITUDE.

negative servitude. *Civil law.* A real servitude allowing a person to prohibit the servient landowner from exercising a right. • For example, a negative servitude, such as *jus ne luminibus officiatur*, prevents an owner of land from building in a way that blocks light from reaching another person's house.

nonapparent servitude. *Civil law.* A predial servitude that is not obvious because there are no exterior signs of its existence. • An example is a prohibition against building above a certain height. Cf. *apparent servitude.*

personal servitude. A servitude granting a specific person certain rights in property.

positive servitude. *Civil law.* A real servitude allowing a person to do something on the servient landowner's property, such as entering the property.

predial servitude. See *servitude appurtenant.*

private servitude. A servitude vested in a particular person. • Examples include a landowner's personal right-of-way over an adjoining piece of land or a right granted to one person to fish in another's lake.

public servitude. A servitude vested in the public at large or in some class of indeterminate individuals. • Examples include the right of the public to a highway over privately owned land and the right to navigate a river the bed of which belongs to some private person.

servitude appurtenant. A servitude that is not merely an encumbrance of one piece of land but is accessory to another piece; the right of using one piece of land for the benefit of another, such as the right of support for a building. — Also termed *real servitude*; *predial* (or *praedial*) *servitude*; *landed servitude.*

servitude in gross. A servitude that is not accessory to any dominant tenement for whose benefit it exists but is merely an encumbrance on a given piece of land.

urban servitude. A servitude appertaining to the building and construction of houses in a city, such as the right to light and air.

2. The condition of being a servant or slave <under the 15th Amendment, an American citizen's right to vote cannot be denied on account of race, color, or previous condition of servitude>. **3.** The condition of a prisoner who has been sentenced to forced labor <penal servitude>.

involuntary servitude. The condition of one forced to labor — for pay or not — for another by coercion or imprisonment.

servitus (**sər**-vi-təs), *n.* [Latin fr. *servire* "to serve"] *Roman law.* **1.** Slavery; bondage. **2.** A servitude; an easement. Pl. ***servitutes.***

servitus actus (**sər**-vi-təs **ak**-təs). [Latin "the servitude of driving cattle"] *Roman law.* A type of right-of-way; a servitude entitling one to walk, ride, or drive animals over another's property.

servitus altius non tollendi (**sər**-vi-təs **al**-shee-əs non tə-**len**-dɪ). [Latin "the servitude of not building higher"] *Roman law.* A servitude allowing a person to prevent a neighbor from building a higher house.

servitus aquae ducendae (**sər**-vi-təs **ak**-wee d[y]oo-**sen**-dee). [Latin "the servitude of leading water"] *Roman law.* A servitude allowing one to bring water to property through another's land, as by a canal.

servitus aquae educendae (**sər**-vi-təs **ak**-wee ee-d[y]oo-**sen**-dee). [Latin "the servitude of leading off water"] *Roman law.* A servitude entitling a person to discharge water onto another's land.

servitus aquae hauriendae (**sər**-vi-təs **ak**-wee haw-ree-**en**-dee). [Latin "the servitude of drawing water"] *Roman law.* A servitude entitling a person to draw water from another's spring or well. — Also termed *servitus aquae haustus.*

servitus fluminis (**sər**-vi-təs **floo**-mə-nəs). [Latin "the servitude of a stream of rainwater"] *Roman law.* A servitude consisting in the right to divert rainwater as opposed to drip (*stillicidium*) onto another's land.

servitus fumi immittendi (**sər**-vi-təs **fyoo**-mI im-ə-**ten**-dI). [Latin "the servitude of discharging smoke"] *Roman law.* A servitude allowing a person's chimney smoke to be directed over a neighbor's property.

servitus itineris (**sər**-vi-təs I-**tin**-ər-is). [Latin "the servitude of way"] *Roman law.* A servitude allowing one to walk, ride, or be carried by horse over another's property, but not to drive animals across it.

servitus luminum (**sər**-vi-təs **loo**-mə-nəm). [Latin "the servitude of lights"] *Roman law.* A servitude entitling one to receive light from a neighbor's land, as by building windows in a common wall to light a room.

servitus ne luminibus officiatur (**sər**-vi-təs nee loo-**min**-ə-bəs ə-fish-ee-**ay**-tər). [Latin "the servitude not to hinder light"] *Roman law.* A servitude preventing someone's light from being obstructed by a neighbor's building.

servitus ne prospectui officiatur (**sər**-vi-təs nee prə-**spek**-too-I ə-fish-ee-**ay**-tər). [Latin "the servitude not to intercept one's prospect"] *Roman law.* A servitude entitling someone to an unobstructed view.

servitus oneris ferendi (**sər**-vi-təs **on**-ə-ris fə-**ren**-dI). [Latin "the servitude of bearing weight"] *Roman law.* The servitude allowing a person's building to rest on a neighbor's building, wall, or pillar.

servitus pascendi (**sər**-vi-təs pa-**sen**-dI). [Latin "the servitude of pasturing"] *Roman law.* A servitude allowing one to pasture cattle on another's land. — Also termed *jus pascendi*.

servitus pecoris ad aquam adpulsum (**sər**-vi-təs **pek**-ə-ris ad **ak**-wəm ad-**pəl**-səm). [Latin "the servitude to drive cattle to water"] *Roman law.* A servitude allowing one to drive cattle to water across another's land.

servitus praedii rustici (**sər**-vi-təs **pree**-dee-I **rəs**-ti-sI). [Latin "the servitude of a country estate"] *Roman law.* A rural servitude; a servitude attached to land, as in *servitus pecoris ad aquam adpulsam*.

servitus praedii urbani (**sər**-vi-təs **pree**-dee-I ər-**bay**-nI). [Latin "the servitude of an urban estate"] *Roman law.* An urban servitude; a servitude attached to a building, as in *servitus oneris ferendi*.

servitus praediorum (**sər**-vi-təs pree-dee-**or**-əm). [Latin "praedial servitude"] *Roman law.* A burden on one estate for the benefit of another. See *servitude appurtenant* under SERVITUDE (1).

servitus projiciendi (**sər**-vi-təs prə-jish-ee-**en**-dI). [Latin "the servitude of projecting"] *Roman law.* An urban servitude allowing a projection from one's building into the open space of a neighbor's property.

servitus stillicidii (**sər**-vi-təs stil-ə-**sid**-ee-I). [Latin "the servitude of drip"] *Roman law.* A servitude allowing water to drip from one's house onto the house or ground of a neighbor. Cf. AQUAE IMMITTENDAE; DRIP RIGHTS.

servitus tigni immittendi (**sər**-vi-təs **tig**-nI im-ə-**ten**-dI). [Latin "the servitude of letting in a beam"] *Roman law.* An urban servitude allowing one to insert beams into a neighbor's wall.

servitus viae (**sər**-vi-təs **vI**-ee). [Latin "the servitude of road way"] *Roman law.* The right to use a road over another's land. • It is broader than and includes the *servitus actus* and *servitus itineris*.

servus (**sər**-vəs), *n.* [Latin] **1.** *Roman law.* A slave. **2.** *Hist.* A bondman; a servant. Cf. INGENUUS; LATINI JUNIANI.

sess, *n.* See CESS.

sessio (**sesh**-ee-oh), *n.* [Latin "a sitting"] *Hist.* A session; a sitting, as in *sessio parliamenti* ("the sitting of Parliament").

session. 1. A sitting together or meeting of a court, legislature, or other deliberative body so that it can conduct business <the court's spring session>. — Also termed (for a court) *sitting*. See TERM (5). **2.** The period within any given day during which such a body is assembled and performing its duties <court is in session>.

biennial session. A legislative session held every two years. • Most state legislatures have biennial sessions, usu. held in odd-numbered years.

closed session. **1.** A session to which parties not directly involved are not admitted. **2.** *Military law.* A period during a court-martial when the members (or the judge, if trial is before a military judge) deliberate alone. — Also termed *closed court*.

extraordinary session. See *special session*.

extra session. See *special session*.

joint session. The combined meeting of two legislative bodies (such as the House of Representatives and the Senate) to pursue a common agenda.

lame-duck session. A post-election legislative session in which some of the participants are voting during their last days as elected officials. See LAME DUCK.

open session. **1.** A session to which parties not directly involved are admitted. **2.** *Military law.* The period during a court-martial in which all participants are in the courtroom. • Generally, the public may attend a court-martial's open session.

plenary session. A meeting of all the members of a deliberative body, not just a committee.

quarter session. **1.** *English law.* The meetings held four times a year by a county's justices of the peace to transact business, including trying certain criminal and civil matters as specified by statute. • The quarter sessions were abolished in 1971 and replaced by the Crown Court system. **2.** *Scots law.* A meeting formerly held four times a year by the justices to review criminal sentences. — Abbr. Q.S.

regular session. A session that takes place at fixed intervals or specified times.

special session. A legislative session, usu. called by the executive, that meets outside its regular term to consider a specific issue or to reduce backlog. — Also termed *extra session*; *extraordinary session.*

session laws. 1. A body of statutes enacted by a legislature during a particular annual or biennial session. **2.** The softbound booklets containing these statutes. — Also termed *acts of assembly*; *blue books*; *sheet acts.*

set-aside, *n.* Something (such as a percentage of funds) that is reserved or put aside for a specific purpose.

set aside, *vb.* (Of a court) to annul or vacate (a judgment, order, etc.) <the judge refused to set aside the default judgment>.

setback, *n. Real estate.* The minimum amount of space required between a lot line and a building line <a 12-foot setback>. • Typically contained in zoning ordinances or deed restrictions, setbacks are designed to ensure that enough light and ventilation reach the property and to keep buildings from being erected too close to property lines.

set down, *vb.* To schedule (a case) for trial or hearing, usu. by making a docket entry.

se te fecerit securum (see tee **fes**-ər-it si-**kyoor**-əm). [Latin] See SI FECERIT TE SECURUM.

set forth. See SET OUT.

seti. *Mining law.* A lease.

set of exchange. *Commercial law.* A single bill of lading drawn in a set of parts, each of which is valid only if the goods have not been delivered against any other part. • Bills may be drawn in duplicate or triplicate, the first part being "first of exchange," the second part being "second of exchange," and so on. When one part has been paid, the other parts become void.

setoff, *n.* **1.** A defendant's counterdemand against the plaintiff, arising out of a transaction independent of the plaintiff's claim. **2.** A debtor's right to reduce the amount of a debt by any sum the creditor owes the debtor; the counterbalancing sum owed by the creditor. — Also written *set-off.* — Also termed (in civil law) *compensation*; *stoppage.* — **set off,** *vb.* See COUNTERCLAIM; OFFSET. Cf. RECOUPMENT (3).

> "Set-off signifies the subtraction or taking away of one demand from another opposite or cross demand, so as to distinguish the smaller demand and reduce the greater by the amount of the less; or, if the opposite demands are equal, to extinguish both. It was also, formerly, sometimes called stoppage, because the amount to be set-off was *stopped* or deducted from the cross demand." Thomas W. Waterman, *A Treatise on the Law of Set-Off, Recoupment, and Counter Claim* § 1, at 1 (2d ed. 1872).

> "Before considering the counter-claim, a brief reference to 'the set-off' as known in former practice is necessary. By the common law, the setting off of one demand against another in the same action was unknown. If A had a cause of action in debt against B, and B had another cause of action in debt in equal amount against A, each must bring his action. One could not be set off against the other. This was changed by statute in England in 1729, by a provision which, somewhat enlarged and modified, has been generally adopted in this country." Edwin E. Bryant, *The Law of Pleading Under the Codes of Civil Procedure* 250–51 (2d ed. 1899).

> "Set-off is defined to be a counter-demand, generally of a liquidated debt *growing out of an independent transaction* for which an action might be maintained by the defendant against the plaintiff." Eugene A. Jones, *Manual of Equity Pleading and Practice* 65 n.42 (1916).

set out, *vb.* To recite, explain, narrate, or incorporate (facts or circumstances) <set out the terms of the contract>. — Also termed *set forth.*

set over, *vb.* To transfer or convey (property) <to set over the land to the purchaser>.

setting, *n.* The date and time established by a court for a trial or hearing <the plaintiff sought a continuance of the imminent setting>.

special setting. A preferential setting on a court's calendar, usu. reserved for older cases or cases given priority by law, made either on a party's motion or on the court's own motion. • For example, some jurisdictions authorize a special setting for cases involving a party over the age of 70. — Also termed *special trial setting*; *trial-setting preference.*

settled estate. See ESTATE.

settlement, *n.* **1.** The conveyance of property — or of interests in property — to provide for one or more beneficiaries, usu. members of the settlor's family, in a way that differs from what the beneficiaries would receive as heirs under the statutes of descent and distribution <in marriage settlements, historically, the wife waived her right to claim dower or to succeed to her husband's property>. **2.** An agreement ending a dispute or lawsuit <the parties reached a settlement the day before trial>. **3.** Payment, satisfaction, or final adjustment <the seller shipped the goods after confirming the buyer's settlement of the account>. **4.** CLOSING <the settlement on their first home is next Friday>. **5.** *Wills & estates.* The complete execution of an estate by the executor <the settlement of the tycoon's estate was long and complex>. — **settle,** *vb.*

final settlement. Wills & estates. A court order discharging an executor's duties after an estate's execution.

full settlement. A settlement and release of all pending claims between the parties.

judicial settlement. The settlement of a civil case with the help of a judge who is not assigned to adjudicate the dispute. • Parties sometimes find this procedure advantageous because it capitalizes on judicial experience in evaluating the settlement value of a claim.

nuisance settlement. A settlement in which the defendant pays the plaintiff purely for economic reasons — as opposed to any notion of responsibility — because without the settlement the defendant would spend more money in legal fees and expenses caused by protracted litigation than in paying the settlement amount. • The money paid in such a settlement is often termed *nuisance money.*

out-of-court settlement. The settlement and termination of a pending suit, arrived at without the court's participation.

strict settlement. Hist. A property settlement that aimed to keep the estate within the family by creating successive interests in tail and shielding remainders from destruction by the interposition of a trust.

structured settlement. A settlement in which the defendant agrees to pay periodic sums to the plaintiff for a specified time.

viatical settlement (vɪ-**at**-ə-kəl). [fr. Latin *viaticus* "relating to a road or journey"] A transaction in which a terminally or chronically ill person sells the benefits of a life-insurance policy to a third party in return for a lump-sum cash payment equal to a percentage of the policy's face value. • Viatical settlements are common with AIDS patients, many of whom sell their policies at a 20% to 40% discount, depending on life expectancy. When the insured (called the "viator") dies, the investor receives the insurance benefit.

voluntary settlement. A property settlement made without valuable consideration — other than love and affection — from the beneficiary.

settlement class. See CLASS (4).

settlement credit. *Civil procedure.* A court's reduction of the amount of a jury verdict — or the effect of the verdict on nonsettling defendants — to account for settlement funds the plaintiff has received from former defendants or from other responsible parties.

settlement date. See DATE.

settlement-first method. A means by which to apply a settlement credit to a jury verdict, by first reducing the amount of the verdict by subtracting the amount of all settlements the plaintiff has received on the claim, then reducing the remainder by the percentage of the plaintiff's comparative fault. See SETTLEMENT CREDIT. Cf. FAULT-FIRST METHOD.

settlement option. See OPTION.

settlement sheet. See CLOSING STATEMENT (2).

settlement statement. See CLOSING STATEMENT (2).

settlement value. See VALUE.

settler. 1. A person who occupies property with the intent to establish a residence. • The term is usu. applied to an early resident of a country or region. **2.** SETTLOR.

settle up, *vb.* To collect, pay, and turn over debts and property (of a decedent, bankrupt, or insolvent business).

settlor (**set**-lər). **1.** A person who makes a settlement of property; esp., one who sets up a trust. — Also termed *creator*; *donor*; *trustor*; *grantor*; *founder*. **2.** A party to an instrument. — Also spelled (in both senses) *settler*.

set up, *vb.* To raise (a defense) <the defendant set up the insanity defense on the murder charge>.

Seventeenth Amendment. The constitutional amendment, ratified in 1913, transferring the power to elect U.S. senators from the state legislatures to the states' voters.

Seventh Amendment. The constitutional amendment, ratified with the Bill of Rights in 1791, guaranteeing the right to a jury trial in federal civil cases that are traditionally considered to be suits at common law and that have an amount in controversy exceeding $20.

seven-years'-absence rule. The principle that a person who has been missing without explanation for at least seven years is legally presumed dead. Cf. ENOCH ARDEN LAW.

> "[I]n the United States, it is quite generally held or provided by statute that a presumption of death arises from the continued and unexplained absence of a person from his home or place of residence without any intelligence from or concerning him for the period of 7 years. The presumption has been regarded as a procedural expedient and a rule of evidence." 22A Am. Jur. 2d *Death* § 551, at 527 (1988).

severability. See BLUE-PENCIL TEST.

severability clause. A provision that keeps the remaining provisions of a contract or statute in force if any portion of that contract or statute is judicially declared void or unconstitutional. — Also termed *saving clause*; *separability clause*. See *severable contract* under CONTRACT.

severable contract. See CONTRACT.

severable statute. See STATUTE.

several, *adj.* **1.** (Of a person, place, or thing) more than one or two but not a lot <several witnesses>. **2.** (Of liability, etc.) separate; particular; distinct, but not necessarily independent <a several obligation>. **3.** (Of things, etc.) different; various <several settlement options>.

several action. See *separate action* under ACTION.

several contract. See *severable contract* under CONTRACT.

several count. See COUNT.

several covenant. See COVENANT (1).

several demises. See DEMISE.

several fishery. See FISHERY (1).

several inheritance. See INHERITANCE.

several liability. See LIABILITY.

severally, *adj.* Distinctly; separately <severally liable>.

several obligation. See OBLIGATION.

several-remedies rule. A procedural rule that tolls a statute of limitations for a plaintiff who has several available forums (such as a workers'-compensation proceeding and the court system) and who timely files in one forum and later proceeds in another forum, as long as the defendant is not prejudiced.

several tenancy. See TENANCY.

severalty (**sev**-[ə]-rəl-tee). The state or condition of being separate or distinct <the individual landowners held the land in severalty, not as joint tenants>.

severance, *n.* **1.** The act of cutting off; the state of being cut off. **2.** The separation of claims, by the court, of multiple parties either to permit separate actions on each claim or to allow certain interlocutory orders to become final. — Also termed *severance of actions*; *severance of claims*. Cf. *bifurcated trial* under TRIAL. **3.** The termination of a joint tenancy, usu. by converting it into a tenancy in common. **4.** The removal of anything (such as crops or minerals) attached or affixed to real property, making it personal property rather than a part of the land. — **sever,** *vb.* — **severable,** *adj.*

severance damages. See DAMAGES.

severance of actions. See SEVERANCE (2).

severance of claims. See SEVERANCE (2).

severance pay. Money (apart from back wages or salary) paid by an employer to a dismissed employee. • Such a payment is often made in exchange for a release of any claims that the employee might have against the employer. — Also termed *separation pay*; *dismissal compensation*.

severance tax. See TAX.

seward. See CUSTOS MARIS.

sewer service. See SERVICE (2).

sex. **1.** The sum of the peculiarities of structure and function that distinguish a male from a female organism. **2.** Sexual intercourse. **3.** SEXUAL RELATIONS (2).

sex discrimination. See DISCRIMINATION.

sexual abuse. See ABUSE.

sexual activity. See SEXUAL RELATIONS.

sexual assault. See ASSAULT.

sexual battery. See BATTERY.

sexual harassment. A type of employment discrimination consisting in verbal or physical abuse of a sexual nature. See HARASSMENT.

hostile-environment sexual harassment. Sexual harassment in which a work environment is created where an employee is subject to unwelcome verbal or physical sexual behavior that is either severe or pervasive. • This type of harassment might occur, for example, if a group of coworkers repeatedly e-mailed pornographic pictures to a colleague who found the pictures offensive.

quid pro quo sexual harassment. Sexual harassment in which the satisfaction of a sexual demand is used as the basis of an employment decision. • This type of harassment might occur, for example, if a boss fired or demoted an employee who refused to go on a date with the boss.

same-sex harassment. See HARASSMENT.

sexually transmitted disease. A disease transmitted only or chiefly by engaging in sexual acts with an infected person. • Common examples are syphilis and gonorrhea. — Abbr. STD. — Also termed *venereal disease*.

sexual offense. See OFFENSE (1).

sexual orientation. A person's predisposition or inclination toward a particular type of sexual activity or behavior; heterosexuality, homosexuality, or bisexuality. • There has been a trend in recent years to make sexual orientation a protected class, esp. in employment and hate-crime statutes.

sexual relations. **1.** Sexual intercourse. **2.** Physical sexual activity that does not necessarily culminate in intercourse. • Sexual relations usu. involve the touching of another's breast, vagina, penis, or anus. Both persons (the toucher and the person touched) engage in sexual relations. — Also termed *sexual activity*.

SF. See *sinking fund* under FUND (1).

S/F. *abbr.* STATUTE OF FRAUDS.

SG. *abbr.* **1.** SOLICITOR GENERAL. **2.** SURGEON GENERAL.

shack. *Hist.* The straying and escaping of cattle out of their owner's land into other unenclosed land; an intercommoning of cattle.

shadow jury. See JURY.

shadow stock plan. See PHANTOM STOCK PLAN.

shakedown. **1.** An extortion of money using threats of violence or, in the case of a police officer, threats of arrest. **2.** See *shakedown search* under SEARCH.

shakedown search. See SEARCH.

shakeout, *n.* An elimination of weak or nonproductive businesses in an industry, esp. during a period of intense competition or declining prices.

shall, *vb.* **1.** Has a duty to; more broadly, is required to <the requester shall send notice> <notice shall be sent>. **2.** Should (as often interpreted by courts) <all claimants shall request mediation>. **3.** May <no person shall enter the building without first signing the roster>. **4.** Will (as a future-tense verb) <the debtor shall then be released from all debts>. **5.** Is entitled to <the secretary shall be reim-

bursed for all expenses>. • Only sense 1 is acceptable under strict standards of drafting.

sham, *n.* **1.** Something that is not what it seems; a counterfeit. **2.** A person who pretends to be something that he or she is not; a faker. — **sham,** *vb.* — **sham,** *adj.*

sham affidavit. See AFFIDAVIT.

sham defense. See DEFENSE (1).

shame sanction. See SANCTION.

sham exception. An exception to the *Noerr-Pennington* doctrine whereby a company that petitions the government will not receive First Amendment protection or an exemption from the antitrust laws if its intent in petitioning the government is really an effort to harm its competitors rather than to obtain favorable governmental action. — Also termed *sham petitioning*; *sham litigation.* See NOERR-PENNINGTON DOCTRINE.

shaming sentence. See *shame sanction* under SANCTION.

sham litigation. See SHAM EXCEPTION.

sham marriage. See MARRIAGE (1).

sham petitioning. See SHAM EXCEPTION.

sham plea. See *sham pleading* under PLEADING (1).

sham pleading. See PLEADING (1).

sham prosecution. See PROSECUTION.

sham transaction. An agreement or exchange that has no independent economic benefit or business purpose and is entered into solely to create a tax advantage (such as a deduction for a business loss). • The Internal Revenue Service is entitled to ignore the purported tax benefits of a sham transaction.

shanghaiing (shang-**hI**-ing). The act or an instance of coercing or inducing someone to do something by fraudulent or other wrongful means; specif., the practice of drugging, tricking, intoxicating, or otherwise illegally inducing a person to work aboard a vessel, usu. to secure advance money or a premium. — Also termed *shanghaiing sailors.* 18 USCA § 2194.

share, *n.* **1.** An allotted portion owned by, contributed by, or due to someone <Sean's share of the partnership's profits>. **2.** One of the definite number of equal parts into which the capital stock of a corporation or joint-stock company is divided <the broker advised his customer to sell the stock shares when the price reaches $29>. • A share represents an equity or ownership interest in the corporation or joint-stock company. Cf. STOCK (4); SECURITY (4).

share, *vb.* **1.** To divide (something) into portions. **2.** To enjoy or partake of (a power, right, etc.).

share account. See *share-draft account* under ACCOUNT.

share acquisition. The acquisition of a corporation by purchasing all or most of its outstanding shares directly from the shareholders; TAKEOVER. — Also termed *share-acquisition transaction*; *stock acquisition*; *stock-acquisition transaction*. Cf. ASSET ACQUISITION.

share and share alike. To divide (assets, etc.) in equal shares or proportions; to engage in per capita division. See PER CAPITA.

share certificate. See STOCK CERTIFICATE.

sharecropping. An agricultural arrangement in which a landowner leases land and equipment to a tenant who, in turn, gives the landlord a portion of the crop as rent. — **sharecropper,** *n.*

shared-appreciation mortgage. See MORTGAGE.

shared custody. See *joint custody* under CUSTODY (2).

shared-equity mortgage. See MORTGAGE.

share draft. See DRAFT.

share-draft account. See ACCOUNT.

shareholder. One who owns or holds a share or shares in a company, esp. a corporation. — Also termed *shareowner*; (in a corporation) *stockholder.*

controlling shareholder. A shareholder who is in a position to influence the corporation's activities because the shareholder either owns a majority of outstanding shares or owns a smaller percentage but a significant number of the remaining shares are widely distributed among many others.

dummy shareholder. A shareholder who owns stock in name only for the benefit of the true owner, whose identity is usu. concealed.

majority shareholder. A shareholder who owns or controls more than half the corporation's stock.

minority shareholder. A shareholder who owns less than half the total shares outstanding and thus cannot control the corporation's management or singlehandedly elect directors.

shareholder-control agreement. See POOLING AGREEMENT.

shareholder derivative suit. See DERIVATIVE ACTION (1).

shareholder oppression. See OPPRESSION (4).

shareholder proposal. A proposal by one or more corporate stockholders to change company policy or procedure. • Ordinarily, the corporation informs all stockholders about the proposal before the next shareholder meeting.

shareholder resolution. See RESOLUTION (2).

shareholders' equity. See OWNERS' EQUITY.

shareholder's liability. See LIABILITY.

shareholder voting agreement. See POOLING AGREEMENT.

shareowner. See SHAREHOLDER.

shares outstanding. See *outstanding stock* under STOCK.

share split. See STOCK SPLIT.

share-warrant to bearer. A warrant providing that the bearer is entitled to a certain amount of fully paid stock shares. • Delivery of the warrant operates as a transfer of the shares of stock.

shark repellent. A measure taken by a corporation to discourage hostile takeover attempts. • Examples include issuing new shares of stock, acquiring expensive assets, and adopting a poison-pill defense. — Also termed *takeover defense*. See POISON PILL. Cf. PORCUPINE PROVISION.

sharp, *adj.* (Of a clause in a mortgage, deed, etc.) empowering the creditor to take immediate and summary action upon the debtor's default.

sharp practice. Unethical action and trickery, esp. by a lawyer. — Also termed (archaically) *unhandsome dealing.* — **sharp practitioner,** *n.*

shave, *vb.* **1.** To purchase (a negotiable instrument) at a greater than usual discount rate. **2.** To reduce or deduct from (a price).

sheet acts. See SESSION LAWS.

shelf issue. See ISSUE (2).

shelf registration. See REGISTRATION (2).

shelf security. See SECURITY.

shell corporation. See CORPORATION.

Shelley's Case, Rule in. See RULE IN SHELLEY'S CASE.

shelter, *n.* See TAX SHELTER <the shelter saved the taxpayer over $2,000 in taxes>. — **shelter,** *vb.*

shelter doctrine. *Commercial law.* The principle that a person to whom a holder in due course has transferred commercial paper, as well as any later transferee, will succeed to the rights of the holder in due course. • As a result, transferees of holders in due course are generally not subject to defenses against the payment of an instrument. This doctrine ensures the free transferability of commercial paper. Its name derives from the idea that the transferees "take shelter" in the rights of the holder in due course.

shepardize, *vb.* **1.** (*often cap.*) To determine the subsequent history of (a case) by using a printed or computerized version of *Shepard's Citators.* **2.** Loosely, to check the precedential value of (a case) by the same or similar means. — **shepardization, shepardizing,** *n.*

sheriff. A county's chief peace officer, usu. elected, who in most jurisdictions acts as custodian of the county jail, executes civil and criminal process, and carries out judicial mandates within the county.

deputy sheriff. An officer who, acting under the direction of a sheriff, may perform most of the duties of the sheriff's office. • Although *undersheriff* is broadly synonymous with *deputy sheriff*, writers have sometimes distinguished between the two, suggesting that a deputy is appointed for a special occasion or purpose, while an undersheriff is permanent. — Also termed *undersheriff*; *general deputy*; *vice-sheriff*.

sheriff's deed. See DEED.

sheriff's jury. See JURY.

sheriff's sale. See SALE.

Sherman Antitrust Act. A federal statute, passed in 1890, that prohibits direct or indirect interference with the freely competitive interstate production and distribution of goods. • This Act was amended by the Clayton Act in 1914. 15 USCA §§ 1–7. — Often shortened to *Sherman Act*.

shield law. **1.** A statute that affords journalists the privilege not to reveal confidential sources. See *journalist's privilege* under PRIVILEGE (3). **2.** A statute that restricts or prohibits the use, in rape or sexual assault cases, of evidence about the past sexual conduct of the victim. — Also termed (in sense 2) *rape shield law*; *rape shield statute*.

> "The 'rape shield law.' At common law the character of the woman as to chastity or unchastity was held to be admissible in evidence on the theory that it had probative value in determining whether she did or did not consent. Defense counsel, in unrestrained zeal for an acquittal, took advantage of this to the point that it often seemed as if it was the victim of the rape, rather than the perpetrator, who was on trial.... A typical 'rape shield statute' does not prevent the introduction of any relevant and otherwise admissible evidence, but requires that the relevancy of any evidence of the previous sexual conduct of the complaining witness must be determined in a pretrial hearing before the judge in camera." Rollin M. Perkins & Ronald N. Boyce, *Criminal Law* 206 (3d ed. 1982).

shifting, *adj.* (Of a position, place, etc.) changing or passing from one to another <a shifting estate>.

shifting clause. At common law, a clause under the Statute of Uses prescribing a substituted mode of devolution in the settlement of an estate. See STATUTE OF USES.

shifting income. A device used by a taxpayer in a high tax bracket to shelter income by moving the income to another (usu. a spouse or child) in a lower tax bracket, and esp. by forming a Clifford trust. See *Clifford trust* under TRUST.

shifting risk. *Insurance.* The changing risk covered under an insurance policy insuring a stock of goods or similar property that varies in amount and composition in the course of trade.

shifting stock of merchandise. Merchandise inventory subject to change by purchases and sales in the course of trade.

shifting the burden of proof. In litigation, the transference of the duty to prove a fact from one party to the other; the passing of the duty to produce evidence in a case from one side to another as the case progresses, when one side has made a prima facie showing on a point of evidence, requiring the other side to rebut it by contradictory evidence. See BURDEN OF PROOF.

shifting trust. See TRUST.

shifting use. See USE (4).

shill. A person who poses as an innocent bystander at a confidence game but actually serves as a decoy for the perpetrators of the scheme.

shingle theory. *Securities.* The notion that a broker-dealer must be held to a high standard of conduct because by engaging in the securities business ("hanging out a shingle"), the broker-dealer implicitly represents to the world that the conduct of all its employees will be fair and meet professional norms.

> "[I]n judging the appropriate standard of care that attaches to a broker-dealer in recommending securities to his or her customers and in dealing with the customers' accounts, the Commission has relied upon the 'shingle theory.' The shingle theory is but an extension of the common law doctrine of 'holding out.' When brokers hold themselves out as experts either in investments in general or in the securities of a particular issuer, they will be held to a higher standard of care in making recommendations." Thomas Lee Hazen, *The Law of Securities Regulation* § 10.6, at 423 (2d ed. 1994).

shin plaster. *Hist. Slang.* **1.** A bank note that has greatly depreciated in value, esp. the paper money of the Republic of Texas in relation to the U.S. dollar. **2.** Paper money in denominations less than one dollar.

ship, *n.* A type of vessel used or intended to be used in navigation. See VESSEL.

chartered ship. A ship specially hired to transport the goods of only one person or company.

general ship. A ship that is put up for a particular voyage to carry the goods of any persons willing to ships goods on it for that voyage.

ship, *vb.* To send (goods, documents, etc.) from one place to another, esp. by delivery to a carrier for transportation.

ship broker. *Maritime law.* **1.** The business agent of a shipowner or charterer; an intermediary between an owner or charterer and a shipper. **2.** One who negotiates the purchase and sale of a ship.

shipmaster. See MASTER OF A SHIP.

shipment. 1. The transportation of goods; esp., the delivery of goods to a carrier and subsequent issuance of a bill of lading. **2.** The goods so shipped; an order of goods.

shipment contract. See CONTRACT.

Ship Mortgage Act. A federal law regulating mortgages on ships registered as U.S. vessels by, among other things, providing for enforcement of maritime liens in favor of those who furnish supplies or maintenance to the vessels. 46 USCA §§ 911 et seq.

shipowner-negligence doctrine. The principle that a shipowner is liable for an assault on a crew member if the crew member was assaulted by a superior, in the context of an activity undertaken for the benefit of the ship's business, and if the ship's officers could reasonably have foreseen the assault.

shipper. 1. One who ships goods to another. **2.** One who tenders goods to a carrier for transportation.

shipping articles. *Maritime law.* A document (provided by a master of a vessel to the mariners) detailing voyage information, such as the voyage term, the number of crew, and the wage rates. 46 USCA § 10302.

shipping document. Any paper that covers a shipment in trade, such as a bill of lading or letter of credit.

shipping law. See LAW OF SHIPPING.

shipping order. A copy of the shipper's instructions to a carrier regarding the disposition of goods to be transported.

ship's husband. *Maritime law.* A person appointed to act as general agent of all the coowners of a ship, as by contracting for all necessary services, equipment, and supplies. Cf. EXERCITOR.

ship's papers. *Maritime law.* The papers that a vessel is required to carry to provide the primary evidence of the ship's national character, ownership, nature and destination of cargo, and compliance with navigation laws. • This evidence includes certificates of health, charterparty, muster-rolls, licenses, and bills of lading.

shipwreck. *Maritime law.* **1.** A ship's wreckage. **2.** The injury or destruction of a vessel because of circumstances beyond the owner's control, rendering the vessel incapable of carrying out its mission.

shire. A county in Great Britain (esp. England), originally made up of many hundreds but later consisting of larger divisions set off by metes and bounds.

shire-reeve. See REEVE.

***Shively* presumption** (**shɪv**-lee). The doctrine that any prestatehood grant of public property does not include tidelands unless the grant specifically indicates otherwise. *Shively v. Bowlby*, 152 U.S. 1, 14 S.Ct. 548 (1894); *United States v. Holt State Bank*, 270 U.S. 49, 46 S.Ct. 197 (1925). See EQUAL-FOOTING DOCTRINE.

shock, *n.* A profound and sudden disturbance of the physical or mental senses; a sudden and violent physical or mental impression depressing the body's vital forces, as by a sudden injury or medical procedure.

mental shock. Shock caused by agitation of the mental senses and resulting in extreme grief or joy, as by winning the lottery or witnessing the horrific death of a family member. Cf. EMOTIONAL DISTRESS.

physical shock. Shock caused by agitation of the physical senses, as from a sudden violent blow, impact, collision, or concussion.

shock incarceration. See INCARCERATION.

shock probation. See PROBATION.

shop, *n.* A business establishment or place of employment; a factory, office, or other place of business.

agency shop. A shop in which a union acts as an agent for the employees, regardless of their union membership.

closed shop. A shop in which the employer, by agreement with a union, hires and retains in employment only union members in good standing. • Closed shops were made illegal under the federal Labor–Management Relations Act. Cf. *closed union* under UNION.

open shop. A shop in which union membership is not a condition of employment. See RIGHT-TO-WORK LAW. Cf. *open union* under UNION.

preferential shop. A shop in which union members are given preference over nonunion members in employment matters.

union shop. A shop in which the employer may hire nonunion employees on the condition that they join a union within a specified time (usu. at least 30 days).

shop-book rule. *Evidence.* An exception to the hearsay rule permitting the admission into evidence of original bookkeeping records if the books' entries were made in the ordinary course of business and the books are introduced by somebody who maintains them.

shop books. Records of original entry maintained in the usual course of business by a shopkeeper, trader, or other businessperson. — Also termed *books of account*; *account books.*

shop committee. A union committee that resolves employee complaints within a union shop. See *union shop* under SHOP.

shoplifting, *n.* Theft of merchandise from a store or business; specif., larceny of goods from a store or other commercial establishment by willfully taking and concealing the merchandise with the intention of converting the goods to one's personal use without paying the purchase price. See LARCENY. — **shoplift,** *vb.*

> "Shoplifting is a form of larceny .... As a practical matter, however, the difficulty of proving the wrongful taking and the felonious intent requisites for a conviction under the general larceny statutes, together with the risk of retributory civil action against the shopkeeper consequent to acquittal of an accused shoplifter, have caused shoplifting to be established as a specific statutory crime in many jurisdictions." 50 Am. Jur. 2d *Larceny* § 71, at 79–80 (1995).

shop-right doctrine. The principle that an employer is entitled to a nonexclusive free license to use an employee's invention that the employee developed in the course of employment while using the employer's materials.

shop steward. See STEWARD (2).

shore. 1. Land lying between the lines of high- and low-water mark; lands bordering on the shores of navigable waters below the line of ordinary high water. **2.** Land adjacent to a body of water regardless of whether it is below or above the ordinary high- or low-water mark. — Also termed *shore land.*

short, *adj.* **1.** Not holding at the time of sale the security or commodity that is being sold in anticipation of a fall in price <the trader was short at the market's close>. **2.** Of or relating to a sale of securities or commodities not in the seller's possession at the time of sale <a short position>. See *short sale* under SALE. Cf. LONG.

short, *adv.* By a short sale <sold the stock short>. See *short sale* under SALE.

short, *vb.* To sell (a security or commodity) by a short sale <shorted 1,000 shares of Pantheon stock>. See *short sale* under SALE.

short-form agreement. *Labor law.* A contract usu. entered into by a small independent contractor whereby the contractor agrees to be bound by the terms of a collective-bargaining agreement negotiated between a union and a multiemployer bargaining unit.

short-form merger. See MERGER.

short interest. *Securities.* In a short sale, the number of shares that have not been purchased for return to lenders. See *short sale* under SALE.

short lease. See LEASE.

short position. The position of an investor who borrowed stock to make a short sale but has not yet purchased the stock to repay the lender. See *short sale* under SALE.

short sale. See SALE.

short sale against the box. See SALE.

short summons. See SUMMONS.

short-swing profits. Profits made by a corporate insider on the purchase and sale (or sale and purchase) of company stock within a six-month period. • These profits are subject to being returned to the company.

short-term capital gain. See CAPITAL GAIN.

short-term debt. See DEBT.

short-term loan. See LOAN.

short-term security. See SECURITY.

short-term trading. Investment in securities only to hold them long enough to profit from market-price fluctuations.

short-term trust. See *Clifford trust* under TRUST.

short title. See TITLE (3).

short ton. See TON.

shotgun instruction. See ALLEN CHARGE.

shotgun pleading. See PLEADING (1).

show, *vb.* To make (facts, etc.) apparent or clear by evidence; to prove.

show-cause order. See ORDER (2).

show-cause proceeding. A usu. expedited proceeding on a show-cause order. — Also termed *rule to show cause*; *summary process*; *summary procedure*; *expedited proceeding*.

shower (**shoh**-ər), *n.* A person commissioned by a court to take jurors to a place so that they may observe it as they consider a case on which they are sitting. See VIEW (3).

showing, *n.* The act or an instance of establishing through evidence and argument; proof <a prima facie showing>.

show trial. A trial, usu. in a nondemocratic country, that is staged primarily for propagandistic purposes, with the outcome predetermined.

showup, *n.* A pretrial identification procedure in which a suspect is confronted with a witness to or the victim of a crime. • Unlike a lineup, a showup is a one-on-one confrontation. Cf. LINEUP.

shrinkage. The reduction in inventory caused by theft, breakage, or waste.

shrink-wrap license. See LICENSE.

shutdown. A cessation of work production, esp. in a factory.

shut-in royalty. See ROYALTY (2).

shuttle diplomacy. See DIPLOMACY.

shyster (**shɪs**-tər). A person (esp. a lawyer) whose business affairs are unscrupulous, deceitful, or unethical.

si actio (sɪ **ak**-shee-oh), *n.* [Latin] *Hist.* The closing statement in a defendant's plea demanding judgment.

sic (sik). [Latin "so, thus"] Spelled or used as written. • *Sic*, invariably bracketed and usu. set in italics, is used to indicate that a preceding word or phrase in a quoted passage is reproduced as it appeared in the original document <"that case peeked [*sic*] the young lawyer's interest">.

sick leave. 1. An employment benefit allowing a worker time off for sickness, either with or without pay, but without loss of seniority or other benefits. **2.** The time so taken by an employee.

sickness and accident insurance. See *health insurance* under INSURANCE.

si constet de persona (sɪ **kon**-stet dee pər-**soh**-nə). [Latin] If it is certain who is the person meant.

si contingat (sɪ kon-**ting**-at). [Law Latin] If it happens. • This term was formerly used to describe conditions in a conveyance.

sicut alias (**sɪ**-kət **ay**-lee-əs), *n.* [Latin "as at another time"] *Hist.* A second writ issued when the first one was not executed.

> "But where a defendant absconds, and the plaintiff would proceed to an outlawry against him, an original writ must then be sued out regularly, and after that a *capias*. And if the sheriff cannot find the defendant upon the first writ . . . there issues out an *alias* writ, and after that a *pluries*, to the same effect as the former: only after these words 'we command you,' this clause is

inserted, 'as we have *formerly*,' or, 'as we have *often* commanded you;' '*sicut* alias' ...." 3 William Blackstone, *Commentaries on the Laws of England* 283 (1768).

sicut me Deus adjuvet (**sik**-ət mee **dee**-əs **aj**-ə-vet). [Latin] So help me God.

side, *n.* **1.** The position of a person or group opposing another <the law is on our side>. **2.** Either of two parties in a transaction or dispute <both sides put on a strong case>. **3.** *Archaic.* The field of a court's jurisdiction <equity side> <law side>.

sidebar. 1. A position at the side of a judge's bench where counsel can confer with the judge beyond the jury's earshot <the judge called the attorneys to sidebar>. **2.** SIDEBAR CONFERENCE <during the sidebar, the prosecutor accused the defense attorney of misconduct>. **3.** A short, secondary article within or accompanying a main story in a publication <the sidebar contained information on related topics>.

sidebar comment. An unnecessary, often argumentative remark made by an attorney or witness, esp. during a trial or deposition. — Often shortened to *sidebar.* — Also termed *sidebar remark.*

sidebar conference. 1. A discussion among the judge and counsel, usu. over an evidentiary objection, outside the jury's hearing. — Also termed *bench conference.* **2.** A discussion, esp. during voir dire, between the judge and a juror or prospective juror. — Often shortened to *sidebar.*

sidebar remark. See SIDEBAR COMMENT.

sidebar rule. *Hist. English law.* An order or rule allowed by the court without formal application, such as an order to plead within a particular time. • Formerly, the rules or orders were made on the motion of the attorneys at the sidebar in court.

side judge. See JUDGE.

side lines. 1. The margins of something, such as property. **2.** A different type of business or goods than one principally engages in or sells. **3.** *Mining law.* The boundary lines of a mining claim not crossing the vein running on each side of it. — Also written *sidelines.* Cf. END LINES.

sidenote. See MARGINAL NOTE.

side reports. 1. Unofficial volumes of case reports. **2.** Collections of cases omitted from the official reports.

sidesman. *Eccles. law.* A church officer who originally reported to the bishop on clerical and congregational misdeeds, including heretical acts, and later became a standing officer whose duties gradually devolved by custom on the churchwarden. — Also termed *synodsman; questman.*

Sierra–Mobile **doctrine.** See MOBILE–SIERRA DOCTRINE.

si fecerit te securum (sI **fes**-ər-it tee si-**kyoor**-əm). [Law Latin] *Hist.* If he has made you secure. • These were the initial words of a writ ordering the sheriff, upon receipt of security from the plaintiff, to compel the defendant's appearance in court. — Also spelled (erroneously) *se te fecerit securum.*

sight. A drawee's acceptance of a draft <payable after sight>. • The term *after sight* means "after acceptance."

sight draft. See DRAFT.

sigil (**sij**-əl), *n.* A seal or an abbreviated signature used as a seal; esp., a seal formerly used by civil-law notaries.

sigillum (si-**jil**-əm), *n.* [Latin] A seal, esp. one impressed on wax.

sigla (**sig**-lə), *n.* [Latin] *Roman law.* Abbreviations and signs used in writing.

sign, *vb.* **1.** To identify (a record) by means of a signature, mark, or other symbol with the intent to authenticate it as an act or agreement of the person identifying it <both parties signed the contract>. **2.** To agree with or join <the commissioner signed on for a four-year term>.

signal. 1. A means of communication, esp. between vessels at sea or between a vessel and the shore. • The international code of signals assigns arbitrary meanings to different arrangements of flags or light displays. **2.** In the citation of legal authority, an abbreviation or notation supplied to indicate some basic fact about the authority. • For example, according to the *Bluebook*, the signal *See* means that the cited authority directly states or supports the proposition, while *Cf.* means that the cited authority supports a proposition analogous to (but slightly different from) the main proposition. For these and other signals, see *The Bluebook: A Uniform System of Citation* § 1.2, at 22–24 (16th ed. 1996). — Also termed (in sense 2) *citation signal.*

signatorius anulus (sig-nə-**tor**-ee-əs **an**-yə-ləs), *n.* [Latin] *Roman law.* A signet ring.

signatory (**sig**-nə-tor-ee), *n.* A party that signs a document, personally or through an agent, and thereby becomes a party to an agreement <eight countries are signatories to the treaty>. — **signatory,** *adj.*

signature. 1. A person's name or mark written by that person or at the person's direction. **2.** *Commercial law.* Any name, mark, or writing used with the intention of authenticating a document. UCC §§ 1–201(39), 3–401(b). — Also termed *legal signature.*

> "The signature to a memorandum may be any symbol made or adopted with an intention, actual or apparent, to authenticate the writing as that of the signer." Restatement (Second) of Contracts § 134 (1979).

digital signature. A secure, digital code attached to an electronically transmitted message that uniquely identifies and authenticates the sender. • Digital signatures are esp. important for electronic commerce and are a key component of many electronic message-authentication schemes. Several states have passed legislation recognizing the legality of digital signatures. See E-COMMERCE.

***facsimile signature.* 1.** A signature that has been prepared and reproduced by mechanical or photographic means. **2.** A signature on a document that has been transmitted by a fascimile machine. See FAX.

private signature. *Civil law.* A signature made on a document (such as a will) that has not been witnessed or notarized.

unauthorized signature. A signature made without actual, implied, or apparent authority. • It includes a forgery. UCC § 1–201(43).

signature card. A financial-institution record consisting of a customer's signature and other information that assists the institution in monitoring financial transactions, as by comparing the signature on the record with signatures on checks, withdrawal slips, and other documents.

signature crime. See CRIME.

signature evidence. See EVIDENCE.

signature loan. See LOAN.

signed, sealed, and delivered. In a certificate of acknowledgment, a statement that the instrument was executed by the person acknowledging it. — Often shortened to *sealed and delivered.*

signet. 1. *Civil law.* An elaborate hand-drawn symbol (usu. incorporating a cross and the notary's initials) formerly placed at the base of notarial instruments, later replaced by a seal. **2.** *Scots law.* A seal used to authenticate summonses in civil matters before the Court of Session.

significant-relationship theory. See CENTER-OF-GRAVITY DOCTRINE.

significavit (sig-ni-fi-**kay**-vit), *n.* [Latin "he has signified"] *Eccles. law.* **1.** A bishop's certificate that a person has been in a state of excommunication for more than 40 days. **2.** A notice to the Crown in chancery, based on the bishop's certificate, whereby a writ *de contumace capiendo* (or, earlier, a writ *de excommunicato capiendo*) would issue for the disobedient person's arrest and imprisonment. See DE CONTUMACE CAPIENDO.

signum (**sig**-nəm), *n.* [Latin] *Roman law.* **1.** A sign; a seal.

> "Signum. (On written documents.) A seal (a stamp) put on to close a document in order to make its contents inaccessible to unauthorized persons and protect against forgery, or at the end of it after the written text. In the latter case the seal (without or with a signature) indicated that the sealer recognized the written declaration as his .... *Signum* is also the seal of a witness who was present at the making of a document." Adolf Berger, *Encyclopedic Dictionary of Roman Law* 707 (1953).

2. An indication of something seen or otherwise perceived by the senses, such as a bloodstain on a murder suspect. Pl. **signa.**

si ita est (sɪ ɪ-tə est). [Latin] If it be so. • This phrase was formerly used in a mandamus writ to order a judge to affix a seal to a bill of exceptions, if the facts were accurately stated.

si judicas, cognosce (sɪ **joo**-di-kəs, kog-**nos**-ee). [Latin] If you judge, inquire.

silence, *n.* **1.** A restraint from speaking. • In criminal law, silence includes an arrestee's statements expressing the desire not to speak and requesting an attorney. **2.** A failure to reveal something required by law to be revealed. See *estoppel by silence* under ESTOPPEL. — **silent,** *adj.*

silent confirmation. See CONFIRMATION.

silentiary (sI-len-shee-**air**-ee), *n.* **1.** *Roman law.* An official who maintains order in the imperial palace and on the imperial council; a chamberlain. **2.** *Hist.* An officer who is sworn to silence about state secrets; esp., a privy councillor so sworn. **3.** *Hist.* A court usher who maintains order and esp. silence in the court. — Also termed *silentiarius.*

silent partner. See PARTNER.

silent record. See RECORD.

silent-witness theory. *Evidence.* A method of authenticating and admitting evidence (such as a photograph), without the need for a witness to verify its authenticity, upon a sufficient showing of the reliability of the process of producing the evidence, including proof that the evidence has not been altered.

silk gown. 1. The professional robe worn by Queen's Counsel. **2.** One who is a Queen's Counsel. — Often shortened (in sense 2) to *silk.* Cf. STUFF GOWN.

silver certificates. U.S. paper money formerly in circulation and redeemable in silver. • Silver certificates have been replaced by Federal Reserve notes, which are not so redeemable.

silver parachute. See TIN PARACHUTE.

silver-platter doctrine. *Criminal procedure.* The principle that a federal court could allow the admission of evidence obtained illegally by a state police officer as long as a federal officer did not participate in or request the search. • The Supreme Court rejected this doctrine in *Elkins v. United States*, 364 U.S. 206, 80 S.Ct. 1437 (1960).

similar happenings. *Evidence.* Events that occur at a time different from the time in dispute and are therefore usu. inadmissible except to the extent that they provide relevant information on issues that would be fairly constant, such as the control of and conditions on land on the day in question.

similar sales. See SALE.

similiter (si-**mil**-i-tər). [Latin "similarly"] *Common-law pleading.* A party's written acceptance of an opponent's issue or argument; a set form of words by which a party accepts or joins in an issue of fact tendered by the other side. See *joinder of issue* (2) under JOINDER.

simony (**sim**-ə-nee *or* **sI**-mə-nee), *n.* [fr. Latin *simonia* "payment for things spiritual," fr. the proper name *Simon Magus* (see below)] *Hist. Eccles. law.* The unlawful practice of giving or receiving money or gifts in exchange for spiritual promotion; esp., the unlawful buying or selling of a right to present clergy to a vacant benefice.

> "By *simony*, the right of presentation to a living is forfeited, and vested *pro hac vice* in the crown. Simony is the corrupt presentation of any one to an ecclesiastical benefice for money, gift, or reward. It is so called from the resemblance it is said to bear to the sin of Simon Magus, though the purchasing of holy orders seems to approach nearer to his offence. It was by the canon law a very grievous crime: and is so much the more odious, because, as sir Edward Coke observes, it is ever accompanied with perjury; for the presentee is sworn to have committed no simony." 2 William Blackstone, *Commentaries on the Laws of England* 278 (1766).

> "Simony is an offence which consists in the buying and selling of holy orders, and any bond or contract involving simony is illegal and void." John Indermaur, *Principles of the Common Law* 195 (Edmund H. Bennett ed., 1st Am. ed. 1878).

simple, *adj.* **1.** (Of a crime) not accompanied by aggravating circumstances. Cf. AGGRAVATED. **2.** (Of an estate or fee) inheritable by the owner's heirs with no conditions concerning tail. **3.** (Of a contract) not made under seal.

simple agreement. See AGREEMENT.

simple assault. See ASSAULT.

simple average. See *particular average* under AVERAGE.

simple battery. See BATTERY.

simple bond. See BOND (2).

simple contract. See *parol contract* (2) under CONTRACT.

simple-contract debt. See DEBT.

simple interest. See INTEREST (3).

simple kidnapping. See KIDNAPPING.

simple larceny. See LARCENY.

simple listing. See *open listing* under LISTING (1).

simple majority. See MAJORITY.

simple mortgage clause. See *open mortgage clause* under MORTGAGE CLAUSE.

simple negligence. See NEGLIGENCE (1).

simple obligation. See OBLIGATION.

simple resolution. See RESOLUTION (1).

simple robbery. See ROBBERY.

simple state. See *unitary state* under STATE (1).

simple-tool rule. The principle that an employer has no duty to warn its employees of dangers that are obvious to everyone involved, and has no duty to inspect a tool that is within the exclusive control of an employee when that employee is fully acquainted with the tool's condition.

simple trust. See TRUST.

simplex (**sim**-pleks), *adj.* [Latin] Simple; pure; unconditional.

simplex dictum. See DICTUM.

simplex passagium (**sim**-pleks pə-**say**-jee-əm). [Law Latin] *Hist.* Simple passage (to the holy land alone). • This type of pilgrimage served as an excuse for absence from court during the Crusades. — Also termed *simplex peregrinatio.* Cf. IN GENERALI PASSAGIO.

simpliciter (sim-**plis**-i-tər), *adv.* [Latin] **1.** In a simple or summary manner; simply. **2.** Absolutely; unconditionally; per se.

simplified employee pension plan. See EMPLOYEE BENEFIT PLAN.

simplum (**sim**-pləm). [Latin] *Roman law.* The single value of something. Cf. DUPLUM.

simulated contract. See CONTRACT.

simulated fact. A fabricated fact intended to mislead; a lie.

simulated judgment. See JUDGMENT.

simulated sale. See SALE.

simulated transaction. See *simulated sale* under SALE.

simulatio latens (sim-yə-**lay**-shee-oh **lay**-tenz). [Latin "hidden pretence"] *Hist.* Feigned enhancement of illness, as when symptoms are present but not nearly as severe as is pretended.

simulation. 1. An assumption of an appearance that is feigned, false, or deceptive. **2.** *Civil law.* A feigned, pretended act, usu. to mislead or deceive. **3.** See *simulated contract* under CONTRACT.

simul cum (**sɪ**-məl kəm). [Latin] Together with. • This phrase was formerly used in an indictment or other instrument to indicate that a defendant had committed an injury jointly with others unknown.

simul et semel (**sɪ**-məl et **sem**-əl). [Latin] Together at one time.

simultaneous death. See DEATH.

simultaneous-death act. A statute providing that when two persons die under circumstances making it impossible to determine the order of their deaths (as in a common disaster), each person is presumed to have survived the other for purposes of distributing their respective estates. • Many states' simultaneous-death acts have been amended to require that a person survive the decedent by at least 120 hours to qualify as an heir or beneficiary. See COMMORIENTES.

simultaneous-death clause. A clause in a will providing for the disposition of property in the event of a simultaneous death. See *simultaneous death* under DEATH.

sine (**sɪ**-nee or **sin**-ay), *prep.* [Latin] Without.

sine animo revertendi (**sɪ**-nee **an**-ə-moh ree-vər-**ten**-dɪ). [Latin] Without the intention of returning. See *animus revertendi* under ANIMUS.

sine assensu capituli (**sɪ**-nee ə-**sen**-s[y]oo kə-**pich**-[y]ə-lɪ), *n.* [Law Latin "without the consent of the chapter"] *Hist.* A writ for a successor to recover land that the former bishop, abbot, or prior had alienated without the chapter's permission.

sine consideratione curiae (**sI**-nee kən-sid-ə-ray-shee-**oh**-nee **kyoor**-ee-I). [Law Latin] Without the judgment of the court.

sinecure (**sI**-nə-kyoor *or* **sin**-ə-kyoor). [fr. Latin *sine cura* "without duties"] *Hist.* A post without any duties attached; an office for which the holder receives a salary but has no responsibilities. — **sinecural** (**sI**-nə-kyoor-əl *or* sI-nə-**kyoor**-əl), *adj.*

sine decreto (**sI**-nee di-**kree**-toh). [Latin] Without a judge's authority.

sine die (**sI**-nee **dI**-ee *or* **dI** *or* **sin**-ay **dee**-ay). [Latin "without day"] With no day being assigned (as for resumption of a meeting or hearing). See GO HENCE WITHOUT DAY.

sine hoc quod (**sI**-nee hok **kwod**). [Law Latin] Without this, that. See ABSQUE HOC.

sine numero (**sI**-nee **n[y]oo**-mər-oh). [Law Latin "without number"] Countless; without limit.

sine prole (**sI**-nee **proh**-lee). [Latin] Without issue. • This phrase was used primarily in genealogical tables. — Abbr. s.p.

sine qua non (**sI**-nee kway **non** *or* **sin**-ay kwah **nohn**), *n.* [Latin "without which not"] An indispensable condition or thing; something on which something else necessarily depends.

single, *adj.* **1.** Unmarried <single tax status>. **2.** Consisting of one alone; individual <single condition> <single beneficiary>.

single-act statute. See LONG-ARM STATUTE.

single adultery. See ADULTERY.

single bill. See *bill single* under BILL (7).

single bond. See *bill obligatory* under BILL (7).

single combat. See DUEL (2).

single condition. See CONDITION (2).

single-controversy doctrine. See ENTIRE-CONTROVERSY DOCTRINE.

single creditor. See CREDITOR.

single-criminal-intent doctrine. See SINGLE-LARCENY DOCTRINE.

single-date-of-removal doctrine. *Civil procedure.* The principle that the deadline for removing a case from state court to federal court is 30 days from the day that any defendant receives a copy of the state-court pleading on which the removal is based. • If a later-served defendant seeks to remove a case to federal court more than 30 days after the day any other defendant received the pleading, the removal is untimely even if effectuated within 30 days after the removing defendant received the pleading. One theory underlying this doctrine is that all defendants must consent to remove a case to federal court, and a defendant who has waited longer than 30 days to remove does not have the capacity to consent to removal. 28 USCA § 1446(b). See NOTICE OF REMOVAL.

single demise. See DEMISE.

single-entry bookkeeping. See BOOKKEEPING.

single-filing rule. *Civil-rights law.* The principle that an administrative charge filed by one plaintiff in a civil-rights suit (esp. a Title VII suit) will satisfy the administrative-filing requirements for all coplaintiffs who are making claims for the same act of discrimination. • But this rule will not usu. protect a coplaintiff's claims if the coplaintiff also filed an administrative charge, against the same employer, in which different discriminatory acts were complained of, because the administrative agency (usu. the EEOC) and the employer are entitled to rely on the allegations someone makes in an administrative charge.

single-impulse plan. See SINGLE-LARCENY DOCTRINE.

single-juror instruction. See JURY INSTRUCTION.

single-larceny doctrine. *Criminal law.* The principle that the taking of different items of property either belonging to the same or different owners at the same time and place constitutes one act of larceny if the theft is part of one larcenous plan, as when it involves essentially one continuous act or if control over the property is exercised simultaneously. • The intent of the thief determines the number of occurrences. — Also termed *single-impulse plan*; *single-larceny rule*; *single-criminal-intent doctrine.*

single-name paper. A negotiable instrument signed by only one maker and not backed by a surety.

single obligation. See OBLIGATION.

single original. An instrument executed singly, not in duplicate.

single-premium insurance. See INSURANCE.

single-publication rule. The doctrine that a plaintiff in a libel suit against a publisher has only one claim for each mass publication, not a claim for every book or issue in that run.

single-purpose project. A facility that is designed, built, and used for one reason only, such as to generate electricity. • This term most often refers to large, complex, expensive projects such as power plants, chemical-processing plants, mines, and toll roads. Projects of this type are often funded through project financing, in which a special-purpose entity is established to perform no function other than to develop, own, and operate the facility, the idea being to limit the number of the entity's creditors and thus provide protection for the project's lenders. See *project financing* under FINANCING; SPECIAL-PURPOSE ENTITY; BANKRUPTCY-REMOTE ENTITY.

single-recovery rule. See ONE-SATISFACTION RULE.

singular, *adj.* **1.** Individual; each <all and singular>. **2.** *Civil law.* Of or relating to separate interests in property, rather than the estate as a whole <singular succession>.

singular successor. See SUCCESSOR.

singular title. See TITLE (2).

sinking fund. See FUND (1).

sinking-fund bond. See BOND (3).

sinking-fund debenture. See DEBENTURE.

sinking-fund depreciation method. See DEPRECIATION METHOD.

sinking-fund reserve. See RESERVE.

sinking-fund tax. See TAX.

si non omnes (sɪ non **om**-neez). [Latin "if not all"] *Hist.* A writ allowing two or more judges to proceed in a case if the whole commission cannot be present on the assigned day.

sin tax. See TAX.

SIPA (**see**-pə). *abbr.* SECURITIES INVESTOR PROTECTION ACT.

si paret (sɪ **par**-et). [Latin] If it appears. • In Roman law, this phrase was part of the praetor's formula by which judges were appointed and told how they were to decide.

SIPC. *abbr.* SECURITIES INVESTOR PROTECTION CORPORATION.

si prius (sɪ **prɪ**-əs). [Law Latin] If before. • This phrase is used in a writ summoning a jury.

si quis (sɪ **kwis**). [Latin] *Roman law.* If any one. • This term was used in praetorian edicts. In England, it was also mentioned in notices posted in parish churches requesting anyone who knows of just cause why a candidate for holy orders should not be ordained to inform the bishop.

SIR. *abbr.* SELF-INSURED RETENTION.

si recognoscat (sɪ rek-əg-**nos**-kat). [Latin "if he acknowledges"] *Hist.* A writ allowing a creditor to obtain money counted — that is, a specific sum that the debtor had acknowledged in county court to be owed.

sister. A female with the same parents as another.

sister corporation. See CORPORATION.

sister-in-law. **1.** The sister of one's spouse. **2.** The wife of one's brother. **3.** The wife of one's spouse's brother.

sistership exclusion. See EXCLUSION (3).

sistren, *n.* Sisters, esp. those considered spiritual kin (such as female colleagues on a court). Cf. BRETHREN.

sit, *vb.* **1.** (Of a judge) to occupy a judicial seat <Judge Wilson sits on the trial court for the Eastern District of Arkansas>. **2.** (Of a judge) to hold court or perform official functions <is the judge sitting this week?>. **3.** (Of a court or legislative body) to hold proceedings <the U.S. Supreme Court sits from October to June>.

sit-down strike. See STRIKE.

site. 1. A place or location; esp., a piece of property set aside for a specific use. **2.** SCITE.

site plan. A proposal for the development or use of a particular piece of real property. • Some zoning ordinances require a developer to present a site plan to the city council, and to receive council approval, before certain projects may be completed.

sitting, *n.* A court session; esp., a session of an appellate court.

en banc sitting. A court session in which all the judges (or a quorum) participate. See EN BANC.

in camera sitting. A court session conducted by a judge in chambers or elsewhere outside the courtroom. See IN CAMERA.

situation. 1. Condition; position in reference to circumstances <dangerous situation>. **2.** The place where someone or something is occupied; a location <situation near the border>.

situation of danger. See DANGEROUS SITUATION.

situs (sɪ-təs). [Latin] The location or position (of something) for legal purposes, as in *lex situs*, the law of the place where the thing in issue is situated.

Six Clerks. *Hist.* A collective name for the clerks of the English Court of Chancery who filed pleadings and other papers. • The office was abolished in 1842, and its duties transferred to the Clerk of Enrollments in Chancery and to the Clerks of Records and Writs.

Sixteenth Amendment. The constitutional amendment, ratified in 1913, allowing Congress to tax income.

Sixth Amendment. The constitutional amendment, ratified with the Bill of Rights in 1791, guaranteeing in criminal cases the right to a speedy and public trial by jury, the right to be informed of the nature of the accusation, the right to confront witnesses, the right to counsel, and the right to compulsory process for obtaining favorable witnesses.

sixth-sentence remand. See REMAND.

sixty clerks. See SWORN CLERKS IN CHANCERY.

sixty-day notice. *Labor law.* Under the Taft–Hartley Act, the 60–day advance notice required for either party to a collective-bargaining agreement to reopen or terminate the contract. • During this period, strikes and lockouts are prohibited. 29 USCA § 158(d)(1).

S.J.D. See DOCTOR OF JURIDICAL SCIENCE.

skeleton bill. See BILL (7).

skeleton bill of exceptions. See BILL (2).

skill. Ability; proficiency, esp. the practical and familiar knowledge of the principles and processes of an art, science, or trade, combined with the ability to apply them appropriately, with readiness and dexterity.

skilled witness. See *expert witness* under WITNESS.

skilled work. See WORK.

skip bail. See JUMP BAIL.

skip person. *Tax.* A beneficiary who is more than one generation removed from the transferor and to whom assets are conveyed in a generation-skipping transfer. IRC (26 USCA) § 2613(a). See GENERATION-SKIPPING TRANSFER.

> "Since a skip person is necessary to trigger a generation-skipping tax, it is important to have a precise definition of 'skip person.' In most cases, it suffices to say that a skip person is a person who is two or more generations younger than the transferor." John K. McNulty, *Federal Estate and Gift Taxation in a Nutshell* 63 (5th ed. 1994).

skiptracing agency. A service that locates persons (such as delinquent debtors, missing heirs, witnesses, stockholders, bondholders, etc.) or missing assets (such as bank accounts).

S.L. *abbr.* **1.** Session law. See SESSION LAWS. **2.** Statute law.

slamming. The practice by which a long-distance telephone company wrongfully appropriates a customer's service from another company, usu. through an unauthorized transfer or by way of a transfer authorization that is disguised as something else, such as a form to sign up for a free vacation.

slander, *n.* **1.** A defamatory statement expressed in a transitory form, esp. speech. • Damages for slander — unlike those for libel — are not presumed and thus must be proved by the plaintiff (unless the defamation is slander per se). **2.** The act of making such a statement. — **slander,** *vb.* — **slanderous,** *adj.* See DEFAMATION. Cf. LIBEL (1).

> "Although libel and slander are for the most part governed by the same principles, there are two important differences: (1) Libel is not merely an actionable tort, but also a criminal offence, whereas slander is a civil injury only. (2) Libel is in all cases actionable *per se*; but slander is, save in special cases, actionable only on proof of actual damage. This distinction has been severely criticised as productive of great injustice." R.F.V. Heuston, *Salmond on the Law of Torts* 139 (17th ed. 1977).

slander per quod. Slander that does not qualify as slander per se, thus forcing the plaintiff to prove special damages.

slander per se. Slander for which special damages need not be proved because it imputes to the plaintiff any one of the following: (1) a crime involving moral turpitude, (2) a loathsome disease (such as a sexually transmitted disease), (3) conduct that would adversely affect one's business or profession, or (4) unchastity (esp. of a woman).

slanderer, *n.* One who commits slander.

slander of goods. See DISPARAGEMENT.

slander of title. A false statement, made orally or in writing, that casts doubt on another person's ownership of property. See DISPARAGEMENT.

slander per quod. See SLANDER.

slander per se. See SLANDER.

SLAPP (slap). *abbr.* A strategic lawsuit against public participation — that is, a suit brought by a developer, corporate executive, or elected official to stifle those who protest against some type of high-dollar initiative or who take an adverse position on a public-interest issue (often involving the environment). — Also termed *SLAPP suit.*

slate. A list of candidates, esp. for political office or a corporation's board of directors.

slavery. 1. A situation in which one person has absolute power over the life, fortune, and liberty of another. **2.** The practice of keeping individuals in such a state of bondage or servitude. • Slavery was outlawed by the 13th Amendment to the U.S. Constitution.

> "Slavery was a big problem for the Constitution makers. Those who profited by it insisted on protecting it; those who loathed it dreaded even more the prospect that to insist on abolition would mean that the Constitution would die aborning. So the Framers reached a compromise, of sorts. The words 'slave' and 'slavery' would never be mentioned, but the Constitution would safeguard the 'peculiar institution' from the abolitionists." Jethro K. Lieberman, *The Evolving Constitution* 493 (1992).

slavery, badge of. See BADGE OF SLAVERY.

slay, *vb.* To kill (a person), esp. in battle.

slayer's rule. The doctrine that neither a person who kills another nor the killer's heirs can share in the decedent's estate.

SL/C. See *standby letter of credit* under LETTER OF CREDIT.

SLC. *abbr.* SPECIAL LITIGATION COMMITTEE.

sleeper. A security that has strong market potential but is underpriced and lacks investor interest.

sleeping partner. See *secret partner* under PARTNER.

sliding scale. A pricing method in which prices are determined by a person's ability to pay.

slight care. See CARE.

slight diligence. See DILIGENCE.

slight evidence. See EVIDENCE.

slight negligence. See NEGLIGENCE.

slip-and-fall case. 1. A lawsuit brought by a plaintiff for injuries sustained in slipping and falling, usu. on the defendant's property. **2.** Loosely, any minor case in tort.

slip decision. See *slip opinion* under OPINION (1).

slip law. An individual pamphlet in which a single enactment is printed immediately after its passage but before its inclusion in the general laws (such as the session laws or the *U.S. Statutes at Large*). — Also termed *slip-law print.*

slip opinion. See OPINION (1).

slough. **1.** (sloo) An arm of a river, separate from the main channel. **2.** (slow) A bog; a place filled with deep mud.

slowdown. An organized effort by workers to decrease production to pressure the employer to take some desired action.

slump, *n.* A temporary downturn in the economy and in the stock market in particular, characterized by falling market prices.

slush fund. Money that is set aside for undesignated purposes, often corrupt ones, and that is not subject to financial procedures designed to ensure accountability.

Small Business Administration. A federal agency that assists and protects the interests of small businesses, often by making low-interest loans. — Abbr. SBA.

small-business concern. A business qualifying for an exemption from freight undercharges because it is independently owned and operated and is not dominant in its field of operation, with limited numbers of employees and business volume. 15 USCA § 632. — Often shortened to *small business*.

small-business corporation. See CORPORATION.

Small Business Investment Act. A federal law, originally enacted in 1958, under which investment companies may be formed and licensed to supply long-term equity capital to small businesses. • The statute is implemented by the Small Business Administration. 15 USCA §§ 661 et seq.

small-business investment company. A corporation created under state law to provide long-term equity capital to small businesses, as provided under the Small Business Investment Act and regulated by the Small Business Administration. 15 USCA §§ 661 et seq. — Abbr. SBIC.

small claim. A claim for damages at or below a specified monetary amount. See *small-claims court* under COURT.

small-claims court. See COURT.

small-debts court. See *small-claims court* under COURT.

small-estate probate. See PROBATE.

small-loan act. A state law fixing the maximum legal rate of interest and other terms on small, short-term loans by banks and finance companies.

small-loan company. See *consumer finance company* under FINANCE COMPANY.

smart money. **1.** Funds held by sophisticated, usu. large investors who are considered capable of minimizing risks and maximizing profits <the smart money has now left this market>. **2.** See *punitive damages* under DAMAGES <although the jury awarded only $7,000 in actual damages, it also awarded $500,000 in smart money>.

Smith Act. A 1948 federal antisedition law that criminalizes advocating the forcible or violent overthrow of the government. 18 USCA § 2385.

> "The Smith Act is aimed at the advocacy and teaching of concrete action for the forcible overthrow of the government, and not at advocacy of principles divorced from action. The essential distinction is that those to whom the advocacy is addressed must be urged to do something, now or in the future, rather than merely to believe in something." 70 Am. Jur. 2d *Sedition, Etc.* § 63, at 59 (1987).

smoking gun. A piece of physical or documentary evidence that conclusively impeaches an adversary on an outcome-determinative issue or destroys the adversary's credibility.

smuggling, *n.* The crime of importing or exporting illegal articles or articles on which duties have not been paid. — **smuggle,** *vb.* See CONTRABAND.

sober, *adj.* **1.** (Of a person) not drunk. **2.** (Of a person) regularly abstinent or moderate in the use of intoxicating liquors. **3.** (Of a situation, person, etc.) serious; grave. **4.** (Of facts, arguments, etc.) basic; unexaggerated. **5.** (Of a person) rational; having self-control.

sobrestadia. See ESTADIA.

sobriety checkpoint. A part of a roadway at which police officers maintain a roadblock to stop motorists and ascertain whether the drivers are intoxicated.

sobriety test. A method of determining whether a person is intoxicated. • Among the common sobriety tests are coordination tests and the use of mechanical devices to measure the blood alcohol content of a person's breath sample. See BREATHALYZER.

field sobriety test. A motor-skills test administered by a peace officer during a stop to determine whether a suspect has been driving while intoxicated. • The test usu. involves checking the suspect's speaking ability or coordination (as by reciting the alphabet or walking in a straight line). — Abbr. FST.

sobrini (sə-**brI**-nI), *n.* [Latin] *Roman law.* Children of first cousins; second cousins.

soca (**sok**-ə *or* **soh**-kə), *n.* [Law Latin] *Hist.* A seigniory granted the privilege of holding a tenant's court.

socage (**sok**-ij). *Hist.* A type of tenure in which a tenant held lands in exchange for providing the lord husbandry-related (rather than military) service. • Socage, the great residuary tenure, was any free tenure that did not fall within the definition of knight-service, serjeanty, or frankalmoin. Cf. KNIGHT-SERVICE; VILLEINAGE.

> "If they [the peasant's duties] were fixed — for instance, helping the lord with sowing or reaping at specified times — the tenure was usually called *socage.* This was originally the tenure of *socmen*; but it became ... a generic term for all free services other than knight-service, serjeanty, or spiritual service." J.H. Baker, *An Introduction to English Legal History* 260 (3d ed. 1990).

free socage. Socage in which the services were both certain and honorable. • By the statute 12 Car. 2, ch. 24 (1660), all the tenures by knight-service were, with minor exceptions, converted into free socage. — Also termed *free and common socage*; *liberum socagium.*

villein socage (**vil**-ən). Socage in which the services, though certain, were of a baser nature than those provided under free socage.

socager (**sok**-ij-ər). A tenant by socage; SOCMAN.

socer (**soh**-sər), *n.* [Latin] *Roman law.* A father-in-law.

social contract. The express or implied agreement between citizens and their government by which individuals agree to surrender certain freedoms in exchange for mutual protection; an agreement forming the foundation of a political society. • The term is primarily associated with political philosophers, such as Thomas Hobbes, John Locke, and esp. Jean Jacques Rousseau, though it can be traced back to the Greek Sophists.

social cost. See COST (1).

social guest. See GUEST.

social harm. See HARM.

social insurance. See INSURANCE.

social justice. See JUSTICE (1).

Social Security Act. A federal law, originally established in 1935 in response to the Great Depression, creating a system of benefits, including old-age and survivors' benefits, and establishing the Social Security Administration. 42 USCA §§ 401–433.

Social Security Administration. A federal agency created by the Social Security Act to institute a national program of social insurance. — Abbr. SSA.

social-service state. See STATE (1).

socida (sə-**sI**-də), *n.* [Latin] *Civil law.* A contract of bailment by which the bailee assumes the risk of loss; specif., a bailment by which a person delivers animals to another for a fee, on the condition that if any animals perish, the bailee will be liable for the loss.

societas (sə-**sI**-ə-tas), *n.* [Latin] *Roman law.* A partnership between two or more people agreeing to share profits and losses; a partnership contract.

societas leonina (sə-**sI**-ə-tas lee-ə-**nI**-nə), *n.* [Latin "partnership with a lion"] *Roman law.* An illegal partnership in which the profits are distributed to only a few partners to the exclusion of the others; a partnership in which one person takes the lion's share. — Also termed *leonina societas.*

> "But an arrangement by which one party should have *all* the gain was not recognized as binding; it was considered as contrary to the nature and purposes of the *societas,* the aim of which was gain for all the parties concerned. Such an arrangement the lawyers called *societas leonina,* a partnership like that which the lion in the fable imposed upon the cow, the sheep, and the she-goat, his associates in the chase." James Hadley, *Introduction to Roman Law* 231–32 (1881).

societas navalis (sə-**sI**-ə-tas nə-**vay**-lis), *n.* [Latin] *Hist.* A naval partnership; an assembly of vessels for mutual protection. — Also termed *admiralitas.*

societas universorum bonorum (sə-**sɪ**-ə-tas yoo-ni-vər-**sor**-əm bə-**nor**-əm), *n. Hist.* An entire partnership, including all the individual partners' property.

société (soh-see-ay-**tay**), *n.* [French] *French law.* A partnership.

société anonyme (soh-see-ay-**tay** an-aw-**neem**), *n.* [French] *French law.* An incorporated joint-stock company.

société d'acquêts (soh-see-ay-**tay** dah-**kay**), *n.* [French] *French law.* A written agreement between husband and wife designating community property to be only that property acquired during marriage.

société en commandite (soh-see-ay-**tay** aw*n* koh-maw*n*-**deet**), *n.* [French] *French law.* A limited partnership.

société en nom collectif (soh-see-ay-**tay** aw*n* naw*n* koh-lek-**teef**), *n.* [French] *French law.* A partnership in which all members are jointly and severally liable for the partnership debts; an ordinary partnership.

société en participation (soh-see-ay-**tay** aw*n* pahr-tee-see-pah-**syawn**), *n. French law.* A joint venture.

société par actions (soh-see-ay-**tay** pahr ak-**syawn**), *n. French law.* A joint-stock company.

society. 1. A community of people, as of a state, nation, or locality, with common cultures, traditions, and interests.

civil society. The political body of a state or nation; the body politic.

2. An association or company of persons (usu. unincorporated) united by mutual consent, to deliberate, determine, and act jointly for a common purpose. **3.** The general love, affection, and companionship that family members share with one another.

sociological jurisprudence. See JURISPRUDENCE.

sociology of law. See *sociological jurisprudence* under JURISPRUDENCE.

sociopath, *n.* See PSYCHOPATH. — **sociopathy,** *n.* — **sociopathic,** *adj.*

socius (**soh**-shee-əs), *n.* [Latin] *Roman law.* **1.** A business partner. **2.** An accomplice; an accessory. **3.** A political ally. Pl. ***socii*** (**soh**-shee-ɪ).

socius criminis (**soh**-shee-əs **krim**-ə-nis). An associate in crime; an accomplice.

sockman. See SOCMAN.

socman (**sok**-mən). *Hist.* A person who holds land by socage tenure. — Also spelled *sokeman*; *sockman.* — Also termed *socager*; *gainor.* See SOCAGE.

socmanry (**sok**-mən-ree). *Hist.* **1.** Free tenure by socage. **2.** Land and tenements held only by simple services; land enfranchised by the sovereign from ancient demesne. • The tenants were socmen. **3.** The state of being a socman.

socna (**sok**-nə). *Hist.* A privilege; a liberty; a franchise.

Socratic method. A technique of philosophical discussion — and of law-school instruction — by which the questioner (a law professor) questions one or more followers (the law students), building on each answer with another question, esp. an analogy incorporating the answer. • This method takes its name from the Greek philosopher Socrates, who lived in Athens from about 469–399 B.C. His method is a traditional one in law schools, primarily because it forces law students to think through issues rationally and deductively — a skill required in the practice of law. Most law professors who employ this method call on students randomly, an approach designed to teach students to think quickly, without stage fright.

> "[Socrates] himself did not profess to be capable of teaching anything, except consciousness of ignorance.... He called his method of discussion (the *Socratic method*) *obstetrics* ... because it was an art of inducing his interlocutors to develop their own ideas under a catechetical system." 5 *The Century Dictionary and Cyclopedia* 5746 (rev. ed. 1914).

SODDI defense (**sahd**-ee). *Slang.* The some-other-dude-did-it defense; a claim that somebody else committed a crime, usu. made by a criminal defendant who cannot identify the third party.

sodomy (**sod**-ə-mee), *n.* **1.** Oral or anal copulation between humans, esp. those of the same sex. **2.** Oral or anal copulation between a human and an animal; bestiality. — Also termed *buggery*; *crime against nature*; *abominable and detestable crime against nature*; *unnatural offense*; *unspeakable crime*; (archaically) *sodomitry.* — **sodomize,** *vb.* — **sodomitic,** *adj.* — **sodomist, sodomite,** *n.* Cf. PEDERASTY.

> "Sodomitry is a carnal copulation against nature; to wit, of man or woman in the same sex, or of either of them with beasts." Sir Henry Finch, *Law, or a Discourse Thereof* 219 (1759).

> "Sodomy was not a crime under the common law of England but was an ecclesiastical offense only. It was made a felony by an English statute so early that it is a common-law felony in this country, and statutes expressly making it a felony were widely adopted. 'Sodomy' is a generic term including both 'bestiality' and 'buggery.'" Rollin M. Perkins & Ronald N. Boyce, *Criminal Law* 465 (3d ed. 1982).

aggravated sodomy. Criminal sodomy that involves force or results in serious bodily injury to the victim in addition to mental injury and emotional distress. • Some laws provide that sodomy involving a minor is automatically aggravated sodomy.

SOF. *abbr.* STATUTE OF FRAUDS.

soft currency. See CURRENCY.

soft dollars. 1. *Securities.* The credits that brokers give their clients in return for the clients' stock-trading business. **2.** The portion of an equity investment that is tax-deductible in the first year. Cf. HARD DOLLARS.

soft goods. See GOODS.

soft law. 1. Collectively, rules that are neither strictly binding nor completely lacking in legal significance. **2.** *Int'l law.* Guidelines, policy declarations, or codes of conduct that set standards of conduct but are not directly enforceable.

soft market. See MARKET.

soft sell. A low-key sales practice characterized by sincerity and professionalism. Cf. HARD SELL.

so help me God. The final words of the common oath. • The phrase is a translation, with a change to first person, of the Latin phrase *ita te Deus adjuvet* "so help you God." See ITA TE DEUS ADJUVET.

soil bank. A federal agricultural program in which farmers are paid to not grow crops or to grow noncommercial vegetation, to preserve the quality of the soil and stabilize commodity prices by avoiding surpluses.

soit (swah). [Law French] Be; let it be. • This term was used in English-law phrases, esp. to indicate the will of the sovereign in a formal communication with Parliament.

soit baile aux commons (swah **bayl** oh **kom**-ənz). [Law French] Let it be delivered to the commons. • This is an indorsement on a bill sent to the House of Commons.

soit baile aux seigneurs (swah **bayl** oh sen-**yərz**). [Law French] Let it be delivered to the lords. • This is an indorsement on a bill sent to the House of Lords.

soit droit fait al partie (swah **droyt** [*or* **drwah**] **fayt** [*or* **fay**] ahl pahr-**tee**). [Law French] *Hist.* Let right be done to the party. • This phrase is written on a petition of right and subscribed by the Crown.

soit fait comme il est desire (swah **fay**[**t**] **kawm** eel ay day-zeer-**ay**). [Law French] Let it be as it is desired. • This is the phrase indicating royal assent to a private act of Parliament.

sojourn (**soh**-jərn), *n.* A temporary stay by someone who is not just passing through a place but is also not a permanent resident <she set up a three-month sojourn in France>. — **sojourn** (**soh**-jərn *or* soh-**jərn**), *vb.* — **sojourner** (**soh**-jər-nər *or* soh-**jər**-nər), *n.*

sokeman. See SOCMAN.

soke-reeve (**sohk**-reev). *Hist.* The lord's rent-collector in the soca.

solar day. See DAY.

solar easement. See EASEMENT.

solarium (sə-**lair**-ee-əm), *n.* [Latin fr. *solum* "soil"] *Roman law.* Rent paid for building on public land; ground rent.

solar month. See MONTH.

solatium (sə-**lay**-shee-əm), *n.* [Latin "solace"] *Scots law.* Compensation; esp., damages allowed for hurt feelings or grief, as distinguished from damages for physical injury.

Soldiers' and Sailors' Civil Relief Act. A federal law, originally enacted in 1940, protecting the civil rights of persons in military service, as by modifying their civil liability, placing limits on interest rates charged against their obligations, and prescribing specific procedures for claims made against them. 50 USCA app. §§ 501 et seq.

soldier's will. See WILL.

sold note. **1.** See NOTE. **2.** See CONFIRMATION SLIP.

sole-actor doctrine. *Agency.* The rule charging a principal with knowledge of the agent's actions, even if the agent acted fraudulently.

sole and separate use. See *entire use* under USE (4).

sole and unconditional owner. See OWNER.

sole cause. See CAUSE (1).

sole corporation. See CORPORATION.

sole custody. See CUSTODY (2).

solemn admission. See *judicial admission* under ADMISSION (1).

solemnes legum formulae (sə-**lem**-neez **lee**-gəm **for**-myə-lee). [Latin] *Roman law.* Legal formalities required in early Roman law, esp. in civil as opposed to praetorian law.

solemnitas attachiamentorum (sə-**lem**-ni-tas ə-tach-ee-ə-men-**tor**-əm). [Law Latin] *Hist.* The formality required in issuing attachments of property.

solemnity (sə-**lem**-nə-tee). **1.** A formality (such as a ceremony) required by law to validate an agreement or action <solemnity of marriage>. **2.** The state of seriousness or solemn respectfulness or observance <solemnity of contract>.

solemnity of contract. The concept that two people may enter into any contract they wish and that the resulting contract is enforceable if formalities are observed and no defenses exist.

solemnization. The performance of a formal marriage ceremony before witnesses, as distinguished from a clandestine or common-law marriage.

solemnize (**sol**-əm-nɪz), *vb.* To enter into (a marriage, contract, etc.) by a formal act, usu. before witnesses. — **solemnization** (sol-əm-ni-**zay**-shən), *n.*

solemn occasion. In some states, the serious and unusual circumstance in which the supreme court is constitutionally permitted to render advisory opinions to the remaining branches of government, as when the legislature doubts the legality of proposed legislation and a determination must be made to allow the legislature to exercise its functions. • Some factors that have been considered in determining if a solemn occasion exists include whether an important question of law is presented, whether the question is urgent, whether the matter is ripe for an opinion, and whether the court has enough time to consider the question.

solemn war. See WAR.

sole practitioner. A lawyer who practices law without any partners or associates. — Also termed *solo practitioner.* — Often shortened to *solo.*

sole proprietorship. **1.** A business in which one person owns all the assets, owes all the liabilities, and operates in his or her personal capacity. **2.** Ownership of such a business. — Also termed *individual proprietorship.*

sole-source rule. In a false-advertising action at common law, the principle that a plaintiff may not recover unless it can demonstrate that it has a monopoly in the sale of goods possessing the advertised trait, because only then is it clear that the plaintiff would be harmed by the defendant's advertising.

sole use. See *entire use* under USE (4).

solicitation, *n.* **1.** The act or an instance of requesting or seeking to obtain something; a request or petition <a solicitation for volunteers to handle at least one pro bono case per year>. **2.** The criminal offense of urging, advising, commanding, or otherwise inciting another to commit a crime <convicted of solicitation of murder>. • Solicitation is an inchoate offense distinct from the solicited crime. — Also termed *criminal solicitation*; *incitement.* Cf. ATTEMPT (2). **3.** An offer to pay or accept money in exchange for sex <the prostitute was charged with solicitation>. **4.** An attempt or effort to gain business <the attorney's solicitations took the form of radio and television ads>. • The Model Rules of Professional Conduct place certain prohibitions on lawyers' direct solicitation of potential clients. **5.** *Securities.* A request for a proxy; a request to execute, not execute, or revoke a proxy; the furnishing of a form of proxy; or any other communication to security holders under circumstances reasonably calculated to result in the procurement, withholding, or revocation of a proxy. — **solicit,** *vb.*

solicitation for bids. See INVITATION TO NEGOTIATE.

solicitation of bribe. The crime of asking or enticing another to commit bribery. 18 USCA § 201. See BRIBERY.

solicitee. One who is solicited. See SOLICITATION.

soliciting agent. See AGENT.

solicitor. 1. A person who seeks business or contributions from others; an advertiser or promoter. **2.** A person who conducts matters on another's behalf; an agent or representative. **3.** The chief law officer of a governmental body or a municipality. **4.** In the United Kingdom, a legal adviser who consults with clients and prepares legal documents but is not generally heard in High Court or (in Scotland) Court of Session unless specially licensed. Cf. BARRISTER. **5.** See *special agent* under INSURANCE AGENT.

solicitor general. The second-highest-ranking legal officer in a government (after the attorney general); esp., the chief courtroom lawyer for the executive branch. — Abbr. SG. Pl. **solicitors general.**

solidarity. The state of being jointly and severally liable (as for a debt). See *solidary obligation* under OBLIGATION.

solidary (**sol**-ə-der-ee), *adj.* (Of a liability or obligation) joint and several. See JOINT AND SEVERAL.

> "It is a single debt of £100 owing by each of them, in such fashion that each of them may be compelled to pay the whole of it, but that when it is once paid by either of them, both are discharged from it. Obligations of this description may be called solidary, since in the language of Roman law, each of the debtors is bound *in solidum* instead of *pro parte*; that is to say, for the whole, and not for a proportionate part. A solidary obligation, therefore, may be defined as one in which two or more debtors owe the same thing to the same creditor." John Salmond, *Jurisprudence* 462–63 (Glanville L. Williams ed., 10th ed. 1947).

solidary liability. See LIABILITY.

solidary obligation. See OBLIGATION.

solidum (**sol**-ə-dəm), *n.* [Latin] *Roman law.* A whole; an undivided thing. See SOLIDARY.

solinum (sə-**lI**-nəm), *n.* [Law Latin] *Hist.* **1.** Slightly less than two and a half plowlands. **2.** A single plowland.

solitary confinement. Separate confinement that gives a prisoner extremely limited access to other people; esp., the complete isolation of a prisoner.

solo, *n.* See SOLE PRACTITIONER.

solo practitioner. See SOLE PRACTITIONER.

solum italicum (**soh**-ləm I-**tal**-ə-kəm), *n.* [Latin "Italian land"] *Roman law.* Land in Italy (an extension of the old *ager Romanus*) usu. held by one having full ownership and power to transfer the property by formal methods, such as *mancipatio*. Cf. *solum provinciale*.

solum provinciale (**soh**-ləm prə-vin-shee-**ay**-lee), *n.* [Latin "provincial land"] *Roman law.* Provincial land (an extension of the old *ager Publicus*) ultimately held by the Emperor or state, with private holders having only a possessory title without the right to transfer the property by formal methods, as distinguished from *solum italicum*. • Justinian abolished all distinctions between the two, simplifying the conveyance of both types of land. Cf. SOLUM ITALICUM.

> "Ownership of provincial land. The *dominium* of this was in Caesar or the *populus* according as it was an imperial or a senatorial province .... The holders were practically owners, but as they were not *domini* formal methods of transfer were not applicable. The holdings were however transferable informally .... The case disappeared when Justinian abolished the distinction between Italic and provincial land. Not all land in the provinces was *solum provinciale*: many provincial communities were given *ius italicum*, the chief result being that the land was in the *dominium* of the holder and not of the State, so that it could be transferred and claimed at law by civil law methods." W.W. Buckland, *A Textbook of Roman Law: From Augustus to Justinian* 190 (Peter Stein ed., 3d ed. 1963).

solutio (sə-**loo**-shee-oh), *n.* [Latin fr. *solvere* "to pay"] *Roman law.* Payment of an obligation; satisfaction.

solutio indebiti (sə-**loo**-shee-oh in-**deb**-ə-tI). [Latin "payment of what is not owing"] *Roman law.* Payment of a nonexistent debt. • If the payment was made by a mistake of fact, the recipient had a duty to give back the money.

solutio obligationis (sə-**loo**-shee-oh ob-li-gay-shee-**oh**-nis). *Roman law.* The unfastening of a legal bond, so that a party previously bound need not perform any longer. Cf. VINCULUM JURIS.

solutus (sə-**loo**-təs). [Latin fr. *solvere* "to loose"] **1.** *Roman law.* Set free; released from confinement. **2.** *Scots law.* Purged, esp. in reference to counsel.

solvabilité (sawl-vah-beel-ee-**tay**), *n.* [French] *French law.* Solvency.

solvency, *n.* The ability to pay debts as they come due. — **solvent,** *adj.* Cf. INSOLVENCY.

solvendo esse (sol-**ven**-doh **es**-ee). [Latin] *Hist.* To be solvent; to be able to pay an obligation.

solvendum in futuro (sol-**ven**-dəm in f[y]oo-**t[y]oor**-oh). [Latin "to be paid in the future"] *Hist.* (Of a debt) due now but payable in the future.

solvere (**sol**-və-ree), *vb.* [Latin "to unbind"] *Roman law.* To pay (a debt); to release (a person) from an obligation.

solvere poenas (səl-**veer**-ee **pee**-nəs). [Latin] *Hist.* To pay the penalty.

solvit (**sol**-vit). [Latin] He paid; paid.

solvit ad diem (**sol**-vit ad **dɪ**-əm). [Law Latin "he paid on the day"] *Hist.* In a debt action, a plea that the defendant paid the debt on the due date.

solvit ante diem (**sol**-vit **an**-tee **dɪ**-əm). [Law Latin "he paid before the day"] *Hist.* In a debt action, a plea that the defendant paid the money before the due date.

solvit post diem (**sol**-vit pohst **dɪ**-əm). [Law Latin "he paid after the day"] *Hist.* In a debt action on a bond, a plea that the defendant paid the debt after the due date but before commencement of the lawsuit.

somnambulism (sahm-**nam**-byə-liz-əm). Sleepwalking. • Generally, a person will not be held criminally responsible for an act performed while in this state.

somnolentia (sahm-nə-**len**-shee-ə). **1.** The state of drowsiness. **2.** A condition of incomplete sleep resembling drunkenness, during which part of the faculties are abnormally excited while the others are dormant; the combined condition of sleeping and wakefulness producing a temporary state of involuntary intoxication. • To the extent that it destroys moral agency, somnolentia may be a defense to a criminal charge.

son. 1. A person's male child. **2.** An immediate male descendant. **3.** An adopted male child or dependent. **4.** Loosely, any young male person.

son assault demesne (sohn ə-**sawlt** di-**mayn**). [French "his own assault"] The plea of self-defense in a tort action, by which the defendant alleges that the plaintiff originally engaged in an assault and that the defendant used only the force necessary to repel the plaintiff's assault and to protect person and property. See SELF-DEFENSE.

son-in-law. The husband of one's daughter.

Son-of-Sam law. A state statute that prohibits a convicted criminal from profiting by selling his or her story rights to a publisher or filmmaker. • State law usu. authorizes prosecutors to seize royalties from a convicted criminal and to place the money in an escrow account for the crime victim's benefit. Such a law was first enacted in New York in 1977, in response to the lucrative book deals that publishers offered David Berkowitz, the serial killer who called himself "Son of Sam." In 1992, the U.S. Supreme Court declared New York's Son-of-Sam law unconstitutional as a content-based speech regulation, prompting many states to amend their laws in an attempt to avoid constitutionality problems. *Simon & Schuster, Inc. v. New York State Crime Victims Bd.*, 502 U.S. 105, 112 S.Ct. 501 (1992).

sonticus (**sahn**-ti-kəs), *n.* [Latin] *Roman law.* Serious, more than trivial. • The term was used in the Twelve Tables to refer to a serious illness (*morbus sonticus*) that gave a defendant a valid reason not to appear in court.

soror (**sor**-or), *n.* [Latin] *Roman law.* A sister.

sororicide (sə-**ror**-ə-sɪd). **1.** The act of killing one's own sister. **2.** A person who kills his or her sister.

sors (sors), *n.* [Latin] **1.** *Roman law.* A lot; a chance. **2.** *Scots law.* A partnership's capital. **3.** *Hist.* Principal, as distinguished from interest. **4.** *Hist.* Something recovered in an action, as distinguished from mere costs.

sortition (sor-**tish**-ən), *n.* [fr. Latin *sortiri* "to cast lots"] *Roman law.* The drawing of lots, used, for example, in selecting judges for a criminal trial. — Also termed *sortitio.*

sound, *adj.* **1.** (Of health, mind, etc.) good; whole; free from disease or disorder. **2.** (Of property) good; marketable. **3.** (Of discretion) exercised equitably under the circumstances. — **soundness,** *n.*

sound, *vb.* **1.** To be actionable (in) <her claims for physical injury sound in tort, not in contract>. **2.** To be recoverable (in) <his tort action sounds in damages, not in equitable relief>.

sound health. See HEALTH.

source, *n.* The originator or primary agent of an act, circumstance, or result <she was the source of the information> <the side business was the source of income>.

source of law. Something (such as a constitution, treaty, statute, or custom) that provides authority for legislation and for judicial decisions; a point of origin for law or legal analysis. — Also termed *fons juris.*

> "The term 'sources of law' is ordinarily used in a much narrower sense than will be attributed to it here. In the literature of jurisprudence the problem of 'sources' relates to the question: Where does the judge obtain the rules by which to decide cases? In this sense, among the sources of law will be commonly listed: statutes, judicial precedents, custom, the opinion of experts, morality, and equity. In the usual discussions these various sources of law are analyzed and some attempt is made to state the conditions under which each can appropriately be drawn upon in the decision of legal controversies. Curiously, when a legislature is enacting law we do not talk about the 'sources' from which it derives its decision as to what the law shall be, though an analysis in these terms might be more enlightening than one directed toward the more restricted function performed by judges. Our concern here will be with 'sources' in a much broader sense than is usual in the literature of jurisprudence. Our interest is not so much in sources of laws, as in sources of law. From whence does the law generally draw not only its content but its force in men's lives?" Lon L. Fuller, *Anatomy of the Law* 69 (1968).

> "In the context of legal research, the term 'sources of law' can refer to three different concepts which should be distinguished. One, sources of law can refer to the origins of legal concepts and ideas.... Two, sources of law can refer to governmental institutions that formulate legal rules.... Three, sources of law can refer to the published manifestations of the law. The books, computer databases, microforms, optical disks, and other media that contain legal information are all sources of law." J. Myron Jacobstein & Roy M. Mersky, *Fundamentals of Legal Research* 1–2 (5th ed. 1990).

South Eastern Reporter. A set of regional lawbooks that, being part of the West Group's National Reporter System, contain every published decision from Georgia, North Carolina, South Carolina, Virginia, and West Virginia, from 1887 to date. • The first series ran from 1887 to 1939; the second series is the current one. — Abbr. S.E.; S.E.2d.

Southern Reporter. A set of regional lawbooks that, being part of the West Group's National Reporter System, contain every published decision from Alabama, Florida, Louisiana, and Mississippi, from 1887 to date. • The first series ran from 1887 to 1941; the second series is the current one. — Abbr. So.; So.2d.

South Western Reporter. A set of regional lawbooks that, being part of the West Group's National Reporter System, contain every published decision from Arkansas, Kentucky, Missouri, Tennessee, and Texas, from 1886 to date. • The first series ran from 1886 to 1928; the second series is the current one. — Abbr. S.W.; S.W.2d.

sovereign, *n.* **1.** A person, body, or state vested with independent and supreme authority. **2.** The ruler of an independent state. — Also spelled *sovran.* See SOVEREIGNTY.

sovereign immunity. See IMMUNITY (1).

sovereign people. The political body consisting of the collective number of citizens and qualified electors who possess the powers of sovereignty and exercise them through their chosen representatives.

sovereign political power. See POLITICAL POWER.

sovereign power. The power to make and enforce laws.

sovereign right. A unique right possessed by a state or its agencies that enables it to carry out its official functions for the public benefit, as distinguished from certain proprietary rights that it may possess like any other private person.

sovereign state. A state that possesses an independent existence, being complete in itself, without being merely part of a larger whole to whose government it is subject; a political community whose members are bound together by the tie of common subjection to some central authority, whose commands those members must obey. — Also termed *independent state.* Cf. CLIENT STATE.

part-sovereign state. A political community in which part of the powers of external sovereignty are exercised by the home government, and part are vested in or controlled by some other political body or bodies. • Such a state is not fully independent because by the conditions of its existence it is not allowed full freedom of action in external affairs.

sovereignty (**sahv**-[ə-]rin-tee). **1.** Supreme dominion, authority, or rule. **2.** The supreme political authority of an independent state. **3.** The state itself.

"It is well to [distinguish] the senses in which the word Sovereignty is used. In the ordinary popular sense it means Supremacy, the right to demand obedience. Although the idea of actual power is not absent, the prominent idea is that of some sort of title to exercise control. An ordinary layman would call that person (or body of persons) Sovereign in a State who is obeyed because he is acknowledged to stand at the top, whose will must be expected to prevail, who can get his own way, and make others go his, because such is the practice of the country. Etymologically the word of course means merely superiority, and familiar usage applies it in monarchies to the monarch, because he stands first in the State, be his real power great or small." James Bryce, *Studies in History and Jurisprudence* 504–05 (1901).

external sovereignty. The power of dealing on a nation's behalf with other national governments.

internal sovereignty. The power that rulers exercise over their own subjects.

sovran. See SOVEREIGN.

s.p. *abbr.* **1.** SINE PROLE. **2.** Same principle; same point. • This notation, when inserted between two citations, indicates that the second involves the same principles as the first.

space arbitrage. See ARBITRAGE.

spado (**spay**-doh), *n.* [Latin] *Roman law.* **1.** A eunuch. **2.** One who is incapable of sexual intercourse by reason of impotence. Pl. ***spadones*** (spə-**doh**-neez).

sparsim (**spahr**-sim). [Latin] *Hist.* Scattered; here and there. • This term was used in several cases — for example, when an action to recover for waste not only when the injury was complete, but also when the injury was partial or scattered.

"And if waste be done *sparsim*, or here and there, all over a wood, the whole wood shall be recovered; or if in several rooms of a house, the whole house shall be forfeited; because it is impracticable for the reversioner to enjoy only the identical places wasted, when lying interspersed with the other. But if waste be done only in one end of a wood (or perhaps in one room of a house) if that can be conveniently separated from the rest, that part only is the *locus vastatus*, or thing wasted, and that only shall be forfeited to the reversioner." 2 William Blackstone, *Commentaries on the Laws of England* 283–84 (1766).

spatae placitum (**spay**-tee **plas**-ə-təm), *n.* [Latin "the plea of the sword"] *Hist.* During the reign of Henry II, a court providing swift justice in military matters.

SPE. *abbr.* SPECIAL-PURPOSE ENTITY.

speaker. 1. One who speaks or makes a speech <the slander claim was viable only against the speaker>. **2.** The president or chair of a legislative body, esp. the House of Representatives <Speaker of the House>.

speaking demurrer. See DEMURRER.

speaking motion. See MOTION.

speaking objection. See OBJECTION.

speaking statute. See STATUTE.

spec. *abbr.* SPECIFICATION.

special, *adj.* **1.** Of, relating to, or designating a species, kind, or individual thing. **2.** (Of a statute, rule, etc.) designed for a particular purpose. **3.** (Of powers, etc.) unusual; extraordinary.

special acceptance. See ACCEPTANCE (4).

special act. See *special law* under LAW.

special administration. See ADMINISTRATION.

special administrator. See ADMINISTRATOR (1).

special agency. See AGENCY (1).

special agent. See AGENT; INSURANCE AGENT.

special agreement. See *ad hoc compromis* under COMPROMIS.

special allocatur. See ALLOCATUR.

special appearance. See APPEARANCE.

special assessment. See ASSESSMENT.

special-assessment bond. See *special-tax bond* under BOND (3).

special assumpsit. See ASSUMPSIT.

special attorney. See *special counsel* under COUNSEL.

special authority. See AUTHORITY (1).

special bail. See *bail to the action* under BAIL (3).

special bailiff. See BAILIFF.

special benefit. See BENEFIT.

special calendar. See CALENDAR (2).

special case. See *case reserved* (1) under CASE.

special charge. See *special instruction* under JURY INSTRUCTION.

special-circumstances rule. See SPECIAL-FACTS RULE.

special committee. See COMMITTEE.

special contract. See CONTRACT.

special-contract debt. See DEBT.

special counsel. See COUNSEL.

special count. See COUNT.

special court-martial. See COURT-MARTIAL.

special covenant against encumbrances. See COVENANT (4).

special custom. See *local custom* under CUSTOM.

special damages. See DAMAGES.

special demurrer. See DEMURRER.

special deposit. See DEPOSIT (2).

special deputy. See DEPUTY.

special deterrence. See DETERRENCE.

special diligence. See DILIGENCE.

special district. See DISTRICT.

special dividend. See *extraordinary dividend* under DIVIDEND.

special-duty doctrine. *Torts.* The rule that a governmental entity (such as a state or municipality) can be held liable for an individual plaintiff's injury when the entity owed a duty to the plaintiff but not to the general public. • This is an exception to the public-duty doctrine. The special-duty doctrine applies only when the plaintiff has reasonably relied on the governmental entity's assumption of the duty. — Also termed *special-duty exception*. See PUBLIC-DUTY DOCTRINE.

special-duty exception. **1.** SPECIAL-DUTY DOCTRINE. **2.** SPECIAL-ERRAND DOCTRINE.

special election. See ELECTION.

special employee. See *borrowed employee* under EMPLOYEE.

special employer. See EMPLOYER.

special-errand doctrine. The principle that an employee will be covered by workers' compensation for injuries occurring while the employee is on a journey or special duty for the employer away from the workplace. • This is an exception to the general rule that an employee is not covered for injuries occurring away from work. — Also termed *special-duty exception*; *special-mission exception*. See GOING-AND-COMING RULE.

special exception. **1.** A party's objection to the form rather than the substance of an opponent's claim, such as an objection for vagueness or ambiguity. See DEMURRER. Cf. *general exception* (1) under EXCEPTION (1). **2.** An allowance in a zoning ordinance for special uses that are considered essential and are not fundamentally incompatible with the original zoning regulations. — Also termed (in sense 2) *conditional use*; *special use*. Cf. VARIANCE (2).

special execution. See EXECUTION.

special executor. See EXECUTOR.

special-facts rule. *Corporations.* The principle that a director or officer has a fiduciary duty to disclose material inside information to a shareholder when engaging in a stock transaction under special circumstances, as when the shareholder lacks business acumen, the shares are closely held with no readily ascertainable market value, or the director or officer instigated the transaction. • This is an exception to the "majority rule." — Also termed *special-circumstances rule*. Cf. MAJORITY RULE (2).

special finding. See FINDING OF FACT.

special franchise. See FRANCHISE (2).

special grand jury. See GRAND JURY.

special guaranty. See GUARANTY.

special guardian. See GUARDIAN.

special-hazard rule. The principle that an employee is covered by workers' compensation for injuries received while traveling to or from work if the route used contains unique risks or hazards and is not ordinarily used by the public except in dealing with the employer. • This is an exception to the general rule that an employee is not covered for injuries occurring during the employee's commute. See GOING-AND-COMING RULE. Cf. SPECIAL-MISSION EXCEPTION.

special imparlance. See IMPARLANCE.

special indorsement. See INDORSEMENT.

special injunction. See INJUNCTION.

special instruction. See JURY INSTRUCTION.

special-interest group. An organization that seeks to influence legislation or government policy in favor of a particular interest or issue, esp. by lobbying. — Also termed *special interest*.

special interrogatory. See INTERROGATORY.

special issue. **1.** See ISSUE (1). **2.** See *special interrogatory* under INTERROGATORY.

specialist. **1.** A lawyer who has been board-certified in a specific field of law. See BOARD OF LEGAL SPECIALIZATION. **2.** *Securities.* A securities-exchange member who makes a market in one or more listed securities. • The exchange assigns securities to various specialists and expects them to maintain a fair and orderly market as provided by SEC standards.

special judge. See JUDGE.

special jurisdiction. See *limited jurisdiction* under JURISDICTION.

special jury. See JURY.

special law. See LAW.

special legacy. See *specific legacy* under LEGACY.

special letter of credit. See LETTER OF CREDIT.

special lien. See *particular lien* under LIEN.

special limitation. See LIMITATION.

special litigation committee. *Corporations.* A committee of independent corporate directors assigned to investigate the merits of a shareholder derivative suit and, if appropriate, to recommend maintaining or dismissing the suit. — Abbr. SLC. — Also termed *independent investigation committee*; *authorized committee*. See DERIVATIVE ACTION.

special malice. See *particular malice* under MALICE.

special master. See MASTER.

special matter. See MATTER.

special meaning. See SECONDARY MEANING.

special meeting. See MEETING.

special message. See MESSAGE.

special-mission exception. See SPECIAL-ERRAND DOCTRINE.

special mortgage. See MORTGAGE.

special motion. See MOTION.

special-needs analysis. *Criminal procedure.* A balancing test used by the Supreme Court to determine whether certain searches (such as administrative, civil-based, or public-safety searches) impose unreasonably on individual rights.

special occupant. See OCCUPANT.

special offering. See OFFERING.

special owner. See OWNER.

special partner. See *limited partner* under PARTNER.

special partnership. See PARTNERSHIP.

special permit. See SPECIAL-USE PERMIT.

special plea. See PLEA (3).

special pleader. See PLEADER.

special pleading. 1. The common-law system of pleading that required the parties to exchange a series of court papers (such as replications, rebutters, and surrebutters) setting out their contentions in accordance with hypertechnical rules before a case could be tried. • Often, therefore, cases were decided on points of pleading and not on the merits. **2.** The art of drafting pleadings under this system. **3.** An instance of drafting such a pleading. **4.** A responsive pleading that does more than merely deny allegations, as by introducing new matter to justify an otherwise blameworthy act. **5.** An argument that is unfairly slanted toward the speaker's viewpoint because it omits unfavorable facts or authorities and develops only favorable ones.

special plea in bar. See PLEA IN BAR.

special plea in error. At common law, a plea alleging some extraneous matter as a ground for defeating a writ of error (such as a release or expiration of the time within which error can be brought), to which the plaintiff in error must reply or demur.

special power. See POWER.

special power of appointment. See *limited power of appointment* under POWER OF APPOINTMENT.

special power of attorney. See POWER OF ATTORNEY.

special prayer. See PRAYER FOR RELIEF.

special privilege. See PRIVILEGE (1).

special proceeding. See PROCEEDING.

special property. See PROPERTY.

special prosecutor. See PROSECUTOR.

special-purpose entity. A business established to perform no function other than to develop, own, and operate a large, complex project (usu. called a *single-purpose project*), esp. so as to limit the number of creditors claiming against the project. • A special-purpose entity provides additional protection for project lenders, which are usu. paid only out of the money generated by the entity's business, because there will be fewer competing claims for that money and because the entity will be less likely to be forced into bankruptcy. A special-purpose entity will sometimes issue securities instead of just receiving a direct loan. — Abbr. SPE. — Also termed *special-purpose vehicle* (SPV). See BANKRUPTCY-REMOTE ENTITY; SINGLE-PURPOSE PROJECT; *project financing* under FINANCING.

special-purpose vehicle. See SPECIAL-PURPOSE ENTITY.

special reference. See REFERENCE.

special registration. See REGISTRATION (1).

special relationship. A nonfiduciary relationship having an element of trust, arising esp. when one person trusts another to exercise a reasonable degree of care and the other knows or ought to know about the reliance. Cf. FIDUCIARY RELATIONSHIP.

special-relationship doctrine. The theory that if a state has assumed control over an individual sufficient to trigger an affirmative duty to protect that individual (as in an involuntary hospitalization or custody), then the state may be liable for the harm inflicted on the individual by a third party. • This is an exception to the general principle prohibiting members of the public from suing state employees for failing to protect them from third parties. — Also termed *special-relationship exception*. Cf. DANGER-CREATION DOCTRINE.

special replication. See REPLICATION.

special reprisal. See REPRISAL.

special retainer. See RETAINER.

special rule. See RULE.

special-sensitivity rule. See EGGSHELL-SKULL RULE.

special session. See SESSION.

special setting. See SETTING.

special statute. See STATUTE.

special tail. See *tail special* under TAIL.

special tax. See TAX.

special-tax bond. See BOND (3).

special term. See TERM (5).

special traverse. See TRAVERSE.

special trial setting. See *special setting* under SETTING.

special trust. See *active trust* under TRUST.

specialty. 1. See *contract under seal* under CONTRACT. **2.** See DOCTRINE OF SPECIALTY. **3.** *Eminent domain.* Unique property (such as a church or cemetery) that is essentially not marketable, so that its value for condemnation purposes is determined by measuring the property's reproduction cost less any depreciation. — Also termed (in sense 3) *specialty property.*

specialty bar. See BAR.

specialty contract. See *contract under seal* under CONTRACT.

specialty debt. See *special-contract debt* under DEBT.

specialty doctrine. See DOCTRINE OF SPECIALTY.

specialty property. See SPECIALTY (3).

special use. See SPECIAL EXCEPTION (2).

special-use permit. A zoning board's authorization to use property in a way that is identified as a special exception in a zoning ordinance. • Unlike a variance, which is an authorized violation of a zoning ordinance, a special-use permit is a permitted exception. — Abbr. SUP. — Also termed *conditional-use permit*; *special permit.* See SPECIAL EXCEPTION (2). Cf. VARIANCE.

special-use valuation. See VALUATION.

special verdict. See VERDICT.

special warranty. See WARRANTY (1).

special warranty deed. See DEED.

specie (**spee**-shee). See IN SPECIE.

species (**spee**-sheez). A taxonomic class of organisms uniquely distinguished from other classes by shared characteristics and usu. by an inability to interbreed with members of other classes.

endangered species. A species in danger of becoming extinct; esp., under federal law, a species that is in danger of extinction throughout all or a significant part of its range. • Federal law excludes from the definition a species of the class Insecta if the Environmental Protection Agency determines that it constitutes a pest whose protection would present a significant risk to the human population. 50 CFR § 81.1(c).

threatened species. A species that, within the foreseeable future, is likely to become an endangered species throughout all or a significant part of its range. 16 USCA § 1532(20).

specific, *adj.* **1.** Of, relating to, or designating a particular or defined thing; explicit <specific duties>. **2.** Of or relating to a particular named thing <specific item>. **3.** Conformable to special requirements <specific performance>. — **specificity** (spes-ə-**fis**-i-tee), *n.* — **specifically,** *adv.*

specificatio (spes-ə-fi-**kay**-shee-oh), *n.* [Latin fr. *species* "form" + *facere* "to make"] *Roman & civil law.* A giving of form to materials; making something new from existing property. See ACCESSION.

> "***Specificatio.*** This may be described as acquisition of a new thing by making it, out of materials wholly or partly belonging to another person. We shall deal only with the case in which the materials are wholly another's. There was in classical law a conflict of opinion on this topic .... Justinian tells us that there had been a *media sententia* according to which it belonged to the maker if (i) it was irreducible to its former state, and (ii) it really was a *nova species*, where *species* means thing. And this view he adopts as law." W.W. Buckland, *A Manual of Roman Private Law* 143 (2d ed. 1953).

specification. 1. The act of making a detailed statement, esp. of the measurements, quality, materials, or other items to be provided under a contract. **2.** The statement so made. **3.** *Patents.* A patent applicant's written description of how an invention is constructed and used. Cf.

CLAIM (6). **4.** *Military law.* A statement of charges against one who is accused of a military offense. **5.** The acquisition of title to materials belonging to another person by converting those materials into a new and different form, as by changing grapes into wine, lumber into shelving, or corn into liquor. • The effect is that the original owner of the materials loses the property rights in them and is left with a right of action for their original value. — Abbr. spec.

specific bequest. See BEQUEST.

specific denial. See DENIAL.

specific deposit. See *special deposit* under DEPOSIT (2).

specific devise. See DEVISE.

specific enforcement. See *primary right* under RIGHT.

specific guaranty. See GUARANTY.

specific intent. See INTENT (1).

specific jurisdiction. See JURISDICTION.

specific legacy. See LEGACY.

specific legatee. See LEGATEE.

specific lien. See LIEN.

specific performance. A court-ordered remedy that requires precise fulfillment of a legal or contractual obligation when monetary damages are inappropriate or inadequate, as when the sale of real estate or a rare article is involved. • Specific performance is an equitable remedy that lies within the court's discretion to award whenever the common-law remedy is insufficient, either because damages would be inadequate or because the damages could not possibly be established. — Also termed *specific relief.*

> "In essence, the remedy of specific performance enforces the execution of a contract according to its terms, and it may therefore be contrasted with the remedy of damages, which is compensation for non-execution. In specific performance, execution of the contract is enforced by the power of the Court to treat disobedience of its decree as contempt, for which the offender may be imprisoned until he is prepared to comply with the decree. Actually, ... it is not strictly accurate to say that the Court enforces execution of the contract according to its terms, for the Court will not usually intervene until default upon the contract has occurred, so that enforcement by the Court is later in time than performance carried out by the person bound, without the intervention of the Court." G.W. Keeton, *An Introduction to Equity* 304 (5th ed. 1961).

specific remedy. See REMEDY.

specific tax. See TAX.

specific traverse. See *common traverse* under TRAVERSE.

spectrograph. An electromagnetic machine that analyzes sound, esp. a human voice, by separating and mapping it into elements of frequency, time lapse, and intensity (represented by a series of horizontal and vertical bar lines) to produce a final voiceprint. See VOICEPRINT.

speculation, *n.* **1.** The buying or selling of something with the expectation of profiting from price fluctuations <he engaged in speculation in the stock market>. **2.** The act or practice of theorizing about matters over which there is no certain knowledge <the public's speculation about the assassination of John F. Kennedy>. — **speculate,** *vb.* — **speculative,** *adj.*

speculative damages. See DAMAGES.

speculative risk. See RISK.

speculative security. See SECURITY.

speculator. A knowledgeable, aggressive investor who trades securities to profit from fluctuating market prices.

speech. 1. The expression or communication of thoughts or opinions in spoken words; something spoken or uttered. See FREEDOM OF SPEECH.

commercial speech. Communication (such as advertising and marketing) that involves only the commercial interests of the speaker and the audience, and is therefore afforded lesser First Amendment protection than social, political, or religious speech. Cf. *pure speech.*

corporate speech. Speech deriving from a corporation and protected under the First Amendment. • It does not lose protected status simply because of its corporate source.

hate speech. Speech that carries no meaning other than the expression of hatred for some group, such as a particular race, esp. in circumstances where the communication is likely to provoke violence. Cf. *group libel* under LIBEL.

pure speech. Words or conduct limited in form to what is necessary to convey the idea. • This type of speech is given the greatest constitutional protection. Cf. *commercial speech*; *symbolic speech*.

seditious speech. Speech advocating the violent overthrow of government. See SEDITION.

symbolic speech. Conduct that expresses opinions or thoughts, such as a hunger strike or the wearing of a black armband. • Symbolic speech does not enjoy the same constitutional protection that pure speech does. — Also termed *speech-plus*. Cf. *pure speech*.

2. *English law*. An opinion delivered by a Law Lord; JUDGMENT (2).

Speech or Debate Clause. The clause of the U.S. Constitution giving members of Congress immunity for statements made during debate in either the House or the Senate. • This immunity is extended to other areas where it is necessary to prevent impairment of deliberations and other legitimate legislative activities, such as subpoenaing bank records for an investigation. U.S. Const. art. I, § 6., cl. 1. — Also termed *Speech and Debate Clause*. See *congressional immunity* under IMMUNITY (1).

speech-plus. See *symbolic speech* under SPEECH.

speedy execution. See EXECUTION.

speedy remedy. See REMEDY.

speedy trial. *Criminal procedure*. A trial that the prosecution, with reasonable diligence, begins promptly and conducts expeditiously. • The Sixth Amendment secures the right to a speedy trial. In deciding whether an accused has been deprived of that right, courts generally consider the length of the delay, the reason for the delay, and the prejudice to the accused.

Speedy Trial Act of 1974. A federal statute establishing time limits for carrying out the major events (such as information, indictment, arraignment, and trial commencement) in the prosecution of federal criminal cases. 18 USCA §§ 3161–3174.

spending power. See POWER.

spendthrift, *n*. One who spends lavishly and wastefully; a profligate. — **spendthrift,** *adj*.

spendthrift trust. See TRUST.

sperate (**speer**-ət), *adj*. *Archaic*. (Of a debt) recoverable; not hopeless. • In determining whether a debt could be collected, consideration was formerly given to whether the debt was *desperate* or *sperate*.

spes accrescendi (**speez** ak-rə-**sen**-dɪ). [Latin "hope of accrual"] Hope of acquiring an extra share of a legacy or inheritance by survival.

spes recuperandi (**speez** ri-k[y]oo-pə-**ran**-dɪ). [Latin "hope of recovery"] Hope of recovering a prize, as from a captured vessel.

spes successionis (**speez** sək-sesh-ee-**oh**-nis). [Latin "hope of succession"] Hope of succeeding to a right.

> "A mere *spes successionis* must be distinguished from a contingent right. If Matilda has nursed her invalid friend for thirty years, she may have every hope of succeeding to the property, but she has no right." George Whitecross Paton, *A Textbook of Jurisprudence* 306 (G.W. Paton & David P. Derham eds., 4th ed. 1972).

Spielberg **doctrine.** *Labor law*. The policy of the National Labor Relations Board to defer to an arbitrator's decision regarding a contract dispute if (1) the decision is not repugnant to the National Labor Relations Board, (2) the arbitration proceedings provided a hearing as fair as would have been provided before the NLRB, and (3) the contract requires binding arbitration. *Spielberg Mfg. Co.*, 112 NLRB Dec. (CCH) 86 (1955). Cf. COLLYER DOCTRINE.

> "In Spielberg Mfg. Co. (1955), the Board announced its policy of dismissing an unfair labor practice complaint in deference to an arbitration award already rendered, provided the arbitral procedures were fair and the award was not repugnant to the policies of the Labor Act.... The Supreme Court in several cases cited the Board's deferral policy with approval, noting that the Board has discretion to respect an arbitration award and that arbitration of disputes contributes to industrial peace and stability." Robert A. Gorman, *Basic Text on Labor Law: Unionization and Collective Bargaining* 751 (1976).

spigurnel (spig-ər-**nel**), *n*. *Hist*. An early officer of the Chancery, equivalent to the Sealer of the king's writs in later times.

spillover. See EXTERNALITY.

spillover theory. The principle that a severance must be granted only when a defendant can show that trial with a codefendant would substantially prejudice the defendant's case, as when the jury might wrongly use evidence against the defendant.

"The spillover theory involves the question of whether a jury's unfavorable impression of a defendant against whom the evidence is properly admitted will influence the way the jurors view a codefendant .... The test ... is whether the jury can keep separate the evidence that is relevant to each defendant and render a fair and impartial verdict." 22A C.J.S. *Criminal Law* § 571, at 190–91 (1989).

spin-off, *n.* **1.** A corporate divestiture in which a division of a corporation becomes an independent company and stock of the new company is distributed to the corporation's shareholders. **2.** The company created by this divestiture. Cf. SPLIT-OFF; SPLIT-UP.

spirit of the law. The general meaning or purpose of the law, as opposed to its literal content. Cf. LETTER OF THE LAW.

spiritual, *adj.* Of or relating to ecclesiastical rather than secular matters <spiritual corporation>.

spiritual corporation. See CORPORATION.

spiritual court. See *ecclesiastical court* under COURT.

spiritual lord. An archbishop or bishop having a seat in the House of Lords.

spiritual tenure. See TENURE.

spital (**spit**-əl). *Archaic.* A hospital. — Also termed *spittle.*

spite fence. A fence erected solely to annoy a neighbor, as by blocking the neighbor's view or preventing the neighbor from acquiring an easement of light <the court temporarily enjoined the completion of the 25–foot spite fence>.

spittle. See SPITAL.

split, *vb.* **1.** To divide (a cause of action) into segments or parts. **2.** To issue two or more shares for each old share without changing the shareholder's proportional ownership interest. See STOCK SPLIT.

split-dollar insurance. See INSURANCE.

split fund. See *dual fund* under MUTUAL FUND.

split-funded plan. See EMPLOYEE BENEFIT PLAN.

split gift. See GIFT.

split income. See INCOME.

split-interest trust. See *charitable-remainder trust* under TRUST.

split-level statute. See STATUTE.

split-off, *n.* **1.** The creation of a new corporation by an existing corporation that gives its shareholders stock in the new corporation in return for their stock in the original corporation. **2.** The corporation created by this process. Cf. SPIN-OFF; SPLIT-UP.

split order. See ORDER (4).

split sentence. See SENTENCE.

splitting a cause of action. Separating parts of a demand and pursuing it piecemeal; presenting only a part of a claim in one lawsuit, leaving the rest for a second suit. • This practice has long been considered procedurally impermissible.

split-up, *n.* The division of a corporation into two or more new corporations. • The shareholders in the original corporation typically receive shares in the new corporations, and the original corporation goes out of business. Cf. SPIN-OFF; SPLIT-OFF.

split verdict. See VERDICT.

spoils of war. See BOOTY (1).

spoils system. The practice of awarding government jobs to supporters and friends of the victorious political party. Cf. MERIT SYSTEM.

spoliation (spoh-lee-**ay**-shən), *n.* **1.** The intentional destruction, mutilation, alteration, or concealment of evidence, usu. a document. • If proved, spoliation may be used to establish that the evidence was unfavorable to the party responsible. **2.** The seizure of personal or real property by violent means; the act of pillaging. **3.** The taking of a benefit properly belonging to another. **4.** *Eccles. law.* The wrongful deprivation of a cleric of his benefice. — **spoliate** (**spoh**-lee-ayt), *vb.* — **spoliator** (**spoh**-lee-ay-tər), *n.*

spolium (**spoh**-lee-əm), *n.* [Latin] *Roman law.* Something illegally and violently taken from another. • The plural *spolia* was more common than the singular.

Spondesne? Spondeo (**spon**-deez **spon**-dee-oh). [Latin] *Roman law.* Do you agree to undertake? I undertake. • This was a common phrase used to create a stipulation. See STIPULATIO.

spondet peritiam artis (**spon**-det pə-**rish**-ee-əm **ahr**-tis). [Latin "he guarantees his professional skill"] *Hist.* He promised to use the skill of his art. • This phrase is used in construction contracts to indicate an implied agreement to perform in a workmanlike manner.

sponsalia (spon-**say**-lee-ə), *n.* [Latin] *Hist.* A betrothal; an espousal. — Also termed *stipulatio sponsalitia.*

sponsalia per verba de futuro (spon-**say**-lee-ə pər **vər**-bə dee f[y]oo-**t**[**y**]**oor**-oh). [Latin "espousals by words about the future"] *Hist.* A promise to marry in the future.

> "[A] promise to marry in the future (*sponsalia per verba de futuro*) gave rise only to an executory contract of marriage. The regular way of executing the contract was to solemnise the marriage, using present words. But the Canon law acknowledged that it could also be turned into the indissoluble bond of present matrimony by physical consummation .... Thus, in the absence of carnal copulation, the validity of a marriage had come to depend on whether the contract was by words *de praesenti* or *de futuro* .... It is hardly surprising that it gave rise to so much wrangling and fraud, and that the commonest species of matrimonial suit in the medieval consistory courts was to interpret and enforce 'espousals'." J.H. Baker, *An Introduction to English Legal History* 546 (3d ed. 1990).

sponsio (**spon**-shee-oh), *n.* [Latin] *Roman law.* An undertaking in the form of an answer to a question in a *stipulatio*, esp. by way of suretyship. See STIPULATIO.

sponsio judicialis (**spon**-shee-oh joo-dish-ee-**ay**-lis). [Latin] *Roman law.* A formal promise that the judge is entitled to acquire by virtue of his office.

sponsio ludicra (**spon**-shee-oh **loo**-di-krə). [Latin "a laughable promise"] **1.** *Civil law.* An informal understanding that is not enforceable. **2.** *Scots law.* An obligation that a court will not enforce because it does not concern a serious subject; e.g., a gambling agreement.

sponsion (**spon**-shən), *n.* [fr. Latin *sponsere* "to engage"] **1.** The formal pledge by which a person becomes a surety. **2.** *Int'l law.* An ultra vires promise of an official agent (such as a general in wartime), requiring later ratification by the principal. **3.** *Roman law.* A form of adpromission accessory to an oral contract. • Only Roman citizens could make this type of adpromission. See ADPROMISSION. — **sponsional** (**spon**-shən-əl), *adj.*

sponsor. 1. One who acts as a surety for another. **2.** A legislator who proposes a bill. **3.** *Civil law.* One who voluntarily intervenes for another without being requested to do so.

spontaneous declaration. *Evidence.* A statement that is made without time to reflect or fabricate and that is related to the circumstances of the perceived occurrence. — Also termed *spontaneous statement*; *spontaneous exclamation*; *spontaneous utterance.* See EXCITED UTTERANCE; PRESENT SENSE IMPRESSION.

sponte oblata (**spon**-tee ə-**blay**-tə). [Latin "freely offered"] *Hist.* A gift to the Crown.

sports franchise. See FRANCHISE (3).

sportula (**spor**-chə-lə), *n.* [Latin] *Roman law.* **1.** A present; a donation, as to the poor. **2.** A fee paid to certain officials for performing judicial duties. — Also termed *sportella.*

spot, *adj.* Made, paid, or delivered immediately <a spot sale> <spot commodities>.

spot market. See MARKET.

spot price. See PRICE.

spot zoning. See ZONING.

spousal abuse. See ABUSE.

spousal allowance. See ALLOWANCE (1).

spousal consortium. See CONSORTIUM.

spousal privilege. See *marital privilege* under PRIVILEGE.

spousals. *Hist.* Mutual promises to marry.

spousal support. See ALIMONY.

spouse. One's husband or wife by lawful marriage; a married person.

spouse-breach. See ADULTERY.

spray trust. See *sprinkling trust* under TRUST.

spread, *n.* **1.** *Banking.* The difference between the interest rate that a financial institution must pay to attract deposits and the rate at which money can be loaned. **2.** *Securities.* The difference between the highest price a buyer will pay for a security (the *bid price*) and the lowest price at which a seller will sell a security (the *asked price*). **3.** *Securities.* The simultaneous buying and selling of one or more options or futures contracts on the same security in order to profit from the price difference. **4.** In investment banking, the difference between the price the underwriter pays the issuer of the security and the price paid by the public in the initial offering. • The spread compensates the underwriter for its services; it is made up of the manager's fee, the underwriter's discount, and the selling-group concession or discount. — Also termed (in sense 4) *gross spread*; *underwriting spread*.

spread eagle. See STRADDLE.

spreadsheet. A multicolumned worksheet used esp. by accountants and auditors to summarize and analyze financial transactions.

springing use. See USE (4).

spring tide. See TIDE.

sprinkling trust. See TRUST.

spurious (**spyoor**-ee-əs), *adj.* **1.** Deceptively suggesting an erroneous origin; fake <spurious trademarks>. **2.** Of doubtful or low quality <spurious goods that fell apart>. **3.** *Archaic.* Of illegitimate birth <spurious offspring>.

spurious bank bill. See *spurious banknote* under BANKNOTE.

spurious banknote. See BANKNOTE.

spurious class action. See CLASS ACTION.

spurius (**sp[y]oor**-ee-əs), *n.* [Latin] *Roman law.* A bastard; the offspring of unlawful intercourse. See NOTHUS.

SPV. *abbr.* Special-purpose vehicle. See SPECIAL-PURPOSE ENTITY.

spy. One who secretly observes and collects secret information or intelligence about what another government or company is doing or plans to do; one who commits espionage. See ESPIONAGE.

square, *n.* **1.** A certain portion of land within a city limit. — Also termed *block.* **2.** A space set apart for public use. **3.** In a government survey, an area measuring 24 by 24 miles.

squatter. 1. A person who settles on property without any legal claim or title. **2.** A person who settles on public land under a government regulation allowing the person to acquire title upon fulfilling specified conditions.

squatter's rights. The right to acquire title to real property by adverse possession, or by preemption of public lands. See ADVERSE POSSESSION.

squeeze-out, *n.* An action taken in an attempt to eliminate or reduce a minority interest in a corporation. Cf. FREEZE-OUT.

ss. *abbr.* **1.** Sections. **2.** *Subscripsi* (i.e., signed below). **3.** Sans (i.e., without). **4.** (Erroneously) scilicet.

> "Many possible etymologies have been suggested for this mysterious abbreviation. One is that it signifies *scilicet* (= namely, to wit), which is usually abbreviated *sc.* or *scil.* Another is that *ss.* represents '[t]he two gold letters at the ends of the chain of office or "collar" worn by the Lord Chief Justice of the King's Bench ....' Max Radin, *Law Dictionary* 327 (1955). Mellinkoff suggests that the precise etymology is unknown: 'Lawyers have been using *ss* for nine hundred years and still are not sure what it means.' David Mellinkoff, *The Language of the Law* 296 (1963). In fact, though, it is a flourish deriving from the Year Books — an equivalent of the paragraph mark: '¶.' Hence Lord Hardwicke's statement that *ss.* is nothing more than a division mark. See *Jodderrell v. Cowell*, 95 Eng. Rep. 222, 222 (K.B. 1737) .... An early formbook writer incorporated it into his forms, and ever since it has been mindlessly perpetuated by one generation after another." Bryan A. Garner, *A Dictionary of Modern Legal Usage* 825 (2d ed. 1995).

SSA. *abbr.* SOCIAL SECURITY ADMINISTRATION.

SSI. *abbr.* SUPPLEMENTAL SECURITY INCOME.

SSS. *abbr.* SELECTIVE SERVICE SYSTEM.

stabilize, *vb.* **1.** To make firm or steadfast <to stabilize the ship>. **2.** To maintain a particular level or amount <stabilize prices>.

stable stand. *Hist.* In forest law, a person found standing in a forest either with a bow bent, ready to shoot a deer, or close to a tree with greyhounds on a leash and ready to slip, being presumptive evidence of an intent to steal the Crown's deer.

stacking. 1. *Insurance.* The process of obtaining benefits from a second policy on the same claim when recovery from the first policy alone would be inadequate.

judicial stacking. The principle that a court can construe insurance policies to permit stacking, under certain circumstances, when the policies do not specifically provide for stacking but public policy is best served by permitting it.

policy stacking. Stacking that is permitted by the express terms of an insurance policy.

2. A gerrymandering technique in which a large political or racial group is combined in the same district with a larger opposition group. Cf. CRACKING; PACKING.

staff attorney. 1. A lawyer who works for a court, usu. in a permanent position, on matters such as reviewing motions, screening docketing statements, preparing scheduling orders, and examining habeas corpus petitions. • Staff attorneys do not rule on motions or decide cases, but they review, research, and recommend proposed rulings to judges, as well as drafting the orders implementing those rulings. **2.** An inhouse lawyer for a corporation.

staff judge advocate. See JUDGE ADVOCATE.

stagflation (stag-**flay**-shən), *n.* A period of slow economic growth or recession characterized by high inflation, stagnant consumer demand, and high unemployment. — **stagflationary,** *adj.*

staggered board of directors. See BOARD OF DIRECTORS.

stagiarius (stay-jee-**air**-ee-əs), *n.* [Latin] *Hist.* **1.** *Eccles. law.* A resident canon; an ecclesiastic bound to keep terms of residence. **2.** A stagiary; a law student keeping terms before admission to the bar.

stake, *n.* **1.** Something (such as property) deposited by two or more parties with a third party pending the resolution of a dispute; the subject matter of an interpleader. **2.** An interest or share in a business venture. **3.** Something (esp. money) bet in a wager, game, or contest. **4.** A boundary marker used in land surveys.

stakeholder. 1. A disinterested third party who holds money or property, the right to which is disputed between two or more other parties. See INTERPLEADER. **2.** A person who has an interest or concern in a business or enterprise, though not necessarily as an owner. **3.** One who holds the money or valuables bet by others in a wager.

stale check. See CHECK.

stale claim. A claim that is barred by the statute of limitations or the defense of laches. — Also termed *stale demand.*

stalking. 1. The act or an instance of following another by stealth. **2.** The offense of following or loitering near another, often surreptitiously, with the purpose of annoying or harassing that person or committing a further crime such as assault or battery. • Some statutory definitions include an element that the person being stalked must reasonably feel harassed, alarmed, or distressed about personal safety or the safety of one or more persons for whom that person is responsible. And some definitions stipulate that acts such as telephoning another and remaining silent during the call amount to stalking.

stallage (**stawl**-ij), *n. Hist.* **1.** The right to erect stalls in public markets. **2.** The cost for that right.

stamp, *n.* An official mark or seal placed on a document, esp. to indicate that a required tax (such as duty or excise tax) has been paid.

stamp acts. English statutes requiring and regulating stamps on deeds, contracts, legal papers, bills, or other documents.

stamp duty. *Hist.* A tax raised by requiring stamps sold by the government to be affixed to designated documents, thus forming part of the perpetual revenue. See *stamp tax* under TAX.

> "A fifth branch of the perpetual revenue consists in the stamp duties, which are a tax imposed upon all parchment and paper whereon any legal proceedings, or private instruments of almost any nature whatsoever, are written; and also upon licenses . . . and pamphlets containing less than six sheets of paper. These imposts are very various, according to the nature of the thing stamped, rising gradually from a penny to ten pounds." 1 William Blackstone, *Commentaries on the Laws of England* 312–13 (1765).

stamp tax. See TAX.

standard, *n.* **1.** A model accepted as correct by custom, consent, or authority <what is the standard in the ant-farm industry?>. **2.** A criterion for measuring acceptability, quality, or accuracy <the attorney was making a nice living — even by New York standards>. — **standard,** *adj*.

objective standard. A legal standard that is based on conduct and perceptions external to a particular person. • In tort law, for example, the reasonable-person standard is considered an objective standard because it does not require a determination of what the defendant was thinking.

subjective standard. A legal standard that is peculiar to a particular person and based on the person's individual views and experiences. • In criminal law, for example, premeditation is determined by a subjective standard because it depends on the defendant's mental state.

standard deduction. See DEDUCTION.

standard-form contract. See CONTRACT.

standard instruction. See JURY INSTRUCTION.

standard mortgage clause. See MORTGAGE CLAUSE.

standard of care. *Torts*. In the law of negligence, the degree of care that a reasonable person should exercise. See CARE (2).

standard of need. In public-assistance law, the total subsistence resources required by an individual or family unit as determined by a state and, when unsatisfied by available resources, entitles the individual or family unit to public assistance.

standard of proof. The degree or level of proof demanded in a specific case, such as "beyond a reasonable doubt" or "by a preponderance of the evidence." See BURDEN OF PERSUASION.

standard policy. See INSURANCE POLICY.

standby commitment. An arrangement between an underwriter and an issuer of securities whereby the underwriter agrees, for a fee, to buy any unsold shares remaining after the public offering. — Also termed *standby underwriting agreement*.

standby counsel. See COUNSEL.

standby letter of credit. See LETTER OF CREDIT.

standby underwriting. See UNDERWRITING.

standby underwriting agreement. See STANDBY COMMITMENT.

standing, *n*. A party's right to make a legal claim or seek judicial enforcement of a duty or right. • To have standing in federal court, a plaintiff must show (1) that the challenged conduct has caused the plaintiff actual injury, and (2) that the interest sought to be protected is within the zone of interests meant to be regulated by the statutory or constitutional guarantee in question. — Also termed *standing to sue*. Cf. JUSTICIABILITY.

> "Have the appellants alleged such a personal stake in the outcome of the controversy as to assure that concrete adverseness which sharpens the presentation of issues upon which the court so largely depends for illumination of difficult constitutional questions? This is the gist of the question of standing." *Baker v. Carr*, 369 U.S. 186, 204, 82 S.Ct. 691, 703 (1962) (Brennan, J.).

> "The word *standing* is rather recent in the basic judicial vocabulary and does not appear to have been commonly used until the middle of our own century. No authority that I have found introduces the term with proper explanations and apologies and announces that henceforth *standing* should be used to describe who may be heard by a judge. Nor was there any sudden adoption by tacit consent. The word appears here and there, spreading very gradually with no discernible pattern. Judges and lawyers found themselves using the term and did not ask why they did so or where it came from." Joseph Vining, *Legal Identity* 55 (1978).

third-party standing. Standing held by someone claiming to protect the rights of others.

standing aside a juror. The prosecution practice of provisionally placing a juror aside until the panel is exhausted, without providing a reason, instead of challenging the juror or showing cause. • The practice originally developed as a method of avoiding the Challenge of Jurors Act (1305), which prohibited the Crown from challenging a juror without showing cause. A similar practice was formerly used in Pennsylvania.

standing by. 1. The awaiting of an opportunity to respond, as with assistance. **2.** Silence or inaction when there is a duty to speak or act; esp., the tacit possession of knowledge under circumstances requiring the possessor to reveal the knowledge. See *estoppel by silence* under ESTOPPEL.

standing committee. See COMMITTEE.

Standing Committee on Rules of Practice and Procedure. A group of judges, lawyers, and legal scholars appointed by the Chief Justice of the United States to advise the Judicial Conference of the United States on possible amendments to the procedural rules in the various federal courts and on other issues relating to the operation of the federal courts. 28 USCA § 331.

> "[Under 28 USCA § 331], the Judicial Conference of the United States has created a Standing Committee on Rules of Practice and Procedure and has authorized the appointment from time to time of various advisory committees. These committees make recommendations regarding amendments of the rules to the Judicial Conference, which in turn transmits those recommendations it approves to the Supreme Court. Under this new plan, as under the machinery in effect from 1934 to 1956, the Court retains the ultimate responsibility for the adoption of amendments to the rules." 4 Charles Alan Wright & Arthur R. Miller, *Federal Practice and Procedure* § 1007, at 35 (2d ed. 1987).

standing master. See MASTER.

standing mortgage. See *interest-only mortgage* under MORTGAGE.

standing offer. See OFFER.

standing order. See ORDER (2).

standing seised to uses. Holding title for the benefit or use of another, such as a relative in consideration of blood or marriage. • A covenant to stand seised to uses is a type of conveyance that depends on the Statute of Uses for its effect. — Often shortened to *seised to uses*. See STATUTE OF USES.

standing to sue. See STANDING.

stand mute. 1. (Of a defendant) to refuse to enter a plea to a criminal charge. • Standing mute is treated as a plea of not guilty. **2.** (Of any party) to raise no objections.

standstill agreement. Any agreement to refrain from taking further action; esp., an agreement by which a party agrees to refrain from further attempts to take over a corporation (as by making no tender offer) for a specified period, or by which financial institutions agree not to call bonds or loans when due.

stand trial. To submit to a legal proceeding, esp. a criminal prosecution.

staple (**stay**-pəl). *Hist.* **1.** A key commodity such as wool, leather, tin, lead, butter, or cheese (collectively termed *the staple*). **2.** A town appointed by the Crown as an exclusive market for staple products. See STATUTE STAPLE.

Star Chamber. 1. *Hist.* An English court having broad civil and criminal jurisdiction at the king's discretion and noted for its secretive, arbitrary, and oppressive procedures, including compulsory self-incrimination, inquisitorial investigation, and the absence of juries. • The Star Chamber was abolished in 1641 because of its abuses of power. — Also termed *Court of Star Chamber*. **2.** (*usu. l.c.*) Any secretive, arbitrary, or oppressive tribunal or proceeding.

stare decisis (**stahr**-ee di-**sɪ**-sis *or* **stair**-ee), *n.* [Latin "to stand by things decided"] The doctrine of precedent, under which it is necessary for a court to follow earlier judicial decisions when the same points arise again in litigation. See PRECEDENT; NON QUIETA MOVERE. Cf. RES JUDICATA; LAW OF THE CASE.

> "The rule of adherence to judicial precedents finds its expression in the doctrine of stare decisis. This doctrine is simply that, when a point or principle of law has been once officially decided or settled by the ruling of a competent court in a case in which it is directly and necessarily involved, it will no longer be considered as open to examination or to a new ruling by the same tribunal, or by those which are bound to follow its adjudications, unless it be for urgent reasons and in exceptional cases." William M. Lile et al., *Brief Making and the Use of Law Books* 321 (3d ed. 1914).

> "The general orthodox interpretation of *stare decisis* . . . is *stare rationibus decidendis* ('keep to the *rationes decidendi* of past cases'), but a narrower and more literal interpretation is sometimes employed. To appreciate this narrower interpretation it is necessary to refer . . . to Lord Halsbury's assertion that a case is only authority for what it actually decides. We saw that situations can arise in which all that is binding is the decision. According to Lord Reid, such a situation arises when the *ratio decidendi* of a previous case is obscure, out of accord with authority or established principle, or too broadly expressed." Rupert Cross & J.W. Harris, *Precedent in English Law* 100–01 (4th ed. 1991).

stare decisis et non quieta movere (**stair**-ee di-**sɪ**-sis et non kwɪ-**ee**-tə moh-**veer**-ee). [Latin] To stand by things decided, and not to disturb settled points. See STARE DECISIS.

stare in judicio (**stair**-ee in joo-**dish**-ee-oh). [Latin] *Hist.* To appear before a tribunal as either a plaintiff or a defendant.

star paging, *n.* **1.** A method of referring to a page in an earlier edition of a book, esp. a legal source. • This method correlates the pagination of the later edition with that of the earlier (usu. the first) edition. **2.** By extension, the method of displaying on a computer screen the page breaks that occur in printed documents such as law reports and law reviews. — Also termed *star pagination*. — **star page,** *n.*

starr (stahr), *n.* [fr. Latin *starrum* fr. Hebrew *sh'tar* "a writing"] *Hist.* A Jewish contract (esp. for release of an obligation) that Richard I declared to be invalid unless it was placed in a lawful repository, the largest being in the king's Exchequer at Westminster. — Also termed *starra.*

> "It is well known that, before the banishment of the Jews under Edward I, their contracts and obligations were denominated in our ancient records *starra* or *starrs*, from a corruption of the Hebrew word, *shetàr*, a covenant.... These starrs, by an ordinance of Richard the first ... were commanded to be enrolled and deposited in chests under three keys in certain places; one, and the most considerable, of which was in the king's exchequer at Westminster .... [T]he room at the exchequer, where the chests containing these starrs were kept, was probably called the *starr-chamber*, and, when the Jews were expelled the kingdom, was applied to the use of the king's council, when sitting in their judicial capacity." 4 William Blackstone, *Commentaries on the Laws of England* 263 n.a (1769).

stash, *vb.* To hide or conceal (money or property).

stat. *abbr.* STATUTE.

state, *n.* **1.** The political system of a body of people who are politically organized; the system of rules by which jurisdiction and authority are exercised over such a body of people <separation of church and state>. — Also termed *political society*. Cf. NATION.

> "A state or political society is an association of human beings established for the attainment of certain ends by certain means. It is the most important of all the various kinds of society in which men unite, being indeed the necessary basis and condition of peace, order, and civilisation. What then is the difference between this and other forms of association? In what does the state differ from such other societies as a church, a university, a joint-stock company, or a trade union? The difference is clearly one of *function*. The state must be defined by reference to such of its activities and purposes as are essential and characteristic." John Salmond, *Jurisprudence* 129 (Glanville L. Williams ed., 10th ed. 1947).

> "A state is an *institution*, that is to say, it is a system of relations which men establish among themselves as a means of securing certain objects, of which the most fundamental is a system of order within which their activities can be carried on. Modern states are territorial; their governments exercise control over persons and things within their frontiers, and today the whole of the habitable world is divided between about seventy of these territorial states. A state should not be confused with the whole community of persons living on its territory; it is only one among a multitude of other institutions, such as churches and corporations, which a community establishes for securing different objects, though obviously it is one of tremendous importance; none the less it is not, except in the ideology of totalitarianism, an all-embracing institution, not something from which, or within which, all other institutions and associations have their being; many institutions, e.g. the Roman Catholic Church, and many associations, e.g. federations of employers and of workers, transcend the boundaries of any single state." J.L. Brierly, *The Law of Nations* 118 (5th ed. 1955).

composite state. A state that comprises an aggregate or group of constituent states.

dependent state. See *nonsovereign state.*

federal state. A composite state in which the sovereignty of the entire state is divided between the central or federal government and the local governments of the several constituent states; a union of states in which the control of the external relations of all the member states has been surrendered to a central government so that the only state that exists for international purposes is the one formed by the union. Cf. *confederation of states* under CONFEDERATION.

imperial state. *Archaic.* A composite state in which a common or central government possesses in itself the entire sovereignty, so that the constituent states possess no portion of this sovereignty.

nonsovereign state. A state that is a constituent part of a greater state that includes both it and one or more others, and to whose government it is subject; a state that is not complete and self-existent. — Also termed *dependent state.*

police state. A state in which the political, economic, and social life of its citizens is subject to repressive governmental control and arbitrary uses of power by the ruling elite, which uses the police as the instrument of control; a totalitarian state.

simple state. See *unitary state.*

social-service state. A state that uses its power to create laws and regulations to provide for the welfare of its citizens.

sovereign state. See SOVEREIGN STATE.

unitary state. A state that is not made up of territorial divisions that are states themselves. — Also termed (archaically) *simple state.*

2. An institution of self-government within a larger political entity; esp., one of the constituent parts of a nation having a federal government <the 50 states>. — Also termed *nonsovereign state*. **3.** (*often cap.*) The prosecution as the representative of the people <the State rests its case>.

state action. Anything done by a government; esp., in constitutional law, an intrusion on a person's rights (esp. civil rights) either by a governmental entity or by a private requirement that can be enforced only by governmental action (such as a racially restrictive covenant, which requires judicial action for enforcement).

state-action doctrine. *Antitrust.* The principle that the antitrust laws do not prohibit a state's anticompetitive acts, or official acts directed by a state. *Parker v. Brown*, 317 U.S. 341, 63 S.Ct. 307 (1943). — Also termed *Parker doctrine.* See MIDCAL TEST.

state auditor. The appointed or elected official responsible for overseeing state fiscal transactions and auditing state-agency accounts. See AUDIT.

state bank. See BANK.

state bar association. See BAR ASSOCIATION.

state bond. See BOND (3).

state-compulsion test. *Civil-rights law.* The rule that a state is responsible for discrimination that a private party commits while acting under the requirements of state law, as when a restaurant owner is required by state law to refuse service to minorities. *Adickes v. S.H. Kress & Co.*, 398 U.S. 144, 90 S.Ct. 1598 (1970). See SYMBIOTIC-RELATIONSHIP TEST; NEXUS TEST.

state court. See COURT.

state criminal. See CRIMINAL.

stated, *adj.* **1.** Fixed; determined; settled <at the stated time> <settlement for a stated amount>. **2.** Expressed; declared <stated facts>.

stated account. See *account stated* under ACCOUNT.

stated capital. See CAPITAL.

State Department. An executive department, headed by the Secretary of State, responsible for analyzing, making recommendations on, and carrying out matters of foreign policy (including trade relations, environmental concerns, and human-rights issues), as by negotiating treaties and other international agreements, and representing the United States in the United Nations and other international organizations. — Also termed *Department of State.* 22 USCA §§ 2651–2728.

stated interest rate. See *nominal rate* under INTEREST RATE.

stated meeting. See *annual meeting* under MEETING.

stated rate. See *nominal rate* under INTEREST RATE.

stated term. See *general term* under TERM (5).

stated value. See PAR VALUE.

state government. See GOVERNMENT.

state law. A body of law in a particular state consisting of the state's constitution, statutes, regulations, and common law. Cf. FEDERAL LAW.

stateless person. *Int'l law.* A natural person who is not considered a national by any country. • The Stateless Persons Convention (1954) provides these people with certain protections, as well as obliging them to abide by the laws of the country where they reside.

> "It is, of course, quite possible that a person may be without any nationality, in which case he is referred to as a *stateless person.*" Oscar Svarlien, *An Introduction to the Law of Nations* 428 (1955).

statement. 1. *Evidence.* A verbal assertion or nonverbal conduct intended as an assertion. **2.** A formal and exact presentation of facts. **3.** *Criminal procedure.* An account of a person's (usu. a suspect's) knowledge of a crime, taken by the police pursuant to their investigation of the offense. Cf. CONFESSION.

consonant statement. A prior declaration of a witness, testified to by a person to whom the declaration was made and allowed into evidence only after the witness's testimony has been impeached. • This type of evidence would, but for the impeachment of the witness, be inadmissible hearsay.

false statement. See FALSE STATEMENT.

financial statement. See FINANCIAL STATEMENT.

incriminating statement. A statement that tends to establish the guilt of an accused.

prior consistent statement. See PRIOR CONSISTENT STATEMENT.

prior inconsistent statement. See PRIOR INCONSISTENT STATEMENT.

sworn statement. **1.** A statement given under oath; an affidavit. **2.** A contractor-builder's listing of suppliers and subcontractors, and their respective bids, required by a lending institution for interim financing.

voluntary statement. A statement free from duress, coercion, or inducement.

Statement and Account Clause. The clause of the U.S. Constitution requiring the regular publication of the receipts and expenditures of the federal government. U.S. Const. art. I, § 9, cl. 7.

statement of account. **1.** A report issued periodically (usu. monthly) by a bank to a customer, providing certain information on the customer's account, including the checks drawn and cleared, deposits made, charges debited, and the account balance. — Also termed *bank statement*. **2.** A report issued periodically (usu. monthly) by a creditor to a customer, providing certain information on the customer's account, including the amounts billed, credits given, and the balance due. — Also termed *account statement*.

statement of affairs. **1.** STATEMENT OF FINANCIAL AFFAIRS. **2.** A balance sheet showing immediate liquidation values (rather than historical costs), usu. prepared when insolvency is imminent.

statement of claim. **1.** COMPLAINT (1). **2.** *English law*. A plaintiff's initial pleading in a civil case; DECLARATION (7).

statement of condition. See BALANCE SHEET.

statement of confession. See CONFESSION OF JUDGMENT.

statement of defense. The assertions by a defendant; esp., in England, the defendant's answer to the plaintiff's statement of claim.

statement of facts. A party's written presentation of the facts leading up to or surrounding a legal dispute, usu. recited toward the beginning of a brief.

agreed statement of facts. A narrative statement of facts that is stipulated to be correct by the parties and is submitted to a tribunal for a ruling. • When the narrative statement is filed on appeal instead of a report of the trial proceedings, it is called an *agreed statement on appeal*.

statement of financial affairs. *Bankruptcy*. A document that an individual or corporate debtor must file to answer questions about its past and present financial status, including any previous bankruptcy, the location of any current accounts, and its recent or current debt. — Also termed *statement of affairs*.

statement of financial condition. See BALANCE SHEET.

statement of financial position. See BALANCE SHEET.

statement of income. See INCOME STATEMENT.

statement of intention. *Bankruptcy*. A preliminary statement filed by the debtor in a Chapter 7 case, in which the debtor details whether property secured by consumer debt will be retained or surrendered and whether the property is claimed as exempt. • The statement usu. must be filed before the first creditors' meeting or within 30 days from the petition-filing date, whichever is earlier. 11 USCA § 521.

statement of particulars. See BILL OF PARTICULARS.

state of art. See STATE OF THE ART.

state officer. See OFFICER (1).

state of mind. **1.** The condition or capacity of a person's mind; MENS REA. **2.** Loosely, a person's reasons or motives for committing an act, esp. a criminal act.

state-of-mind exception. *Evidence*. The principle that an out-of-court declaration of an existing motive is admissible, even when the declarant cannot testify in person. • This principle constitutes an exception to the hearsay rule.

state of nature. The lack of a politically organized society. • The term is a fictional construct for the period in human history predating any type of political society.

> "[W]e may make use of the contrast, familiar to the philosophy of the seventeenth and eighteenth centuries,

between the civil state and the state of nature. This state of nature is now commonly rejected as one of the fictions which flourished in the era of the social contract, but such treatment is needlessly severe. The term certainly became associated with much false or exaggerated doctrine touching the golden age, on the one hand, and the *bellum omnium contra omnes* of Hobbes, on the other, but in itself it nevertheless affords a convenient mode for the expression of an undoubted truth. As long as there have been men, there has probably been some form of human society. The state of nature, therefore, is not the absence of society, but the absence of a society so organised on the basis of physical force as to constitute a state. Though human society is coeval with mankind, the rise of political society, properly so called, is an event in human history." John Salmond, *Jurisprudence* 103–04 (Glanville L. Williams ed., 10th ed. 1947).

state of the art. *Products liability.* The level of pertinent scientific and technical knowledge existing at the time of a product's manufacture, and the best technology reasonably available at the time the product was sold. — Also termed *state of art.* — **state-of-the-art,** *adj.*

"While the statutes in effect in some jurisdictions speak in terms of a state of the art defense, statutes in other jurisdictions provide that state of the art evidence is admissible or may be considered by the trier of fact by statute, and that in determining whether a product was in a defective condition or unreasonably dangerous at the time it left the control of the manufacturer or seller, consideration is given to the state of scientific and technical knowledge available to the manufacturer or seller at the time the product was placed on the market, and to the customary designs, methods, standards, and techniques of manufacturing, inspecting, and testing used by other manufacturers or sellers of similar products." 63A Am. Jur. 2d *Products Liability* § 1319, at 472 (1997).

state of the case. The posture of litigation as it develops, as in discovery, at trial, or on appeal.

State of the Union. See *Presidential message* under MESSAGE.

state of war. A situation in which war has been declared or armed conflict is in progress.

state paper. 1. A document prepared by or relating to a state or national government and affecting the administration of that government in its political or international relations. **2.** A newspaper officially designated for the publication of public statutes, resolutions, notices, and advertisements.

state paper office. *Hist.* An office established in London in 1578, headed by the Clerk of the Papers, to maintain custody of state documents.

state police. The department or agency of a state government empowered to maintain order, as by investigating and preventing crimes, and making arrests.

state police power. The power of a state to enforce laws for the health, welfare, morals, and safety of its citizens, if enacted so that the means are reasonably calculated to protect those legitimate state interests.

state's attorney. See DISTRICT ATTORNEY.

state seal. See *great seal* under SEAL.

state secret. A governmental matter that would be a threat to the national defense or diplomatic interests of the United States if revealed, and is therefore protected against disclosure by a witness in an ordinary judicial proceeding.

state-secrets privilege. See PRIVILEGE (3).

state's evidence. See EVIDENCE.

state's evidence, turn. See TURN STATE'S EVIDENCE.

state sovereignty. The right of a state to self-government; the supreme authority exercised by each state.

states' rights. Under the Tenth Amendment, rights neither conferred on the federal government nor forbidden to the states.

state tax. See TAX.

state trial. See TRIAL.

stateway, *n.* A governmental policy or law. • This term is formed on the analogy of *folkway.*

statim (**stay**-tim). [Latin] *Hist.* Immediately; at the earliest possible time when an act might lawfully be completed.

station. 1. Social position or status. See STATUS. **2.** A place where military duties are performed or military goods are stored. **3.** A headquarters, as of a police department. **4.** A place where both freight and passengers are received for transport or delivered after transport. **5.** *Civil law.* A place where ships may safely travel.

Stationers' Company. *Hist.* An association of stationers and their successors, established in

London in 1557 and entrusted, by order of the Privy Council, with censorship of the press.

Stationers' Hall. *Hist.* The hall of the Stationers' Company, established in London in 1553, at which every person claiming a copyright was required to register as a condition precedent to filing an infringement action.

> "Accordingly 'Entered at Stationers' Hall' on the title page of books was a form of warning to pirates that the owner of the copyright could and might sue. This requirement disappeared with the Copyright Act, 1911." David M. Walker, *The Oxford Companion to Law* 1182 (1980).

Stationery Office. *Hist. English law.* A government office established in 1786 as a department of the treasury, to supply government offices (including Parliament) with stationery and books, and to print and publish government papers. — Also termed *Her Majesty's Stationery Office.*

stationhouse. **1.** A police station or precinct. **2.** The lockup at a police precinct. See *cash bail* under BAIL (1).

stationhouse bail. See *cash bail* under BAIL.

statist (**stay**-tist). **1.** *Archaic.* A statesman; a politician. **2.** A statistician.

statistical-decision theory. A method for determining whether a panel of potential jurors was selected from a fair cross-section of the community, by calculating the probabilities of selecting a certain number of jurors from a particular group to analyze whether it is statistically probable that the jury pool was selected by mere chance. • This method has been criticized because a pool of potential jurors is not ordinarily selected by mere chance; potential jurors are disqualified for a number of legitimate reasons. See FAIR-CROSS-SECTION REQUIREMENT; ABSOLUTE DISPARITY; COMPARATIVE DISPARITY; DUREN TEST.

statuliber (stach-ə-**lɪ**-bər), *n.* [Latin] *Roman law.* A person whose freedom under a will is made conditional or postponed; a person who will be free at a particular time or when certain conditions are met. — Also written *statu liber* (**stay**-t[y]oo **lɪ**-bər).

> "The *statuliber* is one who has freedom arranged to take effect on completion of a period or fulfillment of a condition. Men become *statuliberi* as a result of an express condition, or by the very nature of the case. The meaning of 'express condition' presents no problem. The status arises from the very nature of the case when men are manumitted for the purpose of defrauding a creditor; for so long as it is uncertain whether the creditor will use his right, the men remain *statuliberi*, since fraud is taken in the *lex Aelia Sentia* to involve actual damage." *Digest of Justinian* 40.7.1 (Paul, ad Sabinum 5).

status. **1.** A person's legal condition, whether personal or proprietary; the sum total of a person's legal rights, duties, liabilities, and other legal relations, or any particular group of them separately considered <the status of a landowner>. **2.** A person's legal condition regarding personal rights but excluding proprietary relations <the status of a father> <the status of a wife>. **3.** A person's capacities and incapacities, as opposed to other elements of personal status <the status of minors>. **4.** A person's legal condition insofar as it is imposed by the law without the person's consent, as opposed to a condition that the person has acquired by agreement <the status of a slave>.

> "By the status (or standing) of a person is meant the position that he holds with reference to the rights which are recognized and maintained by the law — in other words, his capacity for the exercise and enjoyment of legal rights." James Hadley, *Introduction to Roman Law* 106 (1881).

> "The word 'status' itself originally signified nothing more than the position of a person before the law. Therefore, every person (except slaves, who were not regarded as persons, for legal purposes) had a *status*. But, as a result of the modern tendency towards legal equality formerly noticed, differences of *status* became less and less frequent, and the importance of the subject has greatly diminished, with the result that the term *status* is now used, at any rate in English Law, in connection only with those comparatively few classes of persons in the community who, by reason of their conspicuous differences from normal persons, and the fact that by no decision of their own can they get rid of these differences, require separate consideration in an account of the law. But professional or even political differences do not amount to *status*; thus peers, physicians, clergymen of the established Church, and many other classes of persons, are not regarded as the subjects of *status*, because the legal differences which distinguish them from other persons, though substantial, are not enough to make them legally abnormal. And landowners, merchants, manufacturers, and wage-earners are not subjects of the Law of Status, though the last-named are, as the result of recent legislation, tending to approach that position." Edward Jenks, *The Book of English Law* 109 (P.B. Fairest ed., 6th ed. 1967).

status, law of. See LAW OF STATUS.

status crime. See CRIME.

status de manerio (**stay**-təs dee mə-**neer**-ee-oh). [Law Latin "the state of a manor"] *Hist.* The assembly of tenants to attend the lord's court.

status offender. See OFFENDER.

status offense. See OFFENSE (1).

status of irremovability. *Hist.* A pauper's right not to be removed from a parish after residing there for one year.

status quo (**stay**-təs *or* **stat**-əs **kwoh**). [Latin] The situation that currently exists.

status quo ante (**stay**-təs **kwoh an**-tee). [Latin] The situation that existed before something else (being discussed) occurred.

statutable (**stach**-ə-tə-bəl), *adj.* **1.** Prescribed or authorized by statute. **2.** Conformed to the legislative requirements for quality, size, amount, or the like. **3.** (Of an offense) punishable by law. See STATUTORY.

statute. A law passed by a legislative body. — Abbr. s.; stat.

> "[W]e are not justified in limiting the statutory law to those rules only which are promulgated by what we commonly call 'legislatures.' Any positive enactment to which the state gives the force of a law is a 'statute,' whether it has gone through the usual stages of legislative proceedings, or has been adopted in other modes of expressing the will of the people or other sovereign power of the state. In an absolute monarchy, an edict of the ruling sovereign is statutory law. Constitutions, being direct legislation by the people, must be included in the statutory law, and indeed they are examples of the highest form that the statute law can assume. Generally speaking, treaties also are statutory law, because in this country, under the provisions of the United States Constitution, treaties have not the force of law until so declared by the representatives of the people." William M. Lile et al., *Brief Making and the Use of Law Books* 8 (3d ed. 1914).

affirmative statute. A law requiring that something be done; one that directs the doing of an act. Cf. *negative statute.*

codifying statute. A law that purports to be exhaustive in restating the whole of the law on a particular topic, including prior caselaw as well as legislative provisions. • Courts generally presume that a codifying statute supersedes prior caselaw. Cf. *consolidating statute.*

compiled statutes. Laws that have been arranged by subject but have not been substantively changed; COMPILATION. Cf. *revised statutes.*

> "The term 'compiled statutes' is properly applied to a methodical arrangement, without revision or reenactment, of the existing statutes of a State, all the statutes on a given subject being collected in one place. The work is usually performed by private persons; and the former statutes, as they were before the compilation, remain the authority." Frank Hall Childs, *Where and How to Find the Law* 12 (1922).

consolidating statute. A law that collects the legislative provisions on a particular subject and embodies them in a single statute, often with minor amendments and drafting improvements. • Courts generally presume that a consolidating statute leaves prior caselaw intact. Cf. *codifying statute.*

> "A distinction of greater importance in this field is that between consolidating and codifying statutes. A consolidating statute is one which collects the statutory provisions relating to a particular topic, and embodies them in a single Act of Parliament, making only minor amendments and improvements. A codifying statute is one which purports to state exhaustively the whole of the law on a particular subject (the common law as well as previous statutory provisions).... The importance of the distinction lies in the courts' treatment of the previous case law, the existence of special procedural provisions with regard to consolidating statutes and the existence of a presumption that they do not change the law." Rupert Cross, *Statutory Interpretation* 5 (1976).

criminal statute. A law that defines, classifies, and sets forth punishment for specific crimes. — Also termed *criminal code.*

declaratory statute. A law enacted to clarify prior law by reconciling conflicting judicial decisions or by explaining the meaning of a prior statute.

directory statute. A law that indicates only what should be done, with no provision for enforcement. Cf. *mandatory statute.*

disabling statute. A law that limits or curbs certain rights.

enabling statute. A law that permits what was previously prohibited or that creates new powers; esp., a congressional statute conferring powers on an executive agency to carry out various delegated tasks. — Also termed *enabling act.*

expository statute. A law enacted to explain the meaning of a previously enacted law.

general statute. A law pertaining to an entire community or all persons generally. — Also termed *public statute.* See PUBLIC LAW (2).

imperfect statute. A law that prohibits, but does not render void, an objectionable transaction. • Such a statute provides a penalty for disobedience without depriving the violative transaction of its legal effect.

local statute. See LOCAL LAW (1), (2).

mandatory statute. A law that requires a course of action as opposed to merely permitting it. Cf. *directory statute.*

negative statute. A law prohibiting something; a law expressed in negative terms. Cf. *affirmative statute.*

nonclaim statute. **1.** STATUTE OF LIMITATIONS. **2.** A law extinguishing a claim that is not timely asserted, esp. in the context of another proceeding. • An example is a statutory deadline for a creditor to file a claim in a probate proceeding. Unlike a statute of limitations, most nonclaim statutes are not subject to tolling.

organic statute. A law that establishes an administrative agency or local government. — Also termed *organic act.* Cf. ORGANIC LAW.

penal statute. A law that defines an offense and prescribes its corresponding fine, penalty, or punishment. — Also termed *penal law; punitive statute.*

perpetual statute. A law containing no provision for repeal, abrogation, or expiration at a future time.

personal statute. *Civil law.* A law that primarily affects a person's condition or status (such as a statute relating to capacity or majority) and affects property only incidentally.

private statute. See *special statute.*

prospective statute. A law that applies to future events.

public statute. See PUBLIC LAW (2).

punitive statute. See *penal statute.*

real statute. *Civil law.* A law primarily affecting the operation, status, and condition of property, and addressing persons only incidentally.

reference statute. A law that incorporates and adopts by reference provisions of other laws.

remedial statute. A law that affords a remedy.

retrospective statute. A law that applies to past events.

revised statutes. Laws that have been collected, arranged, and reenacted as a whole by a legislative body. — Abbr. Rev. Stat.; R.S. See CODE (1). Cf. *compiled statutes.*

revival statute. A law that provides for the renewal of actions, of wills, and of the legal effect of documents.

severable statute. A law that remains operative in its remaining provisions even though a portion of the law is declared unconstitutional.

single-act statute. See LONG-ARM STATUTE.

speaking statute. A statute to be interpreted in light of the understanding of its terms prevailing at the time of interpretation.

special statute. A law that applies only to specific individuals, as opposed to everyone. — Also termed *private statute.*

> "It is ancient wisdom, tracing back at least as far as the Roman taboo against the *privilegium*, that laws ought to be *general*, they ought to be addressed, not to particular persons, but to persons generally or to classes of persons (say, 'all householders'). Accordingly, a number of American states have inserted in their constitutions prohibitions against 'private or special' statutes. These have given rise to endless difficulties." Lon L. Fuller, *Anatomy of the Law* 102–03 (1968).

split-level statute. A law that has connected with it officially promulgated explanatory materials, so that courts are left with two levels of documents to construe.

statute of frauds. See STATUTE OF FRAUDS.

temporary statute. **1.** A law that specifically provides that it is to remain in effect for a fixed, limited period. **2.** A law (such as an appropriation statute) that, by its nature, has only a single and temporary operation.

validating statute. A law that is amended either to remove errors or to add provisions to conform to constitutional requirements. — Also termed *validation statute.*

statute book. A bound collection of statutes, usu. as part of a larger set of books containing a complete body of statutory law, such as the United States Code Annotated.

statute fair. *Hist.* A fair during which the fixed labor rates are announced and laborers of both sexes offer themselves for hire. — Also termed *mop.*

statute law. See STATUTORY LAW.

statute merchant. *Hist.* **1.** (*cap.*) One of two 13th-century statutes establishing procedures to better secure and recover debts by, among other things, providing for a commercial bond that, if not timely paid, resulted in swift execution on the lands, goods, and body of the debtor. 13 Edw., ch. 6 (1283); 15 Edw., ch. 6 (1285). • These statutes were repealed in 1863. **2.** The commercial bond so established. Cf. STATUTE STAPLE.

> "It is not a little remarkable that our common law knew no process whereby a man could pledge his body or liberty for payment of a debt .... Under Edward I, the tide turned. In the interest of commerce a new form of security, the so-called 'statute merchant,' was invented, which gave the creditor power to demand the seizure and

imprisonment of his debtor's body." 2 Frederick Pollock & Frederic W. Maitland, *The History of English Law Before the Time of Edward I* 596–97 (2d ed. 1899).

statute mile. See MILE (1).

Statute of Accumulations. *Hist.* A statute forbidding the accumulation, beyond a certain period, of property settled by deed or will. 39 & 40 Geo. 3, ch. 98 (1800).

Statute of Allegiance de Facto. *Hist.* A statute requiring subjects to give allegiance to the actual (de facto) king, and protecting them in so doing. 11 Hen. 7, ch. 1.

Statute of Amendments and Jeofails (jef-aylz). *Hist.* One of several 15th- and 16th-century statutes allowing a party who acknowledges a pleading error to correct it. 1 Hen. 5, ch. 5 (1413); 32 Hen. 8, ch. 30 (1540); 37 Hen. 8, ch. 6 (1545). See JEOFAIL.

Statute of Anne. *Hist.* **1.** The Copyright Act of 1709, which first granted copyright protection to book authors. 8 Anne, ch. 19 (1709). **2.** The statute that modernized the English bankruptcy system and first introduced the discharge of the debtor's existing debts. 4 Anne, ch. 17 (1705).

statute of bread and ale. See ASSISA PANIS ET CEREVISIAE.

statute of distribution. A state law regulating the distribution of an estate among an intestate's heirs and relatives.

Statute of Elizabeth. *Hist.* The Bankrupts Act of 1705, which contained provisions against conveyances made to defraud creditors. 13 Eliz., ch. 5.

statute of frauds. 1. (*cap.*) An English statute enacted in 1677 declaring certain contracts judicially unenforceable (but not void) if they are not committed to writing and signed by the party to be charged. • The statute was entitled "An Act for the Prevention of Frauds and Perjuries" (29 Car. 2, ch. 3). — Also termed *Statute of Frauds and Perjuries*.

"The best known, and until recently, most important, Act prescribing written formalities for certain contracts only required that those contracts should be evidenced in writing, or to put it another way, that the contract would be unenforceable in a Court (but not void) in the absence of writing. This was the Statute of Frauds 1677, sections 4 and 17 of which required written evidence of a somewhat curious list of contracts. Today, all that is left of these provisions is that part of section 4, which requires contracts of guarantee to be evidenced in writing, and section 40 of the Law of Property Act 1925 (replacing another part of section 4), which deals with contracts of sale of an interest in land." P.S. Atiyah, *An Introduction to the Law of Contract* 141 (3d ed. 1981).

2. A statute (based on the English Statute of Frauds) designed to prevent fraud and perjury by requiring certain contracts to be in writing and signed by the party to be charged. • Statutes of frauds traditionally apply to the following types of contracts: (1) a contract for the sale or transfer of an interest in land, (2) a contract that cannot be performed within one year of its making, (3) a contract for the sale of goods valued at $500 or more, (4) a contract of an executor or administrator to answer for a decedent's debt, (5) a contract to guarantee the debt or duty of another, and (6) a contract made in consideration of marriage. UCC § 2–201. — Abbr. S/F; SOF.

"[T]he primary theory of statutes of frauds, past and present, is that they are means to the end of preventing successful courtroom perjury. The means to this end is simply the requirement of a writing signed by the party to be charged.... [B]ut the statute of frauds writing requirement is ... so far from any kind of guarantee against successful perjury that it is inappropriate even to call it a means to fraud prevention at all." 1 James J. White & Robert S. Summers, *Uniform Commercial Code* § 2–8, at 82 (4th ed. 1995).

Statute of Frauds and Perjuries. See STATUTE OF FRAUDS (1).

Statute of Gloucester (glos-tər). *Hist.* A statute providing for the award of costs in legal actions. 6 Edw., ch. 1 (1278).

statute of limitations. 1. A statute establishing a time limit for suing in a civil case, based on the date when the claim accrued (as when the injury occurred or was discovered). • The purpose of such a statute is to require diligent prosecution of known claims, thereby providing finality and predictability in legal affairs and ensuring that claims will be resolved while evidence is reasonably available and fresh. — Also termed *nonclaim statute*.

"Statutes of limitations, like the equitable doctrine of laches, in their conclusive effects are designed to promote justice by preventing surprises through the revival of claims that have been allowed to slumber until evidence has been lost, memories have faded, and witnesses have disappeared." *Order of R.R. Telegraphers v. Railway Express Agency*, 321 U.S. 342, 348–49, 64 S.Ct. 582, 586 (1944).

2. A statute establishing a time limit for prosecuting a crime, based on the date when the offense occurred. Cf. STATUTE OF REPOSE.

"The purpose of a statute of limitations is to limit exposure to criminal prosecution to a certain fixed period of time following the occurrence of those acts the legislature had decided to punish by criminal sanctions. Such a limitation is designed to protect individuals from having to defend themselves against charges when the basic facts have become obscured by the passage of time and to minimize the danger of official punishment because of acts in the far-distant past. Such a time limit may also have the salutary effect of encouraging law enforcement officials promptly to investigate suspected criminal activity." *Toussie v. United States*, 397 U.S. 112, 90 S.Ct. 858 (1970).

statute of mortmain. See MORTMAIN STATUTE.

statute of repose. A statute that bars a suit a fixed number of years after the defendant acts in some way (as by designing or manufacturing a product), even if this period ends before the plaintiff has suffered any injury. Cf. STATUTE OF LIMITATIONS.

"A statute of repose . . . limits the time within which an action may be brought and is not related to the accrual of any cause of action; the injury need not have occurred, much less have been discovered. Unlike an ordinary statute of limitations which begins running upon accrual of the claim, the period contained in a statute of repose begins when a specific event occurs, regardless of whether a cause of action has accrued or whether any injury has resulted." 54 C.J.S. *Limitations of Actions* § 4, at 20–21 (1987).

Statute of Uses. *Hist.* An English statute of 1535 that converted the equitable title held by a cestui que use (i.e., a beneficiary) to a legal one in order to make the cestui que use liable for feudal dues, as only a legal owner (the *feoffee to uses*) could be. • This statute was the culmination of a series of enactments designed by the Tudors to stop the practice of creating uses in land that deprived feudal lords of the valuable incidents of feudal tenure. The statute discouraged the granting of property subject to another's use by deeming the person who enjoys the use to have legal title with the right of absolute ownership and possession. So after the statute was enacted, if A conveyed land to B subject to the use of C, then C became the legal owner of the land in fee simple. Ultimately, the statute was circumvented by the courts' recognition of the use of equitable trusts in land-conveyancing. See CESTUI QUE USE; GRANT TO USES; USE (4).

"The Statute of 27 H.8. hath advanced Uses, and hath established Surety for him that hath the Use against the Feoffees: for before the Statute the Feoffees were Owners of the Land, but now it is destroyed, and the *cestuy que use* is the Owner of the same: before the Possession ruled the Use, but since the Use governeth the Possession." William Noy, *A Treatise of the Principal Grounds and Maxims of the Laws of This Nation* 73 (4th ed. 1677; repr. C. Sims ed., 1870).

Statute of Westminster the First. See WESTMINSTER THE FIRST, STATUTE OF.

statute of wills. 1. (*cap.*) An English statute (enacted in 1540) that established the right of a person to devise real property by will. — Also termed *Wills Act*. **2.** A state statute, usu. derived from the English statute, providing for testamentary disposition in that jurisdiction.

Statute of Winchester. See WINCHESTER, STATUTE OF.

Statute of York. See YORK, STATUTE OF.

statute roll. *Hist.* A roll upon which a statute was formally entered after receiving the royal assent.

Statutes at Large. An official compilation of the acts and resolutions that become law from each session of Congress, printed in chronological order.

statute staple. *Hist.* **1.** A 1353 statute establishing procedures for settling disputes among merchants who traded in staple towns. • The statute helped merchants receive swift judgments for debt. Cf. STATUTE MERCHANT. **2.** A bond for commercial debt. • A statute staple gave the lender a possessory right in the land of a debtor who failed to repay a loan. See STAPLE.

"A popular form of security after 1285 . . . was the . . . 'statute staple' — whereby the borrower could by means of a registered contract charge his land and goods without giving up possession; if he failed to pay, the lender became a tenant of the land until satisfied. . . . The borrower under a statute or recognizance remained in possession of his land, and it later became a common practice under the common-law forms of mortgage likewise to allow the mortgagor to remain in possession as a tenant at will or at sufferance of the mortgagee." J.H. Baker, *An Introduction to English Legal History* 354 (3d ed. 1990).

statuti (stə-**t[y]oo**-tɪ). [Latin] *Roman law.* Licensed advocates whose names are inscribed in registers of matriculation, forming part of the college of advocates. Cf. SUPERNUMERARII.

statuto mercatorio. See DE STATUTO MERCATORIO.

statutory (**stach**-ə-tor-ee), *adj.* **1.** Of or relating to legislation <statutory interpretation>. **2.**

Legislatively created <the law of patents is purely statutory>. **3.** Conformable to a statute <a statutory act>.

statutory action. See ACTION.

statutory agent. See AGENT.

statutory arson. See ARSON (2).

statutory bond. See BOND (2), (3).

statutory burglary. See BURGLARY.

statutory construction. **1.** The act or process of interpreting a statute. **2.** Collectively, the principles developed by courts for interpreting statutes. — Also termed *statutory interpretation*. See CONSTRUCTION (2).

> "[T]here is not, and probably never can be, anything meriting the description of a coherent body of case-law on statutory interpretation as a whole as distinct from the interpretation of a particular statute." Rupert Cross, *Statutory Interpretation* 39 (1976).

statutory crime. See CRIME.

statutory damages. See DAMAGES.

statutory dedication. See DEDICATION.

statutory deed. See DEED.

statutory employee. See EMPLOYEE.

statutory employer. See EMPLOYER.

statutory exception. See EXCEPTION (2).

statutory exposition. A statute's special interpretation of the ambiguous terms of a previous statute <the statute contained a statutory exposition of the former act>.

statutory extortion. See EXTORTION.

statutory forced share. See ELECTIVE SHARE.

statutory foreclosure. See *power-of-sale foreclosure* under FORECLOSURE.

statutory guardian. See GUARDIAN.

statutory instrument. A British administrative regulation or order.

statutory interpretation. See STATUTORY CONSTRUCTION.

statutory law. The body of law derived from statutes rather than from constitutions or judicial decisions. — Also termed *statute law*; *legislative law*; *ordinary law*. Cf. COMMON LAW (1); CONSTITUTIONAL LAW.

statutory lien. See LIEN.

statutory merger. See MERGER.

statutory obligation. See OBLIGATION.

statutory omnibus clause. *Insurance.* An omnibus clause provided by statute. See OMNIBUS CLAUSE (1).

statutory partnership association. See PARTNERSHIP ASSOCIATION.

statutory penalty. See PENALTY.

statutory presumption. See PRESUMPTION.

statutory rape. See RAPE.

statutory redemption. See REDEMPTION.

statutory release. *Hist.* A conveyance superseding the compound assurance by lease and release, created by the Conveyance by Release Without Lease Act of 1841 (St. 4 & 5 Vict., ch. 21).

statutory right of redemption. The right of a mortgagor in default to recover property after a foreclosure sale by paying the principal, interest, and other costs that are owed, together with any other measure required to cure the default. • This statutory right exists in many states but is not uniform. See REDEMPTION.

statutory share. See ELECTIVE SHARE.

statutory staple. *Hist.* A writ to seize the lands, goods, and person of a debtor for forfeiting a statute staple. See STATUTE STAPLE.

statutory successor. The person to whom all corporate assets pass upon a corporation's dissolution according to the statute of the state of incorporation applicable at the time of the dissolution. See Restatement (Second) of Conflict of Laws § 388 cmt. a (1971).

statuto stapulae. See DE STATUTO STAPULAE.

statutum (stə-**t**[**y**]**oo**-təm), *adj*. Established; determined.

statutum, *n*. **1.** *Hist*. An act of Parliament, esp. one that has been approved by the monarch. Cf. ACTUS (2). **2.** *Roman law*. An ordinance; esp., an imperial law.

Statutum de Nova Custuma (stə-**t**[**y**]**oo**-təm dee **noh**-və **kəs**-chə-mə *or* kəs-tyə-mə). See CARTA MERCATORIA.

stay, *n*. **1.** The postponement or halting of a proceeding, judgment, or the like. **2.** An order to suspend all or part of a judicial proceeding or a judgment resulting from that proceeding. — Also termed *stay of execution*. — **stay,** *vb*. — **stayable,** *adj*.

automatic stay. *Bankruptcy*. A bar to all judicial and extrajudicial collection efforts against the debtor or the debtor's property. • The policy behind the automatic stay, which is effective upon the filing of the bankruptcy petition, is that all actions against the debtor should be halted pending the determination of creditors' rights and the orderly administration of the debtor's assets free from creditor interference. — Also termed *automatic suspension*.

stay of execution. See STAY.

stay-put rule. *School law*. The principle that a child must remain in his or her current educational placement while an administrative claim under the Individuals with Disabilities Education Act (usu. for an alternative placement or for mainstreaming) is pending. 20 USCA § 1415(j).

STB. *abbr*. Surface Transportation Board. See INTERSTATE COMMERCE COMMISSION.

STD. *abbr*. SEXUALLY TRANSMITTED DISEASE.

steady course. *Maritime law*. A ship's path that can be readily ascertained either because the ship is on a straight heading or because the ship's future positions are easy to plot based on the ship's current position and movements.

steal, *vb*. **1.** To take (personal property) illegally with the intent to keep it unlawfully. **2.** To take (something) by larceny, embezzlement, or false pretenses.

stealth. 1. *Hist*. Theft; an act or instance of stealing. • Etymologically, this term is the noun corresponding to the verb *steal*.

> "Stealth is the wrongful taking of goods without pretence of title: and therefore altereth not the property, as a trespass doth, so as upon an appeal the party shall rehave them." Sir Henry Finch, *Law, or a Discourse Thereof* 210 (1759).

2. Surreptitiousness; furtive slyness.

stellionatus (stel-ee-ə-**nay**-təs *or* stel-yə-). [Latin "underhand dealing"] *Roman & Scots law*. Conduct that is fraudulent but does not fall within a specific class of offenses. • This term applies primarily to fraudulent practices in the sale or hypothecation of land. — Also termed (in Scots law) *stellionate*. Cf. COZENING.

> "Though *pignus* and hypothec are almost different names for the same thing, there were differences. Hypothec was used mainly for land, which cannot be removed. A thing could be pledged only to one, but successive hypothecs might be created over a thing. There was no fraud in this but it was the offence of *stellionatus* to give a hypothec without declaring existing hypothecs." W.W. Buckland, *A Manual of Roman Private Law* 355 (2d ed. 1953).

> "STELLIONATE ... is a term applied, in the law of Scotland, either to any crime which, though indictable, goes under no general denomination, and is punishable arbitrarily, or to any civil delinquency of which fraud is an ingredient. Those, *e.g.*, who grant double conveyances of the same subject, are guilty of this crime ... and are punishable arbitrarily in their persons and goods, besides becoming infamous." William Bell, *Bell's Dictionary and Digest of the Law of Scotland* 940 (George Watson ed., 1882).

stepchild. The child of one's spouse by a previous marriage.

stepfather. The husband of one's mother by a later marriage. — Formerly also termed *vitricus*.

step-in-the-dark rule. *Torts*. The contributory-negligence rule that a person who enters a totally unfamiliar area in the darkness has a duty, in the absence of unusual stress, to refrain from proceeding until first ascertaining the existence of any dangerous obstacles. See *contributory negligence* under NEGLIGENCE.

stepmother. The wife of one's father by a later marriage.

stepped-up basis. See BASIS.

step-rate-premium insurance. See INSURANCE.

step-transaction doctrine. A method used by the Internal Revenue Service to determine tax liability by viewing the transaction as a whole, and disregarding one or more nonsubstantive, intervening transactions taken to achieve the final result. — Also termed *step-transaction approach*.

sterling, *adj*. **1.** Of or conforming to a standard of national value, esp. of English money or metal <a pound sterling>. **2.** (Of an opinion, value, etc.) valuable; authoritative <a sterling report>.

stet (stet), *n*. [Latin "let it stand"] **1.** An order staying legal proceedings, as when a prosecutor determines not to proceed on an indictment and places the case on a stet docket. • The term is used chiefly in Maryland. **2.** An instruction to leave a text as it stands.

stet processus (stet prə-**ses**-əs), *n*. [Law Latin "let the process stand"] *Hist*. **1.** A record entry, similar to a *nolle prosequi*, by which the parties agree to stay further proceedings. **2.** The agreement between the parties to stay those proceedings. • This was typically used by a plaintiff to suspend an action rather than suffer a nonsuit.

stevedore (**stee**-və-dor). *Maritime law*. A person employed in the loading and unloading of vessels. Cf. SEAMAN.

steward. 1. A person appointed in place of another. **2.** A union official who represents union employees and who oversees the carrying out of union contracts. — Also termed (in sense 2) *union steward*; *shop steward*.

steward of all England. *Hist*. An officer vested with various powers, including the power to preside over the trial of peers.

steward of a manor. *Hist*. An officer who handles the business matters of a manor, including keeping the court rolls and granting admittance to copyhold lands.

Steward of Chiltern Hundreds (**chil**-tərn). *English law*. Formerly, a royal officer charged with protecting residents from robbers and thieves who hid in the hundreds' wooded areas. • A member of Parliament can now use the office as a way to resign from office (something forbidden by statute) by accepting in lieu of a Parliamentary seat a royal appointment as Steward of Chiltern Hundreds. By law, a member of Parliament may not accept certain Crown appointments without forfeiting his or her seat, so once a member secures an appointment as Steward of Chiltern Hundreds — an office that is now only a sinecure — he or she is removed from Parliament. A resignation from the office of Steward completes the resignation process.

stickering. *Securities*. The updating of a prospectus by affixing stickers that contain the new or revised information. • Stickering avoids the expense of reprinting an entire prospectus.

stickler. *Hist*. An arbitrator.

stickup. An armed robbery in which the victim is threatened by the use of weapons. — Also termed *holdup*. See *armed robbery* under ROBBERY.

stifling of a prosecution. An agreement, in exchange for money or other advantage, to abstain from prosecuting a person.

stigma-plus doctrine. The principle that defamation by a government official is not actionable as a civil-rights violation unless the victim suffers not only embarrassment but also the loss of a property interest (such as continued employment in a government job).

stillicidium (stil-ə-**sid**-ee-əm). [Latin fr. *stilla* "a drop" + *cadere* "to fall"] *Roman law*. See AQUAE IMMITTENDAE.

sting. An undercover operation in which law-enforcement agents pose as criminals to catch actual criminals engaging in illegal acts.

stint. 1. *English law*. A limited number <a stint of common>.

> "All these species, of pasturable common, may be and usually are limited as to number and time; but there are also commons without stint, and which last all the year." 2 William Blackstone, *Commentaries on the Laws of England* 34 (1766).

2. The task for the day or work <he has done his stint>.

stipend (**stɪ**-pend *or* -pənd). **1.** A salary or other regular, periodic payment. **2.** A tribute to support the clergy, usu. consisting of payments in money or grain.

stipendiary estate (stɪ-**pen**-dee-er-ee). See ESTATE.

stipendiary magistrate. See MAGISTRATE.

stipendium (stI-**pen**-dee-əm), *n.* [Latin] *Roman law.* A soldier's regular pay. Cf. SALARIUM.

stipes (**stI**-peez), *n.* [Latin "a trunk"] *Hist.* Family stock; a source of descent or title. Pl. ***stipites*** (**stip**-ə-teez).

stipital (**stip**-i-təl), *adj.* See STIRPITAL.

stipulated authority. See *express authority* under AUTHORITY (1).

stipulated damages. See *liquidated damages* under DAMAGES.

stipulated judgment. See *agreed judgment* under JUDGMENT.

stipulatio (stip-yə-**lay**-shee-oh), *n.* [Latin] *Roman law.* An oral contract requiring a formal question and reply, binding the replier to do what was asked. • It is essential that both parties speak, and that the reply directly conforms to the question asked and is made with the intent to enter into a contractual obligation. No consideration is required. See *actio ex stipulatu* under ACTIO.

> "[I]t must be remembered that the law-forms used by the Romans had their origin in times when writing was neither easy nor common. It is not surprising, therefore, that among them a form of spoken words, a verbal contract, should hold the place which among us is occupied by written notes. This form ... *stipulatio* — was of a very simple character, consisting only of a question asked by one party, and an answer returned by the other .... Such forms as *Spondesne mihi decem aureos dare* (do you engage to give me ten aurei, or gold-pieces): answer, *Spondeo* (I engage) ...." James Hadley, *Introduction to Roman Law* 210 (1881).

> "The oldest Roman contract was the *stipulatio*, an oral promise made by an answer to an immediately preceding question, with the promisor using the same verb. The contract was unilateral. Only one party, the promisor, was legally liable, and he was bound strictly by the words used." Alan Watson, *Ancient Law and Modern Understanding* 96 (1998).

stipulatio aquiliana (stip-yə-**lay**-shee-oh ə-kwil-ee-**ay**-nə). [Latin] *Roman law.* A type of *stipulatio* used to collect and discharge all the liabilities owed by a single contract.

> "[*S*]*tipulatio Aquiliana*, a device credited to Aquilius Gallus, of Cicero's time. Where two persons with complex relations between them desired to square or simplify their accounts they could work out the items and arrive at the balance .... This balance being paid or otherwise arranged, each party would then make with the other this *stipulatio*, which was a comprehensive formula .... This would novate all the claims and turn them into a single promise, for an *incertum*. These mutual stipulations might then be released by *acceptilatio*." W.W. Buckland, *A Manual of Roman Private Law* 348 (2d ed. 1953).

stipulatio juris (stip-yə-**lay**-shee-oh **joor**-is). [Latin "stipulatio as to the law"] The parties' agreement on a question of law or its applicability. • The court is not bound to accept the stipulation if it is erroneous. But the parties are allowed to stipulate the law to be applied to a dispute.

stipulation (stip-yə-**lay**-shən), *n.* **1.** A material condition or requirement in an agreement; esp., a factual representation that is incorporated into a contract as a term <breach of the stipulation regarding payment of taxes>. • Such a contractual term often appears in a section of the contract called "Representations and Warranties." **2.** A voluntary agreement between opposing parties concerning some relevant point <the plaintiff and defendant entered into a stipulation on the issue of liability>. • A stipulation relating to a pending judicial proceeding, made by a party to the proceeding or the party's attorney, is binding without consideration.

> "Breach of a stipulation should not be confused with *misrepresentation*, which is a false statement made before or at the time the contract is made, and which induces the contract; only if it is incorporated into the contract does it become a stipulation or term, the breach of which will entitle the injured party to pursue the usual remedies which are available where there has been a breach of a warranty or of a condition." 1 E.W. Chance, *Principles of Mercantile Law* 239 (P.W. French ed., 13th ed. 1950).

> "Stipulations with respect to matters of form and procedure serve the convenience of the parties to litigation and often serve to simplify and expedite the proceeding. In some cases they are supported by the policy of favoring compromise in order to reduce the volume of litigation. Hence they are favored by the courts and enforced without regard to consideration." Restatement (Second) of Contracts § 94 cmt. a (1981).

3. *Roman law.* A formal contract by which a promisor (and only the promisor) became bound by oral question and answer. • By the sixth century A.D., stipulations were exclusively in written form. — **stipulate** (**stip**-yə-layt), *vb.* — **stipulative** (**stip**-yə-lə-tiv), *adj.*

stipulation pour autrui (**poor** oh-troo-**ee**). [French "for other persons"] *Civil law.* A contractual provision that benefits a third party and gives the third party a cause of action against the promisor for specific performance. See *third-party beneficiary* under BENEFICIARY.

stipulatio sponsalitia (stip-yə-**lay**-shee-oh spon-sə-**lish**-ee-ə). See SPONSALIA.

stipulative definition. See DEFINITION.

stipulator. **1.** One who makes a stipulation. **2.** *Civil law.* The promisee in a stipulation pour autrui, accepting the promise of a benefit to a third party.

stirpal (**stər**-pəl), *adj.* See STIRPITAL.

stirpes (**stər**-peez). *pl.* STIRPS.

stirpital (**stər**-pə-təl), *adj.* Of or relating to per stirpes distribution. — Also termed *stipital*; *stirpal.* See PER STIRPES.

stirps (stərps), *n.* [Latin "stock"] A branch of a family; a line of descent. Pl. **stirpes** (**stər**-peez). See PER STIRPES.

stock, *n.* **1.** The original progenitor of a family; a person from whom a family is descended <George Harper, Sr. was the stock of the Harper line>. **2.** A merchant's goods that are kept for sale or trade <the car dealer put last year's models on sale to reduce its stock>. **3.** The capital or principal fund raised by a corporation through subscribers' contributions or the sale of shares <Acme's stock is worth far more today than it was 20 years ago>. **4.** A proportional part of a corporation's capital represented by the number of equal units (or shares) owned, and granting the holder the right to participate in the company's general management and to share in its net profits or earnings <Julia sold her stock in Pantheon Corporation>. See SHARE (2). Cf. SECURITY (4).

assented stock. Stock that an owner deposits with a third person according to an agreement by which the owner voluntarily accepts a change in the corporation's securities.

assessable stock. Stock that is subject to resale by the issuer if the holder fails to pay any assessment levied on it.

authorized stock. See *capital stock* (1).

bailout stock. Nontaxable preferred stock issued to stockholders as a dividend. • Bailout stock is issued to gain favorable tax rates by distributing corporate earnings at capital gains rates rather than by distributing dividends at ordinary income rates. This practice is now prohibited by the Internal Revenue Code. IRC (26 USCA) § 306.

barometer stock. A stock whose price fluctuates according to market conditions; an individual stock considered to be indicative of the strength of the market in general. — Also termed *bellwether stock.*

blank stock. *Securities.* Stock with voting powers and rights set by the issuer's board of directors after the stock has been sold.

blue-chip stock. See BLUE CHIP.

bonus stock. A stock share that is issued for no consideration, as an enticement to buy some other type or class of security. • It is considered a type of watered stock. — Also termed *bonus share.*

book-value stock. Stock offered to executives at a book-value price, rather than at its market value. • The stock is offered with the understanding that when its book value has risen, the company will buy back the stock at the increased price or will make payments in stock equal to the increased price.

callable preferred stock. Preferred stock that may be repurchased by the issuing corporation at a prestated price, usu. at or slightly above par value.

capital stock. **1.** The total number of shares of stock that a corporation may issue under its charter or articles of incorporation, including both common stock and preferred stock. • A corporation may increase the amount of capital stock if the owners of a majority of the outstanding shares consent. — Also termed *authorized stock*; *authorized capital stock*; *authorized stock issue*; *authorized shares.* **2.** The total par value or stated value of this stock; CAPITALIZATION (4). **3.** See *common stock.*

common stock. A class of stock entitling the holder to vote on corporate matters, to receive dividends after other claims and dividends have been paid (esp. to preferred shareholders), and to share in assets upon liquidation. • Common stock is often called *capital stock* if it is the corporation's only class of stock outstanding. — Also termed *ordinary shares.* Cf. *preferred stock.*

convertible stock. See *convertible security* under SECURITY.

corporate stock. An equity security issued by a corporation.

cumulative preferred stock. Preferred stock that must pay dividends in full before common shareholders may receive any dividend. • If the corporation omits a dividend in a particular year or period, it is carried over to the next year or period and must be paid before the common shareholders receive any payment. — Also termed *cumulative stock*; *cumulative preference share.*

deferred stock. Stock whose holders are entitled to dividends only after the corporation has met some other specified obligation, such as the discharge of a liability or the payment of a dividend to preferred shareholders.

discount stock. A stock share issued for less than par value. • Discount stock is considered a type of watered stock, the issuance of which may impose liability on the recipient for the difference between the par value and the cash amount paid. — Also termed *discount share.*

donated stock. Stock donated to a charity or given to a corporation by its own stockholders, esp. for resale.

equity stock. Stock of any class having unlimited dividend rights, regardless of whether the stock is preferred.

floating stock. Stock that is offered for sale on the open market and that has not yet been purchased; the number of outstanding shares available for trading.

full-paid stock. Stock on which no further payments can be demanded by the issuing company. — Also termed *paid-up stock.*

glamour stock. A stock with great public interest because of a real or imagined potential for fast growth or high earnings. — Also termed *growth stock*; *performance stock.*

growth stock. **1.** Stock issued by a growth company. • Because a growth company usu. reinvests a large share of its income back into the company, growth stock pays relatively low dividends, though its price usu. has a relatively high appreciation in market value over time. **2.** See *glamour stock.*

guaranteed stock. Preferred stock whose dividend is guaranteed by someone (usu. a parent corporation) other than the issuer.

guarantee stock. A fixed, nonwithdrawal investment in a building-and-loan association. • This type of stock guarantees to all other investors in the association a fixed dividend or interest rate. See BUILDING-AND-LOAN ASSOCIATION.

guaranty stock. A savings-and-loan association's stock yielding dividends to the holders after dividends have been paid to the depositors.

hot stock. See *hot issue* under ISSUE (2).

inactive stock. A low-volume stock.

income stock. A stock with a history of high yields or dividend payments (e.g., public utilities and well-established corporations).

issued stock. Capital stock that has been authorized and sold to subscribers, but may be reacquired, such as treasury stock.

letter stock. See *restricted security* under SECURITY.

listed stock. See *listed security* under SECURITY.

margin stock. See *marginable security* under SECURITY.

nonassessable stock. Stock owned by a holder whose potential liability is limited to the amount paid for the stock and who cannot be charged additional funds to pay the issuer's debts. • Stock issued in the United States is usu. nonassessable.

noncumulative preferred stock. Preferred stock that does not have to pay dividends that are in arrears. • Once a periodic dividend is omitted, it will not be paid. — Also termed *noncumulative stock.*

nonparticipating preferred stock. Preferred stock that does not give the shareholder the right to additional earnings — usu. surplus common-stock dividends — beyond those stated in the preferred contract.

nonvoting stock. Stock that has no voting rights attached to it under most situations.

no-par stock. Stock issued without a specific value assigned to it. • For accounting purposes, it is given a legal or stated value that has little or no connection to the stock's market value. — Also termed *no-par-value stock.* — Sometimes shortened to *no par.*

outstanding stock. Stock that is held by investors and has not been redeemed by the issuing corporation. — Also termed *outstanding capital stock*; *shares outstanding.*

participating preferred stock. Preferred stock whose holder is entitled to receive stated dividends and to share with the common shareholders in any additional distributions of earnings.

participation stock. Stock permitting the holder to participate in profits and surplus.

par-value stock. Stock originally issued for a fixed value derived by dividing the total value of capital stock by the number of shares to be issued. • The par value does not bear a necessary relation to the actual stock value because of the part surplus plays in the valuation.

penny stock. An equity security that is not traded in established markets, represents no tangible assets, or has average revenues less than required for trading on an exchange. • Typically, a penny stock is highly speculative and can be purchased for less than $5 a share.

performance stock. See *glamour stock.*

phantom stock. Imaginary stock that is credited to a corporate executive account as part of the executive's compensation package. See PHANTOM STOCK PLAN.

preferred stock. A class of stock giving its holder a preferential claim to dividends and to corporate assets upon liquidation but that usu. carries no voting rights. — Also termed *preference shares.* Cf. *common stock.*

premium stock. Stock that carries a premium for trading, as in the case of short-selling.

prior preferred stock. Preferred stock that has preference over another class of preferred stock from the same issuer. • The preference usu. relates to dividend payments or claims on assets.

public stock. **1.** See *public security* under SECURITY. **2.** Stock of a publicly traded corporation.

reacquired stock. See *treasury stock.*

redeemable stock. Preferred stock that can be called by the issuing corporation and retired.

registered stock. See *registered security* under SECURITY.

restricted stock. See *restricted security* under SECURITY.

retired stock. See *treasury stock.*

subscribed stock. A stockholder's equity account showing the capital that will be contributed when the subscription price is collected. See SUBSCRIPTION (2).

tainted stock. Stock owned or transferred by a person disqualified from serving as a plaintiff in a derivative action. • A good-faith transferee is also disqualified from filing a derivative action.

treasury stock. Stock issued by a company but then reacquired and either canceled or held. • Some states have eliminated this classification and treat such stock as if it is authorized but unissued. — Also termed *treasury security*; *reacquired stock*; *retired stock.*

unissued stock. Stock that is authorized by the corporate charter but not yet distributed.

unlisted stock. See *unlisted security* under SECURITY.

volatile stock. Stock subject to wide and rapid fluctuations in price. — Also termed *yo-yo stock.*

voting stock. Stock that entitles the holder to vote in the corporation's election of officers and on other matters put to a vote. — Also termed *voting security.*

watered stock. Stock issued with a par value greater than the value of the corporation's assets.

> "The term 'watered stock' is a colorful common law phrase describing the situation where shareholders receive shares without paying as much for them as the law requires.... Much of the early common law relating to watered shares concerned the liability of shareholders receiving watered shares to pay the additional consideration needed to 'squeeze out the water.' ... [It now] seems clear that a shareholder is liable to the corporation if he or she pays less for the shares than the consideration fixed by the directors, and this liability is measured by the difference between the fixed consideration and the amount actually paid." Robert W. Hamilton, *The Law of Corporations in a Nutshell* 120–21 (3d ed. 1991).

whisper stock. The stock of a company that is rumored to be the target of a takeover attempt.

yo-yo stock. See *volatile stock.*

stock acquisition. See SHARE ACQUISITION.

stock-appreciation right. (*usu. pl.*) A right, typically granted in tandem with a stock option, to be paid the option value (usu. in cash) when exercised along with the simultaneous cancellation of the option. — Abbr. SAR.

stock association. See *joint-stock company* under COMPANY.

stock attribution. See ATTRIBUTION.

stock bailout. A stock redemption in the form of a preferred stock dividend.

stock bonus plan. A special type of profit-sharing plan in which the distribution of benefits is in the form of the employer-company's own stock.

stockbroker. One who buys or sells stock as agent for another. — Also termed *account executive*; *account representative.*

stock certificate. An instrument evidencing ownership of a bond or shares of stock. — Also termed *certificate of stock*; *share certificate.*

stock clearing. The actual exchange of money and stock between buyer and seller, typically performed by a clearing corporation.

stock clearing corporation. A New York Stock Exchange subsidiary that is a central agency for securities deliveries and payments between member firms.

stock control. A system of inventory management by which a business maintains perpetual records of its inventory.

stock corporation. See CORPORATION.

stock dividend. See DIVIDEND.

stock exchange. See SECURITIES EXCHANGE.

stockholder. See SHAREHOLDER.

stockholder derivative suit. See DERIVATIVE ACTION (1).

stockholder of record. The person who is listed in the issuer's books as the owner of stock on the record date. — Also termed *holder of record*; *owner of record*; *record owner*. See *record date* under DATE.

stockholders' equity. See OWNERS' EQUITY.

stockholder's liability. See *shareholder's liability* under LIABILITY.

stock insurance company. See INSURANCE COMPANY.

stock in trade. **1.** The inventory carried by a retail business for sale in the ordinary course of business. **2.** The tools and equipment owned and used by a person engaged in a trade. **3.** The equipment and other items needed to run a business.

stockjobber. See JOBBER (2).

stockjobbing, *n.* The business of dealing in stocks or shares; esp., the buying and selling of stocks and bonds by jobbers who operate on their own account. — Also termed *stockjobbery*.

stock-law district. A district in which cattle or other stock are prohibited from running free.

stock life-insurance company. See INSURANCE COMPANY.

stock manipulation. See MANIPULATION.

stock market. See MARKET (4), (5).

stock merger. See MERGER.

stock note. See NOTE (1).

stock option. **1.** An option to buy or sell a specific quantity of stock at a designated price for a specified period regardless of shifts in market value during the period. **2.** An option that allows a corporate employee to buy shares of corporate stock at a fixed price or within a fixed period. • Such an option is usu. granted as a form of compensation and can qualify for special tax treatment under the Internal Revenue Code. — Also termed (in sense 2) *employee stock option*; *incentive stock option* (ISO).

nonqualified stock option. A stock-option plan that does not receive capital-gains tax treatment, thus allowing a person to buy stock for a period (often ten years) at or below the market price.

qualified stock option. A now-rare stock-option plan that allows a person to buy stock for a period (often five years) at the market price, the stock being subject to capital-gains tax treatment.

stock-option contract. See CONTRACT.

stock-parking, *n.* See PARKING.

stock power. A power of attorney permitting a person, other than the owner, to transfer ownership of a security to a third party. — Also termed *stock/bond power*.

stock-purchase plan. An arrangement by which an employer corporation allows employees to purchase shares of the corporation's stock.

stock redemption. See REDEMPTION (3).

stock repurchase. See REDEMPTION (3).

stock-repurchase plan. A program by which a corporation buys back its own shares in the open market, usu. when the corporation believes the shares are undervalued.

stock right. See SUBSCRIPTION RIGHT.

stocks, *n.* A punishment device consisting of two boards that together form holes for trapping an offender's feet and hands. — Formerly also termed *cippi*. Cf. BILBOES (1); PILLORY.

stock split. The issuance of two or more new shares in exchange for each old share without changing the proportional ownership interests of each shareholder. • For example, a 3–for–1 split would give an owner of 100 shares a total of 300 shares, or 3 shares for each share previously owned. A stock split lowers the price per share and thus makes the stock more attractive to potential investors. — Also termed *share split*.

reverse stock split. A reduction in the number of a corporation's shares by calling in all outstanding shares and reissuing fewer shares having greater value.

stock subscription. See SUBSCRIPTION (2).

stock swap. See SWAP.

stock-transfer agent. See AGENT.

stock-transfer tax. See TAX.

stock warrant. See SUBSCRIPTION WARRANT.

stolen property. Goods acquired by larceny, robbery, or theft.

stop, *n.* Under the Fourth Amendment, a temporary restraint that prevents a person from walking away.

stop and frisk, *n.* A police officer's brief detention, questioning, and search of a person for a concealed weapon when the officer reasonably suspects that the person has committed or is about to commit a crime. • The stop and frisk, which can be conducted without a warrant or probable cause, was held constitutional by the Supreme Court in *Terry v. Ohio*, 392 U.S. 1, 88 S.Ct. 1868 (1968). — Also termed *investigatory stop*; *Terry stop*. See REASONABLE SUSPICION.

stopgap zoning. See *interim zoning* under ZONING.

stop-limit order. See *stop order* under ORDER (4).

stop-list. *Antitrust.* An illegal means by which manufacturers sometimes attempt to enforce price maintenance, by having suppliers agree among themselves not to supply any party who competes actively and breaks anticompetitive price "rules."

stop-loss insurance. See INSURANCE.

stop-loss order. See *stop order* under ORDER (4).

stop-notice statute. A law providing an alternative to a mechanic's lien by allowing a contractor, supplier, or worker to make a claim against the construction lender and, in some instances, the owner for a portion of the undisbursed construction-loan proceeds. See *mechanic's lien* under LIEN.

stop order. 1. See ORDER (4). **2.** An SEC order that suspends a registration statement containing false, incomplete, or misleading information. **3.** A bank customer's order instructing the bank not to honor one of the customer's checks. — Also termed (in sense 3) *stop-payment order*.

stoppage, *n.* **1.** An obstruction or hindrance to the performance of something <stoppage of goods or persons in transit for inspection>. **2.** *Civil law.* SETOFF <stoppage in pay for money owed>.

stoppage *in transitu* (in **tran**-si-t[y]oo *or* **tranz**-i-t[y]oo). The right that a seller of goods has, under certain circumstances, to regain the possession of those goods even though the seller has already parted with them under a contract for sale. • This right traditionally applies when goods are consigned wholly or partly on credit from one person to another, and the consignee becomes bankrupt or insolvent before the goods arrive — in which event the consignor may direct the carrier to deliver the goods to someone other than the consignee (who can no longer pay for them). — Also termed *stoppage in transit*.

stop-payment order. See STOP ORDER (3).

store, *n.* **1.** A place where goods are deposited to be purchased or sold. **2.** (*usu. pl.*) A supply of articles provided for the subsistence and accommodation of a ship's crew and passengers. **3.** A place where goods or supplies are stored for future use; a warehouse.

public store. A government warehouse administratively maintained, as for the storage of imported goods or military supplies.

store, *vb.* To keep (goods, etc.) in safekeeping for future delivery in an unchanged condition.

stowage (**stoh**-ij). *Maritime law.* **1.** The storing, packing, or arranging of cargo on a vessel to protect the goods from friction, bruising, or water damage during a voyage. • The bill of lading will often prescribe the method of stowage to be used. **2.** The place (such as a ship's hull) where goods are stored. **3.** The goods so stored. **4.** A fee paid for the storage of goods; a storage fee.

stowaway. A person who hides on board an outgoing or incoming vessel or aircraft to obtain free passage. 18 USCA § 2199.

STR. *abbr.* SUSPICIOUS-TRANSACTION REPORT.

straddle, *n.* In securities and commodities trading, a situation in which an investor holds contracts to buy and to sell the same security or commodity, thus ensuring a loss on one of the contracts. • The aim of this strategy is to defer gains and use losses to offset other taxable income. — Also termed *spread eagle*; *combination*. — **straddle,** *vb.*

straight annuity. See ANNUITY.

straight bankruptcy. See CHAPTER 7.

straight bill of lading. See BILL OF LADING.

straight deductible. See DEDUCTIBLE.

straight letter of credit. See LETTER OF CREDIT.

straight life annuity. See *nonrefund annuity* under ANNUITY.

straight life insurance. See *whole life insurance* under INSURANCE.

straight-line depreciation method. See DEPRECIATION METHOD.

straight-line interest. See *simple interest* under INTEREST (3).

straight mortgage. See MORTGAGE.

straight sentence. See *determinate sentence* under SENTENCE.

straight-term mortgage. See *interest-only mortgage* under MORTGAGE.

straight voting. See *noncumulative voting* under VOTING.

stramineus homo (strə-**min**-ee-əs **hoh**-moh). [Latin "man of straw"] See STRAW MAN.

strand, *n.* A shore or bank of an ocean, lake, river, or stream.

stranding, *n. Maritime law.* A ship's drifting, driving, or running aground on a strand.

accidental stranding. Stranding as a result of natural forces, as in wind and waves. • The type of stranding that occurs determines the method of apportioning the liability for any resulting losses. See *general average* and *special average* under AVERAGE. — Also termed *involuntary stranding*.

> "Damage to a vessel from involuntary stranding or wreck, and the cost of repairs, are particular average only. Where, however, the ship and cargo are exposed to a common peril by the accidental stranding, the expenses of unloading and taking care of the cargo, rescuing the vessel, reloading the cargo, and other expenses other than repairs requisite to enable the vessel to proceed on the voyage, are brought into general average, provided the vessel and cargo were saved by the same series of measures during the continuance of the common peril which created the joint necessity for the expenses." 70 Am. Jur. 2d *Shipping* § 961, at 1069 (1987).

voluntary stranding. Stranding to avoid a more dangerous fate or for fraudulent purposes.

> "The loss occurring when a ship is voluntarily run ashore to avoid capture, foundering, or shipwreck is to be made good by general average contribution, if the ship is afterwards recovered so as to be able to perform its voyage, as such a claim is clearly within the rule that whatever is sacrificed for the common benefit of the associated interests shall be made good by all the interests exposed to the common peril which were saved from the common danger by the sacrifice .... A vessel cannot, however, claim contribution founded on even a voluntary stranding made necessary by ... unseaworthiness or the negligence of those in charge, except in pursuance of a valid agreement to that effect." 70 Am. Jur. 2d *Shipping* § 961, at 1069 (1987).

stranger. 1. One who is not party to a given transaction <she was a stranger to the agreement>. **2.** One not standing toward another in some relation implied in the context <the trustee was negotiating with a stranger>.

stranger in blood. 1. One not related by blood, such as a relative by affinity. **2.** Any person not within the consideration of natural love and affection arising from a relationship.

stratagem. A trick or deception to obtain an advantage, esp. in a military conflict.

strategic alliance. A coalition formed by two or more persons in the same or complementary businesses to gain long-term financial, operational, and marketing advantages without jeopardizing competitive independence <through their strategic alliance, the manufacturer and distributor of a co-developed product shared development costs>. Cf. JOINT VENTURE; PARTNERSHIP.

stratocracy (strə-**tok**-rə-see). A military government.

strator (**stray**-tər). *Hist.* A surveyor of the highways.

straw bail. See *bail common* under BAIL (3).

straw bond. See BOND (2).

straw man. 1. A fictitious person, esp. one that is weak or flawed. **2.** A tenuous and exaggerated counterargument that an advocate puts forward for the sole purpose of disproving it. — Also termed *straw-man argument*. **3.** A third party used in some transactions as a temporary transferee to allow the principal parties to accomplish something that is otherwise impermissible. **4.** A person hired to post a worthless bail bond for the release of an accused. — Also termed *stramineus homo*.

stray remarks. *Employment law.* Statements to or about an employee by a coworker or supervisor, concerning the employee's race, sex, age, national origin, or other status, that are either objectively or subjectively offensive, but that do not represent harassment or discrimination by the employer because of (1) their sporadic, unsystematic, and unofficial nature, (2) the circumstances in which they were made, or (3) their not showing any intention to hamper the employee's continued employment. — Also termed *stray comments*.

stream. Anything liquid that flows in a line or course; esp., a current of water consisting of a bed, bank, and watercourse, usu. emptying into other bodies of water but not losing its character even if it breaks up or disappears.

private stream. A watercourse, the bed, channel, or waters of which are exclusively owned by private parties.

stream-of-commerce theory. 1. The principle that a state may exercise personal jurisdiction over a defendant if the defendant places a product in the general marketplace and the product causes injury or damage in the forum state, as long as the defendant also takes other acts to establish some connection with the forum state, as by advertising there or by hiring someone to serve as a sales agent there. *Asahi Metal Indus. Co., Ltd. v. Superior Court of California*, 480 U.S. 102, 107 S.Ct. 1026 (1987). **2.** The principle that a person who participates in placing a defective product in the general marketplace is strictly liable for harm caused by the product. Restatement (Second) of Torts § 402A (1979).

street. A road or public thoroughfare used for travel in an urban area, including the pavement, shoulders, gutters, curbs, and other areas within the street lines.

> "Strictly speaking, a 'street' is a public thoroughfare in an urban community such as a city, town, or village, and the term is not ordinarily applicable to roads and highways outside of municipalities. Although a street, in common parlance, is equivalent to a highway, it is usually specifically denominated by its own proper appellation. . . . Whether a particular highway is to be regarded as a 'street' within the meaning of that term as used in a statute must, of course, be resolved by construction." 39 Am. Jur. 2d *Highways, Streets, and Bridges* § 8, at 588–89 (1999).

street crime. See CRIME.

street gang. See GANG.

street name. A brokerage firm's name in which securities owned by another are registered. • A security is held by a broker in street name (at the customer's request) to simplify trading because no signature on the stock certificate is required. A street name may also be used for securities purchased on margin. The word "street" in this term is a reference to Wall Street.

strepitus judicialis (**strep**-ə-təs joo-dish-ee-**ay**-lis), *n.* [Law Latin] *Hist.* Disruptive behavior in court.

strict, *adj.* **1.** Narrow; restricted <strict construction>. **2.** Rigid; exacting <strict statutory terms>. **3.** Severe <strict punishment>. **4.** Absolute; requiring no showing of fault <strict liability>.

strict construction. See CONSTRUCTION.

strict constructionism, *n.* The doctrinal view of judicial construction holding that judges should interpret a document or statute (esp. one involving penal sanctions) according to its literal terms, without looking to other sources to ascertain the meaning. — Also termed *strict construction*; *literal canon*; *literal rule*; *textualism*. — **strict constructionist,** *n.*

strict foreclosure. See FORECLOSURE.

stricti juris (**strik**-tI **joor**-is). [Latin] Of strict right of law; according to the exact law, without extension or enhancement in interpretation. • This term was often applied to servitudes because they are a restriction on the free exercise of property rights.

strict interpretation. See INTERPRETATION.

strictissimi juris (strik-**tis**-ə-mI **joor**-is). [Latin] Of the strictest right or law; to be interpreted in the strictest manner. • This term was usu. applied to certain statutes, esp. those imposing penalties or restraining natural liberties.

strict liability. See LIABILITY.

strict-liability crime. See CRIME.

strictly ministerial duty. See DUTY (2).

stricto jure (**strik**-toh **joor**-ee). [Latin] In strict law.

strict products liability. See PRODUCTS LIABILITY.

strict scrutiny. *Constitutional law.* The standard applied to suspect classifications (such as race) in equal-protection analysis and to fundamental rights (such as voting rights) in due-process analysis. • Under strict scrutiny, the state must establish that it has a compelling interest that justifies and necessitates the law in question. See COMPELLING-STATE-INTEREST TEST; SUSPECT CLASSIFICATION; FUNDAMENTAL RIGHT. Cf. INTERMEDIATE SCRUTINY; RATIONAL-BASIS TEST.

strict settlement. See SETTLEMENT.

strict test. *Evidence.* The principle that disclosure of a privileged document, even when inadvertent, results in a waiver of the attorney-client privilege regarding the document, unless all possible precautions were taken to protect the document from disclosure. Cf. LENIENT TEST; HYDRAFLOW TEST.

strictum jus (**strik**-təm **jəs**). See JUS STRICTUM.

strict underwriting. See *standby underwriting* under UNDERWRITING.

strike, *n.* **1.** An organized cessation or slowdown of work by employees to compel the employer to meet the employees' demands. Cf. LOCKOUT; BOYCOTT; PICKETING.

ca'canny strike (kah-**kan**-ee *or* kaw-). A strike in which the workers remain on the job but work at a slower pace to reduce their output.

economic strike. A strike resulting from an economic dispute with the employer (such as a wage dispute); a dispute for reasons other than unfair labor practices. • An employer can permanently replace an economic striker but cannot prevent the worker from coming back to an unreplaced position simply because the worker was on strike.

general strike. A strike organized to affect an entire industry.

illegal strike. **1.** A strike using unlawful procedures. **2.** A strike to obtain unlawful objectives, as in a strike to force an employer to stop doing business with a particular company.

jurisdictional strike. A strike resulting from a dispute between members of different unions over work assignments.

outlaw strike. See *wildcat strike.*

quickie strike. See *wildcat strike.*

recognition strike. A strike by workers seeking to force their employer to acknowledge the union as their collective-bargaining agent. • After the National Labor Relations Act was passed in 1935, recognition strikes became unnecessary. Under the Act, the employer is required to recognize an NLRB-certified union for bargaining purposes. — Also termed *organizational strike.*

secondary strike. A strike against an employer because that employer has business dealings with another employer directly involved in a dispute with the union. See *secondary boycott* under BOYCOTT; *secondary picketing* under PICKETING.

sit-down strike. A strike in which employees occupy the workplace but do not work.

sympathy strike. A strike by union members who have no grievance against their own employer but who want to show support for another union involved in a labor dispute.

wildcat strike. A strike not authorized by a union or in violation of a collective-bargaining agreement. — Also termed *outlaw strike*; *quickie strike.*

2. The removal of a prospective juror from the jury panel <a peremptory strike>. See CHAL-

LENGE (2). **3.** A failure or disadvantage, as by a criminal conviction <a strike on one's record>.

strike, *vb.* **1.** (Of an employee or union) to engage in a strike <the flight attendants struck to protest the reduction in benefits>. **2.** To remove (a prospective juror) from a jury panel by a peremptory challenge or a challenge for cause <the prosecution struck the panelist who indicated an opposition to the death penalty>. See *peremptory challenge* under CHALLENGE. **3.** To expunge, as from a record <motion to strike the prejudicial evidence>.

strikebreaker. See SCAB.

strike down. To invalidate (a statute); to declare void.

strike fund. A union fund that provides benefits to its members who are on strike, esp. for subsistence while the members are not receiving wages.

strike off. **1.** (Of a court) to order (a case) removed from the docket. **2.** (Of an auctioneer) to announce, usu. by the falling of the hammer, that an item has been sold.

strike price. See PRICE.

strike suit. See SUIT.

striking a jury. The selecting of a jury out of all the candidates available to serve on the jury; esp., the selecting of a special jury. See *special jury* (1) under JURY.

striking off the roll. See DISBARMENT.

striking price. See *strike price* under PRICE.

strip, *n.* **1.** The act of separating and selling a bond's coupons and corpus separately. **2.** The act of a tenant who, holding less than the entire fee in land, spoils or unlawfully takes something from the land.

STRIP (strip). *abbr.* SEPARATE TRADING OF REGISTERED INTEREST AND PRINCIPAL OF SECURITIES.

strip search. See SEARCH.

strong-arm clause. A provision of the Bankruptcy Code allowing a bankruptcy trustee to avoid a security interest that is not perfected when the bankruptcy case is filed. 11 USCA § 544(a)(1).

strongly corroborated. (Of testimony) supported from independent facts and circumstances that are powerful, satisfactory, and clear to the court and jury.

strong mark. See TRADEMARK.

strong market. See *bull market* under MARKET.

strong trademark. See TRADEMARK.

struck jury. See JURY.

structural alteration. See ALTERATION.

structural unemployment. See UNEMPLOYMENT.

structure. **1.** Any construction, production, or piece of work artificially built up or composed of parts purposefully joined together <a building is a structure>. **2.** The organization of elements or parts <the corporate structure>. **3.** A method of constructing parts <the loan's payment structure was a financial burden>.

structured security. See SECURITY.

structured settlement. See SETTLEMENT.

study release. A program that allows a prisoner to be released for a few hours at a time to attend classes at a nearby college or technical institution. — Also termed *study furlough*.

stuff gown. **1.** The professional robe worn by barristers of the outer bar who have not been appointed Queen's Counsel. **2.** A junior barrister. Cf. SILK GOWN.

stultify, *vb.* **1.** To make (something or someone) appear stupid or foolish <he stultified opposing counsel's argument>. **2.** To testify about one's own lack of mental capacity. **3.** To contradict oneself, as by denying what one has already alleged.

stultiloquium (stəl-ti-**loh**-kwee-əm). [fr. Latin *stultus* "foolish" + *loqui* "to speak"] *Hist.* A frivolous pleading punishable by fine. • This may have been the origin of the beaupleader. See BEAUPLEADER.

stumpage (**stəmp**-ij). **1.** The timber standing on land. **2.** The value of the standing timber. **3.** A license to cut the timber. **4.** The fee paid for the right to cut the timber.

stuprum (**st[y]oo**-prəm), *n.* [Latin] *Roman & civil law.* Illegal sexual intercourse with a woman, usu. a virgin or widow, or with a male (pederasty).

> "The law refers to *stuprum* and adultery indiscriminately and with rather a misuse of terms. But properly speaking adultery is committed with a married woman, the name being derived from children conceived by another (*alter*); *stuprum*, however, is committed against a virgin or a widow; the Greeks call it corruption." *Digest of Justinian* 48.5.6.1 (Papinian, De Adulteriis 1).

style, *n.* **1.** A case name or designation <the style of the opinion is *Connor v. Gray*>. Cf. CAPTION (1). **2.** *Scots law.* A form of writ or deed used in conveyancing. • A book of styles is essentially a formbook; a typical Scottish example is John Hendry's *Styles of Deeds and Instruments* (2d ed. 1862).

suable, *adj.* **1.** Capable of being sued <a suable party>. **2.** Capable of being enforced <a suable contract>. — **suability,** *n.*

suapte natura (s[y]oo-**ap**-tee nə-**t[y]oor**-ə). [Latin] In its own nature — as in *suapte natura sterilia* ("barren of its own nature").

sua sponte (**s[y]oo**-ə **spon**-tee). [Latin "of one's own accord; voluntarily"] Without prompting or suggestion; on its own motion <the court took notice sua sponte that it lacked jurisdiction over the case>.

sub (səb). [Latin] Under; upon.

subagent. See AGENT.

subaltern (səb-**awl**-tərn), *n.* An inferior or subordinate officer.

sub ballivus (səb bə-**lI**-vəs), *n.* [Law Latin] *Hist.* An undersheriff; a sheriff's deputy. See BALLIVUS.

subchapter-C corporation. See *C corporation* under CORPORATION.

subchapter-S corporation. See *S corporation* under CORPORATION.

sub colore juris (səb kə-**lor**-ee **joor**-is). [Latin] Under color of right; under an appearance of right.

subcommittee. A committee subdivision that reports to and performs duties on behalf of a regular committee.

sub conditione (səb kən-dish-ee-**oh**-nee). [Law Latin] Under condition. • This term creates a condition in a deed.

subcontract. See CONTRACT.

subcontractor. One who is awarded a portion of an existing contract by a contractor, esp. a general contractor. • For example, a contractor who builds houses typically retains subcontractors to perform specialty work such as installing plumbing, laying carpet, making cabinetry, and landscaping — each subcontractor is paid a somewhat lesser sum than the contractor receives for the work.

sub curia (səb **kyoor**-ee-ə). [Latin] Under law.

sub disjunctione (səb dis-jəngk-shee-**oh**-nee). [Latin] In the alternative.

subditus (**səb**-də-təs). [Latin] *Hist.* Someone under another's power; a vassal.

subdivision, *n.* **1.** The division of a thing into smaller parts. **2.** A parcel of land in a larger development. — **subdivide,** *vb.*

illegal subdivision. The division of a tract of land into smaller parcels in violation of local subdivision regulations, as when a developer begins laying out streets, installing sewer and utility lines, and constructing houses without the authorization of the local planning commission.

legal subdivision. The governmentally approved division of a tract of land into smaller parcels using ordinary and legally recognized methods for surveying and platting land and publicly recording the results.

subdivision exaction. A charge that a community imposes on a subdivider as a condition for permitting recordation of the subdivision map and sale of the subdivided parcels.

subdivision map. A map that shows how a parcel of land is to be divided into smaller lots, and generally showing the layout and utilities.

subinfeudate (səb-in-**fyoo**-dayt), *vb. Hist.* (Of a subvassal) to grant lands to another to hold as his vassal rather than his superior. — Also termed *subinfeud* (səb-in-**fyood**).

> "[A] more common method of obtaining the annual quota of knights was to *subinfeudate* portions of the baronial lands to individual knights in exchange for their obligations to spend a fixed portion of time annually in the king's or baron's service. A knight who so received a portion of a baron's land would hold *of* his baron in much the same way as the baron held *of* the king." Thomas F. Bergin & Paul G. Haskell, *Preface to Estates in Land and Future Interests* 4 (2d ed. 1984).

subinfeudation (səb-in-fyoo-**day**-shən), *n. Hist.* The system under which the tenants in a feudal system granted smaller estates to their tenants, who in turn did the same from their pieces of land. Cf. INFEUDATION; SUPERINFEUDATION.

subinfeudatory (səb-in-**fyoo**-də-tor-ee), *n.* A tenant holding lands by subinfeudation.

subjacent (səb-**jay**-sənt), *adj.* Located underneath or below <the land's subjacent support>.

subjacent support. See SUPPORT.

subject, *n.* **1.** One who owes allegiance to a sovereign and is governed by that sovereign's laws <the monarchy's subjects>.

> "Speaking generally, we may say that the terms subject and citizen are synonymous. Subjects and citizens are alike those whose relation to the state is personal and not merely territorial, permanent and not merely temporary. This equivalent, however, is not absolute. For in the first place, the term subject is commonly limited to monarchical forms of government, while the term citizen is more specially applicable in the case of republics. A British subject becomes by naturalisation a citizen of the United States of America or of France. In the second place, the term citizen brings into prominence the rights and privileges of the status, rather than its correlative obligations, while the reverse is the case with the term subject. Finally it is to be noticed that the term subject is capable of a different and wider application, in which it includes all members of the body politic, whether they are citizens (*i.e.*, subjects *stricto sensu*) or resident aliens. All such persons are subjects, all being subject to the power of the state and to its jurisdiction, and as owing to it, at least temporarily, fidelity and obedience." John Salmond, *Jurisprudence* 133 (Glanville L. Williams ed., 10th ed. 1947).

natural-born subject. A person born within the dominion of a monarchy, esp. England. Cf. NATIONAL.

2. The matter of concern over which something is created <the subject of the statute>. — Also termed (in sense 2) *subject matter*.

subject, *adj.* Referred to above; having relevance to the current discussion <the subject property was then sold to Smith>.

subjection. 1. The act of subjecting someone to something <their subjection to torture was unconscionable>. **2.** The condition of a subject in a monarchy; the obligations surrounding such a person <a subject, wherever residing, owes fidelity and obedience to the Crown, while an alien may be released at will from all such ties of subjection>. **3.** The condition of being subject, exposed, or liable; liability <the defendants' subjection to the plaintiffs became clear shortly after the trial began>. — Also termed (in sense 3) *liability*; *susceptibility*.

subjective, *adj.* **1.** Based on an individual's perceptions, feelings, or intentions, as opposed to externally verifiable phenomena <the subjective theory of contract — that the parties must have an actual meeting of the minds — is not favored by most courts>. **2.** Personal; individual <subjective judgments about popular music>. Cf. OBJECTIVE.

subjective ethics. See MORAL RELATIVISM.

subjective meaning. See MEANING.

subjective novation. See NOVATION.

subjective standard. See STANDARD.

subjective theory of contract. The doctrine (now largely outmoded) that a contract is an agreement in which the parties have a subjective meeting of the minds. — Often shortened to *subjective theory*. See MEETING OF THE MINDS. Cf. OBJECTIVE THEORY OF CONTRACT.

subject matter. The issue presented for consideration; the thing in which a right or duty has been asserted; the thing in dispute. See CORPUS (2). — Sometimes written (as a noun) *subject-matter*. — **subject-matter,** *adj.*

subject-matter jurisdiction. See JURISDICTION.

subject-matter test. A method of determining whether an employee's communication with a corporation's lawyer was made at the direction of the employee's supervisors and in the course and scope of the employee's employment, so as to be protected under the attorney-client privilege, despite the fact that the employee is not a member of the corporation's control group. *Harper & Row Pubs., Inc. v. Decker*, 423 F.2d 487 (7th Cir. 1970), *aff'd per curiam by equally divided Court*, 400 U.S. 348, 91 S.Ct. 479 (1971). — Also termed *Decker test*. Cf. CONTROL-GROUP TEST.

subject of a right. 1. The owner of a right; the person in whom a legal right is vested. **2.** OBJECT OF A RIGHT.

subject to open. Denoting the future interest of a class of people when this class is subject to a possible increase or decrease in number.

sub judice (səb **joo**-di-see *also* suub **yoo**-di-kay), *adv*. [Latin "under a judge"] Before the court or judge for determination; at bar <in the case sub judice, there have been no out-of-court settlements>. • Legal writers sometimes use "case sub judice" where "the present case" would be more comprehensible.

subjugation. See DEBELLATIO.

sublease, *n*. A lease by a lessee to a third party, conveying some or all of the leased property for a shorter term than that of the lessee, who retains a reversion in the lease. — Also termed *subtenancy* and (esp. in England) *underlease*. — **sublease, sublet,** *vb*.

sublessee. A third party who receives by lease some or all of the leased property from a lessee. — Also termed *subtenant* and (esp. in England) *undertenant*.

sublessor. A lessee who leases some or all of the leased property to a third party. — Also termed (esp. in England) *underlessor*.

sublicense. A license granting a portion or all of the rights granted to the licensee under an original license.

submission, *n*. **1.** A yielding to the authority or will of another <his resistance ended in an about-face: complete submission>. **2.** A contract in which the parties agree to refer their dispute to a third party for resolution <in their submission to arbitration, they referred to the rules of the American Arbitration Association>. **3.** An advocate's argument <neither the written nor the oral submissions were particularly helpful>. — **submit,** *vb*.

submission bond. See BOND (2).

submission date. See DATE.

submission to a finding. The admission to facts sufficient to warrant a finding of guilt. — Also termed *admission to sufficient facts*.

submission to the jury. The process by which a judge gives a case to the jury for its consideration and verdict, usu. occurring after all evidence has been presented, arguments have been completed, and instructions have been given.

sub modo (səb **moh**-doh). [Latin] Subject to conditions or qualifications <the riparian landowner enjoys the property *sub modo*, i.e., subject to the right of the public to reserve enough space for levees, public roads, and the like>.

submortgage. A mortgage created when a person holding a mortgage as security for a loan procures another loan from a third party and pledges the mortgage as security; a loan to a mortgagee who puts up the mortgage as collateral or security for the loan.

sub nomine (səb **nom**-ə-nee). [Latin] Under the name. • This phrase, typically in abbreviated form, is often used in a case citation to indicate that there has been a name change from one stage of the case to another, as in *Guernsey Memorial Hosp. v. Secretary of Health and Human Servs.*, 996 F.2d 830 (6th Cir. 1993), *rev'd sub nom. Shalala v. Guernsey Memorial Hosp.*, 514 U.S. 87, 115 S.Ct. 1232 (1995). — Abbr. *sub nom*.

subordinate (sə-**bor**-də-nit), *adj*. **1.** Placed in or belonging to a lower rank, class, or position <a subordinate lien>. **2.** Subject to another's authority or control <a subordinate lawyer>.

subordinate (sə-**bor**-də-nayt), *vb*. To place in a lower rank, class, or position; to assign a lower priority to <subordinate the debt to a different class of claims>.

subordinated bond. See BOND (3).

subordinate debenture. See DEBENTURE.

subordinate debt. See DEBT.

subordinate legislation. See LEGISLATION.

subordinate officer. See OFFICER (1).

subordinate political power. See POLITICAL POWER.

subordination, *n.* The act or an instance of moving something (such as a right or claim) to a lower rank, class, or position <subordination of a first lien to a second lien>.

subordination agreement. See AGREEMENT.

subordination clause. A covenant in a junior mortgage enabling the first lien to keep its priority in case of renewal or refinancing.

suborn (sə-**born**), *vb.* **1.** To induce (a person) to commit an unlawful or wrongful act, esp. in a secret or underhanded manner. **2.** To induce (a person) to commit perjury. **3.** To obtain (perjured testimony) from another. — **subornation** (səb-or-**nay**-shən), *n.* — **suborner** (sə-**bor**-nər), *n.*

subornation of perjury. The crime of persuading another to commit perjury. — Sometimes shortened to *subornation.*

subpartnership. See PARTNERSHIP.

sub pede sigilli (səb **pee**-dee si-**jil**-I). [Latin] Under the foot of the seal.

subpoena (sə-**pee**-nə), *n.* [Latin "under penalty"] A writ commanding a person to appear before a court or other tribunal, subject to a penalty for failing to comply. — Also spelled *subpena.* Pl. **subpoenas.**

alias subpoena (**ay**-lee-əs sə-**pee**-nə). A subpoena issued after an initial subpoena has failed.

subpoena ad testificandum (sə-**pee**-nə ad tes-tə-fi-**kan**-dəm). [Law Latin] A subpoena ordering a witness to appear and give testimony.

subpoena duces tecum (sə-**pee**-nə **d[y]oo**-seez **tee**-kəm *also* **doo**-səz **tay**-kəm). [Law Latin] A subpoena ordering the witness to appear and to bring specified documents or records.

subpoena, *vb.* **1.** To call before a court or other tribunal by subpoena <subpoena the material witnesses>. **2.** To order the production of (documents or other things) by subpoena duces tecum <subpoena the corporate records>. — Also spelled *subpena.*

subpoenal (sə-**pee**-nəl), *adj.* Required or done under penalty, esp. in compliance with a subpoena.

sub potestate (səb poh-tes-**tay**-tee). [Latin] Under the power of another, as in a child or other person not *sui juris.* See SUI JURIS.

subreptio (səb-**rep**-shee-oh). [Latin "surreptitious removal"] *Roman law.* **1.** Theft. **2.** The obtaining of a grant from the emperor under false pretenses. — Also termed (in French law) *subreption.*

subrogate (**səb**-rə-gayt), *vb.* To substitute (a person) for another regarding a legal right or claim.

subrogation (səb-rə-**gay**-shən), *n.* **1.** The substitution of one party for another whose debt the party pays, entitling the paying party to rights, remedies, or securities that would otherwise belong to the debtor. • For example, a surety who has paid a debt is, by subrogation, entitled to any security for the debt held by the creditor and the benefit of any judgment the creditor has against the debtor, and may proceed against the debtor as the creditor would. **2.** The principle under which an insurer that has paid a loss under an insurance policy is entitled to all the rights and remedies belonging to the insured against a third party with respect to any loss covered by the policy. See EQUITY OF SUBROGATION. Cf. ANTISUBROGATION RULE.

> "Subrogation is equitable assignment. The right comes into existence when the surety becomes obligated, and this is important as affecting priorities; but such right of subrogation does not become a cause of action until the debt is fully paid. Subrogation entitles the surety to use any remedy against the principal which the creditor could have used, and in general to enjoy the benefit of any advantage that the creditor had, such as a mortgage, lien, power to confess judgment, to follow trust funds, to proceed against a third person who has promised either the principal or the creditor to pay the debt." Laurence P. Simpson, *Handbook on the Law of Suretyship* 205 (1950).

> "Subrogation simply means substitution of one person for another; that is, one person is allowed to stand in the shoes of another and assert that person's rights against the defendant. Factually, the case arises because, for some justifiable reason, the subrogation plaintiff has paid a debt owed by the defendant." Dan B. Dobbs, *Law of Remedies* § 4.3, at 404 (2d ed. 1993).

conventional subrogation. Subrogation that arises by contract or by an express act of the parties.

legal subrogation. Subrogation that arises by operation of law or by implication in equity to prevent fraud or injustice. • Legal subrogation usu. arises when (1) the paying party has a liability, claim, or fiduciary relationship with the debtor, (2) the party pays to fulfill a legal duty or because of public policy, (3) the paying party is a secondary debtor, (4) the paying party is a surety, or (5) the party pays to protect its own rights or property. — Also termed *equitable subrogation*.

subrogative (**səb**-rə-gay-tiv), *adj*. Of or relating to subrogation <subrogative rights>. — Also termed *subrogatory*; *subrogational*.

subrogee (səb-rə-**jee**). One who is substituted for another in having a right, duty, or claim. • An insurance company frequently becomes a subrogee after paying a policy claim, as a result of which it is then in a position to sue a tortfeasor who injured the insured or otherwise caused damages.

subrogor (səb-rə-**gor**). One who allows another to be substituted for oneself as creditor, with a transfer of rights and duties.

sub rosa (səb **roh**-zə), *adj*. [Latin "under the rose"] *Hist*. Confidential; secret; not for publication.

sub salvo et securo conductu (səb **sal**-voh et si-**kyoor**-oh kən-**dək**-t[y]oo). [Law Latin] *Hist*. Under safe and secure conduct. • This phrase was used in writs of habeas corpus.

subscribed capital. See CAPITAL.

subscribed stock. See STOCK.

subscribing witness. See WITNESS.

subscriptio (səb-**skrip**-shee-oh), *n*. [Latin] *Roman law*. **1.** A signature, esp. a name written under or at the bottom of a document to authenticate it. **2.** A signature to a will, required in certain cases in addition to the seals of witnesses.

subscription, *n*. **1.** The act of signing one's name on a document; the signature so affixed. **2.** *Securities*. A written contract to purchase newly issued shares of stock or bonds. — Also termed (in connection with stock) *stock subscription*. **3.** An oral or a written agreement to contribute a sum of money or property, gratuitously or with consideration, to a specific person or for a specific purpose. — Also termed (in sense 3) *subscription contract*. — **subscribe,** *vb*. — **subscriber,** *n*.

subscription contract. See SUBSCRIPTION (3).

subscription list. An enumeration of subscribers to an agreement, periodical, or service.

subscription price. The price at which investors can buy shares in a new stock offering before the shares are offered to the public.

subscription privilege. See PREEMPTIVE RIGHT.

subscription right. A certificate evidencing a shareholder's right (known as a *preemptive right*) to purchase newly issued stock before the stock is offered to the public. • Subscription rights have a market value and are actively traded because they allow the holder to purchase stock at favorable prices. — Also termed *stock right*. See PREEMPTIVE RIGHT.

subscription warrant. An instrument granting the holder a long-term (usu. a five- to ten-year) option to buy shares at a fixed price. • It is commonly attached to preferred stocks or bonds. — Also termed *warrant*; *stock warrant*.

subsellia (səb-**sel**-ee-ə), *n*. [Latin fr. *sub* "under" and *sella* "seat"] *Roman law*. Lower seats in a courtroom, usu. occupied by the parties or their witnesses, as distinguished from the seat of the tribunal.

subsequent, *adj*. (Of an action, event, etc.) occurring later; coming after something else.

subsequent-advance rule. *Bankruptcy*. The principle that a preferential transfer by the debtor will not be avoided or rescinded by the debtor's bankruptcy trustee if (1) the creditor extended new value to the debtor after receiving the preferential transfer, (2) the new value is unsecured, and (3) the new value remains unpaid after its transfer. 11 USCA § 547(c)(4).

subsequent creditor. See CREDITOR.

subsequent negligence. See NEGLIGENCE.

subsequent-negligence doctrine. See LAST-CLEAR-CHANCE DOCTRINE.

subsequent remedial measure. (*usu. pl.*) *Evidence*. An action taken after an event, which, if taken before the event, would have reduced the likelihood of the event's occurrence. • Evidence of subsequent remedial measures is not admissible to prove negligence, but it may be admitted to prove ownership, control, feasibility, or the like. Fed. R. Evid. 407.

subservant. See *subagent* under AGENT.

subsidiary (səb-**sid**-ee-er-ee), *adj.* Subordinate; under another's control. See *subsidiary corporation* under CORPORATION.

subsidiary, *n.* See *subsidiary corporation* under CORPORATION.

subsidiary corporation. See CORPORATION.

subsidiary merger. See *triangular merger* under MERGER.

subsidy, *n.* **1.** A grant, usu. made by the government, to any enterprise whose promotion is considered to be in the public interest. **2.** A specific financial contribution by a foreign government or public entity conferring a benefit on exporters to the United States. • Such a subsidy is countervailable under 19 USCA §§ 1671, 1677. — **subsidize,** *vb.*

sub sigillo (səb si-**jil**-oh). [Latin "under the seal (of confession)"] *Hist.* In the strictest confidence.

sub silentio (səb si-**len**-shee-oh). [Latin] Under silence; without notice being taken; without being expressly mentioned (such as precedent *sub silentio*).

subsistence. Support; means of support. See NECESSARIES.

sub spe reconciliationis (səb **spee** rek-ən-sil-ee-ay-shee-**oh**-nis). [Latin] *Hist.* Under the hope of reconcilement.

substance. 1. The essence of something; the essential quality of something, as opposed to its mere form <matter of substance>. **2.** Any matter, esp. an addictive drug <illegal substance> <abuse of a substance>.

substantial-capacity test. *Criminal law.* The Model Penal Code's test for the insanity defense, stating that a person is not criminally responsible for an act if, as a result of a mental disease or defect, the person lacks substantial capacity either to appreciate the criminality of the conduct or to conform the conduct to the law. • This test combines elements of both the *McNaghten* rules and the irresistible-impulse test by allowing consideration of both volitional and cognitive weaknesses. This test was formerly used by the federal courts and many states, but since 1984 many jurisdictions (including the federal courts) — in response to the acquittal by reason of insanity of would-be presidential assassin John Hinckley — have narrowed the insanity defense and adopted a new test resembling the *McNaghten* rules, although portions of the substantial-capacity test continue to be used. Model Penal Code § 4.01. — Also termed *Model Penal Code test*; *MPC test*; *American Law Institute test*; *ALI test.* See INSANITY DEFENSE.

substantial-certainty test. *Copyright.* The test for deciding whether a second work was copied from the first. • The question is whether a reasonable observer would conclude with substantial certainty that the second work is a copy.

substantial-compliance rule. See SUBSTANTIAL-PERFORMANCE DOCTRINE.

substantial-continuity doctrine. A principle for holding a successor corporation liable for the acts of its predecessor corporation, if the successor maintains the same business as the predecessor, with the same employees, doing the same jobs, for the same supervisors, under the same working conditions, and using the same production processes to produce the same products for the same customers. — Also termed *continuity-of-enterprise doctrine.* Cf. MERE-CONTINUATION DOCTRINE.

substantial damages. See DAMAGES.

substantial equivalent. *Patents.* The same essential thing as the patented item, so that if two devices do the same work in substantially the same way, they are equivalent, even though they differ in name, form, or shape. — Also termed *substantial equivalent of a patented device.*

substantial evidence. See EVIDENCE.

substantial-evidence rule. The principle that a reviewing court should uphold an administrative body's ruling if it is supported by evidence on which the administrative body could reasonably base its decision.

substantial-factor test. *Torts.* The principle that causation exists when the defendant's conduct is an important or significant contributor to the plaintiff's injuries. Cf. BUT-FOR TEST.

substantial justice. See JUSTICE (1).

substantially justified. (Of conduct, a position, etc.) having a reasonable basis in law and in fact. • Under the Equal Access to Justice Act, a prevailing party in a lawsuit against the government will be unable to recover its attorney's fees if the government's position is substantially justified.

substantial performance. See PERFORMANCE.

substantial-performance doctrine. The equitable rule that, if a good-faith attempt to perform does not precisely meet the terms of the agreement, the agreement will still be considered complete if the essential purpose of the contract is accomplished. • Courts may allow a remedy for minimal damages caused by the deviance. — Also termed *substantial-compliance rule*. Cf. PERFECT-TENDER RULE.

> "There has arisen in the United States an indefinite doctrine sometimes referred to as that of substantial performance. It is a doctrine that deals not with performance of a duty as a discharge thereof but with performance by the plaintiff as a condition precedent to the active duty of performance by the defendant. Where a defendant is sued for non-performance he cannot avoid paying damages by showing that he substantially performed or came near performing or gave something equally good; but he can always successfully defend if in fact some condition precedent to his own duty has not been fulfilled by the plaintiff." William R. Anson, *Principles of the Law of Contract* 422 (Arthur L. Corbin ed., 3d Am. ed. 1919).

substantial right. See RIGHT.

substantial similarity. *Copyright.* A strong resemblance between a copyrighted work and an alleged infringement, thereby creating an inference of unauthorized copying. • The standard for substantial similarity is whether an ordinary person would conclude that the alleged infringement has appropriated nontrivial amounts of the copyrighted work's expressions. See DERIVATIVE WORK.

comprehensive nonliteral similarity. Similarity evidenced by the copying of the protected work's general ideas or structure (such as a movie's plot) without using the precise words or phrases of the work. — Also termed *pattern similarity*.

fragmented literal similarity. Similarity evidenced by the copying of verbatim portions of the protected work.

substantial-step test. *Criminal law.* The Model Penal Code's test for determining whether a person is guilty of attempt, based on the extent of the defendant's preparation for the crime, the criminal intent shown, and any statements personally made that bear on the defendant's actions. Model Penal Code § 5.01(1)(c). See ATTEMPT (2).

substantiate, *vb.* To establish the existence or truth of (a fact, etc.), esp. by competent evidence; to verify.

substantive consolidation. See CONSOLIDATION.

substantive crime. See *substantive offense* under OFFENSE (1).

substantive due process. See DUE PROCESS.

substantive evidence. See EVIDENCE.

substantive law (**səb**-stən-tiv). The part of the law that creates, defines, and regulates the rights, duties, and powers of parties. Cf. PROCEDURAL LAW.

> "So far as the administration of justice is concerned with the application of remedies to violated rights, we may say that the substantive law defines the remedy and the right, while the law of procedure defines the modes and conditions of the application of the one to the other." John Salmond, *Jurisprudence* 476 (Glanville L. Williams ed., 10th ed. 1947).

substantive offense. See OFFENSE (1).

substantive right. See RIGHT.

substantive rule. See LEGISLATIVE RULE.

substantive unconscionability. See UNCONSCIONABILITY.

substitute, *n.* **1.** One who stands in another's place <a substitute for a party>. See SUBSTITUTION OF PARTIES. **2.** *Civil law.* A person named in a will as heir to an estate after the estate has been held and then passed on by another specified person (called the *institute*). — **substitute,** *vb.*

substitute amendment. See AMENDMENT (1).

substituted agreement. See NOVATION.

substituted basis. See BASIS.

substituted contract. See CONTRACT.

substituted executor. See EXECUTOR.

substituted-judgment doctrine. The rule allowing a person (such as a family member or a conservator) or a court to make a decision about medical treatment on behalf of one who is incompetent and unable to make his or her own decisions.

substituted service. See SERVICE (2).

substitute gift. See GIFT.

substitutio haeredis (səb-stə-**t[y]oo**-shee-oh hə-**ree**-dis). [Latin] *Roman law.* The substitution of an heir who, under certain circumstances, took the place of the original heir, as when the original heir declined an estate.

substitution. 1. A designation of a person or thing to take the place of another person or thing. **2.** The process by which one person or thing takes the place of another person or thing. **3.** *Roman law.* The nomination of a person to take the place of a previously named heir who has refused or failed to accept an inheritance. — Also termed *common substitution*; *vulgar substitution.* **4.** *Roman law.* The nomination of a person to take as heir in place of, or to succeed, a descendant who is under the age of puberty and in the potestas of the testator, if the descendant has failed to take the inheritance or has died before reaching puberty. • This type of substitution was also known as a *pupillary substitution.* If a descendant of any age failed to take by reason of lunacy, the substitution was known as an *exemplary substitution* or *quasi-pupillary substitution.* **5.** *Roman law.* A testator's designation of a person to whom the property was to be given by the person named as heir, or by the heir of that person. — Also termed *fideicommissary substitution.* See FIDEICOMMISSUM. **6.** *Civil law.* The designation of a person to succeed another as beneficiary of an estate, usu. involving a fideicommissum. — Also termed *fideicommissary substitution.*

substitutional, *adj.* Capable of taking or supplying the position of another <substitutional executor> <substitutional issue>. — Also termed *substitutionary.*

substitutional gift. See *substitute gift* under GIFT.

substitutional legacy. See LEGACY.

substitutional remedy. See REMEDY.

substitutionary. See SUBSTITUTIONAL.

substitutionary evidence. See *secondary evidence* under EVIDENCE.

substitution-of-judgment doctrine. *Administrative law.* The standard for reviewing an agency's decision, by which a court uses its own independent judgment in interpreting laws and administrative regulations — rather than deferring to the agency — when the agency's interpretation is not instructive or the regulations do not involve matters requiring the agency's expertise.

substraction (səb-**strak**-shən), *n.* The secret misappropriation of property, esp. from a decedent's estate.

subsume (səb-**s[y]oom**), *vb.* To judge as a particular instance governed by a general principle; to bring (a case) under a broad rule. — **subsumption** (səb-**səmp**-shən), *n.*

sub suo periculo (səb **s[y]oo**-oh pə-**rik**-[y]ə-loh). [Law Latin] *Hist.* At his own risk.

subsurety (səb-**shuur**[-ə]-tee). A person whose undertaking is given as additional security, usu. conditioned not only on nonperformance by the principal but also on nonperformance by an earlier promisor as well; a surety with the lesser liability in a subsuretyship.

subsuretyship (səb-**shuur**[-ə]-tee-ship). The relation between two (or more) sureties, in which a principal surety bears the burden of the whole performance that is due from both sureties; a relationship in which one surety acts as a surety for another.

subsurface right. 1. A landowner's right to the minerals and water below the property. **2.** A like right, held by another through grant by, or purchase from, a landowner. See MINERAL RIGHT. Cf. SURFACE RIGHT.

subtenancy. See SUBLEASE.

subtenant. See SUBLESSEE.

subterfuge (**səb**-tər-fyooj). A clever plan or idea used to escape, avoid, or conceal something <a subterfuge to avoid liability under a statute>.

subterranean water. See WATER.

subtraction. **1.** The process of deducting one number from another number to determine the difference. **2.** *Hist.* The act of neglecting a duty or service that one party owes to another, esp. one that arises out of land tenure.

> "Subtraction, which is the fifth species of injuries affecting a man's real property, happens, when any person who owes any suit, duty, custom, or service to another, withdraws or neglects to perform it. It differs from a disseisin, in that *this* is committed without any denial of the right, consisting merely in non-performance; *that* strikes at the very title of the party injured, and amounts to an ouster or actual dispossession. Subtraction however, being clearly an injury, is remediable by due course of law: but the remedy differs according to the nature of the services; whether they be due by virtue of any tenure, or by custom only." 3 William Blackstone, *Commentaries on the Laws of England* 230 (1768).

subtraction of conjugal rights. *Hist.* The act of a husband and wife unlawfully living apart.

suburbani (səb-ər-**bay**-nɪ), *n.* [Latin] *Hist.* Husbandmen.

subvention (səb-**ven**-shən). A grant of financial aid or assistance; a subsidy.

subversion. The process of overthrowing, destroying, or corrupting <subversion of legal principles> <subversion of the government>.

Subversive Activities Control Act of 1950. See MCCARRAN ACT.

subversive activity. A pattern of acts designed to overthrow a government by force or other illegal means.

successful party. See *prevailing party* under PARTY (2).

successio (sək-**sesh**-ee-oh), *n.* [Latin] *Roman law.* A succession to something, as to an estate by will or by the laws of intestacy.

successio in universum jus (sək-**ses[h]**-ee-oh in yoo-ni-**vər**-səm **jəs**). [Latin "succession to universal right"] *Roman law.* The succession on death of the entirety of a deceased person's assets and liabilities. See HEREDITAS JACENS.

succession, *n.* **1.** The act or right of legally or officially taking over a predecessor's office, rank, or duties. **2.** The acquisition of rights or property by inheritance under the laws of descent and distribution; DESCENT (1). — **succeed,** *vb.*

hereditary succession. Succession by the common law of descent. See DESCENT; TESTATE SUCCESSION; INTESTATE SUCCESSION.

intestate succession. See INTESTATE SUCCESSION.

irregular succession. Succession by special laws favoring certain persons or the state, rather than heirs (such as testamentary heirs) under the ordinary laws of descent.

legal succession. The succession established by law, usu. in favor of the nearest relation of a deceased person.

natural succession. Succession between natural persons, as in descent on the death of an ancestor.

testamentary succession. *Civil law.* Succession resulting from the institution of an heir in a testament executed in the legally required form.

testate succession. See TESTATE SUCCESSION.

universal succession. *Civil law.* Succession to an entire estate of another, living or dead (though usu. the latter). • This type of succession carries with it the predecessor's liabilities as well as assets.

vacant succession. *Civil law.* **1.** A succession that fails either because there are no known heirs or because the heirs have renounced the estate. **2.** An estate that has suffered such a failure.

3. The right by which one group, in replacing another group, acquires all the goods, movables, and other chattels of a corporation. **4.** The continuation of a corporation's legal status despite changes in ownership or management. — Also termed *artificial succession.* — **successor,** *n.*

perpetual succession. The continuous succession of a corporation — despite changes in shareholders and officers — for as long as the corporation legally exists.

> "As a general rule, the words 'perpetual succession,' as used in charters, often in connection with a further provision limiting the period of corporate existence to a certain number of years, mean nothing more than that the corporation shall have continuous and uninterrupted succession so long as it shall continue to exist as a corporation, and are not intended to define its duration." 18 Am. Jur. 2d *Corporations* § 69, at 883 (1985).

successional, *adj.* Of or relating to acquiring rights or property by inheritance under the laws of descent and distribution.

succession tax. See *inheritance tax* (1) under TAX.

successive, *adj.* **1.** *Archaic.* (Of an estate) hereditary. **2.** (Of persons, things, appointments, etc.) following in order; consecutive.

successive tortfeasors. See TORTFEASOR.

successor. 1. A person who succeeds to the office, rights, responsibilities, or place of another; one who replaces or follows another. **2.** A corporation that, through amalgamation, consolidation, or other assumption of interests, is vested with the rights and duties of an earlier corporation.

particular successor. *Civil law.* One who succeeds to rights and obligations that pertain only to the property conveyed.

singular successor. One who succeeds to a former owner's rights in a single piece of property.

universal successor. One who succeeds to all the rights and powers of a former owner, as with an intestate estate or an estate in bankruptcy.

successor fiduciary. See FIDUCIARY.

successor in interest. One who follows another in ownership or control of property. • A successor in interest retains the same rights as the original owner, with no change in substance.

successor trustee. See TRUSTEE (1).

such, *adj.* **1.** Of this or that kind <she collects a variety of such things>. **2.** That or those; having just been mentioned <a newly discovered Fabergé egg will be on auction next week; such egg is expected to sell for more than $500,000>.

sudden-and-accidental pollution exclusion. See *pollution exclusion* under EXCLUSION (3).

sudden-emergency doctrine. See EMERGENCY DOCTRINE (1).

sudden heat of passion. See HEAT OF PASSION.

sudden-onset rule. The principle that medical testimony is unnecessary to prove causation of the obvious symptoms of an injury that immediately follows a known traumatic incident.

sudden passion. See HEAT OF PASSION.

sudden-peril doctrine. See EMERGENCY DOCTRINE (1).

sue, *vb.* To institute a lawsuit against (another party).

sue-and-labor clause. *Marine insurance.* A provision providing that the marine insurer will cover the costs incurred by the insured in protecting the covered property from damage or minimizing actual damages to the property. — Also termed *rescue clause.*

> "Some insurance today is written against 'all risks' .... Besides the perils clause ... recovery under the policy can be had on the entirely separate 'sue and labor' clause .... Under this clause, the underwriter may become liable for certain charges incurred by the assured in caring for the insured property, whether or not there is any actual loss or damage. Where sue-and-labor charges are incurred and loss also occurs, the underwriter may become liable for more than the policy amount, which limits only a claim for loss of or damage to the goods or vessel." Grant Gilmore & Charles L. Black, Jr., *The Law of Admiralty* § 2–10, at 75 (2d ed. 1975).

sue facts. Facts that determine whether a party should bring a lawsuit; esp., facts determining whether a shareholder-derivative action should be instituted under state law.

sue out, *vb.* To apply to a court for the issuance of (a court order or writ).

suffer, *vb.* **1.** To experience or sustain physical or emotional pain, distress, or injury <suffer grievously><suffer damages>. **2.** To allow or permit (an act, etc.) <to suffer a default>.

sufferance (**səf**-ər-ənts *or* **səf**-rənts). **1.** Toleration; passive consent. **2.** The state of one who holds land without the owner's permission. See *tenancy at sufferance* under TENANCY. **3.** A license implied from the omission to enforce a right.

sufferance wharves. *Hist. English law.* Wharves designated by the Commissioner of the Customs to receive goods before any duties must be paid.

sufferentia pacis (səf-ə-**ren**-shee-ə **pay**-sis), *n.* [Latin] A grant of peace; a truce; an armistice.

suffering a recovery. *Hist.* A conveyor's act of allowing, for the purposes of a conveyance, a fictitious action to be brought by the conveyee and a judgment to be recovered for the land in question.

sufficiency-of-evidence test. 1. The guideline for a grand jury considering whether to indict a suspect: if all the evidence presented were uncontradicted and unexplained, it would warrant a conviction by the fact-trier. **2.** A standard for reviewing a criminal conviction on appeal, based on whether enough evidence exists to justify the fact-trier's finding of guilt beyond a reasonable doubt. — Also termed *sufficiency-of-the-evidence test.*

sufficient, *adj.* Adequate; of such quality, number, force, or value as is necessary for a given purpose <sufficient consideration> <sufficient evidence>.

sufficient cause. 1. See *good cause* under CAUSE (2). **2.** PROBABLE CAUSE.

sufficient consideration. See CONSIDERATION.

sufficient evidence. See *satisfactory evidence* under EVIDENCE.

suffragan (**səf**-rə-gən). A titular bishop ordained to aid and assist a bishop of the diocese in the church business; a deputy or assistant bishop. • Suffragans were originally appointed only to replace absent bishops and were called *chorepiscopi* ("bishops of the county"), as distinguished from the regular bishops of the city or see.

suffrage (**səf**-rij). **1.** The right or privilege of casting a vote at a public election. — Also termed RIGHT TO VOTE.

> "In the United States suffrage is a privilege, franchise or trust conferred by the people upon such persons as it deems fittest to represent it in the choice of magistrates or in the performance of political duties which it would be inexpedient or inconvenient for the people to perform in a body. The person upon whom the franchise is conferred is called an elector or voter. No community extends suffrage to all persons, but places such restrictions upon it as may best subserve the ends of government." George W. McCrary, *A Treatise on the American Law of Elections* § 1, at 2 (Henry L. McCune ed., 4th ed. 1897).

2. A vote; the act of voting.

suffragium (sə-**fray**-jee-əm), *n.* [Latin] *Roman law.* **1.** A vote; the right to vote. **2.** A recommendation of someone for a special privilege or office.

suggested retail price. See PRICE.

suggestibility, *n.* The readiness with which a person accepts another's suggestion. — **suggestible,** *adj.*

suggestio falsi (səg-**jes**-tee-oh **fal**-sɪ *or* **fawl**-sɪ). [Latin] A false representation or misleading suggestion. Cf. SUPPRESSIO VERI.

suggestion, *n.* **1.** An indirect presentation of an idea <the client agreed with counsel's suggestion to reword the warranty>. **2.** *Procedure.* A statement of some fact or circumstance that will materially affect the further proceedings in the case <suggestion for rehearing en banc>. — **suggest** (for sense 1), *vb.*

suggestion of bankruptcy. A pleading by which a party notifies the court that the party has filed for bankruptcy and that, because of the automatic stay provided by the bankruptcy laws, the court cannot legally take further action in the case.

suggestion of death. A pleading filed by a party, or the party's representatives, by which the court is notified that a party to a suit has died.

suggestion of error. An objection made by a party to a suit, indicating that the court has committed an error or that the party wants a rehearing of a particular issue.

suggestive interrogation. See LEADING QUESTION.

suggestive question. See LEADING QUESTION.

suggestive trademark. See TRADEMARK.

sui (**s[y]oo**-ɪ). [Latin] *Roman law.* A person's direct descendants who were unemancipated.

suicide, *n.* **1.** The act of taking one's own life. — Also termed *self-killing*; *self-destruction*; *self-slaughter*; *self-murder*; *felony de se.*

assisted suicide. The intentional act of providing a person with the medical means or the medical knowledge to commit suicide. — Also termed *assisted self-determination.* Cf. EUTHANASIA.

attempted suicide. An unsuccessful suicidal act.

2. A person who has taken his or her own life. — **suicidal,** *adj.*

suicide clause. *Insurance.* A life-insurance-policy provision either excluding suicide as a risk or limiting the liability of the insurer in the event of a suicide to the total premiums paid.

suicide letter of credit. See *clean letter of credit* under LETTER OF CREDIT.

sui generis (**s[y]oo**-I *or* **soo**-ee **jen**-ə-ris). [Latin "of its own kind"] Of its own kind or class; unique or peculiar.

sui heredes (**s[y]oo**-I hə-**ree**-deez). [Latin] *Roman law*. One's own heirs. — Also spelled *sui haeredes*.

> "If a man died without a will, his property went to his *sui heredes* (own heirs, direct heirs), that is, to the persons who were previously under his *potestas*, but were released from it by his death. If he had adopted as son a person not connected with him by birth, that person was included among the *sui heredes*; on the other hand, a son by birth whom he had emancipated was ... excluded from the *sui heredes* ...." James Hadley, *Introduction to Roman Law* 134 (1881).

sui juris (**s[y]oo**-I *or* **soo**-ee **joor**-is). [Latin "of one's own right; independent"] **1.** Of full age and capacity. **2.** Possessing full social and civil rights.

suit. Any proceeding by a party or parties against another in a court of law; CASE. — Also termed *lawsuit*; *suit at law*. See ACTION.

ancillary suit (**an**-sə-ler-ee). An action, either at law or in equity, that grows out of and is auxiliary to another suit and is filed to aid the primary suit, to enforce a prior judgment, or to impeach a prior decree. — Also termed *ancillary bill*; *ancillary proceeding*; *ancillary process*.

blackmail suit. A suit filed by a party having no genuine claim but hoping to extract a favorable settlement from a defendant who would rather avoid the expenses and hassles of litigation.

class suit. See CLASS ACTION.

derivative suit. See DERIVATIVE ACTION (1).

plenary suit (**plee**-nə-ree *or* **plen**-ə-ree). An action that proceeds on formal pleadings under rules of procedure. Cf. *summary proceeding* under PROCEEDING.

strike suit. A suit (esp. a derivative action), often based on no valid claim, brought either for nuisance value or as leverage to obtain a favorable or inflated settlement.

suit at law. A suit conducted according to the common law or equity, as distinguished from statutory provisions. • Under the current rules of practice in federal and most state courts, the term *civil action* embraces an action both at law and in equity. Fed. R. Civ. P. 2.

suit of a civil nature. A civil action. See *civil action* under ACTION.

suitable, *adj.* (Of goods, etc.) fit and appropriate for their intended purpose.

suitas (**s[y]oo**-ə-tas), *n.* [Law Latin] The status of a proper heir.

suit at law. See SUIT.

suit for exoneration. A suit in equity brought by a surety to compel the debtor to pay the creditor. • If the debtor has acted fraudulently and is insolvent, a suit for exoneration may include further remedies to ensure that the debtor's assets are applied equitably to the debtor's outstanding obligations. — Also termed *suit to compel payment*.

suit money. Attorney's fees and court costs allowed or awarded by a court; esp., in some jurisdictions, a husband's payment to his wife to cover her reasonable attorney's fees in a divorce action.

suitor. 1. A party that brings a lawsuit; a plaintiff or petitioner. **2.** An individual or company that seeks to take over another company.

Suitors' Deposit Account. An account consisting of suitors' fees paid in the Court of Chancery that, by the Chancery Act of 1872, were to be invested in government securities bearing interest at 2% per annum on behalf of the investing suitor, unless the suitor directed otherwise.

Suitors' Fee Fund. *Hist.* A fund consisting largely of fees generated by the Court of Chancery out of which the court officers' salaries and expenses were paid. • In 1869 the fund was transferred to the Commissioners for the Reduction of the National Debt.

suit papers. See COURT PAPERS.

suit *pro laesione fidei* (proh lee-zhee-**oh**-nee **fI**-dee-I), *n.* [Latin "for injury to faith"] *Hist. Eccles. law.* A suit in ecclesiastical court for spiritual offenses against conscience, nonpayment of debts, or a civil breach of contract. • This attempt to turn the ecclesiastical courts into courts of equity was abolished in 1164.

Suits in Admiralty Act. A federal law giving injured parties the right to sue the government in admiralty. 46 USCA app. §§ 741–752.

suit to compel payment. See SUIT FOR EXONERATION.

sum. **1.** A quantity of money. **2.** *English law.* A legal summary or abstract; a compendium; a collection. • Several treatises are called *sums.*

sum certain. **1.** Any amount that is fixed, settled, or exact. **2.** *Commercial law.* In a negotiable instrument, a sum that is agreed on in the instrument or a sum that can be ascertained from the document.

summa injuria (**səm**-ə in-**joor**-ee-ə). [Latin] The greatest injury or injustice.

summa potestas (**səm**-ə pə-**tes**-təs), *n.* [Latin "sum or totality of power"] The final authority or power in government.

summary, *n.* **1.** An abridgment or brief. **2.** A short application to a court without the formality of a full proceeding.

summary, *adj.* **1.** Short; concise <a summary account of the events on March 6>. **2.** Without the usual formalities; esp., without a jury <a summary trial>. **3.** Immediate; done without delay <the new weapon was put to summary use by the military>. — **summarily** (**səm**-ər-ə-lee *or* sə-**mair**-ə-lee), *adv.*

summary adjudication. See *partial summary judgment* under SUMMARY JUDGMENT.

summary conviction. See CONVICTION.

summary court-martial. See COURT-MARTIAL.

summary disposition. See SUMMARY JUDGMENT.

summary eviction. See EVICTION.

summary judgment. A judgment granted on a claim about which there is no genuine issue of material fact and upon which the movant is entitled to prevail as a matter of law. • This procedural device allows the speedy disposition of a controversy without the need for trial. Fed. R. Civ. P. 56. — Also termed *summary disposition*; *judgment on the pleadings.* See JUDGMENT.

partial summary judgment. A summary judgment that is limited to certain issues in a case and that disposes of only a portion of the whole case. — Also termed *summary adjudication.*

summary-judgment motion. See MOTION FOR SUMMARY JUDGMENT.

summary jurisdiction. See JURISDICTION.

summary jury trial. See TRIAL.

summary offense. See OFFENSE (1).

summary plan description. Under ERISA, an outline of an employee benefit plan, containing such information as the identity of the plan administrator, the requirements for eligibility and participation in the plan, circumstances that may result in disqualification or denial of benefits, and the identity of any insurers responsible for financing or administering the plan. • A summary plan description must generally be furnished to all employee-benefit-plan participants and beneficiaries. 29 USCA § 1022.

summary procedure. See SHOW-CAUSE PROCEEDING.

summary proceeding. See PROCEEDING.

summary process. See PROCESS.

summary trial. See *summary proceeding* under PROCEEDING.

summation. See CLOSING ARGUMENT.

summer associate. See CLERK (4).

summer clerk. See CLERK (4).

summing up. See CLOSING ARGUMENT.

summon, *vb.* To command (a person) by service of a summons to appear in court. — Also termed *summons.*

summoneas (sə-**moh**-nee-əs), *n.* [Law Latin "you are to summon"] *Hist.* A writ ordering a party to appear in court.

summoner. *Hist.* A petty officer charged with summoning parties to appear in court. See NUNTIUS.

> "But process, as we are now to consider it, is the method taken by the law to compel a compliance with the original writ, of which the primary step is by giving the party notice to obey it. This notice is given . . . by *summons*; which is a warning to appear in court . . . given to the defendant by two of the sheriff's messengers called *summoners*, either in person or left at his house or land." 3

William Blackstone, *Commentaries on the Laws of England* 279 (1768).

summonitio (səm-ə-**nish**-ee-oh), *n.* [Law Latin fr. Latin *summonere* "to summon"] *Hist.* A summons.

summonitores scaccarii (səm-ən-ə-**tor**-eez skə-**kair**-ee-I). [Law Latin] *Hist.* Exchequer officers who assisted in revenue collections by summoning defaulters to court.

summons, *n.* **1.** Formerly, a writ directing a sheriff to summon a defendant to appear in court. **2.** A writ or process commencing the plaintiff's action and requiring the defendant to appear and answer. **3.** A notice requiring a person to appear in court as a juror or witness. **4.** *English law.* The application to a common-law judge upon which an order is made. Pl. **summonses.**

alias summons. A second summons issued after the original summons has failed for some reason.

John Doe summons. **1.** A summons to a person whose name is unknown at the time of service. **2.** *Tax.* A summons from the Internal Revenue Service to a third party to provide information on an unnamed, unknown taxpayer with potential tax liability. — Also termed *third-party record-custodian summons.*

short summons. A summons having a response time less than that of an ordinary summons, usu. served on a fraudulent or nonresident debtor.

summons, *vb.* **1.** SUMMON. **2.** To request (information) by summons.

"The horrible expression 'summonsed for an offence' (turning the noun 'summons' into a verb) has now become accepted usage, but 'summoned' remains not only allowable but preferable." Glanville Williams, *Learning the Law* 15 n.28 (11th ed. 1982).

summum bonum (**səm**-əm **boh**-nəm *also* **suum**-uum **baw**-nuum). [Latin] The greatest good.

summum jus (**səm**-əm **jəs**). [Latin] The highest law.

sumner (**səm**-nər), *n. Hist.* A summoning officer, esp. in an ecclesiastical court. See SUMMONER.

sum-of-the-years'-digits depreciation method. See DEPRECIATION METHOD.

sum payable. An amount due; esp., the amount for which the maker of a negotiable instrument becomes liable and must tender in full satisfaction of the debt.

sumptuary law (**səmp**-choo-er-ee). **1.** A statute, ordinance, or regulation that limits the expenditures that people can make for personal gratification or ostentatious display. **2.** More broadly, any law whose purpose is to regulate conduct thought to be immoral, such as prostitution, gambling, or drug abuse.

Sunday-closing law. See BLUE LAW.

Sunday law. See BLUE LAW.

sundries (**sən**-dreez). Miscellaneous items that may be considered together, without being separately specified or identified.

sundry (**sən**-dree), *adj.* Separate; diverse; various.

sunk cost. See COST (1).

sunset law. A statute under which a governmental agency or program automatically terminates at the end of a fixed period unless it is formally renewed.

sunshine committee. An official or quasi-official committee whose proceedings and work are open to public access.

sunshine law. A statute requiring a governmental department or agency to open its meetings or its records to public access. — Also termed *open-meeting law*; *public-meeting law*; *open-door law.*

suo nomine (**s[y]oo**-oh **nom**-ə-nee). [Latin] In one's own name.

suo periculo. See SUB SUO PERICULO.

SUP. *abbr.* SPECIAL-USE PERMIT.

sup. ct. *abbr.* SUPREME COURT.

super (**s[y]oo**-pər). [Latin] Above; over; higher.

super altum mare (**s[y]oo**-pər **al**-təm **mair**-ee *or* **mahr**-ee). [Latin] On the high sea.

supercargo. *Maritime law.* A person specially employed and authorized by a cargo owner to sell cargo that has been shipped and to purchase returning cargo, at the best possible prices; the commercial or foreign agent of a merchant.

> "Supercargoes are persons employed by commercial companies or by private merchants to take charge of the cargoes they export to foreign countries, to sell them there to the best advantage, and to purchase proper commodities to relade the ships on their return home. They usually go out with the ships on board of which the goods are embarked, and return home with them, and in this they differ from factors who live abroad .... The supercargo is the agent of the owners, and disposes of the cargo and makes purchases under their general instructions on his own responsibility." 70 Am. Jur. 2d *Shipping* § 886, at 1025 (1987).

superductio (s[y]oo-pər-**dək**-shee-oh). [Latin] *Roman law.* The obliteration of part of a will or other document by writing on top of something erased within it.

superfeudation. See SUPERINFEUDATION.

superficiarius (s[y]oo-pər-fish-ee-**air**-ee-əs), *n.* [Latin] *Roman law.* A person who had a hereditary and alienable right to a building on another's land subject to the payment of an annual rent.

superficies (s[y]oo-pər-**fish**-ee-eez *or* -**fish**-eez), *n.* [Latin "surface"] *Roman & civil law.* **1.** The surface of the ground. **2.** An improvement that stands on the surface of the ground, such as a building. **3.** The right of a *superficiarius*.

Superfund. **1.** The program that funds and administers the cleanup of hazardous-waste sites through a trust fund (financed by taxes on petroleum and chemicals and a new tax on corporations) created to pay for cleanup pending reimbursement from the liable parties. **2.** The popular name for the act that established this program — the Comprehensive Environmental Response, Compensation, and Liability Act of 1980 (CERCLA). See CERCLA.

superinfeudation. *Hist.* The granting of one or more feuds out of a feudal estate. — Also termed *superfeudation*. Cf. SUBINFEUDATION.

> "Whatever may be the proper view of its origin and legal nature, the best mode of vividly picturing to ourselves the feudal organisation is to begin with the basis, to consider the relation of the tenant to the patch of soil which created and limited his services — and then to mount up, through narrowing circles of super-feudation, till we approximate to the apex of the system." Henry S. Maine, *Ancient Law* 88 (17th ed. 1901).

superinstitution. *Eccles. law.* The institution of one person in an office that already has an incumbent, as when two individuals claim a benefice by adverse titles.

superintendent. A person with the power to direct activities; a manager.

superintending control. See CONTROL.

superior, *adj.* (Of a rank, office, power, etc.) higher; elevated; possessing greater power or authority; entitled to exert authority or command over another <superior estate> <superior force> <superior agent>. — **superior,** *n.*

superior agent. See *high-managerial agent* under AGENT.

superior commissioned officer. See OFFICER (2).

superior court. See COURT.

superior fellow servant. See FELLOW SERVANT.

superior force. See FORCE MAJEURE; VIS MAJOR.

superior knowledge. See KNOWLEDGE.

superjurare (s[y]oo-pər-juu-**rair**-ee). [Latin "to overswear"] *Hist.* To swear too strenuously. • This describes the situation in which an obviously guilty criminal attempted to avoid conviction by producing oaths of several parties but was convicted by an overwhelming number of witnesses.

superlien. A statutory lien that is superior to all existing liens and all later-filed liens on the same property. • Superliens are sometimes granted to a state's environmental-protection agency. Several states — such as Arkansas, Connecticut, Massachusetts, New Hampshire, New Jersey, and Tennessee — have enacted statutes creating superliens on property owned by a party responsible for environmental cleanup.

supermajority. See MAJORITY.

supernumerarii (s[y]oo-pər-n[y]oo-mə-**rair**-ee-I). [Latin "persons above the number"] *Roman law.* Advocates who were unregistered and not attached to a particular bar; advocates who were in excess of the permitted number. Cf. STATUTI.

superoneratio (s[y]oo-pər-on-ə-**ray**-shee-oh). [Law Latin] *Hist.* **1.** The act or practice of surcharging a common. **2.** The placement of more cattle on a common than is allowed; over-stocking.

superoneratione pasturae. See DE SUPERONERATIONE PASTURAE.

superplusagium (s[y]oo-pər-plə-**say**-jee-əm), *n.* [Law Latin] *Hist.* A surplus; a remainder.

super praerogativa regis (**s**[**y**]**oo**-pər pri-rog-ə-**tI**-və **ree**-jis), *n.* [Law Latin] *Hist.* A writ against the king's tenant's widow for marrying without royal permission.

superpriority. *Bankruptcy.* The special priority status granted by the court to a creditor for extending credit to a debtor or trustee that cannot obtain unsecured credit from a willing lender. • This priority may be either an administrative claim outranking other administrative claims or, if certain statutory requirements are met, a security interest in property. 11 USCA § 364(c)(1).

supersede, *vb.* **1.** To annul, make void, or repeal by taking the place of <the 1996 statute supersedes the 1989 act>. **2.** To invoke or make applicable the right of supersedeas against (an award of damages) <what is the amount of the bond necessary to supersede the judgment against her?>. — **supersession** (for sense 1), *n.*

supersedeas (soo-pər-**seed**-ee-əs), *n.* [Latin "you shall desist"] A writ or bond that suspends a judgment creditor's power to levy execution, usu. pending appeal. — Also termed *writ of supersedeas.* Pl. **supersedeases** (soo-pər-**see**-dee-əs-iz).

supersedeas bond. See BOND (2).

superseding cause. See CAUSE (1).

super statuto (**s**[**y**]**oo**-pər stə-**t**[**y**]**oo**-toh), *n.* [Law Latin] *Hist.* A writ against tenants-in-chief who transferred their land without the king's permission in violation of the Statute of Westminster II, chs. 12 & 13.

super statuto de articulis cleri (**s**[**y**]**oo**-pər stə-**t**[**y**]**oo**-toh dee ahr-**tik**-yə-lis **kleer**-I), *n.* [Law Latin] *Hist.* A writ against a sheriff who unlawfully distrains goods.

super statuto facto pour seneschal et marshal de roy (**s**[**y**]**oo**-pər stə-**t**[**y**]**oo**-toh **fak**-toh poor sen-ə-**shahl** ay mahr-[ə-]**shahl** də **roy**), *n.* [Law Latin] *Hist.* A writ to restrain the court of the Marshalsea from interfering in matters outside the court's jurisdiction.

super statuto versus servantes et laboratores (**s**[**y**]**oo**-pər stə-**t**[**y**]**oo**-toh **vər**-səs sər-**van**-teez et lab-ər-ə-**tor**-eez), *n.* [Law Latin] *Hist.* **1.** A writ against someone who employs laborers who unlawfully left former employments. **2.** A writ against a person who refused to work at the required wage.

superstitious use. See USE (1).

supervening cause. See *intervening cause* under CAUSE (1).

supervening negligence. See *subsequent negligence* under NEGLIGENCE.

supervening-negligence doctrine. See LAST-CLEAR-CHANCE DOCTRINE.

supervision, *n.* The act of managing, directing, or overseeing persons or projects. — **supervise,** *vb.* — **supervisory** (soo-pər-**vI**-zə-ree), *adj.*

supervisor, *n.* **1.** One having authority over others; a manager or overseer. • Under the National Labor Relations Act, a supervisor is any individual having authority to hire, transfer, suspend, lay off, recall, promote, discharge, discipline, and handle grievances of other employees, by exercising independent judgment. **2.** The chief administrative officer of a town or county. — **supervisorial** (soo-pər-vI-**zor**-ee-əl), *adj.*

supervisory authority. *Military law.* An officer who, exercising general court-martial jurisdiction, reviews summary and special court-martial trial records after the convening authority has reviewed them.

supervisory control. The control exercised by a higher court over a lower court, as by prohibiting the lower court from acting extrajurisdictionally and by reversing its extrajurisdictional acts. See MANDAMUS.

supplemental, *adj.* Supplying something additional; adding what is lacking <supplemental rules>.

supplemental affidavit. See AFFIDAVIT.

supplemental bill. See BILL (2).

supplemental bill in nature of bill of review. See *bill in the nature of a bill of review* under BILL (2).

supplemental claim. See CLAIM (4).

supplemental complaint. See COMPLAINT.

supplemental jurisdiction. See JURISDICTION.

supplemental pleading. See PLEADING (1).

Supplemental Rules for Certain Maritime and Admiralty Claims. See MARITIME JURISDICTION.

supplemental security income. Monthly income provided under a program administered by the Social Security Administration to a qualified person as defined by Social Security regulations, including a person who is disabled or over the age of 65. — Abbr. SSI.

supplemental surety. See SURETY.

supplementary proceeding. See PROCEEDING.

suppletory oath (sәp-lә-tor-ee). See OATH.

suppliant (**sәp**-lee-әnt). One who humbly requests something; specif., the actor in a petition of right.

supplicatio (sәp-li-**kay**-shee-oh), *n.* [Latin] *Roman law.* **1.** A petition to the emperor requesting him to decide a case in the first instance or, sometimes, to reopen a case in which no appeal is normally allowed.

> "Another mode was *supplicatio*, petition to the Emperor by a private person, not allowed when the question was already before a court or had been decided and not properly appealed. It was mainly used to bring matters before the Emperor or his delegate, in first instance, where for any reason it was unlikely that justice would be done, e.g. where the claimant was humble and the opponent a '*potentior*,' or where the claimant was of too high rank to go before the ordinary court, or the decision was of an unappealable magistrate." W.W. Buckland, *Elementary Principles of the Roman Private Law* 671 (1912).

2. A petition for a pardon on a first offense. **3.** *Hist.* A pleading similar to a rejoinder.

supplicavit (sәp-li-**kay**-vit). *Hist.* A writ issuing out of the King's Bench or Chancery for taking sureties of the peace, obligating a person to be on good behavior for a specified period. • It is commonly directed to the justices of the peace who are hesitant to intervene in their judicial capacities. See *surety of the peace* under SURETY.

> "Any justices of the peace, by virtue of their commission, or those who are *ex officio* conservators of the peace ... may demand such security according to their own discretion: or it may be granted at the request of any subject, upon due cause shewn .... Or, if the justice is averse to act, it may be granted by a mandatory writ, called a *supplicavit*, issuing out of the court of king's bench or chancery; which will compel the justice to act, as a ministerial and not as a judicial officer ...." 4 William Blackstone, *Commentaries on the Laws of England* 250 (1769).

supplicium (sә-**plish**-ee-әm), *n.* [Latin "atonement"] *Roman law.* A punishment. • *Ultimum supplicium* is the death penalty.

supplier, *n.* A person engaged, directly or indirectly, in the business of making a product available to consumers.

supplies, *n.* **1.** Means of provision or relief; stores available for distribution. **2.** In parliamentary proceedings, the annual grant voted on by the House of Commons for maintaining the Crown and various public services.

supply, *n.* The amount of goods produced or available at a given price.

aggregate supply. The total amount of goods and services generated in an economy during a specific period.

supply curve. A line on a price-output graph showing the relationship between a good's price and the quantity supplied at a given time.

support, *n.* **1.** Sustenance or maintenance; esp., articles such as food and clothing that allow one to live in the degree of comfort to which one is accustomed. See MAINTENANCE (5); NECESSARIES. **2.** Basis or foundation. **3.** The right to have one's ground braced so that it does not cave in because of another landowner's actions. — **support,** *vb.*

lateral support. The right to have one's land supported by the land that lies next to it. — Also termed *easement of natural support.*

subjacent support. The right to have one's land supported by the earth that lies underneath it.

support obligation. A secondary obligation or letter-of-credit right that supports the payment or performance of an account, chattel paper, general intangible, document, healthcare-insurance receivable, instrument, or investment property. UCC § 9–102(a)(53).

support order. A court decree requiring a party in a divorce proceeding or a paternity proceeding to make payments to maintain a child or spouse, including medical, dental, and educational expenses.

foreign support order. An out-of-state support order.

support price. See PRICE.

support trust. See TRUST.

supposition (səp-ə-**zish**-ən), *n.* An assumption that something is true, without proof of its veracity; the act of supposing. — **suppose,** *vb.* — **supposable,** *adj.*

suppress, *vb.* To put a stop to, put down, or prohibit; to prevent (something) from being seen, heard, known, or discussed <the defendant tried to suppress the incriminating evidence>. — **suppression,** *n.* — **suppressible, suppressive,** *adj.*

suppression hearing. See HEARING.

suppression of evidence. 1. A trial judge's ruling that evidence that a party has offered should be excluded because it was illegally acquired. **2.** The destruction of evidence or the refusal to give evidence at a criminal proceeding. • This is usu. considered a crime. See OBSTRUCTION OF JUSTICE. **3.** The prosecution's withholding from the defense of evidence that is favorable to the defendant.

suppressio veri (sə-**pres**[**h**]-ee-oh **veer**-ɪ). [Latin] Suppression of the truth; a type of fraud. Cf. SUGGESTIO FALSI.

supra (**s**[**y**]**oo**-prə). [Latin "above"] Earlier in this text; used as a citational signal to refer to a previously cited authority. Cf. INFRA.

supralegal, *adj.* Above or beyond the law <a supralegal sovereign>.

supranational, *adj.* Free of the political limitations of nations.

supra protest. (Of a debt) under protest. See PROTEST (3).

supra riparian (**soo**-prə ri-**pair**-ee-ən *or* rɪ-). Upper riparian; higher up the stream. • This phrase describes the estate, rights, and duties of a riparian owner whose land is situated nearer the source of a stream than the land it is compared to.

supremacy. The position of having the superior or greatest power or authority.

Supremacy Clause. The clause in Article VI of the U.S. Constitution declaring that all laws made in furtherance of the Constitution and all treaties made under the authority of the United States are the "supreme law of the land" and enjoy legal superiority over any conflicting provision of a state constitution or law. See PREEMPTION.

supremacy of law. See RULE OF LAW.

supreme, *adj.* (Of a court, power, right, etc.) highest; superior to all others.

supreme court. 1. (*cap.*) SUPREME COURT OF THE UNITED STATES. **2.** An appellate court existing in most states, usu. as the court of last resort. **3.** In New York, a court of general jurisdiction with trial and appellate divisions. • The Court of Appeals is the court of last resort in New York. — Abbr. S.C.; S.Ct.; Sup. Ct.

Supreme Court of Appeals. The highest court in West Virginia.

Supreme Court of Errors. *Hist.* The court of last resort in Connecticut. • The court is now called the *Supreme Court.*

Supreme Court of Judicature. The highest court in England and Wales, consisting of the High Court of Justice, the Court of Appeal, and the Crown Court. • The Supreme Court was created under the Judicature Act of 1873 that consolidated the existing superior courts, including the High Court of Chancery, the court of Queen's Bench, the court of Exchequer, the High Court of Admiralty, the court of Probate, and the London court of Bankruptcy.

Supreme Court of the United States. The court of last resort in the federal system, whose members are appointed by the President and approved by the Senate. • The Court was established in 1789 by Article III of the U.S.

Constitution, which vests the Court with the "judicial power of the United States." — Often shortened to *Supreme Court*. — Also termed *United States Supreme Court*.

Supreme Judicial Court. The highest appellate court in Maine and Massachusetts.

supreme law of the land. 1. The U.S. Constitution. **2.** Acts of Congress made according to the U.S. Constitution. **3.** U.S. treaties.

supreme legislation. See LEGISLATION.

supreme power. See *sovereign political power* under POLITICAL POWER.

sur (sər). [Law French] *Hist.* Upon. • This term appears in various phrases, such as *sur cognizance de droit* ("upon acknowledgment of right").

surcharge, *n.* **1.** An additional tax, charge, or cost, usu. one that is excessive. **2.** An additional load or burden. **3.** A second or further mortgage. **4.** The omission of a proper credit on an account. **5.** The amount that a court may charge a fiduciary that has breached its duty. **6.** An overprint on a stamp, esp. one that changes its face value. **7.** The overstocking of an area with animals. — **surcharge,** *vb.*

surcharge, *vb.* **1.** To impose an additional (usu. excessive) tax, charge, or cost. **2.** To impose an additional load or burden. **3.** (Of a court) to impose a fine on a fiduciary for breach of duty. **4.** To overstock (an area) with animals.

second surcharge. To overstock (a common) a second time for which a writ of second surcharge was issued.

surcharge and falsify. To scrutinize particular items in an account to show items that were not credited as required (to surcharge) and to prove that certain items were wrongly inserted (to falsify). • The courts of chancery usu. granted plaintiffs the opportunity to surcharge and falsify accounts that the defendant alleged to be settled.

sur cui ante divortium (sər kI [*or* kwI *or* kwee] **an**-tee də-**vor**-shee-əm). See CUI ANTE DIVORTIUM.

sur cui in vita (sər kI [*or* kwI *or* kwee] in **vI**-tə). See CUI IN VITA.

sur disclaimer. *Hist.* A writ brought by a lord against a tenant who has disclaimed tenure, to recover the land.

surdus (**sər**-dəs). [Latin] *Roman law.* A deaf person. • A wholly deaf or dumb person could not lawfully make a will before the time of Justinian, who changed the law.

surety (**shuur**[-ə]-tee). **1.** A person who is primarily liable for the payment of another's debt or the performance of another's obligation. • Although a surety is similar to an insurer, one important difference is that a surety often receives no compensation for assuming liability. A surety differs from a guarantor, who is liable to the creditor only if the debtor does not meet the duties owed to the creditor; the surety is directly liable. Cf. GUARANTOR.

> "The words surety and guarantor are often used indiscriminately as synonymous terms; but while a surety and a guarantor have this in common, that they are both bound for another person, yet there are points of difference between them which should be carefully noted. A surety is usually bound with his principal by the same instrument, executed at the same time and on the same consideration. He is an original promisor and debtor from the beginning, and is held ordinarily to know every default of this principal. Usually the surety will not be discharged, either by the mere indulgence of the creditor to the principal, or by want of notice of the default of the principal, no matter how much he may be injured thereby. On the other hand, the contract of the guarantor is his own separate undertaking, in which the principal does not join. It is usually entered into before or after that of the principal, and is often founded on a separate consideration from that supporting the contract of the principal." 1 George W. Brandt, *The Law of Suretyship and Guaranty* § 2, at 9 (3d ed. 1905).

> "A surety, in the broad sense, is one who is liable for the debt or obligation of another, whether primarily or secondarily, conditionally or unconditionally. In other words, the term surety includes anyone who is bound on an obligation which, as between himself and another person who is bound to the obligee for the same performance, the latter obligor should discharge. In this sense, suretyship includes all accessorial obligations. By such terminology, guarantors and indorsers are kinds of sureties.... A surety, in the narrow sense, is one who is liable in form primarily on the debt or obligation of another. His obligation is accessorial to that of the principal debtor, but it is direct and not conditioned on the principal debtor's default. In this sense, suretyship differs from guaranty and indorsement, which are conditional, secondary obligations.... The word surety is in the majority of American decisions used in the narrower sense to indicate a primary obligation to pay another's debt, to distinguish it from the secondary obligation of a guarantor. This terminology has the advantage of indicating by the use of the one word 'surety' an obligation which is at once one to pay another's debt, but which at the same time is not conditioned upon another's default." Laurence P. Simpson, *Handbook on the Law of Suretyship* 6, 8–9 (1950).

accommodation surety. See *voluntary surety*.

compensated surety. A surety who is paid for becoming obliged to the creditor. • A bonding company is a typical example of a compensated surety. — Also termed *commercial surety*.

cosurety. See COSURETY.

gratuitous surety. A surety who is not compensated for becoming obliged to the creditor. • Perhaps the most common example is the parent who signs as a surety for a child.

subsurety. See SUBSURETY.

supplemental surety. A surety for a surety.

surety of the peace. *Hist.* A surety responsible for ensuring that a person will not commit a future offense. • It is required of one against whom there are probable grounds to suspect future misbehavior. See SUPPLICAVIT.

voluntary surety. A surety who receives no consideration for the promise to act as a surety. — Also termed *accommodation surety*.

2. A formal assurance; esp., a pledge, bond, guarantee, or security given for the fulfillment of an undertaking.

surety and fidelity insurance. See *fidelity insurance* under INSURANCE.

surety bond. See BOND (2).

surety company. See COMPANY.

surety insurance. See *guaranty insurance* under INSURANCE.

surety of the peace. See SURETY.

suretyship. 1. The legal relation that arises when one party assumes liability for a debt, default, or other failing of a second party. • The liability of both parties begins simultaneously. In other words, under a contract of suretyship, a surety becomes a party to the principal obligation. **2.** The lending of credit to aid a principal who does not have sufficient credit. • The purpose is to guard against loss if the principal debtor were to default. **3.** The position or status of a surety.

involuntary suretyship. A suretyship that arises incidentally, when the chief object of the contract is to accomplish some other purpose.

personal suretyship. A suretyship in which the surety is answerable in damages.

real suretyship. A suretyship in which specified property can be taken, but the surety is not answerable in damages.

suretyship by operation of law. A suretyship that the law creates when a third party promises a debtor to assume and pay the debt that the debtor owes to a creditor.

voluntary suretyship. A suretyship in which the chief object of the contract is to make one party a surety.

surface. 1. The top layer of something, esp. of land. **2.** *Mining law.* An entire portion of land, including mineral deposits, except those specifically reserved. • The meaning of the term varies, esp. when used in legal instruments, depending on the language used, the intention of the parties, the business involved, and the nature and circumstances of the transaction. **3.** *Mining law.* The part of the geologic section lying over the minerals in question.

surface right. A landowner's right to the land's surface and to all substances below the surface that are not defined as minerals. • The surface right is subject to the mineral owner's right to use the surface. — Also termed *surface interest*. Cf. MINERAL RIGHT; SUBSURFACE RIGHT.

Surface Transportation Board. See INTERSTATE COMMERCE COMMISSION.

surface water. See *diffused surface water* under WATER.

Surgeon General. 1. The chief medical officer of the U.S. Public Health Service or of a state public-health agency. **2.** The chief officer of the medical departments in the armed forces. — Abbr. SG.

surmise (sər-**mɪz**), *n.* **1.** An idea based on weak evidence; conjecture. **2.** *Hist.* A suggestion, esp. to a court. **3.** *Hist. Eccles. law.* An allegation in the complaint. • A collateral surmise is a surmise of a fact not contained in the libel. See LIBEL (3).

surplice fees (**sər**-plis **feez**). *Eccles. law.* Fees paid to clergy for performing occasional duties, such as marriages, funerals, and baptisms.

surplus. 1. The remainder of a thing; the residue or excess. **2.** The excess of receipts over disbursements. **3.** Funds that remain after a partnership has been dissolved and all its debts paid. **4.** A corporation's net worth, beyond the par value of capital stock. — Also termed *overplus*.

accumulated surplus. Earnings in excess of a corporation's capital and liabilities.

acquired surplus. The surplus gained by the purchase of another business.

appreciation surplus. See *revaluation surplus*.

appropriated surplus. **1.** The portion of surplus earmarked for a specific purpose. — Also termed *reserved surplus*. **2.** See *appropriated retained earnings* under EARNINGS.

capital surplus. **1.** All surplus (such as paid-in surplus or donated surplus) not arising from the accumulation of profits; a company's surplus other than earned surplus, usu. created by financial reorganization or gifts. **2.** See *paid-in surplus*.

donated surplus. **1.** Assets (such as stock) contributed to a corporation. **2.** The increase in the shareholders' equity account resulting from such a contribution.

earned surplus. See *retained earnings* under EARNINGS.

initial surplus. The surplus that appears on the financial statement at the beginning of an accounting period, but that does not reflect the operations for the statement's period.

paid-in surplus. The surplus gained by the sale, exchange, or issuance of capital stock at a price above par value. — Also termed *capital surplus*; *premium on capital stock*.

reserved surplus. See *appropriated surplus* (1).

restricted surplus. A surplus with a limited or restricted use; esp., the portion of retained earnings that cannot be distributed as dividends. • The restriction is usu. due to preferred dividends in arrears, a covenant in a loan agreement, or some decision of the board of directors. See *retained earnings* under EARNINGS.

revaluation surplus. Surplus that is gained when assets are reappraised at a higher value. — Also termed *appreciation surplus*.

trade surplus. The excess of merchandise exports over merchandise imports during a specific period. Cf. *trade deficit* under DEFICIT.

unearned surplus. *Corporations*. The total of amounts assigned to shares in excess of stated capital, surplus arising from a revaluation of assets above cost, and contributions other than for shares, whether from shareholders or others.

surplusage (**sər**-pləs-ij). **1.** Redundant words in a statute or other drafted document; language that does not add meaning <the court must give effect to every word, reading nothing as mere surplusage>. **2.** Extraneous matter in a pleading <allegations that are irrelevant to the case will be treated as surplusage>.

> "Surplusage is to be avoided. The perfection of pleading is to combine the requisite certainty and precision with the greatest possible brevity of statement. 'Surplusage' . . . includes matter of any description which is unnecessary to the maintenance of the action or defense. The rule requires the omission of such matter in two instances: (1) Where the matter is wholly foreign and irrelevant to the merits of the case. (2) When, though not wholly foreign, such matter need not be stated." Benjamin J. Shipman, *Handbook of Common-Law Pleading* § 316, at 514 (Henry Winthrop Ballantine ed., 3d ed. 1923).

surplus earnings. See EARNINGS.

surplus-lines insurance. See INSURANCE.

surplus profit. See PROFIT.

surplus revenue. See *appropriated retained earnings* under EARNINGS.

surplus water. See WATER.

surprise. An occurrence for which there is no adequate warning or that affects someone in an unexpected way. • In a trial, the procedural rules are designed to limit surprise — or trial by ambush — as much as possible. For example, the parties in a civil case are permitted to conduct discovery, to determine the essential facts of the case and the identities of possible witnesses, and to inspect relevant documents. At trial, if a party calls a witness who has not been previously identified, the witness's testimony may be excluded if it would unfairly surprise and prejudice the other party. And if a party has diligently prepared the case and is nevertheless taken by surprise on a material point at trial, that fact can sometimes be grounds for a new trial or for relief from the judgment under Rules 59 and 60 of the Federal Rules of Civil Procedure.

surrebuttal (sər-ri-**bət**-əl). The response to the opposing party's rebuttal in a trial or other proceeding; a rebuttal to a rebuttal <called two extra witnesses in surrebuttal>.

surrebutter (sər-ri-**bət**-ər). *Common-law pleading*. The plaintiff's answer of fact to the defendant's rebutter.

surrejoinder (sər-ri-**joyn**-dər). *Common-law pleading.* The plaintiff's answer to the defendant's rejoinder. See REPLICATION.

"Where the common-law system of pleading is in force, the pleadings do not terminate with the plaintiff's replication. The defendant may interpose a rejoinder to the replication, and the plaintiff a surrejoinder to the defendant's rejoinder. Then follows the rebutter, which in turn may be met by a surrebutter." 61A Am. Jur. 2d *Pleading* § 193, at 192 (1981).

surrender, *n.* **1.** The act of yielding to another's power or control. **2.** The giving up of a right or claim; RELEASE (1). **3.** The return of an estate to the person who has a reversion or remainder, so as to merge the estate into a larger estate. **4.** *Commercial law.* The delivery of an instrument so that the delivery releases the deliverer from all liability. **5.** A tenant's relinquishment of possession before the lease has expired, allowing the landlord to take possession and treat the lease as terminated. — **surrender,** *vb.*

surrender by bail. A surety's delivery of a prisoner, who had been released on bail, into custody.

surrender by operation of law. An act that is an equivalent to an agreement by a tenant to abandon property and the landlord to resume possession, as when the parties perform an act so inconsistent with the landlord-tenant relationship that surrender is presumed, or when a tenant performs some act that would not be valid if the estate continued to exist.

surrenderee. One to whom a surrender is made. See SURRENDER.

surrenderer. See SURRENDEROR.

surrender of a criminal. An officer's delivery of a prisoner to the authorities in the appropriate jurisdiction. See EXTRADITION; RENDITION.

surrender of a preference. *Bankruptcy.* The yielding of a voidable conveyance, transfer, assignment, or encumbrance by a creditor to the trustee as a condition of allowing the creditor's claim.

surrender of charter. *Corporations.* The dissolution of a corporation by a formal yielding of its charter to the state under which it was created and the subsequent acceptance of that charter by the state.

"The surrender of a charter can be made only by some formal, solemn act of the corporation, and will be of no avail until accepted by the government. There must be the same agreement of the parties to dissolve that there was to form the compact. It is the acceptance which gives efficacy to the surrender. Consent of the state is sometimes given by general statute." 19 Am. Jur. 2d *Corporations* § 2738, at 546 (1986).

surrender of copyhold. *Hist.* The transfer by a tenant of a copyhold estate by yielding it to the lord in trust for the transferee according to the terms in the surrender. • In normal practice, the tenant went to the steward of the manor and delivered a rod, a glove, or other customary symbol, thereby conveying to the lord (through the steward) all interest and title to the estate, in trust, to be then granted by the lord to the transferee. See COPYHOLD.

surrenderor. One who surrenders; esp., one who yields up a copyhold estate for conveyance. — Also spelled *surrenderer.* See COPYHOLD.

surrender to uses of will. *Hist.* A required yielding of a copyhold interest passed by will to the will's uses. • The requirement was abolished by St. 55 Geo. 3, ch. 192.

surrender value. See *cash surrender value* under VALUE.

surreptitious (sər-əp-**tish**-əs), *adj.* (Of conduct) unauthorized and clandestine; stealthily and usu. fraudulently done <surreptitious interception of electronic communications is prohibited under wiretapping laws>.

surreptitious-entry warrant. See WARRANT (1).

surrogate (**sər**-ə-git), *n.* **1.** A substitute; esp., a person appointed to act in the place of another <in his absence, Sam's wife acted as a surrogate>. **2.** PROBATE JUDGE <the surrogate held that the will was valid>. — **surrogacy** (**sər**-ə-gə-see), **surrogateship,** *n.*

surrogate court. See *probate court* under COURT.

surrogate mother. **1.** A woman who carries a child to term on behalf of another woman and then assigns her parental rights to that woman and the father. **2.** A person who carries out the role of a mother.

surrogate parent. A person who carries out the role of a parent by court appointment or the voluntary assumption of parental responsibilities.

surrogate-parenting agreement. An agreement in which the surrogate mother agrees to carry a child to term on behalf of another woman and then assign her parental rights to that woman and the father.

surrogate's court. See *probate court* under COURT.

surrounding circumstances. The facts underlying an act, injury, or transaction — usu. one at issue in a legal proceeding.

sursise (sər-**sIz**). [Law French] *Hist.* Neglect; omission.

sursum reddere (**sər**-səm **red**-ər-ee), *vb.* [Law Latin] *Hist.* In conveyancing, to render up or surrender (property rights, etc.).

sursum redditio (**sər**-səm rə-**dish**-ee-oh). [Law Latin] *Hist.* In conveyancing, a surrender of an estate by mutual agreement.

surtax. See TAX.

surtax exemption. 1. An exclusion of an item from a surtax. **2.** An item or an amount not subject to a surtax. See *surtax* under TAX.

surveillance (sər-**vay**-lənts), *n.* Close observation or listening of a person or place in the hope of gathering evidence. — **surveil** (sər-**vayl**), *vb.*

survey, *n.* **1.** A general consideration of something; appraisal <a survey of the situation>. **2.** The measuring of a tract of land and its boundaries and contents; a map indicating the results of such measurements <the lender requires a survey of the property before it will issue a loan>.

government survey. A survey made by a governmental entity of tracts of land (as of townships and sections and quarter-sections of land). — Also termed (when conducted by the federal government) *congressional survey.*

topographical survey. A survey that determines a property's elevation above sea level.

3. A governmental department that carries out such measurements <please obtain the boundaries from survey>. **4.** A poll or questionnaire, esp. one examining popular opinion <the radio station took a survey of the concert audience>. **5.** A written assessment of a vessel's current condition. — Also termed *survey of a vessel.* — **survey,** *vb.*

surveyor (sər-**vay**-ər), *n.* One who surveys land and buildings. — **surveyorship,** *n.*

surveyor of the port. *Hist.* A U.S. customs revenue officer appointed for each principal port of entry to oversee the inspection and valuation of imports. • The office was abolished in 1953.

survival action. A lawsuit brought on behalf of a decedent's estate for injuries or damages incurred by the decedent immediately before dying. • A survival action derives from the claim that a decedent who had survived would have had — as opposed to the claim that beneficiaries might have in a wrongful-death action. Cf. WRONGFUL-DEATH ACTION.

survival statute. A law that modifies the common law by allowing certain actions to continue in favor of a personal representative after the death of the party who could have originally brought the action; esp., a law that provides for the estate's recovery of damages incurred by the decedent immediately before death. Cf. DEATH STATUTE.

surviving, *adj.* Remaining alive; living beyond the happening of an event so as to entitle one to a distribution of property or income <surviving spouse>. See SURVIVAL ACTION.

surviving corporation. See CORPORATION.

surviving partner. See PARTNER.

surviving spouse. A spouse who outlives the other spouse.

survivor. 1. One who outlives another. **2.** A trustee who administers a trust after the cotrustee has been removed, has refused to act, or has died.

survivorship. 1. The state or condition of being the one person out of two or more who remains alive after the others die. **2.** The right of a surviving party having a joint interest with others in an estate to take the whole. See RIGHT OF SURVIVORSHIP.

survivorship annuity. See ANNUITY.

survivorship policy. See INSURANCE POLICY.

susceptibility. See SUBJECTION (3).

suspect, *n.* A person believed to have committed a crime or offense.

suspect class. A group identified or defined in a suspect classification.

suspect classification. *Constitutional law.* A statutory classification based on race, national origin, or alienage, and thereby subject to strict scrutiny under equal-protection analysis. • Examples of suspect classifications are a law permitting only U.S. citizens to receive welfare benefits and a law setting quotas for the government's hiring of minority contractors. See STRICT SCRUTINY. Cf. FUNDAMENTAL RIGHT.

quasi-suspect classification. A statutory classification based on gender or legitimacy, and therefore subject to intermediate scrutiny under equal-protection analysis. • Examples of quasi-suspect classifications are a law permitting alimony for women only and a law providing for an all-male draft. See INTERMEDIATE SCRUTINY.

suspend, *vb.* **1.** To interrupt; postpone; defer <the fire alarm suspended the prosecutor's opening statement>. **2.** To temporarily keep (a person) from performing a function, occupying an office, holding a job, or exercising a right or privilege <the attorney's law license was suspended for violating the Model Rules of Professional Conduct>.

suspendatur per collum (səs-pen-**day**-tər pər **kahl**-əm). [Law French] *Hist.* Let him be hanged by the neck. • This phrase was written by a judge in the margin of the sheriff's calendar, opposite the name of a prisoner who had been sentenced to death. — Abbr. *sus. per coll.*

> "And now the usage is, for the judge to sign the calendar, or list of all the prisoners' names, with their separate judgments in the margin, which is left with the sheriff. As, for capital felony, it is written opposite to the prisoner's name, 'hanged by the neck;' formerly, in the days of Latin and abbreviation, '*sus. per coll.*' for '*suspendatur per collum.*' And this is the only warrant that the sheriff has for so material an act as taking away life of another." 4 William Blackstone, *Commentaries on the Laws of England* 396 (1769).

suspended sentence. See SENTENCE.

suspense. The state or condition of being suspended; temporary cessation <a suspense of judgment>.

suspense reserve. See *appropriated retained earnings* under EARNINGS.

suspension. 1. The act of temporarily delaying, interrupting, or terminating something <suspension of business operations> <suspension of a statute>. **2.** The state of such delay, interruption, or termination <corporate transfers were not allowed because of the suspension of business>. **3.** The temporary deprivation of a person's powers or privileges, esp. of office or profession <suspension of her bar license>. **4.** The temporary withdrawal from employment, as distinguished from permanent severance <suspension from teaching without pay>. **5.** *Eccles. law.* An ecclesiastical censure that can be temporary or permanent, and partial or complete. See DEPRIVATION. **6.** *Scots law.* The process of staying a judgment pending an appeal to the Supreme Court.

suspension of arms. See TRUCE.

suspension of trading. The temporary cessation of all trading of a particular stock on a stock exchange because of some abnormal market condition.

suspensive appeal. See APPEAL.

suspensive condition. See CONDITION (2).

suspensive veto. See *suspensory veto* under VETO.

suspensory veto. See VETO.

sus. per coll. *abbr.* SUSPENDATUR PER COLLUM.

suspicion. The imagination or apprehension of the existence of something wrong based only on slight or no evidence, without definitive proof. See REASONABLE SUSPICION.

suspicious-activity report. A form that, as of 1996, a financial institution must complete and submit to federal regulatory authorities if it suspects that a federal crime has occurred in the course of a monetary transaction. • This form superseded two earlier forms, the criminal-referral form and the suspicious-transaction report. — Abbr. SAR.

suspicious character. In some states, a person who is strongly suspected or known to be a habitual criminal and therefore may be arrested or required to give security for good behavior.

suspicious-transaction report. A checkbox on IRS Form 4789 formerly (1990–1995) requiring banks and other financial institutions to report transactions that might be relevant to a violation of the Bank Secrecy Act or its regulations or that might suggest money-laundering or tax evasion. • This checkbox, like the criminal-referral form, has since been superseded by the suspicious-activity report. — Abbr. STR.

sustain, *vb.* **1.** To support or maintain, esp. over a long period <enough oxygen to sustain life>. **2.** To nourish and encourage; lend strength to <she helped sustain the criminal enterprise>. **3.** To undergo; suffer <Charles sustained third-degree burns>. **4.** (Of a court) to uphold or rule in favor of <objection sustained>. **5.** To substantiate or corroborate <several witnesses sustained Ms. Sipes's allegation>. **6.** To persist in making (an effort) over a long period <he sustained his vow of silence for the last 16 years of his life>. — **sustainment, sustentation,** *n.* — **sustainable,** *adj.*

suthdure (suuth-**door**). *Hist. Eccles. law.* The south door of a church, where purgations and other acts were performed and complaints were heard and resolved.

suum cuique tribuere (**s[y]oo**-əm **k[w]ɪ**-kwee tri-**byoo**-ər-ee), *vb.* [Latin] *Roman law.* To render to every person his due. • This was one of the three general precepts in which Justinian expressed the requirements of the law. Cf. ALTERUM NON LAEDERE; HONESTE VIVERE.

suus haeres (**s[y]oo**-əs **heer**-eez). [Latin] *Roman law.* A proper heir.

suus judex (**s[y]oo**-əs **joo**-deks). [Law Latin] *Hist.* A proper judge in a cause.

suzerain (**soo**-zə-rin *or* -rayn), *n.* [Law French] **1.** *Hist.* A Crown tenant; a tenant *in capite* holding an estate immediately of the Crown. **2.** *Int'l law.* A nation that exercises control over another nation's foreign relations. — Also spelled *suzereign.*

suzerainty (**soo**-zə-rin-tee *or* -rayn-tee). **1.** *Hist.* The power of a feudal overlord to whom fealty is due. See FEALTY. **2.** *Int'l law.* The dominion of a nation that controls the foreign relations of another nation but allows it autonomy in its domestic affairs.

> "At the present time there appears to be no instance of a relation between states which is described as a suzerainty. The term was applied to the relation between Great Britain and the South African Republic, and also to that between Turkey and Bulgaria from 1878 to 1909, but it seems likely to disappear from diplomatic terminology." J.L. Brierly, *The Law of Nations* 128 (5th ed. 1955).

suzereign. See SUZERAIN.

swamp and overflowed land. See LAND.

swap, *n. Commercial law.* **1.** An exchange of one security for another. **2.** A financial transaction between two parties, usu. involving an intermediary or dealer, in which payments or rates are exchanged over a specified period and according to specified conditions.

currency swap. An agreement to swap specified payment obligations denominated in one currency for specified payment obligations denominated in a different currency.

stock swap. In a corporate reorganization, an exchange of one corporation's stock for another corporation's stock.

swarf money. *Hist.* A payment made in lieu of the service of maintaining a lord's castle.

swear, *vb.* **1.** To administer an oath to (a person). **2.** To take an oath. **3.** To use obscene or profane language.

swearing contest. See SWEARING MATCH.

swearing-in, *n.* The administration of an oath to a person who is taking office or testifying in a legal proceeding. See OATH.

swearing match. A dispute in which determining a vital fact involves the credibility choice between one witness's word and another's — the two being irreconcilably in conflict and there being no other evidence. • In such a dispute, the fact-finder is generally thought to believe the more reputable witness, such as a police officer over a convicted drug-dealer. — Also termed *swearing contest*; *oath against an oath.*

swearing the peace. *Hist.* The giving of proof to a magistrate that one fears for one's own safety, so that the magistrate will order the troublemaker to keep the peace by issuing a supplicavit. See SUPPLICAVIT.

swear out, *vb.* To obtain the issue of (an arrest warrant) by making a charge under oath <Franklin swore out a complaint against Sutton>.

sweat equity. Financial equity created in property by the owner's labor in improving the property <the lender required the homeowner to put 300 hours of sweat equity into the property>.

sweating. *Criminal procedure.* The illegal interrogation of a prisoner by use of threats or similar means to extort information.

sweatshop. A business where the employees are overworked and underpaid in extreme conditions; esp., in lawyer lingo, a law firm that requires associates to work so hard that they barely (if at all) maintain a family or social life — though the firm may, in return, pay higher salaries.

sweeping, *adj.* **1.** Comprehensive in scope <a sweeping objection><sweeping legislation>. **2.** Overwhelming <sweeping voter turnout>.

Sweeping Clause. See NECESSARY AND PROPER CLAUSE.

sweepstakes. **1.** A race (esp. a horse race) in which the winner's prize is the sum of the stakes contributed by the various competitors. **2.** A contest, often for promotional purposes, that awards prizes based on the random selection of entries. • State and federal laws prohibit conducting a sweepstakes as a scheme to obtain money or property through the mail by false representations. 39 USCA § 3005.

sweetener. **1.** An inducement offered to a brokerage firm to enter into an underwriting arrangement with an issuer. **2.** A special stock feature (such as convertibility) that enhances the stock's marketability.

sweetheart deal. A collusive agreement; esp., a collective-bargaining agreement made as a result of collusion between an employer and a union representative, usu. allowing the employer to pay lower wages in exchange for payoffs to the union representative.

swein (swayn). *Hist.* A forest freeholder. — Also spelled *swain.*

sweinmote (**swayn**-moht). *Hist.* A forest court held three times a year, before verderors as judges and freeholders of the forest as jurors, to try forest offenses. — Also spelled *swainmote*; *swanimote*; *swainemote*; *swaingemote.*

> "The court of *sweinmote* is to be holden before the verderors, as judges, by the steward of the sweinmote thrice in every year .... The principal jurisdiction of this court is, first, to enquire into the oppressions and grievances committed by the officers of the forest ... and, secondly, to receive and try presentments certified from the court of attachments against offences in vert and venison." 3 William Blackstone, *Commentaries on the Laws of England* 72 (1768).

swell, *n.* **1.** An expansion in the bulk of something <a swell resulting from defective canning procedures>. **2.** A gradual rise of something <a swell of damages>. **3.** A large, unbroken wave; the collective waves, particularly following a storm <a rough swell caused the shipwreck>.

swift witness. See WITNESS.

swindle, *vb.* **1.** To cheat (a person) out of property <Johnson swindled Norton out of his entire savings>. **2.** To cheat a person out of (property) <Johnson swindled Norton's entire savings out of him>. — **swindle,** *n.* — **swindling,** *n.*

swindler. A person who willfully defrauds or cheats another.

swing loan. See *bridge loan* under LOAN.

swing vote. The vote that determines an issue when all other voting parties, such as appellate judges, are evenly split.

switching. In mutual funds, the practice of selling shares in one fund to buy shares in another.

swoling (**swuul**-ing). *Hist.* The quantity of land that can be plowed in a year; a hide of land. — Also spelled *suling* (**suul**-ing); *sulung* (**suu**-luung). — Also termed *swoling of land.*

sworn brothers. *Hist.* Persons who, by mutual oaths, swear to share in each other's fortunes.

sworn clerks in chancery. *Hist.* Certain officers in the Court of Chancery who assist the six principal clerks by performing clerical tasks, including keeping records and making copies of pleadings. • The offices were abolished in 1842 by the Court of Chancery Act. St. 5 & 6 Vict., ch. 103. — Also termed *sixty clerks.*

sworn statement. See STATEMENT.

SYD. *abbr.* Sum of the years' digits. See *sum-of-the-years'-digits depreciation method* under DEPRECIATION METHOD.

syllabus (**sil**-ə-bəs). **1.** An abstract or outline of a topic or course of study. **2.** HEADNOTE. Pl. **syllabuses, syllabi** (**sil**-ə-bɪ).

symbiotic-relationship test. The standard by which a private person may be considered a state actor — and may be liable for violating someone's constitutional rights — if the relationship between the private person and the government is so close that they can fairly be said to be acting jointly. • Private acts by a private person do not generally create liability for violating someone's constitutional rights. But if a private person violates someone's constitutional rights while engaging in state action, the private person, and possibly the government, can be held liable. State action may be shown by proving that the private person and the state have a mutually dependent (symbiotic) relationship. For example, a restaurant in a public parking garage was held to have engaged in discriminatory state action by refusing to serve African–Americans. *Burton v. Wilmington Parking Authority*, 365 U.S. 715, 81 S.Ct. 856 (1961). There, the Court found a symbiotic relationship because the restaurant relied on the garage for its existence and significantly contributed to the municipal parking authority's ability to maintain the garage. But the symbiotic-relationship test is strictly construed. For example, the fact that an entity receives financial support from — or is heavily regulated by — the government is probably insufficient to show a symbiotic relationship. Thus, although a state had granted a partial monopoly to a public utility, the Court refused to find a symbiotic relationship between them. *Jackson v. Metropolitan Edison Co.*, 419 U.S. 345, 95 S.Ct. 449 (1974). See JOINT-PARTICIPATION TEST. Cf. STATE-COMPULSION TEST; NEXUS TEST.

symbolaeography (sim-bə-lee-**og**-rə-fee). The art of drafting legal instruments.

symbolic, *adj.* (Of a signature) consisting of a symbol or mark. Cf. ONOMASTIC (2); HOLOGRAPH.

symbolic delivery. See DELIVERY.

symbolic speech. See SPEECH.

symbolum animae (**sim**-bə-ləm **an**-ə-mee). [Latin] *Hist.* A mortuary. See MORTUARY (2).

sympathy strike. See STRIKE.

synallagmatic contract. See CONTRACT.

syndic (**sin**-dik), *n.* [French "governmental representative"] **1.** An agent (esp. of a government or corporation) appointed to transact business for others. **2.** *Civil law.* A bankruptcy trustee.

syndicalism (**sin**-di-kə-liz-əm), *n.* A direct plan or practice implemented by trade-union workers seeking to control the means of production and distribution, esp. by using a general strike. — **syndicalist,** *n.*

criminal syndicalism. Any doctrine that advocates or teaches the use of illegal methods to change industrial or political control.

syndicate (**sin**-di-kit), *n.* A group organized for a common purpose; esp., an association formed to promote a common interest, carry out a particular business transaction, or (in a negative sense) organize criminal enterprises. — **syndicate** (**sin**-di-kayt), *vb.* — **syndication** (sin-di-**kay**-shən), *n.* — **syndicator** (**sin**-di-kay-tər), *n.* See ORGANIZED CRIME.

buying syndicate. A group of investment bankers who share the risk in underwriting a securities issue.

syndicating. 1. The act or process of forming a syndicate. **2.** The gathering of materials for newspaper publication from various writers and distribution of the materials at regular intervals to newspapers throughout the country for publication on the same day.

syndicus (**sin**-di-kəs), *n.* [Latin "advocate" fr. Greek *syn-* "with" + dike "lawsuit"] *Roman law.* One chosen (by a corporate body such as a municipality, college, etc.) to represent it at law. See SYNDIC.

synergism (**sin**-ər-jiz-əm), *n. Patents.* **1.** A combination of known elements or functions that create a result greater than the sum of the individual elements or functions. • Demonstrating that synergism exists is sometimes useful in proving nonobviousness. **2.** A patentable device that produces a new or different function or an unusual or surprising consequence. — Also termed *synergy*; *synergistic result.* — **synergistic** (sin-ər-**jis**-tik), **synergetic** (sin-ər-**jet**-ik), *adj.*

synod (**sin**-əd). *Eccles. law.* An ecclesiastical council lawfully assembled to determine church matters; esp., a meeting of several adjoining presbyteries in the Presbyterian church.

diocesan synod (dy-**os**-ə-sən). A synod composed of clergy from one diocese.

general synod. A synod composed of bishops from all nations. — Also termed *universal synod.*

national synod. A synod composed of clergy from a single nation.

provincial synod. A synod composed of clergy from a single province. — Also termed *convocation.*

synodal (**sin**-ə-dəl), *n.* **1.** A collection of ordinances of diocesan synods. **2.** A tribute of money given by clergy to a bishop at the Easter visitation.

synodales testes (sin-ə-**day**-leez **tes**-teez), *n.* [Law Latin "synods-men"] *Hist.* Persons who gave evidence at synods, informing them of misconduct by clergy or laity.

synodsman. See SIDESMAN.

synopsis (si-**nop**-sis), *n.* A brief or partial survey; a summary or outline; HEADNOTE. — **synopsize** (si-**nop**-sɪz), *vb.*

synthetic lease. See LEASE.

synthetic rule. See QUANTITATIVE RULE.

systematic jurisprudence. See *expository jurisprudence* under JURISPRUDENCE.

systematic violation. *Civil-rights law.* An employer's policy or procedure that is discriminatory against an employee. • Such a policy or procedure will usu. be considered a continuing violation. So an employee's claim of unlawful discrimination will not be barred as untimely as long as some discriminatory effect of the policy or procedure occurs within the limitations period (e.g., 300 days for a Title VII claim). Cf. SERIAL VIOLATION.

T

T. *Hist.* **1.** A letter branded on the base of the thumb of a person who claimed the benefit of clergy to prevent the person from claiming it again. • This practice was formally abolished by the Criminal Statutes (England) Repeal Act of 1827. **2.** In Pennsylvania, a letter sewn onto the left sleeve of a convicted thief. • This letter — required by a 1698 statute — had to be at least four inches high and of a different color from the rest of the garment.

TAB. *abbr.* TAX-ANTICIPATION BILL.

table, *vb.* To postpone consideration of (a pending bill or proposal) with no commitment to resume consideration unless the motion to table specifies a later date or time.

tableau of distribution. *Civil law.* A list of creditors of an insolvent estate, stating what each is entitled to.

table of authorities. See INDEX OF AUTHORITIES.

table of cases. An alphabetical list of cases cited, referred to, or digested in a legal textbook, volume of reports, or digest, with references to the section, page, or paragraph where each case appears.

tabula rasa (**tab**-yə-lə **rah**-zə). [Latin "scraped tablet"] A blank tablet ready for writing; a clean slate. Pl. ***tabulae rasae*** (**tab**-yə-lee-**rahs**-I).

tabulis exhibendis. See DE TABULIS EXHIBENDIS.

T-account. An accounting form shaped like the letter *T*, with the account's name above the horizontal line, debits to the left of the vertical line, and credits to the right.

tacit (**tas**-it), *adj.* **1.** Implied but not actually expressed; implied by silence or silent acquiescence <a tacit understanding> <a tacit admission>. **2.** *Civil law.* Arising by operation of law; constructive <a tacit mortgage> <tacit relocation>. — **tacitly,** *adv.*

tacit acceptance. *Civil law.* An acceptance of an inheritance, indicated by the heir's doing some act that shows an intent to accept it and that the heir would have no right to do except in that capacity.

tacit admission. See *implied admission* under ADMISSION.

tacit contract. See CONTRACT.

tacit dedication. See DEDICATION.

tacit hypothecation. See HYPOTHECATION.

tacit law. See LAW.

tacit mortgage. See *legal mortgage* under MORTGAGE.

tacit relocation. *Civil law.* The implied or constructive renewal of a lease, usu. on a year-to-year basis, when the landlord and tenant have failed to indicate their intention to have the lease terminated at the end of the original term.

tacit-relocation doctrine. The principle under which a lease is presumed to continue (usu. for a one-year period) beyond its expiration date because of the parties' failure to indicate that the agreement should terminate at the stipulated date.

tacit remission. See REMISSION.

tack, *vb.* **1.** To add (one's own period of land possession) to a prior possessor's period to establish continuous adverse possession for the statutory period. **2.** To annex (a junior lien) to a first lien to acquire priority over an intermediate lien.

tacking. 1. The joining of consecutive periods of possession by different persons to treat the periods as one continuous period; esp., the adding of one's own period of land possession to that of a prior possessor to establish continuous adverse possession for the statutory period. See

ADVERSE POSSESSION. **2.** The joining of a junior lien with the first lien in order to acquire priority over an intermediate lien.

Taft–Hartley Act. See LABOR–MANAGEMENT RELATIONS ACT.

Taft–Hartley fund. See *joint-welfare fund* under FUND (1).

tail, *n.* The limitation of an estate so that it can be inherited only by the fee owner's issue or class of issue. See FEE TAIL; ENTAIL.

tail female. A limitation to female heirs.

tail general. A tail limited to the issue of a particular person, but not to that of a particular couple. — Also termed *general tail.*

tail male. A limitation to male heirs.

tail special. A tail limited to specified heirs of the donee's body. — Also termed *special tail.*

"Estates-tail are either *general*, or *special* .... Tenant in tail-special is where the gift is restrained to certain heirs ... and does not go to all of them in general. And this may happen in several ways. I shall instance in only one: as where lands and tenements are given to a man and the *heirs of his body, on Mary his now wife to be begotten*; here no issue can inherit, but such special issue as is engendered, between them two; not such as the husband may have by another wife: and therefore it is called special tail." 2 William Blackstone, *Commentaries on the Laws of England* 113–14 (1766).

taint, *n.* **1.** A conviction of felony. **2.** A person so convicted. See ATTAINDER.

taint, *vb.* **1.** To imbue with a noxious quality or principle. **2.** To contaminate or corrupt. **3.** To tinge or affect slightly for the worse. — **taint,** *n.*

tainted evidence. See EVIDENCE.

tainted stock. See STOCK.

take, *vb.* **1.** To obtain possession or control, whether legally or illegally <it's a felony to take that property without the owner's consent>. **2.** To seize with authority; to confiscate or apprehend <take the suspect into custody>. **3.** (Of a federal or state government) to acquire (property) for public use; condemn <the state took the land under its eminent-domain powers>. **4.** To acquire possession by virtue of a grant of title, the use of eminent domain, or other legal means; esp., to receive property by will or intestate succession <the probate code indicates the proportions according to which each heir will take>. See TAKING. **5.** To claim one's rights under <she took the Fifth Amendment>.

take away, *vb. Hist.* To entice or persuade (a female under the age of 18) to leave her family for purposes of marriage, prostitution, or illicit sex. See ABDUCTION (2).

take back, *vb.* To revoke; to retract.

take by stealth. To steal (personal property); to pilfer or filch.

take care of. 1. To support or look after (a person). **2.** To pay (a debt). **3.** To attend to (some matter).

take delivery. To receive something purchased or ordered; esp., to receive a commodity under a futures contract or spot-market contract, or to receive securities recently purchased.

take effect, *vb.* **1.** To become operative or executed. **2.** To be in force; to go into operation.

take-home pay. Gross wages or salary reduced by deductions such as income taxes, social-security taxes, voluntary contributions, and union dues; the net amount of a paycheck.

take-it-or-leave-it contract. See *adhesion contract* under CONTRACT.

take-nothing judgment. See JUDGMENT.

take-or-pay contract. See CONTRACT.

takeover. The acquisition of ownership or control of a corporation. ● A takeover is typically accomplished by a purchase of shares or assets, a tender offer, or a merger.

friendly takeover. A takeover that is approved by the target corporation's board of directors.

hostile takeover. A takeover that is resisted by the target corporation's board of directors.

takeover bid. An attempt by outsiders to wrest control from the incumbent management of a target corporation.

takeover defense. See SHARK REPELLENT.

takeover offer. See TENDER OFFER.

taker, *n.* A person who acquires; esp., one who receives property by will, by power of appointment, or by intestate succession.

first taker. A person who receives an estate that is subject to a remainder or executory devise.

taker in default. A person designated by a donor to receive property under a power of appointment if the donee fails to exercise that power.

take the witness. You may now question the witness. • This phrase is a lawyer's courtroom announcement that ends one side's questioning and prompts the other side to begin its questioning. Synonymous phrases are *your witness* and *pass the witness.*

take up, *vb.* **1.** To pay or discharge (a note). **2.** To retire (a negotiable instrument); to discharge one's liability on (a negotiable instrument), esp. the liability of an indorser or acceptor. **3.** To purchase (a note).

taking, *n.* **1.** *Criminal & tort law.* The act of seizing an article, with or without removing it, but with an implicit transfer of possession or control.

constructive taking. An act that does not equal an actual appropriation of an article but that does show an intention to convert it, as when a person entrusted with the possession of goods starts using them contrary to the owner's instructions.

2. *Constitutional law.* The government's actual or effective acquisition of private property either by ousting the owner and claiming title or by destroying the property or severely impairing its utility. • There is a taking of property when government action directly interferes with or substantially disturbs the owner's use and enjoyment of the property. — Also termed *constitutional taking.* See CONDEMNATION (2); EMINENT DOMAIN.

actual taking. A physical appropriation of an owner's property by an entity clothed with eminent-domain authority.

de facto taking (di **fak**-toh). A taking in which an entity clothed with eminent-domain power substantially interferes with an owner's use, possession, or enjoyment of property.

taking a case from the jury. See *directed verdict* under VERDICT.

Takings Clause. The Fifth Amendment provision that prohibits the government from taking private property for public use without fairly compensating the owner. See EMINENT DOMAIN.

taking the Fifth. See PLEADING THE FIFTH.

tales (**tay**-leez *or* taylz). [Latin, pl. of *talis* "such," in the phrase *tales de circumstantibus* "such of the bystanders"] **1.** A supply of additional jurors, usu. drawn from the bystanders at the courthouse, summoned to fill a panel that has become deficient in number because of juror challenges or exemptions. **2.** A writ or order summoning these jurors.

tales-juror. See TALESMAN.

talesman (**taylz**-mən *or* **tay**-leez-mən). *Archaic.* **1.** A person selected from among the bystanders in court to serve as a juror when the original jury panel has become deficient in number. **2.** VENIREMEMBER. — Also termed *tales-juror.*

talisman (**tal**-is-mən), *n.* A charm, amulet, or other physical thing supposedly capable of working wonders <private property is not some sacred talisman that can never be touched by the state — it can be taken for public use as long as the owner is justly compensated>. — **talismanic** (tal-is-**man**-ik), *adj.*

tally. 1. *Hist.* A stick cut into two parts and marked with notches to show what was due between a debtor and creditor.

> "The tally, used as a receipt for money or chattels, was a narrow wooden stick with notches of varying dimensions to represent the amount received. After the notches had been cut, the stick was split lengthwise into two unequal pieces. The longer, which contained a stump or handle and was called the 'stock,' was given to the person making the payment, and the shorter, a flat strip called the 'foil,' to the other party. If the sum involved was disputed, the two pieces could be fitted one to the other to see if they would 'tally.'" C.H.S. Fifoot, *History and Sources of the Common Law: Tort and Contract* 223 (1949).

> "A thousand pounds was marked by cutting out the thickness of the palm of the hand, a hundred by the breadth of the thumb, a score by the breadth of the little finger, one pound by that of a swelling barley-corn .... The terminology has left a permanent imprint on our language. If you lent money to the Bank of England, tallies were cut for the amount: the Bank kept the foil and you received the stock; you thus held 'Bank Stock' of the amount recorded upon it. When the form of cheque was adopted, it was not indeed called a foil, but the part retained by the payer is still the counterfoil; and the word 'cheque' itself goes back ultimately to the same root as 'exchequer.'" Reginald L. Poole, *The Exchequer in the Twelfth Century* 86–93 (1912).

> "From early times tallies were used in the Exchequer and this lasted until 1826. The burning of a large quantity of old tallies led to the burning down of the old Houses of Parliament." David M. Walker, *The Oxford Companion to Law* 1207 (1980).

2. Anything used to record an account. **3.** An account; a score.

Talmud (**tahl**-muud *or* **tal**-məd), *n.* A work embodying the civil and canonical law of the Jewish people. — **Talmudic** (tahl-**moo**-dik *or* tal-), *adj.*

TAM. *abbr.* TECHNICAL ADVICE MEMORANDUM.

tame, *adj.* (Of an animal) domesticated; accustomed to humans.

tamper, *vb.* **1.** To meddle so as to alter (a thing); esp., to make changes that are illegal, corrupting, or perverting. **2.** To interfere improperly; to meddle.

tampering, *n.* The act or an instance of engaging in improper or underhanded dealings, esp. in an attempt to influence. • Tampering with a witness or jury is a criminal offense. See OBSTRUCTION OF JUSTICE; EMBRACERY.

TAN. See *tax-anticipation note* under NOTE (1).

tangible, *adj.* **1.** Having or possessing physical form. **2.** Capable of being touched and seen; perceptible to the touch; capable of being possessed or realized. **3.** Capable of being understood by the mind.

tangible asset. See ASSET.

tangible chattel paper. See CHATTEL PAPER.

tangible cost. See COST (1).

tangible evidence. See *demonstrative evidence* under EVIDENCE.

tangible personal property. See PROPERTY.

tangible property. See PROPERTY.

tapper, *n.* **1.** A person who approaches another for money; a beggar. **2.** By extension, a thief.

tapping, *n.* See WIRETAPPING.

tare (tair), *n.* **1.** A deficiency in the weight or quantity of merchandise resulting from including its container's weight in the total. **2.** An allowance or abatement of a certain weight or quantity that a seller makes to the buyer because of the container's weight. Cf. TRET.

target benefit plan. See EMPLOYEE BENEFIT PLAN.

target corporation. See CORPORATION.

target offense. See *object offense* under OFFENSE.

target price. See PRICE.

target witness. See WITNESS.

tariff, *n.* **1.** A schedule or system of duties imposed by a government on imported or exported goods. • In the United States, tariffs are imposed on imported goods only. **2.** A duty imposed on imported or exported goods under such a system. See DUTY (4).

antidumping tariff. A tariff equaling the difference between the price at which the product is sold in the exporting country and the price at which the importer will sell the product in the importing country. • These tariffs are designed to prevent foreign businesses from artificially lowering their prices and gaining unfair advantages outside their home market. See ANTIDUMPING LAW.

autonomous tariff. A tariff set by legislation rather than by commercial treaty.

discriminatory tariff. A tariff containing duties that are applied unequally to different countries or manufacturers.

preferential tariff. A tariff that favors the products of one country over those of another. Cf. MOST-FAVORED-NATION CLAUSE.

protective tariff. A tariff designed primarily to give domestic manufacturers economic protection against price competition from abroad, rather than to generate revenue.

retaliatory tariff. A tariff imposed to pressure another country into removing its own tariffs or making trade concessions.

revenue tariff. A tariff enacted solely or primarily to raise revenue.

3. A fee that a public utility or telecommunications company may assess for its services. • The tariffs that a provider may charge are limited by statute. **4.** A schedule listing the rates charged for services provided by a public utility, the U.S. Postal Service, or a business (esp. one that must by law file its rates with a public agency). — **tariff,** *vb.*

joint tariff. A rate schedule established by two or more carriers covering shipments between places requiring the use of facilities owned by those carriers.

tax, *n.* A monetary charge imposed by the government on persons, entities, or property to yield public revenue. • Most broadly, the term embraces all governmental impositions on the person, property, privileges, occupations, and enjoyment of the people, and includes duties, imposts, and excises. Although a tax is often thought of as being pecuniary in nature, it is not necessarily payable in money. — **tax,** *vb.*

> "Taxes are the enforced proportional contributions from persons and property, levied by the state by virtue of its sovereignty for the support of government and for all public needs. This definition of taxes, often referred to as 'Cooley's definition,' has been quoted and indorsed, or approved, expressly or otherwise, by many different courts. While this definition of taxes characterizes them as 'contributions,' other definitions refer to them as 'imposts,' 'duty or impost,' 'charges,' 'burdens,' or 'exactions'; but these variations in phraseology are of no practical importance." 1 Thomas M. Cooley, *The Law of Taxation* § 1, at 61–63 (Clark A. Nichols ed., 4th ed. 1924).

accrued tax. A tax that has been incurred but not yet paid or payable.

accumulated-earnings tax. A penalty tax imposed on a corporation that has retained its earnings in an effort to avoid the income-tax liability arising once the earnings are distributed to shareholders as dividends. — Also termed *excess-profits tax*; *undistributed-earnings tax*.

admission tax. A tax imposed as part of the price of being admitted to a particular event.

ad valorem tax. A tax imposed proportionally on the value of something (esp. real property), rather than on its quantity or some other measure.

> "[A]n ad valorem tax is a tax of a fixed proportion of the value of the property with respect to which the tax is assessed, and requires the intervention of assessors or appraisers to estimate the value of such property before the amount due from each taxpayer can be determined." 71 Am. Jur. 2d *State and Local Taxation* § 20, at 355 (1973).

alternative minimum tax. A flat tax potentially imposed on corporations and higher-income individuals to ensure that those taxpayers do not avoid all income-tax liability by using exclusions, deductions, and credits. — Abbr. AMT. — Also termed *minimum tax*.

amusement tax. A tax on a ticket to a concert, sporting event, or the like. • The tax is usu. expressed as a percentage of the ticket price.

capital-gains tax. A tax on income derived from the sale of a capital asset. • The federal income tax on capital gains typically has a more favorable tax rate — now 28% for an individual and 34% for a corporation — than the maximum tax rate on ordinary income. See CAPITAL GAIN.

capital-stock tax. **1.** A tax on capital stock in the hands of a stockholder. **2.** A state tax for conducting business in the corporate form, usu. imposed on out-of-state corporations for the privilege of doing business in the state. • The tax is usu. assessed as a percentage of the par or assigned value of a corporation's capital stock.

capitation tax. See *poll tax*.

classified tax. A tax system in which different rates are assessed against different types of taxed property.

collateral-inheritance tax. A tax levied on the transfer of property by will or intestate succession to a person other than the spouse, a parent, or a descendant of the decedent.

consumption tax. A tax imposed on sale of goods to be consumed and services.

death tax. An estate tax or inheritance tax.

delinquent tax. A tax not paid when due.

direct tax. A tax that is imposed on property, as distinguished from a tax on a right or privilege. • Ad valorem and property taxes are direct taxes.

documentary stamp tax. See *stamp tax*.

erroneous tax. **1.** A tax levied without statutory authority. **2.** A tax on property not subject to taxation. **3.** A tax levied by an officer who lacks authority to levy the tax. — Also termed *illegal tax*.

estate tax. A tax imposed on property transferred by will or by intestate succession. Cf. *inheritance tax*.

estimated tax. A tax paid quarterly by a taxpayer not subject to withholding (such as a self-employed person) based on either the previous year's tax liability or an estimate of the current year's tax liability.

excess-profits tax. **1.** A tax levied on profits that are beyond a business's normal profits. • This type of tax is usu. imposed only in times of national emergency (such as war) to discourage profiteering. **2.** See *accumulated-earnings tax*.

excise lieu property tax. A tax on the gross premiums received and collected by designated classes of insurance companies.

excise tax. See EXCISE.

export tax. A tax levied on merchandise and goods shipped or to be shipped out of a country.

flat tax. A tax whose rate remains fixed regardless of the amount of the tax base. • Most sales taxes are flat taxes. — Also termed *proportional tax*. Cf. *progressive tax*; *regressive tax*.

floor tax. A tax imposed on distilled spirits stored in a warehouse.

franchise tax. A tax imposed on the privilege of carrying on a business (esp. as a corporation), usu. measured by the business's income. See FRANCHISE.

general tax. **1.** A tax that returns no special benefit to the taxpayer other than the support of governmental programs that benefit all. **2.** A property tax or an ad valorem tax that is imposed for no special purpose except to produce public revenue. Cf. *special assessment* under ASSESSMENT.

generation-skipping tax. A tax on a property transfer that skips a generation. • The tax limits the use of generation-skipping techniques as a means of avoiding estate taxes.

generation-skipping transfer tax. A gift or estate tax imposed on a generation-skipping transfer or a generation-skipping trust. — Also termed *generation-skipping tax*; *transfer tax*. IRC (26 USCA) §§ 2601–2663. See DIRECT SKIP; GENERATION-SKIPPING TRANSFER; *generation-skipping trust* under TRUST; TAXABLE DISTRIBUTION; TAXABLE TERMINATION.

gift tax. A tax imposed when property is voluntarily and gratuitously transferred. • Under federal law, the gift tax is imposed on the donor, but some states tax the donee.

graduated tax. See *progressive tax*.

gross-income tax. A tax on gross receipts rather than on net profits; an income tax without allowance for expenses or deductions. — Also termed *gross-receipts tax*.

head tax. **1.** See *poll tax*. **2.** HEAD MONEY (3).

hidden tax. A tax that is paid, often unknowingly, by someone other than the person or entity on whom it is levied; esp., a tax imposed on a manufacturer or seller (such as a gasoline producer) who passes it on to consumers in the form of higher sales prices.

highway tax. A tax raised to pay for the construction, repair, and maintenance of highways.

holding-company tax. A federal tax imposed on undistributed personal-holding-company income after allowing deductions for such things as dividends paid. IRC (26 USCA) § 545. — Also termed *personal-holding-company tax*.

illegal tax. See *erroneous tax*.

income tax. A tax on an individual's or entity's net income. • The federal income tax — governed by the Internal Revenue Code — is the federal government's primary source of revenue, and many states have income taxes as well. Cf. *property tax*; EXCISE.

indirect tax. A tax on a right or privilege, such as an occupation tax or franchise tax.

inheritance tax. **1.** A tax imposed on a person who inherits property from another (unlike an estate tax, which is imposed on the decedent's estate). • There is no federal inheritance tax, but some states provide for one (though it is deductible under the federal estate tax). — Also termed *succession tax*. Cf. *estate tax*. **2.** Loosely, an estate tax.

intangible tax. A state tax imposed on the privilege of owning, transferring, devising, or otherwise dealing with intangible property.

interest-equalization tax. A tax imposed on a U.S. citizen's acquisition of stock issued by a foreign issuer or a debt obligation of a foreign obligor, but only if the obligation did not mature within a year. • This tax was repealed in the mid-1970s. IRC (26 USCA) § 4911.

kiddie tax. A federal tax imposed on a child's unearned income at the parents' tax rate if the parents' rate is higher and if the child is under 14 years of age.

land tax. See *property tax*.

legacy tax. A tax on the privilege of inheriting property by will or by succession.

lieu tax. A tax imposed as a substitute for another.

luxury tax. An excise tax imposed on high-priced items that are not deemed necessities (such as cars costing more than a specified amount). Cf. *sin tax*.

minimum tax. See *alternative minimum tax*.

nanny tax. A federal social-security tax imposed on the employer of a domestic employee if the employer pays that employee more than a specified amount in total wages in a year. • The term, which is not a technical legal phrase, was popularized in the mid-1990s, when several of President Clinton's nominees were found not to have paid the social-security tax for their nannies.

occupation tax. An excise tax imposed for the privilege of carrying on a business, trade, or profession. • For example, many states require lawyers to pay an occupation tax. — Also termed *occupational tax.*

payroll tax. **1.** A tax payable by an employer based on its payroll (such as a social-security tax or an unemployment tax). **2.** A tax collected by an employer from its employees' gross pay (such as an income tax or a social-security tax). See *withholding tax.*

per capita tax. See *poll tax.*

personal-holding-company tax. See *holding-company tax.*

personal-property tax. A tax on personal property (such as jewelry or household furniture) levied by a state or local government.

poll tax. A fixed tax levied on each person within a jurisdiction. • The 24th Amendment prohibits the federal and state governments from imposing poll taxes as a condition for voting. — Also termed *per capita tax*; *capitation tax*; *capitation*; *head tax.*

premium tax. A state tax paid by an insurer on payments made by the insurer on behalf of an insured.

privilege tax. A tax on the privilege of carrying on a business or occupation for which a license or franchise is required.

progressive tax. A tax structured so that the tax rate increases as the tax base increases. • Most income taxes are progressive, meaning that higher income is taxed at a higher rate. — Also termed *graduated tax.* Cf. *regressive tax*; *flat tax.*

property tax. A tax levied on the owner of property (esp. real property), usu. based on the property's value. • Local governments often impose property taxes to finance school districts, municipal projects, and the like. — Also termed (specif.) *land tax.* Cf. *income tax*; EXCISE.

proportional tax. See *flat tax.*

regressive tax. A tax structured so that the tax rate decreases as the tax base increases. • A flat tax (such as the typical sales tax) is usu. considered regressive — despite its constant rate — because it is more burdensome for low-income taxpayers than high-income taxpayers. Cf. *progressive tax*; *flat tax.*

repressive tax. See *sin tax.*

sales tax. A tax imposed on the sale of goods and services, usu. measured as a percentage of their price. — Also termed *retail sales tax.* See *flat tax.*

> "While the term 'sales tax' encompasses a large variety of levies, the term often refers to the 'retail sales tax,' where the tax is separately stated and collected on a transaction-by-transaction basis from the consumer; although the economic burden of the sales tax falls upon the consumer, the seller has the statutory duty to collect the tax for the taxing jurisdiction." 68 Am. Jur. 2d *Sales and Use Tax* § 1, at 11 (1993).

self-employment tax. The social-security tax imposed on the net earnings of a self-employed person.

service-occupation tax. A tax imposed on persons who sell services, usu. computed as a percentage of net cost of the tangible personal property transferred as an incident to the sale.

severance tax. A tax imposed on the value of oil, gas, timber, or other natural resources extracted from the earth.

sinking-fund tax. A tax to be applied to the repayment of a public loan.

sin tax. An excise tax imposed on goods or activities that are considered harmful or immoral (such as cigarettes, liquor, or gambling). — Also termed *repressive tax.* Cf. *luxury tax.*

special tax. **1.** A tax levied for a unique purpose. **2.** A tax (such as an inheritance tax) that is levied in addition to a general tax.

specific tax. A tax imposed as a fixed sum on each article or item of property of a given class or kind without regard to its value.

stamp tax. A tax imposed by requiring the purchase of a revenue stamp that must be affixed to a legal document (such as a deed or note) before the document can be recorded. — Also termed *documentary-stamp tax.*

state tax. **1.** A tax — usu. in the form of a sales or income tax — earmarked for state, rather than federal or municipal, purposes. **2.** A tax levied under a state law.

stock-transfer tax. A tax levied by the federal government and by some states on the transfer or sale of shares of stock. — Often shortened to *transfer tax.*

> "Some state statutes impose special taxes, usually in the form of a stamp tax, upon sales and agreements for sale and other transfers of stock in corporations. Such a tax is in the nature of an excise tax on the transfer. Taxes on the issuance and transfer of corporate stock, commonly known as 'stock transfer taxes' and payable by means of stamps, are constitutional, as within the power of state

governments." 71 Am. Jur. 2d *State and Local Taxation* § 643, at 896 (1973).

succession tax. See *inheritance tax.*

surtax. An additional tax imposed on something being taxed or on the primary tax itself.

tonnage tax. See TONNAGE DUTY.

transfer tax. **1.** A tax imposed on the transfer of property, esp. by will, inheritance, or gift. • The federal estate-and-gift tax is sometimes referred to as the *unified transfer tax* (or the *unified estate-and-gift tax*) because lifetime gifts and death gifts are treated equally under the same tax laws. **2.** See *stock-transfer tax.*

undistributed-earnings tax. See *accumulated-earnings tax.*

unemployment tax. A tax imposed on an employer by state or federal law to cover the cost of unemployment insurance. • The Federal Unemployment Tax Act (FUTA) provides for a tax based on a percentage of employee earnings but allows a credit for amounts paid in state unemployment taxes.

unitary tax. A tax of income earned locally by a business that transacts business through an affiliated company outside the state. See UNITARY BUSINESS.

unrelated-business-income tax. A tax levied on a not-for-profit organization's taxable income, such as advertising revenue from a publication.

use tax. A tax imposed on the use of certain goods that are bought outside the taxing authority's jurisdiction. • Use taxes are designed to discourage the purchase of products that are not subject to the sales tax.

value-added tax. A tax assessed at each step in the production of a commodity, based on the value added at each step by the difference between the commodity's production cost and its selling price. • A value-added tax — which is popular in several European countries — effectively acts as a sales tax on the ultimate consumer. — Abbr. VAT.

windfall-profits tax. A tax imposed on a business or industry as a result of a sudden increase in profits. • An example is the tax imposed on oil companies in 1980 for profits resulting from the Arab oil embargo of the 1970s.

window tax. *Hist. English law.* A tax imposed on a house containing a certain number of windows (usu. more than six). • It was established under the Taxation Act of 1695 and replaced with a tax on inhabited houses established under the House Tax of 1851. See HOUSE-DUTY.

withholding tax. A portion of income tax that is deducted from salary, wages, dividends, or other income before the earner receives payment. • The most common example is the income tax and social-security tax withheld by an employer from an employee's pay.

taxable, *adj.* **1.** Subject to taxation <interest earned on a checking account is taxable income>. **2.** (Of legal costs or fees) assessable <expert-witness fees are not taxable court costs>.

taxable distribution. A generation-skipping transfer from a trust to the beneficiary (i.e., the *skip person*) that is neither a direct skip nor a taxable termination. See GENERATION-SKIPPING TRANSFER; *generation-skipping transfer tax* under TAX; *generation-skipping trust* under TRUST; SKIP PERSON.

taxable estate. See ESTATE.

taxable gift. See GIFT.

taxable income. See INCOME.

taxable termination. A taxable event that occurs when (1) an interest in a generation-skipping trust property terminates (as on the death of a skip person's parent who possessed the interest), (2) no interest in the trust is held by a nonskip person, and (3) a distribution may be made to a skip person. • Before the creation of taxable terminations in 1976, a taxpayer could create a trust that paid income to a child for life, then to that child's child for life, and so on without incurring an estate or gift tax liability. See GENERATION-SKIPPING TRANSFER; *generation-skipping transfer tax* under TAX; *generation-skipping trust* under TRUST; SKIP PERSON.

taxable year. See TAX YEAR.

tax accounting. The accounting rules and methods used in determining a taxpayer's liability.

tax-anticipation bill. A short-term obligation issued by the U.S. Treasury to meet the cash-flow needs of the government. • Corporations can tender these bills at par value to make quarterly tax payments. — Abbr. TAB.

tax-anticipation note. See NOTE (1).

tax-anticipation warrant. See WARRANT (2).

tax assessment. See ASSESSMENT (3).

tax assessor. See ASSESSOR (1).

taxation. The imposition or assessment of a tax; the means by which the state obtains the revenue required for its activities.

double taxation. **1.** The imposition of two taxes on the same property during the same period and for the same taxing purpose. **2.** The imposition of two taxes on one corporate profit; esp., the structure of taxation employed by Subchapter C of the Internal Revenue Code, under which corporate profits are taxed twice, once to the corporation when earned and once to the shareholders when the earnings are distributed as dividends. **3.** *Int'l law*. The imposition of comparable taxes in two or more states on the same taxpayer for the same subject matter or identical goods.

equal and uniform taxation. A tax system in which no person or class of persons in the taxing district — whether it be a state, city, or county — is taxed at a different rate from others in the same district on the same value or thing.

pass-through taxation. The taxation of an entity's owners for the entity's income without taxing the entity itself. • Partnerships and S corporations are taxed under this method. — Also termed *conduit taxation*.

tax audit. See AUDIT.

tax avoidance. The act of taking advantage of legally available tax-planning opportunities in order to minimize one's tax liability. Cf. TAX EVASION.

tax base. The total property, income, or wealth subject to taxation in a given jurisdiction; the aggregate value of the property being taxed by a particular tax. Cf. BASIS (2).

tax basis. See BASIS (2).

tax-benefit rule. The principle that if a taxpayer recovers a loss or expense that was deducted in a previous year, the recovery must be included in the current year's gross income to the extent that it was previously deducted. — Also termed *tax-benefit doctrine*.

tax bracket. A categorized level of income subject to a particular tax rate under federal or state law <28% tax bracket>.

tax certificate. An instrument issued to the buyer of property at a tax sale, certifying the sale and entitling the buyer to a tax deed and possession of the property upon the expiration of the redemption period. • If the property is redeemed, the tax certificate is voided. See REDEMPTION PERIOD; *tax sale* under SALE. Cf. *tax deed* under DEED.

tax court. **1.** TAX COURT, U.S. **2.** In some states, a court that hears appeals in nonfederal tax cases and can modify or change any valuation, assessment, classification, tax, or final order appealed from.

Tax Court, U.S. A federal court that hears appeals by taxpayers from adverse IRS decisions about tax deficiencies. • The Tax Court was created in 1942, replacing the Board of Tax Appeals. — Abbr. T.C.

tax credit. An amount subtracted directly from one's total tax liability, dollar for dollar, as opposed to a deduction from gross income. — Often shortened to *credit*. Cf. DEDUCTION (2).

child- and dependent-care tax credit. A tax credit available to a person who is employed full-time and who maintains a household for a dependent child or a disabled spouse or dependent.

earned-income credit. A refundable federal tax credit on the earned income of a low-income worker with dependent children. • The credit is paid to the taxpayer even if it exceeds the total tax liability.

foreign tax credit. A tax credit against U.S. income taxes for a taxpayer who earns income overseas and has paid foreign taxes on that income. See FOREIGN-EARNED-INCOME EXCLUSION.

investment tax credit. A tax credit intended to stimulate business investment in capital goods by allowing a percentage of the purchase price as a credit against the taxpayer's income taxes. • The Tax Reform Act of 1986 generally repealed this credit retroactively for most property placed in service after January 1, 1986.

unified credit. A tax credit applied against the federal unified transfer tax. • The 1999 credit is $211,300, meaning that an estate worth up to $650,000 passes to the heirs free of any federal estate tax. The credit will gradually increase so that, after 2005, it will be

$345,800, meaning that no federal estate tax will be due on an estate worth up to $1 million. — Also termed *unified estate-and-gift tax credit.*

tax deduction. See DEDUCTION (2).

tax deed. See DEED.

tax-deferred, *adj.* Not taxable until a future date or event <a tax-deferred retirement plan>.

tax-deferred annuity. See *403(b) plan* under EMPLOYEE BENEFIT PLAN.

tax deficiency. See DEFICIENCY.

tax-deficiency notice. See NINETY-DAY LETTER.

tax evasion. The willful attempt to defeat or circumvent the tax law in order to illegally reduce one's tax liability. • Tax evasion is punishable by both civil and criminal penalties. — Also termed *tax fraud.* Cf. TAX AVOIDANCE.

tax-exempt, *adj.* **1.** Not legally subject to taxation <a tax-exempt charity>. **2.** Bearing interest that is free from income tax <tax-exempt municipal bonds>. — Also termed *tax-free.*

tax-exempt bond. See BOND (3).

tax ferret. A private person engaged in the business of searching for taxable property that has somehow not been taxed.

tax foreclosure. See FORECLOSURE.

tax fraud. See TAX EVASION.

tax-free, *adj.* See TAX-EXEMPT.

tax-free exchange. A transfer of property that the tax law specifically exempts from income-tax consequences. • For example, a transfer of property to a controlled corporation under IRC (26 USCA) § 351(a) and a like-kind exchange under IRC (26 USCA) § 1031(a).

tax haven. A country that imposes little or no tax on the profits from transactions carried on in that country.

tax home. A taxpayer's principal business location, post, or station. • Travel expenses are tax-deductible only if the taxpayer is traveling away from home.

tax incentive. A governmental enticement, through a tax benefit, to engage in a particular activity, such as the mortgage financing of real-estate sales.

tax-increment financing. A technique used by a municipality to finance commercial developments usu. involving issuing bonds to finance land acquisition and other up-front costs, and then using the additional property taxes generated from the new development to service the debt. — Abbr. TIF.

taxing district. A district — constituting the whole state, a county, a city, or other smaller unit — throughout which a particular tax or assessment is ratably apportioned and levied on the district's inhabitants.

taxing power. See POWER.

tax injunction act. A federal law prohibiting a federal court from interfering with the assessment or collection of any state tax where the state affords a plain, speedy, and efficient remedy in its own courts. 28 USCA § 1341.

tax law. **1.** INTERNAL REVENUE CODE. **2.** The area of legal study dealing with taxation.

tax lease. See LEASE.

tax levy. See LEVY (1).

tax liability. The amount that a taxpayer legally owes after calculating the applicable tax; the amount of unpaid taxes.

tax lien. See LIEN.

tax loophole. See LOOPHOLE.

tax-loss carryback. See CARRYBACK.

tax-loss carryforward. See CARRYOVER.

tax-loss carryover. See CARRYOVER.

tax negligence. See NEGLIGENCE.

tax-option corporation. See *S corporation* under CORPORATION.

taxpayer. One who pays or is subject to a tax.

taxpayers' bill of rights. Federal legislation granting taxpayers specific rights when dealing with the Internal Revenue Service, such as the right to have representation and the right to receive written notice of a levy 30 days before enforcement.

taxpayers' lists. Written exhibits required of taxpayers in some taxing districts, listing all property owned by them and subject to taxation, used as a basis for assessment and valuation. Cf. ROLL (2).

taxpayer-standing doctrine. *Constitutional law.* The principle that a taxpayer has no standing to sue the government for allegedly misspending the public's tax money unless the taxpayer can demonstrate a personal stake and show some direct injury.

tax-preference items. Certain items that, even though deducted in arriving at taxable income for regular tax purposes, must be considered in calculating a taxpayer's alternative minimum tax. See *alternative minimum tax* under TAX.

tax rate. A mathematical figure for calculating a tax, usu. expressed as a percentage.

average tax rate. A taxpayer's tax liability divided by the amount of taxable income.

marginal tax rate. In a progressive-tax scheme, the rate applicable to the last dollar of income earned by the taxpayer. • This concept is useful in calculating the tax effect of receiving additional income or claiming additional deductions. See TAX BRACKET.

tax-rate schedule. A schedule used to determine the tax on a given level of taxable income and based on a taxpayer's status (for example, married filing a joint income-tax return). — Also termed *tax table.*

tax rebate. See TAX REFUND.

tax redemption. See REDEMPTION.

tax refund. Money that a taxpayer overpaid and is thus returned by the taxing authority. — Also termed *tax rebate.*

tax return. An income-tax form on which a person or entity reports income, deductions, and exemptions, and on which tax liability is calculated. — Often shortened to *return.* — Also termed *income-tax return.*

amended return. A return filed after the original return, usu. to correct an error in the original.

consolidated return. A return that reflects combined financial information for a group of affiliated corporations.

false return. See FALSE RETURN (2).

information return. A return, such as a W–2, filed by an entity to report some economic information other than tax liability.

joint return. A return filed together by spouses. • A joint return can be filed even if only one spouse had income, but each spouse is usu. individually liable for the tax payment.

separate return. A return filed by each spouse separately, showing income and liability. • Unlike with a joint return, each spouse is individually liable only for taxes due on the separate return.

tax roll. See ROLL (2).

tax sale. See SALE.

tax shelter, *n.* A financial operation or investment strategy (such as a partnership or real-estate investment trust) that is created primarily for the purpose of reducing or deferring income-tax payments. • The Tax Reform Act of 1986 — by restricting the deductibility of passive losses — sharply limited the effectiveness of tax shelters. — Often shortened to *shelter.* — **tax-sheltered,** *adj.*

tax-sheltered annuity. See *403(b) plan* under EMPLOYEE BENEFIT PLAN.

tax situs (**sɪ**-təs). A state or jurisdiction that has a substantial connection with assets that are subject to taxation.

tax-straddle rule. The rule that a taxpayer may not defer a tax liability by investing a short-term capital gain in a commodities future or option (i.e., investment vehicles whose values formerly did not have to be reported at the end of the year) to create the appearance of a loss in the current tax year. • This practice has been greatly restricted by the requirement that gains and losses on commodities transactions must be reported based on their value at year end. IRC (26 USCA) § 165(c)(2).

tax table. See TAX-RATE SCHEDULE.

tax title. See TITLE (2).

tax warrant. See WARRANT (1).

tax write-off. A deduction of depreciation, loss, or expense.

tax year. The period used for computing federal or state income-tax liability, usu. either the calendar year or a fiscal year of 12 months ending on the last day of a month other than December. — Also termed *taxable year*.

TBC. *abbr.* Trial before the court. See *bench trial* under TRIAL.

T-bill. *abbr.* TREASURY BILL.

T-bond. *abbr.* TREASURY BOND.

T.C. *abbr.* TAX COURT.

T.C. memo. *abbr.* A memorandum decision of the U.S. Tax Court.

teamwork. Work done by a team; esp., work by a team of animals as a substantial part of one's business, such as farming, express carrying, freight hauling, or transporting material. • In some jurisdictions, animals (such as horses) that work in teams are exempt from execution on a civil judgment.

tear-me-open license. See *shrink-wrap license* under LICENSE.

TECA (tee-kə). *abbr.* TEMPORARY EMERGENCY COURT OF APPEALS.

technical adjustment. A brief change in the general upward or downward trend of stock-market prices, such as a short rally during a bull market.

Technical Advice Memorandum. A publication issued by the national office of the IRS, usu. at a taxpayer's request, to explain some complex or novel tax-law issue. — Abbr. TAM.

technical error. See *harmless error* under ERROR.

technical mortgage. See MORTGAGE.

telecopier. See FAX (2).

teleological interpretation. See *purposive construction* under CONSTRUCTION.

teller. 1. A bank clerk who deals directly with customers by receiving and paying out money. **2.** A vote-counter at an election.

Teller in Parliament. One of the members of the British House of Commons — two from government and two from the opposition — appointed by the Speaker to count votes.

teller's check. See CHECK.

temperance. 1. Habitual moderation regarding the indulgence of the natural appetites and passions; restrained or moderate indulgence (esp. of alcoholic beverages). **2.** Abstinence.

temporality. 1. Civil or political power, as distinguished from ecclesiastical power. **2.** (*usu. pl.*) The secular properties or revenues of an ecclesiastic.

temporal lord. See LORD.

temporary, *adj.* Lasting for a time only; existing or continuing for a limited (usu. short) time; transitory.

temporary administration. See ADMINISTRATION.

temporary alimony. See ALIMONY.

temporary allegiance. See ALLEGIANCE.

temporary damages. See DAMAGES.

temporary detention. See *pretrial detention* under DETENTION.

temporary disability. See DISABILITY (1).

Temporary Emergency Court of Appeals. A special U.S. court created in 1971 with exclusive jurisdiction over appeals from federal district courts concerning price and other economic controls begun in the 1950s and 1960s. • The court consists of eight district and circuit judges appointed by the Chief Justice. Although called "temporary," the court was still active through the end of the 20th century. — Abbr. TECA.

temporary fiduciary. See FIDUCIARY.

temporary frustration. See FRUSTRATION.

temporary injunction. See *preliminary injunction* under INJUNCTION.

temporary insanity. See INSANITY.

temporary insider. See INSIDER.

temporary judge. See *visiting judge* under JUDGE.

temporary nuisance. See NUISANCE.

temporary perfection. See PERFECTION.

temporary restraining order. A court order preserving the status quo until a litigant's application for a preliminary or permanent injunction can be heard. • A temporary restraining order may sometimes be granted without notifying the opposing party in advance. — Abbr. TRO. — Often shortened to *restraining order*. Cf. INJUNCTION.

temporary statute. See STATUTE.

temporary total disability. See DISABILITY (1).

temporary ward. See WARD.

tenancy. 1. The possession or occupancy of land by right or title, esp. under a lease; a leasehold interest in real estate. **2.** The period of such possession or occupancy. See ESTATE.

at-will tenancy. See *tenancy at will*.

common tenancy. See *tenancy in common*.

cotenancy. A tenancy with two or more coowners who have unity of possession. • Examples are a joint tenancy and a tenancy in common.

entire tenancy. A tenancy possessed by one person, as opposed to a joint or common tenancy. See *tenancy by the entirety*.

general tenancy. A tenancy that is not of fixed duration under the parties' agreement.

holdover tenancy. See *tenancy at sufferance*.

joint tenancy. A tenancy with two or more coowners who take identical interests simultaneously by the same instrument and with the same right of possession. • A joint tenancy differs from a tenancy in common because each joint tenant has a right of survivorship to the other's share (in some states, this right must be clearly expressed in the conveyance — otherwise, the tenancy will be presumed to be a tenancy in common). See UNITY (2); RIGHT OF SURVIVORSHIP. Cf. *tenancy in common*.

> "The rules for creation of a joint tenancy are these: The joint tenants must get their interests at the same time. They must become entitled to possession at the same time. The interests must be physically undivided interests, and each undivided interest must be an equal fraction of the whole — e.g., a one-third undivided interest to each of three joint tenants. The joint tenants must get their interests by the same instrument — e.g., the same deed or will. The joint tenants must get the same kinds of estates — e.g., in fee simple, for life, and so on." Thomas F. Bergin & Paul G. Haskell, *Preface to Estates in Land and Future Interests* 55 (2d ed. 1984).

life tenancy. See *life estate* under ESTATE.

periodic tenancy. A tenancy that automatically continues for successive periods — usu. month to month or year to year — unless terminated at the end of a period by notice. • A typical example is a month-to-month apartment lease. This type of tenancy originated through court rulings that, when the lessor received a periodic rent, the lease could not be terminated without reasonable notice. — Also termed *tenancy from period to period*; *periodic estate*; *estate from period to period*; (more specif.) *month-to-month tenancy* (or *estate*); *year-to-year tenancy* (or *estate*).

several tenancy. A tenancy that is separate and not held jointly with another person.

tenancy at sufferance. A tenancy arising when a person who has been in lawful possession of property wrongfully remains as a holdover after his or her interest has expired. • A tenancy at sufferance takes the form of either a tenancy at will or a periodic tenancy. — Also termed *holdover tenancy*; *estate at sufferance*. See HOLDING OVER.

tenancy attendant on the inheritance. A tenancy for a term that is vested in a trustee in trust for the owner of the inheritance. — Also termed *tenancy attendant on an inheritance*.

tenancy at will. A tenancy in which the tenant holds possession with the landlord's consent but without fixed terms (as for duration or rent). • Such a tenancy may be terminated by either party upon fair notice. — Also termed *at-will tenancy*; *estate at will*.

tenancy by the entirety (en-tI-ər-tee). A joint tenancy that arises between husband and wife when a single instrument conveys realty to both of them but nothing is said in the deed or will about the character of their ownership. • This type of tenancy exists in only a few states. — Also termed *tenancy by the entireties*; *estate by the entirety*; *estate by the entireties*.

"Where [tenancy by the entirety] is recognized, it may exist only between a husband and a wife. It resembles, in most respects, the joint tenancy. The only major difference is that a tenant by the entirety may not destroy the other spouse's right of survivorship by transferring his or her interest to another. Whether a tenant by the entirety may transfer *any* interest to a third party — for example, the right of present possession or the contingent right of survivorship — is a matter on which the states differ. Most take the view that no interest may be transferred. The husband and wife may, of course, together convey their estate to a third person. If they *both* wish to convert their tenancy into a tenancy in common or a joint tenancy, they may do so. Upon the death of a tenant by the entirety, no interest passes, in theory, to the surviving spouse. As was true of the joint tenancy, the survivor's ownership is thought simply to expand to absorb the relinquished ownership of the decedent." Thomas F. Bergin & Paul G. Haskell, *Preface to Estates in Land and Future Interests* 55 (2d ed. 1984).

"Tenancy by the entireties is a form of joint tenancy. It resembles joint tenancy in that upon the death of either husband or wife the survivor automatically acquires title to the share of the deceased spouse. Like a joint tenancy, also, it is necessary for the creation of a tenancy by the entireties that the husband and wife acquire title by the same deed or will." Robert Kratovil, *Real Estate Law* 198 (6th ed. 1974).

tenancy by the rod. See COPYHOLD.

tenancy by the verge. See COPYHOLD.

tenancy for a term. A tenancy whose duration is known in years, weeks, or days from the moment of its creation. — Also termed *tenancy for a period*; *tenancy for years*; *term for years*; *term of years*; *estate for a term*; *estate for years*; *lease for years*.

tenancy from period to period. See *periodic tenancy*.

tenancy in common. A tenancy by two or more persons, in equal or unequal undivided shares, each person having an equal right to possess the whole property but no right of survivorship. — Also termed *common tenancy*; *estate in common*. Cf. *joint tenancy*.

"The central characteristic of a tenancy in common is simply that each tenant is deemed to own by himself, with most of the attributes of independent ownership, a physically undivided part of the entire parcel." Thomas F. Bergin & Paul G. Haskell, *Preface to Estates in Land and Future Interests* 54 (2d ed. 1984).

tenancy in coparcenary. See COPARCENARY.

tenancy in gross. A tenancy for a term that is outstanding — that is, one that is unattached to or disconnected from the estate or inheritance, such as one that is in the hands of some third party having no interest in the inheritance.

tenancy in tail. See FEE TAIL.

tenancy par la verge. See *tenancy by the rod*.

year-to-year tenancy. See *periodic tenancy*.

tenancy at sufferance. See TENANCY.

tenancy attendant on the inheritance. See TENANCY.

tenancy at will. See TENANCY.

tenancy by the entirety. See TENANCY.

tenancy by the rod. See COPYHOLD.

tenancy by the verge. See COPYHOLD.

tenancy for a period. See *tenancy for a term* under TENANCY.

tenancy for a term. See TENANCY.

tenancy for years. See *tenancy for a term* under TENANCY.

tenancy in common. See TENANCY.

tenancy in coparcenary. See COPARCENARY.

tenancy in gross. See TENANCY.

tenancy in tail. See FEE TAIL.

tenancy par la verge (pahr lə **vərj**). See COPYHOLD.

tenant, *n.* **1.** One who holds or possesses lands or tenements by any kind of right or title. See TENANCY.

customary tenant. A tenant holding by the custom of the manor. • Over time, customary tenants became known as *copyhold tenants*. See COPYHOLD.

"The lord has a court; in that court the tenant in villeinage, even though he be personally unfree, appears as no mere tenant at will, but as holding permanently, often heritably, on fairly definite terms. He is a customary tenant, *customarius, consuetudinarius*; he holds according to the custom of the manor.... Then gradually ... [d]ealings with villein tenements are set forth upon the rolls of the lord's court; the villein tenement is conceived to be holden 'by roll of court,' or even 'by copy of court roll,' and the mode of conveyance serves to mark off the most beneficial of villeinholds from the most onerous of freeholds.... In Henry III's time this process which secured for the tenant in villeinage a written, a registered title, and gave him the name of 'copyholder,' was but beginning...." 2 Frederick Pollock & Frederic

W. Maitland, *The History of English Law Before the Time of Edward I* 361, 375 (2d ed. 1899).

dominant tenant. The person who holds a dominant estate and therefore benefits from an easement. Cf. *servient tenant*.

holdover tenant. A person who remains in possession of real property after a previous tenancy (esp. one under a lease) expires, thus giving rise to a tenancy at sufferance. — Sometimes shortened to *holdover*. See *tenancy at sufferance* under TENANCY.

illusory tenant. **1.** A fictitious person who, as the landlord's alter ego, subleases an apartment to permit the landlord to circumvent rent-law regulations. **2.** A tenant whose business is to sublease rent-controlled apartments.

life tenant. See LIFE TENANT.

particular tenant. A tenant of a limited estate taken out of a fee. See *particular estate* under ESTATE.

prime tenant. A commercial or professional tenant with an established reputation that leases substantial, and usu. the most preferred, space in a commercial development. • A prime tenant is important in securing construction financing and in attracting other desirable tenants.

quasi-tenant. A sublessee that the new tenant or reversioner allows to hold over.

servient tenant. The person who holds a servient estate and is therefore burdened by an easement. Cf. *dominant tenant*.

tenant by the verge. See COPYHOLDER.

tenant for life. See *life tenant*.

tenant in chief. *Hist.* A person who held land directly of the king. — Also termed *tenant in capite*. See IN CAPITE.

tenant in common. One of two or more tenants who hold the same land by unity of possession but by separate and distinct titles, with each person having an equal right to possess the whole property but no right of survivorship. See *tenancy in common* under TENANCY.

tenant in demesne (di-**mayn** *or* di-**meen**). A feudal tenant who holds land of, and owes services to, a tenant in service.

tenant in service. A feudal tenant who grants an estate to another (a *tenant in demesne*) and is therefore entitled to services from the latter.

2. One who pays rent for the temporary use and occupation of another's land under a lease or similar arrangement. See LESSEE. **3.** *Archaic.* The defendant in a real action (the plaintiff being called a *demandant*). See *real action* under ACTION.

tenantable repair. A repair that will render premises fit for present habitation. See HABITABILITY.

tenant by the verge. See COPYHOLDER.

tenant for life. See LIFE TENANT.

tenant in capite. See *tenant in chief* under TENANT.

tenant in chief. See TENANT.

tenant in common. See TENANT.

tenant in demesne. See TENANT.

tenant in service. See TENANT.

tenantlike, *adj.* In accordance with the rights and obligations of a tenant, as in matters of repairs, waste, etc.

tenant par la verge. See COPYHOLDER.

tenant-right. *English law.* A tenant's right, upon termination of the tenancy, to payment for unexhausted improvements made on the holding. • This right is governed by the Agricultural Holdings Act of 1986.

tenantry. A body or group of tenants.

tenant's fixture. See FIXTURE.

tend, *vb.* **1.** To be disposed toward (something). **2.** To serve, contribute, or conduce in some degree or way; to have a more or less direct bearing or effect. **3.** To be directed or have a tendency to (an end, object, or purpose).

ten-day rule. The doctrine that one who sells goods on credit and then learns that the buyer is insolvent has ten days after the buyer receives the goods to demand their return. • The seller has even longer to demand return if the buyer has made a written representation of solvency to the seller within three months before delivery.

tender, *n.* **1.** An unconditional offer of money or performance to satisfy a debt or obligation <a

tender of delivery>. • The tender may save the tendering party from a penalty for nonpayment or nonperformance or may, if the other party unjustifiably refuses the tender, place the other party in default.

tender of delivery. A seller's putting and holding conforming goods at the buyer's disposition and giving the buyer any notification reasonably necessary to take delivery. • The manner, time, and place for tender are determined by the agreement and by Article 2 of the Uniform Commercial Code.

2. Something unconditionally offered to satisfy a debt or obligation. **3.** *Contracts.* Attempted performance that is frustrated by the act of the party for whose benefit it is to take place. • The performance may take the form of either a tender of goods or a tender of payment. Although this sense is quite similar to sense 1, it differs in making the other party's refusal part of the definition itself.

perfect tender. A seller's tender that meets the contractual terms entered into with the buyer concerning the quality and specifications of the goods sold.

4. An offer or bid put forward for acceptance <a tender for the construction contract>. **5.** Something that serves as a means of payment, such as coin, banknotes, or other circulating medium; money <legal tender>. — **tender,** *vb.*

tender, plea of. See PLEA OF TENDER.

tender of delivery. See TENDER (1).

tender offer. A public offer to buy a minimum number of shares directly from a corporation's shareholders at a fixed price, usu. at a substantial premium over the market price, in an effort to take control of the corporation. — Also termed *takeover offer*; *takeover bid.* Cf. *public-exchange offer* under OFFER.

cash tender offer. A tender offer in which the bidder offers to pay cash for the target's shares, as opposed to offering other corporate shares in exchange. • Most tender offers involve cash.

creeping tender offer. The gradual purchase of a corporation's stock at varying prices in the open market. • This takeover method does not involve a formal tender offer, although the SEC may classify it as such for regulatory purposes.

tender of issue. *Common-law pleading.* A form attached to a traverse, by which the traversing party refers the issue to the proper mode of trial.

> "[I]t is the object of all pleadings to bring the parties, in the course of their mutual altercations, to an issue that is a single entire point, affirmed on the one side and denied on the other; and it is to effect this object that the above rule was established. There can be no arrival at this point until one or the other of the parties, by the conclusion of his pleading, offers an issue for the acceptance of his opponent, and this offer is called the 'tender of issue.' " Benjamin J. Shipman, *Handbook of Common-Law Pleading* § 254, at 446 (Henry Winthrop Ballantine ed., 3d ed. 1923).

tender of performance. An offer to perform, usu. necessary to hold the defaulting party to a contract liable for breach.

tender-years doctrine. *Family law.* The doctrine holding that custody of very young children (usu. five years of age and younger) should generally be awarded to the mother in a divorce unless she is found to be unfit. • This doctrine has been rejected in most states and replaced by a presumption of joint custody.

tenement. 1. Property (esp. land) held by freehold; an estate or holding of land.

dominant tenement. See *dominant estate* under ESTATE.

servient tenement (**sər**-vee-ənt). See *servient estate* under ESTATE.

2. A house or other building used as a residence.

tenement house. A low-rent apartment building, usu. in poor condition and at best meeting only minimal safety and sanitary conditions.

tenendum (tə-**nen**-dəm). A clause in a deed designating the kind of tenure by which the things granted are to be held. — Also termed *tenendum clause*. Cf. HABENDUM CLAUSE (1).

10–K. A financial report filed annually with the SEC by a registered corporation. • The report typically includes an audited financial statement, a description of the corporation's business and financial condition, and summaries of other financial data. — Also termed *Form 10–K*. Cf. 8–K.

Tennessee Valley Authority. A government-owned corporation, created in 1933, that conducts a unified program of resource development to advance economic growth in the Tennessee Valley region. • The Authority's activities include flood control, navigation development, electric-power production, fertilizer development, recreation improvement, and forestry-and-wildlife development. Though its power program is financially self-supporting, the Authority's other programs are financed primarily by congressional appropriations. — Abbr. TVA.

ten-percent bond. See BOND (2).

10–Q. An unaudited financial report filed quarterly with the SEC by a registered corporation. • The 10–Q is less detailed than the 10–K. — Also termed *Form 10–Q*.

tentative trust. See *Totten trust* under TRUST.

Tenth Amendment. The constitutional amendment, ratified as part of the Bill of Rights in 1791, providing that any powers not constitutionally delegated to the federal government, nor prohibited to the states, are reserved for the states or the people. — Also termed *Reserved Power Clause*.

1031 exchange (**ten**-thər-tee-**wən**). A like-kind exchange of property that is exempt from income-tax consequences under IRC (26 USCA) § 1031.

tenure (**ten**-yər), *n.* **1.** A right, term, or mode of holding lands or tenements in subordination to a superior. • In feudal times, real property was held predominantly as part of a tenure system. **2.** A particular feudal mode of holding lands, such as socage, gavelkind, villeinage, and frankalmoign.

base tenure. *Hist.* The holding of property in villeinage rather than by military service or free service. See VILLEINAGE (1).

copyhold tenure. See COPYHOLD.

lay tenure. *Hist.* Any tenure not held through religious service, such as a base tenure or a freehold tenure. Cf. *tenure by divine service*.

military tenure. A tenure that bears some relation to military service, such as knight service, grand serjeanty, and cornage.

spiritual tenure. A tenure that bears some relation to religious exercises, such as frankalmoign and tenure by divine service.

tenure ad furcam et flagellum (ad **fər**-kəm et flə-**jel**-əm). [Latin] *Hist.* Tenure by gallows and whip. • This was the meanest of the servile tenures — the bondman was at the disposal of the lord for life and limb.

tenure by divine service. *Hist.* A tenure obligating the tenant to perform an expressly defined divine service, such as singing a certain number of masses or distributing a fixed sum of alms. Cf. *lay tenure*.

3. A status afforded to a teacher or professor as a protection against summary dismissal without sufficient cause. • This status has long been considered a cornerstone of academic freedom. **4.** More generally, the legal protection of a long-term relationship, such as employment. — **tenurial** (ten-**yuur**-ee-əl), *adj.*

tenured faculty. The members of a school's teaching staff who hold their positions for life or until retirement, and who may not be discharged except for cause.

tenure in capite. See IN CAPITE.

term, *n.* **1.** A word or phrase; esp., an expression that has a fixed meaning in some field <term of art>. **2.** A contractual stipulation <the delivery term provided for shipment within 30 days>. See CONDITION (3).

fundamental term. **1.** A contractual provision that must be included for a contract to exist; a contractual provision that specifies an essential purpose of the contract, so that a breach of the provision through inadequate performance makes the performance not only defective but essentially different from what had been promised. **2.** A contractual provision that must be included in the contract to satisfy the statute of frauds. — Also termed *essential term*; *vital term*.

"During the 1950s and 1960s there flourished another species of term called the fundamental term. A fundamental term was said to be a term which was so important and central to a contract that if it was broken, the innocent party always had some remedy, *even if the contract contained an exemption clause* protecting the guilty party from liability. This doctrine served a useful purpose in helping to protect consumers from unreasonably wide exemption clauses. It was first used most extensively in contracts of hire-purchase where vehicles were often let to consumers under contracts containing the widest possible exemptions from liability." P.S. Atiyah, *An Introduction to the Law of Contract* 151 (3d ed. 1981).

implied term. A provision not expressly agreed to by the parties but instead read into the contract by a court as being implicit. • An implied term should not, in theory, contradict the contract's express terms.

nonfundamental term. Any contractual provision that is not regarded as a fundamental term. — Also termed *nonessential term*; *nonvital term*.

3. (*pl.*) Provisions that define an agreement's scope; conditions or stipulations <terms of sale>. **4.** A fixed period of time; esp., the period for which an estate is granted <term for years>.

attendant term. A long period (such as 1,000 years) specified as the duration of a mortgage, created to protect the mortgagor's heirs' interest in the land by not taking back title to the land once it is paid for, but rather by assigning title to a trustee who holds the title in trust for the mortgagor and the mortgagor's heirs. • This arrangement gives the heirs another title to the property in case the interest they inherited proves somehow defective. These types of terms have been largely abolished. See *tenancy attendant on the inheritance* under TENANCY.

satisfied term. A term of years in land that has satisfied the purpose for which it was created before the term's expiration.

term for deliberating. The time given a beneficiary to decide whether to accept or reject an inheritance or other succession.

term in gross. A term that is unattached to an estate or inheritance. See *tenancy in gross* under TENANCY.

unexpired term. The remainder of a period prescribed by law or provided for in a lease.

5. The period or session during which a court conducts judicial business <the most recent term was busy indeed>. — Also termed (in sense 5) *term of court*. See SESSION.

additional term. A distinct, added term to a previous term.

adjourned term. A continuance of a previous or regular term but not a separate term; the same term prolonged.

general term. A regular term of court — that is, the period during which a court ordinarily sits. — Also termed *stated term*.

regular term. A term of court begun at the time appointed by law and continued, in the court's discretion, until the court lawfully adjourns.

special term. A term of court scheduled outside the general term, usu. for conducting extraordinary business.

stated term. See *general term*.

term probatory. *Eccles. law.* The period given to the promoter of an ecclesiastical suit to produce witnesses and prove the case.

term to conclude. *Eccles. law.* A deadline imposed by the judge for all parties to renounce any further exhibits and allegations.

term to propound all things. *Eccles. law.* A deadline imposed by the judge for the parties to exhibit all evidence supporting their positions.

6. *Hist. English law.* One of the four periods in a year during which the courts are in session to conduct judicial business. • Terms came into use in the 13th century, and their dates varied. The four terms — Hilary, Easter, Trinity, and Michaelmas — were abolished by the Judicature Acts of 1873–1875, and the legal year was divided into sittings and vacations. Terms are still maintained by the Inns of Court to determine various time periods and dates, such as a call to the bar or observance of a Grand Day.

term bond. See BOND (3).

term fee. *English law.* A sum that a solicitor may charge a client, and that the client (if successful) may recover from the losing party, payable for each term in which any proceedings following the summons take place.

term for deliberating. See TERM (4).

term for years. See *tenancy for a term* under TENANCY.

terminable interest. An interest that may be terminated upon the lapse of time or upon the occurrence of some condition.

terminable property. Property (such as a leasehold) whose duration is not perpetual or indefinite but that is limited in time or liable to terminate on the happening of an event.

terminal disclaimer. See DISCLAIMER (4).

terminate, *vb.* **1.** To put an end to; to bring to an end. **2.** To end; to conclude.

termination, *n.* **1.** The act of ending something <termination of the partnership by winding up its affairs>.

termination of conditional contract. The act of putting an end to all unperformed portions of a conditional contract.

termination of employment. The complete severance of an employer–employee relationship.

2. The end of something in time or existence; conclusion or discontinuance <the insurance policy's termination left the doctor without

liability coverage>. — **terminate,** *vb.* — **terminable,** *adj.*

termination hearing. *Family law.* A hearing to determine whether parental rights will be taken away from parents of a child who has become the court's ward, usu. because of parental neglect or abuse.

termination proceeding. An administrative action to end a person's or entity's status or relationship. • For example, the International Banking Act authorizes the International Banking Board to institute a termination proceeding when a foreign bank or its U.S. agency or branch is convicted of money-laundering. 12 USCA § 3105(e).

terminer. See OYER AND TERMINER.

term in gross. See TERM (4).

term life insurance. See INSURANCE.

term loan. See LOAN.

term of art. **1.** A word or phrase having a specific, precise meaning in a given specialty, apart from its general meaning in ordinary contexts. • Examples in law include *and his heirs* and *res ipsa loquitur*. **2.** Loosely, a jargonistic word or phrase. — Also termed *word of art.*

term-of-art canon. In statutory construction, the principle that if a term has acquired a technical or specialized meaning in a particular context, the term should be presumed to have that meaning if used in that context.

term of court. See TERM (5).

term of office. The period during which an elected officer or appointee may hold office, perform its functions, and enjoy its privileges and emoluments.

term of years. See *tenancy for a term* under TENANCY.

termor (**tər**-mər). A person who holds lands or tenements for a term of years or for life.

term policy. See INSURANCE POLICY.

term probatory. See TERM (5).

terms. See YEAR BOOKS.

term sheet. *Securities.* A document setting forth all information that is material to investors about the offering but is not disclosed in the accompanying prospectus or the confirmation.

abbreviated term sheet. A term sheet that includes (1) the description of the securities as required by Item 202 of SEC Regulation S–K, or a good summary of that information; and (2) all material changes to the issuer's affairs required to be disclosed on SEC Form S–3 or F–3, as applicable.

termtime. The time of the year when a court is in session.

term to conclude. See TERM (5).

term to propound all things. See TERM (5).

terra nullius (**ter**-ə **nəl**-ee-əs), *n.* [Latin "the land of no one"] A territory not belonging to any particular country.

terre-tenant (**tair**-ten-ənt). **1.** One who has actual possession of land; the occupant of land. **2.** One who has an interest in a judgment debtor's land after the judgment creditor's lien has attached to the land (such as a subsequent purchaser). — Also spelled *tertenant* (**tər**-ten-θnt). — Also termed *land-tenant.*

territorial, *adj.* Having to do with a particular geographical area.

territorial court. See COURT.

territorialism. The traditional approach to choice of law, whereby the place of injury or of contract formation determines which state's law will be applied in a case. See CHOICE OF LAW.

territorial jurisdiction. See JURISDICTION.

territorial law. The law that applies to all persons within a given territory regardless of their citizenship or nationality. Cf. PERSONAL LAW.

territorial property. Land and water over which a state has jurisdiction and control, whether the legal title is held by the state or by a private individual or entity. • Lakes and waters wholly within a state are generally its property, as is the marginal sea within the three-mile limit, but bays and gulfs are not always recognized as state property.

territorial sea. See *territorial waters* under WATER.

territorial waters. See WATER.

territory, *n.* **1.** A geographical area included within a particular government's jurisdiction; the portion of the earth's surface that is in a state's exclusive possession and control.

non-self-governing territory. *Int'l law.* A territory that is governed by another country. • These types of territories are rarely allowed representation in the governing country's legislature.

trust territory. *Int'l law.* A territory governed under the United Nations' international trusteeship system; a territory administered by the United Nations or a member state for the political, economic, educational, and social advancement of its inhabitants.

2. A part of the United States not included within any state but organized with a separate legislature (such as Guam and the U.S. Virgin Islands). — **territorial,** *adj.* Cf. COMMONWEALTH; DEPENDENCY.

territory of a judge. The territorial jurisdiction of a particular court. See JURISDICTION (3).

terrorism, *n.* The use or threat of violence to intimidate or cause panic, esp. as a means of affecting political conduct. — **terrorist,** *adj.* & *n.*

terroristic threat. See THREAT.

***Terry* stop.** See STOP AND FRISK.

tertenant. See TERRE-TENANT.

tertius gaudens (**tər**-shee-əs **gaw**-denz). [Latin "a rejoicing third"] A third party who profits when two others dispute.

testable, *adj.* **1.** Capable of being tested <a testable hypothesis>. **2.** Capable of making a will <an 18-year-old person is testable in this state>. **3.** Capable of being transferred by will <today virtually all property is considered testable>.

test action. See *test case* under CASE.

testacy (**tes**-tə-see), *n.* The fact or condition of leaving a valid will at one's death. Cf. INTESTACY.

testament (**tes**-tə-mənt). **1.** A will disposing of personal property. Cf. DEVISE (4). **2.** WILL (1).

inofficious testament. *Civil law.* A will that does not dispose of property to the testator's natural heirs; esp., a will that deprives the heirs of a portion of the estate to which they are entitled by law. — Also termed *inofficious will*; *unofficious will.*

mystic testament. See *mystic will* under WILL.

officious testament. *Civil law.* A will that disposes of property to the testator's family; a will that reserves the legitime for the testator's children and other natural heirs. — Also termed *officious will.* See LEGITIME.

testamentary (tes-tə-**men**-tə-ree *or* -tree), *adj.* **1.** Of or relating to a will or testament <testamentary intent>. **2.** Provided for or appointed by a will <testamentary guardian>. **3.** Created by a will <testamentary gift>.

testamentary capacity. See CAPACITY (3).

testamentary class. See CLASS (3).

testamentary gift. See GIFT.

testamentary guardian. See GUARDIAN.

testamentary heir. See HEIR.

testamentary intent. See INTENT (1).

testamentary power of appointment. See POWER OF APPOINTMENT.

testamentary succession. See SUCCESSION.

testamentary trust. See TRUST.

testamentary trustee. See TRUSTEE (1).

testamenti factio (tes-tə-**men**-tɪ **fak**-shee-oh). [Latin "right to make a testament"] *Roman law.* **1.** Broadly, the capacity to take part in a will, as testator, heir, or witness. **2.** The capacity to make a will. • This term is sometimes known as "active" *testamenti factio* or *testamenti factio activa*, though the latter phrase was not known to the Roman law. **3.** The capacity to receive property by will. • This is also known as "passive" *testamenti factio* or *testamenti fac-*

tio passiva, though the latter phrase was (like *testamenti factio activa*) unknown to the Roman law. **4.** The capacity to witness a will.

testamentum holografum (tes-tə-**men**-təm hol-ə-**graf**-əm). [Latin] See *holographic will* under WILL.

testamentum in procinctu (tes-tə-**men**-təm in prə-**singk**-t[y]oo). [Latin] *Roman law*. A will made by a soldier while preparing for battle.

testamentum militum (tes-tə-**men**-təm **mil**-ə-təm). [Latin] See *soldier's will* under WILL.

testate (**tes**-tayt), *adj*. Having left a will at death <she died testate>. Cf. INTESTATE.

testate, *n*. See TESTATOR.

testate succession. The passing of rights or property by will. Cf. INTESTATE SUCCESSION.

testation (te-**stay**-shən). **1.** The disposal of property by will; the power to dispose of property by will. **2.** *Archaic*. Attestation; a witnessing.

testator (**tes**-tay-tər *also* te-**stay**-tər). A person who has made a will; esp., a person who dies leaving a will. • Because this term is usu. interpreted as applying to both sexes, *testatrix* has become archaic. — Also termed *testate*. Cf. INTESTATE.

testatrix (te-**stay**-triks *or* **tes**-tə-triks). *Archaic*. A female testator. • In modern usage, a person who leaves a will is called a testator, regardless of sex.

testatum (tes-**tay**-təm). [Latin "attested"] *Hist*. A writ issued in a county where a defendant or a defendant's property is located when venue lies in another county. • This writ, when issued after a ground writ, allowed the seizure of the defendant or the defendant's property in another county. — Also termed *testatum bill*; *testatum writ*; *latitat* (**lat**-ə-tat). Cf. *ground writ* under WRIT.

> "But if the defendant had removed into another county, the next process the plaintiff might sue out against him was a *testatum bill*, directed to the sheriff thereof, which soon gained the name of a *latitat*, from that word being within it." 1 George Crompton, *Practice Common-Placed: Rules and Cases of Practice in the Courts of King's Bench and Common Pleas* xxxv (3d ed. 1787).

testatus (tes-**tay**-təs), *n*. [Latin] *Civil law*. See TESTATOR.

test case. See CASE.

teste (**tes**-tee). [Latin *teste meipso* "I myself being a witness"] In drafting, the clause that states the name of a witness and evidences the act of witnessing.

testifier. One who testifies; WITNESS. — Also termed (archaically) *testificator* (**tes**-tə-fi-kay-tər).

testify, *vb*. **1.** To give evidence as a witness <she testified that the Ford Bronco was at the defendant's home at the critical time>. **2.** (Of a person or thing) to bear witness <the incomplete log entries testified to his sloppiness>.

testifying expert. See EXPERT.

testimonial evidence. See TESTIMONY; EVIDENCE.

testimonial immunity. See IMMUNITY (3).

testimonial incapacity. See INCAPACITY.

testimonial privilege. See PRIVILEGE (1).

testimonial proof. See PROOF.

testimonium clause. A provision at the end of an instrument (esp. a will) reciting the date when the instrument was signed, by whom it was signed, and in what capacity. • This clause traditionally begins with the phrase "In witness whereof." Cf. ATTESTATION CLAUSE.

testimony, *n*. Evidence that a competent witness under oath or affirmation gives at trial or in an affidavit or deposition. — Also termed *personal evidence*. — **testimonial,** *adj*.

affirmative testimony. Testimony about whether something occurred or did not occur, based on what the witness saw or heard at the time and place in question. — Also termed *positive testimony*. See *direct evidence* under EVIDENCE.

cumulative testimony. Identical or similar testimony by more than one witness, and usu. by several, offered by a party usu. to impress the jury with the apparent weight of proof on that party's side. • The trial court typically limits cumulative testimony.

dropsy testimony. A police officer's false testimony that a fleeing suspect dropped an illegal substance that was then confiscated by the police and used as probable cause for arresting the suspect. • Dropsy testimony may be given when an arrest has been made without probable cause, as when illegal substances have been found through an improper search.

expert testimony. See *expert evidence* under EVIDENCE.

false testimony. Testimony that is untrue. • This term is broader than *perjury*, which has a state-of-mind element. Unlike *perjury*, *false testimony* does not denote a crime. — Also termed *false evidence*.

interpreted testimony. Testimony translated because the witness cannot communicate in the language of the tribunal.

lay opinion testimony. Evidence given by a witness who is not qualified as an expert but who testifies to opinions or inferences. • In federal court, the admissibility of this testimony is limited to opinions or inferences that are rationally based on the witness's perception and that will be helpful to a clear understanding of the witness's testimony or the determination of a fact in issue. Fed. R. Evid. 701.

negative testimony. See *negative evidence* under EVIDENCE.

nonverbal testimony. A photograph, drawing, map, chart, or other depiction used to aid a witness in testifying. • The witness need not have made it, but it must accurately represent something that the witness saw. See *demonstrative evidence* under EVIDENCE.

opinion testimony. Testimony based on one's belief or idea rather than on direct knowledge of the facts at issue. • Opinion testimony from either a lay witness or an expert witness may be allowed in evidence under certain conditions. See *opinion evidence* under EVIDENCE.

positive testimony. See *direct evidence* (1) under EVIDENCE.

testimony de bene esse (dee **bee**-nee **es**-ee *also* day **ben**-ay **es**-ay). Testimony taken because it is in danger of being lost before it can be given at a trial or hearing, usu. because of the impending death or departure of the witness. • Such testimony is taken in aid of a pending lawsuit, while testimony taken under a bill to perpetuate testimony is taken in anticipation of future litigation. See *deposition de bene esse* under DEPOSITION.

written testimony. **1.** Testimony given out of court by deposition. • The recorded writing, signed by the witness, is considered testimony. **2.** In some administrative agencies and courts, direct narrative testimony that is reduced to writing, to which the witness swears at a hearing or trial before cross-examination takes place in the traditional way.

testing clause. *Scots law.* The clause in a formal written instrument or deed by which it is authenticated according to the forms of law. • Traditionally, the clause states the name and address of the writer, the number of pages in the instrument, the names and addresses of the witnesses, the name and address of the person who penned the instrument, and the date and place of signing.

test oath. See *oath of allegiance* under OATH.

test-paper. In Pennsylvania, a paper or instrument shown to the jury as evidence.

textbook digest. A legal text whose aim is to set forth the law of a subject in condensed form, with little or no criticism or discussion of the authorities cited, and no serious attempt to explain or reconcile apparently conflicting decisions.

textualism. See STRICT CONSTRUCTIONISM.

thalweg (**tahl**-vayk *or* -veg). **1.** A line following the lowest part of a (usu. submerged) valley. **2.** The middle of the primary navigable channel of a waterway, constituting the boundary between states. — Also termed *midway*.

live thalweg. The part of a river channel that is most followed, usu. at the middle of the principal channel. *Louisiana v. Mississippi*, 466 U.S. 96, 104 S.Ct. 1645 (1984).

Thayer presumption. A presumption that requires the party against whom the presumption operates to come forward with evidence to rebut the presumption, but that does not shift the burden of proof to that party. James B. Thayer, *A Preliminary Treatise on Evidence* 31–44 (1898). • Most presumptions that arise in civil trials in federal court are interpreted in this way. Fed. R. Evid. 301. Cf. MORGAN PRESUMPTION.

The Federalist. See FEDERALIST PAPERS.

theft, *n.* **1.** The felonious taking and removing of another's personal property with the intent of depriving the true owner of it; larceny. **2.** Broadly, any act or instance of stealing, including larceny, burglary, embezzlement, and false pretenses. • Many modern penal codes have consolidated such property offenses under the name "theft." See LARCENY.

> "[T]he distinctions between larceny, embezzlement and false pretenses serve no useful purpose in the criminal law but are useless handicaps from the standpoint of the administration of criminal justice. One solution has been to combine all three in one section of the code under the name of 'larceny.' This has one disadvantage, however, because it frequently becomes necessary to add a modifier to make clear whether the reference is to common-law larceny or to statutory larceny. To avoid this difficulty some states have employed another word to designate a statutory offense made up of a combination of larceny, embezzlement, and false pretenses. And the word used for this purpose is 'theft.' 'Theft' is not the name of any common-law offense. At times it has been employed as a synonym of 'larceny,' but for the most part has been regarded as broader in its general scope. Under such a statute it is not necessary for the indictment charging theft to specify whether the offense is larceny, embezzlement or false pretenses." Rollin M. Perkins & Ronald N. Boyce, *Criminal Law* 389–90 (3d ed. 1982).

cybertheft. See CYBERTHEFT.

theft by deception. The use of deception to obtain another's property.

theft by false pretext. The use of a false pretext to obtain another's property.

theft of services. The act of obtaining services from another by deception, threat, coercion, stealth, mechanical tampering, or using a false token or device.

theft-bote (**theft**-boht). See BOTE (2).

theft by deception. See THEFT.

theft by false pretext. See THEFT.

theft of services. See THEFT.

theftuous (**thef**-choo-əs), *adj.* **1.** (Of an act) characterized by theft. **2.** (Of a person) given to stealing. — Also spelled *theftous.*

thence, *adv.* **1.** From that place; from that time. • In surveying, and in describing land by courses and distances, this word, preceding each course given, implies that the following course is continuous with the one before it <south 240 feet to an iron post, thence west 59 feet>. **2.** On that account; therefore.

thence down the river. With the meanders of a river. • This phrase appears in the field notes of patent surveyors, indicating that the survey follows a meandering river unless evidence shows that the meander line as written was where the surveyor in fact ran it. See MEANDER LINE.

theocracy (thee-**ok**-rə-see). **1.** Government of a state by those who are presumably acting under the immediate direction of God or some other divinity. **2.** A state in which power is exercised by ecclesiastics.

Theodosian Code (thee-ə-**doh**-shən). See CODEX THEODOSIANUS.

theolonio. See DE THEOLONIO.

theory of law. The legal premise or set of principles on which a case rests.

theory-of-pleading doctrine. The principle — now outmoded — that one must prove a case exactly as pleaded. • Various modern codes and rules of civil procedure have abolished this strict pleading-and-proof requirement. • For example, Fed. R. Civ. P. 15 allows amendment of pleadings to conform to the evidence.

theory of the case. A comprehensive and orderly mental arrangement of principles and facts, conceived and constructed for the purpose of securing a judgment or decree of a court in favor of a litigant; the particular line of reasoning of either party to a suit, the purpose being to bring together certain facts of the case in a logical sequence and to correlate them in a way that produces in the decision-maker's mind a definite result or conclusion favored by the advocate. See CAUSE OF ACTION (1).

therapeutic abortion. See ABORTION.

therapeutic relief. See RELIEF.

thereabout, *adv.* Near that time or place <Schreuer was seen in Rudolf Place or thereabout>.

thereafter, *adv.* Afterward; later <Skurry was thereafter arrested>.

thereat, *adv.* **1.** At that place or time; there. **2.** Because of that; at that occurrence or event.

thereby, *adv.* By that means; in that way <Blofeld stepped into the embassy and thereby found protection>.

therefor, *adv.* For it or them; for that thing or action; for those things or actions <she lied to Congress but was never punished therefor>.

therefore, *adv.* **1.** For that reason; on that ground or those grounds <a quorum was not

present; therefore, no vote was taken>. **2.** To that end <she wanted to become a tax lawyer, and she therefore applied for the university's renowned LL.M. program in tax>. — Also termed *thereupon*.

therefrom, *adv.* From that, it, or them <Hofer had several financial obligations to Ricks, who refused to release Hofer therefrom>.

therein, *adv.* **1.** In that place or time <the Dallas/Fort Worth metroplex has a population of about 3 million, and some 20,000 lawyers practice therein>. **2.** Inside or within that thing; inside or within those things <there were 3 school buses with 108 children therein>.

thereinafter, *adv.* Later in that thing (such as a speech or document) <the book's first reference was innocuous, but the five references thereinafter were libelous per se>.

thereof, *adv.* Of that, it, or them <although the disease is spreading rapidly, the cause thereof is unknown>.

thereon, *adv.* On that or them <Michaels found the online reports of the cases and relied thereon instead of checking the printed books>. — Also termed *thereupon*.

thereto, *adv.* To that or them <the jury awarded $750,000 in actual damages, and it added thereto another $250,000 in punitive damages>. — Also termed *thereunto*.

theretofore, *adv.* Up to that time <theretofore, the highest award in such a case has been $450,000>.

thereunder, *adv.* Under that or them <on the top shelf were three books, and situated thereunder was the missing banknote> <section 1988 was the relevant fee statute, and the plaintiffs were undeniably proceeding thereunder>.

thereunto, *adv.* See THERETO.

thereupon, *adv.* **1.** Immediately; without delay; promptly <the writ of execution issued from the court, and the sheriff thereupon sought to find the judgment debtor>. **2.** THEREON. **3.** THEREFORE.

***Thibodaux* abstention** (**tib**-ə-doh). See ABSTENTION.

thief. One who steals, esp. without force or violence; one who commits theft or larceny. See THEFT.

common thief. A thief who has been convicted of theft or larceny more than once. — Also termed *common and notorious thief.*

thieve, *vb.* To steal; to commit theft or larceny. See THEFT.

thin capitalization. See CAPITALIZATION.

thin corporation. See CORPORATION.

thing. 1. A material object regarded as the subject matter of a right, whether it is a material object or not; any subject matter of ownership within the sphere of proprietary or valuable rights. • Things are divided into three categories: (1) things real or immovable, such as land, tenements, and hereditaments, (2) things personal or movable, such as goods and chattels, and (3) things having both real and personal characteristics, such as a title deed and a tenancy for a term. The civil law divided things into corporeal (*tangi possunt*) and incorporeal (*tangi non possunt*).

corporeal thing. The subject matter of corporeal ownership; a material object. — Also termed *res corporalis*.

incorporeal thing. The subject matter of incorporeal ownership; any proprietary right apart from the right of full dominion over a material object. — Also termed *res incorporalis*.

thing in action. See *chose in action* under CHOSE.

thing in possession. See *chose in possession* under CHOSE.

2. Anything that is owned by someone as part of that person's estate or property. — Also termed *res*; *chose*.

thing in action. See *chose in action* under CHOSE.

thing in possession. See *chose in possession* under CHOSE.

things personal. See *personal property* (1) under PROPERTY.

things real. See REAL THINGS.

thin market. See MARKET.

thin-skull rule. See EGGSHELL-SKULL RULE.

Third Amendment. The constitutional amendment, ratified as part of the Bill of Rights in 1791, prohibiting the quartering of soldiers in private homes except during wartime.

third cousin. See COUSIN.

third degree, *n.* The process of extracting a confession or information from a suspect or prisoner by prolonged questioning, the use of threats, or physical torture <the police gave the suspect the third degree>.

third-degree instruction. See ALLEN CHARGE.

third party, *n.* One who is not a party to a lawsuit, agreement, or other transaction but who is somehow involved in the transaction; someone other than the principal parties. — Also termed *outside party.* — **third-party,** *adj.* See PARTY.

third-party, *vb.* To bring (a person or entity) into litigation as a third-party defendant <seeking indemnity, the defendant third-partied the surety>.

third-party action. See ACTION.

third-party beneficiary. See BENEFICIARY.

third-party-beneficiary contract. See CONTRACT.

third-party check. A check that the payee indorses to another party — for example, a customer check that the payee indorses to a supplier. • A person who takes a third-party check in good faith and without notice of a security interest can be a holder in due course.

third-party complaint. See COMPLAINT.

third-party defendant. A party brought into a lawsuit by the original defendant.

third-party equity lease. See *leveraged lease* under LEASE.

third-party insurance. See *liability insurance* under INSURANCE.

third-party plaintiff. A defendant who files a pleading in an effort to bring a third party into the lawsuit. See *third-party complaint* under COMPLAINT.

third-party practice. See IMPLEADER.

third-party record-custodian summons. See *John Doe summons* under SUMMONS.

third-party standing. See STANDING.

third possessor. *Civil law.* A person who acquires mortgaged property but is not personally bound by the obligation secured by the mortgage.

Third World. The group of underdeveloped nations (esp. in Africa and Asia) not aligned with major powers, whether Western democracies (i.e., the *First* — or *Free* — *World*) or countries that were formerly part of the Soviet bloc (i.e., the *Second World*).

Third World country. See DEVELOPING COUNTRY.

Thirteenth Amendment. The constitutional amendment, ratified in 1865, that abolished slavery and involuntary servitude.

> "The thirteenth amendment is fairly unique in two respects. First, it contains an absolute bar to the existence of slavery or involuntary servitude; there is no requirement of 'state action.' Thus it is applicable to individuals as well as states .... Secondly, like the fourteenth and fifteenth amendments, it contains an enforcement clause, enabling Congress to pass all necessary legislation." John E. Nowak & Ronald D. Rotunda, *Constitutional Law* § 15.6, at 918 (4th ed. 1991).

30(b)(6) deposition. See DEPOSITION.

thirty-day letter. A letter that accompanies a revenue agent's report issued as a result of an Internal Revenue Service audit or the rejection of a taxpayer's claim for refund and that outlines the taxpayer's appeal procedure before the Internal Revenue Service. • If the taxpayer does not request any such procedure within the 30-day period, the IRS will issue a statutory notice of deficiency. Cf. NINETY-DAY LETTER.

threat, *n.* **1.** A communicated intent to inflict harm or loss on another or on another's property, esp. one that might diminish a person's freedom to act voluntarily or with lawful consent <the kidnapper's threat was that if the magnate did not meet the demands, his son would never be seen again>.

terroristic threat. A threat to commit any crime of violence with the purpose of (1) terrorizing another, (2) causing the evacuation of a building, place of assembly, or facility of public transportation, (3) causing serious public inconvenience, or (4) recklessly disregarding the risk of causing such terror or inconvenience.

2. An indication of an approaching menace <the threat of bankruptcy>. **3.** A person or thing that might well cause harm <Mrs. Harrington testified that she had never viewed her husband as a threat>. — **threaten,** *vb.* — **threatening,** *adj.*

threatened species. See SPECIES.

three estates, the. See ESTATES OF THE REALM.

341 meeting. See *creditors' meeting* under MEETING.

three-judge court. See COURT.

three-mile limit. The distance of one marine league or three miles offshore, usu. recognized as the limit of territorial jurisdiction.

three-strikes law. A statute prescribing an enhanced sentence, esp. life imprisonment, for a repeat offender's third felony conviction. • About half the states have enacted a statute of this kind. — Also termed *three-strikes-and-you're-out law.*

three wicked sisters. *Slang.* The three doctrines — contributory negligence, the fellow-servant rule, and assumption of the risk — used by 19th-century courts to deny recovery to workers injured on the job.

> "These three common law defenses, contributory negligence, fellow servant rule, and assumption of the risk, became known as the 'three wicked sisters,' because of their preclusive effect on the ability of injured workers to recover.... By precluding application of the traditional respondeat superior concept for acts of fellow servants and by presuming that workers assumed the risks associated with their employment, courts made it extremely difficult for employees to recover from their employers for the increasing number of work-related injuries.... By the late 1800s, courts began to recognize the harsh results generated by rote application of the fellow servant, assumption of the risk, and contributory negligence doctrines." Mark A. Rothstein et al., *Employment Law* § 7.2, at 404 (1994).

thrift institution. See SAVINGS-AND-LOAN ASSOCIATION.

through bill of lading. See BILL OF LADING.

through lot. A lot that abuts a street at each end.

through rate. The total shipping cost when two or more carriers are involved.

throwback rule. *Tax.* **1.** In the taxation of trusts, a rule requiring that an amount distributed in any tax year that exceeds the year's distributable net income must be treated as if it had been distributed in the preceding year. • The beneficiary is taxed in the current year although the computation is made as if the excess had been distributed in the previous year. If the trust did not have undistributed accumulated income in the preceding year, the amount of the throwback is tested against each of the preceding years. IRC (26 USCA) §§ 665–668. **2.** A taxation rule requiring a sale that would otherwise be exempt from state income tax (because the state to which the sale would be assigned for apportionment purposes does not have an income tax, even though the seller's state does) to be attributed to the seller's state and thus subjected to a state-level tax. • This rule applies only if the seller's state has adopted a throwback rule.

throw out, *vb.* To dismiss (a claim or lawsuit).

thumbprint. See FINGERPRINT.

ticket, *n.* **1.** A certificate indicating that the person to whom it is issued, or the holder, is entitled to some right or privilege <she bought a bus ticket for Miami>. **2.** CITATION (2) <he got a speeding ticket last week>. **3.** BALLOT (2) <they all voted a straight-party ticket>.

ticket of leave. *Archaic.* The English equivalent of parole.

ticket-of-leave man. A convict who has obtained a ticket of leave.

ticket speculator. A person who buys tickets and then resells them for more than their face value; a scalper.

tidal, *adj.* Affected by or having tides. • For a river to be "tidal" at a given spot, the water need not necessarily be salt, but the spot must be one where the tide, in the ordinary and regular course of things, flows and reflows.

tide. The rising and falling of seawater that is produced by the attraction of the sun and moon, uninfluenced by special winds, seasons, or other circumstances that create meteorological and atmospheric meteorological tides; the ebb and flow of the sea. • Tides are used to measure a shore's upland boundary.

mean high tide. The average of all high tides, esp. over a period of 18.6 years. — Also termed *ordinary high tide*.

mean lower low tide. The average of lower low tides over a fixed period.

mean low tide. The average of all low tides — both low and lower low — over a fixed period.

neap tide (neep). A tide, either high tide or low tide, that is lower than average because it occurs during the first or last quarter of the moon, when the sun's attraction partly counteracts the moon's.

ordinary high tide. See *mean high tide*.

spring tide. A tide, either high tide or low tide, that is higher than average because it occurs during the new moon and full moon.

tideland. Land between the lines of the ordinary high and low tides, covered and uncovered successively by the ebb and flow of those tides; land covered and uncovered by the ordinary tides.

tidesman. *English law*. A customhouse officer appointed to watch or attend upon ships until the customs are paid. • A tidesman boards a ship at its arrival in the mouth of the Thames and comes up with the tide. See CUSTOMHOUSE.

tidewater. Water that falls and rises with the ebb and flow of the tide. • The term is not usu. applied to the open sea, but to coves, bays, and rivers.

tideway. Land between high- and low-water marks.

tie, *n*. **1.** In connection with an election, an equal number of votes for each candidate. **2.** An equal number of votes cast for and against a particular measure by a legislative or deliberative body. • In the U.S. Senate, the Vice President has the deciding vote in the event of a tie. U.S. Const. art. I, § 3.

tied product. See TYING ARRANGEMENT (1).

tie-in arrangement. See TYING ARRANGEMENT.

tiered partnership. See PARTNERSHIP.

TIF. *abbr*. TAX-INCREMENT FINANCING.

tight, *adj*. *Slang*. (Of a note, bond, mortgage, lease, etc.) characterized by summary and stringent clauses providing the creditor's remedies in case of default.

TILA. *abbr*. Truth in Lending Act. See CONSUMER CREDIT PROTECTION ACT.

tillage (**til**-ij), *n*. A place tilled or cultivated; land under cultivation as opposed to land lying fallow or in pasture.

till-tapping. *Slang*. Theft of money from a cash register.

timber easement. See EASEMENT.

timber lease. See LEASE.

timber rights. See *timber easement* under EASEMENT.

time. 1. A measure of duration. **2.** A point in or period of duration at or during which something is alleged to have occurred. **3.** *Slang*. A convicted criminal's period of incarceration.

flat time. A prison term that is to be served without the benefit of time-reduction allowances for good behavior and the like.

time arbitrage. See ARBITRAGE.

time-bar, *n*. A bar to a legal claim arising from the lapse of a defined length of time, esp. one contained in a statute of limitations. — **time-barred,** *adj*.

time-bargain. See FUTURES CONTRACT.

time bill. See *time draft* under DRAFT.

time charter. See CHARTER (4).

time deposit. See DEPOSIT (2).

time draft. See DRAFT.

time immemorial. 1. A point in time so far back that no living person has knowledge or proof contradicting the right or custom alleged to have existed since then. • At common law, that time was fixed as the year 1189. — Also termed *time out of memory*; *time out of mind*. Cf. LEGAL MEMORY. **2.** A very long time.

time insurance. See INSURANCE.

time is of the essence. See OF THE ESSENCE.

time letter of credit. See LETTER OF CREDIT.

time loan. See *term loan* under LOAN.

time note. See NOTE (1).

time order. See ORDER (4).

time out of memory. See TIME IMMEMORIAL.

time out of mind. See TIME IMMEMORIAL.

time-place-or-manner restriction. *Constitutional law.* A government's limitation on when, where, or how a public speech or assembly may occur, but not on the content of that speech or assembly. • As long as such restrictions are narrowly tailored to achieve a legitimate governmental interest, they do not violate the First Amendment. — Also written *time, place, or manner restriction.* — Also termed *time-place-and-manner restriction.* See PUBLIC FORUM.

time policy. See INSURANCE POLICY.

time-price differential. 1. A figure representing the difference between the current cash price of an item and the total cost of purchasing it on credit. **2.** The difference between a seller's price for immediate cash payment and a different price when payment is made later or in installments.

time-sharing, *n.* Joint ownership or rental of property (such as a vacation condominium) by several persons who take turns occupying the property. — Also termed *time-share.* — **time-share,** *vb.*

timesheet. An attorney's daily record of billable and nonbillable hours, used to generate clients' bills. See BILLABLE HOUR.

time unity. See *unity of time* under UNITY.

time value. The price associated with the length of time that an investor must wait until an investment matures or the related income is earned. Cf. YIELD TO MATURITY.

timocracy (tɪ-**mok**-rə-see). **1.** An aristocracy of property; government by propertied, relatively rich people. **2.** A government in which the rulers' primary motive is the love of honor.

tin parachute. An employment-contract provision that grants a corporate employee (esp. one below the executive level) severance benefits in the event of a takeover. • These benefits are typically less lucrative than those provided under a golden parachute. — Also termed *silver parachute.* Cf. GOLDEN PARACHUTE.

tip, *n.* **1.** A piece of special information; esp., in securities law, advance or inside information passed from one person to another. See INSIDE INFORMATION; INSIDER TRADING. **2.** A gratuity for service given. • Tip income is taxable. IRC (26 USCA) § 61(a).

tippee. *Securities.* A person who acquires material nonpublic information from someone in a fiduciary relationship with the company to which that information pertains.

tipper. *Securities.* A person who possesses material inside information and who selectively discloses that information for trading or other personal purposes <the tippee traded 5,000 shares after her conversation with the tipper>.

tippling house. See *public house* under HOUSE.

tipstaff. A court crier. Pl. **tipstaves, tipstaffs.** See CRIER.

tip-stave. See SERVITOR OF BILLS.

tithe (tɪth), *n.* **1.** A tenth of one's income, esp. in reference to a religious or charitable gift. **2.** *Hist.* A small tax or assessment, esp. in the amount of one-tenth. — **tithe,** *vb.*

great tithe. (*usu. pl.*) A tithe paid in kind and therefore considered more valuable than other tithes. • The great tithes often consisted of corn, peas, beans, hay, and wood.

mixed tithes. Tithes consisting of natural products, such as milk or wool, obtained or cultivated by human effort.

> "A second species of incorporeal hereditaments is that of tithes . . . the first species being usually called *predial*, as of corn, grass, hops, and wood; the second *mixed*, as of wool, milk, pigs, etc., consisting of natural products, but nurtured and preserved in part by the care of man; and of these the tenth must be paid in gross: the third *personal*, as of manual occupations, trades, fisheries, and the like; and of these only the tenth part of the clear gains and profits is due." 2 William Blackstone, *Commentaries on the Laws of England* 24 (1766).

vicarial tithe (vI-**kair**-ee-əl). A small tithe payable to a vicar.

tithe of agistment (ə-**jist**-mənt). *Hist.* A church-levied charge on grazing land. • The tithe was paid by the occupier of the land rather than the person whose cattle grazed on the land. See AGISTMENT.

tithing. See DECENNARY.

title. 1. The union of all elements (as ownership, possession, and custody) constituting the legal right to control and dispose of property; the legal link between a person who owns property and the property itself <no one has title to that land>. **2.** Legal evidence of a person's ownership rights in property; an instrument (such as a deed) that constitutes such evidence .

absolute title. An exclusive title to land; a title that excludes all others not compatible with it. See *fee simple absolute* under FEE SIMPLE.

adverse title. A title acquired by adverse possession. See ADVERSE POSSESSION.

after-acquired title. Title held by a person who bought property from a seller who acquired title only after purporting to sell the property to the buyer. See AFTER-ACQUIRED TITLE DOCTRINE.

bad title. **1.** See *defective title.* **2.** See *unmarketable title.*

clear title. **1.** A title free from any encumbrances, burdens, or other limitations. **2.** See *marketable title.* — Also termed *good title.*

defeasible title. A title voidable on the occurrence of a contingency, but not void on its face.

defective title. A title that cannot legally convey the property to which it applies, usu. because of some conflicting claim to that property. — Also termed *bad title.*

derivative title. **1.** A title that results when an already existing right is transferred to a new owner. **2.** The general principle that a transferee of property acquires only the rights held by the transferor and no more.

dormant title. A title in real property held in abeyance.

doubtful title. A title that exposes the party holding it to the risk of litigation with an adverse claimant. See *unmarketable title.*

equitable title. A title that indicates a beneficial interest in property and that gives the holder the right to acquire formal legal title. Cf. *legal title.*

good title. **1.** A title that is legally valid or effective. **2.** See *clear title* (1). **3.** See *marketable title.*

imperfect title. A title that requires a further exercise of the granting power to pass land in fee, or that does not convey full and absolute dominion.

Indian title. See INDIAN TITLE.

just title. In a case of prescription, a title that the possessor received from someone whom the possessor honestly believed to be the real owner, provided that the title was to transfer ownership of the property.

legal title. A title that evidences apparent ownership but does not necessarily signify full and complete title or a beneficial interest. Cf. *equitable title.*

lucrative title. *Civil law.* A title acquired without giving anything in exchange for the property; title by which a person acquires anything that comes as a clear gain, as by gift, descent, or devise. • Because lucrative title is usu. acquired by gift or inheritance, it is treated as the separate property of a married person. Cf. *onerous title.*

marketable title. A title that a reasonable buyer would accept because it appears to lack any defect and to cover the entire property that the seller has purported to sell. — Also termed *merchantable title*; *clear title*; *good title.*

nonmerchantable title. See *unmarketable title.*

onerous title (**on**-ər-əs). **1.** *Civil law.* A title acquired by giving valuable consideration for the property, as by paying money or performing services. **2.** A title to property that is acquired during marriage through a spouse's skill or labor and is therefore treated as community property. Cf. *lucrative title.*

original title. A title that creates a right for the first time.

> "The catching of fish is an original title of the right of ownership, whereas the purchase of them is a derivative title. The right acquired by the fisherman is newly created; it did not formerly exist in any one." John Salmond, *Jurisprudence* 345 (Glanville L. Williams ed., 10th ed. 1947).

paramount title. **1.** *Archaic.* A title that is the source of the current title; original title. **2.** A title that is superior to another title or claim on the same property.

particular title. *Civil law.* A title acquired from an ancestor by purchase, gift, or inheritance before or after the ancestor's death.

perfect title. **1.** FEE SIMPLE. **2.** A grant of land that requires no further act from the legal authority to constitute an absolute title to the land. **3.** A title that does not disclose a patent defect that may require a lawsuit to defend it. **4.** A title that is good both at law and in equity. **5.** A title that is good and valid beyond all reasonable doubt.

presumptive title. A title of the lowest order, arising out of the mere occupation or simple possession of property without any apparent right, or any pretense of right, to hold and continue that possession.

record title. A title as it appears in the public records after the deed is properly recorded. — Also termed *title of record*; *paper title.*

singular title. The title by which one acquires property as a singular successor.

tax title. A title to land purchased at a tax sale.

title by descent. A title that one acquires by law as an heir of the deceased owner.

title by devise. A title created by will.

title by prescription. A title acquired by prescription. See PRESCRIPTION (2).

title defective in form. A title for which some defect appears on the face of the deed. • Title defective in form cannot be the basis of prescription.

title of entry. The right to enter upon lands.

title of record. See *record title.*

universal title. A title acquired by a conveyance causa mortis of a stated portion of all the conveyor's property interests so that on the conveyor's death the recipient stands as a universal successor.

unmarketable title. A title that a reasonable buyer would refuse to accept because of possible conflicting interests in or litigation over the property. — Also termed *bad title*; *unmerchantable title*; *nonmerchantable title.*

3. The heading of a statute or other legal document <the title of the contract was "Confidentiality Agreement">.

long title. The full, formal title of a statute, usu. containing a brief statement of legislative purpose.

short title. The abbreviated title of a statute by which it is popularly known; a statutory nickname.

4. A subdivision of a statute or code <Title IX>. **5.** An appellation of office, dignity, or distinction <after the election, he bore the title of mayor for the next four years>.

title, abstract of. See ABSTRACT OF TITLE.

title, action to quiet. See *action to quiet title* under ACTION.

title, chain of. See CHAIN OF TITLE.

title, cloud on. See CLOUD ON TITLE.

title, color of. See COLOR OF TITLE (1).

title, covenant for. See *covenant for title* under COVENANT (4).

title, document of. See DOCUMENT OF TITLE.

title, indicia of. See INDICIA OF TITLE.

title, muniment of. See MUNIMENT OF TITLE.

title, root of. See ROOT OF TITLE.

title, warranty of. See *warranty of title* under WARRANTY (2).

Title VII of the Civil Rights Act of 1964. A federal law that prohibits employment discrimination and harassment on the basis of race, sex, pregnancy, religion, and national origin, as well as prohibiting retaliation against an employee who opposes illegal harassment or discrimination in the workplace. • This term is often referred to simply as Title VII. 42 USCA §§ 2000e et seq.

Title IX of the Educational Amendments of 1972. A federal statute generally prohibiting sex discrimination and harassment by educational facilities that receive federal funds. • This term is often referred to simply as Title IX. 20 USCA §§ 1681 et seq.

title by descent. See TITLE (2).

title by devise. See TITLE (2).

title by prescription. See TITLE (2).

title company. See COMPANY.

title deed. See DEED.

title defective in form. See TITLE (2).

title-guaranty company. See *title company* under COMPANY.

title insurance. See INSURANCE.

title jurisdiction. See TITLE THEORY.

title member. See *name partner* under PARTNER.

title of entry. See TITLE (2).

title of record. See *record title* under TITLE (2).

title of right. A court-issued decree creating, transferring, or extinguishing rights. • Examples include a decree of divorce or judicial separation, an adjudication of bankruptcy, a discharge in bankruptcy, a decree of foreclosure against a mortgagor, an order appointing or removing a trustee, and a grant of letters of administration. In all the examples listed, the judgment operates not as a remedy but as a title of right.

title opinion. See OPINION (2).

title registration. A system of registering title to land with a public registry, such as a county clerk's office. See TORRENS SYSTEM.

title retention. A form of lien, in the nature of a chattel mortgage, to secure payment of a loan given to purchase the secured item.

title search. An examination of the public records to determine whether any defects or encumbrances exist in a given property's chain of title. • A title search is typically conducted by a title company or a real-estate lawyer at a prospective buyer's or mortgagee's request.

title standards. Criteria by which a real-estate title can be evaluated to determine whether it is defective or marketable. • Many states, through associations of conveyancers and real-estate attorneys, have adopted title standards.

title state. See TITLE THEORY.

title theory. *Property law.* The idea that a mortgage transfers legal title of the property to the mortgagee, who retains it until the mortgage has been satisfied or foreclosed. • Only a few American states — known as *title states, title jurisdictions,* or *title-theory jurisdictions* — have adopted this theory. Cf. LIEN THEORY.

title transaction. A transaction that affects title to an interest in land.

title unity. See *unity of title* under UNITY.

T-note. *abbr.* TREASURY NOTE.

to-have-and-to-hold clause. See HABENDUM CLAUSE.

token, *n.* **1.** A sign or mark; a tangible evidence of the existence of a fact. **2.** A sign or indication of an intention to do something, as when a buyer places a small order with a vendor to show good faith with a view toward later placing a larger order.

toll, *n.* **1.** A sum of money paid for the use of something; esp., the consideration paid to use a public road, highway, or bridge. **2.** A charge for a long-distance telephone call.

toll, *vb.* **1.** To annul or take away <toll a right of entry>. **2.** (Of a time period, esp. a statutory one) to stop the running of; to abate <toll the limitations period>.

tollage (**toh**-lij). **1.** Payment of a toll. **2.** Money charged or paid as a toll. **3.** The liberty or franchise of charging a toll.

tolling agreement. An agreement between a potential plaintiff and a potential defendant by which the defendant agrees to extend the statutory limitations period on the plaintiff's claim, usu. so that both parties will have more time to resolve their dispute without litigation.

tolling statute. A law that interrupts the running of a statute of limitations in certain situations, as when the defendant cannot be served with process in the forum jurisdiction.

tolt (tohlt). *Hist.* A writ for removing a case pending in a court baron to a county court. — Also termed *writ of tolt.*

> "Where the disputed interest in the land was not a fee held of the king in chief but a fee held of a 'mesne lord' the writ was directed to him bidding him do full right between the parties in the matter of the land in question under pain of the case being removed from his court to the sheriff's court if he failed to do justice. This removal was effected (if necessary) by the process known as 'tolt' under which a sheriff on a complaint to him in his county court of a failure of the lord to do justice ordered his bailiff to attend the lord's court and take away the

plaint into the county court." Geoffrey Radcliffe & Geoffrey Cross, *The English Legal System* 38 (G.J. Hand & D.J. Bentley eds., 6th ed. 1977).

tombstone. *Securities.* An advertisement (esp. in a newspaper) for a public securities offering, describing the security and identifying the sellers. • The term gets its name from the ad's traditional black border and plain print. — Also termed *tombstone advertisement*; *tombstone ad.* Cf. PROSPECTUS.

ton. A measure of weight fixed at either 2,000 pounds avoirdupois or 20 hundredweights, each hundredweight being 112 pounds avoirdupois.

long ton. Twenty long hundredweight (2,240 pounds), or 1.016 metric tons.

short ton. Twenty short hundredweight (2,000 pounds), or 0.907 metric tons.

ton mile. In transportation, a measure equal to the transportation of one ton of freight one mile.

tonnage (**tən**-ij). **1.** The capacity of a vessel for carrying freight or other loads, calculated in tons. **2.** The total shipping tonnage of a country or port. **3.** TONNAGE DUTY.

tonnage duty. A charge or impost for bringing a ship into port, usu. assessed on the basis of the ship's weight. • U.S. Const. art. I, § 10, cl. 3 prohibits the states from levying tonnage duties. — Also termed *tonnage tax*; *tonnage.* See DUTY (4).

tonnage-rent. A rent reserved by a mining lease or similar transaction, consisting of a royalty on every ton of minerals extracted from the mine.

tonnage tax. See TONNAGE DUTY.

tonsure. *Hist.* The shaving of a person's (usu. a cleric's) head. • Serjeants-at-law supposedly wore coifs to conceal their shaved heads.

tontine (**ton**-teen *or* ton-**teen**), *n.* **1.** A financial arrangement in which a group of participants share in the arrangement's advantages until all but one has died or defaulted, at which time the whole goes to that survivor. **2.** A financial arrangement in which an entire sum goes to the contributing participants still alive and not in default at the end of a specified period.

tontine policy. See INSURANCE POLICY.

top-hat plan. See PENSION PLAN.

top lease. See LEASE.

top management. See MANAGEMENT.

topographical survey. See SURVEY.

torpedo doctrine. See ATTRACTIVE-NUISANCE DOCTRINE.

Torrens system (**tor**-ənz *or* **tahr**-ənz). A system for establishing title to real estate in which a claimant first acquires an abstract of title and then applies to a court for the issuance of a title certificate, which serves as conclusive evidence of ownership. • This system — named after Sir Robert Torrens, a 19th-century reformer of Australian land laws — has been adopted in the United States by several counties with large metropolitan areas. — Also termed *Torrens title system.*

tort (tort). **1.** A civil wrong for which a remedy may be obtained, usu. in the form of damages; a breach of a duty that the law imposes on everyone in the same relation to one another as those involved in a given transaction. **2.** (*pl.*) The branch of law dealing with such wrongs.

"To ask concerning any occurrence 'Is this a crime or is it a tort?' is — to borrow Sir James Stephen's apt illustration — no wiser than it would be to ask concerning a man 'Is he a father or a son?' For he may well be both." J.W. Cecil Turner, *Kenny's Outlines of Criminal Law* 543 (16th ed. 1952).

"We may . . . define a tort as a civil wrong for which the remedy is a common-law action for unliquidated damages, and which is not exclusively the breach of a contract or the breach of a trust or other merely equitable obligation." R.F.V. Heuston, *Salmond on the Law of Torts* 13 (17th ed. 1977).

"It might be possible to define a tort by enumerating the things that it is not. It is not crime, it is not breach of contract, it is not necessarily concerned with property rights or problems of government, but is the occupant of a large residuary field remaining if these are taken out of the law. But this again is illusory, and the conception of a sort of legal garbage-can to hold what can be put nowhere else is of no help. In the first place, tort is a field which pervades the entire law, and is so interlocked at every point with property, contract and other accepted classifications that, as the student of law soon discovers, the categories are quite arbitrary. In the second, there is a central theme, or basis or idea, running through the cases of what are called torts, which, although difficult to put into words, does distinguish them in greater or less degree from other types of cases." W. Page Keeton et al., *The Law of Torts* § 1, at 2–3 (5th ed. 1984).

constitutional tort. A violation of one's constitutional rights by a government officer, redressable by a civil action filed directly against the officer. • A constitutional tort committed under color of state law (such as a civil-rights violation) is actionable under 42 USCA § 1983.

dignatory tort (**dig**-nə-tor-ee). A tort involving injury to one's reputation or honor. • In the few jurisdictions in which courts use the phrase *dignatory tort* (such as Maine), defamation is commonly cited as an example.

government tort. A tort committed by the government through an employee, agent, or instrumentality under its control. • The tort may or may not be actionable, depending on whether the government is entitled to sovereign immunity. A tort action against the U.S. government is regulated by the Federal Tort Claims Act, while a state action is governed by the state's tort claims act. See FEDERAL TORT CLAIMS ACT; *sovereign immunity* under IMMUNITY (1).

intentional tort. A tort committed by someone acting with general or specific intent. • Examples include battery, false imprisonment, and trespass to land. — Also termed *willful tort.* Cf. NEGLIGENCE.

maritime tort. A tort committed on navigable waters. See JONES ACT.

mass tort. A civil wrong that injures many people. • Examples include toxic emissions from a factory, the crash of a commercial airliner, and contamination from an industrial-waste-disposal site. Cf. *toxic tort.*

negligent tort. A tort committed by failure to observe the standard of care required by law under the circumstances. See NEGLIGENCE.

personal tort. A tort involving or consisting in an injury to one's person, reputation, or feelings, as distinguished from an injury or damage to real or personal property.

prenatal tort. **1.** A tort committed against a fetus. • If born alive, a child can sue for injuries resulting from tortious conduct predating the child's birth. **2.** Loosely, any of several torts relating to reproduction, such as those giving rise to wrongful-birth actions, wrongful-life actions, and wrongful-pregnancy actions.

prima facie tort (**prī**-mə **fay**-shee-ee *or* -shee *or* -shə). An unjustified, intentional infliction of harm on another person, resulting in damages, by one or more acts that would otherwise be lawful. • Some jurisdictions have established this tort to provide a remedy for malicious deeds — esp. in business and trade contexts — that are not actionable under traditional tort law.

property tort. A tort involving damage to property.

public tort. A minor breach of the law (such as a parking violation) that, although it carries a criminal punishment, is considered a civil offense rather than a criminal one because it is merely a prohibited act (*malum prohibitum*) and not inherently reprehensible conduct (*malum in se*). — Also termed *civil offense.* Cf. *civil wrong* under WRONG; *public delict* under DELICT.

quasi-tort. A wrong for which a nonperpetrator is held responsible; a tort for which one who did not directly commit it can nonetheless be found liable, as when a master is held liable for a tort committed by a servant. — Also spelled *quasi tort.* See *vicarious liability* under LIABILITY; RESPONDEAT SUPERIOR.

sanctions tort. See SANCTIONS TORT.

toxic tort. A civil wrong arising from exposure to a toxic substance, such as asbestos, radiation, or hazardous waste. • A toxic tort can be remedied by a civil lawsuit (usu. a class action) or by administrative action. Cf. *mass tort.*

willful tort. See *intentional tort.*

tortfeasor (**tort**-fee-zər). One who commits a tort; a wrongdoer.

concurrent tortfeasors. Two or more tortfeasors whose simultaneous actions cause injury to a third party. • Such tortfeasors are jointly and severally liable.

consecutive tortfeasors. Two or more tortfeasors whose actions, while occurring at different times, combine to cause a single injury to a third party. • Such tortfeasors are jointly and severally liable.

joint tortfeasors. Two or more tortfeasors who contributed to the claimant's injury and who may be joined as defendants in the same lawsuit. See *joint and several liability* under LIABILITY.

successive tortfeasors. Two or more tortfeasors whose negligence occurs at different times and causes different injuries to the same third party.

tortious (**tor**-shəs), *adj.* **1.** Constituting a tort; wrongful <tortious conduct>. **2.** In the nature of a tort <tortious cause of action>.

tortious battery. See BATTERY (2).

tortious interference with contractual relations. A third party's intentional inducement of a contracting party to break a contract, causing damage to the relationship between the contracting parties. — Also termed *unlawful interference with contractual relations*; *interference with a contractual relationship*; *inducement of breach of contract*; *procurement of breach of contract*.

tortious interference with prospective advantage. An intentional, damaging intrusion on another's potential business relationship, such as the opportunity of obtaining customers or employment. — Also termed *interference with a business relationship*.

tort reform. A movement to reduce the amount of tort litigation, usu. involving legislation that restricts tort remedies or that caps damages awards (esp. for punitive damages). • Advocates of tort reform argue that it lowers insurance and healthcare costs and prevents windfalls, while opponents contend that it denies plaintiffs the recovery they deserve for their injuries.

torture, *n.* The infliction of intense pain to the body or mind to punish, to extract a confession or information, or to obtain sadistic pleasure. — **torture,** *vb.*

total, *adj.* **1.** Whole; not divided; full; complete. **2.** Utter; absolute.

total assignment. See ASSIGNMENT (2).

total breach. See BREACH OF CONTRACT.

total disability. See DISABILITY (1).

total-disability insurance. See *general-disability insurance* under INSURANCE.

total eviction. See EVICTION.

total failure of consideration. See FAILURE OF CONSIDERATION.

total incorporation. See INCORPORATION.

totality-of-the-circumstances test. *Criminal procedure.* A standard for determining whether hearsay (such as an informant's tip) is sufficiently reliable to establish probable cause for an arrest or search warrant. • Under this test — which replaced *Aguilar–Spinelli*'s two-pronged approach — the reliability of the hearsay is weighed by focusing on the entire situation as described in the probable-cause affidavit, and not on any one specific factor. *Illinois v. Gates*, 462 U.S. 213, 103 S.Ct. 2317 (1983). Cf. AGUILAR–SPINELLI TEST.

total loss. See LOSS.

total repudiation. See REPUDIATION.

Totten trust. See TRUST.

touch, *vb. Marine insurance.* To stop at a port, usu. for a brief period.

touch and stay. *Marine insurance.* An insurer's giving to the insured the right to stop and remain at certain designated points in the course of the voyage. • A vessel that has the power to touch and stay at a place must confine itself strictly to the terms of the permission given, and any deviation during a stay — for example, by shipping or landing goods — will discharge the underwriters, unless the vessel has permission to trade as well as to touch and stay.

tout court (too **koor**), *adv.* [French "simply, without qualification"] Very briefly; without explanation.

towage (**toh**-ij), n. **1.** The act or service of towing ships and vessels, usu. by means of a small vessel called a *tug*. **2.** The charge for such a service.

toward, *adj.* **1.** In the direction of; on a course or line leading to (some place or something). **2.** Coming soon; not long before.

to wit (too **wit**), *adv. Archaic.* That is to say; namely <the district attorney amended the complaint to include embezzlement, to wit, "stealing money that the company had entrusted to the accused">. — Sometimes spelled *to-wit*; *towit*.

town. 1. A center of population that is larger and more fully developed than a village, but that (traditionally speaking) is not incorporated as a city. **2.** The territory within which this population lives. **3.** Collectively, the people who live within this territory. Cf. CITY.

> "A town is a precinct anciently containing ten families, whereupon in some countries they are called tithings, within one of which tithings every man must be dwelling, and find sureties for his good behaviour, else he that taketh him into his house is to be amerced in the leet." Sir Henry Finch, *Law, or a Discourse Thereof* 80 (1759).

town-bonding act. A law authorizing a town, county, or other municipal corporation to issue its corporate bonds for the purpose of aiding in construction, often of railroads. — Also termed *town-bonding law*.

town clerk. An officer who keeps the records, issues calls for town meetings, and performs the duties of a secretary to the town's political organization.

town collector. A town officer charged with collecting the taxes assessed by a town.

town commissioner. A member of the board of administrative officers charged with managing the town's business.

town crier. *Hist.* A town officer responsible for making proclamations related to town business.

town hall. A building that houses the offices of a town's government.

townhouse. A dwelling unit having usu. two or three stories and often connected to a similar structure by a common wall and (particularly in a planned-unit development) sharing and owning in common the surrounding grounds. — Also termed *townhome*.

town meeting. 1. A legal meeting of a town's qualified voters for the administration of local government or the enactment of legislation. • Town meetings of this type are common in some New England states. **2.** More generally, any assembly of a town's citizens for the purpose of discussing political, economic, or social issues. **3.** Modernly, a televised event in which one or more politicians meet and talk with representative citizens about current issues.

town order. An official written direction by the auditing officers of a town, directing the treasurer to pay a sum of money. — Also termed *town warrant*.

town purpose. A municipal project or expenditure that concerns the welfare and advantage of the town as a whole.

township. 1. In a government survey, a square tract six miles on each side, containing thirty-six square miles of land. **2.** In some states, a civil and political subdivision of a county.

township trustee. One of a board of officers to whom, in some states, a township's affairs are entrusted.

townsite. A portion of the public domain segregated by proper authority and procedure as the site for a town.

town treasurer. An officer responsible for maintaining and disbursing town funds.

town warrant. See TOWN ORDER.

toxic, *adj.* Having the character or producing the effects of a poison; produced by or resulting from a poison; poisonous. — Also termed *toxical*.

toxicant (**tok**-si-kənt), *n.* A poison; a toxic agent; any substance capable of producing toxication or poisoning.

toxicate, *vb. Archaic.* To poison. See INTOXICATION.

toxicology (tok-si-**kol**-ə-jee). The branch of medicine that concerns poisons, their effects, their recognition, their antidotes, and generally the diagnosis and therapeutics of poisoning; the science of poisons. — **toxicological** (tok-si-kə-**loj**-i-kəl), *adj.*

toxic tort. See TORT.

toxic waste. See WASTE (2).

toxin, *n.* **1.** Broadly, any poison or toxicant. **2.** As used in pathology and medical jurisprudence, any diffusible alkaloidal substance — such as the ptomaines, abrin, brucin, or serpent venoms — and esp. the poisonous products of disease-producing bacteria.

traces. See *retrospectant evidence* under EVIDENCE.

tracing, *n.* **1.** The process of tracking property's ownership or characteristics from the time of its origin to the present. **2.** SKIPTRACING. **3.** A mechanical copy or facsimile of an original, produced by following its lines with a pen or pencil through a transparent medium. — **trace,** *vb.*

tract. A specified parcel of land <a 40-acre tract>.

tract index. See INDEX (1).

trade, *n.* **1.** The business of buying and selling or bartering goods or services; COMMERCE.

inland trade. Trade wholly carried on within a country, as distinguished from foreign commerce.

precarious trade. Int'l law. Trade by a neutral country between two belligerent powers, allowed to exist at the latter's sufferance.

2. A transaction or swap. **3.** A business or industry occupation; a craft or profession. — **trade,** *vb.*

trade acceptance. See ACCEPTANCE (4).

trade agreement. 1. An agreement — such as the North American Free Trade Agreement — between two or more nations concerning the buying and selling of each nation's goods. **2.** See COLLECTIVE-BARGAINING AGREEMENT.

trade and commerce. Every business occupation carried on for subsistence or profit and involving the elements of bargain and sale, barter, exchange, or traffic.

trade association. See ASSOCIATION.

trade deficit. See DEFICIT.

trade discount. See DISCOUNT.

trade dispute. 1. A dispute between two countries arising from tariff rates or other matters related to international commerce. **2.** A dispute between an employer and employees over pay, working conditions, or other employment-related matters. • An employee who leaves during a trade dispute is not entitled to benefits under the Unemployment Insurance Act.

trade dress. The overall appearance and image in the marketplace of a product or a commercial enterprise. • For a product, trade dress typically comprises packaging and labeling. For an enterprise, it typically comprises design and decor. If a trade dress is distinctive and nonfunctional, it may be protected under trademark law.

trade embargo. See EMBARGO (3).

trade fixture. See FIXTURE.

trade gap. See *trade deficit* under DEFICIT.

trade libel. A false statement that disparages the quality or reputation of another's product or business. See DISPARAGEMENT.

trademark, *n.* **1.** A word, phrase, logo, or other graphic symbol used by a manufacturer or seller to distinguish its product or products from those of others. • The main purpose of a trademark is to guarantee a product's genuineness. In effect, the trademark is the commercial substitute for one's signature. To receive federal protection, a trademark must be (1) distinctive rather than merely descriptive, (2) affixed to a product that is actually sold in the marketplace, and (3) registered with the U.S. Patent and Trademark Office. In its broadest sense, the term *trademark* includes a servicemark. — Often shortened to *mark.* Cf. SERVICEMARK. **2.** The body of law dealing with how businesses distinctively identify their products. See LANHAM ACT.

> "The protection of trade-marks is the law's recognition of the psychological function of symbols. If it is true that we live by symbols, it is no less true that we purchase goods by them. A trade-mark is a merchandising shortcut which induces a purchaser to select what he wants, or what he has been led to believe he wants. The owner of a mark exploits this human propensity by making every effort to impregnate the atmosphere of the market with the drawing power of a congenial symbol. Whatever the means employed, the aim is the same — to convey through the mark, in the minds of potential customers, the desirability of the commodity upon which it appears. Once this is attained, the trade-mark owner has something of value. If another poaches upon the commercial magnetism of the symbol he has created, the owner can obtain legal redress." *Mishawaka Rubber & Woolen Mfg. Co. v. S.S. Kresge Co.*, 316 U.S. 203, 205, 62 S.Ct. 1022, 1024 (1942) (Frankfurter, J.).

> "A trademark functions on three different levels: as an indication of origin or ownership, as a guarantee of constancy of the quality or other characteristics of a product or service, and as a medium of advertisement. Thus, a trademark guarantees, identifies, and sells the product or service to which it refers. These three facets of a trademark — of differing importance at different times, in different lines of business and for different products or services — are somewhat correlative. The classical function, that of identification, has been primarily responsible for molding the development of trademark law. The significance of the guarantee function has been somewhat exaggerated, while the implications of the advertisement function still await full recognition in the law." 3 Rudolf Callmann, *The Law of Unfair Competition, Trademarks and Monopolies* § 17.01, at 2 (4th ed. 1998).

arbitrary trademark. A trademark containing common words that do not describe or suggest any characteristic of the product to which the trademark is assigned. — Also termed *arbitrary mark.*

certification trademark. See CERTIFICATION TRADEMARK.

collective trademark. See COLLECTIVE MARK.

descriptive trademark. See DESCRIPTIVE MARK.

fanciful trademark. A trademark consisting of a made-up or coined word; a distinctive trademark or tradename having no independent meaning. • This type of mark is considered inherently distinctive and thus protected at common law, and is eligible for trademark registration from the time of its first use. — Also termed *fanciful mark*; *fanciful term*; *coined term*.

> "Arbitrary or fanciful marks convey nothing about the nature of the product except through knowledge of the market. For instance, Kodak conveys nothing about photographic equipment except to those knowledgeable about that trade." Arthur R. Miller & Michael H. Davis, *Intellectual Property in a Nutshell* 168 (2d ed. 1990).

geographically descriptive trademark. A trademark that uses a geographic name to indicate where the goods are grown or manufactured. • This type of mark is protected at common law, and can be registered only on proof that it has acquired distinctiveness over time. See SECONDARY MEANING.

registered trademark. A trademark that has been filed and recorded with the Patent and Trademark Office. • A federally registered trademark is usu. marked by the symbol "®" so that the trademark owner can collect treble damages or the defendant's profits for an infringement. If the symbol is not used, the owner can still collect these damages or profits by proving that the defendant actually knew that the mark was registered.

strong trademark. An inherently distinctive trademark that is used — usu. by the owner only — in a fictitious, arbitrary, and fanciful manner, and is therefore given greater protection than a weak mark under the trademark laws.

suggestive trademark. A trademark that suggests rather than describes the particular characteristics of a product, thus requiring a consumer to use imagination to draw a conclusion about the nature of the product. • A suggestive trademark is entitled to protection without proof of secondary meaning. See SECONDARY MEANING.

weak trademark. A trademark that is a meaningful word in common usage or that merely describes or suggests a product. • This type of trademark is entitled to protection only if it has acquired distinctiveness over time. See SECONDARY MEANING.

trademark infringement. See INFRINGEMENT.

trade meaning. See SECONDARY MEANING.

tradename. **1.** A name, style, or symbol used to distinguish a company, partnership, or business (as opposed to a product or service); the name under which a business operates. • A tradename is a means of identifying a business — or its products or services — to establish goodwill. It symbolizes the business's reputation. **2.** A trademark that was not originally susceptible to exclusive appropriation but has acquired a secondary meaning. — Also termed *commercial name*.

trade or business. *Tax.* Any business or professional activity conducted by a taxpayer with the objective of earning a profit. • If the taxpayer can show that the primary purpose and intention is to make a profit, the taxpayer may deduct certain expenses as trade-or-business expenses under the Internal Revenue Code.

trader. **1.** A merchant; a retailer; one who buys goods to sell them at a profit. **2.** One who sells goods substantially in the form in which they are bought; one who has not converted them into another form of property by skill and labor. **3.** One who, as a member of a stock exchange, buys and sells securities on the exchange floor either for brokers or on his or her own account. **4.** One who buys and sells commodities and commodity futures for others or for his or her own account in anticipation of a speculative profit.

trade secret. **1.** A formula, process, device, or other business information that is kept confidential to maintain an advantage over competitors; information — including a formula, pattern, compilation, program, device, method, technique, or process — that (1) derives independent economic value, actual or potential, from not being generally known or readily ascertainable by others who can obtain economic value from its disclosure or use, and (2) is the subject of reasonable efforts, under the circumstances, to maintain its secrecy. • This definition states the majority view, which is found in the Uniform Trade Secrets Act.

> "The concept of protecting trade secrets is related to the principles of trademark and patent law. The scope of trade secret protection, however, goes well beyond that of patent law. Unlike patent law, protection under trade secret law is not tied to the information's novelty; rath-

er, the essence of a trade secret is its relative secrecy. Additionally, unlike patent law, trade secret law draws less from property principles, and more from the equitable principles surrounding confidential relationships." Mark A. Rothstein et al., *Employment Law* § 8.18, at 516 (1994).

"The difficulty with defining 'trade secrets' in the abstract is that there are so many ways to go about it. In large part, this is a reflection of the fact that the law of trade secrets, unlike the law of patents or copyright, is a creature of the common law rather than of statute. In trying to impose a moral solution on cases of apparent breach of confidence, judges have juggled competing policy interests while trying to draw a line of protection that would lead to the result that they believed was right.... In other words, the development of trade secret law has been a bit chaotic ...." James Pooley, *Trade Secrets* § 1.01, at 1–1 to 1–3 (1998).

2. Information that (1) is not generally known or ascertainable, (2) provides a competitive advantage, (3) has been developed at the plaintiff's expense and is used continuously in the plaintiff's business, and (4) is the subject of the plaintiff's intent to keep it confidential. • This definition states the minority view, which is found in the Restatement of Torts § 757 cmt. b (1939).

trade surplus. See SURPLUS.

trade union. See UNION.

trade usage. See USAGE.

trading. The business of buying and selling, esp. of commodities and securities.

day trading. The act or practice of buying and selling stock shares or other securities on the same day, esp. over the Internet, usu. for the purpose of making a quick profit on the difference between the buying price and the selling price.

secondary trading. The buying and selling of securities in the market between members of the public, involving neither the issuer nor the underwriter of the securities.

trading corporation. See CORPORATION.

trading partnership. See PARTNERSHIP.

trading voyage. See VOYAGE.

trading with the enemy. The federal offense of carrying on commerce with a nation or with a subject or ally of a nation with which the United States is at war.

traditio brevi manu (trə-**dish**-ee-oh **bree**-vɪ **man**-yoo). [Latin] *Roman law.* The surrender of the mediate possession of a thing to the person who is already in immediate possession of it. • This is a type of constructive delivery in which a delivery to the mediate possessor and redelivery to the immediate possessor are unnecessary. For the other two types of constructive delivery, see ATTORNMENT; CONSTITUTUM POSSESSORIUM.

"The first [type of constructive delivery] is that which the Roman lawyers termed *traditio brevi manu*, but which has no recognised name in the language of English law.... If, for example, I lend a book to someone, and afterwards, while he still retains it, I agree with him to sell it to him, or to make him a present of it, I can effectually deliver it to him in fulfilment of this sale or gift, by telling him that he may keep it. It is not necessary for him to go through the form of handing it back to me and receiving it a second time from my hands." John Salmond, *Jurisprudence* 306 (Glanville L. Williams ed., 10th ed. 1947).

tradition. 1. Past customs and usages that influence or govern present acts or practices. **2.** The delivery of an item or an estate.

traditional public forum. See PUBLIC FORUM.

traditionary evidence. See EVIDENCE.

traduce (trə-**d[y]oos**), *vb.* To slander; calumniate. — **traducement,** *n.*

traffic, *n.* **1.** Commerce; trade; the sale or exchange of such things as merchandise, bills, and money. **2.** The passing or exchange of goods or commodities from one person to another for an equivalent in goods or money. **3.** People or things being transported along a route. **4.** The passing to and fro of people, animals, vehicles, and vessels along a transportation route.

traffic, *vb.* To trade or deal in (goods, esp. illicit drugs or other contraband) <trafficking in heroin>.

traffic balance. The balance of moneys collected in payment for transporting passengers and freight.

traffic regulation. A prescribed rule of conduct for traffic; a rule intended to promote the orderly and safe flow of traffic.

traitor, *n.* **1.** A person who commits treason against his or her country. **2.** One who betrays a person, a cause, or an obligation. — **traitorous,** *adj*.

tramp, *n*. A person who roams about from place to place, begging or living without labor or visible means of support; a vagrant.

tramp corporation. See CORPORATION.

tramp steamer. A ship that is not scheduled to sail between prearranged ports of call but that stops at those ports for which it has cargo.

tranche (transh), *n*. [French "slice"] *Securities*. **1.** A bond issue derived from a pooling of similar debt obligations. • A tranche usu. differs from other issues by maturity date or rate of return. **2.** A block of bonds designated for sale in a foreign country. — Also spelled *tranch*; *trench*. See COLLATERALIZED MORTGAGE OBLIGATION.

transact, *vb*. **1.** To carry on or conduct (negotiations, business, etc.) to a conclusion <transact business>. **2.** *Civil law*. To settle (a dispute) by mutual concession. See TRANSACTION (4). **3.** To carry on or conduct negotiations or business <refuses to transact with the enemy>.

transaction, *n*. **1.** The act or an instance of conducting business or other dealings. **2.** Something performed or carried out; a business agreement or exchange. **3.** Any activity involving two or more persons. **4.** *Civil law*. An agreement that is intended by the parties to prevent or end a dispute and in which they make reciprocal concessions. — **transactional,** *adj*.

closed transaction. *Tax*. A transaction in which an amount realized on a sale can be established for the purpose of stating a gain or loss.

colorable transaction. A sham transaction having the appearance of authenticity; a pretended transaction <the court set aside the colorable transaction>.

transactional immunity. See IMMUNITY (3).

transactional lawyer. See LAWYER.

transaction causation. See CAUSATION.

transaction cost. See COST (1).

transaction-or-occurrence test. A test used to determine whether, under Fed. R. Civ. P. 13(a), a particular claim is a compulsory counterclaim. • Four different tests have been suggested: (1) Are the legal and factual issues raised by the claim and counterclaim largely the same? (2) Would res judicata bar a later suit on the counterclaim in the absence of the compulsory-counterclaim rule? (3) Will substantially the same evidence support or refute both the plaintiff's claim and the counterclaim? (4) Are the claim and counterclaim logically related? See *compulsory counterclaim* under COUNTERCLAIM.

transaction slip. See CONFIRMATION SLIP.

transcribe, *vb*. To make a written or typed copy of (spoken material, esp. testimony).

transcript, *n*. A handwritten, printed, or typed copy of testimony given orally; esp., the official record of proceedings in a trial or hearing, as taken down by a court reporter. — Also termed *report of proceedings*; *reporter's record*.

transcription. 1. The act or process of transcribing. **2.** Something transcribed; a transcript.

transcript of proceedings. A compilation of all documents relating to a bond issue, typically including the notices, affidavits of notices, a bond resolution (or bond ordinance), official statement, trust indenture and loan agreements, and minutes of meetings of all authorizing bodies.

transeunt cum universitate (**tran**-see-ənt kəm yoo-ni-vər-sə-**tay**-tee). [Latin] *Hist*. They are transferred with the whole estate.

transfer, *n*. **1.** Any mode of disposing of or parting with an asset or an interest in an asset, including the payment of money, release, lease, or creation of a lien or other encumbrance. • The term embraces every method — direct or indirect, absolute or conditional, voluntary or involuntary — of disposing of or parting with property or with an interest in property, including retention of title as a security interest and foreclosure of the debtor's equity of redemption. **2.** Negotiation of an instrument according to the forms of law. • The four methods of transfer are by indorsement, by delivery, by assignment, and by operation of law. **3.** A conveyance of property or title from one person to another.

constructive transfer. A delivery of an item — esp. a controlled substance — by someone other than the owner but at the owner's direction.

incomplete transfer. *Tax.* A decedent's inter vivos transfer that is not completed for federal estate-tax purposes because the decedent retains significant powers over the property's possession or enjoyment. • Because the transfer is incomplete, some or all of the property's value will be included in the transferor's gross estate. IRC (26 USCA) §§ 2036–2038.

inter vivos transfer (**in**-tər **vI**-vohs *or* -**vee**-vohs). A transfer of property made during the transferor's lifetime.

transfer in contemplation of death. See *gift causa mortis* under GIFT.

transfer in fraud of creditors. A conveyance of property made in an attempt to prevent the transferor's creditors from making a claim to it.

transfer, *vb.* **1.** To convey or remove from one place or one person to another; to pass or hand over from one to another, esp. to change over the possession or control of. **2.** To sell or give.

transferable (trans-**fər**-ə-bəl), *adj.* Capable of being transferred, together with all rights of the original holder.

transferable letter of credit. See LETTER OF CREDIT.

transfer agent. See AGENT.

transferee. One to whom a property interest is conveyed.

transferee liability. *Tax.* The liability of a transferee to pay taxes owed by the transferor. • This liability is limited to the value of the asset transferred. The Internal Revenue Service can, for example, force a donee to pay the gift tax when the donor who made the transfer cannot pay it. IRC (26 USCA) §§ 6901–6905.

transfer in contemplation of death. See *gift causa mortis* under GIFT.

transfer in fraud of creditors. See TRANSFER.

transfer of a case. The removal of a case from the jurisdiction of one court or judge to another by lawful authority. — Also termed *transfer of a cause.* See REMOVAL (2).

transfer of venue. See CHANGE OF VENUE.

transferor. One who conveys an interest in property.

transfer payment. (*usu. pl.*) A governmental payment to a person who has neither provided goods or services nor invested money in exchange for the payment. • Examples include unemployment compensation and welfare payments.

transfer price. See PRICE.

transferred intent. See INTENT (1).

transferred-intent doctrine. The rule that if one person intends to harm a second person but instead unintentionally harms a third, the first person's criminal or tortious intent toward the second applies to the third as well. • Thus, the offender may be prosecuted for an intent crime or sued by the third person for an intentional tort. See INTENT.

transferred malice. See MALICE.

Transfers to Minors Act. See UNIFORM TRANSFERS TO MINORS ACT.

transfer tax. See TAX.

transfer warranty. See WARRANTY (2).

transgression. *Archaic.* See MISDEMEANOR.

transgressione, ad audiendum et terminandum (trans-gres[h]-ee-**oh**-nee, ad aw-dee-**en**-dəm et tər-mə-**nan**-dəm). See DE TRANSGRESSIONE, AD AUDIENDUM ET TERMINANDUM.

transgressive trust. See TRUST.

transient (**tran**-shənt), *adj.* Temporary; impermanent; passing away after a short time.

transient, *n.* A person or thing whose presence is temporary or fleeting.

transient foreigner. One who visits a country without the intent to remain.

transient jurisdiction. See JURISDICTION.

transient merchant. A trader who sells merchandise at a temporary location without intending to become a permanent merchant in that place.

transient person. One who has no legal residence within a jurisdiction for the purpose of a state venue statute.

transit, *n.* **1.** The transportation of goods or persons from one place to another. **2.** Passage; the act of passing.

transitive covenant. See COVENANT (1).

transitory (**tran**-sə-tor-ee *or* **tran**-zə-), *adj.* That passes from place to place; capable of passing or being changed from one place to another.

transitory action. See ACTION.

transitory wrong. See WRONG.

transit passage. *Int'l law.* The right of a vessel or airplane to exercise freedom of navigation and overflight solely for the purpose of continuous and expeditious transit between one part of the high seas or an exclusive economic zone and another part of the high seas or an exclusive economic zone. — Also termed *right of transit passage.* Cf. INNOCENT PASSAGE.

translation, *n.* **1.** The reproduction in one language of a book, document, or speech into another language. **2.** *Archaic.* The transfer of property. **3.** *Eccles. law.* The removal of a bishop from one diocese to another.

translative (trans- *or* tranz-**lay**-tiv), *adj.* Making or causing a transfer or conveyance.

translative fact. See FACT.

transmission. *Civil law.* The passing of an inheritance to an heir.

transmit, *vb.* **1.** To send or transfer (a thing) from one person or place to another. **2.** To communicate.

transmittal letter. A nonsubstantive letter that establishes a record of delivery, such as a letter to a court clerk advising that a particular pleading is enclosed for filing. • Lawyers have traditionally opened transmittal letters with the phrase "Enclosed please find," even though that phrasing has been widely condemned in business-writing handbooks since the late 19th century. A transmittal letter may properly begin with a range of openers as informal as "Here is" to the more formal "Enclosed is." — Also termed *cover letter.*

transnational law. 1. General principles of law recognized by civilized nations. Cf. INTERNATIONAL LAW. **2.** The amalgam of common principles of domestic and international law dealing esp. with problems arising from agreements made between sovereign states and foreign private parties. **3.** The problems to which such principles apply.

transport, *vb.* To carry or convey (a thing) from one place to another.

transportation, *n.* **1.** The movement of goods or persons from one place to another by a carrier. **2.** *Criminal law.* A type of punishment that sends the criminal out of the country to another place (usu. a penal colony) for a specified period. Cf. DEPORTATION.

transshipment. *Maritime law.* The act of taking cargo out of one ship and loading it on another. — **transship,** *vb.*

trap, *n.* **1.** A device for capturing animals, such as a pitfall, snare, or machine that shuts suddenly. **2.** Any device or contrivance by which one may be caught unawares; stratagem; snare. **3.** *Torts.* An ultrahazardous hidden peril of which the property owner or occupier, but not a licensee, has knowledge. • A trap can exist even if it was not designed or intended to catch or entrap anything.

trashing. DECONSTRUCTION.

travaux préparatoires (tra-**voh** pray-par-ə-**twah**[**r**]**z**). [French "preparatory works"] Materials used in preparing the ultimate form of an agreement or statute, and esp. of an international treaty; materials constituting a legislative history. See LEGISLATIVE HISTORY.

travel-accident insurance. See INSURANCE.

Travel Act. A federal law that prohibits travel in interstate or foreign commerce to further unlawful gambling, prostitution, extortion, bribery, or arson, as well as illegal transactions involving liquor or narcotics. 18 USCA § 1952.

traveled place. A place where the public has, in some manner, acquired the legal right to travel.

traveler, *n.* A person who passes from place to place, for any reason.

traveler's check. See CHECK.

traveler's letter of credit. See LETTER OF CREDIT.

travel expense. See EXPENSE.

traverse (**trav**-ərs), *n. Common-law pleading.* A formal denial of a factual allegation made in the opposing party's pleading <Smith filed a traverse to Allen's complaint, asserting that he did not knowingly provide false information>. — **traverse** (**trav**-ərs *or* trə-**vərs**), *vb.* See DENIAL.

> "It is said that the technical term *traverse*, from *transverto*, to turn over, is applied to an issue taken upon an indictment for a misdemeanor, and means nothing more than turning over or putting off the trial to a following session or assize; and that thus it is that the officer of the court asks the party whether he is ready to try then, or will *traverse* to the next session; though some have referred its meaning originally to the denying or taking issue upon an indictment, without reference to the delay of trial, and which seems more correct." 1 Joseph Chitty, *A Practical Treatise on the Criminal Law* 486 (2d ed. 1826).

common traverse. A traverse consisting of a tender of issue — that is, a denial accompanied by a formal offer for decision of the point denied — with a denial that expressly contradicts the terms of the allegation traversed. — Also termed *specific traverse*.

> "The common or specific traverse is an express denial of a particular allegation in the opposing pleading in the terms of the allegation, accompanied by a tender of issue or formal offer of the point denied for trial." Benjamin J. Shipman, *Handbook of Common-Law Pleading* § 168, at 303 (Henry Winthrop Ballantine ed., 3d ed. 1923).

cumulative traverse. A traverse that analyzes a proposition into its constituent parts and traverses them cumulatively. • It amounts to the same thing as traversing the one entire proposition, since the several parts traversed must all make up one entire proposition or point.

general traverse. A denial of all the facts in an opponent's pleading.

special traverse. A denial of one material fact in an opponent's pleading; a traverse that explains or qualifies the denial. • The essential parts of a special traverse are an inducement, a denial, and a verification.

specific traverse. See *common traverse*.

traverse jury. See *petit jury* under JURY.

traverser, *n.* One who traverses or denies a pleading.

treachery, *n.* A deliberate and willful betrayal of trust and confidence.

treason, *n.* The offense of attempting to overthrow the government of the state to which one owes allegiance, either by making war against the state or by materially supporting its enemies. — Also termed *high treason*; *alta proditio*. — **treasonable, treasonous,** *adj.* Cf. SEDITION.

> "The judgment of *high treason* was, until very lately, an exception to the merciful tenor of our judgments. The least offensive form which is given in the books is, that the offender 'be carried back to the place from whence he came, and from thence to be drawn to the place of execution, and be there hanged by the neck, and cut down alive, and that his entrails be taken out and burned before his face, and his head cut off, and his body divided into four quarters, and his head and quarters disposed of at the king's pleasure.' Some of the precedents add other circumstances, of still more grossness and aggravation. But this horrible denunciation was very seldom executed in its more terrible niceties." 1 Joseph Chitty, *A Practical Treatise on the Criminal Law* 702 (2d ed. 1826).

petty treason. *Archaic.* Murder of one's employer or husband. • Until 1828, this act was considered treason under English law. — Also spelled *petit treason*.

> "The frequent reference to *high* treason is a carry-over from an ancient division of the offense that has long since disappeared. In the feudal stage of history the relation of lord to vassal was quite similar to the relation of king to subject. The relation of husband to wife came to be regarded in the same category, as also did the relation of master to servant, and that of prelate to clergyman. And just as it was *high* treason to kill the king, so a malicious homicide was *petit* treason if it involved a killing of (originally, lord by vassal, and later) husband by wife, master by mistress or servant, or prelate by clergyman. When the special brutality provided by the common law for the punishment of petit treason disappeared, this crime became merged with murder and only one crime of treason remained." Rollin M. Perkins & Ronald N. Boyce, *Criminal Law* 498–99 (3d ed. 1982).

treasonable misdemeanor. *English law.* An act that is likely to endanger or alarm the monarch, or disturb the public peace in the presence of the monarch. Cf. TREASON FELONY.

treason felony. *English law.* An act that shows an intention of committing treason, unaccompanied by any further act to carry out that intention. • This offense usu. results in life imprisonment rather than the death penalty. Cf. TREASONABLE MISDEMEANOR.

Treas. Reg. *abbr.* TREASURY REGULATION.

treasurer. A corporate or governmental officer who receives, maintains custody of, invests, and disburses funds.

treasure trove. [Law French "treasure found"] Valuables (usu. gold or silver) found hidden in the ground or other private place, the owner of which is unknown. • At common law, the finder of a treasure trove was entitled to title against all except the true owner.

> "Treasure hid in the earth, not upon the earth, nor in the sea, and coin though not hidden, being found is the king's; we call it treasure trove." Sir Henry Finch, *Law, or a Discourse Thereof* 177 (1759).

> "Treasure trove consists essentially of articles of gold and silver, intentionally hidden for safety in the earth or in some secret place, the owner being unknown, although it is probable that the category might include articles made from the required metals buried in the ground for other purposes, for example in connection with an ancient sepulture. In the United States, the state has never claimed title to lost property by virtue of its character as treasure trove, and it has been stated that the law relating thereto is merged with that of lost goods generally, although there is authority for the proposition that while treasure trove in the United States belongs to the finder, found goods not of that character go to the owner of the *locus in quo*." Ray Andrews Brown, *The Law of Personal Property* § 13, at 27–28 (2d ed. 1955).

Treasuries. Debt obligations of the federal government backed by the full faith and credit of the government. See TREASURY BILL; TREASURY BOND; TREASURY CERTIFICATE; TREASURY NOTE.

treasury. 1. A place or building in which stores of wealth are kept; esp., a place where public revenues are deposited and kept and from which money is disbursed to defray government expenses. **2.** (*cap.*) TREASURY DEPARTMENT.

Treasury, First Lord. See FIRST LORD OF THE TREASURY.

Treasury Bench. In the British House of Commons, the first row of seats on the right hand of the speaker. • The Treasury Bench is occupied by the First Lord of the Treasury or principal minister of the Crown.

Treasury bill. A short-term debt security issued by the federal government, with a maturity of 13, 26, or 52 weeks. • These bills — auctioned weekly or quarterly — pay interest in the form of the difference between their discounted purchase price and their par value at maturity. — Abbr. T-bill.

Treasury bond. A long-term debt security issued by the federal government, with a maturity of 10 to 30 years. • These bonds are considered risk-free, but they usu. pay relatively little interest. — Abbr. T-bond.

treasury certificate. An obligation of the federal government maturing in one year and on which interest is paid on a coupon basis.

Treasury Department. A federal department — created by Congress in 1789 — whose duties include formulating and recommending financial, tax, and fiscal policies, serving as the federal government's financial agent, and manufacturing coins and currency.

Treasury note. An intermediate-term debt security issued by the federal government, with a maturity of two to ten years. • These notes are considered risk-free, but they usu. pay relatively little interest. — Abbr. T-note.

Treasury Regulation. A regulation promulgated by the U.S. Treasury Department to explain or interpret a section of the Internal Revenue Code. • Treasury Regulations are binding on all taxpayers. — Abbr. Treas. Reg.

treasury security. See *treasury stock* under STOCK.

treasury share. See *treasury stock* under STOCK.

treasury stock. See STOCK.

treasury warrant. See WARRANT (2).

treating-physician rule. The principle that a treating physician's diagnoses and findings about the degree of a social-security claimant's impairment are binding on an administrative-law judge in the absence of substantial contrary evidence.

treaty. 1. A formally signed and ratified agreement between two nations or sovereigns; an international agreement concluded between two or more states in written form and governed by international law. • A treaty is not only the law in each state but also a contract between the signatories. — Also termed *accord*; *convention*; *covenant*; *declaration*; *pact*. Cf. EXECUTIVE AGREEMENT.

commercial treaty. A bilateral or multilateral treaty concerning trade or other mercantile activities. • Such a treaty may be general in nature, as by supplying the framework of long-term commercial relations. Or it may be specific, as by detailing the conditions of particular branches of trade or other commercial transactions. Sometimes a treaty of this kind deals with an individual project, such as a guaranty agreement.

dispositive treaty (dis-**poz**-ə-tiv). A treaty by which a country takes over territory by impressing a special character on it, creating something analogous to a servitude or easement in private law.

guaranty treaty. An agreement between countries directly or indirectly establishing a unilateral or reciprocal guarantee. — Also termed *quasi-guarantee treaty*; *pseudo-guarantee treaty*.

> "In many instances where the term 'guarantee' is used in international treaties, the contracting parties merely intend to underline their willingness to comply with the obligation they have entered into. Obligations of this kind do not fall within the concept of guarantee in the proper sense of the term. In this particular respect, the expression 'pseudo-guarantees' or 'quasi-guarantee treaties' is used." George Ress, "Guarantee Treaties," in 2 *Encyclopedia of Public International Law* 634 (1995).

nonproliferation treaty. A treaty forbidding the transfer of nuclear weapons from a country with a nuclear arsenal to one that does not have nuclear-weapons capability. • The first such treaty was reached in 1968, and now more than 100 nations have agreed to its terms. — Also termed *nuclear-nonproliferation treaty*.

peace treaty. A treaty signed by heads of state to end a war. — Also termed *treaty of peace*.

pseudo-guarantee treaty. See *guaranty treaty*.

quasi-guarantee treaty. See *guaranty treaty*.

2. A contract or agreement between insurers providing for treaty reinsurance. See *treaty reinsurance* under REINSURANCE.

Treaty Clause. The constitutional provision giving the President the power to make treaties, with the advice and consent of the Senate. U.S. Const. art. II, § 2.

treaty-created law. See CONVENTIONAL LAW.

treaty-made law. See CONVENTIONAL LAW.

treaty of peace. See *peace treaty* under TREATY.

treaty of reinsurance. See REINSURANCE TREATY.

treaty power. The President's constitutional authority to make treaties, with the advice and consent of the Senate. See TREATY CLAUSE.

treaty reinsurance. See REINSURANCE.

treble damages. See DAMAGES.

trebucket (**tree**-bək-it). See CASTIGATORY.

trend. A long-term price pattern in the stock market generally or in a particular stock.

major trend. A long-term trend of the stock market; a general increase or decrease of stock prices over an extended period. — Also termed *fundamental trend*.

market trend. The direction of stock-market prices over a several-month period.

trespass (**tres**-pəs *or* **tres**-pas), *n.* **1.** An unlawful act committed against the person or property of another; esp., wrongful entry on another's real property. **2.** At common law, a legal action for injuries resulting from an unlawful act of this kind. **3.** *Archaic.* MISDEMEANOR. — **trespass,** *vb.* — **trespassory** (**tres**-pə-sor-ee), *adj.*

> "The term trespass has been used by lawyers and laymen in three senses of varying degrees of generality. (1) In its widest and original signification it includes any wrongful act — any infringement or transgression of the rule of right. This use is common in the Authorised Version of the Bible, and was presumably familiar when that version was first published. But it never obtained recognition in the technical language of the law, and is now archaic even in popular speech. (2) In a second and narrower signification — its true legal sense — the term means any legal wrong for which the appropriate remedy was a writ of trespass — *viz.* any direct and forcible injury to person, land, or chattels. (3) The third and narrowest meaning of the term is that in which, in accordance with popular speech, it is limited to one particular kind of trespass in the second sense — *viz.* the tort of trespass to land (trespass *quare clausum fregit*)." R.F.V. Heuston, *Salmond on the Law of Torts* 4 (17th ed. 1977).

> "Before the word 'misdemeanor' became well established the old writers tended to use the word 'trespass' to indicate an offense below the grade of felony. And it was used at times by Blackstone for this purpose, as in the phrase 'treason, felony, or trespass.' " Rollin M. Perkins & Ronald N. Boyce, *Criminal Law* 405 (3d ed. 1982).

continuing trespass. A trespass in the nature of a permanent invasion on another's rights, such as a sign that overhangs another's property.

criminal trespass. **1.** A trespass on property that is clearly marked against trespass by signs or fences. **2.** A trespass in which the trespasser remains on the property after being ordered off by a person authorized to do so.

innocent trespass. A trespass committed either unintentionally or in good faith.

joint trespass. A trespass that two or more persons have united in committing, or that some have actually committed while others commanded, encouraged, or directed it.

permanent trespass. A trespass consisting of a series of acts, done on consecutive days, that are of the same nature and that are renewed or continued from day to day, so that the acts in the aggregate form one indivisible harm.

trespass ab initio (ab i-**nish**-ee-oh). An entry on land that, though begun innocently or with a privilege, is deemed a trespass from the beginning because of conduct that abuses the privilege.

trespass by relation. A trespass committed when the plaintiff had a right to immediate possession of land but had not yet exercised that right. • When the plaintiff takes possession, a legal fiction treats the plaintiff as having had possession ever since the accrual of the right of entry. This is known as *trespass by relation* because the plaintiff's possession relates back to the time when the plaintiff first acquired a right to possession.

trespass de bonis asportatis (dee **boh**-nis as-pər-**tay**-tis). [Latin "trespass for carrying goods away"] **1.** A wrongful taking of chattels. • This type of trespassory taking was also an element of common-law larceny. **2.** At common law, an action to recover damages for the wrongful taking of chattels. — Often shortened to *trespass de bonis*. — Also termed *trespass to personal property*.

trespass on the case. At common law, an action to recover damages that are not the immediate result of a wrongful act but rather a later consequence. • This action was the precursor to a variety of modern-day tort claims, including negligence, nuisance, and business torts. — Often shortened to *case*. — Also termed *action on the case*; *breve de transgressione super casum*.

> "The most important of the writs framed under the authority of the statute of Westminster 2 is that of 'trespass on the case,' to meet cases analogous to trespass in delict, but lacking the element of direct or immediate force or violence. This writ gave a form of action in which the court was enabled to render judgment of damages in cases of fraud, deceit, negligence, want of skill, defamation oral or written, and all other injurious acts or omissions resulting in harm to person or property, but wanting the *vi et armis*, the element of direct force and violence, to constitute trespass." Edwin E. Bryant, *The Law of Pleading Under the Codes of Civil Procedure* 7 (2d ed. 1899).

> "Common law recognizes a distinction between the actions of trespass vi et armis (or simply trespass) and trespass on the case. This distinction has been expressed by stating that a tort committed by the direct application of force is remediable by an action for trespass, while a tort accomplished indirectly is a matter for trespass on the case. Other authority makes the distinction on the basis of the defendant's intent, stating that trespass involves a willful and deliberate act while trespass on the case contemplates an act or omission resulting from negligence." 1 Am. Jur. 2d *Actions* § 23, at 738 (1994).

trespass quare clausum fregit (**kwair**-ee-**klaw**-zəm-**free**-jit). [Latin "why he broke the close"] **1.** A person's unlawful entry on another's land that is visibly enclosed. • This tort consists of doing any of the following without lawful justification: (1) entering upon land in the possession of another, (2) remaining on the land, or (3) placing or projecting any object upon it. **2.** At common law, an action to recover damages resulting from another's unlawful entry on one's land that is visibly enclosed. — Also termed *trespass to real property*; *trespass to land*; *quare clausum querentis fregit*. See *trespass vi et armis*.

> "Every unwarrantable entry on another's soil the law entitles a trespass by *breaking his close*; the words of the writ of trespass commanding the defendant to shew cause, *quare clausum querentis fregit*. For every man's land is in the eye of the law enclosed and set apart from his neighbour's: and that either by a visible and material fence, as one field is divided from another by a hedge; or, by an ideal invisible boundary, existing only in the contemplation of law, as when one man's land adjoins to another's in the same field. And every such entry or breach of a man's close carries necessarily along with it some damage or other: for, if no other special loss can be assigned, yet still the words of the writ itself specify one general damage, viz. the treading down and bruising his herbage." 3 William Blackstone, *Commentaries on the Laws of England* 209–10 (1768).

trespass to chattels. The act of committing, without lawful justification, any act of direct physical interference with a chattel possessed by another. • The act must amount to a direct forcible injury.

trespass to land. See *trespass quare clausum fregit* (2).

trespass to personal property. See *trespass de bonis asportatis*.

trespass to real property. See *trespass quare clausum fregit* (2).

trespass to try title. **1.** In some states, an action for the recovery of property unlawfully withheld from an owner who has the immediate right to possession. **2.** A procedure under which a claim to title may be adjudicated.

trespass vi et armis (**vI** et **ahr**-mis). [Latin "with force and arms"] **1.** At common law, an action for damages resulting from an intentional injury to person or property, esp. if by violent means; trespass to the plaintiff's person, as in illegal assault, battery, wounding, or imprisonment, when not under color of legal process, or when the battery, wounding, or imprisonment was in the first instance lawful, but unnecessary violence was used or the imprisonment continued after the process had ceased to be lawful. • This action also lay for injury to relative rights, such as menacing tenants or servants, beating and wounding a spouse, criminal conversation with or seducing a wife, or debauching a daughter or servant. **2.** See *trespass quare clausum fregit*. • In this sense, the "force" is implied by the "breaking" of the close (that is, an enclosed area), even if no real force is used.

trespass ab initio. See TRESPASS.

trespass by relation. See TRESPASS.

trespass de bonis asportatis. See TRESPASS.

trespasser. One who commits a trespass; one who intentionally and without consent or privilege enters another's property. • In tort law, a landholder owes no duty to unforeseeable trespassers. Cf. INVITEE; LICENSEE (2).

> "The word 'trespasser' has an ugly sound, but it covers the wicked and the innocent. The burglar and the arrogant squatter are trespassers, but so are all sorts of comparatively innocent and respectable persons such as a walker in the countryside who unhindered strolls across an open field. Perhaps much of the trouble in this area has arisen from 'the simplistic stereotype' of the definition. The courts are therefore beginning to recognise that the duty of the occupier may vary according to the nature of the trespasser." R.F.V. Heuston, *Salmond on the Law of Torts* 278 (17th ed. 1977).

innocent trespasser. One who enters another's land unlawfully, but either inadvertently or believing in a right to do so.

trespass for mesne profits. *Hist.* An action — supplementing an action for ejectment — brought against a tenant in possession to recover the profits wrongfully received during the tenant's occupation.

trespass on the case. See TRESPASS.

trespass quare clausum fregit. See TRESPASS.

trespass to chattels. See TRESPASS.

trespass to land. See *trespass quare clausum fregit* under TRESPASS.

trespass to personal property. See *trespass de bonis asportatis* under TRESPASS.

trespass to real property. See *trespass quare clausum fregit* under TRESPASS.

trespass to try title. See TRESPASS.

trespass vi et armis. See TRESPASS.

tret (tret), *n.* An allowance or abatement of a certain weight or quantity that a seller makes to a buyer because of water or dust that may be mixed with a commodity. Cf. TARE.

triable, *adj.* Subject or liable to judicial examination and trial <a triable offense>.

triable either way. *English law.* (Of an offense) prosecutable either in the Crown Court or in a magistrates' court.

> "The criminal courts in England and Wales are the magistrates' courts and the Crown Court. Those offences considered least serious are summary offences, triable only in the magistrates' courts. Those offences considered most serious are triable only on indictment, in the Crown Court. A large number of offences, such as theft and most burglaries, are 'triable either way,' in a magistrates' court or the Crown Court. For these offences the defendant can elect to be tried at the Crown Court, where there is a judge and jury. If the defendant does not wish a Crown Court trial, the magistrates may decide (having heard representations from the prosecutor) that the case is so serious that it should be committed to the Crown Court for trial." Andrew Ashworth, *Principles of Criminal Law* 16 (1991).

trial. A formal judicial examination of evidence and determination of legal claims in an adversary proceeding.

bench trial. A trial before a judge without a jury. • The judge decides questions of fact as well as questions of law. — Also termed *trial to the bench*; *nonjury trial*; *trial before the court* (abbr. TBC); *judge trial*.

bifurcated trial. A trial that is divided into two stages, such as for guilt and punishment or for liability and damages. — Also termed *two-stage trial*. Cf. SEVERANCE (2).

fair trial. See FAIR TRIAL.

joint trial. A trial involving two or more parties; esp., a criminal trial of two or more persons for the same or similar offenses.

judge trial. See *bench trial*.

jury trial. A trial in which the factual issues are determined by a jury, not by the judge. — Also termed *trial by jury*.

mock trial. See MOCK TRIAL.

nonjury trial. See *bench trial*.

political trial. A trial (esp. a criminal prosecution) in which either the prosecution or the defendant (or both) uses the proceedings as a platform to espouse a particular political belief; a trial of a person for a political crime. See SHOW TRIAL.

separate trial. **1.** *Criminal procedure*. The individual trial of each of several persons jointly accused of a crime. Fed. R. Crim. P. 14. **2.** *Civil procedure*. Within a single action, a distinct trial of a separate claim or issue — or of a group of claims or issues — ordered by the trial judge, usu. to conserve resources or avoid prejudice. Fed. R. Civ. P. 42(b). Cf. SEVERANCE.

show trial. See SHOW TRIAL.

speedy trial. See SPEEDY TRIAL.

state trial. A trial for a political offense.

summary jury trial. A settlement technique in which the parties argue before a mock jury, which then reaches a nonbinding verdict that will assist the parties in evaluating their positions.

trial at bar. *Hist*. A trial before all the judges of the court in which the proceedings take place. — Also termed *trial at the bar*.

trial at nisi prius (**nI**-sI **prI**-əs). *Hist*. A trial before the justices of assize and nisi prius in the county where the facts are alleged to have occurred, and from which county the jurors have been summoned.

trial before the court. See *bench trial*.

trial by battle. See TRIAL BY COMBAT.

trial by certificate. *Hist*. A trial in which the issue is decided on evidence in the form of witnesses' certificates of what they individually know.

trial by combat. See TRIAL BY COMBAT.

trial by inspection. *Hist*. A trial in which the judge decided the dispute by individual observation and investigation, without the benefit of a jury.

trial by jury. See *jury trial*.

trial by ordeal. See ORDEAL.

trial by record. *Hist*. A trial in which, a record having been pleaded by one party and denied by the other, the record is inspected in order to decide the dispute, no other evidence being admissible. See NUL TIEL RECORD.

trial by the country. See *trial per pais*.

trial per pais (pər **pay** *or* **pays**). [Law French "trial by the country"] Trial by jury. — Also termed *trial by the country*. Cf. CONCLUSION TO THE COUNTRY; GOING TO THE COUNTRY; PATRIA (3).

trial to the bench. See *bench trial*.

trifurcated trial. A trial that is divided into three stages, such as for liability, general damages, and special damages.

two-stage trial. See *bifurcated trial*.

trial at bar. See TRIAL.

trial at nisi prius. See TRIAL.

trial before the court. See *bench trial* under TRIAL.

trial brief. Counsel's written submission, usu. just before trial, outlining the legal issues before the court and arguing one side's position.

trial by certificate. See TRIAL.

trial by combat. *Hist*. A trial that is decided by personal battle between the disputants, common in Europe and England during the Middle Ages; specif., a trial in which the person accused fought with the accuser, the idea being that God would give victory to the person in the right. • This method was introduced into England by the Normans after 1066, but it was a widely detested innovation and was little used. It became obsolete several centuries before being formally abolished in 1818, having been replaced in practice by the grand assize and indictment. — Also termed *trial by battle*; *trial by wager of battle*; *judicial combat*; *duel*; *duellum*; *wager of battle*; *ornest*; *vadiatio duelli*; *wehading*. See JUDICIUM DEI.

trial by inspection. See TRIAL.

trial by jury. See *jury trial* under TRIAL.

trial by oath. See COMPURGATION.

trial by ordeal. See ORDEAL.

trial by record. See TRIAL.

trial by the country. See *trial per pais* under TRIAL.

trial by the record. A trial in which one party insists that a record exists to support its claim and the opposing party denies the existence of such a record. • If the record can be produced, the court will consider it in reaching a verdict — otherwise, it will rule for the opponent.

trial by wager of battle. *Hist.* See TRIAL BY COMBAT.

trial calendar. See DOCKET (2).

trial counsel. See COUNSEL.

trial court. See COURT.

trial de novo (dee *or* di **noh**-voh). A new trial on the entire case — that is, on both questions of fact and issues of law — conducted as if there had been no trial in the first instance.

trial examiner. See ADMINISTRATIVE-LAW JUDGE.

trial franchise. See FRANCHISE (4).

trial judge. See JUDGE.

trial jury. See *petit jury* under JURY.

trial on the merits. A trial on the substantive issues of a case, as opposed to a motion hearing or interlocutory matter.

trial per pais. See TRIAL.

trial-setting preference. See *special setting* under SETTING.

trial to the bench. See *bench trial* under TRIAL.

trial-type hearing. See ADMINISTRATIVE PROCEEDING.

triangular merger. See MERGER.

tribal land. A part of an Indian reservation that is not allotted to or occupied by individual Indians but is held as the common land of the tribe. Cf. INDIAN LAND.

tribunal (trI-**byoo**-nəl). **1.** A court or other adjudicatory body. **2.** The seat, bench, or place where a judge sits.

tributary (**trib**-yə-ter-ee), *n.* A stream flowing directly or indirectly into a river.

tribute (**trib**-yoot), *n.* **1.** An acknowledgment of gratitude or respect. **2.** A contribution that a sovereign raises from its subjects to defray the expenses of state. **3.** Money paid by an inferior sovereign or state to a superior one to secure the latter's friendship and protection.

tributum (tri-**byoo**-təm). [Latin] *Roman law.* Originally, a war tax; later, a regular tax on land or persons.

trier of fact. See FACT-FINDER.

trifurcated trial. See TRIAL.

trigamy (**trig**-ə-mee), *n.* The act of marrying a person while legally married to someone else and bigamously married to yet another.

> "Trigamy, literally three marriages, is often used for a special situation. 'Trigamy,' in the sense of the special problem of the third wife, stems from the premise that invalidity of the alleged prior marriage is a good defense to a charge of bigamy. Thus in a bigamy prosecution a so-called common-law marriage can be relied upon to establish either the first or second marriage, if it is recognized in the jurisdiction as giving rise to the marital status, but cannot be relied upon where it is not so recognized. A logical result is that a charge of bigamy may be defeated by showing that the alleged prior marriage, relied upon to support the charge, was itself void because of an even earlier marriage existing at the time — as was held about 1648 in Lady Madison's Case. For example, **D** marries **A**, and afterward while **A** is alive marries **B**, and still later when **A** is dead but **B** alive, marries **C**. The marriage to **C** is not bigamy because the marriage to **B** was bigamous and void." Rollin M. Perkins & Ronald N. Boyce, *Criminal Law* 458 (3d ed. 1982).

tripartite (trI-**pahr**-tIt), *adj.* Involving, composed of, or divided into three parts or elements <a tripartite agreement>.

triple damages. See *treble damages* under DAMAGES.

triple net lease. See *net-net-net lease* under LEASE.

triple trigger. *Insurance.* A theory of coverage providing that all insurers on a risk from the day a claimant is first exposed to an injury-producing product (such as asbestos) — beyond the last exposure — to the date of diagnosis or death, whichever occurs first, must cover the loss. — Also termed *continuous trigger*. Cf. ACTUAL-INJURY TRIGGER; EXPOSURE THEORY; MANIFESTATION THEORY.

tristis successio (**tris**-tis sək-**ses**[**h**]-ee-oh). See *hereditas luctuosa* under HEREDITAS.

triverbial days (trɪ-**vər**-bee-əl). See *dies fasti* under DIES.

trivial, *adj.* Trifling; inconsiderable; of small worth or importance.

TRO (tee-ahr-**oh**). *abbr.* TEMPORARY RESTRAINING ORDER.

trover (**troh**-vər). A common-law action for the recovery of damages for the conversion of personal property, the damages generally being measured by the value of the property. — Also termed *trover and conversion.* Cf. DETINUE; REPLEVIN.

> "Trover may be maintained for all kinds of personal property, including legal documents, but not where articles are severed from land by an adverse possessor, at least until recovery of possession of the land. It lies for the misappropriation of specific money, but not for breach of an obligation to pay where there is no duty to return specific money." Benjamin J. Shipman, *Handbook of Common-Law Pleading* § 43, at 99 (Henry Winthrop Ballantine ed., 3d ed. 1923).

truancy (**troo**-ən-see), *n.* The act or state of shirking responsibility; esp., willful and unjustified failure to attend school by one who is required to attend. — **truant,** *adj.* & *n.*

truancy officer. An official responsible for enforcing laws mandating school attendance for minors of specified ages (usu. 16 and under). — Also termed *truant officer*; *attendance officer.*

truce. *Int'l law.* A suspension or temporary cessation of hostilities by agreement between belligerent powers. — Also termed *armistice*; *ceasefire*; *suspension of arms.*

true admission. See *judicial admission* under ADMISSION.

true and correct. Authentic; accurate; unaltered <we have forwarded a true and correct copy of the expert's report>. — Also termed *true and exact.*

true bill, *n.* A grand jury's notation that a criminal charge should go before a petty jury for trial <the grand jury returned a true bill, and the state prepared to prosecute>. — Also termed *billa vera.* Cf. NO BILL.

true-bill, *vb.* To make or deliver a true bill on <the grand jury true-billed the indictment>.

true copy. See COPY.

true residue. See CLEAR RESIDUE.

true value. See *fair market value* under VALUE.

true-value rule. The rule requiring that one who subscribes for and receives corporate stock must pay par value for it, in either money or its equivalent, so that a corporation's real assets square with its books. • If true value is less than par value, the stock is deemed unpaid for to the full extent of the difference, and the affected shareholder is liable to creditors for the difference, notwithstanding the directors' good faith.

true verdict. See VERDICT.

trust, *n.* **1.** The right, enforceable solely in equity, to the beneficial enjoyment of property to which another person holds the legal title; a property interest held by one person (the *trustee*) at the request of another (the *settlor*) for the benefit of a third party (the *beneficiary*). • For a trust to be valid, it must involve specific property, reflect the settlor's intent, and be created for a lawful purpose. **2.** A fiduciary relationship regarding property and subjecting the person with title to the property to equitable duties to deal with it for another's benefit; the confidence placed in a trustee, together with the trustee's obligations toward the property and the beneficiary. • A trust arises as a result of a manifestation of an intention to create it. See FIDUCIARY RELATIONSHIP. **3.** The property so held; TRUST FUND. **4.** A business combination that aims at monopoly. See ANTITRUST.

> "[A] trust involves three elements, namely, (1) a trustee, who holds the trust property and is subject to equitable duties to deal with it for the benefit of another; (2) a beneficiary, to whom the trustee owes equitable duties to deal with the trust property for his benefit; (3) trust property, which is held by the trustee for the beneficiary." Restatement (Second) of Trusts § 2 cmt. h (1959).

> "One must distinguish, ... [in] countries where English is spoken, between a wide and a narrow sense of the word 'trust.' In the wide sense a trust exists when property is to be held or administered by one person on behalf of another or for some purpose other than his own benefit.... In the narrow or strict sense a trust exists when the creator of the trust ... hands over or is bound to hand over the control of an asset which, or the proceeds of which, is to be administered by another (the trustee or administrator) in his capacity as such for the benefit of some person (beneficiary) other than the trustee or for some impersonal object. A trust in this sense is a species of the genus 'trust' in the wide sense." Tony Honoré, *The South African Law of Trusts* §§ 1–2, at 1–3 (3d ed. 1985).

"Some courts and legal writers have defined a trust as a certain kind of right that the beneficiary has against the trustee, or a certain kind of interest that the beneficiary has against the trustee, or a certain kind of interest that the beneficiary has in the trust property, thus looking at it from the point of view of the beneficiary. While it is true that the beneficiary has the right or interest described, the trust is something more than the right or interest of the beneficiary. The trust is the whole juridical device: the legal relationship between the parties with respect to the property that is its subject matter, including not merely the duties that the trustee owes to the beneficiary and to the rest of the world, but also the rights, privileges, powers, and immunities that the beneficiary has against the trustee and against the rest of the world. It would seem proper, therefore, to define the trust either as a relationship having certain characteristics stated in the definition or perhaps as a juridical device or legal institution involving such a relationship." 1 Austin W. Scott & William F. Fratcher, *The Law of Trusts* § 2.4, at 42 (4th ed. 1987).

accumulation trust. A trust in which the trustee must accumulate income and gains from sales of trust assets for ultimate disposition when the trust terminates. • Many states restrict the time over which accumulations may be made or the amount that may be accumulated.

active trust. A trust in which the trustee has some affirmative duty of management or administration besides the obligation to transfer the property to the beneficiary. — Also termed *special trust*. Cf. *passive trust*.

alimony trust. A trust in which the husband transfers to the trustee property from which the wife, as beneficiary, will be supported after a divorce or separation.

annuity trust. A trust from which the trustee must pay a sum certain annually to one or more beneficiaries for their respective lives or for a term of years, and must then either transfer the remainder to or for the use of a qualified charity or retain the remainder for such a use. • The sum certain must not be less than 5% of the initial fair market value of the property transferred to the trust by the donor. A qualified annuity trust must comply with the requirements of IRC (26 USCA) § 664.

bank-account trust. See *Totten trust*.

blended trust. A trust in which the beneficiaries are a group, with no member of the group having a separable individual interest. • Courts rarely recognize these trusts.

blind trust. A trust in which the settlor places investments under the control of an independent trustee, usu. to avoid a conflict of interest.

bond trust. A trust whose principal consists of bonds that yield interest income.

business trust. A form of business organization, similar to a corporation, in which investors receive transferable certificates of beneficial interest (instead of stock shares). — Also termed *Massachusetts trust*; *common-law trust*.

"The business trust was developed in Massachusetts from 1910 to 1925 to achieve limited liability and to avoid restrictions then existing there on a corporation's acquiring and developing real estate, by adoption of the trust device. . . ." Henry G. Henn & John R. Alexander, *Laws of Corporations* § 58, at 117 (3d ed. 1983).

bypass trust. A trust into which a decedent's estate passes, so that the surviving heirs get a life estate in the trust rather than the property itself, in order to avoid estate taxes on an estate larger than the tax-credit-sheltered amount ($650,000 in 1999, increasing to $1 million after 2005). — Also termed *credit-shelter trust*. See *unified credit* under TAX CREDIT.

charitable remainder annuity trust. A charitable-remainder trust in which the beneficiaries receive for a specified period a fixed payment of 5% or more of the fair market value of the original principal, after which the remaining principal passes to charity.

charitable-remainder trust. A trust that consists of assets that are designated for a charitable purpose and that are paid over to the trust after the expiration of a life estate or intermediate estate. — Also termed *split-interest trust*.

charitable trust. A trust created to benefit a specific charity, specific charities, or the general public rather than a private individual or entity. • Charitable trusts are often eligible for favorable tax treatment. — Also termed *public trust*; *charitable use*. See CY PRES. Cf. *private trust*.

Claflin trust. See *indestructible trust*.

Clifford trust. An irrevocable trust, set up for at least ten years and a day, whereby income from the trust property is paid to the beneficiary but the property itself reverts back to the settlor when the trust expires. • These trusts were often used by parents — with their children as beneficiaries — to shelter investment income, but the Tax Reform Act of 1986 eliminated the tax advantage by imposing the kiddie tax and by taxing the income of settlors with a reversionary interest that exceeds 5% of the trust's value. This term gets its name from *Helvering v. Clifford*, 309 U.S. 331, 60 S.Ct. 554 (1940). — Also termed *short-term trust*.

common-law trust. See *business trust.*

community trust. See COMMUNITY TRUST.

complete voluntary trust. See *executed trust.*

complex trust. **1.** A trust having elaborate provisions. **2.** See *discretionary trust.*

constructive trust. A trust imposed by a court on equitable grounds against one who has obtained property by wrongdoing, thereby preventing the wrongful holder from being unjustly enriched. • Such a trust creates no fiduciary relationship. — Also termed *implied trust*; *involuntary trust*; *trust de son tort*; *trust ex delicto*; *trust ex maleficio*; *remedial trust*; *trust in invitum.* Cf. *resulting trust.*

> "A constructive trust is the formula through which the conscience of equity finds expression. When property has been acquired in such circumstances that the holder of the legal title may not in good conscience retain the beneficial interest, equity converts him into a trustee." *Beatty v. Guggenheim Exploration Co.*, 122 N.E. 378, 380 (N.Y. 1919) (Cardozo, J.).

> "It is sometimes said that when there are sufficient grounds for imposing a constructive trust, the court 'constructs a trust.' The expression is, of course, absurd. The word 'constructive' is derived from the verb 'construe,' not from the verb 'construct.' ... The court construes the circumstances in the sense that it explains or interprets them; it does not construct them." 5 Austin W. Scott & William F. Fratcher, *The Law of Trusts* § 462.4 (4th ed. 1987).

contingent trust. An express trust depending for its operation on a future event.

credit-shelter trust. See *bypass trust.*

custodial trust. A revocable trust in which the trustee manages property in the event of the disability of the primary beneficiary, usu. intended for use by elderly property owners. • This type of trust is sometimes used as a will substitute to avoid probate in disposing of trust property when the primary beneficiary dies.

destructible trust. A trust that can be destroyed by the happening of an event or by operation of law.

directory trust. **1.** A trust that is not completely and finally settled by the instrument creating it, but only defined in its general purpose and to be carried into detail according to later specific directions. **2.** See *fixed trust.*

direct trust. See *express trust.*

discretionary trust. A trust in which the trustee alone decides whether or how to distribute the trust property or its income to the beneficiary. • The beneficiary, in other words, has no say in the matter.

donative trust. A trust requiring no payment of consideration by a beneficiary.

dry trust. **1.** A trust that merely vests legal title in a trustee and does not require that trustee to do anything. **2.** See *passive trust.*

educational trust. A trust to found, endow, or support a school.

equipment trust. See EQUIPMENT TRUST.

estate trust. A trust all or part of the income of which is to be accumulated during the surviving spouse's life and added to the trust property, with the accumulated income and trust property being paid to the estate of the surviving spouse at death. • This type of trust is commonly used to qualify property for the marital deduction.

ex delicto trust (də-**lik**-toh). A trust that is created for an illegal purpose, esp. to prevent the settlor's creditors from collecting their claims out of the trust property.

executed trust. A trust in which the estates and interests in the subject matter of the trust are completely limited and defined by the instrument creating the trust and require no further instruments to complete them. — Also termed *complete voluntary trust.*

executory trust (eg-**zek**-yə-tor-ee). A trust in which the instrument creating the trust is intended to be provisional only, and further conveyances are contemplated by the trust instrument before the terms of the trust can be carried out. — Also termed *imperfect trust.*

express active trust. An active trust created under a will that confers upon the executor authority to generally manage the estate property and pay over the net income to the devisees or legatees.

express private passive trust. A trust in which land is conveyed to or held by one person in trust for another, without any power being expressly or impliedly given to the trustee to take actual possession of the land or exercise any ownership rights over it, except at the beneficiary's direction.

express trust. A trust created with the settlor's express intent, usu. declared in writing; an ordinary trust as opposed to a resulting trust or a constructive trust. — Also termed *direct trust.*

fixed trust. A trust in which the trustee may not exercise any discretion over the trust's management or distributions. — Also termed *directory trust*; *nondiscretionary trust.*

foreign-situs trust (-**sɪ**-təs). A trust that owes its existence to foreign law. • For tax purposes, this type of trust is treated as a nonresident alien individual.

foreign trust. A trust created and administered under foreign law.

generation-skipping trust. A trust that is established to transfer (usu. principal) assets to a skip person (a beneficiary more than one generation removed from the settlor). • The transfer is often accomplished by giving some control or benefits (such as trust income) of the assets to a nonskip person, often a member of the generation between the settlor and skip person. This type of trust is subject to a generation-skipping transfer tax. IRC (26 USCA) §§ 2601 et seq. See DEEMED TRANSFEROR; GENERATION-SKIPPING TRANSFER; *generation-skipping transfer tax* under TAX; SKIP PERSON.

governmental trust. **1.** A type of charitable trust established to provide a community with facilities ordinarily supplied by the government, esp. by a municipality, and to promote purposes that are sufficiently beneficial to the community to justify permitting the property to be perpetually devoted to those purposes. • Examples of such facilities include public buildings, bridges, streets, parks, schools, and hospitals. **2.** A type of charitable trust established for general governmental or municipal purposes, such as defraying the expenses of a governmental entity or paying the public debt. Restatement (Second) of Trusts §§ 373, 374 (1959).

grantor trust. A trust in which the settlor retains control over the trust property or its income to such an extent that the settlor is taxed on the trust's income. See *Clifford trust*.

honorary trust. A trust that is legally invalid and unenforceable because it lacks a proper beneficiary. • Examples include trusts that honor dead persons, maintain cemetery plots, or benefit animals.

Illinois land trust. See *land trust*.

illusory trust. An arrangement that looks like a trust but, because of powers retained in the settlor, has no real substance and is not a completed trust.

imperfect trust. See *executory trust*.

implied trust. See *constructive trust*.

indestructible trust. A trust that, because of the settlor's wishes, cannot be prematurely terminated by the beneficiary. — Also termed *Claflin trust*.

insurance trust. A trust whose principal consists of insurance policies or their proceeds.

inter vivos trust (**in**-tər **vI**-vohs *or* **-vee**-vohs). A trust that is created and takes effect during the settlor's lifetime. — Also termed *living trust*. Cf. *testamentary trust*.

investment trust. See *investment company* under COMPANY.

involuntary trust. See *constructive trust*.

irrevocable trust (i-**rev**-ə-kə-bəl). A trust that cannot be terminated by the settlor once it is created. • In most states, a trust will be deemed irrevocable unless the settlor specifies otherwise.

land trust. A land-ownership arrangement by which a trustee holds both legal and equitable title to land while the beneficiary retains the power to direct the trustee, manage the property, and draw income from the trust. — Also termed *Illinois land trust*; *naked land trust*.

life-insurance trust. A trust consisting of one or more life-insurance policies payable to the trust when the insured dies.

limited trust. A trust created for a limited period. Cf. *perpetual trust*.

liquidating trust. A trust designed to be liquidated as soon as possible. • An example is a trust into which a decedent's business is placed to safeguard the business until it can be sold.

living trust. See *inter vivos trust*.

marital-deduction trust. A testamentary trust created to take full advantage of the marital deduction; esp., a trust entitling a spouse to lifetime income from the trust and sufficient control over the trust to include the trust property in the spouse's estate at death.

Massachusetts trust. See *business trust*.

Medicaid-qualifying trust. A trust that is deemed to have been created in an effort to reduce someone's assets so that the person may qualify for Medicaid, and that will be included as an asset for purposes of determining the person's eligibility. • Someone who wants to apply and qualify for Medicaid, but who has too many assets to qualify, will sometimes set up a trust — or have a spouse or custodian set up a trust — using the applicant's own assets, under which the applicant may be the beneficiary of all or part of the payments from the trust, which are distributed by a trustee with discretion to make trust payments to the applicant. Such a trust may be presumed to have been established for the purpose of attempting to qualify for Medicaid, and may be counted as an asset of the applicant, resulting in a denial of benefits.

ministerial trust. See *passive trust.*

mixed trust. A trust established to benefit both private individuals and charities.

naked land trust. See *land trust.*

naked trust. See *passive trust.*

nominal trust. See *passive trust.*

nominee trust. **1.** A trust in which the beneficiaries have the power to direct the trustee's actions regarding the trust property. **2.** An arrangement for holding title to real property under which one or more persons or corporations, under a written declaration of trust, declare that they will hold any property that they acquire as trustees for the benefit of one or more undisclosed beneficiaries.

nondiscretionary trust. See *fixed trust.*

oral trust. **1.** A trust created by the settlor's spoken statements as opposed to a written agreement. • Trusts of real property must usu. be in writing (because of the statute of frauds), but trusts of personal property usu. can be created orally. — Also termed *parol trust.* **2.** A trust created by operation of law, such as a resulting trust or a constructive trust.

passive trust. A trust in which the trustee has no duty other than to transfer the property to the beneficiary. — Also termed *dry trust*; *nominal trust*; *simple trust*; *naked trust*; *ministerial trust.* Cf. *active trust.*

pension trust. An employer-funded pension plan; esp., a pension plan in which the employer transfers to trustees amounts sufficient to cover the benefits payable to the employees.

perpetual trust. A trust that is to continue as long as the need for it continues, such as for the lifetime of a beneficiary or the term of a particular charity. Cf. *limited trust.*

personal trust. See *private trust.*

pourover trust. An inter vivos trust that receives property (usu. the residual estate) from a will upon the testator's death. Cf. *pourover will* under WILL.

power-of-appointment trust. A trust, used to qualify property for the marital deduction, under which property is left in trust for the surviving spouse. • The trustee must distribute income to the spouse for life, and the power of appointment is given to the spouse or to his or her estate.

precatory trust (**prek**-ə-tor-ee). A trust that the law will recognize to carry out the wishes of the testator or grantor even though the statement in question is in the nature of an entreaty or recommendation rather than a positive command.

presumptive trust. See *resulting trust.*

private trust. A trust created for the financial benefit of one or more designated beneficiaries rather than for the public benefit; an ordinary trust as opposed to a charitable trust. • Three elements must be present for a private trust: (1) sufficient words to create it, (2) a definite subject matter, and (3) a certain or ascertained object. — Also termed *personal trust.* Cf. *charitable trust.*

protective trust. A trust that is designed to protect the trust property to ensure the continued support of the beneficiary.

> "In a broad sense, a spendthrift, support, or other similarly protective trust is one created to provide a fund for the maintenance of the beneficiary and at the same time to secure it against the beneficiary's improvidence or incapacity." 76 Am. Jur. 2d *Trusts* § 121 (1992).

public trust. See *charitable trust.*

purchase-money resulting trust. A resulting trust that arises when one person buys property but directs the seller to transfer the property and its title to another. • The buyer is the beneficiary, and the holder is the trustee. — Abbr. PMRT.

QTIP trust (**kyoo**-tip). A testamentary trust established to transfer assets between spouses when one spouse dies. • Under this trust, the assets — referred to as the qualified-terminable-interest property (QTIP) — are considered part of the surviving spouse's estate and are therefore not subject to the estate tax on the decedent spouse's estate.

real-estate investment trust. See REAL-ESTATE INVESTMENT TRUST.

reciprocal trust. A trust arrangement between two parties in which one party is beneficiary of a trust established by the other party, and vice versa. • Such trusts are common between husband and wife.

remedial trust. See *constructive trust.*

resulting trust. A trust imposed by law when property is transferred under circumstances suggesting that the transferor did not intend for the transferee to have the beneficial interest in the property. — Also termed *implied trust*; *presumptive trust.* Cf. *constructive trust.*

revocable trust (**rev**-ə-kə-bəl). A trust in which the settlor reserves the right to terminate the trust and recover the trust property and any undistributed income.

savings-account trust. See *Totten trust.*

savings-bank trust. See *Totten trust.*

secret trust. A testamentary trust giving property to a legatee or devisee who orally promises to hold it in trust for another person.

self-settled trust. A trust in which the settlor is also the person who is to receive the benefits from the trust, usu. set up in an attempt to protect the trust assets from creditors. • In most states, such a trust will not protect trust assets from the settlor's creditors. Restatement (Second) of Trusts § 156 (1959).

shifting trust. An express trust providing that, upon a specified contingency, it may operate in favor of an additional or substituted beneficiary.

short-term trust. See *Clifford trust.*

simple trust. **1.** A trust that must distribute all income as it accrues. **2.** See *passive trust.*

special trust. See *active trust.*

spendthrift trust. A trust that prohibits the beneficiary's interest from being assigned and also prevents a creditor from attaching that interest.

split-interest trust. See *charitable-remainder trust.*

sprinkling trust. A trust in which the trustee has discretion to decide how much will be given to each beneficiary. — Also termed *spray trust.*

support trust. A trust in which the trustee pays to the beneficiary only as much trust income as the trustee believes is needed for the beneficiary's support. • As with a spendthrift trust, the beneficiary's interest cannot be assigned or reached by creditors.

tentative trust. See *Totten trust.*

testamentary trust (tes-tə-**men**-tə-ree *or* -tree). A trust that is created by a will and takes effect when the settlor (testator) dies. — Also termed *trust under will.* Cf. *inter vivos trust.*

Totten trust. A revocable trust created by one's deposit of money in one's own name as a trustee for another. • A Totten trust is commonly used to indicate a successor to the account without having to create a will. — Also termed *tentative trust*; *bank-account trust*; *savings-account trust*; *savings-bank trust.*

> "A deposit by one person of his own money, in his own name as trustee for another, standing alone, does not establish an irrevocable trust during the lifetime of the depositor. It is a tentative trust merely, revocable at will, until the depositor dies or completes the gift in his lifetime by some unequivocal act or declaration, such as delivery of the pass book or notice to the beneficiary. In case the depositor dies before the beneficiary without revocation, or some decisive act or declaration of disaffirmance, the presumption arises that an absolute trust was created as to the balance on hand at the death of the depositor." *In re Totten*, 179 N.Y. 112, 125–26 (1904) (Vann, J.).

transgressive trust. A trust that violates the rule against perpetuities.

trust de son tort. See *constructive trust.*

trust ex delicto. See *constructive trust.*

trust ex maleficio. See *constructive trust.*

trust in invitum. See *constructive trust.*

trust under will. See *testamentary trust.*

unit-investment trust. **1.** A trust in which funds are pooled and invested in income-producing securities. • Units of the trust are sold to investors, who maintain an interest in the trust in proportion to their investment. **2.** An investment company that gives a shareholder an undivided interest in a fixed pool of securities held by the trustee. • This type of company can be organized in several ways (as by trust indenture, contract of custodianship or agency, or similar instrument), but is most commonly organized with a trust indenture. Such a company does not have a board of directors and issues only redeemable securities, each of which represents an undivided interest in a unit of specified securities. 15 USCA § 80a–4. See *investment company* under COMPANY.

unitrust. See UNITRUST.

vertical trust. *Antitrust.* A combination that gathers together under a single ownership a number of businesses or plants engaged in successive stages of production or marketing.

voluntary trust. **1.** A trust that is not founded on consideration. • One having legal title to property may create a voluntary trust by (1) declaring that the property is to be held in trust for another, and (2) transferring the legal title to a third person who acts as trustee. **2.** An obligation arising out of a personal confidence reposed in, and voluntarily accepted by, one for the benefit of another.

voting trust. A trust in which corporate stockholders transfer their shares to a trustee for the purpose of creating a voting bloc. • The stockholders still receive dividends under such an arrangement. Cf. VOTING GROUP.

"At common law there was great suspicion of voting trusts. One commentator described a voting trust as 'little more than a vehicle for corporate kidnapping.' This attitude has largely disappeared. State statutes now uniformly recognize the validity of voting trusts and they have received a more hospitable judicial reception." Robert W. Hamilton, *The Law of Corporations in a Nutshell* 199 (3d ed. 1991).

wasting trust. A trust in which the trust property is gradually depleted by periodic payments to the beneficiary.

trust agreement. See *declaration of trust* (2) under DECLARATION (1).

trustbuster, *n.* A person — esp. a federal officer — who seeks the dissolution of trusts under the antitrust laws. See TRUST (1).

trust certificate. See EQUIPMENT TRUST CERTIFICATE.

trust company. See COMPANY.

trust deed. 1. See *declaration of trust* (2) under DECLARATION. **2.** See *deed of trust* under DEED.

trust de son tort (də sawn [*or* son] **tor**[**t**]). See *constructive trust* under TRUST.

trust distribution. See DISTRIBUTION.

trustee (trəs-**tee**), *n.* **1.** One who, having legal title to property, holds it in trust for the benefit of another and owes a fiduciary duty to that beneficiary. • Generally, a trustee's duties are to convert to cash all debts and securities that are not qualified legal investments, to reinvest the cash in proper securities, to protect and preserve the trust property, and to ensure that it is employed solely for the beneficiary, in accordance with the directions contained in the trust instrument.

bare trustee. A trustee of a passive trust. • A bare trustee has no duty other than to transfer the property to the beneficiary. See *passive trust* under TRUST.

corporate trustee. A corporation that is empowered by its charter to act as a trustee, such as a bank or trust company.

indenture trustee. A trustee named in a trust indenture and charged with holding legal title to the trust property; a trustee under an indenture.

joint trustee. See COTRUSTEE.

judicial trustee. A trustee appointed by a court to execute a trust.

quasi-trustee. One who benefits from a breach of a trust to a great enough degree to become liable as a trustee.

successor trustee. A trustee who succeeds an earlier trustee, usu. as provided in the trust agreement.

testamentary trustee (tes-tə-**men**-tə-ree *or* -tree). A trustee appointed by or acting under a will; one appointed to carry out a trust created by a will.

trustee ad litem (ad **lI**-tem *or* -təm). A trustee appointed by the court.

trustee de son tort (də sawn [*or* son] **tor**[**t**]). A person who, without legal authority, administers a living person's property to the detriment of the property owner. See *constructive trust* under TRUST.

trustee ex maleficio (eks mal-ə-**fish**-ee-oh). A person who is guilty of wrongful or fraudulent conduct and is held by equity to the duty of a trustee, in relation to the subject matter, to prevent him or her from profiting from the wrongdoing.

2. *Bankruptcy.* An officer of the court who is elected by creditors or appointed by a judge to act as the representative of a bankruptcy estate. • The trustee's duties include (1) collecting and reducing to cash the assets of the estate, (2) operating the debtor's business with court approval if appropriate to preserve the value of business assets, (3) examining the debtor at a meeting of creditors, (4) filing inventories and making periodic reports to the court on the financial condition of the estate, (5) investigating the debtor's financial affairs, (6) examining proofs of claims and objecting to improper claims, (7) furnishing information relating to the bankruptcy to interested parties, and (8) opposing discharge through bankruptcy, if advisable. — Also termed (in sense 2) *bankruptcy trustee*; *trustee in bankruptcy*.

interim trustee. A bankruptcy trustee appointed to perform all the functions and duties of a trustee until the regular trustee is selected and qualified. • Before the meeting of creditors, the interim trustee often preliminarily investigates the debtor's assets and financial affairs.

trustee, *vb.* **1.** To serve as trustee. **2.** To place (a person or property) in the hands of one or more trustees. **3.** To appoint (a person) as trustee, often of a bankrupt's estate in order to restrain a creditor from collecting moneys due. **4.** To attach (the effects of a debtor) in the hands of a third person.

trustee, U.S. See UNITED STATES TRUSTEE.

trustee ad litem. See TRUSTEE (1).

trustee de son tort. See TRUSTEE (1).

trustee ex maleficio. See TRUSTEE (1).

trustee in bankruptcy. See BANKRUPTCY TRUSTEE.

trustee process. See FACTORIZING PROCESS.

trusteeship. 1. The office, status, or function of a trustee. **2.** *Int'l law.* Administration or supervision of a territory by one or more countries, esp. under a U.N. commission. Cf. MANDATE (6).

trust estate. See CORPUS (2).

trust ex delicto. See *constructive trust* under TRUST.

trust ex maleficio. See *constructive trust* under TRUST.

trust fund. The property held in a trust by a trustee; CORPUS (2).

common trust fund. A trust fund set up within a bank trust department to combine the assets of numerous small trusts to achieve greater investment diversification. • Common trust funds are regulated by state law.

trust-fund doctrine. The principle that the assets of an insolvent company, including paid and unpaid subscriptions to the capital stock, are held as a trust fund to which the company's creditors may look for payment of their claims. • The creditors may follow the property constituting this fund, and may use it to reduce the debts, unless it has passed into the hands of a bona fide purchaser without notice. — Also termed *trust-fund theory*.

trust indenture. See INDENTURE.

Trust Indenture Act. A federal law, enacted in 1939, designed to protect investors of certain types of bonds by requiring that (1) the SEC approve the trust indenture, (2) the indenture include certain protective clauses and exclude certain exculpatory clauses, and (3) the trustees be independent of the issuing company. 15 USCA §§ 77aaa et seq.

trust in invitum (in in-vɪ-təm). See *constructive trust* under TRUST.

trust instrument. See *declaration of trust* under DECLARATION.

trust legacy. See LEGACY.

trust officer. A trust-company official responsible for administering funds held by the company as a trustee.

trustor. One who creates a trust; SETTLOR (1).

trust ownership. See OWNERSHIP.

trust process. See PROCESS (1).

trust property. See CORPUS (2).

trust receipt. 1. A pre-UCC security device — now governed by Article 9 of the Code — consisting of a receipt stating that the wholesale buyer has possession of the goods for the benefit of the financier. • Today there must usu. be a security agreement coupled with a filed financing statement. **2.** A method of financing commercial transactions by which title passes directly from the manufacturer or seller to a banker or lender, who as owner delivers the goods to the dealer on whose behalf the banker or lender is acting, and to whom title ultimately goes when the banker's or lender's primary right has been satisfied.

trust res (reez *or* rays). See CORPUS (2).

trust territory. See TERRITORY.

trust under will. See *testamentary trust* under TRUST.

trusty, *n.* A convict or prisoner who is considered trustworthy by prison authorities and therefore given special privileges.

truth. 1. A fully accurate account of events; factuality. **2.** *Defamation.* An affirmative defense by which the defendant asserts that the alleged defamatory statement is substantially accurate.

Truth in Lending Act. See CONSUMER CREDIT PROTECTION ACT. — Abbr. TILA.

try, *vb.* To examine judicially; to examine and resolve (a dispute) by means of a trial.

try title. The judicial examination of a title. See TRESPASS TO TRY TITLE; *action to quiet title* under ACTION.

TSCA. *abbr.* Toxic Substances Control Act. 42 USCA §§ 2601 et seq.

Tucker Act. A federal law enacted in 1887 to ameliorate the inadequacies of the original authority of the Court of Claims by extending that court's jurisdiction to include (1) claims founded on the Constitution, a federal statute, or a federal regulation, and (2) damage claims in cases not arising in tort.

turncoat witness. See WITNESS.

turnkey, *adj.* **1.** (Of a product) provided in a state of readiness for immediate use <a turnkey computer network>. **2.** Of, relating to, or involving a product provided in this manner <a turnkey contract>.

turnkey, *n.* A jailer; esp., one charged with keeping the keys to a jail or prison.

turnkey contract. See *engineering, procurement, and construction contract* under CONTRACT.

turnover duty. *Maritime law.* A shipowner's obligation to provide safe working conditions and to give notice of any nonobvious hazards regarding instruments and areas that the shipowner turns over to the stevedore and longshoremen while the ship is being loaded or unloaded. — Cf. ACTIVE-OPERATIONS DUTY; INTERVENTION DUTY.

turnover order. See ORDER (2).

turn state's evidence, *vb.* To cooperate with prosecutors and testify against other criminal defendants <after hours of intense negotiations, the suspect accepted a plea bargain and agreed to turn state's evidence>.

turntable doctrine. See ATTRACTIVE-NUISANCE DOCTRINE. • This term gets its name from the enticing yet dangerous qualities of railroad turntables, which have frequently been the subject of personal-injury litigation.

turpitude (**tər**-pə-t[y]ood). See MORAL TURPITUDE.

tutela (t[y]oo-**tee**-lə), *n.* [Latin "tutelage"] *Roman law.* A type of guardianship either for those not having reached puberty (*tutela impuberum*) or for women (*tutela mulierum*). • The guardian was called the *tutor*, the ward the *pupillus*. Cf. CURA.

tutelage (**t[y]oo**-tə-lij), *n.* **1.** The act of protecting or guiding; guardianship. **2.** *Int'l law.* The state of being under the care and management of an international organization such as the League of Nations or United Nations. • This term applies, for example, to the status of a people who do not yet benefit from a fully operational government of their own — such as people displaced by war and living in a territory that will in the future be given its autonomy.

tutor, *n.* **1.** One who teaches; esp., a private instructor. **2.** *Civil law.* A guardian of a minor; a person appointed to have the care of the minor's person and estate. • The guardian of a minor past a certain age is called a *curator* and has duties somewhat different from those of a tutor.

tutorship. *Civil law.* The office and power of a tutor; the power that an individual has, *sui juris*, to take care of one who cannot care for himself or herself. • The four types of tutorship are (1) tutorship by nature, (2) tutorship by will, (3) tutorship by the effect of the law, and (4) tutorship by judicial appointment. La. Civ. Code art. 247.

tutorship by nature. **1.** Tutorship of a minor child that belongs by right to a surviving parent. **2.** Tutorship of a minor child that belongs to the parent under whose care the child has been placed following divorce or judicial separation. • If the parents are awarded joint custody, both have cotutorship and equal authority, privileges, and responsibilities. La. Civ. Code art. 250.

tutorship by will. Tutorship that is created (1) by the will of the parent who dies last, or (2) by any declaration of the surviving father or mother (or the parent who is the curator of the other spouse), executed before a notary and two witnesses. La. Civ. Code art. 257.

TVA. *abbr.* TENNESSEE VALLEY AUTHORITY.

Twelfth Amendment. The constitutional amendment, ratified in 1804, that altered the electoral-college system by separating the balloting for presidential and vice-presidential candidates.

twelve-day rule. *Criminal procedure.* A rule in some jurisdictions requiring that a person charged with a felony be given a preliminary examination no later than 12 days after the arraignment on the original warrant.

twelve-month liquidation. See LIQUIDATION.

Twelve Tables. *Roman law.* The earliest surviving legislation enacted by the Romans, written on 12 tablets in the 5th century B.C. • The Tables set out all the main rights and duties of Roman citizens, including debtors' rights, family law, criminal law, wills, torts, and public law. They substituted a written body of laws, easily accessible and binding on all citizens of Rome, for an unwritten usage accessible to only a few. The law of the Twelve Tables was also known as the *Lex Duodecim Tabularum.*

> "The Twelve Tables continued to be recognized for many centuries as the fundamental law of the Romans; they did not formally lose this character until it was taken from them by the legislation of Justinian." James Hadley, *Introduction to Roman Law* 74–75 (1881).

Twentieth Amendment. The constitutional amendment, ratified in 1933, that changed the date of the presidential and vice-presidential inaugurations from March 4 to January 20, and the date for congressional convention from March 4 to January 3, thereby eliminating the short session of Congress, during which a number of members sat who had not been reelected to office. — Also termed *lame-duck amendment.*

Twenty-fifth Amendment. The constitutional amendment, ratified in 1967, that established rules of succession for the presidency and vice presidency in the event of death, resignation, or incapacity.

Twenty-first Amendment. The constitutional amendment, ratified in 1933, that repealed the 18th Amendment (which established national Prohibition) and returned the power to regulate alcohol to the states.

Twenty-fourth Amendment. The constitutional amendment, ratified in 1964, that prohibits the federal and state governments from restricting the right to vote in a federal election because of one's failure to pay a poll tax or other tax.

Twenty-second Amendment. The constitutional amendment, ratified in 1951, that prohibits a person from being elected President more than twice (or, if the person succeeded to the office with more than half the predecessor's term remaining, more than once).

Twenty-seventh Amendment. The constitutional amendment, ratified in 1992, that prevents a pay raise for senators and representatives from taking effect until a new Congress convenes. • This amendment was proposed as part of the original Bill of Rights in 1789, but it took 203 years for the required three-fourths of the states to ratify it.

Twenty-sixth Amendment. The constitutional amendment, ratified in 1971, that sets the minimum voting age at 18 for all state and federal elections.

Twenty-third Amendment. The constitutional amendment, ratified in 1961, that allows District of Columbia residents to vote in presidential elections.

twisting, *n.* An insurance agent's or company's misrepresenting or misstating facts, or giving an incomplete comparison of policies, to induce an insured to give up a policy in one company and buy another company's policy.

two-dismissal rule. The rule that a notice of voluntary dismissal operates as an adjudication on the merits — not merely as a dismissal without prejudice — when filed by a plaintiff who has already dismissed the same claim in another court.

two-issue rule. The rule that if multiple issues were submitted to a trial jury and at least one of them is error-free, the appellate court should presume that the jury based its verdict on the proper issue — not on an erroneous one — and should therefore affirm the judgment.

two-stage trial. See *bifurcated trial* under TRIAL.

two-tier offer. A two-step technique by which a bidder tries to acquire a target corporation, the first step involving a cash tender offer and the second usu. a merger in which the target company's remaining shareholders receive securities from the bidder (these securities ordinarily being less favorable than the cash given in the first step).

two-witness rule. 1. The rule that, to support a perjury conviction, two independent witnesses (or one witness along with corroborating evidence) must establish that the alleged perjurer gave false testimony. **2.** The rule, as stated in the U.S. Constitution, that no person may be convicted of treason without two witnesses to the same overt act — or unless the accused confesses in open court. U.S. Const. art. IV, § 2, cl. 2.

tying, *adj. Antitrust.* Of or relating to an arrangement whereby a seller sells a product to a buyer only if the buyer purchases another product from the seller <tying agreement>.

tying arrangement. *Antitrust.* **1.** A seller's agreement to sell one product or service only if the buyer also buys a different product or service. • The product or service that the buyer wants to buy is known as the *tying product* or *tying service*; the different product or service that the seller insists on selling is known as the *tied product* or *tied service*. Tying arrangements may be illegal under the Sherman or Clayton Act if their effect is too anticompetitive. **2.** A seller's refusal to sell one product or service unless the buyer also buys a different product or service. — Also termed *tying agreement*; *tie-in*; *tie-in arrangement*. Cf. RECIPROCAL DEALING.

tying product. See TYING ARRANGEMENT (1).

tyranny, *n.* Arbitrary or despotic government; the severe and autocratic exercise of sovereign power, whether vested constitutionally in one ruler or usurped by that ruler by breaking down the division and distribution of governmental powers. — **tyrannical, tyrannous,** *adj.*

tyrant, *n.* A sovereign or ruler, legitimate or not, who wields power unjustly and arbitrarily to oppress the citizenry; a despot.

U

U3C. *abbr.* UNIFORM CONSUMER CREDIT CODE.

U.B. *abbr.* Upper Bench. See *bancus superior* under BANCUS.

uberrimae fidei (yoo-**ber**-ə-mee **fi**-dee-ɪ). [Latin] Of the utmost good faith. See *contract uberrimae fidei* under CONTRACT.

uberrima fides (yoo-**ber**-ə-mə **fɪ**-deez), *n.* [Latin] Utmost good faith <a contract requiring *uberrima fides*>.

ubi (**yoo**-bɪ *or* **oo**-bee). [Latin] Where.

ubi re vera (**yoo**-bɪ ree **veer**-ə). [Latin] Where in reality; when in truth or in point of fact.

ubi supra (**yoo**-bɪ **s**[**y**]**oo**-prə). [Latin] Where stated above.

UCC. *abbr.* **1.** UNIFORM COMMERCIAL CODE. **2.** UNIVERSAL COPYRIGHT CONVENTION.

UCC battle of the forms. See BATTLE OF THE FORMS.

UCCC. *abbr.* UNIFORM CONSUMER CREDIT CODE.

UCCJA. *abbr.* UNIFORM CHILD CUSTODY JURISDICTION ACT.

UCMJ. *abbr.* UNIFORM CODE OF MILITARY JUSTICE.

UCP. *abbr.* UNIFORM CUSTOMS AND PRACTICE FOR COMMERCIAL DOCUMENTARY CREDITS.

UCR. *abbr.* UNIFORM CRIME REPORTS.

UDITPA. *abbr.* UNIFORM DIVISION OF INCOME FOR TAX PURPOSES ACT.

UFCA. *abbr.* UNIFORM FRAUDULENT CONVEYANCES ACT.

UFTA. *abbr.* UNIFORM FRAUDULENT TRANSFER ACT.

UGMA. See UNIFORM TRANSFERS TO MINORS ACT.

U.K. *abbr.* UNITED KINGDOM.

ukase (yoo-**kays** *or* **yoo**-kays). A proclamation or decree, esp. of a final or arbitrary nature. • This term originally referred to a decree issued by a Russian czar.

ullage (**əl**-ij). The amount that a cask of liquid lacks from being full.

ulna ferrea (**əl**-nə **fer**-ee-ə). [Law Latin "iron ell"] *Hist.* An iron measuring device, approximately a yard in length, kept in the Exchequer as a standard measure.

ulnage (**əl**-nij). Alnage. See ALNAGER.

ulterior intent. See INTENT (1).

ultima ratio (**əl**-ti-mə **ray**-shee-oh). [Latin] The final argument; the last resort; the means last to be resorted to.

ultimate fact. See FACT.

ultimate issue. See ISSUE (1).

ultimatum (əl-tə-**may**-təm), *n.* The final and categorical proposal made in negotiating a treaty, contract, or the like. • An ultimatum implies that a rejection might lead to a break-off in negotiations or, in international law, to a cessation of diplomatic relations or even to war. Pl. **ultimatums.**

ultimus heres (**əl**-ti-məs **heer**-eez). See HERES.

ultrahazardous activity. See ABNORMALLY DANGEROUS ACTIVITY.

ultra mare (**əl**-trə **mair**-ee *or* **mahr**-ee). [Latin] See BEYOND SEAS.

ultra reprises (**əl**-trə ri-**prɪz**-iz). After deduction of expenses; net.

ultra vires (əl-trə **vI**-reez *also* **veer**-eez), *adj.* Unauthorized; beyond the scope of power allowed or granted by a corporate charter or by law <the officer was liable for the firm's ultra vires actions>. — Also termed *extra vires.* — **ultra vires,** *adv.* Cf. INTRA VIRES.

umbrella limited partnership. See PARTNERSHIP.

umbrella-partnership real-estate investment trust. See REAL-ESTATE INVESTMENT TRUST.

umbrella policy. See INSURANCE POLICY.

umpirage (**əm**-pIr-ij). **1.** The office or authority of an umpire. **2.** The decision (such as an arbitral award) of an umpire.

umpire. An impartial person appointed to make an award or a final decision, usu. when a matter has been submitted to arbitrators who have failed to agree. • An arbitral submission may provide for the appointment of an umpire.

un-, *prefix.* **1.** Not <unassignable>. **2.** Contrary to; against <unconstitutional>.

U.N. *abbr.* UNITED NATIONS.

unaccrued, *adj.* Not due, as rent on a lease.

unalienable, *adj.* See INALIENABLE.

unanimous (yoo-**nan**-ə-məs), *adj.* **1.** Agreeing in opinion; being in complete accord <the judges were unanimous in their approval of the recommendation>. **2.** Arrived at by the consent of all <a unanimous verdict>.

unanimous-consent calendar. See CONSENT CALENDAR (2).

unascertained duty. See DUTY (4).

unauthorized, *adj.* Done without authority; specif. (of a signature or indorsement), made without actual, implied, or apparent authority. UCC § 1-201(43).

unauthorized completion. *Commercial law.* The act of filling in missing information in a negotiable instrument either without any authority to do so or beyond the authority granted. • Unauthorized completion is a personal defense, so it can be raised against any later holder of the instrument who does not have the rights of a holder in due course. See *personal defense* under DEFENSE (3).

unauthorized indorsement. See INDORSEMENT.

unauthorized practice of law. See PRACTICE OF LAW.

unauthorized signature. See SIGNATURE.

unauthorized use of a vehicle. See JOYRIDING.

unavailability, *n.* The status or condition of not being available, as when a witness is exempted by court order from testifying. • Unavailability is recognized under the Federal Rules of Evidence as an exclusion to the hearsay rule. Fed. R. Evid. 804.

una voce (**yoo**-nə **voh**-see). [Latin] With one voice; unanimously; without dissent.

unavoidable accident. See ACCIDENT.

unavoidable-accident doctrine. *Torts.* The rule holding no party liable for an accident that was not foreseeable and that could not have been prevented by the exercise of reasonable care. • The modern trend is for courts to ignore this doctrine, relying instead on the basic concepts of duty, negligence, and proximate cause. — Also termed *inevitable-accident doctrine.*

unavoidable casualty. See *unavoidable accident* under ACCIDENT.

unavoidable cause. See CAUSE (1).

unavoidable danger. See DANGER.

unborn beneficiary. See BENEFICIARY.

unborn child. See CHILD.

unborn-widow rule. The legal fiction, assumed under the rule against perpetuities, that a beneficiary's widow is not alive at the testator's death, and thus a succeeding life estate to her voids any remainders because the interest would not vest within the perpetuities period. See RULE AGAINST PERPETUITIES.

unbroken, *adj.* Not interrupted; continuous <unbroken possession by the adverse possessor>.

unbundling rules. *Telecommunications.* Regulations passed by the Federal Communications Commission to effectuate the local-competition requirements of the Telecommunications Act of 1996, which requires local-exchange carriers to provide access to elements of local-exchange networks on an unbundled (i.e., separated) basis. 47 USCA § 251; 47 CFR pt. 51. See NETWORK ELEMENT.

uncertain damages. See DAMAGES.

uncertified security. See SECURITY.

uncia (ən-shee-ə). [Latin] **1.** *Roman law.* One-twelfth of the *as* (a pound or, by analogy, an estate or inheritance). • The English word *ounce* is derived from this term. Cf. AS; BES. **2.** *Hist.* A measure of land used in a royal charter. • The size of an *uncia* is unclear, but it may have measured 1,200 square feet (i.e., 12 *modii*). **3.** Generally, the proportion of one-twelfth.

unciarius heres (ən-shee-**air**-ee-əs **heer**-eez). [Latin] *Roman law.* An heir to one-twelfth of an estate or inheritance.

unclean-hands doctrine. See CLEAN-HANDS DOCTRINE.

uncollected funds. A credit, such as an increase in the balance of a checking or other deposit account in a bank, given on the basis of a check or other right to payment that has not yet been received from the drawee or other payor.

unconditional, *adj.* Not limited by a condition; not depending on an uncertain event or contingency.

unconditional delivery. See DELIVERY.

unconditional discharge. See DISCHARGE (7).

unconditional heir. See HEIR.

unconditional pardon. See *absolute pardon* under PARDON.

unconditional promise. See PROMISE.

unconscionability (ən-kon-shə-nə-**bil**-ə-tee). **1.** Extreme unfairness. **2.** The principle that a court may refuse to enforce a contract that is unfair or oppressive because of procedural abuses during contract formation or because of overreaching contractual terms, esp. terms that are unreasonably favorable to one party while precluding meaningful choice for the other party. • Because unconscionability depends on circumstances at the time the contract is formed, a later rise in market price is irrelevant.

> "Traditionally, a bargain was said to be unconscionable in an action at law if it was 'such as no man in his senses and not under delusion would make on the one hand, and as no honest and fair man would accept on the other;' damages were then limited to those to which the aggrieved party was 'equitably' entitled. *Hume v. United States*, 132 U.S. 406, [10 S.Ct. 134] (1889), quoting *Earl of Chesterfield v. Janssen*, 2 Ves. Sen. 125, 155, 28 Eng. Rep. 82, 100 (Ch. 1750). Even though a contract was fully enforceable in an action for damages, equitable remedies such as specific performance were refused where 'the sum total of its provisions drives too hard a bargain for a court of conscience to assist.' *Campbell Soup Co. v. Wentz*, 172 F.2d 80, 84 (3d Cir. 1948). Modern procedural reforms have blurred the distinction between remedies at law and in equity. For contracts for the sale of goods, Uniform Commercial Code § 2–302 states the rule of this Section without distinction between law and equity. Comment 1 to that section adds, 'The principle is one of the prevention of oppression and unfair surprise . . . and not of disturbance of allocation of risks because of superior bargaining power.' " Restatement (Second) of Contracts § 208 cmt. b (1981).

> "Nowhere among the [Uniform Commercial] Code's many definitions is there one of *unconscionability*. That the term is incapable of precise definition is a source of both strength and weakness." E. Allan Farnsworth, *Contracts* § 4.28, at 310 (1982).

procedural unconscionability. Unconscionability resulting from improprieties in contract formation (such as oral misrepresentations or disparities in bargaining position) rather than from the terms of the contract itself. • This type of unconscionability suggests that there was no meeting of the minds.

substantive unconscionability. Unconscionability resulting from actual contract terms that are unduly harsh, commercially unreasonable, and grossly unfair given the existing circumstances.

unconscionable (ən-**kon**-shə-nə-bəl), *adj.* **1.** (Of a person) having no conscience; unscrupulous <an unconscionable used-car salesman>. **2.** (Of an act or transaction) showing no regard for conscience; affronting the sense of justice, decency, or reasonableness <the contract is void as unconscionable>. Cf. CONSCIONABLE.

unconscionable agreement. See AGREEMENT.

unconscionable contract. See *unconscionable agreement* under AGREEMENT.

unconscious, *adj.* Without awareness; not conscious. • A person who commits a criminal act while unconscious may be relieved from liability for the act.

unconstitutional, *adj.* Contrary to or in conflict with a constitution, esp. the U.S. Constitution <the law is unconstitutional because it violates the First Amendment's free-speech guarantee>. Cf. NONCONSTITUTIONAL.

unconstitutional-conditions doctrine. The principle that a government may not condition the receipt of government benefits on the recipient's surrender of constitutional rights (esp. First Amendment rights). • For example, a television station that receives public funds cannot be forced to refrain from endorsing political candidates.

uncontrollable, *adj.* Incapable of being controlled.

uncontrollable impulse. See IMPULSE.

uncontrolled-securities-offering distribution. See *securities-offering distribution* under DISTRIBUTION.

uncore prist (ən[g]-kor **prist**). [Law French "still ready"] *Hist.* A plea by which a party alleges readiness to pay or perform what is justly demanded.

> "Yet sometimes, after tender and refusal of a debt, if the creditor harasses his debtor with an action, it then becomes necessary for the defendant to acknowledge the debt, and plead the tender; adding, that . . . he is still ready, *uncore prist*, to discharge it. . . ." 3 William Blackstone, *Commentaries on the Laws of England* 303 (1768).

uncounseled, *adj.* Without the benefit or participation of legal counsel <an uncounseled conviction> <an uncounseled defendant>.

uncovered option. See *naked option* under OPTION (4).

unde nihil habet (ən-dee **nɪ**-hil **hay**-bət). [Law Latin "whereof she has nothing"] *Hist.* A writ of dower for a widow where no dower had been assigned to her within the time allowed by law.

undercapitalization. See CAPITALIZATION.

undercover agent. See AGENT.

undercurrent of surface stream. Water that moves slowly through the bed of a stream or lands under or immediately adjacent to the stream. • This water is considered part of the surface stream. — Also termed *underflow of surface stream*.

underdeveloped country. See DEVELOPING COUNTRY.

underflow of surface stream. See UNDERCURRENT OF SURFACE STREAM.

underinsurance. An agreement to indemnify against property damage up to a certain amount but for less than the property's full value.

underinsured-motorist coverage. Insurance that pays for losses caused by a driver who negligently damages the insured but does not have enough liability insurance to cover the damages. Cf. UNINSURED-MOTORIST COVERAGE.

underlease. See SUBLEASE.

underlessor. See SUBLESSOR.

under protest. See PROTEST.

undersheriff. See *deputy sheriff* under SHERIFF.

undersigned, *n.* A person whose name is signed at the end of a document <the undersigned agrees to the aforementioned terms and conditions>.

understand, *vb.* To apprehend the meaning of; to know <the testator did not understand what he was signing>.

understanding, *n.* **1.** The process of comprehending; the act of a person who understands something. **2.** One's personal interpretation of an event or occurrence. **3.** An agreement, esp. of an implied or tacit nature.

under submission. Being considered by the court; under advisement <the case was under submission in the court of appeals for more than two years>.

undertake, *vb.* **1.** To take on an obligation or task <he has undertaken to chair the committee on legal aid for the homeless>. **2.** To give a formal promise; guarantee <the merchant undertook that the goods were waterproof>. **3.** To act as surety for (another); to make oneself responsible for (a person, fact, or the like) <her

husband undertook for her appearance in court>.

undertaking, *n.* **1.** A promise, pledge, or engagement. **2.** A bail bond.

undertenant. See SUBLESSEE.

under the influence. (Of a driver, pilot, etc.) deprived of clearness of mind and self-control because of drugs or alcohol. See DRIVING UNDER THE INFLUENCE.

Undertreasurer of England. *Hist.* An officer immediately subordinate to the Lord High Treasurer.

under-tutor. *Civil law.* A person appointed by a court to represent a minor under the care of a tutor whenever the interests of the minor conflict with that of the tutor. See TUTORSHIP.

underwriter. 1. INSURER. **2.** One who buys stock from the issuer with an intent to resell it to the public; a person or entity, esp. an investment banker, who guarantees the sale of newly issued securities by purchasing all or part of the shares for resale to the public.

> "The term 'underwriter' derives its meaning from former British insurance practices. When insuring their cargo shippers would seek out investors to insure their property. The insurers would add their signatures and would write their names under those of the shipper; hence the term 'underwriters.' Both in terms of the insurance industry and the securities markets, the concept of underwriting has expanded significantly since its inception." Thomas Lee Hazen, *The Law of Securities Regulation* § 2.1, at 57 (2d ed. 1994).

chartered life underwriter. An underwriter who has satisfied the requirements set forth by The American College (formerly The American College of Life Underwriters) to be designated a life insurance underwriter. — Abbr. CLU.

underwriting, *n.* **1.** The act of assuming a risk by insuring it; the insurance of life or property. See INSURANCE. **2.** The act of agreeing to buy all or part of a new issue of securities to be offered for public sale. — **underwrite,** *vb.*

best-efforts underwriting. Underwriting in which an investment banker agrees to direct, but not guarantee, the public sale of the issuer's securities. • The underwriter, or selling group, sells the securities as agent for the issuer, and any unsold securities are never issued.

firm-commitment underwriting. Underwriting in which the underwriter agrees to buy all the shares to be issued and remain financially responsible for any securities not purchased. • The underwriter, or underwriting group, buys the securities from the issuer and resells them as principal. In this type of underwriting, securities that cannot be sold to the public are owned by the underwriter, and the issuer is paid for those securities as well as the others.

standby underwriting. Underwriting in which the underwriter agrees, for a fee, to buy from the issuer any unsold shares remaining after the public offering. — Also termed *strict underwriting.*

underwriting agreement. See AGREEMENT.

underwriting spread. See SPREAD.

undesirable discharge. See DISCHARGE (8).

undigested offering. See OFFERING.

undisclosed agency. See AGENCY (1).

undisclosed principal. See PRINCIPAL (1).

undisputed, *adj.* Not questioned or challenged; uncontested.

undisputed fact. See FACT.

undistributed-earnings tax. See *accumulated-earnings tax* under TAX.

undistributed profit. See *retained earnings* under EARNINGS.

undivided interest. An interest held under the same title by two or more persons, whether their rights are equal or unequal in value or quantity. — Also termed *undivided right*; *undivided title.* See *joint tenancy* and *tenancy in common* under TENANCY.

undivided profit. See *accumulated profit* under PROFIT.

undivided right. See UNDIVIDED INTEREST.

undivided title. See UNDIVIDED INTEREST.

undocumented alien. See *illegal alien* under ALIEN.

undue, *adj.* **1.** *Archaic.* Not yet owed; not currently payable <an undue debt>. **2.** Excessive or unwarranted <undue burden> <undue influence>.

undue-burden test. *Constitutional law.* The Supreme Court test stating that a law regulating abortion will be struck down if it places a substantial obstacle in the path of a woman's right to obtain an abortion. • This test replaced the "trimester analysis," set forth in *Roe v. Wade*, in which the state's ability to restrict abortion increased after each trimester of pregnancy. *Planned Parenthood of Southeastern Pa. v. Casey*, 505 U.S. 833, 112 S.Ct. 2791 (1992).

undue influence. 1. The improper use of power or trust in a way that deprives a person of free will and substitutes another's objective. • Consent to a contract, transaction, relationship, or conduct is voidable if the consent is obtained through undue influence.

> "Undue influence is unfair persuasion of a party who is under the domination of the person exercising the persuasion or who by virtue of the relation between them is justified in assuming that the person will not act in a manner inconsistent with his welfare." Restatement (Second) of Contracts § 177(1) (1981).

> "When at the turn of the twentieth century, the common law doctrine of duress was expanded to provide relief for coercion irrespective of the means of coercion, much of the work of undue influence became unnecessary. The doctrine has a much more specialized role today, although often enough the precedents decided when the more general doctrine prevailed are cited and quoted to the general confusion of the profession. Today the gist of the doctrine is unfair persuasion rather than coercion. Euphoria rather than fear is often, but certainly not always, the state of mind of the party unduly influenced." John D. Calamari & Joseph M. Perillo, *The Law of Contracts* § 9–9, at 351–52 (3d ed. 1987).

2. *Wills & estates.* Coercion that destroys a testator's free will and substitutes another's objectives in its place. • When a beneficiary actively procures the execution of a will, a presumption of undue influence may be raised, based on the confidential relationship between the influencer and the testator. — Also termed *improper influence.* See COERCION; DURESS.

undue prejudice. See PREJUDICE.

unearned income. See INCOME.

unearned increment. See INCREMENT.

unearned interest. See INTEREST (3).

unearned premium. See PREMIUM (1).

unearned-premium reserve. See RESERVE.

unearned surplus. See SURPLUS.

unemployment. The state or condition of being unemployed.

structural unemployment. Unemployment resulting from a shift in the demand for a particular product or service.

unemployment compensation. See COMPENSATION.

unemployment insurance. See INSURANCE.

unemployment tax. See TAX.

unenacted law. See LAW.

unencumbered (ən-in-**kəm**-bərd), *adj.* Without any burdens or impediments <unencumbered title to property>.

unenforceable, *adj.* (Of a contract) valid but incapable of being enforced. Cf. VOID; VOIDABLE.

unenforceable contract. See CONTRACT.

unequal, *adj.* Not equal in some respect; uneven <unequal treatment under the law>.

unequivocal (ən-i-**kwiv**-ə-kəl), *adj.* Unambiguous; clear; free from uncertainty.

unerring (ən-**ər**-ing *also* ən-**er**-ing), *adj.* Incapable of error; infallible.

unessential mistake. See MISTAKE.

unethical, *adj.* Not in conformity with moral norms or standards of professional conduct. See LEGAL ETHICS.

unexpected, *adj.* Happening without warning; not expected.

unexpired term. See TERM (4).

unfair competition. 1. Dishonest or fraudulent rivalry in trade and commerce; esp., the practice of endeavoring to substitute one's own goods or products in the market for those of another by means of imitating or counterfeiting the name, brand, size, shape, or other distinctive characteristic of the article or its packaging. **2.** The body of law protecting the first user of such a name, brand, size, shape, or other distinctive characteristic against an imitating or counterfeiting competitor.

unfair hearing. See HEARING.

unfair labor practice. Any conduct prohibited by state or federal law governing the relations among employers, employees, and labor organizations. • Examples of unfair labor practices by an employer include (1) interfering with protected employee rights, such as the right to self-organization, (2) discriminating against employees for union-related activities, (3) retaliating against employees who have invoked their rights, and (4) refusing to engage in collective bargaining. Examples of unfair labor practices by a labor organization include causing an employer to discriminate against an employee, engaging in an illegal strike or boycott, causing an employer to pay for work not to be performed (i.e., featherbedding), and refusing to engage in collective bargaining. 29 USCA §§ 151–169.

unfair persuasion. *Contracts.* A type of undue influence in which a stronger party achieves a result by means that seriously impair the weaker party's free and competent exercise of judgment. • Unfair persuasion is a lesser form of undue influence than duress and misrepresentation. The two primary factors to be considered are the unavailability of independent advice and the susceptibility of the person persuaded. See UNDUE INFLUENCE (1).

unfair surprise. A situation in which a party, having had no notice of some action or proffered evidence, is unprepared to answer or refute it.

unfair trade. An inequitable business practice; esp. the act or an instance of a competitor's repeating of words in a way that conveys a misrepresentation that materially injures the person who first used the words, by appropriating credit of some kind earned by the first user.

unfit, *adj.* **1.** Unsuitable; not adapted or qualified for a particular use or service <the buyer returned the unfit goods to the seller and asked for a refund>. **2.** *Family law.* Morally unqualified; incompetent <the judge found her to be an unfit mother and awarded custody to the father>.

unforeseen, *adj.* Not foreseen; not expected <unforeseen circumstances>.

unfriendly suitor. See CORPORATE RAIDER.

unhandsome dealing. *Archaic.* See SHARP PRACTICE.

unharmed, *adj.* Not injured or damaged.

unica taxatio (**yoo**-nə-kə tak-**say**-shee-oh). [Law Latin "a single taxation"] *Hist.* The practice of having the jury assess damages against a defaulting defendant as well as a defendant who contests the case.

unifactoral obligation. See OBLIGATION.

unified bar. See *integrated bar* under BAR.

unified credit. See TAX CREDIT.

unified estate-and-gift tax. See *transfer tax* under TAX.

unified estate-and-gift tax credit. See *unified credit* under TAX CREDIT.

unified transfer tax. See *transfer tax* under TAX.

uniform, *adj.* Characterized by a lack of variation; identical or consistent.

uniform act. A law drafted with the intention that it will be adopted by all or most of the states; esp., UNIFORM LAW. Cf. MODEL ACT.

Uniform Child Custody Jurisdiction Act. An act, in force in all states, that sets out a standard (based on the child's residence in and connections with the state) by which a state court determines whether it has jurisdiction over a particular child-custody matter or whether it must recognize a custody decree issued by another state's court. — Abbr. UCCJA. Cf. PARENTAL KIDNAPPING PREVENTION ACT.

Uniform Code of Military Justice. 1. CODE OF MILITARY JUSTICE. **2.** A model code promulgated by the National Conference of Commissioners on Uniform State Laws to govern state military forces when not in federal service. 11 U.L.A. 335 et seq. (1974). — Abbr. UCMJ.

Uniform Commercial Code. A uniform law that governs commercial transactions, including sales of goods, secured transactions, and negotiable instruments. • The Code has been adopted in some form by every state. — Abbr. UCC.

Uniform Consumer Credit Code. A uniform law designed to simplify and modernize the consumer credit and usury laws, to improve consumer understanding of the terms of credit transactions, to protect consumers against unfair practices, and the like. • This Code has been adopted by only a few states. — Abbr. UCCC; U3C. — Also termed *Consumer Credit Code.* See CONSUMER CREDIT PROTECTION ACT.

Uniform Controlled Substances Act. A uniform act, adopted by many states and the federal government, governing the sale, use, and distribution of drugs. 21 USCA §§ 801 et seq.

Uniform Crime Reports. A series of annual criminological studies (each entitled *Crime in the United States*) prepared by the FBI. • The reports include data on eight index offenses, statistics on arrests, and information on offenders, crime rates, and the like. — Abbr. UCR.

Uniform Customs and Practice for Commercial Documentary Credits. A publication of the International Chamber of Commerce that codifies widespread customs of bankers and merchants relating to the mechanics and operation of letters of credit. • Courts look to this publication to supplement and help interpret primary sources of credit law, such as UCC Article 5. — Abbr. UCP.

Uniform Deceptive Trade Practices Act. A type of Baby FTC Act that provides monetary and injunctive relief for a variety of unfair and deceptive acts, such as false advertising and disparagement. See BABY FTC ACT.

Uniform Division of Income for Tax Purposes Act. A uniform law, adopted by some states, that provides criteria to assist in assigning the total taxable income of a multistate corporation among the various states. — Abbr. UDITPA.

Uniform Divorce Recognition Act. A uniform code adopted by some states regarding full-faith-and-credit issues that arise in divorces.

Uniform Enforcement of Foreign Judgments Act. A uniform state law giving the holder of a foreign judgment the right to levy and execute as if it were a domestic judgment.

Uniform Fraudulent Conveyances Act. A model act adopted in 1918 to deal with issues arising from fraudulent conveyances by insolvent persons. • This act differentiated between conduct that was presumed fraudulent and conduct that required an actual intent to commit fraud. — Abbr. UFCA.

Uniform Fraudulent Transfer Act. A model act designed to bring uniformity among the states regarding the definition of, and penalties for, fraudulent transfers. • This act was adopted in 1984 to replace the Uniform Fraudulent Conveyances Act. — Abbr. UFTA.

Uniform Gifts to Minors Act. See UNIFORM TRANSFERS TO MINORS ACT.

Uniformity Clause. The clause of the U.S. Constitution requiring the uniform collection of federal taxes. U.S. Const. art. I, § 8, cl. 1.

Uniform Law. An unofficial law proposed as legislation for all the states to adopt exactly as written, the purpose being to promote greater consistency among the states. • All the uniform laws are promulgated by the National Conference of Commissioners on Uniform State Laws. For a complete collection, see *Uniform Laws Annotated.*

Uniform Law Commissioners. See NATIONAL CONFERENCE OF COMMISSIONERS ON UNIFORM STATE LAWS.

Uniform Partnership Act. A model code promulgated in 1914 to bring uniformity to state laws governing general and limited partnerships. • The act was adopted by almost all the states, but has been superseded in several of them by the Revised Uniform Partnership Act (1994). — Abbr. UPA.

Uniform Principal and Income Act. A uniform code adopted by some states governing allocation of principal and income in trusts and estates.

Uniform Reciprocal Enforcement of Support Act. A uniform law providing a procedure by which an alimony or child-support decree issued by one state can be enforced against a former spouse who resides in another state. — Abbr. URESA.

Uniform Transfers to Minors Act. A uniform law — adopted by most states — providing for the transfer of property to a minor, permitting a custodian acting in a fiduciary capacity to manage investments and apply the income from the property for the minor's support. — Abbr. UTMA. — Also termed *Transfers to Minors Act.* — Formerly also termed *Uniform*

Gifts to Minors Act (UGMA); *Gifts to Minors Act*.

unify, *vb.* To cause to become one; to form into a single unit.

unigeniture (yoo-nə-**jen**-ə-chər). *Archaic.* The fact of being an only child.

unilateral (yoo-nə-**lat**-ər-əl), *adj.* One-sided; relating to only one of two or more persons or things <unilateral mistake>.

unilateral act. See ACT (2).

unilateral contract. See CONTRACT.

unilateral mistake. See MISTAKE.

unimproved land. **1.** Land that has never been improved. **2.** Land that was once improved but has now been cleared of all buildings and structures.

unincorporated association. See ASSOCIATION (3).

unindicted coconspirator. See *unindicted conspirator* under CONSPIRATOR.

unindicted conspirator. See CONSPIRATOR.

uninsured-motorist coverage. Insurance that pays for the insured's injuries and losses negligently caused by a driver who has no liability insurance. Cf. UNDERINSURED-MOTORIST COVERAGE.

unintentional act. See ACT (2).

uninterrupted-adverse-use principle. See CONTINUOUS-ADVERSE-USE PRINCIPLE.

unio (**yoo**-nee-oh). *Eccles. law.* A consolidation of two churches into one.

union, *n.* An organization formed to negotiate with employers, on behalf of workers collectively, about job-related issues such as salary, benefits, hours, and working conditions. • Unions generally represent skilled workers in trades and crafts. — Also termed *labor union*; *labor organization*; *organization*. — **unionize,** *vb.* — **unionist,** *n.*

closed union. A union with restrictive membership requirements, such as high dues and long apprenticeship periods. Cf. *closed shop* under SHOP.

company union. **1.** A union whose membership is limited to the employees of a single company. **2.** A union under company domination.

craft union. A union composed of workers in the same trade or craft, such as carpentry or plumbing, regardless of the industry in which they work. — Also termed *horizontal union*.

federal labor union. A local union directly chartered by the AFL–CIO.

horizontal union. See *craft union*.

independent union. A union that is not affiliated with a national or international union.

industrial union. A union composed of workers in the same industry, such as shipbuilding or automobile manufacturing, regardless of their particular trade or craft. — Also termed *vertical union*.

international union. A parent union with affiliates in other countries.

local union. A union that serves as the local bargaining unit for a national or international union.

multicraft union. A union composed of workers in different industries.

national union. A parent union with locals in various parts of the United States.

open union. A union with minimal membership requirements. Cf. *open shop* under SHOP.

trade union. A union composed of workers of the same or of several allied trades; a craft union.

vertical union. See *industrial union*.

union certification. A determination by the National Labor Relations Board or a state agency that a particular union qualifies as the bargaining representative for a segment of a company's workers — a bargaining unit — because it has the support of a majority of the workers in the unit. — Also termed *certification of bargaining agent*; *certification of labor union*.

union contract. See LABOR AGREEMENT.

union givebacks. See CONCESSION BARGAINING.

Union Jack. The common name of the national flag of the United Kingdom, combining the national flags of England, Scotland, and Ireland. • The Union Jack was originally a small union flag flown from the jack-staff at the bow of a vessel. It is different from the Royal Standard, which bears the royal arms and is the Queen's personal flag.

union mortgage clause. See *standard mortgage clause* under MORTGAGE CLAUSE.

union rate. See RATE.

union-security clause. A provision in a union contract intended to protect the union against employers, nonunion employees, and competing unions.

union shop. See SHOP.

union steward. See STEWARD.

unissued stock. See STOCK.

unit. The number of shares, often 100, that a given stock is normally traded in.

unital (**yoo**-nə-təl), *adj.* Of or relating to legal relations that exist between only two persons. Cf. MULTITAL.

> "The relations of the *cestui que trust* with the trustee are *in personam* or 'unital,' and the same is true of a contract beneficiary and the promisor . . . ." William R. Anson, *Principles of the Law of Contract* 326 n.1 (Arthur L. Corbin ed., 3d Am. ed. 1919).

unitary business (**yoo**-nə-ter-ee). *Tax.* A business that has subsidiaries in other states or countries and that calculates its state income tax by determining what portion of a subsidiary's income is attributable to activities within the state, and paying taxes on that percentage.

unitary state. See STATE (1).

unitary tax. See TAX.

unitas actus (**yoo**-ni-tas **ak**-təs). [Latin] *Roman law.* Unity of action, esp. in the execution of a will, which must not be interrupted by any intervening act.

unitas juris (**yoo**-ni-tas **joor**-is). [Latin] Unity of right.

unit cost. See COST (1).

unit depreciation method. See DEPRECIATION METHOD.

unite, *vb.* **1.** To combine or join to form a whole. **2.** To act in concert or in a common cause.

United Kingdom. A country in Europe comprising England, Scotland, Wales, and Northern Ireland, but not the Isle of Man or the Channel Islands. — Abbr. U.K.

United Nations. An international organization formed in 1945 to establish a global community with the goals of preventing war, providing justice, and promoting human rights and welfare. — Abbr. U.N.

United States Attorney. A lawyer appointed by the President to represent, under the direction of the Attorney General, the federal government in civil and criminal cases in a federal judicial district. — Also termed *United States District Attorney*. Cf. DISTRICT ATTORNEY.

United States Claims Court. See UNITED STATES COURT OF FEDERAL CLAIMS.

United States Code. A multivolume published codification of federal statutory law. • In a citation, it is abbreviated as USC, as in 42 USC § 1983.

United States Code Annotated. A multivolume publication of the complete text of the United States Code with historical notes, cross-references, and casenotes of federal and state decisions construing specific Code sections. — Abbr. USCA.

United States Commissioner. See COMMISSIONER.

United States court. See *federal court* under COURT.

United States Court of Appeals. A federal appellate court having jurisdiction to hear cases in one of the 13 judicial circuits of the United States (the First Circuit through the Eleventh Circuit, plus the District of Columbia Circuit and the Federal Circuit). — Also termed *circuit court.*

United States Court of Appeals for the Armed Forces. The primary civilian appellate tribunal responsible for reviewing court-martial convictions from all the military services. 10 USCA §§ 941–950. — Formerly also termed *Court of Military Appeals*.

United States Court of Appeals for the Federal Circuit. An intermediate-level appellate court with jurisdiction to hear appeals in patent cases, various actions against the United States to recover damages, cases from the U.S. Court of Federal Claims, the U.S. Court of International Trade, the U.S. Court of Veterans Appeals, the Merit Systems Protection Board, and some administrative agencies. • The Court originated in the 1982 merger of the Court of Customs and Patent Appeals and the U.S. Court of Claims (although the trial jurisdiction of the Court of Claims was given to a new U.S. Claims Court). — Abbr. Fed. Cir.

United States Court of Federal Claims. A specialized federal court created under Article I of the Constitution in 1982 (with the name *United States Claims Court*) as the successor to the Court of Claims, and renamed in 1992 as the United States Court of Federal Claims. • It has original, nationwide jurisdiction to render a money judgment on any claim against the United States founded on the Constitution, a federal statute, a federal regulation, an express or implied-in-fact contract with the United States, or any other claim for damages not sounding in tort. — Also termed *Court of Claims* (abbr. Cl. Ct.).

United States Court of International Trade. A court with jurisdiction over any civil action against the United States arising from federal laws governing import transactions or the eligibility of workers, firms, and communities for adjustment assistance under the Trade Act of 1974 (19 USCA §§ 2101–2495). • Its exclusive jurisdiction also includes actions to recover customs duties, to recover on a customs bond, and to impose certain civil penalties for fraud or negligence. See 28 USCA §§ 1581–1584. — Also termed *International Trade Court*; (formerly) *U.S. Customs Court*.

United States Court of Veterans Appeals. A federal appellate court that has exclusive jurisdiction to review decisions of the Board of Veterans Appeals. • The Court was created in 1988, and appeals from its decisions are to the U.S. Court of Appeals for the Federal Circuit. — Abbr. CVA.

United States currency. See CURRENCY.

United States Customs Court. A court that formerly heard cases involving customs and duties. • Abolished in 1980, its responsibilities have been taken over by the United States Court of International Trade. See UNITED STATES COURT OF INTERNATIONAL TRADE.

United States District Attorney. See UNITED STATES ATTORNEY.

United States District Court. A federal trial court having jurisdiction within its judicial district. — Abbr. U.S.D.C.

United States Magistrate Judge. A federal judicial officer who hears civil and criminal pretrial matters and who may conduct civil trials or criminal misdemeanor trials. 28 USCA §§ 631–639. — Also termed *federal magistrate* and (before 1990) *United States Magistrate*.

United States Marshal. See MARSHAL.

United States of America. A federal republic formed after the War of Independence and made up of 48 conterminous states, plus the state of Alaska and the District of Columbia in North America, plus the state of Hawaii in the Pacific.

United States officer. See OFFICER (1).

United States person. A U.S. resident or national (with the exception of one living outside the United States who is employed by someone who is not a United States person), a domestic American concern, and any foreign subsidiary or affiliate of a domestic concern with operations controlled by the domestic concern. • Under antiboycott regulatory controls, no United States person may participate in a secondary boycott or discrimination against Jews and others by members of the League of Arab States. 50 USCA app. § 2415(2).

***United States Reports*.** The official printed record of U.S. Supreme Court cases. • In a citation, it is abbreviated as U.S., as in 388 U.S. 14 (1967).

United States Supreme Court. See SUPREME COURT OF THE UNITED STATES.

United States Tax Court. See TAX COURT, U.S.

United States trustee. A federal official who is appointed by the Attorney General to perform administrative tasks in the bankruptcy process, such as appointing bankruptcy trustees in Chapter 7 and Chapter 11 cases. See BANKRUPTCY TRUSTEE.

unit-investment trust. See TRUST.

unitization (yoo-nə-tə-**zay**-shən), *n. Oil & gas.* The aggregation of two or more separately owned oil-producing properties to form a single property that can be operated as a single entity under an arrangement for sharing costs and revenues. — **unitize** (**yoo**-nə-tɪz), *vb.* Cf. COMMUNITIZATION.

unit-ownership act. A state law governing condominium ownership.

unit price. See PRICE.

unit pricing. A system in which contract items are priced per unit rather than on the basis of a flat contract price.

unit rule. A method of valuing securities by multiplying the total number of shares held by the sale price of one share sold on a licensed stock exchange, ignoring all other facts about value.

unitrust. A trust from which a fixed percentage of the fair market value of the trust's assets, valued annually, is paid each year to the beneficiary.

units-of-output depreciation method. See DEPRECIATION METHOD.

units-of-production method. *Tax.* An accounting method in which the depreciation provision is computed at a fixed rate per product unit, based on an estimate of the total number of units that the property will produce during its service life. • This method is used in the oil-and-gas industry when the total number of units of production (i.e., barrels in a reserve) can be accurately estimated.

unity, *n.* **1.** The fact or condition of being one in number; oneness. **2.** At common law, a requirement for the creation of a joint tenancy. • The four unities are interest, possession, time, and title. — **unitary,** *adj.* See *joint tenancy* under TENANCY.

unity of interest. The requirement that all joint tenants' interests must be identical in nature, extent, and duration. — Also termed *interest unity.*

unity of possession. The requirement that each joint tenant must be entitled to possession of the whole property. — Also termed *possession unity.*

unity of time. The requirement that all joint tenants' interests must vest at the same time. — Also termed *time unity.*

unity of title. The requirement that all joint tenants must acquire their interests under the same instrument. — Also termed *title unity.*

unity of seisin (**see**-zin). The merging of seisin in one person, brought about when the person becomes seised of a tract of land on which he or she already has an easement.

universal agency. See *general agency* under AGENCY (1).

universal agent. See AGENT.

Universal Copyright Convention. An international convention, first adopted in the United States in 1955, by which signatory countries agree to give the published works of a member country the same protection as that given to works of its own citizens. — Abbr. UCC.

Universal Declaration of Human Rights. An international bill of rights approved by the United Nations in December 1948, being that body's first enumeration of human rights and fundamental freedoms. • The preamble states that "recognition of the inherent dignity and of the equal and inalienable rights of all members of the human family is the foundation of freedom, justice and peace in the world." The Declaration contains a lengthy list of rights and fundamental freedoms. For the full text of the Declaration, see Appendix C.

> "The Universal Declaration is the first comprehensive human rights instrument to be proclaimed by a universal international organization. Because of its moral status and the legal and political importance it has acquired over the years, the Declaration ranks with the Magna Carta, the French Declaration of the Rights of Man and the American Declaration of Independence as a milestone in mankind's struggle for freedom and human dignity. Its debt to all these great historical documents is unmistakable." Thomas Buergenthal, *International Human Rights in a Nutshell* 29–30 (2d ed. 1995).

universal defense. See *real defense* under DEFENSE (4).

universal life insurance. See INSURANCE.

universal malice. See MALICE.

universal partnership. See PARTNERSHIP.

universal succession. See SUCCESSION.

universal successor. See SUCCESSOR.

universal synod. See *general synod* under SYNOD.

universal title. See TITLE (2).

universitas (yoo-ni-**vər**-sə-tas). [Latin] *Roman law*. A union of persons considered as a whole; a corporation.

universitas facti (yoo-ni-**vər**-sə-tas **fak**-tI). [Law Latin] A plurality of corporeal things of the same kind regarded as a whole, such as a herd of cattle.

universitas juris (yoo-ni-**vər**-sə-tas **joor**-is). [Latin] *Roman & civil law*. The whole of a person's rights and liabilities; the totality of a person's legal relations.

> "A *universitas juris* is a collection of rights and duties united by the single circumstance of their having belonged at one time to some one person." Henry S. Maine, *Ancient Law* 148 (17th ed. 1901).

universitas personarum (yoo-ni-**vər**-sə-tas pər-sə-**nay**-rəm). [Latin] *Roman & civil law*. A group of people that are legally considered an entity, such as a college or corporation.

universitas rerum (yoo-ni-**vər**-sə-tas **reer**-əm). [Latin] *Roman & civil law*. A whole collection of things; a variety of individual things that are together regarded by the law as a whole. See JUS RERUM.

> "In the time of Justinian the *universitas rerum*, or *universitas iuris* (both expressions are used) is a somewhat abstract conception: it means the sum or whole of a man's legal position so far as it concerns the *ius rerum*. The conception is important in law only on the occasions, of which death is by far the most important, on which the *universitas* passes from one to another.... The expression *universitas rerum* is also used in another sense, to denote any collection of objects considered as a whole." W.W. Buckland, *A Manual of Roman Private Law* 172 (2d ed. 1953).

universus (yoo-ni-**vər**-səs). [Latin] The whole; all together.

unjudicial, *adj*. Not becoming of or appropriate to a judge.

unjust, *adj*. Contrary to justice; not just.

unjust enrichment. 1. The retention of a benefit conferred by another, without offering compensation, in circumstances where compensation is reasonably expected. **2.** A benefit obtained from another, not intended as a gift and not legally justifiable, for which the beneficiary must make restitution or recompense. **3.** The area of law dealing with unjustifiable benefits of this kind.

unlaw, *n*. **1.** A violation of law; an illegality. **2.** Lawlessness.

> "But lawlessness is often a superficial phenomenon and whenever the duke was strong enough to keep the peace then law revived. We hear the same of England: times of 'unlaw' alternate with times of law." 1 Frederick Pollock & Frederic W. Maitland, *The History of English Law Before the Time of Edward I* 68–69 (2d ed. 1898).

3. *Scots law*. A fine; a penalty.

unlawful, *adj*. **1.** Not authorized by law; illegal <in some cities, jaywalking is unlawful>. **2.** Criminally punishable <unlawful entry>. **3.** Involving moral turpitude <the preacher spoke to the congregation about the unlawful activities of gambling and drinking>. — **unlawfully,** *adv*.

unlawful act. Conduct that is not authorized by law; a violation of a civil or criminal law.

unlawful assembly. See ASSEMBLY.

unlawful condition. See CONDITION (2).

unlawful detainer. See DETAINER.

unlawful-detainer proceeding. An action to return a wrongfully held tenancy (as one held by a tenant after the lease has expired) to its owner. See *unlawful detainer* under DETAINER.

unlawful entry. 1. The crime of entering another's property, by fraud or other illegal means, without the owner's consent. **2.** An alien's crossing of a border into a country without proper documents.

unlawful force. See FORCE.

unlawful interference with contractual relations. See TORTIOUS INTERFERENCE WITH CONTRACTUAL RELATIONS.

unlawful picketing. See PICKETING.

unlawful sexual intercourse. See RAPE.

unless lease. See LEASE.

unlimited, *adj*. Without restriction or limitation.

unliquidated, *adj*. Not previously specified or determined <unliquidated damages>.

unliquidated claim. See CLAIM (3).

unliquidated damages. See DAMAGES.

unliquidated debt. See DEBT.

unlisted security. See SECURITY.

unlisted stock. See *unlisted security* under SECURITY.

unlivery. *Maritime law*. The unloading of cargo at its intended destination.

unmarketable title. See TITLE (2).

unmarried, *adj*. Not married; single.

unmerchantable title. See *unmarketable title* under TITLE (2).

unnatural offense. See SODOMY.

unnatural will. See WILL.

unnavigable, *adj*. See INNAVIGABLE.

unnecessary, *adj*. Not required under the circumstances; not necessary.

unnecessary hardship. *Zoning*. A ground for granting a variance, based on the impossibility or prohibitive expense of conforming the property or its use to the zoning regulation. See VARIANCE (2).

uno actu (**yoo**-noh **ak**-t[y]oo). [Latin] In a single act; by one and the same act.

unoccupied, *adj*. **1.** (Of a building) not occupied; vacant. **2.** (Of a person) not busy; esp., unemployed.

unofficious will. See *inofficious testament* under TESTAMENT.

uno flatu (**yoo**-noh **flay**-t[y]oo). [Latin] In one breath.

unpaid dividend. See DIVIDEND.

unperfected security interest. See SECURITY INTEREST.

unprecedented (ən-**pres**-ə-dent-id), *adj*. Never before known; without any earlier example.

unpremeditation. The lack of premeditation.

unprofessional conduct. See CONDUCT.

unqualified indorsement. See INDORSEMENT.

unqualified opinion. See OPINION (2).

unques (**ən**[**g**]-kweez), *adv*. [Law French] Ever; always.

unques prist (**ən**[**g**]-kweez **prist**). [Law French] Always ready. • This is another form of *tout temps prist*.

unrealized loss. See *paper loss* under LOSS.

unrealized profit. See *paper profit* under PROFIT.

unrealized receivable. An amount earned but not yet received. • Unrealized receivables have no income-tax basis for cash-basis taxpayers.

unreasonable, *adj*. **1.** Not guided by reason; irrational or capricious. **2.** Not supported by a valid exception to the warrant requirement <unreasonable search and seizure>.

unreasonable compensation. See COMPENSATION.

unreasonable decision. An administrative agency's decision that is so obviously wrong that there can be no difference of opinion among reasonable minds about its erroneous nature.

unreasonable refusal to submit to operation. *Workers' compensation*. An injured employee's refusal to submit to a necessary surgical procedure. • This refusal is grounds for terminating the employee's workers'-compensation benefits.

unreasonable restraint of trade. See RESTRAINT OF TRADE.

unreasonable restraint on alienation. See RESTRAINT ON ALIENATION (1).

unreasonable search. See SEARCH.

unrebuttable, *adj.* Not rebuttable <an unrebuttable presumption>.

unrecorded, *adj.* Not recorded; esp., not filed in the public record <unrecorded deed>.

unregistered security. See *restricted security* under SECURITY.

unrelated business income. See INCOME.

unrelated-business-income tax. See TAX.

unrelated offense. See OFFENSE (1).

unresponsive answer. *Evidence.* A response from a witness (usu. at a deposition or hearing) that is irrelevant to the question asked.

unrestricted indorsement. See *unrestrictive indorsement* under INDORSEMENT.

unrestrictive indorsement. See INDORSEMENT.

unrestrictive interpretation. See INTERPRETATION.

unreviewable, *adj.* Incapable of being legally or judicially reviewed <the claim is unreviewable on appeal>.

unsatisfied-judgment fund. See FUND (1).

unseaworthy, *adj.* (Of a vessel) unable to withstand the perils of an ordinary voyage. Cf. SEAWORTHY.

unsecured bail bond. See BOND (2).

unsecured bond. See DEBENTURE (3).

unsecured claim. See CLAIM (5).

unsecured creditor. See CREDITOR.

unsecured debt. See DEBT.

unsecured note. See NOTE (1).

unskilled work. See WORK.

unsolemn will. See WILL.

unsound, *adj.* **1.** Not healthy; esp., not mentally well <unsound mind>. **2.** Not firmly made; impaired <unsound foundation>. **3.** Not valid or well founded <unsound argument>.

unspeakable crime. See SODOMY.

unsworn, *adj.* Not sworn <an unsworn statement>.

unsworn declaration under penalty of perjury. See DECLARATION (8).

untenantable (ən-**ten**-ən-tə-bəl), *adj.* Not capable of being occupied or lived in; not fit for occupancy <the city closed the untenantable housing project>.

unthrift. *Archaic.* A prodigal; a spendthrift.

untimely, *adj.* Not timely <an untimely answer>.

untrue, *adj.* **1.** (Of something said) not correct; inaccurate. **2.** (Of a person) not faithful or true (to a standard or belief).

***unus nullus* rule** (**yoo**-nəs **nəl**-əs). *Civil law.* The evidentiary principle that the testimony of only one witness is given no weight. Cf. HALF-PROOF (1).

unvalued policy. See INSURANCE POLICY.

unworthy, *adj.* *Civil law.* (Of an heir) not entitled to inherit from a person because of a failure in a duty to that person.

unwritten constitution. See CONSTITUTION.

unwritten evidence. See EVIDENCE.

unwritten law. Law that, although never enacted in the form of a statute or ordinance, has the sanction of custom. • The term traditionally includes caselaw. — Also termed *jus non scriptum*; *jus ex non scripto*; *lex non scripta*; *jus moribus constitutum*.

> "[T]he very words of the court promulgating the opinion and making the decision do not determine absolutely the rule of law but . . . the rule of law is ascertained by discovering what general proposition was essential to the result reached, and by using the words of the opinion as a mere aid in the ascertaining of that rule, so that, although opinions are written, the authoritative rules derived from them are sometimes not written, but are ascertained by the use of reason, causing case law to be classed as unwritten law — lex non scripta, to use the

Latin phrase." William M. Lile et al., *Brief Making and the Use of Law Books* 335 (3d ed. 1914).

"In the common law it is not too much to say that the judges are always ready to look behind the words of a precedent to what the previous court was trying to say, or to what it would have said if it could have foreseen the nature of the cases that were later to arise, or if its perception of the relevant factors in the case before it had been more acute. There is, then, a real sense in which the written words of the reported decisions are merely the gateway to something lying behind them that may be called, without any excess of poetic license, 'unwritten law.' " Lon L. Fuller, *Anatomy of the Law* 145 (1968).

unwritten will. See *nuncupative will* under WILL.

UPA. *abbr.* UNIFORM PARTNERSHIP ACT.

up-front performance bond. See PERFORMANCE BOND.

UPL. *abbr.* Unauthorized practice of law <the state bar's UPL committee>. See *unauthorized practice of law* under PRACTICE OF LAW.

Upper Bench. See *bancus superior* under BANCUS.

upper chamber. See CHAMBER.

upper court. See *court above* under COURT.

upper estate. See *dominant estate* under ESTATE.

upper management. See *top management* under MANAGEMENT.

UPREIT (**əp**-rɪt). See *umbrella-partnership real-estate investment trust* under REAL-ESTATE INVESTMENT TRUST.

upset bid. See BID (1).

upset price. See PRICE.

upstreaming. A parent corporation's use of a subsidiary's cash flow or assets for purposes unrelated to the subsidiary.

upstream merger. See MERGER.

upward departure. See DEPARTURE.

u.r. *abbr.* UTI ROGAS.

urban, *adj.* Of or relating to a city or town; not rural.

urban planning. See LAND-USE PLANNING.

urban renewal. The process of redeveloping urban areas by demolishing or repairing existing structures or by building new facilities on areas that have been cleared in accordance with an overall plan.

urban servitude. See SERVITUDE (1).

urbs (ərbz). [Latin] *Roman law.* **1.** A city or town. **2.** The city of Rome.

ure (yoor). [fr. Old French *oeuvre*] Custom; practice; exercise.

URESA (yə-**ree**-sə). *abbr.* UNIFORM RECIPROCAL ENFORCEMENT OF SUPPORT ACT.

U.S. *abbr.* **1.** United States. **2.** UNITED STATES REPORTS.

usage. 1. A well-known, customary, and uniform practice, usu. in a specific profession or business. See CUSTOM (1). Cf. CONVENTION (3).

"A 'usage' is merely a customary or habitual practice; a 'convention' is a practice that is established by general tacit consent. 'Usage' denotes something that people are accustomed to do; 'convention' indicates that they are accustomed to do it because of a general agreement that it is the proper thing to do." Herbert W. Horwill, *The Usages of the American Constitution* 22 (1925).

"Although rules of law are often founded on usage, usage is not in itself a legal rule but merely habit or practice in fact. A particular usage may be more or less widespread. It may prevail throughout an area, and the area may be small or large — a city, a state or a larger region. A usage may prevail among all people in the area, or only in a special trade or other group. Usages change over time, and persons in close association often develop temporary usages peculiar to themselves." Restatement (Second) of Contracts § 219 cmt. a (1981).

general usage. A usage that prevails throughout a country or particular trade or profession; a usage that is not restricted to a local area.

immemorial usage. A usage that has existed for a very long time; longstanding custom. See TIME IMMEMORIAL.

trade usage. A practice or method of dealing having such regularity of observance in a region, vocation, or trade that it justifies an expectation that it will be observed in a given transaction; a customary practice or set of practices relied on by persons conversant in, or connected with, a trade or business. •

While a course of performance or a course of dealing can be established by the parties' testimony, a trade usage is usu. established by expert testimony. — Also termed *usage of trade*. Cf. COURSE OF DEALING; COURSE OF PERFORMANCE.

"The existence and scope of a usage of trade are to be determined as questions of fact. If a usage is embodied in a written trade code or similar writing the interpretation of the writing is to be determined by the court as a question of law. Unless otherwise agreed, a usage of trade in the vocation or trade in which the parties are engaged or a usage of trade of which they know or have reason to know gives meaning to or supplements or qualifies their agreement." Restatement (Second) of Contracts § 222 (1981).

2. See *conventional custom* under CUSTOM.

usance (**yoo**-zənts). The time allowed for the payment of a foreign bill of exchange, sometimes set by custom but now usu. by law.

usance credit. See *time letter of credit* under LETTER OF CREDIT.

USC. *abbr.* UNITED STATES CODE.

USCA. *abbr.* UNITED STATES CODE ANNOTATED.

U.S. citizen. See *national of the United States* under NATIONAL.

U.S. Customs Court. See COURT OF INTERNATIONAL TRADE.

U.S.D.C. *abbr.* UNITED STATES DISTRICT COURT.

use (yoos), *n.* **1.** The application or employment of something; esp., a long-continued possession and employment of a thing for the purpose for which it is adapted, as distinguished from a possession and employment that is merely temporary or occasional <the neighbors complained to the city about the owner's use of the building as a dance club>.

accessory use. *Zoning.* A use that is dependent on or pertains to a main use.

adverse use. A use without license or permission. Cf. ADVERSE POSSESSION.

beneficial use. *Property.* The right to use property and all that makes that property desirable or habitable, such as light, air, and access, even if someone else owns the legal title to the property.

collateral use. *Intellectual property.* The legal use of a trademark by someone other than the trademark owner, whereby the other party must clearly identify itself, the use of the trademark, and the absence of affiliation with the trademark owner.

conditional use. *Zoning.* A use of property subject to special controls and conditions. • A conditional use is one that is suitable to a zoning district, but not necessarily to every location within that district. — Also termed *special exception.*

conforming use. *Zoning.* The use of a structure or of the land in conformity with the uses permitted under the zoning classifications of a particular area, such as the building of a single-family dwelling in a residential zone.

double use. *Patents.* An application of a known principle or process to a new use without leading to a new result or product.

exclusive use. **1.** *Trademarks.* The right to use a specific mark without exception, and to prevent another from using a confusingly similar mark. **2.** *Property.* The right of an adverse user to a property, exercised independently of any similar rights held by others; one of the elements of a prescriptive easement. See USER.

experimental use. *Patents.* **1.** The use or sale of an invention by the inventor for experimental purposes. **2.** A defense to liability for patent infringement when the infringement took place only to satisfy curiosity or to complete an experiment, rather than for profit.

highest and best use. *Real estate.* In valuing property, the use that will generate the most profit; esp. used to determine the fair market value of property subject to eminent domain. — Often shortened to *best use.* — Also termed *most suitable use.*

incidental use. *Zoning.* Land use that is dependent on or affiliated with the land's primary use.

most suitable use. See *highest and best use.*

nonconforming use. *Zoning.* Land use that is impermissible under current zoning restrictions but that is allowed because the use existed lawfully before the restrictions took effect.

public use. **1.** *Property.* The public's beneficial right to use property or facilities subject to condemnation. See CONDEMNATION (2). **2.** *Patents.* Any use of or offer to use a completed or operative invention in a nonsecret, natural, and intended manner. • A patent is invalid if the invention was in public use more than one year before the patent's application date.

reasonable use. Use of one's property for an appropriate purpose that does not unreasonably interfere with another's use of property. See REASONABLE-USE THEORY.

regular use. *Insurance.* A use that is usual, normal, or customary, as opposed to an occasional, special, or incidental use. • This term often appears in automobile-insurance policies in the definition of a *nonowned automobile* — that is, an automobile not owned by or furnished for the regular use of the insured. Nonowned automobiles are excluded from coverage under most liability policies.

superstitious use. A designation or use of property for religious purposes not legally recognized or tolerated (such as gifts either favoring an unrecognized religion or supporting the saying of prayers for the dead).

2. A habitual or common practice <drug use>. **3.** A purpose or end served <the tool had several uses>. **4.** A benefit or profit; esp., the right to take profits from land owned and possessed by another; the equitable ownership of land to which another person holds the legal title <cestui que use>. See CESTUI QUE USE. — **use** (yooz), *vb.*

contingent use. A use that would be a contingent remainder if it had not been limited by way of use. • An example is a transfer "to A, to the use of B for life, with the remainder to the use of C's heirs." — Also termed *future use.*

entire use. A use of property that is solely for the benefit of a married woman. • When used in the habendum of a trust deed for the benefit of a married woman, this phrase operates to keep her husband from taking anything under the deed. — Also termed *entire benefit*; *sole use*; *sole and separate use.*

executed use. *Hist.* A use that results from the combining of the equitable title and legal title of an estate, done to comply with the Statute of Uses' mandate that the holder of an estate be vested with legal title to ensure the holder's liability for feudal dues. See STATUTE OF USES.

executory use. See *springing use.*

future use. See *contingent use.*

official use. *Hist.* A use imposing a duty on a person holding legal title to an estate on behalf of another, such as a requirement that a feoffee to uses sell the estate and apportion the proceeds among several beneficiaries. • The Statute of Uses eliminated this type of use.

permissive use. *Hist.* A passive use resorted to before passage of the Statute of Uses in 1535 to avoid an oppressive feudal law (such as mortmain) by naming one person as the legal owner of property while allowing another to possess the property and enjoy the benefits arising from it.

present use. *Hist.* A use that has an immediate existence and that is subject to the Statute of Uses.

resulting use. A use created by implication and remaining with the grantor when the conveyance lacks consideration.

secondary use. See *shifting use.*

separate use. See *entire use.*

shifting use. A use arising from the occurrence of a certain event that terminates the preceding use. • In the following example, C has a shifting use that arises when D makes the specified payment: "to A for the use of B, but then to C when D pays $1,000 to E." This is a type of conditional limitation. — Also termed *secondary use.* See *conditional limitation* under LIMITATION.

sole use. See *entire use.*

springing use. A use that arises on the occurrence of a future event. • In the following example, B has a springing use that vests when B marries: "to A for the use of B when B marries." — Also termed *executory use.*

use/derivative-use immunity. See *use immunity* under IMMUNITY (3).

usee. See USE PLAINTIFF.

useful, *adj. Patents.* (Of an invention) having a practical application.

> "When applied to a machine, 'useful' means that the machine will accomplish its purpose practically when applied in industry. The word is given a practical and not a speculative meaning." 60 Am. Jur. 2d *Patents* § 131 (1987).

useful life. The estimated length of time that depreciable property will generate income. • Useful life is used to calculate depreciation and amortization deductions. — Also termed *depreciable life.* See DEPRECIATION METHOD.

use immunity. See IMMUNITY (3).

use in commerce. *Trademarks.* Actual use of a trademark in the sale of goods or services. • Use of a trademark in commerce is a prerequisite to trademark registration.

useless-gesture exception. *Criminal procedure.* An exception to the knock-and-announce rule by which police are excused from having to announce their purpose before entering the premises to execute a warrant when it is evident from the circumstances that the authority and purpose of the police are known to those inside. See KNOCK-AND-ANNOUNCE RULE.

use plaintiff. *Common-law pleading.* A plaintiff for whom an action is brought in another's name. • For example, when the use plaintiff was an assignee ("A") of a chose in action and had to sue in someone else's name, the assignor ("B") would appear first on the petition's title: "B for the Use of A against C." — Also termed *usee.*

user (**yooz**-ər). **1.** The exercise or employment of a right or property <the neighbor argued that an easement arose by his continuous user over the last 15 years>. Cf. NONUSER.

user de action (**yoo**-zər **dak**-shən). [Law French] The pursuing or bringing of an action.

2. Someone who uses a thing <the stapler's last user did not put it away>.

end user. The ultimate consumer for whom a product is designed.

user fee. A charge assessed for the use of a particular item or facility.

Uses, Statute of. See STATUTE OF USES.

use tax. See TAX.

use value. See VALUE.

use variance. See VARIANCE (2).

usher, *n.* A doorkeeper responsible for maintaining silence and order in some English courts.

U.S. Magistrate. See UNITED STATES MAGISTRATE JUDGE.

U.S. national. See *national of the United States* under NATIONAL.

U.S.-owned foreign corporation. See CORPORATION.

usque ad (**əs**-kwee ad). [Law Latin] As far as; up to; until.

usque ad coelum (**əs**-kwee ad **see**-ləm). [Latin] Up to the sky <the owner of land also owns the space above the surface *usque ad coelum*>.

usual, *adj.* **1.** Ordinary; customary. **2.** Expected based on previous experience.

usuary (**yoo**-zhoo-er-ee). *Civil law.* A person who has the use (*usus*) of a thing to satisfy personal and family needs; a beneficiary. — Also termed (in Roman law) *usuarius.*

usucaption (yoo-zə-**kap**-shən), *n. Civil law.* The acquisition of ownership by prescription. — Also termed *usucapio* (yoo-zə-**kay**-pee-oh); *usucapion* (yoo-zə-**kay**-pee-on *or* -ən). — **usucapt,** *vb.* See PRESCRIPTION (1).

> "There is no principle in all law which the moderns, in spite of its beneficial character, have been so loath to adopt and to carry to its legitimate consequences as that which was known to the Romans as Usucapion, and which has descended to modern jurisprudence under the name of Prescription." Henry S. Maine, *Ancient Law* 236 (17th ed. 1901).

usufruct (**yoo**-zə-frəkt), *n. Roman & civil law.* A right to use another's property for a time without damaging or diminishing it, although the property might naturally deteriorate over time. • In Roman law, the usufruct was considered an encumbrance. In modern civil law, the owner of the usufruct is similar to a life tenant, and the owner of the thing burdened is the *naked owner.* — Also termed *usufructus*; *perfect usufruct*; (in Scots law) *life-rent.* Cf. HABITATION (3).

> "*Usufructus* is . . . the right of using and enjoying property belonging to another provided the substance of the property remained unimpaired. More exactly, a usufruct was the right granted to a man personally to use and enjoy, usually for his life . . . , the property of another which, when the usufruct ended, was to revert intact to the *dominus* or his heir. It might be for a term of years, but even here it was ended by death, and in the case of a corporation (which never dies) Justinian fixed the period at 100 years. A usufruct might be in land or buildings, a slave or beast of burden, and in fact in anything except things which were destroyed by use . . . , the reason, of course, being that it was impossible to restore such things at the end of the usufruct intact . . . ." R.W. Leage, *Roman Private Law* 181–82 (C.H. Ziegler ed., 2d ed. 1930).

legal usufruct. A usufruct established by operation of law, such as the right of a surviving spouse to property owned by the deceased spouse.

quasi-usufruct. A right to consume things that would otherwise be useless, such as money or food. • Unlike a perfect usufruct, a quasi-usufruct actually involves alteration and diminution of the property used. — Also termed *imperfect usufruct*.

"The Roman jurists, therefore, would not acknowledge a usufruct of money; though, in their desire to carry out the wishes of testators, they came at length to recognize a quasi-usufruct. For testators, being seldom learned in the law, would often set forth as legacies in their wills the usufruct of a designated sum .... In such a case the person named as legatee was allowed to receive the amount ... on giving security that when he died the same amount should be paid out of his own estate to the *heres*, the heir of the testator. The relation here, though bearing some resemblance to the usufruct, was really quite different; the person who received the money became absolute owner of it; the heir had no ownership, nothing but the assurance of receiving an equal amount at some future time." James Hadley, *Introduction to Roman Law* 193 (1881).

usufructuary (yoo-zə-**frək**-choo-er-ee), *adj*. Of or relating to a usufruct; of the nature of a usufruct.

usufructuary, *n*. A person who has the right to the benefits of another's property; one having the right to a usufruct.

usura (yoo-**s[y]oor**-ə). [Latin] *Civil law*. **1.** Money paid for the use of money; interest. **2.** USURY. Pl. ***usurae*** (yoo-**s[y]oor**-ee).

usurae centesimae (yoo-**s[y]oor**-ee sen-**tes**-ə-mee). [Latin] Interest at the rate of 12% per year (1% per month), normally the highest rate allowed by law. • The Romans calculated interest rates by dividing the principal sum into one hundred parts, with one part being payable monthly as interest.

usura manifesta (yoo-**s[y]oor**-ə man-ə-**fes**-tə). [Latin] Manifest or open usury.

usura maritima (yoo-**s[y]oor**-ə mə-**rit**-ə-mə). [Latin] Interest taken on a bottomry or respondentia bond, proportioned to the risk and so not restricted by a usury law.

usurarius (yoo-s[y]ə-**rair**-ee-əs). [Law Latin] *Hist*. A usurer.

usura velata (yoo-**s[y]oor**-ə və-**lay**-tə). [Latin] Veiled or concealed usury.

usurious (yoo-**zhuur**-ee-əs), *adj*. **1.** Practicing usury <a usurious lender>. **2.** Characterized by usury <a usurious contract>.

usurpatio (yoo-sər-**pay**-shee-oh). [Latin] *Roman law*. The interruption of usucaption by loss of possession or a lawsuit by the real owner.

usurpation (yoo-sər-**pay**-shən *or* yoo-zər-**pay**-shən), *n*. The unlawful seizure and assumption of another's position, office, or authority. — **usurp** (yoo-**sərp** *or* yoo-**zərp**), *vb*.

usurpation of advowson (ad-**vow**-zən). *Hist*. An injury consisting in the absolute ouster or dispossession of the patron from the advowson. • This happens when a stranger, without the right to do so, presents a clerk who is installed in office. See ADVOWSON.

usury (**yoo**-zhə-ree) *n*. **1.** Historically, the lending of money with interest. **2.** Today, the charging of an illegal rate of interest. **3.** An illegally high rate of interest. — **usurious** (yoo-**zhuur**-ee-əs), *adj*. — **usurer** (**yoo**-zhər-ər), *n*.

usury law. A law that prohibits moneylenders from charging illegally high interest rates.

usus (**yoo**-səs *or* **yoo**-zəs). [Latin "use"] *Roman law*. **1.** The right to use another's property, without the right to the produce (*fructus*) of the thing. • *Usus* was a personal servitude; it gave the holder a right in rem. Cf. USUFRUCT.

"It is essentially a fraction of a usufruct, *usus* without the *fructus*. In strictness, there was no right to any fruits but this was somewhat relaxed in practice. The usuary of a house might consume the fruits of the gardens in his household, but he might not sell them, as a usufructuary might." W.W. Buckland, *A Manual of Roman Private Law* 165 (2d ed. 1953).

2. A marriage brought about by the acquisition of marital power (*manus*) over the wife through an uninterrupted cohabitation of one year with the intention of living as husband and wife. • *Usus* was the first method of creating a marriage with *manus* (*confarreatio* and *coemptio* being the other two) to pass out of use. Cf. CONFARREATIO; COEMPTIO.

"*Usus* is the acquisition of [power over] a wife by *possession* and bears the same relation to *coemptio* as usucapion to a mancipation. A Roman citizen who bought some object of property and got possession of it, but not ownership, because he neglected to go through the mancipation prescribed by *jus civile*, might nevertheless become owner by usucapion, *i.e.* lapse of time; thus if the object was a movable, continuous possession for one year made him *dominus*. In like manner, if a man lived with a woman whom he treated as his wife, but whom he had not married by *coemptio* (or *confarreatio*), and the cohabitation lasted without interruption for a year, then at the end of that period the man acquired [power over] the woman as his wife, she passed to him *in manum* ...." R.W. Leage, *Roman Private Law* 100 (C.H. Ziegler ed., 2d ed. 1930).

usus bellici (**yoo**-səs [*or* -zəs] **bel**-ə-sɪ). [Latin] *Int'l law*. Warlike objects or uses. • This phrase refers to items that, though not inherently of a military nature, are considered contraband because they are used by a belligerent to support its war effort.

Usus Feudorum (**yoo**-səs [*or* -zəs] fyoo-**dor**-əm). See FEUDORUM LIBRI.

ut currere solebat (ət **kər**-ər-ee sə-**lee**-bat). [Latin] As it was wont to run. • This referred to the course of a stream.

ut de feodo (ət dee **fee**-ə-doh *or* **fyoo**-doh). [Law Latin] As of fee.

uterine (**yoo**-tər-in), *adj.* Born of the same mother but different fathers.

uterine brother. See BROTHER.

uterque (yoo-**tər**-kwee). [Latin] Each of two; both (considered separately).

uterque nostrum. See UTRUMQUE NOSTRUM.

utfangthief (**ət**-fang-theef). See OUTFANGTHIEF.

ut hospites (ət **hos**-pə-teez). [Latin] As guests.

uti (**yoo**-tɪ), *vb.* [Latin] *Civil law.* To use.

uti frui (**yoo**-tɪ **froo**-ɪ). [Latin] *Civil law.* To have the full use and enjoyment of a thing, without damage to its substance.

utilis (**yoo**-tə-lis), *adj.* [Latin] *Civil law.* Useful; beneficial; equitable. • This word appeared in phrases such as *actio utilis* (**ak**-shee-oh **yoo**-tə-lis), meaning "equitable action."

utilitarian-deterrence theory. The legal theory that a person should be punished only if it is for the good of society — that is, only if the punishment would further the prevention of future harmful conduct. See *hedonistic utilitarianism* under UTILITARIANISM. Cf. RETRIBUTIVISM.

utilitarianism. A philosophy that the goal of public action should be the greatest happiness to the greatest number of people.

hedonistic utilitarianism. The theory that the validity of a law should be measured by determining the extent to which it would promote the greatest happiness to the greatest number of citizens. • This theory is found most prominently in the work of Jeremy Bentham, whose "Benthamite utilitarianism" greatly influenced legal reform in nineteenth-century Britain. Hedonistic utilitarianism generally maintains that pleasure is intrinsically good and pain intrinsically bad. Therefore, inflicting pain, as by punishing a criminal, is justified only if it results in a net increase of pleasure by deterring future harmful behavior. — Also termed *Benthamism.* See *utilitarian-deterrence theory*; BENTHAMITE. Cf. RETRIBUTIVISM.

utility. 1. The quality of serving some function that benefits society. **2.** *Patents.* Capacity to perform a function or attain a result claimed for protection as intellectual property. • In patent law, utility is one of the three basic requirements of patentability, the others being nonobviousness and novelty. **3.** A business enterprise that performs essential public service and that is subject to governmental regulation.

public utility. A company that provides necessary services to the public, such as telephones, electricity, and water. • Most utilities operate as monopolies but are subject to governmental regulation.

utility fund. See MUTUAL FUND.

utility patent. See PATENT (3).

ut infra (ət **in**-frə *also* uut). [Latin] As below.

uti possidetis (**yoo**-tɪ pah-si-**dee**-tis). [Latin] **1.** *Int'l law.* The doctrine that old administrative boundaries will become international boundaries when a political subdivision achieves independence. **2.** *Roman law.* An interdict ordering the parties to a lawsuit to maintain the possession of real property as it stands pending a decision on who owns it. Cf. UTRUBI.

uti rogas (**yoo**-tɪ **roh**-gas *or* -gəs). [Latin] *Roman law.* As you ask. • This was inscribed on a ballot to indicate a vote in favor of a bill or candidate. — Abbr. *u.r.*

utlagare (**ət**-lag-ə-ree *or* ət-lə-**gair**-ee), *vb.* [Law Latin] *Hist.* To put (an offender) outside the protection of the law. Cf. INLAGARE; OUTLAWRY (2).

utlagation (ət-lə-**gay**-shən), *n.* [Law Latin] *Hist.* The act of placing an offender outside the protection of the law; outlawry. — Also termed *utlagatio.* Cf. INLAGATION; OUTLAWRY (2).

utlagatus (ət-lə-**gay**-təs). [Latin] *Hist.* An outlawed person; an outlaw. — Also spelled *utlagatum*.

utlage (**ət**-lahzh *or* -lij). [Law French] An outlaw.

utlagh (**ət**-law). [Old English] *Hist.* A person outside the protection of the law; an outlaw.

utland (**ət**-lənd) [Old English] *Hist.* The outer portion of a lord's demesne, used to support the lord's tenants. — Also termed *delantal* (di-**lan**-təl). Cf. INLAND (2).

utlesse (**ət**-lis). *Hist.* An escape of a felon out of prison.

UTMA. *abbr.* UNIFORM TRANSFERS TO MINORS ACT.

utmost care. See *highest degree of care* under DEGREE OF CARE.

utrubi (**ət**-rə-bɪ). [Latin] *Civil law.* An interdict for maintaining the status quo of possession of movable property pending a ruling to determine its rightful owner. Cf. UTI POSSIDETIS.

utrumque nostrum (yoo-**trəm**-kwee **nos**-trəm). [Latin] Each of us. • This phrase usu. appeared in bonds. The accusative form is *uterque nostrum*.

ut supra (ət **s[y]oo**-prə *also* uut). [Latin] As above.

utter, *vb.* **1.** To say, express, or publish <don't utter another word until your attorney is present>. **2.** To put or send (a document) into circulation; esp., to circulate (a forged note) as if genuine <she uttered a counterfeit $50 bill at the grocery store>. — **utterance** (for sense 1), **uttering** (for sense 2), *n.*

utter, *adj.* Complete; absolute; total <an utter denial>.

utter bar. See OUTER BAR.

utter barrister. See *outer barrister* under BARRISTER.

uttering. The crime of presenting a false or worthless instrument with the intent to harm or defraud. — Also termed *uttering a forged instrument*. See FORGERY.

uxor (**ək**-sor). [Latin] Wife. — Abbr. *ux.* See ET UX.

uxore rapta et abducta (ək-**sor**-ee [*also* əg-**zor**-ee] **rap**-tə et ab-**dək**-tə). See DE UXORE RAPTA ET ABDUCTA.

uxorial (ək-**sor**-ee-əl *or* əg-**zor**-), *adj.* Of, relating to, or characteristic of a wife <uxorial property>.

uxoricide (ək-**sor**-ə-sɪd *or* əg-**zor**-). **1.** The murder of one's wife. **2.** A man who murders his wife.

v. *abbr.* **1.** VERSUS. — Also abbreviated *vs.* **2.** Volume. — Also abbreviated *vol.* **3.** Verb. — Also abbreviated *vb.* **4.** (*cap.*) Victoria — the Queen of England from 1837 to 1901. **5.** *Vide.* • This Latin term, meaning "see," is used in some phrases such as *quod vide* "which see," abbreviated *q.v.* **6.** *Voce* (**voh**-see). • This Latin term means "voice."

VA. *abbr.* VETERANS AFFAIRS, DEPARTMENT OF.

vacancy, *n.* **1.** The state or fact of a lack of occupancy in an office, post, or piece of property. **2.** The time during which an office, post, or piece of property is not occupied. **3.** An unoccupied office, post, or piece of property; an empty place. • Although the term sometimes refers to an office or post that is temporarily filled, the more usual reference is to an office or post that is unfilled even on a temporary basis. An officer's misconduct does not create a vacancy even if a suspension occurs; a vacancy, properly speaking, does not occur until the officer is officially removed.

vacancy clause. *Insurance.* A special indorsement allowing premises to be unoccupied beyond the period stipulated in the original insurance policy, so that the insurance remains in effect during an extension period, often for a reduced amount.

vacant, *adj.* **1.** Empty; unoccupied <a vacant office>. • Courts have sometimes distinguished *vacant* from *unoccupied*, holding that *vacant* means completely empty while *unoccupied* means not routinely characterized by the presence of human beings. **2.** Absolutely free, unclaimed, and unoccupied <vacant land>. **3.** (Of an estate) abandoned; having no heir or claimant. — The term implies either abandonment or nonoccupancy for any purpose.

vacantia (və-**kan**-sh[ee]-ə). See *bona vacantia* under BONA.

vacantia bona (və-**kan**-sh[ee]-ə **boh**-nə). See *bona vacantia* under BONA.

vacant succession. See SUCCESSION (2).

vacate, *vb.* **1.** To nullify or cancel; make void; invalidate <the court vacated the judgment>. Cf. OVERRULE. **2.** To surrender occupancy or possession; to move out or leave <the tenant vacated the premises>.

vacatio (və-**kay**-shee-oh). *Civil law.* Exemption; immunity; privilege; dispensation.

vacation, *n.* **1.** The act of vacating <vacation of the office> <vacation of the court's order>. **2.** The period between one term of court and the beginning of the next; the space of time during which a court holds no sessions. • The traditional vacations in England were Christmas vacation, beginning December 24 and ending January 6; Easter vacation, beginning Good Friday and ending Easter Tuesday; Whitsun vacation, beginning on the Saturday before and ending the Tuesday after Whitsunday (i.e., Pentecost, the seventh Sunday after Easter); and the long vacation, beginning August 13 and ending October 23. **3.** Loosely, any time when a given court is not in session. **4.** *Eccles. law.* The act or process by which a church or benefice becomes vacant, as on the death or resignation of the incumbent, until a successor is appointed. — Also termed (in sense 4) *vacatura.*

vacation barrister. See BARRISTER.

vacatur (və-**kay**-tər), *n.* [Law Latin "it is vacated"] **1.** The act of annulling or setting aside. **2.** A rule or order by which a proceeding is vacated.

vacatura (vay-kə-**t[y]oor**-ə), *n.* VACATION (4).

vacua possessio (**vak**-yoo-ə pə-**zes[h]**-ee-oh). [Latin "a vacant possession"] *Roman & civil law.* Free and unburdened possession, which a seller must give to a purchaser.

vacuus (**vak**-yoo-əs), *adj.* [Latin] *Hist.* Empty; void; vacant; unoccupied.

vades (**vay**-deez), *n.* [Latin pl. of *vas* "a surety"] Pledges, sureties, bail; esp., security for a criminal defendant's appearance in court.

vadiare duellum (vad-ee-**air**-ee d[y]oo-**el**-əm), *vb.* [Law Latin "to wage the duellum"] *Hist.* To give pledges mutually for engaging in trial by combat.

vadiare legem (vad-ee-**air**-ee **lee**-jəm), *vb.* [Law Latin "to wage law"] *Hist.* To give security to make one's law on a day assigned.

vadiatio (vad-ee-**ay**-shee-oh), *n.* [Law Latin] *Hist.* Wager. Cf. INVADIATIO.

vadiatio duelli (vad-ee-**ay**-shee-oh d[y]oo-**el**-I). [Law Latin "wager of battle"] See TRIAL BY COMBAT.

vadiatio legis (vad-ee-**ay**-shee-oh **lee**-jis). [Law Latin "wager of law"] See WAGER OF LAW.

vadimony (vad-ə-**moh**-nee). *Roman law.* **1.** A guarantee (originally backed by sureties) that a litigant would appear in court. **2.** A solemn promise to this effect. — Also termed *vadimonium.*

vadium (**vay**-dee-əm). [Law Latin "pledge, bail, security"] *Hist.* **1.** Security by a pledge of property.

vadium mortuum (**vay**-dee-əm **mor**-choo-əm). [Law Latin "dead pledge"] A mortgage. • This was considered a "dead pledge" because an estate was given as security by the borrower, who granted to the lender the estate in fee, on the condition that if the money were not repaid at the specified time, the pledged estate would continue as the lender's — it would be gone from, or "dead" to, the borrower (mortgagor). — Also termed *mortuum vadium.* See MORTGAGE.

vadium vivum (**vay**-dee-əm **vI**-vəm). [Law Latin "live pledge"] A living pledge, which exists when an estate is granted until a debt is paid out of its proceeds. • The pledge was so called because neither the money nor the lands were lost; it was a "living pledge" because the profits of the land were constantly paying off the debt. — Also termed *vivum vadium*; *vif-gage.*

2. Wages; salary.

vadium ponere (**vay**-dee-əm **poh**-nə-ree), *vb. Hist.* To take bail for the appearance of a person in court.

vagabond (**vag**-ə-bond), *n. Archaic.* A homeless wanderer without means of honest livelihood; VAGRANT. • This term became archaic over the course of the 20th century, as vagrants won the right not to be forcibly removed from cities. In the 1980s and 1990s, vagabonds came to be known as *street people* and *homeless people*, or *the homeless.* — Also termed *vagabundus* (vag-ə-**bən**-dəs).

> "[A]ll idle persons or vagabonds [are] ... divided into three classes, *idle* and *disorderly* persons, *rogues* and *vagabonds*, and *incorrigible rogues*; — all these are offenders against the good order, and blemishes in the government, of any kingdom. They are therefore all punished ... rogues and vagabonds with whipping and imprisonment not exceeding six months ...." 4 William Blackstone, *Commentaries on the Laws of England* 170 (1769).

vagabondage (**vag**-ə-bon-dij). **1.** The condition of a vagabond. **2.** Vagabonds as a class. — Also termed (in sense 1) *vagabondism*; (in senses 1 & 2) *vagabondry.*

vagabundus (vag-ə-**bən**-dəs). [Law Latin] See VAGABOND.

vagrancy (**vay**-grən-see), *n.* **1.** The state or condition of wandering from place to place without a home, job, or means of support. • Vagrancy is generally considered a course of conduct or a manner of living rather than a single act. But under some statutes, a single act has been held sufficient to constitute vagrancy; one court held, for example, that the act of prowling about and creeping up on parked cars and their occupants at night, under circumstances suggesting an intent to commit a crime, constitutes vagrancy. See *Smith v. Drew*, 26 P.2d 1040 (Wash. 1933). Many state laws prohibiting vagrancy have been declared unconstitutionally vague. — Also termed *vagrantism.* **2.** An instance of such wandering. Cf. LOITERING.

> "Vagrancy is a status resulting from misconduct and in the form of a socially harmful condition or mode of life which has been defined and made punishable by law. Until recently it was a misdemeanor, or group of misdemeanors, in most states." Rollin M. Perkins & Ronald N. Boyce, *Criminal Law* 494 (3d ed. 1982).

vagrant, *adj.* **1.** Of, relating to, or characteristic of a vagrant; inclined to vagrancy. **2.** Nomadically homeless.

vagrant, *n.* **1.** At common law, anyone belonging to the several classes of idle or disorderly persons, rogues, and vagabonds. **2.** One who, not having a settled habitation, strolls from place to place; a homeless, idle wanderer. • The term often refers to one who spends time in idleness or immorality, having no property and without any visible means of support. Under some statutes, a vagrant is an offender against or menace to the public peace, usu. liable to become a public burden. — Also termed *vagabond.* See VAGABOND.

vagrantism. See VAGRANCY.

vague, *adj.* **1.** Imprecise; not sharply outlined; indistinct. **2.** (Of words) broadly indefinite; not clearly or concretely expressed; uncertain. **3.** Characterized by haziness of thought.

vagueness. 1. Uncertain breadth of meaning <the phrase "within a reasonable time" is plagued by vagueness — what is reasonable?>. • Though common in writings generally, vagueness raises due-process concerns if legislation does not provide fair notice of what is required or prohibited, so that enforcement might well become arbitrary. **2.** Loosely, ambiguity. See AMBIGUITY.

vagueness doctrine. *Constitutional law.* The doctrine — based on the Due Process Clause — requiring that a criminal statute state explicitly and definitely what acts are prohibited, so as to provide fair warning and preclude arbitrary enforcement. — Also termed *void-for-vagueness doctrine.* Cf. OVERBREADTH DOCTRINE.

valentia (və-**len**-shee-ə), *n.* [Law Latin from Latin *valere* "to be of value"] *Hist.* Value; worth. • In old indictments for larceny, this term often appeared to express the value of the things taken.

valid, *adj.* **1.** Legally sufficient; binding <a valid contract>. **2.** Meritorious <that is a valid conclusion based on the facts presented in this case>. — **validate,** *vb.* — **validation, validity,** *n.*

valid agreement. See *valid contract* under CONTRACT.

validating statute. See STATUTE.

valid contract. See CONTRACT.

valise diplomatique (və-**lees** di-ploh-ma-**teek**). See DIPLOMATIC POUCH.

valor (**val**-ər), *n.* [Latin] *Hist.* Value; worth; rate; a valuation. — Also spelled *valour.* See AD VALOREM.

valor beneficiorum (**val**-ər ben-ə-fish-ee-**or**-əm). [Law Latin] *Hist.* The value of all ecclesiastical benefices and spiritual preferments.

valor maritagii (**val**-ər mar-ə-**tay**-jee-ɪ). [Latin] *Hist.* The value of a marriage. • Under ancient tenures, this was the amount that a female ward forfeited to a guardian when the guardian had offered her a marriage without disparagement (inequality), and she refused. In feudal law, the guardian in chivalry had the right of tendering to a minor ward a suitable match, without disparagement. If the ward refused, she forfeited the value of the marriage (*valor maritagii*) to the guardian. — Also termed (in the accusative) *valorem maritagii*; (Scots law) *avail of marriage.*

> "If an infant ward of a guardian in chivalry refused a match tendered by the guardian, he or she forfeited the value of the marriage (*valorem maritagii*) to the guardian; that is, so much as a jury would assess, or any one would *bona fide* give to the guardian for such an alliance." 2 Alexander M. Burrill, *A Law Dictionary and Glossary* 572–73 (2d ed. 1867).

valuable, *adj.* Worth a good price; having financial or market value.

valuable consideration. See CONSIDERATION.

valuable improvement. See IMPROVEMENT.

valuable papers. Documents that, upon a person's death, are important in carrying out the decedent's wishes and in managing the estate's affairs. • Examples include a will, title documents, stock certificates, powers of attorney, letters to be opened on one's death, and the like. Some statutes require that, to be effective, a holographic will devising realty be found among the decedent's valuable papers.

valuation, *n.* **1.** The process of determining the value of a thing or entity. **2.** The estimated worth of a thing or entity. — **value, valuate,** *vb.*

assessed valuation. The value that a taxing authority gives to property and to which the tax rate is applied.

special-use valuation. An executor's option of valuating real property in an estate, esp. farmland, at its current use rather than for its highest potential value.

valuation date. See ALTERNATE VALUATION DATE.

valuation list. *Hist.* An inventory of all the ratable hereditaments in a parish, each item in the inventory recording the name of the occupier, the owner, the property, the extent of the property, the gross estimated rental, and the ratable value. • The list was traditionally prepared by the overseers of each parish.

value, *n.* **1.** The monetary worth or price of something; the amount of goods, services, or money that something will command in an exchange.

actual cash value. *Insurance.* **1.** Replacement cost minus normal depreciation. **2.** See *fair market value.*

actual market value. See *fair market value.*

actual value. See *fair market value.*

agreed value. A property's value that is fixed by agreement of the parties with the property. • An example is a list of property values contained in an insurance policy.

annual value. **1.** The net yearly income derivable from a given piece of property. **2.** One year's rental value of property, less costs and expenses.

book value. See BOOK VALUE.

cash surrender value. *Insurance.* The amount of money payable when an insurance policy having cash value, such as a whole-life policy, is redeemed before maturity or death. — Abbr. CSV. — Also termed *surrender value.*

cash value. See *full cash value.*

clear annual value. The net annual value of property, after payment of taxes, interest on mortgages, and other charges.

clear market value. See *fair market value.*

clear value. *Tax.* For purposes of an inheritance tax, whatever remains of an estate after all claims against it have been paid.

fair market value. The price that a seller is willing to accept and a buyer is willing to pay on the open market and in an arm's-length transaction; the point at which supply and demand intersect. — Abbr. FMV. — Also termed *actual value*; *actual cash value*; *actual market value*; *cash value*; *clear market value*; *fair and reasonable value*; *fair cash market value*; *fair cash value*; *fair market price*; *fair value*; *full value*; *just value*; *market value*; *salable value*; *true value.*

"[A] forced sale price is not fair value though it may be used as evidence on the question of fair value. Likewise, the fair value of saleable assets is not what they would sell for in the slow process of the debtor's trade as if the debtor were continuing business unhampered. The general idea of fair value is the amount of money the debtor could raise from its property in a short period of time, but not so short as to approximate a forced sale, if the debtor operated as a reasonably prudent and diligent businessman with his interests in mind, especially a proper concern for the payment of his debts." David G. Epstein et al., *Bankruptcy* § 6–18, at 307 (1993).

fair value. See *fair market value.*

full cash value. Market value for property tax purposes; estimated value derived by standard appraisal methods. — Also termed *cash value.*

full value. See *fair market value.*

future value. The value, at some future time, of a present sum or a series of payments of money, calculated at a specific interest rate.

going-concern value. The value of a commercial enterprise's assets or the enterprise itself as an active business with future earning power, as opposed to the liquidation value of the business or its assets. • Going-concern value includes, for example, goodwill. — Also termed *going value.* Cf. GOODWILL.

highest proved value. In a trover action, the greatest value (as proven by the plaintiff) that the converted property reached from the time of the conversion until trial. • This is the most that a plaintiff is entitled to recover.

intrinsic value. The inherent value of a thing, without any special features that might alter its market value. • The instrinsic value of a silver coin, for example, is simply the value of the silver within it.

just value. See *fair market value.*

liquidation value. **1.** The value of a business or of an asset when it is sold in liquidation, as opposed to being sold in the ordinary course of business. **2.** See *liquidation price* under PRICE.

market value. See *fair market value.*

most-suitable-use value. See *optimal-use value.*

net value. **1.** *Insurance.* The excess of policyholder payments over the yearly cost of insurance; the part of an insured's annual premium that, according to actuarial tables, the insurer must set apart to meet the insurer's obligations to the insured. — Also termed *reserve.* **2.** The fair market value of shares of stock.

new value. **1.** A value (such as money) that is newly given. **2.** The value obtained by taking a security, such as collateral, for any debt other than a preexisting debt.

optimal-use value. *Tax.* The highest and best use of a thing from an economic standpoint. • If a farm is worth more as a potential shopping center, the shopping-center value will control even if the transferee (that is, a donee or heir) continues to use the property as a farm. — Also termed *most-suitable-use value*.

par value. See PAR VALUE.

present value. See PRESENT VALUE.

residual value. See *salvage value*.

salable value. See *fair market value*.

salvage value. The value of an asset after it has become useless to the owner; the amount expected to be obtained when a fixed asset is disposed of at the end of its useful life. • Salvage value is used, under some depreciation methods, to determine the allowable tax deduction for depreciation. And under the UCC, when a buyer of goods breaches or repudiates the contract of sale, the seller may, under certain circumstances, either complete the manufacture of any incomplete goods or cease the manufacture and sell the partial product for scrap of salvage value. UCC § 2–704(2). — Also termed *residual value*; *scrap value*. See DEPRECIATION.

scrap value. See *salvage value*.

settlement value. The present value of a claim if settled immediately as opposed to pursuing it further through litigation.

surrender value. See *cash surrender value*.

true value. See *fair market value*.

use value. A value established by the utility of an object instead of its value upon selling or exchanging it.

value received. See VALUE RECEIVED.

2. The significance, desirability, or utility of something. **3.** Sufficient contractual consideration. — **value,** *vb.* — **valuation,** *n.*

> "Value also includes paying or securing a preexisting debt, and in this regard value is broader than common-law consideration. Thus, a debtor receives value in satisfying an antecedent claim (as by paying an overdue account or an outstanding loan or by transferring property to vindicate a preexisting interest in it) or in providing collateral for a previously unsecured creditor. It makes no difference that the debtor got nothing new, in terms of property added to her estate, at the time of the transfer." David G. Epstein et al., *Bankruptcy* § 6–49, at 374 (1993).

value-added tax. See TAX.

value date. The date when the proceeds of a bill of exchange (e.g., a check) or of a foreign-exchange transaction (e.g., a sale of dollars for euros) become available for use. — Also termed *here and there*.

valued policy. See INSURANCE POLICY.

valued-policy law. A statute requiring insurance companies to pay the full amount of the insurance to the insured in the event of a total loss, regardless of the true value of the property at the time of loss.

valuer. See APPRAISER.

value received. Consideration that has been delivered. • This phrase is commonly used in a bill of exchange or promissory note to show that it was supported by consideration.

valuta (və-**loo**-tə), *n.* [Italian fr. Latin] Value; worth; esp., the value of a currency in relation to that of the currency of some other country.

valvasor (**valv**-ə-sor), *n.* [Law Latin] *Hist.* A principal vassal who, though not holding directly of the sovereign, held of those who did so; a vassal of the second degree or rank. — Also spelled *valvassor*. See VAVASOR.

VA mortgage. See MORTGAGE.

vandal. [fr. Latin *Vandalus*, a member of the Germanic tribe known as Vandals] A malicious destroyer or defacer of works of art, monuments, buildings, or other property.

vandalism, *n.* **1.** Willful or ignorant destruction of public or private property, esp. of artistic, architectural, or literary treasures. **2.** The actions or attitudes of one who maliciously or ignorantly destroys or disfigures public or private property; active hostility to anything that is venerable or beautiful. — **vandalize,** *vb.* — **vandalistic,** *adj.*

vara (**vah**-rah). A Spanish–American measure of length equal to about 33 inches. • Local usage varies, so that it may sometimes be more and sometimes less than 33 inches. In Mexican land grants, the measure is equal to 32.9927 inches.

variable annuity. See ANNUITY.

variable annuity contract. See CONTRACT.

variable cost. See COST (1).

variable life insurance. See INSURANCE.

variable rate. See INTEREST RATE.

variable-rate mortgage. See *adjustable-rate mortgage* under MORTGAGE.

variance. 1. A difference or disparity between two statements or documents that ought to agree; esp., in criminal procedure, a difference between the allegations in a charging instrument and the proof actually introduced at trial. — Also termed *variation*.

fatal variance. A variance that either deprives the defendant of fair notice of the charges or exposes the defendant to the risk of double jeopardy. • Such a variance is grounds for reversing a conviction.

immaterial variance. A variance that is too slight to mislead or prejudice the defendant, and is thus harmless error.

2. A license or official authorization to depart from a zoning law. — Also termed (in sense 2) *zoning variance*. Cf. SPECIAL EXCEPTION (2); SPECIAL-USE PERMIT.

area variance. A variance that permits deviation from zoning requirements about construction and placement, but not from requirements about use.

use variance. A variance that permits deviation from zoning requirements about use.

varrantizatio (və-ran-ti-**zay**-shee-oh), *n.* [Law Latin] *Hist. Scots law.* A warranty.

vas (vas), *n. Civil law.* A pledge or surety; esp., a surety in a judicial proceeding, whether civil or criminal. Pl. **vades.**

vassal (**vas**-əl), *n.* [fr. Law Latin *vassallus*] *Hist.* The grantee of a fief, feud, or fee; a feudal tenant. Cf. FREEMAN.

arriere vassal (a-ree-**air vas**-əl). *Hist.* The vassal of a vassal.

vassalage (**vas**-əl-ij), *n. Hist.* **1.** The state of being a vassal or feudatory. — Also termed *vasseleria*. **2.** The service required of a vassal. — Also termed *vassaticum*; *main-rent*. **3.** The territory held by a vassal; a fief or fee. **4.** Vassals collectively. **5.** The dominion or authority of a feudal superior over vassals. **6.** Political servility; subjection.

vassallus (**vas**-ə-ləs), *n.* [Law Latin] *Hist.* A feudal tenant. Cf. VASSUS.

vassal state. *Int'l law.* A state that is supposed to possess only those rights and privileges that have been granted to it by a more powerful state.

vassaticum (və-**sat**-ə-kəm). [Law Latin] See VASSALAGE (2).

vasseleria (vas-ə-**leer**-ee-ə). [Law Latin] See VASSALAGE (1).

vassus (**vas**-əs), *n.* [Law Latin] *Hist.* A feudal tenant that held immediately of the king. Cf. VASSALLUS.

vasto. See DE VASTO.

vastum (**vas**-təm), *n. Hist.* WASTE.

vastum forestae vel bosci (**vas**-təm for-**es**-tee vel **bahs**-I). *Hist.* Waste of a forest or wood.

VAT. See *value-added tax* under TAX.

vauderie (**vaw**-dər-ee). *Hist.* Sorcery; witchcraft.

vavasor (**vav**-ə-sor), *n.* [Law Latin] *Hist.* The vassal or tenant of a baron; one who held under a baron and also had subtenants. — Also spelled *vavasour* (**vav**-ə-suur). Cf. VALVASOR.

vavasory (**vav**-ə-sor-ee), *n.* [fr. Law Latin *vavasoria*] *Hist.* The lands held by a vavasor.

VC. *abbr.* VICE-CHANCELLOR.

VCC. *abbr.* VICE-CHANCELLOR'S COURT.

v.e. *abbr.* VENDITIONI EXPONAS.

veal-money. *Hist.* The annual rent paid by tenants of the manor of Bradford, in the county of Wiltshire, in lieu of veal formerly paid in kind.

vectigal (vek-**tI**-gəl), *n. Roman & civil law.* **1.** A tax, esp. an import or export duty, paid to the state. **2.** An annual ground rent paid in kind or in money. Pl. ***vectigalia*** (vek-tə-**gay**-lee-ə).

vectigal judiciarium (vek-**tI**-gəl joo-dish-ee-**air**-ee-əm), *n.* A tax or fine to defray the expenses of maintaining courts of justice.

vectura (vek-**t[y]oor**-ə). *Hist. Maritime law.* Freight.

vehicle (**vee**-ə-kəl), *n.* Something used as an instrument of conveyance; any conveyance used in transporting passengers or merchandise by land, water, or air.

vehicular (vee-**hik**-yə-lər), *adj.* Of or relating to a vehicle or vehicles.

vehicular homicide. See HOMICIDE.

vein, *n. Mining law.* A continuous body of mineral or mineralized rock, filling a seam or fissure in the earth's crust, within defined boundaries that clearly separate it from surrounding rock.

discovery vein. The primary vein for the purpose of locating a mining claim.

vejour (və-**zhoor**), *n.* [Law French fr. Law Latin *visores* "viewers"] *Hist.* **1.** One of several persons sent by the court to examine a place in question to help in the decision-making process. **2.** A person sent to view those who excuse themselves from court on grounds of illness, to see whether they are actually so sick that they cannot appear or whether they are malingering. — Also spelled *veyor*; *veyour*; *vayowr*; *veiour*; *veighor*.

vel non (vel **non**). [Latin "or not"] Or the absence of it (or them) <this case turns solely on the finding of discrimination vel non>.

venal (**vee**-nəl), *adj.* **1.** (Of a person) capable of being bribed. **2.** Ready to sell one's services or influence for money or other valuable consideration, usu. for base motives. **3.** Of, relating to, or characterized by corrupt bargaining. **4.** Broadly, purchasable; for sale.

vend, *vb.* **1.** To transfer to another for money or other thing of value. • The term is not commonly applied to real estate, although its derivatives (*vendor* and *vendee*) are. **2.** To make an object of trade, especially by hawking or peddling. **3.** To utter publicly; to say or state; to publish broadly.

vendee. A purchaser, usu. of real property; a buyer.

vendetta (ven-**det**-ə), *n.* A private blood feud in which family members seek revenge on a person outside the family (often members of another family); esp., a private war in which the nearest of kin seek revenge for the slaying of a relative.

vend. ex. *abbr.* VENDITIONI EXPONAS.

vendible, *adj.* Sellable; fit or suitable to be sold.

venditae (**ven**-də-tee). [fr. Latin *vendere* "to sell"] *Hist.* A tax on things sold in markets and at public fairs.

venditio (ven-**dish**-ee-oh). [Latin] *Roman & civil law.* **1.** A sale; VENDITION. **2.** A contract of sale. • In this sense, the term is short for *emptio et venditio*. See EMPTIO. **3.** Broadly, any contract by which the ownership of something may be transferred for value.

vendition, *n.* The act of selling; a sale. — Also termed *venditio*.

venditioni exponas (ven-dish-ee-**oh**-nI eks-**poh**-nəs). [Latin "you are to expose for sale"] A writ of execution requiring a sale to be made. • The writ is directed to a sheriff when he has levied upon goods under a *fieri facias* but has made return that they remain unsold for lack of buyers. In some jurisdictions, a *venditioni exponas* is issued to require a sale of lands seized under an earlier writ, after they have been condemned or passed upon by inquisition. Abbr. *vend. ex.*; *v.e.*

venditor (**ven**-də-tər), *n. Hist.* See VENDOR.

venditor regis (**ven**-də-tər **ree**-jis). [Latin] *Hist.* The king's seller; esp., the person who sold goods and chattels that had been seized or distrained to answer a debt due to the king.

venditrix (**ven**-də-triks), *n. Hist.* A female vendor.

vendor. A seller, usu. of real property. — Also termed *venditor*.

itinerant vendor. A vendor who travels from place to place selling goods.

vendor's lien. See LIEN.

vendue (ven-**d[y]oo** *or* **ven**-d[y]oo). *Hist.* **1.** A sale; esp., a sale at public auction. **2.** See *execution sale* under SALE.

vendue master. *Hist.* See AUCTIONEER.

venereal disease. See SEXUALLY TRANSMITTED DISEASE.

venery (**ven**-ə-ree). *Archaic.* **1.** Hunting. **2.** Sexual intercourse.

venia (**vee**-nee-ə), *n.* [Latin] *Hist.* **1.** A penitent's kneeling or assuming a prostrate position on the ground. **2.** A pardon. **3.** The granting of a privilege.

venia aetatis (**vee**-nee-ə i-**tay**-tis). *Roman & civil law.* A privilege granted by a prince or sovereign by virtue of which an underage person is entitled to act as if he or she were of full age.

venial (**vee**-nee-əl), *adj.* (Of a transgression) forgivable; pardonable.

venire (və-**nI**-ree *or* -**neer**-ee *or* -**nIr** *or* -**neer**). **1.** A panel of persons who have been selected for jury duty and from among whom the jurors are to be chosen. — Also termed *array; jury panel; jury pool.* **2.** VENIRE FACIAS.

venire de novo. See *venire facias de novo* under VENIRE FACIAS.

venire facias (və-**nI**-ree [*or* -**neer**-ee *or* -**nIr** *or* -**neer**] **fay**-shee-əs). A writ directing a sheriff to assemble a jury. — Often shortened to *venire.* — Also termed *venire facias juratores* (juur-ə-**tor**-eez).

venire facias ad respondendum (ad ree-spon-**den**-dəm). A writ requiring a sheriff to summon a person against whom an indictment for a misdemeanor has been issued. • A warrant is now more commonly used.

venire facias de novo (dee *or* di **noh**-voh). A writ for summoning a jury panel anew because of some impropriety or irregularity in the original jury's return or verdict so that no judgment can be given on it. • The result of a new venire is a new trial. In substance, the writ is a motion for new trial, but when the party objects to the verdict because of an error in the course of the proceeding (and not on the merits), the form of motion was traditionally for a venire facias de novo. — Often shortened to *venire de novo.*

venire facias tot matronas (tot mə-**troh**-nəs). A writ requiring a sheriff to summon a jury of matrons to execute a writ *de ventre inspiciendo.* See DE VENTRE INSPICIENDO.

veniremember (və-**nI**-ree-mem-bər *or* və-**neer**-ee- *or* və-**neer**-). A prospective juror; a member of a jury panel. — Also termed *venireman; venireperson; talesman.* See TALESMAN.

venit et defendit (**vee**-nit et di-**fen**-dit). [Latin] Comes and defends. • This phrase appeared in old-style defensive pleading.

venit et dicit (**vee**-nit et **dI**-sit). [Latin] Comes and says. • The phrase appeared in old-style pleading. Its remnant still occurs in some American jurisdictions: *Now comes the plaintiff, and respectfully says ....*

vente (vawnt *or* vont). [French] *French law.* A sale; contract of sale.

vente aléatoire (a-lay-ə-**twahr**). A sale subject to an uncertain event.

vente à réméré (ah ray-may-**ray**). A conditional sale, in which the seller reserves the right to redeem or repurchase at the same price. • The term is used in Louisiana and in some parts of Canada.

vente aux enchères (oh-zawn-**shair**). An auction. See AUCTION.

venter (**ven**-tər), *n.* [Latin "womb"] **1.** The womb of a wife or mother. **2.** One of two or more women who are sources of the same man's offspring.

> "**venter** ... is a term nowadays considered objectionable, as it refers to the woman merely as the possessor of a birth canal." Bryan A. Garner, *A Dictionary of Modern Legal Usage* 910 (2d ed. 1995).

ventre inspiciendo. See DE VENTRE INSPICIENDO; *venire facias tot matronas* under VENIRE FACIAS.

venture. An undertaking that involves risk; esp., a speculative commercial enterprise.

venture capital. See CAPITAL.

venturer, *n.* One who risks something in a business enterprise.

venue (**ven**-yoo). [Law French "coming"] *Procedure.* **1.** The proper or a possible place for the trial of a lawsuit, usu. because the place has some connection with the events that have given rise to the lawsuit. **2.** The county or other territory over which a trial court has jurisdiction. Cf. JURISDICTION. **3.** Loosely, the place where a conference or meeting is being held. **4.** In a pleading, the statement establishing the place for trial. **5.** In an affidavit, the designation of the place where it was made.

> "Venue must be carefully distinguished from jurisdiction. Jurisdiction deals with the power of a court to hear and dispose of a given case; in the federal system, it involves questions of a constitutional dimension concerning the basic division of judicial power among the states and between state and federal courts. Venue is of a distinctly lower level of importance; it is simply a statutory device designed to facilitate and balance the objectives of optimum convenience for parties and witnesses

> and efficient allocation of judicial resources." Jack H. Friedenthal et al., *Civil Procedure* § 2.1, at 10 (2d ed. 1993).

> "The distinction must be clearly understood between jurisdiction, which is the power to adjudicate, and venue, which relates to the place where judicial authority may be exercised and is intended for the convenience of the litigants. It is possible for jurisdiction to exist though venue in a particular district is improper, and it is possible for a suit to be brought in the appropriate venue though it must be dismissed for lack of jurisdiction. The most important difference between venue and jurisdiction is that a party may consent to be sued in a district that otherwise would be an improper venue, and it waives its objection to venue if it fails to assert it promptly. This is in striking contrast to subject-matter jurisdiction, which cannot be conferred by the parties, if it has not been granted by Congress, whether by consent, waiver, or estoppel." Charles Alan Wright, *The Law of Federal Courts* § 42, at 257 (5th ed. 1994).

venue, change of. See CHANGE OF VENUE.

venue facts. Facts that need to be established in a hearing to determine whether venue is proper in a given court.

venville (**ven**-vil), *n. Hist.* A tenure peculiar to the area of Dartmoor forest in Devonshire, whereby tenants have certain rights in the forest.

veracious (və-**ray**-shəs), *adj.* Truthful; accurate. — Also termed *veridical.*

veracity (və-**ras**-ət-ee), *n.* **1.** Truthfulness <the witness's fraud conviction supports the defense's challenge to his veracity>. **2.** Accuracy <you called into question the veracity of Murphy's affidavit>. — **veracious** (və-**ray**-shəs), *adj.*

veray (və-**ray**), *adj.* [Law French "true"] *Hist.* True. • This word is an older form of the French *vrai.*

verba (**vər**-bə), *n. pl.* [Latin] Words — esp. oral as opposed to written words.

verbal, *adj.* **1.** Of, relating to, or expressed in words. **2.** Loosely, of, relating to, or expressed in spoken words.

verbal act. See ACT (2).

verbal-act doctrine. The rule that utterances accompanying conduct that might have legal effect are admissible when the conduct is material to the issue and is equivocal in nature, and when the words help give the conduct its legal significance.

verbal contract. See *parol contract* (1) under CONTRACT.

verbal note. *Diplomacy.* An unsigned memorandum informally reminding an official of a pending request, an unanswered question, or the like.

verbal will. See *nuncupative will* under WILL.

verba precaria (**vər**-bə pri-**kair**-ee-ə). [Latin] *Civil law.* **1.** Precatory words. **2.** Words of trust; words of request used in creating a trust.

verbatim ac litteratim (vər-**bay**-tim ak lit-ə-**ray**-tim), *adv.* (vər-**bay**-tim ak li-tər-**ay**-tim). [Latin] Word for word and letter for letter. — Also termed *verbatim et litteratim.* — Also spelled *verbatim ac literatim*; *verbatim et literatim.*

verbi gratia (**vər**-bɪ **gray**-shee-ə). [Latin "for example"] Words for the sake of example. — Abbr. V.G.

verbruikleening (ver-**bruuk**-layn-ing), *n. Roman Dutch law.* A loan for use; COMMODATUM.

verderer (**vər**-dər-ər), *n.* [fr. French *verdier* "caretaker of green things"] *Hist.* A judicial officer who, being in charge of the king's forest, is sworn to preserve the vert (foliage) and venison, to keep the assizes, and to view, receive, and enroll attachments and presentments on matters involving trespass. — Also spelled *verderor.*

> "In all the forests there were a varying number of officers (usually four) elected in the county court, and styled Verderers. Manwood says that they should be 'gentlemen of good account, ability, and living, and well learned in the laws of the forest.' Their chief duty was to attend the forest courts; they served gratuitously; and they were immediately responsible to the crown. Possibly they were regarded as a check upon the Warden, as the coroner was upon the sheriff." 1 William Holdsworth, *A History of English Law* 96 (7th ed. 1956).

verdict. **1.** A jury's finding or decision on the factual issues of a case. **2.** Loosely, in a nonjury trial, a judge's resolution of the issues of a case.

chance verdict. A now-illegal verdict, arrived at by hazard or lot. — Also termed *gambling verdict*; *verdict by lot.*

compromise verdict. A verdict that is reached when jurors concede some issues so they can settle other issues in their favor.

defective verdict. A verdict on which a judgment cannot be based because of irregularities or legal inadequacies.

directed verdict. A judgment entered on the order of a trial judge who takes over the fact-finding role of the jury because the evidence is so compelling that only one decision can reasonably follow or because it fails to establish a prima facie case. — Also termed *instructed verdict.*

excessive verdict. A verdict that results from the jury's passion or prejudice and thereby shocks the court's conscience.

false verdict. A verdict so contrary to the evidence and so unjust that the judge may set it aside.

gambling verdict. See *chance verdict.*

general verdict. A verdict by which the jury finds in favor of one party or the other, as opposed to resolving specific fact questions. Cf. *special verdict.*

general verdict subject to a special case. *Archaic.* A court's verdict rendered without regard to the jury's general verdict, given when a party does not want to put the legal question on the record but merely wants the court to decide on the basis of a written statement of all the facts in the case, prepared for the opinion of the court by counsel on either side, according to the principles of a special verdict, whereupon the court decides the special case submitted and gives judgment accordingly.

general verdict with interrogatories. A general verdict accompanied by answers to written interrogatories on one or more issues of fact that bear on the verdict.

guilty verdict. A jury's formal pronouncement that a defendant is guilty of the charged offense.

instructed verdict. See *directed verdict.*

joint verdict. A verdict covering two or more parties to a lawsuit.

legally inconsistent verdict. A verdict in which the same element is found to exist and not to exist, as when a defendant is acquitted of one offense and convicted of another, when the offenses arise from the same set of facts and an element of the second offense requires proof that the first offense has been committed.

open verdict. A verdict of a coroner's jury finding that the subject "came to his death by means to the jury unknown" or "came to his death at the hands of a person or persons to the jury unknown." ● Such a verdict leaves open either the question whether any crime was committed or the identity of the criminal.

partial verdict. A verdict by which a jury finds a criminal defendant innocent of some charges and guilty of other charges.

perverse verdict. A jury verdict so contrary to the evidence that it justifies the granting of a new trial.

privy verdict (**priv**-ee). *Hist.* A verdict given after the judge has left or adjourned the court, and the jury, having agreed, obtain leave to give their verdict privately to the judge out of court so that the jurors can be delivered from their confinement. ● Such a verdict was of no force unless afterwards affirmed by a public verdict given in open court. This practice has been superseded by that of rendering a sealed verdict.

public verdict. A verdict delivered by the jury in open court.

quotient verdict. An improper verdict that a jury arrives at by totaling their individual damage awards and dividing by the number of jurors.

repugnant verdict. A verdict that contradicts itself in that the defendant is convicted and acquitted of different crimes having identical elements. ● Sometimes the inconsistency occurs in a single verdict (*repugnant verdict*), and sometimes it occurs in two separate verdicts (*repugnant verdicts*). Both terms are used mainly in New York.

responsive verdict. *Civil law.* A verdict that properly answers the indictment with specific findings prescribed by statute, the possible findings being guilty, not guilty, and guilty of a lesser-included offense.

sealed verdict. A written verdict put into a sealed envelope when the jurors have agreed on their decision but when court is not in session at the time. ● Upon delivering a sealed verdict, the jurors may separate. When court convenes again, this verdict is officially returned with the same effect as if the jury had returned it in open court before separating. This type of verdict is useful to avoid detaining the jurors until the next session of court.

special verdict. A verdict that gives a written finding for each issue, leaving the application of the law to the judge. Cf. *general verdict.*

split verdict. **1.** A verdict in which one party prevails on some claims, while the other party prevails on others. **2.** *Criminal law.* A verdict finding a defendant guilty on one charge but innocent on another. **3.** *Criminal law.* A verdict of guilty for one defendant and of not guilty for a codefendant.

true verdict. A verdict that is reached voluntarily — even if one or more jurors freely compromise their views — and not as a result of an arbitrary rule or order, whether imposed by the jurors themselves, the court, or a court officer.

verdict by lot. See *chance verdict.*

verdict contrary to law. A verdict that the law does not authorize a jury to render because the conclusion drawn is not justified by the evidence.

verdict subject to opinion of court. A verdict that is subject to the court's determination of a legal issue reserved to the court upon the trial, so that judgment is ultimately entered depending on the court's ruling on a point of law.

veredicto. See NON OBSTANTE VEREDICTO.

veredictum (ver-ə-**dik**-təm), *n. Hist.* A verdict; a declaration of the truth of a matter in issue, submitted to a jury for trial.

verge (vərj), *n. Hist.* **1.** The area within 12 miles of the place where the king held his court and within which the king's peace was enforced. • This area was commonly referred to as being *in the verge.* The verge got its name from the staff (called a "verge") that the marshal bore. **2.** The compass of the royal court, within which the lord steward and marshal of the king's household had special jurisdiction. — Also termed *Court of Verge.* **3.** The neighborhood of Whitehall, the section of London in which British government offices have traditionally been located. **4.** An uncertain quantity of land from 15 to 30 acres. **5.** A stick or rod by which a person, after holding the stick and swearing fealty, is admitted as a tenant to a copyhold estate. For *tenant by the verge,* see COPYHOLDER. — Also spelled *virge.*

vergens ad inopiam (**vər**-jenz ad in-**oh**-pee-əm), *adj.* [Latin] *Civil law.* Tending to become insolvent.

verger, *n.* One who carries a verge (a rod) as an emblem of office; esp., an attendant on a bishop or justice.

veridical (və-**rid**-ə-kəl). See VERACIOUS.

verification, *n.* **1.** A formal declaration made in the presence of an authorized officer, such as a notary public, by which one swears to the truth of the statements in the document. • Traditionally, a verification is used as a conclusion for all pleadings that do not tender issue. Cf. ACKNOWLEDGMENT (4). **2.** An oath or affirmation that an authorized officer administers to an affiant or deponent. **3.** Loosely, ACKNOWLEDGMENT (5). **4.** See *certified copy* under COPY. **5.** CERTIFICATE OF AUTHORITY. **6.** Any act of notarizing. — **verify,** *vb.* — **verifier,** *n.* Cf. JURAT (1).

verified copy. See *certified copy* under COPY.

verify, *vb.* **1.** To prove to be true; to confirm or establish the truth or truthfulness of; to authenticate. **2.** To confirm or substantiate by oath or affidavit; to swear to the truth of.

verily, *adv. Archaic.* Truly; in fact; certainly.

veritas (**ver**-i-tas *or* -tahs), *n.* [Latin] **1.** Truth. **2.** (*cap.*) An international institution of maritime underwriters for the survey and rating of vessels. • Founded in Belgium in 1828, it moved to Paris in 1832 and has long been represented all over the world. — Also termed *Bureau Veritas.*

verity (**ver**-ə-tee). Truth; truthfulness; conformity to fact.

vermenging (vər-**meng**-ing), *n.* [Dutch "mingling"] The extinction of a debt when the debtor's and the creditor's interests merge, as in a corporate merger.

verna (**vər**-nə). *Hist.* A slave born in the slaveholder's house.

versari (vər-**sair**-I), *vb.* [Latin] **1.** To be employed. **2.** To be conversant.

versari in re illicita (vər-**sair**-I in ree i-**lis**-ə-tə). [Latin] To be engaged in an unlawful activity (as a bar to a claim for damages).

versus, *prep.* Against. — Abbr. v.; vs.

vert (vərt). *Hist.* **1.** Anything that grows and bears green leaves within a forest. **2.** A power, given by royal grant, to cut green wood in a forest.

vertical competition. See COMPETITION.

vertical integration. See INTEGRATION (4).

vertical merger. See MERGER.

vertical nonprivity. See NONPRIVITY.

vertical price-fixing. See PRICE-FIXING.

vertical privity. See PRIVITY.

vertical restraint. See RESTRAINT OF TRADE.

vertical trust. See TRUST.

vertical union. See *industrial union* under UNION.

verus (**veer**-əs), *adj.* [Latin] True; truthful; genuine; actual.

very heavy work. See WORK.

vessel. A ship, brig, sloop, or other craft used — or capable of being used — to navigate on water. • To qualify as a vessel under the Jones Act, the structure's purpose must to some reasonable degree be the transportation of passengers, cargo, or equipment from place to place across navigable waters.

foreign vessel. A vessel owned by residents of, or sailing under the flag of, a foreign nation.

Jones Act vessel. A craft designed or used for transporting cargo or people on navigable waters, or that was being used for navigation at the time of a worker's injury. • For an injured worker to qualify as a seaman, and to be entitled to recover under the Jones Act, the worker must have been assigned to a vessel. A craft qualifies as a vessel if it is designed or used primarily for transportation on navigable waters, or if it was being used for navigational purposes at the time the worker was injured. But if the injury occurred, for example, on a work platform that was securely anchored and had no independent means of navigation, the platform would not qualify as a vessel and a claim under the Jones Act would fail.

public vessel. A vessel owned and used by a nation or government for its public service, whether in its navy, its revenue service, or otherwise.

sea-going vessel. A vessel that — considering its design, function, purpose and capabilities — is normally expected both to carry passengers for hire and to engage in substantial operations beyond the boundary line (set by the Coast Guard) dividing inland waters from the high seas. • Typically excluded from the definition are pleasure yachts, tugs and towboats, fishing boats, and other vessels that do not ordinarily carry passengers for hire.

> "Despite the important role a 'vessel' plays in maritime law, there is no settled definition of the term. Congress has defined a vessel as including 'every description of watercraft or other artificial contrivance used, or capable of being used, as a means of transportation on water.' 1 U.S.C.A. § 3. The Supreme Court has defined vessels as 'all navigable structures intended for transportation.' *Cope v. Vallette Dry-Dock Co.*, 119 U.S. 625 (1887)." Frank L. Maraist, *Admiralty in a Nutshell* 14 (3d ed. 1996).

seaworthy vessel. A vessel that can withstand the ordinary stress of the wind, waves, and other weather that seagoing vessels might ordinarily be expected to encounter. See SEAWORTHY.

vest, *vb.* **1.** To confer ownership of (property) upon a person. **2.** To invest (a person) with the full title to property. **3.** To give (a person) an immediate, fixed right of present or future enjoyment. **4.** *Hist.* To put (a person) into possession of land by the ceremony of investiture. — **vesting,** *n.*

vested, *adj.* Having become a completed, consummated right for present or future enjoyment; not contingent; unconditional; absolute <a vested interest in the estate>.

> "[U]nfortunately, the word 'vested' is used in two senses. Firstly, an interest may be vested *in possession*, when there is a right to present enjoyment, e.g. when I own and occupy Blackacre. But an interest may be vested, even where it does not carry a right to immediate possession, if it does confer a fixed right of taking possession in the future." George Whitecross Paton, *A Textbook of Jurisprudence* 305 (G.W. Paton & David P. Derham eds., 4th ed. 1972).

> "A future interest is *vested* if it meets two requirements: first, that there be no *condition precedent* to the interest's becoming a present estate other than the *natural expiration* of those estates that are prior to it in possession; and second, that it be *theoretically* possible to identify who would get the right to possession if the interest should become a present estate *at any time.*" Thomas F. Bergin & Paul G. Haskell, *Preface to Estates in Land and Future Interests* 66–67 (2d ed. 1984).

vested in interest. Consummated in a way that will result in future enjoyment. • Reversions, vested remainders, and any other future use or executory devise that does not depend on an uncertain period or event are all said to be vested in interest.

vested in possession. Consummated in a way that has resulted in present enjoyment.

vested estate. See ESTATE.

vested gift. See GIFT.

vested interest. See INTEREST (2).

vested legacy. See LEGACY.

vested ownership. See OWNERSHIP.

vested pension. See PENSION.

vested remainder. See REMAINDER.

vested right. See RIGHT.

vestigial words (ve-**stij**-ee-əl). Statutory words and phrases that, through a succession of amendments, have been rendered useless or meaningless. • Courts do not allow vestigial words to defeat the fair meaning of a statute.

vestigium (ve-**stij**-ee-əm). *Archaic.* A vestige, mark, or sign; a trace, track, or impression left by a person or a physical object.

vesting order. A court order passing legal title in lieu of a legal conveyance.

vestita manus (ves-**tI**-tə **may**-nəs), *n.* [Latin "vested hand"] *Hist.* The right hand used in the ceremony of investiture.

vestitive fact (**ves**-tə-tiv). See *dispositive fact* under FACT.

vestry (**ves**-tree). *Eccles. law.* **1.** The place in a church where the priest's robes are deposited. — Also termed *sacristy*. **2.** An assembly of the minister, church wardens, and parishioners to conduct church business.

vestry clerk. *Eccles. law.* An officer appointed to attend vestries and to take minutes of the proceedings.

vesture (**ves**-chər). *Hist.* **1.** The corn, grass, underwood, stubble, or other growth — apart from trees — that covers the land. — Also termed *vestura* (ves-**t[y]oor**-ə); *vestura terrae* (**ter**-ee); *vesture of land*. **2.** Seisin; investiture.

veteran. A person who, having been in military service, has been honorably discharged.

Veterans Affairs, Department of. An independent federal agency that administers benefit programs for veterans and their families. — Abbr. VA. — Also termed *Veterans Administration*.

Veterans Appeals, U.S. Court of. See UNITED STATES COURT OF VETERANS APPEALS.

vetera statuta (**vet**-ə-rə sta-**t[y]oo**-tə), *n. pl.* [Law Latin "ancient statutes"] The statutes from Magna Carta (1215) to the end of Edward II's reign (1327). — Also termed *antiqua statuta* (an-**tI**-kwə stə-**t[y]oo**-tə). Cf. NOVA STATUTA.

vetitive (**vet**-ə-tiv), *adj.* Of, relating to, or having the power to veto.

vetitum namium (**vet**-ə-təm **nay**-mee-əm), *n.* [Law Latin "a prohibited taking"] *Hist.* See NAMIUM VETITUM.

veto (**vee**-toh), *n.* [Latin "I forbid"] **1.** A power of one governmental branch to prohibit an action by another branch; esp., a chief executive's refusal to sign into law a bill passed by the legislature. **2.** VETO MESSAGE. *Pl.* **vetoes**. — **veto,** *vb.*

absolute veto. An unrestricted veto that is not subject to being overridden.

legislative veto. A veto that allowed Congress to block a federal executive or agency action taken under congressionally delegated authority. • The Supreme Court held the legislative veto unconstitutional in *INS v. Chadha*, 462 U.S. 919, 103 S.Ct. 2764 (1983). See DELEGATION DOCTRINE.

liberum veto (**lib**-ər-əm). *Hist.* Formerly in Poland, the right of any single member of the diet to invalidate a measure.

limited veto. See *qualified veto*.

line-item veto. The executive's power to veto some provisions in a legislative bill without affecting other provisions. • The U.S. Supreme Court declared the presidential line-item veto unconstitutional in 1998. See *Clinton v. City of New York*, 524 U.S. 417, 118 S.Ct. 2091 (1998). — Also termed *item veto*.

negative veto. See *qualified veto*.

overridden veto. A veto that the legislature has superseded by again passing the vetoed act, usu. by a supermajority of legislators. • In the federal government, a bill vetoed by the President must receive a two-thirds majority in Congress to override the veto and enact the measure into law.

pocket veto. A veto resulting from the President's failure to sign a bill passed within the last ten days of the legislative session.

qualified veto. A veto that is conclusive unless overridden by an extraordinary majority of the legislature. • This is the type of veto that the President of the United States has. — Also termed *limited veto*; *negative veto*.

suspensory veto (sə-**spen**-sə-ree). A veto that suspends a law until the legislature reconsiders it and then allows the law to take effect if repassed by an ordinary majority. — Also termed *suspensive veto*.

vetoer, *n.* One who vetoes. — Also termed *vetoist*.

veto message. A document communicating the reasons for the executive's not officially approving a proposed law. — Sometimes shortened to *veto*.

veto power. An executive's conditional power to prevent an act that has passed the legislature from becoming law.

vetus jus (**vee**-təs **jəs**). *Roman & civil law.* **1.** The law of the Twelve Tables. See TWELVE TABLES. **2.** Long-established or ancient law. **3.** A law in force before the passage of a later law.

vex, *vb.* To harass, disquiet, and annoy.

vexari (vek-**sair**-I), *vb.* [Latin] To be harassed, vexed, or annoyed.

vexata quaestio (vek-**say**-tə **kwes**-chee-oh). See VEXED QUESTION.

vexation. The injury or damage that is suffered as a result of another's trickery or malice.

vexatious (vek-**say**-shəs), *adj.* (Of conduct) without reasonable or probable cause or excuse; harassing; annoying.

vexatious delay. An insurance company's unjustifiable refusal to pay on an insurance claim, esp. based on a mere suspicion but no hard facts that the claim is ill-founded. — Also termed *vexatious refusal to pay*; *refusal to pay*.

vexatious lawsuit. See VEXATIOUS SUIT.

vexatious proceeding. See VEXATIOUS SUIT.

vexatious refusal to pay. See VEXATIOUS DELAY.

vexatious suit. A lawsuit instituted maliciously and without good cause. — Also termed *vexatious lawsuit*; *vexatious litigation*; *vexatious proceeding*. Cf. MALICIOUS PROSECUTION.

vexed question. 1. A question often argued about but seemingly never settled. **2.** A question or point that has been decided differently by different tribunals and has therefore been left in doubt. — Also termed *vexata quaestio* (vek-**say**-tə **kwes**-tee-oh).

v.g. *abbr.* VERBI GRATIA.

via (**vI**-ə). [Latin "way, road"] Roman & civil law. **1.** A road, way, or right-of-way.

via publica (**vI**-ə **pəb**-li-kə). [Latin] *Roman & civil law.* A public way or road. • The land itself belongs to the public.

2. A type of rural servitude that gave people the right to walk, ride, or drive over another's land. • *Via* encompassed both *iter* (a footpath) and *actus* (a driftway). **3.** *Civil law.* The way in which legal procedures are followed.

via executiva (**vI**-ə eg-zek-yə-**tI**-və). *Civil law.* Executory process whereby the debtor's property is seized, without previous citation, for some reason specified by law, usu. because of an act or title amounting to a confession of judgment.

via ordinaria (**vI**-ə or-di-**nair**-ee-ə). *Civil law.* The ordinary way or process whereby a citation is served and all the usual forms of law are followed.

viable (**vI**-ə-bəl), *adj.* **1.** Capable of living, esp. outside the womb <a viable fetus>. **2.** Capable of independent existence or standing <a viable lawsuit>. — **viability** (vI-ə-**bil**-ə-tee), *n.*

viae servitus (**vI**-ee **sər**-və-təs). [Latin "a servitude of way"] *Roman law.* A right-of-way over another's land.

via executiva. See VIA (3).

via facti (**vI**-ə **fak**-tI), *adv.* [Law Latin "by way of deed"] By force; in a forcible way.

viagère rente. See RENTE VIAGÈRE.

via ordinaria. See VIA (3).

via publica. See VIA (1).

via regia (**vI**-ə **ree**-jee-ə). [Latin "the king's highway"] *Hist.* The highway or common road — called the "king's highway" because the king authorized and protected it.

viatical settlement. See SETTLEMENT.

viatication (vI-at-ə-**kay**-shən). [fr. Latin *viaticus* "relating to a road or journey"] The purchase of a terminally or chronically ill policyholder's life insurance in exchange for a lump-sum payment. See *viatical settlement* under SETTLEMENT.

viator (vI-**ay**-tər). **1.** APPARITOR (1). **2.** A terminally or chronically ill life-insurance policyholder who sells the policy to a third party in return for a lump-sum payment equal to a percentage of the policy's face value.

viatorial privilege. See PRIVILEGE (1).

vi aut clam (**vI** awt **klam**), *adv.* [Latin] By force or covertly.

vicar. 1. One who performs the functions of another; a substitute. **2.** The incumbent of an appropriated impropriated ecclesiastical benefice. Cf. RECTOR.

vicarage (**vik**-ər-ij). **1.** The benefice of a vicar. **2.** The house or household of a vicar. **3.** VICARSHIP.

vicar general. An ecclesiastical officer who helps the archbishop in the discharge of his office.

vicarial tithe (vI-**kair**-ee-əl). See TITHE.

vicarious (vI-**kair**-ee-əs), *adj.* Performed or suffered by one person as substitute for another; indirect; surrogate.

vicarious disqualification. See DISQUALIFICATION.

vicarious infringement. See INFRINGEMENT.

vicarious liability. See LIABILITY.

vicarius apostolicus (vI-**kair**-ee-əs ap-əs-**tahl**-ə-kəs), *n.* [Latin "apostolic vicar"] *Eccles. law.* An officer through whom the Pope exercises authority in remote regions. • This officer is sometimes sent with episcopal functions into provinces where there is no bishop resident or where there has long been a vacancy in the see.

vicarship. The office, function, or duty of a vicar. — Also termed *vicarage.*

vice (**vI**-see *or* **vI**-sə), *prep.* In the place of; in the stead of. • As a prefix, *vice-* (vIs) denotes one who takes the place of.

vice (vIs), *n.* **1.** A moral failing; an ethical fault. **2.** Wickedness; corruption. **3.** Broadly, any defect or failing.

vice-admiralty. 1. The office of a vice-admiral. **2.** *Hist.* A civil officer exercising admiralty jurisdiction within a specific locale.

vice-admiralty court. *Hist.* A tribunal established in British possessions beyond the seas, with jurisdiction over maritime cases, including those related to prize. • The governor of the colony, in the capacity of "vice-admiral," exercised judicial authority in this court.

vice-chamberlain. *Hist.* A great officer under the lord chamberlain. • In the lord chamberlain's absence, the vice-chamberlain would control and command the officers attached to the part of the royal household called the "chamber."

vice-chancellor. A judge appointed to act for the chancellor, esp. in a chancery court. — Abbr. VC.

vice-comes (vI-sə-**koh**-meez), *n.* [Law Latin] *Hist.* **1.** VISCOUNT. **2.** SHERIFF. — Also spelled *vicecomes.*

vicecomital (vI-sə-**kom**-ə-təl). See VICONTIEL.

vice-comitissa (vI-sə-kom-ə-**tis**-ə). See VISCOUNTESS.

vice-commercial agent. *Hist.* In the consular service of the United States, a consular officer who was substituted temporarily to fill the place of a commercial agent who was absent or had been relieved from duty.

vice-consul. A consular officer subordinate to a consul; esp., one who is substituted temporarily to fill the place of a consul who is absent or has been relieved from duty.

career vice-consul. A vice-consul who is a member of the Foreign Service. — Also termed *vice-consul of career.*

noncareer vice-consul. A vice-consul who is not a member of the Foreign Service and who is appointed without examination.

vice crime. See CRIME.

vice-dominus episcopi (vI-sə-**dom**-ə-nəs ə-**pis**-kə-pI). **1.** A vicar general. **2.** A commissary of a bishop.

vicegerent (vIs-**jeer**-ənt). A deputy; lieutenant.

vice-governor, *n.* A deputy or lieutenant governor.

vice-judex (vIs-**joo**-deks). *Hist.* A deputy judge.

vice-marshal. An officer appointed to assist the earl marshal. See EARL MARSHAL.

vice president, *n.* **1.** An officer selected in advance to fill the presidency if the president dies, becomes incapacitated, resigns, or is removed from office. • The Vice President of the United States, who is elected at the same time as the President, serves as presiding officer of the Senate. On the death, incapacity, resignation, or removal of the President, the Vice President succeeds to the presidency. **2.** A corporate officer of mid-level to high rank, usu. having charge of a department. — Also written *vice-president.* — **vice presidency,** *n.* — **vice presidential,** *adj.*

vice principal. See FELLOW-SERVANT RULE.

viceregent, *n.* **1.** A deputy regent; esp., one who acts in the place of a ruler, governor, or sovereign. **2.** More broadly, an officer deputed by a superior or by proper authority to exercise the powers of the higher authority; one with delegated power.

viceroy, *n.* The governor of a kingdom or colony, who rules as the deputy of a monarch. — **viceroyal, viceregal,** *adj.*

vice-sheriff. See *deputy sheriff* under SHERIFF.

vice-treasurer, *n.* A deputy or assistant treasurer.

vicinage (**vis**-ə-nij). [Law French "neighborhood"] **1.** Vicinity; proximity. **2.** The place where a crime is committed or a trial is held; the place from which jurors are to be drawn for trial; esp., the locale from which the accused is entitled to have jurors selected. — Also termed *vicinetum.*

> "Whereas venue refers to the locality in which charges will be brought and adjudicated, vicinage refers to the locality from which jurors will be drawn.... The vicinage concept requires that the jurors be selected from a geographical district that includes the locality of the commission of the crime, and it traditionally also mandates that such district not extend too far beyond the general vicinity of that locality." Wayne R. LaFave & Jerold H. Israel, *Criminal Procedure* § 16.1, at 738–39 (2d ed. 1992).

3. A right of common that neighboring tenants have in a barony or fee.

vicious propensity. An animal's tendency to endanger the safety of persons or property.

vicontiel (vI-**kon**-tee-əl). **1.** Of or relating to a viscount. **2.** Of or relating to a sheriff. — Also spelled *vicountiel.* — Also termed *vicecomital.*

vicontiel rent. *Hist.* Rent that a viscount or sheriff pays for the use of a royal farm.

vicontiels (vI-**kon**-tee-əlz). *Hist.* **1.** Money payable by a viscount or sheriff to the Crown. **2.** Vicontiel rents.

vicontiel writ. See WRIT.

victim, *n.* A person harmed by a crime, tort, or other wrong. — **victimize,** *vb.* — **victimization,** *n.*

victim allocution. See ALLOCUTION.

victim-impact statement. A statement read into the record during sentencing to inform the judge or jury of the financial, physical, and psychological impact of the crime on the victim and the victim's family.

victimless crime. See CRIME.

victualer (**vit**-əl-ər). *Hist.* **1.** A person authorized by law to keep a house of entertainment for the public; a publican. **2.** A person who serves food or drink prepared for consumption on the premises. — Also spelled *victualler.*

victual rent. *Scots law.* A rent paid in grain or its monetary equivalent.

victus (**vik**-təs). *Civil law.* Sustenance; support; a means of living.

vidame (vee-**dam**). [French] *Hist.* In French feudal law, an officer who represented the bishop. • Over time, these officers erected their offices into fiefs and became feudal nobles, such as the *vidame* of Chartres, Rheims, etc. They continued to take their titles from the seat of the bishop whom they represented, even though the lands held by virtue of their fiefs might be situated elsewhere.

vide (**vɪ**-dee *also* **vee**-day). [Latin] See. • This is a citation signal still seen in some texts, esp. in the abbreviated form *q.v.* (*quod vide* "which see"). *Vide ante* or *vide supra* refers to a previous passage in a text; *vide post* or *vide infra* refers to a later passage.

videlicet (vi-**del**-ə-set *or* -sit). [Latin] To wit; that is to say; namely; SCILICET. • The term is used primarily to point out, particularize, or render more specific what has been previously stated in general (or occasionally obscure) language. One common function is to state the time, place, or manner when that is the essence of the matter at issue. — Abbr. *viz.* See VIZ.

vidimus (**vid**-ə-məs), *n.* [Latin "we have seen"] **1.** An inspection of documents, etc. **2.** An abstract, syllabus, or summary. **3.** An attested copy of a document. **4.** INSPEXIMUS.

vidua regis (**vij**-oo-ə **ree**-jis), *n.* [Latin] **1.** The widow of the king. **2.** The widow of a tenant in capite. • In sense 2, she was so called because she was not allowed to marry a second time without the king's permission. She obtained her dower from the king, who was her patron and defender.

viduitatis professio (və-d[y]oo-ə-**tay**-tis prə-**fes**[**h**]-ee-oh), *n.* [Latin] *Hist.* A woman's solemn act of professing that she will live as a single, chaste woman.

viduity (vi-**d**[**y**]**oo**-ə-tee). *Archaic.* Widowhood.

vie (vee). [French] Life. • The term occurs in such Law French phrases as *cestui que vie* and *pur autre vie.*

vi et armis (**vɪ** et **ahr**-mis). [Latin] *Hist.* By or with force and arms. See *trespass vi et armis* under TRESPASS.

> "The words '*with force and arms,*' anciently '*vi et armis,*' were, by the common law, necessary in indictments for offences which amount to an actual disturbance of the peace, or consist, in any way, of acts of violence; but it seems to be the better opinion, that they were never necessary where the offence consisted of a cheat, or nonfeazance, or a mere consequential injury." 1 Joseph Chitty, *A Practical Treatise on the Criminal Law* 240 (2d ed. 1826).

> "***vi et armis*** ... was a necessary part of the allegation, in medieval pleading, that a trespass had been committed with force and therefore was a matter for the King's Court because it involved a breach of the peace. In England, the term survived as a formal requirement of pleading until 1852." Bryan A. Garner, *A Dictionary of Modern Legal Usage* 916 (2d ed. 1995).

view, *n.* **1.** The common-law right of prospect — that is, an outlook from the windows of one's house. **2.** An urban servitude that prohibits the obstruction of the outlook from a person's house. **3.** A jury's inspection of a place relevant to a case it is considering; the act or proceeding by which a tribunal goes to observe an object that cannot be produced in court because it is immovable or inconvenient to remove. • The appropriate procedures are typically regulated by state statute. At common law, and today in many civil cases, the trial judge's presence is not required. The common practice has been for the jury to be conducted to the scene by "showers" who are commissioned for this purpose. Parties and counsel are generally permitted to attend, although this is a matter typically within the trial judge's discretion. Cf. VIEW OF AN INQUEST. **4.** In a real action, a defendant's observation of the thing at issue to ascertain its identity and other circumstances surrounding it. Cf. DEMAND OF VIEW.

viewer. A person, usu. one of several, appointed by a court to investigate certain matters or to examine a particular locality (such as the proposed site of a new road) and to report to the court.

view of an inquest. A jury's inspection of a place or property to which an inquiry or inquest refers. Cf. VIEW (3).

view of frankpledge. *Hist.* The twice-yearly gathering and inspection of every freeman within the district who was more than 12 years old to determine whether each one had taken the oath of allegiance and had found nine freeman pledges for his peaceable demeanor. See FRANKPLEDGE.

vif-gage (**veef**-gayj *or* **vif**-). [Law French] See *vadium vivum* under VADIUM.

vigil. *Eccles. law.* The day before any solemn feast.

vigilance. Watchfulness; precaution; a proper degree of activity and promptness in pursuing one's rights, in guarding them from infraction, and in discovering opportunities for enforcing one's lawful claims and demands.

vigilant, *adj.* Watchful and cautious; on the alert; attentive to discover and avoid danger.

vigilante (vij-ə-**lan**-tee). A person who seeks to avenge a crime by taking the law into his or her own hands.

vigilantism (vij-ə-**lan**-tiz-əm). The act of a citizen who takes the law into his or her own hands by apprehending and punishing suspected criminals.

viis et modis (**vI**-is et **moh**-dis). [Latin] *Eccles. law.* By all ways and means. • In ecclesiastical courts, service of a decree or citation *viis et modis* is equivalent to substituted service in temporal courts. It is opposed to personal service.

vi laica amovenda. See DE VI LAICA AMOVENDA.

vill (vil). *Hist.* **1.** A part into which a hundred or wapentake was divided. **2.** A town or village.

village. 1. Traditionally, a modest assemblage of houses and buildings for dwellings and businesses. **2.** In some states, a municipal corporation with a smaller population than a city. — Also termed (in sense 2) *town*; *borough*.

villanis regis subtractis reducendis (vi-**lay**-nis **ree**-jis səb-**trak**-tis ree-d[y]oo-**sen**-dis), *n.* [Latin "for returning the king's villeins who have been removed"] *Hist.* A writ that lay for the bringing back of the king's bondmen who had been carried away by others out of his manors, where they belonged.

villanum servitium (vi-**lay**-nəm sər-**vish**-ee-əm), *n.* [Latin] *Hist.* See VILLEINAGE (1).

villein (**vil**-ən). *Hist.* A person entirely subject to a lord or attached to a manor, but free in relation to all others; a serf. • At the time of the Domesday Inquest (shortly after the Norman Conquest), about 40% of households were marked as belonging to villeins: they were the most numerous element in the English population. Cf. FREEMAN.

> ***villein in gross.*** A villein who was annexed to the person of the lord, and transferable by deed from one owner to another.
>
> ***villein regardant*** (ri-**gahr**-dənt). A villein annexed to the manor of land.

villeinage (**vil**-ə-nij). *Hist.* **1.** The holding of property through servitude to a feudal lord; a servile type of tenure in which a tenant was obliged to render to a lord base services. Cf. KNIGHT-SERVICE; SOCAGE. **2.** A villein's status, condition, or service. — Also spelled *villenage*; *villainage*; *villanage*.

> "At the lower level the services were not always defined. The duties of the peasant were chiefly agricultural. If they were unfixed, so that the lord might in theory demand all manner of work, the tenure was 'unfree' and was called *villeinage*." J.H. Baker, *An Introduction to English Legal History* 260 (3d ed. 1990).

> ***privileged villeinage.*** Villeinage in which the services to be performed were certain, though of a base and servile nature.
>
> ***pure villeinage.*** Villeinage in which the services were not certain, but the tenant was obliged to do whatever he was commanded whenever the command came.

villein in gross. See VILLEIN.

villein regardant. See VILLEIN.

villein service. *Hist.* A base service that a villein performed, such as working on the lord's land on certain days of the week (usu. two to four). • These services were not considered suitable to a man of free and honorable rank. — Also termed *villein servitium*. See WEEK-WORK.

villein socage (**sok**-ij). See SOCAGE.

villenous judgment (**vil**-ə-nəs). *Hist.* A judgment that deprived a person of his *libera lex*, as a result of which he was discredited and disabled as a juror and witness, forfeited his goods and chattels and land, had his houses razed and trees uprooted, and went to prison. — Also spelled *villainous judgment*.

vinagium (vi-nay-**jee**-əm). A payment in kind of wine as rent for a vineyard.

vinculación (vin-koo-lah-**syohn**). *Spanish law.* An entail.

vinculo (**ving**-kyə-loh). *Spanish law.* The bond of marriage. See *divorce a vinculo matrimonii* under DIVORCE.

vinculum juris (**ving**-kyə-ləm **joor**-is), *n.* [Latin "a bond of the law"] *Roman law.* The tie that legally binds one person to another; legal bond; obligation. Cf. SOLUTIO OBLIGATIONIS.

vindex (**vin**-deks). [Latin] *Civil law.* A defender.

vindicare (vin-di-**kair**-ee), *vb.* [Latin "to claim or challenge"] *Hist.* To demand as one's own; to assert a right in or to (a thing); to assert or claim ownership of (a thing).

vindicate, *vb.* **1.** To clear (a person or thing) from suspicion, criticism, blame, or doubt <the serial killer will never be vindicated in the minds of the victims' families>. **2.** To assert, maintain, or affirm (one's interest) by action <the claimants sought to vindicate their rights through a class-action proceeding>. **3.** To defend (one's interest) against interference or encroachment <the borrower vindicated its interest in court when the lender attempted to foreclose>. **4.** To clear from censure or suspicion by means of demonstration. **5.** *Roman & civil law.* To assert a legal right to (a thing); to seek recovery of (a thing) by legal process <Antony Honoratus attempted to vindicate the sword he had lent his cousin>. — **vindication,** *n.* — **vindicator,** *n.*

vindicatio (vin-di-**kay**-shee-oh), *n.* [Latin "claim"] **1.** *Roman law.* An action by the owner to recover property. **2.** *Civil law.* The claiming of a thing as one's own; the assertion of a right in or title to a thing.

vindicatio servitutis (vin-di-**kay**-shee-oh sər-və-**t[y]oo**-tis). [Latin "claim of servitude"] *Roman law.* An action against the owner of land on which the plaintiff claims a servitude. — Also termed *actio confessoria.*

vindicatory part (**vin**-də-kə-tor-ee). The portion of a statute that sets forth the penalty for committing a wrong or neglecting a duty.

vindicta (vin-**dik**-tə), *n. Roman law.* **1.** A rod or wand. **2.** By extension, a legal act by which a person holding a rod or wand manumitted a slave.

vindictive damages. See *punitive damages* under DAMAGES.

vindictive prosecution (vin-**dik**-tiv). The practice of singling a person out for prosecution under a law or regulation because the person has exercised a constitutionally protected right. Cf. *selective enforcement* under ENFORCEMENT.

viocontiel writ. See WRIT.

viol (vyohl), *n.* [French] *French law.* Rape; indecent assault.

violation, *n.* **1.** An infraction or breach of the law; a transgression. **2.** The act of breaking or dishonoring the law; the contravention of a right or duty. **3.** Rape; ravishment. **4.** Under the Model Penal Code, a public-welfare offense. • In this sense, a violation is not a crime. See Model Penal Code § 1.04(5). — **violate,** *vb.* — **violative** (**vɪ**-ə-lay-tiv), *adj.* — **violator,** *n.*

violence. Unjust or unwarranted use of force, usu. accompanied by fury, vehemence, or outrage; physical force unlawfully exercised with the intent to harm. • Some courts have held that violence in labor disputes is not limited to physical contact or injury, but may include picketing conducted with misleading signs, false statements, erroneous publicity, and veiled threats by words and acts.

domestic violence. Violence between members of a household, usu. spouses; an assault or other violent act committed by one member of a household against another. See BATTERED-CHILD SYNDROME; BATTERED-WOMAN SYNDROME.

violent, *adj.* **1.** Of, relating to, or characterized by strong physical force <violent blows to the legs>. **2.** Resulting from extreme or intense force <violent death>. **3.** Vehemently or passionately threatening <violent words>.

violent crime. See CRIME.

violent death. See DEATH.

violent offense. A crime characterized by extreme physical force, such as murder, forcible rape, and assault and battery with a dangerous weapon. — Also termed *violent felony.*

violent profits. *Scots law.* Rents or profits of an estate kept by a holdover tenant who has already been warned by the landlord not to keep them.

vir (veer), *n.* **1.** An adult male; a man. **2.** A husband. • In the Latin phrases and maxims that once pervaded English law, *vir* generally means "husband," as in the expression *vir et uxor* (corresponding to the Law French *baron et feme*).

vires (**vɪ**-reez), *n.* **1.** Natural powers; forces. **2.** Granted powers, esp. when limited. See ULTRA VIRES; INTRA VIRES.

vir et uxor (**veer** et **ək**-sor). [Latin] Husband and wife.

virga (**vər**-gə). *Hist.* A rod or staff; esp., a rod as an ensign of office.

virgata (vər-**gay**-tə). **1.** A quarter of an acre of land. See ACRE. **2.** A quarter of a hide of land. See HIDE.

virgata regia (vər-**gay**-tə **ree**-jee-ə). [Latin "king's verge"] *Hist.* The bounds of the king's household, within which the court of the steward had jurisdiction.

virga terrae (**vər**-gə **ter**-ee), *n.* [Latin "branch of land"] *Hist.* A variable measure of land ranging from 20 to 40 acres. — Also termed *virgata terrae*. See YARDLAND.

virge. See VERGE.

viridario eligendo (vir-ə-**dair**-ee-oh el-ə-**jen**-doh). *Hist.* A writ for choice of a verderer in the forest.

virile share. *Civil law.* An amount that an obligor owes jointly and severally with another. — Also termed *virile portion*.

virilia (və-**ril**-ee-ə *or* vɪ-**ril**-ee-ə), *n.pl.* [Latin] The male genitals.

virtual adoption. See *adoption by estoppel* under ADOPTION.

virtual representation. A party's maintenance of an action on behalf of others with a similar interest, as a class representative does in a class action.

virtual-representation doctrine. The principle that a judgment may bind a person who is not a party to the litigation if one of the parties is so closely aligned with the nonparty's interests that the nonparty has been adequately and effectively represented by the party in court. • Under this doctrine, for instance, a judgment in a case naming only the husband as a party can be binding on his wife as well. See RES JUDICATA.

virtute cujus (vər-**t[y]oo**-tee **k[y]oo**-jəs), *adv.* [Latin] *Hist.* By virtue whereof. • This phrase began the clause in a pleading that attempted to justify an entry onto land by alleging that it was by virtue of an order from one entitled that the entry took place.

virtute officii (vər-**t[y]oo**-tee ə-**fish**-ee-ɪ), *adv.* [Latin] *Hist.* By virtue of his (or her) office; by the authority invested in one as the incumbent of a particular office. • An officer acts *virtute officii* when carrying out some official authority as the incumbent of an office.

vis (vis). [Latin "power"] **1.** Any force, violence, or disturbance relating to a person or property. **2.** The force of law. • Thus *vim habere* ("to have force") is to be legally valid. Pl. ***vires.***

visa (**vee**-zə). An official indorsement made out on a passport, showing that it has been examined and that the bearer is permitted to proceed; a recognition by the country in which a passport-holder wishes to travel that the holder's passport is valid. • A visa is generally required for the admission of aliens into the United States. 8 USCA §§ 1181, 1184. — Also termed (archaically) *visé* (**vee**-zay *or* vi-**zay**).

vis ablativa (**vis** ab-lə-**tɪ**-və), *n.* [Latin "ablative force"] *Civil law.* Force exerted in taking something away from another.

vis absoluta (**vis** ab-sə-**loo**-tə). Physical compulsion.

> "The difference is between compulsion of the will (*vis compulsiva*) which results in an act though not of free volition, and physical compulsion (*vis absoluta*) in which the unavoidable movement is no act at all." Rollin M. Perkins & Ronald N. Boyce, *Criminal Law* 1054–55 (3d ed. 1982).

vis armata (**vis** ahr-**may**-tə), *n.* [Latin "armed force"] *Hist.* Force exerted by means of weapons. Cf. VIS INERMIS.

vis-à-vis (**veez**-ə-**vee**). [French "face to face"] **1.** *prep.* In relation to; opposite to <the creditor established a preferred position vis-à-vis the other creditors>. **2.** *adv.* Facing each other; opposite <that defense is possible in all intrafamilial legal relationships, esp. parent vis-à-vis child>.

vis clandestina (**vis** klan-des-**tI**-nə), *n.* [Latin "clandestine force"] *Hist.* Force furtively used, esp. at night.

vis compulsiva (**vis** kom-pəl-**sI**-və), *n.* [Latin "compulsive force"] *Hist.* Force exerted to compel another to do something involuntarily; menacing force exerted by terror.

viscount (**vI**-kownt). **1.** The title of the fourth rank of European nobility. • In the British peerage, viscount is placed between the dignity of earl and baron. **2.** *Hist.* A sheriff.

viscountess (**vI**-kown-tis). The wife of a viscount. — Also termed *vice-comitissa.*

vis divina (**vis** di-**vI**-nə), *n. Civil law.* Divine or superhuman force; VIS MAJOR.

visé. See VISA.

vis expulsiva (**vis** eks-pəl-**sI**-və), *n.* [Latin "expulsive force"] *Hist.* Force used to expel or dispossess another.

vis exturbativa (**vis** eks-tər-bə-**tI**-və), *n.* [Latin "eliminating force"] *Hist.* Force used to thrust out another, esp. when two claimants are contending for possession.

vis fluminis (**vis floo**-mə-nis), *n.* [Latin "the force of a river"] *Civil law.* The force exerted by a stream or river; waterpower.

visible, *adj.* **1.** Perceptible to the eye; discernible by sight. **2.** Clear, distinct, and conspicuous.

visible means of support. An apparent method of earning a livelihood. • Vagrancy statutes have long used this phrase to describe those who have no ostensible ability to support themselves.

vis illicita (**vis** il-**lis**-ə-tə). See VIS INJURIOSA.

vis impressa (**vis** im-**pres**-ə), *n.* [Latin "impressed force"] The original act of force from which an injury arises, as distinguished from the proximate (or immediate) force.

vis inermis (**vis** in-**ər**-mis), *n.* [Latin] Unarmed force. Cf. VIS ARMATA.

vis injuriosa (**vis** in-joor-ee-**oh**-sə), *n.* [Latin "injurious force"] *Hist.* Wrongful force. — Also termed *vis illicita.*

vis inquietativa (**vis** in-kwI-ə-tə-**tI**-və), *n.* [Latin "disquieting force"] *Civil law.* Force that prevents another from using his or her possession quietly and in peace.

visit, *n. Int'l law.* A naval officer's boarding an ostensibly neutral merchant vessel from another state to exercise the right of search. • This right is exercisable when suspicious circumstances exist, as when the vessel is suspected of involvement in piracy. — Also termed *visitation.* See RIGHT OF SEARCH.

visitation (viz-ə-**tay**-shən). **1.** Inspection; superintendence; direction; regulation. **2.** *Family law.* A noncustodial parent's period of access to a child. • Although the noncustodial parent is responsible for the care of the child during visits, visitation differs from custody because noncustodial parent and child do not live together as a family unit. **3.** The process of inquiring into and correcting corporate irregularities. **4.** VISIT.

visitation books. *Hist.* Books compiled by the heralds, when royal progresses were solemnly and regularly made into every part of the kingdom, to inquire into the state of families and to register whatever marriages and descents were verified to them upon oath.

visitation order. An order establishing the visiting times for a noncustodial parent with his or her children.

visitation right. **1.** *Family law.* A noncustodial parent's or grandparent's court-ordered privilege of spending time with a child or grandchild who is living with another person, usu. the custodial parent. **2.** *Int'l law.* A belligerent nation's right to go upon and search a neutral vessel to find out whether it is carrying contraband or is otherwise engaged in nonneutral service. • If it is doing either of these things, the searchers may seize the contraband and carry out an appropriate punishment. — Also termed *right of visitation.*

visitatorial (viz-ə-tə-**tor**-ee-əl), *adj.* See VISITORIAL.

visiting judge. See JUDGE.

visitor. **1.** A person who goes or comes to a particular person or place. **2.** A person appointed to visit, inspect, inquire into, and correct corporate irregularities.

visitorial (viz-ə-**tor**-ee-əl), *adj*. Of or relating to on-site inspection or supervision. — Also termed *visitatorial*.

visitor of manners. A regarder's office in the forest.

vis laica (**vis lay**-ə-kə), *n*. [Latin "lay force"] *Hist*. An armed force used in holding possession of a church.

vis licita (**vis lis**-ə-tə), *n*. [Latin] Lawful force.

vis major (**vis may**-jər), *n*. [Latin "a superior force"] **1.** A greater or superior force; an irresistible force; FORCE MAJEURE. **2.** A loss that results immediately from a natural cause without human intervention and that could not have been prevented by the exercise of prudence, diligence, and care. — Also termed *vis divina*; *superior force*.

visne (veen *or* **veen**-ee). Neighborhood; at common law, the district from which juries were drawn; VICINAGE.

vis perturbativa (**vis** pər-tər-bə-**tI**-və), *n*. [Latin "perturbing force"] *Hist*. Force used between persons contending for possession of something.

vis proxima (**vis prahk**-sə-mə), *n*. [Latin "proximate force"] *Hist*. Immediate force.

vis simplex (**vis sim**-pleks), *n*. [Latin "simple force"] *Hist*. Mere force; sheer force.

VISTA (**vis**-tə). [fr. "Volunteers in Service to America"] A federal program established in 1964 to provide volunteers to help improve the living conditions of people in the poorest areas of the United States, its possessions, and Puerto Rico.

visus (**vI**-səs *or* **vI**-zəs), *n*. [Latin] *Hist*. An inspection of a place, person, or thing. See VIEW (3), (4).

vital statistics. Public records — usu. relating to matters such as births, marriages, deaths, diseases, and the like — that are statutorily mandated to be kept by a city, state, or other governmental subdivision. • On the admissibility of vital statistics, see Fed. R. Evid. 803(9).

vital term. See *fundamental term* under TERM (2).

vitiate (**vish**-ee-ayt), *vb*. **1.** To impair; to cause to have no force or effect <the new statute vitiates any common-law argument that the plaintiffs might have>. **2.** To make void or voidable; to invalidate either completely or in part <fraud vitiates a contract>. **3.** To corrupt morally <Mr. Lawrence complains that his children were vitiated by their governess>. — **vitiation,** *n*. — **vitiator,** *n*.

vitilitigate (vit-ə-**lit**-ə-gayt), *vb*. [fr. Latin *vitilitigare* "to quarrel disgracefully"] *Archaic*. To litigate merely from quarrelsome motives; to carry on a lawsuit in an unduly contentious, wrangling way. — **vitilitigation,** *n*. — **vitilitigious** (vit-ə-li-**tij**-əs), *adj*.

vitious intromission. See INTROMISSION.

vitium clerici (**vish**-ee-əm **kler**-ə-sI). [Latin] See *clerical error* under ERROR.

vitium scriptoris (**vish**-ee-əm skrip-**tor**-is), *n*. [Latin "the mistake of a scribe"] *Hist*. A clerical error in writing.

vitricus (**vi**-trə-kəs), *n*. [Latin] *Hist*. A stepfather.

viva aqua (**vI**-və **ak**-wə), *n*. [Latin "living water"] *Hist*. Running water; water that comes from a spring or fountain.

viva pecunia (**vI**-və pi-**kyoo**-nee-ə), *n*. [Latin "living money"] *Hist*. Cattle, which obtained this name during the Saxon period, when they were received as money, usu. at regulated prices.

viva voce (**vI**-və **voh**-see *also* **vee**-və), *adv*. [Law Latin "with living voice"] By word of mouth; orally. • When referring to votes, the term signifies voting by speech outcry as opposed to voting by a ballot. When referring to the examination of witnesses, the term is contrasted with answering written questions or providing evidence by affidavit.

vivum vadium (**vI**-vəm **vay**-dee-əm). See *vadium vivum* under VADIUM.

viz. (viz). *abbr*. [Latin *videlicet*] Namely; that is to say <the defendant engaged in fraudulent activities, *viz*., misrepresenting his gross income, misrepresenting the value of his assets, and forging his wife's signature>.

vocabula artis (voh-**kab**-yə-lə **ahr**-tis), *n.* [Latin] Words of art. See TERM OF ART.

vocare ad curiam (voh-**kair**-ee ad **kyoor**-ee-əm), *vb.* [Latin] To summon to court.

vocatio in jus (voh-**kay**-shee-oh in **jəs**), *n.* [Latin] *Roman law.* A plaintiff's oral summoning of a defendant to go before a magistrate. • The *vocatio in jus* occurred when the plaintiff would summon the defendant in formal words to accompany the plaintiff.

vocation. A person's regular calling or business; one's occupation or profession.

vociferatio (voh-sif-ə-**ray**-shee-oh), *n.* [Latin] *Hist.* An outcry; HUE AND CRY.

voco (**voh**-koh). [Latin "I call"] *Hist.* I summon; I vouch. See VOCATIO IN JUS.

Voconian law (və-**koh**-nee-in). See LEX VOCONIA.

voice exemplar. A sample of a person's voice used for the purpose of comparing it with a recorded voice to determine whether the speaker is the same person. • Although voiceprint identification was formerly inadmissible, the trend in recent years has been toward admissibility. See Fed. R. Evid. 901. Cf. VOICEPRINT.

voiceprint. A distinctive pattern of curved lines and whorls that are made by a machine that measures human vocal sounds for the purpose of identifying an individual speaker. • Like fingerprints, voiceprints are thought to be unique to each person.

void, *adj.* **1.** Of no legal effect; null. • The distinction between *void* and *voidable* is often of great practical importance. Whenever technical accuracy is required, *void* can be properly applied only to those provisions that are of no effect whatsoever — those that are an absolute nullity. — **void, avoid,** *vb.* — **voidness,** *n.*

facially void. (Of an instrument) patently void upon an inspection of the contents. — Also termed *void on its face.*

void ab initio (ab i-**nish**-ee-oh). Null from the beginning, as from the first moment when a contract is entered into. • A contract is void ab initio if it seriously offends law or public policy, in contrast to a contract that is merely voidable at the election of one party to the contract.

void for vagueness. **1.** (Of a deed or other instrument affecting property) having such an insufficient property description as to be unenforceable. **2.** (Of a penal statute) establishing a requirement or punishment without specifying what is required or what conduct is punishable, and therefore void because violative of due process. — Also termed *void for indefiniteness.*

2. VOIDABLE. • Although sense 1 above is the strict meaning of *void,* the word is often used and construed as bearing the more liberal meaning of "voidable."

voidable, *adj.* Valid until annulled; esp., (of a contract) capable of being affirmed or rejected at the option of one of the parties. • This term describes a valid act that may be voided rather than an invalid act that may be ratified. — **voidability,** *n.*

> "Most of the disputed questions in the law of infancy turn upon the legal meaning of the word 'voidable' as applied to an infant's acts. The natural meaning of the word imports a valid act which may be avoided, rather than an invalid act which may be confirmed, and the weight of authority as well as reason points in the same direction. Certainly, so far as executed transfers of property are concerned the authority of the decisions clearly supports this view." 1 Samuel Williston, *The Law Governing Sales of Goods* § 12, at 28 (3d ed. 1948).

> "The promise of an infant surety is voidable as distinguished from void. The infant may expressly disaffirm or assert the defense of infancy when sued at any time before the expiration of a reasonable time after majority." Laurence P. Simpson, *Handbook on the Law of Suretyship* 82 (1950).

voidable agreement. See *voidable contract* under CONTRACT.

voidable contract. See CONTRACT.

voidable judgment. See JUDGMENT.

voidable marriage. See MARRIAGE (1).

voidable preference. See PREFERENTIAL TRANSFER.

voidable promise. See PROMISE.

voidable transfer. See PREFERENTIAL TRANSFER.

void agreement. See *void contract* under CONTRACT.

voidance, *n.* The act of annulling, canceling, or making void. — Also termed *avoidance.*

void contract. See CONTRACT.

void for indefiniteness. See *void for vagueness* under VOID.

void for vagueness. See VOID.

void-for-vagueness doctrine. See VAGUENESS DOCTRINE; *void for vagueness* under VOID.

void judgment. See JUDGMENT.

void legacy. See LEGACY.

void marriage. See MARRIAGE (1).

void on its face. See *facially void* under VOID.

void process. See PROCESS.

voir dire (vwahr **deer** *also* vor **deer** *or* vor **dɪr**), *n.* [Law French "to speak the truth"] **1.** A preliminary examination of a prospective juror by a judge or lawyer to decide whether the prospect is qualified and suitable to serve on a jury. **2.** A preliminary examination to test the competence of a witness or evidence. **3.** *Hist.* An oath administered to a witness requiring that witness to answer truthfully in response to questions. — Also spelled *voire dire.* — Also termed *voir dire exam*; *examination on the voir dire.* — **voir dire,** *vb.*

voiture (vwah-**t[y]oor**), *n.* Carriage; transportation by carriage.

volatile stock. See STOCK.

volatility. In securities markets, the quality of having sudden and extreme price changes.

volens (**voh**-lenz), *adj.* [Latin] Willing. See NOLENS VOLENS.

volenti non fit injuria (voh-**len**-tɪ non fit in-**joor**-ee-ə). [Law Latin "a person is not wronged by that to which he or she consents"] The principle that a person who knowingly and voluntarily risks danger cannot recover for any resulting injury. • This is the type of affirmative defense that must be pleaded under Fed. R. Civ. P. 8(c). — Often shortened to *volenti.* See ASSUMPTION OF THE RISK.

volition (və-**lish**-ən *or* voh-), *n.* **1.** The ability to make a choice or determine something. **2.** The act of making a choice or determining something. **3.** The choice or determination that someone makes. — **volitional,** *adj.*

volitional test. See IRRESISTIBLE-IMPULSE TEST.

Volstead Act (**vol**-sted). A federal statute enacted in 1919 to prohibit the manufacture, sale, or transportation of liquor. • Sponsored by Andrew Joseph Volstead of Minnesota, a famous Prohibitionist, the statute was passed under the 18th Amendment to the U.S. Constitution. When the 21st Amendment repealed the 18th Amendment in 1933, the Volstead Act was voided.

volume discount. See DISCOUNT.

volumen (vol-**yoo**-mən), *n.* [Latin "a rolled-up thing"] *Civil law.* A volume.

volumus (**vol**-ə-məs), *vb.* [Latin] *Hist.* We will; it is our will. • This was the first word of a clause in royal writs of protection and letters patent. It uses the royal *we* — the plural first person by which monarchs have traditionally spoken.

voluntarily, *adv.* Intentionally; without coercion.

voluntarius daemon (vol-ən-**tair**-ee-əs **dee**-mən), *n.* [Law Latin "voluntary madman"] *Hist.* A drunkard; one who has voluntarily contracted madness by intoxication.

voluntary, *adj.* **1.** Done by design or intention <voluntary act>. **2.** Unconstrained by interference; not impelled by outside influence <voluntary statement>. **3.** Without valuable consideration; gratuitous <voluntary gift>. **4.** Having merely nominal consideration <voluntary deed>. — **voluntariness,** *n.*

voluntary abandonment. See ABANDONMENT (2).

voluntary appearance. See APPEARANCE.

voluntary arbitration. See ARBITRATION.

voluntary assignment. See *general assignment* under ASSIGNMENT.

voluntary association. See ASSOCIATION (3).

voluntary bankruptcy. See BANKRUPTCY.

voluntary bar. See BAR.

voluntary bond. See BOND (3).

voluntary conveyance. See CONVEYANCE.

voluntary courtesy. An act of kindness performed by one person toward another, from the free will of the doer, without any previous request or promise of reward made by the person who is the object of the act. • No promise of remuneration arises from such an act.

voluntary deposit. See DEPOSIT (6).

voluntary discontinuance. See NONSUIT.

voluntary dismissal. See DISMISSAL (1).

voluntary dissolution. See DISSOLUTION.

voluntary escape. See ESCAPE (3).

voluntary euthanasia. See EUTHANASIA.

voluntary exposure to unnecessary danger. An intentional act that, from the standpoint of a reasonable person, gives rise to an undue risk of harm. • The phrase implies a conscious, deliberate exposure of which one is consciously willing to take the risk.

voluntary ignorance. Willful obliviousness; an unknowing or unaware state resulting from the neglect to take reasonable steps to acquire important knowledge.

voluntary intoxication. See INTOXICATION.

voluntary jurisdiction. See JURISDICTION.

voluntary lien. See LIEN.

voluntary manslaughter. See MANSLAUGHTER.

voluntary petition. See PETITION.

voluntary pilot. *Maritime law.* A ship pilot who controls a ship with the permission of the vessel's owner. • The vessel's owner is personally liable for damage resulting from a collision caused by a voluntary pilot. Cf. COMPULSORY PILOT.

> "If a vessel is in the hands of a harbor pilot at the time of the collision, the question arises whether the fault of the pilot is imputed to the vessel owner or operator. American law draws an unwarranted distinction between the 'voluntary pilot,' who is taken on voluntarily, and the 'compulsory pilot,' who is mandated by a statute or local regulation. The voluntary pilot is considered to be the same as any crew member, and his fault is fully attributable to the vessel owner. A compulsory pilot's fault, however, cannot be imputed to the shipowner personally; the doctrine of *respondeat superior* does not apply. At most, the vessel is liable *in rem* since the compulsory pilot's negligence is attributable to the ship. The distinction makes little sense in that it throws the loss upon potentially innocent parties and ignores the fact that the vessel owner commonly carries insurance against this liability. In any collision case, therefore, care should be taken to assert a maritime lien and to sue the vessel *in rem* if a compulsory pilot may be involved." Thomas J. Schoenbaum, *Admiralty and Maritime Law* § 13-1, at 450-51 (1987).

voluntary respite. See RESPITE.

voluntary sale. See SALE.

voluntary search. See SEARCH.

voluntary settlement. See SETTLEMENT.

voluntary statement. See STATEMENT.

voluntary stranding. See STRANDING.

voluntary surety. See SURETY.

voluntary suretyship. See SURETYSHIP.

voluntary trust. See TRUST.

voluntary waste. See WASTE (1).

voluntas (və-**lən**-tas), *n.* [Latin] *Hist.* **1.** Volition, purpose, or intention; a feeling or impulse that prompts the commission of an act. **2.** A will by which a testator plans to dispose of an estate; WILL.

volunteer. **1.** A voluntary actor or agent in a transaction; esp., a person who, without an employer's assent and without any justification from legitimate personal interest, helps an employee in the performance of the employer's business. **2.** The grantee in a voluntary conveyance; a person to whom a conveyance is made without any valuable consideration. See *voluntary conveyance* under CONVEYANCE. **3.** *Military law.* A person who enters military service voluntarily and is then subject to the same rules as other soldiers. Cf. DRAFT (2).

Volunteers in Service to America. See VISTA.

vote, *n.* **1.** The expression of one's preference or opinion by ballot, show of hands, or other type of communication <the Republican candidate received more votes than the Democratic candidate>. **2.** The total number of votes cast in an election <the incumbent received 60% of the vote>. **3.** The act of voting, usu. by a legislative body <the Senate postponed the vote on the gun-control bill>. — **vote,** *vb.*

vote dilution. See DILUTION (3).

vote of no confidence. See NO-CONFIDENCE VOTE.

voter. 1. A person who engages in the act of voting. **2.** A person who has the qualifications necessary for voting. — Also termed (in sense 2) *legal voter.*

voting. The casting of votes for the purpose of deciding an issue.

absentee voting. Participation in an election by a qualified voter who is unable to appear at the polls on election day; the practice of allowing voters to participate in this way.

class voting. A method of shareholder voting by which different classes of shares vote separately on fundamental corporate changes that affect the rights and privileges of that class. — Also termed *voting by class*; *voting by voting group.*

cumulative voting. A system for electing corporate directors whereby a shareholder may multiply his or her number of shares by the number of open directorships and cast the total for a single candidate or a select few candidates. • Cumulative voting enhances the ability of minority shareholders to elect at least one director.

majority voting. A system for electing corporate directors whereby each shareholder is allowed one vote for each director, who can win with a simple majority.

noncumulative voting. A corporate voting system in which a shareholder is limited in board elections to voting no more than the number of shares he or she owns for a single candidate. • The result is that a majority shareholder will elect the entire board of directors. — Also termed *straight voting.*

voting by class. See *class voting.*

voting by voting group. See *class voting.*

voting agreement. See POOLING AGREEMENT.

voting by class. See *class voting* under VOTING.

voting by voting group. See *class voting* under VOTING.

voting group. 1. A classification of shareholders by the type of stock held for voting on corporate matters. **2.** Collectively, the shareholders falling within such a classification.

Voting Rights Act. The federal law that guarantees a citizen's right to vote, without discrimination based on race, color, or previous condition of servitude. • The U.S. Attorney General is authorized to bring suit for preventive relief to protect this right. 42 USCA §§ 1971–1974.

voting security. See *voting stock* under STOCK.

voting stock. See STOCK.

voting-stock rights. A stockholder's right to vote stock in the affairs of the company. • Most commonly, holders of common stock have one vote for each share. Holders of preferred stock usu. have the right to vote when preferred dividends are in default for a specified period.

voting trust. See TRUST.

voting-trust certificate. A certificate issued by a voting trustee to the beneficial holders of shares held by the voting trust. • A voting-trust certificate may be as readily transferable as the underlying shares; it carries with it all the incidents of ownership except the power to vote. See *voting trust* under TRUST.

votum (**voh**-təm), *n.* [Latin] *Hist.* A vow; a promise. See *dies votorum* under DIES.

vouch, *vb.* **1.** To answer for (another); to personally assure <the suspect's mother vouched for him>. **2.** To call upon, rely on, or cite as authority; to substantiate with evidence <counsel vouched the mathematical formula for determining the statistical probability>. **3.** *Hist.* To call into court to warrant and defend, usu. in a fine and recovery. See FINE (1). **4.** *Hist.* To authenticate (a claim, etc.) by vouchers.

vouchee (vow-**chee**), *n.* *Hist.* **1.** A person vouched into court; one who has been vouched over. See VOUCH OVER. **2.** A person cited as authority in support of some fact.

voucher, *n.* **1.** Confirmation of the payment or discharge of a debt; a receipt. **2.** A written or printed authorization to disburse money. **3.** *Hist.* A person who calls on another person (the vouchee) as a witness, esp. in support of a warranty of title. **4.** *Hist.* The tenant in a writ of right.

voucher to warranty. *Hist.* The calling into court of a person who has warranted lands, by the person warranted, to come and defend a lawsuit.

vouching-in. **1.** At common law, a procedural device by which a defendant may give notice of suit to a third party who is liable over to the defendant on the subject-matter of the suit, so that the third party will be bound by the court's decision. • Although this device has been largely replaced by third-party practice, it still remains marginally available under the Federal Rules of Civil Procedure. *Humble Oil & Refining Co. v. Philadelphia Ship Maintenance Co.*, 444 F.2d 727, 735 (3d Cir. 1971). **2.** The invitation of a person who is liable to a defendant in a lawsuit to intervene and defend so that, if the invitation is denied and the defendant later sues the person invited, the latter is bound by any determination of fact common to the two lawsuits. See UCC § 2–607. **3.** IMPLEADER.

vouch over, *vb.* To cite (a person) into court in one's stead.

voyage. *Maritime law.* The passing of a vessel by sea from one place, port, or country to another. • Courts generally hold that the term includes the entire enterprise, not just the route.

foreign voyage. A voyage to a port or place within the territory of a foreign nation. • If the voyage is from one port in a foreign country to another port in the same country, it is considered a foreign voyage.

freighting voyage. A voyage that involves a vessel's transporting cargo between terminal points.

trading voyage. A voyage that contemplates a vessel's touching and stopping at various ports to traffic in, buy and sell, or exchange commodities on the owners' and shippers' account.

voyage charter. See CHARTER (4).

voyage insurance. See INSURANCE.

voyage policy. See INSURANCE POLICY.

voyeur (voy-**yər** *also* vwah-**yər**), *n.* A person who observes something without participating; esp., one who gains pleasure by secretly observing another's sexual acts.

voyeurism. Gratification derived from observing the sexual organs or acts of others, usu. secretly. — **voyeuristic,** *adj.*

vs. *abbr.* VERSUS.

vulgaris purgatio (vəl-**gair**-is pər-**gay**-shee-oh), *n.* [Law Latin] See ORDEAL (1).

vulgar purgation. See PURGATION.

vulgar substitution. See SUBSTITUTION (3).

vulgo concepti (**vəl**-goh kən-**sep**-tɪ), *n.* [Latin] *Hist.* Illegitimate children; bastards.

vulgo quaesiti (**vəl**-goh kwi-**sɪ**-tɪ), *n.* [Latin] *Hist.* Spurious children; the offspring of promiscuity, so that the true fathers are unknowable.

vulture fund. See MUTUAL FUND.

W–2 form. *Tax.* A statement of earnings and taxes withheld (including federal, state, and local income taxes and FICA tax) during a given tax year. • The W–2 is prepared by the employer, provided to each employee, and filed with the Internal Revenue Service. Cf. W–4 FORM.

W–4 form. *Tax.* A form that indicates the number of personal exemptions an employee is claiming and that is used by the employer in determining the amount of income to be withheld from the employee's paycheck for federal-income tax purposes. — Also termed *Employee's Withholding Allowance Certificate.* Cf. W–2 FORM.

wacreour (wah-**kroor**), *n.* [Law French] *Hist.* A vagrant.

***Wade* hearing.** *Criminal law.* A pretrial hearing in which the defendant contests the validity of his or her out-of-court identification. • If the court finds that the identification was tainted by unconstitutional methods, the prosecution cannot use the identification and must link the defendant to the crime by other means. *United States v. Wade,* 388 U.S. 218, 87 S.Ct. 1926 (1967).

wadia (**way**-dee-ə), *n.* [Law Latin] *Hist.* Pledges.

wadset, *n. Scots law.* **1.** A mortgage. **2.** A pledge or pawn.

wadset, *vb. Scots law.* **1.** To mortgage. **2.** To pledge.

wafter (**waf**-tər), *n.* [Law Latin "convoyer"] *Hist.* An English naval officer appointed under Edward IV to protect fishermen, esp. on the coast of Norfolk and Suffolk. — Also spelled *waftor.*

waga (**way**-gə), *n.* [Law Latin] *Hist.* A measure of weight; a measure of goods.

wage, *n.* (*usu. pl.*) Payment for labor or services, usu. based on time worked or quantity produced. Cf. SALARY.

covered wages. Wages on which a person is required to pay social-security taxes.

current wages. Wages for the current period; wages that are not past due.

front wages. Prospective compensation paid to a victim of job discrimination until the denied position becomes available.

minimum wage. The lowest permissible hourly rate of compensation for labor, as established by federal statute and required of employers engaged in interstate commerce. 29 USCA § 206.

noncovered wages. Wages on which a person is not required to pay social-security taxes.

real wages. Wages representing the true purchasing power of the dollar, derived by dividing a price index into money wages.

wage, *vb.* **1.** To engage in (a war, etc.). **2.** *Archaic.* To give security for (a performance, etc.). Cf. GAGE.

wage-and-hour law. A law (such as the federal Fair Labor Standards Act) governing minimum wages and maximum working hours for employees.

wage and price controls. A system of government-mandated maximum prices that can be charged for different goods and services or paid to various workers in different jobs.

wage-and-price freeze. See FREEZE.

wage assignment. See ASSIGNMENT (2).

wage-earner's plan. See CHAPTER 13.

wager, *n.* **1.** Money or other consideration risked on an uncertain event; a bet or gamble. **2.** A promise to pay money or other consideration on the occurrence of an uncertain event. **3.** See *wagering contract* under CONTRACT. — **wager,** *vb.* — **wagerer,** *n.*

wagering contract. See CONTRACT.

wager of battle. See TRIAL BY COMBAT.

wager of law. *Hist.* A method of proof in which a person defends against a claim by swearing that the claim is groundless, and by enlisting others (*compurgators*) to swear to the defendant's credibility. — Also termed *gager del ley* (**gay**-jər del **lay**); *vadiatio legis* (vad-ee-**ay**-shee-oh **lee**-jis). See COMPURGATION.

wager policy. See INSURANCE POLICY.

Wagner Act. See NATIONAL LABOR RELATIONS ACT.

wagonage (**wag**-ə-nij). **1.** Transportation by a wagon. **2.** The fee for carriage by wagon. **3.** A group of wagons.

waif (wayf), *n.* A stolen article thrown away by a thief in flight, usu. through fear of apprehension. • At common law, the rule was that if a waif is seized by a public officer or private person before the owner reclaims it, the title vests in the Crown, but today the general rule is that a waif passes to the state in trust for the true owner, who may regain it by proving ownership.

> "Waifs, *bona waviata*, are goods stolen, and waived or thrown away by the thief in his flight, for fear of being apprehended. These are given to the king by the law, as a punishment upon the owner, for not himself pursuing the felon, and taking away his goods from him. And therefore if the party robbed do his diligence immediately to follow and apprehend the thief (which is called making fresh *suit*) or do convict him afterwards, or procure evidence to convict him, he shall have his goods again." 1 William Blackstone, *Commentaries on the Laws of England* 286–87 (1765).

wainable (**way**-nə-bəl), *adj. Archaic.* (Of land) plowable; tillable.

wainage (**way**-nij), *n. Hist.* The plow, team, and other implements used by a person (esp. a villein) to cultivate the soil; instruments of husbandry. — Also termed *wainagium*; *waynagium* (way-**nay**-jee-əm).

wait-and-see principle. A modification to the rule against perpetuities, under which a court may determine the validity of a contingent future interest based on whether it actually vests within the perpetuities period, rather than on whether it possibly could have vested outside the period. — Also termed *second-look doctrine*.

waiting clerk. *Hist.* An officer who waits in attendance on the court of chancery. • The office of the waiting clerk was abolished in 1842 by the Court of Chancery Act. St. 5 & 6 Vict. ch. 103.

waiting period. A period that must expire before some legal right or remedy can be enjoyed or enforced. • For example, many states have waiting periods for the issuance of marriage licenses or the purchase of handguns.

waive (wayv), *n. Archaic.* A woman who has by her conduct deprived herself of the protection of the law; a female outlaw. • The term "outlaw" usu. referred only to a male. See OUTLAW.

waive, *vb.* **1.** To abandon, renounce, or surrender (a claim, privilege, right, etc.); to give up (a right or claim) voluntarily. • Ordinarily, to waive a right one must do it knowingly — with knowledge of the relevant facts. **2.** To refrain from insisting on (a strict rule, formality, etc.); to forgo.

waiver (**way**-vər), *n.* **1.** The voluntary relinquishment or abandonment — express or implied — of a legal right or advantage <waiver of notice>. • The party alleged to have waived a right must have had both knowledge of the existing right and the intention of forgoing it. Cf. ESTOPPEL.

> "The term *waiver* is one of those words of indefinite connotation in which our legal literature abounds; like a cloak, it covers a multitude of sins." William R. Anson, *Principles of the Law of Contract* 419 (Arthur L. Corbin ed., 3d Am. ed. 1919).

> " 'Waiver' is often inexactly defined as 'the voluntary relinquishment of a known right.' When the waiver is reinforced by reliance, enforcement is often said to rest on 'estoppel.' . . . Since the more common definition of estoppel is limited to reliance on a misrepresentation of an existing fact, reliance on a waiver or promise as to the future is sometimes said to create a 'promissory estoppel.' The common definition of waiver may lead to the incorrect inference that the promisor must know his legal rights and must intend the legal effect of the promise. But . . . it is sufficient if he has reason to know the essential facts." Restatement (Second) of Contracts § 84 cmt. b (1981).

> "Although it has often been said that a waiver is 'the intentional relinquishment of a known right,' this is a misleading definition. What is involved is not the relinquishment of a right and the termination of a reciprocal duty but the excuse of the nonoccurrence or of a delay in the occurrence of a condition of a duty." E. Allan Farnsworth, *Contracts* § 8.5, at 561 (1982).

express waiver. A voluntary and intentional waiver.

implied waiver. A waiver evidenced by a party's decisive, unequivocal conduct reasonably inferring the intent to waive.

> "An implied waiver may arise where a person has pursued such a course of conduct as to evidence an intention to waive a right, or where his conduct is inconsistent with any other intention than to waive it. Waiver may be inferred from conduct or acts putting one off his guard and leading him to believe that a right has been waived. Mere silence, however, is no waiver unless there is an obligation to speak." 28 Am. Jur. 2d *Estoppel and Waiver* § 160, at 845–46 (1966).

prospective waiver. A waiver of something that has not yet occurred, such as a contractual waiver of future claims for discrimination upon settlement of a lawsuit.

2. The instrument by which a person relinquishes or abandons a legal right or advantage <the plaintiff must sign a waiver when the funds are delivered>.

lien waiver. A written and signed waiver of a subcontractor's mechanic's lien rights, usu. submitted to enable the owner or general contractor to receive a draw on a construction loan.

waiver by election of remedies. A defense arising when a plaintiff has sought two inconsistent remedies and by a decisive act chooses one of them, thereby waiving the other.

waiver of claims and defenses. **1.** The intentional relinquishment by a maker, drawer, or other obligor under a contract of the right to assert against the assignee any claims or defenses the obligor has against the assignor. **2.** The contractual clause providing for such a waiver.

waiver of defenses. *Real estate.* A document by which a mortgagor acknowledges that the mortgage is good and valid for the full amount of the mortgage note. • This document ensures that the mortgagor has no defenses to the mortgage. — Also termed *estoppel certificate*; *no-setoff certificate*; *declaration of no defenses*.

waiver of exemption. **1.** A debtor's voluntary relinquishment of the right to an exemption from a creditor's levy or sale of any part of the debtor's personal property by judicial process. **2.** The contractual clause expressly providing for such a waiver.

waiver of immunity. The act of giving up the right against self-incrimination and proceeding to testify. See IMMUNITY (3).

waiver-of-premium clause. *Insurance.* A provision for a waiver of premium payments after the insured has been disabled for a specified length of time, such as six months.

waiver of protest. A relinquishment by a party to a negotiable instrument of the formality of protest in case of dishonor. See PROTEST (2).

waiver of tort. The election to sue in quasi-contract to recover the defendant's unjust benefit, instead of suing in tort to recover damages. See *implied-in-law contract* under CONTRACT.

> "A person upon whom a tort has been committed and who brings an action for the benefits received by the tortfeasor is sometimes said to 'waive the tort.' " Restatement of Restitution § 525 (1937).

> " 'Waiver of tort' is a misnomer. A party only waives a tort in the sense that he elects to sue in quasi-contract to recover the defendant's unjust benefit rather than to sue in tort to recover damages; he has a choice of alternative remedies. But the tort is not extinguished. Indeed it is said that it is a *sine qua non* of both remedies that he should establish that a tort has been committed." Lord Goff of Chieveley & Gareth Jones, *The Law of Restitution* 605 (3d ed. 1986).

waivery. *Hist.* The act of putting a woman outside the protection of the law. • At common law, a woman could not be "outlawed" because she was not considered "in law" — that is, she could not undertake legal proceedings on her own. By Bracton's day, the effect of outlawing a woman was achieved by "waiving" her — the act being called *waivery*.

walk, *vb. Slang.* **1.** To be acquitted <though charged with three thefts, Robinson walked each time>. **2.** To escape any type of real punishment <despite the seriousness of the crime, Selvidge spent only two nights in jail, and when convicted had to pay a fine of only $750: he walked>.

walker, *n. Hist.* A forester who inspects an assigned area of land.

walkout. **1.** STRIKE. **2.** Loosely, the act of leaving a work assignment, meeting, or other event as a show of protest.

wall. An erection of stone, brick, or other material raised to varying heights, esp. inside or surrounding a building, for privacy, security, or enclosure.

ancient wall. A party wall that has stood for at least 20 years, thus giving each party an easement right to refuse to allow the other party to remove or substantially change the wall.

party wall. A wall that divides two adjoining, separately owned properties and that is shared by the two property owners as tenants in common. — Also termed *common wall.*

wallia (**wahl**-ee-ə), *n.* [Law Latin] *Hist.* A wall (such as a mound or bank) erected in marshy areas for protection against the sea; a seawall.

Walsh–Healey Act. A federal law, enacted in 1936, stipulating that government contractors must: (1) pay their workers no less than the prevailing minimum wage; (2) observe the eight-hour day and 40–hour workweek (with time-and-a-half for work exceeding those hours); (3) employ no convict labor and no females under 18 or males under 16 years of age; and (4) maintain sanitary working conditions. 41 USCA §§ 35 et seq.

wampum (**wom**-pəm), *n. Hist.* Indian money consisting of shells, beads, or animal pelts. • In 1637, it became the first medium of exchange for the New England colonies by order of the General Court of Massachusetts, because England had not provided the colonies with a standard of exchange. The Court ordered that "wampampege should passe at 6 a penny for any sum under 12d." Wampum was used as the medium of exchange, esp. for small transactions, until 1652 when the General Court ordered the first metallic currency.

wanlass (**wahn**-ləs). *Hist.* An ancient form of tenure requiring the tenant to drive deer to a stand so that the lord can take a shot. — Also spelled *wanlace.*

wantage (**wahnt**-ij), *n.* A deficiency of something; specif., a vessel's deficiency of not being full, due to leakage.

want of consideration. The lack of consideration for a contract. See CONSIDERATION. Cf. FAILURE OF CONSIDERATION.

want of jurisdiction. A court's lack of power to act in a particular way or to give certain kinds of relief. • A court may have no power to act at all, may lack authority over a person or the subject matter of a lawsuit, or may have no power to act until the prerequisites for its jurisdiction have been satisfied. — Also termed *lack of jurisdiction.* See JURISDICTION.

want of prosecution. Failure of a litigant to pursue the case <dismissal for want of prosecution>. — Also termed *lack of prosecution*; *no progress.* — Abbr. w.o.p.

want of repair. A defective condition, such as a condition on a highway making it unsafe for ordinary travel.

wanton (**wahn**-tən), *adj.* Unreasonably or maliciously risking harm while being utterly indifferent to the consequences. • In criminal law, *wanton* usu. connotes malice (in the criminal-law sense), while *reckless* does not. Cf. RECKLESS; WILLFUL.

> "Wanton differs from reckless both as to the actual state of mind and as to the degree of culpability. One who is acting recklessly is fully aware of the unreasonable risk he is creating, but may be trying and hoping to avoid any harm. One acting wantonly may be creating no greater risk of harm, but he is not trying to avoid it and is indifferent to whether harm results or not. Wanton conduct has properly been characterized as 'vicious' and rates extreme in the degree of culpability. The two are not mutually exclusive. Wanton conduct is reckless plus, so to speak." Rollin M. Perkins & Ronald N. Boyce, *Criminal Law* 879–80 (3d ed. 1982).

wanton and reckless misconduct. See *wanton misconduct* under MISCONDUCT.

wanton misconduct. See MISCONDUCT.

wanton negligence. See *gross negligence* under NEGLIGENCE.

wantonness, *n.* Conduct indicating that the actor is aware of the risks but indifferent to the results. • Wantonness usu. suggests a greater degree of culpability than recklessness, and it often connotes malice in criminal-law contexts. — **wanton,** *adj.* Cf. RECKLESSNESS.

wapentake (**wahp**-ən-tayk *or* **wap**-), *n.* [fr. Saxon *waepen* "weapons" + *tac* "touch"] *Hist.* In some English counties, a division corresponding to the hundred or ward in other counties. See HUNDRED. **2.** The court within such a division. **3.** A bailiff who works in such a court.

war. 1. Hostile conflict by means of armed forces, carried on between nations, states, or rulers, or sometimes between parties within the same nation or state; a period of such conflict <the Gulf War>.

civil war. An internal armed conflict between people of the same nation; esp. (usu. cap.), the war from 1861 to 1865, resulting from the Confederate states' attempted secession from the Union.

imperfect war. A war limited in terms of places, persons, and things.

mixed war. A war between a nation and private individuals.

perfect war. A war involving an entire nation against another.

private war. A war between private persons.

public war. A war between two nations under authority of their respective governments.

solemn war. A war formally declared — esp. by public declaration — by one country against another.

2. A dispute or competition between adversaries <fare wars are common in the airline industry>. **3.** A struggle to solve a pervasive problem <America's war against drugs>.

warantizare. See WARRANTIZARE.

war clause. U.S. Const. art. I, § 8, cl. 11–14, giving Congress the power to declare war. See WAR POWER.

war contribution. *Int'l law.* An extraordinary payment imposed by an occupying power on the population of an occupied territory during wartime. — Often shortened to *contribution.*

war crime. Conduct that violates international laws governing war. • Examples of war crimes are the killing of hostages, abuse of civilians in occupied territories, abuse of prisoners of war, and devastation that is not justified by military necessity.

ward. 1. A person, usu. a minor, who is under a guardian's charge or protection. See GUARDIAN.

permanent ward. A ward who has been assigned a permanent guardian, the rights of the natural parents having been terminated by a juvenile court.

temporary ward. A minor who is under the supervision of a juvenile court but whose parents' parental rights have not been terminated.

ward-in-chancery. *Hist.* An infant under the superintendence of the chancellor.

ward of admiralty. *Hist.* A seaman, so called because of the legal view that a seaman, in contractual matters, should be treated as a beneficiary and the other contracting party as a fiduciary due to their perceived inequitable bargaining positions.

ward of the state. A person who is housed by, and receives protection and necessities from, the government.

2. A territorial division in a city, usu. defined for purposes of city government. **3.** The act of guarding or protecting something or someone. **4.** *Archaic.* One who guards. **5.** CASTLE-GUARD. — Formerly also termed *warda.*

warda (**wor**-də), *n.* [Law Latin] *Hist.* Wardship; guardianship.

wardage. See WARDPENNY.

warden. A person in charge of something <game warden> <port warden>; esp., the official in charge of a prison or jail <prison warden>.

warden of the cinque ports (singk ports). *Hist.* A magistrate with jurisdiction over the five cinque ports. • This office was created in imitation of the Roman policy of strengthening coasts against enemies. The warden, formally called the Lord Warden, presided over the Court of the Lord Warden of the Cinque Ports, which was created in the 14th century and, over time, variously exercised civil, equity, and admiralty jurisdiction. — Formerly termed *guardian of the cinque ports.* See CINQUE PORTS.

ward-horn. *Hist.* The duty of keeping watch and ward with a horn to blow in the event of a surprise. See WATCH AND WARD.

ward-in-chancery. See WARD.

wardite. *Hist.* A fine that a tenant was required to pay upon failing to fulfill the duty of castle-guard. See CASTLE-GUARD.

wardmote (**word**-moht). *Hist.* **1.** A court maintained in every London ward. — Also termed *wardmote court*; *inquest.* **2.** A meeting of a ward.

ward of admiralty. See WARD.

wardpenny, *n. Hist.* **1.** Money paid in lieu of military service. **2.** Money paid to the sheriff or castellains in exchange for watching and warding a castle. — Also termed *wardage*; *warth.*

wardship. 1. Guardianship of a person, usu. a minor. **2.** The condition of being a ward. **3.** *Hist.* The right of the feudal lord to guardianship of a deceased tenant's minor heir until the heir reached the age of majority.

wardship in chivalry. Wardship as incident to the tenure of knight-service.

wardship in copyholds. Wardship by which the lord is guardian of an infant tenant by special custom.

wardstaff, *n. Hist.* A staff carried by an authority; esp., a constable's or watchman's staff.

wardwit, *n. Hist.* **1.** An immunity or exemption from the duty of warding or contributing to warding. **2.** A fine for failing to watch and ward. — Also termed *warwit*; *wardwite*.

warectare (wor-ək-**tair**-ee), *vb.* [Law Latin "to let lie fallow"] *Hist.* To plow land in the spring and then let it lie fallow for a better wheat crop the next year.

warehouse. A building used to store goods and other items.

bonded warehouse. A special type of private warehouse used to store products subject to customs duties. See WAREHOUSE SYSTEM.

warehouse book. A book used by merchants to account for quantities of goods received, shipped, and in stock.

warehouseman. See WAREHOUSER.

warehouseman's lien. See *warehouser's lien* under LIEN.

warehouser. One who, as a business, keeps or stores the goods of another for a fee. • The transaction in which a warehouser engages is a bailment for the benefit of both parties, and the bailee is liable for ordinary negligence. — Also termed *warehouseman*. See BAILEE.

warehouse receipt. A document evidencing title to goods stored with someone else; esp., a receipt issued by a person engaged in the business of storing goods for a fee. • A warehouse receipt, which is considered a document of title, may be a negotiable instrument and is often used for financing with inventory as security. See BAILMENT.

warehouser's lien. See LIEN.

warehouse system. A system of maintaining bonded warehouses so that importers can either store goods for reexportation without paying customs duties or store the goods without paying duties until the goods are removed for domestic consumption. See *bonded warehouse* under WAREHOUSE.

warehousing. 1. A mortgage banker's holding of mortgages until the resale market improves. **2.** A corporation's giving of advance notice of a tender offer to institutional investors, who can then buy stock in the target company before public awareness of the takeover inflates the stock's price. See TENDER OFFER.

warfare. 1. The act of engaging in war or military conflict. See WAR. **2.** Loosely, the act of engaging in any type of conflict.

biological warfare. The use of biological or infectious agents in war, usu. by delivering them via airplanes or ballistic missiles.

economic warfare. **1.** A hostile relationship between two or more countries in which at least one tries to damage the other's economy for economic, political, or military ends. **2.** The collective measures that might be taken to achieve such ends.

guerrilla warfare. Hostilities that are conducted by individuals or small groups who are usu. not part of an organized army and who fight by means of surprise attacks, ambushes, and sabotage. • Formerly, it was thought that the hostilities had to be conducted in enemy-occupied territory. Typically, guerrilla warfare is carried out only when geographical conditions are favorable and when the civilian population is at least partly cooperative.

land warfare. Hostilities conducted on the ground, as opposed to at sea or in the air.

WARN (worn). *abbr.* WORKER ADJUSTMENT AND RETRAINING NOTIFICATION ACT.

warning. The pointing out of a danger, esp. to one who would not otherwise be aware of it. • State and federal laws (such as 21 USCA § 825) require warning labels to be placed on potentially dangerous materials, such as drugs and equipment.

warnistura (wor-nə-**st[y]oor**-ə), *n.* [Law Latin] *Hist.* Furniture; provision.

warnoth (**wor**-noht). *Hist.* A defunct custom by which a tenant who failed to pay rent on a set day had to pay double the amount due, and on failing a second time had to pay triple (and so on).

war power. The constitutional authority of Congress to declare war and maintain armed forces

(U.S. Const. art. I, § 8, cls. 11–14), and of the President to conduct war as commander-in-chief (U.S. Const. art. II, § 2, cl. 1).

war-powers resolution. A resolution passed by Congress in 1973 (over the President's veto) restricting the President's authority to involve the United States in foreign hostilities without congressional approval, unless the United States or one of its territories is attacked. 50 USCA §§ 1541–1548.

warrant, *n.* **1.** A writ directing or authorizing someone to do an act, esp. one directing a law enforcer to make an arrest, a search, or a seizure.

administrative warrant. A warrant issued by a judge at the request of an administrative agency. • This type of warrant is sought to conduct an administrative search. See *administrative search* under SEARCH.

anticipatory search warrant. See SEARCH WARRANT.

arrest warrant. A warrant, issued only on probable cause, directing a law-enforcement officer to arrest and bring a person to court. — Also termed *warrant of arrest.*

bench warrant. A warrant issued directly by a judge to a law-enforcement officer, esp. for the arrest of a person who has been held in contempt, has been indicted, has disobeyed a subpoena, or has failed to appear for a hearing or trial.

blanket search warrant. See SEARCH WARRANT.

commitment warrant. See *warrant of commitment.*

death warrant. A warrant authorizing a warden or other prison official to carry out a death sentence. • A death warrant typically sets the time and place for a prisoner's execution.

distress warrant. **1.** A warrant authorizing a court officer to distrain property. See DISTRESS. **2.** A writ allowing an officer to seize a tenant's goods for failing to pay rent due to the landlord.

escape warrant. **1.** A warrant directing a peace officer to rearrest an escaped prisoner. **2.** *Hist.* A warrant granted to retake a prisoner who had escaped from a royal prison after being committed there. • The warrant was obtained on affidavit from the judge of the court in which the action had been brought, and was directed to all sheriffs throughout England, commanding them to retake and commit the prisoner to the nearest jail.

extradition warrant. A warrant for the return of a fugitive from one jurisdiction to another. Cf. *rendition warrant.*

fugitive warrant. A warrant that authorizes law-enforcement officers to take into custody a person who has fled from one state to another to avoid prosecution or punishment.

general warrant. **1.** *Hist.* A warrant issued by the English Secretary of State for the arrest of the author, printer, or publisher of a seditious libel, without naming the persons to be arrested. • General warrants were banned by Parliament in 1766.

> "A practice had obtained in the secretaries office ever since the restoration, grounded on some clauses in the acts for regulating the press, of issuing *general* warrants to take up (without naming any person in particular) the authors, printers and publishers of such obscene or seditious libels, as were particularly specified in the warrant. When those acts expired in 1694, the same practice was inadvertently continued, in every reign and under every administration, except the four last years of queen Anne, down to the year 1763: when such a warrant being issued to apprehend the authors, printers and publishers of a certain seditious libel, its validity was disputed; and the warrant was adjudged by the whole court of king's bench to be void, in the case of Money *v.* Leach. *Trin.* 5 *Geo. III. E.R.* After which the issuing of such general warrants was declared illegal by a vote of the house of commons." 4 William Blackstone, *Commentaries on the Laws of England* 288 n.i (1769).

2. A warrant that gives a law-enforcement officer broad authority to search and seize unspecified places or persons; a search or arrest warrant that lacks a sufficiently particularized description of the person or thing to be seized or the place to be searched. • General warrants are unconstitutional because they fail to meet the Fourth Amendment's specificity requirements.

> "But though there are precedents of general warrants to search all suspected places for stolen goods, these are not at common law legal, because it would be extremely dangerous to leave it to the discretion of a common officer to arrest what person, or search what houses he thinks fit. And in the great case of Money v. Leach, it was declared by Lord Mansfield, that a warrant to search for, and secure the person and papers of the author, printer and publisher of a libel, is not only illegal in itself, but is so improper on the face of it, that it will afford no justification to an officer acting under its sanction. And by two resolutions of the House of Commons such general warrants were declared to be invalid." 1 Joseph Chitty, *A Practical Treatise on the Criminal Law* 66 (2d ed. 1826).

justice's warrant. See *peace warrant.*

landlord's warrant. A type of distress warrant from a landlord to seize the tenant's goods, to sell them at public sale, and to compel the tenant to pay rent or observe some other lease stipulation. See DISTRAIN; DISTRESS.

no-knock search warrant. See SEARCH WARRANT.

outstanding warrant. An unexecuted arrest warrant.

peace warrant. A warrant issued by a justice of the peace for the arrest of a specified person. — Also termed *justice's warrant.*

preliminary warrant. A warrant to bring a person to court for a preliminary hearing on probable cause.

rendition warrant. A warrant requesting the extradition of a fugitive from one jurisdiction to another. Cf. *extradition warrant.*

search warrant. See SEARCH WARRANT.

surreptitious-entry warrant. A warrant that authorizes a law officer to enter and observe an ongoing criminal operation (such as an illegal drug lab).

tax warrant. An official process that is issued for collecting unpaid taxes and under which property may be seized and sold.

warrant of arrest. See *arrest warrant.*

warrant of commitment. A warrant committing a person to custody. — Also termed *commitment warrant.*

warrant upon indictment or information. An arrest warrant issued at the request of the prosecutor for a defendant named in an indictment or information. Fed. R. Crim. P. 9.

2. A document conferring authority, esp. to pay or receive money.

deposit warrant. A warehouse receipt used as security for a loan.

dock warrant. See DOCK RECEIPT.

interest warrant. An order drawn by a corporation on its bank directing the bank to pay interest to a bondholder.

municipal warrant. An order to draw money from a municipality's treasury for the payment of the municipality's expenses or debts.

tax-anticipation warrant. A warrant that is issued to raise public money and that is payable out of tax receipts when collected.

treasury warrant. An order in the form of a check on which government disbursements are paid.

3. An order by which a drawer authorizes someone to pay a particular sum of money to another.

county warrant. A warrant drawn by a county official, directing the county treasurer to pay a sum of money out of county funds to bearer, to a named individual, or to the named individual's order.

4. SUBSCRIPTION WARRANT.

warrant, *vb.* **1.** To guarantee the security of (realty or personalty, or a person) <the store warranted the safety of the customer's jewelry>. **2.** To give warranty of (title); to give warranty of title to (a person) <the seller warrants the property's title to the buyer>. **3.** To promise or guarantee <warrant payment>.

> "Even today lawyers use the verb 'to warrant' meaning to promise without necessarily indicating that the promise is a warranty." P.S. Atiyah, *An Introduction to the Law of Contract* 145 n.1 (3d ed. 1981).

4. To justify <the conduct warrants a presumption of negligence>. **5.** To authorize <the manager warranted the search of the premises>.

Warrant Clause. The clause of the Fourth Amendment to the U.S. Constitution requiring that warrants be issued on probable cause.

warrant creditor. See CREDITOR.

warrantee (wor-ən-**tee** *or* wahr-). A person to whom a warranty is given.

warrantia chartae. See DE WARRANTIA CHARTAE.

warrantia custodiae (wə-**ran**-shee-ə kə-**stoh**-dee-ee), *n.* [Law Latin] *Hist.* A writ for a purchaser of land held in knight's service against the seller (and heirs), who had warranted that the land was free of wardship when a wardship was later claimed.

warrantia diei. See DE WARRANTIA DIEI.

warrantizare (wor-ən-tə-**zair**-ee), *vb.* [Law Latin] *Hist.* To warrant by covenant (in a deed of conveyance) to defend the grantee's title and possession. — Also spelled *warantizare.*

warrantless arrest. See ARREST.

warrantless search. See SEARCH.

warrant of arrest. See *arrest warrant* under WARRANT (1).

warrant of attorney. 1. POWER OF ATTORNEY (1). **2.** *Hist.* Written authority given by a client to a lawyer to appear in court and to confess judgment in favor of a specified party. • It usu. instructed the attorney not to bring any action, seek a writ of error, or file a bill in equity that might delay the judgment. The warrant was typically given as security for an obligation on which judgment was authorized. Cf. CONFESSION OF JUDGMENT; COGNOVIT.

> "A warrant of attorney was not required to be under seal, though it generally was so. In order to guard against any imposition in procuring debtors to execute warrants of attorney or *cognovits* in ignorance of the effect of such instruments, it is provided that a warrant of attorney to confess judgment in any personal action, or *cognovit actionem*, given by any person, shall not be of any force, unless there is present some attorney of one of the superior courts on behalf of such person, expressly named by him and attending at his request, to inform him of the nature and effect of such warrant or cognovit, before the same is executed . . . ." Joshua Williams, *Principles of the Law of Personal Property* 125 (11th ed. 1881).

warrant of commitment. See WARRANT (1).

warrant officer. See OFFICER (2).

warrantor (**wor**-ən-tor *or* -tər *or* **wahr**-). A person who gives a warranty.

warrant recall, *n.* A procedure for removing from government computers information about canceled warrants in order to avoid repeated or mistaken arrests.

warrant to sue and defend. *Hist.* **1.** Written authority given by a client to a lawyer to authorize commencement or defense of a lawsuit. **2.** A special warrant from the Crown authorizing a party to appoint an attorney to sue or defend on the party's behalf.

warrant upon indictment or information. See WARRANT (1).

warranty (**wor**-ən-tee *or* **wahr**-), *n.* **1.** *Property.* A covenant by which the grantor in a deed promises to secure to the grantee the estate conveyed in the deed, and pledges to compensate the grantee with other land if the grantee is evicted by someone having better title. • The covenant is binding on the grantor's heirs. See COVENANT (4). Cf. *quitclaim deed* under DEED.

collateral warranty. A warranty that is made by a stranger to the title, and that consequently runs only to the covenantee and not to the land.

general warranty. A warranty against the claims of all persons.

lineal warranty. *Hist.* A warranty existing when an heir derives title to land from the warrantor; a warranty from the same ancestor as the one from whom the land derived.

special warranty. A warranty against any person's claim made by, through, or under the grantor or the grantor's heirs.

2. *Contracts.* An express or implied promise that something in furtherance of the contract is guaranteed by one of the contracting parties; esp., a seller's promise that the thing being sold is as represented or promised. • A warranty differs from a representation in four principal ways: (1) a warranty is an essential part of a contract, while a representation is usu. only a collateral inducement, (2) a warranty is always written on the face of the contract, while a representation may be written or oral, (3) a warranty is conclusively presumed to be material, while the burden is on the party claiming breach to show that a representation is material, and (4) a warranty must be strictly complied with, while substantial truth is the only requirement for a representation. Cf. CONDITION (3).

> "[T]wo points must be borne in mind. In the first place, the words 'condition' and 'warranty' are not invariably kept as distinct as accuracy of definition demands; and in insurance law especially 'warranty' is very commonly used in the sense ascribed to 'condition' . . . . In the second place, the injured party, if he chooses to waive his right to repudiate the contract on breach of a condition, may still bring an action for such damages as he has sustained." William R. Anson, *Principles of the Law of Contract* 223 (Arthur L. Corbin ed., 3d Am. ed. 1919).

> "The distinction between conditions and warranties is relatively modern so far as the terminology is concerned, and it will be found that in the older cases the word 'warranty' is frequently used to mean any term of the contract. There is some ground for regretting the modern usage. The difference between a condition and a warranty is that a breach of the former gives the innocent party the option of treating the whole contract as discharged, while a breach of the latter merely entitles the innocent party to claim damages, but does not discharge him from performing his own duties under the contract. In other words, the right to the other party's performance is conditional upon conditions (but not warranties) being performed." P.S. Atiyah, *An Introduction to the Law of Contract* 145–46 (3d ed. 1981).

as-is warranty. A warranty that goods are sold with all existing faults. See AS IS.

construction warranty. A warranty from the seller or building contractor of a new home that the home is free of structural, electrical, plumbing, and other defects and is fit for its intended purpose.

deceptive warranty. A warranty containing false or fraudulent representations or promises.

express warranty. A warranty created by the overt words or actions of the seller. • Under the UCC, an express warranty is created by any of the following: (1) an affirmation of fact or promise made by the seller to the buyer relating to the goods that becomes the basis of the bargain; (2) a description of the goods that becomes part of the basis of the bargain; or (3) a sample or model made part of the basis of the bargain. UCC § 2–313.

extended warranty. An additional warranty often sold with the purchase of consumer goods (such as appliances and motor vehicles) to cover repair costs not otherwise covered by a manufacturer's standard warranty, by extending either the standard-warranty coverage period or the range of defects covered. — Also termed *extended service warranty*; *extended service contract*.

full warranty. A warranty that fully covers labor and materials for repairs. • Under federal law, the warrantor must remedy the consumer product within a reasonable time and without charge after notice of a defect or malfunction. 15 USCA § 2304. Cf. *limited warranty*.

implied warranty. A warranty arising by operation of law because of the circumstances of a sale, rather than by the seller's express promise.

implied warranty of fitness for a particular purpose. A warranty — implied by law if the seller has reason to know of the buyer's special purposes for the property — that the property is suitable for those purposes. — Sometimes shortened to *warranty of fitness*.

> "Those unfamiliar with the differences between the warranty of merchantability (fitness for the *ordinary* purposes for which such goods are used) and the warranty of fitness for a *particular* purpose often confuse the two; one can find many opinions in which the judges used the terms 'merchantability' and 'fitness for a particular purpose' interchangeably. Such confusion under the Code is inexcusable." 1 James J. White & Robert S. Summers, *Uniform Commercial Code* § 9–10, at 527 (4th ed. 1995).

implied warranty of habitability. In a residential lease, a warranty from the landlord to the tenant that the leased property is fit to live in and that it will remain so during the term of the lease. — Also termed *covenant of habitability*.

implied warranty of merchantability. A warranty that the property is fit for the ordinary purposes for which it is used. — Sometimes shortened to *warranty of merchantability*.

limited warranty. A warranty that does not fully cover labor and materials for repairs. • Under federal law, a limited warranty must be clearly labeled as such on the face of the warranty. Cf. *full warranty*.

personal warranty. A warranty arising from an obligation to pay all or part of the debt of another.

presentment warranty. An implied promise concerning the title and credibility of an instrument, made to a payor or acceptor upon presentment of the instrument for payment or acceptance. UCC §§ 3–417, 3–418, 4–207(1).

transfer warranty. **1.** An implied promise concerning the title and credibility of an instrument, made by a transferor to a transferee and, if the transfer is by indorsement, to remote transferees. UCC §§ 3–417, 4–207. **2.** A warranty made by a transferee of a document of title upon a transfer of the document for value to the immediate transferee. UCC § 7–507.

warranty ab initio (ab i-**nish**-ee-oh). An independent subsidiary promise whose breach does not discharge the contract, but gives to the injured party a right of action for the damage sustained as a result of the breach. Cf. *warranty ex post facto*.

warranty against infringement. A merchant seller's warranty that the goods being sold do not violate any patent, copyright, trademark, or similar claim. • The warranty does not arise if the buyer provides the seller with the specifications for the goods purchased.

warranty ex post facto (eks pohst **fak**-toh). A broken condition for which the injured party could void the contract, but decides instead to continue the contract, with a right of action for the broken condition (which amounts to a breached warranty). See CONDITION (2). Cf. *warranty ab initio*.

warranty of actual title. See *warranty of title*.

warranty of assignment. An assignor's implied warranty that he or she (1) has the rights assigned, (2) will do nothing to interfere with those rights, and (3) knows of nothing that impairs the value of the assignment.

warranty of authorship. *Copyright.* An author's contractual warranty that the work is an original work by that author.

warranty of merchantability. See *implied warranty of merchantability*.

warranty of title. A warranty that the seller or assignor of property has title to that property, that the transfer is rightful, and that there are no liens or other encumbrances beyond those that the buyer or assignee is aware of at the time of contracting. • This warranty arises automatically whenever anyone sells goods. — Also termed *warranty of actual title*.

written warranty. A warranty made in writing; specif., any written affirmation or promise by a supplier of a consumer product to a buyer (for purposes other than resale), forming the basis of the bargain and providing that the material or workmanship is free of defects or will be repaired or replaced free of charge if the product fails to meet the required specifications. 15 USCA § 2301.

Y2K warranty. See Y2K WARRANTY.

3. *Insurance.* A pledge or stipulation by the insured that the facts relating to the person insured, the thing insured, or the risk insured are as stated.

affirmative warranty. A warranty — express or implied — that facts are as stated at the beginning of the policy period. • An affirmative warranty is usu. a condition precedent to the policy taking effect.

executory warranty. A warranty that arises when an insured undertakes to perform some executory stipulation, such as a promise that certain acts will be done or that certain facts will continue to exist.

promissory warranty. A warranty that facts will continue to be as stated throughout the policy period, such that a failure of the warranty provides the insurer with a defense to a claim under the policy. — Also termed *continuing warranty*.

warranty ab initio. See WARRANTY (2).

warranty against infringement. See WARRANTY (2).

warranty deed. See DEED.

warranty ex post facto. See WARRANTY (2).

warranty of actual title. See *warranty of title* under WARRANTY (2).

warranty of assignment. See WARRANTY (2).

warranty of authorship. See WARRANTY (2).

warranty of title. See WARRANTY (2).

warren (**wor**-ən *or* **wahr**-ən). **1.** A place for the preservation of certain wildlife (such as pheasants, partridges, or rabbits). **2.** A privilege to keep wildlife or game in a warren. **3.** The area to which the privilege extends.

free warren. A warren privilege giving the grantee the sole right to kill the wildlife to the extent of the grantee's warren area. — Also termed *libera warrena*.

> "*Free warren* is a . . . franchise, erected for preservation or custody . . . of beasts and fowls of warren; which being *ferae naturae*, every one had a right to kill as he could; but upon the introduction of the forest laws . . . these animals being looked upon as royal game and the sole property of our savage monarchs, this franchise of free warren was invented to protect them; by giving the grantee a sole and exclusive power of killing such game . . . on condition of his preventing other persons. A man therefore that has the franchise of warren is in reality no more than a royal gamekeeper; but no man, not even a lord of a manor, could by common law justify sporting on another's soil, or even on his own, unless he had the liberty of free warren." 2 William Blackstone, *Commentaries on the Laws of England* 38–39 (1766).

war-risk insurance. See INSURANCE.

Warsaw Convention. *Int'l law.* A treaty (to which the United States is a party) negotiated in Warsaw, Poland, in 1929, consisting of uniform rules governing claims made for personal injuries arising out of international air travel. Cf. MONTREAL AGREEMENT.

> "Under the [Warsaw] Convention . . . air carriers are absolutely liable up to a preset monetary ceiling for any accident in which a passenger suffers bodily injury or death, as long as the accident took place on board the aircraft or in the process of any of the operations of embarking or disembarking. The Convention limits the liability of the carrier for each passenger to the sum of 125,000 francs, unless the carrier and passenger by special contract agree to a higher limit of liability, or unless it can be established that the carrier has been guilty of 'willful misconduct.' The Convention contains a two-year time limitation for bringing suit, and also absolves the carrier from liability upon a showing of due care on its part." 8A Am. Jur. 2d *Aviation* § 149, at 160–61 (1997).

warth. See WARDPENNY.

warwit. See WARDWIT.

war zone. *Int'l law.* A designated area, on land or at sea, within which the rights of neutral countries are not respected by belligerent countries.

wash, *n.* The shallow part of a river or the arm of a sea; the sand, rocks, and gravel washed down by a mountain stream and deposited on level land near the mouth of a canyon.

wash sale. See SALE.

wash transaction. See *wash sale* under SALE.

waste, *n.* **1.** Permanent harm to real property committed by a tenant (for life or for years) to the prejudice of the heir, the reversioner, or the remainderman. • In the law of mortgages, any of the following acts by the mortgagor may constitute waste: (1) physical damage, whether intentional or negligent, (2) failure to maintain and repair, except for repair of casualty damage or damage caused by third-party acts, (3) failure to pay property taxes or governmental assessments secured by a lien having priority over the mortgage, so that the payments become delinquent, (4) the material failure to comply with mortgage covenants concerning physical care, maintenance, construction, demolition, or casualty insurance, or (5) keeping the rents to which the mortgagee has the right of possession. — Also termed *vastum.*

> "The old action of waste was a mixed action, being founded in part on the statute of Gloucester (A.D. 1278), which provided that 'he which shall be attainted of waste shall lose the thing wasted, and moreover shall recompense thrice as much as the waste shall be taxed at.' The action was to recover the land in which waste had been done and the treble damages. The statute of Gloucester was imported into this country, but many variant statutes now regulate the subject." Edwin E. Bryant, *The Law of Pleading Under the Codes of Civil Procedure* 13 (2d ed. 1899).

active waste. See *commissive waste.*

affirmative waste. See *commissive waste.*

ameliorating waste (ə-**meel**-yə-ray-ting). A lessee's unauthorized change to the physical character of a lessor's property — technically constituting waste, but in fact resulting in improvement of the property. • Generally, equity will not enjoin such waste. — Also termed *ameliorative waste.*

commissive waste (kə-**mis**-iv). Waste caused by the affirmative acts of the tenant. — Also termed *active waste*; *affirmative waste*; *voluntary waste.*

double waste. *Hist.* The destruction occurring when a tenant having a duty to repair allows a house to deteriorate, and then unlawfully cuts down timber to repair it.

equitable waste. An abuse of the privilege of nonimpeachability for waste at common law, for which equity will restrain the commission of willful, destructive, malicious, or extravagant waste; esp., waste caused by a life tenant who, although ordinarily not responsible for permissive waste, flagrantly damages or destroys the property.

> "A life tenant with the benefit of an express exemption from liability for voluntary waste will nevertheless be restrained in equity from committing acts of flagrant destruction to the premises; hence the (seemingly paradoxical) term, 'equitable waste'. A life tenant who has engaged in, or who threatens to engage in, reprehensible acts of voluntary waste will not be permitted unconscientiously to shield behind his legal right to commit waste to the detriment of those next entitled to enjoyment of the property, for this would be to abuse the legal right." Peter Butt, *Land Law* 114–15 (2d ed. 1988).

permissive waste. A tenant's failure to make normal repairs to property so as to protect it from substantial deterioration.

voluntary waste. Waste resulting from some positive act of destruction. See *commissive waste.*

> "*Voluntary waste.* This involves some positive act of injury to the property, diminishing its value for the person next in succession; it is a deliberate and active change to the property. Examples are altering the character of premises by demolishing internal walls and fittings or opening and working a mine on the land (but not working a mine already opened, for the pre-existence of the mine shows an intention on the part of the grantor that the profits from the mine are to be enjoyed by the life tenant). A life tenant is liable for voluntary waste, unless the instrument conferring the interest expressly exempts liability for voluntary waste." Peter Butt, *Land Law* 114 (2d ed. 1988).

2. Refuse or superfluous material, esp. that remaining after a manufacturing or chemical process <toxic waste>.

hazardous waste. Waste that — because of its quantity, concentration, or physical, chemical, or infectious characteristics — may cause or significantly contribute to an increase in mortality or otherwise harm human health or the environment. 42 USCA § 6903(5). — Also termed *hazardous substance.*

toxic waste. Hazardous, poisonous substances, such as dichlorodiphenyltrichloroethane (DDT). • Most states regulate the handling and disposing of toxic waste, and several federal statutes (such as the Comprehensive Environmental Response Compensation and Liability Act of 1980 (CERCLA), 42 USCA §§ 9601–9657) regulate the use, transportation, and disposal of toxic waste.

waste book. A merchant's book for making rough entries of transactions before posting them into a journal. — Also termed *blotter.*

wastewater. See WATER.

wasting asset. See ASSET.

wasting property. A right to or an interest in something that is consumed in its normal use, such as a wasting asset, a leasehold interest, or a patent right.

wasting trust. See TRUST.

wastor, *n. Hist.* A type of thief, mentioned in Stat. 4 Hen. 4, ch. 27.

watch, *n. Maritime law.* **1.** A division of a ship's crew <port or starboard watch>. **2.** The division of the day into time periods of service by officers and the crew <four-hour watch>.

watch, *vb. Hist.* To stand guard during the night.

watch and ward, *n. Hist.* A feudal duty that some tenants had to keep guard through continuous vigilance. • The phrase denotes keeping guard by night (*watch*) and by day (*ward*). — Also termed *watching and warding*.

water. 1. The transparent liquid that is a chemical compound of hydrogen and oxygen (H_2O). **2.** A body of this liquid, as in a stream, river, lake, or ocean.

backwater. Water in a stream that, because of a dam or obstruction, cannot flow forward and sometimes flows back.

coast water. Tidewater navigable by an ocean vessel; all water opening directly or indirectly into the ocean and navigable by a vessel coming in from the ocean. — Also termed *coastal water*.

developed water. Water brought to the surface and made available for use by the party claiming the water rights.

diffused surface water. Water, such as rainfall runoff, that collects and flows on the ground but does not form a watercourse. • Surface water is usu. subject to different regulations from water flowing in a watercourse. — Often shortened to *surface water*. See COMMON-ENEMY DOCTRINE; WATERCOURSE.

excess water. Water that is flowing in a stream in addition to what may be termed adjudicated waters; any water not needed for the reasonable beneficial uses of those having priority rights. — Also termed *surplus water*.

floodwater. Water that escapes from a watercourse in large volumes and flows over adjoining property in no regular channel.

foreign water. Water belonging to another nation or subject to another jurisdiction.

inland waters. See INTERNAL WATERS.

internal waters. See INTERNAL WATERS.

navigable water. See NAVIGABLE WATER.

navigable water of the United States. See NAVIGABLE WATER.

percolating water. Water that oozes or seeps through the soil without a defined channel (such as rainwater or other water that has lost its status as part of a stream). • Percolating water usu. constitutes part of the land on which it is found.

posted water. (*usu. pl.*) A body of water that is reserved for the exclusive use of the person who owns the land surrounding it. • The owner secures the exclusive use by posting a notice prohibiting others from using the water.

private water. Nonnavigable water owned and controlled by one or more individuals and not subject to public use.

public water. Water adapted for purposes of navigation or public access.

subterranean water. Water naturally flowing, lying in an immovable body, or percolating beneath the earth's surface.

surplus water. **1.** Water running off irrigated ground; water not consumed by the irrigation process. **2.** See *excess water*.

territorial waters. The waters under a state's or nation's jurisdiction, including both inland waters and surrounding sea (traditionally within three miles of the coastline). — Also termed *marine belt*; *maritime belt*.

tidewater. See TIDEWATER.

wastewater. **1.** Water that escapes from the canals, ditches, or other receptacles of the lawful claimant; water that is not used by the appropriator and is permitted to run off the appropriator's property. **2.** Water that is left over, esp. after a chemical or manufacturing process.

water bayley (**bay**-lee). *Hist.* An officer (mentioned in the colony laws of New Plymouth in A.D. 1671) who primarily collects dues for fish taken out of the colony's waters.

watercourse. A body of water flowing in a reasonably definite channel with bed and banks. — Also termed *waterway*.

"Once water joins a watercourse it becomes subject to state control; in appropriation states it becomes available for appropriation to private uses according to state law .... [A] watercourse could be defined to include not only rivers and lakes, but every tiny brook flowing into them, all the gullies through which water flows to the brooks, the snowpack and rainfall that feed them, and the evaporating or transpiring water in the process of forming clouds. But we need not require scientists to trace water to such remote sources because it would be beyond the ability of governments to regulate these sources. Legal definitions are intended to define a point beyond which a state does not regulate water use. Usually that point is when water is not in a 'natural stream'." David H. Getches, *Water Law in a Nutshell* 106–107 (3d ed. 1997).

ancient watercourse. A watercourse in a channel that has existed from time immemorial.

artificial watercourse. A man-made watercourse, usu. to be used only temporarily. • If the watercourse is of a permanent character and has been maintained for a sufficient length of time, it may be considered a natural watercourse to which riparian rights can attach.

"An artificial waterway or stream may, under some circumstances, have the characteristics and incidents of a natural watercourse. In determining the question, three things seem generally to be taken into consideration by the courts: (1) whether the way or stream is temporary or permanent; (2) the circumstances under which it was created; and (3) the mode in which it has been used and enjoyed." 78 Am. Jur. 2d *Waters* § 196, at 644 (1975).

natural watercourse. A natural stream of water flowing in a specific direction within a reasonably definite natural channel with banks. • A *natural watercourse* does not include surface water, which often flows intermittently and in an indefinite channel. In addition, a natural stream is distinguished from an artificial ditch or canal, which is typically not the subject of riparian rights. See RIPARIAN RIGHTS; WATER.

water district. A geographical subdivision created by a state or local government entity to provide the public with a water supply.

watered stock. See STOCK.

waterfront, *n.* Land or land with buildings fronting a body of water.

watergage, *n.* **1.** A seawall. **2.** An instrument used to measure water.

watergavel, *n. Hist.* A fee paid for a benefit (such as fishing) obtained from a body of water.

watermark. 1. A mark indicating the highest or lowest point to which water rises or falls.

***high-water mark.* 1.** The shoreline of a sea reached by the water at high tide. • The high-water mark is usu. computed as a mean or average high tide and not as the extreme height of the water. **2.** In a freshwater lake created by a dam in an unnavigable stream, the highest point on the shore to which the dam can raise the water in ordinary circumstances. **3.** In a river not subject to tides, the line that the river impresses on the soil by covering it long enough to deprive it of agricultural value. — Also termed *high-water line.*

***low-water mark.* 1.** The shoreline of a sea marking the edge of the water at the lowest point of the ordinary ebb tide. **2.** In a river, the point to which the water recedes at its lowest stage.

2. The transparent design or symbol seen when paper is held up to the light, usu. to indicate the genuineness of the document or the document's manufacturer.

water ordeal. See ORDEAL.

waterpower. 1. The force obtained by converting water into energy. **2.** The riparian owner's right consisting of the fall in the stream as it passes over or through the riparian owner's land; the difference of the level between the surface where the stream first touches one's land and the surface where the water leaves the land.

water right. (*often pl.*) The right to use water from a natural stream or from an artificial canal for irrigation, power, domestic use, and the like; RIPARIAN RIGHT. — Also termed *aquatic right.*

waterscape, *n.* An aqueduct or passage for water.

waterway. See WATERCOURSE.

waveson (**wayv**-sən), *n. Hist.* Goods that float on the sea after a shipwreck. Cf. FLOTSAM; JETSAM; LAGAN.

wax scot (wak **skot**), *n. Hist.* A duty on wax candles used in churches, usu. paid twice a year. — Also termed *cerage* (**seer**-ij); *ceratium* (si-**ray**-shee-əm).

way. 1. A passage or path. **2.** A right to travel over another's property. See RIGHT-OF-WAY.

private way. **1.** The right to pass over another's land. **2.** A way provided by local authorities primarily to accommodate particular individuals (usu. at the individual's expense) but also for the public's passage.

way of necessity. See *implied easement* under EASEMENT.

waybill. See BILL OF LADING.

way-going crop. A grain crop, formerly sown by a tenant during a tenancy (esp. in Pennsylvania), that did not ripen until after expiration of the lease. • In the absence of an express agreement to the contrary, the tenant was entitled to the crop.

way-leave, *n.* **1.** A right-of-way (usu. created by an express grant) over or through land for the transportation of minerals from a mine or quarry. **2.** The royalty paid for such a right.

waynagium (way-**nay**-jee-əm). See WAINAGE.

way of necessity. See *implied easement* under EASEMENT.

ways-and-means committee. A legislative committee that determines how money will be raised for various governmental purposes.

WC. *abbr.* WORKERS' COMPENSATION.

W.D. *abbr.* Western District, in reference to U.S. judicial districts.

weak mark. See TRADEMARK (1).

weak trademark. See TRADEMARK.

wealreaf (**weel**-reef), *n. Archaic.* The robbery of a dead person in a grave.

wealth. 1. A large quantity of something. **2.** The state of having abundant financial resources; affluence.

wealth maximization. An economic situation in which a change in the allocation of resources benefits the winner — i.e., the one who gains from the allocation — more than it harms the loser. — Also termed *Kaldor-Hicks efficiency*; *potential Pareto superiority*.

weapon. An instrument used or designed to be used to injure or kill someone.

concealed weapon. A weapon that is carried by a person but that is not visible by ordinary observation.

dangerous weapon. An object or device that, because of the way it is used, is capable of causing serious bodily injury.

deadly weapon. Any firearm or other device, instrument, material, or substance that, from the manner it is used or is intended to be used, is calculated or likely to produce death. — Also termed *lethal weapon.* Cf. DANGEROUS INSTRUMENTALITY.

deadly weapon per se. A weapon that is deadly in and of itself or would ordinarily result in death by its use <a gun is a deadly weapon>. — Also termed *per se deadly weapon.*

lethal weapon. See *deadly weapon.*

wear, *n.* [fr. Saxon *were* "a taking"] *Hist.* A dam made of stakes interlaced by twigs of willows that are placed across a river to more easily accommodate the netting of fish. — Also termed *weir.*

wear and tear. Deterioration caused by ordinary use <the tenant is not liable for normal wear and tear to the leased premises>. — Also termed *fair wear and tear.*

> " 'Fair wear' is the deterioration caused by the reasonable use of the premises; 'fair tear' is the deterioration caused by the ordinary operation of natural forces. A tenant's repairing covenant commonly exempts the tenant from the obligation to repair damage characterisable as 'fair wear and tear' (sometimes called 'reasonable wear and tear'). In the absence of such an exempting provision, a covenant to repair requires the repairing of damage characterisable as fair wear and tear. Where a covenant to repair exempts the tenant from liability for 'fair wear and tear', he is not responsible for deterioration or dilapidation caused by 'the reasonable use of the house by the tenant and the ordinary operation of natural forces.' " Peter Butt, *Land Law* 256 (2d ed. 1988).

natural wear and tear. The depreciation of property resulting from its ordinary and reasonable use.

Webb–Pomerene Act. A federal law, originally enacted in 1918, that provides a qualified exemption for an export business against the prohibitions of the antitrust laws. 15 USCA §§ 61 et seq.

> "The Webb–Pomerene Act was passed to aid and encourage our manufacturers and producers to extend our foreign trade. Congress believed that American firms needed the power to form joint export associations in

order to compete with foreign cartels, but while Congress was willing to create an exemption from the antitrust laws to serve this narrow purpose, the exemption created by the Webb–Pomerene Act was carefully hedged in to avoid substantial injury to domestic interests. Organization under the Webb–Pomerene Act does not give an export association the right to agree with foreign competitors to fix prices . . . or establish exclusive markets . . . ." 54 Am. Jur. 2d *Monopolies and Restraints of Trade* § 262, at 298 (1996).

wedding. See MARRIAGE CEREMONY.

wedge principle. The principle that an act is wrong in a specific instance if, when raised to a general level of conduct, it would injure humanity.

"[T]here is the familiar argument from the 'wedge principle,' which is used to deny the possibility of looking at particular circumstances in applying moral rules." Glanville Williams, *The Sanctity of Life and the Criminal Law* 315 (1957).

wedlock. The state of being married; matrimony.

week. 1. A period of seven consecutive days beginning on either Sunday or Monday. **2.** Any consecutive seven-day period.

weekend sentence. See *intermittent sentence* under SENTENCE.

week-work. *Hist.* In feudal times, the obligation of a tenant to work two to four days in every week for his lord during the greater part of the year, and four or five during the summer months. See VILLEIN SERVICE.

wehading. See TRIAL BY COMBAT.

weighage (**way**-ij). A duty or other payment required in return for weighing merchandise.

weight. A measure of heaviness; a measure of the quantity of matter.

gross weight. The total weight of a thing, including its contents and any packaging.

net weight. The total weight of a thing, after deducting its container, its wrapping, and any other extraneous matter.

weight of the evidence. The persuasiveness of some evidence in comparison with other evidence <because the verdict is against the great weight of the evidence, a new trial should be granted>. See BURDEN OF PERSUASION. Cf. MANIFEST WEIGHT OF THE EVIDENCE; PREPONDERANCE OF THE EVIDENCE.

weir. See WEAR.

welching. See WELSHING.

welfare. 1. Well-being in any respect; prosperity.

corporate welfare. Governmental financial assistance given to a large company, usu. in the form of a subsidy.

general welfare. The public's health, peace, morals, and safety.

public welfare. A society's well-being in matters of health, safety, order, morality, economics, and politics.

2. A system of social insurance providing assistance to those who are financially in need, as by providing food stamps and family allowances.

Welfare Clause. See GENERAL WELFARE CLAUSE.

welfare state. A nation in which the government undertakes various social insurance programs, such as unemployment compensation, old-age pensions, family allowances, food stamps, and aid to the blind or deaf. — Also termed *welfare-regulatory state.*

well, *adv.* In a legally sufficient manner; unobjectionable <well-pleaded complaint>.

well, *adj. Marine insurance.* (Of a vessel) in good condition; safe and sound <the vessel was warranted well on January 1>.

well, *n.* A hole or shaft sunk into the earth to obtain a fluid, such as water, oil, or natural gas.

limited-capacity well. An oil or gas well that is limited to producing only a portion of its monthly allowable because of market demand.

well-knowing, *adj.* Intentional <a well-knowing act or omission>. ● This term was formerly used in a pleading to allege scienter. See SCIENTER.

well-pleaded complaint. See COMPLAINT.

welshing. 1. The act or an instance of evading an obligation, esp. a gambling debt. **2.** The common-law act of larceny in which one receives a deposit to be paid back with additional money depending on the outcome of an event (such as a horse race) but at the time of the deposit the depositee intends to cheat and defraud the depositor by absconding with the money. • Although this term is sometimes thought to be a slur against those hailing from Wales, etymologists have not been able to establish this connection. Authoritative dictionaries record the origin of the term as being unknown. — Also termed *welching*. — **welsh,** *vb*. — **welsher,** *n*.

Welsh mortgage. See MORTGAGE.

wend, *n. Hist.* A large section of land; a perambulation; a circuit.

wergild (**wər**-gild). *Hist.* The fixed value of a person's life, being the amount that a homicide's kindred must pay to the kindred of the slain person so as to avoid a blood feud. — Also spelled *wergeld*; *weregild*; *wehrgeld*. See EFFUSIO SANGUINIS; LEODES.

Westlaw. A West Group database for computer-assisted legal research, providing online access to legal resources, including federal and state caselaw, statutes, regulations, and legal periodicals. — Abbr. WL.

Westminster Confession (**west**-min-stər). A document containing a statement of religious doctrine, originating at a conference of British and continental Protestant divines at Westminster in 1643, and becoming the basis of the Scottish Presbyterian Church.

Westminster the First, Statute of. *Hist.* An English statute divided into 51 chapters (later correlating to separate acts of Parliament), including provisions (1) protecting the property of the church from the violence and spoliation of the Crown and nobles; (2) providing for the freedom of popular elections; (3) enforcing the rules contained in Magna Carta against excessive fines; (4) enumerating and correcting the abuses of tenures (esp. concerning marriages of wards); (5) regulating the levying of tolls; (6) correcting and restraining the powers of the royal escheator and other officers; (7) amending the criminal law (esp. by classifying rape as a most grievous, though not capital, offense); and (8) making criminal and civil procedures more expeditious and less costly. 3 Edw. (1275).

West-Saxon law. A system of rules introduced by the West Saxons and one of the three principal legal systems prevailing in England in the beginning of the 11th century. • It was observed primarily in southern English counties from Kent to Devonshire. — Also termed *West-Saxon lage*. See MERCENLAGE; DANELAW.

wharf. A structure on the shores of navigable waters, to which a vessel can be brought for loading or unloading.

private wharf. One that can be used only by its owner or lessee.

public wharf. One that can be used by the public.

wharfage (**worf**-ij), *n. Hist.* **1.** The fee paid for landing, loading, or unloading goods on a wharf. **2.** The accommodation for loading or unloading goods on a wharf.

wharfinger (**wor**-fin-jər), *n. Hist.* The owner or occupier of a wharf; one who keeps a wharf to receive merchandise for forwarding or delivery to a consignee.

wharfing out, right of. See RIGHT OF WHARFING OUT.

Wharton rule ([**h**]**wor**-tən). *Criminal law.* The doctrine preventing conspiracy prosecution for a crime that necessarily involves the participation of two or more persons, such as illegal gambling. • But if an additional person participates so as to enlarge the scope of the agreement, all the actors may be charged with conspiracy. The doctrine takes its name from the influential criminal-law author Francis Wharton (1820–1889). — Also termed *Wharton's rule*; *concert-of-action rule*.

wheel. *Hist.* **1.** An instrument of torture used in medieval Europe, consisting of a wheel or cross on which a criminal was bound with arms and legs extended, while the criminal's bones were broken one by one with an iron bar, usu. until death. **2.** The torture itself.

wheelage ([**h**]**weel**-ij), *n. Hist.* A duty or toll for a vehicle to pass over certain property.

wheel conspiracy. See CONSPIRACY.

when-issued security. See SECURITY.

whereabouts, *n*. The general locale where a person or thing is <her whereabouts are unknown> <the Joneses' present whereabouts is a closely guarded secret>. • As the examples illustrate, this noun, though plural in form, may be construed with either a plural or a singular verb. — **whereabouts,** *adv.* & *conj.*

whereas, *conj.* **1.** While by contrast; although <McWilliams was stopped at 10:08 p.m. wearing a green hat, whereas the assailant had been

identified at 10:04 p.m. wearing a black hat>. **2.** Given the fact that; since <Whereas, the parties have found that their 1994 agreement did not adequately address incidental expenses . . . ; and Whereas, the parties have now decided in an equitable sharing of those expenses . . . ; Now, Therefore, the parties agree to amend the 1994 agreement as follows. . . .>. • In sense 2, *whereas* is used to introduce contractual recitals and the like, but modern drafters increasingly prefer a simple heading, such as "Recitals" or "Preamble," and in that way avoid the legalistic *whereases*. — **whereas** (recital or preamble), *n.*

whereat, *conj.* **1.** At or toward which <the point whereat he was aiming>. **2.** As a result of which; whereupon <Pettrucione called Bickley a scurrilous name, whereat a fistfight broke out>.

whereby, *conj.* By which; through which; in accordance with which <the treaty whereby the warring nations finally achieved peace>.

wherefore, premises considered. For all these reasons; for the reason or reasons mentioned above.

wherefrom, *conj.* From which <the students sent two faxes to the president's office, wherefrom no reply ever came>.

wherein, *conj.* **1.** In which; where <the jurisdiction wherein Lynn practices>. **2.** During which <they listened intently at the concert, wherein both of them became convinced that the composer's "new" work was a fraud>. **3.** How; in what respect <Fallon demanded to know wherein she had breached any duty>. — **wherein,** *adv.*

whereof, *conj.* **1.** Of what <Judge Wald knows whereof she speaks>. **2.** Of which <citations whereof even the most responsible are far afield from the true issue>. **3.** Of whom <judges whereof only the most glowing words might be said>.

whereon, *conj.* On which <the foundation whereon counsel bases this argument>. — Also termed *whereupon.*

whereto, *conj.* To what place or time <at first, Campbell did not know whereto he was being taken>. — Also termed *whereunto.* — **whereto,** *adv.*

whereupon, *conj.* **1.** WHEREON <the precedent whereupon the defense bases its argument>. **2.** Soon after and as a result of which; and then <a not-guilty verdict was announced, whereupon a riot erupted>.

wherewith, *conj.* By means of which <the plaintiff lacked a form of action wherewith to state a compensable claim>.

whim. A passing fancy; an impulse <the jury was instructed to render a verdict based solely on the evidence, not on a whim>.

whipping, *n.* A method of corporal punishment formerly used in England and a few American states, consisting of inflicting long welts on the skin, esp. with a whip.

whisper stock. See STOCK.

whistleblower, *n.* An employee who reports employer illegality to a governmental or law-enforcement agency. • Federal and state laws protect whistleblowers from employer retaliation. — **whistleblowing,** *n.*

whistleblower act. A federal or state law protecting employees from retaliation for disclosing employer illegality, such as during an investigation by a regulatory agency. • Federal laws containing whistleblower provisions include the Occupational Safety and Health Act (29 USCA § 660), CERCLA (42 USCA § 9610), and the Air Pollution and Control Act (42 USCA § 7622).

whiteacre. A fictitious tract of land used in legal discourse (esp. law-school hypotheticals) to discuss real-property issues. See BLACKACRE.

white book. 1. *Hist.* (*cap.*) ALBUS LIBER. **2.** A government report bound in white, common esp. in European and papal affairs.

whitecapping. The criminal act of threatening a person — usu. a member of a minority group — with violence in an effort to compel the person either to move away or to stop engaging in a certain business or occupation. • *Whitecapping* statutes were originally enacted to curtail the activities of the Ku Klux Klan.

white-collar crime. A nonviolent crime usu. involving cheating or dishonesty in commercial matters. • Examples include fraud, embezzlement, bribery, and insider trading.

whitehorse case. *Slang.* A reported case with facts virtually identical to those of the instant case, so that the disposition of the reported case should determine the outcome of the instant case. — Also termed *horse case*; *goose case*; *gray mule case*. Cf. ON ALL FOURS.

white knight. A person or corporation that rescues the target of an unfriendly corporate takeover, esp. by acquiring a controlling interest in the target corporation or by making a competing tender offer. — Also termed *friendly suitor*. See TAKEOVER. Cf. CORPORATE RAIDER.

Whiteley rule. See FELLOW-OFFICER RULE.

White model. *Labor law.* A method for determining whether a union member's state-law claim against the employer is preempted by federal law, by focusing on whether state law permits the claim to be waived by a private contract. • In *Lingle v. Norge Division of Magic Chef, Inc.*, 486 U.S. 399, 108 S.Ct. 1877 (1988), the Supreme Court held that a union member's state-law retaliatory-discharge claim was not preempted by the Labor–Management Relations Act because the claim could be resolved without interpreting the collective-bargaining agreement. There are at least two models for applying the *Lingle* test: the White model, which focuses on whether the claim is negotiable or nonnegotiable (that is, whether state law allows the claim to be waived by a private contract) and the Marcus model, which focuses on the independence of the claim in relation to the collective-bargaining agreement. Under the White model, all negotiable claims (those waivable by private contract) are necessarily preempted because their resolution will require an interpretation of the collective-bargaining agreement. A nonnegotiable claims (one that state law does not permit to be waived by private contract) will be preempted only if its resolution requires an interpretation of the collective-bargaining agreement. The White model is named for the author of the law-review article in which it was proposed. Rebecca Homer White, *Section 301's Preemption of State Law Claims: A Model for Analysis*, 41 Ala. L. Rev. 377 (1990). Cf. MARCUS MODEL. See LINGLE TEST.

white rent. *Hist.* A feudal rent paid in silver, rather than in work, grain, or money baser than silver. Cf. BLACK RENT.

white slavery. The practice of forcing a female (or, rarely, a male) to engage in commercial prostitution. • Trafficking in white slavery is prohibited by the Mann Act (18 USCA §§ 2421–2424).

White Slave Traffic Act. See MANN ACT.

whole blood. See *full blood* under BLOOD.

whole law. The law applied by a forum court in a multistate or multinational case after referring to its own choice-of-law rules.

whole life insurance. See INSURANCE.

wholesale, *n.* The sale of goods or commodities usu. for resale by a retailer, as opposed to a sale to the ultimate consumer. — **wholesale,** *vb.* — **wholesale,** *adj.* Cf. RETAIL.

wholesale dealer. One who sells goods in gross to retail dealers rather than selling in smaller quantities directly to consumers.

wholesale price. See PRICE.

wholesale price index. See PRODUCER PRICE INDEX.

wholesaler. One who buys large quantities of goods and resells them in smaller quantities to retailers or other merchants, who in turn sell to the ultimate consumer.

whole-statute rule. The principle of statutory construction that a statute should be considered in its entirety, and that the words used within it should be given their ordinary meanings unless there is a clear indication to the contrary.

wholly, *adv.* Not partially; fully; completely.

wholly and permanently disabled, *adj. Insurance.* (Of an insured) completely and continuously unable to perform work for compensation or profit.

wholly dependent, *adj. Workers' compensation.* (Of a person) deriving full support from a worker's wages.

wholly destroyed, *adj. Insurance.* (Of a building) so damaged that it is no longer capable of being classified as a building, although some parts may remain intact.

wholly disabled, *adj. Insurance.* (Of a person) unable to perform the substantial and material acts necessary to carry on a business or occupation in the customary and usual manner.

widow, *n.* A woman whose husband has died and who has not remarried.

widower. A man whose wife has died and who has not remarried.

widower's allowance. See *spousal allowance* under ALLOWANCE.

widow's allowance. See *spousal allowance* under ALLOWANCE.

widow's election. See RIGHT OF ELECTION.

wifa (**wɪ**-fə), *n.* [Law Latin] *Hist.* A mark or sign; esp., a landmark showing exclusive occupation or to prohibit an entry.

wife's equity. See EQUITY TO A SETTLEMENT.

wife's settlement. See EQUITY TO A SETTLEMENT.

wildcat strike. See STRIKE.

wild deed. See DEED.

Wild's Case, Rule in. See RULE IN WILD'S CASE.

will, *n.* **1.** Wish; desire; choice <employment at will>. **2.** A document by which a person directs his or her estate to be distributed upon death <there was no mention of his estranged brother in the will>. — Also termed *testament*; *will and testament.* — **will,** *vb.*

> "The word 'will' has two distinct meanings. The first, and strict, meaning is metaphysical, and denotes the sum of what the testator wishes, or 'wills,' to happen on his death. The second, and more common, meaning is physical, and denotes the document or documents in which that intention is expressed." Anthony R. Mellows, *The Law of Succession* 6 (3d ed. 1977).

ambulatory will. A will that can be altered during the testator's lifetime.

antenuptial will. See *prenuptial will.*

closed will. See *mystic will.*

conditional will. A will that depends on the occurrence of an uncertain event for the will to take effect.

conjoint will. See *joint will.*

contingent will. A will that takes effect only if a specified event occurs.

counter will. See *mutual will.*

double will. See *mutual will.*

duplicate will. A will executed in duplicate by a testator who retains one copy and gives the second copy to another person. • The rules applicable to wills apply to both wills, and upon application for probate, both copies must be tendered into the registry of the probate court.

holographic will (hol-ə-**graf**-ik). A will that is entirely handwritten by the testator. • In many states, a holographic will is valid even if not witnessed. — Also termed *olographic will.*

inofficious will. See *inofficious testament* under TESTAMENT.

international will. A will that is executed according to formalities provided in an international treaty or convention, and that will be valid although it may be written in a foreign language by a testator domiciled in another country.

invalid will. A will that fails to make an effective disposition of property.

joint and mutual will. A will executed by two or more people — to dispose of property they own separately, in common, or jointly — requiring the surviving testator to dispose of the property in accordance with the terms of the will, and showing that the devises are made in consideration of one another. • The word "joint" indicates the form of the will. The word "mutual" describes the substantive provisions. — Also termed *joint and reciprocal will.*

joint will. A single will executed by two or more testators, usu. disposing of their common property by transferring their separate titles to one devisee. — Also termed *conjoint will.*

last will. The most recent will of a deceased; the instrument ultimately fixing the disposition of real and personal property at the testator's death.

living will. See LIVING WILL.

lost will. An executed will that cannot be found at the testator's death. • Its contents can be proved by parol evidence in many jurisdictions, but in some states a lost will creates a rebuttable presumption that it has been revoked.

mariner's will. See *soldier's will.*

mutual will. (*usu. pl.*) One of two separate wills in which two persons, usu. a husband and wife, establish identical or similar testamentary provisions disposing of their estates in favor of each other. • It is also possible (though rare) for the testators to execute a single mutual will, as opposed to separate ones. And it is possible (though, again, rare) for more than two parties to execute mutual wills. — Also termed *reciprocal will*; *counter will*; *double will*; *mutual testament*.

mystic will. *Civil law.* A secret will signed by the testator, sealed and delivered to a notary in the presence of three to seven witnesses, accompanied by the testator's declaration that it is a valid will. • The notary is then required to indorse on the envelope containing the will a statement of all the facts surrounding the transaction, and this is signed by the notary and all the witnesses. — Also termed *mystic testament*; *secret will*; *secret testament*; *closed will*; *closed testament*; *sealed will*; *sealed testament*.

nonintervention will. A will that authorizes the executor to settle and distribute the estate without court supervision.

notarial will. A will executed by a testator in the presence of two witnesses and a notary public.

nuncupative will (**nəng**-kyə-pay-tiv *or* nəng-**kyoo**-pə-tiv). An oral will made in contemplation of imminent death from an injury recently incurred. • Nuncupative wills are invalid in most states, but in those states allowing them, the amount that may be conveyed is usu. limited by statute, and they traditionally apply only to personal property. — Also termed *oral will*; *unwritten will*; *verbal will*.

> "Nuncupative (i.e., oral) wills are by statute in almost all States required to be proved by two (sometimes three) witnesses, who were present and heard the testamentary words." John H. Wigmore, *A Students' Textbook of the Law of Evidence* 299 (1935).

olographic will. See *holographic will*.

oral will. A will made by the spoken declaration of the testator and usu. dependent on oral testimony for proof.

pourover will (**por**-oh-vər). A will giving money or property to an existing trust. Cf. *pourover trust* under TRUST.

prenuptial will (pree-**nəp**-shəl). A will executed before marriage. • At common law, marriage automatically revoked a spouse's will, but modern statutes usu. provide that marriage does not revoke a will (although divorce does). Unif. Probate Code § 2–508. — Also termed *antenuptial will*.

reciprocal will. See *mutual will*.

sealed will. See *mystic will*.

seaman's will. See *soldier's will*.

secret will. See *mystic will*.

self-proved will. A will proved by the testator's affidavit instead of by the live testimony of attesting witnesses.

soldier's will. A soldier's informal oral or written will that is usu. valid despite its noncompliance with normal statutory formalities, as long as the soldier was in actual service at the time the will was made. — Also termed *seaman's will*; *mariner's will*; *military testament*.

unnatural will. A will that distributes the testator's estate to strangers rather than to the testator's relatives, without apparent reason.

unofficious will. See *inofficious testament* under TESTAMENT.

unsolemn will. *Civil law.* A will in which an executor is not named.

unwritten will. See *nuncupative will*.

verbal will. See *nuncupative will*.

will contest. *Wills & estates.* The litigation of a will's validity, usu. based on allegations that the testator lacked capacity or was under undue influence.

willful, *adj.* Voluntary and intentional, but not necessarily malicious. — Sometimes spelled *wilful.* — **willfulness,** *n.* Cf. WANTON.

> "The word 'wilful' or 'wilfully' when used in the definition of a crime, it has been said time and again, means only intentionally or purposely as distinguished from accidentally or negligently and does not require any actual impropriety; while on the other hand it has been stated with equal repetition and insistence that the requirement added by such a word is not satisfied unless there is a bad purpose or evil intent." Rollin M. Perkins & Ronald N. Boyce, *Criminal Law* 875–76 (3d ed. 1982).

> "Almost all of the cases under [Bankruptcy Code § 523(a)(6)] deal with the definition of the two words 'willful' and 'malicious.' Initially one might think that willful and malicious mean the same thing. If they did, Congress should have used one word and not both. Most courts feel compelled to find some different meaning for each of them." David G. Epstein et al., *Bankruptcy* § 7–30, at 531 (1993).

willful and malicious injury. *Bankruptcy.* Under the statutory exception to discharge, damage to another entity (such as a creditor) caused by a debtor intentionally performing a wrongful act — without just cause or excuse — that the debtor knew was certain or substantially certain to cause injury. 11 USCA § 523(a)(6).

willful and wanton misconduct. Conduct committed with an intentional or reckless disregard for the safety of others, as by failing to exercise ordinary care to prevent a known danger or to discover a danger. — Also termed *willful indifference to the safety of others.*

willful and wanton negligence. See *gross negligence* (2) under NEGLIGENCE.

willful blindness. Deliberate avoidance of knowledge of a crime, esp. by failing to make a reasonable inquiry about suspected wrongdoing despite being aware that it is highly probable. • A person acts with willful blindness, for example, by deliberately refusing to look inside an unmarked package after being paid by a known drug dealer to deliver it. Willful blindness creates an inference of knowledge of the crime in question.

willful, continued, and obstinate desertion. See *obstinate desertion* under DESERTION.

willful indifference to the safety of others. See WILLFUL AND WANTON MISCONDUCT.

willful infringement. See INFRINGEMENT.

willful misconduct. See MISCONDUCT.

willful misconduct of employee. The deliberate disregard by an employee of the employer's interests, including its work rules and standards of conduct, justifying a denial of unemployment compensation if the employee is terminated for the misconduct.

willful murder. See MURDER.

willful neglect. See NEGLECT.

willful negligence. See *gross negligence* under NEGLIGENCE.

willfulness. A condition shown by the intentional disregard of a known duty necessary to another's safety of person or property, and the complete lack of care for another's life, person, or property. — Also termed *legal willfulness.*

willful tort. See *intentional tort* under TORT.

willful wrong. See *intentional wrong* under WRONG.

Williams Act. A federal statute, enacted in 1968, that amended the Securities Exchange Act of 1934 by requiring investors who own more than 5% of a company's stock to furnish certain information to the SEC and to comply with certain requirements when making a tender offer.

Wills Act. 1. STATUTE OF WILLS (1). **2.** An 1837 English statute that allowed people to dispose of every type of property interest by will and that required every will to be attested by two witnesses. — Also termed (in sense 2) *Lord Langdale's Act.*

will substitute. A document or instrument that attempts to dispose of an estate in the same or similar manner as a will, such as a trust or a life-insurance plan.

Winchester, Statute of. *Hist.* A statute passed in the 13th year of the reign of Edward I, requiring every man to provide himself with armor to keep the peace, recognizing and regulating the offices of high and petty constables, organizing the police, and enforcing the old Saxon police laws. • It was repealed in 1827 by the Criminal Statutes (England) Repeal Act. St. 7 & 8 Geo. 4, ch. 27.

Winchester measure. *Hist.* The standard weights and measures of England, originally kept at Winchester.

windfall. An unanticipated benefit, usu. in the form of a profit and not caused by the recipient.

windfall-profits tax. See TAX.

winding up, *n.* The process of settling accounts and liquidating assets in anticipation of a partnership's or a corporation's dissolution. Cf. DISSOLUTION (3). — **wind up,** *vb.* — **wind up,** *n.*

window-dressing. The deceptive arrangement of something, usu. facts or appearances, to make it appear more attractive or favorable. • The term is often used to describe the practice of some financial managers, esp. some managers of mutual funds, to sell certain positions at the end of a quarter to make an investment's quarterly performance appear better than it actually was.

window tax. See TAX.

wire fraud. See FRAUD.

wiretapping, *n.* Electronic or mechanical eavesdropping, usu. done by law-enforcement officers under court order, to listen to private conversations. • Wiretapping is regulated by federal and state law. — **wiretap,** *vb.* — **wiretap,** *n.* — Often shortened to *tapping.* See BUGGING; EAVESDROPPING. Cf. PEN REGISTER.

wish, *vb.* **1.** To desire; to hope. **2.** To will; to devise; to give.

witan (**wit**-ən). [Anglo–Saxon "wise men"] *Hist.* The members of the king's council who sat to assist the king in administrative and judicial matters. • Among the members were ealdormen, bishops, abbots, high officers, and occasionally the king's friends and relatives.

witchcraft. The practices of a witch, esp. in black magic; sorcery. • Under the Witchcraft Act of 1541 (33 Hen. 8, ch. 8) and the Witchcraft Act of 1603 (1 Jac. ch. 12), witchcraft was a felony punishable by death without benefit of clergy. These acts were repealed in 1736, and the last execution in England for witchcraft occurred in 1716. In the United States, the most conspicuous (and nearly the last) persecution for witchcraft occurred in Salem, Massachusetts, where some 20 people were hanged for this offense in 1692.

wite (wɪt). *Hist.* A penal fine exacted by the Crown or other authority for a serious crime, such as murder. — Also spelled *wyte.*

witenagemot (**wit**-ə-nə-gə-moht). [Anglo–Saxon "a meeting of the wise"] *Hist.* A national assembly of noblemen, high ecclesiastics, and other great thanes of England who advised and aided the kin in the general administration of the government. • Its composition depended on the will of the king. It passed out of existence with the Norman Conquest (1066). Although it was a precursor to the British Parliament, that was a separate growth — not a continuation of the witenagemot. — Also spelled *witenagemot*; *wittenagemot*; *witanagemote.*

witepenny. *Hist.* In early English law, money paid in satisfaction of a wite.

with all deliberate speed. See DELIBERATE SPEED, WITH ALL.

with all faults. See AS IS.

withdrawal, *n.* **1.** The act of taking back or away; removal <withdrawal of consent>. **2.** The act of retreating from a place, position, or situation <withdrawal from the moot-court competition>. **3.** The removal of money from a depository <withdrawal of funds from the checking account>. **4.** RENUNCIATION (2) <withdrawal from the conspiracy to commit arson>. — **withdraw,** *vb.*

withdrawal of charges. The removal of charges by the one bringing them, such as a prosecutor. See NOLLE PROSEQUI.

withdrawal of counsel. An attorney's termination of his or her role in representing a party in a lawsuit. • An attorney usu. must obtain the court's permission to withdraw from a case. Such permission is usu. sought by a written motion (1) explaining the reason for the requested withdrawal (often, a conflict between attorney and client over a matter such as strategy or fees), and (2) stating whether the client agrees.

withdrawing a juror. The act or an instance of removing a juror, usu. to obtain a continuance in a case or, sometimes in English practice, to end the case, as when the case has settled, the parties are too anxious to proceed to verdict, or the judge recommends it because the action is not properly before the court.

withdrawing record. A plaintiff's removing of the *nisi prius* or trial record to prevent the case from being tried, usu. either before the jury is sworn or afterwards with the consent of defense counsel.

withernam (**with**-ər-nahm), *n.* [fr. Saxon *weder* "other" + *naam* "a taking"] *Hist.* A reciprocal taking or distress in place of a previous one. See CAPIAS IN WITHERNAM.

withersake (**with**-ər-sayk). *Archaic.* An enemy; esp., a deliberately faithless renegade.

withheld sentence. See *suspended sentence* under SENTENCE.

withholding, *n.* **1.** The practice of deducting a certain amount from a person's salary, wages, dividends, winnings, or other income, usu. for tax purposes; esp., an employer's practice of taking out a portion of an employee's gross earnings and paying that portion to the government for income-tax and social-security purposes. **2.** The money so deducted. — **withhold,** *vb.*

withholding of evidence. The act or an instance of obstructing justice by stifling or suppressing evidence knowing that it is being sought in an official investigation or a judicial proceeding. See OBSTRUCTION OF JUSTICE.

withholding tax. See TAX.

without day. See GO HENCE WITHOUT DAY.

without delay. 1. Instantly; at once. **2.** Within the time reasonably allowed by law.

without impeachment of waste. (Of a tenant) not subject to an action for waste; not punishable for waste. • This clause is inserted in a lease to give a tenant the right to take certain actions (such as cutting timber) without being held liable for waste. But a tenant cannot abuse the right and will usu. be held liable for maliciously committing waste. — Also termed *absque impetitione vasti.*

without notice. Lacking actual or constructive knowledge. • To be a bona fide purchaser, one must buy something "without notice" of another's claim to the item or of defects in the seller's title. To be a holder in due course, one must take a bill or note "without notice" that it is overdue, has been dishonored, or is subject to a claim. UCC § 3-302(a)(2). See *bona fide purchaser* under PURCHASER.

without prejudice, *adv.* Without loss of any rights; in a way that does not harm or cancel the legal rights or privileges of a party <dismissed without prejudice>. See *dismissal without prejudice* under DISMISSAL.

without recourse. (In an indorsement) without liability to subsequent holders. • With this stipulation, one who indorses an instrument indicates that he or she has no further liability to any subsequent holder for payment. — Also termed *sans recours.*

without reserve. Of or relating to an auction at which an item will be sold for the highest bid price.

without this, that. See ABSQUE HOC.

with prejudice, *adv.* With loss of all rights; in a way that finally disposes of a party's claim and bars any future action on that claim <dismissed with prejudice>. See *dismissal with prejudice* under DISMISSAL.

with recourse, *adv.* (In an indorsement) with liability to subsequent holders. • With this stipulation, one who indorses an instrument indicates that he or she remains liable to the holder for payment.

with reserve. Of or relating to an auction at which an item will not be sold unless the highest bid exceeds a minimum price.

with strong hand. With force. • In common-law pleading, this term implies a degree of criminal force, esp. as used in forcible-entry statutes.

witness, *n.* **1.** One who sees, knows, or vouches for something <a witness to the accident>. **2.** One who gives testimony, under oath or affirmation (1) in person, (2) by oral or written deposition, or (3) by affidavit <the prosecution called its next witness>. — **witness,** *vb.*

> "The term 'witness,' in its strict legal sense, means one who gives evidence in a cause before a court; and in its general sense includes all persons from whose lips testimony is extracted to be used in any judicial proceeding, and so includes deponents and affiants as well as persons delivering oral testimony before a court or jury." 97 C.J.S. *Witnesses* § 1, at 350 (1957).

> "Every witness is an editor: he tells you not everything he saw and heard, for that would be impossible, but what he saw and heard and found significant, and what he finds significant depends on his preconceptions." Patrick Devlin, *The Criminal Prosecution in England* 66 (1960).

accomplice witness. An accomplice in a criminal act. • A codefendant cannot be convicted solely on the testimony of an accomplice witness.

adverse witness. See *hostile witness.*

alibi witness. A witness who testifies that the defendant was in a location other than the scene of the crime at the relevant time; a witness that supports the defendant's alibi.

attesting witness. One who vouches for the authenticity of another's signature by signing an instrument that the other has signed <proof of the will requires two attesting witnesses>.

character witness. A witness who testifies about another person's character traits or community reputation. See *character evidence* under EVIDENCE.

competent witness. A witness who is legally qualified to testify. • A lay witness who has personal knowledge of the subject matter of the testimony is competent to testify. Fed. R. Evid. 601–602.

corroborating witness. A witness who confirms or supports someone else's testimony.

credible witness. A witness whose testimony is believable.

disinterested witness. A witness who is legally competent to testify and has no private interest in the matter at issue.

expert witness. A witness qualified by knowledge, skill, experience, training, or education to provide a scientific, technical, or other specialized opinion about the evidence or a fact issue. Fed. R. Evid. 702–706. — Also termed *skilled witness*. See EXPERT; *DAUBERT* TEST.

going witness. *Archaic*. A witness who is about to leave a court's jurisdiction, but not the country. • An example is the witness who leaves one state to go to another.

grand-jury witness. A witness who is called to testify in a matter under inquiry by a grand jury.

hostile witness. A witness who is biased against the examining party or who is unwilling to testify. • A hostile witness may be asked leading questions on direct examination. Fed. R. Evid. 611(c). — Also termed *adverse witness*.

interested witness. A witness who has a direct and private interest in the matter at issue.

lay witness. A witness who does not testify as an expert and who therefore may only give an opinion or make an inference that is based on firsthand knowledge and helpful in understanding the testimony or in determining facts. Fed. R. Evid. 701.

material witness. A witness who can testify about matters having some logical connection with the consequential facts, esp. if few others, if any, know about those matters.

prosecuting witness. A person who files the complaint that triggers a criminal prosecution and whose testimony the prosecution usu. relies on to secure a conviction.

qualified witness. A witness who, by explaining the manner in which a company's business records are made and kept, is able to lay the foundation for the admission of business records under an exception to the hearsay rule. Fed. R. Evid. 803(6).

rebuttal witness. A witness who contradicts or attempts to contradict evidence previously presented.

res gestae witness. A witness who, having been at the scene of an incident, can give a firsthand account of what happened. See RES GESTAE.

skilled witness. See *expert witness*.

subscribing witness. One who witnesses the signatures on an instrument and signs at the end of the instrument to that effect.

swift witness. See *zealous witness*.

target witness. **1.** The person who has the knowledge that an investigating body seeks. **2.** A witness who is called before a grand jury and against whom the government is also seeking an indictment.

turncoat witness. A witness whose testimony was expected to be favorable but who becomes (usu. during the trial) a hostile witness.

zealous witness (**zel**-əs). A witness who is unduly zealous or partial to one side of a lawsuit and shows bias through extreme readiness to answer questions or volunteer information advantageous to that side. — Also termed *swift witness*.

witness box. See WITNESS STAND.

witnesseth, *vb*. Shows; records. • This term, usu. set in all capitals, commonly separates the preliminaries in a contract, up through the recitals, from the contractual terms themselves, but modern drafters increasingly avoid it as an antiquarian relic. Traditionally, the subject of this verb was *This Agreement*: the sentence, boiled down, was *This Agreement witnesseth* [i.e., shows or records] *that, whereas* [*the parties have agreed to contract with one another*], *the parties therefore agree as follows* .... Many modern contracts erroneously retain the *Witnesseth* even though a new verb appears in the preamble: *This Agreement is between* [one party and the other party]. After the preamble is a period, followed by an all-capped WITNESSETH. It is an example of a form retained long after its utility, and most lawyers do not know what it means or even what purpose it once served.

witness fee. See FEE (1).

witnessing part. See ATTESTATION CLAUSE.

witness jurat. See JURAT.

witness-protection program. A federal or state program in which a person who testifies against a criminal is assigned a new identity and relocated to another part of the country to avoid retaliation by anyone convicted as a result of that testimony. • The Federal Witness Protection Program was established by the Organized Crime Control Act of 1970 and is administered by the marshals of the U.S. Justice Department.

witness stand. The space in a courtroom, usu. a boxed area, occupied by a witness while testifying. — Often shortened to *stand*. — Also termed *witness box*.

witness tampering. The act or an instance of obstructing justice by intimidating, influencing, or harassing a witness before or after the witness testifies. • Several state and federal laws, including the Victim and Witness Protection Act of 1982 (18 USCA § 1512), provide criminal penalties for tampering with witnesses or other persons in the context of a pending investigation or official proceeding. See OBSTRUCTION OF JUSTICE.

witword (**wit**-wərd). *Hist.* A legally allowed claim; esp., the right to vindicate ownership or possession by one's affirmation under oath.

wobbler. *Slang.* A public offense that may be either a felony or a misdemeanor.

wolf's head. *Hist.* An outlaw, who was formerly often referred to as carrying a wolf's head (*caput lupinum*) and to be no more than a wild beast or wolf who could be slain and whose head could be carried to the king. — Also termed *woolferthfod*. See OUTLAW.

> "Outlawry is the last weapon of ancient law, but one that it must often use. As has been well said, it is the sentence of death pronounced by a community which has no police constables or professional hangmen. To pursue the outlaw and knock him on the head as though he were a wild beast is the right and duty of every law-abiding man. 'Let him bear the wolf's head:' this phrase is in use even in the thirteenth century." 1 Frederick Pollock & Frederic W. Maitland, *The History of English Law Before the Time of Edward I* 476 (2d ed. 1898).

Women's Suffrage Amendment. See NINETEENTH AMENDMENT.

wood-corn, *n. Hist.* A quantity of oats or grain paid by customary tenants to a lord for the privilege of picking up dead or broken wood.

wood-geld (**wuud**-geld). *Hist.* **1.** Money paid for the privilege of taking wood from a forest. **2.** Immunity from paying money for this privilege. — Also termed *pudzeld*.

wood-leave. *Hist.* A license or right to cut down, remove, and use standing timber.

wood-mote (**wuud**-moht). See COURT OF ATTACHMENTS.

Wood-Plea Court. *Hist.* A court held twice a year in Clun Forest, in Shropshire, to determine matters of wood and agistments.

woodshedding. See HORSESHEDDING.

woodward (**wuud**-word), *n. Hist.* A forest officer who patrols and protects the forest.

woolferthfod. See WOLF'S HEAD.

word of art. See TERM OF ART.

words actionable in themselves. Language that is libelous or slanderous per se. See *slander per se* under SLANDER; *libel per se* under LIBEL.

words of limitation. Language in a deed or will — often nonliteral language — describing the extent or quality of an estate. • For example, under long-standing principles of property law, the phrasing "to A and her heirs" creates a fee simple and does not give anything to A's heirs. See LIMITATION (4).

words of negotiability. See NEGOTIABLE WORDS.

words of procreation (proh-kree-**ay**-shən). Language in a deed essential to create an estate tail, such as an estate "to A and the heirs of his body."

words of purchase. Language in a deed or will designating the persons who are to receive the grant. • For example, the phrasing "to A for life with a remainder to her heirs" creates a life estate in A and a remainder in A's heirs. See PURCHASE (2).

work, *n.* **1.** Physical and mental exertion to attain an end, esp. as controlled by and for the benefit of an employer; labor.

additional work. **1.** Work that results from a change or alteration in plans concerning the work required, usu. under a construction contract; added work necessary to meet the performance goals under a contract. **2.** See *extra work*.

extra work. In construction law, work not required under the contract; something done or furnished in addition to the contract's requirements; work entirely outside and independent of the contract and not contemplated by it. • A contractor is usu. entitled to charge for extra work consisting of labor and materials not contemplated by or subsumed within the original contract, at least to the extent that the property owner agrees to a change order. Materials and labor not contemplated by the contract, but that are required by later changes in the plans and specifications, are considered to be extra work. — Also termed *additional work.*

heavy work. Work that involves frequent lifting and carrying of large items. • Under the Social Security Administration regulations for describing a worker's physical limitations, heavy work involves lifting no more than 100 pounds, with frequent lifting or carrying of objects weighing up to 50 pounds. 20 CFR § 404.1567(d).

light work. Work that involves some limited lifting and moving. • Under the Social Security Administration regulations for describing a worker's physical limitations, light work includes walking, standing, sitting while pushing or pulling arm or leg controls, and lifting no more than 20 pounds, with frequent lifting or carrying of objects that weigh up to 10 pounds. 20 CFR § 404.1567(b).

medium work. Work that involves some frequent lifting and moving. • Under the Social Security Administration regulations for describing a worker's physical limitations, medium work includes lifting up to 50 pounds, with frequent lifting or carrying of objects weighing up to 25 pounds. 20 CFR § 404.1567(c).

sedentary work. Work that involves light lifting and only occasional walking or standing. • Under the Social Security Administration regulations for describing a worker's physical limitations, sedentary work involves lifting of no more than ten pounds, occasionally carrying small items such as docket files and small tools, and occasional standing or walking. 20 CFR § 404.1567(a).

semi-skilled work. Work that may require some alertness and close attention, such as inspecting items or machinery for irregularities, or guarding property or people against loss or injury. 20 CFR § 404.1568(b). — Also written *semiskilled work.*

skilled work. Work requiring the worker to use judgment, deal with the public, analyze facts and figures, or work with abstract ideas at a high level of complexity. 20 CFR § 404.1568(c).

unskilled work. Work requiring little or no judgment, and involving simple tasks that can be learned quickly on the job. 20 CFR § 404.1568(a).

very heavy work. Work that involves frequent lifting of very large objects and frequent carrying of large objects. • Under the Social Security Administration regulations for describing a worker's physical limitations, very heavy work involves lifting 100 pounds or more, and frequent lifting or carrying of objects weighing 50 pounds or more. 20 CFR § 404.1567(e).

2. *Copyright.* An original expression, in fixed or tangible form (such as paper, audiotape, or computer disk), that may be entitled to common-law or statutory copyright protection. • A work may take many different forms, including art, sculpture, literature, music, crafts, software, and photography.

work, *vb.* **1.** To exert effort; to perform, either physically or mentally <lawyers work long hours during trial>. **2.** To function properly; to produce a desired effect <the strategy worked>. **3.** *Patents.* To develop and commercially exploit (the invention covered by a patent) <the patent owner failed to work the patent>.

> "A patentee has the *exclusive* right to *make, use,* or *sell* the invention. 35 U.S.C.A. § 154. The right includes the right to *refrain* from making, using, or selling the invention. In many foreign countries, the inventor is obliged to 'work' the patent and if he does not do so, he can be required to grant a compulsory license to others who wish to exploit the invention. But an American patentee is under no such duty, although there are antitrust implications involved in the failure to work a patent." Arthur R. Miller & Michael H. Davis, *Intellectual Property in a Nutshell* 128–29 (2d ed. 1990).

work and labor. *Hist.* A common count in an action of *assumpsit* for the work and labor performed and materials furnished by the plaintiff. See ASSUMPSIT.

worker. One who labors to attain an end; esp., a person employed to do work for another.

Worker Adjustment and Retraining Notification Act. A federal law that requires an employer to provide notice of a plant closing or mass layoff, 60 days before the closing or layoff, to the employees, the state-dislocated-workers unit, and the chief elected official of the unit of local government where the plant closing or layoff is to occur. 29 USCA §§ 2101–2109. — Abbr. WARN.

workers' compensation. A system of providing benefits to an employee for injuries occurring in the scope of employment. • Most workers'-compensation statutes both hold the employer strictly liable and bar the employee from suing in tort. — Also termed *workmen's compensation; employers' liability.* — Abbr. WC.

> "Workers' compensation laws were designed to provide employees with expansive protection against the conse-

> quences of employment-related injuries. Injured workers no longer had to establish negligence attributable to their employer in order to obtain legal redress. They merely had to demonstrate that their conditions arose out of and during the course of their employment." Mark A. Rothstein et al., *Employment Law* § 7.3, at 406 (1994).

workers'-compensation board. An agency that reviews cases arising under workers'-compensation statutes and administers the related rules and regulations. — Also termed *workers'-compensation commission.*

> "Workers' compensation boards ... are tribunals ... of limited and special jurisdiction and have only such authority and power as have been conferred upon them by express grant, or by implication as necessary and incidental to the full exercise of their authority. The functions of such agencies may include the settlement of disputes with respect to the right to and the amount of compensation, the supervision of voluntary settlements or agreements, the collection and administration of compensation funds, and the supervision and regulation of matters pertaining to compensation insurance." 82 Am. Jur. 2d *Workers' Compensation* § 56, at 65 (1992).

workfare. A system of requiring a person receiving a public-welfare benefit to earn that benefit by performing a job provided by a government agency.

work for hire. *Copyright.* A copyrightable work produced either by an employee within the scope of employment or by an independent contractor under a written agreement; esp., a work specially ordered or commissioned for use as (1) a contribution to a collective work, (2) a translation, (3) a supplementary work, (4) a part of a movie or other audiovisual work, (5) a compilation, (6) an instructional text, (7) a test, (8) answer material for a test, or (9) an atlas. • If the work is produced by an independent contractor, the parties must agree expressly in writing that the work will be a work for hire. The employer or commissioning party owns the copyright. — Also termed *work made for hire.*

work furlough (**fər**-loh). A prison-treatment program allowing an inmate to be released during the day to work in the community. See WORK-RELEASE PROGRAM.

work-furlough program. See WORK-RELEASE PROGRAM.

workhouse. A jail for criminals who have committed minor offenses and are serving short sentences.

working capital. See CAPITAL.

working capital acceptance. See *finance bill* under BILL (6).

working control. See CONTROL.

working interest. *Oil & gas.* The right to the mineral interest granted by an oil-and-gas lease. • The term is so called because the lessee acquires the right to work on the lease property to search, develop, and produce oil and gas, and the obligation to pay all costs. See ROYALTY. — Also termed *leasehold interest*; *operating interest.*

working papers. 1. WORK PERMIT. **2.** *Accounting.* The records kept by an independent auditor of the procedures followed, tests performed, information obtained, and conclusions reached in an audit.

work-in-process. A product being manufactured or assembled but not yet completed. — Also termed *work-in-progress.*

work made for hire. See WORK FOR HIRE.

workmen's compensation. See WORKERS' COMPENSATION.

work of necessity. Work reasonably essential to the public's economic, social, or moral welfare as determined by the community standards at a particular time, and excepted from the operation of blue laws. See BLUE LAW.

workout, *n.* **1.** The act of restructuring or refinancing overdue loans. **2.** *Bankruptcy.* A debtor's agreement, usu. negotiated with a creditor or creditors out of court, to reduce or discharge the debt. — **work out,** *vb.*

work permit. An alien's documentary work authorization from the Immigration and Naturalization Service. • Under the Immigration Reform and Control Act of 1986, it is illegal for an employer to hire an alien who lacks a work permit. 8 USCA § 1324(a)(1). — Also termed *working papers.*

work product. Tangible material or its intangible equivalent — in unwritten or oral form — that was either prepared by or for a lawyer or prepared for litigation, either planned or in progress. • Work product is generally exempt from discovery or other compelled disclosure. The term is also used to describe the products of a party's investigation or communications concerning the subject matter of a lawsuit if made (1) to assist in the prosecution or defense of a pending suit, or (2) in reasonable anticipation of litigation. — Also termed *attorney work product*.

work-product privilege. See WORK PRODUCT.

work-product rule. The rule providing for qualified immunity of an attorney's work product from discovery or other compelled disclosure. Fed. R. Civ. P. 26(b)(3). • The exemption was primarily established to protect an attorney's litigation strategy. *Hickman v. Taylor*, 329 U.S. 495, 67 S.Ct. 385 (1947). — Also termed *work-product immunity*; *work-product privilege*; *work-product exemption*.

> "Although the work-product rule has often been spoken of as creating a 'privilege,' it is a qualified one that does not grant full immunity from discovery. To the extent the term 'privilege' causes confusion between the work-product rule and the absolute privilege for confidential communications between attorney and client, it is important to keep in mind this distinction.... Rule 26(b)(3) provides that work-product material is subject to discovery 'only upon a showing that the party seeking discovery has substantial need of the materials in the preparation of the party's case and that the party is unable without undue hardship to obtain the substantial equivalent of the materials by other means.' " 8 Charles Alan Wright et al., *Federal Practice and Procedure* § 2025, at 371, 373–74 (2d ed. 1994).

work-release program. A correctional program allowing a prison inmate — primarily one being readied for discharge — to hold a job outside prison. — Also termed *work-furlough program*. See HALFWAY HOUSE.

works. 1. A mill, factory, or other establishment for manufacturing or other industrial purposes; a manufacturing plant; a factory. **2.** Any building or structure on land.

new works. *Civil law.* A structure newly commenced on a particular estate. • A denunciation of new works is a remedy allowed for an adjacent landowner whose property will be injured if the structure is completed.

public works. Structures (such as roads or dams) built by the government for public use and paid for by public funds.

work stoppage. A cessation of work; STRIKE.

world. 1. The planet Earth <the world has limited natural resources>. **2.** All the Earth's inhabitants; the public generally <the world will benefit from this discovery>. **3.** All persons who have a claim or acquire an interest in a particular subject matter <a judgment *in rem* binds all the world>.

World Bank. A U.N. bank established in 1945 to provide loans that aid in economic development, through economically sustainable enterprises. • Its capital derives from U.N. member states' subscriptions and by loans on the open market. — Also termed *International Bank for Reconstruction and Development*.

World Court. See INTERNATIONAL COURT OF JUSTICE.

worldly, *adj.* Of or relating to the present state of existence; temporal; earthly <worldly possessions>. See SECULAR.

worship. 1. Any form of religious devotion or service showing reverence for a divine being.

public worship. **1.** Worship conducted by a religious society according to the society's system of ecclesiastical authority, ritual propriety, and rules and regulations. **2.** Worship under public authority. **3.** Worship in a public place, without privacy or concealment. **4.** Worship allowed by all members of the public equally.

2. *English law.* A title of honor or dignity used in addressing certain magistrates or other high officers.

wort (wərt), *n. Archaic.* A country farm; a curtilage. — Also termed *worth*.

worth, *n.* **1.** The monetary value of a thing; the sum of the qualities that render a thing valuable and useful, expressed in the current medium of exchange. **2.** The emotional or sentimental value of something. **3.** The total wealth held by a person or entity. **4.** WORT.

worthier-title doctrine. 1. *Hist.* At common law, the doctrine holding that if a beneficiary of a will would receive an identical interest as an heir under the laws of intestacy, the person takes the interest as an heir rather than as a beneficiary. • The doctrine has been abolished in most states. **2.** *Property.* The doctrine that favors a grantor's intent by construing a grant as a reversion in the grantor instead of as a remainder in the grantor's heirs. See REMAINDER; REVERSION.

worthiest blood, *n. Hist.* A descendant that, in a given legal system, is given preference in the laws of descent. See PRIMOGENITURE.

> "Thus sons shall be admitted before daughters; or, as our male lawgivers have somewhat uncomplaisantly expressed it, the worthiest blood shall be preferred. As if John Stiles hath two sons, Matthew and Gilbert, and two

daughters, Margaret and Charlotte, and dies; first Matthew, and (in case of his death without issue) then Gilbert shall be admitted to the succession in preference to both the daughters." 2 William Blackstone, *Commentaries on the Laws of England* 213 (1766).

worthless, *adj*. Totally lacking worth; of no use or value.

worthless check. See *bad check* under CHECK.

worthless person. *Archaic*. A person who owns nothing.

worthless security. See SECURITY.

worthy, *adj*. Having worth; possessing merit; valuable.

wounded feelings. Injuries resulting from insults, indignity, or humiliation, as distinguished from the usual mental pain and suffering consequent to physical injury.

wounding. 1. An injury, esp. one involving a rupture of the skin. **2.** An injury to feelings or reputation. **3.** *Hist*. An aggravated type of assault and battery in which one person seriously injures another.

wraparound mortgage. See MORTGAGE.

wreck, *n*. **1.** SHIPWRECK. **2.** Goods cast ashore from a wrecked vessel and not claimed by the owner within a specified period (such as one year).

wreckfree, *adj*. (Of a port, etc.) exempt from the forfeiture of shipwrecked goods and vessels to the Crown.

writ (rit). A court's written order, in the name of a state or other competent legal authority, commanding the addressee to do or refrain from doing some specified act.

"[W]rits have a long history. We can trace their formal origin to the Anglo-Saxon formulae by which the king used to communicate his pleasure to persons and courts. The Anglo-Norman writs, which we meet with after the Conquest, are substantially the Anglo-Saxon writs turned into Latin. But what is new is the much greater use made of them, owing to the increase of royal power which came with the Conquest." W.S. Holdsworth, *Sources and Literature of English Law* 20 (1925).

alias writ. An additional writ issued after another writ of the same kind in the same case. • It derives its name from a Latin phrase that formerly appeared in alias writs: *sicut alias praecipimus*, meaning "as we at another time commanded." Cf. *alias execution* under EXECUTION.

alternative writ. A common-law writ commanding the person against whom it is issued either to do a specific thing or to show cause why the court should not order it to be done.

close writ. *Hist*. **1.** A royal writ sealed because the contents were not deemed appropriate for public inspection. Cf. *patent writ*; CLAUSE ROLLS. **2.** A writ directed to a sheriff instead of to a lord.

concurrent writ. A duplicate of an original writ (esp. a summons), issued either at the same time as the original writ or at any time while the original writ is valid.

counterpart writ. A copy of an original writ, to be sent to a court in another county when a defendant resides in, or is found in, that county.

extraordinary writ. A writ issued by a court exercising unusual or discretionary power. • Examples are certiorari, habeas corpus, mandamus, and prohibition. — Also termed *prerogative writ*.

ground writ. *Hist*. A writ issued in a county having venue of an action in order to allow a writ of *capias ad satisfaciendum* or of *fieri facias* to be executed in a county where the defendant or the defendant's property was found. • These two writs could not be executed in a county other than the county having venue of the action until a ground writ and then a *testatum* writ were first issued. This requirement was abolished in 1852. Cf. TESTATUM.

judicial writ. **1.** A writ issuing from the court to which the original writ was returnable; a writ issued under the private seal of the court and not under the great seal of England. Cf. *original writ*. **2.** Any writ issued by a court.

junior writ. A writ issued at a later time than a similar writ, such as a later writ issued by a different party or a later writ on a different claim against the same defendant.

optional writ. At common law, an original writ issued when the plaintiff seeks specific damages, such as payment of a liquidated debt. • The writ commands the defendant either to do a specified thing or to show why the thing has not been done.

original writ. A writ commencing an action and directing the defendant to appear and answer. • In the United States, this writ has been largely superseded by the summons. At common law, this type of writ was a mandatory letter issuing from the court of chancery under the great seal, and in the king's name, directed to the sheriff of the county where the injury was alleged to have occurred, containing a summary statement of the cause of complaint, and requiring the sheriff in most cases to command the defendant to satisfy the claim or else appear in court to account for not satisfying it. — Sometimes shortened to *original*. See SUMMONS.

patent writ (**pay**-tənt). *Hist.* An open writ; one not closed or sealed up. Cf. *close writ.*

peremptory writ (pər-**emp**-tə-ree). At common law, an original writ issued when the plaintiff seeks only general damages, as in an action for trespass. • The writ, which is issued only after the plaintiff gives security for costs, directs the sheriff to have the defendant appear in court.

pluries writ. See PLURIES.

prerogative writ. See *extraordinary writ.*

testatum writ (tes-**tay**-təm). See TESTATUM.

vicontiel writ (vɪ-**kon**-tee-əl). *Hist.* A writ triable in the county court. • In the 13th–14th centuries, civil litigation could originate in the county court either by oral plaint or by a writ from the Chancery ordering the sheriff to do justice in a case. The writ that began such a proceeding was called *vicontiel* because it was addressed to the sheriff. See VICONTIEL (2).

> "*Vicontiel writs* were of two sorts, the one founded on *Torts*, the other on *Contracts*. The *vicontiel* writs adapted for torts, were those of *trespass*, *replegiari facias*, *nuisance*, and others of the like nature; and those of matters of contract were called writs of *justicies*, which was a command to the sheriff to do justice between the parties. . . ." 1 George Crompton, *Practice Common-Placed: Rules and Cases of Practice in the Courts of King's Bench and Common Pleas* vii–viii (3d ed. 1787).

writ *de haeretico comburendo*. See DE HAERETICO COMBURENDO.

write-down, *vb. Accounting.* To transfer a portion of the cost of an asset to an expense account because the asset's value has decreased.

write off, *vb.* To remove (an asset) from the books, esp. as a loss or expense <the partnership wrote off the bad debt>.

writer of the tallies. *English law.* An officer of the Exchequer who writes on the tallies the letters of tellers' bills. See TALLY.

Writer to the Signet. *Scots law.* A member of the oldest and leading society of Scottish solicitors, originally a clerk in the Scottish Secretary of State's office responsible for preparing warrants, writs, charters, and precepts.

write-up, *n.* **1.** A memorandum of a conference between an employer and an employee, usu. held to discuss the employee's poor work performance or a disciplinary action against the employee. **2.** A publication (such as a newspaper article) about a particular person, thing, or event.

write-up, *vb. Accounting.* To increase the valuation of an asset in a financial statement to reflect current value. • With a few minor exceptions, this is generally not permitted.

writing, *n.* Any intentional recording of words in a visual form, whether in the form of handwriting, printing, typewriting, or any other tangible form.

writing obligatory, *n.* A bond; a written obligation, as technically described in a pleading.

writ of *ad quod damnum*. See AD QUOD DAMNUM.

writ of aiel (**ay**-əl). See AIEL (2).

writ of assistance. 1. A writ to enforce a court's decree transferring real property, the title of which has been previously adjudicated. **2.** *Hist.* A writ issued by the Court of Exchequer ordering the sheriff to assist in collecting a debt owed the Crown. **3.** *Hist.* In colonial America, a writ issued by a superior colonial court authorizing an officer of the Crown to enter and search any premises suspected of containing contraband. • The attempted use of this writ in Massachusetts — defeated in 1761 — was one of the acts that led to the American Revolution.

writ of association. *Hist. English law.* A writ whereby certain persons (usu. the clerk of assize and subordinate officers) were directed to associate themselves with the justices and serjeants so that there would be an adequate supply of commissioners for the assizes.

writ of attachment. See ATTACHMENT (3).

writ of capias. See CAPIAS.

writ of certiorari. See CERTIORARI.

writ of conspiracy. *Hist.* A writ against one who conspired to injure the plaintiff, esp. by indicting the plaintiff for treason or felony. • Under common law, all other circumstances of conspiracy were actions on the case.

writ of *coram nobis*. See CORAM NOBIS.

writ of *coram vobis*. See CORAM VOBIS.

writ of course. A writ issued as a matter of course or granted as a matter of right. — Also termed *writ of right*.

writ of covenant. *Hist.* A writ for one claiming damages as a result of a breach of a promise under seal or other covenant. — Also termed *breve de conventione* (breev *or* **bree**-vee dee kən-ven-shee-**oh**-nee).

> "The writ of covenant (*breve de conventione*) is not mentioned by Glanvill; but it appears within a short time after the publication of his book and already in the early years of Henry III. It can be had 'as of course,' at all events when the tenement that is in question is of small value. Before Henry's death it has become a popular writ .... The great majority of actions of covenant are brought merely in order that they may be compromised. We doubt whether any principle was involved in the choice; but may infer that the procedure instituted by this writ was cheap and expeditious for those who wished to get to their final concord." 2 Frederick Pollock & Frederic W. Maitland, *The History of English Law Before the Time of Edward I* 216–17 (2d ed. 1899).

writ of debt. See DEBT (4).

writ of deceit. *Hist.* A writ against one who deceives and damages another by acting in the other's name.

writ of deliverance. See DELIVERANCE (3).

writ of detinue. A writ in an action for detinue. See DETINUE.

writ of dower. 1. DE DOTE UNDE NIHIL HABET. **2.** A widow's writ of *right of dower* providing her the remainder of the dower to which she is entitled after part of it had been assigned by the tenant.

writ of ejectment. The writ in an action of ejectment for the recovery of land. See EJECTMENT.

writ of entry. A writ that allows a person wrongfully dispossessed of real property to enter and retake the property.

writ of error. 1. A writ issued by an appellate court directing a lower court to deliver the record in the case for review. Cf. ASSIGNMENT OF ERROR.

> "The writ of error is the most common of all the forms of remedial process available to an unsuccessful party after a final determination of the merits of the action, and is in common use in this country at the present time, where the common-law modes of procedure are followed. Its object ... is to obtain a reversal of the judgment, either by reason of some error in fact affecting the validity and regularity of the legal decision itself, or on account of some mistake or error in law, apparent upon the face of the record, from which the judgment appears to have been given for the wrong party." Benjamin J. Shipman, *Handbook of Common-Law Pleading* § 337, at 538 (Henry Winthrop Ballantine ed., 3d ed. 1923).

writ of error coram nobis. See CORAM NOBIS.

writ of error coram vobis. See CORAM VOBIS.

2. *Hist.* A writ issued by a chancery court, at the request of a party who was unsuccessful at trial, directing the trial court either to examine the record itself or to send it to another court of appellate jurisdiction to be examined, so that some alleged error in the proceedings may be corrected.

writ of escheat. *Hist.* A writ allowing a lord to take possession of lands that had escheated to him. See ESCHEAT (1).

writ of estrepement (e-**streep**-mənt). See DE ESTREPAMENTO.

writ of execution. See EXECUTION (4).

writ of *exigi facias*. See EXIGI FACIAS.

writ of extent. See EXTENT (2).

writ of formedon. See FORMEDON.

writ of habeas corpus. See HABEAS CORPUS.

writ of injunction. See INJUNCTION.

writ of inquiry. *Hist.* A writ ordering the sheriff to empanel a jury and act as judge in a trial held to determine the amount of damages suffered by a plaintiff who has won a default judgment on an unliquidated claim.

writ of mainprise. See MAINPRISE (2).

writ of mandamus. See MANDAMUS.

writ of mesne (meen). See DE MEDIO.

writ of ne exeat. See NE EXEAT REPUBLICA.

writ of possession. A writ issued to recover the possession of land.

writ of praecipe. See PRAECIPE (1).

writ of prevention. A writ to prevent the filing of a lawsuit. See QUIA TIMET.

writ of privilege. *Hist.* A writ to enforce or maintain a privilege; esp., a writ to secure the release of a person who, though entitled to privilege from arrest, is arrested in a civil suit.

writ of proclamation. *Hist.* A writ, issued at the time an *exigent* was issued, ordering the sheriff of the county of a defendant's residence to make three proclamations of outlawry in a public and notorious place a month before the outlawry is declared. See OUTLAW.

writ of prohibition. See PROHIBITION (2).

writ of protection. **1.** A writ to protect a witness in a judicial proceeding who is threatened with arrest. **2.** A writ exempting anyone in the Crown's service from arrest in a civil proceeding for a year and a day.

writ of *quare impedit*. See QUARE IMPEDIT.

writ of quominus. See QUOMINUS.

writ of *quo warranto*. See QUO WARRANTO.

writ of rebellion. See COMMISSION OF REBELLION.

writ of recaption. *Hist.* A writ allowing a plaintiff to recover goods and damages from a defendant who makes a second distress while a replevin action for a previous distress is pending. See RECAPTION.

writ of replevin. See REPLEVIN (2).

writ of restitution. **1.** The process of enforcing a civil judgment in a forcible-entry-and-detainer action or enforcing restitution on a verdict in a criminal prosecution for forcible entry and detainer.

> "In some states, following the British statutes, the prosecutor may have a writ of restitution for the premises immediately on the rendition of a verdict of guilty on an indictment for forcible entry and detainer; and the operation of such writ of restitution is not suspended by an appeal by the defendant." 35 Am. Jur. 2d *Forcible Entry and Detainer* § 61, at 931 (1967).

2. A common-law writ issued when a judgment is reversed, whereby the prevailing party is restored all that was lost as a result of the judgment.

writ of review. A general form of process issuing from an appellate court to bring up for review the record of the proceedings in the court below; the common-law writ of certiorari.

writ of right. See WRIT OF COURSE.

writ of second deliverance. See DELIVERANCE (4).

writ of sequestration. A writ ordering that a court be given custody of something, or ordering that something not be taken from the jurisdiction, such as the collateral for a promissory note. • Such a writ is usu. issued during litigation, often so that the object will be available for attachment or execution after judgment.

writ of summons. *English law.* A writ by which, under the Judicature Acts of 1873–1875, all actions were commenced. See SUMMONS.

writ of supersedeas. See SUPERSEDEAS.

writ of supervisory control. A writ issued to correct an erroneous ruling made by a lower court either when there is no appeal or when an appeal cannot provide adequate relief and the ruling will result in gross injustice.

writ of threats. See SECURITATE PACIS.

writ of tolt (tohlt). See TOLT.

writ of trial. *Hist. English law.* By the Civil Procedure Act of 1835, a writ ordering an action brought in a superior court to be tried in an inferior court or before the undersheriff. • It was superseded by the County Courts Act of 1867, ch. 142, § 6 authorizing a defendant, in certain cases, to obtain an order that an action is to be tried in a county court. St. 3 & 4 Will. 4, ch. 42.

writ of waste. *Hist.* A writ to recover damages against a tenant who committed waste. See WASTE (1).

> "After waste had been actually committed, the ancient corrective remedy, in a court of common law, was by a

writ of waste for the recovery of the place wasted, and treble damages as a compensation for the injury done to the inheritance." 78 Am. Jur. 2d *Waste* § 29, at 417 (1975).

writ *pro retorno habendo* (proh ri-**tor**-noh hə-**ben**-doh), *n.* [Law Latin "for return to be had"] *Hist.* A writ ordering the return of goods to a defendant who, upon the plaintiff's default, obtained a favorable judgment in a replevin action.

writ system. The common-law procedural system under which plaintiff commenced an action by obtaining the appropriate type of original writ.

written contract. See CONTRACT.

written directive. See ADVANCE DIRECTIVE.

written law. Statutory law, together with constitutions and treaties, as opposed to judge-made law. — Also termed *jus scriptum*; *lex scripta*.

written testimony. See TESTIMONY.

written warranty. See WARRANTY (2).

wrong, *n.* Breach of one's legal duty; violation of another's legal right. — **wrong,** *vb.*

"A wrong may be described, in the largest sense, as anything done or omitted contrary to legal duty, considered in so far as it gives rise to liability." Frederick Pollock, *A First Book of Jurisprudence* 68 (1896).

"A wrong is simply a wrong act — an act contrary to the rule of right and justice. A synonym of it is injury, in its true and primary sense of *injuria* (that which is contrary to *jus*) . . . ." John Salmond, *Jurisprudence* 227 (Glanville L. Williams ed., 10th ed. 1947).

civil wrong. A violation of noncriminal law, such as a tort, a breach of contract or trust, a breach of statutory duty, or a defect in performing a public duty; the breach of a legal duty treated as the subject matter of a civil proceeding. Cf. CRIME.

continuing wrong. An ongoing wrong that is capable of being corrected by specific enforcement. • An example is the nonpayment of a debt.

intentional wrong. A wrong in which the *mens rea* amounts to intention, purpose, or design. — Also termed *willful wrong*.

legal wrong. An act that is a violation of the law; an act authoritatively prohibited by a rule of law.

moral wrong. An act that is contrary to the rule of natural justice. — Also termed *natural wrong*.

positive wrong. A wrongful act, wilfully committed.

private wrong. An offense committed against a private person and dealt with at the instance of the person injured.

public wrong. An offense committed against the state or the community at large, and dealt with in a proceeding to which the state is itself a party. • Not all public wrongs are crimes. For example, a person that breaches a contract with the government commits a public wrong, but the offense is a civil one, not a criminal one.

real wrong. An injury to the freehold.

transitory wrong. A wrong that, once committed, belongs to the irrevocable past. • An example is defamation.

willful wrong. See *intentional wrong*.

wrong of negligence. A wrong in which the *mens rea* is a form of mere carelessness, as opposed to wrongful intent.

wrong of strict liability. A wrong in which a *mens rea* is not required because neither wrongful intent nor culpable negligence is a necessary condition of responsibility.

wrongdoer, *n.* One who violates the law <both criminals and tortfeasors are wrongdoers>. — **wrongdoing,** *n.*

wrongful, *adj.* **1.** Characterized by unfairness or injustice <wrongful military invasion>. **2.** Contrary to law; unlawful <wrongful termination>. **3.** (Of a person) not entitled to the position occupied <wrongful possessor>. — **wrongfully,** *adv.*

wrongful act. See WRONGFUL CONDUCT.

wrongful-birth action. A lawsuit brought by parents against a doctor for failing to advise them prospectively about the risks of their having a child with birth defects.

wrongful-conception action. See WRONGFUL-PREGNANCY ACTION.

wrongful conduct. An act taken in violation of a legal duty; an act that unjustly infringes on another's rights. — Also termed *wrongful act*.

wrongful-death action. A lawsuit brought on behalf of a decedent's survivors for their damages resulting from a tortious injury that caused the decedent's death. — Also termed *death action*; *death case*. Cf. SURVIVAL ACTION.

wrongful-death statute. A statute authorizing a decedent's personal representative to bring a wrongful-death action for the benefit of certain beneficiaries.

wrongful discharge. See DISCHARGE (7).

wrongful-discharge action. A lawsuit brought by an ex-employee against the former employer, alleging that the termination of employment violated a contract or was illegal. — Also termed *wrongful-termination action*.

wrongful dishonor, *n*. A refusal to accept or pay (a negotiable instrument) when it is properly presented and is payable. Cf. DISHONOR.

wrongful garnishment. See GARNISHMENT.

wrongful levy. See LEVY.

wrongful-life action. A lawsuit brought by or on behalf of a child with birth defects, alleging that but for the doctor-defendant's negligent advice, the parents would not have conceived the child, or if they had, they would have aborted the fetus to avoid the pain and suffering resulting from the child's congenital defects. • Most jurisdictions reject these claims.

wrongful-pregnancy action. A lawsuit brought by a parent for damages resulting from a pregnancy following a failed sterilization. — Also termed *wrongful-conception action*.

wrongful process. See ABUSE OF PROCESS.

wrongful-termination action. See WRONGFUL-DISCHARGE ACTION.

wrong of negligence. See WRONG.

wrong of strict liability. See WRONG.

wyte (wɪt). *Hist.* **1.** An immunity from an amercement. See AMERCEMENT. **2.** See WITE.

X

X. *abbr.* **1.** EX DIVIDEND. **2.** EX RIGHTS. **3.** EX DISTRIBUTION. **4.** EX WARRANTS.

X. 1. A mark serving as the signature of a person who is physically handicapped or illiterate. • The signer's name usu. appears near the mark, and if the mark is to be notarized as a signature, two signing witnesses are ordinarily required in addition to the notary public. **2.** A symbol equivalent to "by" when used in giving dimensions, as in 3 x 5 inches. **3.** A mark placed on a document (such as an application) to indicate a selection, such as "yes" or "no"; esp., a mark on a ballot to indicate a vote.

XD. *abbr.* EX DIVIDEND.

XDIS. *abbr.* EX DISTRIBUTION.

xenodochium (zen-ə-də-**kI**-əm *or* -**dok**-ee-əm), *n.* [fr. Greek *xenos* "a guest" + *docheus* "receiver"] *Roman law.* **1.** A publicly licensed inn. **2.** The reception of strangers; hospitality. **3.** A hospital. — Also termed *xenodochion*; *xenodocheum*; *xenodochy*.

XQ. See *cross-question* under QUESTION (1).

XR. *abbr.* EX-RIGHTS.

XW. *abbr.* EX-WARRANTS.

xylon (**zI**-lon), *n.* [fr. Greek *xulon* "wood"] *Archaic.* A Greek punishment apparatus similar to stocks.

XYY-chromosome defense. *Criminal law.* A defense, usu. asserted as the basis for an insanity plea, whereby a male defendant argues that his criminal behavior is due to the genetic abnormality of having an extra Y chromosome, which causes him to have uncontrollable aggressive impulses. • Most courts have rejected this defense because its scientific foundations are uncertain. See INSANITY DEFENSE. — Also termed *XYY defense*.

> "As one commentator has suggested . . . 'an attorney defending an XYY individual will be required to call upon both a geneticist and a psychiatrist to give expert testimony. The geneticist's role would be to testify with respect to the individual's genetic structure, any distinguishing characteristics which are relevant to an insanity defense, and the result of family studies designated to determine the influence of genetics and environment on the development of this individual. The psychiatrist's testimony would focus upon the defendant's mental capacity or condition.' But in the absence of sound medical support for an XYY defense, courts are understandably unsympathetic to defense efforts to obtain such expert testimony." Wayne R. LaFave & Austin W. Scott, Jr., *Criminal Law* § 4.8, at 380 (2d ed. 1986) (quoting Note, 57 Geo. L.J. 892, 902–03 (1969)).

XYY syndrome. The abnormal presence of an extra Y chromosome in a male, theoretically resulting in increased aggressiveness and antisocial behavior often resulting in criminal conduct. See XYY-CHROMOSOME DEFENSE.

Y2K warranty. *abbr.* Year 2000 warranty; a warranty that software, hardware, or a product having computer hardware or software components will function properly on and after January 1, 2000.

yardland, *n. Hist.* A variable quantity of land, often 20 acres. — Also termed *virgata terrae* (vər-**gay**-tə **ter**-ee).

yardstick theory. *Antitrust.* A method of determining damages for lost profits (and sometimes overcharges) whereby a corporate plaintiff identifies a company similar to the plaintiff but without the impact of the antitrust violation. Cf. BEFORE-AND-AFTER THEORY; MARKET-SHARE THEORY.

> "To the extent that either the markets or firms being compared are dissimilar, the yardstick theory will not produce a trustworthy estimate of what the plaintiff would have earned but for the defendant's conduct. The method therefore works best in markets that are both local and relatively homogeneous." Herbert Hovenkamp, *Economics and Federal Antitrust Law* § 16.7, at 454 (1985).

yea and nay (**yay** / **nay**). Yes and no. • In old records, this was a mere assertion and denial without the necessity of an oath.

year. 1. Twelve calendar months beginning January 1 and ending December 31. — Also termed *calendar year.* **2.** Twelve calendar months beginning at any point.

half-year. In legal computation, a period of 182 days.

natural year. *Hist.* The period of 365 days and about 6 hours, or the time it takes the earth to orbit the sun.

Year 2000 warranty. See Y2K WARRANTY.

year and a day. The common-law time limit fixed for various purposes, such as claiming rights, exemptions, or property (such as rights to wreckage or estrays) or for prosecuting certain acts — so called because a year was formerly counted to include the first and last day, meaning that a year from January 1 was December 31, so a year and a day would then mean a full year from January 1 through January 1. — Also termed *year and day*; (formerly in Scots law) *zeir and day.* See YEAR-AND-A-DAY RULE; YEAR, DAY, AND WASTE.

year-and-a-day rule. *Criminal law.* The common-law principle that an act causing death is not homicide if the death occurs more than a year and a day after the act was committed. • In Latin, the phrase *year and a day* was commonly rendered *annus et dies.*

> "It has long been the rule that no one can be convicted of the murder or manslaughter of another person who does not die within a year and a day of the blow received or other cause of death. 'Day' was here added merely to indicate that the 365th day after that of the injury must be included. Such an indication was rendered necessary by an old rule (now obsolete) that, in *criminal* law, in reckoning a period 'from' the doing of any act, the period was (in favour of prisoners) to be taken as beginning on the very day when this act was done." J.W. Cecil Turner, *Kenny's Outlines of Criminal Law* 105 (16th ed. 1952).

> "The phrase 'year and a day,' in this test [for proving causation of a person's death], means no more than a year. The accepted method of computing time today is by excluding the first day and including the last. Thus a year from January first is the first day of the following January. In ancient times, however, there was a tendency to include both the first day and the last day so that a year from January first was thought of as the thirty-first of the following December, and 'the day was added that there might be a whole year.' The use of this peculiar phrase to mean just a year in the homicide cases has found expression in some of the statutes. Other enactments have wisely dropped this ancient jingle." Rollin M. Perkins & Ronald N. Boyce, *Criminal Law* 778 (3d ed. 1982).

> "Several centuries ago, when doctors knew very little about medicine, the judges created an absolute rule of law: one cannot be guilty of murder if the victim lives for a year and a day after the blow. The difficulty in proving that the blow caused the death after so long an interval was obviously the basis of the rule. Now that doctors know infinitely more, it seems strange that the year-and-a-day rule should survive to the present, but it has done so in most of the American states, either by judicial decision or by statute." Wayne R. LaFave & Austin W. Scott, Jr., *Criminal Law* § 3.12, at 299 (2d ed. 1986).

year and day. See YEAR AND A DAY.

Year Books. *Hist.* Books of cases anonymously and fairly regularly reported covering primarily the period from the reign of Edward I to the time of Henry VIII. • The title "Year Books" derives from their being grouped under the regnal years of the sovereigns in whose reigns the reported cases were cited. The reports were probably originally prepared by law teachers and students and later by professional reporters or scribes. — Also written *Year-Books*; *yearbooks*; *yearbooks*. — Also termed *terms*.

> "[F]rom 1300 there is a continuous stream of reports of arguments in the common Pleas. The reports were written in Anglo-French, the language of courtly speech. Their authorship is unknown, and they are referred to by the generic name 'year-books' .... If we have to account for their beginning, the most likely explanation is that they arose from a case-method of instruction in the law school which served the apprentices of the Bench before the emergence of the inns of court .... For the same reason, the contemporary value of the earliest reports lay not in their historical authenticity as precedents but in the ideas and suggestions which they contained .... Once the age of experiment was over, the reports settled into a more uniform and at times apparently single series .... The year-books did not end at any fixed date. What has usually been taken as their end is the result of two concurrent factors: the advent of printing, and the practice of identifying reports by the name of the author." J.H. Baker, *An Introduction to English Legal History* 205–07 (3d ed. 1990).

year, day, and waste. *Hist.* A right of the Crown to the profits and waste for a year and a day of the land of persons convicted of petty treason or felony (unless the lord made redemption), after which the Crown had to restore the property to the lord of the fee. The right was abrogated by the Corruption of Blood Act of 1814. — Also termed (in Law French) *ann, jour, et wast*; (in Law Latin) *annus, dies, et vastum*.

year-end dividend. See DIVIDEND.

year in mourning. See ANNUM LUCTUS.

Year of Our Lord. See ANNO DOMINI.

year-to-year tenancy. See *periodic tenancy* under TENANCY.

yeas and nays. The affirmative and negative votes on a bill or resolution before a legislative body.

yellow-dog contract. An employment contract forbidding membership in a labor union. • Such a contract is generally illegal under federal and state law.

yeoman (**yoh**-mən). **1.** *Hist.* An attendant in a royal or noble household. **2.** *Hist.* A commoner; a freeholder (under the rank of gentleman) who holds land yielding 40 shillings per year.

> "A *yeoman* is he that hath free land of forty shillings by the year; who was thereby qualified to serve on juries, vote for knights of the shire, and do any other act, where the law requires one that is *probus et legalis homo* [an upright and law-abiding man]." 1 William Blackstone, *Commentaries on the Laws of England* 394 (1765).

3. *English law.* One who owns and cultivates property. **4.** A petty officer performing clerical work in the U.S. Navy. — Also sometimes spelled *yoman*.

yeoman of the guard. A member of a corps of officers whose primary duties are to ceremonially guard the English royal household. • A yeoman is usu. at least six feet tall, is of the best rank under the gentry, and is generally exempt from arrest on civil process. — Also termed *yeoman of the guard of the royal household*.

yeomanry. 1. The collective body of yeomen. **2.** Volunteer cavalry units in Great Britain, later transferred to the Territorial Army.

yeven (**yev**-ən *or* **yiv**-ən). *Hist.* Given; dated. — Also spelled *yeoven* (**yoh**-vən).

***Yick Wo* doctrine** (yik **woh**). The principle that a law or ordinance that gives a person or entity absolute discretion to give or withhold permission to carry on a lawful business is in violation of the 14th Amendment to the U.S. Constitution. *Yick Wo v. Hopkins*, 118 U.S. 356, 6 S.Ct. 1064 (1886).

yield, *n.* Profit expressed as a percentage of the investment. — Also termed *yield on investment*; *return*. See RATE OF RETURN.

coupon yield. The annual interest paid on a security (esp. a bond) divided by the security's par value. — Also termed *nominal yield*.

current yield. The annual interest paid on a security (esp. a bond) divided by the security's current market price.

discount yield. The yield on a security sold at a discount.

earnings yield. The earnings per share of a security divided by its market price. • The higher the ratio, the better the investment yield. — Also termed *earnings-price ratio*. Cf. PRICE-EARNINGS RATIO.

net yield. The profit or loss on an investment after deducting all appropriate costs and loss reserves.

nominal yield. See *coupon yield*.

yield, *vb.* **1.** To give up, relinquish, or surrender (a right, etc.) <yield the floor>. **2.** *Hist.* To perform a service owed by a tenant to a lord <yield and pay>. See YIELDING AND PAYING.

yield on investment. See YIELD.

yield spread. The differences in yield between various securities issues.

yield to maturity. The rate of return from an investment if the investment is held until it matures. — Abbr. YTM. Cf. TIME VALUE.

yokelet (yohk-lit), *n. Hist.* A small farm requiring only one yoke of oxen to till it.

yoman. See YEOMAN.

York, custom of. *Hist.* A custom prevalent in York whereby a male intestate's effects were divided according to the doctrine of *pars rationabilis* ("a reasonable part") — that is, one-third each to the widow, children, and administrator, one-half to the administrator if the man was married but had no children or was single but had children, or all to the administrator if the man was single with no children.

York, Statute of. *Hist.* An English statute passed in York in the twelfth year of Edward II's reign, and including provisions on the subject of attorneys, witnesses, and the taking of inquests by nisi prius.

York–Antwerp rules. A set of rules relating to the settlement of maritime losses and disputes arising from bills of lading. • Although these rules have no statutory authority, they are incorporated into almost all bills of lading.

***Younger* abstention.** See ABSTENTION.

young offender. See *youthful offender* under OFFENDER.

your Honor. A title customarily used when directly addressing a judge or other high official. Cf. HIS HONOR.

your witness. See TAKE THE WITNESS.

youthful offender. See OFFENDER.

yo-yo stock. See *volatile stock* under STOCK.

YTM. *abbr.* YIELD TO MATURITY.

Z

zap. See INTERSUBJECTIVE ZAP.

ZBA. *abbr.* ZERO-BRACKET AMOUNT.

Z-bond. See *accrual bond* under BOND (3).

zealous witness. See WITNESS.

zeir and day (yeer). See YEAR AND DAY. • *Zeir* is an obsolete graphic variant of *year*.

zero-bracket amount. A tax deduction formerly available to all individual taxpayers, regardless of whether they itemized their deductions. • In 1944 this was replaced by the standard deduction. — Abbr. ZBA. See *standard deduction* under DEDUCTION.

zero-coupon bond. See BOND (3).

zero-coupon security. See SECURITY.

zero-rate mortgage. See MORTGAGE.

zetetic (zi-**tet**-ik), *adj. Hist.* Proceeding by inquiry; investigative. — Also spelled *zetetick*.

zipper clause. An integration clause, esp. in a labor agreement. See INTEGRATION CLAUSE.

zone. 1. An area that is different or is distinguished from surrounding areas <zone of danger>. **2.** An area in a city or town that, through zoning regulations, is under particular restrictions as to building size, land use, and the like <the capitol is at the center of the height-restriction zone>.

holding zone. Temporary, low-density zoning used until a community determines how the area should be rezoned.

zone-of-danger rule. *Torts.* The doctrine allowing the recovery of damages for negligent infliction of emotional distress if the plaintiff was both located in the dangerous area created by the defendant's negligence and frightened by the risk of harm.

zone of employment. *Workers' compensation.* The physical place of employment within which an employee, if injured there, can receive compensation. Cf. SCOPE OF EMPLOYMENT.

zone of interests. The class or type of interests or concerns that a statute or constitutional guarantee is intended to regulate or protect. • To have standing to challenge a ruling (esp. of an administrative agency), the plaintiff must show that the specific injury suffered comes within the zone of interests protected by the statute on which the ruling was based.

zone of privacy. *Constitutional law.* A range of fundamental privacy rights that are implied in the express guarantees of the Bill of Rights. See PENUMBRA; RIGHT OF PRIVACY.

zone search. See SEARCH.

zoning, *n.* The legislative division of a region, esp. a municipality, into separate districts with different regulations within the districts for land use, building size, and the like. — **zone,** *vb.*

aesthetic zoning. Zoning designed to preserve the aesthetic features or values of an area.

bonus zoning. See *incentive zoning*.

cluster zoning. Zoning that favors planned-unit development by allowing a modification in lot size and frontage requirements under the condition that other land in the development be set aside for parks, schools, or other public needs. — Also termed *density zoning*. See PLANNED-UNIT DEVELOPMENT.

conditional zoning. Zoning in which a governmental body (without definitively committing itself) grants a zoning change subject to conditions that are usu. not imposed on similarly zoned property.

> "Conditions imposed are designed to protect adjacent land from the loss of use value which might occur if the newly authorized use was permitted without restraint of any kind. Thus, conditional zoning seeks to minimize the potentially deleterious effect of a zone change on neighboring properties through reasonably conceived conditions which harmonize the landowner's need for rezon-

ing with the public interest." 83 Am. Jur. 2d *Zoning and Planning* § 218, at 193 (1992).

contract zoning. **1.** Zoning according to an agreement, by which the landowner agrees to certain restrictions or conditions in exchange for more favorable zoning treatment. • This type of contract zoning is usu. considered an illegal restraint of the government's police power, because by private agreement, the government has committed itself to a particular type of zoning. **2.** Rezoning of property to a less restrictive classification subject to the landowner's agreement to observe specified limitations on the use and physical development of the property that are not imposed on other property in the zone. • This device is esp. used when property is located in a more restrictive zone that borders on a less restrictive zone.

cumulative zoning. A method of zoning in which any use permitted in a higher-use, less intensive zone is permissible in a lower-use, more intensive zone. • For example, under this method, a house could be built in an industrial zone but a factory could not be built in a residential zone.

density zoning. See *cluster zoning*.

Euclidean zoning (yoo-**klid**-ee-ən). Zoning by specific and uniform geographical division. • This type of zoning takes its name from the Supreme Court case that approved it: *Village of Euclid v. Ambler Realty Co.*, 272 U.S. 365, 47 S.Ct. 114 (1926).

exclusionary zoning. Zoning that excludes a specific class type of business from a district.

floating zoning. Zoning that creates exceptional-use districts, as needed, within ordinary zoned districts.

incentive zoning. A relaxation in zoning restrictions (such as density limits) that offer an incentive to a developer to provide certain public benefits (such as building low-income housing units). — Also termed *bonus zoning*.

interim zoning. Temporary emergency zoning pending revisions to existing ordinances or the development of a final zoning plan. — Also termed *stopgap zoning*.

inverse zoning. Zoning that attempts to disperse particular types of property use rather than concentrate them.

partial zoning. Zoning that affects only a portion of a municipality's territory, and that is usu. invalid because it contradicts the comprehensive zoning plan. — Also termed *piecemeal zoning*.

private zoning. The use of restrictive covenants in private agreements to restrict the use and occupancy of real property. • Private zoning often covers such things as lot size, building lines, architectural specifications, and property uses.

reverse spot zoning. Zoning of a large area of land without regard for the zoning of a small piece of land within that area.

"When parcels around a given property are rezoned to allow for higher uses leaving an island of less intensive use, reverse spot zoning is the result." Donald G. Hagman & Julian Conrad Juergensmeyer, *Urban Planning and Land Development Control Law* § 5.4, at 136 (2d ed. 1986).

spot zoning. Zoning of a particular piece of land without regard for the zoning of the larger area surrounding the land.

"To the popular mind, spot zoning means the improper permission to use an 'island' of land for a more intensive use than permitted on adjacent properties. The popular definition needs several qualifications .... The set of facts usually involves an 'island' of more intensive use than surrounding property .... Usually the 'island' is small .... Furthermore, the term is not properly applied to development permission that comes about by variance or special exception. Rather, the term refers to a legislative act, such as a rezoning, or to a situation in which the 'island' is created by the original ordinance." Donald G. Hagman & Julian Conrad Juergensmeyer, *Urban Planning and Land Development Control Law* § 5.4, at 136 (2d ed. 1986).

stopgap zoning. See *interim zoning*.

zoning map. The map that is created by a zoning ordinance and shows the various zoning districts.

zoning ordinance. A city ordinance that regulates the use to which land within various parts of the city may be put. • It allocates uses to the various districts of a municipality, as by allocating residences to certain parts and businesses to other parts. A comprehensive zoning ordinance usu. regulates the height of buildings and the proportion of the lot area that must be kept free from buildings.

zoning variance. See VARIANCE (2).

zygnomic (zig-**noh**-mik), *adj.* Of, relating to, or involving an act whose evolution directly abridges the freedom of a person who bears a duty in the enjoyment of a legal advantage. • This rather abstract term was coined by the philosopher Albert Kocourek in his book *Jural Relations* (1927). Cf. MESONOMIC.

zygocephalum (zɪ-gə-**sef**-ə-ləm), *n.* [Greek fr. *zygo-*"yoke, pair" + *kephalos* "head"] *Hist.* A measure of land, esp. the amount that can be plowed in one day.

zygostates (zɪ-goh-**stay**-teez), *n.* [Greek] *Roman law.* An officer who resolved controversies over weight; a public weigher.

Appendix A

Legal Maxims

In the first edition of this dictionary, published in 1891, Henry Campbell Black remarked that the book contained "a complete collection of legal maxims," adding: "These have not been grouped in one body, but distributed in their proper alphabetical order through the book. This is believed to be the more convenient arrangement" (p. iv). Although it might indeed have been more convenient for readers who knew the maxims they wanted to look up—as 19th-century readers might have been apt to—spreading Latin sentences throughout the book is decidedly inconvenient for most dictionary users today. We have therefore collected them for ease of reference.

Of course, many scholars have long been intolerant of those who use maxims to decide cases. As James Fitzjames Stephen, one of the great 19th-century legal scholars, incisively put it before Black's work appeared:

> It seems to me that legal maxims in general are little more than pert headings of chapters. They are rather minims than maxims, for they give not a particularly great but a particularly small amount of information. As often as not, the exceptions and disqualifications to them are more important than the so-called rules.[1]

Other scholars have been equally derisive.[2]

But there is an element of fun in legal maxims: they sometimes express surprising insights—and these from ancient writers. Though they will not clinch arguments, they will delight many readers who have a historical bent.

This collection of maxims has been carefully researched and retranslated by two classicists, Edwin Carawan and Alison Parker, whose splendid work has made the collection a reliable work of scholarship. Their bibliography of works cited appears on page 1701.

—B.A.G.

1. 2 James Fitzjames Stephen, *History of the Criminal Law of England* 94 n.1 (1883).

2. For a collection of critical comments, see Garner, *A Dictionary of Modern Legal Usage* 552 (2d ed. 1995.)

Ab abusu ad usum non valet consequentia. A conclusion about the use of a thing from its abuse is invalid.

Ab assuetis non fit injuria. No injury is done by things long acquiesced in.

Abbreviationum ille numerus et sensus accipiendus est ut concessio non sit inanis. Such number and sense is to be given to abbreviations that the grant may not be void.

Absentem accipere debemus eum qui non est eo loco in quo petitur. We must consider a person absent who is not in that place in which he is sought.

Absentia ejus qui reipublicae causa abest neque ei neque alii damnosa esse debet. The absence of a person who is abroad in service to the state ought to be prejudicial neither to that person nor to another. Dig. 50.17.140.

Absoluta sententia expositore non indiget. A simple proposition needs no expositor.

Abundans cautela non nocet. Abundant caution does no harm.

Accessorium non ducit, sed sequitur, suum principale. An accessory does not lead, but follows, its principal.

Accessorius sequitur naturam sui principalis. An accessory follows the nature of his principal.

Accipere quid ut justitiam facias non est tam accipere quam extorquere. To accept anything as a reward for doing justice is rather extorting than accepting.

Accusare nemo debet se, nisi coram Deo. No one is obliged to accuse himself, except before God.

Accusator post rationabile tempus non est audiendus, nisi se bene de omissione excusaverit. A person who makes an accusation after a reasonable time has passed is not to be heard unless the person makes a satisfactory excuse for the omission.

A communi observantia non est recedendum. There should be no departure from common observance (or usage).

Acta exteriora indicant interiora secreta. Outward acts indicate the thoughts hidden within.

Acta in uno judicio non probant in alio nisi inter easdem personas. Things done in one action cannot be taken as evidence in another, unless it is between the same parties.

Actio non datur non damnificato. An action is not given to one who is not injured.

Actio non facit reum, nisi mens sit rea. An act does not make a person guilty unless the mind is guilty. • Properly, *Actus non reum* (q.v.).

Actionum genera maxime sunt servanda. The kinds of actions are especially to be preserved.

Actio personalis moritur cum persona. A personal action dies with the person.

Actio quaelibet it sua via. Every action proceeds in its own course.

Actore non probante, reus absolvitur. If the plaintiff does not prove his case, the defendant is acquitted.

Actori incumbit onus probandi. The burden of proof rests upon the plaintiff.

Actor qui contra regulam quid adduxit non est audiendus. A pleader ought not to be heard who advances a proposition contrary to the rule (of law).

Actor sequitur forum rei. The plaintiff follows the forum of the thing in dispute.

Actus curiae neminem gravabit. An act of the court will prejudice no one.

Actus Dei nemini facit injuriam. An act of God does wrong to no one. • That is, no one is responsible in damages for inevitable accidents.

Actus inceptus cujus perfectio pendet ex voluntate partium revocari potest; si autem pendet ex voluntate tertiae personae, vel

ex contingenti, revocari non potest. An act already begun whose completion depends upon the will of the parties may be recalled; but if it depends on consent of a third person or on a contingency, it cannot be recalled.

Actus judiciarius coram non judice irritus habetur; de ministeriali autem a quocunque provenit ratum esto. A judicial act before one not a judge (or without jurisdiction) is void; as to a ministerial act, from whomsoever it proceeds, let it be valid.

Actus legis nemini est damnosus. An act of the law prejudices no one.

Actus legis nemini facit injuriam. An act of the law does no one wrong.

Actus legitimi non recipiunt modum. Acts required by law admit of no qualification.

Actus me invito factus non est meus actus. An act done (by me) against my will is not my act.

Actus non reum facit nisi mens sit rea. An act does not make a person guilty unless his mind (or intention) is guilty. 3 Co. Inst. 54; 107.

Actus repugnans non potest in esse produci. A repugnant act cannot be brought into being (that is, cannot be made effectual).

Actus servi, in iis quibus opera ejus communiter adhibita est, actus domini habetur. The act of a servant in those things in which he is usually employed is considered the act of his master.

Additio probat minoritatem. An addition proves inferiority. • That is, if it be said that a person has a fee tail, it is less than if the person has the fee.

Ad ea quae frequentius accidunt jura adaptantur. The laws are adapted to those cases that occur more frequently.

A digniori fieri debet denominatio et resolutio. The denomination and explanation ought to be derived from the more worthy.

Adjuvari quippe nos, non decipi, beneficio oportet. Surely we ought to be helped by a benefit, not be entrapped by it.

Ad officium justiciariorum spectat unicuique coram eis placitanti justitiam exhibere. It is the duty of justices to administer justice to everyone pleading before them.

Ad proximum antecedens fiat relatio, nisi impediatur sententia. A relative is to be referred to the nearest antecedent, unless prevented by the sense.

Ad quaestiones facti non respondent judices; ad quaestiones legis non respondent juratores. Judges do not answer questions of fact; jurors do not answer questions of law.

Ad quaestiones legis judices, et non juratores, respondent. Judges, and not jurors, answer questions of law.

Ad recte docendum oportet primum inquirere nomina, quia rerum cognitio a nominibus rerum dependet. In order rightly to comprehend a thing, it is necessary first to inquire into the names, for a right knowledge of things depends upon their names.

Adversus extraneos vitiosa possessio prodesse solet. Possession though faulty is usually sufficient against outsiders. • Prior possession is a good title of ownership against all who cannot show a better.

Ad vim majorem vel ad casus fortuitos non tenetur quis, nisi sua culpa intervenerit. No one is held to answer for the effects of superior force or accidents, unless his own fault has contributed.

Aedificare in tuo proprio solo non licet quod alteri noceat. It is not lawful to build upon one's own land what may be injurious to another.

Aedificatum solo solo cedit. What is built upon the land goes with the land.

Aedificia solo cedunt. Buildings go with the land.

Aequior est dispositio legis quam hominis. The law's disposition is more impartial than man's.

Aequitas agit in personam. Equity acts upon the person.

Aequitas est correctio legis generaliter latae qua parte deficit. Equity is the correction of some part of the law where by reason of its generality it is defective.

Aequitas ignorantiae opitulatur, oscitantiae non item. Equity assists ignorance but not complacency (or carelessness).

Aequitas non facit jus, sed juri auxiliatur. Equity does not create a right, but aids the right.

Aequitas sequitur legem. Equity follows the law.

Aequitas supervacua odit. Equity abhors superfluous things.

Aequum et bonum est lex legum. What is equitable and good is the law of laws.

Aestimatio praeteriti delicti ex postremo facto nunquam crescit. The assessment of a past offense never increases from a subsequent fact.

Affectio tua nomen imponit operi tuo. Your motive gives a name to your act.

Affectus punitur licet non sequatur effectus. The intention is punished even if the object is not achieved.

Affinis mei affinis non est mihi affinis. A person connected by marriage to someone connected by marriage to me is no connection of mine.

Affirmanti, non neganti, incumbit probatio. The proof is incumbent upon the one who affirms, not on the one who denies.

Affirmantis est probare. The person who affirms must prove.

Agentes et consentientes pari poena plectentur. Acting and consenting parties will be liable to the same punishment.

A jure suo cadunt. They fall from their right. • That is, they lose their right.

A justitia (quasi a quodam fonte) omnia jura emanant. From justice, as from a fountain, all rights flow.

Aliena negotia exacto officio geruntur. The business of another is conducted with scrupulous attention.

Alienatio licet prohibeatur, consensu tamen omnium in quorum favorem prohibita est potest fieri; et quilibet potest renunciare juri pro se introducto. Even if alienation is prohibited, it may yet take place by the consent of all in whose favor it is prohibited; it is in the power of anyone to renounce a right introduced for his own benefit.

Alienatio rei praefertur juri accrescendi. Alienation of property is favored over the right to accumulate.

A l'impossible nul n'est tenu. No one is bound to do what is impossible.

Aliquid conceditur ne injuria remaneat impunita quod alias non concederetur. Something is conceded that otherwise would not be conceded, so that a wrong not remain unpunished.

Aliquis non debet esse judex in propria causa, quia non potest esse judex et pars. A person ought not to be judge in his own cause, because he cannot act both as judge and party.

Aliud est celare, aliud tacere. To conceal is one thing, to be silent another.

Aliud est distinctio, aliud separatio. Distinction is one thing, separation another.

Aliud est possidere, aliud esse in possessione. It is one thing to possess, another to be in possession.

Aliud est vendere, aliud vendenti consentire. To sell is one thing, to give consent to the seller another.

Allegans contraria non est audiendus. A person making contradictory allegations is not to be heard.

Allegans suam turpitudinem non est audiendus. A person alleging his own wrong is not to be heard.

Allegari non debuit quod probatum non relevat. What is not relevant if proved ought not to have been alleged.

Allegatio contra factum non est admittenda. An allegation contrary to the deed (or fact) is not admissible.

Alterius circumventio alii non praebet actionem. A deception practiced upon one person does not give a cause of action to another.

Alternativa petitio non est audienda. An alternative petition is not to be heard.

Ambigua responsio contra proferentem est accipienda. An ambiguous answer is to be taken against the party who offers it.

Ambiguis casibus semper praesumitur pro rege. In doubtful cases the presumption is always in favor of the king.

Ambiguitas contra stipulatorem est. A dubious expression is construed against the party using it.

Ambiguitas verborum latens verificatione suppletur; nam quod ex facto oritur ambiguum verificatione facti tollitur. A latent ambiguity in wording is resolved by evidence; for whatever ambiguity arises from an extrinsic fact is resolved by extrinsic evidence.

Ambiguitas verborum patens nulla verificatione excluditur. A patent ambiguity is not removed by extrinsic evidence (or is never helped by averment).

Ambiguum placitum interpretari debet contra proferentem. An ambiguous plea ought to be interpreted against the party pleading it.

Ambulatoria est voluntas defuncti usque ad vitae supremum exitum. The will of a decedent is ambulatory (that is, can be altered) until the last moment of life.

Angliae jura in omni casu libertati dant favorem. The laws of England are favorable in every case to liberty.

Animus ad se omne jus ducit. The mind brings every right unto itself. • Often explained: It is to the intention that all law applies.

Animus hominis est anima scripti. The intention of the person is the soul of the instrument.

Anniculus trecentesimo sexagesimo-quinto die dicitur, incipiente plane non exacto die, quia annum civiliter non ad momenta temporum sed ad dies numeramur. We call a child a year old on the 365th day, when the day is clearly begun but not ended, because we calculate the civil year not by moments, but by days.

Annua nec debitum judex non separat ipse. Even the judge apportions neither annuities nor debt.

Annus est mora motus quo suum planeta pervolvat circulum. A year is the duration of the motion by which a planet revolves through its orbit.

Annus inceptus pro completo habetur. A year begun is held as completed. • Said to be of very limited application.

A non posse ad non esse sequitur argumentum necessarie negative, licet non affirmative. From impossibility to nonexistence the inference follows necessarily in the negative, though not in the affirmative.

Apices juris non sunt jura. Legal niceties are not law.

A piratis aut latronibus capti liberi permanent. Those captured by pirates or robbers remain free.

A piratis et latronibus capta dominium non mutant. Things captured by pirates or robbers do not change their ownership.

Applicatio est vita regulae. The application is the life of a rule.

Aqua cedit solo. The water goes with the ground. • A grant of the land includes the water on it.

Aqua currit et debet currere ut currere solebat. Water runs and ought to run as it was wont to run.

Arbitramentum aequum tribuit cuique suum. A just arbitration renders to each his own.

Arbitrium est judicium. An award is a judgment.

Arbor dum crescit; lignum dum crescere nescit. It is a tree while it is growing; wood when it cannot grow.

A rescriptis valet argumentum. An argument from rescripts (i.e., original writs in the register) is valid.

Argumentum ab auctoritate est fortissimum in lege. An argument drawn from authority is the strongest in law.

Argumentum ab impossibili plurimum valet in lege. An argument deduced from an impossibility has the greatest validity in law.

Argumentum ab inconvenienti plurimum valet in lege. An argument drawn from what is unsuitable (or improper) has the greatest validity in law. Co. Litt. 66a.

Argumentum a divisione est fortissimum in jure. An argument based on a subdivision of the subject is most powerful in law.

Argumentum a majori ad minus negative non valet; valet e converso. An argument from the greater to the lesser is of no force in the negative; conversely (in the affirmative) it is valid.

Argumentum a simili valet in lege. An argument by analogy (from a similar case) has force in law.

Arma in armatos sumere jura sinunt. The laws permit taking up arms against the armed.

Assignatus utitur jure auctoris. An assignee is clothed with the rights of the principal.

A summo remedio ad inferiorem actionem non habetur regressus neque auxilium. From the highest remedy to an inferior action there is no recourse or assistance.

Auctoritates philosophorum, medicorum et poetarum sunt in causis allegandae et tenendae. The authoritative opinions of philosophers, physicians, and poets are to be adduced and regarded in causes.

Aucupia verborum sunt judice indigna. Quibbling over words is unworthy of a judge.

Audi alteram partem. Hear the other side. • No one should be condemned unheard.

A verbis legis non est recedendum. From the words of the law there is to be no departure.

Baratriam committit qui propter pecuniam justitiam baractat. A person is guilty of barratry who sells justice for money.

Bastardus non potest habere haeredem nisi de corpore suo legitime procreatum. A bastard cannot have an heir unless it be one lawfully begotten of his own body.

Bastardus nullius est filius, aut filius populi. A bastard is nobody's son, or the son of the people.

Bello parta cedunt reipublicae. Things acquired in war go to the state.

Benedicta est expositio quando res redimitur a destructione. Blessed is the exposition when a thing is saved from destruction.

Beneficium invito non datur. A privilege or benefit is not granted against a person's will.

Beneficium non datum nisi propter officium. A remuneration is not given, unless on account of a duty performed.

Beneficium non datur nisi officii causa. A benefice is not granted except on account or in consideration of duty.

Beneficium principis debet esse mansurum. The benefaction of a prince ought to be be lasting.

Benigne faciendae sunt interpretationes chartarum, ut res magis valeat quam pereat; et quaelibet concessio fortissime contra donatorem interpretanda est. Deeds should be subject to liberal interpretation, so that the matter may take effect rather than fail; and every grant is to be taken most strongly against the grantor.

Benigne faciendae sunt interpretationes propter simplicitatem laicorum, ut res magis valeat quam pereat; et verba intentioni, non e contra, debent inservire. Constructions (of written instruments) are to be made liberally, for the simplicity of laymen, in order that the matter may have effect rather than fail (or become void); and words must be subject to the intention, not the intention to the words.

Benignior sententia in verbis generalibus seu dubiis est preferenda. The more favorable construction is to be preferred in general or doubtful expressions.

Benignius leges interpretandae sunt quo voluntas earum conservetur. Laws are to be more liberally interpreted so that their intent may be preserved.

Bigamus seu trigamus, etc., est qui diversis temporibus et successive duas seu tres uxores habuit. A bigamus or trigamus, etc., is one who has had two or more wives in succession, each at a different time. 3 Co. Inst. 88.

Bis dat qui cito dat. He pays twice who pays promptly.

Bis idem exigi bona fides non patitur, et in satisfactionibus non permittitur amplius fieri quam semel factum est. Good faith does not allow the same thing to be exacted twice; and in satisfying claims, it is not permitted that more should be done after satisfaction has once been rendered.

Bonae fidei non congruit de apicibus juris disputare. It is incompatible with good faith to insist on the extreme subtleties of the law.

Bonae fidei possessor in id tantum quod ad se pervenerit tenetur. A possessor in good faith is liable only for that which he himself has obtained (literally, what has come to him). 2 Co. Inst. 285.

Bona fide possessor facit fructus consumptos suos. A possessor in good faith is entitled to the fruits (or produce) that he consumes.

Bona fides exigit ut quod convenit fiat. Good faith demands that what is agreed upon shall be done.

Bona fides non patitur ut bis idem exigatur. Good faith does not allow payment to be exacted twice for the same thing.

Boni judicis est ampliare jurisdictionem (or justitiam). It is the role of a good judge to enlarge (or use liberally) his jurisdiction (or remedial authority).

Boni judicis est ampliare justitiam. It is the role of a good judge to enlarge or extend justice.

Boni judicis est causas litium dirimere. It is the role of a good judge to remove causes of litigation.

Boni judicis est judicium sine dilatione mandare executioni. It is the role of a good judge to render judgment for execution without delay.

Boni judicis est lites dirimere, ne lis ex lite oriatur. It is the role of a good judge to dispose of litigations so that one suit should not grow from another. 5 Coke 31a.

Bonum defendentis ex integra causa; malum ex quolibet defectu. A good outcome for the defendant comes from a sound case; a bad outcome from some defect.

Bonum necessarium extra terminos necessitatis non est bonum. A thing good from necessity is not good beyond the limits of the necessity.

Bonus judex secundum aequum et bonum judicat, et aequitatem stricto juri praefert. A good judge decides according to fairness and the good and prefers equity to strict law.

Breve ita dicitur, quia rem de qua agitur, et intentionem petentis, paucis verbis breviter enarrat. A writ is called a "breve" because it briefly states, in few words, the matter in dispute, and the object of the party seeking relief.

Breve judiciale debet sequi suum originale, et accessorium suum principale. A judicial writ ought to follow its original, and an accessory its principal.

Breve judiciale non cadit pro defectu formae. A judicial writ does not fail for a defect of form.

Brevia, tam originalia quam judicialia, patiuntur anglica nomina. Writs, original as well as judicial, bear English names.

Cancellarii angliae dignitas est, ut secundus a rege in regno habetur. The dignity of the chancellor of England is (such) that he is considered in the realm from the sovereign.

Carcer ad homines custodiendos, non ad puniendos, dari debet. Imprisonment should be imposed for keeping people in confinement, not for punishing them (further). Co. Litt. 260a.

Carcer non supplicii causa sed custodiae constitutus. A prison is established not for the sake of punishment, but for detention under guard.

Casus fortuitus non est sperandus, et nemo tenetur divinare. A chance event is not to be expected, and no one is bound to foresee it.

Casus fortuitus non est supponendus. A chance event is not to be presumed.

Casus omissus et oblivioni datus dispositioni communis juris relinquitur. A case omitted and forgotten (not provided for in statute) is left to the disposal of the common law.

Casus omissus pro omisso habendus est. A case omitted is to be held as (intentionally) omitted.

Catalla juste possessa amitti non possunt. Chattels rightly possessed cannot be lost.

Catalla reputantur inter minima in lege. Chattels are considered in law among things of least consequence.

Causa causae est causa causati. The cause of a cause is the cause of the effect.

Causa causantis causa est causati. The cause of the thing causing is the cause of the effect.

Causa ecclesiae publicis aequiparatur; et summa est ratio quae pro religione facit. The cause of the church is equal to public causes; and paramount is the reason that acts in favor of religion.

Causae dotis, vitae, libertatis, fisci sunt inter favorabilia in lege. Causes of dower, life, liberty, revenue are among the things favored in law.

Causae ecclesiae publicis causis aequiparantur. The causes of the church are equal to public causes.

Causa et origo est materia negotii. The cause and origin of a matter are the substance of it. • "The law regards the original act": as in the case of a man who attempts suicide in madness, but dies after regaining sanity; such is not suicide. 1 Coke 99.

Causa patet. The reason is obvious.

Causa proxima non remota spectatur. The immediate and not the remote cause is considered.

Causa vaga et incerta non est causa rationabilis. A vague and uncertain cause is not a reasonable cause.

Caveat emptor. Let the buyer beware.

Caveat emptor qui ignorare non debuit quod jus alienum emit. Let the buyer beware; for he ought not act in ignorance when he buys what another has right to.

Caveat venditor. Let the seller beware.

Caveat viator. Let the traveler beware.

Cavendum est a fragmentis. Beware of fragments.

Certa debet esse intentio et narratio et certum fundamentum et certa res quae deducitur in judicium. The design and narration ought to be certain, the foundation certain, and the matter certain that is brought into court to be tried.

Certum est quod certum reddi potest. That is certain which can be rendered certain.

Cessante causa, cessat effectus. The cause ceasing, the effect ceases.

Cessante ratione legis cessat et ipsa lex. When the reason of the law ceases, the law itself also ceases.

Cessante statu primitivo, cessat derivativus. When the original estate comes to an end, the derivative estate is also at an end.

Cessa regnare, si non vis judicare. Cease to reign if you wish not to adjudicate.

C'est le crime qui fait la honte, et non pas véchafaud. It is the crime that causes the shame, and not the scaffold.

Cestuy que doit inheriter al pére doit inheriter al fils. The person who should have inherited from the father should also inherit from the son.

Chacea est ad communem legem. A chase (or hunting ground) exists by common law.

Charta de non ente non valet. A deed of a thing not in being is not valid.

Charta non est nisi vestimentum donationis. A deed is nothing else than the vestment (or clothing) of a gift.

Chartarum super fidem, mortuis testibus, ad patriam de necessitudine recurrendum est. (A dispute) regarding the veracity of deeds, with the witnesses dead, must necessarily be referred to the country (or jury).

Chirographum apud debitorem repertum praesumitur solutum. When the evidence (or voucher) is found in the debtor's possession, the debt is presumed to be paid.

Chirographum non extans praesumitur solutum. When the evidence of a debt is not in existence, it is presumed to have been discharged.

Circuitus est evitandus. Circuity (roundabout proceeding) is to be avoided.

Circuitus est evitandus; et boni judicis est lites dirimere, ne lis ex lite oriatur. Circuity is to be avoided; and it is the role of a good judge to determine (or dispose of) litigations so that one lawsuit may not arise from another.

Citatio est de juri naturali. A summons is by natural right.

Citationes non concedantur priusquam exprimatur super qua re fieri debet citatio. Citations should not be granted before it is stated about what matter the citation is to be made.

Clam delinquens magis punitur quam palam. A person who does wrong secretly is punished more severely than one who acts openly. 8 Coke 127.

Clam factum id videtur esse, quod quisque, quum controversiam haberet, habiturumve se putaret, fecit. That is considered done secretly which someone did when he had a legal dispute or thought he would have one.

Clausulae inconsuetae semper inducunt suspicionem. Unusual clauses always arouse suspicion.

Clausula generalis de residuo non ea complectitur quae non ejusdem sint generis cum iis quae speciatim dicta fuerant. A general clause of remainder does not embrace those things that are not of the same kind as those that had been specially mentioned.

Clausula generalis non refertur ad expressa. A general clause does not refer to things expressly mentioned.

Clausula quae abrogationem excludit ab initio non valet. A clause that precludes abrogation is invalid from the beginning.

Clausula vel dispositio inutilis per praesumptionem remotam vel causam ex post facto non fulcitur. A useless clause or disposition is not supported by a remote presumption or by a cause arising afterwards. • A useless clause or disposition is one that expresses no more than the law by intendment would have supplied; it is not supported by a remote presumption or foreign intendment of some purpose, in regard whereof it might be material, or by a cause arising afterwards that may induce an operation of those idle words.

Cogitationis poenam nemo meretur. No one deserves punishment for his thoughts.

Cogitationis poenam nemo patitur. No one is punished for his thoughts.

Cognomen majorum est ex sanguine tractum, hoc intrinsecum est; agnomen extrinsecum ab eventu. The cognomen is derived from the blood of ancestors and is intrinsic; an agnomen (or honorary title) arises from an event, and is extrinsic.

Cohaeredes una persona censentur, propter unitatem juris quod habent. Coheirs are deemed as one person, on account of the unity of right that they possess.

Collegium est societas plurium corporum simul habitantium. A college is a society of several people dwelling together.

Commenda est facultas recipiendi et retinendi beneficium contra jus positivum a suprema potestate. A commendam is the power of receiving and retaining a benefice contrary to positive law, by supreme authority.

Commercium jure gentium commune esse debet et non in monopolium et privatum paucorum quaestum convertendum. Commerce, by the law of nations, ought to be common and not converted into a monopoly and the private gain of a few.

Commodum ex injuria sua non habere debet. (The wrongdoer) should not derive any benefit from his own wrong.

Communis error facit jus. A common error (one often repeated) makes law.

Communis error non facit jus. A common error does not make law.

Compendia sunt dispendia. Abridgments are hindrances. Shortcuts or time-saving measures are often a loss. • Coke continues, *Melius est petere fontes*. Co. Litt. 305b.

Compromissarii sunt judices. Arbitrators are judges.

Compromissum ad similitudinem judiciorum redigitur. A compromise is brought into affinity with judgments.

Conatus quid sit non definitur in jure. What an attempt is, is not defined in law.

Concessio per regem fieri debet de certitudine. A grant by the king ought to be made of a certainty. • Coke explains, "If the king grants to me that I shall not be sheriff, without showing of what county, it is void for uncertainty." 9 Coke 46b.

Concessio versus concedentem latam interpretationem habere debet. A grant ought to have a liberal interpretation against the grantor.

Concordare leges legibus est optimus interpretandi modus. To make laws agree with laws is the best mode of interpreting them.

Concordia parvae res crescunt et opulentia lites. Small means increase by concord and litigations by opulence.

Conditio beneficialis, quae statum construit, benigne secundum verborum intentionem est interpretanda; odiosa autem quae statum destruit stricte, secundum verborum proprietatem, accipienda. A beneficial condition that creates an estate ought to be construed favorably, according to the intention of the words; but a condition that destroys an estate is odious and ought to be construed according to the strict sense of the words.

Conditio dicitur cum quid in casum incertum qui potest tendere ad esse aut non esse confertur. It is called a condition when something is given for an uncertain event that may or may not come into existence.

Conditio illicita habetur pro non adjecta. An unlawful condition is considered unconnected.

Conditiones quaelibet odiosae; maxime autem contra matrimonium et commercium. Any conditions are odious, but especially those against matrimony and commerce.

Conditio praecedens adimpleri debet prius quam sequatur effectus. A condition precedent ought to be fulfilled before the effect can follow.

Confessio facta in judicio omni probatione major est. A confession made in court is of greater effect than any proof.

Confessus in judicio pro judicato habetur et quodammodo sua sententia damnatur. A person who has confessed his guilt when arraigned is considered to have been tried and is, as it were, condemned by his own sentence.

Confirmare est id quod prius infirmum fuit simul firmare. To confirm is to make firm at once what before was not firm.

Confirmare nemo potest priusquam jus ei acciderit. No one can confirm before the right accrues to him.

Confirmatio est nulla ubi donum praecedens est invalidum. A confirmation is null where the preceding gift is invalid.

Confirmatio omnes supplet defectus, licet id quod actum est ab initio non valuit. Confirmation supplies all defects, even if that which has been done was not valid at the beginning.

Confirmat usum qui tollit abusum. One confirms a use who removes an abuse.

Conjunctio mariti et feminae est de jure naturae. The union of husband and wife derives from the law of nature.

Conscientia dicitur a con et scio, quasi scire cum Deo. Conscience is so called from con and scio, to know, as it were, with God.

Consecratio est periodus electionis; electio est praeambula consecrationis. Consecration is the termination of election; election is the preamble of consecration.

Consensus est voluntas plurium ad quos res pertinet, simul juncta. Consent is the conjoint will of several people to whom the thing belongs.

Consensus facit legem. Consent makes law. • A contract constitutes law between the parties agreeing to be bound by it.

Consensus, non concubitus, facit matrimonium. Consent, not coition (or sharing a bed), constitutes marriage.

Consensus, non concubitus, facit nuptias vel matrimonium, et consentire non possunt ante annos nubiles. Consent, not coition (or sharing a bed), constitutes nuptials or marriage, and persons cannot consent before marriageable years.

Consensus tollit errorem. Consent removes an error. • A person cannot object to something he has consented to.

Consensus voluntas multorum ad quos res pertinet simul juncta. Consent is the united will of several interested in one subject matter.

Consentientes et agentes pari poena plectentur. Those consenting and those perpetrating will receive the same punishment.

Consentire matrimonio non possunt infra (ante) annos nubiles. Persons cannot consent to marriage before marriageable years.

Consequentiae non est consequentia. The consequence of a consequence does not exist.

Consilia multorum quaeruntur (requiruntur) in magnis. The advice of many is sought in great affairs.

Consortio malorum me quoque malum facit. The company of wicked men makes me also wicked.

Constitutiones tempore posteriores potiores sunt his quae ipsas praecesserunt. Later laws prevail over those that preceded them.

Constitutum esse eam domum unicuique nostrum debere existimari, ubi quisque sedes et tabulas haberet, suarumque rerum constitutionem fecisset. It is a settled principle that what ought to be considered the home of each of us is where he has his dwelling, keeps his records, and has established his business.

Constructio legis non facit injuriam. The construction of the law does not work an injury.

Consuetudo contra rationem introducta potius usurpatio quam consuetudo appellari debet. A custom introduced against reason ought rather to be called a usurpation than a custom.

Consuetudo debet esse certa. Custom ought to be fixed.

Consuetudo debet esse certa, nam incerta pro nulla (nullius) habetur. Custom ought to be fixed, for if variable it is held as null (or of no account).

Consuetudo est altera lex. Custom is another law.

Consuetudo est optimus interpres legum. Custom is the best expounder of the law.

Consuetudo et communis assuetudo vincit legem non scriptam, si sit specialis; et interpretatur legem scriptam, si lex sit generalis. Custom and common usage overcome the unwritten law if it is special; and interpret the written law if the law is general.

Consuetudo ex certa causa rationabili usitata privat communem legem. Custom observed by reason of a certain and reasonable cause supersedes the common law.

Consuetudo, licet sit magnae auctoritatis, nunquam tamen praejudicat manifestae veritati. A custom, even if it is of great authority, is never prejudicial to plain truth.

Consuetudo loci observanda est. The custom of the place is to be observed.

Consuetudo manerii et loci observanda est. The custom of a manor and place is to be observed.

Consuetudo neque injuria oriri neque tolli protest. A custom can neither arise nor be abolished by a wrong.

Consuetudo non habitur (trahitur) in consequentiam. Custom is not held as (or drawn into) a precedent.

Consuetudo praescripta et legitima vincit legem. A prescriptive and lawful custom overrides the law.

Consuetudo regni Angliae est lex Angliae. The custom of the kingdom of England is the law of England.

Consuetudo semel reprobata non potest amplius induci. A custom once disallowed cannot again be introduced.

Consuetudo tollit communem legem. Custom takes away the common law.

Consuetudo vincit communem legem. Custom overrules common law.

Consuetudo volentes ducit, lex nolentes trahit. Custom leads the willing; law drags the unwilling.

Contemporanea expositio est optima et fortissima in lege. A contemporaneous exposition is the best and most powerful in the law. • A statute is best explained by following the construction put upon it by judges who lived at the time it was made, or soon after.

Contestatio litis eget terminos contradictarios. An issue requires terms of contradiction. • (That is, there can be no issue without an affirmative on one side and a negative on the other.)

Contractus est quasi actus contra actum. A contract is, as it were, act against act.

Contractus ex turpi causa vel contra bonos mores nullus est. A contract founded on a wrongful consideration or against good morals is null.

Contractus legem ex conventione accipiunt. Contracts receive legal validity from the agreement of the parties.

Contra legem facit qui id facit quod lex prohibit; in fraudem vero qui, salvis verbis legis, sententiam ejus circumvenit. A person acts contrary to the law who does what the law prohibits; a person acts in fraud of the law who, without violating the wording, circumvents the intention. Dig. 1.3.29.

Contra negantem principia non est disputandum. There is no disputing against one who denies first principles.

Contra non valentem agere nulla currit praescriptio. No prescription runs against a person unable to act (or bring an action).

Contrariorum contraria est ratio. The reason of contrary things is contrary.

Contra veritatem lex nunquam aliquid permittit. The law never allows anything contrary to truth.

Contrectatio rei alienae animo furandi est furtum. Touching or taking another's property with an intention of stealing is theft.

Conventio omnis intelligitur clausula rebus sic stantibus. Every contract is to be understood as being based on the assumption of things remaining as they were (that is, at the time of its conclusion).

Conventio privatorum non potest publico juri derogare. An agreement of private persons cannot derogate from public right. • That is, it cannot prevent the application of general rules of law, or render valid any contravention of law.

Conventio vincit legem. The express agreement of the parties overrides the law.

Convicia si irascaris tua divulgas; spreta exolescunt. If you are moved to anger by insults, you spread them abroad; if despised, they die out.

Copulatio verborum indicat acceptationem in eodem sensu. Coupling words together shows that they ought to be understood in the same sense.

Corporalis injuria non recipit aestimationem de futuro. A personal injury does not receive satisfaction from proceedings yet in the future.

Corpus humanum non recipit aestimationem. The person of a human being can have no price put on it.

Creditorum appellatione non hi tantum accipiuntur qui pecuniam crediderunt, sed omnes quibus ex qualibet causa debetur. Under the name of creditors are included not only those who have lent money, but also all to whom a debt is owed from any cause.

Crescente malitia crescere debet et poena. With increase of malice, punishment ought also to increase.

Crimen falsi dicitur, cum quis illicitus, cui non fuerit ad hoea data auctoritas, de sigillo regis rapto vel invento brevia cartasve consignaverit. It is called "crimen falsi" when anyone to whom power has not been given for such purposes has illicitly signed writs or grants with the king's seal, either stolen or found.

Crimen laesae majestatis omnia alia crimina excedit quoad poenam. The crime of treason exceeds all other crimes in its punishment.

Crimen omnia ex se nata vitiat. Crime taints everything that springs from it.

Crimen trahit personam. The crime brings with it the person. • That is, the commission of a crime gives the courts of the place where it is committed jurisdiction over the person of the offender.

Crimina morte extinguuntur. Crimes are extinguished by death.

Cuicunque aliquid conceditur, conceditur etiam et id sine quo res ipsa non esse potuit. To whomever anything is granted, that also is granted without which the thing itself could not exist.

Cuicunque aliquis quid concedit concedere videtur et id sine quo res ipsa esse non potuit. To whomever anyone grants a thing he is considered also to grant that without which the thing itself could not be (the sine qua non). 11 Coke 52.

Cui jurisdictio data est, ea quoque concessa esse videntur sine quibus jurisdictio explicari non potest. To whom jurisdiction is given, those things also are considered to be granted without which the jurisdiction cannot be exercised. • That is, the grant of jurisdiction implies the grant of all powers necessary to its exercise.

Cui jus est donandi eidem et vendendi et concedendi jus est. A person who has a right to give has also a right to sell and to grant.

Cuilibet in arte sua perito est credendum. Credence should be given to a person skilled in his art (that is, when speaking of matters connected with that art).

Cuilibet licit juri pro se introducto renunciare. Anyone may waive or renounce the benefit of a principle or rule of law that exists only for his protection.

Cui licet quod majus non debet quod minus est non licere. A person who has authority to do the more important act ought not to be debarred from doing what is of less importance.

Cui pater est populus non habet ille patrem. That person to whom the people is father has not a father.

Cuique in sua arte credendum est. Everyone is to be believed in his own area of expertise.

Cujus est commodum, ejus debet esse incommodum. The person who has the advantage should also have the disadvantage.

Cujus est commodum, ejus est onus. The person who has the benefit has also the burden.

Cujus est dare, ejus est disponere. The person who has a right to give has the right of disposition. • That is, the bestower of a gift has a right to regulate its disposal.

Cujus est divisio, alterius est electio. When one of two parties has the division (of an estate), the other has the choice (of the shares). • In partition between coparceners, where the division is made by the eldest, the rule in English law is that she shall choose her share last.

Cujus est dominium, ejus est periculum. The risk lies upon the owner.

Cujus est instituere, ejus est abrogare. Whoever can institute can also abrogate.

Cujus est solum, ejus est usque ad coelum. The person who owns the soil owns up to the sky. • One who owns the surface of the ground owns, or has an exclusive right to everything that is upon or above it to an indefinite height.

Cujus est solum, ejus est usque ad coelum et ad inferos. Whoever owns the soil owns everything up to the sky and down to the depths.

Cujus juris (i.e., jurisdictionis) est principale, ejusdem juris erit accessorium. An accessory matter is subject to the same jurisdiction as its principal.

Cujus per errorem dati repetitio est, ejus consulto dati donatio est. A thing given by mistake can be recovered; if given purposely, it is a gift. Dig. 50.17.53.

Cujusque rei potissima pars est principium. The principal part of everything is the beginning.

Culpa caret qui scit sed prohibere non potest. A person is free of blame who knows but cannot prevent.

Culpae poena par esto. Let the punishment be equal to the crime.

Culpa est immiscere se rei ad se non pertinenti. It is a fault for anyone to meddle in a matter not pertaining to him.

Culpa lata dolo aequiparatur. Gross negligence is equivalent to fraud.

Culpa tenet (teneat) suos auctores. A fault binds (or should bind) its own authors.

Cum actio fuerit mere criminalis, institui poterit ab initio criminaliter vel civiliter. When an action is purely criminal, it can be instituted from the beginning either criminally or civilly.

Cum adsunt testimonia rerum, quid opus est verbis? When the proofs of facts are present, what need is there of words?

Cum aliquis renunciaverit societati, solvitur societas. When any partner has renounced the partnership, the partnership is dissolved.

Cum confitente sponte mitius est agendum. One making a voluntary confession is to be dealt with more leniently.

Cum de lucro duorum quaeritur melior est causa possidentis. When there is a question of gain between two people, the cause of the possessor is the better.

Cum duo inter se pugnantia reperiuntur in testamento, ultimum ratum est. When two clauses in a will are found to be contradictory, the last in order prevails.

Cum duo jura concurrunt in una persona, aequum est ac si essent in duobus. When two rights meet in one person, it is the same as if they were in two persons.

Cum in corpore dissentitur, apparet nullam esse acceptionem. When there is a disagreement in the substance, there is clearly no acceptance.

Cum in testamento ambigue aut etiam perperam scriptum, est benigne interpretari, et secundum id quod credible est cogitatum credendum est. When an ambiguous or even an erroneous expression occurs in a will, it should be construed liberally, and in accordance with the testator's probable meaning.

Cum legitimae nuptiae factae sunt, patrem liberi sequuntur. Children born under a legitimate marriage follow the condition of the father.

Cum par delictum est duorum, semper oneratur petitor, et melior habetur possessoris causa. Where two parties are equally at fault, the claimant always is at the disadvantage, and the party in possession has the better cause.

Cum quod ago non valet ut ago, valeat quantum valere potest. When that which I do is of no effect as I do it, let it have as much effect as it can (that is, in some other way).

Curatus non habet titulum. A curate has no title (to tithes).

Curia cancellariae officina justitiae. The court of chancery is the workshop of justice.

Curia parliamenti suis propriis legibus subsistit. The court of parliament is governed by its own laws.

Curiosa et captiosa interpretatio in lege reprobatur. An overnice and captious interpretation in the law is rejected.

Currit tempus contra desides et sui juris contemptores. Time runs against the indolent and those who are not mindful of their rights.

Cursus curiae est lex curiae. The practice of the court is the law of the court.

Custome serra prise stricte. Custom shall be construed strictly.

Custos statum haeredis in custodia existentis meliorem, non deteriorem, facere potest. A guardian can make the estate of an heir living under his guardianship better, not worse.

Damnum sine injuria esse potest. There can be damage without any act of injustice.

Dans et retinens nihil dat. One who gives and yet retains (possession) does not give effectually (literally, gives nothing).

Da tua dum tua sunt, post mortem tunc tua non sunt. Give the things which are yours while they are yours; after death they are not yours.

Datur digniori. It is given to the more worthy.

Debet esse finis litium. There ought to be a limit to litigation.

Debet quis juri subjacere ubi delinquit. Any offender should be subject to the law of the place where he offends.

Debet sua cuique domus esse perfugium tutissimum. Every person's house should be his safest refuge.

Debile fundamentum fallit opus. A weak foundation frustrates the work (built on it).

Debita sequuntur personam debitoris. Debts follow the person of the debtor. • That is, debts belong to no locality and may be collected wherever the debtor can be found.

Debitor non praesumitur donare. A debtor is not presumed to make a gift.

Debitorum pactionibus creditorum petitio nec tolli nec minui potest. The creditors' suit can be neither quashed nor diminished by the contracts of their debtors.

Debitum et contractus sunt nullius loci. Debt and contract belong to no particular place.

Deceptis, non decipientibus, jura subveniunt. The laws help persons who have been deceived, not those deceiving.

Decet (tamen) principem servare leges quibus ipse servatus est. It is proper (nonetheless) for the prince to preserve the laws by which he himself is preserved.

Decimae de decimatis solvi non debent. Tithes ought not to be paid from that which is given for tithes.

Decimae de jure divino et canonica institutione pertinent ad personam. Tithes belong to the parson by divine right and canonical institution.

Decimae non debent solvi ubi non est annua renovatio, et ex annuatis renovantibus simul semel. Tithes ought not to be paid where there is not an annual renovation, and from annual renovations once only.

Decipi quam fallere est tutius. It is safer to be deceived than to deceive.

Decreta conciliorum non ligant reges nostros. The decrees of councils do not bind our kings.

Deficiente uno sanguine, non potest esse haeres. For lack of one blood, he cannot be heir. • Coke explains, "The blood of the father and of the mother are but one inheritable blood, and both are necessary to procreation of an heir." 3 Coke 41.

De fide et officio judicis non recipitur quaestio, sed de scientia sive sit error juris sive facti. The good faith and honesty of purpose of a judge cannot be questioned, but his knowledge may be impugned if there is an error either of law or of fact.

De jure decimarum, originem ducens de jure patronatus, tunc cognitio spectat at legem civilem, i.e., communem. With regard to the right of tithes, deducing its origin from the right of the patron, then the cognizance of them belongs to the civil law, i.e., common law.

De jure judices, de facto juratores, respondent. The judges answer regarding the law, the jury on the facts.

Delegata potestas non potest delegari. A delegated authority cannot be delegated.

Delegatus non potest delegare. A delegate (or deputy) cannot appoint another.

Delicatus debitor est odiosus in lege. A luxurious debtor is hateful in the law.

Delinquens per iram provocatus puniri debet mitius. A wrongdoer provoked by anger ought to be punished less severely. 3 Co. Inst. 55.

De majori et minori non variant jura. Concerning greater and lesser, rights do not vary (or justice does vary).

De minimis non curat lex. The law does not notice or concern itself with trifling matters.

De molendino de novo erecto non jacet prohibitio. A prohibition does not lie against a newly erected mill.

De morte hominis nulla est cunctatio longa. When the death of a human being is concerned, no delay is long.

Denominatio fieri debet a dignioribus. Denomination should be made from the more worthy.

De nomine proprio non est curandum cum in substantia non erretur; quia nomina mutabilia sunt, res autem immobiles. As to the proper name, it is not to be regarded when there is no error in substance; because names are changeable, but things are immutable.

De non apparentibus et non existentibus eadem est ratio. The rule is the same respecting things that do not appear and things that do not exist.

De nullo quod est sua natura indivisibile et divisionem non patitur nullam partem habebit vidua, sed satisfaciat ei ad valentiam. A widow shall have no part from that which in its own nature is indivisible and is not susceptible of division; but let (the heir) satisfy her with an equivalent.

De nullo tenemento, quod tenetur ad terminum, fit homagii; fit tamen inde fidelitatis sacramentum. For no tenement that is held for a term is there the oath of homage, but there is the oath of fealty.

Derivativa potestas non potest esse major primitiva. Power that is derived cannot be greater than that from which it is derived.

Derogatur legi cum pars detrahitur; abrogatur legi, cum prorsus tollitur. There is derogation from a law when part of it is taken away; there is abrogation of a law when it is abolished entirely.

Designatio justiciariorum est a rege; jurisdictio vero ordinaria a lege. The appointment of justices is by the king, but their ordinary jurisdiction is by the law.

Designatio unius est exclusio alterius, et expressum facit cessare tacitum. The designation of one is the exclusion of the other; and what is expressed prevails over what is implied.

De similibus ad similia eadem ratione procedendum est. From like things to like things we are to proceed by the same rule. • That is, we are allowed to argue from the analogy of cases.

De similibus idem est judicium. Concerning like things the judgment is the same.

Deus solus haeredem facere potest, non homo. God alone, and not man, can make an heir.

Dies dominicus non est juridicus. Sunday is not a judicial day.

Dies inceptus pro completo habetur. A day begun is held as complete.

Dies incertus pro conditione habetur. An uncertain day is considered as a condition.

Dilationes in lege sunt odiosae. Delays in law are odious.

Discretio est discernere per legem quid sit justum. Discretion is to discern through law what is just.

Discretio est scire per legem quid sit justum. Discretion consists in knowing what is just in law.

Disparata non debent jungi. Dissimilar things ought not to be joined.

Dispensatio est mali prohibiti provida relaxatio, utilitate seu necessitate pensata; et est de jure domino regi concessa, propter impossibilitatem praevidendi de omnibus particularibus. A dispensation is the provident relaxation of a malum prohibitum weighed from utility or necessity; and it is conceded by law to the king on account of the impossibility of foreknowledge concerning all particulars.

Dispensatio est vulnus, quod vulnerat jus commune. A dispensation is a wound, because it wounds a common right.

Disseisinam satis facit qui uti non permittit possessorem, vel minus commode, licet omnino non expellat. A person commits disseisin if he does not permit the possessor to enjoy, or makes the possessor's enjoyment less useful, even if the disseisor does not expel the possessor altogether. Co. Litt. 331.

Dissimilium dissimilis est ratio. Of dissimilars the rule is dissimilar.

Dissimulatione tollitur injuria. Injury is wiped out by reconciliation.

Distinguenda sunt tempora; aliud est facere, aliud perficere. Times must be distinguished; it is one thing to do a thing, another to complete it.

Distinguenda sunt tempora; distingue tempora, et concordabis leges. Times are to be distinguished; distinguish times, and you will harmonize laws.

Divinatio, non interpretatio, est quae omnino recedit a litera. It is a guess, not interpretation, that altogether departs from the letter.

Divortium dicitur a divertendo, quia vir divertitur ab uxore. Divorce is so called from divertendo, because a man is diverted from his wife.

Dolo facit qui petit quod redditurus est. A person acts with deceit who seeks what he will have to return.

Dolo malo pactum se non servaturum. An agreement induced by fraud will not preserve itself (will not stand).

Dolosus versatur in generalibus. A deceiver deals in generalities.

Dolum ex indiciis perspicuis probari convenit. Fraud should be proved by clear proofs.

Dolus auctoris non nocet successori. The fraud of a predecessor does not prejudice the successor.

Dolus circuitu non purgatur. Fraud is not purged by circuity.

Dolus est machinatio, cum aliud dissimulat aliud agit. Deceit is an artifice, since it pretends one thing and does another.

Dolus et fraus nemini patrocinentur (patrocinari debent). Deceit and fraud should excuse or benefit no one (they themselves require some excuse).

Dolus latet in generalibus. Fraud lurks in generalities.

Dolus versatur in generalibus. Fraud deals in generalities.

Dominium non potest esse in pendenti. The right of property cannot be in abeyance.

Dominus capitalis loco haeredis habetur, quoties per defectum vel delictum extinguitur sanguis sui tenentis. The supreme lord takes the place of the heir, as often as the blood of the tenant is extinct through deficiency or crime.

Dominus non maritabit pupillum nisi semel. A lord cannot give a ward in marriage but once.

Dominus rex nullum habere potest parem, multo minus superiorem. The king cannot have an equal, much less a superior.

Domus sua cuique est tutissimum refugium. Everyone's house is his safest refuge.

Domus tutissimum cuique refugium atque receptaculum sit. Everyone's house should be his safest refuge and shelter.

Dona clandestina sunt semper suspiciosa. Clandestine gifts are always suspicious.

Donari videtur quod nullo jure cogente conceditur. That is considered to be given which is granted when no law compels.

Donatio non praesumitur. A gift is not presumed.

Donationum alia perfecta, alia incepta et non perfecta; ut si donatio lecta fuit et concessa, ac traditio nondum fuerit subsecuta. Some gifts are perfect, others incipient and not perfect; for example, if a gift were read and agreed to, but delivery had not then followed.

Donatio perficitur possessione accipientis. A gift is rendered complete by the possession of the receiver.

Donatio principis intelligitur sine praejudicio tertii. A gift of the prince is understood without prejudice to a third party.

Donator nunquam desinit possidere antequam donatarius incipiat possidere. A donor never ceases to have possession until the donee obtains possession.

Dormiunt aliquando leges, nunquam moriuntur. Laws sometimes sleep but never die.

Dos de dote peti non debet. Dower ought not to be sought from dower.

Dos rationabilis vel legitima est cujuslibet mulieris de quocunque tenemento tertia pars omnium terrarum et tenementorum, quae vir suus tenuit in dominio suo ut de feodo, etc. Reasonable or legitimate dower belongs to every woman of a third part of all the lands and tenements of which her husband was seised in his demesne, as of fee, etc.

Doti lex favet; praemium pudoris est, ideo parcatur. The law favors dower; it is the reward of chastity; therefore let it be preserved.

Do ut des. I give that you may give.

Do ut facias. I give that you may do.

Droit ne done pluis que soit demaunde. The law gives no more than is demanded.

Droit ne poet pas morier. Right cannot die.

Duas uxores eodem tempore habere non licet. It is not lawful to have two wives at one time.

Duo non possunt in solido unam rem possidere. Two cannot possess one thing each in entirety.

Duorum in solidum dominium vel possessio esse non potest. Ownership or possession in entirety cannot belong to two persons.

Duo sunt instrumenta ad omnes res aut confirmandas aut impugnandas, ratio et auctoritas. There are two instruments for confirming or impugning everything: reason and authority.

Duplicationem possibilitatis lex non patitur. The law does not allow a duplication of possibility.

Eadem causa diversis rationibus coram judicibus ecclesiasticis et secularibus ventilatur. The same cause is argued upon different principles before ecclesiastical and secular judges.

Eadem est ratio, eadem est lex. (If) the reason is the same, the law is the same.

Eadem mens praesumitur regis quae est juris et quae esse debet, praesertim in dubiis. The mind of the sovereign is presumed to be the same as that of the law, and the same as what it ought to be, especially in ambiguous matters.

Ea est accipienda interpretatio quae vitio caret. That interpretation is to be received that is free from fault.

Ea quae commendandi causa in venditionibus dicuntur, si palam appareant venditorem non obligant. Those things that, by way of commendation, are stated at sales, if they are openly apparent, do not bind the seller.

Ea quae dari impossibilia sunt, vel quae in rerum natura non sunt, pro non adjectis habentur. Those things that cannot be given, or that are not in the nature of things, are considered as not added (as no part of the agreement).

Ea quae in curia nostra rite acta sunt debitae executioni demandari debent. Those things that are properly transacted in our court ought to be committed to a due execution.

Ea quae raro accidunt non temere in agendis negotiis computantur. Those things that rarely happen are not to be taken into account in the transaction of business, without sufficient reason.

Ecclesia ecclesiae decima solvere non debet. A church should not pay tithes to a church.

Ecclesia est domus mansionalis omnipotentis dei. The church is the mansionhouse of the omnipotent God.

Ecclesia est infra aetatem et in custodia domini regis, qui tenetur jura et haereditates ejusdem manu tenere et defendere. The church is underage and in the custody of the king, who is bound to uphold and defend its rights and inheritances.

Ecclesia fungitur vice minoris; meliorem conditionem suam facere potest, deteriorem nequaquam. The church enjoys the privilege of a minor; it can make its own condition better but not worse.

Ecclesiae magis favendum est quam personae. The church is to be more favored than the parson (or an individual).

Ecclesia non moritur. The church does not die.

Effectus sequitur causam. The effect follows the cause.

Ei incumbit probatio qui dicit, non qui negat. The burden of the proof rests upon the person who affirms, not the one who denies.

Ei nihil turpe, cui nihil satis. Nothing is immoral to the person to whom nothing is enough.

Eisdem modis dissolvitur obligatio quae nascitur ex contractu, vel quasi, quibus contrahitur. An obligation that arises from a contract or quasi contract is dissolved in the same ways in which it is contracted.

Ejus est interpretari cujus est condere. It is that person's to interpret whose it is to enact.

Ejus est nolle, qui potest velle. A person who can will (exercise volition) has a right to refuse to will (withhold consent).

Ejus est non nolle qui potest velle. A person may consent tacitly who can consent expressly.

Ejus est periculum cujus est dominium aut commodum. He who has the dominion or advantage has the risk.

Ejus nulla culpa est cui parere necesse sit. No guilt attaches to a person who is compelled to obey.

Electa una via, non datur recursus ad alteram. When one way has been chosen, no recourse is given to another.

Electio est interna libera et spontanea separatio unius rei ab alia, sine compulsione, consistens in animo et voluntate. Election is an internal, free, and spontaneous separation of one thing from another, without compulsion, consisting in intention and will.

Electiones fiant rite et libere sine interruptione aliqua. Let elections be made in due form and freely, without any interruption.

Electio semel facta, et placitum testatum, non patitur regressum. An election once made, and a plea witnessed (or intent shown), allows no going back.

Emptor emit quam minimo potest; venditor vendit quam maximo potest. The buyer buys for as little as possible; the vendor sells for as much as possible.

En eschange il covient que les estates soient egales. In an exchange it is desirable that the estates be equal.

Enitia pars semper praeferenda est propter privilegium aetatis. The part of the elder sister is always to be preferred on account of the privilege of age.

Enumeratio infirmat regulam in casibus non enumeratis. Enumeration disaffirms the rule in cases not enumerated.

Enumeratio unius est exclusio alterius. Specification of one thing is an exclusion of the other.

Eodem ligamine quo ligatum est dissolvitur. An obligation is dissolved by the same bond by which it is contracted.

Eodem modo quo oritur, eodem modo dissolvitur. It is discharged in the same way as it is created.

Eodem modo quo quid constituitur, dissolvitur. In the same way as anything is constituted, it is dissolved (or destroyed). 6 Coke 53.

Equitas sequitur legem. Equity follows the law.

Errores ad sua principia referre est refellere. To refer errors to their origin is to refute them.

Errores scribentis nocere non debent. The mistakes of the scribe (or copyist) ought to do no harm.

Error fucatus nuda veritate in multis est probabilior; et saepenumero rationibus vincit veritatem error. Error artfully colored is in many instances more probable than naked truth; and frequently error conquers truth by argumentation.

Error juris nocet. An error of law injures.

Error nominis nunquam nocet, si de identitate rei constat. Mistake in the name never injures if the identity of the thing is certain.

Error qui non resistitur approbatur. An error that is not resisted is approved.

Error scribentis nocere non debet. The error of a scribe (or copyist) ought not to injure.

Erubescit lex filios castigare parentes. The law blushes when children correct their parents.

Est aliquid quod non oportet etiam si licet; quicquid vero non licet certe non oportet. There is that which is not proper, even though permitted; but whatever is not permitted is certainly not proper.

Est autem jus publicum et privatum quod ex naturalibus praeceptis aut gentium aut civilibus est collectum; et quod in jure scripto jus appellatur, id in lege Angliae rectum esse dicitur. Public and private law is that which is collected either from natural precepts of the (law of) nations or from civil precepts; and that which in the civil law is called jus is said in the law of England to be right. Co. Litt. 558.

Est autem vis legem simulans. Violence may also put on the mask of law.

Est boni judicis ampliare jurisdictionem. It is the role of a good judge to extend the jurisdiction.

Est ipsorum legislatorum tanquam viva vox. The voice of the legislators themselves is like a living voice. • That is, the provisions of a statute are to be understood and interpreted as practical rules for real circumstances. Coke adds, *Rebus et non verbis legem imponimus*. 10 Coke 101.

Estoveria sunt ardendi, arandi, construendi et claudendi. Estovers (tenants' rights to material at hand) are for burning, plowing, building, and fencing.

Est quiddam perfectius in rebus licitis. There is something more perfect in things that are permitted.

Eum qui nocentem infamat, non est aequum et bonum ob eam rem condemnari; delicta enim nocentium nota esse oportet et expedit. It is not just and proper that one who speaks ill of a bad person should be condemned on that account; for it is fitting and expedient that the wrongdoings of bad people should be known.

Eventus varios res nova semper habet. A novel matter always produces various results.

Ex antecedentibus et consequentibus fit optima interpretatio. The best interpretation is made from what precedes and what follows.

Exceptio ejus rei cujus petitur dissolutio nulla est. There is no exception based on the very matter for which a solution is being sought.

Exceptio falsi est omnium ultima. The exception for falsehood is last of all.

Exceptio firmat regulam in casibus non exceptis. An exception affirms the rule in cases not excepted.

Exceptio firmat regulam in contrarium. An exception affirms an opposite rule.

Exceptio nulla est versus actionem quae exceptionem perimit. There is no exception against an action that extinguishes the exception.

Exceptio probat regulam de rebus non exceptis. An exception proves a rule concerning things not excepted.

Exceptio quae firmat legem exponit legem. An exception that confirms the law expounds the law.

Exceptio quoque regulam declarat. The exception also declares the rule.

Exceptio semper ultima ponenda est. An exception is always to be put last.

Excessus in jure reprobatur. Excess in law is condemned.

Excessus in re qualibet jure reprobatur communi. Excess in anything at all is condemned by common law.

Excusat aut extenuat delictum in capitalibus, quod non operatur idem in civilibus. That excuses or extenuates a wrong in capital causes which does not have the same effect in civil suits.

Ex diuturnitate temporis omnia praesumuntur solenniter esse acta. From length of time, all things are presumed to have been done in due form.

Ex dolo malo non oritur actio. An action does not arise from a fraud.

Executio est executio juris secundum judicium. Execution is the execution of the law according to the judgment.

Executio est finis et fructus legis. Execution of the law is its end and fruition.

Executio legis non habet injuriam. Execution of the law cannot work an injury.

Ex facto jus oritur. The law arises out of the fact.

Ex frequenti delicto augetur poena. Punishment increases with repeated offense. 2 Co. Inst. 479.

Ex maleficio non oritur contractus. A contract does not arise out of an illegal act.

Ex malis moribus bonae leges natae sunt. Good laws are born from evil morals.

Ex multitudine signorum colligitur identitas vera. From a great number of signs true identity is ascertained.

Ex nihilo nihil fit. From nothing nothing comes.

Ex nudo pacto non oritur actio. No action arises on a contract without a consideration.

Ex pacto illicito non oritur actio. From an illicit contract no action arises.

Expedit rei publicae ne sua re quis male utatur. It is to the advantage of the state that a person should not make bad use of his own property.

Expedit rei publicae ut sit finis litium. It is to the advantage of the state that there should be a limit to litigation.

Experientia per varios actus legem facit. Experience through various acts makes law.

Expositio quae ex visceribus causae nascitur, est aptissima et fortissima in lege. An exposition that springs from the vitals of a cause is the fittest and most powerful in law.

Expressa nocent, non expressa non nocent. Things expressed do harm; things not expressed do not.

Expressa non prosunt quae non expressa proderunt. There is no benefit in expressing what will benefit when unexpressed.

Expressio eorum quae tacite insunt nihil operatur. The expression of those things that are tacitly implied is of no consequence.

Expressio unius est exclusio alterius. The expression of one thing is the exclusion of another. • Also termed *Inclusio unius est exclusio alterius* or *enumeratio unius est exclusio alterius*.

Expressum facit cessare tacitum. Something expressed nullifies what is unexpressed.

Ex procedentibus et consequentibus optima fit interpretatio. The best interpretation is made from things proceeding and following (i.e., the context).

Exterus non habet terras. An alien holds no lands.

Extincto subjecto, tollitur adjunctum. When the substance is gone, the adjunct disappears.

Ex tota materia emergat resolutio. The construction or explanation should arise out of the whole subject matter.

Extra legem positus est civiliter mortuus. An outlaw is dead as a citizen.

Extra territorium jus dicenti impune non paretur. One who gives a judgment outside his jurisdiction is disobeyed with impunity. • There is no punishment for disobeying. Dig. 2.1.20.

Extra territorium jus dicenti non paretur impune. One who gives a judgment outside his jurisdiction is not obeyed with impunity. • Anyone who executes such a judgment may be punished. 10 Coke 77.

Extremis probatis praesumuntur media. Extremes having been proved, intermediate things are presumed.

Ex turpi causa non oritur actio. No action arises out of a wrongful consideration.

Ex turpi contractu non oritur actio. No action arises from a wrongful contract.

Facinus quos inquinat aequat. Guilt makes equal those whom it stains.

Facio ut des. I do that you may give.

Facio ut facias. I do that you may do.

Facta sunt potentiora verbis. Deeds (or facts) are more powerful than words.

Facta tenent multa quae fieri prohibentur. Deeds contain many things that are prohibited to be done.

Factum a judice quod ad ejus officium non spectat, non ratum est. A judge's act that does not pertain to his office is of no force.

Factum cuique suum, non adversario, nocere debet. Anyone's act should injure himself, not his adversary.

Factum infectum fieri nequit. What is done cannot be undone.

Factum negantis nulla probatio. No proof is incumbent on a person who denies a fact.

Factum non dicitur quod non perseverat. That is not said to be done which does not last.

Factum unius alteri nocere non debet. The deed of one should not hurt the other.

Facultas probationum non est angustanda. The capability of offering proofs is not to be narrowed.

Falsa demonstratione legatum non perimi. A legacy is not destroyed by an incorrect description.

Falsa demonstratio non nocet, cum de corpore (persona) constat. False description does not injure or vitiate, provided the thing or person intended has once been sufficiently described. • Mere false description does not make an instrument inoperative.

Falsa grammatica non vitiat concessionem. False or bad grammar does not vitiate a grant. • Neither false Latin nor false English will make a deed void when the intent of the parties plainly appears.

Falsa orthographia sive falsa grammatica non vitiat concessionem. Error in spelling or grammar does not vitiate a grant.

Falsus in uno, falsus in omnibus. False in one thing, false in everything.

Fama, fides, et oculus non patiuntur ludum. Reputation, plighted faith, and eyesight do not endure deceit.

Fama, quae suspicionem inducit, oriri debet apud bonos et graves, non quidem malevolos et maledicos, sed providas et fide dignas personas, non semel sed saepius, quia clamor minuit et defamatio manifestat. Report, which induces suspicion, ought to arise from good and grave men; not, indeed, from malevolent and malicious men, but from cautious and credible persons; not only once, but frequently, for clamor diminishes, and defamation manifests.

Fatetur facinus qui judicium fugit. A person who flees judgment confesses guilt.

Fatuus, apud jurisconsultos nostros, accipitur pro non compos mentis; et fatuus dicitur, qui omnino desipit. "Fatuous," among our jurisconsults, is applied to a man not of sound mind; one is also called "fatuous" who is altogether foolish.

Fatuus praesumitur qui in proprio nomine errat. A person is presumed to be incompetent who makes a mistake in his own name (that is, does not know his own name).

Favorabilia in lege sunt fiscus, dos, vita, libertas. The treasury, dower, life, and liberty are things favored in law.

Favorabiliores rei potius quam actores habentur. Defendants are rather to be favored than plaintiffs.

Favorabiliores sunt executiones aliis processibus quibuscunque. Executions are preferred to all other processes whatever.

Favores ampliandi sunt; odia restringenda. Favorable inclinations are to be enlarged; animosities restrained.

Felonia, ex vi termini, significat quodlibet capitale crimen felleo animo perpetratum. Felony, by force of the term, signifies any capital crime perpetrated with a malicious intent.

Felonia implicatur in quolibet proditione. Felony is implied in every treason.

Feodum est quod quis tenet ex quacunque causa, sive sit tenementum sive redditus. A fee is what anyone holds from whatever cause, whether tenement or rent.

Feodum simplex quia feodum idem est quod haereditas, et simplex idem est quod legituum vel purum; et sic feodum simplex idem est quod haereditas legitima vel haereditas pura. "Fee simple" is so called because fee is the same as inheritance and simple is the same as lawful or pure; and thus fee simple is the same as a lawful inheritance or a pure inheritance.

Festinatio justitiae est noverca infortunii. The hurrying of justice is the stepmother of misfortune.

Fiat justitia ruat caelum. Let justice be done, though the heaven should fall.

Fiat prout fieri consuevit, nil temere novandum. Let it be done as it is accustomed to be done; let no innovation be made rashly.

Fictio cedit veritati; fictio juris non est ubi veritas. Fiction yields to truth; where the truth appears, there is no fiction of law.

Fictio est contra veritatem, sed pro veritate habetur. Fiction is contrary to the truth, but it is regarded as truth.

Fictio juris non est ubi veritas. Where truth is, fiction of law does not exist.

Fictio legis inique operatur alicui damnum vel injuriam. Fiction of law works unjustly if it works loss or injury to anyone.

Fictio legis neminem laedit. A fiction of law injures no one.

Fides est obligatio conscientiae alicujus ad intentionem alterius. A trust is an obligation of conscience of one to the will of another.

Fides servanda est. Faith must be observed. • An agent must not violate the confidence reposed in him or her.

Fides servanda est; simplicitas juris gentium praevaleat. Faith is to be preserved; the simplicity of the law of nations should prevail.

Fieri non debet, sed factum valet. It ought not to be done, but if done it is valid.

Filiatio non potest probari. Filiation cannot be proved. • That is, the husband is presumed to be the father of a child born during coverture.

Filius est nomen naturae, sed haeres nomen juris. "Son" is a name of nature, but "heir" a name of law.

Filius in utero matris est pars viscerum matris. A child in the mother's womb is part of the mother's vitals.

Finis est amicabilis compositio et finalis concordia ex concensu et concordia domini regis vel justiciarum. A fine is an amicable settlement and decisive agreement by consent and agreement of our lord, the king, or his justicies.

Finis finem litibus imponit. A fine puts an end to litigation.

Finis rei attendendus est. The end of a thing is to be attended to.

Finis unius diei est principium alterius. The end of one day is the beginning of another.

Firmior et potentior est operatio legis quam dispositio hominis. The operation of law is firmer and more powerful than the will of man.

Flumina et portus publica sunt, ideoque jus piscandi omnibus commune est. Rivers and ports are public; and therefore the right of fishing is common to all.

Foeminae ab omnibus officiis civilibus vel publicis remotae sunt. Women are excluded from all civil and public charges or offices.

Foeminae non sunt capaces de publicis officiis. Women are not qualified for public offices.

Forma dat esse. Form gives being.

Forma legalis forma essentialis. Legal form is essential form.

Forma non observata, infertur adnullatio actus. When form is not observed, a nullity of the act is inferred.

Forstellarius est pauperum depressor, et totius communitatis et patriae publicus inimicus. A forestaller is an oppressor of the poor, and a public enemy of the whole community and the country.

Fortior est custodia legis quam hominis. The custody of the law is stronger than that of man.

Fortior et potentior est dispositio legis quam hominis. The disposition of the law is stronger and more powerful than that of man.

Fractionem diei non recipit lex. The law does not regard a fraction of a day.

Frater fratri uterino non succedit in haereditate paterna. A brother shall not succeed a uterine brother in the paternal inheritance.

Fraus est celare fraudem. It is a fraud to conceal a fraud.

Fraus est odiosa et non praesumenda. Fraud is odious and not to be presumed.

Fraus et dolus nemini patrocinari debent. Fraud and deceit should excuse no one.

Fraus et jus nunquam cohabitant. Fraud and justice never dwell together.

Fraus latet in generalibus. Fraud lies hidden in general expressions.

Fraus meretur fraudem. Fraud deserves fraud.

Frequentia actus multum operatur. The frequency of an act has much effect. • Continual usage establishes a right.

Fructus augent haereditatem. Fruits enhance an inheritance.

Fructus pendentes pars fundi videntur. Hanging fruits are considered part of the parcel of land.

Fructus perceptos villae non esse constat. It is agreed that gathered fruits are not a part of the farm.

Frumenta quae sata sunt solo cedere intelliguntur. Grain that has been sown is understood to belong to the soil.

Frustra agit qui judicium prosequi nequit cum effectu. A person sues in vain who cannot prosecute his judgment with effect.

Frustra est potentia quae nunquam venit in actum. Power that never comes to be exercised is useless.

Frustra expectatur eventus cujus effectus nullus sequitur. An event is vainly awaited from which no effect follows.

Frustra feruntur leges nisi subditis et obedientibus. Laws are made to no purpose except for those who are subject and obedient.

Frustra fit per plura quod fieri potest per pauciora. That is done vainly through many measures if it can be accomplished through fewer.

Frustra legis auxilium quaerit qui in legem committit. Vainly does a person who offends against the law seek the help of the law.

Frustra petis quod mox es restiturus. Vainly you seek what you are soon to restore.

Frustra petis quod statim alteri reddere cogeris. Vainly you seek what you will immediately be compelled to give back to another.

Frustra probatur quod probatum non relevat. It is useless to prove what if proved would not aid the matter in question.

Furiosi nulla voluntas est. An insane person has no will.

Furiosus absentis loco est. An insane person is considered as absent.

Furiosus nullum negotium contrahere (gerere) potest (quia non intelligit quod agit). An insane person cannot make a contract (because he doesn't understand what he is doing).

Furiosus solo furore punitur. An insane person is punished by insanity alone.

Furiosus stipulari non potest nec aliquod negotium agere, qui non intelligit quid agit. An insane person who knows not what he does cannot make a bargain or transact any business.

Furor contrahi matrimonium non sinit, quia consensu opus est. Insanity prevents marriage from being contracted, because consent is needed.

Furtum est contrectatio rei alienae fraudulenta, cum animo furandi, invito illo domino cujus res illa fuerat. Theft is the fraudulent handling of another's property, with an intention of stealing, against the will of the proprietor, whose property it had been.

Furtum non est ubi initium habet detentionis per dominium rei. There is not theft where the holder has a beginning of detention (began holding the object) through ownership of the thing.

Generale dictum generaliter est interpretandum. A general expression is to be construed generally.

Generale nihil certi implicat. A general expression implies nothing certain.

Generale tantum valet in generalibus quantum singulare in singulis. What is general has as much validity among things general as what is particular does among things particular.

Generalia praecedunt, specialia sequuntur. Things general precede; things special follow.

Generalia specialibus non derogant. Things general do not restrict (or detract from) things special.

Generalia sunt praeponenda singularibus. General things are to be put before particular things.

Generalia verba sunt generaliter intelligenda. General words are to be understood in a general sense.

Generalibus specialia derogant. Things special restrict things general.

Generalis clausula non porrigitur ad ea quae antea specialiter sunt comprehensa. A general clause does not extend to those things that have been previously provided for specifically.

Generalis regula generaliter est intelligenda. A general rule is to be understood generally.

Glossa viperina est quae corrodit viscera textus. It is a poisonous gloss that gnaws away the vitals of the text.

Grammatica falsa non vitiat chartam. False grammar does not vitiate a deed.

Gravius est divinam quam temporalem laedere majestatem. It is more serious to hurt divine than temporal majesty.

Habemus optimum testem, confitentem reum. We have the best witness, a confessing defendant.

Haeredem Deus facit, non homo. God, and not man, makes the heir.

Haeredipetae suo propinquo vel extraneo, periculoso sane custodi, nullus committatur. Let no ward be entrusted to the next heir in succession, whether his own relation or a stranger, as the next heir is surely a dangerous guardian. Co. Litt. 88b.

Haereditas est successio in universum jus quod defunctus habuerat. Inheritance is the succession to every right possessed by the late possessor.

Haereditas nihil aliud est quam successio in universum jus, quod defunctus habuerat. The right of inheritance is nothing other than the faculty of succeeding to all the rights of the deceased.

Haereditas nunquam ascendit. An inheritance never ascends.

Haeredum appellatione veniunt haeredes haeredum in infinitum. By the title of heirs, come the heirs of heirs to infinity.

Haeres est alter ipse, et filius est pars patris. An heir is another self, and a son is a part of the father.

Haeres est aut jure proprietatis aut jure representationis. A person is an heir by either right of property or right of representation.

Haeres est eadem persona cum antecessore. The heir is the same person as the ancestor.

Haeres est nomen collectivum. "Heir" is a collective noun.

Haeres est nomen juris, filius est nomen naturae. "Heir" is a term of law; "son" is one of nature.

Haeres est pars antecessoris. An heir is a part of the ancestor.

Haeres haeredis mei est meus haeres. The heir of my heir is my heir.

Haeres legitimus est quem nuptiae demonstrant. The lawful heir is the one whom the marriage indicates (i.e., who is born in wedlock).

Haeres minor uno et viginti annis non respondebit, nisi in casu dotis. An heir under 21 years of age is not answerable, except in the matter of the dower.

Hoc servabitur quod initio convenit. That shall be preserved which is useful in the beginning.

Home ne sera puny pur suer des briefes en court le roy, soit il a droit ou a tort. A person shall not be punished for suing out writs in the king's court, whether the person is right or wrong.

Hominum causa jus constitutum est. Law was established for the benefit of humankind.

Homo potest esse habilis et inhabilis diversis temporibus. A person may be capable and incapable at different times.

Homo vocabulum est naturae; persona juris civilis. "Man" (homo) is a term of nature; "person" (persona), a term of civil law.

Hora non est multum de substantia negotii, licet in appello de ea aliquando fiat mentio. The hour is not of much consequence to the substance of business, although in appeal it is sometimes mentioned.

Hostes sunt qui nobis vel quibus nos bellum decernimus; caeteri proditores vel praedones sunt. Enemies are those upon whom we declare war, or who declare it against us; all others are traitors or pirates.

Ibi semper debet fieri triatio ubi juratores meliorem possunt habere notitiam. A trial should always be held where the jurors can have the best information.

Id certum est quod certum reddi potest. That is certain which can be made certain.

Id certum est quod certum reddi potest, sed id magis certum est quod de semetipso est certum. That is certain which can be made certain, but that is more certain which is certain of itself.

Idem agens et patiens esse non potest. The same person cannot be both agent and patient (i.e., the doer and person to whom the thing is done).

Idem est facere et nolle prohibere cum possis. It is the same thing to commit an act and to refuse to prohibit it when you can.

Idem est facere et non prohibere cum possis; et qui non prohibit cum prohibere possit in culpa est (aut jubet). It is the same thing to commit an act and not to prohibit it when you can; and he who does not prohibit when he can prohibit is at fault (or does the same as ordering it to be done).

Idem est nihil dicere et insufficienter dicere. It is the same thing to say nothing and not to say enough. • To say a thing in an insufficient manner is the same as not to say it at all. Applied to the plea of a prisoner.

Idem est non esse et non apparere. It is the same thing not to be as not to appear. • What does not appear on the record is considered nonexistent.

Idem est non probari et non esse; non deficit jus sed probatio. It is the same thing not to be proved and not to exist; the law is not deficient but the proof.

Idem est scire aut scire debere aut potuisse. To be bound to know or to have been able to know is the same as to know.

Idem non esse et non apparere. It is the same thing not to exist and not to appear.

Idem semper antecedenti proximo refertur. Idem (the same) always refers to the nearest antecedent.

Identitas vera colligitur ex multitudine signorum. True identity is collected from a great number of signs.

Id perfectum est quod ex omnibus suis partibus constat. That is perfect which is complete in all its parts.

Id possumus quod de jure possumus. We are able to do that which we can do lawfully.

Id quod est magis remotum non trahit ad se quod est magis junctum, sed e contrario in omni casu. That which is more removed does not draw to itself what is more closely joined, but to the contrary in every case.

Id quod nostrum est sine facto nostro ad alium transferri non potest. What belongs to us cannot be transferred to another without our act (or deed).

Id solum nostrum quod debitis deductis nostrum est. That alone is ours which is ours after debts have been deducted.

Id tantum possumus quod de jure possumus. We can do only what we can lawfully do.

Ignorantia eorum quae quis scire tenetur non excusat. Ignorance of those things that anyone is bound to know does not excuse.

Ignorantia excusatur non juris sed facti. Ignorance of fact is excused but not ignorance of law.

Ignorantia facti excusat, ignorantia juris non excusat. Ignorance of fact excuses; ignorance of law does not excuse. • Every person must be considered cognizant of the law; otherwise, there is no limit to the excuse of ignorance.

Ignorantia judicis est calamitas innocentis. The ignorance of the judge is the misfortune of the innocent.

Ignorantia juris non excusat. Ignorance of the law does not excuse.

Ignorantia juris quod quisque scire tenetur neminem excusat. Ignorance of the law, which everyone is bound to know, excuses no one.

Ignorantia juris sui non praejudicat juri. Ignorance of one's right does not prejudice the right.

Ignorantia legis neminem excusat. Ignorance of law excuses no one.

Ignorantia praesumitur ubi scientia non probatur. Ignorance is presumed where knowledge is not proved.

Ignorare legis est lata culpa. To be ignorant of the law is gross neglect of it.

Ignoratis terminis artis, ignoratur et ars. Where the terms of an art are unknown, the art is also unknown.

Ignoscitur ei qui sanguinem suum qualiter redemptum voluit. A person is forgiven who chose to purchase his own blood (or life) upon any terms whatsoever. • Whatever a person may do under the fear of losing life or limb will not be held binding upon him in law. 1 Bl. Com. 127.

Illud quod alias licitum non est, necessitas facit licitum, et necessitas inducit privilegium quod jure privatur. That which is not otherwise lawful, necessity makes lawful; and necessity brings in as a privilege what is denied by right. 10 Coke 61.

Illud quod alteri unitur extinguitur, neque amplius per se vacare licet. That which is united to another is extinguished, nor can it again be detached.

Immobilia situm sequuntur. Immovables follow (the law of) their locality.

Imperii majestas est tutelae salus. The majesty of the empire is the safety of its protection.

Imperitia culpae annumeratur. Unskillfulness is considered a fault (as blamable conduct or neglect).

Imperitia est maxima mechanicorum poena. Unskillfulness is the greatest punishment of mechanics (i.e., from its effect in making them liable to those by whom they are employed).

Impersonalitas non concludit nec ligat. Impersonality neither concludes nor binds.

Impius et crudelis judicandus est qui libertati non favet. A person is to be judged impious and cruel who does not favor liberty.

Impossibilium nulla obligatio est. There is no obligation to perform impossible things.

Impotentia excusat legem. Powerlessness excuses (or dispenses with) law. • The impossibility of doing what is required by the law excuses nonperformance or nonenforcement. 2 Bl. Com. 127.

Impunitas continuum affectum tribuit delinquendi. Impunity provides a constant inclination to wrongdoing. 4 Coke 45.

Impunitas semper ad deteriora invitat. Impunity invites (an offender) to ever worse offenses.

In aequali jure melior est conditio possidentis. When the parties have equal rights, the condition of the possessor is the better.

In alta proditione nullus potest esse accessorius sed principalis solummodo. In high treason no one can be an accessory but only a principal.

In alternativis electio est debitoris. The debtor has the choice among alternatives.

In ambigua voce legis ea potius accipienda est significatio quae vitio caret; praesertim cum etiam voluntas legis ex hoc colligi possit. In an ambiguous expression of the law, the meaning will be preferred that is free of defect, especially when the intent of the law can be gathered from it.

In ambiguis casibus sempter praesumitur pro rege. In doubtful cases the presumption is always in favor of the king.

In ambiguis orationibus maxime sententia spectanda est ejus qui eas protulisset. In ambiguous expressions, the opinion (or meaning) of the person who made them is chiefly to be regarded.

In ambiguo sermone non utrumque dicimus sed id duntaxat quod volumus. When the language we use is ambiguous, we do not use it in a double sense, but merely in the sense that we intend.

In Anglia non est interregnum. In England there is no interregnum. • The heir to the throne is understood to succeed from the instant of his predecessor's death or removal.

In atrocioribus delictis punitur affectus licet non sequatur effectus. In the more atrocious crimes, the intent (or attempt) is punished even if the effect does not follow.

In casu extremae necessitatis omnia sunt communia. In a case of extreme necessity, everything is in common.

Incaute factum pro non facto habetur. An alteration done carelessly (inadvertently) will be taken as not done. Dig. 28.4.1.

Incendium aere alieno non exuit debitorem. A fire does not release a debtor from his debt.

Incerta pro nullis habentur. Things uncertain are considered as nothing.

Incerta quantitas vitiat actum. An uncertain quantity vitiates the act.

Incivile est, nisi tota lege prospecta, una aliqua particula ejus proposita, judicare vel respondere. It is improper, unless the whole law has been examined, to give judgment or advice upon any single clause of it.

Incivile est, nisi tota sententia inspecta, de aliqua parte judicare. It is improper to give an opinion on any part of a passage without examining the whole.

In civilibus ministerium excusat, in criminalibus non item. In civil matters, agency (or service) excuses, but not so in criminal matters.

In claris non est locus conjecturis. In obvious instances there is no room for conjectures.

Inclusio unius est exclusio alterius. See *Expressio unius est exclusio alterius*.

Incolas domicilium facit. Literally, the domicile makes the residents. • That is, the principal place of residence establishes legal residency. Often rendered conversely, *Incola domicilium facit* (residence creates domicile).

In commodato haec pactio, ne dolus praestetur, rata non est. In a loan for use (*commodatum*), a pact excluding liability for fraud is invalid. • Often extended to contracts for loans in general. Dig. 13.6.17.

Incommodum non solvit argumentum. An inconvenience does not solve (or demolish) an argument.

In conjunctivis oportet utramque partem esse veram. In conjunctive constructions, each part must be true.

In consimili casu consimile debet esse remedium. In a similar case, the remedy should be similar.

In consuetudinibus non diuturnitas temporis sed soliditas rationis est consideranda. In customs, not length of time but the soundness of the reason should be considered.

In contractibus, benigna; in testamentis, benignior; in restitutionibus, benignissima interpretatio facienda est. In contracts, the interpretation or construction should be liberal; in wills, more liberal; in restitutions, most liberal.

In contractibus, rei veritas potius quam scriptura perspici debet. In contracts, the truth of the matter ought to be regarded rather than the writing.

In contractibus tacite insunt quae sunt moris et consuetudinis. In contracts, matters of custom and usage are tacitly implied. • A contract is understood to contain the customary clauses, although they are not expressed.

In contrahenda venditione, ambiguum pactum contra venditorem interpretandum est. In the contract of sale, an ambiguous agreement is to be interpreted against the seller.

In conventionibus, contrahentium voluntas potius quam verba spectari placuit. In agreements, the intention of the contracting parties should be regarded more than their words.

Incorporalia bello non adquiruntur. Incorporeal things are not acquired by war.

In criminalibus probationes debent esse luce clariores. In criminal cases, the proofs ought to be clearer than light.

In criminalibus sufficit generalis malitia intentionis cum facto paris gradus. In criminal cases, a general malice of intention is sufficient if combined with an act of equal or corresponding degree.

In criminalibus voluntas reputabitur pro facto. In criminal matters, the intent will be reckoned as the deed. • In criminal attempts or conspiracy, the intention is considered in place of the act. 3 Inst. 106.

Inde datae leges ne fortior omnia posset. Laws were made lest the stronger should have unlimited power.

Indefinitum aequipollet universali. The undefined is equivalent to the whole.

Indefinitum supplet locum universalis. The undefined supplies the place of the whole.

Independenter se habet assecuratio a viaggio navis. The route insured is distinct from the voyage of the ship.

Index animi sermo. Speech is the index of the mind.

Indictment de felony est contra pacem domini regis, coronam et dignitatem suam, in genere et non in individuo; quia in Anglia non est interregnum. Indictment for felony is against the peace of our lord the king, his crown and dignity, in general and not in his individual person; because in England there is no interregnum.

In disjunctivis sufficit alteram partem esse veram. In disjunctive constructions, it is sufficient if either part is true.

In dubiis benigniora praeferenda sunt. In doubtful cases, the more liberal constructions are to be preferred.

In dubiis magis dignum est accipiendum. In doubtful cases, the more worthy is to be accepted.

In dubiis non praesumitur pro testamento. In doubtful cases, there is not presumption in favor of the will.

In dubio, haec legis constructio quam verba ostendunt. In a doubtful case, the construction of the law is what the words indicate.

In dubio, pars mitior est sequenda. In a doubtful case, the gentler course is to be followed.

In dubio, pro lege fori. In a doubtful case, the law of the forum (is to be favored).

In dubio, sequendum quod tutius est. In a doubtful case, the safer course is to be followed.

In eo quod plus sit semper inest et minus. The lesser is always included in the greater.

Inesse potest donationi modus, conditio sive causa; ut modus est; si conditio; quia causa. In a gift there may be manner, condition, or cause; as (*ut*) introduces a manner; if (*si*), a condition; because (*quia*), a cause.

In expositione instrumentorum, mala grammatica, quod fieri potest, vitanda est. In the construction of instruments, bad grammar is to be avoided as much as possible.

In facto quod se habet ad bonum et malum magis de bona quam de malo lex intendit. In an act (or deed) that may be considered good or bad, the law looks more to the good than to the bad.

Infans non multum a furioso distat. An infant does not differ much from a lunatic.

In favorabilibus magis attenditur quod prodest quam quod nocet. In things favored, what does good is more regarded than what does harm.

In favorem vitae, libertatis, et innocentiae omnia praesumuntur. All presumptions are in favor of life, liberty, and innocence.

In fictione juris semper aequitas existit. In a fiction of law there is always equity. • A legal fiction is always consistent with equity.

In fictione juris semper subsistit aequitas. In a legal fiction equity always abides (or prevails).

Infinitum in jure reprobatur. That which is endless is condemned in law.

In generalibus versatur error. Error dwells in general expressions.

In genere quicunque aliquid dicit, sive actor sive reus, necesse est ut probat. In general, whoever alleges anything, whether plaintiff or defendant, must prove it.

In haeredes non solent transire actiones quae poenales ex maleficio sunt. Penal actions arising from anything of a criminal nature do not pass to heirs.

In his enim quae sunt favorabilia animae, quamvis sunt damnosa rebus, fiat aliquando extentio statuti. In things that are favorable to the spirit, though injurious to property, an extension of the statute should sometimes be made.

In his quae de jure communi omnibus conceduntur, consuetudo alicujus patriae vel loci non est alleganda. In those things that by common right are conceded to all, the custom of a particular country or place is not to be adduced.

Iniquissima pax est anteponenda justissimo bello. The most unjust peace is to be preferred to the justest war.

Iniquum est alios permittere, alios inhibere mercaturam. It is inequitable to permit some to trade and to prohibit others to do so.

Iniquum est aliquem rei sui esse judicem. It is unjust for anyone to be judge in his own cause.

Iniquum est ingenuis hominibus non esse liberam rerum suarum alienationem. It is unjust for freeborn individuals not to have the free disposal of their own property.

In judiciis minori aetati succurritur. In judicial proceedings, allowance is made for a minor (in age).

In judicio non creditur nisi juratis. In court no one is trusted except those sworn.

In jure non remota causa, sed proxima, spectatur. In law, the proximate, and not the remote, cause is regarded.

Injuria fit ei cui convicium dictum est, vel de eo factum carmen famosum. An injury is done to the person of whom an insult was said, or concerning whom an infamous song was made.

Injuria non excusat injuriam. A wrong does not excuse a wrong.

Injuria non praesumitur. A wrong is not presumed.

Injuria propria non cadet beneficium facientis. No benefit shall accrue to a person from his own wrongdoing.

Injuria servi dominum pertingit. The servant's wrongdoing reaches the master. • The master is liable for injury done by his servant.

Injustum est, nisi tota lege inspecta, de una aliqua ejus particula proposita judicare vel respondere. It is unjust to give judgment or opinion concerning any particular clause of a law without having examined the whole law.

In majore summa continetur minor. In the greater sum is contained the less.

In maleficiis voluntas spectatur, non exitus. In criminal offenses, the intention is regarded, not the event.

In maleficio ratihabitio mandato comparatur. In delict (or tort), ratification is equivalent to authorization. Dig. 43.16.1.15.

In maxima potentia minima licentia. In the greatest power there is the least license.

In mercibus illicitis non sit commercium. Let there be no commerce in illicit goods.

In novo casu novum remedium apponendum est. In a novel case a new legal remedy must be applied.

In obscuris inspici solere quod verisimilius est, aut quod plerumque fieri solet. In obscure cases it is usual to regard what is more probable or what is more often done.

In obscuris quod minimum est sequimur. In obscure cases, we follow what is least so.

In odium spoliatoris omnia praesumuntur. Everything is presumed to the prejudice of the despoiler.

In omni actione ubi duae concurrunt districtiones, videlicet in rem et in personam, illa districtio tenenda est quae magis timetur et magis ligat. In every action where two distresses (or forms of distraint) concur, that is in rem and in personam, the distraint is to be chosen that is more dreaded and that binds more firmly. Bracton 372.

In omnibus contractibus, sive nominatis sive innominatis, permutatio continetur. In all contracts, whether express or implied, there must be something given in exchange. 2 Bl. Com. 444.

In omnibus (fere) poenalibus judiciis, et aetati et imprudentiae succurritur. In almost all penal judgments, allowance is made for age (or youth) and lack of discretion. Dig. 50.17.108.

In omnibus obligationibus, in quibus dies non ponitur, praesenti die debetur. In all obligations, when no date is fixed (for performance), the thing is due the same day.

In omnibus quidem, maxime tamen in jure, aequitas spectanda sit. In all affairs indeed, but especially in those that concern the administration of justice, equity should be regarded.

In omni re nascitur res quae ipsam rem exterminat. In everything, the thing is born that ends the thing itself.

In pari causa possessor potior haberi debet. When two parties have equal claims, the possessor should be considered the stronger.

In pari causa potior est conditio possidentis. When two parties have equal claims, the position of the possessor is the stronger.

In pari delicto melior est conditio possidentis. When both parties are equally at fault, the position of the possessor is the better.

In pari delicto potior est conditio defendentis. Where both parties are equally in the wrong, the position of the defendant is the stronger.

In poenalibus causis benignius interpretandum est. In penal cases, the more liberal interpretation is to be made.

In praeparatoriis ad judicium favetur actori. In things preparatory to trial, the plaintiff is favored.

In praesentia majoris potestatis, minor potestas cessat. In the presence of the superior power, the minor power ceases.

In pretio emptionis et venditionis naturaliter licet contrahentibus se circumvenire. In setting the price for buying and selling, it is naturally allowed to the contracting parties to get the better of each other.

In propria causa nemo judex. No one can be judge in his own cause.

In quo quis delinquit, in eo de jure est puniendus. In whatever matter one offends, in that the person is rightfully to be punished. • Coke refers to forfeiture of the office abused. Co. Litt. 233b.

In rebus manifestis errat qui auctoritates legum allegat; quia perspicua vera non sunt probanda. A person errs who adduces authorities on the law in matters self-evident; because obvious truths need not be proved.

In re communi neminem dominorum jure facere quicquam, invito altero, posse. In common property no one of the coproprietors can do (or make) anything against the will of the other. Dig. 10.3.28.

In re dubia benigniorem interpretationem sequi non minus justius est quam tutius. In a doubtful matter, to follow the more liberal interpretation is as much the more just as it is the safer course.

In re dubia magis infitiatio quam affirmatio intelligenda. In a doubtful matter, the negation is to be understood rather than the affirmation.

In re lupanari testes lupanares admittentur. In a matter concerning a brothel, prostitutes will be admitted as witnesses.

In re pari potiorem causam esse prohibentis constat. Where the parties have equal rights (in common property), it is an established principle that the one prohibiting has the stronger cause. Dig. 10.3.28.

In re propria iniquum admodum est alicui licentiam tribuere sententiae. It is extremely unjust to assign anyone the privilege of judgment in his own cause.

In republica maxime conservanda sunt jura belli. The laws of war must be especially preserved in the state.

In restitutionem, non in poenam, haeres succedit. The heir succeeds to the restitution, not the penalty.

In restitutionibus benignissima interpretatio facienda est. The most favorable construction is to be made in restitutions.

Insanus est qui, abjecta ratione, omnia cum impetu et furore facit. The person is insane who, having cast aside reason, does everything with violence and rage.

In satisfactionibus non permittitur amplius fieri quam semel factum est. In payments, it is not permitted that more be received than has been received once for all (i.e., after payment in full).

Instans est finis unius temporis et principium alterius. An instant is the end of one time and the beginning of another.

In stipulationibus cum quaeritur quid actum sit, verba contra stipulatorem interpretanda sunt. In agreements, when there is a question whether action has been taken, the terms are to be interpreted against the party offering them. Dig. 45.1.38.18.

In stipulationibus id tempus spectatur quo contrahimus. In agreements, there is regard to the time at which we reach agreement.

In suo quisque negotio hebetior est quam in alieno. Everyone is less perceptive (of flaws) in his own business than in that of another.

Intentio caeca mala. A concealed intention is an evil one.

Intentio inservire debet legibus, non leges intentioni. The intention ought to be subject to the laws, not the laws to the intention.

Intentio mea imponit nomen operi meo. My intent gives a name to my act.

Inter alios res gestas aliis non posse praejudicium facere saepe constitutum est. It has been often decided that matters transacted between other parties cannot cause prejudice (to those who were not involved).

Inter arma silent leges. Amid the arms of war the laws are silent.

Interdum venit ut exceptio quae prima facie justa videtur tamen inique noceat. It sometimes happens that a plea that seems prima facie just is nevertheless injurious and unfair.

Interest reipublicae ne maleficia remaneant impunita. It is in the interest of the state that crimes not remain unpunished.

Interest reipublicae ne sua quis male utatur. It is in the interest of the state that no one misuse his own property.

Interest reipublicae quod homines conserventur. It is in the interest of the state that people should be protected.

Interest reipublicae res judicatas non rescindi. It is in the interest of the state that judgments already given not be rescinded.

Interest reipublicae suprema hominum testamenta rata haberi. It is in the interest of the state that a person's last will should be held valid.

Interest reipublicae ut carceres sint in tuto. It is in the interest of the state that prisons should be secure.

Interest reipublicae ut pax in regno conservetur et quaecunque paci adversentur provide declinentur. It is in the interest of the state to preserve peace in the kingdom and prudently to decline whatever is adverse to it.

Interest reipublicae ut quilibet re sua bene utatur. It is in the interest of the state that each person make good use of his own property.

Interest reipublicae ut sit finis litium. It is in the interest of the state that there be a limit to litigation.

Interpretare et concordare leges legibus est optimus interpretandi modus. To interpret and reconcile laws so they harmonize is the best mode of construction.

Interpretatio fienda est ut res magis valeat quam pereat. Such a construction should be made that the measure may take effect rather than fail.

Interpretatio talis in ambiguis semper fienda est ut evitetur inconveniens et absurdum. In ambiguities, a construction should always be found such that what is unsuitable and absurd may be avoided.

Interruptio multiplex non tollit praescriptionem semel obtentam. Repeated interruptions do not remove a prescription (or acquisition by long use) once it has been obtained.

In testamentis plenius testatoris intentionem scrutamur. In wills we examine the intention of the testator more fully.

In testamentis plenius voluntates testantium interpretantur. In wills the intentions of the testators are more fully (or liberally) construed.

Intestatus decedit qui aut omnino testamentum non fecit aut non jure fecit, aut id quod fecerat ruptum irritumve factum est, aut nemo ex eo haeres exstitit. A person dies intestate who either has made no will at all or has not made it legally, or when the will that he had made has been annulled or become ineffectual, or when there is no living heir.

In toto et pars continetur. In the whole the part also is included.

In traditionibus scriptorum (chartarum) non quod dictum est, sed quod gestum (factum) est, inspicitur. In the delivery of writings (deeds), not what is said but what is done is to be considered.

Inutilis labor et sine fructu non est effectus legis. Useless and fruitless labor is not the effect of law.

Inveniens libellum famosum et non corrumpens punitur. A person who discovers a libel and does not destroy it is punished.

In veram quantitatem fidejussor teneatur, nisi pro certa quantitate accessit. Let the surety be held for the true amount unless he agreed for a certain amount.

In verbis non verba sed res et ratio quaerenda est. In wording, it is not the words but the substance and the meaning that is to be sought.

Invito beneficium non datur. No benefit is given to one unwilling. • No one is obliged to accept a benefit against his consent. Dig. 50.17.69.

In vocibus videndum non a quo sed ad quid sumatur. In discourse it is not the point from which but the end to which it is drawn that should be regarded.

Ipsae leges cupiunt ut jure regantur. The laws themselves desire that they should be governed by right.

Ira furor brevis est. Anger is a short insanity.

Ita lex scripta est. So the law is written.

Ita semper fiat relatio ut valeat dispositio. Let the relation be so made that the disposition may stand.

Iter est jus eundi, ambulandi hominis; non etiam jumentum agendi vel vehiculum. A way is a right of going or walking for a human being, and does not include the right of driving a beast of burden or a carriage.

Judex aequitatem semper spectare debet. A judge ought always to regard equity.

Judex ante oculos aequitatem semper habere debet. A judge ought always to have equity before his eyes.

Judex bonus nihil ex arbitrio suo faciat nec propositione domesticae voluntatis, sed juxta leges et jura pronunciet. A good judge should do nothing from his own preference or from the prompting of his private desire; but he should pronounce according to law and justice.

Judex damnatur cum nocens absolvitur. The judge is condemned when the guilty party is acquitted.

Judex debet judicare secundum allegata et probata. The judge ought to give judgment according to the allegations and the proofs.

Judex est lex loquens. The judge is the speaking law.

Judex habere debet duos sales, salem sapientiae, ne sit insipidus, et salem conscientiae, ne sit diabolus. A judge should have two salts: the salt of wisdom, lest he be foolish; and the salt of conscience, lest he be devilish.

Judex non potest esse testis in propria causa. A judge cannot be a witness in his own cause.

Judex non potest injuriam sibi datum punire. A judge cannot punish a wrong done to himself.

Judex non reddit plus quam quod petens ipse requirit. The judge does not give more than the plaintiff himself demands.

Judicandum est legibus non exemplis. Judgment must be given by the laws, not by examples.

Judices non tenentur exprimere causam sententiae suae. Judges are not bound to explain the reason of their judgments.

Judicia in curia regis non adnihilentur, sed stent in robore suo quousque per errorem aut attinctam adnullentur. Let judgments in the king's court not be invalidated but remain in force until annulled by error or attaint. 2 Inst. 360.

Judicia in deliberationibus crebro maturescunt, in accelerato processu nunquam. Judgments often ripen in the course of deliberation, never in hurried proceeding. 2 Inst. 210.

Judicia posteriora sunt in lege fortiora. The later decisions are stronger in law.

Judicia sunt tanquam juris dicta, et pro veritate accipiuntur. Judgments are, as it were, the dicta (or sayings) of the law, and are received as truth.

Judiciis posterioribus fides est adhibenda. Trust should be put in the later decisions.

Judici officium suum excedenti non paretur. A judge who exceeds his office (or jurisdiction) is not obeyed.

Judici satis poena est quod Deum habet ultorem. It is punishment enough for a judge that he has God to take vengeance upon him.

Judicis est in pronuntiando sequi regulam, exceptione non probata. It is the proper role of a judge in rendering his decision to follow the rule, when the exception has not been proved.

Judicis est judicare secundum allegata et probata. It is the proper role of a judge to decide according to the allegations and proofs.

Judicis est jus dicere, non dare. It is the the proper role of a judge to state the right, not to endow it. • Generally interpreted, it is the duty of the judge to administer justice and not to make law.

Judicis officium est opus diei in die suo perficere. It is the duty of a judge to finish the work of each day within that day.

Judicis officium est ut res ita tempora rerum quaerere; quaesito tempore tutus eris. It is the duty of a judge to inquire into the timing of events as much as the matters themselves; by inquiring into the time, you will be safe.

Judicium a non suo judice datum nullius est momenti. A judgment given by a person who is not its proper judge (not in the proper jurisdiction) is of no consequence. 10 Coke 76.

Judicium est quasi juris dictum. Judgment is, as it were, a pronouncement of the right (or a saying of the law).

Judicium non debet esse illusorium, suum effectum habere debet. A judgment ought not to be illusory (or deceptive); it ought to have its proper effect. 2 Co. Inst. 341.

Judicium redditur in invitum, in praesumptione legis. In presumption of law, a judgment is given against one's will.

Judicium semper pro veritate accipitur. A judgment is always taken for truth.

Juncta juvant. Things joined together are helpful.

Jura ecclesiastica limitata sunt infra limites separatos. Ecclesiastical laws are limited within separate bounds.

Jura eodem modo destituuntur quo constituuntur. Laws are abrogated or repealed by the same means by which they are made.

Juramentum est indivisibile, et non est admittendum in parte verum et in parte falsum. An oath is indivisible; it is not to be accepted as partly true and partly false.

Jura naturae sunt immutabilia. The laws of nature are unchangeable.

Jura publica anteferenda privatis. Public rights are to be preferred to private.

Jura publica ex privato promiscue decidi non debent. Public rights ought not to be determined in confusion, from private considerations. • In Coke's example, the validity of a sheriff's warrant is not affected by a dispute among the parties. Co. Litt. 181b.

Jurare est Deum in testem vocare, et est actus divini cultus. To swear is to call God to witness, and is an act of religion.

Jura regis specialia non conceduntur per generalia verba. The special rights of the king are not granted by general words.

Jura sanguinis nullo jure civili dirimi possunt. The rights of blood (or kinship) cannot be destroyed by any civil law.

Juratores debent esse vicini, sufficientes et minus suspecti. Jurors ought to be neighbors, of sufficient means and free from suspicion (literally, less suspected).

Juratores sunt judices facti. The jurors are the judges of fact.

Juratus creditur in judicio. In judgment a person who has sworn an oath is believed.

Jure naturae aequum est neminem cum alterius detrimento et injuria fieri locupletiorem. By the law of nature, it is just that no one should be enriched to the detriment and injury of another.

Juri non est consonum quod aliquis accessorius in curia regis convincatur antequam aliquis de facto fuerit attinctus. It is not consonant to justice that any accessory should be convicted in the king's court before anyone has been attainted of the fact (i.e., under sentence of attainder for committing the act). • The accessory should not be convicted before the principal is proved guilty. 2 Co. Inst. 183.

Jurisdictio est potestas de publico introducta, cum necessitate juris dicendi. Jurisdiction is a power introduced for the public good, on account of the necessity of dispensing justice.

Juris effectus in executione consistit. The effect of law (or of a right) consists in the execution.

Juris ignorantia est cum jus nostrum ignoramus. It is ignorance of law when we do not know our own right.

Juris praecepta sunt haec, honeste vivere, alterum non laedere, suum cuique tribuere. These are the precepts of the law: to live honorably, not to injure another, to render to each person his due.

Jurisprudentia est divinarum atque humanarum rerum notitia, justi atque injusti scientia. Jurisprudence is the knowledge of things divine and human, the science of the just and the unjust. Just. Inst. 1.1.1.

Jurisprudentia legis communis Angliae est scientia socialis et copiosa. The jurisprudence of the common law of England is a social science comprehensive in scope.

Juris quidem ignorantiam cuique nocere, facti verum ignorantiam non nocere. Ignorance of law is prejudicial to everyone, but ignorance of fact is not.

Jus accrescendi inter mercatores locum non habet, pro beneficio commercii. For the good of commerce, the right of survivorship has no place among merchants.

Jus accrescendi praefertur oneribus. The right of survivorship is preferred to incumbrances.

Jus accrescendi praefertur ultimae voluntati. The right of survivorship is preferred to a last will.

Jus civile est quod sibi populus constituit. The civil law is what a people has established for itself.

Jus descendit, et non terra. A right descends, and not the land.

Jus dicere (et) non jus dare. To state the right (and) not to endow it. • Generally interpreted, to declare the law (and) not to make it.

Jus est ars boni et aequi. Law is the science of what is good and just.

Jus est norma recti; et quicquid est contra normam recti est injuria. The law is the rule of right; and whatever is contrary to the rule of right is an injury.

Jus et fraus nunquam cohabitant. Right and fraud never abide together.

Jus ex injuria non oritur. A right does not arise from a wrong.

Jus in re inhaerit ossibus usufructuarii. A right in the thing cleaves to the person (literally, the bones) of the usufructuary.

Jusjurandi forma verbis differt, re convenit; hunc enim sensum habere debet, ut Deus invocetur. The form of taking an oath differs in language, but agrees in meaning; for it ought to have this sense, that God is invoked.

Jusjurandum inter alios factum nec nocere nec prodesse debet. An oath made between third parties ought neither to hurt nor to profit.

Jus naturale est quod apud homines eandem habet potentiam. Natural right is that which has the same force among (all) mankind.

Jus non habenti tute non paretur. It is safe not to obey a person who has no right.

Jus publicum privatorum pactis mutari non potest. A public right cannot be changed by agreements of private parties.

Jus quo universitates utuntur est idem quod habent privati. The right that corporations exercise is the same as the right that individuals possess.

Jus respicit aequitatem. Law regards equity.

Jus superveniens auctori accrescit successori. An additional or enhanced right for the possessor accrues to the successor.

Justitia est constans et perpetua voluntas jus suum cuique tribuendi. Justice is a steady and unceasing disposition to render to every person his due.

Justitia est virtus excellens et Altissimo complacens. Justice is an excellent virtue and pleasing to the Most High.

Justitia firmatur solium. By justice the throne is strengthened.

Justitia nemini neganda est. Justice is to be denied to no one.

Justitia non est neganda, non differenda. Justice is not to be denied or delayed.

Justitia non novit patrem nec matrem, solum veritatem spectat justitia. Justice knows neither father nor mother; justice looks to truth alone.

Justum non est aliquem antenatum mortuum facere bastardum, qui pro tota vita sua pro legitimo habetur. It is not just to make a bastard after his death an elder child who all his life has been accounted legitimate.

Jus vendit quod usus approbavit. The law dispenses what use has approved.

La conscience est la plus changeante des régles. Conscience is the most changing of rules.

La ley favour la vie d'un home. The law favors a man's life.

La ley favour l'inheritance d'un home. The law favors a man's inheritance.

La ley voit plus tost suffer un mischiefe que un inconvenience. The law will sooner suffer a mischief than an inconvenience.

Lata culpa dolo aequiparatur. Gross negligence is equivalent to fraud.

Le contrat fait la loi. The contract makes the law.

Legatos violare contra jus gentium est. It is contrary to the law of nations to do violence to ambassadors.

Legatum morte testatoris tantum confirmatur, sicut donatio inter vivos traditione sola. A legacy is confirmed by the death of the testator, in the same manner as a gift from a living person is by delivery alone.

Legatus regis vice fungitur a quo destinatur, et honorandus est sicut ille cujus vicem gerit. An ambassador fills the place of the king by whom he is sent, and is to be honored as he is whose place he fills.

Legem enim contractus dat. The contract gives the law.

Legem terrae amittentes perpetuam infamiae notam inde merito incurrunt. Those who lose the law of the land thereby justly incur an eternal stigma of infamy.

Leges Angliae sunt tripartitae: jus commune, consuetudines, ac decreta comitiorum. The laws of England are threefold: common law, customs, and decrees of parliament.

Leges figendi et refigendi consuetudo est periculosissima. The practice of adding and annulling laws is a most dangerous one. 4 Coke pref.

Leges humanae nascuntur, vivunt, et moriuntur. Laws that humans have made are born, live, and die.

Leges naturae perfectissimae sunt et immutabiles; humani vero juris conditio semper in infinitum decurrit, et nihil est in eo quod perpetuo stare possit. The laws of nature are most perfect and immutable; but the condition of human law is an unending succession, and there is nothing in it that can stand forever.

Leges non verbis sed rebus sunt impositae. Laws are imposed on affairs, not words.

Leges posteriores priores contrarias abrogant. Subsequent laws repeal prior conflicting ones.

Leges suum ligent latorem. Laws should bind their own author.

Leges vigilantibus, non dormientibus subveniunt. The laws aid those who keep watch, not those who sleep (that is, the vigilant, not the negligent).

Legibus sumptis desinentibus, lege naturae utendum est. Where man-made laws fail, the law of nature must be used.

Legis constructio non facit injuriam. The construction of law does not do wrong.

Legis interpretatio legis vim obtinet. The interpretation of law obtains the force of law.

Legislatorum est viva vox, rebus et non verbis legem imponere. The voice of legislators is a living voice, to impose laws on (actual) affairs and not on (mere) words.

Legis minister non tenetur, in executione officii sui, fugere aut retrocedere. The minister of the law is not bound, in the execution of his office, either to flee or to retreat.

Legitime imperanti parere necesse est. One who commands lawfully must be obeyed.

Legitimus haeres et filius est quem nuptiae demonstrant. A lawful son and heir is he whom the marriage declares to be lawful.

Le ley de Dieu et ley de terre sont tout un, et l'un et l'autre preferre et favour le common et publique bien del terre. The law of God and the law of the land are all one; and both promote and favor the common and public good of the land.

Le ley est le plus haut enheritance que le roy ad, car par le ley, il mesme et touts ses sujets sont rules, et si le ley ne fuit, nul roy ne nul enheritance serra. The law is the highest inheritance that the king possesses; for by the law both he and all his subjects are ruled; and if there were no law, there would be neither king nor inheritance.

Le salut du peuple est la suprême loi. The safety of the people is the highest law.

Les fictions naissent de la loi, et non la loi des fictions. Fictions arise from the law, and not law from fictions.

Les lois ne se chargent de punir que les actions exterieures. Laws undertake to punish only outward actions.

Lex aequitate gaudet. Law delights in equity.

Lex aequitate gaudet; appetit perfectum; est norma recti. The law delights in equity: it covets perfection; it is a rule of right.

Lex aliquando sequitur aequitatem. The law sometimes follows equity.

Lex Angliae est lex misericordiae. The law of England is a law of mercy.

Lex Angliae non patitur absurdum. The law of England does not allow an absurdity.

Lex Angliae nunquam matris sed semper patris conditionem imitari partum judicat. The law of England rules that the offspring always follows the condition of the father, never that of the mother.

Lex Angliae nunquam sine parliamento mutari potest. The law of England can never be changed without (act of) parliament.

Lex beneficialis rei consimili remedium praestat. A beneficial law affords a remedy in a similar case.

Lex citius tolerare vult privatum damnum quam publicum malum. The law would sooner endure a private loss than a public evil.

Lex contra id quod praesumit probationem non recipit. The law accepts no proof against that which it presumes.

Lex deficere non potest in justitia exhibenda. The law cannot fail in dispensing justice.

Lex de futuro, judex de praeterito. The law (provides) for the future, the judge for the past.

Lex dilationes semper exhorret. The law always abhors delays.

Lex est ab aeterno. The law is from eternity.

Lex est dictamen rationis. Law is the dictate of reason.

Lex est norma recti. Law is a rule of right.

Lex est ratio summa, quae jubet quae sunt utilia et necessaria, et contraria prohibet. Law is the highest form of reason, which commands what is useful and necessary and forbids the contrary.

Lex est sanctio sancta, jubens honesta et prohibens contraria. Law is a sacred sanction, commanding what is right and prohibiting the contrary.

Lex est tutissima cassis; sub clypeo legis nemo decipitur. Law is the safest helmet; under the shield of the law no one is deceived.

Lex favet doti. The law favors dower.

Lex fingit ubi subsistit aequitas. Law creates a fiction where equity abides.

Lex intendit vicinum vicini facta scire. The law presumes that one neighbor knows the actions of another.

Lex judicat de rebus necessario faciendis quasi re ipsa factis. The law judges of things that must necessarily be done as if actually done.

Lex necessitatis est lex temporis, i.e., instantis. The law of necessity is the law of time, i.e., time present.

Lex neminem cogit ad vana seu inutilia peragenda. The law forces no one to do vain or useless things.

Lex neminem cogit ostendere quod nescire praesumitur. The law forces no one to make known what he is presumed not to know.

Lex nemini facit injuriam. The law does wrong to no one.

Lex nemini operatur iniquum, nemini facit injuriam. The law works an injustice to no one and does wrong to no one.

Lex nil facit frustra, nil jubet frustra. The law does nothing in vain and commands nothing in vain.

Lex non a rege est violanda. The law is not to be violated by the king.

Lex non cogit ad impossibilia. The law does not compel to impossible ends.

Lex non curat de minimis. The law is not concerned with matters of least consequence.

Lex non deficit in justitia exhibenda. The law does not fail in showing justice.

Lex non exacte definit, sed arbitrio boni viri permittit. The law does not define exactly, but trusts in the judgment of a good man.

Lex non favet votis delicatorum. The law does not favor the wishes of the fastidious.

Lex non intendit aliquid impossibile. The law does not intend anything impossible.

Lex non patitur fractiones et divisiones statuum. The law does not tolerate fractions and divisions of estates. 1 Coke 87a.

Lex non praecipit inutilia, quia inutilis labor stultus. The law does not command useless things, because useless labor is foolish.

Lex non requirit verificari quod apparet curiae. The law does not require that to be proved which is apparent to the court.

Lex plus laudatur quando ratione probatur. The law is more praised when it is consonant with reason.

Lex posterior derogat priori. A later statute repeals an earlier one.

Lex prospicit, non respicit. The law looks forward, not backward.

Lex punit mendaciam. The law punishes falsehood.

Lex rejicit superflua, pugnantia, incongrua. The law rejects superfluous, contradictory, and incongruous things.

Lex reprobat moram. The law disapproves of delay.

Lex respicit aequitatem. Law regards equity.

Lex scripta si cesset, id custodiri oportet quod moribus et consuetudine inductum est; et, si qua in re hoc defecerit, tunc id quod proximum et consequens ei est; et, si id non appareat, tunc jus quo urbs Romana utitur servari oportet. If the written law fails, that which is drawn from manners and custom ought to be observed; and, if that is in any manner defective, then what is next and consistent with it; and, if that does not appear, then the law that Rome uses should be followed.

Lex semper dabit remedium. The law will always give a remedy.

Lex semper intendit quod convenit rationi. The law always intends what is agreeable to reason.

Lex spectat naturae ordinem. The law regards the order of nature.

Lex succurrit ignoranti. The law assists the ignorant.

Lex succurrit minoribus. The law assists minors.

Lex uno ore omnes alloquitur. The law speaks to all with one mouth.

Lex vigilantibus, non dormientibus, subvenit. Law aids the watchful, not the sleeping.

Liberata pecunia non liberat offerentem. The return of money does not free the party presenting it (from liability).

Libertas est naturalis facultas ejus quod cuique facere libet, nisi quod de jure aut vi prohibetur. Liberty is the natural power of doing whatever one pleases, except what is prevented by law or force.

Libertas inaestimabilis res est. Liberty is a priceless good.

Libertas non recipit aestimationem. Freedom does not admit of valuation.

Libertas omnibus rebus favorabilior est. Liberty is more favored than all things.

Libertates regales ad coronam spectantes ex concessione regum a corona exierunt. Royal franchises relating to the Crown have emanated from the Crown by grant of kings.

Libertinum ingratum leges civiles in pristinam servitutem redignunt; sed leges Angliae semel manumissum semper liberum judicant. The civil laws reduce an ungrateful freedman to his original slavery; but the laws of England regard a person once manumitted as ever after free.

Liberum corpus nullam recipit aestimationem. The body of a free person allows no price to be set upon it. Dig. 9.3.7.

Liberum est cuique apud se explorare an expediat sibi consilium. Everyone is free to ascertain for himself whether a recommendation is advantageous to him.

Librorum appellatione continentur omnia volumina, sive in charta, sive in membrana sint, sive in quavis alia materia. Under the name of books are contained all volumes, whether upon paper, or on parchment, or on any other material.

Licet dispositio de interesse futuro sit inutilis, tamen potest fieri declaratio praecedens quae sortiatur effectum interveniente novo actu. Even if the grant of a future interest is inoperative, yet a declaration precedent may be made that may take effect, provided a new act intervenes.

Licita bene miscentur, formula nisi juris obstet. Lawful acts are well joined together, unless some form of law prevents it.

Ligeantia est quasi legis essentia; est vinculum fidei. Allegiance is, as it were, the essence of the law; it is the bond of faith.

Ligeantia naturalis nullis claustris coercetur, nullis metis refraenatur, nullis finibus premitur. Natural allegiance is restrained by no barriers, curbed by no bounds, compressed by no limits.

Ligna et lapides sub armorum appellatione non continentur. Sticks and stones are not contained under the name of arms.

Linea recta est index sui et obliqui; lex est linea recta. A right line is an index of itself and of an oblique; law is a right line. Co. Litt. 158b.

Linea recta semper praefertur transversali. The right line is always preferred to the collateral.

Literae patentes regis non erunt vacuae. Letters patent of the king will not be void.

Litis nomen omnem actionem significat, sive in rem, sive in personam sit. The word "lis" (a lawsuit) signifies every action, whether it is in rem or in personam.

Litus est quousque maximus fluctus a mari pervenit. The shore is where the highest wave from the sea has reached.

L'obligation sans cause, ou sur une fausse cause, ou sur cause illicite, ne peut avoir aucun effet. An obligation without consideration, or upon a false consideration, or upon unlawful consideration, cannot have any effect.

Locus contractus regit actum. The place of the contract governs the act.

Locus pro solutione reditus aut pecuniae secundum conditionem dimissionis aut obligationis est stricte observandus. The place for the payment of rent or money is to be strictly observed according to the condition of the lease or obligation.

Longa patientia trahitur ad consensum. Long sufferance is construed as consent.

Longa possessio est pacis jus. Long possession is a right of peace.

Longa possessio jus parit. Long possession begets a right.

Longa possessio parit jus possidendi et tollit actionem vero domino. Long possession produces the right of possession and deprives the true owner of his action.

Longum tempus et longus usus qui excedit memoriam hominum sufficit pro jure. Long time and long use beyond the memory of men suffice for right.

Loquendum ut vulgus, sentiendum ut docti. We should speak as the common people; we should think as the learned.

L'ou le ley done chose, la ceo done remedie a vener a ceo. Where the law gives a right, it gives a remedy to recover.

Lubricum linquae non facile trahendum est in poenam. A slip of the tongue ought not to be easily subject to punishment.

Lucrum facere ex pupilli tutela tutor non debet. A guardian ought not to make money out of the guardianship of his ward.

Lunaticus, qui gaudet in lucidis intervallis. A person is (still) a lunatic who enjoys lucid intervals.

Magis de bono quam de malo lex intendit. The law favors a good rather than a bad construction. • When an agreement's words are susceptible of both a favorable and unfavorable meaning, the former is adopted. Thus, a bond conditioned to assign all offices will be construed to apply to assignable offices.

Magister rerum usus; magistra rerum experientia. Use is the master of things; experience is the mistress of things.

Magna Charta et Charta de Foresta sont appelés les deux grandes charters. Magna Carta and the Charter of the Forest are called the two great charters.

Magna culpa dolus est. Great fault (or gross negligence) is equivalent to fraud.

Magna negligentia culpa est; magna culpa dolus est. Great negligence is fault; great fault is fraud.

Maihemium est homicidium inchoatum. Mayhem is incipient homicide.

Maihemium est inter crimina majora minimum, et inter minora maximum. Mayhem is the least of great crimes, and the greatest among small.

Maihemium est membri mutilatio, et dici poterit, ubi aliquis in aliqua parte sui corporis effectus sit inutilis ad pugnandum. Mayhem is the mutilation of a limb, and can be said (to occur) when a person is injured in any part of his body so as to be useless in a fight.

Major continet in se minus. The greater includes the less.

Majore poena affectus quam legibus statuta est non est infamis. A criminal afflicted with a greater punishment than is provided by law is not infamous. 4 Co. Inst. 66.

Major haereditas venit unicuique nostrum a jure et legibus quam a parentibus. A greater inheritance comes to every one of us from right and the laws than comes from parents.

Majori summae minor inest. The lesser is included in the greater sum.

Major numerus in se continet minorem. The greater number contains in itself the less.

Majus dignum trahit ad se minus dignum. The more worthy draws to itself the less worthy.

Majus est delictum seipsum occidere quam alium. It is a greater crime to kill one's self than another.

Mala grammatica non vitiat chartam; sed in expositione instrumentorum mala grammatica quoad fieri possit evitanda est. Bad grammar does not vitiate a deed; but in the construction of instruments, bad grammar, as far as possible, is to be avoided.

Maledicta expositio quae corrumpit textum. It is a cursed construction that corrupts the text.

Maleficia non debent remanere impunita, et impunitas continuum affectum tribuit delinquendi. Evil deeds ought not to remain unpunished, and impunity affords continual incitement to wrongdoing. 4 Coke 45.

Maleficia propositis distinguuntur. Evil deeds are distinguished by their evil purposes.

Malitia est acida, est mali animi affectus. Malice is sour; it is the quality of a bad mind.

Malitia supplet aetatem. Malice makes up for age.

Malitiis hominum est obviandum. The malicious designs of men must be thwarted. • Also found as *Malum hominum est obviandum.*

Malum non habet efficientem sed deficientem causam. Evil has not an efficient but a deficient cause.

Malum non praesumitur. Evil is not presumed.

Malum quo communius eo pejus. The more common the evil, the worse.

Malus usus est abolendus. An evil custom ought to be abolished.

Mandata licita strictam recipiunt interpretationem, sed illicita latam et extensam. Lawful commands receive a strict interpretation, but unlawful ones receive a wide and an expansive interpretation.

Mandatarius terminos sibi positos transgredi non potest. A mandatary cannot exceed the bounds of his authority.

Mandatum nisi gratuitum nullum est. Unless a mandate is gratuitous (without payment), it is not a mandate.

Manifesta probatione non indigent. Obvious facts are not in need of proof.

Maris et faeminae conjunctio est de jure naturae. The union of male and female is founded on the law of nature.

Matrimonia debent esse libera. Marriages ought to be free.

Matrimonium subsequens tollit peccatum praecedens. A subsequent marriage removes preceding fault.

Matter en ley ne serra mise en bouche del jurors. Matter of law shall not be put into the mouths of jurors.

Maturiora sunt vota mulierum quam virorum. The wishes of women are of quicker maturity than those of men. • That is, women arrive earlier at eligibility for marriage. 6 Coke 71.

Maxime ita dicta quia maxima est ejus dignitas et certissima auctoritas, atque quod maxime omnibus probetur. A maxim is so called because its dignity is chiefest and its authority is the most certain, and because it is most approved by all.

Maxime paci sunt contraria vis et injuria. The greatest enemies to peace are force and wrong.

Maximus erroris populus magister. The people are the greatest master of error.

Meliorem conditionem suam facere potest minor, deteriorem nequaquam. A minor can improve or make his condition better, but in no way worse.

Melior est causa possidentis. The cause of the possessor is preferable.

Melior est conditio defendentis. The condition of the defendant is the better.

Melior est conditio possidentis et rei quam actoris. Better is the condition of the possessor, and that of the defendant (is better) than that of the plaintiff.

Melior est conditio possidentis, ubi neuter jus habet. Better is the condition of the possessor where neither of the two has the right.

Melior est justitia vere praeveniens quam severe puniens. Justice that truly prevents a crime is better than that which severely punishes it.

Melius est in tempore occurrere quam post causam vulneratum remedium quaerere. It is better to oppose in time than to seek a remedy after a wrong has been inflicted. • Coke introduces this maxim with the phrase *ne per negligentiam damnum incurrat*: "lest he incur damage through negligence." 2 Co. Inst. 299.

Melius est jus deficiens quam jus incertum. Law that is deficient is better than law that is uncertain.

Melius est omnia mala pati quam malo consentire. It is better to suffer every wrong than to consent to wrong.

Melius est recurrere quam male currere. It is better to run back than to run wrong (or badly). • It is better to retrace one's steps than to proceed improperly.

Mens testatoris in testamentis spectanda est. In wills, the intention of the testator is to be regarded.

Mentiri est contra mentem ire. To lie is to go against the mind.

Mercis appellatio ad res mobiles tantum pertinet. The term "merchandise" belongs to movable things only.

Mercis appellatione homines non contineri. Under the name of merchandise human beings are not included.

Merito beneficium legis amittit qui legem ipsam subvertere intendit. A person deservedly loses the protection of the law who attempts to overturn the law itself.

Merx est quidquid vendi potest. Merchandise is whatever can be sold.

Meum est promittere, non dimittere. It is mine to promise, not to discharge.

Minatur innocentibus qui parcit nocentibus. A person threatens the innocent who spares the guilty.

Minima poena corporalis est major qualibet pecuniaria. The smallest bodily punishment is greater than any pecuniary one.

Minime mutanda sunt quae certam habuerunt interpretationem. Things that have had a fixed interpretation are to be altered as little as possible.

Minimum est nihilo proximum. The least is next to nothing.

Minor ante tempus agere non potest in casu proprietatis, nec etiam convenire. A minor before majority cannot act in a case of property, nor even agree.

Minor jurare non potest. A minor cannot take an oath.

Minor minorem custodire non debet; alios enim praesumitur male regere qui seipsum regere nescit. A minor ought not be guardian of a minor, for he is presumed to govern others ill who does not know how to govern himself.

Minor non tenetur respondere durante minori aetati, nisi in causa dotis, propter favorem. A minor is not bound to answer during his minority, except as a matter of favor in a cause of dower.

Minor qui infra aetatem 12 annorum fuerit utlagari non potest nec extra legem poni, quia ante talem aetatem, non est sub lege aliqua nec in decenna. A minor who is under 12 years of age cannot be outlawed nor placed beyond the law, because before such age he is not under any law nor in a decennary.

Minor septemdecim annis non admittitur fore executorem. A person under 17 years of age is not admitted to be an executor.

Minus solvit qui tardius solvit; nam et tempore minus solvitur. A person pays too little who pays too late; for, from the delay, the payment is less.

Misera est servitus ubi jus est vagum aut incertum. It is a miserable slavery where the law is vague or uncertain.

Mitius imperanti melius paretur. The more mildly one commands, the better is he obeyed.

Mobilia non habent situm. Movables have no fixed site or locality.

Mobilia personam sequuntur, immobilia situm. Movable things follow the person; immovable ones, their locality.

Mobilia sequuntur personam. Movables follow the person.

Modica circumstantia facti jus mutat. A small circumstance attending an act alters the right.

Modus de non decimando non valet. A prescription not to pay tithes is void.

Modus et conventio vincunt legem. Customary form and the agreement of the parties overcome the law. • One of the first principles relative to the law of contract. 2 Coke 73.

Modus legem dat donationi. Custom (or form) gives law to a gift.

Moneta est justum medium et mensura rerum commutabilium, nam per medium monetae fit omnium rerum conveniens et justa aestimatio. Money is the just medium and measure of all exchangeable things, for by the medium of money a suitable and just estimation of all things is made.

Monetandi jus comprehenditur in regalibus quae nunquam a regio sceptro abdicantur. The right of coining is included among those rights of royalty that are never relinquished by the kingly scepter.

Mora reprobatur in lege. Delay is disapproved of in law.

Mors dicitur ultimum supplicium. Death is called the extreme penalty.

Mors omnia solvit. Death dissolves all things.

Mortis momentum est ultimum vitae momentum. The moment of death is the last moment of life.

Mortuus exitus non est exitus. A dead issue is not issue. • That is, a child born dead is no child.

Mos retinendus est fidelissimae vetustatis. A custom of the truest antiquity is to be retained.

Mulcta damnum famae non irrogat. A fine does not impose a loss of reputation.

Multa conceduntur per obliquum quae non conceduntur de directo. Many things are conceded indirectly that are not allowed directly.

Multa fidem promissa levant. Many promises lessen confidence.

Multa ignoramus quae nobis non laterent si veterum lectio nobis fuit familiaris. We are ignorant of many things that would not be hidden from us if the reading of old authors were familiar to us.

Multa in jure communi contra rationem disputandi pro communi utilitate introducta sunt. Many things have been introduced into the common law, with a view to the public good, that are contrary to logical reasoning. Co. Litt. 70b.

Multa multo exercitatione facilius quam regulis percipies. You will perceive many things much more easily by practice than by rules.

Multa non vetat lex quae tamen tacite damnavit. The law does not forbid many things that yet it has silently condemned.

Multa transeunt cum universitate quae non per se transeunt. Many things pass with the whole that would not pass separately.

Multi multa, nemo omnia novit. Many men know many things; no one knows everything.

Multiplex et indistinctum parit confusionem; et quaestiones quo simpliciores, eo lucidiores. Multiplicity and indistinctness produce confusion: the simpler questions are, the more lucid they are.

Multiplicata transgressione crescat poenae inflictio. The infliction of punishment should increase with the repetition of the offense. Coke continues, *Ex frequenti delicto augetur poena* (q.v.). 2 Co. Inst. 479.

Multitudinem decem faciunt. Ten make a multitude.

Multitudo errantium non parit errori patrocinium. The multitude of those who err does not produce indulgence for error.

Multitudo imperitorum perdit curiam. A multitude of ignorant practitioners destroys a court.

Multo utilius est pauca idonea effundere, quam multis inutilibus homines gravari. It is much more useful to pour forth a few suitable things than to burden mankind with many useless things.

Natura appetit perfectum, ita et lex. Nature aspires to perfection, and so does the law.

Naturae vis maxima; natura bis maxima. The force of nature is greatest; (and, as some say,) nature is doubly greatest. 2 Co. Inst. 564.

Natura fide jussionis sit strictissimi juris et non durat vel extendatur de re ad rem, de persona ad personam, de tempore ad tempus. The nature of the contract of suretyship is strictissimi juris, and does not endure or should not be extended from thing to thing, from person to person, or from time to time.

Naturale est quidlibet dissolvi eo modo quo ligatur. It is natural for a thing to be dissolved in the same way in which it is bound.

Natura non facit saltum, ita nec lex. Nature makes no leap, and neither does the law.

Natura non facit vacuum, nec lex supervacuum. Nature makes no vacuum, and the law nothing purposeless.

Nec curia deficeret in justitia exhibenda. Nor should the court be deficient in showing justice.

Necessarium est quod non potest aliter se habere. That is necessary which cannot be otherwise.

Necessitas est lex temporis et loci. Necessity is the law of time and place.

Necessitas excusat aut extenuat delictum in capitalibus, quod non operatur idem in civilibus. Necessity excuses or extenuates delinquency in capital cases, but does not have the same effect in civil cases.

Necessitas facit licitum quod alias non est licitum. Necessity makes lawful what otherwise is unlawful.

Necessitas inducit privilegium quoad jura privata. Necessity creates a privilege with regard to private rights.

Necessitas non habet legem. Necessity has no law.

Necessitas publica major est quam privata. Public necessity is greater than private necessity.

Necessitas quod cogit defendit. Necessity defends what it compels.

Necessitas sub lege non continetur, quia quod alias non est licitum necessitas facit licitum. Necessity is not restrained by law; since what otherwise is not lawful necessity makes lawful.

Necessitas vincit legem. Necessity overcomes the law.

Necessitas vincit legem; legum vincula irridet. Necessity overcomes the law; it laughs at the fetters of laws.

Nec tempus nec locus occurrit regi. Neither time nor place thwarts the king.

Nec veniam effuso sanguine casus habet. Where blood has been spilled, the case is unpardonable.

Nec veniam, laeso numine, casus habet. Where the Divinity has been insulted, the case is unpardonable.

Negatio conclusionis est error in lege. The denial of a conclusion is error in law.

Negatio destruit negationem, et ambae faciunt affirmationem. A negative destroys a negative, and both make an affirmative.

Negatio duplex est affirmatio. A double negative is an affirmative.

Negligentia semper habet infortuniam comitem. Negligence always has misfortune for a companion.

Neminem laedit qui jure suo utitur. A person who exercises his own rights injures no one.

Neminem oportet esse sapientiorem legibus. No one ought to be wiser than the laws.

Nemo admittendus est inhabilitare seipsum. No one is allowed to incapacitate himself.

Nemo agit in seipsum. No one acts against himself.

Nemo alienae rei, sine satisdatione, defensor idoneus intelligitur. No one is considered a competent defender of another's property, without security.

Nemo alieno nomine lege agere potest. No one can sue at law in the name of another.

Nemo aliquam partem recte intelligere potest, antequam totum iterum atque iterum perlegerit. No one can properly understand any part of a thing until he has read through the whole again and again.

Nemo allegans suam turpitudinem audiendus est. No one testifying to his own wrong is to be heard as a witness.

Nemo bis punitur pro eodem delicto. No one is punished twice for the same offense.

Nemo cogitationis poenam patitur. No one suffers punishment for his thoughts.

Nemo cogitur rem suam vendere, etiam justo pretio. No one is bound to sell his property, even for a just price.

Nemo contra factum suum (proprium) venire potest. No one can contradict his own deed. 2 Co. Inst. 66.

Nemo damnum facit, nisi qui id fecit quod facere jus non habet. No one does damage except the person who did what he has no right to do.

Nemo dare potest quod non habet. No one can give that which he does not have.

Nemo dat qui non habet. No one gives who does not possess.

Nemo debet bis puniri pro uno delicto. No one ought to be punished twice for the same offense.

Nemo debet bis vexari pro eadem causa. No one should be twice troubled for the same cause.

Nemo debet bis vexari pro una et eadem causa. No one ought to be twice troubled for one and the same cause.

Nemo debet bis vexari, si constet curiae quod sit pro una et eadem causa. No one ought to be twice troubled, if it appears to the court that it is for one and the same cause of action.

Nemo debet esse judex in propria causa. No one should be judge in his own cause.

Nemo debet immiscere se rei alienae ad se nihil pertinenti. No one should interfere in another's business that does not at all concern him.

Nemo debet in communione invitus teneri. No one should be retained in a partnership against his will.

Nemo debet locupletari aliena jactura. No one ought to be enriched at another's expense.

Nemo debet locupletari ex alterius incommodo. No one ought to be enriched out of another's disadvantage.

Nemo debet rem suam sine factu aut defectu suo amittere. No one should lose his property without his own act or negligence.

Nemo de domo sua extrahi potest. No one can be dragged (taken by force) from his own house. Dig. 50.17.103.

Nemo duobus utatur officiis. No one should exercise two offices.

Nemo ejusdem tenementi simul potest esse haeres et dominus. No one can be at the same time heir and lord of the same tenement.

Nemo enim aliquam partem recte intelligere possit antequam totum iterum atque iterum perlegerit. No one may be able rightly to understand one part before he has again and again read through the whole.

Nemo est haeres viventis. No one is an heir of someone living.

Nemo est supra leges. No one is above the laws.

Nemo ex alterius facto praegravari debet. No one ought to be burdened in consequence of another's act.

Nemo ex consilio obligatur. No one is bound for the advice he gives.

Nemo ex dolo suo proprio relevetur aut auxilium capiat. Let no one be relieved or gain advantage by his own fraud.

Nemo ex proprio dolo consequitur actionem. No one acquires a right of action from his own wrong (or deception).

Nemo ex suo delicto meliorem suam conditionem facere potest. No one can improve his condition by his own wrong.

Nemo inauditus condemnari debet, si non sit contumax. No one ought to be condemned unheard, unless he is obstinate (in refusing to appear).

Nemo in propria causa testis esse debet. No one can be a witness in his own cause.

Nemo jus sibi dicere potest. No one can give judgment for himself.

Nemo militans Deo implicetur secularibus negotiis. No one warring for God should be troubled by secular business.

Nemo nascitur artifex. No one is born an expert. • Wisdom in the law is acquired only through diligent study. Co. Litt. 97b.

Nemo patriam in qua natus est exuere, nec ligeantiae debitum ejurare possit. No one can cast off his native land or refuse the obligation of allegiance to it.

Nemo plus commodi haeredi suo relinquit quam ipse habuit. No one leaves a greater asset to his heir than he had himself.

Nemo plus juris ad alienum transferre potest quam ipse haberet. No one can transfer to another a greater right than he himself might have. Dig. 50.17.54.

Nemo potest contra recordum verificare per patriam. No one can verify by the country against a record. • Certain matters of record cannot be contested in court. 2 Co. Inst. 380.

Nemo potest esse dominus et haeres. No one can be both owner and heir.

Nemo potest esse simul actor et judex. No one can be at the same time suitor and judge.

Nemo potest esse tenens et dominus. No one can be at the same time tenant and landlord (of the same tenement).

Nemo potest exuere patriam. No one can cast off his own country.

Nemo potest facere per alium quod per se non potest. No one can do through another what he cannot do by himself.

Nemo potest facere per obliquum quod non potest facere per directum. No one can do indirectly what he cannot do directly.

Nemo potest mutare consilium suum in alterius injuriam. No one can change his purpose to the injury of another.

Nemo potest nisi quod de jure potest. No one is able to do a thing, unless he can do it lawfully.

Nemo potest plus juris ad alium transferre quam ipse habet. No one can transfer to another a greater right than he himself (actually) has. Co. Litt. 309.

Nemo potest sibi debere. No one can owe to himself.

Nemo praesens nisi intelligat. One is not present unless he understands.

Nemo praesumitur alienam posteritatem suae praetulisse. No one is presumed to have preferred another's posterity to his own.

Nemo praesumitur donare. No one is presumed to make a gift.

Nemo praesumitur esse immemor suae aeternae salutatis, et maxime in articulo mortis. No one is presumed to be forgetful of his eternal welfare, and especially at the point of death.

Nemo praesumitur ludere in extremis. No one is presumed to trifle at the point of death.

Nemo praesumitur malus. No one is presumed to be bad.

Nemo prohibetur plures negotiationes sive artes exercere. No one is prohibited from exercising several kinds of business or arts.

Nemo prohibetur pluribus defensionibus uti. No one is forbidden to employ several defenses.

Nemo prudens punit ut praeterita revocentur, sed ut futura praeveniantur. No one who is wise gives punishment so that past deeds may be revoked, but so that future deeds may be prevented.

Nemo punitur pro alieno delicto. No one is punished for the crime or wrong of another.

Nemo punitur sine injuria, facto, seu defalta. No one is punished unless for some wrong, act, or default.

Nemo qui condemnare potest absolvere non potest. No one who can condemn is unable to acquit.

Nemo sibi esse judex vel suis jus dicere debet. No one ought to be his own judge or to administer justice in cases where his relations are concerned.

Nemo sine actione experitur, et hoc non sine breve sive libello conventionali. No one goes to trial without an action, and no one can bring an action without a writ or bill.

Nemo tenetur ad impossibile. No one is bound to an impossibility.

Nemo tenetur armare adversarium contra se. No one is bound to arm his adversary against himself.

Nemo tenetur divinare. No one is bound to foretell the future.

Nemo tenetur edere instrumenta contra se. No one is bound to produce writings against himself.

Nemo tenetur informare qui nescit sed quisquis scire quod informat. No one who is ignorant of a thing is bound to give information of it, but everyone is bound to know what he gives information of.

Nemo tenetur jurare in suam turpitudinem. No one is bound to swear to his own criminality.

Nemo tenetur prodere seipsum. No one is bound to betray himself. • In other words, no one can be compelled to incriminate himself.

Nemo tenetur seipsum accusare. No one is bound to accuse himself.

Nemo tenetur seipsum infortuniis et periculis exponere. No one is bound to expose himself to misfortune and dangers.

Nemo tenetur seipsum prodere. No one is bound to betray himself.

Nemo unquam judicet in se. Let no one ever be a judge in his own cause.

Nemo unquam vir magnus fuit sine aliquo divino afflatu. No one was ever a great man without some divine inspiration.

Nemo videtur fraudare eos qui sciunt et consentiunt. No one is considered as deceiving those who know and consent.

Neque leges neque senatus consulta ita scribi possunt ut omnes casus qui quandoque inciderint comprehendantur; sed sufficit ea quae plerumque accidunt contineri. Neither laws nor acts of senate can be so written as to include all cases that have happened at any time; it is sufficient that those things that usually occur are encompassed. Dig. 1.3.10. pr.

Ne quid in loco publico vel itinere fiat. Let nothing be done (put or erected) in a public place or way. • The title of an interdict in the Roman law.

Nigrum nunquam excedere debet rubrum. The black should never go beyond the red. • That is, the text of a statute should never be read in a sense more comprehensive than the rubric, or title.

Nihil aliud potest rex quam quod de jure potest. The king can do nothing but what he can do legally.

Nihil consensui tam contrarium est quam vis atque metus. Nothing is so opposite to consent as force and fear.

Nihil dat qui non habet. A person gives nothing who has nothing.

Nihil de re accrescit ei qui nihil in re quando jus accresceret habet. Nothing from a property accrues to a person who had no interest in the property when the right accrued. Co. Litt. 188.

Nihil dictum quod non dictum prius. Nothing is said that was not said before.

Nihil est enim liberale quod non idem justum. For there is nothing generous that is not at the same time just.

Nihil est magis rationi consentaneum quam eodem modo quodque dissolvere quo conflatum est. Nothing is more consonant to reason than that everything should be dissolved in the same way as it was made.

Nihil facit error nominis cum de corpore constat. An error in the name is nothing when there is certainty as to the person.

Nihil habet forum ex scena. The court has nothing to do with what is not before it.

Nihil infra regnum subditos magis conservat in tranquilitate et concordia quam debita legum administratio. Nothing better preserves the subjects of the realm in tranquillity and concord than a due administration of the laws. 2 Co. Inst. 158.

Nihil iniquius quam aequitatem nimis intendere. Nothing is more unjust than to extend equity too far.

Nihil in lege intolerabilius est (quam) eandem rem diverso jure censeri. Nothing in law is more intolerable than that the same case should be subject (in different courts) to different views of the law.

Nihil magis justum est quam quod necessarium est. Nothing is more just than what is necessary.

Nihil nequam est praesumendum. Nothing wicked is to be presumed.

Nihil perfectum est dum aliquid restat agendum. Nothing is perfect while something remains to be done.

Nihil peti potest ante id tempus quo per rerum naturam persolvi possit. Nothing can be demanded before the time when, in the nature of things, it can be paid.

Nihil possumus contra veritatem. We have no power against truth.

Nihil praescribitur nisi quod possidetur. There is no prescription for what is not possessed.

Nihil quod est contra rationem est licitum. Nothing that is against reason is lawful.

Nihil quod est inconveniens est licitum. Nothing that is improper is lawful. Co. Litt. 66a.

Nihil simul inventum est et perfectum. Nothing is invented and perfected at the same moment.

Nihil tam conveniens est naturali aequitati quam unumquodque dissolvi eo ligamine quo ligatum est. Nothing is so consonant with natural equity as that each thing should be dissolved by the same means as it was bound.

Nihil tam conveniens est naturali aequitati quam voluntatem domini volentis rem suam in alium transferre ratam haberi. Nothing is more conformable to natural equity than to confirm the will of an owner who desires to transfer his property to another.

Nihil tam naturale est quam eo genere quidque dissolvere quo colligatum est. Nothing is so natural as that an obligation should be dissolved by the same principle by which it was contracted.

Nihil tam naturale est quam eo genere quidque dissolvere quo colligatum est; ideo verborum obligatio verbis tollitur; nudi consensus obligatio contrario consensu dissolvitur. Nothing is so natural as to dissolve anything in the way in which it was bound together; therefore the obligation of words is taken away by words; the obligation of mere consent is dissolved by the contrary consent.

Nihil tam proprium imperio quam legibus vivere. Nothing is so becoming to authority as to live according to the law.

Nil agit exemplum litem quod lite resolvit. A precedent accomplishes nothing if it settles one dispute by raising another.

Nil facit error nominis cum de corpore vel persona constat. An error in the name is immaterial when the body or person is certain.

Nil sine prudenti fecit ratione vetustas. Antiquity did nothing without a good reason.

Nil temere novandum. Nothing should be rashly changed.

Nimia certitudo certitudinem ipsam destruit. Too great certainty destroys certainty itself.

Nimia subtilitas in jure reprobatur. Too much subtlety in law is condemned.

Nimia subtilitas in jure reprobatur, et talis certitudo certitudinem confundit. Too great subtlety is disapproved of in law, and such certainty confounds certainty.

Nimium altercando veritas amittitur. By too much quarreling truth is lost.

Nobiles magis plectuntur pecunia, plebes vero in corpore. The higher classes are more punished in money, but the lower in person.

Nobiles sunt qui arma gentilitia antecessorum suorum proferre possunt. The gentry are those who are able to produce the heraldic arms of their own ancestors.

Nobiliores et benigniores praesumptiones in dubiis sunt praeferendae. When in doubt, the more generous and kind presumptions are to be preferred.

Nobilitas est duplex, superior et inferior. There are two sorts of nobility, the higher and the lower.

Nomen est quasi rei notamen. A name is, as it were, the distinctive sign (or signifier) of a thing.

Nomen non sufficit si res non sit de jure aut de facto. A name does not suffice if the thing does not exist by law or by fact.

Nomina si nescis, perit cognitio rerum. If you do not know the names of things, the knowledge of things themselves perishes.

Nomina si nescis, perit cognitio rerum; et nomina si perdas, certe distinctio rerum perditur. If you do not know the names of things, the knowledge of things themselves perishes; and, if you lose the names, the distinction of the things is certainly lost.

Nomina sunt mutabilia, res autem immobiles. Names are mutable, but things immutable.

Nomina sunt notae rerum. Names are the marks of things.

Nomina sunt symbola rerum. Names are the symbols of things.

Non accipi debent verba in demonstrationem falsam, quae competunt in limitationem veram. Words ought not to be accepted to import a false description when they are consistent with a true definition.

Non alio modo puniatur aliquis, quam secundum quod se habet condemnatio. A person may not be punished otherwise than according to what the sentence enjoins.

Non aliter a significatione verborum recedi oportet quam cum manifestum est aliud sensisse testatorem. We must depart from the (ordinary) significance of words only when it is evident that the testator had a different understanding. Dig. 32.69. pr.

Non auditur perire volens. One who wishes to perish is not heard.

Non bis in idem (or imperative, ne bis in idem). Not twice for the same thing. • That is, a person shall not be twice tried for the same crime. This maxim of the civil law expresses the same principle as the familiar rule against "double jeopardy."

Non concedantur citationes priusquam exprimatur super qua re fieri decet citatio. Summonses should not be granted before it is expressed upon what ground a summons should be issued.

Non consentit qui errat. A person who errs does not consent.

Non dat qui non habet. A person who does not have does not give.

Non debeo melioris conditionis esse quam auctor meus a quo jus in me transit. I ought not to be in better condition than the person to whose rights I succeed.

Non deberet alii nocere quod inter alios actum esset. A person ought not to be injured by what has taken place between other parties.

Non debet actori licere quod reo non permittitur. What is not permitted to the defendant ought not to be allowed to the plaintiff.

Non debet adduci exceptio ejus rei cujus petitur dissolutio. An exception (or plea) should not be made upon the very matter of which a determination is sought (in the case at hand).

Non debet alii nocere quod inter alios actum est. A person ought not to be prejudiced by what has been done between others.

Non debet alteri per alterum iniqua conditio inferri. An unfair condition ought not to be brought upon one person by the act of another.

Non debet cui plus licet quod minus est non licere. A person who is permitted to do the greater thing ought not to be forbidden to do the lesser.

Non debet dici tendere in praejudicium ecclesiasticae liberatatis quod pro rege et republica necessarium videtur. What seems necessary for the king and the state ought not to be said to tend to the prejudice of spiritual liberty.

Non decet homines dedere causa non cognita. It is unbecoming to surrender people when no cause has been shown.

Non decipitur qui scit se decipi. A person is not deceived who knows himself to be deceived.

Non definitur in jure quid sit conatus. What an attempt is, is not defined in law.

Non differunt quae concordant re, tametsi non in verbis iisdem. Those things that agree in substance, even if not in the same words, do not differ.

Non dubitatur, etsi specialiter venditor evictionem non promiserit, re evicta, ex empto competere actionem. It is certain that even if the vendor has not given a special guarantee, an action ex empto lies against him, if the purchaser is evicted.

Non efficit affectus nisi sequatur effectus. The intention amounts to nothing unless some effect follows.

Non erit alia lex Romae, alia Athaenis; alia nunc, alia posthac; sed et omnes gentes, et omni tempore, una lex, et sempiterna, et immortalis continebit. There will not be one law at Rome, another at Athens; one law now, another hereafter; but one eternal and immortal law shall bind together all nations throughout all time.

Non est arctius vinculum inter homines quam jusjurandum. There is no closer (or firmer) link among men than an oath.

Non est certandum de regulis juris. There is no disputing rules of law.

Non est consonum rationi quod cognitio accessorii in curia christianitatis impediatur, ubi cognitio causae principalis ad forum ecclesiasticum noscitur pertinere. It is unreasonable that the cognizance of an accessory matter should be impeded in an ecclesiastical court, when the cognizance of the principal cause is admitted to appertain to an ecclesiastical court.

Non est disputandum contra principia negantem. There is no disputing against a person who denies first principles.

Non est justum aliquem antenatum post mortem facere bastardum qui toto tempore vitae suae pro legitimo habebatur. It is not just to make an elderborn a bastard after his death, who during his lifetime was accounted legitimate.

Non est novum ut priores leges ad posteriores trahantur. It is not an innovation to adapt earlier laws to later ones. Dig. 1.3.26.

Non est recedendum a communi observantia. There should be no departure from a common observance.

Non est regula quin fallat. There is no rule that may not deceive (or disappoint).

Non est reus nisi mens sit rea. A person is not guilty unless his mind is guilty.

Non est singulis concedendum quod per magistratum publice possit fieri, ne occasio sit majoris tumultus faciendi. That is not to be conceded to private persons which can be publicly done by the magistrate, lest it be the occasion of greater tumult.

Non exemplis sed legibus judicandum est. Not by examples but by the laws must judgment be made.

Non ex opinionibus singulorum, sed ex communi usu, nomina exaudiri debent. Names of things ought to be understood according to common usage, not according to the opinions of individuals.

Non facias malum ut inde veniat bonum. You are not to do evil that good may come of it.

Non impedit clausula derogatoria quo minus ab eadem potestate res dissolvantur a qua constituuntur. A derogatory clause does not prevent things from being dissolved by the same power by which they were originally made.

Non in legendo sed in intelligendo leges consistunt. The laws consist not in reading but in understanding.

Non jus ex regula, sed regula ex jure. The law does not arise from the rule (or maxim), but the rule from the law.

Non jus, sed seisina facit stipitem. Not right, but seisin, makes a stock (from which the inheritance must descend).

Non licet quod dispendio licet. That which is permitted only at a loss is not permitted.

Non nasci et natum mori paria sunt. Not to be born and to be born dead are equivalent.

Non obligat lex nisi promulgata. A law is not binding unless it has been promulgated.

Non observata forma, infertur adnullatio actus. When the form has not been observed, an annulment of the act is inferred.

Non officit conatus nisi sequatur effectus. An attempt does not harm unless a consequence follows.

Non omne damnum inducit injuriam. Not every loss produces an injury (i.e., gives a right to action).

Non omne quod licet honestum est. Not everything that is permitted is honorable.

Non omnium quae a majoribus nostris constituta sunt ratio reddi potest. Reason cannot always be given for the institutions of our ancestors.

Non pertinet ad judicem secularem cognoscere de iis quae sunt mere spiritualia an-

nexa. It belongs not to the secular judge to take cognizance of things that are merely spiritual.

Non possessori incumbit necessitas probandi possessiones ad se pertinere. It is not incumbent on the possessor of property to prove that his possessions belong to him.

Non potest adduci exceptio ejusdem rei cujus petitur dissolutio. An exception cannot be brought upon the same matter whose determination is at issue (in the action at hand).

Non potest probari quod probatum non relevat. That cannot be proved which, when proved, is irrelevant.

Non potest quis sine brevi agere. No one can sue without a writ.

Non potest rex gratiam facere cum injuria et damno aliorum. The king cannot confer a favor that occasions injury and loss to others.

Non potest rex subditum renitentem onerare impositionibus. The king cannot load a subject with impositions against his consent.

Non potest videri desisse habere qui nunquam habuit. A person cannot be considered as having ceased to have a thing who never had it.

Non praestat impedimentum quod de jure non sortitur effectum. A thing that has no effect in law is not an impediment.

Non quod dictum est, sed quod factum est, inspicitur. Not what has been said but what has been done is regarded.

Non refert an quis assensum suum praefert verbis an rebus ipsis et factis. It is immaterial whether a person gives assent by words or by acts themselves and deeds.

Non refert quid ex aequipollentibus fiat. It does not matter which of two equivalents happens.

Non refert quid notum sit judici, si notum non sit in forma judicii. It matters not what is known to the judge if it is not known to him judicially.

Non refert verbis an factis fit revocatio. It does not matter whether a revocation is made by words or by acts.

Non respondebit minor, nisi in causa dotis, et hoc pro favore doti. A minor shall not answer except in a case of dower, and here in favor of dower.

Non solent quae abundant vitiare scripturas. Superfluous expressions do not usually vitiate writings.

Non solum quid licet sed quid est conveniens considerandum, quia nihil quod inconveniens est licitum. Not only what is permitted but what is proper is to be considered, because nothing improper is lawful.

Non sunt longa ubi nihil est quod demere possis. There is no prolixity where there is nothing that you can omit.

Non temere credere est nervus sapientae. Not to believe rashly is the sinew of wisdom.

Non valebit felonis generatio nec ad haereditatem paternam vel maternam; si autem ante feloniam generationem fecerit, talis generatio succedit in haereditate patris vel matris a quo non fuerit felonia perpetrata. The offspring of a felon cannot succeed either to a maternal or paternal inheritance; but if the felon had offspring before the felony, the offspring may succeed to the inheritance of the father or mother by whom no felony was committed.

Non valet confirmatio, nisi ille, qui confirmat, sit in possessione rei vel juris unde fieri debet confirmatio; et eodem modo, nisi ille cui confirmatio fit sit in possessione. Confirmation is not valid unless the person who confirms is in possession either of the thing or of the right of which confirmation is to be made, and, in like manner, unless that person to whom confirmation is made is in possession.

Non valet donatio nisi subsequatur traditio. A gift is not valid unless delivery (or transference) follows.

Non valet exceptio ejusdem rei cujus petitur dissolutio. An exception based on the very matter of which the determination is sought is not valid.

Non valet impedimentum quod de jure non sortitur effectum. An impediment that does not derive its effect from the law has no force.

Non verbis sed ipsis rebus leges imponimus. Not upon words, but upon affairs themselves do we impose laws.

Non videntur qui errant consentire. They who err are not considered as consenting.

Non videntur rem amittere quibus propria non fuit. They are not considered as losing a thing if it was not their own.

Non videtur consensum retinuisse si quis ex praescripto minantis aliquod immutavit. If a person has changed anything at the demand of a party threatening, he is not considered to have maintained his consent.

Non videtur perfecte cujusque id esse quod ex casu auferri potest. A thing is not considered completely to belong to anyone if it can be taken from him by chance (or occasion).

Non videtur quisquam id capere quod ei necesse est alii restituere. A person is not considered to acquire property in a thing that he must restore to another. Dig. 50.17.51.

Non videtur vim facere qui jure suo utitur et ordinaria actione experitur. A person is not judged to use force who exercises his own right and proceeds by ordinary action.

Noscitur a sociis. It is known from its associates.

Noscitur ex socio qui non cognoscitur ex se. A person who is not known for himself is known from his associate.

Notitia dicitur a noscendo; et notitia non debet claudicare. Notice is named from knowledge; and notice ought not to limp (that is, be imperfect).

Nova constitutio futuris formam imponere debet, non praeteritis. A new enactment ought to impose form upon what is to come, not upon what is past. • A new regulation should not apply retroactively but from its enactment. 2 Co. Inst. 292.

Novatio non praesumitur. A novation is not presumed.

Novitas non tam utilitate prodest quam novitate perturbat. Novelty does not as much benefit by its utility as it disturbs by its novelty.

Novum judicium non dat novum jus, sed declarat antiquum. A new judgment does not make a new right, but declares the old.

Novum judicium non dat novum jus, sed declarat antiquum; quia judicium est juris dictum, et per judicium jus est noviter revelatum quod diu fuit velatum. A new judgment does not make a new right, but declares the old; because adjudication is the declaration of a right, and by adjudication the right is newly revealed which has long been hidden. 10 Coke 42.

Noxa caput sequitur. The injury follows the head or person. • Liability to make good an injury caused by a slave attaches to the master. Dig. 2.14.7.4.

Nuda pactio obligationem non parit. A naked agreement (i.e., without consideration) does not create an obligation. Dig. 2.14.7.4.

Nuda ratio et nuda pactio non ligant aliquem debitorem. Bare reason and naked agreement do not bind any debtor.

Nudum pactum est ubi nulla subest causa praeter conventionem; sed ubi subest causa, fit obligatio, et parit actionem. Naked agreement (nudum pactum) is where there is no consideration besides the agreement; but when there is a consideration, an obligation is created and it gives a right of action.

Nudum pactum ex quo non oritur actio. Naked agreement (nudum pactum) is that from which no action arises.

Nul charter, nul vente, ne nul done vault perpetualment, si le donor n'est seise al temps de contracts de deux droits, sc. del droit de possession et del droit de properite. No grant, no sale, no gift, is valid forever unless the donor, at the time of the contract, is seised of two rights, namely, the right of possession and the right of property.

Nulla curia quae recordum non habet potest imponere finem neque aliquem mandare carceri; quia ista spectant tantummodo ad curias de recordo. No court that does not have a record can impose a fine or commit any person to prison; because those powers look only to courts of record.

Nulla emptio sine pretio esse potest. There can be no sale without a price.

Nulla impossibilia aut inhonesta sunt praesumenda; vera autem et honesta et possibilia. No impossible or dishonorable things are to be presumed; but things true, honorable, and possible.

Nulla pactione effici potest ne dolus praestetur. No agreement is sufficient to effect that there be no liability for fraud. Dig. 2.14.27.3.

Nulla virtus, nulla scientia locum suum et dignitatem conservare potest sine modestia. Without moderation, no virtue, no knowledge can preserve its place and dignity.

Nulle régle sans faute. There is no rule without fault.

Nulle terre sans seigneur. No land without a lord.

Nulli enim res sua servit jure servitutis. No one can have a servitude over his own property.

Nullius hominis auctoritas apud nos valere debet, ut meliora non sequeremur si quis attulerit. The authority of no person ought to have (such) power among us that we should not follow better (opinions) if anyone presents them.

Nulli vendemus, nulli negabimus, aut differemus rectum vel justitiam. We shall sell to no one, deny to no one, or delay to no one, equity or justice.

Nullum crimen majus est inobedientia. No crime is greater than disobedience.

Nullum exemplum est idem omnibus. No example is the same for all purposes.

Nullum iniquum est praesumendum in jure. Nothing unjust is to be presumed in law.

Nullum matrimonium, ibi nulla dos. No marriage, there no dower.

Nullum simile est idem. Nothing that is like another is the same. • That is, no likeness is exactly identical.

Nullum simile est idem nisi quatuor pedibus currit. Nothing similar is identical, unless it run on all fours.

Nullum simile quatuor pedibus currit. No simile runs upon four feet (on all fours). • No simile holds in every respect.

Nullum tempus aut locus occurrit regi. No time or place bars the king.

Nullum tempus occurrit regi. Lapse of time does not bar the right of the Crown. • Literally, no time runs against the king.

Nullum tempus occurrit reipublicae. No time runs against the commonwealth (or state).

Nullus alius quam rex possit episcopo demandare inquisitionem faciendam. No other than the king can command the bishop to make an inquisition.

Nullus commodum capere potest de injuria sua propria. No one can gain advantage by his own wrong.

Nullus debet agere de dolo, ubi alia actio subest. Where another form of action is given, no one ought to sue in the action de dolo.

Nullus dicitur accessorius post feloniam sed ille qui novit principalem feloniam fecisse, et illum receptavit et comfortavit. No one is called an accessory after the fact but that person who knew the principal to have committed a felony, and received and comforted him.

Nullus dicitur felo principalis nisi actor aut qui praesens est, abettans aut auxilians actorem ad feloniam faciendam. No one is called a principal felon except the party actually committing the felony, or the party who was present aiding and abetting the perpetrator in its commission.

Nullus idoneus testis in re sua intelligitur. No one is understood to be a competent witness in his own cause.

Nullus jus alienum forisfacere potest. No one can forfeit another's right.

Nullus recedat e curia cancellaria sine remedio. Let no one depart from the court of chancery without a remedy.

Nullus videtur dolo facere qui suo jure utitur. No one is to be regarded as acting by fraud who exercises his legal right.

Nul ne doit s'enrichir aux depens des autres. No one ought to enrich himself at the expense of others.

Nul prendra advantage de son tort demesne. No one shall take advantage of his own wrong.

Nul sans damage avera error ou attaint. No one shall have error or attaint unless there has been damage.

Nunquam crescit ex post facto praeteriti delicti aestimatio. The valuation (or assessment of damage) for a past offense is never increased by what happens subsequently. Dig. 50.17.138.1.

Nunquam decurritur ad extraordinarium sed ubi deficit ordinarium. One never resorts to the extraordinary but when the ordinary fails.

Nunquam fictio sine lege. There is no fiction without law.

Nunquam nimis dicitur quod nunquam satis dicitur. What is never sufficiently said is never said too much.

Nunquam praescribitur in falso. There is never prescription in case of falsehood (or forgery).

Nunquam res humanae prospere succedunt ubi negliguntur divinae. Human affairs never prosper when divine ones are neglected.

Nuptias non concubitus sed consensus facit. Not sharing a bed but consent makes the marriage.

Obedientia est legis essentia. Obedience is the essence of the law.

Obtemperandum est consuetudini rationabili tanquam legi. A reasonable custom is to be obeyed like law.

Occupantis fiunt derelicta. Things abandoned become the property of the (first) occupant.

Odiosa et inhonesta non sunt in lege praesumenda. Odious and dishonest acts are not to be presumed in law.

Odiosa non praesumuntur. Odious things are not presumed.

Officia judicialia non concedantur antequam vacent. Judicial offices ought not to be granted before they are vacant.

Officia magistratus non debent esse venalia. The offices of magistrates ought not to be sold.

Officit conatus si effectus sequatur. The attempt becomes of consequence if the effect follows.

Officium nemini debet esse damnosum. An office ought to be injurious to no one.

Omissio eorum quae tacite insunt nihil operatur. The omission of those things that are silently implied is of no consequence.

Omne actum ab intentione agentis est judicandum. Every act is to be judged by the intention of the doer.

Omne crimen ebrietas et incendit et detegit. Drunkenness both inflames and reveals every crime.

Omne jus aut consensus fecit, aut necessitas constituit, aut firmavit consuetudo. Every right has been derived from consent, established by necessity, or confirmed by custom.

Omne magis dignum trahit ad se minus dignum, quamvis minus dignum sit antiquius. Every worthier thing draws to it the less worthy, even if the less worthy is more ancient.

Omne magnum exemplum habet aliquid ex iniquo, quod publica utilitate compensatur. Every great example has some portion of evil, which is compensated by its public utility.

Omne majus continet in se minus. Every greater thing contains in itself the less.

Omne majus dignum continet in se minus dignum. Every more worthy thing contains in itself the less worthy.

Omne majus minus in se complectitur. Every greater thing embraces in itself the lesser.

Omne principale trahit ad se accessorium. Every principal thing draws to itself the accessory.

Omne quod solo inaedificatur solo cedit. Everything that is built on the soil belongs to the soil.

Omne sacramentum debet esse de certa scientia. Every oath ought to be founded on certain knowledge.

Omnes actiones in mundo infra certa tempora habent limitationem. All actions in the world are limited within certain periods.

Omnes licentiam habere his quae pro se indulta sunt renunciare. All have liberty to renounce these things that have been granted in their favor.

Omnes prudentes illa admittere solent quae probantur iis qui in arte sua bene versati sunt. All prudent people are accustomed to admit those things that are approved by those who are skilled in their profession.

Omne testamentum morte consummatum est. Every will is consummated by death.

Omnia delicta in aperto leviora sunt. All crimes committed openly are considered lighter.

Omnia praesumuntur contra spoliatorem. All presumptions are against one who wrongfully dispossesses another (a despoiler).

Omnia praesumuntur legitime facta donec probetur in contrarium. All things are presumed to be done legitimately until the contrary is proved.

Omnia praesumuntur rite et solemniter esse acta. All things are presumed to have been rightly and regularly done.

Omnia praesumuntur rite et solemniter esse acta donec probetur in contrarium. All things are presumed to have been done regularly and with due formality until the contrary is proved.

Omnia quae jure contrahuntur contrario jure pereunt. All obligations contracted under a law are destroyed by a law to the contrary.

Omnia quae sunt uxoris sunt ipsius viri. All things that are the wife's belong to her husband.

Omnia rite esse acta praesumuntur. All things are presumed to have been done in due form.

Omnis conclusio boni et veri judicii sequitur ex bonis et veris praemissis et dictis juratorum. Every conclusion of a good and true judgment follows from good and true premises and the verdicts of jurors.

Omnis consensus tollit errorem. Every consent removes an error. 2 Co. Inst. 123.

Omnis definitio in jure civili periculosa est, parum est enim ut non subverti possit. Every definition in the civil law is dangerous, for there is very little that cannot be overthrown.

Omnis exceptio est ipsa quoque regula. Every exception is itself also a rule.

Omnis indemnatus pro innoxio legibus habetur. Every uncondemned person is held by the law as innocent.

Omnis innovatio plus novitate perturbat quam utilitate prodest. Every innovation disturbs by its novelty more than it benefits by its usefulness.

Omnis interpretatio si fieri potest ita fienda est in instrumentis, ut omnes contrarietates amoveantur. Every interpretation of instruments is to be made, if it can be, so that all contradictions may be removed.

Omnis interpretatio vel declarat, vel extendit, vel restringit. Every interpretation explains, or extends, or restricts.

Omnis nova constitutio futuris (temporibus) formam imponere debet, non praeteritis. Every new statute ought to prescribe a form for the future, not the past.

Omnis persona est homo, sed non vicissim. Every person is a human being, but not every human being a person.

Omnis privatio praesupponit habitum. Every privation presupposes possession. • "Every discontinuance is a privation . . . and he cannot discontinue that estate which he never had." Co. Litt. 339a.

Omnis querela et omnis actio injuriarum limitata est infra certa tempora. Every plaint and every action for injuries is limited within fixed times.

Omnis ratihabitio retrotrahitur et mandato priori aequiparatur. Every subsequent ratification has a retrospective effect and is equivalent to a prior command.

Omnis regula suas patitur exceptiones. Every rule of law allows its own exceptions.

Omnium contributione sarciatur quod pro omnibus datum est. What has been given for all should be compensated by the contribution of all.

Omnium rerum quarum usus est, potest esse abusus, virtute solo excepta. Of everything of which there is a use, there can be abuse, virtue alone excepted.

Opinio quae favet testamento est tenenda. That opinion is to be followed which favors the will.

Oportet quod certa res deducatur in judicium. A thing, to be brought to judgment, must be definite.

Oportet quod certa sit res quae venditur. A thing, to be sold, must be definite.

Optima enim est legium interpres consuetudo. Custom is the best interpreter of laws. Dig. 1.3.37.

Optima est lex quae minimum relinquit arbitrio judicis; optimus judex qui minimum sibi. It is the best law that leaves the least to the discretion of the judge; the best judge is he who leaves least to himself.

Optimam esse legem quae minimum relinquit arbitrio judicis; id quod certitudo ejus praestat. The law is the best that leaves the least discretion to the judge; this advantage results from its certainty.

Optima statuti interpretatrix est (omnibus particulis ejusdem inspectis) ipsum statutum. The best interpreter of a statute is (when all the separate parts of it have been considered) the statute itself.

Optimus interpres rerum usus. Usage is the best interpreter of things.

Optimus interpretandi modus est sic leges interpretare ut leges legibus accordant. The best mode of interpreting laws is to make laws agree with laws.

Optimus judex qui minimum sibi. He is the best judge who (leaves) the least to his own discretion.

Optimus legum interpres consuetudo. Custom is the best interpreter of laws.

Ordine placitandi servato, servatur et jus. When order of pleading has been preserved, the law is also preserved.

Origine propria neminem posse voluntate sua eximi manifestum est. It is manifest that no one by his own will can be stripped of his origin (or be banished from his place of origin).

Origo rei inspici debet. The origin of a thing ought to be regarded.

Pacta conventa quae neque contra leges neque dolo malo inita sunt, omni modo observanda sunt. Contracts that have been entered neither illegally nor with fraud must in all respects be observed.

Pacta dant legem contractui. Agreements give law to the contract.

Pacta privata juri publico derogare non possunt. Private contracts cannot restrict (or take away from) public law.

Pacta quae contra leges constitutionesque vel contra bonos mores fiunt nullam vim habere, indubitati juris est. It is a matter of unquestionable law that contracts against the laws and statutes, or against moral standards, have no force.

Pacta quae turpem causam continent non sunt observanda. Contracts founded upon an immoral consideration are not to be observed.

Pactis privatorum juri publico non derogatur. There is no derogation from public law by private contracts.

Pacto aliquid licitum est quod sine pacto non admittitur. By agreement (or contract) something is permitted that, without agreement, is not allowed. • Coke continues, "but not in violation of public law." Co. Litt. 166.

Parens est nomen generale ad omne genus cognationis. "Parent" is a general name for every kind of relationship.

Parentum est liberos alere etiam nothos. It is the role of parents to support their children even when illegitimate.

Paria copulantur paribus. Similar things unite with similar.

Paribus sententiis reus absolvitur. When opinions are evenly divided, the defendant is acquitted. 4 Co. Inst. 64.

Par in parem imperium non habet. An equal has no power over an equal.

Parte quacumque integrante sublata, tollitur totum. When any essential part has been removed, the whole is removed (or destroyed).

Partus ex legitimo thoro non certius noscit matrem quam genitorem suum. The offspring of a legitimate bed does not know his mother more certainly than his father.

Partus sequitur ventrem. The offspring follows the condition of the mother (literally, the womb).

Parum est latam esse sententiam, nisi mandetur executioni. It is not enough that judgment has been given if it is not committed to execution.

Parum proficit scire quid fieri debet si non cognoscas quomodo sit facturum. It does little good to know what ought to happen, if you do not know how it will take effect.

Pater est quem nuptiae demonstrant. The father is the man whom the marriage indicates. • This expresses the idea that a child born to a married woman is presumed begotten by her husband.

Pater is est quem nuptiae demonstrant. The father is he whom the marriage indicates.

Patria laboribus et expensis non debet fatigari. A jury ought not to be wearied with labors and expenses.

Patria potestas in pietate debet, non in atrocitate consistere. Parental authority should consist in devotion, not dread.

Peccata contra naturam sunt gravissima. Offenses against nature are the most serious.

Peccatum peccato addit qui culpae quam facit patrocinium defensionis adjungit. A person adds one offense to another, who, when he commits a crime, joins to it the protection of a defense.

Pendente lite nihil innovetur. During litigation, let nothing be changed.

Per alluvionem id videtur adici, quod ita paulatim adicitur ut intelligere non possimus quantum quoque momento temporis adiciatur. That is considered "added by alluvion" which accumulates so gradually that we cannot tell how much is added at any one moment of time. Dig. 41.1.7.1.

Perfectum est cui nihil deest secundum suae perfectionis vel naturae modum. That is perfect which lacks nothing according to the measure of its perfection or nature.

Periculosum est res novas et inusitatas inducere. It is dangerous to introduce new and unaccustomed things.

Periculum rei venditae, nondum traditae, est emptoris. The purchaser assumes the risk for a thing sold, but not yet delivered.

Perjuri sunt qui servatis verbis juramenti decipiunt aures eorum qui accipiunt. Those who preserve the words of an oath but deceive the ears of those who accept it are perjurors. • Coke adds, "By ancient law of England, in all oathes equivocation is utterly condemned." 3 Co. Inst. 166.

Perpetua lex est nullam legem humanam ac positivam perpetuam esse; et clausula

quae abrogationem excludit ab initio non valet. It is a perpetual law that no human or positive law can be perpetual; and a clause in a law that precludes abrogation is void from the outset.

Per rationes pervenitur ad legitimam rationem. By reasoning we come to legal reason.

Per rerum naturam factum negantis nulla probatio est. By the nature of things, a person who denies a fact is not bound to give proof.

Persona conjuncta aequiparatur interesse proprio. A personal connection is equivalent to one's own interest.

Persona est homo cum statu quodam consideratus. A person is a human being considered with reference to a certain status.

Personae vice fungitur municipium et decuria. Towns and boroughs act in the role of persons.

Personalia personam sequuntur. Personal things follow the person.

Perspicua vera non sunt probanda. Plain truths are not to be proved.

Per varios actus legem experientia facit. In the course of various acts, experience frames the law.

Pirata est hostis humani generis. A pirate is an enemy of the human race.

Placita negativa duo exitum non faciunt. Two negative pleas do not form an issue.

Plena et celeris justitia fiat partibus. Let the parties have full and speedy justice.

Pluralis numerus est duobus contentus. The plural number is satisfied with two.

Plures cohaeredes sunt quasi unum corpus, propter unitatem juris quod habent. Several coheirs are as one body, by reason of the unity of right that they possess.

Plures participes sunt quasi unum corpus in eo quod unum jus habent. Several coheirs (or parceners) are as one body in that they have one right. Co. Litt. 164.

Plus exempla quam peccata nocent. Examples hurt more than offenses.

Plus peccat auctor quam actor. The instigator of a crime is a worse offender than the perpetrator.

Plus valet unus oculatus testis quam auriti decem. One eyewitness is better than ten ear-witnesses.

Plus vident oculi quam oculus. Several eyes see more than one.

Poena ad paucos, metus ad omnes perveniat. Let punishment be inflicted on a few, dread upon all.

Poenae potius molliendae quam exasperandae sunt. Punishments should rather be softened than aggravated.

Poenae sunt restringendae. Punishments should be restrained.

Poena ex delicto defuncti haeres teneri non debet. The heir ought not to be bound by a penalty for the crime of the deceased.

Poena non potest, culpa perennis erit. Punishment cannot be, guilt will be, perpetual.

Poena suos tenere debet actores et non alios. Punishment should take hold of the guilty (who commit the wrong), and not others. Bracton 380b.

Poena tolli potest, culpa perennis erit. The punishment can be removed, but the guilt will be perpetual.

Politiae legibus, non leges politiis, adaptandae. Politics are to be adapted to the laws, not the laws to politics.

Ponderantur testes, non numerantur. Witnesses are weighed, not counted.

Posito uno oppositorum negatur alterum. One of two opposite positions having been affirmed, the other is denied.

Possessio est quasi pedis positio. Possession is, as it were, the position of the foot.

Possessio fratris de feodo simplici facit sororem esse haeredem. Possession by the brother in fee simple makes the sister an heir.

Possessio pacifica per annos 60 facit jus. Peaceable possession for 60 years gives a right.

Posteriora derogant prioribus. Later things restrict (or detract from) earlier ones.

Posthumus pro nato habetur. A posthumous child is considered as though born (before the father's death).

Postliminium fingit eum qui captus est semper in civitate fuisse. Postliminy (restoration of rights) imagines that a person who has been captured has never left the state. • A person captured by the enemy, who later returns, is restored to all his former rights. Just. Inst. 1.12.5.

Potentia debet sequi justitiam, non antecedere. Power ought to follow, not to precede, justice.

Potentia inutilis frustra est. Useless power is in vain.

Potentia non est nisi ad bonum. Power is not conferred but for the (public) good.

Potestas stricte interpretatur. A power should be strictly interpreted.

Potestas suprema seipsum dissolvere potest, ligare non potest. Supreme power can dissolve (or release), but cannot bind, itself.

Potest quis renunciare, pro se et suis, jus quod pro se introductum est. A person may relinquish, for himself and his heirs, a right that was introduced for his own benefit.

Potior est conditio defendentis. Stronger is the condition of the defendant (than that of the plaintiff).

Potior est conditio possidentis. Stronger is the condition of the possessor.

Praedium servit praedio. Land is under servitude to land. • A servitude is not a personal right, but attaches to the dominant tenement.

Praepropera consilia raro sunt prospera. Hasty counsels are seldom prosperous.

Praescriptio est titulus ex usu et tempore substantiam capiens ab auctoritate legis. Prescription is a title derived from usage and time, given substance by the authority of law. Co. Litt. 113.

Praescriptio et executio non pertinent ad valorem contractus, sed ad tempus et modum actionis instituendae. Prescription and execution do not affect the validity of the contract, but affect the time and manner of bringing an action.

Praesentare nihil aliud est quam praesto dare seu offerre. To present is nothing other than to give or offer on the spot.

Praesentia corporis tollit errorem nominis, et veritas nominis tollit errorem demonstrationis. The presence of the body cancels an error in the name; the truth of the name cancels an error in the description.

Praestat cautela quam medela. Prevention is better than cure.

Praesumatur pro justitia sententiae. Let there be a presumption of sentence's justice.

Praesumitur pro legitimatione. There is a presumption in favor of legitimacy.

Praesumptio ex eo quod plerumque fit. A presumption arises from what generally happens.

Praesumptiones sunt conjecturae ex signo verisimili ad probandum assumptae. Presumptions are conjectures based upon indications of probable truth, assumed for the purpose of establishing proof.

Praesumptio violenta plena probatio. Forceful presumption is full proof.

Praesumptio violenta valet in lege. Forceful presumption is effective in law.

Praetextu liciti non debet admitti illicitum. What is illegal ought not to be admitted under pretext of legality.

Praxis judicum est interpres legum. The practice of the judges is the interpreter of the laws.

Pretium succedit in locum rei. The price takes the place of the thing sold.

Prima pars aequitatis aequalitas. The first part of equity is equality.

Primo executienda est verbi vis, ne sermonis vitio obstruatur oratio, sive lex sine argumentis. The force of a word is to be first examined, lest by the fault of diction the sentence be destroyed or the law be without arguments.

Princeps et respublica ex justa causa possunt rem meam auferre. The king and the commonwealth can take away my property for just cause.

Princeps legibus solutus est. The emperor is not bound by statutes. Dig. 1.3.31.

Principalis debet semper excuti antequam perveniatur ad fideijussores. The principal should always be exhausted before resorting to the sureties.

Principia probant, non probantur. Principles prove; they are not proved.

Principiis obsta. Oppose beginnings. • Oppose a thing in its inception in order to have any success against it.

Principiorum non est ratio. There is no reasoning of principles.

Principium est potissima pars cujusque rei. The beginning is the most powerful part of each thing.

Prior tempore, potior jure. Earlier in time, stronger in right.

Privatio praesupponit habitum. Deprivation presupposes possession.

Privatis pactionibus non dubium est non laedi jus caeterorum. There is no doubt that the rights of others (not party to the agreement) cannot be prejudiced by private agreements.

Privatorum conventio juri publico non derogat. An agreement of private persons does not derogate from public law.

Privatum commodum publico cedit. Private yields to public advantage.

Privatum incommodum publico bono pensatur. Private disadvantage is made up for by public good.

Privilegium est beneficium personale et extinguitur cum persona. A privilege is a benefit belonging to a person, and it dies with the person.

Privilegium est quasi privata lex. A privilege is, as it were, a private law.

Privilegium non valet contra rempublicam. A privilege has no force against the commonwealth.

Probandi necessitas incumbit illi qui agit. The necessity of proving rests upon the one who sues (or claims some right). Just. Inst. 2.20.5.

Probationes debent esse evidentes, (id est) perspicuae et faciles intelligi. Proofs ought to be evident, (that is) clear and easily understood.

Probatis extremis, praesumitur media. When the extremes have been proved, the intermediate proceedings are presumed.

Processus legis est gravis vexatio; executio legis coronat opus. The process of the law is heavy hardship; the execution of the law crowns (or rewards) the work.

Prohibetur ne quis faciat in suo quod nocere possit alieno. It is prohibited for anyone to do on his own property what may injure another's.

Proles sequitur sortem paternam. The offspring follows the condition of the father.

Propinquior excludit propinquum; propinquus remotum; et remotus remotiorem. A nearer relation excludes a near one; a near relation excludes one distant (or removed); a distant relative excludes one yet more removed. Co. Litt. 10.

Propositio indefinita aequipollet universali. An indefinite proposition is equal to a general one.

Pro possessione praesumitur de jure. From possession arises a presumption of right.

Pro possessore habetur qui dolo injuriave desiit possidere. A person is considered a possessor who has ceased possession through fraud or injury.

Proprietas totius navis carinae causam sequitur. The property of the whole ship follows the condition of the keel.

Proprietates verborum observandae sunt. The proprieties (i.e., proper meanings) of words are to be observed.

Prosecutio legis est gravis vexatio; executio legis coronat opus. Litigation is a heavy hardship, but execution of the law crowns (or rewards) the work.

Protectio trahit subjectionem, subjectio protectionem. Protection brings submission; submission (brings) protection.

Proviso est providere praesentia et futura, non praeterita. A proviso is to provide for things present and future, not past.

Prudenter agit qui praecepto legis obtemperat. A person acts prudently who obeys the precept of law.

Pueri sunt de sanguine parentum, sed pater et mater non sunt de sanguine puerorum. Children are of the blood of their parents, but the father and mother are not of the blood of their children.

Pupillus pati posse non intelligitur. A pupil is not considered able to suffer. • That is, a pupil is not competent to permit or do what would be prejudicial to him. Dig. 50.17.110.2.

Quae ab hostibus capiuntur, statim capientium fiunt. Things taken from public enemies immediately become the property of the captors.

Quae ab initio inutilis fuit institutio, ex post facto convalescere non potest. An institution void in the beginning cannot acquire validity by a subsequent act.

Quae ab initio non valent, ex post facto convalescere non possunt. Things invalid from the beginning cannot be made valid by a subsequent act.

Quae accessionum locum obtinent, extinguuntur cum principales res peremptae fuerint. When the principal is extinguished, those things that are accessory to it are also extinguished. Dig. 33.8.2.

Quae ad unum finem locuta sunt, non debent ad alium detorqueri. What speaks to one purpose ought not to be twisted to another.

Quae cohaerent personae a persona separari nequeunt. Things that belong to the person cannot be separated from the person.

Quae communi legi derogant stricte interpretantur. (Statutes) that derogate from the common law should be strictly construed.

Quae contra rationem juris introducta sunt, non debent trahi in consequentiam. Things introduced contrary to the reason of the law ought not to be drawn into precedents. • "We do find divers precedents ... which are utterly against law and reason and for that void." 12 Coke 75.

Quaecunque intra rationem legis inveniuntur, intra legem ipsam esse judicantur. Whatever appears within the reason of the law is considered within the law itself.

Quae dubitationis causa tollendae inseruntur communem legem non laedunt. Whatever is inserted for the purpose of removing doubt does not hurt the common law.

Quae dubitationis tollendae causa contractibus inseruntur jus commune non laedunt. Clauses inserted in agreements to remove ambiguity do not prejudice the general law. Dig. 50.17.81.

Quae incontinenti (vel certo) fiunt inesse videntur. Things that are done immediately (or with certainty) are considered part of the same transaction. Co. Litt. 236b.

Quae in curia acta sunt rite agi praesumuntur. What is done in court is presumed to be rightly done.

Quae in partes dividi nequeunt solida a singulis praestantur. Things (such as services) that cannot be divided into parts are rendered entire by each severally.

Quae inter alios acta sunt nemini nocere debent, sed prodesse possunt. Transactions between others can benefit, but should not injure, anyone who is not party to them.

Quae in testamento ita sunt scripta ut intelligi non possint, perinde sunt ac si scripta non essent. Things that are so written in a will that they cannot be understood are as if they had not been written.

Quae legi communi derogant non sunt trahenda in exemplum. Things that derogate (or detract) from the common law are not to be drawn into precedent.

Quae legi communi derogant stricte interpretantur. Things that derogate (or detract) from the common law are construed strictly.

Quaelibet concessio fortissime contra donatorem interpretanda est. Every grant is to be construed most strongly against the grantor.

Quaelibet jurisdictio cancellos suos habet. Every jurisdiction has its boundaries.

Quaelibet poena corporalis, quamvis minima, major est qualibet poena pecuniaria. Every corporal punishment, although the very least, is greater than any pecuniary punishment.

Quae mala sunt inchoata in principio vix bono peraguntur exitu. Things bad in the commencement seldom end well.

Quae non fieri debent, facta valent. Things that ought not to be done are held valid when they have been done.

Quae non valeant singula, juncta juvant. Things that may not avail individually have effect when united.

Quae praeter consuetudinem et morem majorum fiunt, neque placent neque recta videntur. What is done contrary to the custom and usage of our ancestors neither pleases nor is considered right.

Quae propter necessitatem recepta sunt, non debent in argumentum trahi. Things that are accepted as a matter of necessity ought not to be brought into the argument. Dig. 50.17.162.

Quaeras de dubiis, legem bene discere si vis. Inquire into doubtful points if you wish to understand the law well.

Quaere de dubiis, quia per rationes pervenitur ad legitimam rationem. Inquire into doubtful points, because through reasoning we arrive at legal reason.

Quaerere dat sapere quae sunt legitima vere. To investigate is the way to know what things are truly lawful.

Quae rerum natura prohibentur nulla lege confirmata sunt. What is prohibited by the nature of things can be confirmed by no law.

Quae singula non prosunt, juncta juvant. Things that are of no advantage individually are helpful when taken together.

Quae sunt minoris culpae sunt majoris infamiae. Offenses that are of lesser guilt are of greater infamy.

Qualitas quae inesse debet, facile praesumitur. A quality that ought to be inherent is easily presumed.

Quam longum debet esse rationabile tempus, non definitur in lege, sed pendet ex discretione justiciariorum. How long a time should be "reasonable" the law does not define; it depends on the discretion of the judges.

Quam rationabilis debet esse finis, non definitur, sed omnibus circumstantiis inspectis pendet ex justiciariorum discretione. How reasonable a fine should be is not defined, but depends on the discretion of the judges, after all the circumstances have been considered.

Quamvis aliquid per se non sit malum, tamen si sit mali exempli, non est faciendum. Although in itself a thing may not be bad, yet if it serves as a bad example, it is not to be done.

Quamvis lex generaliter loquitur, restringenda tamen est, ut cessante ratione et ipsa cessat. Although a law speaks generally, it must bear some restriction, since the law ceases (or loses effect) when the reason ceases.

Quando aliquid conceditur, conceditur id sine quo illud fieri non possit. When anything is granted, that also is granted without which it cannot take effect.

Quando aliquid mandatur, mandatur et omne per quod pervenitur ad illud. When anything is commanded, everything by which it can be accomplished is also commanded.

Quando aliquid per se non sit malum, tamen si sit mali exempli, non est faciendum. When anything by itself is not evil, and yet if it is an example for evil, it is not to be done.

Quando aliquid prohibetur ex directo, prohibetur et per obliquum. When anything is prohibited directly, it is also prohibited indirectly.

Quando aliquid prohibetur, prohibetur omne per quod devenitur ad illud. When anything is prohibited, everything by which it is arrived at is prohibited.

Quando aliquis aliquid concedit, concedere videtur et id sine quo res uti non potest. When a person grants a thing, he is supposed to grant that also without which the thing cannot be used.

Quando charta continet generalem clausulam, posteaque descendit ad verba specialia quae clausulae generali sunt consentanea, interpretanda est charta secundum verba specialia. When a deed contains a general clause, and afterwards descends to special words that are consistent with the general clause, the deed is to be construed according to the special words.

Quando de una et eadem re, duo onerabiles existunt, unus, pro insufficientia alterius, de integro onerabitur. When two persons are liable concerning one and the same thing, if one makes default, the other must bear the whole liability.

Quando dispositio referri potest ad duas res, ita quod secundum relationem unam vitiatur et secundum alteram utilis sit, tum facienda est relatio ad illam ut valeat dispositio. When a disposition can refer to two matters, so that according to one reference it would be void and by another it would be effective, reference must be made to the latter, so that the disposition may take effect.

Quando diversi desiderantur actus ad aliquem statum perficiendum, plus respicit lex actum originalem. When different acts are required to the formation of any estate, the law chiefly regards the original act.

Quando duo jura concurrunt in una persona, aequum est ac si essent in diversis. When two rights run together in one person, it is the same as if they were in separate persons.

Quando jus domini regis et subditi concurrunt, jus regis praeferri debet. When the right of the sovereign king and of the subject run together (or clash), the right of the king ought to be preferred.

Quando lex aliquid alicui concedit, concedere videtur id sine quo res ipsa esse non potest. When the law grants anything to anyone, it is considered to grant that without which the thing itself cannot be (the sine qua non). 5 Coke 47.

Quando lex aliquid alicui concedit, omnia incidentia tacite conceduntur. When the law gives anything to anyone, it gives tacitly all that is incident to it.

Quando lex est specialis, ratio autem generalis, generaliter lex est intelligenda. When the law is special, but its reason is general, the law is to be understood generally.

Quando licit id quod majus, videtur licere id quod minus. When the greater is allowed, the lesser is considered to be allowed also.

Quando plus fit quam fieri debet, videtur etiam illud fieri quod faciendum est. When more is done than ought to be done, that at least is considered as performed that should have been performed.

Quando quod ago non valet ut ago, valeat quantum valere potest. When what I do does not have effect as I do it, let it have as much effect as it can.

Quando res non valet ut ago, valeat quantum valere potest. When the thing is of no force as I do it, let it have as much as it can have.

Quando verba et mens congruunt, non est interpretationi locus. When the words and the mind agree, there is no room for interpretation.

Quando verba statuti sunt specialia, ratio autem generalis, generaliter statutum est intelligendum. When the words of a statute are special, but the reason for it general, the statute is to be construed generally.

Quemadmodum ad quaestionem facti non respondent judices, ita ad quaestionem juris non respondent juratores. In the same manner that judges do not answer questions of fact, so jurors do not answer questions of law.

Qui accusat integrae famae sit et non criminosus. Let the one who accuses be of honest reputation and not implicated in a crime.

Qui acquirit sibi acquirit haeredibus. A person who acquires for himself acquires for his heirs.

Qui adimit medium dirimit finem. A person who takes away the means destroys the end.

Qui aliquid statuerit parte inaudita altera, aequum licet dixerit, haud aequum fecerit. One who has decided anything without hearing the other party, even though he has said what is right, has done wrong.

Qui alterius jure utitur, eodem jure uti debet. A person who uses the right of another ought to use the same right.

Qui bene distinguit bene docet. One who distinguishes well teaches well.

Qui bene interrogat bene docet. One who questions well teaches well.

Qui cadit a syllaba cadit a tota causa. One who fails in a syllable fails in his whole cause.

Qui concedit aliquid, concedere videtur et id sine quo res ipsa esse non potuit (sine quo concessio est irrita). A person who grants anything is considered as granting that without which the thing itself could not be (without which the grant is invalid). • More precisely, *Cuicunque aliquis quid concedit* (q.v.). 11 Coke 52.

Qui confirmat nihil dat. A person who confirms gives nothing.

Qui contemnit praeceptum, contemnit praecipientem. A person who shows contempt for the precept shows contempt for the author (or advocate) or it.

Quicquid acquiritur servo, acquiritur domino. Whatever is acquired by the servant is acquired for the master.

Quicquid demonstratae rei additur satis demonstratae frustra est. Whatever is added to the description of a thing already sufficiently described is of no effect.

Quicquid est contra normam recti est injuria. Whatever is against the rule of right is a wrong.

Quicquid in excessu actum est, lege prohibetur. Whatever is done in excess is prohibited by law.

Quicquid judicis auctoritati subjicitur, novitati non subjicitur. Whatever is subject to the authority of a judge is not subject to innovation.

Quicquid plantatur solo, solo cedit. Whatever is affixed to the soil belongs to it.

Quicquid recipitur, recipitur secundum modum recipientis. Whatever is received is received according to the direction of the recipient.

Quicquid solvitur, solvitur secundum modum solventis. Whatever is paid is paid according to the direction of the payer.

Qui cum alio contrahit, vel est vel debet esse non ignarus conditionis ejus. A party who contracts with another either is or ought to be cognizant of that party's condition. • Otherwise, he is not excusable. Dig. 50.17.19.

Qui dat finem dat media ad finem necessaria. A person who gives an end gives the necessary means to that end.

Qui destruit medium destruit finem. A person who destroys the means destroys the end.

Qui doit inheriter al pére, doit inheriter al fitz. One who ought to inherit from the father ought to inherit from the son.

Quidquid enim sive dolo et culpa venditoris accidit in eo venditor securus est. For concerning anything that occurs without deceit and guilt on the part of the vendor, the vendor is secure.

Quid sit jus, et in quo consistit injuria, legis est definire. What constitutes right, and wherein lies the injury, it is the function of the law to declare.

Quid turpi ex causa promissum est non valet. A promise arising from a wrongful cause is invalid.

Quieta non movere. Not to disturb what is settled.

Qui evertit causam evertit causatum futurum. One who overthrows the cause overthrows its future effects.

Qui ex damnato coitu nascuntur, inter liberos non computentur. They who are born of an illicit union should not be counted among children.

Qui facit id quod plus est, facit id quod minus est, sed non convertitur. A person who does that which is more does that which is less, but not vice versa.

Qui facit per alium facit per se. A person who acts through another acts himself. • The acts of an agent are considered the acts of the principal.

Qui habet jurisdictionem absolvendi, habet jurisdictionem ligandi. One who has jurisdiction for dissolving (an obligation) has jurisdiction to bind.

Qui haeret in litera, haeret in cortice. One who clings to the letter clings to the shell (or surface).

Qui ignorat quantum solvere debeat, non potest improbus videri A person who does not know what he ought to pay cannot be regarded as dishonest. • Also in reverse order: *Non potest improbus videri qui ignorat quantum solvere debeat*. Dig. 50.17.99.

Qui in jus dominiumve alterius succedit jure ejus uti debet. One who succeeds to another's right or property ought to use that person's right. • That is, the successor has the same rights and liabilities as attached to that property or interest in the hands of the assignor.

Qui in utero est, pro jam nato habetur quoties de ejus commodo quaeritur. A child in the womb is considered as born, whenever there is a question of benefit to the child.

Qui jure suo utitur, nemini facit injuriam. A person who exercises his proper right harms no one.

Qui jussu judicis aliquod fecerit non videtur dolo malo fecisse, quia parere necesse est. A person who has done anything by order of a judge is not considered to have acted in fraud, because it is necessary to obey.

Quilibet potest renunciare juri pro se inducto. Anyone may renounce a right introduced for his own benefit.

Qui male agit odit lucem. A person who does wrong hates the light (of discovery).

Qui mandat ipse fecisse videtur. A person who commands (a thing to be done) is considered to have done it himself.

Qui melius probat, melius habet. The party who gives better proof has the better (right). • Often rendered, he who proves more recovers more.

Qui nascitur sine legitimo matrimonio, matrem sequitur. A child who is born out of lawful matrimony follows the condition of the mother.

Qui non cadunt in constantem virum, vani timores sunt aestimandi. Those fears are considered vain (or frivolous) that do not affect a man of stable character.

Qui non habet, ille non dat. Who has not gives not.

Qui non habet in aere, luat in corpore, ne quis peccetur impune. Let him who has not (the wherewithal to pay) in money pay in his person (i.e., by corporal punishment), lest anyone be wronged with impunity.

Qui non habet potestatem alienandi habet necessitatem retinendi. A person who has not the power of alienating is obliged to retain.

Qui non improbat approbat. A person who does not disapprove approves.

Qui non negat fatetur. A person who does not deny admits.

Qui non obstat quod obstare potest, facere videtur. A person who does not prevent what he can prevent is considered to act.

Qui non prohibet cum prohibere possit, jubet. A person who does not forbid when he can forbid commands.

Qui non prohibet quod prohibere potest, assentire videtur. A person who does not forbid what he can forbid is considered to assent.

Qui non propulsat injuriam quando potest infert. A person who does not repel an injury when he can brings it on.

Qui obstruit aditum destruit commodum. A person who obstructs an entrance destroys a conveniency.

Qui omne dicit nihil excludit. A person who says all excludes nothing.

Qui parcit nocentibus innocentes punit. A person who spares the guilty punishes the innocent.

Qui peccat ebrius, luat sobrius. Let him who offends while drunk be punished when sober.

Qui per alium facit per seipsum facere videtur. A person who does anything through another is considered as doing it himself.

Qui per fraudem agit frustra agit. A person who acts fraudulently acts in vain.

Qui potest et debet vetare, tacens jubet. A person who can and ought to forbid a thing (as much as) orders it, if he keeps silent.

Qui primum peccat ille facit rixam. Who first offends causes the quarrel.

Qui prior est tempore potior est jure. The person who is prior in time is stronger in right.

Qui pro me aliquid facit, mihi fecisse videtur. A person who does something in my behalf is considered to have done it to me (for me). • "To do a service for a man is to do it to him." 2 Co. Inst. 500.

Qui providet sibi, providet haeredibus. A person who provides for himself provides for his heirs.

Qui rationem in omnibus quaerunt rationem subvertunt. They who seek a reason for everything subvert reason.

Qui sciens solvit indebitum donandi consilio id videtur fecisse. A person who knowingly pays what is not due is considered to have done it with the intention of making a gift.

Qui semel actionem renunciaverit, amplius repetere non potest. A litigant who has once renounced his action cannot bring it any longer.

Qui semel malus, semper praesumitur esse malus in eodem genere. A person who is once bad is always presumed to be bad in the same kind of affair.

Qui sentit commodum, sentire debet et onus. A person who feels the benefit ought also to feel the burden.

Qui sentit onus, sentire debet et commodum. A person who feels the burden ought also to feel the benefit.

Quisquis est qui velit jurisconsultus haberi, continuet studium, velit a quocunque doceri. Whoever there is who wishes to be regarded as a jurisconsult (legal expert) should prolong his study and be willing to be taught by everyone.

Qui tacet consentire videtur. A party who is silent appears to consent.

Qui tacet consentire videtur ubi tractatur de ejus commodo. A party who is silent is considered as assenting, when his advantage is debated.

Qui tacet non utique fatetur, sed tamen verum est eum non negare. A person who is silent does not indeed confess, but yet it is true that he does not deny.

Qui tardius solvit minus solvit. A person who pays too late pays less (than he ought).

Qui vult decipi, decipiatur. Let one who wishes to be deceived be deceived.

Quod ab initio non valet, (in) tractu temporis non convalescet. What is ill from the outset will not be cured by passage of time.

Quod ad jus naturale attinet, omnes homines aequales sunt. All men are equal as far as natural law is concerned.

Quod aedificatur in area legata cedit legato. Whatever is built upon land given by will passes with the gift of the land.

Quod alias bonum et justum est, si per vim vel fraudem petatur, malum et injustum efficitur. What is otherwise good and just, if it is sought by force or fraud, becomes bad and unjust.

Quod alias non fuit licitum necessitas licitum facit. Necessity makes lawful what otherwise was unlawful.

Quod approbo non reprobo. What I approve I do not disapprove.

Quod a quoque poenae nomine exactum est id eidem restituere nemo cogitur. What has been exacted from someone as a penalty no one is obliged to restore to him.

Quod attinet ad jus civile, servi pro nullis habentur, non tamen et jure naturali, quia, quod ad jus naturale attinet, omnes homines aequali sunt. So far as the civil law is concerned, slaves are not reckoned as nonentities, but not so by natural law, for so far as regards natural law, all men are equal.

Quod constat clare, non debet verificari. What is clearly agreed need not be proved.

Quod constat curiae, opere testium non indiget. What appears true to the court needs not the help of witnesses.

Quod contra juris rationem receptum est, non est producendum ad consequentias. What has been admitted against the reason of the law ought not to be drawn into precedents.

Quod contra legem fit, pro infecto habetur. What is done contrary to the law is considered as not done.

Quodcunque aliquis ob tutelam corporis sui fecerit jure id fecisse videtur. Whatever one does in defense of his person, he is considered to have done legally.

Quod datum est ecclesiae, datum est Deo. What has been given to the church has been given to God.

Quod demonstrandi causa additur rei satis demonstratae, frustra fit. What is added for the sake of demonstration to a thing sufficiently demonstrated is done to no purpose.

Quod dubitas, ne feceris. When in doubt, do not do it.

Quod enim semel aut bis existit, praetereunt legislatores. Legislators pass by that which happens but once or twice.

Quod est ex necessitate nunquam introducitur, nisi quando necessarium. What is introduced of necessity is never introduced except when necessary.

Quod est inconveniens aut contra rationem non permissum est in lege. What is unsuitable or contrary to reason is not allowed in law.

Quod est necessarium est licitum. What is necessary is lawful.

Quod fieri debet facile praesumitur. That which ought to be done is easily presumed.

Quod fieri non debet, factum valet. What ought not to be done, when done, is valid.

Quod inconsulto fecimus, consultius revocemus. What we have done without due consideration we should revoke with better consideration.

Quod initio non valet, tractu temporis non valet. What is void in the beginning does not become valid by passage of time.

Quod initio vitiosum est non potest tractu temporis convalescere. What is defective in origin cannot be mended by passage of time.

Quod in jure scripto jus appellatur, id in lege Angliae rectum esse dicitur. What in the civil law (literally, written law) is called jus, in the law of England is said to be rectum (right).

Quod in minori valet, valebit in majori; et quod in majori non valet, nec valebit in minori. What avails in the less will avail in the greater; and what does not avail in the greater will not avail in the less.

Quod in uno similium valet, valebit in altero. What avails in one of two similar things will avail in the other.

Quod ipsis, qui contraxerunt, obstat, et successoribus eorum obstabit. That which bars those who have contracted will bar their successors also.

Quod jussu alterius solvitur pro eo est quasi ipsi solutum esset. That which is paid at the bidding of another has the same effect as if it had been paid to that person himself. • The party who has a debt paid for him is in the same position as though the money were paid to him directly. Dig. 17.180.

Quod meum est, sine facto sive defectu meo amitti seu in alium transferri non potest. What is mine cannot be lost or transferred to another without my own act or default.

Quod meum est sine me auferri non potest. What is mine cannot be taken away without me (i.e., my consent).

Quod minus est in obligationem videtur deductum. That which is the lesser is held to be imported into the contract.

Quod naturalis ratio inter omnes homines constituit, vocatur jus gentium. What natural reason has established among all men is called the law of nations.

Quod necessarie intelligitur id non deest. What is necessarily understood is not lacking.

Quod necessitas cogit, defendit. What necessity compels, it justifies.

Quod non apparet non est, et non apparet judicialiter ante judicium. What appears not does not exist, and nothing appears judicially before judgment.

Quod non capit Christus, capit fiscus. What Christ (or the church) does not take, the treasury takes.

Quod non habet principium non habet finem. What has no beginning has no end.

Quod non legitur non creditur. What is not read is not believed.

Quod non valet in principali, in accessorio seu consequenti non valebit; et quod non valet in magis propinquo, non valebit in magis remoto. What is not valid in the principal will not be valid in the accessory or consequence; and what has no effect in the nearer instance will be of no effect in the more remote.

Quod nullius esse potest, id ut alicujus fieret nulla obligatio valet efficere. What can belong to no one no agreement (or obligation) can make property of anyone. Dig. 50.17.182.

Quod nullius est, est domini regis. That which belongs to nobody belongs to our lord the king.

Quod nullius est id ratione naturali occupanti conceditur. What belongs to no one, by natural reason becomes property of the first occupant. Dig. 41.1.3.

Quod nullum est, nullum producit effectum. That which is null produces no effect.

Quod omnes tangit, ab omnibus debet supportari. What touches (or concerns) all ought to be supported by all.

Quod per me non possum, nec per alium. What I cannot do in person, I also cannot do through the agency of another.

Quod per recordum probatum non debet esse negatum. What is proved by the record ought not to be denied.

Quod populus postremum jussit, id jus ratum esto. What the people have last enacted, let that be the established law.

Quod principi placuit legis habet vigorem; utpote cum lege regia, quae de imperio ejus lata est, populus ei et in eum omne suum imperium et potestatem conferat. A decision of the emperor has the force of law; for, by the royal law that has been made concerning his authority, the people have conferred upon him all their sovereignty and power. Dig. 1.4.1.

Quod prius est verius est; et quod prius est tempore potius est jure. What is prior is truer; and what comes earlier in time is stronger in right.

Quod pro minore licitum est et pro majore licitum est. What is lawful in the lesser is also lawful in the greater.

Quod pure debetur praesenti die debetur. That which is due unconditionally is due the same day.

Quodque dissolvitur eodem modo quo ligatur. In the same manner that anything is bound, it is unbound.

Quod quis ex culpa sua damnum sentit, non intelligitur damnum sentire. The damage that any person suffers by his own fault he is not considered to suffer as damage. Dig. 50.17.203.

Quod quisquis norit, in hoc se exerceat. Let every one employ himself in what he knows.

Quod quis sciens indebitum dedit hac mente, ut postea repeteret, repetere non potest. What one has paid knowing that it is not owed, with the intention of reclaiming it afterwards, he cannot recover. Dig. 12.6.50.

Quod remedio destituitur ipsa re valet si culpa absit. What is without a remedy is by that very fact valid if there is no fault.

Quod semel aut bis existit praetereunt legislatores. Legislators pass over what happens (only) once or twice.

Quod semel meum est amplius meum esse non potest. What is once mine cannot be any more completely mine.

Quod semel placuit in electione, amplius displicere non potest. That which in making his election a man has once decided, he cannot afterwards disavow.

Quod solo inaedificatur solo cedit. Whatever is built on the soil goes with the soil.

Quod sub certa forma concessum vel reservatum est, non trahitur ad valorem vel compensationem. That which has been granted or reserved under a certain form is not to be drawn into valuation or compensation.

Quod subintelligitur non deest. What is understood is not lacking.

Quod tacite intelligitur deesse non videtur. What is tacitly understood does not appear to be lacking.

Quod vanum et inutile est, lex non requirit. The law does not require what is vain and useless.

Quod vero contra rationem juris receptum est, non est producendum ad consequentias. But what has been admitted contrary to the reason of law ought not to be drawn into precedents.

Quo ligatur, eo dissolvitur. As a thing is bound, so it is unbound.

Quo modo quid constituitur eodem modo dissolvitur. In whatever mode a thing is constituted, in the same manner it is dissolved.

Quorum praetextu nec auget nec minuit sententiam, sed tantum confirmat praemissa. "Quorum praetextu" neither increases nor diminishes the meaning, but only confirms what went before.

Quotiens dubia interpretatio libertatis est, secundum libertatem respondendum erit. Whenever there is an interpretation doubtful as to liberty (or slavery), the decision must be in favor of liberty.

Quotiens idem sermo duas sententias exprimit, ea potissimum accipiatur quae rei gerendae aptior est. Whenever the same words express two meanings, that is to be taken most strongly which is the better fitted for carrying out the proposed end.

Quoties in stipulationibus ambigua oratio est, commodissimum est id accipi quo res de quo agitur in tuto sit. Whenever in stipulations the expression is ambiguous, it is most proper to give it that interpretation by which the subject matter may be in safety.

Quoties in verbis nulla est ambiguitas, ibi nulla expositio contra verba expressa fienda est. Whenever there is no ambiguity in the words, then no exposition contrary to the words is to be made.

Quum de lucro duorum quaeratur, melior est conditio possidentis. When there is a question of gain (to one) of two parties, the condition of the possessor is the better.

Quum in testamento ambigue aut etiam perperam scriptum est, benigne interpretari et secundum id quod credible est cogitatum, credendum est. When in a will an ambiguous or even an erroneous expression occurs, it should be construed liberally and in accordance with what is thought the probable meaning (of the testator).

Quum principalis causa non consistit, ne ea quidem quae sequuntur locum habent. When the principal cause does not stand, neither do the accessories (or consequences) obtain.

Ratihabitio mandato aequiparatur. Ratification is equal to a command.

Ratio est formalis causa consuetudinis. Reason is the source and formal cause of custom.

Ratio est legis anima, mutata legis ratione mutatur et lex. Reason is the soul of the law; when the reason of the law has been changed, the law is also changed.

Ratio et auctoritas duo clarissima mundi lumina. Reason and authority are the two brightest lights in the world.

Ratio in jure aequitas integra. Reason in law is perfect equity.

Ratio legis est anima legis. The reason of the law is the soul of the law.

Ratio non clauditur loco. Reason is not confined to any place.

Ratio potest allegari deficiente lege, sed vera et legalis et non apparens. A reason can be adduced when the law is defective, but it must be a true and legal reason, and not specious (or apparent).

Receditur a placitis juris potius quam injuriae et delicta maneant impunita. One departs from settled rules of law, rather than let crimes and wrongs remain unpunished.

Recorda sunt vestigia vetustatis et veritatis. Records are vestiges of antiquity and truth.

Recurrendum est ad extraordinarium quando non valet ordinarium. We must have recourse to what is extraordinary when what is ordinary fails.

Reddenda singula singulis. Each must be put in each separate place. • That is, the several terms or items apply distributively, or each to its proper object.

Regula est, juris quidem ignorantiam cuique nocere, facti vero ignorantiam non nocere. The rule is that ignorance of the law is harmful (or prejudicial) to anyone, but ignorance of a fact is not. • Ignorance of a fact may excuse a party from the legal consequences of his conduct, but not ignorance of law.

Regula pro lege, si deficit lex. If the law is inadequate, the maxim serves in its place.

Regulariter non valet pactum de re mea non alienanda. As a rule, a contract not to alienate my property is not binding.

Reipublicae interest voluntates defunctorum effectum sortiri. It is in the interest of the state that the wills of the dead should have their (intended) effect.

Rei turpis nullum mandatum est. There is no mandate for a thing immoral (or illegal). • Hence, there is no action for failing to act upon such a mandate. Dig. 17.1.6.3.

Relatio est fictio juris et intenta ad unum. Relation is a fiction of law, and intended for one thing. • Coke explains, "Relatio is a fiction of law to make a nullity of a thing ab initio"; obstacles are removed for the one purpose, *ut res magis valeat*, that the matter have effect. 3 Coke 28.

Relatio semper fiat ut valeat dispositio. Reference should always be made in such a manner that a disposition (in a will) may have effect.

Relativorum cognito uno, cognoscitur et alterum. Of things relating to each other, one being known, the other is also known.

Religio sequitur patrem. Religion follows the father. • The father's religion is prima facie the infant's religion.

Remissius imperanti melius paretur. A person commanding not too strictly is better obeyed.

Remoto impedimento, emergit actio. When the impediment has been removed, the action arises.

Repellitur a sacramento infamis. An infamous person is prevented from taking an oath.

Repellitur exceptione cedendarum actionum. (The litigant) is defeated by the plea that the actions have been assigned.

Reprobata pecunia liberat solventem. Money refused releases the person paying (or offering payment).

Reputatio est vulgaris opinio ubi non est veritas. Reputation is a common opinion where there is no certain knowledge.

Rerum ordo confunditur, si unicuique jurisdictio non servetur. The order of things is confounded if the proper jurisdiction of each is not maintained.

Rerum progressus ostendunt multa, quae in initio praecaveri seu praevideri non possunt. The course of events reveals many things that in the beginning could not be guarded against or foreseen.

Rerum suarum quilibet est moderator et arbiter. Every one is the manager and disposer of his own matters.

Res accendent lumina rebus. Matters will throw light upon (other) matters.

Res accessoria sequitur rem principalem. An accessory follows its principal.

Res denominatur a principaliori parte. A thing is named from its more essential (or primary) part.

Reservatio non debet esse de proficuis ipsis quia ea conceduntur, sed de redditu novo extra proficua. A reservation ought not to be of the annual increase itself, because it is granted, but of new rent apart from the annual increase.

Res est misera ubi jus est vagum et incertum. It is a miserable state of things where the law is vague and uncertain.

Res generalem habet significationem, quia tam corporea, quam incorporea, cujuscunque sunt generis naturae sive speciei, comprehendit. The word "things" has a general signification, because it comprehends corporeal as well as incorporeal objects, of whatever sort, nature, or species.

Resignatio est juris proprii spontanea refutatio. Resignation is the spontaneous relinquishment of one's own right.

Res inter alios acta alteri nocere non debet. Things done between others ought not to injure an outsider (not party to them).

Res inter alios judicatae nullum aliis praejudicium faciunt. Matters adjudged in the lawsuits of others do not prejudice those who were not parties to them.

Res judicata facit ex albo nigrum, ex nigro album, ex curvo rectum, ex recto curvum. A matter adjudged makes white black; black white; the crooked straight; the straight crooked.

Res judicata pro veritate accipitur. A matter adjudged is taken for truth.

Res nullius naturaliter fit primi occupantis. A thing that has no owner naturally belongs to the first taker.

Resoluto jure concedentis, resolvitur jus concessum. When the right of the grantor has been extinguished, the right granted is extinguished.

Res periit domino suo. The destruction of the thing is a loss to its owner.

Res per pecuniam aestimatur, et non pecunia per res. The value of a thing is estimated by its worth in money, and the value of money is not estimated by reference to things.

Respiciendum est judicanti nequid aut durius aut remissius constituatur quam causa deposcit; nec enim aut severitatis aut clementiae gloria affectanda est. The person judging must see to it that nothing should be either more severely or more leniently construed than the cause itself demands; neither for severity nor clemency is glory to be sought after.

Respondeat raptor, qui ignorare non potuit quod pupillum alienum abduxit. Let the ravisher answer, for he could not be ignorant that he has taken away another's ward.

Respondeat superior. Let the principal answer.

Responsio unius non omnino audiatur. The answer of one witness should not be heard at all.

Res propria est quae communis non est. A thing is private that is not common.

Res quae intra praesidia perductae nondum sunt quanquam ab hostibus occupatae, ideo postliminii non egent, quia dominum nondum mutarunt ex gentium jure. Things that have not yet been brought within the enemy's camp, although held by the enemy, do not need the fiction of postliminy on this account, because their ownership by the law of nations has not yet changed.

Res sacra non recipit aestimationem. A sacred thing does not admit of valuation.

Res sua nemini servit. No one can have a servitude over his own property.

Res transit cum suo onere. The thing passes with its burden.

Reus excipiendo fit actor. The defendant by a plea (or exception) becomes plaintiff.

Reus laesae majestatis punitur, ut pereat unus ne pereant omnes. A traitor is punished that one may die lest all perish.

Re, verbis, scripto, consensu, traditione, junctura vestes sumere pacta solent. Compacts usually take their clothing from the thing itself, from words, from writings, from consent, from delivery, from the joining together.

Rex non debet esse sub homine sed sub Deo et lege. The king should not be under the authority of man, but of God and the law.

Rex non potest fallere nec falli. The king cannot deceive or be deceived.

Rex non potest peccare. The king can do no wrong.

Rex nunquam moritur. The king never dies.

Riparum usus publicus est jure gentium, sicut ipsius fluminis. The use of riverbanks is by the law of nations public, like that of the stream itself.

Roy n'est lie per ascun statute, si il ne soit expressement nosme. The king is not bound by any statute, if he is not expressly named.

Sacramentum habet in se tres comites, veritatem justitiam et judicium: veritas habenda est in jurato; justitia et judicium in judice. An oath has in it three components—truth, justice, and judgment: truth in the party swearing, justice and judgment in the judge (administering the oath).

Sacramentum si fatuum fuerit, licet falsum, tamen non committit perjurium. A foolish oath, though false, does not make perjury.

Sacrilegus omnium praedonum cupiditatem et scelerem superat. A sacrilegious person surpasses the greed and wickedness of all other robbers.

Saepe constitutum est res inter alios judicatas aliis non praejudicare. It has often been settled that matters adjudged between others ought not to prejudice those who were not parties.

Saepenumero ubi proprietas verborum attenditur, sensus veritatis amittitur. Frequently where propriety of words is given attention, the meaning of truth is lost.

Saepe viatorem nova, non vetus, orbita fallit. Often it is the new track, not the old one, that deceives the traveler.

Salus populi (est) suprema lex. The safety of the people is the supreme law. • The phrase is sometimes put in the imperative: *Salus populi suprema lex esto* (let the safety of the people be the supreme law).

Salus reipublicae suprema lex. The safety of the state is the supreme law.

Salus ubi multi consiliarii. Where there are many counselors, there is safety.

Sanguinis conjunctio benevolentia devincit homines et caritate. A tie of blood overcomes human beings through benevolence and family affection.

Sapiens incipit a fine, et quod primum est in intentione, ultimum est in executione. A wise person begins from the end, and what is first in intention is last in execution.

Sapiens omnia agit cum consilio. A wise man does everything advisedly.

Sapientia legis nummario pretio non est aestimanda. No price in money is to be put upon the wisdom of the law.

Sapientis judicis est cogitare tantum sibi esse permissum, quantum commissum et creditum. It is the mark of a wise judge to suppose that he is permitted only so much as has been committed and entrusted to him.

Satius est petere fontes quam sectari rivulos. It is better to seek the sources than to follow tributaries.

Scientia sciolorum est mixta ignorantia. The knowledge of smatterers is ignorance diluted.

Scientia utrimque par pares contrahentes facit. Equal knowledge on both sides makes the contracting parties equal.

Scienti et volenti non fit injuria. A wrong is not done to one who knows and assents to it.

Scire debes cum quo contrahis. You ought to know with whom you make an agreement.

Scire et scire debere aequiparantur in jure. To know a thing and to be bound to know it are regarded in law as equivalent.

Scire leges non hoc est verba earum tenere, sed vim et potestatem. To know the laws is to observe not their (mere) words, but their force and power.

Scire proprie est rem ratione et per causam cognoscere. To know properly is to know a thing in its reason and by its cause.

Scribere est agere. To write is to act.

Scriptae obligationes scriptis tolluntur, et nudi consensus obligatio contrario consensu dissolvitur. Written obligations are undone by writing, and the obligation of mere consent (or naked agreement) is dissolved by a bare consent to the contrary.

Secta est pugna civilis, sicut actores armantur actionibus, et quasi accinguntur gladiis, ita rei (e contra) muniuntur exceptionibus, et defenduntur quasi clypeis. A suit is a civil battle; just as the plaintiffs are armed with actions and, as it were, girded with swords, so (against them) the defendants are fortified with pleas, and defended as though by shields.

Secta quae scripto nititur a scripto variari non debet. A suit that relies upon a writing ought not to vary from the writing.

Secundum naturam est commoda cujusque rei eum sequi quem sequentur incommoda. It is according to nature that the advantages in any matter should come to the person to whom the disadvantages will attend.

Securius expediuntur negotia commissa pluribus, et plus vident oculi quam oculus. Business entrusted to several people is done more reliably, and (several) eyes see more than (one) eye does.

Seisina facit stipitem. Seisin makes the stock.

Semel civis semper civis. Once a citizen, always a citizen.

Semel malus semper praesumitur esse malus in eodem genere. Whoever is once bad is presumed to be so always in the same kind of affair.

Semper in dubiis benigniora praeferenda sunt. In dubious cases, the more favorable constructions are always to be preferred.

Semper in dubiis id agendum est, ut quam tutissimo loco res sit bona fide contracta, nisi quum aperte contra leges scriptum est. Always in doubtful cases that is to be done by which a bona fide contract may be in the safest condition, except when it has been drawn up clearly contrary to law.

Semper in obscuris quod minimum est sequimur. In obscure cases we always follow what is least obscure.

Semper in stipulationibus et in caeteris contractibus id sequimur quod actum est. In stipulations and other contracts, we always follow what was done (or agreed to). Dig. 50.17.34.

Semper ita fiat relatio ut valeat dispositio. Let the reference always be so made that the disposition may avail.

Semper necessitas probandi incumbit ei qui agit. The necessity of proving always rests upon the claimant.

Semper praesumitur pro legitimatione puerorum, et filiatio non potest probari. The presumption is always in favor of legitimacy of children, and filiation cannot be proved.

Semper praesumitur pro negante. The presumption is always in favor of the one who denies.

Semper praesumitur pro sententia. The presumption is always in favor of a judgment (or sentence).

Semper qui non prohibet pro se intervenire mandare creditur. A person who does not prohibit the intervention of another in his behalf is always believed to authorize it.

Semper sexus masculinus etiam faemininum continet. The masculine gender always includes the feminine as well. Dig. 32.63.

Semper specialia generalibus insunt. Special clauses are always included in general ones.

Senatores sunt partes corporis regis. Senators are part of the body of the king.

Sensus verborum est anima legis. The meaning of words is the spirit of the law.

Sensus verborum est duplex, mitis et asper, et verba semper accipienda sunt in mitiore sensu. The meaning of words is twofold, mild and harsh; and words are always to be received in their milder sense.

Sensus verborum ex causa dicendi accipiendus est, et sermones semper accipiendi sunt secundum subjectam materiam. The sense of words is to be taken from the occasion of speaking them, and discourses are always to be interpreted according to the subject matter.

Sententia a non judice lata nemini debet nocere. A judgment pronounced by one who is not a judge should harm no one.

Sententia contra matrimonium nunquam transit in rem judicatam. A sentence against marriage never becomes a final judgment (i.e., res judicata).

Sententia facit jus, et legis interpretatio legis vim obtinet. The judgment creates the right, and the interpretation of the law obtains the force of law.

Sententia facit jus, et res judicata pro veritate accipitur. The judgment creates the right, and what is adjudicated is taken for truth.

Sententia interlocutoria revocari potest, definitiva non potest. An interlocutory judgment may be revoked, but not a final one.

Sententia non fertur de rebus non liquidis. Judgment is not given upon matters that are not clear.

Sequi debet potentia justitiam, non praecedere. Power should follow justice, not precede it.

Sermo index animi. Speech is an index of the mind.

Servanda est consuetudo loci ubi causa agitur. The custom of the place where the action is brought is to be observed.

Servitia personalia sequuntur personam. Personal services follow the person (of the lord). • Such "personal services" were those "annexed to the person of the Mesne, as homage, fealty, etc." 2 Co. Inst. 374.

Si a jure discedas, vagus eris et erunt omnia omnibus incerta. If you depart from the law, you will wander (without a guide), and everything will be in a state of uncertainty to everyone.

Si alicujus rei societas sit et finis negotio impositus est, finitur societas. If there is a partnership in any matter, and the business is ended, the partnership ceases.

Si aliquid ex solemnibus deficiat, cum aequitas poscit subveniendum est. If anything is lacking from formal requirements, when equity requires, it will be supplied.

Si assuetis mederi possis, nova non sunt tentanda. If you can be relieved by accustomed remedies, new ones should not be tried.

Sic enim debere quem meliorem agrum suum facere, ne vicini deteriorem faciat. Everyone ought so to improve his land as not to injure his neighbor's.

Sic interpretandum est ut verba accipiantur cum effectu. Such an interpretation is to be made that the words may be taken with effect.

Sic utere tuo ut alienum non laedas. So use your own as not to injure another's property.

Sicut natura nil facit per saltum, ita nec lex. Just as nature does nothing with a leap, so neither does the law.

Si duo in testamento pugnantia reperientur, ultimum est ratum. If two conflicting provisions are found in a will, the latter is decisive.

Sigillum est cera impressa, quia cera sine impressione non est sigillum. A seal is a piece of wax impressed, because wax without an impression is not a seal.

Si judicas, cognosce. If you judge, understand.

Silent leges inter arma. Laws are silent amid arms.

Si meliores sunt quos ducit amor, plures sunt quos corrigit timor. If the better are those whom love leads, the greater number are those whom fear corrects.

Similitudo legalis est casuum diversorum inter se collatorum similis ratio; quod in uno similium valet, valebit in altero. Legal similarity is a similar reason that governs various cases when compared with each other, for what avails in one similar case will avail in the other.

Simplex commendatio non obligat. A simple recommendation does not bind.

Simplex et pura donatio dici poterit ubi nulla est adjecta conditio nec modus. A gift is said to be pure and simple when no condition or qualification has been annexed.

Simplicitas est legibus amica, et nimia subtilitas in jure reprobatur. Simplicity is a friend to the laws, and too much subtlety in law is condemned.

Sine possessione usucapio procedere non potest. Without possession, prescription (Roman usucapio) cannot proceed.

Singuli in solidum tenentur. Each individual is bound for the whole.

Si non appareat quid actum est, erit consequens ut id sequamur quod in regione in qua actum est frequentatur. If it is not clear what was done (or agreed upon), the consequence will be that we follow what is commonly done in the place where the agreement was made. Dig. 50.17.34.

Si nulla sit conjectura quae ducat alio, verba intelligenda sunt ex proprietate, non grammatica sed populari ex usu. If there is no inference that leads to a different result, words are to be understood according to their proper meaning, not in a grammatical but in a popular and ordinary sense.

Si plures conditiones ascriptae fuerunt donationi conjunctim, omnibus est parendum; et ad veritatem copulative requiritur quod utraque pars sit vera, si divisim, quilibet vel alteri eorum satis est obtemperare; et in disjunctivis, sufficit alteram partem esse veram. If several conditions are conjunctively written in a gift, the whole of them must be complied with; and with respect to their truth, it is necessary that every part be true, taken jointly: if the conditions are separate, it is sufficient to comply with either one or the other of them; and being disjunctive, that one or the other be true.

Si plures sint fidejussores, quotquot erunt numero, singuli in solidum tenentur. If there are more sureties than one, however many they will be in number, they are individually liable for the whole.

Si quidem in nomine, cognomine, praenomine, agnomine legatarii testator erraverit, cum de persona constat, nihilominus valet legatum. If the testator has erred in the name, cognomen, praenomen, or title of the legatee, when there is certainty about the person, the legacy is nonetheless valid.

Si quid universitati debetur, singulis non debetur, nec quod debet universitas singuli debent. If anything is due to a corporation, it is not due to the individual members of it, nor do the members individually owe what the corporation owes.

Si quis cum totum petiisset partem petat, exceptio rei judicatae vocet. If anyone sues for a part when he should have sued for the whole, the judgment should constitute res judicata (against another suit).

Si quis custos fraudem pupillo fecerit, a tutela removendus est. If a guardian commits fraud against his ward, he is to be removed from the guardianship.

Si quis praegnantem uxorem reliquit, non videtur sine liberis decessisse. If anyone dies leaving his wife pregnant, he is not considered as having died childless.

Si quis unum percusserit cum alium percutere vellet, in felonia tenetur. If a person kills one when he meant to kill another, he is held guilty of felony.

Si suggestio non sit vera, literae patentes vacuae sunt. If the suggestion is not true, the letters patent are void.

Sive tota res evincatur, sive pars, habet regressum emptor in venditorem. If the property is taken from him by eviction, whether whole or in part, the purchaser has an action against the vendor. Dig. 21.2.1.

Socii mei socius meus socius non est. The partner of my partner is not my partner.

Sola ac per se senectus donationem, testamentum aut transactionem non vitiat. Old age does not alone and of itself vitiate gift, will or transaction.

Solemnitates juris sunt observandae. The solemnities of law must be observed.

Solo cedit quod solo implantatur. What is planted in the soil belongs to the soil.

Solo cedit quod solo inaedificatur. Whatever is built on the soil belongs to the soil.

Solus Deus haeredem facit. God alone makes the heir.

Solutio pretii emptionis loco habetur. The payment of the price stands in the place of a sale.

Solvendo esse nemo intelligitur nisi qui solidum potest solvere. No one is understood to be in a state of solvency except the one who can pay all that he owes. Dig. 50.16.114.

Solvitur adhuc societas etiam morte socii. A partnership is also dissolved by the death of a partner.

Solvitur eo ligamine quo ligatur. It is released by the bond with which it is bound.

Spes impunitatis continuum affectum tribuit delinquendi. The hope of impunity supplies a constant inclination to wrongdoing.

Spoliatus debet ante omnia restitui. A party forcibly deprived of possession ought first of all to have restitution.

Spoliatus episcopus ante omnia debet restitui. A bishop despoiled of his see ought, above all, to be restored.

Spondet peritiam artis. He promises (to use) the skill of his art. • That is, he engages to do the work in a skillful manner.

Sponte virum fugiens mulier et adultera facta, doti sua careat, nisi sponsi sponte retracta. A woman leaving her husband of her own accord and committing adultery should lose her dower, unless she is taken back by her husband of his own accord.

Stabit praesumptio donec probetur in contrarium. A presumption will stand until proof is given to the contrary.

Stare decisis et non quieta movere. Literally, to stand by previous decisions and not to disturb settled matters. • To adhere to precedents, and not to depart from established principles.

Stat pro ratione voluntas. The will stands in place of a reason.

Stat pro ratione voluntas populi. The will of the people stands in place of a reason.

Statuta pro publico commodo late interpretantur. Statutes made for the public advantage ought to be broadly construed.

Statuta suo clauduntur territorio, nec ultra territorium disponunt. Statutes are confined to their own territory and have no extraterritorial effect.

Statutum affirmativum non derogat communi legi. An affirmative statute does not take away from the common law.

Statutum generaliter est intelligendum quando verba statuti sunt specialia, ratio autem generalis. A statute is to be understood generally when the words of the statute are special but its reason is general.

Statutum speciale statuto speciali non derogat. One special statute does not take away from another special statute.

Sublata causa tollitur effectus. Remove the cause and the effect ceases.

Sublata veneratione magistratuum, respublica ruit. When respect for magistrates has been destroyed, the commonwealth perishes.

Sublato fundamento, cadit opus. When the foundation has been removed (or demolished), the structure collapses.

Sublato principali, tollitur adjunctum. When the principal has been taken away, the adjunct is also taken away.

Succurritur minori; facilis est lapsus juventutis. Aid is given to a minor; easy is the slip-up of youth (i.e., youth is liable to err).

Summa caritas est facere justitiam singulis et omni tempore quando necesse fuerit. The greatest charity is to do justice to each individual and at every time when it is necessary.

Summa est lex quae pro religione facit. The highest law is the one that acts on behalf of religion.

Summa ratio est quae pro religione facit. The highest reason is that which acts in favor of religion. • Also found in indirect form, *Summam esse rationem quae pro religione facit.*

Summum jus, summa injuria. The highest right is the utmost injury. • That is, law too rigidly interpreted produces the greatest injustice.

Superficies solo cedit. The surface goes with the land. • That is, whatever is attached to the land forms part of it.

Superflua non nocent. Superfluities do no injury.

Suppressio veri, expressio falsi. Suppression of the truth (is equivalent to) the expression of what is false.

Suppressio veri, suggestio falsi. Suppression of the truth (is equivalent to) the suggestion of what is false.

Surplusagium non nocet. Extraneous matter does no harm. • Superfluous allegations, not proper to the case, should have no effect.

Tacita quaedam habentur pro expressis. Certain things though unexpressed are considered as expressed.

Talis interpretatio semper fienda est ut evitetur absurdum, et inconveniens, et ne judicium sit illusorium. Interpretation is always to be made in such a manner that what is absurd and improper is avoided, and so that the judgment is not a mockery.

Talis non est eadem, nam nullum simile est idem. "Such" is not "the same," for nothing similar is the same thing.

Tantum bona valent, quantum vendi possunt. Things are worth as much as they can be sold for.

Tantum concessum quantum scriptum. So much is granted as is written.

Tantum habent de lege, quantum habent de justitia. (Precedents) have value in the law to the extent that they represent justice.

Tantum operatur fictio in casu ficto quantum veritas in casu vero. A legal fiction operates to the same extent and effect in the supposed case as the truth does in a real case.

Tantum praescriptum quantum possessum. There is only prescription insofar as there has been possession.

Tempus enim modus tollendi obligationes et actiones, quia tempus currit contra desides et sui juris contemptores. For time is a means of destroying obligations and actions, because time runs against those who are inactive and show little respect for their own rights.

Tempus ex suapte natura vim nullam effectricem habet. Time, of its own nature, has no effectual force.

Tempus mortis inspiciendum. (One must) look to the time of death.

Tenor est qui legem dat feudo. It is the tenor that gives law to the fee. • That is, the tenor of the feudal grant regulates its effect and extent.

Terminus annorum certus debet esse et determinatus. A term of years ought to be certain and definite (with a fixed end).

Terminus et (ac) feodum non possunt constare simul in una eademque persona. Term and fee cannot both be vested in one and the same person at the same time.

Terra manens vacua occupanti conceditur. Land lying unoccupied is given to the occupant.

Terra transit cum onere. Land passes with the incumbrances.

Testamenta latissimam interpretationem habere debent. Wills ought to have the broadest interpretation.

Testamentum est voluntatis nostrae justa sententia, de eo quod quis post mortem suam fieri velit. A testament is the just expression of our will concerning that which anyone wishes done after his death. • Or, as Blackstone renders it, a testament is "the legal declaration of a man's intentions which he wills to be performed after his death." 2 Bl. Com. 499.

Testamentum omne morte consummatum. Every will is completed by death.

Testatoris ultima voluntas est perimplenda secundum veram intentionem suam. The last will of a testator is to be fulfilled according to his true intention.

Testibus deponentibus in pari numero, dignioribus est credendum. When the number of witnesses giving testimony is equal on both sides, the more trustworthy are to be believed.

Testibus, non testimoniis, credendum est. The witnesses must be believed, not (simply) their testimony.

Testimonia ponderanda sunt, non numeranda. Testimonies are to be weighed, not counted.

Testis de visu praeponderat aliis. An eyewitness outweighs others.

Testis nemo in sua causa esse potest. No one can be a witness in his own cause.

Testis oculatus unus plus valet quam auriti decem. One eyewitness is worth more than ten earwitnesses.

Testmoignes ne poent testifier le negative, mes l'affirmative. Witnesses cannot testify to a negative; they must testify to an affirmative.

Timores vani sunt aestimandi qui non cadunt in constantem virum. Those fears must be considered vain (or frivolous) that do not affect a man of steady character.

Titius haeres esto. Let Titius be my heir. • Titius was the Roman counterpart of John Doe.

Titulus est justa causa possidendi id quod nostrum est. Title is the just cause of possessing that which is ours.

Tolle voluntatem et erit omnis actus indifferens. Take away the will, and every action will be indifferent.

Totum praefertur unicuique parti. The whole is preferred to any single part.

Tout ce que la loi ne defend pas est permis. Everything that the law does not forbid is permitted.

Toute exception non surveillée tend à prendre la place du principe. Every exception not watched tends to assume the place of the principle.

Tractent fabrilia fabri. Let smiths perform the work of smiths.

Traditio loqui facit chartam. Delivery makes the deed (document) speak.

Traditionibus et usucapionibus, non nudis pactis, transferuntur rerum dominia. Rights of property are transferred by delivery and by prescription (founded on lengthy possession), not by naked agreements.

Traditio nihil amplius transferre debet vel potest ad eum qui accipit quam est apud eum qui tradit. Delivery neither can nor should transfer anything more to the recipient than is in possession of the one who delivers.

Trado tibe ecclesiam. I deliver this church (or living) to you.

Transgressione multiplicata, crescat poenae inflictio. When transgression is repeated, let the infliction of punishment be increased. 2 Co. Inst. 479.

Transit in rem judicatam. It passes into a judgment.

Transit terra cum onere. The land passes with its burdens.

Tres faciunt collegium. Three form a corporation.

Triatio ibi semper debet fieri ubi juratores meliorem possunt habere notitiam. Trial ought always to be held where the jurors can have the better information.

Triennalis pacificus possessor beneficii est inde securus. The undisturbed possessor of a benefice for three years is thereafter secure (from challenge).

Turpis est pars quae non convenit cum suo toto. The part is bad that does not accord with its whole.

Tuta est custodia quae sibimet creditur. The guardianship is secure that is entrusted to itself alone.

Tutius erratur ex parte mitiori. It is safer to err on the gentler side (or on the side of leniency).

Tutius est rei incumbere quam personae. It is safer to rely upon a thing than upon a person. • Real security is safer than personal security.

Tutius semper est errare in acquietando quam in puniendo, ex parte misericordiae quam ex parte justitiae. It is always safer to err in acquitting than in punishing, (and) on the side of mercy than of justice.

Tutor incertus dari non potest. An uncertain person cannot be given or appointed as tutor.

Tutor in rem suam auctor fieri non potest. A tutor cannot act for his own interest.

Tutor praesumitur intus habere, ante redditas rationes. A tutor is presumed to have funds in his own hands until his accounts have been rendered.

Tutor rem pupilli emere non potest. A tutor cannot purchase the property of his ward.

Ubi aliquid conceditur, conceditur et id sine quo res ipsa esse non potest. When anything is granted, that also is granted without which the thing itself cannot exist.

Ubi aliquid impeditur propter unum, eo remoto, tollitur impedimentum. When anything is impeded by reason of one thing, when that is removed, the impediment is removed.

Ubi cessat remedium ordinarium, ibi decurritur ad extraordinarium. When a common remedy ceases to be of service, recourse is had to an extraordinary one.

Ubi culpa est, ibi poena subesse debet. Where the fault is, there the punishment should be imposed.

Ubicunque est injuria, ibi damnum sequitur. Wherever there is a legal wrong, there damage follows.

Ubi damna dantur victus victori in expensis condemnari debet. Where damages are awarded, the party that did not succeed ought to be adjudged to pay expenses for the party that prevailed.

Ubi eadem ratio, ibi idem jus. Where there is the same reason, there is the same law.

Ubi eadem ratio, ibi idem jus; et de similibus idem est judicium. Where there is the same reason, there is the same law; and the same judgment should be rendered on comparable facts.

Ubi est forum, ibi ergo est jus. Where the forum (or place of jurisdiction) is, there accordingly is the law.

Ubi et dantis et accipientis turpitudo versatur, non posse repeti dicimus; quotiens autem accipientis turpitudo versatur, repeti posse. Where there is misconduct on the part of both giver and receiver, we say the thing cannot be recovered; but as often as the misconduct is on the side of the receiver (alone), it can be recovered.

Ubi factum nullum, ibi fortia nulla. Where there is no fact, there are no strong points.

Ubi jus, ibi remedium. Where there is a right, there is a remedy.

Ubi jus incertum, ibi jus nullum. Where the right is uncertain, there is no right.

Ubi lex aliquem cogit ostendere causam, necesse est quod causa sit justa et legitima.

Where the law compels someone to show cause, it is necessary that the cause be just and legal.

Ubi lex deest, praetor supplet. Where the law is deficient, the praetor supplies the deficiency.

Ubi lex est specialis et ratio ejus generalis, generaliter accipienda est. Where the law is special and the reason of it is general, it ought to be taken as general.

Ubi lex non distinguit, nec nos distinguere debemus. Where the law does not distinguish, we ought not to distinguish.

Ubi major pars est, ibi totum. Where the greater part is, there is the whole.

Ubi matrimonium, ibi dos. Where there is marriage, there is dower.

Ubi non adest norma legis, omnia quasi pro suspectis habenda sunt. Where there is no rule of law, everything must be held, as it were, suspect.

Ubi non est condendi auctoritas, ibi non est parendi necessitas. Where there is no authority to establish (a rule), there is no necessity to obey.

Ubi non est directa lex, standum est arbitrio judicis, vel procedendum ad similia. Where there is not direct law, one must rely on the judgment of the judge or refer to similar cases.

Ubi non est lex, ibi non est transgressio quoad mundum. Where there is not law, there is not transgression, as far as this world is concerned.

Ubi non est manifesta injustitia, judices habentur pro bonis viris, et judicatum pro veritate. Where there is no manifest injustice, the judges are to be regarded as honest men, and their judgment as truth.

Ubi non est principalis, non potest esse accessorius. Where there is no principal, there can be no accessory.

Ubi nulla est conjectura quae ducat alio, verba intelligenda sunt ex proprietate non grammatica sed populari ex usu. Where there is no inference that would lead in another direction, the words are to be understood according to their proper meaning, not strictly according to grammar but according to popular usage.

Ubi nullum matrimonium, ibi nulla dos. Where there is no marriage, there is no dower.

Ubi onus ibi emolumentum. Where the burden is, there is the profit or advantage.

Ubi periculum, ibi et lucrum collocatur. Where the risk is, there also the profit accrues.

Ubi pugnantia inter se in testamento juberentur, neutrum ratum est. When two directions conflicting with each other were given in a will, neither is held valid.

Ubi quid generaliter conceditur, inest haec exceptio, si non aliquid sit contra jus fasque. Where a thing is granted in general terms, this exception is implied: if there is not anything contrary to law and right.

Ubi quis delinquit ibi punietur. Where anyone commits an offense, there will he be punished.

Ubi verba conjuncta non sunt, sufficit alterutrum esse factum. Where words are not conjoined, it is enough that one or another (of the things enumerated) has been done.

Ultima voluntas testatoris est perimplenda secundum veram intentionem suam. The last will of a testator is to be fulfilled according to his true intention.

Ultimum supplicium esse mortem solam interpretamur. We consider death alone to be the extreme punishment.

Ultra posse non potest esse et vice versa. What is beyond possibility cannot exist, and the reverse (what cannot exist is not possible).

Una persona vix potest supplere vices duarum. One person can scarcely supply the place of two.

Unaquaeque gleba servit. Every lump of earth (on the land) is subject to the servitude.

Uniuscujusque contractus initium spectandum est et causa. The beginning and cause of each and every contract must be considered.

Unius omnino testis responsio non audiatur. Let the evidence of one witness not be heard at all.

Universalia sunt notiora singularibus. Things universal are better known than things particular.

Universitas vel corporatio non dicitur aliquid facere nisi id sit collegialiter deliberatum, etiamsi major pars id faciat. A university or corporation is not said to take any action unless the action was resolved by it as a body, even if a greater part of the body should act.

Un ne doit prise advantage de son tort demesne. One should not take advantage from his own wrong.

Uno absurdo dato, infinita sequuntur. When one absurdity has been allowed, an infinity follows.

Unumquodque dissolvitur eodem ligamine quo ligatur. Everything is dissolved by the same binding by which it is bound together.

Unumquodque eodem modo dissolvitur quo colligatur. Any obligation is discharged in the same manner as it is constituted.

Unumquodque eodem modo quo colligatum est dissolvitur. In the same manner in which anything was bound, it is loosened.

Unumquodque est id quod est principalius in ipso. That which is the principal part of a thing is the thing itself.

Unumquodque ligamen dissolvitur eodem ligamine qui et ligatur. Every obligation is dissolved in the same manner in which it is contracted.

Unumquodque principiorum est sibimet ipsi fides; et perspicua vera non sunt probanda. Each and every one of the general principles is its own pledge of trust, and plain truths need not be proved.

Unusquisque debet esse gnarus conditionis ejus cum quo contrahit. Everyone ought to be cognizant of the condition of the person with whom he makes contract.

Usucapio constituta est ut aliquis litium finis esset. Prescription (Roman usucapio) was instituted that there might be some end to lawsuits. Dig. 41.10.5.

Usus est dominium fiduciarium. Use is a fiduciary ownership.

Usus fit ex iteratis actibus. Usage arises from repeated acts.

Utile per inutile non vitiatur. What is useful is not vitiated by the useless.

Ut poena ad paucos, metus ad omnes perveniat. So that punishment afflict few, (and) fear affect all. • Blackstone cites Cicero (pro Cluentio 46) emphasizing deterrence. 4 Bl. Com. 11.

Ut res magis valeat quam pereat. That the matter may have effect rather than fail.

Uxor et filius sunt nomina naturae. Wife and son are names of nature.

Uxor non est sui juris sed sub potestate viri. A wife is not in her own right (i.e., she cannot act independently), but under the power of her husband.

Uxor sequitur domicilium viri. A wife follows the domicile of her husband.

Vagabundum nuncupamus eum qui nullibi domicilium contraxit habitationis. We call the person a vagabond who has acquired nowhere a domicile of residence.

Valeat quantum valere potest. Let it have effect as far as it can have effect.

Vana est illa potentia quae nunquam venit in actum. Vain is that power that never comes into action.

Vani timores sunt aestimandi, qui non cadunt in constantem virem. Those fears are to be considered groundless that do not affect a man of steady character.

Vani timoris justa excusatio non est. There is no legal excuse based on a groundless fear.

Velle non creditur qui obsequitur imperio patris vel domini. A person is not presumed to act of his own will who obeys the orders of his father or his master.

Vendens eandem rem duobus falsarius est. A vendor is fraudulent if he sells the same thing to two (separate) buyers.

Veniae facilitas incentivum est delinquendi. Ease of winning pardon is an incentive to committing crime.

Verba accipienda sunt secundum subjectam materiam. Words are to be interpreted according to the subject matter.

Verba accipienda ut sortiantur effectum. Words are to be taken so that they may have some effect.

Verba aequivoca ac in dubio sensu posita intelliguntur digniori et potentiori sensu. Equivocal words and those in a doubtful sense are understood in the more suitable and more effective sense.

Verba aliquid operari debent—debent intelligi ut aliquid operentur. Words ought to have some effect—words ought to be understood so as to have some effect.

Verba aliquid operari debent; verba cum effectu sunt accipienda. Words ought to have some effect; words must be taken so as to have effect.

Verba artis ex arte. Terms of art (should be explained) from the art.

Verba chartarum fortius accipiuntur contra proferentem. The words of deeds are taken most strongly against the person offering them.

Verba cum effectu accipienda sunt. Words must be taken so as to have effect.

Verba currentis monetae tempus solutionis designant. The words "current money" refer to the time of payment.

Verba debent intelligi cum effectu. Words ought to be understood with effect.

Verba debent intelligi ut aliquid operentur. Words ought to be so understood that they may have some effect.

Verba dicta de persona intelligi debent de conditione personae. Words spoken of the person are to be understood of the condition of the person.

Verba generalia generaliter sunt intelligenda. General words are to be understood generally.

Verba generalia restringuntur ad habilitatem rei vel aptitudinem personae. General words are limited to the capability of the subject matter or the aptitude of the person.

Verba generalia restringuntur ad habilitatem rei vel personae. General words are limited to the capability of the subject matter or of the person.

Verba illata (relata) inesse videntur. Words referred to are considered as if incorporated.

Verba in differenti materia per prius, non per posterius, intelligenda sunt. Words referring to a different subject are to be understood by what goes before, not by what follows.

Verba intelligenda sunt in casu possibili. Words are to be understood in reference to a possible case.

Verba intentioni, et non e contra, debent inservire. Words should be subject to the intention, not the reverse.

Verba ita sunt intelligenda, ut res magis valeat quam pereat. Words are to be so understood that the matter may have effect rather than fail.

Verba mere aequivoca, si per communem usum loquendi in intellectu certo sumuntur, talis intellectus praeferendus est. When words are purely equivocal, if by common usage of speech they are taken in a certain meaning, such meaning is to be preferred.

Verba nihil operari melius est quam absurde. It is better that words should have no effect than an absurd effect.

Verba non tam intuenda quam causa et natura rei, ut mens contrahentium ex eis potius quam ex verbis appareat. The words (of a contract) are not to be looked to so much as the cause and nature of the matter, so that the intention of the contracting parties may appear from these rather than from the (mere) words.

Verba offendi possunt, imo ab eis recedere licet, ut verba ad sanum intellectum reducantur. The words can be faulted—indeed, it is permitted to depart from them, in order that the words may be restored to a sensible meaning.

Verba ordinationis, quando verificari possunt in sua vera significatione, trahi ad extraneum intellectum non debent. When the words of an ordinance can be made true in their true signification, they ought not to be warped to a foreign meaning.

Verba posteriora propter certitudinem addita, ad priora quae certitudine indigent, sunt referunda. Later words added for the purpose of certainty are to be referred to preceding words in which certainty is wanting.

Verba pro re et subjecta materia accipi debent. Words should be taken most in favor of the thing and the subject matter.

Verba quae aliquid operari possunt non debent esse superflua. Words that can have some effect ought not to be (treated as) superfluous.

Verba quantumvis generalia ad aptitudinem restringuntur, etiamsi nullam aliam paterentur restrictionem. Words, howsoever general, are confined to fitness (i.e., to harmonize with the subject matter), even if they would bear no other restriction.

Verba relata hoc maxime operantur per referentiam ut in eis inesse videntur. Words to which reference is made have, by the reference, this particular effect, that they are considered to be incorporated in those (clauses). • Words to which reference is made in an instrument have the same effect and operation as if they were inserted in the clause referring to them.

Verba relata inesse videntur. Words to which reference is made are considered incorporated.

Verba secundum materiam subjectam intelligi nemo est qui nescit. There is no one who does not know that words should be understood according to the subject matter.

Verba semper accipienda sunt in mitiori sensu. Words are always to be taken in their milder sense.

Verba strictae significationis ad latam extendi possunt, si subsit ratio. Words of a strict signification can be given a wide signification if there is reason for it.

Verba sunt indices animi. Words are indications of the intention.

Verbis standum ubi nulla ambiguitas. One must abide by the words where there is no ambiguity.

Verbum imperfecti temporis rem adhuc imperfectam significat. The verb in the imperfect tense indicates a matter as yet incomplete.

Veredictum quasi dictum veritatis; ut judicium quasi juris dictum. A verdict is, as it were, the saying of the truth, in the same manner that a judgment is the saying of the law (or right).

Veritas demonstrationis tollit errorem nominis. The truth of the description removes the error of the name.

Veritas habenda est in juratore; justitia et judicium in judice. Truth is the desideratum in a juror; justice and judgment in a judge.

Veritas nihil veretur nisi abscondi. Truth fears nothing but to be hidden.

Veritas nimium altercando amittitur. By too much quarreling the truth is lost.

Veritas nominis tollit errorem demonstrationis. The truth of the name takes away the error of the description.

Veritatem qui non libere pronunciat, proditor est veritatis. One who does not speak the truth freely is a traitor to the truth.

Via antiqua via est tuta. The old way is the safe way.

Via trita est tutissima. The beaten road is the safest.

Via trita, via tuta. The beaten way is the safe way.

Vicarius non habet vicarium. A deputy does not have a deputy.

Vicini viciniora praesumuntur scire. Neighbors are presumed to know things of the immediate vicinity.

Videtur qui surdus et mutus ne poet faire alienation. A deaf and mute person is considered not to be able to alienate.

Vigilantibus et non dormientibus jura subveniunt. The laws aid the vigilant, not those who sleep.

Vim vi repellere licet, modo fiat moderamine inculpatae tutelae, non ad sumendam vindictam, sed ad propulsandam injuriam. It is lawful to repel force by force; but let it be done with the self-control of blameless defense—not to take revenge, but to repel injury.

Viperina est expositio quae corrodit viscera textus. That is a viperous exposition that gnaws away the innards of the text.

Vir et uxor censentur in lege una persona. Husband and wife are considered one person in law.

Vis legibus est inimica. Force is inimical to the laws.

Vitium clerici nocere non debet. A clerical error ought not to prejudice.

Vitium est quod fugi debet, ne, si rationem non invenias, mox legem sine ratione esse clames. It is a fault that ought to be avoided, that if you do not discover the reason, you quickly exclaim that the law is without reason.

Vix ulla lex fieri potest quae omnibus commoda sit, sed si majori parti prospiciat, utilis est. Scarcely any law can be made that is advantageous to all; but if it benefits the majority, it is useful.

Vocabula artium explicanda sunt secundum definitiones prudentium. Terms of art are to be explained according to the definitions of those who are experienced in that art.

Volenti non fit injuria. There is no injury to one who consents.

Voluit sed non dixit. The person willed but did not say.

Voluntas donatoris in charta doni sui manifeste expressa observetur. The will of the donor, if clearly expressed in the deed of his gift, should be observed.

Voluntas et propositum distinguunt maleficia. The will and the purpose distinguish crimes.

Voluntas facit quod in testamento scriptum valeat. The will (of the testator) gives validity to what is written in the will.

Voluntas in delictis non exitus spectatur. In offenses, the will and not the outcome is regarded.

Voluntas reputatur pro facto. The will is to be taken for the deed.

Voluntas testatoris ambulatoria est usque ad mortem. The will of a testator is ambulatory right up until his death. • That is, he may change it at any time.

Voluntas testatoris habet interpretationem latam et benignam. The will of the testator should receive a broad and liberal interpretation.

Voluntas ultima testatoris est perimplenda secundum veram intentionem suam. The last will of a testator is to be fulfilled according to his true intention.

Vox emissa volat; litera scripta manet. The uttered voice flies; the written letter remains.

Maxims Bibliography

Bl. Com. = Blackstone, William. *Commentaries on the Laws of England*. 4 vols. Reprinted Chicago and London: University of Chicago Press, 1979. From the 1st ed. Oxford: Clarendon Press 1765–1769.

Bracton = Bracton, Henry de. *De Legibus et Consuetudinibus Angliae*. G.E. Woodbine ed.; S.E. Thorne transl. 4 vols. Cambridge, Mass.: Harvard University Press, 1968.

Coke = *The Reports of Sir Edward Coke*. J.H. Thomas & J.F. Fraser eds. 13 parts in 6 vols. London: Butterworth, 1826.

Co. Litt. = Coke, Sir Edward. *The First Part of the Institutes of the Laws of England, or A Commentarie upon Littleton*. 2 vols. Reprinted New York and London: Garland, 1979. From the 1st ed. London: Societe of Stationers, 1628.

Co. Inst. = Coke, Sir Edward. *The Institutes of the Laws of England*. Parts 2–4, in 4 vols. Reprinted Buffalo, N.Y.: William S. Hein, 1986. From the edition of London: Brooke, 1797.

Dig. = *The Digest of Justinian*. T. Mommsen et al. 4 vols. Philadelphia: University of Pennsylvania Press, 1985.

Just. Inst. = *Justinian's Institutes*. P. Krueger ed.; P. Birks & G. McLeod trans. Ithaca, N.Y.: Cornell University Press, 1987.

Appendix B

The Constitution of the United States of America

We the People of the United States, in Order to form a more perfect Union, establish Justice, insure domestic Tranquility, provide for the common defence, promote the general Welfare, and secure the Blessings of Liberty to ourselves and our Posterity, do ordain and establish this Constitution for the United States of America.

Article I

Section 1. All legislative Powers herein granted shall be vested in a Congress of the United States, which shall consist of a Senate and House of Representatives.

Section 2. The House of Representatives shall be composed of Members chosen every second Year by the People of the several States, and the Electors in each State shall have the Qualifications requisite for Electors of the most numerous Branch of the State Legislature.

No Person shall be a Representative who shall not have attained to the Age of twenty five Years, and been seven Years a Citizen of the United States, and who shall not, when elected, be an Inhabitant of that State in which he shall be chosen.

Representatives and direct Taxes shall be apportioned among the several States which may be included within this Union, according to their respective Numbers, which shall be determined by adding to the whole Number of free Persons, including those bound to Service for a Term of Years, and excluding Indians not taxed, three fifths of all other Persons. The actual Enumeration shall be made within three Years after the first Meeting of the Congress of the United States, and within every subsequent Term of ten Years, in such Manner as they shall by Law direct. The Number of Representatives shall not exceed one for every thirty Thousand, but each State shall have at Least one Representative; and until such enumeration shall be made, the State of New Hampshire shall be entitled to chuse three, Massachusetts eight, Rhode Island and Providence Plantations one, Connecticut five, New York six, New Jersey four, Pennsylvania eight, Delaware one, Maryland six, Virginia ten, North Carolina five, South Carolina five, and Georgia three.

When vacancies happen in the Representation from any State, the Executive Authority thereof shall issue Writs of Election to fill such Vacancies.

The House of Representatives shall chuse their Speaker and other Officers; and shall have the sole Power of Impeachment.

Section 3. The Senate of the United States shall be composed of two Senators from each State, chosen by the Legislature thereof, for six Years; and each Senator shall have one Vote.

Immediately after they shall be assembled in Consequence of the first Election, they shall be divided as equally as may be into three Classes. The Seats of the Senators of the first Class shall be vacated at the Expiration of the Second Year, of the second Class at the Expiration of the fourth Year, and of the third Class at the Expiration of the sixth Year, so that one third may be chosen every second Year; and if Vacancies happen by Resignation, or otherwise, during the Recess of the Legislature of any State, the Executive thereof may make temporary Appointments until the next Meeting of the Legislature, which shall then fill such Vacancies.

No Person shall be a Senator who shall not have attained to the Age of thirty Years, and been nine Years a Citizen of the United States, and who shall not, when elected, be an Inhabitant of that State for which he shall be chosen.

The Vice President of the United States shall be President of the Senate, but shall have no Vote, unless they be equally divided.

The Senate shall chuse their other Officers, and also a President pro tempore, in the Absence of the Vice President, or when he shall exercise the Office of President of the United States.

The Senate shall have the sole Power to try all Impeachments. When sitting for that Purpose, they shall be on Oath or Affirmation. When the President of the United States is tried, the Chief Justice shall preside: And no Person shall be convicted without the Concurrence of two thirds of the Members present.

Judgment in Cases of Impeachment shall not extend further than to removal from Office, and disqualification to hold and enjoy any Office of honor, Trust or Profit under the United States: but the Party convicted shall nevertheless be liable and subject to Indictment, Trial, Judgment and Punishment, according to Law.

Section 4. The Times, Places and Manner of holding Elections for Senators and Representatives, shall be prescribed in each State by the Legislature thereof; but the Congress may at any time by Law make or alter such Regulations, except as to the Places of chusing Senators.

The Congress shall assemble at least once in every Year, and such Meeting shall be on the first Monday in December, unless they shall by Law appoint a different Day.

Section 5. Each House shall be the Judge of the Elections, Returns and Qualifications of its own Members, and a Majority of each shall constitute a Quorum to do Business; but a smaller Number may adjourn from day to day, and may be authorized to compel the Attendance of absent Members, in such Manner, and under such Penalties as each House may provide.

Each House may determine the Rules of its Proceedings, punish its Members for disorderly Behavior, and, with the Concurrence of two thirds, expel a Member.

Each House shall keep a Journal of its Proceedings, and from time to time publish the same, excepting such Parts as may in their Judgment require Secrecy; and the Yeas and Nays of the Members of either House on any question shall, at the Desire of one fifth of those Present, be entered on the Journal.

Neither House, during the Session of Congress, shall, without the Consent of the other, adjourn for more than three days, nor to any other Place than that in which the two Houses shall be sitting.

Section 6. The Senators and Representatives shall receive a Compensation for their Services, to be ascertained by Law, and paid out of the Treasury of the United States. They shall in all Cases, except Treason, Felony and Breach of the Peace, be privileged from Arrest during their Attendance at the Session of their respective Houses, and in going to and returning from the same; and for any Speech or Debate in either House, they shall not be questioned in any other Place.

No Senator or Representative shall, during the Time for which he was elected, be appointed to any civil Office under the Authority of the United States, which shall have been created, or the Emoluments whereof shall have been encreased during such time; and no Person holding any Office under the United States, shall be a Member of either House during his Continuance in Office.

Section 7. All Bills for raising Revenue shall originate in the House of Representatives; but the Senate may propose or concur with Amendments as on other Bills.

Every Bill which shall have passed the House of Representatives and the Senate, shall, before it become a Law, be presented to the President of the United States; If he approve he shall sign it, but if not he shall return it, with his Objections to the House in which it shall have originated, who shall enter the Objections at large on their Journal, and proceed to reconsider it. If after such Reconsideration two thirds of that House shall agree to pass the

Bill, it shall be sent, together with the Objections, to the other House, by which it shall likewise be reconsidered, and if approved by two thirds of that House, it shall become a Law. But in all such Cases the Votes of both Houses shall be determined by yeas and nays, and the Names of the Persons voting for and against the Bill shall be entered on the Journal of each House respectively. If any Bill shall not be returned by the President within ten Days (Sundays excepted) after it shall have been presented to him, the Same shall be a Law, in like Manner as if he had signed it, unless the Congress by their Adjournment prevent its Return, in which Case it shall not be a Law.

Every Order, Resolution, or Vote to which the Concurrence of the Senate and House of Representatives may be necessary (except on a question of Adjournment) shall be presented to the President of the United States; and before the Same shall take Effect, shall be approved by him, or being disapproved by him, shall be repassed by two thirds of the Senate and House of Representatives, according to the Rules and Limitations prescribed in the Case of a Bill.

Section 8. The Congress shall have Power To lay and collect Taxes, Duties, Imposts and Excises, to pay the Debts and provide for the common Defence and general Welfare of the United States; but all Duties, Imposts and Excises shall be uniform throughout the United States;

To borrow Money on the credit of the United States;

To regulate Commerce with foreign Nations, and among the several States, and with the Indian Tribes;

To establish an uniform Rule of Naturalization, and uniform Laws on the subject of Bankruptcies throughout the United States;

To coin Money, regulate the Value thereof, and of foreign Coin, and fix the Standard of Weights and Measures;

To provide for the Punishment of counterfeiting the Securities and current Coin of the United States;

To establish Post Offices and post Roads;

To promote the Progress of Science and useful Arts, by securing for limited Times to Authors and Inventors the exclusive Right to their respective Writings and Discoveries;

To constitute Tribunals inferior to the supreme Court;

To define and punish Piracies and Felonies committed on the high Seas, and Offences against the Law of Nations;

To declare War, grant Letters of Marque and Reprisal, and make Rules concerning Captures on Land and Water;

To raise and support Armies, but no Appropriation of Money to that Use shall be for a longer Term than two Years;

To provide and maintain a Navy;

To make Rules for the Government and Regulation of the land and naval Forces;

To provide for calling forth the Militia to execute the Laws of the Union, suppress Insurrections and repel Invasions;

To provide for organizing, arming, and disciplining, the Militia, and for governing such Part of them as may be employed in the Service of the United States, reserving to the States respectively, the Appointment of the Officers, and the Authority of training the Militia according to the discipline prescribed by Congress;

To exercise exclusive Legislation in all Cases whatsoever, over such District (not exceeding ten Miles square) as may, by Cession of particular States, and the Acceptance of Congress, become the Seat of the Government of the United States, and to exercise like Authority over all Places purchased by the Consent of the Legislature of the State in which the Same shall be, for the Erection of Forts, Magazines, Arsenals, dock-Yards, and other needful Buildings;—And

To make all Laws which shall be necessary and proper for carrying into Execution the foregoing Powers, and all other Powers vested by this Constitution in the Government of the United States, or in any Department or Officer thereof.

Section 9. The Migration or Importation of Such Persons as any of the States now existing shall think proper to admit, shall not be prohibited by the Congress prior to the Year one thousand eight hundred and eight, but a Tax or duty may be imposed on such Importation, not exceeding ten dollars for each Person.

The Privilege of the Writ of Habeas Corpus shall not be suspended, unless when in Cases of Rebellion or Invasion the public Safety may require it.

No Bill of Attainder or ex post facto Law shall be passed.

No Capitation, or other direct, Tax shall be laid, unless in Proportion to the Census or Enumeration herein before directed to be taken.

No Tax or Duty shall be laid on Articles exported from any State.

No Preference shall be given by any Regulation of Commerce or Revenue to the Ports of one State over those of another: nor shall Vessels bound to, or from, one State, be obliged to enter, clear, or pay Duties in another.

No Money shall be drawn from the Treasury, but in Consequence of Appropriations made by Law; and a regular Statement and Account of the Receipts and Expenditures of all public Money shall be published from time to time.

No Title of Nobility shall be granted by the United States: And no Person holding any Office of Profit or Trust under them, shall, without the Consent of the Congress, accept of any present, Emolument, Office, or Title, of any kind whatever, from any King, Prince, or foreign State.

Section 10. No State shall enter into any Treaty, Alliance, or Confederation; grant Letters of Marque and Reprisal; coin Money; emit Bills of Credit; make any Thing but gold and silver Coin a Tender in Payment of Debts; pass any Bill of Attainder, ex post facto Law, or Law impairing the Obligation of Contracts, or grant any Title of Nobility.

No State shall, without the Consent of the Congress, lay any Imposts or Duties on Imports or Exports, except what may be absolutely necessary for executing its inspection Laws: and the net Produce of all Duties and Imposts, laid by any State on Imports or Exports, shall be for the Use of the Treasury of the United States; and all such Laws shall be subject to the Revision and Controul of the Congress.

No State shall, without the Consent of Congress, lay any Duty of Tonnage, keep Troops, or Ships of War in time of Peace, enter into any Agreement or Compact with another State, or with a foreign Power, or engage in War, unless actually invaded, or in such imminent Danger as will not admit of delay.

Article II

Section 1. The executive Power shall be vested in a President of the United States of America. He shall hold his Office during the Term of four Years, and, together with the Vice President, chosen for the same Term, be elected, as follows:

Each State shall appoint, in such Manner as the Legislature thereof may direct, a Number of Electors, equal to the whole Number of Senators and Representatives to which the State may be entitled in the Congress: but no Senator or Representative, or Person holding an Office of Trust or Profit under the United States, shall be appointed an Elector.

The Electors shall meet in their respective States, and vote by Ballot for two Persons, of whom one at least shall not be an Inhabitant of the same State with themselves. And they shall make a List of all the Persons voted for, and of the Number of Votes for each; which List they shall sign and certify, and transmit sealed to the Seat of the Government of the United States, directed to the President of the Senate. The President of the Senate shall, in the Presence of the Senate and House of Representatives, open all the Certificates, and the Votes shall then be counted. The Person having the greatest Number of Votes shall be the President, if such Number be a Majority of the whole Number of Electors appointed; and if there be more than one who have such Majority, and have an equal Number of Votes, then the House of Representatives shall immediately chuse by Ballot one of them for President; and if no Person have a Majority, then from the five highest on the List the said House shall in like Manner chuse the President. But in chusing the President, the Votes shall be taken by States, the Representation from each State having one Vote; A quorum for this Purpose shall consist of a Member or Members from two thirds of the States, and a Majority of all the States shall be necessary to a Choice. In every Case, after the Choice of the President, the Person having the greater Number of Votes of the Electors shall be the Vice President. But if there should remain two or more who have equal Votes, the Senate shall chuse from them by Ballot the Vice President.

The Congress may determine the Time of chusing the Electors, and the Day on which they shall give their Votes; which Day shall be the same throughout the United States.

No Person except a natural born Citizen, or a Citizen of the United States, at the time of the Adoption of this Constitution, shall be eligible to the Office of President; neither shall any Person be eligible to that Office who shall not have attained to the Age of thirty five Years, and been fourteen Years a Resident within the United States.

In Case of the Removal of the President from Office, or of his Death, Resignation or Inability to discharge the Powers and Duties of the said Office, the Same shall devolve on the Vice President and the Congress may by Law provide for the Case of Removal, Death, Resignation or Inability, both of the President and Vice President, declaring what Officer shall then act as President, and such Officer shall act accordingly, until the Disability be removed, or a President shall be elected.

The President shall, at stated Times, receive for his Services, a Compensation, which shall neither be increased nor diminished during the Period for which he shall have been elected, and he shall not receive within that Period any other Emolument from the United States, or any of them.

Before he enter on the Execution of his Office, he shall take the following Oath or Affirmation: "I do solemnly swear (or affirm) that I will faithfully execute the Office of President of the United States, and will to the best of my Ability, preserve, protect and defend the Constitution of the United States."

Section 2. The President shall be Commander in Chief of the Army and Navy of the United States, and of the Militia of the several States, when called into the actual Service of the United States; he may require the Opinion, in writing, of the principal Officer in each of the Executive Departments, upon any Subject relating to the Duties of their respective Offices and he shall have Power to grant Reprieves and Pardons for Offences against the United States, except in Cases of Impeachment.

He shall have Power, by and with the Advice and Consent of the Senate, to make Treaties, provided two thirds of the Senators present concur; and he shall nominate, and by and with the Advice and Consent of the Senate, shall appoint Ambassadors, other public Ministers and Consuls, Judges of the supreme Court, and all other Officers of the United States, whose Appointments are not herein otherwise provided for, and which shall be established by Law: but the Congress may by Law vest the Appointment of such inferior Officers, as they think proper, in the President alone, in the Courts of Law, or in the Heads of Departments.

The President shall have Power to fill up all Vacancies that may happen during the Recess of the Senate, by granting Commissions which shall expire at the End of their next Session.

Section 3. He shall from time to time give to the Congress Information of the State of the Union, and recommend to their Consideration such Measures as he shall judge necessary and expedient; he may, on extraordinary Occasions, convene both Houses, or either of them, and in Case of Disagreement between them, with Respect to the Time of Adjournment, he may adjourn them to such Time as he shall think proper; he shall receive Ambassadors and other public Ministers; he shall take Care that the Laws be faithfully executed, and shall Commission all the Officers of the United States.

Section 4. The President, Vice President and all civil Officers of the United States, shall be removed from Office on Impeachment for, and Conviction of, Treason, Bribery, or other high Crimes and Misdemeanors.

Article III

Section 1. The judicial Power of the United States, shall be vested in one supreme Court, and in such inferior Courts as the Congress may from time to time ordain and establish. The Judges, both of the supreme and inferior Courts, shall hold their Offices during good Behaviour, and shall, at stated Times, receive for their Services a Compensation, which shall not be diminished during their Continuance in Office.

Section 2. The judicial Power shall extend to all Cases, in Law and Equity, arising under this Constitution, the Laws of the United States, and Treaties made, or which shall be made, under their Authority;—to all Cases affecting Ambassadors, other public Ministers and Consuls;—to all Cases of admiralty and maritime Jurisdiction;—to Controversies to which the United States shall be a Party;—to Controversies between two or more States;—between a State and Citizens of another State;—between Citizens of different States;—between Citizens of the same State claiming Lands under the Grants of different States, and between a State, or the Citizens thereof, and foreign States, Citizens or Subjects.

In all Cases affecting Ambassadors, other public Ministers and Consuls, and those in which a State shall be a Party, the supreme Court shall have original Jurisdiction. In all the other Cases before mentioned, the supreme Court shall have appellate Jurisdiction, both as to Law and Fact, with such Exceptions, and under such Regulations as the Congress shall make.

The trial of all Crimes, except in Cases of Impeachment, shall be by Jury; and such Trial shall be held in the State where the said Crimes shall have been committed; but when not committed within any State, the Trial shall be at such Place or Places as the Congress may by Law have directed.

Section 3. Treason against the United States, shall consist only in levying War against them, or, in adhering to their Enemies, giving them Aid and Comfort. No Person shall be convicted of Treason unless on the Testimony of two Witnesses to the same overt Act, or on Confession in open Court.

The Congress shall have Power to declare the Punishment of Treason, but no Attainder of Treason shall work Corruption of Blood, or Forfeiture except during the Life of the Person attainted.

Article IV

Section 1. Full Faith and Credit shall be given in each State to the public Acts, Records, and judicial Proceedings of every other State. And the Congress may by general Laws prescribe the Manner in which such Acts, Records and Proceedings shall be proved, and the Effect thereof.

Section 2. The Citizens of each State shall be entitled to all Privileges and Immunities of Citizens in the several States.

A Person charged in any State with Treason, Felony, or other Crime, who shall flee from Justice, and be found in another State, shall on demand of the executive Authority of the State from which he fled, be delivered up, to be removed to the State having Jurisdiction of the Crime.

No Person held to Service or Labour in one State, under the Laws thereof, escaping into another, shall, in Consequence of any Law or Regulation therein, be discharged from such Service or Labour, but shall be delivered up on Claim of the Party to whom such Service or Labour may be due.

Section 3. New States may be admitted by the Congress into this Union; but no new State shall be formed or erected with the Jurisdiction of any other State; nor any State be formed by the Junction of two or more States, or Parts of States, without the Consent of the Legislatures of the States concerned as well as of the Congress.

The Congress shall have Power to dispose of and make all needful Rules and Regulations respecting the Territory or other Property belonging to the United States; and nothing in this Constitution shall be so construed as to Prejudice any Claims of the United States, or of any particular State.

Section 4. The United States shall guarantee to every State in this Union a Republican Form of Government, and shall protect each of them against Invasion; and on Application of the Legislature, or of the Executive (when the Legislature cannot be convened) against domestic Violence.

Article V

The Congress, whenever two thirds of both Houses shall deem it necessary, shall propose Amendments to this Constitution, or, on the Application of the Legislatures of two thirds of the several States, shall call a Convention for proposing Amendments, which, in either Case, shall be valid to all Intents and Purposes, as Part of this Constitution, when ratified by the Legislatures of three fourths of the several States, or by Conventions in three fourths thereof, as the one or the other Mode of Ratification may be proposed by the Congress; Provided that no Amendment which may be made prior to the Year One thousand eight hundred and eight shall in any Manner affect the first and fourth Clauses in the Ninth Section of the first Article; and that no State, without its Consent, shall be deprived of its equal Suffrage in the Senate.

Article VI

All Debts contracted and Engagements entered into, before the Adoption of this Constitution, shall be as valid against the United States under this Constitution, as under the Confederation.

This Constitution, and the Laws of the United States which shall be made in Pursuance thereof; and all Treaties made, or which shall be made, under the Authority of the United States, shall be the supreme Law of the Land; and the Judges in every State shall be bound thereby, any Thing in the Constitution or Laws of any State to the Contrary notwithstanding.

The Senators and Representatives before mentioned, and the Members of the several State Legislatures, and all executive and judicial Officers, both of the United States and of the several States, shall be bound by Oath or Affirmation, to support this Constitution; but no religious Test shall ever be required as a Qualification to any Office or public Trust under the United States.

Article VII

The Ratification of the Conventions of nine States, shall be sufficient for the Establishment of this Constitution between the States so ratifying the Same.

ARTICLES IN ADDITION TO, AND AMENDMENT OF, THE CONSTITUTION OF THE UNITED STATES OF AMERICA, PROPOSED BY CONGRESS, AND RATIFIED BY THE LEGISLATURES OF THE SEVERAL STATES PURSUANT TO THE FIFTH ARTICLE OF THE ORIGINAL CONSTITUTION.

Amendment I [1791]

Congress shall make no law respecting an establishment of religion, or prohibiting the free exercise thereof; or abridging the freedom of speech, or of the press; or the right of the people peaceably to assemble, and to petition the Government for a redress of grievances.

Amendment II [1791]

A well regulated Militia, being necessary to the security of a free State, the right of the people to keep and bear Arms, shall not be infringed.

Amendment III [1791]

No Soldier shall, in time of peace be quartered in any house, without the consent of the Owner, nor in time of war, but in a manner to be prescribed by law.

Amendment IV [1791]

The right of the people to be secure in their persons, houses, papers, and effects, against unreasonable searches and seizures, shall not be violated, and no Warrants shall issue, but upon probable cause, supported by Oath or affirmation, and particularly describing the place to be searched, and the persons or things to be seized.

Amendment V [1791]

No person shall be held to answer for a capital, or otherwise infamous crime, unless on a presentment or indictment of a Grand Jury, except in cases arising in the land or naval forces, or in the Militia, when in actual service in time of War or public danger; nor shall any person be subject for the same offence to be twice put in jeopardy of life or limb; nor shall be compelled in any criminal case to be a witness against himself, nor be deprived of life, liberty, or property, without due process of law; nor shall private property be taken for public use, without just compensation.

Amendment VI [1791]

In all criminal prosecutions, the accused shall enjoy the right to a speedy and public trial, by an impartial jury of the State and district wherein the crime shall have been committed, which district shall have been previously ascertained by law, and to be informed of the nature and cause of the accusation; to be confronted with the witnesses against him; to have compulsory process for obtaining witnesses in his favor, and to have the Assistance of Counsel for his defence.

Amendment VII [1791]

In Suits at common law, where the value in controversy shall exceed twenty dollars, the right of trial by jury shall be preserved, and no fact tried by jury, shall be otherwise re-examined in any Court of the United States, than according to the rules of the common law.

Amendment VIII [1791]

Excessive bail shall not be required, nor excessive fines imposed, nor cruel and unusual punishments inflicted.

Amendment IX [1791]

The enumeration in the Constitution, of certain rights, shall not be construed to deny or disparage others retained by the people.

Amendment X [1791]

The powers not delegated to the United States by the Constitution, nor prohibited by it to the States, are reserved to the States respectively, or to the people.

Amendment XI [1798]

The Judicial power of the United States shall not be construed to extend to any suit in law or equity, commenced or prosecuted against one of the United States by Citizens of another State, or by Citizens or Subjects of any Foreign State.

Amendment XII [1804]

The Electors shall meet in their respective states and vote by ballot for President and Vice-President, one of whom, at least, shall not be an inhabitant of the same state with themselves; they shall name in their ballots the person voted for as President, and in distinct ballots the person voted for as Vice-President, and they shall make distinct lists of all persons voted for as President, and of all persons voted for as Vice-President, and of the number of votes for each, which lists they shall sign and certify, and transmit sealed to the seat of the government of the United States, directed to the President of the Senate;—The President of the Senate shall, in the presence of the Senate and House of Representatives, open all the certificates and the votes shall then be counted;—The person having the greatest number of votes for President, shall be the President, if such number be a majority of the whole number of Electors appointed; and if no person have such majority, then from the persons having the highest numbers not exceeding three on the list of those voted for as President, the House of Representatives shall choose immediately, by ballot, the President. But in choosing the President, the votes shall be taken by states, the representation from each state having one vote; a quorum for this purpose shall consist of a member or members from two-thirds of the states, and a majority of all the states shall be necessary to a choice. And if the House of Representatives shall not choose a President whenever the right of choice shall devolve upon them before the fourth day of March next following, then the Vice-President shall act as President, as in the case of the death or other constitutional disability of the President.—The person having the greatest number of votes as Vice-President, shall be the Vice-President, if such number be a majority of the whole number of Electors appointed, and if no person have a majority, then from the two highest numbers on the list, the Senate shall choose the Vice-President; a quorum for the purpose shall consist of two-thirds of the whole number of Senators, and a majority of the whole number shall be necessary to a choice. But no person constitutionally ineligible to the office of President shall be eligible to that of Vice-President of the United States.

Amendment XIII [1865]

Section 1. Neither slavery nor involuntary servitude, except as a punishment for crime whereof the party shall have been duly convicted, shall exist within the United States, or any place subject to their jurisdiction.

Section 2. Congress shall have power to enforce this article by appropriate legislation.

Amendment XIV [1868]

Section 1. All persons born or naturalized in the United States, and subject to the jurisdiction thereof, are citizens of the United States and of the State wherein they reside. No State shall make or enforce any law which shall abridge the privileges or immunities of citizens of the United States; nor shall any State deprive any person of life, liberty, or property, without due process of law; nor deny to any person within its jurisdiction the equal protection of the laws.

Section 2. Representatives shall be apportioned among the several States according to their respective numbers, counting the whole number of persons in each State, excluding

Indians not taxed. But when the right to vote at any election for the choice of electors for President and Vice President of the United States, Representatives in Congress, the Executive and Judicial officers of a State, or the members of the Legislature thereof, is denied to any of the male inhabitants of such State, being twenty-one years of age, and citizens of the United States, or in any way abridged, except for participation in rebellion, or other crime, the basis of representation therein shall be reduced in the proportion which the number of such male citizens shall bear to the whole number of male citizens twenty-one years of age in such State.

Section 3. No person shall be a Senator or Representative in Congress, or elector of President and Vice President, or hold any office, civil or military, under the United States, or under any State, who, having previously taken an oath, as a member of Congress, or as an officer of the United States, or as a member of any State legislature, or as an executive or judicial officer of any State, to support the Constitution of the United States, shall have engaged in insurrection or rebellion against the same, or given aid or comfort to the enemies thereof. But Congress may by a vote of two-thirds of each House, remove such disability.

Section 4. The validity of the public debt of the United States, authorized by law, including debts incurred for payment of pensions and bounties for services in suppressing insurrection or rebellion, shall not be questioned. But neither the United States nor any State shall assume or pay any debt or obligation incurred in aid of insurrection or rebellion against the United States, or any claim for the loss or emancipation of any slave; but all such debts, obligations and claims shall be held illegal and void.

Section 5. The Congress shall have power to enforce, by appropriate legislation, the provisions of this article.

Amendment XV [1870]

Section 1. The right of citizens of the United States to vote shall not be denied or abridged by the United States or by any State on account of race, color, or previous condition of servitude.

Section 2. The Congress shall have power to enforce this article by appropriate legislation.

Amendment XVI [1913]

The Congress shall have power to lay and collect taxes on incomes, from whatever source derived, without apportionment among the several States, and without regard to any census or enumeration.

Amendment XVII [1913]

[1] The Senate of the United States shall be composed of two Senators from each State, elected by the people thereof, for six years; and each Senator shall have one vote. The electors in each State shall have the qualifications requisite for electors of the most numerous branch of the State legislatures.

[2] When vacancies happen in the representation of any State in the Senate, the executive authority of such State shall issue writs of election to fill such vacancies: *Provided,* That the legislature of any State may empower the executive thereof to make temporary appointments until the people fill the vacancies by election as the legislature may direct.

[3] This amendment shall not be so construed as to affect the election or term of any Senator chosen before it becomes valid as part of the Constitution.

Amendment XVIII [1919]

Section 1. After one year from the ratification of this article the manufacture, sale, or transportation of intoxicating liquors within, the importation thereof into, or the exportation thereof from the United States and all territory subject to the jurisdiction thereof for beverage purposes is hereby prohibited.

Section 2. The Congress and the several States shall have concurrent power to enforce this article by appropriate legislation.

Section 3. This article shall be inoperative unless it shall have been ratified as an amendment to the Constitution by the legislatures of the several States, as provided in the Constitution, within seven years from the date of the submission hereof to the States by the Congress.

Amendment XIX [1920]

[1] The right of citizens of the United States to vote shall not be denied or abridged by the United States or by any State on account of sex.

[2] Congress shall have power to enforce this article by appropriate legislation.

Amendment XX [1933]

Section 1. The terms of the President and Vice President shall end at noon on the 20th day of January, and the terms of Senators and Representatives at noon on the 3d day of January, of the years in which such terms would have ended if this article had not been ratified; and the terms of their successors shall then begin.

Section 2. The Congress shall assemble at least once in every year, and such meeting shall begin at noon on the 3d day of January, unless they shall by law appoint a different day.

Section 3. If, at the time fixed for the beginning of the term of the President, the President elect shall have died, the Vice President elect shall become President. If the President shall not have been chosen before the time fixed for the beginning of his term, or if the President elect shall have failed to qualify, then the Vice President elect shall act as President until a President shall have qualified; and the Congress may by law provide for the case wherein neither a President elect nor a Vice President elect shall have qualified, declaring who shall then act as President, or the manner in which one who is to act shall be selected, and such person shall act accordingly until a President or Vice President shall have qualified.

Section 4. The Congress may by law provide for the case of the death of any of the persons from whom the House of Representatives may choose a President whenever the right of choice shall have devolved upon them, and for the case of the death of any of the persons from whom the Senate may choose a Vice President whenever the right of choice shall have devolved upon them.

Section 5. Sections 1 and 2 shall take effect on the 15th day of October following the ratification of this article.

Section 6. This article shall be inoperative unless it shall have been ratified as an amendment to the Constitution by the legislatures of three-fourths of the several States within seven years from the date of its submission.

Amendment XXI [1933]

Section 1. The eighteenth article of amendment to the Constitution of the United States is hereby repealed.

Section 2. The transportation or importation into any State, Territory, or possession of the United States for delivery or use therein of intoxicating liquors, in violation of the laws thereof, is hereby prohibited.

Section 3. This article shall be inoperative unless it shall have been ratified as an amendment to the Constitution by conventions in the several States, as provided in the Constitution, within seven years from the date of the submission hereof to the States by the Congress.

Amendment XXII [1951]

Section 1. No person shall be elected to the office of the President more than twice, and no person who has held the office of President, or acted as President, for more than two years of a term to which some other person was elected President shall be elected to the office of President more than once. But this Article shall not apply to any person holding the office of President when this Article was proposed by the Congress, and shall not prevent any person who may be holding the office of President, or acting as President, during the term within which this Article becomes operative from holding the office of President or acting as President during the remainder of such term.

Section 2. This article shall be inoperative unless it shall have been ratified as an amendment to the Constitution by the legislatures of three-fourths of the several States within seven years from the date of its submission to the States by the Congress.

Amendment XXIII [1961]

Section 1. The District constituting the seat of Government of the United States shall appoint in such manner as the Congress may direct:

A number of electors of President and Vice President equal to the whole number of Senators and Representatives in Congress to which the District would be entitled if it were a State, but in no event more than the least populous state; they shall be in addition to those appointed by the states, but they shall be considered, for the purposes of the election of President and Vice President, to be electors appointed by a state; and they shall meet in the District and perform such duties as provided by the twelfth article of amendment.

Section 2. The Congress shall have power to enforce this article by appropriate legislation.

Amendment XXIV [1964]

Section 1. The right of citizens of the United States to vote in any primary or other election for President or Vice President, for electors for President or Vice President, or for Senator or Representative in Congress, shall not be denied or abridged by the United States or any State by reason of failure to pay any poll tax or other tax.

Section 2. The Congress shall have power to enforce this article by appropriate legislation.

Amendment XXV [1967]

Section 1. In the case of the removal of the President from office or of his death or resignation, the Vice President shall become President.

Section 2. Whenever there is a vacancy in the office of the Vice President, the President shall nominate a Vice President who shall take office upon confirmation by a majority vote of both Houses of Congress.

Section 3. Whenever the President transmits to the President pro tempore of the Senate and the Speaker of the House of Representatives his written declaration that he is unable to discharge the powers and duties of his office, and until he transmits to them a written declaration to the contrary, such powers and duties shall be discharged by the Vice President as Acting President.

Section 4. Whenever the Vice President and a majority of either the principal officers of the executive departments or of such other body as Congress may by law provide, transmit to the President pro tempore of the Senate and the Speaker of the House of Representatives their written declaration that the President is unable to discharge the powers and duties of his office, the Vice President shall immediately assume the powers and duties of the office as Acting President.

Thereafter, when the President transmits to the President pro tempore of the Senate and the Speaker of the House of Representatives his written declaration that no inability exists, he shall resume the powers and duties of his office unless the Vice President and a majority of either the principal officers of the executive department or of such other body as Congress may by law provide, transmit within four days to the President pro tempore of the Senate and the Speaker of the House of Representatives their written declaration that the President is unable to discharge the powers and duties of his office. Thereupon Congress shall decide the issue, assembling within forty-eight hours for that purpose if not in session. If the Congress, within twenty-one days after receipt of the latter written declaration, or, if Congress is not in session, within twenty-one days after Congress is required to assemble, determines by two-thirds vote of both Houses that the President is unable to discharge the powers and duties of his office, the Vice President shall continue to discharge the same as Acting President; otherwise, the President shall resume the powers and duties of his office.

Amendment XXVI [1971]

Section 1. The right of citizens of the United States, who are eighteen years of age or older, to vote shall not be denied or abridged by the United States or by any State on account of age.

Section 2. The Congress shall have power to enforce this article by appropriate legislation.

Amendment XXVII [1992]

No Law, varying the compensation for the services of the Senators and Representatives, shall take effect, until an election of Representatives shall have intervened.

Appendix C

Universal Declaration of Human Rights

On December 10, 1948, the General Assembly of the United Nations adopted and proclaimed the Universal Declaration of Human Rights, the full text of which appears in the following pages. Following this historic act, the Assembly called upon all Member countries to publicize the text of the Declaration and "to cause it to be disseminated, displayed, read and expounded principally in schools and other educational institutions, without distinction based on the political status of countries or territories."

Preamble

Whereas recognition of the inherent dignity and of the equal and inalienable rights of all members of the human family is the foundation of freedom, justice and peace in the world,

Whereas disregard and contempt for human rights have resulted in barbarous acts which have outraged the conscience of mankind, and the advent of a world in which human beings shall enjoy freedom of speech and belief and freedom from fear and want has been proclaimed as the highest aspiration of the common people,

Whereas it is essential, if man is not to be compelled to have recourse, as a last resort, to rebellion against tyranny and oppression, that human rights should be protected by the rule of law,

Whereas it is essential to promote the development of friendly relations between nations,

Whereas the peoples of the United Nations have in the Charter reaffirmed their faith in fundamental human rights, in the dignity and worth of the human person and in the equal rights of men and women and have determined to promote social progress and better standards of life in larger freedom,

Whereas Member States have pledged themselves to achieve, in cooperation with the United Nations, the promotion of universal respect for and observance of human rights and fundamental freedoms,

Whereas a common understanding of these rights and freedoms is of the greatest importance for the full realization of this pledge,

Now, Therefore
THE GENERAL ASSEMBLY
proclaims
THIS UNIVERSAL DECLARATION OF HUMAN RIGHTS
as a common standard of achievement for all peoples and all nations, to the end that every individual and every organ of society, keeping this Declaration constantly in mind, shall strive by teaching and education to promote respect for these rights and freedoms and by progressive measures, national and international, to secure their universal and effective recognition and observance, both among the peoples of Member States themselves and among the peoples of territories under their jurisdiction.

Article 1. All human beings are born free and equal in dignity and rights. They are endowed with reason and conscience and should act towards one another in a spirit of brotherhood.

Article 2. Everyone is entitled to all the rights and freedoms set forth in this Declaration, without distinction of any kind, such as race, colour, sex, language, religion, political or other opinion, national or social origin, property, birth or other status. Furthermore, no distinction shall be made on the basis of the political, jurisdictional or international status of the country or territory to which a person belongs, whether it be independent, trust, non-self-governing or under any other limitation of sovereignty.

Article 3. Everyone has the right to life, liberty and security of person.

Article 4. No one shall be held in slavery or servitude; slavery and the slave trade shall be prohibited in all their forms.

Article 5. No one shall be subjected to torture or to cruel, inhuman or degrading treatment or punishment.

Article 6. Everyone has the right to recognition everywhere as a person before the law.

Article 7. All are equal before the law and are entitled without any discrimination to equal protection of the law. All are entitled to equal protection against any discrimination in violation of this Declaration and against any incitement to such discrimination.

Article 8. Everyone has the right to an effective remedy by the competent national tribunals for acts violating the fundamental rights granted him by the constitution or by law.

Article 9. No one shall be subjected to arbitrary arrest, detention or exile.

Article 10. Everyone is entitled in full equality to a fair and public hearing by an independent and impartial tribunal, in the determination of his rights and obligations and of any criminal charge against him.

Article 11. (1) Everyone charged with a penal offence has the right to be presumed innocent until proved guilty according to law in a public trial at which he has had all the guarantees necessary for his defence.

(2) No one shall be held guilty of any penal offence on account of any act or omission which did not constitute a penal offence, under national or international law, at the time when it was committed. Nor shall a heavier penalty be imposed than the one that was applicable at the time the penal offence was committed.

Article 12. No one shall be subjected to arbitrary interference with his privacy, family, home or correspondence, nor to attacks upon his honour and reputation. Everyone has the right to the protection of the law against such interference or attacks.

Article 13. (1) Everyone has the right to freedom of movement and residence within the borders of each State.

(2) Everyone has the right to leave any country, including his own, and to return to his country.

Article 14. (1) Everyone has the right to seek and to enjoy in other countries asylum from persecution.

(2) This right may not be invoked in the case of prosecutions genuinely arising from nonpolitical crimes or from acts contrary to the purposes and principles of the United Nations.

Article 15. (1) Everyone has the right to a nationality.

(2) No one shall be arbitrarily deprived of his nationality nor denied the right to change his nationality.

Article 16. (1) Men and women of full age, without any limitation due to race, nationality or religion, have the right to marry and to found a family. They are entitled to equal rights as to marriage, during marriage and at its dissolution.

(2) Marriage shall be entered into only with the free and full consent of the intending spouses.

(3) The family is the natural and fundamental group unit of society and is entitled to protection by society and the State.

Article 17. (1) Everyone has the right to own property alone as well as in association with others.

(2) No one shall be arbitrarily deprived of his property.

Article 18. Everyone has the right to freedom of thought, conscience and religion; this right includes freedom to change his religion or belief, and freedom, either alone or in community with others and in public or private, to manifest his religion or belief in teaching, practice, worship and observance.

Article 19. Everyone has the right to freedom of opinion and expression; this right includes freedom to hold opinions without interference and to seek, receive and impart information and ideas through any media and regardless of frontiers.

Article 20. (1) Everyone has the right to freedom of peaceful assembly and association.

(2) No one may be compelled to belong to an association.

Article 21. (1) Everyone has the right to take part in the government of his country, directly or through freely chosen representatives.

(2) Everyone has the right to equal access to public service in his country.

(3) The will of the people shall be the basis of the authority of government; this shall be expressed in periodic and genuine elections which shall be by universal and equal suffrage and shall be held by secret vote or by equivalent free voting procedures.

Article 22. Everyone, as a member of society, has the right to social security and is entitled to realization, through national effort and international cooperation and in accordance with the organization and resources of each State, of the economic, social and cultural rights indispensable for his dignity and the free development of his personality.

Article 23. (1) Everyone has the right to work, to free choice of employment, to just and favourable conditions of work and to protection against unemployment.

(2) Everyone, without any discrimination, has the right to equal pay for equal work.

(3) Everyone who works has the right to just and favourable remuneration ensuring for himself and his family an existence worthy of human dignity, and supplemented, if necessary, by other means of social protection.

(4) Everyone has the right to form and to join trade unions for the protection of his interests.

Article 24. Everyone has the right to rest and leisure, including reasonable limitation of working hours and periodic holidays with pay.

Article 25. (1) Everyone has the right to a standard of living adequate for the health and well-being of himself and of his family, including food, clothing, housing and medical care and necessary social services, and the right to security in the event of unemployment, sickness, disability, widowhood, old age or other lack of livelihood in circumstances beyond his control.

(2) Motherhood and childhood are entitled to special care and assistance. All children, whether born in or out of wedlock, shall enjoy the same social protection.

Article 26. (1) Everyone has the right to education. Education shall be free, at least in the elementary and fundamental stages. Elementary education shall be compulsory. Technical and professional education shall be made generally available and higher education shall be equally accessible to all on the basis of merit.

(2) Education shall be directed to the full development of the human personality and to the strengthening of respect for human rights and fundamental freedoms. It shall promote understanding, tolerance and friendship among all nations, racial or religious groups, and shall further the activities of the United Nations for the maintenance of peace.

(3) Parents have a prior right to choose the kind of education that shall be given to their children.

Article 27. (1) Everyone has the right freely to participate in the cultural life of the community, to enjoy the arts and to share in scientific advancement and its benefits.

(2) Everyone has the right to the protection of the moral and material interests resulting from any scientific, literary or artistic production of which he is the author.

Article 28. Everyone is entitled to a social and international order in which the rights and freedoms set forth in this Declaration can be fully realized.

Article 29. (1) Everyone has duties to the community in which alone the free and full development of his personality is possible.

(2) In the exercise of his rights and freedoms, everyone shall be subject only to such limitations as are determined by law solely for the purpose of securing due recognition and respect for the rights and freedoms of others and of meeting the just requirements of morality, public order and the general welfare in a democratic society.

(3) These rights and freedoms may in no case be exercised contrary to the purposes and principles of the United Nations.

Article 30. Nothing in this Declaration may be interpreted as implying for any State, group or person any right to engage in any activity or to perform any act aimed at the destruction of any of the rights and freedoms set forth herein.

Appendix D

Time Chart of the United States Supreme Court †

The following table is designed to aid the user in identifying the composition of the Court at any given time in American history. Each listing is headed by the Chief Justice, whose name is italicized. Associate Justices are listed following the Chief Justice in order of seniority. In addition to dates of appointment, the table provides information on political-party affiliation. Following each Justice is a symbol representing his party affiliation at the time of appointment:

F = Federalist
DR = Democratic Republican (Jeffersonian)
D = Democrat
W = Whig
R = Republican
I = Independent

1789
- Jay (F)
- J. Rutledge (F)
- Cushing (F)
- Wilson (F)
- Blair (F)

1790-91
- *Jay* (F)
- J. Rutledge (F)
- Cushing (F)
- Wilson (F)
- Blair (F)
- Iredell (F)

1792
- *Jay* (F)
- Cushing (F)
- Wilson (F)
- Blair (F)
- Iredell (F)
- T. Johnson (F)

1793-94
- *Jay* (F)
- Cushing (F)
- Wilson (F)
- Blair (F)
- Iredell (F)
- Paterson (F)

1795
- *J. Rutledge* (F)*
- Cushing (F)
- Wilson (F)
- Blair (F)
- Iredell (F)
- Paterson (F)

1796-97
- *Ellsworth* (F)
- Cushing (F)
- Wilson (F)
- Iredell (F)
- Paterson (F)
- S. Chase (F)

1798-99
- *Ellsworth* (F)
- Cushing (F)
- Iredell (F)
- Paterson (F)
- S. Chase (F)
- Washington (F)

1800
- *Ellsworth* (F)
- Cushing (F)
- Paterson (F)
- S. Chase (F)
- Washington (F)
- Moore (F)

1801-03
- *J. Marshall* (F)
- Cushing (F)
- Paterson (F)
- S. Chase (F)
- Washington (F)
- Moore (F)

1804-05
- *J. Marshall* (F)
- Cushing (F)
- Paterson (F)
- S. Chase (F)
- Washington (F)
- W. Johnson (DR)

1806
- *J. Marshall* (F)
- Cushing (F)
- S. Chase (F)
- Washington (F)
- W. Johnson (DR)
- Livingston (DR)

1807-10
- *J. Marshall* (F)
- Cushing (F)
- S. Chase (F)
- Washington (F)
- W. Johnson (DR)
- Livingston (DR)
- Todd (DR)

1811-22
- *J. Marshall* (F)
- Washington (F)
- W. Johnson (DR)
- Livingston (DR)
- Todd (DR)
- Duval (DR)
- Story (DR)

1823-25
- *J. Marshall* (F)
- Washington (F)
- W. Johnson (DR)
- Todd (DR)
- Duval (DR)
- Story (DR)
- Thompson (DR)

1826-28
- *J. Marshall* (F)
- Washington (F)
- W. Johnson (DR)
- Duval (DR)
- Story (DR)
- Thompson (DR)
- Trimble (DR)

1829
- *J. Marshall* (F)
- Washington (F)
- W. Johnson (DR)
- Duval (DR)
- Story (DR)
- Thompson (DR)
- McLean (D)

1830-34
- *J. Marshall* (F)
- W. Johnson (DR)
- Duval (DR)
- Story (DR)
- Thompson (DR)
- McLean (D)
- Baldwin (D)

1835
- *J. Marshall* (F)
- Duval (DR)
- Story (DR)
- Thompson (DR)
- McLean (D)
- Baldwin (D)
- Wayne (D)

1836
- *Taney* (D)
- Story (DR)
- Thompson (DR)
- McLean (D)
- Baldwin (D)
- Wayne (D)
- Barbour (D)

1837-40
- *Taney* (D)
- Story (DR)
- Thompson (DR)
- McLean (D)
- Baldwin (D)
- Wayne (D)
- Barbour (D)
- Catron (D)
- McKinley (D)

1841-43
- *Taney* (D)
- Story (DR)
- Thompson (DR)
- McLean (D)
- Baldwin (D)
- Wayne (D)
- Catron (D)
- McKinley (D)
- Daniel (D)

1844
- *Taney* (D)
- Story (DR)
- McLean (D)
- Baldwin (D)
- Wayne (D)
- Catron (D)
- McKinley (D)
- Daniel (D)

† Source: Ducat and Chase, *Constitutional Interpretation*, 4th Edition, published in 1988 by West Publishing Co.

1845
Taney (D)
McLean (D)
Wayne (D)
Catron (D)
McKinley (D)
Daniel (D)
Nelson (D)
Woodbury (D)

1846-50
Taney (D)
McLean (D)
Wayne (D)
Catron (D)
McKinley (D)
Daniel (D)
Nelson (D)
Woodbury (D)
Grier (D)

1851-52
Taney (D)
McLean (D)
Wayne (D)
Catron (D)
McKinley (D)
Daniel (D)
Nelson (D)
Grier (D)
Curtis (W)

1853-57
Taney (D)
McLean (D)
Wayne (D)
Catron (D)
Daniel (D)
Nelson (D)
Grier (D)
Curtis (W)
Campbell (D)

1858-60
Taney (D)
McLean (D)
Wayne (D)
Catron (D)
Daniel (D)
Nelson (D)
Grier (D)
Campbell (D)
Clifford (D)

1861
Taney (D)
McLean (D)
Wayne (D)
Catron (D)
Nelson (D)
Grier (D)
Campbell (D)
Clifford (D)

1862
Taney (D)
Wayne (D)
Catron (D)
Nelson (D)
Grier (D)
Clifford (D)
Swayne (R)
Miller (R)
Davis (R)

1863
Taney (D)
Wayne (D)
Catron (D)
Nelson (D)
Grier (D)
Clifford (D)
Swayne (R)
Miller (R)
Davis (R)
Field (D)

1864-65
S. P. Chase (R)
Wayne (D)
Catron (D) * *
Nelson (D)
Grier (D)
Clifford (D)
Swayne (R)
Miller (R)
Davis (R)
Field (D)

1866
S. P. Chase (R)
Wayne (D) * *
Nelson (D)
Grier (D)
Clifford (D)
Swayne (R)
Miller (R)
Davis (R)
Field (D)

1867-69
S. P. Chase (R)
Nelson (D)
Grier (D)
Clifford (D)
Swayne (R)
Miller (R)
Davis (R)
Field (D)

1870-71
S. P. Chase (R)
Nelson (D)
Clifford (D)
Swayne (R)
Miller (R)
Davis (R)
Field (D)
Strong (R)
Bradley (R)

1872-73
S. P. Chase (R)
Clifford (D)
Swayne (R)
Miller (R)
Davis (R)
Field (D)
Strong (R)
Bradley (R)
Hunt (R)

1874-76
Waite (R)
Clifford (D)
Swayne (R)
Miller (R)
Davis (R)
Field (D)
Strong (R)
Bradley (R)
Hunt (R)

1877-79
Waite (R)
Clifford (D)
Swayne (R)
Miller (R)
Field (D)
Strong (R)
Bradley (R)
Hunt (R)
Harlan (Ky.) (R)

1880
Waite (R)
Clifford (D)
Swayne (R)
Miller (R)
Field (D)
Bradley (R)
Hunt (R)
Harlan (Ky.) (R)
Woods (R)

1881
Waite (R)
Miller (R)
Field (D)
Bradley (R)
Hunt (R)
Harlan (Ky.) (R)
Woods (R)
Matthews (R)
Gray (R)

1882-87
Waite (R)
Miller (R)
Field (D)
Bradley (R)
Harlan (Ky.) (R)
Woods (R)
Matthews (R)
Gray (R)
Blatchford (R)

1888
Fuller (D)
Miller (R)
Field (D)
Bradley (R)
Harlan (Ky.) (R)
Matthews (R)
Gray (R)
Blatchford (R)
L. Lamar (D)

1889
Fuller (D)
Miller (R)
Field (D)
Bradley (R)
Harlan (Ky.) (R)
Gray (R)
Blatchford (R)
L. Lamar (D)
Brewer (R)

1890-91
Fuller (D)
Field (D)
Bradley (R)
Harlan (Ky.) (R)
Gray (R)
Blatchford (R)
L. Lamar (D)
Brewer (R)
Brown (R)

1892
Fuller (D)
Field (D)
Harlan (Ky.) (R)
Gray (R)
Blatchford (R)
L. Lamar (D)
Brewer (R)
Brown (R)
Shiras (R)

1893
Fuller (D)
Field (D)
Harlan (Ky.) (R)
Gray (R)
Blatchford (R)
Brewer (R)
Brown (R)
Shiras (R)
H. Jackson (D)

1894
Fuller (D)
Field (D)
Harlan (Ky.) (R)
Gray (R)
Brewer (R)
Brown (R)
Shiras (R)
H. Jackson (D)
E. White (D)

1895-97
Fuller (D)
Field (D)
Harlan (Ky.) (R)
Gray (R)
Brewer (R)
Brown (R)
Shiras (R)
E. White (D)
Peckham (D)

1998-1901
Fuller (D)
Harlan (Ky.) (R)
Gray (R)
Brewer (R)
Brown (R)
Shiras (R)
E. White (D)
Peckham (D)
McKenna (R)

1902
Fuller (D)
Harlan (Ky.) (R)
Brewer (R)
Brown (R)
Shiras (R)
E. White (D)
Peckham (D)
McKenna (R)
Holmes (R)

1903-05
Fuller (D)
Harlan (Ky.) (R)
Brewer (R)
Brown (R)
E. White (D)
Peckham (D)
McKenna (R)
Holmes (R)
Day (R)

1906-08
Fuller (D)
Harlan (Ky.) (R)
Brewer (R)
E. White (D)
Peckham (D)
McKenna (R)
Holmes (R)
Day (R)
Moody (R)

1909
Fuller (D)
Harlan (Ky.) (R)
Brewer (R)
E. White (D)
McKenna (R)
Holmes (R)
Day (R)
Moody (R)
Lurton (D)

1910-11
E. White (D)
Harlan (Ky.) (R)
McKenna (R)
Holmes (R)
Day (R)
Lurton (D)
Hughes (R)
Van Devanter (R)
J. Lamar (D)

1912-13
E. White (D)
McKenna (R)
Holmes (R)
Day (R)
Lurton (D)
Hughes (R)
Van Devanter (R)
J. Lamar (D)
Pitney (R)

1914-15
E. White (D)
McKenna (R)
Holmes (R)
Day (R)
Hughes (R)
Van Devanter (R)
J. Lamar (D)
Pitney (R)
McReynolds (D)

1916-20
E. White (D)
McKenna (R)
Holmes (R)
Day (R)
Van Devanter (R)
Pitney (R)
McReynolds (D)
Brandeis (R) * * *
Clarke (D)

1921
Taft (R)
McKenna (R)
Holmes (R)
Day (R)
Van Devanter (R)
Pitney (R)
McReynolds (D)
Brandeis (R)
Clarke (D)

1922
Taft (R)
McKenna (R)
Holmes (R)
Van Devanter (R)
Pitney (R)
McReynolds (D)
Brandeis (R)
Sutherland (R)
Butler (D)

1923-24
Taft (R)
McKenna (R)
Holmes (R)
Van Devanter (R)
McReynolds (D)
Brandeis (R)
Sutherland (R)
Butler (D)
Sanford (R)

1925-29
Taft (R)
Holmes (R)
Van Devanter (R)
McReynolds (D)
Brandeis (R)
Sutherland (R)
Butler (D)
Sanford (R)
Stone (R)

1930-31
Hughes (R)
Holmes (R)
Van Devanter (R)
McReynolds (D)
Brandeis (R)
Sutherland (R)
Butler (D)
Stone (R)
Roberts (R)

1932-36
Hughes (R)
Van Devanter (R)
McReynolds (D)
Brandeis (R)
Sutherland (R)
Butler (D)
Stone (R)
Roberts (R)
Cardozo (D)

1937
Hughes (R)
McReynolds (D)
Brandeis (R)
Sutherland (R)
Butler (D)
Stone (R)
Roberts (R)
Cardozo (D)
Black (D)

1938
Hughes (R)
McReynolds (D)
Brandeis (R)
Butler (D)
Stone (R)
Roberts (R)
Cardozo (D)
Black (D)
Reed (D)

1939
Hughes (R)
McReynolds (D)
Butler (D)
Stone (R)
Roberts (R)
Black (D)
Reed (D)
Frankfurter (I)
Douglas (D)

1940
Hughes (R)
McReynolds (D)
Stone (R)
Roberts (R)
Black (D)
Reed (D)
Frankfurter (I)
Douglas (D)
Murphy (D)

1941-42
Stone (R)
Roberts (R)
Black (D)
Reed (D)
Frankfurter (I)
Douglas (D)
Murphy (D)
Byrnes (D)
R. Jackson (D)

1943-44
Stone (R)
Roberts (R)
Black (D)
Reed (D)
Frankfurter (I)
Douglas (D)
Murphy (D)
R. Jackson (D)
W. Rutledge (D)

1945
Stone (R)
Black (D)
Reed (D)
Frankfurter (I)
Douglas (D)
Murphy (D)
R. Jackson (D)
W. Rutledge (D)
Burton (R)

1946-48
Vinson (D)
Black (D)
Reed (D)
Frankfurter (I)
Douglas (D)
Murphy (D)
R. Jackson (D)
W. Rutledge (D)
Burton (R)

1949-52
Vinson (D)
Black (D)
Reed (D)
Frankfurter (I)
Douglas (D)
R. Jackson (D)
Burton (R)
Clark (D)
Minton (D)

1953-54
Warren (R)
Black (D)
Reed (D)
Frankfurter (I)
Douglas (D)
R. Jackson (D)
Burton (R)
Clark (D)
Minton (D)

1955
Warren (R)
Black (D)
Reed (D)
Frankfurter (I)
Douglas (D)
Burton (R)
Clark (D)
Minton (D)
Harlan (N.Y.) (R)

1956
Warren (R)
Black (D)
Reed (D)
Frankfurter (I)
Douglas (D)
Burton (R)
Clark (D)
Harlan (N.Y.) (R)
Brennan (D)

1957
Warren (R)
Black (D)
Frankfurter (I)
Douglas (D)
Burton (R)
Clark (D)
Harlan (N.Y.) (R)
Brennan (D)
Whittaker (R)

1958-61
Warren (R)
Black (D)
Frankfurter (I)
Douglas (D)
Clark (D)
Harlan (N.Y.) (R)
Brennan (D)
Whittaker (R)
Stewart (R)

1962-65
Warren (R)
Black (D)
Douglas (D)
Clark (D)
Harlan (N.Y.) (R)
Brennan (D)
Stewart (R)
B. White (D)
Goldberg (D)

1965-67
Warren (R)
Black (D)
Douglas (D)
Clark (D)
Harlan (N.Y.) (R)
Brennan (D)
Stewart (R)
B. White (D)
Fortas (D)

1967-69
Warren (R)
Black (D)
Douglas (D)
Harlan (N.Y.) (R)
Brennan (D)
Stewart (R)
B. White (D)
Fortas (D)
T. Marshall (D)

1969
Burger (R)
Black (D)
Douglas (D)
Harlan (N.Y.) (R)
Brennan (D)
Stewart (R)
B. White (D)
Fortas (D)
T. Marshall (D)

1969-70
Burger (R)
Black (D)
Douglas (D)
Harlan (N.Y.) (R)
Brennan (D)
Stewart (R)
B. White (D)
T. Marshall (D)

1970
Burger (R)
Black (D)
Douglas (D)
Harlan (N.Y.) (R)
Brennan (D)
Stewart (R)
B. White (D)
T. Marshall (D)
Blackmun (R)

1971
Burger (R)
Douglas (D)
Brennan (D)
Stewart (R)
B. White (D)
T. Marshall (D)
Blackmun (R)

1972-75
Burger (R)
Douglas (D)
Brennan (D)
Stewart (R)
B. White (D)
T. Marshall (D)
Blackmun (R)
Powell (D)
Rehnquist (R)

1975-81
Burger (R)
Brennan (D)
Stewart (R)
B. White (D)
T. Marshall (D)
Blackmun (R)
Powell (D)
Rehnquist (R)
Stevens (R)

1981-1986
Burger (R)
Brennan (D)
B. White (D)
T. Marshall (D)
Blackmun (R)
Powell (D)
Rehnquist (R)
J. Stevens (R)
O'Connor (R)

1986-1988
Rehnquist (R)
Brennan (D)
B. White (D)
T. Marshall (D)
Blackmun (R)
Powell (D)
J. Stevens (R)
O'Connor (R)
Scalia (R)

1988-1990
Rehnquist (R)
Brennan (D)
B. White (D)
T. Marshall (D)
Blackmun (R)
J. Stevens (R)
O'Connor (R)
Scalia (R)
Kennedy (R)

1990-1991
Rehnquist (R)
B. White (D)
T. Marshall (D)
Blackmun (R)
J. Stevens (R)
O'Connor (R)
Scalia (R)
Kennedy (R)
Souter (R)

1991-1993
Rehnquist (R)
B. White (D)
Blackmun (R)
J. Stevens (R)
O'Connor (R)
Scalia (R)
Kennedy (R)
Souter (R)
Thomas (R)

1993-1994
Rehnquist (R)
Blackmun (R)
J. Stevens (R)
O'Connor (R)
Scalia (R)
Kennedy (R)
Souter (R)
Thomas (R)
Ginsburg (D)

1994-
Rehnquist (R)
J. Stevens (R)
O'Connor (R)
Scalia (R)
Kennedy (R)
Souter (R)
Thomas (R)
Ginsburg (D)
Breyer (D)

* Rutledge was a recess appointment whose confirmation was rejected by the Senate after the 1795 Term.
** Upon the death of Catron in 1865 and Wayne in 1867 their positions were abolished according to a congressional act of 1866. The Court's membership was reduced to eight until a new position was created by Congress in 1869. The new seat has generally been regarded as a re-creation of Wayne's seat.
*** According to Professor Henry Abraham, "Many—and with some justice—consider Brandeis a Democrat; however, he was in fact a registered Republican when nominated." *Freedom and the Court* 455 (3d ed. 1977).

Appendix E

Federal Circuits Map

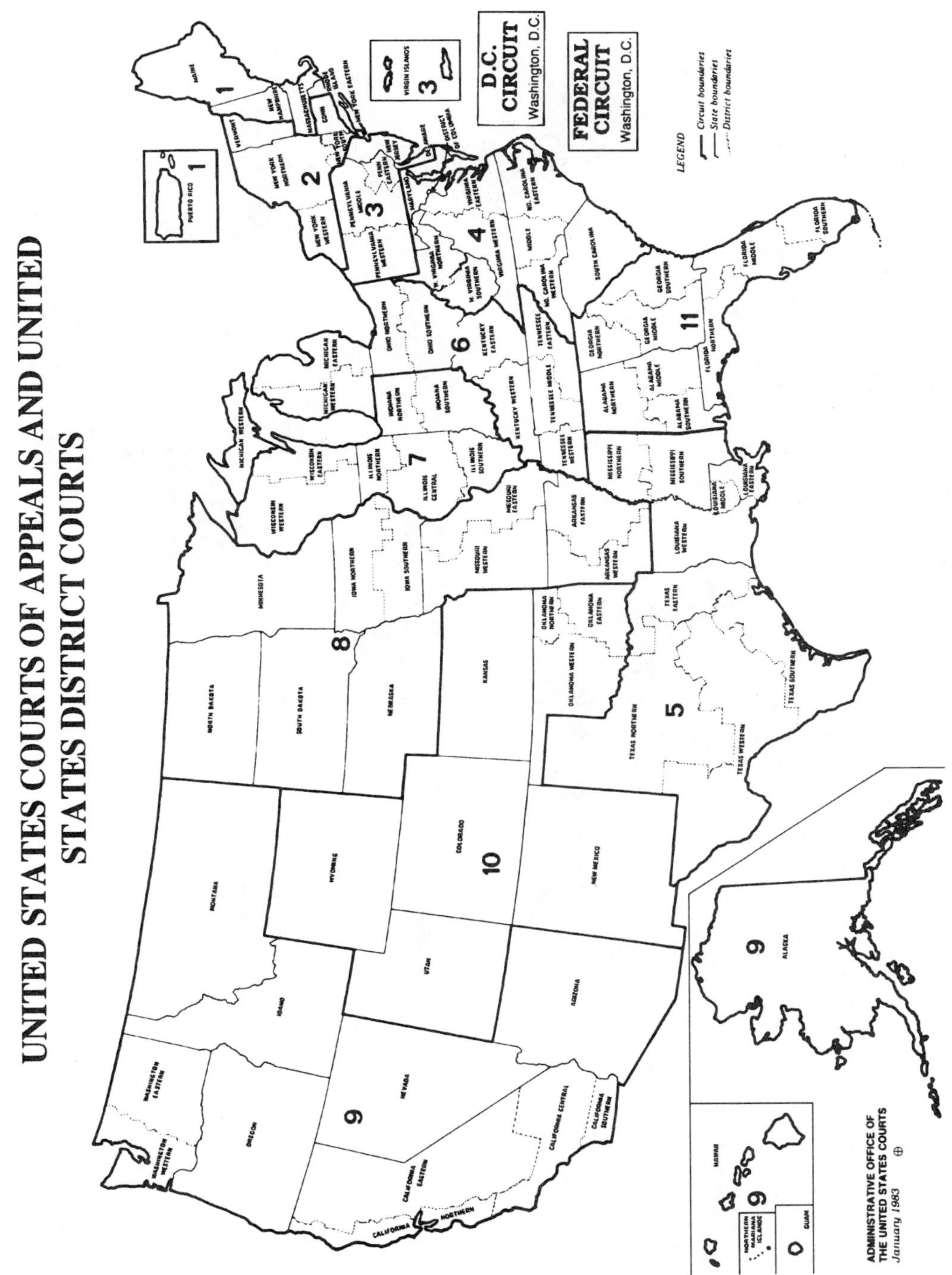

Appendix F

British Regnal Years

Sovereign	Accession	Years in reign
William I	Oct. 14, 1066	21
William II	Sept. 26, 1087	13
Henry I	Aug. 5, 1100	36
Stephen	Dec. 26, 1135	19
Henry II	Dec. 19, 1154	35
Richard I	Sept. 23, 1189	10
John	May 27, 1199	18
Henry III	Oct. 28, 1216	57
Edward I	Nov. 20, 1272	35
Edward II	July 8, 1307	20
Edward III	Jan. 25, 1326	51
Richard II	June 22, 1377	23
Henry IV	Sept. 30, 1399	14
Henry V	Mar. 21, 1413	10
Henry VI	Sept. 1, 1422	39
Edward IV	Mar. 4, 1461	23
Edward V	Apr. 9, 1483	—
Richard III	June 26, 1483	3
Henry VII	Aug. 22, 1485	24
Henry VIII	Apr. 22, 1509	38
Edward VI	Jan. 28, 1547	7
Mary	July 6, 1553	6
Elizabeth I	Nov. 17, 1558	45
James I	Mar. 24, 1603	23
Charles I	Mar. 27, 1625	24
The Commonwealth	Jan. 30, 1649	11
Charles II	May 29, 1660	37
James II	Feb. 6, 1685	4
William and Mary	Feb. 13, 1689	14
Anne	Mar. 8, 1702	13
George I	Aug. 1, 1714	13
George II	June 11, 1727	34
George III	Oct. 25, 1760	60
George IV	Jan. 29, 1820	11
William IV	June 26, 1830	7
Victoria	June 20, 1837	64
Edward VII	Jan. 22, 1901	9
George V	May 6, 1910	25
Edward VIII	Jan. 20, 1936	1
George VI	Dec. 11, 1936	15
Elizabeth II	Feb. 6, 1952	—

Appendix G

List of Works Cited

Ackerman, Bruce A. *Reconstructing American Law* (1984).

Alix, Jay; and Elmer E. Heupel, *Financial Handbook for Bankruptcy Professionals* (1991).

Allen, Carleton K. *Law in the Making* (7th ed. 1964).

American Jurisprudence 2d. 83 vols. (1962–).

American Law and Procedure. 14 vols. (1962).

American Law of Mining. 6 vols. (2d ed. 1984–).

American Law of Property. 7 vols. (1952).

Anderson, Ronald A. *Uniform Commercial Code*. 8 vols. (3d ed. 1981–).

Anderson, William C. *A Dictionary of Law* (1889).

Anson, William R. *Principles of the Law of Contract* (Arthur L. Corbin ed., 3d Am. ed. 1919).

Appleman, John Alan; and Jean Appleman. *Insurance Law and Practice*. 61 vols. (1941–).

Aronson, Robert H.; and Donald T. Weckstein. *Professional Responsibility in a Nutshell* (2d ed. 1991).

Ashworth, Andrew. *Principles of Criminal Law* (1991).

Atiyah, P.S. *An Introduction to the Law of Contract* (3d ed. 1981).

Atkinson, Thomas E. *Handbook of the Law of Wills* (2d ed. 1953).

Austin, John. *The Providence of Jurisprudence Determined*. 3 vols. (Sarah Austin ed., 2d ed. 1861).

Baker, J.H. *An Introduction to English Legal History* (3d ed. 1990).

Baker, J.H. *A Manual of Law French* (1979).

Barclay, Hugh. *A Digest of the Law of Scotland* (3d ed. 1865).

Barron, Jerome A.; and C. Thomas Dienes. *Constitutional Law in a Nutshell* (3d ed. 1995).

Beale, Joseph H. *A Treatise on the Conflict of Laws*. 3 vols. (1935).

Beardsley, Arthur Sydney. *Legal Bibliography and the Use of Law Books* (1937).

Bell, William. *Bell's Dictionary and Digest of the Law of Scotland* (George Watson ed., 7th ed. 1890).

Bentham, Jeremy. *An Introduction to the Principles of Morals and Legislation*. 2 vols. (1823).

Berger, Adolf. *Encyclopedic Dictionary of Roman Law* (1953).

Bergin, Thomas F.; and Paul G. Haskell. *Preface to Estates in Land and Future Interests* (2d ed. 1984).

Bernhardt, Roger. *Real Property in a Nutshell* (3d ed. 1993).

Bispham, George T. *The Principles of Equity* (Joseph D. McCoy ed., 11th ed. 1931).

Black, Henry Campbell. *Handbook on the Construction and Interpretation of the Laws* (1896).

Black, Henry Campbell. *A Treatise on the Law of Judgments*. 2 vols. (2d ed. 1902).

Blackstone, William. *Commentaries on the Laws of England*. 4 vols. (1766–1769).

Block, Dennis J.; et al. *The Business Judgment Rule*. 2 vols. (5th ed. 1998).

Blount, Thomas. *Nomo Lexicon: A Law-Dictionary* (1670).

Boberg, P.Q.R. *The Law of Delict* (1984).

Bouvier, John. *Bouvier's Law Dictionary*. 3 vols. (Francis Rawle ed., 8th ed. 1914).

Boyer, Ralph E.; et al. *The Law of Property* (4th ed. 1991).

Brandt, George W. *The Law of Suretyship and Guaranty*. 2 vols. (3d ed. 1905).

Brierly, J.L. *The Law of Nations* (5th ed. 1955).

Bromberg, Alan R.; and Larry E. Ribstein. *Bromberg and Ribstein on Partnerships*. 4 vols. (1988–).

Brown, Harold. *Franchising Realities and Remedies*. 2 vols. (1993).

Brown, Ray Andrews. *The Law of Personal Property* (2d ed. 1955).

Bryant, Edwin E. *The Law of Pleading Under the Codes of Civil Procedure* (2d ed. 1899).

Bryce, James. *Studies in History and Jurisprudence*. 2 vols. (1901).

Buckland, W.W. *Elementary Principles of the Roman Private Law* (1912).

Buckland, W.W. *A Manual of Roman Private Law* (2d ed. 1953).

Buckland, W.W. *Some Reflections on Jurisprudence* (1945).

Buckland, W.W. *A Textbook of Roman Law* (Peter Stein ed., 3d ed. 1963).

Buergenthal, Thomas. *International Human Rights in a Nutshell* (2d ed. 1995).

Buergenthal, Thomas; and Harold G. Maier. *Public International Law in a Nutshell* (2d ed. 1990).

Burke, Barlow. *Personal Property in a Nutshell* (2d ed. 1993).

Burn, Richard. *A New Law Dictionary*. 2 vols. (1792).

Burnham, Scott J. *Contract Drafting Guidebook* (2d ed. 1992).

Burrill, Alexander M. *A Law Dictionary and Glossary*. 2 vols. (2d ed. 1867).

Burrill, Alexander M. *A Treatise on the Law and Practice of Voluntary Assignments for the Benefit of Creditors* (James Avery Webb ed., 6th ed. 1894).

Burrill, Alexander M. *A Treatise on the Nature, Principles and Rules of Circumstantial Evidence* (1868).

Butt, Peter. *Land Law* (3d ed. 1996).

Calamari, John D.; and Joseph M. Perillo. *The Law of Contracts* (4th ed. 1998).

Callmann, Rudolf. *The Law of Unfair Competition, Trademarks and Monopolies*. 6 vols. (4th ed. 1981–).

Canby, William, Jr. *American Indian Law in a Nutshell* (2d ed. 1988).

Century Dictionary and Cyclopedia, The. 10 vols. (1895).

Chambers, Sir Robert. *A Course of Lectures on the English Law: 1767–1773* (Thomas M. Curley ed. 1986).

Chance, E.W. *Principles of Mercantile Law*. Vol. 1. (P.W. French ed., 13th ed. 1950).

Chance, E.W. *Principles of Mercantile Law*. Vol. 2. (P.W. French ed., 10th ed. 1951).

Childs, Frank Hall. *Where and How to Find the Law* (1922).

Chirelstein, Marvin A. *Concepts and Case Analysis in the Law of Contracts* (1990).

Chisum, Donald S. *Patents*. 13 vols. (1978–).

Chitty, Joseph. *A Practical Treatise on the Criminal Law*. 4 vols. (2d ed. 1826).

Christie, Donna R. *Coastal and Ocean Management Law in a Nutshell* (1994).

Clark, Barkley; and Christopher Smith. *The Law of Product Warranties* (1984).

Clark, David G.; and Earl R. Hutchinson. *Mass Media and the Law* (1970).

Clark, Homer H., Jr. *The Law of Domestic Relations in the United States* (2d ed. 1988).

Clark, William Lawrence. *A Treatise on the Law of Crimes* (Marian Quinn Barnes ed., 7th ed. 1967).

Cohen, Morris R. *Law and the Social Order* (1933).

Cohen, Morris R. *Reason and Law* (1961).

Cooley, Thomas M. *The Law of Taxation*. 4 vols. (Clark A. Nichols ed., 4th ed. 1924).

Cooley, Thomas M. *A Treatise on the Constitutional Limitations* (1868).

Corpus Juris Secundum. 101 vols. (1936–).

Couch, George J. *Couch on Insurance*. 26 vols. (2d ed. 1959–1994).

Cowell, John. *The Interpreter* (1607).

Cowen, Zelman. *Essays on the Law of Evidence* (1956).

Cribbet, John E. *Principles of the Law of Property* (2d ed. 1975).

Crompton, George. *Practice Common-Placed: Rules and Cases of Practice in the Courts of King's Bench and Common Pleas*. 2 vols. (3d ed. 1787).

Cross, Rupert. *Statutory Interpretation* (1976).

Cross, Rupert; and J.W. Harris. *Precedent in English Law* (4th ed. 1991).

Cunningham, Roger A.; et al. *The Law of Property* (2d ed. 1993).

Currie, David P. *Federal Jurisdiction in a Nutshell* (3d ed. 1990).

Curzon, L.B. *English Legal History* (2d ed. 1979).

Dangel, Edward M. *Contempt* (1939).

Daniel, John W. *A Treatise on the Law of Negotiable Instruments*. 3 vols. (Thomas H. Calvert ed., 7th ed. 1933).

Davis, George B. *A Treatise on the Military Law of the United States* (3d ed. 1915).

Decker, Kurt H.; and H. Thomas Felix II. *Drafting and Revising Employment Contracts* (1991).

de Funiak, William Q. *Handbook of Modern Equity* (2d ed. 1956).

Devlin, Patrick. *The Criminal Prosecution in England* (1960).

Devlin, Patrick. *The Enforcement of Morals* (1968).

Devlin, Patrick. *The Judge* (1979).

Dhokalia, R.P. *The Codification of Public International Law* (1970).

Dias, R.W.M.; and B.S. Markesinis. *Tort Law* (2d ed. 1989).

Dickerson, Reed. *The Interpretation and Application of Statutes* (1975).

Digest of Justinian. 4 vols. ([A.D. 533] Theodor Mommsen et al. eds., 1985).

Dobbs, Dan B. *Law of Remedies*. 3 vols. (2d ed. 1993).

Dobbyn, John F. *Insurance Law in a Nutshell* (3d ed. 1995).

Dolan, John F. *The Law of Letters of Credit* (1984).

Drake, Charles D. *A Treatise on the Law of Suits by Attachment in the United States* (7th ed. 1891).

Drinker, Henry S. *Legal Ethics* (1953).

Drone, Eaton S. *A Treatise on the Law of Property in Intellectual Productions* (1879).

Dworkin, Gerald. *Odgers' Construction of Deeds and Statutes* (5th ed. 1967).

Dworkin, Ronald. *Law's Empire* (1986).

Eckstrom's Licensing in Foreign and Domestic Operations. 4 vols. (David M. Epstein ed., 4th ed. 1994–).

Eddy, Jonathan A.; and Peter Winship. *Commercial Transactions* (1985).

Eggleston, Richard. *Evidence, Proof and Probability* (1978).

Elias, Stephen. *Patent, Copyright and Trademark* (1996).

Elliott, Byron K.; and William F. Elliott. *A Treatise on the Law of Railroads*. 6 vols. (3d ed. 1921).

Ely, John Hart. *Democracy and Distrust* (1980).

Encyclopaedia Britannica. 24 vols. (9th ed. 1907).

Encyclopedia of Public International Law. 5 vols. (1992).

Epstein, David G.; and Steve H. Nickles. *Consumer Law in a Nutshell* (2d ed. 1981).

Epstein, David G.; et al. *Bankruptcy* (1993).

Essays on the Civil Law of Obligations (Joseph Dainow ed., 1969).

Estee, Morris M. *Estee's Pleadings, Practice, and Forms*. 3 vols. (Carter P. Pomeroy ed., 3d ed. 1885).

Everest, Lancelot Feilding. *Everest and Strode's Law of Estoppel* (3d ed. 1923).

Faber, Robert C. *Landis on Mechanics of Patent Claim Drafting* (3d ed. 1990).

Farnsworth, E. Allan. *Contracts* (2d ed. 1990).

Fifoot, C.H.S. *History and Sources of the Common Law: Tort and Contract* (1949).

Finch, Sir Henry. *Law, or a Discourse Thereof* (1759).

Fisch, Edith L. *The Cy Pres Doctrine in the United States* (1950).

Fletcher, C. Edward. *Materials on the Law of Insider Trading* (1991).

Fletcher, William Meade. *Fletcher Cyclopedia on the Law of Private Corporations*. 20 vols. (1931–).

Folsom, Ralph H.; and Michael W. Gordon. 2 vols. *International Business Transactions* (1995).

Freund, Ernst. *The Police Power* (1904).

Friedenthal, Jack H.; et al. *Civil Procedure* (2d ed. 1993).

Friedman, Lawrence M. *A History of American Law* (2d ed. 1985).

Frost, Thomas Gold. *A Treatise on Guaranty Insurance* (2d ed. 1909).

Fuller, Lon L. *Anatomy of the Law* (1968).

Fuller, Lon L. *The Morality of Law* (rev. ed. 1969).

Fullinwider, Robert K. *The Reverse Discrimination Controversy* (1980).

Gahan, Frank. *The Law of Damages* (1936).

Garner, Bryan A. *A Dictionary of Modern American Usage* (1998).

Garner, Bryan A. *A Dictionary of Modern Legal Usage* (2d ed. 1995).

Garner, Bryan A. *The Winning Brief* (1999).

Geldart, William. *Introduction to English Law* (D.C.M. Yardley ed., 9th ed. 1984).

Gellhorn, Ernest; and William E. Kovacic. *Antitrust Law and Economics in a Nutshell* (4th ed. 1994).

Gellhorn, Ernest; and Ronald M. Levin. *Administrative Law and Process in a Nutshell* (4th ed. 1997).

Getches, David H. *Water Law in a Nutshell* (3d ed. 1997).

Gilmore, Grant. *The Death of Contract* (1974).

Gilmore, Grant; and Charles L. Black, Jr. *The Law of Admiralty* (2d ed. 1975).

Goff, Robert H.; and Gareth H. Jones. *The Law of Restitution* (3d ed. 1986).

Golding, Martin P. *Philosophy of Law* (1975).

Goldstein, Paul. *Copyright's Highway* (1994).

Golub, I.M.; et al. *COBRA Handbook* (1994).

Goodrich, Herbert F.; and Eugene F. Scoles. *Handbook of the Conflict of Laws* (4th ed. 1964).

Gorman, Robert A. *Basic Text on Labor Law: Unionization and Collective Bargaining* (1976).

Graham, Michael H. *Federal Rules of Evidence in a Nutshell* (3d ed. 1992).

Graveson, R.H. *Conflict of Laws* (7th ed. 1974).

Gray, John Chipman. *The Nature and Sources of the Law* (2d ed. 1921).

Gray, John Chipman. *The Rule Against Perpetuities* (1886).

Grimes, Allen. *The City Attorney: A Practice Manual* (1978).

Hadley, James. *Introduction to Roman Law* (1881).

Hagman, Donald G.; and Julian Conrad Juergensmeyer. *Urban Planning and Land Development Control Law* (2d ed. 1986).

Hall, James Parker. *American Law and Procedure*. 14 vols. (1920–).

Hamilton, Robert W. *Fundamentals of Modern Business* (1989).

Hamilton, Robert W. *The Law of Corporations in a Nutshell* (3d ed. 1991).

Harding, Alan. *A Social History of English Law* (1966).

Harrison, Jeffrey L. *Law and Economics in a Nutshell* 56 (1995).

Hart, H.L.A. *Punishment and Responsibility* 136, 147–48 (1968).

Hart, H.L.A.; and Tony Honoré. *Causation in the Law* (2d ed. 1985).

Hartley, T.C. *The Foundations of European Community Law* (1981).

Hawkland, William D. *Uniform Commercial Code Series*. 15 vols. (1982–).

Hazard, Geoffrey C., Jr.; and Michele Taruffo. *American Civil Procedure: An Introduction* (1993).

Hazen, Thomas Lee. *Treatise on the Law of Securities Regulation*. 3 vols. (3d ed. 1995).

Hemingway, Richard W. *The Law of Oil and Gas* (3d ed. 1991).

Henn, Henry G.; and John R. Alexander. *Laws of Corporations* (3d ed. 1983).

Henson, Ray D. *Handbook on Secured Transactions Under the Uniform Commercial Code* (2d ed. 1979).

Henson, Ray D. *Secured Transactions* (3d ed. 1983).

Heuston, R.F.V. *Salmond on the Law of Torts* (17th ed. 1977).

Hinch, Frederick M. *John's American Notary and Commission of Deeds Manual* (3d ed. 1922).

Holdsworth, William S. *A History of English Law*. 17 vols. (1936–1972).

Holdsworth, William S. *Sources and Literature of English Law* (1925).

Holland, Thomas E. *The Elements of Jurisprudence* (13th ed. 1924).

Holt, J.C. *Magna Carta* (1965).

Honoré, Tony. *About Law* (1995).

Honoré, Tony. *Making Law Bind: Essays Legal and Philosophical* (1987).

Honoré, Tony. *The South African Law of Trusts* (3d ed. 1985).

Horniman, Ivan. *Wharton's Law Lexicon* (13th ed. 1925).

Horwill, Herbert W. *The Usages of the American Constitution* (1925).

Horwitz, Morton J. *The Transformation of American Law, 1780–1860* (1977).

Hovenkamp, Herbert. *Economics and Federal Antitrust Law* (1985).

Hughes, William, Jr. *Federal Practice, Jurisdiction & Procedure*. 19 vols. (1931).

Hunnisett, R.F. *The Medieval Coroner* (1961).

Hynes, J. Dennis. *Agency, Partnership, and the LLC in a Nutshell* (1997).

Ilbert, Courtenay P. *Legislative Methods and Forms* (1901).

Indermaur, John. *Principles of the Common Law* (Edmund H. Bennett ed., 1st Am. ed. 1878).

Israel, Jerold H.; and Wayne R. LaFave. *Criminal Procedure in a Nutshell* (5th ed. 1993).

Jacob, Giles. *A New Law-Dictionary* (8th ed. 1762).

Jacobs, Arnold S. *Opinion Letters in Securities Matters*. 2 vols. (1998–).

Jacobstein, J. Myron; and Roy M. Mersky. *Fundamentals of Legal Research* (5th ed. 1990).

Jenks, Edward. *The Book of English Law* (P.B. Fairest ed., 6th ed. 1967).

Jessup, Philip C. *A Modern Law of Nations* (1949).

Jessup, Philip C. *The Use of International Law* (1959).

Johnson, James D., Jr. *Guide to Louisiana Real Actions, Ten Year and Thirty Year Prescriptions* (1961).

Johnson, Samuel. *A Dictionary of the English Language*. 2 vols. (1755).

Johnstone, Quintin; and Dan Hopson, Jr. *Lawyers and Their Work* (1967).

Jones, Eugene A. *Manual of Equity Pleading and Practice* (1916).

Jones, Leonard A. *A Treatise on the Law of Collateral Securities and Pledges* (Edward M. White rev., 3d ed. 1912).

Jones, Leonard A. *A Treatise on the Law of Mortgages* (5th ed. 1908).

Jowitt, William A. *The Dictionary of English Law* (1959).

Joyce, Howard C. *A Treatise on the Law Relating to Injunctions*. 3 vols. (1909).

Keeton, G.W. *An Introduction to Equity* (5th ed. 1961).

Keeton, Robert E. *Judging* (1990).

Keeton, Robert E.; and Alan I. Widiss. *Insurance Law: A Guide to Fundamental Principles, Legal Doctrines, and Commercial Practices* (1988).

Keeton, W. Page.; et al. *Prosser and Keeton on the Law of Torts* (5th ed. 1984).

Kintner, Earl W.; and Jack L. Lahr. *An Intellectual Property Law Primer* (2d ed. 1982).

Kionka, Edward J. *Torts in a Nutshell* (2d ed. 1992).

Kiralfy, A.K.R. *Potter's Outlines of English Legal History* (5th ed. 1958).

Kraemer, Sandy F. *Solar Law* (1978).

Kratovil, Robert. *Real Estate Law* (6th ed. 1974).

LaFave, Wayne R.; and Jerold H. Israel. *Criminal Procedure* (2d ed. 1992).

LaFave, Wayne R.; and Austin W. Scott, Jr. *Criminal Law* (2d ed. 1986).

LaFave, Wayne R.; and Austin W. Scott, Jr. *Substantive Criminal Law*. 2 vols. (1986–).

Larson, Lex K. *Unjust Dismissal*. 2 vols. (1985–).

Lawrence, T.J. *A Handbook of Public International Law* (10th ed. 1925).

Laycock, Douglas. *The Death of the Irreparable Injury Rule* (1991).

Laycock, Douglas. *Modern American Remedies* (1985).

Leage, R.W. *Roman Private Law* (C.H. Ziegler ed., 2d ed. 1930).

Lee, R.W. *The Elements of Roman Law* (4th ed. 1956).

Leflar, Robert A. *American Conflicts Law* (3d ed. 1977).

Legal Essays in Tribute to Orrin Kip McMurray (Max Radin & Alexander M. Kidd eds., 1935).

Leslie, Douglas L. *Labor Law in a Nutshell* (3d ed. 1992).

Lieberman, Jethro K. *The Evolving Constitution* (1992).

Lile, William M.; et al. *Brief Making and the Use of Law Books* (3d ed. 1914).

Llewellyn, Karl N. *The Common Law Tradition: Deciding Appeals* (1960).

Loewy, Arnold H. *Criminal Law in a Nutshell* (2d ed. 1987).

Lord, Richard A. *A Treatise on the Law of Contracts*. 8 vols. (4th ed. 1990–).

Lovett, William A. *Banking and Financial Institutions Law in a Nutshell* (4th ed. 1997).

Lowe, John S. *Oil and Gas Law in a Nutshell* (3d ed. 1995).

Lynn, Robert J. *The Modern Rule Against Perpetuities* (1966).

Madden, Joseph W. *Handbook of the Law of Persons and Domestic Relations* (1931).

Madden, M. Stuart. *Products Liability*. 2 vols. (2d ed. 1988).

Maine, Henry S. *Ancient Law* (17th ed. 1901).

Maitland, Frederic W. *Domesday Book and Beyond* (1921).

Maitland, Frederic W. *Equity* (A.H. Chaytor & W.J. Whittaker eds., 1909).

Manchester, A.H. *Modern Legal History of England and Wales, 1750–1950* (1980).

Maraist, Frank L. *Admiralty in a Nutshell* (3d ed. 1996).

McCarthy, J. Thomas. *McCarthy on Trademarks and Unfair Competition*. 5 vols. (3d ed. 1992–).

McCormack, David R. *Racketeering Influenced Corrupt Organizations*. 2 vols. (1988–).

McCormick, Charles T. *Handbook on the Law of Damages* (1935).

McCrary, George W. *A Treatise on the American Law of Elections* (Henry L. McCune ed., 4th ed. 1897).

McDonnell, Denis Lane; and John George Monroe. *Kerr on the Law of Fraud and Mistake* (7th ed. 1952).

McNeil, Bruce J. *Nonqualified Deferred Compensation Plans* (1994).

McNulty, John K. *Federal Estate and Gift Taxation in a Nutshell* (5th ed. 1994).

McNulty, John K. *Federal Income Taxation of Individuals in a Nutshell* (5th ed. 1995).

Meador, Daniel John; and Jordana Simone Bernstein. *Appellate Courts in the United States* v (1994).

Mechem, Floyd R. *Outlines of the Law of Agency* (Philip Mechem ed., 4th ed. 1952).

Megarry, Robert E.; and P.V. Baker. *Snell's Principles of Equity* (27th ed. 1973).

Megarry, Robert E.; and H.W.R. Wade. *The Law of Real Property* (5th ed. 1984).

Mellows, Anthony R. *The Law of Succession* (3d ed. 1977).

Menell, Robert L.; and Thomas M. Boykoff. *Community Property in a Nutshell* (2d ed. 1988).

Merwin, Elias. *Principles of Equity and Equity Pleading* (H.C. Merwin ed., 1896).

Meyer, Charles H. *Accounting and Finance for Lawyers in a Nutshell* (1995).

Michie on Banks and Banking. 14 vols. (1931–).

Miller, Arthur R.; and Michael H. Davis. *Intellectual Property in a Nutshell* (2d ed. 1990).

Milsom, S.F.C. *Historical Foundations of the Common Law* (1969).

Minda, Gary. *Postmodern Legal Movements* (1995).

Moliterno, James E.; and John M. Levy. *Ethics of the Lawyer's Work* (1993).

Morton, William K.; and Dale A. Whitman. *Manual of the Law of Scotland* (1896).

Moynihan, Cornelius J. *Introduction to the Law of Real Property* (2d ed. 1988).

Nelson, Grant S. *Real Estate Finance Law* (3d ed. 1994).

New York Institute of Finance. *How the Bond Market Works* (1988).

Nimmer, Melville B.; and David Nimmer. *Nimmer on Copyright*. 10 vols. (1978–1995).

Noonan, John T., Jr. *Bribes* (1984).

Nowak, John E.; and Ronald D. Rotunda. *Constitutional Law* (4th ed. 1991).

Noy, William. *A Treatise of the Principal Grounds and Maxims of the Laws of This Nation* (C. Sims ed. 1870) (4th ed. 1677).

Oakley, John Bilyeu; and Robert S. Thompson. *Law Clerks and the Judicial Process* (1980).

O'Connell, John F. *Remedies in a Nutshell* (2d ed. 1985).

Odean, Kathleen. *High Steppers, Fallen Angels, and Lollipops: Wall Street Slang* (1988).

O'Gallagher, Judith. *Municipal Ordinances* (2d ed. 1998).

Oppenheim, F.L. *International Law* (Hersch Lauter ed., 8th ed. 1955).

Oxford Companion to the Supreme Court of the United States (Kermit L. Hall ed., 1992).

Oxford English Dictionary. 20 vols. (2d ed. 1989).

Page, William H.; and Paul Jones. *A Treatise on the Law of Taxation by Local and Special Assessments*. 2 vols. (1909).

Palgrave, R.H. Inglis. *Palgrave's Dictionary of Political Economy*. 3 vols. (Henry Higgs ed., 2d ed. 1925).

Palmer, George E. *The Law of Restitution*. 4 vols. (1978).

Paton, George Whitecross. *A Textbook of Jurisprudence* (G.W. Paton & David P. Derham eds., 4th ed. 1972).

Patry, William F. *Copyright Law and Practice*. 3 vols. (1994).

Perkins, Rollin M.; and Ronald N. Boyce. *Criminal Law* (3d ed. 1982).

Player, Mack A. *Employment Discrimination Law* (1988).

Player, Mack A. *Federal Law of Employment Discrimination in a Nutshell* (3d ed. 1992).

Plucknett, Theodore F.T. *A Concise History of the Common Law* (5th ed. 1956).

Pocket Lawyer and Family Conveyancer (3d ed. 1833).

Podgor, Ellen S.; and Jerold H. Israel. *White Collar Crime in a Nutshell* (2d ed. 1997).

Pollock, Frederick. *A First Book of Jurisprudence* (1896).

Pollock, Frederick; and Frederic W. Maitland. *History of English Law Before the Time of Edward I*. 2 vols. (2d ed. 1898–1899).

Pollock, Frederick; and Robert Samuel Wright. *An Essay on Possession in the Common Law* (1888).

Polyviou, Polyvios G. *The Equal Protection of the Laws* (1980).

Poole, Reginald L. *The Exchequer in the Twelfth Century* (1912).

Pooley, James. *Trade Secrets* (1998).

Posner, Richard A. *Economic Analysis of Law* (2d ed. 1977).

Posner, Richard A. *The Federal Courts: Crisis and Reform* 1985).

Posner, Richard A. *Law and Literature: A Misunderstood Relation* (1988).

Posner, Richard A. *The Problems of Jurisprudence* (1990).

Pound, Roscoe. *The Development of Constitutional Guarantees of Liberty* (1957).

Pound, Roscoe. *The Formative Era of American Law* (1938).

Pound, Roscoe. *An Introduction to the Philosophy of Law* (rev. ed. 1954).

Powell, Richard R. *Powell on Real Property*. 17 vols. (Patrick J. Rohan ed., 1949–).

Proffatt, John. *A Treatise on the Law Relating to the Office and Duties of Notaries Public* (John F. Tyler & John J. Stephens eds., 2d ed. 1892).

Purver, Jonathan M.; and Lawrence E. Taylor. *Handling Criminal Appeals* (1980).

Quindry, Silvester E. *Bonds & Bondholders Rights & Remedies*. 2 vols. (1934).

Rabin, Edward H. *Fundamentals of Modern Real Property Law* (1974).

Radcliffe, Geoffrey; and Geoffrey Cross. *The English Legal System* (G.J. Hand & D.J. Bentley eds., 6th ed. 1977).

Radin, Max. *Handbook of Anglo-American Legal History* (1936).

Radin, Max. *Handbook of Roman Law* (1927).

Radin, Max. *The Law and You* (1948).

Randolph, Joseph F. *A Treatise on the Law of Commercial Paper*. 3 vols. (2d ed. 1899).

Rapalje, Stewart; and Robert L. Lawrence. *A Dictionary of American and English Law*. 2 vols. (1883).

Rastell, John. *Les Termes de la Ley* (26th ed. 1721).

Ratner, David L. *Securities Regulation in a Nutshell* (4th ed. 1992).

Reilly, John W. *The Language of Real Estate* (2d ed. 1982).

Restatement (Second) of Contracts. 10 vols. (1981).

Restatement of the Law Governing Lawyers (1998).

Restatement of the Law of Restitution (1937).

Restatement (Second) of Torts. 4 vols. (1965–1979).

Restatement (Third) of Torts (1999).

Restatement (Second) of Trusts. 5 vols. (1959).

Reuschlein, Harold Gill; and William A. Gregory. *The Law of Agency and Partnership* (2d ed. 1990).

Rex, Benjamin F. *The Notaries' Manual* (J.H. McMillan ed., 6th ed. 1913).

Reynolds, Osborne M., Jr. *Handbook of Local Government Law* (1982).

Richardson, William P. *The Law of Evidence* (3d ed. 1928).

Rohwer, Claude; and Gordon D. Schaber. *Contracts in a Nutshell* (4th ed. 1997).

Rose, Michael D.; and John C. Chommie. *Federal Income Taxation* (3d ed. 1988).

Rothstein, Mark A. *Occupational Safety and Health Law* 7 (1990).

Rothstein, Mark A.; et al. *Employment Law* (1994).

Sack, Robert D.; and Sandra S. Baron. *Libel, Slander, and Related Problems* (2d ed. 1994).

Safire, William. *Safire's New Political Dictionary* (1993).

Salmond, John. *Jurisprudence* (Glanville L. Williams ed., 10th ed. 1947).

Salsich, Peter W., Jr. *Land Use Regulation* (1991).

Scarman, Leslie. *English Law — the New Dimension* (1974).

Schermers, Henry G. *International Institutional Law*. 3 vols. (1972).

Schoenbaum, Thomas J. *Admiralty and Maritime Law* (1987).

Schwarzenberger, Georg. *Power Politics: A Study of International Society* (2d ed. 1951).

Schwing, Ann Taylor. *California Affirmative Defenses*. 5 vols. (2d ed. 1996).

Schwing, Ann Taylor. *Open Meeting Laws* (2d ed. 1999).

Scott, Austin W.; and William F. Fratcher. *The Law of Trusts*. 12 vols. (4th ed. 1987).

Select Essays in Anglo-American Legal History. 3 vols. (1907–1909).

Shanor, Charles A.; and L. Lynn Hogue. *Military Law in a Nutshell* (2d ed. 1996).

Shapo, Marshall S. *The Duty to Act* (1977).

Shaw, Malcolm N. *International Law* (4th ed. 1997).

Shipman, Benjamin J. *Handbook of Common-Law Pleading* (Henry Winthrop Ballantine ed., 3d ed. 1923).

Shklar, Judith N. *Legalism: Law, Morals, and Political Trials* (1964).

Siegel, David D. *Conflicts in a Nutshell* (2d ed. 1994).

Simes, Lewis M.; and Allan F. Smith. *The Law of Future Interests* (2d ed. 1956).

Simpson, Brian. *An Introduction to the History of the Land Law* (1961).

Simpson, Laurence P. *Handbook on the Law of Suretyship* (1950).

Singer, Norman J. *Sutherland Statutes and Statutory Construction*. 8 vols. (4th ed. 1986).

Sohm, Rudolph. *The Institutes: A Textbook of the History and System of Roman Private Law* (James Crawford Ledlie trans., 3d ed. 1907).

Sohn, Louis B.; and Kristen Gustafson. *The Law of the Sea in a Nutshell* (1984).

Spaht, Katherine S.; and W. Lee Hargrave. *Louisiana Civil Law Treatise: Matrimonial Regimes* (2d ed. 1997).

Speidel, Richard E. *Negotiable Instruments and Check Collection in a Nutshell* (4th ed. 1993).

Speiser, Stuart M. *The Negligence Case: Res Ipsa Loquitur* (1972).

Sprankling, John G.; and Gregory S. Weber. *The Law of Hazardous Wastes and Toxic Substances in a Nutshell* (1997).

Steinberg, Marc I. *Understanding Securities Law* (2d ed. 1996).

Stephen, James Fitzjames. *A Digest of the Law of Evidence* (4th ed. 1881).

Stephenson, Gilbert Thomas. *Wills* (1934).

Story, Joseph. *Commentaries on Equity Jurisprudence* (W.E. Grigsby ed., 1st English ed. 1884).

Sullivan, Lawrence A. *Handbook of the Law of Antitrust* (1977).

Svarlien, Oscar. *An Introduction to the Law of Nations* (1955).

Taylor, Benjamin J.; and Fred Whitney. *Labor Relations Law* (1971).

Taylor, Hannis. *The Science of Jurisprudence* (1908).

Thayer, James B. *A Preliminary Treatise on Evidence at the Common Law* (1898).

Thoreau, Henry David. *Journal of Henry D. Thoreau*. 2 vols. (Bradford Torrey & Francis H. Allen eds., 1962).

Thornton, G.C. *Legislative Drafting* (2d ed. 1979).

Tigar, Michael E. *Federal Appeals: Jurisdiction and Practice* (2d ed. 1993).

Torcia, Charles E. *Wharton's Criminal Law*. 4 vols. (15th ed. 1993).

Treitel, G.H. *The Law of Contract* (8th ed. 1991).

Tribe, Laurence H. *Constitutional Choices* (1985).

Turner, J.W. Cecil. *Kenny's Outlines of Criminal Law* (16th ed. 1952).

Underhill, H.C. *A Treatise on the Law of Wills*. 2 vols. (1900).

United States Attorneys' Manual (1997).

Verplanck, Gulian C. *An Essay on the Doctrine of Contracts* (1825).

Vining, Joseph. *Legal Identity* (1978).

Walker, David M. *The Oxford Companion to Law* (1980).

Walker, David M. *Principles of Scottish Private Law*. 4 vols. (4th ed. 1988).

Walsh, William F. *Outlines of the History of English and American Law* (1924).

Walsh, William F. *A Treatise on Equity* (1930).

Warvelle, George W. *A Treatise on the Principles and Practice of the Action of Ejectment* (1905).

Waterman, Thomas W. *A Treatise on the Law of Set-Off, Recoupment, and Counter Claim* (2d ed. 1872).

Waters, D.W.M. *The Constructive Trust* (1964).

Watson, Alan. *Ancient Law and Modern Understanding* (1998).

Watson, George. *Bell's Dictionary and Digest of the Law of Scotland* (3d ed. 1882).

Weldon, Arthur; and H. Gibson Rivington. *Gibson's Conveyancing* (14th ed. 1933).

White, Alan R. *Grounds of Liability* (1985).

White, James J.; and Robert S. Summers. *Uniform Commercial Code*. 4 vols. (4th ed. 1995).

Wigmore, John Henry. *Evidence*. 13 vols. (John T. McNaughton rev., 1961–1988).

Wigmore, John Henry. *Evidence in Trials at Common Law*. 5 vols. (James H. Chadbourn ed., 4th rev. ed. 1961–).

Wigmore, John Henry. *Problems of Law* (1920).

Wigmore, John Henry. *A Students' Textbook of the Law of Evidence* (1935).

Williams, Glanville. *Criminal Law* (2d ed. 1961).

Williams, Glanville. *Learning the Law* (11th ed. 1982).

Williams, Glanville. *The Sanctity of Life and the Criminal Law* (1957).

Williams, Glanville. *Textbook of Criminal Law* (1978).

Williams, Joshua. *Principles of the Law of Personal Property* (11th ed. 1881).

Williston, Samuel. *The Law Governing Sales of Goods*. 4 vols. (3d ed. 1948).

Williston, Samuel. *A Treatise on the Law of Contracts*. 18 vols. (Walter H.E. Jaeger ed., 3d ed. 1957).

Windeyer, W.J.V. *Lectures on Legal History* (2d ed. 1949).

Winfield, Percy H. *The Chief Sources of English Legal History* (1925).

Wolff, Hans Julius. *Roman Law: An Historical Introduction* (1951).

Wood, H.G. *A Treatise on the Law of Master and Servant* (2d ed. 1886).

Wright, Charles Alan. *The Law of Federal Courts* (5th ed. 1994).

Wright, Charles Alan; et al. *Federal Practice and Procedure*. 55 vols. (1978–1999).